CASES AND MATERIALS ON
THE LAW OF TORTS

Third Edition

By

George C. Christie
James B. Duke Professor of Law
Duke University

James E. Meeks
Professor of Law
Ohio State University

Ellen S. Pryor
Associate Professor of Law
Southern Methodist University

Joseph Sanders
A. A. White Professor of Law
University of Houston

AMERICAN CASEBOOK SERIES®

WEST PUBLISHING CO.
ST. PAUL, MINN., 1997

COPYRIGHT © 1983, 1990 WEST PUBLISHING CO.

COPYRIGHT © 1997 By WEST GROUP
                          610 Opperman Drive
                          P.O. Box 64526
                          St. Paul, MN 55164–0526
                          1–800–328–9352

Library of Congress Cataloging-in-Publication Data

Christie, George C.
    Cases and materials on the law of torts / by George C. Christie,
James E. Meeks. — 3rd ed.
          p.   cm. — (American casebook series)
    Includes index.
    ISBN 0–314–21113–6 (hardcover)
    1. Torts—United States—Cases.   I. Meeks, James E., 1938–   .
II. Title.   III. Series.
KF1249.C48   1997
346.7303—dc21   97–10156
                                                                      CIP

ISBN 0–314–21113–6

*TEXT IS PRINTED ON 10% POST
CONSUMER RECYCLED PAPER*

To Our Spouses and Children

*

Preface

The Third Edition continues the approach of exploring the historical derivation of modern tort law and of describing, where appropriate, how tort law relates to the major jurisprudential debates as to the nature of legal reasoning. The thorough coverage of the evolution of the basic building blocks of modern tort law—the law of negligence and the concept of legal cause—is of course retained. Although some cases have been deleted and a number of new cases have been added, the Third Edition continues to present minimally edited cases so that the book may be used as a vehicle for teaching first-year students the essential techniques of case analysis and legal method.

The chapter on products liability has been substantially revised. While retaining its historical introduction, the bulk of the chapter is now organized around the proposed Restatement (Third) of Torts: Products Liability. A number of new cases include majority and dissenting opinions so that the student can observe the substantial disagreement that still surrounds this important area of tort law. Significant developments in the law regarding alternative feasible design, preemption, and compliance with regulations are noted and discussed. The chapter concludes with a brief note on products liability law in the European Community and Japan.

As in the past, the Third Edition gives substantial attention to how the tort system actually operates. The problems that arise when multiple defendants are present, which have become increasingly more complex with the advent of comparative negligence, have led to the complete reorganization of the relevant chapters and the addition of new cases. There is also significant coverage of the subject of damages. Because so much of the law relating to damages has been affected by legislative tort reforms, and by judicial attention to concerns about a perceived tort-liability crisis, the chapters in which questions of damages assume major importance have been revised to take account of recent legislative and judicial developments.

The chapters dealing with insurance and non-tort alternatives have been substantially revised to take account of recent scholarly and judicial attention to the role of liability insurance in tort litigation. The basic arguments, relating to the existence and magnitude of a tort liability crisis, are set out, as are the tort reforms enacted in response to this perceived crisis. The discussion of non-tort alternatives, such as workers' compensation and no-fault insurance, has been revised to address the increasing public importance of questions such as where to draw the dividing line between workers' compensation and tort, whether workers' compensation should cover mental injury, and whether workers' compensation is itself in need of reform.

The chapter on misrepresentation has been expanded to trace recent developments on liability to parties not in privity with the defendant and to provide some material on the causes of action for tortious interference with contract and tortious interference with prospective business relations. Finally, the thorough coverage of the modern law of defamation, including its history and common-law and constitutional components, is retained.

As can be seen from this brief description of some of the new features of the Third Edition, this casebook covers the law of torts in its entirety. The casebook is divided into 22 chapters and easily permits each instructor to pick and choose what to cover in a torts course. The casebook is thus as suitable for a three hour torts course as it is for a four, five, or six credit course. Because of its breadth and depth of coverage it is also eminently suitable for use in an advanced torts course.

We should finally like to acknowledge the assistance given us by Anne Hickey and Joe Walker of the Duke Law School; Alex Lattin, Dean Pacific and Andy Gardner of the Ohio State Law School; Eric Berkley and Brent Dyer of the Southern Methodist University Law School; and Chris Blanton of the University of Houston Law Center. We would also particularly like to thank Joe (Joseph G.) Walker for preparing the index for this casebook.

GEORGE C. CHRISTIE
Durham, North Carolina

JAMES E. MEEKS
Columbus, Ohio

ELLEN S. PRYOR
Dallas, Texas

JOSEPH SANDERS
Houston, Texas

Summary of Contents

*

Table of Contents

Table of Cases

The principal cases are in bold type. Cases cited or discussed in the text are roman type. References are to pages. Cases cited in principal cases and within other quoted materials are not included.

CASES AND MATERIALS ON
THE LAW OF TORTS
Third Edition

*

Chapter 1

INTRODUCTION

A. GENERAL

1. Some Early History

Torts, as its law-French name suggests, is concerned with what might loosely be called "civil" or "private wrongs." It is one of the oldest branches of our law. Indeed, it would be hard to imagine a community of people, no matter how primitive, that had not evolved some institutional means of handling the injuries that people, interacting on a daily basis, inevitably occasionally inflict upon each other. In our relatively more advanced society, it is commonplace to distinguish between the means by which wrongs are redressed. Some wrongs are redressed under the law of torts; others under the criminal law; and others under both branches of our law. It is characteristic of the early stages of legal development, however, that there is no clear distinction between criminal and tort law. In fact, before the rise of an institutionalized authority able to prosecute and to punish what may be conceived of as public wrongs, the sole legal redress for conduct that we would conceive of as criminal was typically provided by remedies that are much more analogous to modern tort remedies than to modern criminal law. This was certainly to a large extent true of early Roman law[1] and it was even more true of English law during its earliest periods.[2] In pre-conquest England what is generally called an "emendatory" system of justice largely prevailed. To this extent, it was primarily what we would classify as tort law. Under an emendatory system someone injured by another—or in the case of death, the deceased's kinsmen—is entitled to compensation from the aggressor and/or his kinsmen. In this way, it was hoped to achieve the "composition" of the dispute between the parties and their kin and thus prevent recourse to self-help and the development of feuds. In Anglo–Saxon England the amount of compensation (called *"wergild"* where death ensued; *"bot"* where it did not) varied according to the nature of the injury inflicted and the status of the injured person.[3]

1. *See* H. Jolowicz, Historical Introduction to Roman Law 317–27 (1932).

2. *See* 2 W. Holdsworth, A History of English Law 43–54 (3d ed. 1927); 1 F. Pollock & F. Maitland, The History of English Law 46–56 (2d ed. 1898).

3. *But cf.* S. Rubin, Bot *Composition in Anglo–Saxon Law: A Reassessment,* 17 J.Legal History 144 (1996), who, in opposition to

There were, however, features of the emendatory system that prevailed in Anglo–Saxon England that were clearly characteristic of modern criminal law. Thus, in addition to the compensation paid by the wrongdoer to his victim or the victim's kinsmen as a composition for the injury inflicted, the wrongdoer was also obliged to pay a sum known as *"wite"* to the public authority. This sum was probably considered initially as a payment of something in the nature of costs to the public authority that maintained the court to which the matter was referred. In time, however, wite came to be considered as a penalty, and it was paid either to the crown or to someone to whom the crown had granted the right to receive wite, as, for example, a magnate who was granted by the crown the right to hold a court with cognizance of the matters in question.

In addition to this basically emendatory system, there existed in Anglo–Saxon times a residual number of acts that were considered offenses against public authority which could be punished by imposition of wite, and sometimes even corporal punishment, regardless of whether the victim sought any redress. These included offenses against the king's servants, failure to perform military service, and certain serious offenses against public order such as treason, harboring outlaws, attacking dwelling places, or assaulting someone by ambush. Given the customary feebleness of the Anglo–Saxon kings, how these legal prohibitions were enforced is another matter. This, then, was the system of tort and criminal law that existed in England in 1066 at the time of the Norman Conquest.

The Norman conquerors initially made little overt change in the system that they found functioning in England, although the emendatory system inherited from the Anglo–Saxons gradually fell into disuse and in time faded away. Instead, the Normans engrafted upon it a new remedy, that they brought with them from Normandy, called the appeal of felony.[4] It was available only when what we would consider a serious crime was committed. Under this procedure, the injured person—or, in cases involving matters like homicide or rape, a kinsman—brought what came to be considered, for jurisdictional purposes, a civil action against the alleged wrongdoer, although the appeal of felony is, for analytical purposes, more fruitfully considered a criminal and not a civil proceeding. The remedy was hedged in with many procedural requirements. For example, the appellor had to raise the hue and cry among his neighbors who would assist him in pursuing the wrongdoer until he was caught or had outdistanced his pursuers; a formal complaint had to be made, with all diligence, to some administrative official such as the bailiff of the hundred court (the local court) or, after 1194, when this office was probably established, to the Coroner. If these and other procedural steps were properly followed, the appellor (or appellant) in due course then brought his action in a court of competent jurisdiction and trial was by battle. There gradually arose ways by which the appellee (or defendant) could avoid battle and have the matter referred to a jury if he wished, but, in theory at any rate, he could always

the authorities cited in note 2, *supra*, maintains that, unlike *wergild*, *bot* did not vary according to social status other than that of membership in the clergy.

4. For a discussion of the appeal of felony and some additional citations of authority see J. Goebel Jr., Cases and Materials on the Development of Legal Institutions 67–80 (1946).

insist upon it except in a few circumstances such as where the appellant was an infant, a woman, or over 60 years of age. Although it had long since ceased to be a major heading of litigation the appeal of felony was not actually completely abolished until 1819 (59 George III, c. 46).[5] The occasion for its abolishment was an appeal of murder in which the appellee in open court pleaded: "'Not guilty; and I am ready to defend the same by my body.' And thereupon taking his glove off, he threw it upon the floor of the court."[6] Lord Chief Justice Ellenborough and his colleagues ruled that the plea was a good one; whereupon, the appellant refused to proceed further and the defendant was discharged.[7] It was in response to this farce that Parliament abolished both the appeal of felony and trial by battle which had been available not only in appeals but also in certain of the ancient "real" actions by which ownership of land could be litigated.

In 1166, the foundations of a new *criminal* procedure by way of indictment, through what in time came to be called the grand jury, were established by Henry II in the Assize (or statute) of Clarendon. Under this procedure, a jury of twelve men was to be appointed in each county to inquire whether certain crimes had been committed and to present to the itinerant royal justices the names of those suspected of having committed these crimes.[8] At about the same time, the crown started making available to litigants, in *civil* matters, new remedies pursuable before royal judges. In the beginning, these remedies concerned controversies over the use and possession of real property. Prior to this intrusion of royal justice an individual was largely forced to resort to the court of his feudal superior.[9] Except for the great magnates, or tenants in chief, who held land directly from the Crown, resort to the king was originally extremely difficult, and

5. Appeals in some matters had, over the course of time, been abolished by statute and in other situations fell into complete disuse. Appeals of murder, however, persisted probably as a means whereby the relatives of the deceased could pursue a defendant who had been acquitted in a criminal proceeding. It was also a means whereby the deceased's relatives could force a defendant to pay some compensation for causing the deceased's death. *See* 2 W. Holdsworth, A History of English Law 357–64 (1927).

6. Ashford v. Thornton, 1 B. & Ald. 405, 409, 106 Eng.Rep. 149, 150 (K.B.1818).

7. There was a procedure under which *discontinued* appeals could be prosecuted (before a jury) by the Crown. When this was attempted in *Ashford v. Thornton*, the defendant pleaded "*autrefois acquit*" and the plea was accepted as a good one. *Id.* at 460–61, 2 Eng.Rep. at 169. "*Autrefois acquit*" (previously acquitted) was one of the ways of raising at common law what we would call the defense of double jeopardy. How far the previous proceeding must progress before "jeopardy" attaches is still sometimes a disputed point. On the early history of the doctrine of double jeopardy and the relationship between criminal proceedings brought by the Crown and the appeal of a felony, see J. Hunter, *The Development of the Rule*

Against Double Jeopardy, 5 J.Leg.Hist. 1 (1984).

8. The list of crimes was gradually expanded. The trial of the accused was usually by the ordeal, the exact nature of which varied in different parts of the country. After the Fourth Lateran Council, in 1215, withdrew the sanction of the Church from the ordeal, other methods of trial were needed and the trial or petit jury evolved to meet this need. For a discussion of the beginnings and expansion of both the civil and criminal aspects of royal justice, and of the development of the jury as an institution, see 1 W. Holdsworth, A History of English Law 321–50 (7th ed. 1956); 1 F. Pollock & F. Maitland, The History of English Law 136–53 (2d ed. 1898).

9. It was the Normans, of course, who brought feudalism to England. A feudal lord, in theory, was entitled to, and indeed was supposed to, hold a court which all his immediate tenants were obliged to attend. The "court," consisting of lord and free tenants, decided controversies between the tenants or between lord and tenant and advised the lord on the various administrative problems that might arise. The Council of the King was in theory, at least originally, the feudal court of the King and his principal tenants.

then only when one was able to show some extraordinary injustice perpetrated in the feudal courts. Gradually, these new remedies, to which others were in time added, became so attractive that the feudal courts began to disappear. The fees for holding a court became so few that it was no longer worth a lord's time and expense to maintain a court. In this brief sketch of the early history of the common law,[10] we can see the origins of both our modern tort law and our modern criminal law.

From the thirteenth century onward, as royal justice expanded, as the three great common law courts[11] started to take on a distinct and separate identity, as royal justice was increasingly brought into the hinterlands through itinerant justices, sometimes called justices in eyre, the development of criminal and tort law started to diverge more clearly. It is with the development of the law of torts, of course, that we will be concerned. Before continuing this brief review of the historical origins of modern tort law, however, it will be useful to pause for a moment to consider the aims

10. "Common law" is a term of diverse meanings. Depending upon the context it can mean any or all of the following: (1) the law common to all England and not confined to a particular locality—the law enforced in royal courts; (2) a system of law that is developed case-by-case by the courts as opposed to law established by statute; (3) the law of the English speaking world whose origins are in English law as opposed to the law of the continent (or in Scotland) which developed out of Roman law or as opposed to any other system of law whose roots are not in English law. As to meaning (2), the situation is complicated by the fact that much of what we consider of judicial origin probably originated in statutes or royal decrees that are now lost.

11. These were among the institutions that were spun off or developed by the King's Council (the *curia regis*) as more and more of the crown's business was routinized and delegated or referred to committees of experts. The *Court of Exchequer*, was originally an adjunct of the Exchequer which concerned itself with matters concerning the royal revenues. The Exchequer was the first department of government to achieve separate institutional status. The Exchequer can be traced back to at least 1118 and the separate judicial character of some of its business was clearly recognized by 1234. Originally concerned with matters involving royal revenues and local officials who were required to render accounts to the Exchequer, in the course of time the Court of Exchequer emerged as a full-blown common law court. The *Court of Common Bench* (or *Common Pleas*) appears to have been established by royal decree in 1178. It appears to have been a creation of the *curia regis* and not a spinning off of some of its functions. The *Court of King's Bench*, on the other hand, is clearly of conciliar origin and did not achieve separate institutional status until 1234. The difficulty in

tracing the early history of these latter two courts is that there seem to have been periods when two courts existed at the same time with a similar jurisdiction in civil matters and others when we can find evidence of only one such court. Whether there were two courts sitting at the same time depended principally upon whether the king was of age and within the realm (i.e. not in Normandy or elsewhere abroad), in which case some judicial functionaries perambulated through the country with the Crown, while others sat elsewhere, usually in Westminster. One of the complaints of the barons to which King John, in 1215, acceded in the Magna Carta (c. 17) was that "Common pleas shall not follow our court but shall be held in some fixed place." By the middle of the thirteenth century both courts had achieved permanent and distinct institutional status. The Court of Common Pleas was supposed to be the principal forum for actions between private parties; the Court of King's Bench was the forum for criminal matters and civil matters in which the Crown had an interest. The curial origins of King's Bench was preserved in theory, and as late as the 17th century, James I claimed the right to sit in King's Bench. Over the course of time, partly through the use of legal fictions, the jurisdiction of these courts over civil matters became co-extensive except that certain matters involving real property—the so-called real actions—could only be tried in Common Pleas. These separate courts were finally abolished by the Judicature Act of 1873 and their jurisdiction transferred to a new "High Court of Justice" which for a time maintained Queen's Bench, Common Pleas, and Exchequer Divisions. In 1881, the two latter were finally merged into Queen's Bench. The old Court of Chancery, which exercised equitable jurisdiction, was also abolished as a separate court by the 1873 act and made into a division of the High Court of Justice.

of tort law and its philosophical underpinnings, if any. As we will see, these factors will not only influence our views on how the law of torts should develop in the future, but they will also influence how we will interpret the historical development of the law of torts. For, as we shall see, there is probably no branch of the law, except perhaps for the law of real property, which has been so heavily influenced by its course of historical development and none, except perhaps again for the law of real property, in which the modern law can be traced so clearly and continuously to its ancient foundations.

2. *The Aims of the Law of Torts*

It is customary to supply at least four goals for the law of torts. These may be identified as (1) prevention of self-help by victims and their relatives and friends against those who have caused injury, (2) retribution against wrongdoers, (3) deterrence of wrongdoers, and (4) compensation for the victims of wrongdoers. Except for goal number 4, compensation, these are pretty much the same social goals that are given for the criminal law. It has become increasingly common in recent years, however, to focus on compensation as the principle justification of the tort system. Indeed, in 1951, Professor Glanville Williams argued that compensation of victims should be the principal aim of the law of torts.[12] Insofar as the possibility of providing payment of compensation to victims is not a sufficient deterrent, he maintained that the function of deterrence should be relegated to the criminal law. As for the functions of appeasing victims and giving vent to the retributive feelings of society, Professor Williams questioned the ethical propriety of fulfilling these supposed needs. One gathers that he felt that people would be better off if they outgrew the need for such emotional release.

Two comments may be made with regard to this line of argument. First, if compensation is to be the principal justification for retaining the tort system, there is no question that, as Professor Williams recognized, there are far cheaper and more efficient means for compensating injured people than an action in tort with its emphasis on fault and causation and all the panoply of legal machinery necessary for the resolution of such

---

12. G. Williams, *The Aims of the Law of Tort*, 4 Current Legal Problems 137 (1951). We will return to the question of the "aims" of the law of tort in Chapter Three, devoted to the subject of negligence, and again in Chapter Fourteen, when we consider some of the alternatives to the tort system provided by statutorily created compensation schemes such as workmen's compensation and no-fault automobile accident compensation schemes. In these later portions of the casebook we will consider some of the attempts to apply modern economic analysis to the goals and functions of tort liability. Indeed, in recent years, there has been some controversy as to whether the promotion of economic efficiency is itself also a (subsidiary) goal of the law of torts. We shall refer to some of this literature in the course of our later discussion. For the moment however, it will not be necessary for us to explore, in this preliminary portion of the casebook, that additional and complicating factor. On the more general question of the values that the modern tort system is thought to further, the following citations may be helpful when the student has progressed far enough in his studies to attempt to get some theoretical overview of the subject. *See* A. Ehrenzweig, *Negligence Without Fault*, 54 Calif.L.Rev. 1422–77 (1966); J. Fleming, *Is There a Future for Tort?* 44 La.L.Rev. 1193 (1984); G. Fletcher, *Fairness and Utility in Tort Theory*, 85 Harv.L.Rev. 537–73 (1972); G. Fridman, *Punitive Damages in Tort*, 48 Canadian Bar Rev. 373–409 (1970); L. Green, *Tort Law—Public Law in Disguise*, 38 Texas L.Rev. 1–13, 257–69 (1959–60); T. Hadden, *Contract, Tort, and Crime: The Forms of Legal Thought*, 87 Law Q.Rev. 240–60 (1971).

questions. And it is no mere coincidence that those writers who have focused on the need to give compensation to the victims of automobile accidents or to consumers injured by manufactured products have usually argued in favor of some sort of insurance scheme. Indeed, if compensation is the paramount consideration, a general system of social insurance to cover almost all the injuries for which redress is now sought in the tort system is the most logical answer. In point of fact, during the discussion that preceded and accompanied the establishment of the National Health Service and other social welfare schemes by the Post World War II Labour Government of Great Britain, serious consideration was given to some very significant curtailment of the present tort system.[13]

There is a second type of response that can also be made with regard to Professor Williams' thesis that compensation should be the principal focus of tort law and that, except for deterrence which should be left to the criminal law, people should outgrow their need for appeasement and the infliction of retributory punishment. Many people would contend that the history of the last forty years has actually increased the importance of the retributive and appeasing functions of the tort law. In a society that has become not only more complex but is characterized by the individual's confrontation with institutions like government, industrial corporations, unions, and even universities that seem to grow continually larger in response to the demands of modern society, the individual now more than ever needs some means of reasserting his sense of human dignity when he has been humiliated or otherwise wronged by these institutions. Thus, it could be argued, there is an ever-increasing need to allow the individual to recover punitive damages, for example, against government officials who may harass him or otherwise infringe his civil rights. Punitive damages, as we shall see, are awarded, in the discretion of the jury, as assuagement to the plaintiff in order to punish the defendant and bear no necessary relationship to the actual damage caused by the defendant. Those who are uncomfortable with the notion of punitive damages can nevertheless still provide the plaintiff with similar amounts of additional compensation, as we shall also eventually see,[14] by including within the ambit of damages the humiliation and mortification experienced by the victims of such conduct, and by such other devices as "presumed" damages.

3. The Theoretical Structure of Tort Law and Its Capacity to Expand to Cover New Situations

How well the tort system can respond to the demands made upon it to adjust to the needs of modern life will depend to some extent on its theoretical foundations. For example, is there one unitary or "general" theory underlying the entire field of torts such as that "there is no wrong without a remedy," or that "whoever is injured as a result of the fault of another should receive redress," or that "whoever is injured by the

---

13. For a brief description of this discussion and some citation to original sources, *see* W. Friedmann, *Social Insurance and the Principles of Tort Liability*, 63 Harv.L.Rev. 241, 252–58 (1949). The most drastic restriction in the scope of common-law tort remedies, and their replacement by a social insurance scheme, has occurred in New Zealand, culminating with the New Zealand Accident Compensation Act of 1974. The New Zealand act will be discussed at p. 948, *infra*.

14. *See* pp. 1158–59, *infra*.

intentional activities of another should receive redress," etc.? Or, is modern tort law, as the "particular" theory asserts, merely a composite of a set of discrete torts that have evolved over time and which cannot be fully understood or expanded to cover new situations without reference to their particular historical evolution? The controversy over whether there is a law of tort or only a law of torts raged with particular intensity during the first few decades of the twentieth century, although it had been raised as early as 1887 by Sir Frederick Pollock who argued for the "general" theory.[15] Pollock was joined by a number of great legal scholars including A. V. Dicey and P. H. Winfield in England and James Barr Ames in the United States.[16] On the other hand, the "particular" theory was championed by an equally impressive list of scholars, including Sir John Salmond and Arthur Goodhart.[17]

Most contemporary scholars would probably conclude that the particular theory is, from the historical point of view, the correct one.[18] To the extent that the courts are prepared to adopt this view, an advocate who is confronted with a novel situation which he wishes to make the basis for an action for damages will have to try and show a close analogy between his new factual situation and the factual situations dealt with by some one or more traditional torts. For example, in their germinal article on privacy,[19] which was published in 1890, Samuel Warren and Louis Brandeis showed that redress for invasion of privacy could and should be given—and indeed had been given—by the logical extension of existing tort remedies. However, after the acceptance of Warren and Brandeis' thesis that there should nevertheless be even greater legal protection for privacy than that which might be afforded as a logical extension of traditional remedies, a separate tort, invasion of privacy, appeared which took on a life of its own.

If a court is prepared to accept the general theory, it should, from the point of view of logic, be easier to argue for the extension of tort remedies to cover new situations. At the same time, as we have already suggested in the course of speculating as to what this general theory might be, actually stating the general theory in any reasonably concrete form is a difficult if not impossible matter. Furthermore, using the so-called "general" theory to further the expansion of the law of torts to cover new situations can run afoul of the accepted theory of legislative supremacy, namely that the legislatures, not the courts, are to make the basic policy decisions. There will, of course, always be tensions between the so-called legislative and the so-called judicial role. Some of it is inevitable because, in adjudicating, courts inevitably legislate. It is all a question of more or less and, even if there were some broad consensus as to when "judicial legislation" was appropriate and when it was not, it would be hard to state in advance how

15. The Law of Torts, *1–26 (1st ed. 1887).

16. A. Dicey, Note, 18 Law Q.Rev. 1, 4–5 (1902); P. Winfield, *The Foundation of Liability in Tort*, 27 Colum.L.Rev. 1 (1927); F. Ames, *Tort Because of a Wrongful Motive*, 18 Harv.L.Rev. 411 (1905). *See also* J. Smith, *Torts Without Particular Names*, 69 U.Pa. L.Rev. 91 (1921).

17. J. Salmond, Torts 7–13 (2d ed. 1910); A. Goodhart, *The Foundations of Tortious Liability*, 2 Mod.L.Rev. 1 (1938).

18. For a good discussion and evaluation of the respective positions in this controversy, *see* G. Williams, *The Foundations of Tortious Liability*, 1939 Camb.L.J. 111.

19. S. Warren & L. Brandeis, *The Right to Privacy*, 4 Harv.L.Rev. 193 (1890).

this consensus should operate in any particular case. The problem can sometimes become particularly acute in the field of torts because experience has shown that torts is, in a real sense, the grab bag of the law. Whenever a new problem arises as to which it is felt legal redress is required but there is no remedy clearly evident under some other division of the law, such as contracts or real property, almost inevitably those seeking redress will turn to the law of torts, and the question of the underlying theory and aims of the law of torts will be raised anew. To illustrate these methodological points it may be instructive to turn to a famous case in which the resolution of these issues proved to be important. (For a recent case in which a court refused to recognize the tort of "intentional interference with parental custodial rights," *see* Larson v. Dunn, 460 N.W.2d 39 (Minn.1990); and for a recent exhaustive review of cases which considered the question of whether the law of torts should expand to cover new areas, *see* R. Blomquist, *"New Torts": A Critical History, Taxonomy, and Appraisal*, 95 Dick. L. Rev. 23 (1990)).

ROBERSON v. ROCHESTER FOLDING BOX CO.

Court of Appeals of New York, 1902.
171 N.Y. 538, 64 N.E. 442.

* * * From a judgment of the appellate division (71 N.Y.Supp. 876) affirming a judgment in favor of plaintiff overruling a demurrer to the complaint, defendants appeal. Reversed.

* * *

PARKER, C. J. The appellate division has certified that the following questions of law have arisen in this case, and ought to be reviewed by this court: (1) Does the complaint herein state a cause of action at law against the defendants, or either of them? (2) Does the complaint herein state a cause of action in equity against the defendants, or either of them? These questions are presented by a demurrer to the complaint, which is put upon the ground that the complaint does not state facts sufficient to constitute a cause of action.

* * * The complaint alleges that the Franklin Mills Company, one of the defendants, was engaged in a general milling business and in the manufacture and sale of flour; that before the commencement of the action, without the knowledge or consent of plaintiff, defendants, knowing that they had no right or authority so to do, had obtained, made, printed, sold, and circulated about 25,000 lithographic prints, photographs, and likenesses of plaintiff, made in a manner particularly set up in the complaint; that upon the paper upon which the likenesses were printed and above the portrait there were printed, in large, plain letters, the words, "Flour of the Family," and below the portrait, in large capital letters, "Franklin Mills Flour," and in the lower right-hand corner, in smaller capital letters, "Rochester Folding Box Co., Rochester, N.Y."; that upon the same sheet were other advertisements of the flour of the Franklin Mills Company; that those 25,000 likenesses of the plaintiff thus ornamented have been conspicuously posted and displayed in stores, warehouses, saloons, and other public places; that they have been recognized by friends of

the plaintiff and other people, with the result that plaintiff has been greatly humiliated by the scoffs and jeers of persons who have recognized her face and picture on this advertisement, and her good name has been attacked, causing her great distress and suffering, both in body and mind; that she was made sick, and suffered a severe nervous shock, was confined to her bed, and compelled to employ a physician, because of these facts; that defendants had continued to print, make, use, sell, and circulate the said lithographs, and that by reason of the foregoing facts plaintiff had suffered damages in the sum of $15,000. The complaint prays that defendants be enjoined from making, printing, publishing, circulating, or using in any manner any likenesses of plaintiff in any form whatever; for further relief (which it is not necessary to consider here); and for damages.

It will be observed that there is no complaint made that plaintiff was libeled by this publication of her portrait. The likeness is said to be a very good one, and one that her friends and acquaintances were able to recognize. Indeed, her grievance is that a good portrait of her, and therefore one easily recognized, has been used to attract attention toward the paper upon which defendant mill company's advertisements appear. Such publicity, which some find agreeable, is to plaintiff very distasteful, and thus, because of defendants' impertinence in using her picture, without her consent, for their own business purposes, she has been caused to suffer mental distress where others would have appreciated the compliment to their beauty implied in the selection of the picture for such purposes; but, as it is distasteful to her, she seeks the aid of the courts to enjoin a further circulation of the lithographic prints containing her portrait made as alleged in the complaint, and, as an incident thereto, to reimburse her for the damages to her feelings, which the complaint fixes at the sum of $15,000. There is no precedent for such an action to be found in the decisions of this court. Indeed, the learned judge who wrote the very able and interesting opinion in the appellate division said, while upon the threshold of the discussion of the question: "It may be said, in the first place, that the theory upon which this action is predicated is new, at least in instance, if not in principle, and that few precedents can be found to sustain the claim made by the plaintiff, if, indeed, it can be said that there are any authoritative cases establishing her right to recover in this action." Nevertheless that court reached the conclusion that plaintiff had a good cause of action against defendants, in that defendants had invaded what is called a "right of privacy"; in other words, the right to be let alone. Mention of such a right is not to be found in Blackstone, Kent, or any other of the great commentators upon the law; nor, so far as the learning of counsel or the courts in this case have been able to discover, does its existence seem to have been asserted prior to about the year 1890, when it was presented with attractiveness, and no inconsiderable ability, in the Harvard Law Review (volume 4, p. 193) in an article entitled "Rights of a Citizen to His Reputation." The so-called "right of privacy" is, as the phrase suggests, founded upon the claim that a man has the right to pass through this world, if he wills, without having his picture published, his business enterprises discussed, his successful experiments written up for the benefit of others, or his eccentricities commented upon either in handbills, circulars, catalogues, periodicals, or newspapers; and, necessarily, that the things which may not be written and published of him must not be spoken of him by his neighbors, whether the comment be favorable or otherwise. While most persons would much prefer to have a good likeness of themselves appear in a responsible periodical or leading newspaper rather than upon an advertising card or sheet, the doctrine which the courts are asked to create for this case would apply as well to the one publication as to the other, for the principle which a court of equity is asked to assert in support of a recovery in this action is that the right of privacy exists and is enforceable in equity, and that the publication of that which purports to be a portrait of another person, even if obtained upon the street by an impertinent individual with a camera, will be restrained in equity on the ground that an individual has the right to prevent his features from becoming known to those outside of his circle of friends and acquaintances. If such a principle be incorporated into the body of the law through the instrumentality of a court of equity, the attempts to logically apply the principle will necessarily result not only in a vast amount of litigation, but in litigation bordering upon the absurd, for the right of privacy, once established as a legal doctrine, cannot be confined to the restraint of the publication of a likeness, but must necessarily embrace as well the publication of a word picture, a comment upon one's looks, conduct, domestic relations or habits. And, were the right of privacy once legally asserted, it would necessarily be held to include the same things if spoken instead of printed, for one, as well as the other, invades the right to be absolutely let alone. An insult would certainly be in violation of such a right, and with many persons would more seriously wound the feelings than would the publication of their picture. And so we might add to the list of things that are spoken and done day by day which seriously offend the sensibilities of good people to which the principle which the plaintiff seeks to have imbedded in the doctrine of the law would seem to apply. I have gone only far enough to barely suggest the vast field of litigation which would necessarily be opened up should this court hold that privacy exists as a legal right enforceable in equity by injunction, and by damages where they seem necessary to give complete relief.

The legislative body could very well interfere and arbitrarily provide that no one should be permitted for his own selfish purpose to use the picture or the name of another for advertising purposes without his consent. In such event no embarrassment would result to the general body of the law, for the rule would be applicable only to cases provided for by the statute. The courts, however, being without authority to legislate, are required to decide cases upon principle, and so are necessarily embarrassed by precedents created by an extreme, and therefore unjustifiable, application of an old principle. The court below properly said that: "While it may be true that the fact that no precedent can be found to sustain an action in any given case is cogent evidence that a principle does not exist upon which the right may be based, it is not the rule that the want of a precedent is a sufficient reason for turning the plaintiff out of court," provided (I think should be added) there can be found a clear and unequivocal principle of the common law, which either directly or mediately governs it, or which, by analogy or parity of reasoning, ought to govern it. It is undoubtedly true that in the early days of chancery jurisdiction in England the chancellors were accustomed to deliver their judgments without regard to principles or precedents, and in that way the process of building up the system of equity went on, the chancellor disregarding absolutely many established principles of the common law. * * * In their work the chancellors were guided not only by what they regarded as the eternal principles of absolute right, but also by their individual consciences; but after a time, when "the period of infancy was passed, and an orderly system of equitable principles, doctrines, and rules began to be developed out of the increasing mass of precedents, this theory of a personal conscience was abandoned; and 'the conscience,' which is an element of the equitable jurisdiction, came to be regarded, and has so continued to the present day, as a metaphorical term, designating the common standard of civil right and expediency combined, based upon general principles, and limited by established doctrines to which the court appeals, and by which it tests the conduct and rights of suitors,—a juridical, and not a personal, conscience." Pom.Eq.Jur. § 57.

The importance of observing the spirit of this rule cannot be overestimated; for, while justice in a given case may be worked out by a decision of the court according to the notions of right which govern the individual judge or body of judges comprising the court, the mischief which will finally result may be almost incalculable under our system, which makes a decision in one case a precedent for decisions in all future cases which are akin to it in the essential facts. So, in a case like the one before us, which is concededly new to this court, it is important that the court should have in mind the effect upon future litigation and upon the development of the law which would necessarily result from a step so far outside of the beaten paths of both common law and equity, assuming—what I shall attempt to show in a moment—that the right of privacy, as a legal doctrine enforceable in equity, has not, down to this time, been established by decisions. The history of the phrase "right of privacy" in this country seems to have begun in 1890, in a clever article in the Harvard Law Review,—already referred to,—in which a number of English cases were analyzed, and, reasoning by analogy, the conclusion was reached that, notwithstanding the unanimity of the courts in resting their decisions upon property rights in cases where publication is prevented by injunction, in reality such prevention was due to the necessity of affording protection to thoughts and sentiments expressed through the medium of writing, printing, and the arts, which is like the right not to be assaulted or beaten; in other words, that the principle actually involved, though not always appreciated, was that of an inviolate personality, not that of private property. This article brought forth a reply from the Northwestern Review (volume 3, p. 1) urging that equity has no concern with the feelings of an individual, or with considerations of moral fitness, except as the inconvenience or discomfort which the person may suffer is connected with the possession or enjoyment of property, and that the English authorities cited are consistent with such view. Those authorities are now to be examined, in order that we may see whether they were intended to and did mark a departure from the established rule which had been enforced for generations; or, on the other hand, are entirely consistent with it.

The first case is Prince Albert v. Strange, 1 Macn. & G. 25; Id., 2 De Gex & S. 652. The queen and the prince, having made etchings and drawings for their own amusement, decided to have copies struck off from the etched plates for presentation to friends and for their own use. The workman employed, however, printed some copies on his own account, which afterwards came into the hands of Strange, who purposed exhibiting them, and published a descriptive catalogue. Prince Albert applied for an injunction as to both exhibition and catalogue, and the vice chancellor granted it, restraining defendant from publishing, "at least by printing or writing, though not by copy or resemblance," a description of the etchings. An examination of the opinion of the vice chancellor discloses that he found two reasons for granting the injunction, namely, that the property rights of Prince Albert had been infringed, and that there was a breach of trust by the workman in retaining some impressions for himself. The opinion contained no hint whatever of a right of privacy separate and distinct from the right of property.

Pollard v. Photographic Co., 40 Ch.Div. 345, is certainly not an authority for granting an injunction on the ground of threatened injury to the feelings, although it is true, as stated in the opinion of the appellate division, that the court did say in the course of the discussion that the right to grant an injunction does not depend upon the existence of property; but the decision was, in fact, placed upon the ground that there was a breach of an implied contract. The facts, briefly stated, were that a photographer had been applied to by a woman to take her photograph, she ordering a certain number of copies, as is usual in such cases. The photographer made copies for himself, and undertook to exhibit them, and also sold copies to a stationer, who used them as Christmas cards. Their action was restrained by the court on the ground that there was an implied contract not to use the negative for any other purpose than to supply the sitter with copies of it for a price. During the argument of plaintiff's counsel the court asked this question: "Do you dispute that, if the negative likeness were taken on the sly, the person who took it might exhibit copies?" Counsel replied, "In that case there would be no consideration to support a contract."

* * *

In Duke of Queensbury v. Shebbeare, 2 Eden, 329, the Earl of Clarendon delivered to one Gwynne an original manuscript of his father's "Lord Clarendon's History." Gwynne's administrator afterwards sold it to Shebbeare, and the court, upon the application of the personal representatives of Lord Clarendon, restrained its publication on the ground that they had a property right in the manuscript which it was not intended that Gwynne should have the benefit of by multiplying the number of copies in print for profit.

In not one of these cases, therefore, was it the basis of the decision that the defendant could be restrained from performing the act he was doing or threatening to do on the ground that the feelings of the plaintiff would be thereby injured; but, on the contrary, each decision was rested either upon the ground of breach of trust, or that plaintiff had a property right in the subject of litigation which the court could protect.

* * *

The case that seems to have been more relied upon than any other by the learned appellate division in reaching the conclusion that the complaint in this case states a cause of action is Schuyler v. Curtis, 147 N.Y. 434, 42 N.E. 22. * * * In that case certain persons attempted to erect a statue or bust of a woman no longer living, and one of her relatives commenced an action in equity to restrain such erection, alleging that his feelings and the feelings of other relatives of deceased would be injured thereby. At special term an injunction was granted on that ground. 19 N.Y.Supp. 264. The general term affirmed the decision. 64 Hun, 594. This court reversed the judgment, Judge Peckham writing, and, so far as the decision is concerned, therefore, it is not authority for the existence of a right of privacy which entitles a party to restrain another from doing an act which, though not actionable at common law, occasions plaintiff mental distress. In the course of the argument, however, expressions were used which it is now claimed indicate that the court recognized the existence of such a right. A sufficient answer to that contention is to be found in the opinion written on the motion for reargument in Colonial City Traction Co. v. Kingston City R. Co., 154 N.Y. 493, 48 N.E. 900, in which it was said: "It was not our intention to decide any case but the one before us. * * * If, as sometimes happens, broader statements were made by way of argument or otherwise than were essential to the decision of the questions presented, they are the dicta of the writer of the opinion, and not the decision of the court. A judicial opinion, like evidence, is only binding so far as it is relevant; and when it wanders from the point at issue it no longer has force as an official utterance." The question up for decision in the Schuyler Case was whether the relatives could restrain the threatened action of defendants, and not whether Mrs. Schuyler could have restrained it had she been living. The latter question not being before the court, it was not called upon to decide it, and, as we read the opinion, there is no expression in it which indicates an intention either to decide it or to seriously consider it; but, rather, it proceeds upon the assumption that, if such a right did exist in Mrs. Schuyler, her relatives did not succeed to it upon her death. * * *

* * *

An examination of the authorities leads us to the conclusion that the so-called "right of privacy" has not as yet found an abiding place in our jurisprudence, and, as we view it, the doctrine cannot now be incorporated without doing violence to settled principles of law by which the profession and the public have long been guided.

* * *

The judgment of the appellate division and of the special term should be reversed and [the] questions certified answered in the negative. * * *

GRAY, J. (dissenting).

* * *

* * * As I have suggested, that the exercise of this peculiar preventive power of a court of equity is not found in some precisely analogous case, furnishes no valid objection at all to the assumption of jurisdiction if the particular circumstances of the case show the performance, or the threat-

ened performance, of an act by a defendant, which is wrongful, because constituting an invasion, in some novel form, of a right to something which is, or should be conceded to be, the plaintiff's, and as to which the law provides no adequate remedy. It would be a justifiable exercise of power whether the principle of interference be rested upon analogy to some established common-law principle, or whether it is one of natural justice. In an article in the Harvard Law Review of December 15, 1890, which contains an impressive argument upon the subject of the "right of privacy," it was well said by the authors: "That the individual shall have full protection in person and in property is a principle as old as the common law; but it has been found necessary from time to time to define anew the exact nature and extent of such protection. * * * The right to life has come to mean the right to enjoy life,—the right to be let alone; the right to liberty secures the exercise of extensive civil privileges; and the term 'property' has grown to comprise every form of possession, intangible as well as tangible." * * * The proposition is, to me, an inconceivable one that these defendants may, unauthorizedly, use the likeness of this young woman upon their advertisement as a method of attracting widespread public attention to their wares, and that she must submit to the mortifying notoriety, without right to invoke the exercise of the preventive power of a court of equity.

Such a view, as it seems to me, must have been unduly influenced by a failure to find precedents in analogous cases, or some declaration by the great commentators upon the law of a common-law principle which would precisely apply to and govern the action, without taking into consideration that in the existing state of society new conditions affecting the relations of persons demand the broader extension of those legal principles which underlie the immunity of one's person from attack. I think that such a view is unduly restricted, too, by a search for some property which has been invaded by the defendants' acts. Property is not, necessarily, the thing itself which is owned; it is the right of the owner in relation to it. The right to be protected in one's possession of a thing or in one's privileges, belonging to him as an individual, or secured to him as a member of the commonwealth, is property, and as such entitled to the protection of the law. The protective power of equity is not exercised upon the tangible thing, but upon the right to enjoy it; and so it is called forth for the protection of the right to that which is one's exclusive possession as a property right. It seems to me that the principle which is applicable is analogous to that upon which courts of equity have interfered to protect the right of privacy in cases of private writings, or of other unpublished products of the mind. The writer or the lecturer has been protected in his right to a literary property in a letter or a lecture, against its unauthorized publication, because it is property to which the right of privacy attaches. * * * I think that this plaintiff has the same property in the right to be protected against the use of her face for defendant's commercial purposes as she would have if they were publishing her literary compositions. The right would be conceded if she had sat for her photograph; but if her face or her portraiture has a value, the value is hers exclusively, until the use be granted away to the public. Any other principle of decision, in my opinion, is as repugnant to equity as it is shocking to reason.

* * *

The right to grant the injunction does not depend upon the existence of property which one has in some contractual form. It depends upon the existence of property in any right which belongs to a person * * * . It would be, in my opinion, an extraordinary view, which, while conceding the right of a person to be protected against the unauthorized circulation of an unpublished lecture, letter, drawing, or other ideal property, yet would deny the same protection to a person whose portrait was unauthorizedly obtained and made use of for commercial purposes. The injury to the plaintiff is irreparable, because she cannot be wholly compensated in damages for the various consequences entailed by defendants' acts. The only complete relief is an injunction restraining their continuance. Whether, as incidental to that equitable relief, she should be able to recover only nominal damages, is not material, for the issuance of the injunction does not, in such a case, depend upon the amount of the damages in dollars and cents.

* * *

O'BRIEN, CULLEN, and WERNER, JJ., concur with PARKER, C. J. BARTLETT and HAIGHT, JJ., concur with GRAY, J.

Judgment reversed, etc.

Notes

1. The question of privacy has now become a major issue in the law. We shall return to the matter in Chapter Nineteen, *infra*. The particular issue involved in the *Roberson* case was, in 1903, resolved by the New York legislature in favor of granting a cause of action to similarly situated plaintiffs. As we shall see in greater detail in Chapter Nineteen, § 51 of the New York Civil Rights Law, as amended, provides that any person "whose name, portrait or picture is used * * * for advertising purposes or for the purposes of trade without * * * written consent * * * may maintain an equitable action[20] * * * to prevent and restrain the use thereof; and may also sue and recover damages for any injuries sustained by reason of such use." The statute provides for the imposition of "exemplary" (or punitive) damages, in the discretion of the jury, if the defendant shall have acted knowingly. A companion statute, § 50 of the Civil Rights Law, makes it a misdemeanor for defendant to engage in such conduct. Many states, as we shall also see in Chapter Nineteen, have recognized a right of privacy as a matter of common law. A leading case is Pavesich v. New England Life Insurance Co., 122 Ga. 190, 50 S.E. 68 (1905). Although most commentators have applauded the development of a right of privacy, it is now recognized, as we shall again see in Chapter Nineteen, that the enforcement of a right of privacy can infringe upon the interests in free speech protected by the First and Fourteenth Amendments of the United States

---

20. In accordance with the normal terminology one usually speaks of a "suit in equity" and an "action" (for damages) "at law." With the modern merger of law and equity the distinction is less important and it is often ignored in practice. Many scholars and judges, however, still insist on preserving the older terminological distinction and the student may find it desirable, in order to avoid confusion, to follow their example.

Constitution. In England, the right of privacy still receives little protection in situations that cannot easily be subsumed under some of the property and contractual theories discussed in the *Roberson* case. The issue has been a matter that has been intensely studied and debated and various suggestions for legislation have been put forward. One important study was that conducted by the Younger Committee, on which *see* G. Dworkin, *The Younger Committee Report on Privacy*, 36 Mod.L.Rev. 399 (1973). Thus far, however, Parliament has not acted. *See also* W. Pratt, Privacy in Britain (1979).

2. Suppose the Court had decided that Ms. Roberson had a cause of action against the defendants for invasion of her privacy. You will recall that, in addition to asking for an injunction, she also asked for $15,000 in damages most of which was claimed to be compensation for the mental distress and humiliation that she suffered. How did she and her lawyers arrive at that figure? How would a jury determine the amount of damages to which she was entitled? The question of determining the proper award of damages for intangible injuries is a difficult one that will be addressed in Chapter 10 *infra* at p. 763ff. Should there be some relationship between the amount of damages awarded for injury to intangible interests and the amounts awarded for tangible injury? Consider Seffert v. Los Angeles Transit Lines, 56 Cal.2d 498, 15 Cal.Rptr. 161, 364 P.2d 337 (1961). In that case the majority affirmed a judgment, entered on a jury verdict, of $187,903.75 in favor of an injured woman who, at the time of trial, had an anticipated life expectancy of almost 35 years. From the material preserved in the trial record, the appellate court broke down the award as follows: approximately $54,000 represented pecuniary loss in the form of past and future medical expenses and loss of earnings from the time of the accident to the time of trial and possible loss of future earnings; the remaining $134,000 was presumed to be for pain and suffering. At the time, the total judgment was considered unusually large and the defendants, on appeal, claimed that the damages were excessive. In a 4–3 decision, a majority of the Supreme Court of California found no basis upon which to disturb the judgment. Writing for the three dissenters, Justice Traynor noted that the plaintiff had returned to her $375 a month job as a file clerk. Judge Traynor felt that the award was out of line with previous awards for pain and suffering. The majority stressed that the jury was entitled to rely on the evidence that the plaintiff had had to have nine operations, many of them painful, and that she might need to have future operations, as well as the plaintiff's testimony that, although she had gone back to work, she experienced difficulty in standing, walking, or even sitting. As the tort course proceeds and you see more cases in which these issues arise, consider how you would solve these questions as to the proper amount of money that should be awarded for so-called intangible injury, such as, for example, pain and suffering or humiliation.

3. The study of law is preeminently the study of argumentation.[21] One of the chief purposes of law school education is to teach the student how to make an effective argument to a court or other legally trained

---

21. The term "rhetoric," and its derivatives, have unfortunately and undeservedly gained a poor reputation among a large number of people. For this reason it is fashiona-ble to use the less emotionally-ridden term "argumentation" and its derivatives. There is no gainsaying the matter, however; law is a rhetorical discipline.

decision-makers. The appropriateness of any argument depends, of course, in part on the subject matter involved, but the nature of the audience is even more important. An experienced advocate knows that some types of argument appeal to some judges more than they do to others. Depending upon the composition of the court before which he is appearing, he will gauge his argument accordingly.[22] Some particular types of argument, however, are recurrent in legal argumentation. The *Roberson* case has been presented in some detail because it is a rich store of the types of argument that can be presented, on both sides of the issue, when a new type of case is presented to a court.

The nature of informal argumentation is, of course, not only of interest to those who plead in courts of law. It has been a matter of general philosophical interest since at least the time of the ancient Greeks. A complete bibliography would fill many volumes. For those who may wish to explore these questions further, an introduction to the subject and citation to further sources may be obtained in G. Christie, Jurisprudence: Text and Readings on the Philosophy of Law 833–1050 (1973). Throughout the remainder of this book, in editing the cases presented in the text, an attempt will be made to preserve as much as possible of the rhetorical flavor of the court's opinion.

4. The Historical Development of the Modern Law of Torts— Development of the Concept of "Fault"

Most of modern tort law has evolved from two ancient forms of action, trespass and trespass on the case. We have already noted that the reign of Henry II (1154–89) was an important one in the history of the law. As we have seen, the roots of our criminal law and criminal procedure can, for example, be traced back to the Assize of Clarendon in 1166 which established the precursor of the criminal indictment procedure. That same year probably also witnessed the origin of an important new civil remedy, the assize of novel disseisin,[23] a device by which the right to possession of real

22. Whether the arguments presented to courts and then presented by them to justify their decisions are mere rationalizations of decisions previously reached on other grounds or actually a part of the court's decision-making processes, is a question that can never be resolved. Suffice it to say, in the present context, that the tradition of writing judicial decisions which are made available to the public and the need for public acceptance of these decisions require the courts to produce publicly acceptable reasons for their decisions. These factors guarantee that courts must try to produce arguments to support their decisions that the public will accept as plausibly supporting these decisions. Without such support, judicial decisions become judicial fiats and the courts lose their status as legitimate organs of state.

23. "Assize" in this context means, as will be stated shortly in the text, an action pursuant to an "original" writ which was issued out of the royal chancery. The writs were called "original" to distinguish them from the "judicial writs" issued by the courts. Sometimes "assize" is used to refer to the original writ itself. In the assize of novel disseisin the sheriff was ordered, provided the plaintiff furnished proper security, to restore the plaintiff to possession of the land (from which plaintiff claimed to be recently disseised or dispossessed) while a jury of recognitors was impanelled to inquire and report to the royal justices as to whether the plaintiff had, in fact, been recently disseised by the defendant. The possessory assizes were heard by judges or commissioners acting under a commission of assize and their sittings were themselves called assizes. In modern English usage the term "assize" refers to the court (or the time when this court sits or the place where it sits) held by High Court judges on circuit to try criminal cases sent down from the courts at Westminster for a trial before local juries. As we have seen previously "assize" can also mean a statute or ordinance. The word assize comes from the Latin "*assisa*" which originally meant

property could be tried before a royal court and disputed matters of fact would be decided by a jury drawn from the vicinage rather than by wager of law[24] or trial by battle. In the succeeding years a number of other new royal remedies were made available to litigants. Not surprisingly, given the economic and social structure of the times, the very earliest of these remedies all related to disputes over the possession of real property.[25] It was characteristic of these new remedies that their use involved purchase of what was known as an "original" writ from the Royal Chancery.[26] In this regard, it must never be forgotten that, in a feudal society, maintenance of a court and of a system of justice were partially money-making schemes.

In the latter part of the 13th century, a new form of writ came to be discerned, the writ of trespass. Despite an impressive amount of scholarship devoted to the study of its first appearance and its early development, the origins of the writ of trespass are still in dispute. For a substantial period, most scholars thought that trespass had developed out of the older appeals of felony,[27] a conclusion supported by the fact that, until the 17th century, a defendant against whom judgment had been rendered in trespass was subject to paying a fine to the crown, as well. This factor was thought to emphasize the quasi-criminal character of trespass and to make more plausible the theory that trespass arose out of the appeal of felony. The weight of modern scholarship, however, has come to reject the view that trespass arose out of the appeal of felony.[28]

Another theory, urged by some scholars, was that trespass arose out of the assize of novel disseisin and that the purpose of the new action was to provide monetary damages as an ancillary remedy for wrongful deprivation of possession.[29] (The purpose of the assize of novel disseisin, as noted above, was to enable the plaintiff to obtain an order directing the sheriff to restore him to possession of real property). In support of this theory it is noted that the earliest actions for trespass seemed to have concerned instances where damages were sought for unlawful entry into land (tres-

the sitting of a court or other assembly, and then by extension came to refer to the things done at this court or assembly.

24. This was a procedure available in an action for debt whereby the defendant would swear that he did not owe the debt and would bring with him eleven "compurgators" who would swear that they believed that the defendant was telling the truth.

25. *See* 1 F. Pollock & F. Maitland, The History of English Law 144–51 (2d ed. 1898). The very earliest of these assizes was probably the assize *utrum* which strictly speaking involved more than mere possession. It was used to inquire whether (*utrum*) the land in question was held in lay or in ecclesiastical tenure, the determination of which issue dictated whether disputes over the land were cognizable in lay or ecclesiastical courts.

26. *See* note 23, *supra.* In time procedural devices were invented whereby an action was commenced by judicial writ and the origi-

nal writ was obtained subsequently. Eventually the need for an original writ was totally dispensed with.

27. The principal proponent of the traditional or orthodox view was probably Frederic William Maitland. *See* The Forms of Action at Common Law (1936). Among the others who espoused this view were William Holdsworth, in England, and James Barr Ames and Oliver Wendell Holmes, Jr., in the United States. For a list of citations to writers on all sides of this controversy *see* C. Fifoot, History and Sources of the Common Law 44–56 (1949).

28. *See* G. Woodbine, *The Origins of the Action of Trespass*, (Pt. I), 33 Yale L.J. 799 (1924), (Pt. II), 34 Yale L.J. 343 (1925). See particularly Pt. I at 800–07; Pt. II at 360–64. *See also* C. Fifoot, *supra* note 27, at 44–56.

29. This was the position taken by Woodbine, in the articles cited in the preceding note.

pass *quare clausum fregit*, or, more popularly, trespass q.c.f.) or for the carrying away of chattels from land (trespass *de bonis asportatum*, or trespass d.b.a.). It is argued that this evidence shows that trespass was originally developed as an adjunct of the assize of novel disseisin. Others have argued, however, that the fact that money damages might sometimes have been a more appropriate remedy does not show that trespass arose out of novel disseisin. It only shows that trespass may have arisen to meet the inadequacies of this and other remedies. A third theory, which has distinguished modern support, is that trespass developed out of the *querela* (or informal complaints) handed to royal justices, often by poor people. The writ of trespass, it is urged, was the formalization of this procedure.[30]

However it may have arisen, the action of trespass came to be considered the appropriate remedy when the plaintiff alleged that he had been injured as the *immediate* result of some conduct on the part of the defendant. Where the plaintiff's injury was merely a *consequential* effect of the defendant's activities, trespass on the case, whose origins we shall soon also consider, was said to lie. A commonly given illustration concerns persons hurt as the result of the cutting down of a tree. If the tree hit someone as it fell, that person would be able to bring an action for trespass; if a traveler came upon the scene sometime later and tripped over the fallen tree, his remedy, if any, would have to be in trespass on the case. In many cases, however, actually determining what was consequential and what was not was a difficult task. Suppose, as in the famous *Squib Case*, the defendant threw a "squib" (a firecracker) into the street and the plaintiff was injured when the squib exploded after it had been kicked away by the first pedestrian it came close to?[31] The difficulties became even more pronounced with the rise of the industrial revolution and the attempts to impose liability upon an employer for injuries caused by his employees.[32]

Nor should it be thought that the old forms of action and the procedural framework in which they existed presented problems only for plaintiffs. There were problems presented for defendants as well that were exacerbated with the passage of time. Take the case where the defendant's horse, upon which the defendant was riding, had bolted as the result of a sudden noise. The plaintiff was run down by the horse and injured. The plaintiff then brought an action for trespass. What should the defendant now have done? The options open to him at common law were basically two: he could plead the general issue and put the plaintiff to his proof; or the defendant could make some special plea of justification, as to the establishment of the factual basis of which he would have the burden of persuasion. In the case posited, let us suppose that the defendant decided to make the plea that the accident was not his responsibility because the plaintiff had

---

30. *See* C. Fifoot, *supra* note 27, at 50–56. *See also* T. Plucknett, A Concise History of the Common Law 369–73 (5th ed. 1956).

31. *See* Scott v. Shepherd, 3 Wils. 403, 95 Eng.Rep. 1124 (C.P. 1773)(the majority held that trespass would lie).

32. We shall discuss these problems in greater detail in the introduction to Chapter

Three, *infra*. Briefly most actions seeking to impose vicarious liability upon an employer for the torts of his employees had to be brought in trespass on the case, regardless of whether the injuries were immediate or consequential. What if the plaintiff was not sure whether the defendant rather than one of his employees caused the accident?

carelessly placed himself in front of the out-of-control horse. What would have been the result? On essentially these facts, the King's Bench in Gibbons v. Pepper, 1 Ld.Raym. 38, 91 Eng.Rep. 922 (K.B. 1695), rendered judgment for the plaintiff. Why? On the alleged facts, there was no evidence of a battery. Given that the horse was out-of-control, the defendant could not be said to have ridden his horse into the plaintiff. Nevertheless, by making his plea in justification, the defendant had admitted the battery and therefore judgment had to be entered for the plaintiff. What the defendant should have done was to plead the general issue. Then, at the trial, the defendant would have prevailed *if* the proof established the facts pleaded, namely that the defendant's horse, while temporarily out of control, had knocked down the plaintiff. On the other hand, if the defendant had pleaded the general issue, and the proof showed that the defendant had been in control of the animal at the time of the accident but that the plaintiff had been injured due to his own want of due care, the defendant likewise could not have prevailed.[33] On those facts the defendant should have made a special plea in justification. A plea of the general issue only put in issue the question of whether a battery had occurred; it did not put in issue any affirmative defenses which the defendant might have had, and the rigors of common-law pleading, which were designed to sharply limit and define the matters at issue, did not permit a defendant to plead in the alternative. In the nineteenth century, with the improvement of roads and the increased frequency of highway travel and accidents, cases presenting defendants with these difficult choices were becoming more common.

From the point of view of the plaintiff, the importance of the distinction between trespass and trespass on the case lay in two procedural consequences. First, as we have seen, if, in pleading a cause of action, the plaintiff made the wrong choice, he lost. Under the rules governing joinder of actions that then prevailed, a claim based upon case could not be joined in the same action with one based upon trespass. Second, in trespass, detailed allegations of the factual nature of the plaintiff's claim were unnecessary and this procedural advantage extended even to the issue of damages—some damage to the plaintiff was presumed; whereas, in trespass on the case, it was essential to set forth in the pleadings the factual basis of the plaintiff's claim. There were also other asserted differences between the actions, some of which will be noted shortly. With regard to the two differences already mentioned, the first, mistake as to form of pleading, is no longer important with the advent of modern codes of civil procedure. The second difference, the degree of detail required in the pleadings, is still important particularly with regard to the issue of damages. Although the forms of action have long since been abolished, those modern types of actions which are traceable to trespass, such as battery, can, with certain exceptions, still proceed without proof of actual damages. This is not true of actions, such as the modern action for negligence, which have retained many of the features of the old action of trespass on the case. In the modern action of negligence, as we shall see in Chapter Three, below, where we shall discuss in greater detail the breakdown of the old distinction between trespass and trespass on the case, allegation and proof of actual damages are essential—there are no presumed damages.

33. *See* Hall v. Fearnley, 3 Q.B. 919, 114 Eng.Rep. 761 (Q.B. 1842).

As important as the distinction between trespass and trespass on the case came to be, actually tracing the historical origins of trespass on the case is as difficult as tracing the origins of trespass. One view popular among scholars has been that it developed as a result of the statute of Westminster II, 13 Edw. I, c. 24 (1285).[34] This statute, in English translation, provided:

> And whensoever from henceforth it shall happen in the Chancery that in one case a writ is found and in a similar case falling under the same law and needing a similar remedy there is no writ found, the clerks of the Chancery shall agree in making a writ, or they shall adjourn the complainants to the next Parliament and they shall write down the cases in which they cannot agree and refer them to the next Parliament, and a writ shall be made by the consent of those learned in the law; so that from henceforth it shall not befall that the court shall fail those who seek justice.

A more traditional view has been premised on the contention that the chancery clerks improvised even before 1285; they were merely further encouraged in these activities by the first clause of Westminster II.[35] According to these scholars, the action is called "on the case" because the details of the action are set forth with some particularity and not because of the "in a similar case" (*"in consimile casu"*) language. A final and more recent group of scholars contends that Westminster II had no noteworthy role at all in the derivation of trespass on the case.[36] Their argument proceeds upon several lines. First, trespass on the case does not appear as a separate action until late in the reign of Edward III, some 80 years after Westminster II. Second, they argue that, rather than spurring the chancery clerks to greater improvisation, the significance of Westminster II is in its requirement that in cases of doubt the clerks should refer the matter to Parliament. How then did trespass on the case arise? It is suggested by these scholars that case was judicially grafted upon trespass in the latter 14th century and that the action took root and grew during the 15th century, finally separating off completely from trespass in the 16th century.[37]

It may seem surprising that the history of such important aspects of the law should be wrapped in what now appears to be impenetrable obscurity. Not only, however, is the early history of trespass and trespass on the case not well understood, it is also difficult, in the present day and age, to comprehend fully the doctrinal development of these actions, even though this development would seem to be of crucial importance in ascertaining the relationship between fault and liability in our legal system.

34. An important source making this contention is R. Sutton, Personal Actions at Common Law 24–25 (1929). Among the other scholars who have supported this position are Ames, Holmes, Maitland, and Salmond. For further citations see C. Fifoot, *supra* note 27, at 66–78.

35. *See* P. Landon, *The Action on the Case and the Statute of Westminster II*, 52 Law Q.Rev. 68 (1936).

36. E. Dix, *The Origins of the Action of Trespass on the Case*, 46 Yale L.J. 1142 (1937); T. Plucknett, *Case and the Statute of Westminster II*, 31 Colum.L.Rev. 778 (1931). *See also*, C. Fifoot, *supra* note 27, at 66–78.

37. In commenting on the various schools of thought one scholar suggests that we probably shall never be able to ascertain how the action of trespass on the case emerged. H. Potter, Historical Introduction to English Law 267 (2d ed. 1943).

Did our legal system, as many scholars over the past one hundred years have asserted, originally impose liability regardless of fault upon all people whose actions resulted in injury to others? Was it, in other words, based upon what is now often called "absolute liability?" Or, was some element of fault always a part of our legal system and not merely, to a large extent, a nineteenth century development?[38] The action of trespass out of which most of our present day intentional torts have evolved is often associated with the notion of absolute liability, although there are few, if any, torts, at least in the present day, in which liability is really absolute. On the other hand trespass on the case and its modern analogue, the action for negligence are, in the present day, associated with the notion of fault. Certainly the more detailed pleadings of the typical action on the case at common law typically included some allegations of fault, at least in the sense of deviation from community standards. What about the older action of trespass and its less detailed pleadings? Following the view that liability in tort was originally imposed regardless of fault, it has been asserted that trespass began as a form of absolute liability which, over the course of time, came to recognize some excuses which could be raised by the defendant to escape liability.[39] The recognition that fault is an essential part of most actions of tort and that proving fault is part of the plaintiff's affirmative case is, on this view, said to be a nineteenth century development.

The resolution of these issues may, however be more complex and difficult than the conventional wisdom suggests. It is important to recognize that it is misleading to look at the common law, even in the 17th and 18th centuries, through contemporary eyes. For example, as we have already seen, the modern distinction between torts based upon negligently inflicted injuries and those based upon intentionally inflicted injuries does not coincide with the distinction between "case" and trespass. If the damage caused was consequential, the plaintiff was obliged to resort to trespass on the case even if the defendant intended to cause the harm. Conversely, where the damage was direct, the plaintiff had to resort to trespass even if the defendant had merely been negligent. Since some showing of fault or at least of a failure to conform to community standards seems to have always been a part of trespass on the case, was the 19th century recognition that even directly caused injuries are not normally actionable without a showing of either negligence or some (usually) greater

38. Oliver Wendell Holmes, Jr. always questioned whether the early common law was basically a system of liability premised upon the mere causing of damage upon others without any necessity for showing fault. The Common Law 1–38 (1881). Prosser, while noting the view of Holmes and others and while recognizing that the imposition of liability upon the totally innocent defendant was very rare, nevertheless asserts that it was not until the close of the 19th century that the tendency to associate liability with moral blameworthiness was sufficiently widespread to suggest to scholars the necessity that liability must be premised upon fault. W. Prosser, Torts 16–18 (4th ed. 1971). In reaching this conclusion, Prosser relied on the work of Wigmore, Ames, and Holdsworth who, unlike Holmes, contended that at early common law, a man acted at his peril. *See* W. Prosser, *supra* at 17, n. 23. A recent article questioning whether in fact at early common law a man acted at his peril is R. Rabin, *The Historical Development of the Fault Principle. A Reinterpretation*, 15 Ga. L.Rev. 925 (1981). A good review of the early cases is W. Malone, *Ruminations on the Role of Fault in the History of the Common Law of Torts*, 31 La.L.Rev. 1 (1970).

39. *See* Prosser, Wade, & Schwartz, Cases and Materials on Torts 1–3 (6th ed. 1976). *See also* C. Peck, *Negligence and Liability Without Fault in Tort Law*, U.S. Dept. of Transp. Study of Automobile Insurance and Compensation 51–56 (1956).

degree of fault really an innovation or was it merely the spelling out, in the context of the modern jury trial, of what had always been implicit? In this regard, it must be pointed out that among the greatest changes in the English legal system in the past few hundred years has been in the nature of the trial. In the earliest days, the emphasis was almost entirely upon the pleadings. The reports that we have in the Year Books[40] are concerned with the pleading stage of a case. In almost none of the cases in the Year Books do we know what transpired at the trial, or even if there was a so-called trial. The sergeants-at-law, the elite of the English Bar at this period who were appointed by royal writ from senior practicing lawyers, pleaded their cases in the great hall of Westminster; any issues of fact that needed trial were usually tried subsequently and in the country with locally drawn juries.[41] Furthermore, the earliest juries were chosen principally because they were likely to know either what the facts actually were or to report the belief of the community as to the actual facts; the jury could thus respond to the inquiries from the royal justices. There were no trials of issues of fact in the modern sense of the term "trial."[42] The sergeants-at-law often neither knew nor cared about what transpired at this fact-finding stage.

These tremendous difficulties in comprehending exactly what the ancient cases stand for, given the different procedure that prevailed in those days, greatly complicates the attempt to resolve the dispute as to whether the notion of fault has always been a part of our legal system or is merely a recent development which could, perhaps, in time again cease to play a major role in our law. Moreover, the notion of fault is itself an evolving one. Not only do our notions of what is reasonable or blameworthy conduct change over time, but the nature of fault itself is capable of changes. Fault, for example, may mean an individualized, flexible standard that is adjusted to all the circumstances of time and place; or it may refer to deviations from some general standard with little or no concern for the nuances of the particular case. The following cases may be helpful in illustrating the nature of the controversy and what are the underlying issues that are at stake.

---

40. The Year Books were reports, or really notes in law-French apparently taken by legal apprentices, of cases heard by the Courts, sitting in the great hall of Westminster, between the reigns of Edward I (1272–1307) and Henry VIII (1509–47).

41. For an excellent description of the organization of the English legal profession during the formative periods of English law, *see* J. Dawson, The Oracles of the Law 1–99 (1968). It should be pointed out that up until at least the 17th century the Court of Common Pleas was by far the most important of the common law courts. Only sergeants-at-law had the right of audience in this court. Moreover, only sergeants-at-law were eligible for appointment as judges in any of the three common law courts. This requirement was retained into the 19th century, although at the end it became a mere *pro forma* requirement. A prospective judge was appointed a sergeant at the same time he became a judge. The sergeants-at-law followed the custom of wearing a special type of white cap, called a "coif," that covered the top, back, and sides of the head. Hence, the honorary society, with chapters at most American law schools, whose purpose it is to recognize scholastic achievement at law school, is called the "Order of the Coif."

42. It took a long while for the notion of the jury as a body of impartial persons who sat to hear the evidence presented by the parties to evolve. In the 17th century Sir Edward Coke was still able to say that the evidence of witnesses before a jury is not part of a criminal trial; trial is by jury, not by witnesses. *See* T. Plucknett, *supra* note 30, at 435–36. For more on the evolution of the jury in civil as well as criminal cases, *see id.* at 120–38, 433–36.

THE CASE OF THORNS

1466 Year Book, 6 Ed. IV, 7, pl. 18.
(as reported in *Bessey v. Olliott & Lambert*, Sir T.
Raym. 467, 83 Eng.Rep. 244 (C.B. 1661).)

Trespass quare vi & armis clausum fregit, & herbam suam pedibus conculando consumpsit in six acres. The defendant pleads, that he hath an acre lying next the said six acres, and upon it a hedge of thorns, and he cut the thorns, and they *ipso invito* [himself unwilling] fell upon the plaintiff's land, and the defendant took them off as soon as he could, which is the same trespass; and the plaintiff demurred; and adjudged for the plaintiff; for though a man doth a lawful thing, yet if any damage do thereby befall another, he shall answer for it, if he could have avoided it. As if a man lop a tree, and the boughs fall upon another *ipso invito*, yet an action lies. If a man shoot at butts, and hurt another unawares, an action lies. I have land through which a river runs to your mill, and I lop the fallows growing upon the river side, which accidentally stop the water, so as your mill is hindered, an action lies. If I am building my own house, and a piece of timber falls on my neighbor's house and breaks part of it, an action lies. If a man assault me, and I lift up my staff to defend myself, and in lifting it up hit another, an action lies by that person, and yet I did a lawful thing. And the reason of all these cases is because he that is damaged ought to be recompensed. But otherwise it is in criminal cases, for there *actus non facit reum nisi mens sit rea* [the crime is not committed unless there is a criminal intent].

Note

Would you say, in the absence of any other evidence, that a person who cuts off portions of a hedge, which then fall upon the adjoining land of his neighbor, was behaving negligently toward his neighbor?

WEAVER v. WARD

Court of King's Bench, 1616.[a]
Hob. 134, 80 Eng.Rep. 284.

Weaver brought an action of trespass of assault and battery against Ward. The defendant pleaded, that he was amongst others by the commandment of the Lords of the Council a trained soldier in London, of the band of one Andrews captain; and so was the plaintiff, and that they were skirmishing with their musquets charged with powder for their exercise in re militari [in a military matter], against another captain and his band; and as they were so skirmishing, the defendant casualiter & per infortunium & contra voluntatem suam [accidentally and by misfortune and against his will], in discharging of his piece did hurt and wound the plaintiff, which

a. The case is sometimes reported as having been decided in 1617. The case was decided in the Easter term of Fourteen James the First. James the First became king of England on March 24, 1603. The present editors have continued to use what seems to be the more customarily attributed date of 1616. It should also be pointed out that Hobart was Chief Justice of the Court of Common Pleas and occasionally one sees the decision of the case ascribed to Common Pleas. It is thus conceivable that the case may have been heard in that court rather than in King's Bench. Again the present editors have chosen to conform to the more customary usage.

is the same, & c. absque hoc [without this], that he was guilty aliter sive alio modo [otherwise or in another manner]. And upon demurrer by the plaintiff, judgment was given for him; for though it were agreed, that if men tilt or turney in the presence of the King, or if two masters of defence playing their prizes kill one another, that this shall be no felony; or if a lunatick kill a man, or the like, because felony must be done animo felonico [with felonious intent]: yet in trespass, which tends only to give damages according to hurt or loss, it is not so; and therefore if a lunatick hurt a man, he shall be answerable in trespass: and therefore no man shall be excused of a trespass (for this is the nature of an excuse, and not of a justification, prout ei bene licuit [as is rightly permitted to him])except it may be judged utterly without his fault.

As if a man by force take my hand and strike you, or if here the defendant had said, that the plaintiff ran cross his piece when it was discharging, or had set forth the case with the circumstances, so as it had appeared to the Court that it had been inevitable, and that the defendant had committed no negligence to give occasion to the hurt.

BROWN v. KENDALL

Supreme Judicial Court of Massachusetts, 1850.
60 Mass. (6 Cush.) 292.

It appeared in evidence, on the trial, which was before *Wells*, C. J., in the court of common pleas, that two dogs, belonging to the plaintiff and the defendant, respectively, were fighting in the presence of their masters; that the defendant took a stick about four feet long, and commenced beating the dogs in order to separate them; that the plaintiff was looking on, at the distance of about a rod, and that he advanced a step or two towards the dogs. In their struggle, the dogs approached the place where the plaintiff was standing. The defendant retreated backwards from before the dogs, striking them as he retreated; and as he approached the plaintiff, with his back towards him, in raising his stick over his shoulder, in order to strike the dogs, he accidentally hit the plaintiff in the eye, inflicting upon him a severe injury.

Whether it was necessary or proper for the defendant to interfere in the fight between the dogs; whether the interference, if called for, was in a proper manner, and what degree of care was exercised by each party on the occasion; were the subject of controversy between the parties, upon all the evidence in the case, of which the foregoing is an outline.

The defendant requested the judge to instruct the jury, that "if both the plaintiff and defendant at the time of the blow were using ordinary care, or if at that time the defendant was using ordinary care and the plaintiff was not, or if at that time both plaintiff and defendant were not using ordinary care, then the plaintiff could not recover."

The defendant further requested the judge to instruct the jury, that, "under the circumstances, if the plaintiff was using ordinary care and the defendant was not, the plaintiff could not recover, and that the burden of proof on all these propositions was on the plaintiff."

The judge declined to give the instructions, as above requested, but left the case to the jury under the following instructions: "If the defendant, in beating the dogs, was doing a necessary act, or one which it was his duty under the circumstances of the case to do, and was doing it in a proper way; then he was not responsible in this action, provided he was using ordinary care at the time of the blow. If it was not a necessary act; if he was not in duty bound to attempt to part the dogs, but might with propriety interfere or not as he chose; the defendant was responsible for the consequences of the blow, unless it appeared that he was in the exercise of extraordinary care, so that the accident was inevitable, using the word inevitable not in a strict but a popular sense."

"If, however, the plaintiff, when he met with the injury, was not in the exercise of ordinary care, he cannot recover, and this rule applies, whether the interference of the defendant in the fight of the dogs was necessary or not. If the jury believe, that it was the duty of the defendant to interfere, then the burden of proving negligence on the part of the defendant, and ordinary care on the part of the plaintiff, is on the plaintiff. If the jury believe, that the act of interference in the fight was unnecessary, then the burden of proving extraordinary care on the part of the defendant, or want of ordinary care on the part of the plaintiff, is on defendant."

The jury under these instructions returned a verdict for the plaintiff; whereupon the defendant alleged exceptions.

SHAW, C. J. This is an action of trespass, *vi et armis*, brought by George Brown against George K. Kendall, for an assault and battery; and the original defendant having died pending the action, his executrix has been summoned in. The rule of the common law, by which this action would abate by the death of either party, is reversed in this commonwealth by statute, which provides that actions of trespass for assault and battery shall survive. Rev.Sts. c. 93, § 7.

The facts set forth in the bill of exceptions preclude the supposition, that the blow, inflicted by the hand of the defendant upon the person of the plaintiff, was intentional. The whole case proceeds on the assumption, that the damage sustained by the plaintiff, from the stick held by the defendant, was inadvertent and unintentional; and the case involves the question how far, and under what qualifications, the party by whose unconscious act the damage was done is responsible for it. We use the term "unintentional" rather than involuntary, because in some of the cases, it is stated, that the act of holding and using a weapon or instrument, the movement of which is the immediate cause of hurt to another, is a voluntary act, although its particular effect in hitting and hurting another is not within the purpose or intention of the party doing the act.

It appears to us, that some of the confusion in the cases on this subject has grown out of the long-vexed question, under the rule of the common law, whether a party's remedy, where he has one, should be sought in an action of the case, or of trespass. This is very distinguishable from the question, whether in a given case, any action will lie. The result of these cases is, that if the damage complained of is the immediate effect of the act of the defendant, trespass *vi et armis* lies; if consequential only, and not immediate, case is the proper remedy. * * *

In these discussions, it is frequently stated by judges, that when one receives injury from the direct act of another, trespass will lie. But we think this is said in reference to the question, whether trespass and not case will lie, assuming that the facts are such, that some action will lie. These *dicta* are no authority, we think, for holding, that damage received by a direct act of force from another will be sufficient to maintain an action of trespass, whether the act was lawful or unlawful, and neither wilful, intentional, or careless. In the principal case cited, *Leame v. Bray*, the damage arose from the act of the defendant, in driving on the wrong side of the road, in a dark night, which was clearly negligent if not unlawful. In the course of the argument of that case, Lawrence, J., said: "There certainly are cases in the books, where, the injury being direct and immediate, trespass has been holden to lie, though the injury was not intentional." The term "injury" implies something more than damage; but, independently of that consideration, the proposition may be true, because though the injury was unintentional, the act may have been unlawful or negligent, and the cases cited by him are perfectly consistent with that supposition. So the same learned judge in the same case says, "No doubt trespass lies against one who drives a carriage against another, whether done wilfully or not." But he immediately adds, "Suppose one who is driving a carriage is negligently and heedlessly looking about him, without attending to the road when persons are passing, and thereby runs over a child and kills him, is it not manslaughter? and if so, it must be trespass; for every manslaughter includes trespass; " showing what he understood by a case not wilful.

We think, as the result of all the authorities, the rule is correctly stated by Mr. Greenleaf, that the plaintiff must come prepared with evidence to show either that the *intention* was unlawful, or that the defendant was *in fault*; for if the injury was unavoidable, and the conduct of the defendant was free from blame, he will not be liable. 2 Greenl. Ev. §§ 85 to 92 * * * If, in the prosecution of a lawful act, a casualty purely accidental arises, no action can be supported for an injury arising therefrom. * * * In applying these rules to the present case, we can perceive no reason why the instructions asked for by the defendant ought not to have been given; to this effect, that if both plaintiff and defendant at the time of the blow were using ordinary care, or if at that time the defendant was using ordinary care, and the plaintiff was not, or if at that time, both the plaintiff and defendant were not using ordinary care, then the plaintiff could not recover.

In using this term, ordinary care, it may be proper to state, that what constitutes ordinary care will vary with the circumstances of cases. In general, it means that kind and degree of care, which prudent and cautious men would use, such as is required by the exigency of the case, and such as is necessary to guard against probable danger. A man, who should have occasion to discharge a gun, on an open and extensive marsh, or in a forest, would be required to use less circumspection and care, than if he were to do the same thing in an inhabited town, village, or city. To make an accident, or casualty, or as the law sometimes states it, inevitable accident, it must be such an accident as the defendant could not have avoided by the use of the kind and degree of care necessary to the exigency, and in the circumstances in which he was placed.

We are not aware of any circumstances in this case, requiring a distinction between acts which it was lawful and proper to do, and acts of legal duty. There are cases, undoubtedly, in which officers are bound to act under process, for the legality of which they are not responsible, and perhaps some others in which this distinction would be important. We can have no doubt that the act of the defendant in attempting to part the fighting dogs, one of which was his own, and for the injurious acts of which he might be responsible, was a lawful and proper act, which he might do by proper and safe means. If, then, in doing this act, using due care and all proper precautions necessary to the exigency of the case, to avoid hurt to others, in raising his stick for that purpose, he accidentally hit the plaintiff in his eye, and wounded him, this was the result of pure accident, or was involuntary and unavoidable, and therefore the action would not lie. Or if the defendant was chargeable with some negligence, and if the plaintiff was also chargeable with negligence, we think the plaintiff cannot recover without showing that the damage was caused wholly by the act of the defendant, and that the plaintiff's own negligence did not contribute as an efficient cause to produce it.

The court instructed the jury, that if it was not a necessary act, and the defendant was not in duty bound to part the dogs, but might with propriety interfere or not as he chose, the defendant was responsible for the consequences of the blow, unless it appeared that he was in the exercise of extraordinary care, so that the accident was inevitable, using the word not in a strict but a popular sense. This is to be taken in connection with the charge afterwards given, that if the jury believed, that the act of interference in the fight was unnecessary, (that is, as before explained, not a duty incumbent on the defendant,) then the burden of proving extraordinary care on the part of the defendant, or want of ordinary care on the part of plaintiff, was on the defendant.

The court are of opinion that these directions were not conformable to law. If the act of hitting the plaintiff was unintentional, on the part of the defendant, and done in the doing of a lawful act, then the defendant was not liable, unless it was done in the want of exercise of due care, adapted to the exigency of the case, and therefore such want of due care became part of the plaintiff's case, and the burden of proof was on the plaintiff to establish it. * * *

Perhaps the learned judge, by the use of the term extraordinary care, in the above charge, explained as it is by the context, may have intended nothing more than that increased degree of care and diligence, which the exigency of particular circumstances might require, and which men of ordinary care and prudence would use under like circumstances, to guard against danger. If such was the meaning of this part of the charge, then it does not differ from our views, as above explained. But we are of opinion, that the other part of the charge, that the burden of proof was on the defendant, was incorrect. Those facts which are essential to enable the plaintiff to recover, he takes the burden of proving. The evidence may be offered by the plaintiff or by the defendant; the question of due care, or want of care, may be essentially connected with the main facts, and arise from the same proof; but the effect of the rule, as to the burden of proof, is this, that when the proof is all in, and before the jury, from whatever side it comes, and whether directly proved, or inferred from circumstances, if it appears that the defendant was doing a lawful act, and unintentionally hit and hurt the plaintiff, then unless it also appears to the satisfaction of the jury, that the defendant is chargeable with some fault, negligence, carelessness, or want of prudence, the plaintiff fails to sustain the burden of proof, and is not entitled to recover.

New trial ordered.

Notes

1. *Brown v. Kendall* became a "leading case." After *Brown v. Kendall* on whom would the burden of persuasion be on the issue of the plaintiff's own fault or what we would now call the plaintiff's contributory negligence? Is it, to use Shaw, J.'s words, one of "[t]hose facts which are essential to enable the plaintiff to recover"? In Massachusetts the burden was initially placed upon the plaintiff to prove the absence of contributory negligence, Gahagan v. Boston & Lowell Railroad, 83 Mass. (1 Allen) 187 (1861), but in 1914, by statute, the burden of proving contributory negligence was placed upon the defendant. In the nineteenth century there was a split of authority on the issue, with most states placing the burden on the defendant. The majority rule seems logically sounder because it is easier for the defendant to prove a negative than for the plaintiff to prove an affirmative. In the course of time more states have adopted the majority position, see 9 J. Wigmore, Evidence § 2507 (3d ed. 1940). Illinois is one of the states that ostensibly still places the burden upon the plaintiff. One says "ostensibly" because in practice the burden is often treated as one of pleading. Moreover, in particular types of cases, where the plaintiff's pleadings themselves raise the possibility of his being contributorily negligent, for all practical purposes, the burden of persuasion may shift to the plaintiff, even in a state following the majority "rule." *See ibid. See also id.* at § 2485.

2. The term "burden of proof" may, depending on the context, mean (1) the burden of pleading, *i.e.* of raising an issue; (2) the burden of adducing evidence on a point (sometimes called the burden of coming forward); or (3) the burden of persuading the trier of fact (*i.e.* the allocation of the risk of nonpersuasion where the trier of fact is undecided). It is important to keep these possible meanings, and the distinctions upon which they are based, constantly in mind. We shall return to the analysis of the term "burden of proof" at pp. 211–12, below.

3. Although cases like *Brown v. Kendall* settled the question as to whether, in the modern action for negligence, the plaintiff had all three burdens identified in note 2, *supra,* on the issue of the defendant's fault, uncertainty persisted as to whether the same was true in a modern action for trespass to the person. The issue was dramatically presented in Fowler v. Lanning, [1959] 1 Q.B. 426, 2 W.L.R. 241, 1 All E.R. 290. In that case the plaintiff and the defendant had participated in a hunting party at Corfe Castle in Dorset. As described by Diplock, J. (later Lord Diplock), "[t]he statement of claim alleges laconically that at that place and on that date 'the defendant shot the plaintiff' ". The defendant pleaded that the claim " 'is bad in law and discloses no cause of action against him on the ground that the plaintiff does not allege that the said shooting was either intentional or negligent' ". Di-

plock, J., thus felt obliged to decide whether at common law, in an action for trespass, it was necessary for the plaintiff to show that the defendant had intentionally harmed the plaintiff or otherwise was at fault or whether the burden was on the defendant to show that he was not at fault. Since there was no suggestion that the defendant had intentionally shot the plaintiff, the issue boiled down to whether, if an action for an unintended injury were brought on the basis of trespass to the person rather than as a modern action for negligence, the defendant could be forced to show that he was not at fault. At that time it was still possible to choose between these remedies in England. Citing *Weaver v. Ward*, Diplock, J., held that, whether a person acted at his peril in medieval times, and he doubted whether such a proposition ever was true "the strict principal that every man acts at his peril was not applied in the case of trespass to the person" even as long ago as *Weaver v. Ward*. Diplock, J., felt, moreover, that, in the simpler society that existed before the industrial revolution, the assertion that the defendant had injured the plaintiff as a direct consequence of his actions "would normally be prima facie evidence of the defendant's negligence." Furthermore, he noted that, before the Common Law Procedure Act of 1852, the major focus was on the pleadings. This is a point that has been noted earlier in this introductory chapter (p. 23, *supra*), and was used by Shaw, C.J., in *Brown v. Kendall, supra,* to support the conclusion that the earlier cases cited to him for the proposition that all direct injuries were redressable in trespass were, in fact, only concerned with whether, if the plaintiff had an action, it would lie in trespass rather than case. Diplock, J., accordingly held that the onus of proving negligence lay upon the plaintiff whether the action were framed in trespass or negligence. He noted that from the nineteenth century this had always been the case with regard to highway accidents. The only question was whether the highway accidents were illustrative of the general rule or whether they were the so-called exception to the general rule. A result similar to that reached by Diplock, J., had been reached in Walmsley v. Humenick, [1954] 2 D.L.R. 232 (British Columbia). For a discussion of how the common law evolved from a system that focused largely on procedural law to one whose principal focus was substantive law, *see* P. Kelley, *Proximate Cause in Negligence Law: History, Theory, and the Present Darkness*, 69 Wash.U.L.Q. 49, 54–82 (1991).

Fowler v. Lanning was followed by a number of courts in the British Commonwealth, such as, for example, Beals v. Hayward, [1960] N.Z.L.R. 131. On the other hand, the historical analysis of *Fowler v. Lanning* was specifically rejected in *Goshen v. Larin*, 46 D.L.R.3d 137 (Nova Scotia, 1974); Dahlberg v. Naydiuk, 72 W.W.R. 210 (Manitoba, 1969); McHale v. Watson, 111 C.L.R. 384 (High Ct.Aust.1964). In England itself, the Court of Appeal, a few years after *Fowler v. Lanning*, went one step further and held that, where the injury is unintended, the plaintiff's only cause of action is in negligence; trespass to the person will not lie. Letang v. Cooper [1965] 1 Q.B. 232 (C.A.1964).

Whether one agrees with Diplock, J. on the question of whether the plaintiff was required to show that the defendant was at fault in an action for trespass at common law is not, for present purposes, important. What is important is that one appreciate that the law is complex, that it is the product of a long process of historical development, and that it consists of a vast number of particulars. This is not said to frighten the student. It is only to warn the student that it is important for a lawyer to approach generalizations cautiously. The greater the degree of generalization the more cautious one must be. That it is not to say that one should abandon the attempt to generalize; that would be as foolish as it is impossible. One could not organize his experience if he eschewed all generalization. But one must recognize that generalizations are only a means of organizing one's experience; they cannot be treated as if they are in fact the reality of experience. At least in the law, reality consists of much more prosaic things.

Chapter 2

INTENTIONAL TORTS

A. THE CONCEPT OF "INTENT"

RESTATEMENT (SECOND) OF TORTS (1965)

§ 8A. Intent

The word "intent" is used throughout the Restatement of this Subject to denote that the actor desires to cause consequences of his act, or that he believes that the consequences are substantially certain to result from it.

Comment:

* * *

b. All consequences which the actor desires to bring about are intended, as the word is used in this Restatement. Intent is not, however, limited to consequences which are desired. If the actor knows that the consequences are certain, or substantially certain, to result from his act, and still goes ahead, he is treated by the law as if he had in fact desired to produce the result. As the probability that the consequences will follow decreases, and becomes less than substantial certainty, the actor's conduct loses the character of intent, and becomes mere recklessness, as defined in § 500. As the probability decreases further, and amounts only to a risk that the result will follow, it becomes ordinary negligence, as defined in § 282. All three have their important place in the law of torts, but the liability attached to them will differ.

Notes

1. In the *Restatement of Torts* (1939), the definition of intent is contained in the *comment* to § 13, on battery. The definition is substantially the same as that contained in § 8A of the *Restatement (Second)* quoted above, except that the *Restatement* spoke in terms of the actor's "*knowledge*" that a harmful or offensive contact was "substantially certain to be produced." There appears to be no explanation of the change either in the preliminary drafts or in the discussions of the American Law Institute. Do you think there could ever be any difference between results a person *knows* are substantially certain to

occur and those that he believes are substantially certain to occur? Is one standard more susceptible of objective proof than the other?

2. In § 500 *Restatement (Second) of Torts* "reckless" conduct is defined as an act or intentional failure to act under circumstances where the actor knows or has reason to know "of facts which would lead a reasonable man to realize, not only that his conduct creates an unreasonable risk of physical harm to another, but also that such risk is substantially greater than that which is necessary to make his conduct negligent." After thus setting out the "black-letter" law, the *Restatement (Second)* continues with the following explanatory statements:

> Special Note: The conduct described in this Section is often called "wanton or wilful misconduct" both in statutes and judicial opinions. On the other hand, this phrase is sometimes used by courts to refer to conduct intended to cause harm to another.

Comment:

* * *

> f. *Intentional misconduct and recklessness contrasted.* Reckless misconduct differs from intentional wrongdoing in a very important particular. While an act to be reckless must be intended by the actor, the actor does not intend to cause the harm which results from it. It is enough that he realizes or, from facts which he knows, should realize that there is a strong probability that harm may result, even though he hopes or even expects that his conduct will prove harmless. However, a strong probability is a different thing from the substantial certainty without which he cannot be said to intend the harm in which his act results.

3. In the pages that follow we shall study the torts of battery, assault, trespass to land, and trespass to chattels. All these torts can be said to be modern derivatives of the old writ of trespass although, with the modern emphasis on the intent of the defendant rather than the directness of the injury to the plaintiff, these modern torts do not always exactly track their common-law antecedents. Another tort that is derived from the old writ of trespass is *false imprisonment*. A discussion of false imprisonment could thus logically be placed in this section of the casebook. A typical modern case of false imprisonment, however, involves an alleged invasion of the plaintiff's emotional tranquility rather than the physical safety of his person or of his property. Moreover, many modern cases of false imprisonment raise serious constitutional questions concerning the extent to which the state can authorize the arrest of persons suspected of criminal behavior. It therefore seems more appropriate to discuss false imprisonment later in the casebook after we have discussed a number of other so-called "dignitary torts," including the newly developed tort of intentional infliction of emotional distress which has no close common-law antecedent, that also raise some important, albeit different, constitutional questions. Accordingly, we shall postpone a discussion of false imprisonment until Chapter Twenty when we shall consider it in conjunction with the tort of malicious prosecution. It should of course be no cause for surprise that many modern cases include allegations of both false imprisonment and malicious prosecution.

JACKSON v. BRANTLEY

Court of Civil Appeals of Alabama, 1979.
378 So.2d 1109.

HOLMES, JUDGE.

This is an action for damages.

Plaintiff filed suit and the defendants counterclaimed as a result of a collision of plaintiff's automobile with defendants' horse. The jury rendered a verdict in favor of the plaintiff and denied recovery to defendants on the counterclaim. After denial of defendants' post trial motions, defendants appealed.

The dispositive issues on appeal are (1) whether there is sufficient evidence to support the jury's conclusion that the defendants knowingly or willfully put an animal upon a public highway within the meaning of the liability provisions of Code of Ala.1975, § 3–5–3, and (2) whether contributory negligence is a defense to a violation of § 3–5–3.

The record reveals the following: The defendant, Mr. Jackson, Jr., owns livestock which he pastures on leased property. The pasture abuts a paved public highway known as the Mitchell–Young Road.

On January 12, 1977, four of Jackson's horses apparently jumped the fence which surrounds the pasture and went onto the land of Mr. Jones, a nearby neighbor. Mrs. Jones called the defendant and requested that he remove the animals from her property.

The defendant called his father, defendant-Ivy Jackson, Sr., and asked him to round up the animals. Mr. Jackson, Sr., accompanied by a helper, then drove to the Jones's property, arriving there after dark.

Upon arriving at the Jones's property, Jackson, Sr., caught two of the four animals and secured them with halters. The remaining two horses, a gray and a colt, avoided capture attempts. Jackson then instructed his helper to lead the captured animals back to their pasture.

The helper led the two bridled horses down the unpaved driveway of the Jones's property toward the public highway. At this time, the two animals which had avoided capture fell in behind and followed the two bridled animals. Jackson slowly followed behind the four animals in his truck. Although the two horses which had evaded capture were immediately in front of Jackson's truck, neither he nor his helper attempted to secure them with halters prior to proceeding onto the public highway.

The helper, the bridled and unrestrained horses, and Jackson, Sr. turned onto the shoulder of the Mitchell–Young Road. After they had proceeded a short distance, plaintiff's automobile appeared around a curve in the highway and approached them. The horses were apparently startled by the headlights of the oncoming car and the two unbridled animals bolted into the road. Plaintiff's automobile struck and killed the colt.

* * *

The defendants initially contend that pursuant to § 3–5–3, there is insufficient evidence to support the jury's finding that the defendants knowingly or willfully placed livestock on the public highway. Specifically, the defendants contend that plaintiff's evidence at most shows the defendants were negligent or grossly negligent and this is insufficient to carry the burden of proof established by § 3–5–3. We disagree.

> Section 3–5–3 provides in pertinent part: [T]he owner of any * * * animal shall not be liable for any damages to any motor vehicle * * * caused by * * * a collision with such * * * animal, unless it be proven that such owner knowingly or wilfully put or placed such stock upon such public highway * * * where such damages were occasioned.

Our cases hold that in order for a motorist to recover under § 3–5–3, his proof must demonstrate more than negligence or gross carelessness on the part of the defendant. *Carter v. Alman*, 46 Ala.App. 633, 247 So.2d 676 (1971). As Presiding Judge Wright stated in the *Carter* case:

> These cases plainly state that for recovery, a motorist must submit proof that the owner of the feasant beast placed or put it upon the highway with a "designed set purpose, *intention,* or deliberation." Evidence of negligence or gross carelessness is not enough. * * *

Stated alternatively, the statute imposes liability on the owner of livestock for torts which are *intentional, i.e.,* those in which the owner's conduct is purposeful, willful, deliberate, or knowingly done. * * *

While it is beyond doubt that the defendants in this instance would not have been liable for failure to keep the animals within the confines of the pasture, *Carter, supra,* our review of the record indicates that there is ample evidence to support the jury's conclusion that in this instance, the livestock was in fact knowingly placed on the public highway.

At trial, Mr. Jackson, Sr. testified that after his unsuccessful attempt to secure two of the four horses, he and his helper proceeded onto the public highway with the two bridled animals followed by the unrestrained horses as well. On direct examination he stated that prior to entering the highway he made *no attempt* to bridle the pair that were loose.

> Q Now, when those two came up there, did y'all attempt to put a halter on them at that time?
>
> A They wouldn't let us.
>
> Q Did you try to?
>
> A We tried down there at the fence.
>
> Q No, sir, I mean at the time they joined you—
>
> A No, sir.
>
> Q —you didn't try to put a halter on them any more?
>
> A No, sir.

Later, on redirect, Mr. Jackson, Sr. stated:

> Q Now, Mr. Jackson, you intended to put those horses on that shoulder of that road, didn't you?
>
> A That's the only way I knew to get them back there.

*   *   *   *   *   *   *   *

Q   That was your intention, though, wasn't it?

A   I was in hopes they'd follow them.

Based upon this testimony, the defendants' deliberate actions in regard to the horses are such that it can be concluded that they knowingly and intentionally "led" the unfettered livestock onto the public road and thus committed the act proscribed by the express language of § 3–5–3. Put another way, the defendants' acts in this instance legally placed the animals in the road because it is well settled that where, as here, the defendant knows that the consequences of his act are certain or substantially certain to result from his intentional conduct, and he still proceeds, it is considered that he in fact *intended* to produce the consequences which in fact occurred. *See e.g., Restatement (Second) of Torts* § 8A(b)(1965).

* * *

Furthermore, the record reveals that Jackson, Sr. knew that the consequences of his act were certain or substantially certain to result from leading the horses onto the public road. The record shows that this defendant had worked with horses and other livestock for twenty-seven years and that he had, on a prior occasion experienced a similar situation while attempting to round up horses at night in which five animals had been killed by motorists. On direct examination, the following colloquy occurred:

Q   Now, have you had any experience, prior to January of 1977, of rounding up horses that had gotten out at night?

A   Yes, sir, I helped to get some in. Yes, sir.

Q   And several got killed in that roundup, didn't they?

A   Yes, sir.

Q   How many was that?

A   Five.

Q   And was that at night when the cars were running into them?

A   Yes, sir.

Q   Now, you knew then that at night horses were liable to bolt or more likely to bolt in front of cars and their lights, didn't you?

A   Yes, sir, I know they'll do that.

Given this testimony, the jury was warranted in finding that, by virtue of the defendants' intentional conduct, the animals were in fact knowingly and willfully placed upon the highway. *See, e.g., Restatement, supra.*

Defendants next contend that plaintiff's contributory negligence, as demonstrated by the evidence, bars his recovery. As noted below, even though the jury apparently found no contributory negligence on the part of the plaintiff, contributory negligence, as a matter of law, is not a defense to an intentional tort such as the wrong set forth in § 3–5–3.

* * *

For the foregoing reasons, the judgment of the trial court is affirmed.

Notes

1.   In your judgment do the facts set forth in the court's opinion establish that Ivy Jackson, Sr., believed (or knew) that the unbridled horses were substantially certain to follow the bridled horses onto the highway?

2.   As the note immediately preceding the principal case indicates, the term "wanton" is sometimes used as a synonym for intentional conduct. *See* Mountain States Tel. and Tel. Co. v. Horn Tower Constr. Co., 147 Colo. 166, 171, 73, 363 P.2d 175, 178, 79 (1961).   More often, however, as in the Restatements, the term is used as a synonym for "reckless" conduct.   "Fault" is another term which is sometimes ambiguous.   Usually, it means tortious conduct that is either intentional, reckless, or negligent.   At other times, however, the term "fault" is restricted to conduct that is negligent, or reckless or negligent, as opposed to intentional.   The reason for this occasional usage is that not only can conduct be found intentional even where there is no desire to injure the plaintiff, conduct can also be found intentional for purposes of tort law even if the actor is not guilty of any degree of moral fault.   Take a case, for example, where a person mistakenly, but reasonably, believes that he is entering his own house, when in point of fact he is entering someone else's house.   As we shall see shortly, pp. 55–56, infra, this will be a trespass.   Likewise one who shoots at what he reasonably but mistakenly thinks is a wolf, is liable to the owner for trespass to chattels, which will be discussed at pp. 59–60, infra, when it turns out that the animal was someone's dog.   *See* Ranson v. Kitner, 31 Ill.App. 241 (1888).   In both situations, all that is necessary is that the actor should have intended to do what he did, not that he have intended to commit a trespass or have known or even realized that a trespass was even a possible consequence of his actions.

3.   A much cited case on the question of what constitutes "intent" in a civil action is Garratt v. Dailey, 46 Wn.2d 197, 279 P.2d 1091 (1955), 49 Wn.2d 499, 304 P.2d 681 (1956).   In that case, Brian, aged 5 years, nine months, had pulled away a lightly built wood and canvas lawn chair, in order to sit on it himself, while his arthritic maiden aunt was in the process of sitting down upon it.   The boy testified that he picked up the chair, moved it a few feet sideways and seated himself, at which time he discovered the plaintiff was about to sit where the chair formerly had been.   He quickly got up and attempted to move the chair under the plaintiff, but was unable to do so in time.   The case was tried to a judge who found for the defendant because the child did not intend to play a prank on his aunt and he did not intend to injure her.   The first time the case reached the Supreme Court of Washington, that court remanded for a determination of whether the boy knew what the consequences of his moving the chair would be.   The second time the case reached the Supreme Court of Washington, the court affirmed the trial judge's finding, based on the testimony of the Brian's sister, that the boy had known his aunt had begun the slow process of sitting down when he moved the chair and, therefore, that the boy knew with "substantial certainty" that his aunt "would attempt to sit in the place where the chair had been."   Garratt v. Dailey, 49 Wash.2d 499, 304 P.2d 681 (1956).   Do you think Brian was "substantially certain" his aunt would

fall; that she would injure herself? An analogous English case is Wilson v. Pringle, [1987] Q.B. 237, [1986] 3 W.L.R. 1, [1986] 3 All E.R. 440 (C.A. 1986). The question of establishing "intent" when the defendant is a child will be further considered in *Singer v. Marx*, p. 52, *infra*. As *Williams v. Kearby*, p. 61, *infra*, illustrates, some of the same problems are raised in connection with the question of whether insane people are capable of committing intentional torts.

BEAUCHAMP v. DOW CHEMICAL COMPANY

Supreme Court of Michigan, 1986.
427 Mich. 1, 398 N.W.2d 882.

LEVIN, JUSTICE.

The questions presented are whether the exclusive remedy provision of the Workers' Disability Compensation Act bars an employee from commencing a civil action against his employer where the employee alleges (1) that the employer committed an intentional tort against the employee, and (2) that the employer breached its contract to provide a safe work place.

Plaintiff Ronald Beauchamp was employed for two years as a research chemist by defendant Dow Chemical Company. He applied for workers' compensation benefits, alleging impairment of normal bodily functions caused by exposure to tordon, 2, 4–D, and 2, 4, 5–T ("agent orange").

[He] * * * thereafter commenced this civil action against Dow. The complaint alleged that Ronald Beauchamp had been physically and mentally affected by exposure to "agent orange" "and * * * that Dow intentionally assaulted Ronald Beauchamp ..." * * * The circuit court granted summary judgment for Dow on * * * the basis that the complaint failed to state a claim on which relief could be granted."

* * *

We conclude that the contract claim is barred by the exclusive remedy provision and remand for further proceedings on the intentional tort claims.

* * *

The origin and evolution of the workers' compensation act indicates that the legislation, including the exclusive remedy provision, was designed to provide an alternative compensation system respecting accidental and not intentional injuries.

* * *

Although a number of courts have agreed that the exclusivity provision of a workers' compensation act does not preclude employees from bringing intentional tort actions against their employers, the courts have not been able to agree on a definition of "intentional" in this context. Some courts have limited the recovery to so called "true intentional torts," that is, when the employer truly intended the injury as well as the act. Other courts have relied on the standard in the Restatement of Torts, 2d, stating that when the employer intended the act that caused the injury and knew that the injury was substantially certain to occur from the act, the employer has committed an intentional tort. The substantial certainty test has apparently been extended by at least one state to cover substantial likelihood of injury.

The Court of Appeals in the instant case declared, "In, order to allege an intentional tort outside the act, the plaintiff must allege that the employer intended the injury itself and not merely the activity leading to the injury." A number of states have adopted a similar intentional tort test requiring an actual intent to injure.

* * *

The "substantial certainty" line of cases defines intentional tort more broadly. An intentional tort "is not ... limited to consequences which are desired. If the actor knows that the consequences are certain, or substantially certain, to result from his act, and still goes ahead, he is treated by the law as if he had in fact desired to produce the result." Bazley v. Tortorich, 397 So.2d 475, 482, n. 54 (La.1981). It does not matter whether the employer wishes the injury would not occur or does not care whether it occurs. If the injury is substantially certain to occur as a consequence of actions the employer intended, the employer is deemed to have intended the injuries as well. The substantial certainty test tracks the Restatement definition of an intentional tort.

* * *

Another case that might be decided differently had the standard been substantial certainty rather than true intent was Serna v. Statewide Contractors, 6 Ariz.App. 12, 429 P.2d 504 (1967). Two men were killed when a ditch caved in and buried them alive. In the five months preceding the disaster, inspectors had warned that "the sides of the ditch were not sloped properly, the side was sandy, more shoring was needed, and escape ladders should be placed every 25 feet." During that time a cave-in had occurred, burying one of the decedents up to his waist. All warnings were ignored. The court disallowed the action, finding that the act was not "done knowingly and purposely, with the direct object of injuring another." Id. at 15, 429 P.2d 504.

The recent People v. Film Recovery Systems case decided in Illinois adds a new perspective to the different intentional tort standards. The facts in the case were as follows: Film Recovery Systems went into the business of recovering silver from film negatives. This was done by placing the negatives into vats of cyanide. Hydrogen cyanide gas would bubble up from the vats and there was inadequate ventilation. The employer knew about the dangers. The labels on the chemicals being used contained adequate warnings; as a result, the employer hired only employees who could not speak or read English. The workers complained about the fumes daily. In 1981, an inspector had warned that the operation had outgrown the plant. The employer's response was to move the executive offices while tripling the size of the operations. Eventually one worker died and several others were seriously injured because of hydrogen cyanide poisoning. The corporate officers were convicted of involuntary manslaughter.

The facts in this case are a good example of the type of employer conduct that would seem to meet the substantial certainty as well as a substantial likelihood of harm standard. It is questionable, however, whether even this outrageous conduct would constitute a "true intentional tort." The employer did not desire to injure or kill the employees, even though the employer knew with a substantial certainty that his conduct would injure the employees.

Selecting the appropriate intentional tort test is difficult. The problem with the substantial certainty test is that it is difficult to draw the line between substantial certainty and substantial risk. In applying the substantial certainty test, some courts have confused intentional, reckless, and even negligent misconduct, and therefore blurred the line between intentional and accidental injuries. The true intentional tort standard keep the distinction clear.[69]

The problem with the true intentional tort test appears to be that it allows employers to injure and even kill employees and suffer only workers' compensation damages so long as the employer did not specifically intend to hurt the worker. The facts in the Film Recovery System case are a good example. Prohibiting a civil action in such a case "would allow a corporation to 'cost-out' an investment decision to kill workers." Blankenship v. Cincinnati Milacron Chemicals, 69 Ohio St.2d 608, 617, 433 N.E.2d 572 (1982)(Celebrezze, J., concurring).

We adopt the substantial certainty standard. * * * [W]e stress that substantial certainty should not be equated with substantial likelihood. The facts in Serna and Film Recovery System are examples of what would constitute substantial certainty.

* * *

Remanded to the circuit court for further proceedings consistent with this opinion. We do not retain jurisdiction.

[The opinion of Justice Boyle, concurring in part and dissenting in part, is omitted]

Notes

1. In response to the Beauchamp opinion the Michigan legislature amended the worker's compensation statute. The amendment reads in part,

"The right to the recovery of benefits as provided in this act shall be the employee's exclusive remedy against the employer for a personal injury or occupational disease. The only exception to this exclusive remedy is an intentional tort. An intentional tort shall exist only when an employee is injured as a result of a deliberate act of the employer and the employer specifically intended an injury. An employer shall be deemed to have intended to injure if the employer had actual knowledge that an injury was certain to occur and willfully disregarded that knowledge. The issue of whether an act was an intentional tort shall be a question of law for the court." M.C.L. 418.131; M.S.A. 17.237(131).

We shall explore workers compensation statutes in Chapter Fourteen.

69. Still a further complication is the possible difference between the standard or definition of intentional tort and the evidence that would constitute a prima facie case.

2. The Beauchamp court adopted the "substantial certainty" test in part to cover fact patterns such as those described in Serna v. Statewide Contractors and People v. Film Recovery Systems. In your opinion, would those cases be resolved differently after the passage of 418.131?

B. BATTERY AND ASSAULT

MASTERS v. BECKER

Supreme Court of New York, Appellate Division, Second Department, 1964.
22 A.D.2d 118, 254 N.Y.S.2d 633.

CHRIST, JUSTICE.

The single question is whether, with respect to a cause of action for assault, the definition of intent given by the trial court in its charge and in its ruling on an exception and a request to charge constituted reversible error. The court stated that the plaintiffs were required to establish that the infant defendant intended the act that resulted in injury, that she intended to commit an injury, and that she intended the very injury sustained by the infant plaintiff. The court also posed the question: "Can a nine-year old, by her action, intend the injury which resulted in this case?" To all this plaintiffs' counsel took an exception and requested the court to charge that plaintiffs were required to establish only that "the act was done with intent to inflict an offensive bodily contact." The court refused such request to charge and adhered to its previous instructions.

When the injury occurred, the infant plaintiff Susan Masters was about six years of age and the infant defendant Claudia Becker was about nine years of age. They, together with Claudia's sister, were playing on a motor truck in an empty lot, and Susan was standing on a narrow ledge on the outside of the truck's tailgate. Claudia told or at least urged Susan to get off; and Susan refused and cried, saying she was frightened. Then Claudia pried Susan's fingers off the tailgate and Susan fell to the ground, sustaining severe injuries. Claudia's testimony indicated that the reason for her act was to force Susan to give Claudia and her sister their turns to get onto the ledge so that they could jump off.

The correct rule as to intent is set forth in the American Law Institute's Restatement of the Law (Restatement of the Law of Torts, vol. 1, § 16, subd. 1), namely: that intent is established "If an act is done with the intention of inflicting upon another an offensive but not a harmful bodily contact or of putting another in apprehension of either a harmful or offensive bodily contact, and such act causes a bodily contact to the other * * * although the act was not done with the intention of bringing about the resulting bodily harm." * * *

The law as thus stated has been followed in Baldinger v. Banks, 26 Misc.2d 1086, 201 N.Y.S.2d 629 which case was approved by this court in a subsequent connected case (Baldinger v. Consolidated Mut. Ins. Co., 15 A.D.2d 526, 222 N.Y.S.2d 736, aff'd. 11 N.Y.2d 1026, 230 N.Y.S.2d 25, 183 N.E.2d 908 * * *.) There are other consistent decisions to the same effect * * *.

A plaintiff in an action to recover damages for an assault founded on bodily contact must prove only that there was bodily contact; that such contact was offensive; and that the defendant intended to make the contact. The plaintiff is not required to prove that defendant intended physically to injure him. Certainly he is not required to prove an intention to cause the specific injuries resulting from the contact.

Hence, the trial court's rulings and instructions were not in harmony with the law. On the facts a jury could well find that Claudia intended only to force Susan off the truck, without any thought of injuring her. It could also find that Claudia intended the bodily contact she was forcing upon Susan; and that, although this was not harmful in itself, it was offensive to Susan. Under a correct instruction, findings of the presence of such intent would be sufficient for holding Claudia responsible for the ensuing injury. In requiring plaintiffs to establish that Claudia in fact intended an injury and even the very injury that Susan sustained, the trial court was in error. Such instruction imposed on plaintiffs an excessive burden and made it highly improbable that the jury would find in favor of plaintiffs.

In Baldinger v. Banks, supra, where the correct rule was applied, liability was found against an even younger child than Claudia. There, the act of a six-year-old boy was not significantly dissimilar to Claudia's. He resented the four-year-old infant plaintiff's presence on a lawn where he was playing and he pushed her. She fell to the ground and sustained severe injuries. A substantial recovery was awarded against the boy.

As the error in the instant case was highly prejudicial the judgment should be reversed on the law, and a new trial granted, with costs to plaintiffs to abide the event.

Judgment reversed on the law and new trial granted as between the plaintiffs and the infant defendant, with costs to the plaintiffs to abide the event.

Notes

1. The Restatement (Second) of Torts defines a battery as the intentional infliction of either a "harmful contact" (§ 13) or an "offensive contact" (§ 18) with the person of another. The necessary intent is either an intent to cause the harmful or offensive contact or an intent to put the other in "imminent apprehension of such a contact." The intentional putting of another in imminent apprehension of a harmful or offensive contact constitutes the tort of assault. Restatement (Second) of Torts § 21. Again, the requisite intent may be shown by an intent to cause a harmful or offensive contact or by an intention to cause an imminent apprehension of such a contact. For the point that intent does not mean the desire to injure, *see* Vosburg v. Putney, 80 Wis. 523, 50 N.W. 403 (1891)(boy kicks another boy across the aisle in the classroom). In Vosberg, the court noted that had the boys been playing on the school play ground it would have hesitated to hold the plaintiff liable. In the new trial of the instant case, do you think Claudia has a good argument that her touching of Susan was permissible under the "implied license of the playgrounds?" Was Claudia's intent to cause an *offensive* contact or was it to cause a *harmful* contact or was it merely to put the plaintiff in imminent apprehension of a harmful or offensive contact?

2. As the instant case illustrates, it is not uncommon for judges and lawyers to use the phrase "assault and battery" for what is, strictly speaking, a battery. Perhaps the reason for this usage is that most but not all batteries probably involve the putting of the victim in imminent apprehension of a battery. These cases thus present something of a civil analogue of the notion of a lesser included offense in criminal law. Indeed in the criminal law, assault was originally a lesser included offense to battery, but, in the criminal law, assault was historically defined as an attempted battery and not as putting the other in imminent apprehension of a battery. In many jurisdictions, the civil definition of assault has now been added to the traditional attempted battery definition in order to broaden the reach of the crime of assault. Most cases would be decided the same way regardless of which definition was used. There are, however, some cases where the choice of definition will make a difference. Thus, take a case where the defendant points an unloaded revolver at the plaintiff, who is unaware that the revolver is unloaded. Under the attempted battery definition, this is not an assault. Under the civil definition, which focuses on the plaintiff's imminent apprehension of a battery, such conduct would amount to an assault. *See* Lowry v. Standard Oil Co., 63 Cal.App.2d 1, 146 P.2d 57 (1944); Beach v. Hancock, 27 N.H. 223 (1853). On the other hand firing a weapon at an unconscious person would be an assault under the attempted battery definition of criminal law but not under the civil definition which focuses upon the plaintiff's apprehension. *See* Tom v. Lenox Hill Hospital, 165 Misc.2d 313, 627 N.Y.S.2d 874 (Sup.Ct.1995). Of course, if the victim is hit, the conduct will amount to a battery under either the criminal or tort law regardless of whether the victim was aware of what was happening to him. On the differences between the criminal and civil definitions of assault, *see* R. Perkins, An Analysis of Assault and Attempts to Assault, 47 Minn.L.Rev. 71 (1962).

3. In order to constitute a battery the contact need not actually be with the body of the victim. It is enough that contact is made with something that is attached or closely related to a person's body. Knocking a person's hat off his head would thus be a battery as would striking his cane. In Fisher v. Carrousel Motor Hotel, Inc., 424 S.W.2d 627 (Tex.1967) defendant's restaurant employee approached plaintiff, snatched a plate from his hand and "shouted that he, a Negro, could not be served." Held: intentionally grabbing the plate constituted a battery. It has been held that striking a horse upon which a person is riding is a battery (*see* Dodwell v. Burford, 1 Mod.Rep. 24, 86 Eng.Rep. 703 (K.B. 1669)), and there are also cases holding that intentional physical contact with an occupied car constitutes a battery against the occupants. *See* Crossman v. Thurlow, 336 Mass. 252, 143 N.E.2d 814 (1957); Farm Bureau Mutual Automobile Insurance Co. v. Hammer, 177 F.2d 793 (4th Cir.1949). In both the horse and automobile cases, however, the plaintiff was physically injured as the result of the defendant's conduct. Despite the intimation of some commentators, it is not clear that intentional physical contact with a horse or vehicle constitutes a battery against the rider of the horse or the occupants of the vehicle when no injury is caused them. Indeed, in such circumstances, it often might not be accurate to assert that the defendant intended to cause a harmful or offensive bodily contact to a person.

4. Spitting in someone's face would be a prototypical instance of an offensive contact, as would also be kissing a stranger where there is no reason to believe that the stranger has consented to such contact. A certain amount of contact that is an inevitable accompaniment of life, however, such as the

inevitable jostling that takes place in crowded public areas, is not deemed to be offensive. The English cases use the term "hostile" intention to cover the situation where an action will lie despite the absence of an intent to cause a harmful contact with another. For a good review of the types of "physical molestation" that, over a period of 300 years, have been held not to have been committed with hostile intent, *see* Wilson v. Pringle, [1987] Q.B. 237, [1986] 3 W.L.R. 1, [1986] 2 All E.R. 440 (C.A.1986). The following case wrestles with the definition of offensive contact in a contemporary context.

BRZOSKA v. OLSON

Supreme Court of Delaware, 1995.
668 A.2d 1355.

WALSH, JUSTICE, for the majority:

In this appeal from the Superior Court, we confront the question of whether a patient may recover damages for treatment by a health care provider afflicted with Acquired Immunodeficiency Syndrome ("AIDS") absent a showing of a resultant physical injury or exposure to disease. The appellants, plaintiffs below, are 38 former patients of Dr. Raymond P. Owens, a Wilmington dentist who died of AIDS on March 1, 1991. In an action brought against Edward P. Olson, the administrator of Dr. Owens' estate, the plaintiffs sought recovery under theories of negligence, battery, and misrepresentation. After limited discovery, the Superior Court granted summary judgment in favor of Dr. Owens' estate, ruling that, in the absence of a showing of physical harm, plaintiffs were not entitled to recover under any theory advanced. Plaintiffs have appealed only the rulings disallowing recovery on the claims of battery and misrepresentation.

We conclude that the Superior Court correctly ruled that, under the circumstances of Dr. Owens' treatment, there can be no recovery for fear of contracting a disease in the absence of a showing that any of the plaintiffs had suffered physical harm. Specifically, plaintiffs cannot recover under battery as a matter of law because they could not show that their alleged offense was reasonable in the absence of being actually exposed to a disease-causing agent.

* * *

I

Although plaintiffs have alleged that Dr. Owens was aware that he had AIDS for at least ten years, it is clear from the record that it was in March, 1989, that Dr. Owens was advised by his physician that he was HIV-positive. Dr. Owens continued to practice, but his condition had deteriorated by the summer of 1990. Toward the end of 1990, he exhibited open lesions, weakness, and memory loss. In February, 1991, his physician recommended that Dr. Owens discontinue his practice because of deteriorating health. Shortly thereafter, on February 23, Dr. Owens was hospitalized. He remained hospitalized until his death on March 1, 1991.

Shortly after Dr. Owens' death, the Delaware Division of Public Health (the "Division") undertook an evaluation of Dr. Owens' practice and records, in part to determine if his patients had been placed at risk through exposure to HIV. The Division determined that Dr. Owens' equipment, sterilization procedures and precautionary methods were better than average and that he had ceased doing surgery since being diagnosed as HIV-positive in 1989. * * * Of the 630 former patients of Dr. Owens who have been tested, none have tested positive for HIV.

* * *

Plaintiffs' theory of recovery was cast in five counts: (i) negligence; (ii) recklessness; (iii) battery; (iv) fraudulent misrepresentation; and (v) false pretenses. * * * [T]he battery count sought recovery for "unconsented" and "offensive touching."

* * *

Under the Restatement (Second) of Torts, "[a]n actor is subject to liability to another for battery if (a) he acts intending to cause a harmful or offensive contact with the person ... and (b) a harmful contact with the person of the other directly or indirectly results." Restatement (Second) of Torts s 18 (1965). * * * This Court has recognized that, under appropriate factual circumstances, a patient may have a cause of action against a medical practitioner for the tort of battery for acts arising from the practitioner's professional conduct. *See* Newmark v. Williams, Del.Supr., 588 A.2d 1108, 1115 (1991)

In essence, the tort of battery is the intentional, unpermitted contact upon the person of another which is harmful or offensive. Lack of consent is thus an essential element of battery. The intent necessary for battery is the intent to make contact with the person, not the intent to cause harm. In addition, the contact need not be harmful, it is sufficient if the contact offends the person's integrity. "Proof of the technical invasion of the integrity of the plaintiff's person by even an entirely harmless, yet offensive, contact entitles the plaintiff to vindication of the legal right by the award of nominal damages." Prosser and Keeton § 9 at 40. The fact that a person does not discover the offensive nature of the contact until after the event does not, ipso facto, preclude recovery.

Although a battery may consist of any unauthorized touching of the person which causes offense or alarm, the test for whether a contact is "offensive" is not wholly subjective. The law does not permit recovery for the extremely sensitive who become offended at the slightest contact. Rather, for a bodily contact to be offensive, it must offend a reasonable sense of personal dignity. In order for a contact be offensive to a reasonable sense of personal dignity, it must be one which would offend the ordinary person and as such one not unduly sensitive as to his personal dignity. It must, therefore, be a contact which is unwarranted by the social usages prevalent at the time and place at which it is inflicted. * * * The propriety of the contact is therefore assessed by an objective "reasonableness" standard.

Plaintiffs contend that the "touching" implicit in the dental procedures performed by Dr. Owens was offensive because he was HIV-positive. We must therefore determine whether the performance of dental procedures by an HIV-infected dentist, standing alone, may constitute offensive bodily contact for purposes of battery, i.e., would such touching offend a reasonable sense of personal dignity?

* * *

The risk of HIV transmission from a health care worker to a patient during an invasive medical procedure is very remote.

* * *

It is unreasonable for a person to fear infection when that person has not been exposed to a disease. * * * In such circumstances, the fear of contracting AIDS is per se unreasonable without proof of actual exposure to HIV.[9] In our view, the mere fear of contracting AIDS, in the absence of actual exposure to HIV, is not sufficient to impose liability on a health care provider. AIDS phobia, standing alone, cannot form the basis for recovery of damages, even under a battery theory because the underlying causation/harm nexus is not medically supportable.

AIDS is a disease that spawns widespread public misperception based upon the dearth of knowledge concerning HIV transmission. Indeed, plaintiffs rely upon the degree of public misconception about AIDS to support their claim that their fear was reasonable. To accept this argument is to contribute to the phobia. Were we to recognize a claim for the fear of contracting AIDS based upon a mere allegation that one may have been exposed to HIV, totally unsupported by any medical evidence or factual proof, we would open a Pandora's Box of "AIDS-phobia" claims by individuals whose ignorance, unreasonable suspicion or general paranoia cause them apprehension over the slightest of contact with HIV-infected individuals or objects.

* * *

In sum, we find that, without actual exposure to HIV, the risk of its transmission is so minute that any fear of contracting AIDS is per se unreasonable. We therefore hold, as a matter of law, that the incidental touching of a patient by an HIV-infected dentist while performing ordinary, consented-to dental procedures is insufficient to sustain a battery claim in the absence of a channel for HIV infection. In other words, such contact is "offensive" only if it results in actual exposure to the HIV virus. We therefore adopt an "actual exposure" test, which requires a plaintiff to show "actual exposure" to a disease-causing agent as a prerequisite to prevail on a claim based upon fear of contracting disease. Attenuated and speculative allegations of exposure to HIV do not give rise to a legally cognizable claim in Delaware.

* * *

9. In this holding, we recognize that the issue of reasonableness is ordinarily a question of fact for the trier of fact. *See generally* Duphily v. Delaware Electric Cooperative, Inc., Del.Supr., No. 148, 1994, slip op. at 23, Walsh, J. (July 31, 1995). Nevertheless, this Court will decide an issue as a matter of law in those circumstances where only one conclusion can be reached from the application of the legal standard to the undisputed facts. *See* Hercules Powder Co. v. DiSabatino, Del. Supr., 188 A.2d 529, 535 (1963).

The judgment of the Superior Court is AFFIRMED IN PART, RE-VERSED IN PART, and REMANDED for proceedings consistent with this opinion.

DUFFY, JUSTICE (RETIRED), concurring in part and dissenting:

My views differ in several respects from those stated in the majority opinion and, respectfully, I dissent from much of its analysis and I agree with only one of its conclusions.

This is the first AIDS case of its kind to reach this Court and, unhappily, it involves the relationship between an infected health care provider—a dentist—and his patients. Obviously, that implicates serious and sensitive public policy (probably best determined in the legislative process) requiring a delicate balance between the dentist's need and opportunity to continue practicing his profession, and the right of patients (the public) to be protected from AIDS infection—which, as the majority states, is invariably fatal. It is this latter fact of life which gives this case both its pain and its special significance.

The litigation arrived here after the Superior Court had entered a summary judgment for defendant—on limited discovery and without trial on any issue.

The majority opinion makes little, if any, attempt to balance or analyze the respective interests of dentist and patient. Rather, its dispositive focus is on so-called "AIDS-phobia" claims which are based on fear of the virus and nothing more. But that is not this case—which is based on what the dentist did and did not do in his patient contacts. And although there were professional guidance and precautionary measures for health care workers to reduce the risk of HIV transmission, these were advisory only. Thus, in the last analysis, Dr. Owens was his own judge of what he should or should not do in his patient contacts. And the evidence certainly suggests that he acted in his own interest.

* * *

As the majority states, a battery "is the intentional, unpermitted contact upon the person of another which is harmful or offensive." Lack of consent is essential and the contact must offend a reasonable sense of personal dignity:

Relying entirely on national statistics of the most general kind, and with the benefit of hindsight, the majority concludes that any fear of contracting AIDS under the facts of this case is per se unreasonable-without "actual exposure" to the disease. Here there is much more than the "phobia" which the majority condemns as arising from ignorance, unreasonable suspicion, general paranoia or fragile sensibility. Indeed, there is an abundance of evidence from which a jury could conclude that the fears of plaintiffs-or some of them-that they may have contracted a fatal disease were reasonable. Consider the following, which is in the record:

- In March 1989, Dr. Owens knew that he was HIV positive; he continued to practice dentistry, including invasive procedures in which patients bled.

- His physical condition deteriorated in mid–1990.

- Thereafter he had open lesions on his face, arms, hands, legs, ankles and elbows; he scratched a lesion on his elbow, causing it to weep. He exhibited body weakness and memory loss.

- On at least one occasion he cut himself while working on a patient.

- In February 1991 Dr. Owens' own physician recommended that he discontinue practicing. He did not do so. * * *

- On March 13, 1991, Dr. Paul Silverman, the State Epidemiologist, filed a report, which states in part: Towards the end of 1990 [Dr. Owens'] illness seriously interfered with his clinical practice. We know this from several sources. Loss of memory, loss of motor skills, dementia. He cut himself at least once, and there are other accounts of problems which could pose a risk to patients. This became most serious during January and February. He did have lesions on his hand and elbow. Although he consistently gloved, he did not wash between.

* * *

I agree that defendant may do what was done here; that is, offer statistical data to show that patient contact by a dentist with AIDS results in transmission of the disease only in a very small percentage of cases and, for that reason (defendant argues), fear of AIDS from such a contact is not reasonable (and thus the contact is not "offensive" within the legal definition of "battery").

But I do not agree that the statistical data offered in this case is conclusive or dispositive "as a matter of law."

* * *

Finally, as to the battery claim, the majority quotes with approval the standard law on that subject found in both the Restatement (Second) of Torts and in Prosser and Keeton, supra: an actor is liable if he intends to cause an "offensive contact with the person" of another. But the majority creates a special "offensive" requirement for this AIDS case, viz: the contact is not offensive as a matter of law unless it permits "the passage of fluids."

Notes

1. Because of their origins in the writ of trespass, the intentional torts of assault and battery do not require that the plaintiff show actual damages in order to state a cause of action. Thus, spitting in someone's face has been held to constitute a battery. Alcorn v. Mitchell, 63 Ill. 553 (1872). Does the majority opinion require proof of actual physical damages in A.I.D.S. battery cases in Delaware? Should courts begin to require physical damages in all battery cases?

2. On what grounds, exactly, did the court conclude that the touching was not "objectively" offensive? Can Dr. Owens' behavior be distinguished from spitting in someone's face? Consider the following passage from comment c. to Restatement (Second) of Torts § 18:

'Since the essence of plaintiff's grievance consists in the offense to the dignity involved in the unpermitted and intentional invasion of the inviolability of his person and not in any physical harm done to his body, it is not necessary that the plaintiff's actual body be disturbed.'

3.   Ordinarily, as the dissent indicates, the question of whether a particular touching is offense is a question that would be left to the jury. Why do you think the majority refused to allow a jury to decide this question? We will discuss the constantly evolving relationship between judge and jury in Chapter Three.

DICKENS v. PURYEAR

Supreme Court of North Carolina, 1981.
302 N.C. 437, 276 S.E.2d 325.

EXUM, JUSTICE.

Plaintiff's complaint is cast as a claim for intentional infliction of mental distress. It was filed more than one year but less than three years after the incidents complained of occurred. Defendants moved for summary judgment before answer was due or filed. Much of the factual showing at the hearing on summary judgment related to assaults and batteries committed against plaintiff by defendants. Defendants' motions for summary judgment were allowed on the ground that plaintiff's claim was for assault and battery; therefore it was barred by the one-year statute of limitations applicable to assault and battery. G.S. 1–54(3).

The facts brought out at the hearing on summary judgment may be briefly summarized: For a time preceding the incidents in question plaintiff Dickens, a thirty-one year old man, shared sex, alcohol and marijuana with defendants' daughter, a seventeen year old high school student. On 2 April 1975 defendants * * * lured plaintiff into rural Johnston County, North Carolina. Upon plaintiff's arrival defendant Earl Puryear, after identifying himself, * * * pointed a pistol between plaintiff's eyes and shouted "Y'all come on out." Four men wearing ski masks and armed with nightsticks then approached from behind plaintiff and beat him into semi-consciousness. They handcuffed plaintiff to a piece of farm machinery and resumed striking him with nightsticks. Defendant Earl Puryear, while brandishing a knife and cutting plaintiff's hair, threatened plaintiff with castration. During four or five interruptions of the beatings defendant Earl Puryear and the others, within plaintiff's hearing, discussed and took votes on whether plaintiff should be killed or castrated. Finally, after some two hours and the conclusion of a final conference, the beatings ceased. Defendant Earl Puryear told plaintiff to go home, pull his telephone off the wall, pack his clothes, and leave the state of North Carolina; otherwise he would be killed. Plaintiff was then set free.

Plaintiff filed his complaint on 31 March 1978. It alleges that defendants on the occasion just described intentionally inflicted mental distress upon him. * * * Judge Braswell, * * * concluded that plaintiff's claim was barred by G.S. 1–54(3), the one-year statute of limitations applicable to assault and battery. On 29 March 1979 he granted summary judgment in favor of both defendants.

* * *

North Carolina follows common law principles governing assault and battery. An assault is an offer to show violence to another without striking him, and a battery is the carrying of the threat into effect by the infliction of a blow. * * * The interest protected by the action for battery is freedom from intentional and unpermitted contact with one's person; the interest protected by the action for assault is freedom from apprehension of a harmful or offensive contact with one's person. * * * The apprehension created must be one of an immediate harmful or offensive contact, as distinguished from contact in the future.

* * *

Common law principles of assault and battery as enunciated in North Carolina law are also found in the Restatement (Second) of Torts (1965)(hereinafter "the Restatement"). As noted in s 29(1) of the Restatement, "(t)o make the actor liable for an assault he must put the other in apprehension of an *imminent* contact." (Emphasis supplied.) The comment to s 29(1) states: "The apprehension created must be one of imminent contact, as distinguished from any contact in the future. 'Imminent' does not mean immediate, in the sense of instantaneous contact.... It means rather that there will be no significant delay." Similarly, s 31 of the Restatement provides that "(w)ords do not make the actor liable for assault unless together with other acts or circumstances they put the other in reasonable apprehension of an *imminent* harmful or offensive contact with his person." (Emphasis supplied.)

* * *

Again, as noted by Prosser, s 10, p. 40, "(t)hreats for the future ... are simply not present breaches of the peace, and so never have fallen within the narrow boundaries of (assault)." Thus threats for the future are actionable, if at all, not as assaults but as intentional infliction of mental distress.

* * *

Although plaintiff labels his claim one for intentional infliction of mental distress, we agree with the Court of Appeals that "(t)he nature of the action is not determined by what either party calls it...." * * * The nature of the action is determined "by the issues arising on the pleading and by the relief sought," id., and by the facts which, at trial, are proved or which, on motion for summary judgment, are forecast by the evidentiary showing.

Here much of the factual showing at the hearing related to assaults and batteries committed by defendants against plaintiff. The physical beatings and the cutting of plaintiff's hair constituted batteries. The threats of castration and death, being threats which created apprehension of immediate harmful or offensive contact, were assaults. Plaintiff's recovery for injuries, mental or physical, caused by these actions would be barred by the one-year statute of limitations.

The evidentiary showing on the summary judgment motion does, however, indicate that defendant Earl Puryear threatened plaintiff with death in the future unless plaintiff went home, pulled his telephone off the wall, packed his clothes, and left the state. The Court of Appeals characterized this threat as being "an immediate threat of harmful and offensive contact. It was a present threat of harm to plaintiff...."

* * *

The Court of Appeals thus concluded that this threat was also an assault barred by the one-year statute of limitations.

We disagree with the Court of Appeals' characterization of this threat. The threat was not one of imminent, or immediate, harm. It was a threat for the future apparently intended to and which allegedly did inflict serious mental distress; therefore it is actionable, if at all, as an intentional infliction of mental distress.

Reversed in part. Affirmed in part.

Notes

1. The appellate court concluded that the defendant was not entitled to a summary judgment on the plaintiff's intentional infliction of emotional distress claim with respect to the threat of future injury if the plaintiff did not leave town. One of the first cases to adopt this approach on somewhat similar facts was State Rubbish Collectors Association v. Siliznoff, 38 Cal.2d 330, 240 P.2d 282 (1952)(Siliznoff was told that, if he did not accede to the association's demands, he would be beaten up and his trucks would be burned.) The subject of intentional infliction of emotional distress will be discussed in Chapter Seventeen, *infra*.

2. The defendant in the instant case was convicted of a conspiracy to commit simple assault in a separate criminal case. *See* State v. Puryear, 30 N.C.App. 719, 228 S.E.2d 536, appeal dismissed, 291 N.C. 325, 230 S.E.2d 678 (1976).

3. Statutes of limitations require suits to be commenced within a certain period of time. Under North Carolina law, actions for assault and battery must be brought within one year of the alleged tortious act. N.C. Gen. Stat. § 1–54(3)(1994). Actions based on a claim of an intentional infliction of emotional distress are swept up in a general provision that establishes a 3 year limitation period for "criminal conversation, or for any other injury to the person or rights of another, not arising on contract and not hereafter enumerated." N.C. Gen. Stat. § 1–52(5)(1994). Why do you think the legislature provides such a short time for bringing a battery claim?

4. Conditional threats. If, during a heated quarrel, one party puts his hand on his sword and says "If it were not assize-time, I would not take such language from you." Has there been an assault? *See* Tuberville v. Savage, 1 Mod. 3, 86 Eng.Rep. 684 (K.B. 1669). Is there an assault if at one point the defendants show the plaintiffs that they are carrying blackjacks and at a later point in time the defendants threaten to strike the plaintiffs with blackjacks? Cucinotti v. Ortmann, 399 Pa. 26, 159 A.2d 216 (1960).

5. Section 21 of the *Restatement (Second)* defines assaults in terms of "apprehension." It distinguishes apprehension from "fright." Is there an assault if the plaintiff has every reason to believe that bystanders will interfere with the defendant before he is actually able to strike the plaintiff?

C.   TRANSFERRED INTENT

SINGER v. MARX

District Court of Appeal of California, 1956.
144 Cal.App.2d 637, 301 P.2d 440.

ASHBURN, JUSTICE.

Plaintiff Denise Singer, a minor, sues Tim Marx, another minor, for personal injury alleged to have been inflicted upon her (1) through his negligence, and (2) through a battery of her person. She seeks recovery from Tim's parents, Zeppo Marx and Marion Marx, on the theory of their negligent failure to control Tim's known penchant for throwing rocks at other people. Denise's father also sues the parents of Tim for recovery of expenses incurred by him as a result of his child's injury, the charge being negligence upon the part of the parents. The trial judge granted a nonsuit as to both plaintiffs and all causes of action. Plaintiffs appeal.

"Under well-established rules we must, in considering whether the judgment of nonsuit was proper, resolve every conflict in their testimonies in favor of plaintiff, consider every inference which can reasonably be drawn and every presumption which can fairly be deemed to arise in support of plaintiff, and accept as true all evidence adduced direct and indirect which tends to sustain plaintiff's case." * * * In the following discussion the court assumes as established all evidence and all inferences favorable to plaintiffs' causes of action.

On September 13, 1953, Tim Marx was nine years of age. Plaintiff Denise was eight and Barbara Corcoran was also eight. They are the only eyewitnesses to the episode under examination. Tim and Denise were on the front lawn of the Singer residence, which was located on the north side of the street fronting south. Barbara was riding a bicycle back and forth on the pavement. At the time the injury was inflicted upon her Denise was some six, eight or ten feet north of the sidewalk and Tim was to her left and rear about four feet away. The children were not playing any game. Tim had been throwing rocks into or across the street and talking about how far he could throw. Neither girl threw any rocks or clods. Immediately preceding Tim's striking Denise in the eye with a rock, which he admitted, Barbara was riding easterly on the sidewalk and entering upon the Singer property at the west side, about 30 feet from Denise. Tim, who was looking at plaintiff, said to her, "watch Barbie." He had not previously thrown at her or Barbara. Denise looked toward Barbara and then back at Tim and at the same moment was struck in the eye by the rock, which was a flat, rough one about the size of a small hen's egg. Barbara saw him throw at an angle toward her; saw him let go of the rock but did not see it strike plaintiff. Denise heard him say "watch Barbie" and saw him raise his arm in the throw but did not see the rock leave his hand. She was struck immediately in the left eye. The line of throw toward Barbara would pass several feet in front of Denise. For the rock to strike her, one of two things would have to occur, either (1) Tim changed the direction of throw without any warning, or (2) he held the rock too loosely, or let go of it too soon to control its flight, and inadvertently hit Denise. The evidence is susceptible of either of these inferences.

The general proposition that an infant is liable for his torts is established in this state by statute. Civil Code, § 41, says: "A minor * * * is civilly liable for a wrong done by him, but is not liable in exemplary damages unless at the time of the act he was capable of knowing that it was wrongful." That statute, it will be noted, does not imply as an element of liability for compensatory damages the existence of capacity to appreciate the wrongful character of the act. But the cases have engrafted upon it certain reasonable qualifications about to be discussed.

An infant who forcibly invades the person of another is liable for a battery regardless of an intent to inflict injury; the only intent which is necessary is that of doing the particular act in question in this case throwing a rock at somebody. This matter is discussed in Ellis v. D'Angelo, 116 Cal.App.2d 310, at page 316, 253 P.2d 675, at page 678, in which it was held that, although a four-year-old child is, as a matter of law, incapable of negligence, the complaint nevertheless stated a cause of action for battery against the same child. At page 315 of 116 Cal.App.2d, at page 677 of 253 P.2d it is said: "From these authorities and the cases which they cite it may be concluded generally that an infant is liable for his torts even though he lacks the mental development and capacity to recognize the wrongfulness of his conduct so long as he has the mental capacity to have the state of mind necessary to the commission of the particular tort with which he is charged. Thus as between a battery and negligent injury an infant may have the capacity to intend the violent contact which is essential to the commission of battery when the same infant would be incapable of realizing that his heedless conduct might foreseeably lead to injury to another which is the essential capacity of mind to create liability for negligence." * * *

Certainly it cannot be said as a matter of law that Tim did not have sufficient mental capacity to intend the harmful striking of another. If he indicated to both girls that he was throwing at Barbara and then aimed at Denise, whom he hit he was plainly liable to her for a battery.

This matter of intent in a battery case is also discussed in Lopez v. Surchia, 112 Cal.App.2d 314, 246 P.2d 111, which involved an adult defendant who had shot plaintiff and claimed self-defense. At page 318 of 112 Cal.App.2d, at page 113 of 246 P.2d: "'The true rule is that intent is the gist of the action only where the battery was committed in the performance of an act not otherwise unlawful * * *. If the cause of action is an alleged battery committed in the performance of an unlawful or wrongful act, the intent of the wrongdoer to injure is immaterial. In other words, if the defendant did an illegal act which was likely to prove injurious to another, he is answerable for the consequence which directly and naturally resulted from the conduct, even though he did not intend to do the particular injury which followed. * * *'"

While throwing rocks at trees or into the street ordinarily is an innocent and lawful pastime, that same act when directed at another person is wrongful. The evidence at bar (combining that of Barbara with portions of Tim's own testimony) warrants an inference that Tim threw at Barbara and inadvertently struck Denise. In such circumstances the doctrine of "transferred intent" renders him liable to Denise. On this subject the Lopez case, supra, says at page 318 of 112 Cal.App.2d, at page 113 of 246 P.2d: " 'If defendant unlawfully aims at one person and hits another he is guilty of assault and battery on the party he hit, the injury being the direct, natural and probable consequence of the wrongful act. * * *' " The rule is not confined to criminal cases, as argued by respondents.

* * *

We hold that the evidence at bar would sustain an inference that Tim (1) deliberately threw the rock at plaintiff, or (2) threw the rock at Barbara and accidentally struck plaintiff, or (3) negligently held and threw the rock in such manner as to cause the throw to miscarry and thus strike plaintiff. Pursuing this line of thought counsel for respondent Tim argue that: "When one equally reasonable inference supports a plaintiff's prima facie case against an equally reasonable inference supporting the defendant, the plaintiff has not sustained his burden of proof." In support thereof * * * cases are cited: * * *. While they do hold that evidence which is equally susceptible of opposing inferences, one favorable and one unfavorable to the plaintiff, constitutes no proof at all, we are cognizant of no authority to the effect that that is true of evidence susceptible of several inferences all of which point in the same direction, liability of defendant. On principle it seems that whenever the evidence affords room for several inferences favorable to the plaintiff the jury should determine the one to draw, and the plaintiff does not have to elect or to establish one inescapable inference. * * * The plaintiff relying on circumstantial evidence does not have to exclude the possibility of every other reasonable inference possibly derivable from the facts proved. * * *

The granting of a nonsuit in favor of Tim was erroneous.

* * *

[In the remainder of its opinion the court considered the propriety of the nonsuit granted by the trial court in favor of Tim's parents. The crucial issue was whether there was sufficient evidence of negligence in exercising control over a child known "to possess and exercise dangerous proclivities toward other people." On the basis of the testimony of a former neighbor "that she could almost say that she had never seen Tim or his younger brother when they were not throwing rocks" and of evidence that Mrs. Marx had been told by the principal of Tim's school that Tim had thrown clods of earth at her car, the court concluded that a jury could infer that Mrs. Marx had knowledge of her son's proclivities and was negligent in failing to control him. The court concluded however that there was no evidence that Mr. Marx had any personal knowledge of his son's rock-throwing proclivities; the most the evidence showed was that Mr. Marx had been consulted before Tim had been punished for throwing clods of earth at his school principal's car. The court therefore affirmed the nonsuit as to Mr. Marx.]

Note

In the instant case, the infant defendant may have wanted to hit one of the girls with a stone. If he had this morally reprehensible purpose, it does not seem unfair to subject him to full liability for a battery when he misses the girl he was aiming at and hits another girl. Suppose, however, the defendant did not desire to cause a harmful or offensive bodily contact upon anyone, but is nevertheless held to have acted intentionally because he knew that a harmful or offensive bodily contact was substantially certain to occur, as for example in Garratt v. Dailey discussed in the notes on p. 37, *supra*. There, a five year old boy pulled away a chair while his maiden aunt was about to sit in it because the boy wanted to sit in the chair himself. Suppose, while falling down, the maiden aunt had fallen against a third person? Could this person bring an action for battery against the boy on the basis of "transferred intent?" The conventional wisdom is that he can. Cf. Reynolds v. Pierson, 29 Ind.App. 273, 64 N.E. 484 (1902). Does the imposition of liability in such circumstances seem as morally justifiable as in a case like Singer v. Marx? Of course, if the plaintiff suffers any significant injuries, he probably would have the basis of an action for negligence against the defendant, unless the defendant was a young child. As the discussion in Singer v. Marx indicates, there may be occasions when it is difficult to bring an action against a young child on the basis of negligence (i.e. a lack of reasonable care) even though the child is held to be capable of committing an intentional tort. This question will be discussed again in Chapter Three, *infra*. On the question of parental liability for the conduct of their children, *see* Note, Parental Liability for the Torts of their Minor Children: Limits, Logic & Legality, 9 Nova L.Rev. 205 (1984).

D.   TRESPASS TO LAND

1.   *General*

We have already noted, in Chapter One, that, at common law, trespass was distinguished from trespass on the case on the basis of whether the injury suffered by the plaintiff was the direct or indirect consequence of the defendant's tortious conduct. As we have seen, in the nineteenth century this method of legal classification was gradually replaced by one that focused upon whether or not the defendant had intended to injure the plaintiff. The term "trespass" itself largely dropped from the legal vocabulary, except with respect to *intentional* physical invasions of land and *intentional* physical interference with chattels.[1] It must be stressed, however, that the only thing that must be intended is the action that constitutes the invasion of another's land or the action that constitutes the physical interference with the chattels of another. That is, in order for an action for trespass to land to lie, it is not necessary that the defendant have intended to enter the land of the plaintiff. In the area of trespass, as in many other areas of tort law, it is often useful to distinguish between acts that are properly called mistakes and those that are properly called accidents. One who enters the land of another in the mistaken but nevertheless reasonable belief that he is entering onto his own land is nonetheless liable in trespass. As long as the defendant intended to take

---

1. The old common law distinctions can nevertheless still occasionally have some practical importance. In a state where a claim that is based upon a cause of action that would have been trespass to land at common law has a different (usually longer) statute of limitations than actions based upon negligence, it will be necessary to determine whether the defendant's conduct, even if not intentional, would have constituted trespass at common law. *See* Martin v. Union Pacific Railroad, 256 Or. 563, 474 P.2d 739 (1970); Zimmer v. Stephenson, 66 Wn.2d 477, 403 P.2d 343 (1965).

the step which resulted in his entry onto the plaintiff's land, the requisite intention exists.

If the entry upon land is not the result of a voluntary act, that is, the entry is not intentional, as where a person stumbles and falls upon the land of another, no action will lie unless the entry causes damage and even then, in almost all jurisdictions, only if the entry can be shown to be the result of reckless or negligent conduct or of the miscarriage of an abnormally dangerous activity such as blasting. Purely accidental entries, where no fault has been shown and where the accident has not arisen in the course of an abnormally dangerous activity are now generally not actionable regardless of the damage they have caused. *See* Hayes v. Bushey, 160 Me. 14, 196 A.2d 823 (1964).

If an airplane involuntarily and through no fault of the owner or operator crashes or lands upon the land of others, whether the owner or operator of the aircraft will be liable in damages to the possessor of land will depend upon whether aviation is considered an ultrahazardous or abnormally dangerous activity, a topic that will be considered in Chapter Eight, *infra*. If aviation is not considered an ultrahazardous or abnormally dangerous activity, and if the entry is voluntary, as where a plane in distress makes a forced landing, liability for ground damage will depend upon the extent of the *privilege* to enter private property to save life or property. This is a topic that will be considered below.

Once a trespass to land has been shown, the plaintiff has a cause of action for at least nominal damages regardless of whether the plaintiff has suffered any damages and regardless of the good faith of the defendant. These legal doctrines are justified on the ground that they provide a basis for using the tort of trespass to land as a vehicle for trying title to land.[2] How important the action for trespass actually is as a means of determining ownership of land, particularly in the present day, is another question, however. Another justification for allowing an action for trespass to be brought in the absence of actual damages and regardless of the defendant's good faith is the high social value traditionally placed upon the inviolability of a person's real property, and particularly of his home. Thus, the action of trespass is viewed as a means of enhancing the individual's sense of security and of discouraging people from resorting to breaches of the peace in order to protect this important interest.

2. *Privileged Entries Upon the Land of Another*

Not all intentional entries onto the land of another are actionable. Some entries are privileged as, for example, when one enters the land of another with the consent of the possessor. In many everyday situations consent is implied. For example, in Dobrin v. Stebbins, 122 Ill.App.2d 387, 259 N.E.2d 405 (1970) the plaintiff, a door-to-door salesman was attacked by the defendant's dog as he approached the defendant's front door. The court held that in the absence of signs warning salesmen and others to keep off, plaintiff and others who might peaceably come onto the land in

---

2. Strictly speaking, the right of a plaintiff to bring an action for trespass to land is based upon the plaintiff's right to present possession of the land, which is not necessarily the same thing as title. Nevertheless, determining the right to present possession will usually require a determination as to who has title to the land.

this way were not trespassers. Some privileges, however, arise independently of the consent of the person in possession of the land. Later in this chapter we shall, for example, have occasion to consider the defense (or privilege) of necessity under which in some emerging situations, public authorities and also private persons can enter the land of others, and even destroy the real and personal property of others, to avoid greater perils. Other privileges that arise by operation of law, that is privileges that arise regardless of the consent of the possessor, include the privileges long recognized at common law of travelers upon the public highways to enter adjoining land in order to avoid obstructions upon the highway and of the owners of animals being driven upon the public highway to enter adjoining land to recapture animals that have strayed from the highway.

3. *Variant Situations*

Although the core notion of trespass to land is that of unauthorized entry onto the land of another, there are some situations where a person may be held liable in trespass although his initial entry upon the land was lawful. Thus, one who has entered land with the permission of the possessor cannot remain upon the land after the possessor has asked him to leave. If he does not leave the land within a reasonable time after his permission to remain has been revoked, he will be liable in trespass to the possessor of the land. At common law this was known as the doctrine of trespass *ab initio*. *See* The Six Carpenters' Case, 8 Co.Rep. 146a, 77 Eng.Rep. 695 (K.B. 1610). Likewise, if a person has been permitted to place personal property on the land of another and refuses to remove the property within a reasonable time after the permission has been revoked, trespass to land will again lie. *See* Rogers v. Kent Board of County Road Commissioners, 319 Mich. 661, 30 N.W.2d 358 (1947). To permit the removal of the unwanted item, the person entitled to the immediate possession of the chattel is permitted to enter the land in a reasonable manner and within a reasonable time to remove the chattel. *See Restatement (Second) of Torts* § 177.

4. *Extent of the Interest Protected*

The typical trespass case involves an invasion of the possessor's interest in the exclusive possession of the surface area of the land. The possessor's interests, however, include an interest in the subsurface areas of the land as well as the airspace above it. The question is, how extensive is this legally protected interest? A typical case presenting this question is Herrin v. Sutherland, 74 Mont. 587, 241 P. 328, 331–32 (1925), which contains the following useful discussion.

CALLAWAY, C. J.

3. It must be held that when the defendant, although standing upon the land of another, fired a shotgun over plaintiff's premises, dwelling and cattle, he interfered with "the quiet, undisturbed, peaceful enjoyment" of the plaintiff, and thus committed a technical trespass at least. The plaintiff was the owner of the land. "Land," says Blackstone, "in its legal signification has an indefinite extent, upwards as well as downwards; whoever owns the land possesses all the space

upwards to an indefinite extent; such is the maxim of the law."
Cooley's Blackstone, Book II, 18 * * *.

The Court of Appeals of New York, in Butler v. Frontier Telephone Co., 186 N.Y. 486, 79 N.E. 716 (1906), had before it an ejectment
case in which wire, unsupported by any structure resting upon plaintiff's land, was strung over the surface of the ground at a height of
from 20 to 30 feet across the entire width of plaintiff's premises. In
speaking of the extent of the operation of the ancient maxim quoted
above the court said:

> "The surface of the ground is a guide, but not the full
> measure, for within reasonable limitations land includes not only
> the surface but also the space above and the part beneath. Co.
> Litt. 4a; 2 Blackstone's Com. 18; 3 Kent's Com. [14th Ed.] § 401.
> 'Usque ad coelum' is the upper boundary, and while this may not
> be taken too literally, there is no limitation within the bounds of
> any structure yet erected by man. So far as the case before us is
> concerned, the plaintiff as the owner of the soil owned upward to
> an indefinite extent."

Sir Frederick Pollock, in the tenth edition of his valuable work on
Torts, page 363, observes that it has been doubted whether it is a
trespass to pass over land without touching the soil, as one may in a
balloon, or to cause a material object, as a shot fired from a gun, to
pass over it.

> "Lord Ellensborough thought it was not in itself a trespass to
> 'interfere with the column of air superincumbent upon the close,'
> and that the remedy would be by action on the case for any actual
> damage: though he had no difficulty in holding that a man is a
> trespasser who fires a gun on his own land so that the shot fall on
> his neighbor's land"—citing Pickering v. Rudd, 4 Camp. 219–221,
> 16 R.R. 777.

Fifty years later, says Pollock (page 364), "Lord Blackburn inclined to
think differently (Kenyon v. Hart, 6 B. & S. 249, 252, 34 L. J. M. C87, 11
Law Times, 733), and his opinion seems the better." Continuing he
observes:

> "As regards shooting it would be strange if we could object to
> shots being fired point blank across our land only in the event of
> actual injury being caused, and the passage of the foreign object in
> the air above our soil being thus a mere incident and a distinct
> trespass to person or property."

But he concludes that, when taking into account the extreme flight
of projectiles fired from modern artillery which may pass thousands of
feet above the land, the subject is not without difficulty. That shortly
it will become one of considerable importance is indicated by the rapid
approach of the airplane as an instrumentality of commerce, as is
suggested in a valuable note found in 32 Harvard Law Review, 569.
However, it seems to be the consensus of the holdings of the courts in
this country that the air space, at least near the ground, is almost as
inviolable as the soil itself. * * * It is a matter of common knowledge

that the shotgun is a firearm of short range. To be subjected to the danger incident to and reasonably to be anticipated from the firing of this weapon at water fowl in flight over one's dwelling house and cattle would seem to be far from inconsequential, and, while plaintiff's allegations are very general in character, it cannot be said that a cause of action is not stated for nominal damages at least.

It is now settled that, at least since the Air Commerce Act of 1926, 44 Stat. 568, the navigable air space, as defined by regulations promulgated by the Federal Aviation Authority, is within the public domain. *See* United States v. Causby, 328 U.S. 256, 66 S.Ct. 1062, 90 L.Ed. 1206 (1946); . The typical overflight case that reaches litigation involves use of federally designated glidepaths to airports. *See* City of Newark v. Eastern Airlines, 159 F.Supp. 750 (D.N.J.1958). While the use of these glidepaths does not constitute a trespass onto the land of the surface owner, the interference with the surface owner's right to use his land may be so extensive as to amount to a "taking" of property. *See* Griggs v. Allegheny County, 369 U.S. 84, 82 S.Ct. 531, 7 L.Ed.2d 585 (1962)(planes passing as close as 30 feet of the plaintiff's house; noise from airport operations "unbearable;" county required to buy air easement over plaintiff's property). *See also* United States v. Causby, *supra*. If the airport is privately operated, its activities might constitute a nuisance which would entitle the adjoining landowners to damages and in some circumstances, in the discretion of the court, an injunction. The subject of nuisance will be considered in Chapter Fifteen, *infra*. A landowner obviously has a similar interest in exploiting the subsurface potential of his real property or preventing others from doing so without his consent. *See* Edwards v. Sims, 232 Ky. 791, 24 S.W.2d 619 (Ky.App.1930). (plaintiff claimed the Great Onyx Cave ran beneath his land and sought to prohibit owner of land where the cave mouth was located from conducting guided tours through the portion of the cave under plaintiff's land). However, public easements for sewer lines or subways may be so far below the potentially useable subsurface areas of the land as not to constitute a compensable "taking" of property. *See* Boehringer v. Montalto, 142 Misc. 560, 254 N.Y.S. 276 (1931).

E. TRESPASS TO CHATTELS

1. *General*

In modern law, the tort of trespass to chattels covers the intentional physical interference with or destruction of chattels. As with trespass to land, all that is required is that the defendant act voluntarily. A good faith and reasonable belief that the chattels are one's own is no defense. In a classic case, the defendant shot at what he reasonably believed was a wolf. The animal turned out to be a dog owned by the plaintiff and the defendant was held liable for damages. Ranson v. Kitner, 31 Ill.App. 241 (1888). As the *Ranson* case illustrates, animals are considered to be chattels. Although apparently under English law, nominal damages are recoverable for trespass to chattels on the same basis as they may be recovered for trespass to land—*see* Salmond, Torts 92 (17th ed. by R.F.V. Heuston 1977)—this is no longer always the case in the United States. The consensus in this country is that trespass to chattels will lie even if only for nominal damages when the defendant has intentionally *dispossessed* the plaintiff. Where, however, the defendant has merely intentionally *interfered* with the chattel, an action for trespass to chattels will only lie if the plaintiff can show some actual damages. *See Restatement (Second) of Torts* § 218. The damages can consist in physical damage to the chattel itself or in the loss of the use of the chattel for a substantial period of time.

2. *Relationship to Conversion*

The tort of trespass to chattels is closely related to the tort of conversion. Conversion covers the intentional "exercise of dominion or control over a chattel which so seriously interferes with the right of another to control it that the actor may justly be required to pay the other the full value of the chattel." *Restatement (Second) of Torts* § 222A. In other words, under a conversion theory, the defendant is forced to purchase the chattel from the plaintiff. The exercise of dominion can consist of the intentional unauthorized use, destruction, possession, or wrongful disposition of the chattel. *Id.* at § 223. In a case where the defendant intentionally destroys a chattel, the remedy will be the same whether the plaintiff brings his action in trespass to chattels or in conversion. Under both theories the damages will be the fair market value of the chattel at the time of its destruction. Where the chattel is not totally destroyed, however, the remedy under a trespass theory will only be the damage caused to the chattel,[3] that is, as we shall see in Chapter Ten, *infra*, an amount representing the diminution in the chattel's fair market value. In those circumstances a plaintiff might prefer to proceed in conversion if he is able to establish that the defendant has exercised the requisite dominion or control over the plaintiff's property. Similarly, to take a case of unauthorized use of a chattel, conversion will lie, and the defendant will in effect be forced to purchase the chattel, if the unauthorized use "is a serious violation of the right of another to control its use." *Restatement (Second) of Torts* § 227. *See also id.* at § 228. Control that is accompanied by an unauthorized, intentional refusal to return the chattel to its owner, will sometimes constitute a conversion even where the other's possession lasts only a short period of time. In such circumstances, if a court concludes that the defendant was "exercising dominion over [the chattel] in exclusion or defiance of plaintiff's right" it may hold that the defendant has converted the automobile and assess damages accordingly. *See* Russell–Vaughn Ford, Inc. v. Rouse, 281 Ala. 567, 206 S.2d 371 (1968)(automobile salesman asks for the keys to plaintiff's car and mockingly refuses to return them until the police are called). If the unauthorized use is not so serious but nevertheless deprives someone of the use of a chattel for a substantial enough period of time, *i.e.* for a period that is more than *de minimis*, damages, as has already been noted, may be recovered for the temporary loss of the use of the chattel under a trespass to chattels theory. Many of the more interesting modern cases of conversion involve the hypothecation of financial instruments, such as stock certificates. While such instruments are chattels, they are different sorts of chattels from the ones

---

3. In some cases the plaintiff might also be entitled to damages for the loss of the use of the chattel while it is being repaired as well as what might also be called "conse-quential" damages. These are questions that will be discussed in Chapter Ten, *infra*; for present purposes they may be ignored.

generally associated with trespass to chattels. Conversion is thus more fruitfully discussed in connection with other economic torts that typically arise in a commercial context.

F. DEFENSES

1. *Insanity*

WILLIAMS v. KEARBEY

Kansas Court of Appeals, 1989.
13 Kan.App.2d 564, 775 P.2d 670.

DAVIS, JUDGE:

In this case, we are asked to update Kansas tort law by holding that a 1927 Kansas Supreme Court decision no longer states the current tort law in Kansas. That decision held that "[a]n insane person who shoots and kills another is civilly liable in damages to those injured by his tort." Seals v. Snow, 123 Kan. 88, Syl. P 1, 254 P. 348 (1927). We conclude that Seals v. Snow is well grounded in sound public policy and expresses the unanimous view of all jurisdictions considering this question. Thus, we affirm the decision of the trial court.

Defendant Alan Kearbey, a minor, shot and wounded plaintiff Don Harris and plaintiff Daniel Williams, also a minor. Plaintiffs brought this action against Kearbey for battery. The jury found for plaintiffs. It also found, in answer to a special question, that Kearbey was insane at the time. The trial court entered judgment for plaintiffs and Kearbey appeals, arguing: (1) that an insane person should not be held civilly liable for his torts; and (2) that an insane person cannot commit a battery because he is incapable of forming the necessary intent.

Highly summarized, the material facts are as follows: On January 21, 1985, Alan Kearbey, who was then 14 years old, shot several people at Goddard Junior High School. The principal was killed and three other people were wounded. Among the wounded were plaintiff Don Harris, a teacher at the school, and plaintiff Daniel Williams, a student at the school. Both were shot in the leg.

Harris and Williams brought this action against Kearbey, his parents, and the Goddard School District (U.S.D. No. 265). The trial court held that Harris' claim against the school district was barred by the Kansas Workers' Compensation Act and, at the close of plaintiffs' case, granted the school district's motion for a directed verdict against plaintiff Williams based on governmental immunity.

* * *

The court denied Alan Kearbey's motion for a directed verdict on the grounds of insanity.

* * *

1. Whether an Insane Person Should be Held Civilly Liable for His Torts.

* * *

The tort liability of insane persons presents a policy question. In resolving this question, American courts have unanimously chosen to impose liability on an insane person rather than leaving the loss on the innocent victim. Seals v. Snow is a leading case in support of this view.

In Seals v. Snow, Martin Snow shot and killed Arthur Seals. Seals' widow brought an action for wrongful death. Snow answered that he had acted in self-defense. The jury returned a general verdict for the plaintiff, and found in answer to special questions that Snow had not acted in self-defense, that he was insane when he shot Seals, and that he was not able "to distinguish right from wrong" at the time he shot Seals. 123 Kan. at 88–89, 254 P. 348.

On appeal, Snow argued that he should not be held liable for his torts since he was insane. The court responded: "It is conceded that the great weight of authority is that an insane person is civilly liable for his torts. This liability has been based on a number of grounds, one that where one of two innocent persons must suffer a loss, it should be borne by the one who occasioned it. Another, that public policy requires the enforcement of such liability in order that relatives of the insane person shall be led to restrain him and that tort-feasors shall not simulate or pretend insanity to defend their wrongful acts causing damage to others, and that if he was not liable there would be no redress for injuries, and we might have the anomaly of an insane person having abundant wealth depriving another of his rights without compensation." 123 Kan. at 90, 254 P. 348.

Kearbey argues (1) the loss should fall upon plaintiffs rather than himself since he was not capable of avoiding his conduct and, hence, was not at fault; (2) it no longer makes sense to impose liability on an insane person in order to encourage his relatives to confine him since public policy no longer favors confinement of the mentally ill unless the insane person presents a danger to other people, in which case liability should be imposed directly on the insane person's relatives for failing to confine him, rather than on the insane person himself; and (3) concern over feigned insanity is no longer warranted since psychiatrists and psychologists now have improved methods of proving or disproving insanity.

Taking up Kearbey's arguments in reverse order, it is obvious that Kearbey's confidence in modern psychiatry is not widely shared. Comments to the Restatement (Second) of Torts list several valid reasons why liability is still imposed on insane persons. These reasons include: "the unsatisfactory character of the evidence of mental deficiency in many cases, together with the ease with which it can be feigned, the difficulty of estimating its existence, nature and extent; and some fear of introducing into the law of torts the confusion that has surrounded the defense of insanity in the criminal law." Restatement (Second) of Torts s 895J comment a (1977).

Next, Kearbey argues that liability should not be imposed on an insane person in order to encourage his relatives to confine him since public policy no longer favors confinement of the mentally ill. We agree that this is not a particularly strong reason for imposing liability. It is also clear, however, that removing this rationale would not have changed the court's decision in Seals v. Snow.

The main rationale of Seals v. Snow and the one which keys our affirmance of the trial court in this case is that, as between an insane person who injures another and an innocent person, it is more just for the insane person to bear the loss he caused than to visit the loss on the injured person. As stated in Seals v. Snow:

> " 'Undoubtedly, there is some appearance of hardship, even of injustice, in compelling one to respond for that which, for want of the control of reason, he was unable to avoid; that it is imposing upon a person already visited with the inexpressible calamity of mental obscurity an obligation to observe the same care and precaution respecting the rights of others that the law demands of one in the full possession of his faculties. But the question of liability in these cases, as well as in others, is a question of policy; and it is to be disposed of as would be the question whether the incompetent person should be supported at the expense of the public, or of his neighbors, or at the expense of his own estate. If his mental disorder makes him dependent, and at the same time prompts him to commit injuries, there seems to be no greater reason for imposing upon the neighbors or the public one set of these consequences, rather than the other; no more propriety or justice in making others bear the losses resulting from his unreasoning fury, when it is spent upon them or their property, than there would be in calling upon them to pay the expense of his confinement in an asylum, when his own estate is ample for the purpose.' " 123 Kan. at 90–91, 254 P. 348 (quoting 1 Cooley on Torts 172 [3d ed.1906]).

Although the above language is somewhat dated, the reasoning is still well grounded in sound public policy. Someone must bear the loss and, as between the tortfeasor, the injured party, and the general public, sound public policy favors placing the loss on the person who caused it, whether sane or not.

* * *

2. Whether an Insane Person is Capable of Forming the Intent of Bringing about a Harmful or Offensive Bodily Contact that is Necessary to the Tort of Battery.

Kearbey argues that he did not commit the tort of battery because his insanity prevented him from forming the intent necessary for that tort. The prevailing American view as set forth above is that a finding of insanity does not preclude a finding that a defendant acted intentionally. A jury may find that an insane person acted intentionally if he intended to do what he did, even though his reasons and motives were entirely irrational. Restatement (Second of Torts § 895J comment c (1977)); Prosser & Keeton on Torts s 135, p. 1074 (5th ed.1984).

The requirements of the prevailing American view for imposing liability for an intentional tort are satisfied in this case. In finding for the plaintiffs, the jury necessarily found that Alan Kearbey touched or struck the plaintiffs "with the intent of bringing about either a contact or an apprehension of contact, that is harmful or offensive." The fact that Kearbey did not "understand the nature of his acts" or did not "understand that what he was doing was prohibited by law" does not preclude the jury from finding that Kearbey acted intentionally in discharging a weapon in Goddard Junior High School.

Affirmed.

Notes

1. The doctrine that insane persons are liable for their torts has been much criticized over the years in the legal literature. *See e.g.,* F. Bohlen, Liability in Tort of Infants and Insane Persons, 23 Mich.L.Rev. 9 (1924); W. Cook, Mental Deficiency in Relation to Tort, 21 Colum.L.Rev. 333 (1921). Nevertheless, the American decisions are all in accord with the principal case. Polmatier v. Russ, 206 Conn. 229, 537 A.2d 468 (1988). *See also* Bolen v. Howard, 452 S.W.2d 401 (Ky.1970)(a somewhat recent case questioning the wisdom of the doctrine); McGuire v. Almy, 297 Mass. 323, 8 N.E.2d 760 (1937). Bohlen and, to a somewhat less categorical extent, Cook suggest, in their articles cited above, that English law is to the contrary. Admittedly English authority on the point is sparse, but English textbooks indicate that English law is similar to American law on this point. *See* Salmond & Heuston, Torts 415–17 (21st ed. by R. F. V. Heuston & R. A. Buckley, 1996). Where, however, malice in the sense of an improper motive, such as a desire to harm the plaintiff, is an essential part of the tort, as for example it is said to be in actions for malicious prosecution, insanity might be a defense. Likewise, insanity would seem to be a factor mitigating against the award of punitive damages.

2. Where the defendant loses all capacity for voluntary action, such as where he unexpectedly becomes ill, then the defendant will not be held to be capable of forming the requisite intent. *See* Goodrich v. Blair, 132 Ariz. 459, 646 P.2d 890 (Ariz.App.1982)(80 year defendant suffers sudden heart attack while taking driving test and swerves into oncoming traffic); Cohen v. Petty, 65 F.2d 820 (D.C.Cir.1933)(driver faints). *See also* Buckley and Toronto Transp. Comm. v. Smith Transp., [1946] 4 D.L.R. 721 (as a result of syphilis of the brain defendant's driver suddenly became subject to insane delusions that his truck was being controlled by an electric beam). Nevertheless, even in such instances, the defendant may be held liable on a negligence theory if, having reason to know that he was subject to such seizures, he engages in activities that create a high degree of risk to others if he should suddenly suffer a seizure. *See* Reliance Insurance Co. v. Dickens, 279 So.2d 234 (La.App.1973)(epileptic has seizure); Eleason v. Western Casualty and Surety Co., 254 Wis. 134, 35 N.W.2d 301 (1948)(same). *See also* Breunig v. American Family Insurance Co., 45 Wis.2d 536, 173 N.W.2d 619 (1970)(defendant suffered from hallucinations but had lucid moments from which the jury could infer that she was aware that she was likely to have hallucinations). Goldman v. New York Railways, 185 App.Div. 739, 173 N.Y.S. 737 (1919)(defendant's driver kept on operating a street car after he had a dizzy spell; the accident occurred when he suffered another dizzy spell shortly thereafter). For a recent collection of the cases involving the blackout or other sudden unconsciousness of automobile drivers, *see* Storjohn v. Fay, 246 Neb. 454, 519 N.W.2d 521 (1994).

3. The insanity "defense" is in fact a denial that the plaintiff has proven an essential element of his claim, i.e. that the defendant intended to batter the plaintiff. Most defenses, however, accept that the plaintiff has proven each element of the tort, but claim there are other circumstances that vitiate the

plaintiff's right to recover, e.g. the plaintiff consented or the defendant was acting in self defense.

2. Consent

HELLRIEGEL v. THOLL

Supreme Court of Washington, 1966.
69 Wn.2d 97, 417 P.2d 362.

DONWORTH, JUDGE.

This is an appeal by a plaintiff from the dismissal of his complaint at the end of the plaintiff's evidence. Wolf–Jurgen Hellriegel, plaintiff's teen-age son, was seriously injured when three of his friends tried to throw him into Lake Washington during an afternoon spent in water-skiing, sunbathing, and engaging in horseplay. The defendants in the suit are these three teen-age friends of plaintiff's son. Plaintiff sued in his own behalf for recovery of the cost of the medical care for his son, and sued in his son's behalf for the loss of income and for the temporary total disability and the alleged permanent partial disability, as well as for general damages for the alleged negligence and recklessness by which his son was harmed. Before trial, the complaint was amended by changing the grounds of the liability from negligence and recklessness to that of battery.

The only issue on this appeal is the issue decided by the trial court in the granting of the nonsuit—did the plaintiff present sufficient evidence to take the question of liability of any of the three defendants to the jury?

* * *

Certain background against which to consider the sufficiency of appellant's evidence should be stated. On the afternoon of July 26, 1963, appellant's son, Wolf–Jurgen Hellriegel (called Dicka by his friends), a 15- or 16-year-old high school student, joined a group of friends and fellow students at the Mount Baker Beach, on Lake Washington, for an afternoon of waterskiing.

Although there may have been other teenagers coming and going and for a time sunbathing and mingling with them, the group consisted primarily of the 6 witnesses whose testimony was presented to the trial court. * * * Although these witnesses recall the general setting and the incident with varying details and with varying degrees of clarity about what happened, there appears to be no dispute that, in general, the circumstances leading up to the injury of minor appellant Hellriegel occurred approximately as young Hellriegel himself described it.

He stated:

* * *

And somebody started throwing a pillow—I don't know who it was—it was Nina's pillow. And we threw it around, and after a while it got so far out of reach—we were kind of lazy at the time—and we just—I don't think we bothered about it and started throwing grass, and I guess after we tired of throwing grass we got around—talk got around to throwing people into the lake. And after a while of talking like this—I don't know—somebody must have said they could throw me in, or something to this effect, and I stated, "Oh, you couldn't throw me in even if you tried." And with that the three boys, Mike, Greg and John, jumped up and, well, tried to throw me into the water. I struggled for a while and I ended up in a sitting position parallel to the lake, facing, my head facing north, and Mike was behind me. Again, I was in a sitting position and John and Greg had my legs up in the air.

I was trying to get them off, and I had my hands reaching toward my legs when Mike, trying to reach my hands, must have slipped or lost his balance, and he fell on the back of my head and pushed it forward. I heard two cracks like somebody snapping his knuckles, and right after that I lost all control, I couldn't move my legs, and it was kind of a numb sensation all over.

I yelled out, I knew what had happened. I yelled out, "Please, let me down, I am paralyzed."

With that, John and Greg put down my legs and they must have—somehow they must have got them crossed, and Mike got off me as fast as possible. And then I just lay there looking up at the sun. There was a big tree above me. It was getting hot. I didn't notice it, but I figured somebody better put a towel over me. So they did this, and my brother arrived.

* * *

Appellant has assigned error solely to the trial court's determination that there was not sufficient evidence of a battery to establish a prima facie case of liability against respondents. Appellant acknowledges that the basis for the trial court's ruling is shown in the colloquy between counsel and the court just prior to the granting of respondents' motion. The record shows that the trial court ruled that respondents were not liable because:

(1) The actions of respondents in trying to throw appellant's son into the lake were not such as to constitute an offensive touching of his person.

(2) The actions of the respondents were consented to by appellant's son by his participation in the "horseplay" and his statement to the effect that all three of the boys could not throw him into the lake.

If the trial court is correct on either point, its judgment must be affirmed.

We shall first discuss the issue of consent before considering the issue of offensive touching.

It is agreed by all parties to the suit that consent is a defense to battery, except for some exceptions (not presently applicable) when consent cannot be given. The points on which the parties differ is whether the words and actions of Dicka amounted to consent to engage in the horse-play, and whether this consent was broad enough to encompass the events which caused his injury.

First, with regard to the significance of Dicka's words and actions, we agree with the trial court that his words were an invitation to respondents to try to throw him into the water if they thought they could. His statement to them (quoted above) constituted a consent that the boys could *try* to throw him into the lake (as distinguished from a consent to being thrown into the lake) and he thereby assumed the risk that he might be accidentally injured during the horseplay that necessarily would result from their attempt to throw him into the lake and his resistance to such attempt. Even if what he said was in response to someone's statement to the effect "Let's throw Dicka into the lake," his words were an invitation to try, as distinguished from a warning to the other boys *not* to try to throw him in because he did not want to be thrown in and would resist.

The setting in which these words were spoken is the key to their meaning. The boys had been throwing a pillow around, apparently at each other, rather like a ball. They also threw grass when the pillow was thrown out of reach. They were all good friends. No one was angry, nor had anyone tried to withdraw from the horseplay. It was in good-natured fun.

If there had been the slightest indication that Dicka had not wanted to participate in this horseplay but had engaged in it only to the extent necessary to protect himself, then appellant's position might be plausible. However, we have Dicka's own statement that he had joined in the pillow throwing and the grass throwing. Dicka also stated that he and the boy who fell on him, Mike Dorris, were used to wrestling together prior to this accident. Dicka was very athletic and this activity was regarded by all of the boys as "fun." Under the circumstances shown by the evidence, it would be a strained and unreasonable interpretation of Dicka's statement to the boys to construe it as a warning not to try to throw him into the lake, because he did not want to be thrown in, even in fun, and that he would resist such an attempt.

Appellant's counsel argues in his brief that, even if Dicka gave any consent, it was consent to being thrown into the lake, and not a consent to have his neck broken, i.e., that the scope of the consent did not include this battery. Of course, Dicka did not consent to having his neck broken. As we pointed out above, Dicka did not even consent to being thrown into the lake—he consented only to having his three friends *try* to throw him into the lake, while he resisted their attempt. In other words, *he consented to rough and tumble horseplay*.

Appellant's counsel argues in connection with this issue that Restatement, Torts § 53, and *Comment a* clearly show that the particular invasion was not consented to by Dicka. That section reads:

> To constitute a consent, the assent must be to the invasion itself and not merely to the act which causes it.

* * *

Appellant argues (1) that the invasion to which this section refers in the present case is the breaking of Dicka's neck, and (2) that the breaking of his neck was not substantially certain to result from being thrown into the lake, and that, therefore, he did not consent to this invasion. We do not agree with appellant's understanding of what the term "invasion" means as used in § 53 of the Restatement. *Comment b* of that section shows that the "invasion" refers to the intentional acts, such as blows received in a boxing match, and not the injuries which may result from accidents such as accidental slipping, as in the case at bar.

The invasion consented to in this instance, as we stated earlier, was rough and tumble horseplay. The question which § 53 of the Restatement does not answer is, who takes the risk of injury which may, accidentally result from such rough and tumble play? It seems to us that rough and tumble play is like an informal boxing match, which is described in *Comment b* above. The boxer accepts the risk of serious injuries from the blows received. * * * Persons who engage in roughhouse horseplay also accept the risk of accidental injuries which result from participation therein.

* * *

The second question is whether there was evidence of any intentional act which could be called "offensive contact" committed by respondents beyond the limits of that consent? The record is completely barren of any such evidence. The contact (when Mike Dorris slipped and fell onto Dicka) which actually broke Dicka's neck was accidental. All other contact was a part of the rough and tumble play.

Therefore, we must affirm the trial court.

* * *

Notes

1. Consent need not be expressed in words. It can be inferred from the circumstances. Indeed, what is crucial is not so much what the person purportedly consenting intended but what a reasonable person interacting with that individual would conclude under the prevailing circumstances. That is, the law is searching for *apparent* consent. Consent can be either expressly given or implied from the circumstances. For example, suppose the plaintiff, who understands English, is standing in a line of women who are being vaccinated against smallpox on shipboard to meet immigration requirements. When the ship's doctor reaches her, she says nothing. He proceeds to vaccinate her. In O'Brien v. Cunard S. S. Co., 154 Mass. 272, 28 N.E. 266 (1891), it was held that she could not bring an action against the steamship company. The plaintiff claimed that she had already been vaccinated and had not wanted to be vaccinated again.

2. A continuing controversy has surrounded the question of whether or not consent is a defense to a tort action when the conduct consented to is criminal. It has consistently been held that the consent of the victim is no defense to a criminal prosecution. *See, e.g.,* Regina v. Brown, [1994] 1 A.C. 212 (1993), [1993] 2 W.L.R. 556, 2 All E.R. 75; Attorney–General Reference (No. 6 of 1980), [1981] Q.B. 715, 3 W.L.R. 125, 2 All E.R. 1057 (C.A.); Rex v. Donovan, [1934] 2 K.B. 498 (Ct.Crim.App.). Although, English law has always apparently been to the contrary, at one time a majority of American jurisdictions held that consent was likewise no defense to a tort action when the action consented to was criminal in nature, such as when the plaintiff and the defendant agreed to settle their differences in a fist fight.[4] The *Restatement of*

---

4. The fact of consent, however, could be taken into consideration on the question of whether punitive damages should be awarded.

Torts (§ 60), however, took the "minority" position that consent should operate to bar a tort action under those circumstances. Today, there is a distinct split in authority on this point. It is said that a majority of jurisdictions continue to resist the restatement position. *See* Janelsins v. Button, 102 Md.App. 30, 38, 648 A.2d 1039, 1043 (Md.App.1994)

3. Even in a state prepared to accept that consent is a bar to a tort action based on criminal behavior, there will be circumstances where a person injured can bring an action regardless of his consent. These are situations where the public policy of the jurisdiction—largely based upon statutory provisions—is to protect the members of the class of which the plaintiff is a member against their own imprudence. Typical situations are statutes prohibiting the sale of intoxicating beverages to minors, forbidding sexual intercourse with minor females, and safety regulations. *See* Hudson v. Craft, 33 Cal.2d 654, 204 P.2d 1 (1949)(minor injured in carnival boxing exhibition not conducted in accordance with regulations of State Athletic Commission; tort action allowed against promoter).

Consent obtained by fraud or duress or even by the nondisclosure of some material fact will not immunize someone from liability. Liability for sexually transmitted diseases is becoming an increasing subject of litigation. Such litigation raises not only the question of fraudulent disclosure or nondisclosure, but also whether the illegality or assumed immorality of the behavior involved affects the rights and liabilities of the parties. Does the fact that the plaintiff has knowingly engaged in conduct that might be considered illegal or immoral affect the plaintiff's right to complain of the defendant's lack of candor? On these questions *see* R. Prentice and P. Murray, *Liability for Transmission of Herpes: Using Traditional Tort Principles to Encourage Honesty in Sexual Relationships,* 11 J. of Contemp.Law 67 (1984); Katherine Kelly, *The Assumption of Risk Defense and the Sexual Transmission of A.I.D.S.: A Proposal For The Application of Comparative Knowledge,* 143 U. Pa. L. Rev. 1121 (1995). The general trend in the more recent cases seems to be clearly in favor of allowing the action. *See* Doe v. Johnson, 817 F.Supp. 1382 (W.D.Mich.1993); B.N. v. K.K., 312 Md. 135, 538 A.2d 1175 (1988); Kathleen K. v. Robert B., 150 Cal.App.3d 992, 198 Cal.Rptr. 273, 40 A.L.R.4th 1083 (1984). Such actions have even been allowed on a negligence theory. *See* Long v. Adams, 175 Ga.App. 538, 333 S.E.2d 852 (1985). *See also* B.N. v. K.K., *supra.* Note, *Assessing Liability For Negligent Transmission of A.I.D.S.,* 24 Suffolk U. L. Rev. 649 (1990). In the *Kathleen K.* case, *supra,* the defendant unsuccessfully tried to defend on the ground that allowing the action infringed upon his sexual privacy.

4. In Hackbart v. Cincinnati Bengals, Inc., 601 F.2d 516 (10th Cir.1979), *cert. denied,* 444 U.S. 931, 100 S.Ct. 275, 62 L.Ed.2d 188 (1979), the plaintiff Dale Hackbart, a defensive back for the Denver Broncos tried to block Charles "Booby" Clark, an offensive back for the Cincinnati Bengals, during the run back of a pass interception. Clark had been running a pass pattern but the pass was intercepted by another Denver player. While Hackbart was on the ground, according to the findings of the trial court, Clark "acting out of anger and frustration [at losing the game] but without a specific intent to injure * * * stepped forward and struck a blow with his right forearm to the back of the kneeling plaintiff's head and neck." No penalty was called because no official saw the incident, but the game film clearly showed what had occurred. Both players left the field. By the next day the plaintiff was experiencing considerable pain and eventually he sought medical help. It was discovered

that he had suffered a serious fracture of the neck. Trying the case without a jury, the trial judge took note of the fact that many fouls are overlooked and concluded that it was unreasonable to apply what the court of appeals described as "the laws and rules of injury," to professional football. He held in favor of the defendants. The court of appeals reversed. It doubted whether a professional football player either consents to or assumes the risk of being injured by conduct in violation of the rules of football. The court noted the evidence of witnesses that not only is the intentional striking of others prohibited by the rules of football but that it is contrary to the general customs of the game. Accord, in a very similar situation in a hockey game, is Agar v. Canning (1966) 54 W.W.R. 302 (Man.). *See also* Nabozny v. Barnhill, 31 Ill.App.3d 212, 334 N.E.2d 258 (1975) (high school age soccer game). Several cases have been more cautious in extending liability for intentional contact outside the rules of the game for fear that they will chill competition. *See* Turcotte v. Fell, 68 N.Y.2d 432, 510 N.Y.S.2d 49, 502 N.E.2d 964 (N.Y.1986)(horse racing); Gauvin v. Clark, 404 Mass. 450, 537 N.E.2d 94 (Mass.1989)(college hockey). In Hanson v. Kynast, 38 Ohio App.3d 58, 526 N.E.2d 327 (1987) the plaintiff was paralyzed during a college lacrosse game when the defendant flipped him over another player's back causing plaintiff's head to strike the ground. The court held the defendant's act was not intentional, but rather was a reflexive and instinctive reaction.

Several cases have arisen out of athletic injuries in informal settings. *See* Marchetti v. Kalish, 53 Ohio St.3d 95, 559 N.E.2d 699 (1990)(children's game of "kick the can"); Knight v. Jewett, 3 Cal.4th 296, 11 Cal.Rptr.2d 2, 834 P.2d 696 (1992)(social game of touch football). *See* Ray Yasser, *In The Heat Of Competition: Tort Liability Of One Participant To Another: Why Can't Participants Be Required to Be Reasonable?* 5 Seton Hall J. Sport L. 253 (1995).

MULLOY v. HOP SANG

Supreme Court of Manitoba, Appellate Division, 1934.
[1935] 1 W.W.R. 714.

An appeal by plaintiff from the following judgment of Jackson, D.C.J. and a cross-appeal by defendant for increased damages were dismissed by the Appellate Division on March 27, without written reasons.

* * *

JACKSON, D.C.J.—The plaintiff's claim is for professional fees for an operation involving the amputation of the defendant's hand which was badly injured in a motor-car accident. The accident took place near the town of Cardston and the defendant was taken to the hospital there. The plaintiff, a physician and surgeon duly qualified to practice, was called to the hospital and the defendant, being a stranger and unacquainted with the plaintiff, asked him to fix up his hand but not to cut it off as he wanted to have it looked after in Lethbridge, his home city. Later on in the operating room the defendant repeated his request that he did not want his hand cut off. The doctor, being more concerned in relieving the suffering of the patient, replied that he would be governed by the conditions found when the anaesthetic had been administered. The defendant said nothing. As the hand was covered by an old piece of cloth and it was necessary to administer an anaesthetic before doing anything, the doctor was not in a position to advise what should be done. On examination he decided an operation was necessary and the hand was amputated. Dr. Mulloy said the wounds indicated an operation as the condition of the hand was such that delay would mean blood poisoning with no possibility of saving it. In this he was supported by the two other attending physicians. I am, however, not satisfied that the defendant could not have been rushed to Lethbridge where he evidently wished to consult with a physician whom he knew and relied on. Dr. Mulloy took it for granted when the defendant, a Chinaman without much education in English and probably not of any more than average mentality, did not reply or make any objection to his statement that he would be governed by conditions as he found them, that he had full power to go ahead and perform an operation if found necessary. On the other hand, the defendant did not, in my opinion, understand what the doctor meant, and he would most likely have refused to allow the operation if he did. Further, he did not consider it necessary to reply as he had already given explicit instructions.

Under these circumstances I think the plaintiff should have made full explanation and should have endeavoured to get the defendant to consent to an operation, if necessary. It might have been different if the defendant had submitted himself generally to the doctor and had pleaded with him not to perform an operation and the doctor found it necessary to do so afterwards. The defendant's instructions were precedent and went to the root of the employment. The plaintiff did not do the work he was hired to do and must, in my opinion, fail in his action.

The defendant has counterclaimed for damages in the sum of $400, being $150 for an artificial hand and the balance for loss of wages due to the operation and possibly general damages.

In my opinion the operation was necessary and performed in a highly satisfactory manner. Indeed, there was no suggestion otherwise. The damage and loss and the cost of an artificial hand are the results of the accident and not the unauthorized operation. The defendant, however, is, in my opinion, entitled to damages because of the trespass to the person, which at the same time became trespass *ab initio*, having in mind the old case of *The Six Carpenters* (1610) 8 Co. Rep. 146*a*, 77 E.R. 695. The damages are *per se* and should be more than nominal. Personally, I in a similar position might have been able to satisfy myself that the operation was necessary, and that I should be glad to pay the reasonable fee charged, but it was not my hand and the defendant will always no doubt feel that he might have saved the hand if he had consulted with a doctor he knew. While I might have been able to forego my rights, I cannot ask the defendant to do so and he is entitled to rely on his rights. There also must have been some shock to him when he found out his hand had been taken off in the manner in which it was, over and above the ordinary shock from an operation. His damages, should, therefore, be substantial but only sufficient to make them substantial rather than nominal. I place the amount at $50.

The action is dismissed with costs and the defendant is entitled to his costs of the counterclaim.   * * *

Notes

1. The *Hop Sang* case states the traditional doctrine. Accord, Mohr v. Williams, 95 Minn. 261, 104 N.W. 12 (1905)(plaintiff consented to an operation on her right ear; defendant doctor operated on her left ear because he concluded that that ear needed treatment more; defendant held liable, although operation performed competently). Where in the course of an operation under general anaesthesia, however, a situation arises which good surgical practice would require to be treated immediately rather than to wait for the patient to regain consciousness to secure his express consent and then further wait for the patient to recover sufficiently from the effects of the first operation before a second operation may be performed, the patient's consent will be "presumed" in the absence of express instructions from the patient to the contrary. *See* Kennedy v. Parrott, 243 N.C. 355, 90 S.E.2d 754 (1956). Consent will also be presumed in an emergency, for example where a patient needing immediate treatment arrives at a hospital in an unconscious state, although it is customary in such cases to seek to obtain the consent of relatives. For a review of the consent rules in the doctor-patient relationship over the last 150 years. *See* Anthony Szczgiel, *Beyond Informed Consent*, 21 Ohio N.U.L.Rev. 171 (1994).

2. To guard against the possibility of liability it is customary for surgeons to seek a general consent from patients. For example, the following form is currently used in Texas:

DISCLOSURE AND CONSENT
Medical and Surgical Procedures[1]

* *TO THE PATIENT: You have the right, as a patient, to be informed about your condition and the recommended surgical, medical, or diagnostic procedure to be used so that you may make the decision whether or not to undergo the procedure after knowing the risks and hazards involved. This disclosure is not meant to scare or alarm you; it is simply an effort to make you better informed so you may give or withhold your consent to the procedure.*

I voluntarily request Dr. _____ as my physician, and such associates, technical assistants and other health care providers as they may deem necessary, to treat my condition which has been explained to me as:____.

I understand that the following surgical, medical and/or diagnostic procedures are planned for me and I voluntarily consent and authorize these procedures:_____

_____.

I understand that my physician may discover other or different conditions which require additional or different procedures than those planned. I authorize my physician, and such associates, technical assistants and other health care providers to perform such other procedures which are advisable in their professional judgment.

I (do)(do not) consent to the use of blood and blood products as deemed necessary.

I understand that no warranty or guarantee has been made to me as to result or cure.

---

1. This form is authorized by Vernon's Annotated Texas Statutes, art. 4590i, § 6.04.

Just as there may be risks and hazards in continuing my present condition without treatment, there are also risks and hazards related to the performance of the surgical, medical and/or diagnostic procedures planned for me. I realize that common to surgical, medical, and/or diagnostic procedures is the potential for infection, blood clots in veins and lungs, hemorrhage, allergic reaction, and even death. I also realize that the following risks and hazards may occur in connection with this particular procedure:_____

_____.

I understand that anesthesia involves additional risks and hazards but I request the use of anesthetics for the relief and protection from pain during the planned and additional procedures. I realize that anesthesia may have to be changed possibly without explanation to me.

I understand that certain complication may result from the use of any anesthetic including respiratory problems, drug reactions, paralysis, brain damage or even death. Other risks and hazards which may result from the use of general anesthetics range from minor discomfort to injury to vocal cords, teeth or eyes. I understand that other risks and hazards resulting from spinal or epidural anesthetics include headache and chronic pain.

I have been given an opportunity to ask questions about my condition, alternative forms of anesthesia and treatment, risks of non-treatment, the procedures to be used, and the risk and hazards involved, and I believe I have sufficient information to give this informed consent.

I certify this form has been fully explained to me, that I have read it or have had it read to me, that the blank spaces have been filled in, and that I understand its contents.

DATE: _____ TIME: _____ A.M./P.M.

_____
PATIENT/OTHER LEGALLY RESPON-
SIBLE PERSON SIGN

_____
WITNESS

_____.
Name

_____
Address (Street or P.O. Box)

_____
City, State, Zip Code

In Rogers v. Lumbermens Mutual Casualty Co., 119 So.2d 649 (La.App. 1960), the patient consented to an appendectomy. The physician, however, also performed a total hysterectomy. The physician admitted that no emergency existed but he had performed the hysterectomy "as a precautionary measure" because he thought it was "good surgical procedure." The physician relied upon a one sentence general consent form that read as follows:

I hereby authorize the Physician or Physicians in charge to administer such treatment and the surgeon to have administered such anesthetics as found necessary to perform this operation which is advisable in the treatment of this patient.

The court declared the consent form to be so ambiguous as to be "almost completely worthless" and held that the consent form "can have no possible weight under the factual circumstances of the instant case." Although the hysterectomy was skillfully performed, the court held that the plaintiff had not consented to the operation and that such unconsented surgery amounted to an assault and battery. *See also* Millard v. Nagle, 402 Pa.Super. 376, 587 A.2d 10 (1991), *aff'd per curiam* 533 Pa. 410, 625 A.2d 641 (1993).

If a patient consents to an operation to be performed by doctor X, but the surgery is competently performed by another doctor in practice with doctor X, does the patient have a battery claim against the second physician? *See* Perna v. Pirozzi, 92 N.J. 446, 457 A.2d 431 (1983). *See* Cathy Jones, *Autonomy and Informed Consent in Medical Decision Making: Toward a New Self–Fulfilling Prophecy* 47 Wash. & Lee L. Rev. 379 (1990) for a useful discussion of the difference between informed consent law and the actual practice of acquiring informed consent in a hospital setting.

3. As the previous note intimates, most cases turn upon the question of the adequacy of the patient's consent. Typically, a physician is said to have breached the duty to disclose if he or she withholds any facts which are necessary to form the basis of an intelligent consent by the patient. The vagueness of this standard potentially opens the physician to second guessing by any patient dissatisfied with the outcome of a procedure. The Texas Medical Malpractice Act attempts to bring some predictability to this area of law by establishing the Texas Medical Disclosure Panel. The Panel's task is to evaluate various surgical and medical procedures and then outline the precise hazards and risks which must be disclosed to obtain an informed consent. Disclosure of the enumerated risks creates a rebuttable presumption that the physician did not breach a disclosure duty to the patient. Tex. Rev. Civ. Stat. Ann. art. 4590i, §§ 6.01–6.07.

4. The trend in recent cases involving the question of adequacy of disclosure is to treat the case as one involving negligence rather than battery. *See* Canterbury v. Spence, 464 F.2d 772 (D.C.Cir.1972); Miller v. Kennedy, 11 Wn.App. 272, 522 P.2d 852 (1974), *affirmed* 85 Wn.2d 151, 530 P.2d 334 (1975) p. 196, *infra*. This is the approach taken under English law. *See* Sidaway v. Board of Governors of the Bethel Royal Hospital, [1985] A.C. 871, 2 W.L.R. 480, 1 All E.R. 643. Under a negligence theory, the plaintiff must prove that a reasonable patient, if adequately apprised of the risk, would have refused the treatment. The issue of damages will also involve some different considerations. Finally, the question arises as to the relevancy of the custom of the medical profession in advising patients. We will consider this question again in Chapter Three, when we explore the topic of negligence.

5. *Withheld or withdrawn consent.* In the last 30 years many courts have had to wrestle with situations where patients or their families have withheld their consent to treatment that the doctor or hospital believes to be essential to the patient's well being. In re Osborne, 294 A.2d 372 (D.C.App.1972) is typical of one variety of cases. A young father was seriously injured when a tree fell on him. The doctors at the hospital to which he was taken recommended a transfusion with whole blood to counteract internal bleeding. The patient withheld his consent. Instead, he executed a statement refusing the recommended transfusion and releasing the hospital from liability. The patient's decision was supported by his wife and other family members, all of whom were of the Jehovah's Witnesses faith and who believed their religion forbids such transfusions. As the patient's grandfather explained, he "wants to live very much. * * * He wants to live in the Bible's promised new world where life will

never end. A few hours here would nowhere compare to everlasting life." A superior court judge visited the patient in the hospital to ascertain his condition. She determined that he was rational and lucid and proceeded to determine whether there was an "overriding state interest based on the fact that the patient had two young children" who could conceivably become wards of the state if their father died. She determined that they would be well cared for by the family. On direction of the appellate court she had a bedside hearing with the patient and asked him "whether he believed that he would be deprived of the opportunity for 'everlasting life' if transfusion were ordered by the court. His response was, 'Yes.'" Under these circumstances the court refused to order a transfusion. Judge Yeagley, in a concurring opinion, pointed out that although the court was aware of no cases were medical care was refused based on non-religious convictions, in his opinion the outcome was not based solely on religious freedom but on a broader based freedom of choice.

Osborne is but one of a number of cases where Jehovah's Witnesses have refused whole blood transfusions. In all of these cases the patient has been young and otherwise healthy and the prognosis has been that with a transfusion the crisis would pass and the individual would be restored to normal good health. Under these circumstances a few court have ordered transfusions. One of the most notable cases adopting this position is Application of President and Directors of Georgetown College, Inc., 118 U.S.App.D.C 80, 331 F.2d 1000 (1964). Judge Skelley Wright ordered a transfusion in part because the patient was very weak when she repeated to him her desire not to be transfused. It is not clear, however, that she was unable to make a decision.

Most recent opinions share with the *Osborne* and *Georgetown* case the fact that the patient has minor children and the courts are interested in how the children will be supported in the absence of the parent. As the *Georgetown* court noted, since the state ordinarily will not stand by and allow a parent to abandon a child it ought not permit "this most ultimate of voluntary abandonments," 331 F.2d 1000, 1008. Other courts have come close to saying that a patient's wishes should prevail regardless of the potential effect on minor dependents. *See* Fosmire v. Nicoleau, 75 N.Y.2d 218, 551 N.Y.S.2d 876, 551 N.E.2d 77 (1990). Most, however, would probably agree with In re Dubreuil, 629 So.2d 819 (Fla.1993) that the cases demand individual attention and cannot be covered by a blanket rule.

The First Amendment to the United States Constitution states that there shall be no law abridging the free exercise of religion. Should this provision especially privilege religious grounds for refusing medical treatment? Should the state be more willing to intervene if the patient is a single parent? *See* Fosmire v. Nicoleau, 75 N.Y.2d 218, 229, 551 N.Y.S.2d 876, 882, 551 N.E.2d 77, 83 (1990).

6. The preceding cases can be distinguished from another group of cases where the proposed treatment is less routine, or the prognosis for recovery is less hopeful. Courts routinely permit competent but terminally ill patients to refuse treatment. Somewhat more difficult are cases where the patient's quality of life is substantially diminished but the condition is not terminal. The courts have had to deal with "the constantly increasing power of science to keep the human body alive for longer than any reasonable person would want to inhabit it." Cruzan v. Harmon, 497 U.S. 261, 292, 110 S.Ct. 2841, 2859, 111 L.Ed.2d 224 (1990). (Justice Scalia, concurring). In Gray v. Romeo, 697 F.Supp. 580 (D.R.I.1988) the court held that a person has a constitutional right

to refuse medical treatment that, in the context of that case which involved a patient in a "vegetative" state, overrode any competing state interests such as the preservation of life, the protection of the interests of innocent third parties, the prevention of suicide, and the maintenance of the ethical integrity of the medical profession. Similar results have been reached in a number of cases. *See, e.g.* Bouvia v. Superior Ct., 179 Cal.App.3d 1127, 225 Cal.Rptr. 297, 300 (1986)(twenty-eight year old woman with cerebral palsy permitted to refuse treatment); McKay v. Bergstedt, 106 Nev. 808, 801 P.2d 617, 628–32 (Nev.1990)(approving a quadriplegic man's petition to remove a ventilator); Thor v. Superior Court, 5 Cal.4th 725, 21 Cal.Rptr.2d 357, 855 P.2d 375 (1993)(quadriplegic prisoner permitted to refuse life sustaining procedures). *See* 93 A.L.R.3d 67 (1979).

7. *Substituted consent.* The more interesting set of questions raised by the *Gray* case concern who is to decide when the patient is incompetent to make a decision. The situation is further complicated by the fact that what is involved is not so much the termination of medical treatment in the strictest sense but the termination of some method of feeding and "hydrating" a comatose patient. There are a number of cases permitting relatives serving as guardians to secure a court order directing the termination of such life-maintaining services. To reach this result these courts have had to reject, for such patients, any distinction between so-called extraordinary care, such as the transfusion sought to be performed in the *Osborne* case, and simple life maintenance. In addition to the *Gray* case, *see* In re Gardner, 534 A.2d 947 (Me.1987); Brophy v. New England Sinai Hosp. Inc., 398 Mass. 417, 497 N.E.2d 626 (1986), and two influential New Jersey cases, Matter of Conroy, 98 N.J. 321, 486 A.2d 1209 (1985), and In re Quinlan, 70 N.J. 10, 355 A.2d 647 (1976), *cert. denied* 429 U.S. 922, 97 S.Ct. 319, 50 L.Ed.2d 289.

The crucial issue, of course, is the wishes of the patient. Sometimes the patient has foreseen the problem and expressly stated his or her preferences in a "living will" or in some other way. In the absence of some express statement of the patient's wishes, the courts will consider evidence presented by close relatives and friends as to what the patient would have wanted. The court in the *Conroy* case was confronted with an elderly incompetent resident of a nursing home whose guardian was a nephew. There was no evidence of what the patient would have wanted so that what the court called the "subjective test" was not met. Nor, the court concluded, was there sufficient evidence to meet what the court called the "limited-objective" test, namely some evidence that the patient would have refused the treatment *and* clear evidence that the burdens of life with the treatment outweigh the benefits of life to the patient. The court therefore enunciated a "pure-objective test," namely whether "the net burdens of the patient's life with the treatment * * * clearly and markedly outweigh the benefits that the patient derives from life." 98 N.J. at 366, 486 A.2d at 1232.

In two later cases the New Jersey court was confronted with patients who were not only incompetent but were in a "persistent vegetative state." The court ruled that, in such cases, the possible life expectancy of the patient was not important. Rather, relying on *Quinlan,* the court declared that the main focus should be on the possibility of a return to a "cognitive and sapient life" as distinguished from the "forced continuance of * * * biological vegetative existence." Where there is no such possibility the patient's surrogate must exercise his or her best judgment, taking into account what the surrogate knows about the patient and the patient's value system. Matter of Jobes, 108

N.J. 394, 529 A.2d 434 (1987); Matter of Peter, 108 N.J. 365, 529 A.2d 419 (1987).

Occasionally, the courts have refused to allow a guardian to discontinue life support for a patient in a persistent vegetative state. In Mack v. Mack, 329 Md. 188, 219, 618 A.2d 744, 760 (App.1992) the court said: "Nor is this Court prepared to declare, as part of the common law of Maryland, that the feeding of the irreversibly comatose should be stopped, without regard to the patient's desires, on the theory that it is in the best interest of such patients to die." In Mack, however, the family was not of one mind as to what should be done. The most well known refusal to suspend life support occurred in Cruzan v. Harmon, 760 S.W.2d 408 (Mo.1988), 497 U.S. 261, 110 S.Ct. 2841, 111 L.Ed.2d 224 (1990). The guardians of the patient brought declaratory judgment action seeking judicial sanction of their wish to terminate artificial hydration and nutrition. The Missouri Supreme Court rejected the New Jersey line of cases. The United States Supreme Court affirmed, and held; a) the federal constitution did not forbid Missouri from requiring clear and convincing evidence of an incompetent's wishes to the withdrawal of life-sustaining treatment, b) the state Supreme Court did not commit constitutional error in concluding that evidence adduced at trial did not amount to clear and convincing evidence of patient's desire to cease hydration and nutrition, and c) due process did not require the state to accept substituted judgment of close family members absent substantial proof that their views reflected those of patient.

In the *Brophy* case, *supra,* the Massachusetts court held that, although a patient could choose to refuse treatment and die, the hospital was not obliged to participate in the execution of the patient's desires. Rather the hospital was only under an obligation to assist the guardian in transferring the patient to a suitable facility. Both the *Jobes* case and the *Gray* case, *supra* at the beginning of this note, have refused to allow the hospital or nursing home this privilege to refuse to assist in carrying out the decision to terminate treatment. *See* Kathleen Boozang, *Deciding the Fate of Religious Hospitals in the Emerging Health Care Market* 31 Hou. L. Rev. 1429 (1995) for a discussion of the problems that arise when the patient's wishes go against the moral convictions of the doctor or hospital. An important article emphasizing the role of the incompetent patient's family is Nancy Rhoden, *Litigating Life and Death,* 102 Harv.L.Rev. 375 (1988). More than three-fourths of the states now have "living will" statutes which provide a means for people to state their wishes while they are still competent. *See* 49 A.L.R.4th 812 (1986). These statutes are not without their own problems. One set of problems arises from the fact that the statutes typically only cover "terminally ill" patients.

8. There is ample authority that the courts have power to order necessary medical treatment for mental incompetents or for children over the objections of their guardians. Some courts have distinguished the case where the medical treatment was necessary to save a child's life from that in which the treatment was desirable but not essential for preservation of life. For cases on the treatment of children, *see* Annot. 52 A.L.R.3d 1118 (1973). In many states, there are now statutory provisions governing these situations.

More difficult questions are raised in cases in which someone seeks to compel an adult to undergo treatment for the benefit of another person. The typical case involves a pregnant woman. *See* Nancy Rhoden, *The Judge in the Delivery Room: The Emergence of Court–Ordered Caesareans,* 74 Calif. L. Rev. 1951 (1986). *See* In re A.C., 573 A.2d 1235, 1237 (D.C.1990)(en banc)(a competent, terminally-ill pregnant woman may refuse a cesarean which would improve the fetus' chances of survival). A thorough discussion of the many questions raised in this and the preceding notes would range far beyond the scope of a first-year torts course. Many of these questions would be worthwhile subjects of advanced courses or seminars.

3. Self–Defense

a. Defense of Person

LANE v. HOLLOWAY

Court of Appeal, 1967.
[1968] 1 Q.B. 379, [1967] 3 W.L.R. 1003, 3 All E.R. 129.

LORD DENNING M.R. On July 21, 1966, the peace of the ancient borough of Dorchester was disturbed. Mr. Lane, the plaintiff, was a retired gardener aged 64. He was living in a quiet court just off High East Street. Backing onto that court there was a café which was run by a young man, Mr. Holloway, the defendant, aged 23. The people in the court did not like the sound of a juke-box from the café. They also objected because the customers relieved themselves at night in the courtyard. To meet their objection Mr. Holloway began to build some lavatories. But relations were strained. On July 21, 1966, at about 11 o'clock at night Mr. Lane, the 64–year-old, came back from the public house. He stopped outside his door and started talking to his neighbour, Mrs. Brake. Mr. Holloway was in bed drinking a cup of coffee. His wife, hearing Mr. Lane and Mrs. Brake talking, called out to them: "You bloody lot." Mr. Lane replied: "Shut up, you monkey-faced tart." Mr. Holloway sprang up and said: "What did you say to my wife?" He said it twice. Mr. Lane said: "I want to see you on your own," implying a challenge to fight. Whereupon Mr. Holloway came out in his pyjamas and dressing-gown. He walked up the courtyard to the place where Mr. Lane was standing at his door. He moved up close to Mr. Lane in a manner which made Mr. Lane think that he might himself be struck by Mr. Holloway. Whereupon Mr. Lane threw a punch at Mr. Holloway's shoulder. Then Mr. Holloway drew his right hand out of his pocket and punched Mr. Lane in the eye, a very severe blow. Mr. Holloway said: "You hit me first." Mr. Lane said: "If I had two good pins you would not have done this. I shall make a case of it." Mr. Lane was taken to hospital. It was indeed a very severe wound. It needed 19 stitches. He had also to have an operation. He was in hospital for a month. It made worse his chronic glaucoma. The surgeon of the Dorset General Hospital said that in his view the injury was caused by a hard object, not a soft one. He had never seen injuries of this kind caused by a fist. It was suggested that Mr. Holloway must have used a weapon or a hard instrument. But the judge found that that was not so: it was caused by a fist. Nevertheless it caused this very severe injury.

* * *

The first question is: Was there an assault by Mr. Holloway for which damages are recoverable in a civil court? I am quite clearly of opinion that there was. It has been argued before us that no action lies because this was an unlawful fight: that both of them were concerned in illegality; and therefore there can be no cause of action in respect of it. Ex turpi causa oritur non actio. To that I entirely demur. Even if the fight started by being unlawful, I think that one of them can sue the other for damages for a subsequent injury if it was inflicted by a weapon or savage blow out of all proportion to the occasion. I agree that in an ordinary fight with fists there is no cause of action to either of them for any injury suffered. The reason is that each of the participants in a fight voluntarily takes upon himself the risk of incidental injuries to himself. Volenti non fit injuria. But he does not take on himself the risk of a savage blow out of all proportion to the occasion. The man who strikes a blow of such severity is liable in damages unless he can prove accident or self-defence.

In this case the judge found that

> "with a young man of 23 and a man of 64, whom he knows to be somewhat infirm, the young man cannot plead a challenge seriously: nor is he entitled to go and strike him because of an insult hurled at his wife."

I quite agree. Mr. Holloway in anger went much too far. He gave a blow out of proportion to the occasion for which he must answer in damages.

Thus far I entirely agree with the judge. Then the question arises as to the amount of damages. The judge said that

> "to a substantial extent the plaintiff brought the injury on himself: first, by insulting the defendant's wife; secondly, by challenging the defendant to fight; and, thirdly, by striking the first blow. These matters in my judgment must operate to reduce the damages extensively."

He gave a sum of £75, saying it would have been very much higher but for reasons stated.

Now there is an appeal. It is said that the judge ought not to have reduced the damages. The judge had cases before him, both in this country and New Zealand and Canada, where it was held that provocation could be used to reduce the damages. But most of these cases were considered by the High Court of Australia in 1962 in *Fontin v. Katapodis*.[2] The plaintiff struck the defendant with a weapon, a wooden T-square. It broke on his shoulder. There was not much trouble from that. But then the defendant picked up a sharp piece of glass with which he was working and threw it at the plaintiff, causing him severe injury. The judge reduced the damages from £2,850 to £2,000 by reason of the provocation. But the High Court of Australia, including the Chief Justice, Sir Owen Dixon, held that provocation could be used to wipe out the element of exemplary or aggravated damages but could not be used to reduce the actual figure of pecuniary compensation. So they increased the damages to the full £2,850.

I think that the Australian High Court should be our guide. The defendant has done a civil wrong and should pay compensation for the physical damage done by it. Provocation by the plaintiff can properly be used to take away any element of aggravation. But not to reduce the real

2. (1962) 108 C.L.R. 177.

damages. I ought to say in fairness to the judge that he did not have the benefit of the case in the High Court of Australia. We have had the benefit of it.

On the evidence this young man went much too far in striking a blow out of all proportion to the occasion. It must have been a savage blow to produce these consequences. I think the damages ought to be increased from £75 to £300 and I would allow the appeal accordingly.

[The concurring judgments of Salmon and Winn, L.JJ., have been omitted.]

Notes

1. We have already discussed, at p. 68, *supra*, in the notes following *Hellriegel v. Tholl*, the question of whether consent can operate as a defense to a tort action when the conduct consented to amounts to a breach of the peace. The defendant in the *Lane* case had been convicted of "unlawful wounding" in separate criminal proceedings.

2. Although there are some cases to the contrary, *see e.g.* Moore v. Blanchard, 216 La. 253, 43 So.2d 599 (1949), the predominant view in the United States, as in England, is that provocation is not relevant to the issue of compensatory damages. *See* Note, 31 N.C.L.Rev. 147 (1952). Provocation is of course always relevant on the issue of punitive damages.

3. In the United States, except in Louisiana which follows the civil law, an appellate court that is dissatisfied with the adequacy of the damages awarded by the trial court cannot enter an award for what it considers to be the appropriate amount of damages. Rather, the case must be remanded to the trial court for a retrial either of the entire case or of merely the issue of damages. To avoid the inconvenience of a retrial, an appellate court may, however, issue a conditional judgment remanding the case to the trial court for a new trial unless the plaintiff agrees to a reduction of damages (remittitur) or, less frequently and then only in some jurisdictions, unless the defendant agrees to an increase in the damages (additur). We will return to these issues in Chapter Ten, *infra*, when we consider the question of damages.

SILAS v. BOWEN

United States District Court, District of South Carolina, 1967.
277 F.Supp. 314.

DONALD RUSSELL, DISTRICT JUDGE.

This cause came on for trial before me without a jury on the 21st day of November, 1967, upon the issues made by the complaint and answer, and having heard testimony of witnesses and having observed their conduct and demeanor on the stand and having weighed their credibility, and having considered the exhibits, and being fully advised in the premises, * * * I find the facts specially and state my conclusions of law thereon, in the above cause, as follows:

FINDINGS OF FACT

1. Plaintiff is a resident of the State of Missouri. He is a professional basketball player, affiliated with the St. Louis Hawks. At the times involved herein, however, he was engaged in his basic training as a member

of the Missouri National Guard detailed for training at Fort Jackson on the outskirts of the City of Columbia, South Carolina.

2. The defendant is a resident of Columbia, South Carolina, and operates a parking lot just outside one of the main gate entrances to Fort Jackson.

3. About a week before the incident out of which this action arose, the plaintiff and another serviceman, in possession of the car of a third party, brought such car to the parking lot of the defendant and engaged a mechanic who was present at the lot, though not employed by the defendant to make certain repairs to the car. About 11 o'clock on the Saturday following, August 14, 1965, the plaintiff and his fellow-serviceman returned to defendant's parking lot and reclaimed the car, after paying the full repair charges. They then drove in the car to the City of Columbia.

4. Shortly after the plaintiff and his companion reached Columbia, they went to the home of a young woman, who thereafter accompanied them in their travels. Between the time they left the parking lot in the morning and their return late in the afternoon, they drank, according to the plaintiff, beer and had some in the car when they returned to the parking lot.

5. During that afternoon, the plaintiff and his companions noted that the repairs made to the car were not satisfactory and that the clutch thereon was still slipping. They then returned to the parking lot to demand a correction of the condition of the clutch. The plaintiff testified that it was about 1 P.M. when they arrived. However, the records at Fort Jackson conclusively establish that it was about 6 P.M. when they returned.

6. When they arrived at the parking lot, plaintiff's companion was driving. He drove into the parking lot at an excessive speed, indicating undoubtedly his anger at discovering that the car had not been properly repaired.

There seems little question that both the plaintiff and his companion were upset and distinctly annoyed by the failure to repair satisfactorily the car.

It seems equally clear that they had been drinking, even though the plaintiff denied that either of them was drunk. They had been driving around all day, had with them in the car some beer, and it is only credible to assume that they had been drinking such beer during much of the day. At least the defendant, his wife, and one disinterested witness judged them to be under the influence when they arrived at the lot.

7. According to the plaintiff, his companion got out of the car, approached the defendant who was near the door of a small office maintained by him on the lot. He demanded that his car be repaired immediately, and, when the defendant stated that the repairman did not work for him and was not then at the lot, he became insistent, whereupon defendant inquired if he were trying "to be smart." In the meantime, the plaintiff alighted from the car. He testified that he stood by the side of the car, did not approach the defendant, and took no part in the controversy between

his companion and the defendant other than to state to the defendant that they wanted the car fixed at once.

This testimony of the plaintiff is vigorously denied by the defendant, his wife, who was in the small office located on the parking lot, and a disinterested witness who was only a short distance from the parties. According to their testimony, the plaintiff got out of the car along with his companion, and approached the defendant in a threatening manner, cursing and abusing him. Frightened, the defendant, after demanding without success that the plaintiff and his party leave his premises, went into his office and got a shotgun. When he returned with the shotgun, the plaintiff, according to the defendant and his witnesses, told the defendant he was not afraid of the gun, approached the defendant and took the defendant by the shoulder with one hand, with his other hand in his pocket. The defendant claims that, frightened by the action and the language of the plaintiff and believing himself in danger of serious bodily harm, he drew back and fired the gun, not at the plaintiff but towards the ground, hoping that this would induce the plaintiff to withdraw and to cease any threat of serious bodily harm to him. Unquestionably, the defendant was not seeking to kill the plaintiff; in fact, he seems not to have intended to harm the plaintiff, only to frighten him to desist from his assault and it was a mere accident that the shot hit the plaintiff in his foot.

I cannot believe that the plaintiff conducted himself in such a restrained way as he stated. If he had not taken a far more active part in the whole controversy than he indicates—if his companion were the aggressor in the whole transaction and he largely an onlooker, as he testifies—it would seem that his companion, would have been the one involved in the shotgun affair and not the plaintiff.

The testimony of the defendant and his two corroborating witnesses, one of whom it is true, is his wife, seems more credible. According to them, the plaintiff was drinking when he arrived at the parking lot; he was quite belligerent, was cursing, refused to depart when told to leave, approached the defendant in a threatening manner and grabbed him. When the difference in the size and age of the plaintiff and defendant is considered, the situation of the defendant was such to strike fear and terror in the latter. The plaintiff was a young man, a professional athlete, robust, standing some six feet six inches, in perfect physical condition, weighing 225 to 230 pounds. The defendant, on the other hand, was of middle age, weighing about 135 pounds and standing five feet six inches. Facing a threat from the plaintiff, unable to induce him and his companions to leave his premises, already assaulted by the plaintiff, the defendant, under the emergency thus created and with reasonable cause to fear serious bodily harm from an individual so much more overpowering than he, fired his shotgun, not, I am convinced, with the intent of striking the plaintiff, but for the purpose of frightening him into desisting from his attack and into leaving his premises. Unfortunately, the shot, though directed downward towards the ground, struck the plaintiff in the foot. At any rate the defendant sought to use no more force than appeared necessary under the circumstances to protect himself from serious bodily harm.

As a result of his gunshot wound, plaintiff was taken to the hospital at Fort Jackson, where, as a result of the skilled medical attention rendered him, he recovered, without any impairment in the use of his foot, save for slight discomfort in the early months after his release from the hospital.

CONCLUSIONS OF LAW

* * *

The commission of an assault and battery by the defendant on the plaintiff is conceded and defendant seeks exoneration on his affirmative plea of self-defense. In testing such defense, it is necessary at the outset to note the circumstances of the parties at the scene of the controversy. The defendant, at the time of the battery, was at his place of business in the doorway to his office. The plaintiff, though initially perhaps an invitee, had become a trespasser on the defendant's premises as a result of the demand of the defendant that the former vacate the parking lot. Under these circumstances, the legal rights of the parties were:

1. While entry of the defendant's premises by the plaintiff was lawful, the defendant had a plain right to order the plaintiff and his companions to depart; and, when the plaintiff refused to withdraw voluntarily after such demand, to use reasonable force to eject them. * * *

2. While this right to use reasonable force does not ordinarily encompass the use of a deadly weapon, such use will be authorized, by way of self-defense, if the conduct of the trespasser under all the circumstances is such as to produce in the mind of a person of reasonable prudence and courage an apprehension of an assault by such trespasser involving serious bodily harm. * * *

3. As it is stated in 100 A.L.R.2d 1024–1025, "There is no disagreement, however, that a property owner may shoot with impunity where the incursion upon his property is also attended by a threat of personal harm to himself, his family, or others he is entitled to defend. * * * The property owner's reasonable belief that he or his family were in danger of bodily injury would appear to be the touchstone of exoneration in this area of law."

4. In determining whether there was reasonable cause and justification for the use of a deadly weapon in such a situation, all the circumstances must be considered. Accordingly, it is generally stated that a defendant, in his own place of business, where he has a right to be, as the defendant was in this case, is not required to retreat in the face of a threatened assault in order to be able to plead self-defense. * * * Again, while it is well-settled that mere words, however, "abusive, insulting, vexatious or threatening", will not in themselves justify the use of a deadly weapon, such words if "accompanied by an actual offer of physical violence" reasonably warranting fear of serious bodily harm, may be an integral part of a plea of self-defense against liability for an assault and battery. * * * Moreover, in determining whether there was reasonable cause for the apprehension of serious bodily harm, the difference in age, size, and relative physical strength of the parties to the controversy is a proper matter for consideration. * * * As the Court said in State v. Floyd

(1859), 51 N.C. (6 Jones) 392, "One cannot be expected to encounter a lion as he would a lamb."

5. Of course, the defendant, in order to support his plea of self-defense must not have been at fault in provoking the difficulty * * * but, by demanding that the plaintiff and his companions leave his parking lot, the defendant acted within his legal rights and can in no way be regarded as provoking the difficulty in this case. * * *

* * *

In my opinion, the defendant has made out his plea of self-defense under the facts and applicable law, as I have found and concluded. He acted in reasonable apprehension of serious bodily harm and to repel what he reasonably feared would be a serious and dangerous assault by a person of overpowering size.

Let judgment be entered for defendant, * * *.

Notes

1. The fact that the plaintiff may not have desired or in any way intended to harm the defendant is irrelevant. When the issue is defense of person, the law focuses upon how the situation would have appeared to a reasonable person in the defendant's position.

2. The *Restatement (Second) of Torts* § 65 adopts the so-called English common-law rule that resort to deadly force, that is force threatening death or serious bodily injury, cannot be justified if retreat is possible *unless* the defender is attacked within his own dwelling or is defending his own dwelling against intrusion or dispossession. It is said, however, that the majority of American jurisdictions have not adopted this "retreat to the wall" rule. *See* Prosser, Torts 110–11 (4th ed. 1971). *But see* Prosser & Keeton, Torts 127–28 (5th ed. 1984) which refuses to take a position on what is now the majority rule. As the principal case illustrates, there are some states that have adopted some type of intermediate position between the traditional majority view and the doctrine espoused by the *Restatement.*

3. The *Restatement (Second) of Torts* § 76 gives a person the right to use force to protect third persons "under the same conditions and by the same means as those under and by which he is privileged to defend himself if the actor correctly or *reasonably* believes that

> (a) the circumstances are such as to give the third person a privilege of self defense, and

> (b) his [i.e. the actor's] intervention is necessary for the protection of the third person."

The majority of states, however, probably follow an earlier doctrine that one who seeks to justify the use of force, on the grounds of protection of a third person, steps into the shoes of the third person. If the third person would have been privileged to use force, the actor is protected. If the third person would not have been entitled to use force, the actor's mistaken but nevertheless reasonable belief that the third person was so privileged would not be a defense. Take a case where the actor comes across what he reasonably believes is a hold-up. The actor intervenes to help the apparent victim. It turns out that what the actor has witnessed is two people rehearsing for a theatrical performance.   Under the *Restatement* view the actor is still privileged to use reasonable force; under the other view he is not.   There are relatively few cases in the area.   At one time, apparently, the privilege to use force in defense of third persons was limited to the defense of members of one's immediate family or household.

4.   The *Restatement (Second) of Torts* § 143 takes the position that deadly force may not be used in order to prevent the commission of a felony unless the felony is one "threatening death or serious bodily harm or involving the breaking and entry of a dwelling place."   *Restatement (Second) of Torts* § 131, however, reaffirms the traditional common law doctrine that deadly force may be used if reasonably necessary in order to arrest a person for a felony.   The subject of arrest is discussed in some detail at p. 1263f, *infra*.   It should be noted, however, that, in *Tennessee v. Garner,* 471 U.S. 1, 105 S.Ct. 1694, 85 L.Ed.2d 1 (1985), the United States Supreme Court has held that police officers who use deadly force against a fleeing felon are subject to an action under 42 U.S.C. § 1983 for depriving that person of rights guaranteed under the Constitution of the United States unless they can justify the use of deadly force by a reasonable belief that the fleeing felon posed a serious risk of death or serious harm to others.   The fact that the use of deadly force is reasonably believed to be necessary to effect the arrest is not by itself enough to justify resort to such force.

b.   Defense of Property

BROWN v. MARTINEZ

Supreme Court of New Mexico, 1961.
68 N.M. 271, 361 P.2d 152.

MOISE, JUSTICE.

Appellants, being father and son, appeal from a judgment dismissing their claim for damages against appellee growing out of injuries suffered by the son when he was shot in the left leg while engaged with several other boys in a watermelon stealing escapade on appellee's property.

We will refer to the son as appellant, the father being a party to the suit merely to recover items of expense incurred by him for medical and hospital care for the son, and as next friend because of the son's minority.

For a consideration of the issues raised by appellant and necessary for a decision there is no need to set forth the facts in any detail.

It is sufficient to point out that on the night of September 18, 1954, appellant, a 15–year old boy, and two other boys visited appellee's garden patch adjacent to the road for the purpose of stealing melons.   About 8:30 or 9:00 p.m., the next night, being September 19, 1954, appellant with several other boys again went to the farm of appellee for the purpose of stealing watermelons.   While two of the boys entered the melon patch, appellant went to the southeast corner of the property and was in the highway right of way close to the fence when appellee hearing the boys in the patch came out of his house with a rifle in his hand, called to the boys to get out, and seeing the two boys running toward the southwest corner of the property fired the gun toward the southeast to scare them, the bullet striking appellant in the back of the left leg, half way between the ankle and the knee, breaking the bones and coming out of the front of the leg.

* * *

We now come to the determinative issue in the case. In addition to facts related above, the court also found that a considerable quantity of melons were taken or destroyed and that the fence between the patch and the road was damaged, and as a conclusion of law held that on the night in question appellant and the other boys had assembled unlawfully "with the intent to do an unlawful act of force and violence against the property of the defendant (appellee) and to commit an unlawful act against the peace and that they did commit such unlawful acts by trespassing upon the defendant's land with intent and purpose of stealing crops from that land." The court further concluded that appellant and his companions "did unlawfully injure the fence enclosing the lands of defendant (appellee)"; that the appellee "acted reasonably and prudently to prevent any further trespassing against his land and crops" and his actions "did not constitute the use of unnecessary force, malice or wilful or specific intent to injure" appellant or anyone else but was only "such force as was reasonably necessary to eject" the trespassers from the property.

Appellant asserts that the conclusions that defendant acted reasonably and prudently to prevent further trespassing; that he did not use excessive force and was free from malice or wilful intent to injure appellant were error, and further that in firing a high powered rifle under the facts and circumstances here present the court erred in not concluding appellee's actions were wilful and intentional or done with reckless disregard of consequences or in a grossly negligent manner.

There is no question that appellant, together with his companions, was engaged in an illegal undertaking, viz., trespassing on land occupied by appellee and stealing his crop; also that they had done some very minor injury to his fence. The question thus presented is whether or not injury resulting from the use of such force as a rifle to prevent a trespass or loss of property is actionable.

State v. McCracken, 22 N.M. 588, 166 P. 1174, 1176, was a case in which the defendant was charged with murder for killing a trespasser on land attempting to build a fence thereon. This court there said:

> "We do not believe that the law, under such circumstances, would have justified the appellant in using force to the extent of taking human life in order that he might assert his dominion over the property in question. In Wharton on Homicide (3rd Ed.), § 526, it is said:

>> " 'While the law justifies the taking of life when necessary to prevent the commission of a felony, one cannot defend his property, other than his habitation, to the extent of killing the aggressor for the mere purpose of preventing a trespass. Rather than slay the aggressor to prevent a mere trespass, he should yield and appeal to the courts for redress.' "

* * *

State v. Beal, 55 N.M. 382, 234 P.2d 331, 335, should also be noticed. This is a case where a boy, along with some companions, was out at night soaping windows as part of a Halloween prank. The court, while affirming a second degree murder conviction, had the following to say:

"A well founded belief that a known felony was about to be committed will extenuate a homicide committed in prevention of the supposed crime, and this upon a principle of necessity; but when the necessity ceases, and the supposed felon flees, and thereby abandons his proposed design, a killing in pursuit, however well grounded the belief may be that he intended to commit a felony will not extenuate the offense of the pursuer. This extenuation rests upon an actual felony committed, and a necessity for the killing to prevent the escape of the felon. The evidence shows that no felony had been committed. The defendants saw one of the boys running away at the time he stepped out of the trailer door. He ran from his trailer house to the pick-up truck of his father-in-law, saw two more boys run around the side of the grocery store and on up the highway. He then went to the edge of the pavement and began shooting. The last shot in the magazine of his automatic pistol was the fatal one which killed the deceased who was running away and had travelled approximately seventy feet from the premises on the public highway when he was felled."

We are well aware that all the cases cited above and certain other cases hereinafter cited are criminal cases, whereas the present case is civil. We do not consider this fact to make any difference since our study of the authorities convinces us that rules of law governing the liability of appellee for shooting and wounding appellant while stopping a trespass or the theft of watermelons are the same whether the proceedings be civil or criminal. 25 A.L.R. 508, 537.

From that part of the trial court's decision which found damage to appellee's fence and injury to his crop we take it that it was the court's feeling that appellant and his companions had gotten together to violate and were violating § 40–47–12, N.M.S.A.1953, which reads as follows:

"The unlawful cutting, destruction or injury to any fence enclosing in whole or in part any real estate or lands, to which lands any person or persons, company or corporation, has a good and indefeasible title either by grant from the government of Spain or Mexico, or under the laws of the United States or New Mexico, and the unlawful and malicious destruction or injury of any hay, stock, grain, crop, orchard or building on any such land, is hereby declared a felony."

On the other hand, appellant argues that if appellant was guilty of anything it could only have been a misdemeanor and calls our attention to § 40–47–5, N.M.S.A.1953, which reads as follows:

"Every person who shall wilfully commit any trespass, by entering upon the garden, orchard, vineyard, or any other improved land belonging to another, without the permission of the owner thereof, with intent to cut, take, carry away, destroy or injure the trees, grain, grass, hay, fruit, or vegetables there growing, shall be punished by fine not exceeding twenty-five dollars ($25.00), nor less than three dollars ($3.00).''

That there was no sufficient proof of a violation of § 40–47–12, quoted above, at least in so far as the injury to the fence is concerned, would seem to be clear. * * * In simplest terms, the boys were out on a watermelon stealing escapade. They had no intent to injure any fence of appellee even if in going into the melon patch they incidentally did remove some staples holding the fence strands to some posts.

It is interesting to note that although the court found an unlawful injury to the fence he did not couple this with any conclusion that there was an unlawful and malicious destruction or injury of the crop. A reading of the statute makes it clear that for the acts to be felonious the unlawful injury to the fence *and* unlawful and malicious destruction or injury to the crop must coincide. As we interpret the court's findings and conclusions he did not decide that the appellant was guilty of violating § 40–47–12, supra. That the actions proven constituted a violation of § 40–47–5 would seem to be clear. However, these acts were only a misdemeanor. * * *

The court also concluded that the boys assembled unlawfully to do an unlawful act of force and violence against the property of appellee and to commit an unlawful act against the peace and that they did commit such unlawful acts by trespassing. It is clear that by this conclusion the court determined that appellant was guilty of violating § 40–12–10, N.M.S.A. 1953 * * * It will be noted that the acts prohibited in this section are likewise only misdemeanors * * * and the rules hereinafter set forth concerning trespass and misdemeanors generally apply.

The question then becomes one of whether appellee was justified in shooting to prevent a trespass or the stealing of his watermelons, being misdemeanors under the law.

There is an exhaustive note in 25 A.L.R. 508, on the general subject of "Homicide or Assault in Defense of Habitation or Property." At page 542, the note writer states the rule thus:

"While a man may use as much force as is necessary in the defense of his property, it is generally held that, in the absence of the use of force on the part of the intruder, he is not justified in the use of such force as to inflict great bodily harm or to endanger life."

On page 543 appears the following:

"The use of a deadly weapon in the protection of property is generally held, except in extreme cases, to be the use of more than justifiable force, and to render the owner of the property liable, both civilly and criminally, for the assault. * * *"

It is our conclusion that the quotations from State v. McCracken, supra * * * and State v. Beal, supra, are all in accord with these rules. *See also* State v. Terrell, 186 P. 108, 25 A.L.R. 497, being a case involving burglary and defense of habitation where a different rule applies. * * *

We are here met by appellee's argument that it was for the court to determine as a fact whether or not excessive force was used, and although the court denominated it a conclusion, the court found that appellee acted "reasonably and prudently to prevent any further trespassing against his land and crops" and that the force used was only such amount as was "reasonably necessary to eject" appellant and the other boys from the property.

While in no way questioning the rules relied upon by appellee, * * * we do not think that the case here presents a question of fact of whether or not the force used by appellee was reasonable or excessive. Just as in Padilla v. Chavez, 62 N.M. 170, 306 P.2d 1094, it was held that as a matter of law a police officer had no right to shoot to place a misdemeanant under arrest, absent an attempt to inflict bodily harm on the officer, so here, as a matter of law the use of a gun by appellee was not permissible and when appellee did so he became liable to appellant. Also, the trial court did not consider that he was making findings of fact but denominated the determinations complained of as conclusions of law. The conclusions reached were erroneous.

* * *

There is no suggestion in the proof here that appellee in any way felt his safety was threatened. Accordingly, under the facts as proven and found, the appellee acted improperly and is liable for injuries caused in using a gun in the manner he did, and with such unfortunate consequences, in order to drive away trespassers on his property, or to protect his watermelons, or to scare the intruders. * * *

There remains only one additional point that need be noticed. Does it make any difference that the act was not done intentionally, but was in the nature of an accident, the appellee intending to shoot only for the purpose of scaring the trespassers and in a direction where he did not know any boys were present?

Restatement of Law of Torts, § 16, reads as follows:

* * *

"(2) If an act is done with the intention of affecting a third person in the manner stated in Subsection (1), but causes a harmful bodily contact to another, the actor is liable to such other as fully as though he intended so to affect him."

* * * and this is followed by Illustration 3 which is a situation identical to that before us:

"3. A and B are trespassers upon C's land. C sees A but does not see B nor does he know that B is in the neighborhood. C throws a stone at A which misses him. Immediately after C has done so, B raises his head above a wall behind which he has been hiding. The stone misses A but strikes B, putting out his eye. C is liable to B."

* * *

It follows from what has been said that the cause must be reversed and remanded with instructions that the court set aside its order of dismissal; determine appellants' damages; and otherwise proceed in a manner not inconsistent herewith.

It is so ordered.

Notes

1. Do you think the court is correct on the issue of transferred intent?

2. What force might the defendant use to scare the boys away from his watermelons? *See* Restatement (Second) Torts § 81.

3. The *Restatement (Second) of Torts* § 143, as already noted at p. 85, *supra*, takes the position that deadly force can only be used to prevent the commission of a felony if the actor reasonably believes that "the felony cannot otherwise be prevented" and if "the felony * * * is of a type that threatens death or serious bodily harm" *or* involves "the breaking and entry of a dwelling house." *Restatement of Torts* (now *Restatement (Second) of Torts*) § 140, cited in the full report of the principal case, declares that no force at all may be used to prevent the commission of a misdemeanor that does not amount to a serious breach of the peace. This is not to say that, if the threatened misdemeanor constitutes a threat to one's property, one may not use reasonable force to protect one's property but the fact that the threat amounts to a misdemeanor does not give one an independent basis for resorting to force.

3. A *cause célèbre* of recent times was Katko v. Briney, 183 N.W.2d 657 (Iowa 1971), where the plaintiff admitted that he had broken into an "unoccupied boarded-up farmhouse" that had been uninhabited for years searching for antique bottles. When the plaintiff entered a bedroom he was shot in the legs by a "20 gauge spring shotgun." The court affirmed an award of $20,000 actual and $10,000 punitive damages. The case received an enormous amount of publicity, some of it quite emotional. For background on the case *see*, G. Palmer, *Katko v. Briney: A Study in American Gothic*, 56 Ia.L.Rev. 1219 (1971). In the first of the spring gun cases, Ilott v. Wilkes, 3 B. & Ald. 304, 106 Eng.Rep. 674 (C.P.1820), the Court of Common Pleas ruled that the landowner was not liable to a trespassing poacher. The public outcry was so intense that Parliament, in 1827, made the setting of such devices a crime. 7 & 8 Geo. IV, c. 18. In a subsequent case that arose prior to the passage of the act, the court found a way to distinguish *Ilott* and give the trespasser a tort remedy. Bird v. Holbrook, 4 Bing. 628, 130 Eng.Rep. 911 (C.P.1828). There are suggestions in some American cases that notice of the existence of the spring gun will absolve the landowner, but there do not seem to be any cases actually so holding. In State v. Marfaudille, 48 Wash. 117, 92 P. 939 (1907), the court declared that for notice of the spring gun to be a defense, the notice must be so immediate and explicit that the deceased could be said to have committed suicide by proceeding further.

Would the Katko case be decided differently if there were a sign above the building advertising the presence of the spring-gun? What about liability for injury to trespasser caused by unadvertised attack dogs left inside business establishments to guard the premises at night? Does the answer turn on the amount of force the owner would be allowed to use were he present? *See* Restatement (Second) Torts § 85.

4. *Recapture of property*: The *Restatement (Second) of Torts* has several provisions covering the use of force to recapture real property (§§ 88–99) and chattels (§§ 100–111). The court in Giant Food, Inc. v. Mitchell, 334 Md. 633, 640 A.2d 1134, 1139 (Md.App.1994) summarizes the conditions where force may be used to recapture chattels.

1.   The person against whom the force is used has tortiously taken the chattel;

2.   The actor is entitled to immediate possession as against the other;

3.   The recaption is effected promptly;

4.   The actor has first requested the other to return the chattel, or the actor reasonably believes that such a request would be useless, dangerous, or likely to defeat the effective exercise of the privilege;

5.   The force is employed for the purpose of effecting the recaption; and

6.   The force is reasonable.

Under no circumstance may deadly force be used. As the third condition notes, the owner must act "promptly after his dispossession or after his timely discovery of it." (*Restatement (Second) of Torts § 103*). When personal property is involved, the courts recognize a right of "fresh" or "hot pursuit." *See* Hodgeden v. Hubbard, 18 Vt. 504, 46 Am.Dec. 167 (1846).

An attempt to reenter real property that is not sufficiently timely is likely to run against statutes based upon the Statute of Forcible Entry, 5 Richard II, St. 2, c. 2 (1381), and subsequent legislation. These statutes make it a criminal offense to make a forcible entry even against one in wrongful possession. In England these statutes have not been construed to create a civil action on behalf of a wrongful possessor who has been ejected by force, contrary to the statute. The predominant American view, however, is to grant such a person a cause of action against the person making the unlawful forcible entry.

5.   *Repossessions*: The right to use force generally applies to property that has been taken by force or fraud in the first instance, e.g. merchandise taken by a shoplifter. The right of an owner to repossess property legally acquired is more limited. Godwin v. Stanley, 331 S.W.2d 341 (Tex.Civ.App.1959). Today, the Uniform Commercial Code Sec. 9–503 deals with the right of persons holding a secured interest in chattel to repossess it from those who have lost the right of possession because, for example, they have fallen in arrears on their payments. It provides in part: "Unless otherwise agreed a secured party has on default the right to take possession of the collateral. In taking possession a secured party may proceed without judicial process if this can be done without a breach of the peace or may proceed by action." Most jurisdictions interpret this provision and similar statutes to permit a repossession as long as it is accomplished without the express, contemporaneous objection of the buyer. Stealthy, midnight repossessions that involve going onto the property of the buyer are permitted as long as the repossessor is not caught in the act. *See* Hester v. Bandy, 627 So.2d 833 (Miss.1993); MBank El Paso v. Sanchez, 836 S.W.2d 151 (Tex.1992) Absent a breach of the peace, the trespass onto another's land in order to retake the chattel is privileged. *See* Salisbury Livestock Co. v. Colorado Central Credit Union, 793 P.2d 470 (Wyo.1990).

4. *Discipline*

In a number of situations the law gives individuals the privilege to discipline others. The most important examples of this privilege are between parent and child and between teacher and student. Except where parental behavior rises to the level of child abuse, there are few modern cases concerning parental discipline. Suits by a student and his or her parents against a teacher or principal are more frequent. Most cases address the scope of the privilege in the context of corporal punishment. Willoughby v. Lehrbass, 150 Mich.App. 319, 388 N.W.2d 688 (1986)(teacher puts student in a "half-nelson" and marches him to the principal's office); Crews v. McQueen, 192 Ga.App. 560, 385 S.E.2d 712 (1989) (principal fractured eight year old's arm while spanking him); Mathis v. Berrien County School District, 190 Ga.App. 255, 378 S.E.2d 505 (1989) (thirteen year old student diagnosed as suffering from "post traumatic stress disorder" two years after paddling at school); Rinehart v. Board of Education, Western Local School District, 87 Ohio App.3d 214, 621 N.E.2d 1365 (1993)(paddling of twelve year old caused bruises and emotional distress). Statutes or local school regulation may limit or completely eliminate the teacher's privilege to administer corporal punishment. *See* Simms v. School Dist. No. 1, 13 Or.App. 119, 508 P.2d 236 (1973); Simmons v. Vancouver School District No. 37, 41 Wn.App. 365, 704 P.2d 648 (1985). Cases occasionally raise the question of the constitutionality of physical school discipline. *See* Cynthia Denenholz Sweeney, *Corporal Punishment in Public Schools: A Violation of Substantive Due Process?* 33 Hastings L.J. 1245 (1982).

5. *Necessity*

a. *Public Necessity*

United States v. Caltex, Inc., 344 U.S. 149, 73 S.Ct. 200, 97 L.Ed. 157 (1952), involved a claim for compensation for petroleum storage facilities destroyed by United States forces to prevent them from falling into the hands of the advancing Japanese when American and Philippine forces abandoned Manila and retreated to the Bataan peninsula in late December 1941. In denying the claim for compensation, the Court fell back on the long recognized distinction between a taking for use, which must be compensated, and the destruction of property in the course of combat operations for which compensation is not required. In a similar case involving a claim for compensation for petroleum stores and refining and storage facilities destroyed by the British Army when it retreated from Rangoon in early 1942, the House of Lords rejected the distinction. Burmah Oil Co. v. Lord Advocate, [1965] A.C. 75, [1964] 2 W.L.R. 1231, 2 All E.R. 348 (Scot.1964). It could see no difference, from the claimant's point of view, between taking the petroleum for use by the Army and outright destruction of the petroleum stores and facilities to keep them from falling into the hands of the Japanese. Parliament, however, disagreed. In the War Damage Act of 1965 (1965, c. 18), it provided that "[n]o person shall be entitled at common law to receive from the Crown compensation in respect of damage to, or destruction of, property * * * by Acts lawfully done by, or on the authority of, the Crown during, or in contemplation of the outbreak of, a war in which the Sovereign was, or is, engaged." The Act also provided for the dismissal of any pending action for compensation, such as the *Burmah Oil* case itself, which had been remanded for an assessment of the plaintiff's claim. Underlying much of the traditional doctrine is the judgment that, if compensation is to be paid in such circumstances, the question should be decided by the political branches of government.

More recently in National Board of Young Men's Christian Associations v. United States, 395 U.S. 85, 89 S.Ct. 1511, 23 L.Ed.2d 117 (1969), a claim was made for damage caused to buildings in the Panama Canal Zone during riots in January 1964. United States Army troops who had been sent to protect the buildings retreated into the buildings to gain protection from sniper fire. One of the buildings was subsequently set afire by Molotov cocktails and the troops were forced to evacuate the buildings. The other building involved in the claim was heavily damaged by fire bombs after the troops withdrew from this building as well. In affirming rejection of the claims, the Court, per Justice Brennan, held that the occupation of the buildings in the course of trying to protect them was not a taking of property. Nor was the Government liable for any increased damage because of the presence, in the area, of troops who were under attack from angry mobs. Justice Stewart concurred in the Court's opinion and opined that if the troops had used "a building for their own purposes— as a defense bastion or command post—it seems to me this would be a Fifth Amendment taking." Justice Harlan concurred only in the result. Compensation should be payable if the "military had reason to believe that its action placed the property in question in greater peril than if *no* form of protection had been provided at all." Justices Black and Douglas dissented, as they had in the *Caltex* case.

In less dramatic circumstances, it has long been recognized that public authorities have the right to destroy private property in emergency situations, such as destroying buildings to prevent the spread of fire, Surocco v. Geary, 3 Cal. 69, 58 Am.Dec. 385 (1853), destroying the wallpaper in the bedrooms of small pox victims, Seavey v. Preble, 64 Me. 120 (1874), destroying mad dogs, Putnam v. Payne, 13 Johns. (N.Y.) 312 (1816), and destroying commercial elk heard suffering from tuberculosis, South Dakota Department of Health v. Owen, 350 N.W.2d 48 (S.D.1984). In an effort to eradicate the Mediterranean fruit fly that threatened the California citrus industry, the state undertook a widespread aerial spraying campaign. The chemical mixture used caused erosion of the painted surfaces of automobiles. Claims against the state by insurance companies forced to compensate insureds for this damage were rejected on the grounds of public necessity. Farmers Insurance Exchange v. State, 175 Cal.App.3d 494, 221 Cal.Rptr. 225 (1985). Not only is there no common-law right to compensation in these circumstances but the Supreme Court has held, in a case involving the destruction of diseased cedar trees, that there is no compensable claim under the Fourteenth Amendment of the United States Constitution. Miller v. Schoene, 276 U.S. 272, 48 S.Ct. 246, 72 L.Ed. 568 (1928). While in the typical case it is the public authorities that have made and executed the decision to destroy private property to prevent greater public danger, there is authority that, in extreme situations, private citizens can successfully invoke the privilege (or defense) of public necessity. For example, Harrison v. Wisdom, 54 Tenn. 99 (1872), involved private citizens who destroyed merchants' stocks of whiskey and other liquors on the eve of the anticipated entry of the Union Army into Clarksville, Tennessee.

A closer case is presented when the police destroy property in an effort to apprehend felons. In Steele v. City of Houston, 603 S.W.2d 786 (Tex.1980) the police burned the plaintiff's building to the ground in an effort to recapture escaped convicts hiding in the house. In the process of ordering a trial on the merits, the Texas Supreme Court held that the plaintiff could recover the value of his property under a constitutional provision requiring compensation for takings for the public use unless the state could show "great public necessity." The Supreme Court of Minnesota adopted a similar position in Wegner v. Milwaukee Mutual Insurance Co., 479 N.W.2d 38 (Minn.1991). There the police caused extensive damage to a home when they fired tear gas and "flash-bang" grenades into the dwelling in the course of apprehending an armed suspect barricaded within. The court held that the doctrine of public necessity did not insulate the municipality from its liability to pay just compensation to the homeowner.

The Supreme Court of California refused to adopt this position in Customer Company v. City of Sacramento, 10 Cal.4th 368, 41 Cal.Rptr.2d 658, 895 P.2d 900 (1995). As in the Minnesota case, the police caused substantial damage to the plaintiff's store when they fired tear gas into the structure in an effort to apprehend a suspect holed up inside. The court held that store owner could not recover for damage to building and contents on a theory of inverse condemnation in the face of a valid claim of public necessity.

In a notorious exercise of the police power, the Philadelphia Police Department attempted to end the siege of a radical organization called MOVE by dropping an explosive device on the roof of the house in which the group had barricaded itself. The police then prevented the fire department from attempting to control or extinguish the ensuing fire. The conflagration killed 11 persons, including five children, in the residence and destroyed dozens of homes in the vicinity. Is dropping the explosive justified on the basis of public necessity? What of the refusal to fight the fire? See In re City of Philadelphia Litigation, 938 F.Supp. 1278 (E.D.Pa. 1996).

While the cases hold that the public is not legally required to pay for property destroyed pursuant to a valid claim of public necessity, statutory schemes for compensating the owners of destroyed property have been established in many types of situations. For example, municipal ordinances providing compensation to owners of urban real property that has been destroyed to prevent the spread of fire are of long-standing. See Mayor of New York v. Lord, 17 Wend. (N.Y.) 285 (1837). To take another example, the owners of cattle that are required to be destroyed because of foot-and-mouth-disease receive statutory compensation for the loss they have suffered, 21 U.S.C. §§ 114a, 134a. The enactment of a statutory compensation scheme in such circumstances recognizes both that cattle owners are more likely to cooperate with the public authorities if they receive compensation and that, since the benefits of destroying the cattle redound to the public good, the public should bear a large part of the loss.

The *YMCA* case touches the interesting question whether, if the public authorities decide for some reason not to provide fire or police protection to a particular building, and the building is destroyed, the owners of the building have a claim for compensation against the public authorities. Such cases have actually arisen in urban riot situations. In Westminster Investing Corp. v. G. C. Murphy Co., 434 F.2d 521 (D.C.Cir.1970), the court rejected a claim against the District of Columbia which had decided, *inter alia*, not to shoot looters in the disturbances arising out of the April 1968 riots in the District of Columbia; the court concluded that requests for compensation should be addressed to Congress.

b. *Private Necessity*

PLOOF v. PUTNAM

Supreme Court of Vermont, 1908.
81 Vt. 471, 71 A. 188.

MUNSON, J. It is alleged as the ground of recovery that on the 13th day of November, 1904, the defendant was the owner of a certain island in Lake Champlain, and of a certain dock attached thereto, which island and dock were then in charge of the defendant's servant; that the plaintiff was then possessed of and sailing upon said lake a certain loaded sloop, on which were the plaintiff and his wife and two minor children; that there then arose a sudden and violent tempest, whereby the sloop and the property and persons therein were placed in great danger of destruction; that, to save them from destruction or injury, the plaintiff was compelled to, and did, moor the sloop to defendant's dock; that the defendant, by his servant, unmoored the sloop, whereupon it was driven upon the shore by the tempest, without the plaintiff's fault; and that the sloop and its contents were thereby destroyed, and the plaintiff and his wife and children cast into the lake and upon the shore, receiving injuries. This claim is set forth in two counts—one in trespass, charging that the defendant by his servant with force and arms willfully and designedly unmoored the sloop; the other in case, alleging that it was the duty of the defendant by his servant to permit the plaintiff to moor his sloop to the dock, and to permit it to remain so moored during the continuance of the tempest, but that the defendant by his servant, in disregard of this duty, negligently, carelessly, and wrongfully unmoored the sloop. Both counts are demurred to generally.

There are many cases in the books which hold that necessity, and an inability to control movements inaugurated in the proper exercise of a strict right, will justify entries upon land and interferences with personal property that would otherwise have been trespasses. A reference to a few of these will be sufficient to illustrate the doctrine. In Miller v. Fandrye, Poph. 161, trespass was brought for chasing sheep, and the defendant pleaded that the sheep were trespassing upon his land, and that he with a little dog chased them out, and that, as soon as the sheep were off his land, he called in the dog. It was argued that, although the defendant, might lawfully drive the sheep from his own ground with a dog, he had no right to pursue them into the next ground; but the court considered that the defendant might drive the sheep from his land with a dog, and that the nature of a dog is such that he cannot be withdrawn in an instant, and that, as the defendant had done his best to recall the dog, trespass would not lie. In trespass of cattle taken in A., defendant pleaded that he was seised of C. and found the cattle there damage feasant, and chased them towards the pound, and they escaped from him and went into A., and he

presently retook them; and this was held a good plea. 21 Edw. IV, 64;
Vin. Ab. Trespass, H. a, 4, pl. 19. If one have a way over the land of
another for his beasts to pass, and the beasts being properly driven, feed
the grass by morsels in passing, or run out of the way and are promptly
pursued and brought back, trespass will not lie. See Vin. Ab. Trespass, K.
a, pl. 1. A traveler on a highway who finds it obstructed from a sudden
and temporary cause may pass upon the adjoining land without becoming a
trespasser because of the necessity. Henn's Case, W. Jones, 296 * * *. An
entry upon land to save goods which are in danger of being lost or
destroyed by water or fire is not a trespass. 21 Hen. VII, 27; Vin. Ab.
Trespass, H. a, 4, pl. 24, K. a, pl. 3. In Proctor v. Adams, 113 Mass. 376, 18
Am.Rep. 500, the defendant went upon the plaintiff's beach for the purpose
of saving and restoring to the lawful owner a boat which had been driven
ashore, and was in danger of being carried off by the sea; and it was held
no trespass. * * *

This doctrine of necessity applies with special force to the preservation
of human life. One assaulted and in peril of his life may run through the
close of another to escape from his assailant. 37 Hen. VII, pl. 26. One may
sacrifice the personal property of another to save his life or the lives of his
fellows. In Mouse's Case, 12 Co. 63, the defendant was sued for taking and
carrying away the plaintiff's casket and its contents. It appeared that the
ferryman of Gravesend took 47 passengers into his barge to pass to
London, among whom were the plaintiff and defendant; and the barge
being upon the water a great tempest happened, and a strong wind, so that
the barge and all the passengers were in danger of being lost if certain
ponderous things were not cast out, and the defendant thereupon cast out
the plaintiff's casket. It was resolved that in case of necessity, to save the
lives of the passengers, it was lawful for the defendant, being a passenger,
to cast the plaintiff's casket out of the barge; that, if the ferryman
surcharge the barge, the owner shall have his remedy upon the surcharge
against the ferryman, but that if there be no surcharge, and the danger
accrue only by the act of God, as by tempest, without fault of the ferryman,
every one ought to bear his loss to safeguard the life of a man.

It is clear that an entry upon the land of another may be justified by
necessity, and that the declaration before us discloses a necessity for
mooring the sloop. But the defendant questions the sufficiency of the
counts because they do not negative the existence of natural objects to
which the plaintiff could have moored with equal safety. The allegations
are, in substance, that the stress of a sudden and violent tempest compelled
the plaintiff to moor to defendant's dock to save his sloop and the people in
it. The averment of necessity is complete, for it covers not only the
necessity of mooring, but the necessity of mooring to the dock; and the
details of the situation which created this necessity, whatever the legal
requirements regarding them, are matters of proof, and need not be
alleged. It is certain that the rule suggested cannot be held applicable
irrespective of circumstance, and the question must be left for adjudication
upon proceedings had with reference to the evidence or the charge.

The defendant insists that the counts are defective in that they fail to
show that the servant in casting off the rope was acting within the scope of
his employment. It is said that the allegation that the island and dock

were in charge of the servant does not imply authority to do an unlawful act, and that the allegations as a whole fairly indicate that the servant unmoored the sloop for a wrongful purpose of his own, and not by virtue of any general authority or special instruction received from the defendant. But we think the counts are sufficient in this respect. The allegation is that the defendant did this by his servant. The words "willfully, and designedly" in one count, and "negligently, carelessly, and wrongfully" in the other, are not applied to the servant, but to the defendant acting through the servant. The necessary implication is that the servant was acting within the scope of his employment. * * *

Judgment affirmed and cause remanded.

VINCENT v. LAKE ERIE TRANSPORTATION CO.

Supreme Court of Minnesota, 1910.
109 Minn. 456, 124 N.W. 221.

O'BRIEN, J. The steamship Reynolds, owned by the defendant, was for the purpose of discharging her cargo on November 27, 1905, moored to plaintiff's dock in Duluth. While the unloading of the boat was taking place a storm from the northeast developed, which at about 10 o'clock p.m., when the unloading was completed, had so grown in violence that the wind was then moving at 50 miles per hour and continued to increase during the night. There is some evidence that one, and perhaps two, boats were able to enter the harbor that night, but it is plain that navigation was practically suspended from the hour mentioned until the morning of the 29th, when the storm abated, and during that time no master would have been justified in attempting to navigate his vessel, if he could avoid doing so. After the discharge of the cargo the Reynolds signaled for a tug to tow her from the dock, but none could be obtained because of the severity of the storm. If the lines holding the ship to the dock had been cast off, she would doubtless have drifted away; but, instead, the lines were kept fast, and as soon as one parted or chafed it was replaced, sometimes with a larger one. The vessel lay upon the outside of the dock, her bow to the east, the wind and waves striking her starboard quarter with such force that she was constantly being lifted and thrown against the dock, resulting in its damage, as found by the jury, to the amount of $500.

We are satisfied that the character of the storm was such that it would have been highly imprudent for the master of the Reynolds to have attempted to leave the dock or to have permitted his vessel to drift away from it. One witness testified upon the trial that the vessel could have been warped into a slip, and that, if the attempt to bring the ship into the slip had failed, the worse that could have happened would be that the vessel would have been blown ashore upon a soft and muddy bank. The witness was not present in Duluth at the time of the storm, and, while he may have been right in his conclusions, those in charge of the dock and the vessel at the time of the storm were not required to use the highest human intelligence, nor were they required to resort to every possible experiment which could be suggested for the preservation of their property. Nothing more was demanded of them than ordinary prudence and care, and the record in this case fully sustains the contention of the appellant that, in holding the vessel fast to the dock, those in charge of her exercised good judgment and prudent seamanship.

It is claimed by the respondent that it was negligence to moor the boat at an exposed part of the wharf, and to continue in that position after it became apparent that the storm was to be more than usually severe. We do not agree with this position. The part of the wharf where the vessel was moored appears to have been commonly used for that purpose. It was situated within the harbor at Duluth, and must, we think, be considered a proper and safe place, and would undoubtedly have been such during what would be considered a very severe storm. The storm which made it unsafe was one which surpassed in violence any which might have reasonably been anticipated.

The appellant contends by ample assignments of error that, because its conduct during the storm was rendered necessary by prudence and good seamanship under conditions over which it had no control, it cannot be held liable for any injury resulting to the property of others, and claims that the jury should have been so instructed. An analysis of the charge given by the trial court is not necessary, as in our opinion the only question for the jury was the amount of damages which the plaintiffs were entitled to recover, and no complaint is made upon that score.

The situation was one in which the ordinary rules regulating property rights were suspended by forces beyond human control, and if, without the direct intervention of some act by the one sought to be held liable, the property of another was injured, such injury must be attributed to the act of God, and not to the wrongful act of the person sought to be charged. If during the storm the Reynolds had entered the harbor, and while there had become disabled and been thrown against the plaintiffs' dock, the plaintiffs could not have recovered. Again, if while attempting to hold fast to the dock the lines had parted, without any negligence, and the vessel carried against some other boat or dock in the harbor, there would be no liability upon her owner. But here those in charge of the vessel deliberately and by their direct efforts held her in such a position that the damage to the dock resulted, and, having thus preserved the ship at the expense of the dock, it seems to us that her owners are responsible to the dock owners to the extent of the injury inflicted.

In Depue v. Flateau, 100 Minn. 299, 111 N.W. 1, 8 L.R.A. (N.S.) 485, this court held that where the plaintiff, while lawfully in the defendants' house, became so ill that he was incapable of traveling with safety, the defendants were responsible to him in damages for compelling him to leave the premises. If, however, the owner of the premises had furnished the traveler with proper accommodations and medical attendance, would he have been able to defeat an action brought against him for their reasonable worth?

In Ploof v. Putnam, 71 Atl. 188, 20 L.R.A. (N.S.) 152, the Supreme Court of Vermont held that where, under stress of weather, a vessel was without permission moored to a private dock at an island in Lake Champlain owned by the defendant, the plaintiff was not guilty of trespass, and that the defendant was responsible in damages because his representative upon the island unmoored the vessel, permitting it to drift upon the shore, with resultant injuries to it. If, in that case, the vessel had been permitted to remain, and the dock had suffered an injury, we believe the shipowner would have been held liable for the injury done.

Theologians hold that a starving man may, without moral guilt, take what is necessary to sustain life; but it could hardly be said that the obligation would not be upon such person to pay the value of the property so taken when he became able to do so. And so public necessity, in times of war or peace, may require the taking of private property for public purposes; but under our system of jurisprudence compensation must be made.

Let us imagine in this case that for the better mooring of the vessel those in charge of her had appropriated a valuable cable lying upon the dock. No matter how justifiable such appropriation might have been, it would not be claimed that, because of the overwhelming necessity of the situation, the owner of the cable could not recover its value.

This is not a case where life or property was menaced by any object or thing belonging to the plaintiff, the destruction of which became necessary to prevent the threatened disaster. Nor is it a case where, because of the act of God, or unavoidable accident, the infliction of the injury was beyond the control of the defendant, but is one where the defendant prudently and advisedly availed itself of the plaintiffs' property for the purpose of preserving its own more valuable property, and the plaintiffs are entitled to compensation for the injury done.

Order affirmed.

LEWIS, J. I dissent. It was assumed on the trial before the lower court that appellant's liability depended on whether the master of the ship might, in the exercise of reasonable care, have sought a place of safety before the storm made it impossible to leave the dock. The majority opinion assumes that the evidence is conclusive that appellant moored its boat at respondent's dock pursuant to contract, and that the vessel was lawfully in position at the time the additional cables were fastened to the dock, and the reasoning of the opinion is that, because appellant made use of the stronger cables to hold the boat in position, it became liable under the rule that it had voluntarily made use of the property of another for the purpose of saving its own.

In my judgment, if the boat was lawfully in position at the time the storm broke, and the master could not, in the exercise of due care, have left that position without subjecting his vessel to the hazards of the storm, then the damage to the dock, caused by the pounding of the boat, was the result of an inevitable accident. If the master was in the exercise of due care, he was not at fault. The reasoning of the opinion admits that if the ropes, or cables, first attached to the dock had not parted, or if, in the first instance, the master had used the stronger cables, there would be no liability. If the master could not, in the exercise of reasonable care, have anticipated the severity of the storm and sought a place of safety before it became impossible, why should he be required to anticipate the severity of the storm, and, in the first instance, use the stronger cables?

I am of the opinion that one who constructs a dock to the navigable line of waters, and enters into contractual relations with the owner of a vessel to moor at the same, takes the risk of damage to his dock by a boat caught there by a storm, which event could not have been avoided in the exercise of due care and further, that the legal status of the parties in such a case is not changed by renewal of cables to keep the boat from being cast adrift at the mercy of the tempest.

JAGGARD, J., concurs herein.

Notes

1. Following up on the suggestions in the dissent, suppose, in the *Vincent* case, the original ropes had never parted and the ship damaged the pier after the owners of the pier had asked the ship to cast off? Suppose the ship's crew had used extra strong lines to tie up to the dock because they had anticipated the ferocity of the storm?

2. Do you think either of the parties in *Vincent* contemplated that such a situation might arise? Do you think they included a provision covering this eventuality in their contract? In the absence of an explicit bargain, should the law implicitly impose such a provision? Why doesn't the court simply conclude that the potential for incidental damage to the dock was "covered" in the fee the wharf owner charged the Reynolds to dock there?

3. The court, in *Vincent*, appears to suggest that if, in the circumstances of *Ploof v. Putnam*, the sloop had damaged the defendant's property in the course of the attempt of the plaintiff to save the life of his family, he would have been liable for the damage done. This is the position adopted by the *Restatement (Second) of Torts* § 197. There is very little authority on the point. Under the *Restatement* view, in a jurisdiction in which aviation is not treated as an ultrahazardous or abnormally dangerous activity, the owners and operators of an airplane that, without fault on their part, is obliged to make a forced landing would be required to pay for any ground damage. Given the fact that our society values life more than property, this result seems contrary to public policy. It does not seem rational that a pilot who is obliged by an act of God to make a forced landing should be encouraged to hazard his life and those of his passengers because, say, the safest alternative landing place has valuable flower beds on it while nearby vacant land is rockier and less flat. One must note that public authorities clearly have a privilege to destroy property to save life and, in the exercise of that privilege, they are under no common-law duty to pay compensation to the owner of the property. Recognizing a privilege of similar scope for private persons does not seem unwarranted. Consider, for example, the following statement of Devlin, J. [later Lord Devlin]:

> * * * I am not prepared to hold without further consideration that a man is entitled to damage the property of another without compensating him merely because the infliction of such damage is necessary in order to save his own property. I doubt whether the court in such circumstances can be asked to evaluate the relation of the damage done to the property saved, by inquiring, for example, whether it is permissible to do £5,000 worth of damage to a third party in order to save property worth £10,000. In the ordinary case of jettison the property which is sacrificed is the property of a person who is interested in the venture, and an equitable adjustment is made by the application of general average. The same considerations may not apply to the property of a third party who has no

stake in the venture which is being saved. The defence of necessity would, therefore, have called for close examination if in fact it had been based solely on the saving of property and if in law I had thought that the plaintiffs' rights of ownership in the foreshore were unqualified by their proximity to the sea. But, apart from the law, on which I have already expressed my view, the facts of this case, when examined, show that the peril said to justify the discharge of the cargo is that the ship was in imminent danger of breaking her back. The consequence of that would be not merely that the ship herself would become a total loss but that in the circumstances of this case the lives of the crew would have been endangered. The safety of human lives belongs to a different scale of values from the safety of property. The two are beyond comparison and the necessity for saving life has at all times been considered a proper ground for inflicting such damage as may be necessary on another's property.
* * *

Southport Corp. v. Esso Petroleum Co., [1953] 2 All E.R. 1204, 1209–10 (Q.B.). The Court of Appeal reversed the denial of damages on the ground that the ship had gotten into difficulties owing to the negligence of the defendant. The House of Lords, however, accepted the trial judge's finding of no negligence and dismissed the action. [1956] A.C. 218, 2 W.L.R. 81, [1955] 3 All E.R. 864 (1955). None of the appellate judges dissented from Devlin, J.'s assertion that, in the absence of negligence, necessity was a complete defense. *See,* for example, Earl Jowitt's declaration:

> Devlin J. decided that the fact that it was necessary to discharge the oil in the interest of the safety of the crew afforded a sufficient answer to the claim based upon trespass or nuisance. I agree with him in this view and think it unnecessary to consider whether, had this fact not been established, the cause of action in trespass or nuisance would have succeeded.

[1956] A.C. at 235, 2 W.L.R. at 84, [1955] 3 All E.R. at 866. There is also support in American literature for this eminently rational position. *See* R. Keeton, *Conditional Fault in the Law of Torts,* 72 Harv.L.Rev. 401, 415–18, 427–30 (1959); Note, *Incomplete Privilege to Inflict Intentional Invasions of Interests of Property and Personality,* 39 Harv.L.Rev. 307, 318 (1926).

4. Should the necessity defense ever be extended to the taking of human life in situations where one life may be traded for many?

Chapter 3

NEGLIGENCE

A. HISTORICAL DEVELOPMENT

As was indicated in Chapter One most of the traditional intentional torts arose out of the common-law action of trespass.[1] We have already noted, however, that trespass was distinguished from trespass on the case—the other great common-law form of tort action—not on the basis of whether or not the defendant intended to injure the plaintiff but rather on the basis of whether or not the plaintiff's injuries were the direct effect of the defendant's conduct. Admittedly, as we saw in Chapter One, it was often difficult to ascertain whether the plaintiff's injuries were a direct or indirect consequence of the defendant's conduct. This was not, however, the only reason that the old distinctions broke down to be replaced by the modern distinction between intentional injuries and those that were merely caused by the defendant's negligence. There were other difficulties with the old forms of action that, like the distinction between direct and indirect injuries, gradually became more exacerbated in the increasingly industrialized society that England was becoming in the late eighteenth and early nineteenth centuries. It had, for example, long been settled, despite occasional deviations,[2] that in an action against a master for the torts of his servants only trespass on the case would lie regardless of whether the servant himself would have been liable in trespass.[3] The apparent theoretical basis for this doctrine was that the liability of the master was in some ways based upon the master's fault in employing careless servants. On this view of the matter, the master had only indirectly caused the injury to the plaintiff. The master could only be said to have directly caused the plaintiff's injuries if the master had expressly directed the servant to injure the plaintiff in which case the master's liability would be premised not upon vicarious liability for the torts of his servants but upon the master's concert of action in the injuries caused by his servants. In the context of an action against the owner of a carriage for injuries sustained when the carriage ran him over, the plaintiff might be confronted with the following

---

1. *See* p. 18, *supra*.

2. *See* Savignac v. Roome, 6 T.R. 125, 101 Eng.Rep. 470 (K.B. 1794). Among the arcane procedural differences between trespass and trespass on the case mentioned in *Savignac* was the fact that a judgment in trespass of under 40 shillings did not entitle the plain-

tiff to his costs whereas there was no such limitation in case.

3. M'Manus v. Crickett, 1 East 106, 102 Eng.Rep. 43 (K.B. 1800); Morley v. Gaisford, 2 H.Bl. 441, 126 Eng.Rep. 639 (C.P. 1795).

dilemma: if the plaintiff brought the action in trespass on the case and the proof showed that the owner of the carriage was driving, the plaintiff would lose; if the action was brought in trespass and the proof showed that the servant was driving, again the plaintiff would lose. He would be forced to start the action over again in the proper form.[4]

One of the ways adopted by the English courts in the nineteenth century to avoid some of these problems was to hold that, regardless of whether the harm suffered by the plaintiff was immediate or consequential, trespass on the case would lie so long as the harm was not caused willfully.[5] Where the harm was both immediate and willfully caused only trespass would lie. Trespass would also lie as an alternative remedy where the harm was immediate but not willful. In most accident cases, plaintiffs henceforth proceeded in trespass on the case, and since the cause of action was the same, they could now also join the master and the servant as defendants in the same action. The stage was thus set for the eventual evolution of the modern action of negligence. As we saw in Chapter One, however, although the old common-law forms of action were abolished in England and in most American jurisdictions in the latter part of the nineteenth century, it was thought, at least in England, that the plaintiff had alternate remedies for negligently caused immediate injuries. If the plaintiff took the usual course, he pleaded the action in a manner analogous to an action for trespass on the case and the burden of persuasion on the issue of fault was clearly on the plaintiff. If the plaintiff chose, however, he could frame his complaint in a manner analogous to an action for trespass. In this event, it was thought that the burden of persuasion on the issue of fault would be placed upon the defendant. As we saw in Chapter One,[6] *Fowler v. Lanning* held that this was not possible and, in the course of so doing, questioned whether, in point of fact, it ever was the case at common law that the burden of persuasion on the issue of fault in an action for trespass was on the defendant.

B.   THE PLAINTIFF'S PRIMA FACIE CASE

The plaintiff must establish what is called a prima facie case in order to survive a motion to dismiss at the close of the presentation of his evidence. Since the typical negligence action is tried before a judge and a jury, the concept of the prima facie case denotes what the plaintiff must allege and prove in order to get to the jury. The concept will operate, however, even if the case is tried without a jury and the trial judge serves as the trier of fact. In this context, when the plaintiff has established a

---

4. Even if the defendant himself was driving the carriage, there was always the possibility that the defendant might plead the general issue and show that at the moment of impact the horses were out of his control because they had been frightened by loud noises made by third parties. See the discussion of Gibbons v. Pepper, 1 Ld.Raym. 38, 91 Eng.Rep. 922 (K.B. 1695), in Chapter One, *supra*, at 20. The plaintiff would now lose his action in trespass. If, however, the plaintiff had brought an action in case alleging that the defendant had hitched up horses to his carriage that were unmanageable and could not be safely driven on the highway without danger to others, the plaintiff might have won.

5. Williams v. Holland, 2 Bing. 190, 131 Eng.Rep. 848 (C.P. 1833); Moreton v. Hardern, 4 B. & C. 223, 107 Eng.Rep. 1042 (K.B. 1825). The historical development, which has been briefly summarized here, is discussed at length in M. Prichard, *Trespass, Case and the Rule in*, Williams v. Holland, [1964] Cam.L.J. 234.

6. *See* p. 29f, *supra*.

prima facie case the trial judge may no longer decide the case as a matter of law but must, like a jury, weigh the evidence and resolve all the disputed issues of material fact.

In an action for negligence the plaintiff must allege and prove:

1. damage to the plaintiff. Without allegation and proof of actual damages, an action for negligence will not lie. Put another way, an action for negligence cannot be brought merely for nominal damages as a means of vindicating the plaintiff's abstract rights.

2. fault on the part of the defendant. As we shall see this requirement is sometimes interpreted as requiring that the plaintiff must establish a) the existence of a duty on the part of the defendant towards the plaintiff and b) the breach of that duty by the defendant.

3. causation, that is to say establishing that the defendant's fault (or breach of duty) was the legal cause of the plaintiff's damages.

In the nineteenth century many, if not most, jurisdictions also required the plaintiff, as part of his prima facie case, to allege and prove the absence of contributory negligence. On the ground that it is both difficult and unfair to force the plaintiff to prove a negative, most jurisdictions now—Illinois is one of the few exceptions[7]—place the burden of pleading and proving contributory negligence upon the defendant.

The notion of legal fault has been afflicted with what, it is submitted, has been an unnecessary degree of complexity through the insistence of many courts and commentators in almost always pitching discussions of legal fault in terms of a bifurcated approach that seeks to establish first the existence of a duty owed by the defendant to the plaintiff and then proceeds to establish a breach of that duty. As the cases, which will be presented in this chapter will illustrate, however, one normally is considered to have a duty to refrain from exposing others to a reasonably foreseeable risk of injury. In a very real sense the common law has increasingly adopted and built upon Lord Atkin's famous remarks in Donoghue v. Stevenson, [1932] A.C. 562, 580 (Sc.):

> At present I content myself with pointing out that in English law there must be, and is, some general conception of relations giving rise to a duty of care, of which the particular cases found in the books are but instances. The liability for negligence, whether you style it such or treat it as in other systems as a species of "culpa," is no doubt based upon a general public sentiment of moral wrongdoing for which the offender must pay. But the acts or omissions which any moral code would censure cannot in a practical world be treated so as to give a right to every person injured by them to demand relief. In this way rules of law arise which limit the range of complainants and the extent of their remedy. The rule that you are to love your neighbour becomes in law, you must not injure your neighbour; and the lawyer's question, Who is my neighbour? receives a restricted reply. You must take reasonable care to avoid acts or omissions which you can reasonably foresee would be likely to injure your neighbour. Who, then, in law is

---

7. *See* Hardware State Bank v. Cotner, 55 Ill.2d 240, 302 N.E.2d 257 (1973); McRae v. Globetrotter Communications, Inc., 37 Ill. App.3d 408, 346 N.E.2d 1 (1976).

my neighbour? The answer seems to be—persons who are so closely and directly affected by my act that I ought reasonably to have them in contemplation as being so affected when I am directing my mind to the acts or omissions which are called in question * * *

In most contexts the notion of legal fault approximates the common sense notions of fault that underlie the ascriptions of fault and responsibility that people make in ordinary life. That is why many courts usually dispense with the duty analysis, and speak merely in terms of fault, when it has been shown that the defendant has exposed the plaintiff to a reasonably foreseeable risk of injury.[8] Injecting the duty analysis into these types of situations unnecessarily complicates the analysis and gives a certain metaphysical quality to legal reasoning. Under an approach that uses the simpler fault analysis, the notion of duty is reserved for those situations, which still exist in the law and which we shall in due course examine, where for reasons of policy the law does not impose liability when a person injures others through exposing them to a reasonably foreseeable risk of injury. It is in these contexts, where the notion of breach of duty is not equivalent to exposing others to a reasonably foreseeable risk of injury, that the duty concept serves an important purpose. In these contexts, the use of the duty analysis highlights the fact that the notion of legal fault can often be a somewhat technical and artificial concept that should not be confused with common sense notions of fault. Among the contexts in which one is still not always obliged to refrain from exposing others to a foreseeable risk of injury are those involving trespassers on real property and situations involving negligently or even intentionally caused emotional injury.

C. THE STANDARD OF CARE

1. *The Reasonable "Person"*

VAUGHAN v. MENLOVE

Court of Common Pleas, 1837.
3 Bing. (N.C.) 468, 132 Eng.Rep. 490.

The declaration stated, that before and at the time of the grievance and injury, hereinafter mentioned, certain premises, to wit, two cottages with the appurtenances situate in the county of Salop, were respectively in the respective possessions and occupations of certain persons as tenants thereof to the Plaintiff, to wit, one thereof in the possession and occupation of one Thomas Ruscoe as tenant thereof to the Plaintiff, the reversion of and in the same with the appurtenances then belonging to the Plaintiff,

---

8. The cumbersome nature of the duty analysis in the typical personal injury case can be illustrated as follows: Q. Why was the defendant at fault? A. Because he owed a duty to the plaintiff which he breached; Q. Why did the defendant owe the plaintiff a duty? A. Because the activities of the defendant had the potential of exposing the plaintiff to a foreseeable risk of injury; Q. How did the defendant breach that duty? A. Be-

cause he did expose the plaintiff to a foreseeable risk of injury. Contrast the foregoing analysis with the following analysis: Q. Why was the defendant at fault? A. Because he exposed the plaintiff to a foreseeable risk of injury. What is gained by the more elaborate duty analysis? We are, of course, assuming in both illustrations that, as a result of the defendant's activities, the plaintiff has suffered some physical damage.

and the other thereof in the possession and occupation of one Thomas Bickley as tenant thereof to the Plaintiff, the reversion of and in the same with the appurtenances then belonging to the Plaintiff: that the Defendant was then possessed of a certain close near to the said cottages, and of certain buildings of wood and thatch, also near to the said cottages; and that the Defendant was then also possessed of a certain rick or stack of hay before then heaped, stacked, or put together, and then standing, and being in and upon the said close of the Defendant. That on the 1st of August 1835, while the said cottages so were in the occupation of the said tenants, and while the reversion thereof respectively so belonged to the Plaintiff as aforesaid, the said rick or stack of hay of the Defendant was liable and likely to ignite, take fire, and break out into a flame, and there had appeared, and were just grounds to apprehend and believe that the same would ignite, take fire, and break out into a flame; and by reason of such liability, and of the state and condition of the said rick or stack of hay, the same then was and continued dangerous to the said cottages; of which said several premises the Defendant then had notice: yet the Defendant well knowing the premises, but not regarding his duty in that behalf, * * * wrongfully, negligently, and improperly, kept and continued the said rick or stack of hay, so likely and liable to ignite and take fire, and in a state and condition dangerous to the said cottages, although he could, and might, and ought to have removed and altered the same, so as to prevent the same from being and continuing so dangerous as aforesaid; and by reason thereof the said cottages for a long time, to wit, during all the time aforesaid, were in great danger of being consumed by fire. That by reason of the premises, and of the carelessness, negligence, and improper conduct of the Defendant, in so keeping and continuing the said rick or stack, in a state or condition so dangerous as aforesaid, and so liable and likely to ignite and take fire and break out into flame, * * * the said rick or stack of hay of the Defendant, standing in the close of the Defendant, and near the said cottages, did ignite, take fire, and break out into flame, and by fire and flame thence issuing and arising, the said buildings of the Defendant so being of wood and thatch as aforesaid, and so being near to the said rick or stack as aforesaid, were set on fire; and thereby and by reason of the carelessness, negligence, and improper conduct of the Defendant, in so keeping and continuing the said rick or stack in such condition as aforesaid, fire and flame so occasioned as aforesaid by the igniting and breaking out into flame, of the said rick or stack, was thereupon then communicated unto the said cottages in which the Plaintiff was interested as aforesaid, which were thereby then respectively set on fire, and then were consumed, damaged, and wholly destroyed, the cottages being of great value, to wit, the value of 500*l*. And by means of the premises, the Plaintiff was greatly and permanently injured in his said reversionary estate and interest of and in each of them; to the Plaintiff's damage of 500*l*.

At the trial it appeared that the rick in question had been made by the Defendant near the boundary of his own premises; that the hay was in such a state when put together, as to give rise to discussions on the probability of fire: that though there were conflicting opinions on the subject, yet during a period of five weeks, the Defendant was repeatedly warned of his peril; that his stock was insured; and that upon one occasion, being advised to take the rick down to avoid all danger, he said "he would chance it." He made an aperture or chimney through the rick; but in spite, or perhaps in consequence of this precaution, the rick at length burst into flames from the spontaneous heating of its materials; the flames communicated to the Defendant's barn and stables, and thence to the Plaintiff's cottages, which were entirely destroyed.

Patteson J. before whom the cause was tried, told the jury that the question for them to consider, was, whether the fire had been occasioned by gross negligence on the part of the Defendant; adding, that he was bound to proceed with such reasonable caution as a prudent man would have exercised under such circumstances.

A verdict having been found for the Plaintiff, a rule nisi for a new trial was obtained, on the ground that the jury should have been directed to consider, not, whether the Defendant had been guilty of gross negligence with reference to the standard of ordinary prudence, a standard too uncertain to afford any criterion; but whether he had acted bonâ fide to the best of his judgment; if he had, he ought not to be responsible for the misfortune of not possessing the highest order of intelligence. The action under such circumstances, was of the first impression.

Talfourd Serjt. and Whately, shewed cause.

The pleas having expressly raised issues on the negligence of the Defendant, the learned Judge could not do otherwise than leave that question to the jury. The declaration alleges that the Defendant knew of the dangerous state of the rick, and yet negligently and improperly allowed it to stand. The plea of not guilty, therefore, puts in issue the scienter. * * * And the action, though new in specie, is founded on a principle fully established, that a man must so use his own property as not to injure that of others. On the same circuit a defendant was sued a few years ago, for burning weeds so near the extremity of his own land as to set fire to and destroy his neighbours' wood. The plaintiff recovered damages, and no motion was made to set aside the verdict. Then, there were no means of estimating the defendant's negligence, except by taking as a standard, the conduct of a man of ordinary prudence: that has been the rule always laid down, and there is no other that would not be open to much greater uncertainties.

R. V. Richards, in support of the rule.

First, there was no duty imposed on the Defendant, as there is on carriers or other bailees, under an implied contract, to be responsible for the exercise of any given degree of prudence: the Defendant had a right to place his stack as near to the extremity of his own land as he pleased; *Wyatt v. Harrison* (3 B. & Adol. 871): under that right, and subject to no contract, he can only be called on to act bonâ fide to the best of his judgment: if he has done that, it is a contradiction in terms, to inquire whether or not he has been guilty of gross negligence. At all events what would have been gross negligence ought to be estimated by the faculties of the individual, and not by those of other men. The measure of prudence varies so with the varying faculties of men, that it is impossible to say what is gross negligence with reference to the standard of what is called ordinary prudence. In *Crook v. Jadis* (5 B. & Adol. 910), Patteson J. says, "I never

could understand what is meant by parties taking a bill under circumstances which ought to have excited the suspicion of a prudent man:" and
Taunton J., "I cannot estimate the degree of care which a prudent man
should take."

* * *

TINDAL C. J. I agree that this is a case primæ impressionis; but I feel
no difficulty in applying to it the principles of law as laid down in other
cases of a similar kind. Undoubtedly this is not a case of contract, such as
a bailment or the like where the bailee is responsible in consequence of the
remuneration he is to receive: but there is a rule of law which says you
must so enjoy your own property as not to injure that of another; and
according to that rule the Defendant is liable for the consequence of his
own neglect: and though the Defendant did not himself light the fire, yet
mediately, he is as much the cause of it as if he had himself put a candle to
the rick; for it is well known that hay will ferment and take fire if it be not
carefully stacked. It has been decided that if an occupier burns weeds so
near the boundary of his own land that damage ensues to the property of
his neighbour, he is liable to an action for the amount of injury done,
unless the accident were occasioned by a sudden blast which he could not
forsee: *Turbervill v. Stamp* (1 Salk. 13). But put the case of a chemist
making experiments with ingredients, singly innocent, but when combined,
liable to ignite; if he leaves them together, and injury is thereby occasioned
to the property of his neighbour, can any one doubt that an action on the
case would lie?

It is contended, however, that the learned Judge was wrong in leaving
this to the jury as a case of gross negligence, and that the question of
negligence was so mixed up with reference to what would be the conduct of
a man of ordinary prudence that the jury might have thought the latter the
rule by which they were to decide; that such a rule would be too uncertain
to act upon; and that the question ought to have been whether the
Defendant had acted honestly and bonâ fide to the best of his own
judgment. That, however, would leave so vague a line as to afford no rule at
all, the degree of judgment belonging to each individual being infinitely
various: and though it has been urged that the care which a prudent man
would take, is not an intelligible proposition as a rule of law, yet such has
always been the rule adopted in cases of bailment, as laid down in *Coggs v.
Bernard* (2 Ld. Raym. 909). * * * The care taken by a prudent man has
always been the rule laid down; and as to the supposed difficulty of
applying it, a jury has always been able to say, whether, taking that rule as
their guide, there has been negligence on the occasion in question.

Instead, therefore, of saying that the liability for negligence should be
co-extensive with the judgment of each individual, which would be as
variable as the length of the foot of each individual, we ought rather to
adhere to the rule which requires in all cases a regard to caution such as a
man of ordinary prudence would observe. That was in substance the
criterion presented to the jury in this case, and therefore the present rule
must be discharged.

PARK J. I entirely concur in what has fallen from his Lordship.
Although the facts in this case are new in specie, they fall within a

principle long established, that a man must so use his own property as not to injure that of others. * * *

As to the direction of the learned Judge, it was perfectly correct. Under the circumstances of the case it was proper to leave it to the jury whether with reference to the caution which would have been observed by a man of ordinary prudence, the Defendant had not been guilty of gross negligence. After he had been warned repeatedly during five weeks as to the consequences likely to happen, there is no colour for altering the verdict, unless it were to increase the damages.

GASELEE J. concurred in discharging the rule.

VAUGHAN J. The principle on which this action proceeds, is by no means new. It has been urged that the Defendant in such a case takes no duty on himself; but I do not agree in that position: every one takes upon himself the duty of so dealing with his own property as not to injure the property of others. It was, if any thing, too favourable to the Defendant to leave it to the jury whether he had been guilty of gross negligence; for when the Defendant upon being warned as to the consequences likely to ensue from the condition of the rick, said, "he would chance it," it was manifest he adverted to his interest in the insurance office. The conduct of a prudent man has always been the criterion for the jury in such cases: but it is by no means confined to them. In insurance cases, where a captain has sold his vessel after damage too extensive for repairs, the question has always been, whether he had pursued the course which a prudent man would have pursued under the same circumstance. Here, there was not a single witness whose testimony did not go to establish gross negligence in the Defendant. He had repeated warnings of what was likely to occur, and the whole calamity was occasioned by his procrastination.

Rule discharged.

Notes

1. Among the classic treatments of the concept of negligence are H. Terry, *Negligence,* 29 Harv.L.Rev. 40 (1915); H. Edgerton, *Negligence, Inadvertence and Indifference; The Relation of Mental States to Negligence,* 39 Harv.L.Rev. 849 (1926); W. Seavey, *Negligence—Subjective or Objective?,* 41 Harv.L.Rev. 1 (1927). The issues raised by these authors are discussed in 3 F. Harper, F. James, Jr., and O. Gray, Torts 381–466 (1986). *See also* S. Young, *Reconceptualizing Accountability in the Early Nineteenth Century: How the Tort of Negligence Appeared,* 21 Conn.L.Rev. 197 (1989); Note, *Origin of the Modern Standard of Due Care in Negligence,* 1976 Wash.U.L.Q. 447. *Cf.* W.F. Schwartz, *Objective and Subjective Standards of Negligence: Defining the Reasonable Person to Induce Optimal Care and Optimal Populations of Injurers and Victims,* 78 Geo.L.J. 241 (1989) on the question of how modern concerns might affect the choice of the appropriate standard.

2. On the characteristics of the ordinary prudent "man," see F. James, Jr., *The Qualities of the Reasonable Man in Negligence Cases,* 16 Mo.L.Rev. 1 (1951); O. Reynolds Jr., *The Reasonable Man of Negligence Law: A Health Report on the Odious Creature,* 23 Okla.L.Rev. 410 (1970).

DELAIR v. McADOO

Supreme Court of Pennsylvania, 1936.
324 Pa. 392, 188 A. 181.

KEPHART, CHIEF JUSTICE.

Plaintiff brought an action in trespass to recover for damages to his person and property sustained as a result of a collision between his automobile and that owned by the defendant. The accident occurred when defendant, proceeding in the same direction as plaintiff, sought to pass him. As defendant drew alongside of plaintiff, the left rear tire of his car blew out, causing it to swerve and come into contact with the plaintiff's car. The latter's theory at trial was that defendant was negligent in driving with defective tires. The jury found for plaintiff in the sum of $7,500. The court below granted defendant a new trial on the ground that the verdict was excessive, but refused his motion for a judgment n.o.v. Its ruling on the latter motion is here for review.

This case presents but another factual situation presenting in terms of realities the abstract legal principle that the owner of a motor vehicle must exercise such care with respect to it as not to subject others to unreasonable risk of injury from its operation. There are numerous precautions which an owner must take to make that instrumentality reasonably safe and appropriate for use on the public highways. If he chooses to intrust the operation of the vehicle to another, he cannot knowingly place it in the hands of an incompetent driver. * * * And, just as he must guard against the danger arising from the incompetency of the human element, so also must he preclude risks arising from a defective mechanism.

* * *

This court has held that it is negligence to drive an auto equipped with inadequate headlights * * * or with inadequate brakes * * *. A car equipped with tires unfit to meet the strain of travel is likewise governed by the principles applied in these cases. In Mike v. Lian, 322 Pa. 353, 185 A. 775, it was decided that driving an auto with tires in a defective condition did not constitute willful misconduct or wanton negligence * * *, but the problem as to whether the same defect might not amount to want of ordinary care is a novel one in this jurisdiction.

It is common experience that the blow-out of an automobile tire is a hazardous occurrence. A blow-out has a known tendency to cause the vehicle to swerve and become unmanageable, rendering possible injury to others due to the lack of control. * * *

While blow-outs may result from untoward accidents for which no responsibility exists such as from spikes and other causes * * *, where they result from defects in the tire arising from age or wear, there seems little doubt that responsibility should attend the dereliction of the vehicle owner in using such equipment, if the faults would be disclosed on reasonable inspection.

* * *

It has been held in other states that the question whether a particular person is negligent in failing to know that his tires are in too poor a condition for ordinary operation on the highways is a question of fact for the jury. * * * In the instant case the testimony relative to the defect was as follows: A witness for the plaintiff stated that the tire "was worn pretty well through. You could see the tread in the tire—the inside lining." The witness later described this inside lining as the "fabric." The fact that the tire was worn through to and into the fabric over its entire area was corroborated by another witness. The repairman who replaced the tire which had blown out stated that he could see "the breaker strip" which is just under the fabric of a tire. This testimony was contradicted by the defendant.

On a motion for a judgment n.o.v., the testimony must be read in the light most favorable to the plaintiff. * * * It is apparent that a tire so worn that the fabric is exposed is not in a condition for safe driving, and that such a defect will support a finding by a jury of negligence. This conclusion is in accord with that of other jurisdictions which have been confronted with a similar problem. * * * It cannot avail defendant to claim that an ordinary inspection would not have revealed the defect since it was apparent to all of those making an inspection immediately after the accident.

The question was raised at bar whether plaintiff should not have had expert testimony to show that a tire in the condition testified to was dangerous. It would seem, however, that this is a matter as to which the ordinary man's experience is sufficient to enable him to make a sound judgment. * * *

* * * It is an elementary rule that where a court and jury can make their own deductions they must not be made by others. * * *

* * *

A jury is just as well qualified to pass judgment as to the risk of danger in the condition of an article in universal use under a given state of facts as experts. * * * Any ordinary individual, whether a car owner or not, knows that when a tire is worn through to the fabric, its further use is dangerous and it should be removed. When worn through several plies, it is very dangerous for further use. All drivers must be held to a knowledge of these facts. An owner or operator cannot escape simply because he says he does not know. He must know. The hazard is too great to permit cars in this condition to be on the highway. It does not require opinion evidence to demonstrate that a trigger pulled on a loaded gun makes the gun a dangerous instrument when pointed at an individual, nor could one escape liability by saying he did now know it was dangerous. The use of a tire worn through to the fabric presents a similar situation. The rule must be rigid if millions are to drive these instrumentalities which in a fraction of a second may become instruments of destruction to life and property. There is no series of accidents more destructive or more terrifying in the use of automobiles than those which come from "blow-outs." The law requires drivers and owners of motor vehicles to know the condition of those parts which are likely to become dangerous where the flaws or faults would be disclosed by a reasonable inspection. It will assume they do know of the dangers ascertainable by such examination.

Order affirmed.

Notes

1. On what knowledge the reasonable person is expected to have, see Note, 23 Minn.L.Rev. 628 (1939). The standard textual treatments assert that the ordinary person is "presumed" to know certain facts of common experience. This terminology suggests that it would be open to a defendant to introduce rebuttal evidence showing that he did not actually possess that knowledge. Hence the statement in some authorities that there is nothing a person is obliged to know at his peril. At the same time, however, it is also generally recognized that a defendant may be under a "duty to find out," that is to obtain knowledge about the characteristics of the environment in which he lives.

2. One of the classic statements on this subject is that of Oliver Wendell Holmes, Jr.:

> The standards of the law are standards of general application. The law takes no account of the infinite varieties of temperament, intellect, and education which make the internal character of a given act so different in different men. It does not attempt to see men as God sees them, for more than one sufficient reason. In the first place, the impossibility of nicely measuring a man's powers and limitations is far clearer than that of ascertaining his knowledge of law, which has been thought to account for what is called the presumption that every man knows the law. But a more satisfactory explanation is, that, when men live in society, a certain average of conduct, a sacrifice of individual peculiarities going beyond a certain point, is necessary to the general welfare. If, for instance, a man is born hasty and awkward, is always having accidents and hurting himself or his neighbors, no doubt his congenital defects will be allowed for in the courts of Heaven, but his slips are no less troublesome to his neighbors than if they sprang from guilty neglect. His neighbors accordingly require him, at his proper peril, to come up to their standard, and the courts which they establish decline to take his personal equation into account.

O.W. Holmes, Jr., The Common Law, 108 (1881). On the moral justification for holding people to an objective standard of conduct, *see* T. Honoré, *Responsibility and Luck,* 104 L.Q.Rev. 530 (1988).

2. Variations on the "Reasonable 'Man' "Standard

CHARBONNEAU v. MacRURY
Supreme Court of New Hampshire, 1931.
84 N.H. 501, 153 A. 457.

* * *

Case, for negligence. The plaintiff's son and intestate, aged three years, was struck and killed by the defendant Colin's automobile, driven by his minor son, the defendant Elwood. The latter was seventeen years of age and duly licensed. Trial by jury. A nonsuit as to Colin was granted at the close of the plaintiff's evidence. A verdict was returned for the defendant Elwood.

The court charged the jury that the standard by which the defendant's care should be measured was that "of the average person of ordinary prudence acting under like circumstances and conditions." Upon the suggestion of counsel that a defendant minor should not be held to the same degree of care as an adult, the court made the following statement to the jury: "During the course of my instructions to you I told you that the standard by which care on the part of the defendant should be measured would be that of the average person of ordinary prudence acting under like circumstances and conditions. I should like to modify that to this extent: That in judging of the conduct of the defendant, it appearing that he is a minor seventeen or so years of age, * * * his conduct should be judged according to the average conduct of persons of his age and experience. I think I will leave it right there. The standard which you should use in judging of his conduct should be that of the average person of his age and experience." To this the plaintiff excepted.

* * *

SNOW, J.

The plaintiff concedes that the infancy of a person is of material importance in determining whether he has been guilty of contributory negligence, but contends that a minor charged with actionable negligence is to be held to the standard of care of an adult without regard to his non-age and want of experience. While the issue thus presented has been mooted in discussion by writers, there is a dearth of judicial authority directly in point.

The two leading cases dealing with the specific question are Neal v. Gillett (1855) 23 Conn. 437, 442, and Briese v. Maechtle (1911) 146 Wis. 89, 91, 130 N.W. 893, 894, 35 L.R.A.(N.S.) 574, Ann.Cas. 1912C, 176. In the former the defendants, thirteen and sixteen years of age, playing ball by the roadside, were charged with negligently passing a ball so close to the head of the plaintiff's horse as to produce fright and cause the injury. Exception was taken by the defendants to a refusal to charge that the jury were at liberty to take into consideration their age in connection with the other circumstances of the case, and "that the law would not require the same acts of caution, and prudence in a child, as in a man"; and also to the instruction given, namely, that "the age of the defendants was not to be taken into account by the jury in determining the question of negligence as they were only to allow in any event actual damages, this being all the plaintiff claimed." It was there contended by the plaintiff's counsel: (1) That a child incapable of exercising intelligent volition was liable for actual damages committed by him, (2) that cases in which extreme youth had been held to excuse a child from exercising ordinary care were exclusively cases where the child had been plaintiff, and (3) that children of the age of the defendants were bound to exercise the same care as adults. The opinion reads: "A majority of the court are of opinion that the charge was right; though we do not intend to decide whether the distinction taken by the plaintiffs' counsel in regard to the protection which infancy, or 'no-nage,' affords, when claimed by a plaintiff, and when set up by a defendant, is well taken or not, and only remark, that we have been referred to no authority, which directly sanctions such distinction. We place our determination upon a different ground." An obiter dictum to like effect is to be found in Roberts v. Ring, 143 Minn. 151, 153, 173 N.W. 437, 438, where, after stating the rule that, in considering the contributory negligence of a seven year old boy plaintiff the standard is the degree of care commonly exercised by the ordinary boy of his age and maturity, the court remarked: "It would be different if he had caused injury to another. In such a case he could not take advantage of his age or infirmities."

Briese v. Maechtle, supra, was an action in behalf of a boy of nine years of age charging a defendant of ten years with negligent injury inflicted in a collision while playing games with their schoolmates—the plaintiff at marbles and the defendant at tag. The court there said: "Infants may be guilty of actionable negligence, and, even though the defendant was engaged in a perfectly lawful occupation, he may have conducted himself so negligently as to make himself liable for damages resulting from such negligence. Here, however, comes in the marked difference between the tests of negligence as applied to the act of an adult and the same act when committed by a child. The rule is that a child is only required to exercise that degree of care which the great mass of children of the same age ordinarily exercise under the same circumstances, taking into account the experience, capacity, and understanding of the child. * * * This was the measure of the defendant's duty, no greater and no less." The court, reviewing the facts, considered that no one could say that the defendant was doing anything more or less than healthy boys of his age have done from time immemorial, holding in effect that, inasmuch as the defendant's conduct complied with the prescribed standard, there could be no recovery. The case appears to be directly in point for the defendant here.

Dicta supporting the latter view is to be found in several cases. * * *

A like conflict of views appears among legal scholars and text-book writers. Henry T. Terry, in his article on Negligence, 29 Harv.L.Rev. at page 47, says: "The test of reasonableness is what would be the conduct or judgment of what may be called a standard man in the situation of the person whose conduct is in question. * * * Every man, whether he is a standard man or not, is required to act as a standard man would. If by chance he is not such a man, he may * * * make a mistake and act so as to be guilty of legal negligence, though he has used all such care and forethought as he was capable of. In the case of contributory negligence there is an exception to this rule in the case of abnormal persons, such as children and persons of unsound mind. They are not required to act like a standard man, but only to use such judgment as they are capable of. But as to negligence which is not merely contributory, as to negligent wrongs against others, the standard man test applies to their conduct also."

On the other hand, Prof. Bohlen, in his Studies in the Law of Torts (1926) p. 543 (59 Am.L.Rev. 864), says (page 568): "There is a dearth of authority as to the liability of infants or insane persons for harm done to others by acts which would have been negligent in adult or normal persons, but there is a plethora of authority in a field closely allied thereto. * * * The reports are full of cases in which infants have been held incapable of contributory negligence. * * * (Page 570) If our law recognizes infants and insane persons as incapable of exercising that care for their own protection which is required of normal persons as a condition to their right to redress for injuries caused by the wrongful acts of others and relieves them from the penalty which such lack of care would, but for their incapacity, impose, it would be inconsistent and arbitrary to penalize them by requiring them to compensate others whom they injure by conduct, which, though guilty in others, is, by reason of their incapacity, innocent in them. * * * It would therefore seem * * * that where a liability, like that for the impairment of the physical condition of another's body or property, is imposed upon persons capable of fault only if they have been guilty of fault, immaturity of age or mental deficiency which destroys the capacity for fault, should preclude the possibility of liability. * * *''

After discussing the relevancy of evidence of youth in disproof of malice or special intent, Salmond, in his Law of Torts (7th Ed. 1928) p. 82, says: "It would seem that in order to make a child liable for negligence it must be proved that he failed to show the amount of care reasonably to be expected from a child of that age. It is not enough that an adult would have been guilty of negligence had he acted in the same way in the same circumstances. * * *''

* * *

The American Law Institute (Am.L.Inst. Restatement Torts Tent.) § 167, in commenting upon the adopted standard of conduct which it defines as "that of a reasonable man under like circumstances," says: (e) "A child of tender years is not required to conform to the standard of behavior which it is reasonable to expect of an adult, but his conduct is to be judged by the standard of behaviour to be expected from a child of like age, intelligence and experience. * * *.''

Such are the opposing authorities and divergent views where the question has been directly considered, so far as they have come to our attention. However, as indicated in the foregoing excerpts, a "plethora of authority" is to be found in the analogous field of contributory negligence. The reasons there expressed, or impliedly assigned, for limiting the measure of care required of infants in their own protection would, for the most part, support a like limitation in the case of their actionable fault. It is, however, unnecessary to look to other jurisdictions for such analogous authority.

While the specific question of the application of the rule of reasonable conduct to minors charged with primary negligence has not before arisen in this jurisdiction, in the cases where a child's contributory fault has been in issue the conclusion of the court that his infancy is a factor to be considered has been expressed in terms which would apply to his primary as well as to his contributory fault. * * *

There is nothing in the language of these cases which suggests any distinction between the care required of an infant in his own protection and that exacted of him in his conduct toward others. On the contrary, it tends to refute such a distinction. If the law requires a minor for his own protection "to exercise the degree of care and caution of which he is capable" (Buch v. Amory Mfg. Co., supra), * * * it is plain that to exact of him a higher standard of care for the protection of others would be to require him to exceed his capabilities, to transcend the natural expectation, to possess a reason which he did not have and to do what one of his age, experience, opportunity, and capacity would not have done. The law makes no such unreasonable demand. Such a holding would be in the teeth of the expressed attitude of this court in dealing with the infirmities of youth. * * *

Unless infants are to be denied the environment and association of their elders until they have acquired maturity, there must be a living relationship between them on terms which permit the child to act as a child in his stage of development. As well expect a boy to learn to swim without experience in the water as to expect him to learn to function as an adult without contact with his superiors. * * * During the period of his development he must participate in human activities on some basis of reason. Reason requires that indulgence be shown him commensurate with his want of development as indicated by his age and experience. * * * Though strictly speaking it is the resultant qualities reasonably attributable to these factors that measures his want of capacity * * *, it is sufficient, as a practical matter, to speak of age and experience as inclusive of these qualities.

It is error, however, to assume that the law requires reasonable care of adults and not of minors, or applies different measures to the primary and contributory faults of the latter. The law of negligence has for its foundation the rule of reasonable conduct. The general rule is more fully stated as reasonable care under all the circumstances of the particular case. * * * This is the true test or measure in all cases. In applying this rule to the conduct of adults recourse is had to a mythical person called the "standard man" with whose conduct that of the actor is to be compared, namely, the average prudent person placed in his position. * * * While this standard is external * * *, it must necessarily be applied to the actor in the particular situation disclosed by the evidence. It is for the jury to say whether such standard person put in his place, possessed of the same knowledge and means of knowledge that he had of the surrounding circumstances, would or might have done as he did. The knowledge which the actor had, or which he would have had if he had used his faculties, are facts in the light of which he is bound to act as the average prudent person would have acted in his situation. * * * The jury bring to bear their experience in the affairs of life and their knowledge of the motives that govern human action and of the conduct of reasonable prudent men. * * * In other words, possessed of a yardstick with which the law presumes them to be familiar, wholly external to the subject to be surveyed, the jury apply it to the conduct of the party in evidence and determine whether it measures up to the standard. * * * Such is the rule of reasonable conduct and the method of its application to the normal person whether he is charged with primary fault * * * or with contributory negligence. * * * How and why does the rule, or its application, differ if the actor is a minor? And is there anything in the basis for such difference that calls for any distinction between the minor's primary and his contributory fault?

We are told that "the personification of a standard person helps us realize that the actor's conduct is to be compared with that of a human being with all the human failings." 41 Harv.L.Rev. 9. But such standard person is the average prudent adult. In striking this average the law takes into account the failings only of those who have come to maturity. A minor, in the absence of evidence to the contrary, is universally considered to be lacking in judgment. His normal condition is one of recognized incompetency. * * * He is a "human being" subject not only to the ordinary "human failings" but also to those normally incident to immaturity. It is a matter of common knowledge that the normal minor not only lacks the adult's knowledge of the probable consequences of his acts or omissions, but is wanting in capacity to make effective use of such knowledge as he has. His age is a factor in so far as it is a mark of capacity. * * * But other qualities which are ordinarily the product of experience, using the term in its broader sense as inclusive of education and of the understanding that comes from practice and opportunity for observation, are important considerations in determining his ability both to appreciate the dangerous character of his conduct and to avoid its consequences. A danger may be concealed by the obscurity of intelligence due to immaturity as well as by its own inherent obscurity. * * *

It is for these reasons that the law recognizes that indulgence must be shown the minor in appraising the charactor of his conduct. * * * But what is reasonable when the actor is a minor? Manifestly the adult test of the standard man cannot be applied in disregard of the actor's youth and inexperience. Either a new standard denoting the average person of the minor's age and development must be taken as the yardstick, or else allowance must be made for the minor's stage of development as one of the circumstances incident to the application of the general rule of reasonable care. As a practical matter it is not important which course is pursued. This court, however, is inclined to approve the latter both as supporting the theory that reasonable care under all the circumstances is a universal rule, and in the interest of simplicity of applying the law to the facts. The latter course merely requires the jury to apply the accepted rule of reasonable conduct under the circumstances, of which the stage of development of the minor is one, while the former imposes upon the jury the duty first to set up a standard youth for each particular case from the composite factors of age and experience as disclosed in the evidence, and then to apply that standard to the remaining circumstances in proof. * * *

It is a matter of common knowledge that physical and mental maturity is attained by a gradual but generally progressive process of growth from birth, and that the stage at which it is reached varies with the individual. As the factors making for this variation are not alone congenital but result from teaching and experience, it follows that the age at which maturity is in fact reached cannot be determined with mathematical accuracy. The necessities of society, however, require that some age should be considered as prima facie evidence of maturity. The age of twenty-one, which has been accepted by common consent as the basis for the enfranchisement of infants, as fixing his capacity to make contracts and for other purposes, is allowed to mark the supposed border line between immaturity and maturity. This limit is, however, but an approximation of the truth when applied to the individual. This fact must necessarily be recognized in applying the rule of reasonable conduct to infants. If an infant of seventeen years of age, by reason of natural or artificial causes, has acquired the capacity for observation, reasoning, and action of the average prudent adult, this circumstance places him on a parity with the latter. Likewise if his development has progressed only to the stage of the average fourteen year old boy, that circumstance bears on what should be esteemed to be reasonable conduct on his part. In other words, the fundamental rule of reasonable conduct remains constant, but the circumstances of the age and stage of development of the individual in the process of his growth during his minority are important considerations in applying the rule.

* * *

This is consonant with our treatment of the physical infirmities of adults. Ordinarily we do not take into consideration their mental incapacity short of insanity. But their physical defects are circumstances to be considered in the application of the rule. * * * This is because their physical impairments, unlike their mental defects, are susceptible of ascertainment and not because the latter are logically irrelevant. An exception is made in favor of infants because their normal condition is one of incapacity and the state of their progress toward maturity is reasonably capable of determination. So far as defects, whether of adult or minor, can be reasonably ascertained and judged the law recognizes them. As in the case of the physical defect of the blind or one-legged adult, so the mental incapacity imputable to the minor, being deemed capable of proof, is recognized as a factor to be weighed in appraising the character of his conduct. * * * Reasonable conduct is alike demanded of both. The rule of reasonable conduct is constant but the reasonably ascertainable defects of the actor, whether adult or minor, are circumstances to be considered in its application. In neither case does the law make any distinction between the conduct of an actor when charged with actionable fault and when charged with contributory negligence.

* * *

Judgment for the defendant Elwood F. MacRury.

ON MOTION FOR REHEARING.

Attention is called to our omission to deal with the plaintiff's claim in argument that all operators licensed under Pub. Laws 1926, c. 101, §§ 1, 2, 3, are held to the same degree of care. This statute prohibits the operation of a motor vehicle without a license * * *. The plaintiff's contention is based upon a misconception of the design and purport of these provisions. The purpose of the Legislature was the protection of the traveling public. This is accomplished by imposing certain positive limitations of the right to operate cars upon the public highways. * * * Section 3 is a legislative declaration that minors under 16 years of age are incompetent to operate such vehicles, and arbitrarily denies them the right. Section 2 provides a means of assuring a minimum capacity in drivers of motor vehicles by denying the right to all eligible applicants who do not pass the test, whether adults or minors above the prohibited age. The Legislature has not declared that all successful applicants shall be deemed to be of equal capacity and discretion in operating a vehicle. It has not undertaken to deal with the rule of care at all. It neither expressly or impliedly authorizes the trier of facts to disregard the legally ascertainable defects of the actor when material to the issue of his reasonable conduct, whether he be an adult or a minor. The authorized license is not a certificate of the physical perfection of the adult or of the mental maturity of the eligible minor. * * *

Former result affirmed.

Notes

1. A few jurisdictions, by analogy perhaps with the common-law rule that a child under seven is incapable of committing a crime, have held that a child under seven is incapable of negligent conduct. *See, e.g.,* Baker v. Alt, 374 Mich. 492, 132 N.W.2d 614 (1965); Walston v. Greene, 247 N.C. 693, 102 S.E.2d 124 (1958). Some states go further and presume that a child between the ages of seven and fourteen is incapable of negligence but the child may be shown to be capable of negligence. Between the ages of fourteen and twenty-one, a child is presumed to be capable of negligence but the contrary may be shown. *See, e.g.,* Kuhns v. Brugger, 390 Pa. 331, 135 A.2d 395 (1957)(seven to fourteen); Kehler v. Schwenk, 144 Pa. 348, 22 A. 910 (1891). In cases applying these rules the standard of negligence is normally that of a child of the same age and experience so that the actual effect of these supposed special rules is really only to make a child under seven years of age incapable of negligent conduct as a matter of law. It should finally be noted that, even in one of the majority of jurisdictions that purports to follow a more flexible rule, there will often be an age below which a child will be held, as a matter of law, to be incapable of negligence. *See, e.g.,* Christian v. Goodwin, 188 Cal.App.2d 650, 10 Cal.Rptr. 507 (1961)(four years, seven months); Verni v. Johnson, 295 N.Y. 436, 68 N.E.2d 431 (1946)(three years, two months). Indeed, it would be surprising to find a case in which a child under four was held to be capable of negligent conduct.

2. With the age of majority now eighteen for most purposes, the general doctrines premised upon an age of majority of twenty-one will of course have to be somewhat modified, although it should be noted that the courts have always had a tendency to treat "minors" over eighteen as adults. *See, e.g.,* Atlanta Gas Light Co. v. Brown, 94 Ga.App. 351, 94 S.E.2d 612 (1956)(contributory negligence of twenty year old automobile driver); Smith v. Bailey, 91 N.H. 507, 23 A.2d 363 (1941)(nineteen year old automobile driver as defendant). Indeed, in Dorais v. Paquin, 113 N.H. 187, 304 A.2d 369 (1973), without overruling *Charbonneau,* the court held, in a case involving a seventeen year old decided before the effective date of a statute lowering the age of majority to eighteen, that "it is clear * * * that the plaintiff in this case had substantially an adult capacity to appreciate the obvious risk of walking on the wrong side of the road under dark and icy conditions in dark clothing and without a light." Furthermore, in Daniels v. Evans, 107 N.H. 407, 224 A.2d 63 (1966), the court, following a trend to be discussed in the next principal case, had already held a minor driving a car to an adult standard, a result clearly inconsistent with the opinion issued to dispose of the motion for rehearing in *Charbonneau.*

GOSS v. ALLEN

Supreme Court of New Jersey, 1976.
70 N.J. 442, 360 A.2d 388.

SULLIVAN, J.

This case involves a claim for personal injuries and arises out of a skiing accident which occurred at a ski resort in Vermont. Suit was brought in New Jersey because defendant, who was involved in the accident, is a resident of New Jersey.[1] The jury returned a verdict for defendant based on its specific finding that defendant was not negligent. On appeal, the Appellate Division * * * reversed and remanded for a new trial holding that the trial judge committed plain error in his charge to the jury as to the standard of care required of defendant in the circumstances. We reverse and reinstate the judgment for defendant.

* * *

On February 21, 1972, plaintiff, an experienced skier, was serving as a first aid advisor on the ski patrol at the Mad River Glen ski resort in Vermont. The facility includes a beginners slope which near its end makes an abrupt left turn. The accident occurred some 60 feet beyond the end of the slope in a flat area where plaintiff and a friend happened to be standing taking pictures. Plaintiff had been working in the first aid room which is adjacent to the area where plaintiff and her friend were standing.

Defendant, then 17 years of age, was a beginning skier who had limited cross-country skiing experience but had never attempted a downhill run. Nor had he ever been to Mad River Glen before. Upon arrival, defendant was sent to the beginners' slope. However, instead of riding the mechanical T-bar lift to the top, defendant confined his first run to the lower portion of the slope. He walked a quarter of the way up the hill and started to ski down, successfully completing the comparatively short run of 30 feet or so until he came to the abrupt left turn. In attempting to negotiate the turn, defendant lost control over his momentum and direction. He saw the two girls ahead of him but because of the short distance remaining, his efforts to regain control and his lack of experience, he did not call out until he was almost upon the girls. Plaintiff attempted to get out of the way but was unable to do so and was struck and knocked down by defendant.

* * * Counsel have agreed that Vermont law * * * is the same as New Jersey's.

The trial court charged the jury that the standard of care applicable in the case was not the same degree of care required of an adult, but rather that degree of care which a reasonably prudent person of that age (defendant was 17 years of age) would have exercised under the same or similar circumstances. Following a side bar conference, the court supplemented its charge with the following:

"All right. Perhaps I didn't charge as clearly as I thought that I had charged with reference to the duty of a 17 year old. * * * The law imposes on a 17 year old that standard of care that a 17 year old with the experience and background that this 17 year old had. * * *"

---

1. We are advised at oral argument that plaintiff has also filed suit in Vermont against the owner of the ski resort.

There was no exception taken to the charge. As heretofore noted, the jury in answer to an interrogatory submitted to it found the defendant not negligent.

Plaintiff appealed solely on the ground that the jury verdict was against the weight of the evidence. The Appellate Division, however, *sua sponte,* raised the issue of plain error in the court's charge on the applicable standard of care. Following briefing of the issue and oral argument thereon, the Appellate Division reversed and remanded for a new trial finding plain error in the charge. In essence, the Appellant Division held that skiing was an adult activity and that where a child engages in an activity which is normally undertaken by adults, such as skiing, he should be held to the standard of adult skill, knowledge and competence, without allowance for his immaturity. The Appellate Division added that had an adult standard of care been imposed, as it should have been, the jury might well have found defendant negligent.

The Appellate Division determination that defendant, in the circumstances presented, should be held to the standard of care required of an adult was premised on its conclusion that skiing is an activity which may be dangerous to others and is normally undertaken only by adults, and for which adult qualifications are required. See Restatement, Torts 2d, § 283A, Comment c at 16 (1965). We find nothing in the record to support this conclusion. We think it judicially noticeable that skiing as a recreational sport, save for limited hazardous skiing activities, is engaged in by persons of all ages. Defendant's attempt to negotiate the lower end of the beginners' slope certainly cannot be characterized as a skiing activity that as a matter of law was hazardous to others and required that he be held to an adult standard of conduct. * * *

We recognize that certain activities engaged in by minors are so potentially hazardous as to require that the minor be held to an adult standard of care. Driving a motor vehicle, operating a motor boat and hunting would ordinarily be so classified. However, as to the activities mentioned New Jersey law requires that the minor must be licensed and must first demonstrate the requisite degree of adult competence. * * *

We find that the applicable standard of care, correctly charged by the trial court, was that generally applicable to minors. * * * The required standard is that of a reasonable person of like age, intelligence[2] and experience under like circumstances. 42 Am.Jur.2d, *Infants,* § 142 at 136 (1969); *Restatement, Torts* 2d, § 283A at 14 (1965).[3] Among those circumstances, of course, would be the nature of the activity in which the minor was engaged.

Most of the cases which apply this standard have been concerned with the minor's contributory negligence and not primary negligence. It has been suggested that a different standard might well apply where the minor's conduct causes injury to others. See Schulman, "The Standard of

2. Although the charge to the jury in this case omitted the word intelligence, we do not believe the defendant was thereby prejudiced in the light of the charge as a whole and the facts of the case. There was no objection to the charge based on this omission * * *.

3. The *Restatement* Comment states that the rule in § 283A has seldom been applied to anyone over the age of 16 but that no definite line can be drawn.

Care Required of Children," 37 Yale L.J. 618, 619 (1928). While this Court has not previously had occasion to consider this question, the Appellate Division has held that the principles enunciated by this Court regarding the contributory negligence of a child would also apply to a case where the primary negligence of a child is involved. * * * We think that a rational basis exists for applying the same standard whether the issue involves a question of contributory negligence of a child or primary negligence. Moreover, to hold otherwise would further complicate an already difficult area of tort law. The practicalities of the situation weigh heavily in favor of a single standard. See annotation, 97 A.L.R.2d 872, *supra*.

The Appellate Division, while it decided the case on the ground heretofore discussed, also criticized the trial court's application of the standard applicable to children to a 17–year-old person, pointing out that by N.J.S.A. 9:17B–1 *et seq.* (eff. January 1, 1973) every person in this State 18 or more years of age is deemed to be an adult. The Appellate Division could see little sense in holding an 18–year-old person to one standard of care and applying a lesser standard to one 17 years of age.

However, this problem will exist no matter where the line is drawn, whether it be at 10, 14 or 18 years. Since it has to be drawn somewhere, it is not unreasonable to fix it at the age of legal maturity—now 18 in this State—holding those under that age and capable of negligence to the standard of care required of a reasonable person of like age, intelligence and experience under like circumstances. * * *

* * *

The judgment of the Appellate Division is reversed and the judgment of the trial court in favor of defendant is hereby reinstated.

SCHREIBER, J. (dissenting).

The standard of care now made generally applicable to minors does not square with reality, nor does its purported application justify the charge given.

* * *

II

* * *

Under the norm adopted this day where the negligence or contributory negligence of an infant between ages 7 and 18 is in issue, his activity or inactivity is to be measured by a reasonable person of the same age, intelligence and experience under similar circumstances unless the activities "are so potentially hazardous as to require that the minor be held to an adult standard of care." * * * There are several inherent difficulties in and inequitable consequences of this rule.

What criteria are to be employed by the jury to ascertain whether an activity is "potentially hazardous"? If a "potentially hazardous" activity is one which results in serious or permanent injury, then almost any activity might fall within that category. The injured person who has lost the sight of an eye resulting from a carelessly thrown dart, or stone, or firecracker, the death caused by a bicycle, or an individual seriously maimed due to an errant skier—all are indisputable proof of "potentially hazardous" activity. The majority prescribes no guideline except to imply that whenever licensing is required, the "potentially hazardous" test is met.[2] But the State does not impose a licensing requirement on all "potentially hazardous" activities and whether one has a license or not is often not relevant in measuring conduct of a reasonably prudent person. Whether the driver of an automobile is licensed, for example, is not relevant in adjudicating if the automobile was being driven in a reasonable prudent manner. * * *

To the injured party, his loss is the same irrespective of the wrongdoer's date of birth and it is inequitable and unjust that a minor should not be expected to exercise the same degree of care as the mythical reasonable and prudent person, at least when engaged in adult activities.[3] The majority's proposition unnecessarily sanctions the imposition of the burden of young people's hazards on innocent victims. Whenever an infant participates in activities in which adults normally engage, the infant should be held to the adult standard of care. Other courts have not hesitated to do so. * * * Some jurisdictions recognize that children after a certain age [14] are presumably capable of adult discretion. * * *

Inherent in these approaches, either on the basis of activities or on age well below legal adulthood, is recognition of the realism and justness in applying the adult objective standard. In some measure this is probably due to the expansion of experiences and activity of minors, as well as the protection afforded all members of the family by comprehensive liability insurance policies.[4] Functionally, skiing is as much as a sport for people over 18, as under 18. It is no different than golf or cycling. And the hazards to the public whether operating a motor vehicle, power boat, motor scooter, bicycle, tractor or hitting a golf ball, or skiing are self-evident. Third persons may be exposed to serious injury because of the dangers which occur when the activity is not being performed in a reasonably prudent manner by a reasonably prudent person and no sound reason exists for not holding the child defendant to the standard of the reasonably prudent adult. * * *

III

The 18–year-old line drawn today is contrary to policies enunciated by the legislature in regulating some aspects of the conduct of minors in relation to others. A 16–year-old juvenile may be tried as an adult for a homicide, treason, offense against the person in an aggressive, violent and

2. No license is required for a motorized bike, but a ten-speed bike can be pedaled at 25 miles per hour on a flat road. The U.S. Consumer Product Safety Commission reports that there are 500 to 1000 fatalities and about 500,000 permanently crippled each year from bicycle mishaps.

3. Dean Shulman acknowledged that "in some situations a minor is fully as competent as a person over twenty-one and should be held to the same standard of conduct." Shulman, "The Standard of Care Required of Children," 37 Yale L.J. 618 (1928).

4. Payments for child responsibilities are made by adults or insurance companies under policies paid for by adults. James, "Accident Liability Reconsidered: The Impact of Liability Insurance," 57 Yale L.J. 549, 554–556 (1948). In Note, "Torts: Application of Adult Standard of Care to Minor Motor Vehicle Operators," 1962 Duke L.J. 138, 141 it is stated that "Minors are seldom sued in the absence of insurance, because they usually lack sufficient financial resources to make suit worthwhile."

willful manner, or for sale and distribution of narcotics.   N.J.S.A. 2A:4–48.
* * * The 18–year-old line is not consonant with the common law rule that
at age 14 an infant is presumed to have the capacity to be guilty of criminal
intent.   * * * The Restatement, Torts 2d, § 283A, Comment a refers to the
fact that its rule "has seldom been applied to anyone over the age of
sixteen" and "is commonly applied to children of tender years."

The 18–year demarcation line ignores the earlier mental development
of young people.   * * *[a]   Selection of the 16th year is a more reasonable
age at which to draw the line for the individual to be held to an adult
standard of care irrespective of the activity.

IV

I would adopt a rule that an infant 16 years or over would be held to
an adult standard of care and that an infant between ages 7 and 16 would
be rebuttably presumed to have the duty to act, while engaged in an adult
activity, that is, one in which adults normally or usually engage, as a
reasonably prudent person, but that, upon a showing that adult judgmental
capacity for that type of activity is not warranted, the subjective-objective
criteria of the *Restatement* and adopted by the majority be applied.   Application of this rule recognizes the difference between negligence and contributory negligence since the required judgment capacity in foreseeing and
avoiding the hazards created by others may be substantially greater than
that to be comprehended by one's own acts.   * * * If the infant between
ages 7 and 16 is found not to have been occupied in an adult activity, the
Restatement rule adopted by the majority would be applicable.   As to those
16 or over I would apply the adult standard.

I would affirm the judgment of the Appellate Division.

Notes

1.   The *Restatement (Second) of Torts* covers the standard of conduct
expected of a child in § 283A, which was cited in both the majority and
dissenting opinions in *Goss*.   Of particular relevance to the problem now under
consideration is Comment *c* "*Child engaging in adult activity,*" which begins
"[a]n exception to the rule stated in this Section may arise where the child
engages in an activity which is normally undertaken only by adults, and for
which adult qualifications are required."   The comment presents a hypothetical case involving a fourteen year old boy flying an airplane and asserts that
"his age and inexperience would not excuse him from liability for flying it in a
negligent manner."   The comment then continues "[t]he same may be true
where the child drives an automobile."   These are the only two situations
discussed.

a.   [Ed. note].   Schreiber, J., at this point in the text of his opinion quotes the following statement from A. Skolnick, *The Limits of Childhood: Concepts of Child Development and Social Context,* 39 (No. 3) Law & Contemp.Prob. 38, 43 (1975):

Rodman [in "Children Under the Law," 43 Harv.Ed.Rev. 487, 489 (1973)]notes that the law's placement of the dividing line between legal minority and adult status at the age of eighteen or twenty-one years is "artificial and simplistic" because it obscures the dramatic differences among children of different ages and the striking similarities between older children and adults. That observation seems so sound and obvious that it raises the question of how such differences—and also the resemblance between older children and adults—have come to be obscured?

2. In Jackson v. McCuiston, 247 Ark. 862, 448 S.W.2d 33 (1969), a case cited in Schreiber, J.'s, dissent in *Goss,* "a farm boy almost fourteen years old" was held to an adult standard in an action brought for injuries inflicted by the boy while operating a tractor-propelled stalk cutter. The court relied upon an earlier case applying the adult standard to a minor operating a motor vehicle. It will be recalled that the majority in the *Goss* case assumed that hunting would be an adult activity. Nevertheless, in Purtle v. Shelton, 251 Ark. 519, 474 S.W.2d 123 (1971), a divided court held that a seventeen year old boy who accidently shot a hunting companion with a 30.06 rifle was not to be judged by an adult standard. In declining to classify hunting with driving an automobile and operating a stalk cutter, the majority said:

> We have no doubt that deer hunting is a dangerous sport. We cannot say, however, either on the basis of the record before us or on the basis of common knowledge, that deer hunting is an activity normally engaged in by adults only. To the contrary, all the indications are the other way. A child may lawfully hunt without a hunting license at any age under sixteen. Arkansas Game & Fish Commission's 1971–1972 Hunting Regulations, p. 4. We know, from common knowledge, that youngsters only six or eight years old frequently use .22 caliber rifles and other lethal firearms to hunt rabbits, birds, and other small game. We cannot conscientiously declare, without proof and on the basis of mere judicial notice, that only adults normally go deer hunting.

> In refusing to apply an adult standard of care to a minor engaged in hunting deer, we do not imply that a statute to that effect would be unwise. Indeed, we express no opinion upon that question. As judges, we cannot lay down a rule with the precision and inflexibility of a statute drafted by the legislature. If we should declare that a minor hunting deer with a high-powered rifle must in all instances be held to an adult standard of care, we must be prepared to explain why the same rule should not apply to a minor hunting deer with a shotgun, to a minor hunting rabbits with a high-powered rifle, to a twelve-year-old shooting crows with a .22, and so on down to the six-year-old shooting at tin cans with an air rifle. Not to mention other dangerous activities, such as the swinging of a baseball bat, the explosion of firecrackers, or the operation of an electric train. All we mean to say in this case is that we are unwilling to lay down a brand-new rule of law, without precedent and without any logical or practical means of even surmising where the stopping point of the new rule might ultimately be reached.

251 Ark. at 522, 474 S.W.2d at 125–26. In Schomp v. Wilkens, 206 N.J.Super. 95, 501 A.2d 1036 (1985), bicycle riding was held not to be so hazardous an activity as to require minors to be subjected to an adult standard of conduct. Likewise, fire building was held not to be an adult activity in Farm Bureau Ins. Group v. Phillips, 116 Mich.App. 544, 323 N.W.2d 477 (1982). On the other hand, an eleven year old who had played golf regularly for two years and who had taken lessons was held to an adult standard in Neumann v. Shlansky, 58 Misc.2d 128, 294 N.Y.S.2d 628 (County Ct.1968), *affirmed per curiam,* 63 Misc.2d 587, 312 N.Y.S.2d 951 (App.Term 1970), with one judge dissenting, *affirmed per curiam,* 36 A.D.2d 540, 318 N.Y.S.2d 925 (1971).

3. In Dellwo v. Pearson, 259 Minn. 452, 457, 107 N.W.2d 859, 863 (1961), which held a twelve year old operating an outboard motor boat to an adult standard of care, the court, citing a suggestion in an earlier Minnesota case,

opined that "there may be a difference between the standard of care that is required of a child in protecting himself against hazards and the standard that may be applicable when his activities expose others to hazards." When actually forced to make a choice, however, the courts have been almost universally reluctant to disagree with the majority in *Goss* that there is a single standard whether the issue is the negligence of a child defendant or the contributory negligence of a child plaintiff. We are talking of course about the articulated standard and not on whether the trier of fact may in practice be inclined to be more forgiving of contributory negligence—an issue upon which many assertions have been made but little conclusive evidence is available. It should be noted, however, that with the widespread introduction of comparative negligence the perceived pressure for the adoption of a dual standard may abate.

4. *Mentally deficient adults.* Considerable investigation has failed to find any cases in which a mentally deficient adult was not held to the objective reasonable adult standard when the mentally deficient person was a defendant in an action for negligence. *See* Restatement (Second) of Torts § 283B. Conversely, there are a number of cases that have taken the mentally deficient person's diminished capacity into account when the issue was the contributory negligence of a mentally deficient adult plaintiff. *See* Mochen v. State, 43 A.D.2d 484, 352 N.Y.S.2d 290 (1974); Lynch v. Rosenthal, 396 S.W.2d 272 (Mo.App.1965). *But see* Wright v. Tate, 208 Va. 291, 156 S.E.2d 562 (1967). The court in *Wright* relied upon *Restatement (Second) of Torts* § 464(1) which provides that "[u]nless the actor is a child or an insane person, the standard of conduct to which he must conform for his own protection is that of a reasonable man under like circumstances."[9] Most of the cases involving the contributory negligence of a mentally deficient adult, including the three cases just cited, concern a person whose diminished mental capacity was known to the defendant. Should one be totally surprised if a court were to take into account a mentally deficient defendant's diminished mental capacity in an action brought by someone who was well aware of the defendant's diminished mental capacity? For an article on the subject that advocates a subjective approach, regardless of whether negligence or contributory negligence is involved, *see* J. Ellis, *Tort Responsibility of Mentally Disabled Persons,* 1981 Amer. Bar Found.Res.J. 1079. *But see* Note, *Tort Liability of the Mentally Ill in Negligence Actions,* 93 Yale L.J. 153 (1983), taking the position that contemporary attitudes towards the mentally ill as well as empirical research point to an objective standard as being the appropriate approach regardless of whether negligence or contributory negligence is at issue.

5. *Standard applied in emergency situations.* When a person is confronted with a sudden emergency, through no fault of his own, the fact of an emergency and the consequent need for speedy action will be taken into account in determining what it is reasonable to expect of that person. In other words, the reasonable person in an emergency will not be required to exercise the judgment and care of a person who has ample time to reflect about what he ought to do. Some courts describe the emergency doctrine in terms of

9. Where the insane person is a defendant the Restatement (Second) of Torts § 283B does *not* relieve him from legal liability if his conduct does not conform to the "reasonable man" standard. For cases, *see* Annot., 49 A.L.R.3d 189 (1973).

"instinctive action," but the doctrine undoubtedly covers more than purely instinctive reactions. Furthermore, even instinctive action can be negligent. Consider, for example, the following excerpts from the late Judge Magruder's concurring opinion in Whicher v. Phinney, 124 F.2d 929, 932, 933 (1st Cir. 1942):

* * *

The opinion of the court refers to various New Hampshire cases dealing with the special situation where an actor, without previous fault on his part, is faced with a sudden emergency in which he has no time for anything other than "instinctive action." To me the form of statement of the emergency doctrine found in the New Hampshire cases is somewhat confusing, but upon closer examination I suspect that the rule in New Hampshire on this point is not substantially different from that generally laid down in other states.

* * *

The reference to "instinctive action" would seem to introduce a psychological subtlety inappropriate for submission to the jury. The precise meaning of "instinctive action" is difficult enough to define, but it presumably is accompanied by some form of mental activity. The organism apprehends danger and stimulates a muscular response to avert it. This is purposeful action, precipitated by a mental operation, though not on the plane of conscious deliberation. There is no good talking to the jury of behavior patterns, conditioned reflexes, instinctive action, and similar phrases. The point is that when one drives a car on a busy highway, he must be prepared to pay for damages caused to an innocent plaintiff, if his conduct fails to meet an objective standard of ordinary care and skill. This means that in situations of emergency, even where there may not be time for a conscious weighing of alternatives, the driver's behavior pattern, his responses, his skill, must be so educated as to be as good as that of a driver of ordinary competence acting under similar circumstances. No more refinement is practicable for a jury issue. The ordinary formulation of the emergency doctrine enables the jury to make reasonable allowance for the time element in judging the actor's conduct by the traditional standard. Of course, cases of sudden emergency may arise where on the evidence the trial judge should rule as a matter of law that the defendant's response or reaction to the crisis measured up to that of a driver of ordinary competence acting under similar circumstances. Such I believe to be the case here.

Other cases involving the emergency doctrine are Cook v. Thomas, 25 Wis.2d 467, 131 N.W.2d 299 (1964), which suggests that if a motorist has much over five seconds to react, the emergency doctrine cannot be invoked; and Cordas v. Peerless Transportation Co., 27 N.Y.S.2d 198 (City Ct.1941), which involved a cab driver who abandoned his moving taxicab after it had been entered by an armed robber who was attempting to flee from the pursuit of his victim and in which no liability was found.

HALEY v. LONDON ELECTRICITY BOARD

House of Lords, 1964.
[1965] A.C. 778, [1964] 3 W.L.R. 479, 3 All E.R. 185.

LORD REID. My Lords, the appellant became blind many years ago as a result of an accident. He conquered his disability to such an extent that for some years before 1956 he was employed as a telephonist by the London County Council. He lived in a street in South East London and it was his habit to walk unaccompanied from his home for about 100 yards along the pavement and then to get someone to help him to cross the main road where he boarded a bus. With the aid of his white stick he had learned to avoid all ordinary obstacles. On the morning of October 29, 1956, he had walked some 50 yards from his house. On that morning, unknown to him, the respondents' workmen had begun excavating a trench in the pavement, and they had placed an obstacle, which I shall describe in a moment, near the end of the trench. The appellant tripped over it and fell heavily. As a result of his head striking the pavement he has become deaf. He now sues the respondents on the ground of negligence. The case was decided against him by the trial judge and by the Court of Appeal and he now appeals to this House.

The respondents had authority to make this excavation under the Public Utilities Street Works Act, 1950. That Act requires that any such excavation shall be adequately fenced and guarded but the respondents argue that there is no civil liability under that Act for breach of a statutory duty. I need not consider that question because I am of opinion that the appellant is entitled to succeed at common law.

The respondents gave no instructions to their men as to how they were to guard this excavation and gave them no apparatus for that purpose except two notice boards. What the men did was to put the notice boards in such a position in the roadway as to prevent vehicles coming near the kerb and so enable pedestrians to avoid the excavation by walking past it on the roadway. At one end of the excavation they put a pick and shovel on the pavement, and at the end, to which the appellant came, they put a punner. This implement consists of a long handle like a broomstick to one end of which is attached a heavy weight. They put the heavy end on the pavement near the kerb and put the other end on to a railing, which runs along the inside of the pavement, so that it was some two feet above the ground. The handle was therefore sloping up from ground level at the outside to a height of about two feet at the inside of the pavement.

The appellant approached using his stick in the proper way—keeping it in front of him more or less vertical and moving it about so as to detect anything in his way. But he missed the punner handle and his leg caught it about 4½ inches above his ankle or about 8 or 9 inches above the ground. It is not alleged that he was negligent. He gave evidence that he had more than once detected with his stick the railing which the Post Office always use to guard their excavations. A senior Post Office engineer gave evidence that they always guard their excavations with a light fence like a towel rail about two feet high, and that they take into account the protection of blind people. He said that he knew of cases of blind people coming into contact with their fences.   Unfortunately he was not asked whether this fence was effective to protect blind people, but I think that one can infer that it is seeing that the Post Office do have regard to their needs.   Certainly the appellant's view, based on his own experience, is that a fence like that would have prevented his accident.

The trial judge held that what the respondents' men did gave adequate warning to ordinary people with good sight, and I am not disposed to disagree with that.   The excavation was shallow and was to be filled in before nightfall, and the punner (or the pick and shovel) together with the notice boards and the heap of spoil on the pavement beside the trench were, I think, sufficient warning to ordinary people that they should not try to pass along the pavement past the trench.   * * *

On the other hand, if it was the duty of the respondents to have in mind the needs of blind or infirm pedestrians I think that what they did was quite insufficient.   Indeed, the evidence shows that an obstacle attached to a heavy weight and only 9 inches above the ground may well escape detection by a blind man's stick and is for him a trap rather than a warning.

So the question for your Lordships' decision is the nature and extent of the duty owed to pedestrians by persons who carry out operations on a city pavement.   The respondents argue that they were only bound to have in mind or to safeguard ordinary able-bodied people and were under no obligation to give particular consideration to the blind or infirm.   If that is right, it means that a blind or infirm person who goes out alone goes at his peril.   He may meet obstacles which are a danger to him but not to those with good sight because no one is under any obligation to remove or protect them.   And if such an obstacle causes him injury he must suffer the damage in silence.

I could understand the respondents' contention if it was based on an argument that it was not reasonably foreseeable that a blind person might pass along that pavement on that day; or that, although foreseeable, the chance of a blind man coming there was so small and the difficulty of affording protection to him so great that it would have been in the circumstances unreasonable to afford that protection.   Those are well recognised grounds of defence.   But in my judgment neither is open to the respondents in this case.

In deciding what is reasonably foreseeable one must have regard to common knowledge.   We are all accustomed to meeting blind people walking alone with their white sticks on city pavements.   No doubt there are many places open to the public where for one reason or another one would be surprised to see a blind person walking alone, but a city pavement is not one of them.   And a residential street cannot be different from any other.   The blind people we meet must live somewhere and most of them probably left their homes unaccompanied.   It may seem surprising that blind people can avoid ordinary obstacles so well as they do, but we must take account of the facts.   There is evidence in this case about the number of blind people in London[a] and it appears from Government publications

---

a. [Ed. note]. In the speech of Lord Evershed, the number of totally blind people   registered under the National Assistance was stated to be 7,321 in "London as a whole"

that the proportion in the whole country is near one in 500. By no means all are sufficiently skilled or confident to venture out alone but the number who habitually do so must be very large. I find it quite impossible to say that it is not reasonably foreseeable that a blind person may pass along a particular pavement on a particular day.

No question can arise in this case of any great difficulty in affording adequate protection for the blind. In considering what is adequate protection again one must have regard to common knowledge. One is entitled to expect of a blind person a high degree of skill and care because none but the most foolhardy would venture to go out alone without having that skill and exercising that care. We know that in fact blind people do safely avoid all ordinary obstacles on pavements; there can be no question of padding lamp posts as was suggested in one case. But a moment's reflection shows that a low obstacle in an unusual place is a grave danger: on the other hand, it is clear from the evidence in this case and also, I think, from common knowledge that quite a light fence some two feet high is an adequate warning. There would have been no difficulty in providing such a fence here. The evidence is that the Post Office always provide one, and that the respondents have similar fences which are often used. Indeed the evidence suggests that the only reason there was no fence here was that the accident occurred before the necessary fences had arrived. So if the respondents are to succeed it can only be on the ground that there was no duty to do more than safeguard ordinary able-bodied people.

* * *

We were also referred to American authorities. * * * Most are in reports not available here, but it seems clear that widely differing views are expressed. We were informed that there is nothing in the American Restatement on the question we have to decide, and I am unable to determine whether any view on the question can now be said to prevail in the United States.

I can see no justification for laying down any hard-and-fast rule limiting the classes of persons for whom those interfering with a pavement must make provision. It is said that it is impossible to tell what precautions will be adequate to protect all kinds of infirm pedestrians or that taking such precautions would be unreasonably difficult or expensive. I think that such fears are exaggerated * * * It appears to me that the ordinary principles of the common law must apply in streets as well as elsewhere, and that fundamentally they depend on what a reasonable man, careful of his neighbour's safety, would do having the knowledge which a reasonable man in the position of the defendant must be deemed to have. I agree with the statement of law at the end of the speech of Lord Sumner in *Glasgow Corporation v. Taylor*[6]: "a measure of care appropriate to the inability or disability of those who are immature or feeble in mind or body is due from others, who know of or ought to anticipate the presence of such persons within the scope and hazard of their own operations." I would

and 258 in the borough of Woolwich, which was where the accident took place. [1965] A.C. at 798, [1964] 3 W.L.R. at 489, 3 All E.R. at 192.

6. [1922] 1 A.C. 44, 67; 38 T.L.R. 102, H.L.

therefore allow this appeal. The assessment of damages has been deferred and the case must be remitted for such assessment.

* * *

Appeal allowed.

Notes

1. Edward Terrell, Esq., Q.C., was lead counsel for the appellant Haley. He closed his argument with the following statement:

> In conclusion, those who appear on behalf of the appellant are very conscious that they represent not only him but also in a sense, the thousands of blind and partially-sighted persons who are to be seen about our cities and towns. When Lord Atkin posed the famous question "who is my neighbour"? in *Donoghue v. Stevenson*,[10] he was, of course, making a reference to Mosaic Law. The House is reminded of another statement from the same source. The Third Book of Moses, Leviticus, Chapter 19, verse 14: "Thou shalt not curse the deaf, nor put a stumbling block before the blind. * * *"

[1965] A.C. at 788.

2. There are a number of cases holding that a blind person's condition must be taken into account in determining what to expect of the reasonable person in his circumstances. *See, e.g.,* Argo v. Goodstein, 438 Pa. 468, 265 A.2d 783 (1970); Hill v. City of Glenwood, 124 Iowa 479, 100 N.W. 522 (1904). Obviously, a reasonable blind person must take measures to offset his handicap but to ignore his handicap in determining what he must do would be tantamount to imposing upon him a legal obligation not to be blind. Cases involving other *physical* defects are in accord. But typically, in the blind cases, such as the two American cases cited, it has been clear that the defendant had created a condition which would have been dangerous to the average person. The issue has been whether the defendant could be excused because the obviousness of the danger of a completely unprotected and unmarked excavation might have been apparent to, and thus have barred an action by, the average person. The *Haley* case is of particular interest because it was assumed that the defendants had sufficiently marked their excavation so that it presented no unreasonable danger to persons with sight and the issue became not only what standard of conduct the law expected of the blind but also the extent of the obligation if any to anticipate the presence of blind people. In Fletcher v. City of Aberdeen, 54 Wn.2d 174, 338 P.2d 743 (1959), the court declared that there was a duty to anticipate the presence of the blind, but in that case, involving an excavation from which all barriers had been removed, it was again clear that the excavation would have presented an unreasonable danger to persons with sight. Another interesting question is whether one must anticipate that one may come in contact with emotionally disturbed people. *Cf.* Chadwick v. British Railway Board, [1967] 1 W.L.R. 912, 2 All E.R. 945.

3. As the *Haley* case illustrates, once one determines the standard of care expected of a potential plaintiff and the existence of an obligation to anticipate a particular potential plaintiff because of a foreseeable degree of risk to that potential plaintiff, the question becomes what should the defendant, as a

---

10. [1932] A.C. 562, 580.

reasonable person, have done under the circumstances. The *Haley* case thus introduces us to the question of the calculus of risk to which we shall now turn.

3. *The Calculus of Risk*

BARKER v. CITY OF PHILADELPHIA

United States District Court, Eastern District of Pennsylvania, 1955.
134 F.Supp. 231.

LORD, DISTRICT JUDGE.

This action was instituted by Dolores Barker, administratrix of the estate of Robert P. Ebbecke, deceased, to recover damages under the Wrongful Death * * * and Survival Statutes of Pennsylvania * * * for the death of Robert P. Ebbecke, a minor, on August 18, 1952. Plaintiff alleged the minor's death resulted from the negligent operation of one of the City of Philadelphia's trash trucks.

The case was tried before a jury and resulted in verdicts in favor of the estate and the parents of the deceased minor. Defendant has filed the present motion to set aside the verdicts and for judgment n.o.v.

The question is: Should a prudent or reasonably cautious man have foreseen that the alleged negligent act of defendant would result in the injury sustained?

The accident occurred in a densely populated section of the City of Philadelphia. The City maintained a garage for its trash trucks approximately one and one-half blocks from the scene of the accident. The street on which the garage is situated is the same street on which the misfortune occurred. The trucks used this street regularly in traveling to and from the garage. As a result of such use, the drivers of the trucks were thoroughly familiar with the fact that this was a neighborhood of children.

On the east side of the block where the accident occurred is a vacant lot which attracts children from time to time. On the west side of the same block is a City playground where at the time of the accident, "quite a gang of" children were playing.

On the afternoon of the accident, the driver of the City's truck was proceeding down this street to the garage. As he approached the scene where the accident occurred, he came upon another City truck double-parked in the street and headed in the same direction. The driver of the double-parked vehicle motioned that it was all right to proceed around him. Thereupon, the driver of the City truck which was in motion turned out into the extreme left-hand side of the street, in attempting to pass the City vehicle which was parked. While doing so, the driver noticed a huge piece of brown wrapping paper approximately six feet in diameter and two or three feet in height. This paper was lying partially in the gutter and partially on the curb on the east side of the street. The driver stated he did not desire to run over the paper because it might contain broken bottles and thus injure the tires of the truck. He attempted to avoid it by judging the distance between the paper and the City trash truck that was double-parked. After endeavoring to pass between these two objects, he then proceeded on to the garage.

What, in fact, actually happened was that the driver misjudged the truck's position with respect to the paper and ran over it, crushing to death the boy who was under the paper with a playmate.

At the conclusion of the trial, the Court charged the jury in substance as follows:

"In the argument of counsel much has been said as to the foreseeability of the danger on the part of the truck driver. The law as to this is that one cannot be held legally liable for injury to the personal [sic?] [person or?] property of another unless by the exercise of that degree of care and caution which a prudent or reasonably cautious man, acting under similar circumstances, would exert could he have foreseen, not the extent of the injury or damage, or manner in which it occurred, but could have foreseen that some injury or damage to the person or property of another would reasonably be expected to ensue as the result of his action or conduct.

"In this case the question for you to determine as a fact is whether the truck driver acted as a reasonably prudent and cautious man would act in driving his truck under the facts and the evidence as they have been testified to in this case. If he did you should find for the defendant. If he did not your verdict should be for the plaintiff. Could he have foreseen that the injury would reasonably be expected as a result of his conduct? If he could you should find for the plaintiff. If he could not, your verdict should be for the defendant."

To determine if there was negligence, it is necessary to ascertain first if a prudent or reasonably cautious man should have foreseen that his act would cause injury.

Negligence has long been defined generally as the omission to do something which a reasonable man, guided upon those considerations which ordinarily regulate the conduct of human affairs would do, or doing something which a prudent and reasonable man would not do. * * *

* * *

Thus, negligence is a matter of risk—that is to say, of recognizable danger of injury. In most instances, it is caused by an act of heedlessness or carelessness, where the negligent party is unaware of the results which may follow from his act. But it may also exist where he has considered the possible consequences carefully and has exercised his own best judgment as in the present case.

The Restatement of Torts in Section 435, ill. 1, and the Supreme Court of Pennsylvania have adopted the view that a defendant who is negligent must take existing circumstances as he finds them, and may be liable for consequences brought about by his acts, even though they were not reasonably to have been anticipated. Or, as it is sometimes expressed, what he could foresee is important in determining whether he was negligent in the first instance, but not at all decisive in determining the extent of the consequences for which, once negligent, he will be liable. * * *

Applying the law to the facts of the instant case it is readily ascertainable that the driver of the City's truck should have known that some form of injury might ensue if he were to pass over this huge piece of paper. Taking the facts most favorable to the plaintiff, it is a justifiable conclusion to draw that the appearance of the paper, as shown by the fact it was two to three feet in height, would put an ordinarily prudent man on notice that injury might result if he ran over it, and that he should exercise additional precautions to avoid doing so. This is evident by the fact that the driver acknowledged that he was *aware* that something might be under the wrapping paper. Additionally, I believe that this awareness coupled with the fact that the driver was one who consistently handled trash, bundles of paper and similar discarded objects, put him on notice that the nature and position of this object was not of the kind ordinarily encountered in his travels. A person who is employed specifically to collect trash, and does so for a period of time, acquires that additional and somewhat special, knowledge as to the type of ordinary trash set out by inhabitants to be collected.

The evidence shows that the deceased and another little boy were playing "opening envelopes" under this huge piece of paper and that the boys were not sitting absolutely still. The natural tendency of children is to move about causing some movement of the paper.

* * *

Accordingly, under Pennsylvania law a defendant who has failed to exercise reasonable care under the circumstances cannot escape liability for damage upon the ground that he could not have foreseen the particular results of his negligent act. Therefore, in the instant case, it is no defense for the City to say that the driver, who carelessly drove over a piece of paper which for reasons of safety he intended to avoid, did not foresee that a child was under the paper. To allow such a defense would exculpate negligent persons from liability for all but deliberate or wantonly malicious acts.

However, assuming the law requires the driver to have foreseen the possibility of injury, the jury, from the facts in evidence, together with all reasonable inferences in favor of plaintiff, might well have found that the driver should have foreseen the possibility that a child was underneath this object.

* * *

* * * As a matter of fact, the surviving child testified that he had been sitting under the paper with decedent "opening envelopes." The jury may then have concluded that the motion caused by children playing underneath the paper was easily observable by a prudent driver.

The evidence in the case amply supports the jury's verdict that the driver of the truck under these particular circumstances was careless and that his careless act resulted in the decedent's death.

* * *

Accordingly, defendant's motion to set aside the verdicts and for judgment n.o.v. is dismissed.

Notes

1. It is generally agreed that a defendant is legally responsible for (i.e. is the legal cause of) injuries whose extent he could not reasonably have foreseen. It is another question whether, before legal liability can attach, the defendant must not at least have been reasonably able to foresee the general type of injury he has inflicted. This is one of the questions that will be pursued in Chapter 4, *infra,* which is devoted to the issue of causation.

2. Do you agree with Judge Lord that a jury could have found that a reasonable person in the position of the driver of the truck could have reasonably foreseen the presence of a child underneath the paper?

UNITED STATES v. CARROLL TOWING CO.

Circuit Court of Appeals, Second Circuit, 1947.
159 F.2d 169.

[The appeal in this somewhat complex admiralty proceeding involved the allocation of damages from the collision of the barge "Anna C" with a tanker and the consequent sinking of the barge and loss of her cargo of flour which was owned by the United States. The "Anna C," together with a number of other barges, had broken loose from her moorings while the tug "Carroll" was trying to move a nearby barge. The district court had not allocated to the "Anna C" any share of the blame for any part of the loss. The voluminous footnote citations to the cases referred to by Judge Hand have been omitted.]

L. HAND, CIRCUIT JUDGE.

These appeals concern the sinking of the barge, "Anna C," on January 4, 1944, off Pier 51, North River. The Conners Marine Co., Inc., was the owner of the barge, * * *; the Grace Line, Inc., was the charterer of the tug, "Carroll," of which the Carroll Towing Co., Inc., was the owner. * * *

* * *

We cannot, however, excuse the Conners Company for the bargee's failure to care for the barge, and we think that this prevents full recovery. First as to the facts. As we have said, the deckhand and the "harbormaster" jointly undertook to pass upon the "Anna C's" fasts to the pier; and even though we assume that the bargee was responsible for his fasts after the other barges were added outside, there is not the slightest ground for saying that the deckhand and the "harbormaster" would have paid any attention to any protest which he might have made, had he been there. We do not therefore attribute it as in any degree a fault of the "Anna C" that the flotilla broke adrift. Hence she may recover in full against the Carroll Company and the Grace Line for any injury she suffered from the contact with the tanker's propeller, which we shall speak of as the "collision damages." On the other hand, if the bargee had been on board, and had done his duty to his employer, he would have gone below at once, examined the injury, and called for help from the "Carroll" and the Grace Line tug.[a] Moreover, it is clear that these tugs could have kept the barge

---

a. [Ed. note] The reference is to a second tug, the "Grace", owned by the Grace Line which came to the rescue of the flotilla of barges once they had broken loose. The

afloat, until they had safely beached her, and saved her cargo. This would have avoided what we shall call the "sinking damages." Thus, if it was a failure in the Conner Company's proper care of its own barge, for the bargee to be absent, the company can recover only one third of the "sinking" damages from the Carroll Company and one third from the Grace Line. For this reason the question arises whether a barge owner is slack in the care of his barge if the bargee is absent.

As to the consequences of a bargee's absence from his barge there have been a number of decisions; and we cannot agree that it is never ground for liability even to other vessels who may be injured. * * *

It appears from the foregoing review that there is no general rule to determine when the absence of a bargee or other attendant will make the owner of the barge liable for injuries to other vessels if she breaks away from her moorings. However, in any cases where he would be so liable for injuries to others, obviously he must reduce his damages proportionately, if the injury is to his own barge. It becomes apparent why there can be no such general rule, when we consider the grounds for such a liability. Since there are occasions when every vessel will break from her moorings, and since, if she does, she becomes a menace to those about her; the owner's duty, as in other similar situations, to provide against resulting injuries is a function of three variables: (1) The probability that she will break away; (2) the gravity of the resulting injury, if she does; (3) the burden of adequate precautions. Possibly it serves to bring this notion into relief to state it in algebraic terms: if the probability be called P; the injury, L; and the burden, B; liability depends upon whether B is less than L multiplied by P: i.e., whether B<PL. Applied to the situation at bar, the likelihood that a barge will break from her fasts and the damage she will do, vary with the place and time; for example, if a storm threatens, the danger is greater; so it is, if she is in a crowded harbor where moored barges are constantly being shifted about. On the other hand, the barge must not be the bargee's prison, even though he lives aboard; he must go ashore at times. We need not say whether, even in such crowded waters as New York Harbor a bargee must be aboard at night at all; it may be that the custom is otherwise, as Ward, J., supposed in "The Kathryn B. Guinan," supra; and that, if so, the situation is one where custom should control. We leave that question open; but we hold that it is not in all cases a sufficient answer to a bargee's absence without excuse, during working hours, that he has properly made fast his barge to a pier, when he leaves her. In the case at bar the bargee left at five o'clock in the afternoon of January 3rd, and the flotilla broke away at about two o'clock in the afternoon of the following day, twenty-one hours afterwards. The bargee had been away all the time, and we hold that his fabricated story was affirmative evidence that he had no excuse for his absence. At the locus in quo—especially during the short January days and in the full tide of war activity—barges were being constantly "drilled" in and out. Certainly it was not beyond reasonable expectation that, with the inevitable haste and bustle, the work might not be done with adequate care. In such circum-

"Grace" was not involved in any of the legal
proceedings attempting to assess liability for
the damage.

stances we hold—and it is all that we do hold—that it was a fair requirement that the Conners Company should have a bargee aboard (unless he had some excuse for his absence), during the working hours of daylight.

* * *

Decrees reversed and cause remanded for further proceedings in accordance with the foregoing.

Notes

1. Hand, J., first sketched out his now famous formula for ascertaining whether a person was negligent in Conway v. O'Brien, 111 F.2d 611 (2d Cir.1940), *reversed on other grounds* 312 U.S. 492, 61 S.Ct. 634, 85 L.Ed. 969 (1941). That case involved the application of the Vermont "guest" statute, which provided that an automobile guest could not recover against the host-operator unless his injuries were caused by the "gross or wilful negligence of the operator." In the course of the opinion, Hand, J., declared:

> The degree of care demanded of a person by an occasion is the resultant of three factors: the likelihood that his conduct will injure others, taken with the seriousness of the injury if it happens, and balanced against the interest which he must sacrifice to avoid the risk. All these are practically not susceptible of any quantitative estimate, and the second two are generally not so, even theoretically. For this reason a solution always involves some preference, or choice between incommensurables, and it is consigned to a jury because their decision is thought most likely to accord with commonly accepted standards, real or fancied. A statute like that before us presupposes that the answer to the general question has been against the defendant (that is, that his conduct has been inexcusable) but it imposes upon his liability a condition which cannot even be described in quantitative terms; not only must the interest which he would have had to sacrifice be less than the risk to which he subjects others, but it must so far fail to match that risk that some opprobrium or reproach attaches to him.
> * * *

111 F.2d at 612.

2. Consider the following extract from the work of Professor (now Judge) Richard Posner:

> It is time to take a fresh look at the social function of liability for negligent acts. The essential clue, I believe, is provided by Judge Learned Hand's famous formulation of the negligence standard—one of the few attempts to give content to the deceptively simple concept of ordinary care. Although the formulation postdates the period of our primary interest, it never purported to be original but was an attempt to make explicit the standard that the courts had long applied. In a negligence case, Hand said, the judge (or jury) should attempt to measure three things: the magnitude of the loss if an accident occurs; the probability of the accident's occurring; and the burden of taking precautions that would avert it. If the product of the first two terms exceeds the burden of precautions, the failure to take those precautions is negligence. Hand was adumbrating, perhaps unwittingly,[11] an economic meaning of negligence. Discounting

---

11. But it should be noted that Hand was no stranger to economic analysis. See especially United States v. Corn Products Refining Co., 234 Fed. 964 (S.D.N.Y.1916).

(multiplying) the cost of an accident if it occurs by the probability of occurrence yields a measure of the economic benefit to be anticipated from incurring the costs necessary to prevent the accident. The cost of prevention is what Hand meant by the burden of taking precautions against the accident. It may be the cost of installing safety equipment or otherwise making the activity safer, or the benefit forgone by curtailing or eliminating the activity. If the cost of safety measures or of curtailment—whichever cost is lower—exceeds the benefit in accident avoidance to be gained by incurring that cost, society would be better off, in economic terms, to forgo accident prevention. A rule making the enterprise liable for the accidents that occur in such cases cannot be justified on the ground that it will induce the enterprise to increase the safety of its operations. When the cost of accidents is less than the cost of prevention, a rational profit-maximizing enterprise will pay tort judgments to the accident victims rather than incur the larger cost of avoiding liability. Furthermore, overall economic value or welfare would be diminished rather than increased by incurring a higher accident-prevention cost in order to avoid a lower accident cost. If, on the other hand, the benefits in accident avoidance exceed the costs of prevention, society is better off if those costs are incurred and the accident averted, and so in this case the enterprise is made liable, in the expectation that self-interest will lead it to adopt the precautions in order to avoid a greater cost in tort judgments.

One misses any reference to accident avoidance by the victim. If the accident could be prevented by the installation of safety equipment or the curtailment or discontinuance of the underlying activity by the victim at lower cost than any measure taken by the injurer would involve, it would be uneconomical to adopt a rule of liability that placed the burden of accident prevention on the injurer. Although not an explicit part of the Hand formula this qualification, as we shall see, is implicit in the administration of the negligence standard.

Perhaps, then, the dominant function of the fault system is to generate rules of liability that if followed will bring about, at least approximately, the efficient—the cost-justified—level of accidents and safety.[12] Under this view, damages are assessed against the defendant as a way of measuring the costs of accidents, and the damages so assessed are paid over to the plaintiff (to be divided with his lawyer) as the price of enlisting their participation in the operation of the system. Because we do not like to see resources squandered, a judgment of negligence has inescapable overtones of moral disapproval, for it implies that there was a cheaper alternative to the accident. Conversely, there is no moral indignation in the case in which the cost of prevention would have exceeded the cost of the accident. Where the measures necessary to avert the accident would have consumed

---

12. The first systematic attempt to explain a portion of tort law by economic theory was R. H. Coase, The Problem of Social Cost, 3 J. Law & Econ. 1 (1960)(English nuisance law). The extension of the approach to negligence is suggested, but not developed, in Harold Demsetz, Issues in Automobile Accidents and Reparations from the Viewpoint of Economics (June 1968), in Charles O. Gregory and Harry Kalven, Jr., Cases and Materials on Torts 870 (2d ed. 1969); and Guido Calabresi, in The Cost of Accidents, A Legal and Economic Analysis (1970), and in his earlier articles, cited *id.* at 321, has used economic theory to mount an attack on the negligence system. The utility of economic theory in explaining the law of intentional torts is explored in Richard A. Posner, Killing or Wounding To Protect a Property Interest, 14 J. Law & Econ. 201 (1971).

excessive resources, there is no occasion to condemn the defendant for not having taken them.

If indignation has its roots in inefficiency, we do not have to decide whether regulation, or compensation, or retribution, or some mixture of these best describes the dominant purpose of negligence law. In any case, the judgment of liability depends ultimately on a weighing of costs and benefits.

R. Posner, *A Theory of Negligence,* 1 J.Legal Studies 29, 32–34 (1972) (footnotes renumbered). Although Judge Hand's formula has been expressly adopted by many courts and has greatly influenced the *Restatement (Second) of Torts* provisions that will be presented shortly, it has been asserted that the Hand formula is rarely included in jury instructions given in negligence cases. S. Gilles, *The Invisible Hand Formula,* 80 Va.L.Rev. 1015 (1994).

On some of the difficulties of trying to incorporate the Hand analysis of negligence into a coherent and optimal economic theory of liability, see J. Brown, *Toward an Economic Theory of Liability,* 2 J.Legal Studies 323 (1973). In Economic Analysis of Law (2d ed. 1977), Posner discussed a large number of legal issues from the perspective of economics. Among the critical literature generated by the first edition of Posner's book, are A. Leff, *Economic Analysis of Law, Some Realism About Nominalism,* 60 Va.L.Rev. 451 (1974); A. M. Polinsky, *Economic Analysis as a Potentially Defective Product: A Buyer's Guide to Posner's* Economic Analysis of the Law, 87 Harv.L.Rev. 1655 (1974). Posner's book was a good source of citations to further reading on the general subject of the economic analysis of law. Important subsequent work included F. Michelman, *Norms and Normativity in the Economic Theory of Law,* 62 Minn.L.Rev. 1015 (1978); R. Posner, *Some Uses and Abuses of Economics in Law,* 46 U.Chi.L.Rev. 281 (1979). *See also* R. Posner, *A Reply to Some Recent Criticism of the Efficiency Theory of the Common Law,* 9 Hofstra L.Rev. 775 (1981), W. Landes and R. Posner, *The Positive Economic Theory of Tort Law,* 15 Ga.L.Rev. 851 (1981). More recent discussions include R. Cooter, *Prices and Sanctions,* 84 Colum.L.Rev. 1523 (1984); D. Gjerdingen, *The Coase Theorem and the Psychology of Common–Law Thought,* 56 So.Calif.L.Rev. 711 (1983); M. Grady, *A New Positive Economic Theory of Negligence,* 92 Yale L.J. 799 (1983); Note, *The Inefficient Common Law,* 92 Yale L.J. 862 (1983). *See also* S. Shavell, Economic Analysis of Accident Law (1987); M. Grady, *Multiple Tortfeasors and the Economy of Prevention,* 19 J.Legal Studies 653 (1990).

3. In the excerpt from Posner's article quoted above, economic analysis is also used to determine what a rational person would do to minimize costs once the rules of liability have been established. Judge Hand, however, was only trying to use economic analysis to determine how liability should be apportioned in the first place. In a world where transaction costs are nonexistent, or at most minimal, how liability is initially assigned is not important because the parties will have an economic incentive to arrive at the most efficient allocation of accident costs by private arrangements. In the real world, however, where transaction costs are likely to be significant, the initial allocation of legal liability becomes more critical.

4. In determining whether a person was negligent the courts will often consider the social utility of his conduct and the social utility of the interests that have been harmed. Does the Hand formula provide a basis for taking these matters into consideration?

RESTATEMENT (SECOND) OF TORTS (1965)

§ 291. Unreasonableness; How Determined; Magnitude of Risk and Utility of Conduct

Where an act is one which a reasonable man would recognize as involving a risk of harm to another, the risk is unreasonable and the act is negligent if the risk is of such magnitude as to outweigh what the law regards as the utility of the act or of the particular manner in which it is done.

§ 292. Factors Considered in Determining Utility of Actor's Conduct

In determining what the law regards as the utility of the actor's conduct for the purpose of determining whether the actor is negligent, the following factors are important:

    (a) the social value which the law attaches to the interest which is to be advanced or protected by the conduct;

    (b) the extent of the chance that this interest will be advanced or protected by the particular course of conduct;

    (c) the extent of the chance that such interest can be adequately advanced or protected by another and less dangerous course of conduct.

§ 293. Factors Considered in Determining Magnitude of Risk

In determining the magnitude of the risk for the purpose of determining whether the actor is negligent, the following factors are important:

    (a) the social value which the law attaches to the interests which are imperiled;

    (b) the extent of the chance that the actor's conduct will cause an invasion of any interest of the other or of one of a class of which the other is a member;

    (c) the extent of the harm likely to be caused to the interests imperiled:

    (d) the number of persons whose interests are likely to be invaded if the risk takes effect in harm.

PITRE v. EMPLOYERS LIABILITY ASSURANCE CORP.

Court of Appeal of Louisiana, First Circuit, 1970.
234 So.2d 847.

LANDRY, JUDGE.

This appeal by defendants, Employers Liability Assurance Corporation, Ltd. and Maryland Casualty Company, insurers of the Thibodaux Fireman's Fair, is from the judgment of the trial court awarding Mr. and Mrs. Merville N. Pitre damages for the death of their nine and one-half year old son, Anthony Pitre, who died of injuries received when he was struck in the head by the hand of a fair patron winding up to pitch a baseball at a concession stand. The trial court rendered no reasons for judgment. We reverse the judgment and dismiss plaintiffs' actions with prejudice upon finding defendants' insured free of negligence.

Defendants-insurers were sued directly pursuant to LSA–R.S. 22:655.[a]
* * *

* * *

The determinative facts of this case are not in dispute. The unfortunate accident occurred at approximately 8:00 P.M., April 29, 1967, at the baseball concession stand operated at the annual Fireman's Fair conducted upon public school grounds in the City of Thibodaux by the Fire Department. The funds raised are used exclusively to purchase equipment for the companies concerned. It appears that the fairs, which have been held for several successive years, are considerable in scope and grow larger each year. The fair is designed to attract people of all ages. It offers a variety of mechanical rides and amusement devices such as a ferris wheel, merry-go-round, and similar contraptions. Additionally, it offers food in the form of hot dogs, hamburgers and similar fare. Drinks include soft drinks, lemonade and beer. From the record, it is safe to infer the enterprise nets the Fire Department approximately $40,000–$45,000 yearly.

The baseball concession stand consisted of two "alleys" at the rear of which was a canopy type cover of canvas or similar material. At the other end, about 20–25 feet distant, was a counter approximately two feet in height. Beneath the canopy was some sort of rack on which were mounted canvas flaps or dolls which could be knocked down if struck with a baseball. Between the counter and canopy ropes were strung to keep spectators from walking between the counter and the dolls. For the sum of 25¢ a participant was furnished three baseballs from a supply kept on the counter. The object of the game was to knock over the "dolls" and win a prize. Participants were required to stand outside the enclosure and throw from beyond the counter. Beyond the counter there were no barriers, ropes or other devices to restrain the thrower or isolate or separate him from spectators or other patrons attending the fair. Two members of the Fire Department operated the concession from posts which they assumed inside the counter near the restraining side ropes. At no time did the attendants leave the alleys to supervise the activity of a patron standing on the opposite side of the counter to pitch balls.

It is conceded that LeBouef, who was seventeen years of age at the time, in the act of "winding up" to pitch a baseball at the concession, struck young Anthony Pitre in the left temple region.

Insofar as concerns the alleged negligence of the Fire Department, as operator or proprietor of the fair, the pivotal question is was there a duty to in some manner warn spectators and participants of the possible dangers

a. [Ed. note] Louisiana is one of a very few states that permits a direct action against the liability insurance carrier of the person alleged to have injured the plaintiff. In most states, the plaintiff must first secure judgment against the insured before he may take any legal action against the insured's insurance carrier.

inherent in the game, or provide devices to effectively separate and isolate participants from spectators and other participants to prevent injury?

LeBouef's testimony is to the effect he did not see decedent prior to the accident. He acknowledged inadvertently striking the child on the side of the head as he drew his hand behind him to pitch a ball. He recalled that the area near the baseball concession was not particularly crowded. He also observed that there was no expressly designed "pitcher's box" marked off outside the counter to restrict the area from which the participant was required to throw. Neither did he note any type of barrier between participants and mere spectators. The only relevant fact he recalled was that he was throwing overhand when he struck the child.

* * *

Calvin Weber, general chairman of the 1967 Fireman's Fair, testified concerning the organizational structure of the fair. * * * He acknowledged that after the accident, a meeting was held at which safety measures were discussed for the baseball concession at the next fair.

George Everett Henderson, an expert on conducting fairs, testified he has had twenty years experience in the business, the last sixteen as Concessions Manager for Playland Amusements, Incorporated, Pontchartrain Beach, New Orleans. As manager, he is in charge of all concessions at Pontchartrain Beach including design, construction and safety aspects. He has operated approximately 48 similar baseball concessions or stands and at present is operating three such concessions. He noted that safety is not considered as large a problem with concessions of this type as in the case of mechanical rides and amusement devices. He provided such stands with baffles at the end where the targets are situated. The baffles prevented baseballs from ricocheting since experience proved ricocheting balls were the greatest hazard in operating a concession of this nature. His visits to hundreds of similar concessions at other fairs showed the only significant hazard was that incident to ricocheting baseballs. He has never seen or used restraining ropes or barriers to isolate participants from spectators. He conceded that professional fairs draw a line on the ground six feet from the counter and require participants to stand within this line when throwing. He explained that since the thrower must cast down at the targets, the closer the participant is to the target, the less accurate he is because of the trajectory involved at a short distance. The farther away the thrower stands, the more level his trajectory and the greater the accuracy. He noted that the six foot restraining line used by professionals has no relation to safety. He further noted that insurance company safety engineers have always approved the operation of his baseball stands without barriers * * * He also stated that, as a matter of policy, he did not permit very young persons to patronize such a game because they lacked physical strength to knock over the dolls.

Over defendants' objection, the trial court permitted A. J. Naquin, Fire Chief, to testify that the day following the accident, the baseball concession was roped off as a safety precaution.

Admission of this type of evidence was erroneous. Evidence of corrections or improvements following an accident to prevent recurrence of similar incidents is not admissible. Insofar as such corrections tend to constitute an admission of guilt or negligence, they serve to deter one from improving his premises. * * *

* * *

Fault is determined by asking the question: How would a reasonably prudent individual have acted or what precautions would he have taken under the same or similar circumstances? * * * Negligent conduct is determined in the light of the facts and environmental circumstances of each case. * * *

Failure to take every precaution against all foreseeable injury to another does not necessarily constitute negligence. On the contrary, negligence requires that the risk be both foreseeable and unreasonable. * * * Failure to take a particular precaution to guard against injury to another in connection with a risk constitutes negligence only where it appears such a precaution would have been undertaken under the circumstances by a reasonably prudent individual. * * * One is bound to protect against what usually happens or what is likely to happen under the circumstances. * * * Ordinary care requires only that precautions be taken against occurrences that can and should be foreseen; it does not require that one anticipate unusual and improbable, though entirely possible happenings. * * *

Plaintiffs, relying principally upon Gilliam v. Serrano, 162 So.2d 32, maintain that the Fire Department owed the affirmative duty to either warn or guard participants and spectators against the inherent danger of being struck by a person winding up to throw at the targets. * * *

We find Gilliam, above, clearly distinguishable from the case at hand. In Gilliam, the fair operators were operating a mechanical amusement device at a "fair" designed expressly to attract children of pre-school age. In essence, Gilliam holds that where pre-school children are concerned, the operator of amusement devices owes a high degree of care. With this general rule, we are in accord. To hold as plaintiffs urge herein would make operators of amusement devices insurers of the safety of their patrons. Such is not the law. The operator is required only to exercise that degree of care commensurate with foreseeable dangers inherent under the circumstances, including the age bracket of his anticipated patrons. Plaintiff has not shown that children of decedent's age were permitted to participate in the baseball concession involved herein. Mr. Henderson's testimony justifies the assumption that persons of decedent's age were not allowed to indulge in this particular sport.

It is well settled that custom and usage are properly considered in determining whether sufficient care has been taken in a particular instance, but custom and usage are not controlling or decisive since the customary way of doing a thing may be negligent and may create a false standard of care. * * * Here the record shows it is customary only to protect against ricocheting balls. It is not normal or customary to station attendants outside the enclosed concession area nor is it standard procedure to rope off or barricade the pitching area. Although the custom shown does not conclusively establish that the Fire Department discharged its duty to decedent, it is one factor to be considered in determining whether a reasonably prudent person would or should have foreseen the danger of injury from the source encountered here. It does not appear that the same or a similar accident had previously occurred. We find that there were no latent or hidden dangers to spectators in the throwing of baseballs under the circumstances shown. The pitching was conducted openly, in full view of all who watched. It involved forcibly throwing an object which could produce injury if misdirected, but the injury here did not result in this manner. Such danger as attended a participant stepping back, winding up to throw and actually throwing a ball was clearly visible to all.

* * *

The national popularity of baseball as a sport warrants the conclusion that even a nine and one-half year old lad is aware of such danger as attends his remaining in proximity to persons throwing baseballs. Although the type of accident in question is one that was perhaps foreseeable, and certainly of a type possible, its probability of occurrence was not so great as to render the operators negligent for failing to take measures to prevent its happening. As stated above, failure to take precautions does not constitute negligence unless the danger is both foreseeable and unreasonable. Here, such danger as existed was not unreasonable. Here, a nonprofit organization, performing a vital public service, took such precaution as was deemed advisable by persons engaged in a similar enterprise as a business. In this instance, we find that the risk of foreseeable harm to others, and the probability of an accident of this nature occurring is outweighed by the utility of purpose for which the enterprise was conducted.

* * *

Notes

1. As the court in *Pitre* holds, evidence of *post* accident behavior is normally not permitted to be introduced into evidence, although there are exceptions. If the fair operator were a commercial enterprise do you think that, even in the absence of any evidence of prior accidents, the court would have found the operator free from negligence?

2. The question of whether it is reasonable to ignore a foreseeable risk is a troublesome one. The House of Lords was confronted with the issue in Bolton v. Stone, [1951] A.C. 850, 1 All E.R. 1078, where a ball was hit out of a cricket ground and hit a woman standing on the adjoining road outside her home. The road was not very much travelled. Some balls had previously been hit out of the cricket ground, although not very frequently—perhaps six times in twenty-eight years—so that it was impossible to argue that such an occurrence was unforeseeable. However, no previous injuries had ever been inflicted. The defendants were held not liable. Whether the House of Lords would reach the same decision today is not at all clear. Unlike the *Pitre* case, however, it is not immediately obvious what the defendants in the *Bolton* case could have done to make sure that such an accident would not reoccur. No matter how high they made the fence, there was always the possibility some athlete might have been able to hit the ball out of the grounds.

3. Although the impression is difficult to document, one senses that the general public will be judged more leniently than technically trained people engaged in specialized activities.

4. The *Pitre* case is a good transition to the question of how an injured person goes about proving negligence, the question that will be discussed in the next section of this chapter.

4. Establishment of the Standard of Care: The Function of the Judge and the Jury

In principle, the distinct functions of judge and jury are clear. Judges, whether at the trial or the appellate level, decide questions of law; juries decide questions of fact. In order to maintain some control over jury determinations, the question of whether a reasonable jury could make a particular finding has been made a question of law. In this way a trial judge or an appellate court can exercise some control over the jury without, in theory, preempting the jury's function. As the student will see, if he has not already done so, practice does not always measure up to the neat analytical framework established by the generally accepted theory. There are many cases in which judges have disagreed with juries and in which it would be fatuous to maintain that no reasonable person could have arrived at the conclusion reached by the jury on the facts presented. This deviation from the standard theory is explained by noting that some questions decided by a jury, such as "Was the defendant negligent?", are "mixed questions of law and fact." Exactly what is a mixed question of law and fact is another question. For an extended discussion of the epistemological and policy questions underlying this whole area, *see* G. Christie, *Judicial Review of Findings of Fact,* 87 N.W.U.L.Rev. 14 (1992).

In a highly original essay by the late Roy Stone, *The Compleat Wrangler,* 50 Minn.L.Rev. 1001, 1009–10 (1966), the legal universe was broken down into three parts: *alpha* facts, *aleph* facts, and questions of law. *Alpha* facts are those questions that are determined by direct observation and by accepting or rejecting the testimony of witnesses who are reporting their own direct observations. For example, "is the defendant red-haired?" "Was it raining on the night of May 14, 1977?" "Was the plaintiff hit by a large object?" These are questions uniquely suited for jury determination and there would have to be a complete absence of evidentiary support for a jury's verdict before a judge could reject the jury's conclusions on such issues. *Aleph* facts are also questions of fact but they are not decided by direct observation. Questions concerning *aleph* facts arise when doubt remains even after all the evidence is in. The decision will be made not by resort to further reports of direct observations but by reflection. In a negligence action such questions of *aleph* fact would include "Did the defendant behave as a reasonable person?" "Was there an appreciable risk of injury to third persons?" etc. Even what would normally be a question of *alpha* fact can become a question of *aleph* fact if the evidence of direct observation does not resolve the matter. Take the question of whether it was raining on the evening of May 14, 1977. Suppose the reports of direct observers indicate that, on that evening, the condition that the English describe as "spitting" existed. That is, throughout the evening there were periods when a few drops of water fell. How would one characterize this situation? Was it raining or wasn't it? It all depends on what you mean by raining and this question must be determined by reflection not observation. Judges are rather freer in disregarding the conclusions of juries on questions of *aleph* fact *not* because the issues are not questions of fact but because the answers to such questions are not ultimately derived from observation but from reflection. Finally, in Stone's legal universe, there are questions of law that are for the judges alone to decide. These are questions such as "what duty of care does a possessor of land owe to a trespasser?" "Is contributory negligence a complete defense to the plaintiff's action for damages?" Despite its clarity, Stone's analytical framework has not been widely adopted.

Another and more famous legal thinker who rejected the mixed question of law and fact analysis as being inadequate to explain why judges will intrude upon the jury's province more in some situations than in others was Oliver Wendell Holmes, Jr. It was Holmes' position that sometimes juries, as well as judges, exercised a purely law-making or legislative role. Consider the following passages from the writings of Holmes. First, from *The Common Law* 122–24, 126–27 (1881)(footnotes omitted):

* * *

Many have noticed the confusion of thought implied in speaking of such cases as presenting mixed questions of law and fact. No doubt, as has been said above, the averment that the defendant has been guilty of negligence is a complex one: first, that he has done or omitted certain things; second, that his alleged conduct does not come up to the legal standard. And so long as the controversy is simply on the first half, the whole complex averment is plain matter for the jury without special instructions, just as a question of ownership would be where the only dispute was as to the fact upon which the legal conclusion was founded. But when a controversy arises on the second half, the question whether the court or the jury ought to judge of the defendant's conduct is wholly unaffected by the accident, whether there is or is not also a dispute as to what that conduct was. If there is such a dispute, it is entirely possible to give a series of hypothetical instructions adapted to every state of facts which it is open to the jury to find. If there is no such dispute, the court may still take their opinion as to the standard. The problem is to explain the relative functions of court and jury with regard to the latter.

When a case arises in which the standard of conduct, pure and simple, is submitted to the jury, the explanation is plain. It is that the court, not entertaining any clear views of public policy applicable to the matter, derives the rule to be applied from daily experience, as it has been agreed that the great body of the law of tort has been derived. But the court further feels that it is not itself possessed of sufficient practical experience to lay down the rule intelligently. It conceives that twelve men taken from the practical part of the community can aid its judgment. Therefore it aids its conscience by taking the opinion of the jury.

But supposing a state of facts often repeated in practice, is it to be imagined that the court is to go on leaving the standard to the jury forever? Is it not manifest, on the contrary, that if the jury is, on the whole, as fair a tribunal as it is represented to be, the lesson which can be got from that source will be learned? Either the court will find that the fair teaching of experience is that the conduct complained of usually is or is not blameworthy, and therefore, unless explained, is or is not a ground of liability; or it will find the jury oscillating to and fro, and will see the necessity of making up its mind for itself. There is no reason why any other such question should not be settled, as well as that of liability for stairs with smooth strips of brass upon their edges. The exceptions would mainly be found where the standard was rapidly changing, as, for instance, in some questions of medical treatment.

If this be the proper conclusion in plain cases, further consequences ensue. Facts do not often exactly repeat themselves in practice; but cases with comparatively small variations from each other do. A judge who has long sat at *nisi prius* ought gradually to acquire a fund of experience which enables him to represent the common sense of the community in ordinary instances far better than an average jury. He should be able to lead and to instruct them in detail, even where he thinks it desirable, on the whole, to take their opinion. Furthermore, the sphere in which he is able to rule without taking their opinion at all should be continually growing.

* * *

The principal argument that is urged in favor of the view that a more extended function belongs to the jury as matter of right, is the necessity of continually conforming our standards to experience. No doubt the general foundation of legal liability in blameworthiness, as determined by the existing average standards of the community, should always be kept in mind, for the purpose of keeping such concrete rules as from time to time may be laid down conformable to daily life. No doubt this conformity is the practical justification for requiring a man to know the civil law, as the fact that crimes are also generally sins is one of the practical justifications for requiring a man to know the criminal law. But these considerations only lead to the conclusion that precedents should be overruled when they become inconsistent with present conditions; and this has generally happened, except with regard to the construction of deeds and wills. On the other hand, it is very desirable to know as nearly as we can the standard by which we shall be judged at a given moment, and, moreover, the standards for a very large part of human conduct do not vary from century to century.

* * *

It is perfectly consistent with the views maintained in this Lecture that the courts have been very slow to withdraw questions of negligence from the jury, without distinguishing nicely whether the doubt concerned the facts or the standard to be applied. Legal, like natural divisions, however clear in their general outline, will be found on exact scrutiny to end in a penumbra or debatable land. This is the region of the jury, and only cases falling on this doubtful border are likely to be carried far in court. Still, the tendency of the law must always be to narrow the field of uncertainty. That is what analogy, as well as the decisions on this very subject, would lead us to expect.

* * *

Holmes was even more explicit on the law-making role of the jury in his article, *Law in Science and Science in Law,* 12 Harv.L.Rev. 443, 457–60 (1899)(footnotes omitted):

* * * From saying that we will leave a question to the jury to saying that it is a question of fact is but a step, and the result is that at this day it has come to be a widespread doctrine that negligence not only is a question for the jury but is a question of fact. I have heard it urged with great vehemence by counsel, and calmly maintained by professors that, in addition to their wrongs to labor, courts were encroaching upon the province of the jury when they directed a verdict in a negligence case, even in the unobtrusive form of a ruling that there was no evidence of neglect.

I venture to think, on the other hand, now, as I thought twenty years ago, before I went upon the bench, that every time that a judge declines to rule whether certain conduct is negligent or not he avows his inability to state the law, and that the meaning of leaving nice questions to the jury is that while if a question of law is pretty clear we can decide it, as it is our duty to do, if it is difficult it can be decided better by twelve men taken at random from the street. * * *

When we rule on evidence of negligence we are ruling on a standard of conduct, a standard which we hold the parties bound to know beforehand, and which in theory is always the same upon the same facts and not a matter dependent upon the whim of the particular jury or the eloquence of the particular advocate. And I may be permitted to observe that, referring once more to history, similar questions originally were, and to some extent still are, dealt with as questions of law. It was and is so on the question of probable cause in malicious prosecution. It was so on the question of necessaries for an infant. It was so in questions of what is reasonable, as—a reasonable fine, convenient time, seasonable time, reasonable time, reasonable notice of dishonor. It is so in regard to the remoteness of damage in an action of contract. * * *

I do not believe that the jury have any historic or *a priori* right to decide any standard of conduct. I think that the logic of the contrary view would be that every decision upon such a question by the court is an invasion of their province, and that all the law properly is in their breasts. I refer to the subject, however, merely as another matter in which phrases have taken the place of real reasons, and to do my part toward asserting a certain freedom of approach in dealing with negligence cases, not because I wish to quarrel with the existing and settled practice. I think that practice may be a good one, as it certainly is convenient, for Mr. Starkie's reason. There are many cases where no one could lay down a standard of conduct intelligently without hearing evidence upon that, as well as concerning what the conduct was. And although it does not follow that such evidence is for the jury, any more than the question of fact whether a legislature passed a certain statute, still they are a convenient tribunal, and if the evidence to establish a rule of law is to be left to them, it seems natural to leave the conclusion from the evidence to them as well. I confess that in my experience I have not found juries specially inspired for the discovery of truth. I have not noticed that they could see further into things or form a saner judgment than a sensible and well trained judge. I have not found them freer from prejudice than an ordinary judge would be. Indeed one reason why I believe in our practice of leaving questions of negligence to them is what is precisely one of their gravest defects from the point of view of their theoretical function: that they will introduce into their verdict a certain amount—a very large amount, so far as I have observed—of popular prejudice, and thus keep the administration of the law in accord with the wishes and feelings of the community. Possibly such a justification is a little like that which an eminent English barrister gave me many years ago for the distinction between barristers and solicitors. It was in substance that if law was to be practised somebody had to be damned, and he preferred that it should be somebody else.

* * *

Holmes' frank recognition of a law-making role for the jury may be said to enhance the importance of the jury; on the other hand, having characterized part of the role of the jury as law-making, Holmes is now able to justify judicial intrusion into the role of the jury and even to envision wholesale judicial supplanting of the jury's role.

For a more recent exposition of Holmes' view as to both the function of the jury and of the desirability of the courts superseding the jury's role, consider the following opinion by Traynor, J.:

TRAYNOR, JUSTICE (dissenting in part).

I concur in the judgment. I cannot subscribe, however, to the view that when a jury determines standards of care in negligence cases it is simply finding facts. It is a question of law what the rule or standard of conduct should be for adjudging the actions of men as lawful or unlawful and for determining the consequences of those actions. A question of fact relates to what acts or events have occurred or what conditions exist or have existed. * * * Questions of fact in this country, where there is a constitutional right to a jury trial, are for the jury, while questions of law are ordinarily for the judge. In the field of negligence it is common practice for the jury to determine not only the facts but the standard of conduct to be applied within the compass of the rule that the conduct prescribed must be that of a reasonably prudent man under the circumstances. To determine whether given conduct should impose liability or bar a recovery is to make law. If the court has formulated a standard of reasonable conduct that is applicable to the case, the jury's sole concern is to determine whether a person's conduct has met that standard, a question of fact. If the court has not formulated such a standard, it becomes the jury's responsibility to do so, and thereafter to determine whether a person's conduct has met that standard. The decision as to whether the standard should be fixed by the court or left to the jury rests with the appellate courts and turns upon whether the jury would be at an advantage in arriving at a standard by virtue of being a cross-section of the community and therefore representative of the community views and attitudes.

Toschi v. Christian, 24 Cal.2d 354, 364–65, 149 P.2d 848, 854 (1944). Traynor, J., reiterated this point of view in his concurring opinion in Startup v. Pacific Electric Railway, 29 Cal.2d 866, 872–73, 180 P.2d 896, 899–900 (1947).

One of the reasons the question of the role of the jury in negligence actions is a difficult one is the confusion introduced into the law by the notion of duty. In the typical negligence case, does breach of duty mean the same thing as fault, namely the creation of an unreasonable risk of injury, which is basically a factual question albeit what Roy Stone called a question of *aleph* fact, or does breach of duty mean something else? (See the discussion in Section B, above at p. 104). Consider the following statement from the opinion of Friedman, J., writing for the California District Court of Appeal (Third District) in Raymond v. Paradise Unified School District, 218 Cal.App.2d 1, 7–10, 31 Cal.Rptr. 847, 851–52 (1963):

* * *

Implicit in the present appeal is the thesis that this court may nullify the jury's verdict by extracting the vital essence of a duty of care on the school district's part; in other words, that the question of duty is one of law for the court, not a question of fact for the jury. To the extent that existence of a duty of care turns on conflicting evidence as to the reasonable foreseeability of injury, the question may be one for the jury. Initially, however, presence of a duty rests upon factors other than foreseeability, and its existence is primarily for judicial determination. * * * In submitting the question of the school district's negligence to the jury, the trial judge made a preliminary determination that, granted a foreseeable risk, the school district owed a duty of care. (Richards v. Stanley, supra). This determination was one of law, within the range of appellate review.

The concept of duty as a question of law provides a measure for evaluating the appellate decisions on school district negligence which have been cited to us. Generally speaking, each of the proximate cause decisions turns on its own facts and has little value as precedent. * * * A judicial declaration of duty, in contrast, may amount to a statement of law and thus create precedent, more or less influential according to its factual proximity to the case at hand.

An affirmative declaration of duty simply amounts to a statement that two parties stand in such relationship that the law will impose on one a responsibility for the exercise of care toward the other. Inherent in this simple description are various and sometimes delicate policy judgments. The social utility of the activity out of which the injury arises, compared with the risks involved in its conduct; the kind of person with whom the actor is dealing; the workability of a rule of

care, especially in terms of the parties' relative ability to adopt practical means of preventing injury; the relative ability of the parties to
bear the financial burden of injury and the availability of means by
which the loss may be shifted or spread; the body of statutes and
judicial precedents which color the parties' relationship; the prophylac-
tic effect of a rule of liability; in the case of a public agency defendant,
the extent of its powers, the role imposed upon it by law and the
limitations imposed upon it by budget; and finally, the moral impera-
tives which judges share with their fellow citizens—such are the
factors which play a role in the determination of duty. * * * Occasions for judicial determination of a duty of care are infrequent,
because in "run of the mill" accident cases the existence of a duty may
be—and usually is—safely assumed. Here the problem is squarely
presented. * * *

As this discussion has indicated, although there is some broad general
agreement on some general principles, there is a great deal of dispute as to
the exact function of the jury and as to the reason why courts will
sometimes intrude more aggressively into the function of the jury on some
types of questions and not on others. Nevertheless, with some experience,
one can expect to develop a good sense as to when a particular court is
likely to defer to the judgment of a jury and when it will not. One point
should be noted, however; in practice it has not been possible to decide
definitively the question of negligence, even for some discrete grouping of
cases. For example, in Baltimore & Ohio Railroad Co. v. Goodman, 275
U.S. 66, 48 S.Ct. 24, 72 L.Ed. 167 (1927), a jury verdict for the plaintiff was
sustained by the trial court and then by the Sixth Circuit on appeal. The
Supreme Court reversed. Goodman was killed when the truck he was
driving was hit by the defendant's train. In the course of the opinion,
Holmes declared:

* * *

We do not go into further details as to Goodman's precise situation, beyond mentioning that it was daylight and that he was familiar
with the crossing, for it appears to us plain that nothing is suggested
by the evidence to relieve Goodman from responsibility for his own
death. When a man goes upon a railroad track he knows that he goes
to a place where he will be killed if a train comes upon him before he is
clear of the track. He knows that he must stop for the train, not the
train stop for him. In such circumstances it seems to us that if a
driver cannot be sure otherwise whether a train is dangerously near he
must stop and get out of his vehicle, although obviously he will not
often be required to do more than to stop and look. It seems to us that
if he relies upon not hearing the train or any signal and takes no
further precaution he does so at his own risk. If at the last moment
Goodman found himself in an emergency it was his own fault that he
did not reduce his speed earlier or come to a stop. It is true as said in
Flannelly v. Delaware & Hudson Co., 225 U.S. 597, 603, that the
question of due care very generally is left to the jury. But we are
dealing with a standard of conduct, and when the standard is clear it

should be laid down once for all by the Courts. See Southern Pacific Co. v. Berkshire, 254 U.S. 415, 417, 419.

275 U.S. at 69–70, 48 S.Ct. at 25, 72 L.Ed. at 168. Holmes' attempt to justify and extend the "stop, look, and listen" rule nevertheless ultimately failed. In Pokora v. Wabash Railway Co., 292 U.S. 98, 54 S.Ct. 580, 78 L.Ed. 1149 (1934), a case very similar to the *Goodman* case, a unanimous Court reversed the trial court's granting of a directed verdict which had been affirmed by the Seventh Circuit. The following excerpts from the Court's opinion are instructive:

* * *

MR. JUSTICE CARDOZO delivered the opinion of the Court.

John Pokora, driving his truck across a railway grade crossing in the city of Springfield, Illinois, was struck by a train and injured. Upon the trial of his suit for damages, the District Court held that he had been guilty of contributory negligence, and directed a verdict for the defendant. The Circuit Court of Appeals (one judge dissenting) affirmed, 66 F.2d 166, resting its judgment on the opinion of this court in B. & O. R. Co. v. Goodman, 275 U.S. 66. A writ of certiorari brings the case here.

* * *

Standards of prudent conduct are declared at times by courts, but they are taken over from the facts of life. To get out of a vehicle and reconnoitre is an uncommon precaution, as everyday experience informs us. Besides being uncommon, it is very likely to be futile, and sometimes even dangerous. If the driver leaves his vehicle when he nears a cut or curve, he will learn nothing by getting out about the perils that lurk beyond. By the time he regains his seat and sets his car in motion, the hidden train may be upon him. * * * Often the added safeguard will be dubious though the track happens to be straight, as it seems that this one was, at all events as far as the station, about five blocks to the north. A train traveling at a speed of thirty miles an hour will cover a quarter of a mile in the space of thirty seconds. It may thus emerge out of obscurity as the driver turns his back to regain the waiting car, and may then descend upon him suddenly when his car is on the track. Instead of helping himself by getting out, he might do better to press forward with all his faculties alert. So a train at a neighboring station, apparently at rest and harmless, may be transformed in a few seconds into an instrument of destruction. At times the course of safety may be different. One can figure to oneself a roadbed so level and unbroken that getting out will be a gain. Even then the balance of advantage depends on many circumstances and can be easily disturbed. Where was Pokora to leave his truck after getting out to reconnoitre? If he was to leave it on the switch, there was the possibility that the box cars would be shunted down upon him before he could regain his seat. The defendant did not show whether there was a locomotive at the forward end, or whether the cars were so few that a locomotive could be seen. If he was to leave his vehicle near the curb, there was even stronger reason to believe that the space to be covered in going back and forth would make his observations worthless. One must remember that while the traveler turns his eyes in one direction, a train or a loose engine may be approaching from the other.

Illustrations such as these bear witness to the need for caution in framing standards of behavior that amount to rules of law. The need is the more urgent when there is no background of experience out of which the standards have emerged. They are then, not the natural flowerings of behavior in its customary forms, but rules artificially developed, and imposed from without. Extraordinary situations may not wisely or fairly be subjected to tests or regulations that are fitting for the common-place or normal. In default of the guide of customary conduct, what is suitable for the traveler caught in a mesh where the ordinary safeguards fail him is for the judgment of a jury. * * * The opinion in *Goodman's* case has been a source of confusion in the federal courts to the extent that it imposes a standard for application by the judge, and has had only wavering support in the courts of the states. We limit it accordingly.

The judgment should be reversed and the cause remanded for further proceedings in accordance with this opinion.

292 U.S. at 104–106, 54 S.Ct. at 582–83, 78 L.Ed. at 1154–55.

5. *Establishment of the Standard of Care by the Legislature: Violation of Statute*

MARTIN v. HERZOG

Court of Appeals of New York, 1920.
228 N.Y. 164, 126 N.E. 814.

CARDOZO, J. The action is one to recover damages for injuries resulting in death. Plaintiff and her husband, while driving toward Tarrytown in a buggy on the night of August 21, 1915, were struck by the defendant's automobile coming in the opposite direction. They were thrown to the ground, and the man was killed. At the point of the collision the highway makes a curve. The car was rounding the curve, when suddenly it came upon the buggy, emerging, the defendant tells us, from the gloom. Negligence is charged against the defendant, the driver of the car, in that he did not keep to the right of the center of the highway. Highway Law, § 286, subd. 3, and section 332 (Consol.Laws, c. 25). Negligence is charged against the plaintiff's intestate, the driver of the wagon in that he was traveling without lights. Highway Law, § 329a, as amended by Laws 1915, c. 367. There is no evidence that the defendant was moving at an excessive speed. There is none of any defect in the equipment of his car. The beam of light from his lamps pointed to the right as the wheels of his car turned along the curve toward the left; and, looking in the direction of the plaintiff's approach, he was peering into the shadow. The case against him must stand, therefore, if at all upon the divergence of his course from the center of the highway. The jury found him delinquent and his victim blameless. The Appellate Division reversed, and ordered a new trial.

We agree with the Appellate Division that the charge to the jury was erroneous and misleading. The case was tried on the assumption that the hour had arrived when lights were due. It was argued on the same assumption in this court. In such circumstances, it is not important whether the hour might have been made a question for the jury. * * * A controversy put out of the case by the parties is not to be put into it by us. * * * In the body of the charge the trial judge said that the jury could consider the absence of light "in determining whether the plaintiff's intestate was guilty of contributory negligence in failing to have a light upon the buggy as provided by law. I do not mean to say that the absence of light necessarily makes him negligent, but it is a fact for your consideration." The defendant requested a ruling that the absence of a light on the plaintiff's vehicle was "prima facie evidence of contributory negligence." This request was refused, and the jury were again instructed that they might consider the absence of lights as some evidence of negligence, but that it was not conclusive evidence. The plaintiff then requested a charge that "the fact that the plaintiff's intestate was driving without a light is not negligence in itself," and to this the court acceded. The defendant saved his rights by appropriate exceptions.

We think the unexcused omission of the statutory signals is more than some evidence of negligence. It *is* negligence in itself. Lights are intended for the guidance and protection of other travelers on the highway. Highway Law, § 329a. By the very terms of the hypothesis, to omit, willfully or heedlessly, the safeguards prescribed by law for the benefit of another that he may be preserved in life or limb, is to fall short of the standard of diligence to which those who live in organized society are under a duty to conform. That, we think, is now the established rule in this state. * * * Whether the omission of an absolute duty, not willfully or heedlessly, but through unavoidable accident, is also to be characterized as negligence, is a question of nomenclature into which we need not enter, for it does not touch the case before us. There may be times, when, if jural niceties are to be preserved, the two wrongs, negligence and breach of statutory duty, must be kept distinct in speech and thought. * * *

In the conditions here present they come together and coalesce. A rule less rigid has been applied where the one who complains of the omission is not a member of the class for whose protection the safeguard is designed. * * * Some relaxation there has also been where the safeguard is prescribed by local ordinance, and not by statute. * * * Courts have been reluctant to hold that the police regulations of boards and councils and other subordinate officials create rights of action beyond the specific penalties imposed. This has led them to say that the violation of a statute is negligence, and the violation of a like ordinance is only evidence of negligence. An ordinance, however, like a statute, is a law within its sphere of operation, and so the distinction has not escaped criticism. * * * Whether it has become too deeply rooted to be abandoned, even if it be thought illogical, is a question not now before us. What concerns us at this time is that, even in the ordinance cases, the omission of a safeguard prescribed by statute is put upon a different plane, and is held not merely some evidence of negligence, but negligence in itself. * * *

In the case at hand, we have an instance of the admitted violation of a statute intended for the protection of travelers on the highway, of whom the defendant at the time was one. Yet the jurors were instructed in effect that they were at liberty in their discretion to treat the omission of lights either as innocent or as culpable. They were allowed to "consider the default as lightly or gravely" as they would (Thomas, J., in the court below). They might as well have been told that they could use a like discretion in holding a master at fault for the omission of a safety appliance prescribed by positive law for the protection of a workman. Jurors have no dispensing power, by which they may relax the duty that one traveler on the highway owes under the statute to another. It is error to tell them that they have. The omission of these lights was a wrong, and, being wholly unexcused, was also a negligent wrong. No license should have been conceded to the triers of the facts to find it anything else.

We must be on our guard, however, against confusing the question of negligence with that of the causal connection between the negligence and the injury. A defendant who travels without lights is not to pay damages for his fault, unless the absence of lights is the cause of the disaster. A plaintiff who travels without them is not to forfeit the right to damages, unless the absence of lights is at least a contributing cause of the disaster. To say that conduct is negligence is not to say that it is always contributory negligence. * * *

We think, however, that evidence of a collision occurring more than an hour after sundown between a car and an unseen buggy, proceeding without lights, is evidence from which a causal connection may be inferred between the collision and the lack of signals. * * * If nothing else is shown to break the connection, we have a case, prima facie sufficient, of negligence contributing to the result.

There may, indeed, be times when the lights on a highway are so many and so bright that lights on a wagon are superfluous. If that is so, it is for the offender to go forward with the evidence, and prove the illumination as a kind of substituted performance. The plaintiff asserts that she did so here. She says that the scene of the accident was illumined by moonlight, by an electric lamp, and by the lights of the approaching car. Her position is that, if the defendant did not see the buggy thus illumined, a jury might reasonably infer that he would not have seen it anyhow. We may doubt whether there is any evidence of illumination sufficient to sustain the jury in drawing such an inference; but the decision of the case does not make it necessary to resolve the doubt, and so we leave it open. It is certain that they were not required to find that lights on the wagon were superfluous. They might reasonably have found the contrary. They ought, therefore, to have been informed what effect they were free to give, in that event, to the violation of the statute. They should have been told, not only that the omission of the light was negligence, but that it was "prima facie evidence of contributory negligence"; i.e., that it was sufficient in itself unless its probative force was overcome (Thomas, J., in court below) to sustain a verdict that the decedent was at fault. * * *

Here, on the undisputed facts, lack of vision, whether excusable or not, was the cause of the disaster. The defendant may have been negligent in swerving from the center of the road; but he did not run into the buggy purposely, nor was he driving while intoxicated, nor was he going at such a reckless speed that warning would of necessity have been futile. Nothing of the kind is shown. The collision was due to his failure to see at a time when sight should have been aroused and guided by the statutory warnings. Some explanation of the effect to be given to the absence of those warnings, if the plaintiff failed to prove that other lights on the car or the highway took their place as equivalents, should have been put before the jury. The explanation was asked for and refused.

We are persuaded that the tendency of the charge, and of all the rulings, following it, was to minimize unduly, in the minds of the triers of the facts, the gravity of the decedent's fault. Errors may not be ignored as unsubstantial, when they tend to such an outcome. A statute designed for the protection of human life is not to be brushed aside as a form of words, its commands reduced to the level of cautions, and the duty to obey attenuated into an option to conform.

The order of the Appellate Division should be affirmed, and judgment absolute directed on the stipulation in favor of the defendant, with costs in all courts.

[The dissenting opinion of Hogan, J., is omitted. The principal focus of that opinion is the issue of causation.]

Notes

1. Most courts adopt the position espoused by Cardozo, J., in *Martin v. Herzog*, that violation of a criminal statute is conclusive evidence of negligence or negligence *per se*. A minority of jurisdictions takes the position that violation of a criminal statute is merely "evidence of negligence," although cases can be found even in such jurisdictions holding that, in some circumstances, the evidence of negligence provided by a statutory violation may be so strong as to warrant withdrawal of the issue of due care from the jury. This result may be easier to achieve in those jurisdictions which, while rejecting the negligence *per se* approach, treat a statutory violation as *prima facie* evidence of negligence rather than merely as "evidence" of negligence. *See* Davis v. Marathon Oil Co., 64 Ill.2d 380, 1 Ill.Dec. 93, 356 N.E.2d 93 (1976). A good discussion of the state of the law on this subject is contained in Morris, Torts 61–72 (2d ed. by C. Morris and C. R. Morris, Jr. 1980). For a discussion of English law, *see* R. Buckley, *Liability in Tort for Breach of Statutory Duty*, 100 L.Q.Rev. 204 (1984). For one of the classic early treatments of the subject, *see* E. Thayer, *Public Wrong and Private Actions*, 27 Harv.L.Rev. 317 (1914).

2. The standard rubric is that the plaintiff will be able to bring a civil action based upon the violation of a statute if the plaintiff is within the class of persons intended to be protected by the statute and if the damage suffered by the plaintiff is within the type of harm the legislature sought to avert. These are among the questions that will be considered in the subsequent cases and the notes accompanying them. Nevertheless, the question has been asked why, if the legislature has failed to provide for civil liability for violation of a criminal or regulatory statute, the courts should make a violation of the statute the basis of a civil action. In C. Morris, *The Role of Criminal Statutes in Negligence Actions*, 49 Colum.L.Rev. 21 (1949), it is urged that the courts

should not routinely extend tort liability in all instances of statutory violation. While the existence of the statute is obviously relevant, the courts should not automatically extend civil liability when the legislature has, by hypothesis, chosen to remain silent on the issue of civil liability. Stress is often laid upon the fact that, in enacting criminal statutes, the legislature has not addressed itself to the question of civil liability. Given, however, that a high percentage of state legislators are lawyers who must be aware of the tendency of the courts to impose civil liability for statutory violations, is this a reasonable assumption? Two particular classes of cases give rise to the doubts as to whether the courts should be as free in allowing a civil action for a violation of statute as they are. The first type are cases in which the issue arises whether the violation of the statute was an "excused" violation. The assumption underlying the concern expressed in these cases is that there may be situations where the defendant was clearly in breach of the criminal law—he would have no valid defense in a criminal prosecution—but, for the purposes of a civil action, it is maintained that his conduct may nevertheless have been excusable. The second class of cases where doubts arise as to the propriety of courts unreflectively implying a civil cause of action for a statutory violation concerns instances where the statute in question imposes absolute liability, such as some of the statutes requiring a motorist to maintain his brakes in good working order or prohibiting a restauranteur from serving adulterated food. Obviously, cases involving a statute imposing absolute criminal liability are also likely to be cases where the question of excused violation arises, although the issue of excused violations also arises in other contexts. Both sets of questions—those involving the issue of excused violations and those involving the applicability in civil litigation of statutes imposing absolute criminal responsibility—will be discussed in some of the succeeding cases and in the notes following those cases.

3. *Administrative regulations and local ordinances.* As indicated in Cardozo, J.'s, opinion in *Martin v. Herzog,* some courts that are prepared to hold that the violation of a statute is negligence *per se* will treat violations of administrative regulations or of local ordinances as only evidence of negligence. On the other hand, some courts will not make this distinction and will also treat violations of administrative regulations and ordinances as negligence *per se.* For a more extended discussion of the issue, see Morris, Torts at 72–79.

4. The Supreme Court of the United States has now taken a restrictive view as to whether violation of federal regulatory legislation can give rise to a private right of action in federal courts. *See* Cort v. Ash, 422 U.S. 66, 95 S.Ct. 2080, 45 L.Ed.2d 26 (1975); *cf.* Transamerica Mortgage Advisors, Inc. v. Lewis, 444 U.S. 11, 100 S.Ct. 242, 62 L.Ed.2d 146 (1979); Cannon v. University of Chicago, 441 U.S. 677, 99 S.Ct. 1946, 60 L.Ed.2d 560 (1979). One factor that is important for the Court and which will weigh against a private cause of action is whether the asserted federal cause of action is of a type traditionally relegated to state law. This of course is not a factor that is relevant when state courts are deciding whether they should imply a civil cause of action when a state criminal or regulatory statute has been violated. For a discussion, *see* H. M. Foy, III, *Some Reflections on Legislation, Adjudication, and Implied Private Actions in the Federal Courts,* 71 Cornell L.Rev. 501 (1986).

BROWN v. SHYNE

Court of Appeals of New York, 1926.
242 N.Y. 176, 151 N.E. 197.

LEHMAN, J.   The plaintiff employed the defendant to give chiropractic treatment to her for a disease or physical condition. The defendant had no license to practice medicine, yet he held himself out as being able to diagnose and treat disease, and, under the provisions of the Public Health Law (Cons.Laws, c. 45), he was guilty of a misdemeanor. The plaintiff became paralyzed after she had received nine treatments by the defendant. She claims, and upon this appeal we must assume, that the paralysis was caused by the treatment she received. She has recovered judgment in the sum of $10,000 for the damages caused by said injury.

The plaintiff in her complaint alleges that the injuries were caused by the defendant's negligence. If negligence on the part of the defendant caused the injury, the plaintiff may recover the consequent damages. Though the defendant held himself out, and the plaintiff consulted him, as a chiropractor, and not as a regular physician, he claimed to possess the skill requisite for diagnosis and treatment of disease, and in the performance of what he undertook to do he may be held to the degree of skill and care which he claimed to possess. At the trial the plaintiff gave testimony in regard to the manner in which she was treated. She supplemented this testimony by evidence that the treatment was not in accordance with recognized theory or practice; that it produced the injury which followed; and that a person qualified to treat disease should have foreseen that the treatment might have such result. Though her testimony was contradicted, the jury might well have resolved the conflict in her favor, and, if the only question submitted to the jury had been whether or not this evidence showed that plaintiff's injury was caused by the defendant's negligence, the defendant could not complain of any substantial error at the trial. Indeed, it would seem that in some respects the rulings of the trial judge may have been too favorable to the defendant.

At the close of the plaintiff's case the plaintiff was permitted to amend the complaint to allege "that in so treating the plaintiff the defendant was engaged in the practice of medicine contrary to and in violation of the provisions of the Public Health Law of the state of New York in such case made and provided, he at the time of so treating plaintiff not being a duly licensed physician or surgeon of the state of New York."   Thereafter the trial judge charged the jury that they might bring in a verdict in favor of the plaintiff if they found that the evidence established that the treatment given to the plaintiff was not in accordance with the standards of skill and care which prevail among those treating disease.   He then continued:

"This is a little different from the ordinary malpractice case, and I am going to allow you, if you think proper under the evidence in the case, to predicate negligence upon another theory. The public health laws of this state prescribe that no person shall practice medicine unless he is licensed so to do by the board of regents of this state and registered pursuant to statute. * * * This statute to which I have referred is a general police regulation. Its violation, and it has been violated by the defendant, is some evidence, more or less cogent, of negligence which you may consider for what it is worth, along with all the other evidence in the case. If the defendant attempted to treat the plaintiff and to adjust the vertebrae in her spine when he did not possess the requisite knowledge and skill as prescribed by the statute to know what was proper and necessary to do under the circumstances, or how to do it, even if he did know what to do, you can find him negligent."

In so charging the jury that from the violation of the statute the jury might infer negligence which produced injury to the plaintiff, the trial justice in my opinion erred.

The provisions of the Public Health Law prohibiting the practice of medicine without a license granted upon proof of preliminary training, and after examination intended to show adequate knowledge, are of course intended for the protection of the general public against injury which unskilled and unlearned practitioners might cause. If violation of the statute by the defendant was the proximate cause of the plaintiff's injury, then the plaintiff may recover upon proof of violation. If violation of the statute has no direct bearing on the injury, proof of the violation becomes irrelevant. For injury caused by neglect of duty imposed by the penal law there is civil remedy; but, of course, the injury must follow from the neglect.

Proper formulation of general standards of preliminary education and proper examination of the particular applicant should serve to raise the standards of skill and care generally possessed by members of the profession in this state; but the license to practice medicine confers no additional skill upon the practitioner, nor does it confer immunity from physical injury upon a patient if the practitioner fails to exercise care. Here, injury may have been caused by lack of skill or care; it would not have been obviated if the defendant had possessed a license yet failed to exercise the skill and care required of one practicing medicine. True, if the defendant had not practiced medicine in this state, he could not have injured the plaintiff, but the protection which the statute was intended to provide was against risk of injury by the unskilled or careless practitioner, and, unless the plaintiff's injury was caused by carelessness or lack of skill, the defendant's failure to obtain a license was not connected with the injury. The plaintiff's cause of action is for negligence or malpractice. The defendant undertook to treat the plaintiff for a physical condition which seemed to require remedy. Under our law such treatment may be given only by a duly qualified practitioner who has obtained a license.

The defendant in offering to treat the plaintiff held himself out as qualified to give treatment. He must meet the professional standards of skill and care prevailing among those who do offer treatment lawfully. If injury follows through failure to meet those standards, the plaintiff may recover. The provisions of the Public Health Law may result in the exclusion from practice of some who are unqualified. Even a skilled and learned practitioner who is not licensed commits an offense against the state; but against such practitioners the statute was not intended to protect, for no protection was needed, and neglect to obtain a license results in no injury to the patient and, therefore, no private wrong. The purpose of the statute is to protect the public against unfounded assumption of skill by one who undertakes to prescribe or treat for disease. In order to show that the plaintiff has been injured by defendant's breach of the statutory duty, proof must be given that defendant in such treatment did not exercise the care and skill which would have been exercised by qualified practitioners within the state, and that such lack of skill and care caused the injury. Failure to obtain a license as required by law gives rise to no remedy if it has caused no injury. No case has been cited where neglect of a statutory duty has given rise to private cause of action where it has not appeared that private injury has been caused by danger against which the statute was intended to afford protection, and which obedience to the statute would have obviated. It is said that in the case of Karpeles v. Heine, 124 N.E. 101, 227 N.Y. 74, this court held that liability per se arises from breach of the statute which prohibits employment of a child under 16 years of age, but in that case this court merely decided that the statute was intended to protect the child against danger arising from its own lack of foresight in the course of such employment, and that, therefore, an action against the employer by a child unlawfully employed "for injuries arising in the course of such employment and as the proximate result thereof cannot be defeated by his contributory negligence." In that case the court was considering the legal effect of the proven negligence of the child who was unlawfully employed; only upon proof in the present case of negligence on the part of the chiropractor would any analogy be apparent.

It is said that the trial justice did not charge that plaintiff might recover for defendant's failure to obtain a license, but only that failure to obtain a license might be considered "some evidence" of defendant's negligence. Argument is made that, even if neglect of the statutory duty does not itself create liability, it tends to prove that injury was caused by lack of skill or care. That can be true only if logical inference may be drawn from defendant's failure to obtain or perhaps seek a license that he not only lacks the skill and learning which would enable him to diagnose and treat disease generally, but also that he lacks even the skill and learning necessary for the physical manipulation he gave to this plaintiff. Evidence of defendant's training, learning, and skill and the method he used in giving the treatment was produced at the trial, and upon such evidence the jury could base [a] finding either of care or negligence, but the absence of a license does not seem to strengthen [the] inference that might be drawn from such evidence, and a fortiori would not alone be a basis for such inference. Breach or neglect of duty imposed by statute or ordinance may be evidence of negligence only if there is logical connection between the proven neglect of statutory duty and the alleged negligence.

Our decision in the case of People v. Meyer, 147 N.E. 216, 239 N.Y. 608, is not in conflict with these views. The defendant there was charged with causing death by "culpable negligence." * * * We held that the circumstance that the defendant practiced medicine without those qualifications which the law demands as a prerequisite to practice was relevant and material upon the question whether the defendant's proven negligence was venial or culpable. We did not hold that the absence of license tended to prove negligence itself.

For these reasons the judgments should be reversed, and a new trial granted, with costs to abide the event.

CRANE, J. (dissenting). The defendant is a chiropractic practitioner in Utica, N.Y. The plaintiff, a woman about 46 years of age, in March of 1923, was his patient. Through treatment received the plaintiff claims to have become paralyzed, and has brought this action to recover damages. A judgment in her favor has been unanimously affirmed by the Appellate Division, which, however, granted leave to the defendant to come to this court, certifying that in its opinion a question of law was involved which we should review. At the time mentioned Miss Brown had been suffering from laryngitis, and went to the defendant's (Dr. Shyne's) office for treatment. She went there nine times. It was the last treatment that was injurious.

* * *

The plaintiff's complaint, as amended on the trial, alleged the negligence of the defendant, and his violation of the Public Health Law. The defendant upon the trial, and his witnesses, testified that his treatment of vertebrae alignment was according to the established practice and methods of chiropractors, and that by such treatment it was impossible to cause the plaintiff's injuries. There was some evidence to show that the defendant may have been unusually severe and harsh.

The charge of the court to the jury treated the case as one in negligence, and stated the law as applicable to duly licensed physicians; that is, that they were bound to exercise that degree of care and skill generally possessed by members of the profession in the locality where the doctor practiced. The defendant's negligence, he stated, would consist in failing to meet this standard. * * *

* * * The point is presented that the violation of the Public Health Law by the defendant, and his practicing medicine without a license, had nothing to do with this case; was not competent evidence; and should not have been considered by the jury as some evidence of negligence. With this view I do not agree.

The judge fully and completely charged the jury that the defendant was not liable for any of the plaintiff's injuries unless they were the direct and proximate cause of his acts. The evidence was abundant to prove that the plaintiff's paralysis and injuries resulted from the defendant's manipulation and treatment of her back, neck and head. The jury were justified in finding that whatever he did, whether it were proper or improper, resulted in the plaintiff's painful condition. * * *

* * *

The prohibition against practicing medicine without a license was for the very purpose of protecting the public from just what happened in this case. The violation of this statute has been the direct and proximate cause of the injury. The courts will not determine in face of this statute whether a faith healer, a patent medicine man, a chiropractor, or any other class of practitioner acted according to the standards of his own school, or according to the standards of a duly licensed physician. The law, to insure against ignorance and carelessness, has laid down a rule to be followed; namely, examinations to test qualifications and a license to practice. If a man, in violation of this statute, takes his chances in trying to cure disease, and his acts result directly in injury, he should not complain if the law, in a suit for damages, says that his violation of the statute is some evidence of his incapacity.

* * *

Notes

1. In Whipple v. Grandchamp, 261 Mass. 40, 158 N.E. 270 (1927), the court held that a statute requiring physicians to be licensed did provide the basis for a civil action against an unlicensed person by "all persons suffering from harm when the violation of the statute is the proximate cause of their injuries." In that case, however, there was evidence from which a jury could find that the defendant chiropractor had fractured one of the plaintiff's vertebra in the course of his treatment.

2. Statutes requiring the operators of motor vehicles to be licensed have generally been treated the same way that Lehman, J., treated the physician licensing statute in *Brown v. Shyne. See* Annot., 73 A.L.R. 156 (1931). The New Hampshire courts, however, had at one time taken the aberrational position that an unlicensed driver could not bring an action for any injuries he might have received while illegally operating a motor vehicle and was liable for any injuries suffered by others as a result of his illegal operation of a motor vehicle. The New Hampshire legislature amended the statute in 1937 (now N.H.Rev.Stat.Ann. § 263.1 (1982)) to provide that operating a motor vehicle in violation of the licensing provisions "shall be prima facie evidence of * * * unfitness to operate a motor vehicle." The courts consequently retreated from their previous position. *See* Fuller v. Sirois, 97 N.H. 100, 82 A.2d 82 (1951). Along the same line, Massachusetts at one time followed the court-created doctrine that a person driving an unregistered motor vehicle was a trespasser on the highway and, as such, was liable for any injuries he might cause and also barred from recovering for any injuries he might suffer unless those injuries were the result of intentional or reckless conduct. The doctrine was disapproved in Comeau v. Harrington, 333 Mass. 768, 130 N.E.2d 554 (1955), but the court felt any change must be made by the legislature. In 1959, the legislature amended the statutory provisions dealing with the registration of motor vehicles to provide that:

> Violation of this section shall not be deemed to render the motor vehicle or trailer a nuisance or any person a trespasser upon a way and shall not constitute a defense to, or prevent a recovery in, an action of tort for injuries suffered by a person, or for the death of a person, or for damage to property, unless such violation by the person injured or killed or sustaining the damage was in fact a proximate cause of such injury, death or damage, but violation of this section shall be deemed evidence of negligence on the part of the violator.

Annot.L.Mass. c. 90, § 9 (1975). The Massachusetts courts took the position that the 1959 changes were prospective only and did not apply to actions based upon actions occurring prior to the effective date of the amendment. *See* Falvey v. Hamelburg, 347 Mass. 430, 198 N.E.2d 400 (1964).

3. In order for the plaintiff to be able to recover in an action based upon the violation of a statutory duty, he must show not only that his injuries were "caused" by the statutory violation but that the injuries he suffered were of the kind the legislature enacted the statute to guard against. A classic case is Gorris v. Scott, L.R. 9 Ex. 125 (1874). In that case the plaintiff's sheep which were being carried from Hamburg to Newcastle as deck cargo had been washed overboard. In his action the plaintiff relied upon regulations which had been issued pursuant to an act of Parliament and which provided that animals must be confined in pens no larger than 9 feet by 15 feet and that the pens must have "battens or other foot-hold." The Court of Exchequer held that the statute, The Contagious Diseases (Animals) Act, 1869, "was passed merely for sanitary purposes, in order to prevent animals in a state of infectious disease from communicating it to other animals * * *," and sustained a demurrer to the plaintiff's complaint.

4. The courts have differed over the purpose or purposes of statutes or ordinances making it illegal to leave the ignition key in a parked automobile. Some courts have held that at least one purpose of these statutes or ordinances is to protect third persons from the incompetent driving of thieves and have thus used these statutes or ordinances to impose liability upon a motorist who left his key in the ignition. Other courts have refused to impose such liability and have held that these statutes or ordinances were passed merely to protect the owners of motor vehicles or to prevent inadvertent moving of the vehicles. See Annot. 45 A.L.R.3d 787, 800–11 (1972). We shall consider some of these cases at p. 334, *infra*, during our discussion of how questions of causation are affected by the intervening criminal acts of third persons.

5. A somewhat unusual case is Kernan v. American Dredging Co., 355 U.S. 426, 78 S.Ct. 394, 2 L.Ed.2d 382 (1958). In that case a seaman lost his life one night when a kerosene lamp used as a navigation light on a scow ignited vapor arising from petroleum that had accumulated on the surface of the surrounding waters. The lamp had been no more than three feet above water level. Its placement thus violated a navigation rule promulgated by the Coast Guard requiring that scows must display at night a white navigation light "not less than 8 feet above the surface of the water, and [such light] shall be so placed as to show an unbroken light all around the horizon, and shall be of such a character as to be visible on a dark night with a clear atmosphere at a distance of at least 5 miles." The claim of the seaman's widow was dismissed in the district court and this dismissal was affirmed by the Third Circuit. The Supreme Court reversed in a 5–4 decision. Justice Brennan, writing for the majority, stressed that the Jones Act, under which the action had been brought, took the place of workmen's compensation for maritime workers. Accordingly, "the tort doctrine which the lower court applied [which] imposes liability for violation of a statutory duty only where the injury is one which the statute was designed to prevent" was not applicable.

6. Since 1971, N.Y.Civ.Prac. § 4504(d) has provided that in actions for personal injuries, "against a person not authorized to practice medicine under article 131 of the education law," the fact that the person practiced medicine without being authorized to do so "shall be deemed to be prima facie evidence of negligence." Why only prima facie evidence? Is one reason the desire to take into account physicians licensed in other jurisdictions but not in New York?

TEDLA v. ELLMAN

Court of Appeals of New York, 1939.
280 N.Y. 124, 19 N.E.2d 987.

LEHMAN, JUDGE.

While walking along a highway, Anna Tedla and her brother, John Bachek, were struck by a passing automobile, operated by the defendant Ellman. She was injured and Bachek was killed. Bachek was a deaf-mute. His occupation was collecting and selling junk. His sister, Mrs. Tedla, was engaged in the same occupation. They often picked up junk at the incinerator of the village of Islip. At the time of the accident they were walking along "Sunrise Highway" and wheeling baby carriages containing junk and wood which they had picked up at the incinerator. It was about six o'clock, or a little earlier, on a Sunday evening in December. Darkness had already set in. Bachek was carrying a lighted lantern, or, at least, there is testimony to that effect. The jury found that the accident was due solely to the negligence of the operator of the automobile. The defendants do not, upon this appeal, challenge the finding of negligence on the part of the operator. They maintain, however, that Mrs. Tedla and her brother were guilty of contributory negligence as matter of law.

Sunrise Highway, at the place of the accident, consists of two roadways, separated by a grass plot. There are no footpaths along the highway and the center grass plot was soft. It is not unlawful for a pedestrian, wheeling a baby carriage, to use the roadway under such circumstances, but a pedestrian using the roadway is bound to exercise such care for his safety as a reasonably prudent person would use. The Vehicle and Traffic Law (Consol.Laws, c. 71) provides that "Pedestrians walking or remaining on the paved portion, or traveled part of a roadway shall be subject to, and comply with, the rules governing vehicles, with respect to meeting and turning out, except that such pedestrians shall keep to the left of the center line thereof, and turn to their left instead of right side thereof, so as to permit all vehicles passing them in either direction to pass on their right. Such pedestrians shall not be subject to the rules governing vehicles as to giving signals." Section 85, subd. 6. Mrs. Tedla and her brother did not observe the statutory rule, and at the time of the accident were proceeding in easterly direction on the east bound or right-hand roadway. The defendants moved to dismiss the complaint on the ground, among others, that violation of the statutory rule constitutes contributory negligence as matter of law. They did not, in the courts below, urge that any negligence in other respect of Mrs. Tedla or her brother bars a recovery. The trial judge left to the jury the question whether failure to observe the statutory rule was a proximate cause of the accident; he left to the jury no question of other fault or negligence on the part of Mrs. Tedla or her brother, and the defendants did not request that any other question be submitted. Upon this appeal, the only question presented is whether, as matter of law, disregard of the statutory rule that pedestrians shall keep to the left of the center line of a highway constitutes contributory negligence which bars any recovery by the plaintiff.

Vehicular traffic can proceed safely and without recurrent traffic tangles only if vehicles observe accepted rules of the road. Such rules, and especially the rule that all vehicles proceeding in one direction must keep to a designated part or side of the road—in this country the right-hand side—have been dictated by necessity and formulated by custom. The general use of automobiles has increased in unprecedented degree the number and speed of vehicles. Control of traffic becomes an increasingly difficult problem. Rules of the road, regulating the rights and duties of those who use highways, have, in consequence, become increasingly important. The Legislature no longer leaves to custom the formulation of such rules. Statutes now codify, define, supplement, and, where changing conditions suggest change in rule, even change rules of the road which formerly rested on custom. Custom and common sense have always dictated that vehicles should have the right of way over pedestrians and that pedestrians should walk along the edge of a highway so that they might step aside for passing vehicles with least danger to themselves and least obstruction to vehicular traffic. Otherwise, perhaps, no customary rule of the road was observed by pedestrians with the same uniformity as by vehicles; though, in general, they probably followed, until recently, the same rules as vehicles.

Pedestrians are seldom a source of danger or serious obstruction to vehicles and when horse-drawn vehicles were common they seldom injured pedestrians using a highway with reasonable care, unless the horse became unmanageable or the driver was grossly negligent or guilty of willful wrong. Swift-moving motor vehicles, it was soon recognized, do endanger the safety of pedestrians crossing highways, and it is imperative that there the relative rights and duties of pedestrians and of vehicles should be understood and observed. The Legislature in the first five subdivisions of section 85 of the Vehicle and Traffic Law has provided regulations to govern the conduct of pedestrians and of drivers of vehicles when a pedestrian is crossing a road. Until by chapter 114 of the Laws of 1933, it adopted subdivision 6 of section 85, quoted above, there was no special statutory rule for pedestrians walking along a highway. Then for the first time it reversed, for pedestrians, the rule established for vehicles by immemorial custom, and provided that pedestrians shall keep to the left of the center line of a highway.

The plaintiffs showed by the testimony of a State policeman that "there were very few cars going east" at the time of the accident, but that going west there was "very heavy Sunday night traffic." Until the recent adoption of the new statutory rule for pedestrians, ordinary prudence would have dictated that pedestrians should not expose themselves to the danger of walking along the roadway upon which the "very heavy Sunday night traffic" was proceeding when they could walk in comparative safety along a roadway used by very few cars. It is said that now, by force of the statutory rule, pedestrians are guilty of contributory negligence as matter of law when they use the safer roadway, unless that roadway is left of the center of the road. Disregard of the statutory rule of the road and observance of a rule based on immemorial custom, it is said, is negligence which as matter of law is a proximate cause of the accident, though observance of the statutory rule might, under the circumstances of the particular case, expose a pedestrian to serious danger from which he would be free if he followed the rule that had been established by custom. If that be true, then the Legislature has decreed that pedestrians must observe the general rule of conduct which it has prescribed for their safety even under circumstances where observance would subject them to unusual risk; that pedestrians are to be charged with negligence as matter of law for acting as prudence dictates. It is unreasonable to ascribe to the Legislature an intention that the statute should have so extraordinary a result, and the courts may not give to a statute an effect not intended by the Legislature.

The Legislature, when it enacted the statute, presumably knew that this court and the courts of other jurisdictions had established the general principle that omission by a plaintiff of a safeguard, prescribed by statute, against a recognized danger, constitutes negligence as matter of law which bars recovery for damages caused by incidence of the danger for which the safeguard was prescribed. * * *

* * * The "established rule" should not be weakened either by subtle distinctions or by extension beyond its letter or spirit into a field where "by the very terms of the hypothesis" it can have no proper application. At times the indefinite and flexible standard of care of the traditional reasonably prudent man may be, in the opinion of the Legislature, an insufficient measure of the care which should be exercised to guard against a recognized danger; at times, the duty, imposed by custom, that no man shall use what is his to the harm of others provides insufficient safeguard for the preservation of the life or limb or property of others. Then the Legislature may by statute prescribe additional safeguards and may define duty and standard of care in rigid terms; and when the Legislature has spoken, the standard of the care required is no longer what the reasonably prudent man would do under the circumstances but what the Legislature has commanded. That is the rule established by the courts and "by the very terms of the hypothesis" the rule applies where the Legislature has prescribed safeguards "for the benefit of another that he may be preserved in life or limb." In that field debate as to whether the safeguards so prescribed are reasonably necessary is ended by the legislative fiat. Obedience to that fiat cannot add to the danger, even assuming that the prescribed safeguards are not reasonably necessary and where the legislative anticipation of dangers is realized and harm results through heedless or willful omission of the prescribed safeguard, injury flows from wrong and the wrongdoer is properly held responsible for the consequent damages.

The statute upon which the defendants rely is of different character. It does not prescribe additional safeguards which pedestrians must provide for the preservation of the life or limb or property of others, or even of themselves, nor does it impose upon pedestrians a higher standard of care. What the statute does provide is rules of the road to be observed by pedestrians and by vehicles, so that all those who use the road may know how they and others should proceed, at least under usual circumstances. A general rule of conduct—and, specifically, a rule of the road—may accomplish its intended purpose under usual conditions, but, when the unusual occurs, strict observance may defeat the purpose of the rule and produce catastrophic results.

Negligence is failure to exercise the care required by law. Where a statute defines the standard of care and the safeguards required to meet a recognized danger, then, as we have said, no other measure may be applied in determining whether a person has carried out the duty of care imposed by law. Failure to observe the standard imposed by statute is negligence, as matter of law. On the other hand, where a statutory general rule of conduct fixes no definite standard of care which would under all circumstances tend to protect life, limb or property but merely codifies or supplements a common-law rule, which has always been subject to limitations and exceptions; or where the statutory rule of conduct regulates conflicting rights and obligations in manner calculated to promote public convenience and safety, then the statute, in the absence of clear language to the contrary, should not be construed as intended to wipe out the limitations and exceptions which judicial decisions have attached to the common-law duty; nor should it be construed as an inflexible command that the general rule of conduct intended to prevent accidents must be followed even under conditions when observance might cause accidents. We may assume reasonably that the Legislature directed pedestrians to keep to the left of the center of the road because that would cause them to face traffic approaching in that lane and would enable them to care for their own safety better than if the traffic approached them from the rear. We cannot assume reasonably that the Legislature intended that a statute enacted for the preservation of the life and limb of pedestrians must be observed when observance would subject them to more imminent danger.

The distinction in the effect of statutes defining a standard of care or requiring specified safeguards against recognized dangers and the effect of statutes which merely codify, supplement or even change common-law rules or which prescribe a general rule of conduct calculated to prevent accidents but which under unusual conditions may cause accidents, has been pointed out often. Seldom have the courts held that failure to observe a rule of the road, even though embodied in a statute, constitutes negligence as matter of law where observance would subject a person to danger which might be avoided by disregard of the general rule. * * *

The generally accepted rule and the reasons for it are set forth in the comment to section 286 of the Restatement of the Law of Torts: "Many statutes and ordinances are so worded as apparently to express a universally obligatory rule of conduct. Such enactments, however, may in view of their purpose and spirit be properly construed as intended to apply only to ordinary situations and to be subject to the qualification that the conduct prohibited thereby is not wrongful if, because of an emergency or the like, the circumstances justify an apparent disobedience to the letter of the enactment. * * * The provisions of statutes intended to codify and supplement the rules of conduct which are established by a course of judicial decision or by custom, are often construed as subject to the same limitations and exceptions as the rules which they supersede. Thus, a statute or ordinance requiring all persons to drive on the right side of the road may be construed as subject to an exception permitting travellers to drive upon the other side, if so doing is likely to prevent rather than cause the accidents which it is the purpose of the statute or ordinance to prevent."

Even under that construction of the statute, a pedestrian is, of course, at fault if he fails without good reason to observe the statutory rule of conduct. The general duty is established by the statute, and deviation from it without good cause is a wrong and the wrongdoer is responsible for the damages resulting from his wrong. * * *

I have so far discussed the problem of the plaintiffs' right to compensation for the damages caused by defendants' negligence as if it depended solely upon the question of whether the pedestrians were at fault, and I have ignored the question whether their alleged fault was a proximate cause of the accident. In truth, the two questions cannot be separated completely. If the pedestrians had observed the statutory rule of the road they would have proceeded easterly along the roadway on the left of the center grass plot, and then, it must be conceded, they would not have been struck by the automobile in which the defendants were riding, proceeding in the same direction along the roadway on the right. Their presence on the roadway where they were struck was an essential condition of their injury. Was it also as matter of law a proximate cause of the accident? * * * Here the jury might find that the pedestrians avoided a greater, indeed an almost suicidal, risk by proceeding along the east bound roadway; that the operator of the automobile was entirely heedless of the possibility of the presence of pedestrians on the highway; and that a pedestrian could not have avoided the accident even if he had faced oncoming traffic. Under those circumstances the question of proximate cause, as well as the question of negligence, was one of fact.

In each action, the judgment should be affirmed, with costs.

O'BRIEN and FINCH, JJ., dissent on the authority of Martin v. Herzog, 228 N.Y. 164, 126 N.E. 814.

Judgments affirmed.

BARNUM v. WILLIAMS

Supreme Court of Oregon, 1972.
264 Or. 71, 504 P.2d 122.

DENECKE, JUSTICE.

The plaintiff brought this action for damages for personal injuries allegedly incurred when the motorcycle he was driving collided with the car the defendant was driving. The jury found for the defendant and the plaintiff appeals, contending the trial court gave two erroneous instructions.

The collision occurred on a rainy day on Vista Avenue, in Portland. The plaintiff was going uphill and rounding an extremely sharp curve to his left. The defendant was coming downhill. Vista Avenue is divided into two lanes by a yellow line. The line is much closer to the curb on the defendant's side. The jury could have found that the impact occurred on or near the line or on the plaintiff's side of the line. The jury could also have found that when the defendant observed the plaintiff, the plaintiff was riding on the center line and leaning into the turn; the defendant in the narrow lane was near the center line and became apprehensive that they might collide; the defendant applied his brakes and slid into plaintiff's lane and collided with the plaintiff.

The trial court instructed the jury:

"In addition to common law negligence, there is also statutory negligence, which consists of the violation of a law which, for the safety or protection of others, requires certain acts or conduct or forbids certain acts or conduct. Where I call your attention to any such law, a violation of such law is negligence in and of itself; with this exception: If you find that, under all the attending circumstances, a statute cannot or should not be complied with by a person exercising reasonable care for the safety of himself and others, then I instruct you that you may find that the failure to strictly observe the statute should be excused and should not be deemed negligence."

The problem posed by the instruction originates in the difficulties this court and others have had with the application of the statutory negligence per se doctrine.

We have repeatedly held that violation of a law or ordinance is negligence or contributory negligence in itself, i.e., per se. This has been an exception to the usual rule that whether one is negligent depends upon whether one acted as a reasonably prudent person. Under the negligence per se doctrine the question of whether the actor acted as a reasonably prudent person is irrelevant; the only question is, did the actor violate the statute?

Despite our stated adherence to the doctrine that violation of a statute is negligence per se, we could not submerge our deeply-rooted tradition that fault is the basis of liability in tort. In a defective brake case, we stated: "We are now of the opinion that the motor vehicle code was not intended to eliminate the element of fault from the law of torts." McConnell v. Herron, 240 Or. 486, 491, 402 P.2d 726, 729 (1965).

Early in the development of the tort law of motor vehicles we stated the doctrine that violation of a motor vehicle operation statute is negligence per se. At the same time, however, we engrafted the principle of fault into this doctrine. Marshall v. Olson, 102 Or. 502, 511–513, 202 P. 736 (1922). In the *Marshall* case the jury could have found that the defendant turned in violation of a city ordinance. The court observed: "* * * [I]t would be unreasonable to maintain that a man would be culpably negligent under such circumstances, if he turned either to the right or to the left to avoid imminent danger of collision, when the peril could be escaped only by such action, and that, too, without injury to any one else: * * *." 102 Or. at 512–513, 202 P. at 739.

* * *

Most, but not all, of our decisions on this issue have dealt with a situation in which the driver suddenly was faced with a vehicle, a pedestrian, or some other obstacle on his side of the road and reacted by turning into the "wrong side" of the road in violation of the statute. In such cases we have approved instructions to the effect that violation of the statute requiring one to drive on his own side of the road is negligence per se; however, the driver is not negligent if he is faced with an emergency not of his own making and in turning onto the left side of the road acts as a reasonably prudent person would have acted when faced with a similar emergency. * * *

The sudden emergency caused by someone or something in the driver's lane is the factor which most commonly makes a swerve to the "wrong side" of the road the act of a reasonably prudent person. The rule, however, has not been and logically cannot be confined solely to such circumstances.[1]

The presence of an emergency does not change the standard of care; the standard remains reasonable care under the circumstances. If a party acts unreasonably in the face of an emergency, he is negligent; if he acts reasonably, he is not negligent. The emergency is simply one of the circumstances to consider in judging whether the actor behaved reasonably under the circumstances.

* * *

In some of our cases in which a party acted contrary to a traffic statute the driver did not turn onto the "wrong side" in response to an emergency but went onto the "wrong side" for other reasons.

In Tokstad v. Lund, 255 Or. 305, 466 P.2d 938 (1970), the defendant was not faced with an emergency. He slid on packed snow across to the plaintiff's side of the highway. We held: "There was evidence that although the defendant Lund was upon the wrong side of the road when he struck plaintiff's vehicle, the defendant, nevertheless, was acting as a reasonably prudent person." 255 Or. at 307, 466 P.2d at 939.

* * *

In Mennis v. Highland Trucking, Inc., 261 Or. 233, 492 P.2d 464 (1972), the defendant was not faced with an emergency. The defendant was driving a log truck and was on plaintiff's side of the road when he collided with plaintiff. The defendant was on the "wrong side" because the road was narrow and abruptly dropped off on the defendant's side. We held the defendant was not as a matter of law negligent and this issue was properly submitted to the jury. * * *

Because excusing statutory violations solely in instances of emergency is illogical, we would be constantly urged and tempted to circumvent the rule. We continue to consider fault as the basis for imposing liability in automobile litigation. Courts are extremely loath to find a party who has acted reasonably to be negligent or contributorily negligent merely because the party acted contrary to a statute. Because of this ingrained reaction the courts are constantly being asked to create exceptions to the statutory negligence per se rule and the courts are doing so to avoid the seeming harshness of the negligence per se doctrine.

1. The present case may be classified as an emergency case because the defendant was suddenly confronted with the plaintiff riding on the center line leaning toward the defendant and the defendant reacted without time for considered judgment. We prefer, however, to treat it more broadly.

Our experience with this problem extends to cases involving statutory violations other than driving on the wrong side of the road.

* * *

There is no rational basis by which we can hold that in certain instances violation of a statute is not negligence per se if the jury could find the party was acting reasonably, but in other instances violation of a statute is negligence per se regardless of whether the party was acting reasonably.

We consider the present state of the law to be that if a party is in violation of a motor vehicle statute, such a party is negligent as a matter of law unless such party introduces evidence from which the trier of fact could find that the party was acting as a reasonably prudent person under the circumstances. We so hold regardless of whether the circumstances do or do not include facts which the law regards as an emergency.

Another way of stating this is that the violation of a motor vehicle statute creates a presumption of negligence. When the evidence establishes that a party has violated a motor vehicle statute, such a party has the burden of producing evidence that, nevertheless, he was acting reasonably. Without such evidence the party is negligent as a matter of law.
* * *

If the party having such burden produces no evidence of reasonable conduct or the court finds the evidence produced is insufficient to prove reasonable conduct, the court must find the party negligent as a matter of law. If the party produces evidence which the court determines raises a question of fact whether the party acted reasonably, despite violation of the statute, then, the question of the party's negligence is for the jury.

On occasion it will be difficult to decide whether to submit the issue to the jury. However, the court's task in such a case is identical to that imposed in the administration of a judicially set standard of conduct in which the court must also decide whether to submit the issue to the jury or find negligence as a matter of law. For example, in railroad crossing cases this court has set a judicial standard that a train on a crossing is itself adequate warning of its presence and the railroad has no duty to provide further warning, such as a flagman. We have alleviated the sometimes harsh effects of that rule, however, by creating an exception that if a reasonably prudent driver might not observe the train on the crossing, then, the railroad does have a duty to warn the driver of the presence of the train. * * * In such cases the court must decide whether there is evidence from which a jury could find that a reasonably prudent person might not observe the train unless the railroad provided some warning.

The jury in this case could have found that the defendant acted as a reasonably prudent person although his vehicle may have proceeded over the dividing line. For this reason the instruction was not erroneous in substance.

* * *

Affirmed.

McALLISTER, JUSTICE (dissenting).

The majority concludes that under the present state of our law, the violation of a motor vehicle operational statute creates a disputable presumption of negligence which may be rebutted by a showing that the actor, in violating the statute, was acting reasonably. I disagree. In my opinion, our prior cases have established the stricter doctrine of negligence per se, with only limited exceptions.

* * *

In Gum, Adm. v. Wooge, 211 Or. 149, 315 P.2d 119 (1957), the court held that, although violation of the statute requiring a driver to keep on the right half of the road is negligence per se, the statute is not an absolute requirement:

> " * * * where the driver, acting as a reasonably prudent person, turns to the left to avoid a collision with an approaching vehicle traveling in its wrong lane. * * * ''* * *

In Raz v. Mills, 231 Or. 220, 372 P.2d 955 (1962) the court said that if the defendant was not at fault in causing the emergency,

> "* * * then, if the jury should find that there was such an emergency, the defendant might be excused for her failure to remain on her own side of the road." * * *

All of these cases involved violations of operational statutes, and all recognized as an excuse only the existence of an emergency.

Then, in McConnell v. Herron, 240 Or. 486, 402 P.2d 726 (1965), we considered the problem of violations of safety equipment statutes. Drawing on the cases involving operational statutes, we concluded that a limited type of excuse should also be available in equipment statute cases. * * * This standard was later modified to make it clear that the actor need not show literal impossibility of compliance, but need only show that the defect in his equipment could not have been discovered by the exercise of the highest degree of care. * * *

In Pozsgai v. Porter, 249 Or. 84, 435 P.2d 818 (1967) plaintiff contended that defendant, whose vehicle was on the wrong side of the road at the time of the collision, could be excused for a violation of the statute only if it was impossible for him to comply by the exercise of the highest degree of care. We held that the standard adopted in McConnell v. Herron, supra, was not applicable to cases involving operational statutes. The opinion contains the following statement, from which the trial court's instruction in the present case was apparently taken:

> "* * * These cases hold that an individual violating such a statute can excuse his conduct by showing that he could not or should not have complied by the exercise of reasonable care. * * *

Although the cases cited here all involved sudden emergencies, as I have pointed out above, the opinion in *Pozsgai* failed to incorporate that element into the statement of the rule applicable to operational statutes. This was apparently the result of an oversight. *Pozsgai* was a sudden emergency case, and the element of emergency was recognized elsewhere in the opinion. * * *

* * *

In Tokstad v. Lund, 255 Or. 305, 306–307, 466 P.2d 938, 939 (1970), upon which the majority relies, we said:

> "A statute requires a driver to stay upon his own side of the highway and the law in this state is that a violation of a statute is negligence per se. Nevertheless, we have held that a failure to stay upon the right side of the road is not negligence per se if the offending driver went on the wrong side through no fault of his own. Raz v. Mills, * * *; Harrison v. Avedovech, 249 Or. 584, 588–590, 439 P.2d 877 (1968)."

Both *Raz* and *Harrison* were, as pointed out above, sudden emergency cases. *Pozsgai* was not mentioned in the *Tokstad* opinion, and the rationale of the case on this point is not clear. What is clear is that the court's attention was primarily focused on another issue, which determined the disposition of the case. I do not believe that we intended in *Tokstad* to initiate a change in the law of statutory negligence. * * *

In my opinion *Tokstad* should be disapproved or limited to its facts. Our other cases clearly hold that the violation of a motor vehicle operational statute is negligence per se, except when there is evidence from which the jury could find that the actor was confronted with a sudden emergency and, in the face of that emergency, acted reasonably. The instruction given in the present case permitted the jury to excuse a statutory violation if it believed the defendant was acting reasonably, without regard to the existence of an emergency. I believe this instruction was an incorrect statement of the law and, under the facts of this case, was prejudicial to plaintiff. I dissent.

Notes

1. Under the reasoning of the court, how much evidence must a party that pleads an "excused violation" of a statute introduce? Enough to carry the burden of persuasion on the issue of whether he behaved reasonably? Or merely enough to make that issue a jury question? A subsequent Oregon case applying *Barnum v. Williams* is Roach v. Kelly Health Care, Inc., 87 Or.App. 495, 742 P.2d 1190 (1987). The problem of a so-called "excused violation" is a difficult one. One possible method of analysis, which at least has the merit of clarity, is to conclude that there is no such thing as an excused violation. Either the statute has been violated or it has not been violated. What many courts in tort cases call instances of "excused violations" are really situations in which there has been no violation of the criminal statute. *Tedla v. Ellman, supra,* is capable of being analyzed on this basis.

Undoubtedly, courts are reluctant to hold that circumstances urged as an "excuse" to a tort action would constitute a defense to a criminal action because it seems anomalous to construe definitively a criminal statute in a civil action. On the other hand, since the penalties for violating the motor vehicle statutory regulations typically involved in these cases are relatively minor, it is unlikely that the highest court of a state will in fact ever hear a criminal case involving the issue. In two cases decided in 1947, the Supreme Court of

California adopted a position similar to that taken in *Barnum v. Williams*. Satterlee v. Orange Glenn School District, 29 Cal.2d 581, 177 P.2d 279 (1947); Combs v. Los Angeles Railway, 29 Cal.2d 606, 177 P.2d 293 (1947). In both cases, Traynor, J. dissented on the issue of retreating from the negligence per se doctrine. Carter, J. on the other hand took the position in both cases that, once it is conceded that violation of a statute or ordinance does not necessarily bar recovery, there was no sense in talking about presumptions of negligence arising from violation of the statute, since it is now the jury, and not the legislature, which decides on the standard of care. Accordingly, whether or not the defendants were negligent becomes a jury question to be decided by the jury in the same manner as in the typical common-law case where there is no relevant applicable statute. A few years later, in Alarid v. Vanier, 50 Cal.2d 617, 327 P.2d 897 (1958), the California Supreme Court attempted to impose some order on the various ways in which the problem of excused violations had been handled in California. It declared that, "the correct test [in deciding whether or not the violation of a statute is excused] is whether the person who has violated a statute has sustained the burden of showing that he did what might reasonably be expected of a person of ordinary prudence, acting under similar circumstances, who desired to comply with the law. * * *" 50 Cal.2d at 624, 327 P.2d at 900.

Morris, Torts 63–64 (2d ed. by C. Morris and C. R. Morris, Jr. 1980) supports the concept of excused violation, but, recognizing that the widespread application of this doctrine would lead to the jury taking over completely the function ostensibly performed by the legislature, urges the courts to be selective in when they will allow the defendant to raise the issue of "excused violation." Unfortunately, it is hard to articulate exactly when the defense of "excused violation" may properly be raised and when it may not.

2. *Extending the concept of negligence per se by analogy in situations not covered by statute.* In Clinkscales v. Carver, 22 Cal.2d 72, 136 P.2d 777 (1943), the defendant ran a stop sign and killed the plaintiff's intestate. The stop sign had been installed pursuant to an ordinance held invalid in its entirety because of defects in its publication. The defendant was nevertheless held negligent as a matter of law. In a somewhat confusing opinion the court declared that it was adopting the standard formulated by the legislature, even though it was conceded that the criminal prosecution of the defendant was impossible. Perhaps a better way of looking at these situations is to recognize that the community relies on what to all intents and purposes look like valid traffic signs and that for anyone to ignore such a sign in these circumstances is negligence. *Cf.* Rochester v. Bussey, 251 S.C. 347, 162 S.E.2d 841 (1968)(sign announcing a 35 mph speed limit installed by state highway department, although of proper shape, had brown letters on a yellow background instead of black letters on a white background as required by the department's general regulations).

3. *Absolute liability.* What is the effect in a civil action of a statute imposing absolute criminal liability? In situations involving statutes requiring an automobile to have brakes in good working order or to display tail lights at dark the courts have split on whether a defendant who had no reason to know that his automobile was defective was civilly liable on something analogous to a negligence per se theory. *Compare* Taber v. Smith, 26 S.W.2d 722 (Tex.Civ. App.1930)(no civil liability where car's lighting system suddenly went out) *with* Albers v. Ottenbacher, 79 S.D. 637, 116 N.W.2d 529 (1962)(brakes failed in circumstances where the defendant had no reason to believe they would fail;

held negligent as a matter of law).[13]   Since, by hypothesis, such statutes impose criminal liability regardless of fault, these cases are perhaps better analyzed in terms of statutory liability rather than as instances of negligence per se.

Statutes prohibiting the sale of adulterated food have been construed to impose not only absolute or strict criminal liability but also strict civil liability. *See* Doherty v. S. S. Kresge Co., 227 Wis. 661, 278 N.W. 437 (1938).   Statutes imposing an absolute duty upon a limited class of persons for the benefit of a limited class of people or even the general public are more likely to be construed as imposing strict civil liability.   In Ross v. Ross, 294 Minn. 115, 200 N.W.2d 149 (1972), a somewhat unique case, the court not only applied the provisions of the dram shop act against social hosts but seemingly indicated that the act could be the basis of civil as well as criminal liability for the provision of liquor to minors, even in the absence of the host having any reason to know that his guest was a minor.   The imposition of liability upon social hosts was overruled by the Minnesota legislature.   *See* Holmquist v. Miller, 367 N.W.2d 468 (1985).   For the current statute, *see* Minn.Stat.Ann. § 340A.801 (1990).   It should be noted that, when the statute is construed to impose civil liability regardless of fault, the contributory negligence of the plaintiff has been held not to be available as a defense.   See Van Gaasbeck v. Webatuck Central School District, 21 N.Y.2d 239, 287 N.Y.S.2d 77, 234 N.E.2d 243 (1967) (requirement that school bus driver instruct children to cross in front of bus and that driver wait until children reached opposite side of highway).   With the advent of comparative negligence, however, see p. 343, *infra*, the plaintiff's contributory fault may now, in some states, be a partial defense even when a statute is construed as imposing absolute liability.

6. *Proof of Negligence; the Use of Custom and Expert Testimony*

a. *General*

Determining what knowledge a reasonable person would have and evaluating any particular risk as one that a reasonable person would or would not undertake are normally questions for the trier of fact ultimately to determine.   In helping the trier of fact make these determinations, certain kinds of evidence may be both relevant and useful.   One such kind of evidence is that of custom.   "Custom" is a broad term that encompasses not only the unwritten but generally prevailing practices in a community or industry, but also trade rules or standards that have been explicitly adopted by a particular profession or industry.   Unless a custom is of such prevalence that the jury may be entitled to take note of it of their own accord, it is normally necessary to prove the existence of a custom through persons so familiar with the custom and its scope of application that they can be considered experts with regard to it.

One way of defining an expert, in the context of an action for personal injuries, is to say that he is a person who is able to testify before the jury on matters of fact within his special field of knowledge and to express his opinion on a variety of matters. Normally, witnesses are only permitted to

---

13. In Maloney v. Rath, 69 Cal.2d 442, 71 Cal.Rptr. 897, 445 P.2d 513 (1968), the court refused to impose absolute liability upon the owner of a vehicle for defective brakes but nonetheless held her liable for the injuries she had caused on the ground that the duty to maintain the brakes was non-delegable and that therefore she was responsible for the admitted negligence of a mechanic who had serviced her vehicle.

testify regarding what they have seen or heard or otherwise directly experienced themselves. There are inevitably, however, some exceptions. For example, the ordinary person, when called as a witness, is usually permitted to testify that someone was "drunk." Likewise he is generally permitted to estimate that the defendant's car, immediately before the accident, was travelling at, say, 30 miles an hour. The questions of whether the defendant was intoxicated or of how fast he was driving his car are, in a sense, questions of fact; but they are not normally directly observable facts. In permitting the ordinary person to testify as to these matters, he is in reality being permitted to express an opinion based upon certain observed facts. The same considerations apply when a witness is permitted to testify as to the reputation of one of the litigants in his community. But, with the exception of these and other similar instances, the ordinary person is not permitted to testify as to his opinion on the matters in issue. The rationale is that the jury is as capable as the witness of drawing the proper conclusion and that to permit the witness to evaluate the evidence is to invade the province of the jury. Nevertheless, the expert *is* permitted to present his opinions on a variety of matters to the jury because he has special knowledge and experience which is normally not available to the jury.

In the use of expert testimony the first requirement is the qualification of the witness as an expert. This preliminary qualification procedure is carried on before the judge, and is sometimes called the *voir dire*. The witness testifies as to his qualifications and the judge ultimately decides whether the witness is in fact an expert; and, if so, what he is an expert on. The jury will normally be present during some portion of the time when the qualifications of a proposed expert are considered and the jury may be expected to consider the qualifications of the expert in deciding upon the weight to be given to his testimony. A typical use of an expert is to establish the custom of an industry. This sort of testimony is in a sense testimony about matters of "fact" but, as in the case of testimony about whether a person was drunk in the absence of blood tests or breath analysis, the presenting of such testimony actually requires the witness to make a number of evaluations. An expert witness may also be asked to testify as to what is "good engineering practice."[14] In such a case, it is more obvious that the expert is giving opinion evidence than in the case where the expert witness is asked whether the accident would have been avoided if certain precautions had been taken. In some of the earlier cases, it was held that it is improper to ask the expert for an opinion on the ultimate issue in the case, namely whether the defendant exercised due care under the circumstances. But the modern trend, particularly where the matter at issue involves complex technical factors, permits an expert to testify even as to these ultimate issues.[15] Nevertheless, although the

---

14. *See* Beck v. Monmouth Lumber Co., 137 N.J.L. 268, 59 A.2d 400 (1948)(expert permitted to testify as to "good and safe engineering practice"). *See also* Pittsburgh, Shawmut & Northern Railroad v. Lamphere, 137 Fed. 20 (C.C.A.3 1905) (expert permitted to testify as to the "custom of well-regulated railroads").

15. *Compare* Demarais v. Johnson, 90 Mont. 366, 3 P.2d 283 (1931) (expert may not testify as to what "a reasonably careful and prudent person would have done in the way of inspecting the track") *with* Marigold Coal, Inc. v. Thames, 274 Ala. 421, 149 So.2d 276 (1962)(expert permitted to testify that "blasting was improperly done") and Shutka v.

evidence may be admissible the jury is normally still free to reject the expert testimony presented on these or any other contested issues *and* to come to its own conclusion on these issues. There is, however, as we shall see later in this section, one major qualification that must be made to this last statement. In the medical malpractice area, by contrast, the jury is not normally permitted to come to a conclusion at variance with all the expert testimony. Furthermore, in the absence of some expert testimony supporting the plaintiff's position in a medical malpractice case, he normally will not be able to survive a motion for a directed verdict.

b. *Effect of Evidence of Custom*

DEMPSEY v. ADDISON CRANE CO.

United States District Court, District of Columbia, 1965.
247 F.Supp. 584.

HOLTZOFF, DISTRICT JUDGE.

This is an action for personal injuries. As the trial has been without a jury, the Court has separated the issue of liability, reserving the issue of damages to be tried later in the event that the Court reached the conclusion that the defendant was liable to the plaintiff.

The male plaintiff was a pile driver employed on a construction project at the corner of 12th and E Streets in the Northwest section of Washington. The project was then in the excavating stage. On March 27th, 1962 the plaintiff's employer, who was the contractor erecting the building to be located at the site, rented a crane from the defendant, which was a concern in the business of renting and operating cranes for others. The crane arrived early in the morning of that day and was moved on the site of the excavation. The contractor's foreman directed the crane operator to move a welding machine that was located on the site and that apparently was interfering with the progress of the work.

The crane operator and his assistant proceeded to lift the welding machine by means of the crane, to shift it to a different location, and to let it down in the new place indicated. Four pile drivers, including the plaintiff, were holding the machine, each of them holding one corner, in order to prevent it from twisting. Just as the welding machine was about to come to rest in its new location, an auxiliary jib attached to the boom broke loose, fell, and hit and struck two of the pile drivers who were holding the corners of the machine. One of them was killed and the other, who is one of the plaintiffs in this action, was seriously injured.

* * *

At the outset it is necessary to summarize briefly the applicable rules of law of negligence. The defendant was not an insurer of the safety of his apparatus or of anyone coming in contact with or close to it. On the other hand, the defendant was under a duty to use due care in connection with

Pennsylvania Railroad, 74 N.J.Super. 381, 181 A.2d 400 (1962)(expert may testify as to ultimate fact in issue). The *Shutka* case is a good source of citations to the discussion of the issue in the legal treatises on evidence. *Accord* Uniform Rules of Evidence, Rule 56(4).

the apparatus, such care as would be used by a prudent man under similar circumstances and conditions. Failure to use such due care is negligence, and if the negligence is a proximate cause of an injury to someone, the injured party may recover damages from the defendant. What constitutes due care under any particular set of circumstances depends on the risk involved and the hazards connected with the apparatus or activity in question. The degree of care that must be exercised by a person in charge of any apparatus depends upon possible consequences of negligence.

It is claimed in behalf of the plaintiffs that the defendant was negligent in two respects: first, in that he left the auxiliary jib suspended from the boom at a time when the auxiliary jib was not in actual use; and, second, in that the means by which the jib was suspended and the apparatus which attached it to the boom were unsafe. Each of the two charges must be analyzed separately.

The operating member of the crane was a boom about 60 feet long, which could be shifted horizontally and lifted vertically, being raised or lowered at different angles. Attached to the boom was an auxiliary jib about 30 feet long. The purpose of the jib was for use as an extension piece, presumably for tasks for which the boom was not long enough.

It is claimed in behalf of the plaintiffs that it was negligence to permit the auxiliary jib to remain suspended from the boom when the boom was in operation but the jib was not in actual use, and that the safe practice was to detach the jib from the boom under those circumstances and to lay it on some supports to one side. There were expressions of opinion to that effect on the part of some witnesses. The Court reaches the conclusion, however, that the plaintiff has not sustained by a fair preponderance of the evidence the contention that there was any negligence in the failure to detach and remove the jib at the time when the boom was operating merely because the jib was not in actual use at that particular moment.

The second charge of negligence, however, requires greater consideration. That charge is that the means by which the jib was suspended from the boom were unsafe and that this lack of safety caused the accident. In considering this charge of negligence it is necessary to examine the apparatus in detail.

The boom was of metal latticework construction, so to speak, as was also the jib. Two slings were attached to the jib by which the jib was suspended from the boom. In order to hold the jib in place the slings were inserted through apertures in the metal framework of the jib and through similar apertures in the metal framework of the boom. When the boom was raised from a horizontal position, one of the two slings would be above the other. The slings were spaced in such a way as to hold the jib in place. Each sling consisted of a cable ending with a metal hook, one hook being at each end of the cable. The hooks were open at the bottom. They were not closed or fastened in any way. The hooks were suspended or placed on the framework of the boom, thus holding the jib in attachment to the boom.

The accident happened in the following manner. While the boom was at an angle and slowly setting the welding machine on the ground, one of the hooks on the upper sling somehow or other slipped from its connection. This, in turn, increased the load on the lower sling and the lower sling broke. The jib then fell, striking two of the men, as heretofore stated.

There was also in existence an alternative apparatus for attaching the jib to the boom. It consisted of shackles connected together, the shackles being at each end of the sling. In other words, the sling would form a closed loop instead of ending with an open hook at each terminus.

The evidence showed that the apparatus employed in this case was in wide use by the industry at the time of the accident and prior thereto, and, further, that some of the largest concerns in the crane renting business used apparatus of this type. On the other hand, there was also evidence that the alternative apparatus was available and had been in actual use, although on a smaller scale than the one involved in this case. The component parts of the alternative apparatus were readily available in hardware stores and were not expensive.

The slings connecting the jib with the boom are not standard equipment. They are not furnished with the crane, but each crane owner fabricates his own. In this instance the testimony is that the defendant made these slings in its own shop.

* * *

As has been stated, the evidence clearly shows that the apparatus of the type used in this instance was the prevailing apparatus employed in the industry at the time of the accident, although the alternative and the safer apparatus was also utilized, but to a much lesser extent. The fact that a particular apparatus or method is used by the industry is admissible in evidence on the issue of negligence, but it is by no means conclusive. * * *

* * *

The case of The T. J. Hooper (2 Cir.) 60 F.2d 737, an admiralty case, illustrates this point very vividly. The case involved a collision between two vessels, one of which was a coastwise tug. The tug had not been equipped with radio receiving sets and thus had been unable to receive a storm warning that had been broadcast over the radio. It was held that this failure constituted negligence. The opinion was written by Judge Learned Hand, who said, in passing:

> "It is not fair to say that there was a general custom among coastwise carriers so to equip their tugs. One line alone did it; as for the rest, they relied upon their crews, so far as they can be said to have relied at all."

And again he said:

> "Is it a final answer that the business had not yet generally adopted receiving sets? There are, no doubt, cases where courts seem to make the general practice of the calling the standard of proper diligence; we have indeed given some currency to the notion ourselves * * * Indeed in most cases reasonable prudence is in fact common prudence; but

strictly it is never its measure; a whole calling may have unduly lagged in the adoption of new and available devices. It never may set its own tests, however persuasive be its usages."

An accident that is very similar in its facts to that involved in this case confronted the Supreme Court of New Jersey in McComish v. DeSoi, 42 N.J. 274, 200 A.2d 116. * * * The question involved in that case, as it is here, was whether the means of attaching the apparatus to be moved was safe or not. The Court stated, at page 121:

> "What ought to be done is fixed by the standard of reasonable prudence, and in law that requirement remains the same whether it is usually complied with or not. Thus, what is usually done in a particular industry cannot be regarded as what ought to be done unless the conduct and the test are in harmony."

This Court makes an ultimate finding of fact that the means and the apparatus by which the jib was attached to the boom were unsafe as of the date of the accident; that the use of this means constituted negligence on the part of the defendant; and that this negligence was the cause of the injuries to the plaintiff.

* * *

There remains to say a word concerning another case arising out of the same accident. It has been already stated that another workman was killed in the accident. An action was brought by his estate * * *. This action was likewise tried without a jury before another Judge of this Court and terminated in favor of the defendant. The judgment was affirmed by the Court of Appeals in Socash v. Addison Crane Co., D.C.Cir., 346 F.2d 420, on the ground that the questions presented to the trial Judge were questions of fact and that his findings could not be set aside unless clearly erroneous, which they were not.[a] * * *

Naturally, just as two juries may reach different conclusions on the same facts, so may two judges do likewise. Here, however, the evidence in the two actions was not the same. Testimony was presented at this trial which it is understood from counsel had not been introduced in evidence at the trial of the Socash case. It should be noted that the plaintiffs in this case are represented by different counsel than the plaintiff in the Socash case.

Accordingly, the Court concludes that the defendant is liable to the two plaintiffs for the damages sustained by each of them as a result of the accident involved in this action and the trial will be resumed on the issue of damages.

---

a. [Ed. note] In Socash v. Addison Crane Co., 346 F.2d 420 (D.C.Cir.1965), the trial court, trying the case without a jury, found that no negligence had been shown. The appellate court affirmed. Bazelon, J., concurred in the result but did not agree that the finding that the defendant was not negligent was a finding of fact which could not be reversed unless it was "clearly erroneous." Bazelon, J., thought that questions such as "negligence *vel non* are 'mixed questions of law and fact freely reviewable on appeal * * *.'" *Cf.* the earlier discussion on the function of judge and jury in § 4 (p. 145), *supra*.

Notes

1. The T. J. Hooper, 60 F.2d 737 (2d Cir.1932), discussed in Judge Holtzoff's opinion, is the most frequently cited judicial declaration on the weight to be given to evidence of custom. There are some earlier cases declaring that conformity to custom is conclusive proof of due care, see, *e.g.*, Titus v. Bradford, Bordell & Kinzua Railroad, 136 Pa. 618, 20 A. 517 (1890), and even an occasional more recent case so holding, see, *e.g.*, Ellis v. Louisville & Nashville Railroad, 251 S.W.2d 577 (Ky.1952), but such cases are now largely considered judicial curiosities. Under the standard rubric neither compliance with an industry-wide custom nor the failure to comply with such a custom is conclusive evidence of due care or of lack of due care. In actual fact, however, it would be rare to find instances in which a defendant was found to have failed to conform to customary standard but was nevertheless not found negligent. One such rare instance seems to have been Cunningham v. Fort Pitt Bridge Works, 197 Pa. 625, 47 A. 846 (1901). Indeed, the modern tendency is to permit evidence of the defendant's failure to conform to its own safety regulations into evidence, regardless of whether such internal rules do or do not illustrate industry-wide standards. *See* Phillips v. Montgomery Ward & Co., 125 F.2d 248 (5th Cir.1942); Hurley v. Connecticut Co., 118 Conn. 276, 172 A. 86 (1934). In order realistically to expect to succeed in a case where it was shown that the defendant failed to conform to an industry-wide custom, the defendant would have to show that its alternative methods for dealing with a safety problem were safer than the customary standards of the industry. *See* Brown v. Rolls Royce Ltd., [1960] 1 W.L.R. 210, 1 All E.R. 577 (H.L.).

2. In trying to prove negligence, reference is often made to safety codes promulgated by professional or trade organizations, such as the American General Contractors Safety Specifications or safety manuals used by the armed forces in their own activities, none of which are the equivalent of statutorily based safety codes that the courts must take judicial notice of and which are obligatory upon the parties involved in the litigation. The introduction of such codes in evidence is often barred on the ground that they are hearsay. On the other hand, if an expert witness first testifies as to the industry-wide custom and uses these "codes" as illustrative of his conclusions, the modern tendency is to admit the "codes" into evidence. For a good discussion of the problems, see McComish v. DeSoi, 42 N.J. 274, 200 A.2d 116 (1964). A more extended discussion of these questions should be reserved for a course on evidence.

3. As we have seen, in modern law, the standard rubric is that evidence of custom is not conclusive on the issue of due care. Although basically true, this statement requires some emendation. In activities that are engaged in by practically everyone, customary behavior is, for all practical purposes, probably conclusive on the issue of due care. Failing to check the level of the brake fluid in one's car each morning before one uses it may impose a risk of injury upon others and it may, furthermore, be an easy thing to do, but hardly anyone ever does it. It is hard to believe that a jury would find that a motorist's failure to check the level each morning constituted the imposition of an unreasonable risk. The other possible exception to the general doctrine is more important. It has to do with the standard of conduct expected of certain types of professionals, principally doctors but also probably lawyers, whose profession requires the exercise of considerable skill and, more importantly, of judgment. This will be among the questions explored in the next few cases.

c. *Malpractice*

SHILKRET v. ANNAPOLIS EMERGENCY HOSPITAL ASSOCIATION

Court of Appeals of Maryland, 1975.
276 Md. 187, 349 A.2d 245.

LEVINE, JUDGE.

In this appeal, which stems from a negligence action brought against several physicians and a hospital, we are asked to decide upon the proper standard of care to be applied in medical malpractice cases.

At the trial of the case in the Circuit Court for Anne Arundel County, the court (Wray, J.) ruled that the standard to be applied was the "strict locality" rule (the standard of care exercised by physicians in the defendant's own community or locality), and since appellants, who were plaintiffs below, had failed to meet the requirements of that rule, directed a verdict for appellees. The Court of Special Appeals affirmed that decision in an unreported per curiam opinion. * * *

According to the agreed statement of facts filed in lieu of a record extract, the infant plaintiff, Mark Alan Shilkret, was born at the Anne Arundel General Hospital (Anne Arundel) on December 22, 1968, and has been continuously institutionalized since that date because of brain damage that appellants allege resulted from intracranial bleeding caused by negligence at delivery. This was allegedly complicated by subsequent treatment rendered by appellees, the various attending physicians and the hospital. The several physicians who are appellees here include two obstetricians who treated the mother throughout the prenatal stage and then delivered the infant, an anesthesiologist in attendance at birth, and a pediatrician at the hospital who allegedly examined the infant the day after his birth.

At the trial, after excerpts from the depositions of the four defendant-physicians had been admitted in evidence, argument ensued over the applicable standard of care. When the court indicated that it would apply "the strict locality rule," appellants conceded that they could not prove their case against appellees under that standard and requested leave to make a proffer of expert medical testimony which "could meet any other rule in medical negligence cases." They were afforded this opportunity and proceeded with extensive statements of what their two experts, an obstetrician-gynecologist and a neurosurgeon, would say if called as witnesses. Each expert had an impressive curriculum vitae.

The proffered testimony of the obstetrician-gynecologist established that Anne Arundel belongs to the American Hospital Association, one of several members of the accrediting body known as the Joint Commission on Accreditation of Hospitals. It was his opinion that all hospitals belonging to this group meet a national standard in caring for obstetrical patients. At the time of the infant's birth, the witness had been chief of the obstetrical-gynecological services at the U.S. Army Hospital at Aberdeen Proving Ground. He believed that in this branch of medicine, the standards at Anne Arundel were the same as those observed at Aberdeen and at all other accredited hospitals in the United States. Similarly, as a member of the American College of Gynecologists and Obstetricians, and being board certified, he believed that a national standard of care applied to those with the same qualifications. He then detailed how the failure of the four physicians and the hospital to meet the national standards of care applicable to them resulted in the injury to the plaintiff.

The other expert witness whose testimony was proffered would have stated in some detail that he was employed as a neurosurgeon at the National Institutes of Health at Bethesda, Maryland, that a national standard of care is observed in the diagnosis and treatment of neurological diseases, the knowledge of which is also possessed by general practitioners, and that each of the defendants had violated what he believed to be a national standard regarding the care of newborn infants.

Following these proffers, the trial judge granted each appellee's motion for a directed verdict. He adhered to his previously pronounced belief that the "strict locality" standard applies in Maryland, rather than the "national" (in which the standard of care is not tied to a particular geographic locality) or "similar locality" (the standard of care observed by physicians of ordinary skill and care in either the defendant-physician's locality or in a similar community) tests urged by appellants, and therefore ruled that the latter had failed to present a sufficient case for the jury. The Court of Special Appeals affirmed, holding that its own prior cases—and the decisions of this Court—compelled this result. For reasons that follow, we reverse.

The general principles which ordinarily govern in negligence cases also apply in medical malpractice claims. * * * Therefore, as in any other case founded upon negligent conduct, the burden of proof rests upon the plaintiff in a medical malpractice case to show a lack of the requisite skill or care on the part of the defendant. * * * But, whereas the conduct of the average layman charged with negligence is evaluated in terms of the hypothetical conduct of a reasonably prudent person acting under the same or similar circumstances, the standard applied in medical malpractice cases must also take into account the specialized knowledge or skill of the defendant. W. Prosser, Torts § 32 (4th ed. 1971); McCoid, *The Care Required Of Medical Practitioners*, 12 Vand.L.Rev. 549, 558 (1959). The formulation of a standard of care that is consistent with these well established tort principles, but which is fair to both the patient and his physician, has troubled the courts for the past century.

Recently, in Raitt v. Johns Hopkins Hospital, 274 Md. 489, 499–500, 336 A.2d 90 (1975), where we held that an expert medical witness need not necessarily reside or practice in the defendant's community to testify as to the applicable standard of care in a medical malpractice case, we intimated that despite the plethora of reported medical malpractice decisions in Maryland, this Court actually had never been confronted with the need to adopt a standard of care from among the three we have mentioned.

In State, use of Janney v. Housekeeper, 70 Md. 162, 172, 16 A. 382, 384 (1889), the standard of care which this Court applied was "* * * that reasonable degree of care and skill which physicians and surgeons ordinarily exercise in the treatment of their patients * * *." * * * As we noted in *Raitt*, this rule, which makes no reference to the defendant-physician's community, was followed in this state prior to 1962. * * * Indeed, it has been quoted occasionally since 1962. * * *

This Court applied the strict locality rule for the first time in State, use of Solomon v. Fishel, 228 Md. 189, 179 A.2d 349 (1962), the purported authority for this proposition in Maryland. It is important to note, however, that *Fishel* did not turn on the standard of care issue, but dealt with the proper use of hypothetical questions addressed to medical experts and with a jury instruction involving the plaintiff's burden of proof. * * *

The only reported decision to flatly hold that the strict locality rule applies in Maryland is Dunham v. Elder, 18 Md.App. 360, 306 A.2d 568 (1973), which we did not have occasion to review. There, the Court of Special Appeals read *Fishel* to stand for the application of the stricter rule. In applying the same rule in this case, the two courts below relied heavily on *Dunham*, but we hasten to point out that the portents in *Raitt* were not yet available to them.

In any event, we now explicitly decide for the first time this question of the standard of care to be applied in medical malpractice cases. It should hardly come as a surprise that appellants advocate the adoption of the national standard or, alternatively, the similar locality rule. They claim that their proof satisfied both tests. Appellees, on the other hand, contend for the strict locality rule.

In addressing this issue, we note at the outset that we are dealing with two types of defendants, physicians and hospitals.

(1)

The Standard of Care Applicable to Physicians

The earliest traces of the strict locality rule appeared a century ago. Smothers v. Hanks, 34 Iowa 286 (1872); Tefft v. Wilcox, 6 Kan. 46 (1870); Hathorn v. Richmond, 48 Vt. 557, 559 (1876)("such skill as doctors in the same general neighborhood, in the same general lines of practice, ordinarily have and exercise in like cases"). It is an exclusive product of the United States; possibly because of the difference in the size of the two countries, the English courts have never developed such a principle. Waltz, *The Rise And Gradual Fall Of The Locality Rule In Medical Malpractice Litigation*, 18 DePaul L.Rev. 408 (1969). The rule was unquestionably developed to protect the rural and small town practitioner, who was presumed to be less adequately informed and equipped than his big city brother. *Id.* The court reasoned with what was then unassailable logic in *Tefft v. Wilcox, supra*, 6 Kan. at 63–64:

> "* * * In the smaller towns and country, those who practice medicine and surgery, though often possessing a thorough theoretical knowledge of the highest elements of the profession do not enjoy so great opportunities of daily observation and practical operations, where the elementary studies are brought into every day use, as those have who reside in the metropolitan towns, and though just as well informed in the elements and literature of their profession, they should not be expected to exercise that high degree of skill and practical knowledge possessed by those having greater facilities for performing and witness-

ing operations, and who are, or may be constantly observing the various accidents and forms of disease.   * * *' "

In short, the rationale underlying the development of the strict locality rule a century ago was grounded in the manifest inequality existing in that day between physicians practicing in large urban centers and those practicing in remote rural areas.

Ultimately, the rule came under sharp attack on two grounds. First, "[i]t effectively immunized from malpractice liability any doctor who happened to be the sole practitioner in his community. He could be treating bone fractures by the application of wet grape leaves and yet remain beyond the criticism of more enlightened practitioners from other communities." *Waltz, supra* at 411. Secondly, a "conspiracy of silence" in the plaintiff's locality could effectively preclude any possibility of obtaining expert medical testimony. Note, 40 Fordham L.Rev. 435, 438 (1971).

Whatever may have justified the strict locality rule fifty or a hundred years ago, it cannot be reconciled with the realities of medical practice today.[4] "New techniques and discoveries are available to all doctors within a short period of time through medical journals, closed circuit television presentations, special radio networks for doctors, tape recorded digests of medical literature, and current correspondence courses." Note, *An Evaluation, Of Changes In The Medical Standard Of Care*, 23 Vand.L.Rev. 729, 732 (1970). More importantly, the quality of medical school training itself has improved dramatically in the last century. Where early medical education consisted of a course of lectures over a period of six months, which was supplemented by apprenticeships with doctors who had even less formal education, there now exists a national accrediting system which has contributed to the standardization of medical schools throughout the country. *Id.* n. 16.

A distinct minority of states, however, cling to the strict locality rule. * * * Nevertheless, recognizing the significant developments which have occurred in the training and practice of medicine, and the population shifts which have marked the increased urbanization of our society, a majority of American courts have now abandoned the strict locality rule as being too narrow. We, too, conclude that it can be sustained no longer given the current state of medical science.

We have noted that one of the earliest applications of the similar locality rule occurred in *Small v. Howard, supra*, 128 Mass. at 136, where, essentially for the same reasons that have traditionally undergirded the strict locality rule, the court enunciated as the standard: " 'that skill only which physicians and surgeons of ordinary ability and skill, practising in

---

4. The absurdity of coupling the standard of care with the doctor's community is aptly illustrated in Brune v. Belinkoff, 354 Mass. 102, 235 N.E.2d 793 (1968), in which the Supreme Judicial Court of Massachusetts overruled its earlier decision in Small v. Howard, 128 Mass. 131, 35 Am.Rep. 363 (1880), containing one of the first enunciations of the similar locality rule. In *Brune*, which involved an act of alleged malpractice in the City of New Bedford, slightly more than 50 miles from Boston, the trial judge had instructed the jury: " '* * * If, in a given case, it were determined by a jury that the ability and skill of the physician in New Bedford were fifty percent inferior to that which existed in Boston, a defendant in New Bedford would be required to measure up to the standard of skill and competence and ability that is ordinarily found by physicians in New Bedford.' " 235 N.E.2d at 795.

similar localities, with opportunities for no larger experience, ordinarily possess' "; thus the defendant " 'was not bound to possess that high degree of art and skill possessed by eminent surgeons practising in large cities, and making a specialty of the practice of surgery.' "

A plurality, if not a majority, of states apply the similar locality rule. * * *

The similar locality rule answers some of the criticism aimed at the strict locality standard by enabling the plaintiff to obtain expert witnesses from different communities, thus reducing the likelihood of their acquaintance with the defendant. It does not, however, effectively alleviate the other potential problem, a low standard of care in some of the smaller communities, because the standard in similar communities is apt to be the same. Another criticism leveled at the similar locality rule is the difficulty which arises in defining a "similar" locality.[5] For these reasons, the similar locality rule is regarded as no more than a slight improvement over the stricter standard.

These deficiencies in the locality rules and the increasing emphasis on the availability of medical facilities have led some courts to dilute the rules by extending geographical boundaries to include those centers that are readily accessible for appropriate treatment. * * * This expanded rule, expressed in terms of "medical neighborhood" or "medical locality," have paved the way for the national standard. In any event, the trend continues away from standards which rest solely on geographic considerations.

Ever-increasing emphasis on medical specialization has accelerated the erosion of the locality rules and the concomitant emergence of the so-called national standard. Even within the framework of the locality rules, it has been generally accepted that where a physician holds himself out as a specialist, he is held to a higher standard of knowledge and skill than a general practitioner. Some courts, therefore, have abandoned the locality rules for a national standard only as to specialists. * * * This is consistent with the position of the American Law Institute which otherwise adopts the similar locality rule.[8]

Were we to adopt a standard tied to locality for specialists, we would clearly be ignoring the realities of medical life. As we have indicated, the

---

5. One standard which has been applied is geographic proximity between communities, which retains much of the "same" locality flavor. Other courts have considered socio-economic factors such as population, type of economy, size of city, and income of inhabitants. Most courts applying this standard, however, have adopted the view that "similar" locality should be defined in terms of medical factors such as the existence of research and laboratory facilities, medical schools, teaching hospitals and modern equipment in the localities to be compared. The commentators agree that this is the most logical application of the rule when measured against a major reason for its adoption—the availability of resources which will enable the physician to maintain the standard of his practice. * * *

8. "Unless he represents that he has greater or less skill or knowledge, one who undertakes to render services in the practice of a profession or trade is required to exercise the skill and knowledge normally possessed by members of that profession or trade in good standing in similar communities." Restatement (Second) of Torts § 299 A (1965).

Comment d provides:

"An actor undertaking to render services may represent that he has superior skill or knowledge, beyond that common to his profession or trade. * * * Thus a physician who holds himself out as a specialist in certain types of practice is required to have the skill and knowledge common to other specialists. * * *"

various specialties have established uniform requirements for certification. The national boards dictate the length of residency training, subjects to be covered, and the examinations given to the candidates for certification. Since the medical profession itself recognizes national standards for specialists that are not determined by geography, the law should follow suit.

The courts in another group of cases, however, have gone further, and have adopted this same standard of care—one which is not governed by the locality of the defendant—for all physicians regardless of whether they are specialists or not. * * *

We agree with these courts that justification for the locality rules no longer exists. The modern physician bears little resemblance to his predecessors. As we have indicated at length, the medical schools of yesterday could not possibly compare with the accredited institutions of today, many of which are associated with teaching hospitals. But the contrast merely begins at that point in the medical career: vastly superior postgraduate training, the dynamic impact of modern communications and transportation, the proliferation of medical literature, frequent seminars and conferences on a variety of professional subjects, and the growing availability of modern clinical facilities are but some of the developments in the medical profession which combine to produce contemporary standards that are not only much higher than they were just a few short years ago, but also are national in scope.

In sum, the traditional locality rules no longer fit the present-day medical malpractice case.

* * *a

We align ourselves with the Kentucky court and hold that a physician is under a duty to use that degree of care and skill which is expected of a reasonably competent practitioner in the same class to which he belongs, acting in the same or similar circumstances. Under this standard, advances in the profession, availability of facilities, specialization or general practice, proximity of specialists and special facilities, together with all other relevant considerations, are to be taken into account.

(2)

The Standard of Care Applicable to Hospitals

In reviewing some of our medical malpractice decisions earlier, we intimated that neither of the locality rules has been applied in Maryland where a hospital has been the defendant. * * * Equally significant is the absence in our prior cases of any distinction between physicians and hospitals regarding the applicable standard of care. * * * Courts elsewhere have tended to apply the same standards to hospitals that they apply to physicians. * * *

The only case, of which we are aware, to make a distinction of any kind between physicians and hospitals is Duling v. Bluefield Sanitarium, Inc.,

---

a. [Ed. note]. In the portion of its opinion that has been omitted the court considered whether the standard should be phrased in terms of the "average practitioner" (Massachusetts) or the "average competent practitioner" (Washington) or the "reasonably competent practitioner" (Kentucky). It opted for the "reasonably competent practitioner" since numerical average suggests better than 50% and could mislead the jury.

149 W.Va. 567, 142 S.E.2d 754, 764 (1965). There, the court, although adhering to the similar locality rule in medical malpractice cases, held that an action brought against a hospital because of a nurse's carelessness, as distinguished from that of a physician, is founded solely on negligence and want of due care. Hence, the proper standard was held to be "reasonable care."

In Dickinson v. Mailliard, 175 N.W.2d 588, 596, 36 A.L.R.3d 425 (Iowa 1970), the court, in adopting as a standard "that which obtains in hospitals generally under similar circumstances," stated:

> "* * * It is doubtful today if there is any substantial difference from one locality to another in the type of hospital services rendered. Hospitals must now be licensed and accredited. They are subject to statutory regulation. In order to obtain approval they must meet certain standard requirements. * * * It is no longer justifiable, if indeed it ever was, to limit a hospital's liability to that degree of care which is customarily practiced in its own community. * * * [M]any communities have only one hospital. Adherence to such a rule, then, means the hospital whose conduct is assailed is to be measured only by standards which it has set for itself. There is no other hospital to which it may be compared."

We think the same reasoning is apposite here. Hospitals in general, and Anne Arundel in particular, are accredited by the Joint Commission on Accreditation. This group establishes national standards to which all hospitals seeking accreditation must conform. In addition, hospitals in Maryland are subject to a rigorous regulatory scheme which promotes statewide standards. * * * These factors, together with much of what we said earlier regarding physicians, warrant the adoption of a standard of care for hospitals which conforms to that applied in cases against physicians.

We hold, therefore, that a hospital is required to use that degree of care and skill which is expected of a reasonably competent hospital in the same or similar circumstances. As in cases brought against physicians, advances in the profession, availability of special facilities and specialists, together with all other relevant considerations, are to be taken into account.

Here, there was evidence that there is a national standard of care for accredited hospitals in the prenatal, intrapartum and perinatal periods of pregnancy. Similarly, the evidence proffered by appellants showed national standards of care for child delivery, infant care, and the treatment of neurological problems generally, and the measure of vital functions specifically, that are observed by specialists and general practitioners alike. Under our holdings here, this evidence was sufficient to take the standard of care issue to the jury as to all of the appellees. Our review, as we observed at the outset, has been limited to this question. Whether the evidence was sufficient to establish a failure to comply with the applicable standards of care, and, if so, whether said failure directly caused the injuries sustained by the infant plaintiff, are questions which we do not reach here.

[The judgment of the Court of Special Appeals was reversed and the case remanded for a new trial.]

Notes

1. Brune v. Belinkoff, 354 Mass. 102, 235 N.E.2d 793 (1968), which is mentioned several times in *Shilkret*, has become a leading case, but *Brune* does not contain as detailed an examination of the history and development of the law as does the *Shilkret* case. Nor does *Brune* discuss the question of the standards to be applied to hospitals. In *Brune*, the Supreme Judicial Court of Massachusetts declared that a national standard should be applied to general practitioners. In a portion of its opinion that has been omitted, the *Shilkret* court labelled this statement as dictum. Are the portions of *Shilkret* on the standards to be applied to general practitioners also dicta? Once a more general standard is adopted for general practitioners, the paucity of local facilities cuts two ways. On the one hand it may excuse certain less than optimal practices, particularly in emergency situations; on the other hand, such paucity of local resources may impose an obligation on the attending physician to refer the patient to a larger metropolitan area with better medical facilities and more specialists.

2. The same or similar communities rules—many courts treat the latter as a variant of the first rather than as a distinct doctrine—have probably now been abandoned by most jurisdictions in favor of a national standard where specialists are concerned. A more recent case illustrating this trend is Paintiff v. City of Parkersburg, 176 W.Va. 469, 345 S.E.2d 564 (1986) (case involved treatment of a specialist nature but the court's abolition of the "locality" rule was unqualified by any distinction between specialists and general practitioners). Nevertheless, there continue to be cases applying the same or similar locality rules even to specialists. *See* Slezak v. Girzadas, 167 Ill.App.3d 1045, 118 Ill.Dec. 677, 522 N.E.2d 132 (1988)(similar locality rule applied to an orthopedic surgeon); Gibson v. D'Amico, 97 A.D.2d 905, 470 N.Y.S.2d 739 (1983) (strict locality rule applied to an orthopedic surgeon). *See also* Grimes v. Green, 113 Idaho 519, 746 P.2d 978 (1987)(construing a statutory provision). As to general practitioners, although the trend is clearly away from the same or similar locality rules—*see* Capitol Hill Hosp. v. Jones, 532 A.2d 89 (D.C.App. 1987); Paintiff v. City of Parkersburg, *supra*—the majority of states may still be applying the same or similar community standards. *See e.g.* Purtill v. Hess, 111 Ill.2d 229, 95 Ill.Dec. 305, 489 N.E.2d 867 (1986)(general practitioner providing gynecological services); Hickson v. Martinez, 707 S.W.2d 919 (Tex. App.1985). For recent annotations on the subject *see* 99 A.L.R.3d 1133 (1980), which is supplemented annually. One way of eroding the same or similar communities doctrine is to expand the range of expert witnesses who are competent to testify as to the local standard. For example, in Siirila v. Barrios, 398 Mich. 576, 248 N.W.2d 171 (1976), the court indicated that even a specialist could testify—in that case a pediatrician—in an action against a general practitioner charging negligence towards a new-born infant, so long as it could be shown that the specialist was familiar with the standards of general practice in the defendant's community or in similar communities. *See also* Lee v. Andrews, 545 S.W.2d 238 (Tex.Civ.App.1976). In a more recent case, Slezak v. Girzadas, *supra,* the Illinois Court of Appeals allowed a New York surgeon to testify as to the standard of care applicable in Chicago. For the argument that where physicians are minimally compensated, one is not justified in expecting

the same exhaustiveness in treatment and diagnosis, *see* J. Siciliano, *Wealth, Equity and the Unitary Medical Malpractice Standard,* 77 Va.L.Rev. 439 (1991).

HELLING v. CAREY

Supreme Court of Washington, 1974.
83 Wn.2d 514, 519 P.2d 981.

HUNTER, ASSOCIATE JUSTICE.

This case arises from a malpractice action instituted by the plaintiff (petitioner), Barbara Helling.

The plaintiff suffers from primary open angle glaucoma. Primary open angle glaucoma is essentially a condition of the eye in which there is an interference in the ease with which the nourishing fluids can flow out of the eye. Such a condition results in pressure gradually rising above the normal level to such an extent that damage is produced to the optic nerve and its fibers with resultant loss in vision. The first loss usually occurs in the periphery of the field of vision. The disease usually has few symptoms and, in the absence of a pressure test, is often undetected until the damage has become extensive and irreversible.

The defendants (respondents), Dr. Thomas F. Carey and Dr. Robert C. Laughlin, are partners who practice the medical specialty of ophthalmology. Ophthalmology involves the diagnosis and treatment of defects and diseases of the eye.

The plaintiff first consulted the defendants for myopia, nearsightedness, in 1959. At that time she was fitted with contact lenses. She next consulted the defendants in September, 1963, concerning irritation caused by the contact lenses. Additional consultations occurred in October, 1963; February, 1967; September, 1967; October, 1967; May, 1968; July, 1968; August, 1968; September, 1968; and October 1968. Until the October 1968 consultation, the defendants considered the plaintiff's visual problems to be related solely to complications associated with her contact lenses. On that occasion, the defendant, Dr. Carey, tested the plaintiff's eye pressure and field of vision for the first time. This test indicated that the plaintiff had glaucoma. The plaintiff, who was then 32 years of age, had essentially lost her peripheral vision and her central vision was reduced to approximately 5 degrees vertical by 10 degrees horizontal.

Thereafter, in August of 1969, after consulting other physicians, the plaintiff filed a complaint against the defendants alleging, among other things, that she sustained severe and permanent damage to her eyes as a proximate result of the defendants' negligence. During trial, the testimony of the medical experts for both the plaintiff and the defendants established that the standards of the profession for that specialty in the same or similar circumstances do not require routine pressure tests for glaucoma upon patients under 40 years of age. The reason the pressure test for glaucoma is not given as a regular practice to patients under the age of 40 is that the disease rarely occurs in this age group. Testimony indicated, however, that the standards of the profession do require pressure tests if the patient's complaints and symptoms reveal to the physician that glaucoma should be suspected.

The trial court entered judgment for the defendants following a defense verdict. The plaintiff thereupon appealed to the Court of Appeals, which affirmed the judgment of the trial court. * * * The plaintiff then petitioned this Court for review, which we granted.

In her petition for review, the plaintiff's primary contention is that under the facts of this case the trial judge erred in giving certain instructions to the jury and refusing her proposed instructions defining the standard of care which the law imposes upon an ophthalmologist. As a result, the plaintiff contends, in effect, that she was unable to argue her theory of the case to the jury that the standard of care for the specialty of ophthalmology was inadequate to protect the plaintiff from the incidence of glaucoma, and that the defendants, by reason of their special ability, knowledge and information, were negligent in failing to give the pressure test to the plaintiff at an earlier point in time which, if given, would have detected her condition and enabled the defendants to have averted the resulting substantial loss in her vision.

We find this to be a unique case. The testimony of the medical experts is undisputed concerning the standards of the profession for the specialty of ophthalmology. * * * The issue is whether the defendants' compliance with the standard of the profession of ophthalmology, which does not require the giving of a routine pressure test to persons under 40 years of age, should insulate them from liability under the facts in this case where the plaintiff has lost a substantial amount of her vision due to the failure of the defendants to timely give the pressure test to the plaintiff.

The defendants argue that the standard of the profession, which does not require the giving of a routine pressure test to persons under the age of 40, is adequate to insulate the defendants from liability for negligence because the risk of glaucoma is so rare in this age group. The testimony of the defendant, Dr. Carey, however, is revealing as follows:

Q. Now, when was it, actually, the first time any complaint was made to you by her of any field or visual field problem? A. Really, the first time that she really complained of a visual field problem was the August 30th date. [1968] Q. And how soon before the diagnosis was that? A. That was 30 days. We made it on October 1st. Q. And in your opinion, how long, as you now have the whole history and analysis and the diagnosis, how long had she had this glaucoma? A. I would think she probably had it ten years or longer. Q. Now, Doctor, there's been some reference to the matter of taking pressure checks of person over 40. What is the incidence of glaucoma, the statistics, with persons under 40? A. In the instance of glaucoma under the age of 40, is less than 100 to one per cent. The younger you get, the less the incidence. It is thought to be in the neighborhood of one in 25,000 people or less. Q. How about the incidence of glaucoma in people over 40? A. Incidence of glaucoma over 40 gets into the two to three per cent category, and hence, that's where there is this great big difference and that's why the standards around the world has been to check pressures from 40 on.

The incidence of glaucoma in one out of 25,000 persons under the age of 40 may appear quite minimal. However, that one person, the plaintiff in this instance, is entitled to the same protection, as afforded persons over 40, essential for timely detection of the evidence of glaucoma where it can be arrested to avoid the grave and devastating result of this disease. The test is a simple pressure test, relatively inexpensive. There is no judgment factor involved, and there is no doubt that by giving the test the evidence of glaucoma can be detected. The giving of the test is harmless if the physical condition of the eye permits. The testimony indicates that although the condition of the plaintiff's eyes might have at times prevented the defendants from administering the pressure test, there is an absence of evidence in the record that the test could not have been timely given.

Justice Holmes stated in Texas & Pac. Ry. v. Behymer, 189 U.S. 468, 470, 23 S.Ct. 622, 623, 47 L.Ed. 905 (1903):

> What usually is done may be evidence of what ought to be done, but what ought to be done is fixed by a standard of reasonable prudence, whether it usually is complied with or not.

In The T. J. Hooper, 60 F.2d 737, on page 740 (2d Cir.1932), Justice Hand stated:

> [I]n most cases reasonable prudence is in fact common prudence; but strictly it is never its measure; a whole calling may have unduly lagged in the adoption of new and available devices. It never may set its own tests, however persuasive be its usages. *Courts must in the end say what is required; there are precautions so imperative that even their universal disregard will not excuse their omission.*

(Italics ours.)

Under the facts of this case reasonable prudence required the timely giving of the pressure test to this plaintiff. The precaution of giving this test to detect the incidence of glaucoma to patients under 40 years of age is so imperative that irrespective of its disregard by the standards of the ophthalmology profession, it is the duty of the courts to say what is required to protect patients under 40 from the damaging results of glaucoma.

We therefore hold, as a matter of law, that the reasonable standard that should have been followed under the undisputed facts of this case was the timely giving of this simple, harmless pressure test to this plaintiff and that, in failing to do so, the defendants were negligent, which proximately resulted in the blindness sustained by the plaintiff for which the defendants are liable.

There are no disputed facts to submit to the jury on the issue of the defendants' liability. * * *

The judgment of the trial court and the decision of the Court of Appeals is reversed, and the case is remanded for a new trial on the issue of damages only.

UTTER, ASSOCIATE JUSTICE (concurring).

I concur in the result reached by the majority. I believe a greater duty of care could be imposed on the defendants than was established by their profession. The duty could be imposed when a disease, such as glaucoma, can be detected by a simple, well-known harmless test whose results are definitive and the disease can be successfully arrested by early detection, but where the effects of the disease are irreversible if undetected over a substantial period of time.

The difficulty with this approach is that we as judges, by using a negligence analysis, seem to be imposing a stigma of moral blame upon the doctors who, in this case, used all the precautions commonly prescribed by their profession in diagnosis and treatment. Lacking their training in this highly sophisticated profession, it seems illogical for this court to say they failed to exercise a reasonable standard of care. It seems to me we are, in reality, imposing liability, because, in choosing between an innocent plaintiff and a doctor, who acted reasonably according to his specialty but who could have prevented the full effects of this disease by administering a simple, harmless test and treatment, the plaintiff should not have to bear the risk of loss. As such, imposition of liability approaches that of strict liability.

* * *

In applying strict liability there are many situations where it is imposed for conduct which can be defined with sufficient precision to insure that application of a strict liability principle will not produce miscarriages of justice in a substantial number of cases. If the activity involved is one which can be defined with sufficient precision, that definition can serve as an accounting unit to which the costs of the activity may be allocated with some certainty and precision. With this possible, strict liability serves a compensatory function in situations where the defendant is, through the use of insurance, the financially more responsible person. Peck, Negligence and Liability Without Fault in Tort Law, [46 Wash.L.Rev. (1971)] *supra* at 240, 241.

If the standard of a reasonably prudent specialist is, in fact, inadequate to offer reasonable protection to the plaintiff, then liability can be imposed without fault. To do so under the narrow facts of this case does not offend my sense of justice. * * *

The failure of plaintiff to raise this theory at the trial and to propose instructions consistent with it should not deprive her of the right to resolve the case on this theory on appeal. Where this court has authoritatively stated the law, the parties are bound by those principles until they have been overruled. Acceptance of those principles at trial does not constitute a waiver or estop appellants from adapting their cause on appeal to such a rule as might be declared if the earlier precedent is overruled. * * *

Finley and Hamilton, JJ., concur.

Notes

1. The *Helling* case is somewhat unique in that it allows the jury to find the prevailing standard of medical care inadequate. There are some earlier cases where the jury was permitted to find physicians negligent even in the absence of any expert testimony as to the standard of good medical practice but these cases involved instances of clear mistakes. *See, e.g.,* Steinke v. Bell, 32 N.J.Super. 67, 107 A.2d 825 (1954) (dentist removed wrong tooth); Evans v. Roberts, 172 Iowa 653, 154 N.W. 923 (1915)(tongue cut off in operation for

removal of adenoids). One line of cases possibly analogous to *Helling* involves surgical implements, typically sponges, left in the bodies of patients. Attempts by the surgeon to escape liability on the ground that the custom of the profession is to delegate responsibility for counting the implements have been rejected. *See, e.g.*, Ales v. Ryan, 8 Cal.2d 82, 64 P.2d 409 (1936); Ault v. Hall, 119 Ohio St. 422, 164 N.E. 518 (1928). What made these cases worth litigating from the defendants' point of view is the fact that at one time many courts treated the surgeons and nurses as something like independent contractors who were responsible to the patient for their own negligence but not for the negligence of the other members of the operating team. *See, e.g.*, Guell v. Tenney, 262 Mass. 54, 159 N.E. 451 (1928)(surgeon not responsible for failure of nurse to keep accurate sponge count); Hale v. Atkins, 215 Mo.App. 380, 256 S.W. 544 (1923). To avoid this line of cases, the plaintiff would argue that the obligation to make sure that no surgical implements were left in the patient was that of the surgeon. The modern trend, however, is to hold both the surgeon and the hospital responsible for the activities of the operating crew, who are usually employees of the hospital. *See, e.g.*, Tonsic v. Wagner, 458 Pa. 246, 329 A.2d 497 (1974); *cf.* Sparger v. Worley Hosp., Inc., 547 S.W.2d 582 (Tex.1977). With regard to the surgeon, the key factor is the right to control the actions of the other members of the operating team. The surgeon will also be responsible for adequately supervising post-operative care. *See, e.g.*, Bateman v. Rosenberg, 525 S.W.2d 753 (Mo.App.1975).

2. The *Helling* decision has been severely criticized. *See* R. Pearson, *The Role of Custom in Medical Malpractice Cases*, 51 Ind.L.J. 528 (1976). In 1975, the Washington legislature enacted a statute declaring that, in a medical malpractice action, the plaintiff must establish that "the defendant * * * failed to exercise that degree of skill, care and learning possessed [at that time] by other persons in the same profession * * * but in no event shall the provisions of this section apply to an action based on the failure to obtain the informed consent of a patient." Wash.Rev.Code Ann. § 4.24.290. The words in brackets were added in 1983. Why do you think they were added? *See also id.* at § 7.70.040. In Gates v. Jensen, 92 Wn.2d 246, 595 P.2d 919 (1979), a case somewhat similar to *Helling*, the court ruled that the statute did not abrogate "the *Helling* rule" that reasonable prudence may sometimes require a higher standard of care than that followed by the profession. The statute would only apply if the defendant and other ophthalmologists did not *possess* the skill necessary to test for the plaintiff's glaucoma.

3. Utter, J.'s, call for strict liability in medical treatment cases, in his concurrence in *Helling* recalls Traynor, J.'s, call for strict liability in products liability in his concurring opinion in Escola v. Coca Cola Bottling Co., 24 Cal.2d 453, 150 P.2d 436 (1944), quoted at p. 630, *infra*. A similar call for strict liability for the untoward results of medical treatment was made by Tobriner, J., in a concurring opinion in Clark v. Gibbons, 66 Cal.2d 399, 414, 58 Cal.Rptr. 125, 135, 136, 426 P.2d 525, 535, 536 (1967). It remains to be seen whether these calls for strict liability will prove to be as prescient as that of Traynor, J. For a reference to cases rejecting strict liability in medical treatment, *see* A. Belsky, *Injury as a Matter of Law: Is This the Answer to the Wrongful Life Dilemma?*, 22 U.Balt.L.Rev. 185, 258ff (1993). In recent years no-fault plans have been suggested as the way to deal with the problems of patients who are injured in the course of medical treatment. *See* C. Havighurst, *"Medical Adversity Insurance"—Has Its Time Come?*, 1975 Duke L.J. 1233. *See also* J. O'Connell, *Elective No–Fault Liability by Contract—With or Without an En-*

abling Statute, 1975 U.Ill.L.F. 59 (O'Connell's plan would apply to more than just the providers of health-care services). More recent work includes J. O'Connell, *Offers that Can't Be Refused: Foreclosure of Personal Injury Claims by Defendants' Prompt Tender of Claimants' Net Economic Loss*, 77 Nw. U.L.Rev. 589 (1982); J. O'Connell, *Neo-No-Fault Remedies for Medical Injuries: Coordinated Statutory and Contractual Alternatives*, 49 Law & Contemp.Probs. 125 (1986); L. Tancredi, *Designing a No-Fault Alternative*, 49 Law & Contemp.Probs. 277 (1986). A good discussion of the various alternatives proposed is contained in C. Havighurst, Health Care Law and Policy 906–18 (1988). The problem confronting these schemes is that unfortunate results from medical treatment can be regarded either as incidents of the original disease or condition or as the results of some sort of error committed in the healthcare system. Once one eliminates the question of fault, how does one determine which negative outcomes are compensable? Under the Medical Adversity Insurance discussed by Havighurst, representative groups of clinicians would establish in advance a list of potential injuries as a result of treatment that would probably have been avoidable by adequate conformity to accepted medical practice. Persons suffering those complications would be automatically compensated, without being required to prove fault.

4. For a good discussion of the present state of the evolving health care regime in the United States, *see* K. Abraham and P. Weiler, *Enterprise Medical Liability and the Evolution of the American Health Care System*, 108 Harv. L.Rev. 381 (1994). The rising cost of medical malpractice insurance has led to some legislative attempts to regulate the judicial treatment of malpractice claims, by providing, for example, for submission of claims to screening panels and for settlement conferences and sometimes even to limit the amount that may be recovered in actions for malpractice. *See* D. Nye *et al.*, *The Causes of the Medical Malpractice Crisis: An Analysis of Claims Data and Insurance Company Finances*, 76 Geo.L.J. 1495 (1988)(discusses the situation in Florida in some detail); D. Smith, *Battling a Receding Tort Frontier: Constitutional Attacks on Medical Malpractice Laws*, 38 Okla.L.Rev. 195 (1985); M. Redish, *Legislative Response to the Medical Malpractice Insurance Crisis: Constitutional Implications*, 55 Tex.L.Rev. 759 (1977); Commentary, *Medical Malpractice: The Second Wave of "Reform"*, 37 Ala.L.Rev. 419 (1986); Note, *Legislative Responses to the Medical Malpractice Crisis*, 39 Ohio St.L.J. 855 (1978); Comment, *An Analysis of State Legislative Responses to the Medical Malpractice Crisis*, 1977 Duke L.J. 1147. Damage limitations were struck down in Lucas v. United States, 757 S.W.2d 687 (Tex.1988)($500,000 total limit with exception for cost of hospital and other custodial care); Smith v. Department of Ins., 507 So.2d 1080 (Fla.1987)($450,000 limit on non-economic damages); Carson v. Maurer, 120 N.H. 925, 424 A.2d 825 (1980)($250,000 for non-economic loss); Arneson v. Olson, 270 N.W.2d 125 (N.D.1978)($300,000 total recovery); Wright v. Central Du Page Hospital Association, 63 Ill.2d 313, 347 N.E.2d 736 (1976)($500,000 total recovery). The New Hampshire Legislature responded to the *Carson* case by enacting, in 1986, a provision limiting total recovery for non-economic loss in all personal injury actions to $875,000. N.H.Rev.Stat.Ann. 508: 4–d. This statute was held unconstitutional in Brannigan v. Usitalo, 134 N.H. 50, 587 A.2d 1232 (1991). Statutes limiting recovery in malpractice cases have been upheld in Etheridge v. Medical Center Hosps., 237 Va. 87, 376 S.E.2d 525 (1989)($750,000 limit on total recovery; now increased to $1,000,000 for more recent injuries); Fein v. Permanente Med. Group, 38 Cal.3d 137, 211 Cal.Rptr. 368, 695 P.2d 665 (1985) *appeal dismissed*

474 U.S. 892, 106 S.Ct. 214, 88 L.Ed.2d 215 ($250,000 limit on non-economic loss); Prendergast v. Nelson, 199 Neb. 97, 256 N.W.2d 657 (1977)($500,000 total recovery). The subject is discussed again in greater detail in Chapter Ten, p. 781–84, *infra*, which is devoted to the question of damages and in which we shall have occasion to discuss attempts to impose limitations on damages in a broader context than that of merely medical malpractice.

5. For discussion as to why, from the perspective of economics, one might expect to see an increase in malpractice claims see M. Grady, *Why are People Negligent? Technology, Nondurable Precautions, and the Medical Malpractice Explosion,* 82 Nw.U.L.Rev. 293 (1988).

MILLER v. KENNEDY

Court of Appeals of Washington, Division 1, 1974.
11 Wn.App. 272, 522 P.2d 852, *affirmed per curiam* (and adopting Court of Appeals opinion), 85 Wash.2d 151, 530 P.2d 334 (1975).

CALLOW, JUDGE.

The plaintiff, Richard R. Miller, appeals from the trial court's refusal to grant a motion for a new trial or judgment n. o. v. following a verdict for the defendant in a medical malpractice case. * * *

Dr. Kennedy is a board certified specialist in internal medicine, with sub-specialties in heart and nephrology, practicing in Tacoma, Washington. The plaintiff first consulted with Dr. Kennedy on January 14, 1970, complaining of fatigue, lightheadedness, tiring out easily and becoming shortwinded with exercise. Dr. Kennedy examined Mr. Miller, wrote down his medical history and took an electrocardiogram. At that time, Dr. Kennedy found that Mr. Miller had first degree heart block. On January 20, 1970, Mr. Miller returned for further examination and was found to have second and third degree heart block. Mr. Miller was immediately hospitalized and placed in intensive care. On January 26, 1970, Mr. Miller was removed from intensive care and placed in a ward.

Many tests were performed to assist Dr. Kennedy in his efforts to diagnose the cause of Mr. Miller's heart disease. Various tests showed evidence of a kidney problem, and therefore Dr. Kennedy felt that a kidney biopsy was necessary. Witnesses for both parties testified that the decision to perform the biopsy was not malpractice. However, Mr. Miller testified that Dr. Kennedy did not advise him of the risk of the loss of the kidney nor explain the alternative ways of performing biopsies. The plaintiff further testified that he would not have consented to the biopsy had he known there was a risk of loss of the kidney. Dr. Kennedy testified that he did so inform the patient, and this testimony is substantially corroborated by the hospital record and by the prior conduct of the doctor in which he diagramed and explained in detail to Mr. Miller what was happening in his heart.

In performing the biopsy, the biopsy needle was inserted some 3 or 4 centimeters above the intended biopsy site. The kidney is encased in an outer capsule covering, inside of which there is an area called the cortex. The cortex surrounds the medulla which contains the nephrons, which are filtering, absorbing and secreting units doing the essential work of the kidney. The process of forming urine begins when arterial blood flows into a tuft of capillaries, called the glomerulus. The glomerulus is enclosed in a double membrance which leads into a tubule. The glomerulus, membranes and tubule form a single nephron. The glomerulus initially filters out some of the passing blood as do the membranes. The blood fluid then enters the tubule of the nephron where useful sugars, salts and water are reabsorbed by small capillaries and returned to the main bloodstream. The capillaries in turn secrete ammonia through the tubule wall into the fluid remaining which is flowing into the collecting tubule. The resulting comparatively small amount of waste is urine. The medulla area of the kidney contains approximately two and a half million nephrons. Inside the medulla area is the calyceal area, the collecting system of the kidney.

The plaintiff alleged that the biopsy needle was negligently inserted penetrating the calyceal system of the kidney causing damage and injury which eventually resulted in loss of the kidney. The defendant contended that the calyceal area was not punctured and that a small artery may have been injured. There is no dispute in the testimony that the loss of the kidney proximately resulted from the kidney biopsy, that the kidney was healthy prior to the biopsy and that the biopsy specimens were negative as to any of the conditions for which the biopsy was performed. The position of the plaintiff is that the defendant violated the standard of care while the defendant states that the standard of care was met and claims that an unfortunate chance led to the result.

Following the biopsy, the plaintiff remained in the hospital from January 29, 1970, until February 26, 1970, suffering continual bleeding from his kidney and considerable pain. On February 26, 1970, Dr. Kennedy called upon another physician, Dr. Osborne, to examine Mr. Miller. In spite of his weakened condition and extensive bleeding, Mr. Miller was released from the hospital. Mr. Miller was again, at his own insistence, examined by Dr. Osborne, who removed blood clots from his bladder and returned him home. After the condition returned, Mr. Miller was again hospitalized on March 30, 1970. It was suggested that an operation be performed to see if the upper portion of the kidney, where the bleeding was taking place, could be surgically removed in an attempt to save the balance of the kidney. On April 4, the date set for the surgical procedure, Mr. Miller hemorrhaged, and the surgical procedure was expedited. Dr. Osborne performed this surgery, attempted to remove the upper portion of the kidney, but was unable to do so. Finally, he was required to do a complete nephrectomy, removing the entire kidney. Mr. Miller was released from the hospital on April 10, 1970.

* * *

The plaintiff has objected to the instruction given on informed consent claiming it is inadequate under the criteria laid down by ZeBarth v. Swedish Hosp. Medical Center, 81 Wash.2d 12, 499 P.2d 1 (1972), wrongfully places the burden of proving the failure to inform upon the plaintiff and wrongfully imposes on the plaintiff the obligation to prove by medical testimony a breach of a medical standard of disclosure. The plaintiff claims his proposed instruction on informed consent should have been given. * * * In 1972 at the time ZeBarth v. Swedish Hosp. was being decided, Canterbury v. Spence, 150 U.S.App.D.C. 263, 464 F.2d 772 (1972),

Cobbs v. Grant, 8 Cal.3d 229, 104 Cal.Rptr. 505, 502 P.2d 1 (1972) and Wilkinson v. Vesey, 295 A.2d 676 (R.I.1972), as well as other cases, were also in the process of decision. We deem it appropriate to review the plaintiff's assignment of error guided primarily by the pronouncement of our highest court in *ZeBarth* but also to take notice of the decisions reached in other jurisdictions which enlighten this area. We review the instruction given, and the instruction proposed cognizant of the fact that at the time that this case was in trial in 1972, few of the decisions which now reflect the direction of this developing area of the law had yet been published. (Appendix I reflects the plaintiff's proposed instruction and the court's instruction. Both contain misleading flaws and neither is approved in toto.) * * *

The contest over whether the failure to inform a patient of the material risks of a medical procedure constitutes an assault upon the patient or a negligent breach of a physician's duty to acquaint the patient with the perils of each medical course of action has been laid to rest. The performance of an operation without first obtaining any consent thereto may fall within the concepts of assault and battery as an intentional tort, but the failure to tell the patient about the perils he faces is the breach of a duty and is appropriately considered under negligence concepts. * * * As stated in *Wilkinson* 295 A.2d on page 686:

> The prevailing view, however, classifies the physician's duty in this regard as a question of negligence because of the absence of the elements of any wilful intent by the physician to injure his patient.

The relationship between a doctor and his patient is one of trust calling for a recognition by the physician of the ignorance and helplessness of the patient regarding his own physical condition. * * * The duty of the doctor to inform the patient is a fiduciary duty. * * * The patient is entitled to rely upon the physician to tell him what he needs to know about the condition of his own body. The patient has the right to chart his own destiny, and the doctor must supply the patient with the material facts the patient will need in order to intelligently chart that destiny with dignity. * * *

The scope of the duty to disclose information concerning the treatment proposed, other treatments and the risks of each course of action and of no treatment at all is measured by the patient's need to know. The inquiry as to each item of information which the doctor knows or should know about the patient's physical condition is "Would the patient as a human being consider this item in choosing his or her course of treatment?" Cobbs v. Grant referring to the *Canterbury* case states, 104 Cal.Rptr. on page 514, 502 P.2d on page 10:

> The court in Canterbury v. Spence, supra, 464 F.2d 772, 784, bluntly observed: "Nor can we ignore the fact that to bind the disclosure obligation to medical usage is to arrogate the decision on revelation to the physician alone. Respect for the patient's right of self-determination on particular therapy demands a standard set by law for physicians rather than one which physicians may or may not impose upon themselves." Unlimited discretion in the physician is irreconcilable with the basic right of the patient to make the ultimate informed

decision regarding the course of treatment to which he knowledgeably consents to be subjected.

Indeed, it is the prerogative of the patient to choose his treatment. A doctor may not withhold from the patient the knowledge necessary for the exercise of that right. Without it, the prerogative is valueless. * * *

The burden of proving that a physician failed to inform the plaintiff-patient of the available courses of treatment or failed to warn of the consequential hazards of each choice of treatment is on the plaintiff. It is the plaintiff who must initially establish the existence of the elements of an action based on the informed consent doctrine, i.e., the existence of a material risk unknown to the patient, the failure to disclose it, that the patient would have chosen a different course if the risk had been disclosed and resulting injury. * * * The burden of proving a defense when failure to disclose has been established is on the doctor. * * *

* * *

Those elements which are the province of the medical profession must be established by the testimony of medical experts in the field of inquiry. Thus, the existence of the risks and alternatives which were present in the particular physical condition would be beyond the knowledge of the layman and would have to be established by medical testimony. On the other hand, those matters which are not within the special province of the training and experience of doctors may be established by the testimony of any witness with knowledge of the particular inquiry, such as whether the patient knew of the risk or whether the average patient would consider the risk in making a decision. * * * There is no need to prove what other doctors might tell their patients in similar circumstances. The doctor has a duty to disclose the material risks as a matter of law. The testimony of medical experts is not necessary to establish the duty to disclose that which the law requires. Once the existence of a risk has been established by expert medical testimony, there is no need to take the next step and also prove by expert medical testimony that the doctor should have told the patient about the risk. Once it has been established by expert medical testimony that a risk existed, then the existence of the risk is the patient's business; and it is not for the medical profession to establish a criteria for the dissemination of information to the patient based upon what doctors feel the patient should be told. * * * The patient has a right to know and the doctor has the duty to inform the patient whether the doctor wants to or not. The fiduciary duty of the doctor requires disclosure. There is no room for paternalism or for overprotectiveness. * * *

We hold, therefore, that a plaintiff who alleges that a physician failed to warn him of material risks inherent in his treatment, and to advise him of feasible alternatives, need not produce expert medical testimony that it is the custom of physicians in the same or similar localities to give such warnings in comparable cases. The duty to warn and to advise of alternatives does not arise from and is not limited by the custom of physicians in the locality. Rather, it exists as a matter of law if (1) the risk of injury inherent in the treatment is material; (2) there are feasible alternative courses available; and (3) the plaintiff can be advised of the risks and alternatives without detriment to his wellbeing. If there is evidence tending to prove all these elements, the plaintiff is entitled to have his case submitted to the jury under proper instructions. In most cases, expert medical testimony will be necessary to establish each of the three elements.

* * *

The patient is endowed with the right to know each hazard which the usual person would utilize in reaching his decision. When a reasonable person in the patient's position probably would attach significance to the specific risk in deciding on treatment, the risk is material and must be disclosed. * * *

Situations may be envisioned where the disclosure of a risk to a patient would be detrimental to the patient. The existence of such a situation is a matter of defense for the doctor. The doctor may present evidence to justify the failure to disclose by his own testimony or by the testimony of other lay or expert witnesses. The doctor may establish the existence of a standard of nondisclosure by medical experts in his field or practice, but it is for the jury to accept or reject whether any standard of nondisclosure should deprive a patient of his right of self-determination. The situations where there was either no requirement of disclosure or where there was a reason for nondisclosure have been illustrated in Holt v. Nelson, Wash. App., 523 P.2d 211 (1974). Included are mental incompetence, emergencies, and potential physical trauma or mental disturbance to the patient. * * * A review of the defenses reveals that the validity of a defense is considered from the standpoint of concern for the well-being of the patient.

The jury is capable of deciding whether the doctor did not tell the patient about something that should have been revealed. The jury does not need testimony from physicians about the norm of disclosure in the community. The usual conduct of doctors in this matter is not relevant to the establishment of the liability which is imposed by law. The jury, as lay people, are equipped to place themselves in the position of a patient and decide whether, under the circumstances, the patient should have been told. * * *

An instruction outlining the elements of the negligence doctrine of "informed consent" should set forth that it is the duty of a physician or surgeon to disclose to a patient all relevant, material information the patient will need to make an informed decision on whether to consent to or reject the proposed treatment or operation. The jury should also be instructed that the plaintiff-patient must prove by a preponderance of the evidence that (1) the physician failed to inform the patient of a material risk involved in submitting to the proposed course of treatment; (2) the patient consented to the proposed treatment without being aware of or fully informed of the material risks of each choice of treatment and of no treatment at all; (3) a reasonable, prudent patient probably would not have consented to the treatment when informed of the material risks; and (4) the treatment chosen caused injury to the patient. It is also appropriate to instruct the jury that in the event a patient has consented to a proposed treatment or operation, a failure of the physician or surgeon to fully inform the patient of all of the material risks present in his medical situation before obtaining such consent is negligence; and a physician or surgeon is liable for any injury proximately resulting from the treatment if a reasonably prudent person in the patient's position would not have consented to the treatment if adequately informed of all the significant perils.[11]

The instruction given by the court apprised the jury that the physician must disclose all material facts to the patient. However, the instruction was misleading in emphasizing that the duty to inform existed regardless of negligence or the exercise of due care by the physician "in the procedure itself" without making it clear also that the duty to inform of the risks inherent in the treatment existed as a matter of law. The small but important transgression of the instruction is one of misdirection. The instruction also stressed that the plaintiff was required to prove that he, the plaintiff-patient, would not have consented to the treatment had he been fully informed; while the proper approach requires the plaintiff to prove instead that a reasonable person in the plaintiff-patient's position would not have consented. * * * The instruction incorrectly stated the precepts of the law of informed consent. * * *

* * *

Reversed and remanded.

Appendix I

The plaintiff's proposed instruction reads:

You are instructed that a patient has the right to determine what shall be done with his own body. A surgeon must obtain from the patient consent to perform a surgical procedure, such as a kidney biopsy. The consent of the patient must be an informed consent, that is, the physician must inform the patient of all material facts which are necessary to form the basis of an intelligent consent by the patient, and, in that regard, must inform him of the nature and consequences of the procedure and the reasonably foreseeable risks. If the patient inquires further as to any or all risks involved, the physician must make a complete disclosure of all facts and risks. Surgery performed, without disclosure by the surgeon as above described, constitutes an assault and battery. If you find from the evidence that the defendant physician failed to properly inform the plaintiff as above described, and further find that the plaintiff would not have consented to the surgical procedure if he had been informed, and that the plaintiff was injured as a result of submitting to the procedure, then you should find the defendant liable to the plaintiff for the injuries and damages resulting from said surgical procedure.

The court's instruction reads:

---

11. * * * The trial court's instruction was faulty also in telling the jury to consider whether the plaintiff would have consented rather than to consider whether a reasonably prudent patient in the patient's position would have consented.

The instruction proposed by the plaintiff affirmatively stated the duty of the doctor to inform the patient of material risks as a matter of law. This was proper. Its defect was to introduce the concept of surgery without informed consent as imposing liability on an assault and battery theory. That intentional tort theory is accepted currently only where treatment is performed in the absence of any consent at all.

Appropriately, neither the proposed nor the given instruction would have instructed the jury to measure the duty of the doctor to inform his patient of the material risks of treatment against a standard of disclosure established by expert medical testimony.

Under the legal doctrine of "informed consent," a patient may recover from a physician for damages proximately caused by a procedure performed without the patient's "informed consent," irrespective of any negligence or lack of negligence of the physician in the procedure itself.

In order to recover on this basis in this case, plaintiff must prove by a preponderance of the evidence:

    1.   That he was not informed of a reasonably foreseeable risk or that he inquired of defendant as to all risks and was not informed thereof;

    2.   That he would not have consented to the procedure had he been so informed;

    3.   That he has been injured as a proximate result of the procedure.

Appendix II

The *Statement of a Patient's Bill of Rights* as promulgated in 1972 by the American Hospital Association includes the following provisions:

    1.   The patient has the right to considerate and respectful care.

    2.   The patient has the right to obtain from his physician complete current information concerning his diagnosis, treatment, and prognosis in terms the patient can be reasonably expected to understand. When it is not medically advisable to give such information to the patient, the information should be made available to an appropriate person in his behalf. He has the right to know, by name, the physician responsible for his care.

    3.   The patient has the right to receive from his physician information necessary to give informed consent prior to the start of any procedure and/or treatment. Except in emergencies, such information for informed consent should include but not necessarily be limited to the specific procedure and/or treatment, the medically significant risks involved, and the probable duration of incapacitation. Where medically significant alternatives for care or treatment exist, or when the patient requests information concerning medical alternatives, the patient has the right to such information. The patient also has the right to know the name of the person responsible for the procedures and/or treatment.

    4.   The patient has the right to refuse treatment to the extent permitted by law and to be informed of the medical consequences of his action.

* * *

    8.   The patient has the right to obtain information as to any relationship of his hospital to other health care and educational institutions insofar as his care is concerned. The patient has the right to obtain information as to the existence of any professional relationships among individuals, by name, who are treating him.

9. The patient has the right to be advised if the hospital proposes to engage in or perform human experimentation affecting his care or treatment. The patient has the right to refuse to participate in such research projects.

10. The patient has the right to expect reasonable continuity of care. He has the right to know in advance what appointment times and physicians are available and where. The patient has the right to expect that the hospital will provide a mechanism whereby he is informed by his physician of the patient's continuing health care requirements following discharge.

Notes

1. Canterbury v. Spence, 464 F.2d 772 (D.C.Cir.1972), was immediately perceived to be an important case. In describing the physician's duty to disclose the court relied heavily on J. Waltz & T. Scheuneman, *Informed Consent to Therapy*, 64 Nw.U.L.Rev. 628 (1970) and, to a lesser extent, Comment, *Informed Consent in Medical Malpractice*, 55 Cal.L.Rev. 1396 (1967). As the *Miller* case indicates, *Canterbury* was soon expressly followed in a number of jurisdictions. Spottswood Robinson, J., writing for the court in *Canterbury*, made some important observations on the possible exceptions to the physicians duty to disclose:

> Two exceptions to the general rule of disclosure have been noted by the courts. Each is in the nature of a physician's privilege not to disclose, and the reasoning underlying them is appealing. Each, indeed, is but a recognition that, as important as is the patient's right to know, it is greatly outweighed by the magnitudinous circumstances giving rise to the privilege. The first comes into play when the patient is unconscious or otherwise incapable of consenting, and harm from a failure to treat is imminent and outweighs any harm threatened by the proposed treatment. When a genuine emergency of that sort arises, it is settled that the impracticality of conferring with the patient dispenses with need for it. Even in situations of that character the physician should, as current law requires, attempt to secure a relative's consent if possible. But if time is too short to accommodate discussion, obviously the physician should proceed with the treatment.

> The second exception obtains when risk-disclosure poses such a threat of detriment to the patient as to become unfeasible or contraindicated from a medical point of view. It is recognized that patients occasionally become so ill or emotionally distraught on disclosure as to foreclose a rational decision, or complicate or hinder the treatment, or perhaps even pose psychological damage to the patient.[94] Where that is so, the cases have generally held that the physician is armed with a privilege to keep the information from the patient,[95] and we think it clear that portents of that type may justify the physician in action he deems medically warranted. The critical inquiry is whether the physician responded to a sound medical

94. See, *e.g.*, Salgo v. Leland Stanford, Jr. Univ. Bd. of Trustees, * * *, 317 P.2d at 181 (1957); Waltz & Scheuneman, Informed Consent to Therapy, 64 Nw.U.L.Rev. 628, 641–43 (1970).

95. *E.g.*, Roberts v. Wood, 206 F.Supp. 579, 583 (S.D.Ala.1962); Nishi v. Hartwell, 52 Haw. 188, 473 P.2d 116, 119 (1970); * * * Ball v. Mallinkrodt Chem. Works, 53 Tenn. App. 218, 381 S.W.2d 563, 567–568 (1964).

judgment that communication of the risk information would present a threat to the patient's well-being.

The physician's privilege to withhold information for therapeutic reasons must be carefully circumscribed, however, for otherwise it might devour the disclosure rule itself. The privilege does not accept the paternalistic notion that the physician may remain silent simply because divulgence might prompt the patient to forego therapy the physician feels the patient really needs. That attitude presumes instability or perversity for even the normal patient, and runs counter to the foundation principle that the patient should and ordinarily can make the choice for himself. Nor does the privilege contemplate operation save where the patient's reaction to risk information, as reasonably foreseen by the physician, is menacing. And even in a situation of that kind, disclosure to a close relative with a view to securing consent to the proposed treatment may be the only alternative open to the physician.

464 F.2d at 788–89 (some footnotes omitted). The question of whether full disclosure to a "close relative" can affect the legal position of an adult, who has not been adjudged mentally incompetent, is an interesting one that is not without difficulty. On the question of how to measure the physician's duty to inform a patient of the risks of treatment, *see* Annot., 88 A.L.R.3d 1008 (1978). Not only must a physician disclose the risks of side-effects of treatment, but recent cases have also stressed the physician's duty to explain the risks of non-treatment. *See* Truman v. Thomas, 27 Cal.3d 285, 165 Cal.Rptr. 308, 611 P.2d 902 (1980) (woman who refused to have Pap smear and died of cervical cancer). Scholarly discussions include M. Shultz, *From Informed Consent to Patient Choice: A New Protected Interest*, 95 Yale L.J. 219 (1985); T. LeBlang and J. King, *Tort Liability for Non–Disclosure: Physicians Legal Obligations to Disclose Patient Illness and Injury*, 89 Dick.L.Rev. 1 (1984).

In Sidaway v. Governors of the Bethlem Royal Hosp., [1985] A.C. 871, 2 W.L.R. 480, 1 All E.R. 643, the House of Lords, with Lord Scarman dissenting, refused to adopt the perspective enunciated in *Canterbury v. Spence* and reaffirmed that, under English Law, the adequacy of the physician's disclosure would be judged from the perspective of competent and respected professional opinion. Nevertheless several of the Law Lords who formed the majority on this issue were prepared to concede that there might be some situations where the trial judge might conclude that disclosure of a particular risk was so obviously necessary to an informed choice on the part of the patient that no reasonably prudent physician would fail to make that disclosure. It was also conceded that, if the patient makes a specific inquiry, the physician is under an obligation to respond truthfully.

2. In *Canterbury v. Spence*, the court indicated that the action could be brought on either a battery or negligence theory. 464 F.2d at 793–94. As the *Miller* court indicates, subsequent courts dealing with cases involving inadequate consent rather than a total absence of consent seem to prefer the negligence theory. Determining the adequacy of the physician's disclosure from the point of view of the patient rather than the custom of the profession would appear to favor the plaintiff-patient. On the other hand, the use of a negligence rather than a battery theory requires the plaintiff to show some physical injury before he can recover anything at all and also to show that a reasonable patient would have refused the treatment if he had been adequately advised. The movement from battery to negligence in the adequacy of consent

cases is criticized in J. Katz, *Informed Consent—A Fairy Tale? Law's Vision*, 39 U.Pitt.L.Rev. 137 (1977). Katz traces the development of the confused legal treatment of adequacy of consent cases to Salgo v. Leland Stanford, Junior University Board of Trustees, 154 Cal.App.2d 560, 317 P.2d 170 (1957), cited and relied upon by the court in *Canterbury v. Spence*. As we have already seen, *supra* p. 74, under English Law, as expounded in the Sidaway case, *supra*, the adequacy of disclosure is also now considered under a negligence theory. The result of *Miller v. Kennedy*, the principal case, has been essentially codified in Wash.Rev.Code Ann. §§ 7.70.050–7.70.060.

3. In a later chapter, see p. 496, *infra*, we shall discuss the "good-samaritan" statutes which were enacted to encourage the rendition of *emergency* assistance at the scene of an accident. While these statutes may effect the degree of care that a physician is legally obliged to give in an emergency situation—the statutes usually absolve a provider of care unless at least "gross negligence" is shown—they should have no effect upon the physician's duty to disclose to the patient the scope and effect of the treatment. Obviously, however, the existence of an emergency situation will itself have some effect on the adequacy of the physician's efforts to discharge his duty to disclose.

4. *Other types of malpractice.*

a. *Attorneys.* In Lucas v. Hamm, 56 Cal.2d 583, 15 Cal.Rptr. 821, 364 P.2d 685 (1961), *cert. denied* 368 U.S. 987, 82 S.Ct. 603, 7 L.Ed.2d 525 (1962), an attorney prepared a will which violated the rule against perpetuities. The Supreme Court of California affirmed the dismissal of the resulting malpractice action. Given the complexity of the legal issues involved, the fact that the attorney made a mistake did not mean that he was negligent. Subsequently, *Lucas v. Hamm* was distinguished in Smith v. Lewis, 13 Cal.3d 349, 118 Cal.Rptr. 621, 530 P.2d 589 (1975). In that case, the defendant attorney, representing the wife in a divorce action, had failed to claim, as community property, retirement benefits paid to the husband by the State of California and the husband's future retirement benefits from the federal government for service in the National Guard. The court held that at the time he filed the papers in the divorce action (1967), the defendant should have known that the state retirement benefits were community property. As to the federal benefits, the question was more difficult, but the defendant should have known that there was a good chance that the California courts would classify them as community property. When the issue was litigation strategy, there was room for the exercise of judgment but "[t]here is nothing strategic or tactical about ignorance," quoting Pineda v. Craven, 424 F.2d 369, 372 (9th Cir.1970). Clark, J., dissented from the court's decision on the ground that even a better prepared attorney might have made the same mistake as the defendant. It should be noted that, in McCarty v. McCarty, 453 U.S. 210, 101 S.Ct. 2728, 69 L.Ed.2d 589 (1981), the Court held that military pensions are *not* subject to division under state community property laws. In response to strong reactions to that decision, Congress enacted the Uniformed Services Former Spouses' Protection Act, P.L. 97–252, Sept. 8, 1982. This act, the principal provisions of which are codified as 10 U.S.C. § 1408, permits state courts to treat retired pay as the property of either the retired "member" or of the "member and his spouse." It has been held, however, that, under the act, retired pay which has been waived by the member in order to receive disability pay—which the member would want to do, if eligible for disability pay, because disability payments are not subject to federal or state income tax—cannot be treated as community property. Mansell v. Mansell, 490 U.S. 581, 109 S.Ct. 2023, 104

L.Ed.2d 675 (1989). Other provisions of the act concern survivors benefits and medical benefits.

The subject of legal malpractice is discussed in G. Smith. III, *The Locality Standard of Care in Legal Malpractice Actions: What Principles Govern Us When We Break Our Own Rules?*, 3 Geo.J.Legal Ethics 581 (1990); D. Gillen, *Legal Malpractice*, 12 Washburn L.J. 281 (1973); D. Haughey, *Lawyers' Malpractice: A Comparative Appraisal*, 48 Notre Dame Law. 888 (1973)(comparison between legal and medical malpractice). A good discussion of the causation question that so concerned Clark, J., is contained in Note, *The Standard of Proof of Causation in Legal Malpractice Cases*, 63 Cornell L.Rev. 666 (1978). This note proposes that, in place of a "but for" test that is often conjoined with a certainty requirement, the courts should use a "lost substantial possibility of recovery" standard. The note also discusses cases suggesting that, where an attorney is charged with malpractice in conducting a case that the attorney filed as the plaintiff's lawyer, the fact that the attorney himself filed the case shifts the burden of persuasion to the attorney on the issue of whether the original and unsuccessful action was likely to have succeeded on the merits if it had been properly handled. *See also,* J. Koffler, *Legal Malpractice Damages in a Trial Within a Trial—A Critical Analysis of Unique Concepts: Areas of Unconscionability,* 73 Marq.L.Rev. 40 (1989). For the proposal that, for certain routine tasks performed by professional people that do not involve the exercise of discretion and are more akin to administrative duties, strict liability should be imposed, see J. Mallor, *Liability Without Fault for Professional Services: Toward a New Standard of Professional Accountability,* 9 Seton Hall L.Rev. 474 (1978).

There are a number of very significant differences between legal malpractice and medical malpractice. For example, in legal malpractice, the plaintiff is almost always seeking to recover for economic loss unrelated to any physical injury to himself or his property. In addition, there is a good chance that the plaintiff in a legal malpractice case will be someone other than a client of the negligent lawyer. He may, for example, be the beneficiary of a will, as in *Lucas v. Hamm, supra.* Thus, doctrines limiting the recovery of economic loss and restricting the ambit of liability for negligently made statements can limit the extent of liability and the amounts of damages recovered in legal malpractice actions. *See,* W. Probert and R. Hendricks, *Lawyer Malpractice: Duty Relationships beyond Contract,* 55 Notre Dame Law. 708 (1980). An instructive case is Greycas, Inc. v. Proud, 826 F.2d 1560 (7th Cir.1987), a case which involves some interesting questions of professional ethics. In that case, as an accommodation to his brother-in-law who was seeking a loan from the plaintiff, the defendant attorney certified that farm machinery owned by the brother-in-law was currently free of outstanding liens. The defendant made no attempt to examine the records in the county record office. By certifying that he had personally searched the records when in point of fact he had not, the defendant, as Judge Posner writing for the Seventh Circuit pointed out, was undoubtedly guilty of fraud. The plaintiff, however, brought the action under the theories of negligent malpractice and negligent misrepresentation, undoubtedly, as Judge Posner also surmised, to make it possible to bring to bear the defendant's malpractice insurance which probably excluded coverage for intentional torts. The court upheld liability on both counts. Although Illinois restricted an attorney's malpractice liability to third parties to situations in which the primary purpose of the creation of the lawyer/client relationship was either to benefit or to influence the third party, that was precisely the situation in the case before it. The client, the brother-in-law, sought the defendant's assistance to influence the conduct of the plaintiff lender. The subjects of economic loss and negligent misrepresentation will be discussed in later chapters.

b. *Architects.* There has been increasing litigation in recent years against architects. If an architect negligently designs a building there is no longer much doubt that he will be liable to those who are physically injured as a consequence. The difficult problems arise when an architect who has contracted with his principal to supervise construction is charged with negligence in performing that supervision by a third party physically injured as a result of faulty construction. A good discussion of the subject is J. Sweet, *Site Architects and Construction Workers: Brothers and Keepers or Strangers?*, 29 Emory L.J. 289 (1979). A more recent discussion of some of the issues involved in this area is J. Peck and W. Hoch, *Liability of Engineers for Structural Design Errors: State of the Art Considerations in Defining the Standard of Care*, 30 Vill.L.Rev. 403 (1985). *See also* Note, *The Crumbling Tower of Architectural Immunity: Evolution and Expansion of the Liability to Third Parties*, 45 Ohio St.L.J. 217 (1984); Note, *Liability of Architects and Engineers to Third Parties*, 53 Notre Dame Law. 306 (1977).

7. *The Use of Circumstantial Evidence: "Res Ipsa Loquitur"*

a. Historical Roots

BYRNE v. BOADLE

Court of Exchequer, 1863.
2 H. & C. 722, 159 Eng.Rep. 299.

Declaration. For that the defendant, by his servants, so negligently and unskillfully managed and lowered certain barrels of flour by means of a certain jigger-hoist and machinery attached to the shop of the defendant, situated in a certain highway, along which the plaintiff was then passing, that by and through the negligence of the defendant, by his said servants, one of the said barrels of flour fell upon and struck against the plaintiff, whereby the plaintiff was thrown down, wounded, lamed, and permanently injured, and was prevented from attending to his business for a long time, to wit, thence hitherto, and incurred great expense for medical attendance, and suffered great pain and anguish, and was otherwise damnified.

Plea. Not guilty.

At the trial before the learned Assessor of the Court of Passage at Liverpool, the evidence adduced on the part of the plaintiff was as follows:—A witness named Critchley said: "On the 18th July, I was in Scotland Road, on the right side going north, defendant's shop is on that side. When I was opposite to his shop, a barrel of flour fell from a window above in defendant's house and shop, and knocked the plaintiff down. He was carried into an adjoining shop. A horse and cart came opposite the defendant's door. Barrels of flour were in the cart. I do not think the barrel was being lowered by a rope. I cannot say: I did not see the barrel until it struck the plaintiff. It was not swinging when it struck the plaintiff. It struck him on the shoulder and knocked him towards the shop. No one called out until after the accident." The plaintiff said: "On approaching Scotland Place and defendant's shop, I lost all recollection. I felt no blow. I saw nothing to warn me of danger. I was taken home in a cab. I was helpless for a fortnight." (He then described his sufferings.) "I saw the path clear. I did not see any cart opposite defendant's shop." Another witness said: "I saw a barrel falling. I don't know how, but from defendant's." The only other witness was a surgeon, who described the injury which the plaintiff had received. It was admitted that the defendant was a dealer in flour.

It was submitted, on the part of the defendant, that there was no evidence of negligence for the jury. The learned Assessor was of that opinion, and nonsuited the plaintiff, reserving leave to him to move the Court of Exchequer to enter the verdict for him with 50*l*. damages, the amount assessed by the jury.

Littler, in the present term, obtained a rule nisi to enter the verdict for the plaintiff, on the ground of misdirection of the learned Assessor in ruling that there was no evidence of negligence on the part of the defendant; against which

Charles Russell now shewed cause. First, there was no evidence to connect the defendant or his servants with the occurrence. It is not suggested that the defendant himself was present, and it will be argued that upon these pleadings it is not open to the defendant to contend that his servants were not engaged in lowering the barrel of flour. But the declaration alleges that the defendant, by his servants, so negligently lowered the barrel of flour, that by and through the negligence of the defendant, by his said servants, it fell upon the plaintiff. That is tantamount to an allegation that the injury was caused by the defendant's negligence, and it is competent to him, under the plea of not guilty, to contend that his servants were not concerned in the act alleged. * * * Then, assuming the point is open upon these pleadings, there was no evidence that the defendant, or any person for whose acts he would be responsible, was engaged in lowering the barrel of flour. It is consistent with the evidence that the purchaser of the flour was superintending the lowering of it by his servant, or it may be that a stranger was engaged to do it without the knowledge or authority of the defendant. [Pollock, C.B. The presumption is that the defendant's servants were engaged in removing the defendant's flour; if they were not it was competent to the defendant to prove it.] Surmise ought not to be substituted for strict proof when it is sought to fix a defendant with serious liability. The plaintiff should establish his case by affirmative evidence.

Secondly, assuming the facts to be brought home to the defendant or his servants, these facts do not disclose any evidence for the jury of negligence. The plaintiff was bound to give affirmative proof of negligence. But there was not a scintilla of evidence, unless the occurrence is of itself evidence of negligence. There was not even evidence that the barrel was being lowered by a jigger-hoist as alleged in the declaration. [Pollock, C.B. There are certain cases of which it may be said res ipsa loquitur, and this seems one of them. In some cases the Courts have held that the mere fact of the accident having occurred is evidence of negligence, as, for instance, in the case of railway collisions.] On examination of the authorities, that doctrine would seem to be confined to the case of a collision between two trains upon the same line, and both being the property and under the management of the same Company. Such was the case of *Skinner* v. *The London, Brighton and South Coast Railway Company* (5 Exch. 787), where the train in which the plaintiff was ran into another train which had stopped a short distance from a station, in consequence of a luggage train before it having broken down. In that case there must have been negligence, or the accident could not have happened. * * * Later cases have qualified the doctrine of presumptive negligence. In *Cotton* v. *Wood* (8 C.B.N.S. 568) it was held that a Judge is not justified in leaving the case to the jury where the plaintiff's evidence is equally consistent with the absence as with the existence of negligence in the defendant. In *Hammack* v. *White* (11 C.B.N.S. 588, 594), Erle, J., said that he was of opinion "that the plaintiff in a case of this sort was not entitled to have the case left to the jury unless he gives some affirmative evidence that there has been negligence on the part of the defendant." [Pollock, C.B. If he meant that to apply to all cases, I must say, with great respect, that I entirely differ from him. He must refer to the mere nature of the accident in that particular case. Bramwell, B. No doubt, the presumption of negligence is not raised in every case of injury from accident, but in some it is. We must judge of the facts in a reasonable way; and regarding them in that light we know that these accidents do not take place without a cause, and in general that cause is negligence.] The law will not presume that a man is guilty of a wrong. It is consistent with the facts proved that the defendant's servants were using the utmost care and the best appliances to lower the barrel with safety. Then why should the fact that accidents of this nature are sometimes caused by negligence raise any presumption against the defendant? There are many accidents from which no presumption of negligence can arise. [Bramwell, B. Looking at the matter in a reasonable way it comes to this—an injury is done to the plaintiff, who has no means of knowing whether it was the result of negligence; the defendant, who knows how it was caused, does not think fit to tell the jury.] Unless a plaintiff gives some evidence which ought to be submitted to the jury, the defendant is not bound to offer any defence. The plaintiff cannot, by a defective proof of his case, compel the defendant to give evidence in explanation. [Pollock, C.B. I have frequently observed that a defendant has a right to remain silent unless a primâ facie case is established against him. But here the question is whether the plaintiff has not shewn such a case.] In a case of this nature, in which the sympathies of a jury are with the plaintiff, it would be dangerous to allow presumption to be substituted for affirmative proof of negligence.

Littler appeared to support the rule, but was not called upon to argue.

Pollock, C.B. We are all of opinion that the rule must be absolute to enter the verdict for the plaintiff. The learned counsel was quite right in saying that there are many accidents from which no presumption of negligence can arise, but I think it would be wrong to lay down as a rule that in no case can presumption of negligence arise from the fact of an accident. Suppose in this case the barrel had rolled out of the warehouse and fallen on the plaintiff, how could he possibly ascertain from what cause it occurred? It is the duty of persons who keep barrels in a warehouse to take care that they do not roll out, and I think that such a case would, beyond all doubt, afford primâ facie evidence of negligence. A barrel could not roll out of a warehouse without some negligence, and to say that a plaintiff who is injured by it must call witnesses from the warehouse to prove negligence seems to me preposterous. So in the building or repairing a house, or putting pots on the chimneys, if a person passing along the road is injured by something falling upon him, I think the accident alone would be primâ facie evidence of negligence. Or if an article calculated to cause damage is put in a wrong place and does mischief, I think that those whose duty it was to put it in the right place are primâ facie responsible, and if there is any state of facts to rebut the presumption of negligence, they must prove them. The present case upon the evidence comes to this, a man is passing in front of the premises of a dealer in flour, and there falls down upon him a barrel of flour. I think it apparent that the barrel was in the custody of the defendant who occupied the premises, and who is responsible for the acts of his servants who had the controul of it; and in my opinion the fact of its falling is primâ facie evidence of negligence, and the plaintiff who was injured by it is not bound to shew that it could not fall without negligence, but if there are any facts inconsistent with negligence it is for the defendant to prove them.

Bramwell, B. I am of the same opinion.

Channell, B. I am of the same opinion. The first part of the rule assumes the existence of negligence, but takes this shape, that there was no evidence to connect the defendant with the negligence. The barrel of flour fell from a warehouse over a shop which the defendant occupied, and therefore primâ facie he is responsible. Then the question is whether there was any evidence of negligence, not a mere scintilla, but such as in the absence of any evidence in answer would entitle the plaintiff to a verdict. I am of opinion that there was. I think that a person who has a warehouse by the side of a public highway, and assumes to himself the right to lower from it a barrel of flour into a cart, has a duty cast upon him to take care that persons passing along the highway are not injured by it. I agree that it is not every accident which will warrant the inference of negligence. On the other hand, I dissent from the doctrine that there is no accident which will in itself raise a presumption of negligence. In this case I think that there was evidence for the jury, and that the rule ought to be absolute to enter the verdict for the plaintiff.

Pigott, B. I am of the same opinion.

Rule absolute.

Notes

1. Lawyers speak of circumstantial evidence when proof of fact *Y* is also proof of another fact, *Z*. For example suppose *A* and *B* are alone in a room. A

loud noise is heard. People immediately break into the room and find *A* dead from a bullet wound and *B* holding a smoking gun. Proof of these facts is certainly strong evidence that *B* shot and killed *A*. That circumstantial evidence may be used in proving a contested issue of fact in courts is an unexceptionable proposition. Certainly, *Byrne v. Boadle*, was not necessary to establish this almost self-evident proposition. What Chief Baron Pollock's casual use of the Latin phrase "res ipsa loquitur"—the thing speaks for itself— gave birth to is a doctrine that sanctions the use of circumstantial evidence in a very particular manner. In the normal circumstantial evidence case, the evidence is presented to the jury (or other trier of fact) and counsel will invite the jury to make the particular inferences that he thinks are warranted and that are necessary to the proof of his case. When the doctrine of res ipsa loquitur is invoked, not only may counsel argue that proof of a set of facts, *Y* (usually that an accident occurred that injured the plaintiff), is proof of a set of facts, *Z* (usually that the defendant was negligent and his negligence caused the plaintiff's injury), but the plaintiff is entitled to have the trial judge specifically tell the jury that they may make this inference.

2. *The various "burdens" in the trial of an issue of fact.* In reading the succeeding cases discussing the doctrine of res ipsa loquitur it will be helpful to keep in mind the various "burdens" that come into play in the litigation process. These burdens are sometimes subsumed under the generic term "burden of proof." In order to avoid confusion, however, it has become customary to distinguish among at least three separate burdens that are always present in the trial of an issue of fact. These are: (a) the *burden of pleading* (i.e. of raising the issue); (b) the *burden of coming forward* (with evidence); and (c) the *burden of persuasion.* One way of describing the burden of persuasion is to say that, when the burden of persuasion on a particular issue is placed upon one of the parties, it allocates to that party "the risk of non-persuasion." Thus, deciding upon which party to place the burden of persuasion determines which party bears the risk of equipoise, that is, which party will lose if the trier of fact cannot make up its mind. It is analogous to the rule in baseball that "a tie belongs to the runner." In the normal civil action, all issues of fact are determined by the preponderance of evidence; the person with the burden of persuasion must convince the trier of fact that his version of the facts is more likely than not. The preponderance of the evidence standard is a lesser standard and must be distinguished from both the proof "beyond a reasonable doubt" standard used in criminal cases and the "clear and convincing" evidence standard that is often used in quasi-criminal proceedings to collect fines and sometimes in an ordinary civil action to determine the existence of malice.

Although all three burdens—the burden of pleading, the burden of coming forward with evidence, and the burden of persuasion—are normally on the plaintiff in a civil action, this is not always so. (For example, when an issue is an affirmative defense, as is the case with regard to contributory negligence in most jurisdictions, all three burdens are on the defendant.) In a normal action for negligence, the burden of pleading is initially on the plaintiff. He must initiate the action and explain in his pleadings why the defendant is liable to him. The burden of pleading then shifts to the defendant who is required to answer the plaintiff's allegations. If the defendant does not answer the plaintiff's complaint, the plaintiff is entitled to seek entry of judgment by default. For the action to progress to the trial stage, the defendant must deny at least some of the plaintiff's allegations; otherwise there are no issues for the trier of fact to resolve. The plaintiff is then obliged to come forward with evidence to support his allegations. This evidence may be direct evidence, it may consist of circumstantial evidence, or some combination of both. At the very least, the plaintiff must produce enough evidence to withstand a motion to dismiss at the close of his affirmative case. It is at this stage of the proceeding that the doctrine of res ipsa loquitur begins to have important procedural consequences that influence the subsequent course of the proceedings. For the moment, however, it will be helpful to continue describing the progress of the trial of an issue of fact without taking account of the particular ramifications that flow from the invocation of the doctrine of res ipsa loquitur.

If the plaintiff has survived a motion to dismiss after the conclusion of the presentation of his affirmative case, whether the defendant now comes forward with evidence will depend on how persuasive the defendant feels the plaintiff's case is. If the defendant feels that the plaintiff's evidence is not very persuasive and that his own evidence is not likely to help his cause very much, he may decide not to come forward with any evidence, but take his chance with the trier of fact. If the plaintiff's evidence is of high probative value (i.e., if it is very persuasive), the defendant will be under real practical pressure to come forward with evidence. In a very real sense, the burden of coming forward with evidence has shifted to him. That is, once the plaintiff has made out a convincing case, the defendant must come forward with at least enough evidence to put the issue in the equipoise situation. Since he does not bear the burden of persuasion, he is not obliged to persuade the trier of fact that his version of the facts is more likely than the plaintiff's version. He must only persuade the trier of fact that his version is *at least as likely* as the plaintiff's version, although as a practical matter he will try to ensure success by presenting as persuasive case as he can, just as a prudent batter will try to reach first base before the fielder's throw and make the umpire's task easy rather than be forced to rely on the "tie belongs to the runner" rule.

In the succeeding cases and the notes that follow, we will examine how this normal scenario for the trial of an issue of fact will be affected by the invocation of the doctrine of res ipsa loquitur.

b. The Modern Doctrine

GEORGE FOLTIS, INC. v. CITY OF NEW YORK

Court of Appeals of New York, 1941.
287 N.Y. 108, 38 N.E.2d 455.

Lehman, Chief Judge.

The premises occupied by the plaintiff as a restaurant were damaged by water from a broken water main installed in the street by the city of New York and maintained by it. The break in the water main was discovered in the evening of April 12, 1938. There was a longitudinal split in the "flange part" of the main. The plaintiff produced evidence intended to show that the city failed to shut off the water from the broken water main within a reasonable time after it received notice of the break. It produced no evidence to show the cause of the break and no evidence that the break was due to negligence of the city in the construction or maintenance of the water main unless from the nature of the break in a main constructed and maintained by the city, negligence may be inferred or presumed by application of the rule of res ipsa loquitur.

At the close of the plaintiff's evidence, the defendant moved to dismiss the complaint on the ground that the plaintiff had failed to prove a prima facie case. After some discussion the trial judge stated that in view of conflict of judicial authority he felt that the question of whether the rule of res ipsa loquitur applies should receive more careful consideration than he could give to it at that time. For that reason, he suggested that he should reserve decision upon the defendant's motion to dismiss and that, after hearing the evidence of the defendant he should also reserve decision upon the motions which both parties would make at the close of the whole case, until the jury had answered five questions which he proposed to submit. Both sides acquiesced in that suggestion.

The five questions which the trial judge stated he would submit to the jury are:

"(1) Was the defendant negligent in failing to use reasonable care in the construction of the water main which broke?

"(2) Was the defendant negligent in failing to use reasonable care in maintaining the water main in a reasonably proper state of repair?

"(3) Was the defendant negligent in failing to be reasonably diligent in shutting off the water after receiving notice of the break?

"(4) What is the total amount of damage which the plaintiff sustained in consequence of its property being subjected to contact with water, mud, sand and gravel?

"(5) If your answer to question No. 3 is yes, what is the amount of damage which was caused to the plaintiff in consequence of the failure to shut off the water with reasonable diligence?"

The defendant city then produced evidence sufficient, if credited, to show that it did not fail in any duty to exercise reasonable diligence in shutting off the water after it received notice of the break. Even if without fault there, the city would still be liable for damages caused by the break if the break was due to its negligence, either in the construction or maintenance of the water main. The city produced no evidence to show the cause of the break. It did attempt to prove that whatever may have been the cause of the break, no negligence by the city, either in the construction or maintenance of the pipe, caused or contributed to the injury. For that purpose it produced evidence which, if credited, was sufficient to show that the pipes were new when laid; that field inspectors of the city tested carefully all pipes before they were laid; and that it was their duty to see that the pipes were properly laid. It is undisputed that cast iron pipes do not wear out or become defective from ordinary use for many decades and, perhaps, for centuries; but the length of life of such pipes may be affected by chemicals in the ground as well as in the water.

At the close of the case the defendant made a motion to dismiss the complaint and also for the direction of a verdict. The trial judge reserved decision upon that motion. The plaintiff's attorney then stated: "I have no motions to make. I am not going to join in the motion for a directed verdict. I ask to go to the jury on all the grounds that I have set forth in the memorandum I gave your Honor * * *." Even without a motion by the plaintiff for the direction of a verdict the trial judge would be required to determine whether the rule of res ipsa loquitur could be applied in this case. Without application of that rule it is plain that the evidence is, as matter of law, insufficient to justify any inference that the defendant was negligent either in the construction or maintenance of the broken main and the trial judge would be bound to grant the *defendant's motion* for the direction of a verdict. The trial judge could not, without a motion by the plaintiff, direct a verdict *in favor of the plaintiff* even if he should decide that by application of the rule of res ipsa loquitur the uncontradicted evidence dictated an inference or presumption of negligence on the part of the defendant which had not been refuted and which as matter of law entitled the plaintiff to a verdict for the consequent damages. Failure by the plaintiff to move for the direction of a verdict and acquiescence by the plaintiff in the submission to the jury of the questions whether the defendant had failed to use reasonable care in the construction or maintenance of the water main would have the effect of a concession that upon this record there are questions of fact. If the jury should thereafter decide the questions submitted to it in favor of the defendant the plaintiff would not be in a position to urge, either upon a motion to set aside the verdict or upon an appeal, that as matter of law it was entitled to the direction of a verdict.

In the following colloquy the trial judge pointed out to the plaintiff's attorney that a motion for the direction of a verdict would not have the effect of a submission of questions of fact to the court but that the failure to make such a motion would have the effect of a concession that a question of fact exists which must be submitted to the jury:

"The Court: In order to relieve your mind of any possible difficulty you think you might be in by moving to direct a verdict, I will say now that if you do move to direct a verdict, I will not take that as joining in the motion. I do not think there is any such thing as joining in a motion for a directed verdict except it is done deliberately for the purpose of submitting the questions of fact to the Court.

"Suppose I should ultimately decide that the rule of res ipsa loquitur applies *and the Jury has found a verdict for the defendant, should you not have your record in condition where any Appellate Court could decide either way without the necessity for a new trial?*

"Mr. Klein: I am very grateful to your Honor for the suggestion you have made and putting it in the proper light. Frankly, sir, I had not given that consideration, and with that in mind, then I also join for a directed verdict.

"The Court: You do not join. You made a separate independent motion for a directed verdict.

"Mr. Klein: Yes, sir. I also move for a directed verdict on that issue.

"The Court: I will reserve decision on both. * * *"

The plaintiff cannot now contend that the parties submitted to the court any question of fact if under the rule of res ipsa loquitur the evidence is sufficient to permit, but insufficient to dictate as matter of law, an inference of negligence.

The jury answered the first three questions in the negative, finding that the defendant had not failed to use reasonable care in the construction or maintenance of the water main, nor had it failed to use reasonable diligence in shutting off the water. In answer to the fourth question the jury found that the plaintiff had sustained damages of $2,500. The trial judge, disregarding the findings of the jury in favor of the defendant, held that the rule of res ipsa loquitur applied and, as matter of law, dictated an inference or presumption of negligence. He, therefore, granted the motion of the plaintiff, upon which decision had been reserved, for the direction of a verdict for the amount of damages suffered by the plaintiff, as found by the jury.

We have said that "where the instrumentality which produced an injury is within the exclusive possession and control of the person charged with negligence, and such person has exclusive knowledge of the care exercised in the control and management of that instrumentality, evidence of circumstances which show that the accident would not ordinarily have occurred without neglect of some duty owed to the plaintiff is sufficient to justify an inference of negligence and to shift the burden of explanation to the defendant. * * *" Galbraith v. Busch, 267 N.Y. 230, at page 234, 196 N.E. 36, at page 38. In such circumstances the doctrine of res ipsa loquitur relieves a plaintiff from the burden of producing direct evidence of negligence, but it does not relieve a plaintiff from the burden of proof that the person charged with negligence was at fault. So in the cited case we have also said on the same page: "The doctrine of res ipsa loquitur is not an arbitrary rule. It is rather a common-sense appraisal of the probative value of circumstantial evidence. It requires evidence which shows at least probability that a particular accident could not have occurred without legal wrong by the defendant. To negative every possibility that the accident occurred in some extraordinary manner which would exculpate the defendant is often impossible. In the administration of the law we must be satisfied with proof which leads to a conclusion with probable certainty where absolute logical certainty is impossible. We may be constrained to act upon indecisive evidence where complete proof is impossible. Then the logical probative force of the evidence produced is measured, in part, by the test of whether it is the best evidence available."

We must determine whether the rule of res ipsa loquitur may be applied in accordance with those principles, to the proof tendered in this case; whether, upon "a common-sense appraisal of the probative value" of the circumstantial evidence, measured in part by the test of whether it is the best evidence available, inference of negligence is justified. Here the pipes were in position for almost nine years before any break occurred. In accordance with proper practice they had been laid four feet below the surface. There is no evidence or suggestion that from the time when the pipes were laid there was any warning that the pipes had shifted or deteriorated, and in the absence of such warning the city was certainly under no duty to examine the deeply-buried water mains. The lapse of time before the break occurred presents ground for argument that under the circumstances of this case the break was not due to an original defect, which careful inspection might have revealed, in the pipes or in the manner in which the pipes were laid.

In spite of such arguments the courts in some cases have applied the rule of res ipsa loquitur where the injury occurred from a break in an underground water main and have held that under that rule proof of the break constitutes circumstantial evidence sufficient to establish prima facie that the injury was due to the negligence of the public authorities. * * * In other cases courts have reached the opposite contention. * * *

A "common-sense appraisal of the probative value of circumstantial evidence" excludes the arbitrary use of any rule of thumb. In directing a verdict for the plaintiff in this case the trial judge, Mr. Justice Walter, wrote a notably careful opinion in which he points out that the doctrine of res ipsa loquitur does not mean that the "plaintiff may recover without sustaining the burden of proving negligence by a fair preponderance of the credible evidence. * * * The doctrine merely means that certain occurrences contain within themselves a sufficient basis for an inference of negligence, and it does not differ from ordinary cases of circumstantial evidence except in the respect that the facts and circumstances from which the inference of negligence is drawn are immediately attendant on the occurrence. * * * The doctrine is not confined to any particular class of cases * * *, and the test of its application is whether or not the occurrence does in truth point to negligence of the defendant as the fair and reasonable inference from the occurrence. Where the agency which produces the injury is not within the control of the person charged with negligence, or where the occurrence is one which naturally might occur from causes other than his negligence, the inference of his negligence is not fair and reasonable; but wherever there is a combination of those two conditions, viz., control by the person charged with negligence and improbability of the occurrence having happened if he had been reasonably careful the doctrine applies. * * *"

The fact that the break occurred in a water main which had been buried in the ground for several years weakens the probative value of the evidence, but it does not completely destroy it. Slight differences in the evidence might change the inferences which may fairly be drawn, but we agree with the trial judge that in this case an inference of negligence might reasonably be drawn from the unexplained occurrence of the break. True, more than a remote possibility would still remain that the break may have been the result of causes against which the city could not by vigilance guard, and by stressing one circumstance rather than another the inference that the injury was due to any dereliction of duty by the city may gain or lose in strength. If the city has in its control evidence which would make clear the cause of the break or would show exactly what care it has exercised in the construction and maintenance of the water main, a failure to produce such evidence might be a factor in weighing probabilities. Reasonable men might perhaps differ as to the inference that should be drawn from the occurrence of the break even though the city should offer no proof, but we think that both reason and the weight of authority support the ruling of the trial judge that the defendant's motion at the close of the plaintiff's case to dismiss the complaint should be denied. We agree that under the rule of res ipsa loquitur the plaintiff's proof that its property was damaged by a break in a water main constructed and controlled by the city was sufficient to establish prima facie that the injury was due to negligence of the city.

Though the plaintiff's proof, when it rested, may have been sufficient to establish prima facie the negligence of the defendant, it was certainly not conclusive proof. Even where the rule of res ipsa loquitur is applied, the burden of showing that the injury is due to the negligence of the defendant rests on the plaintiff. The burden never shifts to the defendant, and the plaintiff must sustain its claim by a preponderance of evidence. * * * Here the defendant produced evidence intended to meet the prima facie case established by the plaintiff. The jury is the trier of the facts. If conflicting inferences may be drawn, choice of inference must be made by the jury. Upon all the evidence in this case the jury refused to find that the plaintiff had proven negligence by a preponderance of evidence. Its verdict may not be disregarded unless at the close of the whole case the plaintiff's prima facie proof had become conclusive.

The evidence produced by the defendant, as we have said, did not reveal the cause of the break. No burden rests upon the city to show that. Possible inference arising from the occurrence of the injury, that it was due to the negligence of the city would, of course, be completely rebutted by conclusive affirmative proof that the city had exercised all care reasonably possible in the manner in which it tested the pipes and supervised the laying of the main. Then it would be clear that whatever might have been the cause of the break, it was not due to any dereliction of the defendant. Here the defendant's evidence, even if believed by the jury, might, we may assume, still leave open the possibility that the injury was due to fault in laying the pipe. To that extent the defendant's testimony does not completely rebut the plaintiff's prima facie case. For that reason the trial court has held that without complete rebuttal the inference of negligence becomes conclusive and has directed a verdict in favor of the plaintiff.

The direction of a verdict in favor of the plaintiff might be justified if the rule of res ipsa loquitur created a full presumption in favor of the plaintiff. It is without logical foundation if res ipsa loquitur is only a common-sense rule for the appraisal of the probative force of evidence which enables an injured person, in proper case, to establish prima facie that the injury was caused by the defendant's negligence, though the injured person may be unable to produce direct evidence of want of care in any particular. See Wigmore on Evidence, 3d Ed., § 2509. It has been said by the Supreme Court of the United States that: "Res ipsa loquitur means that the facts of the occurrence warrant the inference of negligence, not that they compel such an inference; that they furnish circumstantial evidence of negligence where direct evidence of it may be lacking, but it is evidence to be weighed, not necessarily to be accepted as sufficient; that they call for explanation or rebuttal, not necessarily that they require it; that they make a case to be decided by the jury, not that they forestall the verdict. Res ipsa loquitur, where it applies, does not convert the defendant's general issue into an affirmative defense. When all the evidence is in, the question for the jury is whether the preponderance is with the plaintiff." Sweeney v. Erving, 228 U.S. 233, 240, 33 S.Ct. 416, 418, 57 L.Ed. 815, Ann.Cas.1914D, 905.

In other jurisdictions, too, the courts have held that even where a defendant does not produce evidence to rebut the plaintiff's prima facie case established by application of the rule of res ipsa loquitur, it is for the jury to determine whether the inference of negligence should be drawn. * * *

Relying upon the authority of Hogan v. Manhattan Ry. Co., 149 N.Y. 23, 25, 43 N.E. 403, the trial judge felt constrained to reject this conclusion and to hold that the rule is different in this State. Disregarding the finding of the jury in favor of the defendant he directed a verdict in favor of the plaintiff because the defendant's evidence, even if credited, fell short of rebutting, in all particulars, the inference that the defendant's negligence caused the injury and because it still left open the possibility that the break may have been due to the negligence of the city in constructing the main. * * *

Though in some other jurisdictions it has been held that where a defendant produces no evidence to rebut an inference or presumption of negligence, arising under the rule of res ipsa loquitur, the court may direct a verdict in plaintiff's favor, in no case has it been held that a verdict may be directed where evidence is presented by the defendant which weakens such inference, even though it does not conclusively rebut it. Very little evidence might suffice to rebut a presumption. * * * There may be cases where the prima facie proof is so convincing that the inference of negligence arising therefrom is inescapable if not rebutted by other evidence. We need not now determine whether that was true in the Hogan case. In most cases it is not true and it is certainly not true here where the plaintiff's evidence, even while unrebutted, left serious doubt whether the break in 1938 was due to conditions which might have been avoided by the exercise of care in 1929.

We should not, however, place our decision in this case upon any narrow ground. A study of the opinions of the appellate courts of this State reveals that judges have used the terms "inference" and"presumption" indiscriminately and without recognition that an "inference" and a "presumption" are not identical in scope or effect. Judicial failure to note the distinction has led to confusion of thought and often to inconsistencies in judicial opinions and decisions. * * * It is perhaps impossible for trial judges to deduce from the opinions or decisions of the appellate court the procedure they should follow when under the rule of res ipsa loquitur the plaintiff has established prima facie that injury was due to the negligence of the defendant and the defendant introduces no evidence in rebuttal. * * * The opinion of Mr. Justice Walter has served to make manifest the fact that the fault for diversity of procedure in the trial courts does not lie there. The time has come to attempt authoritative formulation of the procedural rule, confused in this State as in other jurisdictions by earlier failure to appreciate fully the implications latent in the rule of res ipsa loquitur. * * *

Where a plaintiff establishes prima facie by direct evidence that injury was caused by negligence of the defendant the court may seldom direct a verdict, though the plaintiff's evidence is not contradicted or rebutted by the defendant. In such cases the question of whether the defendant was in fault in what he did or failed to do is ordinarily one of fact to be determined by the jury unless the jury is waived. The practice should be the same where under the rule of res ipsa loquitur the plaintiff establishes prima facie by circumstantial evidence a right to recover.

* * *

The trial judge has submitted to the jury as separate questions (1) whether the defendant was negligent in the construction of the water main, and (2) whether the defendant was negligent in maintaining the water main in a reasonably safe condition. The evidence, even by application of the rule or doctrine of res ipsa loquitur, is insufficient to sustain a finding of negligence in either particular considered separately; it is sufficient to sustain a finding that the break would not have occurred if the defendant had exercised due care in all particulars. The use of such words as "res ipsa loquitur" or an attempt to discuss with a jury whether by application of the rule a "presumption" or an "inference" arises from the evidence might confuse rather than enlighten a jury, but the jury cannot pass intelligently upon the question whether the inference of negligence should be drawn, unless, in language which it can understand, it receives an explanation of why the evidence would permit an inference of negligence, and why the jury may reject such inference if it sees fit.

The same logical difficulty in reconciling the decisions of this court, which inevitably caused confusion as to the procedural effect of the application of the rule or doctrine of res ipsa loquitur, resulted no less inevitably in failure to submit to the jury the decisive question in this case in a form which would enable the jury to exercise its functions in accordance with the principles outlined above. The fault, we have said, does not lie with the trial judge and for the same reasons it does not lie with the parties if they failed by proper exceptions and requests to charge to ask for a more adequate submission of the decisive question. The trial judge has power to grant the plaintiff's motion to set aside the findings of the jury if he concludes that for such reasons there should be a new trial.

The judgments should be reversed and the case remitted to the Trial Term to proceed in accordance with this opinion, with costs in all courts to appellant to abide the event.

[The dissenting opinion of Loughran, J., is omitted. He felt that the parties had agreed to let the trial judge decide the ultimate issue of fact.]

Note

What Judge Lehman called a "full presumption" is not a presumption at all. Wigmore made the point well when he pointed out that the so-called "presumption of innocence" in the criminal law is nothing of the sort. It is not a presumption but rather a rule of law about the ultimate burden of persuasion in a criminal case. *See* 9 J. Wigmore, Evidence § 2511 (3d ed. 1940). Presumptions, on the other hand, are concerned with the weight of evidence. They concern the burden of coming forward with evidence, not the burden of persuasion. Kentucky did at one time follow the practice of actually shifting the burden of persuasion when the doctrine of res ipsa loquitur was successfully invoked, but this practice has now been abandoned in favor of the conventional approach. *Compare* Schechter v. Hann, 305 Ky. 794, 205 S.W.2d 690

(1947) *with* Bell & Koch, Inc. v. Stanley, 375 S.W.2d 696 (Ky.1964). That is not to say, as Judge Lehman noted in *Foltis*, that, in a jurisdiction that will grant the plaintiff a directed verdict in a civil case, the strength of the inference may not be so strong as to warrant directing a verdict for the plaintiff. *See* Moore v. Atchison, Topeka & Santa Fe Railway, 28 Ill.App.2d 340, 171 N.E.2d 393 (1960)(two trains collided head-on on a single track). In such cases, however, the plaintiff receives a directed verdict because he has satisfied the burden of persuasion and not because the burden of persuasion was shifted to the defendant. We will return to these problems again in the notes following the next case.

SWINEY v. MALONE FREIGHT LINES

Court of Appeals of Tennessee, 1976.
545 S.W.2d 112.

GODDARD, JUDGE.

OPINION

This appeal presents two principal questions, the first of which, insofar as we have been able to determine, is one of first impression in this state: (1) Does the doctrine of *res ipsa loquitur* apply where a wheel becomes detached from a moving vehicle, and (2) if so, did the Defendants introduce sufficient proof to entitle them to a directed verdict at the conclusion of all the proof?

The facts are relatively simple and undisputed. Plaintiffs' proof showed that on December 21, 1973, about 1:30 p. m., Davis M. Swiney, Plaintiff–Appellee, was driving his 1967 Chevrolet automobile in a northerly direction on U.S. Highway 11–W in Grainger County just north of Bean Station. He was meeting a tractor-trailer which was leased to Malone Freight Lines and was being operated by Charles Wayne Wilson, Defendants–Appellants, who owned the vehicle in partnership with Marshall Adams. The tractor was equipped in the rear with dual tandem wheels. As the vehicles approached each other the tractor's outside left-rear forward wheel became detached. Mr. Swiney was able to avoid a collision with this wheel, but shortly thereafter a second wheel also became detached and rolled down the highway striking Mr. Swiney's vehicle in the center of the grill. The collision resulted in injuries to Mr. Swiney and damages to his automobile.

At the conclusion of the Plaintiffs' proof the Trial Court, being of the opinion that the facts presented were sufficient to permit the claim to go to the jury under the doctrine of *res ipsa loquitur*, overruled Defendants' motion for a directed verdict.

The Defendants thereupon introduced proof to show that the tractor-trailer in question was returning to its home terminal in Birmingham, Alabama, from a trip to Pittsburgh, Pennsylvania. It was loaded with carpeting which weighed approximately 40,000 pounds. The lug bolts, which held the dual wheels in place, had sheared, causing the wheels to become disengaged. The wheels in question had been inspected on three separate occasions within four days prior to the accident: (1) regular 30–day inspection by Malone Freight Lines four days prior to the accident, (2) inspection on the day of the accident by Defendant Wilson at Salem, Virginia, where he tested the wheels with a "tire billy," (3) inspection on the day of the accident by Tennessee Public Service Commission representatives at the Tennessee–Virginia state line.

Defendant Wilson, who was an experienced truck driver, having driven trucks for seven years and this particular truck seven months, testified that the wheels were last removed some 30 days prior to the accident when new tires were installed. He also testified that he had had no difficulty with the wheels in the seven months that he had driven the truck, and that if the lug nuts became loose a driver could detect it because "when you go into a curve, when you come back to straighten back up with the road it will want to keep on sliding over with you, and it will just twist you can't * * *" When asked by his attorney if one could tell when lug nuts are loose by looking at them, he testified as follows:

A. Yes, you can tell, if they have been loose just a day, you can * * * just any truck driver can look at them and just look at them and tell that they are loose because they'll a rusty ring come out from under every one of them.

Q. All right, now, did you see any rusty rings around those lugs when you looked at them at Salem, Virginia?

A. No.

Fred Massengill, claims manager for Malone Freight Lines, testified as to the procedure used in connection with its regular 30–day inspection; however, Jackie Donaldson, the employee who made the inspection, was not called to testify.

Although as indicated, no Tennessee cases have dealt with the exact factual situation here presented, the Tennessee courts have applied the doctrine in other situations involving motor vehicles—* * *

* * *

Defendants strongly insist, however, that two Tennessee cases are controlling and dispositive of the questions. * * *

* * *

We are of the opinion that neither of these cases is dispositive of the case at bar. As to *Smith*, we cannot equate a tractor wheel, which is removed and replaced at regular and frequent intervals, becoming detached with the sudden breaking of a universal joint or a brake band. Additionally, there was proof that an inspection of the truck (unless it was "torn down") would not have revealed a defect in the universal joint, and that there was no visible or discoverable defect in the brake band. In *Sloan*, the Court specifically found, undoubtedly upon proof adduced in the record, that the accident was caused by a latent defect that could not have been discovered by ordinary inspection.

We accordingly conclude that the doctrine of *res ipsa loquitur*—which, as the courts have often said, is "a common-sense appraisal of the probative value of circumstantial evidence"—is applicable to the case at bar and warranted the jury in finding in favor of the Plaintiffs, unless it can be said, as insisted by the Defendants, that their proof, which is undisputed, shows that the cause of the accident was not due to their negligence.

We note initially that, although some of the cases * * * use the term "inference" which permits the jury to accept or reject defendant's negligence as it may choose and others "presumption" which, in the absence of contrary proof, requires acceptance, it is not necessary in this case for us to determine which is the proper terminology.

We are however required to determine the quantum of proof necessary to entitle the Defendants to a directed verdict where, under the Plaintiffs' proof, the doctrine is applicable; or to put it another way, we are required to determine whether, under all the proof of the case, the doctrine remains applicable.

An older case relied upon by the Defendants disposes of the question in a cursory manner, stating that the doctrine never applies "where the defendant goes forward with proof explaining the cause of the accident." Granert v. Bauer, 17 Tenn.App. 370, 67 S.W.2d 748 (1933).

A more recent case * * * explored the required quantum of proof more carefully and quoted with approval from Prosser on Torts, Second Edition. We adopt as the proper rule the language used in the Fourth Edition which is now available (at page 233):

> If the defendant seeks a directed verdict in his favor, he must produce evidence which will destroy any reasonable inference of negligence, or so completely contradict it that reasonable men could no longer accept it. The evidence necessary to do this will vary with the strength of the inference. It takes more of an explanation to justify a falling elephant than a falling brick, more to account for a hundred defective bottles than for one. If the defendant proves definitely by uncontradicted evidence that the occurrence was caused by some outside agency over which he had no control, that it was of a kind which commonly occurs without negligence on the part of anyone, or that it could not have been avoided by the exercise of all reasonable care, the inference of negligence is no longer permissible, and the verdict is directed for the defendant. The *res ipsa* case has been overthrown by showing that it is not a *res ipsa* case.
>
> But if the defendant merely offers evidence of his own acts and precautions amounting to reasonable care, it is seldom that a verdict can be directed in his favor. The inference from the circumstances remains in the case to contradict his evidence. If he testifies that he used proper care to insulate his wires, to inspect his chandelier, to drive his bus, or to keep defunct mice and wandering insect life out of his bottled beverage, the fact that electricity escaped from the wires, that the chandelier fell, that the bus went into the ditch and the bug was in the bottle, with the background of common experience that such things do not usually happen if proper care is used, may permit reasonable men to find that his witnesses are not to be believed, that the precautions described were not sufficient to conform to the standard required or were not faithfully carried out, and that the whole truth has not been told. It is of course not impossible that proof of proper care may be so overwhelming as to call for a directed verdict,

but in the ordinary case it will not be sufficient to destroy the inference from *res ipsa loquitur*.

Applying this rule, can it be said that the evidence produced by the Defendants destroyed any reasonable inference of negligence, or so completely contradicted it that reasonable minds could no longer accept it? We think not. We readily concede the Defendants have explained the cause of the wheels becoming detached; but they have, in our view, failed to show that the cause was not due to their negligence. It may have been that there were internal structural defects in all of the lug bolts or in a sufficient number to cause them all to shear, and that these defects could not have been detected upon reasonable inspection. No proof however was adduced to this fact, and because the cases suggest the Defendants have the better opportunity to determine and explain the cause, the burden rests with them. Other possible explanations which have not been excluded are (1) the lug bolts became crystalized and subject to shearing because the vehicle had been operated on prior occasions when the lug nuts were not properly tightened, (2) the lug bolts developed fissures which were readily discernable but overlooked by the Defendants' agents in changing tires and making inspections, (3) the lug bolts were weakened by overloading of the truck on prior occasions. We cannot be sure as to any of these possibilities, but we do know that either the Defendants failed to have an expert examine the lug bolts subsequent to the accident or chose not to present the results of such an examination. In view of the foregoing, we are of the opinion that under all the proof the case was properly submitted to the jury under the doctrine of *res ipsa loquitur*.

* * *

For all of the foregoing reasons, the assignments of error are overruled and the Trial Court affirmed. * * *

Sanders, Judge (dissenting).

I must respectfully dissent from the holding in the majority opinion that the doctrine of *res ipsa loquitur* is controlling in this case.

* * *

The fallacy of the rationale in the majority opinion seems to lie in the fact that it places two inferences of negligence upon the Defendants. The effect of the holding is not only that the inference of negligence existed until there was an explanation of why the wheel came off but, after it was shown that it came off because the lug bolts sheared, there then arose a second inference that the Defendants knew, or should have known, they were defective.

* * *

Finally, I cannot agree that the rule quoted from Prosser on Torts has any application to the case at bar. Should this quotation be approved in the context of this case, in my view, we would be establishing an extremely dangerous precedent. We would, in effect, be saying, "Any time a third party is injured as the result of a mechanical failure of a motor vehicle, the jury may infer negligence on the part of the owner or operator unless he can *show due care by overwhelming proof*."

Since the proof shows affirmatively that the accident resulted from the lug bolts' shearing off and the record is devoid of evidence that the Defendants knew or, through the exercise of ordinary care, should have known they were defective, it was, in my view, error for the Trial Court not to direct a verdict in favor of the Defendants.

Notes

1.   The majority opinion in *Swiney* noted that "some of the cases * * * use the term 'inference' which permits the jury to accept or reject defendant's negligence as it may choose and others 'presumption' which, in the absence of contrary proof, requires acceptance." The court felt that "it is not necessary in this case for us to determine which is the proper terminology." What is a *presumption which, in the absence of contrary proof, requires acceptance*? Does the statement mean that the burden of persuasion shifts to the defendant or that the inference is so strong that substantial contrary evidence must be brought forward by the defendant before a rational jury could find in his favor? We have seen, in the note following the *Foltis* case, that Wigmore does not believe that the term presumption can be used to describe the shifting of the burden of persuasion to the defendant. Furthermore, it is hard to find modern cases where it unequivocally appears that the court has used the res ipsa loquitur doctrine to shift the burden of persuasion. The typical modern approach is exemplified in Winter v. Scherman, 57 Hawaii 279, 554 P.2d 1137 (1976). In that case a van driven by the defendant's decedent "failed to negotiate a curve * * * described as fairly gentle and crossed the opposite lane onto the opposite shoulder of the highway." The van then travelled 225 feet on the shoulder, struck a utility pole, overturned, and came to rest 53 feet away from the pole. There were no eyewitnesses to the accident. In a wrongful death action brought by the administrator of the passenger's estate, the jury ruled for the defendant but the trial court granted the plaintiff's motion for judgment n. o. v. The Hawaii Supreme Court declared:

> * * * It has been argued that there is nothing distinctive about the doctrine of res ipsa loquitur, and that the logic used in res ipsa loquitur cases is the same as that in all cases of circumstantial evidence. 2 Harper and James, Torts § 19.5, p. 1079 (1956). We have treated the doctrine as one which, where applicable, raises a rebuttable inference which allows a plaintiff to get his case to the jury. * * *

In the absence of any evidence of how the accident occurred without fault on the part of Appellant's decedent, the parties agree that the circumstances at least raised an inference of negligence which could properly be submitted to the jury. They dispute whether application of the doctrine of res ipsa loquitur raises a presumption of negligence which entitles the plaintiff to a directed verdict in the absence of any evidence rebutting the presumption. We have had occasion to consider these contentions and have refused to be drawn into the argument.

* * * It follows that, although no evidence is introduced which tends to rebut the inference of negligence, the inference arising from the facts of a particular case might not be inescapable and might still be subject to rejection by the jury. In that event, a motion for directed verdict in reliance solely upon the doctrine should be denied. The question becomes whether the evidence is such as to inescapably compel an inference of negligence. We agree with the trial court that the answer must be

affirmative in the present case. Appellant argues that there are reasonable possible explanations of the accident other than negligence, but suggests only the possibilities of "horseplay" in the van, an animal or child in the road or a mechanical defect of some kind in the van. However, there was no evidence whatever supporting these inferences and the most that can be said is that there was no evidence which directly negated them. We conclude that the inference of negligence here is so strong that it could not reasonably have been rejected by the jury in favor of such speculative hypotheses. The trial court did not err in granting judgment for Appellee notwithstanding the verdict. * * *

2. The crucial question in these cases is how much evidence must a defendant come forward with to defeat the invocation of the res ipsa loquitur doctrine, that is to make it error for the trial court to instruct the jury that, from the occurrence of the accident, they may conclude that the defendant was negligent. The question is complicated by the fact that the United States Supreme Court had at one time indicated that a presumption[16] might be used in a criminal case if there was a "rational connection" between the fact proved and the fact to be proved (i.e. the fact to be inferred from the proven fact). *See* Tot v. United States, 319 U.S. 463, 63 S.Ct. 1241, 87 L.Ed. 1519 (1943); *cf.* Mobile, Jackson & Kansas City Railroad v. Turnipseed, 219 U.S. 35, 31 S.Ct. 136, 55 L.Ed. 78 (1910). It was thought by some authorities that the "rational connection" requirement did not mean that proof of fact X must make the existence of fact Y sufficiently probable to satisfy the "beyond a reasonable doubt" test or even that the existence of fact X made fact Y more likely than not. It was only necessary that there be some "strong" probative connection between the two facts. Under this view, in order to avoid the application of a presumption, the defendant was obliged to come forward with enough evidence to show that there was little probative connection between fact X and fact Y. As a practical matter, this was often an almost impossible burden. The Supreme Court has now made it clear, however, that the rational connection test will not suffice. A specific instruction on a legal presumption can only be used in a criminal case when there is a sufficient probative connection between the two facts to permit a reasonable person to conclude that proof of fact X makes the existence of fact Y more likely than not. Furthermore, when fact Y, the fact to be proved, is the ultimate fact to be proved *and* the existence of fact X is the only evidentiary basis for finding fact Y, a specific instruction based upon a legal presumption can only be used in a criminal case when there is sufficient probative connection between X and Y to permit a reasonable person to conclude that proof of X is proof beyond a reasonable doubt of Y. *See* Turner v. United States, 396 U.S. 398, 90 S.Ct. 642, 24 L.Ed.2d 610 (1970); Leary v. United States, 395 U.S. 6, 89 S.Ct. 1532, 23 L.Ed.2d 57 (1969). *See also* County Court of Ulster County v. Allen, 442 U.S. 140, 99 S.Ct. 2213, 60 L.Ed.2d 777 (1979). If the defendant comes forward with enough evidence to make that conclusion questionable, an express instruction on the presumption and its effect cannot be given to the jury. Applying the same type of analysis to a civil case and allowing for the different standard of persuasion applicable to a civil case, a res ipsa loquitur instruction should not be given when proof of

---

16. A common presumption used in the criminal law is that involving knowing possession of recently stolen goods. In most jurisdictions, a jury can be specifically told that, if it is proven that the defendant was in knowing possession of recently stolen goods, it may be inferred that he is a receiver of stolen goods. Indeed, in many jurisdictions the same basic fact will support the inference that the defendant stole the goods in question.

the occurrence of the accident would not permit a reasonable person to conclude that the defendant was negligent. A res ipsa loquitur instruction also should not be given when the proof would not permit a reasonable person to conclude that the defendant's conduct caused the plaintiff's injuries. Thus, to defeat the application of the doctrine and the express instruction to the jury the defendant must come forward with enough evidence to make it doubtful that a reasonable person would find that proof of the occurrence of the accident made it more likely than not that the defendant was negligent or that the defendant's conduct caused the accident. In almost all jurisdictions this is how the doctrine is normally applied. What leads to the confusion in civil cases is that, since the plaintiff's burden of persuasion merely calls for proof that his version of the facts is more likely than not, in order to get the case to the equipoise situation the defendant will have to present a substantial amount of proof, indeed *almost* enough proof to establish that the plaintiff's version of the facts is less likely than not. By contrast, in a criminal case, where the beyond a reasonable doubt test applies, the defendant can defeat the operation of a presumption that operates to establish guilt or innocence by introducing enough evidence to make it impossible to conclude that the inference provided by the presumption has been established beyond a reasonable doubt, even if the inference still remains much more likely than not.

3. It is sometimes said that, if the plaintiff makes some specific allegations of negligence, he cannot also rely on the doctrine of res ipsa loquitur. *See* Sankey v. Williamsen, 180 Neb. 714, 144 N.W.2d 429 (1966). There is no logical reason why this should be so and most courts do not place the plaintiff in this procedural dilemma.

c. Some Special Applications of the Doctrine of Res Ipsa Loquitur

YBARRA v. SPANGARD

Supreme Court of California, 1944.
25 Cal.2d 486, 154 P.2d 687.

GIBSON, CHIEF JUSTICE.

This is an action for damages for personal injuries alleged to have been inflicted on plaintiff by defendants during the course of a surgical operation. The trial court entered judgments of nonsuit as to all defendants and plaintiff appealed.

On October 28, 1939, plaintiff consulted defendant Dr. Tilley, who diagnosed his ailment as appendicitis, and made arrangements for an appendectomy to be performed by defendant Dr. Spangard at a hospital owned and managed by defendant, Dr. Swift. Plaintiff entered the hospital, was given a hypodermic injection, slept, and later was awakened by Drs. Tilley and Spangard and wheeled into the operating room by a nurse whom he believed to be defendant Gisler, an employee of Dr. Swift. Defendant Dr. Reser, the anesthetist, also an employee of Dr. Swift, adjusted plaintiff for the operation, pulling his body to the head of the operating table and, according to plaintiff's testimony, laying him back against two hard objects at the top of his shoulders, about an inch below his neck. Dr. Reser then administered the anesthetic and plaintiff lost consciousness. When he awoke early the following morning he was in his hospital room attended by defendant Thompson, the special nurse, and another nurse who was not made a defendant.

Plaintiff testified that prior to the operation he had never had any pain in, or injury to, his right arm or shoulder, but that when he awakened he felt a sharp pain about half way between the neck and the point of the right shoulder. He complained to the nurse, and then to Dr. Tilley, who gave him diathermy treatments while he remained in the hospital. The pain did not cease but spread down to the lower part of his arm, and after his release from the hospital the condition grew worse. He was unable to rotate or lift his arm, and developed paralysis and atrophy of the muscles around the shoulder. He received further treatments from Dr. Tilley until March, 1940, and then returned to work, wearing his arm in a splint on the advice of Dr. Spangard.

Plaintiff also consulted Dr. Wilfred Sterling Clark, who had X-ray pictures taken which showed an area of diminished sensation below the shoulder and atrophy and wasting away of the muscles around the shoulder. In the opinion of Dr. Clark, plaintiff's condition was due to trauma or injury by pressure or strain applied between his right shoulder and neck.

Plaintiff was also examined by Dr. Fernando Garduno, who expressed the opinion that plaintiff's injury was a paralysis of traumatic origin, not arising from pathological causes, and not systemic, and that the injury resulted in atrophy, loss of use and restriction of motion of the right arm and shoulder.

Plaintiff's theory is that the foregoing evidence presents a proper case for the application of the doctrine of res ipsa loquitur, and that the inference of negligence arising therefrom makes the granting of a nonsuit improper. Defendants take the position that, assuming that plaintiff's condition was in fact the result of an injury, there is no showing that the act of any particular defendant, nor any particular instrumentality, was the cause thereof. They attack plaintiff's action as an attempt to fix liability "en masse" on various defendants, some of whom were not responsible for the acts of others; and they further point to the failure to show which defendants had control of the instrumentalities that may have been involved. Their main defense may be briefly stated in two propositions: (1) that where there are several defendants, and there is a division of responsibility in the use of an instrumentality causing the injury, and the injury might have resulted from the separate act of either one of two or more persons, the rule of res ipsa loquitur cannot be invoked against any one of them; and (2) that where there are several instrumentalities, and no showing is made as to which caused the injury or as to the particular defendant in control of it, the doctrine cannot apply. We are satisfied, however, that these objections are not well taken in the circumstances of this case.

The doctrine of res ipsa loquitur has three conditions: "(1) the accident must be of a kind which ordinarily does not occur in the absence of someone's negligence; (2) it must be caused by an agency or instrumentality within the exclusive control of the defendant; (3) it must not have been due to any voluntary action or contribution on the part of the plaintiff."

Prosser, Torts, p. 295. It is applied in a wide variety of situations, including cases of medical or dental treatment and hospital care. * * *

There is, however, some uncertainty as to the extent to which res ipsa loquitur may be invoked in cases of injury from medical treatment. This is in part due to the tendency, in some decisions, to lay undue emphasis on the limitations of the doctrine, and to give too little attention to its basic underlying purpose. The result has been that a simple, understandable rule of circumstantial evidence, with a sound background of common sense and human experience, has occasionally been transformed into a rigid legal formula, which arbitrarily precludes its application in many cases where it is most important that it should be applied. If the doctrine is to continue to serve a useful purpose, we should not forget that "the particular force and justice of the rule, regarded as a presumption throwing upon the party charged the duty of producing evidence, consists in the circumstance that the chief evidence of the true cause, whether culpable or innocent, is practically accessible to him but inaccessible to the injured person." 9 Wigmore, Evidence, 3d Ed., § 2509, p. 382 * * *. Maki v. Murray Hospital, 91 Mont. 251, 7 P.2d 228, 231. In the last-named case, where an unconscious patient in a hospital received injuries from a fall, the court declared that without the doctrine the maxim that for every wrong there is a remedy would be rendered nugatory, "by denying one, patently entitled to damages, satisfaction merely because he is ignorant of facts peculiarly within the knowledge of the party who should, in all justice, pay them."

The present case is of a type which comes within the reason and spirit of the doctrine more fully perhaps than any other. The passenger sitting awake in a railroad car at the time of a collision, the pedestrian walking along the street and struck by a falling object or the debris of an explosion, are surely not more entitled to an explanation than the unconscious patient on the operating table. Viewed from this aspect, it is difficult to see how the doctrine can, with any justification, be so restricted in its statement as to become inapplicable to a patient who submits himself to the care and custody of doctors and nurses, is rendered unconscious, and receives some injury from instrumentalities used in his treatment. Without the aid of the doctrine a patient who received permanent injuries of a serious character, obviously the result of some one's negligence, would be entirely unable to recover unless the doctors and nurses in attendance voluntarily chose to disclose the identity of the negligent person and the facts establishing liability. * * * If this were the state of the law of negligence, the courts, to avoid gross injustice, would be forced to invoke the principles of absolute liability, irrespective of negligence, in actions by persons suffering injuries during the course of treatment under anesthesia. But we think this juncture has not yet been reached, and that the doctrine of res ipsa loquitur is properly applicable to the case before us.

The condition that the injury must not have been due to the plaintiff's voluntary action is of course fully satisfied under the evidence produced herein; and the same is true of the condition that the accident must be one which ordinarily does not occur unless some one was negligent. We have here no problem of negligence in treatment, but of distinct injury to a healthy part of the body not the subject of treatment, nor within the area covered by the operation. The decisions in this state make it clear that such circumstances raise the inference of negligence and call upon the defendant to explain the unusual result. * * *

The argument of defendants is simply that plaintiff has not shown an injury caused by an instrumentality under a defendant's control, because he has not shown which of the several instrumentalities that he came in contact with while in the hospital caused the injury; and he has not shown that any one defendant or his servants had exclusive control over any particular instrumentality. Defendants assert that some of them were not the employees of other defendants, that some did not stand in any permanent relationship from which liability in tort would follow, and that in view of the nature of the injury, the number of defendants and the different functions performed by each, they could not all be liable for the wrong, if any.

We have no doubt that in a modern hospital a patient is quite likely to come under the care of a number of persons in different types of contractual and other relationships with each other. For example, in the present case it appears that Drs. Smith, Spangard and Tilley were physicians or surgeons commonly placed in the legal category of independent contractors; and Dr. Reser, the anesthetist, and defendant Thompson, the special nurse, were employees of Dr. Swift and not of the other doctors. But we do not believe that either the number or relationship of the defendants alone determines whether the doctrine of res ipsa loquitur applies. Every defendant in whose custody the plaintiff was placed for any period was bound to exercise ordinary care to see that no unnecessary harm came to him and each would be liable for failure in this regard. Any defendant who negligently injured him, and any defendant charged with his care who so neglected him as to allow injury to occur, would be liable. The defendant employers would be liable for the neglect of their employees; and the doctor in charge of the operation would be liable for the negligence of those who became his temporary servants for the purpose of assisting in the operation.

In this connection, it should be noted that while the assisting physicians and nurses may be employed by the hospital, or engaged by the patient, they normally become the temporary servants or agents of the surgeon in charge while the operation is in progress, and liability may be imposed upon him for their negligent acts under the doctrine of respondeat superior. Thus a surgeon has been held liable for the negligence of an assisting nurse who leaves a sponge or other object inside a patient, and the fact that the duty of seeing that such mistakes do not occur is delegated to others does not absolve the doctor from responsibility for their negligence. * * *

It may appear at the trial that, consistent with the principles outlined above, one or more defendants will be found liable and others absolved, but this should not preclude the application of the rule of res ipsa loquitur. The control at one time or another, of one or more of the various agencies or instrumentalities which might have harmed the plaintiff was in the hands of every defendant or of his employees or temporary servants. This, we think, places upon them the burden of initial explanation. Plaintiff was rendered unconscious for the purpose of undergoing surgical treatment by the defendants; it is manifestly unreasonable for them to insist that he identify any one of them as the person who did the alleged negligent act.

The other aspect of the case which defendants so strongly emphasize is that plaintiff has not identified the instrumentality any more than he has the particular guilty defendant. Here, again, there is a misconception which, if carried to the extreme for which defendants contend, would unreasonably limit the application of the res ipsa loquitur rule. It should be enough that the plaintiff can show an injury resulting from an external force applied while he lay unconscious in the hospital; this is as clear a case of identification of the instrumentality as the plaintiff may ever be able to make.

An examination of the recent cases, particularly in this state, discloses that the test of actual exclusive control of an instrumentality has not been strictly followed, but exceptions have been recognized where the purpose of the doctrine of res ipsa loquitur would otherwise be defeated. Thus, the test has become one of right of control rather than actual control. * * * In the bursting bottle cases where the bottler has delivered the instrumentality to a retailer and thus has given up actual control, he will nevertheless be subject to the doctrine where it is shown that no change in the condition of the bottle occurred after it left the bottler's possession, and it can accordingly be said that he was in constructive control. Escola v. Coca Cola Bottling Co., 24 Cal.2d 453, 150 P.2d 436. Moreover, this court departed from the single instrumentality theory in the colliding vehicle cases, where two defendants were involved, each in control of a separate vehicle. See Smith v. O'Donnell, 215 Cal. 714, 12 P.2d 933 * * *.

In the face of these examples of liberalization of the tests for res ipsa loquitur, there can be no justification for the rejection of the doctrine in the instant case. As pointed out above, if we accept the contention of defendants herein, there will rarely be any compensation for patients injured while unconscious. A hospital today conducts a highly integrated system of activities, with many persons contributing their efforts. There may be, e.g., preparation for surgery by nurses and internes who are employees of the hospital; administering of an anesthetic by a doctor who may be an employee of the hospital, an employee of the operating surgeon, or an independent contractor; performance of an operation by a surgeon and assistants who may be his employees, employees of the hospital, or independent contractors; and post surgical care by the surgeon, a hospital physician, and nurses. The number of those in whose care the patient is placed is not a good reason for denying him all reasonable opportunity to recover for negligent harm. It is rather a good reason for re-examination of the statement of legal theories which supposedly compel such a shocking result.

We do not at this time undertake to state the extent to which the reasoning of this case may be applied to other situations in which the doctrine of res ipsa loquitur is invoked. We merely hold that where a plaintiff receives unusual injuries while unconscious, and in the course of medical treatment, all those defendants who had any control over his body or the instrumentalities which might have caused the injuries may properly be called upon to meet the inference of negligence by giving an explanation of their conduct.

The judgment is reversed.

Rehearing denied; TRAYNOR, J., dissenting.

Notes

1. If you were the lawyer representing nurse Thompson, what strategy would you adopt at the new trial? Do you think you would have been successful? In point of fact, on the new trial, the trial judge, trying the case without a jury, ruled against all of the defendants. His decision was affirmed by the California Court of Appeals. 93 Cal.App.2d 43, 208 P.2d 445 (1949). The *Ybarra* case was severely criticized in W. Seavey, *Res Ipsa Loquitur: Tabula in Naufragio*, 63 Harv.L.Rev. 643 (1950). The subject of unexplained injuries that occur in the course of surgery is discussed in E. W. Thode, *The Unconscious Patient: Who Should Bear the Risk of Unexplained Injuries to a Healthy Part of His Body?*, 1969 Utah L.Rev. 1.

2. *Ybarra v. Spangard* would not have been a difficult case if the court had been prepared to hold that all the defendant doctors and nurses were engaged in a joint enterprise. It could then have imposed vicarious liability upon all the joint entrepreneurs for the negligence of the unknown member of the enterprise. But as will be seen *infra*, in Chapter Five, joint enterprise is not a favored theory in the law. In the context of *Ybarra*, many of the members of the enterprise had negligible management rights and the existence of such rights is generally crucial in finding a joint enterprise. As we have already seen, however, a more promising theory, certainly in recent years, might have been to impose responsibility upon the owner of the hospital and the chief surgeon for the activities of the other members of the medical team.

3. The general logical requirements for the application of the doctrine of res ipsa loquitur are: (a) the accident which injured the plaintiff is of a kind that normally does not occur in the absence of someone's negligence and (b) the defendant has had a sufficiently close connection with the instrumentality that caused the injury that it is more likely than not that he is the negligent somebody. As the cases that have been presented illustrate, this second requirement is often restated more stringently by the courts as the requirement that the instrumentality that caused the accident must have been in the "exclusive management and control" of the defendant. This has proven to be too stringent a requirement. Taken literally, the doctrine could not be invoked by a patron of a restaurant when the stool he is sitting on unexpectedly collapses, and there are some older cases which have so held. *See* Kilgore v. Shepard Co., 52 R.I. 151, 158 A. 720 (1932). And then of course, there are the exploding bottle cases where the consumer is the one in possession of the bottle at the time of the accident. To avoid such absurd results, the courts, as Gibson, C.J., noted in his opinion for the court in *Ybarra v. Spangard*, have come up with notions like "the right of control as opposed to actual control" or "constructive control." How meaningful these alternative notions are is another matter. As a matter of logic, all that is needed is a strong probability that the defendant had a sufficiently crucial connection with the instrumentality at the time the negligence most likely occurred to support the inference that it was most likely the defendant's negligence that caused the accident. Control and management of the instrumentality involved are highly probative on that issue but are not logically necessary, and certainly control and management of the instrumentality at the time of the injury are not logically necessary. This

is the position taken by *Restatement (Second) of Torts* § 328D, Comment *g. See also,* Parrillo v. Giroux Co., 426 A.2d 1313 (R.I.1981).

4. What makes a res ipsa loquitur case different from the ordinary case where circumstantial evidence forms part of the proof, is that the jury is specifically instructed that from proof of the accident they may infer that the defendant was negligent and that his negligence caused the plaintiff's injuries. The most usual policy justification for the use of this procedural device is that, since most of the evidence as to exactly what happened is in the possession of the defendant, the doctrine serves as a means of putting pressure on the defendant to come forward with evidence. Is it, however, always essential before the doctrine can be invoked that the defendant must, in theory at least, be in a position to explain the accident? If the paramount consideration is the fairness of forcing the defendant to come forward, then perhaps it is essential that the defendant should be in a position to explain the accident. In that case, management and control, and particularly management and control at the time of the accident, become particularly crucial. But, if the strength of the inference is of equal if not greater importance, then management and control, particularly at the time of the accident, will not be conclusive, although they will still influence the application of the doctrine. If the strength of the inference is a paramount consideration, a court will consider a variety of factors in deciding whether the doctrine of res ipsa loquitur should be applied to the case before it. These factors will include not only the ability of the defendant to explain the accident but also the relative ability of the plaintiff to present further proof upon the cause of the accident. And, during all its deliberations, a court will keep its attention focused on the probative force of the inference of the defendant's negligence from the occurrence of the accident.

Take a case where an airliner takes off for a long journey that is to take place largely over the ocean. The plane never arrives at its destination. In Cox v. Northwest Airlines, Inc., 379 F.2d 893 (7th Cir.1967), *cert. denied* 389 U.S. 1044, 88 S.Ct. 788, 19 L.Ed.2d 836 (1968), the doctrine of res ipsa loquitur was applied against the airline under these circumstances. *See also* Haasman v. Pacific Alaska Air Express, 13 Alaska 439, 100 F.Supp. 1 (D.Alaska 1951), *affirmed sub nom.,* Des Marais v. Beckman, 198 F.2d 550 (9th Cir.1952), *cert. denied* 344 U.S. 922, 73 S.Ct. 388, 97 L.Ed. 710 (1953). The airplane was certainly probably under the management and control of the defendant at the time the airplane was lost, but it is unlikely that this gave the airline much greater knowledge of what happened than was possessed by those bringing wrongful death actions on behalf of the lost passengers. Admittedly, the defendant might have been negligent in the maintenance of the aircraft and this is a matter that the defendant knew more about than the plaintiffs, but is it clear that negligence in maintenance was the most likely cause of the accident? On the other hand, it does seem that negligence in the maintenance *or* operation of the aircraft was the most likely cause. Furthermore, it is unlikely that the plaintiffs could have produced much evidence on why the airplane disappeared.

5. In *Ybarra v. Spangard* the court obviously focused on the policy consideration of forcing the defendant to come forward with proof, even though with regard to some of the defendants, the inference of negligence was very weak, to say the least. This focusing on the desirability of forcing the defendant to come forward with evidence has given rise, at least in California, to the doctrine of "conditional res ipsa loquitur" which has been applied in medical malpractice cases. *See* Clark v. Gibbons, 66 Cal.2d 399, 58 Cal.Rptr.

125, 426 P.2d 525 (1967). The doctrine is applied where (a) there is evidence that the unfortunate results of an operation *could* have been occasioned by negligence and (b) there is some evidence of negligent acts on the part of the defendant that could have caused these unfortunate results but not enough proof to make it more likely than not that the unfortunate results were in fact caused by the defendant's negligence. The use of res ipsa loquitur under these circumstances, which would appear to be a throwback to the "some rational connection" test, is thus "conditioned" upon the plaintiff's lack of access to the evidence that he needs to support his case. How sound do you think this doctrine is? For the argument that *Ybarra* is better understood as a case of group liability and the proposal that group liability should be used more extensively, *see* S. Levmore, *Gomorrah to Ybarra and More: Overextraction and the Puzzle of Immoderate Group Liability*, 81 Va.L.Rev. 1561 (1995).

Chapter 4

CAUSATION

A. CAUSE IN FACT—THE BUT FOR TEST AND THE NOTION OF "SUBSTANTIAL CAUSE"

1. General

In this chapter we shall examine the requirement that the plaintiff, as part of his prima facie case, must prove that the defendant's negligence "caused" his injuries. The quest for a legal cause is usually broken down into two subsidiary inquiries: was the defendant's conduct the *cause in fact* of the plaintiff's injuries? If it was, was the defendant's conduct also the *proximate cause* of the plaintiff's injuries? The discussion of this difficult subject is often complicated by the fact that the term legal cause is sometimes used as a synonym for "proximate cause," and not to cover the entire range of questions considered in deciding the issue of causation.

The ascription of a causal relationship between any two events—say the defendant's negligent conduct and the plaintiff's injuries—is philosophically a very difficult question. The law has tried to avoid the philosophical difficulties involved in the concept of causation but it has not always succeeded in doing so. We ascribe a causal relationship between two events as part of our attempt to understand these events and the degree of interdependence between them. If we cannot ascribe any causal relationship between two events we are forced to conclude that, with respect to each other, they are random. When we say, on the other hand, that we fully comprehended the cause of any particular event, we are saying that, at least in theory, we can recreate the particular event in which we are interested by bringing into existence all the antecedent events which we maintain caused the event in question. Often, however, it is impossible to completely recreate an event, even in theory. Under these circumstances, the focus is upon some prior event, which has occurred and could have been part of the cause of the event in question. For example, the prior event could be the defendant's negligent conduct and the event in question could be the plaintiff's injury. We then try to eliminate every other possible cause, so that by a process of elimination the prior event becomes the most likely cause of the event in question. The defendant's negligent conduct can thus be established as being more likely than not part of the causal chain leading up to the plaintiff's injuries.

In this section we shall examine the requirement that the defendant's conduct must have been the cause in fact of the plaintiff's injuries. This requirement is sometimes described as the *sine qua non* test, that is, "but for" the defendant's conduct, the plaintiff would not have suffered his injuries. In the limiting case, event X is a cause in fact (or "but for" cause) of event Y, if the occurrence of event X is invariably followed by the occurrence of event Y. In the real world, however, that type of one-to-one correlation between two events is not always provable or even possible. As a general matter, therefore, event X can be established as a cause in fact of event Y if (a) there is a sufficiently high statistical correlation between the occurrence of events of type X and the occurrence of events of type Y, and if (b), in the particular case under consideration, there is no other plausible explanation of the occurrence of event Y that does not require the occurrence of event X. As we specify the events in which we are interested with greater and greater specificity, events which had not previously been considered to be causally related may turn out to be causally related after all. Thus, driving a motor vehicle on a straight highway at 80 miles an hour does not appear to have any statistical correlation with the falling of a dead tree upon the car. If, however, we were to particularize our description of the events to include precise time, atmospheric and wind conditions, and the state of decay of the tree, we would eventually reach a description of the events in which there was a correlation between the act of driving in excess of the speed limit and the falling of the tree killing a passenger in the car.

Applying these general notions to the complex set of events involved in the typical action for negligence, the following general conclusions would seem to be warranted: A particular event will be a cause in fact of another event if (a) it can be described as part of a number of antecedent events which culminate in the event under consideration and (b) the absence of this particular antecedent event would diminish the probability of the occurrence of the consequent event. As we shall see, although these conclusions appear to cover the vast range of tort actions, there are some situations where the law finds this test too stringent in that it would prevent a plaintiff from recovering in instances where it is felt that he ought to be able to recover. The cases will reveal how the courts have attempted to deal with the problem. The courts have often attempted to justify their deviation from the rigors imposed by what may be called the "logic of causation" by declaring that they are not concerned with establishing *the* cause or causes of an event—this is the work of a scientist—but rather are concerned with discovering the "substantial cause or causes" of that event.

2. The Cases

KINGSTON v. CHICAGO & NORTHWEST RAILWAY CO.

Supreme Court of Wisconsin, 1927.
191 Wis. 610, 211 N.W. 913.

Action to recover damages caused by a fire. One main line of defendant's railroad extends in a general north and south direction from Gillett,

Wis., to Saunders, Mich., through Bonita. A branch line extends westerly from Bonita to Oconto Company's logging road. The branch runs generally in an east and west direction, and is about ten miles in length. La Fortune's spur is on the branch about two miles west of Bonita. The spur consists of a side track on the south side of and parallel with the branch track. Plaintiff's property was located on a landing, known as Kingston's landing and as the cedar yard, adjacent to and south of the spur track.

On April 29, 1925, a forest fire was burning about one-half to one mile northwesterly, nearly west, of this landing. On the same date another fire was burning about four miles northeast of the landing. On April 30th these two fires united in a region about 940 feet north of the railroad track. The line of fire thus formed after the union was about 40 or 50 rods east and west. It then traveled south and burned plaintiff's property, consisting of logs, timber, and poles on this landing or in the cedar yard. The plaintiff claims that both fires which united were set by the railroad company; one by a locomotive on its main line running north of Bonita, the other by a locomotive on the branch about three miles west of Bonita and about a mile in a westerly direction from the spur.

* * *

Owen, J. The jury found that both fires were set by sparks emitted from locomotives on and over defendant's right of way. Appellant contends that there is no evidence to support the finding that either fire was so set. We have carefully examined the record, and have come to the conclusion that the evidence does support the finding that the northeast fire was set by sparks emitted from a locomotive then being run on and over the right of way of defendant's main line. We conclude, however, that the evidence does not support the finding that the northwest fire was set by sparks emitted from defendant's locomotives or that the defendant had any connection with its origin. * * *

We, therefore, have this situation: The northeast fire was set by sparks emitted from defendant's locomotive. This fire, according to the finding of the jury, constituted a proximate cause of the destruction of plaintiff's property. This finding we find to be well supported by the evidence. We have the northwest fire, of unknown origin. This fire, according to the finding of the jury, also constituted a proximate cause of the destruction of the plaintiff's property. This finding we also find to be well supported by the evidence. We have a union of these two fires 940 feet north of plaintiff's property, from which point the united fire bore down upon and destroyed the property. We, therefore, have two separate, independent, and distinct agencies, each of which constituted the proximate cause of plaintiff's damage, and either of which, in the absence of the other, would have accomplished such result.

It is settled in the law of negligence that any one of two or more joint tort-feasors, or one of two or more wrongdoers whose concurring acts of negligence result in injury, are each individually responsible for the entire damage resulting from their joint or concurrent acts of negligence. This rule also obtains—

"where two causes, each attributable to the negligence of a responsible person, concur in producing an injury to another, either of which causes would produce it regardless of the other, * * * because, whether the concurrence be intentional, actual or constructive, each wrongdoer, in effect, adopts the conduct of his coactor, and for the further reason that it is impossible to apportion the damage or to say that either perpetrated any distinct injury that can be separated from the whole. The whole loss must necessarily be considered and treated as an entirety." Cook v. Minneapolis, St. Paul & Sault Ste. Marie R. Co., 98 Wis. 624, at page 642, 74 N.W. 561, 566.

That case presented a situation very similar to this. One fire, originating by sparks emitted from a locomotive, united with another fire of unknown origin and consumed plaintiff's property. There was nothing to indicate that the fire of unknown origin was not set by some human agency. The evidence in the case merely failed to identify the agency. In that case it was held that the railroad company which set one fire was not responsible for the damage committed by the united fires because the origin of the other fire was not identified. In that case a rule of law was announced, which is stated in the syllabus prepared by the writer of the opinion as follows:

"A fire started by defendant's negligence, after spreading one mile and a quarter to the northeast, near plaintiffs' property, met a fire having no responsible origin, coming from the northwest. After the union, fire swept on from the northwest to and into plaintiffs' property, causing its destruction. Either fire, if the other had not existed, would have reached the property and caused its destruction at the same time. Held:

"(1) That the rule of liability in case of joint wrongdoers does not apply.

"(2) That the independent fire from the northwest became a superseding cause so that the destruction of the property could not, with reasonable certainty, be attributed in whole or in part to the fire having a responsible origin; that the chain of responsible causation was so broken by the fire from the northwest that the negligent fire, if it reached the property at all, was a remote and not the proximate cause of the loss."

Emphasis is placed upon the fact, especially in the opinion, that one fire had "no responsible origin." At other times in the opinion the fact is emphasized that it had no "known responsible origin." The plain inference from the entire opinion is that, if both fires had been of responsible origin, or of known responsible origin, each wrongdoer would have been liable for the entire damage. The conclusion of the court exempting the railroad company from liability seems to be based upon the single fact that one fire had no responsible origin, or no known responsible origin. It is difficult to determine just what weight was accorded to the fact that the origin of the fire was unknown. If the conclusion of the court was founded upon the assumption that the fire of unknown origin had no responsible origin, the conclusion announced may be sound and in harmony with well-settled principles of negligence.

From our present consideration of the subject, we are not disposed to criticise the doctrine which exempts from liability a wrongdoer who sets a fire which unites with a fire originating from natural causes, such as lightning, not attributable to any human agency, resulting in damage. It is also conceivable that a fire so set might unite with a fire of so much greater proportions, such as a raging forest fire, so as to be enveloped or swallowed up by the greater holocaust, and its identity destroyed, so that the greater fire could be said to be an intervening or superseding cause. But we have no such situation here. These fires were of comparatively equal rank. If there was any difference in their magnitude or threatening aspect the record indicates that the northeast fire was the larger fire and was really regarded as the menacing agency. At any rate, there is no intimation or suggestion that the northeast fire was enveloped and swallowed up by the northwest fire. We will err on the side of the defendant if we regard the two fires as of equal rank.

According to well-settled principles of negligence, it is undoubted that, if the proof disclosed the origin of the northwest fire, even though its origin be attributed to a third person, the railroad company, as the originator of the northeast fire, would be liable for the entire damage. There is no reason to believe that the northwest fire originated from any other than human agency. It was a small fire. It had traveled over a limited area. It had been in existence but for a day. For a time it was thought to have been extinguished. It was not in the nature of a raging forest fire. The record discloses nothing of natural phenomena which could have given rise to the fire. It is morally certain that it was set by some human agency.

* * *

Speaking of the decision in the Cook Case, Thompson, in his work on Negligence, § 739, says:

"The conclusion is so clearly wrong as not to deserve discussion. It is just as though two wrongdoers, not acting in concert, or simultaneously, fire shots from different directions at the same person, each shot inflicting a mortal wound. Either wound being sufficient to cause death, it would be a childish casuistry that would engage in a debate as to which of the wrongdoers was innocent on the ground that the other was guilty."

His illustration does not exactly answer the reason which we conceive to underlie the decision in the Cook Case. It would exactly fit it, as we understand the Cook Case, if the one who was known to have fired one of the shots should be permitted to escape liability for death because he who fired the other shot had not been identified, although it was certain that the other shot had been fired by some other human being. We are not disposed to apply the doctrine of the Cook Case to the instant situation. There being no attempt on the part of the defendant to prove that the northwest fire was due to an irresponsible origin—that is, an origin not attributable to a human being—and the evidence in the case affording no reason to believe that it had an origin not attributable to a human being, and it appearing that the northeast fire, for the origin of which the defendant is responsible, was a proximate cause of plaintiff's loss the defendant is responsible for the entire amount of that loss. While under some circumstances a wrongdoer is not responsible for damage which would have occurred in the absence of his wrongful act, even though such wrongful act was a proximate cause of the accident, that doctrine does not obtain "where two causes, each attributable to the negligence of a responsible person, concur in producing an injury to another, either of which causes would produce it regardless of the other." This is because "it is impossible to apportion the damages or to say that either perpetrated any distinct injury that can be separated from the whole," and to permit each of two wrongdoers to plead the wrong of the other as a defense to his own wrongdoing, would permit both wrongdoers to escape and penalize the innocent party who has been damaged by their wrongful acts.

The fact that the northeast fire was set by the railroad company, which fire was a proximate cause of plaintiff's damage, is sufficient to affirm the judgment. This conclusion renders it unnecessary to consider other grounds of liability stressed in respondent's brief.

Judgment affirmed.

Note

Why should it make any difference whether the other fire was set by natural causes or an "unknown human being?"

KRAMER SERVICE v. WILKINS

Supreme Court of Mississippi, 1939.
184 Miss. 483, 186 So. 625.

GRIFFITH, JUSTICE.

Appellant was and is the owner and operator of a large hotel. About 5:30 o'clock P.M. on January 15, 1935, one Clockey registered as a guest and was given a room, to which he was conducted by a bellboy. Mr. Clockey was the district sales representative of an oil company, and appellee was the local representative. The business which brought Clockey to the hotel was to have a conference with appellee. It was the long established custom of the hotel that a guest should have the privilege of inviting to his room any person whom the guest wished to see on business. It was the purpose of Clockey to telephone appellee of his arrival, and expected that a telephone would be in his room.

Soon after entering the room, Clockey discovered that there was no telephone therein, and that the windows could not be raised nor the transom lowered so as to give ventilation. The reason that the guest could not undertake to lower the transom was that there was a break in the glass thereof, the break being described by this witness as cone-shaped and about twenty inches in length at the base, the broken portion clinging nevertheless in the transom.

Clockey was obliged to go to the hotel office in order to telephone appellee, his business associate, which he did in about twenty minutes after he had registered. While on this mission Clockey informed the hotel clerk of the objectionable condition of the room, including a reference to the condition of the transom. The clerk explained that there was a convention in session at the hotel, and that the room assigned was the only one left, but that a better room could be given on the next day.

About two hours later appellee came to Clockey's room in response to the telephone message, and when the business conference was concluded appellee was in the act of leaving the room. When he opened the door, which was done in an ordinary manner, without any violence, the broken piece of the transom fell striking appellee upon the head. Three wounds were thus made upon appellee's head, one of which was a jagged abrasion on the temple.

The foregoing statement of the facts is supported by competent evidence which in the light of the verdict of the jury must be accepted as true. There is further competent evidence to the effect that the condition of unrepair which resulted in the fall of the broken transom glass had existed for a sufficient length of time to charge appellant with responsible notice thereof, and that the condition was such that a reasonably prudent and careful operator should have foreseen the fall of the broken glass and an injury thereby as a likelihood of appreciable weight and moment. * * * There is no reversible error in the record on the issue of liability, and as to that issue the judgment will be affirmed.

But there is plain and serious error in the matter of the amount of the damages. The wound on the temple did not heal, and some months after the injury appellee was advised by his local physician to visit a specialist in skin diseases, which he did in January, 1937, about two years after the injury, and it was then found that at the point where the injury occurred to appellee's temple, a skin cancer had developed, of which a cure had not been fully effected at the time of the trial, some three years after the injury first mentioned.

Appellee sued for a large sum in damages, averring and contending that the cancer resulted from the stated injury; and the jury evidently accepted that contention, since there was an award by the verdict in the sum of twenty thousand dollars. Appellant requested an instruction to the effect that the cancer or any prolongation of the trouble on account thereof should not be taken into consideration by the jury, but this instruction was refused.

Two physicians or medical experts, and only two, were introduced as witnesses, and both were specialists in skin diseases and dermal traumatisms. One testified that it was possible that a trauma such as appellee suffered upon his temple, could or would cause a skin cancer at the point of injury, but that the chances that such a result would ensue from such a cause would be only one out of one hundred cases. The other testified that there is no causal connection whatever between trauma and cancer, and went on to illustrate that if there were such a connection nearly every person of mature age would be suffering with cancer. * * *

It seems therefore hardly to be debatable but that appellant was entitled to the requested instruction as regards the cancer; and since, except as to that element, the verdict could not have been large, the verdict and judgment must be reversed on the issue of the amount of the damages.

There is one heresy in the judicial forum which appears to be Hydra-headed, and although cut off again and again, has the characteristic of an endless renewal. That heresy is that proof that a past event possibly happened, or that a certain result was possibly caused by a past event, is sufficient in probative force to take the question to a jury. Such was never the law in this state, and we are in accord with almost all of the other common-law states. Nearly a half century ago, when our Court stood forth in point of ability never excelled, and when the principles of the jurisprudence of this state were being put into a more definite form than ever before, Chief Justice Campbell said in Railroad v. Cathy, 70 Miss. 332, 337, 12 So. 253: "It is not enough that negligence of the employer and injury to the employe coexisted, but the injury must have been caused by the negligence. * * * 'Post hoc ergo propter hoc' is not sound as evidence or argument. Nor is it sufficient for a plaintiff seeking recovery for alleged negligence by an employer towards an employe to show a possibility that the injury complained of was caused by negligence. Possibilities will not sustain a verdict. It must have a better foundation."

This terse and expressive language had no such limited application as that it governed only in employer and employe cases * * *

Over and over in language to the same effect since that day this rule has been repeated and reaffirmed * * *

Taking the medical testimony in this case in the strongest light in which it could be reasonably interpreted in behalf of the plaintiff, this testimony is that as a possibility a skin cancer could be caused by an injury such as here happened, but as a probability the physicians were in agreement that there was or is no such a probability.

And the medical testimony is conclusive on both judge and jury in this case. That testimony is undisputed that after long and anxious years of research the exact cause of cancer remains unknown—there is no dependably known origin to which it can be definitely traced or ascribed. If, then, the cause be unknown to all those who have devoted their lives to a study of the subject, it is wholly beyond the range of the common experience and observation of judges and jurors, and in such a case medical testimony when undisputed, as here, must be accepted and acted upon in the same manner as is other undisputed evidence; otherwise the jury would be allowed to resort to and act upon nothing else than the proposition post hoc ergo propter hoc, which, as already mentioned, this Court has long ago rejected as unsound, whether as evidence or as argument.

* * *

Affirmed as to liability; reversed and remanded on the issue of the amount of the damages.

Note

According to the court, one of the doctors testified that "it was possible that a trauma such as appellee suffered upon his temple, could or would cause a cancer at the point of injury, but that the chances that such a result would ensue from such a cause would be only one out of one hundred cases." Would you think that the absence of any other possible explanation for the skin cancer produced in the plaintiff in this particular case makes the plausibility of the causal inference greater than one in one hundred in this case?

DALY v. BERGSTEDT

Supreme Court of Minnesota, 1964.
267 Minn. 244, 126 N.W.2d 242.

MURPHY, JUSTICE.

This appeal follows a verdict recovered by plaintiffs' decedent for personal injuries and is from an order denying a new trial and granting indemnity to two of the codefendants against the others. The action was brought by Marie P. Daly against James and Robert Duffy, doing business as Duffy Brothers, who operated a grocery and general retail merchandise store in the village of Rosemount. Also joined as defendants were John H. Bergstedt and George W. Nielsen, doing business as Bergstedt–Nielsen Store Equipment Company, and Richard Hotch, their employee. At the time the plaintiff's alleged injuries were incurred, the Bergstedt–Nielsen company was engaged in installing new equipment in Duffy Brothers place of business. (Mrs. Daly died after trial and respondents Daly have been substituted for her.)

The first issue raised is whether the record establishes that there was a causal connection between the disease of cancer, from which the plaintiff allegedly suffered, and the accident which occurred on the store premises. The second issue is whether the trial court properly allowed indemnity in favor of Duffy Brothers against the appellants, Bergstedt, Nielsen, and Hotch.

From the record it appears that while shopping at Duffy Brothers store on June 26, 1957, Mrs. Daly fell and was injured. She had patronized the store for a number of years. On the day in question she completed her shopping and paid for her merchandise. A clerk placed the merchandise in two large grocery bags. He handed them to Mrs. Daly, one in each arm, and she proceeded to walk down the aisle toward the doorway leading to her car. Along the way her left foot struck a pile of masonite molding placed directly across the aisle, causing her to fall to the floor.

Prior to the fall, Richard Hotch had moved a bundle of molding sheets out into the aisle where Mrs. Daly fell. These sheets were dark in color, as was the floor, and 6 inches in height. The store was open for business as usual during remodeling. It does not appear that special arrangements were made between the Duffys and the contractor with reference to the areas of work while the alterations were being made. Robert Duffy testified that he did not see the masonite in the aisle before the accident and that it had been placed there shortly before Mrs. Daly fell. The aisle was clear when Mrs. Daly entered the store. The statements of Hotch as to how long the masonite had been in the aisle prior to the accident are contradictory. He testified that the pile had been there close to an hour and explained why this was correct. However, this testimony was contrary to an earlier statement made the day after the accident. He then said that Mrs. Daly was in the store when he began working with the masonite and that the stack was in the aisle about 5 minutes before the accident. About a week after the accident, he signed a statement in which he said that the masonite had been in the aisle 15 minutes before the fall.

It appears that immediately after the fall plaintiff was dazed. When she completely regained her senses, she found that she was lying on top of cans of staples contained in the bags. She could not move her left leg or left side and was in severe pain. She was taken to her home and from there transferred to the hospital in Farmington. Five days later it was found that her left leg had been fractured below the knee. Two days after the fall, Mrs. Daly noticed a bruise, a black and blue mark, on her left breast. This black and blue mark was noticed by both the nurses at the hospital and a friend. Mrs. Daly remained in the hospital for 3 weeks. During the following autumn, her leg grew stronger, allowing her to resume some of her normal activities. It appears, however, that recovery from the fracture was slow. During the winter of 1957–1958, she received approximately 20 to 25 physiotherapy treatments to relieve the pain in her leg. Later, both Mrs. Daly and her friend, Mrs. Akin, noticed that the bruise on her left breast was getting yellow. Sometime thereafter, the discoloration completely disappeared. She continued to have a distressed feeling in her left side, especially in her breast. On August 16, 1958, approximately 14 months following the fall, Mrs. Daly found a large lump on her breast located at the same spot as the bruise. On September 2, 1958, further medical examinations disclosed the presence of cancer and the breast was removed by radical mastectomy the next day. After the operation she no longer suffered the pain and discomfort in the left side which she had experienced since the time of the accident. The record indicates that subsequent to this operation, the disease spread to other parts of her body. X-ray and other medical treatments failed to stop the spread of the cancer. Approximately 4 months prior to the accident she had been examined by Dr. Jane Hodgson. At that time her breasts were normal, no tumors or lumps were found, and aside from having some hypertension and being overweight, the plaintiff was in good physical condition.

1. The issue of liability of the parties for such injuries as the plaintiff actually sustained by reason of the fall is not before us. It is strenuously contended by appellants, however, that there is no factual basis in the record to establish a causal connection between the injury and the disease of cancer. In reviewing this question it may be noted at the outset that this court has considered the subject of causation of cancer in numerous workmen's compensation cases. Noting the lack of certainty as to the cause of cancer in general, we said in Pittman v. Pillsbury Flour Mills, Inc., 234 Minn. 517, 524, 48 N.W.2d 735, 739:

"Although the absence of exact medical knowledge on the cause of cancer makes it impossible to say with absolute certainty whether a particular injury caused or aggravated a particular cancer, we are hardly compelled to say that a finding of cause and effect in a given case is without support in the evidence because such tenuous uncertainty exists."

But in the case before us, appellants point to the circumstance that six physicians testified that there was no causal connection, while but one physician expressed the contrary view. Doctors Jane Hodgson, Logan N. Leven, Davitt A. Felder, Roy Swanson, and Ellery M. James, none of whom examined Mrs. Daly after her fall, were all of the opinion that the trauma in the breast could not cause the cancer. Dr. William W. Heck stated that it has never been satisfactorily proved that there is any causal relation between trauma and cancer. On the other hand, Dr. Moses Barron, who testified for the plaintiff, expressed the opinion that cancer could develop from trauma sustained in the fall. Dr. Barron holds to the so-called Ewing view, which postulates that under some circumstances a single trauma may produce a malignant tumor.[2] Following the criteria announced by this medical authority, Ewing, Neoplastic Diseases (4 ed.), Dr. Barron pointed out that Mrs. Daly's case presented a chronological history in which it was found that at no time during the interval between the fall and the discovery of cancer was there a complete or absolute restitution of the injured tissues of the breast to normalcy. He testified that Mrs. Daly had—

"'* * * either noticed the bluish discoloration at the time of the injury and later on she noticed some pain, she couldn't lie on it, and later on she noticed that she'd have distress and discomfort in that breast, until, finally, she had more and more of this discomfort and she went to see a doctor, when a definite nodule was found, which, at the time of the operation, was a very large tumor.

* * *

"So that the whole history here, from the time of the injury to the time when this tumor was found, and according to the statements that were made that the tumor was in the region where the trauma occurred, that it is entirely reasonable to assume that this process that had been going on in the breast from the time of the blow up to the time of the cancer was a continuous course in which these cells were multiplying and gradually a year or sixteen months later produced a mass large enough that could be easily palpated and led to the operation which showed that it was a scirrhus carcinoma of the breast.

* * *

"This is the reason then that I feel, from the history that I heard presented, that it is my opinion that there is a definite causal relationship between the fall and the trauma to the breast to the later development of the cancer which metastasized to the bones."

The point raised by appellants is not new. It arises because of the difference in the medical and legal approach to the question of causation. In the case before us it seems that appellants refuse to recognize that legal determination for responsibility may differ from medical findings as to the cause or source of a disease. In Murray v. Industrial Comm., 87 Ariz. 190, 199, 349 P.2d 627, 633, it was said:

"'* * * The difference in the medical and legal concept of cause results from the obvious differences in the basic problems and exigen-

---

2. Ewing, *The Relation of Trauma to Malignant Tumors*, 40 American Journal of Surgery 30.

cies of the two professions in relation to causation. By reason of his training, the doctor is thinking in terms of a single, precise cause for a particular condition. The law, however, endeavors to reach an inference of reasonable medical certainty, from a given event or sequence of events, and recognizes more than one cause for a particular injurious result."

Here the defendants' experts assert that it cannot be medically established that a single trauma can cause cancer. The thrust of plaintiff's case is that there is not only medical authority to the effect that trauma may produce cancer but, more importantly, that the record establishes legal cause. This concept takes into consideration the entire chain of events from the time of the accident to the time when cancer developed at the exact point of the trauma, including the fact that the accident occurred to a woman in good health and that she was never healthy thereafter. They argue that the inferences from the proven sequence of events provide a reasonable basis for the jury's verdict.

The question raised by appellants was considered in Golob v. Buckingham Hotel, 244 Minn. 301, 304, 69 N.W.2d 636, 639, where it was claimed that a trauma or exertion could not result in thrombosis. We there said:

"* * * It is possible that part of the difficulty in understanding the divergence of views of doctors comes about by virtue of the difference in approach to the question of causation by members of the medical and legal professions. However that may be, until the time comes when medical knowledge has progressed to such a point that experts in the field of medicine can agree, causal relation in determining compensable injury or disease will have to remain in the province of the trier of fact. Where qualified medical witnesses differ as they do here, it ordinarily is not for us on appeal to say that one is so eminently right and the other so clearly wrong that the fact finder was obliged to accept the opinion of one and discard the opinion of the other. The determination of this question is like the determination of any other question of fact, and it must depend to a large extent upon the credibility attached by the trier of facts to the opinion and testimony of the various witnesses who are expressing their opinions."

Moreover, it should be recognized that inferences, if rational and natural, which follow from a sequence of proved events, may be sufficient to establish causal connection without any supporting medical testimony.

We conclude that the record fairly establishes that a question of fact as to causation was presented which question was properly submitted to the jury.

2. Nor do our authorities support the appellants' contention that the verdict here cannot stand because the proof is uncertain and speculative. Much the same objection was presented in Weller v. Northwest Airlines, 239 Minn. 298, 58 N.W.2d 739, where the plaintiff's doctor was of the opinion that the "most likely diagnosis" of the plaintiff's disability was multiple sclerosis, the cause of which is equally as inexplicable as the cause of cancer. We there said * * *:

"It is well settled that a medical expert's opinion need not be free from doubt or capable of demonstration. It is only necessary that it be in his judgment true. * * * The use of the words 'the most likely diagnosis' does not make the testimony speculative or conjectural but merely indicates the problem of all experts that, although their opinion be based upon tests and methods recognized and prescribed by the medical profession, nevertheless there is always the possibility of error.

* * *

"* * * Where there is such a difference of opinion and where the opinion of a reputable medical expert is submitted that in plaintiff's case the trauma which resulted from the accident was a precipitating factor in bringing on the condition, the causal relationship between the accident and the disease described becomes one for the jury's determination."

* * *

Affirmed.

Notes

1. Do you think that the plaintiffs had established that Mrs. Daly's fall was "the cause" of her cancer? It is reported that the overwhelming weight of medical opinion is now "that a single traumatic blow could not cause a malignant tumor," despite what the courts might hold. S. Gross, *Expert Evidence*, 1991 Wis.L.Rev. 1113, 1184. The view that a single traumatic blow could cause cancer first seems to have arisen in worker's compensation cases and then spread to ordinary tort cases such as *Daly*. *See* P. Huber, Galileo's Revenge, 39–56 (1991). Perhaps because of the hardening of medical opinion, there seems to have been a dramatic decrease in the number of such cases that are brought. See *id*. at 55–56. The Gross article, *supra*, contains a good overview of how expert witnesses are used in litigation. On expert evidence and how it bears on the issue of causation in tort cases, *see* A. Marino and L. Marino, *The Scientific Basis of Causality in Toxic Tort Cases*, 21 Dayton L.Rev. 1 (1995). At least in the federal courts, the admissibility of expert evidence is governed by Federal Evidence Rule 702, as interpreted by Daubert v. Merrell Dow Pharmaceuticals, Inc., 509 U.S. 579, 113 S.Ct. 2786, 125 L.Ed.2d 469 (1993).

2. It is increasingly common among legal authorities to stress that the law is only concerned with establishing whether the defendant's conduct was a "substantial cause" of an event and that this is not the same thing as establishing that the defendant's conduct was *the* cause of the event. The *Restatement (Second) of Torts*, §§ 431 *et seq.*, declares that a legal cause must be a "'substantial factor' in bringing about the harm." In Mitchell v. Gonzales, 54 Cal.3d 1041, 1 Cal.Rptr.2d 913, 819 P.2d 872 (1991), the court adopted the *Restatement (Second)*'s substantial factor test and held it was error to use a jury instruction which incorporated a "but for" test of cause in fact. Because the *Restatement (Second)* merges the notion of cause in fact with that of proximate cause, we shall postpone an examination of the *Restatement's* treatment of the subject of causation until the next section when we discuss proximate cause.

SUMMERS v. TICE

Supreme Court of California, 1948.
33 Cal.2d 80, 199 P.2d 1.

CARTER, JUSTICE.

Each of the two defendants appeals from a judgment against them in an action for personal injuries. Pursuant to stipulation the appeals have been consolidated.

Plaintiff's action was against both defendants for an injury to his right eye and face as the result of being struck by a bird shot discharged from a shotgun. The case was tried by the court without a jury and the court found that on November 20, 1945, plaintiff and the two defendants were hunting quail on the open range. Each of the defendants was armed with a 12 gauge shotgun loaded with shells containing 7½ size shot. Prior to going hunting plaintiff discussed the hunting procedure with defendants, indicating that they were to exercise care when shooting and to "keep in line." In the course of hunting plaintiff proceeded up a hill, thus placing the hunters at the points of a triangle. The view of defendants with reference to plaintiff was unobstructed and they knew his location. Defendant Tice flushed a quail which rose in flight to a ten foot elevation and flew between plaintiff and defendants. Both defendants shot at the quail, shooting in plaintiff's direction. At that time defendants were 75 yards from plaintiff. One shot struck plaintiff in his eye and another in his upper lip. Finally it was found by the court that as the direct result of the shooting by defendants the shots struck plaintiff as above mentioned and that defendants were negligent in so shooting and plaintiff was not contributorily negligent.

First, on the subject of negligence, defendant Simonson contends that the evidence is insufficient to sustain the finding on that score, but he does not point out wherein it is lacking. There is evidence that both defendants, at about the same time or one immediately after the other, shot at a quail and in so doing shot toward plaintiff who was uphill from them, and that they knew his location. That is sufficient from which the trial court could conclude that they acted with respect to plaintiff other than as persons of ordinary prudence. The issue was one of fact for the trial court.
* * *

Defendant Tice states in his opening brief, "we have decided not to argue the insufficiency of negligence on the part of defendant Tice." It is true he states in his answer to plaintiff's petition for a hearing in this court that he did not concede this point but he does not argue it. Nothing more need be said on the subject.

Defendant Simonson urges that plaintiff was guilty of contributory negligence and assumed the risk as a matter of law. He cites no authority for the proposition that by going on a hunting party the various hunters assume the risk of negligence on the part of their companions. Such a tenet is not reasonable. It is true that plaintiff suggested that they all "stay in line," presumably abreast, while hunting, and he went uphill at somewhat of a right angle to the hunting line, but he also cautioned that they use care, and defendants knew plaintiff's position. We hold, therefore, that the trial court was justified in finding that he did not assume the risk or act other than as a person of ordinary prudence under the circumstances. * * *

The problem presented in this case is whether the judgment against both defendants may stand. It is argued by defendants that they are not joint tort feasors, and thus jointly and severally liable, as they were not acting in concert, and that there is not sufficient evidence to show which defendant was guilty of the negligence which caused the injuries—the shooting by Tice or that by Simonson. Tice argues that there is evidence to show that the shot which struck plaintiff came from Simonson's gun because of admissions allegedly made by him to third persons and no evidence that they came from his gun. Further in connection with the latter contention, the court failed to find on plaintiff's allegation in his complaint that he did not know which one was at fault—did not find which defendant was guilty of the negligence which caused the injuries to plaintiff.

Considering the last argument first, we believe it is clear that the court sufficiently found on the issue that defendants were jointly liable and that thus the negligence of both was the cause of the injury or to that legal effect. It found that both defendants were negligent and "That as a direct and proximate result of the shots fired by *defendants, and each of them*, a birdshot pellet was caused to and did lodge in plaintiff's right eye and that another birdshot pellet was caused to and did lodge in plaintiff's upper lip." In so doing the court evidently did not give credence to the admissions of Simonson to third persons that he fired the shots, which it was justified in doing. It thus determined that the negligence of both defendants was the legal cause of the injury—or that both were responsible. Implicit in such finding is the assumption that the court was unable to ascertain whether the shots were from the gun of one defendant or the other or one shot from each of them. The one shot that entered plaintiff's eye was the major factor in assessing damages and that shot could not have come from the gun of both defendants. It was from one or the other only.

It has been held that where a group of persons are on a hunting party, or otherwise engaged in the use of firearms, and two of them are negligent in firing in the direction of a third person who is injured thereby, both of those so firing are liable for the injury suffered by the third person, although the negligence of only one of them could have caused the injury. Moore v. Foster, Miss., 180 So. 73; Oliver v. Miles, Miss., 110 So. 666 * * *. The same rule has been applied in criminal cases (State v. Newberg, 129 Or. 564, 278 P. 568, 63 A.L.R. 1225), and both drivers have been held liable for the negligence of one where they engaged in a racing contest causing an injury to a third person. Saisa v. Lilja, 1 Cir., 76 F.2d 380. These cases speak of the action of defendants as being in concert as the ground of decision, yet it would seem they are straining that concept and the more reasonable basis appears in Oliver v. Miles, supra. There two persons were hunting together. Both shot at some partridges and in so doing shot across the highway injuring plaintiff who was travelling on it. The court stated they were acting in concert and thus both were liable.

The court then stated [110 So. 668]: "We think that * * * each is liable for the resulting injury to the boy, although no one can say definitely who actually shot him. *To hold otherwise, would be to exonerate both from liability, although each was negligent, and the injury resulted from such negligence.*" [Emphasis added.] 110 So. p. 668. It is said in the Restatement: "For harm resulting to a third person from the tortious conduct of another, a person is liable if he * * * (b) knows that the other's conduct constitutes a breach of duty and gives substantial assistance or encouragement to the other so to conduct himself, or (c) gives substantial assistance to the other in accomplishing a tortious result and his own conduct, separately considered, constitutes a breach of duty to the third person." (Rest., Torts, sec. 876(b)(c).) Under subsection (b) the example is given: "A and B are members of a hunting party. Each of them in the presence of the other shoots across a public road at an animal, this being negligent as to persons on the road. A hits the animal. B's bullet strikes C, a traveler on the road. A is liable to C." (Rest., Torts, sec. 876(b), Com., Illus. 3.) An illustration given under subsection (c) is the same as above except the factor of both defendants shooting is missing and joint liability is not imposed. It is further said that: "If two forces are actively operating, one because of the actor's negligence, the other not because of any misconduct on his part, and each of itself is sufficient to bring about harm to another, the actor's negligence may be held by the jury to be a substantial factor in bringing it about." (Rest., Torts, sec. 432.) Dean Wigmore has this to say: "When two or more persons by their acts are possibly the sole cause of a harm, or when two or more acts of the same person are possibly the sole cause, and the plaintiff has introduced evidence that the one of the two persons, or the one of the same person's two acts, is culpable, then the defendant has the burden of proving that the other person, or his other act, was the sole cause of the harm. (b) * * * The real reason for the rule that each joint tortfeasor is responsible for the whole damage is the practical unfairness of denying the injured person redress simply because he cannot prove how much damage each did, when it is certain that between them they did all; let them be the ones to apportion it among themselves. Since, then, the difficulty of proof is the reason, the rule should apply whenever the harm has plural causes, and not merely when they acted in conscious concert. * * *" (Wigmore, Select Cases on the Law of Torts, sec. 153.) Similarly Professor Carpenter has said: "[Suppose] the case where A and B independently shoot at C and but one bullet touches C's body. In such case, such proof as is ordinarily required that either A or B shot C, of course fails. It is suggested that there should be a relaxation of the proof required of the plaintiff * * * where the injury occurs as the result of one where more than one independent force is operating, and it is impossible to determine that the force set in operation by defendant did not in fact constitute a cause of the damage, and where it may have caused the damage, but the plaintiff is unable to establish that it was a cause." (20 Cal.L.Rev. 406.)

When we consider the relative position of the parties and the results that would flow if plaintiff was required to pin the injury on one of the defendants only, a requirement that the burden of proof on that subject be shifted to defendants becomes manifest. They are both wrongdoers—both negligent toward plaintiff. They brought about a situation where the negligence of one of them injured the plaintiff, hence it should rest with them each to absolve himself if he can. The injured party has been placed by defendants in the unfair position of pointing to which defendant caused the harm. If one can escape the other may also and plaintiff is remediless. Ordinarily defendants are in a far better position to offer evidence to determine which one caused the injury. This reasoning has recently found favor in this Court. In a quite analogous situation this Court held that a patient injured while unconscious on an operating table in a hospital could hold all or any of the persons who had any connection with the operation even though he could not select the particular acts by the particular person which led to his disability. Ybarra v. Spangard, 25 Cal.2d 486, 154 P.2d 687, 162 A.L.R. 1258. * * *

* * *

Defendants rely upon Christensen v. Los Angeles Electrical Supply Co., 112 Cal.App. 629, 297 P. 614, holding that a defendant is not liable where he negligently knocked down with his car a pedestrian and a third person then ran over the prostrate person. That involves the question of intervening cause which we do not have here. Moreover it is out of harmony with the current rule on that subject * * * and must be deemed disapproved.

* * *

Cases are cited for the proposition that where two or more tort feasors acting independently of each other cause an injury to plaintiff, they are not joint tort feasors and plaintiff must establish the portion of the damage caused by each, even though it is impossible to prove the portion of the injury caused by each. * * * In view of the foregoing discussion it is apparent that defendants in cases like the present one may be treated as liable on the same basis as joint tort feasors and hence the last cited cases are distinguishable inasmuch as they involve independent tort feasors.

In addition to that, however, it should be pointed out that the same reasons of policy and justice shift the burden to each of defendants to absolve himself if he can—relieving the wronged person of the duty of apportioning the injury to a particular defendant, apply here where we are concerned with whether plaintiff is required to supply evidence for the apportionment of damages. If defendants are independent tort feasors and thus each liable for the damage caused by him alone, and, at least, where the matter of apportionment is incapable of proof, the innocent wronged party should not be deprived of his right to redress. The wrongdoers should be left to work out between themselves any apportionment. * * * Some of the cited cases refer to the difficulty of apportioning the burden of damages between the independent tort feasors, and say that where factually a correct division cannot be made, the trier of fact may make it the best it can, which would be more or less a guess, stressing the factor that the wrongdoers are not in a position to complain of uncertainty. * * *

It is urged that plaintiff now has changed the theory of his case in claiming a concert of action; that he did not plead or prove such concert. From what has been said it is clear that there has been no change in theory. The joint liability, as well as the lack of knowledge as to which defendant was liable, was pleaded and the proof developed the case under either theory. We have seen that for the reasons of policy discussed herein, the case is based upon the legal proposition that, under the circumstances here presented, each defendant is liable for the whole damage whether they are deemed to be acting in concert or independently.

The judgment is affirmed.

Notes

1. Does *Summers v. Tice* stand for the proposition that each of the defendants was a cause or a "substantial cause" of the plaintiff's injuries?

2. The hunting party cases could be treated as joint enterprise situations, that is where a group of hunters is acting in concert, they are jointly and severally liable to any third persons injured by the activities of the enterprise. This is in point of fact how the *Restatement of Torts* handled the situation in the illustrations cited by the court. The text of the *Restatement* section cited by the court is as follows:

§ 876. Persons Acting in Concert.

For harm resulting to a third person from the tortious conduct of another, a person is liable if he

(a) orders or induces such conduct, knowing of the conditions under which the act is done or intending the consequences which ensue, or

(b) knows that the other's conduct constitutes a breach of duty and gives substantial assistance or encouragement to the other so to conduct himself, or

(c) gives substantial assistance to the other in accomplishing a tortious result and his own conduct, separately considered, constitutes a breach of duty to the third person.

* * *

Comment on Clause (b):

b. Advice or encouragement to act operates as a moral support to a tortfeasor and if the act encouraged is known to be tortious, it has the same effect upon the liability of the adviser as participation or physical assistance. If the encouragement or assistance is a substantial factor in causing the resulting tort, the one giving it is himself a tortfeasor and is responsible for the consequences of the other's act. This is true both where the act done is an intended trespass (see illustrations 1 and 2) and where it is merely a negligent act (see Illustration 3).

* * *

Illustrations:

1. A and B participate in a riot in which B, although throwing no rocks himself, encourages A to throw rocks. One of these strikes C, a bystander. B is liable to C.

2. A, a policeman, advises other policemen to use illegal methods of coercion upon B. A is liable to B for batteries committed in accordance with the advice.

3. A and B are members of a hunting party. Each of them in the presence of the other shoots across a public road at an animal, this being

negligent as to persons on the road. A hits the animal. B's bullet strikes C, a traveler on the road. A is liable to C.

* * *

In *Summers v. Tice*, however, the person injured was a member of the putative joint enterprise, and not a third party. Describing it only as "[a]n illustration . . . under subsection (c)," the court cites Illustration 9 to *Restatement* § 876 to support its conclusion that it is the fact that both the defendants shot in the direction of the plaintiff rather than that a joint enterprise situation was involved that supports the imposition of liability in Illustration 3. Is the point that simple, however? The full text of Illustration 9 is as follows:

> 9. A and B hunt together *but not in the prosecution of a joint enterprise*. It is not negligent to hunt where they are and neither of them has reason to believe that the other will be negligent. Under the unreasonable belief that it is an animal, A shoots at a moving object which proves to be a man. B is not liable for A's negligent act.

(Emphasis supplied). The *Restatement* thus does not say that liability would not have been imposed if a joint enterprise had been found. Indeed, in Illustration 3, in which liability is imposed upon A, it was assumed that there was conclusive proof that A's bullet could not have hit C, the traveler. Is it, therefore, the joint enterprise or the fact that A fired his weapon that results in A's liability in Illustration 3? It is interesting to note that the District Court of Appeal, whose judgment was vacated when the Supreme Court of California decided to hear the case, held that, under the supposition that both Tice and Simonson fired their weapons, neither could be held liable, and, in doing so, referred to the same portions of the *Restatement* referred to by the Supreme Court of California. The District Court of Appeal noted that Tice testified that he had not fired his weapon, but the trial court had refused to believe his statement. 190 P.2d 963 (1948).

3. As the court itself intimated the result in *Summers v. Tice* is sometimes justified not so much on the ground that A and B both caused C 's injuries but rather on the ground that, under these circumstances, where both defendants were admittedly negligent, the burden of persuasion on the issue of causation shifts to the defendants. It is then open to any of them to prove that he was not the cause of the plaintiff's injuries. Since, however, further proof on the issue of causation is, by hypothesis, most likely unavailable, the effect of this procedural device will be to impose liability upon both defendants on the ground that each of them "caused" the plaintiff's injuries, a conclusion which we know to be logically impossible. The conclusion has been generalized by the *Restatement (Second) of Torts* § 433B(3) to apply in any situation where the "conduct of two or more actors is tortious, and it is proved that harm has been caused to the plaintiff by only one of them, but there is uncertainty as to which one has caused it. * * *" As the number of defendants increases, however, the justification for shifting the burden of persuasion on the issue of causation to the defendants becomes more questionable. Suppose there are seven potential defendants involved in a shooting incident. All of them displayed some lack of care towards the plaintiff, but it is impossible to ascertain which of them caused the plaintiff's injuries. If the probabilities that any one of these defendants was the responsible party are equal, the probability that any particular defendant was responsible is roughly 14 percent. Should a 14 percent probability of being the responsible party be enough to shift the burden

of persuasion to such a defendant on the ground that he was admittedly negligent and might have been the cause in fact of the plaintiff's injuries?

In Hall v. E. I. Du Pont De Nemours & Co., 345 F.Supp. 353, 386 (E.D.N.Y.1972), a complaint filed against six manufacturers of blasting caps, who constituted "substantially the entire blasting cap industry," and their national trade association was upheld against a motion to dismiss. The plaintiffs could not identify who had manufactured the blasting caps that injured them. On the other hand, in Burton v. Waller, 502 F.2d 1261 (5th Cir.1974), *cert. denied* 420 U.S. 964, 95 S.Ct. 1356, 43 L.Ed.2d 442 (1975), the court held that the burden of persuasion on the issue of causation could not be transferred to seven highway patrolmen who had been shown to have negligently fired their weapons during a civil disturbance. Thirty-one other highway patrolmen and two local policemen were also shown to have fired their weapons non-negligently. Subsequently, there were attempts to impose industry-wide liability against the manufacturers of DES, a synthetic estrogen prescribed for pregnant women in the 1940's, 1950's and 1960's to prevent miscarriage. More recently there have been attempts to impose industry-wide liability upon the manufacturers of asbestos products. In the DES and asbestos situations, and even, although to a lesser extent, in the blasting cap cases, one is dealing with so-called "mass-tort" situations in which a number of people over a period of time have been injured by a product manufactured by a number of manufacturers. These situations present many difficult policy issues in addition to the causation issues which are being discussed in this chapter. We shall thus postpone our discussion of these cases, and the policy issues they raise, until Chapter Six, when we shall return to these issues in the context of discussing the apportionment of damages among multiple tortfeasors. By contrast, in *Summers v. Tice* and in *Burton v. Waller* we are concerned with proving causation in contexts in which the very reason each of the defendants has been negligent is because he has created a risk of injury to the particular plaintiff in question. They are not cases where the defendant's tortious conduct consists in being one of a number of persons, some of whom may never have actually endangered the plaintiff at all, who have created a potential for injury to a large and indeterminate number of people. On the general subject of cause in fact, *see* P. Zwier, *"Cause in Fact" in Tort Law: A Philosophical and Historical Examination,* 31 DePaul L.Rev. 769 (1982); W. Malone, *Ruminations on Cause-in-Fact,* 9 Stanf.L.Rev. 60 (1956). For a recent discussion of the problem of apportioning harm, *see* S. Boston, *Apportionment of Harm in Tort Law: A Proposed Restatement,* 21 Dayton L.Rev. 267 (1996).

4. *Other problems of indeterminacy.* A typical situation involves safety precautions that the defendant has admittedly not taken but in which it is not clear that, if the safety precautions had been taken, the injury to the plaintiff would have been avoided. For example, in New York Central R.R. v. Grimstad, 264 Fed. 334 (C.C.A.2 1920), the defendant had not equipped its barge with either life preservers or a life buoy. The appellate court reversed a judgment for the deceased's administratrix because it was "pure conjecture and speculation" whether a life buoy could have saved the deceased, who did not know how to swim. *See also* Ford v. Trident Fisheries Co., 232 Mass. 400, 122 N.E. 389 (1919), which involved an improperly stowed and equipped life boat. The deceased disappeared when he fell from the trawler. The court concluded that "it does not appear that if the boat had been suspended from davits and a different method of propelling it had been used, he could have been rescued."

On the other hand, in Zinnel v. United States Shipping Board Emergency Fleet Corp., 10 F.2d 47 (2d Cir.1925), the court took a more indulgent view on the causation issue. The deceased seaman had drowned after he was washed overboard. The ship had not been equipped with a rope life-line, which might have checked his fall. The appellate court reversed the trial judge's dismissal of the complaint. It declared:

> Nobody could in the nature of things be sure that the intestate would have seized the rope or, if he had not, that it would have stopped his body. But we are not dealing with a criminal case, nor are we justified, where certainty is impossible, in insisting upon it. We cannot say that there was no likelihood that a rope three feet above the deck made by the timber would not have saved the seaman.

Id. at 49 (per L. Hand, J.). *See also* Kirincich v. Standard Dredging Co., 112 F.2d 163 (3d Cir.1940). Did the plaintiff have a stronger case in *Zinnel,* so that a jury would not be forced to resort to conjecture and speculation, or is the case simply inconsistent with the two earlier decisions?

A more difficult case is Haft v. Lone Palm Hotel, 3 Cal.3d 756, 91 Cal.Rptr. 745, 478 P.2d 465 (1970). In that case a father and his five-year-old son drowned in one of the hotel's pools and an action for wrongful death was brought by their survivors. No one else was in the pool at the time of the tragedy. In violation of a California statute, there was neither a lifeguard present nor a sign advising guests of this fact. Other violations of California law were the failure to mark the pool with indications of depth; the absence of a sign warning children not to use the pool without an adult in attendance; the failure to post telephone numbers for ambulance, hospital, fire, police rescue services, physician, and pool operator; the failure to post diagrams describing artificial respiration and mouth-to-mouth resuscitation; and the failure to provide twelve-foot-long life poles. The court held that the failure to provide lifeguard services or, in the alternative, a sign warning of the absence of a lifeguard, shifted the burden of persuasion on the issue of causation onto the defendants. Furthermore, for policy reasons inferred from the statute, the court held that, since the defendants had not posted a sign warning of the absence of a lifeguard, the question of their legal responsibility was to be judged on the basis of their having failed to provide a lifeguard, not on the basis of their failing to post a sign warning users of the absence of a lifeguard. Obviously the plaintiffs were in no position to supply more information on the tragedy. Query if the defendants were in any better position. Still it might be argued that it was the defendant's failure to provide a lifeguard that insured that there would be no witness to the tragedy. *Cf.* Smith v. Americania Motor Lodge, 39 Cal.App.3d 1, 113 Cal.Rptr. 771 (1974). In a recent decision, the House of Lords has shown itself adverse to shifting the burden of persuasion to the defendant when the plaintiff has shown that the negligence of the defendant has increased the likelihood of injury to the plaintiff but has been unable to show that this conclusion is more probable than not. Wilsher v. Essex Area Health Authority, [1988] 1 A.C. 1074, 2 W.L.R. 557, 1 All E.R. 871.

5. *Loss of a chance.* Suppose a person is already subject to some particular risk—say, permanent paralysis or the development of cancer. The defendant, by his admittedly negligent conduct, increases that risk, a situation which could analytically be described as the loss of a chance to avoid permanent

paralysis or cancer. For what damages, if any, should the defendant be liable? The problem could be looked at from the point of view of either damage theory or of causation. If, for example, the loss of a chance were considered a compensable item of damage, the plaintiff's task of proving causation would not be different from that which he is confronted with in a more typical case. The difficult practical problem would be in determining how to value the loss of a chance in monetary terms. This is the approach endorsed in J. King, Jr., *Causation, Evaluation, and Chance in Personal Injury Torts: Preexisting Conditions and Future Consequences,* 90 Yale L.J. 1353 (1981), and which relying on this article, was adopted in McKellips v. Saint Francis Hosp., Inc. 741 P.2d 467 (Okl.1987). On the other hand, if an attempt is made to subject the defendant to the burden of compensating the plaintiff for the entire cost of his injuries if the unfortunate consequences ensue or the plaintiff fails to recover from preexisting injuries, serious problems of causation can arise. Where the plaintiff has been deprived of a more than 50 percent chance of avoiding an injury or of a more than 50 percent chance of recovery, the case can be analogized to one where there is substantial uncertainty on the causation issue but in which a rational trier of fact could conclude, on the balance of probabilities, that the defendant was in fact the cause of the plaintiff's injuries. *See* Hicks v. United States, 368 F.2d 626 (4th Cir.1966). Arguably this is what happened in Hamil v. Bashline, 481 Pa. 256, 392 A.2d 1280 (1978). There the court held that once the plaintiff shows that the defendant physician's failure to diagnose and treat the deceased's heart attack increased the risk of harm to the plaintiff, it was up to the jury and not the experts to determine on the balance of probabilities whether the defendant was indeed the cause of the harm that resulted to the plaintiff. *Hicks* was subsequently construed by the Fourth Circuit to support the proposition that a "substantial possibility of survival" did not mean 51 percent rather than 49 percent. Waffen v. United States Dept. of Health and Human Services, 799 F.2d 911 (4th Cir.1986).

What if, however, the experts agree that the chance of which the plaintiff has been deprived is clearly significantly less than 50 percent? This was the situation presented in Herskovits v. Group Health Co-op. of Puget Sound, 99 Wn.2d 609, 664 P.2d 474 (1983), where it was accepted that, owing to the defendant's negligence, the plaintiff's 39 percent chance of survival was reduced to 25 percent—that is, the plaintiff suffered the loss of a 14 percent chance of avoiding the death from lung cancer that eventually ensued and that even with proper treatment was more likely than not to have occurred. The trial court granted summary judgment for the defendant. The Supreme Court of Washington reversed and remanded the case for trial. There were four opinions in the case, none of which commanded a majority of the nine-member court. Two of the opinions supported the reversal of the trial court and two of the opinions were filed by the three dissenters. Since there was no opinion for the court, the case would have to be presented in its entirety or summarized. A good summary of the arguments presented in *Herskovits,* as well as of the logical and legal issues involved in this difficult area of the law, is contained in Lord MacKay's speech in Hotson v. East Berkshire Area Health Authority, [1987] A.C. 750, 3 W.L.R. 232, 2 All E.R. 909. In *Hotson,* as will be seen, the House of Lords was able to avoid ruling on whether one who was deprived of a chance of recovery was able to recover and, if so, for what.

HOTSON v. EAST BERKSHIRE AREA HEALTH AUTHORITY

House of Lords, 1987.
[1987] A.C. 750, 3 W.L.R. 232, 2 ALL E.R. 909.

LORD BRIDGE OF HARWICH. My Lords, the respondent plaintiff is now 23 years of age. On 26 April 1977, as a schoolboy of 13, whilst playing in the school lunch hour he climbed a tree to which a rope was attached, lost his hold on the rope and fell some 12 feet to the ground. He sustained an acute traumatic fracture of the left femoral epiphysis. Within hours he was taken to St. Luke's Hospital, Maidenhead, for which the appellant health authority ("the authority") was responsible. Members of the hospital staff examined him, but failed to diagnose the injury and he was sent home. For five days he was in severe pain. On 1 May 1977 he was taken to the hospital once more and this time X-rays of his hip yielded the correct diagnosis. He was put on immediate traction, treated as an emergency case and transferred to the Heatherwood Hospital where, on the following day, he was operated on by manipulation and reduction of the fracture and pinning of the joint. In the event the plaintiff suffered an avascular necrosis of the epiphysis. The femoral epiphysis is a layer of cartilage separating the bony head from the bony neck of the femur in a growing body. Avascular necrosis results from a failure of the blood supply to the epiphysis and causes deformity in the maturing head of the femur. This in turn involves a greater or lesser degree of disability of the hip joint with a virtual certainty that it will in due course be aggravated by osteoarthritis developing within the joint.

The plaintiff sued the authority, who admitted negligence in failing to diagnose the injury on 26 April 1977. Simon Brown J. * * * awarded £150 damages for the pain suffered by the plaintiff from 26 April to 1 May 1977 which he would have been spared by prompt diagnosis and treatment. This element of the damages is not in dispute. The authority denied liability for any other element of damages. The judge expressed his findings of fact as follows * * *:

"(1) Even had the health authority correctly diagnosed and treated the plaintiff on 26 April there is a high probability, which I assess as a 75 per cent. risk, that the plaintiff's injury would have followed the same course as it in fact has, that is, he would have developed avascular necrosis of the whole femoral head with all the same adverse consequences as have already ensued and with all the same adverse future prospects. (2) That 75 per cent. risk was translated by the health authority's admitted breach of duty into an inevitability. Putting it the other way, their delay in diagnosis denied the plaintiff the 25 per cent. chance that, given immediate treatment, avascular necrosis would not have developed. (3) Had avascular necrosis not developed, the plaintiff would have made a very nearly full recovery. (4) The reason why the delay sealed the plaintiff's fate was because it allowed the pressure caused by haemarthrosis—the bleeding of ruptured blood vessels into the joint—to compress and thus block the intact but distorted remaining vessels with the result that even had the fall left intact sufficient vessels to keep the epiphysis alive (which, as finding (1) makes plain, I think possible but improbable) such vessels would have become occluded and ineffective for this purpose."

On the basis of these findings he held, as a matter of law, that the plaintiff was entitled to damages for the loss of the 25 per cent. chance that, if the injury had been promptly diagnosed and treated, it would not have resulted in avascular necrosis of the epiphysis and the plaintiff would have made a very nearly full recovery. He proceeded to assess the damages attributable to the consequences of the avascular necrosis at £46,000. Discounting this by 75 per cent., he awarded the plaintiff £11,500 for the lost chance of recovery. The authority's appeal against this element in the award of damages was dismissed by the Court of Appeal * * *. The authority now appeal by leave of your Lordships' House.

* * *

It is here, with respect, that I part company with the judge. The plaintiff's claim was for damages for physical injury and consequential loss alleged to have been caused by the authority's breach of their duty of care. In some cases, perhaps particularly medical negligence cases, causation may be so shrouded in mystery that the court can only measure statistical chances. But that was not so here. On the evidence there was a clear conflict as to what had caused the avascular necrosis. The authority's evidence was that the sole cause was the original traumatic injury to the hip. The plaintiff's evidence, at its highest, was that the delay in treatment was a material contributory cause. This was a conflict, like any other about some relevant past event, which the judge could not avoid resolving on a balance of probabilities. Unless the plaintiff proved on a balance of probabilities that the delayed treatment was at least a material contributory cause of the avascular necrosis he failed on the issue of causation and no question of quantification could arise. But the judge's findings of fact, as stated in the numbered paragraphs (1) and (4) which I have set out earlier in this opinion, are unmistakably to the effect that on a balance of probabilities the injury caused by the plaintiff's fall left insufficient blood vessels intact to keep the epiphysis alive. This amounts to a finding of fact that the fall was the sole cause of the avascular necrosis.

The upshot is that the appeal must be allowed on the narrow ground that the plaintiff failed to establish a cause of action in respect of the avascular necrosis and its consequences. Your Lordships were invited to approach the appeal more broadly and to decide whether, in a claim for damages for personal injury, it can ever be appropriate, where the cause of the injury is unascertainable and all the plaintiff can show is a statistical chance which is less than even that, but for the defendant's breach of duty, he would not have suffered the injury, to award him a proportionate fraction of the full damages appropriate to compensate for the injury as the measure of damages for the lost chance.

There is a superficially attractive analogy between the principle applied in such cases as *Chaplin v. Hicks* [1911] 2 K.B. 786 (award of damages for breach of contract assessed by reference to the lost chance of securing valuable employment if the contract had been performed) and *Kitchen v. Royal Air Force Association* [1958] 1 W.L.R. 563 (damages for solicitors' negligence assessed by reference to the lost chance of prosecuting a successful civil action) and the principle of awarding damages for the lost chance of avoiding personal injury or, in medical negligence cases, for the lost chance of a better medical result which might have been achieved by prompt diagnosis and correct treatment. I think there are formidable difficulties in the way of accepting the analogy. But I do not see this appeal as a suitable occasion for reaching a settled conclusion as to whether the analogy can ever be applied.

As I have said, there was in this case an inescapable issue of causation first to be resolved. But if the plaintiff had proved on a balance of probabilities that the authority's negligent failure to diagnose and treat his injury promptly had materially contributed to the development of avascular necrosis, I know of no principle of English law which would have entitled the authority to a discount from the full measure of damage to reflect the chance that, even given prompt treatment, avascular necrosis might well still have developed. The decisions of this House in *Bonnington Castings Ltd. v. Wardlaw* [1956] A.C. 613 and *McGhee v. National Coal Board* [1973] 1 W.L.R. 1 give no support to such a view.

I would allow the appeal to the extent of reducing the damages awarded to the plaintiff by £11,500 and the amount of any interest on that sum which is included in the award.

* * *

Lord Mackay of Clashfern. My Lords, I have had the advantage of reading in draft the speeches prepared by my noble and learned friends, Lord Bridge of Harwich and Lord Ackner. I agree with them that this appeal should be allowed for the reasons which they have given.

In their printed case the authority first took the position that they were entitled to succeed in this appeal because the plaintiff had not proved that any loss or damage (other than five days' pain and suffering) had been caused by the authority's breach of duty. They also submitted that damages for loss of a chance were not recoverable in tort and at the close of the hearing Mr. Whitfield, for the authority, invited your Lordships to decide this case not only on the ground of fact which he submitted was available but also on the more general ground that damages for loss of a chance could not be awarded. This latter submission has been discussed in the course of the hearing very fully and I wish to add some observations, particularly on that aspect of the case.

When Mr. Williams, who appeared for the plaintiff, was invited to say what he meant by a chance he said that in relation to the facts of this case as found by the judge what was meant by a chance was that if 100 people had suffered the same injury as the plaintiff 75 of them would have developed avascular necrosis of the whole femoral head and 25 would not. This, he said, was an asset possessed by the plaintiff when he arrived at the authority's hospital on 26 April 1977. It was this asset which Mr. Williams submits the plaintiff lost in consequence of the negligent failure of the authority to diagnose his injury properly until 1 May 1977.

* * *

* * * [W]hat was the plaintiff's condition on being first presented at the hospital? Did he have intact sufficient blood vessels to keep the affected epiphysis alive? The judge had evidence from the authority's expert which amounted to an assertion that the probability was 100 per cent. that the fall had not left intact sufficient vessels to keep the epiphysis alive while he had evidence from Mr. Bucknill, for the plaintiff, which, although not entirely consistently, suggested that the probability was perhaps between 40 and 60 per cent., say 50 per cent., that sufficient vessels were left intact to keep the epiphysis alive. The concluding sentence in the judge's fourth finding in fact makes it plain, in my opinion, that he took the view, weighing that testimony along with all the other matters before him, that it was more probable than not that insufficient vessels had been left intact by the fall to maintain an adequate blood supply to the epiphysis and he expressed this balance by saying that it was 75 per cent. to 25 per cent., a result reached perhaps as Mr. Williams suggested by going for a figure midway between the competing estimates given by the parties' experts in evidence. Although various statistics were given in evidence, I do not read any of them as dealing with the particular probability which the judge assessed at 75 per cent. to 25 per cent. In the circumstances of this case the probable effect of delay in treatment was determined by the state of facts existing when the plaintiff was first presented to the hospital. It is not, in my opinion, correct to say that on arrival at the hospital he had a 25 per cent. chance of recovery. If insufficient blood vessels were left intact by the fall he had no prospect of avoiding complete avascular necrosis whereas if sufficient blood vessels were left intact on the judge's findings no further damage to the blood supply would have resulted if he had been given immediate treatment, and he would not have suffered the avascular necrosis.

As I have said, the fundamental question of fact to be answered in this case related to a point in time before the negligent failure to treat began. It must, therefore, be a matter of past fact. It did not raise any question of what might have been the situation in a hypothetical state of facts. To this problem the words of Lord Diplock in *Mallett v. McMonagle* [1970] A.C. 166, 176 apply:

"In determining what did happen in the past a court decides on the balance of probabilities. Anything that is more probable than not it treats as certain."

In this respect this case is the same, in principle, as any other in which the state of facts existing before alleged negligence came into play has to be determined. For example, if a claimant alleges that he sustained a certain fracture in a fall at work and there is evidence that he had indeed fallen at work, but that shortly before he had fallen at home and sustained the fracture, the court would have to determine where the truth lay. If the claimant denied the previous fall, there would be evidence, both for and against the allegation, that he had so fallen. The issue would be resolved on the balance of probabilities. If the court held on that balance that the fracture was sustained at home, there could be no question of saying that since all that had been established was that it was more probable than not that the injury was not work-related, there was a possibility that it was work-related and that this possibility or chance was a proper subject of compensation.

I should add in this context that where on disputed evidence a judge reaches a conclusion on the balance of probabilities it will not usually be easy to assess a specific measure of probability for the conclusion at which he has arrived. As my noble and learned friend Lord Bridge of Harwich observed in the course of the hearing, a judge deciding disputed questions of fact will not ordinarily do it by use of a calculator.

On the other hand, I consider that it would be unwise in the present case to lay it down as a rule that a plaintiff could never succeed by proving loss of a chance in a medical negligence case. In *McGhee v. National Coal Board* [1973] 1 W.L.R. 1 this House held that where it was proved that the failure to provide washing facilities for the pursuer at the end of his shift had materially increased the risk that he would contract dermatitis it was proper to hold that the failure to provide such facilities was a cause to a material extent of his contracting dermatitis and thus entitled him to damages from his employers for their negligent failure measured by his loss resulting from dermatitis. Material increase of the risk of contraction of dermatitis is equivalent to material decrease in the chance of escaping dermatitis. Although no precise figures could be given in that case for the purpose of illustration and comparison with this case one might, for example, say that it was established that of 100 people working under the same conditions as the pursuer and without facilities for washing at the end of their shift 70 contracted dermatitis: of 100 people working in the same conditions as the pursuer when washing facilities were provided for them at the end of the shift 30 contracted dermatitis. Assuming nothing more were known about the matter than that, the decision of this House may be taken as holding that in the circumstances of that case it was reasonable to infer that there was a relationship between contraction of dermatitis in these conditions and the absence of washing facilities and therefore it was reasonable to hold that absence of washing facilities was likely to have made a material contribution to the causation of the dermatitis. * * * In these circumstances I think it unwise to do more than say that unless and until this House departs from the decision in *McGhee* your Lordships cannot affirm the proposition that in no circumstances can evidence of loss of a chance resulting from the breach of a duty of care found a successful claim of damages, although there was no suggestion that the House regarded such a chance as an asset in any sense.

By agreement of the parties we were supplied with a list of American authorities relevant to the questions arising in this appeal, although they were not examined in detail. Of the cases referred to, the one that I have found most interesting and instructive is *Herskovits v. Group Health Cooperative of Puget Sound* (1983) 664 P.2d 474, a decision of the Supreme Court of Washington en banc. In this case the claim arose in respect of Mr. Herskovits' death. He was seen at Group Health Hospital at a time when he was suffering from a tumour but this was not diagnosed on first examination. The medical evidence available suggested that at that stage, assuming the tumour was a stage 1 tumour, the chance of survival for more than five years was 39 per cent. When he was treated later the tumour was a stage 2 tumour and the chance of surviving more than five years was 25 per cent. The defendant moved for summary judgment on the basis that, taking the most favourable view of the evidence that was possible, the case could not succeed. The Superior Court of King County granted the motion. This decision was reversed by a majority on appeal to the Supreme Court. The first judgment for the majority in the Supreme Court was delivered by Dore J. Early in his judgment he read from section 323 of the American *Restatement, Second, Torts*, vol. 2 (1965), which is in these terms:

> "One who undertakes, gratuitously or for consideration, to render services to another which he should recognise as necessary for the protection of the other's person or things, is subject to liability to the other for physical harm resulting from his failure to exercise reasonable care to perform his undertaking, if (a) his failure to exercise such care increases the risk of such harm * * *"

After noting that the Supreme Court of Washington had not faced the issue of whether, under this paragraph, proof that the defendant's conduct had increased the risk of death by decreasing the chances of survival was sufficient to take the issue of proximate cause to the jury he said, at p. 476:

> "Some courts in other jurisdictions have allowed the proximate cause issue to go to the jury on this type of proof * * * These courts emphasised the fact that defendants' conduct deprived the decedents of a 'significant' chance to survive or recover, rather than requiring proof that with absolute certainty the defendants' conduct caused the physical injury. The underlying reason is that it is not for the wrongdoer, who put the possibility of recovery beyond realisation, to say afterward that the result was inevitable * * *. Other jurisdictions have rejected this approach, generally holding that unless the plaintiff is able to show that it was *more likely than not* that the harm was caused by the defendant's negligence, proof of a decreased chance of survival is not enough to take the proximate cause question to the jury. * * * These courts have concluded that the defendant should not be liable where the decedent more than likely would have died anyway."

To the question whether the plaintiff should be allowed, in the case before him, to proceed to a jury he returned an affirmative answer; and gave as the reason, at p. 477:

> "To decide otherwise would be a blanket release from liability for doctors and hospitals any time there was less than a 50 per cent. chance of survival, regardless of how flagrant the negligence."

In support of this reasoning he referred to *Hamil v. Bashline* (1978) 481 Pa. 256; 392 A.2d 1280, a decision of the Pennsylvania Supreme Court, and said:

> "The *Hamil* court distinguished the facts of that case from the general tort case in which a plaintiff alleges that a defendant's act or omission set in motion a force which resulted in harm. In the typical tort case, the 'but for' test, requiring proof that damages or death probably

would not have occurred 'but for' the negligent conduct of the defendant, is appropriate. In *Hamil* and the instant case, however, the defendant's act or omission failed in a *duty* to protect against harm from *another source*. Thus, as the *Hamil* court noted, the fact finder is put in the position of having to consider not only what *did* occur, but also what *might* have occurred."

He goes on to quote from *Hamil,* 481 Pa. 256, 271; 392 A.2d 1280, 1287–1288:

" 'Such cases by their very nature elude the degree of certainty one would prefer and upon which the law normally insists before a person may be held liable. Nevertheless, in order that an actor is not completely insulated because of uncertainties as to the consequence of his negligent conduct, section 323(a) [of the *Restatement, Second, Torts*]tacitly acknowledges this difficulty and permits the issue to go to the jury upon a less than normal threshold of proof.' "

He goes on, at pp. 477–478, to refer to another decision, namely *Hicks v. United States* (1966) 368 F.2d 626, as containing a succinct statement of the relevant doctrine, at p. 632, and quotes:

" 'Rarely is it possible to demonstrate to an absolute certainty what would have happened in circumstances that the wrongdoer did not allow to come to pass. The law does not in the existing circumstances require the plaintiff to show to a *certainty* that the patient would have lived had she been hospitalised and operated on promptly.' "

He refers also to a general observation in the Supreme Court of the United States dealing with a contention similar to that argued before him by the doctors and the hospital. In *Lavender v. Kurn* (1946) 327 U.S. 645, 653 the Supreme Court said:

"It is no answer to say that the jury's verdict involved speculation and conjecture. Whenever facts are in dispute or the evidence is such that fair-minded men may draw different inferences, a measure of speculation and conjecture is required on the part of those whose duty it is to settle the dispute by choosing what seems to them to be the most reasonable inference."

He therefore concluded, at p. 479, that the evidence available which showed at maximum a reduction in the 39 per cent. chance of five years' survival to a 25 per cent. chance of five years' survival was sufficient to allow the case to go to the jury on the basis that the jury would be entitled to infer from that evidence that the delay in treatment was a proximate cause of the decedent's death. He pointed out, however, that causing reduction of the opportunity to recover (also described as a loss of chance) by one's negligence did not necessitate a total recovery against the negligent party for all damages caused by the victim's death. He held that damages should be awarded to the injured party and his family based only on damages caused directly by premature death, such as lost earnings and additional medical expenses and the like.

The approach of Dore J. bears some resemblance to the approach taken by some members of this House in *McGhee v. National Coal Board* [1973] 1 W.L.R. 1, and by Lord Guthrie in *Kenyon v. Bell,* 1953 S.C. 125.

Brachtenbach J. dissented. He warned against the danger of using statistics as a basis on which to prove proximate cause and indicated that it was necessary at the minimum to produce evidence connecting the statistics to the facts of the case. He gave an interesting illustration of a town in which there were only two cab companies, one with three blue cabs and the other with one yellow cab. If a person was knocked down by a cab whose colour had not been observed it would be wrong to suggest that there was a 75 per cent. chance that the victim was run down by a blue cab and that accordingly it was more probable than not that the cab that ran him down was blue and therefore that the company running the blue cabs would be responsible for negligence in the running down. He pointed out that before any inference that it was a blue cab would be appropriate further facts would be required as, for example, that a blue cab had been seen in the immediate vicinity at the time of the accident or that a blue cab had been found with a large dent in the very part of the cab which had struck the victim. He concluded that the evidence available was not sufficient to justify the case going to the jury and noted, at p. 491:

> "The apparent harshness of this conclusion cannot be overlooked. The combination of the loss of a loved one to cancer and a doctor's negligence in diagnosis seems to compel a finding of liability. Nonetheless, justice must be dealt with an even hand. To hold a defendant liable without proof that his actions *caused* plaintiff harm would open up untold abuses of the litigation system."

Pearson J. agreed that the appeal should be allowed but did not agree with the reasoning by which that result was supported by Dore J. Pearson J., after examining the authorities and an academic article,[a] stated that he was persuaded that a middle course between the reasoning of Dore J. and Brachtenbach J. was correct and concluded, at p. 487: "that the best resolution of the issue before us is to recognise the loss of a less than even chance as an actionable injury." He recognised that this also required that the damage payable be determined by the application of that chance expressed as a percentage to the damages that would be payable on establishing full liability.

I have selected references to the views expressed by the judges who took part in this decision to illustrate the variety of views open in this difficult area of the law. These confirm me in the view that it would not be right in the present case to affirm the general proposition for which Mr. Whitfield contended. On the other hand, none of the views canvassed in *Herskovits'* case, 644 P.2d 474, would lead to the plaintiff succeeding in the present case since the judge's findings in fact mean that the sole cause of the plaintiff's avascular necrosis was the injury he sustained in the original fall, and that implies, as I have said, that when he arrived at the authority's hospital for the first time he had no chance of avoiding it. Accordingly, the subsequent negligence of the authority did not cause him the loss of such a chance.

* * *

Appeal allowed.

---

a. [Ed. note] This was the article by Prof. King cited at p. 255, *supra.*

Note

Following Lord MacKay's reasoning, could every loss of a chance of future recovery be turned into a factual inquiry into whether the plaintiff's condition before treatment was or was not such as to make his recovery possible—that is, the more we know of the plaintiff's *ex ante* position, the less we need to speculate upon what might have happened if the defendant had been more careful? Should the defendants in *Herskovits* have argued that the plaintiff's *ex ante* so-called 39 percent "chance" of survival with proper treatment really amounted to a 61 percent probability that at the time of treatment the plaintiff was doomed? For a recent discussion of the few English cases on this subject, *see* H. Reece, *Loses of Chances in the Law,* 59 Mod.L.Rev. 188 (1996).

It is not at all clear how much support can be derived from *Restatement (Second) of Torts* § 323(a) for permitting recovery in the "loss of a chance" cases where the chance is substantially less than a probability or even merely less than a probability. As we will see more clearly in Chapter Seven, *infra,* the provision was adopted by the American Law Institute to answer the question of who had a duty to other people, not to answer the question of the quantum of proof needed to establish that a breach of any such duty actually caused the plaintiff's injuries. Nevertheless, Herskovits v. Group Health Co-op. of Puget Sound, 99 Wn.2d 609, 664 P.2d 474 (1983) was applied in Aasheim v. Humberger, 215 Mont. 127, 695 P.2d 824 (1985), where the court did not expressly state what damages were recoverable but seems to have left open the possibility that, if the jury found that the defendant physician's negligence was "a substantial factor in reducing plaintiff's chances of obtaining a better result," she might recover the full range of damages otherwise recoverable. The issue has now been litigated in over forty states and in the District of Columbia. A slight majority seem to have recognized the possibility that damages might be awarded for the loss of a chance of recovery, at least in some circumstances. *Compare e.g.* McAfee v. Baptist Med. Ctr., 641 So.2d 265 (Ala.1994); Fabio v. Bellomo, 504 N.W.2d 758 (Minn.1993); Jones v. Owings, 318 S.C. 72, 456 S.E.2d 371 (1995); Kramer v. Lewisville Mem. Hosp., 858 S.W.2d 397 (Tex.1993), refusing to recognize such recovery, *with* Thompson v. Sun City Community Hosp., 141 Ariz. 597, 688 P.2d 605 (1984); Blackmon v. Langley, 293 Ark. 286, 737 S.W.2d 455 (1987); Falcon v. Memorial Hosp., 436 Mich. 443, 462 N.W.2d 44 (1990); Wollen v. DePaul Health Ctr., 828 S.W.2d 681 (Mo.1992)(en banc); Perez v. Las Vegas Med. Ctr., 107 Nev. 1, 805 P.2d 589 (1991); McKellips v. St. Francis Hosp., 741 P.2d 467 (Okl.1987). In the *Thompson* and *Blackmon* cases, the plaintiff was awarded full damages; in the other three, the damages were reduced by multiplying them by the percent chance of survival lost owing to the physician's negligence. The cases seem to be all confined to medical malpractice. For example, the Washington Supreme Court has refused to extend its decision in *Herskovits* to legal malpractice. Daugert v. Pappas, 104 Wn.2d 254, 704 P.2d 600 (1985). The issue as posed by the plaintiff was whether the defendant's failure to file an appeal on time deprived the plaintiff of a chance to have a decision of the court of appeals reversed. The court held that the plaintiff was required to show that it would probably have prevailed upon appeal. *See also,* In re Elscint, Ltd. Securities Litigation, 674 F.Supp. 374 (D.Mass.1987)(loss of chance type reasoning not applied to question of whether a causal connection can be traced between a misleading prospectus and the subsequent purchase of shares in the company).

B. PROXIMATE CAUSE

IN RE AN ARBITRATION BETWEEN POLEMIS AND FURNESS, WITHY & CO., LTD.

Court of Appeal, 1921.
[1921] 3 K.B. 560.

Appeal from the judgment of Sankey J. on an award in the form of a special case.

The owners of the Greek steamship *Thrasyvoulos* claimed to recover damages for the total loss of the steamship by fire.

* * *

The vessel by the directions of the charterers or their agents in or about the months of June and July, 1917, loaded at Nantes a part cargo of cement and general cargo for Casablanca, Morocco. She then proceeded to Lisbon and was loaded with further cargo, consisting of cases of benzine and/or petrol and iron for Casablanca and other ports on the Morocco coast. She arrived at Casablanca on July 17, and there discharged a portion of her cargo. The cargo was discharged by Arab workmen and winchmen from the shore supplied and sent on board by the charterers' agents. The cargo in No. 1 hold included a considerable quantity of cases of benzine or petrol which had suffered somewhat by handling and/or by rough weather on the voyage, so that there had been some leakage from the tins in the cases into the hold. On July 21, it had become necessary to shift from No. 1 lower hold a number of the cases of benzine which were required to be taken on by the ship to Safi, and for this purpose the native stevedores had placed heavy planks across the forward end of the hatchway in the 'tween decks, using it as a platform in the process of transferring the cases from the lower hold to the 'tween decks. There were four or five of the Arab shore labourers in the lower hold filling the slings which, when filled, where hove up by means of the winch situated on the upper deck to the 'tween decks level of the platform on which some of the Arabs in the 'tween decks were working. In consequence of the breakage of the cases there was a considerable amount of petrol vapour in the hold. In the course of heaving a sling of the cases from the hold the rope by which the sling was being raised or the sling itself came into contact with the boards placed across the forward end of the hatch, causing one of the boards to fall into the lower hold, and the fall was instantaneously followed by a rush of flames from the lower hold, and this resulted eventually in the total destruction of the ship.

The owners contended (so far as material) that the charterers were liable for the loss of the ship; that fire caused by negligence was not an excepted peril; and that the ship was in fact lost by the negligence of the stevedores, who were the charterers' servants, in letting the sling strike the board, knocking it into the hold, and thereby causing a spark which set fire to the petrol vapour and destroyed the ship.

The charterers contended that fire however caused was an excepted peril; that there was no negligence for which the charterers were responsible, inasmuch as to let a board fall into the hold of the ship could do no harm to the ship and therefore was not negligence towards the owners;

and that the danger and/or damage were too remote—i.e., no reasonable man would have foreseen danger and/or damage of this kind resulting from the fall of the board.

The three arbitrators made the following findings of fact:—

(*a*) That the ship was lost by fire.

(*b*) That the fire arose from a spark igniting petrol vapour in the hold.

(*c*) That the spark was caused by the falling board coming into contact with some substance in the hold.

(*d*) That the fall of the board was caused by the negligence of the Arabs (other than the winchman) engaged in the work of discharging.

(*e*) That the said Arabs were employed by the charterers or their agents the Cie. Transatlantique on behalf of the charterers, and that the said Arabs were the servants of the charterers.

(*f*) That the causing of the spark could not reasonably have been anticipated from the falling of the board, though some damage to the ship might reasonably have been anticipated.

(*g*) There was no evidence before us that the Arabs chosen were known or likely to be negligent.

(*h*) That the damages sustained by the owners through the said accident amount to the sum of 196,165*l*. 1*s*. 11*d*. as shown in the second column of the schedule hereto.

Subject to the opinion of the Court on any questions of law arising the arbitrators awarded that the owners were entitled to recover from the charterers the before-mentioned sum.

If the Court should be of opinion that the above award was wrong, then the arbitrators awarded that the owners should recover nothing from the charterers.

Sankey J. affirmed the award. The charterers appealed.

* * *

BANKES L.J. By a time charterparty dated February 21, 1917, the respondents chartered their vessel to the appellants. * * * The vessel was employed by the charterers to carry a cargo to Casablanca in Morocco. The cargo included a quantity of benzine or petrol in cases. While discharging at Casablanca a heavy plank fell into the hold in which the petrol was stowed, and caused an explosion, which set fire to the vessel and completely destroyed her. The owners claimed the value of the vessel from the charterers, alleging that the loss of the vessel was due to the negligence of the charterers' servants. The charterers contended that they were protected by the exception of fire contained in clause 21 of the charterparty, and they also contended that the damages claimed were too remote. The claim was referred to arbitration and the arbitrators stated a special case for the opinion of the Court. * * * These findings are no doubt intended to raise the question whether the view taken, or said to have been taken, by Pollock C.B. in *Rigby v. Hewitt* [5 Ex. 243] and *Greenland v. Chaplin* [5 Ex. 248], or the view taken by Channell B. and Blackburn J. in *Smith v. London and*

South Western Ry. Co. [L.R. 6 C.P. 21], is the correct one. The doubt which I have indicated in reference to what Pollock C.B. really said is due to the fact that, as reported in the Law Journal [19 L.J. (Ex. 292, 295)], the Chief Baron does not use the words on which reliance is placed and which were quoted with approval by Vaughan Williams L.J. in *Cory v. France.* [[1911] 1 K.B. 122] Assuming the Chief Baron to have been correctly reported in the Exchequer Reports, the difference between the two views is this: According to the one view, the consequences which may reasonably be expected to result from a particular act are material only in reference to the question whether the act is or is not a negligent act; according to the other view, those consequences are the test whether the damages resulting from the act, assuming it to be negligent, are or are not too remote to be recoverable. Sir F. Pollock in his Law of Torts, 11th ed., pp. 39, 40, refers to this difference of view, and calls attention to the fact that the late Mr. Beven, in his book on Negligence, supports the view founded on *Smith v. London and South Western Ry. Co.* In two recent judgments dealing with the question, the view taken by the Court in *Smith v. London and South Western Ry. Co.* has been adopted—namely, by the late President (Sir Samuel Evans) in *H.M.S. London* [[1914] P. 72, 76], and by Lord Sumner in *Weld-Blundell v. Stephens.* [[1920] A.C. 983, 984] In the former case the President said: "The Court is not concerned in the present case with any inquiry as to the chain of causes resulting in the creation of a legal liability from which such damages as the law allows would flow. The tortious act—i.e., the negligence of the defendants, which imposes upon them a liability in law for damages—is admitted. This gets rid at once of an element which requires consideration in a chain of causation in testing the question of legal liability—namely, the foresight or anticipation of the reasonable man. In *Smith v. London and South Western Ry. Co.* Channell B. said: 'Where there is no direct evidence of negligence, the question what a reasonable man might foresee is of importance in considering the question whether there is evidence for the jury of negligence or not * * * but when it has been once determined that there is evidence of negligence, the person guilty of it is equally liable for its consequences, whether he could have foreseen them or not.' And Blackburn J. in the same case said: 'What the defendants might reasonably anticipate is only material with reference to the question, whether the defendants were negligent or not, and cannot alter their liability if they were guilty of negligence' "; and after referring to the various phrases used in connection with remoteness of damages he said: "But it must be remembered, to use the words of a well-known American author (Sedgwick), that 'the legal distinction between what is proximate and what is remote is not a logical one, nor does it depend upon relations of time and space; it is purely practical, the reason for distinguishing between the proximate and remote causes and consequences being a purely practical one'; and again, to use the words of an eminent English jurist (Sir F. Pollock [11th ed., 35, 36]), 'In whatever form we state the rule of "natural and probable consequences," we must remember that it is not a logical definition, but only a guide to the exercise of common sense. The lawyer cannot afford to adventure himself with philosophers in the logical and metaphysical controversies that beset the idea of cause.' " In the latter case Lord Sumner said: "What are 'natural, probable and necessary' consequences? Everything that happens, happens in the order of nature and is therefore 'natural.' Nothing that happens by the free choice of a thinking man is 'necessary,' except in the sense of predestination. To speak of 'probable' consequence is to throw everything upon the jury. It is tautologous to speak of 'effective' cause or to say that damages too remote from the cause are irrecoverable, for an effective cause is simply that which causes, and in law what is ineffective or too remote is not a cause at all. I still venture to think that direct cause is the best expression. Proximate cause has acquired a special connotation through its use in reference to contracts of insurance. Direct cause excludes what is indirect, conveys the essential distinction, which causa causans and causa sine qua non rather cumbrously indicate, and is consistent with the possibility of the concurrence of more direct causes than one, operating at the same time and leading to a common result * * *."

In the present case the arbitrators have found as a fact that the falling of the plank was due to the negligence of the defendants' servants. The fire appears to me to have been directly caused by the falling of the plank. Under these circumstances I consider that it is immaterial that the causing of the spark by the falling of the plank could not have been reasonably anticipated. The appellants' junior counsel sought to draw a distinction between the anticipation of the extent of damage resulting from a negligent act, and the anticipation of the type of damage resulting from such an act. He admitted that it could not lie in the mouth of a person whose negligent act had caused damage to say that he could not reasonably have foreseen the extent of the damage, but he contended that the negligent person was entitled to rely upon the fact that he could not reasonably have anticipated the type of damage which resulted from his negligent act. I do not think that the distinction can be admitted. Given the breach of duty which constitutes the negligence, and given the damage as a direct result of that negligence, the anticipations of the person whose negligent act has produced the damage appear to me to be irrelevant. I consider that the damages claimed are not too remote.

The other point relied upon by the appellants was that the damage having been caused by fire they were protected by clause 21 of the charterparty. * * * Neither shipowner nor charterer can, in my opinion, under this clause claim to be protected against the consequences of his own negligence.

For these reasons I think, that the appeal fails, and must be dismissed with costs.

WARRINGTON L.J. * * *

* * *

The result may be summarised as follows: The presence or absence of reasonable anticipation of damage determines the legal quality of the act as negligent or innocent. If it be thus determined to be negligent, then the question whether particular damages are recoverable depends only on the answer to the question whether they are the direct consequence of the act.
* * *

On the whole in my opinion the appeal fails and must be dismissed with costs.

SCRUTTON L.J.   The steamship *Thrasyvoulos* was lost by fire while being discharged by workmen employed by the charterers. Experienced arbitrators, by whose findings of fact we are bound, have decided that the fire was caused by a spark igniting petrol vapour in the hold, the vapour coming from leaks from cargo shipped by the charterers, and that the spark was caused by the Arab workmen employed by the charterers negligently knocking a plank out of a temporary staging erected in the hold, so that the plank fell into the hold, and in its fall by striking something made the spark which ignited the petrol vapour.

On these findings the charterers contend that they are not liable for two reasons: first, that they are protected by an exception of "fire" which in the charter is "mutually excepted"; secondly, that as the arbitrators have found that it could not be reasonably anticipated that the falling of the board would make a spark, the actual damage is too remote to be the subject of a claim. In my opinion both these grounds of defence fail.

* * *

The second defence is that the damage is too remote from the negligence, as it could not be reasonably foreseen as a consequence. On this head we were referred to a number of well known cases in which vague language, which I cannot think to be really helpful, has been used in an attempt to define the point at which damage becomes too remote from, or not sufficiently directly caused by, the breach of duty, which is the original cause of action, to be recoverable. For instance, I cannot think it useful to say the damage must be the natural and probable result. This suggests that there are results which are natural but not probable, and other results which are probable but not natural. I am not sure what either adjective means in this connection; if they mean the same thing, two need not be used; if they mean different things, the difference between them should be defined. And as to many cases of fact in which the distinction has been drawn, it is difficult to see why one case should be decided one way and one another. Perhaps the House of Lords will some day explain why, if a cheque is negligently filled up, it is a direct effect of the negligence that some one finding the cheque should commit forgery: *London Joint Stock Bank v. Macmillan* [[1918] A.C. 777]; while if some one negligently leaves a libellous letter about, it is not a direct effect of the negligence that the finder should show the letter to the person libelled: *Weld-Blundell v. Stephens*. In this case, however, the problem is simpler. To determine whether an act is negligent, it is relevant to determine whether any reasonable person would foresee that the act would cause damage; if he would not, the act is not negligent. But if the act would or might probably cause damage, the fact that the damage it in fact causes is not the exact kind of damage one would expect is immaterial, so long as the damage is in fact directly traceable to the negligent act, and not due to the operation of independent causes having no connection with the negligent act, except that they could not avoid its results. Once the act is negligent, the fact that its exact operation was not foreseen is immaterial. This is the distinction laid down by the majority of the Exchequer Chamber in *Smith v. London and South Western Ry. Co.*, and by the majority of the Court in Banc in *Rigby v. Hewitt* and *Greenland v. Chaplin*, and approved recently by Lord Sumner in *Weld-Blundell v. Stephens* and Sir Samuel Evans in *H.M.S. London*. In the present case it was negligent in discharging cargo to knock down the planks of the temporary staging, for they might easily cause some damage either to workmen, or cargo, or the ship. The fact that they did directly produce an unexpected result, a spark in an atmosphere of petrol vapour which caused a fire, does not relieve the person who was negligent from the damage which his negligent act directly caused.

For these reasons the experienced arbitrators and the judge appealed from came, in my opinion, to a correct decision, and the appeal must be dismissed with costs.

Appeal dismissed.

PALSGRAF v. LONG ISLAND RAILROAD

Court of Appeals of New York, 1928.
248 N.Y. 339, 162 N.E. 99.

CARDOZO, C.J. Plaintiff was standing on a platform of defendant's railroad after buying a ticket to go to Rockaway Beach. A train stopped at the station, bound for another place. Two men ran forward to catch it. One of the men reached the platform of the car without mishap, though the train was already moving. The other man, carrying a package, jumped aboard the car, but seemed unsteady as if about to fall. A guard on the car, who had held the door open, reached forward to help him in, and another guard on the platform pushed him from behind. In this act, the package was dislodged, and fell upon the rails. It was a package of small size, about fifteen inches long, and was covered by a newspaper. In fact it contained fireworks but there was nothing in its appearance to give notice of its contents. The fireworks when they fell exploded. The shock of the explosion threw down some scales at the other end of the platform many feet away. The scales struck the plaintiff, causing injuries for which she sues.

The conduct of the defendant's guard, if a wrong in its relation to the holder of the package, was not a wrong in its relation to the plaintiff, standing far away. Relatively to her it was not negligence at all. Nothing in the situation gave notice that the falling package had in it the potency of peril to persons thus removed. Negligence is not actionable unless it involves the invasion of a legally protected interest, the violation of a right. "Proof of negligence in the air, so to speak, will not do." Pollock, Torts (11th Ed.) p. 455 * * *. The plaintiff, as she stood upon the platform of the station, might claim to be protected against intentional invasion of her bodily security. Such invasion is not charged. She might claim to be protected against unintentional invasion by conduct involving in the thought of reasonable men an unreasonable hazard that such invasion would ensue. These, from the point of view of the law, were the bounds of her immunity, with perhaps some rare exceptions, survivals for the most part of ancient forms of liability, where conduct is held to be at the peril of the actor. * * * If no hazard was apparent to the eye of ordinary vigilance, an act innocent and harmless, at least to outward seeming, with reference to her, did not take to itself the quality of a tort because it happened to be a wrong, though apparently not one involving the risk of bodily insecurity, with reference to some one else. * * * "The ideas of negligence and duty are strictly correlative." Bowen, L.J., in Thomas v. Quartermaine, 18 Q.B.D. 685, 694. The plaintiff sues in her own right for a wrong personal to her, and not as the vicarious beneficiary of a breach of duty to another.

A different conclusion will involve us, and swiftly too, in a maze of contradictions. A guard stumbles over a package which has been left upon a platform. It seems to be a bundle of newspapers. It turns out to be a can of dynamite. To the eye of ordinary vigilance, the bundle is abandoned waste, which may be kicked or trod on with impunity. Is a passenger at the other end of the platform protected by the law against the unsuspected hazard concealed beneath the waste? If not, is the result to be any different, so far as the distant passenger is concerned, when the guard stumbles over a valise which a truckman or a porter has left upon the walk? The passenger far away, if the victim of a wrong at all, has a cause of action, not derivative, but original and primary. His claim to be protected against invasion of his bodily security is neither greater nor less because the act resulting in the invasion is a wrong to another far removed. In this case, the rights that are said to have been violated, the interests said to have been invaded, are not even of the same order. The man was not injured in his person nor even put in danger. The purpose of the act, as well as its effect, was to make his person safe. If there was a wrong to him at all, which may very well be doubted it was a wrong to a property interest only, the safety of his package. Out of this wrong to property, which threatened injury to nothing else, there has passed, we are told, to the plaintiff by derivation or succession a right of action for the invasion of an interest of another order, the right to bodily security. The diversity of interests emphasizes the futility of the effort to build the plaintiff's right upon the basis of a wrong to some one else. The gain is one of emphasis, for a like result would follow if the interests were the same. Even then, the orbit of the danger as disclosed to the eye of reasonable vigilance would be the orbit of the duty. One who jostles one's neighbor in a crowd does not invade the rights of others standing at the outer fringe when the unintended contact casts a bomb upon the ground. The wrongdoer as to them is the man who carries the bomb, not the one who explodes it without suspicion of the danger. Life will have to be made over, and human nature transformed, before prevision so extravagant can be accepted as the norm of conduct, the customary standard to which behavior must conform.

The argument for the plaintiff is built upon the shifting meanings of such words as "wrong" and "wrongful," and shares their instability. What the plaintiff must show is "a wrong" to herself; i.e., a violation of her own right, and not merely a wrong to some one else, nor conduct "wrongful" because unsocial, but not "a wrong" to any one. We are told that one who drives at reckless speed through a crowded city street is guilty of a negligent act and therefore of a wrongful one, irrespective of the consequences. Negligent the act is, and wrongful in the sense that it is unsocial, but wrongful and unsocial in relation to other travelers, only because the eye of vigilance perceives the risk of damage. If the same act were to be committed on a speedway or a race course, it would lose its wrongful quality. The risk reasonably to be perceived defines the duty to be obeyed, and risk imports relation; it is risk to another or to others within the range of apprehension. Seavey, Negligence, Subjective or Objective, 41 H.L.Rv. 6 * * * This does not mean, of course, that one who launches a destructive force is always relieved of liability, if the force, though known to be destructive, pursues an unexpected path. "It was not necessary that the defendant should have had notice of the particular method in which an accident would occur, if the possibility of an accident was clear to the ordinarily prudent eye." Munsey v. Webb, 231 U.S. 150, 156 * * *. Some acts, such as shooting are so imminently dangerous to any one who may come within reach of the missile however unexpectedly, as to impose a duty of prevision not far from that of an insurer. Even to-day, and much oftener in earlier stages of the law, one acts sometimes at one's peril. * * * Under this head, it may be, fall certain cases of what is known as transferred intent, an act willfully dangerous to A resulting by misadventure in injury to B. * * * These cases aside, wrong is defined in terms of the natural or probable, at least when unintentional. Parrot v. Wells, Fargo & Co. (The Nitro–Glycerine Case) 15 Wall. 524, 21 L.Ed. 206. The range of reasonable apprehension is at times a question for the court, and at times, if varying inferences are possible, a question for the jury. Here, by concession, there was nothing in the situation to suggest to the most cautious mind that the parcel wrapped in newspaper would spread wreckage through the station. If the guard had thrown it down knowingly and willfully, he would not have threatened the plaintiff's safety, so far as appearances could warn him. His conduct would not have involved, even then, an unreasonable probability of invasion of her bodily security. Liability can be no greater where the act is inadvertent.

Negligence, like risk, is thus a term of relation. Negligence in the abstract, apart from things related, is surely not a tort, if indeed it is understandable at all. * * * Negligence is not a tort unless it results in the commission of a wrong, and the commission of a wrong imports the violation of a right, in this case, we are told, the right to be protected against interference with one's bodily security. But bodily security is protected, not against all forms of interference or aggression, but only against some. One who seeks redress at law does not make out a cause of action by showing without more that there has been damage to his person. If the harm was not willful, he must show that the act as to him had possibilities of danger so many and apparent as to entitle him to be protected against the doing of it though the harm was unintended. Affront to personality is still the keynote of the wrong. Confirmation of this view will be found in the history and development of the action on the case. Negligence as a basis of civil liability was unknown to mediaeval law. 8 Holdsworth, History of English Law, p. 449 * * * For damage to the person, the sole remedy was trespass, and trespass did not lie in the absence of aggression, and that direct and personal. * * * Liability for other damage, as where a servant without orders from the master does or omits something to the damage of another, is a plant of later growth. * * * When it emerged out of the legal soil, it was thought of as a variant of trespass, an offshoot of the parent stock. This appears in the form of action, which was known as trespass on the case. * * * The victim does not sue derivatively, or by right of subrogation, to vindicate an interest invaded in the person of another. Thus to view his cause of action is to ignore the fundamental difference between tort and crime. Holland, Jurisprudence (12th Ed.) p. 328. He sues for breach of a duty owing to himself.

The law of causation, remote or proximate, is thus foreign to the case before us. The question of liability is always anterior to the question of the measure of the consequences that go with liability. If there is no tort to be redressed, there is no occasion to consider what damage might be recovered if there were a finding of a tort. We may assume, without deciding, that negligence, not at large or in the abstract, but in relation to the plaintiff, would entail liability for any and all consequences, however novel or extraordinary. * * * cf. Matter of Polemis, L.R. 1921, 3 K.B. 560 * * *. There is room for argument that a distinction is to be drawn according to the diversity of interests invaded by the act, as where conduct negligent in that it threatens an insignificant invasion of an interest in property results in an unforeseeable invasion of an interest of another order, as, e.g., one of bodily security. Perhaps other distinctions may be necessary. We do not go into the question now. The consequences to be followed must first be rooted in a wrong.

The judgment of the Appellate Division and that of the Trial Term should be reversed, and the complaint dismissed, with costs in all courts.

ANDREWS, J. (dissenting). Assisting a passenger to board a train, the defendant's servant negligently knocked a package from his arms. It fell between the platform and the cars. Of its contents the servant knew and could know nothing. A violent explosion followed. The concussion broke some scales standing a considerable distance away. In falling, they injured the plaintiff, an intending passenger.

Upon these facts, may she recover the damages she has suffered in an action brought against the master? The result we shall reach depends upon our theory as to the nature of negligence. Is it a relative concept—the breach of some duty owing to a particular person or to particular persons? Or, where there is an act which unreasonably threatens the safety of others, is the doer liable for all its proximate consequences even where they result in injury to one who would generally be thought to be outside the radius of danger? This is not a mere dispute as to words. We might not believe that to the average mind the dropping of the bundle would seem to involve the probability of harm to the plaintiff standing many feet away whatever might be the case as to the owner or to one so near as to be likely to be struck by its fall. If, however, we adopt the second hypothesis, we have to inquire only as to the relation between cause and effect. We deal in terms of proximate cause, not of negligence.

Negligence may be defined roughly as an act or omission which unreasonably does or may affect the rights of others, or which unreasonably fails to protect one's self from the dangers resulting from such acts. Here I confine myself to the first branch of the definition. Nor do I comment on the word "unreasonable." For present purposes it sufficiently describes that average of conduct that society requires of its members.

There must be both the act or the omission, and the right. It is the act itself, not the intent of the actor, that is important. * * * In criminal law both the intent and the result are to be considered. Intent again is material in tort actions, where punitive damages are sought, dependent on actual malice—not on merely reckless conduct. But here neither insanity nor infancy lessens responsibility. * * *

As has been said, except in cases of contributory negligence, there must be rights which are or may be affected. Often though injury has occurred, no rights of him who suffers have been touched. A licensee or trespasser upon my land has no claim to affirmative care on my part that the land be made safe. * * * Where a railroad is required to fence its tracks against cattle, no man's rights are injured should he wander upon the road because such fence is absent. Di Caprio v. New York Cent. R. Co., 231 N.Y. 94, 131 N.E. 746, 16 A.L.R. 940. An unborn child may not demand immunity from personal harm. * * *

But we are told that "there is no negligence unless there is in the particular case a legal duty to take care, and this duty must be one which is owed to the plaintiff himself and not merely to others." Salmond Torts (6th Ed.) 24. This I think too narrow a conception. Where there is the unreasonable act, and some right that may be affected there is negligence whether damage does or does not result. That is immaterial. Should we drive down Broadway at a reckless speed, we are negligent whether we strike an approaching car or miss it by an inch. The act itself is wrongful. It is a wrong not only to those who happen to be within the radius of danger, but to all who might have been there—a wrong to the public at large. Such is the language of the street. Such the language of the courts when speaking of contributory negligence. Such again and again their language in speaking of the duty of some defendant and discussing proximate cause in cases where such a discussion is wholly irrelevant on any other theory. * * *

Due care is a duty imposed on each one of us to protect society from unnecessary danger, not to protect A, B, or C alone.

It may well be that there is no such thing as negligence in the abstract. "Proof of negligence in the air, so to speak, will not do." In an empty world negligence would not exist. It does involve a relationship between man and his fellows, but not merely a relationship between man and those whom he might reasonably expect his act would injure; rather, a relationship between him and those whom he does in fact injure. If his act has a tendency to harm some one, it harms him a mile away as surely as it does those on the scene. We now permit children to recover for the negligent killing of the father. It was never prevented on the theory that no duty was owing to them. A husband may be compensated for the loss of his wife's services. To say that the wrongdoer was negligent as to the husband as well as to the wife is merely an attempt to fit facts to theory. An insurance company paying a fire loss recovers its payment of the negligent incendiary. We speak of subrogation—of suing in the right of the insured. Behind the cloud of words is the fact they hide, that the act, wrongful as to the insured, has also injured the company. Even if it be true that the fault of father, wife, or insured will prevent recovery, it is because we consider the original negligence, not the proximate cause of the injury. Pollock, Torts (12th Ed.) 463.

In the well-known Polemis Case, [1921] 3 K.B. 560, Scrutton, L.J., said that the dropping of a plank was negligent, for it might injure "workman or cargo or ship." Because of either possibility, the owner of the vessel was to be made good for his loss. The act being wrongful, the doer was liable for its proximate results. Criticized and explained as this statement may have been, I think it states the law as it should be and as it is.   * * *

The proposition is this: Every one owes to the world at large the duty of refraining from those acts that may unreasonably threaten the safety of others. Such an act occurs. Not only is he wronged to whom harm might reasonably be expected to result, but he also who is in fact injured, even if he be outside what would generally be thought the danger zone. There needs be duty due the one complaining, but this is not a duty to a particular individual because as to him harm might be expected. Harm to some one being the natural result of the act, not only that one alone, but all those in fact injured may complain. We have never, I think, held otherwise. Indeed in the Di Caprio Case we said that a breach of a general ordinance defining the degree of care to be exercised in one's calling is evidence of negligence as to every one. We did not limit this statement to those who might be expected to be exposed to danger. Unreasonable risk being taken, its consequences are not confined to those who might probably be hurt.

If this be so, we do not have a plaintiff suing by "derivation or succession." Her action is original and primary. Her claim is for a breach of duty to herself—not that she is subrogated to any right of action of the owner of the parcel or of a passenger standing at the scene of the explosion.

The right to recover damages rests on additional considerations. The plaintiff's rights must be injured, and this injury must be caused by the negligence. We build a dam, but are negligent as to its foundations. Breaking, it injures property down stream. We are not liable if all this happened because of some reason other than the insecure foundation. But, when injuries do result from our unlawful act, we are liable for the consequences. It does not matter that they are unusual, unexpected, unforeseen, and unforeseeable. But there is one limitation. The damages must be so connected with the negligence that the latter may be said to be the proximate cause of the former.

These two words have never been given an inclusive definition. What is a cause in a legal sense, still more what is a proximate cause, depend in each case upon many considerations, as does the existence of negligence itself. Any philosophical doctrine of causation does not help us. A boy throws a stone into a pond. The ripples spread. The water level rises. The history of that pond is altered to all eternity. It will be altered by other causes also. Yet it will be forever the resultant of all causes combined. Each one will have an influence. How great only omniscience can say. You may speak of a chain, or, if you please, a net. An analogy is of little aid. Each cause brings about future events. Without each the future would not be the same. Each is proximate in the sense it is essential. But that is not what we mean by the word. Nor on the other hand do we mean sole cause. There is no such thing.

Should analogy be thought helpful, however, I prefer that of a stream. The spring, starting on its journey, is joined by tributary after tributary. The river, reaching the ocean, comes from a hundred sources. No man may say whence any drop of water is derived. Yet for a time distinction may be possible. Into the clear creek, brown swamp water flows from the left. Later, from the right comes water stained by its clay bed. The three may remain for a space, sharply divided. But at last inevitably no trace of separation remains. They are so commingled that all distinction is lost.

As we have said, we cannot trace the effect of an act to the end, if end there is. Again, however, we may trace it part of the way. A murder at Serajevo may be the necessary antecedent to an assassination in London twenty years hence. An overturned lantern may burn all Chicago. We may follow the fire from the shed to the last building. We rightly say the fire started by the lantern caused its destruction.

A cause, but not the proximate cause. What we do mean by the word "proximate" is that, because of convenience, of public policy, of a rough sense of justice, the law arbitrarily declines to trace a series of events beyond a certain point. This is not logic. It is practical politics. Take our rule as to fires. Sparks from my burning haystack set on fire my house and my neighbor's. I may recover from a negligent railroad. He may not. Yet the wrongful act as directly harmed the one as the other. We may regret that the line was drawn just where it was, but drawn somewhere it had to be. We said the act of the railroad was not the proximate cause of our neighbor's fire. Cause it surely was. The words we used were simply indicative of our notions of public policy. Other courts think differently. But somewhere they reach the point where they cannot say the stream comes from any one source.

Take the illustration given in an unpublished manuscript by a distinguished and helpful writer on the law of torts. A chauffeur negligently collides with another car which is filled with dynamite, although he could not know it. An explosion follows. A, walking on the sidewalk nearby, is killed. B, sitting in a window of a building opposite, is cut by flying glass. C, likewise sitting in a window a block away, is similarly injured. And a further illustration: A nursemaid, ten blocks away, startled by the noise, involuntarily drops a baby from her arms to the walk. We are told that C may not recover while A may. As to B it is a question for court or jury. We will all agree that the baby might not. Because, we are again told, the chauffeur had no reason to believe his conduct involved any risk of injuring either C or the baby. As to them he was not negligent.

But the chauffeur, being negligent in risking the collision, his belief that the scope of the harm he might do would be limited is immaterial. His act unreasonably jeopardized the safety of any one who might be affected by it. C's injury and that of the baby were directly traceable to the collision. Without that, the injury would not have happened. C had the right to sit in his office, secure from such dangers. The baby was entitled to use the sidewalk with reasonable safety.

The true theory is, it seems to me, that the injury to C, if in truth he is to be denied recovery, and the injury to the baby, is that their several injuries were not the proximate result of the negligence. And here not what the chauffeur had reason to believe would be the result of his conduct, but what the prudent would foresee, may have a bearing—may have some bearing, for the problem of proximate cause is not to be solved by any one consideration. It is all a question of expediency. There are no fixed rules to govern our judgment. There are simply matters of which we may take account. We have in a somewhat different connection spoken of "the stream of events." We have asked whether that stream was deflected— whether it was forced into new and unexpected channels. * * * This is rather rhetoric than law. There is in truth little to guide us other than common sense.

There are some hints that may help us. The proximate cause, involved as it may be with many other causes, must be, at the least, something without which the event would not happen. The court must ask itself whether there was a natural and continuous sequence between cause and effect. Was the one a substantial factor in producing the other? Was there a direct connection between them, without too many intervening causes? Is the effect of cause on result not too attenuated? Is the cause likely, in the usual judgment of mankind, to produce the result? Or, by the exercise of prudent foresight, could the result be foreseen? Is the result too remote from the cause, and here we consider remoteness in time and space. * * * Clearly we must so consider, for the greater the distance either in time or space, the more surely do other causes intervene to affect the result. When a lantern is overturned, the firing of a shed is a fairly direct consequence. Many things contribute to the spread of the conflagration—the force of the wind, the direction and width of streets, the character of intervening structures, other factors. We draw an uncertain and wavering line, but draw it we must as best we can.

Once again, it is all a question of fair judgment, always keeping in mind the fact that we endeavor to make a rule in each case that will be practical and in keeping with the general understanding of mankind.

Here another question must be answered. In the case supposed, it is said, and said correctly, that the chauffeur is liable for the direct effect of the explosion, although he had no reason to suppose it would follow a collision. "The fact that the injury occurred in a different manner than that which might have been expected does not prevent the chauffeur's negligence from being in law the cause of the injury." But the natural results of a negligent act—the results which a prudent man would or should foresee—do have a bearing upon the decision as to proximate cause. We have said so repeatedly. What should be foreseen? No human foresight would suggest that a collision itself might injure one a block away. On the contrary, given an explosion, such a possibility might be reasonably expected. I think the direct connection, the foresight of which the courts speak, assumes prevision of the explosion, for the immediate results of which, at least, the chauffeur is responsible.

It may be said this is unjust. Why? In fairness he should make good every injury flowing from his negligence. Not because of tenderness toward him we say he need not answer for all that follows his wrong. We look back to the catastrophe, the fire kindled by the spark, or the explosion. We trace the consequences, not indefinitely, but to a certain point. And to aid us in fixing that point we ask what might ordinarily be expected to follow the fire or the explosion.

This last suggestion is the factor which must determine the case before us. The act upon which defendant's liability rests is knocking an apparently harmless package onto the platform. The act was negligent. For its proximate consequences the defendant is liable. If its contents were broken, to the owner; if it fell upon and crushed a passenger's foot, then to him; if it exploded and injured one in the immediate vicinity, to him also as to A in the illustration. Mrs. Palsgraf was standing some distance away. How far cannot be told from the record—apparently 25 or 30 feet, perhaps less. Except for the explosion, she would not have been injured. We are told by the appellant in his brief, "It cannot be denied that the explosion was the direct cause of the plaintiff's injuries." So it was a substantial factor in producing the result—there was here a natural and continuous sequence—direct connection. The only intervening cause was that, instead of blowing her to the ground, the concussion smashed the weighing machine which in turn fell upon her. There was no remoteness in time, little in space. And surely, given such an explosion as here, it needed no great foresight to predict that the natural result would be to injure one on the platform at no greater distance from its scene than was the plaintiff. Just how no one might be able to predict. Whether by flying fragments, by broken glass, by wreckage of machines or structures no one could say. But injury in some form was most probable.

Under these circumstances I cannot say as a matter of law that the plaintiff's injuries were not the proximate result of the negligence. That is all we have before us. The court refused to so charge. No request was made to submit the matter to the jury as a question of fact, even would that have been proper upon the record before us.

The judgment appealed from should be affirmed, with costs.

POUND, LEHMAN, and KELLOGG, JJ., concur with CARDOZO, C.J.

ANDREWS, J., dissents in opinion in which CRANE and O'BRIEN, JJ., concur.

Judgment reversed, etc.

Notes

1. Cardozo, J.'s, suggestion that "[t]here is room for argument that a distinction is to be drawn according to the diversity of interests invaded by the act, as where conduct negligent in that it threatens an insignificant invasion of an interest in property results in an unforeseeable invasion of an interest of another order, as *e.g.*, one of bodily security" fully reflects the position adopted by *Restatement of Torts* § 281. Insofar as pertinent that provision provides that "[t]he actor is liable for an invasion of an interest of another if: (a) the interest invaded is protected against unintentional invasion, and (b) the conduct of the actor is negligent with respect to such interest or any other similar interest of the other which is protected against unintentional invasion * * *." It is now well-known that Cardozo had attended a conference of the advisors for the *Restatement* after the *Palsgraf* case had been decided in the Appellate Division but before an appeal had been lodged in the New York Court of Appeals. At this meeting, the Reporter, Professor Bohlen, referred to the

Palsgraf case in connection with the draft provision that became § 281 and which took a position opposed to that of the lower New York courts. There was a lively debate and the advisors voted to accept the Reporter's position by a narrow margin. Cardozo listened to the debate but did not participate in it. See W. Prosser, *Palsgraf Revisited*, 52 Mich.L.Rev. 1, 4–5 (1953).* *The Restatement (Second) of Torts* § 281 has now altered this position. If "the actor is negligent with respect to the other," the "actor is liable for an invasion of an interest" of that person if "the interest invaded is protected against unintentional invasion." There is thus no longer any express requirement that the interest invaded be the same or similar to the interest the threat to which made the actor's conduct negligent. See *id. Comment j*.

2. Apparently Andrew, J.'s, illustration from "an unpublished manuscript by a distinguished and helpful writer on the law of torts" refers to a memorandum prepared by Professor Bohlen for the meeting referred to in Note 1, *supra*. Cardozo did participate in the discussion of that memorandum and surprisingly, stating that he was merely expressing a "hunch," took an expansive view of the extent of the liability of a driver who negligently drives into what turns out to be dynamite. See R. Keeton, *A Palsgraf Anecdote*, 56 Tex.L.Rev. 513 (1978).

3. The *Palsgraf* case, and particularly Cardozo's opinion, has engendered a great deal of comment through the years. For a detailed bibliography see J. Noonan, Persons and Masks of the Law 191–92 (1976). Nevertheless, despite the prominence that the *Palsgraf* case has had in academic discussions, it has had surprisingly little practical effect in the decision of actual cases.

4. In *Palsgraf*, Cardozo surmised that, if negligence towards Mrs. Palsgraf had been found, liability would have followed under the direct cause test of the *Polemis* case. Is it plausible to contend that Cardozo resorted to the duty analysis of negligence because he wished to avoid imposing liability upon the defendant as would have been required by the direct cause test? By resorting to the negligence analysis did Cardozo really avoid the difficult causal question? If legal cause is defined in terms of the actualization of foreseeable risks, clearly he has not.

5. Andrew, J.'s, suggestion that questions of proximate cause all boil down to questions of policy to be decided on the basis of common sense has considerable surface appeal. Whether the injunction to apply common sense is a sufficient guide to judges in deciding disputed cases is another matter. In the *Palsgraf* case, thirteen judges were involved in its various stages (one trial judge, five judges in the Appellate Division and seven in the Court of Appeals). Of these seven supported the jury verdict in Mrs. Palsgraf's favor and six ruled for the defendant. Unfortunately for Mrs. Palsgraf, four of those six were in the Court of Appeals. If the judges had all agreed that common sense was the ultimate rule of decision, do you think that they would have been more likely to agree on the result?

Andrew, J., writing in 1928, speculated that a "murder at Serajevo [*sic*]may be the necessary antecedent to an assassination in London twenty years hence." The Archduke Francis Ferdinand, heir to the Hapsburg throne, was of course assassinated in Sarajevo on June 28, 1914. It is interesting to note that, on October 9, 1934, King Alexander of Yugoslavia and the foreign minister of France, Barthou, were assassinated in Marseilles.

6. On the actual merits of the *Palsgraf* case, is it so clear to a person considering the facts of the case today that the conduct of the defendant's servants could not reasonably be foreseen to pose any risk of injury to Mrs.

---

* As this book was going to press, the editors were advised that Professor Andrew L. Kaufman, in a biography of Cardozo scheduled for publication in the spring of 1998, questions whether Cardozo was at any such meeting and even whether such a meeting ever took place.

Palsgraf? See Judge Friendly's remarks in the *Kinsman Transit Co.* case, reprinted at p. 301, *infra*.

OVERSEAS TANKSHIP (U.K.) LTD. v. MORTS DOCK & ENGINEERING CO., LTD. (THE WAGON MOUND)

Privy Council, 1961.
[1961] A.C. 388, 2 W.L.R. 126, 1 All E.R. 404.

Appeal * * * from an order of the Full Court of the Supreme Court of New South Wales * * * dismissing an appeal by the appellants, Overseas Tankship (U.K.) Ltd., from a judgment of Kinsella J. * * *.

The following facts are taken from the judgment of the Judicial Committee: In the action the respondents sought to recover from the appellants compensation for the damage which its property known as the Sheerlegs Wharf, in Sydney Harbour, and the equipment thereon had suffered by reason of fire which broke out on November 1, 1951. For that damage they claimed that the appellants were in law responsible.

The relevant facts can be comparatively shortly stated inasmuch as not one of the findings of fact in the exhaustive judgment of the trial judge had been challenged.

The respondents at the relevant time carried on the business of ship-building, ship-repairing and general engineering at Morts Bay, Balmain, in the Port of Sydney. They owned and used for their business the Sheerlegs Wharf, a timber wharf about 400 feet in length and 40 feet wide, where there was a quantity of tools and equipment. In October and November, 1951, a vessel known as the *Corrimel* was moored alongside the wharf and was being refitted by the respondents. Her mast was lying on the wharf and a number of the respondents' employees were working both upon it and upon the vessel itself, using for that purpose electric and oxy-acetylene welding equipment.

At the same time the appellants were charterers by demise of the *s.s. Wagon Mound*, an oil-burning vessel, which was moored at the Caltex Wharf on the northern shore of the harbour at a distance of about 600 feet from the Sheerlegs Wharf. She was there from about 9 a. m. on October 29 until 11 a. m. on October 30, 1951, for the purpose of discharging gasolene products and taking in bunkering oil.

During the early hours of October 30, 1951, a large quantity of bunkering oil was, through the carelessness of the appellants' servants, allowed to spill into the bay, and by 10.30 on the morning of that day it had spread over a considerable part of the bay, being thickly concentrated in some places and particularly along the foreshore near the respondents' property. The appellants made no attempt to disperse the oil. The *Wagon Mound* unberthed and set sail very shortly after.

When the respondents' works manager became aware of the condition of things in the vicinity of the wharf he instructed their workmen that no welding or burning was to be carried on until further orders. He inquired of the manager of the Caltex Oil Company, at whose wharf the *Wagon Mound* was then still berthed, whether they could safely continue their operations on the wharf or upon the *Corrimal*. The results of the inquiry coupled with his own belief as to the inflammability of furnace oil in the open led him to think that the respondents could safely carry on their operations. He gave instructions accordingly, but directed that all safety precautions should be taken to prevent inflammable material falling off the wharf into the oil.

For the remainder of October 30 and until about 2 p. m. on November 1 work was carried on as usual, the condition and congestion of the oil remaining substantially unaltered. But at about that time the oil under or near the wharf was ignited and a fire, fed initially by the oil, spread rapidly and burned with great intensity. The wharf and the *Corrimal* caught fire and considerable damage was done to the wharf and the equipment upon it.

The outbreak of fire was due, as the judge found, to the fact that there was floating in the oil underneath the wharf a piece of débris on which lay some smouldering cotton waste or rag which had been set on fire by molten metal falling from the wharf: that the cotton waste or rag burst into flames: that the flames from the cotton waste set the floating oil afire either directly or by first setting fire to a wooden pile coated with oil, and that after the floating oil became ignited the flames spread rapidly over the surface of the oil and quickly developed into a conflagration which severely damaged the wharf.

* * *

1961. January 18. The judgment of their Lordships was delivered by Viscount Simonds, who stated the facts set out above and continued: The trial judge also made the all-important finding, which must be set out in his own words: "The raison d'être of furnace oil is, of course, that it shall burn, but I find the defendant did not know and could not reasonably be expected to have known that it was capable of being set afire when spread on water." This finding was reached after a wealth of evidence, which included that of a distinguished scientist, Professor Hunter. It receives strong confirmation from the fact that at the trial the respondents strenuously maintained that the appellants had discharged petrol into the bay on no other ground than that, as the spillage was set alight, it could not be furnace oil. An attempt was made before their Lordships' Board to limit in some way the finding of fact, but it is clear that it was intended to cover precisely the event that happened.

One other finding must be mentioned. The judge held that apart from damage by fire the respondents had suffered some damage from the spillage of oil in that it had got upon their slipways and congealed upon them and interfered with their use of the slips. He said: "The evidence of this damage is slight and no claim for compensation is made in respect of it. Nevertheless it does establish some damage, which may be insignificant in comparison with the magnitude of the damage by fire, but which nevertheless is damage which, beyond question, was a direct result of the escape of the oil." It is upon this footing that their Lordships will consider the question whether the appellants are liable for the fire damage. That consideration must begin with an expression of indebtedness to Manning J. for his penetrating analysis of the problems that today beset the question of liability for negligence. In the year 1913 in the case of *H.M.S. London*,[1] a case to which further reference will be made, Sir Samuel Evans P. said: "The doctrine of legal causation, in reference both to the creation of liability and to the measurement of damages, has been much discussed by judges and commentators in this country and in America. Vast numbers of learned and acute judgments and disquisitions have been delivered and written upon the subject. It is difficult to reconcile the decisions; and the views of prominent commentators and jurists differ in important respects. It would not be possible or feasible in this judgment to examine them in anything approaching detail." In the near half-century that has passed since the learned President spoke those words the task has not become easier, but it is possible to point to certain landmarks and to indicate certain tendencies which, as their Lordships hope, may serve in some measure to simplify the law.

It is inevitable that first consideration should be given to the case of *In re Polemis and Furness Withy & Co. Ltd.* which will henceforward be referred to as *Polemis*. For it was avowedly in deference to that decision and to decisions of the Court of Appeal that followed it that the Full Court was constrained to decide the present case in favour of the respondents. In doing so Manning J., after a full examination of that case, said: "To say that the problems, doubts and difficulties which I have expressed above render it difficult for me to apply the decision in *In re Polemis* with any degree of confidence to a particular set of facts would be a grave understatement. I can only express the hope that, if not in this case, then in some other case in the near future, the subject will be pronounced upon by the House of Lords or the Privy Council in terms which, even if beyond my capacity fully to understand, will facilitate, for those placed as I am, its everyday application to current problems." This cri de coeur would in any case be irresistible, but in the years that have passed since its decision *Polemis* has been so much discussed and qualified that it cannot claim, as counsel for the respondents urged for it, the status of a decision of such long standing that it should not be reviewed.

What, then, did *Polemis* decide? Their Lordships do not propose to spend time in examining whether the issue there lay in breach of contract or in tort. That might be relevant for a tribunal for which the decision was a binding authority: for their Lordships it is not.   * * *

There can be no doubt that the decision of the Court of Appeal in *Polemis* plainly asserts that, if the defendant is guilty of negligence, he is responsible for all the consequences whether reasonably foreseeable or not. The generality of the proposition is perhaps qualified by the fact that each of the Lords Justices refers to the outbreak of fire as the direct result of the negligent act. There is thus introduced the conception that the negligent actor is not responsible for consequences which are not "direct," whatever that may mean. It has to be asked, then, why this conclusion should have been reached. The answer appears to be that it was reached upon a consideration of certain authorities, comparatively few in number, that were cited to the court. Of these, three are generally regarded as having influenced the decision. The earliest in point of date was *Smith v. London*

---

1. [1914] P. 72, 76; 30 T.L.R. 196.

& *South Western Railway Co.*[3] In that case it was said that "when it has been once determined that there is evidence of negligence, the person guilty of it is equally liable for its consequences, whether he could have foreseen them or not": see *per* Channell B. Similar observations were made by other members of the court. Three things may be noted about this case: the first, that for the sweeping proposition laid down no authority was cited; the second, that the point to which the court directed its mind was not unforeseeable damage of a different kind from that which was foreseen, but more extensive damage of the same kind; and the third, that so little was the mind of the court directed to the problem which has now to be solved that no one of the seven judges who took part in the decision thought it necessary to qualify in any way the consequences for which the defendant was to be held responsible. It would perhaps not be improper to say that the law of negligence as an independent tort was then of recent growth and that its implications had not been fully examined. The second case was *H.M.S. London*, which has already been referred to. There the statement in *Smith's* case was followed, Sir Samuel Evans citing Blackburn J.: "What the defendants might reasonably anticipate is only material with reference to the question whether the defendants were negligent or not, and cannot alter their liability if they were guilty of negligence." This proposition, which provides a different criterion for determining liability and compensation, goes to the root of the matter and will be discussed later. It was repeated by Lord Sumner in the third case which was relied on in *Polemis*, namely, *Weld-Blundell v. Stephens.*[7] In that case the majority of their Lordships, of whom Lord Sumner was one, held, affirming a decision of the Court of Appeal, that the plaintiff's liability for damages in certain libel actions did not result from an admitted breach by the defendant of the duty that he admittedly owed to him. Lord Dunedin (another of the majority) decided the case on the ground that there was there no evidence which entitled the jury to give the affirmative answer that they did to the question as put to them that the actions of libel and damages recovered were the "natural and probable consequences" of the proved negligence of the defendant. Lord Wrenbury (the third of the majority) summed up his view of the case by saying[8]: "I am quite unable to follow the proposition that the damages given in the libel actions are in any way damages resulting from anything which Stephens did in breach of duty." Lord Sumner, whose speech their Lordships, like others before them, have not found in all respects easy to follow, said[9]: "What a defendant ought to have anticipated as a reasonable man is material when the question is whether or not he was guilty of negligence, that is, of want of due care according to the circumstances. This, however, goes to culpability, not to compensation." But this observation followed a passage in which His Lordship, directing his mind to the problem of causation, had asked what were "natural, probable and necessary consequences," and had expressed the view that "direct cause" was the best expression. Adopting that test he rejected the plaintiff's claim as too remote. The question of foreseeability became irrelevant and the passage cited from his speech was unneces-

---

3. (1870) L.R. 6 C.P. 14.

7. [1920] A.C. 956, 983; 36 T.L.R. 640, H.L.

8. [1920] A.C. 956, 999.

9. Ibid. 984.

sary to his decision. Their Lordships are constrained to say that this dictum (for such it was) perpetuated an error which has introduced much confusion into the law.

Before going forward to the cases which followed *Polemis*, their Lordships think it desirable to look back to older authorities which appear to them to deserve consideration. In two cases, *Rigby v. Hewitt*[10] and *Greenland v. Chaplin*,[11] Pollock C.B. affirmed[12] (stating it to be his own view only and not that of the court) that he entertained "considerable doubt whether a person who is guilty of negligence is responsible for all the consequences which may under any circumstances arise and in respect of mischief which could by no possibility have been foreseen and which no reasonable person would have anticipated." It was not necessary to argue this question and it was not argued.

Next, one of many cases may be cited which show how shadowy is the line between so-called culpability and compensation. In *Sharp v. Powell*[13] the defendant's servant in breach of the Police Act washed a van in a public street and allowed the waste water to run down the gutter towards a grating leading to the sewer about 25 yards off. In consequence of the extreme severity of the weather the grating was obstructed by ice and the water flowed over a portion of the causeway and froze. There was no evidence that the defendant knew of the grating being obstructed. The plaintiff's horse, while being led past the spot, slipped upon the ice and broke its leg. The defendant was held not to be liable. The judgment of Bovill C.J. is particularly valuable and interesting. "No doubt," he said, "one who commits a wrongful act is responsible for the ordinary consequences which are likely to result therefrom; but, generally speaking, he is not liable for damage which is not the natural or ordinary consequence of such an act unless it be shown that he knows or has reasonable means of knowing that consequences not usually resulting from the act are by reason of some existing cause likely to intervene so as to occasion damage to a third person. Where there is no reason to expect it, and no knowledge in the person doing the wrongful act that such a state of things exists as to render the damage probable, if injury does result to a third person it is generally considered that the wrongful act is not the proximate cause of the injury so as to render the wrongdoer liable to an action." Here all the elements are blended, "natural" or "ordinary consequences," "foreseeability," "proximate cause." What is not suggested is that the wrongdoer is liable for the consequences of his wrongdoing whether reasonably foreseeable or not, or that there is one criterion for culpability, another for compensation. It would, indeed, appear to their Lordships that, unless the learned Chief Justice was making a distinction between "one who commits a wrongful act" and one who commits an act of negligence, the case is not reconcilable with *Polemis*. In that case it was not dealt with except in a citation from *Weld-Blundell v. Stephens*.

Mention should also be made of *Cory & Son Ltd. v. France Fenwick & Co. Ltd.*[16] In that case Vaughan Williams L.J., citing the passage from the

10. (1850) 5 Exch. 240.

11. Ibid. 243.

12. Ibid. 248.

13. (1872) L.R. 7 C.P. 258.

16. [1911] 1 K.B. 114; 27 T.L.R. 18, C.A.

judgment of Pollock C.B. in *Greenland v. Chaplin* which has already been read, said: "I do not myself suppose that although, when these propositions were originally laid down, they were not intended as positive judgments but as opinions of the learned judge, there would be any doubt nowadays as to their accuracy." And Kennedy L.J. said of the same passage, "with that view of the law no one would venture to quarrel." Some doubt was expressed in *Polemis* as to whether the citation of which these learned judges so emphatically approved was correct. That is irrelevant. They approved that which they cited and their approval has high authority. It is probable in any case that it had not occurred to them that there was any such dichotomy as was suggested in *Polemis*. * * * The impression that may well be left on the reader of the scores of cases in which liability for negligence has been discussed is that the courts were feeling their way to a coherent body of doctrine and were at times in grave danger of being led astray by scholastic theories of causation and their ugly and barely intelligible jargon.

Before turning to the cases that succeeded it, it is right to glance at yet another aspect of the decision in *Polemis*. Their Lordships, as they have said, assume that the court purported to propound the law in regard to tort. But up to that date it had been universally accepted that the law in regard to damages for breach of contract and for tort was, generally speaking, and particularly in regard to the tort of negligence, the same. Yet *Hadley v. Baxendale*[20] was not cited in argument nor referred to in the judgments in *Polemis*. This is the more surprising when it is remembered that in that case, as in many another case, the claim was laid alternatively in breach of contract and in negligence. If the claim for breach of contract had been pursued, the charterers could not have been held liable for consequences not reasonably foreseeable. It is not strange that Sir Frederick Pollock said that Blackburn and Willes JJ. would have been shocked beyond measure by the decision that the charterers were liable in tort: see Pollock on Torts, 15th ed., p. 29. Their Lordships refer to this aspect of the matter not because they wish to assert that in all respects today the measure of damages is in all cases the same in tort and in breach of contract, but because it emphasises how far *Polemis* was out of the current of contemporary thought. The acceptance of the rule in *Polemis* as applicable to all cases of tort directly would conflict with the view theretofore generally held.

If the line of relevant authority had stopped with *Polemis*, their Lordships might, whatever their own views as to its unreason, have felt some hesitation about overruling it. But it is far otherwise. It is true that both in England and in many parts of the Commonwealth that decision has from time to time been followed; but in Scotland it has been rejected with determination. It has never been subject to the express scrutiny of either the House of Lords or the Privy Council, though there have been comments upon it in those Supreme Tribunals. Even in the inferior courts judges have, sometimes perhaps unwittingly, declared themselves in a sense adverse to its principle. Thus Asquith L.J. himself, who in *Thurogood v. Van*

---

20.   (1854) 9 Exch. 341.

den Berghs & Jurgens Ltd.[21] had loyally followed *Polemis*, in *Victoria Laundry (Windsor) Ltd. v. Newman Industries Ltd.*,[22] holding that a complete indemnity for breach of contract was too harsh a rule, decided that "the aggrieved party is only entitled to recover such part of the loss actually resulting as was at the time of the contract reasonably foreseeable as liable to result from the breach." It is true that in that case the Lord Justice was dealing with damages for breach of contract. But there is nothing in the case to suggest, nor any reason to suppose, that he regarded the measure of damage as different in tort and breach of contract. The words "tort" and "tortious" have perhaps a somewhat sinister sound but, particularly where the tort is not deliberate but is an act of negligence, it does not seem that there is any more moral obliquity in it than in a perhaps deliberate breach of contract, or that the negligent actor should suffer a severer penalty. In *Minister of Pensions v. Chennell*[24] Denning J. (as he then was) said: "Foreseeability is as a rule vital in cases of contract; and also in cases of negligence, whether it be foreseeability in respect of the person injured as in *Palsgraf v. Long Island Railway* (discussed by Professor Goodhart in his Essays, p. 129), *Donoghue v. Stevenson* and *Bourhill v. Young*, or in respect of intervening causes as in *Aldham v. United Dairies (London) Ltd.* and *Woods v. Duncan*. It is doubtful whether *In re Polemis and Furness Withy & Co.* can survive these decisions. If it does, it is only in respect of neglect of duty to the plaintiff which is the immediate or precipitating cause of damage of an unforeseeable kind." Their Lordships would with respect observe that such a survival rests upon an obscure and precarious condition.

Instances might be multiplied of deviation from the rule in *Polemis*, but their Lordships think it sufficient to refer to certain later cases in the House of Lords and then to attempt to state what they conceive to be the true principle. In *Glasgow Corporation v. Muir*[31] Lord Thankerton said that it had long been held in Scotland that all that a person can be bound to foresee are the reasonable and probable consequences of the failure to take care judged by the standard of the ordinary reasonable man, while Lord MacMillan said that "It is still left to the judge to decide what, in the circumstances of the particular case, the reasonable man would have had in contemplation, and what, accordingly, the party sought to be made liable ought to have foreseen." Here there is no suggestion of one criterion for determining culpability (or liability) and another for determining compensation. In *Bourhill v. Young*[34] the double criterion is more directly denied. There Lord Russell of Killowen said: "In considering whether a person owes to another a duty a breach of which will render him liable to that other in damages for negligence, it is material to consider what the defendant ought to have contemplated as a reasonable man. This consideration may play a double role. It is relevant in cases of admitted negligence (where the duty and breach are admitted) to the question of remoteness of

21. [1951] 2 K.B. 537; [1951] 1 T.L.R. 557; [1951] 1 All E.R. 682, C.A.

22. [1949] 2 K.B. 528; 65 T.L.R. 274; [1949] 1 All E.R. 997, C.A.

24. [1947] K.B. 250, 253; 62 T.L.R. 753; [1946] 2 All E.R. 719.

31. [1943] A.C. 448; 59 T.L.R. 266; [1943] 2 All E.R. 44, H.L.

34. [1943] A.C. 92; [1942] 2 All E.R. 396, H.L.

damage, i.e., to the question of compensation not to culpability, but it is also relevant in testing the existence of a duty as the foundation of the alleged negligence, i.e., to the question of culpability not to compensation." This appears to be in flat contradiction to the rule in *Polemis* and to the dictum of Lord Sumner in *Weld-Blundell v. Stephens*.

From the tragic case of *Woods v. Duncan*,[37] the facts of which are too complicated to be stated at length, some help may be obtained. There Viscount Simon analysed the conditions of establishing liability for negligence and stated them to be (1) that the defendant failed to exercise due care, (2) that he owed the injured man the duty to exercise due care, and (3) that his failure to do so was the cause of the injury in the proper sense of the term. He held that the first and third conditions were satisfied, but inasmuch as the damage was due to an extraordinary and unforeseeable combination of circumstances the second condition was not satisfied. Be it observed that to him it was one and the same thing whether the unforeseeability of damage was relevant to liability or compensation. To Lord Russell of Killowen in the same case the test of liability was whether the defendants (Cammell Laird & Co. Ltd.) could reasonably be expected to foresee that the choking of a test cock (itself undoubtedly a careless act) might endanger the lives of those on board; Lord Macmillan asked whether it could be said that they, the defendants, ought to have foreseen as reasonable people that if they failed to detect and rectify the clogging of the hole in the door the result might be that which followed, and later, identifying, as it were, reasonable foreseeability with causation, he said: "The chain of causation, to borrow an apposite phrase, would appear to be composed of missing links."

Enough has been said to show that the authority of *Polemis* has been severely shaken though lip-service has from time to time been paid to it. In their Lordships' opinion it should no longer be regarded as good law. It is not probable that many cases will for that reason have a different result, though it is hoped that the law will be thereby simplified, and that in some cases, at least, palpable injustice will be avoided. For it does not seem consonant with current ideas of justice or morality that for an act of negligence, however slight or venial, which results in some trivial foreseeable damage the actor should be liable for all consequences however unforeseeable and however grave, so long as they can be said to be "direct." It is a principle of civil liability, subject only to qualifications which have no present relevance, that a man must be considered to be responsible for the probable consequences of his act. To demand more of him is too harsh a rule, to demand less is to ignore that civilised order requires the observance of a minimum standard of behaviour.

This concept applied to the slowly developing law of negligence has led to a great variety of expressions which can, as it appears to their Lordships, be harmonised with little difficulty with the single exception of the so-called rule in *Polemis*. For, if it is asked why a man should be responsible for the natural or necessary or probable consequences of his act (or any other similar description of them) the answer is that it is not because they are natural or necessary or probable, but because, since they have this

37. [1946] A.C. 401.

quality, it is judged by the standard of the reasonable man that he ought to have foreseen them. Thus it is that over and over again it has happened that in different judgments in the same case, and sometimes in a single judgment, liability for a consequence has been imposed on the ground that it was reasonably foreseeable or, alternatively, on the ground that it was natural or necessary or probable. The two grounds have been treated as coterminous, and so they largely are. But, where they are not, the question arises to which the wrong answer was given in *Polemis*. For, if some limitation must be imposed upon the consequences for which the negligent actor is to be held responsible—and all are agreed that some limitation there must be—why should that test (reasonable foreseeability) be rejected which, since he is judged by what the reasonable man ought to foresee, corresponds with the common conscience of mankind, and a test (the "direct" consequence) be substituted which leads to nowhere but the never-ending and insoluble problems of causation. "The lawyer," said Sir Frederick Pollock, "cannot afford to adventure himself with philosophers in the logical and metaphysical controversies that beset the idea of cause." Yet this is just what he has most unfortunately done and must continue to do if the rule in *Polemis* is to prevail. A conspicuous example occurs when the actor seeks to escape liability on the ground that the "chain of causation" is broken by a "nova causa" or "novus actus interveniens."

The validity of a rule or principle can sometimes be tested by observing it in operation. Let the rule in *Polemis* be tested in this way. In the case of *Liesbosch*[39] the appellants, whose vessel had been fouled by the respondents, claimed damages under various heads. The respondents were admittedly at fault; therefore, said the appellants, invoking the rule in *Polemis*, they were responsible for all damage whether reasonably foreseeable or not. Here was the opportunity to deny the rule or to place it secure upon its pedestal. But the House of Lords took neither course; on the contrary, it distinguished *Polemis* on the ground that in that case the injuries suffered were the "immediate physical consequences" of the negligent act. It is not easy to understand why a distinction should be drawn between "immediate physical" and other consequences, nor where the line is to be drawn. It was perhaps this difficulty which led Denning L.J. in *Roe v. Minister of Health*[40] to say that foreseeability is only disregarded when the negligence is the immediate or *precipitating* cause of the damage. This new word may well have been thought as good a word as another for revealing or disguising the fact that he sought loyally to enforce an unworkable rule.

In the same connection may be mentioned the conclusion to which the Full Court finally came in the present case. Applying the rule in *Polemis* and holding therefore that the unforeseeability of the damage by fire afforded no defence, they went on to consider the remaining question. Was it a "direct" consequence? Upon this Manning J. said: "Notwithstanding that, if regard is had separately to each individual occurrence in the chain of events that led to this fire, each occurrence was improbable and, in one sense, improbability was heaped upon improbability. I cannot escape from

---

39. [1933] A.C. 449; 49 T.L.R. 289, H.L.   **40.** [1954] 2 Q.B. 66, 85; [1954] 2 W.L.R. 915; [1954] 2 All E.R. 131, C.A.

the conclusion that if the ordinary man in the street had been asked, as a matter of common sense, without any detailed analysis of the circumstances, to state the cause of the fire at Mort's Dock, he would unhesitatingly have assigned such cause to spillage of oil by the appellant's employees." Perhaps he would, and probably he would have added: "I never should have thought it possible." But with great respect to the Full Court this is surely irrelevant, or, if it is relevant, only serves to show that the *Polemis* rule works in a very strange way. After the event even a fool is wise. But it is not the hindsight of a fool; it is the foresight of the reasonable man which alone can determine responsibility. The *Polemis* rule by substituting "direct" for "reasonably foreseeable" consequence leads to a conclusion equally illogical and unjust.

At an early stage in this judgment their Lordships intimated that they would deal with the proposition which can best be stated by reference to the well-known dictum of Lord Sumner: "This however goes to culpability not to compensation." It is with the greatest respect to that very learned judge and to those who have echoed his words, that their Lordships find themselves bound to state their view that this proposition is fundamentally false.

It is, no doubt, proper when considering tortious liability for negligence to analyse its elements and to say that the plaintiff must prove a duty owed to him by the defendant, a breach of that duty by the defendant, and consequent damage. But there can be no liability until the damage has been done. It is not the act but the consequences on which tortious liability is founded. Just as (as it has been said) there is no such thing as negligence in the air, so there is no such thing as liability in the air. Suppose an action brought by A for damage caused by the carelessness (a neutral word) of B, for example, a fire caused by the careless spillage of oil. It may, of course, become relevant to know what duty B owed to A, but the only liability that is in question is the liability for damage by fire. It is vain to isolate the liability from its context and to say that B is or is not liable, and then to ask for what damage he is liable. For his liability is in respect of that damage and no other. If, as admittedly it is, B's liability (culpability) depends on the reasonable foreseeability of the consequent damage, how is that to be determined except by the foreseeability of the damage which in fact happened—the damage in suit? And, if that damage is unforeseeable so as to displace liability at large, how can the liability be restored so as to make compensation payable?

But, it is said, a different position arises if B's careless act has been shown to be negligent and has caused some foreseeable damage to A. Their Lordships have already observed that to hold B liable for consequences however unforeseeable of a careless act, if, but only if, he is at the same time liable for some other damage however trivial, appears to be neither logical nor just. This becomes more clear if it is supposed that similar unforeseeable damage is suffered by A and C but other foreseeable damage, for which B is liable, by A only. A system of law which would hold B liable to A but not to C for the similar damage suffered by each of them could not easily be defended. Fortunately, the attempt is not necessary. For the same fallacy is at the root of the proposition. It is irrelevant to the question whether B is liable for unforeseeable damage that he is liable for foreseeable damage, as irrelevant as would the fact that he had trespassed on Whiteacre be to the question whether he has trespassed on Blackacre. Again, suppose a claim by A for damage by fire by the careless act of B. Of what relevance is it to that claim that he has another claim arising out of the same careless act? It would surely not prejudice his claim if that other claim failed: it cannot assist it if it succeeds. Each of them rests on its own bottom, and will fail if it can be established that the damage could not reasonably be foreseen. We have come back to the plain common sense stated by Lord Russell of Killowen in *Bourhill v. Young.* As Denning L.J. said in *King v. Phillips*[42]: "there can be no doubt since *Bourhill v. Young* that the test of *liability for shock* is foreseeability of *injury by shock.*" Their Lordships substitute the word "fire" for "shock" and endorse this statement of the law.

Their Lordships conclude this part of the case with some general observations. They have been concerned primarily to displace the proposition that unforeseeability is irrelevant if damage is "direct." In doing so they have inevitably insisted that the essential factor in determining liability is whether the damage is of such a kind as the reasonable man should have foreseen. This accords with the general view thus stated by Lord Atkin in *Donoghue v. Stevenson*[43]: "The liability for negligence, whether you style it such or treat it as in other systems as a species of 'culpa,' is no doubt based upon a general public sentiment of moral wrongdoing for which the offender must pay." It is a departure from this sovereign principle if liability is made to depend solely on the damage being the "direct" or "natural" consequence of the precedent act. Who knows or can be assumed to know all the processes of nature? But if it would be wrong that a man should be held liable for damage unpredictable by a reasonable man because it was "direct" or "natural," equally it would be wrong that he should escape liability, however "indirect" the damage, if he foresaw or could reasonably foresee the intervening events which led to its being done: cf. *Woods v. Duncan.* Thus foreseeability becomes the effective test. In reasserting this principle their Lordships conceive that they do not depart from, but follow and develop, the law of negligence as laid down by Baron Alderson in *Blyth v. Birmingham Waterworks Co.*[45]

It is proper to add that their Lordships have not found it necessary to consider the so-called rule of "strict liability" exemplified in *Rylands v. Fletcher*[46] and the cases that have followed or distinguished it. Nothing that they have said is intended to reflect on that rule.

One aspect of this case remains to be dealt with. The respondents claim, in the alternative, that the appellants are liable in nuisance if not in negligence. Upon this issue their Lordships are of opinion that it would not be proper for them to come to any conclusion upon the material before them and without the benefit of the considered view of the Supreme Court. On the other hand, having regard to the course which the case has taken, they do not think that the respondents should be finally shut out from the opportunity of advancing this plea, if they think fit. They therefore

42. [1953] 1 Q.B. 429, 441.   **45.** (1856) 11 Exch. 781, 784.

43. [1932] A.C. 562, 580.   **46.** (1868) L.R. 3 H.L. 330, H.L.

propose that on the issue of nuisance alone the case should be remitted to the Full Court to be dealt with as may be thought proper.

Their Lordships will humbly advise Her Majesty that this appeal should be allowed, and the respondents' action so far as it related to damage caused by the negligence of the appellants be dismissed with costs, but that the action so far as it related to damage caused by nuisance should be remitted to the Full Court to be dealt with as that court may think fit. The respondents must pay the costs of the appellants of this appeal and in the courts below.

Notes

1. Weld–Blundell v. Stephens, [1920] A.C. 956, to which frequent reference was made in both *Polemis* and *Wagon Mound*, involved a complex factual situation. Weld–Blundell, the plaintiff, had sent a letter to his accountant, Stephens, in which he made some serious charges of impropriety against officials of a company in which he had invested considerable amounts of money. Stephens, who was asked to investigate the matter, handed the letter to his partner and asked him to look into the question. Stephens' partner went to the company's offices to make inquiries. The partner, unfortunately, forgot the letter at the company's offices. The letter was found by the company's office manager who showed it to two of the company officials whose propriety the plaintiff had attacked in the letter. These men then successfully brought libel actions against the plaintiff. Whereupon the plaintiff brought an action against his accountant for "negligence in the custody of * * * [the] letter." The jury found for the plaintiff but the verdict was set aside by the trial judge. The Court of Appeal reversed the trial judge and held that the action was maintainable but also held, with Scrutton, L.J., dissenting, that the plaintiff was not entitled to anything more than nominal damages because the libel actions were the result of the plaintiff's own wrongful act in publishing a malicious libel. The plaintiff then took the case to the House of Lords seeking entry of judgment on the jury's verdict. The House of Lords in a 3–2 decision affirmed the judgment of the Court of Appeal on the ground that the plaintiff's liability for damages in the libel actions was not the "result" of the defendant's negligence.

2. The Privy Council is a direct descendant of the old Curia Regis (see Chapter One, *supra* at n. 11). With the establishment of the common law courts and the development of Parliament, the Privy Council came by the end of the medieval period to be considered as mainly an executive body through which the King carried on the day-to-day business of government. The Council, however, retained some judicial functions including cases which were beyond the jurisdiction of the common-law courts, although by the beginning of the sixteenth century some of this jurisdiction came to be vested in the Court of Chancery. During the Tudor and early Stuart periods the large amount of judicial work caused a gradual separation between the administrative functions of the Council and its judicial functions. Since, when acting in a judicial capacity, it usually sat in a building in the Palace of Westminster called the "Starred Chamber," it came to be called "The Court of Star Chamber." In 1641, however, Parliament deprived the Council of its jurisdiction in England (16 Car. I, c. 10). The Council, however, retained its jurisdiction over the dominions of the Crown outside England. Originally this meant little more than the Channel Islands but, with establishment of the British Empire, the

judicial business of the Council sufficiently increased to require the establishment of a statutory Judicial Committee of the Privy Council to hear those appeals. Although most components of the British Empire have become completely independent states, a number of them which are still part of the British Commonwealth of Nations have retained the right to appeal to the Privy Council in London as the apex of their judicial system. Canada, however, has completely abolished appeals to the Privy Council. By virtue of the Australia Act of 1986, Australia has now done the same. The 1986 act abolished appeals to the Privy Council from the Australian state courts. Previous legislation, in 1975, abolished appeals to the Privy Council from the High Court of Australia, a federal court. New Zealand, for the moment, still retains the right of appeal to the Privy Council. The theory underlying the Privy Council's jurisdiction from these otherwise independent nations is that it is the prerogative of the Crown to entertain applications for redress from its subjects. That is why the Privy Council renders its decisions in the form of advice to the Crown as to how to dispose of the appeal. It is also why it is the custom to render only one opinion, except in the rare cases where there are dissents. Unlike the House of Lords, the Privy Council has never held that it is bound by its own decisions. The decisions of the Privy Council are not in theory binding upon English courts. Nevertheless, since the members of the Judicial Committee are largely drawn from the judges who sit in the House of Lords, the decisions of the Privy Council are treated as similarly authoritative. In reading the tort decisions of the Privy Council, one senses the perpetuation of the older notion, especially prevalent in the nineteenth century, that there was one common law, at least among English-speaking peoples, whether they were in Australia, England, or the United States. There is still a fairly strong undercurrent of this view throughout the legal profession, which is why these cases are so widely referred to, even in the United States.

HUGHES v. LORD ADVOCATE

House of Lords (Sc.), 1963.
[1963] A.C. 837, 2 W.L.R. 779, 1 All E.R. 705.

* * *

LORD GUEST. My Lords, in November, 1958, some Post Office employees had opened a manhole in Russell Road, Edinburgh, for the purpose of obtaining access to a telephone cable. The manhole from which the cover had been removed was near the edge of the roadway. A shelter tent had been erected over the open manhole. The manhole was some nine feet deep and a ladder had been placed inside the manhole to give access to the cable. Around the area of the site had been placed four red warning paraffin lamps. The lamps were lit at 3.30 p.m. About 5 p.m. or 5.30 p.m. the Post Office employees left the site for a tea break for which purpose they went to an adjoining Post Office building. Before leaving they removed the ladder from the manhole and placed it on the ground beside the shelter and pulled a tarpaulin cover over the entrance to the shelter, leaving a space of two feet to two feet six inches between the lower edge of the tarpaulin and the ground. The lamps were left burning.

After they left, the appellant, aged eight, and his uncle, aged ten, came along Russell Road and decided to explore the shelter. According to the findings of the Lord Ordinary, the boys picked up one of the red lamps, raised up the tarpaulin sheet and entered the shelter. They brought the ladder into the shelter with a view to descending into the manhole. They also brought a piece of rope which was not Post Office equipment, tied the rope to the lamp and, with the lamp, lowered themselves into the manhole. They both came out carrying the lamp. Thereafter, according to the evidence, the appellant tripped over the lamp, which fell into the hole. There followed an explosion from the hole with flames reaching a height of thirty feet. With the explosion the appellant fell into the hole and sustained very severe burning injuries.

In an action by the pursuer directed against the Lord Advocate, as representing the Postmaster–General, on the ground that the accident was due to the fault of the Post Office employees in failing to close the manhole before they left or to post a watchman while they were away the Lord Ordinary assoilzied the respondent. His judgment was affirmed by a majority of the First Division, Lord Carmont dissenting.

Before the Lord Ordinary and the Division a preliminary point was taken by the respondent that the appellant was a trespasser in the shelter and that the Post Office employees therefore owed no duty to take precautions for his safety. This point was not persisted in before this House and it is therefore unnecessary to say anything about it.

The Lord Ordinary, after a very careful analysis of the evidence, has found that the cause of the explosion was as a result of the lamp which the appellant knocked into the hole being so disturbed that paraffin escaped from the tank, formed vapour and was ignited by the flame. The lamp was recovered from the manhole after the accident; the tank of the lamp was half out and the wick-holder was completely out of the lamp. This explanation of the accident was rated by the experts as a low order of probability. But as there was no other feasible explanation it was accepted by the Lord Ordinary, and this House must take it as the established cause.

The Lord Ordinary has held that the presence of children in the shelter and in the manhole ought reasonably to have been anticipated by the Post Office employees. His ground for so holding was that the lighted lamps in the public street adjacent to a tented shelter in which there was an open manhole provided an allurement which would have been an attraction to children passing along the street.

I pause here to observe that the respondent submitted an argument before the Division and repeated in this House that, having regard to the evidence, the presence of children in Russell Road on that day, which was a Saturday, could not reasonably have been anticipated. The argument received only the support of the Lord President in the court below. It was founded on the fact that Russell Road is a quiet road and has no dwelling-house fronting it, the nearest house being four hundred yards away and the evidence of the Post Office employees that they were never bothered with children. This contention was rejected by the Lord Ordinary, who was in a better position than we are to judge of its validity. Having regard to the fact that this was a public street in the heart of the city there was no necessity, in my view, for the appellant to prove the likelihood of children being present. If the respondent had to establish the unlikelihood of the presence of children, his evidence fell far short of any such situation. It was entirely dependent on the experience of the Post Office employees during the preceding five days of the week. They had no previous experience of traffic at any other time. The Lord Ordinary, in my view, was well entitled to reach the conclusion which he did.

The next step in the Lord Ordinary's reasoning was that it was reasonable to anticipate that danger would be likely to result from the children's interference with the red lamps and their entrance to the shelter. He has further held that in these circumstances "the normal dangers of such children falling into the manhole or being in some way injured by a lamp, particularly if it fell or broke, were such that a reasonable man would not have ignored them." This view of the evidence was not, as I read the judgments, dissented from in the Inner House. Reference may be particularly made to Lord Guthrie's remarks, where he says: "The Lord Ordinary had held that it should have been anticipated that a boy might in the circumstances fall into the manhole and sustain injuries by burning from the paraffin lamp." It seems to have been accepted by both parties in the hearing before the Division that burning injuries might reasonably have been foreseen. But whether this be the position, there was ample evidence upon which the conclusion could be drawn that there was a reasonable probability of burning injuries if the children were allowed into the shelter with the lamp.

The Solicitor–General endeavoured to limit the extent of foreseeability in this connection by references to certain passages in the evidence regarding the safety of the red paraffin lamps. It might very well be that paraffin lamps by themselves, if left in the open, are not potentially dangerous even to children. But different considerations apply when they are found in connection with a shelter tent and a manhole, all of which are allurements to the inquisitive child. It is the combination of these factors which renders the situation one of potential danger.

In dismissing the appellant's claim the Lord Ordinary and the majority of the judges of the First Division reached the conclusion that the accident which happened was not reasonably foreseeable. In order to establish a coherent chain of causation it is not necessary that the precise details leading up to the accident should have been reasonably foreseeable: it is sufficient if the accident which occurred is of a type which should have been foreseeable by a reasonably careful person * * * or as Lord Mackintosh expressed it in the *Harvey* case, the precise concatenation of circumstances need not be envisaged. Concentration has been placed in the courts below on the explosion which, it was said, could not have been foreseen because it was caused in a unique fashion by the paraffin forming into vapour and being ignited by the naked flame of the wick. But this, in my opinion, is to concentrate on what is really a non-essential element in the dangerous situation created by the allurement. The test might better be put thus: Was the igniting of paraffin outside the lamp by the flame a foreseeable consequence of the breach of duty? In the circumstances, there was a combination of potentially dangerous circumstances against which the Post Office had to protect the appellant. If these formed an allurement to children it might have been foreseen that they would play with the lamp, that it might tip over, that it might be broken, and that when broken the paraffin might spill and be ignited by the flame. All these steps in the chain of causation seem to have been accepted by all the judges in the courts below as foreseeable. But because the explosion was the agent which caused the burning and was unforeseeable, therefore the accident, according to them, was not reasonably foreseeable. In my opinion, this reasoning is fallacious. An explosion is only one way in which burning can be caused. Burning can also be caused by the contact between liquid paraffin and a naked flame. In the one case paraffin vapour and in the other case liquid paraffin is ignited by fire. I cannot see that these are two different types of accident. They are both burning accidents and in both cases the injuries would be burning injuries. Upon this view the explosion was an immaterial event in the chain of causation. It was simply one way in which burning might be caused by the potentially dangerous paraffin lamp. I adopt, with respect, Lord Carmont's observation in the present case: "The defender cannot, I think, escape liability by contending that he did not foresee all the possibilities of the manner in which allurements—the manhole and the lantern—would act upon the childish mind."

The respondent relied upon the case of *Muir v. Glasgow Corporation*[29] and particularly on certain observations by Lords Thankerton and Macmillan. There are, in my view, essential differences between the two cases. The tea urn was, in that case, not like the paraffin lamp in the present circumstance, a potentially dangerous object. Moreover, the precise way in which the tea came to be spilled was never established and, as Lord Romer said: "It being thus unknown what was the particular risk that materialised, it is impossible to decide whether it was or was not one that should have been within the reasonable contemplation of Mrs. Alexander or of some other agent or employee of the appellants, and it is, accordingly, also impossible to fix the appellants with liability for the damage that the respondents sustained."

I have therefore reached the conclusion that the accident which occurred and which caused burning injuries to the appellant was one which ought reasonably to have been foreseen by the Post Office employees and that they were at fault in failing to provide a protection against the appellant entering the shelter and going down the manhole.

I would allow the appeal.

Notes

1. The decision in *Hughes* was unanimous. Lord Guest gave one of the five speeches in the House of Lords in the case. Lord Guest's speech was chosen for inclusion in this book because two of the other law lords specifically said that they endorsed his views.

2. Because the *Hughes* case arose in Scotland some of the terminology may seem strange to American or even English law students. Some definitions, largely taken from Black's Law Dictionary, may therefore be helpful:

    a. assoilzied—to be acquitted.

    b. Lord Advocate—the principal law officer of the Crown in Scotland. Actions brought in Scotland against the Government are nominally brought against the Lord Advocate.

29. [1943] A.C. 448, 467.

c. Lord Ordinary—the judge presiding at the Court of Sessions, the principal trial court in Scotland.

d. Inner House—the Chambers (in the Parliament House in Edinburgh) where the "First Division" (an appellate court) of the Court of Sessions sits and hence an alternate name for the First Division.

DOUGHTY v. TURNER MANUFACTURING CO., LTD.

Court of Appeal, 1963.
[1964] 1 Q.B. 518, 2 W.L.R. 240, 1 All E.R. 98.

Appeal from STABLE J., sitting at Stafford Assizes.

The following statement of facts is taken substantially from the judgment of Lord Pearce. The plaintiff, William James Doughty, was employed by the defendants, Turner Manufacturing Co. Ltd., in their factory, and on October 10, 1960, had been sent to deliver a message to the foreman who was working in the heat treatment room. In that room there stood two baths or cauldrons 3 ft. 10 ins. high and 3 ft. 4 ins. square. They had thick walls intended to resist great heat so that the internal area of each bath was only 1 ft. 6 ins. by 2 ft. 7 ins. Into those baths was placed sodium cyanide powder. Two upright electrodes, lowered by chains into the bath, passed an electric current through the powder which became a molten liquid and attained the very great heat of 800 degrees centigrade, eight times the heat of boiling water. The process consisted of subjecting metal parts to heat by immersing them in the liquid. In order to conserve the heat in each bath there were two loose covers which rested side by side over it. Those covers were made of a compressed compound of asbestos and cement known as sindanyo which, at that time, was thought to be a safe and suitable material for such a purpose. It had been so used in England and the United States for over 20 years. The defendants bought the covers for the particular purpose from the reputable manufacturers of the baths (Electric Resistance Furnace Co. Ltd.).

Immediately before the accident the subject-matter of the action, the electrodes in the bath, were being changed by a workman standing on the side of the bath. He, or some other of the four workmen in the vicinity, must have inadvertently knocked the loose asbestos cement cover so that it slid into the bath and disappeared from sight beneath the molten liquid. Nobody regarded that as a dangerous matter or withdrew from the neighbourhood of the bath. Two men actually moved closer to peer into the bath and see what had happened. After an interval of between one and two minutes the molten liquid erupted from the bath, injuring the bystanders by its great heat and setting fire to objects on which it fell. The plaintiff was at that moment standing by the side of the foreman not far from the bath, and suffered personal injuries as a result of the eruption.

The reason for the eruption was discovered by experiments which Imperial Chemical Industries Ltd., which had installed similar covers, carried out as a result of this accident. It then appeared that whenever any cover made of compound asbestos cement was immersed in the molten liquid and subjected to a temperature of over 500 degrees it created such an eruption. At that temperature the compound, which contained hydrogen and oxygen, underwent a chemical change which either created or released water. This water turned to steam and produced an explosion or eruption which threw some of the hot molten liquid out of the bath. Thus the immersion of the cover in the bath was inevitably followed by an eruption of liquid from the bath. The same result would occur if something that contained actual moisture in it (as opposed to what might be called the potential moisture which was thus precipitated by great heat) was immersed; if, for instance, this cover, which was porous and capable of holding water, had been immersed when wet. But it was not suggested that this particular cover contained actual moisture at the time of the accident, since it had been standing in the hot room for some days beforehand.

The plaintiff sued the defendants for damages in respect of his injuries on the ground of negligence. The judge held that the defendants did not appreciate that the immersion of the cover in the liquid would produce an explosion and he held that they were not to blame for not appreciating it. He said: "The result simply is this that if, for example, the bath contained an amount of this substance and it exploded whilst it was being used in the ordinary way, I think the defendants would have escaped liability." That was clearly right.

He went on to hold, however, that it must have been common knowledge that there were substances which, if dropped into such immense heat, would produce an explosion, although not all substances would do so; and that, therefore, "every possible precaution should be taken to see that nothing was dropped into the bath which could have that result." He, therefore, held that the inadvertence of one of the defendants' workmen in upsetting the cover into the bath was "negligent in the true sense of the word; that is to say, it constituted an actionable wrong." He accordingly held the defendants liable in negligence and awarded the plaintiff £150 damages.

The defendants appealed.

Lord Pearce stated the facts and continued: No authorities were cited to the judge at the trial and in the light of the judgment of the Privy Council in *Overseas Tankship (U.K.) Ltd. v. Morts Dock and Engineering Co. Ltd. (The Wagon Mound),* which important case gave such a different complexion to cases where seemingly harmless acts result in unforeseeble calamities, I think that the judge, if it had been called to his attention in the present case, might have reached a different conclusion. * * *

In the present case the evidence showed that nobody supposed that an asbestos cement cover could not safely be immersed in the bath. The judge took the view, which Mr. James concedes was correct, that if the defendants had deliberately immersed this cover in the bath as part of the normal process, they could not have been held liable for the resulting explosion. The fact that they inadvertently knocked it into the bath cannot of itself convert into negligence that which they were entitled to do deliberately. In the then state of their knowledge, for which the judge, rightly on the evidence, held them in no way to blame, the accident was not foreseeable. In spite of Mr. James' able argument, I am of opinion that they cannot, therefore, be held liable for negligence.

Mr. James has further argued that * * * the defendants are liable on grounds similar to those on which the House of Lords, while following the reasoning of *The Wagon Mound,* upheld a judgment for the infant plaintiff in *Hughes v. Lord Advocate.* * * * Their Lordships held * * * that although the exact chain of events was unforeseeable, the type of accident and the injuries "though perhaps different in degree, did not differ in kind from injuries which might have resulted from an accident of a foreseeable nature * * *" (See Lord Reid's speech.) * * *

In the present case the potential eruptive qualities of the covers when immersed in great heat were not suspected and they were not a known source of danger, but Mr. James argues that the cause of injury was the escape of the hot liquid from the bath, and that injury through the escape of liquid from the bath by splashing was foreseeable. The evidence showed that splashes caused by sudden immersion, whether of the metal objects for which it was intended or any other extraneous object, were a foreseeable danger which should be carefully avoided. The falling cover might have ejected the liquid by a splash and in the result it did eject the liquid, though in a more dramatic fashion. Therefore, he argues, the actual accident was merely a variant of foreseeable accidents by splashing. It is clear, however, both by inference and by one explicit observation, that the judge regarded splashes as being in quite a different category. Moreover, according to the evidence, it seems that the cover never did create a splash: it appears to have slid into the liquid at an angle of some 45 degrees and dived obliquely downwards. Further, it seems somewhat doubtful whether the cover falling only from a height of four or six inches, which was the difference in level between the liquid and the sides, could have splashed any liquid outside the bath. And when (if ever) the plaintiff was in the area in which he could be hit by a mere splash (apparently the liquid being heavy, if splashed, would not travel further than a foot from the bath) the cover had already slid into the liquid without splashing. Indeed, it seems from the plaintiff's evidence that when he first came on to the scene the cover was already half in and half out of the liquid. On broader grounds, however, it would be quite unrealistic to describe this accident as a variant of the perils from splashing. The cause of the accident, to quote Lord Reid's words, was "the intrusion of a new and unexpected factor." There was an eruption due to chemical changes underneath the surface of the liquid as opposed to a splash caused by displacement from bodies falling on to its surface. In my judgment, the reasoning in *Hughes v. Lord Advocate* cannot be extended far enough to cover this case.

I have great sympathy with the plaintiff who suffered injury through no fault of his own. But, in my judgment, the defendants cannot, on the evidence, be held guilty of negligence, and I would accordingly allow the appeal and enter judgment for the defendants.

[The concurring judgment of Harman L.J. has been omitted]

* * *

DIPLOCK L.J. * * * The cover was of a type designed for use with the furnace and had been widely so used in the trade for upwards of 20 years. The use of a cover made of this material presents, it is now known, two risks of injury to persons in the vicinity of the furnace. The first risk, which it shares with any other solid object of similar weight and size, is that if it is allowed to drop on to the hot liquid in the bath with sufficient momentum it may cause the liquid to splash on to persons within about one foot from the bath and injure them by burning. The second risk is that if it becomes immersed in a liquid, the temperature of which exceeds 500 degrees centigrade, it will disintegrate and cause an under-surface explosion which will eject the liquid from the bath over a wide area and may cause injury by burning to persons within that area.

The former risk was well known (that was foreseeable) at the time of the accident; but it did not happen. It was the second risk which happened and caused the plaintiff damage by burning. The crucial finding by the judge, in a characteristically laconic judgment, was that this was not a risk of which the defendants at the time of the accident knew, or ought to have known. This finding, which was justified by the evidence and has not been assailed in this appeal, would appear to lead logically to the conclusion that in causing, or failing to prevent, the immersion of the cover in the liquid, the defendants, by their servants, were in breach of no duty of care owed to the plaintiff, for this was not an act or omission which they could reasonably foresee was likely to cause him damage.

The judge, nevertheless, found the defendants liable. His ratio decidendi, which was somewhat elliptically expressed, can, I think, be fairly expanded into the following findings of fact and propositions of law: (1) It was common knowledge that some substances (viz., those which were chemically unstable at 800 degrees and upon disintegration at that temperature formed, among other things, a gas) would cause an explosion upon immersion in the liquid cyanide. (2) It was common knowledge that other substances (viz., those which were chemically inert at 800 degrees) would not cause an explosion upon immersion in the liquid cyanide. (3) Therefore, the defendants were under a duty to all persons whom they ought reasonably to foresee might be within the area within which they would be likely to sustain damage if an explosion occurred to take every possible precaution to see that nothing was immersed in the liquid cyanide which in fact, whether or not they knew or ought to have known it, could cause an explosion. (4) The plaintiff was a person whom the defendants ought reasonably to have foreseen might be within the area which he would be likely to sustain damage if an explosion occurred. (5) The defendants did not take every possible precaution to ensure that the cover was not immersed in the liquid cyanide. They used it in a place where it might inadvertently be caused to fall into the liquid cyanide and become immersed therein. (6) One of the defendants' servants in fact inadvertently caused the cover to fall into the liquid cyanide and become immersed therein, thereby causing an explosion whereby the plaintiff sustained damage. (7) Therefore, the damage was the result of the defendants' breach of the duty which they owed to the plaintiff.

With great respect the fallacy in this reasoning appears to me to lie in the proposition of law in paragraph (3). It means, in effect, that the defendants could only use the furnace at their peril, for the whole purpose of its use was to immerse in it substances which were chemically inert at 800 degrees. If the judge's proposition is correct, the mere fact of an explosion consequent upon the immersion of some substance in the liquid would render the defendants liable, however meticulous the care they had taken to see that the substance was chemically inert at 800 degrees, for the fact of the explosion would show that the substance "could" cause one.

This is to impose on the defendants a "strict liability" analogous to the duty to prevent a dangerous thing escaping from his land which, under the rule laid down in *Rylands v. Fletcher,*[15] is owed by an occupier of land to persons who are likely to be injured by its escape. An attempt to import into the general law of negligence a similar strict liability upon persons carrying on an ultra-hazardous activity was made in *Read v. J. Lyons & Co. Ltd.,*[16] and was negatived by the House of Lords.

There is no room today for mystique in the law of negligence. It is the application of common morality and common sense to the activities of the common man. He must take reasonable care to avoid acts or omissions which he can reasonably foresee would be likely to injure his neighbour; but he need do no more than this. If the act which he does is not one which he could, if he thought about it, reasonably foresee would injure his neighbour it matters not whether he does it intentionally or inadvertently. The judge's finding, uncontested on appeal, that in the state of knowledge as it was at the time of the accident the defendants could not reasonably have foreseen that the immersion of the asbestos cement cover in the liquid would be likely to injure anyone must lead to the conclusion that they would have been under no liability to the plaintiff if they had intentionally immersed the cover in the liquid. The fact that it was done inadvertently cannot create any liability, for the immersion of the cover was not an act which they were under any duty to take any care to avoid.

It was, however, argued by Mr. James for the plaintiff that, even though the risk of explosion upon immersion of the cover was not one which the defendants could reasonably foresee, the plaintiff can, nevertheless, recover because one of the defendants' servants inadvertently either knocked the cover into the liquid or allowed it to slip in, thus giving rise to a foreseeable risk of splashing the hot liquid on to the plaintiff and injuring him by burning. The actual damage sustained by the plaintiff was damage of the same kind, that is by burning, as could be foreseen as likely to result from knocking the cover into the liquid or allowing it to slip in, and Mr. James contended that this was sufficient to impose a duty on the defendants owed to the plaintiff to take reasonable care to avoid knocking the cover into the liquid, or allowing it to slip in, and that the plaintiff's damage flowed from their breach of this duty. Such a proposition might, before *Overseas Tankship (U.K.) Ltd. v. Morts Dock and Engineering Co. Ltd. (The Wagon Mound)*, have been supported by *In re Polemis, and Furness, Withy & Co. Ltd.*, but the decision of the Court of Appeal is no longer law. Mr. James relied principally on *Hughes v. Lord Advocate*, a case in which the House of Lords treated *The Wagon Mound* as correctly stating the law, but distinguished it on the facts. I do not think that this authority assists him. * * *

15. L.R. 3 H.L. 330. [Ed. note. *Rylands v. Fletcher* is reprinted at p. 528, *infra,* as part of the discussion of "strict liability."]

16. [1947] A.C. 156; 62 T.L.R. 646; [1946] 2 All E.R. 471, H.L.

But in the present case the defendants' duty owed to the plaintiff in relation to the only foreseeable risk, that is of splashing, was to take reasonable care to avoid knocking the cover into the liquid or allowing it to slip in in such a way as to cause a splash which would injure the plaintiff. Failure to avoid knocking it into the liquid, or allowing it to slip in, was of itself no breach of duty to the plaintiff. It is not clear on the evidence whether the dropping of the cover on to the liquid caused any splash at all. The judge made no finding on this. * * * However that may be, it is incontrovertible that, even if there was some slight splash when the cover fell on to the liquid, the plaintiff was untouched by it and it caused him no injury. There was thus, in the circumstances of this case, no breach of duty to the plaintiff involved in inadvertently knocking the cover into the liquid or inadvertently allowing it to slip in.

For these reasons I would accordingly allow this appeal.

Appeal allowed with costs.

Notes

1. Suppose there had been a smaller passage of time between the immersion of the cover and the explosion. Would you expect a different result?

2. If the plaintiff had been standing within the area where he might have been hit by an anticipated splash, would it have made any difference (assuming, as in the actual case, that there was no splash on impact but only an explosion after the sindanyo cover had been heated to 500° C.)?

PETITION OF KINSMAN TRANSIT CO.

United States Court of Appeals, Second Circuit, 1964.
338 F.2d 708, *cert. denied,* 380 U.S. 944, 85 S.Ct. 1026, 13 L.Ed.2d 963 (1965).

FRIENDLY, CIRCUIT JUDGE:

* * *

The Buffalo River flows through Buffalo from east to west, with many turns and bends, until it empties into Lake Erie. Its navigable western portion is lined with docks, grain elevators, and industrial installations; during the winter, lake vessels tie up there pending resumption of navigation on the Great Lakes, without power and with only a shipkeeper aboard. About a mile from the mouth, the City of Buffalo maintains a lift bridge at Michigan Avenue. Thaws and rain frequently cause freshets to develop in the upper part of the river and its tributary, Cazenovia Creek; currents then range up to fifteen miles an hour and propel broken ice down the river, which sometimes overflows its banks.

On January 21, 1959, rain and thaw followed a period of freezing weather. The United States Weather Bureau issued appropriate warnings which were published and broadcast. Around 6 P.M. an ice jam that had formed in Cazenovia Creek disintegrated. Another ice jam formed just west of the junction of the creek and the river; it broke loose around 9 P.M.

The MacGilvray Shiras, owned by The Kinsman Transit Company, was moored at the dock of the Concrete Elevator, operated by Continental Grain Company, on the south side of the river about three miles upstream of the Michigan Avenue Bridge. She was loaded with grain owned by Continental. The berth, east of the main portion of the dock, was exposed in the sense that about 150 of the Shiras' forward end, pointing upstream, and 70 of her stern—a total of over half her length—projected beyond the dock. This left between her stem and the bank a space of water seventy-five feet wide where the ice and other debris could float in and accumulate. The position was the more hazardous in that the berth was just below a bend in the river, and the Shiras was on the inner bank. None of her anchors had been put out. From about 10 P.M. large chunks of ice and debris began to pile up between the Shiras' starboard bow and the bank; the pressure exerted by this mass on her starboard bow was augmented by the force of the current and of floating ice against her port quarter. The mooring lines began to part, and a "deadman," to which the No. 1 mooring cable had been attached, pulled out of the ground—the judge finding that it had not been properly constructed or inspected. About 10:40 P.M. the stern lines parted, and the Shiras drifted into the current. During the previous forty minutes, the shipkeeper took no action to ready the anchors by releasing the devil's claws; when he sought to drop them after the Shiras broke loose, he released the compressors with the claws still hooked in the chain so that the anchors jammed and could no longer be dropped. The trial judge reasonably found that if the anchors had dropped at that time, the Shiras would probably have fetched up at the hairpin bend just below the Concrete Elevator, and that in any case they would considerably have slowed her progress, the significance of which will shortly appear.

Careening stern first down the S-shaped river, the Shiras, at about 11 P.M., struck the bow of the Michael K. Tewksbury, owned by Midland Steamship Line, Inc. The Tewksbury was moored in a relatively protected area flush against the face of a dock on the outer bank just below a hairpin bend so that no opportunity was afforded for ice to build up between her port bow and the dock. Her shipkeeper had left around 5 P.M. and spent the evening watching television with a girl friend and her family. The collision caused the Tewksbury's mooring lines to part; she too drifted stern first down the river, followed by the Shiras. The collision caused damage to the Steamer Druckenmiller which was moored opposite the Tewksbury.

Thus far there was no substantial conflict in the testimony; as to what followed there was. Judge Burke found, and we accept his findings as soundly based, that at about 10:43 P.M., Goetz, the superintendent of the Concrete Elevator, telephoned Kruptavich, another employee of Continental, that the Shiras was adrift; Kruptavich called the Coast Guard, which called the city fire station on the river, which in turn warned the crew on the Michigan Avenue Bridge, this last call being made about 10:48 P.M. Not quite twenty minutes later the watchman at the elevator where the Tewksbury had been moored phoned the bridge crew to raise the bridge. Although not more than two minutes and ten seconds were needed to elevate the bridge to full height after traffic was stopped, assuming that the motor started promptly, the bridge was just being raised when, at 11:17 P.M., the Tewksbury crashed into its center. The bridge crew consisted of an operator and two tenders; a change of shift was scheduled for 11 P.M. The inference is rather strong, despite contrary testimony, that the operator on the earlier shift had not yet returned from a tavern when the telephone call from the fire station was received; that the operator on the second shift did not arrive until shortly before the call from the elevator where the Tewksbury had been moored; and that in consequence the bridge was not raised until too late.

The first crash was followed by a second, when the south tower of the bridge fell. The Tewksbury grounded and stopped in the wreckage with her forward end resting against the stern of the Steamer Farr, which was moored on the south side of the river just above the bridge. The Shiras ended her journey with her stern against the Tewksbury and her bow against the north side of the river. So wedged, the two vessels substantially dammed the flow, causing water and ice to back up and flood installations on the banks with consequent damage as far as the Concrete Elevator, nearly three miles upstream. Two of the bridge crew suffered injuries. Later the north tower of the bridge collapsed, damaging adjacent property.

Judge Burke concluded that Continental and the Shiras had committed various faults discussed below; that the faults of the Shiras were without the privity or knowledge of her owner, thus entitling Kinsman to limit its liability, 46 U.S.C. § 183; that the Tewksbury and her owner were entitled to exoneration; and that the City of Buffalo was at fault for failing to raise the Michigan Avenue Bridge. The City was not faulted for the manner in which it had constructed and maintained flood improvements on the river and on Cazenovia Creek, or for failing to dynamite the ice jams. For the damages sustained by the Tewksbury and the Druckenmiller in the collisions at the Standard Elevator dock, Judge Burke allowed those vessels to recover equally from Continental and from Kinsman, jointly and severally, subject however, to the latter's right to limit liability. He held the City, Continental and Kinsman equally liable jointly and severally (again subject to Kinsman's limitation of liability) for damages to persons and property sustained by all others as a result of the disaster at the bridge. But, on the basis of the last clear chance rule, he held the City solely liable for damages sustained by the other tort-feasors, to wit, the Shiras and Continental as operator of the Concrete Elevator, and refused to allow recovery by the City against them.

* * *

We thus come to what we consider the most serious issues: (I) Whether the City of Buffalo was at fault for failing to raise the bridge on learning of the prospective advent of the Shiras and the Tewksbury; (II) the consequences of the time relation of the City's failure to the prior faults of the Shiras and Continental; and (III) the effect of the allegedly unexpectable character of the events leading to much of the damage—and here of the Palsgraf case, infra.

I. THE CITY'S FAILURE TO RAISE THE BRIDGE

If this were a run of the mine negligence case, the City's argument against liability for not promptly raising the Michigan Avenue Bridge would be impressive: All the vessels moored in the harbor were known to be without power and incapable of controlled movement save with the aid of tugs. The tugs had quit at 4 P.M.; they were not docked in the river, and would not undertake after quitting time to tow a vessel into or out of the inner harbor. Since the breaking loose of a ship was not to be anticipated, it would have been consistent with prudence for the City to relieve the bridge crews of their duties. Neglect by the crews ought not subject the City to liability merely because, out of abundance of caution, it had ordered them to be present when prudence did not so require. The case is unlike those in which a railway or a city, having undertaken to give warning signals at a crossing although under no duty to do so, is held liable to a plaintiff who relied on the absence of warning when it failed to continue its practice. * * * It would be nonsense to suppose that Continental and the Shiras did what they did, and didn't what they didn't, in reliance on the bridge operators being sufficiently alert to avert disaster if the Shiras should break loose.

Buffalo's adversaries answer with § 4 of the Bridge Act of 1906, 33 U.S.C. § 494, which requires, inter alia, that if a bridge over a navigable stream "shall be constructed with a draw, then the draw shall be opened promptly by the persons owning or operating such bridge upon reasonable signal for the passage of boats and other water craft." Buffalo replies that this general language cannot reasonably be construed to require that all drawbridges over all navigable streams in all fifty states shall be tended at all times of day or night, summer or winter, despite the near certainty that no traffic will approach. Alternatively it is arguable that a signal given when no traffic was to be expected would not be a "reasonable signal" unless this gave the bridge owner reasonable time to get someone down to the bridge to open it. However, an older statute, 28 Stat. 362 (1894), as amended, 33 U.S.C. § 499, makes it "the duty of all persons owning, operating, and tending the drawbridges * * * across the navigable rivers and other waters of the United States, to open, or cause to be opened, the draws of such bridges under such rules and regulations as in the opinion of the Secretary of the Army the public interests require * * *." The section goes on to authorize the promulgation of such regulations by the Secretary of the Army and to make it a misdemeanor to delay unreasonably the opening of a draw after reasonable signal. Pursuant to this authority, the Corps of Engineers promulgated 33 C.F.R. § 203.707, as follows:

"(a) The Michigan Avenue bridges across Buffalo River and Buffalo Ship Canal will not be required to open for the passage of vessels from 7:00 to 7:30 a. m., 8:00 to 8:30 a. m., 3:45 to 4:30 p. m., and 5:15 to 6:00 p. m.

* * *

"(d) The closed periods prescribed in this section shall not be effective on Sundays and on New Year's day * * * [and other holidays].

"(e) The draws of these bridges shall be opened promptly on signal for the passage of any vessel at all times during the day or night except as otherwise provided in this section." [None of the unquoted subsections provide otherwise.]

It is possible to read this statute and the regulations thereunder as creating by implication a cause of action, irrespective of negligence, for any person, or at least for any ship, injured by their breach. * * *

* * * The effect of the Corps of Engineers' regulation was to withdraw decision as to when the bridge might be left untended from what would otherwise have been a permissible area for exercise of the City's prudent, judgment. * * * Indeed, Buffalo exercised no judgment contrary to the regulation; the fault lay in its employees' failure to carry out the United States' commands and those of their employer.

II.   The Time Relation of the City's Failure to the
Prior Faults of the Shiras and Continental

All three parties held liable complain of the effect which the judge gave to the failure of the City to raise the bridge.   Kinsman and Continental contend that the City's failure insulates them from liability for damages to others resulting from the collision at the bridge; the City objects to the imposition of sole liability for damage to the Shiras and to Continental and to the exoneration of these parties from liability for destruction of the bridge.

We speedily overrule the objections of Kinsman and Continental.   Save for exceptions which are not here pertinent, an actor whose negligence has set a dangerous force in motion is not saved from liability for harm it has caused to innocent persons solely because another has negligently failed to take action that would have avoided this.   * * * As against third persons, one negligent actor cannot defend on the basis that the other had "the last clear chance."   * * * The contrary argument grows out of the discredited notion that only the last wrongful act can be a cause—a notion as faulty in logic as it is wanting in fairness.   The established principle is especially appealing in admiralty which will divide the damages among the negligent actors or non-actors.

On the other hand, we disagree with the judge's holding that because the City had "the last clear chance," Kinsman and Continental as plaintiffs against it are absolved of their negligence and the City as plaintiff is left without recourse against them.   Here, as in the case of the injuries to persons not at fault, the damages should be divided.   * * *

* * *

None of the cases in which this Court has applied the last clear chance rule to impose sole liability in admiralty is at all analogous to this one; indeed we doubt whether this case would come within the principle as generally applied at common law.   * * *

* * *

III.   The Allegedly Unexpectable Character of
the Events Leading to Much of the Damage

The very statement of the case suggests the need for considering Palsgraf v. Long Island R.R. * * * and the closely related problem of liability for unforeseeable consequences.

In Sinram v. Pennsylvania R.R., 61 F.2d 767, 770 (2 Cir.1932), which received Palsgraf into the admiralty, Judge Learned Hand characterized the issue in that case as "whether, if A. omitted to perform a positive duty to B., C., who had been damaged in consequence, might invoke the breach, though otherwise A. owed him no duty; in short, whether A. was chargeable for the results to others of his breach of duty to B." Thus stated, the query rather answers itself; Hohfeld's analysis tells us that once it is concluded that A. had no duty to C., it is simply a correlative that C. has no right against A. The important question is what was the basis for Chief Judge Cardozo's conclusion that the Long Island Railroad owed no "duty" to Mrs. Palsgraf under the circumstances.

Certainly there is no general principle that a railroad owes no duty to persons on station platforms not in immediate proximity to the tracks, as would have been quickly demonstrated if Mrs. Palsgraf had been injured by the fall of improperly loaded objects from a passing train. * * * Neither is there any principle that railroad guards who jostle a package-carrying passenger owe a duty only to him; if the package had contained bottles, the Long Island would surely have been liable for injury caused to close bystanders by flying glass or spurting liquid. The reason why the Long Island was thought to owe no duty to Mrs. Palsgraf was the lack of any notice that the package contained a substance demanding the exercise of any care toward anyone so far away; Mrs. Palsgraf was not considered to be within the area of apparent hazard created by whatever lack of care the guard had displayed to the anonymous carrier of the unknown fireworks.[5] * * *

We see little similarity between the Palsgraf case and the situation before us. The point of Palsgraf was that the appearance of the newspaper-wrapped package gave no notice that its dislodgement could do any harm save to itself and those nearby, and this by impact, perhaps with consequent breakage, and not by explosion, in contrast, a ship insecurely moored in a fast flowing river is a known danger not only to herself but to the owners of all other ships and structures down-river, and to persons upon them. No one would dream of saying that a shipowner who "knowingly and wilfully" failed to secure his ship at a pier on such a river "would not have threatened" persons and owners of property downstream in some manner.[6] The ship owner and the wharfinger in this case having thus

---

5. There was exceedingly little evidence of negligence of any sort. The only lack of care suggested by the majority in the Appellate Division was that instead of endeavoring to assist the passenger, the guards "might better have discouraged and warned him not to board the moving train." * * * Chief Judge Cardozo said: "The man was not injured in his person nor even put in danger. The purpose of the act, as well as its effect, was to make his person safe. If there was a wrong to him at all, which may very well be doubted, it was a wrong to a property interest only, the safety of his package." * * * Judge Andrews' dissent said the Long Island had been negligent * * * but did not state in what respect.

How much ink would have been saved over the years if the Court of Appeals had reversed Mrs. Palsgraf's judgment on the basis that there was no evidence of negligence at all!

6. The facts here do not oblige us to decide whether the Shiras and Continental could successfully invoke Palsgraf against claims of owners of shore-side property upstream from the Concrete Elevator or of non-riparian property other than the real and personal property which was sufficiently close to the bridge to have been damaged by the fall of the towers.

owed a duty of care to all within the reach of the ship's known destructive power, the impossibility of advance identification of the particular person who would be hurt is without legal consequence. * * * Similarly the foreseeable consequences of the City's failure to raise the bridge were not limited to the Shiras and the Tewksbury. Collision plainly created a danger that the bridge towers might fall onto adjoining property, and the crash of two uncontrolled lake vessels, one 425 feet and the other 525 feet long, into a bridge over a swift ice-ridden stream, with a channel only 177 feet wide, could well result in a partial damming that would flood property upstream. As to the City also, it is useful to consider, by way of contrast, Chief Judge Cardozo's statement that the Long Island would not have been liable to Mrs. Palsgraf had the guard wilfully thrown the package down. If the City had deliberately kept the bridge closed in the face of the on-rushing vessels, taking the risk that they might not come so far, no one would give house-room to a claim that it "owed no duty" to those who later suffered from the flooding. Unlike Mrs. Palsgraf, they were within the area of hazard.

The case is quite different from this Court's ruling in Sinram, where a tug which had negligently rammed a barge was held free of liability for the loss of coal that the bargee subsequently allowed to be loaded into his barge without first having inspected her for damage. That case illustrates the principle, noted in Judge Hand's opinion, 61 F.2d at 771, "that there must be a terminus somewhere, short of eternity, at which the second party becomes responsible in lieu of the first," * * *

Since all the claimants here met the Palsgraf requirement of being persons to whom the actors owed a "duty of care," we are not obliged to reconsider whether that case furnishes as useful a standard for determining the boundaries of liability in admiralty for negligent conduct as was thought in Sinram, when Palsgraf was still in its infancy. But this does not dispose of the alternative argument that the manner in which several of the claimants were harmed, particularly by flood damage, was unforeseeable and that recovery for this may not be had—whether the argument is put in the forthright form that unforeseeable damages are not recoverable or is concealed under a formula of lack of "proximate cause."[8]

So far as concerns the City, the argument lacks factual support. Although the obvious risks from not raising the bridge were damage to itself and to the vessels, the danger of a fall of the bridge and of flooding would not have been unforeseeable under the circumstances to anyone who gave them thought. And the same can be said as to the failure of Kinsman's shipkeeper to ready the anchors after the danger had become apparent. The exhibits indicate that the width of the channel between the Concrete Elevator and the bridge is at most points less than two hundred fifty feet. If the Shiras caught up on a dock or vessel moored along the shore, the current might well swing her bow across the channel so as to block the ice floes, as indeed could easily have occurred at the Standard Elevator dock where the stern of the Shiras struck the Tewksbury's bow.

---

8. It is worth underscoring that the *ratio decidendi* in Palsgraf was that the Long Island was not required to use *any* care with respect to the package vis-a-vis Mrs. Palsgraf; Chief Judge Cardozo did not reach the issue of "proximate cause" for which the case is often cited. * * *

At this point the channel scarcely exceeds two hundred feet, and this was further narrowed by the presence of the Druckenmiller moored on the opposite bank. Had the Tewksbury's mooring held, it is thus by no means unlikely that these three ships would have dammed the river. Nor was it unforeseeable that the drawbridge would not be raised since, apart from any other reason, there was no assurance of timely warning. What may have been less foreseeable was that the Shiras would get that far down the twisting river, but this is somewhat negated both by the known speed of the current when freshets developed and by the evidence that, on learning of the Shiras' departure, Continental's employees and those they informed foresaw precisely that.

Continental's position on the facts is stronger. It was indeed foreseeable that the improper construction and lack of inspection of the "deadman" might cause a ship to break loose and damage persons and property on or near the river—that was what made Continental's conduct negligent. With the aid of hindsight one can also say that a prudent man, carefully pondering the problem, would have realized that the danger of this would be greatest under such water conditions as developed during the night of January 21, 1959, and that if a vessel should break loose under those circumstances, events might transpire as they did. But such *post hoc* step by step analysis would render "foreseeable" almost anything that has in fact occurred; if the argument relied upon has legal validity, it ought not be circumvented by characterizing as foreseeable what almost no one would in fact have foreseen at the time.

The effect of unforeseeability of damage upon liability for negligence has recently been considered by the Judicial Committee of the Privy Council, Overseas Tankship (U.K.) Ltd. v. Morts Dock & Engineering Co. (The Wagon Mound), * * * The Committee there disapproved the proposition, thought to be supported by Re Polemis and Furness, Withy & Co. Ltd., * * * "that unforeseeability is irrelevant if damage is 'direct.'" We have no difficulty with the result of The Wagon Mound, in view of the finding * * * that the appellant had no reason to believe that the floating furnace oil would burn * * *. On that view the decision simply applies the principle which excludes liability where the injury sprang from a hazard different from that which was improperly risked * * *. Although some language in the judgment goes beyond this, we would find it difficult to understand why one who had failed to use the care required to protect others in the light of expectable forces should be exonerated when the very risks that rendered his conduct negligent produced other and more serious consequences to such persons than were fairly foreseeable when he fell short of what the law demanded. Foreseeability of danger is necessary to render conduct negligent; where as here the damage was caused by just those forces whose existence required the exercise of greater care than was taken—the current, the ice, and the physical mass of the Shiras, the incurring of consequences other and greater than foreseen does not make the conduct less culpable or provide a reasoned basis for insulation.[9] See Hart and Honoré, Causation in the Law, 234–48 (1959). The oft encoun-

9. * * *

This principle supports the judgment for the defendant in the recent case of Doughty v. Turner Mfg. Co., [1964] 2 W.L.R. 240 (C.A.). * * *

tered argument that failure to limit liability to foreseeable consequences may subject the defendant to a loss wholly out of proportion to his fault seems scarcely consistent with the universally accepted rule that the defendant takes the plaintiff as he finds him and will be responsible for the full extent of the injury even though a latent susceptibility of the plaintiff renders this far more serious than could reasonably have been anticipated. * * *

The weight of authority in this country rejects the limitation of damages to consequences foreseeable at the time of the negligent conduct when the consequences are "direct," and the damage, although other and greater than expectable, is of the same general sort that was risked. * * * Other American courts, purporting to apply a test of foreseeability to damages, extend that concept to such unforeseen lengths as to raise serious doubt whether the concept is meaningful;[10] indeed, we wonder whether the British courts are not finding it necessary to limit the language of The Wagon Mound as we have indicated.[11]

We see no reason why an actor engaging in conduct which entails a large risk of small damage and a small risk of other and greater damage, of the same general sort, from the same forces, and to the same class of persons, should be relieved of responsibility for the latter simply because the chance of its occurrence, if viewed alone, may not have been large enough to require the exercise of care. By hypothesis, the risk of the lesser harm was sufficient to render his disregard of it actionable; the existence of a less likely additional risk that the very forces against whose action he was required to guard would produce other and greater damage than could have been reasonably anticipated should inculpate him further rather than limit his liability. This does not mean that the careless actor will always be held for all damages for which the forces that he risked were a cause in fact. Somewhere a point will be reached when courts will agree that the link has become too tenuous—that what is claimed to be consequence is only fortuity. Thus, if the destruction of the Michigan Avenue Bridge had delayed the arrival of a doctor, with consequent loss of a patient's life, few judges would impose liability on any of the parties here, although the agreement in result might not be paralleled by similar unanimity in reasoning; perhaps in the long run one returns to Judge Andrews' statement in Palsgraf * * *. "It is all a question of expediency, * * * of fair judgment, always keeping in mind the fact that we endeavor to make a rule

---

10. An instance is In re Guardian Casualty Co., 253 App.Div. 360, 2 N.Y.S.2d 232 (1st Dept.), aff'd, 278 N.Y. 674, 16 N.E.2d 397 (1938), where the majority gravely asserted that a foreseeable consequence of driving a taxicab too fast was that a collision with another car would project the cab against a building with such force as to cause a portion of the building to collapse twenty minutes later, when the cab was being removed, and injure a spectator twenty feet away. Surely this is "straining the idea of foreseeability past the breaking point," Bohlen, Book Review, 47 Harv.L.Rev. 556, 557 (1934), at least if the matter be viewed as of the time of the negligent act, as the supposedly symmetrical test of The Wagon Mound demands, * * *. On the other hand, if the issue of foreseeability is viewed as of the moment of impact, see Seavey, Mr. Justice Cardozo and the Law of Torts, 52 Harv.L.Rev. 372, 385 (1939), the test loses functional significance since at that time the defendant is no longer able to amend his conduct so as to avert the consequences.

11. * * * [Friendly, J., discussed the reasoning in Hughes v. Lord Advocate and concluded:] This comes very close to saying that where the damage was of the sort that was risked, foreseeability is not required.

in each case that will be practical and in keeping with the general understanding of mankind." It would be pleasant if greater certainty were possible, * * * but the many efforts that have been made at defining the *locus* of the "uncertain and wavering line," * * * are not very promising; what courts do in such cases makes better sense than what they, or others, say. Where the line will be drawn will vary from age to age; as society has come to rely increasingly on insurance and other methods of loss-sharing, the point may lie further off than a century ago. Here it is surely more equitable that the losses from the operators' negligent failure to raise the Michigan Avenue Bridge should be ratably borne by Buffalo's taxpayers than left with the innocent victims of the flooding; yet the mind is also repelled by a solution that would impose liability solely on the City and exonerate the persons whose negligent acts of commission and omission were the precipitating force of the collision with the bridge and its seque-lae. We go only so far as to hold that where, as here, the damages resulted from the same physical forces whose existence required the exercise of greater care than was displayed and were of the same general sort that was expectable, unforeseeability of the exact developments and of the extent of the loss will not limit liability. Other fact situations can be dealt with when they arise.

MOORE, CIRCUIT JUDGE (concurring and dissenting):

I do not hesitate to concur with Judge Friendly's well-reasoned and well-expressed opinion as to limitation of Kinsman's liability, the extent of the liability of the City of Buffalo, Continental and Kinsman for the damages suffered by the City, the Shiras, the Tewksbury, the Druckenmiller and the Farr and the division of damages.

I cannot agree, however, merely because "society has come to rely increasingly on insurance and other methods of loss-sharing" that the courts should, or have the power to, create a vast judicial insurance company which will adequately compensate all who have suffered damages. Equally disturbing is the suggestion that "[H]ere it is surely more equitable that the losses from the operators' negligent failure to raise the Michigan Avenue Bridge should be ratably borne by Buffalo's taxpayers than left with the innocent victims of the flooding." Under any such principle, negligence suits would become further simplified by requiring a claimant to establish only his own innocence and then offer, in addition to his financial statement, proof of the financial condition of the respective defendants. Judgment would be entered against the defendant which court or jury decided was best able to pay. Nor am I convinced that it should be the responsibility of the Buffalo taxpayers to reimburse the "innocent victims" in their community for damages sustained. In my opinion, before financial liability is imposed, there should be some showing of legal liability.

Unfortunate though it was for Buffalo to have had its fine vehicular bridge demolished in a most unexpected manner, I accept the finding of liability for normal consequences because the City had plenty of time to raise the bridge after notice was given. Bridges, however, serve two purposes. They permit vehicles to cross the river when they are down; they permit vessels to travel on the river when they are up. But no bridge builder or bridge operator would envision a bridge as a dam or as a dam potential.

By an extraordinary concatenation of even more extraordinary events, not unlike the humorous and almost-beyond-all-imagination sequences depicted by the famous cartoonist, Rube Goldberg, the Shiras with its companions which it picked up en route did combine with the bridge demolition to create a very effective dam across the Buffalo River. Without specification of the nature of the damages, claims in favor of some twenty persons and companies were allowed * * * resulting from the various collisions and from "the damming of the river at the bridge, the backing up of the water and ice upstream, and the over-flowing of the banks of the river and flooding of industrial installations along the river banks." (Sup. Finding of Fact #26a.)

My dissent is limited to that portion of the opinion which approves the awarding of damages suffered as a result of the flooding of various properties upstream. I am not satisfied with reliance on hindsight or on the assumption that since flooding occurred, therefore, it must have been foreseeable. In fact, the majority hold that the danger "of flooding would not have been unforeseeable under the circumstances to anyone who gave them thought." But believing that "anyone" might be too broad, they resort to that most famous of all legal mythological characters, the reasonably "prudent man." Even he, however, "carefully pondering the problem," is not to be relied upon because they permit him to become prudent "[W]ith the aid of hindsight."

The majority, in effect, would remove from the law of negligence the concept of foreseeability because, as they say, "[T]he weight of authority in this country rejects the limitation of damages to consequences foreseeable at the time of the negligent conduct when the consequences are 'direct.'" Yet lingering thoughts of recognized legal principles create for them lingering doubts because they say: "This does not mean that the careless actor will always be held for all damages for which the forces that he risked were a cause in fact. Somewhere a point will be reached when courts will agree that the link has become too tenuous—that what is claimed to be consequence is only fortuity." The very example given, namely, the patient who dies because the doctor is delayed by the destruction of the bridge, certainly presents a direct consequence as a factual matter yet the majority opinion states that "few judges would impose liability on any of the parties here," under these circumstances.

In final analysis the answers to the questions when the link is "too tenuous" and when "consequence is only fortuity" are dependent solely on the particular point of view of the particular judge under the particular circumstances. In differing with my colleagues, I must be giving "unconscious recognition of the harshness of holding a man for what he could not conceivably have guarded against, because human foresight could not go so far." (L. Hand, C.J., in Sinram v. Pennsylvania R. Co. * * *) If "foreseeability" be the test, I can foresee the likelihood that a vessel negligently allowed to break its moorings and to drift uncontrolled in a rapidly flowing river may well strike other ships, piers and bridges. Liability would also result on the "direct consequence" theory. However, to me the fortuitous circumstance of the vessels so arranging themselves as to create a dam is much "too tenuous."

The decisions bearing on the foreseeability question have been so completely collected in three English cases[1] that no repetition of the reasoning pro and con of this principle need be made here. To these cases may be added the many American cases cited in the majority opinion which to me push the doctrine of foreseeability to ridiculous lengths—ridiculous, I suppose, only to the judge whose "human foresight" is restricted to finite limits but not to the judge who can say: It happened; *ergo,* it must have been foreseeable. The line of demarcation will always be "uncertain and wavering," Palsgraf v. Long Island R.R., * * * but if, concededly, a line exists, there must be areas on each side. The flood claimants are much too far on the non-liability side of the line. As to them, I would not award any recovery even if the taxpayers of Buffalo are better able to bear the loss.

Notes

1. The traditional admiralty rule of equal division of damages among negligent parties that was applied in the *Kinsman* case has now been replaced by a rule apportioning damages on the basis of degree of fault. United States v. Reliable Transfer Co., 421 U.S. 397, 95 S.Ct. 1708, 44 L.Ed.2d 251 (1975). This judicial change has now brought American practice into accord with the rule followed by most maritime countries since the Brussels Convention of 1910, which the United States never ratified.

2. Is Friendly, J., in *Kinsman,* suggesting that the Privy Council would not have allowed the up-stream riparian owners to recover for the damage caused by the flooding of their property? Do you think Friendly has properly understood the test of causation being evolved by the English courts?

3. Because the Buffalo River was closed to navigation for almost two months after the accident, one grain company was unable to move grain, that it was contractually bound to deliver, to the appropriate dock. To fulfill its obligation grain had to be supplied from other sources at increased expense. Another grain company that owned grain carried aboard the Farr, which had broken loose from her moorings, was forced to incur increased expenses to unload the ship. Judge Burke, the trial judge, treated the claims of these parties as ones for negligent interference with contractual relations and held that no recovery could be had in tort on that theory. The Court of Appeals, per Kaufman, J., affirmed but on different grounds. Petition of Kinsman Transit Co., 388 F.2d 821 (2d Cir.1968). It refused to rely on the traditional distinction between physical damage and purely economic harm. Instead it relied on notions of causation. The key portions of the court's opinion are as follows:

> Numerous principles have been suggested to determine the point at which a defendant should no longer be held legally responsible for damage caused "in fact" by his negligence. See Prosser, supra, 282–329; 2 Harper and James, supra, 1132–61; Hart and Honoré, Causation in the Law, chs. VI and IX (1959). Such limiting principles must exist in any system of jurisprudence for cause and effect succeed one another with the same certainty that night follows day and the consequences of the simplest act

1. In re Polemis and Furness, Withy & Co., [1921] 3 K.B. 560 (C.A.); Overseas Tankship (U.K.), Ltd. v. Morts Dock & Engineering Co., Ltd. (The Wagon Mound), [1961] 1 All E.R. 404; Miller Steamship Company, Pty., Ltd. v. Overseas Tankship (U.K.) Ltd., [1963] 1 Lloyd's Law List Rep. 402 (Sup.Ct., New South Wales).

may be traced over an ever-widening canvas with the passage of time. In Anglo–American law, as Edgerton has noted, "[e]xcept only the defendant's intention to produce a given result, no other consideration so affects our feeling that it is or is not just to hold him for the result so much as its foreseeability" Legal Cause, 72 U.Pa.L.Rev. 211, 352 (1924). * * *

When the instant case was last here, we held—although without discussion of the Cargill and Cargo Carriers claims—that it was a foreseeable consequence of the negligence of the City of Buffalo and Kinsman Transit Company that the river would be dammed. It would seem to follow from this that it was foreseeable that transportation on the river would be disrupted and that some would incur expenses because of the need to find alternative routes of transportation or substitutes for goods delayed by the disaster. It may be that the specific manner was not foreseeable in which the damages to Cargill and Cargo Carriers would be incurred but such strict foreseeability—which in practice would rarely exist except in hindsight—has not been required. Hart and Honoré, supra at 233.

On the previous appeal we stated aptly: "somewhere a point will be reached when courts will agree that the link has become too tenuous—that what is claimed to be consequence is only fortuity." * * * We believe that this point has been reached with the Cargill and Cargo Carriers claims. Neither the Gillies nor the Farr suffered any direct or immediate damage for which recovery is sought. The instant claims occurred only because the downed bridge made it impossible to move traffic along the river.[7] Under all the circumstances of this case, we hold that the connection between the defendants' negligence and the claimants' damages is too tenuous and remote to permit recovery. "The law does not spread its protection so far." Holmes, J., in Robins Dry Dock, supra, 275 U.S. at 309, 48 S.Ct. at 135.[8]

In the final analysis, the circumlocution, whether posed in terms of "foreseeability," "duty," "proximate cause," "remoteness," etc. seems unavoidable. As we have previously noted, 338 F.2d at 725, we return to Judge Andrews' frequently quoted statement in Palsgraf v. Long Island R. R. * * *: "It is all a question of expediency * * * of fair judgment, always keeping in mind the fact that we endeavor to make a rule in each case that will be practical and in keeping with the general understanding of mankind."

7. The claim of Cargo Carriers is the more troublesome of the two because the Farr was struck by either the Shiras or the Tewksbury and where there is physical damage to a vessel the owner can recover for the loss of its use until repairs are completed. * * * But apparently Cargo Carriers has not sought recovery for physical damage to the Farr. And, as we understand the facts, the Farr could have been unloaded without additional expense were it not for the fact that the tugs which ordinarily are used to break up ice jams were caught below the Michigan Avenue Bridge.

8. Although to reason by example is often merely to restate the problem, the following illustration may be an aid in explaining our result. To anyone familiar with N.Y. traffic there can be no doubt that a foreseeable result of an accident in the Brooklyn Battery Tunnel during rush hour is that thousands of people will be delayed. A driver who negligently caused such an accident would certainly be held accountable to those physically injured in the crash. But we doubt that damages would be recoverable against the negligent driver in favor of truckers or contract carriers who suffered provable losses because of the delay or to the wage earner who was forced to "clock in" an hour late. And yet it was surely foreseeable that among the many who would be delayed would be truckers and wage earners.

Has Kaufman ended up, in spite of his protestations, by retreating to the distinction between physical damage and pure economic loss unaccompanied by any physical injury?

OVERSEAS TANKSHIP (U.K.) LTD. v. THE MILLER STEAMSHIP CO. PTY. (THE WAGON MOUND NO. 2)

Privy Council, 1966.
[1967] 1 A.C. 617, [1966] 3 W.L.R. 498, 2 All E.R. 709.

1966. May 25. The judgment of the Board was delivered by Lord Reid.

This is an appeal from a judgment of Walsh J. dated October 10, 1963, in the Supreme Court of New South Wales in commercial cases by which he awarded to the respondents sums of £80,000 and £1,000 in respect of damage from fire sustained by their vessels *Corrimal* and *Audrey D* on November 1, 1951. These vessels were then at Sheerlegs Wharf, Morts Bay, in Sydney Harbour undergoing repairs. The appellant was charterer by demise of a vessel, the *Wagon Mound,* which in the early hours of October 30, 1951, had been taking in bunkering oil from Caltex Wharf not far from Sheerlegs Wharf. By reason of carelessness of the *Wagon Mound* engineers a large quantity of this oil overflowed from the *Wagon Mound* onto the surface of the water. Some hours later much of the oil had drifted to and accumulated round Sheerlegs Wharf and the respondents' vessels. About 2 p.m. on November 1 this oil was set alight: the fire spread rapidly and caused extensive damage to the wharf and to the respondents' vessels.

An action was raised against the present appellant by the owners of Sheerlegs Wharf on the ground of negligence. On appeal to the Board it was held that the plaintiffs were not entitled to recover on the ground that it was not foreseeable that such oil on the surface of the water could be set alight: *Overseas Tankship (U.K.) Ltd. v. Morts Dock and Engineering Co. (The Wagon Mound (No. 1)).* The issue of nuisance was also raised but their Lordships did not deal with it: they remitted this issue to the Supreme Court and their Lordships now understand that the matter was not pursued there in that case.

In the present case the respondents sue alternatively in nuisance and negligence. Walsh J. had found in their favour in nuisance but against them in negligence. Before their Lordships the appellant appeals against his decision on nuisance and the respondents appeal against his decision on negligence.

Their Lordships are indebted to that learned judge for the full and careful survey of the evidence which is set out in his judgment. Few of his findings of fact have been attacked, and their Lordships do not find it necessary to set out or deal with the evidence at any length. But it is desirable to give some explanation of how the fire started before setting out the learned judge's findings.

In the course of repairing the respondents' vessels the Morts Dock Co., the owners of Sheerlegs Wharf, were carrying out oxyacetylene welding and cutting. This work was apt to cause pieces or drops of hot metal to fly off and fall in the sea. So when their manager arrived on the morning of

October 30 and saw the thick scum of oil round the wharf he was apprehensive of fire danger and he stopped the work while he took advice. He consulted the manager of Caltex wharf and after some further consultation he was assured that he was safe to proceed: so he did so, and the repair work was carried on normally until the fire broke out on November 1. Oil of this character with a flash point of 170° F. is extremely difficult to ignite in the open. But we now know that that is not impossible. There is no certainty about how this oil was set alight, but the most probable explanation, accepted by Walsh J., is that there was floating in the oil-covered water some object supporting a piece of inflammable material, and that a hot piece of metal fell on it when it burned for a sufficient time to ignite the surrounding oil.

The findings of the learned trial judge are as follows:

"(1) Reasonable people in the position of the officers of the *Wagon Mound* would regard the furnace oil as very difficult to ignite upon water. (2) Their personal experience would probably have been that this had very rarely happened. (3) If they had given attention to the risk of fire from the spillage, they would have regarded it as a possibility, but one which could become an actuality only in very exceptional circumstances. (4) They would have considered the chances of the required exceptional circumstances happening whilst the oil remained spread on the harbour waters as being remote. (5) I find that the occurrence of damage to the plaintiff's property as a result of the spillage was not reasonably foreseeable by those for whose acts the defendant would be responsible. (6) I find that the spillage of oil was brought about by the careless conduct of persons for whose acts the defendant would be responsible. (7) I find that the spillage of oil was a cause of damage to the property of each of the plaintiffs. (8) Having regard to those findings, and because of finding (5), I hold that the claim of each of the plaintiffs, framed in negligence, fails."

Having made these findings Walsh J. went on to consider the case in nuisance. There is no doubt that the carelessness of the appellant's servants in letting this oil overflow did create a public nuisance by polluting the waters of Sydney Harbour. And also there can be no doubt that anyone who suffered special damage from that pollution would have had an action against the appellant. But the special damage sustained by the respondents was caused, not by pollution, but by fire. So, having held in finding (5) that risk of fire was not reasonably foreseeable, Walsh J. had to consider whether foreseeability has any place in the determination of liability for damage caused by nuisance. He made an extensive survey of the case-law and said that the principles which he found there

"suggest that a plaintiff may set up a case, depending upon the following steps. The defendant has committed a 'wrongful' act in that it has created a public nuisance by polluting the harbour waters with oil. As a result of the presence of that 'nuisance' (*i.e.*, of the oil) the plaintiff has suffered damage over and above that suffered by others. This gives the plaintiff an action, subject only to proof that there is the requisite relationship between the presence of that nuisance and the injury, so that it can be said that the injury suffered was direct. It matters not that the injury was different in kind from a fouling of the ship by the polluted waters."

Then, coming to the words used by the judges in numerous cases of nuisance, he said that

"by and large, the judgments are not expressed in terms of the concept of foreseeability. The term used again and again is 'direct.' It is true that other expressions are also used, but one does not find, in express terms, any testing of the matter by what the defendant might have contemplated or might have foreseen."

And later added:

"I do not find in the case law on nuisance, up to the time of *The Wagon Mound* decision, any authority for the view that liability depends on foreseeability."

Their Lordships must now make their own examination of the case-law. They find the most striking feature to be the variety of words used: and that is not very surprising because in the great majority of cases the facts were such that it made no difference whether the damage was said to be the direct or the natural or the probable or foreseeable result of the nuisance. The word "natural" is found very often and it is peculiarly ambiguous. It can and often does mean a result which one would naturally expect, i.e., which would not be surprising: or it can mean the result at the end of a chain of causation unbroken by any conscious act, the result produced by so-called natural laws however surprising or even unforeseeable in the particular case. Another word frequently used is "probable." It is used with various shades of meaning. Sometimes it appears to mean more probable than not, sometimes it appears to include events likely but not very likely to occur, sometimes it has a still wider meaning and refers to events the chance of which is anything more than a bare possibility, and sometimes, when used in conjunction with other adjectives, it appears to serve no purpose beyond rounding off a phrase.

* * *

In their Lordships' judgment the cases point strongly to there being no difference as to the measure of damages between nuisance and negligence but they are not conclusive. So it is desirable to consider the question of principle.

* * *

Comparing nuisance with negligence the main argument for the respondent was that in negligence foreseeability is an essential element in determining liability and therefore it is logical that foreseeability should also be an essential element in determining the amount of damages: but negligence is not an essential element in determining liability for nuisance and therefore it is illogical to bring in foreseeability when determining the amount of damages. It is quite true that negligence is not an essential element in nuisance. Nuisance is a term used to cover a wide variety of tortious acts or omissions and in many negligence in the narrow sense is not essential. An occupier may incur liability for the emission of noxious fumes or noise although he has used the utmost care in building and using his premises. The amount of fumes or noise which he can lawfully emit is a question of degree and he or his advisers may have miscalculated what can be justified. Or he may deliberately obstruct the highway adjoining his premises to a greater degree than is permissible, hoping that no one will object. On the other hand the emission of fumes or noise or the obstruction of the adjoining highway may often be the result of pure negligence on his part: there are many cases * * * where precisely the same facts will establish liability both in nuisance and in negligence. And although negligence may not be necessary, fault of some kind is almost always necessary and fault generally involves foreseeability, e.g., * * * the fault is in failing to abate the nuisance of the existence of which the defender is or ought to be aware as likely to cause damage to his neighbour. * * * The present case is one of creating a danger to persons or property in navigable waters (equivalent to a highway) and there it is admitted that fault is essential—in this case the negligent discharge of the oil.

"But how are we to determine whether a state of affairs in or near a highway is a danger? This depends, I think, on whether injury may reasonably be foreseen. If you take all the cases in the books, you will find that if the state of affairs is such that injury may reasonably be anticipated to persons using the highway it is a public nuisance" (per Lord Denning M.R. in Morton v. Wheeler [30]).

So in the class of nuisance which includes this case foreseeability is an essential element in determining liability.

It could not be right to discriminate between different cases of nuisance so as to make foreseeability a necessary element in determining damages in those cases where it is a necessary element in determining liability, but not in others. So the choice is between it being a necessary element in all cases of nuisance or in none. In their Lordships' judgment the similarities between nuisance and other forms of tort to which The Wagon Mound (No. 1) applies far outweigh any differences, and they must therefore hold that the judgment appealed from is wrong on this branch of the case. It is not sufficient that the injury suffered by the respondents' vessels was the direct result of the nuisance if that injury was in the relevant sense unforeseeable.

It is now necessary to turn to the respondents' submission that the trial judge was wrong in holding that damage from fire was not reasonably foreseeable. In The Wagon Mound (No. 1) the finding on which the Board proceeded was that of the trial judge: "the defendant did not know and could not reasonably be expected to have known that [the oil] was capable of being set afire when spread on water." In the present case the evidence led was substantially different from the evidence led in The Wagon Mound (No. 1) and the findings of Walsh J. are significantly different. That is not due to there having been any failure by the plaintiffs in The Wagon Mound (No. 1) in preparing and presenting their case. The plaintiffs there were no doubt embarrassed by a difficulty which does not affect the present plaintiffs. The outbreak of the fire was consequent on the act of the manager of the plaintiffs in The Wagon Mound (No. 1) in resuming oxy-acetylene welding and cutting while the wharf was surrounded by this oil.

30. C.A., No. 33 of 1956, January 31, 1956 (unreported).

So if the plaintiffs in the former case had set out to prove that it was foreseeable by the engineers of the *Wagon Mound* that this oil could be set alight, they might have had difficulty in parrying the reply that this must also have been foreseeable by their manager. Then there would have been contributory negligence and at that time contributory negligence was a complete defence in New South Wales.

The crucial finding of Walsh J. in this case is in finding (5): that the damage was "not reasonably foreseeable by those for whose acts the defendant would be responsible." That is not a primary finding of fact but an inference from the other findings, and it is clear from the learned judge's judgment that in drawing this inference he was to a large extent influenced by his view of the law. The vital parts of the findings of fact which have already been set out in full are (1) that the officers of the *Wagon Mound* "would regard furnace oil as very difficult to ignite upon water"—not that they would regard this as impossible; (2) that their experience would probably have been "that this had very rarely happened"—not that they would never have heard of a case where it had happened, and (3) that they would have regarded it as a "possibility, but one which could become an actuality only in very exceptional circumstances"—not, as in *The Wagon Mound (No. 1)*, that they could not reasonably be expected to have known that this oil was capable of being set afire when spread on water. The question which must now be determined is whether these differences between the findings in the two cases do or do not lead to different results in law.

In *The Wagon Mound (No. 1)* the Board were not concerned with degrees of foreseeability because the finding was that the fire was not foreseeable at all. So Lord Simonds had no cause to amplify the statement that the "essential factor in determining liability is whether the damage is of such a kind as the reasonable man should have foreseen." But here the findings show that some risk of fire would have been present to the mind of a reasonable man in the shoes of the ship's chief engineer. So the first question must be what is the precise meaning to be attached in this context to the words "foreseeable" and "reasonably foreseeable."

Before *Bolton v. Stone*[33] the cases had fallen into two classes: (1) those where, before the event, the risk of its happening would have been regarded as unreal either because the event would have been thought to be physically impossible or because the possibility of its happening would have been regarded as so fantastic or far-fetched that no reasonable man would have paid any attention to it—"a mere possibility which would never occur to the mind of a reasonable man" (*per* Lord Dunedin in *Fardon v. Harcourt-Rivington*[34])—or (2) those where there was a real and substantial risk or chance that something like the event which happens might occur, and then the reasonable man would have taken the steps necessary to eliminate the risk.

Bolton v. Stone posed a new problem. There a member of a visiting team drove a cricket ball out of the ground onto an unfrequented adjacent public road and it struck and severely injured a lady who happened to be

33. [1951] A.C. 850 * * *.   **34.** (1932) 146 L.T. 391.

standing in the road. That it might happen that a ball would be driven onto this road could not have been said to be a fantastic or far-fetched possibility: according to the evidence it had happened about six times in 28 years. And it could not have been said to be a far-fetched or fantastic possibility that such a ball would strike someone in the road: people did pass along the road from time to time. So it could not have been said that, on any ordinary meaning of the words the fact that a ball might strike a person in the road was not foreseeable or reasonably foreseeable—it was plainly foreseeable. But the chance of its happening in the foreseeable future was infinitesimal. A mathematician given the data could have worked out that it was only likely to happen once in so many thousand years. The House of Lords held that the risk was so small that in the circumstances a reasonable man would have been justified in disregarding it and taking no steps to eliminate it.

But it does not follow that, no matter what the circumstances may be, it is justifiable to neglect a risk of such a small magnitude. A reasonable man would only neglect such a risk if he had some valid reason for doing so, e.g., that it would involve considerable expense to eliminate the risk. He would weigh the risk against the difficulty of eliminating it. If the activity which caused the injury to Miss Stone had been an unlawful activity, there can be little doubt but that *Bolton v. Stone* would have been decided differently. In their Lordships' judgment *Bolton v. Stone* did not alter the general principle that a person must be regarded as negligent if he does not take steps to eliminate a risk which he knows or ought to know is a real risk and not a mere possibility which would never influence the mind of a reasonable man. What that decision did was to recognise and give effect to the qualification that it is justifiable not to take steps to eliminate a real risk if it is small and if the circumstances are such that a reasonable man, careful of the safety of his neighbour, would think it right to neglect it.

In the present case there was no justification whatever for discharging the oil into Sydney Harbour. Not only was it an offence to do so, but it involved considerable loss financially. If the ship's engineer had thought about the matter, there could have been no question of balancing the advantages and disadvantages. From every point of view it was both his duty and his interest to stop the discharge immediately.

It follows that in their Lordships' view the only question is whether a reasonable man having the knowledge and experience to be expected of the chief engineer of the *Wagon Mound* would have known that there was a real risk of the oil on the water catching fire in some way: if it did, serious damage to ships or other property was not only foreseeable but very likely. Their Lordships do not dissent from the view of the trial judge that the possibilities of damage "must be significant enough in a practical sense to require a reasonable man to guard against them" but they think that he may have misdirected himself in saying

> "there does seem to be a real practical difficulty, assuming that some risk of fire damage was foreseeable, but not a high one, in making a factual judgment as to whether this risk was sufficient to attract liability if damage should occur."

In this difficult chapter of the law decisions are not infrequently taken to apply to circumstances far removed from the facts which gave rise to them and it would seem that here too much reliance has been placed on some observations in *Bolton v. Stone* and similar observations in other cases.

In their Lordships' view a properly qualified and alert chief engineer would have realised there was a real risk here and they do not understand Walsh J. to deny that. But he appears to have held that if a real risk can properly be described as remote it must then be held to be not reasonably foreseeable. That is a possible interpretation of some of the authorities. But this is still an open question and on principle their Lordships cannot accept this view. If a real risk is one which would occur to the mind of a reasonable man in the position of the defendant's servant and which he would not brush aside as far-fetched, and if the criterion is to be what that reasonable man would have done in the circumstances, then surely he would not neglect such a risk if action to eliminate it presented no difficulty, involved no disadvantage, and required no expense.

In the present case the evidence shows that the discharge of so much oil onto the water must have taken a considerable time, and a vigilant ship's engineer would have noticed the discharge at an early stage. The findings show that he ought to have known that it is possible to ignite this kind of oil on water, and that the ship's engineer probably ought to have known that this had in fact happened before. The most that can be said to justify inaction is that he would have known that this could only happen in very exceptional circumstances. But that does not mean that a reasonable man would dismiss such a risk from his mind and do nothing when it was so easy to prevent it. If it is clear that the reasonable man would have realised or foreseen and prevented the risk, then it must follow that the appellant is liable in damages. The learned judge found this a difficult case: he says that this matter is "one upon which different minds would come to different conclusions." Taking a rather different view of the law from that of the judge, their Lordships must hold that the respondents are entitled to succeed on this issue.

The judgment appealed from is in the form of a verdict in favour of the respondents upon the claim based upon nuisance, a verdict in favour of the appellant on the claim based upon negligence, and a direction that judgment be entered for the respondents in the sums of £80,000 and £1,000 respectively. The result of their Lordships' findings is that the direction that judgment be entered for the respondents must stand but that the appeal against the verdict in favour of the respondents and the cross-appeal against the verdict in favour of the appellant must both be allowed.

Accordingly, their Lordships will humbly advise Her Majesty that the appeal and the cross-appeal should be allowed and that the judgment for the respondents in the sums of £80,000 and 1,000 should be affirmed. The appellant must pay two-thirds of the respondents' costs in the appeal and cross-appeal.

Notes

1. The Privy Council justified the different result in *The Wagon Mound No. 2*, by stressing that "the evidence led in *The Wagon Mound No. 1*" was

"significantly different" from that led in *The Wagon Mound No. 2*. This was accepted as the reason for the difference in the trial judges' findings in the two cases. The Privy Council surmised that the plaintiffs in *The Wagon Mound No. 1* were embarrassed by the problem of the possible contributory negligence of their works manager which, at the time, would have been a complete bar to their action. This is a point that is stressed in A. Goodhart, *The Brief Life Story of The Direct Consequence Rule in English Tort Law*, 53 Va.L.Rev. 857, 867 (1967). It is true that, at least as appears from the lower court decisions in both cases, more evidence was introduced in *The Wagon Mound No. 2* than in *The Wagon Mound No. 1*. *Compare* [1963] 1 Lloyds' List Law Rep. 402 *with* [1958] 1 Lloyds' List Law Rep. 575. It is not at all clear from an examination of these reports however that Kinsella, J. in the earlier case regarded the probabilities any differently than Walsh, J., in the latter case. Kinsella, J., it will be recalled, found that "the defendant did not know, and could not be expected to have known that it [the furnace oil] was capable of being set on fire when spread on water" whereas in the latter case Walsh, J., who found the fire "not reasonably foreseeable" also found that "if they had given attention to the risk of fire from the spillage, they would have regarded it as a possibility, but one which could become an actuality only in very exceptional circumstances." These are indeed different ultimate findings, but whether they reflected a different view of the facts is another matter.[1] Consider the following extracts from Kinsella, J.'s, judgment in *The Wagon Mound No. 1*:

> On the question of the volume of furnace oil on the water and its inflammability, the plaintiff called Captain Craven, an Inspector, employed by the Maritime Services Board, who said that he went on board the *Wagon Mound* about 10:30 a.m. on Oct. 30. He saw heavy black oil on the deck, on the sides of the ship and a large quantity on the waters of the harbour extending over a considerable area—some of it in thick concentration. He had a conversation with the master who told him there had been an overflow of oil. The master also said that he would leave authority with his agents to act on his behalf—naming Mr. Durack—in any proceedings against him for breach of regulations in permitting oil to escape into the harbour. Mr. Durack was manager of the Caltex Oil Installation at Mort's Bay. Captain Craven was asked by Mr. Taylor: "Was this furnace oil a fire hazard, on this day?" He replied: "No, it was not."

> Mr. Parkin, works manager of the plaintiff company, gave evidence that, when he arrived at the works before 8 o'clock on the morning of Oct. 30, he saw a very large quantity of heavy oil floating in the vicinity of the caisson, along the foreshores and across the dock. It had got on to the slipways and had congealed on them, thereby interfering with the plaintiff's use of the slips. It extended under the Sheerlegs Wharf and around the *Corrimal*.

> He immediately issued instructions that no welding was to be done until further orders, and then telephoned the manager of Caltex Wharf, Mr. Durack, who came to the plaintiff's premises about 10 a.m. He assured Mr. Parkin that the oil was quite safe for normal work to continue. Mr. Parkin thereupon directed that normal work be resumed, including the use of electric torches and oxy-welding apparatus, and this work was continued until the outbreak of fire in the afternoon of Nov. 1.

---

1. It appears from *The Wagon Mound No. 2* that the engineers of the defendant, the people whose reasonable foresight was in question, were never called as witnesses in either case. [1963] 1 Lloyds' List Law Rep. at 413.

He said that, on that day, about 2 p.m., he was in his office when he received a telephone call from Mr. Durack who asked his permission to bring someone over to inspect the damage to the plaintiff's property, and that, before he could answer, Mr. Durack exclaimed: "Good Lord, your place has gone up in flames."

The witness then described the nature and extent of the fire as he observed it.

In cross-examination, he said that the condition as to oil was much the same from the morning of Oct. 30 until the outbreak of fire on Nov. 1, and that, during that period, burning was being done by his men with electric torches and with oxy-acetylene welders on the wharf, and that welding had been done on a staging between the *Corrimal* and the wharf.

Notwithstanding his evidence that when he saw the oil he ordered burning and welding work to be suspended until he was told by Mr. Durack that it was safe to carry on, Mr. Parkin was asked by Mr. Taylor for his opinion as to the safety of furnace oil in the open. He replied "reasonably safe" and, being asked to amplify that, said that he thought, in the light of his experience, that it would be nearly impossible to ignite it in the open.

* * *

I find that the oil which escaped was furnace oil of the order of 170° F. flash point, that is to say, oil which was delivered by the Vacuum Oil Company on Oct. 30. If I be wrong in this, I would hold that the oil which escaped was ordinary furnace oil with a flash point in the range from 150° F. to 190° F. It follows that the plaintiff has proved only that ordinary furnace oil escaped from the *Wagon Mound*, and, on that, its case must stand or fall.

I turn now to the scientific evidence as to the incidents and other characteristics of the oil.

Professor Hunter, whom I have mentioned earlier, is Professor of Chemical Engineering at the University of Sydney. He is a Fellow of the Institute of Petroleum, and was awarded his Doctorate of Philosophy by the University of Birmingham for a thesis on the refining of petrol. He was, for a time, research assistant in the department of fuel in the Royal Naval College at Greenwich; from 1931 to 1937, he was senior lecturer in the department of petroleum engineering and refining in the University of Birmingham; for some years he was consultant to the Anglo–Iranian Oil Company; he was, during the war, consultant to the Ministry of Aircraft Production in England, in relation to incendiary bombs, flame throwers and fuel barriers around the English coast, and was concerned in consideration of methods of igniting oil on the surface of the English Channel in the event of invasion.

In connection with the present case, he has recently carried out more than 300 experiments on the ignition of furnace oil floating on sea water. For these he used furnace oil of flash point 170° F. obtained from the Vacuum Oil Company. He said that the results would have been substantially the same with oil within the flash-point range of 150° F. to 190° F. as would the opinion which he expressed as to its inflammability.

In his experiments, he found it virtually impossible for furnace oil less than ¹⁄₁₆th of an inch thick on sea water to catch fire. He could not ignite it in the course of his experiments.

With oil ⅛th of an inch thick he tried various means of igniting it, but succeeded only with two, a roman candle (which emits a jet of very hot sparks) and an oxy-acetylene flame held 6 in. from the oil. When the thickness of the oil was increased to a quarter of an inch, it was lit by these two methods and also by red hot coke. Attempts to light floating oil by dropping molten metal on to it all failed. A large number of tests were carried out, the results of which were tabulated and put in evidence. I do not find it necessary to analyse them. Professor Hunter said that after the tests were carried out, and as a result of them, he came to the view that the oil which escaped from the *Wagon Mound* could have been fired by a wick. To quote his words:

> There must have been a wick present, floating on the oil, and, further, the wick must have been burning and probably fanned by a breeze not more than 20 miles an hour.

He defined a wick as a substance floating on oil, partly submerged in the oil and partly above it which is lit and burns above the oil. He conducted a number of tests with various substances, particularly hessian and cotton waste, and found them effective wicks. He formed the conclusion "that an oily cotton waste would be an ideal wick for igniting the fuel oil and one would be almost certain to get it ignited by such an oily cotton waste if that oily cotton was on fire."

He then described tests in which molten metal from oxy-welding processes fell distances from 3 ft. to 10½ ft. on to cotton waste floating on a raft in sea water, and ignited it in every case. The tests showed also that the oily waste, when so lit, set fire to the floating oil ⅛th of an inch thick.

He was questioned as to the probability of the fire on Nov. 1 having been ignited by a wick, and he said that it certainly could have been ignited by that means, and that the only other means which he could think of were by holding an oxy-torch near the surface of the oil, by holding a roman candle over the surface of the oil, or by putting extremely hot coke on the surface of the oil. These methods need not concern us.

I find that the oil which caught fire was ordinary furnace oil with flash point of the order of 170° F.; that immediately before the outbreak of the fire there was floating in the oil underneath the wharf a piece of debris on which lay some smouldering cotton waste or rag which had been set on fire by molten metal falling from the wharf; that the cotton waste or rag burst into flames; that it was close to a wooden pile coated with oil; that the flames from the cotton waste or rag set the floating oil on fire either directly or by first setting fire to the wooden pile; and that after the floating oil became ignited the flames spread rapidly over the surface of the oil and quickly developed into a conflagration which severely damaged the wharf. In this last finding, I have not overlooked the doubts expressed by Professor Hunter as to whether the fire of floating furnace oil could have so quickly spread as some witnesses described it.

I find also that the oil which escaped had done some damage to the property of the plaintiff before the fire occurred, in that it had got on the slipways and interfered with the plaintiff's use of the slips, and had caused a suspension of the operations of burning and welding for some hours.

The evidence of this damage is slight and no claim for compensation is made in respect of it. Nevertheless, it does establish some damage, which may be insignificant in comparison with the magnitude of the damage by fire, but which, nevertheless, is damage which, beyond question, was a direct result of the escape of the oil.

The question of foreseeability of fire damage from the furnace oil has been debated at length. I have referred to the evidence led by the plaintiff that, prior to this occurrence, furnace oil was regarded as safe. In addition, the following evidence was led by Mr. Meares from Professor Hunter:

> Q.: As you indicated, prior to doing the tests you would not have thought that this oil was a fire hazard? A.: Not a serious hazard. Q.: I suppose you would say now in the light of what you know that if you had a quantity of furnace oil of flash point 150° F. to 190° F. beneath a wharf in circumstances where it was of the depth on the water of more than $\frac{1}{16}$th of an inch that it would, in your opinion, constitute a fire hazard? A.: I think I can best answer that by putting it this way: the fire hazard under those circumstances depends on the habits of the people working on the wharf rather than the oil itself. * * * Q.: If there is fuel oil not more than $\frac{1}{16}$th of an inch then you don't have to consider fire risk, whatever they are doing on the wharf? A.: That is right. Q.: What I suggest is, if you increase the height of it above $\frac{1}{16}$th of an inch, there is then something under the wharf that is a fire danger that was not there before? A.: If the oil is there entirely by itself, it does not constitute a fire danger but if it is oil plus floating wicks it is then a fire danger.

This evidence I interpret to mean that before he made his tests and, of course, before he knew of the subject fire, the Professor did not regard floating oil as a serious hazard in any circumstances; and that, in the light of knowledge gleaned from his tests, he now regards it as not being dangerous in itself, but capable of being made dangerous by people who are working near it. These latter remarks throw no light on the problem, as they would apply equally to every substance which is capable of being set on fire.

I feel bound, on the evidence, to come to the conclusion that, prior to this fire, furnace oil in the open was generally regarded as safe, and that, in the light of knowledge at that time, the defendant's servants and agents reasonably so regarded it. Mr. Taylor urged that the fire in Fremantle Harbour in which the steamship *Panamanian* was damaged (*Eastern Asia Navigation Company, Ltd. v. Fremantle Harbour Trust Commissioners and the Commonwealth of Australia*, (1950) 83 C.L.R. 358), would be notorious among owners of oil-burning ships. The suggestion has some merit, but, in the absence of any evidence, I am not satisfied that the incident was, in 1951, known generally in the mercantile world, or, in particular, to the defendant or its agents.

The *raison d' être* of furnace oil is, of course, that it shall burn, but I find that the defendant did not know, and could not reasonably be expected to have known, that it was capable of being set on fire when spread on water.

[1958] 1 Lloyds' List Law Rep. 578–82.[2] The skepticism of the present editors about whether the trial judges in the two *Wagon Mound* cases took a different view of the facts is shared by other observers. Professor J.C. Smith, a Canadian, concludes that there was "no essential difference in the finding of fact. * * *" J. Smith, Liability in Negligence 109 (1984).

2. Despite the statement by Friendly, J., in *Kinsman Transit Co., supra,* the late Professor Prosser concluded that, in America, "the conclusion may well be drawn that while there are still rearguard actions, and cases that do not fit, the 'scope of the foreseeable risk' is on its way to ultimate victory as the criterion of what is 'proximate,' if it has not already achieved it." W. Prosser, Torts 267 (4th ed. 1971). At the same time Prosser also argued that the test "lacks all clarity and precision," because "[i]n one sense, almost nothing is entirely unforeseeable, since there is a very slight mathematical chance, recognizable in advance, that even the most freakish accident which is possible will occur, particularly if it has ever happened in history before." *Ibid.* Prosser therefore approved the language of the *Restatement (Second) of Torts* § 435(2), of which he was the Reporter, which provides:

> The actor's conduct may be held not to be a legal cause of harm to another where after the event and looking back from the harm to the actor's negligent conduct, it appears to the court highly extraordinary that it should have brought about the harm.

While this provision seems to bring foreseeability into the determination of legal cause—the *Restatement,* except for this provision, seems to adopt a direct cause approach—the provision also appears to give the court an escape when the accident, although foreseeable, might be considered to be a bizarre one. Would the accident in *Hughes* be sufficiently bizarre? What about the eggshell skull cases where the defendant is said to take the plaintiff as he finds him? *See* Smith v. Leech Brain & Co., Ltd., [1962] 2 Q.B. 405, 2 W.L.R. 148, [1961] 3 All E.R. 1159; McCahill v. New York Transportation Co., 201 N.Y.

---

2. Compare the following extract from the judgment of Walsh, J., in *The Wagon Mound No. 2*:

On the defendant's side, I think it is an important fact that fuel oil fires on water had been (so far as the evidence shows) very infrequent occurrences. It seems likely that the average experienced seagoing man would either have known of no such occurrence or, at the most, would have known of one or two isolated ones apart from wartime disasters. Whether or not the man in the street would have said, upon hearing of such a fire, "I never should have thought it possible" ([1961] A.C., at p. 424; [1961] 1 Lloyd's Rep., at p. 10), the average master or engineer, on the *Wagon Mound,* would probably have said, before the fire, "I have never experienced such a thing." This is not conclusive, but I think it is important.

I am disposed to think that, in trying to assess what would have been in the mind of the reasonable ship's officer on this occasion, I should alike reject the view that he would have rejected outright all possibility of a fire risk (as would Captain Moss) and the view that he would have seen the spillage as creating a great danger of fire (as would Captain Murcheson). His state of mind would have been between these extremes, but closer to the former than to the latter. Perhaps one may get fairly close to what might have been the state of mind of the average master by reflecting upon the opinions of Captain Newton and Captain Forrest, which I have quoted. If he was like Captain Newton he would have seen fire as a possibility, but only in very exceptional circumstances. It would not have "occupied his mind." He would have thought the large fire or explosion, which he might think of as a way in which it could be brought about, as quite a remote possibility. If he was like Captain Forrest, he would have seen some risk of fire and been "uneasy about it." He would not have considered it as "an immediate risk or a risk requiring immediate action." He would have thought that the possibility was "normally, slight".

[1963] 1 Lloyd's List Law Rep. at 425.

221, 94 N.E. 616 (1911). *See also* G. Bahr and B. Graham, *The Thin Skull Plaintiff Concept: Evasive or Persuasive,* 15 Loy.(L.A.)L.Rev. 409 (1982).

3. In opposition to the customary analysis of causation in negligence cases, stands the work of the late Professor Leon Green. According to Green, causation only enters the decision of a negligence case with regard to the issue of was there a "causal connection" between the defendant's conduct and the plaintiff's injury. Neither the foreseeability test nor the direct consequence test is determinative of this issue.

The crucial issues in the trial of an action for negligence are, for Green, the issues of duty and breach of duty. On these issues, it is for the judge to decide as a matter of policy whether the defendant owed the plaintiff a duty. Foreseeability of harm or risk is an important component of this inquiry but not the only one. If the judge finds the existence of a duty and if there is a causal relation between the defendant's conduct and the plaintiff's harm, the jury must make the crucial decision as to whether the particular defendant has been negligent to the particular plaintiff. The jury will consider many of the factors already considered by the judge in determining the existence of a duty but they will do so only by considering these factors in relation to the parties to the litigation. It is the jury's function to consider whether *"under all the circumstances present in the case before them,* (including the multitude of causal factors) the defendant's conduct was negligent and whether he should be penalized for his conduct or whether the plaintiff should bear his loss without compensation." *See* L. Green, *The Causal Relation Issue in Negligence Law,* 60 Mich.L.Rev. 543, 571–72 (1962). *See also The Duty Problem in Negligence Cases,* 28 Colum.L.Rev. 1014 (1928); *The Duty Problem in Negligence Cases: II,* 29 Colum.L.Rev. 255 (1929); *Foreseeability in Negligence Law,* 61 Colum.L.Rev. 1401 (1961). Green had earlier sketched out his ideas, in text book form, in Rationale of Proximate Cause (1927).

4. The subject of legal causation has been discussed in numerous articles and several books. Among the latter are H.L.A. Hart & A. Honore, Causation in the Law (1959)(2d ed. 1985); R. Keeton, Legal Cause in the Law of Torts (1963). A good more recent discussion is P. Kelly, *Proximate Cause in Negligence Law: History, Theory, and the Present Darkness,* 69 Wash.U.L.Q. 49 (1991).

C. INTERVENING CAUSES AS SUPERSEDING CAUSES

GLASGOW REALTY CO. v. METCALFE

Court of Appeals of Kentucky, 1972.
482 S.W.2d 750.

EDWARD P. HILL, JR., JUDGE.

This appeal is from a judgment entered on the verdict of a jury which awarded appellee, Vivian Metcalfe, $47,500 damages for personal injuries she claimed resulted from appellant's negligence in maintaining a glass window in one of its third-floor apartments.

Appellant is the owner of a three-story building that stands flush with the sidewalk on the public square and in sight of the courthouse in Glasgow, Kentucky. The first floor is leased to merchants, the second floor as offices, and the third floor is divided into apartments.

On August 1, 1969, nine-year-old Marty Stout, in the company of his parents, went to one of the third-floor apartments to visit Marty's grandmother. Finding the place uninteresting, Marty wandered into a nearby apartment occupied by the William Mayo family. On this day the merchants of Glasgow were having a "Sidewalk Sale Day," which attracted a large crowd to the public square. Young Marty Stout raised, or discovered raised, a lower sash of one of the windows immediately above the sidewalk on the public square. He naturally proceeded to enjoy his high perch by attracting the attention of interested and curious youngsters below by "hollering" to them. His conduct did not meet with the approval of seventeen-year-old Linda Mayo, one of the occupants of the apartment. She proceeded to pull the raised sash down to its proper position to abate Marty's conduct. The latter placed both hands against the glass, either to prevent the closing of the window, or to assist Linda in closing it. Thereupon, the glass of the lower sash broke and fell to the sidewalk, striking an awning above the first floor causing the glass to further shatter. Numerous people, including appellee, were milling about the sidewalk when the glass fell. The crowd stampeded to avoid the falling glass. Some unknown person ran into appellee, Vivian L. Metcalfe, and knocked her down, as a result of which she received a fractured hip and numerous lacerations. Although appellee was only 52 years of age at the time, her injuries proved to be more serious than anticipated. She required constant care for over seven months and proved special damages of about $7,500. The testimony indicated that she is 25 to 35 percent permanently disabled.

Appellant presents five grounds for reversal of the judgment, the first of which is that it was entitled to a directed verdict.

The chain of events in the instant case suggests a number of interesting legal questions, such as of intervening and superseding cause and the foreseeability of the consequences of a defectively maintained glass window. First, however, we should get to the basic, fundamental question of appellant's duty with respect to the maintenance of the glass window in question, and then determine from the facts whether appellant violated that duty.

Before discussing appellant's duty, we should get a birds-eye view of the situation. The glass window in question was in a third-floor apartment where children were known to live. It was immediately above the sidewalk where pedestrians were known to be and had a right to be. A screen or storm window had been installed but was useless at the time due to the fact that the screen was out. The window cords at the lower sash were broken and inoperative.

Unquestionably it was the duty of appellant to inspect its building for dangerous conditions that were likely to result in injury to persons using the sidewalk below.

* * *

From the foregoing evidence, two salient facts emerge: First, it is clear from the admission of appellant's manager that there was a failure to inspect the condition of the window in question; secondly, the condition of the window was defective to the extent that at least some of the putty was gone from around the glass, and the screen was out. These facts made a jury issue on the question of appellant's negligence in the maintenance of the premises in question. * * *

* * *

Although appellant does not list the subject of intervening or superseding cause, except to complain that its offered instruction relative to intervening cause was refused by the court, since a substantial part of appellant's brief and a large part of the appellee's brief are devoted to the subject, we consider it appropriate to go into the question in some depth. The intervening cause refers to the action of Marty Stout in placing both hands against the glass window, as a result of which the glass or a part of it broke and fell to the street. There is no way the force applied by Marty can be measured. The fact that portions of the glass remained in the sash after part of it fell out is some evidence that considerable force was applied by Marty, and it is also some evidence that not all of the glass was unsupported (by putty or metal pins). Anyway, we think from all the evidence and all the circumstances that Marty's act constituted a "contributing cause of the accident." The question then is whether the contributing cause relieves appellant of liability.

We go to Restatement of the Law (Torts) 2d § 439, for some light on the subject. Therein it is written:

"If the effects of the actor's negligent conduct actively and continuously operate to bring about harm to another, the fact that the active and substantially simultaneous operation of the effects of a third person's innocent, tortious, or criminal act is also a substantial factor in bringing about the harm does not protect the actor from liability."

This court in Parker v. Redden, Ky., 421 S.W.2d 586, 595, said:

"The principle involved here is simply the basic principle of the law of intervening or superseding causes—that the original negligent actor is not relieved of liability by the subsequent negligent acts of another if the subsequent acts might reasonably have been foreseen. * * *"

Before concluding this opinion, we should discuss another phase of this case that has been treated in the briefs although not listed specifically in the "questions presented" part of the briefs. That phase relates to the question of liability for the "unforeseeable consequences" of what the jury found to be negligence on the part of appellant.

Appellant argues that even if it was guilty of some fault it could not anticipate or foresee that a stranger would come into its building and apply sufficient force to break out a glass window, and further that appellant would not reasonably foresee the extent of injury from falling, shattered glass, or that plaintiff would sustain a freak injury by being trampled over by the stampeding crowd.

This question was ably discussed in Miller v. Mills, Ky., 257 S.W.2d 520, 522, wherein the court said:

"We think it is clear that so far as foreseeability enters into the question of liability for negligence, it is not required that the particular, precise form of injury be foreseeable—it is sufficient if the probability of injury of some kind to persons within the natural range of effect of the alleged negligent act could be foreseen. * * *"

The judgment is affirmed.

Notes

1. Where the type of intervening negligent act is at all foreseeable, even if the specific intervening act is not, the original tortfeasor will normally be held liable for the plaintiff's injuries. *See* Gossett v. Burnett, 251 S.C. 548, 164 S.E.2d 578 (1968)(The defendant bank negligently set off an alarm. A police car speeding to the scene negligently crashed into the plaintiff's car. Held: defendant's demurrer overruled); Gibson v. Garcia, 96 Cal.App.2d 681, 216 P.2d 119 (1950)(defendant street railway's electric power pole was negligently permitted to become rotten. The plaintiff was injured when the pole fell after being struck by a negligent motorist. Held: defendant's demurrer overruled); Gilbert v. New Mexico Construction Co., 39 N.M. 216, 44 P.2d 489 (1935)(The defendant negligently broke a water main. While the water pressure was reduced, a fire extensively damaged the plaintiff's house. The city's negligence in not increasing the water pressure after repairs were complete was held not to supersede the defendant's original negligence).

2. Where the intervening negligence is considered unforeseeable, the originally negligent party will usually escape liability. The grossness of the intervening negligence will be a factor considered by the courts in determining its foreseeability. In McLaughlin v. Mine Safety Appliances Co., 11 N.Y.2d 62, 226 N.Y.S.2d 407, 181 N.E.2d 430 (1962), heat blocks supplied by firemen were used by a nurse on the plaintiff, a drowning victim. Because the blocks were not wrapped in cloth before application, the plaintiff was badly burned. The court held that the warnings placed on the blocks themselves by the defendant manufacturer were inadequate. Nevertheless a representative of the distributor of the blocks had warned the firemen during a demonstration of the need to wrap the blocks before application. It was held that the gross negligence of the firemen in failing to warn the nurse was not foreseeable. Do you agree that a manufacturer could not foresee that information conveyed during a demonstration would not be relayed to an attending nurse at the scene of an emergency?

In Mahone v. Birmingham Electric Co., 261 Ala. 132, 73 So.2d 378 (1954), the defendant's bus violated a city ordinance by failing to pull over to the curb before discharging passengers. The plaintiff slipped on a banana peel in the street while alighting from the bus. It was held that the defendant's negligence was not the proximate cause of the plaintiff's injuries because the intervening cause of the accident was not reasonably to be anticipated.

As has already been suggested, the more reckless the intervening act is, the more likely it is to be held to be unforeseeable and to lead to a finding that the original negligence was not the proximate cause of the plaintiff's injuries. The greater moral culpability of the intervening party is probably also a factor that might lead to assigning sole causal responsibility to him.

3. *Restatement (Second) of Torts* § 439, quoted by the court in the *Glasgow Realty Co.* case is concerned with situations in which the effects of the defendant's negligence "actively and continuously operate" up until the time of injury. The section, in other words, is concerned with situations in which the original negligence and the intervening factors are "in substantially simultaneous operation." (*See Comment a* to § 439). An illustration would be a case in which a motorist negligently swerves and forces an oncoming car into the

path of a stolen vehicle racing along at 90 miles per hour. Many observers would classify the situation involved in the *Glasgow Realty Co.* case as one in which the defendant's conduct was not substantially simultaneous in operation with that of the intervening party but was rather "antecedent" to the intervening conduct. In such circumstances, the traditional tendency of the courts has been to hold the intervening criminal acts of a third person to be a superseding cause of the plaintiff's injuries. *See Restatement (Second) of Torts* § 448. This difficult problem will be discussed in the next case and in the notes following. In the *Glasgow Realty Co.* case, there was of course no suggestion that either the nine-year-old Marty Stout or the unknown person who ran into the plaintiff were engaged in criminal conduct.

BRAUER v. NEW YORK CENTRAL & HUDSON RIVER RAILROAD

Court of Errors and Appeals of New Jersey, 1918.
91 N.J.L. 190, 103 A. 166.

SWAYZE, J. This is a case of a grade crossing collision. We are clear that the questions of negligence and contributory negligence were for the jury. If there were nothing else, the testimony of the plaintiff as to signals of the flagman would carry the case to the jury. The only question that has caused us difficulty is that of the extent of the defendant's liability. The complaint avers that the horse was killed, and the wagon and harness and the cider and barrels with which the wagon was loaded were destroyed. What happened, was that as a result of the collision, aside from the death of the horse and the destruction of the wagon, the contents of the wagon, consisting of empty barrels and a keg of cider, were scattered, and probably stolen by people at the scene of the accident. The driver, who was alone in charge for the plaintiff, was so stunned that one of the railroad detectives found him immediately after the collision in a fit. There were two railroad detectives on the freight train to protect the property it was carrying against thieves, but they did nothing to protect the plaintiff's property. The controversy on the question of damages is as to the right of the plaintiff to recover the value of the barrels, cider, and blanket. An objection was based solely on the ground that the complaint alleged that they were destroyed; counsel said "there is no use proving value unless they were destroyed." We think that, if they were taken by thieves, they were destroyed as far as was important to the case; at least the averment was sufficient to justify the evidence and the charge, since the case was fully tried. It is now argued that the defendant's negligence was not in any event the proximate cause of the loss of this property, since the act of the thieves intervened. The rule of law exempting the one guilty of the original negligence from damage due to an intervening cause is well settled. The difficulty lies in the application. Like the question of proximate cause, this is ordinarily a jury question. * * * Del. Lack. & West. R. R. Co. v. Salmon, 39 N.J.Law, 299, 23 Am.Rep. 214. In his opinion in the last-named case Justice Depue, speaking for this court, says that the cases in which the responsibility is laid on the original wrongdoer, though intervening agencies without his fault have interposed, are quite numerous, and he adds that they are only instances of the application of the principle of Scott v. Shephard, 2 W.Bl. 892. He refers to a number of cases by way of illustration. We have recently held that a recovery can be had although death resulted from overexertion by the decedent herself before she had completely recovered from the result of the accident. * * *

A more recent English case than those cited by Justice Depue in the Salmon Case is Englehart v. Farrant & Co., [1897] 1 Q.B. 240. There the defendant employed a man to drive a cart, with instructions not to leave it. A lad 17 years old, for whose acts it was held the defendant was not responsible, went along to deliver parcels to defendant's customers. The driver left the cart and went into a house. During his absence the lad drove on, and came into collision with plaintiff's carriage. It was held that the negligence of the driver in leaving the cart was the effective cause of the damage, and that the defendant was liable. Lord Esher said:

> "If a stranger interferes, it does not follow that the defendant is liable; but equally it does not follow that because a stranger interferes the defendant is not liable if the negligence of a servant of his is an effective cause of the accident."

In a later Massachusetts case the defendant was held not liable where it had allowed a platform to become saturated with oil, and fire resulted to the plaintiff's damage by a stranger throwing a match on the ground underneath the platform. Stone v. Boston & A. R. Co., 171 Mass. 536, 51 N.E. 1, 41 L.R.A. 794. The opinion contains an abundant citation of authorities on both sides of the line of cleavage.

* * *

We think these authorities justified the trial judge in his rulings as to the recovery of the value of the barrels, cider, and blanket. The negligence which caused the collision resulted immediately in such a condition of the driver of the wagon that he was no longer able to protect his employer's property; the natural and probable result of his enforced abandonment of it in the street of a large city was its disappearance; and the wrongdoer cannot escape making reparation for the loss caused by depriving the plaintiff of the protection which the presence of the driver in his right senses would have afforded.

"The act of a third person," said the Supreme Court of Massachusetts, "intervening and contributing a condition necessary to the injurious effect of the original negligence, will not excuse the first wrongdoer, if such act ought to have been foreseen." Lane v. Atlantic Works, 111 Mass. 136.

A railroad company which found it necessary or desirable to have its freight train guarded by two detectives against thieves is surely chargeable with knowledge that portable property left without a guard was likely to be made off with. Again, strictly speaking, the act of the thieves did not intervene between defendant's negligence and the plaintiff's loss; the two causes were to all practical intent simultaneous and concurrent; it is rather a case of a joint tort than an intervening cause. * * * An illustration will perhaps clarify the case. Suppose a fruit vendor at his stand along the street is rendered unconscious by the negligence of the defendant, who disappears, and boys in the street appropriate the unfortunate vendor's stock in trade; could the defendant escape liability for their value? We can hardly imagine a court answering in the affirmative. Yet the case is but little more extreme than the jury might have found the present case.

The judgment is affirmed, with costs.

GARRISON, J. [joined by four other judges] (dissenting). The collision afforded an opportunity for theft of which a thief took advantage, but I cannot agree that the collision was therefore the proximate cause of loss of the stolen articles. Proximate cause imports unbroken continuity between cause and effect, which, both in law and in logic, is broken by the active intervention of an independent criminal actor. This established rule of law is defeated if proximate cause is confounded with mere opportunity for crime. A maladjusted switch may be the proximate cause of the death of a passenger who was killed by the derailment of the train or by the fire or collision that ensued, but it is not the proximate cause of the death of a passenger who was murdered by a bandit who boarded the train because of the opportunity afforded by its derailment. This clear distinction is not met by saying that criminal intervention should be foreseen, for this implies that crime is to be presumed, and the law is directly otherwise.

There should be a new trial upon the question of damages, to which end the judgment should be reversed.

Notes

1. The *Brauer* case is a well-known early case allowing recovery against a negligent defendant despite the intervening intentional criminal acts of a third person. Another frequently cited early case is Watson v. Kentucky & Indiana Bridge & Railroad, 137 Ky. 619, 126 S.W. 146 (1910). In the *Watson* case a tank car carrying gasoline had derailed owing to the negligence of the defendants. As a result, gasoline spilled out over the surrounding streets and accumulated in puddles. Some three hours later, an identified third person lit a cigar and threw the still lit match down on the street. There was an explosion that "threw appellant from his bed and almost demolished his house, from the ruins of which he was taken unconscious and bleeding with a fractured jaw and one cheek nearly torn from his face." The trial judge directed a verdict for the defendants. The appellate court returned the case to the trial court for a new trial. It declared that if the third person "inadvertently or negligently lighted and threw the match in the gas," the plaintiff's injuries were attributable to the defendants' antecedent negligence. On the other hand, "if * * * the act of * * * [the third person] in lighting the match and throwing it into the vapor or gas arising from the gasoline was malicious, and done for the purpose of causing the explosion, we do not think appellees would be responsible. * * *" The court continued:

> The mere fact that the concurrent cause or intervening act was unforeseen will not relieve the defendant guilty of the primary negligence from liability, but if the intervening agency is something so unexpected or extraordinary as that he could not or ought not to have anticipated it, he will not be liable, and certainly he is not bound to anticipate the criminal acts of others by which damage is inflicted and hence is not liable therefor.

How would one reconcile the *Brauer* case with the *Watson* case? British courts have struggled with the same problems. For a recent discussion of the subject by the House of Lords, *see* Smith v. Littlewoods Organization Ltd., [1987] A.C. 241, 2 W.L.R. 480, 1 All E.R. 710 (Sc.). In Graham v. Keuchel, 847 P.2d 342

(Okl.1993), a woman became pregnant despite the defendant doctors' instructions not to become pregnant. The woman was Rh-negative and knew that she was. The negligence of the defendants consisted in not administering an anti-sensitization drug after a prior miscarriage. The plaintiff gave birth to a Rh-positive child who died shortly after birth. The court held that it was a jury question whether the mother had *willfully* become pregnant with full knowledge of the possible consequences. The trial court had instructed the jury that the mother's conduct relieved the doctors of liability if, with knowledge of the consequences she elected to become pregnant. A judgment for the defendants entered on a jury verdict was reversed and the case was remanded for a new trial.

2. In Williams v. State, 308 N.Y. 548, 127 N.E.2d 545 (1955), a prisoner escaped from a minimum security state prison farm. The escaped prisoner apparently forced Williams, a local farmer, to drive him out of the area. Although he had not been physically attacked, Williams suffered severe emotional stress which, in turn, caused a brain hemorrhage. Williams died the next day. In an action against the State of New York by Williams' estate, the court held that "[f]rom nothing in the record and exhibits below can we derive any basis for the foreseeability of his (i.e. the prisoner's) conduct toward Williams." Consequently the court reversed a judgment rendered for the estate. The court noted that the prisoner although convicted of attempted robbery had only used a toy pistol. The prisoner had been recommitted for parole violation but the violation merely consisted in failing to report to his parole officer. On the other hand, in Hicks v. United States, 511 F.2d 407 (D.C.Cir.1975), the United States was held liable to the estate of a deceased woman whose husband had been released from St. Elizabeth's hospital and soon thereafter killed her. The husband had, over a ten year period, "been arrested for drunkenness, disorderly conduct or assault at least sixteen times." He had last been arrested on a warrant for assault secured by his wife on the grounds that he had kicked, choked and beaten her and threatened to murder her. The criminal charges were disposed of by a *nolle prosequi* entered by the United States Attorney's office on the basis of a competency report prepared by the hospital which concluded that, if the accused had committed a crime it was the result of "acute brain syndrome due to alcoholic intoxication" from which he was now recovered. Pursuant to her request, the wife was warned that her husband had been released. A few days later he was again arrested for intoxication. He was released on condition he accept outpatient treatment. A month later he came to the family home. When his wife told him he could not stay, he shot and killed her. The court held that the competency report had been negligently prepared and affirmed a judgment against the United States.

Traditionally, social hosts who provide alcoholic beverages to their guests have not been held liable for injuries that may be caused by their inebriated adult guests, in the absence of some provision in the dram-shop statutes— which, moreover, often apply, or are held to apply, only to those who sell alcoholic beverages. The most frequent type of case, of course, involves automobile accidents. There have, however, in recent years been several cases in which such liability has been extended to social hosts. *See, e.g.,* Kelly v. Gwinnell, 96 N.J. 538, 476 A.2d 1219 (1984)(partially overruled by N.J.S.A. §§ 2A: 15–5.6, 15–5.7 which provides that hosts are not responsible to guests for injuries resulting from the guest's intoxication and limits liability to persons injured by intoxicated guests to instances where the host provided alcohol to a "visibly intoxicated" guest); McGuiggan v. New England Tel. & Tel. Co., 398 Mass. 152, 496 N.E.2d 141 (1986); Hart v. Ivey, 332 N.C. 299, 420 S.E.2d 174

(1992). A similar decision in California, Coulter v. Superior Court, 21 Cal.3d 144, 145 Cal.Rptr. 534, 577 P.2d 669 (1978), was expressly overturned by the California legislature, which specifically declared that the proximate cause of the resulting injury was the consumption of the alcoholic beverage by the intoxicated person. *See* West's Ann.Cal.Bus. & Prof.Code § 25602c(b)(c); West's Ann.Cal.Civil Code § 1714(b). *See also* Holmquist v. Miller, 367 N.W.2d 468 (Minn.1985), which interpreted the Minnesota legislature's deletion of the word "giving" from the dram-shop act to amount to a legislative overruling of Ross v. Ross, 294 Minn. 115, 200 N.W.2d 149 (1972).

3. A frequently recurring type of situation has involved the effect of ordinances or statutes making it unlawful to leave keys in the ignition of an automobile left on the public streets. The issue has arisen in actions brought by persons who have been injured by automobiles driven by car thieves. The cases are usually argued in terms of whether the intent of the statute was to protect persons like the plaintiffs or to cut down on car thefts for the conservation of police resources or the protection of either insurance companies or teenagers who might be tempted to joy ride. The cases have split. *Compare* Ross v. Hartman, 139 F.2d 14 (D.C.App.1943), *cert. denied* 321 U.S. 790, 64 S.Ct. 790, 88 L.Ed. 1080 (1944) *and* Ney v. Yellow Cab Co., 2 Ill.2d 74, 117 N.E.2d 74 (1954), allowing recovery, *with* Meihost v. Meihost, 29 Wis.2d 537, 139 N.W.2d 116 (1966) *and* Galbraith v. Levin, 323 Mass. 255, 81 N.E.2d 560 (1948), denying recovery. The latter seems to be the most common result and it has been also the result reached in the absence of a statute or ordinance, at least where there are no unusual circumstances indicating that it would be especially dangerous to leave the keys in a car left in a particular location. *See* Richards v. Stanley, 43 Cal.2d 60, 271 P.2d 23 (1954);[a] Liney v. Chestnut Motors, Inc., 421 Pa. 26, 218 A.2d 336 (1966). Although often questioned, *Richards v. Stanley* continues to be applied. *See* Archer v. Sybert, 167 Cal.App.3d 722, 213 Cal.Rptr. 486 (1985). For a review of what might be considered unusual circumstances so as to increase the foreseeability that the automobile might be stolen, *see* Palma v. United States Industrial Fasteners, Inc., 36 Cal.3d 171, 203 Cal.Rptr. 626, 681 P.2d 893 (1984). The court, in *Palma*, noted, in footnote 13 to its opinion, that it had "no occasion" to reach the question of whether *Richards v. Stanley* enjoyed continued viability. In Dean v. General Motors Corp., 301 F.Supp. 187 (E.D.La.1969), a car was stolen by a teenager using a screwdriver to pry off the cap of the ignition lock. The court held that, even if it could be held that the lock had been negligently designed, the actions of the thief, who was involved in an accident a day later, were an intervening superseding cause.

4. *Suicide.* These cases involve a person initially injured by the defendant who later commits suicide. Is the original tortfeasor responsible for the enhanced damages resulting from the injured person's death by suicide? The cases seem to turn on the question of whether the deceased exercised a free and deliberate choice or whether, because of his injuries, the deceased was not really aware of what he was doing or was incapable of controlling his acts. In Exxon Corp. v. Brecheen, 526 S.W.2d 519 (Tex.1975), the driver of a tank truck had been injured when a loading chute became loose and let loose a stream of oil which hit him in the face and knocked him to the ground. Some two years and nine months later, he committed suicide. While the court was not prepared to accept that merely because he committed suicide one could con-

---

a. There was in fact a municipal ordinance which had been violated, but the ordinance expressly declared that its violation should have no effect in civil litigation. The court therefore treated the case as one involving common-law liability.

clude that he did so because of mental disturbance caused by the accident, it nevertheless affirmed a judgment in favor of the deceased driver's survivors which included damages for wrongful death. The court noted that the deceased had exhibited evidence of mental disturbance from the day after the accident until the time of his death. There was psychiatric testimony that he had become schizophrenic and "unable to think in the manner that a normal person would." *See also* Fuller v. Preis, 35 N.Y.2d 425, 363 N.Y.S.2d 568, 322 N.E.2d 263 (1974).

5. *Acts of God.* To the extent that these are considered to be reasonably foreseeable, they will not serve to cut off the responsibility of a negligent defendant. *Compare* Klinefelter v. S. J. Groves & Sons Co., 8 Ill.App.3d 989, 291 N.E.2d 227 (1972) *with* Chase v. Washington Water Power Co., 62 Idaho 298, 111 P.2d 872 (1941). In the *Klinefelter* case a car which hit a deer rolled over the embankment of the road into a ravine. In an action against the road contractor alleging faulty design of the embankment, it was held that the actions of the deer were unforeseeable. In the *Chase* case, on the other hand, the wingtips of two hawks sparring with each other joined a high voltage power line with a guy wire with the result that a fire was started that destroyed the plaintiff's barn. The court noted the necessity of care in the design and maintenance of high voltage lines and that it was foreseeable that many causes could have caused the wires, spaced as they were, to come together. The defendant was accordingly held liable.

6. *Aggravation of Injuries.* It is generally held that one who negligently injures another is also responsible for any aggravation of injuries suffered by the plaintiff during the course of medical treatment, even if the injuries are aggravated owing to the negligence of the attending physicians. *See* Thompson v. Fox, 326 Pa. 209, 192 A. 107 (1937); Elliott v. Kansas City, 174 Mo. 554, 74 S.W. 617 (1903). *See also* City of Covington v. Keal, 280 Ky. 237, 133 S.W.2d 49 (1939). Liability is justified on the ground that such aggravation of injuries is a foreseeable consequence of the original tortfeasor's negligence. Obviously, if the subsequent aggravation of injuries is caused by intentional conduct or by some particularly foolhardy type of treatment, the courts will be inclined to cut off the original tortfeasor's liability on the ground that the aggravation of the plaintiff's injuries was unforeseeable. The original tortfeasor has likewise been held liable for the aggravation of the plaintiff's injuries when, because of the plaintiff's original injuries, say a broken leg, he is subsequently re-injured while attempting to manage on his own, say, in the example posited, slipping while trying to walk with crutches. *See, e.g.,* Squires v. Reynolds, 125 Conn. 366, 5 A.2d 877 (1939); Wagner v. Mittendorf, 232 N.Y. 481, 134 N.E. 539 (1922). In a few extreme cases, the original tortfeasor has even been held liable when the plaintiff's injuries were aggravated when the ambulance he was riding in was involved in a road accident. *See* State ex rel. Smith v. Weinstein, 398 S.W.2d 41 (Mo.App.1965); Lucas v. City of Juneau, 127 F.Supp. 730 (D.C.Alaska 1955). These cases would be easier to assimilate with underlying theory if they involved ambulances speeding the plaintiff to a hospital but that does not appear to have been the situation in either of the cases cited. Indeed, in the *Lucas* case the second accident occurred 18 days later when it was decided to transfer the plaintiff to a hospital in Seattle. The accident occurred en route to the airport. While one might be able to foresee that an ambulance might be involved in an accident, it cannot be said that such accidents are more likely than an accident that might occur while the plaintiff was driving to a motion picture theater. In other words, unlike the situation where the plaintiff's

injuries are aggravated by his physician's malpractice, the original tortfeasor did not increase the chances of the plaintiff's being injured by the activity of riding in a motor vehicle.

7. *Rescuers*. On the theory that "danger invites rescue," the original tortfeasor has been held liable for injuries suffered by those going to the rescue of those imperiled or injured by the original tortfeasor. *See* Wagner v. International Railway, 232 N.Y. 176, 133 N.E. 437 (1921). The liability will attach even if the interest threatened is a property interest and even if the person threatened or injured is responsible for his own predicament. Thus, in Talbert v. Talbert, 22 Misc.2d 782, 199 N.Y.S.2d 212 (1960), a father who tried to commit suicide was liable for injuries suffered by his son while attempting to rescue him.

When the injured rescuer is a so-called "professional rescuer," such as a fireman or policeman, however, there are a number of cases denying recovery. *See* Walters v. Sloan, 20 Cal.3d 199, 142 Cal.Rptr. 152, 571 P.2d 609 (1977)(policeman); Maltman v. Sauer, 84 Wn.2d 975, 530 P.2d 254 (1975)(crew of Army rescue helicopter); Krauth v. Geller, 31 N.J. 270, 157 A.2d 129 (1960)(fireman). A number of reasons are given for this result including the doctrine of assumption of the risk. To some extent, however, the doctrine of assumption of the risk should also operate against a non-professional rescuer. At any rate, where a professional rescuer is injured as the result of a risk which is inherent in the rescue activity in which he is employed, he is likely to be denied recovery against a person whose negligence created the danger. The doctrine is sometimes known as the "fireman's rule" because it originated in cases denying recovery to firemen who were injured on premises which they had entered in order to fight a fire. The aspects of the doctrine that relate specifically to the liability of owners and occupiers of premises will be discussed again in Chapter 7, *infra*. In Hubbard v. Boelt, 28 Cal.3d 480, 169 Cal.Rptr. 706, 620 P.2d 156 (1980), the doctrine was held to preclude recovery even when the defendant's conduct was reckless. As will be described, *infra*, that has now been changed by statute. In *Hubbard* a policeman was injured in a high-speed automobile chase. On the other hand, in Mahoney v. Carus Chemical Co., 102 N.J. 564, 510 A.2d 4 (1986), the doctrine was held *not* to bar recovery for injuries caused by willful and wanton behavior. For a discussion of when the doctrine is applicable in New Jersey, *see* Rosa v. Dunkin' Donuts of Passaic, 122 N.J. 66, 583 A.2d 1129 (1991). In Lipson v. Superior Court, 31 Cal.3d 362, 182 Cal.Rptr. 629, 644 P.2d 822 (1982), the doctrine was interpreted as not to preclude recovery when the plaintiff fireman was injured because of an act of negligence independent of that which was the occasion for the fireman to be called to the premises in the first place. By statute, Cal.Civil Code § 1714.9, California now provides that, once a person knows or should know that a policeman or fireman is present, that person is liable for injuries suffered by the policeman or fireman as a result of that person's subsequent "willful acts" or negligence. *See* Gibb v. Stetson, 199 Cal.App.3d 1008, 245 Cal.Rptr. 283 (1988). In a subsequent case, the fireman's rule was held not to apply to private security guards, although actions by such persons might, in some circumstances, be defeated by the doctrine of assumption of risk. Neighbarger v. Irwin Industries, Inc., 8 Cal.4th 532, 34 Cal.Rptr.2d 630, 882 P.2d 347 (1994). The doctrine was abolished in Oregon in Christensen v. Murphy, 296 Or. 610, 678 P.2d 1210 (1984). The doctrine has not been recognized in England. Ogwo v. Taylor, [1988] A.C. 431 (1987), [1987] 3 W.L.R. 1145, 3 All E.R. 961.

Chapter 5

PLAINTIFF'S CONDUCT AS A CONTRIBUTING CAUSE

Up to now, we have generally concentrated on a conventional lawsuit between an injured plaintiff and a defendant charged with responsibility for causing plaintiff's injury. However, often, as we have already seen, injury cases are much more complicated, with many potential defendants who have in some way contributed to plaintiff's injury. Moreover, plaintiff's conduct may have also contributed to the injury. In the next two chapters we take up some of the many problems raised by these more complicated situations. Over the history of the common law, the courts, and to some extent, the legislative branches had come to resolution on many of these problems with clear cut legal rules recognized by most courts. However, in the past few years there has been a revolutionary change, still in process in many states, in the whole range of these rules. Involved are the common law defenses based upon the conduct of the plaintiff that contributes to the injury, as well as the manner in which the responsibility for the injury is apportioned among the possible responsible parties, including the plaintiff. We will start in this chapter with plaintiff's contributory conduct. In the next chapter we turn to the evolution of the law regarding multiple defendants and then review the interrelationships between the two chapters.

A. CONTRIBUTORY NEGLIGENCE

Until about 30 years ago, almost all states recognized the doctrine of contributory negligence. If the plaintiff was found to have been at fault to any degree in causing the accident, the plaintiff's behavior was a complete defense to a negligence action. In the intervening years, however, at least forty-six states and the United States in many tort related federal statutory actions, have adopted some general form of comparative negligence, in which the plaintiff, although partially at fault in causing the accident may be able to recover some damages. Because the common law doctrine still exists substantially unaltered in some states[1] and because many of the

---

1. The principal bastion of the old common law doctrine that contributory negligence is a complete defense to an action based on negligence is the southeast United States. Alabama, Maryland, the District of Columbia, Virginia, and North Carolina have thus far not adopted the doctrine of comparative negligence for most tort actions. Howev-

subsequent developments require understanding of the common law doctrine, we will begin with a review of contributory negligence as it existed, until recently, in most jurisdictions in this country. Understand also that the definition of contributory negligence has not, for the most part, been altered with the adoption of comparative negligence. Only the amount of damages that the plaintiff can recover has changed.

BUTTERFIELD v. FORRESTER

King's Bench, 1809.
11 East 60, 103 Eng.Rep. 926.

This was an action on the case for obstructing a highway, by means of which obstruction the plaintiff, who was riding along the road, was thrown down with his horse, and injured, & c. At the trial before Bayley J. at Derby, it appeared that the defendant, for the purpose of making some repairs to his house, which was close by the road side at one end of the town, had put up a pole across this part of the road, a free passage being left by another branch or street in the same direction. That the plaintiff left a public house not far distant from the place in question at 8 o'clock in the evening in August, when they were just beginning to light candles, but while there was light enough left to discern the obstruction at 100 yards distance: and the witness, who proved this, said that if the plaintiff had not been riding very hard he might have observed and avoided it: the plaintiff however, who was riding violently, did not observe it, but rode against it, and fell with his horse and was much hurt in consequence of the accident; and there was no evidence of his being intoxicated at the time. On this evidence Bayley J. directed the jury, that if a person riding with reasonable and ordinary care could have seen and avoided the obstruction; and if they were satisfied that the plaintiff was riding along the street extremely hard, and without ordinary care, they should find a verdict for the defendant: which they accordingly did.

Vaughan Serjt. now objected to this direction, on moving for a new trial; and referred to Buller's Ni. Pri. 26(a), where the rule is laid down, that "if a man lay logs of wood across a highway; though a person may with care ride safely by, yet if by means thereof my horse stumble and fling me, I may bring an action."

BAYLEY J. The plaintiff was proved to be riding as fast as his horse could go, and this was through the streets of Derby. If he had used ordinary care he must have seen the obstruction; so that the accident appeared to happen entirely from his own fault.

LORD ELLENBOROUGH C.J. A party is not to cast himself upon an obstruction which has been made by the fault of another, and avail himself of it, if he do not himself use common and ordinary caution to be in the right. In cases of persons riding upon what is considered to be the wrong side of the road, that would not authorise another purposely to ride up against them. One person being in fault will not dispense with another's

er, in Virginia and North Carolina, as in some other states, there is legislation applying comparative negligence to certain actions, for example, those brought by employees of railroads engaged in intrastate commerce. These statutes are similar to the Federal Employer's Liability Act, which will be discussed later in this chapter.

using ordinary care for himself. Two things must concur to support this action, an obstruction in the road by the fault of the defendant, and no want of ordinary care to avoid it on the part of the plaintiff.

Per Curiam. Rule refused.

Notes

1. Among the early cases in which the plaintiff's contributory negligence barred his recovery against a negligent defendant are: Fowler v. Adam, 2 Taunt. 314, 127 Eng.Rep. 1098 (C.P.1810); Smith v. Smith, 19 Mass. (2 Pick.) 621 (1824); Pennsylvania Railroad Co. v. Aspell, 23 Pa. 147 (1854). In the *Aspell* case, the trial court had instructed the jury that the plaintiff's "imprudence" might be considered in assessing damages—a suggestion found in several early cases—but the Supreme Court of Pennsylvania held that the plaintiff's action was completely barred and this became the prevailing rule. This is the aspect of the doctrine that has been changed substantially by the advent of comparative fault. That will be taken up in detail later in this chapter.

2. As previously noted in Chapter One, *supra* (p. 29), most states now place the burden of persuasion on the issue of contributory negligence upon the defendant (and this remains true with the advent of comparative negligence). In other words, contributory negligence is treated as an affirmative defense. See Preliminary Draft of *Restatement (Third) of Torts: Apportionment of Liability* § 5.[2] In the nineteenth century most states made proof of the absence of contributory negligence part of the plaintiff's case.

3. As we have seen in *Martin v. Herzog, supra* p. 153, violation of a statute can constitute contributory negligence as a matter of law. *See also* Southern Pacific Co. v. Castro, 493 S.W.2d 491 (Tex.1973).

4. Contributory negligence will normally also be a defense to an action based upon the defendant's violation of a statutory duty. It will not, however, be a defense to an action based upon a violation of a statute if (i) the statute imposes absolute liability, *i.e.* requires no scienter on the part of the defendant, see Jenkins v. Chicago & Eastern Illinois Railroad, 5 Ill.App.3d 954, 284 N.E.2d 392 (1972); (ii) the statute is aimed at protecting a limited class of persons against their own imprudence, such as children or intoxicated persons, see Zerby v. Warren, 297 Minn. 134, 210 N.W.2d 58 (1973); or (iii) the plaintiff is a workman injured as a result of the violation of a factory safety act, see Koenig v. Patrick Construction Corp., 298 N.Y. 313, 83 N.E.2d 133 (1948). These three categories often overlap.

5. As already indicated at pp. 125–26 *supra*, the issue of contributory negligence is supposed to be governed by the same objective standard that is used to determine whether a defendant has been negligent. *Compare Restatement (Second) of Torts* § 464 *with id.* § 483. This principle is continued in the Preliminary Draft of the *Restatement (Third) of Torts: Apportionment of Liability* § 4. Section 464 of the *Restatement (Second)* nevertheless does have a *caveat* on the question of the contributory negligence of insane persons. As already noted in the more detailed discussion at p. 126, *supra*, Mochen v. State,

---

2. The Preliminary Draft of the Restatement (Third) of Torts: Apportionment of Liability is at the time this casebook is being written at an early stage in the process of consideration by the American Law Institute. Nevertheless it will be cited extensively in these two chapters as representing the current thinking of at least its co-reporters and probably a large part of the tort lawyers' community.

43 A.D.2d 484, 352 N.Y.S.2d 290 (1974), is indeed an explicit holding that a person with severe mental disability or retardation is only required to exercise the care for his own person of which he is capable. Beyond this, however, there are some judicial intimations that it may be appropriate for a jury to judge plaintiffs and defendants by different standards. *See* Stubbs v. Pancake Corner of Salem, 254 Or. 220, 458 P.2d 676 (1969). The suggestion is that it is less heinous to threaten one's own safety than to threaten the safety of others. *See also* Seattle First National Bank v. Shoreline Concrete Co., 91 Wn.2d 230, 238, 588 P.2d 1308, 1314 (1978). But is this really so? As we have seen, one who carelessly places himself in physical danger may be liable to someone who is injured while trying to rescue him. With the advent of comparative fault, there would seem to be less reason to want to judge the conduct of the plaintiff and the defendant by different standards. The use of different standards would also make it more difficult to compare the fault of the plaintiff with that of the defendant. The proposed *Restatement (Third)*, reflects these ideas. It explicitly rejects the modification of the standard as to plaintiff's conduct. See the Preliminary Reporter's Notes to § 4, providing that the same standard used for assessing defendant's conduct will also be used to assess the plaintiff's.

SMITHWICK v. HALL & UPSON CO.

Supreme Court of Errors of Connecticut, 1890.
59 Conn. 261, 21 A. 924.

TORRANCE, J. The general question reserved for our advice in this case is whether the plaintiff, upon the facts found, is entitled to the substantial damages or only to the nominal damages found by the court below. Inasmuch as that court has expressly found that the negligence of the defendant caused or contributed to the injury for which the plaintiff seeks to recover, the decision of the above general question depends upon this single point, namely, whether the acts and conduct of the plaintiff, as set forth upon the record, constitute or amount to such contributory negligence on his part as will bar his right to substantial damages. The facts found, so far as they bear upon the question for decision, are in substance the following: The plaintiff was a workman in the service of the defendant, and at the time of the injury complained of was engaged in helping to store ice for the defendant in a certain brick building. In doing this work the plaintiff stood upon a platform about 5 feet wide and 17 feet long, raised 15 feet above the ground, and extending from the west side of the building easterly to a point about 2 feet east of the door or aperture through which the ice was taken into the building. A stout plank of suitable height and strength extended along the outer side of the platform as far as the west side of the door, and served as a protective railing or guard to that portion of the platform. In front of the door, and east of it, the platform was without guard or railing of any kind. A short time prior to the injury the foreman of the defendant stationed the plaintiff on the platform just west of the door, and inside the railing, and showed him what his duties were there, and told him 'not to go upon the east end of the platform east of the slide and door, as it was not safe to stand there.' He did not tell the plaintiff why it was not safe, but the danger which he had in mind was the narrowness and unrailed condition of the platform, and the liability by inadvertence to misstep or fall or slip off, the latter being aggravated by the liability of the platform to become slippery from broken ice. These dangers were all manifest. The peril resulting from the accident which happened to the building was not in contemplation. After the foreman went away the plaintiff, in spite of the orders so given to him, and for reasons of his own apparently, went over to the east end of the platform, and worked there. It is found that there was no sufficient reason or excuse for the change of position. One of his fellow-workmen, seeing the plaintiff in that place, told him that 'it was not safe, and to stand on the other side,' but the plaintiff, notwithstanding such warning, remained at work there. While so at work the brick wall of the building above the platform, in consequence of the negligence of the defendant, gave way, the brick falling upon the platform, and thence to the ground. The plaintiff was struck by portions of the descending mass, and fell to the earth. He was either knocked off, or his fall, in the condition in which he stood, was inevitable; indeed, had he not fallen when he did, his injuries, which were very serious, would have been worse. Most of the injuries which he actually sustained were occasioned by the fall. The plaintiff had no knowledge that the wall would be likely to fall, or was in any way unsafe, and it is found that "no fault or negligence can be imputed to him in this regard." In contemplation of the peril from the falling wall, it is found that "the spot where the plaintiff stood could not have been considered more dangerous than the place where he was directed to stand, though in fact most of the brick fell upon the side where he stood, and the result demonstrated, therefore, that the other side would have been safer in the event which occurred."

Upon these facts the defendant contends that the plaintiff, in going to and remaining on the east end of the platform, contrary to the orders and in spite of the warning given him, and in view of the obvious and manifest danger in so doing, was guilty of such contributory negligence as bars him of his right to recover more than nominal damages. If the plaintiff's injuries had resulted from any of the perils and dangers attendant upon the mere fact of his standing and working on the east end of the platform, which were obvious and manifest to any one in his place, which were in the mind of the foreman when he told the plaintiff not to go there, and in view of which his fellow-workman warned him, then this claim of the defendant would be a valid one. But upon the facts found it is without foundation. The injury to the plaintiff was not the result of any such dangers, but was caused through the negligence of the defendant by the falling walls. This was a source of danger of which he had no knowledge whatever. He was justified in supposing that the wall was safe, and would not be likely to fall upon him, no matter where he stood on the platform. He had no reason to anticipate even the slightest danger from that source before or after he changed his position. This being so, he could be guilty of no negligence with respect to this source of danger by changing his position contrary to orders; for negligence presupposes a duty of taking care, and this, in turn, presupposes knowledge or its legal equivalent. With respect to that danger, the plaintiff, upon the facts found, must be held to have acted as any reasonably careful man would have acted under the same circumstances. In changing his position contrary to orders, he voluntarily took the risk of all perils and dangers which a man of ordinary care in his place ought to have known or could reasonably have anticipated; but as to dangers arising through the defendant's negligence from other sources,—dangers which he was not bound to anticipate and of whose existence he had no knowledge,— he took no risk and assumed no duty of taking care. It was the duty of the defendant, on the facts found, to warn the plaintiff against the danger from the falling wall. Now, the act or omission of a party injured, which amounts to what is called "contributory negligence," must be a negligent act or omission, and in the production of the injury it must operate as a proximate cause, or one of the proximate causes, and not merely as a condition. In the case at bar the conduct of the plaintiff, as we have seen, was, with respect to the danger from the falling wall, not negligent, for the want of knowledge or its equivalent on the part of the plaintiff. Nor was his conduct, legally considered, a cause of the injury. It was a condition, rather. If he had not changed his position, he might not have been hurt. And so, too, if he had never been born, or had remained at home on the day of the injury, it would not have happened; yet no one would claim that his birth, or his not remaining at home that day, can in any just or legal sense be deemed a cause of the injury. The court below has found that the plaintiff's fall in the position in which he stood was due to the giving way of the wall, and that most of his injuries were occasioned by the fall. His position there, upon the facts found can no more be considered as a cause of the injury, than it could be in a case where the defendant, in doing some act near the platform without the plaintiff's knowledge, had negligently knocked him to the ground, or had negligently hit him with a stone. Had the injury been occasioned by a misstep or slip from the platform by the carelessness of the plaintiff, or for the want of a railing, the casual connection between the change of position and the injury would, legally speaking, be quite obvious; but, from a legal point of view, no such connection exists between the change of position and the giving way of the wall.

The plaintiff had full knowledge of and was abundantly cautioned against certain particular sources of peril and danger, and he voluntarily neglected the warnings and took the risk of those perils and dangers. He was injured through the negligence of the defendant from an entirely different source of danger, of which he knew and could know nothing, and of whose existence it was the duty of the defendant to warn him. Under these circumstances, the failure or neglect to heed the warning does not constitute contributory negligence. * * * The defendant seems to claim, however, that, although some of the plaintiff's injuries were caused by falling bricks, yet most of them were caused by his fall; and that, as he probably would not have fallen had he remained behind the railing, he contributed to his injury by placing himself where, in case of such accident, there was nothing to prevent his fall. Whether the claim that he would probably not have fallen had he remained where he was stationed be true or not, must forever remain matter of conjecture. But if its truth could be demonstrated it would not, as we have seen, change the relation of the plaintiff's act to the legal cause of his injury, or make that act, from a legal stand-point, a contributing cause when it was but a condition. And if the claim means that the plaintiff by his act increased the injury merely, then, if this were true, it would not be such contributory negligence as would defeat the action. To have that effect it must be an act or omission which contributes to the happening of the act or event which caused the injury. An act or omission that merely increases or adds to the extent of the loss or injury will not have that effect, though, of course, it may affect the amount of damages recovered in a given case. * * * This claim, however, on the facts found, is wholly without foundation. The plaintiff is entitled to judgment in his favor for $1,000, and the superior court is so advised. The other judges concurred.

B. COMPARATIVE NEGLIGENCE

1. *Historical Background*

There seems always to have been some lingering dissatisfaction with the doctrine that a plaintiff who was contributorily negligent in any way that proximately contributed to his own injuries was totally barred from receiving any legal redress for those injuries. During the nineteenth century the courts in a few states experimented with some form of judicially created comparative negligence but these tentative beginnings were largely overruled by the end of that century. For example, *compare* Galena & Chicago Union Railroad v. Jacobs, 20 Ill. 478 (1858) *with* City of Lanark v. Dougherty, 153 Ill. 163, 38 N.E. 892 (1894). In *Galena,* the court had allowed a plaintiff to recover all his damages if his negligence was slight when compared with that of the defendant. Other jurisdictions allowed the plaintiff to recover if the negligence was not only slight but also causally remote. *See, e.g.,* Bejach v. Colby, 141 Tenn. 686, 214 S.W. 869 (1919); Atchison, Topeka & Santa Fe Railroad v. Morgan, 31 Kan. 77, 1 P. 298 (1883). A number of jurisdictions in the late nineteenth century, nevertheless adopted statutes permitting railroad workers to recover against their employers despite their own negligence.[3] These culminated in the Federal Employers Liability Act of 1908, 35 Stat. 65, as amended 45 U.S.C. §§ 51 ff. These employer liability acts are typically instances of the "pure" form of comparative negligence, namely instances where, at least theoretically, a worker can recover a proportion of the damages regardless of whether he was more negligent than the defendant-employer. That is, an employee 99% at fault would be entitled to recover 1% of the damages from the defendant-employer.

Beginning with Mississippi in 1910 (now Miss.Code 1972, § 11–7–15) a few states enacted general comparative negligence statutes. The Mississippi statute is of the "pure" type. By 1960, perhaps half a dozen states had some form of general comparative negligence scheme. Under the schemes adopted in Nebraska in 1913 (now Neb.Rev.Stat. § 25–21,185) and by South Dakota in 1941 (now S.D. Codified Laws 20–9–2) the plaintiff can recover a proportion of the damages if his negligence is "slight" and that of the defendant "gross" in comparison.[4] Wisconsin, Arkansas (now Ark. Code of 1987 Ann. § 16–64–122) and Georgia, by extension of railroad legislation, adopted schemes under which the plaintiff could recover a proportionate amount of the damages if his negligence were "less than"

3. The states that adopted such statutes include Iowa, Kentucky, North Carolina, South Carolina, and Virginia.

4. For comment see R. Johnson, *Comparative Negligence—The Nebraska View,* 36 Neb.L.Rev. 240 (1957); Note, 7 S.D.L.Rev. 114 (1962).

that of the defendant.[5] Maine (Me.Rev.Stat.Ann. tit. 14, § 156) and Colorado (Colo.Rev.Stat.Ann. § 13–21–111(1)) joined this group in the mid–1960's. Because of the frequent tendency of juries to find both sides equally at fault, the Wisconsin scheme has been since amended to permit the plaintiff to recover a proportionate share of the damages if his negligence is less than or equal to that of the defendant (Wis.Stat.Ann. § 895.045 (West)). Finally, on the federal level the rule of equal division of damages among negligent parties was applied in admiralty. *See, e.g.,* The Schooner Catharine, 58 U.S. (17 How.) 170, 15 L.Ed. 233 (1855).[6] Attempts to secure judicial adoption of comparative negligence prior to the 1970's were generally unsuccessful. A well-known attempt occurred in Maki v. Frelk, 40 Ill.2d 193, 239 N.E.2d 445 (1968), in which the Supreme Court of Illinois reversed a decision of the Illinois Court of Appeals adopting comparative negligence. 85 Ill.App.2d 439, 229 N.E.2d 284 (1967). The Supreme Court of Illinois declared that any such far-reaching change in the law should be left to the legislature. As will be noted at p. 354, *infra*, the Illinois Supreme Court did eventually adopt comparative negligence in 1981.

2. *The Tide of Judicial Change*

HOFFMAN v. JONES

Supreme Court of Florida, 1973.
280 So.2d 431.

ADKINS, JUSTICE.

* * *

The question certified by the District Court of Appeal is:

"Whether or not the Court should replace the contributory negligence rule with the principles of comparative negligence?"

The District Court of Appeal answered the certified question in the affirmative and reversed the trial court in the case *sub judice* for following the precedent set down by this Court in Louisville and Nashville Railroad Co. v. Yniestra, 21 Fla. 700 (1886). This early case specifically held the contributory negligence rule to be the law of Florida, and it has uniformly been followed by the courts of the State ever since. The District Court of Appeal attempted, therefore, to overrule all precedent of this Court in the area of contributory negligence and to establish comparative negligence as the proper test. In so doing, the District Court has exceeded its authority.

* * * To allow a District Court of Appeal to overrule controlling precedent of this Court would be to create chaos and uncertainty in the judicial forum, particularly at the trial level. Ever since the District Court ren-

---

5. *See, e.g.,* R. Campbell, *Ten Years of Comparative Negligence,* [1941] Wis.L.Rev. 289. As we shall see below, the Wisconsin scheme has now been modified to permit a plaintiff to recover if his negligence is less than or equal to that of the defendant. Note, 11 Ark.L.Rev. 391 (1957). The Georgia scheme was explained in Smith v. American Oil Co., 77 Ga.App. 463, 49 S.E.2d 90 (1948).

6. Now overruled by United States v. Reliable Transfer Co., 421 U.S. 397, 95 S.Ct. 1708, 44 L.Ed.2d 251 (1975). The Court opted for a "pure" system of comparative negligence.

dered its opinion there has been great confusion and much delay in the trial courts of the District Court of Appeal, Fourth District, while the attorneys and judges alike have been awaiting our decision in this case.

We point out that the mere certification to this Court by a District Court of Appeal that its decision involves a question of great public interest does not vest this Court with jurisdiction. If neither party involved petitioned here for a writ of certiorari, we would not have jurisdiction to answer the question certified or to review the District Court's action.

This is not to say that the District Courts of Appeal are powerless to seek change; they are free to certify questions of great public interest to this Court for consideration, and even to state their reasons for advocating change. They are, however, bound to follow the case law set forth by this Court.

Prior to answering the question certified, we must also consider our own power and authority to replace the rule of contributory negligence with that of comparative negligence. It has been suggested that such a change in the common law of Florida is properly within the province only of the Legislature, and not of the courts. We cannot agree.

The rule that contributory negligence is an absolute bar to recovery was—as most tort law—a judicial creation, and it was specifically judicially adopted in Florida in Louisville and Nashville Railroad Co. v. Yniestra, *supra*. Most scholars attribute the origin of this rule to the English case of Butterfield v. Forrester, 11 East 60, 103 Eng.Rep. 926 (K.B.1809), although as much as thirty years later—in Raisin v. Mitchell, 9 Car. & P. 613, 173 Eng.Rep. 979 (C.P.1839)—contributory negligence was held not to be a complete bar to recovery. Maloney, From Contributory to Comparative Negligence: A Needed Law Reform, 11 U.Fla.L.Rev. 135, 141–142 (1958). Although "contributory negligence" itself had been mentioned in some earlier cases, our research reveals that prior to 1809 (as well as for a time after that date) there was no clear-cut, common law rule that contributory negligence was a complete defense to an action based on negligence. Most probably, the common law was the same in this regard as English maritime law and the civil law—i.e., damages were apportioned when both plaintiff and defendant were at fault. See Maloney, *supra,* page 152. Many authorities declare that early references to "contributory negligence" did not concern contributory negligence as we are familiar with it—i.e., lack of due care by the plaintiff which contributes to his injuries—but that it originally meant a plaintiff's own negligent act which was the effective, *direct cause* of the accident in which he was injured. E. G. Turk, Comparative Negligence on the March, 28 Chi–Kent L.Rev. 189, p. 196 (1950).

Prior to Butterfield v. Forrester, *supra,* there was no clear-cut pronouncement of the contributory negligence rule, so it must be said that "judicial thinking" culminated in the implicit pronouncement of the contributory negligence rule in the 1809 decision of Butterfield v. Forrester, *supra.* In view of the fact that prior to *Butterfield* contributory negligence was a matter of judicial thought rather than judicial pronouncement, it cannot be said that the common law was "clear and free from doubt," so as to make it a part of the statute law of this State by virtue of Fla.Stat., § 2.01, F.S.A.

As we stated in Duval v. Thomas, 114 So.2d 791, 795 (Fla.1959), it is "only when the common law is plain that we must observe it." We also said in this case,

> "[W]hen grave doubt exists of a true common law doctrine * * * we may, as was written in Ripley v. Ewell, supra, [61 So.2d 420], exercise a 'broad discretion' taking 'into account the changes in our social and economic customs and present day conceptions of right and justice.'"

Even if it be said that the present bar of contributory negligence is a part of our common law by virtue of prior judicial decision, it is also true from *Duval* that this Court may change the rule where great social upheaval dictates. It has been modified in many instances by judicial decision, such as those establishing the doctrines of "last clear chance," "appreciable degree" and others. * * * In a large measure the rule has been transfigured from any "statutory creation" by virtue of our adoption of the common law (if such it were) into decisional law by virtue of various court refinements. We have in the past, with hesitation, modified the common law in justified instances, and this is as it should be. Randolph v. Randolph, 146 Fla. 491, 1 So.2d 480 (1941), modified the common law doctrine that gave a father the superior right to the custody of a child; Banfield v. Addington, 104 Fla. 661, 140 So. 893 (1932), removed the common law exemption of a married woman from causes of action based on contract or mixed contracts in tort.

In Waller v. First Savings & Trust Co., 103 Fla.1025, 138 So. 780 (1931), this Court refused to follow the common law principle that an action for personal injuries was abated upon the death of the tortfeasor, the Court saying:

> "This court has expressly recognized the principle that in specific instances certain rules which were admittedly a part of the old English common law did not become a part of the Florida common law, because contrary to our customs, institutions, or intendments of our statutes on other subjects." (p. 784)

* * * Gates v. Foley, 247 So.2d 40 (Fla.1971), established the right of a wife to recover for the loss of consortium as a result of her husband's injuries. This decision * * * abrogated a common law principle, saying:

> "It may be argued that any change in this rule should come from the Legislature. No recitation of authority is needed to indicate that this Court has not been backward in overturning unsound precedent in the area of tort law. *Legislative action could, of course, be taken, but we abdicate our own function, in a field peculiarly nonstatutory, when we refuse to reconsider an old and unsatisfactory court-made rule.*" (Emphasis supplied) 247 So.2d 40, p. 43

All rules of the common law are designed for application to new conditions and circumstances as they may be developed by enlightened commercial and business intercourse and are intended to be vitalized by practical application in advanced society. One of the most pressing social problems facing us today is the automobile accident problem, for the bulk of tort litigation involves the dangerous instrumentality known as the automobile. Our society must be concerned with accident prevention and compensation of victims of accidents. The Legislature of Florida has made great progress in legislation geared for accident prevention. The prevention of accidents, of course, is much more satisfying than the compensation of victims, but we must recognize the problem of determining a method of securing just and adequate compensation of accident victims who have a good cause of action.

The contemporary conditions must be met with contemporary standards which are realistic and better calculated to obtain justice among all of the parties involved, based upon the circumstances applying between them at the time in question. The rule of contributory negligence as a complete bar to recovery was imported into the law by judges. Whatever may have been the historical justification for it, today it is almost universally regarded as unjust and inequitable to vest an entire accidental loss on one of the parties whose negligent conduct combined with the negligence of the other party to produce the loss. If fault is to remain the test of liability, then the doctrine of comparative negligence which involves apportionment of the loss among those whose fault contributed to the occurrence is more consistent with liability based on a fault premise.

We are, therefore, of the opinion that we do have the power and authority to reexamine the position we have taken in regard to contributory negligence and to alter the rule we have adopted previously in light of current "social and economic customs" and modern "conceptions of right and justice."

Use of the terms "contributory negligence" and "comparative negligence" is slightly confusing. The two theories now commonly known by these terms both recognize that negligence of a plaintiff may play a part in causing his injuries and that the damages he is allowed to recover should, therefore, be diminished to some extent. The "contributory negligence" theory, of course, *completely* bars recovery, while the "comparative negligence" theory is that a plaintiff is prevented from recovering only that proportion of his damages for which he is responsible.

The demise of the absolute-bar theory of contributory negligence has been urged by many American scholars in the law of torts. It has been abolished in almost every common law nation in the world, including England—its country of origin—and every one of the Canadian Provinces. Some form of comparative negligence now exists in Austria, France, Germany, Portugal, Switzerland, Italy, China, Japan, Persia, Poland, Russia, Siam and Turkey. Maloney, *supra,* page 154.

Also, our research reveals that sixteen states have so far adopted some form of the comparative negligence doctrine.

One reason for the abandonment of the contributory negligence theory is that the initial justification for establishing the complete defense is no longer valid. It is generally accepted that, historically, contributory negligence was adopted "to protect the essential growth of industries, particularly transportation." Institute of Judicial Administration, Comparative Negligence—1954 Supplement, at page 2. Modern economic and social customs, however, favor the individual, not industry.

We find that none of the justifications for denying any recovery to a plaintiff, who has contributed to his own injuries to any extent, has any validity in this age.

Perhaps the best argument in favor of the movement from contributory to comparative negligence is that the latter is simply a more equitable system of determining liability and a more socially desirable method of loss distribution. The injustice which occurs when a plaintiff suffers severe injuries as the result of an accident for which he is only slightly responsible, and is thereby denied any damages, is readily apparent. The rule of contributory negligence is a harsh one which either places the burden of a loss for which two are responsible upon only one party or relegates to Lady Luck the determination of the damages for which each of two negligent parties will be liable. When the negligence of more than one person contributes to the occurrence of an accident, each should pay the proportion of the total damages he has caused the other party.

In an effort to ameliorate the harshness of contributory negligence, other doctrines have evolved in tort law such as "gross, willful, and wanton" negligence, "last clear chance" and the application of absolute liability in certain instances. Those who defend the doctrine of contributory negligence argue that the rule is also not as harsh in its practical effect as it is in theory. This is so, they say, because juries tend to disregard the instructions given by the trial judge in an effort to afford some measure of rough justice to the injured party. We agree with Dean Maloney that,

> "[T]here is something basically wrong with a rule of law that is so contrary to the settled convictions of the lay community that laymen will almost always refuse to enforce it, even when solemnly told to do so by a judge whose instructions they have sworn to follow.   * * *

> "[T]he disrespect for law engendered by putting our citizens in a position in which they feel it is necessary to deliberately violate the law is not something to be lightly brushed aside; and it comes ill from the mouths of lawyers, who as officers of the courts have sworn to uphold the law, to defend the present system by arguing that it works because jurors can be trusted to disregard that very law." 11 U.Fla.L.Rev. 135, pp. 151–152 (1958).

In Connolly v. Steakley, 197 So.2d 524, 537 (Fla.1967), Mr. Justice O'Connell referred to contributory negligence as a "primitive device for achieving justice as between parties who are both at fault." Even Mr. Chief Justice McWhorter, in authoring the decision which specifically held the contributory negligence doctrine to be the law of this State, referred to it as "unjust and inequitable." Louisville and Nashville Railroad Co. v. Yniestra, *supra*, 21 Fla. p. 738.

Eighty-seven years after that decision, we find ourselves still laboring under a rule of law that has long been recognized as inequitable. The Legislature did enact a statute in 1887 which applied the principle of comparative negligence to railroad accidents. We held the statute unconstitutional under the due process and equal protection clauses of the Federal and State constitutions because it was of limited scope and not of *general* application. Georgia Southern & Florida Railway Co. v. Seven–Up Bottling Co., 175 So.2d 39 (Fla.1965). Our Legislature again addressed the problem in 1943, when a comparative negligence statute of general application was passed by both houses. This bill was vetoed by the Governor and the Legislature would not override the veto. Senate Journal, Regular Session, 1943, pp. 716–717. One man thus prevented this State from now operating under a much more equitable system of recovery for negligent personal injuries and property damage. Since that "defeat," the Legislature has done little to discard the harsh and inequitable contributory negligence rule, perhaps because it considers the problem to be a judicial one.

Since we definitely consider the problem to be a judicial one, we feel the time has come for this Court to join what seems to be a trend toward almost universal adoption of comparative negligence. A primary function of a court is to see that legal conflicts are equitably resolved. In the field of tort law, the most equitable result that can ever be reached by a court is the equation of liability with fault. Comparative negligence does this more completely than contributory negligence, and we would be shirking our duty if we did not adopt the better doctrine.

Therefore, we now hold that a plaintiff in an action based on negligence will no longer be denied any recovery because of his contributory negligence.

If it appears from the evidence that both plaintiff and defendant were guilty of negligence which was, in some degree, a legal cause of the injury to the plaintiff, this does not defeat the plaintiff's recovery entirely. The jury in assessing damages would in that event award to the plaintiff such damages as in the jury's judgment the negligence of the defendant caused to the plaintiff. In other words, the jury should apportion the negligence of the plaintiff and the negligence of the defendant; then, in reaching the amount due the plaintiff, the jury should give the plaintiff only such an amount proportioned with his negligence and the negligence of the defendant. * * *

This rule should not be construed so as to entitle a person to recover for damage in a case where the proof shows that the defendant could not by the exercise of due care have prevented the injury, or where the defendant's negligence was not a legal cause of the damage. Stated differently, there can be no apportionment of negligence where the negligence of the defendant is not directly a legal cause of the result complained of by the plaintiff. A plaintiff is barred from recovering damages for loss or injury caused by the negligence of another only when the plaintiff's negligence is the sole legal cause of the damage, or the negligence of the plaintiff and some person or persons other than the defendant or defendants was the sole legal cause of the damage.

If plaintiff and defendant are both at fault, the former may recover, but the amount of his recovery may be only such proportion of the entire damages plaintiff sustained as the defendant's negligence bears to the combined negligence of both the plaintiff and the defendant. For example, where it is found that the plaintiff's negligence is at least equal to that of the defendant, the amount awarded to the plaintiff should be reduced by one-half from what it otherwise would have been.

The doctrine of last clear chance would, of course, no longer have any application in these cases. * * *

We decline herein to dissect and discuss all the possible variations of comparative negligence which have been adopted in other jurisdictions. Countless law review commentaries and treatises can be found which have covered almost every conceivable mutation of the basic doctrine. Suffice it to say that we consider the "pure form" of comparative negligence—as we have phrased it above—to be the most equitable method of allocating damages in negligence actions.

In the usual situation where the negligence of the plaintiff is at issue, as well as that of the defendant, there will undoubtedly be a counterclaim filed. The cross-plaintiff (just as plaintiff in the main suit) guilty of some degree of negligence would be entitled to a verdict awarding him such damages as in the jury's judgment were proportionate with his negligence and the negligence of cross-defendant. This could result in two verdicts— one for plaintiff and one for cross-plaintiff. In such event the Court should enter one judgment in favor of the party receiving the larger verdict, the amount of which should be the difference between the two verdicts. This is in keeping with the long recognized principles of "set off" in contract litigation. The Court's primary responsibility is to enter a judgment which reflects the true intent of the jury, as expressed in its verdict or verdicts.

In rare cases the net result of two such claims will be that the party more responsible for an accident will recover more than the party less responsible. On the surface, this might seem inequitable. However, using an extreme example, let us assume that a plaintiff is 80 per cent responsible for an automobile accident and suffers $20,000 in damages, and that the defendant—20 per cent responsible—fortunately suffers no damages. The liability of the defendant in such a case should not depend upon what damages he *suffered*, but upon what damages he *caused*. If a jury found that this defendant had been negligent and that his negligence, in relation to that of the plaintiff, was 20 per cent responsible for causing the accident then he should pay 20 per cent of the total damages, regardless of the fact that he has been fortunate enough to not be damaged personally.

Petitioners in this cause, and various amicus curiae who have filed briefs, have raised many points which they claim we must consider in adopting comparative negligence, such as the effects of such a change on the concept of "assumption of risk," and no "contribution" between joint tortfeasors. We decline to consider all those issues, however, for two reasons. One reason is that we already have a body of case law in this State dealing with comparative negligence, under our earlier railroad statute. Much of this case law will be applicable under the comparative negligence rule we are now adopting generally.

The other reason is that it is not the proper function of this Court to decide unripe issues, without the benefit of adequate briefing, not involving an actual controversy, and unrelated to a specific factual situation.

We are fully confident that the trial court judges of this State can adequately handle any problems created by our change to a comparative negligence rule as these problems arise. The answers to many of the problems will be obvious in light of the purposes for which we adopt the rule stated above:

(1) To allow a jury to apportion fault as it sees fit between negligent parties whose negligence was part of the legal and proximate cause of any loss or injury; and

(2) To apportion the total damages resulting from the loss or injury according to the proportionate fault of each party.

In accomplishing these purposes, the trial court is authorized to require special verdicts to be returned by the jury and to enter such judgment or judgments as may truly reflect the intent of the jury as expressed in any verdict or verdicts which may be returned.

We recognize the thousands of pending negligence cases affected by this decision. In fact, the prospect of a general upheaval in pending tort litigation has always been a deterring influence in considering the adoption of a comparative negligence rule. * * * We feel the trial judges of this State are capable of applying this comparative negligence rule without our setting guidelines in anticipation of expected problems. The problems are more appropriately resolved at the trial level in a practical manner instead of a theoretical solution at the appellate level. The trial judges are granted broad discretion in adopting such procedure as may accomplish the objectives and purposes expressed in this opinion.

Determining the time when the comparative negligence rule shall be applied at the trial level presents another problem. The confusion created by the premature adoption of the comparative negligence rule by the District Court of Appeal is further exemplified by the fact that some trial judges, relying on the decision, have applied the rule in the trial of many cases. Other trial judges have conducted their trials in accordance with the law of contributory negligence.

Under the circumstances, we hold that this opinion shall be applied as follows:

1. As to those cases in which the comparative negligence rule has been applied, this opinion shall be applicable.

2. As to those cases already commenced, but in which trial has not yet begun, this opinion shall be applicable.

3. As to those cases in which trial has already begun or in which verdict or judgment has already been rendered, this opinion shall not be applicable, unless the applicability of the comparative negligence rule was appropriately and properly raised during some stage of the litigation.

4. As to those cases on appeal in which the applicability of the comparative negligence rule has been properly and appropriately made a question of appellate review, this opinion shall be applicable.

5. This opinion shall be applicable to all cases commenced after the decision becomes final.

The certified question having now been answered in full, this cause is remanded to the District Court of Appeal, Fourth District, to be further remanded to the Circuit Court for a new trial.

In order to finalize the determination of the question in this case as expeditiously as possible, this decision is made effective immediately and a petition for rehearing will not be allowed.

It is so ordered.

ROBERTS, JUSTICE (dissenting).

I must respectfully dissent from the majority opinion in this cause. My primary concern is whether this Court is empowered to reject and replace the established doctrine of contributory negligence by judicial decree.

The sovereign powers of this State are divided into three coordinate branches of government—legislative, judicial and executive—by the Constitution of Florida, Article II, Section 3. Our Constitution specifically prohibits a person belonging to one of such branches from exercising any powers "appertaining to either of the other branches unless expressly provided herein." This Court has been diligent in preserving and maintaining the doctrine of separation of powers, which doctrine was imbedded in both the state and federal constitutions at the threshhold of constitutional democracy in this country, and under which doctrine the judiciary has no power to make statutory law. * * * It is the statutory law of this state that,

> "The common and statute laws of England which are of a general and not a local nature, with the exception hereinafter mentioned, down to the fourth day of July, 1776, are declared to be of force in this state; provided, the said statutes and common law be not inconsistent with the constitution and laws of the United States and the acts of the legislature of this state." Florida Statutes, Section 2.01, F.S.A.

The doctrine of contributory negligence was a part of the common law of England prior to July 4, 1776, and therefore, is part of the common law of this state pursuant to Florida Statutes, Section 2.01, F.S.A., and is secure from the desires of this Court to supplant it by the doctrine of comparative negligence, provided that it is not inconsistent with the Constitution and laws of the United States and the Constitution and acts of the Legislature of this state. * * * Furthermore, we have held that courts are bound by the rule of stare decisis to follow common law as it has been judicially declared in previously adjudicated cases. * * *

The question presently before this Court is whether this Court should replace the doctrine of contributory negligence with the concept of comparative negligence. Sub judice, by applying the doctrine of contributory negligence, the trial court correctly followed the precedent set down by this Court in Louisville and Nashville Railroad Co. v. Yniestra, 21 Fla. 700 (1886), and its progeny. This Court in *Yniestra* recognized and described contributory negligence as "the law as it unquestionably stands," * * *.

Although the case of Butterfield v. Forrester, 11 East 60, 103 Eng.Rep. 926 (K.B.1809), is recognized as a leading case in the area of contributory negligence, such case was not the first pronouncement of the common law doctrine of contributory negligence. * * *

The brief opinions of Bayley, J. and Lord Ellenborough in *Forrester* were merely a restatement of the concept of common law contributory negligence. If this case was the origin of common law contributory negligence, then clearly it would not have been adopted as part of the statutory law of this state through Florida Statutes, Section 2.01, F.S.A., because that decision was rendered subsequent to July 4, 1776.

I note with much interest the comment by Wex S. Malone in, "The Formative Era of Contributory Negligence," 41 Illinois Law Review, 151, to the following effect:

> "The concise opinions of Bayley and Lord Ellenborough in Butter-field v. Forrester (1809) afford no indication that either of those judges felt at the time that he was charting new paths for law."

Contributory negligence was adopted much earlier as a part of the common law. In Bayly v. Merrell, Cro.Jac. 386, 79 Eng.Rep. 331 (1606), the Court explicated,

> "[I]f he doubted of the weight thereof, he might have weighed it; and was not bound to give credence to another's speech; *and being his own negligence*, he is without remedy." (Emphasis supplied) * * *

Charles Beach in 1882 traced the doctrine of contributory negligence back to its origin in his treatise on contributory negligence, wherein he set out,

> "Our Anglo–American law of Negligence, including, as of course, that of Contributory Negligence, has come down to us, in ordinary generation, from the civil law of imperial Rome. It is a part of that great debt which the common law owes to the classical and the scholastic jurisprudence." Beach on Contributory Negligence, § 1, p. 1 (1882). * * *

Although he expressed a personal view of dislike for the operation of the principle of contributory negligence, Chief Justice McWhorter recognized in Louisville and Nashville Railroad Co. v. Yniestra, supra, the inability of this Court to change the common law rule of contributory negligence when he applied the existing law required to the facts of the case before him. He observed,

> "The law, in cases at least where human life is concerned, certainly needs *legislative* revision." (Emphasis supplied) 21 Fla. 700, p. 738.

By virtue of Florida Statutes, Section 2.01, contributory negligence is in force and said doctrine can be modified or replaced only by legislation to the contrary. Interposition of judicial power to make a legislative change in a statute which the Legislature on numerous occasions has refused to do is a clear invasion of the legislative.

In fine, the primary question is not whether or not the law of contributory negligence should be changed, but rather, who should do the changing. Contributory negligence was recognized in the common law as far back as A.D. 1606 and made a part of the statute law of this State in A.D. 1829, and thus far not changed by statute. If such a fundamental change is to be made in the law, then such modification should be made by the legislature where proposed change will be considered by legislative committees in public hearing where the general public may have an opportunity to be heard and should not be made by judicial fiat. Such an excursion into the field of legislative jurisdiction weakens the concept of separation of powers and our tripartite system of government.

For the foregoing reasons, I respectfully dissent.

Notes

1. What do you think of the constitutional theory that permits the majority to dismiss the failure of comparative negligence to be adopted in 1943: "One man thus prevented this state from now operating under a much more equitable system. * * *"?

2. This case illustrates again the point made in *Fowler v. Lanning* in Chapter One, *supra* (p. 29), namely the difficulty of establishing what the common law was, particularly in areas in which the old forms of action dictated the procedure. Moreover, it was not until the late eighteenth and early nineteenth centuries that the great volume of highway cases that presented these issues started reaching the courts.

3. If contributory negligence is to be traced to *Butterfield v. Forrester*, is it not fatuous to maintain—as the majority's opinion indicates some have maintained—that contributory negligence was adopted to promote industrial development (and particularly railroad development)? On a more concrete level, it has been asserted that the historical evidence does not support this relatively crude kind of economic determinism. *See* G. Schwartz, *Tort Law and the Economy in Nineteenth–Century America: A Reinterpretation*, 90 Yale L.J. 1717 (1981).

4. "Fla.Stat., § 201, F.S.A." mentioned in the majority's opinion and quoted in the dissent is what is called a *reception statute*. Such statutes started to be enacted after the break with Great Britain in order to establish what were to be the rules of decision in the courts of the newly independent states. July 4, 1776, the date adopted by Florida, is one of the typical dates chosen. Virginia distinguishes between the common law and statutes. The current Virginia version of these statutes provides for the continuance in force of the common law of England "insofar as it is not repugnant to the Bill of Rights and Constitution of this state" and of acts of Parliament "in aid of the common law prior to the fourth year of the reign of James the First" (1607). Va.Code 1950, §§ 1–10 and 1–11. *See also* Colo.Rev.Stat. 2–4–211. In its constitution of 1777, New York opted for April 19, 1775 (§ 35) for both common law and statutes, but subsequent legislation deprived English and colonial statutes of any force as legislation. N.Y.—McKinney's Gen.Construct.Law §§ 70–72.

5. *Hoffman v. Jones* was followed by four other judicial abrogations of the traditional rule that contributory negligence is a complete defense. *See e.g.*, Kaatz v. State, 540 P.2d 1037 (Alaska 1975); Li v. Yellow Cab Co., 13 Cal.3d 804, 119 Cal.Rptr. 858, 532 P.2d 1226 (1975); Kirby v. Larson, 400 Mich. 585, 256 N.W.2d 400 (1977), as extended in Placek v. City of Sterling Heights, 405 Mich. 638, 275 N.W.2d 511 (1979); Alvis v. Ribar, 85 Ill.2d 1, 52 Ill.Dec. 23, 421 N.E.2d 886 (1981). In 1991 and 1992, two more states adopted comparative negligence by judicial decision: Nelson v. Concrete Supply Co., 303 S.C. 243, 399 S.E.2d 783 (1991); McIntyre v. Balentine, 833 S.W.2d 52 (Tenn.1992). Both adopted modified systems, however similar to that presented in the *Bradley* case, which follows next. The Supreme Court of Alabama recently considered making the change and decided not to. Williams v. Delta Int'l Machinery Corp., 619 So.2d 1330 (Ala.1993). Most states that have adopted comparative negligence, however, have done so by statute.

BRADLEY v. APPALACHIAN POWER CO.

Supreme Court of Appeals of West Virginia, 1979.
163 W.Va. 332, 256 S.E.2d 879.

MILLER, JUSTICE:

In these two cases, which have been consolidated on appeal, we are asked to re-examine and ameliorate the common law doctrine of contributory negligence.

In each case the plaintiff sought by way of an instruction to utilize the doctrine of comparative negligence to avoid the defense of contributory negligence. The tendered instruction was rejected and the usual contributory negligence instruction was given, with the jury returning a verdict for the defendant in each case.

I

The doctrine of contributory negligence is generally thought to have originated in the English common law in Butterfield v. Forrester, 11 East 60, 103 Eng.Rep. 926 (K.B.1809), where the plaintiff, a horseman, was barred from recovery for his injuries when his horse ran into a pole. The pole had been left projecting onto the public road by the defendant, an adjoining landowner who was repairing his house.[7]

There can be no doubt that the doctrine of contributory negligence was judicially created.

There is an almost universal dissatisfaction among leading scholars of tort law with the harshness of the doctrine of contributory negligence. Neither intensive scholarship nor complex legal arguments need be advanced to demonstrate its strictness. A plaintiff can, if the jury is faithful to the contributory negligence instruction it receives, be barred from recovery if his negligence "contributed in the slightest degree" to the accident. * * * Thus, our system of jurisprudence, while based on concepts of justice and fair play, contains an anomaly in which the slightest negligence of a plaintiff precludes any recovery and thereby excuses the defendant from the consequences of all of his negligence, however great it may be.

There have been several judicial modifications of the severity of contributory negligence. Under the doctrine of last clear chance, the plaintiff's contributory negligence is excused if it can be shown that the defendant had the last opportunity to avoid the accident. * * *

The defense of contributory negligence is also not available where the defendant is found to be guilty of wanton and wilful misconduct. * * *

---

7. At least one commentator has questioned whether Butterfield v. Forrester, 11 East 60, 103 Eng.Rep. 926 (K.B.1809), was the first common law contributory negligence case. W. S. Malone in "The Formative Era of Contributory Negligence," 41 Ill.L.Rev. 151 (1946), states:

"The concise opinions of Bayley and Lord Ellenborough in *Butterfield v. Forrester* (1809) afford no indication that either of those judges felt at the time that he was charting new paths for the law."

Justice Roberts, dissenting in Hoffman v. Jones, 280 So.2d 431, 442 (Fla.1973), makes this assertion:

"Contributory negligence was adopted much earlier as a part of the common law.... Bayly v. Merrel, Cro.Jac. 386, 79 Eng.Rep. 331 (1606)...."

This result is justified on what is roughly a comparative negligence theory, whereby the intentional tort of the defendant makes trivial the simple negligence of the plaintiff. Perhaps this same explanation may also be the basis for barring contributory negligence where the defendant is subject to strict liability * * *.

In some instances the doctrine of contributory negligence is not available where the defendant violates a statute clearly designed for the protection of the plaintiff. * * *.

Legislatures in a number of states have enacted comparative negligence statutes of one variety or another. The basic framework of these statutes is to permit a negligent plaintiff to recover so long as his negligence does not exceed some established percentage, usually 50 percent.[8] Such statutes require that his recovery be reduced by the percentage of contributory negligence found to exist.

Four states—Alaska, California, Florida, and Michigan—have by judicial decision abolished the doctrine of contributory negligence and substituted in its place a "pure" comparative negligence concept. Under this principle, a plaintiff may recover regardless of the degree of his contributory negligence, but the jury is required to reduce his award in proportion to his contributory negligence.

Most commentators and the four courts which have adopted the pure comparative negligence position are critical of the 50 percent approach, primarily on the basis that it involves the drawing of an arbitrary line beyond which contributory negligence can still be asserted as a bar to the plaintiff's action. The basis of this criticism is expressed in Li v. Yellow Cab Co., 13 Cal.3d 804, 827–28, 119 Cal.Rptr. 858, 874–75, 532 P.2d 1226, 1242–43 (1975):

"We have concluded that the 'pure' form of comparative negligence is that which should be adopted in this state. In our view the '50 percent' system simply shifts the lottery aspect of the contributory negligence rule to a different ground. As Dean Prosser has noted, under such a system '[i]t is obvious that a slight difference in the proportionate fault may permit a recovery; and there has been much justified criticism of a rule under which a plaintiff who is charged with 49 percent of a total negligence recovers 51 percent of his damages, while one who is charged with 50 percent recovers nothing at all.' " [Footnotes omitted]

The difficulty with the pure comparative negligence rule, however, is that it focuses solely on the hypothetical "plaintiff" without recognizing that once pure comparative negligence is embraced, all parties whose negligence or fault combined to contribute to the accident are automatically potential plaintiffs unless a particular party is found to be 100 percent at fault.

The fundamental justification for the pure comparative negligence rule is its fairness in permitting everyone to recover to the extent he is not at fault. Thus, the eye of the needle is "no fault," and we are asked not to

---

8. Four states—Mississippi, New York, Rhode Island and Washington—have by statute adopted "pure" comparative negligence, whereby the plaintiff can recover so long as he is not 100 percent negligent.

think about the larger aspect—the camel representing "fault." It is difficult, on theoretical grounds alone, to rationalize a system which permits a party who is 95 percent at fault to have his day in court as a plaintiff because he is 5 percent fault-free.

The practical result of such a system is that it favors the party who has incurred the most damages regardless of his amount of fault or negligence. To illustrate, a plaintiff who has sustained a moderate injury with a potential jury verdict of $20,000, and who is 90 percent fault-free, may be reluctant to file suit against a defendant who is 90 percent, at fault, but who has received severe injuries and whose case carries a potential of $800,000 in damages from a jury verdict. In this situation, even though the defendant's verdict is reduced by his 90 percent fault to $80,000, it is still far in excess of the plaintiff's potential recovery of $18,000.[9]

While it can be conceded that there is an obvious injustice in the current contributory negligence rule which bars recovery no matter how slight the plaintiff's negligence, nevertheless the pure comparative negligence rule seems equally extreme at the other end of the spectrum. None of the courts which have adopted the pure comparative negligence rule have discussed the problems addressed above, and are content to rest their holdings on the following syllogism: (1) the contributory negligence rule is draconian in its operation; (2) the legislative solution of apportioning the plaintiff's fault up to 50 percent is an arbitrary line-drawing lottery;[10] (3) therefore, the pure comparative negligence rule is fairer.

The Michigan court in Kirby v. Larson, 400 Mich. 585, 637–41, 256 N.W.2d 400, 425–27 (1977), besides relying heavily on *Li v. Yellow Cab Co.*, supra, quotes at length from United States v. Reliable Transfer Co., 421 U.S. 397 (1975), where the United States Supreme Court abandoned its divided damages rule in admiralty in favor of apportioned damages based on the respective fault of the involved vessels. It may be seriously questioned whether an admiralty rule involving damage to vessels has much relevance to the common law doctrine of contributory negligence.[11]

9. The courts which have adopted the pure comparative negligence rule have not discussed this type of result. They also appear to proceed on the unstated assumption that all accidents will be covered by sufficient insurance to pay all the verdicts stemming from a multi-party accident. This premise is never documented. If we consider the text illustration and assume the plaintiff has a modest insurance limit of $50,000 for any one injury, the potential exposure to an $80,000 net verdict in favor of the 90–percent-at-fault, but seriously damaged defendant, creates a substantial practical bar to a suit. It is doubtful that a competent attorney would advise the plaintiff to sue, since the plaintiff's claim has a maximum jury potential of $20,000, which nets $18,000 when reduced by his 10 percent fault or contributory negligence. This leaves the plaintiff with a potential $12,000 uninsured exposure even after he recovers his $18,000 and pays it to the defendant along with his $50,000 worth of insurance to satisfy the defendant's $80,000 net verdict.

10. The argument that the difference between recovery at 49 percent contributory negligence and no recovery at 50 percent or above is an arbitrary line, is probably more theoretical than real. It is doubtful that any jury will be able to slice contributory negligence so thinly, a point which Prosser notes in his article *Comparative Negligence* in 41 Cal.L.Rev. at 25. In all probability, when the contributory negligence rises near the 50 percent level the jury will conclude that plaintiff is guilty of such substantial contributory negligence that it will fix his percentage at 50 or higher to bar his recovery.

11. As noted in 2 Am.Jur.2d *Admiralty* § 1 (1962), the development of admiralty in England was independent of the common law courts and against their opposition. * * * Apart from the federal statutory rights noted below, the traditional maritime remedy for injured seamen was a suit for maintenance and cure—basically medical and per diem support—which arises out of neither contract

The history of the common law is one of gradual judicial development and adjustment of the case law to fit the changing conditions of society. We see no practical benefit to be gained by the radical break from the common law's tort-fault methodology that the pure comparative negligence rule requires. There are basic inequities inherent in the pure comparative negligence rule and its resulting singular emphasis on the amount of damages and insurance coverage as the ultimate touchstone of the viability of instituting a suit.[12]

We do not accept the major premise of pure comparative negligence that a party should recover his damages regardless of his fault, so long as his fault is not 100 percent. Without embarking on an extended philosophical discussion of the nature and purpose of our legal system, we do state that in the field of tort law we are not willing to abandon the concept that where a party substantially contributes to his own damages, he should not be permitted to recover for any part of them. We do recognize that the present rule that prohibits recovery to the plaintiff if he is at fault in the slightest degree is manifestly unfair, and in effect rewards the substantially negligent defendant by permitting him to escape any responsibility for his negligence.

Our present judicial rule of contributory negligence is therefore modified to provide that a party is not barred from recovering damages in a tort action so long as his negligence or fault does not equal or exceed the combined negligence or fault of the other parties involved in the accident. To the extent that our prior contributory negligence cases are inconsistent with this rule, they are overruled.

II

Some explanation is warranted as to how this new rule operates. We do not intend to consider exhaustively all the particular ramifications of the new rule, since they are best resolved within the particular factual framework of the individual case.

We do state what may be the obvious, that the sum of the negligence of all the parties to a given accident cannot exceed 100 percent. Furthermore, it will be the jury's obligation to assign the proportion or degree of this total negligence among the various parties, beginning with the plaintiff.

nor tort, but rather as an incident of their status. The only other remedy was under the doctrine of unseaworthiness, a doctrine akin to a breach of warranty action founded on the duty to have a seaworthy vessel, in which negligence was not a factor. * * *

Kirby also quotes note 13 of *United States v. Reliable Transfer Co.,* * * * where the Supreme Court mentions the statutory, comparative negligence rule in the Jones Act, 46 U.S.C. § 688, and in the Death on the High Seas Act, 46 U.S.C. § 766. However, since these statutes give relief only to the injured seamen and are not designed to permit the employer-defendant to countersue, they have no real analogy to the pure comparative negligence rule, whereby the defendant may also be a plaintiff. The same is true under the Federal Employers Liability Act, 45 U.S.C. § 51, *et seq.*

12. We acknowledge that in any legal system permitting recovery of damages, the amount actually recovered ultimately depends on the financial solvency of the defendant. To create, however, as does the pure comparative negligence rule, a system where plaintiff's decision to sue may depend not on the degree to which he is free from fault but on his financial ability to withstand the countersuit, is to emphasize unduly the damage aspect and to obscure the relative fault of the parties.

The requirements of proximate cause have not been altered by the new rule. Consequently, before any party is entitled to recover, it must be shown that the negligence of the defendant was the proximate cause of the accident and subsequent injuries. The same is true of contributory fault or negligence. Before it can be counted against a plaintiff, it must be found to be the proximate cause of his injuries.

The jury should be required by general verdict to state the total or gross amount of damages of each party whom they find entitled to a recovery, and by special interrogatory the percentage of fault or contributory negligence, if any, attributable to each party. After the verdicts have been accepted, the trial court will calculate the net amount by deducting the party's percentage of fault from his gross award. To this extent, we follow the mechanics of the jury verdict award employed by the courts which have adopted pure comparative negligence, which is compatible with most of the statutory approaches. V. Schwartz, *Comparative Negligence* (1974), § 17.4, at 282, *et seq.*

Our comparative negligence rule has no effect on the plaintiff's right to sue only one of several joint tortfeasors. However, as we pointed out in Haynes v. City of Nitro, W.Va., 240 S.E.2d 544 (1977), the joint tortfeasor so sued may implead the other joint tortfeasors as third-party defendants. *Haynes* established that there is an inchoate right of contribution between joint tortfeasors in advance of judgment except where the act is *malum in se*. Thus, while the original defendant may have to respond only to the plaintiff for the latter's damages, the defendant in the third-party action can have these damages apportioned among the third-party defendants.

Haynes enables a joint tortfeasor to institute a third-party action before judgment in order to bring in the other joint tortfeasors to have them share in any liability that he may be found to have with regard to the plaintiff. * * * *Haynes* is designed to moderate the inequity which existed in our law that enabled the plaintiff to cast the entire responsibility for an accident on one of several joint tortfeasors by deciding to sue only him.

Neither our comparative negligence rule nor *Haynes* is designed to alter our basic law which provides for joint and several liability among joint tortfeasors after judgment. * * * Most courts which have considered the question after either a statutory or judicial adoption of some form of comparative negligence have held that the plaintiff can sue one or more joint tortfeasors, and if more than one is sued and a joint judgment is obtained, he may collect the entire amount from any one of the defendants. * * *

Our comparative negligence rule does not change the right of a joint tortfeasor to obtain a *pro tanto* credit on the plaintiff's judgment for monies obtained by the plaintiff in a settlement with another joint tortfeasor. * * *

Since we have not completely abolished the doctrine of contributory negligence, we recognize that in appropriate circumstances the doctrine of last clear chance is still available. In the case of an intentional tort, contributory negligence is not a defense. * * * Therefore, comparative negligence would not come into play, and the plaintiff would recover his damages undiminished by any contributory negligence.

By way of summary, we believe that moderating the harshness of our contributory negligence rule achieves a more satisfactory balance in the allocation of fault as it relates to recovery in our tort system. Our comparative negligence rule still bars the substantially negligent plaintiff[13] from obtaining a recovery, but it does permit the plaintiff who is more than slightly at fault to recover his injuries diminished by his percentage of contributory negligence. The rule is an intermediate position between the absolute bar of the present contributory negligence rule and the almost total permissiveness of the pure comparative negligence rule. It represents a considerable improvement over the present rule without undertaking a radical change in our present fault-based tort system, as would be the case with pure comparative negligence.

III

Finally, we address the question of the applicability of the rule here announced to cases now pending. * * *

In the four states which have adopted pure comparative negligence, a rule which we consider to be a much more radical departure than our new rule, two states [Alaska and Florida] have accorded what amounts to full retroactivity to their decision. * * * In *Kirby v. Larson,* * * * the Michigan court limited the applicability of its pure comparative negligence rule "to the present case and to those cases filed after the date of this decision." However, in Placek v. City of Sterling Heights, 405 Mich. 638, 275 N.W.2d 511, 521–22 (1979), the court acknowledged that the retroactivity rule of *Kirby* was too restrictive, and decided to extend complete retroactivity to its pure comparative negligence rule.

California, in *Li v. Yellow Cab Co.,* * * * accorded retroactivity of its pure comparative negligence rule to cases which had not reached the trial stage prior to the date of the *Li* opinion, but denied it as to other cases on appeal.

We thus find that the cases have generally extended retroactivity to the pure comparative negligence rule. * * * Under the foregoing analysis of retroactivity, we hold that the new rule of comparative negligence is fully retroactive.

For the foregoing reasons, the judgment in each case is reversed and the cases are remanded for further proceedings not inconsistent with this opinion.

Reversed and remanded.

3. *Some Representative Statutes*

THE FEDERAL EMPLOYERS LIABILITY ACT OF 1908

35 Stat. 66, as amended 45 U.S.C. §§ 53 and 54.

§ 53. **Contributory negligence; diminution of damages**

In all actions on and after April 22, 1908 brought against any such common carrier by railroad under or by virtue of any of the provisions of

---

13. From a purely mechanical standpoint, our new rule of comparative negligence means that where plaintiff's contributory negligence is equal to or above 50 percent of the combined negligence of the parties to the accident, he is barred from recovery. This obviously is the meaning of the phrase, "substantially negligent plaintiff."

this chapter to recover damages for personal injuries to an employee, or where such injuries have resulted in his death, the fact that the employee may have been guilty of contributory negligence shall not bar a recovery, but the damages shall be diminished by the jury in proportion to the amount of negligence attributable to such employee: *Provided*, That no such employee who may be injured or killed shall be held to have been guilty of contributory negligence in any case where the violation by such common carrier of any statute enacted for the safety of employees contributed to the injury or death of such employee.

§ 54. Assumption of risks of employment

In any action brought against any common carrier under or by virtue of any of the provisions of this chapter to recover damages for injuries to, or the death of, any of its employees, such employee shall not be held to have assumed the risks of his employment in any case [where such injury or death resulted in whole or in part from the negligence of any of the officers, agents, or employees of such carrier; and no employee shall be held to have assumed the risks of his employment in any case] where the violation by such common carrier of any statute enacted for the safety of employees contributed to the injury or death of such employee.[14]

ARKANSAS CODE OF 1987 ANNOTATED

§ 16–64–122. Comparative fault.

(a) In all actions for damages for personal injuries or wrongful death or injury to property in which recovery is predicated upon fault, liability shall be determined by comparing the fault chargeable to a claiming party with the fault chargeable to the party or parties from whom the claiming party seeks to recover damages.

(b)(1) If the fault chargeable to a party claiming damages is of a lesser degree than the fault chargeable to the party or parties from whom the claiming party seeks to recover damages, then the claiming party is entitled to recover the amount of his damages after they have been diminished in proportion to the degree of his own fault.

(2) If the fault chargeable to a party claiming damages is equal to or greater in degree than any fault chargeable to the party or parties from whom the claiming party seeks to recover damages, then the claiming party is not entitled to recover such damages.

(c) The word "fault" as used in this section includes any act, omission, conduct, risk assumed, breach of warranty, or breach of any legal duty which is a proximate cause of any damages sustained by any party.

NEW YORK CIVIL PRACTICE LAW & RULES (McKinney)

§ 1411. Damages recoverable when contributory negligence or assumption of risk is established

In any action to recover damages for personal injury, injury to property, or wrongful death, the culpable conduct attributable to the claimant or

---

14. The words in brackets were added in 1939 (53 Stat. 1404). (In 1920, the Jones Act made the provisions of the FELA applicable to actions brought against his employer by "any seaman" injured in the course of his employment. (46 U.S.C. app. § 688)).

to the decedent, including contributory negligence or assumption of risk, shall not bar recovery, but the amount of damages otherwise recoverable shall be diminished in the proportion which the culpable conduct attributable to the claimant or decedent bears to the culpable conduct which caused the damages.

WISCONSIN STATUTES ANNOTATED (West)

§ 895.045 Contributory negligence

Contributory negligence shall not bar recovery in an action by any person or his legal representative to recover damages for negligence resulting in death or in injury to person or property, if such negligence was not greater than the negligence of the person against whom recovery is sought, but any damages allowed shall be diminished in the proportion to the amount of negligence attributable to the person recovering.

UNIFORM COMPARATIVE FAULT ACT
Approved 1977, amended 1979.

Section 1.   [Effect of Contributory Fault]

(a) In an action based on fault seeking to recover damages for injury or death to person or harm to property, any contributory fault chargeable to the claimant diminishes proportionately the amount awarded as compensatory damages for an injury attributable to the claimant's contributory fault, but does not bar recovery. This rule applies whether or not under prior law the claimant's contributory fault constituted a defense or was disregarded under applicable legal doctrines, such as last clear chance.

(b) "Fault" includes acts or omissions that are in any measure negligent or reckless toward the person or property of the actor or others, or that subject a person to strict tort liability. The term also includes breach of warranty, unreasonable assumption of risk not constituting an enforceable express consent, misuse of a product for which the defendant otherwise would be liable, and unreasonable failure to avoid an injury or to mitigate damages. Legal requirements of causal relation apply both to fault as the basis for liability and to contributory fault.

[The remaining sections of the Uniform Comparative Fault Act deal with various subsidiary problems that will be taken up in the next chapter and will be considered further there.]

The statutory change in the law of Great Britain is:

LAW REFORM (CONTRIBUTORY NEGLIGENCE) ACT OF 1945
8 and 9 Geo. 6, C. 28, as amended.

An Act to amend the law relating to contributory negligence
and for purposes connected therewith

1.—(1) Where any person suffers damages as the result partly of his own fault and partly of the fault of any other person or persons, a claim in respect of that damage shall not be defeated by reason of the fault of the person suffering the damage, but the damages recoverable in respect thereof shall be reduced to such extent as the court thinks just and equitable having regard to the claimant's share in the responsibility for the damage:

Provided that—

(a) this subsection shall not operate to defeat any defence arising under a contract;

(b) where any contract or enactment providing for the limitation of liability is applicable to the claim, the amount of damages recoverable by the claimant by virtue of this subsection shall not exceed the maximum limit so applicable.

(2) Where damages are recoverable by any person by virtue of the foregoing subsection subject to such reduction as is therein mentioned, the court shall find and record the total damages which would have been recoverable if the claimant had not been at fault.

* * *

(5) Where, in any case to which subsection (1) of this section applies, one of the persons at fault avoids liability to any other such person or his personal representative by pleading the Limitation Act 1939, or any other enactment limiting the time within which proceedings may be taken, he shall not be entitled to recover any damages from that other person or representative by virtue of the said subsection.

(6) Where any case to which subsection (1) of this section applies is tried with a jury, the jury shall determine the total damages which would have been recoverable if the claimant had not been at fault and the extent to which those damages are to be reduced.

Notes

1. In addition to New York, Louisiana (LSA Civ.Code art. 2323), Mississippi (Miss.Code 1972, § 11–7–15), Rhode Island (R.I.Gen.L.1956, § 9–20–4), and Washington (Wash.Rev.Code Ann. § 4.22.005) have adopted statutory "pure" comparative negligence schemes. Most states with statutory schemes, as can be seen in the succeeding notes, have opted for one of the modified schemes.

2. The Arkansas ("less than") form of modified comparative negligence has been adopted also in Colorado (Colo.Rev.Stat. 13–21–111(1)); Idaho (Idaho Code § 6–801); Kansas (Kan.Stat.Ann. 60–258a); Maine (Me.Rev.Stat.Ann. tit. 14, § 156); North Dakota (N.D.Cent.Code 32.03.2–02); and Utah (Utah Code Ann.1953, 78–27–38).

3. The most popular form of statutory comparative negligence is the Wisconsin ("not greater than" i.e. less than or equal to) formula. This form has also been adopted in, e.g., Connecticut (Conn.Gen.Stat.Ann. § 52–572h); Hawaii (Hawaii Rev.Stat. § 663–31); Iowa (Iowa Code Ann. § 668.3); Massachusetts (Mass.Gen.Law Ann. c. 231, § 85); Minnesota (Minn.Stat.Ann. § 604.01 (West)); Montana (Mont.Code Ann. § 27–1–702); Nevada (Nev.Rev. Stat. 41.141); New Hampshire (N.H.Rev.Stat.Ann. 507:7–d); New Jersey (N.J.Stat.Ann. 2A:15–5.1 (West)); Ohio (Ohio Rev. Code Ann. § 2315.19); Oklahoma (Okla.Stat.Ann. tit. 23, § 13); Oregon (Or.Rev.Stat. 18.470); Penn-

sylvania (42 Pa.Cons.Stat.Ann. § 7102 (Purdon)); Texas (V.T.C.A., Civ.Prac. & Rem.Code § 33.001); Vermont (Vt.Stat.Ann. tit. 12, § 1036); and Wyoming (Wyo.Stat.1977, § 1–1–109).

4. Some Problems That Have Arisen in the Application of Comparative Negligence

a. While comparative negligence is the general term still in use to describe these various approaches to the treatment of plaintiff's conduct, the terms comparative fault and, more recently comparative responsibility have become more accurate in many situations. Comparative approaches have been applied in many states to cases other than those involving mere negligence, including not only, as we will see, intentional behavior, but also, in some states, strict liability contexts where there is no fault at all. See, e.g., Daly v. General Motors Corp., 20 Cal.3d 725, 144 Cal.Rptr. 380, 575 P.2d 1162 (1978)(applying comparative responsibility to strict products liability cases discussed *infra*, p. 712); *Restatement (Third) of Torts: Apportionment of Liability* § 1 (Preliminary Draft #2).

The obvious operational problem is what to include in the comparison. The Preliminary Draft of the *Restatement (Third) of Torts: Apportionment of Liability* in the Comment to § 9 provides:

> When assigning percentages of responsibility to parties or other relevant persons, the fact finder should consider the relative character and nature of each person's conduct, including how culpable or reprehensible was the conduct, how egregious was the failure to meet the applicable legal standard, and how extensively the conduct contributed as a proximate cause of the harm.

Most of statutes assign responsibility on the basis of the relative *degree* of fault. In several states, however, the comparison process expressly includes consideration of the causal contribution of each party to the total amount of damages suffered (*see, e.g.*, the Kansas, New Hampshire, and Vermont statutes). *See also* Lovesee v. Allied Development Corp., 45 Wis.2d 340, 173 N.W.2d 196 (1970).

b. It should come as no surprise that the advent of comparative fault has not prevented the application of *res ipsa loquitur*, with appropriate modifications. *See, e.g.*, Gordon v. Westinghouse Electric Corp., 42 Colo. App. 426, 599 P.2d 953 (1979); Cramer v. Mengerhausen, 275 Or. 223, 550 P.2d 740 (1976); Turk v. H. C. Prange Co., 18 Wis.2d 547, 119 N.W.2d 365 (1963).

c. What has been the practical impact of comparative negligence on the cost of liability insurance? Thus far there is little information available. What information is available is presented in the following description of a report submitted by a "study committee" of the North Carolina Research Commission:

> The committee, created pursuant to a joint resolution of the House and Senate, was instructed to "determine the cost and effects of changing from the current system to a comparative negligence tort

system" * * * and "to determine what laws should govern in negligence cases when both parties are, to some extent, negligent."

* * *

The committee first undertook "to determine the cost and effects of changing from the current system to a comparative negligence tort system". It was determined that some form of comparative negligence has been adopted either by legislative action or by judicial decision in thirty-five states and that no state which had adopted comparative negligence had ever abandoned the concept. Questionnaires were sent to the Insurance Commissioner of each of the thirty-five states which have adopted comparative negligence asking if the adoption of comparative negligence had (1) no impact, (2) caused a slight increase, (3) caused a moderate increase, or (4) caused a significant increase in insurance premiums. Twenty-four states responded to the questionnaire of which twelve indicated there had been no impact, six indicated that there was insufficient data to estimate the impact and six indicated a slight increase. It is significant to note that no state indicated either a moderate or significant increase in insurance premiums after the adoption of comparative negligence.

In addition to this survey, the committee staff contacted the major national insurance associations including the Insurance Information Institute, Insurance Services Office, Alliance of American Insurors, American Insurance Association, National Association of Independent Insurors and the North Carolina Association of Defense Attorneys to determine whether they had figures or were aware of published studies on possible effects of comparative negligence laws on liability insurance costs. None of these associations were able to supply the committee with any historical figures or statistics which shed any light on an actual increase in insurance rates attributable to the adoption of comparative negligence.

* * *

Warlick, 13 Trial Briefs of the N.C. Academy of Trial Lawyers 1–3 (No. 1, 1st quarter, 1981). For a critique of this study and the suggestion that its conclusions may be wrong, see Gardner, Contributory Negligence, Comparative Negligence, & Stare Decisis in North Carolina, 18 Campbell L. Rev. 1 (1996).

MARTEL v. MONTANA POWER CO.

Montana Supreme Court, 1988.
231 Mont. 96, 752 P.2d 140.

HUNT, JUSTICE:

Plaintiff Martel appeals the jury's special verdict finding the defendant Montana Power Company (MPC) 25% negligent; himself 75% negligent; and setting his damages at $290,000. He also appeals the order denying his motion for a new trial.

We affirm in part, reverse in part and remand with instructions.
* * *

On July 7, 1979, Terry Martel suffered permanent injuries as a result of being electrocuted when some portion of his body came within a few inches of an electric power transmission line carrying 100,000 volts. Martel testified that he had two beers with friends after they arrived at the old Piedmont Substation south of Whitehall, Montana. Martel was 19 at the time of the accident. The substation sits at the end of a short road off a county roadway.

After one other person climbed the tower, Martel also climbed it. A dispute in the facts exists as to whether Martel reached out to the line but the evidence is clear he did not touch the line. In any event, his proximity to the line caused electricity from the line to arc to his body causing serious injury.

The substation has a tower which supports the transmission line. The tower is crossed with metal brackets and sits on top of a concrete footing sunk in the ground. To climb it one must take a step from the ground to the footing, then to a bracket 17″ from the concrete footing, then to another bracket 2′ 3¾″ above, then to a bolt step 4′ 6¼″ above that. Beyond that is a series of bolt steps leading to the top of the tower. No barricades surrounded the tower. A wooden sign was near the tower. The sign had been painted over but the word "danger" was still visible.

The Milwaukee Road built the substation prior to 1920 and MPC acquired it in 1974. MPC employees drove by the tower site at least once a month to examine the site. One employee and the Whitehall town marshal Rand McLester offered testimony that neither had ever seen children or any other unauthorized people on the tower. * * *

Near the end of the plaintiff's case-in-chief the trial court ruled that plaintiff established a prima facie case of willful or wanton misconduct on the part of defendant power company. Although the court instructed the jury that they could find that MPC had acted willfully or wantonly, the court refused plaintiff's proposed instruction that comparative negligence was not an issue if they found the defendant had acted willfully or wantonly. The trial court correctly refused this instruction.

We said in Derenberger v. Lutey (1983), 207 Mont. 1, 674 P.2d 485, 487–88, 40 St.Rep. 902, 906, that comparative negligence is inapplicable when the action is based on willful and wanton misconduct. In that case, we made a distinction between conduct that is willful and wanton and conduct that is merely negligent. When the defendant's conduct is willful and wanton, the plaintiff's own mere negligence could not be used to offset his recovery. We now conclude that this distinction is faulty and expressly overrule Derenberger.

Prior to the enactment of comparative negligence, the rule preventing comparison of willful and wanton conduct and mere negligence served to ameliorate the harshness of the defense of contributory negligence which would bar all recovery to the plaintiff. Fortunately, we now operate under a scheme of comparative negligence where there is no danger of a plaintiff's slight negligence barring all recovery against a willful and wanton or grossly negligent defendant. See § 27–1–702, MCA as enacted in 1975 and amended in 1983. The rationale for the rule in Derenberger no longer exists.

It is more appropriate, then, as Justice Gulbrandson pointed out in his concurring and dissenting opinion in Derenberger, to adopt the interpretation from the state where our comparative negligence statute originated. The Wisconsin Supreme Court ruled that negligence in all its forms, gross, willful and wanton or ordinary, can be compared to and offset by each other under its comparative negligence statute. Bielski v. Schulze (1962), 16 Wis.2d 1, 114 N.W.2d 105, 111–114. In 1975, Montana adopted the Wisconsin statute. We hold, therefore, that all forms of conduct amounting to negligence in any form including but not limited to ordinary negligence, gross negligence, willful negligence, wanton misconduct, reckless conduct, and heedless conduct, are to be compared with any conduct that falls short of conduct intended to cause injury or damage. The trial court is affirmed on this issue. * * *

Since 1917, the legislature has incorporated the NESC [National Electrical Safety Code] in one form or another into the Montana statutes and requires utilities in Montana to construct, install and maintain lines and equipment so as to reduce hazards to life as far as practicable. Section 69–4–201, MCA * * * The manner in which the footing, braces and channel irons were configured to provide access to the bolt ladder that led to the top of the tower is a matter of construction and design standards, as is the matter of installing barriers around towers or signs. The standards of the NESC should not be limited to a narrow meaning of the word "construction" but should imply an obligation to comply with the standards in the broader sense of "design" as well. Although MPC did not initially construct the tower it must still bring its "design" within the NESC standards. This duty may also include elements of maintenance. * * *

One of the purposes of the NESC is to ensure the safeness of electrical systems that have life-threatening capabilities. If a utility can avoid complying with these standards by purchasing constructed lines and towers instead of constructing them itself, the NESC becomes ineffectual. It is unlikely that the legislature intended such a result when it incorporated the NESC into § 69–4–201, MCA. We have recognized that a violation of statutes intended to protect the public is negligence per se. Stepanek v. Kober Const. (Mont.1981), 625 P.2d 51, 55, 38 St.Rep. 385, 391. We therefore * * * hold that violations of maintenance and design standards intended to protect the public are also negligence per se. However, to be complete the trial court should inform the jury that in this action a violation of law is of no consequence unless it contributed as a proximate cause to an injury found by the jury to have been suffered by the plaintiff. * * *

Was it error for the trial court to refuse to tell the jury the effect of comparative negligence on the verdict?

We hold that it was error. The applicable statute, § 27–1–702, MCA (1978), provides that a plaintiff may recover damages for injury if the plaintiff's "negligence was not greater than the negligence of the person against whom recovery is sought, but any damages allowed shall be diminished in the proportion to the amount of negligence attributable to the person recovering." The purpose of this statute is to remove the harsh treatment of contributory negligence on the part of plaintiff under the old scheme that prevented any recovery for any negligence of the plaintiff.

MPC argues that the scale may have gone too far the other way, and juries informed of the legal effect of comparative negligence are overly generous to the negligent plaintiff. It argues that the jury's determination of damages will reflect the jury's sympathies for the plaintiff's injuries rather than reflect its computation of actual damages sustained and offset by the plaintiff's own negligence.

In opposition, Martel argues that juries, not informed of the legal effect of their apportionment of negligence, operate in the dark. This, he argues, makes it impossible to tell whether the amount of damages awarded is based on the jury's determination of actual damages or whether it is infected with speculation about the effect of its apportionment of negligence.

We have held that the jury can objectively consider the facts before it. Owens v. Parker Drilling Co. (1984), 207 Mont. 446, 676 P.2d 162, 166, 41 St.Rep. 66, 71. In fact, we have refused to order a new trial based upon the reasons defendant gives. In North v. Bunday (Mont.1987), 735 P.2d 270, 277, 44 St.Rep. 627, 636, we expressly recognized the integrity of the jury in determining negligence percentages when we stated:

> We cannot impugn the integrity of the jury that it indulged in that kind of manipulation. The single duty of the jury in this case was to determine the applicable percentages of negligence, if such negligence existed. We cannot order a new trial in this case upon the mere speculation that if the jury could foresee the precise effect of their factual determination, even though not called on to determine damages, their factual determination would be different from what they decided.

We are persuaded by appellant's argument that the jury speculated about the effect of its percentage determinations. During deliberations the jury sent a note to the judge, "Do the percentages in question #4 apply to monetary compensation in question #5?" The judge answered, "Dear Folks: You must answer each question separately by 8 or more of your number."

We think Montana juries can and should be trusted with the information about the consequences of their verdict. Other jurisdictions have considered this question and have come to differing conclusions. An excellent review of the holdings in those jurisdictions is set forth in the Idaho case of Seppi v. Betty (1978), 99 Idaho 186, 579 P.2d 683. After a lengthy discussion, the Idaho Supreme Court concluded that it is naive to believe that jurors do not speculate about the effect of their answers. To end speculation, the Idaho court said juries should be informed of the effect of their answers. * * * The Idaho court tempered its position by giving the trial court the discretion not to inform the jury in those cases where the issues are so complex or uncertain that the jury would only be confused. * * *

We adopt the reasoning of the Idaho Supreme Court and hold that under the circumstances of this case the jury should have been informed of the effect of its verdict. * * *

We affirm in part, reverse in part and remand.

Notes

1. A question that frequently came up before the advent of comparative negligence was whether the plaintiff's contributory negligence would bar recovery if the defendants conduct was more blameworthy. It was generally held that plaintiff's contributory negligence was not a defense if the defendant's conduct was intentional, wilful or wanton misconduct, or even grossly negligent conduct. This exception to the contributory negligence rule was a halfway house in the transition from contributory to comparative fault. For a recent rearticulation of this position, see Burke v. 12 Rothschild's Liquor Mart, 148 Ill.2d 429, 170 Ill.Dec. 633, 593 N.E.2d 522 (1992), in which the court, based partially upon the Illinois comparative fault act, held that the legislature had not intended to change the prevailing rule that plaintiff's contributory fault was not a defense if the defendant's fault was intentional or wilful or wanton misconduct.

2. *Gross negligence* is generally treated as a type of negligence and subject to the comparative treatment.[15] As to reckless or "wilful" conduct short of intentional conduct, the cases are divided, as noted in the *Martel* case. Several federal courts have ruled that there has been no change from the earlier rule in this regard, i.e., that plaintiff's negligent behavior was not even a partial defense to wilful and wanton misconduct. *See* Vargus v. Pitman Space Mf'g Co., 510 F.Supp. 116 (E.D.Pa.1981), *affirmed per curiam* 673 F.2d 1304 (3d Cir.), *affirmed on rehearing* 675 F.2d 73 (3d Cir.1982); Honeywell v. American Standards Testing Bureau, Inc., 851 F.2d 652 (3d Cir.1988). The state courts have split on this issue. Decisions declaring that the adoption of comparative negligence does not abrogate the common-law doctrines with respect to wilful and wanton misconduct include: Davies v. Butler, 95 Nev. 763, 602 P.2d 605 (1979); Draney v. Bachman, 138 N.J.Super. 503, 351 A.2d 409 (1976); Burke v. 12 Rothschild's Liquor Mart, 148 Ill.2d 429, 170 Ill.Dec. 633, 593 N.E.2d 522 (1992)(based in part on the wording of the Illinois statute). Cases agreeing with *Martel* and holding that wilful and wanton conduct is subject to comparative fault analysis include: Vining v. City of Detroit, 162 Mich.App. 720, 413 N.W.2d 486 (1987); Sorensen v. Allred, 112 Cal.App.3d 717, 169 Cal.Rptr. 441 (1980);[16] Wing v. Morse, 300 A.2d 491 (Me.1973). The Illinois court has distinguished between types of wilful and reckless misconduct, allowing comparisons in some cases but not in others. Poole v. City of Rolling Meadows, 167 Ill.2d 41, 212 Ill.Dec. 171, 656 N.E.2d 768 (1995).

3. Normally one guilty of intentionally injuring another has not been thought able to take advantage of a comparative fault scheme to reduce the damages assessed against him. However, there are an increasing number of

---

15. In Pedernales Electric Cooperative, Inc. v. Schulz, 583 S.W.2d 882 (Tex.Civ.App. 1979), the court treated gross negligence as a type of negligence, which was therefore subject to the comparison process, but at the same time allowed the assessment of punitive damages because of the defendant's gross negligence.

16. The soundness of this decision was questioned in Coudriet v. Southland Corp., 198 Cal.App.3d 849, 244 Cal.Rptr. 69 (1988), a decision that, by order of the Supreme Court of California, was not officially published.

cases that treat even intentional cases under comparative fault. See, e.g., Hickey v. Zezulka, 440 Mich. 1203, 487 N.W.2d 106 (1992); Blazovic v. Andrich, 124 N.J. 90, 590 A.2d 222 (1991); Barth v. Coleman, 118 N.M. 1, 878 P.2d 319 (N.M.1994). See also Comeau v. Lucas, 90 A.D.2d 674, 455 N.Y.S.2d 871 (4th Dept.1982); Jordan v. Britton, 128 A.D.2d 315, 515 N.Y.S.2d 678 (4th Dept.1987). The New York statute is unique in that it expressly refers to the "culpable conduct" of the parties rather than to their "negligence" or "fault." The Preliminary Draft (No. 2) of the *Restatement (Third) of Torts: Apportionment of Liability* includes all degrees of fault under the comparative scheme, including intentional behavior. The preliminary Reporters Notes to § 1 state that:

> Applying comparative responsibility to intentional torts is not the majority rule, but it commands a plurality among the courts that have addressed the question and has growing support, especially in cases apportioning damages among defendants. (Id. at 24–25.)

4. Before the advent of comparative negligence, when the plaintiff charged the defendant with a greater degree of fault than simple negligence but the jury found that the plaintiff's conduct measured up to the same degree of fault as the defendant's, the plaintiff would be completely barred from recovery. For example, consider the unhappy fate of Frank Elliott when he attempted to charge wanton and wilful misconduct by the defendant to save himself from his own negligent behavior. As reported by the Pennsylvania Supreme Court, the facts were as follows:

> At about 10:30 a.m., May 27, 1943, a clear day, plaintiff, a paper hanger by trade, was at the northwest corner of Haverford Avenue and Preston Street when he heard and saw a fire engine about a block away on Preston Street approaching southward toward Haverford Avenue; it was returning to the fire house on the northeast corner of Preston Street and Haverford Avenue. He also saw a street car approaching from the west on Haverford Avenue. He testified that on seeing the fire engine, he 'went out in the middle of the street [Haverford Avenue] and I stood there right in the middle of the car track' and 'waved to the trolley car' which was then 'at 41st and Haverford Avenue.' The distance between him and 41st Street was 421 feet. He was familiar with the neighborhood. He gave the speed of the trolley car as 'about 25 or 30 miles an hour.' At first he was 'facing the trolley car' but after a while he turned, facing northward, and 'waved for the fire engine to come on, and the trolley car kept moving toward me.' The car 'was coming about the same speed, around 30 miles an hour.' When the car struck him he was 'looking toward the fire engine.' The car stopped within its own length. The plaintiff had an unobstructed view as there was no other traffic on Haverford Avenue between 41st Street and the plaintiff. He testified that he had been facing the approaching car until it was between Budd Street and Ludwick Street, when he 'turned around and had my hands up and waved for the fire engine to come on * * *.' Budd Street was 232 feet from Preston Street where plaintiff stood and Ludwick Street was 75 feet from there. At the time he turned from facing the street car it must then have been at some point within the 232 feet distance between Budd and Preston Streets and must reach him within five or six seconds at the rate at which he said it was moving.

There was no reason why he remained standing in the car track to give the signals he described; he was not asked to give them. He appears to have volunteered to 'flag' the fire engine into Haverford Avenue. There is nothing to show that such 'flagging' was needed nor that the motorman on the street car should have known what plaintiff intended by 'waving' his arms. He might have given his signals just as well and in perfect safety while standing in the Avenue outside the range of the rapidly approaching car. He continued to stand in the tracks although a step or two would have taken him out of danger. By remaining on the track he also endangered the street car passengers.

* * *

Plaintiff's reckless conduct bars recovery for the result of defendant's wanton misconduct for the same reason that contributory negligence constitutes a defense to an action based on mere negligence. Contributory negligence is a defense because it introduces in a case a new cause of plaintiff's injury making defendant's negligence no longer the legal cause. So in this case, defendant's wanton misconduct, as a legal cause of injury, was superseded by plaintiff's wanton or reckless misconduct which became the legal cause of his injury.

Elliott v. Philadelphia Transp. Co., 356 Pa. 643, 645–648, 53 A.2d 81, 82–83 (1947). How would you characterize the plaintiff's behavior? How would you characterize the behavior of the trolley motorman? According to Justice Stearne, who dissented from the majority affirmance of a trial court j.n.o.v. for the defendant, "After the accident, the driver of the fire truck asked the motorman: 'What is the idea of hitting that man? Didn't you see that man?' The motorman replied: 'Sure, I saw the man, but what the hell is he doing on the track?'" 356 Pa. at 649, 53 A.2d at 84. Does this change your assessment?

5. These issues of fault of both parties arise frequently in connection with actions brought by passengers injured while riding with intoxicated drivers. The driver will defend on the ground that the passenger was contributorily negligent to ride in a vehicle driven by a person who had consumed alcoholic beverages. The plaintiff will respond by arguing that he or she did not appreciate how drunk the defendant really was and/or that the defendant behaved particularly recklessly. *See, e.g.,* Harlow v. Connelly, 548 S.W.2d 143 (Ky.App.1977); Cole v. Woods, 548 S.W.2d 640 (Tenn.1977). The issue also comes up in cases in which the action is against the provider of the alcoholic beverages to the plaintiff. In Ewing v. Cloverleaf Bowl, 20 Cal.3d 389, 143 Cal.Rptr. 13, 572 P.2d 1155 (1978), the defendant's bartender served a twenty-one year old man (boy?) 10 shots of 151 proof rum. He died the next day. It was held that a jury could find that the bartender's continued serving of such a potent drink to a hopelessly intoxicated person was reckless conduct which made the contributory negligence of the drinker irrelevant. For contrasting approaches under comparative negligence regimes, see Estate of Kelley v. Moguls, Inc., 160 Vt. 531, 632 A.2d 360 (1993)(the estate of the drunken driver was allowed to sue the vendor and the jury was permitted to allocate fault between the driver and the vendor under the comparative negligence statute), and Estate of Kelly v. Falin, 127 Wash.2d 31, 896 P.2d 1245 (1995)(the intoxicated driver's estate was not permitted to sue the vendor because that would encourage irresponsible drunk driving).

6. *Guest Statutes.* A number of states have "guest statutes," which restrict the right of a person who has been gratuitously furnished automobile transportation to bring an action against the owner or driver for injuries caused by the negligent operation of the vehicle. In some states, in order to recover from the host, the plaintiff must show gross negligence; in others—which are more typical—the injured passenger must go further and show wilful and wanton misconduct (*i.e.* recklessness). In a few states a similar result was reached by judicial decision. The effect of statutes requiring the plaintiff to show recklessness is to place the plaintiff in such actions in the same posture as a plaintiff in an ordinary personal injury action who has been shown to be contributorily negligent. Indeed, one can find cases under the guest statutes where the contributory negligence of the plaintiff was conceded and, regardless of the existence of the guest statute, recovery could only be had if the plaintiff could show recklessness. *See* Williams v. Carr, 68 Cal.2d 579, 68 Cal.Rptr. 305, 440 P.2d 505 (1968). That case involved a situation where the plaintiff had been out drinking with the defendant and fell asleep on the drive home. The accident occurred a few miles from home. The court held that a jury could find that the driver's continuing to drive after he had momentarily dozed off constituted recklessness.

What is the impact of the adoption of comparative responsibility upon guest statutes? Smith & Pitts, *Comparative Fault: A Primer*, 54 Ala. Law. 56 (1963), states:

> Some have argued that the adoption of comparative fault should impliedly repeal the guest statute. While the guest statute in a comparative fault case could produce some unkind results, no court in any state has held the adoption of comparative fault has impliedly repealed a guest statute.

7. The use of aggravated degrees of negligence in a limited class of cases has been attacked as a denial of the equal protection of the laws under both the federal constitution and the applicable state constitutions. In Brown v. Merlo, 8 Cal.3d 855, 106 Cal.Rptr. 388, 506 P.2d 212 (1973), the California guest statute was held to be unconstitutional under both the federal and California constitutions. The reasoning of the *Brown* case was followed in a number of other jurisdictions but it has also been rejected in a number of jurisdictions, including Cannon v. Oviatt, 520 P.2d 883 (Utah 1974), *appeal dismissed for want of a substantial federal question*, 419 U.S. 810, 95 S.Ct. 24, 42 L.Ed.2d 37 (1974). Since the *Cannon* decision and two subsequent decisions in which the Supreme Court likewise dismissed the appeals, most decisions striking down guest statutes have relied exclusively on the provisions of state constitutions. For cases subsequent to *Cannon*, with extensive citation to the earlier decisions, see Bierkamp v. Rogers, 293 N.W.2d 577 (Iowa 1980); Nehring v. Russell, 582 P.2d 67 (Wyo.1978).

5. *Last Clear Chance*

The doctrine of last clear chance developed very early in the history of contributory negligence. It recognized that negligently caused injuries often resulted from a sequence of events. The courts tried to allocate legal blame for the injury to the last party that had a chance to avoid the accident under the last clear chance doctrine. It worked primarily as a device to soften the impact of plaintiff's contributory negligence when the defendant had perceived the perilous position of the plaintiff (or in some manifestations of the doctrine, could have perceived) and could have avoided the accident by the exercise of reasonable care. This sequential analysis was very effective at putting the burden on the party who was the best accident avoider in many situations. The first case to articulate this idea was Davies v. Mann, 10 M. & W. 546, 152 Eng.Rep. 588 (Exch. 1842). In England the doctrine that evolved out of *Davies v. Mann* is called "the last opportunity rule."

RESTATEMENT (SECOND) OF TORTS (1965)

§ 479. Last Clear Chance: Helpless Plaintiff

A plaintiff who has negligently subjected himself to a risk of harm from the defendant's subsequent negligence may recover for harm caused thereby if, immediately preceding the harm,

(a) the plaintiff is unable to avoid it by the exercise of reasonable vigilance and care, and

(b) the defendant is negligent in failing to utilize with reasonable care and competence his then existing opportunity to avoid the harm, when he

(i) knows of the plaintiff's situation and realizes or has reason to realize the peril involved in it or

(ii) would discover the situation and thus have reason to realize the peril, if he were to exercise the vigilance which it is then his duty to the plaintiff to exercise.

§ 480. Last Clear Chance: Inattentive Plaintiff

A plaintiff who, by the exercise of reasonable vigilance, could discover the danger created by the defendant's negligence in time to avoid the harm to him, can recover if, but only if, the defendant

(a) knows of the plaintiff's situation, and

(b) realizes or has reason to realize that the plaintiff is inattentive and therefore unlikely to discover his peril in time to avoid the harm, and

(c) thereafter is negligent in failing to utilize with reasonable care and competence his then existing opportunity to avoid the harm.

Notes

1. The most common theoretical justification for the last clear chance doctrine is a causal one. Because she/he has had the last clear chance, the defendant's conduct is the proximate cause of the accident. The causal theory works in the case of the helpless plaintiff; it breaks down when the plaintiff is merely inattentive.

2. When the plaintiff is helpless *and* the defendant actually discovers the plaintiff's peril, almost all American jurisdictions permitted the plaintiff to recover, even if they otherwise purported to reject the doctrine of last clear chance. In these situations in which the plaintiff's helplessness had been discovered some courts were prepared to characterize the defendant's conduct as "willful and wanton." Where the plaintiff was helpless but the defendant did not actually discover the plaintiff's peril a majority of jurisdictions would apply the doctrine but, many jurisdictions would not accept the *Restatement*'s position. *See* Cartwright v. Harris, 400 N.E.2d 1192 (Ind.App.1980); Kumku-

mian v. City of New York, 305 N.Y. 167, 111 N.E.2d 865 (1953). Likewise, where the plaintiff is inattentive *and* the defendant is aware of the plaintiff's situation a majority of courts would follow the *Restatement* position. It is said that Missouri followed the so-called "humanitarian doctrine" under which a defendant might be liable for injuring an inattentive plaintiff even if the defendant were also inattentive. *See* Banks v. Morris & Co., 302 Mo. 254, 257 S.W. 482 (1924)(where the defendant is under a duty to maintain a look out, negligence in doing so may constitute "constructive notice" of the plaintiff's inattentiveness). The application of the doctrine in subsequent cases was discussed in Pankey v. Claywell, 417 S.W.2d 9 (Mo.App.1967).

3. It should be obvious, upon reflection, that a person who would be a defendant in a § 480 situation and who fails to take evasive action could become a plaintiff in a § 479 situation if he becomes helpless—*i.e.* unable to do anything about the situation—before the other party. Given the different performance characteristics of various automobiles this is a real possibility.

4. Note that the *Restatement* talks in terms of the defendant's "then existing opportunity to avoid the harm." In a much criticized decision the Privy Council applied the English last opportunity rule in a situation where an electric railroad car was unable to stop after the engineer discovered the plaintiff because the brake on the car was out of order. British Columbia Electric Ry. v. Loach, [1916] 1 A.C. 719. The American cases, as indicated by the *Restatement,* generally rejected this result. See Andersen v. Bingham & Garfield Railway, 117 Utah 197, 214 P.2d 607 (1950).

5. As a matter of logic, if *last clear chance* is considered as based on notions of causation, as when it is applied in the case of a helpless plaintiff, its continued existence is not necessarily inconsistent with comparative fault. *See, e.g., Bradley v. Appalachian Power Co., supra* p. 355; Street v. Calvert, 541 S.W.2d 576 (Tenn.1976); Vlach v. Wyman, 78 S.D. 504, 104 N.W.2d 817 (1960). *See also* Davies v. Swan Motor Co., [1949] 2 K.B. 291, 1 All E.R. 620 (C.A.). Nevertheless the predominant view has been that last clear chance does not survive the introduction of comparative fault. This was the approach taken in *Hoffman v. Jones, supra* p. 344. *See also* Kaatz v. State, 540 P.2d 1037 (Alaska 1975); Li v. Yellow Cab Co. of Calif., 13 Cal.3d 804, 119 Cal.Rptr. 858, 532 P.2d 1226 (1975); Davies v. Butler, 95 Nev. 763, 602 P.2d 605 (1979); de Anda v. Blake, 562 S.W.2d 497 (Tex.Civ.App.1978). In practice the evidence and argument regarding the sequential ability of the parties to avoid the accident are still quite relevant and admissible but is directed not at a "winner take all" situation but to an allocation of the fault between the two parties. *See, e.g.,* Macon v. Seaward Construction Co., 555 F.2d 1 (1st Cir.1977); Cushman v. Perkins, 245 A.2d 846 (Me.1968); Danculovich v. Brown, 593 P.2d 187 (Wyo. 1979). One other difference—before comparative negligence, the party relying on the last clear chance doctrine could get a specific charge to the jury regarding application of the doctrine. Under comparative negligence, the predominant view is that a specific charge becomes unnecessary.

C. ASSUMPTION OF THE RISK

LaFRENZ v. LAKE COUNTY FAIR BOARD

Court of Appeals of Indiana, 1977.
172 Ind.App. 389, 360 N.E.2d 605.

HOFFMAN, JUDGE.

On August 19, 1972, Linda LaFrenz was fatally injured when an automobile participating in a demolition derby jumped a barrier striking her. At the time of the occurrence, the decedent was standing in the pit area. Before entering the pit area, decedent had executed an instrument entitled, "WAIVER AND RELEASE FROM LIABILITY AND INDEMNITY AGREEMENT." Appellant David LaFrenz, Administrator of the Estate of Linda LaFrenz, filed a complaint to recover damages from the various defendants. Defendants-appellees Lake County Fair Board and Variety Attractions, Inc. moved for summary judgment based on the release. Such motions were sustained by the trial court on October 24, 1974.

Appellant brings this appeal contending that there are genuine issues of material fact which preclude the entry of summary judgment. Appellant asserts that these fact issues involve the decedent's state of mind as to whether she knowingly and willingly assumed the risk and as to whether she knowingly and willingly signed the release.

Appellant David LaFrenz testified in his deposition that a demolition derby was to be held at the Lake County Fair on August 19, 1972. Approximately four to six weeks prior to August 19, 1972, Linda LaFrenz signed an entry blank to participate in the demolition derby. She had attended demolition derbies previously. In 1970 she observed a demolition derby from the grandstand, and in 1971 she worked in a booth selling tickets. She was aware of the nature of a demolition derby in that the cars would crash into each other.

On August 19, 1972, the demolition derby was scheduled for two sessions—one in the afternoon and another in the evening. Linda LaFrenz was in the pit area during both sessions. She signed documents to be in the pit area as opposed to the grandstand area. She executed a document entitled, "WAIVER AND RELEASE FROM LIABILITY AND INDEMNITY AGREEMENT" which stated that in consideration of being permitted in the "RESTRICTED AREA"[17] she agreed to release the appellees "from all liability to the Undersigned, his personal representatives, assigns, heirs and next of kin for all loss or damage, and any claim or demands therefor, on account of injury to the person or property or resulting in death to the Undersigned, whether caused by the negligence of Releasees or otherwise while the Undersigned is upon the Restricted Area." The agreement also contained a provision in which Linda LaFrenz agreed to indemnify and hold the Releasees harmless for "any loss, liability, damage or cost they may incur due to the presence of the Undersigned in or about the Restricted Area and whether caused by the negligence of the Releasees or otherwise."

Linda LaFrenz was issued a pit pass for the evening session after signing in. She obtained the pit pass to assist her husband, David LaFrenz, as a helper or mechanic.

Later that evening, while standing in the pit area, an automobile participating in the demolition derby jumped the arena barrier striking Linda LaFrenz. She subsequently died from these injuries.

---

17. The "RESTRICTED AREA" was defined as being "the area to which admission for the general public is prohibited, including but not limited to the pit area, racing surface and infield, including walkways, concessions and other appurtenances therein."

At the time of the occurrence, Linda LaFrenz was twenty-six years of age, had graduated from high school, and had attended two years as a part-time student at Indiana University Northwest.

Before considering whether the release bars recovery in the immediate case, the public policy ramifications of exculpatory agreements should be examined. In this respect, parties are generally permitted to agree in advance that one is under no obligation of care for the benefit of the other, and shall not be liable for the consequences of conduct which would otherwise be negligent. * * *

Thus, in the absence of legislation to the contrary, there is ordinarily no public policy which prevents parties from contracting as they see fit. Consequently, it is not against public policy to enter into an agreement which exculpates one from the consequences of his own negligence. * * *

Other jurisdictions which have addressed the question in the context of race track release forms have upheld the validity of the releases as against challenges that such were against public policy. * * *

However, there are several exceptions to the general rule that exculpatory clauses are not against public policy. For example, the Legislature has recently enacted a statute declaring all agreements in construction or design contracts (except highway contracts), which purport to indemnify the promisee against liability arising from the sole negligence or wilful misconduct of the promisee, void as against public policy. IC 1971, 26–2–5–1 (Burns Supp.1976).

Prosser, in his work on torts, notes several other exceptions to the general rule. One proviso is that the relationship of the parties must be such that their bargaining be free and open. Thus where one party is at such an obvious disadvantage in bargaining power that the effect of the contract is to put him at the mercy of the other's negligence, the contract is void as against public policy. This proviso is applicable on this basis between employer and employee. Prosser, *Law of Torts, supra,* § 68, at 442 (4th Ed. 1971).

A second exception noted by Prosser arises in transactions affecting the public interest, such as public utilities, common carriers, innkeepers, and public warehousemen. *Id.* at 443. Likewise it is against public policy in Indiana for a railway company, acting as a common carrier, to contract for indemnity against its own tort liability when it is performing either a public or quasi public duty such as that owing to a shipper, passenger, or servant. * * *

This exception has been extended to other professional bailees who are under no public duty but who deal with the public, such as garagemen, owners of parking lots, and of parcel checkrooms, on the ground that the indispensable need for their services deprives the customer of all real equal bargaining power. * * *

Prosser finally notes that exculpatory agreements are not construed to cover the more extreme forms of negligence or any conduct which constitutes an intentional tort. * * *

The leading case in Indiana on exculpatory provisions is Weaver v. American Oil Co., *supra* (1971), 257 Ind. 458, 276 N.E.2d 144, 49 A.L.R.3d

306, wherein our Supreme Court struck down an exculpatory clause in a commercial lease arrangement. The court * * * stated:

> "When a party can show that the contract, which is sought to be enforced, was in fact an unconscionable one, due to a prodigious amount of bargaining power on behalf of the stronger party, which is used to the stronger party's advantage and is unknown to the lesser party, causing a great hardship and risk on the lesser party, the contract provision, or the contract as a whole, if the provision is not separable, should not be enforceable on the grounds that the provision is contrary to public policy. The party seeking to enforce such a contract has the burden of showing that the provisions were explained to the other party and *came to his knowledge* and there was in fact a *real and voluntary meeting of the minds and not merely an objective meeting.*"

The court went on to explain that it did not mean to infer that parties may not make contracts exculpating one of his negligence, but that it must be done "knowingly and willingly."

In the case at bar, there was no unequal bargaining power between the parties. The decedent was under no compulsion, economic or otherwise, to be in the restricted pit area. * * *

Likewise, the activity did not exhibit any of the characteristics of one affected with the public interest. In *Winterstein v. Wilcom, supra,* the court quoted from Tunkl v. Regents of University of California (1963), 60 Cal.2d 92, 32 Cal.Rptr. 33, 37–38, 383 P.2d 441, at 445–46, 6 A.L.R.3d 693, as listing the criteria for determining whether particular contracts are affected with the public interest, as follows:

> " 'Thus the attempted but invalid exemption involves a transaction which exhibits some or all of the following characteristics. It concerns a business of a type generally thought suitable for public regulation. The party seeking exculpation is engaged in performing a service of great importance to the public, which is often a matter of practical necessity for some members of the public. The party holds himself out as willing to perform this service for any member of the public who seeks it, or at least for any member coming within certain established standards. As a result of the essential nature of the service, in the economic setting of the transaction, the party invoking exculpation possesses a decisive advantage of bargaining strength against any member of the public who seeks his services. In exercising a superior bargaining power the party confronts the public with a standardized adhesion contract of exculpation, and makes no provision whereby a purchaser may pay additional reasonable fees and obtain protection against negligence. Finally, as a result of the transaction, the person or property of the purchaser is placed under the control of the seller, subject to the risk of carelessness by the seller or his agents.' "

Winterstein v. Wilcom, supra, notes a further refinement in instances where a safety statute enacted for the protection of the public is violated. The rationale is that the obligation and the right created by the statute are public ones which are not within the power of any private individual to waive.

We must therefore turn to an examination of the release to determine whether such was "knowingly and willingly" made. The "WAIVER AND RELEASE FROM LIABILITY AND INDEMNITY AGREEMENT" clearly reveals that its sole purpose was to relieve the appellees of liability which may arise from permitting appellant's decedent to be in the restricted pit area. The release was to include all liability which may arise on account of injury to person or property whether caused by the negligence of appellees or otherwise. This situation is different from that which arose in *Weaver* in which the clause there in question *"was in fine print and contained no title heading* which would have identified it as an indemnity clause." (At 462 of 257 Ind., at 147 of 276 N.E.2d.) Moreover, in the case at bar, each and every signature line contains printing in bold, black print approximately ³⁄₁₆th inch, stating "THIS IS A RELEASE." Such printing is placed upon the signature line in such a manner that one who signs the instrument is superimposing his signature over such printing. Thus, the uncontroverted facts indicate that the decedent did execute the "WAIVER AND RELEASE FROM LIABILITY AND INDEMNITY AGREEMENT"; the form and language of the agreement explicitly refers to the appellees' negligence; and the decedent could not have signed the instrument without seeing the wording "THIS IS A RELEASE." Thus the form and language is so conspicuous that reasonable men could not reach different conclusions on the question whether the deceased "knowingly and willingly" signed the document. * * *

Appellant asserts that decedent may have been misinformed concerning the nature of the agreement. In his deposition, Ronald Halcomb, Sr., the driver of the automobile which struck decedent, testified that someone, whom he assumed to be an official, stated that the form was an insurance form.

Appellant, however, was with decedent when she signed in for the evening session. He did not assert that such a representation was made.

Thus, we are faced with a situation in which appellant is attempting to raise an inference that such representations were made to the decedent by showing that similar representations were made to others.

However, this assertion alone would not be sufficient to establish a genuine issue of material fact involving misrepresentation. Generally proof of representations made by appellees to persons other than the decedent does not tend to establish that such representations were made to decedent.

Affirmed.

Notes

1. Cases involving agreements like that involved in the *LaFrenz* case are often classified under the rubric "express assumption of risk," as distinguished from those cases involving merely an "implied assumption of risk" where there has been no conscious prior agreement between the parties. The adoption of comparative negligence does not seem to have made any change in the judicial treatment of "express assumption of risk." *See, e.g.,* Schlobohm v. Spa Petite, Inc., 326 N.W.2d 920 (Minn.1982); Hammer v. Road America, Inc., 614 F.Supp. 467 (E.D.Wis.1985); Haines v. St. Charles Speedway, Inc., 689 F.Supp. 964

(E.D.Mo.1988); Arbegast v. Board of Education, 65 N.Y.2d 161, 490 N.Y.S.2d 751, 480 N.E.2d 365 (1985). See also Council Draft (No. 1), *Restatement (Third) of Torts: Apportionment of Liability* § 2.

2. But what constitutes an "express" assumption of the risk? Express assumption of the risk continues to be a complete defense because the "contract" between the parties relieves the defendant of responsibility. Thus the theory is premised upon an enforceable contract. See Diamond, *Assumption of Risk after Comparative Negligence: Integrating Contract Theory into Tort Doctrine,* 52 Ohio St.L.J. 717 (1991). As the *Turkl* case holds, as discussed in the next note, such contracts will not be enforced when they contravene public policy. But assuming no such problem, what does "express" mean? All agree that it includes situations in which the agreement is in writing. But is it limited to written expressions? What about oral agreements or agreements based purely upon what can be implied from conduct. These may also be enforceable contracts under usual contract law analysis but if the expression of consent to shift the responsibility for the risk involved is communicated orally or by conduct does that take it out of the "express" category? Keep this question in mind as you read the cases that follow. Few cases have directly dealt with this problem of definition but it is clear that when the agreement has to be implied from conduct, the courts will generally not use a contract analysis but rather treat the case as an implied assumption of the risk and deal with it under comparative responsibility. How should the following case be handled? Plaintiff parks his car on a parking lot that contains a very prominent sign that says "Cars are left on this lot at owner's risk." An employee of the defendant lot owner negligently runs into plaintiff's car. Plaintiff sues the lot owner. *Cf.* Allright, Inc. v. Schroeder, 551 S.W.2d 745 (Tex.Civ.App.1977).

3. Tunkl v. Regents of the University of California, 60 Cal.2d 92, 32 Cal.Rptr. 33, 383 P.2d 441 (1963), mentioned in *LaFrenz,* involved a release signed by a patient at the defendant's hospital which exculpated the defendant from any liability on account of any negligence of its staff employees if the defendant exercised due care in selecting those employees. As noted in the *LaFrenz* case, that agreement was declared contrary to public policy. In Tenants Council of Tiber Island–Carrollsburg Square v. DeFranceaux, 305 F.Supp. 560 (D.D.C.1969), the defendant landlord refused to issue passes entitling tenants to use the pool unless they signed agreements assuming the risk of personal injury. The court declared the agreement unlawful and enjoined the defendant's efforts to make the tenants sign it. For a recent discussion of developments in this area, *see* A. Cava and D. Wiesner, *Rationalizing a Decade of Judicial Responses to Exculpatory Clauses*, 28 Santa Clara L.Rev. 611 (1988).

4. A 1995 case involved a plaintiff that was a guest at the defendants' ski resort. He had signed a general release before skiing. He was injured when he skied into a metal pole that was part of the control maze for a ski lift line. The court held the release invalid. It found its coverage clearly applicable to the situation but refused to enforce it on public policy grounds.

> The defendants' area is a facility open to the public. They advertise and invite skiers and nonskiers of every level of skiing ability to their premises for the price of a ticket * * *. In Vermont, a business owner has a duty "of active care to make sure that its premises are in safe and suitable condition for its customers." * * * The business invitee "ha[s] a right to

assume that the premises, aside from obvious dangers, [are] reasonably safe for the purpose for which he [is] upon them, and that proper precaution [has] been taken to make them so." * * * The policy rationale is to place responsibility for maintenance of the land on those who own or control it, with the ultimate goal of keeping accidents to the minimum level possible. Defendants, not recreational skiers, have the expertise and opportunity to foresee and control hazards, and to guard against the negligence of their agents and employees. They alone can properly maintain and inspect their premises, and train their employees in risk management. They alone can insure against risk and effectively spread the cost of insurance among their thousands of customers. Skiers, on the other hand, are not in a position to discover and correct risks of harm, and they cannot insure against the ski area's negligence.

Dalury v. S–K–I, Ltd., 670 A.2d 795 (Vt.1995). (The duty owed by possessors of land to business invitees will be taken up in more detail in Section C of Chapter Seven, *infra*.) The court also discussed a Vermont statute providing that "a person who takes part in any sport accepts as a matter of law the damages that inhere therein insofar as they are obvious and necessary." The court held that "A ski area's own negligence * * * is neither an inherent risk nor an obvious and necessary one in the sport of skiing." *See also* Eder v. Lake Geneva Raceway, Inc., 187 Wis.2d 596, 523 N.W.2d 429 (App.1994)(involving spectators injured at a motor bike racetrack); Wagenblast v. Odessa Sch. Dist. No. 105–157–166J, 110 Wn.2d 845, 758 P.2d 968 (Wash.1988)(release involving interscholastic athletics violated public policy); Kyriazis v. University of W.Va., 192 W.Va. 60, 450 S.E.2d 649 (W.Va.1994)(holding release related to university-sponsored rugby club invalid on public policy grounds); Hiett v. Lake Barcroft Community Ass'n, 244 Va. 191, 418 S.E.2d 894 (Va.1992)(a case involving a "Teflon Man Triathlon" competition; the court said: "To hold that it was competent for one party to put the other parties to the contract at the mercy of its own misconduct * * * can never be lawfully done").

A case almost identical to *LaFrenz* is Allabach v. Santa Clara County Fair Assoc., Inc., 46 Cal.App.4th 1007, 54 Cal.Rptr.2d 330 (1996). Other cases agreeing with *LaFrenz* and enforcing the release include, *e.g.*, Jones v. Dressel, 623 P.2d 370 (Colo.1981)(involving a parachute jump); Milligan v. Big Valley Corp., 754 P.2d 1063 (Wyo.1988)(involving an "Ironman Decathlon" competition); Barnes v. New Hampshire Karting Ass'n, Inc. 128 N.H. 102, 509 A.2d 151 (1986).

5. Can a parent agree to relieve the defendant of responsibility for the risk posed to a minor? Frequently parents must sign a release before a child is permitted to engage in sporting activity. See Scott v. Pacific West Mountain Resort, 119 Wn.2d 484, 834 P.2d 6 (1992)(refusing to enforce a parent signed release for skiing). What about a spouse waiving responsibility for another spouse? See Huber v. Hovey, 501 N.W.2d 53 (Iowa 1993)(refusing to enforce the release).

6. Most courts are exacting in requiring that the release be very clear as to both what activities are covered and what the risks are. For an example of a release that passed muster, *see* Krazek v. Mountain River Tours, Inc., 884 F.2d 163 (4th Cir.1989). *See*, generally, Boehm v. Cody Country Chamber of Commerce, 748 P.2d 704 (Wyo.1987).

7. Courts will generally not honor a release when conduct more blame-worthy than negligence is involved, no matter how clear the release. *See* Sommer v. Federal Signal Corp., 79 N.Y.2d 540, 583 N.Y.S.2d 957, 593 N.E.2d 1365 (1992).

HEROD v. GRANT

Supreme Court of Mississippi, 1972.
262 So.2d 781.

PATTERSON, JUSTICE:

This is an appeal from a judgment of the Circuit Court of Montgomery County wherein the appellee was awarded $15,000 in damages for injuries received by him in falling from the appellant's truck. We reverse.

On the evening of October 24, 1969, Joseph Grant, plaintiff below, and Eddie Earl Herod, defendant below, engaged in a common enterprise to rid the appellee's bean field of predatory wild animals. Each equipped himself with a headlight and a rifle and at approximately 10:00 p.m. ventured into the appellee's bean field in the appellant's pickup truck. In scanning the field they observed a deer and the appellee seated himself in a cross-legged position upon a tool box situated in the bed of the truck immediately to the rear of the cab. The appellant then drove the truck not more than fifteen to twenty miles per hour along the rows of the field which had been combined that afternoon by the appellee. The deer, when it became illuminated by the lights of the truck and the headlights of the occupants, was twice fired upon by the appellee to no avail when the weapon jammed. He then obtained the rifle of the appellant in furtherance of his defense of the field when the deer, which had been running parallel to the truck, veered toward the vehicle, motivating the appellant, according to the appellee, to suddenly increase the speed of the truck in an attempt to run over the deer. This action, as well as a slight turn of the vehicle by the appellant, caused the appellee to fall from the tool box to the ground, seriously injuring him.

The testimony of the appellant is substantially the same with the exception that he denies the truck was rapidly accelerated or sharply turned from its path.

The sole issue before the Court is whether the appellee, by engaging in this activity, assumed the attendant risk attached to the endeavor.

In Elias v. New Laurel Radio Station, Inc., 245 Miss. 170, 146 So.2d 558 (1962), and Dendy v. City of Pascagoula, 193 So.2d 559 (Miss.1967), we quoted with approval the rule relative to the necessary elements of assumption of risk as set forth in 19 Mississippi Law Journal, Negligence–Automobile Accidents–Assumption of Risk as a Defense–Contributory Negligence Distinguished, at 370 (1948), wherein it is stated:

> * * * The elements which must be found in order to constitute a defense of assumption of risk are generally stated in some such terms as the following: (1) Knowledge on the part of the injured party of a condition inconsistent with his safety; (2) appreciation by the injured party of the danger in the condition; and (3) a deliberate and voluntary choice on the part of the injured party to expose his person to that

danger in such a manner as to register assent on the continuance of the dangerous condition.   * * *

The critical question for this Court to answer is whether the plaintiff comprehended a knowledge of the risk involved in riding in the rear of the truck. We have stated that the assumption of risk is governed by the subjective standard of the plaintiff himself whereas contributory negligence is measured by the objective standard of a reasonable man, and that the assumption of risk is a jury question in all but the clearest cases.

In considering subjective knowledge, 1 Blashfield Automobile Law and Practice, section 64.3 (3d Ed. 1965), stated that:

> Subjective knowledge is more difficult to prove. Plaintiff may always claim he did not know of the facts creating the risk, or that he did not comprehend the risk involved. Evidence contradicting this is difficult to secure. The jury, having no external standard by which to judge his knowledge, must determine whether he is telling the truth. However, the courts have indicated a willingness to override such contentions of plaintiff where they find that any person of ordinary intelligence must, as a matter of law, have known and appreciated the risk.   * * *

The case of De Winne v. Waldrep, 101 Ga.App. 570, 114 S.E.2d 455 (1960), presents a fact situation remarkably similar to that of the case at bar. In *De Winne* a party fell or was thrown from the back of a pickup while driving through open fields and hunting deer. The Georgia Court of Appeals held that one who knowingly and voluntarily takes a risk of injury to his person, the danger of which is so obvious that the act of taking such risk is and of itself amounts to a failure to exercise ordinary care and diligence for his own safety, cannot hold another liable for damages for injuries thus occasioned. The case at bar clearly presents a stronger fact situation for application of the assumption of risk doctrine than *De Winne* for the reason the parties here were defending, or hunting, at night and travelling through a cultivated field traversed by plowed rows.

We are of the opinion that Joseph Grant, by hunting deer from a seated position upon a tool box in the bed of the truck in the late evening hours in a cultivated field, assumed the risk that the vehicle might either pass over rough ground or that it might be accelerated or swerved in the excitement of the chase, or a combination thereof, none lending itself to safety, but rather all pointing directly to a precarious position from which injury could very easily flow. There being no relationship of master and servant, the appellee, a mature and reasonable man, assumed the risk of the endeavor for which no liability extends to the defendant.

We are of the opinion the trial court should have sustained the defendant's motion for a directed verdict at the conclusion of the plaintiff's testimony.

Reversed and rendered.

Notes

1. The notion of assumption of the risk at one time was widely used to restrict recoveries by workers in dangerous occupations against their employ-

ers. Much of this litigation has now been absorbed by worker's compensation law. To the extent it has not, as the court in *Herod v. Grant* recognized, the employment situation is one where the courts are now reluctant to find an assumption of the risk—either on the ground that the employee did not truly understand the risk or, more commonly, that the employee's action was not voluntary.

The type of assumption of risk involved in *Herod v. Grant,* namely, that in which the plaintiff can be said to have been negligent in exposing himself to the risk of being injured, is the one that is most likely to have been absorbed by the concept of comparative negligence. It should be noted, however, that Mississippi was one of the first states to adopt a general scheme of comparative negligence, and yet assumption of risk survives there. As the *Herod* court noted, assumption of risk also survives in Georgia, where comparative negligence has roots in the nineteenth century. It has, moreover, recently been held that it is still an open question in Pennsylvania whether the type of assumption of risk in which the plaintiff has unreasonably exposed himself to a risk of injury has been abolished by introduction of comparative negligence. *See* Berman v. Radnor Rolls, Inc., 374 Pa.Super. 118, 133–36, 542 A.2d 525, 532–33 (1988).

2. *Herod v. Grant* is a good illustration of how what is ostensibly a subjective determination—awareness of the risk—inevitably in the course of judicial decision-making comes to be made by reference to objective criteria, namely, what a rational person would clearly have understood about his situation. The nexus of course is that what a rational person would have understood is probative of what this particular plaintiff understood.

3. In England what is characterized by American courts as assumption of risk is part of the general doctrine of *volenti non fit injuria.* For a good description of the evolution of English law on the issue see T. Ingman, *A History of the Defence of Volenti Non Fit Injuria,* [1981] Juridical Rev. 1.

JONES v. THREE RIVERS MANAGEMENT CORP.

Supreme Court of Pennsylvania, 1978.
483 Pa. 75, 394 A.2d 546.

ROBERTS, JUSTICE.

Appellant Evelyn M. Jones brought an action of trespass in the Court of Common Pleas of Allegheny County against appellee Pittsburgh Athletic Company, Inc., holder of the Pittsburgh Pirates baseball franchise, and appellee Three Rivers Management Corporation, a wholly owned subsidiary of the Pittsburgh Athletic Company, Inc., which manages Three Rivers Stadium. A jury found appellees negligent and awarded appellant damages of $125,000. The Superior Court held that appellant failed to establish a prima facie case and reversed and remanded for entry of judgment notwithstanding the verdict as to both appellees. We granted allowance of appeal and now reverse.

I

Appellant was injured at Three Rivers Stadium, Pittsburgh, on July 16, 1970, the sport facility's inaugural day. Two interior concourses, or walkways, encircle the stadium on its second level. One concourse, at the outer circumference of the stadium and away from the playing field, houses concessions and restrooms. The other, located behind the seating and scoreboard areas, runs, in part, directly behind and above "right field." Built into the concourse wall above right field, are large openings through which pedestrians may look out over the field and stands. Ramps lead patrons from this second walkway to the seating areas overlooking the field of play. Appellant was standing in this second walkway in the vicinity of one of the large right field openings when she was struck in the eye by a ball hit during batting practice.

Appellant's evidence established that the stadium's structure requires pedestrians interested in looking out onto the playing field to stop or to divert their attention away from the path of the concourse. Appellant testified that as she entered the right field area of the concourse, she directed her attention away from the walkway, approached one of the right field openings and scanned the playing field. She testified that, although she saw some activity on the field, she was not aware that batting practice had begun and did not see home plate.[18] After this stop, she decided not to continue around the walkway, but to walk back to get some food in the "concession" concourse. Appellant turned away from the field of play, started back, and almost immediately heard a cry of "Watch!" As she turned, again, toward the field, she was struck in the eye by a batted ball. Appellant testified, in addition, that she was a fan of the Pittsburgh Pirates and that she had attended many of the "home" games played at Forbes Field, the Pirates' former stadium. The day she was injured marked her first visit to Three Rivers Stadium. She testified that in Forbes Field patrons were not exposed to batted balls until they had left the walkways and emerged onto ramps in the seating area.

In response to appellant's case, appellees presented no evidence. Instead, they moved for both nonsuits and directed verdicts. The trial court denied the motions and submitted the case to the jury. After the jury's verdict for appellant, the trial court denied appellees' motions for judgments notwithstanding the verdict.

On appeal, a majority of the Superior Court held that appellant failed to meet her burden of proving negligence and that the trial court erred in denying the motions for judgments n. o. v. Judge Spaeth filed an opinion concurring in part and dissenting in part which Judge Hoffman joined. Judge Spaeth agreed with the result as to the Pittsburgh Athletic Co., Inc. He concluded, however, that appellant presented sufficient evidence to reach the jury on the question of appellee Three Rivers Management Corp.'s liability.

II

Appellees in this appeal argue only that appellant has not established a prima facie case of negligence and that, in the alternative, appellees' defense of assumption of the risk precludes appellant's recovery. Appellees contend that the outcome in this case is controlled by "the universal rule" that batted balls in baseball stadiums do not present an unreasonable risk of harm, and thus, do not create liability in trespass for negligence.

---

18. The testimony leaves open whether home plate was visible from the place where appellant originally scanned the field.

Appellant concedes the existence of such a rule, but maintains that its application is limited to injuries which occur during games and regularly scheduled batting practice sessions. Appellant maintains that any injury which occurs on a concourse behind the stands, from which the injured party could not and did not see the source of danger, and which results from an unusually early batting practice falls outside the scope of the above rule.

This Court has never considered the liability of a baseball stadium operator for damages incurred by a patron in the grandstand or bleachers, struck by a batted ball. There are, however, settled principles which apply to all cases involving a place of amusement for which admission is charged. An operator of such an establishment is not an insurer of his patrons. E.g., Taylor v. Churchill Valley Country Club, 425 Pa. 266, 269, 228 A.2d 768, 769 (1967) citing Haugh v. Harris Bros. Am. Co., 315 Pa. 90, 172 A. 145 (1934). Rather, he will be liable for injuries to his patrons only where he fails to "use reasonable care in the construction, maintenance, and management of [the facility], *having regard to the character of the exhibitions given and the customary conduct of patrons invited.*" Id. (emphasis added in *Taylor*). * * *

Thus, this Court affirmed a directed verdict for a defendant golf club sued on the ground that it was negligent not to provide screening over an area on the golf course where a caddy was exposed to flying golf balls, *Taylor*, supra. The Court granted a judgment n. o. v. to a defendant movie theatre operator where the plaintiff patron alleged no more than that his injury was caused by the lighting conditions, or degree of darkness, ordinarily necessary to show a movie, Beck v. Stanley Co. of America, 355 Pa. 608, 50 A.2d 306 (1947). * * *.

And we granted a judgment n. o. v. to an amusement park, holding no liability for injuries allegedly suffered from slipping in the seat of a roller coaster equipped with individual seat belts and large handrails, when the coaster went through a steep turn. * * *

The Superior Court has applied these principles to two baseball cases in which spectators seated in the stands during games have been struck by batted balls. In Iervolino v. Pittsburgh Athletic Co., 212 Pa.Super. 330, 243 A.2d 490 (1968)(allocatur refused), Superior Court directed entry of a judgment n. o. v. where plaintiff contended it was negligent "to invite a patron to a sports event and view a baseball game from a position where she was exposed to a hard projectile traveling 94½ feet in a split second," but did not go on to also establish that exposure to this risk resulted from any deviation from established custom in a baseball stadium.

The Superior Court has also directed entry of a judgment n. o. v. where plaintiff's allegations were "tantamount to a request for a holding that a baseball club must at its peril always have available a seat behind the screen whenever a patron requests one." Schentzel v. Philadelphia National League Club, 173 Pa.Super. 179, 96 A.2d 181 (1953).[19]

19. In *Schentzel*, the Superior Court cited with approval the opinion of the Supreme Court of Minnesota in Brisson v. Minneapolis Baseball & Athletic Assn., 185 Minn. 507, 240 N.W. 903 (1932). *Brisson* held a baseball stadium operator had no duty to provide screened seats for all spectators in the stands exposed to batted balls. Instead, it held the

Recovery is not granted to those who voluntarily expose themselves to the kind of risks involved in *Iervolino,* supra, and *Schentzel,* supra, by participating in or viewing the activity. We have therefore regularly granted or affirmed judgments n. o. v. in cases involving places of amusement where the plaintiff alleges no more than injury caused by a risk inherent in the activity in question. Only when the plaintiff introduces adequate evidence that the amusement facility in which he was injured deviated in some relevant respect from established custom will it be proper for an "inherent-risk" case to go to the jury. The Superior Court has articulated this principle:

> "In this case, plaintiff produced no evidence tending to show that defendant's screening of certain sections of its grandstand deviated from that customarily employed at other baseball parks. The courts of this Commonwealth have adhered to general usage as a test of negligence with respect to methods and appliances employed in business and have held that in the absence of proof by plaintiff that defendant deviated from ordinary standards the question of negligence is not for the jury. * * * 'While customary methods do not furnish a conclusive or controlling test of negligence or justify a practice obviously laden with danger, they are nevertheless to be considered as factors of measurement of due care.' "

Schentzel, 173 Pa. at 185, 96 A.2d at 184. * * *

Movies must be seen in a darkened room, roller coasters must accelerate and decelerate rapidly and players will bat balls into the grandstand. But even in a "place of amusement" not every risk is reasonably expected. The rationale behind the rule that the standard of reasonable care does not impose a duty to protect from risks associated with baseball, naturally limits its application to those injuries incurred as a result of risks any baseball spectator must and will be held to anticipate. Goade v. Benevolent and Protective Order of Elks, 213 Cal.App.2d 189, 28 Cal.Rptr. 669 (1963), in explaining the difference between the risk of being struck by a batted ball and a flying baseball bat, observes:

> "In baseball, a sport often referred to as our 'national pastime,' it has been held that the spectator as a matter of law assumes the risk of being hit by a fly ball. * * * But when a spectator is hit by a flying baseball bat the doctrine of assumption of the risk is not applied. * * * The difference in the treatment of these two baseball spectators is explained by the fact that it is a matter of 'common knowledge' that

reasonable care standard satisfied when a screen is provided over the most dangerous part of the grandstand, and a reasonable number of people are protected by it.

Similar results have been reached in other jurisdictions considering liability to a patron injured in the stands by a batted ball. * * *

Although courts are in agreement that a ballpark patron must establish more than injury by a batted ball while in the stands to avoid a dismissal or a directed verdict, they variously describe the rationale for this result. * * *

Although "assumption of the risk" language is used, the issue is not one of the plaintiff's subjective consent to assume the risks of defendant's negligent conditions, but rather whether defendant was negligent in failing to protect plaintiff from certain risks. * * *

fly balls are a common, frequent and expected occurrence in this well-known sport, and it is not a matter of 'common knowledge' that flying baseball bats are common, frequent or expected."

Thus, "no-duty" rules, apply only to risks which are "common, frequent and expected," *Goade,* supra, and in no way affect the duty of theatres, amusement parks and sports facilities to protect patrons from foreseeably dangerous conditions not inherent in the amusement activity. Patrons of baseball stadiums have recovered when injured by a swinging gate while in their grandstand seats, * * * by tripping over a beam at the top of a grandstand stairway, * * * and by falling into a hole in a walkway, under a grandstand, used to reach refreshment stands, * * *. In these cases, just as in the "flying baseball bat" case, * * * the occurrence causing injury was not "a common, frequent and expected" part of the game of baseball. Therefore, there is no bar to finding the defendant negligent. Further, in such cases, there is no burden on the plaintiff to introduce evidence with respect to established custom of baseball stadiums.[20] * * *

III

The central question, then, is whether appellant's case is governed by the "no-duty" rule applicable to common, frequent and expected risks of baseball or by the ordinary rules applicable to all other risks which may be present in a baseball stadium. To settle this question, we must determine whether one who attends a baseball game as a spectator can properly be charged with anticipating as inherent to baseball the risk of being struck by a baseball while properly using an interior walkway.

The openings built into the wall over right field are an architectural feature of Three Rivers Stadium which are not an inherent feature of the spectator sport of baseball. They are not compelled by or associated with the ordinary manner in which baseball is played or viewed.[21] The principles underlying our rules barring recovery in amusement facility cases, e.g., *Taylor,* supra (flying golf balls); *Beck,* supra (ordinary degree of darkness in a movie theatre); *Wood,* supra (roller coaster), cannot extend to the kind of risk of harm claimed present here. Like the swinging gate, * * * the dangerous grandstand stairway, * * * and the hole in the floor of the stadium walkway, * * * these concourse openings simply cannot be characterized as "part of the spectator sport of baseball." It, therefore, cannot be concluded that recovery is foreclosed to appellant who was struck while standing in an interior walkway of Three Rivers Stadium. The Superior Court was in error when it extended to appellant, standing in this walkway, the no-duty rule applicable to patrons in the stands. The no-duty rule was improperly applied.[22]

20. The question of whether a risk is properly to be anticipated cannot be answered by looking to whether exposure to such risks is customary in the trade. This would permit defendant/stadium operators to avoid liability for universally prevalent negligent conditions, an undesirable result. * * *

21. Indeed, appellees did not challenge appellant's testimony that a patron was protected in the walkways at Forbes Field.

22. In view of our holding, we need not determine the significance, if any, of the hour at which batting practice was held on the inaugural day of the stadium.

Order of the Superior Court reversed and judgment for appellant reinstated.

Notes

1. In Lee v. National League Baseball Club of Milwaukee, 4 Wis.2d 168, 89 N.W.2d 811 (1958), a patron seated in a box-seat was trampled by fans chasing a foul ball. In affirming a judgment for the plaintiff, the court noted that the ushers normally present in the box-seat area had been withdrawn. It also noted that, since there was no record of a comparable injury to a spectator from fans chasing foul balls, the plaintiff could not be held to have any knowledge of the risk. Nevertheless, there had been sufficient incidents of unruly behavior on the part of fans chasing foul balls in the past to put the defendant on notice that someone might be trampled. Suppose the plaintiff had been sitting in the general admission section? The baseball cases are collected in 91 A.L.R.3d 24 (1979).

2. Suppose, in the *Jones* case, the plaintiff was aware of the danger of being hit by batted balls, from having watched baseball on television, but had never attended a professional baseball game in person. Should she have still recovered if she had been hit on the walkway? Taking the facts as they were, should she have been able to recover if she had been hit just as she emerged from the walkway into the stands? Should the normal baseball case where the plaintiff loses be classified as a no-duty case or one where the plaintiff has assumed the risk? If there is no duty, then the knowledge of the particular plaintiff is irrelevant, although the knowledge of a "typical" spectator would be relevant in determining the scope of what the defendant ought to have anticipated. *See* Gunther v. Charlotte Baseball, Inc., 854 F.Supp. 424 (D.S.C.1994)(spectator struck in face by foul ball assumed risk even though she had never before attended baseball game); Bellezzo v. State, 174 Ariz. 548, 851 P.2d 847 (App.1992)(being struck by foul ball was open and obvious risk). For cases holding that baseball park had fulfilled its duty by providing protected seating, *see* Arnold v. City of Cedar Rapids, 443 N.W.2d 332 (Iowa 1989); Dent v. Texas Rangers Ltd., 764 S.W.2d 345 (Tex.App.1989). *But see* Yates v. Chicago National League Ball Club, Inc., 230 Ill.App.3d 472, 172 Ill.Dec. 209, 595 N.E.2d 570 (1992).

Suppose all baseball parks removed the screens from behind home plate in order to make the game more realistic and no fans were admitted who did not appreciate the risks. If a fan sitting behind home plate were injured, how should any subsequent personal injury action against the ballpark be analyzed?

3. A leading English case on the liability of participants to spectators is Wooldridge v. Sumner, [1963] 2 Q.B. 43 (1962), [1962] 3 W.L.R. 616, 2 All E.R. 978 (C.A.). The *Wooldridge* case suggests that it is the job of participants to strive as best they can to win and that they incur no liability to spectators for accidental injuries they may inflict in the course of those efforts. What if the participants were aware that the arena in which they were competing had inadequate safety precautions? The question of the liability of a competitor to other competitors for intentional misconduct has been discussed in *Hackbart v. Cincinnati Bengals, Inc., supra*, p. 69. *Ordway v. Superior Court, infra*, p. 395, presents the question of the liability of a competitor to fellow competitors for negligent behavior.

AUCKENTHALER v. GRUNDMEYER

Supreme Court of Nevada, 1994.
110 Nev. 682, 877 P.2d 1039.

PER CURIAM:

FACTS

Appellant Lori S. Auckenthaler ("Auckenthaler") and several other individuals were riding horses in an area north of Reno, known as Red Rock. The individuals were participating in the "field training" of dogs owned by co-respondent Steven Grundmeyer ("Grundmeyer"). Field training is an exercise where dogs are led through a prearranged course marked by the random placement of birds. Co-respondent Jody White ("White") was a member of the group and was riding a horse owned by Grundmeyer named "Bum." White and Grundmeyer were specifically involved in the training expedition and the other riders were at the event as observers. The ride was purely recreational, and none of the participants obtained any compensation or commercial gain from the activity.

During the ride, Bum was acting antsy and nervous and had been threatening to kick other horses that ventured into his proximity. Bum had been recently gelded. Auckenthaler was injured when the horse she was riding strayed too close to Bum. Bum turned and kicked at Auckenthaler's horse, striking Auckenthaler in the leg.

Auckenthaler filed a negligence suit against both White and Grundmeyer. She alleged that White was negligent in continuing to ride a horse that was temperamental and exhibiting dangerous behavior. Auckenthaler also alleged that Grundmeyer was negligent for supplying White with a horse Grundmeyer knew was aggressive and anxious.

White and Grundmeyer moved for summary judgment. * * * The district court * * * summarily dismissed Auckenthaler's complaint. The court adopted the California standard and reasoned that Auckenthaler "ha[d] not alleged or presented any evidence that defendants intentionally tried to hurt plaintiff or that defendants engaged in conduct which was so reckless as to be totally outside the range of ordinary activities involved in the horseback riding and dog training sport."

Auckenthaler appeals from summary judgment and argues that the district court erred by adopting a reckless or intentional standard of care because such a reduced standard affronts Nevada's abolition of implied assumption of risk. We agree and accordingly reverse the district court's judgment.

DISCUSSION

* * * In granting summary judgment in favor of Grundmeyer and White, the district court adopted the standard of care for participants in a recreational event that was applied in two California Supreme Court companion decisions: Knight v. Jewett, 3 Cal.4th 296, 11 Cal.Rptr.2d 2, 834 P.2d 696 (1992), and Ford v. Gouin, 3 Cal.4th 339, 11 Cal.Rptr.2d 30, 834 P.2d 724 (1992). In Knight, plaintiff was injured while participating in an informal game of touch football. Defendant jumped up to intercept a

pass and tumbled down on top of plaintiff's hand. * * * Plaintiff sued defendant for negligence. In affirming summary judgment for defendant, the California high court noted that an "overwhelming majority of the cases, both within and outside California ... have concluded that it is improper to hold a sports participant liable to a coparticipant for ordinary careless conduct committed during the sport." * * * The court then established the general proposition that in sporting activities, liability can only be imposed "where the participant intentionally injures another player or engages in conduct that is so reckless as to be totally outside the range of the ordinary activity involved in the sport." * * * The court ultimately held that plaintiff could not prove that defendant had engaged in this type of conduct.

In Ford, the California Supreme Court extended the reckless or intentional legal standard of care to participants in a recreational activity. Plaintiff was injured in a water skiing accident when he struck a tree limb. [Ed. note: the plaintiff was skiing barefoot and backwards in a relatively narrow channel.] Plaintiff sued the driver of the boat for negligence, claiming that he drove the boat too close to the shore of the waterway. The court upheld summary judgment in favor of defendant, concluding that plaintiff could not prove that he had been injured by intentional or reckless behavior. * * *

The purpose of this differing standard of care was succinctly articulated by a more recent California case:

> By eliminating liability for unintended accidents, the doctrine ensures that the fervor of athletic competition will not be chilled by the constant threat of litigation from every misstep, sharp turn and sudden stop. On a larger scale, participation in amateur athletics is a socially desirable activity that improves the mental and physical well-being of its participants.

Stimson v. Carlson, 11 Cal.App.4th 1201, 14 Cal.Rptr.2d 670, 673 (1992).

As in Knight and Ford, and pursuing the same policy goals as articulated in Stimson, the district court in the case at bar ruled that Auckenthaler did not present any evidence establishing that she was injured as a result of reckless or intentional conduct. The sole issue on appeal is whether the district court erred by deviating from Nevada's ordinary negligence rubric and adopting this California standard.

* * * Before analyzing * * * Auckenthaler's argument, it is necessary to understand the different types of the assumption of risk affirmative defense and certain nuances of corresponding California law. Assumption of risk is divided into two separate categories: express and implied. Express assumption of risk is essentially a contract where the plaintiff signs a document and openly agrees to hold the defendant harmless for known and inherent dangers of a particular activity.

Implied assumption of risk has three different sub-categories. The first, often referred to as primary implied assumption of risk, occurs when the plaintiff voluntarily accepts known risks involved in a particular situation, and the defendant has no duty of care with respect to the plaintiff. The classic example is the spectator at a baseball game who impliedly understands that the players have no duty to refrain from hitting a ball into the stands. The second variety of implied assumption of risk is characterized by the plaintiff voluntarily encountering a known risk created by the defendant's negligence. An example is where the plaintiff continues to use a defective lawn mower that he knows is defective because the inconvenience of repair outweighs the added risk of injury. The third variety of implied assumption of risk is where the plaintiff unreasonably accepts a known threat of danger in pursuing a particular course of conduct. This situation would exist if the plaintiff takes an unnecessary and expedient shortcut to his destination, confronting known hazards along the way. * * *

It seems undisputed that the facts of the instant case present a situation much like primary implied assumption of risk. Horseback riding is a recreational or sporting activity that has inherent dangers. By choosing to participate, the plaintiff impliedly consents to the inherent risks of the activity and the defendant has no duty or a reduced duty to protect the plaintiff.

If the accident at issue had occurred in California, there is no doubt Auckenthaler would be barred from recovery. Even though the California legislature has adopted pure comparative negligence, the state still recognizes the viability of primary implied assumption of risk as an affirmative defense. * * * Conversely, the California high court has held that secondary implied assumption of risk (the latter two sub-categories described above) has been subsumed by the state's comparative negligence framework. * * * Due to this dichotomous precedent, California courts are struggling to define what constitutes primary and secondary aspects of the affirmative defense. To a large extent, the Knight and Ford decisions are geared toward defining the difference between the two legal concepts.

As Auckenthaler correctly argues on appeal, the principles described in Knight and Ford and utilized by the district court in granting summary judgment are inapplicable in Nevada. The holding and rationale of those decisions are infected by California's recognition of primary implied assumption of risk. The reckless or intentional standard of care applied in California is simply another way of determining that the plaintiff assumed the risk of injury. In either instance, the plaintiff is summarily barred from recovery. Such a reduced standard affronts Nevada law because, unlike California, Nevada precedent has abrogated all forms of implied assumption of risk. Accordingly, we conclude that the district court erred by adopting California's reckless or intentional standard of care for participants in recreational activities.

This conclusion is supported and, in fact, mandated by our holding and accompanying rationale in Mizushima. In Mizushima [v. Sunset Ranch, 103 Nev. 259, 737 P.2d 1158 (1987)], plaintiff and a friend went to a commercial stable and rented horses for a horseback riding excursion. Plaintiff was thrown from her mount and severely injured when the horse she was riding bolted back to the stable toward the end of the ride. Plaintiff sued the stable for negligence, claiming that it failed to provide a safe riding environment. At trial, the district court instructed the jury regarding the affirmative defense of assumption of risk. The jury returned a defense verdict. * * *

We reversed on appeal, holding that implied assumption of risk had been subsumed by Nevada's comparative negligence statute. * * * All three forms of the defense were unduly confusing, and examples of such conduct were best examined utilizing traditional principles of comparative negligence:

> In our view, it is equally clear that *any* variety of an implied assumption of risk is merely circumlocution for the preclusive form of contributory negligence the statute sought to eliminate. No matter how the assumption of risk scenario is depicted, *it is translatable into a degree of negligent conduct by the plaintiff. . . .*
>
> The defense of assumption of risk is not favored. [Footnote omitted.] It continues to vex and confuse as a masquerade for contributory negligence. Moreover, *it focuses on a lack of duty in the defendant* rather than the more compelling issue of comparative breach of duty by the parties. In that regard, the doctrine faces backward, emphasizing escape more than accountability and inertia more than progress. In short, *we are unable to ascertain any productive reason why any species of implied assumption of risk should survive the beneficent purposes and effect of Nevada's comparative negligence statute.*

[*Mizushima*] at 263–64, 737 P.2d at 1161 (emphasis added).

In a footnote, we expanded upon this rationale and added the following:

> We perceive no valid reason for leaving primary implied assumption of risk intact. In virtually every instance, including the injured spectator, liability can be analyzed in the context of the conduct of the actor and the injured party, weighed against a standard of care dictated by the circumstances. Thus, there is no arbitrary bar to recovery and no sweeping exemption from duty accorded a defendant. *The determination of duty is left to the jury* as a factor in the comparative negligence analysis.

Id. at 264, 737 P.2d at 1161 n. 7 (emphasis added).

This language not only abrogated implied assumption of risk as an affirmative defense, but also established that every future implied assumption of risk type case would be resolved by applying a traditional negligence standard of care. The negligence standard is sufficiently flexible to accommodate liability issues underlying all recreational injury cases. There is no reduction in the defendant's standard of care (e.g., reckless or intentional), nor is there any fictitious undertaking that the defendant does not owe a duty to the plaintiff. As we noted in Mizushima, implied assumption of risk cases improperly "*[focus] on a lack of duty in the defendant* rather than the more compelling issue of comparative breach of duty by the parties." Id. at 264, 737 P.2d at 1161 (emphasis added). Whether the defendant has failed to act reasonably in the particular circumstances is not an issue of law, but is a matter for the jury to decide. * * *

Grundmeyer and White try to overcome the foregoing analysis by arguing public policy. They warn that applying an ordinary negligence standard to the case at issue will translate into a flood of future litigation between participants in sporting and recreational activities. They maintain that such an occurrence would have a chilling effect on sports participation within Nevada. * * * To combat this policy dilemma, Grundmeyer and White claim that this court should adopt a reckless or intentional standard of care. This is the approach followed by a number of states that have examined the issue. * * * See, e.g., Knight, 11 Cal.Rptr.2d at 16, 834 P.2d at 710; Pfister v. Shusta, 256 Ill.App.3d 186, 194 Ill.Dec. 618, 627 N.E.2d 1260 (1994)(reckless standard applied to game where participants kicked can in college dormitory); Oswald v. Township High School Dist. No. 214, 84 Ill.App.3d 723, 40 Ill.Dec. 456, 406 N.E.2d 157 (1980)(reckless standard applied to gym class basketball game); Gauvin v. Clark, 404 Mass. 450, 537 N.E.2d 94 (1989)(reckless standard applied to college hockey game); Moe v. Steenberg, 275 Minn. 448, 147 N.W.2d 587 (1966)(reckless standard applied to ice skating injury); Ross v. Clouser, 637 S.W.2d 11 (Mo.1982)(applying reckless standard of care to church softball game); and Marchetti v. Kalish, 53 Ohio St.3d 95, 559 N.E.2d 699 (1990)(reckless standard applied to game of "kick the can"). Moreover, the reckless standard of care is not only followed in California, where the state still clings to some form of assumption of risk, but is also applied in other states where assumption of risk has been subsumed by statutory comparative negligence. See, e.g., Kabella v. Bouschelle, 100 N.M. 461, 465, 672 P.2d 290, 294 (1983)(public policy demands that a reduced standard of care governs cases involving recreational sporting injuries); Connell v. Payne, 814 S.W.2d 486 (Tex.Ct.App.1991).

We are not persuaded. First, the negligence standard is a more attractive alternative to resolving these types of cases. The standard is malleable and the jury simply examines each case to determine whether the defendant acted unreasonably under the circumstances. Within the factual climate of recreational activities or even sporting events, the question posed is whether the defendant participated in a reasonable manner and within the rules of the game or in accordance with the ordinary scope of the activity. See Lestina v. West Bend Mut. Ins. Co., 176 Wis.2d 901, 501 N.W.2d 28 (1993)(finder of fact determines whether defendant is liable for injury occurring in a sporting event utilizing an ordinary negligence standard of care); see also LaVine v. Clear Creek Skiing Corp., 557 F.2d 730 (10th Cir.1977)(negligence standard applied to snow skiers); Gray v. Houlton, 671 P.2d 443 (Colo.Ct.App.1983)(negligence standard applied to snow skiing accident); Babych v. McRae, 41 Conn.Supp. 280, 567 A.2d 1269 (1989)(negligence standard applied to hockey game); Duke's GMC, Inc. v. Erskine, 447 N.E.2d 1118 (Ind.Ct.App.1983)(negligence standard applied to golf injury); and Crawn v. Campo, 266 N.J.Super. 599, 630 A.2d 368 (App.Div.1993)(negligence standard applied to softball game), leave to appeal granted, 134 N.J. 557, 636 A.2d 516 (1993). This approach is straightforward and avoids the confusion related to tinkering with standards of care and defining what types of activities qualify for the differing legal treatment. At a practical level, this court avoids creating a wilderness of confusing and disjunctive precedent in this area of the law. * * *

Finally, claims regarding a potential flood of litigation and the chilling effect upon participation in recreational activities seem overstated. We have found very few cases allowing recovery for sports injuries based upon ordinary negligence principles. When properly applied, the negligence standard strikes the proper balance between vigorous participation in sports and accommodating litigants injured by unreasonable behavior.

* * * The underlying facts of this case, and all forthcoming similar cases, are to be examined by utilizing simple negligence rubric. Applying the negligence standard on appeal, it is clear that Auckenthaler presented enough evidence to overcome summary judgment. Accordingly, we reverse the district court's ruling and remand for further proceedings consistent with this opinion.

Notes

1. With the advent of comparative negligence, the general trend has been either to abolish assumption of risk as a separate defense or to merge it with the notion of comparative fault. Nevertheless, a number of jurisdictions that have adopted comparative fault continue to recognize assumption of risk as a separate defense. Other cases continuing to recognize assumption of risk in comparative negligence jurisdictions include Singleton v. Wiley, 372 So.2d 272 (Miss.1979); Kennedy v. Providence Hockey Club, Inc., 119 R.I. 70, 376 A.2d 329 (1977); Blum v. Brichacek, 191 Neb. 457, 215 N.W.2d 888 (1974); Bugh v. Webb, 231 Ark. 27, 328 S.W.2d 379 (1959). When assumption of risk is used to describe the situation where it is held that the defendant has not been negligent towards the plaintiff (i.e. had no "duty"), comparative negligence has generally effected no change in the law. *See, e.g.*, Marchetti v. Kalish, 53 Ohio St.3d 95, 559 N.E.2d 699 (1990)("Where individuals engage in recreational or sports activities, they assume the ordinary risks of the activity and cannot recover for any injury unless it can be shown that the other participant's actions were either 'reckless' or 'intentional' * * *"); Armstrong v. Mailand, 284 N.W.2d 343 (Minn.1979); Sunday v. Stratton Corp., 136 Vt. 293, 390 A.2d 398 (1978); Becker v. Beaverton School District, 25 Or.App. 879, 551 P.2d 498 (1976); Akins v. Glens Falls City School District, 53 N.Y.2d 325, 441 N.Y.S.2d 644, 424 N.E.2d 531 (1981). *But see* Zambito v. Southland Recreation Enterprises, Inc., 383 So.2d 989 (Fla.App.1980).

2. As the *Auckenthaler* case and the cases cited in the previous note suggest, there is a very distinct split between those states that follow the *Auckenthaler* case and include primary assumption of risk in the comparative negligence calculation and those that treat it as an absence of duty on the part of the defendant or, perhaps, an absence of negligence on the part of the defendant as a matter of law because no duty of reasonable care was owed. In Blackburn v. Dorta, 348 So.2d 287 (Fla.1977) the court stated:

> The term primary assumption of risk is simply another means of stating that the defendant was not negligent, either because he owed no duty to the plaintiff in the first instance, or because he did not breach the duty owed.

The critical difference is who decides whether the plaintiff's conduct bars the plaintiff completely or whether it just reduces the plaintiff's recovery. If it is an absence of duty, that is normally regarded as a question of law for the court. If it is just whether the plaintiff was negligent under the circumstances, it is a question for the jury.

3. It should be pointed out that a number of jurisdictions abolished assumption of risk as a separate defense before—and in some instances well before—they adopted comparative negligence. For example, New Jersey adopted comparative negligence by statute in 1973, at least ten years after the Supreme Court of New Jersey completely abolished assumption of risk as a separate defense. In Meistrich v. Casino Arena Attractions, Inc., 31 N.J. 44, 155 A.2d 90 (1959), followed by McGrath v. American Cyanamid Co., 41 N.J. 272, 196 A.2d 238 (1963), the New Jersey Supreme Court purported to abolish totally all forms of implied assumption of risk, which it defined as situations in which there was neither an "express contract not to sue for injury * * * [nor] actual consent * * * as, for example, participation in a *contact* sport." 31 N.J. 44, 48, 155 A.2d at 93. (Emphasis supplied.) In *Blackburn v. Dorta, supra*, the Supreme Court of Florida purported to do likewise. An extremely influential and often cited article is F. James, Jr., *Assumption of Risk*, 61 Yale L.J. 141 (1952). This was followed by F. James, Jr., *Assumption of Risk: Unhappy Reincarnation*, 78 Yale L.J. 185 (1968), which lamented the *Restatement (Second) of Torts* (1965) continued recognition of the defense (§§ 496A–496G). The late Professor James was one of the ardent proponents of abolishing all but express assumption of risk. It remains to be seen whether most jurisdictions will find it possible to adopt this position. Specifically, it all boils down to the question of whether it is advisable, or even possible, to reduce all situations not involving an "express agreement" or "actual consent" to instances of either "no duty" on the part of the defendant or "contributory negligence" on the part of the plaintiff. For the argument that this is not possible, see K. Simons, *Assumption of Risk and Consent in the Law of Torts: A Theory of Full Preference*, 67 B.U.L.Rev. 213 (1987). The drafters of the *Restatement (Third) of Torts: Apportionment of Liability* have been struggling with this issue. In Preliminary Draft (No. 2), the reporters included a § 3 that provided as follows:

§ 3   Implied Assumption of Risk and Consent

A person's voluntary choice to engage in conduct that reflects a full preference to accept a risk of harm fully known to the person bars recovery for that harm.

Looking back over the cases you have read, how would they be dealt with under this section? Is that a desirable approach? This provision was abandoned in the next draft, Council Draft (No. 1).

4. Consider the following case: A person has been seriously injured and is in danger of bleeding to death. A relative puts the injured person in his automobile and races towards the nearest hospital. Upon approaching a red light at an intersection the relative honks his horn and enters the intersection. The automobile is struck by a vehicle driven by an inattentive motorist who was also driving 10 miles over the speed limit and who is unable to stop in time. The relative is severely injured. Is it not possible that a rational trier of facts could find that the relative behaved reasonably under the circumstances? Would it also not seem odd to conclude that the inattentive, speeding motorist had no duty towards someone in the relative's situation? Should the relative therefore be permitted to recover against the motorist? If not, why not?

5. In Ordway v. Superior Court, 198 Cal.App.3d 98, 243 Cal.Rptr. 536 (1988), it was held that implied assumption of risk remains a viable defense after the adoption of comparative fault in California. The plaintiff, Judy Casella, was a veteran jockey who had ridden in 500 professional horse races

without incident. She was thrown from her mount and further injured when her horse fell and rolled over her during a quarterhorse race. Her injuries occurred after a horse owned by Ordway tangled with another horse which then stumbled in front of Casella's horse. The California Horse Racing Board determined that the jockey riding the first horse violated the rules of the Board by crossing over without sufficient clearance. He was suspended for five racing days. Casella sued the riders, trainers, and owners of the other horses. The California District Court of Appeal cited a similar New York case, Turcotte v. Fell, 68 N.Y.2d 432, 510 N.Y.S.2d 49, 502 N.E.2d 964 (1986). Turcotte, the plaintiff jockey, had won the Triple Crown riding Secretariat in 1973 and had ridden in over 22,000 races. He was injured and rendered a paraplegic as a result of a collision between several horses shortly after the start of a race at Belmont. Turcotte claimed that the defendant jockey violated the New York Racing Association rules and that the defendant New York Racing Association was itself liable for negligently maintaining the portion of the race track near the starting gate. The court ruled that summary judgment should be granted in favor of all the defendants "because by participating in the race plaintiff *consented* that the duty of care owed him by the defendants was no more than a duty to avoid reckless or intentionally harmful conduct." 68 N.Y.2d 432 at 437, 510 N.Y.S.2d at 52, 502 N.E.2d at 967. (Emphasis supplied.) In the California case, plaintiff Casella's assertion that "I did not consider at the time of this race that I was participating in a dangerous activity" was dismissed by the court as "disingenuous." 198 Cal.App.3d 98, 111, 243 Cal.Rptr. at 544. Are these jockey cases more accurately described as cases of "actual consent," as seems to have been the position taken by the New York court, or are they better described as indications that "implied assumption of risk" still remains a viable defense in many situations, even after the adoption of comparative fault?

In another California case, the plaintiff, a private security guard, was injured when a car, driven by a person whom the guard had ordered to leave a roped-off parking area, became entangled in the rope barrier. A majority of the court held that the plaintiff's action was barred by the doctrine of reasonable implied assumption of risk. Novicke v. Vons Grocery Co., 260 Cal.Rptr. 694 (1989)(not officially published). *Cf.* Von Beltz v. Stuntman, Inc., 207 Cal. App.3d 1467, 255 Cal.Rptr. 755 (1989) (stuntwoman).

D. AVOIDABLE CONSEQUENCES, THE "SEAT BELT" DE-FENSE, AND MITIGATION OF DAMAGES

Often plaintiff's behavior before an accident or after an accident may affect the damages suffered by the plaintiff. In both situations the plaintiff may be held to have the responsibility to take *reasonable* action to avoid the behavior that exacerbates the injuries that the defendant's negligence would have otherwise caused. In general, before the advent of comparative negligence, many courts were not very receptive to these defenses, although the courts would occasionally allow them, especially in the case of a duty to mitigate after the accident, for example by taking reasonable actions to seek and follow medical treatment. This reluctance was based, in part, on the idea that the plaintiff should have no duty to anticipate or reduce the consequences of the defendant's negligence. Moreover, the defendant might avoid any responsibility for his/her negligence.

Much legal attention, both case and statute, has been directed at one example involving pre-accident negligence on the part of the plaintiff.

What effect, if any, should be given to the fact that a plaintiff may not have been wearing a seat belt at the time of his injury in an automobile accident? A similar issue arises with regard to the wearing of a protective helmet when riding a motorcycle. Most states now require seat belt use by statute. Similarly several states passed mandatory helmet laws for motorcyclists. In many of those states, however, the mandatory use laws were repealed as a result of political pressure. One might expect that most courts would hold that either violation of a mandatory use law would be contributory negligence per se or, irrespective of the statute, that it should be a jury question whether failure to wear seat belts or helmets was unreasonable conduct on the part of the plaintiff, barring recovery of those damages that could be shown to have resulted from failure to wear the protective gear.

As one might guess the interest group politics on these issues in recent years have had a significant affect upon the law. Several states, in adopting mandatory seat belt laws, explicitly provided that the evidence of the violation of the statute could not be used in civil cases to prove contributory negligence. *See, e.g.,* Conn. Gen. Stat. § 14–100a(c)(4). Several cases, even without statutes, took the same position, relying, in part, upon the idea articulated above: that the plaintiff owes no duty to the defendant to minimize the affect of the defendant's negligence by taking protective measures. Fischer v. Moore, 183 Colo. 392, 517 P.2d 458 (1973); Swajian v. General Motors Corp., 559 A.2d 1041 (R.I.1989).

In some other states, however, either by judicial decision or statute, some reduction in damages is possible for the plaintiff's failure to wear a seat belt. When consideration of the plaintiff's failure to wear a seat belt is permitted by statute, most jurisdictions only allow a limited apportionment of damages for failure to wear a seat belt. *See e.g.* Iowa Code Ann. § 321.445(4)(b)(2)(West)(Supp.1989)(five percent); Mich.Comp.L.Ann. § 257.710e(5)(Supp.1989)(five percent). The New York statute, on the other hand, places no limit on the amount that may be apportioned. N.Y.—McKinney's Veh. & Traf.L. § 1229–c(8).

On the general subject, *see* L. Schwartz, *The Seat Belt Defense and Mandatory Seat Belt Usage: Law, Ethics, and Economics,* 24 Idaho L.Rev. 275 (1988); R. Ackerman, *The Seat Belt Defense Reconsidered: A Return to Accountability in Tort Law?,* 36 Defense L.J. 607 (1987); R. Cochran, Jr., *New Seat Belt Defense Issues: The Impact of Air Bags and Mandatory Seat Belt Use Statutes on the Seat Belt Defense, and the Basis of Damage Reduction Under the Seat Belt Defense,* 73 Minn.L.Rev. 1369 (1989). As to English law, *see* Froom v. Butcher, [1976] Q.B. 286 (C.A.1975), [1975] 3 W.L.R. 379, 3 All E.R. 520.

With the advent of comparative responsibility, courts have increasing come to the conclusion that the evidence of plaintiff's behavior ought to be admissible and then the jury should be allowed to assign the appropriate degree of responsibility of each party. This is the position taken in the Preliminary Draft (No. 2) of the *Restatement (Third) of Torts: Apportionment of Liability,* § 4 (see Comment b and the Reporters' Notes). *See* Waterson v. General Motors Corp., 111 N.J. 238, 544 A.2d 357 (1988), in which the court held that a jury could reduce the plaintiff's recovery owing to her failure to wear her seat belt. In Casenote, 102 Harv.L.Rev. 925 (1989), the *Waterson* case is criticized for not making failure to wear a seat belt a complete bar to recovery for damages that would otherwise have been avoidable. Other cases applying comparative responsibility law include, Hutchins v. Schwartz, 724 P.2d 1194 (Alaska 1986) and Duncan v. Cessna Aircraft Co., 665 S.W.2d 414 (Tex.1984).

With respect to the motorcycle helmet situation, a similar split of authority exists. Denying admission of the evidence as irrelevant are Kealoha v. County of Hawaii, 74 Haw. 308, 844 P.2d 670 (1993); Dare v. Sobule, 674 P.2d 960 (Colo.1984). Failure to wear a helmet was admitted on the issue of damages in Dean v. Holland, 76 Misc.2d 517, 350 N.Y.S.2d 859 (1973). *See also* Halvorson v. Voeller, 336 N.W.2d 118 (N.D.1983); Minn. Stat. § 169.974(6)(1986); Warfel v. Cheney, 157 Ariz. 424, 758 P.2d 1326 (App.1988). In the *Warfel* case the court said

> A helmetless rider who is injured and brings an action to recover in tort must bear the consequences of the free choice not to wear a helmet by reduction of damages in the amount the jury determines the helmet would have reduced the injuries.

For a good, but now somewhat dated, discussion of the issue, see Comment, *Helmetless Motorcyclists—Easy Riders Facing Hard Facts: The Rise of the Motorcycle Helmet Defense*, 41 Ohio St.L.J. 233 (1980).

The issue of mitigation after an accident has not been quite so controversial but does raise some other problems. The *Restatement (Second) of Torts,* § 918 requires reasonable action to mitigate. *See also* Moulton v. Alamo Ambulance Service, 414 S.W.2d 444 (Tex.1967). Preliminary Draft (No. 2) of the new *Restatement,* § 4, includes the duty to mitigate within the comparative responsibility concept. An example used is a plaintiff that is negligently injured, suffering a broken leg. Plaintiff then goes skiing on the broken leg one week after it is set. Plaintiff is reinjured, delaying return to work by two weeks. The *Restatement* provides that this evidence is admissible to allow the jury to reduce defendant's responsibility for the damages associated with the re-injury. This approach leaves the relative blame for subsequent injury or failure to mitigate to be assessed by the jury.

This issue also arises in the context of a negligently injured person refusing medical treatment. The classic case is the refusal to have a blood transfusion for religious reasons. A similar issue was presented in the context of intentional torts earlier. *See, supra*, pp. 74–76. The draft of the new *Restatement* would presumably leave this issue to the jury to resolve. But it could be argued that the plaintiff's action, given the plaintiff's religious beliefs, was reasonable as a matter of law.

One should note, finally, that if the plaintiff's action is egregious enough, the court may hold that that action is a superceding, proximate cause of the accident and relieve the defendant of all responsibility. *See,* for example, Exxon Co. v. Sofec, Inc., ___ U.S. ___, 116 S.Ct. 1813, 135 L.Ed.2d 113 (1996).

Chapter 6

RESPONSIBILITY OF MULTIPLE PARTIES, INCLUDING THE PLAINTIFF

A. INTRODUCTION

We have already encountered several cases in which there were two or more defendants involved. For example, you may want to go back and look at Ybarra v. Spangard, p. 226, Summers v. Tice, p. 247 and Petition of Kinsman Transit Co., p. 301. Cases in which the plaintiff chooses to sue two or more defendants occur in two very different situations. The first is where a defendant is held legally responsible for the tortious conduct of another who is the one actually at fault in causing the injury. This is referred to as "vicarious liability". In these cases suit against the primary tortfeasor, the party that has actually caused the injury, may be useless, frequently, although not always, because that party does not have the financial resources to satisfy a judgment. In situations where vicarious liability exists, the law has provided another defendant, usually one that is more likely to have the financial ability to pay the damages, to insure that the plaintiff will be compensated.[1]

The other common situation in which the plaintiff sues more than one defendant arises in situations in which more than one party has allegedly caused plaintiff an indivisible injury. This situation is covered by the law of "joint tortfeasors". The liability is said to be "joint and several."

Also at the end of this chapter we will take up some relatively recent theories of group liability applicable in certain kinds of situations.

Closely related to vicarious liability and joint and several liability are the law of indemnity and the law of contribution, respectively. The law of indemnity involves the right of one held vicariously liable for the acts of the primary tortfeasor to be "indemnified" for all of the damages paid to the plaintiff. Contribution involves the right of one defendant, who has had to pay a judgment to the plaintiff, to recover some portion of those damages from other joint tortfeasors.

---

1. The person or persons vicariously liable could at common law, and usually today, be joined in one action with the person or persons for whose tort they are responsible.

Today, vicarious liability and indemnity law remain more-or-less as they developed historically at common law. Joint and several liability and the law governing contribution, on the other hand, have been evolving of late, especially to take into account other changes in the law of torts; for example, the adoption in most states of some form of comparative fault and the development of liability based primarily upon degrees of fault.

In reading the material that follows, consider the following hypothetical. Paul is driving down the street. Suddenly a car driven by David negligently pulls out in front of him. He slams on his brakes and stops before hitting David. However, Abby, in a car following Paul, has been driving too closely to stop and runs into the rear of Paul causing serious injury to him. Assume that all agree that Paul's damages amount to $500,000. Also assume that Abby is seventeen years old, a student who has virtually no income or assets. She was, however, driving her father's car, with his permission.

Incidentally, if Abby and her father came to your office seeking to retain you as their lawyer, could you ethically represent both?

B. VICARIOUS LIABILITY

1. *In the Employment Context*

The basic idea of holding someone responsible for the wrongful acts of another has a long and complex history. In many legal systems, indiscriminate revenge has been a common component, holding the group responsible for the acts of any of its members. Specifically, one was generally held responsible for the harmful acts of one's servants or slaves. This approach started to change in the fourteenth century in England and by the sixteenth century the master was only liable if the servant was operating under the express command or consent of the master. Applied strictly, as the rule was by the seventeenth century, the master became a primary tortfeasor, rather than vicariously liable, because of his direct involvement in the tortious act. By the end of the seventeenth century, during a period of growing commercial activity, however, such a cramped view of the extent of the master's liability became increasingly inadequate. *See* Winfield & Jolowicz on Torts 550–51 (11th ed. W. Rogers 1979).

In Tuberville v. Stampe, 1 Salk 13, 1 Ld. Raymond 264, 91 Eng.Rep. 1072 (K.B.1697), Lord Chief Justice Holt finally declared that the master was liable not only for acts which he had expressly commanded but also for acts done by his implied command such as could be inferred from the general authority the servant had been given to execute the tasks given him by the master. From this beginning the modern doctrine evolved that an employer is liable for the actions of employees done within the scope of their employment. In such circumstances the employer is said to be *vicariously liable* for the torts of the employee and the term "vicarious liability" has come to be used as the generic name for this kind of liability. In the context of the employee/employer relationship, the concept of vicarious liability has come to be known as the doctrine of *respondeat superior*.

Over time the emphasis has shifted from actions done within the "scope" of the employee's employment to the broader category of actions that are done within the "course" of an employee's employment.[2] The verbal change has had to do with the problem of "frolic and detour."[3] Take an employee who is told to drive a truck from city *A* to city *B*, fifty miles away. The employee drives thirty miles out of his way to visit a friend in city *C* and negligently injures someone while engaged in this digression. If the deviation from the assigned route is considered sufficiently great to be classified as a "frolic" on the part of the employee, the employer may not be liable for the accident in these circumstances. But as the relative extent of the deviation diminishes, so that the digression becomes a mere "detour," the chances of the employer being held liable increase. Similarly, some of the early cases would not extend the employer's liability to intentional or "wilful" torts that were committed by an employee that could not be said to be authorized by the employer. *See* Prosser & Keeton on Torts 505 (5th ed. 1984). But, at least since the mid-nineteenth century, the courts have been prepared to hold that a master can be liable for intentional torts, however unauthorized, if they are committed by the employee in furtherance of the employer's business purpose. In a leading English case, for example, the employer was held liable when its bus driver crowded a competitor's bus off the road. Limpus v. London & General Omnibus Co., 1 H. & C. 526, 32 L.J.Ex. 34, 158 Eng.Rep. 993 (Ex. Ch. 1862).

In some situations, even if the employee's acts can be said to have no possible relations to the business, actions of employees in the course of their employment have led to liability on the part of their employer. There are, for example, several American cases in which a taxicab or other transportation company has been held liable for the rape of a passenger by an employee. *See* Co-op Cab Co. v. Singleton, 66 Ga.App. 874, 19 S.E.2d 541 (1942); Berger v. Southern Pacific Co., 144 Cal.App.2d 1, 300 P.2d 170 (1956).

Absent applicable statutory provision, on the other hand, some courts have been unwilling to extend the idea to cover other sexual molestation situations. *See* John R. v. Oakland Unified School District, 48 Cal.3d 438, 256 Cal.Rptr. 766, 769 P.2d 948 (1989), where a divided court held that the school district could not be held vicariously liable for the alleged sexual molestation of a boy by his mathematics teacher. Cases imposing and rejecting liability in similar and analogous situations are cited in notes 7 and 8 of the majority opinion. The case was remanded for a determination whether the school district had been negligent in the hiring and supervision of the teacher. A similar, later California case, Lisa M. v. Henry Mayo Newhall Memorial Hosp., 12 Cal.4th 291, 48 Cal.Rptr.2d 510, 907 P.2d 358 (1995), involved a suit against a hospital claiming vicarious liability for the

---

2. The term "course of employment" has been subject to considerable judicial development in worker's compensation where the issue is whether an injury suffered by an employee is covered by the employer's worker's compensation coverage. *See* 1 A. Larson, Workmen's Compensation Ch. IV (1985 ed.). Worker's compensation cases are a fruitful source of analogy in tort cases concerned with the extent of an employer's vicarious liability for the torts of employees.

3. In Joel v. Morison, 6 C. & P. 501, 503, 172 Eng.Rep. 1338, 1339 (Exch.1834), Baron Parke declared that a master is not responsible for the torts of a servant who is not engaged in his business but who is "going on a frolic of his own." On the other hand, as the succeeding text indicates, the master will be responsible for accidents negligently caused by the servant in the course of taking a detour while performing the assigned tasks.

acts of an ultrasound technician who sexually molested a patient. The court stated:

> The nexus required for respondeat superior liability—that the tort be engendered by or arise from the work—is to be distinguished from "but for" causation. That the employment brought the tortfeasor and victim together in time and place is not enough. * * * As with non-sexual assaults, a sexual tort will not be considered engendered by the employment unless its motivating emotions were fairly attributable to work-related events or conditions.

In addition to the "scope of employment" issue, there is much litigation regarding whether the person causing the injury is an employee (or servant) at all. Vicarious responsibility usually does not apply to non-employee agents of the employer, that is, to so-called "independent contractors." As a result there is a great deal of litigation surrounding the definition of these relationships. *See* Prosser & Keeton, Torts 508–16 (5th ed. 1984). If someone hires a taxicab to get to the airport, that person is not responsible for the negligent acts of the taxicab driver en route. In relation to the person hiring the taxicab, the driver will be considered an "independent contractor." On the other hand if the person who hires the taxicab starts to take an active part in the enterprise—say by telling the driver: "Get me to the airport and forget about the speed limit"—then the person hiring the cab may be responsible for the driver's negligent or reckless driving. The whole rationale for the "independent contractor" doctrine is that the employer justifiably relies on the skill of the contractor and does not enter into any active control of the execution of the enterprise.

Over the years, however, the notion of non-delegable duties has arisen to impose liability in a number of situations upon a person who employs an independent contractor. Non-delegable duties typically arise when a person contracts for the performance of dangerous activities such as blasting or excavating. Thus, one who hires an independent contractor to perform any such dangerous activities will be liable for the negligence of the contractor, particularly if the activities result in making some place open to the public dangerous for public use. If the activity is sufficiently dangerous to be called ultrahazardous or abnormally dangerous, the employer of the contractor will also be subjected to the doctrines governing strict liability when the activity miscarries. (*See* Chapter Eight, *infra*). Finally, anyone who is under a duty to maintain land or chattels in a condition that is safe with regard to others is under an obligation to exercise reasonable care in inspecting the completed work of his contractor to determine whether the land or chattels are in a reasonably safe condition; the duty to inspect cannot be delegated. The owner of an office building and a car rental company would be typical instances of persons subject to such non-delegable duties.

Despite some criticism of the idea of the employer's vicarious liability over the years, *see* for example, O.W. Holmes, Jr., *Agency,* 4 Harv.L.Rev. 345, 5 Harv.L.Rev. 1 (1891), and some suggestion that the doctrine was based in the negligence of the employer in the choice of employees, *see* Sharrod v. London & N.W.RY., 4 Exch. 580, 585, 154 Eng.Rep. 1345 1348

(Ex.1849)(Per Parke, B.), the modern trend has unquestionably been in the direction of extending vicarious liability of employers. This trend has been consistent with modern approaches furthering the objectives of compensation and enterprise liability and the relative ease of insuring against the injury, thus spreading the risk and cost of such injuries.

2. *Other Situations Involving Vicarious Liability*

The concept of vicarious liability extends beyond the employer/employee relationship and encompasses activities which involve the pursuit of common purposes that are perfectly lawful. Many of these activities are classified under the rubric, *joint enterprise*. Typically these situations arise in commercial settings when two or more individuals or firms contract to form some kind of joint venture. A partnership would be one type of such joint enterprise. The ends of the partnership or other joint venture might be some specific project or the operation of a continuing business. A law partnership would be an example of the latter situation. In all these situations the general partners or other joint venturers would be legally responsible for any torts committed by the other partners or joint venturers in the course of furthering the common activity. A primary reason for incorporating an enterprise, or choosing some other form of limited liability organizational form permitted by statute, is to escape the full range of risks of vicarious liability for the acts of others.

A joint enterprise can exist in the law, however, even in the absence of an express agreement setting out the purposes and scope of the joint enterprise. Because the classification of an activity as a joint enterprise leads to the vicarious liability of the joint entrepreneurs for the actions of each other, the modern tendency of the courts is to limit the reach of the joint enterprise classification in those situations where there has been no express agreement among the parties. Thus, if two or more friends decide to drive from city *A* to city *B* to see an art exhibit, that fact alone will not change the act of driving from *A* to *B* into a joint enterprise so as to make all of the friends liable in tort if the driver of the car negligently injures someone on the way. In other words, the agreement to share the driving and the expenses will not be enough to make the activity a joint enterprise.

Before a joint enterprise will be found, the courts will insist upon some evidence that the people involved in the activity each had reserved a voice in the management of the activity. Thus, where four school teachers had agreed to tour the western states during their summer vacation and to share the expenses and driving, the court found a joint enterprise because the teachers had agreed that they would decide their itinerary as they proceeded on the basis of a majority vote. *See* Murphy v. Keating, 204 Minn. 269, 283 N.W. 389 (1939). *See also Restatement (Second) of Torts* § 491, *Comment C* (1964) which stresses "(1) an agreement, express or implied, among the members of the group; (2) a common purpose to be carried out by the group; (3) a community of pecuniary interest in that purpose, among the members; and (4) *an equal right to a voice in the direction of the enterprise, which gives an equal right of control.*" (Emphasis supplied). It should finally be noted that the joint enterprise doctrine is generally only applied to govern the relationship between members of the enterprise and outsiders. It normally does not come into play when one member of the enterprise is suing another. *See* Prosser & Keeton on Torts 521–22 (5th ed. 1984).

A distinct situation arose in the law with the advent of the automobile. Courts and legislatures struggled to place financial responsibility on the automobile's owner to cover torts committed by those who drive the automobile with the owner's consent.[4] The purpose has been to provide a party able, usually because of the presence of insurance, to pay the damages and reflects the fact that drivers other than the owner are frequently judgment proof. One of the earliest moves in this direction was the judicial creation, in about a dozen states, of the *family purpose* doctrine. Under this doctrine a person who owns an automobile and permits the members of the household to use it, has been deemed to have obtained and provided the vehicle for a "family purpose." In effect, the members of the owner's household using the vehicle with his permission for their own pleasure or convenience are considered to be the servants of the owner in the pursuit of this "family purpose." Overlapping this doctrine is the doctrine developed in a number of states that, if the owner of the automobile is present, he is deemed to have a sufficient right of control over the driver to make the driver the agent of the owner. Thus the effect of these devices is to make the owner responsible for the torts of the driver. There are so many variations in these doctrines from state to state that it is not worth pursuing the matter further in a first-year torts case-book. For a more extended textual discussion, see Prosser & Keeton on Torts 522–29 (5th ed. 1984).

At least a dozen states have dealt with the automobile situation more directly by enacting legislation imposing vicarious liability upon the owner of a vehicle for torts committed by persons driving the vehicle with the owner's consent. Owner's liability has even been found under this type of statute when the car was entrusted to a parking lot attendant. *See* Carter v. Travelers Ins. Co., 113 A.D.2d 178, 495 N.Y.S.2d 168 (1985). For the purposes of illustrating these "owner responsibility" statutes, consider the following New York and North Carolina statutes:

§ 388. Negligence in use or operation of vehicle attributable to owner

1. Every owner of a vehicle used or operated in this state shall be liable and responsible for death or injuries to person or property resulting from negligence in the use or operation of such vehicle, in the business of such owner or otherwise, by any person using or operating the same with the permission, express or implied, of such owner.

N.Y. [Veh. & Traf.] Law § 388 (Westlaw 1996).

§ 20–71.1. Registration evidence of ownership; ownership evidence of defendant's responsibility for conduct of operation.

(a) In all actions to recover damages for injury to the person or to property or for the death of a person, arising out of an accident or

---

4. The handling of this issue under no-fault insurance schemes, now adopted in a number of states, is discussed in Chapter Fourteen, *infra*.

collision involving a motor vehicle, proof of ownership of such motor vehicle at the time of such accident or collision shall be prima facie evidence that said motor vehicle was being operated and used with the authority, consent, and knowledge of the owner in the very transaction out of which said injury or cause of action arose.

N.C. Gen. Stat. § 20–71.1(a)(Westlaw 1996).[5]

3. *Indemnity*

The common law allowed a vicariously liable party to seek indemnity from the primary tortfeasor. Under the concept of indemnity, the party satisfying the claim of the plaintiff is entitled to recover the entire amount that he has paid from the party against whom indemnity is granted. The paradigm case of indemnity arises where there has been no concert of action nor any independent acts contributing to an indivisible result but rather one person is merely vicariously liable for the torts of another, such as an employer for the torts of his employee or, in many states, the owner of a motor vehicle for the negligence of the driver. In these situations the person who is vicariously liable for the torts of another is not considered to be guilty of any fault in the context of any action for reimbursement he may bring against the person for whose torts he is vicariously liable. The vicarious liability rules are designed to ensure that the injured party can get compensation. The indemnity rule is designed to promote the deterrent and punishment functions by placing the cost of the accident, when possible, on the person really at fault.

Usually the primary party will be sued along with the vicariously responsible party, in which case the underlying liability of the primary party is established and that party has notice and the opportunity to defend. When this is true the indemnity action is relatively simple. However, when, for example, the vicariously liable party settles the suit with the plaintiff and then seeks indemnity, the indemnity plaintiff must establish that the indemnity defendant received proper and timely notice of settlement, that the indemnity defendant was in fact liable, and that the settlement was fair and reasonable. Unlike the modern law of contribution, to which we will shortly turn, release by the plaintiff of one defendant also operates as a release of the other defendant since there is only one claim against either defendant. *See* Mamalis v. Atlas Van Lines, 522 Pa. 214, 560 A.2d 1380 (1989).

The concept of indemnity has been extended, in many jurisdictions, to cover the situation where one of the defendants may be said to be merely "passively" negligent while the other defendant was "actively" negligent. This type of indemnity is sometimes referred to as "equitable indemnity" or "implied indemnity." As a typical example, consider the case where one defendant is liable to the plaintiff for negligently manufacturing an item and the other defendant, the retailer, is jointly liable to the plaintiff for failing to inspect the item. If the plaintiff secures satisfaction of the judgment from the second defendant who was guilty of merely "passive"

---

5. In North Carolina, when physically present in the vehicle, the owner is normally considered to have the right to control the driver and will thus be responsible for the driver's negligence irrespective of the presumption in this section. *See* Randall v. Rogers, 262 N.C. 544, 138 S.E.2d 248 (1964).

negligence, this passively negligent defendant may seek indemnity for the entire amount that was paid the plaintiff from the first defendant who negligently manufactured the item. The principle has also been used in products liability-strict liability cases. *See* Promaulayko v. Johns Manville Sales Corp., 116 N.J. 505, 562 A.2d 202 (1989) for a full discussion of the policies involved. See generally, 79 ALR 4th 278. In several states, this active-passive distinction has now been abolished as those states have modified the law of indemnity and contribution to reflect the adoption of comparative fault. Preliminary Draft (No. 2) of the *Restatement (Third) of Torts: Apportionment of Liability* § 30 does away with the active-passive distinction except as to parties held vicariously liable in the chain of distribution of products under products liability law. The Reporter's Notes in Comment e. states:

> These doctrines were developed and [the] vast majority of the cases employing them arose prior to the adoption of comparative responsibility. They could be justified as avoiding the harsh effect of pro rata contribution when one of the tortfeasors was substantially more culpable than the other. These doctrines are no longer needed under comparative responsibility. In fact, their all or nothing approach is inconsistent with the goals of comparative responsibility.

See, e.g., American Motorcycle Ass'n v. Superior Court, 20 Cal.3d 578, 146 Cal.Rptr. 182, 578 P.2d 899 (1978); Cella Barr Asso., Inc. v. Cohen, 177 Ariz. 480, 868 P.2d 1063 (App.1994). *But see,* Hiway 20 Terminal, Inc. v. Tri–County Agri–Supply, Inc., 232 Neb. 763, 443 N.W.2d 872 (Neb.1989). The Uniform Contribution Among Tortfeasors Act, *infra,* does not alter any rights of indemnity. However, the Connecticut Supreme Court has held that the Connecticut products liability statute replaced the common law of indemnity with comparative responsibility for products liability cases. Kyrtatas v. Stop & Shop Inc., 205 Conn. 694, 535 A.2d 357 (1988).

4. *Imputed Contributory/Comparative Negligence*

WATSON v. REGIONAL TRANSPORTATION DISTRICT

Supreme Court of Colorado, 1988.
762 P.2d 133.

Lohr, Justice.

Jayma Watson (Watson) suffered severe injuries to her right leg and foot when the motorcycle on which she was riding as a passenger collided with a bus owned and operated by the Regional Transportation District (RTD). The motorcycle was operated by Watson's husband, Randy. Watson brought a negligence action against RTD. A jury determined that she had suffered damages in the amount of $100,000 and that fifty-one percent of the damages were caused by the negligence of RTD and forty-nine percent by the negligence of Randy Watson. The trial court ruled that the negligence of Watson's husband must be imputed to her and entered judgment in favor of Watson and against RTD in the sum of $51,000. Watson appealed * * *. We conclude that the negligence of Watson's husband should not have been imputed to her * * *. We therefore remand the case to the * * * trial court for a new trial.

I.

This case arose out of a traffic accident that occurred on April 23, 1982, in Boulder, Colorado. Watson and her husband were traveling west on their motorcycle on Arapahoe Avenue at a distance behind an RTD bus. The bus stopped for a stoplight at 33rd Street and began a right turn after the light changed. Before completing the turn, the bus stopped again. Watson's husband applied the brakes on the motorcycle when he saw the bus stop. The motorcycle skidded sixty-three feet and struck the rear of the bus.

At the time of the accident, the Watsons were running errands * * *. Although Jayma Watson owned the motorcycle jointly with her husband, she did not have an operator's license and did not know how to operate the motorcycle.

Watson brought an action against RTD * * *. Prior to trial, RTD moved for summary judgment. In the motion, RTD argued that the accident was caused solely by the negligence of Watson's husband. RTD further argued that Randy Watson's negligence must be imputed to Jayma Watson as a matter of law, "since Jayma Watson is the joint owner of the motorcycle, was a passenger on the motorcycle at the time of the rear-end collision, and Mr. and Mrs. Watson were proceeding to an agreed upon destination for a common purpose." RTD also argued that "[t]here is no evidence or facts which demonstrate any negligence on the part of [RTD] at the time the rear-end collision occurred."

II.

A.

This case presents an issue concerning the circumstances under which the negligence of the operator of a motor vehicle should be imputed to a passenger in a negligence action brought by the passenger against a third party to recover damages for personal injuries. * * * [In] *Moore v. Skiles,* 130 Colo. 191, 274 P.2d 311 (1954), the plaintiff was injured when the truck driven by her husband in which she was riding as a passenger was involved in an accident with another vehicle. The couple owned the truck jointly. The plaintiff subsequently brought an action in negligence against the driver of the other vehicle. The trial court instructed the jury that the contributory negligence of the plaintiff's husband must be imputed to the plaintiff. In assessing the correctness of the instruction, we stated the following rule:

> Where, as here, joint ownership of the car is shown; where joint occupancy and possession of the vehicle is admitted, and where the occupant-owners of the car use it upon a joint mission, the driver will be presumed to be driving for himself and as an agent for the other present joint owner.

Moore v. Skiles is somewhat typical of those cases in which contributory or comparative negligence is imputed because of the existence of a "joint enterprise" between the parties. Generally speaking, a joint enterprise is an undertaking to carry out a small number of acts or objectives, which is entered into by associates under such circumstances that all have an equal voice in directing the conduct of the enterprise. The law then considers that each is the agent or servant of the others, and that the act of any one within the scope of the enterprise is to be charged vicariously against the rest. * * *

Moore v. Skiles has been followed in cases subsequently decided by this court and the Colorado Court of Appeals. * * * In *Lasnetske v. Parres,* we elaborated on the right of the passenger-owner or co-owner to control the driver—the right that underpins the imputation of negligence of the driver to the passenger:

> The 'right to exercise control' is not dependent upon the ability of the passenger to actually drive the vehicle. It is not contemplated that a co-owning passenger in exercising his right to control will physically wrest the wheel from the driver. Rather, verbal admonition, suggestions or even outright commands are the usual methods whereby the co-owning passenger exercises his right to control. It is a well-known fact that some of the better 'back seat' drivers are those who know little, or nothing, about the actual driving of the vehicle, but can nonetheless still offer friendly advice, if not flat commands, to the driver.

148 Colo. at 78, 365 P.2d at 254.

Watson urges us to reconsider the rule of *Moore v. Skiles*. She argues that an owner who is a passenger in a motor vehicle has no practical ability to exercise control over the driver and that there is no basis in logic or in policy for imputing the driver's negligence to the passenger under such circumstances. This issue has occupied the attention of many courts and commentators, and we now revisit the rule of *Moore v. Skiles* with the guidance provided by those authorities.

B.

Imputed negligence is a form of vicarious liability and represents one exception to the rule in our system of tort liability that individuals are responsible for their own negligence, but not that of another. *See* 4 F. Harper, F. James, Jr., & O. Gray, *The Law of Torts* § 23.1 (2d ed. 1986) * * *. The rule, as applied in the present context, undoubtedly rests on the legal fiction "that an owner-passenger reserves a right to control over the physical details of driving or that the driver consents to submit himself to the control of a 'back-seat driver.' " * * * This fiction perhaps bore some resemblance to reality before the advent of the automobile, when a passenger on a wagon pulled by a team of horses could assume control of the team from the driver. * * * Today, however, "there is no longer any basis for assuming that the passenger, no matter what his relationship to the driver may be, has the capacity to assert control over or direct the operation of a moving automobile." * * *

The rule of imputed negligence in motor vehicle cases, and the fictional right to control upon which it is based, arose as a result of and still find their primary justifications in considerations of public policy. Earlier in the twentieth century the growing injury toll from traffic accidents prompted a search for financially responsible defendants. * * * The search ultimately led to the employment of the doctrine of imputed negligence in motor vehicle cases, whereby liability was imposed on the defendant owner-passenger of a vehicle based upon the negligence of the driver, even though the owner-passenger was free from negligence. * * * The salient rationale underlying the doctrine, as it relates to defendant owner-passengers, is that since automobiles are expensive, the owner is more likely to be able to pay any damages than the driver, who may be entirely impecunious; and that the owner is the obvious person to carry the necessary insurance to cover the risk, and so to distribute any losses among motorists as a class. * * * Thus, the negligence of a driver was imputed to the defendant owner-passenger to provide the injured party with a financially responsible source of recovery. * * * Courts justified the doctrine either by reference to the parties' legal relationship (*e.g.,* master-servant, principal-agent or joint enterprise) or simply in terms of the all-encompassing "right to control." * * *

The imputation of a driver's negligence to an owner-passenger, however, was later recognized in circumstances in which the owner-passenger sought recovery from a third party for injuries suffered. *Reed v. Hinderland,* 660 P.2d at 469. Absent a basis in policy or logic, but in order to provide symmetry between cases involving defendants' and plaintiffs' negligence, courts employed the rule of imputed negligence "both ways." *Johnson v. Los Angeles–Seattle Motor Express, Inc.,* 222 Or. 377, 352 P.2d 1091, 1094–95 (1960); Harper, James and Gray § 23.1. Paradoxically, the "both-ways" rationale led courts to take a rule that departed from the common law in response to a call for wider liability and to employ that rule to curtail liability by expanding the scope of the defense of contributory negligence. * * *

The "both-ways" rule of imputed contributory negligence has attracted criticism from courts and commentators pointing out its logical infirmities and questionable policy consequences. As a result, although many courts have adopted a rule similar to that of *Moore v. Skiles* and have adhered to it, others have either declined in the first instance to impute contributory negligence of a driver to an owner-passenger seeking recovery from a third party for negligent infliction of injuries, or have retreated from the doctrine after initially adopting it. * * *

We conclude that the rule of imputed comparative negligence, as expressed in *Moore v. Skiles,* is based upon a legal fiction unsupported by, and in direct opposition to, valid policy considerations. We are persuaded that the better rule is that an owner-passenger's recovery for injuries negligently inflicted by a third party should be limited only if the owner-passenger herself is negligent and if that negligence is a proximate cause of her injury. As one commentator has stated:

> The whole doctrine of vicarious liability stems from considerations other than the defendant's personal fault, for it assumes his innocence. * * * If the principle of liability or disability for individualized fault is taken as the norm, and vicarious liability or disability is regarded as an exceptional solution (to be justified only for reasons of policy sufficient in each case to warrant the exception), then there would be little justification indeed for imputing negligence to an innocent plaintiff in most cases.

Harper, James and Gray § 23.6, at 441–42. The very considerations upon which the doctrine of imputed negligence rests are absent in the case of imputed comparative negligence where the owner is an injured passenger in his own car. *See Weber v. Stokely–Van Camp, Inc.*, 144 N.W.2d at 543. The sole virtue of the both ways test "is that it is logical and symmetrical. Important legal rights ought to have better footing than mere architectural symmetry." * * * In fact, the rule of imputed comparative negligence if applied to defeat or reduce recovery by an injured owner-passenger, only serves to frustrate the goal of broadened liability upon which the doctrine was originally based. * * * A "rule which so incongruously shields conceded wrongdoing bears a heavy burden of justification." *Kalechman*, 353 N.Y.S.2d at 419–20, 308 N.E.2d at 890–91 (quoting *Badigian v. Badigian*, 9 N.Y.2d 472, 215 N.Y.S.2d 35, 38, 174 N.E.2d 718, 721 (1961)). In short, symmetry is an insufficient justification for continued adherence to a rule of law that is at odds with logic and policy.

C.

The logical and practical shortcomings of the rule of imputed comparative negligence are apparent when applied to the facts of this case. The fictional "joint enterprise" upon which the Watsons embarked was simply the decision to run a couple of errands and then ride to Longmont. From this "joint enterprise" and Watson's co-ownership of the motorcycle arises a second fiction: that Jayma Watson had a "right to control" Randy Watson's actions. Jayma Watson's "right to control" leads to the third fiction: that Randy Watson was her agent. "This top heavy structure tends to fall of its own weight." Prosser and Keeton § 72, at 522. Moreover, as a practical matter any attempt on Jayma Watson's part to interfere with Randy Watson's driving at the time of the accident likely would have constituted negligence on her part as well.

We therefore hold that the driver's negligence may not be imputed to an owner-passenger so as to limit the owner-passenger's recovery in an action in negligence. The owner-passenger's recovery shall be affected only if she is personally negligent, and if that negligence is a proximate cause of her injuries. In so holding, we overrule *Moore v. Skiles* and the cases that have followed it.

Notes

1. One of the leading cases abolishing imputed contributory negligence is Kalechman v. Drew Auto Rental, Inc., 33 N.Y.2d 397, 353 N.Y.S.2d 414, 308 N.E.2d 886 (1973). That case involved imputation of the negligence of the deceased driver to a passenger who had rented the car and therefore "had dominion and control" over the driver. The suit was against the car rental agency, which, under a New York statute, was vicariously liable for the negligence of the driver. The court held that the negligence of the driver would not be imputed to the passenger to block the action against the owner.

2. The introduction of the "both-ways" test was initially considered not only intellectually more satisfying but also as a reform measure. At one time there were cases in which the contributory negligence of a bus driver was imputed to a passenger, that of a bailee to a bailor, and that of a parent to a child whom the parent had negligently supervised. These were all situations in which it was only contributory negligence that was being imputed; the passen-

ger was not vicariously liable for the negligence of the driver, nor the bailor for the negligence of the bailee, nor the child for the negligence of a parent. For the history of these doctrines, see F. James, Jr., *Imputed Contributory Negligence,* 14 La.L.Rev. 340 (1954). The passenger/bus driver cases were overruled in the latter nineteenth century. Texas was apparently the last state, in the absence of a statute, to impute the contributory negligence of a bailee to a bailor. It repudiated this doctrine in Rollins Leasing Corp. v. Barkley, 531 S.W.2d 603 (Tex.1975). Maine appears to be the last state to abolish imputation of the negligence of a parent to a child suing a third party for his/her injury. LaBier v. Pelletier, 665 A.2d 1013 (Me.1995). In most of these situations today, the defendant can, of course, implead the negligent parent, spouse, bailee, etc. as a co-defendant. The rule was never used to impute the negligence of the primary tortfeasor to the vicariously liable party in an action by that party for indemnity.

The problems with the both-ways test started to surface when vicarious liability began to expand. We have already noted, for example, the owner responsibility statutes and caselaw holding the owner responsible for accidents caused by those driving with permission or pursuant to a "family purpose." Most such statutes and caselaw have been construed not to impute the driver's contributory negligence to the owner bringing an action for damage to his interest, at least when the owner is not present in the vehicle so as to bring into play any "right of control" doctrine. Thus in this area, at least, most states have carved out an exception to the both-ways rule for automobile accident cases.

Preliminary Draft (No. 2) of the *Restatement (Third) of Torts: Apportionment of Liability,* § 6, reflects this approach. While it continues to use the both-ways rule, imputing the contributory negligence in most tort situations, it carves out an exception in the automobile accident cases. Thus, in most cases, except automobile accident cases, where the third party's negligence would be imputed to the vicariously liable party in his or her posture as a defendant, it will also be imputed as contributory negligence when that party is suing as plaintiff. Of course, with comparative negligence, only that portion of the responsibility assigned by the jury to the primary tortfeasor will be imputed in any case.

One very important area in which imputed contributory negligence arises is derivative actions, such as wrongful death and claims for lose of consortium. These will be taken up in Chapter 11, *infra.*

3. The areas in which imputed contributory negligence has retained most of its original force are the employer/employee relationship and, by analogy, those situations in which the courts are prepared to find a joint enterprise.

C. JOINT AND SEVERAL LIABILITY

Under traditional principles, when two or more people acting in pursuit of a common purpose engage in tortious activity towards some other person, each of the persons engaged in the common enterprise will be liable to the injured party for the entire damages. Thus the plaintiff has the choice of suing one or more of the joint tortfeasors and, once judgment is secured, collecting the damages against any one or more of the defendants.[6] In this way the law gives the plaintiff the maximum opportunity to

---

6. As we will see later in this chapter, although the plaintiff may receive a judgment or judgments against a number of defendants, the plaintiff is only entitled to one

collect damages against one or more of the defendants and the law does not much care who ends up having to pay since all of the defendants have been determined to be wrongdoers and to have caused plaintiff's injury. To use the conventional legal terms, all the participants in a common enterprise are classified as *joint tortfeasors* and they will each be *severally* liable for satisfying the plaintiff's judgment.

So long as the defendant has joined in the enterprise, each member of the enterprise will be liable even if he or she did not personally commit any of the acts that injured the plaintiff. *See* Sir John Heydon's Case, 11 Co.Rep. 5, 77 Eng.Rep. 1150 (K.B.1613). The early cases typically involved situations where two or more persons had agreed (or "conspired") to do some illegal act, such as beat up the plaintiff. Over the course of time, cases arose in which there was no express agreement to engage in the illegal activity. For example, motorists who engage in a spontaneous drag race have been treated as joint tortfeasors. *See, e.g.,* Bierczynski v. Rogers, 239 A.2d 218 (Del.1968); Nelson v. Nason, 343 Mass. 220, 177 N.E.2d 887 (1961). In other words, an agreement to engage in illegal conduct can be implied from the surrounding circumstances.

At common law two or more tortfeasors could not be joined as defendants in the same action unless there were either some concert of action or the situation was one involving vicarious liability.[7] This state of the law imposed substantial difficulties upon plaintiffs who suffered one indivisible injury from the conduct of two independent tortfeasors, and such types of situations rapidly multiplied in the course of the nineteenth century with the improvement in roads and consequent increase in road traffic attendant upon the industrial revolution. A typical instance would be a case in which the plaintiff was forced to swerve his horse drawn wagon to avoid a negligent driver of another wagon and then was struck by another negligently driven wagon. At common law although the plaintiff suffered one indivisible injury he could not join the two negligent drivers in one action. The plaintiff would have to bring separate actions against each of them.[8]

"satisfaction" of the claim. Once the claim has been paid in full—as by the satisfaction of the judgment against one of the defendants—the plaintiff may not enforce any judgment or judgments pertaining to the same claim entered against the other members of the enterprise. What the rights of the various defendants are among themselves will be explored in the section of this chapter dealing with contribution. For the moment, it may be helpful to be aware of the fact that, although the law has greatly changed over the last 100 years, at common law there was no contribution among joint tortfeasors; whoever paid the plaintiff's claim had no remedies against the other tortfeasors. Put another way the plaintiff had, and incidentally still has in most situations, complete discretion in deciding which defendant against whom to enforce the judgment. At common law, joint tortfeasors had to be sued in one action, and in England this was the law until well into the twentieth century, but in the United States, from a much earlier time, an unsatisfied judgment against one joint tortfeasor did not bar action against a joint tortfeasor who had not been joined in the previous action.

7. In the vicarious liability situation the person or persons vicariously liable could be joined in one action with the person or persons for whose torts they were responsible.

8. The plaintiff would be forced into this expedient if he were unable (or not sure that he would be able) to recover satisfaction for all of his injuries from one of the potential defendants.

In England, it was not until the early twentieth century that the courts construed the procedural reforms of the late nineteenth century to have changed this state of affairs.[9] In the United States, however, the situation began to be altered with the adoption of the Field Code in New York in 1848 and the adoption of similar codes of civil procedure in many other states. These codes were gradually interpreted to permit joinder of defendants responsible for indivisible injuries even though the plaintiff is technically asserting separate causes of action against these defendants because they were not acting in concert. At the present day, persons who have been responsible for causing single indivisible injuries to a particular plaintiff will for all intents and purposes be regarded as the equivalent of joint tortfeasors. They may thus be joined in a single action and, if found to have tortiously contributed to the plaintiff's injuries, will be jointly and severally liable to the plaintiff. The interesting modern question concerns the issue of when have the defendants, although acting independently, contributed to one indivisible set of injuries.

MADDUX v. DONALDSON

Supreme Court of Michigan, 1961.
362 Mich. 425, 108 N.W.2d 33.

SMITH, JUSTICE.

Once again we consider the problem of damages when the car in which plaintiffs are riding is struck first by one automobile and then, almost simultaneously, by another.

The plaintiffs are Fred Maddux, his wife, and infant daughter. They were driving in an easterly direction on US–112, near Clinton, Michigan, in a Ford pickup. It had been raining and the pavement was wet. Paul Bryie was following them, both cars traveling at speeds between 35 and 40 miles per hour. As the cars approached a bend in the road, Mr. Maddux observed a car some 1500 feet away, skidding towards him, sideways, "in a swinging motion, in an arc" at a high rate of speed. He tried to get beyond a certain point on the highway before the skidding car reached it but was unsuccessful. The 2 cars collided, with extensive damage to both.

While plaintiffs' car was stopped, with its occupants injured, it was struck again almost immediately, this time by the car following. Again the impact was substantial; Mr. Bryie considered his car to be a total loss.

The cases against the skidding driver, William Donaldson, was [sic] discontinued by plaintiffs. The court subsequently dismissed the cases of Mrs. Maddux and her daughter against Mr. Bryie, the driver of the following car, on the ground that "there is no evidence of damage before this jury from which any inference can be drawn in relation to the responsibility of Paul Bryie." Mr. Maddux's case was dismissed on the ground that he was guilty of contributory negligence as a matter of law. [This ruling was reversed in a part of the opinion that is omitted.]

We now reach the problem of the plaintiff whose injuries have resulted from successive impacts, to all intents and purposes concurrent. This is

9. Bullock v. London General Omnibus Co., [1907] 1 K.B. 264 (C.A.1906).

one of the most baffling of our current legal problems, critical because of the extensive use of expressways upon which large numbers of cars travel at high speeds in close proximity to one another. As to the issue presented, the courts are in the most serious conflict, our own Court dividing 3 ways among the 6 justices sitting the last time the issue was before us. The difficulty arises from the fact that we do not have a "joint" tort in the ordinary sense of the word, and thus it is argued that there cannot be joint and several liability. There has been no breach of any "joint" duty owed the plaintiffs by the 2 automobile drivers who successively collided with their car. Obviously the 2 did not act in concert. Nor is the joint enterprise doctrine applicable, nor master-servant, nor principal-agent. Actually what we have is injury to plaintiffs resulting from the independent and tortious acts of 2 tortfeasors.

There is authority, in this situation, that plaintiff must separate the injuries, ascribing some to one tortfeasor and the balance to the other * * *. Such authority concludes that if plaintiff cannot make such differentiation he cannot recover from either. This type of decision is well illustrated by the case of Adams v. Hall, 1829, 2 Vt. 9. In this case an owner of sheep suffered loss to his flock through the depredations of 2 dogs. The owners he sued jointly. It was shown at the trial, however, that they were not joint owners. In addition, there was no testimony as to which dog killed which sheep. In approving a non-suit it was held that neither owner was liable for the actions of the other's dog, merely because they "did the mischief in company."

However defensible such a result may have been in this and cases similar in principle in an agrarian economy shortly after the American Revolution (and even this is open to question) we do not regard it as precedent governing the liability of automobile owners in what are known as "chain collisions" on today's highways. It should be unnecessary to spell out the differences between the social problems presented or the judicial policies involved in their solution. When we impose upon an injured plaintiff the necessity of proving which impact did which harm in a chain collision situation, what we are actually expressing is a judicial policy that it is better that a plaintiff, injured through no fault of his own, take nothing, than that a tortfeasor pay more than his theoretical share of the damages accruing out of a confused situation which his wrong has helped to create. The mere statement of the policy exposes its aberrations. It is at war with at least the last hundred years of judicial progress. It is, in addition, as Dean Wigmore has pointed out,[10] utterly inconsistent with the *ratio decidendi* of precedents going back at least to the year 1613[11] when the rule of joint and several liability dispensed with the necessity of plaintiff's proof of just which ruffian inflicted which injury when he was set upon by three. The reason behind the rule was impossibility, the impossibility of plaintiff's proving the origin of each of his injuries. Where the same impossibility exists today, our sensitivity to plaintiff's injury should be no less than that of the King's Bench to its plaintiff, whose "wounding (which in truth was in a cruel and barbarous manner) at Fakenham in

10. Wigmore, Joint–Tortfeasors and Severance of Damages, 17 Ill.L.Rev. 458 [1922–23].

11. Heydon's Case (K.B.1613) 11 Co.Rep. 5a (77 Eng.Rep. 1150).

Norfolk" was held to impose joint and several liability upon the defendants. It is clear that there is a manifest unfairness in "putting on the injured party the impossible burden of proving the specific shares of harm done by each. * * * Such results are simply the law's callous dullness to innocent sufferers. One would think that the obvious meanness of letting wrong-doers go scot free in such cases would cause the courts to think twice and to suspect some fallacy in their rule of law."[12]

The fallacy involved turns upon the word "divisible." In the case before us, at the conclusion of the 2 impacts, Mrs. Maddux suffered from a fracture of the right femur, of the left patella, and of the right radius ulna, in addition to multiple lacerations of the face. She had passed blood in her urine, suffered an eye injury, and, withal, came psychiatric difficulties, possibly "of an organic toxic basis." Are such injuries divisible? Theoretically, they may be, possibly they are. We may hypothesize situations in which some participant in the tragedy remains uninjured and observant, or in which the force and direction of the impacts are so markedly different that a reasonable allocation of harm to them may be made. But these cases would present no difficulty. The challenging situation is the one before us, involving 2 substantial impacts with multiple injuries, in respect of which a jury would be well justified in concluding that the plaintiff's various injuries may not be identified as to origin. As a matter of fact it may be utterly unrealistic to insist that the plaintiff is suffering merely from a series of wounds, separable either legally or medically. Actually the plaintiff may suffer from a composite injury, the ingredients of which are impossible to identify in origin and impracticable to isolate in treatment. Thus in the case before us, was the blood in the urine the result of the first impact or the second? Will the psychiatric treatment be related to the fracture of the femur, or to the multiple lacerations of the face, with its "jagged facial scars," or to the overall condition?

* * * It is our conclusion that if there is competent testimony, adduced either by plaintiff or defendant, that the injuries are factually and medically separable, and that the liability for all such injuries and damages, or parts thereof, may be allocated with reasonable certainty to the impacts in turn, the jury will be instructed accordingly and mere difficulty in so doing will not relieve the triers of the facts of this responsibility.[13] This merely follows the general rule that "where the independent concurring acts have caused distinct and separate injuries to the plaintiff, or where some reasonable means of apportioning the damages is evident, the courts generally will not hold the tort-feasors jointly and severally liable."[14]

But if, on the other hand, the triers of the facts conclude that they cannot reasonably make the division of liability between the tortfeasors, this is the point where the road of authority divides.

12. Wigmore, Joint–Tortfeasors and Severance of Damages, 17 Ill.L.Rev. 458, 459 [1922–23].

13. "This does not mean that the question is always one of fact. Indeed, it is easy to conceive the case of chain vehicular pile-up where, as a matter of law, the last or next to last negligent motorist is shown as having caused no damage to the precedently injured plaintiff." Meier v. Holt, 347 Mich. 430, 441, 80 N.W.2d 207, 215 [1956] (Black, J., concurring).

14. 1 Harper and James, Torts, § 10.1, at 694.

It is pointed out, also, that one impact took place some 30 seconds after the other. The fact that one wrong takes place a few seconds after the other is without legal significance. What is significant is that the injury is indivisible. The blows of the ruffians referred to in Heydon's case, supra, need not necessarily have fallen upon the victim at the same instant of time, and undoubtedly did not. The reason for the rule as to joint liability for damages was the indivisibility of the injuries, not the timing of the various blows. As a matter of fact, a distinguished English authority has stated that concurrence, in the law of torts, has no reference to time, except that both torts must precede the damage. Carefully reasoned American cases fully support this view. The conclusion seems inescapable unless we take the position that "concurrent" actually means "simultaneous," a position for which there is no well-reasoned authority.

Many years ago, a Justice, in speaking for this Court, put a pregnant question. He asked, in a case in which joint liability in tort was urged, whether or not the plaintiff "who has thus suffered the wrong" was entitled to a remedy, or whether "the difficulties and dangers [of the suit] are to be thrown upon those presumably in the wrong rather than upon him who was not in fault?" He continued "If in either view injustice is likely to be done should not the defendants assume or be charged with the risk? Is there, however, likely to be any injustice done in holding them jointly liable? I think not."[15] Nor do we.

Here, then, is the essence of the problem—Where is the likelihood of injustice? We think it is in denying the blameless victim of traffic chain collision any recovery whatever. We perceive no reason why his tortfeasors should escape liability because of the very complexity of the injury created by their wrong.

There is no merit in additional points raised. The case is reversed and remanded for new trial. Costs to appellants.

CARR, JUSTICE (dissenting). [DETHMERS, C.J. and KELLY, J. concurred in the dissent.]

The rule has been consistently recognized in Michigan, as well as in other States, that a tortfeasor may not be held liable for damages for an injury not caused by such defendant's wrongful conduct.

It will be noted that we are not dealing in these cases with the possible liability of a first tortfeasor for injuries sustained by plaintiff as the result of subsequent acts by others. Conceivably the facts in such a case might justify the conclusion that the first wrongdoer's conduct had set in motion a chain of circumstances, that should have been foreseen by him, involving the theory of continuing negligence or other sufficient reason for not applying the doctrine of subsequent independent acts of negligence on the part of another. Neither do we have a case of joint tortfeasors or of concurrent acts by two or more parties resulting in an injury. As plaintiff Fred Maddux testified, approximately 30 seconds elapsed between his collision with the Donaldson car and the subsequent impact by the automobile of defendant Bryie. A number of injuries were sustained by each of the parties, but the proofs failed to indicate what specific injuries were

15. Cuddy v. Horn, 46 Mich. 596, 603, 10 N.W. 32, 34 (1881).

caused by each impact. In fact, there was a dearth of proof that defendant Bryie, with whose liability we are solely concerned in the instant cases, was responsible for any of the injuries sustained by Mrs. Maddux or the daughter.

The application of [the majority approach] would obviously result in relieving a plaintiff bringing action against two or more successive tortfeasors of the duty of proving his case against each in order to be entitled to recover damages therefrom. Under ordinary circumstances at least a plaintiff might consider that a joint and several judgment against both or all of the defendants would be preferable to separate recoveries against them based on evidence. This might well result in forcing a defendant to assume the burden of showing liability of one of his co-defendants in order to avoid a judgment against himself.

Notes

1. The insurance company that had insured "Donaldson, the skidding driver," had become insolvent while this case was pending. 362 Mich. at 437, 108 N.W.2d at 39 (portion of Carr, J.'s, dissenting opinion not reprinted above). This is undoubtedly the reason the action against Donaldson was discontinued by the plaintiffs who filed a claim in the receivership proceedings instituted against the insolvent insurance carrier. Under the rule prevailing in Michigan prior to the *Maddux* case, could the plaintiffs have recovered their entire damages from Donaldson, assuming that Donaldson was found negligent and had sufficient resources to pay the judgment?

2. The result reached in the *Maddux* case has received support in subsequent cases in other jurisdictions, particularly when the successive injuries are so contemporaneous. *See, e.g.*, Mathews v. Mills, 288 Minn. 16, 178 N.W.2d 841 (1970); Holtz v. Holder, 101 Ariz. 247, 418 P.2d 584 (1966). *See also* Maroulis v. Elliott, 207 Va. 503, 151 S.E.2d 339 (1966) and Apodaca v. Haworth, 206 Cal.App.2d 209, 23 Cal.Rptr. 461 (1962), which reached the same result without reference to *Maddux*. *See*, Prosser & Keeton on Torts 347–53 (5th ed. 1984).

3. The *Restatement (Second) of Torts* covers the problem in the following sections:

§ 879. Concurring or Consecutive Independent Acts

> If the tortious conduct of each of two or more persons is a legal cause of harm that cannot be apportioned, each is subject to liability for the entire harm, irrespective of whether their conduct is concurring or consecutive.

§ 881. Distinct or Divisible Harms

> If two or more persons, acting independently, tortiously cause distinct harms or a single harm for which there is a reasonable basis for division according to the contribution of each, each is subject to liability only for the portion of the total harm that he has himself caused.

In the Comments to both sections, reference is made to Section 433A for a definition of when a harm is single and indivisible. That section provides as follows:

§ 433A. Apportionment of Harm to Causes

(1) Damages for harm are to be apportioned among two or more causes where

(a) there are distinct harms, or

(b) there is a reasonable basis for determining the contribution of each cause to a single harm.

(2) Damages for any other harm cannot be apportioned among two or more causes.

4. In Watts v. Smith, 375 Mich. 120, 134 N.W.2d 194 (1965) plaintiff was a passenger in an automobile that was struck from behind in the morning on the way to work and then again in the afternoon on the way home from work. After the morning accident the plaintiff "felt a generalized pain in his head and back," but continued to work and sought no medical attention. After the afternoon collision plaintiff went home "with pain in his neck and back". The next day, while continuing to try to work, he sought medical attention. Plaintiff then brought an action against both drivers. The court held that it was permissible to sue both parties in the same action and, if the injury was found by the jury to be indivisible under the *Maddux* rule, to be awarded a full judgment against both.

5. In Yaklin v. Stanley, 42 Mich.App. 157, 201 N.W.2d 347 (1972), the plaintiff suffered some apparently slight injuries when her automobile was struck in the rear by an automobile negligently driven by the defendant. She was then much more seriously injured in an altercation with the defendant after the initial accident. The plaintiff brought an action against the defendant for both negligence and battery. The defendant was insured against injuries due to negligence but not against injuries inflicted by his intentional torts. On the strength of *Maddux v. Donaldson* the court upheld a jury verdict rendering "a single verdict on both counts," when the jury found it could not apportion the damages between the negligence count and the battery count.

6. In Goodman v. Stafford, 20 Mich.App. 631, 174 N.W.2d 593 (1969), the court refused to apply *Maddux* when the issue was not one of damages but which of two motorists was negligent. The plaintiff was a passenger in one of two cars involved in a collision and she brought an action against both drivers. She was obliged to prove negligence on the part of either or both of the drivers she sued. She could not succeed on a theory that one of them must have been negligent. Refer back to Kingston v. Chicago & Northwest Railway Co., p. 224 and Summers v. Tice, p. 247 *supra*. Do those cases involve a different issue? Are they distinguishable?

7. In Michie v. Great Lakes Steel Division, National Steel Corp., 495 F.2d 213 (6th Cir.1974), cert. denied 419 U.S. 997, 95 S.Ct. 310, 42 L.Ed.2d 270, the federal court held that, under Michigan law, each of the defendants could be jointly and severally liable for maintaining a nuisance. It was thus possible for the plaintiffs to aggregate their claims against each of the defendants to meet the $10,000 jurisdictional amount then required for federal diversity jurisdiction. The court recognized that Michigan law historically had not treated independent polluters as joint tortfeasors and that *Restatement of Torts* § 881 required apportionment in nuisance cases. The federal court felt, however, that, although *Maddux* and *Watt v. Smith* were multiple collision cases, the Michigan courts would apply the same type of reasoning to nuisance cases. One might point out, however, that although *Restatement (Second) of Torts*

§ 881 no longer makes any special provisions for nuisance cases in the black letter, that section does refer to *Restatement (Second) of Torts* § 433A on the issue of when damages are divisible. *Comment d* to Section 433A provides as follows:

> *d. Divisible harm.* There are other kinds of harm which, while not so clearly marked out as severable into distinct parts, are still capable of division upon a reasonable and rational basis, and of fair apportionment among the causes responsible. Thus where the cattle of two or more owners trespass upon the plaintiff's land and destroy his crop, the aggregate harm is a lost crop, but it may nevertheless be apportioned among the owners of the cattle, on the basis of the number owned by each, and the reasonable assumption that the respective harm done is proportionate to that number. Where such apportionment can be made without injustice to any of the parties, the court may require it to be made.
>
> Such apportionment is commonly made in cases of private nuisance, where the pollution of a stream, or flooding, or smoke or dust or noise, from different sources, has interfered with the plaintiff's use or enjoyment of his land. Thus where two or more factories independently pollute a stream, the interference with the plaintiff's use of the water may be treated as divisible in terms of degree, and may be apportioned among the owners of the factories, on the basis of evidence of the respective quantities of pollution discharged into the stream.

Be that as it may, in Oakwood Homeowners Association v. Ford Motor Co., 77 Mich.App. 197, 258 N.W.2d 475 (1977), the Michigan Court of Appeals accepted *Michie* as accurately stating the law of Michigan in air pollution cases.

8. Prosser & Keeton, Torts 351 (5th ed. 1984) states:

> The choice among different rules may have significant implications with respect to who bears the risk of financial irresponsibility of one or more tortfeasors. Three different types of outcomes may be identified: first, denying relief on the ground that the plaintiff has failed to meet a burden of proof on causation; second, imposing entire liability on each of two or more wrongdoers, allowing them to be sued jointly or severally; or, third, apportioning liability in some manner. If entire liability is imposed on each wrongdoer, an injured person may in fact recover full damages if any one of the wrongdoers is financially responsible, even though others are not. If instead liability is apportioned, the injured person bears the risk of financial irresponsibility of each wrongdoer. (Footnotes omitted.)

These concepts will be elaborated upon *infra* as they relate to contribution.

9. In recent years a number of states have started to move away from the concept of joint and several liability. The move has been to substitute the rule of "several" liability, that is, each defendant under all circumstances is only responsible for its own allocated share of liability. The importance of this shift becomes clearer when we look at the rules of contribution, to be taken up shortly. Note, however, that the change has only occurred when the defendants act independently of each other. If true joint action is found, joint and several liability will still be the governing rule.

Approximately fourteen states have not significantly changed the application of joint and several liability. This includes the five jurisdictions that have not adopted comparative negligence. All of the other states have abolished joint and several liability, at least in some significant situations. The modifications have followed a number of different paths in different states. About fourteen states have either explicitly changed the law in their comparative responsibility statute or their courts have held that the adoption of comparative fault leads to a complete repudiation of joint and several liability, even when the plaintiff is not contributorily negligent. *See, e.g.,* Dix & Assoc. Pipeline Contractors, Inc. v. Key, 799 S.W.2d 24 (Ky.1990); McIntyre v. Balentine, 833 S.W.2d 52 (Tenn.1992); S.H.A. 735 ILCS 5/2–1117 (1995); Utah Code Ann. § 78–27–38 (1992); Vt. Stat. Ann. tit. 12 § 1036 (1973).

Others states, either as a result of case law or legislation, have abolished joint and several liability only when the plaintiff was partially at fault. Price v. Southwestern Bell Tel. Co., 812 P.2d 1355 (Okl.1991). The rationale for this distinction rests upon the idea that if the plaintiff is not at fault at all, the plaintiff should still be able to recover all his/her damages from any of the guilty defendants. However if the plaintiff is also at fault, the plaintiff should carry at least some of the consequences of the inability to collect a share from another responsible party. Some states abolished joint and several liability for defendants whose share of the responsibility is found to be below a certain percentage. For example, in Iowa joint and several liability is abolished for those defendants "who are found to bear less than fifty percent of the total fault assigned to all parties". Iowa Code Ann. § 668.4 (West).

In some states, the abolition of joint and several liability only applied in certain tort actions or situation. For example, some statutory changes only applied to product liability suits or cases involving medical malpractice. In others joint and several liability was abolished except in certain kinds of actions, such as pollution cases.

Finally, some states have retained joint and several liability for economic damages but abolished it in whole or in part for non-economic damages, such as pain and suffering. The New York statute provides an example:

§ 1600. Definitions

As used in this article the term "non-economic loss" includes but is not limited to pain and suffering, mental anguish, loss of consortium or other damages for non-economic loss.

§ 1601. Limited liability of persons jointly liable

1. Notwithstanding any other provision of law, when a verdict or decision in an action or claim for personal injury is determined in favor of a claimant in an action involving two or more tortfeasors jointly liable or in a claim against the state and the liability of a defendant is found to be fifty percent or less of the total liability assigned to all persons liable, the liability of such defendant to the claimant for non-economic loss shall not exceed that defendant's equitable share determined in accordance with the relative culpability of each person causing or contributing to the total liability for non-economic loss; provided, however that the culpable conduct of any person not a party to the action shall not be considered in determining any equitable share herein if the claimant proves that with due diligence he was unable to obtain jurisdiction over such person in said action * * *.

N.Y. McKinney's Civ.Prac.Law §§ 1600, 1601. For a description of the similar Montana statute, *see* Newville v. State Dep't of Family Servs., 267 Mont. 237, 883 P.2d 793, 799 (1994).

Ohio's recently adopted, new statutory scheme retains traditional joint and several liability only for economic damages and even then only when a defendant has been found at least 50% responsible. The statute also provides that the jury shall allocate responsibility among not only the parties to the suit, but also any other person or entity which was partially responsible for causing the injury. For any defendant whose responsibility is found to be less than 50%, the plaintiff can only recover that defendant's proportionate share times the total economic damages found. With regard to non-economic damages, any defendant is only liable for his/her proportionate share no matter what the degree of responsibility found. Ohio Rev. Code § 2307.31 (Anderson 1997).

A few states have also retained joint and several liability when the total damages do not exceed a certain amount, say $25,000 dollars, but abolish it for damages that exceed that amount.

Florida's modification of the law, referred to in the majority opinion in the *Disney World*, case *infra*, p. 430, is one example of the complexity of statutory treatment of these issues. It now provides that: "[T]he court shall enter judgment against each party liable on the basis of such party's percentage of fault and not on the basis of the doctrine of joint and several liability." However, three categories of exceptions significantly modify this abrogation: (1) joint and several liability shall still apply for economic damages "with respect to any party [defendant] whose percentage of fault equals or exceeds that of a particular claimant"; (2) joint and several liability shall still apply "to any action brought by any person to recover actual economic damages resulting from pollution, to any action based upon an intentional tort, or to any cause of action as to which application of the doctrine of joint and several liability is specifically provided by [other sections of the Florida statutes]; and (3) joint and several liability shall still apply "to all actions in which the total amount of damages does not exceed $25,000." § 768.81, West's Fla.Stat. (Supp.1986).

This modification of joint and several liability was part of a general tort "reform" statute. While certain other aspects were held unconstitutional, the modification of joint and several liability was held constitutional in Smith v. Department of Ins., 507 So.2d 1080 (Fla.1987). The court there said:

> The real question in the joint and several liability problem is who should pay the damages caused by an insolvent tortfeasor. The problem is substantially compounded when the plaintiff is also at fault. In addressing this difficult issue, the legislature chose not to abolish joint and several liability in it entirety. Instead, the doctrine was modified by this act and continues to exist as to economic damages when a defendant's negligence is equal to or exceeds the plaintiff's. In this circumstance, each defendant is liable for only his own percentage share of *noneconomic* damages. * * *

> [The legislature] found no need to abrogate the doctrine in cases under $25,000. In answering the question of who should pay damages for the insolvent tortfeasor, the legislature chose a middle ground: both the plaintiff and the solvent defendant.

Id. at 1091.

The end result of these moves in recent years makes it almost impossible to generalize about the applicable law. To further complicate matters, the courts in some states have found some of these changes to violate the state constitution, especially since some of these changes were part of a broader tort reform agenda that raised constitutional questions. One simply most look in each state to see what changes have occurred. Academic discussion of the issue includes R. Wright, *Allocating Liability Among Multiple Responsible Causes: A Principled Defense of Joint and Several Liability for Actual Harm and Risk Exposure,* 21 U.C. Davis L.Rev. 1141 (1988) which was in turn attacked in A. Twerski, *The Joint Tortfeasor Legislative Revolt: A Rational Response to the Critics,* 22 U.C.Davis L.Rev. 1125 (1989). *See also* the further exchange between Professors Wright and Twerski in *id.* at 1147, 1161.

10. *The effect of a settlement and release.* At common law a settlement with any defendant, which released the defendant from further liability, was viewed as satisfying the liability of all the joint defendants to the plaintiff and therefore such a settlement agreement released all defendants from further liability. For an example of how this rule worked, *see, e.g.,* Thompson v. Fox, 326 Pa. 209, 192 A. 107 (1937). The rule had the obvious effect of discouraging settlements unless all of the defendants were parties to the agreement. While following the common law rule, many courts tried to circumvent its effect in order to encourage settlement. One method developed for avoiding the harsh doctrine was the "covenant not to sue." In return for a settlement from one joint tortfeasor, the plaintiff, rather than giving a release from liability, instead promised not to bring an action on the underlying claim against that defendant. The need to resort to such technical devices has now been obviated in many states by adoption of the Uniform Contribution Among Tortfeasors Act, in one form or another. The major provision will be set forth below.

D. CONTRIBUTION AMONG JOINT TORTFEASORS

As noted above, at common law there was no right on the part of one defendant, held liable for an injury, to get contribution or partial payment of the judgment from another defendant, even though the other defendant had also been held liable. The leading common-law case is Merryweather v. Nixan, 8 Term.Rep. 186, 101 Eng.Rep. 1337 (K.B.1799). Although English law confined this harsh doctrine to cases of intentional or wilful wrongdoing, the American cases generally applied it to all cases involving joint tortfeasors. In most American jurisdictions the rule against contribution has now been abolished or modified. This has occurred principally by statute but in some jurisdictions by judicial decision. Early contribution statutes typically allowed contribution only among joint tortfeasors against whom the plaintiff had secured judgment. If the plaintiff had chosen not to include all of the potential defendants in the action, the party or parties satisfying the judgment could not secure contribution from the joint tortfeasors who had not been joined as defendants in the action. Many jurisdictions have now greatly expanded the range of situations in which contribution can be obtained among joint tortfeasors and allow the defendant to join other potential defendants.

UNIFORM CONTRIBUTION AMONG TORTFEASORS ACT

§ 1. [Right to Contribution]

(a) Except as otherwise provided in this Act, where two or more persons become jointly or severally liable in tort for the same injury to person or property or for the same wrongful death, there is a right of contribution among them even though judgment has not been recovered against all or any of them.

(b) The right of contribution exists only in favor of a tortfeasor who has paid more than his pro rata share of the common liability, and his total recovery is limited to the amount paid by him in excess of his pro rata share. No tortfeasor is compelled to make contribution beyond his own pro rata share of the entire liability.

(c) There is no right of contribution in favor of any tortfeasor who has intentionally [wilfully or wantonly] caused or contributed to the injury or wrongful death.

(d) A tortfeasor who enters into a settlement with a claimant is not entitled to recover contribution from another tortfeasor whose liability for the injury or wrongful death is not extinguished by the settlement nor in respect to any amount paid in a settlement which is in excess of what was reasonable.

(e) A liability insurer, who by payment has discharged in full or in part the liability of a tortfeasor and has thereby discharged in full its obligation as insurer, is subrogated to the tortfeasor's right of contribution to the extent of the amount it has paid in excess of the tortfeasor's pro rata share of the common liability. This provision does not limit or impair any right of subrogation arising from any other relationship.

(f) This Act does not impair any right of indemnity under existing law. Where one tortfeasor is entitled to indemnity from another, the right of the indemnity obligee is for indemnity and not contribution, and the indemnity obligor is not entitled to contribution from the obligee for any portion of his indemnity obligation.

(g) This Act shall not apply to breaches of trust or of other fiduciary obligation.

§ 2.   [Pro Rata Shares]

In determining the pro rata shares of tortfeasors in the entire liability (a) their relative degrees of fault shall not be considered; (b) if equity requires the collective liability of some as a group shall constitute a single share; and (c) principles of equity applicable to contribution generally shall apply.

§ 3.   [Enforcement]

(a) Whether or not judgment has been entered in an action against two or more tortfeasors for the same injury or wrongful death, contribution may be enforced by separate action.

(b) Where a judgment has been entered in an action against two or more tortfeasors for the same injury or wrongful death, contribution may be enforced in that action by judgment in favor of one against other judgment defendants by motion upon notice to all parties to the action.

(c) If there is a judgment for the injury or wrongful death against the tortfeasor seeking contribution, any separate action by him to enforce contribution must be commenced within one year after the judgment has become final by lapse of time for appeal or after appellate review.

(d) If there is no judgment for the injury or wrongful death against the tortfeasor seeking contribution, his right of contribution is barred unless he has either (1) discharged by payment the common liability within the statute of limitations period applicable to claimant's right of action against him and has commenced his action for contribution within one year after payment, or (2) agreed while action is pending against him to discharge the common liability and has within one year after the agreement paid the liability and commenced his action for contribution.

(e) The recovery of a judgment for an injury or wrongful death against one tortfeasor does not of itself discharge the other tortfeasors from liability for the injury or wrongful death unless the judgment is satisfied. The satisfaction of the judgment does not impair any right of contribution.

(f) The judgment of the court in determining the liability of the several defendants to the claimant for an injury or wrongful death shall be binding as among such defendants in determining their right to contribution.

§ 4. [Release or Covenant Not to Sue]

When a release or a covenant not to sue or not to enforce judgment is given in good faith to one of two or more persons liable in tort for the same injury or the same wrongful death:

(a) It does not discharge any of the other tortfeasors from liability for the injury or wrongful death unless its terms so provide; but it reduces the claim against the others to the extent of any amount stipulated by the release or the covenant, or in the amount of the consideration paid for it, whichever is the greater; and,

(b) It discharges the tortfeasor to whom it is given from all liability for contribution to any other tortfeasor.

Notes

1. As originally drafted in 1939, what is now § 4(b)(originally § 5) provided that a release given to one joint tortfeasor did not relieve that person from liability for contribution to the other joint tortfeasors unless the release stipulated that the liability of the other joint tortfeasors was to be reduced by the pro rata share of the joint tortfeasor who had settled in return for a release from the plaintiff. The purpose of that provision was to prevent one joint tortfeasor, either in collusion with the plaintiff or otherwise, from settling for a very small amount and saddling the other joint tortfeasors with most of the liability. The provision had the effect, however, of discouraging settlements. The present § 4(b) was then substituted in the 1955 revision of the act. It attempts to limit collusive minimal settlements with some of the defendants with its requirement that the release or covenant not to sue be "given in good faith."

2. The Uniform Act in § 2 provides for pro rata shares to be paid when contribution is allowed. Thus a defendant that is only found to be slightly at fault will still have to contribute a full pro rata share of the damages. Parallel to the development of comparative negligence as applied to responsibility as between the plaintiff and defendant, taken up in the previous chapter, there has been a general move toward changing the law of contribution to make each defendant liable for his/her proportionate share of the liability based upon the jury's determination of the degrees of fault or responsibility. [Leave aside for the moment what happens if one or more defendant's share is uncollectible.] In some states this result was reached by case law, *see* Bielski v. Schulze, 16

Wis.2d 1, 114 N.W.2d 105 (1962), in others it has come as a result of the interpretation of comparative fault statutes, *see* Prudential Life Ins. Co. v. Moody, 696 S.W.2d 503 (Ky.1985); Brown v. Keill, 224 Kan. 195, 580 P.2d 867 (1978). *See also* Sitzes v. Anchor Motor Freight, Inc., 169 W.Va. 698, 289 S.E.2d 679 (1982), in which the court said:

> The basic purpose of the joint and several liability rule is to permit the injured plaintiff to select and collect the full amount of his damages against one or more joint tortfeasors. This rule however need not preclude a right of comparative contribution between the joint tortfeasors *inter se*. The purpose of this latter rule is to require the joint tortfeasors to share in contribution based upon the degree of fault that each has contributed to the accident. There is a definite trend in the field of tort law toward allocation of judgmental liability between the joint tortfeasors *inter se*. It is thought to be fairer to require them to respond in damages based on their degrees of fault.

Id. at 707, 289 S.E.2d at 685.

The Uniform Comparative Fault Act, *infra,* promulgated in 1977, also adopts this approach and announces in a comment that its provisions supercede the Uniform Contribution Among Tortfeasors Act § 2.

E.   TYING IT ALL TOGETHER

The interrelationship of these various rules of law dealing with multiple defendants and plaintiffs also partially at fault raises very intricate problems. Now in the preliminary stages of drafting is the new *Restatement (Third) of Torts: Apportionment of Liability*, which attempts to deal with these various problems. As this book goes to press, the Preliminary Draft presents five different optional approaches, reflected in the laws of the different states. These approaches reflect the differences in approach to the abolition of joint and several liability discussed *supra,* pp. 419–22. The Uniform Comparative Fault Act has also tried to deal with many of these problems. The first section, defining comparative fault, appears *supra,* p. 362. The remainder of the act deals with the various questions of effect upon other legal rules, such as contribution. Those provisions follow:

Section 2.   [Apportionment of Damages]

(a) In all actions involving fault of more than one party to the action, including third-party defendants and persons who have been released under Section 6, the court, unless otherwise agreed by all parties, shall instruct the jury to answer special interrogatories or, if there is no jury, shall make findings, indicating:

(1) the amount of damages each claimant would be entitled to recover if contributory fault is disregarded; and

(2) the percentage of the total fault of all of the parties to each claim that is allocated to each claimant, defendant, third-party defendant, and person who has been released from liability under Section 6. For this purpose the court may determine that two or more persons are to be treated as a single party.

(b) In determining the percentages of fault, the trier of fact shall consider both the nature of the conduct of each party at fault and the extent of the causal relation between the conduct and the damages claimed.

(c) The court shall determine the award of damages to each claimant in accordance with the findings, subject to any reduction under Section 6, and enter judgment against each party liable on the basis of rules of joint-and-several liability. For purposes of contribution under Sections 4 and 5, the court also shall determine and state in the judgment each party's equitable share of the obligation to each claimant in accordance with the respective percentages of fault.

(d) Upon motion made not later than [one year] after judgment is entered, the court shall determine whether all or part of a party's equitable share of the obligation is uncollectible from that party, and shall reallocate any uncollectible amount among the other parties, including a claimant at fault, according to their respective percentages of fault. The party whose liability is reallocated is nonetheless subject to contribution and to any continuing liability to the claimant on the judgment.

Section 3. [Set-off]

A claim and counterclaim shall not be set off against each other, except by agreement of both parties. On motion, however, the court, if it finds that the obligation of either party is likely to be uncollectible, may order that both parties make payment into court for distribution. The court shall distribute the funds received and declare obligations discharged as if the payment into court by either party had been a payment to the other party and any distribution of those funds back to the party making payment had been a payment to him by the other party.

Section 4. [Right of Contribution]

(a) A right of contribution exists between or among two or more persons who are jointly and severally liable upon the same indivisible claim for the same injury, death, or harm, whether or not judgment has been recovered against all or any of them. It may be enforced either in the original action or by a separate action brought for that purpose. The basis for contribution is each person's equitable share of the obligation, including the equitable share of a claimant at fault, as determined in accordance with the provisions of Section 2.

(b) Contribution is available to a person who enters into a settlement with a claimant only (1) if the liability of the person against whom contribution is sought has been extinguished and (2) to the extent that the amount paid in settlement was reasonable.

Section 5. [Enforcement of Contribution]

(a) If the proportionate fault of the parties to a claim for contribution has been established previously by the court, as provided by Section 2, a party paying more than his equitable share of the obligation, upon motion, may recover judgment for contribution.

(b) If the proportionate fault of the parties to the claim for contribution has not been established by the court, contribution may be enforced in a separate action, whether or not a judgment has been rendered against either the person seeking contribution or the person from whom contribution is being sought.

(c) If a judgment has been rendered, the action for contribution must be commenced within [one year] after the judgment becomes final. If no judgment has been rendered, the person bringing the action for contribution either must have (1) discharged by payment the common liability within the period of the statute of limitations applicable to the claimant's right of action against him and commenced the action for contribution within [one year] after payment, or (2) agreed while action was pending to discharge the common liability and, within [one year] after the agreement, have paid the liability and commenced an action for contribution.

Section 6.   [Effect of Release]

A release, covenant not to sue, or similar agreement entered into by a claimant and a person liable discharges that person from all liability for contribution, but it does not discharge any other persons liable upon the same claim unless it so provides. However, the claim of the releasing person against other persons is reduced by the amount of the released person's equitable share of the obligation, determined in accordance with the provisions of Section 2.

Notes

1. The Commissioners Prefatory Note to the Uniform Act states that the comparative fault act is intended to replace the Uniform Contribution Among Tortfeasors Act. The Uniform Comparative Fault Act, however, has not been adopted in its entirety by any jurisdiction. Iowa (Iowa Code Ann. §§ 668.1–668.14) and Washington (West's R.C.W.A. 4.22.005–4.22.926) are listed in the Uniform Laws Annotated (Vol. 12, Supp.1989 at 39) as having, with some modifications, adopted the major provisions of the act.[16] In addition, Kentucky and Missouri, which have adopted comparative negligence by judicial decision, have taken the Uniform Comparative Fault Act as a model or guide to be followed in applying comparative fault in those states. Hilen v. Hays, 673 S.W.2d 713 (Ky.1984); Wemyss v. Coleman, 729 S.W.2d 174 (Ky.1987); Gustafson v. Benda, 661 S.W.2d 11 (Mo.1983); Lippard v. Houdaille Industries, Inc., 715 S.W.2d 491, 492–93 (Mo.1986); Allison v. Sverdrup & Parcel and Assoc. Inc., 738 S.W.2d 440, 452 (Mo.App.1987). Finally, a number of other states have adopted variations on this scheme, at least for some torts.

2. It should be noted that the Uniform Comparative Fault Act does not alter the common-law rule of joint and several liability of all joint tortfeasors. If the plaintiff is not guilty of any contributory fault, the plaintiff can enforce the entire judgment against any of the defendants held liable. If the plaintiff has been contributorily negligent the problem becomes more complicated. On

---

16. How helpful a characterization this is of Iowa is perhaps open to question. Major differences between the Uniform Act and the Iowa statute include the following. Under the Iowa statute (§ 668.3), if the plaintiff's fault is greater than that of all the defendants combined, contributory negligence continues to operate as a total bar. In addition, if a defendant's share of the fault is less than 50 percent of the total fault assigned to all the parties, that defendant is not subject to joint and several liability. The Iowa statutory comparative fault scheme was adopted in response to the judicial abolition of contributory negligence in favor of pure comparative negligence in Goetzman v. Wichern, 327 N.W.2d 742 (Iowa 1982).

the one hand the Act retains the concept of joint and several liability; on the other, it also adopts the principle of reallocation (§ 2(d)). The Commissioners' Comment handles the matter as follows:

> *Joint and Several Liability and Equitable Shares of the Obligation.* The common law rule of joint-and-several liability of joint tortfeasors continues to apply under this Act. This is true whether the claimant was contributorily negligent or not. The plaintiff can recover the total amount of his judgment against any defendant who is liable.
>
> The judgment for each claimant also sets forth, however, the equitable share of the total obligation to the claimant for each party, based on his established percentage of fault. This indicates the amount that each party should eventually be responsible for as a result of the rules of contribution. Stated in the judgment itself, it makes the information available to the parties and will normally be a basis for contribution without the need for a court order arising from motion or separate action.
>
> *Reallocation.* Reallocation of the equitable share of the obligation of a party takes place when his share is uncollectible.
>
> Reallocation takes place among all parties at fault. This includes a claimant who is contributorily at fault. It avoids the unfairness both of the common law rule of joint-and-several liability, which would cast the total risk of uncollectibility upon the solvent defendants, and of a rule abolishing joint-and-several liability, which would cast the total risk of uncollectibility upon the claimant.
>
> *Control by the court.* The total of the several percentages of fault for the plaintiff and all defendants, as found in the special interrogatories, should add up to 100%. Whether the court will inform the jury of this will depend upon the local practice.
>
> The court should be able to exercise any usual powers under existing law of setting aside or modifying a verdict if it is internally inconsistent or shows bias or prejudice, etc. On the same basis as the remittitur principle, a court might indicate its intent to set aside a percentage allocation unless the parties agreed to a somewhat different one.

3. There are, then, a wide variety of approaches among the states to these various issues of application. With regard to dealing with defaulting defendants' shares there are three general approaches: (1) the burden falls upon the remaining defendants (this is the conventional result under traditional joint and several liability); (2) the burden falls upon the plaintiff because the defaulted share is simply uncollectible and responsibility is not shifted to others (this happens under "several" liability schemes, meaning that each defendant can only be held for his/her own share); (3) the default share gets redistributed among all of the parties, including the plaintiff, if the plaintiff was partially at fault (the scheme adopted in the Uniform Comparative Fault Act). The reason for a default can be one of several, including immunity from suit, such as intra-family immunity; employer-employee immunity under workers compensation; governmental immunity, to the extent that it still exist in some jurisdiction; or partial or total insolvency. These situations also raise various procedural problems that affect the substantive reach of the contribution scheme, such as problems of party jurisdiction, notice and joinder, but these problems are not taken up here in any detail.

4. Consider carefully how the Uniform Acts treat the question of settlement and release. Who carries the risk that a settlement with only some of the defendants before trial will provide either a greater or lesser amount than the share of liability assigned to the settling party by the jury? And who does the jury include in its assignment of responsibility—only the parties to the suit? all potentially responsible parties? Should a defendant be able to join parties that the plaintiff does not chose to sue, if the absent party may also be partially responsible? Preliminary Draft (No. 2) of the *Restatement (Third) of Torts: Apportionment of Liability*, Topic 2, in a combination of sections tries to provide answers to all these questions in a way that makes it as fair as possible to all concerns.

Section 6 of the Uniform Comparative Fault Act makes some alterations in the effect of a release upon the right of contribution. The reasons for the change are explained as follows in the Commissioners' Comment:

> *Effect of release on right of contribution.* The question of the contribution rights of tortfeasors A and B against tortfeasor C, who settled and obtained a release or covenant not to sue admits of three answers: (1) A and B are still able to obtain contribution against C, despite the release, (2) A and B are not entitled to contribution unless the release was given not in good faith but by way of collusion, and (3) the plaintiff's total claim is reduced by the proportionate share of C. Each of the three solutions has substantial disadvantages, yet each has been adopted in one of the uniform acts. The first solution was adopted by the 1939 Uniform Contribution Act. Its disadvantage is that it discourages settlements; a tortfeasor has no incentive to settle if he remains liable for contribution. The second solution was adopted by the 1955 Contribution Act. While it theoretically encourages settlements, it may be unfair to the other defendants and if the good-faith requirement is conscientiously enforced settlements may be discouraged.
>
> The third solution is adopted in this Section. Although it may have some tendency to discourage a claimant from entering into a settlement, this solution is fairly based on the proportionate-fault principle.

On the broader questions of the effects of settlement and releases in multi-party litigation see J. Adams, *Settlements After Li: But Is It "Fair"?*, 10 Pac.L.J. 729 (1979); H. Boone, *Multiple-Party Litigation and Comparative Negligence*, 45 Ins.Coun.J. 335 (1978); N. Hensley, *Multiple Party Litigation in Comparative Negligence: Incomplete Resolution of Joinder and Settlement Problems*, 32 S.W.L.J. 669 (1978); Comment, *Comparative Fault and Settlement in Joint Tortfeasor Cases: A Plea for Principle Over Policy*, 16 San Diego L.Rev. 833 (1979).

In Charles v. Giant Eagle Markets, 513 Pa. 474, 522 A.2d 1 (1987) the plaintiff had reached settlement with one joint defendant. The jury then brought in a verdict against the other joint defendant. The settlement with D–1 was for more than its pro rata share of the total verdict. The court held that the plaintiff was entitled to the pro rata share assigned to D–2, as well as the settlement amount negotiated with D–1, even though this produced a total recovery almost $4000 above the total jury award. Preliminary Draft (No. 2) of the *Restatement (Third) of Torts: Apportionment of Liability*, § 28A and § 28C also adopts this position with the rationale that the plaintiff takes the risk of a low settlement, and therefore should get the benefit of a high settlement.

5. One problem in cases involving situation in which the plaintiff is partially at fault involves the right of set-off. It will be recalled that in *Hoffman v. Jones,* the court stated, *supra,* p. 350, that, in a case where both the plaintiff and a counterclaiming defendant were injured and were both at fault, the trial judge should enter one judgment for the net amount due the party receiving the greatest verdict. Where both parties are uninsured this certainly seems just. Where they are insured against third party liability, however, the effect of this solution is to give a windfall to the insurance companies. In Stuyvesant Insurance Co. v. Bournazian, 342 So.2d 471 (Fla.1976), the court declared that set-offs are only to be made when the parties are uninsured or to insured parties to the extent the amounts awarded exceed the policy limits. In a subsequent case, State Farm Mutual Automobile Insurance Co. v. Eberhardt, 374 So.2d 1113 (Fla.App.1979), an uninsured motorist brought an action against an insured motorist who counterclaimed. The uninsured motorist was awarded the larger verdict. The trial court accordingly set-off the verdicts and entered a judgment for the excess in favor of the uninsured motorist. The court of appeal reversed and directed that there should be no set-offs. Otherwise, in such a situation, an insured motorist might never recover anything. Oregon (Or. Rev. Stat. 18.470) and Rhode Island (R.I. Gen. L. 1956 § 9–20–4.1) comparative fault statutes prohibit set-offs. Note the treatment of this problem in § 3 of the Uniform Comparative Fault Act, *supra.* The problem is dealt with in § 10 of the Preliminary Draft (No. 2) of *Restatement (Third) of Torts: Apportionment of Liability,* which provides different rules depending upon the insurance coverage present. *See also* Levy, *Pure Comparative Negligence: Set–Offs, Multiple Defendants and Loss Distribution,* 11 U.S.F.L.Rev. 405 (1977).

The *Walt Disney* case that follows illustrates in a dramatic way some of these problems. Ask yourself how the case would have been decided under the various legal approaches we have seen. The case is now hypothetical for two reasons: first, Florida has since abolished intra-spousal immunity (Waite v. Waite, 618 So.2d 1360 (Fla.1993)); and, second, Florida has abolished joint and several liability in certain situations, as noted *supra,* p. 421.

WALT DISNEY WORLD CO. v. WOOD

Supreme Court of Florida, 1987.
515 So.2d 198.

GRIMES, JUSTICE.

Aloysia Wood was injured in November 1971 at the grand prix attraction at Walt Disney World (Disney), when her fiance,[17] Daniel Wood, rammed from the rear the vehicle which she was driving. Aloysia Wood filed suit against Disney, and Disney sought contribution from Daniel Wood. After trial, the jury returned a verdict finding Aloysia Wood 14% at fault, Daniel Wood 85% at fault, and Disney 1% at fault. The jury assessed Wood's damages at $75,000. The court entered judgment against Disney for 86% of the damages. Disney subsequently moved to alter the judgment to reflect the jury's finding that Disney was only 1% at fault. The court denied the motion. On appeal, the fourth district affirmed the judgment on the basis of this Court's decision in *Lincenberg v. Issen,* 318 So.2d 386 (Fla.1975).

---

17. Wood married her fiance prior to this action.

In *Hoffman v. Jones,* 280 So.2d 431 (Fla.1973), this Court discarded the rule of contributory negligence, which Florida had followed since at least 1886, and adopted the pure comparative negligence standard. *See Smith v. Department of Insurance,* 507 So.2d 1080 (Fla.1987)(tracing the evolution of contributory and comparative negligence); *Louisville & N.R.R. v. Yniestra,* 21 Fla. 700 (1886)(establishing contributory negligence on the part of a prospective plaintiff as a bar to any recovery against a defendant). In adopting comparative negligence, this Court expressly declared two purposes for the change in judicial policy:

(1) To allow a jury to apportion fault as it sees fit between negligent parties whose negligence was part of the legal and proximate cause of any loss or injury; and

(2) To apportion the total damages resulting from the loss or injury according to the proportionate fault of each party. * * *

Thereafter, in *Lincenberg v. Issen,* a faultless plaintiff obtained a verdict in which the jury determined that one defendant was 85% percent negligent and the other defendant was 15% negligent. * * * [T]his Court concluded that the rationale of *Hoffman v. Jones* dictated the elimination of the rule against contribution among joint tortfeasors. The Court then said that since "'no contribution' is no longer a viable principle in Florida, we were confronted with the problem of determining what procedure will most fully effectuate the principle that each party should pay the proportion of the total damages he has caused to the other party, and we considered several alternatives." *Lincenberg,* * * *. At this point, the Court stated in footnote 2 that among the alternatives considered was pure apportionment whereby the plaintiff may recover judgment against codefendants only for the percentage of damages caused by the negligence of each individual defendant. However, the Court noted that the legislature had just passed section 768.31, Florida Statutes (1975), which provided for contribution among joint tortfeasors and interpreted the statute as retaining the "full, joint, and several liability of joint tortfeasors to the plaintiff." Thus, the Court held:

The plaintiff is entitled to a measurement of his full damages and the liability for these damages should be apportioned in accordance with the percentage of negligence as it relates to the total of all the defendants. The negligence attributed to the defendants will then be apportioned on a pro rata basis without considering relative degrees of fault although the multiparty defendants will remain jointly and severally liable for the entire amount. * * *

The real issue before us is whether we should now replace the doctrine of joint and several liability with one in which the liability of codefendants to the plaintiff is apportioned according to each defendant's respective fault. According to Disney, this Court in *Hoffman* set for itself the goal of creating a tort system that fairly and equitably allocated damages according to the degrees of fault. Therefore, a defendant should only be held responsible to the extent of his fault in the same way as a plaintiff under comparative negligence.

Joint and several liability is a judicially created doctrine. * * * This Court may alter a rule of law where great social upheaval dictates its necessity. * * * The "social upheaval" which is said to have occurred here is the fundamental alteration of Florida tort law encompassed by the adoption of comparative negligence. Following the adoption of comparative negligence, some states have passed laws eliminating joint and several liability, and the courts of several others have judicially abolished the doctrine. *E.g., Brown v. Keill*, 224 Kan. 195, 580 P.2d 867 (1978); *Bartlett v. New Mexico Welding Supply, Inc.*, 98 N.M. 152, 646 P.2d 579 (Ct.App.), *cert. denied*, 98 N.M. 336, 648 P.2d 794 (1982); *Laubach v. Morgan*, 588 P.2d 1071 (Okla.1978).[18] The Kansas Supreme Court in *Brown v. Keill* reasoned:

> There is nothing inherently fair about a defendant who is 10% at fault paying 100% of the loss, and there is no social policy that should compel defendants to pay more than their fair share of the loss. Plaintiffs now take the parties as they find them. If one of the parties at fault happens to be a spouse or a governmental agency and if by reason of some competing social policy the plaintiff cannot receive payment for his injuries from the spouse or agency, there is no compelling social policy which requires the codefendant to pay more than his fair share of the loss. The same is true if one of the defendants is wealthy and the other is not.

Brown, 224 Kan. at 203, 580 P.2d at 874.

On the other hand, the majority of courts which have faced the issue in jurisdictions with comparative negligence have ruled that joint and several liability should be retained. *E.g., Arctic Structures, Inc. v. Wedmore*, 605 P.2d 426 (Alaska 1979); *American Motorcycle Ass'n v. Superior Court*, 20 Cal.3d 578, 578 P.2d 899, 146 Cal.Rptr. 182 (1978); *Tucker v. Union Oil Co.*, 100 Idaho 590, 603 P.2d 156 (1979); *Coney v. J.L.G. Industries, Inc.*, 97 Ill.2d 104, 73 Ill.Dec. 337, 454 N.E.2d 197 (1983); *Kirby Bldg. Sys. v. Mineral Explorations*, 704 P.2d 1266 (Wyo.1985). The Illinois Supreme Court in *Coney v. J.L.G. Industries, Inc.* gave four reasons justifying the retention of joint and several liability:

> (1) The feasibility of apportioning fault on a comparative basis does not render an indivisible injury "divisible" for purposes of the joint and several liability rule. A concurrent tortfeasor is liable for the whole of an indivisible injury when his negligence is a proximate cause of that damage. In many instances, the negligence of a concurrent tortfeasor may be sufficient by itself to cause the entire loss. The mere fact that it may be possible to assign some percentage figure to the relative culpability of one negligent defendant as compared to another does not in any way suggest that each defendant's negligence is not a proximate cause of the entire indivisible injury.

> (2) In those instances where the plaintiff is not guilty of negligence, he would be forced to bear a portion of the loss should one of the tortfeasors prove financially unable to satisfy his share of the damages.

---

18. [Ed. note.] If the plaintiff is blameless, however, so that the comparative fault statute does not come into play, the common-law rule of joint and several liability will continue to apply to the defendants. Boyles v. Oklahoma Nat. Gas Co., 619 P.2d 613 (Okl.1980).

(3) Even in cases where a plaintiff is partially at fault, his culpability is not equivalent to that of a defendant. The plaintiff's negligence relates only to a lack of due care for his own safety while the defendant's negligence relates to a lack of due care for the safety of others; the latter is tortious, but the former is not.

(4) Elimination of joint and several liability would work a serious and unwarranted deleterious effect on the ability of an injured plaintiff to obtain adequate compensation for his injuries.

The desirability of abolishing joint and several liability in Florida has also been debated for years both in and out of the legislative halls. *See* Note, *Modification of the Doctrine of Joint and Several Liability: Who Bears the Risk?*, 11 Nova L.J. 165 (Fall 1986). In 1986 the legislature substantially modified the doctrine of joint and several liability as part of its comprehensive tort reform law. § 768.81, Fla.Stat. (Supp.1986). The fact that the new statute did not entirely abolish the doctrine but provided for apportionment of fault only under certain circumstances further indicates the complexity of the problem and suggests there may be no one resolution of the issue which will satisfy the competing interests involved.

While recognizing the logic in Disney's position, we cannot say with certainty that joint and several liability is an unjust doctrine or that it should necessarily be eliminated upon the adoption of comparative negligence. In view of the public policy considerations bearing on the issue, this Court believes that the viability of the doctrine is a matter which should best be decided by the legislature. Consequently, we approve the decision of the district court of appeal.

It is so ordered.

[Dissent omitted.]

Notes

1. Should the jury be told in the instructions about the law of joint and several liability in a case such as this? The states split on informing the jury of the consequences of their allocation of responsibility.

2. Would the result in the *Disney World* case clearly come out differently after the changes in Florida dealing with joint and several liability law, set out above (p. 421)?

3. Assume that both Daniel and Aloysia Wood had come to your office together, explained their situation, and ask you to represent them in the case against Disney World. Could you ethically represent both? Even if they told you that they could not afford two attorneys?

Problem

Assume that there is a multiple party accident in which A and B are injured. C, D, and E are also involved. A's injuries amount to $100,000 and B's to $50,000. E settles before trial with A and B each getting $5000. The case goes to trial and the jury returns a verdict finding A 10% responsible, B 10% responsible, C 40% responsible, D 20% responsible, and E 20% responsible. Assume that D is insolvent and his/her share of the damages are uncollectible. To complicate things a little further, assume that each of A and B's damages were 50% economic and 50% non-economic. Under the various approaches outlined above what would the problems be and who would ultimately get what?

F.   RECENT DEVELOPMENTS IN GROUP LIABILITY

SINDELL v. ABBOTT LABORATORIES

Supreme Court of California, 1980.
26 Cal.3d 588, 163 Cal.Rptr. 132, 607 P.2d 924, *cert. denied*,
449 U.S. 912, 101 S.Ct. 285, 66 L.Ed.2d 140 (1980).

MOSK, JUSTICE.

This case involves a complex problem both timely and significant: may a plaintiff, injured as the result of a drug administered to her mother during pregnancy, who knows the type of drug involved but cannot identify the manufacturer of the precise product, hold liable for her injuries a maker of a drug produced from an identical formula?

Plaintiff Judith Sindell brought an action against eleven drug companies and Does 1 through 100, on behalf of herself and other women similarly situated. The complaint alleges as follows:

Between 1941 and 1971, defendants were engaged in the business of manufacturing, promoting, and marketing diethylstilbesterol (DES), a drug which is a synthetic compound of the female hormone estrogen. The drug was administered to plaintiff's mother and the mothers of the class she represents,[19] for the purpose of preventing miscarriage. In 1947, the Food and Drug Administration authorized the marketing of DES as a miscarriage preventative, but only on an experimental basis, with a requirement that the drug contain a warning label to that effect.

DES may cause cancerous vaginal and cervical growths in the daughters exposed to it before birth, because their mothers took the drug during pregnancy. The form of cancer from which these daughters suffer is known as adenocarcinoma, and it manifests itself after a minimum latent period of 10 or 12 years. It is a fast-spreading and deadly disease, and radical surgery is required to prevent it from spreading. DES also causes adenosis, precancerous vaginal and cervical growths which may spread to other areas of the body. The treatment for adenosis is cauterization, surgery, or cryosurgery. Women who suffer from this condition must be monitored by biopsy or colposcopic examination twice a year, a painful and expensive procedure. Thousands of women whose mothers received DES during pregnancy are unaware of the effects of the drug.

In 1971, the Food and Drug Administration ordered defendants to cease marketing and promoting DES for the purpose of preventing miscarriages, and to warn physicians and the public that the drug should not be used by pregnant women because of the danger to their unborn children.

During the period defendants marketed DES, they knew or should have known that it was a carcinogenic substance, that there was a grave

---

19. The plaintiff class alleged consists of "girls and women who are residents of California and who have been exposed to DES before birth and who may or may not know that fact or the dangers" to which they were exposed. Defendants are also sued as representatives of a class of drug manufacturers which sold DES after 1941.

danger after varying periods of latency it would cause cancerous and precancerous growths in the daughters of the mothers who took it, and that it was ineffective to prevent miscarriage. Nevertheless, defendants continued to advertise and market the drug as a miscarriage preventative. They failed to test DES for efficacy and safety; the tests performed by others, upon which they relied, indicated that it was not safe or effective. In violation of the authorization of the Food and Drug Administration, defendants marketed DES on an unlimited basis rather than as an experimental drug, and they failed to warn of its potential danger.

Because of defendants' advertised assurances that DES was safe and effective to prevent miscarriage, plaintiff was exposed to the drug prior to her birth. She became aware of the danger from such exposure within one year of the time she filed her complaint. As a result of the DES ingested by her mother, plaintiff developed a malignant bladder tumor which was removed by surgery. She suffers from adenosis and must constantly be monitored by biopsy or colposcopy to insure early warning of further malignancy.

The first cause of action alleges that defendants were jointly and individually negligent in that they manufactured, marketed and promoted DES as a safe and efficacious drug to prevent miscarriage, without adequate testing or warning, and without monitoring or reporting its effects.

A separate cause of action alleges that defendants are jointly liable regardless of which particular brand of DES was ingested by plaintiff's mother because defendants collaborated in marketing, promoting and testing the drug, relied upon each other's tests, and adhered to an industry-wide safety standard. DES was produced from a common and mutually agreed upon formula as a fungible drug interchangeable with other brands of the same product; defendants knew or should have known that it was customary for doctors to prescribe the drug by its generic rather than its brand name and that pharmacists filled prescriptions from whatever brand of the drug happened to be in stock.

Each cause of action alleges that defendants are jointly liable because they acted in concert, on the basis of express and implied agreements, and in reliance upon and ratification and exploitation of each other's testing and marketing methods.

Plaintiff seeks compensatory damages of $1 million and punitive damages of $10 million for herself. For the members of her class, she prays for equitable relief in the form of an order that defendants warn physicians and others of the danger of DES and the necessity of performing certain tests to determine the presence of disease caused by the drug, and that they establish free clinics in California to perform such tests.

Defendants demurred to the complaint. While the complaint did not expressly allege that plaintiff could not identify the manufacturer of the precise drug ingested by her mother, she stated in her points and authorities in opposition to the demurrers filed by some of the defendants that she was unable to make the identification, and the trial court sustained the demurrers of these defendants without leave to amend on the ground that plaintiff did not and stated she could not identify which defendant had manufactured the drug responsible for her injuries. Thereupon, the court dismissed the action. This appeal involves only five of ten defendants named in the complaint * * *

This case is but one of a number filed throughout the country seeking to hold drug manufacturers liable for injuries allegedly resulting from DES prescribed to the plaintiffs' mothers since 1947. According to a note in the Fordham Law Review, estimates of the number of women who took the drug during pregnancy range from 1½ million to 3 million. Hundreds, perhaps thousands, of the daughters of these women suffer from adenocarcinoma, and the incidence of vaginal adenosis among them is 30 to 90 percent. (Comment, *DES and a Proposed Theory of Enterprise Liability* (1978) 46 Fordham L.Rev. 963, 964–967 [hereafter Fordham Comment].) * * *

We begin with the proposition that, as a general rule, the imposition of liability depends upon a showing by the plaintiff that his or her injuries were caused by the act of the defendant or by an instrumentality under the defendant's control. The rule applies whether the injury resulted from an accidental event * * * or from the use of a defective product. * * *

There are, however, exceptions to this rule. Plaintiff's complaint suggests several bases upon which defendants may be held liable for her injuries even though she cannot demonstrate the name of the manufacturer which produced the DES actually taken by her mother. The first of these theories, classically illustrated by *Summers v. Tice* (1948) 33 Cal.2d 80, 199 P.2d 1, places the burden of proof of causation upon tortious defendants in certain circumstances. The second basis of liability emerging from the complaint is that defendants acted in concert to cause injury to plaintiff. There is a third and novel approach to the problem, sometimes called the theory of "enterprise liability," but which we prefer to designate by the more accurate term of "industry-wide" liability, which might obviate the necessity for identifying the manufacturer of the injury-causing drug. We shall conclude that these doctrines, as previously interpreted, may not be applied to hold defendants liable under the allegations of this complaint. However, we shall propose and adopt a fourth basis for permitting the action to be tried, grounded upon an extension of the *Summers* doctrine.

I

Plaintiff places primary reliance upon cases which hold that if a party cannot identify which of two or more defendants caused an injury, the burden of proof may shift to the defendants to show that they were not responsible for the harm. This principle is sometimes referred to as the "alternative liability" theory.

The celebrated case of *Summers v. Tice,* supra, * * * a unanimous opinion of this court, best exemplifies the rule. In *Summers,* the plaintiff was injured when two hunters negligently shot in his direction. It could not be determined which of them had fired the shot which actually caused the injury to the plaintiff's eye, but both defendants were nevertheless held jointly and severally liable for the whole of the damages. We reasoned that both were wrongdoers, both were negligent toward the plaintiff, and that it would be unfair to require plaintiff to isolate the defendant responsible, because if the one pointed out were to escape liability, the other might also, and the plaintiff-victim would be shorn of any remedy. In these circumstances, we held, the burden of proof shifted to the defendants, "each to absolve himself if he can." * * * We stated that under these or similar circumstances a defendant is ordinarily in a "far better position" to offer evidence to determine whether he or another defendant caused the injury.

The rule developed in *Summers* has been embodied in the Restatement of Torts. (Rest.2d Torts, § 433B, subsec. (3).)[20] Indeed, the *Summers* facts are used as an illustration * * *.

Defendants assert that these principles are inapplicable here. First, they insist that a predicate to shifting the burden of proof under *Summers–Ybarra* is that the defendants must have greater access to information regarding the cause of the injuries than the plaintiff, whereas in the present case the reverse appears.

Plaintiff does not claim that defendants are in a better position than she to identify the manufacturer of the drug taken by her mother or, indeed, that they have the ability to do so at all, but argues, rather, that *Summers* does not impose such a requirement as a condition to the shifting of the burden of proof. In this respect we believe plaintiff is correct.

In *Summers,* the circumstances of the accident themselves precluded an explanation of its cause. To be sure, *Summers* states that defendants are "[o]rdinarily * * * in a far better position to offer evidence to determine which one caused the injury" than a plaintiff * * *, but the decision does not determine that this "ordinary" situation was present. Neither the facts nor the language of the opinion indicate that the two defendants, simultaneously shooting in the same direction, were in a better position than the plaintiff to ascertain whose shot caused the injury. As the opinion acknowledges, it was impossible for the trial court to determine whether the shot which entered the plaintiff's eye came from the gun of one defendant or the other. Nevertheless, burden of proof was shifted to the defendants.

Here, as in *Summers,* the circumstances of the injury appear to render identification of the manufacturer of the drug ingested by plaintiff's mother impossible by either plaintiff or defendants, and it cannot reasonably be said that one is in a better position than the other to make the identification. Because many years elapsed between the time the drug was taken and the manifestation of plaintiff's injuries she, and many other daughters of mothers who took DES, are unable to make such identification. Certainly there can be no implication that plaintiff is at fault in failing to do so— the event occurred while plaintiff was *in utero,* a generation ago.[21]

20. Section 433B, subsection (3) of the Restatement provides: "Where the conduct of two or more actors is tortious, and it is proved that harm has been caused to the plaintiff by only one of them, but there is uncertainty as to which one has caused it, the burden is upon each such actor to prove that he has not caused the harm." The reason underlying the rule is "the injustice of permitting proved wrongdoers, who among them have inflicted an injury upon the entirely innocent plaintiff, to escape liability merely because the nature of their conduct and the resulting harm has made it difficult or impossible to prove which of them has caused the harm." (Rest.2d Torts, § 433B, com. f, p. 446.)

21. Defendants maintain that plaintiff is in a better position than they are to identify the manufacturer because her mother might recall the name of the prescribing physician or the hospital or pharmacy where the drug originated, and might know the brand and strength of dosage, the appearance of the medication, or other details from which the manufacturer might be identified, whereas

On the other hand, it cannot be said with assurance that defendants have the means to make the identification. In this connection, they point out that drug manufacturers ordinarily have no direct contact with the patients who take a drug prescribed by their doctors. Defendants sell to wholesalers, who in turn supply the product to physicians and pharmacies. Manufacturers do not maintain records of the persons who take the drugs they produce, and the selection of the medication is made by the physician rather than the manufacturer. Nor do we conclude that the absence of evidence on this subject is due to the fault of defendants. While it is alleged that they produced a defective product with delayed effects and without adequate warnings, the difficulty or impossibility of identification results primarily from the passage of time rather than from their allegedly negligent acts of failing to provide adequate warnings. * * *

It is important to observe, however, that while defendants do not have means superior to plaintiff to identify the maker of the precise drug taken by her mother, they may in some instances be able to prove that they did not manufacture the injury-causing substance. In the present case, for example, one of the original defendants was dismissed from the action upon proof that it did not manufacture DES until after plaintiff was born.

Thus we conclude that the fact defendants do not have greater access to information which might establish the identity of the manufacturer of the DES which injured plaintiff does not per se prevent application of the *Summers* rule.

Nevertheless, plaintiff may not prevail in her claim that the *Summers* rationale should be employed to fix the whole liability for her injuries upon defendants, at least as those principles have previously been applied. There is an important difference between the situation involved in *Summers* and the present case. There, all the parties who were or could have been responsible for the harm to the plaintiff were joined as defendants. Here, by contrast, there are approximately 200 drug companies which made DES, any of which might have manufactured the injury-producing drug.

Defendants maintain that, while in *Summers* there was a 50 percent chance that one of the two defendants was responsible for the plaintiff's injuries, here since any one of 200 companies which manufactured DES might have made the product which harmed plaintiff, there is no rational basis upon which to infer that any defendant in this action caused plaintiff's injuries, nor even a reasonable possibility that they were responsible.

These arguments are persuasive if we measure the chance that any one of the defendants supplied the injury-causing drug by the number of possible tortfeasors. In such a context, the possibility that any of the five defendants supplied the DES to plaintiff's mother is so remote that it would be unfair to require each defendant to exonerate itself. There may be a substantial likelihood that none of the five defendants joined in the action made the DES which caused the injury, and that the offending producer not named would escape liability altogether. While we propose, *infra,* an adaptation of the rule in *Summers* which will substantially

they possess none of this information. As we point out in footnote 12, we assume for purposes of this appeal that plaintiff cannot point to any particular manufacturer as the producer of the DES taken by her mother.

overcome these difficulties, defendants appear to be correct that the rule, as previously applied, cannot relieve plaintiff of the burden of proving the identity of the manufacturer which made the drug causing her injuries.[22]

II

The second principle upon which plaintiff relies is the so-called "concert of action" theory. Preliminarily, we briefly describe the procedure a drug manufacturer must follow before placing a drug on the market. Under federal law as it read prior to 1962, a new drug was defined as one "not generally recognized as * * * safe." (§ 102, 76 Stat. 781 (Oct. 10, 1962).) Such a substance could be marketed only if a new drug application had been filed with the Food and Drug Administration and had become "effective." If the agency determined that a product was no longer a "new drug," i.e., that it was "generally recognized as * * * safe," (21 U.S.C.A. § 321, subd. (p)(1)) it could be manufactured by any drug company without submitting an application to the agency. According to defendants, 123 new drug applications for DES had been approved by 1952, and in that year DES was declared not to be a "new drug," thus allowing any manufacturer to produce it without prior testing and without submitting a new drug application to the Food and Drug Administration.

With this background we consider whether the complaint states a claim based upon "concert of action" among defendants. The elements of this doctrine are prescribed in section 876 of the Restatement of Torts. The section provides, "For harm resulting to a third person from the tortious conduct of another, one is subject to liability if he (a) does a tortious act in concert with the other or pursuant to a common design with him, or (b) knows that the other's conduct constitutes a breach of duty and gives substantial assistance or encouragement to the other so to conduct himself, or (c) gives substantial assistance to the other in accomplishing a tortious result and his own conduct, separately considered, constitutes a breach of duty to the third person." With respect to this doctrine, Prosser states that "those who, in pursuance of a common plan or design to commit a tortious act, actively take part in it, or further it by cooperation or request, or who lend aid or encouragement to the wrongdoer, or ratify and adopt his acts done for their benefit, are equally liable with him. [¶] Express agreement is not necessary, and all that is required is that there be a tacit understanding * * *." (Prosser, Law of Torts (4th ed. 1971), sec. 46, p. 292.)

The gravamen of the charge of concert is that defendants failed to adequately test the drug or to give sufficient warning of its dangers and

---

22. *Garcia v. Joseph Vince Co.,* supra, 84 Cal.App.3d 868, 148 Cal.Rptr. 843, relied upon by defendants, presents a distinguishable factual situation. The plaintiff in *Garcia* was injured by a defective saber. He was unable to identify which of two manufacturers had produced the weapon because it was commingled with other sabers after the accident. In a suit against both manufacturers, the court refused to apply the *Summers* rationale on the ground that the plaintiff had not shown that either defendant had violated a duty to him. Thus in *Garcia,* only one of the two defendants was alleged to have manufactured a defective product, and the plaintiff's inability to identify which of the two was negligent resulted in a judgment for both defendants. (See also *Wetzel v. Eaton,* supra, 62 F.R.D. 22.) Here, by contrast, the DES manufactured by all defendants is alleged to be defective, but plaintiff is unable to demonstrate which of the defendants supplied the precise DES which caused her injuries.

that they relied upon the tests performed by one another and took advantage of each others' promotional and marketing techniques. These allegations do not amount to a charge that there was a tacit understanding or a common plan among defendants to fail to conduct adequate tests or give sufficient warnings, and that they substantially aided and encouraged one another in these omissions.

The complaint charges also that defendants produced DES from a "common and mutually agreed upon formula," allowing pharmacists to treat the drug as a "fungible commodity" and to fill prescriptions from whatever brand of DES they had on hand at the time. It is difficult to understand how these allegations can form the basis of a cause of action for wrongful conduct by defendants, acting in concert. The formula for DES is a scientific constant. It is set forth in the United States Pharmacopoeia, and any manufacturer producing that drug must, with exceptions not relevant here, utilize the formula set forth in that compendium. * * *

What the complaint appears to charge is defendants' parallel or imitative conduct in that they relied upon each others' testing and promotion methods. But such conduct describes a common practice in industry: a producer avails himself of the experience and methods of others making the same or similar products. Application of the concept of concert of action to this situation would expand the doctrine far beyond its intended scope and would render virtually any manufacturer liable for the defective products of an entire industry, even if it could be demonstrated that the product which caused the injury was not made by the defendant.

None of the cases cited by plaintiff supports a conclusion that defendants may be held liable for concerted tortious acts. They involve conduct by a small number of individuals whose actions resulted in a tort against a single plaintiff, usually over a short span of time, and the defendant held liable was either a direct participant in the acts which caused damage, or encouraged and assisted the person who directly caused the injuries by participating in a joint activity. * * *

[See] *Agovino v. Kunze,* supra, 181 Cal.App.2d 591, 5 Cal.Rptr. 534, in which liability was imposed upon a participant in a drag race, * * *. There is no allegation here that each defendant knew the other defendants' conduct was tortious toward plaintiff, and that they assisted and encouraged one another to inadequately test DES and to provide inadequate warnings. Indeed, it seems dubious whether liability on the concert of action theory can be predicated upon substantial assistance and encouragement given by one alleged tortfeasor to another pursuant to a tacit understanding to fail to perform an act. Thus, there was no concert of action among defendants within the meaning of that doctrine.

III

A third theory upon which plaintiff relies is the concept of industry-wide liability, or according to the terminology of the parties, "enterprise liability." This theory was suggested in *Hall v. E.I. Du Pont de Nemours & Co., Inc.* (E.D.N.Y.1972) 345 F.Supp. 353. In that case, plaintiffs were 13 children injured by the explosion of blasting caps in 12 separate incidents which occurred in 10 different states between 1955 and 1959. The defendants were six blasting cap manufacturers, comprising virtually the entire blasting cap industry in the United States, and their trade association. There were, however, a number of Canadian blasting cap manufacturers which could have supplied the caps. The gravamen of the complaint was that the practice of the industry of omitting a warning on individual blasting caps and of failing to take other safety measures created an unreasonable risk of harm, resulting in the plaintiffs' injuries. The complaint did not identify a particular manufacturer of a cap which caused a particular injury.

The court reasoned as follows: there was evidence that defendants, acting independently, had adhered to an industry-wide standard with regard to the safety features of blasting caps, that they had in effect delegated some functions of safety investigation and design, such as labelling, to their trade association, and that there was industry-wide cooperation in the manufacture and design of blasting caps. In these circumstances, the evidence supported a conclusion that all the defendants jointly controlled the risk. Thus, if plaintiffs could establish by a preponderance of the evidence that the caps were manufactured by one of the defendants, the burden of proof as to causation would shift to all the defendants. The court noted that this theory of liability applied to industries composed of a small number of units, and that what would be fair and reasonable with regard to an industry of five or ten producers might be manifestly unreasonable if applied to a decentralized industry composed of countless small producers.

Plaintiff attempts to state a cause of action under the rationale of *Hall*. She alleges joint enterprise and collaboration among defendants in the production, marketing, promotion and testing of DES, and "concerted promulgation and adherence to industry-wide testing, safety, warning and efficacy standards" for the drug. We have concluded above that allegations that defendants relied upon one another's testing and promotion methods do not state a cause of action for concerted conduct to commit a tortious act. Under the theory of industry-wide liability, however, each manufacturer could be liable for all injuries caused by DES by virtue of adherence to an industry-wide standard of safety.

In the Fordham Comment, the industry-wide theory of liability is discussed and refined in the context of its applicability to actions alleging injuries resulting from DES. The author explains causation under that theory as follows, "* * * [T]he industrywide standard becomes itself the cause of plaintiff's injury, just as defendants' joint plan is the cause of injury in the traditional concert of action plea. Each defendant's adherence perpetuates this standard, which results in the manufacture of the particular, unidentifiable injury-producing product. Therefore, each industry member has contributed to plaintiff's injury." * * *

The Comment proposes seven requirements for a cause of action based upon industry-wide liability,[23] and suggests that if a plaintiff proves these

---

23. The suggested requirements are as follows:

1. There existed an insufficient, industry-wide standard of safety as to the manufacture of the product.

2. Plaintiff is not at fault for the absence of evidence identifying the causative agent but, rather, this absence of proof is due to defendant's conduct.

elements, the burden of proof of causation should be shifted to the defendants, who may exonerate themselves only by showing that their product could not have caused the injury.

We decline to apply this theory in the present case. At least 200 manufacturers produced DES; *Hall,* which involved 6 manufacturers representing the entire blasting cap industry in the United States, cautioned against application of the doctrine espoused therein to a large number of producers. (345 F.Supp. at p. 378.) Moreover, in *Hall,* the conclusion that the defendants jointly controlled the risk was based upon allegations that they had delegated some functions relating to safety to a trade association. There are no such allegations here, and we have concluded above that plaintiff has failed to allege liability on a concert of action theory.

Equally important, the drug industry is closely regulated by the Food and Drug Administration, which actively controls the testing and manufacture of drugs and the method by which they are marketed, including the contents of warning labels. To a considerable degree, therefore, the standards followed by drug manufacturers are suggested or compelled by the government. Adherence to those standards cannot, of course, absolve a manufacturer of liability to which it would otherwise be subject. * * * But since the government plays such a pervasive role in formulating the criteria for the testing and marketing of drugs, it would be unfair to impose upon a manufacturer liability for injuries resulting from the use of a drug which it did not supply simply because it followed the standards of the industry.

IV

If we were confined to the theories of *Summers* and *Hall,* we would be constrained to hold that the judgment must be sustained. Should we require that plaintiff identify the manufacturer which supplied the DES used by her mother or that all DES manufacturers be joined in the action, she would effectively be precluded from any recovery. As defendants candidly admit, there is little likelihood that all the manufacturers who made DES at the time in question are still in business or that they are subject to the jurisdiction of the California courts. There are, however, forceful arguments in favor of holding that plaintiff has a cause of action.

In our contemporary complex industrialized society, advances in science and technology create fungible goods which may harm consumers and which cannot be traced to any specific producer. The response of the courts can be either to adhere rigidly to prior doctrine, denying recovery to those injured by such products, or to fashion remedies to meet these changing needs. * * * [W]e acknowledge that some adaptation of the rules of causation and liability may be appropriate in these recurring circumstances. The Restatement comments that modification of the *Summers* rule may be necessary in a situation like that before us. * * *

3. A generically similar defective product was manufactured by all the defendants.

4. Plaintiff's injury was caused by this defect.

5. Defendants owed a duty to the class of which plaintiff was a member.

6. There is clear and convincing evidence that plaintiff's injury was caused by a product made by one of the defendants. For example, the joined defendants accounted for a high percentage of such defective products on the market at the time of plaintiff's injury.

7. All defendants were tortfeasors.

The most persuasive reason for finding plaintiff states a cause of action is that advanced in *Summers:* as between an innocent plaintiff and negligent defendants, the latter should bear the cost of the injury. Here, as in *Summers,* plaintiff is not at fault in failing to provide evidence of causation, and although the absence of such evidence is not attributable to the defendants either, their conduct in marketing a drug the effects of which are delayed for many years played a significant role in creating the unavailability of proof.

From a broader policy standpoint, defendants are better able to bear the cost of injury resulting from the manufacture of a defective product. As was said by Justice Traynor in *Escola,* "[t]he cost of an injury and the loss of time or health may be an overwhelming misfortune to the person injured, and a needless one, for the risk of injury can be insured by the manufacturer and distributed among the public as a cost of doing business." (24 Cal.2d p. 462, 150 P.2d p. 441; see also Rest.2d Torts, § 402A, com. c, pp. 349–350.) The manufacturer is in the best position to discover and guard against defects in its products and to warn of harmful effects; thus, holding it liable for defects and failure to warn of harmful effects will provide an incentive to product safety. * * * These considerations are particularly significant where medication is involved, for the consumer is virtually helpless to protect himself from serious, sometimes permanent, sometimes fatal, injuries caused by deleterious drugs.

Where, as here, all defendants produced a drug from an identical formula and the manufacturer of the DES which caused plaintiff's injuries cannot be identified through no fault of plaintiff, a modification of the rule of *Summers* is warranted. As we have seen, an undiluted *Summers* rationale is inappropriate to shift the burden of proof of causation to defendants because if we measure the chance that any particular manufacturer supplied the injury-causing product by the number of producers of DES, there is a possibility that none of the five defendants in this case produced the offending substance and that the responsible manufacturer, not named in the action, will escape liability.

But we approach the issue of causation from a different perspective: we hold it to be reasonable in the present context to measure the likelihood that any of the defendants supplied the product which allegedly injured plaintiff by the percentage which the DES sold by each of them for the purpose of preventing miscarriage bears to the entire production of the drug sold by all for that purpose. Plaintiff asserts in her briefs that Eli Lilly and Company and 5 or 6 other companies produced 90 percent of the DES marketed. If at trial this is established to be the fact, then there is a corresponding likelihood that this comparative handful of producers manufactured the DES which caused plaintiff's injuries, and only a 10 percent likelihood that the offending producer would escape liability.[24]

24. The Fordham Comment explains the connection between percentage of market share and liability as follows: "[I]f X Manufacturer sold one-fifth of all the DES prescribed for pregnancy and identification could be made in all cases, X would be the sole defendant in approximately one-fifth of all cases and liable for all the damages in those cases. Under alternative liability, X would be joined in all cases in which identification could not be made, but liable for only one-fifth of the total damages in these cases. X would pay the same amount either way. Although the correlation is not, in practice,

If plaintiff joins in the action the manufacturers of a substantial share of the DES which her mother might have taken, the injustice of shifting the burden of proof to defendants to demonstrate that they could not have made the substance which injured plaintiff is significantly diminished. While 75 to 80 percent of the market is suggested as the requirement by the Fordham Comment * * *, we hold only that a substantial percentage is required.

The presence in the action of a substantial share of the appropriate market also provides a ready means to apportion damages among the defendants. Each defendant will be held liable for the proportion of the judgment represented by its share of that market unless it demonstrates that it could not have made the product which caused plaintiff's injuries. In the present case, as we have seen, one DES manufacturer was dismissed from the action upon filing a declaration that it had not manufactured DES until after plaintiff was born. Once plaintiff has met her burden of joining the required defendants, they in turn may cross-complaint against other DES manufacturers, not joined in the action, which they can allege might have supplied the injury-causing product.

Under this approach, each manufacturer's liability would approximate its responsibility for the injuries caused by its own products. Some minor discrepancy in the correlation between market share and liability is inevitable; therefore, a defendant may be held liable for a somewhat different percentage of the damage than its share of the appropriate market would justify. It is probably impossible, with the passage of time, to determine market share with mathematical exactitude. But just as a jury cannot be expected to determine the precise relationship between fault and liability in applying the doctrine of comparative fault * * *, the difficulty of apportioning damages among the defendant producers in exact relation to their market share does not seriously militate against the rule we adopt. As we said in *Summers* with regard to the liability of independent tortfeasors, where a correct division of liability cannot be made "the trier of fact may make it the best it can." * * *

We are not unmindful of the practical problems involved in defining the market and determining market share,[25] but these are largely matters of proof which properly cannot be determined at the pleading stage of these proceedings. Defendants urge that it would be both unfair and contrary to public policy to hold them liable for plaintiff's injuries in the absence of proof that one of them supplied the drug responsible for the damage. Most of their arguments, however, are based upon the assumption that one manufacturer would be held responsible for the products of another or for those of all other manufacturers if plaintiff ultimately prevails. But under the rule we adopt, each manufacturer's liability for an injury would be

perfect [footnote omitted], it is close enough so that defendants' objections on the ground of fairness lose their value." (Fordham Comment, supra, at p. 94.)

25. Defendants assert that there are no figures available to determine market share, that DES was provided for a number of uses other than to prevent miscarriage and it would be difficult to ascertain what proportion of the drug was used as a miscarriage preventative, and that the establishment of a time frame and area for market share would pose problems.

approximately equivalent to the damages caused by the DES it manufactured.

The judgments are reversed.

RICHARDSON, JUSTICE, dissenting.

* * * "market share" thesis may be paraphrased. Plaintiffs have been hurt by *someone* who made DES. Because of the lapse of time no one can prove who made it. Perhaps it was not the named defendants who made it, but they did make some. * * * Plaintiffs have suffered injury and defendants are wealthy. There should be a remedy. Strict products liability is unavailable because the element of causation is lacking. Strike that requirement and label what remains "alternative" liability, "industry-wide" liability, or "market share" liability, proving thereby that if you hit the square peg hard and often enough the round holes will really become square, although you may splinter the board in the process.

The foregoing result is directly contrary to long established tort principles. Once again, in the words of Dean Prosser, the applicable rule is: "[Plaintiff] must introduce evidence which affords a reasonable basis for the conclusion that it is more likely than not that the conduct of the defendant was a substantial factor in bringing about the result. *A mere possibility of such causation is not enough;* and when the matter remains one of pure speculation or conjecture, or the probabilities are at best evenly balanced, it becomes the duty of the court to direct a verdict for the defendant." * * *

The injustice inherent in the majority's new theory of liability is compounded by the fact that plaintiffs who use it are treated far more favorably than are the plaintiffs in routine tort actions. In most tort cases plaintiff knows the identity of the person who has caused his injuries. In such a case, plaintiff, of course, has no option to seek recovery from an entire industry or a "substantial" segment thereof, but in the usual instance can recover, if at all, only from the particular defendant causing injury. Such a defendant may or may not be either solvent or amenable to process. Plaintiff in the ordinary tort case must take a chance that defendant can be reached and can respond financially. On what principle should those plaintiffs who wholly fail to prove any causation, an essential element of the traditional tort cause of action, be rewarded by being offered both a wider selection of potential defendants and a greater opportunity for recovery?

It seems to me that liability in the manner created by the majority must inevitably inhibit, if not the research or development, at least the dissemination of new pharmaceutical drugs. * * *

I believe that the scales of justice tip against imposition of this new liability because of the foregoing elements of unfairness to some defendants who may have had nothing whatever to do with causing any injury, the unwarranted preference created for this particular class of plaintiffs, the violence done to traditional tort principles by the drastic expansion of liability proposed, the injury threatened to the public interest in continued unrestricted basic medical research as stressed by the Restatement, and the other reasons heretofore expressed.

CLARK and MANUEL, JJ., concur.

Notes

1. DES cases have been handled in several state and federal courts. In addition to the causation problems, the DES cases raise significant product liability questions, a topic that will be taken up in Chapter 9. The courts have had to face the problem of identifying the specific defendant responsible for the plaintiff's injury in virtually every case. The results have been mixed. Five basic theories have been tried and most have received at least some judicial support but none have received broad recognition as the proper solution to the problem.

2. The alternative liability theory of *Summers v. Tice* has been rejected by most courts for the reasons given in *Sindell.* However, in Abel v. Eli Lilly & Co., 418 Mich. 311, 343 N.W.2d 164, *cert. denied,* 469 U.S. 833, 105 S.Ct. 123, 83 L.Ed.2d 65 (1984), the court adopted a modified version of alternative liability:

> Perhaps the most fundamental, and arguably the most important, factual difference between *Summers* and this case is that in *Summers* each defendant was negligent toward the sole plaintiff; each could have caused the injury to the plaintiff although only one in fact did so. Here, the plaintiffs do not even claim that each of the defendants was negligent toward each of the plaintiffs. Therefore, each of the defendants in this case could not have caused injury to each of the plaintiffs. Stated differently, in *Summers,* each defendant was negligent toward *the* plaintiff; here, each defendant was negligent toward *a* plaintiff, but each defendant was not negligent toward *each* plaintiff. Thus, all defendants were not negligent toward each plaintiff, and each defendant could not have caused each plaintiff's injury.

> Although the rationale of the alternative liability theory in *Summers* is not squarely applicable to this DES litigation, partly because the facts of the two cases are so distinctly different, the theory as first detailed in *Summers* can nevertheless be tailored to accommodate the unique facts of this case, and in fairness ought to be. It should be understood, however, that in approving application of alternative liability to this case, we are not only extending the *policy* of traditional alternative liability as espoused in *Summers* to accommodate the facts; we are actually fashioning and approving a new DES-unique version of alternative liability.

> The requirements which the plaintiffs must meet * * * [are f]irst, it must be shown that all the defendants have acted tortiously * * *; second, that the plaintiffs have been harmed by the conduct of one of the defendants (in order to support this second requirement, the plaintiffs must bring before the court all the actors who may have caused the injury in fact); third, that the plaintiffs, through no fault of their own, are unable to identify which actor caused the injury. * * *

> We also restrict, for the time being, the use of this theory of recovery to those allegations sounding in negligence. Plaintiffs may not resort to the theory for warranty allegations or for strict liability allegations.

> Plaintiffs' ability to meet these conditions precedent will allow them to avail themselves of DES-modified alternative liability, thus relieving them of the traditional burden of proof of causation in fact. We emphasize that

although plaintiffs are absolved of identifying specifically the tortfeasor who caused each specific harm, their burden of proof as to other aspects of causation is not lessened.

In that connection, as necessary corollaries of shifting the burden of proving causation in fact and the requirement that plaintiffs bring all potential tortfeasors before the Court, the plaintiffs are required to prove the following:

1) that all defendants distributed or manufactured one or more of the three drugs involved: DES, DSD, or dienestrol;

2) that the female plaintiffs' mothers ingested DES, DSD, or dienestrol * * *;

3) that the female plaintiffs' mothers ingested DES, DSD, or dienestrol manufactured or distributed in Michigan; and

4) that DES, DSD, and dienestrol each caused the type of injury of which the plaintiffs complain; that is, plaintiffs must prove that these three drugs are essentially identical in their injury-producing results. * * *

In sum, alternative liability will be applied in cases in which all defendants have acted tortiously, but only one unidentifiable defendant caused plaintiff's injury. If a plaintiff brings all the possible defendants into court and establishes the other elements of the underlying cause of action, the court should equitably shift an onerous burden of causation in fact to the defendants. If the defendants are unable to exonerate themselves, joint and several liability results. * * *

Id. at 330–34, 343 N.W.2d at 172–74.

3. The concert of action theory has also been rejected by most courts for the reasons given in *Sindell,* but again the Michigan Supreme Court, in the *Abel* case held that the theory was appropriate if the plaintiff could prove joint action on the part of the defendants.

Here plaintiffs have alleged that defendants acted together in negligently manufacturing and promoting drugs which were ineffective and dangerous, were inadequately tested, and were distributed without sufficient warnings. These allegations are sufficient to withstand summary judgment.

Id. at 338, 343 N.W.2d at 176.

A similar approach was taken in Bichler v. Eli Lilly & Co., 79 A.D.2d 317, 436 N.Y.S.2d 625 (1981)(affirmed, partly on procedural grounds, 55 N.Y.2d 571, 450 N.Y.S.2d 776, 436 N.E.2d 182 (1982)). However, recently New York adopted the *Sindell* market share approach, also in a DES case. Hymowitz v. Eli Lilly & Co., 73 N.Y.2d 487, 541 N.Y.S.2d 941, 539 N.E.2d 1069, *cert. denied* 493 U.S. 944, 110 S.Ct. 350, 107 L.Ed.2d 338 (1989). The court after exploring the difficulties of using market shares within the state, opted to use national market shares.

4. The enterprise or industry-wide liability approach of *Hall* has generally been held inapplicable because of the number of potential defendants involved in the DES cases.

5. Martin v. Abbott Laboratories, 102 Wn.2d 581, 689 P.2d 368 (1984) follows the *Sindell* market share approach with some modification. *See also,*

Conley v. Boyle Drug Co., 570 So.2d 275 (Fla.1990); Gorman v. Abbott Lab., 599 A.2d 1364 (R.I.1991).

6. Wisconsin has taken yet a different approach, referred to as the risk contribution approach. Collins v. Eli Lilly Co., 116 Wis.2d 166, 342 N.W.2d 37, *cert. denied,* 469 U.S. 826, 105 S.Ct. 107, 83 L.Ed.2d 51 (1984):

> Article I, sec. 9 of the Wisconsin Constitution provides, in part, that "[e]very person is entitled to a certain remedy in the laws for all injuries, or wrongs which he may receive in his person, property, or character." We have interpreted this provision of the constitution in the following manner: "'When an adequate remedy or forum does not exist to resolve disputes or provide due process, the courts, under the Wisconsin Constitution, can fashion an adequate remedy.' " * * *

> Although the defendants in this case may not have acted in concert under the concert of action theory, all participated in either gaining approval of DES for use in pregnancy or in producing or marketing DES in subsequent years. Each defendant contributed to the *risk* of injury to the public and, consequently, the risk of injury to individual plaintiffs such as Therese Collins. Thus each defendant shares, in some measure, a degree of culpability in producing or marketing what the FDA, many scientists, and medical researchers ultimately concluded was a drug with possibly harmful side effects. Moreover, as between the injured plaintiff and the possibly responsible drug company, the drug company is in a better position to absorb the cost of the injury. The drug company can either insure itself against liability, absorb the damage award, or pass the cost along to the consuming public as a cost of doing business. We conclude that it is better to have drug companies or consumers share the cost of the injury than to place the burden solely on the innocent plaintiff. Finally, the cost of damages awards will act as an incentive for drug companies to test adequately the drugs they place on the market for general medical use. This incentive is especially important in the case of mass-marketed drugs because consumers and their physicians in most instances rely upon advice given by the supplier and the scientific community and, consequently, are virtually helpless to protect themselves from serious injuries caused by deleterious drugs.

> Practical considerations favor permitting the plaintiff to proceed, at least initially, against one defendant. One alternative would be to require the plaintiff, as in *Sindell,* to join as defendants "a substantial share" of the producers and marketers of DES. We conclude that this is unworkable because of the problems * * * inherent in trying to establish the relevant market and each defendant's share of that market. Another alternative would be to require the defendant to join a "reasonable number" of possibly liable defendants. We cannot, however, define what that "reasonable number" would be because there are so many potentially liable drug companies. Moreover, either alternative would waste judicial resources by requiring an initial determination of whether the plaintiff has joined a sufficient number of defendants. We also conclude that the defendant is in a better position than the plaintiff to determine which other drug companies may share liability. We recognize that many drug companies do not have relevant records, but they, as participants in the DES market, presumably have more information or potential access to relevant information than does the plaintiff.

Id. at 182, 191, 342 N.W.2d at 45, 49–50.

The risk contribution approach is carefully explored in Robinson, *Multiple Causation in Tort Law: Reflections on the DES Cases,* 68 Va.L.Rev. 713 (1982). *See also,* Robinson & Abraham, *Collective Justice in Tort Law,* 78 Va. L. Rev. 1481 (1992).

7. Several state and federal courts have rejected these approaches in DES and related cases. *See, e.g.,* Gray v. United States, 445 F.Supp. 337 (S.D.Tex.1978)(plaintiff sued both Eli Lilly & Co. and the United States); Tidler v. Eli Lilly & Co., 95 F.R.D. 332 (D.D.C.1982)(applying Maryland and D.C. law); Smith v. Eli Lilly & Co., 137 Ill.2d 222, 148 Ill.Dec. 22, 560 N.E.2d 324 (1990)(holding that such a substantial deviation from existing tort principles was for the legislature); Mulcahy v. Eli Lilly & Co., 386 N.W.2d 67 (Iowa 1986); Payton v. Abbott Labs, 386 Mass. 540, 437 N.E.2d 171 (1982)(at least on the facts presented); Zafft v. Eli Lilly & Co., 676 S.W.2d 241 (Mo.1984).

SHACKIL v. LEDERLE LABORATORIES

Supreme Court of New Jersey, 1989.
116 N.J. 155, 561 A.2d 511.

CLIFFORD, J.

This is a medical-malpractice and products-liability action arising out of the 1972 inoculation of the infant plaintiff with a combined diphtheria-pertussis-tetanus vaccine, commonly known as DPT vaccine. Despite extensive discovery, plaintiffs were unable to identify the manufacturer of the DPT vaccine administered to the infant plaintiff. The issue is whether, in the context of childhood vaccinations, New Jersey should substitute for the element of causation-in-fact a theory of "market share" liability, thereby shifting to defendant manufacturers the burden of proof on the issue of causation.

We conclude that the imposition of a theory of collective liability in this case would frustrate overarching public-policy and public-health considerations by threatening the continued availability of needed drugs and impairing the prospects of the development of safer vaccines. Moreover, we are satisfied that an alternative compensation scheme established by Congress, entitled the National Childhood Vaccine Injury Act of 1986, 42 *U.S.C.A.* §§ 300aa–1 to–34 (West Supp.1988), will fulfill in large measure the goal of providing compensatory relief to vaccine-injured plaintiffs.

We therefore reverse the judgment of the Appellate Division and reinstate summary judgment in favor of defendant manufacturers.

I

Underlying this appeal is a profound human tragedy. On October 24, 1972, two days before her second birthday, plaintiff Deanna Marrero was given a final "booster" shot of a DPT vaccine by Dr. Feld, defendant pediatrician. Plaintiff Clara Morgan Shackil, the child's mother, noticed that within twenty-four hours of the inoculation Deanna displayed symptoms of extreme pain. The rapid deterioration of her condition resulted in the loss of her then-acquired verbal, motor, and mental capacities. Deanna, now eighteen years of age, has been diagnosed as having chronic

encephalopathy and severe retardation. She is institutionalized and requires constant care.

In April 1985, thirteen years after the inoculation that allegedly caused
plaintiff's condition, Deanna Marrero and her parents brought suit against
Dr. Feld and Lederle Laboratories, one of the manufacturers of DPT during
1971–72. The complaint asserted theories of negligence, breach of warranty, misrepresentation, and strict liability based on design defect. Plaintiffs'
delay in filing suit was occasioned by the fact that it was not until 1984
that Mrs. Shackil became aware of the linkage between brain damage and
the pertussis portion of the DPT vaccine.

Largely because of the extensive time that had elapsed between the
inoculation and the lawsuit, plaintiffs were unable to establish that Lederle
Laboratories in fact manufactured the vaccine that caused Deanna's injuries. The pediatrician, Dr. Feld, retained no records that would have
revealed the brand name of the vaccine administered, and his pharmacist is
no longer alive. In his deposition, Dr. Feld testified that he had used
Lederle's vaccine "for the most part"; however, he also indicated that on
occasion he had used DPT vaccines manufactured by Eli Lilly, Wyeth
Laboratories, Parke–Davis, and Pitman–Moore. Dr. Feld did not mention
the name of National Drug Company, the only remaining manufacturer of
DPT at the time of Deanna's inoculation.

Plaintiffs amended their complaint to include the additional manufacturers referred to in Dr. Feld's deposition but not National Drug Company.
After several months of discovery, however, plaintiffs were still unable to
identify the manufacturer of the vaccine administered to Deanna. Consequently, defendants Lederle, Eli Lilly, Wyeth, and Parke–Davis moved for
summary judgment based on plaintiffs' failure to satisfy an essential
element of a *prima facie* case—the identity of the manufacturer and
distributor of the DPT dosage.

Relying on *Namm v. Charles E. Frosst & Co.,* 178 *N.J.Super.* 19, 427
*A.*2d 1121 (App.Div.1981), the trial court granted defendant manufacturers'
motions for summary judgment and entered orders dismissing the complaints as to those defendants. The Appellate Division granted leave to
appeal and reversed. * * *

Our primary focus is on whether plaintiffs have demonstrated that a
theory of market-share liability should be applied to the facts of this case to
allow plaintiffs' claims against defendant manufacturers to proceed. Because this appeal emanates from a motion for summary judgment, we must
construe the pleadings and papers in the light most favorable to the
nonmoving party, in this case the plaintiffs. * * * Therefore, we will
assume that the vaccines manufactured by defendants were defectively
designed and that Deanna's injuries were directly caused by a DPT inoculation and not from a hereditary immunological or neurological disorder,
issues that would potentially surface at later stages of this litigation. *See,
e.g., Niemiera v. Schneider,* 114 *N.J.* 550, 554, 555 *A.*2d 1112 (1989)(noting
possibility of independent cause of plaintiffs' injuries, unrelated to DPT
inoculation); *Feldman v. Lederle Laboratories, supra,* 97 *N.J.* at 429, 479
*A.*2d 374 (whether a prescription drug is "unavoidably unsafe," and there-

fore subject to § 402A of the Restatement (Second) of Torts comment k protection, is to be determined on a case-by-case basis).

II

At the center of this appeal is the traditional element of causation-in-fact, "that reasonable connection between the act or omission of the defendant and the damages which plaintiff has suffered." W. Keeton, D. Dobbs, R. Keeton & D. Owen, *Prosser & Keeton on the Law of Torts* § 41 at 263 (5th ed. 1984) [hereinafter *Prosser & Keeton*]. The purpose of the causation-in-fact requirement, besides assigning blameworthiness to culpable parties, is to limit the scope of potential liability and thereby encourage useful activity that would otherwise be deterred if there were excessive exposure to liability. Fischer, "Products Liability—An Analysis of Market Share Liability," 34 *Vand.L.Rev.* 1623, 1628–29 (1981) * * *. Although proof of causation-in-fact is ordinarily an indispensable ingredient of a *prima facie* case, exceptions have nevertheless arisen that have allowed plaintiffs to shift to defendant or a group of defendants the burden of proof on the causation issue. Those exceptions include "concert of action," with its offspring, "enterprise liability"; alternative liability; and market-share liability. In fact, the theory that we are urged to adopt in this case, modified market-share liability, is essentially an extension of the alternative-liability theory. The concert-of-action exception nevertheless warrants brief comment.

Without embarking on an analysis of the merits in or the inherent problems of applying concert-of-action theory to prescription drugs, we are persuaded that the theory is not applicable to this case. There are no allegations that the manufacturers of DPT had a "tacit understanding" or "common plan" to produce a defective product or not to conduct adequate tests on the vaccine. Indeed, unlike the producers of DES, for example, each of the manufacturers involved in this case made the DPT vaccine by a different process, protected by patent or trade secret. Each process was separately licensed by the Food and Drug Administration (FDA) under established guidelines for the production of the vaccine. 21 *C.F.R.* § 620.1 to 620.6 (1988) * * *. In addition, each lot of the DPT vaccine was separately tested by the office of Biologics Research and Reviews, a division of the FDA. 21 *C.F.R.* 620.6 (1988). Application of "concert of action" to this case "would [therefore] expand the doctrine far beyond its intended scope and would render virtually any manufacturer liable for the defective products of an entire industry, even if it could be demonstrated that the product which caused the injury was not made by the defendant." *Sindell v. Abbott Laboratories,* 26 *Cal.*3d 588, 605, 163 *Cal.Rptr.* 132, 607 *P.*2d 924, 933 * * *. [The court next discussed *Summers v. Tice, Sindell v. Abbott Laboratories* and the development of market share liability, noting the cases that have followed *Sindell* and those that have rejected it.]

Among the questions left unanswered in *Sindell* was the question of whether market-share liability was intended to apply to claims other than DES. That issue has frequently arisen in the context of asbestos litigation, where in most cases market-share liability is held inapplicable for public-policy reasons, *see, e.g., Thompson v. Johns–Manville Corp.,* 714 *F.*2d 581 (5th Cir.1983); * * * *Goldman v. Johns–Manville Sales Corp.,* 33 Ohio

St.3d 40, 514 *N.E.*2d 691 (1987)(refusing to apply *Sindell* to asbestos products on grounds that there was a difference between risks associated with asbestos and that it would be inherently unfair to hold companies accountable for market share) * * *.

At present, there are three reported cases addressing the question of whether to apply a theory of market-share liability to a vaccine case. Of these three only one involves the theory urged in this case, that is, that the vaccine is defectively designed. Thus, in *Senn v. Merrell–Dow Pharmaceuticals, Inc.,* 305 *Or.* 256, 751 *P.*2d 215 (1988), the Oregon Supreme Court rejected a theory of market-share liability against two DPT manufacturers in the context of a design-defect claim on grounds that the "adoption of any theory of alternative liability requires a profound change in fundamental tort principles," which was perceived as more properly in the domain of the legislature. *Id.* at 271, 751 *P.*2d 223.

The other two cases involve the imposition of market-share liability in respect of a vaccine based on a manufacturing defect, a theory not relied on in this case. Nevertheless, those cases warrant our attention. In *Sheffield v. Eli Lilly & Co., supra,* 144 *Cal.App.*3d 583, 192 *Cal.Rptr.* 870, plaintiff's claim against the manufacturers of the Salk polio vaccine was summarily dismissed for failure to identify the defendant who had supplied the injury-causing vaccine. Plaintiffs appealed, urging the application of market-share liability.

The California Court of Appeals held that the rationale of *Sindell* was inapplicable for several reasons. First, the alleged defect related to the method in which the vaccine was processed (the "infectivity potential of the virus" had not been destroyed) and not to the design of the product, as was the case in *Sindell. Id.* at 594, 192 *Cal.Rptr.* at 876. The court explained:

> Here, unlike *Sindell,* the injuries did not result from the use of a drug generally defective when used for the purpose it was marketed, but because some manufacturer made and distributed a defective product. The product that allegedly injured plaintiffs was itself not a unit of a total generic pharmaceutical product but a deviant defective vaccine. [Ibid.]

The court reasoned that it would be unfair to hold four innocent manufacturers responsible for an injury caused by the one tortfeasor who manufactured the defective dosage. *Id.* at 599, 192 *Cal.Rptr.* at 880 * * *.

The second reason why *Sindell* was inapplicable to the polio-vaccine context of *Sheffield* was that the "delay in discovering the alleged causation was in no way related to the nature of the defective product or any other act or omission of the unknown tortfeasor," again unlike *Sindell,* where the "delay was occasioned because the potential for harm was latent and did not manifest itself for many years." *Id.* 144 *Cal.App.*3d at 594, 192 *Cal.Rptr.* at 877.

Lastly, the *Sheffield* court was of the view that an application of *Sindell* to the facts of the case would subvert the important public policy of encouraging swift production and marketing of new pharmaceutical products. *Id.* 144 *Cal.App.*3d at 597–98, 192 *Cal.Rptr.* at 878–79. Specifically, the court noted that if market-share liability had been generally prevalent during the development of the poliomyelitis vaccine, manufacturers would have been reluctant to proceed with the distribution of the vaccine, and consequently thousands of polio sufferers would not have been saved by the Salk vaccine program. *Id.* 144 *Cal.App.*3d at 599, 192 *Cal.Rptr.* at 880.

If *Sheffield* clarifies the question of whether market-share liability is applicable to vaccines that are defective because of manufacturing flaws, then the decision in *Morris v. Parke, Davis & Co.,* 667 *F.Supp.* 1332, (C.D.Cal.1987) beclouds it. In *Morris,* a federal district court in California reasoned that *Sheffield* 's prohibition against the application of market-share liability was limited to only one type of manufacturing defect: that involving one unit that deviates from ostensibly identical units. *Id.* at 1341. *Sheffield* was inapplicable, according to the *Morris* court, to manufacturing defects shared by an industry "resulting from common (perhaps for reasons of economy) substandard means of production, storage and transportation or marketing." *Id.* at 1342. The court then went on to impose market-share liability on the manufacturers of DPT vaccines insofar as their vaccines contained this second type of manufacturing defect.

The court in *Morris* therefore focused only on the first point made in *Sheffield:* that market share liability was inappropriate for a manufacturing defect case. As a consequence, the court managed to elude the other two grounds on which *Sheffield* was premised: the fact that the delay in discovering the defect was unrelated to the nature of DPT, and the important public policy considerations attendant on expanding liability to needed pharmaceutical products. * * *

Moreover, we are not convinced that the *Morris* court was correct in classifying the defect as stemming from the manufacturing process. *See Cepeda v. Cumberland Eng'g Co., Inc.,* 76 *N.J.* 152, 169, 386 *A.2d* 816 (1978)(pointing up the distinction between manufacturing defects and defects of design). Although the court in *Morris* later stated that it was "irrelevant * * * whether the defect which caused the plaintiff's injuries is common to the products of all the defendant manufacturers because it was a design defect or because it was a manufacturing defect [shared by an industry]," 667 *F.Supp.* at 1342, that statement is at odds with the court's earlier pronouncement that plaintiff's design-defect claims had been dismissed on grounds that comment k of the *Restatement (Second) of Torts* § 402A was applicable. *Id.* at 1334 n. 1. As such, the analysis in *Morris* lacks persuasive force.

III

With the foregoing in mind, we proceed to the question of whether New Jersey should expand current principles of tort law to adopt risk-modified market-share liability in the DPT context. Preliminarily, we must address the issue of whether DPT is a "generic product" that is uniformly harmful and therefore amenable to a market-share analysis. However, the central consideration on which our decision is essentially premised is whether as a matter of sound public policy this Court should modify traditional tort theory to allow plaintiffs' design-defect claims to proceed. * * *

A determination of whether DPT is "uniformly harmful" must rest on a full understanding of the product involved in this appeal. DPT is a biological product made from three separate components: diphtheria toxoid, tetanus toxoid, and pertussis vaccine, each of which stimulates the production of antibodies that protect the body against those childhood diseases. Two major kinds of preparations used to produce immunity are the toxoid type (diphtheria and tetanus), and the whole-cell type (pertussis). Toxoid preparations contain small amounts of the toxins produced by certain bacteria, chemically treated to stimulate immunity without causing disease symptoms. The diphtheria and tetanus portions of the DPT vaccine are therefore not the source of any harmful side-effects. Instead, it is the pertussis portion of the DPT vaccine, made from a whole-cell type of preparation, that harbors the alleged defect.

Apparently because of the complex nature of the pertussis organism, the poisonous substances produced by the bacteria have been difficult to isolate. Consequently, the vaccine that was developed, still in use today, is made from a whole-cell type of vaccine preparation in which whole cells have simply been isolated and inactivated. This type of vaccine preparation is cruder than the toxoid-type preparation, and has been accompanied by adverse reactions varying from local to systemic. The injury alleged in this case—acute encephalopathy—represents a severe injury that is estimated to occur once in every 110,000 doses of the vaccine. *Staff of the House Subcomm. on Health and the Environment of the House Comm. on Energy and Commerce, 99th Cong., 2d Sess., Report on Childhood Immunizations* 25 (Comm.Print 1986)(hereinafter *Comm.Print*).

Two other methods of vaccinating against pertussis should be mentioned. The first alternative method, which was on the market under the trade name Tri–Solgen at the time of Deanna's inoculation, is a "split-cell" or "soluble" vaccine, in which cells of the pertussis have been split or fragmented by a chemical process. It is unclear whether that method removed the poisonous substances from the organism, or what portions of the pertussis cell remained in the vaccine. However, according to one of the clinicians who conducted early tests on the product, Tri–Solgen produced a "high degree of antibody response and markedly lower incidence of systemic and local reactions." Weihl, "Extracted Pertussis Antigen," 106 *American Journal of Diseases of Children* 210–15 (1963).

According to plaintiffs, however, Tri–Solgen too was defectively designed inasmuch as the vaccine did not completely eradicate the dangerous toxins inherent in pertussis. Plaintiffs refer us to another method of pertussis vaccination, developed by the Japanese, in which all of the toxins have allegedly been eliminated. This "acellular" method of pertussis vaccination has been in widespread use in Japan since 1981 but is not licensed in the United States. Its over-all safety and clinical efficacy have not been formally reported.

At the time of Deanna's inoculation, five DPT manufacturers were producing a whole-cell pertussis vaccine, whereas one, Eli Lilly, was producing a split-cell vaccine. The products were clearly not identical because Eli Lilly's Tri–Solgen engendered a lower risk of harm. Nevertheless, the Appellate Division lead opinion swept all producers into one market share, placing the burden on Eli Lilly to prove that its product was less dangerous. Although we reserve decision on the general appropriateness of including products with differing degrees of risk in a market-share analysis, we are wary of the inclusion, in the lead opinion below, of Tri–Solgen inasmuch as the product may have represented the "state of the art" in vaccine design at the time of the inoculation. *See, e.g., N.J.S.A.* 2A:58C–3(a)(1)(providing that "state of the art" is an absolute defense in products-liability actions).

We are not persuaded, however, that the remaining whole-cell vaccines were also inappropriate for market-share analysis solely because they were made from a biological, as opposed to a chemical, formula. Although the vaccines were separately patented or carried separate trade names, there is sufficient evidence that pediatricians used the whole-cell products interchangeably. One notable study, conducted on vaccines produced by Wyeth, Connaught, Lederle, and Parke–Davis, concluded that there was no significant difference in the rates of more serious reactions by vaccine manufacturers. Baraff, Cody, Cherry, "DPT–Associated Reactions: An Analysis by Injection Site, Manufacturers, Prior Reactions and Dose," 73 *Pediatrics* 31 (Jan.1984). Indeed, any differences that were observed were for less-serious reactions and appeared to be related to differences in vaccine lots rather than in the specific vaccines. *Ibid.*

We turn, then, from the arguments that have been premised on technical distinctions between DES and DPT to the thrust of this appeal: the public-policy and public-health considerations that would accompany the imposition of market-share liability in this context.

IV

This Court has adopted the basic tenet that "[t]he torts process, like the law itself, is a human institution designed to accomplish certain social objectives." *People Express Airlines, Inc. v. Consolidated Rail Corp.,* 100 N.J. 246, 254, 495 A.2d 107 (1985). One of the primary objectives is to ensure "that innocent victims have avenues of legal redress, absent a contrary, overriding public policy." *Id.* at 254–55, 495 A.2d 107. Thus, implicit in any decision to broaden liability in order to provide compensation is a judgment that the goals of public policy will likewise be served. *See, e.g., Kelly v. Gwinnell,* 96 N.J. 538, 545, 476 A.2d 1219 (1984)(imposition of social-host liability is consistent with overall social goal of reducing drunken driving) * * *. In this case, however, we are presented with a difficult circumstance in which societal goals, in encouraging the use and development of needed drugs, would be thwarted by the imposition of unlimited liability on manufacturers in order to provide compensation to those injured by their products.

We deem it a matter of paramount importance that this case involves a vaccine—a product regarded as essential to the public welfare. [The court then discusses the public policy reasons for rejecting the market share approach in this kind of public health context. The court also discusses congressional attention to these issues and passage of the National Childhood Vaccine Injury Act of 1986, which adopts a strict liability remedy, but limits damages recoverable.] * * *

In this case plaintiffs had the option of withdrawing their state tort-law claim without prejudice and filing a claim for compensation under the Act. * * *

[U]nder the Act, attorneys consulted about a vaccine-related injury are required to inform their clients of the availability of compensation * * *.

Instead of pursuing that remedy under the Act, however, plaintiffs have chosen the more hazardous and cumbersome route of attempting to reshape tort-law theory to encompass their claim. They remind us that if we affirm the order of summary judgment, and thereby disallow collective liability in this instance, they will then be precluded from filing a claim under the Act. See 42 *U.S.C.A.* § 300aa–11(a)(5)(A) & (B). But that predicament, admittedly harsh, was a risk of which they were well aware and one that they willingly encountered. It therefore cannot form the basis of a determination by this Court to allow market-share liability or any modification thereof. The aim of the Act has always been to make vaccine liability more predictable by attracting claimants like these plaintiffs, whose legal position is tenuous, *before* they received a final determination by a court of law. No statutory purpose would be served if all potential claimants were permitted to cast the die first in a lawsuit and then turn to the Act in the event they were denied relief.

In sum, the existence of the Act is critical in this case for several reasons. First, it illustrates the complex nature of the problem underlying this appeal, which cannot be resolved simply by expanding tort-law theory. Second, it made available a means of compensatory relief for this plaintiff, which, although potentially smaller than a jury award might have been, was nonetheless certain. Lastly, it satisfies the tort goal of encouraging safer products, inasmuch as the Act establishes a national program for the research and development of safer vaccines.

V

The foregoing discussion should make clear that our opinion is confined solely to the context of vaccines. It should not be read as forecasting an inhospitable response to the theory of market-share liability in an appropriate context, perhaps one in which its application would be consistent with public policy and where no other remedy would be available. This case, the Court's first exposure to market-share liability, may therefore come to represent the exception rather than the rule.

Reversed.

[The dissent is omitted.]

Notes

1. In most of the cases, except the DES cases, in which the various theories of liability discussed in *Sindell* and *Shackil* have been attempted, the courts have rejected them in recent years for a variety of reasons. For example, the plaintiffs in the asbestos litigation frequently face problems similar to those faced in the DES cases in identifying specifically responsible defendants and one lower federal court found the market-share theory applicable. Hardy v. Johns–Manville Sales Corp., 509 F.Supp. 1353 (E.D.Tex.1981), *reversed on other grounds* 681 F.2d 334 (5th Cir.1982). The various theories have been rejected, however, in, *e.g.,* Thompson v. Johns–Manville Sales Corp., 714 F.2d 581 (5th Cir.1983), *cert. denied*, 465 U.S. 1102, 104 S.Ct. 1598, 80 L.Ed.2d 129 (1984); *In re* Related Asbestos Cases, 543 F.Supp. 1152 (N.D.Cal. 1982); Vigiolto v. Johns–Manville Corp., 643 F.Supp. 1454 (W.D.Pa.1986), aff'd

826 F.2d 1058 (3d Cir.1987); Goldman v. Johns–Manville Sales Corp., 33 Ohio St.3d 40, 514 N.E.2d 691 (1987); Gaulding v. Celotex Corp., 772 S.W.2d 66 (Tex.1989). In Case v. Fibreboard Corp., 743 P.2d 1062 (Okl.1987), the court drew the following distinctions:

> Although the market share theory of liability adopted in *Sindell* has been advanced as a basis of possible liability in asbestos related lawsuits where a plaintiff could not name the manufacturers of the products he was exposed to, it has been met with consistent disapproval. * * * It is of major importance that *Sindell* was decided in the context of a product that was truly fungible. DES was produced from a single formula and produced injury when used in a singular context; i.e. when given to pregnant women. Asbestos, on the other hand, is a name applied to a family of minerals, each member of which carries a different degree of risk * * *. "The asbestos family consists of more than 30 different minerals of fibrous structure. * * *"

> Compounding the variables arising from the presence of different minerals with different risk factors is the fact that asbestos is present in more than three thousand products commonly found in the home and work environments * * *

> Thus the degree of risk arising from exposure to asbestos may differ not only depending on the form of the mineral encountered but on the form of the product in which it is encountered.

> Because the market share liability theory is a theory which eliminates proof of causation of injury for public policy reasons, it must also be clearly founded in facts which support the link between the injury suffered and the risk to which the plaintiff was exposed. In the DES arena this cause and effect connection was clear cut. In the application to asbestos related injuries there are more complications * * *.

> In the asbestos related injury area however, as we have seen, the problem of balancing the contributions of each manufacturer to the risk of injury to a particular plaintiff are incalculably difficult when that plaintiff cannot furnish identification of a known tort-feasor. Unlike the DES cases, the injury does not arise at a specific time which can be related to a known ingestion of a dangerous substance. Asbestos products retain their hazardous characteristics throughout their use and injury may occur from any exposure. This is illustrated by facts alleged in this case in which plaintiffs relate that injury may have occurred not from the installation of new materials, which might be identifiable as to manufacture, but from the ripping-out of old materials, installed at unknown dates. * * *

743 P.2d at 1064–67.

Other situations in which the approaches have been suggested and rejected include Santiago v. Sherwin Williams Co., 3 F.3d 546 (1st Cir.1993)(involving exposure to lead-based paint; applying Mass. law); Hurt v. Philadelphia Housing Auth., 806 F.Supp. 515 (E.D.Pa.1992)(involving lead-based paint; applying Pa. law); Griffin v. Tenneco Resins, Inc., 648 F.Supp. 964 (W.D.N.C.1986)(exposure to dyes; applying North Carolina law); Klein v. Council of Chemical Ass'ns, 587 F.Supp. 213 (E.D.Pa.1984)(involving printing supplies alleged to cause cancer); Bly v. Tri–Continental Ind., Inc., 663 A.2d 1232 (D.C.1995)(exposure to benzene); Senn v. Merrell–Dow Pharmaceuticals Inc., 305 Or. 256, 751 P.2d 215 (Or.1988)(involving the DPT vaccine); Cummins v. Firestone Tire & Rubber Co., 344 Pa.Super. 9, 495 A.2d 963 (1985) (involving an exploding tire rim assembly).

2. Cases that have at least gotten beyond a motion to dismiss on the pleadings include Hamilton v. ACCU–TEK, 1996 WL 230136, *amended and superseded,* 935 F.Supp. 1307 (E.D.N.Y.1996)(involving fire arms; applying N.Y. law); Wheeler v. Raybestos–Manhattan, 8 Cal.App.4th 1152, 11 Cal. Rptr.2d 109 (1992)(involving asbestos fibers used to make brake products); Smith v. Cutter Biological, Inc., 72 Haw. 416, 823 P.2d 717 (1991)(involving AIDS-contaminated blood). In the latter case the court said that, assuming all of the defendants were proven to have been negligent, it was important to adapt the rules of causation so that innocent plaintiffs would not go remediless.

3. One issue left open by *Sindell* was what proportion of the total damages to which the plaintiff was found entitled would each defendant have to pay, particularly in situations in which not all the potential defendants were joined in the lawsuit, for example, where a potential defendant was bankrupt or otherwise not amenable to suit. This has been a critical issue in several of the later cases. The California Supreme Court clarified its position on the question in Brown v. Superior Court (Abbott Laboratories), 44 Cal.3d 1049, 245 Cal. Rptr. 412, 751 P.2d 470 (1988). The court held that the defendants were severally liable. Thus each defendant would only be responsible for that portion of the total damages equal to that defendant's market share. The plaintiff would have to shoulder the loss caused by not being able to reach some defendants. Martin v. Abbott Laboratories, 102 Wn.2d 581, 689 P.2d 368 (1984), reached a similar solution. More recently Hymowitz v. Eli Lilly & Co., 73 N.Y.2d 487, 541 N.Y.S.2d 941, 539 N.E.2d 1069, *cert. denied* 493 U.S. 944, 110 S.Ct. 350, 107 L.Ed.2d 338 (1989), adopted the same approach.

4. What should be the responsibility of the Shackil family lawyer for the decision to sue rather than file a claim under the National Childhood Vaccine Injury Act of 1986? What if the lawyer had not bothered to consult the federal act and did not know of the provisions in it cited by the court near the end of the opinion that had the effect of cutting off any recovery from the special fund? What if the lawyer knew of this but did not bother to tell the Shackils because he thought the chance of getting a much larger recovery from the New Jersey courts was very substantial (and would, of course, enhance the lawyer's fee)? What if the lawyer had informed them of the risk but had assured them that the New Jersey court "had such a liberal reputation in these kinds of cases that they had a very good chance of winning much higher damages by taking the tort suit route in his/her professional opinion"?

5. The issues raised in this chapter have been the subject of some interesting legal-economics literature. See S. Shavell, *Uncertainty Over Causation and the Determination of Civil Litigation,* 28 J. of L. & Econ. 587 (1985); G. Robinson, *Multiple Causation in Tort Law: Reflection on the DES Cases,* 68 Va.L.Rev. 713 (1982); W. Landes & R. Posner, *Joint and Multiple Tortfeasors: An Economic Analysis,* 9 J. of Legal Stud. 517 (1980).

Chapter 7

SPECIAL SITUATIONS

For the most part, we have been assuming thus far that the plaintiff owed a general duty of reasonable care to avoid foreseeable injury to the plaintiff. There are, however, a number of situations in which that general duty concept does not apply or, at least, did not apply historically. In this chapter we shall examine types of situations in which a defendant is relieved of any legal liability for failing to take reasonable steps to help, protect, or otherwise avoid injuries to others. In these types of situations, the notion of breach of duty requires more than failing to take reasonable care for the safety of others.

A. THE FAILURE TO AID

1. General

YANIA v. BIGAN

Supreme Court of Pennsylvania, 1959.
397 Pa. 316, 155 A.2d 343.

Benjamin R. Jones, Justice.

A bizarre and most unusual circumstance provides the background of this appeal.

On September 25, 1957 John E. Bigan was engaged in a coal strip-mining operation in Shade Township, Somerset County. On the property being stripped were large cuts or trenches created by Bigan when he removed the earthen overburden for the purpose of removing the coal underneath. One cut contained water 8 to 10 feet in depth with side walls or embankments 16 to 18 feet in height; at this cut Bigan had installed a pump to remove the water.

At approximately 4 p.m. on that date, Joseph F. Yania, the operator of another coal strip-mining operation, and one Boyd M. Ross went upon Bigan's property for the purpose of discussing a business matter with Bigan, and, while there, were asked by Bigan to aid him in starting the pump. Ross and Bigan entered the cut and stood at the point where the pump was located. Yania stood at the top of one of the cut's side walls and then jumped from the side wall—a height of 16 to 18 feet—into the water and was drowned.

Yania's widow, in her own right and on behalf of her three children, instituted wrongful death and survival actions against Bigan contending Bigan was responsible for Yania's death. Preliminary objections, in the nature of demurrers, to the complaint were filed on behalf of Bigan. The court below sustained the preliminary objections; from the entry of that order this appeal was taken.

The complaint avers negligence in the following manner: (1) "The death by drowning of * * * [Yania] was caused entirely by the acts of [Bigan] * * * in *urging, enticing, taunting and inveigling* [Yania] to jump into the water, which [Bigan] knew or ought to have known was of a depth of 8 to 10 feet and dangerous to the life of anyone who would jump therein" (emphasis supplied); (2) "* * * [Bigan] violated his obligations to a business invitee in not having his premises reasonably safe, and not warning his business invitee of a dangerous condition and to the contrary urged, induced and inveigled [Yania] into a dangerous position and a dangerous act, whereby [Yania] came to his death"; (3) "After [Yania] was in the water, a highly dangerous position, having been induced and inveigled therein by [Bigan], [Bigan] failed and neglected to take reasonable steps and action to protect or assist [Yania], or extradite [Yania] from the dangerous position in which [Bigan] had placed him". Summarized, Bigan stands charged with three-fold negligence: (1) by urging, enticing, taunting and inveigling Yania to jump into the water; (2) by failing to warn Yania of a dangerous condition on the land, i.e. the cut wherein lay 8 to 10 feet of water; (3) by failing to go to Yania's rescue after he had jumped into the water.[1]

Appellant initially contends that Yania's descent from the high embankment into the water and the resulting death were caused "entirely" by the spoken words and blandishments of Bigan delivered at a distance from Yania. The complaint does not allege that Yania slipped or that he was pushed or that Bigan made any *physical* impact upon Yania. On the contrary, the only inference deducible from the facts alleged in the complaint is that Bigan, by the employment of cajolery and inveiglement, caused such a *mental* impact on Yania that the latter was deprived of his volition and freedom of choice and placed under a compulsion to jump into the water. Had Yania been a child of tender years or a person mentally deficient then it is conceivable that taunting and enticement could constitute actionable negligence if it resulted in harm. However, to contend that such conduct directed to an adult in full possession of all his mental faculties constitutes actionable negligence is not only without precedent but completely without merit. * * *

Appellant next urges that Bigan, as the possessor of the land, violated a duty owed to Yania in that his land contained a dangerous condition, i.e. the water-filled cut or trench, and he failed to warn Yania of such condition. Yania was a business invitee in that he entered upon the land for a common business purpose for the mutual benefit of Bigan and himself * * *. As possessor of the land, Bigan would become subject to liability to Yania for any physical harm caused by any artificial or natural condition

---

1. So far as the record is concerned we must treat the 33 year old Yania as in full possession of his mental faculties at the time he jumped.

upon the land (1) if, and only if, Bigan knew or could have discovered the condition which, if known to him he should have realized involved an unreasonable risk of harm to Yania, (2) if Bigan had no reason to believe Yania would discover the condition or realize the risk of harm and (3) if he invited or permitted Yania to enter upon the land without exercising reasonable care to make the condition reasonably safe or give adequate warning to enable him to avoid the harm. * * * The inapplicability of this rule of liability to the instant facts is readily apparent.

The *only* condition on Bigan's land which could possibly have contributed in any manner to Yania's death was the water-filled cut with its high embankment. Of this condition there was neither concealment nor failure to warn, but, on the contrary, the complaint specifically avers that Bigan not only requested Yania and Boyd to assist him in starting the pump to remove the water from the cut but "led" them to the cut itself. If this cut possessed any potentiality of danger, such a condition was as obvious and apparent to Yania as to Bigan, both coal strip-mine operators. Under the circumstances herein depicted Bigan could not be held liable in this respect.

Lastly, it is urged that Bigan failed to take the necessary steps to rescue Yania from the water. The mere fact that Bigan saw Yania in a position of peril in the water imposed upon him no legal, although a moral, obligation or duty to go to his rescue unless Bigan was legally responsible, in whole or in part, for placing Yania in the perilous position. * * * The complaint does not aver any facts which impose upon Bigan legal responsibility for placing Yania in the dangerous position in the water and, absent such legal responsibility, the law imposes on Bigan no duty of rescue.

Recognizing that the deceased Yania is entitled to the benefit of the presumption that he was exercising due care and extending to appellant the benefit of every well pleaded fact in this complaint and the fair inferences arising therefrom, yet we can reach but one conclusion: that Yania, a reasonable and prudent adult in full possession of all his mental faculties, undertook to perform an act which he knew or should have known was attended with more or less peril and it was the performance of that act and not any conduct upon Bigan's part which caused his unfortunate death.

Order affirmed.

Notes

1. Section 314 of the *Restatement (Second) of Torts* summarizes the result of *Yania* and similar cases as follows:

> The fact that the actor realizes or should realize that action on his part is necessary for another's aid or protection does not of itself impose upon him a duty to take such action.

This doctrine is at least partly premised upon the now much eroded distinction between nonfeasance (i.e. failure to act) and misfeasance (i.e. acting improperly). A classic case is Thorne v. Deas, 4 Johns. (N.Y.) 84 (1809), where one co-owner gratuitously promised his partner that he would obtain insurance on their ship. He in fact never did so, in order to save on the insurance premium. Unfortunately, the ship was lost at sea. The court held that failure to act on a gratuitous promise was not subject to legal redress. The modern doctrine of promissory estoppel (*see Restatement (Second) of Contracts* § 90) is designed to ameliorate the harsh effects of this doctrine. The *Restatement (Second) of Torts* (§§ 323, 324A) declares that there is liability in tort for negligent failure to perform a gratuitous undertaking if there is at least some partial performance and the failure to perform increases the risk of harm or leads to harm because of reliance on the promise. There is a *caveat* as to whether complete failure to enter upon performance leads to any liability. A case upon which the *Restatement* position is based is Marsalis v. La Salle, 94 So.2d 120 (La.App. 1957). In that case the defendant's cat had bitten the plaintiff. The defendant promised to confine the cat so that it could be ascertained whether the cat was rabid. After a few days, owing to the defendant's negligence, the cat wandered off. The plaintiff underwent the Pasteur treatment and suffered a painful reaction to the treatment. The cat subsequently returned and was found not to be rabid. Although there were other bases upon which liability could have been premised, including the fact that the plaintiff had been bitten while in the defendant's store and that the cat belonged to the defendant, the court imposed liability on the basis of failure to perform the gratuitous undertaking.

In this borderland between contracts and torts, many cases have considered the obligation of physicians who had in some way "promised" to render medical services but in fact failed to do anything when called upon to perform. Early cases absolved the physician, *see* Hurley v. Eddingfield, 156 Ind. 416, 59 N.E. 1058 (1901), but recent cases have imposed liability. *See* Hiser v. Randolph, 126 Ariz. 608, 617 P.2d 774 (App.1980)("On call" doctor refused to attend plaintiff in hospital emergency room), partially overruled on other grounds, Thompson v. Sun City Community Hospital, Inc., 141 Ariz. 597, 688 P.2d 605 (1984).

2. The common-law doctrine that one has no duty to aid others has, not surprisingly, been much criticized. A classic article is J. Ames, *Law and Morals*, 22 Harv.L.Rev. 97 (1908). Ames proposed the imposition of *civil* liability for failing to rescue someone in distress when there is no risk of harm to the rescuer. *See also* F. Bohlen, *The Moral Duty to Aid Others as a Basis of Tort Liability*, 56 U.Pa.L.Rev. 217, 316 (1908). Ames' proposal is criticized in R. Epstein, *A Theory of Strict Liability*, 2 J.Legal Studies 151, 197–203 (1973). Epstein argues that applying tests of reasonableness to a defendant's conduct in these situations seriously infringes personal freedom. A number of European countries have provisions in their penal codes requiring a person to render assistance, under certain circumstances, to persons in distress. Some of these provisions only apply in cases of threatened death; others apply more generally to situations where a person is in danger of bodily harm. For citations and some discussion of these statutes see A. Rudzinski, *The Duty to Rescue: A Comparative Analysis*, in The Good Samaritan and the Law 91 (J. Ratcliffe ed. 1966). The texts of these statutes are set forth in an appendix to the Rudzinski article. *Id.* at 125. More recent works include E. Weinrib, *The Case for a Duty to Rescue*, 90 Yale L.J. 247 (1980); J. Henderson, *Process Constraints in Torts*, 67 Cornell L.Rev. 901 (1982)(criticizing Weinrib); A. Woozley, *A Duty to Rescue: Some Thoughts on Criminal Liability*, 69 Va.L.Rev. 1273 (1983); S. Levmore, *Waiting for Rescue: An Essay on the Evolution and Incentive Structure of the Law of Affirmative Obligations*, 72 Va.L.Rev. 879 (1986); J. Adler, *Relying Upon the Reasonableness of Strangers: Some Observations About the Current State of Common Law Affirmative Duties to Aid or Protect Others*, 1991 Wis. L. Rev. 867. S. Heyman, *Foundations of the Duty to Rescue*, 47 Vand. L. Rev. 673 (1994), is a recent review of the cases and literature on this topic.

In 1967 Vermont became the first state to enact such legislation. The text of the Vermont statute is as follows:

§ 519. Emergency medical care

(a) A person who knows that another is exposed to grave physical harm shall, to the extent that the same can be rendered without danger or peril to himself or without interference with important duties owed to others, give reasonable assistance to the exposed person unless that assistance or care is being provided by others.

(b) A person who provides reasonable assistance in compliance with subsection (a) of this section shall not be liable in civil damages unless his acts constitute gross negligence or unless he will receive or expects to receive remuneration. Nothing contained in this subsection shall alter existing law with respect to tort liability of a practitioner of the healing arts for acts committed in the ordinary course of his practice.

(c) A person who willfully violates subsection (a) of this section shall be fined not more than $100.00.

Vt.Stat.Ann. tit. 12, § 519. Note that paragraph (b) immunizes a person rendering gratuitous assistance from liability for anything less than gross negligence. We shall return to this aspect of the Vermont law later in this section when we discuss "Good Samaritan" laws (pp. 496–501, *infra*). For a description of the circumstances surrounding the adoption of the Vermont statute, see M. Franklin, *Vermont Requires Rescue: A Comment*, 25 Stanf. L.Rev. 51 (1972). The only relevant case cited in the annotations to this statute is State v. Joyce, 139 Vt. 638, 433 A.2d 271 (1981), in which the court held that the statute did not impose any duty upon a bystander to intervene in a fight. In 1983, Minnesota enacted a statute requiring that "[a] person at the scene of an emergency who knows that another person is exposed to or has suffered grave physical harm shall, to the extent that the person can do so without danger or peril to self or others, give reasonable assistance to the exposed person" and making a violation of this duty a petty misdemeanor. Minn.Stat.Ann. § 604.01 (1995). For a discussion of this statute, *see* Note, *The Duty to Rescue and the Good–Samaritan Statute*, 8 Hamline L.Rev. 231 (1985). Several states have enacted statutes requiring those who witness the commission of certain crimes to report the crime to the appropriate authorities as soon as reasonably practicable. *See, e.g.*, Mass.Gen.Laws Annot. c. 268, § 40, adopted in 1983 (applies to aggravated rape, rape, murder, manslaughter, and armed robbery); Gen.Laws R.I.1956, § 11–37–3.1 *et seq.*, also adopted in 1983 (applies to first-degree sexual assault or attempted first-degree sexual assault and requires a signed complaint by the victim). There is virtually no case support for creating a tort remedy from these criminal statutes.

The only case that seems unequivocally to recognize something like a general duty in tort law to assist others is Soldano v. O'Daniels, 141 Cal.App.3d 443, 190 Cal.Rptr. 310 (1983), in which an action for wrongful death was brought against a restaurant which was across the street from a bar in which the decedent was shot. One of the other patrons of the bar had come into the restaurant and asked a restaurant employee to phone the police or to allow him to use the restaurant's phone to call the police because a man was being threatened at the bar. The employee refused. The court gave many policy reasons for allowing the complaint to survive a motion for summary judgment. It also relied on § 327 of the *Restatement (Second) of Torts*, which provides that one who knows that a third person is giving necessary assistance to another to prevent physical harm and then negligently prevents that third person from giving such aid is subject to liability. The court relied on a scope note, which introduces the *Restatement*'s treatment of the topic of preventing assistance by third persons, in which it is noted that one can prevent a third person from rendering assistance to another by preventing a person from using something to aid a person in danger. A subsequent case, Clarke v. Hoek, 174 Cal.App.3d 208, 219 Cal.Rptr. 845 (1985), in which the court held that a physician observing[2] an operation performed by another surgeon had no duty to intervene in the operation on behalf of the patient, distinguished *Soldano* on the basis of its reliance on § 327. It is hard to see how § 327 has any relevance in any of these cases, because it seems to describe a situation in which the obstructing party is destroying or preventing access to an item which the person seeking to aid the victim has a right to use. The whole question in *Soldano* was whether, in point of fact, the third party had a right to the use of the defendant's telephone. In Stangle v. Fireman's Fund Ins. Co., 198 Cal.App.3d 971, 244 Cal.Rptr. 103 (1988), the court did not follow *Soldano* in a case in which the defendant's employee refused to allow someone to call the police immediately after a $50,000 ring had been stolen on the ground that *Soldano* is not applicable to cases involving danger to property.

3. The common-law has gradually come to recognize an obligation to act to help others in a variety of circumstances. In note 1, *supra*, we noted how in some circumstances a promise, even a gratuitous one, can be the basis of imposing an obligation. An obligation to help has been imposed in three other kinds of situations. First there are those situations in which there is some pre-existing type of *status* relationship between the person in peril and the person upon whom one is attempting to impose an affirmative duty to help. There are then those situations where an obligation is imposed upon someone who, whether tortiously or not, has placed the helpless person in the predicament in which he finds himself. Finally, there is the situation in which someone who was under no duty to do so comes to the aid of a helpless person and is then charged with having been negligent in rendering his assistance. We will consider these situations in turn.

2. *"Special" Relationships*

RESTATEMENT (SECOND) OF TORTS (1965)

§ 314 A. Special Relations Giving Rise to Duty to Aid or Protect

(1) A common carrier is under a duty to its passengers to take reasonable action

　　(a) to protect them against unreasonable risk of physical harm, and

　　(b) to give them first aid after it knows or has reason to know that they are ill or injured, and to care for them until they can be cared for by others.

(2) An innkeeper is under a similar duty to his guests.

---

2. The observing physician was there to screen the surgeon performing the operation, who was applying for staff privileges at the hospital where the operation was performed.

(3) A possessor of land who holds it open to the public is under a similar duty to members of the public who enter in response to his invitation.

(4) One who is required by law to take or who voluntarily takes the custody of another under circumstances such as to deprive the other of his normal opportunities for protection is under a similar duty to the other.

Caveat:

The Institute expresses no opinion as to whether there may not be other relations which impose a similar duty.

Comment:

b.   This Section states exceptions to the general rule, stated in § 314, that the fact that the actor realizes or should realize that his action is necessary for the aid or protection of another does not in itself impose upon him any duty to act.   The duties stated in this Section arise out of special relations between the parties, which create a special responsibility, and take the case out of the general rule.   The relations listed are not intended to be exclusive, and are not necessarily the only ones in which a duty of affirmative action for the aid or protection of another may be found.   There may be other such relations, as for example that of husband and wife, where the duty is recognized by the criminal law, but there have as yet been no decisions allowing recovery in tort in jurisdictions where negligence actions between husband and wife for personal injuries are permitted.   The question is therefore left open by the Caveat * * *.   The law appears, however, to be working slowly toward a recognition of the duty to aid or protect in any relation of dependence or of mutual dependence.

d.   The duty to protect the other against unreasonable risk of harm extends to risks arising out of the actor's own conduct, or the condition of his land or chattels.   It extends also to risks arising from forces of nature or animals, or from the acts of third persons, whether they be innocent, negligent, intentional, or even criminal.   (See § 302 B).   It extends also to risks arising from pure accident, or from the negligence of the plaintiff himself, as where a passenger is about to fall off a train, or has fallen.   The duty to give aid to one who is ill or injured extends to cases where the illness or injury is due to natural causes, to pure accident, to the acts of third persons, or to the negligence of the plaintiff himself, as where a passenger has injured himself by clumsily bumping his head against a door.

f.   The defendant is not required to take any action until he knows or has reason to know that the plaintiff is endangered, or is ill or injured.   He is not required to take any action beyond that which is reasonable under the circumstances.   In the case of an ill or injured person, he will seldom be required to do more than give such first aid as he reasonably can, and take reasonable steps to turn the sick man over to a physician, or to those who will look after him and see that medical assistance is obtained.   He is not required to give any aid to one who is in the hands of apparently competent persons who have taken charge of him, or whose friends are present and apparently in a position to give him all necessary assistance.

§ 314 B. Duty to Protect Endangered or Hurt Employee

(1) If a servant, while acting within the scope of his employment, comes into a position of imminent danger of serious harm and this is known to the master or to a person who has duties of management, the master is subject to liability for a failure by himself or by such person to exercise reasonable care to avert the threatened harm.

(2) If a servant is hurt and thereby becomes helpless when acting within the scope of his employment and this is known to the master or to a person having duties of management, the master is subject to liability for his negligent failure or that of such person to give first aid to the servant and to care for him until he can be cared for by others.

Comment:

a. This Section duplicates § 512 of the Restatement of Agency, Second. For Comments, see that Restatement.

The Section is inserted in this Restatement in order to supplement and complete what is said in § 314 A.

Notes

1. Sections 314A and 314B did not have any analogue in the *Restatement of Torts* published in 1934. They reflect an evolution of the law in the intervening thirty year period.

2. The obligation of common carriers to help their passengers is one of the earliest obligations recognized by the law. Some of the earlier cases suggest a possible distinction between a passenger who became ill on a train and a passenger who was ill when he boarded the train, as to whom there would be no obligation, see New Orleans, Jackson & Great Northern Railroad Co. v. Statham, 42 Miss. 607, 97 Am.Dec. 478 (1869), but the distinction was not developed in later cases.

3. The obligation arising out of the relationship of possessors of land to business invitees, such as that between a storeowner and his patrons, is one of the later special situations to be recognized. Cases such as L. S. Ayres & Co. v. Hicks, 220 Ind. 86, 40 N.E.2d 334 (1942), which is often cited in support of such an obligation, can be explained on other grounds. In *Hicks* not only was the infant plaintiff an invitee, but he was also injured by the defendant's escalator. As we shall see later in this section, this latter factor has a significant bearing upon whether a duty to help will be imposed. A case relying on § 314A and clearly recognizing an obligation to help in the business invitee situation is Lloyd v. S. S. Kresge Co., 85 Wis.2d 296, 270 N.W.2d 423 (App.1978). Butler v. Acme Markets, Inc., 89 N.J. 270, 445 A.2d 1141 (1982), involves a patron who was robbed in a store's parking lot after doing her evening's shopping. The parking area was well lit but there nevertheless had been seven muggings in the parking lot during the preceding year, five of which had occurred in the evening during the preceding four months. Similar cases in other jurisdictions include Isaacs v. Huntington Memorial Hosp., 38 Cal.3d 112, 211 Cal.Rptr. 356, 695 P.2d 653 (1985); Nallan v. Helmsley–Spear, Inc., 50 N.Y.2d 507, 429 N.Y.S.2d 606, 407 N.E.2d 451 (1980); Erickson v. Curtis Investment Co., 447 N.W.2d 165 (Minn.1989)(involving a rape in a large parking garage). However, in Ann M. v. Pacific Plaza Shopping Center, 6 Cal.4th 666, 25 Cal.Rptr.2d 137, 863 P.2d 207 (1993), the Supreme Court of California narrowed the reach of

this duty by limiting it to situations where the danger was clearly foreseeable, which usually can be shown only by prior similar incidents on the premises. *See also*, Wright v. Webb, 234 Va. 527, 362 S.E.2d 919 (1987). In Toscano Lopez v. McDonald's, 193 Cal.App.3d 495, 238 Cal.Rptr. 436 (1987), it was held that the fact that the defendant fast-food restaurant had not adopted the security precautions taken by other business establishments in the comparatively high-crime area in which the restaurant was located did not lead to liability to the victims of a maniacal mass murderer who killed twenty-one people and wounded eleven others at the restaurant. More recently, in Kentucky Fried Chicken of Cal., Inc. v. Superior Court, 14 Cal.4th 814, 927 P.2d 1260, 59 Cal.Rptr.2d 756 (1997), the court ruled, with three dissents, that a patron, who allegedly suffered mental distress when she was held hostage by an armed robber while a store employee hesitated in handing over the money in the cash register, had no cause of action against the store owner. Discussions of the issues include F. Zacharias, *The Politics of Torts,* 95 Yale L.J. 698 (1986); Comment, *Business Inviters' Duty to Protect Invitees from Criminal Acts,* 134 U.Pa.L.Rev. 883 (1986); D. Robertson, *Negligence Liability for Crimes and Intentional Torts Committed by Others,* 67 Tul.L.Rev. 135 (1992).

There are also a few cases imposing a duty on property owners to help persons who, as we shall see later in this chapter, would have been considered licensees or social guests at common law. *See, e.g.,* Lindsey v. Miami Development Corp., 689 S.W.2d 856 (Tenn.1985); Grimes v. Hettinger, 566 S.W.2d 769 (Ky.App.1978); Hutchinson v. Dickie, 162 F.2d 103 (6th Cir.1947)(boat owner has duty to rescue guest who fell overboard).

FARWELL v. KEATON

Supreme Court of Michigan, 1976.
396 Mich. 281, 240 N.W.2d 217.

LEVIN, JUSTICE.

There is ample evidence to support the jury determination that David Siegrist failed to exercise reasonable care after voluntarily coming to the aid of Richard Farwell and that his negligence was the proximate cause of Farwell's death. We are also of the opinion that Siegrist, who was with Farwell the evening he was fatally injured and, as the jury found, knew or should have known of his peril, had an affirmative duty to come to Farwell's aid.[3]

I

On the evening of August 26, 1966, Siegrist and Farwell drove to a trailer rental lot to return an automobile which Siegrist had borrowed from a friend who worked there. While waiting for the friend to finish work, Siegrist and Farwell consumed some beer.

Two girls walked by the entrance to the lot. Siegrist and Farwell attempted to engage them in conversation; they left Farwell's car and followed the girls to a drive-in restaurant down the street.

---

3. The trial judge instructed the jury to determine whether Siegrist had voluntarily undertaken to render aid and, if he had, whether he acted reasonably in discharging that duty. Whether Siegrist be charged with the duty of a voluntary rescuer or the duty of a companion, the standard of care—whether he acted reasonably under all the circumstances—is the same and the instruction given was adequate.

The girls complained to their friends in the restaurant that they were being followed. Six boys chased Siegrist and Farwell back to the lot. Siegrist escaped unharmed, but Farwell was severely beaten. Siegrist found Farwell underneath his automobile in the lot. Ice was applied to Farwell's head. Siegrist then drove Farwell around for approximately two hours, stopping at a number of drive-in restaurants. Farwell went to sleep in the back seat of his car. Around midnight Siegrist drove the car to the home of Farwell's grandparents, parked it in the driveway, unsuccessfully attempted to rouse Farwell, and left. Farwell's grandparents discovered him in the car the next morning and took him to the hospital. He died three days later of an epidural hematoma.

At trial, plaintiff contended that had Siegrist taken Farwell to the hospital, or had he notified someone of Farwell's condition and whereabouts, Farwell would not have died. A neurosurgeon testified that if a person in Farwell's condition is taken to a doctor before, or within half an hour after, consciousness is lost, there is an 85 to 88 per cent chance of survival. Plaintiff testified that Siegrist told him that he knew Farwell was badly injured and that he should have done something.

The jury returned a verdict for plaintiff and awarded $15,000 in damages. The Court of Appeals reversed, finding that Siegrist had not assumed the duty of obtaining aid for Farwell and that he neither knew nor should have known of the need for medical treatment.

II

Two separate, but interrelated questions are presented:

A. Whether the existence of a duty in a particular case is always a matter of law to be determined solely by the Court?

B. Whether, on the facts of this case, the trial judge should have ruled, as a matter of law, that Siegrist owed no duty to Farwell?

A.

"A duty, in negligence cases, may be defined as an obligation, to which the law will give recognition and effect, to conform to a particular standard of conduct toward another." Prosser, Torts (4th ed.), § 53, p. 324.

The existence of a duty is ordinarily a question of law. However, there are factual circumstances which give rise to a duty. The existence of those facts must be determined by a jury.[4] * * *

B.

Without regard to whether there is a general duty to aid a person in distress, there is a clearly recognized legal duty of every person to avoid any affirmative acts which may make a situation worse. "[I]f the defendant does attempt to aid him, and takes charge and control of the situation, he is regarded as entering voluntarily into a relation which is attended with

---

4. Of course, merely labeling a question as one of "law" or "fact" does not solve the dilemma.

"No two terms of legal science have rendered better service, than 'law' and 'fact' * * *. They readily accommodate themselves to any meaning we desire to give them * * *. What judge has not found refuge in them? The man who could succeed in defining them would be a public enemy." Green, Judge and Jury, p 270.

responsibility. Such a defendant will then be liable for a failure to use reasonable care for the protection of the plaintiff's interests." Prosser, *supra*, § 56, pp 343–344. "Where performance clearly has been begun, there is no doubt that there is a duty of care." *Id* 346.

In a case such as the one at bar, the jury must determine, after considering all the evidence, whether the defendant attempted to aid the victim. If he did, a duty arose which required defendant to act as a reasonable person.

There was ample evidence to show that Siegrist breached a legal duty owed Farwell. Siegrist knew that Farwell had been in a fight, and he attempted to relieve Farwell's pain by applying an ice pack to his head. While Farwell and Siegrist were riding around, Farwell crawled into the back seat and laid down. The testimony showed that Siegrist attempted to rouse Farwell after driving him home but was unable to do so.

In addition, Farwell's father testified to admissions made to him by Siegrist:

> "Q. What did Mr. Siegrist say, how did the conversation go?
>
> "A. I asked him why he left Ricky [the deceased] in the driveway of his grandfather's home.
>
> "Q. What did he say?
>
> "A. He said, *'Ricky was hurt bad, I was scared.'* I said, *'Why didn't you tell somebody, tell his grandparents?'* He said, *'I know I should have, I don't know.'*" (Emphasis added).

III

Siegrist contends that he is not liable for failure to obtain medical assistance for Farwell because he had no duty to do so.

Courts have been slow to recognize a duty to render aid to a person in peril. Where such a duty has been found, it has been predicated upon the existence of a special relationship between the parties; in such a case, if defendant knew or should have known of the other person's peril, he is required to render reasonable care under all the circumstances.

In Depue v. Flateau, 100 Minn. 299, 111 N.W. 1 (1907), the Supreme Court of Minnesota reversed an order of the trial court dismissing the cause of action and said that if the defendants knew their dinner guest was ill, it was for the jury to decide whether they were negligent in refusing his request to spend the night and, propping him on his wagon with the reins thrown over his shoulder, sending him toward home.

The Sixth Circuit Court of Appeals, in Hutchinson v. Dickie, 162 F.2d 103, 106 (C.A.6, 1947), said that a host had an affirmative duty to attempt to rescue a guest who had fallen off his yacht. The host controlled the only instrumentality of rescue. The Court declared that to ask of the host anything less than that he attempt to rescue his guest would be "so shocking to humanitarian considerations and the commonly accepted code of social conduct that the courts in similar situations have had no difficulty in pronouncing it to be a legal obligation."

Farwell and Siegrist were companions on a social venture. Implicit in such a common undertaking is the understanding that one will render assistance to the other when he is in peril if he can do so without endangering himself. Siegrist knew or should have known when he left Farwell, who was badly beaten and unconscious, in the back seat of his car that no one would find him before morning. Under these circumstances, to say that Siegrist had no duty to obtain medical assistance or at least to notify someone of Farwell's condition and whereabouts would be "shocking to humanitarian considerations" and fly in the face of "the commonly accepted code of social conduct." "[C]ourts will find a duty where, in general, reasonable men would recognize it and agree that it exists."[5]

Farwell and Siegrist were companions engaged in a common undertaking; there was a special relationship between the parties. Because Siegrist knew or should have known of the peril Farwell was in and could render assistance without endangering himself he had an affirmative duty to come to Farwell's aid.

The Court of Appeals is reversed and the verdict of the jury reinstated.

FITZGERALD, JUSTICE (dissenting).

The unfortunate death of Richard Farwell prompted this wrongful death action brought by his father against defendant, David Siegrist, a friend who had accompanied Farwell during the evening in which the decedent received injuries which ultimately caused his death three days later. The question before us is whether the defendant, considering his relationship with the decedent and the activity they jointly experienced on the evening of August 26–27, 1966, by his conduct voluntarily or otherwise assumed, or should have assumed, the duty of rendering medical or other assistance to the deceased. We find that defendant had no obligation to assume, nor did he assume, such a duty.

Defendant did not voluntarily assume the duty of caring for the decedent's safety. Nor did the circumstances which existed on the evening of August 26, 1966, impose such a duty. Testimony revealed that only a qualified physician would have reason to suspect that Farwell had suffered an injury which required immediate medical attention. The decedent never complained of pain and, in fact, had expressed a desire to retaliate against his attackers. Defendant's inability to arouse the decedent upon arriving at his grandparents' home does not permit us to infer, as does plaintiff, that defendant knew or should have known that the deceased was seriously injured.[6] While it might have been more prudent for the defendant to insure that the decedent was safely in the house prior to leaving, we cannot say that defendant acted unreasonably in permitting Farwell to

5. Prosser, *supra*, § 53, p 327.

6. It is at this point—plaintiff's unsuccessful attempt to arouse the decedent in the driveway—that counsel, during oral argument, believes that defendant volunteered to aid the decedent. Yet no affirmative act by defendant indicated that he assumed the responsibility of rendering assistance to the
decedent. Consequently, there could be no *discontinuance* of aid or protection which left decedent in a worse position than when the alleged "volunteering" occurred. This would make operative the concession of plaintiff that where no duty is owed, the refusal to act cannot form the basis for an action in negligence.

spend the night asleep[7] in the back seat of his car.

The close relationship between defendant and the decedent is said to establish a legal duty upon defendant to obtain assistance for the decedent. No authority is cited for this proposition other than the public policy observation that the interest of society would be benefited if its members were required to assist one another. This is not the appropriate case to establish a standard of conduct requiring one to legally assume the duty of insuring the safety of another. Recognizing that legal commentaries have expressed moral outrage at those decisions which permit one to refuse aid to another whose life may be in peril, we cannot say that, considering the relationship between these two parties and the existing circumstances, defendant acted in an unreasonable manner.[8]

Plaintiff believes that a legal duty to aid others should exist where such assistance greatly benefits society and only a reasonable burden is imposed upon those in a position to help. He contends further that the determination of the existence of a duty must rest with the jury where questions of foreseeability and the relationship of the parties are primary considerations.

* * * We must reject plaintiff's proposition which elevates a moral obligation to the level of a legal duty where, as here, the facts within defendant's knowledge in no way indicated that immediate medical attention was necessary and the relationship between the parties imposes no affirmative duty to render assistance. * * * The posture of this case does not permit us to create a legal duty upon one to render assistance to another injured or imperiled party where the initial injury was not caused by the person upon whom the duty is sought to be imposed.

The relationship of the parties and the question of foreseeability does not require that the jury, rather than the court, determine whether a legal duty exists. We are in agreement with the general principle advanced by plaintiff that the question of negligence is one of law for the court only when the facts are such that all reasonable men must draw the same conclusion. However, this principle becomes operative only after the court establishes that a legal duty is owed by one party to another. * * *

The Court of Appeals properly decided as a matter of law that defendant owed no duty to the deceased.

We would affirm.

COLEMAN, J., concurs.

---

7. Defendant had no way of knowing that it was the severity of the head injury suffered by the decedent which caused him to crawl in the back seat and apparently fall asleep. The altercation combined with the consumption of several beers could easily permit defendant to conclude that decedent was simply weary and desired to rest.

8. Were a special relationship to be the basis of imposing a legal duty upon one to insure the safety of another, it would most probably take the form of "co-adventurers" who embark upon a hazardous undertaking with the understanding that each is mutually dependent upon the other for his own safety. There is no evidence to support plaintiff's position that decedent relied upon defendant to provide any assistance whatsoever. A situation where two persons are involved in an altercation provoked by the party ultimately injured, the extent of which was unknown to the other, whose subsequent conduct included drinking beer and a desire to retaliate against his attackers would not fall within this category.

Notes

1. The question of how far the duty recognized in the *Farwell* case extends has been considered in a number of subsequent cases decided by the Michigan Court of Appeals. Only a few years after *Farwell,* in Holloway v. Martin Oil Service, Inc., 79 Mich.App. 475, 262 N.W.2d 858 (1977), the court dealt with a case in which the employee of a gas station sold some gasoline in a "one- or two-gallon container" to some obviously intoxicated men who claimed they had run out of gas. The men used this gasoline to set fire to a dance hall from which they had been ejected. The court held that it would have been prepared to impose liability if, in their intoxicated state, they had hit someone with their automobile, but the defendants owed no duty to any people who were injured in the fire set by these men. In Swartz v. Huffmaster Alarms Systems, Inc., 145 Mich.App. 431, 377 N.W.2d 393 (1985), the court dealt with the case of someone who was described as being an "alcoholically impaired," "anxious" patron of a restaurant who had limited vision and who, upon leaving the restaurant after dinner, was run over while he was crossing a highway. The court held that the restaurant owed him no duty to prevent this accident. Dumka v. Quaderer, 151 Mich.App. 68, 390 N.W.2d 200 (1986), involved a young man who had been ejected from a rollerskating rink because he was under the influence of alcohol and Quaaludes. The young man's friends put him in a car, which they parked 300 feet from the defendant's roller rink. The defendant's employees permitted these friends to leave and reenter the premises when they went out to check on their friend. Eventually the young man wandered off and could not immediately be found. His body was subsequently discovered a day later, lying in the snow. He had died of shock and exposure. The court held that the roller rink had never assumed any duty to help the young man, and, even if it had, it had fulfilled its duty by putting him into the custody of his friends. Finally, in Sierocki v. Hieber, 168 Mich.App. 429, 425 N.W.2d 477 (1988), the court again found against liability. In that case two elderly people lived together. One of them, the defendant in the case, was aware that the other person was starting to lose her mental faculties. The court held that the defendant was under no obligation to try to prevent her from driving—as, for example, by hiding her car keys. The plaintiff was someone who had been injured by her erratic driving. The *Schwarz* and *Dumka* cases are more like *Farwell* in that they involved the question of a duty to an impaired or helpless plaintiff. The other two cases involved duties to third persons and thus involve the more general questions involved in the next principal case, *Thompson v. County of Alameda.*

2. Once one undertakes to help an injured person one is under an obligation not to be negligent in assisting that person. An often-cited case is Zelenko v. Gimbel Brothers, Inc., 158 Misc. 904, 287 N.Y.S. 134 (1935), *affirmed per curiam,* 247 App.Div. 867, 287 N.Y.S. 136 (1936). In that case the plaintiff's intestate was taken ill in the defendant's store. It was alleged that the defendant's employees came to her assistance and then left her alone for six hours in the store's infirmary. On the assumption that the defendant owed the deceased no duty at all, merely because she became ill in its store, the court held that once the defendant came to her assistance "the defendant must not omit to do what an ordinary man would do in performing the task." The court noted that "[i]f defendant had left plaintiff's intestate alone, beyond doubt some bystander who would be influenced more by charity than by legalistic duty would have summoned an ambulance." We shall return to the question of what obligation is owed by someone who comes to the aid of a helpless

person. (*See* p. 492, *infra*). In particular we will be concerned with whether the extent of this obligation is merely to refrain from worsening the helpless person's plight or whether there is an obligation to take whatever reasonable measures are possible to help.

3. When the courts find an obligation to help arising out of some preexisting status relationship, rather than because one has come forward to assist a helpless person, is it a defense to an action based on negligence that one has not placed the other person in a worse situation nor prevented others from helping him?

THOMPSON v. COUNTY OF ALAMEDA

Supreme Court of California, 1980.
27 Cal.3d 741, 167 Cal.Rptr. 70, 614 P.2d 728.

RICHARDSON, JUSTICE.

Plaintiffs appeal from a judgment of dismissal entered in favor of defendant County of Alameda (County) after County's general demurrer was sustained without leave to amend. We will affirm the judgment.

For purposes of this appeal, those factual allegations of the complaint which are properly pleaded are deemed admitted by defendant's demurrer. * * * We recite the gravamen of plaintiffs' causes of action as contained in their amended complaint. Plaintiffs, husband and wife, and their minor son lived in the City of Piedmont, a few doors from the residence of the mother of James F. (James), a juvenile offender. Prior to the incident in question, James had been in the custody and under the control of County and had been confined in a county institution under court order. County knew that James had "latent, extremely dangerous and violent propensities regarding young children and that sexual assaults upon young children and violence connected therewith were a likely result of releasing [him] into the community." County also knew that James had "indicated that he would, if released, take the life of a young child residing in the neighborhood." (James gave no indication of which, if any, young child he intended as his victim.) County released James on temporary leave into his mother's custody at her home, and "[a]t no time did [County] advise and/or warn [James' mother], the local police and/or parents of young children within the immediate vicinity of [James' mother's] house of the known facts * * *." Within 24 hours of his release on temporary leave, James murdered plaintiffs' son in the garage of James' mother's home.

The complaint further alleges that the death was caused by County's "reckless, wanton and grossly negligent" actions in releasing James into the community (first cause of action); failing to advise and/or warn James' mother, the local police, or "parents of young children within the immediate vicinity" of the residence of James' mother (second cause of action); failing to exercise due care in maintaining custody and control over James through his mother in her capacity as County's agent (third cause of action); and failing to exercise reasonable care in selecting James' mother to serve as County's agent in maintaining custody and control over James (fourth cause of action).

We consider, nonsequentially, the validity of each of the alleged causes of action.[9]

* * *

III.   DUTY TO WARN THE LOCAL POLICE, THE NEIGHBORHOOD PARENTS, OR THE JUVENILE'S CUSTODIAN

We now examine the principal and most troublesome contentions of plaintiffs, namely, that County is liable for its failure to warn the local police and the parents of neighborhood children that James was being released or, alternatively, to warn James' mother of his expressed threat. We first inquire whether there would be liability in the absence of immunity * * * and determine initially whether in any event County had a duty to warn for the protection of plaintiffs.

It is a fundamental proposition of tort law that one is liable for injuries caused by a failure to exercise reasonable care. We have said, however, that in considering the existence of "duty" in a given case several factors require consideration including "the foreseeability of harm to the plaintiff, the degree of certainty that the plaintiff suffered injury, the closeness of the connection between the defendant's conduct and the injury suffered, the moral blame attached to the defendant's conduct, the policy of preventing future harm, the extent of the burden to the defendant and consequences to the community of imposing a duty to exercise care with resulting liability for breach, and the availability, cost, and prevalence of insurance for the risk involved. [Citations.]" (Rowland v. Christian (1968) 69 Cal.2d 108, 113, 70 Cal.Rptr. 97, 100, 443 P.2d 561, 564 * * *.) When public agencies are involved, additional elements include "the extent of [the agency's] powers, the role imposed upon it by law and the limitations imposed upon it by budget; * * *" (Raymond v. Paradise Unified School Dist. (1963) 218 Cal.App.2d 1, 8, 31 Cal.Rptr. 847, 852 * * *.)

Bearing in mind the foregoing controlling considerations, we examine the propriety of imposing on those responsible for releasing or confining criminal offenders a duty to warn of the release of a potentially dangerous offender who, as here, has made a generalized threat to a segment of the population. Our earlier rulings in Johnson v. State of California, supra, 69 Cal.2d 782, 73 Cal.Rptr. 240, 447 P.2d 352, and Tarasoff v. Regents of University of California, supra, 17 Cal.3d 425, 131 Cal.Rptr. 14, 551 P.2d 334, furnish considerable guidance in our inquiry and plaintiffs rely heavily on both cases in support of their view that County had an affirmative duty to warn someone (the police, the offender's parent, or neighborhood parents) of the dangers arising from James' release.

In *Johnson*, the state, acting through a Youth Authority placement officer, placed a minor with "homicidal tendencies and a background of violence and cruelty" in the plaintiff's home. Following his attack on the plaintiff, she sued the state. In sustaining plaintiff's cause of action, we

---

9. [Ed. note] The court held that the county was immune from liability for the exercise by county employees of their discretion in deciding to release James and in selecting James' mother as his custodian. The claim that the county was liable for its failure adequately to supervise the activities of James' mother, while acting as his custodian, was likewise dismissed on the same grounds.

held "[a]t the outset, we can dispose summarily of the contention, not strenuously pressed by defendant, that the judgment should be affirmed because the state owed no duty of care to plaintiff. As the party placing the youth with Mrs. Johnson, the state's relationship to plaintiff was such that its duty extended to warning of latent, dangerous qualities suggested by the parolee's history or character. [Citations.] These cases impose a duty upon those who create a *foreseeable peril*, not readily discoverable by endangered persons, to warn them of such potential peril. Accordingly, the state owed a duty to inform Mrs. Johnson of any matter that its agents knew or should have known that might endanger the Johnson family * * *." * * *

In *Johnson* we emphasized the *relationship* between the state and plaintiff-victim, and the fact that the state by its conduct placed the specific plaintiff in a position of clearly foreseeable danger. In contrast with the situation in *Johnson*, in which the risk of danger focused precisely on plaintiff, here County bore no special and continuous relationship with the specific plaintiffs nor did County knowingly place the specific plaintiffs' decedent into a foreseeably dangerous position. Thus the reasoning of our holding in *Johnson* would not sustain the complaint in this action.

Likewise in *Tarasoff* we were concerned with the duty of therapists, after determining that a patient posed a serious threat of violence, to protect the "foreseeable victim of that danger." * * * In reaching the conclusion that the therapists had a duty to warn either "the endangered party or those who can reasonably be expected to notify him. * * *" * * * we relied on an exception to the general rule that one owes no duty to control the conduct of another. * * * As declared in section 315 of the Restatement, such a duty may arise if "(a) a special relation exists between the actor and the third person which imposes a duty upon the actor to control the third person's conduct, or (b) a special relation exists between the actor and the other which gives the other a right to protection."

We noted in *Tarasoff* that a special relationship existed between the defendant therapists and the patient which "*may* support affirmative duties for the benefit of third persons." * * * The *Tarasoff* decedent was the known and specifically foreseeable and identifiable victim of the patient's threats. We concluded that under such circumstances it was appropriate to impose liability on those defendants for failing to take reasonable steps to protect her.

In *Tarasoff*, in reference to the police defendants who had been requested by defendant therapists to detain the patient, we further held that the police had no duty of care to the decedent because there was no "special relationship" between them and either the victim or the patient. We also rejected any application of the principle enunciated in the Restatement to the effect that "If the actor does an act, and subsequently realizes or should realize that it has created an unreasonable risk of causing physical harm to another, he is under a duty to exercise reasonable care to prevent the risk from taking effect." (Rest.2d Torts, supra, § 321.) We reasoned that "The assertion of a cause of action against the police defendants under this theory would raise difficult problems of causation and of public policy," * * *

We recognized in *Tarasoff* that "the open and confidential character of psychotherapeutic dialogue encourages patients to express threats of violence, few of which are ever executed. Certainly a therapist should not be encouraged routinely to reveal such threats; such disclosures could seriously disrupt the patient's relationship with his therapist and with the persons threatened." * * * We further concluded that "the therapist's obligations to his patient require that he not disclose a confidence unless such disclosure is necessary to avert danger to others, and even then that he do so discreetly, and in a fashion that would preserve the privacy of his patient to the fullest extent compatible with the prevention of the threatened danger." * * * Thus, we made clear that the therapist has no *general* duty to warn of each threat. Only if he "does in fact determine, or under applicable professional standards reasonably should have determined, that a patient poses a serious danger of violence to others, [does he bear] a duty to exercise reasonable care to protect the *foreseeable victim* of that danger." * * * Although the intended victim as a precondition to liability need not be specifically named, he must be "readily identifiable." * * *

Unlike *Johnson* and *Tarasoff*, plaintiffs here have alleged neither that a direct or continuing relationship between them and County existed through which County placed plaintiffs' decedent in danger, nor that their decedent was a foreseeable or readily identifiable target of the juvenile offender's threats. Under such circumstances, while recognizing the continuing obligation of County, as with all public entities, to exercise reasonable care to protect *all* of its citizens, we decline to impose a blanket liability on County for failing to warn plaintiffs, the parents of other neighborhood children, the police or James' mother of James' threat. As will appear, our conclusion is based in part on policy considerations and in part upon an analysis of "foreseeability" within the context of this case.

By their very nature parole and probation decisions are inherently imprecise. According to a recent study by the California Probation Parole and Correction Association, during 1977 in California a total of 315,143 persons (225,331 adults and 89,912 juveniles) were supervised on probation. (The Future of Probation, A Report of the CPPCA Committee on the Future of Probation (Jul. 1979) p. 15.) During the same year, cases removed from probation because of violations totaled 13.4 percent in the superior courts, 14.8 percent in the lower courts, and 11.5 percent in the juvenile courts. (*Id.*, at pp. 27–28.) Additionally, a large number of parole violations occur. National parole violation rates reflect that 18–20 percent of parolees fail on one-year follow-up, 25 percent on two-year follow-up, and 26 percent on three-year follow-up. (*Id.*, at p. 35.) Although we fully recognize that not all violations involve new or violent offenses, a significant proportion do.

Notwithstanding the danger illustrated by the foregoing statistics, parole and probation release nonetheless comprise an integral and continuing part in our correctional system authorized by the Legislature, serving the public by rehabilitating substantial numbers of offenders and returning them to a productive position in society. The result, as we observed in *Johnson*, is that "each member of the general public who chances to come into contact with a parolee bear[s] the risk that the rehabilitative effort will fail * * *." * * * The United States Supreme Court very recently reached a similar conclusion in Martinez v. State of Cal. (1980) 444 U.S. 277, 281, 100 S.Ct. 553, 557, 62 L.Ed.2d 481. In *Martinez*, the high court rejected a contention that the California governmental immunity statutes * * * deprived plaintiffs' decedent of her life without due process of law because of a parole decision that led indirectly to her death. * * * The Supreme Court observed that "the basic risk that repeat offenses may occur is always present in any parole system." * * *

Bearing in mind the ever present danger of parole violations, we nonetheless conclude that public entities and employees have no affirmative duty to warn of the release of an inmate with a violent history who has made *nonspecific threats of harm directed at nonspecific victims*. Obviously aware of the risk of failure of probation and parole programs the Legislature has nonetheless as a matter of public policy elected to continue those programs even though such risks must be borne by the public. * * *

Similar general public policy considerations were described in a recent analysis of the *Tarasoff* issue. The author reasoned: "Assume that one person out of a thousand will kill. Assume also that an exceptionally accurate test is created which differentiates with 95% effectiveness those who will kill from those who will not. If 100,000 people were tested, out of the 100 who would kill 95 would be isolated. Unfortunately, out of the 99,900 who would not kill, 4,995 people would also be isolated as potential killers. In these circumstances, it is clear that we could not justify incarcerating all 5,090 people. If, in the criminal law, it is better that ten guilty men go free than that one innocent man suffer, how can we say in the civil commitment area that it is better that fifty-four harmless people be incarcerated lest one dangerous man be free? [Citation.]" (Comment, *Tarasoff and the Psychotherapist's Duty to Warn* (1975) 12 San Diego L.Rev. 932, 942–943, fn. 75.)

Furthermore, we foresee significant practical obstacles in the imposition of a duty in the form that plaintiffs seek, concluding that it would be unwieldy and of little practical value. As previously indicated a large number of persons are released and supervised on probation and parole each year in this state. Notification to the public at large of the release of each offender who has a history of violence and who has made a generalized threat at some time during incarceration or while under supervision would, in our view, produce a cacophony of warnings that by reason of their sheer volume would add little to the effective protection of the public.

The issues herein presented are difficult and we are very sensitive to the tragic consequences herein presented, and the necessity, to the extent possible, of preventing their repetition. Plaintiffs assert that if County had made the requested warnings, a different result would have ensued. * * *

We are skeptical of any net benefit which might flow from a duty to issue a generalized warning of the probationary release of offenders. In our view, the generalized warning sought to be required here would do little to increase the precautions of any particular members of the public who already may have become conditioned to locking their doors, avoiding dark and deserted streets, instructing their children to beware of strangers and taking other precautions. By their very numbers the force of the multiple warnings required to accompany the release of all probationers with a potential for violence would be diluted as to each member of the public who by such release thereby becomes a potential victim. Such a warning may also negate the rehabilitative purposes of the parole and probation system by stigmatizing the released offender in the public's eye.

Unlike members of the general public, in *Tarasoff* and *Johnson* the potential victims were specifically known and designated individuals. The warnings which we therein required were directed at making those individuals aware of the danger to which they were uniquely exposed. The threatened targets were precise. In such cases, it is fair to conclude that warnings given discreetly and to a limited number of persons would have a greater effect because they would alert those particular targeted individuals of the possibility of a specific threat pointed at them. In contrast, the warnings sought by plaintiffs would of necessity have to be made to a broad segment of the population and would be only general in nature. In addition to the likelihood that such generalized warnings when frequently repeated would do little as a practical matter to stimulate increased safety measures, as we develop below, such extensive warnings would be difficult to give.

a.) *Warning the Police.* In our view, warnings to the police as urged by plaintiffs ordinarily would be of little benefit in preventing assaults upon members of the public by dangerous persons unless we were simultaneously and additionally to impose a concurrent duty on the police to act upon such warnings. As we noted in *Tarasoff*, supra, no such duty to act exists.
* * *

In a somewhat parallel situation, we note that the Legislature has expressly spoken in requiring those who have been convicted of certain sex crimes to inform the police of their presence in the community. (See Pen. Code, § 290.) No similar requirement exists for other kinds of offenders or for persons temporarily released on probation or parole. Furthermore, even section 290 does not require the police to take any specific action to warn the community of the offender's presence, or to supervise the offender's movements. All that is required under the section is recordkeeping by the police which, at the discretion of the police, may be utilized when appropriate. Similar recordkeeping which would be required if regular and numerous warnings such as are requested here were given to the police would create a mass of paper, the upkeep and review of which might well divert police personnel from more effective activities.

Thus, unlike the situation in *Tarasoff*, requiring warning to the police ordinarily would result in no benefit to any potential victims of possible violence.

b.) *Warnings to Parents of Neighborhood Children.* In similar fashion, requiring the releasing agent to warn all neighborhood parents of small children that a potentially dangerous offender had been released in the area would require an expenditure of time and limited resources that parole and probation agencies cannot spare and would be of questionable value. The magnitude of the problem may be understood in the light of statistics contained in the above cited CPPCA report. In 1978 California probation departments employed a total of 18,331 persons, including professional probation officers, group counselors, clerical staff, business management professionals, psychiatrists, psychologists, medical specialists, other treatment personnel, and 5,156 part-time or volunteer staff members. As previously noted, these personnel exercised supervision over 315,000 probationers "on the streets" during that year. * * *

Furthermore, such notice might substantially jeopardize rehabilitative efforts both by stigmatizing released offenders and by inhibiting their release. It is also possible that, in addition, parole or probation authorities would be far less likely to authorize release given the substantial drain on their resources which such warnings might require. A stated public policy favoring innovative release programs would be thwarted. * * *

c.) *Warning to the Juvenile's Mother.* Finally, notification to the offender's mother of James' threat in our opinion would not have the desired effect of warning potential victims, at least in a case such as that herein presented. In the usual instance we doubt that the mother of the juvenile offender would be likely voluntarily to inform other neighborhood parents or children that her son posed a general threat to their welfare, thereby perhaps thwarting any rehabilitative effort, and also effectively stigmatizing both the mother and son in the community. The imposition of an affirmative duty on the County to warn a parent of generalized threats without additionally requiring, in turn, some affirmative action by the parent would prove ineffective.

The dissent speculates that the mother "might" have taken special care to control her son had she been warned of James' threats, inferring thereby that she would have maintained such constant surveillance over her son as to prevent any possible harm. Such attenuated conjecture, however, cannot alone support the imposition of civil liability. This is particularly true inasmuch as the County's original decision to release James from close confinement into the obviously less restrictive custody of his mother is a decision we already hold is immunized from liability.

* * * Furthermore, it is contrary to the very purpose of such a release to speculate that a mother in whose care a nearly 18–year-old offender has been temporarily placed would thereby assume the constant minute-to-minute supervision that would have been required to prevent the tragedy.

In summary, whenever a potentially dangerous offender is released and thereafter commits a crime, the possibility of the commission of that crime is statistically foreseeable. Yet the Legislature has concluded that the benefits to society from rehabilitative release programs mandate their continuance. Within this context and for policy reasons the duty to warn depends upon and arises from the existence of a prior threat to a specific identifiable victim. * * * Despite the tragic events underlying the present complaint, plaintiffs' decedent was not a known, identifiable victim, but rather a member of large amorphous public group of potential targets. Under these circumstances we hold that County had no affirmative duty to warn plaintiffs, the police, the mother of the juvenile offender, or other local parents.

The judgment of dismissal is affirmed.

TOBRINER, JUSTICE, dissenting.

I dissent from the conclusion in part III of the majority opinion that plaintiffs' complaint states no cause of action arising from Alameda County's negligence in failing to warn James' mother that he might harm neighborhood children. * * *

* * * Although both *Johnson v. State of California* * * * and *Tarasoff v. Regents of University of California* * * * involved a failure to warn an identifiable victim, the reasoning of those decisions cannot be confined to that narrow scope. Instead, the cases stand for the principle that a special relationship, such as that between the state and a person in its custody, establishes a duty to use reasonable care to avert danger to foreseeable victims. If the victim can be identified in advance, a warning to him may discharge that duty; if he cannot be identified, reasonable care may require other action. But the absence of an identifiable victim does not postulate the absence of a duty of reasonable care.

Our opinion in *Tarasoff* makes clear that failure to warn a victim who is identifiable does not constitute an essential element of the cause of action. We noted that the duty of care requires the defendant "to take one or more of various steps, depending upon the nature of the case. Thus it may call for him to warn the intended victim or others likely to apprise the victim of the danger, to notify the police, or to take whatever other steps are reasonably necessary under the circumstances." * * *

At no point did we hold that such duty of care runs only to identifiable victims. We cited numerous examples to the contrary. * * * One example makes the point particularly clear: "[a] doctor must * * * warn a patient if the patient's condition or medication renders certain conduct, such as driving a car, dangerous to others." * * * It would be absurd to confine that duty to motorists or pedestrians whom the doctor could identify in advance.

Thus under the reasoning of *Tarasoff* and the principles of tort law endorsed in the case, the proper inquiry turns on whether Jonathan Thompson was a foreseeable victim. The complaint alleges that James had threatened to "take the life of a young child residing in the neighborhood"; since Jonathan falls within that description his killing was clearly a foreseeable consequence of James' release and subsequent lack of supervision. Whether Jonathan was also an identifiable victim is relevant not to the existence of a duty of care, but only to whether a warning to Jonathan personally was a reasonable means of discharging that duty. If, as the majority claim, a warning to the neighborhood families was not a reasonable way to reduce the danger, the fact cannot absolve the state of the duty to employ other methods. In particular, it cannot absolve the state from its failure to warn James' mother so that she could exercise proper care in observing and supervising James and thereby preventing the harm that ensued.

Thus no precedent supports the majority's unique attempt to limit the imposition upon defendant of a duty of due care to warn only to a situation in which a person commits a tort upon a victim who can be identified in advance of the wrongful conduct. Even the reading of precedent most favorable to the majority will reveal only that most, but not all, prior cases did involve identifiable victims. Thus the majority position must stand, if it can stand at all, upon the policy considerations it advances.

In sum, the policy considerations discussed by the majority relate to the discretionary decision whether to grant parole or probation, the wisdom of civil commitment of dangerous persons, and the practical problems of warning large classes of possible victims. It is striking how little relevance these considerations have to the present case. None bear significantly on the question whether the County should have warned James' mother.

I believe that as a matter of law and common sense the County, before it released James to his mother's custody, had a duty to tell her of his homicidal threats and inclinations. The complaint alleges that the County's failure to warn her was negligent, and proximately caused Jonathan's death. Thus under settled principles of tort law as explained in our prior opinion in *Tarasoff*, the complaint states a cause of action. I would therefore reverse the judgment dismissing plaintiffs' complaint and remand the cause to the superior court for further proceedings.

Notes

1. It should be noted that Tobriner, J., wrote the opinions for the court in Johnson v. State of California, 69 Cal.2d 782, 73 Cal.Rptr. 240, 447 P.2d 352 (1968) and Tarasoff v. Regents of the University of California, 17 Cal.3d 425, 131 Cal.Rptr. 14, 551 P.2d 334 (1976). The failure to give the warning required by *Tarasoff* was held to give a cause of action for emotional distress to a child who was seated next to his mother when she was shot by the defendant-psychotherapists' patient, who had told his therapists that he intended to inflict serious bodily injury upon her. Hedlund v. Superior Court, 34 Cal.3d 695, 194 Cal.Rptr. 805, 669 P.2d 41 (1983). For a case very similar to *Tarasoff* in another jurisdiction, *see* Peck v. Counseling Service of Addison County, Inc., 146 Vt. 61, 499 A.2d 422 (1985)(psychotherapist has duty to warn parents of patient of his threat to burn down their barn). As indicated in the majority's opinion in *Thompson*, the *Tarasoff* decision has met some severe criticism from commentators,[10] but has also been praised. *See* P. Lake, *Revisiting Tarasoff*, 58 Alb. L. Rev. 97 (1994). On the general subject, *see also* Note, *Professional Obligation and the Duty to Rescue: When Must a Psychiatrist Protect His Patient's Intended Victim?*, 91 Yale L.J. 1430 (1982).

2. Does the distinction between the foreseeability of harm to identifiable individuals and the mere foreseeability of harm to unknown persons make

---

10. Other critical reactions include, A. Stone, *The Tarasoff Decisions: Suing Psychotherapists to Safeguard Society*, 90 Harv. L.Rev. 358 (1976); Note, 14 Calif.W.L.Rev. 153 (1978); Note, 31 Stanf.L.Rev. 165 (1978); Note, 48 U.Colo.L.Rev. 283 (1977). *See also* the earlier, J. Fleming and B. Maximore, *The Patient or His Victim: The Therapists Dilemma*, 62 Calif.L.Rev. 1025 (1974). A principal criticism is the effect of the decision on the therapist-patient relationship. For a favorable response see Note, 29 Hast.L.Rev. 179 (1977). The reference in the Stone article to the "*Tarasoff* Decisions" is to the fact that the original opinion handed down in *Tarasoff* was vacated. There is no mention of this fact in the second *Tarasoff* opinion, which is the one discussed in *Thompson*. The original *Tarasoff* opinion is unofficially reported at 13 Cal.3d 177, 118 Cal.Rptr. 129, 529 P.2d 553 (1974). In its original opinion the court, writing through Tobriner, J., held that there might have been a duty to warn on the part of the police who had questioned the person who eventually killed Ms. Tarasoff. The suggestion was that the police intervention in the case might have deterred the eventual killer from seeking therapy and thus increased the risk to Tarasoff. In its second opinion, the court merely noted that the police did not have a special relationship either with the killer or Tarasoff, his victim, to impose any duty to warn upon them.

sense? By holding that the basic decision to release people on parole is a policy determination for which public authorities are not legally accountable, the court was not obliged to consider some of the more basic questions of public policy. From the societal point of view, is the ultimate issue whether a proper warning would have prevented the tragic death of the Thompson boy? Is Tobriner, J., arguing that it would have? Or, is the basic issue whether the public authorities, having adopted a certain policy on parole, should pay for the foreseeable damages that this policy might cause members of the public? For the contention that governmental entities should be strictly liable by analogy to the liability imposed upon those who engage in abnormally dangerous activities, see Note, *Holding Governments Strictly Liable for the Release of Dangerous Parolees*, 55 N.Y.U.L.Rev. 907 (1980). Would such a policy discourage release on parole?

3. In Davidson v. City of Westminster, 32 Cal.3d 197, 185 Cal.Rptr. 252, 649 P.2d 894 (1982), decided subsequently to the *Thompson* case, the Supreme Court of California held that the police were not liable for failing to warn a patron of a laundromat, who was subsequently stabbed by a person whom they then had under surveillance, that the person under surveillance was suspected of prior assaults with a knife.

4. Contrary to the *Thompson* case, in Division of Corrections v. Neakok, 721 P.2d 1121 (Alaska 1986), the court held that the state could be held liable for negligence in failing to adequately structure and supervise the parole of a prisoner *and* for failing to warn the prisoner's family and the residents of the isolated community of less than a hundred in which he lived of his dangerous proclivities when under the influence of alcohol. Nevertheless, most courts seem unwilling to impose a general duty to warn. It has been held, for example, that the duty is owed to the public at large, not to particular individuals. *See* Hurst v. Ohio Dep't of Rehabilitation & Correction, 72 Ohio St.3d 325, 650 N.E.2d 104 (1995)(no duty to injured plaintiff for negligence in not informing state-wide law enforcement agencies of a parole violation order). Cases involving defendants who are governmental units may also involve the issue of governmental immunity, taken up in Chapter 22.

While the courts are understandably reluctant to impose duties to warn an indefinite class of people, there has not been the same hesitation in imposing liability upon psychiatric institutions which have released patients who subsequently injure third parties. *See, e.g.,* Hamman v. County of Maricopa, 161 Ariz. 58, 775 P.2d 1122 (1989); Perreira v. Colorado, 768 P.2d 1198 (Colo. 1989); Durflinger v. Artiles, 234 Kan. 484, 673 P.2d 86 (1983); *but cf.,* Boulanger v. Pol, 258 Kan. 289, 900 P.2d 823 (1995)(no duty to warn when plaintiff knew of danger and patient was released from voluntary, as opposed to involuntary, commitment). *See also,* Brady v. Hopper, 570 F.Supp. 1333 (D.Colo.1983), *affirmed* 751 F.2d 329 (10th Cir.1984)(litigation by some of the victims of John Hinckley; although liability not imposed, possibility of liability in appropriate case recognized). Is there any practical difference between this approach and imposing a duty to warn? On the other hand, in Sherrill v. Wilson, 653 S.W.2d 661 (Mo.1983), the court held that the physicians at a state mental institution did not owe a duty to the general public in deciding which involuntary patients should be released on a two-day pass. *See also,* Lamb v. Hopkins, 303 Md. 236, 492 A.2d 1297 (1985)(in which it was held that probation officers who failed to report to the supervising judge alcohol-related moving violations by a probationer owed no duty to the parents of a child who was injured by the probationer while he was driving under the influence).

State legislatures are increasingly adopting statutes that require notification to area residents of the release of certain prisoner from jail or prison. For example, Ohio recently passed a statute applicable to defined sex offenders that requires notification to the local law enforcement agency in the area in which the releasee plans to settle. It is not clear whether negligence in following the statute's command may give an injured party a private cause of action. *See* Ohio Rev. Code Ann. §§ 2950–2958.

5. In recent years several cases have been brought under the federal statute, 28 U.S.C. § 1983, charging that the failure of a public official or entity to take some affirmative action has deprived the plaintiff of a constitutional right. The courts have been very reluctant to find liability in these cases for a number of reasons. *See*, DeShaney v. Winnebago County Dept. of Social Services, 489 U.S. 189, 109 S.Ct. 998, 103 L.Ed.2d 249 (1989). Clearly one of the concerns is the reluctance to "federalize" this area of tort law. However, there has been substantial scholarly support for the idea. We will examine "constitutional torts" in more detail in Chapter 21. *See generally*, B. Armacost, *Affirmative Duties, Systemic Harms, and the Due Process Clause*, 94 Mich. L. Rev. 982 (1996).

EISEL v. BOARD OF EDUCATION OF MONTGOMERY COUNTY

Court of Appeals of Maryland, 1991.
324 Md. 376, 597 A.2d 447.

RODOWSKY, JUDGE.

The legal theory advanced by the plaintiff in this wrongful death and survival action is that school counselors have a duty to intervene to attempt to prevent a student's threatened suicide. The specific question presented is whether the duty contended for may be breached by junior high school counselors who fail to inform a parent of suicidal statements attributed to the parent's child by fellow students where, when the counselors sought to discuss the subject, the adolescent denied ever making the statements. The circuit court granted summary judgment for the defendants, premised on the absence of any duty. As explained below, we shall hold that summary judgment was erroneously entered.

The decedent, Nicole Eisel (Nicole), was a thirteen year old student at Sligo Middle School in Montgomery County. She and another thirteen year old girl consummated an apparent murder-suicide pact on November 8, 1988. Nicole's father, Stephen Eisel (Eisel), brought the instant action. His amended complaint alleges negligence on the part of two counselors at Nicole's school, among others.

* * *

The amended complaint avers that Nicole became involved in satanism, causing her to have an "obsessive interest in death and self-destruction." During the week prior to the suicide, Nicole told several friends and fellow students that she intended to kill herself. Some of these friends reported Nicole's intentions to their school counselor, Morgan, who relayed the information to Nicole's school counselor, Jones. Morgan and Jones then questioned Nicole about the statements, but Nicole denied making them. Neither Morgan nor Jones notified Nicole's parents or the school administration about Nicole's alleged statements of intent. Information in the record suggests that the other party to the suicide pact shot Nicole before shooting herself. The murder-suicide took place on a school holiday in a public park at some distance from Sligo Middle School. The other party to the pact attended another school.

III

There is no direct Maryland precedent on the issue before us. We have not been cited to, nor have we found, any decision by any other court that deals with the issue of duty on substantially similar facts. Before the circuit court the defendants' argument that the counselors owed no duty to intervene rested largely on language in judicial decisions that defendants say are analogous.

On the issue of duty Eisel argued that, by the School Board's own policy, counselors were required to contact the parents of any child who had expressed suicidal thoughts. Eisel pointed to deposition testimony on that subject by the principal, who said: "If the student is in danger, of course, you take care of that first. Then the next thing you do would be to notify a parent. If the student is in no apparent danger, you will notify the parent."

There appear to be two broad categories of cases in which a person may be held liable for the suicide of another. The first type occurs when the defendant's conduct actually causes the suicide, as when a negligent driver causes head injuries that lead to psychosis. See Fuller v. Preis, 35 N.Y.2d 425, 322 N.E.2d 263, 363 N.Y.S.2d 568 (1974). It is not contended here that Nicole's suicide was caused, in that sense, by the defendants' conduct.

The second type of case holds that a special relationship between a defendant and the suicidal person creates a duty to prevent a foreseeable suicide. For instance, many courts have held that a hospital or a prison that has custody over a person who commits suicide may be liable if the suicide was foreseeable. See Annotation, Civil Liability for Death by Suicide, 11 A.L.R.2d 751, §§ 13.5–14 (1950 & Supp.1985). In State ex rel. Shockey v. Washington Sanitarium & Hosp., 223 Md. 554, 557, 165 A.2d 764, 765–66 (1960), we said: "[T]here is a duty upon a sanitarium or hospital to exercise such care in looking out for and protecting a patient as the circumstances, including known mental and physical conditions, may reasonably require. Failure to do so may be negligence, and if suicide is a proximate result of the negligence, recovery may be had under the wrongful death statute...."

At least one case has concluded that a professional therapist may be held liable when a patient commits suicide, even if the therapist or the therapist's hospital does not have custody over the patient. Bellah v. Greenson, 81 Cal.App.3d 614, 620, 146 Cal.Rptr. 535, 538 (1978); but see Nally v. Grace Community Church of the Valley, 47 Cal.3d 278, 295–96, 763 P.2d 948, 958, 253 Cal.Rptr. 97, 107–08 (1988)(limiting Bellah), cert. denied, 490 U.S. 1007, 109 S.Ct. 1644, 104 L.Ed.2d 159 (1989). Liability against therapists for outpatient suicides is rarely imposed, e.g., Farwell v. Un, 902 F.2d 282 (4th Cir.1990)(applying Maryland law); Comment, Civil

Liability for Causing or Failing to Prevent Suicide, 12 Loy.L.A.L.Rev. 967, 993 (1979), and some commentators have suggested that liability under these circumstances should never be imposed. See id. at 993 & n. 142.

Recent attempts to extend the duty to prevent suicide beyond custodial or therapist-patient relationships have failed. For instance, the Supreme Court of California refused to impose a duty on a church pastor to refer a twenty-four year old suicidal counselee to a mental health professional. Nally, 47 Cal.3d at 299–300, 763 P.2d at 960–61, 253 Cal.Rptr. at 110. Although on its facts Nally dealt only with religious counselors, the court appeared to extend its no-duty rule to all "nontherapist counselors," who were defined as "persons other than licensed psychotherapists, who counsel others concerning their emotional and spiritual problems." * * *

In McLaughlin v. Sullivan, 123 N.H. 335, 461 A.2d 123 (1983), a jail prisoner killed himself within twelve hours of incarceration after his conviction on burglary and drug charges. The administrator of the suicide's estate sued his attorney for legal malpractice. The Supreme Court of New Hampshire held that the attorney had no duty to prevent the suicide because she neither had custody or control over the defendant nor did she have the "expertise or the training necessary to judge or foresee that a client will commit suicide." * * * In Krieg v. Massey, 239 Mont. 469, 781 P.2d 277 (1989), an apartment manager had reason to believe an elderly tenant was suicidal and attempted to remove the tenant's handgun, but ultimately left it within the tenant's reach. The court found the manager had no duty to prevent the subsequent suicide because she was not in a custodial relationship with the tenant.

Probably the closest case, factually, to the matter before us is Bogust v. Iverson, 10 Wis.2d 129, 102 N.W.2d 228 (1960). The parents of a college student who killed herself sued a college professor-counselor. The suicide occurred about six weeks after the counselor suggested terminating counseling sessions with the student. The court held that the counselor had no duty to secure psychiatric treatment for the student or advise her parents of her emotional state because the plaintiff had alleged no facts showing that the counselor was apprised that the student had suicidal tendencies. One commentator has cited this ruling as potentially establishing a duty when such facts are alleged. See Comment, supra, 12 Loy.L.A.L.Rev. at 991.

The custody rule is extended, arguably unjustifiably, well beyond the confines of the instant matter in Sneider v. Hyatt Corp., 390 F.Supp. 976 (N.D.Ga.1975). That court refused to grant summary judgment for a hotel company which claimed it could not be liable for the death of a registered guest who jumped from the twenty-first floor of the hotel. The plaintiff had alleged that the hotel's management was aware that the hotel had become an "attractive location for suicides," and that the decedent was inebriated, had no luggage and was seen by hotel employees wandering in a confused state on the twenty-first floor. The court acknowledged that a hotel has less control over a customer than does a hospital over a patient. Nonetheless, the court refused to decide that the hotel had no duty at all. * * *

A number of factors distinguish the instant matter from those cases finding an absence of any duty, reviewed above, in which the custodial relationship between the suicide victim and the defendant was other than that of hospital and patient or jailer and prisoner. Eisel's claim involves suicide by an adolescent. The negligence relied on is a failure to communicate to the parent the information allegedly possessed by the defendants concerning the child's contemplated suicide, not a failure by the school authorities physically to prevent the suicide by exercising custody and control over Nicole. The theory of Eisel's case is that he could have exercised his custody and control, as parent, over Nicole, had he been warned, and inferentially, that there was nothing known to the counselors about Eisel's relationship with Nicole that would make such a warning unreasonable. * * *

Further, we have recognized

"the doctrine that the relation of a school vis a vis a pupil is analogous to one who stands in loco parentis, with the result that a school is under a special duty to exercise reasonable care to protect a pupil from harm, Segerman v. Jones, 256 Md. 109, 123–24, 259 A.2d 794, 801 (1969); Restatement (Second) of Torts § 320 at 130 (1965); 2 Harper and James, The Law of Torts § 18.7 at 1058 (1956). * * *

Lunsford v. Board of Educ., 280 Md. 665, 676, 374 A.2d 1162, 1168 (1977) (footnote omitted). [11]

Finally, the relationship of school counselor and pupil is not devoid of therapeutic overtones. The "Counselor Job Description," published by the Department of Professional Personnel of the Board lists the first two "[p]riorities of the counseling profession" to be: "1. Counseling with individuals and groups concerning school adjustment, physical and emotional development, educational planning, and career awareness. . . ." "2. Identifying students with significant problems and taking steps to provide help for these students." * * *

Given the peculiar mix of factors presented, it is an open question whether there is a duty to attempt to prevent an adolescent's suicide, by reasonable means, including, in this case, by warning the parent. Therefore, we must analyze whether we should recognize a duty in this case.

IV

A tort duty is "an expression of the sum total of those considerations of policy which lead the law to say that the plaintiff is entitled to protection." * * * "[A]mong the variables to be considered in determining whether a tort duty should be recognized are: '[T]he foreseeability of harm to the plaintiff, the degree of certainty that the plaintiff suffered the injury, the closeness of the connection between the defendant's conduct and the injury suffered, the moral blame attached to the defendant's conduct, the policy of preventing future harm, the extent of the burden to the defendant and consequences to the community of imposing a duty to exercise care

---

11. The harm in Lunsford was an assault and battery, inflicted on a student who was en route to his home after having been released from school, where there was evidence that the school authorities knew of the danger. The jury verdict was for the defendant. This Court found no error in the proceedings. Two dissenting judges believed it was error to submit the issue of contributory negligence to the jury.

with resulting liability for breach, and the availability, cost and prevalence of insurance for the risk involved.' " Village of Cross Keys, Inc. v. United States Gypsum Co., 315 Md. 741, 752, 556 A.2d 1126, 1131 (1989)(quoting Tarasoff v. Regents of Univ. of Calif., 17 Cal.3d 425, 434, 551 P.2d 334, 342, 131 Cal.Rptr. 14, 22 (1976)). * * *

A. FORESEEABILITY AND CERTAINTY OF HARM

Foreseeability is the most important variable in the duty calculus * * * and without it there can be no duty to prevent suicide. * * * Here Nicole's suicide was foreseeable because the defendants allegedly had direct evidence of Nicole's intent to commit suicide. That notice to the defendants distinguishes this case from Bogust v. Iverson, 10 Wis.2d 129, 102 N.W.2d 228, where the counselor had no notice of contemplated suicide.

The degree of certainty that Eisel and Nicole suffered the harm foreseen is one hundred percent.

Nor would reasonable persons necessarily conclude that the harm ceased to be foreseeable because Nicole denied any intent to commit suicide when the counselors undertook to draw out her feelings, particularly in light of the alleged declarations of intent to commit suicide made by Nicole to her classmates. "An adolescent who is thinking of suicide is more likely to share these feelings with a friend than with a teacher or parent or school guidance counselor. But, we all—parents, teachers, administrators, service providers and friends—can learn what the warning signs are and what to do." 3 Maryland Office for Children and Youth, Monthly Memo, at 3 (Apr.1986). Jurors, as triers of fact, may well conclude that the quoted point of view is consistent with their own experiences with adolescents. On the other hand, when the facts of this case are fully developed, the court may conclude that the duty did not arise, or jurors may conclude that it had not been negligently breached.

B. POLICY OF PREVENTING FUTURE HARM

The General Assembly has made it quite clear that prevention of youth suicide is an important public policy, and that local schools should be at the forefront of the prevention effort. * * * A Youth Suicide Prevention School Programs Act (the Act) was enacted by Chapter 122 of the Acts of 1986, codified as Md.Code (1978, 1989 Repl.Vol.), §§ 7–4A–01 through 7–4A–06 of the Education Article (EA). The uncodified preamble to the Act states that "[t]he rate of youth suicide has increased more than threefold in the last two decades," and that "[o]ver 5,000 young Americans took their lives [in 1985], including over 100 young people in Maryland...."

Further legislative findings and declarations are set forth in EA § 7–4A–01. "A statewide Youth Suicide Prevention School Program is essential to address" the problem. § 7–4A–01(1). "County suicide prevention and crisis center agencies along with local education agencies are best suited for developing and implementing programs for statewide youth suicide prevention." § 7–4A–01(5). Section 7–4A–03(a)(1) provides for a statewide Youth Suicide Prevention School Program administered by the State Department of Education in cooperation with, inter alia, participating local education agencies. Any program established under the Act "shall

... [t]rain school personnel in individual and school wide strategies for teenage suicide prevention." EA § 7–4A–04(c)(2).

In 1987 the Maryland State Department of Education (the Department) published its "YOUTH SUICIDE PREVENTION SCHOOL PROGRAM for the Public Schools of Maryland." It presented goals, objectives and strategies for youth suicide prevention, intervention and "postvention," i.e., "coping with the aftermath of a student's attempted suicide, or completed suicide." Id. at 2.

Nicole's school had a suicide prevention program prior to her death. * * * [T]he superintendent produced, inter alia, a memorandum dated February 18, 1987, from the office of the principal to the staff of Sligo Middle School on the subject of "Suicide Prevention." It consists of a top sheet setting forth the "steps [that] must be followed."[12] The top sheet is supplemented by materials on other pages reproduced from various sources. These materials include lists of the methods of, and motives for, suicide and important warning signs ("[A]lmost all who have committed suicide have communicated their intent beforehand."). Part IX lists ten answers to the question, "How Can You Help In A Suicidal Crisis ?" Answer D is:

> "Tell others—As quickly as possible, share your knowledge with parents, friends, teachers or other people who might be able to help. Don't worry about breaking a confidence if someone reveals suicidal plans to you. You may have to betray a secret to save a life."

There is no indication in the Act that the Legislature intended to create a statutorily based cause of action against school counselors who negligently fail to intervene in a potential suicide. Nevertheless, holding counselors to a common law duty of reasonable care to prevent suicides when they have evidence of a suicidal intent comports with the policy underlying this Act.

C. CLOSENESS OF CONNECTION BETWEEN CONDUCT AND INJURY

This factor is the proximate cause element of a negligence action considered on the macroscale of policy. Consideration is given to whether, across the universe of cases of the type presented, there would ordinarily be so little connection between breach of the duty contended for, and the allegedly resulting harm, that a court would simply foreclose liability by holding that there is no duty. The defendants in the instant matter argue the closeness of connection factor from two aspects, superseding cause and remoteness.

The defendants say that the law considers suicide to be "a deliberate, intentional and intervening act which precludes a finding that a given defendant is responsible for the harm." Brief of Appellees at 6. Defen-

---

12. The description of the steps, in relevant part, reads: "1. Notify the appropriate grade level counselor and administrator immediately. 2. It will be the grade level administrator's responsibility to call a team meeting.... 3. The committee will decide jointly as to the next steps—i.e., contacting parents, outside agencies, etc. 4. Reminders: (a) Our counselors are trained to counsel with a youngster who is contemplating suicide; there are also full-time professionals who are available. (b) Confidentiality is not an issue—it makes for more sense to pick up the pieces of a teacher/pupil relationship after the crisis is over. (c) The student should not be left alone at any time."

dants cite McLaughlin v. Sullivan, 123 N.H. at 339, 461 A.2d at 125, where the court held that an attorney's alleged malpractice, in not requesting a stay of sentence or bail pending appeal in a criminal case, could not have been the proximate cause of the client's suicide in jail during the first day of confinement following conviction. Here, however, we deal with the relationship between an adolescent and school counselors who allegedly were informed that the adolescent was suicidal. Legally to categorize all suicides by adolescents as knowing and voluntary acts which insulate the death, as a matter of law, from all other acts or omissions which might operate, in fact, as causes of the death is contrary to the policy manifested by the Act. The Act does not view these troubled children as standing independently, to live or die on their own. In a failure to prevent suicide case, Maryland tort law should not treat an adolescent's committing suicide as a superseding cause when the entire premise of the Act is that others, including the schools, have the potential to intervene effectively.

The defendants also argue that "[i]n blaming the Board and the school counselors for his daughter's death, [Eisel], at most, makes out a case for a remote cause, one which is speculative and inconclusive." * * * [T]his issue of causation in fact is not before us on this appeal. Obviously, when the factual skeleton, on which the duty issue has been presented to us, has been fleshed out with evidence at trial, causation may be a question for the jury, or it may develop that, as a matter of law, any causal connection has been severed by some fact, other than that death was essentially self-inflicted.

D. MORAL BLAME

Moral blame as a factor to be weighed in deciding whether to recognize a legal duty in tort is less than an intent to cause harm. This factor considers the reaction of persons in general to the circumstances. Is it the sense of the community that an obligation exists under the circumstances? Certainly if classmates of Nicole found her lying on the floor of a lavatory, bleeding from slashed wrists, and those students told one or more teachers of the emergency, society would be outraged if the teachers did nothing and Nicole bled to death. Here, the information allegedly received by the counselors involved intent, not a description of physical facts. The distinction does not form a bright line separating duty from the absence of duty. The youth suicide prevention programs provided for by the Act call for awareness of, and response to, emotional warning signs, thus evidencing a community sense that there should be intervention based on emotional indicia of suicide. * * * The harm that may result from a school counselor's failure to intervene appropriately when a child threatens suicide is total and irreversible for the child, and severe for the child's family. It may be that the risk of any particular suicide is remote if statistically quantified in relation to all of the reports of suicidal talk that are received by school counselors. We do not know. But the consequence of the risk is so great that even a relatively remote possibility of a suicide may be enough to establish duty. * * * See Council of Co–Owners Atlantis Condominium, Inc. v. Whiting–Turner Contracting Co., 308 Md. 18, 35 & n. 5, 517 A.2d 336, 345 & n. 5 (1986)(recognizing a duty against architects, enforceable by recovery for economic loss, if building conditions present a clear risk of death or personal injury).

Moreover, when the risk of death to a child is balanced against the burden sought to be imposed on the counselors, the scales tip overwhelmingly in favor of duty. Certainly the physical component of the burden on the counselors was slight. Eisel claims only that a telephone call, communicating information known to the counselors, would have discharged that duty here. We agree.

The counselors argue that there are elements of confidentiality and discretion in their relationships with students that would be destroyed by the imposition of a duty to notify parents of all reports of suicidal statements. Confidentiality does not bar the duty, given that the school policy explicitly disavows confidentiality when suicide is the concern.

The defendants further point out that counselors are required to exercise discretion when dealing with students. Their discretion, however, cannot be boundless when determining whether to treat a student as a potential suicide. Discretion is relevant to whether the standard of conduct has been breached under the circumstances of a given case. Discretion does not create an absolute immunity, which would be the effect of denying any duty. * * * "Changing social conditions lead constantly to the recognition of new duties." Prosser & Keeton on The Law of Torts § 53, at 359 (5th ed. 1984)(footnote omitted); see, e.g., B.N. v. K.K., 312 Md. 135, 538 A.2d 1175 (1988)(transmission of herpes).

Considering the growth of this tragic social problem in the light of the factors discussed above, we hold that school counselors have a duty to use reasonable means to attempt to prevent a suicide when they are on notice of a child or adolescent student's suicidal intent. On the facts of this case as developed to date, a trier of fact could conclude that that duty included warning Eisel of the danger. [Judgment reversed and case remanded. Concurring opinion omitted.]

Notes

1. In Hoyem v. Manhattan Beach City School District, 22 Cal.3d 508, 150 Cal.Rptr. 1, 585 P.2d 851 (1978), a sharply divided California Supreme Court (4–3) held that a school district could be liable for injuries suffered by a truant during school hours. Starting from the undoubtedly correct premise that the school district had a responsibility to supervise children on school premises, the majority, in an opinion written by Tobriner, J., held that, if the plaintiff's truancy resulted from negligent on-site supervision, injuries suffered during the period of truancy were recoverable. Once even a relatively young child leaves school for the day, however, it has been held that the school district owes the child no duty to protect it against traffic accidents. Searcy v. Hemet Unified School Dist., 177 Cal.App.3d 792, 223 Cal.Rptr. 206 (1986)(six-year-old child injured at least a quarter of a mile from the school premises while taking a "short-cut" home). In Doe v. Taylor Ind. School Dist., 15 F.3d 443 (5th Cir.), *cert. denied*,___ U.S. ___, 115 S.Ct. 70, 130 L.Ed.2d 25 (1994), the court found a duty on the part of school officials to "supervise" a teacher when they were aware that the teacher may have sexually molested students in the past and had been aware for several months of his conduct with the plaintiff-student.

2. There are a number of cases holding that as a general proposition, which as we shall see is developing a number of exceptions, a landlord has no duty to protect tenants or others lawfully on the premises from the criminal

acts of third persons. Goldberg v. Housing Authority of the City of Newark, 38 N.J. 578, 186 A.2d 291 (1962); Smith v. Chicago Housing Authority, 36 Ill.App.3d 967, 344 N.E.2d 536 (1976). On the other hand, in Johnston v. Harris, 387 Mich. 569, 198 N.W.2d 409 (1972), it was held that the landlord could be held responsible if the condition of the premises increased the risk of criminal assault. In that case the vestibule of a four-apartment building was unlit and the outside door was unlocked. A similar, frequently cited case is Kline v. 1500 Massachusetts Avenue Apartment Corp., 439 F.2d 477 (D.C.Cir. 1970). In that case, in holding in favor of the plaintiff on the merits, the court stressed that the landlord was on notice that crime was on the increase in the area and that in recent years the landlord had dispensed with a doorman. The landlord furthermore no longer insured that the front desk was always attended, and one entrance was frequently left unlocked. The court held that the plaintiff, who was injured in 1966, was at least entitled to the security arrangements prevailing in 1959 when she first moved into the building. As to the possible cost of upgrading security, the court concluded:

> Granted, the discharge of this duty of protection by landlords will cause, in many instances, the expenditure of large sums for additional equipment and services, and granted, the cost will be ultimately passed on to the tenant in the form of increased rents. This prospect, in itself, however, is no deterrent to our acknowledging and giving force to the duty, since without protection the tenant already pays in losses from theft, physical assault and increased insurance premiums.

> The landlord is entirely justified in passing on the cost of increased protective measures to his tenants, but the rationale of compelling the landlord to do it in the first place is that he is the only one who is in a position to take the necessary protective measures for overall protection of the premises, which he owns in whole and rents in part to individual tenants.

439 F.2d at 488. Relying on *Kline*, the *Goldberg* case—which involved the robbery of a milkman delivering milk to a public housing project—was distinguished in Braitman v. Overlook Terrace Corp., 68 N.J. 368, 346 A.2d 76 (1975). In that case, the defendant had unreasonably failed, after notice of the condition, to fix a broken dead lock. The landlord was held liable when the apartment was robbed. *See also* Trentacost v. Brussel, 82 N.J. 214, 412 A.2d 436 (1980); Aaron v. Havens, 758 S.W.2d 446 (Mo.1988). *But see*, Bartley v. Sweetser, 319 Ark. 117, 890 S.W.2d 250 (1994)(landlord does not have duty to tenant to make the premises safe from other's criminal conduct).

3. The "Duty" of Those Whose Conduct Has Injured or Threatened Injury to Others

Until well into the twentieth century, the prevailing doctrine was that if one through no fault of his own injured another, he was under no legal obligation to come to the aid of the injured person. *See, e.g.*, Turbeville v. Mobile Light & Railroad Co., 221 Ala. 91, 127 So. 519 (1930); Union Pacific Railway v. Cappier, 66 Kan. 649, 72 P. 281 (1903); Griswold v. Boston & Maine Railroad, 183 Mass. 434, 67 N.E. 354 (1903). When the *Restatement of Torts* appeared in 1934, it reflected this state of the law in Section 322 which, as stated in the title, only imposed a "duty to aid another made helpless by tortious conduct." At the same time, in Section 321, the *Restatement* recognized that, if one "does an act, which at the time he has no reason to believe will involve an unreasonable risk of causing bodily harm to another," he might nonetheless be liable for negligence in failing to take reasonable steps to prevent "the risk from taking effect" once he realizes or should realize that he has created an unreasonable risk of injury to another. *Cf.* Simonsen v. Thorin, 120 Neb. 684, 234 N.W. 628 (1931); Montgomery v. National Convoy and Trucking Co., 186 S.C. 167, 195 S.E. 247 (1938).

The law has evolved considerably since the publication of the *Restatement*. The courts were undoubtedly influenced by the enactment, in almost all jurisdictions, of hit and run statutes which require motorists who are involved in accidents to stop and render assistance regardless of whether the accident was legally their fault.[13] The *Restatement (Second) of Torts* reflects this development. Section 322 was redrafted to impose a "duty to aid another harmed by the actor's conduct." Even if the harm was not caused by the actor's tortious conduct he is nevertheless "under a duty to exercise reasonable care to prevent * * * further harm" to anyone rendered helpless by the initial accident. Cases applying this doctrine include Rains v. Heldenfels Brothers, 443 S.W.2d 280 (Tex.Civ.App.1969); Tubbs v. Argus, 140 Ind.App. 695, 225 N.E.2d 841 (1967); *cf.* L. S. Ayres & Co. v. Hicks, 220 Ind. 86, 40 N.E.2d 334 (1942). Should it make any difference if the legal cause of the original accident, which rendered the plaintiff helpless, was the negligence of the plaintiff?

4. The "Duty" of a Volunteer Rescuer

PARVI v. CITY OF KINGSTON

Court of Appeals of New York, 1977.
41 N.Y.2d 553, 394 N.Y.S.2d 161, 362 N.E.2d 960.

Fuchsberg, J.

This appeal brings up for review the dismissal, at the end of the plaintiff's case, of two causes of action, both of which arise out of the same somewhat unusual train of events. One is for false imprisonment and the other for negligence. The judgment of dismissal was affirmed by the Appellate Division by a vote of three to two. The issue before us, as to each count, is whether a prima facie case was made out. We believe it was.

Sometime after 9:00 p.m. on the evening of May 28, 1972, a date which occurred during the Memorial Day weekend, two police officers employed by the defendant City of Kingston responded in a radio patrol car to the rear of a commercial building in that city where they had been informed some individuals were acting in a boisterous manner. Upon their arrival, they found three men, one Raymond Dugan, his brother Dixie Dugan and the plaintiff, Donald C. Parvi. According to the police, it was the Dugan

---

13. In California v. Byers, 402 U.S. 424, 91 S.Ct. 1535, 29 L.Ed.2d 9 (1971), a motorist who failed to stop and give his name, as required by statute after being involved in an accident causing property damage, challenged his conviction on the ground that application of the statute to him would potentially require him to incriminate himself of a traffic offense. The Court, with three dissenters, rejected this contention on the ground that possible incrimination of traffic offenses was not the purpose or likely effect of the statute. The companion California provisions dealing with bodily injury or death are Cal. Vehicle Code §§ 20001 & 20003.

brothers who alone were then engaged in a noisy quarrel. When the two uniformed officers informed the three they would have to move on or be locked up, Raymond Dugan ran away; Dixie Dugan chased after him unsuccessfully and then returned to the scene in a minute or two; Parvi, who the police testimony shows had been trying to calm the Dugans, remained where he was.

In the course of their examinations before trial, read into evidence by Parvi's counsel, the officers described all three as exhibiting, in an unspecified manner, evidence that they "had been drinking" and showed "the effects of alcohol". They went on to relate how, when Parvi and Dixie Dugan said they had no place to go, the officers ordered them into the police car and, pursuing a then prevailing police "standard operating procedure", transported the two men outside the city limits to an abandoned golf course located in an unlit and isolated area known as Coleman Hill. Thereupon the officers drove off, leaving Parvi and Dugan to "dry out". This was the first time Parvi had ever been there. En route they had asked to be left off at another place, but the police refused to do so.

No more than 350 feet from the spot where they were dropped off, one of the boundaries of the property adjoins the New York State Thruway. There were no intervening fences or barriers other than the low Thruway guardrail intended to keep vehicular traffic on the road. Before they left, it is undisputed that the police made no effort to learn whether Parvi was oriented to his whereabouts, to instruct him as to the route back to Kingston, where Parvi had then lived for 12 years, or to ascertain where he would go from there. From where the men were dropped, the "humming and buzzing" of fast-traveling, holiday-bound automobile traffic was clearly audible from the Thruway; in their befuddled state, which later left Parvi with very little memory of the events, the men lost little time in responding to its siren song. For, in an apparent effort to get back, by 10:00 p.m. Parvi and Dugan had wandered onto the Thruway, where they were struck by an automobile operated by one David R. Darling. Parvi was severely injured, Dugan was killed. (Parvi elected not to appeal from the dismissal of his cause of action against Darling, who originally had been joined as an additional defendant.)

The Cause of Action for Negligence

The Appellate Division upheld the dismissal of the negligence cause on the ground that it was not reasonably foreseeable that a person who is under the influence of alcohol will walk approximately 350 feet in the dead of night and climb over a guardrail onto the New York Thruway. Before treating with that issue, we prefer to give our attention to the more fundamental question of the basic duty owed by the city to the plaintiff in this situation, a question somewhat obscured by the jargon of negligence terminology (Green, The Duty Problem in Negligence Cases, 28 Col.L.Rev. 1014, 29 Col.L.Rev. 255).

In that connection, we do not believe it aids our analysis of the negligence count to speculate on the duty of a police officer to arrest or not to arrest intoxicated persons. Instead, we confront directly the duty of police officers to persons under the influence of alcohol who are already in their custody, as was the case here once Parvi was compelled to enter the police car. The case law is clear that even when no original duty is owed to the plaintiff to undertake affirmative action, once it is voluntarily undertaken, it must be performed with due care. * * * As Restatement of Torts 2d (§ 324) puts it, "One who, being under no duty to do so, takes charge of another who is helpless adequately to aid or protect himself is subject to liability to the other for any bodily harm caused to him by (a) the failure of the actor to exercise reasonable care to secure the safety of the other while within the actor's charge or (b) the actor's discontinuing his aid or protection, if by so doing, he leaves the other in a worse position than when the actor took charge of him".

Comment *g* to that section makes it evident that this duty cannot be fulfilled by placing the helpless person in a position of peril equal to that from which he was rescued. So it tells us that "if the actor has succeeded in removing the other from a position of danger to one of safety, he cannot change his position for the worse by unreasonably putting him back into the same peril, or into a new one."

We return now to the question of whether it was reasonably foreseeable that Parvi, who appeared sufficiently intoxicated for the police to take action, when set down in the dead of night in a lonely rural setting within 350 feet of a superhighway, whose traffic noises were sure to make its presence known, might wander onto the road. To state the question is to answer it. To be sure, much has to depend on what the jury finds to have been the state of his sobriety and the nature of the surrounding physical and other circumstances. But traditionally these are the kind of matters suitable for jury determination rather than for the direction of a verdict * * *.

Finally, a word of clarification may be in order as to the legal role of plaintiff's voluntary intoxication. To accept the defendant's argument, that the intoxication was itself the proximate cause of Parvi's injury as a matter of law, would be to negate the very duty imposed on the police officers when they took Parvi and Dugan into custody. It would be to march up the hill only to march down again. The clear duty imposed on the officers interdicts such a result if, as the jury may find, their conduct was unreasonable. * * * For it is the very fact of plaintiff's drunkenness which precipitated the duty once the officers made the decision to act.

Accordingly, the order of the Appellate Division should be reversed, both causes of action reinstated and a new trial ordered, with leave to the defendant, if so advised, to move at Trial Term for leave to amend its answer to affirmatively plead a defense of justification to the cause of action for false imprisonment.

BREITEL, CHIEF JUDGE (dissenting).

I dissent. On no view of the facts should plaintiff, brought to causing his own serious injury by his voluntary intoxication, be allowed to recover from the City of Kingston for damages suffered when he wandered onto the New York State Thruway and was struck by an automobile. His attack is the familiar one of the good Samaritan, in the persons of two police officers, for not having, in retrospect, done enough.

The order of the Appellate Division should be affirmed, and the action stand dismissed.

Plaintiff's negligence claim is equally without merit. The police officers had no duty to leave Parvi absolutely free from danger in any form. Instead, they owed plaintiff only a duty to exercise ordinary care. * * * That duty was discharged by leaving plaintiff at a camping ground equipped with "lean-to" shelters and removed from the holiday bustle of the city, where Parvi had been drinking for the past two or three days. Since it was not foreseeable that Parvi, rather than "sleeping off" his intoxication, would wander away, climb over a guardrail, and be struck by an automobile on the New York State Thruway, there was no breach of duty, no negligence, and hence, no liability * * *. If, perchance, he was in search of more drinks, there was no chance of giving him absolute safety except by locking him up. It should not be the rule, common to an era long well past, that every drunkard must be locked up on being observed as intoxicated in public.

In removing Parvi and Dugan from the center of town, the police officers were performing a recognized public function. In his intoxicated state, Parvi, with his companions, was creating a public nuisance. It had been a long-standing practice in Kingston to transport publicly intoxicated people out of the center of town. The practice was followed in this case, and it is not, in a smaller city (population 25,544), an inherently unreasonable way of dealing with public intoxication. It avoids the humiliation and degradation to the offender, of maintaining him in jail. It is a commonplace that it is no longer acceptable, albeit it still continues, to treat the intoxicated and alcoholic in this fashion, as one does criminals.

Moreover, transplanting plaintiff from the center of town to an isolated area on the outskirts was protective of plaintiff himself. While a man in an intoxicated state can always be a hazard to himself, he is much more so when located in the center of town, in the midst of city streets, railroad tracks, molesters, muggers, street vehicles, and without shelter, than he would be in an isolated area. But one may not deprive him of reasonable access, after he recovers his sobriety, to food and other necessities. Had the police placed the two men out of reasonable access to any road, the isolation would have been inhumane. And any road would under some circumstances be dangerous. At least, the Thruway was bordered by a guardrail, and the record does not indicate the distance to the other accessible roads, including the road by which they reached Coleman Hill.

Restatement, Torts 2d, defines an act as negligent when it involves a risk of harm "of such magnitude as to outweigh what the law regards as the utility of the act or of the particular manner in which it is done" (§ 291). Here, the risk was slight; the police officers obviously considered safety in choosing the camping site to deposit the two men, and reasonably regarded the site as safe. More significant, by removing Parvi from town, they removed him from a place of greater danger, and halted a public nuisance as well. The police conduct, therefore, was not unreasonable under the Restatement test. * * * The same analysis applies under section 324 of Restatement, Torts 2d, dealing with the duty of one who takes charge of helpless persons, since the officers materially improved plaintiff's position by removing him from town.

Since, therefore, there was no breach of duty to plaintiff, as a matter of law, the negligence count, too, was properly dismissed.

There is hubris in the bringing of an action of this kind. Parvi is one of a pair of drinkers, derelicts perhaps, engaged in making a public nuisance of themselves in the center of a small Hudson River Valley city on a holiday weekend. The police of that city, a tiny force, are not sisters of charity or baby-sitters.

Basically, the legal issues in this case are not difficult. And the justice issues are even less so. A drunken man, a pitiable character, is found with his companions in the middle of town. Sympathetic police officers offer to take the men any where they choose, but the poor fellows have no place to go. So, rather than locking them up for a holiday weekend, the officers deposit the men in a suburban setting, where some shelter is available. The officers are thanked for their kindness. But, in the end, the efforts of the officers are to no avail, as the drunken men wander away from safety and into danger. A tragedy, certainly. A miscalculation, perhaps. But even with the aid of hindsight, the facts in this case are not the stuff on which tort liability may be premised.

Accordingly, I dissent, and vote to affirm the order of the Appellate Division.

Notes

1. There are cases that state categorically that, for a voluntary rescuer to be liable in tort, the rescuer must worsen the helpless person's plight. *See* United States v. DeVane, 306 F.2d 182 (5th Cir.1962) (negligence of Coast Guard in transcription of radio messages led to delay in starting rescue search). *See also* Mendoza v. White Stores, Inc., 488 P.2d 90 (Colo.App.1971).

2. Suppose *B* is floundering in the ocean 100 yards from shore. *A*, the only other person present, goes to *B*'s rescue and gradually brings him to within 20 feet of the shore. If *A* now discontinues his rescue efforts and *B* drowns, would *A* escape liability under *Restatement (Second) of Torts* § 324? After all not only did *A* not worsen *B*'s situation; *A* materially improved *B*'s situation. Is such a result justifiable either from the point of view of morality or public policy?

3. A possible analogous situation concerns a lessor's negligent making of repairs on leased premises. *Restatement (Second) of Torts* § 362 (repeating the treatment of this subject in the *Restatement of Torts*) imposes liability only when the lessor has, unknown to the lessee, made the premises more dangerous or given them a deceptive appearance of safety. There are cases rejecting this position and holding the lessor liable for the negligent repair of premises regardless of whether the premises were made more dangerous or given a deceptive appearance of safety. *See* Bartlett v. Taylor, 351 Mo. 1060, 174 S.W.2d 844 (1943).

4. *Good-Samaritan Statutes.* In 1959 California enacted the first "good-samaritan" statute. Passage of the act was apparently prompted by an incident at Lake Tahoe where a skier, who broke her leg, was left lying in the snow for a considerable period of time despite the fact that there were many

skiers in the area, some of whom were physicians. *See* Note, 42 Ore.L.Rev. 328 (1963). The statutes are prompted by the assumption that it is the fear of tort liability that deters the rendition of emergency treatment, especially by physicians, despite the fact that there are few, if any, reported cases in which a physician has been held liable for rendering emergency first aid. Some of the earlier statutes applied only to physicians and other medically trained personnel. More recent statutes apply more generally; the Wisconsin statute reprinted below is perhaps the most typical. There are presently some sort of good-samaritan statutes in all fifty states and the District of Columbia. The original California good-samaritan statute, West's Ann.Calif.Bus. & Prof.Code § 2144, provided that "[n]o person licensed under [chapter 4] * * *, who in good faith renders emergency care at the scene of the emergency, shall be liable for any civil damages as a result of any acts or omissions by such a person in rendering the emergency care." The statute made no exception for reckless or grossly negligent treatment. Persons licensed under chapter 4 include physicians and surgeons, drugless practitioners, podiatrists, and osteopaths. Dentists and nurses are not licensed under chapter 4. Neither, of course, are out-of-state physicians.[14] In 1963 similar provisions were enacted to deal with dentists and nurses. West's Ann.Calif.Bus. & Prof.Code §§ 1627.5 (dentists), 2727.5 (nurses only immunized if not guilty of gross negligence). Subsequently, provisions were added which cover firemen, policemen, paramedics, etc., usually conditioning immunity on the absence of gross negligence. *See, e.g.,* West's Ann.Calif.Health & Safety Code §§ 1799.107 & 1799.108. In addition, a provision was adopted in 1984 ostensibly giving total immunity from liability to anyone who removes or attempts to remove "food that has become stuck in another person's throat" and who does so "in accordance with instructions adopted by the [California] department" of health services. West's Ann.Calif.Health & Safety Code § 114180(d). Complete immunity from liability has also been purportedly given to any person who "renders emergency care at the scene of an emergency," which is defined as not including "emergency departments and other places where medical care is usually offered." West's Ann.Calif.Health & Safety Code § 1799.102. The complexity of the California situation with different standards of immunity being applied to different categories of persons in different situations can be illustrated by looking at the original California statute, which applies only to licensed physicians and which has over the years been amended and expanded. The current provisions are as follows:

West's Ann. Calif. Bus. & Prof. Code:

§ 2395. Emergency care at scene of accident

No licensee, who in good faith renders emergency care at the scene of an emergency, shall be liable for any civil damages as a result of any acts or omissions by such person in rendering the emergency care.

"The scene of an emergency" as used in this section shall include, but not be limited to, the emergency rooms of hospitals in the event of a medical disaster. "Medical disaster" means a duly proclaimed state of emergency or local emergency declared pursuant to the California Emergency Services Act (Chapter 7 (commencing with Section 8550) of Division 1 of Title 2 of the Government Code).

---

14. In 1980 a provision was inserted expressly declaring that nothing in chapter 4 "prohibits [medical] service in the case of emergency, or the domestic administration of family remedies." Calif.Bus. & Prof.Code § 2058. But, although such services are not prohibited, they do not receive the benefit of the good-samaritan provisions.

Acts or omissions exempted from liability pursuant to this section shall include those acts or omissions which occur after the declaration of a medical disaster and those which occurred prior to such declaration but after the commencement of such medical disaster. The immunity granted in this section shall not apply in the event of a willful act or omission.

§ 2395.5. Licensee serving on on-call basis in hospital emergency room; emergency obstetrical services; exceptions to protections; liability of hospital

(a) A licensee who serves on an on-call basis to a hospital emergency room, who in good faith renders emergency obstetrical services to a person while serving on-call, shall not be liable for any civil damages as a result of any negligent act or omission by the licensee in rendering the emergency obstetrical services. The immunity granted by this section shall not apply to acts or omissions constituting gross negligence, recklessness, or willful misconduct.

(b) The protections of subdivision (a) shall not apply to the licensee in any of the following cases:

(1) Consideration in any form was provided to the licensee for serving, or the licensee was required to serve, on an on-call basis to the hospital emergency room. In either event, the protections of subdivision (a) shall not apply unless the hospital expressly, in writing, accepts liability for the licensee's negligent acts or omissions.

(2) The licensee had provided prior medical diagnosis or treatment to the same patient for a condition having a bearing on or relevance to the treatment of the obstetrical condition which required emergency services.

(3) Before rendering emergency obstetrical services, the licensee had a contractual obligation or agreement with the patient, another licensee, or a third-party payer on the patient's behalf to provide obstetrical care for the patient, or the licensee had a reasonable expectation of payment for the emergency services provided to the patient.

(c) Except as provided in subdivision (b), nothing in this section shall be construed to affect or modify the liability of the hospital for ordinary or gross negligence.

§ 2396. Emergency care for complication arising from prior care by another

No licensee, who in good faith upon the request of another person so licensed, renders emergency medical care to a person for medical complication arising from prior care by another person so licensed, shall be liable for any civil damages as a result of any acts or omissions by such licensed person in rendering such emergency medical care.

§ 2397. Emergency situations in licensee's office or hospital; failure to inform patient; causes; definitions

(a) A licensee shall not be liable for civil damages for injury or death caused in an emergency situation occurring in the licensee's office or in a hospital on account of a failure to inform a patient of the possible consequences of a medical procedure where the failure to inform is caused by any of the following:

(1) The patient was unconscious.

(2) The medical procedure was undertaken without the consent of the patient because the licensee reasonably believed that a medical procedure should be undertaken immediately and that there was insufficient time to fully inform the patient.

(3) A medical procedure was performed on a person legally incapable of giving consent, and the licensee reasonably believed that a medical procedure should be undertaken immediately and that there was insufficient time to obtain the informed consent of a person authorized to give such consent for the patient.

(b) This section is applicable only to actions for damages for injuries or death arising because of a licensee's failure to inform, and not to actions for damages arising because of a licensee's negligence in rendering or failing to render treatment.

(c) As used in this section:

(1) "Hospital" means a licensed general acute care hospital as defined in subdivision (a) of Section 1250 of the Health and Safety Code.

(2) "Emergency situation occurring in the licensee's office" means a situation occurring in an office, other than a hospital, used by a licensee for the examination or treatment of patients, requiring immediate services for alleviation of severe pain, or immediate diagnosis and treatment of unforeseeable medical conditions, which, if not immediately diagnosed and treated, would lead to serious disability or death.

(3) "Emergency situation occurring in a hospital" means a situation occurring in a hospital, whether or not it occurs in an emergency room, requiring immediate services for alleviation of severe pain, or immediate diagnosis and treatment of unforeseeable medical conditions, which, if not immediately diagnosed and treated, would lead to serious disability or death.

(d) Nothing in this article shall be construed to authorize practice by a podiatrist beyond that set forth in Section 2473.

§ 2398. Community college or high school athletic event or contest; voluntary emergency medical assistance to participant

No licensee, who in good faith and without compensation renders voluntary emergency medical assistance to a participant in a community college or high school athletic event or contest, at the site of the event or contest, or during transportation to a health care facility, for an injury suffered in the course of such event or contest, shall be liable for any civil damages as a result of any acts or omissions by such person in rendering such voluntary medical assistance. The immunity granted by this section shall not apply to acts or omissions constituting gross negligence.

––––––––

Wisconsin initially enacted a good-samaritan statute in 1963 that extended only to licensed physicians. It too has since been amended several times and has in the process also become more complex. The current version, Wis.Stat. Ann. 895.48 (West), now reads as follows:

895.48. Civil liability exemption; emergency care, health care at athletic events and hazardous substances

(1) Any person who renders emergency care at the scene of any emergency or accident in good faith shall be immune from civil liability for his or her acts or omissions in rendering such emergency care. This immunity does not extend when employes trained in health care or health care professionals render emergency care for compensation and within the scope of their usual and customary employment or practice at a hospital or other institution equipped with hospital facilities, at the scene of any emergency or accident, en route to a hospital or other institution equipped with hospital facilities or at a physician's office.

[The statute goes on to provide that any physician, chiropractor, dentist, emergency medical technician, physician assistant, or registered nurse] who renders voluntary health care to a participant in an athletic event or contest sponsored by a nonprofit corporation [a private or public school, or a public agency] is immune from civil liability for his or her acts or omissions in rendering that care if all of the following conditions exist:

> (a) The health care is rendered at the site of the event or contest, during transportation to a health care facility from the event or contest, or in a locker room or similar facility immediately before, during or immediately after the event or contest.

> (b) the [person] does not receive compensation for the health care, other than reimbursement for expenses.

The California statute has been construed not to apply to a doctor who was "on call" to supply surgical care to emergency patients, *see* Colby v. Schwartz, 78 Cal.App.3d 885, 144 Cal.Rptr. 624 (1978), since such a person does not need an inducement to provide emergency care, although it has also been held that a hospital can be the scene of an emergency even in the absence of a medical disaster. *See* Burciaga v. St. John's Memorial Hosp., 187 Cal.App.3d 710, 232 Cal.Rptr. 75 (1986)(pediatrician visiting patients in the hospital responded to a call from the delivery room for a pediatrician). *See also* Kearns v. Superior Court, 204 Cal.App.3d 1325, 252 Cal.Rptr. 4 (1988); McKenna v. Cedars of Lebanon Hosp., 93 Cal.App.3d 282, 155 Cal.Rptr. 631 (1979). West's Ann.Calif.Bus. & Prof.Code § 2395.5, *supra,* added in 1988, is obviously, at least in part, a response to *Colby v. Schwartz, supra.* Is it an effective response? A discussion of the California statute is contained in Comment, *California's Good Samaritan Protection for Physicians during Hospital Emergencies: An Argument for an Affirmative Duty,* 15 Western State U.L.Rev. 759 (1988). For citations to, and an overview of, the various statutes in this area, *see* Comment, *Good Samaritan Laws—Legal Disarray: An Update,* 38 Mercer L.Rev. 1439 (1987).[15]

How probable is it that good-samaritan statutes like those of California and Wisconsin will increase the likelihood that people will render emergency help to others? Would you think that the complexity of the California statutory scheme might itself actually serve as a deterrent to anyone who might ever take the time to try to study that scheme? Do you think it is the possibility of tort liability that deters volunteer rescuers or is it the reluctance of busy people to accept responsibility for staying with the injured party until he can be transferred to a suitable hospital? The problem may be more acute for a physician

---

15. *See also* Vt.Stat.Ann. tit. 12, § 519(b), reprinted at p. 463, *supra.*

who might feel obliged to remain with the injured person until the physician is assured that the proper care is being given. To the extent these considerations bear on the decision to render emergency assistance, good-samaritan statutes will be of limited success in changing people's behavior patterns.

B. NEGLIGENT INFLICTION OF EMOTIONAL DISTRESS

DZIOKONSKI v. BABINEAU

Supreme Judicial Court of Massachusetts, 1978.
375 Mass. 555, 380 N.E.2d 1295.

WILKINS, JUSTICE.

These appeals require us to reexamine the question whether a person who negligently causes emotional distress which leads to physical injuries may be liable for those injuries even if the injured person neither was threatened with nor sustained any direct physical injury. At the heart of the plaintiffs' claims is the argument that this court should abandon the so called "impact" rule of Spade v. Lynn & Boston R.R., 168 Mass. 285, 290, 47 N.E. 88 (1897), which denies recovery for physical injuries arising solely from negligently caused mental distress. We agree that the rule of the *Spade* case should be abandoned. Our inquiry does not cease at that point, however, because we must determine what new limits of liability are appropriate and how those limits affect the plaintiffs' decedents, parents of a child alleged to have been injured by the defendants' negligence.

These appeals, transferred here on our own motion, come to us following the allowance of the defendants' motions to dismiss for failure to state claims on which relief can be granted. * * * For the purpose of considering the propriety of the allowance of these motions, we summarize the allegations of each complaint.

On October 24, 1973, Norma Dziokonski, a minor, alighted from a motor vehicle, used as a school bus, on Route 117 in Lancaster. That motor vehicle was owned by the defendant Pelletier and operated by the defendant Kroll. A motor vehicle owned and operated by the defendant Babineau struck Norma as she was crossing the road. The complaints allege the negligence of each defendant on various grounds.

The complaint filed by the administratrix of the estate of Lorraine Dziokonski (Mrs. Dziokonski) alleges that Mrs. Dziokonski was the mother of Norma and that she "lived in the immediate vicinity of the accident, went to the scene of the accident and witnessed her daughter lying injured on the ground." Mrs. Dziokonski "suffered physical and emotional shock, distress and anguish as a result of the injury to her daughter and died while she was a passenger in the ambulance that was driving her daughter to the hospital." This complaint alleges one count for wrongful death and one count for conscious suffering against each of the three defendants.

The complaint filed by the administratrix of the estate of Anthony Dziokonski (Mr. Dziokonski) alleged the facts previously set forth and added that he was the father of Norma and the husband of Mrs. Dziokonski. Mr. Dziokonski "suffered an aggravated gastric ulcer, a coronary occlusion, physical and emotional shock, distress and anguish as a result of the injury to his daughter and the death of his wife and his death was caused thereby." This complaint similarly alleged a count for wrongful death and one count for conscious suffering against each of the three defendants.[16]

THE SPADE CASE

We start with an analysis of *Spade v. Lynn & Boston R.R.* * * *, which announced a principle of tort law that has been limited and refined by our subsequent decisions but not heretofore abandoned. Margaret Spade had been a passenger on a crowded car of the Lynn & Boston Railroad Company late one Saturday night in February, 1895. She was so frightened by the negligent conduct of an employee of the defendant in removing an unruly passenger from the car that she sustained emotional shock and consequent physical injury. The trial judge instructed the jury that, when physical injury results from fear or nervous shock, "there may be a recovery for that bodily injury, and for all the pain, mental or otherwise, which may arise out of that bodily injury." * * * The jury returned a verdict for Mrs. Spade, but this court held that the judge's charge misstated the law.

We acknowledged that fright might cause physical injury and that "it is hard on principle" to say why there should not be recovery even for the mental suffering caused by a defendant's negligence. * * * The court concluded, however, that "in practice it is impossible satisfactorily to administer any other rule." * * * We noted that recovery for fright or distress of mind alone is barred and, that being so, there can be no recovery for physical injuries caused solely by mental disturbance. * * * It was said to be unreasonable to hold persons bound to anticipate and guard against fright and its consequences and thought that a contrary rule would "open a wide door for unjust claims." * * *

Subsequent Treatment of the Spade Rule in Massachusetts.

In Smith v. Postal Tel. Cable Co., 174 Mass. 576, 577–578, 55 N.E. 380 (1899), which applied the *Spade* rule to a case involving a claim of gross negligence, Chief Justice Holmes, speaking for the court, said that the point decided in the *Spade* case "is not put as a logical deduction from the general principles of liability in tort, but as a limitation of those principles upon purely practical grounds." *Id.* Later, he described the *Spade* rule as "an arbitrary exception, based upon a notion of what is practicable." Homans v. Boston Elevated Ry., 180 Mass. 456, 457, 62 N.E. 737 (1902).

Consistently and from its inception, the *Spade* rule has not been applied to deny recovery where immediate physical injuries result from negligently induced fright or emotional shock. Thus, recovery has been allowed "[w]hen the fright reasonably induces action which results in external injury." Cameron v. New England Tel. & Tel. Co., 182 Mass. 310, 312, 65 N.E. 385, 386 (1902)(defendant's negligent blasting caused the plaintiff to faint and sustain physical harm). Freedman v. Eastern Mass.

---

16. Neither complaint involves any claim on behalf of Norma for her own injuries. We do not know whether an action has been brought by or on behalf of Norma, nor whether the circumstances are such that under the no-fault law (St.1970, c. 670), she has no enforceable claim against any defendant. * * *

St. Ry., 299 Mass. 246, 250, 12 N.E.2d 739 (1938)(plaintiff's shoulder injured when she jumped to escape impending danger). * * *

Moreover, recovery for emotionally based physical injuries, sometimes described as "parasitic claims," has been allowed in tort cases founded on traditional negligent impact. * * * Thus, where the plaintiff sustained direct physical injuries as a result of the defendant's negligence and the plaintiff also sustained paralysis, perhaps resulting solely from nervous shock, we did not require the plaintiff to prove that the nervous shock or paralysis was a consequence of the direct physical injuries. *Homans v. Boston Elevated Ry.* * * *. We note that allowing recovery for emotionally based physical injuries unrelated to the physical consequences of the negligently caused impact also presents the threat of "unjust claims" * * * or, perhaps more exactly, the threat of exaggerated claims.

We have declined to apply the *Spade* rule to workmen's compensation claims. * * *

We have never applied the *Spade* rule to bar recovery for intentionally caused emotional distress. The *Spade* opinion itself recognized that the result might be different if the defendant's conduct had been intentional and not negligent. * * * We left that question open in *Smith v. Postal Tel. Cable Co.,* * * * and it so remained until 1971, when we decided George v. Jordan Marsh Co., 359 Mass. 244, 268 N.E.2d 915 (1971).

The *George* case involved allegations that, in their debt collection practices, the defendants intentionally caused emotional distress to the plaintiff and, as a result, her health deteriorated and she suffered two heart attacks. We held that "one who, without a privilege to do so, by extreme and outrageous conduct intentionally causes severe emotional distress to another, with bodily harm resulting from such distress, is subject to liability for such emotional distress and bodily harm." * * * We expressly left open the question now before us, whether there could be liability for negligent conduct causing emotional distress resulting in bodily injury. * * *

The question of liability for intentionally or recklessly caused severe emotional distress in the absence of bodily harm came before us in Agis v. Howard Johnson Co., 371 Mass. 140, 355 N.E.2d 315 (1976). There, we held that a complaint alleging extreme outrageous, and unprivileged conduct by the defendant stated a cause of action in favor of both the female plaintiff who sustained emotional distress but no bodily harm and her husband for loss of consortium. We rejected arguments that we should deny recovery for emotional distress where there is no physical injury because of the insurmountable difficulties of proof and the danger of fraudulent or frivolous claims. Although we recognized these problems, we rejected them as an absolute bar in all such cases and concluded that these were proper matters for consideration by the trier of fact in the adversary, trial process. * * *[17]

17. We left open the question of liability for mental anguish or emotional distress without physical injuries in McDonough v. Whalen, 365 Mass. 506, 516–518, 313 N.E.2d 435 (1974), where the plaintiff's claim was based on negligent conduct (in construction of a septic system) and not, as in the *George* and *Agis* cases, on intentional or reckless conduct. We concluded that, even if there were liability for negligent conduct causing

Although many industrial States initially required some impact as a basis for liability for physical harm resulting from fright, that rule has been abandoned in more recent times to the point where it has been said that "the courts which deny all remedy in such cases are fighting a rearguard action." W. Prosser, Torts § 54, at 333 (4th ed. 1971). As we have already indicated, we think the *Spade* rule should be abandoned. The threat of fraudulent claims cannot alone justify the denial of recovery in all cases. Whether a plaintiff's injuries were a reasonably foreseeable consequence of the defendant's negligence and whether the defendant caused those injuries are best left to determination in the normal manner before the trier of fact.

Recovery for Injuries Arising From Concern over Harm to Another.

The abandonment of the *Spade* rule is only the beginning in the process of determining whether the complaints in these cases state valid claims for relief. The typical case involving physical harm resulting from emotional distress concerns a person who was put in fear for his own safety as a result of alleged negligence of the defendant. Here, neither Mr. nor Mrs. Dziokonski was threatened with direct, contemporaneous injury as a result of the negligence of any defendant. Thus, we must consider the extent to which any defendant in this case may be held liable to the father or the mother, each of whom sustained physical injuries as a result of emotional distress over injuries incurred by their child.[18]

The weight of authority in this country would deny recovery in these cases. * * * Thus, as we fall back from the *Spade* rule, we could find comfort in numbers in denying recovery in these cases. We conclude, however, that we should not adopt a rule which absolutely denies recovery to every parent for whatever negligently caused, emotionally based physical injuries result from his concern over the safety of or injury to his injured child.

The arguments against imposing liability for a parent's injuries from shock and fear for his child have been stated clearly and forcefully in numerous opinions. * * * The reasons advanced for not permitting recovery are principally that (1) there is still a difficulty of proof of causation which has not been mitigated by any change in technology or medical science, (2) no logical justification exists for limiting recovery solely to parents who are affected physically by fear for the safety of an injured child, and (3) the extension of liability will impose an inordinate burden on defendants. In short, under this view, liability should be denied for injuries from shock and fear for another's safety regardless of (a) the relationship of the plaintiff to the accident victim, (b) the plaintiff's proximity to the accident, or (c) whether the plaintiff observed either the accident or its immediate consequences.

emotional distress without physical injuries, evidence that the plaintiff suffered gagging sensations and "got a little nervous and uptight * * *" * * * was insufficient evidence of emotional distress to justify recovery. * * * Because the appeals before us involve emotionally based physical injuries, again, we need not decide the question left open in the *McDonough* and *George* cases.

18. Mr. Dziokonski's injuries are alleged to be the product of his distress over learning of his daughter's injuries and of the death of his wife.

Until 1968, the nearly unanimous weight of authority in this country denied recovery for emotionally based physical injuries resulting from concern for the safety of another where the plaintiff was not himself threatened with contemporaneous injury. * * *

The "zone of danger" rule has something to commend it as a measure of the limits of liability. It permits a relatively easy determination of the persons who might recover for emotionally caused bodily injury by including only those to whom contemporaneous bodily harm of some sort might reasonably have been foreseen. It is arguably reasonable to impose liability for the physical consequences of emotional distress where the defendant's negligent conduct might have caused physical injury by direct impact but did not. The problem with the zone of danger rule, however, is that it is an inadequate measure of the reasonable foreseeability of the possibility of physical injury resulting from a parent's anxiety arising from harm to his child. The reasonable foreseeability of such a physical injury to a parent does not turn on whether that parent was or was not a reasonable prospect for a contemporaneous injury because of the defendant's negligent conduct. Although the zone of danger rule tends to produce more reasonable results than the *Spade* rule and provides a means of limiting the scope of a defendant's liability, it lacks strong logical support.

In 1968, the Supreme Court of California, by a divided court (four to three), broke the solid ranks, overruled its decision in *Amaya v. Home Ice, Fuel & Supply Co.*, * * * and held that a cause of action was properly stated on behalf of a mother, in no danger herself, who witnessed her minor daughter's death in a motor vehicle accident allegedly caused by the defendant's negligence, and who sustained emotional disturbance and shock to her nervous system which caused her physical and mental pain and suffering. Dillon v. Legg, 68 Cal.2d 728, 69 Cal.Rptr. 72, 441 P.2d 912 (1968). An intermediate appellate court in California has since applied the reasoning of *Dillon v. Legg* to permit recovery by a mother who came on the scene of the accident but did not witness it. Archibald v. Braverman, 275 Cal.App.2d 253, 79 Cal.Rptr. 723 (1969). That court said, "Manifestly, the shock of seeing a child severely injured immediately after the tortious event may be just as profound as that experienced in witnessing the accident itself." *Id.* at 256, 79 Cal.Rptr. at 725.[19]

Some tendency toward allowing recovery seems to be developing. The Supreme Court of Rhode Island has reached the same conclusion as the California Supreme Court in *Dillon v. Legg*, on substantially similar facts. D'Ambra v. United States, 114 R.I. 643, 338 A.2d 524 (1975). The results in these cases have the general support of commentators. * * * In Leong v. Takasaki, 55 Haw. 398, 399, 520 P.2d 758, 760 (1974), the Supreme Court of Hawaii held that a complaint stated a cause of action "for nervous shock and psychic injuries suffered without accompanying physical impact or resulting physical consequences" when the plaintiff, a ten-year old boy, witnessed from a distance of several feet the death of his stepfather's

19. In Krouse v. Graham, 19 Cal.3d 59, 76, 137 Cal.Rptr. 863, 872, 562 P.2d 1022, 1031 (1977), the California Supreme Court accepted the view of the *Archibald* case, saying "We confirm the propriety of the expression in *Archibald, supra*, that the *Dillon* requirement of 'sensory and contemporaneous observance of the accident' does not require a *visual* perception of the impact causing the death or injury" (emphasis in original).

mother who was struck by a motor vehicle driven by the defendant. In Toms v. McConnell, 45 Mich.App. 647, 207 N.W.2d 140 (1973), the Michigan Court of Appeals held that a mother alleged a cause of action where, from outside the zone of danger, she saw her daughter struck by the defendant's vehicle after her daughter alighted from a school bus and, as a result, the mother sustained significant depression. * * *

It is not argued seriously here, nor has it been regularly a basis for decisions denying liability, that the threat of fraudulent claims requires the adoption of a rule denying recovery to a parent who sustains physical harm from distress over peril to his child. * * * The facts of cases of this character involve tortious injury to the child and substantial physical consequences to the parent. The tortfeasor is not confronted with the results of a fleeting instance of fear or excitement of which he might be unaware and against which he would be unable to present a defense. The fact that some claims might be manufactured or improperly expanded cannot justify the wholesale rejection of all claims. Of course, there is no suggestion that the physical injuries to Mr. and Mrs. Dziokonski were contrived. We have rejected the idea that tort liability in particular classes of cases must be denied because of the threat of fraud. * * *[20] We have chosen to leave the detection of fraud and collusion to the adversary process. * * *

The fact that the causal connection between a parent's emotional response to peril to his child and the parent's resulting physical injuries is difficult to prove or disprove cannot justify denying all recovery. No one asserts, and we have never claimed, that physical reactions to emotional responses do not occur. * * * We have recognized liability for exclusively emotional reactions to tortious conduct in particular circumstances * * *.[21] We have upheld claims of the character involved here, as so called "parasitic" claims, where they are accompanied by a traditional form of tortious injury. * * * Indeed, certain elements of pain and suffering, recoverable in almost all personal injury actions, may be as tenuous causally as the harm for which recovery is sought in these cases.

The scope of duty in tort is often defined in terms of the reasonable foreseeability of the harm to the plaintiff resulting from the defendant's negligent conduct. Sometimes, liability is predicated on a judicial characterization that the defendant owed a duty to the plaintiff, or that the defendant's negligence was the proximate cause of the plaintiff's injury, or that the defendant is liable for the natural and probable consequences of his conduct. Each of these characterizations is actually a conclusion and is not a helpful guide to arriving at the proper answer in a given set of circumstances. We think reasonable foreseeability is a proper starting point in determining whether an actor is to be liable for the consequences of his negligence. Measured by this standard, it is clear that it is reasonably foreseeable that, if one negligently operates a motor vehicle so as to injure a person, there will be one or more persons sufficiently attached

20. [Ed. note] The court here refers to recent cases abrogating, in the context of motor vehicle accidents, inter-spousal and parent/child immunity from suit. *See* Chapter 22, *infra.*

21. [Ed. note] The court here refers to cases recognizing the action for intentional infliction of mental distress. *See* Chapter 17, *infra.*

emotionally to the injured person that he or they will be affected. See Tobin v. Grossman, 24 N.Y.2d 609, 615, 301 N.Y.S.2d 554, 249 N.E.2d 419 (1969), where the New York Court of Appeals acknowledged this fact but denied recovery for other reasons. The problem, however, is that the class of persons vicariously affected by the tortfeasor's conduct may be large. This concern has prompted many courts to deny all liability. * * * They perceive no logical place at which to impose reasonable limits on the scope of a defendant's liability without going to the full extent of reasonable foreseeability, which would produce, as they see it, a risk of liability disproportionate to the defendant's culpability. The result has been that, as a matter of policy, courts have decided not to give full effect to reasonable foreseeability and have adopted limitations on liability, such as the impact rule or the zone of danger rule.[22]

Every effort must be made to avoid arbitrary lines which "unnecessarily produce incongruous and indefensible results." Mone v. Greyhound Lines, Inc., 368 Mass. 354, 365, 331 N.E.2d 916, 922 (1975)(Braucher, J., dissenting). The focus should be on underlying principles. *Id.* In cases of this character, there must be both a substantial physical injury and proof that the injury was caused by the defendant's negligence. Beyond this, the determination whether there should be liability for the injury sustained depends on a number of factors, such as where, when, and how the injury to the third person entered into the consciousness of the claimant, and what degree there was of familial or other relationship between the claimant and the third person. * * * It does not matter in practice whether these factors are regarded as policy considerations imposing limitations on the scope of reasonable foreseeability (see R. E. Keeton, Legal Cause in the Law of Torts 66 [1963]), or as factors bearing on the determination of reasonable foreseeability itself. The fact is that, in cases of this character, such factors are relevant in measuring the limits of liability for emotionally based injuries resulting from a defendant's negligence. In some instances, it will be clear that the question is properly one for the trier of fact, while in others the claim will fall outside the range of circumstances within which there may be liability.

With these considerations in mind, we conclude that the allegations concerning a parent who sustains substantial physical harm as a result of severe mental distress over some peril or harm to his minor child caused by the defendant's negligence state a claim for which relief might be granted, where the parent either witnesses the accident or soon comes on the scene while the child is still there. This conclusion is not inconsistent with opinions of the highest courts in California * * *, Hawaii * * *,[23] and

22. Keating, J., dissenting alone in *Tobin v. Grossman, supra* * * * , urged that there was no reason to place any restraints on reasonable foreseeability where there was "stringent evidence of causation and of actual injury."

23. The Supreme Court of Hawaii may be read to have gone further than other courts. However, that court has denied recovery to one who was not located a reasonable distance from the scene of the accident. Kelley v. Kokua Sales & Supply, Ltd., 56 Haw. 204, 532 P.2d 673 [1975]. That result is expressed in part on the ground that the consequences were not reasonably foreseeable (death in California following word of the death in Hawaii of the deceased's daughter and granddaughter). That court also states, however, that no duty of care applies to one who was not located within a reasonable distance from the scene of the accident.

Rhode Island * * *,[24] and of informed commentators on the subject. * * *

On this premise, we think it clear that the complaint concerning Mrs. Dziokonski states a claim which withstands a motion to dismiss. The allegations of the complaint concerning Mr. Dziokonski, however, are far more indefinite. We do not know where, when or how Mr. Dziokonski came to know of the injury to his daughter and the death of his wife. We do not have a clear indication of the relationship of his discovery of this information to any mental distress and physical injury he sustained. We cannot say, as matter of law, that, within the scope of the allegations of the complaint concerning Mr. Dziokonski, there are no circumstances which could conceivably justify recovery. Consequently, we conclude that neither of the complaints should be dismissed for failure to state a claim.

Judgments reversed.

QUIRICO, JUSTICE (dissenting).

Although I am in full agreement with the court in its conclusion that *Spade v. Lynn & Boston R. R.*, * * * should be overruled, I do not believe that liability should be extended to the degree described by the court in its opinion here. Therefore, I dissent from the reversal of the dismissal of the complaints of the two plaintiffs.

It is my view that liability for negligently causing emotional distress that results in physical injury should be extended as far as would be allowed by the rule of the Restatement (Second) of Torts § 313 (1965). That section, while allowing recovery under some circumstances, provides that no recovery may be had for "illness or bodily harm of another which is caused by emotional distress arising solely from harm or peril to a third person, unless the negligence of the actor has otherwise created an unreasonable risk of bodily harm to the other." I would agree also that if, contrary to the facts in the present cases, a parent[25] had been present at the time of the alleged negligent conduct which caused the injury, and such parent had suffered emotional distress and resulting physical injury, then he or she should recover regardless of whether they were within the zone of risk of bodily harm created by the negligent act. * * * I do not believe, however, that liability should be extended further to allow recovery by a parent who comes on the scene of an accident after an injury has occurred to the child but before the child is removed. It is my opinion that we should not prescribe rules that allow or deny recovery by the parent on the basis of the speed and efficiency of an ambulance team in responding to an accident call, or on the haste with which a parent can be notified and rushed to the accident scene.

Notes

1. In Mitchell v. Rochester Railway, 151 N.Y. 107, 45 N.E. 354 (1896), the New York Court of Appeals decided that no action could lie in negligence for physical injuries caused by fright in the absence of any physical impact. In that case the team of horses pulling one of the defendant's horse cars turned

24. In each of these cases, however, the plaintiff witnessed the accident.

25. Although a parent was involved in the present cases, I believe the rule should apply similarly if a spouse or other close relative witnessed negligent conduct and injury.

towards the plaintiff as she was standing upon a crosswalk waiting to board another of the defendant's cars. When the horses were brought to a stop "she stood between the horses' heads." The plaintiff "testified that from fright and excitement caused by the approach and proximity of the team she became unconscious, and also that the result was a miscarriage, and consequent illness." There was "medical testimony * * * to the effect that the mental shock which she then received was sufficient to produce that result." The court noted that the weight of authority was against recovery. It also declared "[i]f the right of recovery in this class of cases should be once established, it would naturally result in a flood of litigation in cases where the injury may be easily feigned * * * and where the damages must rest upon mere conjecture or speculation." Displaying, however, less willingness to rely merely upon public policy grounds, as had the early Massachusetts cases, such as Spade v. Lynn & Boston Railroad, 168 Mass. 285, 47 N.E. 88 (1897), discussed in *Dziokonski*, the New York court continued:

> Moreover, it cannot be properly said that the plaintiff's miscarriage was the proximate result of the defendant's negligence. * * * The injuries to the plaintiff were plainly the result of an accidental or unusual combination of circumstances, which could not have been reasonably anticipated * * * and hence her damages were too remote to justify a recovery in this action. These considerations lead to the conclusion that no recovery can be had for injuries sustained by fright occasioned by the negligence of another, where there is no immediate personal injury.

2. *Mitchell* and *Spade* became leading cases in establishing what was for a time the universal American doctrine that no action would lie for negligent infliction of mental suffering absent some physical impact. An earlier Privy Council case, Victorian Railway Commissioners v. Coultas, 13 App.Cas. 222 (1888), had reached the same conclusion, but in Dulieu v. White & Sons, [1901] 2 K.B. 669, Kennedy, J., refused to follow that lead. In a case factually very similar to *Mitchell*, and in which both *Mitchell* and *Spade* were cited by the defendant's counsel, and discussed in his judgment, Kennedy, J., held that an action would lie, at least where the plaintiff feared for her own safety rather than for that of her husband who was standing close-by.

The requirement that the plaintiff must fear for his/her own safety was relaxed in Hambrook v. Stokes Brothers, [1925] 1 K.B. 141 (C.A.). Thereafter the English cases talked in terms of reasonable foreseeability of injury. It was thus determined that it was not reasonably foreseeble that a "fish-wife," who alighted from a tram and saw the mangled remains of a motorcyclist who had just been killed after negligently ramming into the tram, would deliver a still-born child. Bourhill v. Young, [1943] A.C. 92 (Sc.). Their Lordships' speeches are unclear as to whether the case stands for the proposition that mental distress was not a foreseeable consequence of the motorcyclist's negligence or whether the plaintiff's idiosyncratic condition in being eight months pregnant made her an unforeseeable plaintiff. Subsequently, in King v. Phillips, [1953] 1 Q.B. 429 (C.A.), a mother who heard her son scream and looked out her window to see her son's tricycle under a taxicab some 70 or 80 yards away was held to be "outside the range of reasonable anticipation." The boy, it developed, was fortunately not injured. But, subsequently, in Boardman v. Sanderson, [1964] 1 W.L.R. 1317 (C.A.), recovery was allowed to a father who had stepped inside a garage office to pay a bill, heard his son scream, and came out to find the wheel of an automobile resting on the boy's foot. The father helped to release his son. Then in Chadwick v. British Railway Board, [1967] 1 W.L.R.

912 (Q.B.), a man who had been asked to help rescue the victims of a ghastly train wreck developed severe mental symptoms and eventually died. In a wrongful death action one defense was that the man had had some mental illness some 20 years previously necessitating his brief confinement in a mental institution and that therefore this made him an idiosyncratic or unforeseeable plaintiff. In allowing recovery, the court rejected the argument. It noted his long period of normal life and observed that, in the modern world, it was generally recognized that the presence of some degree of mental problems was not all that unusual.

3. Courts in the United States were slow to follow the lead of the English courts. While a number of states were prepared to abandon the impact requirement, they adopted in its place a "zone of danger" requirement. The plaintiff, himself or herself, had to be directly threatened with physical injury.[26] A leading case illustrating this stage of legal development is Waube v. Warrington, 216 Wis. 603, 258 N.W. 497 (1935), which noted with approval the movement away from the impact requirement but expressly disapproved of the extension of liability made by *Hambrook v. Stokes Brothers* to include those whose own personal safety had not been threatened. However, Wisconsin has now abandoned the zone of danger rule in favor of the general rule of foreseeability, discussed in note 4, below. Bowen v. Lumbermens Mut. Cas. Co., 183 Wis.2d 627, 517 N.W.2d 432 (1994).

Although it had become a minority position in America the impact rule lingered. It was finally repudiated by New York in Battalla v. State, 10 N.Y.2d 237, 219 N.Y.S.2d 34, 176 N.E.2d 729 (1961), in a 4–3 decision. Pennsylvania was an even later convert. Niederman v. Brodsky, 436 Pa. 401, 261 A.2d 84 (1970). Perhaps surprisingly, the impact rule has been recently strongly reaffirmed in Oregon. Hammond v. Central Lane Communications Center, 312 Or. 17, 816 P.2d 593 (1991), noted at 71 Or. L. Rev. 219 (1992).

4. The first American case to extend liability beyond the zone of physical danger was Dillon v. Legg, 68 Cal.2d 728, 69 Cal.Rptr. 72, 441 P.2d 912 (1968). In *Dillon*, the defendant had negligently run over and killed a young girl while she was crossing the street. The accident was witnessed by the girl's mother and sister. The sister was arguably within the zone of danger; the mother was not. Writing for the majority Tobriner, J., began by noting the incongruity of allowing the sister to bring an action for negligent infliction of mental distress but denying a cause of action to the mother who was only a few feet further away. In holding that the mother had stated a valid cause of action, the court set down the following guidelines:

> We note, first, that we deal here with a case in which plaintiff suffered a shock which resulted in physical injury and we confine our ruling to that case. In determining, in such a case, whether defendant should reasonably foresee the injury to plaintiff, or, in other terminology, whether defendant

---

26. In applying this doctrine, one controversy concerned whether the person within the zone of danger who suffered the mental shock must have actually feared for his own safety rather than for the safety of someone else, as a mother might suffer fright at the prospect of injury to her child without focusing on the danger to herself. Although one might think that this would be a somewhat sterile controversy—of concern only to academics—the distinction has been insisted upon in several cases. *See* Strazza v. McKittrick, 146 Conn. 714, 156 A.2d 149 (1959); Klassa v. Milwaukee Gas Light Co., 273 Wis. 176, 77 N.W.2d 397 (1956). Interestingly, both cases have recently been overruled and the distinction relied upon abandoned. See Clohessy v. Bachelor, 237 Conn. 31, 675 A.2d 852 (1996) and Bowen v. Lumbermens Mut. Cas. Co., 183 Wis.2d 627, 517 N.W.2d 432 (1994).

owes plaintiff a duty of due care, the courts will take into account such factors as the following: (1) Whether plaintiff was located near the scene of the accident as contrasted with one who was a distance away from it. (2) Whether the shock resulted from a direct emotional impact upon plaintiff from the sensory and contemporaneous observance of the accident, as contrasted with learning of the accident from others after its occurrence. (3) Whether plaintiff and the victim were closely related, as contrasted with an absence of any relationship or the presence of only a distant relationship.

The evaluation of these factors will indicate the *degree* of the defendant's foreseeability: obviously defendant is more likely to foresee that a mother who observes an accident affecting her child will suffer harm than to foretell that a stranger witness will do so. Similarly, the degree of foreseeability of the third person's injury is far greater in the case of his contemporaneous observance of the accident than that in which he subsequently learns of it. The defendant is more likely to foresee that shock to the nearby, witnessing mother will cause physical harm than to anticipate that someone distant from the accident will suffer more than a temporary emotional reaction. All these elements, of course, shade into each other; the fixing of obligation, intimately tied into the facts, depends upon each case.

In light of these factors the court will determine whether the accident and harm was *reasonably* foreseeable. Such reasonable foreseeability does not turn on whether the particular defendant as an individual would have in actuality foreseen the exact accident and loss; it contemplates that courts, on a case-to-case basis, analyzing all the circumstances, will decide what the ordinary man under such circumstances should reasonably have foreseen. The courts thus mark out the areas of liability, excluding the remote and unexpected.

5. *Dillon v. Legg* was soon followed in Rodrigues v. State, 52 Hawaii 156, 472 P.2d 509 (1970), where recovery for the negligent infliction of mental distress was permitted in a case where the defendant's negligence had never directly threatened anyone's safety but merely led to property damage. In that case, owing to the state highway department's negligence in maintaining a drainage culvert, the plaintiffs' dream house was flooded shortly before they were to move in. The case is somewhat *sui generis*.[27] *Dillon* was rejected, however, in Tobin v. Grossman, 24 N.Y.2d 609, 301 N.Y.S.2d 554, 249 N.E.2d 419 (1969). In *Tobin*, although the complaint alleged that the mother had seen the accident, it developed that she had not in fact done so. Rather the mother heard the screech of brakes. She then went immediately to the scene of the accident, which was a few feet away, and saw her injured child lying on the ground. Writing for the court Chief Judge Breitel declared:

> The problem of unlimited liability is suggested by the unforeseeable consequence of extending recovery for harm to others than those directly

27. *But cf.* Hunsley v. Giard, 87 Wn.2d 424, 553 P.2d 1096 (1976), a case distinguishable on its facts because there were people in the house when a car crashed into it and the plaintiff suffered some bruises when a floor collapsed, in which the court approved *Rodrigues'* extension of liability to foreseeable victims of foreseeable risks. In Campbell v. Animal Quarantine Station, 63 Hawaii 557, 632 P.2d 1066 (1981), the court affirmed, on the basis of *Rodrigues*, an award of $1,000 to the plaintiffs and three of their four children, for their emotional suffering from learning that their family dog had suffocated, owing to the defendant's negligence, while in quarantine.

involved in the accident. If foreseeability be the sole test, then once liability is extended the logic of the principle would not and could not remain confined. It would extend to older children, fathers, grandparents, relatives, or others *in loco parentis*, and even to sensitive caretakers, or even any other affected bystanders. Moreover, in any one accident, there might well be more than one person indirectly but seriously affected by the shock of injury or death to the child.

The factor of unduly burdensome liability is a kind of dollars-and-cents argument. It does not vanish, however, by reference to wide-spread or compulsory insurance. Constantly advancing insurance costs can become an undue burden as well, and the aggregate recoveries in a single accident of this kind are not likely to stay within ordinary, let alone, compulsory insurance liability limits.

The final and most difficult factor is any reasonable circumscription, within tolerable limits required by public policy, of a rule creating liability. Every parent who loses a child or whose child of any age suffers an injury is likely to sustain grievous psychological trauma, with the added risk of consequential physical harm. Any rule based solely on eyewitnessing the accident could stand only until the first case comes along in which the parent is in the immediate vicinity but did not see the accident. Moreover, the instant advice that one's child has been killed or injured, by telephone, word of mouth, or by whatever means, even if delayed, will have in most cases the same impact. The sight of gore and exposed bones is not necessary to provide special impact on a parent. Again, the logical difficulty of excluding the grandparent, the relatives, or others *in loco parentis*, and even the conscientious and sensitive caretaker, from a right to recover, if in fact the accident had the grave consequences claimed, raises subtle and elusive hazards in devising a sound rule in this field.

This case is particularly illustrative—just because the pretrial examination reveals that if the pleaded cause of action is sustained the trial court will be faced not with an eyewitness mother, but with one who comes upon the scene immediately following the accident.

Beyond practical difficulties there is a limit to attaining essential justice in this area. While it may seem that there should be a remedy for every wrong, this is an ideal limited perforce by the realities of this world. Every injury has ramifying consequences, like the ripplings of the waters, without end. The problem for the law is to limit the legal consequences of wrongs to a controllable degree. The risks of indirect harm from the loss or injury of loved ones is pervasive and inevitably realized at one time or another. Only a very small part of that risk is brought about by the culpable acts of others. This is the risk of living and bearing children. It is enough that the law establishes liability in favor of those directly or intentionally harmed.

The suggestion in *Tobin v. Grossman* that recovery might be allowed to someone who witnessed injury to another and who was also threatened with physical injury was expressly adopted by the New York Court of Appeals in Bovsun v. Sanperi, 61 N.Y.2d 219, 473 N.Y.S.2d 357, 461 N.E.2d 843 (1984). The Appellate Division more recently has held that the mother of twins, one of which was delivered stillborn and the other of which died an hour after birth, could not recover for the negligent infliction of emotional distress. Sceusa v. Mastor, 135 A.D.2d 117, 525 N.Y.S.2d 101 (4th Dept.1988). The cesarean operation by which the infants had been delivered was held not to be a "threat of physical injury" to the mother.

Initially most courts that considered the issue opted to follow the lead of *Tobin* and rejected *Dillon v. Legg*. *See* Note, *Negligent Infliction of Mental Distress: Reaction to* Dillon v. Legg *in California and Other States*, 25 Hast.L.J. 1248 (1974); Note, *Negligent Infliction of Emotional Distress: Keeping* Dillon *in Bounds*, 37 W. & L.L.Rev. 1235 (1980). *See also* Rickey v. Chicago Transit Authority, 98 Ill.2d 546, 75 Ill.Dec. 211, 457 N.E.2d 1 (1983). In recent years, however, a growing number of jurisdictions have, like Massachusetts in *Dziokonski*, accepted *Dillon*. *See, e.g.*, Sinn v. Burd, 486 Pa. 146, 404 A.2d 672 (1979); Portee v. Jaffee, 84 N.J. 88, 417 A.2d 521 (1980); Barnhill v. Davis, 300 N.W.2d 104 (Iowa 1981); Culbert v. Sampson's Supermarkets, Inc., 444 A.2d 433 (Me.1982); Ramirez v. Armstrong, 100 N.M. 538, 673 P.2d 822 (1983); Paugh v. Hanks, 6 Ohio St.3d 72, 451 N.E.2d 759 (1983); Clohessy v. Bachelor, 237 Conn. 31, 675 A.2d 852 (1996). For an overview of the subject, *see* K. Turezyn, *When Circumstances Provide a Guarantee of Genuineness: Permitting Recovery for Pre–Impact Emotional Distress*, 28 B.C.L.Rev. 881 (1987). For a review of the law in California, *see* Comment, *Clarifying California's Approach to Claims of Negligent Infliction of Emotional Distress*, 39 U.S.F.L. Rev. 227 (1995).

6. If a jurisdiction is prepared to abandon the zone of physical danger requirement, is there any justification for restricting recovery to (close?) relatives? In Leong v. Takasaki, 55 Hawaii 398, 520 P.2d 758 (1974), recovery was allowed in favor of a step-grandchild. But in Drew v. Drake, 110 Cal. App.3d 555, 168 Cal.Rptr. 65 (1980), recovery was denied to a woman who had witnessed "the killing in a vehicular collision caused by respondent's negligence" of her "de facto spouse" with whom she had lived "continuously for three years." The question finally was decided by the Supreme Court of California in Elden v. Sheldon, 46 Cal.3d 267, 250 Cal.Rptr. 254, 758 P.2d 582 (1988). In that case, the plaintiff and a woman with whom the plaintiff alleged he had an "unmarried cohabitation relationship which was both stable and significant and parallel to a marital relationship" were riding together in the same car when the accident which killed the woman occurred. The Supreme Court of California upheld dismissal of the complaint. Except perhaps for the relationships of foster parents and foster children and for step-parenting relationships, the court was not prepared to extend liability beyond nuclear family relationships. New Jersey, on the other hand, has allowed an unmarried cohabitant (a fiance) to recover, Dunphy v. Gregor, 136 N.J. 99, 642 A.2d 372 (1994). *See also*, Note, *The Right of a Cohabitant to Recover in Tort: Wrongful Death, Negligent Infliction of Emotional Distress and Loss of Consortium*, 32 U. Louisville J. Fam. L. 531 (1993–94).

In adopting the zone of danger approach, the United States Supreme Court has allowed a railroad employee who witnessed the death of a fellow worker to recover for negligent infliction of emotional injury under the Federal Employers' Liability Act, but did not allow other workers who had not been on the scene to recover. Consolidated Rail Corp. v. Gottshall, 512 U.S. 532, 114 S.Ct. 2396, 129 L.Ed.2d 427 (1994).

7. In *Dillon v. Legg, supra*, the court declared:

> We further note, at the outset, that defendant has interposed the defense that the contributory negligence of the mother, the sister, and the child contributed to the accident. If any such defense is sustained and

defendant found not liable for the death of the child because of the contributory negligence of the mother, sister or child, we do not believe that the mother or sister should recover for the emotional trauma which they allegedly suffered. In the absence of the primary liability of the tort-feasor for the death of the child, we see no ground for an independent and secondary liability for claims for injuries by third parties. The basis for such claims must be adjudicated liability and fault of defendant; that liability and fault must be the foundation for the tort-feasor's duty of due care to third parties who, as a consequence of such negligence, sustain emotional trauma.

Leaving aside the modifications that would have to be made now that California has adopted comparative negligence (*see* Chapter Five, *supra*), why should the negligence of the primary victim affect the recovery of the bystander? As the dissent of Burke, J., pointed out, California no longer imputes negligence in husband-wife and parent-child situations. At most, to the extent permitted by the growing abrogation of tort immunity in those situations, the bystander might also have an action against the relative whose negligence contributed to the event which caused the bystander's mental distress. Nevertheless, in *Portee v. Jaffee*, *supra* note 5, the New Jersey Supreme Court declared

> * * * To allow a plaintiff seeking damages for emotional injuries to recover a greater proportion than the injured party would surely create liability in excess of the defendant's fault. We therefore hold that any recovery for emotional harm resulting from perceiving the death or serious injury to another shall be reduced by the proportion of the injured party's negligence, as well as, of course, any contributory negligence of the plaintiff himself.

The general issues involving derivative actions will be looked at in depth in Chapter 11.

8. Almost all the cases involve situations in which what we have called the primary victim was either killed or seriously injured. Indeed in *Portee v. Jaffee*, *supra* note 5, the New Jersey court insisted that the bystander would have no cause of action if this were not the case. *See also*, Clohessy v. Bachelor, 237 Conn. 31, 675 A.2d 852 (1996). Nevertheless, in *Barnhill v. Davis*, *supra* note 5, the plaintiff was driving one car and was followed by his mother driving another car. Owing to the defendant's negligence, there was a collision with the mother's car. The mother was "slightly bruised." The plaintiff son alleged that "he * * * suffered emotional distress because of his fear for his mother's safety. He contends the emotional distress has caused pain in his back and legs, dizziness, and difficulty in sleeping." The Iowa court held that the son had stated a cause of action. The issue was whether "a reasonable person in the position of the bystander would believe, and the bystander did believe, that the direct victim of the accident would be seriously injured or killed."

9. The important English case, McLoughlin v. O'Brian, [1983] A.C. 410 (1982), [1982] 2 W.L.R. 982, 2 All E.R. 298, involved

> a very serious and tragic road accident which occurred on October 19, 1973, near Withersfield, Suffolk. The appellant's husband, Thomas McLoughlin, and three of her children, George, aged 17, Kathleen, aged 7, and Gillian, nearly 3, were in a Ford motor car: George was driving. A fourth child, Michael, then aged 11, was a passenger in a following motor car driven by Mr. Pilgrim: this car did not become involved in the accident.

* * * It is admitted that the accident to the Ford car was caused by the respondents' negligence. It is necessary to state what followed in full detail.

As a result of the accident, the appellant's husband suffered bruising and shock; George suffered injuries to his head and face, cerebral concussion, fractures of both scapulae and bruising and abrasions; Kathleen suffered concussion, fracture of the right clavicle, bruising, abrasions and shock; Gillian was so seriously injured that she died almost immediately.

At the time, the appellant was at her home about two miles away; an hour or so afterwards the accident was reported to her by Mr. Pilgrim, who told her that he thought George was dying, and that he did not know the whereabouts of her husband or the condition of her daughter. He then drove her to Addenbrooke's Hospital, Cambridge. There she saw Michael, who told her that Gillian was dead. She was taken down a corridor and through a window she saw Kathleen, crying, with her face cut and begrimed with dirt and oil. She could hear George shouting and screaming. She was taken to her husband who was sitting with his head in his hands. His shirt was hanging off him and he was covered in mud and oil. He saw the appellant and started sobbing. The appellant was then taken to see George. The whole of his left face and left side was covered. He appeared to recognise the appellant and then lapsed into unconsciousness. Finally, the appellant was taken to Kathleen who by now had been cleaned up. The child was too upset to speak and simply clung to her mother. There can be no doubt that these circumstances, witnessed by the appellant, were distressing in the extreme and were capable of producing an effect going well beyond that of grief and sorrow.

* * * At the trial, the judge assumed, for the purpose of enabling him to decide the issue of legal liability, that the appellant subsequently suffered the condition of which she complained. This was described as severe shock, organic depression and a change of personality. Numerous symptoms of a physiological character are said to have been manifested. The details were not investigated at the trial, the court being asked to assume that the appellant's condition had been caused or contributed to by shock, as distinct from grief or sorrow, and that the appellant was a person of reasonable fortitude.

Disagreeing with the trial judge and the Court of Appeal, who had ruled for the respondents, the House of Lords held that the plaintiff had stated a cause of action. The plaintiff was analogized to one who came upon the immediate aftermath of an accident and also to a rescuer. On the latter point, see Chadwick v. British Railway Board, [1967] 1 W.L.R. 912, 2 All E.R. 945, where recovery was allowed on behalf of a rescuer in a particularly gory rail accident. The closeness of the relationship of the plaintiff to the victim and her proximity to the accident were all relevant factors. In the Court of Appeal, [1981] 2 W.L.R. 1014 (1980), which ruled against the plaintiff, Stephenson and Griffiths, L.JJ., expressed the view that the mental injury of survivors would be prolonged and even exacerbated by the anxieties of litigation. Do you think there is any validity to this point?

Dillon v. Legg was cited and discussed by the British judges but *Dziokonski* was not brought to their attention. Whether someone who did not actually witness the accident can recover for negligent infliction of emotional distress was an issue that for many years had escaped a ruling by the Supreme Court of

California. Finally, however, in Thing v. La Chusa, 48 Cal.3d 644, 257 Cal.Rptr. 865, 771 P.2d 814 (1989), that court ruled that a woman, who neither saw nor heard the accident, but became aware of the injury to her son when she was told by her daughter, and who rushed to the scene to see her bloody and unconscious child, whom she believed was dying, lying on the road, could not recover for the negligent infliction of emotional distress. The court reaffirmed the *Dillon* restrictions limiting recovery to close relatives who are present at the "injury-producing event" and who are aware that this event is causing injury to the victim. To recover, moreover, such persons must suffer "serious emotional distress"—that is, a reaction beyond that which would be anticipated in a disinterested witness. The court rejected the suggestion in Ochoa v. Superior Court, 39 Cal.3d 159, 216 Cal.Rptr. 661, 703 P.2d 1 (1985), that the *Dillon* requirements are not absolutely essential in all cases. The *Ochoa* case involved a mother who pleaded with the authorities in a juvenile hall in which her son was being held, to release him into her custody so that she could take him to her own doctor. The boy died of pneumonia, which had been misdiagnosed at first as a cold and later as the flu. The mother was held to have a cause of action for the emotional trauma she suffered in watching her sick boy being denied adequate treatment. The mother was surprisingly subsequently characterized in the *Thing* case as having been a direct victim of the defendant's negligence. *Cf.* p. 527, *infra.* Finally, in Kelley v. Kokua Sales & Supply Ltd., 56 Hawaii 204, 532 P.2d 673 (1975), mentioned in *Dziokonski, supra,* a man who suffered a fatal heart attack in California upon learning of the death of his daughter and granddaughter in a vehicular accident in Hawaii was held not to be a foreseeable victim of that accident.

Should actions seeking recovery on the basis of strict liability for the sale of defective products also provide a basis for recovering for "mere" emotional distress? There are a few cases holding that bystanders could recover for injury to relatives in such circumstances. *See* Shepard v. Superior Court, 76 Cal.App.3d 16, 142 Cal.Rptr. 612 (1977); Walker v. Clark Equipment, 320 N.W.2d 561 (Iowa 1982). *See also* Kately v. Wilkinson, 148 Cal.App.3d 576, 195 Cal.Rptr. 902 (1983) (wife and child of boat owner were held to be "users" of the product and thus were able to state a claim for direct injuries when a friend of the daughter was killed owing to an alleged defect in the boat). *But see* Rahn v. Gerdts, 119 Ill.App.3d 781, 74 Ill.Dec. 378, 455 N.E.2d 807 (1983). For a good discussion of the subject, *see* J. Silverman, *Recovery for Emotional Distress in Strict Products Liability,* 61 Chi–Kent L.Rev. 545 (1985).

MOLIEN v. KAISER FOUNDATION HOSPITALS
Supreme Court of California, 1980.
27 Cal.3d 916, 167 Cal.Rptr. 831, 616 P.2d 813.

Mosk, Justice.

To what extent should the law permit recovery of damages for the negligent infliction of emotional or mental distress unaccompanied by physical injury? We consider this question in two contexts, both presented by an action charging defendants with erroneously diagnosing plaintiff's wife as suffering from an infectious social disease.

Appealing from a judgment entered after a demurrer was sustained, plaintiff asks us to decide whether he may recover for negligently inflicted emotional distress and for loss of consortium, occasioned by emotional injury to his wife. As will appear, in the light of contemporary knowledge we conclude that emotional injury may be fully as severe and debilitating as physical harm, and is no less deserving of redress; the refusal to recognize a cause of action for negligently inflicted injury in the absence of some physical consequence is therefore an anachronism. We further conclude that it is no less regressive to deny recovery for loss of consortium simply because the plaintiff's spouse has suffered a disabling but non-physical injury. Accordingly, the judgment must be reversed and plaintiff permitted to go to trial.

Plaintiff Stephen H. Molien filed this action against Kaiser Foundation Hospitals (Kaiser) and Thomas Kilbridge, M.D. (Kaiser and Dr. Kilbridge are hereafter sometimes referred to collectively as defendants.) The amended complaint sets forth two causes of action. * * *

The principal allegations of the first cause of action are as follows: Plaintiff and his wife, Valerie G. Molien, are members of the Kaiser Health Plan. Mrs. Molien went to Kaiser for a routine multiphasic physical examination. There, Dr. Kilbridge, a Kaiser staff physician, negligently examined and tested her, and subsequently advised her she had contracted an infectious type of syphilis. The diagnosis was erroneous, as she did not in fact have the disease. Nevertheless she was required to undergo treatment for syphilis, including the administration of massive and unnecessary doses of penicillin. As a result of defendants' conduct she suffered "injury to her body and shock and injury to her nervous system."

Defendants knew plaintiff husband would learn of the diagnosis, as they instructed Mrs. Molien to so advise him. Thereafter plaintiff was required to undergo blood tests himself in order to ascertain whether he had contracted syphilis and was the source of his wife's purported infection. The tests revealed that he did not have the disease.

As a result of the negligently erroneous diagnosis, plaintiff's wife became upset and suspicious that he had engaged in extra-marital sexual activities; tension and hostility arose between the two, "causing a break-up of their marriage and the initiation of dissolution proceedings."

Defendants knew or should have known their diagnosis that plaintiff's wife had syphilis and that he might also have the disease would cause him emotional distress. He has in fact suffered "extreme emotional distress" as a result of the negligent misdiagnosis. Additionally, he has incurred medical expenses for counseling in an effort to save the marriage.

The second cause of action, after incorporating by reference all the allegations of the first, alleges that as a consequence of defendants' acts plaintiff has been deprived of the "love, companionship, affection, society, sexual relations, solace, support, and services" of his wife.

The prayer is for damages for mental suffering and loss of consortium, together with medical expenses. The trial court sustained general demurrers to both causes of action, and plaintiff appealed from the ensuing judgment of dismissal.

II

We turn now to the merits of the appeal and first address plaintiffs' contention that he has stated a cause of action for the negligent infliction of emotional distress. Defendants maintain this issue is governed by Dillon v. Legg (1968) 68 Cal.2d 728, 69 Cal.Rptr. 72, 441 P.2d 912; they emphasize that plaintiff was not present when the doctor announced the erroneous diagnosis, but learned of it later from his wife. As we shall explain, however, defendants rely too heavily on *Dillon*: the case is apposite, but not controlling.

A

It must be remembered, however, that in *Dillon* the plaintiff sought recovery of damages she suffered as a percipient witness to the injury of a third person, and the three guidelines there noted served as a limitation on that particular cause of action. * * * Here, by contrast, plaintiff was himself a direct victim of the assertedly negligent act. By insisting that the present facts fail to satisfy the first and second of the *Dillon* criteria, defendants urge a rote application of the guidelines to a case factually dissimilar to the bystander scenario. In so doing, they overlook our explicit statement in *Dillon* that an obligation hinging on foreseeability "must necessarily be adjudicated only upon a case-by-case basis. * * * [N]o immutable rule can establish the extent of that obligation for every circumstance in the future." * * *

Hence the significance of *Dillon* for the present action lies not in its delineation of guidelines fashioned for resolution of the precise issue then before us; rather, we apply its general principle of foreseeability to the facts at hand, much as we have done in other cases presenting complex questions of tort liability. * * *

In the case at bar the risk of harm to plaintiff was reasonably foreseeable to defendants. It is easily predictable that an erroneous diagnosis of syphilis and its probable source would produce marital discord and resultant emotional distress to a married patient's spouse; Dr. Kilbridge's advice to Mrs. Molien to have her husband examined for the disease confirms that plaintiff was a foreseeable victim of the negligent diagnosis. Because the disease is normally transmitted only by sexual relations, it is rational to anticipate that both husband and wife would experience anxiety, suspicion, and hostility when confronted with what they had every reason to believe was reliable medical evidence of a particularly noxious infidelity.

We thus agree with plaintiff that the alleged tortious conduct of defendant was directed to him as well as to his wife. Because the risk of harm to him was reasonably foreseeable we hold, in negligence parlance, that under these circumstances defendants owed plaintiff a duty to exercise due care in diagnosing the physical condition of his wife. There remains the question whether plaintiff is barred from recovery by the fact that he suffered no physical injury.

B

* * * Whether legal protection should extend to the interest in emotional tranquility has been a subject of controversy not only in California,

but elsewhere: "No general agreement has yet been reached as to the liability for negligence resulting in fright, shock, or other 'mental suffering,' or its physical consequences." (Prosser, Torts (4th ed. 1971) § 54, p. 327.) The issue, not novel, has inspired numerous and substantial scholarly expositions since the turn of the century. * * *

As early as 1896, this court recognized that mental suffering "constitutes an aggravation of damages when it naturally ensues from the act complained of." (Sloane v. Southern Cal. Ry. Co. (1896) 111 Cal. 668, 680, 44 P. 320, 322.) But such suffering alone, we said, would not afford a right of action. (*Ibid.*) We pondered the question whether a nervous disorder suffered by the plaintiff after she was wrongfully put off a train was a physical or a mental injury * * *. "* * * It is a matter of general knowledge that an attack of sudden fright, or an exposure to imminent peril, has produced in individuals a complete change in their nervous system, and rendered one who was physically strong and vigorous weak and timid. Such a result must be regarded as an injury to the body rather than to the mind, even though the mind be at the same time injuriously affected." (*Ibid.*)

The foundation was thus laid, nearly a century ago, for two beliefs that have since been frequently reiterated: first, recovery for emotional distress must be relegated to the status of parasitic damages; and second, mental disturbances can be distinctly classified as either psychological or physical injury. That medical science and particularly the field of mental health have made much progress in the 20th century is manifest; yet, despite some noteworthy exceptions, the principles underlying the decision in *Sloane* still pervade the law of negligence.

The present state of the law is articulated in BAJI No. 12.80 (6th ed. 1977): "There can be no recovery of damages for emotional distress unaccompanied by physical injury where such emotional distress arises only from negligent conduct. * * *"

Plaintiff urges that we recognize the concept of negligent infliction of emotional distress as an independent tort. In this inquiry we first seek to identify the rationale for the *Sloane* rule. None appears in the opinion, possibly because the court classified the plaintiff's condition, "nervous paroxysm," as a physical injury, and hence had no need to justify a denial of recovery for psychological injury alone. Neither did the *Espinosa* court provide any justification for its rejection of the plaintiff's attempt to "subvert the ancient rule that mental suffering alone will not support an action for damages based upon negligence." (114 Cal.App.2d at p. 234, 249 P.2d at p. 844.) Therefore, we must look elsewhere.

The primary justification for the requirement of physical injury appears to be that it serves as a screening device to minimize a presumed risk of feigned injuries and false claims. * * * Such harm is believed to be susceptible of objective ascertainment and hence to corroborate the authenticity of the claim.

Although most courts still adhere to the early view, the scholars assert that such artificial barriers to recovery are unnecessary. Thus Dean Prosser explains that "the difficulty is not insuperable. Not only fright and shock, but other kinds of mental injury are marked by definite physical symptoms, which are capable of clear medical proof. It is entirely possible to allow recovery only upon satisfactory evidence and deny it when there is nothing to corroborate the claim, or to look for some guarantee of genuineness in the circumstances of the case. The problem is one of proof, and it will not be necessary to deny a remedy in all cases because some claims may be false." (Prosser, *op. cit. supra,* at p. 328 * * *.)

The foregoing analysis was expressly adopted by the New York Court of Appeals when it held that "Freedom from mental disturbance is now a protected interest in this State." (Ferrara v. Galluchio (1958) 5 N.Y.2d 16, 176 N.Y.S.2d 996, 999, 152 N.E.2d 249, 252.) The case involved a medical malpractice action brought by a patient who, after receiving negligently administered X-ray treatments from the defendants, consulted a dermatologist who advised her to exercise certain precautions because the area of the X-ray burn might become cancerous. The plaintiff alleged she developed a severe "cancerphobia" and sought damages for mental anguish. In affirming a jury verdict for the plaintiff, the New York high court deemed it "entirely plausible, under such circumstances, that plaintiff would undergo exceptional mental suffering over the possibility of developing cancer." * * *

Ferrara represents a view not generally followed in California. Our courts have instead devised various means of compensating for the infliction of emotional distress, provided there is some assurance of the validity of the claim. As we have seen, physical injury, whether it occurs contemporaneously with or is a consequence of emotional distress, provides one such guarantee. * * * Another arises when the plaintiff asserts an independent cause of action apart from personal injury. Thus in a suit against an insurer for damages resulting from its wrongful refusal to settle a claim against the insured within the policy limits, the plaintiff was permitted to recover for mental distress as well as for pecuniary loss. * * *

Finally, intentional torts will support an award of damages for emotional distress alone, but only in cases involving "extreme and outrageous intentional invasions of one's mental and emotional tranquility." * * * As we explained in State Rubbish etc. Assn. v. Siliznoff (1952) 38 Cal.2d 330, 338, 240 P.2d 282, it is the outrageous conduct that serves to insure that the plaintiff experienced serious mental suffering and convinces the courts of the validity of the claim.

We thus reach the crucial question whether continued adherence to the venerable rule that would bar recovery in this case is warranted. Although we recognize a need to guard against fraudulent claims, we are not persuaded that the presently existing artificial lines of demarcation are the only appropriate means of attaining this goal. * * *

The Hawaii Supreme Court confronted the issue forthrightly and discarded the traditional rule that there can be no recovery for the negligent infliction of emotional distress alone. (Rodrigues v. State (1970) 52 Haw. 156, 472 P.2d 509.) It explained that "Courts which have administered claims of mental distress incident to an independent cause of action are just as competent to administer such claims when they are raised as an independent ground for damages." * * * Moreover, defendants will not be exposed to potentially unlimited liability for invasions of emotional tranquility that are trivial and transient if recovery is limited to claims of serious mental distress. The court therefore adopted as its standard: "serious mental distress may be found where a reasonable man, normally constituted, would be unable to adequately cope with the mental stress engendered by the circumstances of the case." * * *

The *Rodrigues* court further noted the "multiplication of psychic stimuli" that society presently faces, and the "increasing widespread knowledge of the debilitating effect mental distress may have on an individual's capacity to carry on the functions of life." * * * Accordingly, the court recognized that "the interest in freedom from negligent infliction of serious mental distress is entitled to independent legal protection. We hold, therefore, that there is a duty to refrain from the negligent infliction of serious mental distress." * * *

We agree that the unqualified requirement of physical injury is no longer justifiable. It supposedly serves to satisfy the cynic that the claim of emotional distress is genuine. Yet we perceive two significant difficulties with the scheme. First, the classification is both overinclusive and under-inclusive when viewed in the light of its purported purpose of screening false claims. It is overinclusive in permitting recovery for emotional distress when the suffering accompanies or results in any physical injury whatever, no matter how trivial. If physical injury, however slight, pro-vides the ticket for admission to the courthouse, it is difficult for advocates of the "floodgates" premonition to deny that the doors are already wide open * * *.

The second defect in the requirement of physical injury is that it encourages extravagant pleading and distorted testimony. Thus it has been urged that the law should provide a remedy for serious invasions of emotional tranquility, "otherwise the tendency would be for the victim to exaggerate symptoms of sick headaches, nausea, insomnia, etc., to make out a technical basis of bodily injury, upon which to predicate a parasitic recovery for the more grievous disturbance, the mental and emotional distress she endured." (Magruder, *Mental and Emotional Disturbance in the Law of Torts* (1936) 49 Harv.L.Rev. 1033, 1059 * * *.)

Furthermore, as we observed in *Sloane v. Southern Cal. Ry. Co.*, supra, * * * the border between physical and emotional injury is not clearly delineated. In 1896 we deemed a "nervous shock or paroxysm" to be distinguishable from mere mental anguish. Today, the notion that physical harm includes "shock to the nervous system" is an accepted aspect of our law of negligence. (See BAJI No. 12.71 (6th ed. 1977).) The Restatement, too, attempts to draw the distinction: "The rule [precluding recovery for negligently caused emotional distress alone] applies to all forms of emotional disturbance, including temporary fright, nervous shock, nausea, grief, rage, and humiliation. The fact that these are accompanied by transitory, non-recurring physical phenomena, harmless in themselves, such as dizziness, vomiting, and the like, does not make the actor liable where such phenomena are in themselves inconsequential and do not amount to any substantial bodily harm. On the other hand, long continued nausea or headaches may amount to physical illness, which is bodily harm; and even long continued mental disturbance * * * may be classified by the courts as illness, notwithstanding [its] mental character. This becomes a medical or psychiatric problem, rather than one of law." (Rest.2d Torts, § 436A; com. c.)

In our view the attempted distinction between physical and psychological injury merely clouds the issue. The essential question is one of proof; whether the plaintiff has suffered a serious and compensable injury should not turn on this artificial and often arbitrary classification scheme. We thus agree with the view of the *Rodrigues* court: "In cases other than where proof of mental distress is of a medically significant nature, [citations] the general standard of proof required to support a claim of mental distress is some guarantee of genuineness in the circumstances of the case." * * * This standard is not as difficult to apply as it may seem in the abstract. As Justice Traynor explained in this court's unanimous opinion in *State Rubbish etc. Assn. v. Siliznoff*, supra, * * * the jurors are best situated to determine whether and to what extent the defendant's conduct caused emotional distress, by referring to their own experience. In addition, there will doubtless be circumstances in which the alleged emotional injury is susceptible of objective ascertainment by expert medical testimony. * * * To repeat: this is a matter of proof to be presented to the trier of fact. The screening of claims on this basis at the pleading stage is a usurpation of the jury's function.

More than half a century ago Roscoe Pound recognized that claims of emotional distress were capable of verification by means more precise than the then-prevailing requirement of physical impact; we think his logic applies equally to the present requirement of physical injury: "In reality [the impact requirement] was a practical rule, growing out of the limitations of trial by jury, the difficulty of proof in cases of injuries manifest subjectively only and the backwardness of our knowledge with respect to the relations of mind and body. In view of the danger of imposition, the courts, on a balance of the interests involved, refused to go beyond cases where there was a voucher for the truth of the plaintiff's claim * * *. With the rise of modern psychology the basis of this caution in securing an important element of the interest of personality was removed." (Pound, Interpretations of Legal History (1923) pp. 120–121.)

For all these reasons we hold that a cause of action may be stated for the negligent infliction of serious emotional distress. Applying these principles to the case before us, we conclude that the complaint states such a cause of action. The negligent examination of Mrs. Molien and the conduct flowing therefrom are objectively verifiable actions by the defendants that foreseeably elicited serious emotional responses in the plaintiff and hence serve as a measure of the validity of plaintiff's claim for emotional distress. * * *

It follows that the trial court erred in sustaining the demurrer to the cause of action for emotional distress.

III

The court also erred in sustaining the demurrer to the cause of action for loss of consortium. Both parties focus, appropriately, on our decision in Rodriguez v. Bethlehem Steel Corp., supra, 12 Cal.3d 382, 115 Cal.Rptr. 765, 525 P.2d 669, in which this cause of action had its genesis in

California. After rejecting a number of arguments against such recovery, we held that "each spouse has a cause of action for loss of consortium, as defined herein, caused by a negligent or intentional injury to the other spouse by a third party." * * *

The negligently inflicted injury in *Rodriguez* consisted of an extensive and permanent paralysis of the plaintiff's husband caused when he was struck on the head by a falling pipe weighing over 600 pounds. Defendants now urge that we limit the general principle there announced to the factual context in which it arose, and hold that the cause of action for loss of consortium requires severe physical injury to the nonplaintiff spouse. But nowhere in our opinion did we restrict its rule to the particular facts then before us. Defendants think it significant that we referred to Mr. Rodriguez's condition as a "severely disabling injury" and understood the personal loss suffered by the spouse of a "severely disabled person." * * * These simple descriptive phrases, however, will not support the inference defendants seek to draw: obviously a person may become "severely disabled" mentally no less than physically, and the resulting detriment to that individual's spouse is no less serious than if the disability were an impairment of mobility or other bodily function.[28]

Two years after *Rodriguez* the Massachusetts Supreme Court addressed this issue directly and recognized a cause of action for loss of consortium arising out of severe emotional distress intentionally inflicted on the plaintiff's spouse: "the underlying purpose of such an action is to compensate for the loss of the companionship, affection and sexual enjoyment of one's spouse, and it is clear that these can be lost as a result of psychological or emotional injury as well as from actual physical harm." (Agis v. Howard Johnson Company (1976) 371 Mass. 140, 355 N.E.2d 315, 320.) The same reasoning applies when, as here, the alleged injury is negligently inflicted.[29]

Finally, defendants present no persuasive reasons to justify their proposal to limit recovery for loss of consortium to cases in which the plaintiff's spouse suffers severe physical injury. Indeed, we perceive compelling grounds for not drawing this line. It is true our opinion in *Rodriguez* contemplates injury to the nonplaintiff spouse that is sufficiently serious and disabling to raise the inference that the conjugal relationship is more than superficially or temporarily impaired. As we earlier explained, however, it is irrefutable that certain psychological injuries can be no less

28. We are aware of the allegation herein that Mrs. Molien suffered "injury to her body and shock and injury to her nervous system." Thus defendants contend that neither trivial physical injury nor emotional injury is adequate to support a cause of action for loss of consortium. But since we have concluded above that the distinction between physical injury and emotional distress is no longer defensible, we do not uphold the present cause of action solely on the ground that *some* physical injury was alleged.

29. There is a paucity of authority from other jurisdictions. An Alabama court held, with no analysis, that the cause of action for

loss of consortium is "premised upon a physical injury suffered by the spouse." (Slovensky v. Birmingham News Co., Inc. (Ala.Civ. App.1978) 358 So.2d 474, 477.) In New York a plaintiff was apparently permitted to recover for loss of consortium when his wife developed a "cancerphobia" caused by the defendants' negligent medical malpractice. The propriety of the award, however, was not before the Court of Appeals when it reviewed the judgment in favor of the wife for her own mental anguish. (Ferrara v. Galluchio, supra, 5 N.Y.2d 16, 176 N.Y.S.2d at p. 998, 152 N.E.2d 249.)

severe and debilitating than physical injuries. We could accept defendants' position only by rejecting the manifest truth that a marital relationship can be grievously injured when one spouse suffers a traumatically induced neurosis, psychosis, chronic depression, or phobia.

Whether the degree of harm suffered by the plaintiff's spouse is sufficiently severe to give rise to a cause of action for loss of consortium is a matter of proof. When the injury is emotional rather than physical, the plaintiff may have a more dificult task in proving negligence, causation, and the requisite degree of harm; but these are questions for the jury, as in all litigation for loss of consortium. In *Rodriguez* we acknowledged that the loss is "principally a form of mental suffering" * * * but nevertheless declared our faith in the ability of the jury to exercise sound judgment in fixing compensation. (*Ibid.*) We reaffirm that faith today.

CLARK, JUSTICE, dissenting.

I dissent.

Our court today allows—for the first time—a money award against one who unintentionally disturbs the mental tranquillity of another.

Because such disturbances are commonplace in our complex society, because they cannot be objectively observed or measured, but mainly because it is for the Legislature to create new causes of action and to fix the limits of recovery, this court has until today refused the invitation to open wide the door to damage claims fraught with potential abuse.

Good reason exists for denying recovery for plaintiffs' claim although the majority appear to acknowledge none. * * *[30] The requirement of a concurrence of physical injury with claimed emotional distress is a safeguard eliminating spurious claims for negligently inflicted mental distress. That safeguard is now abandoned in favor of newly declared standards designed by the majority opinion to limit recoveries under their new, independent tort. A plaintiff claiming his or her mental tranquillity has been disturbed can now recover " 'where proof of mental distress is of a medically significant nature,' "or the claim of mental distress is supported by " 'some guarantee of genuineness in the circumstances of the case.' " * * * In applying these standards, jurors are said to be "best situated to determine whether and to what extent the defendant's conduct caused emotional distress, by referring to their own experience." * * * Such standards are nonstandards, opening wide the door to abuse.

The majority incorrectly rely on *State Rubbish etc. Assn. v. Siliznoff* * * * for their contention that jurors are best situated to determine if a defendant's conduct causes emotional distress warranting recovery of damages pursuant to standards fixed by today's majority. However, *Siliznoff* deals with *intentional* infliction of fright, the court stating that jurors are

30. The majority are encouraged to today's decision by Dean Prosser's longstanding advocacy. (*Ante,* pp. 835, 836–837.) However, even he recognizes the reasons for the current rule, stating immediately before language quoted by the majority (*ante,* at p. 836): "It is now more or less generally conceded that the only valid objection against recovery for mental injury is the danger of vexatious suits and fictitious claims, which has loomed very large in the opinions as an obstacle. The danger is a real one, and must be met. Mental disturbance is easily simulated, and courts which are plagued with fraudulent personal injury claims may well be unwilling to open the door to an even more dubious field." (Prosser, Torts (4th ed. 1971) § 54, p. 328.)

"ordinarily in a better position * * * to determine whether *outrageous conduct* results in mental distress than whether that distress in turn results in physical injury." * * * A different and difficult medical question is presented when the resulting *traumatic effect* of mental distress must be determined. It is this question which the majority would depend on jurors to answer. Relying on a medical study (Smith, *Relations of Emotions to Injury and Disease* (1944) 30 Va.L.Rev. 193), this court concluded in *Amaya* that questions of the effects of emotional distress would not be easy ones for jurors. "Here that 'difficult medical question' cannot be so easily avoided. In the cited article * * * Dr. Smith * * * concludes (1) that 'a majority of persons claiming injury from psychic causes possessed subnormal resistance to [psychic] stimuli'; (2) that 'In only 55 of the 301 cases surveyed could we say actual causation was proved by a preponderance of substantial and credible evidence'; and (3) that hence 'The skeptical courts were * * * correct in doubting whether adequate criteria of proof existed in this field to make administration of a remedy feasible. Law, in a commendable desire to be forward looking, outran scientific standards. Taking all cases decided between 1850 and 1944 * * * the net balance of justice would have been greater had all courts denied damages for injury imputed to psychic stimuli alone.' " * * * No empirical evidence exists and the record fails to establish that psychiatrists and jurors have since become better equipped to evaluate the traumatic effects of psychic stimuli.

The resolution of conflicts the majority would leave to jurors, "as doctors well know * * * often borders on fancy when the causation of alleged psychoneural disorders is at issue. * * * Much timeliness remains in Dr. Smith's warning (*id.*, at p. 212 of 30 Va.L.Rev.) that 'eagerness to be progressive may cause extravagant credulity and injury to scientific standards of proof.' Extravagant credulity, of course, means ultimate injustice." * * *

The fundamental problem is not foreseeing (by unguided hindsight) the consequences of unintentional conduct, but rather realistically limiting liability for those consequences. "It is unthinkable that any one shall be liable to the end of time for all the results that follow in endless sequence from his single act. Causation cannot be the answer; in a very real sense the consequences of an act go forward to eternity, and back to the beginning of the world." (Prosser, *Palsgraf Revisited* (1953) 52 Mich. L.Rev. 1, 24.) In a system compensating injury based on fault, consideration must be given to the "moral blame attached to the defendant's conduct" * * * in fixing liability. When the defendant's act is merely negligent rather than intentional, lesser moral blame attaches, cautioning against extending liability. * * * Liability should be proportionate to the actor's culpability, having in mind the utility and necessity of the conduct negligently performed. Where, as here, imposition of liability is far disproportionate to the degree of culpability, we do a disservice to the public— who must ultimately bear the cost—by sanctioning claims for hurt feelings.[31]

31. The majority's new cause of action will surely suggest to even the less ingenious a vehicle for avoiding prior limitations on certain causes of actions. For instance, while we have not for some time recognized a cause for alienation of affections—an intentional tort—the net effect of today's judgment is to permit recovery for emotional distress and

The signatories to the majority opinion have—in cases where the balance has weighed more heavily in favor of liability than in the instant case—refused for policy reasons to extend liability. In Borer v. American Airlines (1977) 19 Cal.3d 441, 138 Cal.Rptr. 302, 563 P.2d 858, this court noted that "foreseeable injury to a legally recognized relationship" does not necessarily postulate a cause of action, and that "social policy must at some point intervene to delimit liability. * * * 'Every injury has ramifying consequences, like the ripplings of the waters, without end. The problem for the law is to limit the legal consequences of wrongs to a controllable degree.' " * * *[32] The author of today's majority opinion has also properly cautioned against imposition of new burdens on the courts: "As Chief Justice Burger lamented in United States v. Richardson (1974) 418 U.S. 166: 'As our society has become more complex, our numbers more vast, our lives more varied, and our resources more strained, citizens increasingly request the intervention of the courts on a greater variety of issues than at any period of our national development.' " (Carsten v. Psychology Examining Committee of the Board of Medical Quality Assurance (1980) 27 Cal.3d 793, p. 801, 166 Cal.Rptr. 844, p. 849, 614 P.2d 258, p. 281, fn. 2.)

The majority's creation of new consequences for old acts is wrong. The judgment should be affirmed.

Notes

It remains to be seen whether the *Molien* case represents the wave of the future with regard to the expansion of the range of the cause of action for negligent infliction of mental distress. The question whether conduct which might be said directly to injure one person may also be said to be "directed" towards another is an exceedingly difficult one. There have always been cases that have allowed recovery for mental distress by relatives for the mishandling of a corpse. Indeed a cause of action for such conduct is expressly recognized by *Restatement (Second) of Torts* § 868. Somewhat comparable situations involve the failure to deliver telegrams announcing the death of close relatives. *See, e.g.,* Russ v. Western Union Tel. Co., 222 N.C. 504, 23 S.E.2d 681 (1943); *cf.,* Western Union Tel. Co. v. Thomas, 209 Ala. 657, 96 So. 873 (1923). By analogy to these cases, in Johnson v. State, 37 N.Y.2d 378, 372 N.Y.S.2d 638, 334 N.E.2d 590 (1975), a daughter was allowed to bring an action for emotional distress when she had been erroneously advised, by the state hospital in which her senile mother was living, that her mother had died. Whether or not these cases can always be said to represent conduct directed towards the plaintiffs, in many situations, such as in the case of corpses and to a lesser extent incompetent human beings, if the relative cannot sue for what might be considered to be socially undesirable conduct on the part of the defendant, then no one can. Even in the case of the undelivered telegrams, if the recipient is unable to bring an action, the only person who could bring an action would be the sender who

---

loss of consortium caused by even the negligent alienation of plaintiff's wife's affections by defendant. And in a case of slander where the plaintiff is unable to establish all conditions to recovery for this intentional tort, cannot he now obtain relief by alleging his mental tranquility was disturbed—even negligently—by defendant's utterances?

32. [Ed. note] The *Borer* case refused to recognize a cause of action for loss of parental consortium. The plaintiffs were the nine children of a woman injured by the fall of a lighting fixture in the defendant's terminal at Kennedy Airport in New York.

contracted with the telegraph company, and presumably his damages would be largely limited to the cost of the telegram.

In deciding when someone has been the direct victim of tortious conduct that has injured another person, the California courts, subsequent to *Molien*, seem to have adopted the criterion of whether the plaintiff could be considered some kind of third-party beneficiary of a contract for the provision of medical services, as was the case in *Molien* itself. *See* Newton v. Kaiser Hosp., 184 Cal.App.3d 386, 228 Cal.Rptr. 890 (1986); Marchand v. Superior Court, 200 Cal.App.3d 1121, 246 Cal.Rptr. 531 (1988), *review granted*, 250 Cal.Rptr. 267, 758 P.2d 595 (1988). In Ochoa v. Superior Court, 39 Cal.3d 159, 216 Cal.Rptr. 661, 703 P.2d 1 (1985), also discussed at p. 516, *supra*, a woman who watched her son suffer from the defendant juvenile hall's failure to treat him for pneumonia was held to have a cause of action for emotional distress that arose from her witnessing this failure to treat; but it was expressly held that she did *not* have a cause of action under *Molien* because she was not a direct victim of the defendant's inaction. *See also* Cordts v. Boy Scouts of America, Inc., 205 Cal.App.3d 716, 252 Cal.Rptr. 629 (1988)(mother whose two sons were sexually molested by scout leader was held not to be a direct victim of the tortious conduct). *Cf.* Frame v. Kothari, 115 N.J. 638, 560 A.2d 675 (1989)(Parents could not recover for emotional distress against a physician who had misdiagnosed the condition of their child who had been injured in a fall and who eventually died; recovery limited to damages for wrongful death). In Marlene F. v. Affiliated Psychiatric Med. Clinic, Inc., 48 Cal.3d 583, 257 Cal.Rptr. 98, 770 P.2d 278 (1989), on the other hand, a mother whose son was claimed to have been sexually abused by a therapist, who had been counselling both the mother and the son, was held to have a cause of action for negligent infliction of emotional distress under the "direct victim" theory of *Molien*.

In Burgess v. Superior Court, 2 Cal.4th 1064, 9 Cal.Rptr.2d 615, 831 P.2d 1197 (1992), the California court said:

> The board language of the *Molien* decision coupled with its perceived failure to establish criteria for characterizing a plaintiff as a "direct victim" rather than a "bystander" has subjected *Molien* to criticism from various sources, including this court. The great weight of this criticism has centered upon the perception that *Molien* introduced a new method for determining the existence of a duty, limited only by the concept of foreseeability. To the extent that *Molien* * * * stands for this proposition, it should not be relied upon and its discussion of duty is limited to its facts.

In Huggins v. Longs Drug Stores California, Inc., 6 Cal.4th 124, 862 P.2d 148, 24 Cal.Rptr.2d 587 (1993), the pharmacy defendant had given directions on a prescription for the son of the plaintiffs indicating five times the dosage ordered by the doctor. The parents sued to recover for their emotional distress from having unwittingly injured their son by giving him the overdose. They claimed to be "direct" victims of the pharmacy's negligence. The court held, however, that the legal duties imposed upon pharmacists did not include the duty to avoid emotional injury to parents of the patient. The duties reached only to the patient, himself or herself, even when the pharmacist was aware that the patient was an infant and that the parents would be administering the drug. The court concluded:

> If a child is seriously injured by erroneous medical treatment caused by professional negligence, the parent is practically certain to suffer correspondingly serious emotional distress. But even if it were deemed

reasonably foreseeable to a pediatrician, or a pharmacist, that a parent's realization of unwitting participation in the child's injury would by itself be a source of significant emotional distress from guilt, anxiety, or otherwise, that foreseeability would not warrant our establishing a new right of recovery for intangible injury. (See Thing v. La Chusa, supra, 48 Cal.3d 644, 666–667, 257 Cal.Rptr. 865, 771 P.2d 814; Bily v. Arthur Young & Co., supra, 3 Cal.4th 370, 398–399, 11 Cal.Rptr.2d 51, 834 P.2d 745.)

The duty that the Court of Appeal would impose upon pharmacists would inevitably enlarge the potential liabilities of practically all providers of medical goods and services obtained by parents solely for the treatment of their children, or by other caregivers solely for the treatment of dependent family members. All those providers, unlike the providers of care to competent adult patients, would be exposed to new claims of emotional distress allegedly incurred in administering the prescribed medication or treatment to the patient. That expansion of potential liability not only would increase medical malpractice insurance costs but also would tend to "inject undesirable self-protective reservations" impairing the provision of optimal care to the patient. * * *

Because plaintiffs were not the patients for whom defendant dispensed the prescribed medication, they cannot recover as direct victims of defendant's negligence.

What is left of *Molien* after these decision? The significant retreat from the possible reach of the *Molien* opinion in these later cases, reflects, at least in part, the dramatic change in the make-up of the California Supreme Court during this period.

BOYLES v. KERR

Supreme Court of Texas, 1993.
855 S.W.2d 593.

OPINION ON MOTION FOR REHEARING

PHILLIPS, CHIEF JUSTICE.

Respondent's motion for rehearing is overruled. Our opinion of December 2, 1992, is withdrawn and the following is substituted in its place.

This is a suit for the negligent infliction of emotional distress. We hold that there is no general duty in Texas not to negligently inflict emotional distress. A claimant may recover mental anguish damages only in connection with defendant's breach of some other legal duty. Because Respondent proceeded below only on the theory of negligent infliction of emotional distress, we reverse the judgment of the court of appeals in her favor. 806 S.W.2d 255. However, in the interest of justice, we remand for a new trial.

I

On August 10, 1985, Petitioner Dan Boyles, Jr., then seventeen, covertly videotaped nineteen-year-old Respondent Susan Leigh Kerr engaging in sexual intercourse with him. Although not dating steadily, they had known each other a few months and had shared several previous sexual encounters. Kerr testified that she had not had sexual intercourse prior to her relationship with Boyles.

Kerr and Boyles, who were both home in Houston for the summer, had made plans to go out on the night of the incident. Before picking Kerr up, Boyles arranged with a friend, Karl Broesche, to use the Broesche house for sexual intercourse with Kerr. Broesche suggested videotaping the activity, and Boyles agreed. Broesche and two friends, Ray Widner and John Paul Tamborello, hid a camera in a bedroom before Kerr and Boyles arrived. After setting up the camera, the three videotaped themselves making crude comments and jokes about the activity that was to follow. They left with the camera running, and the ensuing activities were recorded.

Boyles took possession of the tape shortly after it was made, and subsequently showed it on three occasions, each time at a private residence. Although he showed the tape to only ten friends, gossip about the incident soon spread among many of Kerr and Boyles' friends in Houston. Soon many students at Kerr's school, Southwest Texas State University, and Boyles' school, the University of Texas at Austin, also became aware of the story. Kerr did not learn of the video until December 1985, long after she and Boyles had stopped seeing each other. After she confronted him, Boyles eventually admitted what he had done and surrendered the tape to Kerr. No copies had been made.

Kerr alleges that she suffered humiliation and severe emotional distress from the videotape and the gossip surrounding it. At social gatherings, friends and even casual acquaintances would approach her and comment about the video, wanting to know "what [she] was going to do" or "why did [she] do it." The tape stigmatized Kerr with the reputation of "porno queen" among some of her friends, and she claimed that the embarrassment and notoriety affected her academic performance. Kerr also claimed that the incident made it difficult for her to relate to men, although she testified to having had subsequent sexually-active relationships. Eventually, she sought psychological counselling.

Kerr sued Boyles, Broesche, Widner and Tamborello, alleging intentional invasion of privacy, negligent invasion of privacy, and negligent (but not intentional) infliction of emotional distress. Before the case was submitted to the jury, however, Kerr dropped all causes of action except for negligent infliction of emotional distress. The jury returned a verdict for Kerr on that claim, assessing $500,000 in actual damages. The jury also found that all defendants were grossly negligent, awarding an additional $500,000 in punitive damages, $350,000 of which was assessed against Boyles. The trial court rendered judgment in accordance with the jury's verdict. * * *

II

Initially, we must determine whether negligent infliction of emotional distress constitutes an independent cause of action in Texas. Kerr claims that we recognized a broad right to recover for negligently inflicted emotional distress in St. Elizabeth Hospital v. Garrard, 730 S.W.2d 649 (Tex.1987). Boyles contends that the Garrard holding is limited to the particular facts of that case.

In Garrard, a hospital negligently disposed of the Garrards' stillborn baby in an unmarked, common grave without the plaintiffs' knowledge or consent. The Garrards sued for negligent infliction of emotional distress, without alleging that they suffered any physical injury. This Court nonetheless concluded that they had stated a cause of action. We determined that "Texas first recognized the tort of negligent infliction of mental anguish in Hill v. Kimball, 76 Tex. 210, 13 S.W. 59 (1890)." 730 S.W.2d at 652. This tort, we said, had been administered under traditional tort concepts, subject only to a refinement on the element of damages: the mental suffering is not compensable unless it manifests itself physically. Id. After determining that the physical manifestation requirement was arbitrary because it "denies court access to persons with valid claims they could prove if permitted to do so," id., we proceeded to abolish it. 730 S.W.2d at 654.

The Court then proceeded, we believe, to create a general duty not to inflict reasonably foreseeable emotional distress. The Court said: Clearly, freedom from severe emotional distress is an interest which the law should serve to protect. * * * Having recognized that an interest merits protection, it is the duty of this court to continually monitor the legal doctrines of this state to insure the public is free from unwarranted restrictions on the right to seek redress for wrongs committed against them. * * * Thus, we hold that proof of physical injury resulting from mental anguish is no longer an element of the common law action for negligent infliction of mental anguish. * * * Four justices joined in the judgment, but concurred on the grounds that the same result could be reached under the traditional Texas rule allowing emotional distress damages arising from the mishandling of a corpse. * * * The liability standard under this new tort, however, was never entirely clear. Garrard seemed to indicate that "trivial" emotional distress should not be compensated, * * * and similarly that the law should protect against "severe" emotional distress. * * * Rather than articulating any threshold level of severity, however, the Court concluded that "[j]urors are best suited to determine whether and to what extent the defendant's conduct caused compensable mental anguish by referring to their own experience." * * *

While the holding of Garrard was correct, we conclude that its reasoning was based on an erroneous interpretation of Hill v. Kimball, and is out of step with most American jurisdictions. Therefore, we overrule the language of Garrard to the extent that it recognizes an independent right to recover for negligently inflicted emotional distress. Instead, mental anguish damages should be compensated only in connection with defendant's breach of some other duty imposed by law. This was the basis for recovery prior to Garrard, which expanded the scope of liability based on a misconstruction of Hill v. Kimball.

In Hill, a pregnant woman suffered a miscarriage when she witnessed the defendant severely beating two men in her yard. The woman sued for her physical injuries under negligence, claiming that the emotional trauma of witnessing the beatings produced the miscarriage and that the defendant should have reasonably anticipated the danger to her. The Court found that the plaintiff had stated a cause of action. The basis, however, was the physical injury she had suffered, together with her allegation of foreseeability. The Court reasoned as follows: That a physical personal injury may be produced through a strong emotion of the mind there can be no doubt. The fact that it is more difficult to produce such an injury through the operation of the mind than by direct physical means affords no sufficient ground for refusing compensation, in an action at law, when the injury is intentionally or negligently inflicted. * * * Here, according to the allegations of the petition, the defendant has produced a bodily injury by means of that emotion, and it is for that injury that the recovery is sought. * * *

The Court considered only whether the plaintiff could recover for her physical injuries, not whether she could otherwise recover for her emotional distress or mental anguish caused by witnessing the beatings. Furthermore, the Court noted that liability would depend on "whether, under the circumstances, and with the lights before him, a reasonably prudent man would have anticipated the danger to her or not." Id. In other words, the defendant was negligent if he should have known that he was imposing an unreasonable risk of physical injury to the plaintiff, not if he merely should have anticipated that the plaintiff would suffer emotional distress.

Hill, therefore, did not recognize a cause of action for negligent infliction of emotional distress. It merely recognized the right to recover for physical injuries under standard negligence principles, notwithstanding that the physical injury is produced indirectly through emotional trauma. Garrard thus did not merely modify Hill, but created an entirely new cause of action.

The dissent vigorously denounces our abolition of the tort created in Garrard, calling it "controlling precedent" that contains a "rather clear pronouncement" of a new tort affirming "the respect for human dignity." 855 S.W.2d at 608, 607, 605 (Doggett, J., dissenting on rehearing). Garrard, however, ill deserves the lofty pedestal to which the dissent has belatedly elevated it. Even today, the justices of this Court cannot agree on the extent of Garrard 's reach, see infra at 604 (Gonzalez, J., concurring on motion for rehearing), and we have never embraced its broad holding. Thus, in Freeman v. City of Pasadena, 744 S.W.2d 923 (Tex.1988), we limited the bystander cause of action to those persons meeting the criteria of Dillon v. Legg, 68 Cal.2d 728, 69 Cal.Rptr. 72, 80, 441 P.2d 912, 920 (1968), without even citing Garrard as a potential basis for broader liability. * * * Further, the Court held in Reagan v. Vaughn, 804 S.W.2d 463, 466–67 (Tex.1990), that a child could not recover mental anguish damages resulting from a severe injury to a parent, without considering Garrard as a basis for recovery. * * * In fact, this Court has never upheld a recovery under the Garrard tort. * * *

Considering our opinions and those of other Texas courts, as well as the law in most American jurisdictions, Garrard could fairly be characterized as an anomaly rather than a landmark. * * *

By overruling the language of Garrard, we hold only that there is no general duty not to negligently inflict emotional distress. Our decision does not affect a claimant's right to recover mental anguish damages caused by defendant's breach of some other legal duty. See, e.g., Fisher v. Coastal Transp. Co., 149 Tex. 224, 230 S.W.2d 522 (1950)(negligent infliction of direct physical injury); Moore v. Lillebo, 722 S.W.2d 683 (Tex.1986)(wrongful death); Fisher v. Carrousel Motor Hotel, Inc., 424 S.W.2d 627 (Tex.1967)(battery); Stuart v. Western Union Tel. Co., 66 Tex. 580, 18 S.W. 351 (1885)(failure of telegraph company to timely deliver death message); Billings v. Atkinson, 489 S.W.2d 858 (Tex.1973) (invasion of privacy); Leyendecker & Assocs., Inc. v. Wechter, 683 S.W.2d 369 (Tex.1984)(defamation); Pat H. Foley & Co. v. Wyatt, 442 S.W.2d 904 (Tex.Civ.App.—Houston [14th Dist.] 1969, writ ref'd n.r.e.) (negligent handling of corpse).

Also, our holding does not affect the right of bystanders to recover emotional distress damages suffered as a result of witnessing a serious or fatal accident. Texas has adopted the bystander rules originally promulgated by the California Supreme Court in Dillon v. Legg. * * * The policy concerns that require limiting the emotional distress cause of action in the direct victim case generally do not apply in the bystander case. Before a bystander may recover, he or she must establish that the defendant has negligently inflicted serious or fatal injuries on the primary victim. * * *

We also are not imposing a requirement that emotional distress manifest itself physically to be compensable. As explained in Garrard, the sole purpose of the physical manifestation rule is to ensure the genuineness of claims for emotional distress. * * * Garrard criticized this requirement as both under- and overinclusive, id., and we agree. See Julie A. Davies, Direct Actions for Emotional Harm: Is Compromise Possible?, 67 Wash. L.Rev. 1, 24–25 (1992)(the physical manifestation rule "has been criticized on the ground that it has no obvious relation to emotional harm"). Where emotional distress is a recognized element of damages for breach of a legal duty, the claimant may recover without demonstrating a physical manifestation of the emotional distress. This has long been the rule, even before Garrard. * * *

Most other jurisdictions do not recognize a general duty not to negligently inflict emotional distress. Many limit recovery by requiring proof of a physical manifestation.[33] Others allow recovery where the claimant establishes the breach of some independent duty.[34] A few jurisdictions recognize a general right to recover for negligently inflicted emotional distress,[35] but these jurisdictions are squarely in the minority.

We find the experience in California to be instructive. In Molien v. Kaiser Foundation Hospitals, 27 Cal.3d 916, 167 Cal.Rptr. 831, 838–39, 616 P.2d 813, 820–21 (1980), the California Supreme Court abolished the physical injury requirement, apparently creating an independent cause of action for negligently inflicted "serious" emotional distress. Nine years later, however, the court declared that "the negligent causing of emotional distress is not an independent tort....", Marlene F. v. Affiliated Psychiatric Medical Clinic, Inc., 48 Cal.3d 583, 257 Cal.Rptr. 98, 101, 770 P.2d 278, 281 (1989), and that damages are recoverable only where there is a "breach of a duty owed the plaintiff that is assumed by the defendant or imposed on

33. [Ed. note] citing cases from 23 states.

34. [Ed. note] citing cases from 4 states.

35. See Taylor v. Baptist Medical Ctr., Inc., 400 So.2d 369 (Ala.1981); Montinieri v. Southern New England Tel. Co., 175 Conn. 337, 398 A.2d 1180 (1978); Rodrigues v. State, 52 Haw. 156, 472 P.2d 509 (1970); Gammon v. Osteopathic Hosp. of Maine, Inc., 534 A.2d 1282 (Me.1987); Johnson v. Supersave Markets, Inc., 211 Mont. 465, 686 P.2d 209 (1984); Bass v. Nooney Co., 646 S.W.2d 765 (Mo.1983); Johnson v. Ruark Obstetrics and Gynecology Assoc., 327 N.C. 283, 395 S.E.2d 85 (1990); Schultz v. Barberton Glass Co., 4 Ohio St.3d 131, 447 N.E.2d 109 (1983).

the defendant as a matter of law, or that arises out of a relationship between the two." * * * In another case decided shortly after Marlene F., the California Supreme Court further explained as follows:

> [I]t is clear that foreseeability of the injury alone is not a useful "guideline" or a meaningful restriction on the scope of the [negligent infliction of emotional distress] action. The Dillon experience confirms, as one commentator observed, that "[f]oreseeability proves too much.... Although it may set tolerable limits for most types of physical harm, it provides virtually no limit on liability for nonphysical harm." [citing Rabin, Tort Recovery for Negligently Inflicted Economic Loss: A Reassessment, 37 Stan.L.Rev. 1513, 1526 (1985)]. It is apparent that reliance on foreseeability of injury alone in finding a duty, and thus a right to recover, is not adequate when the damages sought are for an intangible injury. In order to avoid limitless liability out of all proportion to the degree of a defendant's negligence, and against which it is impossible to insure without imposing unacceptable costs on those among whom the risk is spread, the right to recover for negligently caused emotional distress must be limited. Thing v. La Chusa, 48 Cal.3d 644, 257 Cal.Rptr. 865, 877–78, 771 P.2d 814, 826–27 (1989).

Last year, the court confirmed that Molien should not be relied on as creating an independent tort for negligent infliction of emotional distress, but that recovery may lie "where a duty arising from a preexisting relationship is negligently breached." Burgess v. Superior Court, 2 Cal.4th 1064, 9 Cal.Rptr.2d 615, 619, 831 P.2d 1197, 1201 (1992). In Burgess, the plaintiff sued her obstetrician for emotional distress caused by the doctor's negligent delivery of the plaintiff's child. The court viewed the claim as a traditional professional malpractice cause of action, which, under California law, supported mental anguish damages. * * * The duty allegedly breached was that arising from the doctor-patient relationship. * * *

Some courts have recognized an independent cause of action for "serious" or "severe" emotional distress. See Schultz v. Barberton Glass Co., 4 Ohio St.3d 131, 447 N.E.2d 109 (1983); Bass v. Nooney Co., 646 S.W.2d 765 (Mo.1983); Rodrigues v. State, 52 Haw. 156, 472 P.2d 509 (1970). This standard, however, fails to delineate meaningfully those situations where recovery should be allowed. As one commentator has explained:

> It is difficult to imagine how a set of rules could be developed and applied on a case-by-case basis to distinguish severe from nonsevere emotional harm. Severity is not an either/or proposition; it is rather a matter of degree. Thus, any attempt to formulate a general rule would almost inevitably result in a threshold requirement of severity so high that only a handful would meet it, or so low that it would be an ineffective screen. A middle-ground rule would be doomed, for it would call upon courts to distinguish between large numbers of cases factually too similar to warrant different treatment. Such a rule would, of course, be arbitrary in its application.

Richard N. Pearson, Liability to Bystanders for Negligently Inflicted Emotional Harm—A Comment on the Nature of Arbitrary Rules, 34 U.Fla. L.Rev. 477, 511 (1982).

We therefore reverse the judgment of the court of appeals in favor of Kerr on the ground of negligent infliction of emotional distress.

* * * The dissent also would find a duty based on a "special relationship" between the parties. We agree that certain relationships may give rise to a duty which, if breached, would support an emotional distress award. * * * [Citing cases dealing with corpes and telegraph messages, referred to earlier in the opinion.] However, there must be some specific duty of care that, under the law, arises from the relationship. The dissent can point to no such duty in this case. The law has heretofore not sought to impose specific legal duties based solely on a personal relationship, even an intimate one. The duties that Boyles owed to Kerr included the general duty not to willfully invade the other's privacy and the duty not to intentionally inflict emotional distress by outrageous conduct. It is unnecessary to recognize some other "special duty" based on the parties' intimate relationship to provide a basis for recovery. * * *

In rejecting negligent infliction of emotional distress as an independent cause of action, we stated in the original opinion that "[t]ort law cannot and should not attempt to provide redress for every instance of rude, insensitive or distasteful behavior, even though it may result in hurt feelings, embarrassment, or even humiliation." We made clear, however, that we did not consider Boyles' conduct to fall into that category, stating in part as follows:

> The tort system can and does provide a remedy against those who engage in such conduct. But an independent cause of action for negligent infliction of emotional distress would encompass conduct far less outrageous than that involved here, and such a broad tort is not necessary to allow compensation in a truly egregious case such as this.

We denied recovery not because Boyles breached no duty toward Kerr, but because the only theory which she chose to assert—negligent infliction of emotional distress—was overly broad and would encompass other cases involving merely rude or insensitive behavior. We reaffirm that conclusion today. * * *

Kerr cannot recover based on the cause of action under which she proceeded. It may well be, however, that she failed to assert and preserve alternative causes of action because of her reliance on our holding in Garrard. We have broad discretion to remand for a new trial in the interest of justice where it appears that a party may have proceeded under the wrong legal theory. * * * Remand is particularly appropriate where the losing party may have presented his or her case in reliance on controlling precedent that was subsequently overruled. * * * It is even more appropriate where we have also subsequently given formal recognition to a cause of action which might be applicable to the facts of this case. See Twyman, supra (expressly recognizing the tort of intentional infliction of emotional distress). We therefore reverse the judgment of the court of appeals and remand this cause to the trial court for a new trial.

Concurring opinion on rehearing by GONZALEZ, J.

* * *

In Texas, a home owners policy covers only accidents or careless conduct and excludes intentional acts. Ms. Kerr's lawyers may have believed that if they obtained a judgment declaring that Boyles' conduct came within the rubric of "negligence" (inadvertence or carelessness), they could tap the homeowners policies owned by the parents of Boyles and the other defendants. Thus, this case has a lot to do with a search for a "deep pocket" who can pay. If the purpose of awarding damages is to punish the wrongdoer and deter such conduct in the future, then the individuals responsible for these reprehensible actions are the ones who should suffer, not the people of Texas in the form of higher insurance premiums for home owners.

This case has nothing to do with gender-based discrimination or an assault on women's rights.[36] There is no reason, other than stereotype, to assume that emotional distress is unique only to women. In fact, as noted in Justice Cornyn's plurality opinion in Twyman v. Twyman, 855 S.W.2d 619, 623 (Tex.1993), almost as many men as women have brought claims for negligent infliction of emotional distress. Furthermore, women as well as men will have to pay higher premiums for their home owners policies if the dissenting justices' views were to prevail.

In sum, Susan Kerr does not need this amorphous cause of action in order to obtain a judgment against the parties actually responsible for her traumatic experience. I concur in the Court's judgment and opinion.

[The hard-hitting dissenting opinions by Justice Doggert are omitted.]

Notes

1. In the bystander cases the English courts have never insisted on the mental distress manifesting itself in physical illness. Citing *Molien*, the California Supreme Court, in Hedlund v. Superior Court, 34 Cal.3d 695, 194 Cal.Rptr. 805, 669 P.2d 41 (1983), ruled that the requirement of physical injury had been abolished in bystander cases. Other American cases dispensing with this requirement and insisting instead that the mental distress be "serious" include Chizmar v. Mackie, 896 P.2d 196 (Alaska 1995); Sinn v. Burd, 486 Pa. 146, 404 A.2d 672 (1979); Barnhill v. Davis, 300 N.W.2d 104 (Iowa 1981); Johnson v. Ruark Obstetrics & Gynecology Assoc., 327 N.C. 283, 395 S.E.2d 85, *reh'g denied,* 327 N.C. 644, 399 S.E.2d 133 (1990); Paugh v. Hanks, 6 Ohio St.3d 72, 451 N.E.2d 759 (1983); St. Elizabeth Hosp. v. Garrard, 730 S.W.2d 649 (Tex.1987)(overruled, as we have just seen, by the *Boyles* case, only on the direct injury issues); Bowen v. Lumbermens Mut. Cas. Co., 183 Wis.2d 627, 517 N.W.2d 432 (1994). *See also* Portee v. Jaffee, 84 N.J. 88, 417 A.2d 521 (1980)(case involved physical injury as a result of mental shock but court does not state that this is necessary). In the *Burgess* case, noted above, the California court, while retreating from the full reach of the *Molien* opinion, explicitly upheld *Molien's* holding that a plaintiff need not show a physical injury or impact. *See also*, Potter v. Firestone Tire & Rubber Co., 6 Cal.4th 965, 25 Cal.Rptr.2d 550, 863 P.2d 795 (1993).

---

36. [Ed. note] The original opinion of the court had received considerable adverse publicity and criticism, partially from "feminist" groups.

2. This more modern position, that physical injury is not a prerequisite of recovery, has introduced a new issue. Several recent cases have dealt with whether a plaintiff can recover for negligent infliction of mental distress when the plaintiff has possibly been exposed to a serious or fatal disease, such as AIDS or cancer, but has either not yet developed any symptoms or has subsequently tested negative. The majority of courts have denied liability, at least where the plaintiff is unable to prove actual exposure, as opposed to the possibility of exposure. *See, e.g.,* Barrett v. Danbury Hosp., 232 Conn. 242, 654 A.2d 748 (1995); K.A.C. v. Benson, 527 N.W.2d 553 (Minn.1995); Carroll v. Sisters of St. Francis Health Services, 868 S.W.2d 585 (Tenn.1993); Funeral Services by Gregory v. Bluefield Community Hospital, 186 W.Va. 424, 413 S.E.2d 79 (1991), *overruled on other grounds,* Courtney v. Courtney, 190 W.Va. 126, 437 S.E.2d 436 (1993)(dealing with the appropriate statute of limitations); Hare v. State, 173 A.D.2d 523, 570 N.Y.S.2d 125 (1991), *appeal denied,* 78 N.Y.2d 859, 575 N.Y.S.2d 455, 580 N.E.2d 1058 (1991). Ohio, in an AIDS exposure case, has gone even further and required that the plaintiff have faced the actual *physical* peril, exposure to the possibility of contracting the disease is not enough. Heiner v. Moretuzzo, 73 Ohio St.3d 80, 652 N.E.2d 664 (1995). Two cases that have recognized the cause of action are Faya v. Almaraz, 329 Md. 435, 620 A.2d 327 (1993); Marchica v. Long Island R.R. Co., 31 F.3d 1197 (2d Cir.1994), *cert. denied,* 513 U.S. 1079, 115 S.Ct. 727, 130 L.Ed.2d 631 (1995)(applying the Federal Employers Liability Act).

The issue has also come up in cases involving exposure to toxic wastes. In Potter v. Firestone Tire & Rubber Co., 6 Cal.4th 965, 25 Cal.Rptr.2d 550, 863 P.2d 795 (1993), the California Supreme Court said that "A toxic ingestion or exposure, without more, does not provide a basis for fearing future physical injury or illness that the law is prepared to recognize as reasonable", in an action to recover for negligent infliction of emotional distress. The court did indicate that the injury might be recoverable under other causes of action.

3. In jurisdictions requiring the mental distress to manifest itself in physical injury, inability to sleep, nausea, loss of appetite, and dizziness have generally not been held to be bodily harm or physical injury. *See Restatement (Second) of Torts* § 436A, Comment *c,* quoted in the majority opinion in *Molien.* But a nervous breakdown or the prolonged presence of such symptoms that seriously interferes with a person's ability to pursue a normal life style has been considered to be enough of a showing of physical injury or bodily harm. *Ibid. See also* Daley v. LaCroix, 384 Mich. 4, 179 N.W.2d 390 (1970). Extremely attenuated physical symptoms were held to be sufficient in Quill v. Trans World Airlines, Inc., 361 N.W.2d 438 (Minn.App.1985), which involved distress occasioned when defendant's plane, which had been cruising at 39,000 feet, rolled over and dove 34,000 feet in an uncontrolled spin that lasted for approximately 40 seconds. *But see* Leaon v. Washington County, 397 N.W.2d 867, 874–75 (Minn.1986), where the plaintiff's face was forced into contact with the private parts of a nude dancer at a stag party, which led to the plaintiff temporarily losing weight and becoming "depressed" and experiencing "feelings of anger, fear, and bitterness." These allegations of physical symptoms were insufficient to support a claim for negligent infliction of emotional distress. *See also* State by Woyke v. Tonka Corp., 420 N.W.2d 624 (Minn.App. 1988) (allegation by couple on whose property toxic chemicals were illegally stored that they no longer slept together and that the woman lost hair were insufficient; recovery limited to physical injury to farm).

C. OWNERS AND OCCUPIERS OF LAND[37]

EARNEST v. REGENT POOL, INC.

Supreme Court of Alabama, 1972.
288 Ala. 63, 257 So.2d 313.

McCALL, JUSTICE.

In this case, the father sues to recover damages for the wrongful death of his nine year old son, allegedly drowned in the swimming pool of the defendant, Regent Pool, Inc., a corporation.

The gravamen of this count is laid in the averments that the defendant's premises, upon which the swimming pool was located, were, for a long time prior to the accident, constantly and persistently visited by members of the public, including children, who used them as a play area, that the defendant knew of this practice or use, or should have known of it, that the defendant was negligent in causing or allowing the swimming pool to be in a dangerous and defective condition, as described in the above count, without providing or maintaining an adequate fence or safeguard around the premises to prevent children from entering them and playing in and about the pool, and in not posting signs to warn them of the dangerous and defective condition of the pool.

The plaintiff does not proceed upon the attractive nuisance doctrine in this count. He submits that the attraction of the dangerous condition on the defendant's premises is merely evidentiary and relevant only to the question of negligence.

It is to be noted from reading the count that the perimeter of the defendant's premises was surrounded by a fence. There is no allegation as to how the deceased entered the fenced-in area, only that the fence was inadequate to prevent children from entering upon the premises and playing in and about the area of the pool. It seems to us that any kind of invitation to enter the enclosed area is countered by the existence of a fence. The fence which surrounded the perimeter of the premises informs those who come thereon that what lies beyond is private. * * *

A toleration of trespassers does not alter their status. * * *

Therefore for aught appearing the deceased was a trespasser on the defendant's premises at the time of his unfortunate death. The law has long been settled in this state that a child, as well as an adult, may be a trespasser. * * * And the general rule is that the only duty owed to a trespasser is not to willfully or wantonly injure him, * * * or negligently injure him after his peril is discovered. * * *

Of course, the attractive nuisance doctrine cannot apply under the facts presented in this count because the swimming pool, the dangerous condition complained of, is patent and obvious to a trespasser. It is well settled in Alabama that where the danger from the instrumentality which caused the injury is patent and obvious the doctrine of attractive nuisance is inapplicable. * * *

---

37. The *Restatement* and *Restatement (Second) of Torts* use the term "possessor of land" to encompass both owners and occupiers.

While Alabama adopted the turntable doctrine in Alabama Great So. R. R. Co. v. Crocker, 131 Ala. 584, 31 So. 561, this so called attractive nuisance doctrine has never been extended in Alabama to bodies of water. * * * And thus, our courts have declined to protect children, not invitees, from water hazards.

* * * Alabama recognizes no exception, in the case of a child trespasser, to the conventional rule that a landowner is not liable to a trespasser on his land, when the trespasser is injured or drowns in a water hazard. * * * In each case where the child was a trespasser, either the complaint was held demurrable, or the affirmative charge for defendant was held properly given or that it should have been given.

The plaintiff now urges us to discard our former holdings in such cases and adopt the rule, announced in The Restatement of Torts, 2d, § 339, entitled "Artificial Conditions Highly Dangerous to Trespassing Children." That section provides as follows:

"A possessor of land is subject to liability for physical harm to children trespassing thereon caused by an artificial condition upon the land if

"(a) the place where the condition exists is one upon which the possessor knows or has reason to know that children are likely to trespass, and

"(b) the condition is one of which the possessor knows or has reason to know and which he realizes or should realize will involve an unreasonable risk of death or serious bodily harm to such children, and

"(c) the children because of their youth do not discover the condition or realize the risk involved in intermeddling with it or in coming within the area made dangerous by it, and

"(d) the utility to the possessor of maintaining the condition and the burden of eliminating the danger are slight as compared with the risk to children involved, and

"(e) the possessor fails to exercise reasonable care to eliminate the danger or otherwise to protect the children."

Were we to adopt the rule stated in § 339, supra, we would in effect overrule well settled decisions of long standing which hold that where the doctrine of attractive nuisance is not applicable because the danger is patent and obvious to a trespassing child, no exception will be made to the conventional rule in his case. Since our cases do not support the application of the rule of law announced in § 339 of The Restatement of Torts, we are unwilling to apply it and thus establish a different concept of duty owing from landowners to trespassing children from that now existing in this state. Therefore, we adhere to our holding in Alabama Great So. R. R. Co. v. Green, supra, and affirm the decision of the trial court sustaining the defendant's demurrer to count one.

Affirmed.

Notes

1. People who enter (or remain on) the land of others have been traditionally placed in one of three categories. These categories and the legal conse-

quences they entail will be further described in the ensuing cases. To facilitate the discussion, these categories may be briefly described as follows:

a. *Trespassers*—persons who enter or remain on land without the owner's consent or without some other legally recognized privilege. For example, as we have seen in Chapter Two, *supra*, the law recognizes a privilege to enter land adjoining a public highway when such entry is necessary to avoid an obstruction on the highway. People who enter land by virtue of a legally recognized privilege receive the same legal protection as is afforded to licensees.

b. *Licensees*—persons who enter or remain on land with the consent of the owner or occupier of the land, but who are not invitees.

c. *Invitees*—these are principally people who are "invited" to enter or remain on land for a purpose that directly or indirectly involves some kind of business dealings with the possessor. Such persons are often called "business invitees." In recent years there has been increasing recognition of a class of "public invitees," i.e. persons who, as members of the public, are "invited" to enter or remain on land which has been held open to the public.

2. The common-law doctrine limiting the owner's or occupier's duty to *known* trespassers was in many jurisdictions extended to *constant* trespassers, in some situations. For example, if the owner or occupier of land were aware that people were constantly trespassing on a limited area of the land and if the owner or occupier were engaged in a highly dangerous activity or maintained a highly dangerous artificial condition on that portion of the land, he would be liable for failing to take reasonable steps to avoid injuring such constant trespassers as a result of the dangerous activity or for failing to warn of the highly dangerous artificial condition of the land. *See Restatement (Second) of Torts* §§ 336–37. This extension was undoubtedly facilitated by the fact that injuries caused under such circumstances would seem to have been recklessly inflicted and the analogy to injuring known trespassers would be very close.

3. The common-law rules describing the duty of an owner or occupier of land to trespassers originally made no distinction between the duty owed children and adults. In some jurisdictions this is still the case. In addition to the *Earnest* case, *see* McKinney v. Hartz & Restle Realtors, Inc., 31 Ohio St.3d 244, 510 N.E.2d 386 (1987); Osterman v. Peters, 260 Md. 313, 272 A.2d 21 (1971). Several states, however, have modified this approach. The first major break in the rule treating child trespassers no differently from adult trespassers occurred in what came to be called the "railroad turntable" cases. *See* Sioux City & Pacific R. R. v. Stout, 84 U.S. (17 Wall.) 657, 21 L.Ed. 745 (1873). This gave rise to the so-called "attractive nuisance" doctrine. Justice Holmes declined to apply the doctrine in United Zinc & Chemical Co. v. Britt, 258 U.S. 268, 42 S.Ct. 299, 66 L.Ed. 615 (1922), because the acid pond in an abandoned smelter in which the children in question were poisoned was not visible from outside the property. They thus could not be said to have trespassed because they were "attracted" by a dangerous condition maintained by the defendant. Once they had trespassed in such circumstances they took the premises as they found them. As the *Earnest* case indicates, the *Restatement (Second) of Torts* § 339 has extended the liability of owner and occupiers of land beyond the so-called attractive nuisance situations. One should finally note, however, that the *Restatement (Second)* provisions quoted in *Earnest* only apply to "artificial conditions." *Restatement (Second) of Torts* § 339 has the following *caveat*: "The Institute expresses no opinion to whether the rule stated in this Section may not apply to natural conditions of the land." In the comments it noted

that "the case law thus far indicates that it does not apply." *Id.* at Comment *p.*

WHALEY v. LAWING

Supreme Court of Alabama, 1977.
352 So.2d 1090.

ALMON, JUSTICE.

Plaintiff Robert B. Whaley sued defendants Lloyd and Mary Lawing for injuries sustained when a redwood sundeck on the home of defendants collapsed. The thrust of plaintiff's complaint is that the defendants were wantonly negligent in allowing the plaintiff, a social guest in their home, on the sundeck which they knew was unstable and dangerous. After presentation of the plaintiff's case, the trial court directed a verdict in favor of the defendants. Plaintiff appeals citing several grounds for reversal.

Initially, plaintiff urges the court to reevaluate and abolish the traditional distinctions between trespassers, licensees, and invitees in land occupancy cases. It is sufficient to point out that in light of our recent decision in McMullan v. Butler, 346 So.2d 950 (Ala., 1977), the status of trespasser, licensee, and invitee will continue to be viable classifications under Alabama law.

Third, and most significantly, plaintiff maintains that the trial court committed reversible error in directing a verdict for the defendant since there was a scintilla of evidence supporting the material elements of plaintiff's case. That evidence, when viewed in a light most favorable to the plaintiff, reveals that the defendants Lloyd and Mary Lawing purchased a newly constructed home in Jefferson County in 1972. Attached to the rear of this house was an elevated redwood sundeck which was accessible either through a door entering the den or a staircase leading up from the ground. During the year and a half prior to its collapse, the sundeck was continuously and extensively used. For example, the sundeck was used on numerous occasions for social gatherings, and at times as many as 16 people occupied the deck simultaneously. Both defendants testified that at no time during this period did they notice or feel anything wrong with the deck. At no time did anyone complain about the safety of the deck. The plaintiff and his wife testified that they had experienced a slight bounce and vibration of the sundeck, but they never mentioned it to the defendants. Indeed, the plaintiffs continued to use the sundeck on their own initiative, and often in lieu of other entrances, during their subsequent visits to the defendant's home. In an affidavit, the Lawing's maid stated that the deck wobbled so badly that she wouldn't use it, but in a subsequent deposition she denied having made such a statement and testified that she walked on the sundeck every day she was at work. On the day the deck collapsed the plaintiff was concededly a guest in the defendant's home and voluntarily went on the sundeck with his wife and child. Upon the collapse of the deck, plaintiff sustained injuries to his back.

In order to constitute wantonness, a failure to act must be accompanied by knowledge that someone is probably imperilled, and the failure to act must be in reckless disregard of the consequences. * * * The most crucial element of wantonness is knowledge, and that element need not be shown by direct evidence; rather, it may be made to appear by showing circumstances from which the fact of knowledge is a legitimate inference. * * * With respect to a directed verdict, if a legitimate inference furnishes a scintilla of evidence in support of the theory of the complaint, then the question must go to the jury. * * *

Plaintiff contends that because he and his wife noticed a vibration in the deck, a reasonable inference can be drawn that the defendants also noticed the vibration. Such an inference, although somewhat tenuous, is nevertheless reasonable and legitimate. However, to support the charge of wantonness, an inference must also be drawn that the defendants investigated the wobble and determined it to be the result of defective and dangerous construction and not merely a vibration incident to any elevated structure. Further, an inference must be drawn that the defendants had knowledge that such defective construction was likely to result in the collapse of the structure. In view of the uncontroverted evidence of the extensive, heavy, and uneventful use of the sundeck during the previous year and a half, we feel that these additional inferences exceed the bounds of reasonableness and legitimacy. The directed verdict was not in error.

Finally, we have considered plaintiff's other contentions on appeal and find no error in the trial court's judgment.

The judgment in this cause is therefore affirmed.

Notes

1. Despite the frequent reiteration of the terms "wilful and wanton," if a licensee can show knowledge of a dangerous condition on the part of the owner or occupier, liability will normally lie if the owner or occupier fails to correct the danger or fails to warn of the danger. *See Restatement (Second) of Torts* § 342. The *Restatement (Second)* also provides for liability if the owner or occupier "has reason to know" of the dangerous condition. In either event, if the danger is obvious, the owner or occupier has no duty to warn and this is true even if the licensee's failure to discover the peril is not due to any negligence on his part. A frequently given example is a social guest driving on a private road who fails to see a pothole because his attention has been distracted by the screams of a child who has been bitten by an insect. *See Restatement (Second) of Torts* § 342, Illustration 1.

2. The duty to either remove hidden dangers or warn of their presence is in addition to the duty not to either intentionally or negligently injure the guest as a result of activities being carried out on the land. This is the duty owed to known trespassers and it, of course, extends to persons who enter the land with the consent of the owner or occupier. At common law, one would thus normally be liable for negligent action that causes injury to a person lawfully on the property, but one would not be liable if the injury were caused by the passive condition of the premises unless the injured person were an invitee.

LUNNEY v. POST

District Court of Appeal of Florida, 1971.
248 So.2d 504.

WALDEN, JUDGE.

Plaintiff-appellant, Bernice Lunney, in her amended complaint alleged she was injured in defendant's home while taking a Garden Club sponsored tour of defendant's property. The trial judge instructed the jury that plaintiff was a licensee and the jury found for defendant on that basis. We believe that instruction to be in error and therefore reverse.

Defendant,[38] an honorary Garden Club member, graciously allowed her estate to be included in a Garden Club tour of showplace homes. Defendant received no tangible benefit. The Garden Club charged $5.00 for the tour which plaintiff paid.

Plaintiff arrived at defendant's home on a rainy afternoon. One of the rooms open to the public was the library. It was a dim day and the room was dimly lighted. None of defendant's numerous servants were present in the library. Defendant had installed a vinyl material over her valuable Oriental rugs. This vinyl was, according to testimony, unsuitable for the use assigned it. It bubbled and wrinkled when put into extensive use, as it was that day.

Mrs. Lunney walked into the library, left and returned with her friends. She tripped on the plastic and fractured her hip.

At the trial recovery hinged on the amount of care defendant would be expected to take in the given situation. If plaintiff was declared a licensee, defendant only had a duty to refrain from wanton negligence or willful misconduct. If plaintiff was a business invitee, defendant had a duty to keep the premises in a reasonably safe condition. * * *

The jury, over objection, was instructed that plaintiff was a licensee. Plaintiff's counsel's request for instructions that plaintiff was a business invitee or alternatively that it was a decision for the jury, was denied. The jury found that defendant had not breached her duty to a licensee.

We will not deny that pre–1970 Florida law contains numerous decisions in the area of business invitees and licensees. We feel that in a case such as this a rigid adherence to those decisions would be unjust to plaintiff.

There are three theories concerning invitees in this country today. There are also definite trends.

1. The original Restatement of Torts divided visitors on land into three categories, trespassers, licensees and business invitees. A trespasser came without permission and was owed little duty of care. The licensee came with permission as a social guest. He must be protected against willful and wanton negligence. The business invitee came with an express or implied invitation and for the mutual economic or business benefit of the property owner. It was expected the premises would be made reasonably

---

38. [Ed. note] The defendant was the late Marjorie Merriweather Post.

safe for him. Those states following this classification, including Florida until recently, have called the test for business invitees the *mutual benefit test*. * * *

Using this test customers in stores, hotel guests, even people visiting friends at hotels and hospitals have been held business invitees. But using the same test plaintiff would be a licensee. There was no mutual economic benefit, defendant received nothing, even though the Garden Club did.

It has been often stated that this test is too narrow. Our case bears this out. Clearly plaintiff was invited as a member of the public not as a social guest, and clearly she paid for this invitation. If this case involved a theater, a ball park with an admission fee, plaintiff would be a business invitee. Yet because of the set-up of the tour, and the peculiar relationship of the parties, facts beyond plaintiff's control and knowledge, she can not recover. In fact, plaintiff, not knowing where her money went, had every right to assume she was an invitee of Mrs. Post. She was positive she was not a social guest.

The restrictive nature of the mutual benefit theory leads the courts to graft exceptions. "It may be argued that the courts which have adopted the economic benefit test in striving for what seemed to be a desirable result * * * have so attenuated the concept * * * as to leave it little real content. The test must under many circumstances turn upon a determination of the visitor's subjective state of mind." 95 A.L.R.2d 993, Annotation: Invitee Status—Test.

2. The second test for invitees comes from the 2nd Restatement of Torts, § 332, which states:

"(1) An invitee is either a public invitee or a business visitor.

"(2) A public invitee is a person who is invited to enter or remain on land as a member of the public for a purpose for which the land is held open to the public.

"(3) A business visitor is a person who is invited to enter or remain on land for a purpose directly or indirectly connected with business dealings with the possessor of the land."

Under this theory plaintiff would be an invitee. While she had no business with defendant, she was invited to enter or remain on land as a member of the public for a purpose for which the land was held open to the public.

This test is broader than the mere economic benefit test but does not dispute that, if an economic benefit is present, the person is prima facie an invitee.

Courts are receiving the new test with wide acceptance. Prosser in his Law of Torts, 3rd Edition, states that "the second theory is now accepted by the great majority of the courts; and many visitors from whose presence no shadow of pecuniary benefit is to be found are held to be invitees." Prosser continues that when premises are thrown open to the public assurances of reasonable care are ordinarily given. This test has been called the *invitation test*. It can be said to be a setting out in words what many courts have already been doing through a distortion of the economic benefit test.

Numerous jurisdictions have adopted the invitation test, often in combination with the benefit test.   * * *

Florida, too, has recognized the value of the invitation test. In Smith v. Montgomery Ward Co., Fla.App.1970, 232 So.2d 195, this court said,

"Although superficially the more restricted economic benefit test seems plausible and satisfactory, it is ill-founded for several reasons. For one thing, making the purpose of the visit determinative of the plaintiff's status enables him to clothe himself with an invitee's garments merely by proper allegations in his pleadings. * * *

"There are too many instances where the economic benefit theory has been strained to the breaking point. Yet the courts have determined to be invitees a friend or child accompanying a customer into his store, * * * or a person who goes with another to a railroad station to see him off, * * *. Or the person who goes to a bank to change a five-dollar bill. * * * If benefit is conferred upon the occupier by such visits as these, it is certainly on bases more tenuous than those which often may be found in the case of a social guest whose status has always been considered that of a licensee. * * *

"For the obvious reasons alluded to above, we are disposed not to accept the economic benefit theory as the sole test in Florida, since the invitation theory serves well the broad principles of negligence." (Citations omitted.)

It thus appears a large crack has appeared in the veneer of previous Florida law on invitees. We agree heartily with this new concept.

3.   While the trend is toward adoption of the invitation test there is a sub-trend away from all tests. This non-test would substitute for the various technical rules the broad test of reasonable care under the circumstances. The status of the injured person would have some bearing, in the light of the facts giving rise to such status, but it would not be determinative. * * *

The leading case adopting this view is Rowland v. Christian, 1968, 69 Cal.2d 108, 70 Cal.Rptr. 97, 443 P.2d 561. The court concluded that the proper test to be applied to the liability of the possessor of land is whether in the management of his property he has acted as a reasonable man in view of the probability of injury to others. The court also said that

"A man's life or limb does not become less worthy of protection by the law nor a loss less worthy of compensation under the law because he has come upon the land of another without permission or with permission but without a business purpose. Reasonable people do not ordinarily vary their conduct depending upon such matters, and to focus upon the status of the injured party as a trespasser, licensee, or invitee in order to determine the question whether the landowner has a duty of care, is contrary to our modern social mores and humanitarian values. * * *"

* * *

While this court finds much merit in such a position, we can foresee difficulties in such a case by case approach. This non-test has been explored mainly to bring to light the liberal atmosphere which is fast covering this whole area of the law.

So what is this court to do? Given the law as it stood in Florida before Smith v. Montgomery Ward & Co., supra, we can, as has been done so many times previously, create a fiction or a distortion within the framework of the mutual benefit test. Mrs. Lunney received benefit. The Garden Club received the fee. It could be fairly said that Mrs. Post donated, as was her charitable and benevolent custom, her share of the entrance fee to the Garden Club. Mrs. Post was an honorary club member and as such was interested in its well being and smooth functioning. She was an indirect beneficiary of the club's financial stability. Therefore, there was mutual economic benefit and plaintiff was a business invitee.

This court faces the issue squarely and adopts what we conceive to be the better and majority law as expressed by the Restatement of Torts, Second, and the opinion in Smith v. Montgomery Ward & Co., supra. We feel quite strongly that plaintiff was an invitee and find no reason, aside from the unusual facts in this isolated case, why she should be deprived of an opportunity for recovery because defendant's negligence fits through a loophole of Florida law.

Before pursuing the invitee theories to their conclusion for this case, we discuss another facet, Mrs. Post's relationship with the Garden Club. She was not a lessor because there was no interest in land transferred. She was a licensor, having given the Garden Club permission to use her home for a limited time and purpose. * * *

Lessors normally do not have liability for injuries occurring on the property of the lessee. There are exceptions, however, such as common passages and grounds kept up by the lessor, dangerous pre-existing conditions known to the lessor and special duties put on the lessor by contract, lease or other agreement. * * *

In the case at hand we can only analogize the liability of a lessor to the liability of the licensor. Mrs. Post would normally be at least partially relieved of liability. However, in this case she refused all offers of assistance from the Garden Club. She hired extra servants rather than using the club personnel. She did not use the regular carpet covering the club suggested, but rather procured her own. She handled the lighting in the library.

Under such circumstances her active participation and her control of the whole operation would make her an invitor and responsible for acts and omissions of negligence occurring upon her premises. This would definitely be the case for lessors and we find no reason why it should not be extended to licensors.

Upon reflection and for the reasons stated, we believe that the requirements of law and justice would be best served by a reversal and remand with instructions to submit the issues of negligence and contributory negligence to the jury again, along with an instruction that Mrs. Lunney was an invitee.

In conclusion, this court is basing its reversal on the following points:

1. The adoption of the invitation theory as expressed in the Second Restatement of Torts is more reasonable, realistic and as this case so ably demonstrates, more just. Plaintiff was without question an invitee. She should have an opportunity to recover as such.

2. If the invitation test be unacceptable then we hold plaintiff to be a business invitee as a matter of law. There was mutual economic benefit between Mrs. Post and Mrs. Lunney. Therefore, the benefit test is satisfied.

For the foregoing reasons the judgment is reversed and the cause remanded for a new trial consistent with the views herein expressed.

Reversed and remanded.

REED, JUDGE (dissenting).

There are two Florida Supreme Court opinions dealing with the definition of an invitee and neither has been overruled or receded from.... If, therefore, we adopt the invitation theory, we will place ourselves in a position of conflict with McNulty v. Hurley.

It is my view that the jurisprudence of our state will be better served if the district courts of appeal do not attempt to overrule prior decisions of the Florida Supreme Court in a headlong rush to extend financial liability to every injured person who presents an appealing claim. In a difficult case where controlling precedent seems to be outmoded, the better approach for us to take is to apply the controlling precedent established by the Florida Supreme Court and *then offer to certify the decision*. In this way the law as applied by the district courts of appeal will admit of some degree of predictability, while uniformity and soundness of principle may be achieved through a liberal use of the certification procedure. * * *

For the foregoing reason, I respectfully dissent.

QUESTION CERTIFIED

Ordered that the opinion of this court filed April 19, 1971, is hereby certified to be one which passes upon a question of great public interest. F.A.R.4.5(c)(6), 32 F.S.A.; further,

Ordered that the question certified is as follows:

"Under the facts and circumstances revealed in this opinion, did the plaintiff, Mrs. Lunney, occupy the status of an invitee under either (1) the invitation test stated in Second Restatement of Torts, § 332, and the case of Smith v. Montgomery Ward Co., Fla.App.1970, 232 So.2d 195, or (2) under the economic benefit test promulgated in McNulty v. Hurley, Fla.1957, 97 So.2d 185?"

Notes

1. The Florida Supreme Court upheld the decision of the District Court of Appeal. It specifically concluded:

Part (1) of the certified question is answered in the affirmative. We recede from the McNulty economic or mutual benefit test mentioned in

Part (2). The Decision of the District Court of Appeal * * * is approved and the writ is discharged.

Post v. Lunney, 261 So.2d 146, 150 (Fla.1972). In Wood v. Camp, 284 So.2d 691 (Fla.1973), the Supreme Court of Florida abolished the distinction between invitees and licensees such as social guests who might be said to have been expressly or impliedly *invited* upon the premises by the possessor of the land. The traditional distinction, however, would still apply to those persons who did not fit into any of these categories, but would nevertheless have been held to be licensees, not trespassers, at common law.

2. There is substantial authority for the position that police and firefighters who enter private property in the furtherance of their official duties are merely licensees. *See* Prosser and Keeton, Torts 429–32 (5th ed. 1984). The rule, usually referred to as the "firemen's rule", is reviewed and the caselaw explored in Kreski v. Modern Wholesale Elec. Supply Co., 429 Mich. 347, 415 N.W.2d 178 (1987). *See also*, Zanghi v. Niagara Frontier Transp. Comm., 85 N.Y.2d 423, 626 N.Y.S.2d 23, 649 N.E.2d 1167 (1995). Wisconsin applied the rule to bar a nurse from recovering from an Alzheimer patient in her care. California refused to apply the rule to privately employed firefighters, however. Neighbarger v. Irwin Indus., Inc., 8 Cal.4th 532, 34 Cal.Rptr.2d 630, 882 P.2d 347 (1994). Missouri refused to apply the rule to a volunteer ambulance attendant. Krause v. U.S. Truck Co., Inc., 787 S.W.2d 708 (Mo.1990). There are, nevertheless, some modern cases classifying police and firefighters as invitees. *See, e.g.*, Dini v. Naiditch, 20 Ill.2d 406, 170 N.E.2d 881 (1960). New Jersey abolished the firemen's rule by statute. N.J.S.A. 2A:62A–21. *See* Boyer v. Anchor Disposal, 135 N.J. 86, 638 A.2d 135 (1994). This is the position taken by the *Restatement (Second) of Torts* § 345(2). It should be noted that insofar as a court is prepared to abandon the different treatment of licensees and invitees in favor of a standard of reasonable conduct under the circumstances it no longer makes much difference whether a policeman or fireman is classified as a licensee or invitee. Classifying policemen and firemen as invitees, or even taking the bolder step of abolishing any distinction between licensees and invitees, will not necessarily improve the chances of police officers and firefighters recovering for their injuries. As we saw at p. 336, *supra*, there is a broader doctrine which treats professional rescuers as having, in effect, assumed certain risks of their employment and which often prevents their recovering damages for injuries incurred in performing their duties.

SCURTI v. CITY OF NEW YORK

Court of Appeals of New York, 1976.
40 N.Y.2d 433, 387 N.Y.S.2d 55, 354 N.E.2d 794.

WACHTLER, JUDGE.

Today the court has held that the liability of a landowner to one injured upon his property should be governed, not by the ancient and antiquated distinctions between trespassers, licensees, and invitees decisive under common law, but rather by the standard applicable to negligence cases generally, i.e., the "standard of reasonable care under the circumstances where by foreseeability shall be a measure of liability" (Basso v. Miller, 40 N.Y.2d 233, 241, 386 N.Y.S.2d 564, 568, 352 N.E.2d 868, 872). This case involves the further application of that standard and consideration of those factors, conclusive under prior law, which may continue to have some relevance in determining a landowner's liability for injury to one who concededly entered his property without permission.

On June 26, 1968 John Scurti, a 14–year-old high school student accompanied by another boy, entered a railroad yard through a hole in the fence at the rear of a playground located in Glen Ridge Park in Queens County. He then climbed on the top of a freight car on mainline track No. 5 and was electrocuted when he came in contact with a high-voltage catenary wire used to supply power to the locomotives.

This suit, commenced by Scurti's father as administrator of his son's estate and in his individual capacity, seeks damages for wrongful death, pain and suffering and loss of services. At the trial there was proof that the defendant New York Connecting Railroad Co. owns the yard and the tracks; that the defendants Penn Central Co., New York, New Haven and Hartford Railroad Co. and its trustees own the train and operate mainline track No. 5 and two others pursuant to a trackage agreement with Connecting; and that the defendant Metropolitan Transit Authority (MTA) and its subsidiary Long Island Railroad Co. (LIRR) operate diesel engines in the area, which are controlled from a tower located several hundred yards from the scene of the accident.

There was also proof that the fence through which the boys entered the railroad yard is part of Glen Ridge Park which is owned and maintained by the City of New York as a recreational area and playground; that there are several holes in the fence and that on both sides there are well-worn paths leading to these openings which were made and utilized by children in the area. Furthermore it was stipulated that in this particular yard four teenagers were electrocuted or seriously injured by overhead high-tension wires on four separate occasions—August, 1964, July, 1965, April, 1968 and May, 1968—prior to Scurti's death in June of 1968. It is conceded that Scurti did not have permission to enter the yard or to climb upon the train.

At the end of the plaintiff's case the court dismissed the complaint on the ground that Scurti was a trespasser on the railroad's property at the time of his death. On this appeal the defendants claim that this determination, affirmed by a divided court at the Appellate Division, was correct. In addition the MTA and the LIRR urge that there was no basis under any standard for holding them liable for the injury. The City of New York, it should be noted, argues that the railroads breached no duty owed to the trespasser, apparently on the theory that the city cannot be held liable for contributing to the injury if the other defendants are immune.

The order of the Appellate Division should be modified. With the elimination of the special immunities conferred on landowners, their liability to persons injured on their property depends on the reasonableness of their conduct under all the facts and circumstances. However even under that standard there is no basis for holding the MTA or the LIRR liable in this case. They did not own or control the yard, the tracks, the train or the high-tension wires in the area. They were simply bystanders who ran diesel—not electric powered—trains in the yard, and their activities had nothing to do with Scurti's death. The order of the Appellate Division should be affirmed insofar as it dismissed the complaint against the LIRR and the MTA.

As to the other defendants however, there should be a new trial. They owned or operated the instrumentalities which caused or contributed to the boy's death and the jury could find that under the circumstances, they failed to use reasonable care to avoid a foreseeable injury. And since there must be a new trial it is appropriate to indicate at least in general terms, how this trial should differ from a trial held under prior law, and what factors conclusive under prior law, may continue to have some relevance in determining the liability of a landowner for injury to one who concededly entered the property without permission.

The starting point at common law was the fact that the injury, no matter how foreseeable, had occurred on the defendant's property. At a time when landowners were a dominant class and ownership of land was considered akin to a sacred right, the fact that the plaintiff was a trespasser was of the utmost importance. This attitude was reflected in the law which, in its practical application, valued the rights and privileges of ownership "over the lives and limbs of trespassers" * * *. Thus the landowner was held to owe no duty to a trespasser other than the obligation to refrain from willfully or wantonly injuring him * * *. This simply proscribed certain criminal or quasi-criminal acts such as shooting * * * setting traps * * *, and did little more than serve as a reminder that it was not open season on trespassers.

Later, as the general theory of tort liability developed in response to a heightened awareness of the value of human life, new reasons were found to justify the landowner's immunity. It was said, for instance, that there was little likelihood that one would enter another's property without permission and thus the trespasser was not foreseeable * * *. It was also argued that a landowner should be entitled to develop his property in the most profitable way, and any requirement that he alter the condition of his property or curtail his activities in order to protect intruders would create unreasonable burdens inhibiting enjoyment or profitable use of the land. * * * And finally it was urged that one who enters without permission knowing that the property was not prepared for him assumes the risk or is guilty of contributory negligence as a matter of law * * *.

All of these hypotheses obviously have some probative value. But the facts in a particular case might show that trespassers were foreseeable or even foreseen; that the injury could have been prevented by a minimal effort on the part of the landowner; and that there was no basis for finding that the trespasser proceeded in the face of a known danger or was guilty of contributory negligence. To say that the hypothetical factors are always present and thus entitled to conclusive effect in all cases is the purest legal fiction, particularly unrealistic in the case of the infant trespasser.

This was a harsh rule with harsh results and over the years the courts created a number of exceptions. Thus for instance, distinctions were drawn between plaintiffs who were trespassers, licensees and invitees * * *, with trespassers being further subdivided into discovered and undiscovered trespassers * * *. Defendants were divided into owners and nonowners * * *; the subspecies being nonowners using the premises for their own convenience * * * and nonowners acting on the owner's behalf * * *.

There was a basic distinction drawn between injuries caused by active negligence, i.e., dangerous activities * * * and passive negligence, i.e., dangerous conditions * * *. The variations included mere defects * * * and inherently dangerous conditions * * *, dangerous conditions obvious to the owner and those not obvious to the owner * * *, dangerous attractions on private premises * * * and dangerous attractions on the public highway * * *.

Many of these distinctions were undoubtedly based on considerations which have some probative value in terms of the general theory of tort liability. Thus it has been noted that the distinction between "active" and "passive" negligence was probably based on the notion that it was generally easier and thus more reasonable to expect a landowner to abate an activity than it is to correct a dangerous condition existing on the property (Hughes, Duties to Trespassers, 68 Yale L.J. 633, 698). This may well be true in most cases but certainly not in all and to turn it into an immutable rule applicable in all cases, once again, permits the legal fiction to dominate the facts.

Under the standard of reasonable care adopted by the court today the factors which sustained the landowner's immunity and inspired the exceptions under prior law will no longer be considered decisive. But, as indicated, most of them have some probative value and to that extent they will continue to have some relevance in determining whether, under all the facts and circumstances, there has been a breach of duty.

The fact that the injury occurred on the defendant's property is certainly a relevant circumstance in assessing the reasonableness of the defendant's conduct. The defendant has the right to use his property and to develop it for his profit and enjoyment. That often means that he must conduct dangerous activities or permit dangerous instruments and conditions to exist on the premises. However under those circumstances he must take reasonable measures to prevent injury to those whose presence on the property can reasonably be foreseen. Whether the threat is posed by a dangerous condition or a dangerous activity is of little significance in itself. It may have some bearing on the effort required to prevent the injury, but that depends on the facts of the particular case. In this connection it is important to note that the elimination of the immunity conferred by prior law should not pose an unreasonable burden on the use of the property since all that is now required is the exercise of reasonable care under the circumstances * * *. The defendant can always show that it would have been unduly burdensome to have done more * * *.

The fact that the plaintiff entered without permission is also a relevant circumstance * * *. It may well demonstrate that the plaintiff's presence was not foreseeable at the time and place of the injury. However the likelihood of one entering without permission depends on the facts of the case including the location of the property in relation to populated areas, its accessibility and whether there have been any prior incidents of trespassing in the area where the injury occurred. The age of the plaintiff is also significant in view of the "well-known propensities of children to climb about and play" (Collentine v. City of New York, 279 N.Y. 119, 125, 17 N.E.2d 792, 795). And, of course, the fact that the entry was unauthorized may be of little or no importance if the plaintiff's presence was discovered by the owner in time to avoid the injury.

This does not mean that every case involving injury on private property raises a factual question for the jury's consideration. In any negligence case the court must always determine as a threshold matter whether the facts will support an inference of negligence or lack of negligence * * *. However in this particular case the question of the reasonableness of the parties' conduct cannot be resolved as a matter of law.

In sum, several of the factors considered decisive under prior law may be usefully integrated into the general theory of tort liability so as to provide standards and guidelines in determining a landowner's liability. With this in mind the order of the Appellate Division should be modified by reversing and granting a new trial with respect to all defendants except the Metropolitan Transit Authority and the Long Island Railroad Co., and affirmed as to them.

BREITEL, CHIEF JUDGE (concurring in part and dissenting in part).

I would reinstate the complaint against the City of New York for the negligent maintenance of its park fence all but abutting on the railroad yard with its overhead electric wires and boxcars used for play by children and adolescents. I would otherwise affirm the dismissal of the complaint against the various railroad defendants.

For the reasons indicated in my concurring opinions in Barker v. Parnossa, Inc., 39 N.Y.2d 926, 386 N.Y.S.2d 576, 352 N.E.2d 880, and in Basso v. Miller, 40 N.Y.2d 233, 386 N.Y.S.2d 564, 352 N.E.2d 868, decided herewith, there is neither need nor desirability to work a wholesale abandonment of rules and principles in order to resolve the issues in this and the cases being decided by the court at the same time. It is not in the grand tradition of the common law to do so. Most important, it is dangerous because abrupt departures in the development of the common law are not likely to be free of policy error and are disruptive of the law's stability. Evolutionary development of the law continues to be the lodestar for judicial innovation in the law, burdened as it is by the braking process of *stare decisis* and the obligation to preserve predictability. Similar inhibitions, for obvious reasons, do not apply to the legislative process, where error may be summarily corrected.

On this view, this case too is resolvable justly and predictably by the principles applicable to child trespassers and the maintenance of public parks and in accord with the rules which have evolved in this State and a vast majority of the jurisdictions in the United States. This is provided, of course, that one is not improperly diverted by nomenclature and classification, which are but symbols at best of the realities to which the law must address itself.

To apply the principles already discussed in my concurring opinion in *Barker v. Parnossa (supra)* it is appropriate to treat first with the liability of the railroad defendants. In the *Barker* case, the view was taken by me that the rules applicable to child trespassers elsewhere in the United States and restated in Restatement of Torts 2d, as it had indeed been restated in the first Restatement, were in fact applicable in this State, albeit never avowed.

* * *[39]

Decedent was concededly a trespasser on the applicable railroad's property. His status is not, however, dispositive. The railroad knew that children regularly left the city's park through the fence and climbed onto the boxcars. Indeed, four children had previously been electrocuted in the same manner as Scurti; one child had been electrocuted only one month before. Thus, the railroad knew that children were likely to trespass on its property.

Moreover, in light of the four previous electrocutions, the railroad should have realized that, under the circumstances, the electric wires involved an unreasonable risk of death to trespassing children.

While there is no fixed age limit at which a child is presumed to realize the risk involved in intermeddling with a condition existing on the land, courts have generally denied liability when the child is over 14 years of age * * *. Decedent was almost 15 years of age at the time of his death and had completed his first year of high school. One of his contemporaries testified that he was aware of the danger presented by the high-tension wires. While this is persuasive evidence that decedent should have realized the dangers in playing on the boxcar, it would be essentially a question of fact whether he appreciated the danger presented by the overhead wires, provided however the other bases for liability existed. * * *

In contradistinction to the *Barker* case (*supra*), the balance of the conflicting social policies of freedom to use one's land and the desire to protect children must here be struck in favor of the railroad. The property was in constant, productive use as a railroad switching yard. Railroad police patrolled the area and chased the children when they could. The railroad could reasonably expect the city to maintain its fence and was under no duty to erect one of its own (Railroad Law, § 52). Under the circumstances, the only further precaution which could have been taken was to shut down the operations of the electric railway, which, in fact, was eventually done for reasons or on bases not developed. Thus, the utility to the railroad of maintaining the electric railway and the burden of eliminating the danger were great indeed when compared to the risk to the child involved * * *. Hence, the trial court was correct in dismissing the complaint with respect to the railroads and the Metropolitan Transportation Authority.

The propriety of the dismissal of the complaint with respect to the city is, however, another matter. Decedent's status as a trespasser on the railroad property is irrelevant * * *. The city owes to those who use its parks a duty of ordinary care against foreseeable danger * * *. What degree of care is "reasonable" is ordinarily a jury question * * *.

In this case, the city was aware or should have been aware that children would come to its park, and, through holes in the fence and over a

---

39. [Ed. note]. In the material omitted Breitel, C. J., quoted the text of Restatement (Second) of Torts § 339. This provision is set forth in the *Earnest* case at p. 538, *supra*.

"well beaten" path, regularly would go onto the immediately adjoining railroad property to play on the boxcars. The fence separating the park from the railroad property was in an almost constant state of gross disrepair. No warning signs were posted by the city, nor was a parkkeeper on guard regularly to prevent the fences from being cut or the children from going onto the railroad's property. The accident in this case occurred around 4 p.m. on a June afternoon. Most important, the city was aware that four similar accidents had occurred, and thus could reasonably foresee a recurrence of tragedy. Yet it took no precautions whatsoever. Hence, it was a question of fact, at the very least, whether the city failed to exercise reasonable care.

JASEN, J. (dissenting).

I concur with Chief Judge Breitel's analysis of the issue of the railroads' liability. I cannot, however, subscribe to the proposition that the city was responsible, as a matter of law, for the injuries sustained by the plaintiff's interstate. The city did erect a fence between its playground and the adjoining railroad property and made continuing efforts to maintain it. The difficulty was that the children, in order to use the railroad property as a shortcut route to school, kept cutting holes in the fence. The only way to have maintained an adequate childproof barrier between the playground and the railroad property was to station parkkeepers on the playground on a permanent basis. Under the circumstances, I believe that such a requirement would be unreasonably burdensome. The city provided a playground that in itself was reasonably safe and secure and made efforts to prevent children from crossing from the playground to the railroad property. The city is not an insurer against injury arising from activities conducted, or conditions existing, on adjoining or neighboring property. * * *

Notes

1. In Basso v. Miller, 40 N.Y.2d 233, 386 N.Y.S.2d 564, 352 N.E.2d 868 (1976), referred to in the majority's opinion and Chief Judge Breitel's opinion, the plaintiff was one of a group of people recruited by a patron of a scenic park to rescue another patron who had fallen into a crevice when he had left the main path leading up the hillside upon which the scenic park was located. The plaintiff was injured when the motorcycle upon which he was riding as a passenger overturned after running into a pothole. The issue was originally framed as to whether the plaintiff, as a volunteer rescuer, was a licensee or an invitee. The Court of Appeals instead used the case as the occasion for abandoning the traditional common-law classifications in favor of a duty of reasonable care under the circumstances. Chief Judge Breitel, joined by Judge Jasen, concurred in a separate opinion on the ground that the plaintiff was a public invitee and it was thus unnecessary to consider whether the common law scheme should be jettisoned.

2. The movement to abandon completely the determinative effect of the common-law classifications was begun in Rowland v. Christian, 69 Cal.2d 108, 70 Cal.Rptr. 97, 443 P.2d 561 (1968). That case involved a social guest, i.e. someone who at common law would have been considered a licensee. The trial judge had granted judgment in favor of the defendant, the tenant in whose apartment the plaintiff was a social guest. He had been injured "while using the bathroom fixtures, suffering severed tendons and nerves of his right hand."

In reversing the trial judge's disposition of the case, the court ruled that liability should be determined by "whether in the management of his property he [i.e. the possessor] has acted as a reasonable man in view of the probability of injury to others, and although the plaintiff's status as a trespasser, licensee, or invitee may in the light of the facts giving rise to such status have some bearing on the question of liability, the status is not determinative." Burke, J., joined by McComb, J., dissented. In the concluding portions of his dissent, he declared:

> Liability for negligence turns upon whether a duty of care is owed, and if so, the extent thereof. Who can doubt that the corner grocery, the large department store, or the financial institution owes a greater duty of care to one whom it has invited to enter its premises as a prospective customer of its wares or services than it owes to a trespasser seeking to enter after the close of business hours and for a nonbusiness or even an antagonistic purpose? I do not think it unreasonable or unfair that a social guest (classified by the law as a licensee, as was plaintiff here) should be obliged to take the premises in the same condition as his host finds them or permits them to be. Surely a homeowner should not be obliged to hover over his guests with warnings of possible dangers to be found in the condition of the home (e.g., waxed floors, slipping rugs, toys in unexpected places, etc., etc.). Yet today's decision appears to open the door to potentially unlimited liability despite the purpose and circumstances motivating the plaintiff in entering the premises of another, and despite the caveat of the majority that the status of the parties may "have some bearing on the question of liability * * *," whatever the future may show that language to mean.

> In my view, it is not a proper function of this court to overturn the learning, wisdom and experience of the past in this field. Sweeping modifications of tort liability law fall more suitably within the domain of the Legislature, before which all affected interests can be heard and which can enact statutes providing uniform standards and guidelines for the future.

3. In addition to *Basso v. Miller, supra,* note 1, *Rowland v. Christian* was followed in Pickard v. City of Honolulu, 51 Haw. 134, 452 P.2d 445 (1969); Mile High Fence Co. v. Radovich, 175 Colo. 537, 489 P.2d 308 (1971); Mariorenzi v. Joseph DiPonte, Inc., 114 R.I. 294, 333 A.2d 127 (1975); Ouellette v. Blanchard, 116 N.H. 552, 364 A.2d 631 (1976); Cates v. Beauregard Elec. Co-op., 328 So.2d 367 (La.1976), *cert. denied* 429 U.S. 833, 97 S.Ct. 97, 50 L.Ed.2d 98 (1976); Webb v. City of Sitka, 561 P.2d 731 (Alaska 1977). *Cf.* Kermarec v. Compagnie Generale Transatlantique, 358 U.S. 625, 79 S.Ct. 406, 3 L.Ed.2d 550 (1959), which held that the common law distinction between licensees and invitees did not apply in admiralty. The pace of change has slackened in recent years. About fifteen jurisdictions have opted to follow *Rowland* completely or in part.

4. Although England has now totally abolished the common-law distinctions in favor of a duty to take "such steps as are reasonable in all the circumstances," Occupiers Liability Act, 1984, c. 3, the initial change in English law was to abolish the distinction between licensees and invitees. Occupiers Liability Act, 5 & 6 Eliz. 2, c. 31 (1957). This partial change from the common law has been the approach followed in a number of American jurisdictions. *See, e.g.,* O'Leary v. Coenen, 251 N.W.2d 746 (N.D.1977); Antoniewicz v. Reszcynski, 70 Wis.2d 836, 236 N.W.2d 1 (1975); Mounsey v. Ellard, 363 Mass. 693, 297 N.E.2d 43 (1973); Jones v. Hansen, 254 Kan. 499, 867 P.2d 303

(1994); Poulin v. Colby College, 402 A.2d 846 (Me.1979); *cf.* Burrell v. Meads, 569 N.E.2d 637 (Ind.1991) (social guests to be treated as invitees)*. Smith v. Arbaugh's Restaurant, Inc., 469 F.2d 97 (D.C.Cir.1972), *cert. denied,* 412 U.S. 939, 93 S.Ct. 2774, 37 L.Ed.2d 399 (1973), a case involving someone on the borderline between a licensee and an invitee, was broad enough to eliminate the common law treatment of trespassers but in Alston v. Baltimore & Ohio Railroad, 433 F.Supp. 553 (D.D.C.1977), it was read as merely abolishing the common law distinction between licensees and invitees. This reading was reaffirmed in Holland v. Baltimore & O.R.R., 431 A.2d 597 (D.C.App.1981). Many courts have, however, refused to change the traditional common law. *See, e.g.,* Light v. Ohio University, 28 Ohio St.3d 66, 502 N.E.2d 611 (1986).

5. *Recreational land.* Over 40 states have enacted statutes limiting the liability of the owners of land that is used for recreational purposes. Citations to these statutes are contained in J. Barratt, *Good Sports and Bad Lands: The Application of Washington's Recreational Use Statute Limiting Landowners Liability,* 53 Wash.L.Rev. 1 (1977). Most of these statutes are patterned after a model law proposed by the Council of State Governments. Typically, these statutes provide that, except when some kind of entrance fee is charged, there is no liability for unintentional injuries suffered by those who enter on the land, except when the landowner has willfully or maliciously "failed to guard or warn against a dangerous condition, use, structure or activity." *See, e.g.,* Cal.Civil Code § 846 (West Supp.1989), first enacted in 1963. Bragg v. Genesee County Agricultural Soc., 84 N.Y.2d 544, 620 N.Y.S.2d 322, 644 N.E.2d 1013 (1994)(discussing the New York statute). These statutes have generated a great deal of litigation in recent years testing the outer boundaries of the immunity. In some states the property must be held open for general public use. *See* Loyer v. Buchholz, 38 Ohio St.3d 65, 526 N.E.2d 300 (1988)(interpreting the Ohio statute). While probably most statutes apply equally to privately and publicly owned premises, some states have held that the statute was not intended to apply to publicly owned property. *See* Monteville v. Terrebonne Parish Consolidated Government, 567 So.2d 1097 (La.1990).

6. *Liability to persons outside of the land.* A possessor of land is responsible for taking reasonable measures to prevent excavations, structures, and other artificial conditions on his land from endangering persons outside his land. *See Restatement (Second) of Torts* §§ 364–66, 368. This is particularly true if the land is adjacent to a public highway. In Sprecher v. Adamson Companies, 30 Cal.3d 358, 178 Cal.Rptr. 783, 636 P.2d 1121 (1981), a case involving a mud slide in Southern California, this liability was extended to natural conditions on undeveloped land. The only previous cases of liability on a negligence theory to persons outside the land for what might be called a natural condition appear to have involved trees in residential areas or on land adjacent to public highways.

SARGENT v. ROSS

Supreme Court of New Hampshire, 1973.
113 N.H. 388, 308 A.2d 528.

KENISON, CHIEF JUSTICE.

The question in this case is whether the defendant landlord is liable to the plaintiff in tort for the death of plaintiff's four-year-old daughter who

---

* The court noted that, traditionally, social guests were not treated as invitees because they came "only to receive their hosts' hospitality and therefore have no right to expect that the hosts will take more precautions for their safety than the hosts would normally take for the safety of members of their own households." *Id.* at 643.

fell to her death from an outdoor stairway at a residential building owned by the defendant in Nashua. The defendant resided in a ground-floor apartment in the building, and her son and daughter-in-law occupied a second story apartment serviced by the stairway from which the child fell. At the time of the accident the child was under the care of the defendant's daughter-in-law who was plaintiff's regular baby-sitter.

Plaintiff brought suit against the daughter-in-law for negligent supervision and against the defendant for negligent construction and maintenance of the stairway which was added to the building by the defendant about eight years before the accident. There was no apparent cause for the fall except for evidence that the stairs were dangerously steep, and that the railing was insufficient to prevent the child from falling over the side. The jury returned a verdict for the daughter-in-law but found in favor of the plaintiff in her action against the defendant landlord. The defendant seasonably excepted to the denial of her motions for a nonsuit, directed verdict, judgment n.o.v., and to have the verdict set aside, and all questions of law were reserved and transferred to this court by *Dunfey*, J.

Claiming that there was no evidence that the defendant retained control over the stairway, that it was used in common with other tenants, or that it contained a concealed defect, defendant urges that there was accordingly no duty owing to the deceased child for the defendant to breach. This contention rests upon the general rule which has long obtained in this and most other jurisdictions that a landlord is not liable, except in certain limited situations, for injuries caused by defective or dangerous conditions in the leased premises. * * * The plaintiff does not directly attack this rule of nonliability but instead attempts to show, rather futilely under the facts, defendant's control of the stairway. She also relies upon an exception to the general rule of nonliability, to wit, that a landlord is liable for injuries resulting from his negligent repair of the premises. * * * The issue, as framed by the parties, is whether the rule of nonliability should prevail or whether the facts of this case can be squeezed into the negligent repair or some other exception to the general rule of landlord immunity.

General principles of tort law ordinarily impose liability upon persons for injuries caused by their failure to exercise reasonable care under all the circumstances. * * * A person is generally negligent for exposing another to an unreasonable risk of harm which foreseeably results in an injury. * * * But, except in certain instances, landlords are immune from these simple rules of reasonable conduct which govern other persons in their daily activities. This "quasi-sovereignty of the landowner" (2 Harper and James, Law of Torts 1495 (1956))finds its source in an agrarian England of the dark ages. * * * Due to the untoward favoritism of the law for landlords, it has been justly stated that "the law in this area is a scandal." Quinn and Phillips, The Law of Landlord–Tenant: A Critical Evaluation of the Past with Guidelines for the Future, 38 Ford.L.Rev. 225 (1969). * * * But courts and legislatures alike are beginning to reevaluate the rigid rules of landlord-tenant law in light of current needs and principles of law from related areas. * * * "Justifiable dissatisfaction with the rule" of landlord tort immunity * * * compels its reevaluation in a case such as this where we are asked either to apply the rule, and hold the landlord harmless for a foreseeable death resulting from an act of negligence, or to broaden one of the existing exceptions and hence perpetuate an artificial and illogical rule. * * *

One court recognized at an early date that ordinary principles of tort liability ought to apply to landlords as other persons. "The ground of liability upon the part of a landlord when he demises dangerous property has nothing special to do with the relation of landlord and tenant. It is the ordinary case of liability for personal misfeasance, which runs through all the relations of individuals to each other." Wilcox v. Hines, 100 Tenn. 538, 548–549, 46 S.W. 297, 299 (1898). Most courts, however, while recognizing from an early date that "the law is unusually strict in exempting the landlord from liability" (Bowe v. Hunking, 135 Mass. 380, 386 (1883)), sought refuge from the rigors of the rule by straining other legal principles such as deceit * * * and by carving out exceptions to the general rule of nonliability. * * * Thus, a landlord is now generally conceded to be liable in tort for injuries resulting from defective and dangerous conditions in the premises if the injury is attributable to (1) a hidden danger in the premises of which the landlord but not the tenant is aware, (2) premises leased for public use, (3) premises retained under the landlord's control, such as common stairways, or (4) premises negligently repaired by the landlord. * * *

As is to be expected where exceptions to a rule of law form the only basis of liability, the parties in this action concentrated at trial and on appeal on whether any of the exceptions applied, particularly whether the landlord or the tenant had control of the stairway. * * * The determination of the question of which party had control of the defective part of the premises causing the injury has generally been considered dispositive of the landlord's liability. * * * This was a logical modification to the rule of nonliability since ordinarily a landlord can reasonably be expected to maintain the property and guard against injuries only in common areas and other areas under his control. A landlord, for example, cannot fairly be held responsible in most instances for an injury arising out of the tenant's negligent maintenance of the leased premises. * * * But the control test is insufficient since it substitutes a facile and conclusive test for a reasoned consideration of whether due care was exercised under all the circumstances. * * *

There was evidence from which the jury could find that the landlord negligently designed or constructed a stairway which was dangerously steep or that she negligently failed to remedy or adequately warn the deceased of the danger. A proper rule of law would not preclude recovery in such a case by a person foreseeably injured by a dangerous hazard solely because the stairs serviced one apartment instead of two. But that would be the result if the control test were applied to this case, since this was not a "common stairway" or otherwise under the landlord's control. * * * While we could strain this test to the limits and find control in the landlord * * *, as plaintiff suggests, we are not inclined to so expand the fiction since we agree that "it is no part of the general law of negligence to exonerate a defendant simply because the condition attributable to his negligence has passed beyond his control before it causes injury * * *." 2 Harper and James, Law of Torts § 27.16, at 1509 (1956) * * *.

The anomaly of the general rule of landlord tort immunity and the inflexibility of the standard exceptions, such as the control exception, is pointedly demonstrated by this case. A child is killed by a dangerous condition of the premises. Both husband and wife tenants testify that they could do nothing to remedy the defect because they did not own the house nor have authority to alter the defect. But the landlord claims that she should not be liable because the stairs were not under her control. Both of these contentions are premised on the theory that the other party should be responsible. So the orthodox analysis would leave us with neither landlord nor tenant responsible for dangerous conditions on the premises. This would be both illogical and intolerable, particularly since neither party then would have any legal reason to remedy or take precautionary measures with respect to dangerous conditions. In fact, the traditional "control" rule actually discourages a landlord from remedying a dangerous condition since his repairs may be evidence of his control. * * * Nor can there be serious doubt that ordinarily the landlord is best able to remedy dangerous conditions, particularly where a substantial alteration is required. * * *

* * * In fact, the issue of control is relevant to the determination of liability only insofar as it bears on the question of what the landlord and tenant reasonably should have believed in regard to the division of responsibility for *maintaining* the premises in a safe condition. The basic claim in this case involves only the design or construction of the steps; the maintenance of the stairs was not seriously in issue, except perhaps concerning the lack of precautions, since the evidence was clear that the stairway was dry and free of debris. The inquiry should have centered upon the unreasonableness of the pitch of the steps and the unreasonableness of failing to take precautionary measures to reduce the danger of falls.

Similarly, the truly pertinent questions involved in determining who should bear responsibility for the loss in this case were clouded by the question of whether the accident was caused by a hidden defect or secret danger. * * * The mere fact that a condition is open and obvious, as was the steepness of the steps in this case, does not preclude it from being unreasonably dangerous, and defendants are not infrequently "held liable for creating or maintaining a perfectly obvious danger of which plaintiffs are fully aware." 2 Harper and James, *supra* at 1493 * * *. Additionally, while the dangerous quality of the steps might have been obvious to an adult, the danger and risk would very likely be imperceptible to a young child such as the deceased. * * * The obviousness of the risk is primarily relevant to the basic issue of a plaintiff's contributory negligence. * * * Here, the trial court properly withdrew the issue of the contributory negligence of the deceased from the jury because of the child's very young age. * * *

Finally, plaintiff's reliance on the negligent repairs exception to the rule of nonliability * * * would require us to broaden the exception to include the negligent construction of improvements to the premises. We recognize that this would be no great leap in logic * * *, but we think it more realistic instead to consider reversing the general rule of nonliability (Note, 62 Harv.L.Rev. 669 (1949))since "[t]he exceptions have * * * produced a twisting of legal concepts which seems undesirable." *Id.* at

676. * * * The emphasis on control and other exceptions to the rule of nonliability, both at trial and on appeal, unduly complicated the jury's task and diverted effort and attention from the central issue of the unreasonableness of the risk.

In recent years, immunities from tort liability affording "special protection in some types of relationships have been steadily giving way" in this and other jurisdictions. * * * We think that now is the time for the landlord's limited tort immunity to be relegated to the history books where it more properly belongs.

This conclusion springs naturally and inexorably from our recent decision in Kline v. Burns, 111 N.H. 87, 276 A.2d 248 (1971). *Kline* was an apartment rental claim suit in which the tenant claimed that the premises were uninhabitable. Following a small vanguard of other jurisdictions, we modernized the landlord-tenant contractual relationship by holding that there is an implied warranty of habitability in an apartment lease transaction. As a necessary predicate to our decision, we discarded from landlord-tenant law "that obnoxious legal cliché, *caveat emptor*." * * * In so doing, we discarded the very legal foundation and justification for the landlord's immunity in tort for injuries to the tenant or third persons. * * *

To the extent that Kline v. Burns did not do so, we today discard the rule of "caveat lessee" and the doctrine of landlord nonliability in tort to which it gave birth. We thus bring up to date the other half of landlord-tenant law. Henceforth, landlords as other persons must exercise reasonable care not to subject others to an unreasonable risk of harm. * * * A landlord must act as a reasonable person under all of the circumstances including the likelihood of injury to others, the probable seriousness of such injuries, and the burden of reducing or avoiding the risk. * * * The questions of control, hidden defects and common or public use, which formerly had to be established as a prerequisite to even considering the negligence of a landlord, will now be relevant only inasmuch as they bear on the basic tort issues such as the foreseeability and unreasonableness of the particular risk of harm. * * *

The abiding respect of this court for precedent and stability in the law is balanced by an appreciation of the need for responsible growth and change in rules that have failed to keep pace with modern developments in social and juridical thought. * * *

Our decision will shift the primary focus of inquiry for judge and jury from the traditional question of "who had control?" to a determination of whether the landlord, and the injured party, exercised due care under all the circumstances. Perhaps even more significantly, the ordinary negligence standard should help insure that a landlord will take whatever precautions are reasonably necessary under the circumstances to reduce the likelihood of injuries from defects in his property. "It is appropriate that the landlord who will retain ownership of the premises and any permanent improvements should bear the cost of repairs necessary to make the premises safe * * *." Kline v. Burns, * * *.

Although the trial court's instructions to the jury in the instant case were cast according to the traditional exceptions of control and hidden danger, the charge clearly set forth the elements of ordinary negligence which were presented by the court as a prerequisite to a finding of liability on either issue. Thus, the jury could find that the defendant was negligent in the design or construction of the steep stairway or in failing to take adequate precautionary measures to reduce the risk of injury. We have carefully reviewed the record and conclude that there is sufficient evidence, on the basis of the principles set forth above, to support the verdict of the jury which had the benefit of a view. * * * Both plaintiff and the wife tenant testified that the stairs were too steep, and the husband tenant testified that his wife complained to him of this fact. While the defendant landlord did not testify, the jury could find that she knew that this steep stairway was frequently used by the young children for whom her daughter-in-law was the regular, daily babysitter. In any event, the use of these steps by young children should have been anticipated by the defendant. * * *

The verdict of the jury is sustained * * *.

Notes

1. *Sargent v. Ross* has received a limited following. In Brennan v. Cockrell Investments, Inc., 35 Cal.App.3d 796, 111 Cal.Rptr. 122 (1973), the court applied the doctrine of *Sargent v. Ross* on the ground that it was a natural development of the trend of California law. This conclusion was confirmed by the California Supreme Court in Becker v. IRM Corp., 38 Cal.3d 454, 213 Cal.Rptr. 213, 698 P.2d 116 (1985).[40] Subsequent lower-court cases, however, have held that *Becker* is not applicable to the lease of commercial property. See Muro v. Superior Court, 184 Cal.App.3d 1089, 229 Cal.Rptr. 383 (1986). *See also* Edwards v. Comstock Ins. Co., 205 Cal.App.3d 1164, 252 Cal.Rptr. 807 (1988). *Sargent v. Ross* was also followed in Pagelsdorf v. Safeco Insurance Co. of America, 91 Wis.2d 734, 284 N.W.2d 55 (1979) and now seems to be the law in Massachusetts as a result of the cumulative effect of King v. G & M Realty Corp., 373 Mass. 658, 370 N.E.2d 413 (1977); Crowell v. McCaffrey, 377 Mass. 443, 386 N.E.2d 1256 (1979); Young v. Garwacki, 380 Mass. 162, 402 N.E.2d 1045 (1980). For more recent cases, *see* Mansur v. Eubanks, 401 So.2d 1328 (Fla.1981); Stephens v. Stearns, 106 Idaho 249, 678 P.2d 41 (1984); Bellikka v. Green, 306 Or. 630, 762 P.2d 997 (1988); *cf.*, Turpel v. Sayles, 101 Nev. 35, 692 P.2d 1290 (1985).

2. The landlord's duty to maintain common areas traditionally did not include a duty to correct natural conditions, including removal of natural accumulations of snow and ice, but there has been some movement away from that position. *See, e.g.*, Geise v. Lee, 84 Wn.2d 866, 529 P.2d 1054 (1975); Isaacson v. Husson College, 297 A.2d 98 (Me.1972). Other courts have adhered to the traditional rule. *See, e.g.*, Sullivan v. Town of Brookline, 416 Mass. 825, 626 N.E.2d 870 (1994). In Rutkauskas v. Hodgins, 120 N.H. 788, 423 A.2d 291 (1980), the court ruled that *Sargent v. Ross* did not apply in a case where the plaintiff complained that the design of a building led to an accumulation of ice and snow on the public sidewalk adjoining the building.

3. As indicated in the court's opinion in *Sargent v. Ross*, a person who leased land to another for a purpose that involves the admission of the public (such as the lease of an auditorium or sports arena) is responsible for taking

---

40. As noted below, *Becker* has been overruled to the extent that it imposed strict liability upon the owner of the premises, but the court specifically adherred to the *Becker* approach as applied to a negligence claim.

reasonable care to discover and remedy any dangerous condition if the lessor has reason to know that the public will be admitted "before the land is put in a safe condition." *Restatement (Second) of Torts* § 359. With this exception, at common law, a lessee largely took the premises as they were. The lessor was, however, obliged to warn the lessee of any conditions known to the lessor[41] which presented an unreasonable risk to persons on the property and which the lessee was unlikely to discover on his own. Needless to say, the landlord could not try to conceal any dangerous conditions that he knew about.

As also indicated in *Sargent v. Ross*, a number of jurisdictions have now read into a lease of residential property an implied warranty of habitability. Under this warranty, a lessor will be strictly liable for any unsafe condition existing in the premises at the time they are leased. However, Becker v. IRM Corp., 38 Cal.3d 454, 213 Cal.Rptr. 213, 698 P.2d 116 (1985), basing liability on a strict product liability basis has recently been overruled on this issue. Peterson v. Superior Court, 10 Cal.4th 1185, 43 Cal.Rptr.2d 836, 899 P.2d 905 (1995). Significant cases holding for strict liability include Lemle v. Breeden, 51 Haw.i 426, 462 P.2d 470 (1969); Javins v. First National Realty Corp., 428 F.2d 1071 (D.C.Cir.1970), *cert. denied* 400 U.S. 925, 91 S.Ct. 186, 27 L.Ed.2d 185 (1970); Old Town Development Co. v. Langford, 349 N.E.2d 744 (Ind.App. 1976), case dismissed as moot (after the parties settled the case), 267 Ind. 177, 369 N.E.2d 404 (1977). Given the Oregon legislature's adoption of a statutory requirement of habitability, however, the Oregon Supreme Court refused to recognize a broader common-law, strict-liability claim based on an implied-warranty-of-habitability theory. Bellikka v. Green, 306 Or. 630, 762 P.2d 997 (1988). In Frobig v. Gordon, 124 Wn.2d 732, 881 P.2d 226 (1994), the court held that a landlord was not liable to a third party injured by wild animals kept by the tenant. The subject of strict liability will be discussed in the next two chapters.

4. The *Restatement (Second) of Torts* § 362 limits the landlord's liability when he has negligently repaired premises in the possession of the lessee, to those situations where, unknown to the lessee, the landlord has either made the premises more dangerous or given them a deceptive appearance of safety. In Bartlett v. Taylor, 351 Mo. 1060, 174 S.W.2d 844 (1943), the court rejected this limitation on the extent of a landlord's liability for negligence in making the repairs. *Cf.* the discussion in the first part of this chapter dealing with affirmative duties to assist others.

41. *Restatement (Second) of Torts* § 358 also imposes liability when the lessor "has   reason to know."

Chapter 8

STRICT LIABILITY

A. ANIMALS

DUREN v. KUNKEL

Supreme Court of Missouri, 1991.
En Banc.
814 S.W.2d 935.

HOLSTEIN, JUDGE.

Defendant Ohmer Kunkel, Jr., appeals from a judgment awarding plaintiff Bernard Duren $100,000 for personal injuries sustained when Duren was attacked by a bull owned by Kunkel. Following opinion by the Missouri Court of Appeals, Western District, transfer was granted to this Court. Reversed and remanded.

* * *

Kunkel contends the trial court should have sustained his motions for directed verdict and judgment notwithstanding the verdict because the evidence was insufficient to prove the bull in question had a dangerous propensity. * * *In reviewing a ruling on motions for directed verdict and judgment notwithstanding the verdict, the evidence is taken in a light most favorable to the verdict. The prevailing party is entitled to the benefit of all reasonable inferences favorable to the verdict, and evidence unfavorable to the verdict is disregarded. The recital of the facts is made with these standards in mind.

* * *

In May of 1986, Kunkel bought a limousin bull at a sale. The bull was mature, weighing about 1800 pounds. Kunkel told Duren that he got the bull "a little cheaper" because the bull "acted up" in the sale ring.[1] The exact nature of the bull's conduct was not disclosed, but Duren understood "acting up" to mean trying to climb a fence, snorting and pawing. Kunkel had the bull delivered to his farm. After the bull arrived at the farm, Kunkel kept it in a separate pen for two or three days until it "settled down."

---

1. Kunkel claimed he did not make the statement. However, that claim must be dis- counted along with other testimony inconsistent with the verdict.

On June 27, 1987, Duren was at Kunkel's farm assisting in separating cattle in preparation for castrating and immunizing calves. Duren and Kunkel owned neighboring farms. They had often exchanged work of that kind. The calves were separated from the cows and the limousin bull was left with the calves in a corral. Kunkel wanted the bull moved because of his concern that the bull would "get together" with a longhorn bull that was just "over the fence" from the corral where the limousin bull was located. Kunkel directed Duren to move the bull out of the corral. To do so required that the bull be moved past and very near where the calves had been castrated. The castration of between fifteen to twenty calves had left a quantity of blood on the ground. Duren proceeded as directed.

Acting alone, Duren drove the bull to a point about six feet from where the blood was on the ground. At that point, the bull turned and attacked Duren. Duren was knocked unconscious and sustained substantial and permanent injuries.

Expert testimony was presented as to the general character of bulls and limousin bulls in particular. Plaintiff's primary expert witness was Dr. J.W. Smith, a veterinarian with over forty-six years experience in a large animal practice. He had contact with herds all over the area on a daily basis. According to him, limousin bulls are the most aggressive of all beef breeds. Dr. Smith testified that all bulls are dangerous, but limousins tend to be more aggressive and active than other breeds. He stated that most bulls react aggressively in the presence of blood and it would be especially dangerous for one man to attempt to move a bull alone. The safe method, according to Dr. Smith, would require that there be more than one man or a few cows with the bull. In addition, an experienced cattle farmer testified that the smell of blood excites bulls, and driving a bull near fresh blood causes a bull to be more excitable and dangerous.

* * *

The law in Missouri has long been that one who harbors a domestic animal with dangerous propensities known to the owner may be held liable even without a showing of negligence on the part of the owner. The Missouri rule, and that followed in most jurisdictions, is:

> A possessor of a domestic animal that he knows or has reason to know has dangerous propensities abnormal to its class is subject to liability for harm done by the animal to another, although he has exercised the utmost care to prevent it from doing harm.

Restatement (Second) of Torts, § 509(1)(1977). Rules imposing liability for harm caused by domestic animals find their origin in authority no less ancient than the Pentateuch.[2]

The rule requiring actual or constructive knowledge of an abnormal dangerous propensity of a domestic animal has been rigidly applied to defeat recovery. The majority of these cases involved a dog bite. For

---

2. "And if an ox gores a man or a woman to death, the ox shall surely be stoned and its flesh shall not be eaten; but the owner of the ox shall go unpunished. If, however, an ox was previously in the habit of goring, and its owner has been warned, yet he does not confine it, and it kills a man or a woman, the ox shall be stoned and its owner also shall be put to death." Exodus 21:28–29 (New American Standard Translation).

example, knowledge by the owner that a dog chased and snapped at children on bicycles and fought with other dogs was insufficient to establish a dangerous propensity. [citation omitted] Evidence that a dog was seen barking and lunging from a chain when people would get where they could be seen was held insufficient.

* * *

The rationale for requiring somewhat stringent proof of the owner's actual or constructive knowledge of a domestic animal's vicious propensity is primarily one of public policy. If actual or constructive knowledge is shown, the rule is one of strict liability, not requiring fault by the owner. *Prosser and Keeton on Torts*, 5th Ed. (1984) § 76. In the case of dogs, they have "earned and merited acceptance as man's best friend." *State ex rel. Kroger Co. v. Craig*, 329 S.W.2d 804, 808 (Mo.App.1959).[3] The dog's social utility justifies permitting the owner a degree of freedom from potential liability. Other domestic animals, though naturally somewhat dangerous, also have utility to human beings:

> Bulls are more dangerous than cows and steers; stallions are more dangerous than mares or geldings; rams are more dangerous than ewes and lambs. However, these animals have been kept for stud purposes from time immemorial so that the particular danger involved in their dangerous tendencies has become a normal incident of civilized life ... [T]he virility which makes them dangerous is necessary for their usefulness in performing their function in the socially essential breeding of livestock, [and] justifies the risk involved in their keeping. Therefore the law has not regarded bulls, stallions and rams as being abnormally dangerous animals to be kept under the strict liability stated in this section. Restatement (Second) of Torts, § 509, Comment *e* (1977).

Applying the above principles, here the evidence demonstrated that the bull "acted up" at a sale over a year prior to the accident, that it needed a few days to "settle down" after arriving at the Kunkel farm, and that Kunkel was concerned the bull might breach a fence on the date of the plaintiff's injury. In addition, the evidence demonstrates that limousin bulls are naturally disposed to be aggressive, particularly when exposed to the smell of blood. Even giving plaintiff the benefit of every reasonable inference, the evidence falls short of establishing that Kunkel knew or should have known that the bull in question had a vicious propensity different from other bulls of its breed or class. Thus, a case for strict liability was not established.

Plaintiff's brief on appeal raises a distinct question. That question is whether plaintiff should have been permitted to submit a claim based on a theory of ordinary negligence due to defendant's failure to provide sufficient personnel to drive the bull from the corral.

* * *

---

3. For the literary minded, the Craig case contains Judge Stone's history of mankind's longstanding relationship with the dog.

Defendant's position is that the owner of a domestic animal is immune from liability in the absence of actual or constructive knowledge of the animal's abnormally vicious propensities, even though the owner was in some respect negligent. That is not the law. In *Alexander v. Crotchett*, the most recent Missouri case involving injuries inflicted by a bull, the court of appeals first rejected the claim of strict liability. However, it went on to say, "Plaintiff claims that he was an invitee of defendant's on the latter's premises. We think that is correct and that defendant's liability is measured by its duty to an invitee." 124 S.W.2d at 537. The duty owed to invitees includes the duty to eliminate or warn of dangerous conditions of which the defendant knows or in the exercise of reasonable care should have known.

* * *

The cases are consistent with the general law on the subject:

> Except for animal trespass, one who possesses or harbors a domestic animal that he does not know or have reason to know to be abnormally dangerous, is subject to liability for harm done by the animal if, but only if . . . he is negligent in failing to prevent the harm.

Restatement (Second) of Torts, § 518. Clearly, one who owns or possesses a bull may be found to have actual or constructive knowledge of the animal's normally dangerous propensities and be required to take reasonable steps to prevent foreseeable harm to invitees and employees. Viewed in the light most favorable to plaintiff, a submissible case of negligence is shown.

* * *

Accordingly, the judgment is reversed and the cause is remanded for a new trial on the issue of negligence based on defendant's duty to plaintiff as an invitee or employee.

Notes

1. *Strict liability* (or *absolute liability* as it is sometimes called) is liability without *proof* of fault. As the court in *Duren* indicates, in any given case it should not be assumed that the defendant was without fault. Under either a strict liability or a negligence theory the causal link between the defendant and the plaintiff's injury must still be established.

2. The liability of the possessor of abnormally dangerous domestic animals or wild animals is one of the oldest forms of strict liability. *Restatement (Second) of Torts* § 506 (2) defines a domestic animal as "an animal that is by custom devoted to the service of mankind at the time and in the place where it is kept." As the principal case notes, the dangerousness posed by a domestic animal must in some way be abnormal for the breed. *See* Jividen v. Law, 194 W.Va. 705, 461 S.E.2d 451, 461 (W.Va.1995)("we conclude that traits like rambunctiousness and friskiness are insufficient to impose strict liability.")

3. Wild animals are defined by the restatement as creatures that are not devoted to the service of mankind. One of the first modern English wild animal cases involved a pet monkey. May v. Burdett, 9 Q.B. 101, 115 Eng.Rep. 1213 (1846). A leading modern case is Behrens v. Bertram Mills Circus, Ltd., [1957] 2 Q.B. 1, 2 W.L.R. 404, 1 All E.R. 503 (elephant). Typical American cases include Collins v. Otto, 149 Colo. 489, 369 P.2d 564 (1962)(coyote); Isaacs

v. Powell, 267 So.2d 864 (Fla.App.1972)(chimpanzee). There are occasional cases that are hard to reconcile with the general rules set out in the *Restatement*. For example, in Hansen v. Brogan, 145 Mont. 224, 400 P.2d 265 (1965), it was held that the keeper of a wild buffalo would only be liable if he were shown to have been negligent.

A number of states now have statutory definitions of wild and domestic animals, sometimes leading to interesting results. *See* Ollhoff v. Peck, 177 Wis.2d 719, 503 N.W.2d 323 (App.1993)(Plaintiff, a visitor to a petting zoo, was bit by muskellunge when he put his hand in a pond in order to pet the fish. Wisconsin statute imposes strict liability for only listed wild animals, not including fish.); Gallick v. Barto, 828 F.Supp. 1168 (M.D.Pa.1993)(ferret).

Can a wild animal ever become domesticated so that its owners are no longer strictly liable for an injury it causes? *See* Pate v. Yeager, 552 S.W.2d 513 (Tex.Civ.App.1977)("Mr. Jim," three pound pet monkey bit plaintiff, a four year old visitor to the home of the monkey's owners.)

4. *Restatement (Second) of Torts* § 517 declares that the "rules of strict liability do not apply when the possession of the animal is in pursuance of a duty imposed upon the possessor as a public officer or employee or as a common carrier." *See* City and County of Denver v. Kennedy, 29 Colo.App. 15, 476 P.2d 762 (Colo.App.1970)(city not strictly liable). What about animals in private zoos or animal parks? *See* Cowden v. Bear Country, Inc., 382 F.Supp. 1321 (D.S.D.1974); Burns v. Gleason, 819 F.2d 555 (5th Cir.1987).

5. As § 506 illustrates, what will be considered a wild animal depends upon the local circumstances. Prosser cites a Burmese case in which an elephant used as a draft animal was held not to be a wild animal. Maung Kyan Dun v. Ma Kyian, 2 Upper Burma Rulings 570 (Civ.1900), cited in Prosser & Keeton, Torts 543, 547 (5th ed. 1984).

6. *Restatement (Second) Torts* § 507(2) limits strict liability "to harm that results from a dangerous propensity that is characteristic of wild animals of the particular class, or of which the possessor knows or has reason to know." *Restatement (Second) Torts* § 509(2) similarly limits strict liability for domestic animals to harms "that result from the abnormally dangerous propensity of which the possessor knows or has reason to know." Thus, there are several nineteenth century cases denying liability when horses were frightened by the mere sight of a wild animal. *See, e.g.,* Bostock–Ferari Amusement Co. v. Brocksmith, 34 Ind.App. 566, 73 N.E. 281 (1905)(bear); Scribner v. Kelly, 38 Barb. (N.Y.) 14 (1862)(elephant).

7. The requirement that the owner of a domestic animal must have knowledge of its abnormally dangerous propensities before strict liability will attach is sometimes termed the "one bite" rule. In point of fact, of course, the animal need not actually have bitten anyone to have put its possessor on notice of its dangerous propensities.

The liability of dog owners may be affected by local "leash laws" or ordinances which make it unlawful to allow dogs to run loose. Furthermore, some states have enacted statutes making the owner liable for harm done by a dog, even if the owner has no knowledge of the animal's vicious tendencies. *See, e.g.* Fl. St. § 767.04

> The owner of any dog that bites any person while such person is on or in a public place, or lawfully on or in a private place, including the property of the owner of the dog, is liable for damages suffered by persons bitten,

regardless of the former viciousness of the dog or the owners' knowledge of such viciousness. . . .

In Jones v. Utica Mutual Insurance Co., 463 So.2d 1153 (Fla.1985), the plaintiff, age 12, and defendant's son tied defendant's German Shepard, Shane, to a small wagon. Shane spotted plaintiff's dog and chased after it. As Shane ran past the plaintiff, the wagon struck the boy, causing a permanent injury to his leg. What result under the statute? *See* Nicholes v. Lorenz, 396 Mich. 53, 237 N.W.2d 468 (1976)(construing the Michigan "dog bite" statute); Jones v. Manhart, 120 Ariz. 338, 585 P.2d 1250 (App.1978)(construing the Arizona statute).

8. At common law, the possessor of livestock was strictly liable for the trespassing of the animals upon the land of neighbors. *See Restatement (Second) of Torts* § 504. The only exception was for animals that strayed on to adjoining land while being driven along the highway. *See* Goodwyn v. Cheveley, 4 H. & N. 631, 157 Eng.Rep. 989 (Exch.1859); Tillett v. Ward, 10 Q.B.D. 17 (1882); *Restatement (Second) of Torts* § 505. *See also* Tonawanda Railroad v. Munger, 5 Denio (N.Y.) 255 (1848), *affirmed* 4 N.Y. 349 (1850). Furthermore, as we saw in Chapter Two, *supra* p. 57, the possessor had a privilege to enter that adjoining land to recapture the straying animals. At the same time, failure to remove the animals within a reasonable time would lead to liability.

The common-law rule making a person strictly liable for trespassing livestock met with some opposition in the United States, particularly in the Western states. Either by statute or judicial decision a number of jurisdictions adopted a "fencing out" rule, namely one that put the onus upon the adjoining landowner to put up a "sufficient" fence to keep out a neighbor's livestock. If the animals broke the fence, there would be liability; if there was no fence, there would be no liability. *See* Robinson v. Kerr, 144 Colo. 48, 355 P.2d 117 (1960), which held that such a statute only applied to property damage; as to personal injuries the traditional common law applied. As the country became more densely settled the modern trend has been back towards the common-law rule requiring a person to keep his livestock from trespassing upon a neighbor's land. Some states, indeed, have adopted "fencing-in" statutes. The effect of a "fencing-in" statute, however, is different from the common-law rule because if the defendant constructs a fence that meets the statutory standard, he is not liable if the animal escapes. *See* Overbey v. Poteat, 206 Tenn. 146, 332 S.W.2d 197 (1960).

An interesting question is whether farmers and ranchers alter their behavior depending on whether they live under a "fencing out" or "fencing in" rule. *See* Robert Ellickson, Order Without Law: How Neighbors Settle Disputes. Cambridge: Harvard U. Press. (1991); Kenneth Vogel, The Coase Theorem and California Animal Trespass Law, 16 J. Legal. Stud. 149 (1987). *See also*, the discussion of the Coase Theorem at the end of this chapter.

9. *Restatement (Second) Torts* § 515 enunciates the rule, which it adopts in all cases of strict liability, that the contributory negligence of the plaintiff is no defense to an action for harm done by animals for which the possessor is strictly liable. Only if the plaintiff has assumed the risk of harm will the action be barred. *See* Sandy v. Bushey, 124 Me. 320, 128 A. 513 (1925); Marshall v. Ranne, 511 S.W.2d 255 (Tex.1974)(hog); Franken v. City of Sioux Center, 272 N.W.2d 422 (Iowa 1978)(tiger); Keyser v. Phillips Petroleum Co. 287 So.2d 364 (Fla.App.1973)(snakes). As we shall see below, in Chapter Nine, however, many states that have adopted comparative negligence now permit contributory

negligence to be a partial defense to an action for strict liability for defective products. Parity of reasoning would dictate that contributory negligence should be a partial defense in other types of strict liability, including that involving the keeping of animals. Some courts now have determined that their comparative responsibility statute applies to strict liability actions involving wild animals or abnormally dangerous domestic animals. *See* Mills v. Smith, 9 Kan.App.2d 80, 673 P.2d 117 (1983); Arbegast v. Board of Education, 65 N.Y.2d 161, 490 N.Y.S.2d 751, 480 N.E.2d 365 (1985).

B. DANGEROUS ACTIVITIES

FLETCHER v. RYLANDS

Exchequer Chamber, 1866.
L.R. 1. Ex. 265.

[The plaintiff operated the Red House Colliery in Lancaster. The defendants operated the Ainsworth Mill nearby. In order to guarantee a constant water supply for their mill, the defendants engaged a respected and competent engineering firm to construct a mill pond on the defendant's property. While excavating for the bed of the mill pond, the independent contractors came across five old shafts descending vertically into the ground. The shafts were filled with soil. Unbeknownst to the contractors, these shaft were part of old coal workings under the site of the future reservoir. The contractors proceeded to build the pond on top of the shafts. As the pond began to fill, the weight of the water caused the soil in one of the shafts to give way. On the morning of December 11, 1860 water burst into the old abandoned workings and travelled underground beneath adjacent property until it entered into and flooded the Red House Colliery.]

The judgment of the Court (Willes, Blackburn, Keating, Mellor, Montague Smith, and Lush, JJ.) was delivered by Blackburn, J. This was a special case stated by an arbitrator, under an order of nisi pruis, in which the question for the court is stated to be whether the plaintiff is entitled to recover any, and, if any, what damages from the defendants, by reason of the matters therein before stated.

In the Court of Exchequer, the Chief Barron and Martin, B., were of opinion that the plaintiff was not entitled to recover at all, Bramwell, B. being of a different opinion. The judgment in the Exchequer was consequently given for the defendants, in conformity with the opinion of the majority of the court. The only question argued before us was whether this judgment was right, nothing being said about the measure of damages in case the plaintiff should be held entitled to recover. We have come to the conclusion that the opinion of Bramwell, B., was right, and that the answer to the question should be that the plaintiff was entitled to recover damages from the defendants, by reason of the matters stated in the case, and consequently, that the judgment below should be reversed, but we cannot at present say to what damages the plaintiff is entitled.

* * *

It is found that the defendants, personally, were free from all blame, but that in fact proper care and skill was not used by the persons employed by them, to provide for the sufficiency of the reservoir, with reference to these shafts.

* * *

The plaintiff, though free from all blame on his part, must bear the loss, unless he can establish that it was the consequence of some default for which the defendants are responsible. The question of law therefore arises, what is the obligation which the law casts on a person who, like the defendants, lawfully brings on his land something which, though harmless whilst it remains there, will naturally do mischief if it escape out of his land. It is agreed on all hands that he must take care to keep in that which he has brought on the land and keeps there, in order that it may not escape and damage his neighbours, but the question arises whether the duty which the law casts upon him, under such circumstances, is an absolute duty to keep it in at his peril, or is, as the majority of the Court of Exchequer have thought, merely a duty to take all reasonable and prudent precautions, in order to keep it in, but no more. If the first be the law, the person who has brought on his land and kept there something dangerous, and failed to keep it in, is responsible for all the natural consequences of its escape. If the second be the limit of his duty, he would not be answerable except on proof of negligence, and consequently would not be answerable for escape arising from any latent defect which ordinary prudence and skill could not detect.

Supposing the second to be the correct view of the law, a further question arises subsidiary to the first, viz., whether the defendants are not so far identified with the contractors whom they employed, as to be responsible for the consequences of their want of care and skill in making the reservoir in fact insufficient with reference to the old shafts, of the existence of which they were aware, though they had not ascertained where the shafts went to.

We think that the true rule of law is, that the person who for his own purposes brings on his lands and collects and keeps there anything likely to do mischief if it escapes, must keep it in at his peril, and, if he does not do so, is primâ facie answerable for all the damage which is the natural consequence of its escape. He can excuse himself by shewing that the escape was owing to the plaintiff's default; or perhaps that the escape was the consequence of vis major, or the act of God; but as nothing of this sort exists here, it is unnecessary to inquire what excuse would be sufficient. The general rule, as above stated, seems on principle just. The person whose grass or corn is eaten down by the escaping cattle of his neighbour, or whose mine is flooded by the water from his neighbour's reservoir, or whose cellar is invaded by the filth of his neighbour's privy, or whose habitation is made unhealthy by the fumes and noisome vapours of his neighbour's alkali works, is damnified without any fault of his own; and it seems but reasonable and just that the neighbour, who has brought something on his own property which was not naturally there, harmless to others so long as it is confined to his own property, but which he knows to be mischievous if it gets on his neighbour's, should be obliged to make good the damage which ensues if he does not succeed in confining it to his own property. But for his act in bringing it there no mischief could have accrued, and it seems but just that he should at his peril keep it there so that no mischief may accrue, or answer for the natural and anticipated consequences. And upon authority, this we think is established to be the law whether the things so brought be beasts, or water, or filth, or stenches.

The case that has most commonly occurred, and which is most frequently to be found in the books, is as to the obligation of the owner of cattle which he has brought on his land, to prevent their escaping and doing mischief. The law as to them seems to be perfectly settled from early times; the owner must keep them in at his peril, or he will be answerable for the natural consequences of their escape; that is with regard to tame beasts, for the grass they eat and trample upon, though not for any injury to the person of others, for our ancestors have settled that it is not the general nature of horses to kick, or bulls to gore;[a] but if the owner knows that the beast has a vicious propensity to attack man, he will be answerable for that too.

* * *

* * * No case has been found in which the question as to the liability for noxious vapours escaping from a man's works by inevitable accident has been discussed, but the following case will illustrate it. Some years ago several actions were brought against the occupiers of some alkali works at Liverpool for the damage alleged to be caused by the chlorine fumes of their works. The defendants proved that they at great expense erected contrivances by which the fumes of chlorine were condensed, and sold as muriatic acid, and they called a great body of scientific evidence to prove that this apparatus was so perfect that no fumes possibly could escape from the defendants' chimneys. On this evidence it was pressed upon the jury that the plaintiff's damage must have been due to some of the numerous other chimneys in the neighbourhood; the jury, however, being satisfied that the mischief was occasioned by chlorine, drew the conclusion that it had escaped from the defendants' works somehow, and in each case found for the plaintiff. No attempt was made to disturb these verdicts on the ground that the defendants had taken every precaution which prudence or skill could suggest to keep those fumes in, and that they could not be responsible unless negligence were shewn; yet, if the law be as laid down by the majority of the Court of Exchequer, it would have been a very obvious defence. If it had been raised, the answer would probably have been that the uniform course of pleading in actions on such nuisances is to say that the defendant caused the noisome vapours to arise on his premises, and suffered them to come on the plaintiff's, without stating there was any want of care or skill in the defendant, and that the case of *Tenant v. Goldwin*[1] shewed that this was founded on the general rule of law, that he whose stuff it is must keep it that it may not trespass. There is no difference in this respect between chlorine and water; both will, if they

---

a. [Ed. note] Since Blackburn, J.'s, statement, the common law evolved to permit an *occupier* of land to recover without proof of negligence for personal injuries if he were trampled by trespassing cattle. *See Wormald v. Cole*, [1954] 1 Q.B. 614, 2 W.L.R. 613, 1 All E.R. 683. *See also Restatement (Second) of Torts* § 504, Comments *f* and *g*. Comment *g* declares that "any trespassing bull may be expected to attack and gore any other animal or any person who gets in his way."

1. 1 Salk. 21, 360; 2 Ld. Raym. 1089; 6 Mod. 311.

escape, do damage, the one by scorching, and the other by drowning, and he who brings them there must at his peril see that they do not escape and do that mischief. What is said by Gibbs, C. J., in *Sutton v. Clarke*,[2] though not necessary for the decision of the case, shews that very learned judge took the same view of the law that was taken by Lord Holt. But it was further said by Martin, B., that when damage is done to personal property, or even to the person, by collision, either upon land or at sea, there must be negligence in the party doing the damage to render him legally responsible; and this is no doubt true, and as was pointed out by Mr. Mellish during his argument before us, this is not confined to cases of collision, for there are many cases in which proof of negligence is essential, as for instance, where an unruly horse gets on the footpath of a public street and kills a passenger: *Hammack v. White*[3]; or where a person in a dock is struck by the falling of a bale of cotton which the defendant's servants are lowering, *Scott v. London Dock Company*[4]; and many other similar cases may be found. But we think these cases distinguishable from the present. Traffic on the highways, whether by land or sea, cannot be conducted without exposing those whose persons or property are near it to some inevitable risk; and that being so, those who go on the highway, or have their property adjacent to it, may well be held to do so subject to their taking upon themselves the risk of injury from that inevitable danger; and persons who by the licence of the owner pass near to warehouses where goods are being raised or lowered, certainly do so subject to the inevitable risk of accident. In neither case, therefore, can they recover without proof of want of care or skill occasioning the accident; and it is believed that all the cases in which inevitable accident has been held an excuse for what primâ facie was a trespass, can be explained on the same principle, viz., that the circumstances were such as to shew that the plaintiff had taken that risk upon himself. But there is no ground for saying that the plaintiff here took upon himself any risk arising from the uses to which the defendants should choose to apply their land. He neither knew what these might be, nor could he in any way control the defendants, or hinder their building what reservoirs they liked, and storing up in them what water they pleased, so long as the defendants succeeded in preventing the water which they there brought from interfering with the plaintiff's property.

Judgment for the plaintiff.

RYLANDS v. FLETCHER

House of Lords, 1868.
L.R. 3 E. & I. App. 330.

THE LORD CHANCELLOR (LORD CAIRNS):—

* * *a

My Lords, the principles on which this case must be determined appear to me to be extremely simple. The Defendants, treating them as the

2. 6 Taunt. at p. 44.
3. 11 C.B.(N.S.) 588; 31 L.J.(C.P.) 129.
4. H. & C. 596; 34 L.J.(Ex.) 17, 220.

a. [Ed. note] In the material omitted Lord Cairns stated the facts and prior history of the case.

owners or occupiers of the close on which the reservoir was constructed, might lawfully have used that close for any purpose for which it might in the ordinary course of the enjoyment of land be used; and if, in what I may term the natural user of that land, there had been any accumulation of water, either on the surface or underground, and if, by the operation of the laws of nature, that accumulation of water had passed off into the close occupied by the Plaintiff, the Plaintiff could not have complained that that result had taken place. If he had desired to guard himself against it, it would have lain upon him to have done so, by leaving, or by interposing, some barrier between his close and the close of the Defendants in order to have prevented that operation of the laws of nature.

As an illustration of that principle, I may refer to a case which was cited in the argument before your Lordships, the case of *Smith v. Kenrick* in the Court of Common Pleas.[1]

On the other hand if the Defendants, not stopping at the natural use of their close, had desired to use it for any purpose which I may term a non-natural use, for the purpose of introducing into the close that which in its natural condition was not in or upon it, for the purpose of introducing water either above or below ground in quantities and in a manner not the result of any work or operation on or under the land,—and if in consequence of their doing so, or in consequence of any imperfection in the mode of their doing so, the water came to escape and to pass off into the close of the Plaintiff, then it appears to me that that which the Defendants were doing they were doing at their own peril; and, if in the course of their doing it, the evil arose to which I have referred, the evil, namely, of the escape of the water and its passing away to the close of the Plaintiff and injuring the Plaintiff, then for the consequence of that, in my opinion, the Defendants would be liable. As the case of *Smith v. Kenrick* is an illustration of the first principle to which I have referred, so also the second principle to which I have referred is well illustrated by another case in the same Court, the case of *Baird v. Williamson*,[2] which was also cited in the argument at the Bar.

My Lords, these simple principles, if they are well founded, as it appears to me they are, really dispose of this case.

The same result is arrived at on the principles, referred to by Mr. Justice *Blackburn* in his judgment, in the Court of Exchequer Chamber, where he states the opinion of that Court as to the law in these words: * * *a

My Lords, in that opinion, I must say I entirely concur. Therefore, I have to move your Lordships that the judgment of the Court of Exchequer Chamber be affirmed, and that the present appeal be dismissed with costs.

Lord Cranworth:—

My Lords, I concur with my noble and learned friend in thinking that the rule of law was correctly stated by Mr. Justice *Blackburn* in delivering

---

1. 7 C.B. 515.

2. 15 C.B.(N.S.) 317.

a. [Ed. note] Lord Cairns here quotes verbatim the entire paragraph beginning:

"We think that the true rule of law is * * *," reprinted at p. 569 *supra*.

the opinion of the Exchequer Chamber. If a person brings, or accumulates, on his land anything which, if it should escape, may cause damage to his neighbour, he does so at his peril. If it does escape, and cause damage, he is responsible, however careful he may have been, and whatever precautions he may have taken to prevent the damage.

In considering whether a Defendant is liable to a Plaintiff for damage which the Plaintiff may have sustained, the question in general is not whether the Defendant has acted with due care and caution, but whether his acts have occasioned the damage. This is all well explained in the old case of *Lambert v. Bessey*, reported by Sir *Thomas Raymond*.[1] And the doctrine is founded on good sense. For when one person, in managing his own affairs, causes, however innocently, damage to another, it is obviously only just that he should be the party to suffer. He is bound *sic uti suo ut non lædat alienum*. This is the principle of law applicable to cases like the present, and I do not discover in the authorities which were cited anything conflicting with it.

The doctrine appears to me to be well illustrated by the two modern cases in the Court of Common Pleas referred to by my noble and learned friend. I allude to the two cases of *Smith v. Kenrick*, and *Baird v. Williamson*. In the former the owner of a coal mine on the higher level worked out the whole of his coal, leaving no barrier between his mine and the mine on the lower level, so that the water percolating through the upper mine flowed into the lower mine, and obstructed the owner of it in getting his coal. It was held that the owner of the lower mine had no ground of complaint. The Defendant, the owner of the upper mine, had a right to remove all his coal. The damage sustained by the Plaintiff was occasioned by the natural flow or percolation of water from the upper strata. There was no obligation on the Defendant to protect the Plaintiff against this. It was his business to erect or leave a sufficient barrier to keep out the water, or to adopt proper means for so conducting the water as that it should not impede him in his workings. The water, in that case, was only left by the Defendant to flow in its natural course.

But in the later case of *Baird v. Williamson* the Defendant, the owner of the upper mine, did not merely suffer the water to flow through his mine without leaving a barrier between it and the mine below, but in order to work his own mine beneficially he pumped up quantities of water which passed into the Plaintiff's mine in addition to that which would have naturally reached it, and so occasioned him damage. Though this was done without negligence, and in the due working of his own mine, yet he was held to be responsible for the damage so occasioned. It was in consequence of his act, whether skilfully or unskilfully performed, that the Plaintiff had been damaged, and he was therefore held liable for the consequences. The damage in the former case may be treated as having arisen from the act of God; in the latter, from the act of the Defendant.

Applying the principle of these decisions to the case now before the House, I come without hesitation to the conclusion that the judgment of the Exchequer Chamber was right. The Plaintiff had a right to work his coal through the lands of Mr. *Whitehead*, and up to the old workings. If

1. Sir T. Raym. 421.

water naturally rising in the Defendants' land (we may treat the land as the land of the Defendants for the purpose of this case) had by percolation found its way down to the Plaintiff's mine through the old workings, and so had impeded his operations, that would not have afforded him any ground of complaint. Even if all the old workings had been made by the Plaintiff, he would have done no more than he was entitled to do; for, according to the principle acted on in *Smith v. Kenrick*, the person working the mine, under the close in which the reservoir was made, had a right to win and carry away all the coal without leaving any wall or barrier against *Whitehead's* land. But that is not the real state of the case. The Defendants, in order to effect an object of their own, brought on to their land, or on to land which for this purpose may be treated as being theirs, a large accumulated mass of water, and stored it up in a reservoir. The consequence of this was damage to the Plaintiff, and for that damage, however skilfully and carefully the accumulation was made, the Defendants, according to the principles and authorities to which I have adverted, were certainly responsible.

I concur, therefore, with my noble and learned friend in thinking that the judgment below must be affirmed, and that there must be judgment for the Defendant in Error.

Judgment of the Court of Exchequer Chamber affirmed.

Notes

1. As we have seen in Chapter Six, supra (p. 402), in modern law there would have been no difficulty in holding John Rylands (and his partner Jehu Horrocks) liable for the negligence of the contractors whom they had hired to build the reservoir for them. Building such a reservoir would have had sufficient possibilities for mischief, if done carelessly, to bring into play what is now generally known as the doctrine of "non-delegable duties." The judges who heard the various phases of *Rylands v. Fletcher* were reluctant to decide this issue. English law did not begin to clearly resolve the matter until Bower v. Peate, 1 Q.B.D. 321 (1876).

2. Barron Bramwell and Baron Martin in the Court of Exchequer disagreed as to whether the defendant's could prevail under a trespass cause of action. Martin believed that the damage in this case was mediate or consequential and, therefore, trespass would not lie. He did not give any reason for his position. Why might he have arrived at this conclusion?

3. Blackburn's judgment has been praised as a masterpiece of judicial craftsmanship. Consider the following quotation from a standard English treatise on torts:

> * * * Blackburn J. did not intend to make new law[i] in *Rylands v. Fletcher*; he made a generalization which covered the cases of absolute liability which had survived the general "moralization" of the law in the eighteenth and nineteenth centuries. In the language of Wigmore, these cases of liability without fault "wandered about, unhoused and unshepherded, except for a casual attention, in the pathless fields of jurisprudence, until

---

i. This was Blackburn J.'s own opinion: "I wasted much time in the preparation of the judgment in *Rylands v. Fletcher* if I did not succeed in showing that the law held to govern it had been law for at least 300 years"; Ross v. Fedden (1872) 26 L.T. 966, 968.

they were met by the master-mind of Mr. Justice Blackburn, who guided them to the safe fold where they have since rested. In a sentence epochal in its consequences this judge co-ordinated them all in their true category."[ii]

Salmond on Torts 358 (19th ed. by R. F. V. Heuston & R.S. Buckley 1987) (footnotes renumbered).

4. In applying *Rylands v. Fletcher*, English law has thus far insisted upon an escape of the mischievous element. *See* Read v. J. Lyons & Co., [1947] 1 A.C. 156 (1946), [1946] 2 All E.R. 471. In that case a munitions factory blew up injuring the plaintiff who was a government inspector. She was injured on the defendant's premises and denied recovery in the absence of proof of fault.

5. *Proximate Cause.* Strict liability, either with respect to animals or dangerous activities, is an alternative to negligence. It is an answer to the question of what duty an individual owes fellow citizens. As we noted earlier, under either strict liability or negligence theory the plaintiff must still show a causal line between the defendant and the plaintiff's injury. Not only must there be a cause-in-fact relationship, courts may impose proximate cause limitations on liability.

Recently, in Cambridge Water Co. Ltd. v. Eastern Counties Leather, [1994] 2 A.C. 264, [1994] 1 All E.R. 53 the House of Lords had occasion to revisit the scope of *Rylands v Fletcher* in this regard. The water company sued Eastern Counties Leather for contaminating its underground water supply with the solvent perchloroethelene (PCE) that the defendant used from the 1960s to 1976 to degrease pelts in its tanning works. The trial court found that the contamination was the result of PCEs accidently spilled on the floor during the tanning process. The court also found that seepage down through the tanning floor and into the chalk aquifer beneath was not foreseeable, nor was it foreseeable that the seepage might create an environmental hazard. 1 A.C. at 294. The trial judge dismissed the plaintiff's claim under *Rylands*, but the cause of action was reinstated by the Court of Appeals. The issue before the House of Lords was one of first impression: whether damages must be foreseeable before one can be held liable under the rule in Rylands v. Fletcher. Lord Goff of Chieveley's speech was concurred in by all of the Law Lords who heard the case. Lord Goff's speech was in two parts. First, in England the rule in *Rylands* is an extension of the law of nuisance rather than a totally new principle of strict liability. This was the import of the *Read* case, which required an escape onto the land of another (invading the other's use of the land) in order for a cause of action to lie under *Rylands*. Second, foreseeability of harm is required under a nuisance claim, which, recall, was the conclusion of the Privy Council in Overseas Tankship (U.K.) Ltd. v. Miller Steamship Co. Pty. (The Wagon Mound No.2). [Ed. note: Wagon Mound No. 2 is reprinted on page 314]. Therefore Lord Goff concluded, the plaintiff was not strictly liable for the PCE damage because of the absence of proximate cause (foreseeable damages). [1994] 1 A.C. at 307.

After reading the remainder of this chapter, the reader should ask what similar causal limitations the American courts have put on the scope of strict liability for abnormally dangerous activities.

ii. "Responsibility for Tortious Acts" (1894) 7 Harv.L.Rev. 441, 454. But Lord Simon has said that "it appears to me logically unnecessary and historically incorrect to refer to all these instances as deduced from one common principle": Read v. Lyons [1947] A.C. 156, 167.

5. As to the scope of *Rylands v. Fletcher* in English law, we may close with this general statement of the principle of that case set down in Salmond (most footnotes omitted):

> Blackburn J.'s statement, basing liability on the defendant's artificial accumulation of the thing in question, was expressly approved in the House of Lords. But difficulty has arisen because Lord Cairns, probably unconsciously,[60] laid down another principle, distinguishing the natural from the non-natural user of land, and holding that in the latter case only was the liability absolute. This is to substitute a different principle from that adopted by Blackburn J. Its advantage is that it converts a rigid into a flexible rule, and enables the court by determining what is or is not a natural user of land to give effect to its own view of social and economic needs. Its disadvantage is that it has produced a bewildering series of decisions on the meaning of non-natural use. What is the natural use of land? Is it natural to build a house on it, or to light a fire? Is it natural to keep cattle on land? This must be one of the oldest methods of using land, but in Blackburn J.'s view it is quite logical to impose strict liability because the cattle have been artificially collected. But in Lord Cairns' view it is necessary to say that cattle-keeping is non-natural. Again, it has been held not to be natural to spray crops with herbicide from an aircraft: the activity of destroying weeds is as old as nature itself, but it seems odd today to insist that the hoe should be the only method used. Finally, if, contrary to earlier authorities, it is now the law that there is liability in nuisance for things naturally on the land, the distinction is even less helpful.

> "Extraordinary," "exceptional," "abnormal," are words that are sometimes used in substitution for "non-natural," and they suggest the true principle underlying the doctrine. It is a question of fact, subject to a ruling of the judge whether the particular object can be dangerous or the particular use can be non-natural, and in deciding this question all the circumstances of the time and place and practice of mankind must be taken into consideration so that what might be regarded as dangerous or non-natural may vary according to those circumstances. So today the collection of toxic waste on a rubbish tip, which escapes from it in solution in percolating water, and poisons water on the plaintiff's premises, is probably unlawful at common law as well as by statute.

Salmond on Torts 365–67 (19th ed. by R. F. V. Heuston & R.A. Buckley 1987).

LOSEE v. BUCHANAN

Commission of Appeals of New York, 1873.
51 N.Y. 476.

Appeal by defendants, Coe S. Buchanan and Daniel A. Bullard, from an order of the General Term of the Supreme Court in the fourth judicial district, reversing a judgment entered in their favor upon a verdict. * * *

The action was brought to recover damages occasioned by the explosion of a steam boiler, while the same was owned and being used by the

---

60. Lord Cairns merely seems to have been attempting to restate in his own words Blackburn J.'s point that it was the accumulation or collection by the defendant which was the basis of liability. What Blackburn J. had in mind was the distinction between "natural water" and "artificial water," which is not the same as the distinction between ordinary and extraordinary user.

Saratoga Paper Company, at their mill, situated in the village of Schuylerville, Saratoga county. The boiler exploded on the 13th day of February, 1864, by means whereof it was projected and thrown on to the plaintiff's premises, and through several of his buildings, thereby injuring and damaging the same, and destroying personal property therein.

Buchanan and Bullard were joined with the paper company as defendants in the action, on the ground that they were trustees, stockholders and agents of the corporation, and superintending its business as such, and therefore jointly liable with the company in the action. The Clutes, who manufactured the boiler, were also made defendants, on the ground that they made it in a negligent manner, in consequence of which negligence the boiler exploded.

The case was twice tried. * * *

Upon the second trial * * *a verdict was rendered against the paper company for $2,703.36 damages, and in favor of the defendants Buchanan and Bullard. The plaintiff moved for a new trial on the minutes of the judge, as to the defendants Buchanan and Bullard; the motion was denied, and judgment entered on the verdict in favor of Buchanan and Bullard.

Further facts appear in the opinion.

E. F. Bullard for the appellant Buchanan. Defendants had a right to use steam on their premises, and are not liable for any consequential injury therefrom, unless they were guilty of negligence. * * *

A. Pond for the respondent. Proof of negligence was not necessary to establish defendants' liability, and proof that there was no negligence is inadmissible. * * * Defendants were bound to know that the boilers were safe before using them, and for failing in that respect are liable irrespective of all questions of negligence. * * *

EARL, C. * * *

The claim on the part of the plaintiff is, that the casting of the boiler upon his premises by the explosion was a direct trespass upon his right to the undisturbed possession and occupation of his premises, and that the defendants are liable just as they would have been for any other wrongful entry and trespass upon his premises.

I do not believe this claim to be well founded, and I will briefly examine the authorities upon which mainly an attempt is made to sustain it.

We are also cited to a class of cases holding the owners of animals responsible for injuries done by them. * * * As to [wild animals and animals with known dangerous propensities], the owner can usually restrain and keep them under control, and if he will keep them he must do so. If he does not, he is responsible for any damages which their well known disposition leads them to commit. I believe the liability to be based upon the fault which the law attributes to him, and no further actual negligence need be proved than the fact that they are at large unrestrained. But if I am mistaken as to the true basis of liability in such cases, the body of laws in reference to live animals, which is supposed to be just and wise, considering the nature of the animals and the mutual rights and interests of the owners and others, does not furnish analogies absolutely controlling in reference to inanimate property.

Blackstone (vol. 3, p. 209) says, "that whenever an act is directly and immediately injurious to the person or property of another, and therefore necessarily accompanied with some force, an action of trespass *vi et armis* will lie;" for "the right of *meum* and *tuum* or property in lands being once established, it follows as a necessary consequence that this right must be exclusive; that is, that the owner may retain to himself the sole use and occupation of his soil. Every entry, therefore, thereon without the owner's leave, and especially contrary to his express order, is a trespass or transgression." The learned author was here laying down the distinction between an action of trespass and trespass on the case, and asserting the rule that in the former action the injury must be direct and immediate, and accompanied with some force, whereas in the latter action it could be indirect and consequential. He was also manifestly speaking of a direct entrance by one upon the lands of another. He was laying down a general rule that every unauthorized entrance upon the land of another is a trespass. This was sufficiently accurate for the enunciation of a general rule. Judges and legal writers do not always find it convenient, practicable or important, in laying down general rules, to specify all the limitations and exceptions to such rules. The rule, as thus announced, has many exceptions, even when one makes a personal entry upon the lands of another. I may enter my neighbor's close to succor his beast whose life is in danger; to prevent his beasts from being stolen or to prevent his grain from being consumed or spoiled by cattle; or to carry away my tree which has been blown down upon his land, or to pick up my apples which have fallen from my trees upon his land, or to take my personal property which another has wrongfully taken and placed there, or to escape from one who threatens my life. (Bacon's Abridgment, Trespass, F.) Other illustrations will be given hereafter.

By becoming a member of civilized society, I am compelled to give up many of my natural rights, but I receive more than a compensation from the surrender by every other man of the same rights, and the security, advantage and protection which the laws give me. So, too, the general rules that I may have the exclusive and undisturbed use and possession of my real estate, and that I must so use my real estate as not to injure my neighbor, are much modified by the exigencies of the social state. We must have factories, machinery, dams, canals and railroads. They are demanded by the manifold wants of mankind, and lay at the basis of all our civilization. If I have any of these upon my lands, and they are not a nuisance and are not so managed as to become such, I am not responsible for any damage they accidentally and unavoidably do my neighbor. He receives his compensation for such damage by the general good, in which he shares, and the right which he has to place the same things upon his lands. I may not place or keep a nuisance upon my land to the damage of my neighbor, and I have my compensation for the surrender of this right to use my own as I will by the similar restriction imposed upon my neighbor for my benefit. I hold my property subject to the risk that it may be unavoidably or accidentally injured by those who live near me; and as I move about upon the public highways and in all places where other persons may lawfully be, I take the risk of being accidentally injured in my person by them without fault on their part. Most of the rights of property, as well as of person, in the social state, are not absolute but relative, and they must be so arranged and modified, not unnecessarily infringing upon natural rights, as upon the whole to promote the general welfare.

I have so far found no authorities and no principles which fairly sustain the broad claim made by the plaintiff, that the defendants are liable in this action without fault or negligence on their part to which the explosion of the boiler could be attributed.

But our attention is called to a recent English case, decided in the Exchequer Chamber, which seems to uphold the claim made. In the case of *Fletcher v. Rylands* (1 Exchequer, 265, Law Reports) [the court here gives the essential facts of that case] * * * [i]t was held, reversing the judgment of the Court of Exchequer, that the defendants were liable for the damage so caused, upon the broad doctrine that one who, for his own purposes, brings upon his land, and collects and keeps there, anything likely to do mischief if it escapes, must keep it at his peril, and, if he does not do so, is *prima facie* answerable for all the damage which is the natural consequence of its escape. * * * This conclusion is reached by the learned judge mainly by applying to the case the same rule of liability to which owners are subjected by the escape of their live animals. As I have shown above, the rules of law applicable to live animals should not be applied to inanimate property. That case was appealed to the House of Lords and affirmed (3 H.L. [Law Rep.], 330), and was followed in *Smith v. Fletcher* (20 W.R., 987).

It is sufficient, however, to say that the law, as laid down in those cases, is in direct conflict with the law as settled in this country. Here, if one builds a dam upon his own premises and thus holds back and accumulates the water for his benefit, or if he brings water upon his premises into a reservoir, in case the dam or the banks of the reservoir give away and the lands of a neighbor are thus flooded, he is not liable for the damage without proof of some fault or negligence on his part. * * *

The true rule is laid down in the case of *Livingston v. Adams* [8 Cowen (N.Y.) 175 (1828)] as follows: "Where one builds a mill-dam upon a proper model, and the work is well and substantially done, he is not liable to an action though it break away, in consequence of which his neighbor's dam and mill below are destroyed. Negligence should be shown in order to make him liable."

In support of the plaintiff's claim in this action the rule has been invoked that, where one of two innocent parties must suffer, he who puts in motion the cause of the injury must bear the loss. But, as will be seen by the numerous cases above cited, it has no application whatever to a case like this.

This examination has gone far enough to show that the rule is, at least in this country, a universal one, which, so far as I can discern, has no exceptions or limitations, that no one can be made liable for injuries to the person or property of another without some fault or negligence on his part.

In this case the defendants had the right to place the steam boiler upon their premises. It was in no sense a nuisance, and the jury have found that they were not guilty of any negligence. The judgment in their favor should, therefore, have been affirmed at the General Term, unless there were errors in the charge, or refusal to charge, of the judge who presided at the trial, and these alleged errors I will now briefly examine. [No error was found.]

Notes

1. Did Judge Earl adequately distinguish the animal cases from the facts in this case?

2. A more recent American case rejecting *Rylands v. Fletcher* is Turner v. Big Lake Oil Co., 128 Tex. 155, 96 S.W.2d 221 (1936). In the *Turner* case, salt water that had been pumped to the surface and stored in man-made ponds in the course of producing oil had somehow escaped from those ponds and eventually polluted natural waterholes some six miles away that were used by livestock. The court held that, in the absence of proof of negligence, there could be no liability. The court distinguished *Rylands v. Fletcher* on the ground that "England is a pluvial country where * * *abundant rains make the storage of water unnecessary," whereas West Texas is "an arid * * *region" where water from the infrequent rainfall or water that is pumped from the ground must be accumulated in artificial basins. Much more on point, the court noted a further distinction between England and Texas.

> Again, in England there are no oil wells, no necessity for using surface storage facilities for impounding and evaporating salt waters therefrom. In Texas the situation is different. Texas has many great oil fields, tens of thousands of wells in almost every part of the state. Producing oil is one of our major industries. One of the by-products of oil production is salt water, which must be disposed of without injury to property or the pollution of streams. The construction of basins or ponds to hold this salt water is a necessary part of the oil business.

On this analysis, would Blackburn impose strict liability on Big Lake Oil? Would Cairns? How would these two judges have decided *Losee*?

3. Relying upon the earlier case of Hay v. Cohoes County, 2 N.Y. (2 Comst.) 159 (1849), the New York Court of Appeals held a blaster liable for the death of a woman traveling on a highway, the fragment that killed her having been hurled over 400 feet from the site of the blasting. Sullivan v. Dunham, 161 N.Y. 290, 55 N.E. 923 (1900). The trial judge had charged the jury that negligence need not be shown in order to permit the recovery. The Court of Appeals affirmed a judgment in favor of the personal representative of the deceased. In the course of its judgment the court quoted with approval a statement from the *Hay* case that, if a person engaged in excavating could not accomplish his purpose without casting debris upon the land of his neighbor, "he must abandon that mode of using his property, or be held responsible for all damages resulting therefrom." In *Sullivan*, *Losee* was distinguished as involving an accidental explosion.

4. Recall that the Barons who first heard *Rylands* disagreed as to whether the invasion of the plaintiff's mine by the water constituted a trespass. The old common law distinction between trespass and trespass on the case continued in early American strict liability blasting cases. If an explosion caused a objects to be cast upon the plaintiff's land, this was a trespass and the blaster would be

held strictly liable. If, on the other hand, the blast only caused vibration damages, this was thought to be an indirect injury and the plaintiff would be required to prove that the defendant acted negligently. In Booth v. Rome, Watertown & Ogdensburg Terminal Railroad, 140 N.Y. 267, 35 N.E. 592 (1893), the Court of Appeals held that where the damage caused by blasting came about as the result of concussion rather than from the throwing of debris, no recovery could be had without proof of negligence. Following Exner v. Sherman Power Const. Co., 54 F.2d 510 (2d Cir.1931), American courts increasingly imposed strict liability for both types of harm. *See* Harper v. Regency Development Company, Inc. 399 So.2d 248 (Ala.1981). However, the distinction between damage caused by debris and that caused by vibration survived in New York for over seventy-five years until it was abandoned in Spano v. Perini Corp., 25 N.Y.2d 11, 302 N.Y.S.2d 527, 250 N.E.2d 31 (1969). It should be noted that even before *Booth* was overruled, the Court of Appeals had permitted evidence of injury by concussions resulting from blasting as proof that the blasting had been negligently performed. *See* Schlansky v. Augustus V. Riegel, Inc., 9 N.Y.2d 493, 215 N.Y.S.2d 52, 174 N.E.2d 730 (1961).

5. Eventually, most American jurisdictions embraced the doctrine of absolute liability that originated in *Rylands v. Fletcher*. Since the *Restatement* and *Restatement (Second) of Torts* have largely supplied the vocabulary in which that doctrine is discussed in the United States, we will accordingly proceed to examine their treatment of the subject.

RESTATEMENT OF TORTS (1938)

§ 519. Miscarriage of Ultrahazardous Activities Carefully Carried On

Except as stated in §§ 521–4, one who carries on an ultrahazardous activity is liable to another whose person, land or chattels the actor should recognize as likely to be harmed by the unpreventable miscarriage of the activity for harm resulting thereto from that which makes the activity ultrahazardous, although the utmost care is exercised to prevent the harm.

§ 520. Definition of Ultrahazardous Activity.

An activity is ultrahazardous if it

(a) necessarily involves a risk of serious harm to the person, land or chattels of others which cannot be eliminated by the exercise of the utmost care, and

(b) is not a matter of common usage.

Notes

1. As can be seen, in the *Restatement*'s initial treatment of the subject in 1938, whether an activity was to be classed as ultrahazardous depended on two features: the dangerousness of the activity and the extent of its usage. In addition to capturing something of Lord Cairn's notion of "non-natural use," the "common usage" exception also excluded the possibility that an activity like automobile driving might be considered ultrahazardous and thus subjected to a regime of strict liability.

2. In applying § 520, the conceptually difficult questions revolved around the common usage exception. In Luthringer v. Moore, 31 Cal.2d 489, 190 P.2d

1 (1948), for example, the plaintiff was injured when hydrocyanic acid gas, used by a professional fumigator to fumigate the basement of a restaurant, seeped into an adjoining pharmacy in which the plaintiff was employed. It was argued that fumigation was a common activity. The court held, however, that the gas "may be used commonly by fumigators but they are few in number and are engaged in a specialized activity." This conclusion tracked Comment *e* to § 520 which declared that activities like the "manufacture, storage, transportation, and use of high explosives, although necessary to the construction of many public and private works, are carried on by a comparatively small number of persons and, therefore, are not matters of common usage." In a later California case involving the slippage of a man-made hillside landfill onto the plaintiff's property, a district court of appeal held that such a method of construction in Southern California could be conducted in a manner that avoided risk to others *and*, furthermore, was a matter of common usage. Beck v. Bel Air Properties, 134 Cal.App.2d 834, 286 P.2d 503 (1955).

The question of the scope and effect of the common usage exception were considered again in Loe v. Lenhardt, 227 Or. 242, 362 P.2d 312 (1961). The case involved damage to crops from the aerial spraying (or "crop-dusting") of adjacent apple orchards. The court noted the high degree of danger from the aerial spraying of chemicals. The court responded briefly to the argument that aerial spraying was a common activity:

> However common may be the practice of spraying chemicals by airplane, the prevalence of the practice does not justify treating the sprayer and the "sprayee" as the law of negligence treats motorists, leaving each to fend for himself unless one can prove negligence against the other. * * *

227 Or. at 253, 362 P.2d at 318. The suggestion is that perhaps the question of the ultrahazardous nature of an activity should turn solely upon the relative dangerousness of the activity. As we shall shortly see, the *Restatement (Second)* adopted a somewhat different approach.

3. Since many of the other problems such as the extent of liability and the possible defenses to an action for the miscarriage of dangerous activities are treated in substantially the same way under the *Restatement (Second)*, we shall examine these issues in conjunction with the following discussion.

RESTATEMENT (SECOND) OF TORTS, TENTATIVE DRAFT NO. 10 (1964)

§ 520. Abnormally Dangerous Activities

[The text of this section as finally officially issued in 1977 is set forth below (p. 585)]

Note to Institute: The Council, and all of the Advisers, agree with the change. The following observations are offered in explanation:

1. Volume 1 of the Restatement started out talking about an "extrahazardous activity." In Volume III, for no visible reason, this became "ultrahazardous." The two were obviously intended to mean the same thing. But "ultra" does not mean extra, or even excessive. It means surpassing, going entirely beyond. The dictionary meaning of "ultrahazardous" is something going beyond hazardous, surpassing all risk. It is the wrong word, since we are still in the field of risk, and the defendant is held

liable only within the scope of the risk created. See the limitations on the liability in § 519. This is a minor objection to the term.

2. "Ultrahazardous," as it is defined in the old Section, is misleading. There is probably no activity whatever, unless it be the use of atomic energy, which is not perfectly safe if the *utmost* care is used—which would of course include the choice of an absolutely safe place to carry it on. Blasting is perfectly safe with the right explosives, if it is carried on with small enough charges in the right place. Supersonic jet aviation is quite safe, except for the participants, if it is carried on over an empty part of the Pacific, or the Antarctic continent. The same is true of all of the other activities usually included within this category.

3. The thing which stands out from the cases is that the important thing about the activity is not that it is extremely dangerous in itself, but that it is abnormally so in relation to its surroundings. A magazine of explosives is a matter of strict liability if it is located in the midst of a city or other thickly settled area. * * *It is not, if it is located in the middle of the desert.[a] * * *

The same is true of the storage of gasoline, or other inflammable liquids, in large quantities. In a populated area this is a matter of strict liability. * * *But in an isolated area it is not. * * *

The blasting cases point in all directions, largely because of the initial distinction between trespass and case, and between thrown rocks and concussion, which is now pretty well discredited. On their facts the cases divide fairly well along the lines that blasting in a city, or in close proximity to a highway or to very valuable property, is a matter for strict liability, while blasting on an uninhabited mountainside is not. This distinction has been made expressly in a good many cases. * * *

Compare also the cases of oil and gas wells in the middle of thickly settled communities, which have been held to be a matter of strict liability. * * * The Texas and Oklahoma cases rejecting the strict liability all have arisen in open country, with no particularly valuable property near. * * *

The same distinction is found in the cases of water stored in quantity, as in a reservoir. Rylands v. Fletcher was a case of a reservoir in Lancashire, which was primarily coal mining country; and the basis of the decision in the House of Lords was clearly that this was a "non-natural" use of the particular land. All the subsequent English decisions have borne out this interpretation of the case. Where water is stored in large quantity in dangerous location in a city, there has been strict liability. * * *

But where the water is collected in a rural area, with no particularly valuable property near, there has been no strict liability. * * *

4. In addition, there are a number of cases in which strict liability has been imposed upon activities not extremely dangerous in themselves, but abnormally so because of their location and relation to their surroundings. For example, the following:

a. [Ed. note] None of the cases cited as illustrating this proposition involved blasting in a desert.

Shipley v. 50 Associates, (1869) 101 Mass. 251, 3 Am.Rep. 346, affirmed in (1870) 106 Mass. 194, 8 Am.Rep. 318. Roof so constructed as to collect ice and shed it all at once onto the highway.

Hannem v. Pence, (1889) 40 Minn. 127, 41 N.W. 657. The same.

Gorham v. Gross, (1878) 125 Mass. 232, 28 Am.Rep. 224. Unsafe party wall so constructed as to fall onto plaintiff's land.

Shiffman v. Order of St. John, [1936] 1 All Eng.Rep. 557. Unsafe flagpole erected on public land where crowd expected to congregate, and children had access to it.

Chichester Corp. v. Foster, [1906] 1 K.B. 167. Ten ton traction engine driven along highway, which crushed conduits under the street.

Gas Light & Coke Co. v. Vestry of St. Mary Abbott's, (1885) 15 Q.B.D. 1. The same as to an exceptionally heavy steam roller.

The English courts have had little trouble with all this, because it has been recognized from the beginning that Rylands v. Fletcher is limited to a "non-natural" activity, and that "non-natural" means inappropriate to the place where it is carried on. Much of the rejection of that case by what is now a dwindling minority of the American jurisdictions has been due to the prevalence of the idea that activities must be classified as such, and that if there is strict liability for an activity at all, there must always be strict liability for it in all places and under all circumstances. This is certainly not true.

The Advisers and the Council all agree that "ultrahazardous" is to be discarded. Since it appears to be impossible to formulate a "definition" which will include both the use of atomic energy and a water tank in the wrong place, the decision has been: (1) to refer to "abnormally dangerous" activities, borrowing the term from § 509 as to domestic animals, and (2) to state this Section in terms of factors to be taken into account, relying on the Comments for explanation.

Notes

1. The late Dean Prosser was the Reporter who prepared and presented this portion of the draft *Restatement (Second)* to the American Law Institute for its approval. The excerpts presented are a good illustration of Prosser's style of argument. He presented overwhelming citation of cases (which considerations of space have forced us largely to omit) to make his point.

2. Since §§ 519–20 of the *Restatement* restricted liability to those "the actor should recognize as *likely* to be harmed by the unpreventable miscarriage of the activity * * *" did it not make the circumstances in which the activity was carried on relevant? Is the dispute therefore merely semantic? Moreover are there not a number of activities, such as the storage and transportation of toxic wastes, which experience indicates to have an element of danger that cannot be totally removed? Finally, what is meant by activities "not extremely dangerous in themselves, but abnormally so because of their location * * *"?

RESTATEMENT (SECOND) OF TORTS (1977)

§ 519. General Principle

(1) One who carries on an abnormally dangerous activity is subject to liability for harm to the person, land or chattels of another resulting from the activity, although he has exercised the utmost care to prevent the harm.

(2) This strict liability is limited to the kind of harm, the possibility of which makes the activity abnormally dangerous.

§ 520. Abnormally Dangerous Activities

In determining whether an activity is abnormally dangerous, the following factors are to be considered:

(a) existence of a high degree of risk of some harm to the person, land or chattels of others;

(b) likelihood that the harm that results from it will be great;

(c) inability to eliminate the risk by the exercise of reasonable care;

(d) extent to which the activity is not a matter of common usage;

(e) inappropriateness of the activity to the place where it is carried on; and

(f) extent to which its value to the community is outweighed by its dangerous attributes.

KLEIN v. PYRODYNE CORP.

Supreme Court of Washington, En Banc, 1991.
117 Wn.2d 1, 810 P.2d 917.

GUY, JUSTICE.

The plaintiffs in this case are persons injured when an aerial shell at a public fireworks exhibition went astray and exploded near them. The defendant is the pyrotechnic company hired to set up and discharge the fireworks. The issue before this court is whether pyrotechnicians are strictly liable for damages caused by fireworks displays. We hold that they are.

Defendant Pyrodyne Corporation (Pyrodyne) is a general contractor for aerial fireworks at public fireworks displays. Pyrodyne contracted to procure fireworks, to provide pyrotechnic operators, and to display the fireworks at the Western Washington State Fairgrounds in Puyallup, Washington on July 4, 1987. All operators of the fireworks display were Pyrodyne employees acting within the scope of their employment duties.

* * *

During the fireworks display, one of the 5–inch mortars was knocked into a horizontal position. From this position a shell inside was ignited and discharged. The shell flew 500 feet in a trajectory parallel to the earth and exploded near the crowd of onlookers. Plaintiffs Danny and Marion

Klein were injured by the explosion. Mr. Klein's clothing was set on fire, and he suffered facial burns and serious injury to his eyes.

The parties provide conflicting explanations of the cause of the improper horizontal discharge of the shell. Pyrodyne argues that the accident was caused by a 5–inch shell detonating in its above-ground mortar tube without ever leaving the ground. Pyrodyne asserts that this detonation caused another mortar tube to be knocked over, ignited, and shot off horizontally. In contrast, the Kleins contend that the misdirected shell resulted because Pyrodyne's employees improperly set up the display. They further note that because all of the evidence exploded, there is no means of proving the cause of the misfire.

* * *

The trial court denied Pyrodyne's summary judgment motion regarding the Kleins' strict liability claim, holding that Pyrodyne was strictly liable without fault and ordering summary judgment in favor of the Kleins on the issue of liability. Pyrodyne appealed the order of partial summary judgment to the Court of Appeals, which certified the case to this court. Pyrodyne is appealing solely as to the trial court's holding that strict liability is the appropriate standard of liability for pyrotechnicians. A strict liability claim against pyrotechnicians for damages caused by fireworks displays presents a case of first impression in Washington.

Analysis

I

Fireworks Displays as Abnormally Dangerous Activities

The Kleins contend that strict liability is the appropriate standard to determine the culpability of Pyrodyne because Pyrodyne was participating in an abnormally dangerous activity.

* * *

The modern doctrine of strict liability for abnormally dangerous activities derives from *Fletcher v. Rylands*, 159 Eng.Rep. 737 (1865), rev'd, 1 L.R.-Ex. 265, [1866] All E.R. 1, 6, *aff'd sub nom. Rylands v. Fletcher*, 3 L.R.-H.L. 330, [1868] All E.R. 1, 12, in which the defendant's reservoir flooded mine shafts on the plaintiff's adjoining land. Rylands v. Fletcher has come to stand for the rule that "the defendant will be liable when he damages another by a thing or activity unduly dangerous and inappropriate to the place where it is maintained, in the light of the character of that place and its surroundings." W. Keeton, D. Dobbs, R. Keeton & D. Owen, *Prosser and Keeton on Torts* § 78, at 547–48 (5th ed. 1984).

The basic principle of *Rylands v. Fletcher* has been accepted by the Restatement (Second) of Torts (1977). *See generally Prosser and Keeton* § 78, at 551 (explaining that the relevant Restatement sections differ in some respects from the *Rylands* doctrine). Section 519 of the Restatement provides that any party carrying on an "abnormally dangerous activity" is strictly liable for ensuing damages. The test for what constitutes such an activity is stated in section 520 of the Restatement. Both Restatement sections have been adopted by this court, and determination of whether an activity is an "abnormally dangerous activity" is a question of law. *New*

Meadows Holding Co. v. Washington Water Power Co., 102 Wash.2d 495, 500, 687 P.2d 212 (1984); *Langan v. Valicopters, Inc.*, 88 Wash.2d 855, 567 P.2d 218 (1977); *Siegler v. Kuhlman*, 81 Wash.2d 448, 502 P.2d 1181 (1972), *cert. denied*, 411 U.S. 983, 93 S.Ct. 2275, 36 L.Ed.2d 959 (1973).

Section 520 of the Restatement lists six factors that are to be considered in determining whether an activity is "abnormally dangerous". The factors are as follows: (a) existence of a high degree of risk of some harm to the person, land or chattels of others; (b) likelihood that the harm that results from it will be great; (c) inability to eliminate the risk by the exercise of reasonable care; (d) extent to which the activity is not a matter of common usage; (e) inappropriateness of the activity to the place where it is carried on; and (f) extent to which its value to the community is outweighed by its dangerous attributes. Restatement (Second) of Torts § 520 (1977).* * * [T]he comments to section 520 explain how these factors should be evaluated:

> Any one of them is not necessarily sufficient of itself in a particular case, and ordinarily several of them will be required for strict liability. On the other hand, it is not necessary that each of them be present, especially if others weigh heavily. Because of the interplay of these various factors, it is not possible to reduce abnormally dangerous activities to any definition. The essential question is whether the risk created is so unusual, either because of its magnitude or because of the circumstances surrounding it, as to justify the imposition of strict liability for the harm that results from it, even though it is carried on with all reasonable care.

Restatement (Second) of Torts § 520, comment *f* (1977). Examination of these factors persuades us that fireworks displays are abnormally dangerous activities justifying the imposition of strict liability.

We find that the factors stated in clauses (a), (b), and (c) are all present in the case of fireworks displays. Any time a person ignites aerial shells or rockets with the intention of sending them aloft to explode in the presence of large crowds of people, a high risk of serious personal injury or property damage is created. That risk arises because of the possibility that a shell or rocket will malfunction or be misdirected. Furthermore, no matter how much care pyrotechnicians exercise, they cannot entirely eliminate the high risk inherent in setting off powerful explosives such as fireworks near crowds.

The dangerousness of fireworks displays is evidenced by the elaborate scheme of administrative regulations with which pyrotechnicians must comply. Pyrotechnicians must be licensed to conduct public displays of special fireworks. * * * The necessity for such regulations demonstrates the dangerousness of fireworks displays.

Pyrodyne argues that if the regulations are complied with, then the high degree of risk otherwise inherent in the displays can be eliminated. Although we recognize that the high risk can be reduced, we do not agree that it can be eliminated. Setting off powerful fireworks near large crowds remains a highly risky activity even when the safety precautions mandated by statutes and regulations are followed. The Legislature appears to agree, for it has declared that in order to obtain a license to conduct a public fireworks display, a pyrotechnician must first obtain a surety bond or a certificate of insurance, the amount of which must be at least $1,000,000 for each event.

The factors stated in clauses (a), (b), and (c) together, and sometimes one of them alone, express what is commonly meant by saying an activity is ultrahazardous. Restatement (Second) of Torts § 520, comment *h* (1977). As the Restatement explains, however, "[l]iability for abnormally dangerous activities is not ... a matter of these three factors alone, and those stated in Clauses (d), (e), and (f) must still be taken into account." Restatement (Second) of Torts § 520, comment *h* (1977); *see also New Meadows Holding Co. v. Washington Water Power Co., supra,* 102 Wash.2d at 504, 687 P.2d 212 (Pearson, J., concurring) ("strict liability ... may not be imposed absent the presence of at least one of the factors stated in clauses (d), (e), and (f)").

The factor expressed in clause (d) concerns the extent to which the activity is not a matter "of common usage". The Restatement explains that "[a]n activity is a matter of common usage if it is customarily carried on by the great mass of mankind or by many people in the community." Restatement (Second) of Torts § 520, comment *i* (1977). As examples of activities that are not matters of common usage, the Restatement comments offer driving a tank, blasting, the manufacture, storage, transportation, and use of high explosives, and drilling for oil. The deciding characteristic is that few persons engage in these activities. Likewise, relatively few persons conduct public fireworks displays. Therefore, presenting public fireworks displays is not a matter of common usage.

Pyrodyne argues that the factor stated in clause (d) is not met because fireworks are a common way to celebrate the 4th of July. We reject this argument. Although fireworks are frequently and regularly enjoyed by the public, few persons set off special fireworks displays. Indeed, the general public is prohibited by statute from making public fireworks displays insofar as anyone wishing to do so must first obtain a license. RCW 70.77.255.

The factor stated in clause (e) requires analysis of the appropriateness of the activity to the place where it was carried on. In this case, the fireworks display was conducted at the Puyallup Fairgrounds. Although some locations—such as over water—may be safer, the Puyallup Fairgrounds is an appropriate place for a fireworks show because the audience can be seated at a reasonable distance from the display. Therefore, the clause (e) factor is not present in this case.

The factor stated in clause (f) requires analysis of the extent to which the value of fireworks to the community outweighs its dangerous attributes. We do not find that this factor is present here. This country has a long-standing tradition of fireworks on the 4th of July. That tradition suggests that we as a society have decided that the value of fireworks on the day celebrating our national independence and unity outweighs the risks of injuries and damage.

In sum, we find that setting off public fireworks displays satisfies four of the six conditions under the Restatement test; that is, it is an activity that is not "of common usage" and that presents an ineliminably high risk of serious bodily injury or property damage. We therefore hold that conducting public fireworks displays is an abnormally dangerous activity justifying the imposition of strict liability.

This conclusion is consistent with the results reached in cases involving damages caused by detonating dynamite. This court has recognized that parties detonating dynamite are strictly liable for the damages caused by such blasting. *See Foster v. Preston Mill Co.*, 44 Wash.2d 440, 443, 268 P.2d 645 (1954); *see also Bringle v. Lloyd*, 13 Wash.App. 844, 537 P.2d 1060 (1975); *Erickson Paving Co. v. Yardley Drilling Co.*, 7 Wash.App. 681, 502 P.2d 334 (1972). There are a number of similarities between fireworks and dynamite. Both activities involve licensed experts intentionally igniting for profit explosives that have great potential for causing damage. Moreover, after the explosion no evidence remains as to the original explosive. The notable difference between fireworks and dynamite is that with fireworks the public is invited to watch the display and with dynamite the public is generally prohibited from being near the blasting location. Because detonating dynamite is subject to strict liability, and because of the similarities between fireworks and dynamite, strict liability is also an appropriate standard for determining the standard of liability for pyrotechnicians for any damages caused by their fireworks displays.

II

PUBLIC POLICY AND STRICT LIABILITY FOR FIREWORKS DISPLAYS

Policy considerations also support imposing strict liability on pyrotechnicians for damages caused by their public fireworks displays, although such considerations are not alone sufficient to justify that conclusion. Most basic is the question as to who should bear the loss when an innocent person suffers injury through the nonculpable but abnormally dangerous activities of another. In the case of public fireworks displays, fairness weighs in favor of requiring the pyrotechnicians who present the displays to bear the loss rather than the unfortunate spectators who suffer the injuries. In addition,

> [t]he rule of strict liability rests not only upon the ultimate idea of rectifying a wrong and putting the burden where it should belong as a matter of abstract justice, that is, upon the one of the two innocent parties whose acts instigated or made the harm possible, but it also rests on problems of proof:

> One of these common features is that the person harmed would encounter a difficult problem of proof if some other standard of liability were applied. For example, the disasters caused by those who engage in abnormally dangerous or extra-hazardous activities frequently destroy all evidence of what in fact occurred, other than that the activity was being carried on. Certainly this is true with explosions of dynamite, large quantities of gasoline, or other explosives.

Siegler v. Kuhlman, 81 Wash.2d 448, 455, 502 P.2d 1181 (1972), *cert. denied*, 411 U.S. 983, 93 S.Ct. 2275, 36 L.Ed.2d 959 (1973)(quoting Peck, *Negligence and Liability Without Fault in Tort Law*, 46 Wash.L.Rev. 225, 240 (1971)). In the present case, all evidence was destroyed as to what caused the misfire of the shell that injured the Kleins. Therefore, the problem of proof this case presents for the plaintiffs also supports imposing strict liability on Pyrodyne.

III

STATUTORY STRICT LIABILITY FOR FIREWORKS

As well as holding Pyrodyne strictly liable on the basis that fireworks displays are abnormally dangerous activities, we also hold that RCW 70.77.285 imposes statutory strict liability. The statute, which mandates insurance coverage to pay for all damages resulting from fireworks displays, establishes strict liability for any ensuing injuries.

* * *

CONCLUSION

We hold that Pyrodyne Corporation is strictly liable for all damages suffered as a result of the July 1987 fireworks display. Detonating fireworks displays constitutes an abnormally dangerous activity warranting strict liability. Public policy also supports this conclusion. Furthermore, RCW 70.77.285 mandates the payment of all damages caused by fireworks displays, regardless of whether those damages were due to the pyrotechnicians' negligence. This establishes the standard of strict liability for pyrotechnicians. Therefore, we affirm the decision of the trial court.

DORE, C.J., and BRACHTENBACH, DURHAM, ANDERSEN and UTTER, JJ., concur.

DOLLIVER, JUDGE (concurring).

I concur fully with the result reached by the majority. In my opinion the statute, RCW 70.77.285, is decisive. While I harbor some belief the Legislature may not have intended the result reached by the majority, legislative intent is irrelevant when the language of the statute is plain on its face.

I am not in agreement, however, with the analysis reached by the majority relative to the application of Restatement (Second) of Torts § 520 (1977), which characterizes fireworks displays as "abnormally dangerous". Even if I agreed with the Restatement analysis, I believe it is an act of supererogation and need not and should not be contained in the opinion. Where there is one good reason—and it is surely present here—there is no necessity for multiple reasons.

I first note that no other jurisdiction has adopted a common law rule of strict liability for fireworks displays. While this state regularly does things differently from its companion jurisdictions and, indeed, its uniqueness is many times a source of justifiable pride, extreme care should be exercised before embarking on a new doctrine foreign to this state as well as to all others.

A party engaging in an abnormally dangerous activity is strictly liable for any damages which might ensue. * * * The majority points to Restatement (Second) of Torts § 520 (1977) with its six factors to be considered in determining whether an activity is "abnormally dangerous".

* * *

The majority claims factors (a), (b), (c), and (d) are present while factors (e) and (f) are not present. I agree factors (e) and (f) do not apply for the reasons given by the majority. I also agree factors (a) and (b) are present. Where I disagree with the majority is in whether factors (c) and (d) are present. The majority says yes, I say no.

Fireworks, no less than motor vehicles, for example, are high risk instrumentalities. In reality, all instrumentalities inevitably involve some degree of risk. Nothing in human life is risk free. The real issue is whether the hazard can be reduced to acceptable limits. This analysis is particularly apt where, as here, the likelihood of injury to significant numbers of persons is great unless the risk is significantly reduced. Blasting at some remove from civilization is one thing; public, urban fireworks displays are another matter.

It is apparent the Legislature, recognizing the dangers of public fireworks displays, attempted to regulate comprehensively fireworks displays. * * * The Legislature has made the determination, through the legislative process, that in fact the "high degree of risk" inherent in public fireworks displays can adequately be reduced by the "reasonable care" required by the statute. This being so, I do not believe this court should use a random case, as here, to tamper with this legislative judgment. Factor (c) has not been met.

In discussing factor (d), the majority states that since "few persons set off special fireworks displays" they are not a matter of common usage. * * * I believe the majority misconstrues factor (d). The Restatement comment on clause (d) discusses activities carried on by only a few persons, e.g., blasting, the transportation of high explosives, the drilling of oil wells. What is significant is that each of the activities used for illustrative purposes is not only an activity which is not a matter of common usage, but it is also a solitary activity. In contrast to the large crowds which attend public fireworks displays, the examples listed in comment d are not for spectators and are done away from the public. Comment *d*, Restatement (Second) of Torts § 520, at 40 (1977). The viewing of a public fireworks display is in fact, in the words of the comment on clause (d), "customarily carried on by the great mass of mankind or by many people in the community." Comment *i*, at 39. None of the examples in the comment are in any way similar to public fireworks displays. While it is true the setting up and setting off of the fireworks in public displays are done by very few people, the more important "activity" is viewing the fireworks display. I would find factor (d) is not met.

I also disagree with the majority's treatment of the six factors as acting only in favor of strict liability. Properly construed, each of the factors may also mitigate against strict liability. In *New Meadows*, we expressly stated, "Factors (d), (e), and (f) clearly weigh against imposition of strict liability." *New Meadows*, 102 Wash.2d at 502, 687 P.2d 212. The majority concedes "the value of fireworks to the community outweighs its dangerous attributes." * * * Properly construed, therefore, factor (f) is not merely a nullity in the strict liability analysis, but should actually mitigate against the imposition of strict liability.

Thus, by my analysis, only two of the six factors in section 520 are met and one factor weighs against strict liability. The penultimate paragraph in the comment on clause (c) states:

> A combination of the factors stated in Clauses (a), (b) and (c), or sometimes any one of them alone, is commonly expressed by saying that the activity is "ultrahazardous," or "extra-hazardous." Liability for abnormally dangerous activities is not, however, a matter of these three factors alone, and those stated in Clauses (d), (e), and (f) must still be taken into account. (Italics mine.) Comment *h*, at 39. * * *

I would hold pyrotechnicians licensed under RCW Ch. 70.77 are not strictly liable for damages caused by fireworks displays.

* * *

Thus, while I agree with the result reached by the majority, I would confine the opinion to that which is contained in part II in its opinion.

SMITH, J., and CALLOW, J., PRO TEM., concur.

Notes

1. The plaintiff in *Klein v. Pyrodyne Corp.* was not an adjoining landowner. Rather, he was a spectator who had come to enjoy the show. This, of course, is a departure from the Rylands roots of abnormally dangerous activities law which turned on questions of incompatible land use. How far might this trend continue in the future? The most recent Supplement to the *Prosser & Keeton* treatise offers some thoughts on this issue.

> Both the facts in Rylands and the rule formulation in that case tended to focus strict liability claims on cases of incompatible land use. Under the Restatement formulations of the rule, the focus is on the danger of the activity, so that it becomes possible to assert strict liability claims in cases that have little or no relationship to the way in which land is being exploited. This has led to a small furor of cases in which it is claimed that the sale of normal non-defective[1] handguns is itself a strict liability activity, so that the seller should be responsible for any injuries caused by the guns. With one notable exception,[2] this claim has been rejected. Courts have also rejected similar claims that beer, because of its potential for excessive consumption, is abnormally dangerous,[3] and likewise the claim that non-defective but dangerous equipment calls for strict liability.[4] Although strict liability has been rejected in most of these cases, they reflect a pressure to recognize that strict liability is not limited to activities involving land use.

1. If the gun is defective and it is the defect that causes injury, the manufacturer may be liable, not under an "abnormal danger" theory of strict liability, but under the rules for products liability * * *. [Footnotes are renumbered.]

2. Kelley v. R.G. Industries, Inc., 1985, 304 Md. 124, 497 A.2d 1143, 44 A.L.R.4th 563. * * * [*But see*] Moore v. R.G. Industries, Inc., 9th Cir.1986, 789 F.2d 1326 and Shipman v. Jennings Firearms, Inc., 11th Cir.1986, 791 F.2d 1532. [Ed. note:] *See* *also* Miller v. Civil Constructors, 272 Ill. App.3d 263, 651 N.E.2d 239 (Ill.App.1995)(bystander shot by stray bullet from a firing range in an old quarry. Held: discharge of firearms not an abnormally dangerous activity.)

3. Maguire v. Pabst Brewing Co., Iowa 1986, 387 N.W.2d 565 * * *.

4. Fallon v. Indian Trail School, 1986, 148 Ill.App.3d 931, 102 Ill.Dec. 479, 500 N.E.2d 101 * * * (trampoline at school).

Prosser & Keeton, Torts 83 (5th ed. 1988 Pocket Part).

2. Under the approach taken by the *Restatements*, the fact that the activity miscarries because of a so-called "act of God" will not prevent strict liability from attaching. It will be recalled, however, that Blackburn, J., in *Rylands v. Fletcher*, opined that it might be a defense "that the escape was the consequence of vis major, or the act of God. * * *" There is very little authority on the question. What little there is supports Blackburn, J., rather than the *Restatements*. For example, in Golden v. Amory, 329 Mass. 484, 109 N.E.2d 131 (1952), a dike overflowed as the result of the 1938 hurricane. In reaffirming Massachusetts' adherence to *Rylands v. Fletcher*, the court held there was no liability because the damage had been caused by "the act of God." *See also* Wheatland Irrigation District v. McGuire, 537 P.2d 1128, 1140 (Wyo. 1975); Jacoby v. City of Gillette, 62 Wyo. 487, 174 P.2d 505 (1946); Sutliff v. Sweetwater Water Co., 182 Cal. 34, 186 P. 766 (1920). Dean Prosser wished to change the *Restatement's* position to reflect this judicial authority, *Restatement (Second) of Torts*, Tent. Draft No. 10 (1964) at p. 82, but his views did not prevail.

3. As the *Klein* court noted, *Restatement (Second) of Torts* § 520 comment *f* offered up the following advice as to how courts might apply the six factor test:

> Any one of them is not necessarily sufficient of itself in a particular case, and ordinarily several of them will be required for strict liability. On the other hand, it is not necessary that each of them be present, especially if others weigh heavily.

Similarly, comment *l*. notes:

> Whether the activity is an abnormally dangerous one is to be determined by the court, upon consideration of all the factors listed in this Section, and the weight given to each that it merits upon the fact in evidence.

Are these comprehensible statements? How do the *Klein* majority and concurring opinions weight the factors? The next case demonstrates other ways in which courts may approach § 520 and the range of arguments it seems to permit.

4. *Klein* follows the *Restatement* position that whether something is an abnormally dangerous activity is a question for the court, not the jury. *See Restatement (Second) of Torts* § 520, comment *l* (1977). The primary reason the *Restatement* gives for this rule is that, unlike a jury's decision in a negligence case, the classification of an activity as "abnormally dangerous" could destroy an entire industry. But, of course, a ruling that a product, say an airliner, is negligently designed could also destroy an industrial enterprise. Furthermore, as we shall see in the next chapter, in actions brought on a theory of strict liability for defective products, in a majority of states the issue of whether the product is defective *is* submitted to the jury. Why should strict liability under an abnormally dangerous activity theory be treated differently from strict liability for a defective product? Finally, if, as the Comment suggests, each case is to be decided by weighing the specific factors involved in it, each case will be *sui generis* and one need have no fear that an individual decision, whether made by a judge or by a jury, might ruin an entire industry.

INDIANA HARBOR BELT R.R. CO.
v. AMERICAN CYANAMID CO.

United States Court of Appeals, Seventh Circuit, 1990.
916 F.2d 1174.

POSNER, CIRCUIT JUDGE.

American Cyanamid Company, the defendant in this diversity tort suit governed by Illinois law, is a major manufacturer of chemicals, including acrylonitrile, a chemical used in large quantities in making acrylic fibers, plastics, dyes, pharmaceutical chemicals, and other intermediate and final goods. On January 2, 1979, at its manufacturing plant in Louisiana, Cyanamid loaded 20,000 gallons of liquid acrylonitrile into a railroad tank car that it had leased from the North American Car Corporation. The next day, a train of the Missouri Pacific Railroad picked up the car at Cyanamid's siding. The car's ultimate destination was a Cyanamid plant in New Jersey served by Conrail rather than by Missouri Pacific. The Missouri Pacific train carried the car north to the Blue Island railroad yard of Indiana Harbor Belt Railroad, the plaintiff in this case, a small switching line that has a contract with Conrail to switch cars from other lines to Conrail, in this case for travel east. The Blue Island yard is in the Village of Riverdale, which is just south of Chicago and part of the Chicago metropolitan area.

The car arrived in the Blue Island yard on the morning of January 9, 1979. Several hours after it arrived, employees of the switching line noticed fluid gushing from the bottom outlet of the car. The lid on the outlet was broken. After two hours, the line's supervisor of equipment was able to stop the leak by closing a shut-off valve controlled from the top of the car. No one was sure at the time just how much of the contents of the car had leaked, but it was feared that all 20,000 gallons had, and since acrylonitrile is flammable at a temperature of 30 degrees Fahrenheit or above, highly toxic, and possibly carcinogenic, the local authorities ordered the homes near the yard evacuated. The evacuation lasted only a few hours, until the car was moved to a remote part of the yard and it was discovered that only about a quarter of the acrylonitrile had leaked. Concerned nevertheless that there had been some contamination of soil and water, the Illinois Department of Environmental Protection ordered the switching line to take decontamination measures that cost the line $981,022.75, which it sought to recover by this suit.

One count of the two-count complaint charges Cyanamid with having maintained the leased tank car negligently. The other count asserts that the transportation of acrylonitrile in bulk through the Chicago metropolitan area is an abnormally dangerous activity, for the consequences of which the shipper (Cyanamid) is strictly liable to the switching line, which bore the financial brunt of those consequences because of the decontamination measures that it was forced to take. After the district judge denied Cyanamid's motion to dismiss the strict liability count, the switching line moved for summary judgment on that count—and won.

* * *

The question whether the shipper of a hazardous chemical by rail should be strictly liable for the consequences of a spill or other accident to the shipment en route is a novel one in Illinois ...   * * *

* * *

The parties agree that the question whether placing acrylonitrile in a rail shipment that will pass through a metropolitan area subjects the shipper to strict liability is, as recommended in Restatement (Second) of Torts § 520, comment *l* (1977), a question of law, so that we owe no particular deference to the conclusion of the district court. They also agree * * * that the Supreme Court of Illinois would treat as authoritative the provisions of the Restatement governing abnormally dangerous activities. The key provision is section 520, which sets forth six factors to be considered in deciding whether an activity is abnormally dangerous and the actor therefore strictly liable.

The roots of section 520 are in nineteenth-century cases. The most famous one is *Rylands v. Fletcher*, but a more illuminating one in the present context is *Guille v. Swan*, 19 Johns. (N.Y.) 381 (1822). A man took off in a hot-air balloon and landed, without intending to, in a vegetable garden in New York City. A crowd that had been anxiously watching his involuntary descent trampled the vegetables in their endeavor to rescue him when he landed. The owner of the garden sued the balloonist for the resulting damage, and won. Yet the balloonist had not been careless. In the then state of ballooning it was impossible to make a pinpoint landing.

Guille is a paradigmatic case for strict liability. (a) The risk (probability) of harm was great, and (b) the harm that would ensue if the risk materialized could be, although luckily was not, great (the balloonist could have crashed into the crowd rather than into the vegetables). The confluence of these two factors established the urgency of seeking to prevent such accidents. (c) Yet such accidents could not be prevented by the exercise of due care; the technology of care in ballooning was insufficiently developed. (d) The activity was not a matter of common usage, so there was no presumption that it was a highly valuable activity despite its unavoidable riskiness. (e) The activity was inappropriate to the place in which it took place—densely populated New York City. The risk of serious harm to others (other than the balloonist himself, that is) could have been reduced by shifting the activity to the sparsely inhabited areas that surrounded the city in those days. (f) Reinforcing (d), the value to the community of the activity of recreational ballooning did not appear to be great enough to offset its unavoidable risks.

These are, of course, the six factors in section 520. They are related to each other in that each is a different facet of a common quest for a proper legal regime to govern accidents that negligence liability cannot adequately control. The interrelations might be more perspicuous if the six factors were reordered. One might for example start with (c), inability to eliminate the risk of accident by the exercise of due care. The baseline common law regime of tort liability is negligence. When it is a workable regime, because the hazards of an activity can be avoided by being careful (which is to say, nonnegligent), there is no need to switch to strict liability. Sometimes, however, a particular type of accident cannot be prevented by taking care but can be avoided, or its consequences minimized, by shifting the activity in which the accident occurs to another locale, where the risk or harm of an accident will be less ((e)), or by reducing the scale of the activity in order to minimize the number of accidents caused by it ((f)). Shavell, *Strict Liability versus Negligence*, 9 J. Legal Stud. 1 (1980). By making the actor strictly liable—by denying him in other words an excuse based on his inability to avoid accidents by being more careful—we give him an incentive, missing in a negligence regime, to experiment with methods of preventing accidents that involve not greater exertions of care, assumed to be futile, but instead relocating, changing, or reducing (perhaps to the vanishing point) the activity giving rise to the accident. The greater the risk of an accident ((a)) and the costs of an accident if one occurs ((b)), the more we want the actor to consider the possibility of making accident-reducing activity changes; the stronger, therefore, is the case for strict liability. Finally, if an activity is extremely common ((d)), like driving an automobile, it is unlikely either that its hazards are perceived as great or that there is no technology of care available to minimize them; so the case for strict liability is weakened.

The largest class of cases in which strict liability has been imposed under the standard codified in the Second Restatement of Torts involves the use of dynamite and other explosives for demolition in residential or urban areas. Restatement, supra, § 519, comment *d*. Explosives are dangerous even when handled carefully, and we therefore want blasters to choose the location of the activity with care and also to explore the feasibility of using safer substitutes (such as a wrecking ball), as well as to be careful in the blasting itself. Blasting is not a commonplace activity like driving a car, or so superior to substitute methods of demolition that the imposition of liability is unlikely to have any effect except to raise the activity's costs.

Against this background we turn to the particulars of acrylonitrile. Acrylonitrile is one of a large number of chemicals that are hazardous in the sense of being flammable, toxic, or both; acrylonitrile is both, as are many others. A table in the record, drawn from Glickman & Harvey, Statistical Trends in Railroad Hazardous Material Safety, 1978 to 1984, contains a list of the 125 hazardous materials that are shipped in highest volume on the nation's railroads. Acrylonitrile is the fifty-third most hazardous on the list. Number 1 is phosphorus (white or yellow), and among the other materials that rank higher than acrylonitrile on the hazard scale are anhydrous ammonia, liquified petroleum gas, vinyl chloride, gasoline, crude petroleum, motor fuel antiknock compound, methyl and ethyl chloride, sulphuric acid, sodium metal, and chloroform. The plaintiff's lawyer acknowledged at argument that the logic of the district court's opinion dictated strict liability for all 52 materials that rank higher than acrylonitrile on the list, and quite possibly for the 72 that rank lower as well, since all are hazardous if spilled in quantity while being shipped by rail. Every shipper of any of these materials would therefore be strictly liable for the consequences of a spill or other accident that occurred while the material was being shipped through a metropolitan area. The plaintiff's lawyer further acknowledged the irrelevance, on her view of the case, of the fact that Cyanamid had leased and filled the car that spilled the acrylonitrile; all she thought important is that Cyanamid introduced the product into the stream of commerce that happened to pass through the Chicago metropolitan area. Her concession may have been incautious. One might want to distinguish between the shipper who merely places his goods on his loading dock to be picked up by the carrier and the shipper who, as in this case, participates actively in the transportation. But the concession is illustrative of the potential scope of the district court's decision.

No cases recognize so sweeping a liability. Several reject it, though none has facts much like those of the present case. * * *

Siegler v. Kuhlman, 81 Wash.2d 448, 502 P.2d 1181 (1972), also imposed strict liability on a transporter of hazardous materials, but the circumstances were again rather special. A gasoline truck blew up, obliterating the plaintiff's decedent and her car. The court emphasized that the explosion had destroyed the evidence necessary to establish whether the accident had been due to negligence; so, unless liability was strict, there would be no liability—and this as the very consequence of the defendant's hazardous activity. * * *

So we can get little help from precedent, and might as well apply section 520 to the acrylonitrile problem from the ground up. To begin with, we have been given no reason, whether the reason in Siegler or any other, for believing that a negligence regime is not perfectly adequate to remedy and deter, at reasonable cost, the accidental spillage of acrylonitrile from rail cars. Acrylonitrile could explode and destroy evidence, but of course did not here, making imposition of strict liability on the theory of the Siegler decision premature. More important, although acrylonitrile is flammable even at relatively low temperatures, and toxic, it is not so corrosive or otherwise destructive that it will eat through or otherwise damage or weaken a tank car's valves although they are maintained with due (which essentially means, with average) care. No one suggests, therefore, that the leak in this case was caused by the inherent properties of acrylonitrile. It was caused by carelessness—whether that of the North American Car Corporation in failing to maintain or inspect the car properly, or that of Cyanamid in failing to maintain or inspect it, or that of the Missouri Pacific when it had custody of the car, or that of the switching line itself in failing to notice the ruptured lid, or some combination of these possible failures of care. Accidents that are due to a lack of care can be prevented by taking care; and when a lack of care can (unlike *Siegler*) be shown in court, such accidents are adequately deterred by the threat of liability for negligence.

It is true that the district court purported to find as a fact that there is an inevitable risk of derailment or other calamity in transporting "large quantities of anything." This is not a finding of fact, but a truism: anything can happen. The question is, how likely is this type of accident if the actor uses due care? For all that appears from the record of the case or any other sources of information that we have found, if a tank car is carefully maintained the danger of a spill of acrylonitrile is negligible. If this is right, there is no compelling reason to move to a regime of strict liability, especially one that might embrace all other hazardous materials shipped by rail as well. This also means, however, that the amici curiae who have filed briefs in support of Cyanamid cry wolf in predicting "devastating" effects on the chemical industry if the district court's decision is affirmed. If the vast majority of chemical spills by railroads are preventable by due care, the imposition of strict liability should cause only a slight, not as they argue a substantial, rise in liability insurance rates, because the incremental liability should be slight. The amici have momentarily lost sight of the fact that the feasibility of avoiding accidents simply by being careful is an argument against strict liability.

This discussion helps to show why *Siegler* is indeed distinguishable ... There are so many highway hazards that the transportation of gasoline by truck is, or at least might plausibly be thought, inherently dangerous in the sense that a serious danger of accident would remain even if the truck driver used all due care (though Hawkins and other cases are contra). * * * the plaintiff in this case has not shown that the danger of a comparable disaster to a tank car filled with acrylonitrile is as great and might have similar consequences for proof of negligence.

* * *

The district judge and the plaintiff's lawyer make much of the fact that the spill occurred in a densely inhabited metropolitan area. Only 4,000 gallons spilled; what if all 20,000 had done so? Isn't the risk that this might happen even if everybody were careful sufficient to warrant giving the shipper an incentive to explore alternative routes? Strict liability would supply that incentive. But this argument overlooks the fact that, like other transportation networks, the railroad network is a hub-and-spoke system. And the hubs are in metropolitan areas. Chicago is one of the nation's largest railroad hubs. In 1983, the latest year for which we have figures, Chicago's railroad yards handled the third highest volume of hazardous-material shipments in the nation. East St. Louis, which is also in Illinois, handled the second highest volume. With most hazardous chemicals (by volume of shipments) being at least as hazardous as acrylonitrile, it is unlikely—and certainly not demonstrated by the plaintiff—that they can be rerouted around all the metropolitan areas in the country, except at prohibitive cost. Even if it were feasible to reroute them one would hardly expect shippers, as distinct from carriers, to be the firms best situated to do the rerouting. Granted, the usual view is that common carriers are not subject to strict liability for the carriage of materials that make the transportation of them abnormally dangerous, because a common carrier cannot refuse service to a shipper of a lawful commodity. Restatement, *supra*, § 521. Two courts, however, have rejected the common carrier exception. If it were rejected in Illinois, this would weaken still further the case for imposing strict liability on shippers whose goods pass through the densely inhabited portions of the state.

The difference between shipper and carrier points to a deep flaw in the plaintiff's case. Unlike *Guille*, and unlike *Siegler*, and unlike the storage cases, beginning with Rylands itself, here it is not the actors—that is, the transporters of acrylonitrile and other chemicals—but the manufacturers, who are sought to be held strictly liable. A shipper can in the bill of lading designate the route of his shipment if he likes, 49 U.S.C. § 11710(a)(1), but is it realistic to suppose that shippers will become students of railroading in order to lay out the safest route by which to ship their goods? Anyway, rerouting is no panacea. Often it will increase the length of the journey, or compel the use of poorer track, or both. When this happens, the probability of an accident is increased, even if the consequences of an accident if one occurs are reduced; so the expected accident cost, being the product of the probability of an accident and the harm if the accident occurs, may rise. It is easy to see how the accident in this case might have been prevented at reasonable cost by greater care on the part of those who handled the tank car of acrylonitrile. It is difficult to see how it might have been prevented at reasonable cost by a change in the activity of transporting the chemical. This is therefore not an apt case for strict liability.

* * *

In emphasizing the flammability and toxicity of acrylonitrile rather than the hazards of transporting it, as in failing to distinguish between the active and the passive shipper, the plaintiff overlooks the fact that ultra-hazardousness or abnormal dangerousness is, in the contemplation of the law at least, a property not of substances, but of activities: not of acrylonitrile, but of the transportation of acrylonitrile by rail through populated areas. Natural gas is both flammable and poisonous, but the operation of a natural gas well is not an ultrahazardous activity. Whatever the situation under products liability law (section 402A of the Restatement), the manufacturer of a product is not considered to be engaged in an abnormally dangerous activity merely because the product becomes dangerous when it is handled or used in some way after it leaves his premises, even if the danger is foreseeable.[a] The plaintiff does not suggest that Cyanamid should switch to making some less hazardous chemical that would substitute for acrylonitrile in the textiles and other goods in which acrylonitrile is used. Were this a feasible method of accident avoidance, there would be an argument for making manufacturers strictly liable for accidents that occur during the shipment of their products (how strong an argument we need not decide). Apparently it is not a feasible method.

The relevant activity is transportation, not manufacturing and shipping. This essential distinction the plaintiff ignores. But even if the plaintiff [sic] is treated as a transporter and not merely a shipper, it has not shown that the transportation of acrylonitrile in bulk by rail through populated areas is so hazardous an activity, even when due care is exercised, that the law should seek to create—perhaps quixotically—incentives to relocate the activity to nonpopulated areas, or to reduce the scale of the activity, or to switch to transporting acrylonitrile by road rather than by rail, perhaps to set the stage for a replay of *Siegler v. Kuhlman*. It is no more realistic to propose to reroute the shipment of all hazardous materials around Chicago than it is to propose the relocation of homes adjacent to the Blue Island switching yard to more distant suburbs. It may be less realistic. Brutal though it may seem to say it, the inappropriate use to which land is being put in the Blue Island yard and neighborhood may be,

---

a. [Ed. note] We will discuss *Restatement (Second) Torts* § 402A in Chapter Nine, *infra*.

not the transportation of hazardous chemicals, but residential living. The analogy is to building your home between the runways at O'Hare.

The briefs hew closely to the Restatement, whose approach to the issue of strict liability is mainly allocative rather than distributive. By this we mean that the emphasis is on picking a liability regime (negligence or strict liability) that will control the particular class of accidents in question most effectively, rather than on finding the deepest pocket and placing liability there. At argument, however, the plaintiff's lawyer invoked distributive considerations by pointing out that Cyanamid is a huge firm and the Indiana Harbor Belt Railroad a fifty-mile-long switching line that almost went broke in the winter of 1979, when the accident occurred. Well, so what? A corporation is not a living person but a set of contracts the terms of which determine who will bear the brunt of liability. Tracing the incidence of a cost is a complex undertaking which the plaintiff sensibly has made no effort to assume, since its legal relevance would be dubious. We add only that however small the plaintiff may be, it has mighty parents: it is a jointly owned subsidiary of Conrail and the Soo line.

The case for strict liability has not been made. Not in this suit in any event. We need not speculate on the possibility of imposing strict liability on shippers of more hazardous materials, such as * * * bombs . . .

* * *

[The case] is not over now. But with damages having been fixed at a relatively modest level by the district court and not challenged by the plaintiff, and a voluminous record having been compiled in the summary judgment proceedings, we trust the parties will find it possible now to settle the case. Even the Trojan War lasted only ten years.

The judgment is reversed (with no award of costs in this court) and the case remanded for further proceedings, consistent with this opinion, on the plaintiff's claim for negligence.

REVERSED AND REMANDED, WITH DIRECTIONS.

Notes

1. The District Court's opinion imposing strict liability on Cyanamid emphasized factor (e) of *Restatement (Second) of Torts* § 520, inappropriateness of the activity to the place where it is carried on, e.g. shipping toxic materials so close to a residential neighborhood.

Cyanamid provides an extended list of reasons why it thinks transporting acrylonitrile by rail, if dangerous, is not abnormally so under the Restatement standard. In its opinion, the risk of harm is small and the likelihood of extensive injury is also low because the chemical can be transported safely with the exercise of reasonable care. Indeed, millions of gallons of it are shipped safely every year, which in Cyanamid's lexicon makes the activity one of common usage. It also points forcefully to the many useful products made from acrylonitrile to contend that the activity of shipping it is valuable.

However, perhaps the single most important factor in determining whether or not an activity is abnormally dangerous is what the Restatement calls the "inappropriateness" of bringing the danger to the particular place where the damage occurred.

Indiana Harbor Belt R.R. Co.v. American Cyanamid Co., 662 F.Supp. 635, 641 (N.D.Ill.1987). Around which factor did Judge Posner build his analysis? Whose opinion is truer to the Rylands heritage?

2. In a part of his opinion that has been omitted, Judge Posner noted that the plaintiff might have overcome the destruction of the evidence in *Siegler v. Kuhlman* by basing a negligence claim on the doctrine of *res ipsa loquitur.* Would the application of *res ipsa* have resolved the *Klein* case without resort to an abnormally dangerous activity analysis? Would *res ipsa* be appropriate in the present case? *See*, Indiana Harbor Belt R.R. Co. v. American Cyanamid Co., 1991 WL 206079 (N.D.Ill.).

3. Ground damage caused by the hot-air balloon in *Guille v. Swan* was thought to be an appropriate occasion for the application of strict liability in 1868, in part because the activity was not one of common usage. The first *Restatement of Torts* (1934) adopted the position that aviation was an ultrahazardous activity. By the time the second restatement was adopted, states had begun to reject this position. *See* Boyd v. White, 128 Cal.App.2d 641, 276 P.2d 92 (Cal.App. 1954); Wood v. United Air Lines, 32 Misc.2d 955, 223 N.Y.S.2d 692 (1961), *affirmed mem.*, 16 A.D.2d 659, 226 N.Y.S.2d 1022, *appeal dismissed*, 11 N.Y.2d 1053, 230 N.Y.S.2d 207, 184 N.E.2d 180 (1962). Disregarding this trend, the Second Restatement retained strict liability for ground damage from aircraft.

§ 520A Ground Damage From Aircraft

If physical harm to land or to persons or chattels on the ground is caused by the ascent, descent or flight of aircraft, or by the dropping or falling of an object from the aircraft,

(a) the operator of the aircraft is subject to liability for the harm, even though he has exercised the utmost care to prevent it, and

(b) the owner of the aircraft is subject to similar liability if he has authorized or permitted the operation.

The contrary trend, however, continues unabated. By the time the Washington Supreme Court opted for a negligence standard in 1987, it reported that only six states retained strict liability. Crosby v. Cox Aircraft Co., 109 Wn.2d 581, 746 P.2d 1198 (1987). The Crosby court justified its decision with the following analysis:

> We have discovered no cases relying on *Restatement (Second) of Torts* § 520A. That section is said to be a "special application" of § 519 and § 520(a-f), which impose strict liability on persons engaging in abnormally dangerous activities. An analysis of the individual factors listed in § 520 further persuades us that strict liability is inappropriate here.
>
> Factor (a) of § 520 requires that the activity in question contain a "high degree of risk of some harm to the person, land or chattels of others." No such showing has been made. Indeed, statistics indicate that air transportation is far safer than automobile transportation. Factor (b) speaks to the gravity of the harm—that is, in the unlikely event that an airplane accident occurs, whether there is a "likelihood that the [resulting harm] will be great." It is apparent that this possibility is present. However, this must be further evaluated in light of factor (c), which speaks

of the "inability to eliminate the risk by the exercise of reasonable care." Given the extensive governmental regulation of aviation, and the continuing technological improvements in aircraft manufacture, maintenance and operation, we conclude that the overall risk of serious injury from ground damage can be sufficiently reduced by the exercise of due care. Finally, factors (d), (e), and (f) do not favor the imposition of strict liability. Aviation is an activity of "common usage", it is appropriately conducted over populated areas, and its value to the community outweighs its dangerous attributes. Indeed, aviation is an integral part of modern society.

Crosby v. Cox Aircraft Co., 109 Wn.2d 581, 587–88, 746 P.2d 1198, 1201 (Wash.1987); 73 A.L.R.4th 416. Is strict liability for ground damage caused by aircraft really such a bad idea? *See*, William K. Jones, Strict Liability for Hazardous Enterprise, 92 Colum. L. Rev. 1705, 1747 (1992).

4. As the principal cases indicate, the application of the factors listed in *Restatement (Second) of Torts* § 520 is an uncertain process, in part because courts may not give equal weight to each of the factors. Most cases, however, involve a relatively small group of activities.

a) *Blasting:* Blasting is the quintessential example of an abnormally dangerous activity. Most courts impose strict liability for either blasting or the storage of explosives. *See* Exner v. Sherman Power Const. Co., 54 F.2d 510 (2d Cir.1931); Bedell v. Goulter, 199 Or. 344, 261 P.2d 842 (Or.1953); Yukon Equipment v. Fireman's Fund Insurance Co., 585 P.2d 1206 (Alaska 1978); Harper v. Regency Development Company, Inc., 399 So.2d 248 (Ala.1981); Green v. Ensign–Bickford Co., 25 Conn.App. 479, 595 A.2d 1383 (Conn.App.1991); Continental Insurance Co. v. Great Lakes Dredge & Dock Co., 163 Misc.2d 594, 624 N.Y.S.2d 335 (Sup. Ct., App. Term 1994)

b) *Transportation and Storage of Gasoline*: In Yommer v. McKenzie, 255 Md. 220, 257 A.2d 138 (1969) the court dealt with the seepage of gasoline from the storage tank of a gasoline station that had contaminated the well of a close neighbor. The court said:

> The fifth and perhaps most crucial factor under the Institute's guidelines as applied to this case is the appropriateness of the activity in the particular place where it is being carried on. No one would deny that gasoline stations as a rule do not present any particular danger to the community. However, when the operation of such activity involves the placing of a large tank adjacent to a well from which a family must draw its water for drinking, bathing and laundry, at least that aspect of the activity is inappropriate to the locale, even when equated to the value of the activity.

255 Md. at 225, 257 A.2d at 140; accord City of Northglenn, Colo. v. Chevron U.S. A. Inc., 519 F.Supp. 515 (D.Colo., 1981); *see also* McLane v. Northwest Natural Gas Co. 255 Or. 324, 467 P.2d 635 (Or.1970)(storage of large amounts of natural gas in a populated area is an activity which should be classed as 'abnormally dangerous', within doctrine of strict liability).

On the contrary, in Walker Drug Company, Inc. v. La Sal Oil Company, 902 P.2d 1229 (Utah 1995) the Utah Supreme Court found the storage of gasoline in underground tanks at filling stations not to be abnormally dangerous.

> Applying [the six factors listed in Restatement (Second) of Torts § 520] to the facts of the instant case, we conclude that La Sal and Rio Vista were not engaged in an abnormally dangerous activity in operating their gas stations. The Walkers argue that operating a gas station with underground gasoline storage tanks and lines is abnormally dangerous because of the possibility that the tanks and lines will leak and that, if a leak occurs, the resulting contamination is likely to be extensive. However, the Walkers do not contend that the risk of leakage is great, and we are not convinced that the risk cannot be eliminated by the exercise of reasonable care. Moreover, it is undisputed that defendants' gas stations are located in an area of Moab where the operation of a gas station is common, appropriate, and of significant value to the community. Accordingly, we conclude that La Sal and Rio Vista were not engaged in an abnormally dangerous activity in operating their gas stations.

902 P.2d at 1233. *See* Hudson v. Peavey Oil Co., 279 Or. 3, 566 P.2d 175 (1977) for a similar analysis.

The transportation of large quantities of gasoline is, of course, another matter. In Siegler v. Kuhlman, 81 Wn.2d 448, 502 P.2d 1181 (1972), *cert. denied* 411 U.S. 983, 93 S.Ct. 2275, 36 L.Ed.2d 959 (1973), discussed in *Klein* and *Indiana Harbor Belt R.R.*, about five thousand gallons of gasoline spilled onto a highway when the trailer of a gasoline tanker truck broke loose. The gasoline exploded when the plaintiff's decedent's car drove through the pool of gasoline. The court held that transportation of "great quantities" of gasoline on the public highways is extremely dangerous and was therefore an abnormally dangerous activity. Citing *Yommer*, it concluded that if strict liability were appropriate there, *a fortiori*, it was appropriate in the case before the court.

c) *Impoundments*: The storage of water in reservoirs is only rarely declared to be an abnormally dangerous activity. Clark–Aiken Co. v. Cromwell–Wright Co. 367 Mass. 70, 323 N.E.2d 876 (1975). However, strict liability is frequently imposed if the escape is of something more noisome than water. *See, e.g.* Branch v. Western Petroleum, Inc. 657 P.2d 267 (Utah 1982)(waste water from an oil well); Bunyak v. Clyde J Yancey and Sons Dairy, Inc. 438 So.2d 891 (Fla.App.1983)(thousands of gallons of liquified cow manure); Cities Service Co. v. State, 312 So.2d 799 (Fla.App. 1975)("one billion gallons of phosphate slimes").

d) *The application of poisons*: Strict liability for the application of poisons comes in several guises. Some courts have concluded that crop-dusting is an abnormally dangerous activity. Langan v. Valicopters, Inc., 88 Wash.2d 855, 567 P.2d 218 (Wash.1977); Loe v. Lenhardt, 227 Or. 242, 362 P.2d 312 (Or.1961)(aerial spraying is extrahazardous activity). *But see* Bennett v. Larsen Co., 118 Wis.2d 681, 348 N.W.2d 540 (Wis.1984)(ground application of pesticides not an ultrahazardous activity). Fumigation has also been deemed an ultrahazardous activity. Luthringer v. Moore, 31 Cal.2d 489, 190 P.2d 1 (Cal.1948); Old Island Fumigation, Inc. v. Barbee, 604 So.2d 1246 (Fla.App.1992).

e) *Landfills and Toxic Waste:* Landfills present a complex problem. Older landfills contain toxic substances such as vinyl chloride that may seep into and contaminate surrounding ground water. The organizations that operated the landfill or that deposited their waste into the landfill may have been following all existing regulations and no one appreciated the risk they were creating. Are such activities abnormally dangerous, such that the owners and depositors should be strictly liable? The courts have given conflicting answers. In Fortier v. Flambeau Plastics Co., 164 Wis.2d 639, 476 N.W.2d 593 (Wis.App.1991) and Sunnyside Seed Farms, Inc. v. Refuse Hideaway, Inc., 193 Wis.2d 638, 537 N.W.2d 433 (Wis.App.1995) the Wisconsin courts concluded that depositing volatile organic chemicals in these landfills was a common usage, that the community deemed these landfills to be an appropriate place for the activity, and at the time the landfills were in use the community felt the value of the fill to the community outweighed the danger. Therefore, even though the fills created a substantial risk, they were not abnormally dangerous activities. On the other hand, the New Jersey Supreme Court found the dumping of mercury to be an abnormally dangerous activity in Environmental Protection v. Ventron Corp. 94 N.J. 473, 468 A.2d 150 (1983). Recently, a Connecticut Superior Court found that depositing toxic substances in a landfill between 1920 and 1967 constituted an abnormally dangerous activity, even though the court concluded that this was common usage and not inappropriate at the place and time. Barnes v. General Electric Co.1995 WL 447904 (Conn. Super. Ct. 1995).

Statutory considerations are now the focus of toxic waste liability. The Comprehensive Environmental Response Compensation and Liability Act (CERCLA), 42 U.S.C. §§ 9601 et seq., 9607 (a)(the "Superfund Act") imposes strict liability on entities that released substances into superfund sites and on the owners of the sites as well. Private persons who are injured by releases may seek reimbursement for reasonable clean up costs. *See* Michael D. Green, *Successors and CERCLA: The Imperfect Analogy to Products Liability and an Alternative Proposal*, 87 Nw. U. L. Rev. 897 (1993).

f) *Atomic energy.* One might note another important statutory form of strict liability for the miscarriage of dangerous activities. Under the Price–Anderson Act, 42 U.S.C. § 2210, an insurance scheme is set up for accidents involving nuclear reactors. The Act imposes a $560,000,000 limitation of liability. The Act authorizes the Nuclear Regulatory Commission to provide, and the Commission has so provided, that neither acts of God, nor the intentional acts of third persons, nor any kind of official immunity, nor contributory negligence, nor assumption of risk are defenses to the strict liability imposed by the Act. 10 C.F.R. § 140.91. The limitation of liability was attacked as inadequate but it was upheld in Duke Power Co. v. Carolina Environmental Study Group, Inc., 438 U.S. 59, 98 S.Ct. 2620, 57 L.Ed.2d 595 (1978).

5. *Common Usage.* Determining what constitutes common usage remains a very difficult task. In Langan v. Valicopters, Inc., 88 Wn.2d 855, 567 P.2d 218 (Wash.1977), the defendant's crop dusting operation for neighboring farmers caused some pesticides to fall on the plaintiff's crop, thus preventing him from marketing his crops as "organically grown." In assessing whether the defendant should be held to a strict liability standard the court made the following statement concerning the "common usage" criterion.

Although we recognize that prevalence of crop dusting and acknowledge that it is ordinarily done in large portions of the Yakima Valley, it is carried on by only a comparatively small number of persons (approximately 287 aircraft were used in 1975) and it is not a matter of common usage.

Seven years after *Valicopter* the Washington Supreme Court decided New Meadows Holding Co. v. Washington Water Power Co., 102 Wn.2d 495, 687 P.2d 212 (Wash.1984). In *New Meadows* the plaintiff was seriously injured and his home was blown up due to a gas leak from a 2–inch underground gas transmission line owned by the defendant. As part of its analysis as to whether the underground transmission of natural gas was an abnormally dangerous activity, the court considered whether this was a matter of common usage appropriate to the place where it was carried on. Answering this question in the affirmative, the court made the following observation.

In its brief, the American Gas Association estimates approximately 160 million people use gas for residential needs. About 35 percent of the total energy used by industry is provided by natural gas ... and 720,900 miles of distribution pipelines crisscross communities in every state and the District of Columbia, including 10,062 miles in Washington state * * *.

687 P.2d at 216.

Are these two analyses compatible? How should courts address the "common usage" factor? *See Restatement (Second) Torts* § 520, comment *i*.

6. *Value to the community.* How should courts interpret factor (f) of § 520, the extent to which an activity's value to the community is outweighed by its dangerous attributes? Does this mean that very dangerous, but also very valuable activities should not be subjected to strict liability? Consider the following comment in a leading torts treatise:

Among the factors to be considered, one deserves special note, the value of the activity to the community. In a sense this factor has already been discounted in making the decision to impose strict liability on an activity. Thus in Comment *b* to Section 520 it is explained, in distinguishing strict liability from negligence: "The rule stated in § 519 is applicable to an activity which is carried on with all reasonable care, and which is of such utility that the risk which is involved in it cannot be regarded as so great or so unreasonable as to make it negligence to carry on the activity at all. (*See* § 282.) If the utility of the activity does not justify the risk which it creates, it may be negligence merely to carry it on, and the rule stated in this Section is not necessary to subject the defendant to liability for harm resulting from it."

The justification for strict liability, in other words, is that useful but dangerous activities must pay their own way. There is nothing in this reasoning which would exempt *very* useful activities from the rule, as is shown by the granting of compensation even where the activity is of such paramount importance to society that it justifies the exercise of eminent domain. And if the law were to embrace wholly the principle of strict liability and its underlying rationale, there would be no place for the consideration of this factor. But this is not the present case. Tort law today contains two opposing strains or principles, strict liability and liability based on fault. It is not surprising, therefore, that any attempt to draw a line between them (which is being done in Section 520) should contain factors which would be irrelevant if one principle or the other alone were being consistently pursued.

Fowler V. Harper, Fleming James, Jr., and Oscar S. Gray, *The Law of Torts* (2d ed.) Vol. 3. p. 213–14 (1986). For an interesting theoretical discussion of the relationship of strict liability and negligence *See* George Fletcher, Fairness and Utility in Tort Theory, 85 Harv.L.Rev. 537 (1972).

7. Recently, the Australian High Court, concluded that, "the rule in Rylands v. Fletcher, with all its difficulties, uncertainties, qualifications, and exceptions, should now be seen, for the purposes of the common law of this country, as absorbed by the principles of ordinary negligence. Under those principles, a person who takes advantage of his or her control of premises to introduce a dangerous substance, to carry on a dangerous activity, or to allow another to do one of those things, owes a duty of reasonable care to avoid a reasonably foreseeable risk of injury or damage to the person or property of another." Burnie Port Authority v. General Jones Pty. Ltd. 179 C.L.R. 520, 556–57 (1994). By its decision, the court hoped to escape the "rough sea of contradictory authority" as to the circumstances where the *Rylands* rule should apply. Are the seas any calmer on this side of the Pacific?

FOSTER v. PRESTON MILL CO.

Supreme Court of Washington, 1954.
44 Wn.2d 440, 268 P.2d 645.

HAMLEY, JUSTICE.

Blasting operations conducted by Preston Mill Company frightened mother mink owned by B. W. Foster, and caused the mink to kill their kittens. Foster brought this action against the company to recover damages. His second amended complaint, upon which the case was tried, sets forth a cause of action on the theory of absolute liability, and, in the alternative, a cause of action on the theory of nuisance.

After a trial to the court without a jury, judgment was rendered for plaintiff in the sum of $1,953.68. The theory adopted by the court was that, after defendant received notice of the effect which its blasting operations were having upon the mink, it was absolutely liable for all damages of that nature thereafter sustained. The trial court concluded that defendant's blasting did not constitute a public nuisance, but did not expressly rule on the question of private nuisance. Plaintiff concedes, however, that, in effect, the trial court decided in defendant's favor on the question of nuisance. Defendant appeals.

Respondent's mink ranch is located in a rural area one and one-half miles east of North Bend, in King county, Washington. The ranch occupies seven and one half acres on which are located seven sheds for growing mink. The cages are of welded wire, but have wood roofs covered with composition roofing. The ranch is located about two blocks from U.S. highway No. 10, which is a main east-west thoroughfare across the state. Northern Pacific Railway Company tracks are located between the ranch and the highway, and Chicago, Milwaukee, St. Paul & Pacific Railroad Company tracks are located on the other side of the highway about fifteen hundred feet from the ranch.

The period of each year during which mink kittens are born, known as the whelping season, begins about May 1st. The kittens are born during a period of about two and one-half weeks, and are left with their mothers until they are six weeks old. During this period, the mothers are very excitable. If disturbed by noises, smoke, or dogs and cats, they run back and forth in their cages and frequently destroy their young. However, mink become accustomed to disturbances of this kind, if continued over a period of time. This explains why the mink in question were apparently not bothered, even during the whelping season, by the heavy traffic on U.S. highway No. 10, and by the noise and vibration caused by passing trains. There was testimony to the effect that mink would even become accustomed to the vibration and noise of blasting, if it were carried on in a regular and continuous manner.

Appellant and several other companies have been engaged in logging in the adjacent area for more than fifty years. Early in May, 1951, appellant began the construction of a road to gain access to certain timber which it desired to cut. The road was located about two and one-quarter miles southwest of the mink ranch, and about twenty-five hundred feet above the ranch, along the side of what is known as Rattlesnake Ledge.

It was necessary to use explosives to build the road. The customary types of explosives were used, and the customary methods of blasting were followed. The most powder used in one shooting was one hundred pounds, and usually the charge was limited to fifty pounds. The procedure used was to set off blasts twice a day—at noon and at the end of the work day.

Roy A. Peterson, the manager of the ranch in 1951, testified that the blasting resulted in "a tremendous vibration, is all. Boxes would rattle on the cages." The mother mink would then run back and forth in their cages and many of them would kill their kittens. Peterson also testified that on two occasions the blasts had broken windows.

Appellant's expert, Professor Drury Augustus Pfeiffer, of the University of Washington, testified as to tests made with a pin seismometer, using blasts as large as those used by appellant. He reported that no effect on the delicate apparatus was shown at distances comparable to those involved in this case. He said that it would be impossible to break a window at two and one-fourth miles with a hundred-pound shot, but that it could cause vibration of a lightly-supported cage. It would also be audible. Charles E. Erickson, who had charge of the road construction for appellant in 1951, testified that there was no glass breakage in the portable storage and filing shed which the company kept within a thousand feet of where the blasting was done. There were windows on the roof as well as on the sides of this shed.

Before the 1951 whelping season had far progressed, the mink mothers, according to Peterson's estimate, had killed thirty-five or forty of their kittens. He then told the manager of appellant company what had happened. He did not request that the blasting be stopped. After some discussion, however, appellant's manager indicated that the shots would be made as light as possible. The amount of explosives used in a normal shot was then reduced from nineteen or twenty sticks to fourteen sticks.

Officials of appellant company testified that it would have been impractical to entirely cease road-building during the several weeks required for the mink to whelp and wean their young. Such a delay would have made it necessary to run the logging operation another season, with attendant expense. It would also have disrupted the company's log production schedule and consequently the operation of its lumber mill.

In this action, respondent sought and recovered judgment only for such damages as were claimed to have been sustained as a result of blasting operations conducted after appellant received notice that its activity was causing loss of mink kittens.

The primary question presented by appellant's assignments of error is whether, on these facts, the judgment against appellant is sustainable on the theory of absolute liability.

There is a division of judicial opinion as to whether the doctrine of absolute liability should apply where the damage from blasting is caused, not by the casting of rocks and debris, but by concussion, vibration, or jarring. * * * This court has adopted the view that the doctrine applies in such cases. * * *.

However the authorities may be divided on the point just discussed, they appear to be agreed that strict liability should be confined to consequences which lie within the extraordinary risk whose existence calls for such responsibility. * * *

This restriction which has been placed upon the application of the doctrine of absolute liability is based upon considerations of policy. As Professor Prosser has said:

"* * *It is one thing to say that a dangerous enterprise must pay its way within reasonable limits, and quite another to say that it must bear responsibility for every extreme of harm that it may cause. The same practical necessity for the restriction of liability within some reasonable bounds, which arises in connection with problems of 'proximate cause' in negligence cases, demands here that some limit be set. * * * This limitation has been expressed by saying that the defendant's duty to insure safety extends only to certain consequences. More commonly, it is said that the defendant's conduct is not the 'proximate cause' of the damage. But ordinarily in such cases no question of causation is involved, and the limitation is one of the policy underlying liability." Prosser on Torts, 457, § 60.

Applying this principle to the case before us, the question comes down to this: Is the risk that any unusual vibration or noise may cause wild animals, which are being raised for commercial purposes, to kill their young, one of the things which make the activity of blasting ultrahazardous?

We have found nothing in the decisional law which would support an affirmative answer to this question. The decided cases, as well as common experience, indicate that the thing which makes blasting ultrahazardous is the risk that property or persons may be damaged or injured by coming into direct contact with flying debris, or by being directly affected by vibrations of the earth or concussions of the air.

Where, as a result of blasting operations, a horse has become frightened and has trampled or otherwise injured a person, recovery of damages has been upheld on the theory of negligence. * * * But we have found no case where recovery of damages caused by a frightened farm animal has been sustained on the ground of absolute liability.

If, however, the possibility that a violent vibration, concussion, or noise might frighten domestic animals and lead to property damages or personal injuries be considered one of the harms which makes the activity of blasting ultrahazardous, this would still not include the case we have here.

The relatively moderate vibration and noise which appellant's blasting produced at a distance of two and a quarter miles was no more than a usual incident of the ordinary life of the community. * * * The trial court specifically found that the blasting did not unreasonably interfere with the enjoyment of their property by nearby landowners, except in the case of respondent's mink ranch.

It is the exceedingly nervous disposition of mink, rather than the normal risks inherent in blasting operations, which therefore must, as a matter of sound policy, bear the responsibility for the loss here sustained. We subscribe to the view expressed by Professor Harper (30 Mich.L.Rev. 1001, 1006, supra) that the policy of the law does not impose the rule of strict liability to protect against harms incident to the plaintiff's extraordinary and unusual use of land. This is perhaps but an application of the principle that the extent to which one man in the lawful conduct of his business is liable for injuries to another involves an adjustment of conflicting interests. * * *

In Madsen v. East Jordan Irrigation Co., 101 Utah 552, 125 P.2d 794, recovery was denied under facts very similar to those of the instant case, on the ground that the mother mink's intervention broke the chain of causation.

It is our conclusion that the risk of causing harm of the kind here experienced, as a result of the relatively minor vibration, concussion, and noise from distant blasting, is not the kind of risk which makes the activity of blasting ultrahazardous. The doctrine of absolute liability is therefore inapplicable under the facts of this case, and respondent is not entitled to recover damages.

The judgment is reversed.

Notes

1. What if the blasting were done close enough to the mink ranch so that there was a real possibility that the vibrations from the blasting could break the windows of the mink ranch's buildings although in point of fact no windows were broken? Should the owner of the ranch be able to recover for the kittens killed by their mothers on the ground that you take your victim as you find him? What if, under the circumstances just described, vibration from the blasting actually does break the windows of the ranch buildings? Should there now be recovery for the death of the mink kittens?

2. If you believe that there should be no recovery on a strict liability theory for the death of the mink kittens under any of the circumstances

described in note 1, why should there be recovery if the blasting is done negligently and recovery is sought under a negligence theory?

3. In a case remarkably similar to *Foster*, the noise and vibrations from defendant's blasting injured animals on plaintiff's mink farm. Gronn v. Rogers Construction, Inc. 221 Or. 226, 230, 350 P.2d 1086, 1088 (Or.1960) Reaching the same outcome, the court said, "Defendant's [blasting] is classified as ultrahazardous because of the potential physical damage resulting from the force of an explosion, not because of the 'psychological' effect it may have on either human beings or animals." This language, of course, tracks the language in § 519 of the first Restatement which limited liability to harms "from that which makes the activity ultrahazardous." As we saw on page 585, the Second Restatement § 519 similarly limits the scope of strict liability. Another Restatement section bears on these cases as well.

§ 524   A Plaintiff's Abnormally Sensitive Activity

> There is no strict liability for harm caused by an abnormally dangerous activity if the harm would not have resulted but for the abnormally sensitive character of the plaintiff's activity.

Do § 524A and § 519(2) always lead to the same result? *See* Great Lakes Dredging and Dock Co. v. Sea Gull Operating Corp., 460 So.2d 510 (Fla.App. 1984).

4. Suit against the United States on a strict liability claim has not been permitted. The Federal Torts Claims Act, which waives sovereign immunity for action involving a "negligent or wrongful act or omission", has been held not to include claims based on strict liability. Laird v. Nelms, 406 U.S. 797, 92 S.Ct. 1899, 32 L.Ed.2d 499 (1972), reprinted at p. 1322, *infra*.

5. As in the case with wild animals, the *Second Restatement* permits a defendant in an abnormally dangerous activity case to raise the defense of the assumption of the risk, but not the plaintiff's contributory negligence. *See* §§ 423–524. Few courts have addressed question of whether the movement to comparative negligence should lead to a different outcome in abnormally dangerous activity cases. In Maddy v. Vulcan Materials, 737 F.Supp. 1528, 1541 (D.Kan.1990) the court followed the Uniform Comparative Fault Act's position that comparative fault principles are applicable in cases involving ultrahazardous activities.

6. Some very interesting literature, prompted in part by attention to strict liability, explores the underlying theory of much of tort law. Specifically it addresses the underlying economic effect and moral justification for strict liability, in comparison with other tort concepts. *See, e.g.*, Guido Calabresi & Jon T. Hirschoff, *Toward a Test of Strict Liability in Torts,* 81 Yale L.J. 1055 (1972)(which builds upon extensive earlier work by Dean Calabresi); Richard Epstein, *A Theory of Strict Liability,* 2 J.Legal Studies 151 (1973); George Fletcher, *Fairness and Utility in Tort Theory,* 85 Harv.L.Rev. 537 (1972); Keith N. Hylton, *A Missing Markets Theory of Tort Law,* 90 Nw. U. L. Rev. 977 (1996); William K. Jones, *Strict Liability for Hazardous Enterprise,* 92 Colum. L. Rev. 1705 (1992); Louis Kaplow and Steven Shavell, *Property Rules Versus Liability Rules: An Economic Analysis,* 109 Harv. L. Rev. 713 (1996); James E. Krier and Stewart J. Schwab, *Property Rules and Liability Rules: The Cathedral in Another Light,* 70 N.Y.U. L. Rev. 440 (1995); Richard A. Posner, Economic Analysis of Law 160–164 (3d ed. 1986); Gary Schwartz, *The Vitality*

of Negligence and the Ethics of Strict Liability, 15 Ga.L.Rev. 963 (1981); Steven Shavell, *Strict Liability versus Negligence,* 9 J.Legal Studies 1 (1980).

7. In an analysis which contributed to his winning the Nobel Prize in Economics, Ronald Coase argued that under certain circumstances the law's choice of liability rules will not alter the efficient allocation of resources. Ronald H. Coase, *The Problem of Social Cost,* 3 J. Law and Econ. 1 (1960). These circumstances include, a) zero transaction costs, i.e. perfectly costless bargaining between parties, b) the alienability of entitlements, i.e. individuals are free to buy and sell the rights and obligations imposed by the liability rule, c) the absence of wealth effects, and d) profit-maximizing bargainers. *See* Herbert Hovenkamp, *Marginal Utility and the Coase Theorem,* 75 Cornell L. Rev. 783, 785 (1990). Under these circumstances, once a liability rule is assigned the parties will bargain to the same efficient result, regardless of to whom it the rule was assigned.

The *Foster* facts may be used to illustrate this point. Coase begins with the central observation that it is incorrect to say simply that the blasting causes injury to the mink. The causation is "reciprocal" in the sense that it is the joint presence of both the logging and the mink ranch that is a prerequisite to any damage. If liability is placed on the mink rancher, the damage to his animals is a cost added to the cost of production of pelts. The blasting caused his costs to rise. If, on the other hand, the liability is placed on the logger, the damage to the minks is a cost added to the cost of logging. The existence of nearby minks caused the price of logging to increase.

In order to see how the Theorem applies to this and similar competing land use circumstances, it is useful to imagine two different situations: one in which blasting is worth more to the logger than the damage it causes the mink rancher, and another in which blasting is worth less to the logger than the mink damage it causes. The first situation would exist if blasting is worth $100 to the logger (*i.e.* is $100 cheaper than any alternative way of building logging roads), but costs $90 worth of injuries to the mink rancher. The efficient allocation of resources is to continue to blast, for this creates $100 in value at a $90 cost. If the legal system were to force the logger to cease this method of construction, the collective wealth of the rancher and the logger would be $10 less. However, if the logger only has to pay damages to the rancher for the injuries he causes, he will continue to blast, for blasting is still $10 cheaper ($100 savings less the $90 he must pay the rancher) than his next best alternative. The logger may wish to avoid the cost of litigation and simply pay the rancher directly. He might, for example, pay the rancher $91 for the right to blast and still realize a benefit of $9. If, on the other hand, the law refuses to assign liability to the logger, i.e., he is not legally responsible for injuries to the mink, then the mink rancher will simply have to live with the blasting. It is only worth $90 to him to have the blasting cease, and if he were to offer this sum to the logger, the logger would decline for it is worth $100 to continue blasting.

Now imagine the second situation, where the injuries caused to the minks is greater than the benefits derived from blasting as a method of constructing logging roads. This situation would exist if blasting is $90 cheaper than its alternatives, but costs $100 worth of injuries to the mink rancher. If the logger is liable for the damages he causes the minks, presumably he will turn to another way of building the road, for the cost of blasting ($100 in damages) is not worth the benefit. If, on the other hand, the logger may blast with impunity, the mink rancher will bargain with the logger to cease blasting. For example, the rancher might offer the logger $91 dollars to cease blasting, and still realize a benefit of $9. The central idea of the Coase Theorem is that in both situations, regardless of the initial assignment of liability, the parties achieve the same, efficient allocation resources.

Recall that the parties were unable to reach an agreement about blasting in the *Foster* case. Why do you think they failed to come to an accommodation? Consider the assumptions underlying the Coase Theorem.

The Theorem has generated a large number of articles, criticizing, explaining, and expanding on Coase's analysis. *See* Ian Ayres and Eric Talley, *Solomonic Bargaining: Dividing A Legal Entitlement to Facilitate Coasean Trade*, 104 Yale L.J. 1027 (1995); Robert Cooter, *The Cost of Coase*, 11 J. Legal Stud. 1 (1982); Harold Demsetz, *When Does The Rule Of Liability Matter?* 1 J. Legal Stud. 13 (1972); Donald H. Gjerdingen, *The Coase Theorem and the Psychology of Common–Law Thought,* 56 S. Cal. L. Rev. 711 (1983); Elizabeth Hoffman and Matthew L. Spitzer, *The Coase Theorem: Some Experimental Tests*, 25 J.L. & Econ. 73 (1982); Mark Kelman, Consumption Theory, Production Theory, and Ideology in the Coase Theorem, 52 S. Cal. L. Rev. 669 (1979); Mitchell Polinsky, An Introduction to Law and Economics, 2d ed. (1989).

Chapter 9

PRODUCTS LIABILITY

I. NEGLIGENCE ACTIONS—OVERCOMING THE PRIVITY BARRIER

THOMAS v. WINCHESTER

Court of Appeals of New York, 1852.
6 N.Y. 397.

RUGGLES, CH. J. delivered the opinion of the court. This is an action brought to recover damages from the defendant for negligently putting up, labeling and selling as and for the extract of *dandelion*, which is a simple and harmless medicine, a jar of the extract of *belladonna*, which is a deadly poison; by means of which the plaintiff Mary Ann Thomas, to whom, being sick, a dose of dandelion was prescribed by a physician, and a portion of the contents of the jar, was administered as and for the extract of dandelion, was greatly injured, & c.

The facts proved were briefly these: Mrs. Thomas being in ill health, her physician prescribed for her a dose of dandelion. Her husband purchased what was believed to be the medicine prescribed, at the store of Dr. Foord, a physician and druggist in Cazenovia, Madison county, where the plaintiffs reside.

A small quantity of the medicine thus purchased was administered to Mrs. Thomas, on whom it produced very alarming effects; such as coldness of the surface and extremities, feebleness of circulation, spasms of the muscles, giddiness of the head, dilation of the pupils of the eyes, and derangement of mind. She recovered however, after some time, from its effects, although for a short time her life was thought to be in great danger. The medicine administered was *belladonna, and not dandelion.* The jar from which it was taken was labeled "*½ lb. dandelion, prepared by A. Gilbert, No. 108, John-street, N.Y. Jar 8 oz.*" It was sold for and believed by Dr. Foord to be the extract of dandelion as labeled. Dr. Foord purchased the article as the extract of dandelion from Jas. S. Aspinwall, a druggist at New–York. Aspinwall bought it of the defendant as extract of dandelion, believing it to be such. The defendant was engaged at No. 108 John-street, New–York, in the manufacture and sale of certain vegetable extracts for medicinal purposes, and in the purchase and sale of others. The extracts manufactured by him were put up in jars for sale, and those which he purchased were put up by him in like manner. The jars containing extracts manufactured by himself and those containing extracts purchased by him from others, were labeled alike. Both were labeled like the jar in question, as "prepared by A. Gilbert." Gilbert was a person employed by the defendant at a salary, as an assistant in his business. The jars were labeled in Gilbert's name because he had been previously engaged in the same business on his own account at No. 108 John-street, and probably because Gilbert's labels rendered the articles more salable. The extract contained in the jar sold to Aspinwall, and by him to Foord, was not manufactured by the defendant, but was purchased by him from another manufacturer or dealer. The extract of dandelion and the extract of belladonna resemble each other in color, consistence, smell and taste; but may on careful examination be distinguished the one from the other by those who are well acquainted with these articles. Gilbert's labels were paid for by Winchester and used in his business with his knowledge and assent.

The case depends on the first point taken by the defendant on his motion for a nonsuit; and the question is, whether the defendant, being a remote vendor of the medicine, and there being no privity or connection between him and the plaintiffs, the action can be maintained.[1]

If, in labeling a poisonous drug with the name of a harmless medicine, for public market, no duty was violated by the defendant, excepting that which he owed to Aspinwall, his immediate vendee, in virtue of his contract of sale, this action cannot be maintained. If A. build a wagon and sell it to B., who sells its to C., and C. hires it to D., who in consequence of the gross negligence of A. in building the wagon is overturned and injured, D. cannot recover damages against A., the builder. A.'s obligation to build the wagon faithfully, arises solely out of his contract with B. The public have nothing to do with it. Misfortune to third persons, not parties to the contract, would not be a natural and necessary consequence of the builder's negligence; and such negligence is not an act imminently dangerous to human life.

So, for the same reason, if a horse be defectively shod by a smith, and a person hiring the horse from the owner is thrown and injured in consequence of the smith's negligence in shoeing; the smith is not liable for the injury. The smith's duty in such case grows exclusively out of his contract with the owner of the horse; it was a duty which the smith owed to him alone, and to no one else. And although the injury to the rider may have happened in consequence of the negligence of the smith, the latter was not bound, either by his contract or by any considerations of public policy or safety, to respond for his breach of duty to any one except the person he contracted with.

This was the ground on which the case of *Winterbottom v. Wright*, (10 *Mees. & Welsb.* 109,) was decided. A. contracted with the postmaster general to provide a coach to convey the mail bags along a certain line of road, and B. and others, also contracted to horse the coach along the same line. B. and his co-contractors hired C., who was the plaintiff, to drive the coach. The coach, in consequence of some latent defect, broke down; the

1. [Ed. note] The jury had returned a verdict of $800 against Winchester.

plaintiff was thrown from his seat and lamed. It was held that C. could not maintain an action against A. for the injury thus sustained. The reason of the decision is best stated by Baron Rolfe. A.'s duty to keep the coach in good condition, was a duty to the postmaster general, with whom he made his contract, and not a duty to the driver employed by the owners of the horses.

But the case in hand stands on a different ground. The defendant was a dealer in poisonous drugs. Gilbert was his agent in preparing them for market. The death or great bodily harm of some person was the natural and almost inevitable consequence of the sale of belladonna by means of the false label.

Gilbert, the defendant's agent, would have been punishable for manslaughter if Mrs. Thomas had died in consequence of taking the falsely labeled medicine. Every man who, by his culpable negligence, causes the death of another, although without intent to kill, is guilty of manslaughter. (2 *R.S.* 662, § 19.) * * * Although the defendant Winchester may not be answerable criminally for the negligence of his agent, there can be no doubt of his liability in a civil action, in which the act of the agent is to be regarded as the act of the principal.

In respect to the wrongful and criminal character of the negligence complained of, this case differs widely from those put by the defendant's counsel. No such imminent danger existed in those cases. In the present case the sale of the poisonous article was made to a dealer in drugs, and not to a consumer. The injury therefore was not likely to fall on him, or on his vendee who was also a dealer; but much more likely to be visited on a remote purchaser, as actually happened. The defendant's negligence put human life in imminent danger. Can it be said that there was no duty on the part of the defendant, to avoid the creation of that danger by the exercise of greater caution? or that the exercise of that caution was a duty only to his immediate vendee, whose life was not endangered? * * * The duty of exercising caution in this respect did not arise out of the defendant's contract of sale to Aspinwall. The wrong done by the defendant was in putting the poison, mislabeled, into the hands of Aspinwall as an article of merchandise to be sold and afterwards used as the extract of dandelion, by some person then unknown. The owner of a horse and cart who leaves them unattended in the street is liable for any damage which may result from his negligence. * * * The owner of a loaded gun who puts it into the hands of a child by whose indiscretion it is discharged, is liable for the damage occasioned by the discharge. * * * The defendant's contract of sale to Aspinwall does not excuse the wrong done to the plaintiffs. It was a part of the means by which the wrong was effected. The plaintiffs' injury and their remedy would have stood on the same principle, if the defendant had given the belladonna to Dr. Foord without price, or if he had put it in his shop without his knowledge, under circumstances which would probably have led to its sale on the faith of the label.

In *Longmeid v. Holliday*, (6 *Law and Eq.Rep.* 562) the distinction is recognized between an act of negligence imminently dangerous to the lives of others, and one that is not so. In the former case, the party guilty of the negligence is liable to the party injured, whether there be a contract between them or not; in the latter, the negligent party is liable only to the party with whom he contracted, and on the ground that negligence is a breach of the contract.

The defendant, on the trial, insisted that Aspinwall and Foord were guilty of negligence in selling the article in question for what it was represented to be in the label; and that the suit, if it could be sustained at all, should have been brought against Foord. * * * If the case really depended on the point thus raised, the question was properly left to the jury. But I think it did not. The defendant, by affixing the label to the jar, represented its contents to be dandelion; and to have been "prepared" by his agent Gilbert. The word 'prepared' on the label, must be understood to mean that the article was manufactured by him, or that it had passed through some process under his hands, which would give him personal knowledge of its true name and quality. Whether Foord was justified in selling the article upon the faith of the defendant's label, would have been an open question in an action by the plaintiffs against him, and I wish to be understood as giving no opinion on that point. But it seems to me to be clear that the defendant cannot, in this case, set up as a defense, that Foord sold the contents of the jar as and for what the defendant represented it to be. The label conveyed the idea distinctly to Foord that the contents of the jar was the extract of dandelion; and that the defendant knew it to be such. So far as the defendant is concerned, Foord was under no obligation to test the truth of the representation. * * *

GARDINER, J. concurred in affirming the judgment, on the ground that selling the belladonna without a label indicating that it was a *poison*, was declared a misdemeanor by statute; * * * but expressed no opinion upon the question whether, independent of the statute, the defendant would have been liable to these plaintiffs.

Judgment affirmed.

Notes

1. Winterbottom v. Wright, 10 M. & W. 109, 152 Eng.Rep. 402 (Exch. 1842), which was discussed at some length in Chief Judge Ruggles' opinion in *Thomas v. Winchester*, is the most famous expression of the old common-law privity requirement. The following statement from the judgment of Lord Abinger, C.B., is often cited:

> * * * It is however contended, that this contract being made on behalf of the public by the Postmaster–General, no action could be maintained against him, and therefore the plaintiff must have a remedy against the defendant. But that is by no means a necessary consequence—he may be remediless altogether. There is no privity of contract between these parties; and if the plaintiff can sue, every passenger, or even any person passing along the road, who was injured by the upsetting of the coach, might bring a similar action. Unless we confine the operation of such contracts as this to the parties who entered into them, the most absurd and outrageous consequences, to which I can see no limit, would ensue. * * *

10 M. & W. at 114, 152 Eng.Rep. at 404–05.

2. In Loop v. Litchfield, 42 N.Y. 351 (1870), a circular saw had been constructed with a balance (or fly) wheel which had been improperly cast. The

defect had apparently been pointed out to the original purchaser but was not readily detectable because lead had been used to give the wheel a uniform appearance. Some three years after the saw had been acquired by the original purchaser, it was leased to the plaintiffs' decedent, who was unaware of the problem with the balance wheel. About two years later the wheel burst and killed the decedent. The trial court let the case go to the jury on the theory that the plaintiffs were entitled to recover if the balance wheel was negligently constructed. The General Term reversed a judgment for the plaintiff and the New York Court of Appeals affirmed this reversal. In distinguishing *Thomas v. Winchester*, it declared:

> The appellants recognize the principle of this decision, and seek to bring their case within it, by asserting that the fly wheel in question was a dangerous instrument. Poison is a dangerous subject. Gunpowder is the same. A torpedo is a dangerous instrument as is a spring gun, a loaded rifle or the like. They are instruments and articles in their nature calculated to do injury to mankind, and generally intended to accomplish that purpose. They are essentially, and in their elements, instruments of danger. Not so, however, an iron wheel a few feet in diameter and a few inches in thickness, although one part may be weaker than another.

42 N.Y. at 358–59 (per Hunt, J.). The court also stressed that the wheel had lasted for five years.

Losee v. Clute, 51 N.Y. 494 (1873), involved litigation that arose out of the same accident as that which generated *Losee v. Buchanan*, set out in the text at p. 576, *supra*. In the *Buchanan* case, the plaintiff sought recovery for damage to his property against the owners of the bursting boiler on a *Rylands v. Fletcher* theory of strict liability. In *Losee v. Clute*, the plaintiff brought a negligence action against the manufacturer of the boiler. The court reaffirmed the privity rule, noting that "the opinion of Hunt, J. in Loop v. Litchfield * * * clearly shows that the principle decided in [Thomas v. Winchester] case has no application to this [case]." 51 N.Y. at 497.

3. The next important New York case was Devlin v. Smith, 89 N.Y. 470 (1882). The defendants were Smith, who had contracted to paint the dome of a county court-house, and Stevenson, whom Smith had employed to construct a scaffold upon which the painters would work. Hugh Devlin, the plaintiff's intestate, was one of the painters employed by Smith. The scaffold collapsed hurtling Devlin to his death. The court first held that there was sufficient evidence to go to the jury on the questions of whether the scaffold had been negligently built by Stevenson and of whether that negligence had caused the collapse. The court continued:

> Stevenson undertook to build a scaffold ninety feet in height, for the express purpose of enabling the workmen of Smith to stand upon it to paint the interior of the dome. Any defect or negligence in its construction, which should cause it to give way, would naturally result in these men being precipitated from that great height. A stronger case where misfortune to third persons not parties to the contract would be a natural and necessary consequence of the builder's negligence, can hardly be supposed, nor is it easy to imagine a more apt illustration of a case where such negligence would be an act imminently dangerous to human life. These circumstances seem to us to bring the case fairly within the principle of *Thomas v. Winchester*.

* * *

Loop v. Litchfield (42 N.Y. 351, 1 Am.Rep. 543) was decided upon the ground that the wheel which caused the injury was not in itself a dangerous instrument, and that the injury was not a natural consequence of the defect, or one reasonably to be anticipated. Losee v. Clute (51 N.Y. 494, 10 Am.Rep. 638) was distinguished from *Thomas v. Winchester*, upon the authority of *Loop v. Litchfield*.

89 N.Y. at 477–79. There is no question that *Loop v. Litchfield, supra,* is readily distinguishable on its facts from *Devlin v. Smith. Losee v. Clute, supra,* is much more analogous to *Devlin v. Smith.* Do you think it was proper of Rapallo, J., to dismiss the relevancy of *Losee v. Clute* on the ground that it was decided on the basis of *Loop v. Litchfield*?

MacPHERSON v. BUICK MOTOR CO.

Court of Appeals of New York, 1916.
217 N.Y. 382, 111 N.E. 1050.

CARDOZO, J. The defendant is a manufacturer of automobiles. It sold an automobile to a retail dealer. The retail dealer resold to the plaintiff. While the plaintiff was in the car, it suddenly collapsed. He was thrown out and injured. One of the wheels was made of defective wood, and its spokes crumbled into fragments. The wheel was not made by the defendant; it was bought from another manufacturer. There is evidence, however, that its defects could have been discovered by reasonable inspection, and that inspection was omitted. There is no claim that the defendant knew of the defect and willfully concealed it. * * * The question to be determined is whether the defendant owed a duty of care and vigilance to any one but the immediate purchaser.

The foundations of this branch of the law, at least in this state, were laid in Thomas v. Winchester (6 N.Y. 397). A poison was falsely labeled. The sale was made to a druggist, who in turn sold to a customer. The customer recovered damages from the seller who affixed the label. "The defendant's negligence," it was said, "put human life in imminent danger." A poison falsely labeled is likely to injure any one who gets it. Because the danger is to be foreseen, there is a duty to avoid the injury. Cases were cited by way of illustration in which manufacturers were not subject to any duty irrespective of contract. The distinction was said to be that their conduct, though negligent, was not likely to result in injury to any one except the purchaser. We are not required to say whether the chance of injury was always as remote as the distinction assumes. Some of the illustrations might be rejected to-day. The *principle* of the distinction is for present purposes the important thing.

Thomas v. Winchester became quickly a landmark of the law. In the application of its principle there may at times have been uncertainty or even error. There has never in this state been doubt or disavowal of the principle itself. The chief cases are well known, yet to recall some of them will be helpful. Loop v. Litchfield (42 N.Y. 351) is the earliest. It was the case of a defect in a small balance wheel used on a circular saw. The manufacturer pointed out the defect to the buyer, who wished a cheap article and was ready to assume the risk. The risk can hardly have been an imminent one, for the wheel lasted five years before it broke. In the meanwhile the buyer had made a lease of the machinery. It was held that the manufacturer was not answerable to the lessee. *Loop v. Litchfield* was followed in Losee v. Clute (51 N.Y. 494), the case of the explosion of a steam boiler. That decision has been criticised * * *; but it must be confined to its special facts. It was put upon the ground that the risk of injury was too remote. The buyer in that case had not only accepted the boiler, but had tested it. The manufacturer knew that his own test was not the final one. The finality of the test has a bearing on the measure of diligence owing to persons other than the purchaser * * *.

These early cases suggest a narrow construction of the rule. Later cases, however, evince a more liberal spirit. First in importance is Devlin v. Smith (89 N.Y. 470). The defendant, a contractor, built a scaffold for a painter. The painter's servants were injured. The contractor was held liable. He knew that the scaffold, if improperly constructed, was a most dangerous trap. He knew that it was to be used by the workmen. He was building it for that very purpose. Building it for their use, he owed them a duty, irrespective of his contract with their master, to build it with care.

From *Devlin v. Smith* we pass over intermediate cases and turn to the latest case in this court in which *Thomas v. Winchester* was followed. That case is Statler v. Ray Mfg. Co. (195 N.Y. 478, 480). The defendant manufactured a large coffee urn. It was installed in a restaurant. When heated, the urn exploded and injured the plaintiff. We held that the manufacturer was liable. We said that the urn "was of such a character inherently that, when applied to the purposes for which it was designed, it was liable to become a source of great danger to many people if not carefully and properly constructed."

It may be that *Devlin v. Smith* and *Statler v. Ray Mfg. Co.* have extended the rule of *Thomas v. Winchester*. If so, this court is committed to the extension. The defendant argues that things imminently dangerous to life are poisons, explosives, deadly weapons—things whose normal function it is to injure or destroy. But whatever the rule in *Thomas v. Winchester* may once have been, it has no longer that restricted meaning. A scaffold * * * is not inherently a destructive instrument. It becomes destructive only if imperfectly constructed. A large coffee urn * * * may have within itself, if negligently made, the potency of danger, yet no one thinks of it as an implement whose normal function is destruction. What is true of the coffee urn is equally true of bottles of aerated water (Torgesen v. Schultz, 192 N.Y. 156). We have mentioned only cases in this court. But the rule has received a like extension in our courts of intermediate appeal. * * * We are not required at this time either to approve or to disapprove the application of the rule that was made in these cases. It is enough that they help to characterize the trend of judicial thought.

Devlin v. Smith was decided in 1882. A year later a very similar case came before the Court of Appeal in England (Heaven v. Pender, L.R. [11 Q.B.D.] 503). We find in the opinion of BRETT, M. R., afterwards Lord ESHER (p. 510), the same conception of a duty, irrespective of contract, imposed upon the manufacturer by the law itself: "Whenever one person supplies goods, or machinery, or the like, for the purpose of their being used by another person under such circumstances that every one of ordinary sense would, if he thought, recognize at once that unless he used ordinary care and skill with regard to the condition of the thing supplied or the mode of supplying it, there will be danger of injury to the person or property of him for whose use the thing is supplied, and who is to use it, a duty arises to use ordinary care and skill as to the condition or manner of supplying such thing." He then points out that for a neglect of such ordinary care or skill whereby injury happens, the appropriate remedy is an action for negligence. The right to enforce this liability is not to be confined to the immediate buyer. The right, he says, extends to the persons or class of persons for whose use the thing is supplied. It is enough that the goods "would in all probability be used at once * * * before a reasonable opportunity for discovering any defect which might exist," and that the thing supplied is of such a nature "that a neglect of ordinary care or skill as to its condition or the manner of supplying it would probably cause danger to the person or property of the person for whose use it was supplied, and who was about to use it." On the other hand, he would exclude a case "in which the goods are supplied under circumstances in which it would be a chance by whom they would be used or whether they would be used or not, or whether they would be used before there would probably be means of observing any defect," or where the goods are of such a nature that "a want of care or skill as to their condition or the manner of supplying them would not probably produce danger of injury to person or property." What was said by Lord ESHER in that case did not command the full assent of his associates. His opinion has been criticised "as requiring every man to take affirmative precautions to protect his neighbors as well as to refrain from injuring them" (Bohlen, Affirmative Obligations in the Law of Torts, 44 Am.Law Reg. [N.S.] 341). It may not be an accurate exposition of the law of England. Perhaps it may need some qualification even in our own state. Like most attempts at comprehensive definition, it may involve errors of inclusion and of exclusion. But its tests and standards, at least in their underlying principles, with whatever qualification may be called for as they are applied to varying conditions, are the tests and standards of our law.

We hold, then, that the principle of *Thomas v. Winchester* is not limited to poisons, explosives, and things of like nature, to things which in their normal operation are implements of destruction. If the nature of a thing is such that it is reasonably certain to place life and limb in peril when negligently made, it is then a thing of danger. Its nature gives warning of the consequences to be expected. If to the element of danger there is added knowledge that the thing will be used by persons other than the purchaser, and used without new tests, then, irrespective of contract, the manufacturer of this thing of danger is under a duty to make it carefully. That is as far as we are required to go for the decision of this case. There must be knowledge of a danger, not merely possible, but probable. It is *possible* to use almost anything in a way that will make it dangerous if defective. That is not enough to charge the manufacturer with a duty independent of his contract. Whether a given thing is dangerous may be sometimes a question for the court and sometimes a question for the jury. There must also be knowledge that in the usual course of events the danger will be shared by others than the buyer. Such knowledge may often be inferred from the nature of the transaction. But it is possible that even knowledge of the danger and of the use will not always be enough. The proximity or remoteness of the relation is a factor to be considered. We are dealing now with the liability of the manufacturer of the finished product, who puts it on the market to be used without inspection by his customers. If he is negligent, where danger is to be foreseen, a liability will follow. We are not required at this time to say that it is legitimate to go back of the manufacturer of the finished product and hold the manufacturers of the component parts. To make their negligence a cause of imminent danger, an independent cause must often intervene; the manufacturer of the finished product must also fail in *his* duty of inspection. It may be that in those circumstances the negligence of the earlier members of the series is too remote to constitute, as to the ultimate user, an actionable wrong * * *. We leave that question open. * * * There is here no break in the chain of cause and effect. In such circumstances, the presence of a known danger, attendant upon a known use, makes vigilance a duty. We have put aside the notion that the duty to safeguard life and limb, when the consequences of negligence may be foreseen, grows out of contract and nothing else. We have put the source of the obligation where it ought to be. We have put its source in the law.

* * * Beyond all question, the nature of an automobile gives warning of probable danger if its construction is defective. This automobile was designed to go fifty miles an hour. Unless its wheels were sound and strong, injury was almost certain. It was as much a thing of danger as a defective engine for a railroad. The defendant knew the danger. It knew also that the car would be used by persons other than the buyer. This was apparent from its size; there were seats for three persons. It was apparent also from the fact that the buyer was a dealer in cars, who bought to resell. The maker of this car supplied it for the use of purchasers from the dealer just as plainly as the contractor in *Devlin v. Smith* supplied the scaffold for use by the servants of the owner. The dealer was indeed the one person of whom it might be said with some approach to certainty that by him the car would not be used. Yet the defendant would have us say that he was the one person whom it was under a legal duty to protect. The law does not lead us to so inconsequent a conclusion. Precedents drawn from the days of travel by stage coach do not fit the conditions of travel to-day. The principle that the danger must be imminent does not change, but the things subject to the principle do change. They are whatever the needs of life in a developing civilization require them to be.

In reaching this conclusion, we do not ignore the decisions to the contrary in other jurisdictions. It was held in Cadillac M. C. Co. v. Johnson (221 Fed.Rep. 801) that an automobile is not within the rule of *Thomas v. Winchester*. There was, however, a vigorous dissent. Opposed to that decision is one of the Court of Appeals of Kentucky (Olds Motor Works v. Shaffer, 145 Ky. 616). The earlier cases are summarized by Judge Sanborn in Huset v. J. I. Case Threshing Machine Co. (120 Fed.Rep. 865). Some of them, at first sight inconsistent with our conclusion may be reconciled upon the ground that the negligence was too remote, and that another cause had intervened. But even when they cannot be reconciled, the difference is rather in the application of the principle than in the principle itself. Judge Sanborn says, for example, that the contractor who builds a bridge, or the manufacturer who builds a car, cannot ordinarily foresee injury to other persons than the owner as the probable result * * *. We take a different view. We think that injury to others is to be foreseen not merely as a possible, but as an almost inevitable result. (See the trenchant criticism in Bohlen, *supra*, at p. 351). Indeed, Judge Sanborn concedes that his view is not to be reconciled with our decision in *Devlin v. Smith (supra)*. The doctrine of that decision has now become the settled law of this state, and we have no desire to depart from it.

There is nothing anomalous in a rule which imposes upon A, who has contracted with B, a duty to C and D and others according as he knows or does not know that the subject-matter of the contract is intended for their use. We may find an analogy in the law which measures the liability of landlords. If A leases to B a tumbledown house he is not liable, in the absence of fraud, to B's guests who enter it and are injured. This is because B is then under the duty to repair it, the lessor has the right to suppose that he will fulfill that duty, and, if he omits to do so, his guests must look to him * * *. But if A leases a building to be used by the lessee at once as a place of public entertainment, the rule is different. There injury to persons other than the lessee is to be foreseen, and foresight of the consequences involves the creation of a duty * * *.

We think the defendant was not absolved from a duty of inspection because it bought the wheels from a reputable manufacturer. It was not merely a dealer in automobiles. It was a manufacturer of automobiles. It was responsible for the finished product. It was not at liberty to put the finished product on the market without subjecting the component parts to ordinary and simple tests * * *. Under the charge of the trial judge nothing more was required of it. * * *

Other rulings complained of have been considered, but no error has been found in them.

The judgment should be affirmed with costs.

WILLARD BARTLETT, CH. J. (dissenting). * * *

I do not see how we can uphold the judgment in the present case without overruling what has been so often said by this court and other courts of like authority in reference to the absence of any liability for negligence on the part of the original vendor of an ordinary carriage to any one except his immediate vendee. The absence of such liability was the very point actually decided in the English case of *Winterbottom v. Wright (supra)*, and the illustration quoted from the opinion of Chief Judge Ruggles in *Thomas v. Winchester (supra)* assumes that the law on the subject was so plain that the statement would be accepted almost as a matter of course. In the case at bar the defective wheel on an automobile moving only eight miles an hour was not any more dangerous to the occupants of the car than a similarly defective wheel would be to the occupants of a carriage drawn by a horse at the same speed; and yet unless the courts have been all wrong on this question up to the present time there would be no liability to strangers to the original sale in the case of the horse-drawn carriage.

Notes

1. Cardozo, J., stresses very heavily that New York law on the subject of a manufacturer's liability to third parties was laid down in *Devlin v. Smith* and that the *MacPherson* case is merely an application of the doctrine of *Devlin v. Smith*. Willard Bartlett, Ch. J., in his dissent declares that the court that decided *Devlin v. Smith* would not have found the automobile in *MacPherson* analogous to the scaffold in *Devlin v. Smith* which was some 90 feet high. Which judge do you think has the better of this argument? The *MacPherson* case is a textbook illustration of the technique of legal argument in which a court, when confronted with a potentially controversial decision, asserts that the point at issue was really decided previously. By making this move, the present court rather than being obliged to accept responsibility for its decision can assert that it is merely following the law established by prior courts.

2. Judge Cardozo's opinion in *MacPherson* marked the beginning of the end of the privity rule in products liability cases. Any lingering notion that liability to persons not in privity of contract for negligently manufactured products depends on some finding that the product is in some way potentially dangerous was soon abandoned. All that is necessary is that the product presents a foreseeable risk of physical injury to persons or property, if it should be negligently manufactured. The extensive development of this type of liability is summed up in Dix W. Noel, *Manufacturers' Liability for Negligence*, 33 Tenn.L.Rev. 444 (1966).

3. Once it was generally accepted that an action for negligence would lie against the manufacturer of a defective product, the doctrine of res ipsa loquitur became available to the plaintiff. That is, it was often possible to argue that, since the product was defective, the defect was the result of the defendant's negligence. In Escola v. Coca Cola Bottling Co., 24 Cal.2d 453, 150 P.2d 436 (1944), Traynor, J., in a concurring opinion, argued that the use of res ipsa loquitur in products liability cases was often tantamount to permitting the jury to impose liability without proof of fault. We shall return to Justice Traynor's opinion in *Escola* shortly.

4. *Other remedies—misrepresentation*. In Baxter v. Ford Motor Co., 168 Wash. 456, 12 P.2d 409 (1932); 179 Wash. 123, 35 P.2d 1090 (1934), the defendant advertised that its wind shield was made of "shatter-proof glass." Plaintiff was injured when a rock from a passing car broke his windshield, causing him to lose the sight of one eye. The Washington Supreme Court rejected the defendant's privity defense and ruled that he could rely on Ford's representation to the public that the windshield was shatter-proof. This position was extended in *Restatement (Second) of Torts* § 402B, which deals with liability for misrepresenting a material fact in advertising or other promotional material.

§ 402B. Misrepresentation by Seller of Chattels to Consumer

One engaged in the business of selling chattels who, by advertising, labels, or otherwise, makes to the public a misrepresentation of a material fact concerning the character or quality of a chattel sold by him is subject to liability for physical harm to a consumer of the chattel caused by justifiable reliance upon the misrepresentation, even though

(a) it is not made fraudulently or negligently, and

(b) the consumer has not bought the chattel from or entered into any contractual relation with the seller.

Note that the plaintiff may recover on a § 402B misrepresentation claim even in the absence of manufacturer negligence. An interesting case applying § 402B is Crocker v. Winthrop Laboratories, 514 S.W.2d 429 (Tex.1974). There defendant had represented its painkiller product as "free and safe from all dangers of addiction". Plaintiff had an unforeseeable, idiosyncratic reaction to the drug and became addicted. As we shall see later, the fact that a manufacturer could not know of a danger will often relieve the manufacturer of liability under the strict liability doctrines. The *Crocker* court held, however, that a cause of action based upon misrepresentation would lie even when the manufacturer had no basis in currently available knowledge to know that the statement was untrue.

Judge Cardozo's opinion in *MacPherson* was the capstone of a 75 year struggle with the "citadel" of the privity rule in negligence cases. As we shall see in subsequent chapters, the privity rule has survived in other contexts. *See* William L. Prosser, *The Assault Upon the Citadel (Strict Liability to the Consumer)*, 69 Yale L.J. 1099 (1960).

II. STRICT LIABILITY

A. CONTRACTUALLY BASED REMEDIES—BREACH OF WARRANTY

1. *Introduction*

When there is a direct contractual relationship between the injured plaintiff and the seller of a product, a breach of contract action is possible if the injury has occurred as the result of the breach of an warranty expressly made by the seller or implied by law regarding the nature or condition of the product. Today, warranty law is important to our study of products liability in torts because it played an important role historically in the evolution of tort theory. Moreover, although a majority of the states have now recognized the tort approach, some states have continued to rely upon the contract-warranty approach to the exclusion of the tort remedy. Even in those states recognizing the strict liability action in tort for injuries caused by defective products, lawyers often plead alternatively for breach of warranty and, in most cases, also in negligence.

2. *General Background*

The traditional legal remedy by which a buyer of goods sought to recover from the seller, if the goods proved to be defective, was an action for breach of warranty. Prior to the late eighteenth century any such actions were brought as instances of trespass on the case for deceit or on what we would now call a tort theory. Towards the end of the eighteenth century the action started to become merged with the action for express assumpsit which itself had also evolved out of trespass on the case.

An action for breach of warranty, whether considered as a tort or contract remedy, originally required some kind of express representation, what we would now call an *express* warranty. Gradually, over the course of the nineteenth century a number of *implied* warranties evolved. These were warranties that, in the absence of an effective disclaimer, were read into sales transaction by the courts as a matter of law and which operated as legally enforceable guarantees that the goods sold met certain standards. The two most important of such warranties for our purposes were the implied warranty of fitness for a particular purpose and the implied warranty of merchantability. These types of implied warranties were recognized under the Uniform Sales Act of 1906—eventually adopted in 34 states, the then territories of Alaska and Hawaii, and the District of Columbia—and now under the Uniform Commercial Code which, since 1967, has been in effect in 49 states and the District of Columbia. Portions of the UCC, but not the provisions on sales with which we shall be concerned, have also been adopted by Louisiana.

The implied warranty of fitness for a particular purpose arises when, at the *time of contracting*, the seller has reason to know both the particular purpose for which the goods are required and that the buyer is relying on the seller's skill or judgment [UCC § 2–315 set out below]. The implied warranty of merchantability applies only if the seller is a merchant with regard to goods of that kind [UCC § 2–314 set out below]. For our purposes it suffices to state that, in order to be merchantable, goods must pass without objection in the trade under the contract description and the goods must be fit for the ordinary purposes for which such goods are used. It is obvious that some defective goods may be both not of merchantable quality and not fit for a particular purpose. But there will be instances where the two implied warranties will not both be applicable. Gasoline, for example, can be of merchantable quality even if it is unfit for the particular purpose of starting a fire in your barbecue pit.

Traditionally before an action for breach of an express or implied warranty could be brought there had to be a sale and there had to be privity of contract between the parties. That is, the plaintiff had to have bought the goods from the seller. As people turned to these essentially commercial remedies in order to avoid the need for showing fault as a precondition to recovering damages for physical injuries caused by defective products, pressure developed to relax the privity requirement.

Originally, the UCC abolished the privity requirement only with respect to a very narrow group of individuals. It extended seller warranties to "any natural person who is in the family or household of his buyer or who is a guest in his home if it is reasonable to expect that such person may use, consume or be affected by the goods and who is injured in person by the breach of warranty." In 1966, the sponsors of the UCC provided two alternatives to this provision, which was renamed "Alternative A." "Alternative B" extends a seller's warranties to "any natural person who may reasonably be expected to use, consume or be affected by the goods" and who suffers personal injuries as a result of any breach of warranty. "Alternative C" extends a seller's warranties to "any person * * * who is injured" as a result of any breach of warranty. By 1966, however, judicial solutions to the privity problem were already beginning to be found. As a result, neither Alternative B nor Alternative C was widely adopted.

Presently, the National Conference of Commissioners on Uniform State Laws is considering proposed revisions of parts of Article 2 of the

UCC, including the warranty sections. Current discussion drafts make substantial changes to nearly all of these sections, but the process is not sufficiently far along to be certain what changes ultimately will be proposed.

3. Current State of the Law

UNIFORM COMMERCIAL CODE (1966)

§ 2–313. Express Warranties by Affirmation, Promise, Description, Sample

(1) Express warranties by the seller are created as follows:

(a) Any affirmation of fact or promise made by the seller to the buyer which relates to the goods and becomes part of the basis of the bargain creates an express warranty that the goods shall conform to the affirmation or promise.

(b) Any description of the goods which is made part of the basis of the bargain creates an express warranty that the goods shall conform to the description.

(c) Any sample or model which is made part of the basis of the bargain creates an express warranty that the whole of the goods shall conform to the sample or model.

(2) It is not necessary to the creation of an express warranty that the seller use formal words such as "warrant" or "guarantee" or that he have a specific intention to make a warranty, but an affirmation merely of the value of the goods or a statement purporting to be merely the seller's opinion or commendation of the goods does not create a warranty.

§ 2–314. Implied Warranty: Merchantability; Usage of Trade

(1) Unless excluded or modified (Section 2–316), a warranty that the goods shall be merchantable is implied in a contract for their sale if the seller is a merchant with respect to goods of that kind. Under this section the serving for value of food or drink to be consumed either on the premises or elsewhere is a sale.

(2) Goods to be merchantable must be at least such as

(a) pass without objection in the trade under the contract description; and

(b) in the case of fungible goods, are of fair average quality within the description; and

(c) are fit for the ordinary purposes for which such goods are used; and

(d) run, within the variations permitted by the agreement, of even kind, quality and quantity within each unit and among all units involved; and

(e) are adequately contained, packaged, and labeled as the agreement may require; and

(f) conform to the promises or affirmations of fact made on the container or label if any.

(3) Unless excluded or modified (Section 2–316) other implied warranties may arise from course of dealing or usage of trade.

§ 2–315. Implied Warranty: Fitness for Particular Purpose

Where the seller at the time of contracting has reason to know any particular purpose for which the goods are required and that the buyer is relying on the seller's skill or judgment to select or furnish suitable goods, there is unless excluded or modified under the next section an implied warranty that the goods shall be fit for such purpose.

§ 2–316. Exclusion or Modification of Warranties

(1) Words or conduct relevant to the creation of an express warranty and words or conduct tending to negate or limit warranty shall be construed wherever reasonable as consistent with each other; but subject to the provisions of this Article on parol or extrinsic evidence (Section 2–202) negation or limitation is inoperative to the extent that such construction is unreasonable.

(2) Subject to subsection (3), to exclude or modify the implied warranty of merchantability or any part of it the language must mention merchantability and in case of a writing must be conspicuous, and to exclude or modify any implied warranty of fitness the exclusion must be by a writing and conspicuous. Language to exclude all implied warranties of fitness is sufficient if it states, for example, that "There are no warranties which extend beyond the description on the face hereof."

(3) Notwithstanding subsection (2)

(a) unless the circumstances indicate otherwise, all implied warranties are excluded by expressions like "as is", "with all faults" or other language which in common understanding calls the buyer's attention to the exclusion of warranties and makes plain that there is no implied warranty; and

(b) when the buyer before entering into the contract has examined the goods or the sample or model as fully as he desired or has refused to examine the goods there is no implied warranty with regard to defects which an examination ought in the circumstances to have revealed to him; and

(c) an implied warranty can also be excluded or modified by course of dealing or course of performance or usage of trade.

(4) Remedies for breach of warranty can be limited in accordance with the provisions of this Article on liquidation or limitation of damages and on contractual modification of remedy (Sections 2–718 and 2–719).

Notes

1. The leading case marking the modern development of strict liability under the warranty approach is Henningsen v. Bloomfield Motors, Inc., 32 N.J. 358, 161 A.2d 69 (1960). Mr. Henningsen had bought a new automobile for his wife. Ten days later, while Mrs. Henningsen was driving the car, she was

involved in a one car accident in which the automobile was completely destroyed and she was seriously injured. The accident allegedly occurred as a result of a mechanical failure or defect in the steering mechanism. The Henningsens brought an action based on, among other grounds, breach of warranty. The court examined the modern merchandising approach in some detail and "adapted" warranty law to the consumer interests presented. The court held, in a manner similar to *MacPherson* in the negligence area, that a warranty runs to a foreseeable third party and thus Mrs. Henningsen was covered. Not only was the retail dealer who had sold the car responsible, but also the manufacturer of the automobile.

The court accordingly held that an implied warranty of merchantability and fitness for its intended purpose ran both from the dealer and the manufacturer. Moreover, the efforts of the dealer and manufacturer to disclaim implied warranties were found to be inadequate. They were in small print buried in an unlabeled paragraph on the back of the sales contract. The court further noted that, as a practical matter, the buyer had no choice in the marketing context presented by this case and therefore the disclaimer was not a freely bargained for provision of the contract. In dicta, the court, consistent with UCC § 316, suggested that disclaimers could be valid if clearly stated and prominently displayed in the contract.

2. Several states adopted *Henningsen*, at least to some extent and the UCC provisions, set out above, were greatly influenced by the decision. In most contexts, the decision was soon rendered moot by the development of strict liability under tort theory, to which we will shortly turn. Nevertheless the case is still important in at least two categories of cases.

First, a few states (e.g. Delaware, Massachusetts, North Carolina) have not adopted the torts strict liability approach. *See* Smith v. Fiber Controls Corp., 300 N.C. 669, 268 S.E.2d 504 (1980); Cline v. Prowler Industries of Maryland, Inc., 418 A.2d 968 (Del.1980). In tort law in those states one must still make out a case of negligence, although the courts will generally follow *MacPherson* on the question of privity. Alternatively, one may plead breach of warranty along the lines of the *Henningsen* case.

3. The second class of cases in which the contract-warranty approach to strict liability is still critical are those cases in which the claim is for damage to the product itself or for consequential economic loss. The lines are not always easy to draw, but most courts have held that the tort strict liability remedy is only available for personal injuries and property damage caused by the defective product. For property damage to the product itself and consequential economic loss most courts require the plaintiff to rely upon the UCC warranty provisions instead. Neibarger v. Universal Cooperatives, Inc., 439 Mich. 512, 486 N.W.2d 612 (1992); Florida Power & Light Co. v. Westinghouse Electric Corp., 510 So.2d 899 (Fla.1987); 2000 Watermark Ass'n Inc. v. Celotex Corp., 784 F.2d 1183 (4th Cir.1986)(applying South Carolina law); East River Steamship Corp. v. Transamerica Delaval, Inc., 476 U.S. 858, 106 S.Ct. 2295, 90 L.Ed.2d 865 (1986)(applying admiralty law); Seely v. White Motor Co., 63 Cal.2d 9, 45 Cal.Rptr. 17, 403 P.2d 145 (1965). Indiana has given the same interpretation to its products liability statute. Reed v. Central Soya Company, Inc., 621 N.E.2d 1069 (Ind.1993).

The *Seely* case has been very influential because the opinion was authored by Justice Traynor, one of the principal architects in the development of the tort theory. There the court allowed recovery under the warranty theory but held that the tort remedy was not available. In the *2000 Watermark* case, *supra*, the court said:

> Contract law permits the parties to negotiate the allocation of risk. Even where the law acts to assign risk through implied warranties, it can easily be shifted by the use of disclaimers. No such freedom is available under tort law, which assigns risk as a matter of law. Once assigned, the risk cannot be easily disclaimed. This lack of freedom seems harsh in the context of a commercial transaction, and thus the majority of courts have required that there be injury to person or property before imposing tort liability.

* * *

> If intangible economic loss were actionable under a tort theory, the UCC provisions permitting assignment of risk by means of warranties and disclaimers would be rendered meaningless. It would be virtually impossible for a seller to sell a product "as is" because if the product did not meet the economic expectations of the buyer, the buyer would have an action under tort law. The UCC represents a comprehensive statutory scheme which satisfies the needs of the world of commerce * * *.

To the contrary is Santor v. A & M Karagheusian, Inc., 44 N.J. 52, 207 A.2d 305 (1965). *See also,* City of La Crosse v. Schubert, Schroeder & Assoc., Inc., 72 Wis.2d 38, 240 N.W.2d 124 (1976); Salt River Project Agr. Improvement & Power District v. Westinghouse Electric Corp., 143 Ariz. 368, 694 P.2d 198 (1984)(after applying a balancing approach, the court permitted recovery of both intangible economic loss and damages to the product itself). The West Virginia Supreme Court has held that damage to a product resulting from a sudden calamitous event attributable to a product defect was actionable under tort strict liability. Capitol Fuels Inc. v. Clark Equipment Co., 181 W.Va. 258, 382 S.E.2d 311 (1989). We shall return to this question in Chapter Ten, *infra,* during our discussion of the broader question of when it is possible to recover for economic loss in tort actions generally.

4. When the claim is between two business entities that have a continuing commercial relationship, it is relatively rare to see a products liability claim filed in court when the only injury is the failure of the product to perform as expected. Commonly such claims are handled by some form of mediation or arbitration in order to protect the on-going relationship. *See* Stuart Macaulay, *Non-Contractual Relations in Business: A Preliminary Study,* 28 Am. Soc. Rev. 55 (1963); Thomas Palay, *Comparative Institutional Economics: The Governance of Rail Freight Contracting,* 13 J. Legal Stu. 265 (1984); Cary Coglianese, *Litigating Within Relationships: Disputes and Disturbances in the Regulatory Process,* 30 Law & Soc'y Rev. 735 (1996). In recent years, several states have also passed "lemon laws" of one sort or another, typically dealing with automobiles. These are designed to give the ordinary consumer a relatively easy remedy for products that do not live up to expectations, but which have not caused any physical injury. Frequently, some alternative dispute resolution, such as mediation, is provided in lieu of the traditional tort or contract law suit. *See* Ohio Rev.Code §§ 1345.71–1345.77.

5. If the court had been unwilling in *Henningsen* to strike down the privity barrier in breach of warranty cases, what would the plaintiff have had to show to prove a case based upon negligence?

6. Because plaintiffs frequently plead misrepresentation and warranty theories as part of their products liability cases, the student may find it helpful to consider how one would frame various fact patterns in terms of these different causes of action. Consider the "Golfing Gizmo." As described by the court in Hauter v. Zogarts, 14 Cal.3d 104, 120 Cal.Rptr. 681, 534 P.2d 377 (1975), the Gizmo,

> [I]s a simple device consisting of two metal pegs, two cords—one elastic, one cotton—and a regulation golf ball. After the pegs are driven into the ground approximately 25 inches apart, the elastic cord is looped over them. The cotton cord, measuring 21 feet in length, ties to the middle of the elastic cord. The ball is attached to the end of the cotton cord. When the cords are extended, the Gizmo resembles the shape of a large letter "T," with the ball resting at the base.
>
> The user stands by the ball in order to hit his practice shots. The instruction state that when hit correctly, the ball will fly out and spring back near the point of impact; if the ball returns to the left, it indicates a right hander's "slice"; a shot returning to the right indicates a right-hander's "hook." * * * The label on the shipping carton and the cover of the instruction booklet urge players to " 'drive the ball with full power' and further state: 'COMPLETELY SAFE BALL WILL NOT HIT PLAYER.' "

534 P.2d at 379. The plaintiff, a thirteen year old boy, was seriously injured when he apparently swung under the teed-up ball and his club became entangled in the cotton cord. The ball looped over the club producing a "bolo" effect, and struck the plaintiff in the temple. The plaintiff's mother had purchased the Gismo as a Christmas present. What result under misrepresentation and warranty theories?

7. In a well-known article, *The Model of Rules*, 35 U.Chi.L.Rev. 14 (1967)(reprinted in Taking Rights Seriously 14 (1977)), Ronald Dworkin referred to *Henningsen* as an illustration of a situation in which the settled rules of law dictated a particular solution but in which the court relied upon legal "principles" to reach a result more in accord with its notions of what the law should be, the settled law being that in the absence of fraud contractual disclaimers were valid even against one who had not read the clause. In point of fact, however, prior cases in New Jersey and other jurisdictions, cited in the *Henningsen* opinion, had held disclaimers and limitations in contracts of adhesion invalid. For a critique of Dworkin's thesis, *see* G. Christie, *The Model of Principles,* 1968 Duke L.J. 649.

B. STRICT (DEFECT) LIABILITY IN TORTS

1. *Historical Development*

The first important judicial discussion of strict liability for defective products based upon tort law was in a concurring opinion by Justice Roger Traynor, of the California Supreme Court, in Escola v. Coca Cola Bottling Co., 24 Cal.2d 453, 150 P.2d 436 (1944), referred to *supra,* p. 194. The case involved an exploding pop bottle. The majority had approved a jury verdict based upon a finding of negligence, which in turn had been based upon the use of res ipsa loquitur. Justice Traynor argued that "[i]f public policy demands that a manufacturer of goods be responsible for their quality regardless of negligence there is no reason not to fix that responsibility openly." Justice Traynor went on to argue:

> [P]ublic policy demands that responsibility be fixed wherever it will most effectively reduce the hazards to life and health inherent in defective products that reach the market. It is evident that the manufacturer can anticipate some hazards and guard against the recurrence of others, as the public cannot. Those who suffer injury from defective products are unprepared to meet its consequences. The cost of an injury and the loss of time or health may be an overwhelming misfortune to the person injured, and a needless one, for the risk of injury can be insured by the manufacturer and distributed among the public as a cost of doing business. It is to the public interest to discourage the marketing of products having defects that are a menace to the public. If such products nevertheless find their way into the market it is to the public interest to place the responsibility for whatever injury they may cause upon the manufacturer, who, even if he is not negligent in the manufacture of the product, is responsible for its reaching the market. However intermittently such injuries may occur and however haphazardly they may strike, the risk of their occurrence is a constant risk and a general one. Against such a risk there should be general and constant protection and the manufacturer is best situated to afford such protection.

* * *

As handicrafts have been replaced by mass production with its great markets and transportation facilities, the close relationship between the producer and consumer of a product has been altered. Manufacturing processes, frequently valuable secrets, are ordinarily either inaccessible to or beyond the ken of the general public. The consumer no longer has means or skill enough to investigate for himself the soundness of a product, even when it is not contained in a sealed package, and his erstwhile vigilance has been lulled by the steady efforts of manufacturers to build up confidence by advertising and marketing devices such as trade-marks. Consumers no longer approach products warily but accept them on faith, relying on the reputation of the manufacturer or the trade mark. Manufacturers have sought to justify that faith by increasingly high standards of inspection and a readiness to make good on defective products by way of replacements and refunds. The manufacturer's obligation to the consumer must keep pace with the changing relationship between them; it cannot be escaped because the marketing of a product has become so complicated as to require one or more intermediaries. Certainly there is greater reason to impose liability on the manufacturer than on the retailer who is but a conduit of a product that he is not himself able to test.

The manufacturer's liability should, of course, be defined in terms of the safety of the product in normal and proper use, and should not extend to injuries that cannot be traced to the product as it reached the market.

Nearly 20 years later Traynor wrote the opinion in Greenman that fulfilled his invitation to move to a regime of strict liability.

GREENMAN v. YUBA POWER PRODUCTS, INC.

Supreme Court of California, 1963.
59 Cal.2d 57, 27 Cal.Rptr. 697, 377 P.2d 897.

Traynor, Justice.

Plaintiff brought this action for damages against the retailer and the manufacturer of a Shopsmith, a combination power tool that could be used as a saw, drill, and wood lathe. He saw a Shopsmith demonstrated by the retailer and studied a brochure prepared by the manufacturer. He decided he wanted a Shopsmith for his home workshop, and his wife bought and gave him one for Christmas in 1955. In 1957 he bought the necessary attachments to use the Shopsmith as a lathe for turning a large piece of wood he wished to make into a chalice. After he had worked on the piece of wood several times without difficulty, it suddenly flew out of the machine and struck him on the forehead, inflicting serious injuries. About ten and a half months later, he gave the retailer and the manufacturer written notice of claimed breaches of warranties and filed a complaint against them alleging such breaches and negligence.

After a trial before a jury, the court ruled that there was no evidence that the retailer was negligent or had breached any express warranty and that the manufacturer was not liable for the breach of any implied warranty. Accordingly, it submitted to the jury only the cause of action alleging breach of implied warranties against the retailer and the causes of action alleging negligence and breach of express warranties against the manufacturer. The jury returned a verdict for the retailer against plaintiff and for plaintiff against the manufacturer in the amount of $65,000. The trial court denied the manufacturer's motion for a new trial and entered judgment on the verdict. The manufacturer and plaintiff appeal. Plaintiff seeks a reversal of the part of the judgment in favor of the retailer, however, only in the event that the part of the judgment against the manufacturer is reversed.

Plaintiff introduced substantial evidence that his injuries were caused by defective design and construction of the Shopsmith. His expert witnesses testified that inadequate set screws were used to hold parts of the machine together so that normal vibration caused the tailstock of the lathe to move away from the piece of wood being turned permitting it to fly out of the lathe. They also testified that there were other more positive ways of fastening the parts of the machine together, the use of which would have prevented the accident. The jury could therefore reasonably have concluded that the manufacturer negligently constructed the Shopsmith. The jury could also reasonably have concluded that statements in the manufacturer's brochure were untrue, that they constituted express warranties,[1] and that plaintiff's injuries were caused by their breach.

1. In this respect the trial court limited the jury to a consideration of two statements in the manufacturer's brochure. (1) "WHEN SHOPSMITH IS IN HORIZONTAL POSITION—Rugged construction of frame provides rigid support from end to end. Heavy

The manufacturer contends, however, that plaintiff did not give it notice of breach of warranty within a reasonable time and that therefore his cause of action for breach of warranty is barred by section 1769 of the Civil Code. Since it cannot be determined whether the verdict against it was based on the negligence or warranty cause of action or both, the manufacturer concludes that the error in presenting the warranty cause of action to the jury was prejudicial.

Section 1769 of the Civil Code provides: "In the absence of express or implied agreement of the parties, acceptance of the goods by the buyer shall not discharge the seller from liability in damages or other legal remedy for breach of any promise or warranty in the contract to sell or the sale. But, if, after acceptance of the goods, the buyer fails to give notice to the seller of the breach of any promise or warranty within a reasonable time after the buyer knows, or ought to know of such breach, the seller shall not be liable therefor."

Like other provisions of the uniform sales act * * *, section 1769 deals with the rights of the parties to a contract of sale or a sale. It does not provide that notice must be given of the breach of a warranty that arises independently of a contract of sale between the parties. Such warranties are not imposed by the sales act, but are the product of common-law decisions that have recognized them in a variety of situations. * * *

The notice requirement of section 1769, however, is not an appropriate one for the court to adopt in actions by injured consumers against manufacturers with whom they have not dealt. "As between the immediate parties to the sale [the notice requirement] is a sound commercial rule, designed to protect the seller against unduly delayed claims for damages. As applied to personal injuries, and notice to a remote seller, it becomes a booby-trap for the unwary. The injured consumer is seldom 'steeped in the business practice which justifies the rule,' [James, Product Liability, 34 Texas L.Rev. 44, 192, 197] and at least until he has had legal advice it will not occur to him to give notice to one with whom he has had no dealings." (Prosser, Strict Liability to the Consumer, 69 Yale L.J. 1099, 1150, footnotes omitted). * * *We conclude, therefore, that even if plaintiff did not give timely notice of breach of warranty to the manufacturer, his cause of action based on the representations contained in the brochure was not barred.

Moreover, to impose strict liability on the manufacturer under the circumstances of this case, it was not necessary for plaintiff to establish an express warranty as defined in section 1732 of the Civil Code. A manufacturer is strictly liable in tort when an article he places on the market, knowing that it is to be used without inspection for defects, proves to have a defect that causes injury to a human being. Recognized first in the case of unwholesome food products, such liability has now been extended to a variety of other products that create as great or greater hazards if defective. * * *

Although in these cases strict liability has usually been based on the theory of an express or implied warranty running from the manufacturer to

centerless-ground steel tubing insures perfect alignment of components." (2) "SHOP-SMITH maintains its accuracy because every component has positive locks that hold adjustments through rough or precision work."

the plaintiff, the abandonment of the requirement of a contract between them, the recognition that the liability is not assumed by agreement but imposed by law * * * and the refusal to permit the manufacturer to define the scope of its own responsibility for defective products * * * make clear that the liability is not one governed by the law of contract warranties but by the law of strict liability in tort. Accordingly, rules defining and governing warranties that were developed to meet the needs of commercial transactions cannot properly be invoked to govern the manufacturer's liability to those injured by their defective products unless those rules also serve the purposes for which such liability is imposed.

We need not recanvass the reasons for imposing strict liability on the manufacturer. They have been fully articulated in the cases cited above. * * * The purpose of such liability is to insure that the costs of injuries resulting from defective products are borne by the manufacturers that put such products on the market rather than by the injured persons who are powerless to protect themselves. Sales warranties serve this purpose fitfully at best. * * * In the present case, for example, plaintiff was able to plead and prove an express warranty only because he read and relied on the representations of the Shopsmith's ruggedness contained in the manufacturer's brochure. Implicit in the machine's presence on the market, however, was a representation that it would safely do the jobs for which it was built. Under these circumstances, it should not be controlling whether plaintiff selected the machine because of the statements in the brochure, or because of the machine's own appearance of excellence that belied the defect lurking beneath the surface, or because he merely assumed that it would safely do the jobs it was built to do. It should not be controlling whether the details of the sales from manufacturer to retailer and from retailer to plaintiff's wife were such that one or more of the implied warranties of the sales act arose. * * * To establish the manufacturer's liability it was sufficient that plaintiff proved that he was injured while using the Shopsmith in a way it was intended to be used as a result of a defect in design and manufacture of which plaintiff was not aware that made the Shopsmith unsafe for its intended use.

The judgment is affirmed.

———

Shortly after *Greenman* was decided the American Law Institute promulgated Section 402A.

RESTATEMENT (SECOND) OF TORTS (1965)

§ 402A. Special Liability of Seller of Product for Physical Harm to User or Consumer

(1) One who sells any product in a defective condition unreasonably dangerous to the user or consumer or to his property is subject to liability for physical harm thereby caused to the ultimate user or consumer, or to his property, if

    (a) the seller is engaged in the business of selling such a product, and

(b) it is expected to and does reach the user or consumer without substantial change in the condition in which it is sold.

(2) The rule stated in Subsection (1) applies although

(a) the seller has exercised all possible care in the preparation and sale of his product, and

(b) the user or consumer has not bought the product from or entered into any contractual relation with the seller.

Caveat:

The Institute expresses no opinion as to whether the rules stated in this Section may not apply

(1) to harm to persons other than users or consumers;

(2) to the seller of a product expected to be processed or otherwise substantially changed before it reaches the user or consumer; or

(3) to the seller of a component part of a product to be assembled.

James R. Hackney, Jr., *The Intellectual Origins of American Strict Products Liability: A Case Study in American Pragmatic Instrumentalism*, 39 Am. J. Legal Hist. 443 (1995) offers a fascinating discussion of the intellectual roots of the products liability revolution. For a critique of many of the assumptions underlying *Greenman* and § 402A *see* Alan Schwartz, *The Case Against Strict Liability*, 60 Fordham L. Rev. 819 (1992).

2. *The Parties and the Interests Covered*

Section 402A became the cornerstone of a rapid movement toward "strict" products liability. See, for example, Suvada v. White Motor Co., 32 Ill.2d 612, 210 N.E.2d 182 (1965); McKisson v. Sales Affiliates, Inc., 416 S.W.2d 787 (Tex.1967). The importance of this provision can hardly be overstated. As Professor Vandall put it:

> Only rarely do provisions of the American Law Institute's Restatements of the Law rise to the dignity of holy writ. Even more rarely do individual comments to Restatement sections come to symbolize important, decisive developments that dominate judicial thinking. Nevertheless, section 402A of the Restatement (Second) of Torts is such a provision. Literally thousands upon thousands of products liability decisions in the past thirty years have explicitly referred to, and come to grips with, that section.

Frank J. Vandall, *The Restatement (Third) of Torts, Products Liability, Section 2(B): Design Defect*, 68 Temp. L. Rev. 167 (1995).

A. *Beyond users or consumers—liability to bystanders.* Shortly after § 402 of the *Restatement (Second)* was published in final form, with its *caveat* as to whether liability extended to persons other than those who might be classified as "users or consumers," the cases started to extend strict liability for defective products to "mere bystanders," at least if they were foreseeable victims. *See, e.g.,* Elmore v. American Motors, 70 Cal.2d 578, 75 Cal.Rptr. 652, 451 P.2d 84 (1969); Piercefield v. Remington Arms Co., 375 Mich. 85, 133 N.W.2d 129 (1965). To hold that foreseeable third parties are not within the scope of a strict liability action for defective products is to be caught up in the contractual concerns that gave rise to the original privity problem. A typical case is illustrated by Haumersen v. Ford Motor Co., 257 N.W.2d 7 (Iowa 1977) in which a seven year old boy was killed while playing on a school playground when an automobile using an adjoining street went out of control due to an alleged product defect. The automobile manufacturer was held liable.

B. *Business of Selling.* The comments to § 402A were nearly as important as the black letter in shaping the development of this new approach to products liability. One important comment defined the defendants against whom a § 402A claim might be brought.

> *Comment f. Business of selling.* The rule stated in this Section applies to any person engaged in the business of selling products for use or consumption. It therefore applies to any manufacturer of such a product, to any wholesale or retail dealer or distributor, and to the operator of a restaurant. It is not necessary that the seller be engaged solely in the business of selling such products. Thus the rule applies to the owner of a motion picture theatre who sells popcorn or ice cream, either for consumption on the premises or in packages to be taken home.

> The rule does not, however, apply to the occasional seller of food or other such products who is not engaged in that activity as a part of his business. Thus it does not apply to the housewife who, on one occasion, sells to her neighbor a jar of jam or a pound of sugar. Nor does it apply to the owner of an automobile who, on one occasion, sells it to his neighbor, or even sells it to a dealer in used cars, and this even though he is fully aware that the dealer plans to resell it. The basis for the rule is the ancient one of the special responsibility for the safety of the public undertaken by one who enters into the business of supplying human beings with products which may endanger the safety of their persons and property, and the forced reliance upon that undertaking on the part of those who purchase such goods. This basis is lacking in the case of the ordinary individual who makes the isolated sale, and he is not liable to a third person, or even to his buyer, in the absence of his negligence. An analogy may be found in the provision of the Uniform Sales Act, § 15, which limits the implied warranty of merchantable quality to sellers who deal in such goods; and in the similar limitation of the Uniform Commercial Code, § 2–314, to a seller who is a merchant. This Section is also not intended to apply to sales of the stock of merchants out of the usual course of business, such as execution sales, bankruptcy sales, bulk sales, and the like.

One important consequence of the movement to strict liability was that everyone in the chain of distribution who sells a defective product became a proper defendant. Plaintiffs no longer needed to search out the negligent defendant in the chain of distribution. As Judge Traynor noted in Vandermark v. Ford Motor Co. 61 Cal.2d 256, 391 P.2d 168, 37 Cal.Rptr. 896 (1964): "In some cases the retailer may be the only member of the enterprise reasonably available to the injured plaintiff." When "middlemen" such as a retailers or wholesalers are held strictly liable for a defect caused by the manufacturer they usually have an indemnity claim against the manufacturer. The Texas products liability statute takes this one step further and requires the properly notified manufacturer to indemnify sellers for "court costs and other reasonable expenses, reasonable attorney fees, and any reasonable damages." Tex. Civ. Pract. & Rem. Code. § 82.002(b). The practical effect of this legislation is that the wholesalers and retailers are responsible only when they have been negligent or when the manufacturer has gone out of business or is unreachable through judicial process.

C. *Manufacturers of component parts.* Section 402A's caveat as to whether strict liability extended to the maker of defective component parts was also soon rendered unnecessary. *See, e.g.,* Deveny v. Rheem Manufacturing Co., 319 F.2d 124 (2d Cir.1963); Suvada v. White Motor Co., 32 Ill.2d 612, 210 N.E.2d 182 (1965); Rosenau v. City of New Brunswick, 51 N.J. 130, 238 A.2d 169 (1968). One of the few cases refusing to extend liability to the makers of component parts is Goldberg v. Kollsman Instrument Corp., 12 N.Y.2d 432, 240 N.Y.S.2d 592, 191 N.E.2d 81 (1963).

One must be careful in applying the majority rule, however, because it only applies if the defect in the product causing the injury was in the component part. If the defect was the result of the installation of the component part or the incompatibility of the component with some other aspect of the product, the component part manufacturer will not be liable. *See* Mitchell v. Sky Climber, Inc., 396 Mass. 629, 487 N.E.2d 1374 (1986); Zaza v. Marquess and Nell, Inc., 144 N.J. 34, 675 A.2d 620 (N.J.1996)(interpreting the New Jersey Products Liability Statute). However, if the component part maker knows that the assembler is using the part in a dangerous or inappropriate way and does not warn, the component part maker may be liable. *See* Maake v. Ross Operating Valve Co., 149 Ariz. 244, 717 P.2d 923 (App.1985).

D. *Successor liability.* A more difficult problem has been whether the liability extends to successor corporations after the manufacturer has ceased to exist in the corporate form that it had at the time of the sale of the product. The general rule holds that if there is a merger or consolidation, the successor corporation assumes the liability of the predecessor firm. However, when the manufacturer sells its assets and then ceases business, the liability does not pass to the successor firm unless:

(1) the buyer expressly or impliedly agrees to assume such liability;

(2) the transaction amounts to a *de facto* consolidation or merger;

(3) the buyer corporation is merely a continuation of the seller corporation; or

(4) the transaction is entered into fraudulently for the purpose of escaping liability.

Flaugher v. Cone Automatic Machine Co., 30 Ohio St.3d 60, 62, 507 N.E.2d 331, 334 (1987). *See also* George v. Parke–Davis, 684 F.Supp. 249 (E.D.Wash.1988); Bernard v. Kee Mfg. Co., 409 So.2d 1047 (Fla.1982). California introduced a fifth circumstance under which the successor will be held—when it continues to market the same product line. Ray v. Alad Corp., 19 Cal.3d 22, 136 Cal.Rptr. 574, 560 P.2d 3 (1977). The court reasoned that the successor corporation enjoys the benefits of the good will associated with the product and therefore should bear the burden of the defects as well. This approach has been endorsed in Ramirez v. Amsted Indus., Inc., 86 N.J. 332, 431 A.2d 811 (1981). The reasoning was specifically rejected in the *Flaugher* case, *supra,* on the grounds that "[t]he adoption of the product line theory would cast a potentially devastating burden on business transfers and would convert sales of corporate assets into traps for the unwary." *Id.* at 66, 507 N.E.2d at 337. Most states that have considered the issue have refused to adopt the product line exception. *See* Fish v. Amsted Indus., Inc., 126 Wis.2d 293, 376 N.W.2d 820 (1985); DeLapp v. Xtraman, Inc., 417 N.W.2d 219 (Iowa, 1987); Simoneau v. South Bend Lathe, Inc. 130 N.H. 466, 543 A.2d 407 (1988); Nissen Corp. v. Miller, 323 Md. 613, 594 A.2d 564 (Md.1991).

In the Nissen case, the acquired company maintained its corporate existence for five years after the sale of assets to Nissen. Plaintiff was injured six years after the sale. Do you think rules requiring enterprises to maintain some existence and to post a bond against future tort claims would be a wise policy?

E. *The Sale of Real Estate.* The sale of real estate is not a sale of goods. Nevertheless, the courts have come to recognize an "implied warranty of habitability" in the sale of new housing. Several of the cases have explicitly allowed recovery by persons not in privity with the builder. Schipper v. Levitt & Sons, 44 N.J. 70, 207 A.2d 314 (1965), is a leading case. *See also* Kirk v. Ridgway, 373 N.W.2d 491 (Iowa 1985); Richards v. Powercraft Homes, Inc., 139 Ariz. 242, 678 P.2d 427 (1984); Gupta v. Ritter Homes, Inc., 646 S.W.2d 168 (Tex.1983)(privity of contract unnecessary). *See also*, Lempke v. Dagenais, 130 N.H. 782, 547 A.2d 290 (1988)(overruling an earlier New Hampshire case holding that strict liability only applies to first buyer).

In Becker v. IRM Corp., 38 Cal.3d 454, 213 Cal.Rptr. 213, 698 P.2d 116 (1985), California also applied strict products liability to a landlord of a dwelling unit that contained a latent defect at the time of lease. However, in Peterson v. Superior Court, 10 Cal.4th 1185, 43 Cal.Rptr.2d 836, 899 P.2d 905 (1995), the Supreme Court overruled *Becker*, and refused to hold a hotel owner strictly liable to a guest who slipped in a defective bathtub. The *Becker* case had been virtually alone in imposing strict liability in such cases.

F. *Used goods.* Although there is case authority to the contrary, it is generally thought that one selling used goods is not liable under strict products liability law. The policy objective here seems to be to facilitate a market for inexpensive, used products and is built upon the assumption that the buyer is taking the goods "as is"—a variety of assumption of the risk. Moreover, because sellers of used goods are not in the original chain of distribution they have no direct relationship with the manufacturer and, therefore, are not in a position to influence product safety. Tillman v. Vance Equipment Co., 286 Or. 747, 596 P.2d 1299 (1979); Peterson v. Idaho First National Bank, 117 Idaho 724, 791 P.2d 1303 (Idaho 1990). However, where the seller of used goods extensively modifies the goods before resale, there is an obvious analogy to the status of a manufacturer, especially if the defect is related to the modification. *See* Green v. City of Los Angeles, 40 Cal.App.3d 819, 115 Cal.Rptr. 685 (1974). A difficult case arises when the seller of used goods is "regularly" engaged in that business, as opposed to an occasional transaction, but makes no modification in the goods. This frequently happens in the purchase and resale of used commercial machinery. Indeed the used machinery dealer may never take physical possession of the goods. Here one arguably faces a different policy balance since the seller is in a position to spread the costs over the second hand market, analogous to the manufacturer, but one still has the concern about inhibiting a viable second hand market. Moreover, such a seller is unlikely to be in a position to obtain indemnification from the manufacturer who will claim that the product was not defective when it left the manufacturer's hands. A case holding that in this situation there is no strict products liability and discussing the few cases and secondary authority on the subject is La Rosa v. Superior Court, 122 Cal.App.3d 741, 176 Cal.Rptr. 224 (1981).

G. *Franchisors.* Extending strict products liability to franchisors for sales to customers by a franchisee poses a number of problems. If the franchisor is the manufacturer of the defective product there is no problem. Frequently, however, the franchisor simply furnishes a trade-name, training, recipes or directions and the like. Actual "manufacturing" of the product is done by the franchisee. *See* S. Sandrock, *Tort Liability for a Non–Manufacturing Franchisor for Acts of Its Franchisee,* 48 U.Cin.L.Rev. 699 (1979). A few cases have found liability, the theory being either that sufficient control was exerted or that consumers were brought to rely upon the name of the product as a statement of responsibility. Kosters v. Seven–Up Co., 595 F.2d 347 (6th Cir.1979); City of Hartford v. Associated Construction Co., 34 Conn.Sup. 204, 384 A.2d 390 (1978); Torres v. Goodyear Tire and Rubber Co., 163 Ariz. 88, 786 P.2d 939 (1990).

H. *Non-sales situations—services.* Strict products liability has been extended to a number of non-sales situations. Thus commercial lessors of automobiles have been held strictly liable for supplying defective vehicles. *See, e.g.,* Cintrone v. Hertz Truck Leasing & Rental Service, 45 N.J. 434, 212 A.2d 769 (1965); Price v. Shell Oil Co., 2 Cal.3d 245, 85 Cal.Rptr. 178, 466 P.2d 722 (1970). *See also,* Samuel Friedland Family Enterprises v. Amoroso, 630 So.2d 1067 (Fla.1994)(strict liability applies to hotel and sailboat concession that leased defective sailboat to guest). However, most courts that have passed on the question have rejected strict liability on the part of one who only finances the sale or lease, even in a lease-for-purchase arrangement. *See* Agristor Leasing v. Meuli, 634 F.Supp. 1208 (D.Kan. 1986). Nor do most courts apply strict products liability law to repairers, refurbishers, and installers, usually holding those pursuits to be services and not sales. Barry v. Stevens Equip. Co., 176 Ga.App. 27, 335 S.E.2d 129 (1985). *But see* O'Laughlin v. Minnesota Natural Gas Co., 253 N.W.2d 826 (Minn.1977) (installer).

A large number of activities such as the provision of legal advice have been excluded from the scope of 402A because the defendant's activity was categorized as a "service" rather than a "sale." Difficult cases arise when a product is sold to an individual as part of providing a service. Compare Newmark v. Gimbel's Inc., 54 N.J. 585, 258 A.2d 697 (1969)(defective permanent wave solution used on the plaintiff when she visited a beauty parlor) with Magrine v. Spector, 53 N.J. 259, 250 A.2d 129 (1969)(hypodermic needle used by defendant dentist broke off in plaintiff's gum). Blood transfusions have been the subject of much controversy in this regard, primarily due to litigation with respect to blood transmitted diseases such as hepatitis and A.I.D.S. Because some tainted blood will go undetected even when blood banks exercise the utmost care, the question of whether to impose strict liability for a defective product is presented in a most dramatic situation. Several states have passed statutes that define blood transfusions as a service and not a sale. For example, the Ohio statute provides:

> [T]he procuring, furnishing, donating, processing, distributing, or using human whole blood, plasma, blood products, blood derivatives, and products, corneas, bones, organs, or other human tissue except hair, for the purpose of injecting, transfusing, or transplanting the fluid or body part in another human body, is considered for all purposes as the rendition of a service by every person participating in the act and not a sale of any such fluid or body part. No warranties of any kind or description are applicable to the act.

Ohio Rev. Code § 2108.11. Moreover, the Ohio Products Liability Statute provides that blood and blood products are not a "product" and therefore are not covered by strict products liability. Ohio Rev. Code § 2307.71(L)(2). Blood banks may still be responsible, of course, for negligent conduct. *See* Wadley Research Institute v. Beeson, 835 S.W.2d 689 (Tex.App.1992).

3. *Defining a Defect*

Greenman and the *Restatement (Second) of Torts* § 402A did not alter the elements the plaintiff must prove in order to prevail. They did not abolish the duty requirement. Manufacturers did not become responsible for all injuries caused by their products. The plaintiff must still show that the defendant owed a duty to the plaintiff and breached that duty. The plaintiff must also prove damages and a causal connection between the breach of duty and the damages. As the court in the influential early case of Phillips v. Kimwood Machine Co., 269 Ore. 485, 525 P.2d 1033 (1974) said.

> No one wants absolute liability where all the article has to do is to cause injury. To impose liability there has to be something about the article which makes it dangerously defective without regard to whether the manufacturer was or was not at fault for such condition.

What *Greenman* and § 402A did accomplish was to change the language of duty. They replaced the concept of *negligence* with the concept of *defect*. Over the course of the following 20 years, with many false starts, including occasional flirtations with the possibility of abolishing the requirement of proving a defect, the courts worked out the definition(s) of this new concept within the context of a wide variety of product disappointments. *See* James A. Henderson and Aaron D. Twerski, *Closing the American Products Liability Frontier: The Rejection of Liability Without Defect*, 66 N.Y.U. L. Rev. 1263 (1991).

§ 402A's definition of defectiveness. Two of the most important, comments to § 402A, *g* and *i,* define the key concepts of "defective condition" and "unreasonably dangerous."

g. Defective condition. The rule stated in this Section applies only where the product is, at the time it leaves the seller's hands, in a condition not contemplated by the ultimate consumer, which will be unreasonably dangerous to him. The seller is not liable when he delivers the product in a safe condition, and subsequent mishandling or other causes make it harmful by the time it is consumed. The burden of proof that the product was in a defective condition at the time that it left the hands of the particular seller is upon the injured plaintiff; and unless evidence can be produced which will support the conclusion that it was then defective, the burden is not sustained.

Safe condition at the time of delivery by the seller will, however, include proper packaging, necessary sterilization, and other precautions required to permit the product to remain safe for a normal length of time when handled in a normal manner.

i. Unreasonably dangerous. The rule stated in this Section applies only where the defective condition of the product makes it unreasonably dangerous to the user or consumer. Many products cannot possibly be made entirely safe for all consumption, and any food or drug necessarily involves some risk of harm, if only from over-consumption. Ordinary sugar is a deadly poison to diabetics, and castor oil found use under Mussolini as an instrument of torture. That is not what is meant by "unreasonably dangerous" in this Section. The article sold must be dangerous to an extent beyond that which would be contemplated by the ordinary consumer who purchases it, with the ordinary knowledge common to the community as to its characteristics. Good whiskey is not unreasonably dangerous merely because it will make some people drunk, and is especially dangerous to alcoholics; but bad whiskey, containing a dangerous amount of fusel oil, is unreasonably dangerous. Good tobacco is not unreasonably dangerous merely because the effects of smoking may be harmful; but tobacco containing something like marijuana may be unreasonably dangerous. Good butter is not unreasonably dangerous merely because, if such be the case, it deposits cholesterol in the arteries and leads to heart attacks; but bad butter, contaminated with poisonous fish oil, is unreasonably dangerous.

When § 402A was first drafted it was applicable only to food and drink. These roots are visible in the examples accompanying Comment *i.* Both Comments *g* and *i* adopt a "consumer expectations" test. A product is defective and unreasonably dangerous when the risks it poses are "beyond the contemplation" of the of the ordinary consumer. The consumer expectations test works well when the products under consideration are whiskey and butter. As we shall see, it proved less successful when the courts were confronted with cases involving complex machinery such as automobiles and airplanes.

Why do you think the Restatement required a product to be in a defective condition and also to be unreasonably dangerous to the user? In

Cronin v. J.B.E. Olson Corp., 8 Cal.3d 121, 104 Cal.Rptr. 433, 501 P.2d 1153 (1972) the California Supreme Court rejected the Restatement language. It believed that the "unreasonably dangerous" requirement "has burdened the injured plaintiff with proof of an element which rings of negligence." Moreover, the court felt § 402A was susceptible "to a literal reading which would require the finder of fact to conclude that the product is, first, defective and, second, unreasonably dangerous. A bifurcated standard is of necessity more difficult to prove than a unitary one. But merely proclaiming that the phrase 'defective condition unreasonably dangerous' requires only a single finding would not purge that phrase of its negligence complexion. We think that a requirement that a plaintiff also prove that the defect made the product 'unreasonably dangerous' places upon him a significantly increased burden and represents a step backward in the area pioneered by this court." *Cronin,* 8 Cal.3d at 133, 501 P.2d at 1162, 104 Cal.Rptr. at 442

Given that both "defective condition" and "unreasonably dangerous" are defined in terms of consumer expectations, do you think there is a substantial danger that plaintiffs will lose their lawsuit because they were able to prove only one prong of the "bifurcated standard?" Can you think of a situation where this might occur? What do you think the court meant when it said that the term unreasonably dangerous "rings of negligence?" Do you agree?

The variety of defects. In *MacPherson* and *Escola* the defect was unique to the particular item in question. Mr. MacPherson's Buick had a bad wheel, but not all Buick wheels were alleged to be bad. These came to be known as manufacturing or construction defects. On the other hand, the defect in Mr. Greenman's Shopsmith, the inadequate set-screw, was present in all Shopsmiths. Such defects came to be known as design defects. Neither Justice Traynor's *Greenman* opinion nor the Restatement (Second) § 402A envisions different legal rules for these different types of defect. In time, however, the case law came to recognize three types of defect: manufacture, design, and warning, all with different legal definitions.

In 1991, the American Law Institute began work on a new restatement. The initial focus was on products liability, in part because the case law had moved far beyond the original restatement language. The reporters for the new restatement are James Henderson and Aaron Twerski. Current plans are to complete the project in the Spring of 1997 and publish the product liability restatement in early 1998. The first several sections of Tentative Draft No.2 (March 1995) have now been approved by the membership at the ALI annual meeting. For a discussion of the new Restatement, *see* David G. Owen, The Graying of Products Liability Law: Paths Taken and Untaken In The New Restatement, 61 Tenn. L. Rev. 1241 (1994), and other articles in this symposium issue devoted to the new restatement. There are also symposium issues on the proposed new restatement in volume 21 of W. Mitchell L. Rev. (Winter 1995) and volume 10 Touro. L. Rev. (Fall 1993).

RESTATEMENT (THIRD) OF TORTS: PRODUCTS LIABILITY

(Tentative Draft No. 2, 1995).

§ 1. Liability of Commercial Seller or Distributor for Harm Caused by Defective Products

(a) One engaged in the business of selling or otherwise distributing products who sells or distributes a defective product is subject to liability for harm to persons or property caused by the product defect.

(b) A product is defective if, at the time of sale or distribution, it contains a manufacturing defect, is defective in design, or is defective because of inadequate instructions or warnings.

§ 2. Categories of Product Defect

For purposes of determining liability under § 1;

(a) a product contains a manufacturing defect when the product departs from its intended design even though all possible care was exercised in the preparation and marketing of the product;

(b) a product is defective in design when the foreseeable risks of harm posed by the product could have been reduced or avoided by the adoption of a reasonable alternative design by the seller or other distributor, or a predecessor in the commercial chain of distribution, and the omission of the alternative design renders the product not reasonably safe;

(c) a product is defective because of inadequate instructions or warnings when the foreseeable risks of harm posed by the product could have been reduced or avoided by the provision of reasonable instructions or warnings by the seller or other distributor, or a predecessor in the commercial chain of distribution, and the omission of the instructions or warnings renders the product not reasonably safe.

C. TYPES OF DEFECTS

1. *Manufacturing Defects*

WHITTED v. GENERAL MOTORS CORPORATION

U.S. Court of Appeals, Seventh Circuit, 1995.
58 F.3d 1200.

NORGLE, DISTRICT JUDGE.

John Whitted crashed his 1987 Chevrolet Nova into two trees on January 12, 1993. Whitted sued the manufacturer and seller, New United Motor Manufacturing, Inc., and General Motors Corporation (collectively "Defendants"), in an Indiana state court to recover for his injuries. Defendants removed the matter to the United States District Court for the Southern District of Indiana calling upon that court's diversity jurisdiction. The district court granted Defendants' motion for summary judgment, dismissing the matter. That decision gave rise to this appeal.

I.

John Whitted is a television repairman by trade and, on the date of the accident, he was six feet tall and weighed approximately 265 pounds, his girth is undisclosed. At the time of the collision, the ground was covered with snow, but there was no precipitation. In addition, the road was slick because, as the district court explained, the temperature had risen above freezing during the day but had fallen below freezing in the evening.

On January 12, 1993, Whitted was driving home from work with his seat belt, a single device which included both a shoulder harness and lap belt, securely fastened as he had done so daily for six years. As he negotiated an S-curve, Whitted realized that the wheels of a fast approaching oncoming car were slightly in his lane. The district court found that Whitted was traveling at least 25 m.p.h. as he negotiated the S-curve. To avoid a collision, he moved the 1987 Nova closer to the shoulder on his side of the road. Whitted moved too far and slid off the road and hit two trees. The Nova's speed at the point of impact is not known, nor is the distance travelled from the road over the snow-covered ground to the two trees. The collision thrust Whitted against the steering wheel, which broke, and the windshield, which shattered. Whitted remained within the Nova during the impact. At some point during the accident, the webbing of the seat belt separated while the female clasp (latch plate) remained fastened in the buckle. Whitted sustained fractures to two bones in his lower left arm and cuts to his forehead.

Whitted argued before the district court that the seat belt was defective in violation of Indiana's Strict Product Liability Act. * * * Whitted asserted that the seat belt was defective in that it failed to restrain him.

* * *

Whitted's complaint is based solely on Indiana's Strict Product Liability Act, which is a codification of the Restatement (Second) of Torts s 402A. Ind.Code s 33–1–1.5–1 et seq.

* * *

3. MANUFACTURING

Whitted argues that the mere circumstances of the accident indicate a defect existed at the time the seat belt was manufactured. He contends that Indiana law permits application of the doctrine of res ipsa loquitur to strict liability cases. * * * Whitted reasons that the circumstances surrounding the accident would lend a reasonable jury to infer that the seat belt was defective. The circumstances which he argues would lead a reasonable juror to infer that a defect existed at the time the product left the respective control of each Defendant include (a) a low speed head-on collision, (b) normal use since the purchase of the Nova, (c) his own affidavit that the 1987 seat belt was not dilapidated from use, and (d) a broken seat belt. In substance, Whitted argues that this accident suggests negligence which a reasonable juror would attribute to Defendants.

The doctrine of res ipsa loquitur is a rule of evidence which allows an inference to be drawn from a particular set of facts. The doctrine consists of two elements. First, the doctrine recognizes that under certain rare instances, common sense alone dictates that someone was negligent. Second, the doctrine requires that the injuring instrumentality be in the exclusive control of the defendant at the time of injury. The aspect of control is critical to the theory; the second element recognizes that certain injuring instrumentalities are within the special knowledge and control of the defendant, and that the plaintiff does not have free access to these instrumentalities. The doctrine is one ground in negligence. *See* Byrne v. Boadle, 159 Eng.Rep. 299 (1863). * * *

Of the jurisdictions that allow theories analogous to res ipsa loquitur to prove that a manufacturing defect existed, four methods of proof have evolved. Using the doctrine, a plaintiff should employ one of the following to establish the existence of a manufacturing defect: (1) plaintiff may produce an expert to offer direct evidence of a specific manufacturing defect; (2) plaintiff may use an expert to circumstantially prove that a specific defect caused the product failure; (3) plaintiff may introduce direct evidence from an eyewitness of the malfunction, supported by expert testimony explaining the possible causes of the defective condition; and (4) plaintiff may introduce inferential evidence by negating other possible causes. Again, however, the mere fact that an accident occurred in not enough. Whitted failed to establish any of the above.

This court addressed the question of whether it would be proper to apply a type of res ipsa loquitur rationale to an Indiana product liability case in Smith v. Michigan Beverage Co., 495 F.2d 754, 757 (7th Cir.1974). In that case a bottle exploded and injured the plaintiff. The plaintiff suggested that the res ipsa loquitur doctrine could support the conclusion that a defect existed because the bottle had not been subjected to unusual circumstances. This court responded, "the Indiana doctrine of res ipsa loquitur is not applicable under the circumstances of this case. We decline to adopt a position that will allow the plaintiff to rely on a similar type of presumption in regard to the defect question." The Smith court continued, "there was no objective evidence of an unsafe condition peculiar to this particular bottle and there is no basis for such a presumption. It would be improper to give a jury an opportunity to reach such a conclusion." We did not, however, find that the doctrine may not be applied in all Indiana products cases.

However, although other jurisdictions have applied the evidentiary rule to strict products cases and we have not barred its use, we have recognized the theoretical inconsistencies in fusing the two. Applying Illinois law, that concern was addressed in Welge v. Planters Lifesavers Co., 17 F.3d 209, 211 (7th Cir.1994). In that case, the plaintiff injured himself when a recently purchased glass peanut jar shattered under the plaintiff's normal pressure as he replaced the lid. Chief Judge Posner wrote on behalf of the court and outlined how the doctrine should operate: "The doctrine of res ipsa loquitur teaches that an accident that is unlikely to occur unless the defendant was negligent is itself circumstantial evidence that the defendant was negligent. The doctrine is not strictly applicable to a products liability case because unlike an ordinary accident case the defendant in a products case has parted with possession and control of the harmful object before the accident occurs. But the doctrine merely instantiates the broader principle, which is as applicable to a products case as to any other tort case, that an accident can itself be evidence of liability. If it is the kind of accident that would not have occurred but for a defect in the product, and if it is reasonably plain that the defect was not introduced after the product was sold, the accident is evidence that the product was defective when sold." * * * The Chief Judge concisely articulated how res ipsa loquitur is theoretically incongruous with strict products liability. Again, res ipsa loquitur is a negligence doctrine which focuses on the defendant's care to assess liability, whereas strict products liability focuses on the product only. Furthermore, the second element of res ipsa loquitur, which is critical to the theory, requires that the defendant have control of the instrumentality, whereas the second element of strict products liability requires the product to have left the defendant's control. Without attempting to alloy the two concepts, we glean from the doctrine of res ipsa loquitur the principle that, in certain rare instances, circumstantial evidence may produce reasonable inferences upon which a jury may reasonably find that a defendant manufactured a product containing a defect.

Nevertheless, under the facts of this case, Whitted may not avail himself of the general application of circumstantial evidence. Whitted did not present enough evidence to establish that Defendants retained control or dominion over the seat belt—that is, that six years of invariable use did not disturb Defendants' influence or authority over the product. The evidence adduced on the issue of Defendants' control was that the seat belt appeared to be in good working condition prior to the collision, that the seat belt had never demonstrated problems before, and that the seat belt was not cut or frayed prior to the accident. This is simply not enough to create a reasonable inference. He did not nullify enough of the probable explanations of the seat belt break. Whitted did not negate, for instance, that the seat belt acted properly or that the belt separated at a point in time which decreased his injuries.[6] * * * We find that under the Indiana Strict Product Liability Act a plaintiff may use circumstantial evidence to establish that a manufacturing defect existed only when the plaintiff presents evidence by way of expert testimony, by way of negating other reasonably possible causes, or by way of some combination of the two.

In sum, Whitted failed to produce enough evidence to raise a material issue of fact that the 1987 Chevrolet Nova seat belt broke due to a defect of any sort. Accordingly, we affirm the district court's holding in full.

---

6. Although not argued by the parties, we are aware that 49 C.F.R. s 571.208, S4.1.1.3.1(c) suggests a speed at which seat belts should hold. However, the Code's 30 m.p.h. demarcation is a function of the overall testing conditions: [The vehicle shall,] When it perpendicularly impacts a fixed collision barrier, while moving longitudinally forward at any speed up to and including 30 m.p.h. under the test conditions of S8.1 with anthropomorphic test devices at each front outboard position restrained by Type 2 seat-belt assemblies, experience no complete separation of any load-bearing element of a seat-

belt assembly or anchorage. Nat'l Highway Traffic Safety Admin., 49 C.F.R. s 571.208, S4.1.1.3.1(c)(1994)(emphasis added). It is clear that the speed limit is not to apply to all car accidents, it is not an absolute. For instance, the driver of a car might weigh more or less than the "test dummies," which have their own specific design requirements. In this case, the driver weighed approximately 265 pounds and was traveling at least 25 m.p.h. before he left the road. Given these conditions, it is reasonable to infer that the 1987 Nova seat belt acted as it should have.

Notes

1. Why is res ipsa loquitur "theoretically incongruous with strict products liability?"

2. In the early years of products liability cases under *Restatement (Second) of Torts* § 402A a substantial number of appellate opinions involved manufacturing defects. As the field matured, plaintiffs more frequently advanced design and marketing defects. Most products with obvious manufacturing flaws do not pass inspection and, therefore, never enter the stream of commerce. Products with latent defects are another matter. As Justice Mosk said in his dissent to Daly v. General Motors, Corp., 20 Cal.3d 725, 760, 144 Cal.Rptr. 380, 401, 575 P.2d 1162, 1183 (1978), often such defects are time bombs, waiting to explode at an inappropriate time.

3. The problems that confront plaintiffs in manufacturing defect cases almost uniformly involve proving the existence of a defect at the time the product left the possession of the defendant. The difficulty arises in several forms. In some cases the product is literally destroyed in the accident, leaving little evidence of what went wrong. In the *Welge* case, a glass jar of peanuts smashed as the plaintiff tried to re-fasten the lid. The fragments were preserved and the parties agreed that it must have contained a defect but they could not find the fracture that caused the jar to shatter. More importantly, they did not agree when the defect had come into existence. Not surprisingly, the defendant argued that the defect was introduced due to rough handling and the plaintiff's evidence suggested nothing unusual had happened to the jar. Summary judgment against the plaintiff was held to be inappropriate.

In another group of cases there is a controversy as to whether the defect caused the accident or the accident caused the "defect." For example, in Johnson v. Michelin Tire Corp., 812 F.2d 200 (5th Cir.1987) plaintiff was injured when his car, equipped with four-year-old tires crossed two lanes and ran into a guard rail. The question in the case was whether a defect in the tire caused a blow-out which led to the wreck, or, on the other hand, whether the tire damage was caused by the accident.

4. In most of these situations, the plaintiff must make out a case using circumstantial evidence. The *Restatement (Third) of Torts: Products Liability* (Tentative Draft No. 2, 1995) contains the following provision on circumstantial evidence.

§ 3. Circumstantial Evidence Supporting Inference of Product Defect.

It may be inferred that the harm sustained by the plaintiff was caused by a product defect, without proof of the specific nature of the defect, when:

(a) the incident resulting in the harm was of a kind that ordinarily would occur only as a result of product defect; and

(b) evidence in the particular case supports the conclusion that more probably than not:

(1) the cause of the harm was a product defect rather than other possible causes, including the conduct of the plaintiff and third persons; and

(2) the product defect existed at the time of sale or distribution.

5.   Harrison v. Bill Cairns Pontiac, Inc., 77 Md.App. 41, 549 A.2d 385 (1988) noted five factors to be considered in determining whether a product defect may be inferred from circumstantial evidence: (1) expert testimony on possible causes; (2) the length of time between the sale and the accident; (3) the occurrence of similar accidents in accidents in similar products; (4) the elimination of other causes of the accident; (5) whether the accident is a type that does not happen without a defect. What evidence might the plaintiff in *Whitted* have presented to get to the jury?

2.   Design Defects

CAMACHO v. HONDA MOTOR CO., LTD.

Supreme Court of Colorado, En Banc, 1987.
741 P.2d 1240.

KIRSHBAUM, JUSTICE.

* * *

I

In March 1978, Jaime Camacho purchased a new 1978 Honda Hawk motorcycle, model CV400T2, from a Honda dealer.   In May 1978, while driving the motorcycle through an intersection, Camacho collided with an automobile and sustained serious leg injuries.   Camacho and his wife filed an action against Honda seeking damages for personal injuries, property losses, loss of consortium and exemplary damages.   The action was based on several theories, including strict liability.[3]   The Camachos alleged that the motorcycle was a defectively designed, unreasonably dangerous product under the Restatement (Second) of Torts section 402A because it was not equipped with "crash bars"—tubular steel bars attached to the motorcycle frame to protect the rider's legs in the event of a collision.   They asserted that if such crash bars had been installed on the motorcycle, Camacho's leg injuries would have been mitigated.

Two mechanical engineers employed by the Camachos testified in depositions that, in light of their extensive research work on motorcycle crash bars, including testing conducted for the United States Department of Transportation, the state of the art in mechanical engineering and motorcycle design was such that effective injury-reducing, leg protection devices were feasible in March 1978 and that several manufacturers other than Honda had made such devices available as optional equipment; that, although room for further improvement of crash bars existed in March 1978, crash bars then available from manufacturers other than Honda provided some protection in low-speed collisions and, in particular, would have reduced or completely avoided the serious leg injuries suffered by Camacho;   and that Honda itself had conducted some of the seminal research on crash bars in 1969, as the result of which Honda's engineers

---

3. The Camachos alternatively relied upon theories of negligence and implied warranty of merchantability.   Because the only issue raised in the petition for certiorari concerns the appropriate test for strict liability under the Restatement (Second) of Torts s

402A, we do not address the negligence and implied warranty of merchantability issues. The Camachos also sought recovery from a third party, the driver of the automobile involved in the collision, based on a negligence theory . . .

had concluded that injury-reducing crash bars could be manufactured by strengthening the steel bars which had been tested and providing strong bolts to attach the bars to the motorcycle frame.

Honda moved for summary judgment, arguing that as a matter of law a motorcycle lacking crash bars cannot be deemed unreasonably dangerous. The trial court granted the motion, concluding that (1) because the danger of leg injury was obvious and foreseeable, Honda had no duty to totally alter the nature of its product by installing crash bars; and (2) Honda had no duty under the crashworthiness doctrine to add a safety feature to its product to reduce the severity of injuries resulting from accidents.

In agreeing with the trial court's conclusions, the Court of Appeals held that the determination of whether a product is unreasonably dangerous because of a design defect is to be made on the basis of whether the extent of the danger "would have been fully anticipated by or within the contemplation of" the ordinary user or consumer. Camacho v. Honda Motor Co., 701 P.2d 628, 631 (Colo.App.1985). Because the criteria applied by the trial court and the Court of Appeals are inconsistent with our decisions in Ortho Pharmaceutical Corp. v. Heath, 722 P.2d 410 (Colo. 1986), and Union Supply Co. v. Pust, 196 Colo. 162, 583 P.2d 276 (1978), we reverse and remand for further proceedings.

II

In Roberts v. May, 41 Colo.App. 82, 583 P.2d 305 (1978), the Court of Appeals recognized the applicability of the "crashworthiness" doctrine in Colorado. Under this doctrine, a motor vehicle manufacturer may be liable in negligence or strict liability for injuries sustained in a motor vehicle accident where a manufacturing or design defect, though not the cause of the accident, caused or enhanced the injuries. * * * The doctrine was first recognized in the landmark case of Larsen v. General Motors Corp., 391 F.2d 495 (8th Cir.1968), in which the court noted that a manufacturer's duty encompassed designing and building a product reasonably fit and safe for its intended use, that automobiles are intended for use on the roadways and that injury-producing collisions are a frequent, foreseeable and statistically expectable result of such normal use. Incumbent upon the automobile manufacturer was a duty of reasonable care in the design and manufacture of its product, including a duty to use reasonable care to minimize the injurious effects of a foreseeable collision by employing common sense safety features. The crashworthiness doctrine has been adopted by the vast majority of courts in other jurisdictions which have considered the issue. We agree with the reasoning of those decisions, as did the Court of Appeals in its consideration of this case, and adopt the crashworthiness doctrine for this jurisdiction.

The crashworthiness doctrine has been applied to accidents involving motorcycles. * * * Honda argues, however, that motorcycles are inherently dangerous motor vehicles that cannot be made perfectly crashworthy and, therefore, that motorcycle manufacturers should be free of liability for injuries not actually caused by a defect in the design or manufacture of the motorcycle. We find no principled basis to conclude that liability for failure to provide reasonable, cost-acceptable safety features to reduce the severity of injuries suffered in inevitable accidents should be imposed upon automobile manufacturers but not upon motorcycle manufacturers. The use of motorcycles for transportation over roadways is just as foreseeable as the use of automobiles for such purpose. The crashworthiness doctrine does not require a manufacturer to provide absolute safety, but merely to provide some measure of reasonable, cost-effective safety in the foreseeable use of the product. * * * In view of the important goal of encouraging maximum development of reasonable, cost-efficient safety features in the manufacture of all products, the argument that motorcycle manufacturers should be exempt from liability under the crashworthiness doctrine because serious injury to users of that product is foreseeable must be rejected.

III

In determining the extent of liability of a product manufacturer for a defective product, this court has adopted the doctrine of strict products liability as set forth in the Restatement (Second) of Torts section 402A (1965). * * *

Honda asserts that as a matter of law a motorcycle designed without leg protection devices cannot be deemed "in a defective condition unreasonably dangerous to the user" because the risk of motorcycle accidents is foreseeable to every ordinary consumer and because it is obvious that motorcycles do not generally offer leg protection devices as a standard item. In support of this argument Honda relies on Comment *i* to section 402A, which states in pertinent part:

> *i.* Unreasonably dangerous. The rule stated in this Section applies only where the defective condition of the product makes it unreasonably dangerous to the user or consumer.
>
> · · ·
>
> The article sold must be dangerous to an extent beyond that which would be contemplated by the ordinary consumer who purchases it, with the ordinary knowledge common to the community as to its characteristics. The trial court and the Court of Appeals in essence applied this consumer contemplation test in dismissing the Camachos' claims.

In Cronin v. J.B.E. Olson Corp., 8 Cal.3d 121, 104 Cal.Rptr. 433, 501 P.2d 1153 (1972), the California Supreme Court declined to require an injured person to establish that a product is unreasonably dangerous as a requisite to recovery for injuries in a strict liability design defect context. In Union Supply Co. v. Pust, 196 Colo. 162, 583 P.2d 276 (1978), this court rejected the Cronin rationale, recognizing that requiring a party who seeks recovery on the basis of an alleged defective product to establish that the product is unreasonably dangerous appropriately places reasonable limits on the potential liability of manufacturers. However, we also held in Pust that the fact that the dangers of a product are open and obvious does not constitute a defense to a claim alleging that the product is unreasonably dangerous. We noted that adoption of such a principle would unfairly elevate the assumption of risk defense to a question of law.[6] The obvious

---

6. Where the obviousness of the danger inherent in the ordinary use of a product is not dispositive of whether the product is unreasonably dangerous, the plaintiff's appreci-

and foreseeable consumer contemplation test employed by the trial court and approved by the Court of Appeals is substantially similar to the open and obvious standard specifically rejected in Pust. It is not the appropriate standard in Colorado for measuring whether a particular product is in a defective condition unreasonably dangerous to the consumer or user.

A consumer is justified in expecting that a product placed in the stream of commerce is reasonably safe for its intended use, and when a product is not reasonably safe a products liability action may be maintained. Of course, whether a given product is reasonably safe and, therefore, not unreasonably dangerous, necessarily depends upon many circumstances. Any test, therefore, to determine whether a particular product is or is not actionable must consider several factors. While reference to "reasonable" or "unreasonable" standards introduces certain negligence concepts into an area designed to be free from those concepts, e.g., Barker v. Lull Eng'g Co., 20 Cal.3d 413, 143 Cal.Rptr. 225, 573 P.2d 443 (1978); Turner v. General Motors Corp., 584 S.W.2d 844 (Tex.1979), that difficulty is much less troublesome than are the problems inherent in attempting to avoid dealing with the competing interests always involved in allocating the risk of loss in products liability actions. * * *

These considerations strongly suggest that the consumer contemplation concept embodied in Comment *i*, while illustrative of a particular problem, does not provide a satisfactory test for determining whether particular products are in a defective condition unreasonably dangerous to the user or consumer. In the final analysis, the principle of products liability contemplated by section 402A is premised upon the concept of enterprise liability for casting defective products into the stream of commerce. The primary focus must remain upon the nature of the product under all relevant circumstances rather than upon the conduct of either the consumer or the manufacturer. Total reliance upon the hypothetical ordinary consumer's contemplation of an obvious danger diverts the appropriate focus and may thereby result in a finding that a product is not defective even though the product may easily have been designed to be much safer at little added expense and no impairment of utility. Uncritical rejection of design defect claims in all cases wherein the danger may be open and obvious thus contravenes sound public policy by encouraging design strategies which perpetuate the manufacture of dangerous products.

In Ortho Pharmaceutical Corp. v. Heath, 722 P.2d 410 (Colo.1986), we recently recognized that exclusive reliance upon consumer expectations is a particularly inappropriate means of determining whether a product is

ation of the danger may nonetheless rise to the level of assumption of the risk. Assumption of the risk is an affirmative defense to strict liability, requiring a showing of more than ordinary contributory negligence in that the plaintiff must have voluntarily and unreasonably proceeded to encounter a known danger the specific hazards of which the plaintiff had actual subjective knowledge. * * * Restatement (Second) of Torts section 402A Comment n (1965). The question of whether a plaintiff had actual knowledge of the specific hazards comprising the danger is ordinarily a fact question which should be left for the jury and not precluded by the conclusion that the danger should have been obvious. See, e.g., * * * Hunt v. Harley–Davidson Motor Co., 147 Ga.App. 44, 248 S.E.2d 15 (1978)(plaintiff assumed the risk where he had extensive experience riding motorcycles, both with and without crash bars, was aware of the purpose and utility of crash bars, inquired of their availability at the time of purchase, but failed to place a formal request for their installation at a subsequent date).

unreasonably dangerous under section 402A where both the unreasonableness of the danger in the design defect and the efficacy of alternative designs in achieving a reasonable degree of safety must be defined primarily by technical, scientific information. Moreover, manufacturers of such complex products as motor vehicles invariably have greater access than do ordinary consumers to the information necessary to reach informed decisions concerning the efficacy of potential safety measures. * * *

A product may be unreasonably dangerous due to a manufacturing defect, a design defect or a failure to warn. The question in manufacturing defect cases is whether the product as produced conformed with the manufacturer's specifications. Resolution of whether a particular product is unreasonably dangerous is more difficult in design defect or failure to warn cases, where the product has been manufactured exactly as intended. In Ortho we noted that the following factors are of value in balancing the attendant risks and benefits of a product to determine whether a product design is unreasonably dangerous:

(1) The usefulness and desirability of the product—its utility to the user and to the public as a whole.

(2) The safety aspects of the product—the likelihood that it will cause injury and the probable seriousness of the injury.

(3) The availability of a substitute product which would meet the same need and not be as unsafe.

(4) The manufacturer's ability to eliminate the unsafe character of the product without impairing its usefulness or making it too expensive to maintain its utility.

(5) The user's ability to avoid danger by the exercise of care in the use of the product.

(6) The user's anticipated awareness of the dangers inherent in the product and their avoidability because of general public knowledge of the obvious condition of the product, or of the existence of suitable warnings or instructions.

(7) The feasibility, on the part of the manufacturer, of spreading the loss by setting the price of the product or carrying liability insurance.

Ortho Pharmaceutical Corp. v. Heath, 722 P.2d 410, 414 (relying on Wade, On the Nature of Strict Tort Liability for Products, 44 Miss.L.J. 825, 837–38 (1973)). The factors enumerated in Ortho are applicable to the determination of what constitutes a product that is in a defective unreasonably dangerous condition. By examining and weighing the various interests represented by these factors, a trial court is much more likely to be fair to the interests of both manufacturers and consumers in determining the status of particular products.

The question of the status of the motorcycle purchased by Camacho involves in part the interpretation of mechanical engineering data derived from research and testing—interpretation which necessarily includes the application of scientific and technical principles. In addition, the question posed under the crashworthiness doctrine is not whether the vehicle was obviously unsafe but rather whether the degree of inherent dangerousness could or should have been significantly reduced. The record contains some evidence to support the conclusion that Honda could have provided crash bars at an acceptable cost without impairing the motorcycle's utility or substantially altering its nature and Honda's failure to do so rendered the vehicle unreasonably dangerous under the applicable danger-utility test. It is far from certain, however, that the ultimate answer to this question can be determined on the basis of the limited facts thus far presented to the trial court.

* * *

The Camachos proffered evidence that the Honda Hawk motorcycle could have been equipped with crash bars which would mitigate injuries in low-speed, angled-impact collisions such as the one in which Camacho was involved. The Camachos' expert witnesses' interpretation of research and testing data indicated that the maneuverability of the motorcycle could be retained by making the crash bars no wider than the handlebars, that the stability of the motorcycle could be retained by mounting the crash bars relatively close to the center of gravity and that the addition of crash bars would not impair the utility of the motorcycle as a fuel efficient, open-air vehicle nor impair the safety of the motorcycle in accidents which varied in kind from the accident involving Camacho. These conclusions are all strenuously disputed by Honda. However, precisely because the factual conclusions reached by expert witnesses are in dispute, summary judgment as to whether the design strategies of Honda were reasonable is improper.

The judgment is reversed, and the case is remanded to the Court of Appeals with directions to remand the case to the trial court for further proceedings consistent with the views expressed in this opinion.

Vollack, Justice, dissenting:

Because I believe that the court of appeals correctly affirmed the trial court's order, I respectfully dissent.

The issue before the court is what test should apply in determining whether a product has a design defect causing it to be in a defective condition that is unreasonably dangerous. After arriving at the appropriate test, we must decide whether the court of appeals correctly affirmed the trial court's summary judgment order.

* * *

II.

We have not before decided what test should apply in determining whether a product is "unreasonably dangerous" in a design defect case. I believe the appropriate test is defined in Restatement (Second) of Torts § 402A Comment *i* (1965). Comment *i* states: "The article sold must be dangerous to an extent beyond that which would be contemplated by the ordinary consumer who purchases it, with the ordinary knowledge common to the community as to its characteristics" [hereinafter the consumer contemplation test].

Some jurisdictions have adopted this test; others have adopted it in part or rejected it.

* * *

Other jurisdictions have adopted a variation of the consumer expectation test. Dart v. Wiebe Mfg., Inc., 147 Ariz. 242, 709 P.2d 876 (1985)(where consumer expectation test is sufficient to resolve a case, that test is to be used; where that test "fails to provide a complete answer," application of risk/benefit factors is appropriate). Nichols v. Union Underwear Co., 602 S.W.2d 429 (Ky.1980)(consumer expectation or knowledge is just one factor to be considered by a jury in determining whether a product is unreasonably dangerous). Knitz v. Minster Machine Co., 69 Ohio St.2d 460, 432 N.E.2d 814 (1982)(product is of defective design "if (1) it is more dangerous than an ordinary consumer would expect when used in an intended or reasonably foreseeable manner, or (2) if the benefits of the challenged design do not outweigh the risk inherent in such design.").

Other states have rejected the consumer expectation test. Prentis v. Yale Mfg. Co., 421 Mich. 670, 365 N.W.2d 176 (1984)("[W]e adopt, forthrightly, a pure negligence, risk-utility test in products liability actions against manufacturers of products, where liability is predicated upon defective design."); Turner v. General Motors Corp., 584 S.W.2d 844 (Tex.1979)(risk-utility test will be applied "when the considerations of utility and risk are present in the state of the evidence.").

* * *

The cases discussed demonstrate that states have taken a variety of approaches to resolve this question. Because of the nature of the product here, I believe the appropriate test is the consumer contemplation or consumer expectation test. The facts presented in this case differ from cases which involve the defective condition of products such as automobile brakes, prescription drugs, and gas tanks. With those types of products, the ordinary consumer is not capable of assessing the danger of the product. On the other hand, an ordinary consumer is necessarily aware that motorcycles can be dangerous. The plaintiff had the choice to purchase other motorcycles by other manufacturers which carried additional safety features, and instead elected to purchase this particular motorcycle and ride it without leg protection devices. The conclusion follows that the trial court's ruling and the court of appeals' decision were correct.

* * *

I also believe the majority incorrectly relies on Ortho Pharmaceutical Corp. v. Heath, 722 P.2d 410 (Colo.1986). I believe the risk-benefit test cited by the majority and applied in Ortho is an appropriate test for products such as drugs, because their danger "is defined primarily by technical, scientific information," and because some drugs are unavoidably unsafe in some respect. A consumer of drugs cannot realistically be expected to foresee dangers in prescribed drugs which even scientists find to be complex and unpredictable. On the other hand, the purchaser of a motorcycle knows that the purchase and use of "an economical, open-air, maneuverable form of transportation," maj. op. at 1247, n. 8, presents the risk of accidents and resulting injuries due to the open-air nature of the motorcycle.

Because I believe that the correct test under facts such as these is the consumer-contemplation test, I would affirm the court of appeals' decision. Accordingly, I respectfully dissent.

I am authorized to state that Justice ERICKSON and Justice ROVIRA join in this dissent.

Notes

1. Comment *n* of § 402A, referred to in footnote 6 of the *Camacho* opinion took the position that the contributory negligence of the plaintiff is not a defense in a products liability case when the negligence consists of a failure to discover the defect in the product or to guard against the possibility of a defect. On the other hand, plaintiff's assumption of the risk, i.e. voluntarily and unreasonably proceeding to encounter a known danger, would be a defense. We discuss the general question of plaintiff's behavior below.

2. In an omitted part of the opinion the court says, "Arguably, a warning that injury-reducing crash bars were available as optional equipment or as add-on equipment would render an otherwise unreasonably dangerous motorcycle reasonably safe." *Camacho*, 741 P.2d at 1248. Do you agree?

3. *Consumer expectations versus risk utility.* The Second Restatement's consumer expectation test has slowly been replaced by a risk-utility analysis. Presently, only a handful of states have retained consumer expectations as the sole test in design defect cases.

In Barker v. Lull Eng'g Co., 20 Cal.3d 413, 143 Cal.Rptr. 225, 573 P.2d 443 (1978) the California Supreme Court adopted a two prong test for determining whether a product is defectively designed. The plaintiff could prevail by showing that the product failed to meet the consumer expectation test. Failing that, the consumer could prevail if the risk of the design outweighed its utility. The court shifted the burden of persuasion on this issue to the defendant. Several states adopted the *Barker* two pronged test. However, only a few courts followed the case in shifting the burden of persuasion to the defendant. *See* Caterpillar Tractor Co. v. Beck, 593 P.2d 871 (Alaska 1979).

The scope of *Barker's* consumer-expectation prong was narrowed in Soule v. General Motors Corp., 8 Cal.4th 548, 34 Cal.Rptr.2d 607, 882 P.2d 298 (1994). The *Soule* court held that "the jury may not be left free to find a violation of ordinary consumer expectations whenever it chooses. * * * Instructions based on the ordinary consumer expectations prong of *Barker* are not appropriate where, as a matter of law, the evidence would not support a jury verdict on that theory. * * * The crucial question in each individual case is whether the circumstances of the product's failure permit an inference that the product's design performed below the legitimate commonly accepted minimum safety assumptions of its ordinary consumers." *Soule*, 8 Cal.4th at 567–68, 34 Cal.Rptr.2d at 617–18. The court found the consumer expectations was inappropriate on the facts of *Soule*, which involved a complex claim involving the design of the wheel assembly on the plaintiff's automobile.

In *Soule*, General Motors gave the following reasons for completely abandoning the consumer expectations test in design cases:

First, it defies definition. Second, it focuses not on the objective condition of products, but on the subjective, unstable, and often unreasonable opinions of consumers. Third, it ignores the reality that ordinary consumers know little about how safe the complex products they use can or should be made. Fourth, it invites the jury to isolate the particular consumer, component, accident, and injury before it instead of considering whether the whole product fairly accommodates the competing expectations of all consumers in all situations. Fifth, it eliminates the careful balancing of risks and benefits which is essential to any design issue.

Soule, 8 Cal.4th at 569. Assess the merits of each of these arguments. Which do you think is the strongest?

4. *Obvious defects.* Following Campo v. Scofield, 301 N.Y. 468, 95 N.E.2d 802 (1950), it was held by a number of courts that, if the dangerousness of a product was obvious (or "patent"), there could be no recovery under either a negligence theory or later a strict products liability theory. This insistence that the defect be "latent" could be rationalized under § 402A's requirement that a product be "in a condition not contemplated by the ultimate consumer which will be unreasonably dangerous to him." *Campo* was overruled in Micallef v. Miehle Co., 39 N.Y.2d 376, 384 N.Y.S.2d 115, 348 N.E.2d 571 (1976), and there is little validity now left to the proposition that there is no liability, as a matter of law, for patent defects in manufacturing and design defect cases. As the *Camacho* court suggests, obvious dangers have become a matter to be balanced in the cost-benefit analysis as to whether the product is defective. Some courts, however, may refuse to allow a design defect case to go to the jury on a risk-utility analysis if the product is a "simple" product such as a knife or a lighter. *See* Todd v. Societe BIC ("Todd III"), 21 F.3d 1402 (7th Cir.1994), cert. denied, ___ U.S. ___, 115 S.Ct. 359, 130 L.Ed.2d 312 (1994).

In warning defect cases the obvious danger issue is still alive. The basic idea is that obvious danger conveys its own warning and moots any need for the manufacturer to give warning.

5. *Risk-utility versus negligence.* As Judge Kirshbaum noted in *Camacho,* some courts have been reluctant to move toward a risk-utility standard to judge design defects because they feel that this would be to reintroduce negligence concepts into an area designed to be free of such concepts. On the other hand, some courts have forthrightly stated that a risk-utility analysis in design defect cases is very similar to the negligence test as it was formulated by Learned Hand in *Carroll Towing.* The Michigan Supreme Court took this position in Prentis v. Yale Manufacturing Co., 421 Mich. 670, 365 N.W.2d 176 (1984). The opinion included the following comments about the appropriate test in design defect cases.

Like the courts in every other state, whether a suit is based upon negligence or implied warranty, we require the plaintiff to prove that the product itself is actionable—that something is wrong with it that makes it dangerous. This idea of "something wrong" is usually expressed by the adjective "defective" and the plaintiff must, *in every case, in every jurisdiction,* show that the product was defective. * * *

* * *

At present, questions related to "design defects" and the determination of when a product is defective, because of the nature of its design, appear to be the most agitated and controversial issues before the courts in the field of products liability. * * *

The approaches for determination of the meaning of "defect" in design cases fall into four general categories. The first, usually associated with Dean Wade, employs a negligence risk-utility analysis, but focuses upon whether the manufacturer would be judged negligent if it had known of the product's dangerous condition at the time it was marketed. The second, associated with Dean Keeton, compares the risk and utility of the product at the time of trial. The third focuses on consumer expectations about the product. The fourth combines the risk-utility and consumer-expectation tests. While courts have included many other individual variations in their formulations, the overwhelming consensus among courts deciding defective design cases is in the use of some form of risk-utility analysis, either as an exclusive or alternative ground of liability. Risk-utility analysis in this context always involves assessment of the decisions made by manufacturers with respect to the design of their products.

* * *

The risk-utility balancing test is merely a detailed version of Judge Learned Hand's negligence calculus. See *United States v. Carroll Towing Co.*, 159 F.2d 169, 173 (C.A.2, 1947). * * *

Although many courts have insisted that the risk-utility tests they are applying are not negligence tests because their focus is on the *product* rather than the manufacturer's *conduct,* see, *e.g., Barker v. Lull Engineering Co., Inc.,* 20 Cal.3d 413, 418, 143 Cal.Rptr. 225, 573 P.2d 443 (1978), the distinction on closer examination appears to be nothing more than semantic. As a common-sense matter, the jury weighs competing factors presented in evidence and reaches a conclusion about the judgment or decision (*i.e., conduct*)of the manufacturer. The underlying negligence calculus is inescapable.

Do you agree that the negligence and risk-utility tests are fundamentally the same? At least with respect to design defects, has products liability returned to fault principles? *See* David G. Owen, *The Fault Pit*, 26 Ga. L. Rev. 703 (1992). Not everyone is happy with the move toward a risk utility model. *See* Richard A. Epstein, *The Risks of Risk/Utility*, 48 Ohio St. L.J. 469 (1987)

6. *The time dimension.* As noted in the *Prentis* opinion, Dean Keeton's design defect test weighs the risks and benefits of a product as they are understood at the time of trial, not the time of manufacture. *See* W. Page Keeton, *Product Liability and the Meaning of Defect*, 5 St. Mary's L.J. 30, 34–35 (1973). This test was adopted in Phillips v. Kimwood Machine Co., 269 Or. 485, 525 P.2d 1033 (1974).

A dangerously defective article would be one which a reasonable person would not put into the stream of commerce if he had knowledge of its harmful character. The test, therefore, is whether the seller would be negligent if he sold the article knowing of the risk involved. Strict liability imposed what amounts to constructive knowledge of the condition of the product.

Phillips, 269 Or. at 492, 525 P.2d at 1036.

The time dimension is most important in cases where risks associated with a product are discovered only after manufacture. The *Phillips* court was not confronted with this situation and, therefore, its comment about "constructive knowledge" should not necessarily be interpreted as an endorsement of the Keeton position. Recall that § 1(b) of the *Restatement (Third) of Torts: Products Liability* assesses defectiveness at the time the manufacturer puts the product into the stream of commerce. When risk become known only subsequent to manufacture, the defendant may present a state-of-the-art defense. We will return to state-of-the-art in the section on warning defects. *See* generally, James Henderson, *Coping with the Time Dimension in Products Liability,* 69 Calif.L.Rev. 919 (1981).

7. *Crashworthiness. Camacho* is a crashworthiness case. As explained in Reed v. Chrysler Corp., 494 N.W.2d 224 (Iowa 1992), "The [crashworthiness] doctrine imposes liability on manufacturers for design defects which only enhance injuries rather than cause them. The doctrine is applicable when a design defect, not causally connected to the accident, results in injuries greater than those which would have resulted from the accident had there been no design defect. In other words, enhancement of injuries is the gist of crashworthiness cases, not the precipitating cause of the accident." *Reed,* 494 N.W.2d at 226.

The crashworthiness cases pose very interesting factual situations. Usually the issue arises in a case in which the plaintiff has been a substantial cause of the accident or the one primarily responsible is judgment proof or the accident is one in which no one is at fault. This calls for the plaintiff's attorney to do some imaginative lawyering. Such lawyering has produced many of the crashworthiness cases. In addition to *Camacho, see* Daly v. General Motors Corp., 20 Cal.3d 725, 144 Cal.Rptr. 380, 575 P.2d 1162 (1978)(which appears later in this chapter).

Because the focus of a crashworthiness case is on the enhanced injuries suffered by the plaintiff, the cause of the underlying injury is often considered to be irrelevant. We discuss this issue in the context of the Daly case, *infra* page 712.

RILEY v. BECTON DICKINSON VASCULAR ACCESS, INC.

U.S. District Court, E.D. Pennsylvania, 1995.
913 F.Supp. 879.

MEMORANDUM

TROUTMAN, SENIOR DISTRICT JUDGE.

[T]he plaintiff, a twenty-three year old nurse, contracted the HIV virus as a result of being stuck with an I.V. catheter needle after initiating an I.V. in a patient in the Intensive Care Unit of Community Hospital of Lancaster where she was employed.[7]

Plaintiff asserts that defendant, Becton Dickinson Vascular Access, Inc., is strictly liable for her injury in that the I.V. catheter, an Angiocath manufactured by defendant and used by plaintiff to initiate the I.V., is

7. The device here involved is a peripheral I.V. catheter, which consists of a needle and a slender flexible, hollow tube designed to be inserted into a vein in the patient's arm, hand, leg or foot. The needle is used to gain access to the patient's vein and is then withdrawn through the catheter tubing, which remains attached to the patient's vein for infusion of fluids and/or medications as needed.

unsafe for its intended use because the needle, contaminated by the patient's blood, remains exposed after it is withdrawn from the catheter, thus permitting a needle-stick accident to occur. Plaintiff contends that such design is defective and that an available and feasible alternative design of the catheter, in which the needle is retracted into a plastic sheath as it is withdrawn, would have prevented her accident and consequent injury if she had been using such alternative device at the time the incident in which she was injured occurred.

Presently before the Court is defendant's motion for summary judgment. * * *

* * *

II. STRICT LIABILITY CLAIMS

* * *

[W]hen presented with claims arising under s 402A of the RESTATEMENT (SECOND) OF TORTS, it is necessary for courts applying Pennsylvania law to determine, initially and as a matter of law, whether the product in question is "unreasonably dangerous." Such determination is to be made by weighing the utility of the product against the likelihood and seriousness of the injury claimed and the availability of precautions which might have prevented the injury in order to reach the ultimate conclusion whether, as a matter of social policy, the risk of loss is appropriately placed upon the supplier of the product.

We will first consider the danger inherent in the Angiocath under the unquestionably applicable risk/utility analysis to determine whether the product is unreasonably dangerous in light of its utility and the availability of similarly useful devices which might reduce or eliminate the risk to healthcare workers from exposed I.V. catheter needles. * * *

III. RISK/UTILITY ANALYSIS UNDER PENNSYLVANIA LAW

The parties agree that the Pennsylvania courts have adopted a risk/utility test which requires consideration of the following factors in aid of the determination whether a product is unreasonably dangerous: 1. The usefulness and desirability of the product—its utility to the user and to the public as a whole. 2. The safety aspects of a product—the likelihood that it will cause injury, and the probable seriousness of the injury. 3. The availability of a substitute product which would meet the same need and not be as unsafe. 4. The manufacturer's ability to eliminate the unsafe character of the product without impairing its usefulness or making it too expensive to maintain its utility. 5. The user's ability to avoid danger by the exercise of care in the use of the product. 6. The user's anticipated awareness of the dangers inherent in the product and their avoidability, because of general public knowledge of the obvious condition of the product, or of the existence of suitable warnings or instructions. 7. The feasibility, on the part of the manufacturer, of spreading the loss of setting the price of the product or carrying liability insurance.

* * *

Although the parties agree on the applicable legal standards, they obviously disagree as to the outcome when such standards are properly applied in this action. Upon review of the parties' respective arguments, it appears that their differing conclusions are based upon the different emphasis placed by each party on the various factors.

Plaintiff focuses almost exclusively upon the devastating potential effects of a needle stick accident which, as here, can lead to the transmission of a serious, even deadly, blood-borne disease, as well as upon the ready availability of an alternative design, already on the market, which plaintiff contends is feasible and eliminates the danger inherent in the design of the Angiocath.

Defendant, on the other hand, argues that although each needle stick accident involving HIV exposure is potentially very serious, there are very few accidents given the widespread use of the product. Defendant also contends that the alternative product touted by plaintiff does not meet the same equipment needs as the Angiocath and does not eliminate the potentially serious risk of needle sticks or other blood exposure. * * *

It is difficult, but absolutely essential, for the Court to be completely dispassionate in weighing the risks and benefits of the Angiocath in order to make the required social policy determination concerning the allocation of the risk of loss resulting from an accident such as that here involved. The social policy issue before the Court is not whether plaintiff deserves compensation for a terrible accident, but whether the manufacturer of the device through which she was injured is appropriately subject to liability for the accident, and, therefore, can be required to provide such compensation.

We also note that defendant bears the burden of proof on the threshold determination of allocation of risk and that all of the evidence on the threshold issue must be viewed in the light most favorable to the plaintiff.

It is with these principles firmly in mind that we consider each specific factor of the risk/utility analysis.

A. Utility of the Angiocath to the User and to the Public

It is obvious that many medical procedures depend upon the use of sharp needles to deliver vaccines and medication, to take blood samples, and, as here, to provide a means for intravenous delivery of fluids, nutrients and medicine. Thus, the availability of products such as the Angiocath is absolutely essential to modern medicine. Products which incorporate a sharp needle, therefore, are highly useful to the public as well as to medical professionals, who require devices which function well for their intended purpose, piercing skin and subcutaneous tissue.

* * *

B. Safety Aspects

In analyzing this factor, we consider both the likelihood of injury from use of the product and the probable seriousness of the injury. To make that assessment in this case is somewhat less straightforward than usual in that the term "injury" has several meanings in the present circumstances.

The needle stick itself is an injury of which there is a determinable likelihood, while exposure to HIV or another blood-borne disease is likewise an injury that is more serious but less likely, since most patients are neither HIV positive nor infected with any blood-borne disease. Finally, contracting such a disease is still less likely than exposure thereto, albeit far more serious. Thus, although it is indisputable that all exposures to HIV which result in infection are terribly serious, and, because of the deadly consequences of infection, all needle stick exposures to HIV contaminated blood are serious, it does not follow that all needle stick incidents present a risk of serious injury.[3]

To properly assess this factor in terms of social policy concerns, therefore, the Court must avoid undue consideration of the indisputable fact that whatever the theoretical risk to plaintiff of serious consequent injury from the initial needle stick injury, plaintiff did sustain that most serious of injuries. Nevertheless, that fact alters neither her theoretical risk of serious injury at the time of the initial needle stick injury, nor the theoretical risk of serious injury to all other users of the product in question. To make the requisite social policy determination, which obviously affects every potential user of the Angiocath, the Court must focus on the general, theoretical risks inherent in the use of the product in terms of the likelihood that any needle stick injury involving an Angiocath will result in a serious injury, as that term is used herein, i.e., exposure to HIV/HIV infection.

Calculations from the evidence submitted by both parties to this action indicate that the risks of HIV exposure/HIV infection from an I.V. catheter are quite small. We note, first, that estimates of the rate of HIV infection from HIV exposure range from 0.3—0.47%. * * *

[T]he Court, in order to fulfill our obligation to view the evidence in the light most favorable to the plaintiff, has attempted to calculate the likelihood of HIV exposure/HIV infection from additional data included in evidence submitted by both parties. We begin with the estimate of the number of needle sticks to healthcare workers each year, which ranges from 800,000 to 1,000,000. Next we consider the percentage of all needle sticks attributable to I.V. catheter stylets, which has been documented in a relatively small sample at approximately 2.0%, and was then projected to be approximately 18.4/100,000 uses. Finally, based upon plaintiff's evidence, our estimate of the likely rate of HIV contamination is 2% of all needle sticks. Thus, using the figures most favorable to the plaintiff, 20,000 out of 1,000,000 needle sticks per year are likely to be attributable to an I.V. catheter stylet and 400 such needle sticks are likely to be HIV contaminated. At the previously estimated infection rate of .3—.47%, it appears that

---

3. Our discussion of the risk of injury from a needle stick will be limited to the risk of exposure to and risk of contracting HIV for several reasons: (1) That is the injury involved in this action; (2) actual data available in the record is limited primarily to assessing the risk of exposure to HIV and HBV, (Hepatitis B Virus); (3) although the risk of contracting HBV after exposure via a needle stick is significantly greater than that of contracting HIV, the evidence discloses that healthcare workers can readily protect themselves by receiving the HBV vaccine, which provides over 90% protection from infection for seven years, and which OSHA regulations require hospitals to make available to healthcare workers free of charge.

there are likely to be 1—2 HIV infections to healthcare workers per year from use of all I.V. catheter sets, both conventional and protected.

Stated in other terms, if we assume that there are 18.4 I.V. catheter needle sticks per 100,000 uses of such devices, assume an HIV contamination rate of 2%, and assume the highest likely infection rate, .47%, there could be 17 HIV infections per 1 billion I.V. catheters used, both protected and conventional, or between 8 and 9 infections per 500,000,000 uses of an I.V. catheter set.

* * *

Moreover, we note that the Court's calculations overstate the true risk, since the actual rate of HIV infection from exposure lies somewhere between .3% and .47%. With that consideration in mind, we further note that even using the lower infection rate as an estimate of the incidence of HIV infection from exposure, our projected risk calculation still overstates the actual incidence of HIV infection from defendant's products. Defendant has had only three reports of HIV infection from conventional I.V. catheters since 1981, a period during which defendant estimates that it sold 1.5 billion such devices.

From the available evidence and projections based thereon, the Court concludes that the risk of serious injury from use of an I.V. catheter such as the Angiocath is quite low.

C. Availability of a Safer, Substitute Product

Plaintiff does not argue that there is an acceptable substitute for an I.V. catheter. Plaintiff points out, however, that there is an available substitute for a conventional I.V. catheter which leaves the introducing needle exposed after it is withdrawn from the flexible tube. The ProtectIV, an I.V. catheter manufactured by Critikon, a competitor of defendant, permits the needle to be retracted into a plastic sheath as it is withdrawn from the tube attached to the patient's vein. Indeed, at the time of plaintiff's injury, defendant itself was marketing a similar device known as the Insyte Saf–T–Cath.[7]

A study of 1024 healthcare workers at nine hospitals in 6 states over a period of six months revealed that the incidence of needle sticks was lower with the ProtectIV, i.e., 2.25 injuries per 100,000 compared to 7.48 injuries per 100,000 conventional devices. * * *

Although a reduction in the total number of needle sticks would obviously lessen the likelihood of serious injury, the projected risks of HIV exposure and infection from any one such needle stick are identical to the risks associated with a needle stick from a conventional catheter, since the rate of HIV exposure and infection depend upon the patient population, not the type of I.V. catheter used. Based upon a projected incidence of 2.25 needle sticks per 100,000 uses of a protected catheter, the projected risk of HIV infection from an I.V. catheter needle stick would be reduced from 3.5/500,000,000 uses with a conventional catheter to 2/1,000,000,000 uses

---

7. Defendant's alternative catheter was later withdrawn from the market when an injunction was entered in a patent infringement suit brought by Critikon against Becton–Dickinson.

or 1/500,000,000 uses with a protected catheter. Consequently, it appears that an already small risk might be somewhat reduced, but would not be eliminated, by use of a protected rather than a conventional I.V. catheter.

* * *

[T]he actual experience of one hospital in the use of conventional and protected catheters confirms that the * * * the projected decrease in that risk with the use of a protected catheter is not likely to be achieved in practice until and unless the healthcare workers using the new device become proficient with it. Indeed, such experience indicates that the risk of injury could initially increase.

Such conclusion is supported by anecdotal evidence relating to certain difficulties and drawbacks inherent in the design of the protected catheter which became evident during the early clinical experiences at Community Hospital of Lancaster. We note, e.g., that contrary to plaintiff's argument that the ProtectIV provides "automatic" protection from an exposed needle, the record shows that the introducer needle is retracted into the protective sheath only if the person initiating the I.V. activates that mechanism by sliding the sheath front, over the needle, as the needle is withdrawn through the catheter. Failure to properly engage the mechanism by fully extending the sheath until it "clicks" allows the sharp tip of the needle to remain exposed, which can, and at Community Hospital of Lancaster did, result in a needle stick.[10]

Moreover, the available evidence also discloses that even if the incidence of needle sticks is ultimately somewhat reduced by using the ProtectIV, a healthcare worker's exposure to a patient's blood may not be significantly reduced since more blood escapes from the catheter as the needle is withdrawn than occurs with a conventional I.V. catheter. * * *

Other problems with the ProtectIV were also reported at Community Hospital of Lancaster, such as: faster deterioration of IV sites; failure of the catheters to lock in place because the catheter, not the needle, penetrated the patient's vein; malfunction, such as the needle penetrating the catheter shaft as it was withdrawn; catheter kinking and bending; difficulty using the catheters on infants, small children, elderly patients and others with difficult veins. Many such problems would likely result in the need for additional I.V. initiations, thereby actually increasing the potential for a needle stick by increasing the number of times an I.V. introducer needle is used.

* * *

Finally, the evidence discloses that the experience of Community Hospital of Lancaster appears to be neither unusual nor unique. In a

10. As defendant points out, given the undisputed circumstances of plaintiff's accident and the operation of the ProtectIV, it is not at all certain that she could have avoided the needle stick if she had been using it, since she reacted to a patient's sudden movement by an apparently reflexive movement of her own. It is not possible, therefore, to infer that plaintiff would have been able to completely engage the protective mechanism of the ProtectIV before the incident occurred. Had the needle been suddenly withdrawn from the catheter in response to the patient's movement and the tip remained exposed, a needle stick could have occurred, just as it did when a nurse in the hospital's birthing center failed to fully engage the sheath of the ProtectIV in August, 1993.

September, 1992, article in a publication for healthcare workers, a San Francisco hospital employee stated that the design of the protected catheter requires improvement and described similar complaints and concerns about the protected catheters as those noted by the staff of the Lancaster hospital. * * *

We conclude, therefore, that although the small projected risk of a needle stick might be further reduced by substituting a protected I.V. catheter for a conventional device, assuming that the user is proficient with the new device, the danger of a needle stick cannot be eliminated. Moreover, a reduction in the incidence of needle sticks is by no means assured, and, even if achieved, blood exposure may not be significantly reduced, if at all, due to a generally recognized "backflow" problem which occurs when the needle is withdrawn from the catheter and the I.V. connection is not completed quickly. We further conclude that other design features of the available substitute product render it less effective, in general, than the Angiocath for its intended purpose, since use of the protected catheter may not be appropriate in some situations due to difficulties that cannot be easily overcome, if at all, with certain patients.

Thus, although a substitute for a conventional I.V. catheter is available which may reduce the incidence of needle sticks, it is not entirely certain that such substitute is safer overall when other aspects of the alternative design are considered and it does not appear to be an alternative which can feasibly replace conventional I.V. catheters completely.

D. Elimination of the Unsafe Character of the Product without Impairing Usefulness or Making It Too Expensive

As already discussed in detail in connection with the availability of a safer, comparable product, there is only one substitute for a conventional I.V. catheter on the market at present. With proper use, the alternative product does not leave the introducer needle exposed after it is withdrawn from the catheter. The protective design, however, does not completely eliminate the danger of a needle stick since failure to properly activate the shielding device still leaves the needle exposed, and, in gaining a small safety improvement with respect to the risk of a needle stick, the alternative product creates other problems which do not occur with the use of a conventional I.V. catheter and which render the redesigned product less suitable for some uses.

In addition, the cost of the protected catheter far exceeds that of the conventional device. At the time the Community Hospital of Lancaster first evaluated the ProtectIV in 1992, the cost was $1.40 per unit compared to $.78 for the Angiocath. Moreover, the unit cost of the catheters is not the only cost consideration. As noted, the evidence establishes the need for extensive training with the ProtectIV in order to gain the benefit of somewhat fewer needle sticks and to overcome the problems inherent in other aspects of the product to the greatest possible extent. The additional costs associated with training hundreds of hospital workers prior to introducing the protected device for general use, combined with the potential need for follow-up in-servicing, as occurred at Community Hospital of Lancaster, are also costs associated with use of the alternative product.

Although plaintiff argues that such increased costs of a substitute product are defensible in light of the devastating effects of the injury that she sustained, we note again that we are here concerned with the magnitude of the increased costs in light of the magnitude of the theoretical risks of a needle stick and the consequent costs associated with that risk of injury. In that regard, a discussion of the feasibility and desirability of using products designed to prevent needle sticks noted that "Hospitals should not pay an excessive amount to achieve only a minimal reduction in risk." The authors of the study also suggested an appropriate cost differential based upon the average costs of any needle stick injury: "On average, needlesticks cost an overall 36% above the purchase price of the devices. Thus, a hospital could pay an additional 36% for preventive devices (assuming that they would totally eliminate the costs associated with needle sticks) without increasing total costs."

It is clear, however, that needle sticks, and their associated increased costs, cannot be completely eliminated. Moreover, the authors of the discussion quoted above based their recommendation on the average costs associated with injuries from all types of needles likely to be encountered in a hospital. For present purposes, however, it is more accurate to use the increased needle stick costs associated only with I.V. stylets, which the authors estimate at 10% of the cost of such devices.

Based upon evidence submitted by plaintiff, therefore, it appears that the higher unit cost of a protected catheter would be reasonable in light of its expected benefits if it were 10%–36% above the cost of an unprotected device.

By that measure, it is clear that the unit cost of the ProtectIV, approximately 80% above the cost of the Angiocath, is very high in light of the small benefit likely to be derived from the possible reduction, but not elimination, of the risk of a needle stick. Moreover, the increased unit cost does not include the costs of inservice training or the potential for higher usage due to faster deterioration of I.V. sites.

Thus, we conclude that it is not possible to eliminate the unsafe feature of the Angiocath without impairing its utility since the costs of the only available alternative product are much higher; the risk associated with the allegedly unsafe design cannot be completely eliminated; and there are problems other than the risk of a needle stick associated with the use of the alternative design which require extensive training to diminish and which cannot be entirely eliminated.

E. The User's Ability to Avoid Danger by Exercising Care in the Use of the Product

* * *

We conclude that just as the design of the protected catheter cannot completely prevent needle sticks from the use of I.V. catheters, it is unlikely that even extreme caution and punctilious adherence to recommended procedures can enable a healthcare worker to completely avoid that danger. Nevertheless, it does appear that healthcare facilities and healthcare workers themselves have some ability to reduce the risk inherent in the use of any I.V. catheter by taking appropriate precautions.

F. The User's Anticipated Awareness of the Dangers and Their Avoidability

The sheer size of the record produced in support of and in opposition to the instant motion, including many articles written for healthcare providers concerning the risks of exposure to blood-borne diseases from needle sticks, indicates that there is widespread knowledge of the potential danger of a needle stick accident among healthcare workers. Indeed, plaintiff does not contend that the danger inherent in an exposed needle is hidden, generally unknown to healthcare workers, or that she was personally unaware of such danger.

G. Feasibility on the Part of the Manufacturer of Spreading the Loss

* * *

As plaintiff suggests, a conclusion by the Court that the manufacturer of the Angiocath may be required to assume responsibility for compensating those injured while using it could lead to its withdrawal from the market, or, at least, to such a substantial increase in its cost as to minimize or eliminate the cost differential between the Angiocath and the alternative product, the ProtectIV, potentially leading to increased acceptance of the needle-sheathing design. The Court must, therefore, determine whether, as the plaintiff vigorously contends, that result is desirable and should be encouraged.

Based upon a consideration of all the evidence, we conclude that such a potential manipulation of the market for peripheral I.V. catheters should not be undertaken as a consequence of one of three tragic accidents which occurred during 16 years of experience with defendant's I.V. catheter products by a multitude of healthcare workers, especially where the alternative product is certainly not without its own dangers and other drawbacks and where the product in question appears to be functionally superior to the alternative in all respects other than leaving the needle exposed after it is withdrawn from the catheter.

Moreover, we conclude that in this case, there would be no adverse effect to plaintiff or to the public in general as a result of not shifting the costs of plaintiff's injury to the manufacturer of the product, thereby allowing the costs to remain where they are currently allocated: on the plaintiff's employer via the Workmen's Compensation system. At the time of plaintiff's accident, Community Hospital of Lancaster required the use of the Angiocath by refusing to purchase the alternative product. * * * [I]f the Angiocath was not the best or safest product for plaintiff to use under the circumstances which existed at the time of her accident, the fact that she had no choice but to proceed with the use of a less desirable alternative was due entirely her employer's decision. Hence, it would be unfair to expect the manufacturer of the Angiocath to spread the costs of plaintiff's injury to all users thereof, including those healthcare facilities which might take more care to assure that a variety of products are available to their staffs in order to permit their employees to select the most appropriate device for various circumstances.

* * *

H. Summary

Having examined each factor in the risk/utility analysis which both parties agree is applicable to this case in the light of the available evidence, we conclude that the Angiocath, although dangerous because it is capable of causing serious injury, is not unreasonably dangerous as that term is defined in Pennsylvania law.

* * *

VI. Conclusion

Having carefully considered the extensive evidence, arguments of counsel and other submissions of the parties in connection with a risk/utility analysis undertaken pursuant to Pennsylvania law governing strict liability claims, we conclude that the product in question, the Angiocath peripheral I.V. catheter manufactured and sold by defendant, is not unreasonably dangerous, and, therefore, is not defective as a matter of law. Accordingly, defendant's motion for summary judgment will be granted and judgment will be entered in favor of the defendant.

Order

And now, this 27th day of December, 1995, upon consideration of defendant's Motion for Summary Judgment, and plaintiff's response thereto, IT IS HEREBY ORDERED that the motion is GRANTED.

IT IS FURTHER ORDERED that judgment is entered in favor of the defendant and against the plaintiff.

Notes

1. Why aren't all of the issues discussed by the court properly questions for the jury? Do you think the plaintiff failed to present a prima facie case? Do you believe that the trial court's grant of a summary judgment would be overturned on appeal?

2. At several points in his opinion, Judge Troutman noted that the focus of the risk-utility analysis should be on the theoretical risk of injury to all users of the product, not the particular injury suffered by the plaintiff. Do you agree? Do you believe the average jury would adopt this point of view? Consider the comments of Judge Easterbrook in Carroll v. Otis Elevator Co., 896 F.2d 210 (7th Cir.1990). In *Carroll,* an unidentified child pushed the emergency stop button on an escalator, causing the plaintiff to fall and injure her knee. The plaintiff argued that the escalator was defectively designed because the "emergency stop button was unguarded and unreasonably attractive and operable by children." The jury awarded the plaintiff $43,000.

The *ex post* perspective of litigation exerts a hydraulic force that distorts judgment. Engineers design escalators to minimize the sum of construction, operation, and injury costs. Department stores, which have nothing to gain from maiming their customers and employees, willingly pay for cost-effective precautions. Some persons will be injured when caught in the escalator; these costs go down as emergency stop buttons are easy to find and press. Others will be injured as escalators suddenly stop; these costs will go down as stop buttons are hard to find and press. Escalators move slowly, so stops rarely cause falls (and falls rarely cause serious injuries); passengers with poor balance or frail constitution may protect themselves by holding the handrails. Because the expected costs of stops are small, designers make buttons easy to find and press, to reduce the costs of the rarer, but much more serious, entanglements. The machines they have designed are safer than stairs.

Come the lawsuit, however, the passenger injured by a stop presents himself as a person, not a probability. Jurors see today's injury; persons who would be injured if buttons were harder to find and use are invisible. Although witnesses may talk about them, they are spectral figures, insubstantial compared to the injured plaintiff, who appears in the flesh. * * * [N]o matter how conscientious jurors may be, there is a bias in the system. *Ex post* claims are overvalued and technical arguments discounted in the process of litigation.

Carroll, 896 F.2d at 215–16.

3. The court clearly places much of the responsibility for the plaintiff's injury on her employer. Many products liability cases arise in the employment context, frequently involving machinery by the use of which the plaintiff has been injured. As indicated in the *Riley* opinion, most states have adopted workers' compensation statutes, discussed in more detail in Chapter Fourteen, *infra,* which replace tort law in this situation with a no-fault, statutory remedy. However, these statutes limit the damages that may be recovered. Thus, there is a strong incentive to sue the manufacturer under products liability. Occasionally, these cases have involve situations in which the employer has been given an equipment option and has chosen the less safe design. The manufacturer is nevertheless held liable. Hammond v. International Harvester Co., 691 F.2d 646 (3d Cir.1982)(applying Pennsylvania law). The same result has sometimes occurred where the employer or even the employee has altered the machine to eliminate safety provisions, at least if the machine could have been designed to make such alteration difficult. The theory is that the employer's motive to speed up production by eliminating safety provisions, or pressuring workers to do so, is foreseeable and, when not anticipated in the design of the machine, makes the product defective. *See* Knitz v. Minster Machine Co., 69 Ohio St.2d 460, 432 N.E.2d 814 (1982). What role should employer negligence play in products cases?

4. Perhaps the most controversial provision in *Restatement (Third) of Torts: Products Liability* is § 2's requirement that the plaintiff demonstrate a reasonable alternative design in order to prevail in a design defect case. This position is supported by a substantial number of opinions. *See* General Motors Corp. v. Edwards, 482 So.2d 1176 (Ala.1985); Voss v. Black and Decker Mfgr., 59 N.Y.2d 102, 463 N.Y.S.2d 398, 450 N.E.2d 204 (1983). However, some courts have not explicitly required proof of alternative design, e.g. Thibault v. Sears, Roebuck & Co., 118 N.H. 802, 395 A.2d 843 (1978). Other courts have stated that in some situations the risks associated with a product so outweigh its utility that it is defective even absent an alternative design, e.g. Kallio v. Ford Motor Co., 407 N.W.2d 92, 96–7 (Minn.1987); Banks v. ICI Americas, Inc., 264 Ga. 732, 736, 450 S.E.2d 671, 675 (1994).

O'Brien v. Muskin, 94 N.J. 169, 463 A.2d 298 (1983) adopts this point of view. O'Brien suffered a serious injury when he apparently dove from the roof of a garage into an above-ground swimming pool. His outstretched hands hit the pool bottom and slid apart, allowing his head to strike the bottom of the pool. The plaintiff claimed that the pool was defectively designed because it was lined with vinyl, which became slippery when wet. One of the plaintiff's expert witnesses contended that vinyl should not be used in above-ground pools, even though no alternative was available. The trial court refused to allow the plaintiff's design defect claim go to the jury, but the New Jersey Supreme Court affirmed an appellate court reversal. With respect to design alternatives, the court said:

> The evaluation of the utility of a product also involves the relative need for that product; some products are essentials, while others are luxuries. A product that fills a critical need and can be designed in only one way should be viewed differently from a luxury item. Still other products, including some for which no alternative exists, are so dangerous and of such little use that under the risk-utility analysis, a manufacturer would bear the cost of liability of harm to others. That cost might dissuade a manufacturer from placing the product on the market, even if the product has been made as safely as possible. Indeed, plaintiff contends that above-ground pools with vinyl liners are such products and that manufacturers who market those pools should bear the cost of injuries they cause to foreseeable users.

> A critical issue at trial was whether the design of the pool, calling for a vinyl bottom in a pool four feet deep, was defective. The trial court should have permitted the jury to consider whether, because of the dimensions of the pool and slipperiness of the bottom, the risks of injury so outweighed the utility of the product as to constitute a defect. In removing that issue from consideration by the jury, the trial court erred. To establish sufficient proof to compel submission of the issue to the jury for appropriate fact-finding under risk-utility analysis, it was not necessary for plaintiff to prove the existence of alternative, safer designs. Viewing the evidence in the light most favorable to plaintiff, even if there are no alternative methods of making bottoms for above-ground pools, the jury might have found that the risk posed by the pool outweighed its utility.

O'Brien, 463 A.2d at 306.

New Jersey subsequently passed a products liability statute, which provided in part:

> In any product liability action against a manufacturer or seller for harm allegedly caused by a product that was designed in a defective manner, the manufacturer or seller shall not be liable if: (1) At the time the product left the control of the manufacturer, there was not a practical and technically feasible alternative design that would have prevented the harm without substantially impairing the reasonably anticipated or intended function of the product;

NJ ST 2A: 58C–3(a)(1)

In light of the statute, it is not surprising that the expansive language of *O'Brien* has been reined in by subsequent opinions. In Smith v. Keller Ladder Co., 275 N.J.Super. 280, 645 A.2d 1269 (1994), a jury returned a verdict of $115,000 for the plaintiff who fell off of the defendant's ladder. The appellate court affirmed a trial court j.n.o.v. because the plaintiff "failed to present any evidence suggesting either that there was a reasonably feasible alternative design which would have made defendant's ladder safer, or that the ladder was so dangerous and of so little use that defendant should bear the liability." *Smith*, 645 A.2d at 1271.

The New Jersey statute is one of many that have been passed in recent years, a number of which have also required the plaintiff to present evidence of an alternative design in order to prevail. *See,* e.g., Tx. Civ. Prac. & Rem. Code § 82.005

Design Defects

(a) In a products liability action in which a claimant alleges a design defect, the burden is on the claimant to prove by a preponderance of the evidence that:

(1) there was a safer alternative design; and

(2) the defect was a producing cause of the personal injury, property damage, or death for which the claimant seeks recovery.

(b) In this section, "safer alternative design" means a product design other than the one actually used that in reasonable probability:

(1) would have prevented or significantly reduced the risk of the claimant's personal injury, property damage, or death without substantially impairing the product's utility; and

(2) was economically and technologically feasible at the time the product left the control of the manufacturer or seller by the application of existing or reasonably achievable scientific knowledge.

As a practical matter, in most cases isn't it unlikely that the plaintiff will be able to persuade the trier of fact that the defendant's design is defective without introducing some evidence of a safer alternative?

5. Cigarettes could be thought of as a good example of a product whose risks outweigh its utility even in the absence of an alternative design. In fact, in Horton v. American Tobacco Company, 667 So.2d 1289 (Miss.1995), a jury returned a verdict for the plaintiff on an undifferentiated risk-utility strict liability theory. (However, the jury awarded zero damages because of plaintiff's contributory negligence. Plaintiff admitted that since 1966 he had read and disregarded the warnings on packs of cigarettes. *Id.* at 1290).

In 1993 the Mississippi legislature passed a products liability statute that on its face would prevent such findings in the future by requiring proof of an alternative feasible design. Similarly, earlier New Jersey cases that suggested a plaintiff might proceed with a design defect claim without showing an alternative feasible design (Dewey v. Reynolds Tobacco Co., 216 N.J.Super. 347, 523 A.2d 712 (Law Div.1986), *rev'd in part, aff'd in part,* Dewey v. R.J. Reynolds Tobacco Co., 121 N.J. 69, 577 A.2d 1239 (N.J.1990)) were rendered moot by the New Jersey products liability statute cited above. Courts in other jurisdictions have rejected a general risk/utility test under which a product could be found to be "unreasonable per se," thereby making it a tort to market the product at all. Hite v. R.J. Reynolds Tobacco Co., 396 Pa.Super. 82, 578 A.2d 417 (1990); Kotler v. American Tobacco Co., 926 F.2d 1217, 1225–26 (1st Cir.1990), *vacated,* 505 U.S. 1215, 112 S.Ct. 3019, 120 L.Ed.2d 891 (1992), *reaff'd,* 981 F.2d 7 (1st Cir.1992)(interpreting Massachusetts law); Brown v. R.J. Reynolds Tobacco Co., 852 F.Supp. 8 (E.D.La.1994)(applying Louisiana products liability statute). *See* Gary Schwartz, *Tobacco Liability in the Courts* in SMOKING POLICY: LAW, POLITICS AND CULTURE pp. 131–160 (Robert Rabin & Stephen Sugarman eds., Oxford University Press, 1993); Carl T. Bogus, *War on the Common Law: The Struggle at the Center of Products Liability,* 60 Mo. L. Rev. 1 (1995).

6.   In footnote 7 of the *Riley* opinion, the court notes that the defendant's introduction of a retractable catheter was met with an injunction in a patent infringement claim brought by its competitor. Is it possible for one company to patent the best feasible design and effectively force all other manufacturers to use an inferior design that might be considered defective in subsequent products liability litigation? If a design is patented, does this mean that the design is not "feasible" for other manufacturers? One way to think about this issue is to ask whether strict products liability requires the manufacturer to use the "best" design.

In Lewis v. Coffing Hoist Division, Duff--Norton Co., Inc., 515 Pa. 334, 528 A.2d 590 (1987), the plaintiff was injured when he accidently pushed the "down" button on the control box for an overhead electric chain-hoist. He claimed the design of the control box was defective because the buttons were raised from the surface of the box and, therefore, were too easy to push accidently. He offered two alternative designs, one in which the buttons were recessed into the face of the box and another that had protective flanges around the buttons. The trial court refused to allow defense testimony that ninety percent of the electric hoists around the country lacked a guard around the activating buttons and that the American Society of Mechanical Engineers considered defendant's design to be safe. The Pennsylvania Supreme Court upheld the trial court's rulings and affirmed a jury verdict for the plaintiff.

In dissent, Justice Flaherty argued that strict liability "imposes on suppliers liability for putting an unsafe product on the market. It does not impose liability for failing to make an already safe product somewhat safer, or for failing to utilize the safest of all possible designs. We are simply not dealing with conceptual Platonic ideals of perfection when a jury considers whether any given product is 'safe.'" *Lewis*, 528 A.2d at 594. Do you agree?

7.   The plaintiff must show that the alternative design would have prevented or reduced the harm for which the plaintiff seeks to recover. Comment *c* following § 2 of *Restatement (Third) of Torts: Products Liability* (Tentative Draft No. 2, 1995) notes,

> Thus, even if plaintiff establishes that an alternative design would have provided some added safety, liability is not justified unless that added safety would have prevented or reduced the plaintiff's harm. The more marginal the added safety provided by the plaintiff's suggested alternative design, the less likely it is that the suggested alternative design would have played a sufficiently causal role. Thus, claims based on design defect require that the proposed alternative design provide an increase in safety sufficient to establish causation.

GRUNDBERG v. UPJOHN CO.

Supreme Court of Utah, 1991.
813 P.2d 89.

Durham, Justice:

* * * The issue before us is whether Utah adopts the "unavoidably unsafe products" exception to strict products liability as set forth in Comment k to section 402A of the Restatement (Second) of Torts (1965)("comment k"). This question presents an unanswered issue of law for original disposition by this court.

We hold that a drug approved by the United States Food and Drug Administration ("FDA"), properly prepared, compounded, packaged, and distributed, cannot as a matter of law be "defective" in the absence of proof of inaccurate, incomplete, misleading, or fraudulent information furnished by the manufacturer in connection with FDA approval. We acknowledge that by characterizing all FDA-approved prescription medications as "unavoidably unsafe," we are expanding the literal interpretation of comment k.

The following facts are taken from the federal district court's certification order. Mildred Lucille Coats died at age 83 from gunshot wounds inflicted by her daughter, Ilo Grundberg, on June 19, 1988. Grundberg and Janice Gray, the personal representative of Coat's estate, brought this action, alleging that Grundberg shot her mother as a result of ingesting the drug Halcion, a prescription drug manufactured by defendant Upjohn to treat insomnia.[11]

Plaintiffs allege that Grundberg took a .5 milligram dose of Halcion the day she shot her mother. They allege that this dose was recommended by her physician and was consistent with Upjohn's recommended dosage. Plaintiffs assert that Grundberg shot her mother while in a state of Halcion-induced intoxication, which allegedly included side effects such as depression, psychosis, depersonalization, aggressive assaultive behavior, and homicidal compulsion.

* * * Plaintiffs claim that Upjohn failed to adequately warn about certain adverse side effects of Halcion and that Halcion was defectively designed. The failure-to-warn claim is scheduled for trial. The strict liability claim based on design defect is the subject of Upjohn's pending summary judgment motion, the outcome of which depends on this court's resolution of the certified question.

The parties agree that the Restatement (Second) of Torts section 402A, comment k (1965) and the principles it embodies provide an exemption from strict liability for a claimed design defect in the case of products that are "unavoidably unsafe." * * *

Specifically, the issues we address at the request of the federal court are:

1. Does Utah adopt the "unavoidably unsafe products" exception to strict products liability as set forth in comment k to section 402A of the Restatement (Second) of Torts (1965)?

    (a) If Utah does adopt comment k, should FDA-approved prescription drugs be deemed as a matter of law to have satisfied the "unavoidably unsafe" prerequisite to the comment k exception, or should that determination be made on a case-by-case basis?

    (b) If Utah does adopt comment k, and if it is further determined that its application to FDA-approved prescription drugs ought to be made on a case-by-case basis, is such determination a threshold question for the trial court or a question properly to be presented to the jury?

* * *

11. Halcion is the trade name of the drug triazolam.

In its entirety, comment k reads:

k. *Unavoidably unsafe products.* There are some products which, in the present state of human knowledge, are quite incapable of being made safe for their intended and ordinary use. These are especially common in the field of drugs. An outstanding example is the vaccine for the Pasteur treatment of rabies, which not uncommonly leads to very serious and damaging consequences when it is injected. Since the disease itself invariably leads to a dreadful death, both the marketing and the use of the vaccine are fully justified, notwithstanding the unavoidable high degree of risk which they involve. Such a product, properly prepared, and accompanied by proper directions and warning, is not defective, nor is it unreasonably dangerous. The same is true of many other drugs, vaccines, and the like, many of which for this very reason cannot legally be sold except to physicians, or under the prescription of a physician. It is also true in particular of many new or experimental drugs as to which, because of lack of time and opportunity for sufficient medical experience, there can be no assurance of safety, or perhaps even of purity of ingredients, but such experience as there is justifies the marketing and use of the drug notwithstanding a medically recognizable risk. The seller of such products, again with the qualification that they are properly prepared and marketed, and proper warning is given, where the situation calls for it, is not to be held to strict liability for unfortunate consequences attending their use, merely because he has undertaken to supply the public with an apparently useful and desirable product, attended with a known but apparently reasonable risk.

* * *

We agree with comment k's basic proposition—that there are some products that have dangers associated with their use even though they are used as intended. We also agree that the seller of such products, when the products are properly prepared and marketed and distributed with appropriate warnings, should not be held strictly liable for the "unfortunate consequences" attending their use. Thus, we adopt comment k's basic policy as the law to be applied in this state and must now turn to the issue of how to apply that policy.

* * *

By its terms, comment k excepts unavoidably unsafe products from strict liability only to the extent that the plaintiff alleges a design defect; comment k's immunity from strict liability does not extend to strict liability claims based on a manufacturing flaw or an inadequate warning. The purpose of comment k is to protect from strict liability products that cannot be designed more safely. If, however, such products are mismanufactured or unaccompanied by adequate warnings, the seller may be liable even if the plaintiff cannot establish the seller's negligence.

* * *

Even in the case of a clearly alleged design defect, however, comment k is unclear on the scope of its protection.

* * *

Some courts have applied comment k on a case-by-case basis, conditioning application of the exemption on a finding that the drug is in fact "unavoidably unsafe." see Feldman v. Lederle Laboratories, 97 N.J. 429, 479 A.2d 374, 382–83 (1984)(involving allegations of failure to warn, but stating, "Whether a drug is unavoidably unsafe should be decided on a case-by-case basis. . . .")

California was the first state to fashion a risk/benefit test to determine which drugs are entitled to comment k protection. In Kearl v. Lederle Laboratories, 172 Cal.App.3d 812, 218 Cal.Rptr. 453 (1985), the California Court of Appeal specifically discussed the problems society would face by subjecting drugs to the same accountability as other products, allowing unlimited redress for plaintiffs injured by pharmaceutical products. Such problems, the court noted, include delayed availability of needed drugs and imposition of the costs of research, development, and marketing of new products beyond that which manufacturers, especially small manufacturers, might be willing to risk. (quoting Feldman, 460 A.2d at 209).

The Kearl court expressed discomfort, however, with the "mechanical" method by which many appellate courts had concluded that drugs are entitled to special treatment. Thus, Kearl set forth a risk/benefit analysis to be carried out by the trial court on a case-by-case basis. Under this approach, a product may be deemed unavoidably unsafe and thus exempt from a strict liability design defect cause of action only if the court concludes that (1) the product was intended to provide an exceptionally important benefit, and (2) the risk posed was substantial and unavoidable when distributed.

Idaho adopted and to some extent refined the Kearl approach in Toner v. Lederle Laboratories, 112 Idaho 328, 732 P.2d 297 (1987), a case addressing a suit against the manufacturer of a vaccine to immunize against diphtheria, pertussis, and tetanus ("DPT").

* * *

In direct contrast to those courts applying comment k's immunity on a case-by-case basis are courts holding that all prescription drugs are entitled as a matter of law to the exemption from strict liability claims based on design defect. In Brown v. Superior Court, 44 Cal.3d 1049, 245 Cal.Rptr. 412, 751 P.2d 470 (1988), the court addressed claims brought by plaintiffs who sued drug companies for injuries allegedly arising from their mothers' in utero exposure to diethylstilbestrol, a synthetic hormone marketed for use during pregnancy. The court weighed the problem of whether imposing strict liability on drug manufacturers comports with the traditional goals of tort law, namely, deterrence and cost distribution. The court acknowledged that a drug might be safer if pharmaceutical companies withheld it from the market until scientific skill and knowledge advanced to the point where all dangerous side effects could be discovered. There was concern, however, that this delay, when added to the delay normally required for the FDA to approve a new drug, would not serve the public welfare. The court cited examples of several potentially useful drugs being withdrawn from the market or their availability seriously curtailed because of the liability crisis.

The Brown court acknowledged the appeal of the Kearl cost/benefit approach, yet found the "mini-trial" procedure unworkable because of its negative impact on the development and marketing of new drugs. Another of the Brown court's objections to Kearl was that it left the trial court to hear and resolve mixed questions of law and fact, placing the trial court in the role of fact finder. The court found the cost/benefit test too open-ended and predicted that it would lead to disparate treatment of the same drug by different judges.

The Brown court stressed three public policies mitigating against imposing strict liability for prescription drugs. First, drug manufacturers might stop producing valuable drugs because of lost profits resulting from lawsuits or the inability to secure adequate insurance. Second, consumers have a vested interest in prompt availability of new pharmaceutical products. Imposing strict liability for design defects might cause manufacturers to delay placing new products on the market, even after those products receive FDA approval. Finally, the added expense of insuring against strict liability and additional research programs might cause the cost of medication to increase to the extent that it would no longer be affordable to consumers.

* * *

In reviewing the approaches of other jurisdictions toward strict products liability for design defects in drug products, we are troubled by the lack of uniformity and certainty inherent in the case-by-case approach and fear the resulting disincentive for pharmaceutical manufacturers to develop new products.

* * *

We agree with Brown that the case-by-case method first articulated in Kearl is unworkable. * * * We find the Brown result more in line with the public policy considerations in the important area of pharmaceutical product design. We do not agree, however, with the Brown court's apparent attempt to use the plain language of comment k as the vehicle for exempting all prescription drugs from strict liability rather than relying on the policies underlying that comment.

The American Law Institute's restatements are drafted by legal scholars who attempt to summarize the state of the law in a given area, predict how the law is changing, and suggest the direction the law should take. The restatement serves an appropriate advisory role to courts in approaching unsettled areas of law. We emphasize, however, that section 402A of the Restatement (Second) of Torts, as drafted in 1965, is not binding on our decision in this case except insofar as we explicitly adopt its various doctrinal principles. We agree with the principle comment k embodies, that manufacturers of unavoidably dangerous products should not be liable for a claim of design defect. We are persuaded that all prescription drugs should be classified as unavoidably dangerous in design because of their unique nature and value, the elaborate regulatory system overseen by the

FDA, the difficulties of relying on individual lawsuits as a forum in which to review a prescription drug's design, and the significant public policy considerations noted in Brown. We therefore reach the same conclusion as did the California Supreme Court in Brown, albeit pursuant to a slightly different rationale.

III. UNIQUE CHARACTERISTICS OF DRUGS

* * *

Despite inherent risks, and in contrast to any other product, society has determined that prescription medications provide a unique benefit and so should be available to physicians with appropriate warnings and guidance as to use. The federal government has established an elaborate regulatory system, overseen by the FDA, to control the approval and distribution of these drugs. See 21 U.S.C. §§ 301–393. No other class of products is subject to such special restrictions or protections in our society.

IV. FDA REGULATION

Congress created the FDA to "protect consumers from dangerous products." United States v. Sullivan, 332 U.S. 689, 696, 68 S.Ct. 331, 335, 92 L.Ed. 297 (1948). In its role as "both a health promoter ... and ... a public protector," the FDA employs a comprehensive scheme of premarket screening and post-market surveillance to ensure the safety and efficacy of all licensed medications. 50 Fed.Reg. 7452 (1985).

Before licensing a new medication, the FDA employs an extensive screening mechanism to ensure that the potential benefits of the product outweigh any associated risks. The manufacturer initiates the review by submitting an Investigational New Drug Application ("IND"), containing information about the drug's chemistry, manufacturing, pharmacology, and toxicology. See 21 U.S.C. s 355(b)(1)(Supp.1991); 21 C.F.R. s 312.21 (1990). If the FDA approves the IND, the drug's sponsor may gather data on clinical safety and efficacy needed for a New Drug Application ("NDA"), the formal license application. The NDA must include very detailed reports of all animal studies and clinical testing performed with the drug, reports of any adverse reactions, and any other pertinent information from world-wide scientific literature. 21 U.S.C. s 355(b)(Supp.1991); 21 C.F.R. s 314.50 (1990).

The new drug approval process can require years of testing and review. By the time an NDA is submitted, it often consists of thousands of pages of material describing studies of the drug in several hundred to several thousand patients. See 47 Fed.Reg. 46626 (Oct. 19, 1982). The FDA carefully scrutinizes the data supporting the NDA, requiring "substantial evidence" consisting of adequate and well-controlled investigations. 21 U.S.C. s 355(d)(Supp.1991). The application is reviewed by physicians, pharmacologists, chemists, microbiologists, statisticians, and other professionals within the FDA's National Center for Drugs and Biologics who are experienced in evaluating new drugs. 47 Fed.Reg. 46626 (Oct. 19, 1982). Recommendations by those professionals are then reviewed by management personnel within the National Center for Drugs and Biologics before the FDA makes a final determination to approve or reject the new drug application. Id.

Elaborate premarket screening, however, does not ensure review of approved prescription medications where adverse reactions may appear after extensive preapproval testing. For this reason, the FDA also conducts extensive post-market surveillance. All reports of adverse drug reactions ("ADRs") must be reported to the FDA, regardless of whether the physician, the manufacturer, or others believe the reaction to be drug-related. 21 C.F.R. s 314.80(b). The manufacturer must also periodically submit reports as to what actions it took in response to ADRs and must submit data from any post-marketing studies, reports in the scientific literature, and foreign marketing experience. 21 C.F.R. ss 314.80(b), .80(c). The FDA has authority to enforce these reporting requirements; any failure to comply may subject a manufacturer to civil and criminal penalties. 21 U.S.C. ss 332–34 (1972 & Supp.1991). In response to its surveillance findings, the FDA may require labeling changes or if necessary withdraw NDA approval and thereby revoke the license to market the medication. Id. at s 355(e).

We find this extensive regulatory scheme capable of and appropriate for making the preliminary determination regarding whether a prescription drug's benefits outweigh its risks. The structured follow-up program imposed by law ensures that drugs are not placed on the market without continued monitoring for adverse consequences that would render the FDA's initial risk/benefit analysis invalid. Allowing individual courts and/or juries to continually reevaluate a drug's risks and benefits ignores the processes of this expert regulatory body and the other avenues of recovery available to plaintiffs.

* * *

V. Proper Forum for Risk/Benefit Analysis

Finally, we do not believe that a trial court in the context of a products liability action is the proper forum to determine whether, as a whole, a particular prescription drug's benefits outweighed its risks at the time of distribution. In a case-by-case analysis, one court or jury's determination that a particular drug is or is not "defectively designed" has no bearing on any future case. As a result, differences of opinion among courts in differing jurisdictions leaves unsettled a drug manufacturer's liability for any given drug. Although the FDA may have internal differences of opinion regarding whether a particular new drug application should be approved, the individuals making the ultimate judgment will have the benefit of years of experience in reviewing such products, scientific expertise in the area, and access to the volumes of data they can compel manufacturers to produce. Nor is the FDA subject to the inherent limitations of the trial process, such as the rules of evidence, restrictions on expert testimony, and scheduling demands.[9]

---

9. There is also a certain moral question to be addressed when determining whether a product's benefit outweighs its risk when faced with the reality of an injured plaintiff. For example, in the case of a vaccine, certain benefits of the drug's availability will accrue to group A, the individuals who are prevented from contracting the disease. A smaller number of individuals, however, may contract the disease and react violently to a component of the drug or, as some other result of the drug's properties, suffer terribly. Under a case-by-case approach, courts or juries must ask which is a more significant

One commentator has argued that courts as a whole are unsuited to render responsible judgments in the design defect area generally. See Henderson, Judicial Review of Manufacturers' Conscious Design Choices: The Limits of Adjudication, 73 Colum.L.Rev. 1531 (1973). He argues that decisions in this area are arbitrary due to their "polycentric" nature in which "each point for decision is related to all the others as are the strands of a spider web." Id. at 1536. These issues are difficult to litigate because

> [i]f one strand is pulled, a complex pattern of readjustments will occur throughout the entire web. If another strand is pulled, the relationships among all the strands will again be readjusted. A lawyer seeking to base [an] argument upon established principle and required to address himself in discourse to each of a dozen strands, or issues, would find [the] task frustratingly impossible. Id.

Although we do not accept the notion that courts are unsuited to address design defect claims in any products liability action, we do agree that prescription drug design presents precisely this type of "polycentric" problem. A drug is designed to be effectively administered to specific individuals for one or a number of indications. To determine whether a drug's benefit outweighs its risk is inherently complex because of the manufacturer's conscious design choices regarding the numerous chemical properties of the product and their relationship to the vast physiologic idiosyncracies of each consumer for whom the drug is designed. Society has recognized this complexity and in response has reposed regulatory authority in the FDA. Relying on the FDA's screening and surveillance standards enables courts to find liability under circumstances of inadequate warning, mismanufacture, improper marketing, or misinforming the FDA—avenues for which courts are better suited. Although this approach denies plaintiffs one potential theory on which to rely in a drug products liability action, the benefits to society in promoting the development, availability, and reasonable price of drugs justifies this conclusion.

In light of the strong public interest in the availability and affordability of prescription medications, the extensive regulatory system of the FDA, and the avenues of recovery still available to plaintiffs by claiming inadequate warning, mismanufacture, improper marketing, or misrepresenting information to the FDA, we conclude that a broad grant of immunity from strict liability claims based on design defects should be extended to FDA-approved prescription drugs in Utah.

HALL, C.J., and ZIMMERMAN, J., concur.

STEWART, JUSTICE (dissenting):

I dissent. The majority holds that a drug that is avoidably unsafe to human life or health is exempt from strict liability for design defects if approved by the FDA, even though alternative drugs can provide the same, or even better, therapy, with less risk to life or health. Thus, such FDA-approved drugs as various decongestants, expectorants, deodorants, hair

---

interest: efficacy with respect to group A versus harm to group B? The FDA must ask the same question: Does the benefit of this product outweigh its risk? The distinction is that the FDA is in a more objective and informed posture to make that determination.

growth stimulants, skin moisturizers, and cough and cold remedies,[1] for example, have the same immunity as rabies or polio vaccines or medications essential in the treatment of cancer, heart disease, or AIDS. I see no basis for according drugs used to treat comparatively minor ailments a blanket immunity from strict liability for design defects if they are unreasonably dangerous to those who use them.

* * *

I agree with Justice Huntley of the Idaho Supreme Court, who stated:

[N]o state supreme court has yet become convinced that the FDA has either adequate staffing, expertise, or data base to warrant its being substituted for the judicial system. .... I fear the day when any supreme court can be convinced that an agency such as the FDA, no matter how well-intentioned, can supplant the American judicial system.

Toner v. Lederle Laboratories, 112 Idaho 328, 732 P.2d 297, 313 (1987) (Huntley, J., concurring specially).

* * *

Numerous congressional investigations have demonstrated that the FDA has often approved drugs in complete ignorance of critical information relating to the hazards of such drugs which was contained either in its own files or in the published medical literature, or both.

* * *

In relying on the efficacy of FDA approval procedures as the basis for dispensing with the judicial remedy of product liability, the majority simply ignores FDA failures to protect the public against unnecessary and unacceptable risks.

* * *

Proposals before Congress and rules promulgated by the FDA to make it easier for pharmaceutical companies to obtain FDA approval for new drugs would dilute even further the safety and efficacy standards for FDA approval of drugs. See Note, Regulation of Investigational New Drugs: "Giant Step for the Sick and Dying?", 77 Georgetown L.J. 463 (1988). Perhaps truly unavoidably unsafe drugs intended to treat life-threatening ailments should be more easily available to the public, but a lessening of safety standards is an argument for strict liability, not against. Profit motivation is likely to lead to many more unnecessarily dangerous drugs.

* * *

Certain drugs clearly qualify for comment k exemption, even though the drugs' risk may be comparatively great. A drug's social utility may be so great, for example, a chemotherapeutic agent used for treatment of cancer, that it would obviously qualify for comment k exemption. Other

---

1. The Physicians' Desk Reference (1990 ed.) includes prescription drugs in each of the categories stated in the text.

drugs, such as sleeping compounds or dandruff cures, whose social utility may not be of such a high order, would not automatically qualify.

* * *

The majority opinion states that a case-by-case analysis would leave drug companies uncertain regarding questions of immunity and would result in patchwork verdicts when a drug may be found to be subject to comment k exemption in one case but not subject to the exemption in another case. That consideration has little merit, in my view. We tolerate nonuniformity of result in negligence cases all the time. Nothing this Court does can bring about uniformity of result with respect to drugs. The states are already divided on the issue of whether FDA approval of a drug should confer immunity from design defects, although it appears that no state has gone as far as Utah now does. Suffice to say, a number of courts apply comment k on a case-by-case basis—a task that cannot be avoided even under the majority's position if a strict liability claim is coupled with a negligence claim, as is usually the case.

* * *

In this case, plaintiff Ilo Marie Grundberg was taking a variety of medications for chronic depression and anxiety. Halcion, the medication at issue here, had first been prescribed for Mrs. Grundberg on May 21, 1987. In December 1987, Mrs. Grundberg lost her job and, shortly thereafter, moved with her mother, Mildred Coats, to Hurricane, Utah, where they lived together in a mobile home. On June 19, 1988, Mrs. Grundberg took three medications: Valium, codeine, and Halcion. Later that night, she shot and killed her mother. Mrs. Grundberg was charged with criminal homicide. Because of alienists' reports, the Washington County prosecutor dropped all criminal charges on February 7, 1989. Mrs. Grundberg and Janice Gray, the personal representative of Mrs. Coats' estate, filed this civil action later in 1989. At issue in this case is whether Halcion was the cause of Mrs. Grundberg's bizarre behavior on the night of the homicide.

* * *

[The dissenting opinion of Associate Chief Justice Howe is omitted]

Notes

1. Why do you think Justice Stewart is willing to grant Comment k immunity to chemotherapy drugs used to fight cancer and not to drugs used for more mundane purposes such as fighting dandruff or insomnia? Is it clear that the utility of first type of drug always outweighs its risk?

2. For a review of cases discussing whether products, including drugs, are unavoidably unsafe, see Annotation, Products Liability: What is an "Unavoidably Unsafe" Product, 70 A.L.R.4th 16 (1989 & Supp.1990); Tansy v. Dacomed Corp., 890 P.2d 881 (Okla.1994).

3. Most jurisdictions have refused to conclude that all prescription drugs are unavoidably unsafe. Rather, Comment k is an affirmative defense to be assessed on a case-by-case basis. See Savina v. Sterling Drug, Inc., 247 Kan. 105, 795 P.2d 915, 924 (Kan.1990); White v. Wyeth Lab., 40 Ohio St.3d 390, 533 N.E.2d 748, 752 (Ohio 1988). If a jurisdiction does follow the case-by-case

approach, should the initial determination as to whether the drug is unavoidably unsafe be made by the judge or left to the jury?

A few cases have completely rejected Comment *k* for all drugs. *See* Shanks v. Upjohn Co., 835 P.2d 1189 (Alaska 1992); Allison v. Merck and Co., Inc., 110 Nev. 762, 878 P.2d 948 (1994). One of the reason the Alaska court gave for rejecting Comment *k* was that a risk-benefit test "offers the manufacturers of those products intended to be protected by Comment *k* an opportunity to avoid liability for strict liability claims based on a design defect theory. * * * We recognize that by holding that the liability of drug manufacturers should be measured by the second prong of the Barker test, we are taking a position similar to those jurisdictions which apply Comment k to prescription drugs on a case-by-case basis. However, we arrive at this result without specifically relying on Comment k." *Shanks*, 835 P.2d at 1198. Is Comment *k* an unnecessary redundancy in jurisdictions that have adopted a risk-utility test in design defect cases?

4. Most courts that have considered the question have found that Comment *k* applies to medical devices, especially those which are implanted in the human body. See Harwell v. Amer. Med. Systems, Inc., 803 F.Supp. 1287 (M.D.Tenn.1992) and Tansy v. Dacomed Corp., 890 P.2d 881 (Okl.1994)(penile prosthesis protected under Comment *k*); McKee v. Moore, 648 P.2d 21 (Okl. 1982) and Terhune v. A.H. Robins, 90 Wn.2d 9, 577 P.2d 975 (1978)(Comment *k* applied to an IUD); Phelps v. Sherwood, 836 F.2d 296 (7th Cir.1987) and Brooks v. Medtronic Inc., 750 F.2d 1227 (4th Cir.1984)(pacemaker and heart catheter covered under Comment *k*). But see Hawkinson v. A.H. Robins Co., 595 F.Supp. 1290 (D.Colo.1984)(Dalkon Shield); Coursen v. A.H. Robins, 764 F.2d 1329 (9th Cir.1985)(Dalkon Shield). See 70 A.L.R.4th 16 (1989) for a review of these cases.

5. The *Restatement (Third) of Torts: Products Liability* (Tentative Draft No. 2) takes a different approach to prescription drugs and medical devices.

§ 8 Liability of Commercial Seller or Distributor for Harm Caused by Prescription Drugs and Medical Devices

(a) A manufacturer of a prescription drug or medical device who commercially sells or otherwise distributes a defective product is subject to liability for harm to persons caused by the product defect. A prescription drug or medical device is one that may be legally sold or otherwise distributed only pursuant to a health care provider's prescription.

(b) For purposes of liability under Subsection (a), a product is defective if at the time of sale or distribution:

(1) the drug or medical device contains a manufacturing defect as defined in § 2(a); or;

(2) the drug or medical device is not reasonably safe due to defective design or because of inadequate instructions or warnings.

(c) A prescription drug or medical device is not reasonably safe due to defective design when the foreseeable risks of harm posed by the drug or medical device are sufficiently great in relation to its foreseeable therapeutic benefits so that no reasonable health care provider, knowing of such foreseeable risks and therapeutic benefits, would prescribe the drug or medical device for any class of patients.

(d) A prescription drug or medical device is not reasonably safe because of inadequate instructions or warnings when

(1) reasonable instructions or warnings regarding foreseeable risks of harm posed by the drug or medical device are not provided to prescribing and other health care providers who are in a position to reduce the risks of harm in accordance with the instructions or warnings; or

(2) reasonable instructions or warnings regarding foreseeable risks of harm posed by the drug or medical device are not provided directly to the patient when the manufacturer knew or had reason to know that no health care provider would be in a position to reduce the risk of harm in accordance with the instructions or warnings.

As noted in Comment *f* accompanying § 8,

A defendant prescription drug or device manufacturer defeats plaintiff's design claim by establishing one or more contexts in which its product would be prescribed by a reasonable, informed health care provider. * * * Given this very demanding standard, liability is likely to be imposed only under unusual circumstances. The court has the responsibility to determine when the plaintiff has met the burden of production for this demanding standard.

How does § 8 allocate the burden of proof in prescription drug design defect cases? For one point of view on this question see Tansy v. Dacomed Corp., 890 P.2d 881, 894 (Okl.1994)(concurring opinion of Justice Opala). See Teresa Moran Schwartz, *Prescription Products and the Proposed Restatement (Third)*, 61 Tenn. L. Rev. 1357(1994).

6. *Why are drugs special?* Comment *b* of § 8 offers three rationales for giving special treatment to prescription drugs and medical devices: (1) these products present a unique set of risks and benefits because what may be harmful to one person may provide net benefits to another, (2) governmental regulatory agencies adequately review new prescription drugs and devices, effectively keeping dangerous designs from consumers, (3) there is a "learned intermediary" (a treating physician) between the consumer and the manufacturer who is able to direct the right drugs and devices to the right patients. (We discuss the "learned intermediary rule" in the warning defect section, *infra*).

With respect to the first two rationales, could not the same arguments be made about many other products, including automobiles and motorcycles? How about aircraft?

3. Warning Defects

JOHNSON v. AMERICAN CYANAMID CO.

Supreme Court of Kansas, 1986.
239 Kan. 279, 718 P.2d 1318.

McFARLAND, JUSTICE:

Emil E. Johnson brought this personal injury action alleging he had contracted poliomyelitis as a result of his infant daughter having been vaccinated by defendant physician, Vernon Branson, utilizing Orimune, an oral polio vaccine manufactured by Lederle Laboratories (a division of defendant American Cyanamid Company). Henceforth in the opinion, the manufacturer of the vaccine will be referred to as American Cyanamid. The jury was instructed on comparison of fault as between the two defendants (no issue of fault was submitted as to the plaintiff). The jury assessed 100% of fault against defendant American Cyanamid and awarded $2,000,000.00 actual damages and $8,000,000.00 punitive damages. American Cyanamid appeals from the judgment against it but specifically does not appeal from the jury's finding of zero fault on the part of defendant Branson.

FACTS RELATIVE TO PLAINTIFF'S ILLNESS

On September 26, 1975, plaintiff took his infant daughter Laurie to the child's pediatrician, Dr. Vernon Branson, where Orimune, an oral polio vaccine manufactured by American Cyanamid, was administered to her. The sequence of polio vaccination was completed by additional administration of the same vaccine by the same physician on November 24, 1975, and January 14, 1976. In December of 1975 plaintiff became ill and was admitted to the University of Kansas Medical Center on December 9 where his illness was diagnosed as bulbar paralytic poliomyelitis. Plaintiff contends he is totally disabled as a result of the disease. At trial, it was contested whether or not Laurie's vaccination program was the cause of plaintiff's illness, but this is not an issue on appeal.

HISTORY OF POLIO VACCINES

By virtue of the nature of claims of liability asserted against American Cyanamid, much of the evidence at trial concerned the history of the disease poliomyelitis and efforts to control the disease, namely, the development of vaccines and the federal government's efforts to vaccinate the public. Polio was first identified as a disease in the 19th century. Its occurrence became more frequent and in 1952 it claimed 57,897 victims in the United States alone. The federal government and private medical research facilities commenced an all-out effort to conquer the dreaded killer and crippler of so many children and adults. A major breakthrough occurred when Dr. Jonas Salk developed a killed or "inactivated" polio vaccine. This vaccine must be administered by injection. By 1955 the Salk vaccine was being distributed extensively in the United States and new cases of polio were reduced to less than 5,000 per year by 1959. In the late 1950's a new polio vaccine was developed by Dr. Albert Sabin and was widely tested in Europe. The Sabin vaccine is a live polio vaccine which contains greatly weakened or attenuated polio virus. The Sabin vaccine must be given orally.

Although the Salk vaccine had greatly reduced the incidence of polio, the disease remained a significant health threat and pressure was mounting for a federally funded immunization program to bring the disease under control and, it was hoped, eliminate it. By 1961, the bitter controversy was in full bloom as to which of the two types of vaccines—Sabin or Salk—should be the weapon used in the battle against the disease. At that time only the Salk vaccine was being produced in this country although the Sabin vaccine had been used very successfully in Europe. The American Medical Association urged, in 1961, the use of the Sabin vaccine. The federal government solicited American drug firms to produce the Sabin vaccine. United States manufacturers of the Salk vaccine opposed the introduction of the Sabin vaccine. Three manufacturers agreed to manufacture the Sabin vaccine (including American Cyanamid). The Sabin vaccine rapidly replaced the Salk vaccine in the United States and no Salk vaccine has been manufactured in this country since 1968. American Cyanamid is the only United States firm manufacturing polio vaccine at the present time and it manufactures the Sabin type.

* * *

There are advantages to the Sabin vaccine. It is administered orally— usually on a sugar cube to individuals old enough to eat sugar cubes. The Salk vaccine can only be injected through a needle. The injections are time-consuming and require individual administration by trained medical personnel. Further, injections are less well received by poorly educated persons and resistance thereto is stronger. Additionally, there is substantial medical evidence that the immunity induced by the Sabin vaccine is longer lasting and does not require boosters as may be necessary with the Salk vaccine.

Ironically, the very cause of the longer-lasting immunity of the Sabin vaccine gives rise to the major drawback of this vaccine. The Sabin vaccine must be given orally, as the weakened virus gives immunity by proliferating in the intestines, thereby triggering the body's immune system. For reasons unknown, occasionally, but on a rather predictable ratio of incidence, the virus reproduced in the intestinal tract is a virulent virus, not the weakened Sabin virus. When this occurs, the individual receiving the virus, and persons in close contact with such individual, may acquire polio as a result of the vaccination. This unfortunate event occurs some five to ten times each year in the United States. This risk from the Sabin vaccine has been there from the beginning of its usage. It is a known risk and has been argued at every phase in the long-standing Salk–Sabin controversy.

The very ability of the Sabin vaccine to infest others is, in the broad public health view, a plus factor. Unlike the Salk vaccine, the Sabin vaccine can vaccinate persons in contact with vaccinated persons because the intestines secrete the virus. Usually, the virus so secreted is the same weakened type as was used in the vaccine. Hence, such individuals are vaccinated without actual medical vaccinations. From a public health standpoint, more people can be so vaccinated than could otherwise be reached. Kansas requires polio vaccination before children are admitted to elementary school or state licensed child care centers or preschools.

Being fully informed of this known risk, the federal government approved the Sabin vaccine and purchased large quantities of it for its mass public immunization program. The decision was made that the Sabin vaccine would be the weapon utilized to fight the serious public health problem of polio. The program has been so successful in reducing the incidence of "wild" polio that an individual in the United States now has about the same risk of contracting "wild" polio as he or she does of contracting polio through vaccination or contact with a vaccinee. Virtually all of the Western world utilizes the Sabin vaccine over the Salk vaccine in its public health programs. Finland, by virtue of a recent polio outbreak which included some individuals previously immunized by the Salk vaccine, is now using the Sabin vaccine in its public health program.

* * *

The Sabin-type vaccine was the vaccine of choice recommended by all major health organizations in the United States in 1975. Its production by American Cyanamid was the result of the federal government's solicitation of the firm to manufacture the Sabin vaccine which public health authorities believed, based on a vast array of scientific literature, was necessary to combat a major health problem. The seed strains of virus utilized in the manufacture of the vaccine by American Cyanamid are supplied by the federal government and the vaccine's manufacture is closely monitored by the federal government.

Plaintiff acquired contact polio from his child, the vaccinee. The fact that this type of occurrence would happen on an extremely infrequent, but rather predictable, ratio was known from the time Sabin-type vaccines were introduced. The remote risk of contact polio is inherent in the Sabin-type vaccine and cannot be eliminated. The risk could not be altered by a change in the manufacturing process. The phenomenon of contact polio was not newly discovered information acquired by American Cyanamid and hidden from public view. * * * Plaintiff seeks to impose liability, in the first instance, on what is, in essence, a design defect theory. That is, that the Salk-type vaccine (a killed virus vaccine) is a better product and American Cyanamid should be held liable for producing a Sabin-type vaccine (live virus vaccine) rather than the Salk-type vaccine. Plaintiff is seeking to impose strict liability in tort based upon design defect (the inadequate warning claim of liability will be discussed later). Section 402A of the Restatement (Second) of Torts (1963) states: [The court here quotes § 402A and Comment *k*.]

* * *

Orimune, the Sabin-type vaccine, is an "unavoidably unsafe product" that is an "apparently useful and desirable product, attended with a known but apparently reasonable risk" as a matter of law. Public policy requires that the mere manufacture of the vaccine not be actionable on the ground of design defect. The trial judge should have heard the evidence on this issue outside the presence of the jury and made the determination thereon. There is no claim that the vaccine administered to plaintiff's child was improperly manufactured or that a defective product was delivered. The vaccine was properly prepared and marketed and was exactly what it was intended to be. As a matter of law there is no manufacturing or design defect in the product at issue herein.

This leaves the only possible liability in the adequacy of the warning provided by the manufacturer.

In Wooderson v. Ortho Pharmaceutical Corp., 235 Kan. 387, 681 P.2d 1038, previously cited, this court discusses the duty to warn relative to drugs. As in the case before us, the drug in Wooderson was sold to a physician who, in turn, prescribed/administered the drug to the patient. As recognized in Wooderson, under such circumstances the "learned intermediary" concept comes into play. The manufacturer's duty is to adequately warn the physician of a known risk.

In determining warning issues, the test is reasonableness. To impose liability on a manufacturer, the plaintiff must show negligence on the part of the manufacturer.

* * *

Was the warning adequate as a matter of law? That is, was it a reasonable warning by a manufacturer to a learned intermediary? Was the manufacturer negligent in the warning supplied?

The warning provided herein states:

"ADVERSE REACTIONS

"Individual patients have at times attributed symptoms or conditions to the vaccine by reason of time relationship, but these in general have been minor and apparently unrelated." Expert opinion is in agreement that the administration of live oral poliovirus vaccines is generally an effective and safe method of protecting populations against the natural disease. *Paralytic disease following the ingestion of live poliovirus vaccines has been reported in individuals receiving the vaccine, and* in some instances, in persons who were in close *contact with subjects who had been given live oral poliovirus vaccine.* Fortunately, *such occurrences are rare,* but considering the epidemiological evidence developed with respect to the total group of 'vaccine related cases' it is believed by some that at least some of the cases were caused by the vaccine.

"*The estimated risk of vaccine-induced paralytic disease occurring in vaccinees or those in close contact with vaccinees is extremely low. A total of approximately 30 of such cases were reported for the 8 year period covering 1963 to 1970, during which time about 147,000,000 doses of the vaccine were distributed nationally. Even though this risk is low, it should always be a source of consideration.*" (Emphasis supplied.)

The warning obviously warns that in rare instances a person in close contact with a vaccinee may develop polio. This is exactly what happened to the plaintiff herein. This, then, is not a failure to warn question, but rather a question of the adequacy of the warning. Wooderson v. Ortho Pharmaceutical Corp., 235 Kan. 387, 681 P.2d 1038, previously cited, although couched in terms of an "adequacy of warning" issue, actually involves a failure to warn, as the injury received by plaintiff was not included in the warning.

Plaintiff contends the first paragraph of the warning waters down the total warning. We do not believe so. It deals with what patients have reported rather than scientific fact. If a lay person takes a drug or receives a vaccine and two days later is suffering from an abscessed tooth, an attack of appendicitis, or whatever, he or she tends to link the two occurrences as cause and effect regardless of any medical connection. The paragraph leaves in the possibility some minor side effects reported by patients might be medically possible.

The balance of the warning clearly states the scientific fact that some persons in close contact with vaccinees may develop a paralytic disease from such contact. It is unnecessary to describe to a physician what paralytic disease is and the seriousness of it. The warning then states the chances of this happening are "extremely low." The figures of 30 cases in a particular eight-year period during which time 147,000,000 doses were distributed are included. These figures are consistent with those provided in 1972 by the Public Health Service, and the Advisory Committee on Immunization Practices and were current in 1975 when the vaccine herein was administered.

* * *

Plaintiff contends that the warning was also inadequate because it failed to state that individuals who were not immune to the disease were at greater risk than those who were immune. It hardly takes a medical degree to know that a person immune to a virus cannot acquire the disease. Later warnings spelled this out, but this is not evidence of negligence.

Plaintiff also argues that the warning was inadequate because it did not provide information on alternate vaccines. No Salk-type vaccine was being manufactured in the United States in 1975. Although unclear, there was evidence that a Salk vaccine might have been available at that time through a Canadian source. Sabin-type vaccines were the vaccines of choice and recommended at the time (1975) by all major health organizations involved therein. The general consensus was that the Sabin-type vaccine was superior to the Salk-type vaccine. American Cyanamid had no special knowledge or new information tending to refute this. Further, this is not a case where the drug manufacturer attempted to water down the warning by direct contact with physicians intending to lull the physicians into believing the stated risk was less than the required warning indicated * * *. The warning given herein had been approved by the Federal Drug Administration and was consistent with an overwhelming bulk of the current medical opinion.

We conclude that the trial court erred in denying American Cyanamid's motion for a directed verdict herein. As a matter of law, there was no submissible theory of liability on the part of American Cyanamid.

* * *

As a note of explanation, American Cyanamid originally appealed from the entire verdict, but later specifically dismissed its appeal relative to the jury's finding that Dr. Branson had zero percentage of fault. There was no cross-appeal filed by the plaintiff herein. Does this court have any jurisdiction under these circumstances to remand the case for retrial of the issues between plaintiff and defendant Branson? We believe not. All issues between these two parties were fully litigated in the trial herein, and no party to the appeal claims any error in the trial of said issues.

The judgment against American Cyanamid is reversed.

PRAGER, JUSTICE, dissenting:

I respectfully dissent. By this decision, the majority has denied to the plaintiff his right to trial by jury and has substituted its judgment for that of the jury and the trial judge who heard the testimony of the witnesses and determined the case.

* * *

The law requires that the warning be communicated to the user of the product who may be injured by the use of the product. In situations where a product is sold and delivered to a treating physician, who then administers the product to the patient, the law requires that the manufacturer of the drug provide information and a sufficient warning to the physician who in turn is required to advise the patient or user of the drug of its dangers so that the ultimate user may make an informed decision whether to expose himself or herself to it. In the present case, the evidence is undisputed that the defendant, Dr. Vernon L. Branson, the treating physician, never at any time conveyed to the plaintiff, Emil E. Johnson, any warning whatsoever that the use of Orimune by Mr. Johnson's daughter could transmit paralytic polio either to the child or to Mr. Johnson as the parent and custodian of the child. Both Dr. Branson and Mr. Johnson testified without equivocation that no warning was ever given by the doctor to Johnson.

The evidence was likewise undisputed that some information about the drug and a warning were given by the defendants, American Cyanamid Company and Lederle Laboratories, to Dr. Branson. The primary issue presented to the jury was whether or not the warning was adequate to inform Dr. Branson of the nature of the drug, its dangers, and the possibility of using less dangerous alternatives.

In determining this case, this court must first consider the nature and scope of the warning requirement in mass inoculation cases. In this regard, the cases generally agree that an adequate warning in mass inoculation cases requires that vaccinees be directly informed in clear and simple terms by the drug manufacturer of (1) the reasonably foreseeable risk inherent in the product; (2) reasonable available alternative products and the reasonably foreseeable risks posed by such alternatives; and perhaps—in appropriate cases—(3) the reasonably foreseeable results of remaining untreated.

* * *

This rule is recognized and applied in Kearl v. Lederle Laboratories, 172 Cal.App.3d 812, 218 Cal.Rptr. 453 (1985), * * *. In Kearl, the package of OPV polio vaccine which was sold and delivered by Lederle to the doctor in 1978 contained a one-page warning insert which was described by the Kearl court as follows:

" 'IMPORTANT INFORMATION ABOUT POLIO AND POLIO VAC-CINE. *Please read this carefully.*' The information sheet briefly described polio, stated that the risk of contracting it is very low '[e]ven for someone who is not vaccinated,' and explained inter alia that oral live polio vaccine is '*one* of the best ways to prevent polio' in young children. (Italics added.) It provided: 'POSSIBLE SIDE EFFECTS FROM THE VACCINE: Oral live polio vaccine rarely produces side effects. *However, once in about every 4 million vaccinations, persons who have been vaccinated or who come in close contact with those who*

have recently been vaccinated are permanently crippled and may die.
Even though these risks are very low, they should be recognized. The
risk of side effects from the vaccine must be balanced against the risk
of the disease, both now and in the future.' (Italics added.) The
information sheet suggested that pregnant women should consult a
physician before taking the vaccine, and listed other persons who
should not take the vaccine without consulting a doctor. It then
informed the prospective vaccinee of the alternative vaccine: 'NOTE
ON INJECTABLE (KILLED) POLIO VACCINE: Besides the oral polio
vaccine, there is also a killed polio vaccine given by injection which
protects against polio after several shots. *It has no known risk of
causing paralysis.* Most polio experts do not feel it is as effective as
the oral vaccine for controlling polio in the United States. It is
recommended for persons needing polio vaccination who have low
resistance to infections (or those who live with them) and for unprotected adults traveling to a place where polio is common. It is not
widely used in this country at the present time, but it is available. If
you would like to know more about this type of polio vaccine, please
ask us.' (Italics added.)" pp. 818–19, 218 Cal.Rptr. 453.

* * *

In considering the adequacy or inadequacy of the warning in this case,
the language should be carefully analyzed.

* * *

It seems to me that, from a reading of the warning given in this case, a
reasonable person might conclude that the danger of total paralysis is not
emphasized with the same intensity which is present in the warning which
was found adequate in *Kearl v. Lederle Laboratories*, mentioned heretofore.
*It must also be emphasized that the warning in the present case did not in
any way convey to Dr. Branson the fact that there was a reasonably
available alternative product and the reasonable risks posed by such alternative product.* This element of an adequate warning was considered as
essential by the court in Kearl.

* * *

Dr. Branson was called as a witness. He testified without equivocation
that the 1975 insert involved in this case did not tell him enough. He
testified that he would have liked to have known as a practicing physician
that Lederle was expecting a certain number of contacts to get polio from
the vaccine he was giving to his babies. If he had known about it, he would
have passed the information on to Emil Johnson. He did not consider the
warning adequate, because it was not made clear that the vaccine would
cause paralytic disease. Dr. Branson testified that, since he has learned
about the use of IPV vaccine, he has used it in his practice, and, if Lederle
had told him about IPV vaccine in 1975, he would have done so then. Dr.
Branson, a competent Kansas physician, clearly testified that the warning
provided by the defendants was inadequate. Why has the majority rejected
his testimony as a matter of law?

* * *

I respectfully question how the four-person majority can hold, from the evidence in this case, that no reasonable person could conclude that the warning failed to meet the standard required by law for the protection of the American people. In my judgment, a legitimate fact issue was presented in the case which was for the jury to determine.

* * *

HERD and LOCKETT, JJ., join the foregoing dissenting opinion.

Notes

1. What do you think of the plaintiff's lawyer's failure to appeal the jury verdict in favor of Dr. Branson? Was that malpractice? Remember that he testified very persuasively for the plaintiff and was the plaintiff's personal family doctor.

2. Most courts agree with *Johnson* that in the case of prescription drugs, the manufacturer's obligation to warn extends only to doctors who prescribe the drug. This is referred to as the "learned intermediary" doctrine. *See* Niemiera v. Schneider, 114 N.J. 550, 555 A.2d 1112 (1989); Felix v. Hoffmann–LaRoche, Inc., 540 So.2d 102 (Fla.1989). Some cases have held that there is a duty to warn the consumer directly if the doctor plays a nominal rule in the decision to use the drug. *See* MacDonald v. Ortho Pharmaceutical Corp., 394 Mass. 131, 475 N.E.2d 65 (1985), cert. denied 474 U.S. 920, 106 S.Ct. 250, 88 L.Ed.2d 258; Hill v. Searle Laboratories, 884 F.2d 1064 (8th Cir.1989)(IUD). *But see*, Martin v. Ortho Pharmaceutical Corp., 169 Ill.2d 234, 214 Ill.Dec. 498, 661 N.E.2d 352 (1996)(the existence of a Federal regulation requiring manufacturers to inform patients directly of the risks and benefits involved in the use of oral contraceptives does not create a common law duty to do so. Defendant only had a duty to adequately inform the learned intermediary.)

3. Problems arise in mass immunization situations where the person being immunized is not under the care of some physician. In litigation arising out of the polio immunization campaigns of the 1960's some courts held drug manufacturers to be under an obligation to warn the people participating in the program of the dangers. *See, e.g.,* Davis v. Wyeth Laboratories, Inc., 399 F.2d 121 (9th Cir.1968); Reyes v. Wyeth Laboratories, Inc., 498 F.2d 1264 (5th Cir.1974), cert. denied, 419 U.S. 1096, 95 S.Ct. 687, 42 L.Ed.2d 688.

4. *Read and heed presumption.* A big problem for the plaintiff in such litigation is establishing that, if the warning had been given, the plaintiff might have avoided the injury. In the *Reyes* case, the court held that there was a rebuttable presumption that the consumer would have read a warning provided by the manufacturer and would have acted "so as to minimize the risks." 498 F.2d at 1281. *Accord* Cunningham v. Charles Pfizer & Co., 532 P.2d 1377 (Okl.1974). In *Cunningham* the court nevertheless held that, given the presence of rebutting evidence—12 cases of polio in Tulsa in October and November 1962 and Oklahoma's history as an "epidemic state"—"the issue of whether the plaintiff as a reasonably prudent person would have refused to take the vaccine if adequate warning had been given should have been submitted to the jury." 532 P.2d at 1382.

Most jurisdictions follow *Reyes* and entitle a plaintiff to a rebuttable presumption that he would have read and heeded an adequate warning. *See,* e.g. Coffman v. Keene Corp., 133 N.J. 581, 628 A.2d 710 (1993)(listing the states that have applied the presumption). *But see*, Riley v. American Honda

Motor Co., 259 Mont. 128, 856 P.2d 196 (1993) and Thomas v. Hoffman-LaRoche, Inc. 949 F.2d 806 (5th Cir.1992)(applying Mississippi law). Note that the seller is also entitled to presume that when an adequate warning is given the consumer will read and heed it.

5. The polio cases and the DPT vaccine cases (*see*, e.g. Shackil v. Lederle Laboratories, *supra* p. 449) present a very difficult dilemma in public policy. As noted in most of the cases, one of the great public benefits of the inoculation is the secondary immunization affect communicated to those in close relationship to the person inoculated. The virtual elimination of these diseases in this country is credited in part to that secondary affect. One danger of warning of the statistically slight, and predictable, chance that the receiver of the inoculation, or, as in *Johnson,* someone closely related, will contact the disease is that it may cause many to avoid the inoculation. This leaves not only the individual exposed to the disease, but also, if many behave in this way, it will obstruct the accomplishment of the community objective of mass immunization. One might ask first who should pay for that risk. But also one must ask whether society should deprive the individual of making an informed choice, which entails a meaningful warning. This public policy dilemma is explored to some extent in the *Reyes* case, *supra* note 4. The court in that case came down on the side of informing the recipient of the inoculation of the risk, even if it meant a less effective immunization campaign.

6. In response to this difficult problem, the Congress passed the National Childhood Vaccine Injury Act of 1986, 42 U.S.C.A. §§ 30aa–1 to–34. The statute provides for a system of no-fault compensation for individuals injured by vaccines, but limits recovery for pain and suffering. The Act is funded by a tax on drug manufacturers. Is this a reasonable response to the vaccine problem? Should it be expanded to cover other drugs and other products? *See* Victor E. Schwartz and Liberty Mahshigian, *National Childhood Vaccine Injury Act of 1986: An Ad Hoc Remedy or a Window For The Future?* 48 Ohio St. L. J. 387 (1987).

7. As a result of the litigation surrounding the polio immunization programs, drug manufacturers, in the mid 1970's, were reluctant to participate in swine flu inoculation programs without some sort of adequate insurance coverage. To get the program under way, Congress passed the Swine Flu Act of 1976, 90 Stat. 1113 (1976), under which the United States agreed to accept liability—including strict liability—if such was accepted under the law of the place where "the act or omission occurred." The remedy against the United States was made exclusive. A number of people who participated in the program contracted Guillain–Barre disease, a type of neurological disorder. In the ensuing litigation over $1,000,000,000 in damages was sought against the United States and, in several cases, the constitutionality of the Act was challenged. The constitutionality was upheld in Ducharme v. Merrill–National Laboratories, 574 F.2d 1307 (5th Cir.1978), *cert. denied,* 439 U.S. 1002, 99 S.Ct. 612, 58 L.Ed.2d 677; Dipippa v. United States, 687 F.2d 14 (3d Cir.1982). The swine flu program as well as the general legal problems arising in such mass immunization programs are discussed in N. Appel, *Liability in Mass Immunization Programs,* 1980 B.Y.U.L.Rev. 69. The success of the legislation dealing with the Swine Flu inoculation program was important in the passage of the National Childhood Vaccine Injury Act of 1986, discussed above, although, as we have seen, in that statute the federal remedy does not preempt state remedies.

8. The word "warnings" is often used as a generic term to describe two somewhat different types of information the manufacturer (and others in the chain of distribution) may provide the user. Warnings in the form of safety instructions inform consumers how to minimize any risks associated with the use of the product. Other warnings may simply notify the consumer of an irreducible risk associated with a product, which the consumer can reduce only by choosing not to use the product at all. Which type of "warning" was at issue in the *Johnson* case?

By and large, the duty to provide warnings apprising the user of irreducible risks has been imposed with respect to toxic agents and drugs. It has not expanded to products like automobiles. Why do you think this is the case? See *Restatement (Third) of Torts: Products Liability* (Tentative Draft No. 2, 1995) § 2, Comment *h*.

9. *Adequacy.* The adequacy of warnings and instructions has been a troublesome area of law. As the principal case suggests, after the fact it is often possible to imagine that a somewhat different warning might have caused the plaintiff to take precautions that would have prevented disaster. Questions of adequacy are particularly thorny in cases that do not involve the learned intermediary rule. For example, in Burch v. Amsterdam Corp., 366 A.2d 1079 (D.C.App.1976) the plaintiff was badly burned in an explosion that occurred while he was putting down floor tile using the defendant's mastic adhesive. The warning on the adhesive read as follows:

DANGER! EXTREMELY FLAMMABLE:
See Cautions elsewhere on label.
CAUTION: FLAMMABLE MIXTURE. DO NOT USE NEAR FIRE OR
FLAME
USE WITH ADEQUATE VENTILATION

The plaintiff read the label and checked to see if all flames were out but did not think of the pilot light in the kitchen stove where he was working. The appellate court reversed a trial court summary judgment for the defendant. "Given the potential for serious injury we cannot say as a matter of law that this warning adequately alerted users of the dangers inherent in the product. Among other things, an ordinary user might not have realized that 'near fire or flame' included nearby pilot lights or that fumes and vapors, as well as the adhesive itself, were extremely flammable." *Burch*, 366 A.2d at 1087–88.

Murray v. Wilson Oak Flooring Co., 475 F.2d 129 (7th Cir.1973) also involved a fire that erupted when the vapors of a mastic adhesive were ignited by a pilot light. This time the warning read (in part) as follows:

CAUTION: INFLAMMABLE MIXTURE
DO NOT USE NEAR FIRE OR FLAME

Contains Heptane—use in Well Ventilated Area

Do not smoke—Extinguish flame—including pilot lights.

Reversing a judgment n.o.v. and reinstating a plaintiff verdict, the appellate court said: "We cannot say as a matter of law that the term 'near' was sufficient to inform Murray that his spreading adhesive within four feet of a pilot light located behind a closed door and within eight feet of stove pilot lights three feet off the floor exposed him to the risk of an explosion." *Murray*, 475 F.2d at 132. Do you think you could craft a warning for this product that would result in a directed verdict in similar accidents?

In *Burch*, Chief Judge Reilly dissented. He asked: "if there was a duty to advert expressly to pilot lights in addition to 'fire and flame' , it would seem equally incumbent upon the vendors to devise a label warning against lighted pipes, cigars and cigarettes, vigil lights, candles, sparks from an electric lamp switch, a running fan or motor, and the other myriad of things which could possible ignite vapors." Do you agree, or are pilot lights in a special category?

Is there any warning that the majorities in these two cases are likely to find to be adequate as a matter of law? Perhaps the problem is not one of warnings, but design.

Judicial attitudes toward the costs and benefits of warnings have varied substantially. Compare Moran v. Faberge, Inc., 273 Md. 538, 332 A.2d 11 (1975) with Cotton v. Buckeye Gas Products Co., 840 F.2d 935 (D.C.Cir.1988). In *Moran,* two teenage girls attempted to scent a candle by pouring perfume slightly below the burning flame. The perfume was 82% alcohol and the ensuing fire seriously burned one of the girls. The perfume contained no warnings that it was highly flammable. In reversing a trial court judgment n.o.v. for the defendant, the court made the following comment: "[W]e observe that in cases such as this the cost of giving an adequate warning is usually so minimal, amounting only to the expense of adding some more printing to a label, that this balancing process will almost always weigh in favor of an obligation to warn of latent dangers . . ." *Moran,* 273 Md. at 543–44, 332 a.2d at 15.

In *Cotton*, plaintiff's job was to monitor portable propane heaters used to cure concrete in cold weather and to change propane cylinders supplied by the defendant when they ran low. He failed to close the valves on the used cylinders and stored them near the active heaters. Gas escaped from the used cylinders and badly burned the plaintiff. The cylinders did have a conspicuous label warning that they contained flammable gas and should be stored in a well ventilated area. The label did not warn that gas might escape from used cylinders believed to be empty or instruct the user to shut the valves on used cylinders. However, the cylinders were accompanied by a pamphlet, posted on a bulletin board at the construction site. The pamphlet did instruct the user to close the valve on used cylinders and store them in a well ventilated area. The plaintiff argued that these warnings should have been placed on the cylinders themselves. This time the appellate court affirmed a trial court judgment n.o.v. for the defendant. With respect to the plaintiff's requested warnings, it made the following comment:

> Failure-to-warn cases have the curious property that, when the episode is examined in hindsight, it appears as though addition of warnings keyed to a particular accident would be virtually cost free. What could be simpler than for the manufacturer to add the few simple items noted above? The primary cost is, in fact, the increase in time and effort required for the user to grasp the message. The inclusion of each extra item dilutes the punch of every other item. Given short attention spans, items crowd each other out; they get lost in fine print. Here, in fact, Buckeye responded to the information-cost problem with a dual approach: a brief message on the canisters themselves and a more detailed one in the NLPGA pamphlet * * *.

> Plaintiff's analysis completely disregards the problem of information costs. He asserts that "it would have been neither difficult nor costly for Buckeye to have purchased or created for attachment to its propane

cylinders a clearer, more explicit label, such as the alternatives introduced at trial, warning of propane's dangers and instructing how to avoid them." Brief for Appellant at 25. But he offers no reason to suppose that any alternative package of warnings was preferable. He discounts altogether the warnings in the pamphlet, without even considering what the canister warning would have looked like if Buckeye had supplemented it not only with the special items he is personally interested in—in hindsight—but also with all other equally valuable items (i.e., "equally" in terms of the scope and probability of the danger likely to be averted and the incremental impact of the information on user conduct). If every foreseeable possibility must be covered, "[T]he list of foolish practices warned against would be so long, it would fill a volume." Kerr v. Koemm, 557 F.Supp. 283, 288 n. 2 (S.D.N.Y.1983).

How do these two approaches differ in their assumptions about how humans respond to danger and warnings of danger? *See* Howard Latin, *"Good" Warnings, Bad Products, and Cognitive Limitations*, 41 UCLA L. Rev. 1193 (1994); W. Kip Viscusi, *Individual Rationality, Hazard Warnings, and the Foundations of Tort Law*, 48 Rutgers L. Rev. 625 (1996). Both of these articles report on research assessing how individuals perceive risks and respond to warnings. Experts in areas such as communications psychology and human factors engineering frequently offer testimony on such issues. *See*, e.g. Long v. Deere & Co., 238 Kan. 766, 715 P.2d 1023 (1986).

9. Assessing adequacy. Warnings may suffer from both substantive and procedural inadequacy. A warning is substantively inadequate when it fails provide the consumer with the information necessary to properly assess the risk. A warning may also be "procedurally inadequate." Procedural adequacy involves such things as conspicuousness, i.e. the size and location of warnings, the need for pictorial and other non-verbal warnings such as buzzers or bells, and the adequacy warnings only in English. A number of courts have developed criteria for assessing adequacy. *See*, Pittman v. Upjohn Co., 890 S.W.2d 425 (Tenn.1994); Pavlides v. Galveston Yacht Basin, Inc.,727 F.2d 330, 338 (5th Cir.1984).

[I]n order for a warning to be adequate, it must provide 'a complete disclosure of the existence and extent of the risk involved.' a warning must (1) be designed so it can reasonable be expected to catch the attention of the consumer; (2) be comprehensible and give a fair indication of the specific risks involved with the product; and (3) be of an intensity justified by the magnitude of the risk.

10. *Bulk suppliers.* The learned intermediary rule is an exception to the general rule that the manufacturer must warn the user of risks associated with a product. A second exception has been created for bulk suppliers. Higgins v. E. I. DuPont de Nemours & Co., Inc., 671 F.Supp. 1055 (1987), *aff'd* 863 F.2d 1162 (4th Cir.1988) is a representative case. Plaintiffs sued DuPont, the manufacturer of a paint called Imron claiming it failed to warn them of the paint's possible teratogenic effects. They also sued Eastman Chemical Co. and Union Carbide, two firms that supplied DuPont with the chemical ingredients with which it made Imron. The court granted summary judgment to Eastman and Union Carbide

DuPont manufactured (from various chemicals including the glycol ether acetates supplied by Eastman and Union Carbide), packaged, labeled, and distributed the finished product denominated Imron paint. The facility with which DuPont could communicate an effective labeling warning to its customers is apparent. By comparison, Eastman and Union Carbide supplied in bulk *via* railroad tank cars and tank trucks, vast amounts of liquid chemicals which were subsequently reprocessed and repackaged by DuPont as Imron paint, rendering these bulk suppliers unable, as a practical matter, to communicate any warning to the ultimate purchasers. * * * The suppliers' apparent reliance upon DuPont to communicate an effective warning to its customers was also clearly reasonable.

Higgins, 671 F.Supp. at 1062.

The *Higgins* court considered DuPont to be a sophisticated user who could be relied upon to warn the ultimate consumer. Almost all bulk supplier cases involve a sophisticated user, that is a buyer who appreciates the risks associated with the product. What duty does the bulk supplier have if the buyer is not sophisticated? What if the bulk supplier knows from past experience that the buyer has failed to pass a warning along to the consumer? *See* Hunnings v. Texaco, Inc., 29 F.3d 1480 (11th Cir.1994); *Restatement (Second) of Torts* § 388, Comment *n*.

A large number of lawsuits have been brought against DuPont, the bulk supplier of Teflon to Vitek, a company who used the product to make implants for individuals with problems in their temporomandibular joint, the joint connecting the upper and lower jaw. Over 25,000 TMJ implants were done before trouble arose. The cases are interesting because they involve both bulk supplier and learned intermediary issues. The plaintiffs claim that the bulk supplier should have warned physicians that Teflon was not suitable for this purpose. In almost all cases DuPont has been granted a summary judgment. *See* Edward M. Mansfield, *Reflections on Current Limits on Component and Raw Material Supplier Liability and the Proposed Third Restatement*, 84 Ky. L.J 221 (1995–96).

CATERPILLAR, INC. v. SHEARS

Supreme Court of Texas, 1995.
911 S.W.2d 379.

GONZALEZ, JUSTICE, delivered the opinion of the Court, in which PHILLIPS, CHIEF JUSTICE, HIGHTOWER, HECHT, CORNYN, ENOCH and OWEN, JUSTICES, join.

This is a products liability case. Cipriano Shears, his wife and children sued Caterpillar, Inc. and B.D. Holt Company for personal injuries Shears suffered in a collision of two front-end loaders. The rollover protective structure or "ROPS" for the loader Shears was operating was not installed at the time of the accident. Shears alleged that Caterpillar, the manufacturer of the loader, and B.D. Holt, which sold the loader to Shears' employer, were negligent and strictly liable because the ROPS was designed to be removable, and the defendants did not warn him of the hazards of operating a loader without a ROPS. Based on favorable jury findings, the trial court rendered a judgment for Shears for actual and punitive damages. The court of appeals affirmed the award of actual damages but reversed and rendered a take-nothing judgment as to the punitive damages. For the reasons stated herein, we reverse the judgment of the court of appeals and render judgment that Shears take nothing from Caterpillar and B.D. Holt.

I.

At the time of the accident, Shears was operating a Caterpillar model 920 front-end loader, also called a payloader. It is a four-wheeled, multi-purpose vehicle that is about nineteen feet long and weighs 18,000 pounds. It is used in logging, excavation, construction, mining, material handling, and other industries. The loader has a hydraulic arm in the front which users equip with various devices, typically a bucket for scooping up loose material. Caterpillar manufactured the model 920 with a detachable ROPS as standard equipment. The ROPS on the Caterpillar model 920 is a device with four posts that supports a canopy over and around the driver's seat. Users can remove the ROPS, which weighs 700 pounds, by unbolting twenty-four high-torque bolts and lifting it off with a crane. Removing the ROPS takes twenty or thirty minutes.

In 1979, B.D. Holt, an independent Caterpillar dealer, sold a model 920 front-end loader to Dix Shipping, Inc., which provides stevedore services for the dockyard in Brownsville, Texas. Dix Shipping removed the ROPS in order to use the loaders to unload the cargo of ships with limited clearance between decks. Regulations of the Occupational Safety and Health Administration (OSHA) authorize removing a ROPS for loaders intended for low-clearance use. See 29 C.F.R. s 1918.73(b)(5)(1994). Dix Shipping personnel testified that if the ROPS could not have been otherwise removed, they would have cut it off with a cutting torch.

At the time of the accident, Dix Shipping had hired Shears to move sodium sulphate. Following its transport by railroad to the warehouse, workers unloaded the sulphate onto a conveyer belt, which carried the sulfate into the warehouse and dumped it into a pile. Loader operators moved the sulfate to storage piles in other areas of the warehouse, where it was held until it could be loaded onto ships.

Shears and Jesus Sanchez were using Caterpillar model 920 front-end loaders to move the sulphate from the pile near the conveyer belt to the storage piles. Dix Shipping provided safety personnel to direct Shears' and Sanchez' movements and to keep them in different areas of the warehouse, but blowing sulphate dust limited visibility to a few feet. Shortly before quitting time, Shears stopped his loader to dump a load of sulphate. Sanchez' loader struck Shears' loader from behind, pinning Shears between the seat and the console of the loader and severely injuring him. It is undisputed that if the ROPS that Dix Shipping had removed from Shears' loader had been installed, it would have prevented his injuries.

Shears brought this products liability action against Caterpillar and B.D. Holt, alleging negligence and strict liability. Following trial, the jury found that the defendants failed to warn Shears of the danger of operating a loader without its ROPS: Caterpillar's design of a removable ROPS was unreasonably dangerous; and that both defendants were negligent. Consequently, the jury apportioned causation 0% to Shears, 70% to Caterpillar, and 30% to B.D. Holt. * * *

We first consider the defendants' duty to warn under the theory of strict liability.

II.

This Court has adopted the theory of strict products liability expressed in section 402A of the Restatement (Second) of Torts. McKisson v. Sales Affiliates, Inc., 416 S.W.2d 787, 788–89 (Tex.1967). The law of products liability does not guarantee that a product will be risk free, since most products have some risk associated with their use. The Restatement imposes liability only for products sold "in a defective condition unreasonably dangerous to the user or consumer." RESTATEMENT (SECOND) OF TORTS s 402A(1)(1965)(emphasis added). A product may be unreasonably dangerous because of a defect in manufacturing, design, or marketing. A defendant's failure to warn of a product's potential dangers when warnings are required is a type of marketing defect. Liability will attach if the lack of adequate warnings or instructions renders an otherwise adequate product unreasonably dangerous.

Caterpillar and B.D. Holt contend that they had no duty to warn Shears about operating the loader without its ROPS because the danger, if any, was obvious and therefore a warning would not have prevented the injury. A number of courts have adopted the position that there is no duty to warn of obvious or commonly-known dangers. See, e.g., Hagans v. Oliver Mach. Co., 576 F.2d 97, 102 & n. 5 (5th Cir.1978)(applying Texas law and holding that the manufacturer had no duty to warn of the danger of removing a safety guard from a table saw); * * * Bavuso v. Caterpillar Indus., Inc., 408 Mass. 694, 563 N.E.2d 198, 201 (1990)(concluding there was no duty to warn of the dangers of using a forklift without the overhead guard because the hazard was obvious).

Similarly, this Court has recognized that there is no duty to warn when the risks associated with a particular product are matters "within the ordinary knowledge common to the community." Joseph E. Seagram & Sons, Inc. v. McGuire, 814 S.W.2d 385, 388 (Tex.1991)(holding that there is no duty to warn of the dangers of excessive or prolonged use of alcohol since these dangers are already so widely recognized). Seagram's rationale applies with equal force to products with risks that are obvious to anyone who observes the product. In these circumstances, a warning is not required. Thus, the duty to warn is limited in scope, and applies only to hazards of which the consumer is unaware.

A number of courts have observed that a warning that merely states the obvious would accomplish very little and to the contrary may actually be counterproductive. The fact that a risk is readily apparent serves the same function as a warning. Warnings about obvious hazards are not likely to reduce the chances of injury. Moreover, consumers are prone to ignore warnings of obvious dangers, thereby diminishing the importance given by users to warnings about non-obvious hazards.[2] Thus we hold that the law of products liability does not require a manufacturer or distributer to warn of obvious risks.

---

2. The tentative draft of the Restatement of Torts (Third) also notes that the very obviousness of an obvious risk conveys the same information as do warnings, and that warning of obvious risks tends to undermine the effectiveness of warnings of unobvious risks. See RESTATEMENT (THIRD) OF TORTS: PRODUCTS LIABILITY s 2, at 26–27 (Tentative Draft No. 1, 1994).

The court of appeals did not expressly examine if Caterpillar and B.D. Holt had no duty to warn of obvious risks. However, it concluded that it could not substitute its opinion for that of the jury "about whether the dangers of injury without the ROPS are obvious as a matter of law." 881 S.W.2d at 928. The defendants argue that the court of appeals' analysis conflicts with our holding in Seagram that the existence of a duty to warn of a product's dangers is a question of law.

To understand our holding in Seagram, two aspects of the opinion are particularly important. First, the inquiry whether a recognition of risk "is within the ordinary knowledge common to the community" is an objective standard. Likewise, we conclude that whether a product has obvious dangers requires an objective standard. The determination whether a manufacturer has a duty to warn is made at the time the product leaves the manufacturer. Therefore, courts necessarily must make the judgment of whether a product is unreasonably dangerous from an objective viewpoint. Shears was experienced with the operation of various kinds of heavy equipment. He testified that, although he had seen machinery equipped with a ROPS, he thought it was to protect the operator from the weather, and had no idea of the risks of operating a front-end loader without a ROPS. However, the testimony of one individual does not control a court's determination of whether a risk is open and obvious as a matter of law under an objective standard. Therefore, Shears' subjective testimony that he had no idea the lack of a ROPS was unsafe in a collision is not determinative.

A second important aspect of the Seagram opinion is that we decided whether the risk of injury was common knowledge as a matter of law. (However, we did not foreclose the possibility that in some situations there could be a fact question about whether consumers have common knowledge of risks associated with a product.) We were able to decide Seagram as a matter of law because the dangers of prolonged and excessive use of alcohol were "so well known to the community as to be beyond dispute." The same can be said in the present case about the dangers of using an 18,000–pound front-end loader without its protective equipment. The inquiry is not whether the average person would know that a ROPS makes a loader safer. Rather, the proper inquiry is whether an average person would recognize that operating an industrial vehicle with open sides and top presents a degree of risk of serious harm to the operator. We believe it beyond dispute that the average person, looking at the open cab of a Caterpillar 920 front-end loader, would understand that nothing stands in the way of an intrusion from the rear or above. As a matter of law, Caterpillar and B.D. Holt did not have the duty to warn of the dangers of operating the loader as an open cab without a ROPS.

III.

A number of courts are of the view that obvious risks are not design defects which must be remedied. However, our Court has held that liability for a design defect may attach even if the defect is apparent. Turner, 584 S.W.2d at 850.[3] Determining if a design is unreasonably

---

3. The new Restatement of Torts (Third) draft also takes the position that the absence

dangerous requires balancing the utility of the product against the risks involved in its use.

* * *

Caterpillar designed the model 920 loader for multiple purposes in a wide variety of work environments. * * *

We evaluate whether a product has a design defect in light of the economic and scientific feasibility of safer alternatives. See Boatland of Houston, Inc. v. Bailey, 609 S.W.2d 743, 746 (Tex.1980). The degree of feasibility is one factor courts weigh in balancing the utility of a product versus its risks. However, if there are no safer alternatives, a product is not unreasonably dangerous as a matter of law. * * * Because Shears offered no evidence of a safer design for a loader that could perform the same tasks as the Caterpillar model 920, we hold that this product is not defectively designed as a matter of law.

* * *

V.

A motorcycle could be made safer by adding two additional wheels and a cab, but then it is no longer a motorcycle. A convertible can be made safer by fully enclosing the cab, but then it is just an ordinary car. The law of products liability demands that manufacturers and distributors take feasible steps to make their products reasonably safe. It is not rational, however, to impose liability in such a way as to eliminate whole categories of useful products from the market. If the inherent dangers in a class of products are obvious to a person of ordinary knowledge, there should be no duty to state the obvious. Accordingly, we reverse the judgment of the court of appeals and render judgment that Shears take nothing of Caterpillar, Inc. and B.D. Holt Company.

SPECTOR, JUSTICE, dissenting, joined in Part A by PHILLIPS, CHIEF JUSTICE.

I agree that there is no duty to warn of open and obvious dangers "so well known to the community as to be beyond dispute." Seagram & Sons, Inc. v. McGuire, 814 S.W.2d 385, 388 (Tex.1991). I disagree, however, with the majority's holding that the danger in this case was so indisputably obvious that it justified removal of the issue from the jury's province.

A.

In Seagram, this Court cited a litany of Texas cases indicating that as a matter of law the dangers of alcohol consumption are generally known to the community. The Court also cited a comment in the Restatement noting that the dangers of alcoholism are common knowledge. In addition to these qualifications on its holding, the Court further narrowed its holding by referring to the "judicial notice rule":

> Because Seagram is asking this Court to determine common knowledge as a matter of law, we find the judicial notice rule helpful in providing a standard.

of a duty to warn of an obvious danger does not necessarily mean there is no duty to make the product safer. RESTATEMENT (THIRD), supra note 2, s 2, at 27.

Based in part on this rule, we concluded:

> Consequently, we hold that, because the danger of developing the disease of alcoholism from prolonged and excessive consumption of alcoholic beverages is and has been generally known and recognized, it is within the ordinary knowledge common to the community. Therefore, under the limited circumstances present in this cause, Seagram had no duty to warn or instruct of this particular danger arising from the prolonged and excessive consumption of alcoholic beverages.

This narrow holding was based on a correspondingly narrow view of "common knowledge." * * *

The majority misapplies the Seagram standard when it states that the proper inquiry is "whether an average person would recognize that operating an industrial vehicle with open sides and top presents a degree of serious harm to the operator." Under the test delineated in Seagram, the jury must resolve this issue. To remove the issue from the jury's province, the Court would have to determine that there has been a showing of a "high degree of indisputability" that the risk was commonly known. This is the test in Texas for open and obvious dangers, and Caterpillar has failed to satisfy it.

Unlike the Court in Seagram, the majority cannot cite cases standing for the proposition that the danger associated with the absence of "ROPS" on the vehicle was so commonly known and "highly indisputable" that the Court can take judicial notice that the absence of the safety device posed an open and obvious risk of harm. To the contrary, a number of courts have held that the question of whether the absence of "ROPS" is open and obvious is a fact question for the jury. See, e.g., Young v. Deere & Co., 818 F.Supp. 1420, 1423 (D.Kan.1992); Gann v. International Harvester Co., 712 S.W.2d 100, 106 (Tenn.1986); Caterpillar Tractor Co. v. Donahue, 674 P.2d 1276, 1283 (Wyo.1983).

The danger associated with operating a Caterpillar 920 front-end loader without its safety guards is certainly not common knowledge. * * * An ordinary person looking at a large industrial front-end loader without "ROPS" might well assume that it could withstand a workplace collision without inflicting catastrophic injury.

* * *

For the foregoing reasons, I would not extend Seagram to the facts of this case. I would uphold the jury's determination that Caterpillar's failure to warn was negligent and constituted a marketing defect. Accordingly, I respectfully dissent.

Notes

1. The *Shears* case states the majority rule that the defendant is not required to warn about obvious defects. *See*, e.g. Motley v. Bell Helicopter Textron, Inc., 892 F.Supp. 249 (M.D.Ala.1995)(rotating helicopter swash plate); Smith v. American Motors Sales Corp., 215 Ill.App.3d 951, 159 Ill.Dec. 477, 576 N.E.2d 146 (1991)(driving Jeep CJ–7 with barefoot hanging outside passenger compartment). Comment *i.* of § 2, *Restatement (Third) of Torts: Products*

Liability (Tentative Draft No. 2, 1995), mentioned in the *Shears* opinion, addresses this issue:

> *i. Warnings: obvious and generally known risks.* In general, no duty exists to warn or instruct regarding risks and risk avoidance measures that should be obvious to, or generally known by, foreseeable product users. When a risk is obvious or generally known, the prospective addressee of a warning will or should already know of its existence. Warning of an obvious or generally known risk in most instances will not provide an effective additional measure of safety. Furthermore, warnings that deal with obvious or generally known risks may be ignored by users and consumers and can diminish the significance of warnings about non-obvious, non-generally known risks. Thus, requiring warnings of obvious or generally known risk reduces the efficacy of warnings generally. Where reasonable minds may differ as to whether the risk was obvious or generally known, the issue is to be decided by the trier of fact. The obviousness of risk may bear on the issue of design defect rather than failure to warn.

Also relevant is Comment *k* of *Restatement (Second) of Torts* § 388, a section dealing with the duty of suppliers of chattel to warn users of dangers associated with the chattel under negligence principles.

> Comment *k*. One who supplies a chattel to others to use for any purpose is under a duty to exercise reasonable care to inform them of its dangerous character in so far as it is known to him, or of facts which to his knowledge make it likely to be dangerous, if, but only if, he has no reason to expect that those for whose use the chattel is supplied will discover its condition and realize the danger involved. It is not necessary for the supplier to inform those for whose use the chattel is supplied of a condition which a mere casual looking over will disclose, unless the circumstances under which the chattel is supplied are such as to make it likely that even so casual an inspection will not be made. However, the condition, although readily observable, may be one which only persons of special experience would realize to be dangerous. In such case, if the supplier, having such special experience, knows that the condition involves danger and has no reason to believe that those who use it will have such special experience as will enable them to perceive the danger, he is required to inform them of the risk of which he himself knows and which he has no reason to suppose that they will realize.

2. Do you agree with the *Shears* court that it is "beyond dispute that the average person, looking at the open cab of a Caterpillar 920 front-end loader, would understand that nothing stands in the way of an intrusion from the rear or above?" Is this the right way to phrase the question? Do you think there would be a different outcome if the plaintiff had no previous experience operating the loader? Was he a sophisticated user? Compare *Shears* with Rowson v. Kawasaki Heavy Industries, Ltd., 866 F.Supp. 1221 (N.D.Iowa 1994). In that case the judge concluded that the jury should determine whether a lack of a ROPS on an all-terrain vehicle presented an open and obvious danger. At the time of his accident the plaintiff had never ridden an ATV before. *Rowson,* 866 F.Supp. at 1227.

3. *Duty or causation?* The *Shears* court determined that the defendant had no duty to warn the plaintiff of the open and obvious danger caused by the absence of a ROPS. Many courts have made this a question of causation, i.e.

failure to warn of an obvious defect could not have caused the plaintiff's injury because the plaintiff already possessed the information that would have been conveyed by the warning. *See* Duffee v. Murray Ohio Manufacturing Co., 879 F.Supp. 1078 (D.Kan.1995); Howard v. Poseidon Pools, 72 N.Y.2d 972, 534 N.Y.S.2d 360, 530 N.E.2d 1280 (1988). Is the open and obvious danger issue part of the causal question or part of the duty question? The court in Glittenberg v. Doughboy Recreational Industries, 441 Mich. 379, 491 N.W.2d 208 (1992) addressed this point in a case involving individuals who dove head first into above ground swimming pools.

> Most jurisdictions that have addressed similar cases have been unwilling to impose liability on the pool manufacturer or seller. Summary judgment in favor of the defendant has been based on lack of a causal connection between the alleged negligent failure to warn and the plaintiff's injury. Courts typically focus on the plaintiff's deposition testimony, establishing familiarity with the pool and awareness of the depth of the water in relation to the body, and hence recognition of the need to execute a shallow, flat dive in order to avoid contact with the bottom of the pool and injury. From this, it is concluded that, because the plaintiff was aware of the shallow condition of the pool's water and the dangers inherent in a headfirst dive into observably shallow water, the absence of a warning conveying those very facts could not be a proximate cause of the plaintiff's injuries.

> Although these cases could be decided on the fact specific basis of causation, the temptation to do so or to rely on the observation that a jury should be permitted to determine whether the asserted danger is latent, simply postpones to another day the need to grapple with the more difficult duty analysis. On the record here presented, we find that the plaintiffs' evidence fails to demonstrate the existence of a necessary antecedent to resolution of the causation issue, i.e., that the defendants owe the plaintiffs a duty to warn.

Glittenberg, 441 Mich. at 386–87, 491 N.W.2d at 211.

4. *The ongoing battle between judge and jury.* As the *Glittenberg* court indicates, if a court determines that the question of open and obvious defect is a duty issue then it is more nearly a question of law, and the court may have more latitude in taking the case from the jury. If, on the other hand, open and obvious danger is a question of causation, it is more nearly a factual question for the trier of fact. Throughout this chapter we have seen that some courts have become more aggressive in their willingness to take cases from juries, either through summary judgment, directed verdict, or judgment n.o.v. There is some evidence that this is a general trend. *See* James A. Henderson, Jr. And Theodore Eisenberg, *The Quiet Revolution in Products Liability: An Empirical Study of Legal Change,* 37 UCLA L. Rev. 479 (1990); Theodore Eisenberg and James A. Henderson, Jr., *Inside The Quiet Revolution in Products Liability,* 39 UCLA L. Rev. 731(1992); Philip H. Corboy, *The Not–So–Quiet Revolution: Rebuilding Barriers to Jury Trial in the Proposed Restatement (Third) of Torts: Products Liability,* 61 Tenn. L. Rev. 1043 (1994). Why do you think this is the case?

5. Whether the plaintiff will be able to get to the jury turns on whether the court concludes that reasonable people could disagree as to whether a danger is open and obvious. The cases do not offer an entirely consistent pattern of outcomes. For example, in Landberg v. Ricoh International, 892

F.Supp. 938 (E.D.Mich.1995) the court found that whether fact that copier might tip over if its adjustable leveling legs were removed was a question for the jury. On the other hand, in Grover v. Superior Welding, Inc., 893 P.2d 500 (Okl.1995) the court concluded that the risk of an employee catching her gloved hand in a drill press was an open and obvious danger as a matter of law. For an article that is critical of the courts in this and other warning defect areas, *see* James A. Henderson and Aaron D. Twerski, *Doctrinal Collapse in Products Liability: The Empty Shell of Failure to Warn*, 65 N.Y.U. L. Rev. 265 (1990).

FELDMAN v. LEDERLE LABORATORIES

Supreme Court of New Jersey, 1984.
97 N.J. 429, 479 A.2d 374.

SCHREIBER, J.

* * *

Plaintiff, Carol Ann Feldman, has gray teeth as a result of taking a tetracyline drug, Declomycin. Plaintiff's father, a pharmacist and a medical doctor, prescribed and administered the drug to her when she was an infant to control upper respiratory and other secondary types of infections. Since Dr. Feldman claimed that he had administered Declomycin, suit was instituted against defendant, Lederle Laboratories, which manufactured and marketed Declomycin. The action was presented to the jury on the theory that the defendant was strictly liable, not because the drug was ineffective as an antibiotic, but because defendant had failed to warn physicians of the drug's side effect, tooth discoloration.

* * *

[D]efendant argued that it had complied with the state of the art in its warning literature. It had not warned of possible tooth discoloration because, the defendant claimed, the possibility of that side effect was not known at the time its literature was disseminated.

The jury found for the defendant. * * *

Defendant first marketed Declomycin in 1959. The Physicians' Desk Reference (PDR), a book used by doctors to determine effects of drugs, contains data furnished by drug manufacturers about drugs, their compositions, usages, and reactions. The 1959 PDR entry for Declomycin stated that it had a greater antibiotic potency that made it possible to achieve therapeutic activity with less weight of antibiotic; it had a reduced renal clearance rate that produced a prolongation of the antibacterial levels in the body; and it was therapeutically equally effective as other tetracyclines in infections caused by organisms sensitive to the tetracyclines. The PDR is produced annually. Until the 1965 or 1966 edition, the PDR did not mention that tooth discoloration was a possible side effect of Declomycin. Since 1965 or 1966 the PDR has stated that the drug, when administered to infants and children, could cause tooth discoloration that would be permanent if the drug were given during the developmental stage of the permanent teeth.

Plaintiff, Carol Ann Feldman, was born on February 8, 1960. Her father, Dr. Harold Feldman, asserted that he prescribed Declomycin for her approximately seven or more times from September or October, 1960, when she was eight or nine months old, until the end of 1963.

* * *

Plaintiff's baby teeth were discolored gray-brown. Her permanent teeth were more deeply discolored, being primarily gray. The parties agreed that this discoloration had resulted from use of a tetracycline * * *.

The respective experts, Dr. Bonda for the plaintiff and Dr. Guggenheimer for the defendant, agreed that scientific literature existed by 1960 that referred to tooth staining being caused by tetracycline. Dr. Bonda specifically mentioned a 1956 article by Dr. Andre reciting that tetracycline accumulated in mineralized portions of growing bones and teeth of mice; an article by Dr. Milch in the July, 1957 Journal of the National Cancer Institute reporting that laboratory animals had yellow fluorescents in bones, including teeth, following dosages of tetracycline; a second article by Dr. Milch in the July, 1958 issue of the Journal of Bone and Joint Surgery again describing fluorescents in the bones and incisor teeth of rodents that had been fed tetracycline; a 1959 article by Dr. Swackman noting that of 50 children with cystic fibrosis who had received massive doses of tetracycline, 40 had dark tooth staining; a 1960 letter from Dr. Sigrelli, a Columbia University professor, to the Pediatric Journal observing that patients with cystic fibrosis of the pancreas who had received tetracyclines as an antibiotic suffered severe discoloration of their teeth, possibly as a result of their tetracycline use; a May, 1961 article by Dr. Sigrelli in the New Jersey/New York State Dental Journal containing the same information; and an essay by Dr. Bevlander on "The Effect of the Administration of Tetracycline on the Development of Teeth" in the October, 1961 issue of the Journal of Dental Research reflecting the adverse effect of tetracycline on developing teeth in young laboratory animals. Dr. Bonda concluded the defendant should have begun to investigate the possible effects of all forms of tetracycline on teeth no later than 1956, when the Andre article appeared.

Defendant's expert, Dr. Guggenheimer, on the other hand, noted that before 1962 the literature on tooth discoloration concerned only patients with cystic fibrosis who had been receiving massive doses of tetracyclines. He pointed out that Dr. Milch's papers described only fluorescents, not tooth staining. He testified that Declomycin did not become available until 1959 and that it would take 2½ years for permanent teeth developing in 1959 to erupt. The completion of accurate controlled studies of multiple well-documented cases would have been the only way one could really know whether Declomycin caused tooth discoloration in permanent teeth. Dr. Guggenheimer's testimony is unclear as to whether a correlation between tetracycline and tooth discoloration had been established in 1962. One reading of his testimony indicates that such a correlation was not known to exist and that only by hindsight could that conclusion be drawn. It is also possible to interpret his opinion to be that such correlation had been established in 1962. In any event it is significant that Dr. Guggenheimer gave no opinion as to 1963.

On November 16, 1962, Dr. Swanzey, defendant's Director of Regulatory Agencies Relations, wrote to the Federal Food and Drug Administration

(FDA) that the defendant proposed to add to the labels on all its tetracycline products the following warning: "During therapy tetracyclines may form a stable calcium complex in bone-forming tissue with no known harmful effects. Use of any tetracycline during teeth development in the neonatal period or early childhood may cause discoloration of the teeth." Dr. Swanzey explained that it was not necessary to obtain FDA approval before placing a warning on a label, but it was the practice to do so. On cross-examination, however, he indicated that although no FDA approval was needed to write letters to doctors informing them of this correlation, labeling the product without FDA approval could be considered a misbranding.

The FDA acknowledged receipt of Dr. Swanzey's letter on December 3, 1962, and advised him that the FDA "has been acutely interested by the increasing number of new and/or undesirable effects accompanying or following the use of these products," and would notify the defendant "as soon as any conclusion is reached." Dr. Swanzey telephoned Dr. Barzilai of the FDA, who advised against putting any statement in a circular proposed to be distributed by the defendant and that the FDA had the matter under study. On January 15, 1963, Dr. Swanzey sent to the FDA two articles on bone effects, including a copy of the Bevlander article. Dr. Swanzey also spoke with Dr. Sigrelli, who advised that staining would occur with some tetracyclines, but he had not observed that it occurred with Declomycin.

The FDA, in a letter dated February 4, 1963, proposed that the defendant insert the following warning statement in "all" its tetracycline products: Tetracyclines may form a stable calcium complex in any bone forming tissue with no serious harmful effects reported thus far in humans. However, use of any tetracycline drug during tooth development (= last trimester of pregnancy, neonatal period and early childhood) may cause discoloration of the teeth (= yellow-grey-brownish). This effect occurs mostly during long-term use of the drug but it has also been observed in usual short treatment courses.

Dr. Swanzey responded that the suggested statement was satisfactory and would be incorporated in its literature. He added that he assumed that the directive was applicable to Declomycin as well as other tetracycline drugs. The FDA replied that "[t]here is practically no specific clinical evidence to substantiate such a labeling requirement" for Declomycin and the warning would have to appear only on labeling of other tetracycline drugs. On April 12, 1963, the FDA made it clear that the warning statement was to refer not to tetracyclines generally but only to the specific brand names of the implicated products.

In 1963, the defendant received complaints from eight doctors that Declomycin was causing tooth staining. In May, 1963 the defendant referred the FDA again to the side effect of Declomycin. Commencing in mid-December, 1963, after receipt of FDA approval, it included the same warning in the Declomycin literature as in other tetracyclines.

* * *

The trial court's charge to the jury was directed to * * * whether the defendant knew or should have known of the need to place a warning on its literature accompanying the sale of Declomycin and in the literature distributed to the medical profession. The trial court also stated that if the defendant did not know of the danger of tooth discoloration, and if the application of reasonably developed human skill and foresight consistent with the state of the art and the knowledge of the scientific community existing during the periods in question would not have alerted defendant to the danger, then there would have to be a finding for the defendant. The trial court also charged that the defendant's reliance on the FDA would not serve to relieve defendant of its duty to insert a warning if it knew or should have known of the need for such a warning. No exceptions were taken to the charge.

* * *

[In an omitted portion of the opinion the court addresses the question of whether strict liability applies to prescription drugs. The court determined that Comment *k*. of § 402A should be applied on a case-by-case basis]

III

We commence our strict liability analysis with the now familiar refrain that to establish strict liability a plaintiff must prove that the product was defective, that the defect existed when the product left the defendant's control, and that the defect caused injury to a reasonably foreseeable user. * * *

This is a strict-liability-warning case. The product has been made as the manufacturer intended. The plaintiff does not contend that it contained a manufacturing defect. Declomycin's purpose was to act as did other tetracyclines—as an antibiotic. However, it had several advantages over other antimicrobial therapeutics. The plaintiff does not dispute this. Indeed, there is no evidence that plaintiff's usage of Declomycin was not adequate in this respect. Nor was there any proof that it was improperly designed. The crux of the plaintiff's complaint is that her doctor should have been warned of a possible side effect of the drug in infants, discoloration of teeth.

The failure-to-warn strict liability classification is similar to the improper design category. The manufacturer is under a duty to produce and distribute a product that is reasonably fit, suitable, and safe. It has not met that obligation if it puts a defective article into the stream of commerce that causes injury or damage. * * *

The emphasis of the strict liability doctrine is upon the safety of the product, rather than the reasonableness of the manufacturer's conduct. * * *

* * * Th[e] difference between strict liability and negligence is commonly expressed by stating that in a strict liability analysis, the defendant is assumed to know of the dangerous propensity of the product, whereas in a negligence case, the plaintiff must prove that the defendant knew or should have known of the danger. This distinction is particularly pertinent in a manufacturing defect context.

When the strict liability defect consists of an improper design or warning, reasonableness of the defendant's conduct is a factor in determining liability. The question in strict liability design defect and warning cases is whether, assuming that the manufacturer knew of the defect in the product, he acted in a reasonably prudent manner in marketing the product or in providing the warnings given. Thus, once the defendant's knowledge of the defect is imputed, strict liability analysis becomes almost identical to negligence analysis in its focus on the reasonableness of the defendant's conduct. * * *

Generally, the state of the art in design defect cases and available knowledge in defect warning situations are relevant factors in measuring reasonableness of conduct. Thus * * * we [have] explained that other than assuming that the manufacturer knew of the harmful propensity of the product, the jury could consider "the technological feasibility of manufacturing a product whose design would have prevented or avoided the accident, given the known state of the art." We observed that "the state of the art refers not only to the common practice and standards in the industry but also to the other design alternatives within practical and technological limits at the time of distribution." [W]e again referred to the state of the art as an appropriate factor to be considered by the jury to determine whether feasible alternatives existed when the product was marketed.

Similarly, as to warnings, generally conduct should be measured by knowledge at the time the manufacturer distributed the product. Did the defendant know, or should he have known, of the danger, given the scientific, technological, and other information available when the product was distributed; or, in other words, did he have actual or constructive knowledge of the danger? The Restatement, supra, has adopted this test in Comment j to section 402A, which reads in pertinent part as follows:

> *Directions or warning.* In order to prevent the product from being unreasonably dangerous, the seller may be required to give directions or warning, on the container, as to its use. * * * Where the product contains an ingredient * * * whose danger is not generally known, or if known is one which the consumer would reasonably not expect to find in the product, the seller is required to give warning against it, *if he has knowledge, or by the application of reasonable, developed human skill and foresight should have knowledge*, of the presence of the ingredient and the danger. [Emphasis added.]

Under this standard negligence and strict liability in warning cases may be deemed to be functional equivalents. * * * Constructive knowledge embraces knowledge that should have been known based on information that was reasonably available or obtainable and should have alerted a reasonably prudent person to act. Put another way, would a person of reasonable intelligence or of the superior expertise of the defendant charged with such knowledge conclude that defendant should have alerted the consuming public?

Further, a manufacturer is held to the standard of an expert in the field. A manufacturer should keep abreast of scientific advances. * * *

Furthermore, a reasonably prudent manufacturer will be deemed to know of reliable information generally available or reasonably obtainable in the industry or in the particular field involved. Such information need not be limited to that furnished by experts in the field, but may also include material provided by others. Thus, for example, if a substantial number of doctors or consumers had complained to a drug manufacturer of an untoward effect of a drug, that would have constituted sufficient information requiring an appropriate warning. * * *

This test does not conflict with the assumption made in strict liability design defect and warning cases that the defendant knew of the dangerous propensity of the product, if the knowledge that is assumed is reasonably knowable in the sense of actual or constructive knowledge. A warning that a product may have an unknowable danger warns one of nothing. * * * [T]he manufacturer would [not] be deemed to know of the dangerous propensity of the chattel when the danger was unknowable. In our opinion [Beshada v. Johns–Manville Products Corp., 90 N.J. 191, 447 A.2d 539 (1982)] * * * would not demand a contrary conclusion in the typical design defect or warning case. If *Beshada* were deemed to hold generally or in all cases, particularly with respect to a situation like the present one involving drugs vital to health, that in a warning context knowledge of the unknowable is irrelevant in determining the applicability of strict liability, we would not agree. Many commentators have criticized this aspect of the *Beshada* reasoning and the public policies on which it is based. * * * The rationale of *Beshada* is not applicable to this case. We do not overrule *Beshada*, but restrict Beshada to the circumstances giving rise to its holding. * * *

In strict liability warning cases, unlike negligence cases, however, the defendant should properly bear the burden of proving that the information was not reasonably available or obtainable and that it therefore lacked actual or constructive knowledge of the defect. * * * The defendant is in a superior position to know the technological material or data in the particular field or specialty. The defendant is the expert, often performing self-testing. It is the defendant that injected the product in the stream of commerce for its economic gain. As a matter of policy the burden of proving the status of knowledge in the field at the time of distribution is properly placed on the defendant. * * *

One other aspect with respect to warnings based on subsequently obtained knowledge should be considered. Communication of the new warning should unquestionably be given to prescribing physicians as soon as reasonably feasible. Although a manufacturer may not have actual or constructive knowledge of a danger so as to impose upon it a duty to warn, subsequently acquired knowledge, both actual and constructive, also may obligate the manufacturer to take reasonable steps to notify purchasers and consumers of the newly-discovered danger. * * *

The timeliness of the warning issue is obliquely present in this case. It is possible that Dr. Feldman already had Declomycin on hand when defendant became aware of Declomycin's side effect. If that state of affairs existed, defendant would have had an obligation to warn doctors and others promptly. This most assuredly would include those to whom defendant had already furnished the product. * * * The extent and nature of post-distribution warnings may vary depending on the circumstances, but in the context of this case, the defendant at a minimum would have had a duty of advising physicians, including plaintiff's father, whom it had directly solicited to use Declomycin.

* * *

We reverse and remand for a new trial.

Notes

1. How long after the first hints that there may be a problem with a product should the manufacturer issue a warning? What factors should be considered in making this determination?

2. As noted earlier, state-of-the-art issues arise in both warning defect and design defect cases. Opinion admitting state-of-the-art evidence in warning cases include Anderson v. Owens-Corning Fiberglas Corp., 53 Cal.3d 987, 281 Cal.Rptr. 528, 810 P.2d 549 (1991) and Fibreboard Corp. v. Fenton, 845 P.2d 1168 (Colo.1993). A recent discussion of the state-of-the-art defense in the design defect context can be found in Hughes v. Massey–Ferguson, Inc., 522 N.W.2d 294 (Iowa 1994). See also Boatland of Houston v. Bailey, 609 S.W.2d 743 (Tex.1980). Missouri courts have refused to consider state-of-the-art evidence in design defect cases. *See* Elmore v. Owens–Illinois, Inc., 673 S.W.2d 434 (Mo.1984).

3. The *Beshada* case referred to in *Feldman* rejected a state-of-the-art defense in warning cases. *Beshada* involved a group of plaintiffs suffering from asbestosis, mesothelioma, and other asbestos related diseases. They claimed the defendants failed to warn them of the dangers of exposure to airborne asbestos and the defendants responded that they did not know of the risks at the time the plaintiffs were exposed. The court justified its rejection of the state-of-the-art defense on three grounds: a) denying this defense will maximize the strict liability goal of risk spreading, b) by imposing liability on manufacturers for unknown risks, the courts will create additional incentives to invest in safety research, c) denying the defense will reduce the costs of litigation. With respect to this last point, the court said:

> Proof of what could have been known will inevitably be complicated, costly, confusing, and time consuming. * * * We doubt that juries will be capable of even understanding the concept of scientific knowability, much less be able to resolve such a complex issue. Moreover, we should resist legal rules that will so greatly add to the costs both sides incur in trying a case.

Beshada, 90 N.J. at 207–08, 447 A.2d at 548.

Assess each of these grounds for rejecting a state-of-the-art defense. Most commentators agree with the majority rule set forth in *Feldman*. *See* David Owen, *The Moral Foundation of Products Liability Law: Toward First Principles*, 68 Notre Dame L. Rev. 427 (1993); John Wade, *On the Effect in Product Liability of Knowledge Unavailable Prior to Marketing*, 58 N.Y.U. L. Rev. 734 (1983); Gary Schwartz, *The Vitality of Negligence and the Ethics of Strict Liability*, 15 Ga. L. Rev. 963 (1981). *But see* Ellen Wertheimer, *Unknowable Dangers and the Death of Strict Products Liability: The Empire Strikes Back*, 60 U. Cin. L. Rev. 1183 (1992) for a criticism of the increasing judicial unwillingness to impute knowledge to manufacturers in state-of-the-art cases.

4. *Custom and industry practice.* Courts generally distinguish a state-of-the-art defense from industry custom. In design defect cases, the issue is

usually put as one of feasibility. As the *Hughes* court noted: "custom refers to what was being done in the industry; state-of-the-art refers to what feasibly could have been done." *Hughes, 522 N.W.2d at 295.* The *Boatland* court used similar language: "In our view, 'custom' is distinguishable from 'state of the art.' The state of the art with respect to a particular product refers to the technological environment at the time of its manufacture. This technological environment includes the scientific knowledge, economic feasibility, and the practicalities of implementation when the product was manufactured." *Boatland,* 609 S.W.2d at 748. Likewise, in warning cases the issue is not what warnings firms in the industry actually gave, but what knowledge reasonably should have been possessed concerning the risks associated with the product.

In an omitted part of the *Grundberg v. Upjohn Co.,* 813 P.2d 89 (Utah 1991) opinion, (*supra,* p. 671) the court set forth the standard to which manufacturers should be held in warning cases involving drugs.

> In determining whether a manufacturer has breached that duty [to adequately warn] and the extent to which a manufacturer is required to know of dangers inherent in its drug, it is important to point out that the drug manufacturer is held to be an expert in its particular field and is under a "continuous duty ... to keep abreast of scientific developments touching upon the manufacturer's product and notify the medical profession of any additional side effects discovered from its use." The drug manufacturer is responsible therefore for not only "actual knowledge gained from research and adverse reaction reports," but also for constructive knowledge as measured by scientific literature and other available means of communication. Barson v. E.R. Squibb & Sons, Inc., 682 P.2d 832, 835–36.

Grundberg, 813 P.2d at 98.

5. *Feldman* viewed state-of-the-art as an affirmative defense. *The Restatement (Third) of Torts: Products Liability* (Tentative Draft No. 2, 1995) takes a somewhat different view. § 2(c) requires the manufacturer to provide instructions or warnings only for "foreseeable risks of harm." Comment *l* to § 2 includes the following statement:

> The issue of foreseeability of risk of harm is more complex in the case of products such as prescription drugs, medical devices, and toxic chemicals. Risks attendant to use and consumption of these products may, indeed, be unforeseeable at the time of sale. Unforeseeable risks arising from foreseeable product use or consumption by definition cannot be warned against. Thus, in connection with a claim of inadequate design, instruction, or warning, plaintiff should bear the burden of establishing that the risk in question was known or should have been known to the relevant manufacturing community. The harms that result from unforeseeable risks—for example, in the human body's reaction to a new drug, medical device, or chemical—are not a basis of liability. Of course, a seller bears responsibility to perform reasonable testing prior to marketing a product and to discover risks and risk-avoidance measures that such testing would reveal.

6. *Post Sale duties.* What duty did Lederle have to warn earlier purchasers of it s product once it discovered Declomycin may cause tooth discoloration? This is part of a larger question of a seller's post sale conduct. *The Restatement (Third) of Torts: Products Liability* (Tentative Draft No. 3, 1966) § 18 contains the following provision:

§ 18. Liability of Commercial Seller or Distributor for Harm Caused by Failure to Warn After the Time of Sale

One engaged in the business of selling or otherwise distributing products who sells a product is subject to liability for harm to persons or property caused by the seller's failure to provide a warning after the time of sale when a reasonable person in the seller's position would provide such a warning. A reasonable person would provide a warning after the time of sale when:

(a) the seller knows or reasonably should know that the product poses a substantial risk of harm to persons or property;

(b) those to whom a warning might be provided can be identified and can reasonably be assumed to be unaware of the risk of harm;

(c) a warning can be communicated to, and effectively acted on, by those to whom a warning might be provided; and

(d) the risk of harm is sufficiently great to justify the burden of providing a warning.

For cases supporting this position, *see* Patton v. Hutchinson Wil–Rich Manufacturing Co., 253 Kan. 741, 861 P.2d 1299 (1993); Crowston v. Goodyear Tire & Rubber Co., 521 N.W.2d 401 (N.D.1994). Courts have not been willing to impose a post-sale duty to recall or repair absent some ongoing relationship, e.g. a maintenance contract, between the seller and buyer. *See generally*, Victor Schwartz, *The Post–Sale Duty to Warn: Two Unfortunate Forks in the Road to a Reasonable Doctrine*, 58 N.Y.U. L. Rev. 892 (1983).

How broad is the post-sale duty? Consider the comments of the court in Walton v. Avco Corp., 383 Pa.Super. 518, 530, 557 A.2d 372, 379 (1989).

We do not in this decision hold that there is an absolute continuing duty, year after year, for all manufacturers to warn of a new safety device which eliminates potential hazards. * * * It is beyond reason and good judgment to hold a manufacturer responsible for a duty of annually warning of safety hazards on household items, mass produced and used in every American home, when the product is 6 to 35 years old and outdated by some 20 newer models equipped with every imaginable safety innovation known in the state of art. It would place an unreasonable duty upon these manufacturers if they were required to trace the ownership of each unit sold and warn annually of new safety improvements over a 35 year period. In reaching our decision that Hughes may be held strictly liable for its failure to issue post-sale warnings about the safety of the engine it had installed in its helicopters, we are cognizant of the nature of the helicopter manufacturing industry. A helicopter is not a household good, commonly found in almost any home in this country. It is, instead, a unique and costly product which is manufactured, marketed, and sold to a specialized group of consumers. We believe that Hughes could have communicated safety information and service instructions with relative ease by contacting purchasers of its helicopters, as well as authorized Hughes service centers, through the mail or otherwise.

§ 18 is intended specifically to cover those situations where the courts would not say a product was defective at the time of sale, perhaps because the newly discovered risks were unknowable at that time. If the product was defective at the time of sale, liability exists even in the absence of a post-sale duty to warn and such a warning does not necessarily relieve the seller of liability for any injuries caused by the defect.

D. DEFENSES

1. *Plaintiff's Behavior*

DALY v. GENERAL MOTORS CORPORATION

Supreme Court of California, 1978.
20 Cal.3d 725, 144 Cal.Rptr. 380, 575 P.2d 1162.

RICHARDSON, JUSTICE.

The most important of several problems which we consider is whether the principles of comparative negligence expressed by us in *Li v. Yellow Cab Co.* (1975) 13 Cal.3d 804, 119 Cal.Rptr. 858, 532 P.2d 1226, apply to actions founded on strict products liability. We will conclude that they do. We also inquire whether evidence of "compensating" safety devices install- ed in a motor vehicle by its manufacturer is admissible to offset alleged design deficiencies, and whether, under the particular facts herein, evi- dence of a driver's claimed intoxication or of his asserted failure to use his vehicle's safety equipment may be considered. While agreeing that evi- dence of compensating design characteristics is admissible, we will further determine that under the circumstances herein prejudicial error requiring reversal occurred upon the admission of evidence of the decedent's alleged intoxication and failure to use safety devices in his vehicle.

THE FACTS AND THE TRIAL

Although there were no eyewitnesses, the parties agree, generally, on the reconstruction of the accident in question. In the early hours of October 31, 1970, decedent Kirk Daly, a 36–year–old attorney, was driving his Opel southbound on the Harbor Freeway in Los Angeles. The vehicle, while travelling at a speed of 50–70 miles per hour, collided with and damaged 50 feet of metal divider fence. After the initial impact between the left side of the vehicle and the fence the Opel spun counterclockwise, the driver's door was thrown open, and Daly was forcibly ejected from the car and sustained fatal head injuries. It was equally undisputed that had the deceased remained in the Opel his injuries, in all probability, would have been relatively minor.

Plaintiffs, who are decedent's widow and three surviving minor chil- dren, sued General Motors Corporation, Boulevard Buick, Underwriter's Auto Leasing, and Alco Leasing Company, the successive links in the Opel's manufacturing and distribution chain. The sole theory of plaintiffs' com- plaint was strict liability for damages allegedly caused by a defective product, namely, an improperly designed door latch claimed to have been activated by the impact. It was further asserted that, but for the faulty latch, decedent would have been restrained in the vehicle and, although perhaps injured, would not have been killed. Thus, the case involves a so- called "second collision" in which the "defect" did not contribute to the original impact, but only to the "enhancement" of injury.

At trial the jury heard conflicting expert versions as to the functioning of the latch mechanism during the accident. Plaintiffs' principal witness testified that the Opel's door was caused to open when the latch button on the exterior handle of the driver's door was forcibly depressed by some protruding portion of the divider fence. It was his opinion that the exposed push button on the door constituted a design "defect" which caused injuries greatly in excess of those which Daly would otherwise have sustained. Plaintiffs also introduced evidence that other vehicular door latch designs used in production models of the same and prior years afforded substantially greater protection. Defendants' experts countered with their opinions that the force of the impact was sufficiently strong that it would have caused the door to open resulting in Daly's death even if the Opel had been equipped with door latches of the alternative designs suggested by plaintiffs.

Over plaintiffs' objections, defendants were permitted to introduce evidence indicating that: (1) the Opel was equipped with a seat belt-shoulder harness system, and a door lock, either of which if used, it was contended, would have prevented Daly's ejection from the vehicle; (2) Daly used neither the harness system nor the lock; (3) the 1970 Opel owner's manual contained warnings that seat belts should be worn and doors locked when the car was in motion for "accident security"; and (4) Daly was intoxicated at the time of collision, which evidence the jury was advised was admitted for the limited purpose of determining whether decedent had used the vehicle's safety equipment. After relatively brief deliberations the jury returned a verdict favoring all defendants, and plaintiffs appeal from the ensuing adverse judgment.

Strict Products Liability and Comparative Fault

In response to plaintiffs' assertion that the "intoxication-nonuse" evidence was improperly admitted, defendants contend that the deceased's own conduct contributed to his death. Because plaintiff's case rests upon strict products liability based on improper design of the door latch and because defendants assert a failure in decedent's conduct, namely, his alleged intoxication and nonuse of safety equipment, without which the accident and ensuing death would not have occurred, there is thereby posed the overriding issue in the case, should comparative principles apply in strict products liability actions?

* * * [W]e have recognized that though most forms of contributory negligence do not constitute a defense to a strict products liability action, plaintiff's negligence is a complete defense when it comprises assumption of risk. (*Luque v. McLean* (1972) 8 Cal.3d 136, 145, 104 Cal.Rptr. 443, 501 P.2d 1163; Rest.2d Torts, § 402A, com. b.) * * *

Those counseling against the recognition of comparative fault principles in strict products liability cases vigorously stress, perhaps equally, not only the conceptual, but also the semantic difficulties incident to such a course. The task of merging the two concepts is said to be impossible, that "apples and oranges" cannot be compared, that "oil and water" do not mix, and that strict liability, which is not founded on negligence or fault, is inhospitable to comparative principles. The syllogism runs, contributory negligence was only a defense to negligence, comparative negligence only affects contributory negligence, therefore comparative negligence cannot be a defense to strict liability. * * * While fully recognizing the theoretical and semantic distinctions between the twin principles of strict products liability and traditional negligence, we think they can be blended or accommodated.

The inherent difficulty in the "apples and oranges" argument is its insistence on fixed and precise definitional treatment of legal concepts. In the evolving areas of both products liability and tort defenses, however, there has developed much conceptual overlapping and interweaving in order to attain substantial justice. The concept of strict liability itself, as we have noted, arose from dissatisfaction with the wooden formalisms of traditional tort and contract principles in order to protect the consumer of manufactured goods. Similarly, increasing social awareness of its harsh "all or nothing" consequences led us * * * to moderate the impact of traditional contributory negligence in order to accomplish a fairer and more balanced result. We acknowledged an intermixing of defenses of contributory negligence and assumption of risk and formally effected a type of merger. * * * "We think it clear that the adoption of a system of comparative negligence should entail the merger of the defense of assumption of risk into the general scheme of assessment of liability in proportion to fault in those particular cases in which the form of assumption of risk involved is no more than a variant of contributory negligence." [quoting from *Li*] * * *

Furthermore, the "apples and oranges" argument may be conceptually suspect. It has been suggested that the term "contributory negligence," one of the vital building blocks upon which much of the argument is based, may indeed itself be a misnomer since it lacks the first element of the classical negligence formula, namely, a duty of care owing to another.

* * *

Fixed semantic consistency at this point is less important than the attainment of a just and equitable result. The interweaving of concept and terminology in this area suggests a judicial posture that is flexible rather than doctrinaire.

We pause at this point to observe that where, as here, a consumer or user sues the manufacturer or designer alone, technically, neither fault nor conduct is really compared functionally. The conduct of one party in combination with the product of another, or perhaps the placing of a defective article in the stream of projected and anticipated use, may produce the ultimate injury. In such a case, as in the situation before us, we think the term "equitable apportionment or allocation of loss" may be more descriptive than "comparative fault."

* * * [W]e consider it * * * useful to examine the foundational reasons underlying the creation of strict products liability in California to ascertain whether the purposes of the doctrine would be defeated or diluted by adoption of comparative principles. We imposed strict liability against the manufacturer and in favor of the user or consumer in order to relieve injured consumers "from *problems of proof* inherent in pursuing negligence * * * and warranty * * * remedies, * * *"(*Cronin v. J.B.E. Olson Corp.,*

supra, 8 Cal.3d at p. 133, 104 Cal.Rptr. at p. 442, 501 P.2d at p. 1162, italics added; *Greenman v. Yuba Power Products, Inc., supra,* 59 Cal.2d at p. 63, 27 Cal.Rptr. 697, 377 P.2d 897; *Escola v. Coca Cola Bottling Co.* (1944) 24 Cal.2d 453, 461–462, 150 P.2d 436 (conc. opn. by Traynor, J.).) As we have noted, we sought to place the burden of loss on manufacturers rather than "* * * injured persons *who are powerless to protect themselves * * *.*" (*Greenman, supra,* 59 Cal.2d at p. 63, 27 Cal.Rptr. at p. 701, 377 P.2d at p. 901, italics added; see *Escola, supra,* 24 Cal.2d at p. 462, 150 P.2d 436; *Price v. Shell Oil Co.* (1970) 2 Cal.3d 245, 251, 85 Cal.Rptr. 178, 182, 466 P.2d 722, 726 [*"protection of otherwise defenseless victims* of manufacturing defects and the spreading throughout society of the cost of compensating them"] italics added.)

The foregoing goals, we think, will not be frustrated by the adoption of comparative principles. Plaintiffs will continue to be relieved of proving that the manufacturer or distributor was negligent in the production, design, or dissemination of the article in question. Defendant's liability for injuries caused by a defective product remains strict. The principle of protecting the defenseless is likewise preserved, for plaintiff's recovery will be reduced *only* to the extent that his own lack of reasonable care contributed to his injury. The cost of compensating the victim of a defective product, albeit proportionately reduced, remains on defendant manufacturer, and will, through him, be "spread among society." However, we do not permit plaintiff's own conduct relative to the product to escape unexamined, and as to that share of plaintiff's damages which flows from his own fault we discern no reason of policy why it should, following *Li,* be borne by others. Such a result would directly contravene the principle * * * that loss should be assessed equitably in proportion to fault.

We conclude, accordingly, that the expressed purposes which persuaded us in the first instance to adopt strict liability in California would not be thwarted were we to apply comparative principles. What would be forfeit is a degree of semantic symmetry. However, in this evolving area of tort law in which new remedies are judicially created, and old defenses judicially merged, impelled by strong considerations of equity and fairness we seek a larger synthesis. If a more just result follows from the expansion of comparative principles, we have no hesitancy in seeking it, mindful always that the fundamental and underlying purpose of *Li* was to promote the equitable allocation of loss among all parties legally responsible in proportion to their fault.

A second objection to the application of comparative principles in strict products liability cases is that a manufacturer's incentive to produce safe products will thereby be reduced or removed. While we fully recognize this concern we think, for several reasons, that the problem is more shadow than substance. First, of course, the manufacturer cannot avoid its continuing liability for a defective product even when the plaintiff's own conduct has contributed to his injury. The manufacturer's liability, and therefore its incentive to avoid and correct product defects, remains; its exposure will be lessened only to the extent that the trier finds that the victim's conduct contributed to his injury. Second, as a practical matter a manufacturer, in a particular case, cannot assume that the user of a defective product upon whom an injury is visited will be blameworthy.

Doubtless, many users are free of fault, and a defect is at least as likely as not to be exposed by an entirely innocent plaintiff who will obtain full recovery. In such cases the manufacturer's incentive toward safety both in design and production is wholly unaffected. Finally, we must observe that under the present law, which recognizes assumption of risk as a complete defense to products liability, the curious and cynical message is that it profits the manufacturer to make his product so defective that in the event of injury he can argue that the user had to be aware of its patent defects. To that extent the incentives are inverted. We conclude, accordingly, that no substantial or significant impairment of the safety incentives of defendants will occur by the adoption of comparative principles.

* * *

A third objection to the merger of strict liability and comparative fault focuses on the claim that, as a practical matter, triers of fact, particularly jurors, cannot assess, measure, or compare plaintiff's negligence with defendant's strict liability. We are unpersuaded by the argument and are convinced that jurors are able to undertake a fair apportionment of liability.

We are strengthened in the foregoing conclusion by the federal experience under the maritime doctrine of "unseaworthiness." For decades, seamen have been permitted to recover from shipowners for injuries caused by defects rendering a vessel "unseaworthy." (E.g., *The Osceola* (1903) 189 U.S. 158, 175, 23 S.Ct. 483, 47 L.Ed. 760.) * * *

We find equally unpersuasive a final objection that the merger of the two principles somehow will abolish or adversely affect the liability of such intermediate entities in the chain of distribution as retailers (*Vandermark v. Ford Motor Co.* (1964) 61 Cal.2d 256, 263, 37 Cal.Rptr. 896, 391 P.2d 168), and bailors (*Price v. Shell Oil Co., supra,* 2 Cal.3d 245, 253, 85 Cal.Rptr. 178, 466 P.2d 722.) We foresee no such consequence. Regardless of the identity of a particular defendant or of his position in the commercial chain the basis for his liability remains that he has marketed or distributed a defective product. If, as we believe, jurors are capable of assessing fully and fairly the legal responsibility of a manufacturer on a strict liability basis, no reason appears why they cannot do likewise with respect to subsequent distributors and vendors of the product.

We note that the majority of our sister states which have addressed the problem, either by statute or judicial decree, have extended comparative principles to strict products liability.

Our research discloses that of the more than 30 states which have adopted some form of comparative negligence, three (including California) have done so judicially.

* * *

Moreover, we are further encouraged in our decision herein by noting that the apparent majority of scholarly commentators has urged adoption of the rule which we announce herein. These include, from the academic community: Wade, *A Uniform Comparative Fault Act—What Should It Provide?* (1977) 10 Mich.J.L.Ref. 220; Fleming, *The Supreme Court of*

California 1974–1975—Forward: Comparative Negligence at Last—By Judicial Choice (1976) 64 Cal.L.Rev. 239, 269–271; * * * Wade, *On the Nature of Strict Tort Liability for Products* (1973) 44 Miss.L.J. 825, 850; Noel, *Defective Products; Abnormal Use, Contributory Negligence, and Assumption of Risk* (1972) 25 Vand.L.Rev. 93, 117–118; contra, Levine, *Strict Products Liability and Comparative Negligence: The Collision of Fault and No–Fault* (1977) 14 San Diego L.Rev. 337, 346 et seq.

* * *

Having examined the principal objections and finding them not insurmountable, and persuaded by logic, justice, and fundamental fairness, we conclude that a system of comparative fault should be and it is hereby extended to actions founded on strict products liability. In such cases the separate defense of "assumption of risk," to the extent that it is a form of contributory negligence, is abolished. While, as we have suggested, on the particular facts before us, the term "equitable apportionment of loss" is more accurately descriptive of the process, nonetheless, the term "comparative fault" has gained such wide acceptance by courts and in the literature that we adopt its use herein.

* * *

Retroactivity

* * *

We * * * conclude that, under the particular circumstances, comparative principles cannot be applied retroactively to the instant case in order to justify admission of the intoxication and "nonuse" evidence here challenged. The issue of comparative fault was raised for the first time on appeal, and was never placed in issue by any party at trial herein. No jury instructions on the issue were requested or given. The jury therefore had no basis for evaluating the evidence under correct principles of comparative fault. In the event of retrial, however, the principles herein announced will, of course, apply.

* * *

DEFECT—COMPONENT OR PRODUCT AS A WHOLE?

We examine for the benefit of court and counsel, in the event of retrial, a single remaining contention of plaintiffs.

Plaintiffs challenge a jury instruction which directed that "[i]n determining whether or not the vehicle was defective you should consider all of the equipment on the vehicle including any features intended for the safety of the driver." They urge that only the precise malfunctioning component itself, and alone, may be considered in determining whether injury was caused by a defectively designed product. We disagree, concluding that the issue of defective design is to be determined with respect to the product as a whole, and that the trial court's instruction was correct.

The jury could properly determine whether the Opel's overall design, including safety features provided in the vehicle, made it "crashworthy," thus rendering the vehicle nondefective. Product designs do not evolve in a vacuum, but must reflect the realities of the market place, kitchen, highway, and shop. Similarly, a product's components are not developed in isolation, but as part of an integrated and interrelated whole. Recognizing that finished products must incorporate and balance safety, utility, competitive merit, and practicality under a multitude of intended and foreseeable uses, courts have struggled to evolve realistic tests for defective design which give weight to this necessary balancing. Thus, a number of California cases have recognized the need to "weigh" competing considerations in an overall product design, in order to determine whether the design was "defective." Recently, we ourselves in *Barker v. Lull* (1978) 20 Cal.3d 413, 431, 143 Cal.Rptr. 225, 573 P.2d 443, have described some of the factors to be considered.   * * *

[Concurring and dissenting opinions omitted.]

Notes

1.The problem that seemed so perplexing in theory, comparing the plaintiff's fault to the defendant's defect, has turned out to be a relatively straightforward task in practice.

2. Most jurisdictions have adopted comparative fault principles in products liability cases, either through judicial opinion or legislation. A few "comparative negligence" statutes are, by their terms, limited to negligence cases. *See* Ohio Rev.Code § 2315.19 (Page). Moreover, in its product liability statute, the Ohio legislature provided that both express and implied assumption of the risk would, in most instances, be a complete bar to plaintiff recovery, while contributory negligence would be no bar at all. Ohio Rev.Code § 2315.20. In Bowling v. Heil Co., 31 Ohio St.3d 277, 511 N.E.2d 373 (1987) the Ohio Supreme Court refused to inject a plaintiff's negligence into the law of products liability.

There is a declaration in Murray v. Fairbanks Morse, 610 F.2d 149 (3d Cir.1979)(Virgin Islands) that, in strict products liability actions, the comparison should be on the basis of causal contribution to the injuries, and not on the basis of fault. Texas adopted a comparative causation approach in Duncan v. Cessna Aircraft Co., 665 S.W.2d 414 (Tex.1984); *see also,* Mauch v. Manufacturers Sales & Serv., 345 N.W.2d 338 (N.D.1984).

3. *Apportionment in crashworthiness cases.* Daly is a crashworthiness case. The plaintiffs are only claiming enhancement injuries from General Motors. On retrial, should the court permit the jury to consider Mr. Daly's intoxication in apportioning fault? Should they be allowed to consider the fact that he was not wearing his seat belt? Does your answer change if the plaintiff's injuries are indivisible, i.e., if it is impossible to determine which injuries were caused by the initial crash and which were caused by the automobile's lack of crashworthiness? For different approaches to this issue, *see* Whitehead v. Toyota Motor Corp. 897 S.W.2d 684 (Tenn.1995); Reed v. Chrysler Corp., 494 N.W.2d 224 (Iowa 1992). *See also* the discussion of apportioning damages in Chapter Six, *supra,* at p. 411 ff.

4. *Failure to discover a defect.* Following Comment *n.* to *Restatement (Second) of Torts* § 402A, some courts refuse to apply comparative responsibility when plaintiff's only fault is in failing to discover or guard against a defect in the product. *See* West v. Caterpillar Tractor Co., 336 So.2d 80 (Fla.1976); Keen v. Ashot Ashkelon, Ltd., 748 S.W.2d 91 (Tex.1988).

5. *Assumption of the risk and misuse.* On the other hand, some courts have retained assumption of risk as a complete defense that, if proven, bars the plaintiff from all recovery. *See* Fiske v. MacGregor Division of Brunswick, 464 A.2d 719 (R.I.1983); Bowling v. Heil Co., 31 Ohio St.3d 277, 511 N.E.2d 373 (1987). In addition, some courts have held that misuse of a product is a complete bar to recovery, although it is frequently said that misuse is not a defense at all but rather a failure by the plaintiff to show either causation or defect.

6. The *Restatement (Third) of Torts: Products Liability* (Tentative Draft No. 3, 1996) reflects the majority view on comparative fault while at the same time rejecting any special status for failure to discover or assumption of the risk. All types of plaintiff behavior should be considered when apportioning responsibility. *See* William J. McNichols, *The Relevance of the Plaintiff's Misconduct in Strict Tort Products Liability, The Advent of Comparative Responsibility, and the Proposed Restatement (Third) of Torts*, 47 Okla. L. Rev. 201 (1994).

§ 13. Apportionment of Liability Between or Among Plaintiff, Sellers or Distributors of Defective Products, and Other Tortfeasors

When the conduct of the plaintiff or another person combines with a product defect to cause harm to the plaintiff's person or property and the plaintiff's conduct or that of the other person fails to conform to an applicable standard of care, liability for harm to the plaintiff is apportioned between and among the plaintiff, product seller or distributor, or other tortfeasor pursuant to the applicable rules governing apportionment of liability.

7. While not exactly a defense, Chapter 11 of the U.S. Bankruptcy Code, 11 U.S.C. § 101 *et seq.,* has been increasingly used by corporations facing massive products liability claims. For a look at the effect bankruptcy laws may have on pending product liability claims, *see* Susan S. Ford, *Who Will Compensate the Victims of Asbestos–Related Diseases? Manville's Chapter 11 Fuels the Fire,* 14 Enviro.Law 465 (1983–84); Note, *Strategic Bankruptcies: Class Actions, Classification & the Dalkon Shield Cases,* 7 Cardozo L.Rev. 817 (1985–86); Kesner, *Future Asbestos Related Litigants as Holders of Statutory Claims Under Chapter 11 of the Bankruptcy Code and Their Place in the Johns–Manville Reorganization,* 62 Am.Bankruptcy L.J. 69 (1988).

2. *Preemption*

JOHNSON v. GENERAL MOTORS CORPORATION

U.S. District Court, W.D. Oklahoma, 1995.
889 F.Supp. 451.

MEMORANDUM OPINION AND ORDER

DAVID L. RUSSELL, CHIEF JUDGE.

At issue [is] Defendant, General Motors Corporation's * * * Motion for Partial Summary Judgment on Plaintiffs' "Air Bag" Claim, pursuant to Fed.R.Civ.P. 56(b). This Court's jurisdiction over the instant suit is based upon diversity of citizenship of the parties pursuant to 28 U.S.C. s

1332(a)(1), and is undisputed. For the reasons discussed below, the Court * * * grants Defendant's motion as to Plaintiffs Byron Johnson, III's, and Londa Johnson's "air bag" Claim.

I. Introduction and Statement of the Case.

This is a products liability action. Plaintiff, Byron Johnson, III, was seriously injured when, on January 20, 1993, the 1992 Pontiac Grand Prix (the "Pontiac") which he was driving was struck, virtually "head-on," by another vehicle which had crossed the center line of the highway. Byron Johnson's injuries as a result of the accident included a broken neck, ruptured spleen and fractured pelvis.

* * *

The claims asserted by Plaintiffs focus on issues of the Pontiac's crashworthiness. Generally, Plaintiffs contend the Pontiac was defective in its ability to protect passengers from the increased injuries which often result from "second collisions," i.e., impacts between the passenger and the interior parts of the vehicle immediately following the exterior collision.

* * *

Plaintiffs contend that the Pontiac was defective because it was not equipped with air bags; and because the seat belt assembly failed to adequately restrain a passenger in the event of a sudden stop or crash.

* * *

On January 13, 1995, Defendant moved for judgment on Plaintiffs' "air bag" claim, contending the claim is preempted under the provisions of the Motor Vehicle Safety Act, 49 U.S.C. ss 30101–30169 (the "Safety Act").[9]

* * *

The parties do not dispute the two (2) material facts which are relevant to the issue of pre-emption in this case. First, the parties agree that no air bags were installed in the Pontiac when it left Defendant's possession, custody and control. Second, the parties agree that the regulations promulgated under the authority of the Safety Act (the "Safety Standards") permitted Defendant to choose whether to install air bags in the Pontiac, or to install another type of passenger restraint system. Thus, the parties agree that neither the Safety Act, nor the Safety Standards under that Act, required Defendant to install air bags in the Pontiac.

Plaintiffs contend, however, that Defendant's compliance with federal Safety Standards relating to air bags does not render Defendant exempt from common law liability under state law, if Defendant's failure to install air bags in the Pontiac rendered the vehicle otherwise defective and unreasonably dangerous. See 49 U.S.C. s 30103(e). Plaintiffs ground their

9. Originally titled "The National Traffic and Motor Vehicle Safety Act," and codified at 15 U.S.C. ss 1381–1426, the Safety Act was recently re-codified "without substantive changes" at sections 30101–30169 of Title 49 of the United States Code. See Act of July 5, 1994, Pub.L. No. 103–272, s 1(a)(1994) U.S.C.C.A.N. (108 Stat.) 745. Because the provisions of the Safety Act remain virtually unchanged from the version which appeared in Title 15, this Court will cite to the Safety Act as re-codified in this opinion. However, the case authority relied upon by the Court cites to the Safety Act as it appeared in Title 15 of the United States Code.

"air bag" claim upon the assertion that the Safety Standards set "minimum requirements," and, therefore, they argue that the lack of air bags in the Pontiac rendered the vehicle defective in this case.

Disagreeing, Defendant contends that the pre-emption clause contained in the Safety Act prohibits this Court from considering Plaintiffs' "no air bag" assertions as a basis for Defendant's possible liability. For this proposition, Defendant relies upon Kitts v. General Motors Corp., 875 F.2d 787, 789 (10th Cir.1989), cert. denied, 494 U.S. 1065, 110 S.Ct. 1781, 108 L.Ed.2d 783 (1990), where the United States Court of Appeals for the Tenth Circuit held that a plaintiff's products liability action based upon a manufacturer's failure to install air bags in a motor vehicle, where no air bag is required by federal law, is impliedly pre-empted under the Safety Act.

Because there is no question of fact which is material to Defendant's contention of federal pre-emption on Plaintiff's "air bag" claim, this Court must decide the issue as a matter of law on summary judgment. A review of the applicable provisions of the Safety Act, and recent case authority on the issue of pre-emption, compels the Court to agree, in principle, with Defendant's position, and hold Plaintiff's "air bag" claim to be pre-empted under 49 U.S.C. 30103(b)(1). In so holding, however, the Court departs from the reasoning expressed by the Tenth Circuit in Kitts, and finds Plaintiffs' "air bag" claim to be expressly, rather than impliedly, pre-empted.

The two statutory provisions which have caused the pre-emption question to arise in this case, and to arise in cases coming before other federal courts, are sections 30103(b)(1) and 30103(e) of Title 49 of the United States Code. Section 30103(b)(1), the "Pre-emption Clause," provides:

> When a motor vehicle safety standard is in effect under this chapter, a State or political subdivision of a State may prescribe or continue in effect a standard applicable to the same aspect of performance of a motor vehicle or motor vehicle equipment only if the standard is identical to the standard prescribed under this chapter....

49 U.S.C. s 30103(b)(1)[19] Section 30103(e) of the Safety Act, the "Savings Clause," states:

> Compliance with a motor vehicle safety standard prescribed under this chapter does not exempt a person from liability at common law.

49 U.S.C. s 30103(e)[20] Because it is the responsibility of this Court to interpret these two provisions in a manner which will most fully express Congress' intent in the provisions' enactment, the Court begins its analysis with a review of the provisions' legislative history.

The legislative history of the Safety Act indicates that the Pre-emption Clause was enacted by Congress to assure that the "primary responsibility" for regulating the safety features of motor vehicles was to "fall squarely upon the Federal Government." Accordingly, any state standard applicable to a particular aspect of a motor vehicle which differs from the federal standard was intended by Congress to be preempted.

---

19. Formerly found at 15 U.S.C. s 1392(d).

20. Formerly found at 15 U.S.C. s 1397(k).

Congress did not, however, intend for this pre-emption to "restrict State common law standards of care." Therefore, Congress included the Savings Clause in the Safety Act to assure that common law claims based upon a manufacturer's failure to act with reasonable care were not exempted.

This Court takes the legislative directives contained in the Pre-emption and Savings Clauses to mean precisely what they say, and, consequently, finds little conflict between them. It appears that Congress intended for federal law to dictate the boundaries of a manufacturer's legal duty with respect to certain aspects of a motor vehicle's design and manufacture. State law, however, is permitted to set the standard of care in the exercise of that legal duty.

Accordingly, federal law controls whether a manufacturer, like Defendant, has a legal duty to install an air bag in a vehicle. However, common law may dictate that once the decision in favor of air bag installation is made, the manufacturer exercise reasonable care in such installation. See Perry v. Mercedes Benz of N.A., 957 F.2d 1257, 1264 (5th Cir.1992) (plaintiffs may bring claims for injuries caused by defectively designed and manufactured air bags under 49 U.S.C. s 30103(e)). Thus, the question of pre-emption of Plaintiffs' "air bag" claim in this case should be resolved by determining whether, in permitting Plaintiffs to bring the claim, the Court is likely to create a conflicting legal duty prohibited under section 30103(b)(1), as opposed to a standard of care under state law which is permitted by section 30103(e).

In the instant case, Plaintiffs do not contend Defendant installed an air bag in the Pontiac which was defective. Rather, Plaintiffs assert the Pontiac was defective because Defendant failed to install any air bag. To be successful, Plaintiffs' "air bag" claim must be grounded upon a finding by this Court that, under Oklahoma law, Defendant had a legal duty to install an air bag in the Pontiac, and that the legal duty was breached when Defendant exercised its discretion provided by the Safety Standards and chose to install a seat belt assembly and other safety devices in the air bag's place. Therefore, Plaintiffs can only prevail on the "air bag" claim if a legal duty under state law is recognized by this Court which is more stringent that the legal duty relating to air bags imposed under federal law.

* * *

Looking only to the plain language of the Pre-emption and Savings Clauses, and the legislative history of the Safety Act, it seems clear that Congress intended for such claims as Plaintiff's "air bag" claim to be preempted.

Plaintiffs' "air bag" claim depends upon the creation of a state-imposed, legal standard or duty at common law which directly conflicts with the standard or duty imposed by federal law. This is precisely the kind of circumstance which the Pre-emption Clause contained in the Safety Act was intended to address. Therefore, a finding of express pre-emption of Plaintiffs' "air bag" claim under 49 U.S.C. s 30103(b)(1) seems entirely appropriate. See e.g., Cipollone v. Liggett Group, Inc., 505 U.S. 504, 519–20, 112 S.Ct. 2608, 2619, 120 L.Ed.2d 407, 425–27 (1992)(broad language of pre-emption clause under the amended ("1969") version of the Federal Cigarette Labeling and Advertising Act of 1965, 15 U.S.C. ss 1331–1340, includes standards which may be set by state courts determining common law claims).

However, despite this Court's comfort with the above-stated analysis, other federal courts considering the same issue have had extreme difficulty reaching a similar result. See e.g., Myrick v. Freuhauf Corp., 13 F.3d 1516, 1521 (11th Cir.1994), cert. granted, ___ U.S. ___, 115 S.Ct. 306, 130 L.Ed.2d 218 (1994)(state law claim based upon failure to install anti-lock brakes not expressly pre-empted by Safety Act); Wood v. General Motors Corp., 865 F.2d 395, 419 (1st Cir.1988), cert. denied, 494 U.S. 1065, 110 S.Ct. 1781, 108 L.Ed.2d 782 (1990)(state law claims based upon failure to install air bags are impliedly, but not expressly pre-empted under the Safety Act); Garrett v. Ford Motor Co., 684 F.Supp. 407, 411–2 (D.Md. 1987)(no express pre-emption of "air bag" claim under Safety Act). For example, in Kitts v. General Motors, Corp., 875 F.2d 787, 789 (10th Cir.1989), the Tenth Circuit held that a plaintiff's state law claims based upon a manufacturer's failure to install air bags in a vehicle were not expressly, but were impliedly, pre-empted under the Pre–Emption and Savings Clauses contained in the Safety Act. Thus, the question whether implied or express pre-emption applies to common law claims under the Safety Act has not been uniformly resolved by federal courts.

Nevertheless, whether pre-emption of conflicting common law claims is held to be expressed or implied under the Safety Act, the standing rule of law in the Tenth Circuit is that a plaintiff's state law claim for a manufacturer's failure to install an air bag in a vehicle is pre-empted by federal law. In this Circuit, several post-Kitts cases have held in accord with this rule, and with the underlying reasoning which lead to the rule. Therefore, this Court finds no case authority which indicates the Tenth Circuit would be inclined to change the rule announced in Kitts if confronted with the same issue today.

Despite this, Plaintiffs argue against the Tenth Circuit's rule of pre-emption. In their brief in opposition to Defendant's Rule 56(b) motion on this issue, Plaintiffs correctly point out that the implied pre-emption analysis used by the Tenth Circuit to reach its holding in Kitts was recently rejected by the United States Supreme Court. See Cipollone, 505 U.S. at 516–17, 112 S.Ct. at 2618, 120 L.Ed.2d at 423 (when Congress has included an express pre-emption clause in an act, a court may not engage in an implied pre-emption analysis to broaden its scope). Despite the existence of recent Tenth Circuit authority favoring the Kitts holding, Plaintiffs contend that Cipollone effectively overrules Kitts.

This Court strongly disagrees. The analysis prescribed by the Supreme Court in Cipollone, while admittedly discarding the implied pre-emption approach utilized in Kitts, nevertheless supports the Kitts' holding under the express pre-emption rationale applied by this Court in this opinion.

In Cipollone, the Supreme Court considered whether the prohibitions against state created "requirements" and "obligations" contained in Section 5(b) of the Public Health Cigarette Smoking Act of 1969, 15 U.S.C. ss

1331–1340 (the "Smoking Act"), expressly pre-empts claims for damages brought by plaintiffs under common law. The Supreme Court held common law claims are expressly preempted under the Smoking Act, noting: The phrase "[n]o requirement or prohibition" sweeps broadly and suggests no distinction between positive enactments and common law; to the contrary, those words easily encompass obligations that take the form of common law rules. As we noted in another context, "[state] regulation can be as effectively exerted through an award of damages as through some form of preventive relief. The obligation to pay compensation can be, indeed is designed to be, a potent method of governing conduct and controlling policy." Cipollone, 505 U.S. at 537, 112 S.Ct. at 2628–29, 120 L.Ed.2d at 436–37.

Applying Cipollone by analogy to the instant case, this Court finds the Safety Act's prohibition against state created "standards" contained in 49 U.S.C. s 30103(b)(1) easily encompasses the kind of common law rules and legal duties which would quickly be established if Oklahoma courts permitted plaintiffs to assert products liability claims against motor vehicle manufacturers who failed to install air bags in vehicles because the federal Safety Standards did not require them to do so. Thus, under Cipollone and Kitts, this Court finds Plaintiffs' "air bag" claims to be expressly preempted under the Safety Act. Defendant's motion for partial summary judgment on Plaintiffs' "air bag" claim must therefore be granted.

* * *

III. Conclusion.

Defendant's Motion for Partial Summary Judgment on Plaintiffs' "Airbag" Claim is GRANTED.

IT IS SO ORDERED.

Notes

1. Preemption litigation now sweeps across broad areas of products liability law, involving both design defect and warning defect claims. *See*, e.g. Comeaux v. National Tea Co., 81 F.3d 42 (5th Cir.1996)(alleged inadequate warning accompanying lighter fluid preempted by Federal Hazardous Substances Act); Talbott v. C.R. Bard, Inc., 63 F.3d 25 (1st Cir.1995)(alleged heart catheter defect preempted by the Medical Device Amendments to the Food Drug and Cosmetic Act); Bice v. Leslie's Poolmart, Inc., 39 F.3d 887 (8th Cir.1994)(alleged inadequate labeling on chemical used to maintain swimming pools preempted by Federal Insecticide, Fungicide and Rodenticide Act); Carstensen v. Brunswick Corp., 49 F.3d 430 (8th Cir.)(design defect claim based on lack of propeller guard on boat motor preempted by Federal Boat Safety Act); Cipollone v. Liggett Group, 505 U.S. 504, 112 S.Ct. 2608, 120 L.Ed.2d 407 (1992)(warning defect claims preempted by the Cigarette Labeling and Advertising Act).

2. In Freightliner Corp. v. Myrick, __ U.S. __, 115 S.Ct. 1483, 131 L.Ed.2d 385 (1995) the Supreme Court clarified its *Cipollone* ruling. The existence of an express preemption provision in a statute does not mean that an implied preemption cannot also exist. If a state regulation directly conflicts

with a federal provision, the state rule may be preempted. *Myrick*, 115 S.Ct. At 1488.

3. Medtronic v. Lohr, ___ U.S. ___, 116 S.Ct. 2240, 135 L.Ed.2d 700 (1996) is the most recent Supreme Court statement on preemption. The case involved a failed pacemaker, regulated under the 1976 Medical Device Amendments to the Food and Drug Act. The Amendments contained the following preemption provision:

> [N]o state or political subdivision of a State may establish or continue in effect with respect to a device indented for human use and requirement (1) which is different from, or in addition to, any requirement applicable under [the MDA] to the device, and (2) which related to the safety or effectiveness of the device or to any other matter included in a requirement applicable to the device under [the Act]

21 U.S. C. § 360k(a). A divided court held that the Congress did not intend to preempt the field of medical devices. Specifically, the amendments did not preempt either the plaintiff's negligent design claims nor her manufacturing and labeling claims. In an opinion joined by three other judges, Justice Stevens stated, "It will be rare indeed for a court hearing a common-law cause of action to issue a decree that has 'the effect of establishing a substantive requirement for a specific device.'" 116 S.Ct. at 2259.

Justice O'Connor, writing for four justices, agreed that § 360k(a) did not preempt the Lohr's design defect claim. O'Connor argued, however, that § 360k(a) did preempt their manufacturing claims insofar as these claims would compel Medtronic to comply with requirements different from or in addition to the FDA's Good Manufacturing Practice regulations. Likewise, it would preempt warning defect claims if they required warnings in addition to or different from the labeling requirement imposed by the FDA.

Justice Bryer, writing separately, agreed with the Stevens opinion that none of the Lohr claims were preempted. However, he did not agree that "future incidents of MDA pre-emption of common-law claims will be 'few' or 'rare.'" *Id.* at 2262.

Medtronic reached the Supreme Court following a summary judgment for the defendant. The Court was not confronted with a jury verdict that appeared to place conflicting or additional burdens on the defendant. It did not, therefore, address questions of conflict preemption. If you were advising plaintiff counsel, how would recommend they prosecute their claim so as to minimize the possibility of a successful preemption claim by the defendants after a trial?

The unwillingness of all the judges in *Medtronic* to conclude that design defect claims were precluded by the preemption clause of the MDA is due in large part to the status of the pacemaker under the statute. When the Medical Device Amendments were originally enacted, the Congress mandated that before Class III devices (those that "present a potential unreasonable risk of injury or injury") could be introduced into the market the manufacturer must provide the FDA with "reasonable assurance" that the device is both safe and effective. This requirement was intended to place devices in the same status as prescription drugs and involves a process typically requiring 1,200 hours of review. *Medtronic*, 116 S.Ct. at 2247. However, the statute included a grandfathering provision allowing existing devices to remain on the market until the FDA found the time and resources to conduct a full review. In addition, to prevent the manufacturers of grandfathered devices from monopolizing markets until new devices cleared the pre-marketing assurance process, the statute allowed new devices to be introduced prior to full pre-market approval if they are "substantially equivalent" to pre-existing devices. The average "substantial equivalence" review requires only 20 hours and does not involve an examination of the product's safety and effectiveness. Because of underfunding and the substantial time required for full pre-market approval the vast majority of medical devices have been introduced under the "substantial equivalence" test. The pacemaker involved in this case was introduced through this procedure. Do you think the Court would have held differently on the design defect preemption question if the Medtronic pacemaker had been introduced under the pre-market approval process? *See* Committee of Dental Amalgam Manufacturers v. Stratton, 92 F.3d 807 (9th Cir.1996).

4. Perry v. Mercedes Benz of North America, Inc., 957 F.2d 1257 (5th Cir.1992), cited in Johnson, involved an automobile that in fact did have an airbag. The plaintiff initially failed to notice a stop sign where the street that she was on dead-ended into another street. She then saw a car approaching the intersection on the cross street and concluded she would not be able to stop in time to avoid a collision. She decided to proceed through the intersection and into the ditch on the other side. The driver side air bag did not inflate and the plaintiff was not wearing her seat belt. She struck the steering wheel or windshield and injured her face and mouth. She alleged that the defendant's air bag was defectively designed because it had an unreasonably dangerous "deceleration velocity deployment threshold" i.e. the force that must be caused by the vehicle's sudden deceleration to trigger inflation of the airbag. Mercedes designed the system in Perry's vehicle with a minimum threshold of twelve miles per hour against a rigid barrier.

The Fifth Circuit concluded that the federal regulations that permitted car manufacturers to achieve increased passenger safety either with air bags or seat belts did not preempt a claim that, once having made an air bag election, the defendant employed a defective design. The savings clause in the statute is a clear indication that Congress intended state common law tort law to govern this issue.

Independent of the preemption issue, do you believe the plaintiff will be able to establish an alternative feasible design for the deployment of the air bag? What are the competing design considerations?

5. State supreme courts have been less willing to conclude that the federal government has preempted state law as to air bags. *See* Wilson v. Pleasant, 660 N.E.2d 327 (Ind.1995); Tebbetts v. Ford Motor Co., 140 N.H. 203, 665 A.2d 345 (1995). The *Wilson* court argued that there is no conflict preemption because, assuming *arguendo* that Indiana law requires airbags, this does not conflict with the federal standard inasmuch as the federal standard does not prohibit airbags—it only permits other alternatives. *Wilson*, 660 N.E.2d at 337.

3. *Compliance With Regulations*

Failure to comply with state or government regulations is, of course, often held to be negligence *per se*. The *Restatement (Third) of Torts: Products Liability* (Tentative Draft No 2. 1995) § 7 takes the position that noncompliance with an applicable product safety statute or regulation "renders the product defective with respect to the risks sought to be reduced by the statute or regulation."

As we saw in *Grundberg* (*supra*, p. 671), a number of courts have used comment *k* of the *Restatement of Torts (Second)* § 402A to declare that some or all prescription drugs approved by the Food and Drug Administration are not defectively designed as a matter of law. In these jurisdictions, compliance with FDA regulations provides the pharmaceutical manufacturer with broad immunity. Most courts permit the defendant to introduce compliance evidence as a fact tending to support the defendant's position that its product is non-defective, but the overwhelming majority of courts have said that such evidence is not conclusive. For example, most courts have now held that approval by the Federal Food and Drug Administration, pursuant to the Federal Food, Drug, and Cosmetic Act, 21 U.S.C. § 301 *et seq.* and the Public Health Service Act, 42 U.S.C. § 201 *et seq.*, may be evidence of lack of defect but is not determinative. *See, e.g.,* Feldman v. Lederle Laboratories, 97 N.J. 429, 479 A.2d 374 (1984)(drug); Ferebee v. Chevron Chemical Co., 736 F.2d 1529 (D.C.Cir.1984)(EPA approval of warning under the Federal Insecticide, Fungicide and Rodenticide Act does not compel jury finding that warning adequate). This is the position taken by the proposed *Restatement (Third)*. A few state product liability statutes contain provisions that state compliance with appropriate government standards creates a rebuttable presumption that the product is not defective. For example, the Illinois products liability statute contains the following provision:

> Federal and State standards; presumption. In a product liability action, a product or product component shall be presumed to be reasonably safe if the aspect of the product or product component that allegedly caused the harm was specified or required, or if the aspect is specifically exempted for particular applications or users, by a federal or State statute or regulation promulgated by an agency of the federal or State government responsible for the safety or use of the product before the product was distributed into the stream of commerce.

Il St. Ch. 735 § 5/2–2103 (Supp.1996). *See* Miller v. Lee Apparel Company, Inc., 19 Kan.App.2d 1015, 881 P.2d 576 (1994)(compliance with Federal Flammable Fabrics Act.).

In Dawson v. Chrysler Corp., 630 F.2d 950 (3d Cir.1980), the court, in applying this majority rule, expressed the need for national uniformity in the treatment of design of automobiles but found that the National Traffic & Motor Vehicle Safety Act did not preempt state law. In this regard consider the comments of the West Virginia Supreme court in Blankenship v. General Motors Corp., 185 W.Va. 350, 406 S.E.2d 781, 783, 784 (W.Va. 1991).

> [B]oth the defendant and amicus argue that allowing crashworthiness lawsuits invites juries to second-guess the safety standards promulgated by the National Highway Traffic Safety Administration. Thus, under the common theories of crashworthiness, defendant and amicus argue, different juries will reach different conclusions about the "reasonableness" of safety features, leaving manufacturers in the unenviable position of being unable to predict what juries will deem a

"defective product [that] causes personal injury." Furthermore, defendant and amicus argue, juries may find designs approved by federal regulators "defective," giving the whole regulatory effort a certain Alice in Wonderland quality.

In all of these regards the manufacturers and amicus have strong arguments. Nonetheless, West Virginia is a small rural state with .66 percent of the population of the United States. Although some members of this Court have reservations about the wisdom of many aspects of tort law, as a court we are utterly powerless to make the overall tort system for cases arising in interstate commerce more rational: Nothing that we do will have any impact whatsoever on the set of economic trade-offs that occur in the national economy. And, ironically, trying unilaterally to make the American tort system more rational through being uniquely responsible in West Virginia will only punish our residents severely without, in any regard, improving the system for anyone else.

[P]roduct liability is concerned with spreading the cost of inevitable accidents. Inherent in this cost-spreading function is the collection of what amounts to insurance premiums from all the purchasers of products, and the purchase by manufacturers of commercial insurance or the creation of self insurance funds. * * *

The defendant before us, General Motors, is the largest producer of automobiles in the world. In light of the fact that all of our sister states have adopted a cause of action for lack of crashworthiness, General Motors is already collecting a product liability premium every time it sells a car anywhere in the world, including West Virginia. West Virginians, then, are already paying the product liability insurance premium when they buy a General Motors car, so this Court would be both foolish and irresponsible if we held that while West Virginians must pay the premiums, West Virginians can't collect the insurance after they're injured.

The *Blankenship* opinion is, in part, a call for national standards for products liability law. For several years attempts have been made to get Congress to pass federal legislation, preempting state products liability law. The argument has centered on the need, in a national economy, for manufacturers to have only one legal standard with which to deal. The effort began with a proposed uniform state law proposed by the Commerce Department. In 1996 the Congress did pass a products liability bill, but it was vetoed by President Clinton.

E. RELEVANT STATUTES

An attorney consulted in a potential products liability action would be obliged to examine the growing state and federal regulation of consumer products. Potentially the most pervasive and important legislation of this kind thus far enacted is the Consumer Products Safety Act (now, as amended, 15 U.S.C. §§ 2051–81).

For purposes of a torts lawyer the most important provisions of the Consumer Products Safety Act are those that provide for actions for damages by those persons injured by any violations of the Commission's rules. The Act (15 U.S.C. § 2072) authorizes "[a]ny person who shall sustain injury by reason of any knowing (including willful) violation of a consumer product safety rule * * * or order issued by the Commission" to "sue any person who knowingly (including willfully) violated any such rule." If the plaintiff can meet the jurisdictional amount required for the exercise of federal jurisdiction, the action may be brought in the appropriate federal district court, which is authorized, if "the court determines it to be in the interests of justice" to award the plaintiff in addition to his damages, "the costs of suit, including reasonable attorneys' fees * * * and reasonable expert witness fees." It should be pointed out that, in an action based upon a violation of the Act, the plaintiff is not obliged to litigate the question of the dangerousness or the degree of dangerousness of the product. All the plaintiff must show is the knowing violation of a rule promulgated by the Commission and a sufficient causal connection between that violation and the plaintiff's injuries.

The Act specifically provides that the damage remedy provided "shall be in addition to and not in lieu of any other remedies provided by common law or under Federal or State law" (15 U.S.C. § 2072), and that compliance with a consumer product safety rule "shall not relieve any person from liability at common law or under State statutory law." (15 U.S.C. § 2074). Undoubtedly, however, in an action in the state courts the existence of a federal safety rule will be a highly relevant factor. Many if not most state courts can be expected to treat a violation of the federal rule as negligence *per se* or as an instance in which absolute liability should be imposed.

Another important federal statute for products liability lawyers is the Magnuson–Moss Act of 1975, 15 U.S.C. §§ 2301–2312. The Act was designed to make warranties on consumer products more understandable to consumers and authorizes the Federal Trade Commission to issue regulations implementing the Act's provisions. Written warranties are not required but, if offered, must meet disclosure requirements specified in the regulations. The Act encourages warrantors to establish informal dispute settlement procedures and provides that, where acceptable procedures are established and incorporated in the warranty, a consumer may initiate a civil action only after first resorting to the settlement procedures. 15 U.S.C. § 2310(a).

Many states have now passed tort reform statutes. These measures have varied but in general they have been aimed at (1) limiting non-economic damages; (2) limiting the occasions upon which punitive damages could be awarded; (3) limiting lawyer's fees; (4) limiting the time within which suits can be brought (a statute of repose); (5) defining a product defect to include the state-of-the-art concept and applying it at the point of first sale to a consumer (or a similar point in time); (6) eliminating joint and several liability, at least in comparative negligence states; (7) applying comparative negligence principles in states that have not already done so; (8) making compliance with statutory or administratively set standards a defense; and (9) eliminating suits against retailers or others in the distribution network.

While no legislative action has yet been enacted at the federal level, an increasing number of states have adopted reform legislation incorporating some combination of the above changes. *See, e.g.,* Ohio Rev.Code §§ 2307.71–80, 2315.20 (Page); N.J.Stat.Ann. 2A:58C–1 *et seq.* (West); Tex. Civil Prac. & Rem. Code §§ 33.001 *et seq;* Smith–Hurd Ill. Stat. Ann. Ch. 735 § 5/2–2101 *et seq.* (Supp.1996). Reform efforts are discussed in Joseph Sanders and Craig Joyce, *"Off to the Races": The 1980s Tort Crisis and the Law Reform Process,* 27 Hous. L. Rev. 207(1990)(summarizing tort reform provisions adopted in 48 jurisdictions between 1985 and 1988) and Warren Eginton, *Products Liability Legislation Update,* 4 Prod. Liab. L.J. 181 (1993). *See generally,* Alan Schwartz, *Proposals for Products Liability Reform: A Theoretical Synthesis,* 97 Yale L.J. 353 (1988).

The state legislative reforms of the substantive rules applicable to products liability for the most part have survived constitutional attack. However, statutes of repose and limitations on damages have met mixed reactions. *See* Jones v. Five Star Engineering, Inc., 717 S.W.2d 882 (Tenn.1986)(suit must be filed within 10 years of the product's first sale for use, constitutional); Dague v. Piper Aircraft Corp., 275 Ind. 520, 418 N.E.2d 207 (1981)(within 10 years after delivery to initial user, constitutional); Radke v. H.C. Davis Sons' Manufacturing Co., Inc., 241 Neb. 21, 486 N.W.2d 204 (1992)(within 10 years after product was first sold or leased for use or consumption, constitutional); Hanson v. Williams County, 389 N.W.2d 319 (N.D.1986)(within 10 years from date of purchase or 11 years from date of manufacture, violates equal protection); Kennedy v. Cumberland Engineering Co., 471 A.2d 195 (R.I.1984)(within 10 years, violates access to courts guarantee). *See* Stephen J. Werber, *The Constitutional Dimension of a National Products Liability Statute of Repose,* 40 Vill. L. Rev. 985 (1995)

Statutes of repose are a response to the fact that products liability actions have long "tails." that is many years may pass between the time a product is first put into the stream of commerce and the last lawsuit concerning the product is brought. *See,* George Priest, *The Current Insurance Crisis and Modern Tort Law,* 96 Yale L. J. 1521 (1987) for a discussion of the special problems this creates for insurance markets.

F. PRODUCTS LIABILITY IN THE EUROPEAN COMMUNITY AND JAPAN

1. *The European Economic Union Directive*

The European Economic Union has adopted a Directive providing a uniform code of products liability. O.J.Eur.Comm. (No. L 210) 29–33 (1985). The Directive is a good example of a simple attempt to codify products liability law. A "producer" is liable for damages caused by a defect in his product without proof of negligence. Article 2 of the Directive defines a "product" to "mean all movables." Article 6 defines a "defect."

Article 6.

    1. A product is defective when it does not provide the safety which a person is entitled to expect, taking all circumstances into account, including:

        (a) the presentation of the product;

(b) the use to which it could reasonably be expected that the product would be put;

(c) the time when the product was put into circulation.

2. A product shall not be considered defective for the sole reason that a better product is subsequently put into circulation.

How would you describe the European Directive test for defectiveness in American terms? Do you see any problems with this test?

Article 7 provides the producer with a set of defenses to a products liability claim.

Article 7.

The producer shall not be liable as a result of this Directive if he proves:

(a) that he did not put the product into circulation; or

(b) that, having regard to the circumstances, it is probable that the defects which caused the damage did not exist at the time when the product was put into circulation by him or that this defect came into being afterwards; or

(c) that the product was neither manufactured by him for sale or any form of distribution for economic purpose nor manufactured or distributed by him in the course of his business; or

(d) that the defect is due to compliance of the product with mandatory regulations issued by the public authorities; or

(e) that the state of scientific and technical knowledge at the time when he put the product into circulation was not such as to enable the existence of the defect to be discovered; or

(f) in the case of a manufacturer of a component, that the defect is attributable to the design of the product in which the component has been fitted or the instructions given by the manufacturer of the product.

Article 7(e) establishes what American courts would call a state-of-the-art defense. In Europe this is called "development risk." The development risk defense set forth in Article 7(e) was quite controversial and in response Article 15(1)(b) permits member states to exclude this provision. Member states may "provide * * * that the producer shall be liable even if he proves that the state of scientific and technical knowledge at the time when he put the product into circulation was not such as to enable the existence of a defect to be discovered." *See,* Lori M. Linger, *The Products Liability Directive: A Mandatory Development Risk Defense,* 14 Fordham Int'l L. J. 487 (1991), for a discussion of which alternative member states had adopted as of 1990.

The Directive has the following provision with respect to plaintiff behavior.

Article 8.

* * *

2. The liability of the producer may be reduced or disallowed, when having regard to all the circumstances, the damages is caused both by

a defect in the product and by the fault of the injured person or any person for whom the injured person is responsible.

The Directive has a three year statute of limitations, governed by a discovery rule. It also contains a 10 year statute of repose. For useful discussions of the E.U. directive *see,* Mary J. Davis, *Individual and Institutional Responsibility: A Vision for Comparative Fault in Products Liability,* 39 Vill. L. Rev. 281 (1994); John G. Culhane, *The Limits of Products Liability Reform Within A Consumer Expectation Model: A Comparison of Approaches Taken by the United States and the European Union.* 19 Hastings Int'l & Comp. L. Rev. 1 (1995).

2. Japan

Japan passed a products liability statute in 1994. The statute is modeled on the European Economic Union Directive. As in Europe, a producer is strictly liable for injuries caused by his defective product. Article 2 of the statute defines a defect as a lack of safety which the product should ordinarily provide considering its ordinary use, its specific characteristics, the time it was put on the market, and other considerations. Article 4 provides for a "development risk" defense. As in Europe, there is a three year statute of limitations and a ten year statute of repose. *See* Catherine Dauvergne, *The Enactment of Japan's Product Liability Law,* 28 U.B.C. L. Rev. 403, 413–14 (1994); Anita Bernstein and Paul Fanning, *"Weightier Than A Mountain": Duty, Hierarchy, and the Consumer in Japan,* 29 Vand. J. Transnat'l L. 45 (1996).

Prior to the passage of the products liability statute, Japan had enacted the Consumer Products Safety Act. This 1973 statute created the Products Safety Council which began coordinating a privately ordered, voluntary products liability system. The Council established safety standards for over 100 products. Manufacturers whose products meet the standards attach a S ("safety") label to the goods. In addition, manufactures could opt to attach a SG ("safety goods") label. By doing so, they agreed that their product would be judged by a strict liability standard (i.e. a defectiveness standard) rather than the prevailing negligence standard. *See* J. Mark Ramseyer, *Products Liability Through Private Ordering: Notes on a Japanese Experiment,* 144 U. Pa. L. Rev. 1823 (1996). As Ramseyer notes, this system allows individuals who want to purchase "strict liability" to do so while allowing others who do not choose to pay a higher price for similar goods to rely on a negligence regime. What are the arguments for and against this method of achieving consumer protection against product caused injuries?

Chapter 10

DAMAGES

A. INTRODUCTION

The subject of damages lies at the heart of both the practical workings and the theoretical foundations of the tort system. Practically, damages considerations pervade a tort case from its inception to its conclusion: from the plaintiff's lawyer's choice to accept representation in the plaintiff's case; through negotiation and alternative dispute resolution; through the presentation of proof at trial and the submission of post-trial motions aimed at reducing or adding to the damages findings; and through the drafting of a judgment for a lump sum award or for periodic payment of damages.

Theoretically, tort's traditional approach to damages has come under increasingly intense criticism in recent years. This critique has also found expression in tort reform enactments of legislatures and in some judicial rulings. These enactments include caps on pain and suffering damages, mandatory periodic payment of damages, and elimination or modification of the collateral source rule.

It is no coincidence that the subject of damages receives close attention from both the practitioner and the theorist. Many of the same concerns and issues drive both the practitioner's task with respect to damages and the theoretical discussion about tort damages. The very difficulties of measurement and valuation that occupy lawyers on both sides of the docket also fuel much of the tort reform debate. For example, uncertainty over how to value the nonmonetary aspects of injury is a central feature of both a given lawsuit and the theoretical controversy over the merits of "pain and suffering" damages (Should they exist at all? Should they be capped or "scheduled"?).

Tort reform legislation passed in many states over the past ten years has significantly altered some of the traditional damages doctrines of the tort common law. Thus, the practice and understanding of damages is currently a blend of common law doctrines and statutory provisions. This Chapter will explore both aspects of this blend.

The common law of tort recognizes three distinct categories of damages: nominal, compensatory, and punitive. Although the tort reform enactments of recent years have substantially modified some of the common law doctrines relating to compensatory and punitive damages, tort reform has not erased these three categories of damages or the basic distinctions among them.

Nominal damages are those that are awarded when a particular legal wrong has occurred—such as an intentional tort—and when no actual injury has resulted or when an injury cannot be proved. Nominal damages are usually minor or trivial in amount; their purpose is to symbolize or declare that a right has been violated. In practical terms, one significant aspect of nominal damages is that they can support an award for punitive damages. Thus, a plaintiff who has suffered no actual injury might nonetheless receive a significant monetary judgment if the factfinder awards both nominal and punitive damages. Generally, jurisdictions do not allow nominal damages for negligence alone. By contrast, most jurisdictions do allow nominal damages for intentional torts, defamation, and a variety of other torts.

Compensatory damages are awarded to compensate a party for actual injury or harm. The usually stated aim of compensatory damages—an aim explored in more detail throughout this Chapter—is to place the plaintiff, as far as money can do so, into the position the plaintiff would have occupied if the tortious wrong had never occurred.

Punitive damages are neither nominal nor compensatory. They are awarded to punish the defendant for malicious, outrageous, or highly reckless conduct, and to deter the defendant and others from engaging in similar conduct in the future. Because punitive damages are available only when the defendant has engaged in some level of aggravated wrongdoing, the plaintiff is not entitled to punitive damages simply by showing the required elements of a particular tort. Rather, the plaintiff also must obtain a finding that the defendant engaged in reckless, outrageous, or malicious conduct. The precise standard for finding aggravated conduct differs among jurisdictions.

In addition to these three well-recognized categories of damages, jurisdictions sometimes employ two other labels that primarily have procedural significance: "general damages" and "special damages." In jurisdictions that follow this distinction, the plaintiff need not specifically plead general damages, but must specifically plead special damages. "Special damages" usually are defined as damages that are peculiar to the particular plaintiff or transaction involved in the legal proceeding actually before the court; in addition, the category usually includes the damages that are most readily calculable by objective measures. Lost wages and medical expenses are the prototypical special damages. "General damages" usually are defined as those that are assumed to flow from a particular legal wrong, such as pain and suffering or mental anguish; they also tend to be the damages whose calculation requires greater exercise of discretion from the factfinder.

B. COMPENSATORY DAMAGES FOR NONFATAL PERSONAL INJURY

1. Basic Theories Behind Compensatory Damages

The theoretical case for compensatory damages differs somewhat depending on which major theoretical aim the tort system is seen as serving.

To the extent tort is a mechanism for achieving corrective justice, compensatory damages rest on the notion that the defendant who has caused a loss in some wrongful fashion should repair or compensate that loss, even if this would not necessarily further some instrumental or collective goal such as economic efficiency or distributive justice.

From the other major theoretical perspective—economic efficiency—the important goal is to reduce the overall social costs of accidents, not to achieve individualized corrective justice in a given case. This overall cost reduction aim consists of two strands. The first is deterring those accidents that can be efficiently prevented (under a cost-benefit analysis). In theory, tort damages serve this end, as Professor David Leebron explains:

> While from some perspectives these two goals—compensation and deterrence—often conflict, from an economic viewpoint they walk closely in hand. The basic theory is that the tort system forces activities to internalize the cost of injuries they produce. This, it is argued, will lead to correct cost/benefit decisionmaking on the part of enterprises that cause injuries, as well as the most efficient patterns of consumption and resource allocation. From this economic perspective, the tort system serves two roles. First, it makes relevant factual determinations (such as the failure to exercise due care and causation of the plaintiff's injuries) * * *. Second, it prices goods for which there is, and in many cases is permitted, no market. In other words, the tort system acts as a kind of "shadow pricing" mechanism, determining the cost of certain inputs (injuries), so that correct cost/benefit decisions may be made both by the relevant enterprise and the consumer.

> The problem, of course, is determining the "correct" or "efficient" price. If the tort system overvalues injuries, then business will invest too much in accident prevention. If, on the other hand, the tort system undervalues injuries, then there will be too little investment and hence too many injuries. In most circumstances, the ideal measure of the plaintiff's loss also will be the amount of damages we would want the defendant to anticipate in deciding on the level of safety precautions in which to invest.

David W. Leebron, *Final Moments: Damages For Pain and Suffering Prior to Death*, 64 N.Y.U. L. Rev. 256, 272 (1989)(citations omitted).*

This deterrence reasoning does not require that compensatory damages be awarded to the victim. It requires that the defendant be forced to internalize the full costs of its activities, but a system of administrative fines could do this as well. Practically, of course, payment to the victim is necessary because individual victims would not pursue tort claims if the only outcome were an administrative fine paid to the state.

As noted, deterring some injurious activity is just one strand of reducing overall social costs of accidents. The second strand has to do with those accidents that cannot be efficiently prevented. Even in a world where deterrence levels are optimal, some accidents still will happen, because not all accidents can be efficiently prevented. All car-related

* Reprinted with permission. New York University Law Review.

injuries could be prevented only if society eliminated cars or required everyone to drive slow tanks whose occupants would never be injured.

Although these accidents cannot be efficiently prevented, it may be possible to spread the costs of these accidents in ways that are more efficient than others. For instance, basic intuition and economic theory suggest that an individual suffers less when she incurs a series of small losses over time than when she incurs one large loss at a single moment in time. This is why most of us are willing to pay for insurance. Insurance, then, is a mechanism that does not primarily prevent accidents, but nonetheless can reduce the severity of the impact when an accident occurs.

Tort damages might be seen as a form of insurance. In exchange for paying premiums over time in the form of increased costs on products and services, we purchase a "tort insurance policy" that will award damages to us when certain conditions are met (if we sustain a compensable injury, if we can show fault or the applicable liability standard, if we can show causation, etc.). If this tort insurance policy is a good deal—that is, if it delivers a desirable level of insurance at an acceptable cost—then tort law lowers the costs of accidents not only by preventing them (the deterrence strand) but also by serving as an insurance system that spreads and minimizes the costs of accidents that are not prevented. This "insurance strand," unlike the deterrence strand, does in theory require that the *victim* receive the compensatory award.

Another theoretical aim—distributive justice—sometimes appears in judicial, scholarly, or political discourse. Distributive justice is a catch-all term for any number of theories that argue, usually on grounds of fairness or moral reasoning, for a particular distribution of societal resources. Such a theory might contend, for instance, that society's resources should be allocated in a way that provides for basic satisfaction of every individual's "just wants."

As the next sections will elaborate, tort common law purports to adopt a "full compensation" or restoration measure of damages: the factfinder should award the sum of money that will restore the plaintiff to her pre-injury position, to the extent money can do so. This animating principle results in a damages regime that is in many respects considerably more generous than medical or disability benefits available under any other private or social compensation source, such as social security disability benefits, veterans' disability benefits, workers' compensation benefits, and private medical, disability, or long-term care insurance policies.

Why should society handle so differently the disability problem posed by tortiously caused accidents from the disability problem posed by "natural" illnesses or accidents that happen in the absence of tortious conduct? Consider again the major theoretical aims just discussed: corrective justice, the economic efficiency goal of deterrence, the economic efficiency goal of insuring the costs of injury. Does each (or any) of these in theory require full compensation for all the dimensions of the loss? If not, what level or scope of damages would be proper under the theory?

2. *Categories of Compensable Damages*

In nonfatal personal injury cases, the following categories of compensatory damages are available to the injured person: (1) past and future medical and rehabilitative expenses; (2) past and future lost earning capacity; (3) past and future physical pain and suffering; (4) past and future mental anguish; (5) past and future impairment or disability; and (6) past and future disfigurement. "Impairment" or "disability" typically refers to functional limitations other than reduced wage-earning capacity; examples are the inability or lessened ability to garden, run, or dress oneself. Disfigurement refers to some physical deficit that does not reduce functioning; an obvious example is a scar. As we shall see in Chapter 11, the injured person's spouse, and sometimes her parent or child, also may have a claim for the loss of consortium (or "loss of companionship and society") that the injury has caused.

The precise phrasing of these items differs among jurisdictions. It is possible that a given jurisdiction will subsume items 3, 4, 5, and 6 into the single phrase "pain and suffering and mental anguish." Or a jurisdiction might subsume items 3 and 5 into a single phrase of "pain and suffering." In addition, jurisdictions differ on whether the jury returns an aggregate sum for all past damages and all future damages, or an aggregate sum for each category of past and future damages, or other such variations. Despite these variations, virtually all jurisdictions recognize by some label the plaintiff's ability to recover for the items noted above.

Jurisdictions also differ in how they articulate what sometimes is called "loss of the pleasures of life" or "loss of enjoyment of life." Some jurisdictions list it as a separate category; others allow recovery of it under one or more of the labels noted above.

3. *The Interaction of Damages With Liability*

The compensatory damages finding is separate from the liability finding. In jury trials, the jury is asked to make findings on the elements necessary to establish liability, and in a separate question is asked to assess damages. Litigators on both sides of the docket, and mediators and judges, understand that the evaluation of a case must take into account both of these independent variables: liability and damages. When assessing settlement options, for instances, both sides try to gauge the probability of success on liability, and the range of possible jury findings on damages (for instance, a high realistic prediction might be $1 million, and a low realistic prediction might be $500,000); the parties then value the case according to the expected damages discounted by the probability of success on liability. Thus, a weak liability-high damages case might have a roughly similar settlement value as a strong liability-weak damages case.

4. *Lost Earnings Versus Lost Earning Capacity*

Although courts often refer to the damage category of "lost earnings," the plaintiff is entitled to recover for lost earning capacity, past and future. Proof of the plaintiff's actual lost earnings up to the time of trial has evidentiary relevance, but is not necessarily determinative. The plaintiff might be earning the same amount post-injury as pre-injury, but also might be able to establish that, but for the injury, her wages would have increased even more.

As to loss of future earning capacity, the plaintiff is entitled to the present value of this loss. Calculating this loss involves a number of variables on which disagreement is common: (1) the plaintiff's earning capacity before the injury; (2) the degree to which the plaintiff's earning capacity has been diminished; (3) the period over which this diminished capacity will be experienced, which involves considering the plaintiff's life expectancy and work life expectancy.

As to the third variable, both sides frequently rely on life expectancy tables or worklife tables. In addition, especially for infant plaintiffs or those without an established earning history, wage earning tables of various sorts often are used. Yet these are not determinative, and either side might try to justify departing from the calculations embodied in the tables. Consider the following discussion of the future lost earning capacity of the plaintiff, Nyenpan, who was eight years old at the time of trial.

[D]efendants' expert economist Dr. Bradley Robert Schiller argues that, since [the plaintiff's] father was Liberian and his mother worked in Liberia when he was born, he could not be expected to spend his entire working life in the United States * * *. Aside from the reduced wages he could be expected to receive in Liberia, Dr. Schiller argued that his work life would be shorter by several years. He also believed that, once part of his work life had been spent in Liberia, he would receive less income in the United States. Moreover, Dr. Schiller argued that the appropriate measure of future earnings in the United States for the [plaintiff] (whose mother is white and whose father is black) is the average earnings of black men, not those of all men.

Defendants' argument that Nyenpan's projected earnings should be reduced because he might spend part of his working life in Liberia is not convincing. Insufficient evidence exists to support such a reduction. Furthermore, defendants' argument that average black male earnings are an appropriate measure of Nyenpan's future earnings cannot be accepted, since Nyenpan is half black and half white. Moreover, it would be inappropriate to incorporate current discrimination resulting in wage differences between the sexes or races or the potential for any future such discrimination into a calculation for damages resulting from lost wages. The parties did not cite any precedent on this question. Accordingly, upon request by the Court, Schiller submitted a calculation of the average earnings of all college graduates in the United States without regard to sex or race. Adjusted for changes in worklife expectancy, this calculation resulted in lost wages of $882,692. Dr. Schiller further adjusted this amount to reduce the income amount to earnings, to include FICA payroll taxes in the tax deduction, and to make certain adjustments in the net discount rate, resulting in total lost wages of $573,750. These adjustments appear to be reasonable and were not contested by plaintiffs. The average wages for all persons are lower than average black male wages; thus, the incorporation of women's expected earnings lowers the estimate even further than defendants' estimate. Nevertheless, estimating the plaintiff's future earnings based on the average earnings of all persons appears to be the most accurate means available of eliminating any discriminatory factors.

Wheeler Tarpeh–Doe v. United States, 771 F.Supp. 427, 455–56 (D.D.C. 1991), *rev'd on other grounds*, 28 F.3d 120 (D.C.Cir.1994).

> The [female plaintiff] argues that the utilization of these tables in this case would be inappropriate because they unjustly interdict a consideration of her particular economic condition. At trial, Dr. Reavy, upon cross-examination, indicated that one of the principal contributing factors to the shortened work life expectancy of a female, as reflected in these tables, is the prospect of child-bearing and the concomitant departure from the work force by a woman. In this case, however, the McDonalds did not have any children at the time [the plaintiff], then 33, contracted GBS and, as a result of this illness, it is exceedingly unlikely they ever will. Moreover, as noted, shortly after the onset of her disease, the Plaintiff's husband, Francis, was seriously injured and remains physically disabled for social security purposes. The Plaintiff also testified that she enjoyed her work at Lee Manufacturing and would have continued there if not for her illness. On this latter point, Leo Gutstein, the owner of Lee Manufacturing, testified that [the plaintiff] was a valued employee and a presser position would have remained available to her if she did not become disabled.

McDonald v. United States, 555 F.Supp. 935, 968 (M.D.Pa.1983).

Should racial or sexual differences in standardized life, health, or wage tables ever be allowed to factor into tort litigation? What about standardized life or health tables that take into account other types of differences? Suppose that, in litigation sometime in the future, the plaintiff is shown to have the gene that predisposes her to early Alzheimers', and that the defendant seeks to incorporate this into expert testimony on work life expectancy. Should this be allowed? These types of questions continue to receive extensive discussion in the insurance arena. For introductions, see Kenneth S. Abraham, Distributing Risk 64–100 (1986); Regina Austin, *The Insurance Classification Controversy*, 131 U.Pa.L.Rev. 517 (1983); Deborah A. Stone, *The Struggle for the Soul of Health Insurance*, 18 J. Health Politics, Policy & Law 287 (1993). These classification-related issues, however, have received relatively little attention in the context of the tort system. A recent exception is Martha Chamallas, *Questioning the Use of Race–Specific and Gender–Specific Economic Data in Tort Litigation: A Constitutional Argument*, 63 Ford. L. Rev. 73 (1994).

What if the injury has shortened the plaintiff's life expectancy? The general rule in the United States is that, for purposes of awarding damages for permanent impairment of earning capacity, the plaintiff's life expectancy as of the time of trial is determined without regard to the fact of the accident. In England, loss of future earning capacity was at one time determined on the basis of the plaintiff's physical condition after the accident with an additional sum provided for loss of life expectancy, but this approach has not found favor in the United States and has now been changed. *See* Pickett v. British Rail Eng'g Ltd., [1980] A.C. 136 (1978), [1978] 3 W.L.R. 955, [1979] 1 All E.R. 774. Which approach—the current approach or the former English approach—comports best with a corrective justice, efficient deterrence, or efficient insurance theory of tort?

Another frequently contested variable is what the plaintiff's diminished earning capacity will be over time. The plaintiff need not establish this figure precisely, but the plaintiff is required to submit enough evidence to allow the jury to make a reasonable measure of this item rather than a speculative guess. Consider this standard as applied to the facts in Morris v. Francisco, 238 Kan. 71, 708 P.2d 498 (Kan.1985). The plaintiff, Mary Morris, had cerebral palsy since birth, and when she was seventeen underwent surgery on her hips and ankles to preserve her ability to walk. The surgeon's negligence caused damage to the femoral nerve, leaving her permanently bound to a wheelchair. Morris testified at trial that, before the injury, she had hoped to become a kindergarten teacher or a teacher of children with disabilities. At the time of the trial, she was working in a clerical job, and testified that she now planned to attend night school and become a certified public accountant. Before the case was submitted to the jury, the defendant's lawyer (Mr. McCamish), the plaintiff's lawyer (Mr. Johnson), and the judge discussed whether the jury should be given a damages question on lost earning capacity.

"THE COURT: ... The difficulty as I see in this case, we have a young lady whose aspirations were to be a kindergarten teacher or someone in some capacity to aid or help disabled children. We have no evidence in this case whatsoever as to what such a person could expect to receive by way of income if she had achieved those aspirations. We've had no evidence in this case as to what her prospects of employment would have been in that type of endeavor because of her dexterity problems in her upper limbs, her upper extremities and her speech impairment. It's—she apparently is not only employable but employed at the present time. And her current employer is apparently extremely happy with her.

"MR. JOHNSON: Temporary.

"THE COURT: So we don't know whether her future is any less impaired from the standpoint of income than it was without the—or with the mobility in the lower extremities * * *.

"MR. JOHNSON: I think the difference, Judge, is that—and perhaps the instruction doesn't state it right, but what we're really talking about here is not a specific amount of loss of income, because we knew that we were not going to be able to put anybody really on the stand like an economist or anybody who could really go to that issue; but what we're really talking about here is loss of earning capacity, loss of the ability to have the opportunity to have the same job opportunities and income producing opportunities that she had before.

"And we had evidence from [the vocational counselor], who I think is an experienced person, that her mobility is what is her primary limitation in finding jobs, and it does—in fact, I used those words, does that impair her future earning capacity? And she said yes. So I don't think that an amount—and I don't know what the amount might be that they would put down there—would necessarily have to be directly related to, quote, what she would have made as a kindergarten teacher as opposed to what she's making now.

"THE COURT: If you get into—and the only factor we're dealing with here is loss of income. Either past, present or future. If you're getting into the other aspects that you mentioned, then that goes into the—to what they're going to give her for her disability, for her suffering, disabilities, any accompanying mental anguish.

"MR. JOHNSON: No, the loss of income is derived from the reduced earning capacity. And so—

"THE COURT: But is there any reduced earning capacity?

"MR. JOHNSON: Yes.

"THE COURT: Is it more probably true than not to believe that she has suffered some loss of income?

"MR. JOHNSON: Yes, there's been evidence—there's been evidence of that and there's been no contrary evidence. I mean, I can't have any better evidence than to have—

"THE COURT: There has been possibly some circumstantial evidence, at least, if we consider what her aspirations were—

"MR. JOHNSON: I asked [the vocational counselor] that direct question, Your Honor. I said, based upon your knowledge, experience and training in vocational work, do you have an opinion as to whether this limitation has impaired Amy Morris's earning power compared to what it was? I mean. I couldn't ask the question any different way than that, you know, to get—

"THE COURT: But what is the element of damage? What is the standard of damage? How does this jury arrive at some figure to compensate, other than pure speculation?

"MR. McCAMISH: That's my objection.

"MR. JOHNSON: I don't think they have to engage in pure speculation. They can put down a figure that they believe—and I'll suggest to them a figure * * *. It's not too difficult to present an argument that will give the jury some basis or foundation for coming up with a reasonable determination of what that might be.

"THE COURT: I'm going to let it go to the jury, and then I'll worry about it when they come back.

Id. at 80–81, 708 P.2d at 505–06. Could the plaintiff's lawyer have presented any other type of evidence that would have strengthened the claim for lost earning capacity? Do you agree with the defense lawyer that, given the evidentiary record as it stood, the claim for future lost earning capacity was too speculative to go to the jury? Why did the judge submit the question to the jury, despite the judge's obvious doubts about the evidentiary basis?

Interesting questions arise when the plaintiff still has earning power post-injury but is forced to switch occupations as a result of the injury. Suppose that a medical student is injured and, as a result of the injury, no longer is able to specialize in orthopedic surgery, her original choice. Rather, the medical student goes on to become a pediatrician, which will provide her with an income less than that of the surgical specialty. Should she be able to receive both (1) an award of lost earning capacity (the difference in the earnings potential of the specialties) and (2) an "impairment" award for the fact that she no longer can perform her chosen profession?

Suppose that the student goes on to become a pediatric rheumatologist, a specialty that pays as well as orthopedic surgery. Should she be able to recover for either (1) or (2)? Now suppose that the student drops out of medical school because her only desire was to be a surgeon. She goes on to become a computer programmer, making far less money than would a surgical specialist. Should the defendant be able to argue that the amount for lost earning capacity should be measured by the difference between the surgical specialty and some other medical practice, given that the student could have gone on to become a medical doctor?

5. *Loss of Earning Capacity for Non–Wage–Earners*

An award for lost earning capacity is available even for those who were not in the workforce at the time of injury and who had no plans to work, at least for a good period of the future. A persistent example of this category consists of plaintiffs, traditionally women, who stay out of the paid workforce to care for home and children. Consider a woman who before her injury chooses to remain at home and care for small children. The injury renders her virtually unemployable for the two years between injury and trial, but she would not have worked for pay during that period anyway. Her plans were to re-enter the workforce sometime after her children reached school age. The injury also reduces but does not eliminate her ability to perform household services and to care for her children.

Leaving aside the issue of earnings, all jurisdictions would allow some compensation for the impairment in her ability to perform household services; this is available via two avenues. First, her spouse and sometimes her children will have a claim for the loss of the household services she provided to them. More detail on this appears in Chapter 11's discussion of derivative claims. Second, she herself can recover, under the category of impairment, damages for reductions in the ability to perform various functions, such as her reduced ability to dress herself or reduced mobility. The jury will be instructed not to let these overlap.

Yet what about her claim for lost earning capacity? Many courts will allow this plaintiff to recover for lost earning capacity even for the time (4 or 5 years in our example) during which the woman would have chosen, even if uninjured, not to enter the workforce. Other courts will allow such recovery only to the extent that the plaintiff can prove that she had marketable skills and did intend to enter the labor market. For more detail, see Dan B. Dobbs, 2 Law of Remedies 365–67 (2d ed. 1993). What reasons could support these two different approaches?

When the plaintiff is allowed to recover for lost earning capacity for the time during which she would not have chosen to enter the workforce even if uninjured, two valuation methods have been used: determine the value of the work the plaintiff could have performed outside the home if she had not been injured; or determine the value of the household services that the plaintiff could have performed but for the injury. If the court uses the latter, however, is the court really compensating for lost earning capacity, as distinct from functional impairment?

6. *Future Medical and Rehabilitative Expenses*

In addition to recovery for all medical and rehabilitative expenses reasonably incurred up until the date of trial, the plaintiff is entitled to recover damages representing his estimated future medical and rehabilitative expenses. For purposes of computing future medical expenses, as opposed to computing future damages for loss of earning capacity, it is the plaintiff's post-accident life expectancy, as of the time of trial, that is crucial in determining the period of time over which these future medical expenses will be incurred. Why? In addition, the plaintiff is entitled only to the *present value* of the expenses that he is expected to incur in the future.

Again, several variables often are contested: the time period over which medical and rehabilitative expenses will be incurred, and the nature and price of the medical or rehabilitative services. Consider the following disagreement over the latter variable when the plaintiff became a paraplegic as a result of a vaccination.

> As previously noted, the testimony at trial was, in the Court's view, persuasive in demonstrating that the Plaintiff will require continual nursing care throughout her lifetime to prevent and treat the potential serious complications of her disease. The issue that arises, however, for the Court's determination in awarding damages is the degree or type of nursing care which is reasonably necessary for the Plaintiff. Several options were referred to at trial.

> At the outset, the Court rejects the government's proposal regarding institutionalized care or apartment-type community living for the handicapped for Lucy McDonald. These options were suggested by the Defendant's expert economist, Dr. George Reavy, solely from an economic standpoint and were unsupported by any medical evidence establishing them as feasible alternatives for this particular Plaintiff. On the other hand, Plaintiff herself testified that it is very important for her to stay in her present home; she describes it as being the "family homestead" and the gathering place for her brothers and sisters and their families. Dr. Turchetti, a psychiatrist, opined that such alternatives as proffered by the government would be markedly detrimental to the Plaintiff's emotional condition. He stated that to Lucy McDonald her present home represents security and to strip her away from this would be "cruel". These observations were also confirmed by Joyce Harring, a registered nurse, who is experienced in the care of paraplegics and is presently involved in such treatment with another paraplegic. She testified that institutionalization or handicapped community living would not be a viable alternative for Lucy McDonald because she is "very secure in her own home", and opined that Lucy "would lose the will to go on" if she must live in that environment. Dr. Rhamy also testified that, in his opinion, an extended care treatment center would not be conducive to the normal interpersonal relationship of a husband and wife. Based on this

uncontradicted medical testimony and in a compassionate sense of fairness to the plight of the Plaintiff, the Court concludes that the Defendant's proposals are not a reasonable solution to this Plaintiff's present and future nursing care needs.

Dr. Rhamy testified as to two alternatives, a "low" and "high" nursing care plan for the Plaintiff. The "low" plan consisted of a licensed practical nurse (LPN) for one eight-hour shift and a helper or nurse's aid for the other 16 hours of the day, seven days of the week. The "high" alternative would be an LPN on an around the clock basis, seven days of the week.

* * * Nurse Harring presented a schedule of nursing care for the Plaintiff which, considering all the medical testimony presented regarding the Plaintiff's present physical status and her future medical needs, the Court finds to be the most feasible option in this case. This plan consists of: (1) the services of a RN for one eight-hour shift per day for five days of the week (40 hours per week); (2) the services of an LPN for one eight-hour shift for seven days of the week (56 hours per week); and (3) the services of a nurse's aide or helper for the remaining shift during the week and the extra shift on the weekends (72 hours per week).

McDonald v. United States, 555 F.Supp. 935 (M.D.Pa.1983). Nontort compensation program—such as workers' compensation or veterans' benefits—and private insurance schemes (including health insurance or long-term care insurance) do not usually provide, as did the court's choice here, such generous benefits, so precisely tailored to the plaintiff's particular emotional, medical, and rehabilitative needs. Why is tort law's compensatory approach different?

7. The Collateral Source Rule

The "collateral source rule" refers to the doctrine that prevents a defendant from introducing evidence that the plaintiff has received compensation from independent sources for the damages he is seeking. Where the collateral source rule operates, a plaintiff may recover both from the independent source and from the defendant. Until very recently, the collateral source rule was almost universally followed in the United States.

The rule rests on several rationales. First, even when the rule arguably produces overcompensation of the plaintiff, its defenders argue that the rule is necessary to send the right deterrent signal. Suppose that a worker injured on the job sues the manufacturer of the tool involved in the accident and that the employer's workers' compensation carrier has already paid $50,000 in medical bills and $75,000 (in present value terms) in "disability payments." This is part of the full cost of the loss that the defendant's act produced.

The seriousness of this deterrence concern, however, depends on how significant the collateral source payments are in relation to victims' losses. If the payments represent only a small fraction of most tort judgments, then one could presume that altering the collateral source rule would not significantly lessen deterrence. Patricia Danzon, a respected researcher and economist, concluded that collateral sources cover between 30 and 40 percent of medical malpractice losses. P. Danzon, Medical Malpractice 170 (1985). Does this estimate bolster or assuage the deterrence concern?

Second, on closer inspection, the rule does not always produce the degree of overcompensation that a casual look might suggest. In the workers' compensation example, for instance, who paid for the workers' compensation insurance coverage?

But this argument prompts another challenge to the collateral source rule. If the victim has in some sense already paid for other sources of recovery, should the tort system provide duplicate coverage? A tort system that allows full compensation, without reductions from collateral sources, will cost more than a system that allows such reductions. Is it worth it? Suppose that you had disability insurance coverage with a private disability insurer, which would pay you ⅔ of your income in the event you became totally disabled. Now you have a chance to buy products and services, which come bundled with a "tort insurance policy" that will pay you full damages in the event of wrongful loss, damages that include 100% of your lost income. Would you want to pay again, in the form of a higher price on the good or service, for double coverage of ⅔ of your income stream? Your answer might be that you anticipate some other shortfall; perhaps you believe that the double recovery will help pay the lawyer's contingency fee that will be necessary to finance a tort suit. But, if the reason you are purchasing double disability coverage is to finance the lawsuit, are there better ways by which the tort system could provide financing?

Third, many of the collateral sources usually available—such as first-party property insurance or disability insurance—give the insurer or providing entity (such as a county hospital) a right of "subrogation" as to payments made by tort defendants. So, for instance, if the plaintiff collects $10,000 from her auto collision insurance and then receives the same amount as part of a tort judgment or settlement with the driver who wrecked her car, the insurer will generally be entitled to reimbursement of that amount (less the insurer's fair portion of the expenses for procuring the tort award).

These criticisms have found expression in judicial and, more often, legislative modifications of the collateral source rule in a large majority of states. The modifications vary in shape. A few jurisdictions have abolished the rule outright. *See, e.g.,* Alaska Stat. §§ 09.17.070, 09.55.548 (Supp. 1994); West's Fla.Stat.Ann. § 768.76 (West Supp.1996). Others allow only specified collateral sources to reduce the defendant's tort bill. Examples include allowing only "purely gratuitous" sources to reduce the tort award, see Coyne v. Campbell, 11 N.Y.2d 372, 230 N.Y.S.2d 1, 183 N.E.2d 891 (1962). Some states allow the defendant to introduce evidence of collateral sources, but then allow plaintiffs to introduce evidence of the premiums or other cost that the plaintiff has paid to obtain that collateral benefit. Cal. Civ. Code Ann. § 3333.1 (West Supp. 1996). Plaintiffs have challenged the constitutionality of legislation reforming or abolishing the collateral source rule. More often, the challenges have failed. See, e.g., Fein v. Permanente Med. Group, 38 Cal.3d 137, 211 Cal.Rptr. 368, 695 P.2d 665 (1985). On the general subject, *see* D. Goldsmith, A Survey of the

Collateral Source Rule: *The Effects of Tort Reform and Impact on Multistate Litigation,* 53 J.Air Law & Commerce 799 (1988).

A Reporters' Study of the American Law Institute recommends abolition of the rule with respect to virtually all collateral sources, with the exception of life insurance and insurance for accidental death and dismemberment. These forms of insurance, the Study says, "typically do not provide compensation for out-of-pocket loss." American Law Institute, Reporters' Study on Enterprise Responsibility for Personal Injury, Vol. II, at 177 (1991).

Does partial modification of the collateral source rule make sense in light of the criticisms of the rule? What rationale could explain retaining the collateral source rule for "purely gratuitous" services? Usually, this is understood to mean services rendered at no cost and with no expectation or requirement of reimbursement. An example might be the nursing care rendered by a family member or close friend. And what rationale explains retaining the traditional rule for life insurance or for "dismemberment" policies that do not pay for out-of-pocket losses?

Finally, consider an argument that defendants have begun to make when the plaintiff has sustained a disabling injury that will require special schooling or educational services, such as speech therapy or accommodations in the classroom. Because public schools must by law provide special educational services, some defendants have argued that the jury should be allowed to consider the value of these free educational services in assessing damages. How do the arguments for and against the collateral source rule apply with respect to free special educational services? Should the defendant's ability to admit this evidence turn on whether the plaintiff specifically seeks compensation for the cost of private schooling and private educational services? Does it matter that public funding for special education might suffer cutbacks in the future? For opposing views on the question, compare Williston v. Ard, 611 So.2d 274, 278 (Ala.1992)(disallowing evidence of free public special educational services) with Washington v. Barnes Hospital, 897 S.W.2d 611, 620–21 (Mo.1995)(allowing such evidence after the plaintiff has introduced evidence that special private schooling will be required).

8. *Present Value, Inflation, and Taxes*

Present Value. The calculation of future damages involves three distinct but interrelated complications: present value, inflation, and taxes. Consider a plaintiff whose work life expectancy at the time of trial is 36 years; in each of those years, she will earn less than she would have earned had the injury not occurred. Yet, if her award for lost wage-earning capacity were simply the immediate payment of the sum of these annual deficits, the award would substantially overcompensate her for that loss. So it is necessary to discount that loss to present value.

But at what rate should the future earnings figure be discounted? The larger the discount rate, the lower the lump sum award. If we assume that she could invest the sum at a 10% rather than at an 8% interest rate, then she would need a smaller lump sum than she would need at an 8% rate in order to deliver, over the years, sums matching the loss of earning capacity each year. In theory, the appropriate rate would be the rate that, on the basis of the evidence presented, corresponds to the yield that persons without financial skill could safely secure on their investments. A simplified alternate method of choosing a rate is to ascertain what it would presently cost to purchase with one lump sum payment an annuity for the appropriate amounts, based on the plaintiff's hypothetical life expectancy, from reputable life insurance companies.

In most jurisdictions, it is the jury's task to determine the rate by which to discount the award to present value. A few jurisdictions, however, mandate a particular rate, such as the legal rate of interest. Why should the rate of interest be a jury determination? Why not either announce a particular interest rate for all cases or allow the trial judge to make the choice as a matter of law? Treating the choice as a factfinding decision in each case suggests that factual variations specific to the case are relevant to the choice. Are there such factual variations?

How much guidance should the juries receive as to the choice of discount rate? The detail varies greatly across jurisdictions. Juries in Texas receive only the following question, with no further definition or instruction: "What sum of money, if paid now in cash, would fairly and reasonably compensate" the plaintiff? State Bar of Texas, 3 Pattern Jury Charge 80.02A (1990). A typical instruction defines present value as "that sum which, if invested in reasonably safe investments which an ordinarily prudent person would make, will yield" the amounts equal to the future loss. Ronald W. Eades, Jury Instructions on Damages in Tort Actions 306 (3d ed. 1993).

Other than lost earning capacity, *which* categories of damages should be discounted to present value? Most jurisdictions now require reduction to present value of future medical and rehabilitative expenses, see Thorpe v. Bailey, 386 A.2d 668 (Del.1978), and, in death cases (discussed in more detail later) damages for loss of pecuniary contributions from the deceased. What about damages for pain and suffering, mental anguish, or loss of consortium? Courts split on this. Compare Oberhelman v. Blount, 196 Neb. 42, 241 N.W.2d 355 (Neb.1976)(ruling that trial court did not err in instructing the jury to discount future pain and suffering damages), with Arnold v. Burlington Northern RR Co., 89 Or.App. 245, 748 P.2d 174 (Or.App.1988)(holding that trial court did not err in refusing defendant's requested instruction to discount damages for future pain and suffering).

Why the ambivalence with respect to discounting these categories of damages? The rejection of discounting rests on the view that such discounting would be "artificial and unrealistic because of the imprecise and speculative nature of the elements underlying such determinations." Friedman v. C & S Car Service, 108 N.J. 72, 79, 527 A.2d 871, 875 (1987).

> The application of the present value rule by the jury in making up the amount of damages to be allowed for the deprivation of pecuniary benefits arising from probable future earnings is not only just, but feasible. It is feasible because the jury may from actual past earnings, with other factors in the problem proven, set opposite each year of the estimated life the sum which would probably be earned that year, and in death cases the probable pecuniary benefit to the party complaining

or beneficially interested. These several sums can then be reduced to their present value. No such process is possible in estimating the amount to be allowed for pain and suffering, or for pain and inconvenience. In the matter of pain, suffering, or inconvenience, no books are kept, no inventories made, no balances struck.

Flanigan v. Burlington N., Inc., 632 F.2d 880, 885 (8th Cir.1980), *cert. denied*, 450 U.S. 921 (1981). Does this reasoning lose force in those jurisdictions that allow or require courts to enter "periodic payment" of future damages, including noneconomic damages? In such jurisdictions, as will be explained in more detail later, either the court or the jury assigns a given amount of compensation, including compensation for nonpecuniary losses, for each year of the future.

Inflation. A second complication with assessing future damage awards is whether some account should be taken of the effects of inflation. If inflation does occur over time, then the real purchasing power of each dollar will decline. Thus, if no account is taken of inflation when assessing a lump sum, for example, for future lost wages, then the lump sum will undercompensate the plaintiff.

Yet, though this point is sound in theory, courts have feared that, in practice, accounting for inflation will be too speculative a process. Thus, many courts in the past ignored the possible effects of inflation. Given the sustained high rates of inflation often experienced in the past few years, it is no longer possible to be complacent on this score. Recent years therefore have seen increasing judicial willingness to make some express allowance for inflation. The manner of this allowance has taken several forms.

One method is to allow the parties to introduce evidence about inflation if it is credible. For instance, the plaintiff's economist would be allowed to testify about the annual expected changes in the cost of living over time, and then to adjust upward the estimate of the plaintiff's lost income earning capacity on the premise that the plaintiff would have received cost of living increases. Then, as explained above, the resulting annual sums will be discounted down to present value. For examples, see Steckler v. United States, 549 F.2d 1372 (10th Cir.1977); Lumber Terminals, Inc. v. Nowakowski, 36 Md.App. 82, 373 A.2d 282 (Md.1977).

Other jurisdictions take inflation into account in a very different way, through what has been called a "total offset" approach. Under this approach, future damages are calculated without a reduction to present value, but also without consideration of inflation. The theory is that "inflation diminishes the value of money in an amount approximately equal to that which money, prudently invested, would earn. * * * Any difference would be de minimis. * * *" Mendelsohn v. Anderson, 26 Wash.App. 933, 940, 614 P.2d 693, 697 (1980). Courts also have viewed the approach as more efficient: "Litigators are freed from introducing and verifying complex economic data. Judges and juries are not burdened with complicated, time consuming economic testimony. Finally, * * * the ultimate award is more predictable." Kaczkowski v. Bolubasz, 491 Pa. 561, 421 A.2d 1027, 1038 (1980).

Still another variation, like the total offset method, recognizes that interest earnings and reduced purchasing power somewhat offset each other. Yet, because over time the interest rate has remained slightly higher than inflation rates, this variation does not allow a total offset. Instead, these jurisdictions use an "inflation-adjusted interest rate." That is, they lower the discount rate to take account of the effects of inflation. So, for instance, what would have been a discount rate of 8% is lowered to 1½% or to 2%; the latter two figures, of course, will yield higher lump sum awards. For further discussion of the approach, see Feldman v. Allegheny Airlines, 524 F.2d 384 (2d Cir.1975); Doca v. Marina Mercante Nicaraguense, S.A., 634 F.2d 30 (2d Cir.1980).

What are the reasons for and against giving a greater role to the jury, as does the first approach?

Under English law, except in exceptional cases, no adjustment is made for the possibility of inflation, on the following grounds:

> First, it is pure speculation whether inflation will continue at present, or higher, rates, or even disappear. The only sure comment one may make upon any inflation prediction is that it is as likely to be falsified as to be bourne out by the event. Secondly, * * * inflation is best left to be dealt with by investment policy. It is not unrealistic in modern social conditions, nor is it unjust, to assume that the recipient of a large capital sum by way of damages will take advice as to its investment and use. Thirdly, it is inherent in a system of compensation by way of a lump sum immediately payable, and, I would think, just, that the sum be calculated at current money values, leaving the recipient in the same position as others who have to rely on capital for their support to face the future.

Lim Poh Choo v. Camden and Islington Area Health Authority, [1980] A.C. 174, 193 (1979), [1979] 3 W.L.R. 44, 58, 2 All E.R. 910, 923 (per Lord Scarman). The English courts have been very strict in finding the presence of "exceptional circumstances." *See* Auty v. National Coal Board, [1985] 1 W.L.R. 784, 1 All E.R. 930 (C.A.).

Taxes. Under section 104 of the Internal Revenue Code, 26 U.S.C. § 104(a)(2), compensatory damage awards received for personal injuries are not deemed taxable income. This applies both to actions for personal injury and to actions arising out of death.

Two tax-related issues recur in tort litigation: (1) whether the jury should be instructed that the damages award will not be taxable; and (2) whether the assessment of damages for loss of future earning capacity should take into account the fact that the injured individual would not have received his or her gross income, but only the net income after taxes. In Norfolk & Western Railroad v. Liepelt, 444 U.S. 490, 100 S.Ct. 755, 62 L.Ed.2d 689 (1980), the United States Supreme Court, in a majority opinion authored by Justice Stevens, addressed both issues with respect to tort awards under the Federal Employers' Liability Act, 45 U.S.C. § 51 *et seq.* As can be seen from the following excerpt, the Court gave an affirmative answer to both questions.

> Admittedly there are many variables that may affect the amount of a wage earner's future income-tax liability. The law may change, his family may increase or decrease in size, his spouse's earnings may

affect his tax bracket, and extra income or unforeseen deductions may become available. But future employment itself, future health, future personal expenditures, future interest rates, and future inflation are also matters of estimate and prediction. Any one of these issues might provide the basis for protracted expert testimony and debate. But the practical wisdom of the trial bar and the trial bench has developed effective methods of presenting the essential elements of an expert calculation in a form that is understandable by juries that are increasingly familiar with the complexities of modern life. We therefore reject the notion that the introduction of evidence describing a decedent's estimated after-tax earnings is too speculative or complex for a jury. * * *

                        * * *

* * * [I]t is entirely possible that the members of the jury may assume that a plaintiff's recovery in a case of this kind will be subject to federal taxation, and that the award should be increased substantially in order to be sure that the injured party is fully compensated. * * * [A]s Judge Ely wrote for the Ninth Circuit, "[t]o put the matter simply, giving the instruction [that an award will be tax free] can do no harm, and it can certainly help by preventing the jury from inflating the award and thus overcompensating the plaintiff on the basis of an erroneous assumption that the judgment will be taxable." Burlington Northern, Inc. v. Boxberger, 529 F.2d 284, 297 (1975).

444 U.S. at 494–97, 100 S.Ct. at 758–759. Justices Blackmun and Marshall disagreed with both holdings.

     * * * In my view, by mandating adjustment of the award by way of reduction for federal income taxes that would have been paid by the decedent on his earnings, the Court appropriates for the tortfeasor a benefit intended to be conferred on the victim or his survivors. And in requiring that the jury be instructed that a wrongful-death award is not subject to federal income tax, the Court opens the door for a variety of admonitions to the jury not to "misbehave," and unnecessarily interjects what is now to be federal law into the administration of a trial in a state court.

444 U.S. at 499, 100 S.Ct. at 760 (Blackmun, J., dissenting).

Because the decision interprets a federal statute, most state courts have not interpreted the holding as binding on state tort common law. But a number of state decisions since *Liepelt* have referred to it, sometimes siding with *Liepelt's* conclusions and sometimes not. *Compare* Dennis v. Blanchfield, 48 Md.App. 325, 428 A.2d 80 (Md.App.1981), *modified on other grounds,* 292 Md. 319, 438 A.2d 1330 (Md.1982)(finding *Liepelt* not binding but nonetheless persuasive), *with* Barnette v. Doyle, 622 P.2d 1349 (Wyo.1981)(finding that *Liepelt* does not control and upholding the trial court's refusal to instruct the jury that the award would not be subject to taxation).

9. *Prejudgment Interest*

Once a judgment has been entered, regardless of the type of action in which the judgment has been entered, interest accrues on the unpaid portions of the judgment. "Pre-judgment interest" refers to interest on losses that the plaintiff has incurred before the entry of the judgment, such as a $50,000 hospital bill paid two years before the entry of the judgment. What reasons might support awarding prejudgment interest for such sums? What practical difficulties would the calculation of such interest present? For instance, in theory prejudgment interest should begin to accrue from the time the loss or expense was incurred, yet juries typically are asked only to list the amount of all past damages or various categories of past damages, not precisely when they were incurred. Should pre-judgment interest be allowed on losses such as pain and suffering or mental anguish?

Currently, at least half the states now allow award of prejudgment interest in personal injury claims, either by judicial decision or, more typically, by statute. Some states allow a defendant partially to avoid the payment of prejudgment interest by making an offer of settlement. *E.g.* 42 Pa.Cons.Stat.Ann. Rule 238 (West 1987).

In England, by statute, prejudgment interest is allowed in actions for personal injuries unless the court is satisfied that there are special reasons why no interest should be given. It has been held that with regard to that portion of a damage award which represents future damages—that is, damages that will be incurred after the date of trial—no interest should be awarded for the period prior to trial. Cookson v. Knowles [1979] A.C. 556 (1978), [1978] 2 W.L.R. 978, 2 All E.R. 604.

A comprehensive treatment of prejudgment interest can be found in J. Wilson *et al., Prejudgment Interest in Personal Injury, Wrongful Death and Other Actions,* 30 Trial Lawyers' Guide 105 (1986). Earlier discussions include F. Hare, *Prejudgment Interest in Personal Injury Litigation: A Policy of Fairness,* 5 Am.J.Trial Advocacy 81 (1981); Comment, *Prejudgment Interest: An Element of Damages Not to Be Overlooked,* 8 Cum.L.Rev. 521 (1977). *See also* D. Dobbs, 1 Law of Remedies § 3.6 (1993).

10. *Mass Tort*

Mass tort litigation has posed fundamental challenges to traditional procedural and substantive law relating to torts. One increasingly important issue relates to assessment of damages in mass tort contexts. Although neither tort common law nor tort reform legislation makes use of damages schedules, courts and commentators are increasingly favoring the use of "sampling" with respect to damages in the mass tort context. The basic idea is that courts would allow damages trials of a representative sampling of the claims in the mass tort pool, and then would award the average of the damages to other claims fitting in the same category. For instance, one federal court divided over 2000 plaintiffs in an asbestos class action into five disease categories, including mesothelioma, lung cancer, etc. The court then took a sample of plaintiffs from each disease category—for instance, 25 of the 186 lung cancer victims—and allowed each a trial on his or her damages. Each of these plaintiffs received his or her actual verdict (after post-trial motions). The court then calculated the average verdict in each disease category, and awarded that average amount to all other plaintiffs in the disease category. Cimino v. Raymark Industries, 751 F.Supp. 649 (E.D.Tex.1990). Some scholars argue that this procedure achieves results that are more accurate than a fully individualized trial. This is because any given trial award is "likely to be an over- or under-award relative to the true, or population mean," of possible awards in that trial. Thus, although the verdict in a traditional tort case "appears precise and individualized," in reality it is just a sample of one from a wide population of potential outcomes. "Individualized trials substitute one form of error for another. Therefore, their results may be less accurate than those of a well-conducted aggregated trial." Michael J. Saks & Peter D. Blanck, *Justice Improved: The Unrecognized Benefits of Aggregation and Sampling in the Trial of Mass Torts,* 44 Stan. L. Rev. 815, 839 (1992). Does the process of sampling and aggregating damages conflict with any other values served by an individualized scheme of damage assessment, such as participants' sense that they are playing a meaningful role in the litigation process and have an opportunity to tell their own story of loss?

Another important issue raised by mass tort is the use of the bankruptcy process. In 1982, the Johns Manville Corporation filed a reorganization petition in federal bankruptcy court. The petition was groundbreaking because it did not assert, as does the traditional bankruptcy petition, that debts owed to known creditors warranted bankruptcy. Rather, Manville argued that the value of prospective and still unknown tort claims for asbestos-related disease warranted recourse to the bankruptcy procedure. (Manville estimated its reasonable contingent liability on torts claims arising from exposure to its asbestos products as being over $2 billion, or almost twice its net worth. *See* Wall Street Journal, August 27, 1982, p. 1, col. 6.). Under the federal bankruptcy code, the filing of the petition automatically suspended all personal injury suits and allowed a reorganization of the company's finances, with an eye toward satisfying debts and liabilities. The bankruptcy court created an independent organization, the Manville Personal Injury Settlement Trust, to distribute funds as equitably as possible, balancing the interests of current claimants against those of future and still-unknown claimants. The Trust was in operation for a number of years, until the Second Circuit overruled the district court's and bankruptcy court's approval of the bankruptcy plan. *See* In Re Joint Eastern and Southern District Asbestos Litigation, 982 F.2d 721 (2d. Cir.1992). A.H. Robins also resorted to the bankruptcy mechanism in light of potential liabilities relating to the Dalkon Shield. For history, see In Re A.H. Robins Co., 880 F.2d 709 (4th Cir.), *cert. denied sub nom.* Anderson v. Aetna Casualty & Surety Co., 493 U.S. 959, 110 S.Ct. 377, 107 L.Ed.2d 362 (1989).

For more detail on bankruptcy and mass tort, see M. Roe, *Bankruptcy and Mass Tort,* 84 Colum.L.Rev. 846 (1984); Joan E. Steinman, *Women, Medical Care, and Mass Tort Litigation,* 68 Chicago–Kent L. Rev. 409 (1992); Note, *Mass Tort Claims and the Corporate Tortfeasor: Bankruptcy Reorganization and Legislative Compensation Versus the Common–Law Tort System,* 61 Tex.L.Rev. 1297 (1983).

Mass tort claims also have triggered use of the class action device, although considerable debate surrounds the subject, especially when the class action device is used to settle claims of both current and potential future claimants in mass tort cases. As this book goes to press, the United States Supreme Court is considering what lawyers and academics are deeply divided over, namely the use of settlement class actions in the asbestos context. In Georgine v. Amchem Products, Inc., 83 F.3d 610 (3d Cir.1996), *cert. granted*, ___ U.S. ___, 117 S.Ct. 379, 136 L.Ed.2d 297 (1996), the Third Circuit vacated the trial court's order certifying a class in a "settlement class action." A settlement class action is one in which the court postpones formal class certification until the parties have successfully concluded a settlement. If the parties arrive at a settlement, the court certifies the class for settlement purposes only and notifies the class members of the filing of the class action and the proposed settlement.

In *Georgine*, the plaintiffs filed a complaint in January 1993 on behalf of a class consisting of individuals, and family members of the individuals, exposed to asbestos products produced by one of the defendants. Some of the named plaintiffs had already sustained injury as a result of the exposure; others, however, alleged that they had been exposed but had not yet sustained any asbestos-related condition. On the same day the complaint was filed, the defendants filed an answer. Also on the same day, the defendants and the plaintiffs filed a joint motion seeking conditional class certification for purposes of settlement. The proposed settlement purported to settle all the asbestos-related claims against the defendants that had not been filed before January 15, 1993. It established an administrative procedure for providing compensation for claimants meeting specified exposure and medical criteria. If those criteria were met, then the settlement provided for compensation for four categories of disease: mesothelioma, lung cancer, "other cancers," and "non-malignant conditions" (asbestosis and pleural thickening). The settlement established a range of damages that would be awarded for each disease. Most members of the class would not have the option to pursue tort payments or additional payments beyond the schedule set out in the settlement.

The settlement also set out terms for the "exposure-only" plaintiffs— those who had not yet sustained any asbestos-related condition—as well as plaintiffs with asbestos-related plaques on the lungs but no current physical impairment. These plaintiffs would not receive cash payment for their asserted damages—increased risk of cancer, fear of future injury, and medical monitoring. But the settlement also provided that the statute of limitations for these plaintiffs would be tolled until the time when any such plaintiff developed an impairing illness. In addition, if such plaintiffs sustained a non-malignant condition and received compensation later for it, they would retain the right to file a further claim for any asbestos-related cancer that later developed.

In February 1994, the trial court held a hearing on the proposed settlement. After several months, the trial court approved the settlement and certified the settlement class, holding that the class met the requirements of Federal Rule of Civil Procedure 23, that the settlement was fair and reasonable, and that notice to the class met the requirement of Rule 23 and the due process clause of the United States Constitution. The court then issued a preliminary injunction prohibiting any of the class members from pursuing any claims for asbestos-related personal injury pending the issuance of a final order. (A final judgment had not yet been entered because the insurers for the defendants had not yet approved it.)

Several groups of objectors appealed the trial court's decision to the United States Court of Appeals for the Third Circuit. The following is an excerpt from the Third Circuit's decision.

Every decade presents a few great cases that force the judicial system to choose between forging a solution to a major social problem on the one hand, and preserving its institutional values on the other. This is such a case. It is a class action that seeks to settle the claims of between 250,000 and 2,000,000 individuals who have been exposed to asbestos products against the twenty companies known as the Center for Claims Resolution (CCR). * * * Most notably, the settlement would extinguish asbestos-related causes of action of exposed individuals who currently suffer no physical ailments, but who may, in the future, develop possibly fatal asbestos-related disease. These "futures claims" of "exposure-only" plaintiffs would be extinguished even though they have not yet accrued.

* * *

To obtain class certification, plaintiffs must satisfy all of the requirements of Rule 23(a) and come within one provision of Rule 23(b). * * * Rule 23(a) mandates a showing of (1) numerosity; (2) commonality; (3) typicality; and (4) adequacy of representation: One or more members of a class may sue or be sued as representative parties on behalf of all only if (1) the class is so numerous that joinder of all members is impracticable, (2) there are questions of law or fact common to the class, (3) the claims or defenses of the representative parties are typical of the claims or defenses of the class, and (4) the representative parties will fairly and adequately protect the interests of the class. FED.R.CIV.P. 23(a).

* * *

* * * [T]he class members' claims vary widely in character. Class members were exposed to different asbestos-containing products, for different amounts of time, in different ways, and over different periods. Some class members suffer no physical injury or have only asymptomatic pleural changes, while others suffer from lung cancer, disabling asbestosis, or from mesothelioma—a disease which, despite a latency period of approximately fifteen to forty years, generally kills its victims within two years after they become symptomatic. Each has a different history of cigarette smoking, a factor that complicates the causation inquiry.

The futures plaintiffs especially share little in common, either with each other or with the presently injured class members. It is unclear whether they will contract asbestos-related disease and, if so, what disease each will suffer. They will also incur different medical expenses because their monitoring and treatment will depend on singular circumstances and individual medical histories.

These factual differences translate into significant legal differences. Differences in amount of exposure and nexus between exposure and injury lead to disparate applications of legal rules, including matters of causation, comparative fault, and the types of damages available to each plaintiff.

* * *

Rule 23(a)(4) requires that "the representative parties will fairly and adequately protect the interests of the class." FED.R.CIV.P. 23(a)(4). The adequacy of representation inquiry has two components designed to ensure that absentees' interests are fully pursued. First, the interests of the named plaintiffs must be sufficiently aligned with those of the absentees. * * * This component includes an inquiry into potential conflicts among various members of the class, * * * because the named plaintiffs' interests cannot align with those of absent class members if the interests of different class members are not themselves in alignment. Second, class counsel must be qualified and must serve the interests of the entire class. * * *

Although questions have been raised concerning the second prong of the inquiry, we do not resolve them here. As we have briefly noted above, the objectors have forcefully argued that class counsel cannot adequately represent the class because of a conflict of interest. In the eyes of the objectors, class counsel have brought a collusive action on behalf of the CCR defendants after having been paid over $200 million to settle their inventory of previously filed cases. The objectors also adduce evidence that class counsel, as part of the settlement, have abjured any intention to litigate the claims of any futures plaintiffs. These allegations are, of course, rife with ethical overtones, which have been vigorously debated in the academy. See Symposium, Mass Torts: Serving Up Just Desserts, 80 Cornell L.Rev. 811 (1995). However, Judge Reed resolved this issue in favor of class counsel largely on the basis of fact findings that the objectors have not challenged. * * *

As to the first prong of the inquiry, however, we conclude that serious intra-class conflicts preclude this class from meeting the adequacy of representation requirement. The district court is certainly correct that "the members of the class are united in seeking the maximum possible recovery for their asbestos-related claims." Georgine, 157 F.R.D. at 317 (citation omitted). But the settlement does more than simply provide a general recovery fund. Rather, it makes important judgments on how recovery is to be allocated among different kinds of plaintiffs, decisions that necessarily favor some claimants over others. For example, under the settlement many kinds of claimants (e.g., those with asymptomatic pleural thickening) get no monetary award at all. The settlement makes no provision for medical monitoring or for payment for loss of consortium. The back-end opt out is limited to a few persons per year. The settlement relegates those who are unlucky enough to contract mesothelioma in ten or fifteen years to a modest recovery, whereas the average recovery of mesothelioma plaintiffs in the tort system runs into the millions of dollars. In short, the settlement makes numerous decisions on which the interests of different types of class members are at odds.

The most salient conflict in this class action is between the presently injured and futures plaintiffs. As rational actors, those who are not yet injured would want reduced current payouts (through caps on compensation awards and limits on the number of claims that can be paid each year). The futures plaintiffs should also be interested in protection against inflation, in not having preset limits on how many cases can be handled, and in limiting the ability of defendant companies to exit the settlement. Moreover, in terms of the structure of the alternative dispute resolution mechanism established by the settlement, they should desire causation provisions that can keep pace with changing science and medicine, rather than freezing in place the science of 1993. Finally, because of the difficulty in forecasting what their futures hold, they would probably desire a delayed opt out like the one employed in Bowling v. Pfizer, Inc., 143 F.R.D. 141, 150 (S.D.Ohio 1992) (heart valve settlement allows claimants who ultimately experience heart valve fracture to reject guaranteed compensation and sue for damages at that time).

In contrast, those who are currently injured would rationally want to maximize current payouts. Furthermore, currently injured plaintiffs would care little about inflation-protection. The delayed opt out desired by futures plaintiffs would also be of little interest to the presently injured; indeed, their interests are against such an opt out as the more people locked into the settlement, the more likely it is to survive. * * * In sum, presently injured class representatives cannot adequately represent the futures plaintiffs' interests and vice versa.

* * *

We have concluded that the class certified by the district court cannot pass muster under Rule 23 because it fails the typicality and adequacy of representation requirements of Rule 23(a), as well as the predominance and superiority requirements of Rule 23(b). * * *

The desirability of innovation in the management of mass tort litigation does not escape the collective judicial experience of the panel. But reform must come from the policy-makers, not the courts. Such reform efforts are not, needless to say, without problems, and it is unclear through what mechanism such reform might best be effected. The most direct and encompassing solution would be legislative action. The Congress, after appropriate study and hearings, might authorize the kind of class action that would facilitate the global settlement sought here. Although we have not adjudicated the due process issues raised, we trust that Congress would deal with futures claims in a way that would maximize opt-out rights and minimize due process concerns that could undermine its work. On the other hand, congressional inhospitability to class actions, as reflected in the recently enacted Private Securities Litigation Reform Act of 1995, Pub.L. No. 104–67, 109 Stat. 737 (1995), and by its recently expressed concern about the workload of the federal courts, might not bode well for such a prospect.

In a different vein, Congress might enact compensation-like statutes dealing with particular mass torts. * * *

* * *

Perhaps this case, with its rich matrix of factual and legal issues, will serve as a calipers by which the various proposals before the Rules Committee might be measured. While we hope that these observations are useful, we express doubts that anything less than statutory revisions effecting wholesale changes in the law of mass torts could justify certification of this humongous class. In short, we think that what the district court did here might be ordered by a legislature, but should not have been ordered by a court.

83 F.3d at 617–35.

For entries into this rich debate, see John C. Coffee, Jr., *Class Wars: The Dilemma of the Mass Tort Class Action,* 95 Colum. L. Rev. 1343 (1995); Symposium, *Mass Torts: Serving Up Just Desserts,* 80 Cornell L. Rev. 811 (1995).

11. *Preexisting Injuries, Aggravation of Injury, and Intervening Injuries*

The disability or impairment for which plaintiff seeks compensation from the defendant may, at least in part, have other causal origins. Several different scenarios can occur. First, the defendant's act might aggravate or combine with a preexisting condition to result in a greater level of impairment or disability than what would have resulted without the preexisting condition. Courts often invoke the "eggshell skull" rule in such cases, or state that the defendant "takes his plaintiff as he finds him." But these intonations can be misunderstood; they do not mean that the plaintiff always will recover her full damages.

To illustrate, suppose the defendant causes an injury that, for a person with a healthy back, would cause only a 25% back impairment. ("Impairment" here refers to the reduction in the normal level of functioning, strength, flexibility, and freedom from pain in the back area.) The plaintiff, however, has a preexisting back condition that has resulted in a 30% impairment of the back; the injury inflicted by defendant therefore results in a 90% impairment of the back.

Clearly, the defendant cannot argue that he should have to pay only the damages that would result from a 25% back impairment; that is, the injury's result on a "normal" person. This is probably the core meaning of the eggshell skull rule. But should the rule mean that, in our example, the defendant must pay the full damages associated with a 90% impairment of the back? The answer might turn on which damages are at issue. Suppose, for instance, that the previous 30% back impairment had caused no loss of wages or alteration in plaintiff's vocational status, and that it would not likely have ever reduced the plaintiff's future earning capacity. But the lost wages from the 90% impairment are considerable, as is the future lost wage-earning capacity. Should the plaintiff, then, receive this full amount? By contrast, suppose that the 30% back impairment caused intermittent but severe pain and a need for periodic physical therapy. The

90% impairment causes still more pain and the need for more therapy. Should the plaintiff receive compensation for the full cost of therapy and the full measure of pain she experiences? Finally, if you believe that the reductions in some but not all damages are warranted, how could the jury be instructed appropriately?

Ample cases and other authority state that, in such instances, defendants should have to pay only the damages actually caused by the defendant's act, not those due solely to the preexisting condition. Not surprisingly, however, many appellate opinions have been devoted to reversing judgments rendered after confusing or inappropriate instructions to juries on the point. See 2 M. Minzer, J. Nates, C. Kimball, D. Axelrod & R. Goldstein, Damages in Tort Actions § 15.43 (1992)(collecting cases). Importantly, however, courts often place the risk of evidentiary uncertainty on the defendant: they instruct the jury that, if the evidence is insufficient to allow a particular apportionment, then the defendant must pay the full damages. W. Prosser & R. Keeton, Law of Torts § 52, at 345 (5th ed. 1984).

A second scenario occurs when, after the plaintiff is injured by the defendant, some other injury occurs and aggravates the impairment resulting from the first injury. For instance, suppose the defendant causes a 45% impairment to the plaintiff's back, that plaintiff then sustains another injury, and that the resulting impairment of the back is now 90%. Generally, the plaintiff is entitled to recover only the damages resulting from the 45% impairment. Two main caveats, however, should be noted. First, the first injury might be causally linked—in the actual cause sense—to the second. For instance, the second injury might result from poor medical treatment rendered in an effort to treat the first injury, or the second injury might not have occurred at all were it not for the weakened condition caused by the first. In such cases, plaintiff receives full recovery from the first tortfeasor. Second, as with preexisting impairments, the risk of evidentiary uncertainty may fall on the defendant; trial courts often tell juries that, if it cannot make an apportionment, then the defendant must pay for the full damage.

12. The Aim of Rehabilitation, and the Plaintiff's Obligation to Mitigate Damages

Any compensation program, it would seem, should to the extent possible facilitate rehabilitation of the person who has suffered injury or disease. This topic has received extensive examination with respect to nontort compensation programs such as workers' compensation and social security disability, as Chapter 14 will discuss. Yet whether and how the tort system affects rehabilitation has received surprisingly little attention from scholars or policymakers. Several doctrinal and practical aspects of the tort system potentially bear on the issue.

First, doctrinally, plaintiffs are entitled to recover reasonable medical and rehabilitative costs. Rehabilitative services can include, among many other types, vocational rehabilitation, physical therapy, speech therapy, psychological counseling, and pain control therapies. Just as with medical services, these rehabilitative therapies must be proven to be reasonably necessary for treatment of injuries. Statutes that impose caps on nonpecuniary damages sometimes expressly identify rehabilitative costs as falling in the uncapped category of pecuniary services.

Yet the line between rehabilitative expenses and nonpecuniary losses might not always be so clear. Consider the court's analysis in a case involving a severely burned plaintiff, who was awarded approximately $6000 per year for rehabilitation expenses, including some items (such as speaker telephone and electric toothbrush) that would assist him in performing simple tasks without discomfort. The defendant argued that this award duplicated the award for pain and suffering and mental anguish, and the appellate court agreed in part. "Some items, such as the therapy weights, certainly seem to be medical expenses; others, such as the electric toothbrush, most likely serve only to alleviate suffering. Thus, we remand to the district court to determine which items are compensable medical expenses and which duplicate the award for pain and suffering." Sosa v. M/V Lago Izabal, 736 F.2d 1028, 1034 (5th Cir.1984). Do you agree?

Second, plaintiffs in personal injury contexts, just like plaintiffs in commercial or property loss cases, must take reasonable steps to mitigate damages. (This obligation is sometimes termed the doctrine of "avoidable consequences.") The burden of pleading and proving failure to mitigate is usually the defendant's.

Several factors, however, reduce the chance that a defendant can successfully invoke the doctrine of mitigation. When the plaintiff's conduct presents a close call—that is, when the defendant cannot be very sure that the jury will deem the plaintiff's conduct unreasonable—what is the down side, from the defendant's perspective, of making the argument? In addition, "reasonableness" in this context has in practice become a more subjective than objective standard. The courts have been prepared to concede that the plaintiff's comparative poverty, his aversion to undergoing the pain of treatment, his subjective fears of treatment, and his comparative lack of sophistication are all factors that the jury can consider in deciding the question of reasonableness. See D. Dobbs, 2 Law of Remedies 512 (1993). Is there a principled basis for allowing "reasonableness" in this context to turn so heavily on plaintiff's subjective circumstances, feelings, and motivations, when a more objective standard supposedly governs the determination of the defendant's negligence?

How should religious beliefs factor into the equation? Courts largely have rejected both of the far reaches of the decisional spectrum—allowing religious beliefs to serve as an absolute excuse, or ruling that religious beliefs can never be relevant to the decision of reasonableness. Rather, courts allow the plaintiff to introduce, and the jury to consider, evidence of religious belief as it bears on the reasonableness of the plaintiff's decision. If the jury goes against the plaintiff, courts have held that this does not violate the plaintiff's right to free exercise of religion. For instance, in Munn v. Southern Health Plan, Inc., 719 F.Supp. 525 (N.D.Miss.1989), the court held that applying the doctrine of avoidable consequences to a plaintiff who refused a blood transfusion on religious grounds did not violate the constitutional guarantee of the free exercise of religion.

What reasons could explain treating this issue as a matter for decision case-by-case, by juries? Assessing whether plaintiff's religious beliefs reasonably explain the plaintiff's conduct could end up entailing one or more of several decisions: the veracity of the plaintiff's religious beliefs; the veracity of the plaintiff's factual allegation that the religious beliefs did in fact motivate her conduct in the case; and the value judgment about whether the conduct based on this religious belief was reasonable. Should all these be subject to factfinding case by case?

Other aspects of the tort system also bear on the topic of rehabilitation. The most obvious is delay. Rehabilitation professionals are in agreement that delay tends to undermine rehabilitation. The most obvious reason is that delay in obtaining a particular rehabilitative therapy—such as pain control counseling, physical or occupational therapy—reduces the chance that the therapy, even if obtained later, will be successful. For instance, pain behaviors become more entrenched over time, physical impairments can worsen if physical therapy occurs later rather than sooner.

Delay also might affect rehabilitation in a less obvious way: by lengthening the time during which the prospects for and the precise amount of compensation remain uncertain. When considering this, the first image that might leap to some minds is that of the conscious malingerer, the plaintiff who exaggerates disability, deliberately stays off work, or runs up doctors' bills unnecessarily, like Jack Lemmon in the classic movie *The Fortune Cookie*. But rehabilitation professionals agree that instances of conscious malingering are relatively rare and usually detectable when they occur. For discussion, see Ellen S. Pryor, *Compensation and the Ineradicable Problems of Pain*, 59 Geo. Wash. L. Rev. 239, 280–91 (1991). It is plausible, however, to suppose that the litigation process reinforces disability in less calculated ways. For instance, much of the research in the rehabilitative area stresses the notion of "illness behavior" or "pain behavior," and posits that these behaviors depend on a number of positive and negative reinforcing factors as well as the actual underlying injury or disease. In this respect, consider the common practice by plaintiff's lawyers of asking the plaintiff to record carefully and frequently their pain, their limitations, and their reaction to these. One plaintiff's practice guide, for instance, once supplied the client with a form explaining how this recordkeeping should be done. *See* Association of Trial Lawyers of America, The Anatomy of a Personal Injury Lawsuit 63–64 (2d ed. 1981). Even if rehabilitation professionals might think this is an undesirable practice, should the plaintiff's lawyer drop it?

A settled empirical answer does not yet exist as to the relationship of compensation and rehabilitation. Canvassing many of the studies on compensation programs as they relate to rehabilitation, the Institute of Medicine concluded that "the literature is equivocal on this question and neither dispels nor confirms the common perception that compensation has a negative influence on rehabilitation." Inst. of Medicine, Pain and Disability 248 (1987).

What about the defense lawyer? Suppose that, while the lawsuit is pending, the claimant is in need of physical therapy or pain control measures that might substantially reduce the claimant's final disability. Could the lawyer justifiably advise the defendant to "advance" the money necessary for treatment? The defendant might receive a monetary "credit" off the judgment for such costs if the defendant did choose to advance them. And the plaintiff would not be able to make evidentiary use of the defendant's decision to advance costs. For instance, the plaintiff would not be allowed to argue that this suggested remorse or negligence on the defendant's part.

So why is it so uncommon to see expenses of treatment advanced to plaintiffs? Perhaps plaintiffs have other sources. But some plaintiffs will be uninsured, and many medical (and even workers' compensation) insurance coverages contain big gaps with respect to rehabilitative therapies. Consider the relevance of the plaintiff's case on liability; would liability have to be virtually certain before a defendant could rationally advance expenses? And, even if the plaintiff's case on liability is strong, could defendants gain a strategic advantage in settlement by failing to advance expenses? Why?

Liability insurance might also play a role. For reasons that will become more clear in Chapter 13, insurance profoundly affects the incentives of both defendants and plaintiffs in tort litigation. Insurance funds, and insurance-related legal doctrines, could explain why payment of advanced expenses is not more common.

13. *Judicial Control of Damage Awards, and a Comparative Approach to Assessing Damages*

A trial judge has the authority to set aside a jury verdict if it is against the weight of the evidence. Utilizing this power, a trial judge can thus set aside an award of damages if it is against the weight of the evidence. The authority of appellate courts is usually considered to be more circumscribed. Federal courts of appeals often use a "not monstrous" or not "grossly excessive" test, which is somewhat more deferential than that of many state appellate courts.

If either a trial or appellate court decides to set aside a jury award of damages, the usual practice is to order a new trial. Sometimes, however, the court will issue a conditional order setting aside the jury's award and ordering a new trial unless the plaintiff agrees to some stated lesser amount of damages. This practice is called "remittitur." Although most often utilized by trial courts, it has also been used by appellate courts despite the fact that "appellate remittitur," particularly in the federal courts, has been criticized as an interference with plaintiff's right to trial by a jury. *See* Comment, *Remittitur Review: Constitutionality and Efficiency in Liquidated and Unliquidated Damage Cases*, 43 U.Chi.L.Rev. 376 (1976); Note, *Remittitur Practice in the Federal Courts*, 76 Colum.L.Rev. 299 (1976). In addition, many state courts will occasionally order a new trial unless the defendant agrees to pay greater damages than the jury has awarded. This practice is called "additur." The use of additur in the federal courts has been declared unconstitutional. Dimick v. Schiedt, 293 U.S. 474, 55 S.Ct. 296, 79 L.Ed. 603 (1935).

The tort reform debate has prompted renewed attention to additur-remittitur. Predictably, the attention has focused on whether these judicial controls adequately address perceived excessiveness and variation in jury awards for *nonpecuniary* losses. Defendants argue that additur-remittitur is too seldom employed and too toothless to address perceived problems of excessiveness and variation in nonpecuniary damages. Plaintiffs also have their objections. "[I]t is principally plaintiffs who feel 'blackmailed' by the court when they are forced to surrender a major part of what appears to them a fair award won by the credibility of their testimony and the skill of their counsel. The choice is particularly difficult for plaintiffs who are ill, old, or cannot afford the cost or delay of a new trial." David Baldus, John C. MacQueen, and George Woodworth, *Improving Judicial Oversight of Jury Damage Assessments: A Proposal for the Comparative Additur/Remittitur Review of Awards for Nonpecuniary Harms and Punitive Damages,* 80 Iowa L. Rev. 1109 (1995).

Can the system be meaningfully improved? Consider the two approaches that courts currently use. Under the first and more traditional approach, which most state courts follow, the judge appraises the award solely on the basis of the evidence in the case and his or her judgment; the judge does not look to the verdicts in comparable cases. A second approach, used often in federal courts and in some state courts, examines the jury award in light of other awards in similar cases. Judges using the comparative method rely on their own judgment in selecting which cases are sufficiently similar as to warrant comparison. No defined methodology yet exists as to which or how many cases should be selected, or as to which criteria the comparison should be made.

Why should a comparative analysis be an acceptable method for use by a reviewing trial or appellate judge, even though such an approach is impermissible in the jury trial itself? Perhaps the explanation is that requiring the jury to engage in comparison with prior verdicts would unduly interfere with the jury's ability to exercise judgment in this particular case, or with the plaintiff's right to a jury trial. But then why would use of a comparative methodology for *reviewing* the jury's verdict be any more acceptable? Can the apparent inconsistency be explained by the deferential stance that the reviewing court must take toward the jury's verdict, even when the reviewing judge uses a comparative method?

Another way to resolve the inconsistency would be to allow or require the use of comparative analysis by the jury. One proposal would give juries a limited number of standardized injury "scenarios," with suggested dollar values of noneconomic loss for each scenario. *See* Randall Bovbjerg, Frank Sloan & James Blumstein, *Valuing Life and Limb in Tort: Scheduling "Pain and Suffering,"* 83 Nw. U. L. Rev. 908(1989). No jurisdiction has yet adopted such an approach. What reasons might explain this?

C. NONPECUNIARY DAMAGES

McDOUGALD v. GARBER

Court of Appeals of New York, 1989.
73 N.Y.2d 246, 538 N.Y.S.2d 937, 536 N.E.2d 372.

WACHTLER, CHIEF JUDGE.

This appeal raises fundamental questions about the nature and role of nonpecuniary damages in personal injury litigation. By nonpecuniary damages, we mean those damages awarded to compensate an injured person for the physical and emotional consequences of the injury, such as pain and suffering and the loss of the ability to engage in certain activities. Pecuniary damages, on the other hand, compensate the victim for the economic consequences of the injury, such as medical expenses, lost earnings and the cost of custodial care.

The specific questions raised here deal with assessment of nonpecuniary damages and are (1) whether some degree of cognitive awareness is a prerequisite to recovery for loss of enjoyment of life and (2) whether a jury should be instructed to consider and award damages for loss of enjoyment of life separately from damages for pain and suffering. We answer the first question in the affirmative and the second question in the negative.

I.

On September 7, 1978, plaintiff Emma McDougald, then 31 years old, underwent a Caesarean section and tubal ligation at New York Infirmary. Defendant Garber performed the surgery; defendants Armengol and Kulkarni provided anesthesia. During the surgery, Mrs. McDougald suffered oxygen deprivation which resulted in severe brain damage and left her in a permanent comatose condition. This action was brought by Mrs. McDougald and her husband, suing derivatively, alleging that the injuries were caused by the defendants' acts of malpractice.

A jury found all defendants liable and awarded Emma McDougald a total of $9,650,102 in damages, including $1,000,000 for conscious pain and suffering and a separate award of $3,500,000 for loss of the pleasures and pursuits of life. The balance of the damages awarded to her were for pecuniary damages—lost earnings and the cost of custodial and nursing care. Her husband was awarded $1,500,000 on his derivative claim for the loss of his wife's services. On defendants' posttrial motions, the Trial Judge reduced the total award to Emma McDougald to $4,796,728 by striking the entire award for future nursing care ($2,353,374) and by reducing the separate awards for conscious pain and suffering and loss of the pleasures and pursuits of life to a single award of $2,000,000. * * * Her husband's award was left intact. On cross appeals, the Appellate Division affirmed (135 A.D.2d 80, 524 N.Y.S.2d 192) and later granted defendants leave to appeal to this court.

II.

We note at the outset that the defendants' liability for Emma McDougald's injuries is unchallenged here, except for a claim by Dr. Garber that liability against her was predicated on a theory not asserted in the complaint or bill of particulars. We agree with the Appellate Division, for the reasons stated by that court * * * that Dr. Garber's claim does not warrant a new trial on liability.

Also unchallenged are the awards in the amount of $770,978 for loss of earnings and $2,025,750 for future custodial care—that is, the pecuniary damage awards that survived defendants' posttrial motions.

What remains in dispute, primarily, is the award to Emma McDougald for nonpecuniary damages. At trial, defendants sought to show that Mrs. McDougald's injuries were so severe that she was incapable of either experiencing pain or appreciating her condition. Plaintiffs, on the other hand, introduced proof that Mrs. McDougald responded to certain stimuli to a sufficient extent to indicate that she was aware of her circumstances. Thus, the extent of Mrs. McDougald's cognitive abilities, if any, was sharply disputed.

The parties and the trial court agreed that Mrs. McDougald could not recover for pain and suffering unless she were conscious of the pain. Defendants maintained that such consciousness was also required to support an award for loss of enjoyment of life. The court, however, accepted plaintiffs' view that loss of enjoyment of life was compensable without regard to whether the plaintiff was aware of the loss. Accordingly, because the level of Mrs. McDougald's cognitive abilities was in dispute, the court instructed the jury to consider loss of enjoyment of life as an element of nonpecuniary damages separate from pain and suffering. The court's charge to the jury on these points was as follows:

"If you conclude that Emma McDougald is so neurologically impaired that she is totally incapable of experiencing any unpleasant or painful sensation, then, obviously, she cannot be awarded damages for conscious pain * * *.

"It is for you to determine the level of Emma McDougald's perception and awareness. Suffering relates primarily to the emotional reaction of the injured person to the injury. Thus, for an injured person to experience suffering, there, again, must be some level of awareness. If Emma McDougald is totally unaware of her condition or totally incapable of any emotional reaction, then you cannot award her damages for suffering. * * *

"Damages for the loss of the pleasures and pursuits of life, however, require no awareness of the loss on the part of the injured person. Quite obviously, Emma McDougald is unable to engage in any of the activities which constitute a normal life, the activities she engaged in prior to her injury * * * Loss of the enjoyment of life may, of course, accompany the physical sensation and emotional responses that we refer to as pain and suffering, and in most cases it does. It is possible, however, for an injured person to lose the enjoyment of life without experiencing any conscious pain and suffering. Damages for this item of injury relate not to what Emma McDougald is aware of, but rather to what she has lost. What her life was prior to her injury and what it has been since September 7, 1978 and what it will be for as long as she lives."

We conclude that the court erred, both in instructing the jury that Mrs. McDougald's awareness was irrelevant to their consideration of damages for loss of enjoyment of life and in directing the jury to consider that aspect of damages separately from pain and suffering.

III.

We begin with the familiar proposition that an award of damages to a person injured by the negligence of another is to compensate the victim, not to punish the wrongdoer. * * * The goal is to restore the injured party, to the extent possible, to the position that would have been occupied had the wrong not occurred. * * * To be sure, placing the burden of compensation on the negligent party also serves as a deterrent, but purely punitive damages—that is, those which have no compensatory purpose—are prohibited unless the harmful conduct is intentional, malicious, outrageous, or otherwise aggravated beyond mere negligence * * *.

Damages for nonpecuniary losses are, of course, among those that can be awarded as compensation to the victim. This aspect of damages, however, stands on less certain ground than does an award for pecuniary damages. An economic loss can be compensated in kind by an economic gain; but recovery for noneconomic losses such as pain and suffering and loss of enjoyment of life rests on "the legal fiction that money damages can compensate for a victim's injury" (*Howard v. Lecher,* 42 N.Y.2d 109, 111, 397 N.Y.S.2d 363, 366 N.E.2d 64). We accept this fiction, knowing that although money will neither ease the pain nor restore the victim's abilities, this device is as close as the law can come in its effort to right the wrong. We have no hope of evaluating what has been lost, but a monetary award may provide a measure of solace for the condition created * * *.

Our willingness to indulge this fiction comes to an end, however, when it ceases to serve the compensatory goals of tort recovery. When that limit is met, further indulgence can only result in assessing damages that are punitive. The question posed by this case, then, is whether an award of damages for loss of enjoyment of life to a person whose injuries preclude any awareness of the loss serves a compensatory purpose. We conclude that it does not.

Simply put, an award of money damages in such circumstances has no meaning or utility to the injured person. An award for the loss of enjoyment of life "cannot provide [such a victim] with any consolation or ease any burden resting on him * * * He cannot spend it upon necessities or pleasures. He cannot experience the pleasure of giving it away" (*Flannery v. United States,* 4th Cir., 718 F.2d 108, 111, *cert. denied* 467 U.S. 1226, 104 S.Ct. 2679, 81 L.Ed.2d 874).

We recognize that, as the trial court noted, requiring some cognitive awareness as a prerequisite to recovery for loss of enjoyment of life will result in some cases "in the paradoxical situation that the greater the degree of brain injury inflicted by a negligent defendant, the smaller the award the plaintiff can recover in general damages". The force of this argument, however—the temptation to achieve a balance between injury and damages—has nothing to do with meaningful compensation for the victim. Instead, the temptation is rooted in a desire to punish the defendant in proportion to the harm inflicted. However relevant such retributive symmetry may be in the criminal law, it has no place in the law of civil damages, at least in the absence of culpability beyond mere negligence.

Accordingly, we conclude that cognitive awareness is a prerequisite to recovery for loss of enjoyment of life. We do not go so far, however, as to require the fact finder to sort out varying degrees of cognition and determine at what level a particular deprivation can be fully appreciated. With respect to pain and suffering, the trial court charged simply that there must be "some level of awareness" in order for plaintiff to recover. We think that this is an appropriate standard for all aspects of nonpecuniary loss. No doubt the standard ignores analytically relevant levels of cognition, but we resist the desire for analytical purity in favor of simplicity. A more complex instruction might give the appearance of greater precision but, given the limits of our understanding of the human mind, it would in reality lead only to greater speculation.

We turn next to the question whether loss of enjoyment of life should be considered a category of damages separate from pain and suffering.

IV.

There is no dispute here that the fact finder may, in assessing nonpecuniary damages, consider the effect of the injuries on the plaintiff's capacity to lead a normal life. Traditionally, in this State and elsewhere, this aspect of suffering has not been treated as a separate category of damages; instead, the plaintiff's inability to enjoy life to its fullest has been considered one type of suffering to be factored into a general award for nonpecuniary damages, commonly known as pain and suffering.

Recently, however, there has been an attempt to segregate the suffering associated with physical pain from the mental anguish that stems from the inability to engage in certain activities, and to have juries provide a separate award for each * * *.

Some courts have resisted the effort, primarily on the ground that duplicative and therefore excessive awards would result * * *. Other courts have allowed separate awards, noting that the types of suffering involved are analytically distinguishable (see, e.g., *Rufino v. United States*, 2nd Cir., 829 F.2d 354 [applying its prediction of New York law]; *Thompson v. National R.R. Passenger Corp.*, 6th Cir., 621 F.2d 814, *cert. denied* 449 U.S. 1035, 101 S.Ct. 611, 66 L.Ed.2d 497; *Mariner v. Marsden*, 610 P.2d 6 [Wyo]; *Lebesco v. Southeastern Pa. Transp. Auth.*, 251 Pa.Super. 415, 380 A.2d 848). Still other courts have questioned the propriety of the practice but held that, in the particular case, separate awards did not constitute reversible error * * *.

In this State, the only appellate decisions to address the question are the decision of the Appellate Division, First Department, now under review * * * and the decision of the Second Department in *Nussbaum v. Gibstein*, * * * [decided today]. Those courts were persuaded that the distinctions between the two types of mental anguish justified separate awards and that the potential for duplicative awards could be mitigated by carefully drafted jury instructions. In addition, the courts opined that separate awards would facilitate appellate review concerning the excessiveness of the total damage award.

We do not dispute that distinctions can be found or created between the concepts of pain and suffering and loss of enjoyment of life. If the term "suffering" is limited to the emotional response to the sensation of pain, then the emotional response caused by the limitation of life's activities may be considered qualitatively different * * *. But suffering need not be so limited—it can easily encompass the frustration and anguish caused by the inability to participate in activities that once brought pleasure. Traditionally, by treating loss of enjoyment of life as a permissible factor in assessing pain and suffering, courts have given the term this broad meaning.

If we are to depart from this traditional approach and approve a separate award for loss of enjoyment of life, it must be on the basis that such an approach will yield a more accurate evaluation of the compensation due to the plaintiff. We have no doubt that, in general, the total award for nonpecuniary damages would increase if we adopted the rule. That separate awards are advocated by plaintiffs and resisted by defendants is sufficient evidence that larger awards are at stake here. But a larger award does not by itself indicate that the goal of compensation has been better served.

The advocates of separate awards contend that because pain and suffering and loss of enjoyment of life can be distinguished, they must be treated separately if the plaintiff is to be compensated fully for each distinct injury suffered. We disagree. Such an analytical approach may have its place when the subject is pecuniary damages, which can be calculated with some precision. But the estimation of nonpecuniary damages is not amenable to such analytical precision and may, in fact, suffer from its application. Translating human suffering into dollars and cents involves no mathematical formula; it rests, as we have said, on a legal fiction. The figure that emerges is unavoidably distorted by the translation. Application of this murky process to the component parts of nonpecuniary injuries (however analytically distinguishable they may be) cannot make it more accurate. If anything, the distortion will be amplified by repetition.

Thus, we are not persuaded that any salutary purpose would be served by having the jury make separate awards for pain and suffering and loss of enjoyment of life. We are confident, furthermore, that the trial advocate's art is a sufficient guarantee that none of the plaintiff's losses will be ignored by the jury.

The errors in the instructions given to the jury require a new trial on the issue of nonpecuniary damages to be awarded to plaintiff Emma McDougald. Defendants' remaining contentions are either without merit, beyond the scope of our review or are rendered academic by our disposition of the case.

Accordingly, the order of the Appellate Division, insofar as appealed from, should be modified, with costs to defendants, by granting a new trial on the issue of nonpecuniary damages of plaintiff Emma McDougald, and as so modified, affirmed.

TITONE, JUDGE (dissenting).

The majority's holding represents a compromise position that neither comports with the fundamental principles of tort compensation nor furnishes a satisfactory, logically consistent framework for compensating nonpecuniary loss. Because I conclude that loss of enjoyment of life is an objective damage item, conceptually distinct from conscious pain and suffering, I can find no fault with the trial court's instruction authorizing separate awards and permitting an award for "loss of enjoyment of life" even in the absence of any awareness of that loss on the part of the injured plaintiff. Accordingly, I dissent.

It is elementary that the purpose of awarding tort damages is to compensate the wronged party for the actual loss he or she has sustained * * *.

The capacity to enjoy life—by watching one's children grow, participating in recreational activities, and drinking in the many other pleasures that life has to offer—is unquestionably an attribute of an ordinary healthy individual. The loss of that capacity as a result of another's negligent act is at least as serious an impairment as the permanent destruction of a physical function, which has always been treated as a compensable item under traditional tort principles * * *. Indeed, I can imagine no physical loss that is more central to the quality of a tort victim's continuing life than the destruction of the capacity to enjoy that life to the fullest.

Unquestionably, recovery of a damage item such as "pain and suffering" requires a showing of some degree of cognitive capacity. Such a requirement exists for the simple reason that pain and suffering are wholly subjective concepts and cannot exist separate and apart from the human consciousness that experiences them. In contrast, the destruction of an individual's capacity to enjoy life as a result of a crippling injury is an objective fact that does not differ in principle from the permanent loss of an eye or limb. As in the case of a lost limb, an essential characteristic of a healthy human life has been wrongfully taken, and, consequently, the injured party is entitled to a monetary award as a substitute, if, as the majority asserts, the goal of tort compensation is "to restore the injured party, to the extent possible, to the position that would have been occupied had the wrong not occurred" * * *.

Significantly, this equation does not suggest a need to establish the injured's awareness of the loss. The victim's ability to comprehend the degree to which his or her life has been impaired is irrelevant, since, unlike "conscious pain and suffering," the impairment exists independent of the victim's ability to apprehend it. Indeed, the majority reaches the conclusion that a degree of awareness must be shown only after injecting a new element into the equation. Under the majority's formulation, the victim must be aware of the loss because, in addition to being compensatory, the award must have "meaning or utility to the injured person." * * * This additional requirement, however, has no real foundation in law or logic. "Meaning" and "utility" are subjective value judgments that have no place in the law of tort recovery, where the primary goal is to find ways of quantifying, to the extent possible, the worth of various forms of human tragedy.

Moreover, the compensatory nature of a monetary award for loss of enjoyment of life is not altered or rendered punitive by the fact that the unaware injured plaintiff cannot experience the pleasure of having it. The fundamental distinction between punitive and compensatory damages is that the former exceed the amount necessary to replace what the plaintiff lost * * *. As the Court of Appeals for the Second Circuit has observed, "[t]he fact that the compensation [for loss of enjoyment of life] may inure as a practical matter to third parties in a given case does not transform the nature of the damages" (*Rufino v. United States,* 2nd Cir., 829 F.2d 354, 362).

Ironically, the majority's expressed goal of limiting recovery for nonpecuniary loss to compensation that the injured plaintiff has the capacity to appreciate is directly undercut by the majority's ultimate holding, adopted in the interest of "simplicity," that recovery for loss of enjoyment of life may be had as long as the injured plaintiff has " 'some level of awareness' ", however slight * * *. Manifestly, there are many different forms and levels of awareness, particularly in cases involving brain injury. Further, the type and degree of cognitive functioning necessary to experience "pain and suffering" is certainly of a lower order than that needed to apprehend the loss of the ability to enjoy life in all of its subtleties. Accordingly, the existence of "some level of awareness" on the part of the injured plaintiff says nothing about that plaintiff's ability to derive some comfort from the award or even to appreciate its significance. Hence, that standard does not assure that loss of enjoyment of life damages will be awarded only when they serve "a compensatory purpose," as that term is defined by the majority.

In the final analysis, the rule that the majority has chosen is an arbitrary one, in that it denies or allows recovery on the basis of a criterion that is not truly related to its stated goal. In my view, it is fundamentally unsound, as well as grossly unfair, to deny recovery to those who are completely without cognitive capacity while permitting it for those with a mere spark of awareness, regardless of the latter's ability to appreciate either the loss sustained or the benefits of the monetary award offered in compensation. In both instances, the injured plaintiff is in essentially the same position, and an award that is punitive as to one is equally punitive as to the other. Of course, since I do not subscribe to the majority's conclusion that an award to an unaware plaintiff is punitive, I would have no difficulty permitting recovery to both classes of plaintiffs.

Having concluded that the injured plaintiff's awareness should not be a necessary precondition to recovery for loss of enjoyment of life, I also have no difficulty going on to conclude that loss of enjoyment of life is a distinct damage item which is recoverable separate and apart from the award for conscious pain and suffering. The majority has rejected separate recovery, in part because it apparently perceives some overlap between the two damage categories and in part because it believes that the goal of enhancing the precision of jury awards for nonpecuniary loss would not be advanced. However, the overlap the majority perceives exists only if one assumes, as the majority evidently has * * *, that the "loss of enjoyment" category of damages is designed to compensate only for *"the emotional response* caused by the limitation of life's activities" and *"the frustration* *and anguish caused by* the inability to participate in activities that once brought pleasure" (emphasis added), both of which are highly *subjective* concepts.

In fact, while "pain and suffering compensates the victim for the physical and mental discomfort caused by the injury; * * * loss of enjoyment of life compensates the victim for the limitations on the person's life created by the injury", a distinctly *objective* loss * * *. In other words, while the victim's "emotional response" and "frustration and anguish" are elements of the award for pain and suffering, the "limitation of life's activities" and the "inability to participate in activities" that the majority identifies are recoverable under the "loss of enjoyment of life" rubric. Thus, there is no real overlap, and no real basis for concern about potentially duplicative awards where, as here, there is a properly instructed jury.

Finally, given the clear distinction between the two categories of nonpecuniary damages, I cannot help but assume that permitting separate awards for conscious pain and suffering and loss of enjoyment of life would contribute to accuracy and precision in thought in the jury's deliberations on the issue of damages. * * * In light of the concrete benefit to be gained by compelling the jury to differentiate between the specific objective and subjective elements of the plaintiff's nonpecuniary loss, I find unpersuasive the majority's reliance on vague concerns about potential distortion owing to the inherently difficult task of computing the value of intangible loss. My belief in the jury system, and in the collective wisdom of the deliberating jury, leads me to conclude that we may safely leave that task in the jurors' hands.

---

1. *Guidelines for Assessment and Methods of Argument*

Jury Instructions. As we have seen, jurors are not told about verdict amounts in similar injury cases, nor are they instructed to follow some particular method of measurement. In fact, courts disallow references to verdicts or outcomes in other cases. Instead, for pain and suffering, juries usually are instructed that they should award a sum that would reasonably compensate the plaintiff for her pain and suffering, and that there are no objective guidelines by which to measure this injury. *See* Ronald W. Eades, Jury Instructions on Damages in Tort Actions 321 (3d ed. 1993).

Per Diem Arguments. In arguments to the jury, plaintiff's lawyers often try to use a method of argument known as the "per diem" or "unit of time" argument. Courts remain divided on the method. Probably a quarter to a third of jurisdictions disallow it in all cases, others leave it up to the trial judge's discretion, and many generally allow it. Using the approach, the plaintiff's lawyer will divide into units of time—hours, days, minutes, months, or year—the period that the plaintiff has suffered and will suffer the pain and suffering or mental anguish. Counsel then suggests a dollar figure for each unit of time and multiplies the two figures (dollar value and the number of the units of time). Defendant's lawyers usually dislike the method because it can begin with a modest value (such as $2 an hour for pain and suffering) and yield an extremely high ultimate award.

Why would courts object to use of the method, so long as the jury is not instructed that it *must* use such a method or employ the same figures suggested by trial counsel? One court framed its reasons as follows: "[T]here is no measure by which the amount of pain and suffering * * * can be calculated. * * * The varieties and degrees of pain are almost infinite. * * * It is just as futile to undertake to attach a price tag to each level or plateau. * * * Any effort to do so must become lost in emotion, fancy, and speculation." Botta v. Brunner, 26 N.J. 82, 138 A.2d 713 (1958). But the jury must make the "pricing" decision in some way, by value judgment if not by evidentiary guidance. Why is the suggestion of an evaluative method improper?

Golden Rule Arguments. Another controversial form of argument is known as a "golden rule" argument. All jurisdictions disallow arguments that are obviously of this category. The categorization, however, may not always be so clear. Consider the following arguments. (These and others are collected at 1 M. Minzer, J. Nates, C. Kimball & D. Axelrod, Damages in Tort Actions § 4.72 (1992)).

"All Mrs. Richardson asks you gentlemen to do when you retire to your jury room is to apply the Golden Rule. 'Do unto her as you wish that you would be done.'" Seymour v. Richardson, 194 Va. 709, 75 S.E.2d 77, 81 (1953).

"Any of us would be frustrated and irritable if their spare time was taken away. I know how I would feel if that was taken away from me. Mr. Herring has had something that God has given to him taken away: a healthy, completely accident-free body. That is what he had. Something we all want. Something we all cherish." Klein v. Herring, 347 So.2d 681, 682 (Fla.App.1977).

"Gentlemen, there is no way that you can measure his pain and suffering and the only thing I can suggest for you to do is put yourself in the plaintiff's place and try to figure out how much it would be worth to you to go through the pain and suffering which Mr. Mozo went through." Magid v. Mozo, 135 So.2d 772, 773 (Fla.App.1961).

"Wouldn't you, if your son was injured and you couldn't get some responses or if he has injuries you don't understand and nobody understand, the first thing you're going to want to know as a parent whether male or female, you're going to want to know, 'What can I do for my son? What is the future going to hold for him?'

"I remember when I was a kid growing up hearing, 'Walk a mile in my shoes.' I always thought about that in trying these cases because you have got to in your own mind see what it's like * * *. When you, a normal person, get up, you've got your hopes, all your aspirations, ambitions, you've got all the mental facilities that you have * * *.

"What does [the plaintiff] do on each day that he walks that mile? He knows today and tomorrow morning when he gets up, after you have rendered this verdict, he's going to go to work and he's going to know there is nothing he can do at work except be a helper * * *. He has got to live with that. He can't because they gave him an 84 I.Q. God gave him a 104 I.Q. Their negligence gave him an 84 * * *." LeRetilley v. Harris, 354 So.2d 1213, 1213–14 (Fla.App.1978).

All of these were deemed golden-rule arguments and therefore erroneous; in all but the last instance the error warranted reversal. Courts have explained that golden rule arguments are improper because they "appeal to the prejudice of the jury to abandon their position as fair and impartial jurors and to assume the position of a partisan or claimant in the case." World Wide Tire Co. v. Brown, 644 S.W.2d 144, 146 (Tex.App.1982), quoting Dallas Ry. & Term. Co. v. Smith, 42 S.W.2d 794, 795 (Tex.App. 1931). Does this explanation help explain what is troublesome about each of the quoted arguments? Does the problem lie with the suggestion that the jury should use *no standard other than* "do unto others"? Only the first of the listed arguments does this. Some of the arguments ask the jury to imagine how the plaintiff's loss would feel. Should this be improper? Or is the problem with the suggestion that the *pricing* of the injury should be linked to what the juror herself or himself would want or demand?

Willingness-to-Pay To Avoid Injury. The notion of "what would you demand" to experience a risk of injury, or "what would you pay" to avoid or reduce the risk of injury, forms the basis of methods by which economists value intangible losses, such as pain or the loss of environmental quality. Indeed, federal agencies have made heavy use of such methodologies, beginning with the administration of President Ronald Reagan. For more detail, see Ted R. Miller, *Willingness to Pay Comes of Age: Will the System Survive?*, 83 N.W. U. L. Rev. 876 (1989). But these methodologies do not look at what consumers would pay to avoid a *certain* injury. Rather, they look at what consumers are willing to pay (for example, costs of an airbag) to reduce an *ex ante* risk of injury, or what consumers demand (such as hazard duty pay) to encounter an *ex ante* risk of injury. Should we allow "willingness to pay" or "what would you demand" arguments in tort suits if they are modified to use the notion of risk rather than certain injury? There would be two ways of doing so: allowing the lawyers to use this sort of argument; or allowing the plaintiff to put on expert economic testimony, based on aggregate consumer studies, about the value of certain nonpecuniary losses based on what people are willing to pay to avoid them. This latter approach has received increased judicial attention in recent years. One court described the testimony offered by the expert economist.

[T]he method attempts to get at the value of life by indirection; no one is ever asked "what is the monetary value of living?", because most people would probably respond that life is priceless, scuttling the endeavor. Instead, [the expert] focuses on how much Americans are willing to pay for reductions in health and safety risks, and how much they are compensated for assuming extra risk. This method, according to [the expert's] economic theory, reveals the value we actually place on living, and avoids the astronomical answers people would give in response to a hypothetical question. He relies on three types of willingness-to-pay studies: studies of how much consumers, through the purchase of devices such as smoke detectors and seat belts, pay for increased personal safety; studies of how much more people who assume extra risk (e.g., policemen) are paid because their jobs are dangerous; and studies of cost-benefit analyses conducted in the evaluation of government safety regulation. [The expert] testified that he relied on some 75 such studies in his valuation.

Through this analysis, [the expert] concluded that the value of the enjoyment of a statistically average person's life was $2.3 million in 1988 dollars. (The statistically average person is 31 years old with a 45 year additional life expectancy.) This averages out to approximately a $60,000–per-year value on the enjoyment of life. [The expert] took this figure and multiplied it by the percentage range of Brian's loss of the full experience of life, 66% to 83% (drawn from Dr. Pueschel's calculations). Adjusting for Brian's young age, the plaintiff informs us that [the expert] concluded the value of Brian's lost pleasure of living due to the injuries he suffered in the taxi accident was $2,207,827 to $2,762,227.

Mercado v. Ahmed, 974 F.2d 863, 869 (7th Cir.1992).

Courts have split on the propriety of such testimony, with more courts thus far disallowing it. *Compare* Sena v. New Mexico State Police, 119 N.M. 471, 892 P.2d 604, 610 (App.1995)(stating that, "where an expert witness has been properly qualified, it is not improper for the trial court to permit an economist to testify regarding his or her opinion concerning the economic value of a plaintiff's loss of enjoyment of life") *with* Mercado v. Ahmed, 974 F.2d 863 (7th Cir.1992)(ruling that the trial court did not abuse its discretion in refusing to admit the expert testimony based on this methodology).

As we noted above, the district judge did not believe that [the expert] offered the jury any "expertise" because (1) no consensus among experts supported [the expert's] method of valuing life and (2) [the expert's] research was no more than a compilation of the opinions, expressed through spending decisions, of a large number of Americans as to the value of life. The first criticism is irrefutable: the plaintiff could point to no expert consensus supporting [the expert's] methodology. The second criticism is also on the mark, since [the expert] concedes that his method relies on arriving at a valuation of life based on analyzing the behavior of non-experts.

However, even accepting [the expert's] premise that his method of determining the value of life is different in an important way from submitting the question to a jury because it focuses on observable behavior and not opinion, we have serious doubts about his assertion that the studies he relies upon actually measure how much Americans value life. For example, spending on items like air bags and smoke detectors is probably influenced as much by advertising and marketing decisions made by profit-seeking manufacturers and by government-mandated safety requirements as it is by any consideration by consumers of how much life is worth. Also, many people may be interested in a whole range of safety devices and believe they are worthwhile, but are unable to afford them. More fundamentally, spending on safety items reflects a consumer's willingness to pay to reduce risk, perhaps more a measure of how cautious a person is than how much he or she values life. Few of us, when confronted with the threat, "Your money or your life!" would, like Jack Benny, pause and respond, "I'm thinking, I'm thinking." Most of us would empty our wallets. Why that decision reflects less the value we place on life than whether we buy an airbag is not immediately obvious.

The two other kinds of studies [the expert] relies upon are open to valid and logical criticism as well. To say that the salary paid to those who hold risky jobs tells us something significant about how much we value life ignores the fact that humans are moved by more than monetary incentives. For example, someone who believes police officers working in an extremely dangerous city are grossly undercompensated for the risks they assume might nevertheless take up the badge out of a sense of civic duty to their hometown. Finally, government calculations about how much to spend (or force others to spend) on health and safety regulations are motivated by a host of considerations other than the value of life: is it an election year? how large is the budget deficit? on which constituents will the burden of the regulations fall? what influence and pressure have lobbyists brought to bear? what is the view of interested constituents? And so on.

Mercado v. Ahmed, 974 F.2d 863, 870-71 (7th Cir.1992).

Are you persuaded that such testimony ought to be inadmissible, especially given the fact that opposing counsel could introduce, via cross-examination, the limitations noted by the Seventh Circuit in *Mercado*? Professor Mark Geistfeld recently has taken willingness-to-pay analysis another step. He agrees that market studies of the sort at issue in *Mercado* are severely flawed. But he argues that juries themselves should be instructed to use a willingness-to-pay standard when assessing damages for nonpecuniary losses. He suggests that the following, inter alia, be added to jury instructions on assessing damages for pain and suffering: "[T]he damages award [for pain and suffering] should equal the amount of money that a reasonable person would have accepted as fair compensation for the pain-and-suffering injury when confronted by the risk of suffering that injury." Mark Geistfeld, *Placing a Price on Pain and Suffering: A Method for Helping Juries Determine Tort Damages for Nonmonetary Injuries*, 83 Cal. L. Rev. 773, 842 (1995). Would this standard be subject to any of the concerns noted by the *Mercado* court? Do you think that the standard, if added to the typical jury instruction noted earlier, would yield different results?

2. *Risks and Fears of Incurring Loss in the Future*

Tort settlements and judgments routinely compensate plaintiffs for losses that will occur in the future—expenditures for medical care, lost wages, pain and suffering and mental anguish. Aside from some of the valuation difficulties already discussed—present value, estimating life expectancy, etc.—these claims for future losses have not posed fundamental difficulties for the tort system. Future medical damages can be awarded if there is a reasonable basis for the necessity and amount of such expenses. Anxiety and fear about the risk of incurring these future problems are also compensable if they are "based on a reasonable fear"; for a fear to be reasonable, "it is not necessary to show that the prospect of such an occurrence is a medical certainty or probability. It is sufficient if there is a showing that a substantial possibility exists for such an occurrence." Tamplin v. Star Lumber & Supply Co., 251 Kan. 300, 836 P.2d 1102 (1992). For the purposes of assessing damages for expected future pain and suffering it is of course the plaintiff's projected life expectancy, as of the time of trial, that is important, not his life expectancy had he not been injured. If, however, the plaintiff's injuries have diminished his life expectancy, his awareness of his diminished life expectancy may itself be a compensable form of pain and suffering. *See, e.g.*, Rhone v. Fisher, 224 Md. 223, 167 A.2d 773 (1961); Choicener v. Walters Amusement Agency, 269 Mass. 341, 168 N.E. 918 (1929). The problem of determining the proper compensation for victims of disaster who are aware even for a brief period of time that they are about to die is discussed in D. Beskind, *Fear of Dying*, Trial (*Briefs*) 30 (4th quarter 1989); D. Leebron, *Final Moments: Damages for Pain and Suffering Prior to Death*, 64 N.Y.U.L.Rev. 256 (1989).

The plaintiffs in garden-variety claims for future damages not only *may* seek future damages, but *must* do so. Under traditional tort rules, a plaintiff may not "split" her claim and later seek future damages in a different suit. Rather, she must bring her suit within the statute of limitations, and then seek in that suit all damages flowing from that injury.

Another category of future damage claims is now posing new challenges for courts: when the plaintiff arguably lacks a current disease or injury but alleges that exposure to a toxic substance has increased her risk of contracting an illness.

The most obvious first question is why the worker would want to sue at this time; why not just wait until he or she actually contracts one of the diseases? First, the plaintiff might seek to recover the cost of monitoring, medically, the status of the plaintiff or of obtaining any medical treatments that might be shown to have preventative or therapeutic benefits for those who might contract a particular disease. Second, the plaintiff might face a problem with the statute of limitations. In many jurisdictions, the typical two-year tort statute of limitations is a clock that starts running on the date of "injury" or "occurrence." If "occurrence" could be understood to mean the date of exposure, or if "injury" could be interpreted as the first time when the toxic substance begins to have any physiological effects, then the plaintiff might find that the clock has run out by the time she actually contracts the disease. How could this concern be remedied? In many jurisdictions the statute begins to run when the plaintiff first discovers her disease or should have discovered it.

Third, in a "mass tort" case in which thousands or tens of thousands of claims are filed against a defendant, the exposed yet still uninjured plaintiff might be concerned that the funding (via insurance or the defendant's collectible assets) will be exhausted by the time the plaintiff contracts the illness.

The doctrinal response to this set of problems is still evolving, but courts have tended to agree on a few points. First, under traditional tort rules, if the plaintiff can prove that she has a current injury or disease, then she can recover for the risk of future aggravation or other risks, fear and mental anguish over those future possibilities, and medical monitoring. Some toxic tort claimants have tried to fit themselves within this traditional rubric by contending that they have a current injury or disease, albeit a "subcellular" one—that is, an injury that at present is manifest only in the form of chromosomal breakage or the beginning of a breakdown to the immune system. The success of this strategy depends on whether subcellular damage can constitute a present injury. Courts have treated this as a fact question, to be decided case by case with the help of expert testimony. *See* Werlein v. U.S., 746 F.Supp. 887, 901 (D.Minn.1990), *vacated by agreement on other grounds*, 793 F.Supp. 898 (D.Minn.1992).

Second, if the exposed plaintiff cannot prove a current injury, she still might try to leap over the standard proof hurdle—a greater than 50% likelihood of future injury. If she succeeds, then she can recover full tort damages for the disease. *See* Jackson v. Johns–Manville Sales Corp., 781 F.2d 394 (5th Cir.1986)(over 50 percent chance of incurring cancer).[1] And, when such recovery is allowed, the plaintiff's fear of contracting cancer will also be a compensable item of damage. Third, if the increased likelihood of contracting cancer is low and unquantifiable, the courts have been unwilling to allow plaintiffs to recover anything for the increased risk of incurring cancer. *See* Sterling v. Velsicol Chemical Corp., 855 F.2d 1188 (6th Cir.1988); Ayers v. Jackson Township, 106 N.J. 557, 525 A.2d 287 (1987).

Yet a plaintiff with a low risk of incurring cancer in the future might have current, credible fear and anguish over that risk. Should the plaintiff receive compensation for this current fear and anguish? The California Supreme Court recently rejected the plaintiff's argument that she should be able to recover for current fear if the fear is reasonable under the circumstances. Instead, the court ruled that the plaintiff could recover for current fear if the plaintiff proves that the fear "results from a knowledge, corroborated by reliable medical and scientific opinion, that it is more likely than not that the feared cancer will develop in the future due to the toxic exposure." Potter v. Firestone Tire and Rubber Co., 6 Cal.4th 965, 974, 25 Cal.Rptr.2d 550, 555, 863 P.2d 795, 800 (1993). The court agreed that a plaintiff could reasonably be fearful of cancer when the risk was even lower, but reasoned that "[p]roliferation of fear of cancer claims in California in the absence of meaningful restrictions might compromise the availability and affordability of liability insurance for toxic liability risks." Why is this concern any more pronounced as to this category of claims than as to other varieties of claims for nonpecuniary loss?

What about the costs of medical monitoring or pre-disease treatment? Courts seem increasingly willing to allow compensation for these. The question, according to one recent opinion, is not whether the plaintiff will more likely than not develop the condition in the future, but whether

---

1. *Cf.,* Davis v. Graviss, 672 S.W.2d 928 (Ky.1984)(significant potential of future complications, including meningitis, brain abscess, or other neurological problems, as a result of injury to the skull). This is an interesting and unusual case. It presents the other side of a question we have already examined, *supra,* p. 242, when we were discussing causation. The question there was arguably whether a plaintiff's chances of incurring some complication, which in point of fact was incurred, could be attributed to a particular factor which increased the plaintiff's chance of incurring that complication. In the *Davis* case the complication had not been incurred, and, though the chances of its occurrence were good, no one was prepared to assert that they were more likely than not.

medical monitoring is necessary now. *See* Buckley v. Metro–North Commuter RR, 79 F.3d 1337 (2d Cir.1996) *cert. granted,* 117 S.Ct. 379, 136 L.Ed.2d 297 (1996).

3. *Critiques of Compensation for Nonpecuniary Damages*

One persistent line of attack has been the questionable compensatory value of nonpecuniary damages: money cannot replace or repair mental anguish, the companionship and love of a spouse or child, the experience of pain. Of course, the plaintiff might need money for psychological counseling, pain control therapy, or the replacement of some services that a spouse or parent provided (such as child care or home care), but these are available under pecuniary categories of damages.

One response to this compensatory criticism is that nonpecuniary damages might be used to purchase "substitute" items. For instance, the person who no longer can run or bicycle might instead take up music as a hobby; nonpecuniary damages could help finance this. Interestingly, no jurisdiction directly asks the factfinder to assess damages based upon the cost of substitute items. What could explain why jurisdictions have never directly translated this into a question for the jury? If a key compensatory explanation for nonpecuniary items (such as "pain and suffering" and "impairment") is this notion of purchasing substitutes, why not just ask the factfinder directly to award money for the value of substitutes?

Everyone also understands that, in practice, awards for nonpecuniary damages play a key role in financing the plaintiff's attorney's fee and the expenses of bringing the claim. This is one reason why some tort reform proposals combine the elimination or reduction of nonpecuniary damages with a scheme for delivering compensation for economic damages more quickly and with more certainty to the plaintiff. These proposals are discussed later.

Another possible purpose of nonpecuniary losses is declarative or dignitary. By allowing a monetary award for such damages, society signals or declares that the victim's pain, impairment, and grief have worth and deserve our recognition and protection. But, in the course of sending this signal, do nonpecuniary damages also send a different message? Professor Richard Abel argues that awards for pain and suffering send the message "that every pain suffered can be offset by an equivalent pleasure, which can be bought for money." And damages for injuries to relationships, he continues, "commodify love"; they send "the message that all relationships have a monetary value." Richard A. Abel, *A Critique of Torts,* 37 U.C.L.A. L. Rev. 785, 803–06 (1990). Professor Margaret Radin has also explained the commodification concern that some observers of the tort system might have: "[W]hen we live in a world in which many or most things people need and want are routinely traded as commodities, and when we see dollars systematically being paid to people after they are injured, and in some way 'for' or 'on account of' the injury, we are likely to *come to* conceive of freedom from injury as another commodity bearing exchange value, even if we do not *now* conceive of it that way." Margaret Radin, *Compensation and Commensurability,* 43 Duke L.J. 56, 84 (1993)(emphasis added).

Professor Leslie Bender also laments the potential message that nonpecuniary qualities are possessions or commodities. But she argues that awards for nonpecuniary damages are not the ultimate source of this problem.

> Until we devise other legal remedies that respect all the realties of these injuries and seek to alleviate these harms, how can we blame common law tort or tort victims for following our social norms and translating intangible injuries into the materialistic language of our culture, the language of dollars? * * *

> Monetary damages veer far from the mark in compensating for intangible injuries, but the legal system has been silent about alternatives. Critics have blamed common law tort wrongly for this problem. We should look closer to our core. If we criticize the commodification of injury—a wholly justified criticism—our focus should not be on tort law and tort reform but rather systemic political, economic, and social change. * * *

> * * *

> * * * New kinds of remedies must be developed—remedies that respond to victims' needs for community, care, and relationships, remedies that require corporate officers and responsible individual defendants to perform the physical and emotional caregiving work.

Leslie Bender, *Feminist (Re)Torts: Thoughts on the Liability Crisis, Mass Torts, Power, and Responsibilities,* 1990 Duke L.J. 848, 875, 905–06.

Does the typical jury instruction on pain and suffering, or a jury's response to it, reflect this message that pain, grief, and relationships can be commodified? Or, even if the jury itself does not receive or intend to transmit this message, does the tort system over time nonetheless send a message of commodification?

A third strand of criticism focuses on the practical effects of the traditional approach. Those who contend that the tort system simply produces excessive amounts of compensation usually focus on pain and suffering as the key culprit. A number of studies suggest that awards for nonpecuniary losses make up about fifty percent of the average jury award. Professor Neil Vidmar, however, in his analyses of the data about jury verdicts in the medical malpractice arena, contests the 50% figure and argues that the data do not support that jury damage awards are based on the depth of defendants' pockets, caprice, or sympathy. *See* N. Vidmar, Medical Malpractice and the American Jury 200–01, 259 (1995).

A different practical criticism focuses not on the excessiveness of compensation but on its variability. Several studies have concluded, after controlling for other factors such as differences in the underlying liability facts, that jury verdicts generally achieve "vertical consistency." That is, juries over time and in different places tend to award higher damages for more severe injuries, and lower damages for less severe injuries. Most studies also have found, however, that the tort system does less well at achieving "horizontal consistency"; that is, giving similar valuations to similarly severe injuries. For more detail, *see* Randall Bovbjerg, Frank

Sloan & James Blumstein, *Valuing Life and Limb in Tort: Scheduling "Pain and Suffering,"* 83 Nw.U.L.Rev. 908, 920–26 (1989).

Still another strand of this practical critique aims not so much at the fact of full compensation for nonpecuniary damages, but at the lack of guidance or benchmarks given to the jury or used by trial or appellate judges in reviewing jury awards. Some analysts have suggested using "schedules" for guiding the valuation of nonpecuniary damages. Juries, for instance, could be instructed to compare the plaintiff's injury to a schedule that takes account of severity and age; the schedule also could contain ranges of suggested jury awards, based on past awards in similar cases. For more detail on possible schedules or scales, *see* Paul C. Weiler, Medical Malpractice on Trial 560 (1991); Bovbjerg *et al., supra.* No jurisdiction yet has implemented a schedule approach.

4. *The Insurance Theory Attack on Nonpecuniary Damages*

In recent years, the criticism that nonpecuniary damages have questionable compensatory value has gained momentum. Leading the charge are law and economics scholars focusing on whether tort law advances economic efficiency. Their criticism has focused on the insurance aspect of tort damages, arguing that the tort system—especially its provision for nonpecuniary damages—is an undesirable form of insurance.

This "insurance theory" of damages reasons as follows. When given a free choice, people would not and do not choose to buy insurance for nonpecuniary losses. For instance, we choose to buy homeowner's, health, and disability policies that insure us only for out-of-pocket losses. We do not opt for policies that will pay us money for pain and suffering, or the grief and loss we would suffer at the death of a loved one. This is not because these losses are unreal or unimportant, but because money cannot replace them. So we would not choose to pay money now—in the form of insurance premiums—for a policy that would pay us money for these nonpecuniary losses. Of course, if we were to suffer terrible pain or grief, we all would prefer then—if given the choice post-injury—receiving some money to receiving no money. But this misses the point of the insurance theory. The insurance theory asks whether we would be willing, in advance of injury, to pay premiums for insurance against nonpecuniary losses. For presentations of the theory, *see* American Law Institute, Reporters' Study on Enterprise Responsibility for Personal Injury, Vol. II at 206–11; George L. Priest, *The Current Insurance Crisis and Modern Tort Law,* 96 Yale L.J. 1521, 1556–57 (1987); Alan Schwartz, *Proposals for Products Liability Reform: A Theoretical Synthesis,* 97 Yale L.J. 353, 362–67 (1988).

This insurance critique has not gone unchallenged. An initial question is how well an insurance-driven analysis fits many tort scenarios. The insurance theory starts with the premise that the cost of nonpecuniary loss insurance ultimately falls on consumers; this is why insurance theorists can charge tort with forcing us to buy insurance that we would not choose to buy. Professor Jane Stapleton, though, has argued that in many cases consumers do not bear the full cost of tort damages because corporations face some limits in their ability to pass along these costs to consumers. If consumers do not bear the cost of nonpecuniary loss insurance, then the tort system is not forcing them to pay for insurance that they would not choose. *See* Jane Stapleton, *Tort, Insurance and Ideology*, 58 Modern L. Rev. 820 (1995).

A second challenge focuses on a point that is central to the insurance theory: how do various nonpecuniary losses actually affect individuals' need for money? It might be that some pecuniary losses have the effect, in economic parlance, of increasing the individual's "marginal utility of income." For instance, an injury might force a person to substitute a more expensive activity (such as music) for less expensive activity in which the person no longer can engage (such as tennis or running). To this extent, the injury would raise the marginal utility of money, post-injury. If this were the case, the insurance theorists concede, the rational individual would choose to purchase insurance against the possibility of this loss. By doing so, she could transfer dollars from the pre-injury state (when their marginal utility is lower) to the post-injury state (when their marginal utility would be higher).

Most of the insurance theorists seem to believe, however, that nonpecuniary losses generally will not increase and may even decrease the marginal utility of money. For instance, the person who suffers from severe and chronic pain, post-injury, will derive less benefit from each dollar of income in the post-loss than in the pre-loss state. And so the rational person would not choose, in advance of injury, to pay a premium now (when the value of money is high) simply in order to receive dollars at a time when their marginal utility will be lower.

The still-unanswered question, then, is whether some or all nonpecuniary losses increase, leave unchanged, or actually lower the post-injury value of money to an individual. How could we try to answer the question? Some research has concluded that nonpecuniary losses reduce the marginal utility of money; the research basically draws on the opinions of those without disabilities about what the value of money would be to them if they were to become disabled. Should we rely on the perspective of those without disabilities about what the value of money would be to them in the event of serious disability? For discussion of this issue, *see* Ellen S. Pryor, *The Tort Law Debate, Efficiency, and the Kingdom of the Ill: A Critique of the Insurance Theory of Compensation*, 79 Va. L. Rev. 91, 99–100 (1993).

What about evidence of what individuals actually purchase when given the choice? Consider your own insurance policies. Does any of them provide coverage for nonpecuniary aspects of loss that you might suffer? If not, does this reflect an implicit judgment on your part that the suffering of a nonpecuniary loss would not enhance the value of money post-injury?

A third challenge to the insurance theory is that it assumes a narrow conception of why the "rational individual" might want to purchase insurance. Professors Croley and Hanson have argued that the rational individual, when deciding whether to purchase nonpecuniary loss insurance, would look at something more than just whether the nonpecuniary loss will lower or raise the marginal utility of wealth. Rather, the individual also would seek to protect herself from falling below some overall baseline of utility. Nonpecuniary damages might help provide this baseline protection, and thus the rational consumer might insure herself for nonpecuniary damages to this extent. *See* Steven P. Croley & Jon D. Hanson, *The Nonpecuniary Costs of Accidents: Pain-and-Suffering Damages in Tort Law*, 108 Harv. L. Rev. 1787 (1995).

Still another response to the insurance theory relates to deterrence. Even if nonpecuniary damages reflect a forced overpurchase of insurance, such damages in theory serve a deterrence function by forcing actors to internalize the costs of their activity. Some theorists contend, however, that administrative fines or penalties could take up whatever deterrence slack would result from the elimination or reduction of nonpecuniary damages. In addition, tort's ability to achieve meaningful or optimal deterrence is still under debate. *Compare* Stephen D. Sugarman, *Doing Away With Tort Law*, 73 Cal. L. Rev. 555, 559–91 (1985)(arguing that tort law does a poor job at deterrence), *with* Gary T. Schwartz, *Reality in the Economic Analysis of Law: Does Tort Law Really Deter?*, 42 U.C.L.A. L. Rev. 377 (1994)(arguing that tort law provides something significant by way of deterrence, at least in certain arenas).

If one were to accept the core reasoning of the insurance theory, what sorts of reforms would it support? Would it support eliminating (or reducing) nonpecuniary loss damages in all tort settings—including accidents between strangers—or only in settings such as products or service sales, when the potential defendant can pass along the cost of the "tort insurance policy" by increasing costs of products or services? Does the insurance theory support the elimination of all nonpecuniary loss damages? Tort reform legislation actually has not taken this form, but instead usually employs "caps" on nonpecuniary losses. Does the insurance theory support caps on nonpecuniary damages? Does it support some sort of "scheduled" nonpecuniary damages, which would increase along with the severity of the injury?

5.   *Tort Reform Measures Relating to Nonpecuniary Damages*

Caps on Nonpecuniary Damages. Dozens of states now impose caps on "nonpecuniary" or "noneconomic damages" in tort litigation generally or medical malpractice in particular. In a number of states the cap is $250,000, and in others it is $400,000 or $500,000. Usually, the caps apply despite the severity of the injury; there is no threshold severity that triggers escape from the cap. But there are some exceptions. For instance, the Alaska statute provides a $500,000 cap on noneconomic losses, but states that the limit does not apply to "damages for disfigurement or severe physical impairment." Alaska Stat. § 09.17.010 (1994). Similarly, the Colorado statute states that the cap does apply to "nonpecuniary harm * * * including pain and suffering, inconvenience, emotional stress, and impairment of the quality of life," but does not "limit the recovery of compensatory damages for physical impairment or disfigurement." Colo. Rev. Stat. § 13–21–102.5 (2)(b) & (5)(1988 & 1995). Do the exclusions in the Alaska and Colorado statutes rest on any plausible theoretical or practical rationale?

In many states, plaintiffs have challenged the caps as violating state constitutional provisions relating to due process, open courts, or right to

trial by jury; plaintiffs also have attacked the caps as violating the due
process and equal protection clauses of the United States Constitution.
Challenges based on the United States Constitution have generally been
unavailing. *See, e.g.,* Boyd v. Bulala, 877 F.2d 1191 (4th Cir.1989).
Challenges based on state constitutions have had mixed results, depending
on the wording and scope of the particular state constitution. *Compare*
Knowles v. United States, 1996 SD 10, 544 N.W.2d 183 (S.D.1996)(striking
down cap on due process grounds), with Fein v. Permanente Medical
Group, 38 Cal.3d 137, 211 Cal.Rptr. 368, 695 P.2d 665 (1985)(holding that
the cap on noneconomic damages in medical malpractice cases did not
violate equal protection or due process guarantees); University of Miami v.
Echarte, 618 So.2d 189 (Fla.1993)(holding that, although the statute took
away a previous right to recover full noneconomic damages, it provided a
"commensurate benefit"—the chance for a prompt recovery without the
risk and uncertainty of litigation).

The Effects of Caps. Because caps have been around since the mid–
1970s in medical malpractice contexts, some empirical research has taken
place on the effects of caps. Caps are one of the two reforms that most
significantly reduced insurer losses and premiums (the other was changes
in joint and several liability). The medical malpractice caps enacted in the
mid–1970s reduced the value of the average claim substantially.

It is crucial to understand, however, how these reductions come about.
Most claims will be unaffected by caps, but when caps do affect a claim,
they do so significantly. One study, for instance, found that caps applied
only in 7% of the cases studied, but that the average reduction resulting
from the caps in those cases was more than 70% of the original award.
David Baldus, John C. MacQueen & George Woodworth, *Improving Judicial Oversight of Jury Damages Assessments: A Proposal for the Comparative Additur/Remittur Review of Awards for Nonpecuniary Harms and
Punitive Damages*, 80 Iowa L. Rev. 1109 (1995). Professor Weiler, discussing the effect of caps in the medical arena, points out that "society's
objective of containing the cost of malpractice insurance * * * is pursued
through a policy whose entire burden is imposed on a small number of
relatively young, seriously injured victims of medical negligence." Paul C.
Weiler, Medical Malpractice on Trial 50 (1991).

Suppose that one were persuaded by the various criticisms of nonpecuniary damages outlined above: the excessiveness of verdicts for nonpecuniary damages; the "horizontal variability" of nonpecuniary damages (that
is, significant variation in the amounts awarded for injuries of similar
severity); the questionable compensatory value of nonpecuniary damages;
the commodification concern; and the insurance theory's attack on nonpecuniary damages. To which of these criticisms would caps be an appropriate response? Would some sort of scheduled damage approach, as described earlier, be a more fitting response to any or all of these concerns?
What adjudicative difficulties would schedules raise?

Litigating Under Caps. One attraction of caps to legislatures—in
addition to the promise of alleviating a perceived tort "crisis" of excessive
claims and judgment amounts—has been simplicity. Caps do not require
much modification of the traditional jury charge relating to damages. The

factfinder, of course, has to make separate findings with respect to the pecuniary and the nonpecuniary damages. This means that the factfinder must be given some instruction or definitions about what types of damages are included in each category. Otherwise, however, the cap need not alter the instruction of and deliberation by the jury.

Is it always clear what constitutes "noneconomic" or "nonpecuniary" damages? There seems to be little disagreement in the caselaw, or among lawyers on both sides of the docket, that "rehabilitative" expenses are deemed pecuniary and thus are not capped. This means that courts would allow juries to value, as pecuniary loss, the cost of recreational therapy (the use of adapted equipment to play sports) or adaptations to make a home accessible to the person with a disability. Why do we place on the other side of the line an item such as expenditures for travel, or for taking up a new avocation (such as music) to help replace what was lost?

In some states the cap does not apply to intentional torts. This may increase plaintiff's incentives to plead and pursue claims along intentional tort grounds. An incentive in the opposite direction is already at work, however: the nearly universal exclusion, from insurance coverage, for intentionally caused injuries. (Chapter 13 will discuss this exclusion in more detail.). If the defendant can satisfy a judgment from sources other than insurance, the plaintiff will have greater reason in such states to pursue intentional tort theories. For an example of a plaintiff who escaped the effect of a cap in this way, consider Szkorla v. Vecchione, 8 Cal.App.4th 1427, 283 Cal.Rptr. 219 (1991)(holding that the cap did not apply to the plaintiff's noneconomic damages when the plaintiff had obtained favorable findings on both negligence and battery).

Proposals for Voluntarily Opting Out of or Voluntarily Limiting Nonpecuniary Damages. Scholars such as Professor Jeffrey O'Connell and legislators have proposed a number of schemes that would allow potential victims or potential or actual defendants to opt out of tort's coverage for noneconomic damages. (Some proposals also would allow opting out with respect any tort liability at all.)

Some opt-out proposals would apply only *after* an injury had occurred. For instance, some bills introduced in Congress after the 1994 elections included an "early offer" or "rapid recovery" proposal. Under such proposals, a defendant who makes an early offer to pay, periodically, the full economic costs of tort claims—as they accrue—would be liable only for such costs and attorneys' fees. The defendant would not be liable for noneconomic damages such as pain and suffering. If a claimant rejected the offer, then the claimant could proceed with her tort claim, but under more burdensome standards; for instance, only by proving wanton conduct or by proving fault under a clear and convincing standard of proof.

Florida statutes provide that either a plaintiff or defendant may make an offer to enter into binding arbitration; if the defendant accepts the plaintiff's offer to arbitrate, then noneconomic damages will be limited to a percentage of $250,000, the percentage depending on the amount of disability. If the plaintiff rejects a defendant's offer to settle, then the plaintiff's damages will be limited to no more than $350,000. *See* Fla. Stat. Ch. 766.207(7)(b); 766.207(4).

New Jersey rules for compulsory auto liability insurance now provide that an individual may select either of two tort options: (1) opting out of coverage for nonpecuniary damages, so that the insured will not be able to recover for noneconomic damages and will not be liable for such damages to any individual also selecting this coverage; or (2) opting for the right to recover noneconomic damages, but also being liable for such damages to other drivers. *See* N.J. Rev. Stat. § 39:6A–8 (1990). Which option would you choose, and why?

How do these various opt-out schemes respond to the concern that the elimination of noneconomic damages will leave the plaintiff without the necessary cushion to absorb the costs of attorney's fees and expenses of bringing the claim?

Other opt-out schemes would allow parties, in advance of injury, to agree on limited damages in the event of injury. Should pre-injury opting out be allowed in all settings where the consumer will reap the benefits of the opt-out in the form of reduced prices on goods or services?

D. THE AMERICAN RULE FOR ATTORNEY'S FEES, FEE SHIFT-ING, AND THE CONTINGENCY FEE

Much tort reform attention has centered in recent years on two aspects of the traditional tort regime: (1) the "American rule" on attorney's fee liability, under which each side is liable for its own attorney's fees, whatever the outcome in the case; and (2) the contingency fee arrangement, which finances most plaintiffs' personal injury claims.

1. *The American Rule Versus Loser–pays*

Under the prevailing American rule, each side to the tort suit is responsible for its own attorney's fees and expenses of litigation. Usually the prevailing party is allowed to recover "court costs," but this is a very narrow category of expenses, such as filing fees or charges for court reporters. A standard financing practice has developed for each side of the docket.

On the defense side, many tort defendants are insured under standard forms of liability insurance—whether homeowners', automobile, or general or professional liability policies. All these standard policies actually contain two protections: a promise to pay a judgment or settlement on a covered claim, up to the insurance policy's limits; and a promise to provide a legal defense, uncapped by those limits. The insurer usually pays the defense counsel on some form of hourly basis. For instance, suppose that a driver insured under a $25,000 automobile liability policy is sued, receives legal representation paid for by the insurer and costing a total of $10,000, and eventually is held liable on the claim for a damage amount of $35,000. The insurer will be liable for its full $25,000 policy limits, without any deduction for the $10,000 it has expended on attorney's fees to defend the insured. We will return to this subject in more detail in Chapter 13.

For plaintiffs, no such "litigation insurance" is available. And most injured plaintiffs do not have the means to pay hourly rates for representation. This, along with the American rule, means that the only practical form of legal fee arrangement for plaintiffs is the contingency fee. Under most such arrangements, the plaintiff is obligated to pay the attorney some percentage—usually 33⅓% but sometimes as high as 45%—of any award, whether judgment or settlement. Sometimes the percentages increase depending on the stage at which the case resolves; for instance, 33⅓% for a settlement; 45% if recovery takes place only after trial.

The fee is separate from the issue of expenses, such as payment for experts, documentary services, medical records, etc. (As noted, a narrow category of expenses—"court costs"—are shifted to the losing party.) These expenses can be considerable, especially in complex product and medical malpractice litigation. Under the ABA's Model Rules of Professional Conduct, a lawyer may ethically advance expenses, and then allow repayment to be contingent on the outcome of the matter. ABA Mod. Rules Prof. Cond. 1.8. In practice, most personal injury attorneys understand that advanced expenses are unlikely ever to be paid back if the tort suit ultimately is unsuccessful. When the tort suit is successful, the client is entitled to the sum that remains after (1) deduction of the percentage contingency fee amount; and (2) further subtraction of the expenses.

The American rule on fee arrangements is an exception to the practice that prevails in most European countries. Many state and federal statutory schemes have departed from the American rule in one direction, in favor of plaintiffs. For instance, prevailing plaintiffs in federal civil rights cases and many state consumer protection claims can obtain attorney's fees. In recent years, much scholarly and legislative attention has turned to various forms of "loser pays" approaches to fee-shifting.

These loser-pays proposals build on the two very different criticisms that the traditional approach has attracted: that it produces undercompensation to plaintiffs, and that it fosters excessive and unjustified litigation against defendants. A one-way (in favor of plaintiff) loser-pays approach in theory should address the former concern. Proposals for one-way (in favor of defendant) or two-way fee shifting usually are aimed in part at addressing the latter concern.

Tort reformers certainly have claimed that the system fosters an unreasonable level of claims, but one recent analysis of the available empirical data questions this.

> Taken together, all of these studies suggest that, at the outset of the litigation process, a large number of potential plaintiffs with valid claims never initiate a claim. * * * Note, however, that when the number of claims brought is proportionately so small, even a modest increase in claims is perceived by both defendants and the courts as a huge increase. For example, if the proportion of negligently injured patients who filed claims rose from 4% to 8%, this would double the number of claims, costs of litigation, and compensation paid by defendants and their insurers.

Michael J. Saks, *Do We Really Know Anything About the Behavior of the Tort Litigation System—And Why Not?*, 140 U. Pa. L. Rev. 1147, 1185 (1992).

But even if the rate of claims is low relative to the wrongful injury "base," we should be concerned with whether or not the claims that are

filed are meritorious. Two actors are relevant here: the potential plaintiff
and the plaintiff's lawyer. Under standard economic analysis that posits a
rational actor concerned about maximizing expected wealth, the plaintiff's
decision to sue depends on a comparison of what the suit will cost the
plaintiff (including legal costs) with the "expected judgment." The expected judgment is the amount of damages, discounted by the probability of
success on liability. So, for instance, a case with certain $100,000 damages
but only a 35% chance of success on liability would have an expected
judgment of $35,000. The plaintiff will bring suit if, and only if, his
expected judgment would be at least as large as his expected costs.

Applying this analysis to the American rule versus a two-way loser-
pays approach, the plaintiff will be more willing, under the American rule
than under a loser-pays approach, to bring suit when the plaintiff is not
optimistic about prevailing on liability. This is because under the American rule the plaintiff can usually be certain that he will not bear the
defendant's legal costs. This and other conclusions relating to the impact
of fee-shifting rules are worked out in more detail in Steven Shavell, *Suit,
Settlement and Trial: A Theoretical Analysis Under Alternative Methods
for the Allocation of Legal Costs,* 11 J. Legal Stud. 55 (1982).

Even if this economic analysis accords substantially with how potential
plaintiffs actually behave, would adopting a two-way loser-pays approach
reduce "nonmeritorious" cases without chilling those plaintiffs with "meritorious" claims? An answer to this would turn in part on one's definition
of meritorious. Does this mean only those claims with a greater-than-even
chance of success on liability? How would such a definition be applied to
well-known jurisdictional differences in jury behavior, or variation among
judges? For instance, the same claim that has a 60% chance of obtaining a
liability finding from a jury in one region of a state might have only a 40%
chance in another region. Should the tort system then seek to discourage
the filing of the latter but not the former? And how would this notion of
merit address claims that, at the time of filing, had few prospects of success
on the merits yet ended up winning because they provoked a change in the
law?

A Reporters' Study of the American Law Institute considers the merits
of loser-pays as a response to concerns about frivolous litigation.

> Moreover, it is not clear that the initial intuitive appeal of the recipro-
> cal loser-pays rule should prevail over concerns about fairness to losing
> plaintiffs and disincentives to prospective claimants. An unsuccessful
> party will often have acted reasonably and have done nothing warrant-
> ing condemnation in pursuing a tenable, albeit losing, claim to judg-
> ment. So the loser-pays rule operates as an especially harsh form of
> strict liability when costs are likely to be highest and the loser's
> conduct most reasonable—that is, in closely contested cases.

> * * *

> The deterrent effect of two-way fee shifting is especially strong and
> troubling when prospective plaintiffs are risk averse, as is likely to be
> true of middle-class people with something to lose but not so many
> assets that they can tolerably afford to lose much. * * * The costs of a
> defendant's legal bills are actually borne * * * by all those who

ultimately pay for its insurance coverage or the products and services thereby protected. In our judgment it would be a serious step backward in our system of civil justice to threaten to shift these legal costs to lone individuals who have already been hurt and who are contemplating a suit for the redress that tort law apparently promises them.

American Law Institute, Reporter's Study on Enterprise Responsibility for Personal Injury, Vol. II, at 278–79 (1991).*

2. *The Contingency Fee*

Criticism of the contingency fee focuses on two concerns: that it fosters meritless litigation, and that in practice it allows plaintiff's lawyers to reap huge and inappropriate fees. As to the former, the economic analysis sketched out above would suggest that the contingency fee increases plaintiffs' willingness to sue on claims that in the judgment of many lack merit. In response, defenders point to the interest of access to justice: given the absence of fee-shifting in plaintiff's favor, the contingency fee is for a great many victims the only means of financing the litigation.

Defenders of the contingency fee also point to its role as a screening device. The plaintiff's lawyer in theory will measure the value of the case by calculating the expected damages, discounted by the probability of success in establishing liability. For the lawyer to break even—if the lawyer is on a 33⅓% contingency contract—this value must be three times the cost to the lawyer of pursuing the case. Still, cases with large potential damages and very tenuous liability facts might survive this screening. How this screening process actually works in the world, however, is "another of the more neglected questions in a system that suffers from a lack of hard data at nearly every stage." Michael J. Saks, *Do We Really Know Anything About the Behavior of the Tort Litigation System—And Why Not?*, 140 U. Pa. L. Rev. 1147, 1190 (1992).

The other strand of criticism argues that the contingency fee allows inappropriately large attorneys' fee awards. The charge prompts two questions. First, how wide a lens should we should use when evaluating this charge? If we focus only on individual cases, then certainly there are many cases that have yielded contingency fees grossly disproportionate to the work or risk involved. But success on such cases might be the fuel that allows the lawyer to pursue other cases that, though meritorious, surely might fail. So should our focus be as wide as, but no wider than, the practice of a given individual lawyer? Some plaintiff's lawyers, for instance, eventually make their way into the enviable position of being able to accept only cases with low risk on liability and large damage amounts. This lawyer might be, on the whole, grossly overcompensated in the judgment of many, in light of the time he expends and the risk he assumes. Or should our focus be even wider, on the plaintiff's bar as a whole or on the base of potential claimants as a whole? Such a view might tolerate some grossly overcompensated attorneys if, overall, compensation is not excessive in the aggregate across the plaintiffs' bar.

Second, why shouldn't we presume that current contingency fee arrangements are "optimal" or "efficient," given that they are the product of a free market? Consider a claimant with high damages ($1 million) and a very good liability case (75% chance of success). The expected judgment in this case is $750,000; suppose that the case could be settled after the expenditure of 250 hours. A lawyer who took this case on a 33⅓% basis, then, would make $1000 per hour. In theory, the client should be able to find other lawyers willing to take the case for a smaller percentage. Yet some observers of the current tort scene argue that agreements for less than the standard percentages are rare. Why? Do prospective plaintiffs lack the knowledge to bargain for better terms? Do disparities in bargaining power exist and factor into this? Does the group of plaintiff's lawyers as a whole exert some sort of informal minimum price controls? For contrasting views on this, *compare* Lester Brickman, *Contingency Fees Without Contingencies: Hamlet Without the Prince of Denmark*, 37 U.C.L.A. L. Rev. 29 (1989)(arguing that lawyers have succeeded in preventing a competitive market for contingency fees), *with* Charles Silver, *Control Fees? No, Let the Free Market Do Its Job,* National Law Journal, April 18, 1994, at 17 (arguing that the personal injury plaintiff's lawyers face greater risks and higher costs of advertising and malpractice insurance, and that the free market can do a better job than added regulation at achieving appropriate fees).

The complaint of excessiveness has produced several types of actual or proposed reforms. One consists of "early offer" settlement schemes. The second is regulation of the maximum contingency fees that can be charged in certain circumstances. New Jersey is an example: the lawyer is generally restricted to ⅓ of the first $500,000; 30% of the next $500,000; 25% of the next $500,000; and a "reasonable" fee approved by the trial court on any amount in excess of these sums. N.J.Rules Gen.Application R. 1:21–7 (1996).

E. LUMP–SUM, PERIODIC PAYMENT, AND STRUCTURED SETTLEMENTS

Under the traditional tort approach, a plaintiff who receives a favorable verdict is awarded a single lump-sum amount, to be paid at the time of judgment, for all past and future losses. The same was traditionally true of most settlements. But periodic payments for compensation are now more common, either via periodic payment judgments or via voluntary structured settlements.

Periodic Payment Statutes. Many states by statute now require the periodic payment of at least some future damages in the judgment. The first wave of such statutes appeared as part of the medical malpractice tort reforms beginning in 1975. The next and more general wave of tort reform—in the latter part of the 1980s—has added more. These statutes have been challenged on state constitutional grounds. More often than not, the statutes have survived the challenge. *See* American Bank and Trust Co. v. Community Hosp., 36 Cal.3d 359, 204 Cal.Rptr. 671, 683 P.2d 670 (1984); Adams v. Children's Mercy Hospital, 832 S.W.2d 898 (Mo. 1992). Yet some courts have struck down the statutes. The Arizona Supreme Court, for instance, struck down the Arizona periodic payment statute as violating the state constitution's guarantee that "[n]o law shall be enacted in this State limiting the amount of damages to be recovered for causing the death or injury of any person." *See* Smith v. Myers, 181 Ariz. 11, 887 P.2d 541 (Ariz.1994). The statute violated this guarantee, the court held, in part because it "depriv[es] victims of flexibility in meeting unpredictable expenses." Another problem that the court emphasized is that the statute imposed the risk of insolvency on the tort plaintiff. "Defendants argue that the periodic payment statutes safeguard against this danger by requiring annuity companies to have a certain degree of financial stability before the court can approve funding. Even if an insurer meets statutory qualifications, however, there can be no guarantee of future economic health. The largest and strongest financial institutions may in the long run become insolvent." *Id.* at 545. *See also* Galayda v. Lake Hospital Systems, Inc., 71 Ohio St.3d 421, 644 N.E.2d 298 (Ohio 1994)(striking down Ohio's periodic payment statute as violating the state constitutional right to jury trial and due process).

The statutory provisions vary considerably. Points of variation include whether the statute requires or only encourages periodic scheduling; what amount the verdict must be before scheduling is allowed or required (such as $500,000); and what happens to the payment obligation if the tort plaintiff dies before the life expectancy period on which the jury's original damages finding was premised.

Virtually all the statutes, however, end up entailing three steps. First, the jury renders an award for damages, usually itemized as to past and future, medical and rehabilitative, and possibly other categories as well. Second, the trial judge fashions, according to the prescriptions of the particular statute, a judgment that calls for the periodic payment of some or all future damages. Typically, the statutes require the court's judgment to specify the dollar amount of each payment, when the payments are to take place, and for how long the payments are to continue. This latter point—the duration of the payments—is a key reason for the appeal to defendants of periodic payment. Suppose that an injured plaintiff is expected to sustain a loss of wage-earning capacity and to incur medical expenses until his death; his life expectancy is 35 years. Were the defendant required to pay a lump-sum judgment for future medical and future lost wage earning capacity, then the defendant would have to pay now the present value of 35 years of such losses. This changes under many periodic payment statutes. The statutes often provide that, when the defendant dies, the defendant is relieved of the obligation to pay at least some of the future payments (typically those for noneconomic damages). Third, the defendant then either chooses to "self-fund" this series of payments or, often, may purchase an annuity for this purpose from a life insurance company. The statutes usually require judicial approval of the funding arrangement.

Notice, then, that many of the periodic payment statutes do not eliminate the need for the jury to make difficult assessments about life expectancy, the cost of future medical expenses, or lost wage-earning capacity, etc. The statutes can, however, eliminate the need for the jury to discount future damages. Do the statutes have other benefits? Arguably, if the jury's decision turns out to be an inaccurate prediction and the plaintiff dies sooner than expected, then the periodic payment method allows "correction" for this because the defendant (or payor) need not make some or all of the payments premised on a longer (and incorrect) life expectancy. This improvement in accuracy, however, presumes that the periodic payment schedule devised by the judge is reasonably accurate itself in matching particular payments with particular periods of time.

Now consider the inverse case—when plaintiff lives longer than expected. Should the periodic payment statutes correct for this other error? Most do not. Is there a good practical or theoretical reason for this asymmetry?

For discussion of periodic payment in theory and practice, *see* Roger C. Henderson, *Designing a Responsible Periodic–Payment System for Tort Awards: Arizona Enacts a Prototype*, 32 Ariz. L. Rev. 21 (1994).

Structured Settlements. Voluntary arrangements for periodic payments are usually termed "structured settlements," and their use is increasing. Under a structured settlement, the defendant will pay a lump sum at the time of settlement, and then either purchase or self-fund an annuity that provides payments over time. Usually, at least some of the payments must continue until plaintiff dies; other payments might continue only through the plaintiff's life.

A key attraction of structured settlements for plaintiffs is the tax advantage. Suppose a defendant is willing to spend $2 million to settle a case. If the defendant pays it all in a lump sum, the $2 million itself is not taxable, but the plaintiff will be taxed on all the interest earned on the sum. Now suppose that, instead, the defendant pays $500,000 in a lump sum, and then buys an annuity, at the cost of $1.5 million, that will make a series of monthly and annual payments to plaintiff throughout plaintiff's life. A portion of these payments will include the interest that the insurer (or annuity provider) has been able to earn on investing the $1.5 million paid for the annuity. Yet, if the structure is set up properly, all of the payments over time will be tax free.

When the plaintiff has obtained a periodic payment judgment or a structured settlement, should the attorney's fee be paid completely from the up-front cash payment, completely from the periodic payments, or partially from each?

> As a general rule, the preferable approach is to satisfy the attorney fees immediately out of the cash payment. This is not only the general practice in the community, it makes the most sense as a matter of legislative intent and public policy. The plaintiff's attorney has done what he or she was retained to do once the judgment has been entered. The case is over; the fee is earned. If the fee is to be paid over time out of periodic payments, the attorney may never receive it if the plaintiff should die before the fee is recovered. [Under the statute,] periodic payments cease upon the death of the plaintiff * * * and the judgment in this case so provides. Thus, if the plaintiff's expected life span is cut short, the tortfeasor whose negligence was responsible for the plaintiff's injury receives a windfall at the expense of the attorney whose labor produced the judgment. Indeed, as between the plaintiff, the plaintiff's attorney and the tortfeasor, the tortfeasor stands to gain the most from the deferral of the attorney fee.

Nguyen v. Los Angeles County Harbor/UCLA Med. Ctr., 40 Cal.App.4th 1433, 1444–45 48 Cal.Rptr.2d 301, 306 (1995).

Does this reasoning apply with the same force when the plaintiff's attorney has voluntarily agreed to a structured settlement? In structured settlement contexts, some courts have ruled that, unless the contingency fee contract provides otherwise, the attorney must take his or her percentage out of each payment, as it comes. *See* Cardenas v. Ramsey County, 322 N.W.2d 191 (Minn.1982). Plaintiff's lawyers now increasingly provide, in the contingency fee contract, that the lawyer will be paid his full contingency fee at the time of settlement.

What is the settlement sum against which the percentage fee will be calculated? Surely it is inappropriate to use the sum of the future payments; some form of present value reduction is therefore universally used. But disputes have arisen over how to calculate that value, for purposes of the fee. Consider the following two examples, based on actual but unreported cases.

First, a massive personal injury settlement included a lump-sum payment of $2 million, and payments over time via an annuity that cost the defendant another $6 million. The total cost of the settlement to the defendant, then, was $8 million. Yet experts testified that, given the tax-free nature of the payments, the "present value" to the plaintiff of the annuity was much more than its cost of $6 million. Put another way, if plaintiff had simply been paid $8 million and then had gone out and purchased an annuity for a cost of $6 million, the plaintiff would be taxed for the interest portion of those annuity payments. Under the structured settlement, however, the payments would all be tax free. Experts calculated the present value of this "tax saving" as, approximately, $1.5 million. The plaintiff's lawyer argued that he was entitled to a third of $9.5 million, not just a third of $8 million. Which is the more appropriate value?

In another case, a baby was horribly disabled by misdiagnosis of a serious illness. The child required expensive, lifetime medical care. When the defendants shopped around for an annuity to fund the structured payments that plaintiff's counsel had proposed, the defendants found one reputable life insurer that was willing to provide the annuity for $2 million; every other insurer quoted a price of at least $4 million. The defendants, unsurprisingly, purchased the annuity at the cheaper cost, and also paid a lump sum of $1 million. In fact, the life insurer had made a huge error in the pricing: it had assumed that the child's life expectancy was very short (hence the lower cost), but actually the injury, though severely disabling, was not significantly life-shortening. The plaintiff's lawyer argued that his fee should be a third of $5 million—that is, a third of the sum of the up-front payment of $1 million and the "real" or "accurate" market price for the annuity. The trial judge rejected this, and ruled that the actual cost paid by the defendants was the right figure.

Most courts that have addressed the issue of calculating attorney's fees have agreed that usually the best measure of present value is the cost of the annuity. *See* Schneider v. Kaiser Foundation Hospitals, 215 Cal. App.3d 1311, 264 Cal.Rptr. 227, *overruled on other grounds,* Moncharsh v. Heily & Blase, 3 Cal.4th 1, 10 Cal.Rptr.2d 183, 832 P.2d 899 (1992). Other courts have disagreed that the cost of the annuity should always be the sole measure. *See* Hrimnak v. Watkins, 38 Cal.App.4th 964, 979–80, 45 Cal. Rptr.2d 514, 523–24 (1995).

F. PUNITIVE DAMAGES

1. *The Common Law Approach*

Punitive damages have been the subject of searching judicial, legislative, and scholarly tort reform attention in recent years. Until fairly recently, the substantive and procedural standards governing punitive damages were the result of common law development in state courts. Now, two other influences strongly affect state punitive damages regimes: constitutional boundaries imposed by the United States Constitution, and tort reform legislation.

Under the common law approach, when the evidence shows that defendant's conduct has been "malicious," "wanton," or "oppressive," the jury may, in its discretion, assess punitive (or "exemplary") damages against the defendant as a punishment for his morally reprehensible misconduct. As a practical matter this means that, when defendant's conduct is intentional or reckless, he may be liable for punitive damages, although some courts impose the additional requirement of some showing of actual malice in the form of ill-will or intent to injure. The common law approach imposed few constraints on juries in assessing punitive damages. In some jurisdictions the jury can take into account the plaintiff's legal costs in bringing the action. There are also a number of cases in which evidence of the defendant's net worth was introduced as a tool for assessing the appropriate amount of punitive damages to be assessed against him. Indeed, in some jurisdictions, introduction of such evidence is required before punitive damages may be assessed. Finally, in some jurisdictions, punitive damages can be assessed against a defendant only if he has been found liable for "substantial" compensatory damages. In the majority of states, however, there is no such requirement and substantial punitive damages may be assessed even if only nominal compensatory damages have been awarded. J. Ghiardi and J. Kircher, Punitive Damages: Law and Practice (2 Vols. 1984 and Supps.) is a useful reference work.

2. *Constitutional Challenges*

In recent years, defendants have had some success in asserting constitutional challenges to punitive damages awards. The first round went against defendants. The United States Supreme Court in Browning–Ferris Industries of Vt., Inc. v. Kelco Disposal, Inc., 492 U.S. 257, 109 S.Ct. 2909, 106 L.Ed.2d 219 (1989) held that punitive damage awards, at least when no portion of the award went to the state, could not be challenged under the eighth amendment's prohibition of "excessive fines".

More recent decisions have focused on the due process clause. In Pacific Mut. Life Ins. Co. v. Haslip, 499 U.S. 1, 111 S.Ct. 1032, 113 L.Ed.2d 1 (1991), the Court considered a punitive damages award in an insurance fraud case in Alabama. Although the Court stated that the common law method for assessing punitive damages does not in itself violate due process, particular punitive damages awards might be constitutionally unacceptable under the due process clause. "We need not, and indeed we cannot, draw a mathematical bright line between the constitutionally acceptable and the constitutionally unacceptable that would fit every case. We can say, however, that general concerns of reasonableness and adequate guidance from the court when the case is tried to a jury properly enter the constitutional calculus." 499 U.S. at 18, 111 S.Ct. at 1043. The Court went on to examine (1) the state standards applicable for assessing punitive damages, including jury instructions, post-trial review, and appellate review; and (2) the size of the award in this particular case. As to (1), the court ruled that the scheme imposed "definite and meaningful" restraints on and guidance for the factfinder. As to (2), the court observed that the punitive damages award was more than four times the compensatory award and more than 200 times the plaintiff's out-of-pocket losses. This made the punitive award "close to the line," but the court concluded that the award was not constitutionally impermissible.

Following *Haslip,* numerous state and federal courts have been faced with constitutional challenges to particular punitive damage awards and to various state standards governing the award and review of punitive damages in state courts. Generally, courts have found the challenged award, or challenged state standards, not to violate *Haslip*'s standards. *See* Dunn v. Hovic, 1 F.3d 1371 (3rd Cir.), *cert. denied,* 510 U.S. 1031, 114 S.Ct. 650, 126 L.Ed.2d 608 (1993).

The Supreme Court returned to the due process question in BMW of North America, Inc. v. Gore, ___ U.S. ___, 116 S.Ct. 1589, 134 L.Ed.2d 809 (1996). The plaintiff purchased a new BMW automobile from an authorized dealer in Alabama, and then discovered that the car had been repainted, probably after sustaining minor damage from acid rain during presale transit. The plaintiff sued BMW on various theories, including an Alabama fraud statute. At trial, BMW acknowledged that it had a nationwide policy of not advising its dealers (and therefore of not advising its customers) of any predelivery damage to new cars whenever the cost of repairing the damage did not exceed three percent of the car's retail price. At trial, plaintiff introduced evidenced that BMW had sold 983 refinished cars as new without disclosure of the repainting. Asserting an actual damage estimate of $4,000 per vehicle, plaintiff contended that punitive damages of $4 million would be a proper penalty for selling approximately 1,000 cars without the disclosure. The jury found BMW liable for compensatory damages of $4,000, and punitive damages of $4 million. The trial judge denied BMW's post-trial motion to set aside the punitive damages award. The Alabama Supreme Court reduced the punitive damages award to $2 million on the ground that the jury had improperly multiplied plaintiff's compensatory damages by the number of similar sales across the United States, and not just by the number of similar sales in Alabama.

Justice Stevens authored the majority opinion, which was joined by Justices O'Connor, Kennedy, Souter, and Breyer.

> Punitive damages may properly be imposed to further a State's legitimate interests in punishing unlawful conduct and deterring its repetition. * * * In our federal system, States necessarily have considerable flexibility in determining the level of punitive damages that they

will allow in different classes of cases and in any particular case. * * *
Only when an award can fairly be categorized as "grossly excessive" in
relation to these interests does it enter the zone of arbitrariness that
violates the Due Process Clause of the Fourteenth Amendment. * * *
For that reason, the federal excessiveness inquiry appropriately begins
with an identification of the state interests that a punitive award is
designed to serve. We therefore focus our attention first on the scope
of Alabama's legitimate interests in punishing BMW and deterring it
from future misconduct.

No one doubts that a State may protect its citizens by prohibiting
deceptive trade practices and by requiring automobile distributors to
disclose presale repairs that affect the value of a new car. But the
States need not, and in fact do not, provide such protection in a
uniform manner. Some States rely on the judicial process to formulate
and enforce an appropriate disclosure requirement by applying principles of contract and tort law. Other States have enacted various forms
of legislation that define the disclosure obligations of automobile manufacturers, distributors, and dealers. The result is a patchwork of
rules representing the diverse policy judgments of lawmakers in 50
states.

* * *

We think it follows from these principles of state sovereignty and
comity that a State may not impose economic sanctions on violators of
its laws with the intent of changing the tortfeasors' lawful conduct in
other States. * * * Before this Court Dr. Gore argued that the large
punitive damages award was necessary to induce BMW to change the
nationwide policy that it adopted in 1983. * * * But by attempting to
alter BMW's nationwide policy, Alabama would be infringing on the
policy choices of other States. To avoid such encroachment, the
economic penalties that a State such as Alabama inflicts on those who
transgress its laws, whether the penalties take the form of legislatively
authorized fines or judicially imposed punitive damages, must be
supported by the State's interest in protecting its own consumers and
its own economy. Alabama may insist that BMW adhere to a particular disclosure policy in that State. Alabama does not have the power,
however, to punish BMW for conduct that was lawful where it occurred
and that had no impact on Alabama or its residents. * * * Nor may
Alabama impose sanctions on BMW in order to deter conduct that is
lawful in other jurisdictions.

* * *

Elementary notions of fairness enshrined in our constitutional
jurisprudence dictate that a person receive fair notice not only of the
conduct that will subject him to punishment but also of the severity of
the penalty that a State may impose. * * * Three guideposts, each of
which indicates that BMW did not receive adequate notice of the
magnitude of the sanction that Alabama might impose for adhering to
the nondisclosure policy adopted in 1983, lead us to the conclusion that
the $2 million award against BMW is grossly excessive: the degree of

reprehensibility of the nondisclosure; the disparity between the harm or potential harm suffered by Dr. Gore and his punitive damages award; and the difference between this remedy and the civil penalties authorized or imposed in comparable cases. We discuss these considerations in turn.

* * *

In this case, none of the aggravating factors associated with particularly reprehensible conduct is present. The harm BMW inflicted on Dr. Gore was purely economic in nature. The presale refinishing of the car had no effect on its performance or safety features, or even its appearance for at least nine months after his purchase. BMW's conduct evinced no indifference to or reckless disregard for the health and safety of others. To be sure, infliction of economic injury, especially when done intentionally through affirmative acts of misconduct, * * * or when the target is financially vulnerable, can warrant a substantial penalty. But this observation does not convert all acts that cause economic harm into torts that are sufficiently reprehensible to justify a significant sanction in addition to compensatory damages.

* * *

The second and perhaps most commonly cited indicium of an unreasonable or excessive punitive damages award is its ratio to the actual harm inflicted on the plaintiff. * * * The principle that exemplary damages must bear a "reasonable relationship" to compensatory damages has a long pedigree. * * * Our decisions in both *Haslip* and *TXO* endorsed the proposition that a comparison between the compensatory award and the punitive award is significant.

In *Haslip* we concluded that even though a punitive damages award of "more than 4 times the amount of compensatory damages," might be "close to the line," it did not "cross the line into the area of constitutional impropriety." [Pacific Mut. Life Ins. Co. v. Haslip, 499 U.S. 1, 23–24 (1991)]. *TXO,* following dicta in *Haslip,* refined this analysis by confirming that the proper inquiry is " 'whether there is a reasonable relationship between the punitive damages award and the harm likely to result from the defendant's conduct as well as the harm that actually has occurred.' " [TXO Production Corp. v. Alliance Resources Corp., 509 U.S. 443, 460, 113 S.Ct. 2711, 2721, 125 L.Ed.2d 366 (1993), quoting *Haslip,* 499 U.S. at 21, 111 S.Ct. at 1045]. Thus, in upholding the $10 million award in *TXO,* we relied on the difference between that figure and the harm to the victim that would have ensued if the tortious plan had succeeded. That difference suggested that the relevant ratio was not more than 10 to 1. * * *

The $2 million in punitive damages awarded to Dr. Gore by the Alabama Supreme Court is 500 times the amount of his actual harm as determined by the jury. * * * Moreover, there is no suggestion that Dr. Gore or any other BMW purchaser was threatened with any additional potential harm by BMW's nondisclosure policy. The disparity in this case is thus dramatically greater than those considered in *Haslip* and *TXO.* * * *

Of course, we have consistently rejected the notion that the constitutional line is marked by a simple mathematical formula, even one that compares actual and potential damages to the punitive award. * * * It is appropriate, therefore, to reiterate our rejection of a categorical approach. * * * In most cases, the ratio will be within a constitutionally acceptable range, and remittitur will not be justified on this basis. When the ratio is a breathtaking 500 to 1, however, the award must surely "raise a suspicious judicial eyebrow." [*TXO,* 509 U.S. at 482 (O'Connor, J., dissenting)].

* * *

Comparing the punitive damages award and the civil or criminal penalties that could be imposed for comparable misconduct provides a third indicium of excessiveness. As Justice O'Connor has correctly observed, a reviewing court engaged in determining whether an award of punitive damages is excessive should "accord 'substantial deference' to legislative judgments concerning appropriate sanctions for the conduct at issue." Browning–Ferris Industries of Vt., Inc. v. Kelco Disposal, Inc., 492 U.S., at 301, 109 S.Ct., at 2934 (O'Connor, J., concurring in part and dissenting in part). In *Haslip,* 499 U.S., at 23, 111 S.Ct., at 1046, the Court noted that although the exemplary award was "much in excess of the fine that could be imposed," imprisonment was also authorized in the criminal context. * * * In this case the $2 million economic sanction imposed on BMW is substantially greater than the statutory fines available in Alabama and elsewhere for similar malfeasance.

___ U.S. at ___, 116 S.Ct. at 1595–1604, 134 L.Ed.2d at 822–31.

Justice Scalia, joined by Justice Thomas, dissented.

Today, we see the latest manifestation of this Court's recent and increasingly insistent "concern about punitive damages that 'run wild.'" Pacific Mut. Life Ins. Co. v. Haslip, 499 U.S. 1, 18, 111 S.Ct. 1032, 1043, 113 L.Ed.2d 1 (1991). Since the Constitution does not make that concern any of our business, the Court's activities in this area are an unjustified incursion into the province of state governments.

In earlier cases that were the prelude to this decision, I set forth my view that a state trial procedure that commits the decision whether to impose punitive damages, and the amount, to the discretion of the jury, subject to some judicial review for "reasonableness," furnishes a defendant with all the process that is "due." * * * I do not regard the Fourteenth Amendment's Due Process Clause as a secret repository of substantive guarantees against "unfairness"—neither the unfairness of an excessive civil compensatory award, nor the unfairness of an "unreasonable" punitive award. What the Fourteenth Amendment's procedural guarantee assures is an opportunity to contest the reasonableness of a damages judgment in state court; but there is no federal guarantee a damages award actually be reasonable. * * *

* * *

There is no precedential warrant for giving our judgment priority over the judgment of state courts and juries on this matter. The only support for the Court's position is to be found in a handful of errant federal cases, bunched within a few years of one other, which invented the notion that an unfairly severe civil sanction amounts to a violation of constitutional liberties. These were the decisions upon which the *TXO* plurality relied in pronouncing that the Due Process Clause "imposes substantive limits 'beyond which penalties may not go,' " [509 U.S. at 454]. Although they are our precedents, they are themselves too shallowly rooted to justify the Court's recent undertaking.

* * *

One might understand the Court's eagerness to enter this field, rather than leave it with the state legislatures, if it had something useful to say. In fact, however, its opinion provides virtually no guidance to legislatures, and to state and federal courts, as to what a "constitutionally proper" level of punitive damages might be.

* * *

[The majority opinion] identifies "[t]hree guideposts" that lead it to the conclusion that the award in this case is excessive: degree of reprehensibility, ratio between punitive award and plaintiff's actual harm, and legislative sanctions provided for comparable misconduct. * * * The legal significance of these "guideposts" is nowhere explored, but their necessary effect is to establish federal standards governing the hitherto exclusively state law of damages. Apparently (though it is by no means clear) all three federal "guideposts" can be overridden if "necessary to deter future misconduct," * * *—a loophole that will encourage state reviewing courts to uphold awards as necessary for the "adequat[e] protect[ion]" of state consumers * * *. By effectively requiring state reviewing courts to concoct rationalizations—whether within the "guideposts" or through the loophole—to justify the intuitive punitive reactions of state juries, the Court accords neither category of institution the respect it deserves.

Of course it will not be easy for the States to comply with this new federal law of damages, no matter how willing they are to do so. In truth, the "guideposts" mark a road to nowhere; they provide no real guidance at all. As to "degree of reprehensibility" of the defendant's conduct, we learn that " 'nonviolent crimes are less serious than crimes marked by violence or the threat of violence,' " * * *, and that " 'trickery and deceit' " are "more reprehensible than negligence," * * *. As to the ratio of punitive to compensatory damages, we are told that a " 'general concer[n] of reasonableness ... enter[s] into the constitutional calculus,' " * * *—though even "a breathtaking 500 to 1" will not necessarily do anything more than " 'raise a suspicious judicial eyebrow,' " * * *. And as to legislative sanctions provided for comparable misconduct, they should be accorded " 'substantial deference,' " * * *. One expects the Court to conclude: "To thine own self be true."

These criss-crossing platitudes yield no real answers in no real cases. * * * The Court has constructed a framework that does not genuinely constrain, that does not inform state legislatures and lower courts—that does nothing at all except confer an artificial air of doctrinal analysis upon its essentially ad hoc determination that this particular award of punitive damages was not "fair."

* * *

* * * [I]f the Court is correct, it must be that every claim that a state jury's award of compensatory damages is "unreasonable" (because not supported by the evidence) amounts to an assertion of constitutional injury. * * * And the same would be true for determinations of liability. By today's logic, every dispute as to evidentiary sufficiency in a state civil suit poses a question of constitutional moment, subject to review in this Court. That is a stupefying proposition.

___ U.S. at ___, 116 S.Ct. at 1610–14, 134 L.Ed.2d at 840–46.

Justice Ginsburg, joined by Chief Justice Rehnquist, dissented, focusing in part on the majority opinion's point that the punitive damages verdict represented an impermissible sanction by Alabama of conduct outside the state.

No Alabama authority, it bears emphasis—no statute, judicial decision, or trial judge instruction—ever countenanced the jury's multiplication of the $4,000 diminution in value estimated for each refinished car by the number of such cars (approximately 1,000) shown to have been sold nationwide. The sole prompt to the jury to use nationwide sales as a multiplier came from Gore's lawyer during summation. * * * Nor did BMW's counsel request a charge instructing the jury not to consider out-of-state sales in calculating the punitive damages award. * * *

* * *

In brief, Gore's case is idiosyncratic. The jury's improper multiplication * * * is unlikely to recur in Alabama and does not call for error correction by this Court.

Because the jury apparently (and erroneously) had used acts in other states as a multiplier to arrive at a $4 million sum for punitive damages, the Alabama Supreme Court itself determined " 'the maximum amount that a properly functioning jury could have awarded.' " 646 So.2d, at 630 (HOUSTON, J., concurring specially) (quoting Big B, Inc. v. Cottingham, 634 So.2d 999, 1006 (Ala.1993)). The per curiam opinion emphasized that in arriving at $2 million as "the amount of punitive damages to be awarded in this case, [the court did] not consider those acts that occurred in other jurisdictions." 646 So.2d, at 628 (emphasis in original). As this Court recognizes, the Alabama high court "properly eschewed reliance on BMW's out-of-state conduct and based its remitted award solely on conduct that occurred within Alabama." * * * In sum, the Alabama Supreme Court left standing the jury's decision that the facts warranted an award of punitive damages—a determination not contested in this Court—and the state court concluded that, considering only acts in Alabama, $2 million was "a constitutionally reasonable punitive damages award." * * *

* * *

The Court finds Alabama's $2 million award not simply excessive, but grossly so, and therefore unconstitutional. The decision leads us further into territory traditionally within the States' domain, * * * and commits the Court, now and again, to correct "misapplication of a properly stated rule of law." But cf. S.Ct. Rule 10 ("a petition for a writ of certiorari is rarely granted when the asserted error consists of erroneous factual findings or the misapplication of a properly stated rule of law."). * * * The Court is not well equipped for this mission. Tellingly, the Court repeats that it brings to the task no "mathematical formula," * * * no "categorical approach," * * * no "bright line," * * *. It has only a vague concept of substantive due process, a "raised eyebrow" test, * * * as its ultimate guide. * * *

In contrast to habeas corpus review under 28 U.S.C. § 2254, the Court will work at this business alone. It will not be aided by the federal district courts and courts of appeals. It will be the only federal court policing the area. The Court's readiness to superintend state court punitive damages awards is all the more puzzling in view of the Court's longstanding reluctance to countenance review, even by courts of appeals, of the size of verdicts returned by juries in federal district court proceedings. See generally 11 C. Wright, A. Miller, & M. Kane, Federal Practice and Procedure § 2820 (2d ed. 1995). And the reexamination prominent in state courts * * * and in legislative arenas, * * * serves to underscore why the Court's enterprise is undue. ___ U.S. ___, 116 S.Ct. at 1615–17, 134 L.Ed.2d at 847–50.

3. Punitive Damages and the Tort Liability "Crisis"

There is a fairly widely held view that the imposition of punitive damage awards has contributed to a perceived crisis in the tort system that, by adding to the cost of introducing new products, has adversely affected the United States' ability to compete in the world market. In 1992, a survey of corporate risk managers considered caps on punitive damages and noneconomic damages to be the most important reform issue. See Thomas Koenig & Michael Rustad, *The Quiet Revolution Revisited: An Empirical Study of the Impact of State Tort Reform of Punitive Damages in Products Liability,* 16 Justice Sys. J. 21, 22 (1993). Much of the critical literature on punitive damages has concerned punitive damages assessed in products liability cases. See D. Owen, *Punitive Damages in Products Liability Litigation,* 74 Mich.L.Rev. 1257 (1976); M. Robinson and G. Kane, Jr., *Punitive Damages in Products Liability Cases,* 6 Pepperdine L.Rev. 139 (1978). One of the most famous punitive damage cases is Grimshaw v. Ford Motor Co., 119 Cal.App.3d 757, 174 Cal.Rptr. 348 (1981). Grimshaw was the passenger in a Ford Pinto that burst into flames when it was hit in the rear by another vehicle. There was evidence that Ford was aware of a remediable ($15 per car) design defect in the Pinto. The jury awarded Grimshaw $2,500,000 in compensatory damages and $125,000,000 in punitive damages. As a condition for denying Ford's motion for a new trial, the trial court required Grimshaw to accept a reduction in the amount of punitive damages to $3,500,000. While the trial court concluded that there was sufficient evidence to support the jury's award, it found the jury's award excessive because of the excessive disparity between the punitive and compensatory damages. The trial court's disposition of the case was affirmed on appeal. For an examination of punitive damages by many distinguished scholars, *see* Symposium, 40 Alabama L.Rev. 687–1261 (1989).

A number of empirical studies have tried to determine the frequency with which punitive damages are now being assessed and the economic impact that they have had. One of the more famous of these studies is N. Peterson, S. Sarma and M. Shanley, Punitive Damages, Empirical Findings (1987) published by The Institute for Civil Justice of the RAND Corporation. This study was confined to an in-depth analysis of jury verdicts in Cook County, Illinois and San Francisco, California from 1960 to 1984 and to jury verdicts in other California jurisdictions from 1980 to 1984. The report's findings included the following: (1) the incidence of punitive damage awards (measured by proportion of cases in which such awards are made) and the amount of money (measured in constant 1984 dollars) awarded for punitive purposes have increased substantially over the years; (2) corporate defendants are more likely than individuals or public agencies to be the target of such awards; (3) only about half of the punitive dollars awarded are ultimately paid; (4) personal injury cases were far less likely to result in punitive damage awards than cases involving contract disputes and intentional tort suits (usually civil rights cases); and (4) the ratio of punitive damage awards to compensatory awards in personal injury cases was rarely more than 2:1, a far smaller ratio than in contract and intentional tort cases.

A later study conducted by Professors Koenig and Rustad drew on an even larger sample, and examined the pattern of punitive damages in the wake of state tort reforms. *See* Koenig and Rustad, *supra*. They conclude that: (1) "punitive damages are too rare to be responsible for the variety of evils attributed to them"; (2) any punitive damages problem is confined to a few locales, most of which already have sharply cut back the availability of punitives; (3) the full punitive damages award was collected in less than half the cases; and (4) even the mildest tort reform—such as heightening the burden of proof to a clear-and-convincing standard—has significantly reduced the median size of punitive damage awards outside the asbestos context. If, despite the tort reforms already in place, manufacturers and the medical community continue to withhold new products for fear of punitive damages liability, then "they have been misled by the tort reform rhetoric." *Id.* at 38. For more detail on this latter study and the studies preceding it, *see* Michael Rustad, *In Defense of Punitive Damages in Products Liability: Testing Tort Anecdotes with Empirical Data*, 78 Iowa L. Rev. 1 (1992).

4. Multiple Punitive Awards

A much debated issue is whether, if the plaintiff's action is one of a number of actions arising out of essentially the same tortious conduct—say, an airplane carrying two hundred passengers has crashed or a defectively designed drug has injured 1,000 people or a particular manufacturer's product (such as asbestos) has injured hundreds of thousands—the jury is required to take into account, as a mitigating factor in assessing punitive damages, the fact that the defendant has been or is likely to be assessed punitive damages in these other actions. The argument for requiring the jury to mitigate damages on this basis rests on the notion that, although the defendant should be obliged to compensate all those whom he has injured, he should not be subjected to multiple punishment for essentially a single instance of wrongful conduct. The contrary argument rests on the proposition that each legal action is unique and rests on its own particular facts. *Compare* Roginsky v. Richardson–Merrell, Inc., 378 F.2d 832 (2d Cir.1967) *with* Toole v. Richardson–Merrell, Inc., 251 Cal.App.2d 689, 60 Cal.Rptr. 398 (1967). *See also* Note, *Mass Liability and Punitive Damages Overkill*, 30 Hast.L.J. 1797 (1979). A number of subsequent cases have repeated Judge Friendly's suggestion in *Roginsky* that there must be some limit to the number of times a defendant may be answerable in punitive damages for essentially the same basic conduct, 378 F.2d at 838–42.

One court, in a decision since vacated, ruled that "with respect to those defendants who are able to present competent proof that liability for punitive damages has already been imposed upon them for the conduct alleged to be the basis of a punitive damage claim in this action, the court will dismiss plaintiff's claim for such punitive damages." Juzwin v. Amtorg Trading Corp., 705 F.Supp. 1053 (D.N.J.1989). The court noted that some other proposed solutions to the problem were impractical, such as allowing the defendant to bring to the attention of the jury that it had already been assessed punitive damages in a previous action. Unless there were a bifurcated trial, such an admission would, of course, jeopardize the defendant's case with regard to liability. Even in a bifurcated trial it would not be a strategy without risks to the defendant. *Cf.* Digital & Analog Design Corp. v. The North Supply Co., 44 Ohio St.3d 36, 540 N.E.2d 1358 (1989), in which the court held that "when it is shown that a course of events is governed by a single animus, even though a defendant may be liable for the damages occasioned by a number of torts committed in such course of events, defendants may only be punished by a single award of punitive damages."

What about the *compensatory* concerns raised by multiple punitive awards? Litigants who arrive first will have their compensatory needs met as well as have a good chance of collecting punitive awards. But what if repeated punitive awards to the earlier litigants exhaust the compensatory funds available for later litigants? For a post–*Haslip* discussion of multiple punitive damages awards, as well as a detailed discussion of the appropriate judicial and legislative responses to the issue, *see* Dunn v. Hovic, 1 F.3d 1371 (3rd Cir.1993), *cert. denied*, 510 U.S. 1031, 114 S.Ct. 650, 126 L.Ed.2d 608 (1993).

5. *Legislative Modifications*

Legislative tort reforms also have dramatically altered the punitive damages regime. These include:

— Providing that punitive damages cannot be awarded unless they are supported by "clear and convincing evidence". *See e.g.*, Alaska Stat. 09.17.020 (1996); Cal.Civ.Code Ann. § 3294(a) (West 1996); Minn.Stat.Ann. § 549.20 (West 1996); Ohio Rev.Code § 2307.80(A) (Baldwin 1996).

— Outlawing punitive damages unless specifically provided by statute. *See* N.H.Rev.Stat.Ann. 507:16 (1995).

— Disallowing punitive damages for injuries caused by drugs that have been approved by the F.D.A. unless the manufacturer knowingly misrepresented information supplied to the F.D.A. or willfully withheld pertinent information. *See* N.J.Stat.Ann. 2A:58C–5(c) (West 1996); Ore.Rev.Stat. § 30.927 (1995).

— Authorizing the trial judge to reduce the punitive damage award in the light of previous awards that may have been made against the same defendant for substantially the same conduct. *See e.g.* Mo. Stat.Ann. § 510.263(4) (Vernon 1997); Mont.Code Ann. 27–1–221(7)(c).

— Providing for a bifurcated trial in which the jury at first decides only whether the defendant is liable for punitive damages but assesses them in a second proceeding. *See e.g.*, Mo.Stat.Ann. § 510.263(1) (Vernon 1997)(either party may request a bifurcated trial before the same jury). Mont.Code Ann. 27–1–221(7)(a) (1995); N.J.Stat.Ann. § 2A:15–5.13(a)–(d) (West 1996)(both liability for punitive damages as well as the amount determined in the second proceeding).

— Imposing caps on punitive damages of $350,000. Va.Code § 8.01–38.1 (Michie 1996); Tex.Civil Prac. & Rem.Code Ann. § 41.008 (West 1996)(imposing a limit of $200,000 or four times actual damages, whichever is greater, unless exceptional circumstances can be shown); Ga.Code Ann. § 51–12–5.1(e), (f) and (g)(imposing a limit of $250,000 unless the action is one involving products liability or it is found that the defendant acted or failed to act with specific intent to cause harm).

— Providing that a portion of the punitive damage awards shall be paid into a state fund. *See e.g.* Colo.Rev.Stat. 13–21–102(4)(one-third of award); Fla.Stat.Ann. § 768.73(2) (West 1996)(sixty-five percent of the award is paid to claimant and the remaining thirty-five percent is paid to one of two state funds depending on the nature of the underlying cause of action); Ga.Code Ann. § 51–12–5.1(e) (1996)(seventy-five percent of the amounts awarded in products liability cases); Ill.Rev.Stat. ch. 110, § 512–1207 (1996)(the trial court in its discretion may apportion the award "among the plaintiff, the plaintiff's attorney and the State of Illinois Department of Human Services"); Iowa Code Ann. § 668A.1 (West 1996)(if the defendant's conduct was directed specifically at the claimant, the claimant gets the entire amount; otherwise, after payment of costs and fees, not to exceed twenty-five percent is paid to the claimant with the remainder awarded to a state fund);

Mo.Stat.Ann. § 537.675(2) (Vernon 1997)(fifty percent, after deduction of attorney's fees and expenses, awarded to the state).

6.   *Punitive Damages and Insurance*

In a number of states it is contrary to public policy to insure against possible punitive damages. The states, however, are sharply divided on this issue and many states do permit such insurance. In such states, the liability insurance contract may contain a clause excluding such damages from coverage under the policy. In a state that makes it impossible to insure against liability for punitive damages, such damages must of course be paid directly by the defendant. What are the considerations for and against allowing insurance for punitive damages? On the general subject *see* Allen I. Widiss, *Liability Insurance Coverage for Punitive Damages: Discerning Answers to the Conundrum Created by Disputes Involving Conflicting Public Policies, Pragmatic Considerations and Political Actions,* 39 Vill.L.Rev. 445 (1994). We shall discuss this issue at greater length in Chapter Thirteen, *infra,* at pp. 878–80.

7.   *Taxation of Punitive Damages*

What is now Section 104(a)(2) has always, since its enactment, excluded amounts received on account of personal injuries or sickness from gross income. What about punitive damages? Over the years, the Treasury took conflicting positions as to whether, if awarded in an action for personal injuries or sickness, they too should be excluded from gross income. In 1989, Congress amended § 104(a)(2) to provide that the exclusion did not apply "to any punitive damages in connection with a case not involving physical injury or physical sickness." More recently, in 1996 Congress amended § 104(a)(2) to provide that gross income does not include "the amount of any damages (*other than punitive damages*) received . . . on account of personal injuries or physical sickness." (emphasis supplied) In December 1996, the Court ruled that punitive damages received before the effective date of the 1989 amendments were not excluded by the then version of § 104(a)(2) which excluded from gross income damages "received . . . on account of personal injuries or sickness." O'Gilvie v. United States, ___ U.S. ___, 117 S.Ct. 452, 136 L.Ed.2d 454 (1996). What about cases governed by the 1989 amendment before they were superseded by the 1996 amendments? Incidentally the 1996 amendment to § 104(a) also added an interpretive paragraph which provides that "[f]or purposes of paragraph (2), emotional distress shall not be treated as a physical injury or physical sickness," except to the extent "of the amount received for medical care."

8.   *English Law*

In Rookes v. Barnard, [1964] A.C. 1129, 2 W.L.R. 269, 1 All E.R. 367, the House of Lords materially restricted the availability of "exemplary" damages (to use the usual English terminology). Adopting the reasoning put forth by Lord Devlin in his speech in that case, the House of Lords held that, except where authorized by statute, exemplary damages would only lie in two instances. The first is where "oppressive, arbitrary or unconstitutional action by the servants of the government" is involved; the second is where "the defendant's conduct has been calculated to make a profit for himself." [1964] A.C. at 1226. Lord Devlin continued "* * * the power to award exemplary damages constitutes a weapon that, while it can be used in defence of liberty * * * can also be used against liberty." *Id.* at 1227. Do you think that similar restrictions on the award of exemplary (or punitive) damages should be adopted in the United States? Thus far courts in Australia, New Zealand, and Canada have refused to follow *Rookes v. Barnard. See* Salmond & Heuston, Torts 508, n. 28 (21st ed. R. F. V. Heuston & R. A. Buckley 1996).

G. DAMAGES FOR INJURY TO PROPERTY AND FOR PURE ECONOMIC LOSS

1. *Injury to Property*

Basic Measure. When personal or real property has been tortiously injured, the plaintiff is entitled to damages. If the property is destroyed, the measure of damages is, in theory, the fair market value of the property at the time of its destruction. When the property has been merely damaged, the theoretical measure of damages is the difference between the fair market value of the item immediately before it was damaged and its value after it was damaged. For severely damaged property that is not worth repairing, the test will lead to awarding the plaintiff the difference between the fair market value of the item before it was damaged and its salvage value after the damage has been inflicted. If the damage consists merely in the loss of the use of the item because it has been improperly detained, the appropriate measure of damages is the fair market value of the use of the item for the period during which it was detained. A good definition of "fair market value" is contained in the *Restatements*, which use the term "exchange value" to refer to the same concept. According to *Restatement (Second) of Torts* § 911(2), the exchange value of an item of property "* * * is the amount of money for which * * * [it] could be exchanged or procured if there is a market continuously resorted to by traders. * * *" If there is no such ready market, the exchange value is "* * * the amount that could be obtained in the usual course of finding a purchaser or hirer of similar property. * * *"

Evaluative Options. While the theory of damages dictates comparing the fair market value of an item before and after the defendant's tortious conduct, it is sometimes difficult to establish the fair market value (or exchange value) of an item. This is particularly true of buildings but it may also be true of certain more or less one-of-a-kind chattels. In these situations, *replacement cost,* less accumulated depreciation, might be taken as approximating the so-called fair market value of the item before the accident. If other evidence is unavailable, the courts may look to the *original cost* of the item in ascertaining the fair market value of the item before the accident. In the case of badly damaged property the fair market value of the item after the accident will then be determined by the salvage value of the item.

If a damaged item of property is capable of repair, however, an alternate method of valuation that may be independent of fair market value may be used. Under this alternate method damages will be assessed on the basis of the reasonable *cost of repair* plus the reasonable value of the loss of use of the item until the repairs are completed. Thus, if the item damaged is the plaintiff's car, the plaintiff would be entitled to the reasonable cost of repairing the vehicle together with the reasonable cost of renting a replacement vehicle.

Special Situations. Even after all these tests have been examined there may still be situations in which damaged property has, for the plaintiff, some special value or use that is not reflected in its fair market value or in any of the alternate measures of damage thus far considered. For example, suppose the plaintiff is the owner of a fifteen-year old serviceable automobile and this vehicle is damaged sufficiently by the defendant to make repairing it impractical. Many courts will permit the plaintiff to recover an amount that is greater than the difference between the fair market value of the item before the accident and the salvage value of the item after the accident. More generally, if the property damaged or destroyed is of a type that cannot readily be replaced by a substitute and if this circumstance is not reflected in the fair market value of the item, some compensation for loss of use will be appropriate. There are other more difficult special situations involving items that are uniquely valuable to the plaintiff and which require some adjustment in the damages to be awarded. Take for example, the destruction of a family portrait. Compensation merely based on fair market value will clearly be inadequate. A more prosaic example would be a run-down building which is still habitable and which has a limited use as a storage facility. Based on its capitalized rental value, the structure may have a very low fair market value. On the other hand, if replacement cost less accumulated depreciation were used the plaintiff would be overcompensated. In such a situation many courts would allow the jury to award some intermediate value that takes into account the fact that the building might provide more utility to the plaintiff than is reflected in its rental value.

Consequential Damages. When property is damaged or destroyed, the plaintiff is sometimes also allowed to recover so-called consequential or special damages. Take for example, a case where the plaintiff's car is destroyed or damaged in the countryside and the plaintiff must take a taxicab back home and/or hire a tow truck to take the vehicle to a repair shop. Similarly, take a case where a building is destroyed and the plaintiff must pay to remove the rubble from his land. In all these situations, the plaintiff will be entitled to recover these consequential damages.

Widely Fluctuating Value. When property of widely fluctuating value is destroyed, certain special rules have evolved to take account of this factor. These rules originated in cases involving the conversion of property when the property was more likely to have been taken rather than destroyed; but these rules are also applied to the destruction of widely-fluctuating-in-value property, even when the destruction does not amount to a conversion because there has been no attempt to deprive the owner of dominion over the property. For example, someone negligently burns down a warehouse containing stored wheat, a commodity that does fluctuate widely in value. This is a case of destruction of property that does not involve a conversion of the property destroyed. As we have seen when we were discussing the damages for conversion, a variety of methods have evolved to handle these situations. (*See* Chapter Two, above). The one supported by most commentators and by the *Restatement (Second) of Torts* § 927 gives the plaintiff the greater of either the value at the time of the conversion or destruction of the property or the value reached within a reasonable time during which the plaintiff could have taken reasonable steps to mitigate his damages by replacing the destroyed or converted property. The purpose of these rules is to insure that the plaintiff gets fair damages for his loss but at the same time to prevent him from speculating with the defendant's money, since the plaintiff knows he is guaranteed at least the fair market value at the time of conversion or destruction.

What if the plaintiff claims that he does not have the money to cover his loss? The issue is likely to become acute when the defendant has tortiously damaged the plaintiff's physical property and delay in effective repairs has increased the severity of the damage. In Liesbosch, Dredger (Owners) v. Edison (Owners), [1933] A.C. 449, the House of Lords indicated that the lack of means of the plaintiff, which prevented repair or replacement, was not a factor to be considered in determining the extent of the plaintiff's obligation to mitigate damages. Nevertheless, in Ferguson v. New Zealand Fire Service Comm'n (High Ct.N.Z., Wellington, unreported, April 12, 1983), Eicheleaum, J., held that a man whose truck was damaged and who was unable to continue his hauling business was entitled to recover lost profits. The defendant argued that the plaintiff should have rented a replacement truck, but the plaintiff countered that he was in no financial position to do so. Since some of their lordships' speeches in *Liesbosch* suggested that the impecuniousness of the plaintiff was not reasonably foreseeable, Eicheleaum, J., questioned the continued viability of that case after the *Wagon Mound* cases. Several English cases, while not questioning the continued validity of *Liesbosch,* nonetheless have suggested that the plaintiff's financial position might be relevant if it were either highly foreseeable to the defendant or, given the defendant's refusal to admit liability, reasonable for a prudent person in the plaintiff's position not to embark on repairs until he was assured of a source of funds. *See* Dodd Properties (Kent Ltd.) v. Canterbury City Council, [1980] 1 W.L.R. 433, 1 All E.R. 928 (C.A.1979); Perry v. Sidney Phillips & Son, [1982] 1 W.L.R. 1297, 3 All E.R. 705 (C.A.).[2]

2. *Damages for Pure Economic Loss*

Tort claims for what is often called "pure economic loss" raise interesting and important theoretical as well as practical issues. The term "pure economic loss" refers to claims in which the plaintiff alleges neither personal injury nor physical damage to property, but instead only an economic loss, such as the losses incurred on a bad investment after a tortious misrepresentation, or the business interruption costs necessitated by a malfunctioning and negligently engineered product.

2. The trial court, in ascertaining the date at which the cost of repairs should be determined, took into account the plaintiff's financial inability to undertake repairs under what would otherwise have been considered a reasonable period of time. Perry v. Sidney Phillips & Son, [1982] 1 All E.R. 1005 (Q.B.). For several reasons, including uncertainty as to when he would actually receive a damage award, the plaintiff sold the house while the appeal was pending, and this made this aspect of the case moot.

An exploration of the economic loss rule should begin with several points about what it is not. First, the rule does not mean that all losses that are economic are not recoverable. Lost wages and medical expenses are purely economic losses; damage to property usually is only economic. Yet all these are recoverable when the plaintiff can otherwise establish breach, causation, etc. This is because all these cases involve either an initial personal injury or some type of physical damage to property.

Second, the rule does not mean that tort law altogether exempts wrongful conduct that causes only economic loss. Most jurisdictions, for instance, recognize the tort of professional negligence for attorney and accountant misconduct, as well as claims for tortious interference with contract, misrepresentation, etc. These are usually claims for purely economic losses, yet tort avenues continue to exist for them in most jurisdictions.

Still, the economic loss rule has extensive application. Most jurisdictions follow some version of the rule, and thus bar many claims for pure economic loss. On inspection, one can see that claims for purely economic loss arise in two general types of scenarios: "stranger" contexts and "nonstranger" contexts. Nonstranger contexts are those in which the plaintiff and defendant are in a contractual relationship (such as when a purchaser sues a product manufacturer that sold the product directly to the consumer) or at least are indirectly connected through a market transaction (such as when a consumer sues a product manufacturer that sold the product through a wholesaler or retailer). Stranger contexts are those in which the plaintiff and defendant are not in contractual privity and are not even indirectly connected to the same market transaction (such as when a commercial fisherman sues the oil company whose tanker negligently spilled oil into the ocean and thus harmed the fisherman's income).

RARDIN v. T & D MACHINE HANDLING, INC.

890 F.2d 24 (7th Cir.1989).

Before POSNER, COFFEY, and KANNE, CIRCUIT JUDGES.

POSNER, CIRCUIT JUDGE.

Jack Rardin, the plaintiff, bought for use in his printing business a used printing press from Whitacre–Sunbelt, Inc. for $47,700. The price included an allowance of $1,200 to cover the cost of dismantling the press for shipment and loading it on a truck at Whitacre's premises in Georgia for transportation to Rardin in Illinois. The contract of sale provided that the press was to be "Sold As Is, Where Is," that payment was to be made before the removal of the press from Whitacre's premises, and that Whitacre was to be responsible only for such damage to the press as might be "incurred by reason of the fault or negligence of [Whitacre's] employees, agents, contractors or representatives." To dismantle and load the press, Whitacre hired T & D Machine Handling, Inc., which performed these tasks carelessly; as a result the press was damaged. Not only did Rardin incur costs to repair the press; he also lost profits in his printing business during the time it took to put the press into operating order. He brought this suit against Whitacre, T & D, and others; settled with Whitacre; dismissed all the other defendants except T & D; and now appeals from the dismissal of his case against T & D for failure to state a claim. (The facts we recited are all taken from the complaint.) The only issue is whether Rardin stated a claim against T & D under Illinois law, which the parties agree controls this diversity suit.

* * * The damages that Rardin seeks from T & D are the profits that he lost as a result of the delay in putting the press into operation in his business, a delay caused by T & D's negligence in damaging the press. Rardin could not have sought these damages from Whitacre under the warranty, because consequential damages (of which a loss of profits that is due to delay is the classic example) are not recoverable in a breach of contract suit, with exceptions not applicable here. Rardin had no contract with T & D, and his claim against T & D is a tort claim; consequential damages are the norm in tort law.

We agree with the district judge that Illinois law does not provide a tort remedy in a case such as this. We may put a simpler version of the case, as follows: A takes his watch to a retail store, B, for repair. B sends it out to a watchmaker, C. Through negligence, C damages the watch, and when it is returned to A via B it does not tell time accurately. As a result, A misses an important meeting with his creditors. They petition him into bankruptcy. He loses everything. Can he obtain damages from C, the watchmaker, for the consequences of C's negligence? There is no issue of causation in our hypothetical case; there is none in Rardin's. We may assume that but for C's negligence A would have made the meeting and averted the bankruptcy, just as but for T & D's negligence the press would have arrived in working condition. The issue is not causation; it is duty.

The basic reason why no court (we believe) would impose liability on C in a suit by A is that C could not estimate the consequences of his carelessness, ignorant as he was of the circumstances of A, who is B's customer. In principle, it is true, merely to conclude that C was negligent is to affirm that the costs of care to him were less than the costs of his carelessness to all who might be hurt by it; that, essentially, is what negligence means, in Illinois as elsewhere. So in a perfect world of rational actors and complete information, and with damages set equal to the plaintiff's injury, there would be no negligence: the costs of negligence would be greater to the defendant than the costs of care and therefore it would never pay to be negligent. And if there were no negligence, the scope of liability for negligence would have no practical significance. But all this is a matter of abstract principle, and it is not realistic to assume that every responsible citizen can and will avoid ever being negligent. In fact, all that taking care does is make it less likely that one will commit a careless act. In deciding how much effort to expend on being careful—and therefore how far to reduce the probability of a careless accident—the potential injurer must have at least a rough idea of the extent of liability. C in our example could not form such an idea. He does not know the circumstances of the myriad owners of watches sent him to repair. He cannot know what costs he will impose if through momentary inattention he negligently damages one of the watches in his charge.

Two further points argue against liability. The first is that A could by his contract with B have protected himself against the consequences of C's negligence.   He could have insisted that B guarantee him against all untoward consequences, however remote or difficult to foresee, of a failure to redeliver the watch in working order.   The fact that B would in all likelihood refuse to give such a guaranty for a consideration acceptable to A is evidence that liability for all the consequences of every negligent act is not in fact optimal.   Second, A could have protected himself not through guarantees but simply by reducing his dependence on his watch.   Knowing how important the meeting was he could have left himself a margin for error or consulted another timepiece.   Why impose liability for a harm that the victim could easily have prevented himself?

The present case is essentially the same as our hypothetical example. T & D is in the business of dismantling and loading printing presses.   It is not privy to the circumstances of the owners of those presses.   It did not deal directly with the owner, that is, with Rardin.   It knew nothing about his business and could not without an inquiry that Rardin would have considered intrusive (indeed bizarre) have determined the financial consequences to Rardin if the press arrived in damaged condition.

* * *

We are reinforced in our conclusion that T & D is not liable to Rardin by a series of cases * * * in which the Supreme Court of Illinois has held that damages for "purely economic loss" cannot be recovered in tort cases. The doctrine is not unique to Illinois.   Originating in Chief Justice Traynor's opinion in Seely v. White Motor Co., 63 Cal.2d 9, 45 Cal.Rptr. 17, 403 P.2d 145 (1965), it has become the majority rule (see the thorough discussion of the case law in Spring Motors Distributors, Inc. v. Ford Motor Co., 98 N.J. 555, 489 A.2d 660 (1985)), and was adopted as the rule for admiralty as well in East River S.S. Corp. v. Transamerica Delaval Inc., 476 U.S. 858, 106 S.Ct. 2295, 90 L.Ed.2d 865 (1986).   We need not consider the outer boundaries of the doctrine; it is enough that it bars liability in a suit for lost profits resulting from negligence in carrying out a commercial undertaking.

The doctrine (called in Illinois the Moorman doctrine) rests on the insight * * * that contractual-type limitations on liability may make sense in many tort cases that are not contract cases only because there is no privity of contract between the parties.   The contractual linkage between Rardin and T & D was indirect but unmistakable, and Rardin could as we have said have protected himself through his contractual arrangements with Whitacre, while there was little that T & D could do to shield itself from liability to Whitacre's customer except be more careful—and we have explained why a finding of negligence alone should not expose a defendant to unlimited liability.

* * *

The "economic loss" doctrine of Moorman and of its counterpart cases in other jurisdictions is not the only tort doctrine that limits for-want-of-a-nail-the-kingdom-was-lost liability.   It is closely related to the doctrine, thoroughly discussed in Barber Lines A/S v. M/V Donau Maru, 764 F.2d 50 (1st Cir.1985), that bars recovery for economic loss even if the loss does not arise from a commercial relationship between the parties—even if for example a negligent accident in the Holland Tunnel backs up traffic for hours, imposing cumulatively enormous and readily monetizable costs of delay. See Petition of Kinsman Transit Co., 388 F.2d 821, 825 n. 8 (2d Cir.1968). Admittedly these doctrines are in tension with other doctrines of tort law that appear to expose the tortfeasor to unlimited liability. One is the principle that allows recovery of full tort damages in a personal-injury suit for injury resulting from a defective or unreasonably dangerous product—a form of legal action that arises in a contractual setting and indeed originated in suits for breach of warranty. Another is the principle, also of personal-injury law, that the injurer takes his victim as he finds him and is therefore liable for the full extent of the injury even if unforeseeable—even if the person he runs down is Henry Ford and sustains a huge earnings loss, or because of a preexisting injury sustains a much greater loss than the average victim would have done. Both are doctrines of personal-injury law, however, and there are at least three differences between the personal-injury case and the economic-loss case, whether in a stranger or in a contractual setting. The first difference is that the potential variance in liability is larger when the victim of a tort is a business, because businesses vary in their financial magnitude more than individuals do; more precisely, physical capital is more variable than human capital. The second is that many business losses are offset elsewhere in the system: Rardin's competitors undoubtedly picked up much or all of the business he lost as a result of the delay in putting the press into operation, so that his loss overstates the social loss caused by T & D's negligence. Third, tort law is a field largely shaped by the special considerations involved in personal-injury cases, as contract law is not. Tort doctrines are, therefore, prima facie more suitable for the governance of such cases than contract doctrines are.

* * *

Our conclusion that there is no tort liability in this case does not, therefore, leave buyers in the plaintiff's position remediless. Rardin could have sought guarantees from Whitacre (at a price, of course), but what he could not do was require the tort system to compensate him for business losses occasioned by negligent damage to his property.

* * *

The protracted analysis that we have thought necessary to address the parties' contentions underscores the desirability—perhaps urgency—of harmonizing the entire complex and confusing pattern of liability and nonliability for tortious conduct in contractual settings. But that is a task for the Supreme Court of Illinois rather than for us in this diversity case governed by Illinois law. It is enough for us that Illinois law does not permit a tort suit for profits lost as the result of the failure to complete a commercial undertaking.

AFFIRMED.

Notes

1. *The Economic Loss Rule in Nonstranger Settings.* When applying the economic loss rule in nonstranger settings, most courts have emphasized one

reason in particular: nonstrangers are able, through the law of contract and warranty, to allocate the risks of disappointed economic expectations. Tort law, then, should yield to contract and warranty law in such contexts. *See* East River S.S. Corp. v. Transamerica Delaval Inc., 476 U.S. 858, 106 S.Ct. 2295, 90 L.Ed.2d 865 (1986)(adopting the economic loss rule in admiralty cases). The most commonly litigated nonstranger cases are products liability cases. The majority of jurisdictions apply the economic loss to bar recovery in tort (both negligence and strict liability) if the product defect causes only economic harms or only damage to the product itself. A minority of jurisdictions allow tort claims for products defects that result in solely economic loss, so long as the loss occurred in the context of an "accident-like" event. To illustrate, consider two product scenarios: (1) a wiring defect in an automatic dryer renders the dryer only sporadically operable, thus causing economic costs in the form of a diminished value and the need to spend money at the laundromat; and (2) a wiring defect in the automatic dryer causes a brief fire in the dryer, which is quickly extinguished and thus causes no damage to persons or other property. The majority version of the economic loss rule would bar tort claims in either scenario. *See East River S.S. Corp., supra* (adopting the economic loss rule in admiralty, and rejecting an exception for sudden and calamitous events). The minority version would allow a tort claim in (2) but not (1). *See* Capitol Fuels, Inc. v. Clark Equipment Co., 181 W.Va. 258, 382 S.E.2d 311 (W.Va.1989). What rationales might explain the minority view and majority views?

In nonstranger cases outside the products context—for instance, in the area of services or professional services—courts still apply the economic loss rule, but the precise boundaries of the rule are evolving. One of the biggest areas of uncertainty is whether the economic loss rule applies when the plaintiff can establish an "independent tort"—that is, a tort claim other than a claim in general negligence. An example might be a claim for fraud, for negligent misrepresentation, or for tortious interference with contract. Courts currently are not in agreement on the question. *Compare* Southwestern Bell Tel. Co. v. DeLanney, 809 S.W.2d 493 (Tex.1991)(stating that a tort claim will be available if the plaintiff could establish the elements of some independent tort, other than negligence); Freeman & Mills, Inc. v. Belcher Oil Co., 11 Cal.4th 85, 95, 44 Cal.Rptr.2d 420, 426, 900 P.2d 669, 675 (1995)(concluding that the economic loss caselaw in California suggests courts should limit tort recovery in contract contexts absent an independent tort duty), *with* Hoseline, Inc. v. U.S.A. Diversified Products, Inc., 40 F.3d 1198 (11th Cir.1994) (holding that, if the plaintiff does not sustain personal injury or property damage, then the plaintiff has no tort cause of action for breach of contract, under Florida law, even if he could establish an independent tort such as fraud).

Do the rationales for the economic loss rule, as outlined by Judge Posner, support applying the rule across the board to all tort claims between nonstrangers—including, for instance, claims for attorney malpractice? If not, then which types of tort claims between nonstrangers should escape the reach of the economic loss rule, and why?

For a general discussion of the economic loss rule and the stranger-nonstranger distinction, see William Powers, Jr. & Margaret Niver, *Negligence, Breach of Contract, and the "Economic Loss" Rule,* 23 Tex. Tech L. Rev. 477, 488–89 (1992).

2. *The Economic Loss Rule in Stranger Cases.* Most jurisdictions also apply the economic loss rule in stranger cases. For instance, if a professional

basketball star is negligently run over by a motorist, the injured player can recover for his physical injuries and his loss of earning capacity, but the owner of an arena who suffers diminution in attendance because the star is unable to perform will not have any remedy against the negligent motorist. In these stranger cases, the parties had no opportunity to allocate, via their bargain, the risks of poor performance or negligence. Thus, the nonstranger cases do not so clearly rest on the availability and superiority of the contract regime for allocating loss. Rather, the economic loss rule in such cases is usually grounded in the fear of unlimited and unpredictable liability.

Some important inroads have been made into the economic loss rule in stranger cases. A key case is Union Oil Co. v. Oppen, 501 F.2d 558 (9th Cir.1974) which was decided on the basis of admiralty law and California law which the court treated as pointing to the same result. The case involved a group of commercial fishermen who brought an action against the oil companies responsible for the spillage of oil in the Santa Barbara channel that occurred in January 1969. They claimed damages, *inter alia,* for loss of profits resulting from the reduction in commercial fishing. In a wide-ranging opinion, written by Judge Sneed, the court questioned the traditional rule of denying recovery simply because the injury suffered is labeled "economic loss." Rather customary tort analysis with its strong emphasis on foreseeability should apply. After making this declaration and holding that the commercial fishermen stated a cause of action, Judge Sneed's opinion nevertheless concluded:

> Finally, it must be understood that our holding in this case does not open the door to claims that may be asserted by those, other than commercial fishermen, whose economic or personal affairs were discommoded by the oil spill of January 28, 1969. The general rule urged upon us by defendants has a legitimate sphere within which to operate. Nothing said in this opinion is intended to suggest, for example, that every decline in the general commercial activity of every business in the Santa Barbara area following the occurrences of 1969 constitutes a legally cognizable injury for which the defendants may be responsible. The plaintiffs in the present action lawfully and directly make use of a resource of the sea, *viz.* its fish, in the ordinary course of their business. This type of use is entitled to protection from negligent conduct by the defendants in their drilling operations. Both the plaintiffs and defendants conduct their business operations away from land and in, on and under the sea. Both must carry on their commercial enterprises in a reasonably prudent manner. Neither should be permitted negligently to inflict commercial injury on the other. We decide no more than this.

501 F.2d at 570–71. Since the court in *Oppen* ended by confining its decision to commercial fishermen it could have eschewed any general discussion of the issue of recovery of economic loss and relied on some previous authority that commercial fishermen could recover, on a public nuisance theory, for injury to their business from pollution of public waters. *See, e.g.,* Hampton v. North Carolina Pulp Co., 223 N.C. 535, 27 S.E.2d 538 (1943). *See also* Burgess v. M/V Tamano, 370 F.Supp. 247 (D.Me.1973), *affirmed per curiam,* 559 F.2d 1200 (1st Cir.1977). In Pruitt v. Allied Chemical Corp., 523 F.Supp. 975 (E.D.Va. 1981), however, the federal district court, in a case involving a chemical spill into navigable waters, rejected *Oppen's* attempt to limit recovery of economic loss to commercial fishermen. It held that marina and charterboat owners also could recover economic loss. *Cf.* Masonite Corp. v. Steede, 198 Miss. 530, 23

So.2d 756 (1945). Under this approach, should vacation homeowners be able to recover? How about vacationers whose holiday has been ruined? More recent authority, however, casts some doubt upon any attempt to extend *Oppen* beyond the commercial fishing context. *See* State of Louisiana ex rel. Guste v. M/V Testbank, 752 F.2d 1019 (5th Cir.1985)(*en banc*), *cert. denied* 477 U.S. 903, 106 S.Ct. 3271, 91 L.Ed.2d 562 (1986)(holding that the various plaintiffs in that action, which included shipping interests, marina and boat operators, seafood enterprises, tackle and bait shops, and recreational fisherman, could not recover for pure economic damages, regardless of how the action was characterized). Moreover, insofar as *Oppen* relied on admiralty law, the *East River S.S.* case indicates that *Oppen* was probably incorrectly decided. After initially taking an expansive view of the situations under which pure economic loss could be recovered under English law, the House of Lords has reaffirmed the restrictive, traditional common-law rule. *See* G. Christie, *The Uneasy Place of Principle in Tort Law,* 49 S.M.U. L.Rev. 525 (1996).

Leaving the field of oil and chemical spills, perhaps the most important state case in this area has been J'Aire Corp. v. Gregory, 24 Cal.3d 799, 157 Cal.Rptr. 407, 598 P.2d 60 (1979). That case held that a lessee could recover economic losses against a contractor whose delay in completing a construction project was owing to negligence. The court declared that, in the circumstances of the case, there was a "special relationship" between the plaintiff and the defendant, even though they had no contractual privity. The basis of the special relationship was essentially the high degree of foreseeability of injury to the plaintiff's interests if the construction work was delayed. This case, which has been followed in California, *see, e.g.,* Huang v. Garner, 157 Cal.App.3d 404, 203 Cal.Rptr. 800 (1984), is clearly contrary to the more recent decisions of the House of Lords and Privy Council and also to the United States Supreme Court's decisions in the *Robins Drydock* and *East River S.S.* cases as to the law to be applied in tort cases governed by federal law.

Chapter 11

DERIVATIVE ACTIONS AND FATAL INJURIES

A. LOSS OF CONSORTIUM AND LOSS OF SERVICES IN NON-FATAL PERSONAL INJURY CASES

BERGER v. WEBER

Supreme Court of Michigan, 1981.
411 Mich. 1, 303 N.W.2d 424.

KAVANAGH, JUSTICE.

This action arose out of an automobile collision involving plaintiff Christine Berger and defendant-appellant Albert Weber.[1] It is alleged that as a result of the accident, the plaintiff Christine Berger sustained severe and permanent psychological and physical injuries. Plaintiffs Wayne and Christine Berger filed a complaint on their own behalf and sought damages for medical expenditures, loss of income and loss of consortium. As next friend, Wayne Berger sought damages on behalf of his minor daughter,[2] Denise, for loss of society, companionship, love and affection of her mother Christine Berger.

A jury awarded Wayne and Christine Berger $142,000. The trial court granted defendants' motion for summary judgment as to the issue of liability for the minor daughter's loss of society and companionship. The Court of Appeals affirmed the jury award and reversed the ruling on the child's cause of action, holding that a child may maintain a cause of action for loss of parental society and companionship when a parent is "severely" injured. * * *

We granted leave to speak to the propriety of recognizing a cause of action for loss of parental society and companionship when a parent is negligently injured. After considering the competing policy considerations, we are satisfied that such a cause of action should be enforced.

---

1. This cause of action occurred before the no-fault insurance act, M.C.L. § 500.3101 *et seq.*; M.S.A. § 24.13101 *et seq.*, became effective.

2. Denise Berger was born severely retarded and physically handicapped in October of 1966. She died on July 16, 1977. No claim has been made on behalf of the Bergers' son who was born in November of 1964.

I

Such a cause of action was unknown at common law and only one other jurisdiction recognizes this cause of action.[3]

Lack of precedent cannot absolve a common-law court from responsibility for adjudicating each claim that comes before it on its own merits. * * * Here we must consider the child's claim in light of conditions pertinent to modern society and weigh the reasons urged for denying the cause of action.

II

Plaintiffs assert that denying the action for loss of society and companionship to a child is inconsistent with the public policy of this state. They point out that Michigan has long recognized a cause of action for loss of consortium in favor of spouses[4] and that parents have an independent cause of action for loss of services and other pecuniary damages resulting from negligent injuries to their minor children. * * * In Wycko v. Gnodtke, 361 Mich. 331, 105 N.W.2d 118 (1960), these pecuniary damages were held to include the loss of society and companionship of a child who died from negligently inflicted injuries. More importantly, children may recover for the loss of society and companionship of a parent who is negligently killed under the wrongful death act, M.C.L. § 600.2922; M.S.A. § 27A.2922. They may also recover for such loss under the Dramshop act (M.C.L. § 436.22; M.S.A. § 18.993) * * *

We are satisfied that existing judicial and legislative policies warrant recognizing a child's cause of action for loss of society and companionship of a negligently injured parent. After carefully reviewing the reasons cited by the defendants, we are convinced that they do not justify denying the cause of action the plaintiff seeks.

III

Defendants-appellants urge several reasons for not recognizing a child's cause of action. The first argument is that the differences between the marital relationship and the parent-child relationship call for different treatment. They assert that a spouse's action for loss of consortium is based to a large extent on the impairment or destruction of the sexual relations of the couple and no similar element exists in the child's claim. We are not persuaded that this distinction is significant enough to deny the child's claim. Sexual relations are but one element of the spouse's consortium action. The other elements—love, companionship, affection, society, comfort, services and solace—are similar in both relationships and in each are deserving of protection.

3. Ferriter v. Daniel O'Connell's Sons, Inc., 381 Mass. 507, 413 N.E.2d 690 (1980); Anno.: *Child's Right of Action for Loss of Support, Training, Parental Attention, or the Like, Against a Third Person Negligently Injuring Parent*, 69 A.L.R.3d 528; Borer v. American Airlines, Inc., 19 Cal.3d 441, 138 Cal.Rptr. 302, 563 P.2d 858 (1977). [Ed. note] This case is briefly described at p. 512n, *supra*.

4. * * * Consortium is defined as love, companionship, affection, society, comfort, sexual relations, services, solace and more. * * * The wife's cause of action was created after judicial recognition that the wife's role in the family unit had evolved from the status of servant to the status of equal partner. Therefore, the reasons for denying the wife compensation at common law no longer existed in modern society. * * *

Defendants-appellants next contend that allowing a child to maintain an independent cause of action when his or her parent is negligently injured will result in a burden to the individual defendant and to our court system. Under M.C.L. § 600.5851; M.S.A. § 27A.5851, if a person's claim accrues when he is a minor, he is entitled to bring the cause of action at any time through his 19th birthday. The prospect of multiple suits will discourage settlements.

Multiplicity of actions arising out of the same tortious act are a present reality in tort law. Multiple actions may result whenever a single tortious act injures more than one person or property owned by more than one person. Whenever the persons are minor children the tortfeasor is faced with the minority savings provision in M.C.L. § 600.5851; M.S.A. § 27A.5851.

So too when a new cause of action is created, litigation may be increased. However, as the Court of Appeals aptly pointed out, "[t]he rights of a new class of tort plaintiffs should be forthrightly judged on their own merits, rather than engaging in gloomy speculation as to where it will all end". (Citation omitted.) 82 Mich.App. 199, 210, 267 N.W.2d 124.

Another objection to the child's cause of action raised by defendants-appellants is that it would be anomalous to allow a child to recover for negligent invasion of his family interest when he is specifically prohibited from recovery for intentional, direct invasion of his family interest under M.C.L. § 600.2901(1); M.S.A. § 27A.2901(1), which bars suits for alienation of affections.

We do not regard this as anomalous. One may recover for negligent injury or death of a spouse and a child may recover for the negligent death of a parent even though both be barred from recovery for the intentional, direct invasion of the family interest occasioned by alienation of affection.

We are satisfied that the real anomaly is to allow a child's recovery for the loss of a parent's society and companionship when the loss attends the parent's death but to deny such recovery when the loss attends the parent's injury.

Defendants-appellants ask us not to recognize the child's claim because of the economic burden to the public due to increased insurance premiums. Recognizing the child's cause of action may result in increased insurance costs, but compensating a child who has suffered emotional problems because of the deprivation of a parent's love and affection may provide the child with the means of adjustment to the loss. The child receives the immediate benefit of the compensation, but society will also benefit if the child is able to function without emotional handicap. This may well offset any increase in insurance premiums.

Traditional arguments for not recognizing the child's cause of action claim that the damages to the child are too remote and speculative and that compensating the child will result in double recovery because juries already consider the child when making damage awards to the injured parent.

We are not convinced that the injury to the child is too speculative to award damages. Courts, law review commentators and treatise writers all recognize that the child suffers a genuine loss. While the loss of society and companionship is an intangible loss, juries often are required to calculate damages for intangible loss. Awards are made for pain and suffering, loss of society and companionship in wrongful death actions, and for loss of spousal consortium. Evaluating the child's damages is no more speculative than evaluating these other types of intangible losses.

We agree with the Court of Appeals that because double recovery could result when making awards to parents, this is a further reason for adopting an independent action for the child.

"Rather than having juries make blind calculations of the child's loss in determining an award to the parent, a child's loss could be openly argued in court and the jury could be instructed to consider the child's loss separately. The award would accrue directly to the child rather than be lumped in with that of the parent who may or may not spend it for the child's benefit." (Citation omitted.) 82 Mich.App. 199, 267 N.W.2d 124.

Finally, defendants-appellants urge us to leave this matter to the Legislature. Actions by parents for loss of a child's services and medical expenses and actions for loss of spousal consortium were created and developed by the judiciary. At the present time, children are prevented from recovering for loss of parental consortium by judicial decision. The Court should remove the obstacle. We do not regard the cause of action contemplated here so complex that we should defer action to the Legislature.

IV

The importance of the child to our society merits more than lip service. Convinced that we have too long treated the child as second-class citizen or some sort of nonperson, we feel constrained to remove the disability we have imposed.

We hold today that a child may recover for loss of a parent's society and companionship caused by tortious injury to the parent.

We do not adopt the Court of Appeals limitation to instances of "severely" injured parents of minor children. The need for and extent of limitations beyond those attendant upon the comparable cause of action by a spouse should await demonstration.

Affirmed as modified.

LEVIN, JUSTICE (to reverse).

The issue is whether a child has a cause of action for loss of the society and companionship of a parent who has been negligently injured, but not fatally. Until recently, courts refused to extend the common law to allow a child to maintain such an action. One jurisdiction now allows such an action, and today this Court becomes the second court of last resort to conclude that the common law should be expanded to permit a child to recover money damages for the lost society and companionship of a negligently injured parent.

We would hold with the overwhelming majority of jurisdictions which have considered or reconsidered the question—many in recent years—that such an action should not be authorized and would reverse the decision of the Court of Appeals.

I

Plaintiff Christine Berger was the wife of Wayne Berger and the mother of two children at the time a truck driven by defendant Albert Weber struck her automobile from behind.[5] She suffered no visible injuries as a result of the accident, but she subsequently experienced neck pain, severe headaches and a number of emotional problems. She was treated with medication and physical therapy and was hospitalized for a time.

Christine and Wayne Berger commenced an action seeking damages for Christine's medical expenses, loss of income, and pain and suffering, and Wayne's loss of consortium. The complaint was subsequently amended to allege a cause of action on behalf of the Bergers' minor daughter, Denise,[6] for loss of her mother's society, companionship, love and affection resulting from Christine's injuries. Christine sought judgment in the amount of $750,000 and Wayne and Denise $500,000 each.

The judge, granting defendants' motion for partial summary judgment, dismissed the claim asserted on behalf of Denise. Defendants admitted liability and the question of damages was tried to a jury. Defendants contended that Christine had suffered no more than a neck sprain in the accident and that her subsequent difficulties were caused solely by pre-existing emotional problems.

The jury assessed Christine's damages at $137,000 and Wayne's at $5,000. * * *

II

At common law a husband whose wife had been injured could bring a separate action to recover for his loss of consortium resulting from her injury. Consortium was a loosely defined concept comprised of the husband's rights to "services, society and sexual intercourse of the wife." A father could maintain an action for loss of an injured child's services. But a wife or child could not recover if deprived of a husband's or father's services or society, for the common law recognized no right to such services or society in the "inferior" parties to the relationship.

In most jurisdictions the common law has been altered to permit a wife to recover for loss of consortium. This case presents the question whether a child should be permitted to bring a comparable action.

The advocates of a child's action for loss of what has been termed "parental consortium" maintain that recognition of the child's right to recover is mandated by logic, compassion, and modern sensitivity to the independent identity of the child, the importance of family relationships, and the fairness of compensating persons injured by another's negligent conduct. They point to this Court's eloquent vindication of the wife's

---

5. The truck was owned by defendant Becker Leasing Company, Inc., and was being driven by Weber in the course of his employment with defendant Star of the West Milling Company. The accident occurred on March 13, 1973, before the effective date of the no-fault motor vehicle liability act.

6. Denise Berger was born on October 2, 1966. According to plaintiffs' opening statement at trial, Denise began to have seizures when she was six weeks old. It soon became evident that her mental development would be severely limited and doctors advised the Bergers to institutionalize her. Instead, they chose to care for her at home although she continued to require the attention given an infant.

Denise died on July 16, 1977.

action for loss of consortium and to the wrongful death act, which enables a child to recover for loss of the society and companionship of a deceased parent in a wrongful death action, and assert that justice, public policy, and the Equal Protection Clause require that a child also be allowed to recover for loss of a parent's society and companionship.

The opponents of the proposed cause of action argue that it will (1) spawn multiple lawsuits arising out of the same injury, with consequent multiplication of awards; (2) discourage settlement of parents' claims since the claims of minor children cannot thereby be extinguished; (3) encourage double recovery since juries already take the loss suffered by the injured person's family into account in computing damages; (4) lead to further extensions of tort liability as plaintiffs with other relationships to the injured person seek recognition of their losses; and (5) impose upon the public the unwarranted economic burden of increased insurance premiums to fund insurers' costs in paying and litigating such claims. They also contend (6) that the child's damages are speculative, remote, and not susceptible of monetary compensation; (7) that the child-parent relationship is distinguishable from the marital relationship; and (8) that the Legislature is in the best position to determine whether the new cause of action should be instituted and what limits should be placed upon it.

The Court, building on judicial recognition of causes of action for loss of spousal consortium and for parental loss of a child's services and other pecuniary damages, and on statutes permitting a child to recover for loss of the society and companionship of a deceased parent or where such loss is occasioned by violation of the dramshop act, states that it is "satisfied that existing judicial and legislative policies warrant recognizing a child's cause of action for loss of society and companionship of a negligently injured parent." * * * In contrast with its approach in examining the arguments of the defendants, it does not scrutinize the arguments of proponents of the cause of action and fails to subject them to critical analysis.

III

A

Decisions delineating the extent of tort liability are, however, more than exercises in logic. They are pronouncements of social policy which should reflect the often subtle balance of the interests involved. The Supreme Court of New Jersey observed:

> "[L]ogic (and even abstract justice) must defer to overall policy in the appraisal of the justification for judicial changes in the common law."[7]

Twenty years ago this Court concluded that a wife's interest in compensation for the loss of her injured husband's society and companionship outweighed a negligent defendant's interest in freedom from liability for such loss, although his "liabilities as a result of his negligent act must have some reasonable limitation."[8] Today we balance the interest of an injured person's child in monetary redress for injury to the parent-child relationship against the consequences of imposing yet another potential

7. Russell v. Salem Transportation Co., 61 N.J. 502, 506, 295 A.2d 862 (1972).

8. *Montgomery v. Stephan, supra,* 359 Mich. p. 46, 101 N.W.2d 227.

liability upon a negligent defendant—a liability the additional cost of which will be spread among the citizens of the state through increased insurance premiums. In responding, it is not enough to invoke analogies. An independent re-examination of the policy considerations implicated by the creation of such a separate cause of action is called for.

B

The action for loss of consortium is an historical curiosity. It originated at a time when a husband was considered to possess a proprietary right in his wife's services, and conduct of a third person which impaired her ability to render services was regarded as causing him pecuniary loss. The earliest English cases upholding a husband's right to bring an action for injury to himself resulting from wrongful conduct in respect to his wife involved intentional torts. The complaint alleged, for example, that the defendant had committed an assault and battery upon the wife, or had abducted her. The courts analogized the husband's loss of his wife's "company" to the master's loss of the services of a battered servant.

Recognition of the husband's loss of consortium as an element of damages accompanied the evolution of a variety of actions for intentional interference with the marriage relationship: enticement or harboring (inducing a wife to live apart from her husband); criminal conversation (adultery); alienation of affections.

The question before us emanates from yet another line of cases where the courts, without apparent recognition that they were significantly extending the common law, permitted husbands to recover for loss of consortium resulting from negligently inflicted injury as well as from intentional injury. And, beginning in 1950, a series of American courts extended to wives the right to recover from a negligent tortfeasor for loss of spousal consortium.[9] The first step having been taken, the second logically followed, although equality between husband and wife could as well have been achieved by abolishing the husband's action as by recognizing the wife's.[10]

The soundness of the first step has been questioned,[11] and we should not proceed further along the same path merely because to do so would appear to be logical. Confronted with the question whether a wife should be permitted to recover for loss of consortium, Lord Chief Justice Goddard said:

> "[I]f the matter were now res integra the law, * * * I am tempted to say 'certainly,' would refuse to give an action to the husband merely for loss of consortium due to *negligence*. It is too late now for the courts to deny an action which has existed for hundreds of years. It is

9. The first case to take this step was Hitaffer v. Argonne Co., 87 U.S.App.D.C. 57, 183 F.2d 811 (1950). Subsequent cases are listed in Love, *Tortious Interference With the Parent–Child Relationship: Loss of an Injured Person's Society and Companionship*, 51 Ind.L.J. 590, 596, fn. 20 (1976). Whittlesey v. Miller, 572 S.W.2d 665, 668, fn. 6 (Tex.1978), lists nine states as not yet recognizing the wife's action. Four of those states have since adopted the majority rule. * * *

10. A number of courts, including this one, had at one time concluded that abolition of the husband's action was required by the enactment of statutes recognizing the separate legal existence of married women. See Blair v. Seitner Dry Goods Co., 184 Mich. 304, 313–314, 151 N.W. 724 (1915), overruled by *Montgomery v. Stephan, supra.*

11. Jaffe, *Damages for Personal Injury: The Impact of Insurance*, 18 Law & Contemporary Problems 219, 229 (1953); * * *.

an anomaly at the present day that a husband can obtain damages for an injury to his wife, but *English law is free neither of some anomalies nor of everything illogical, but this is no reason for extending them.*" (Emphasis supplied.)[12]

In a negligence action the plaintiff is almost always a person who alleges personal injury or property damage caused by the defendant's breach of a duty of care. In contrast, a family member who seeks compensation for loss of consortium seeks to recover in respect to physical injury to another.

The jurisprudential concepts of duty and proximate cause, reserved for judicial determination, serve to limit the scope of a defendant's liability for negligence.

* * * What relationship, then, obligates an actor with respect to the interests of a member of an injured person's family so as to create a duty to that person?

While that inquiry was overlooked when the action for loss of consortium became associated with actions for negligent injury to a wife as well as with actions for intentional interference with the marriage relationship, it was much on the minds of the English Lords who refused to permit a wife to bring an action for loss of consortium caused by negligence. The Lords described the husband's action as "an anomaly" "founded on the proprietary right which from ancient times it was considered the husband had in his wife," and remarked upon its inconsistency with general principles regarding the scope of a defendant's liability for the consequences of his negligent actions.

Plaintiffs assert that it is manifestly foreseeable that serious physical injury caused by a tortfeasor's negligence will be accompanied by loss to the victim's immediate family of the society and companionship of the injured person. It is argued that since this Court has, at least implicitly, determined that a wife's or husband's loss is not so remote that it is beyond the ambit of proximate cause and that breach of a duty owed the victim will be deemed a breach of a duty to the victim's spouse, the loss suffered by the victim's children must likewise fall within the sphere of liability.

Foreseeability is not, however, the only criterion for measuring the limits of liability for negligent conduct. It is foreseeable that any injured person will be party to a number of relationships—with the members of his household (who may not form a traditional nuclear family), with relatives, with friends and neighbors, with employer, employees, or co-workers—and that the other party to the relationship will suffer losses, tangible and intangible, should the relationship be interrupted. Lord Goddard observed:

> "It may often happen that an injury to one person may affect another; a servant whose master is killed or permanently injured may lose his employment, it may be of long standing, and the misfortune may come when he is of an age when it would be very difficult for him to obtain other work, but no one would suggest that he thereby acquires a right of action against the wrongdoer."

12. Best v. Samuel Fox & Co., [1952] AC 716, 733.

Even if it is accepted that policy considerations weigh more heavily in favor of recovery where family relationships regarded as fundamental to society are implicated, the anomalous character of the common-law action for loss of consortium[13] should deter us from extending it beyond the marital relationship, "the closest entity recognized by society," to other relationships. There may be appealing analogies between the relationships of husband and wife and parent and child, but "[r]easoning from one analogy to another can carry one into infinity."[14]

The Court does not indicate that it is prepared to draw a line somewhere or anywhere and indeed quotes with approval a statement of the Court of Appeals that " '[t]he rights of a new class of tort plaintiffs should be forthrightly judged on their own merits, rather than engaging in gloomy speculation as to where it will all end,' "—as if the merits of plaintiff's claim can be resolved in the abstract, focusing solely on the justness and fairness from the child's point of view of recognizing a right of recovery in this sympathetic case without regard to countervailing policy considerations and thoughtful consideration of "where it will all end."

The Court's decision does not in terms limit its holding to the creation of a cause of action for *minor* children who lose the society and companionship of an injured parent. Parents often continue to provide their children with society, companionship, nurturance and guidance long after the children themselves become parents. Some children never leave their parents' homes. Other children, whether married or single, become the devoted caretakers and companions of aged parents, whose society and companionship play a prominent role in their lives. The class of cases in which deprivation of parental consortium can be asserted is more extensive than might at first appear.

And now that we recognize a child's cause of action for loss of the society and companionship of a negligently injured parent, will we not also be called upon to compensate a parent's corresponding loss when a child is injured?

The Court's analogy to the wrongful death act suggests that a like analogy may be drawn in future cases where a sibling or other member of "that class who, by law, would be entitled to inherit the personal property of the deceased had he died intestate," and who would therefore be permitted to recover under the wrongful death act if an injured person dies, seeks to recover for loss of the society and companionship of an injured person who survives. Distinctions between the parent-child relationship and other relationships can indeed be made, but the Court's analysis, which minimizes the distinctions that could be drawn in the instant case, holds little promise for drawing such distinctions in other cases. Moreover, the "elements—love, companionship, affection, society, comfort, services and solace—" which the Court identifies as similar in the marital and parent-

---

13. We do not suggest that further extension of the right to recover for loss of consortium should be denied because consortium originated as a property interest. We so conclude, rather, because policy considerations dictate that the circumstances under which one can recover in respect to injury to another should be extremely limited.

14. Production Steel Strip Corp. v. Detroit, 390 Mich. 508, 537, 213 N.W.2d 419 (1973)(opinion of Levin, J.).

child relationships are also present in other relationships: brothers and sisters, a child and a grandparent, or a cohabiting unmarried couple.[15]

The concept of allowing a person to recover for consequential loss resulting from physical injury to another is an idiosyncracy in the law. Reasonable limits on liability for the consequences of negligent acts must be imposed. Upon review of the policy considerations we conclude that they do not favor redrawing the line between liability and non-liability to create a separate cause of action for loss of parental consortium.

IV

It is preferable to minimize the number of actions which can be brought for damages arising out of a single tortious act. The wisdom of creating a new cause of action depends in part upon whether other legal avenues are adequate to redress part or all of the asserted loss. Despite the increased acceptance of the spouse's action for loss of consortium, the extension of tort recovery beyond the primary victim remains the exceptional case. To the extent that a secondary tort victim's loss is likely to be duplicated in the primary victim's recovery, courts should be wary of creating additional claims deriving from the same tortious act, particularly where all injuries are localized within the same family unit.

Today the victim of a personal injury can recover for a broad variety of intangible losses in addition to conventional "pain and suffering." Without intimating a view as to the accuracy of their conclusions, we note that two federal courts, a student commentator, and a practitioner agree that "loss of life's enjoyments constitutes an element of compensable damages under the law of [Michigan]."[16] * * * In fact, if not in form, juries today may compensate personal injury plaintiffs for the overall reduction in the quality of family life, including the impairment of family relationships.

When a close link between two persons is disrupted, it is difficult to distinguish the injury suffered by each. As the California Supreme Court noted: "[T]o ask the jury, even under carefully drafted instructions, to distinguish the loss to the mother from her inability to care for her children from the loss to the children from the mother's inability to care for them may be asking too much."[17] To permit a child to recover for loss of an injured parent's society and companionship while the parent is also compensated for injury to the relationship creates a substantial risk of double recovery because of the difficulty of distinguishing the respective losses of the parties.

As the Supreme Court of New Jersey observed,

15. Loss of society and companionship may not be thought to be significant where the relationship can be characterized as a short-lived "affair." But today some couples, for whatever reasons, continue relationships for many years, perhaps until death do them part. Nor is this a phenomenon observed only among the young; it has been observed that such relationships are increasingly frequent among the elderly, who may seek to form quasi-marital relationships following the death of a spouse.

16. *Pierce v. New York C. R. Co., supra,* [409 F.2d 1392 (6th Cir.1969)] p. 1398, citing *Remey v. Detroit U. R. Co.,* 141 Mich. 116, 104 N.W. 420 (1905)(postponement of marriage), * * *.

17. Borer v. American Airlines, Inc., 19 Cal.3d 441, 448, 138 Cal.Rptr. 302, 307, 563 P.2d 858 (1977).

"The asserted social need for the disputed cause of action may well be qualified, at least in terms of the family as an economic unit, by the practical consideration * * * that reflection of the consequential disadvantages to children of injured parents is frequently found in jury awards to the parents on their own claims under existing law and practice."[18]

Moreover, where the primary victim recovers for his own injuries, the most direct consequences of the accident are compensated and the party at fault does not escape liability. * * *

Courts have generally been willing to tolerate substantial uncertainty in the calculation of damages where such was thought necessary to enable the primary tort victim to receive adequate compensation. That bodily pain and mental anguish defy objective valuation and that money is a poor palliative seem inadequate justifications for denying a victim who has been crippled or disfigured a monetary remedy. In the context of actions not brought by the primary victim, however, objections to the uncertainty of the intangible loss alleged and to the inherent inadequacy of money damages as compensation loom larger, especially since the primary victim may also recover a sum for intangible, uncertain injuries. Considerations which would not deter a court from compensating a primary victim may thus, notwithstanding the anomaly of recovery for spousal consortium, support a refusal further to expand the scope of liability.

Denise Berger's misfortune highlights the difficulties that juries will encounter in valuing loss of parental society and companionship and that courts will face when asked to review jury verdicts. On the one hand, Denise was uniquely dependent on others and her mother necessarily played an overwhelmingly important role in her life; on the other hand, her cognitive faculties—and perhaps her ability to experience loss of her mother's society and companionship—were severely impaired and the range of activities she could share with her mother was drastically limited. Is her loss greater or less than a normal child's? What significance should be attached to the ability of other family members, e.g., her father and brother, to care for her?

In contrast to the intangibility of the alleged injury and the difficulty of appraising it stands the certainty that creating a new basis for recovery will impose an added economic burden upon society. The California Supreme Court observed, "since virtually every serious injury to a parent would engender a claim for loss of consortium on behalf of each of his or her children, the expense of settling or litigating such claims would be sizable."[19] The Supreme Court of New Jersey perceptively described the problem:

"If the claim were allowed there would be a substantial accretion of liability against the tortfeasor arising out of a single transaction (typically the negligent operation of an automobile). Whereas the assertion of a spouse's demand for loss of consortium involves the joining of only a single companion claim in the action with that of the injured person, the right here debated would entail adding as many companion claims as the injured parent had minor children, each such

18. *Russell v. Salem Transportation Co.,* *supra,* 61 N.J. p. 507, 295 A.2d 862.

19. *Id.* [*Borer*], 19 Cal.3d p. 447, 138 Cal. Rptr. 302, 563 P.2d 858.

claim entitled to separate appraisal and award. The defendant's burden would be further enlarged if the claims were founded upon injuries to both parents. Magnification of damage awards to a single family derived from a single accident might well become a serious problem to a particular defendant as well as in terms of the total cost of such enhanced awards to the insured community as a whole."[20]

While the creation of other new causes of action may have affected only a handful of cases and thus generated marginal additional costs, recognizing a separate right of recovery in members of a tort victim's family creates a potential for additional liability in a large number of cases. And a tort victim is likely to have more children than spouses.

The cost of this innovation in the law will be exacerbated if recognition of the cause of action is not limited to cases where, as alleged here, the parent is "severely" injured or disabled for an extended period—the Court eschews such a limitation. Absent some such limitation, claims could be lodged by children whose parent had been hospitalized for a period of months, perhaps even weeks, after an accident, or had been rendered physically incapable of participating in some formerly shared activities. Such claims might outnumber the more substantial ones and exceed them in aggregate dollar amount as well. The administrative expense of reviewing children's claims and the cost of settling or litigating them will be considerable and will require significant increases in insurance premiums.

The Court acknowledges that insurance costs may rise, but suggests that an offsetting benefit for "any" increase may be realized: * * *.

It is doubtful that recognizing a child's cause of action will produce such auspicious results. Because few automobile drivers carry adequate liability insurance, most children who are deprived of a parent's companionship will not be benefitted. Policy limits are likely to be exhausted in the full or partial satisfaction of the injured parent's claim and the spouse's loss of consortium claim, without regard to children's claims for loss of parental consortium. Even fewer drivers have sufficient resources to satisfy such claims themselves. To be sure, some fortunate plaintiffs—for example, a child whose parent happens to be injured in a collision with a common carrier's truck instead of an ordinary citizen's automobile, or in an industrial accident where a third party is responsible, or by a major manufacturer's product—will be able to recover against "deep-pocket" defendants. But in the typical auto accident case, the less serious the parent's injury, the more likely it is that money will be available to pay claims for loss of parental consortium. The benefits of recognizing the child's cause of action will be unevenly and adventitiously distributed, more so than ordinarily.

There is a limit to the range of injuries and the dollar amount of recovery which can be spread across society through the interaction of the tort litigation and insurance systems. Increasing the load on the reparation system by recognizing causes of action in secondary tort victims in addition to the primary victim's action must increase insurance premiums, decrease participation in the system by marginal insureds, and perhaps

20. *Russell v. Salem Transportation Co.,*
supra, 61 N.J. p. 506, 295 A.2d 862.

decrease the amount that an insurer will willingly pay to the primary victim, thereby increasing litigation.

The Court suggests that allowing the child to recover "may provide the child with the means of adjustment to the loss." But it is problematic whether the means of adjustment can be purchased with money, whether awards will be so applied, or whether compensation will be received before the passage of time or the parent's recovery has worked a better adjustment. More accurate than a vision of minor children restored to emotional health by the services of parent substitutes and mental health professionals is the scenario depicted by the California Supreme Court:

> "[M]onetary compensation will not enable plaintiffs to regain the companionship and guidance of a mother; it will simply establish a fund so that upon reaching adulthood, when plaintiffs will be less in need of maternal guidance, they will be unusually wealthy men and women."

The California Supreme Court observed that, where recognition is sought for "a wholly new cause of action, unsupported by statute or precedent," "the inadequacy of monetary damages to make whole the loss suffered, considered in light of the social cost of paying such awards," and of the uncertainty that paying them will produce any social benefit, "constitutes a strong reason for refusing to recognize the asserted claim."[21]

It is significant that, although federal and state courts in approximately 20 jurisdictions have considered the question presented in this case, only one other jurisdiction recognizes a child's right of action for loss of parental society and companionship. While many of the decisions withholding recognition relied upon the lack of common-law precedent, deferred to the legislature, or employed arguments which failed to make an explicit policy judgment, such substantial unanimity of result, even among courts not noted for their timidity in the development of tort law,[22] evidences some consensus regarding the impolicy of subjecting a negligent defendant to liability to members of the victim's family other than the spouse.

V

The Equal Protection Clauses of the United States and Michigan Constitutions do not require recognition of a child's cause of action for loss of parental consortium.

VI

Although we would not permit the child of a negligently injured parent to bring a separate action for loss of the parent's society and companionship, we would permit the injured parent, in his or her own action, to recover certain damages resulting from the effect of the parent's injury upon the child. Injury which removes a parent from the home for a substantial period, or which disables the parent from providing the degree of affection, society and companionship previously provided the child, may necessitate expenditures by the parent to obtain for the child services or

---

21. *Borer v. American Airlines, Inc., supra,* 19 Cal.3d p. 447, 138 Cal.Rptr. 302, 563 P.2d 858.

22. See the opinions of the New Jersey and California Supreme Courts in the *Russell* and *Borer* cases, *supra.*

companionship that the parent would normally have provided. Although the child should have no independent right of recovery, the cost of substitute services should be recoverable in the injured parent's action.

VII

We would reverse the decision of the Court of Appeals and affirm the summary judgment granted by the trial court.

COLEMAN, C. J., and RYAN, J., concur.

Notes

1. *Parental-Child Consortium.* The majority of states continue to refuse to recognize a child's action for the loss of consortium of an injured parent. *See, e.g.,* Salin v. Kloempken, 322 N.W.2d 736 (Minn.1982); De Angelis v. Lutheran Med. Ctr., 58 N.Y.2d 1053, 462 N.Y.S.2d 626, 449 N.E.2d 406 (1983)(*per curiam*); Steiner v. Bell Tel. Co. of Pa., 358 Pa.Super. 505, 517 A.2d 1348 (1986), *affirmed per curiam* 518 Pa. 57, 540 A.2d 266 (1988); Still v. Baptist Hosp., Inc., 755 S.W.2d 807 (Tenn.App.1988). A number of courts that have recognized the child's consortium claim have refused to recognize a parent's consortium claim for injuries to the child. *See* Norman v. Massachusetts Bay Transp. Auth'y, 403 Mass. 303, 529 N.E.2d 139 (1988); Ferriter v. Daniel O'Connell's Sons, Inc., 381 Mass. 507, 413 N.E.2d 690 (1980); Dralle v. Ruder, 124 Ill.2d 61, 124 Ill.Dec. 389, 529 N.E.2d 209 (1988). Among the few cases recognizing a parent's action for the loss of a child's consortium are Shockley v. Prier, 66 Wis.2d 394, 225 N.W.2d 495 (1975);[23] Frank v. Superior Court, 150 Ariz. 228, 722 P.2d 955 (1986). In Sizemore v. Smock, 430 Mich. 283, 422 N.W.2d 666 (1988), the court refused to extend its decision in *Berger v. Weber* to cover the parent's action for the loss of a child's society and companionship.

> The plaintiffs' argument has compelling sympathetic and logical appeal. [The dissenting opinion] relies heavily on the reciprocal nature of the intangible elements protected by the consortium claim in the parent-child context in support of his position. We agree that any attempt to draw a meaningful distinction on the basis of the sentimental aspects of the consortium claim between the parties in the parent-child relationship would be specious and unavoidably futile. Nevertheless, when this Court is confronted with the task of determining whether to expand the scope of a negligent defendant's liability and the conditions of recovery, it must look beyond logical analogies and balance the arguments in support of recognizing a new cause of action against public policy considerations and the social consequences of imposing yet another level of liability.

430 Mich. at 292, 422 N.W.2d at 670. What considerations might justify distinguishing the parental claim for consortium from the child's claim for consortium?

2. *Spousal Consortium.* The cause of action for spousal consortium has evolved over time, in part because the legal and cultural fabric relating to marriage has changed. At common law, the original rationale for the husband's consortium claim was the notion that the man's loss of the wife's domestic services was basically equivalent to the loss of a servant's services. Once the loss of domestic services was shown, and for all intents and purposes

23. Stepparents, however, have been held not to be able to bring such an action. Gar-   rett v. City of New Berlin, 122 Wis.2d 223, 362 N.W.2d 137 (1985).

this loss was presumed, the husband also could recover for loss of companionship and the opportunity to have sexual relations. The husband could also recover in his action any medical expenses he had incurred for his wife; this is because the husband bore a legal obligation to pay for those expenses. (The status of women at common law, to the extent it affects tort law, will be further discussed in Chapter Twenty-two, *infra.*)

Before passage of the married women's property acts of the latter portion of the nineteenth century, the husband was a necessary party in the wife's action for her own injuries. Thus, it became customary to join in the same lawsuit both the wife's injury claim and the husband's consortium claim. For reasons of convenience, this practice continues today despite the wife's legal capacity to bring an action in her own name.

At common law, however, the wife did not have a consortium claim for her husband's injuries. This changed following the passage of the married women's acts. Interestingly, the change did not initially take the direction of granting the wife an action for loss of consortium. Rather, a number of jurisdictions abolished the cause of action for consortium altogether, partly on the theory that the married women's acts gave the wife the sole right to bring an action for loss of earnings and the inability to perform household services. *See, e.g.,* Feneff v. New York Central & Hudson River Railroad Co., 203 Mass. 278, 89 N.E. 436 (1909), *reaffirmed* in Lombardo v. D. F. Frangioso & Co., 359 Mass. 529, 269 N.E.2d 836 (1971), *overruled* in Diaz v. Eli Lilly and Co., 364 Mass. 153, 302 N.E.2d 555 (1973); Helmstetler v. Duke Power Co., 224 N.C. 821, 32 S.E.2d 611 (1945), *overruled* in Nicholson v. Hugh Chatham Memorial Hospital, Inc., 300 N.C. 295, 266 S.E.2d 818 (1980).

With the decision of Hitaffer v. Argonne Co., 183 F.2d 811 (D.C.Cir.1950), the momentum gradually swung the other way. Most states now permit either a husband or a wife to bring an action for loss of the consortium of an injured spouse. In England, the House of Lords refused to extend the loss of consortium action to actions brought by wives. Best v. Samuel Fox & Co., [1952] A.C. 716. In § 2 of the Administration of Justice Act, 1982, c. 53, Parliament completely abolished the husband's action for loss of consortium and also a parent's action for the deprivation of the services of a child, as well as the common-law actions for the deprivation of the services of a menial servant and for the deprivation of the services of a female servant by raping or seducing her.

3. *Categories of Loss Included.* The nomenclature for these types of claims differs among jurisdictions. Some refer to "loss of consortium," others to the "loss of consortium and household services," and still others to "loss of consortium, companionship and society, and services." Whatever the term for the cause of action, virtually all jurisdictions allow the spouse to seek several distinct items of damage: loss of sexual relations, loss of services, and loss of companionship and society. The advent of caps may require jurisdictions to specify more precisely, in jury charges, the elements that traditionally were lumped together under "loss of consortium." For example, the court in Edmonds v. Murphy, 83 Md.App. 133, 170, 573 A.2d 853, 871 (Ct.Sp.App.1990) held that some portions of the consortium damages were subject to the cap, and that some portions were not. "[W]e hold that compensation for * * * services which can, but need not necessarily, be performed by hired help, was not includable within the cap." This decision was affirmed by the Maryland Court of Appeals, 325 Md. 342, 601 A.2d 102 (1992). If you were a trial judge in a

jurisdiction with a cap on "nonpecuniary damages," how would you submit to the jury the damages items for the spouse's derivative claim?

Which types of household services are included? Courts routinely allow compensation for loss of services if the plaintiff expends costs to pay for a replacement; an example would be the cost of child care incurred when the injured spouse no longer can provide those services as fully as before. But is an award of household services available when the noninjured spouse is the one who provides the service, such as taking on a greater role in cooking, cleaning, or child care? Put another way, should compensation be available for any lost services that have a market replacement, or instead should it be limited to those services for which the spouse actually purchases the market replacement? The cases do not speak unanimously on this. Consider the following:

> * * * The defendants maintain that * * the [plaintiffs] are not entitled to compensation for Mrs. Andrus' inability to perform household services because the plaintiffs did not incur any expenses because of this loss.
>
> * * *
>
> [R]ecovery for loss of household services is an item of special damages, requiring proof of a pecuniary loss. However, jurisprudence has also recognized the detrimental effect that one spouse's inability to perform household services can have on a marital relationship and has considered this factor in awarding damages for loss of consortium, even in the absence of pecuniary loss. * * *
>
> Because the Andruses have not shown that they incurred any expenses as a result of Mrs. Andrus' inability to perform household services, the plaintiffs are not entitled to an award for the value of the services as an element of economic loss. However, the effect that Mrs. Andrus' incapacity has had upon the couple's relationship is certainly relevant in determining a proper award for Mr. Andrus' loss of consortium.

Andrus v. Board, 626 So.2d 1224 (La.App.1993). Do you agree?

If the jurisdiction does allow the spouse to recover for loss of household services even if the spouse actually does not incur the expense of obtaining a market replacement, another question arises. Should every item or any degree of lost services be compensable, or should the noninjured spouse not be compensated for having to pick up domestic slack that was his or her "fair share" anyway? Courts do not explicitly articulate the latter as a rule, but consider the following.

> * * * As to the tangible elements of the consortium claim which could be found in the requirement of a spouse to assume greater responsibility for normal household duties or yard work, [the wife] testified that due to her accident her husband had to make his own bed and breakfast, occasionally take out the garbage and take the laundry down to the basement. Although an award on a derivative claim could be premised on such increased chores, we note that the jury could also have determined that his minimal activities were not sufficient to constitute a loss of services as a result of her injuries.

Lolik v. Big V Supermarkets Inc., 210 A.D.2d 703, 620 N.Y.S.2d 167 (1994), *rev'd on other grounds,* 86 N.Y.2d 744, 631 N.Y.S.2d 122, 655 N.E.2d 163 (1995).

4. *Derivative*? The consortium cause of action is generally deemed a "derivative" claim; that is, the consortium claim of one spouse derives from an injury to the other spouse. Most obviously, if one spouse suffers no injury, then the other spouse has no consortium claim. Yet the claim for consortium is also routinely deemed a "separate and independent" claim. Courts often say both that the claim is derivative and that it is separate and independent. *See* Orange County v. Piper, 523 So.2d 196, 198 (Fla.Dist.Ct.App.1988)("loss of consortium is a separate cause of action belonging to the spouse of the injured married partner, and though derivative in the sense of being occasioned by injury to the spouse, it is a direct injury to the spouse who has lost the consortium."); Barchfeld v. Nunley, 395 Pa.Super. 517, 577 A.2d 910, 912 (Pa.Super.Ct.1990)("loss of consortium claim is a derivative of the personal injury claim, but, at the same time, it is separate and distinct from the [physically injured] spouse's personal injury claim."); Torchia v. Aetna Casualty & Sur. Co., 804 S.W.2d 219, 225 (Tex.Ct.App.1991)(although a wife's claim for loss of consortium is derivative because liability of the tortfeasor to her husband must first be established, the claim is nevertheless independent from her husband's negligence action). Courts that use both characterizations might mean that the claim is derivative in the sense that it requires an injury (or a compensable injury) to the other spouse, but that the claim is separately or distinctly "owned" by the spouse bringing the claim. Or the side-by-side existence of these characterizations might mean that the jurisdiction has not fully worked out how "separate" the consortium claim really is.

The characterization matters because a number of thorny questions have arisen about when an obstacle to the injury claim of the injured spouse—such as the injured spouse's contributory negligence, immunity, or release by the injured spouse—will also serve as an obstacle to the consortium claim. Consider first the issue of the injured person's own negligence. Jurisdictions split over whether this should have a reducing effect on the spouse's consortium claim as well. Most jurisdictions conclude that it should, but a substantial minority disagrees. Cases allowing the defense include Lee v. Colorado Dept. of Health, 718 P.2d 221 (Colo.1986); Runcorn v. Shearer Lumber Products, Inc., 107 Idaho 389, 690 P.2d 324 (1984); Eggert v. Working, 599 P.2d 1389 (Alaska 1979); Hamm v. City of Milton, 358 So.2d 121 (Fla.App.1978). Rejecting the applicability of the defense are, among others, Fuller v. Buhrow, 292 N.W.2d 672 (Iowa 1980); Herold v. Burlington Northern, Inc., 761 F.2d 1241 (8th Cir.1985), *cert. denied* 474 U.S. 888, 106 S.Ct. 208, 88 L.Ed.2d 177 (predicting what North Dakota law would be); Christie v. Maxwell, 40 Wash. App. 40, 696 P.2d 1256 (1985); Brann v. Exeter Clinic, Inc., 127 N.H. 155, 498 A.2d 334 (1985); Feltch v. General Rental Co., 383 Mass. 603, 421 N.E.2d 67 (1981).

Courts also have addressed whether the injured spouse's pre-injury or post-injury release of a tort claim, even if effective to release that spouse's tort claim, also bars the other spouse's consortium claim. A few jurisdictions hold that release by the physically injured spouse does apply to the consortium claim. *See* Conradt v. Four Star Promotions, Inc., 45 Wn.App. 847, 728 P.2d 617 (1986). But most courts hold to the contrary. *See* Groves v. Firebird Raceway, Inc., 67 F.3d 306 (9th Cir.1995)(holding to this effect and summarizing caselaw on both pre-injury and post-injury release); Bowen v. Kil–Kare, Inc., 63 Ohio St.3d 84, 585 N.E.2d 384 (1992). These holdings include jurisdictions that have allowed the consortium claim to be reduced by the physically injured spouse's contributory negligence. *See* Groves v. Firebird

Raceway, Inc., 67 F.3d 306 (9th Cir.1995)(predicting that Idaho courts would not allow release by the one spouse to bar the other spouse's consortium claim, even though Idaho courts do allow the consortium claim to be reduced by the other spouse's contributory negligence). Is there any theoretical or practical justification for holding that the defense of contributory negligence is available but not the defense of release?

5. *Cohabiting Adults.* There initially were a few federal diversity cases recognizing a loss of consortium action in situations of cohabiting adults. *See, e.g.,* Bulloch v. United States, 487 F.Supp. 1078 (D.N.J.1980)(couple divorced after twenty years began to cohabit but had not remarried as of time of trial); Sutherland v. Auch Inter–Borough Transit Co., 366 F.Supp. 127 (E.D.Pa.1973)(couple engaged at time of injury and married less than a month after injury). These cases were then followed by Butcher v. Superior Court, 139 Cal.App.3d 58, 188 Cal.Rptr. 503 (1983), which was prepared to recognize the action when the relationship was "stable and significant." In *Butcher* the couple, who claimed to consider themselves as having a "common-law" marriage, had lived together for almost twelve years, had two children together, and even maintained joint bank accounts. Almost all these cases have, however, either been repudiated or not followed. The *Butcher* case was expressly disapproved by the Supreme Court of California in Elden v. Sheldon, 46 Cal.3d 267, 250 Cal.Rptr. 254, 758 P.2d 582 (1988). *But cf.* Dunphy v. Gregor, 136 N.J. 99, 642 A.2d 372 (1994).

B. FATAL INJURIES: WRONGFUL DEATH AND SURVIVAL AC- TIONS

1. *Introduction*

An understanding of fatal injury damages requires some background about the role of statutes in this area. Until the passage of considerable tort reform legislation from the mid–1970s to the present, the law relating to tort damages for non-death injuries was almost entirely the work of common law courts, not statutory enactments by legislatures. The same has never been true of fatal injuries. Rather, in almost every state, whether and to what extent plaintiffs can recover as a result of fatal injuries is governed by statute. This is because, at early common law, death extinguished any tort claim of the decedent, and no family members or loved ones had any claim for damages arising from another's death. Beginning in the nineteenth century, however, virtually every state eventually passed some type of statute or statutes allowing two different types of claims: what usually is termed a "wrongful death" action, and what usually is termed a "survival" action.

Wrongful death statutes usually create a cause of action for certain designated relatives—usually the parents, children, and spouse—for the injuries that the decedent's death has inflicted on them. The first wrongful death statute was Lord Campbell's Act, passed in England in 1846, 9 & 10 Vict. c. 93 (1846). It created a cause of action "for the benefit of the wife, husband, parent and child" of the deceased, and provided that the "jury may give such damages as they may think proportioned to the injury resulting from such death. * * *"

The damages recoverable under wrongful death claims can include, depending on the jurisdiction, any or all of the following: (1) the financial contributions that the decedent would have made to the beneficiary had the beneficiary lived a normal life expectancy (such as the wages that the decedent parent would have spent in feeding, caring for, and educating the child); (2) the services, care and advice of a pecuniary nature that the deceased would have given to the beneficiary (such as child care or home maintenance services rendered by a parent); (3) the beneficiary's loss of companionship and society of the decedent; (4) the grief and anguish experienced by the beneficiary over death; and (5) the loss of the inheritance that the beneficiary would have received if the decedent had lived a normal life span. Jurisdictional variation is substantial. Texas, for instance, allows compensation for all these items; a few jurisdictions allow for only 1 and 2.

A survival claim, by contrast, usually refers to the claim filed by the estate of the decedent for the legally compensable losses that the decedent has suffered. Survival statutes are so named because they provide that some or all tort claims[24] survive the death of the tort victim and become an asset of the estate. This is so whether or not the tortious wrong caused the death. For instance, suppose that a defendant tortiously caused a severe back injury that resulted in considerable pain, medical expenses, and lost wage earning capacity; the victim then dies of an unrelated cause, such as a heart attack, almost two years after sustaining the back injury. The survival statute would allow the person's estate to pursue the back injury claim and seek the damages available for the back injury—two years' worth of lost earnings, pain, and medical expenses. In many other cases, of course, the tortious injury proves to be fatal, either immediately or eventually. Again, the victim's estate can use the survival statute to bring a claim against the tortfeasor for whatever death damages the law allows the estate to recover. These damages differ among jurisdictions, but typically the recoverable damages include: (1) the pre-death conscious pain and suffering and mental anguish that the decedent experienced; (2) the medical expenses caused by the injury; (3) pre-death lost earnings caused by the injury; (4) funeral expenses. For procedural convenience, when the injury results in death, some states provide that the only remedy is under the wrongful death act. After payment of the amounts recoverable by the beneficiaries under the wrongful death action, the remainder of the judgment is paid to the estate. Mich. Comp. Laws Ann. §§ 600.2921–2922.

These descriptions are of the most typical types of survival and wrongful death statutes. A few jurisdictions have wrongful death statutes that measure the compensable damages by the loss to the estate rather than by the loss to the beneficiary or beneficiaries. See Tenn. Code Ann. §§ 20–5–106; 20–5–113; Memphis S.R. Co. v. Cooper, 203 Tenn. 425, 313 S.W.2d 444 (1958).

2. Losses Relating to the Decedent's Earning Power or Wealth

Consider a thirty-five year old married woman and mother of young children, who is in a car crash and sustains injuries that, after a three-day

---

24. The survival statutes often specifically exclude the survivability of defamation actions, malicious prosecution, and invasion of privacy. Contrast Mich.Comp.Laws Ann. § 600.2921 (providing that "[a]ll actions and claims survive death") with N.C.Gen.Stat. § 28a–18–1 (providing that "libel and for slander, except slander of title, * * * [and] false imprisonment * * * do not survive"). On the general subject *see* Note, *Challenging the Exclusion of Libel and Slander from Survival Statutes*, 1984, U.Ill.L.Rev. 423 (1984).

stay in a hospital, prove to be fatal. Let us assume that she earned a salary (including benefits) of $55,000 during the year of her death, and that her work life expectancy would have been another thirty years, with salary and benefit increases along the way. The evidence could show that, of the income she would have earned over those years, some of it (1) would have been spent on the decedent herself; that is, would have gone toward her own personal consumption; (2) would have been spent on feeding, clothing, educating, caring, and supporting in many ways the children, during their years of minority and probably after they reached majority age; (3) would have been spent in support of or on behalf of her spouse (for instance, her income might have helped pay for his continuing education, or for the home in which he lived along with her and the family); (4) would have been spent to help support the expenses of nursing care for her aged parents; (5) would have been spent on persons or causes other than her husband, children, and parents (for instance, friends and charities); and (6) would have been saved over time, yielding some net sum that, at the time when she died after a normal life expectancy, would have been bequeathed to whomever she chose.

Consider how the tort system would handle all these categories if the woman, rather than being fatally injured, had sustained nonfatal but extremely disabling injuries that rendered her virtually unable to earn income for the duration of her life expectancy. All the above categories would be compensable, not necessarily as labeled above, but by means of an award to the woman of a sum of money that represents, discounted to present value, the entirety of her lost future earning capacity. (It is possible that the spousal claim for loss of services might include some of the financial contributions she would have made to her husband, but the point for now is that the tort system, in the nonfatal injury context, would allow full compensation.)

If tort were to aim for full compensation in the death context, would all six dimensions of her lost income stream need to be compensable? Consider the first dimension—the portion of her earnings that would have gone toward her personal consumption. Most jurisdictions do not allow recovery for this item. *See, e.g.*, Sheffield v. Sheffield, 405 So.2d 1314 (Miss.1981). Why? If she is no longer alive to use those sums, then is their absence a loss at all? A loss that should be compensated? Now consider all the other dimensions of her lost income stream. If she is no longer alive, is the absence of those sums a loss?

Once we decide which aspects of the income stream represent losses, then the tort system could allow compensation by two methods. First, the tort system could basically do in the fatal case what it does in the nonfatal case: allow the injured person herself (that is, the estate) to recover a sum that reflects the present value of her lost future earning capacity (less the deduction for personal consumption that applies in death cases). Second, the tort system could split up this scenario into separate claims. For instance, the children, the spouse, and the parents each could have a claim for the financial contributions the mother would have made to them, and for the loss of inheritance. Most jurisdictions follow the latter approach, allowing an award to certain designated beneficiaries of the financial contributions and, perhaps, the loss of inheritance. Does the choice between the approaches matter? If so, what considerations might support each approach?

Deciding how to compensate for the decedent's lost earning stream becomes more complicated when the decedent does not die instantly, but is injured, experiences a loss of earning capacity for some time, and then dies. The typical approach is exemplified in Flowers v. Marshall, 208 Kan. 900, 494 P.2d 1184 (Kan.1972), in which the daughter brought two claims: the survival claim (in the daughter's capacity as legal administrator of the mother's estate), and the wrongful death claim (in the daughter's own capacity as a statutory beneficiary under the wrongful death statute).

The appeal presents a single question—whether recovery may be had in a survival action for loss of earnings and earning capacity beyond the time of the decedent's death where the death was caused by the defendant's negligence? The precise issue is one of first impression here.

* * *

The trial court held that under the survival statute recovery is limited to losses of the victim prior to his death, that is to say, recovery is permitted only for elements of damage occurring prior to death, including the decedent's pain and suffering, medical expenses and loss of time and earnings from the date of injury to the date of death.

* * * The [trial] court expressed concern that if future earnings beyond the time of death were permitted to be recovered in a survival action there could be a duplication of recovery and the effect would be to circumvent the legislative limitation prescribed in the wrongful death statute, considering the two statutes as a part of a single legislative plan or in pari materia.

* * *

* * * The survival statute, where applicable, abrogates the common law rule that a personal right of action dies with the person. It keeps alive in the name of the personal representative the decedent's own cause of action. Loss of earnings or earning capacity is recoverable by the decedent in his lifetime and should he live so long he might recover for that permanent total loss, based upon his life expectancy. On the other hand the decedent's heirs at law may recover for loss of support under the wrongful death act. It cannot be gainsaid that destruction of earning capacity may form the basis for the claim for this loss of support. Hence both statutes can be said to relate to the subject of loss of future earnings and earning capacity and to that extent they must be deemed to be in pari materia and subject to being construed together as complementary enactments.

A doubling up would be involved if recovery based on full loss of future earning capacity were to be allowed in both a survival and a wrongful death action, and this would be true even though the ultimate beneficiaries in the two actions might not always be the same. Such duplication would be punitive to the wrongdoer and we cannot believe the legislature intended such a result, keeping in mind the fact that the survival statute and the wrongful death statute were each enacted to supply a remedy which did not exist at common law, and where, as here, each cause of action is dependent on the same tortious act.

Historically the majority view in other jurisdictions has been that recovery for loss of earnings or earning capacity beyond the time of death was impermissible in a survival action although it must be recognized statutory provisions sometimes are distinctive in the various jurisdictions so as to account for the results reached. The general rule is stated in McCormick on Damages, s 94, p. 337, thus: 'In states where actions may be brought by the personal representative of the deceased under the Survival Act for the injury, and under the Death Act for the death, the damages in the survival action are limited to compensation for injuries actually accruing before death, that is, for the pain and suffering of the injured man and for his loss of earnings and his expenses of care and treatment.'

* * *

Accordingly, we hold that in an action under the survival statute to recover damages for personal injury to plaintiff's decedent who died as result of such injury, recovery may not be had for loss of earnings or earning capacity beyond the time of death.

Id. at 902–04, 494 P.2d at 1186–91.

3. *Loss of Services That Have a Market Replacement, and Losses That Have No Market Replacement*

To continue with our example, the young mother also provided services to family and community that can be monetized fairly easily to the extent that the services have market replacements. For instance, the mother provided volunteer help in her child's classroom once a month and answered calls on a community "crisis" line once every few weeks. The mother also did numerous services in the home and for children and spouse, whether providing child care, cooking, cleaning, homework assistance, driving, etc. Should all these be compensated, and if so via which type of claim—the survival claim of the estate, or the wrongful death claims of family members only?

And, of course, the mother's death will have inflicted many losses for which there is no market substitute. Her family and loved ones will experience grief, anguish, and the loss of a relationship with her. What is the decedent's own loss? If the injury had not proved fatal but only disabling, then tort law would allow compensation, via the categories of "impairment," "loss of life's pleasures," or "pain and suffering," for her reduced ability to engage in the activities and relationships she once valued. Obviously, the decedent no longer can experience life's pleasures and activities. Should this be compensated?

GREEN v. BITTNER

Supreme Court of New Jersey, 1980.
85 N.J. 1, 424 A.2d 210.

WILENTZ, C. J.

In the spring of her senior year at high school, Donna Green was killed in an automobile accident. She was a young woman of average intelligence and cheerful disposition; hard-working and conscientious both at home and at school; level-headed and dependable. As her counsel aptly stated in summation, she was "everybody's daughter," not just meaning normal, but what everybody would want a daughter to be.

This action was brought for her wrongful death under N.J.S.A. 2A:31–1 *et seq.* Liability having been established at a separate trial, the jury in these proceedings were to "give such damages as they shall deem fair and just with reference to the pecuniary injuries resulting from such death * * * to the persons entitled to any intestate personal property of the decedent." N.J.S.A. 2A:31–5. The jury apparently found that Donna's survivors, her parents and brothers and sisters, had suffered no pecuniary loss for they awarded no damages whatsoever. In effect her life was adjudicated worthless to others, in a pecuniary sense.

We reverse. Under the circumstances presented to us, such a verdict is a miscarriage of justice. * * * We remand for a new trial in accordance with this opinion on the issue of damages. We hold that when parents sue for the wrongful death of their child, damages should not be limited to the well-known elements of pecuniary loss such as the loss of the value of the child's anticipated help with household chores, or the loss of anticipated direct financial contributions by the child after he or she becomes a wage earner. We hold that in addition, the jury should be allowed, under appropriate circumstances, to award damages for the parents' loss of their child's companionship as they grow older, when it may be most needed and valuable, as well as the advice and guidance that often accompanies it. As noted later, these other losses will be confined to their pecuniary value, excluding emotional loss. Given this expansion of permissible recovery, a verdict finding no damages for the death of a child should ordinarily be set aside by the trial court and a new trial ordered. To sustain such a verdict "would result in a return to the outmoded doctrine that a child is a liability—not an asset." Bohrman v. Pennsylvania Railroad Co., 23 N.J.Super. 399, 409, 93 A.2d 190 (App.Div.1952). * * *

We intend, by so holding, to give juries in wrongful death cases involving children the same ability to do justice to their parents, within the limits of existing legislation, as they now have under our cases when children lose a parent. By thus expanding the permissible scope of recovery, we also hope to reduce the pressure on juries to award damages for the parents' emotional suffering, unquestionably the most substantial element of damages in these cases, but legally impermissible.

Donna was one of six children in a warm and close family. She was a good student, did her share of household tasks, including babysitting and keeping the younger children busy so that her mother was free to do other things. She worked after school, as well as on weekends and in the summer, and had done so since she was 14. She helped provide for her own material needs and was saving for her forthcoming graduation festivities. She had definite plans to enter college and ultimately to embark on a business career. Although others described her as fun-loving, ebullient and popular, her mother, who concurred, nevertheless characterized her as level-headed. She was always there when she was needed; she always came through. She was a good-hearted, devoted and dependable daughter.

At the close of the evidence the trial court charged the jury that their verdict, in accordance with N.J.S.A. 2A:31–5, was to reflect only past, present and future pecuniary losses to the survivors, including any direct financial contributions that Donna might have made, but was not to compensate for grief and sentimental losses. In addition, the trial judge stated, "the term financial loss also includes the reasonable value of benefits which would have been received by a survivor in the nature of services or assistance or guidance if the decedent had continued to live." He qualified this statement by explaining that the jury should "consider the benefits which Donna bestowed upon the survivors in the form of service or assistance; and * * * the guidance and training afforded by Donna to such survivor infants and the probabilities of whether and how long Donna would continue to have made such contribution to the welfare of other minor children who are now the survivors." As to the parents' losses, the judge stated: "You [the jury] should consider the services that Donna had performed about the household in the past, such as babysitting, cleaning and other types of home chores. In evaluating this claim, you may also consider the likelihood of any additional chores which * * * Donna would have undertaken had she grown older about the house." The jury was further instructed to deduct from the value thus determined the costs of feeding, clothing and educating Donna until her majority. This would have included the $4,000 her father was planning to spend for her college tuition.

After deliberating for approximately an hour and a half, the jury returned a verdict of no damages. Plaintiffs' motion for a new trial on damages was denied. The trial judge concluded that "it would be reasonable for this jury to come to [the] conclusion that the value of her services to babysit or to dry dishes was far exceeded by the cost to the family of feeding, clothing and educating her. The jury in this particular case followed literally the language of the statute and came to the conclusion that they reached." The judge noted that it is unusual for a jury to come in with a verdict of no recovery, and he expressed sympathy with the parents and their shock when they learned of no award for their daughter's death. He concluded, however, that a clear and convincing miscarriage of justice had not occurred. The Appellate Division affirmed this denial in an unreported opinion.

In fairness to the trial court, its instructions to the jury were substantially in accord with present case law. * * * The charge, as is usual in such cases, focused almost exclusively on the value of household chores that Donna might have performed in the future. While there was some reference to the possibility that she might also have rendered "assistance or guidance," subsequent qualification of this phrase must have led the jury to believe that, at least insofar as the parents were concerned, it referred to the same kind of services Donna had performed in the past, namely, household chores. The entire instruction was practically devoid of any suggestion of a different kind of assistance that a parent or sibling might have received from the decedent in the future. There was no reference, for instance, to the pecuniary value of companionship and advice that Donna might perhaps have given her parents as she and they grew older, the caretaking role that she might have fulfilled towards them over time, whether in the sense of actual physical care and companionship in the event of illness or old age, or services and chores performed simply out of a continuing sense of family obligation. As noted above, such a charge was not compelled by prior holdings, nor was it requested by counsel. The evidence, however, could have supported such a charge, and previous cases did not preclude it.[25]

The development of existing case law elsewhere suggests allowance of such damages as "pecuniary injuries" under wrongful death statutes. This development has probably been influenced by the inconsistent treatment in wrongful death cases between a parent's death and a child's death. In the case of a parent's death, in addition to the usual losses clearly having a monetary value, the law allows damages to be awarded to the surviving children for the loss of guidance and counsel which they might otherwise have received from the parent. The cases do not suggest that the calculation of such damages must cease after the child reaches majority. They are based on an ongoing relationship which exists in fact, regardless of any lack of legal duty on the part of the parent to render such guidance and despite the difficulty of placing a dollar value on it. Such damages are regularly allowed despite the total lack of proof of such dollar value and of the probability that such guidance and counsel would in fact have been rendered. * * * *See generally* S. Speiser, *Recovery for Wrongful Death* 2d § 3:47 (1975). For instance, the law has allowed damages for the loss of a mother's training and nurture * * *; and a father's guidance and advice * * *. It has done the same when the loss was that of a grandparent's solicitous care * * *; and even an adult brother's helpful services to a dependent sister * * *. In the case of a child's death, however, those services to be given a dollar value are almost invariably limited to household chores—as distinguished from cases where special circumstances suggest the probability of future financial contributions by the child to his parent, *e.g.*, where a child has exhibited extraordinary talents suggesting substantial earning capacity. * * * Cf. Gluckauf v. Pine Lake Beach Club, Inc., 78 N.J.Super. 8, 187 A.2d 357 (App.Div.1963)(15–year-old decedent had near-genius I.Q. and special aptitude for science); Kopko v. New York Live Poultry Trucking Co., 3 N.J.Misc. 498, 128 A. 870, aff'd, 102 N.J.L. 440, 131 A. 923 (Sup.Ct.1925)(12–year-old violinist had great talent). Some cases allow the jury to consider the possibility of post-majority direct financial help even from what appears to be an average child, given his earnings during minority and the family's special circumstances. * * * Our cases, however, have not recognized that parents whose child is killed

---

25. *But cf.* Cooper v. Shore Electric Co., 63 N.J.L. 558, 567, 44 A.2d 633 (E. & A.1899): "[T]he jury cannot take into consideration mental suffering or loss of society * * *" This proposition is discussed *infra*.

may lose as well the future pecuniary benefit of that child's guidance and counsel, much as the child would have lost theirs had either of them been killed. Nor have they acknowledged the pecuniary value to the parents of the anticipated companionship of the child when the parents are infirm or aged.

As suggested above, other states, sometimes similarly bound by legislation, sometimes by decisional law, have relaxed the strict pecuniary approach to damages for a child's death where its potential for harsh results is substantial. One of the most noteworthy of these efforts has occurred in Michigan. In Wycko v. Gnodtke, 361 Mich. 331, 105 N.W.2d 118 (1960), the Michigan Supreme Court rejected a strict pecuniary loss rule that its courts had engrafted onto a statute that had allowed recovery for losses of a pecuniary nature. The Michigan court pointed out that the era of child labor, and hence the fixation with earnings and services, was over. Rejecting "the bloodless bookkeeping imposed upon our juries by the savage exploitations of the last century," the court held that the worth of a child's life should henceforth be calculated according to his function as part of an ongoing family unit. When *Wycko* was overruled in Breckon v. Franklin Fuel Co., 383 Mich. 251, 174 N.W.2d 836 (1970), the Michigan Legislature responded by incorporating into its Wrongful Death Act a provision that damages may also include recovery for loss of society and companionship, thus affirming the result in *Wycko*. Mich.Stat.Ann. § 27A.2922. [The court here cited cases in Minnesota, Nebraska, and Washington rejecting the strict pecuniary loss rule.] * * * Similar results have occurred in California, Montana, Pennsylvania, South Dakota and the Virgin Islands. *See* S. Speiser, *Recovery for Wrongful Death* 2d § 3:49 at 318 n.3 (1975).

The New York courts, feeling trapped by the strict pecuniary loss limitation set forth in their Wrongful Death Act, have repeatedly criticized the rule and urged the Legislature to change it. * * * *See also* Bell v. Cox, 54 A.D.2d 920, 388 N.Y.S.2d 118 (1976) (change in pecuniary loss test for Legislature or Court of Appeals; nevertheless, $10,000 verdict for death of "loving and considerate" 19–year-old daughter who did not live home with parents held "shockingly inadequate"). * * *

The fact that parents are usually legally entitled to the services of their children until majority seems to have led us in New Jersey to the implicit conclusion that that is the limit of the parents' loss (other than prospective financial contributions). But continuing family relationships—uninterrupted by the death of a family member—encompass more than the exchange of physical chores around the house at various times during the family's history, and even more than direct financial contributions. Perhaps as significant is the apparent absence in infant death cases of the kind of expert testimony that might have helped courts to perceive a greater extent of loss than previously recognized. In any event, we see no reason why the same factual approach used in adult death cases should not be taken when it is a child who has been killed. There is nothing in the statute to distinguish one case from the other: "pecuniary injuries" suffered by the surviving next of kin is the standard for *all* wrongful death cases. N.J.S.A. 2A:31–5. As this Court has said in an infant death case, "the pecuniary injury designated by the statute is nothing more than a deprivation of a reasonable expectation of a pecuniary advantage which would have resulted by a continuance of the life of the deceased," Cooper v. Shore Electric Co., 63 N.J.L. 558, 567, 44 A. 633 (E. & A.1899).   * * *

What services, what activities, could a daughter or son reasonably have been expected to engage in but for their death and to what extent do any of them have monetary value? Just as the law recognizes that a child may continue performing services after age 18, and that monetary contributions may also be received by the parents thereafter when the child becomes productive, it should similarly recognize that the child may, as many do, provide valuable companionship and care as the parents get older. As noted above, our courts have not hesitated to recognize the need of children for physical help and care. Parents facing age or deteriorating health have the same need, and it is usually their children who satisfy that need. Indeed the loss of companionship and advice which a parent suffers when a child is killed will sometimes be as great as the loss of counsel and guidance which a child suffers when a parent is the victim.

Companionship and advice in this context must be limited strictly to their pecuniary element. The command of the statute is too clear to allow compensation, directly or indirectly, for emotional loss. Our cases uniformly so hold. * * *

Companionship, lost by death, to be compensable must be that which would have provided services substantially equivalent to those provided by the "companions" often hired today by the aged or infirm, or substantially equivalent to services provided by nurses or practical nurses.[26] And its value must be confined to what the marketplace would pay a stranger with similar qualifications[27] for performing such services. No pecuniary value may be attributed to the emotional pleasure that a parent gets when it is his or her child doing the caretaking rather than a stranger, although such pleasure will often be the primary value of the child's service, indeed, in reality, its most beneficial aspect. This loss of added emotional satisfaction that would have been derived from the child's companionship is fundamentally similar to the emotional suffering occasioned by the death. Both are emotional rather than "pecuniary injuries," one expressed in terms of actual emotional loss, the other in terms of lost prospective emotional satisfaction. In another sense, the loss of the prospective emotional satisfaction of the companionship of a child when one is older is but one example of the innumerable similar prospective losses occasioned by the child's death—all of which, plus much more, is included in the emotional suffering caused by the death.

26. Hired companions today perform a variety of services, primarily, however, simply keeping the employer company and administering to basic needs. They may prepare and serve meals, do grocery shopping, perform other errands, keep the home tidy, give medicines, make telephone calls, and generally make themselves useful—including making it possible for the employer to be outdoors. Care given by children to aging or infirm parents is often indistinguishable from those services. Children also often provide many of the services ordinarily rendered by practical nurses, such as bathing the bedridden, changing bandages, moving an immobilized patient, administering medication, spoon-feeding invalids, preparing special meals, keeping a sickroom tidy—even removing visitors if they tire the invalid. Companionship, in this sense, however, will not include true nursing services unless the decedent had or was likely to have special training.

27. One such obvious qualification—of pecuniary value—of the deceased child is the knowledge of the parent, his or her habits, likes, dislikes, weaknesses and strengths, all amounting to a complex patient history.

Given this jurisdiction's vastly expanded scope both of tort liability and of recoverable damages—including emotional loss, for instance, when a parent actually witnesses a child's death, Portee v. Jaffee, 84 N.J. 88, 417 A.2d 521 (1980)—we know of no public policy which would prohibit awarding damages that fully compensate for the loss of emotional pleasure in this situation, or indeed for the emotional suffering caused by the death. We recognize that our prohibition against such damages deprives the surviving parent of compensation for the real loss. That prohibition is not a matter of our choice, rather it is fundamental to the legislation.

The loss of guidance, advice and counsel is similarly to be confined to its pecuniary element. It is not the loss simply of the exchange of views, no matter how perceptive, when child and parent are together; it is certainly not the loss of the pleasure which accompanies such an exchange. Rather it is the loss of that kind of guidance, advice and counsel which all of us need from time to time in particular situations, for specific purposes, perhaps as an aid in making a business decision, or a decision affecting our lives generally, or even advice and guidance needed to relieve us from unremitting depression.[28] It must be the kind of advice, guidance or counsel that could be purchased from a business adviser, a therapist, or a trained counselor, for instance. That some of us obtain the same benefit without charge from spouses, friends or children does not strip it of pecuniary value.

Having defined the companionship and advice, loss of which is compensable in an action for the wrongful death of a child, we next address some of the concerns arising from this expansion of recovery in these cases.

Absent special circumstances, it could be claimed that the mere parent-child relationship does not show that it is more probable than not that such services would have been rendered had the child lived. Who knows what the child's circumstances would be or whether the parent would indeed become old or infirm and require such companionship, or need such advice at any time? Given the speculative quality of the inferences, it might further be questioned whether one could realistically attach an estimated pecuniary value to such services. Our answer is, even assuming no special circumstances are proven, that the nature of these cases has led our courts to allow damages even though the inferences, and the estimate of damages, are based on uncertainties. * * * When a parent dies and loss of advice, guidance and counsel is allowed to the surviving children, and when an infant child dies and loss of prospective services is allowed to the parents, the proof that suffices is the parent-child relationship and what we assume the jury can conclude from that relationship alone. Damages are allowed without any showing that the parent had actually been rendering valuable advice, or was likely to do so, or that the child—even if only five months old * * *—was likely to render services around the house. Even in this case the charge of the judge would have allowed the jury to find loss of

---

28. "Clearly, advice and counsel which might have been given appellees by their son in areas of business decisions, family financial decisions, and personal dilemmas which they might encounter, have monetary value." Borak v. Bridge, 524 S.W.2d 773, 776 (Tex.Civ.App.1975)(decedent, a 21-year-old college student, a moral and devoted son); see also Fussner v. Andert, 261 Minn. 347, 113 N.W.2d 355, 359 (1961)(jury must consider value of child's advice, counsel and guidance among other things).

prospective financial contributions, although there was nothing in the record suggesting that Donna would have made such. * * * We acknowledge that it is more likely that parents will render advice and counsel to children than the reverse, and that it is more likely that children will render services about the house when they are minors than that they will provide valuable companionship after the parents become aged or infirm. But we are not about to deny this pecuniary element of prospective companionship and advice from a child because it may be somewhat more conjectural. Our tradition in these cases is to the contrary. Given a normal parent-child relationship, a jury could very well find it is sufficiently probable, had the child lived, that at some point he or she would have rendered the kind of companionship services mentioned herein and, although perhaps even somewhat more conjectural, the kind of advice, guidance and counsel we have described.[29] It will be up to the jury to decide what services would have been rendered, and what their value is, subject to no more or no less control, direction, and guidance from the court than occurs in other wrongful death cases. There need be no showing that companionship and advice will probably be purchased by the parent because of the child's death; it is sufficient that the deceased would have rendered them.

Obviously the use of an expert in these cases could be most helpful, along with such detailed information concerning family circumstances as counsel can provide. * * *

Ascertaining the present value of the prospective services presents no particular problem simply because they will be rendered in the distant future. The same mathematics which allow discounting the value of prospective services to be rendered in two years can be applied to those which may be rendered in twenty.

We do not regard our holding concerning the compensability of loss of companionship as an expansion of recovery in these cases except in the sense that prior cases have not explicitly recognized this element of damage. The loss is within the statutory limit of "pecuniary injuries" and its allowance does not overrule prior cases. * * * In none of these cases, apparently, did counsel attempt to isolate from the ordinary "loss of society and companionship" those elements having a distinctly pecuniary value. * * * The emotional loss flowing from a loss of companionship and society is still beyond the reach of any recovery in a wrongful death action; not so the pecuniary element.

Extension of the scope of recovery in cases involving a child's death should reduce the adverse effect the present restrictive rules probably have on juries. Verdicts in these cases sometimes result from the jury's desire to award the parents something for their emotional suffering (not permitted by law) in view of the severely restricted permissible items of recovery. A compassionate jury, wanting to give the parents something substantial for their emotional loss but being told, in effect, that the measure of

---

29. But compare the degree of speculation suggested by the Appellate Division in another context: "When claim is made by a child of tender years for the death of his parent, it is reasonable to assume, even if he is being supported by one who has no obligation to support him, that at some time before maturity he might have to seek the parent's help." State v. Gosnell, 106 N.J.Super. 279, 284, 255 A.2d 769 (App.Div.1969).

recovery is the value of the household chores that might have been performed less the future cost to the parents of maintaining the child, is inclined to set an unrealistically high value on those household chores. A more conscientious jury will add up the numbers and come in with zero. By allowing the jury realistically to measure these additional elements of the losses which may be suffered by parents when a child is killed, we believe that they will be more likely to return verdicts based upon the judge's charge, rather than, as now, to find a way to do some kind of justice despite the judge's charge. Our expectation is that verdicts will more nearly reflect the actual pecuniary losses suffered.

One further consideration suggests that this extension of recovery is warranted. Parents live longer today; the proportion of people age 65 and over in our population continues to grow. And their children retire earlier, become independent sooner, and free of the obligation to support the grandchildren sooner. We suspect that there are many more children aged 45 to 55 who are faced with their parents' need for care and guidance than there were in the past, and who are able to render such care and guidance along with whatever help they may from time to time give to their emancipated children. Nursing homes are not the only vehicle for this assistance. The parents' need is real, and when a middle-aged son or daughter is not there because of a wrongful death, a prospective pecuniary advantage of the aged or infirm parent has been lost. Another factor is of similar significance: while the death rate of the older part of our population continues to decrease, that of the younger has started to increase.[30]

For the reasons set forth above, the decision of the Appellate Division is reversed and the matter is remanded for a new trial as to damages only.

Notes

1. *Pecuniary loss.* In many American jurisdictions, wrongful death statutes, like the one in Green v. Bittner, used the term "pecuniary loss." As a result, for a long time it was generally impossible to recover anything for the loss of the deceased's companionship. With regard to minor children, the pecuniary loss suffered by the surviving parents and siblings, as measured by the actual services, assistance, and financial contributions that they might have expected to receive had the deceased minor child lived, is likely to be relatively small, if not non-existent. The response to this situation has either been judicial interpretation of pecuniary loss to include loss of companionship or, as is becoming increasingly common, legislative amendment of the statutory scheme.

Nevertheless, as noted in the *Green* case, a declining but still significant number of jurisdictions have refused to depart from a restrictive notion of what constitutes pecuniary loss. The current version of the New York wrongful death statute still talks in terms of "pecuniary injury." N.Y.Est.Powers & Trusts L. § 5–4.3 (McKinney 1995). Colorado is another state in which the concept of pecuniary loss is narrowly construed. *See* Espinoza v. O'Dell, 633 P.2d 455, 464 (Colo.1981), *cert. denied* 456 U.S. 430, 102 S.Ct. 1865, 72 L.Ed.2d

30. *U.S. Dep't of Health and Human Services, Health: United States, 1980* (Public Health Service No. 81–1232)(overall death rate for Americans dropped 20 percent from 1960 to 1978 while the death rate for youths (15–24) rose by 11 percent from 1960 to 1978).

237 (1982). *See also* Beikmann v. International Playtex, Inc., 658 F.Supp. 255 (D.Colo.1987).

In jurisdictions whose wrongful death statutes allow for "actual damages," courts have been more free to depart from the pecuniary approach. An example is the Texas Supreme Court's decision in Sanchez v. Schindler, 651 S.W.2d 249 (Tex.1983), which interpreted the wrongful death statute's reference to "actual damages" to include loss of companionship and society (in both its pecuniary and its nonpecuniary dimensions) and mental anguish.

2. *Mental anguish and Grief.* Many jurisdictions that have departed from the strict pecuniary approach allow the nonpecuniary recovery to include mental anguish and grief. Are you persuaded by the following analysis that these aspects of loss are analytically and practically distinguishable?

> The definitions for mental anguish, and loss of society and companionship, present more difficulty. Some have suggested that these damages necessarily overlap. Both of these awards compensate non-economic losses while pecuniary loss and loss of inheritance damages represent direct economic losses. Mental anguish represents an emotional response to the wrongful death itself. * * * Loss of society, on the other hand, constitutes a loss of positive benefits which flowed to the family from the decedent's having been a part of it. * * * Mental anguish is concerned "not with the benefits [the beneficiaries] have lost, but with the issue of compensating them for their harrowing experience resulting from the death of a loved one." 1 S. Speiser, Recovery for Wrongful Death 2d s 3:52 at 327 (1975). Loss of society asks, "what positive benefits have been taken away from the beneficiaries by reason of the wrongful death?" Mental anguish damages ask about the negative side: "what deleterious effect has the death, as such, had upon the claimants?" *Id.* Mental anguish and loss of society and companionship are distinguishable. * * *

> In the court's charge in wrongful death cases, mental anguish shall be defined as the emotional pain, torment, and suffering that the named plaintiff would, in reasonable probability, experience from the death of the family member. Companionship and society shall be defined as the positive benefits flowing from the love, comfort, companionship, and society the named plaintiff would, in reasonable probability, experience if the decedent lived.

> In awarding damages for mental anguish and loss of society and companionship in a wrongful death case, the trier of fact shall be instructed that it may consider (1) the relationship between husband and wife, or a parent and child; (2) the living arrangements of the parties; (3) any absence of the deceased from the beneficiary for extended periods; (4) the harmony of family relations; and (5) common interests and activities.

> The trier of fact should also be instructed that mental anguish and loss of society and companionship are separate elements of recovery. Damages should not overlap, and no double recovery should be allowed. The jury should be instructed: "in awarding damages for loss of society and companionship, if any, you should not consider the mental anguish, if any, caused by the death of [the deceased]." A corresponding instruction would be appropriate for the damage issues on mental anguish, loss of inheritance, and pecuniary loss.

Moore v. Lillebo, 722 S.W.2d 683, 688 (Tex.1986).

3. *Loss of the Pleasures of Life.* As we saw in Chapter 10, in the nondeath context, the injured person may recover damages for the loss of life's pleasures, either as a separate category of damages or as part of a damage award for "impairment" or "pain and suffering." Most jurisdictions that have considered the issue in the death context have rejected the recoverability of such damages. Several courts have agreed with the rationale of the Pennsylvania Supreme Court:

> Even where the victim survives a compensable injury, this Court has never held that loss of life's pleasures could be compensated other than as a component of pain and suffering. Indeed, the two types of loss are interrelated. * * * Thus, to a large extent it has been the plaintiff's consciousness of his or her inability to enjoy life that we have compensated under the rubric of "loss of life's pleasures". Unlike one who is permanently injured, one who dies as a result of injuries is not condemned to watch life's amenities pass by. Unless we are to equate loss of life's pleasures with loss of life itself, we must view it as something that is compensable only for a living plaintiff who has suffered from that loss. It follows that * * * damages for the pain and suffering that may flow from the loss of life's pleasures should only be recovered for the period of time between the accident and the decedent's death.

Willinger v. Mercy Cloud Catholic Medical Center, 482 Pa. 441, 393 A.2d 1188, 1191 (1978).

A few federal courts have allowed recovery for such damages under federal civil rights statutes. *See* Sherrod v. Berry, 629 F.Supp. 159 (N.D.Ill.1985). The district court's decision in Sherrod was initially affirmed by the Seventh Circuit, but that appellate opinion was subsequently vacated on a motion for rehearing en banc. Sherrod v. Berry, 827 F.2d 195 (7th Cir.1987), *vacated,* 835 F.2d 1222 (7th Cir.1988)(en banc). Upon rehearing en banc, the Seventh Circuit reversed the district court's decision and remanded for a new trial due to error concerning liability issues. Sherrod v. Berry, 856 F.2d 802 (7th Cir.1988)(en banc).

4. *Who May Recover.* What if the beneficiary designated by statute is an especially unappealing one? In Crosby v. Corley, 528 So.2d 1141 (Ala.1988), the Alabama Supreme Court considered a father's right to share in the proceeds of a wrongful death settlement arising from the death of his daughter. The decedent's mother (now divorced from her father) and her siblings all swore in affidavits that the father had a history of drunken physical and mental abuse, as well as sexual abuse of the decedent.

> Only in the situation when the one seeking to share has caused the death of the intestate have the courts disregarded the clear meaning of a distribution statute and fashioned a different result. * * *

> In this case, the father's alleged wrongful conduct did not cause the death of his daughter, and therefore, by receiving his statutorily mandated share of the wrongful death proceeds, he is not profiting from his own wrongful act. Appellees strongly contend, however, that the legislature intended that a parent who continuously abused his child physically, sexually, and mentally should not benefit financially from the child's death. We can find no basis for this conclusion, especially where there has been no termination of parental rights prior to the death of the child.

> The legislature, by mandating that wrongful death proceeds be distributed according to the statute of intestate distribution, necessarily perceived that some beneficiaries would be totally unworthy of inheriting. The

statutory law of intestate succession is not controlled by, nor conditioned upon, equitable considerations of worthiness, fitness, and misconduct, etc. On the contrary, it is controlled by a set of rules that attempt to dispose of the deceased's property in a way the deceased would have had a will been executed, by recognizing the natural law of consanguinity, or of blood, and the natural affections of a person toward those nearest him in that relationship. * * * The distributions listed in the statute mandate who shall inherit, without exceptions. The probate process necessitates such mandates in order to simplify the process and avoid floods of litigation over who the deceased would have intended to inherit.

Crosby v. Corley, 528 So.2d 1141, 1143 (Ala.1988).

Consider again the categories of wrongful death damages that are available in some jurisdictions (listed above). As to which of these categories would the beneficiary's personal qualities, or the quality or nature of the beneficiary's relationship with the decedent, be relevant?

5. *Remarriage.* When a spouse has died, should the other spouse's remarriage be admissible on damages? The great majority of jurisdictions hold that it is not. *See, e.g.,* Seaboard Cost Line RR Co. v. Hill, 270 So.2d 359 (Fla.1972):

Under the [wrongful death] statute and the case law interpreting it, the widow's recoverable damages are all losses occasioned by her husband's death. It, therefore, follows that such damages are not subject to mitigation because their source is the husband's death. Although the hardship imposed upon the widow by her husband's death may be alleviated by a second marriage, the damages flowing from the death of the first husband are in nowise affected.

Is this reasoning convincing? As another rationale for the majority rule, courts have analogized the rule to the collateral source rule. Is this analogy persuasive? Are there other potential justifications for the rule?

6. *Statutes of Limitation.* Most states have special statutes of limitation governing wrongful death actions. A controverted issue is when this statutory period begins to run: at the time of injury or at the time of death? When the statute is unclear, most courts have held that the statute begins to run on the date of death. A related problem is what happens if a person is injured, lingers for a long time and then dies as a result of his original injuries but after the applicable tort statute of limitations has run. There is a conflict of authority on this point. In a jurisdiction where the wrongful death statute closely resembles the provision in Lord Campbell's Act that "whenever the death of a person shall be caused by wrongful act * * * such as would (if death had not ensued) have entitled the party injured to maintain an action * * *" the judicial tendency is to hold the action barred. The ground for doing so is that, the statute of limitations having run, the party injured, at the time of death, could not have maintained an action. *See, e.g.,* Kelliher v. New York Central & Hudson River Railroad Co., 212 N.Y. 207, 105 N.E. 824 (1914).

7. *Limits on Damages Recoverable.* At one time more than twenty states had statutory limitations on the overall amount that could be recovered in a wrongful death action. As recently as 1965 there were over ten states with such limitations. Eventually virtually every state abolished these general limitations. Yet statutes in some states now limit certain types of damages available in death cases. For instance, Kan.Stat.Ann. 60–1903 (1995) limits the

aggregate damages recoverable other than "pecuniary loss sustained by an heir at law" to $100,000. There are similar provisions in other states. Tort reform statutes setting caps on nonpecuniary damages are not always clear about whether they apply in death contexts. *See* United States v. Streidel, 329 Md. 533, 620 A.2d 905 (1993) (holding that the Maryland tort reform statute's cap of $350,000 on noneconomic damages in "personal injury" cases does not apply to wrongful death actions).

8. *The Derivative Nature of the Claim.* The wrongful death claim, like nonfatal consortium claims, is deemed to be derivative. This means that the negligence of the deceased will reduce the beneficiary's recovery, according to the comparative negligence principles of the jurisdiction. A different question is whether the beneficiary's own negligence will have a reducing effect. Most jurisdictions hold that it will, to the extent that the recovery sought is the damages to the beneficiary. If the action is the survival claim of the estate, then a wrongful death beneficiary's negligence usually will not reduce the estate's own recovery.

Chapter 12

FETAL INJURIES, PRECONCEPTION TORTS, AND CHILDREN WITH DISABILITIES

A. PHYSICAL INJURY TO A FETUS

1. When the Child is Born Alive But With a Disability Resulting From the Tortfeasor's Conduct

A fetus might sustain prenatal injuries and then be born alive, with a disability or impairment that results from those injuries; the resulting suit might seek full tort damages for the consequences of the injury. The earliest opinions rejected a cause of action in such cases. Eventually, however, a majority of courts allowed such actions so long as the injuries occurred when the fetus was viable; that is, capable of surviving outside the womb. Currently, most courts reject the viability requirement. This seems sensible not only given how difficult it is to ascertain the exact point of viability for any particular fetus but also as a matter of common sense. Once it is accepted that the fetus has a separate existence from the mother from the moment of conception, the salient factor in any action by the child is the damages it has suffered, not the precise moment when the injury was inflicted.

What if the allegedly negligent actor is the mother? For instance, suppose that the mother's negligent driving causes an accident resulting in prenatal injuries, or that the mother consumes alcohol or drugs and thus causes injury to the fetus and a resulting disability in the child. One obstacle to such suits for many years was the doctrine of intrafamily tort immunities, discussed in more detail in Chapter 22. As the intrafamily tort immunities have fallen, however, courts have had to face squarely the question whether the child in such cases should have a tort claim against the mother. Thus far, a number of courts have denied such a claim. Consider the reasoning in Stallman v. Youngquist, 125 Ill.2d 267, 126 Ill.Dec. 60, 531 N.E.2d 355 (1988), in which a child sued her mother for prenatal injuries allegedly resulting from the negligent driving of the mother.

> This court has never been asked to decide if, by becoming pregnant, a woman exposes herself to a future lawsuit by or on behalf of

the fetus which will become her child. At one time a fetus was seen as only a part of the woman who was the mother of the child. When someone tortiously injured a pregnant woman and her fetus sustained injury as a result, no legal protection would have been extended to the subsequently born child. Today, when the tortious acts of another towards a woman who is or may become pregnant harms a fetus, there is a legally cognizable cause of action for the injury to both the woman and the subsequently born child.

* * *

It is clear that the recognition of a legal right to begin life with a sound mind and body on the part of a fetus which is assertable after birth against its mother would have serious ramifications for all women and their families, and for the way in which society views women and women's reproductive abilities. The recognition of such a right by a fetus would necessitate the recognition of a legal duty on the part of the woman who is the mother; a legal duty, as opposed to a moral duty, to effectuate the best prenatal environment possible. The recognition of such a legal duty would create a new tort: a cause of action assertable by a fetus, subsequently born alive, against its mother for the unintentional infliction of prenatal injuries.

It is the firmly held belief of some that a woman should subordinate her right to control her life when she decides to become pregnant or does become pregnant: anything which might possibly harm the developing fetus should be prohibited and all things which might positively affect the developing fetus should be mandated under penalty of law, be it criminal or civil. Since anything which a pregnant woman does or does not do may have an impact, either positive or negative, on her developing fetus, any act or omission on her part could render her liable to her subsequently born child. While such a view is consistent with the recognition of a fetus' having rights which are superior to those of its mother, such is not and cannot be the law of this State.

A legal right of a fetus to begin life with a sound mind and body assertable against a mother would make a pregnant woman the guarantor of the mind and body of her child at birth. A legal duty to guarantee the mental and physical health of another has never before been recognized in law. Any action which negatively impacted on fetal development would be a breach of the pregnant woman's duty to her developing fetus. Mother and child would be legal adversaries from the moment of conception until birth.

* * *

If a legally cognizable duty on the part of mothers were recognized, then a judicially defined standard of conduct would have to be met. It must be asked, By what judicially defined standard would a mother have her every act or omission while pregnant subjected to State scrutiny? By what objective standard could a jury be guided in determining whether a pregnant woman did all that was necessary in order not to breach a legal duty to not interfere with her fetus' separate and independent right to be born whole? In what way would prejudicial and stereotypical beliefs about the reproductive abilities of women be kept from interfering with a jury's determination of whether a particular woman was negligent at any point during her pregnancy?

* * *

It would be a legal fiction to treat the fetus as a separate legal person with rights hostile to and assertable against its mother. The relationship between a pregnant woman and her fetus is unlike the relationship between any other plaintiff and defendant. No other plaintiff depends exclusively on any other defendant for everything necessary for life itself. No other defendant must go through biological changes of the most profound type, possibly at the risk of her own life, in order to bring forth an adversary into the world. It is, after all, the whole life of the pregnant woman which impacts on the development of the fetus. As opposed to the third-party defendant, it is the mother's every waking and sleeping moment which, for better or worse, shapes the prenatal environment which forms the world for the developing fetus. That this is so is not a pregnant woman's fault: it is a fact of life.

* * *

* * * In holding that no cause of action will lie for maternal prenatal negligence, this court emphasizes that we in no way minimize the public policy favoring healthy newborns. Pregnant women need access to information about the risks inherent in everyday living on a developing fetus and need access to health care for themselves and their developing fetuses. It is, after all, to a pregnant woman's advantage to do all she can within her knowledge and power to bring a healthy child into this world. The way to effectuate the birth of healthy babies is not, however, through after-the-fact civil liability in tort for individual mothers, but rather through before-the-fact education of all women and families about prenatal development.

125 Ill.2d at 275–80, 126 Ill.Dec. at 63–66, 531 N.E.2d at 358–61.

Why would the recognition of such a claim render the mother a "guarantor" of the child's health, any more than the theory of medical malpractice makes physicians the guarantors of patient health? The court identifies a number of problems with devising the standard of care for mothers' behavior. Are these problems significantly different in degree or kind than the problems encountered in applying a standard of care in other contexts? Consider also some practical aspects of these claims. If the claim were filed when the child was still a minor, then a parent or guardian would have to bring the claim on the child's behalf. Presumably, such claims would be most likely when (1) an insurance policy—such as a homeowner's insurance policy—provided a potential source of funding for satisfying a judgment; or (2) an estranged father or relative was critical of the mother's conduct during pregnancy. If the courts were widely to recognize such claims, then insurers might seek to write in exclusions for such claims. But insurers, for a variety of reasons explored in more detail in chapter 13, are often unable to succeed in excluding particular types of tort claims from general liability coverages. Would the recognition of such a right in the fetus suggest that a woman has no right to abort the fetus?

For further discussion of tort claims and regulations relating to a mother's conduct during pregnancy, *see* John A. Robertson, *Procreative Liberty and the Control of Conception, Pregnancy, and Childbirth*, 69 Va. L. Rev. 405 (1983); Note, *The Creation of Fetal Rights: Conflicts With Women's Constitutional Rights to Liberty, Privacy, and Equal Protection*, 95 Yale L.J. 599 (1986).

2. *When There Is No Live Birth*

When, as a result of prenatal injuries, the child is stillborn, in theory a wrongful death or survival action might be available. As Chapter 11 explained in more detail, these causes of action are statutory creations, and so the availability of such claims for fetal injuries depends on statutory construction. A majority of states have interpreted the state's wrongful death statute as extending to fetal injuries resulting in no live birth. A minority, however, requires a live birth. *Compare* Panagopoulous v. Martin, 295 F.Supp. 220 (S.D.W.Va.1969)(allowing the actions without a live birth), *with* Justus v. Atchison, 19 Cal.3d 564, 139 Cal.Rptr. 97, 106, 565 P.2d 122, 131 (1977)(disallowing the action without a live birth), *overruled on other grounds,* Ochoa v. Superior Court, 39 Cal.3d 159, 216 Cal.Rptr. 661, 703 P.2d 1 (1985). On the issue of the wrongful death of a fetus, *see* D. Kader, *The Law of Tortious Prenatal Death Since* Roe v. Wade, 45 Mo.L.Rev. 639 (1980). For an earlier discussion of this and the other issues that will be discussed in this chapter, *see* H. Robertson, Jr., *Toward Rational Boundaries of Tort Liability for Injury to the Unborn: Prenatal Injuries, Preconception Injuries and Wrongful Life*, 1978 Duke L.J. 1401. A more recent comprehensive overview of these and many other related issues is Special Project, *Legal Rights and Issues Surrounding Conception, Pregnancy, and Birth*, 39 Vand.L.Rev. 597–850 (1986).

3. *Bystander Emotional Distress*

Parents of children born with disabilities have sometimes sued for their own emotional distress along the lines of the "bystander" emotional distress recovery recognized in Dillon v. Legg and other cases. This cause of action, in fact, may be the only cause of action potentially available if the child is stillborn and if the jurisdiction's wrongful death and survival statutes require a live birth. In Justus v. Atchison, *supra,* the court refused to allow the fathers of two still-born babies to maintain an action for emotional shock. The fathers were present in the delivery room and they each alleged that the children were still-born because of the negligence of the attending physicians. The court ruled that the fathers, who were voluntarily present, were not sufficiently cognizant of what was transpiring so that it could be said that they actually witnessed the deaths of the fetuses. With regard to children born alive, claims for emotional distress by the parents of children with disabilities were upheld in Haught v. Maceluch, 681 F.2d 291 (5th Cir.1982)(applying Texas law); Speck v. Finegold, 497 Pa. 77, 439 A.2d 110 (1981); Naccash v. Burger, 223 Va. 406, 290 S.E.2d 825 (1982).

4. When the Tortious Conduct That Eventually Causes Injury to the Fetus Occurred Before Conception

The tortious conduct that inflicts injury to the fetus might occur before conception. Courts are still struggling with developing standards for application in such cases. In Hegyes v. Unjian Enterprises, Inc., 234 Cal.App.3d 1103, 286 Cal.Rptr. 85 (1991), the minor plaintiff was born with disabilities that allegedly resulted from injuries her mother had sustained, pre-conception, in a car accident involving another driver. The court, in a lengthy opinion surveying preconception tort cases in other jurisdictions as well as California, concluded that actors owe no duty of care toward yet-to-be-conceived plaintiffs, unless the actor is "a medical professional" or "manufacturer" sued under a product liability theory. Indeed, the court went on to suggest that even these categories would be limited to medical professionals whose "advice and care is directly related to the delivery of a healthy child," and to manufacturers whose products have a particular defect that can cause disabilities in later-conceived children. In other preconception negligence cases, no duty should be recognized, given that "there is an overwhelming need to keep liability within reasonable bounds and to limit the areas of actionable causation by applying the concept of duty." Id. at 1114, 286 Cal.Rptr. at 90.

Would recognition of a duty in cases outside the professional or products liability context lead to a significant rise in claims filed? Presumably, the mother-to-be, if injured herself by the defendant's negligence, would often have her own claim for damages, a claim that might exhaust the limits of any available insurance policy and thus render unlikely a later suit by the child. In addition, the child would have to satisfy traditional actual cause requirements, which often might not be possible.

Courts also have reached mixed results in claims against physicians. Consider two cases with closely similar facts. In both cases, the child was born with severe disabilities resulting from the mother's exposure to rubella during pregnancy. (Such problems can be prevented if a potential mother is tested for immunity to rubella; if she is not immune, she can be vaccinated against it.) In McNulty v. McDowell, 415 Mass. 369, 613 N.E.2d 904 (1993), a woman had gone to a doctor with complaints about bloating and pelvic pain, and the doctor had removed her IUD and advised her to return after her next menstrual period for placement of a different contraceptive device. Instead, the woman became pregnant and gave birth to a child with numerous severe disabilities resulting from rubella. In Monusko v. Postle, 175 Mich.App. 269, 437 N.W.2d 367 (1989), the woman went to a clinic to have her IUD removed and told the physicians that she wished to have another child. She became pregnant, was exposed to rubella, and had a child with severe disabilities.

In *McNulty,* the court rejected "the bright-line rule" proposed by the doctor: that physicians never owe a duty to those yet to be conceived. Instead, the court ruled, "the sparse contacts" in this case between patient and doctor, "and the fact that these contacts were made not in anticipation of pregnancy, but rather to avoid it, are insufficient to establish such a duty." 415 Mass. at 373, 613 N.E.2d at 906. The court in *Monusko,* by contrast, held that a duty did exist:

* * * This case involves a plaintiff who, while not specifically contemplated, would have been the beneficiary of a test and immunization procedure specifically designed to alleviate the harm which resulted in this case. * * * We emphasize the direct connection between the test and immunization procedure and the harm in this case, and the fact that the test and the preconception immunization are specifically designed to prevent rubella syndrome in children that are not yet conceived.

175 Mich. App. at 276–77, 437 N.W.2d at 370.

Should it matter that the initial contact was for the purpose of correcting a problem with the woman's birth control method, especially if the correction required a period of time during which the woman would not be using birth control? Should it matter that the woman specifically conveys her wish or intent to become pregnant? Should the quantity or length of the contacts between patient and doctor play a part in determining the existence of duty, as the court in *McNulty* suggests?

Another category of preconception cases relates to DES. As we saw in Chapter Six, the first round of DES claimants were the daughters of women who had ingested DES during their pregnancies; thus, these claims were not for a "preconception" tort. Now, a "third generation" of DES claimants is appearing: the granddaughters of the women who ingested DES. These plaintiffs have claimed injuries resulting from premature birth that, in turn, resulted from damage to their mother's reproductive system caused by in utero exposure to DES. New York's highest court has rejected these claims, applying earlier New York precedent rejecting a cause of action for preconception torts.

> The nature of the plaintiff's injuries in [both this and the previous case]—birth defects—and their cause—harm to the mothers' reproductive systems before the children were conceived—are indistinguishable for these purposes. They raise the same vexing questions with the same "staggering implications." * * * [T]he cause of action plaintiffs ask us to recognize here could not be confined without the drawing of artificial and arbitrary boundaries. For all we know, the rippling effects of DES exposure may extend for generations. It is our duty to confine liability within manageable limits.

Enright v. Eli Lilly & Co., 77 N.Y.2d 377, 386–87, 570 N.E.2d 198, 203, 568 N.Y.S.2d 550, 555 (N.Y.1991), *cert. denied*, 502 U.S. 868 (1991). The dissenting opinion disagreed with the concerns about overdeterrence and the majority's reading of precedent.

> * * * [T]he majority suggests that permitting a cause of action for Karen Enright could result in "overdeterrence—the possibility that research will be discouraged or beneficial drugs withheld from the market." * * * But * * * [t]he wrongful conduct of the drug companies in producing and marketing DES * * * stopped more than a generation ago when the enormity of the damage from DES became known. * * * But even if deterrence is assumed to be a relevant issue, should we be any less concerned with deterring the development of unsafe drugs which may cause latent damage to the third generation than to the second? * * *

* * * [T]he statement that liability should stop at Karen's mother's generation because it is "commensurate with the risk" is not a statement of an argument or of a legal or policy reason for a particular result. Rather, it is simply a statement of the Court's own policy determination as to where the risk—and, hence, the liability—stops. If, as the majority apparently believes, there are economic and social considerations which require that there be some arbitrary cutoff point in cases of this kind, such a statute of repose could easily be engrafted on the Toxic Tort legislation * * *.

77 N.Y.2d 377, 393–94, 570 N.E.2d 198, 207–08, 568 N.Y.S.2d 550, 559–60 (N.Y.1991)(Hancock, J., dissenting).

5. *The Choice to Become Pregnant as Superseding Cause*

If courts allow suits for preconception conduct that will result in damage to the child, then defendants might argue that the mother's or parents' choice to conceive a child in the face of known danger is a superseding cause. The argument has appeared in several cases in which the child was born with severe problems resulting from the fact that mother had Rh-negative blood and had become "sensitized"—that is, her blood had manufactured antibodies that could attack and destroy the blood cells of a fetus. Sensitization usually can be prevented by giving an Rh-negative mother a drug, Rho-gam, during all pregnancies, and after every miscarriage, abortion, or birth of an Rh-positive fetus or child. When a mother has not received this treatment, then the chances are considerable that, if she becomes pregnant with a fetus whose blood is Rh-positive, the child might be harmed by the sensitization effect.

In Sweeney v. Preston, 642 So.2d 332 (Miss.1994), the plaintiff contended that the doctor—after the plaintiff's first pregnancy—had mistyped her blood as Rh-positive and thus had failed to administer Rhogram to the plaintiff after that first delivery. The plaintiff, after learning of the mistyping and the problems it had created, then went on to conceive and deliver another child, who had Rh factor complications and died two days after delivery. Two years later, the plaintiff conceived another child, who also died shortly after birth as a result of Rh factor complications. The plaintiff alleged that the doctor's mistyping and failure to administer Rhogram resulted in the deaths of the second and third child. The majority opinion was limited to the statute of limitations issue, and held that the suit was not necessarily time-barred, remanding for trial on some facts relating to the limitations issue. The dissenting opinion, however, argued that the cause of action should not be allowed.

* * * Dr. Preston's negligent act, if it occurred, was a single act. After he and the Sweeneys learned of it, there was nothing further Dr. Preston could do except warn. Warning they had. He could not prevent further harm, further injury. That decision was solely for the Sweeneys. They chose the most terrible danger of all, bringing into a life a human being who had little chance of living, and if so, could go through whatever life it had deformed and maimed. That decision was peculiarly one which only the Sweeneys could make, and Dr. Preston should not be held accountable for its consequences.

* * *

The evidence before the circuit court in granting summary judgment was that the Sweeneys deliberately chose for Mrs. Sweeney to become pregnant, it was not an accident. Dr. Preston's negligence, at most, contributed to a certain physical condition in Mrs. Sweeney further impairing her ability to bear a healthy child. It took a deliberate choice followed by a deliberate action by the Sweeneys, however, to produce the harm in this case. If this did not constitute an independent intervening cause, one cannot be envisioned.

Id. at 341–42 (Hawkins, J.).

In Graham v. Keuchel, 847 P.2d 342 (Okl.1993), another case in which the child was born with fatal Rh-related complications, the defendant doctors argued that the mother knew she had been sensitized, had been warned about and understood the dangers, and "willfully engaged in sexual conduct intended to bring about conception with the full resolve of carrying the fetus to term." The court engaged in a lengthy discussion of superseding cause analysis, and concluded that the mother's choice and conduct would be a superseding cause only if (1) she engaged in sexual conduct intended to bring about conception; (2) she knew that her reproductive capacity was impaired; (3) she had been given adequate warnings about the dangers of conceiving in her sensitized condition; and (4) she completely understood the medical risk to herself and to her child if she conceived in a sensitized condition. Given this, the court found that the trial court's instruction to the jury was reversible error, because it instructed the jury that no liability would exist if the mother "elected to become pregnant" with full knowledge and appreciation of the dangers. The quoted phrase was ambiguous, the court found, because it could include something less than "willful" negligence; for instance, the phrase might include predictable failure of birth control, a careless failure to take adequate precautions, or the failure to obtain an abortion.

How should the jury be instructed about the intervening-superseding cause issue?

B. WRONGFUL BIRTH AND WRONGFUL LIFE

BERMAN v. ALLAN

Supreme Court of New Jersey, 1979.
80 N.J. 421, 404 A.2d 8.

PASHMAN, J.

In Gleitman v. Cosgrove, 49 N.J. 22, 227 A.2d 689 (1967), decided 12 years ago, this Court refused to recognize as valid causes of action either a claim for "wrongful life" asserted on behalf of a physically deformed infant or a claim for "wrongful birth" put forth by the infant's parents. Both prayers for relief were premised upon the allegation that had the physician treating Mrs. Gleitman during her pregnancy followed standard medical practice, an abortion would have been procured and the child would never have come into existence. In this case, we are called upon to assess the continued validity of both of our holdings in *Gleitman*.

On September 11, 1975, Paul and Shirley Berman, suing both in their own names and as Guardians *ad litem* for their infant daughter Sharon, instituted the present malpractice action against Ronald Allan and Michael Attardi, medical doctors licensed by the State of New Jersey. Two causes of action were alleged. The first, a claim for damages based upon "wrongful life," was asserted by Mr. Berman on behalf of the infant Sharon. The second, a claim denominated "wrongful birth," sought compensation for injuries suffered by the parents in their own right.

The factual allegations underlying each of these prayers for relief can be briefly summarized. From February 19 until November 3, 1974, Mrs. Berman, while pregnant with Sharon, was under the care and supervision of Drs. Allan and Attardi, both of whom are specialists in gynecology and obstetrics. At the time of her pregnancy, Mrs. Berman was 38 years of age. On November 3, Sharon was born afflicted with Down's Syndrome—a genetic defect commonly referred to as mongolism.

Plaintiffs allege that defendants deviated from accepted medical standards by failing to inform Mrs. Berman during her pregnancy of the existence of a procedure known as amniocentesis. This procedure involves the insertion of a long needle into a mother's uterus and the removal therefrom of a sample of amniotic fluid containing living fetal cells. Through "karyotype analysis"—a procedure in which the number and structure of the cells' chromosomes are examined—the sex of the fetus as well as the presence of gross chromosomal defects can be detected.   * * *

Due to Mrs. Berman's age at the time of her conception, plaintiffs contend that the risk that her child, if born, would be afflicted with Down's Syndrome was sufficiently great that sound medical practice at the time of pregnancy required defendants to inform her both of this risk and the availability of amniocentesis as a method of determining whether in her particular case that risk would come to fruition. Had defendants so informed Mrs. Berman, the complaint continues, she would have submitted to the amniocentesis procedure, discovered that the child, if born, would suffer from Down's Syndrome, and had the fetus aborted.

As a result of defendants' alleged negligence, the infant Sharon, through her Guardian *ad litem*, seeks compensation for the physical and emotional pain and suffering which she will endure throughout life because of her mongoloid condition. Mr. and Mrs. Berman, the child's parents, request damages in their own right both for the emotional anguish which they have experienced and will continue to experience on account of Sharon's birth defect, and the medical and other costs which they will incur in order to properly raise, educate and supervise the child.

On November 4, 1977, the trial judge granted summary judgment in favor of defendants on the ground that plaintiffs had failed to state any actionable claim for relief. In his view, *Gleitman v. Cosgrove, supra*, was dispositive of the issues presented. On December 22, 1977, plaintiffs filed a notice of appeal to the Appellate Division. While the matter was pending before the appellate judges, we directly certified the case to this Court on our own motion. * * *

II

The claim for damages asserted on behalf of the infant Sharon has aptly been labeled a cause of action grounded upon "wrongful life." Sharon does not contend that absent defendants' negligence she would have come into the world in a normal and healthy state. There is no suggestion in either the pleadings below or the medical literature which we have scrutinized that any therapy could have been prescribed which would have decreased the risk that, upon birth, Sharon would suffer from Down's Syndrome. Rather, the gist of the infant's complaint is that had defendants informed her mother of the availability of amniocentesis, Sharon would never have come into existence.

One of the most deeply held beliefs of our society is that life—whether experienced with or without a major physical handicap—is more precious than non-life. See In re Quinlan, 70 N.J. 10, 19 & n. 1, 355 A.2d 647 (1976). Concrete manifestations of this belief are not difficult to discover. The documents which set forth the principles upon which our society is founded are replete with references to the sanctity of life. The federal constitution characterizes life as one of three fundamental rights of which no man can be deprived without due process of law. U.S.Const., Amends. V and XIV. Our own state constitution proclaims that the "enjoying and defending [of] life" is a natural right. N.J.Const. (1947), Art. I, § 1. The Declaration of Independence states that the primacy of man's "unalienable" right to life is a "self-evident truth." Nowhere in these documents is there to be found an indication that the lives of persons suffering from physical handicaps are to be less cherished than those of non-handicapped human beings.

Finally, we would be remiss if we did not take judicial notice of the high esteem which our society accords to those involved in the medical profession. The reason for this is clear. Physicians are the preservers of life.

No man is perfect. Each of us suffers from some ailments or defects, whether major or minor, which make impossible participation in all the activities the world has to offer. But our lives are not thereby rendered less precious than those of others whose defects are less pervasive or less severe.

We recognize that as a mongoloid child, Sharon's abilities will be more circumscribed than those of normal, healthy children and that she, unlike them, will experience a great deal of physical and emotional pain and anguish. We sympathize with her plight. We cannot, however, say that she would have been better off had she never been brought into the world. Notwithstanding her affliction with Down's Syndrome, Sharon, by virtue of her birth, will be able to love and be loved and to experience happiness and pleasure—emotions which are truly the essence of life and which are far more valuable than the suffering she may endure. To rule otherwise would require us to disavow the basic assumption upon which our society is based. This we cannot do.

Accordingly, we hold that Sharon has failed to state a valid cause of action founded upon "wrongful life."

III

The validity of the parents' claim for relief calls into play considerations different from those involved in the infant's complaint. As in the case of the infant, Mr. and Mrs. Berman do not assert that defendants increased the risk that Sharon, if born, would be afflicted with Down's Syndrome. Rather, at bottom, they allege that they were tortiously injured because Mrs. Berman was deprived of the option of making a meaningful decision as to whether to abort the fetus * * *—a decision which, at least during the first trimester of pregnancy, is not subject to state interference, see Roe v. Wade, 410 U.S. 113, 93 S.Ct. 705, 35 L.Ed.2d 147 (1973). They thus claim that Sharon's "birth"—as opposed to her "life"—was wrongful.

Two items of damage are requested in order to redress this allegedly tortious injury: (1) the medical and other costs that will be incurred in order to properly raise, supervise and educate the child; and (2) compensation for the emotional anguish that has been and will continue to be experienced on account of Sharon's condition.

The *Gleitman* majority refused to recognize as valid a cause of action grounded upon wrongful birth. Two reasons underlay its determination. The first related to measure of damages should such a claim be allowed. In its view,

> In order to determine [the parents'] compensatory damages a court would have to evaluate the denial to them of the intangible, unmeasurable, and complex human benefits of motherhood and fatherhood and weigh these against the alleged emotional and money injuries. Such a proposed weighing is * * * impossible to perform * * *. [49 N.J. at 29, 227 A.2d at 693]

Second, even though the Court's opinion was premised upon the assumption that Mrs. Gleitman could have legally secured an abortion, the majority concluded that "substantial [public] policy reasons" precluded the judicial allowance of tort damages "for the denial of the opportunity to take an embryonic life." * * *

In light of changes in the law which have occurred in the 12 years since *Gleitman* was decided, the second ground relied upon by the *Gleitman* majority can no longer stand in the way of judicial recognition of a cause of action founded upon wrongful birth. The Supreme Court's ruling in *Roe v. Wade, supra,* clearly establishes that a woman possesses a constitutional right to decide whether her fetus should be aborted, at least during the first trimester of pregnancy. Public policy now supports, rather than militates against, the proposition that she not be impermissibly denied a meaningful opportunity to make that decision.

As in all other cases of tortious injury, a physician whose negligence has deprived a mother of this opportunity should be required to make amends for the damage which he has proximately caused. Any other ruling would in effect immunize from liability those in the medical field providing inadequate guidance to persons who would choose to exercise their constitutional right to abort fetuses which, if born, would suffer from genetic defects.   * * * Accordingly, we hold that a cause of action founded upon wrongful birth is a legally cognizable claim.

Troublesome, however, is the measure of damages. As noted earlier, the first item sought to be recompensed is the medical and other expenses that will be incurred in order to properly raise, educate and supervise the child. Although these costs were "caused" by defendants' negligence in the sense that but for the failure to inform, the child would not have come into existence, we conclude that this item of damage should not be recoverable. In essence, Mr. and Mrs. Berman desire to retain all the benefits inhering in the birth of the child—*i.e.,* the love and joy they will experience as parents—while saddling defendants with the enormous expenses attendant upon her rearing. Under the facts and circumstances here alleged, we find that such an award would be wholly disproportionate to the culpability involved, and that allowance of such a recovery would both constitute a windfall to the parents and place too unreasonable a financial burden upon physicians.

The parents' claim for emotional damages stands upon a different footing. In failing to inform Mrs. Berman of the availability of amniocentesis, defendants directly deprived her—and, derivatively, her husband—of the option to accept or reject a parental relationship with the child and thus caused them to experience mental and emotional anguish upon their realization that they had given birth to a child afflicted with Down's Syndrome. *See generally*, Note,[1] *supra*, 1978 Duke Law Journal at 1453. We feel that the monetary equivalent of this distress is an appropriate measure of the harm suffered by the parents deriving from Mrs. Berman's loss of her right to abort the fetus. * * *

Unlike the *Gleitman* majority, we do not feel that placing a monetary value upon the emotional suffering that Mr. and Mrs. Berman have and will continue to experience is an impossible task for the trier of fact. In the 12 years that have elapsed since *Gleitman* was decided, courts have come to recognize that mental and emotional distress is just as "real" as physical pain, and that its valuation is no more difficult. Consequently, damages for such distress have been ruled allowable in an increasing number of contexts. * * * Moreover, * * * to deny Mr. and Mrs. Berman redress for their injuries merely because damages cannot be measured with precise exactitude would constitute a perversion of fundamental principles of justice. * * *

Consequently, we hold that Mr. and Mrs. Berman have stated actionable claims for relief. Should their allegations be proven at trial, they are entitled to be recompensed for the mental and emotional anguish they have suffered and will continue to suffer on account of Sharon's condition.

Accordingly, the judgment of the trial court is affirmed in part and reversed in part, and this case remanded for a plenary trial.

HANDLER, J., concurring in part and dissenting in part.

We are called upon in this medical malpractice lawsuit to revisit the sensitive and perplexing problems engendered by the birth of a congenitally

---

1. [Ed. note] The citation is partially incorrect. The cited material is not a student note, but rather an article by Professor H. B. Robertson, Jr.

defective child and the suffering of its parents, aggrieved by the medical doctors who negligently failed to forewarn them of their misfortune. The Court wrestled with these questions some years ago in Gleitman v. Cosgrove, 49 N.J. 22, 227 A.2d 689 (1967) and a majority ruled that neither the parents nor the handicapped child had a sustainable cause of action for injuries, there being no claim that the malpractice in any way caused the birth defects of the child. Today we overrule that decision, at least in part.

The Court now recognizes that the parents of the impaired child have a cause of action for the doctors' breach of duty to render competent medical advice and services and that they are entitled to compensation for their mental and emotional suffering over the birth of their damaged child. I agree with this. However, I hold to a somewhat broader view of mental and emotional injury in these circumstances and would also include as an element of these damages impaired parenthood or parental capacity.

The Court does not, in its opinion, recognize as sustainable a cause of action on behalf of the child. On this, I differ. The child, in my view, was owed directly, during its gestation, a duty of reasonable care from the same physicians who undertook to care for its mother—then expectant—and that duty, to render complete and competent medical advice, was seriously breached. The child, concededly, did not become defective because of the physicians' dereliction; nevertheless, it suffered a form of injury or loss in having been born of parents whose parental capacity may have been substantially diminished by the negligence of their doctors. This is a loss to the child which should be recompensed. For these reasons I concur in part and dissent in part from the opinion of the Court.

A full perception of the mental, emotional—and, I add, moral—suffering of parents in this situation reveals another aspect of their loss. Mental, emotional and moral suffering can involve diminished parental capacity. Such incapacity of the mother and father *qua* parents is brought about by the wrongful denial of a reasonable opportunity to learn of and anticipate the birth of a child with permanent defects, and to prepare for the heavy obligations entailed in rearing so unfortunate an individual. Such parents may experience great difficulty adjusting to their fate and accepting the child's impairment as nature's verdict. * * * While some individuals confronted by tragedy respond magnificently and become exemplary parents, others do not. See *e.g.*, Becker v. Schwartz, 46 N.Y.2d 401, 413 N.Y.S.2d 895, 386 N.E.2d 807 (Ct.App.1978) in which the parents subsequently put their mongoloid child up for adoption, *N.Y. Times*, Feb. 17, 1979, at 23, col. 1. Individuals suffering this form of parental incapacity or dysfunction are denied to a great extent the fuller joys, satisfaction and pride which comes with successful and effective parenting. This may endure for some time during the early developmental years of the child. * * * Impaired parenthood, so understood, constitutes another dimension of the injury and loss suffered by plaintiffs in this case. In this sense, impaired parenthood, together with mental and emotional and moral suffering, should be recognized and compensated as elements of damages.

III

The Court in this case, as in *Gleitman* before it, fails to accord a cause of action to the afflicted infant plaintiff. This denial, I most respectfully urge, is wrong.

Plausibly, the child's injury and loss in the form of diminished childhood can be viewed as a derivative claim based solely on the parents' injury. The great majority of jurisdictions which have considered a child's cause of action for damages as derivative from injuries negligently inflicted on a parent have generally rejected such claims.

No one is contending that any medical procedure consistent with sound medical practice would have served to avert or lessen the physical defects of the infant, which she acquired congenitally, at the moment of conception. But the duty here owed was that of advising the parents fully as to the probability of the impaired physical condition of their unborn child and of the availability of a test which could have proved or disproved that medical prediction. The negligent breach of that duty carried with it the foreseeable consequence that the impaired infant would be born of parents whose parental fitness would be seriously undermined as a result of this professional mishandling, with the equally foreseeable result that the unborn child would be burdened with a diminished childhood. * * *

Clearly the doctors owed a professional duty of care to all of the plaintiffs in this case, the child while unborn as well as her parents. The breach of this duty resulted in discernible injuries to each of the plaintiffs. Some of these losses, those of the parents in the form of mental, emotional and moral injury and impaired parenthood and those of the child in the nature of a diminished childhood, might be hard to sense, difficult to define and puzzling to evaluate. They are, nonetheless, actual and constitute a sound basis for a lawful claim for redress and compensation. I would reverse the summary judgment and remand the litigation to allow the parties to marshall evidence relevant to these issues.

Accordingly, I concur and dissent in part.

Notes

1. *The Parents' Wrongful Birth Claim: In General.* Most courts, like *Berman,* have allowed the parents to pursue at least some categories of damages in a wrongful birth claim, but the courts differ on the allowable damages. Three general categories of damages are at issue: the full costs of raising the child, including costs not specifically necessitated by the disability; the special costs associated with the disability; and the emotional damages experienced by the parents, given the fact that the child has been born with a disability. In contrast to *Berman,* many courts have allowed parents to recover the special expenses, and have disallowed emotional distress recoveries. *See, e.g.,* Smith v. Cote, 128 N.H. 231, 513 A.2d 341 (N.H.1986). The fact that significant doctrinal differences persist is testament to the theoretical and practical complexities explored in *Berman* and in the following notes.

2. *The Parents' Wrongful Birth Claim: The Offset Principle.* Defendants have raised, as to all categories of damages in parents' wrongful birth claims, the "windfall" or "offset" concern noted in *Berman* and articulated in section 920 of the Restatement (Second) of Torts:

§ 920. BENEFIT TO PLAINTIFF RESULTING FROM DEFENDANT'S TORT

When the defendant's tortious conduct has caused harm to the plaintiff or to his property and in so doing has conferred a special benefit to the interest of the plaintiff that was harmed, the value of the benefit conferred is considered in mitigation of damages, to the extent that this is equitable.

Comment:

* * *

b. *Limitation to same interest.* Damages resulting from an invasion of one interest are not diminished by showing that another interest has been benefited. Thus one who has harmed another's reputation by defamatory statements cannot show in mitigation of damages that the other has been financially benefited from their publication * * *, unless damages are claimed for harm to pecuniary interests. * * * Damages for pain and suffering are not diminished by showing that the earning capacity of the plaintiff has been increased by the defendant's act. * * * Damages to a husband for loss of consortium are not diminished by the fact that the husband is no longer under the expense of supporting the wife.

What arguments could the plaintiff and the defendant each present as to why, respectively, the benefit rule should not or should apply as to some or all categories of possible damages in the parents' wrongful birth claim? For discussion of the benefit rule as it bears on claims for wrongful birth, *see* Lininger v. Eisenbaum, 764 P.2d 1202 (Colo.1988).

3. *The Parents' Wrongful Birth Claim: Full Child–Raising Expenses Versus Special Expenses Only.* A number of courts have allowed parents to recover the special costs associated with the disability. A detailed discussion appears in Smith v. Cote, 128 N.H. 231, 513 A.2d 341 (N.H.1986):

The usual rule of compensatory damages in tort cases requires that the person wronged receive a sum of money that will restore him as nearly as possible to the position he would have been in if the wrong had not been committed. * * *

However, "few if any jurisdictions appear ready to apply this traditional rule of damages with full vigor in wrongful birth cases." * * * Although at least one court has ruled that all child-rearing costs should be recoverable, * * * most courts are reluctant to impose liability to this extent. A special rule of damages has emerged; in most jurisdictions the parents may recover only the extraordinary medical and educational costs attributable to the birth defects. * * *

The logic of the "extraordinary costs" rule has been criticized. * * * The rule in effect divides a plaintiff's pecuniary losses into two categories, ordinary costs and extraordinary costs, and treats the latter category as compensable while ignoring the former category. At first glance, this bifurcation seems difficult to justify.

The disparity is explained, however, by reference to the rule requiring mitigation of tort damages. The "avoidable consequences" rule, Restatement (Second) of Torts § 918 (1979), specifies that a plaintiff may not recover damages for "any harm that he could have avoided by the use of reasonable effort or expenditure" after the occurrence of the tort. Rigidly applied, this rule would appear to require wrongful birth plaintiffs to place their children for adoption. *See* Note, *Wrongful Birth: The Avoidance of Consequences Doctrine in Mitigation of Damages,* 53 Fordham L.Rev. 1107 (1985). Because of our profound respect for the sanctity of the family, * * * we are loathe to sanction the application of the rule in these circumstances. If the rule is not applied, however, wrongful birth plaintiffs may receive windfalls. Hence, a special rule limiting recovery of damages is warranted.

Although the extraordinary costs rule departs from traditional principles of tort damages, it is neither illogical nor unprecedented. The rule represents an application in a tort context of the expectancy rule of damages employed in breach of contracts cases. Wrongful birth plaintiffs typically desire a child (and plan to support it) from the outset. It is the defendants' duty to help them achieve this goal. When the plaintiffs' expectations are frustrated by the defendants' negligence, the extraordinary costs rule "merely attempts to put plaintiffs in the position they expected to be in with defendant's help." * * *

Under this view of the problem, ordinary child-rearing costs are analogous to a price the plaintiffs were willing to pay in order to achieve an expected result. According to contract principles, plaintiffs "may not have a return in damages of the price and also receive what was to be obtained for the price." McQuaid v. Michou, 85 N.H. 299, 303, 157 A. 881, 883 (1932). *See* Hawkins v. McGee, 84 N.H. 114, 146 A. 641 (1929). We note that expectancy damages are recoverable in other kinds of tort cases, * * * and that contract principles are hardly unknown in medical malpractice litigation, which has roots in contract as well as in tort. * * * In light of the difficulty posed by tort damages principles in these circumstances, we see no obstacle—logical or otherwise—to use of the extraordinary costs rule. * * *

The extraordinary costs rule ensures that the parents of a deformed child will recover the medical and educational costs attributable to the child's impairment. At the same time it establishes a necessary and clearly defined boundary to liability in this area. * * * Accordingly, we hold that a plaintiff in a wrongful birth case may recover the extraordinary medical and educational costs attributable to the child's deformities, but may not recover ordinary child-raising costs.

Three points stand in need of clarification. First, parents may recover extraordinary costs incurred both before and after their child attains majority. Some courts do not permit recovery of post-majority expenses, on the theory that the parents' obligation of support terminates when the child reaches twenty-one. * * * In New Hampshire, however, parents are required to support their disabled adult offspring. * * *

Second, recovery should include compensation for the extraordinary maternal care that has been and will be provided to the child. Linda alleges that her parental obligations and duties, which include feeding, bathing, and exercising Heather, substantially exceed those of parents of a normal child. One court has ruled that parents "cannot recover for services that they have rendered or will render personally to their own child without incurring financial expense." Schroeder v. Perkel, 87 N.J. 53, 69, 432 A.2d 834, 841 (1981). We see no reason, however, to treat as noncompensable the burdens imposed on a parent who must devote extraordinary time and effort to caring for a child with birth defects. * * * Avoiding these burdens is often among the primary motivations of one who chooses not to bear a child likely to suffer from birth defects. We hold that a parent may recover for his or her ministrations to his or her child to the extent that such ministrations: (1) are made necessary by the child's condition; (2) clearly exceed those ordinarily rendered by parents of a normal child; and (3) are reasonably susceptible of valuation. The trial judge should not allow the jury to consider such a claim unless there is concrete evidence indicating the probable nature and extent of the extra services that will be required. If the issue is submitted to the jury, the trial judge must instruct that damages for this purpose are not to be awarded as an expression of sympathy.

Third, to the extent that the parent's alleged emotional distress results in tangible pecuniary losses, such as medical expenses or counseling fees, such losses are recoverable.

128 N.H. at 243–46, 513 A.2d at 349–50.

Are you convinced by the court's explanation of the special expenses approach? Do you agree with the three points clarifying what the parents may recover? If the parents were not allowed to recover these three items in the wrongful birth claim, would there be any other tort avenue or nontort source (such as health insurance) that could cover such costs?

4. *The Parents' Wrongful Birth Claim: Mental Anguish.* Courts have divided over whether parents should be able to recover emotional damages for the birth of a child with a disability. The *Berman* court allowed such recovery, but other courts have rejected it; sometimes courts have based the rejection on standard doctrinal boundaries relating to emotional distress recoveries, such as the impact rule or bystander recovery rules. See Kush v. Lloyd, 616 So.2d 415 (Fla.1992)(discussing and rejecting application of impact rule). The Kansas Supreme Court has discussed the application of the bystander rules: "We have thus far held [in the bystander line of cases] that visibility of results as opposed to visibility of the tortious act does not give rise to a claim for emotional damages. The child's injury in this case occurred without human fault during development of the fetus; the parents were not aware of the injury at the time. * * * We therefore hold that damages for emotional distress of the parents are not recoverable in a wrongful birth case." Arche v. United States, 247 Kan. 276, 283, 798 P.2d 477, 482 (1990).

Consider again the various arguments, explored in Chapter 10, for and against limiting recovery for nonpecuniary losses. Do these apply with equal or with different force to the question of parental wrongful birth claims for emotional distress?

5. *The Child's Wrongful Life Claim.* Most courts, like *Berman,* have rejected a cause of action by the child for wrongful life. A few courts have allowed the child to recover, under the rubric of this cause of action, the special expenses associated with the disability. See Turpin v. Sortini, 31 Cal.3d 220, 182 Cal.Rptr. 337, 643 P.2d 954 (1982); Procanik v. Cillo, 97 N.J. 339, 478 A.2d 755 (1984). Of course, the child's parents have a legal obligation to support the child, at least through the time of the child's majority age, and so expenses associated with the child's pre-majority years are already recoverable, in most jurisdictions, under the parents' claim for wrongful birth of the child. Yet what about the expenses associated with the disability once the child has reached majority age? One option is to allow allow the child to recover for this, as do the courts in *Turpin* and *Procanik.* Another option, which some courts have chosen, is to allow the parents to recover for expenses associated with the disability and incurred after the child reaches majority age. *See Smith v. Cote,* quoted in note 3 above.

As to either pre-majority or post-majority expenses, allowing these as a damage item to the parents raises concerns about protecting the interests of the child. In one recent case, the concurring judge argued that the wrongful birth action, as currently constituted, offers inadequate protection for the child:

> * * * We should judicially craft [the wrongful birth] claim so that its characteristics require: (1) any sums recovered as damages by the parents for wrongful birth to be placed in a reversionary trust for the use and benefit of the child; and (2) the parents to stand in a fiduciary relationship with the child, with a duty to account for all sums recoverable as damages.
>
> We should mandate the two conditions into the claim for wrongful birth. If we have the authority to recognize the claim, we have the authority to determine its character. The trial court's discretion may be relied upon for establishing the mechanics of the reversionary trust-fiduciary relationship concept on an individual case basis.

Arche v. United States, 247 Kan. 276, 292–93, 798 P.2d 477, 487 (1990) (Six, J., concurring). What dangers is the judge seeking to avert by arguing for these limitations?

6. *Wrongful Life and Right to Die.* The *Berman* opinion, in its discussion of the child's wrongful life claim, cites In re Quinlan, 70 N.J. 10, 355 A.2d 647, *cert. denied* 429 U.S. 922, 97 S.Ct. 319, 50 L.Ed.2d 289 (1976). The case arose from an application requesting the authorization of the father of a 22–year-old girl, after consultations with the attending physician and the hospital's ethics committee, to order the withdrawal of life-support systems. The girl, Karen Quinlan, was completely moribund and had suffered irremedial brain damage. The case was a *cause célèbre. Cf.* the discussion at p. 76 *supra.*

The New Hampshire Supreme Court considered the connection between right to die principles and wrongful life claims when it disallowed wrongful life actions in Smith v. Cote, 128 N.H. 231, 513 A.2d 341 (1986):

> Our reluctance [to recognize the wrongful life claim] is not diminished by the evolving "right to die" doctrine. In a right to die case a court may act to protect an individual's right to choose between a natural death and the prolongation of his life by means of extraordinary medical procedures. The court avoids making an objective judgment as to the value of the plaintiff's life; it strives, instead, to protect the individual's subjective will. Even when the plaintiff is an incompetent, "the court does not arrogate to itself the individual's choice," but instead allows the plaintiff's guardian or surrogate to make that choice on his behalf. Procanik v. Cillo, 97 N.J. 339, 367, 478 A.2d 755, 771 (1984)(Handler, J., concurring in part and dissenting in part).
>
> The same cannot be said of wrongful life cases. At issue is not protection of the impaired child's right to choose nonexistence over life, but whether legal injury has occurred as a result of the defendant's conduct. The necessary inquiry is objective, not subjective; the court cannot avoid assessing the "worth" of the child's life. Simply put, the judiciary has an important role to play in protecting the privacy rights of the dying. It has no business declaring that among the living are people who never should have been born.

128 N.H. at 248–49, 513 A.2d at 352–53.

7. *Healthy But Unplanned Children.* Parents also have sued in tort when a defendant's negligence has led to an unplanned but healthy child. (The

claims sometimes are termed "wrongful conception" but sometimes the label "wrongful life" is used as well.) There is little disagreement that the mother can recover her pregnancy-related expenses (and pain and suffering) as well as the usual tort damages for any pregnancy-related injury she might suffer, such as an infection after a cesearean section. Most courts have disallowed, however, any damages for child-rearing expenses. Some courts have reasoned that as a matter of law a healthy child cannot be deemed a damage or injury. *See* Public Health Trust v. Brown, 388 So.2d 1084 (Fla.Dist.Ct.App.1980). Cockrum v. Baumgartner, 95 Ill.2d 193, 69 Ill.Dec. 168, 447 N.E.2d 385 (1983), *cert. denied,* 464 U.S. 846, 104 S.Ct. 149, 78 L.Ed.2d 139 (1983).

In Hartke v. McKelway, 707 F.2d 1544 (D.C.Cir.1983), the court, in an opinion by Judge Carl McGowan, carved out a middle path. The plaintiff had sought sterilization given her justified concerns that another pregnancy would threaten her health and the health of the potential baby. The sterilization was unsuccessful, and the woman bore a healthy child without suffering any but the usual difficulties of pregnancy.

To say that for reasons of public policy contraceptive failure can result in no damage as a matter of law ignores the fact that tens of millions of persons use contraceptives daily to avoid the very result which the defendant would have us say is always a benefit, never a detriment. Those tens of millions of persons, by their conduct, express the sense of the community. * * *

* * *

Nevertheless, courts have recognized that there is an unusual difficulty in wrongful conception cases in setting the amount of compensation, because the extent, if any, to which the birth of a child is an injury to particular parents is not obvious but will vary depending on their circumstances and aspirations. * * * The parents may in fact have ended up with a child that they adore and that they privately consider to be, on balance, an overwhelming benefit to their lives. * * * This is because the parents may have sought to avoid conception for any of a number of reasons. They may have done so for socio-economic reasons, seeking to avoid disruption of their careers or lifestyle, or to conserve family resources, * * * for eugenic reasons, seeking to avoid the birth of a handicapped child, * * * or for therapeutic reasons, seeking to avoid the dangers to the mother's health of pregnancy and childbirth. * * *

When a couple chooses sterilization solely for therapeutic or eugenic reasons, it seems especially likely that the birth of a healthy child, although unplanned, may be, as it is for most parents, a great benefit to them. In such cases, a court will tend to feel that it is unjust to impose on the defendant doctor the often huge costs of raising the child, and will fear that a jury that did so was motivated by passion or anti-doctor prejudice. Thus, in considering the question of whether childrearing expenses may be recoverable, many courts and commentators have placed great emphasis on the couple's reasons for undergoing sterilization. * * *

We tend to agree that a factfinder should place great weight on a couple's reason for undergoing sterilization in deciding whether the subsequent birth of a child, on balance, constitutes damage to the parents. Their reason for departing from the usual view that childrearing is a positive experience is in effect a calculation of the way in which they anticipate the costs of childbirth to outweigh the benefits. That calculation, untainted by bitterness and greed, or by a sense of duty to a child the parents have brought into the world, is usually the best available evidence of the extent to which the birth of the child has in fact been an injury to them. Thus, for example, where a couple sought sterilization solely for therapeutic or eugenic reasons, there is a presumption raised that the uneventful birth of a healthy child constitutes damage to the parents only to the extent that they experienced abnormal fear of harm to the mother or of the birth of a handicapped child. Courts and juries may assume that the parents treasure the child and that the usual expenses of raising it will be outweighed by the benefits derived.

The presumption raised by the evidence of the parents' reason for seeking sterilization is, however, rebuttable. If it can be shown that the parents' situation has somehow significantly changed since the sterilization—by reliance on presumed infertility in making an income-reducing career change, for example, or by a sudden increase in wealth—it may be that the original calculation of anticipated injury has changed for better or worse. * * * Generally, however, the plaintiff's recovery will most accurately reflect the amount of injury incurred if it is limited to paying for those risks that the plaintiff specifically sought to avoid and that came to pass. * * *

707 F.2d at 147–50.

Virtually all the courts that have allowed recovery of child-rearing expenses apply the rule that the plaintiffs' recovery should be offset by the benefits of the child. *See, e.g.,* Ochs v. Borrelli, 187 Conn. 253, 256 n. 3, 445 A.2d 883, 884 n. 3 (1982); Sherlock v. Stillwater Clinic, 260 N.W.2d 169, 176 (Minn.1977). *Contra,* Custodio v. Bauer, 251 Cal.App.2d 303, 324, 59 Cal.Rptr. 463, 477 (1967); Marciniak v. Lundborg, 153 Wis.2d 59, 450 N.W.2d 243 (1990).

There have been some actions brought by the siblings of unwanted children claiming that, owing to the addition of another child, they have been adversely affected in the amount of care and attention that they would be able to receive from their parents. These actions have been uniformly rejected. *See, e.g.,* Coleman v. Garrison, 349 A.2d 8 (Del.1975); Aronoff v. Snider, 292 So.2d 418 (Fla.App.1974); Cox v. Stretton, 77 Misc.2d 155, 352 N.Y.S.2d 834 (1974)

7. *Abortion.* Abortion rights have proved relevant in several ways to claims for wrongful life, wrongful birth, or wrongful conception. First, with respect to the parents' claim for the wrongful birth of a child with a disability, the parents usually plead, and testify, that they would have obtained an abortion had the defendant not been negligent (if, for instance, the defendant had properly advised the parents that the child had or was likely to have a birth defect). Most courts require this showing. *See* Keel v. Banach, 624 So.2d 1022 (Ala.1993). Assuming that the plaintiffs can testify that, more likely than not, they would have obtained an abortion, it seems unlikely in most cases that defendants could defeat the causation element. Suppose that the parents testified, in depositions before trial, that they "weren't sure" whether they would have obtained an abortion, or that they "probably would not" have sought an abortion. Should the defendant be able to obtain a summary judgment as to the parents' wrongful life claim?

The Missouri Supreme Court, one of the minority of courts that has rejected any parental claim for wrongful birth, criticized the cause of action in part because of these abortion-related proof considerations:

> Those who have practiced family law during the past two decades have with some frequency become painfully aware of the difficulty of satisfactorily determining and knowing the real reason why a given woman may or may not choose to have an abortion. In the wrongful birth action, the right to recovery is based solely on the woman testifying, long after the fact and when it is in her financial interest to do so, that she would have chosen to abort if the physician had but told her of the amniocentesis test. The percentage of women who under pressure refuse to consider abortion, whether for reasons of religious belief, strong motherly instincts, or for other reasons, is sometimes astounding. It would seem that testimony either more verifiable based upon experience or more verifiable by some objective standard should be required as the basis for any action for substantial damages.

Wilson v. Kuenzi, 751 S.W.2d 741, 745–46 (Mo.1988).

What might qualify as testimony that is "more verifiable based on experience" or as "some objective standard," and how difficult would it be for plaintiffs to satisfy these approaches?

Second, when parents sue for failed sterilizations that produce healthy though unplanned children, defendants have argued that the plaintiff's failure to obtain an abortion should bar recovery or at a minimum form the basis of an affirmative defense that the plaintiff failed to take reasonable steps to mitigate damages. These arguments have had some success, but other courts have rejected them. *Compare* Sorkin v. Lee, 78 A.D.2d 180, 181, 434 N.Y.S.2d 300, 301 (1980)(plaintiffs' failure to have abortion barred recovery of childrearing expenses), *with* Johnson v. University Hospitals, 44 Ohio St.3d 49, 540 N.E.2d 1370 (1989)(ruling that a "mother need not mitigate damages by abortion or adoption since a tort victim has no duty to make unreasonable efforts to diminish or avoid prospective damages"). Should the judge give this question of reasonableness to the jury, as some have suggested? *See* Note, Judicial Limitations on Damages Recoverable for the Wrongful Birth of a Healthy Infant, 68 Va.L.Rev. 1311, 1328 (1982)(question of reasonableness of failure to have abortion or place child for adoption is one of fact, not of law).

8. *Negligence That Leads to an Abortion.* Suppose that the doctor's negligence arguably creates a risk of fetal injury, and that the pregnancy is terminated by abortion as a result of this injury. Do the parents have a cause of action, and if so for what damages? Consider Lynch v. Bay Ridge Obstetrical and Gynecological Assoc., 72 N.Y.2d 632, 532 N.E.2d 1239, 536 N.Y.S.2d 11 (N.Y.1988). The plaintiff consulted her gynecologist because she had not had a menstrual period for over three months, and her home pregnancy tests were negative. After the doctor visually examined her but did not give any pregnancy test, he prescribed a hormonal drug. After taking the drug, she learned that she was pregnant. Because the drug was known to have potential harmful effects on the fetus in early stages, she and her husband elected to terminate the pregnancy. She sued the physician, claiming that the doctor's negligence forced her to choose between the risk of having a child with disabilities or having an abortion, which violated her personal, moral, and religious beliefs. The majority allowed the woman's cause of action seeking "physical, psycholog-

ical, and emotional injuries resulting from the abortion and from having to decide whether to undergo it." The majority reasoned that the claim was not a pure emotional distress claim, nor was it a claim for emotional injuries resulting from the birth of a child; instead, the case was akin to a traditional medical malpractice action for physical and emotional injuries.

The dissent argued that the claim should be disallowed because it fell within the category of emotional distress cases and should be governed by the narrow parameters applicable to such actions.

> While acknowledging these principles [from the emotional distress cases], the majority attempts to treat this case as a garden-variety tort action seeking recovery for the physical, as well as emotional, injuries plaintiff sustained as a result of defendants' alleged malpractice * * *. However, the only physical injuries plaintiff was able to allege were the loss of live fetal tissue and blood, coupled with the pain and discomfort, that attends a normal abortion. I do not, of course, intend to minimize or belittle the physical trauma that accompanies many, if not most, abortions. I emphasize this point only to demonstrate that the "physical injury" on which plaintiff's suit is based—including its claim for severe emotional and spiritual damages—is based on really nothing more than an ordinary elective abortion similar to that undergone by thousands of women each year.

> * * * With this decision, the court has effectively embraced a new cause of action for "wrongful infliction of abortion."

72 N.Y.2d at 638, 532 N.E.2d at 1242–43, 536 N.Y.S.2d at 14–15 (Titone, J., dissenting).

Do you think that the claim should be characterized as a traditional medical malpractice action for personal injuries, or as an emotional distress cause of action to be governed by the special parameters of those cases (such as the impact rule, zone of danger)? Can you think of any alternative doctrinal contours for this claim?

9. *Legislative Action.* In response to litigation in this area, a number of states have passed legislation to set certain boundaries on the litigation. For instance, Maine's statute provides that the "birth of a normal, healthy child does not constitute a legally recognizable injury" and there is no cause of action for it (save for recovery of the mother's damages associated with the pregnancy itself); and that damages for wrongful birth are limited to damages associated with the disease or handicap. Me.Rev.Stat.Ann. § 2931 (West 1996).

Pennsylvania's statute, 42 Pa.Cons.Stat. § 8305(a) (1996), provides:

> (a) Wrongful birth.—There shall be no cause of action or award of damages on behalf of any person based on a claim that, but for an act or omission of the defendant, a person once conceived would not or should not have been born. Nothing contained in this subsection shall be construed to prohibit any cause of action or award of damages for the wrongful death of a woman, or on account of physical injury suffered by a woman or child, as a result of an attempted abortion. Nothing contained in this subsection shall be construed to provide a defense against any proceeding charging a health care practitioner with intentional misrepresentation under * * * [various acts] regulating the professional practices of health care practitioners.

10. Recent discussions of the subject in the legal literature include Micheal B. Laudor, *In Defense of Wrongful Life: Bringing Political Theory to the Defense of a Tort*, 62 Ford. L. Rev. 1675 (1994); Shelley A. Ryan, *Wrongful Birth: False Representations of Women's Reproductive Lives*, 78 Minn. L. Rev. 857 (1994); C. Symmons, *Policy Factors in Actions for Wrongful Birth*, 50 Mod.L.Rev. 269 (1987); Special Project, *Legal Rights and Issues Surrounding Conception, Pregnancy, and Birth*, 39 Vand.L.Rev. 597, 724–70 (1986). Compare Comment, *The Trend Toward Judicial Recognition of Wrongful Life: A Dissenting View*, 31 U.C.L.A. L.Rev. 473 (1985), *with* Comment, *Wrongful Life: The Tort That Nobody Wants*, 23 Santa Clara L.Rev. 847 (1983).

Chapter 13

LIABILITY INSURANCE

Tort litigation and liability insurance are, in Professor Kent Syverud's words, "symbiotic institutions." Without tort litigation, the institution of liability insurance would wither away, and without liability insurance many potential tort suits would never be brought. "The insurance industry and the [plaintiffs'] trial lawyers may take potshots at each other in attempts to reform aspects of the relationship, but they cannot afford to shoot to kill." Kent D. Syverud, *The Duty to Settle*, 76 Va. L. Rev. 1113, 1114 (1990). Tort doctrine and liability insurance have evolved together; changes in tort doctrine have affected the shape and scope of insurance, and vice versa.

The United States leads the world in the per capita consumption of liability insurance. American citizens spend in excess of $75 billion per year on liability insurance, which amounts to approximately 2% of the gross national product. "More than 3500 companies employ almost 330,000 workers—agents, brokers, and allied personnel—to sell and service the liability insurance 'product' that we so zealously consume." Kent D. Syverud, *On the Demand for Liability Insurance*, 72 Tex. L. Rev. 1629 (1994). The types of liability insurance most commonly involved in personal injury litigation are automobile, homeowner's, medical professional, and commercial general liability insurance.

This chapter offers an introduction to the fascinating and critical issues posed by the interaction of tort doctrine and liability insurance. (Chapter 14, on existing and proposed alternatives to tort, discusses other forms of insurance, such as workers' compensation insurance and automobile no-fault insurance.) The first two sections of the chapter examine the most basic functions that the liability insurance carrier performs in standard tort litigation: the duties to defend the suit and to pay judgments (part A) and the duty to respond reasonably to settlement offers made by the plaintiff (part B). Part C then considers several other issues relating to the interaction of tort with liability insurance: (1) whether we "overconsume" liability insurance, (2) subrogation, and (3) the process by which insurance carriers calculate the value of tort claims.

A.   THE DUTY TO DEFEND AND THE DUTY TO INDEMNIFY

NORTH STAR MUTUAL INSURANCE CO. v. R.W.

431 N.W.2d 138 (Minn.App.1988).

Heard, considered and decided by FOLEY, P.J., CRIPPEN and SHORT, JJ.

OPINION

FOLEY, JUDGE.

This appeal is from a summary judgment granted in favor of respondent North Star Insurance Company after it had brought a declaratory judgment action against appellant T.F. to determine whether T.F.'s homeowner's insurance policy provided coverage for the negligent transmission of herpes through voluntary consensual sexual intercourse. We reverse and remand for trial.

FACTS

T.F. was insured under a homeowner's policy issued by North Star effective July 9, 1983 through July 9, 1984. In May of 1984, T.F. and R.W., both adults, voluntarily engaged in sexual intercourse at T.F.'s home. Later that month, R.W. was diagnosed as having genital herpes. R.W. claims that T.F. negligently transmitted herpes to her through their sexual intercourse. T.F. acknowledges that after R.W. asked him to submit to a medical exam, he learned that he has herpes. He affirmatively asserts, however, that he did not know that he had herpes at the time that the couple engaged in intercourse.

The complaint specifically alleges that the actions of T.F. were negligent and not intentional. T.F. tendered the defense to North Star which declined coverage and subsequently commenced a declaratory judgment action. The trial court granted summary judgment in favor of North Star dismissing the complaint.

ISSUES

1.   Is the negligent transmission of herpes through voluntary consensual sexual intercourse an accidental occurrence under the homeowner's policy issued by North Star that requires North Star to defend the underlying action?

2.   When an adult insured engages in voluntary consensual sexual intercourse with an adult partner that results in the transmission of a sexual disease, must intent to injure be inferred as a matter of law where there exists a material issue of fact as to whether the disease was negligently transmitted?

3.   Is the duty to defend a claim of negligent transmission of a sexual disease under a homeowner's policy contrary to public policy?

ANALYSIS

* * *

1.   The issue of whether an insurance company, under the terms of a homeowner's policy, has a duty to defend its insured in a claim of negligent

transmission of herpes through voluntary consensual sexual intercourse is one of first impression in Minnesota.

It is well established however, that if any claim is made against an insured which could result in liability for covered damages, the insurer has a duty to defend. United States Fidelity & Guaranty Co. v. Roser, 585 F.2d 932 (8th Cir.1978). Additionally, the Minnesota Supreme Court has held: If any part of the claim is arguably within the scope of coverage afforded by the policy, the insurer should defend and reserve its right to contest coverage based on facts developed at trial. Brown v. State Automobile & Casualty Underwriters, 293 N.W.2d 822, 825–26 (Minn.1980) (emphasis added).

Examination of North Star's Policy Provisions

A. Definition of Bodily Injury

Bodily injury is defined as "bodily harm, sickness or disease to a person including required care, loss of services, and death resulting therefrom." (Emphasis added.) It was conceded at oral argument that herpes is a disease. The language in the policy is clear. Herpes is a disease, and is not specifically excluded from the policy.

B. Liability Provision

Under Coverage L, Personal Liability, the policy provides in part: We pay, up to our limit of liability, all sums for which any insured is legally liable because of bodily injury or property damage caused by an occurrence to which this coverage applies. We will defend any suit seeking damages, provided the suit resulted from bodily injury or property damage not excluded under this coverage. (Emphasis omitted.)

Occurrence is defined in the policy as "an accident, including continuous or repeated exposure to substantially similar conditions." An "accident" is not defined in the policy but has been defined in Minnesota in the landmark case of Hauenstein v. St. Paul–Mercury Indemnity Co., 242 Minn. 354, 65 N.W.2d 122 (1954), as follows: Accident, as a source and cause of damage to property, within the terms of an accident policy, is an unexpected, unforeseen, or undesigned happening or consequence from either a known or an unknown cause. Id. at 358–59, 65 N.W.2d at 126.

Here, T.F. contends that he did not know that he had herpes, and therefore the transmission of herpes to R.W. was an accident. Contrarily, North Star argues that the transmission of a sexual disease is never an accident, and the disease does not occur without wrongful sexual conduct. Our role on appeal is not to measure moral conduct but to determine if, under the facts stated, the duty to defend is required of North Star.

Only one other jurisdiction has considered this issue. In State Farm Fire and Casualty Co. v. Irene S. (Anonymous), 138 A.D.2d 589, 526 N.Y.S.2d 171 (1988), the plaintiff in the underlying action alleged that the defendant had intentionally assaulted and raped her with the intent of transmitting genital herpes. The defendant was covered by a homeowner's policy with language similar to that involved here. There, the New York court held that the defendant had set forth a meritorious defense in that if he proved that the damages sustained by the plaintiff were unintended, the injuries would be covered by the policy, and recognized that at the least, the insurer was obligated to defend in the underlying action, although a decision on the insurer's ultimate responsibility would have to await the trial itself. The court also recognized that it is not legally impossible to find accidental results flowing from intentional causes, i.e., that the resulting damage was unintended although the original act or acts leading to the damages were intentional. Id. at 591, 526 N.Y.S.2d at 173 (citations omitted).

We agree with the reasoning of the New York court. Here, T.F. contends that he did not know that he had herpes on the date that the couple had sexual intercourse. The claim is based in negligence principles. Accordingly, we hold that this is a material issue of fact for a jury to decide. Until this fact question is answered, we hold that the claim is arguably within the scope of coverage, and therefore North Star must defend T.F. in the underlying action. We observe that the duty to defend is broader than the duty to pay, and the obligation to defend is not synonymous with coverage.

2. North Star next contends that as a matter of law, the intentional acts exclusion should apply. The specific provision provides in part: 1. Exclusions that Apply to Both Personal Liability and Medical Payments to Others—This policy does not apply to liability:

* * *

h. caused intentionally by or at the direction of any insured; (Emphasis in original.)

North Star argues that intent to injure is inferred as a matter of law when the insured engages in sexual misconduct even though the claim is based on negligence. To support this argument, North Star cites five Minnesota cases. None of these cases supports North Star's argument that we should infer intent to injure upon the facts here. North Star relies on the following cases.

Fireman's Fund Insurance Co. v. Hill, 314 N.W.2d 834 (Minn.1982). Hill and his wife were foster parents. Hill had been arrested for criminal sexual conduct with a foster child. He engaged in sexual conduct with another boy for 15 months. Hill asserted that he did not intend to harm the boy. The court found that the nature of his conduct was such that an intention to inflict injury could be inferred as a matter of law. Before the abused boy was placed with Hill, the welfare department had confronted Hill with allegations that he had sexually assaulted other foster children. Hill knew that the welfare department viewed his conduct as detrimental to the boy. A psychiatrist testified that if Hill had been confronted with and warned of his activities with other children before having contact with the boy, then he must have realized that his sexual play with him was not in the boy's best interest. The court held that there facts give rise to an inference of intent to inflict injury.

Horace Mann Insurance Co. v. Independent School District No. 656, 355 N.W.2d 413 (Minn.1984). Phillips, a counselor/basketball coach for Independent School District No. 656, allegedly had sexual contact with R.L.E. a high school student who played on the girls basketball team.

Phillips became aware of R.L.E.'s history of drug use and began counseling her. She alleged that he inflicted several sexual contacts upon her during counseling with him and while on the basketball team. After the first alleged contact, she began to exhibit emotional problems more severe than those previously experienced with her drug problems. Since 1979 she experienced severe psychological illness and has required hospitalization on numerous occasions for suicidal tendencies, depression and anorexia. Her medical expenses as of 1983 were approximately $90,000. The court inferred intent to injure from the nature of the acts, nonconsensual sexual contact with a minor.

* * *

Here, North Star is asking us to infer intent as a matter of law in a negligence case involving consenting adults. We decline to do so because there is a remaining material issue of fact to be resolved.

3. North Star argues that it is against public policy to allow coverage here. North Star asserts in support of its position that Minnesota has not recognized a cause of action in tort for the transmission of sexual disease through sexual intercourse. We have, however, recently recognized a cause of action for the fraudulent and negligent transmission of sexual diseases, and in making that decision, we have outlined several important public policy considerations in support of that decision. See R.A.P. v. B.J.P., 428 N.W.2d 103, 106 (Minn.Ct.App.1988)("Minnesota courts have long recognized that the preservation of public health is a matter of great public importance. Legal duties and rules must therefore be designed, whenever possible, to help prevent the spread of dangerous, communicable diseases.")

Next, North Star argues that financial responsibility for sexual misconduct should not be spread among insureds through insurance. We find no merit in this argument. An insurance company can adjust and rewrite its policies to create more specific terms and exclusions. North Star could specifically exclude coverage to policy holders for the transmission of sexual diseases.

Accordingly, we hold that North Star's duty to defend T.F. pursuant to the terms of his homeowner's policy is not contrary to public policy.

DECISION

The decision of the trial court is reversed and remanded for trial of the underlying action. Viewed in the light most favorable to T.F., we hold that North Star's duty to defend T.F. in that action is arguably within the scope of coverage afforded by North Star's policy. The duty to indemnify, however, shall be deferred until a trial on the merits in the underlying action.

REVERSED AND REMANDED.

Notes

1. *Liability Insurance ("Third Party" Insurance) Versus First Party Insurance.* An understanding of insurance begins with the distinction between liability insurance ("third party" insurance) and "first party" insurance. The heart of liability insurance consists of the insurer's promise to pay a *third party*—the injured plaintiff—if the insured causes an injury of the sort covered

under the policy. In contrast, first party insurance is the term that applies to the promise by the insurer to pay *the insured* when the insured himself sustains a loss. Examples include health insurance, property insurance, and disability insurance—all these pay money to the insured when he has sustained a particular loss (medical bills, damaged or burned property, or disability rendering him unable to work). A typical homeowner's insurance policy consists of both first and third party insurance: liability insurance that will indemnify someone injured by the homeowner's actions, and first party insurance for damage to the home.

When significant numbers of people first started purchasing insurance to protect themselves against tort liability to third persons, in the latter part of the nineteenth century, the insurance was typically written as indemnity insurance. That is, the insurance company promised the insured to reimburse him, up to the policy limits, for any loss he might suffer as a result of a tort judgment, arising out of a covered risk, entered against him. Such contracts were open to abuse in that, if the insured were adjudicated a bankrupt after entry of a judgment against him, the insurance company would have no liability under the policy. The abuses are described in Roth v. National Automobile Mutual Casualty Co., 202 App.Div. 667, 195 N.Y.S. 865 (1922). Massachusetts in 1914 and New York in 1918 enacted statutes to prevent these abuses. In Merchants' Mutual Automobile Liability Insurance Co. v. Smart, 267 U.S. 126, 45 S.Ct. 320, 69 L.Ed. 538 (1925), the Court upheld the constitutionality of these statutes. By 1933, about half of the states had enacted such statutes. For these and other reasons the standard policies were changed by the insurance companies from contracts of indemnity into true liability policies. That is, the insurance contract provided that the company would pay on behalf of the insured all sums up to the policy limits "which the insured shall become legally *obligated* to pay" as a result of a covered risk.

The standard policy has traditionally stipulated that no action may be brought against the insurance company until the amount of the insured's obligation to pay has been finally determined by a judgment entered against the insured or a written settlement agreement signed by the insured, the claimant, and the company. Most courts uphold such clauses. Nevertheless in some states, *e.g.*, Louisiana and Wisconsin, by statute the claimant is permitted to join the insurance company as a defendant or even bring a direct action against the insurance carrier without joining the insured as a defendant. Rhode Island by statute permits a direct action against the insurer in some situations in which the defendant cannot be served. *See* Maczuga v. American Universal Insurance Co., 92 R.I. 76, 166 A.2d 227 (1960). In other states joinder or an action only against the insurance company is permitted in certain limited types of situations (*e.g.*, school bus accidents). On the general subject *see* 8 J. Appleman, Insurance §§ 4861–66 (Rev. ed. R. Buckley, 1981).

2. *Standard Liability Policies: The Duty to Defend and the Duty to Indemnify*. Most standard liability policies, such as the liability insurance involved in *North Star*, contain two promises by the insurer: (1) to provide a defense to the insured when the insured is sued on a claim potentially within policy coverage, even if the claim is frivolous (the "duty to defend"); and (2) to pay—up to policy limits—the injured party (or indemnify the insured for his payments to the injured party) for any tort judgment obtained against the insured so long as the judgment is within the scope of the policy's coverage (the "duty to indemnify"). The duty to defend is not capped by the policy limits; only the duty to indemnify is. Suppose, for instance, that the insured with a

$50,000 liability policy is sued on a tort claim, that the insurer spends $15,000 for attorney's fees in defending the case; and that the tort plaintiff obtains a judgment for $75,000. The insurer will be obligated to pay the full $50,000 of the policy amount, notwithstanding the insurer's expense for attorneys' fees.

Why do people purchase these two forms of insurance—insurance against defense costs, and insurance against tort liability? The reason is applicable to all forms of insurance: individuals are generally risk-averse with respect to losses that are significant in relation to the individual's wealth. To take a simplified example, suppose an individual faces a 2% chance that her $100,000 home will burn down. Her "expected loss"—the magnitude of the loss times the probability of its occurrence—is $2,000. So the following two items are an even bet: (1) paying $2000 now, or (2) facing a 2% chance that her home will burn down. A risk-neutral person would have no reason to prefer option 1 over option 2. Yet many individuals prefer option 1, and they implement that preference by paying insurance premiums. Insurers are willing to accept these premiums and to bear the risk not because they are risk-preferring, but because they can use the law of large numbers to their advantage. Insurers can pool together many similar risks to reduce random variation, and then can calculate the premiums that will be necessary to pay claims and still leave room for profit. More detail, as well as a rich discussion of insurance generally, appears in Kenneth S. Abraham, Distributing Risk (1986). Of course, to the extent that an insurer will have to satisfy some or all of the insured's legal obligations, it also has an incentive to try to control and limit the extent of those obligations and thus to manage the insured's legal defense.

3. *Insurance, Deterrence, and Fairness.* Does liability insurance blunt the potential deterrent impact of tort doctrine? This depends on how closely linked the insured's premiums are to the actual risks that the insured's behavior causes. Consider an example from Gary T. Schwartz, *The Ethics and the Economics of Tort Liability Insurance*, 75 Cornell L. Rev. 313 (1990). A manufacturer could alter a product design for a cost of $700 per unit and thereby avoid expected injuries per unit of $1000 (probability times magnitude of potential loss). If liability insurance is priced in a way that is perfectly tailored to the risk, then the manufacturer will know that it can either (1) pay $700 to alter the design, thereby lessening its insurance premium by $1000; or (2) refuse to alter the design and pay an increased premium of $1000. Plainly, the manufacturer would choose the first. But, of course, insurance premiums are not perfectly tailored, for many reasons. Still, "[m]ost liability insurance is written so as to render its premium somewhat responsive to the level of tortious risktaking engaged in by the insured." Schwartz, *supra,* at 363.

How does liability insurance relate to the aim of corrective justice? Does this depend on how well-tailored the insurance is to the risks posed by the insured? Why?

Do you suppose that T.F., the insured in the *North Star* case, paid homeowner's insurance premiums that were linked at all to his sexual conduct? Once insurers realize that their homeowners' policies will cover at least some tort judgments for negligently transmitted sexual diseases, then in theory several options are available. Insurers could: (1) predict the overall risks of such judgments posed by the complete pool of homeowners, and spread that aggregate risk to all homeowners by increasing the premium charged to every homeowner; (2) insert an exclusion in all homeowners' policies for negligence arising out of consensual sexual conduct; (3) charge a higher premium to those homeowners who might predictably be at higher risk for such judgments, just as a higher premium is charged to certain business owners who don't have fire sprinkler systems; or (4) write an exclusion for sexual negligence into most policies, but offer such coverage to insureds willing to pay an extra premium for this coverage.

What are the possible concerns raised by the first and second options? The third option might sound fine in theory, but in practice would it be possible for insurers to identify—except according to crude and perhaps objectionable criteria—which types of people are more at risk for these sorts of tort judgments? The fourth option also might sound promising, but insurers would be wary of it because the law of large numbers generally will not work well with respect to risks that are likely to be very much under the control of the insured. This last point is elaborated in the next note.

4. *The Intentional Injury Exclusion; Exclusions for Punitive Damages.* The term "exclusions" has an unpleasant ring but, to an extent, exclusions allow better risk differentiation and more precisely tailored coverage for insureds. For instance, a homeowner would prefer a policy with an exclusion for products liability coverage: the homeowner knows she has virtually no chance of being found liable as a products manufacturer or supplier, and she would not want to be lumped together in the same risk pool as product suppliers and be charged the resulting higher premium. If there were no exclusions for products liability, then the costs of losses resulting from products injuries would be spread through a risk pool that included not just products manufacturers and suppliers but also homeowners and business owners that have little to do with products.

Unsurprisingly, then, there are many different standardized types of liability coverage with different types of exclusions and coverage. Examples include commercial general liability policies (with or without products liability coverage); director and officer liability policies; and liability policies covering boilers and other machinery. For individuals, the most common types of liability coverage are the liability provisions of automobile policies, and the liability provisions of homeowners' coverage.

Most individual liability coverages, and many commercial coverages, specifically exclude, from the duty to indemnify, injuries expected or intended by the insured. Many of such risks are grouped together under the rubric "moral hazard." Insurers generally desire to exclude such risks for several reasons. First, intentional injuries—as distinct from accidentally produced injuries—are heavily in the control of insureds and thus are less predictable according to the law of large numbers. Second, particularly as to first-party insurance—such as property protection against fire or other types of damage—coverage for intentionally-caused losses would allow the insured to destroy his own property intentionally whenever the insurance proceeds would exceed the valuation of his property. Is this second rationale equally applicable to *liability* insurance coverage for intentional harms?

Is an intentional tort exclusion also understandable from the standpoint of at least some insureds, for at least some conduct? Suppose that you were choosing between two homeowners' insurance policies: Policy A would cover you only for negligently-caused injuries; Policy B would cover you for negligently and intentionally caused injuries, but this policy would cost you a substantially higher premium. Which would you choose, and why?

Closely related to the intentional injury exclusion is the question of coverage for punitive damages. If punitive damages are assessed against an insured on the basis of intentional conduct, then the intentional injury exclusion will apply. The exclusion might not apply, however, if the punitive damages award is based on reckless conduct. Some policies explicitly exclude coverage of punitive damages, in addition to the exclusion for intentional injury. For more detail, *see* Alan I. Widiss, *Liability Insurance Coverage for Punitive Damages? Discerning Answers to the Conundrum Created by Disputes Involving Conflicting Public Policies, Pragmatic Considerations and Political Actions,* 39 Vill. L. Rev. 455 (1994).

5. *Employment Discrimination, Sexual Harassment, and Other Sometimes–Covered Intentional Acts; The Public Policy Exclusion.* The intentional injury exclusion is a common but not universal feature of liability insurance. In recent years, for example, the insurance industry has offered a form of insurance known as "employment practices liability insurance," which covers employment discrimination, sexual harassment, and wrongful termination. One portion of the commonly used "commercial general liability" policy and of certain "excess" or "umbrella" polices contains no exclusion for intentional injury, and some courts have interpreted this to provide coverage for some claims of discrimination and harassment. *See* Union Camp Corp. v. Continental Casualty Co., 452 F.Supp. 565 (S.D.Ga.1978); Clark–Peterson Co. v. Independent Ins. Assoc., 492 N.W.2d 675 (Iowa 1992).

Some courts, however, after finding that a particular policy does provide coverage for certain intentional injuries, have disallowed such coverage on public policy grounds. *See* Rubenstein Lumber Co. v. Aetna Life & Cas. Co., 122 Ill.App.3d 717, 78 Ill.Dec. 541, 462 N.E.2d 660 (1984)(stating that, even if the policy did provide coverage for retaliatory discharge, the provision would be void as against public policy). And certain state statutes set out a public policy exclusion for intentional torts. In California, for instance, an "insurer is not liable for a loss caused by the willful act of the insured * * * but he is not exonerated by the negligence of the insured * * *" Cal. Ins. Code § 553 (West 1996).

If the insurer is willing to sell, and the insured to buy, coverage for intentionally caused harms, why would or should courts nonetheless find it against public policy? Go back to the points made in note 3, and consider whether and why such coverage might raise concerns about deterrence and corrective justice. In light of these concerns, consider three possible lawsuits: (1) a claim against an individual insured (such as a physician under a professional liability policy) for intentional sexual assault; (2) a claim against a corporation, based on vicarious liability, for sexual harassment by one of its employees; and (3) a "disparate impact" discrimination claim contending that the employer's use of certain hiring criteria had the unintended though likely consequence of disadvantaging women applicants. Are public policy concerns about deterrence and corrective justice equally forceful as to all these claims?

The boundaries of the public policy exclusion are still in flux. Some jurisdictions would probably apply the exclusion to all three of the claims just noted; others would not apply it to case 2, and still others would not apply it to cases 2 and 3. For further analysis, *see* Note, *The Public Policy Exclusion and Insurance for Intentional Employment Discrimination*, 92 Mich. L. Rev. 1256 (1994).

The public policy exclusion also comes into play when a particular liability insurance contract is interpreted as providing coverage for punitive damages. Many states by statute or by judicial decision disallow coverage of punitive damages; other states allow such coverage in at least some cases. Once again, the application of a public policy exclusion might differ depending on the nature of the underlying claim, as illustrated in the three patterns above. For further analysis and a thorough account of the jurisdictional postures, *see* Widiss, *supra.*

6. *Duty to Defend When There are Claims of Negligence and Intentional Conduct.* Many tort suits arise from conduct that arguably was intentional, but perhaps was only negligent. A tort plaintiff who was punched in the nose might believe that the injurer acted intentionally, and that alternatively the conduct was at least negligent. The "true" characterization will not be known until the case is adjudicated and the factfinder decides. Thus, this plaintiff may plead in the alternative, and may even submit both theories—negligence and intentional conduct—to the factfinder.

When the alleged puncher is sued, what is the insurer's obligation? Because intentional injury usually is excluded from insurance coverage, the insurer might contend that it has no duty to provide a defense since the plaintiff has pled an excluded theory. Courts almost uniformly reject this option. So long as the plaintiff pleads at least one claim that is potentially within policy coverage, then the insurer must provide a defense. Thus, the duty to defend generally depends on the allegations of the plaintiff's complaint, not on the "true" facts or on the facts as adjudicated. What if the plaintiff, furious at what happened, pleads only an intentional tort theory even though the "true facts" might reveal that the conduct was merely negligent? Many courts, following the California Supreme Court's decision in Gray v. Zurich Ins. Co., 65 Cal.2d 263, 54 Cal.Rptr. 104, 419 P.2d 168 (1966), hold that a duty to defend exists if the plaintiff's pleadings or other facts known to the insurer give rise to a "potential" for a covered claim. Thus, if the facts recounted in a pleading could raise a potential for a covered negligence theory, then the insurer must defend in any event.

In the *North Star* case, the insured, T.F., was sued on a complaint alleging negligence alone, and he tendered the complaint to the carrier requesting a defense. If you were in-house counsel for the carrier, would you advise the carrier that it could deny a defense? That it must provide a defense? Suppose that T.F. had been sued on both a negligence claim and an intentional tort claim, or on an intentional tort theory alone. What would your advice be in this event?

What reasons might explain and support the rules that have evolved about the duty to defend? One way to get at these is to envision the alternative: the carrier is allowed to deny a defense whenever it believes that the "true" facts will show the case really is not covered; the carrier would be liable for breach of the duty to defend only if ultimately (after adjudication in an insurance coverage dispute) the carrier's view of the true facts were rejected by the factfinder. Presumably, we would all pay lower premiums for this type of defense insurance, but the certainty of protection would be diminished. Which version of defense insurance would you prefer?

7. *Pleading With the Aim of Accessing Insurance.* The plaintiff in *North Star* sued T.F. only on a negligence theory. If no insurance considerations had been at stake (if, for instance, T.F. had no insurance or was wealthy enough to

satisfy personally any tort judgment plaintiff had obtained), would plaintiff have pled any differently? Whether T.F.'s actions were intentional or negligent really might have been a close call; the plaintiff might have been genuinely unsure of what the factfinder ultimately might decide. Thus it might make sense to plead on negligence grounds notwithstanding a potential intentional tort action as well. But why would the plaintiff have omitted the intentional tort claim, absent insurance considerations?

Given the possible systemic objectives of tort law—efficiency, corrective justice, recognition of the victim's loss, distributive justice—should we care that, in gray cases, the existence of insurance might cause the tort plaintiff to "underlitigate," that is to characterize intentional conduct as merely negligent? For more detail on the topic, *see* Ellen S. Pryor, *The Stories We Tell: Intentional Harm and the Quest for Insurance Funding,* 75 Tex.L.Rev. (1997).

Despite the general rule that the duty to defend is governed by the plaintiff's allegations and the potential for coverage, insurers in certain patterns of cases have successfully denied a defense despite the plaintiff's artful pleadings. The most common example of this is the significant quantity of litigation arising from adult defendants who have sex with minors; the *North Star* opinion discusses several of these. In these child molestation cases, courts usually infer intent as a matter of law from the basic facts, and thus hold that there is no potential for coverage, notwithstanding plaintiff's allegations that the defendant was negligent. *See* J.C. Penney Casualty Ins. Co. v. M.K., 52 Cal.3d 1009, 278 Cal.Rptr. 64, 804 P.2d 689 (1991). In *J.C. Penney,* the child and mother argued that the molestation was not intentional because the molester meant no harm and was merely acting in a "misguided attempt to show love and affection." *Id.* at 1009, 278 Cal.Rptr. at 65, 804 P.2d at 690. The court nonetheless inferred intent.

8. *The Duty to Indemnify.* The plaintiff in *North Star,* by suing T.F. on a negligence theory, triggered the carrier's duty to defend. But the mere allegation of a covered theory does not trigger the duty to *indemnify or pay.* Rather, North Star would have a duty to indemnify only if (1) a tort judgment against T.F. were entered; and (2) the tort judgment were for an injury that was in fact within the scope of policy coverage—that is, negligent rather than intentional. Why, then, might a tort plaintiff see any advantage to pleading a case in a way that triggers a duty to defend, if this pleading does not also trigger the duty to pay? There are several reasons. First, the very fact that a carrier has to pay defense costs might create some incentive for the carrier to settle the case. Second, in some jurisdictions, a carrier that breaches its duty to defend is considered "estopped" from arguing that it has no duty to pay. This means that pleading the case in a way which triggers a duty to defend might create a back door to insurance coverage, even though the front door— the policy language itself—is closed. These and other reasons are explored more fully in Pryor, *supra.* In most cases, however, if the insurance company acts properly, then the insurer (1) will provide a defense when a potentially covered claim exists, and (2) will be able to avoid paying any judgment that in fact is for an uncovered injury.

Did the court's ruling in *North Star* resolve the duty to defend, the duty to indemnify, or both? What still remains to be determined?

9. *Conflicts of Interest.* Suppose that the plaintiff in *North Star* had sued T.F. for both intentional conduct and negligence, and that the carrier, when it received copies of the plaintiff's pleading against T.F., decided that it had a

duty to defend and hired a lawyer for this purpose. As to the tort litigation, the carrier's interests would conflict with those of T.F., the insured. Both, of course, would like to see the plaintiff lose altogether. But, if the plaintiff were to prevail, the insurer would prefer the judgment to be based on intentional conduct, and the insured—T.F.—would prefer the judgment to be based on negligence. The prevailing rule now is that, when a conflict of interest relating to coverage exists and the conflict may affect how the tort claim is litigated, the carrier must provide "independent counsel." That is, the insurance carrier must pay the lawyer's bills but does not have the right to control or direct the defense or the defense strategy. This is in contrast to the pattern in garden-variety claims where no conflict of interest exists—for instance, when the plaintiff is sued for negligence in causing a car crash and the insurer does not dispute coverage. Then the insurance company will select the defense lawyer and has the right to control the defense.

Suppose North Star had agreed to provide independent counsel to T.F. How would both sides present the case? T.F. and his lawyer would have reason to litigate the case in a way that emphasized negligence and not intentional conduct. The tort plaintiff, too, would have reason to emphasize the negligence case and not the intentional tort case, if insurance funds were the only source of recovery. Suppose, then, that the plaintiff obtained a tort judgment against T.F. on a theory of negligence only. Would this trigger the duty to indemnify, since the theory on which the judgment rested—negligence—was indeed covered? Although some doctrinal differences exist on the question, the general rule now seems to be that the carrier will not be bound to the finding of negligence and will be able to contest—in a separate action on the coverage question—whether or not the injury was intentionally inflicted. Put another way, the finding of negligence in the tort action will not have collateral estoppel effect in the coverage action between the insurance carrier and the insured. For more detail, see Allan D. Windt, Insurance Claims and Disputes, Vol. 1, at 430–31 (3d ed.1995).

The relationship between the insured, the insurance defense counsel, and the insurance carrier is often known as the "tripartite" relationship. It has generated complex and still unsettled questions relating to when an attorney-client relationship exists, what the scope of that relationship is, and what the duties of the attorney are in various insurance defense situations. The American Law Institute is currently drafting a Restatement of the Law Governing Lawyers, and serious disagreement over some of these questions persists. To illustrate some of these questions, suppose that the tort plaintiff brings an action against the insured for injuries arising from a boating accident. The insured defendant forwards the complaint to the insurance company, which then hires insurance defense counsel to represent the insured. Who is or are the client or clients of the insurance defense counsel—the insured only, or also the insurance company? Professor Charles Silver has argued that there is no preordained answer to this question, that attorney-client relationships arise by consensual agreement, and therefore that the defense counsel may have two clients—the insurer and the insured. Yet this view is not universal. For discussion of the views, see Charles Silver, *Does Insurance Defense Counsel Represent the Company or the Insured?*, 72 Tex. L. Rev. 1583 (1994). To continue with our example, suppose the defense counsel works on the case for several months and then learns enough facts from the insured to raise the chance that the boating accident occurred during a "business use" of the boat, and thus possibly is excluded from coverage under the policy. If the defense counsel notifies the insurance company of these facts, this will disadvantage the insured. But if the defense counsel suppresses these facts from the insurance company, this will disadvantage the insurance company. Some have argued that the defense counsel, when presented with a conflict, owes a duty only to the insured or that the duty to the insured overrides the duty to the other client, the insurance company. By contrast, Professors Silver and Syverud have argued that, if both the insured and the insurance company are clients, then the defense counsel owes full ethical and fiduciary duties to both, and must resolve this and other problems under the appropriate rules governing conflicts of interest when an attorney has multiple clients. Their views, as well as background to this and related controversies, are set out in Charles Silver & Kent Syverud, *The Professional Responsibilities of Insurance Defense Lawyers,* 45 Duke L.J. 255 (1995).

B.   THE DUTY TO SETTLE

CRISCI v. SECURITY INSURANCE COMPANY OF NEW HAVEN, CONNECTICUT

Supreme Court of California, 1967.
66 Cal.2d 425, 426 P.2d 173, 58 Cal.Rptr. 13.

PETERS, JUSTICE.

In an action against The Security Insurance Company of New Haven, Connecticut, the trial court awarded Rosina Crisci $91,000 (plus interest) because she suffered a judgment in a personal injury action after Security, her insurer, refused to settle the claim. Mrs. Crisci was also awarded $25,000 for mental suffering. Security has appealed.

June DiMare and her husband were tenants in an apartment building owned by Rosina Crisci. Mrs. DiMare was descending the apartment's outside wooden staircase when a tread gave way. She fell through the resulting opening up to her waist and was left hanging 15 feet above the ground. Mrs. DiMare suffered physical injuries and developed a very severe psychosis. In a suit brought against Mrs. Crisci the DiMares alleged that the step broke because Mrs. Crisci was negligent in inspecting and maintaining the stairs. They contended that Mrs. DiMare's mental condition was caused by the accident, and they asked for $400,000 as compensation for physical and mental injuries and medical expenses.

Mrs. Crisci had $10,000 of insurance coverage under a general liability policy issued by Security. The policy obligated Security to defend the suit against Mrs. Crisci and authorized the company to make any settlement it deemed expedient. * * * Security hired an experienced lawyer, Mr. Healy, to handle the case. Both he and defendant's claims manager believed that unless evidence was discovered showing that Mrs. DiMare had a prior mental illness, a jury would probably find that the accident precipitated Mrs. DiMare's psychosis. And both men believed that if the jury felt that the fall triggered the psychosis, a verdict of not less than $100,000 would be returned.

An extensive search turned up no evidence that Mrs. DiMare had any prior mental abnormality. As a teenager Mrs. DiMare had been in a Washington mental hospital, but only to have an abortion. Both Mrs.

DiMare and Mrs. Crisci found psychiatrists who would testify that the accident caused Mrs. DiMare's illness, and the insurance company knew of this testimony. Among those who felt the psychosis was not related to the accident were the doctors at the state mental hospital where Mrs. DiMare had been committed following the accident. All the psychiatrists agreed, however, that a psychosis could be triggered by a sudden fear of falling to one's death.

The exact chronology of settlement offers is not established by the record. However, by the time the DiMares' attorney reduced his settlement demands to $10,000, Security had doctors prepared to support its position and was only willing to pay $3,000 for Mrs. DiMare's physical injuries. Security was unwilling to pay one cent for the possibility of a plaintiff's verdict on the mental illness issue. This conclusion was based on the assumption that the jury would believe all of the defendant's psychiatric evidence and none of the plaintiff's. Security also rejected a $9,000 settlement demand at a time when Mrs. Crisci offered to pay $2,500 of the settlement.

A jury awarded Mrs. DiMare $100,000 and her husband $1,000. After an appeal * * * the insurance company paid $10,000 of this amount, the amount of its policy. The DiMares then sought to collect the balance from Mrs. Crisci. A settlement was arranged by which the DiMares received $22,000, a 40 percent interest in Mrs. Crisci's claim to a particular piece of property, and an assignment of Mrs. Crisci's cause of action against Security. Mrs. Crisci, an immigrant widow of 70, became indigent. She worked as a babysitter, and her grandchildren paid her rent. The change in her financial condition was accompanied by a decline in physical health, hysteria, and suicide attempts. Mrs. Crisci then brought this action.

The liability of an insurer in excess of its policy limits for failure to accept a settlement offer within those limits was considered by this court in Comunale v. Traders & General Ins. Co., 50 Cal.2d 654, 328 P.2d 198, 68 A.L.R.2d 883. It was there reasoned that in every contract, including policies of insurance, there is an implied covenant of good faith and fair dealing that neither party will do anything which will injure the right of the other to receive the benefits of the agreement; that it is common knowledge that one of the usual methods by which an insured receives protection under a liability insurance policy is by settlement of claims without litigation; that the implied obligation of good faith and fair dealing requires the insurer to settle in an appropriate case although the express terms of the policy do not impose the duty; that in determining whether to settle the insurer must give the interests of the insured at least as much consideration as it gives to its own interests; and that when 'there is great risk of a recovery beyond the policy limits so that the most reasonable manner of disposing of the claim is a settlement which can be made within those limits, a consideration in good faith of the insured's interest requires the insurer to settle the claim.' * * *

In determining whether an insurer has given consideration to the interests of the insured, the test is whether a prudent insurer without policy limits would have accepted the settlement offer. * * *

Several cases, in considering the liability of the insurer, contain language to the effect that bad faith is the equivalent of dishonesty, fraud, and concealment. * * * Obviously a showing that the insurer has been guilty of actual dishonesty, fraud, or concealment is relevant to the determination whether it has given consideration to the insured's interest in considering a settlement offer within the policy limits. The language used in the cases, however, should not be understood as meaning that in the absence of evidence establishing actual dishonesty, fraud, or concealment no recovery may be had for a judgment in excess of the policy limits. Comunale v. Traders & General Ins. Co., supra, 50 Cal.2d 654, 658—659, 328 P.2d 198, makes it clear that liability based or an implied covenant exists whenever the insurer refuses to settle in an appropriate case and that liability may exist when the insurer unwarrantedly refuses an offered settlement where the most reasonable manner of disposing of the claim is by accepting the settlement. Liability is imposed not for a bad faith breach of the contract but for failure to meet the duty to accept reasonable settlements, a duty included within the implied covenant of good faith and fair dealing. Moreover, * * * recovery may be based on unwarranted rejection of a reasonable settlement offer and * * * the absence of evidence, circumstantial or direct, showing actual dishonesty, fraud, or concealment is not fatal to the cause of action.

Amicus curiae argues that, whenever an insurer receives an offer to settle within the policy limits and rejects it, the insurer should be liable in every case for the amount of any final judgment whether or not within the policy limits. As we have seen, the duty of the insurer to consider the insured's interest in settlement offers within the policy limits arises from an implied covenant in the contract, and ordinarily contract duties are strictly enforced and not subject to a standard of reasonableness. Obviously, it will always be in the insured's interest to settle within the policy limits when there is any danger, however slight, of a judgment in excess of those limits. Accordingly the rejection of a settlement within the limits where there is any danger of a judgment in excess of the limits can be justified, if at all, only on the basis of interests of the insurer, and, in light of the common knowledge that settlement is one of the usual methods by which an insured receives protection under a liability policy, it may not be unreasonable for an insured who purchases a policy with limits to believe that a sum of money equal to the limits is available and will be used so as to avoid liability on his part with regard to any covered accident. In view of such expectation an insurer should not be permitted to further its own interests by rejecting opportunities to settle within the policy limits unless it is also willing to absorb losses which may result from its failure to settle.

The proposed rule is a simple one to apply and avoids the burdens of a determination whether a settlement offer within the policy limits was reasonable. The proposed rule would also eliminate the danger that an insurer, faced with a settlement offer at or near the policy limits, will reject it and gamble with the insured's money to further its own interests. Moreover, it is not entirely clear that the proposed rule would place a burden on insurers substantially greater than that which is present under existing law. The size of the judgment recovered in the personal injury action when it exceeds the policy limits, although not conclusive, furnishes an inference that the value of the claim is the equivalent of the amount of the judgment and that acceptance of an offer within those limits was the most reasonable method of dealing with the claim.

Finally, and most importantly, there is more than a small amount of elementary justice in a rule that would require that, in this situation where the insurer's and insured's interests necessarily conflict, the insurer, which may reap the benefits of its determination not to settle, should also suffer the detriments of its decision. On the basis of these and other considerations, a number of commentators have urged that the insurer should be liable for any resulting judgment where it refuses to settle within the policy limits. * * *

We need not, however, here determine whether there might be some countervailing considerations precluding adoption of the proposed rule because, under Comunale v. Traders & General Ins. Co., supra, 50 Cal.2d 654, 328 P.2d 198, and the cases following it, the evidence is clearly sufficient to support the determination that Security breached its duty to consider the interests of Mrs. Crisci in proposed settlements. Both Security's attorney and its claims manager agreed that if Mrs. DiMare won an award for her psychosis, that award would be at least $100,000. Security attempts to justify its rejection of a settlement by contending that it believed Mrs. DiMare had no chance of winning on the mental suffering issue. That belief in the circumstances present could be found to be unreasonable. Security was putting blind faith in the power of its psychiatrists to convince the jury when it knew that the accident could have caused the psychosis, that its agents had told it that without evidence of prior mental defects a jury was likely to believe the fall precipitated the psychosis, and that Mrs. DiMare had reputable psychiatrists on her side. Further, the company had been told by a psychiatrist that in a group of 24 psychiatrists, 12 could be found to support each side.

The trial court found that defendant 'knew that there was a considerable risk of substantial recovery beyond said policy limits' and that 'the defendant did not give as much consideration to the financial interests of its said insured as it gave to its own interests.' That is all that was required. The award of $91,000 must therefore be affirmed.

We must next determine the propriety of the award of Mrs. Crisci of $25,000 for her mental suffering. In Comunale v. Traders & General Ins. Co., supra, 50 Cal.2d 654, 663, 328 P.2d 198, 203, it was held that an action of the type involved here sounds in both contract and tort and that 'where a case sounds both in contract and tort the plaintiff will ordinarily have freedom of election between an action of tort and one of contract. An exception to this rule is made in suits for personal injury caused by negligence, where the tort character of the action is considered to prevail (citations), but no such exception is applied in cases, like the present one, which relate to financial damage (citations).' * * *

Fundamental in our jurisprudence is the principle that for every wrong there is a remedy and that an injured party should be compensated for all damage proximately caused by the wrongdoer. Although we recognize exceptions from these fundamental principles, no departure should be sanctioned unless there is a strong necessity therefor.

The general rule of damages in tort is that the injured party may recover for all detriment caused whether it could have been anticipated or not. * * * In accordance with the general rule, it is settled in this state that mental suffering constitutes an aggravation of damages when it naturally ensues from the act complained of, and in this connection mental suffering includes nervousness, grief, anxiety, worry, shock, humiliation and indignity as well as physical pain. * * * Such awards are not confined to cases where the mental suffering award was in addition to an award for personal injuries; damages for mental distress have also been awarded in cases where the tortious conduct was an interference with property rights without any personal injuries apart from the mental distress.

We are satisfied that a plaintiff who as a result of a defendant's tortious conduct loses his property and suffers mental distress may recover not only for the pecuniary loss but also for his mental distress. No substantial reason exists to distinguish the cases which have permitted recovery for mental distress in actions for invasion of property rights. The principal reason for limiting recovery of damages for mental distress is that to permit recovery of such damages would open the door to fictitious claims, to recovery for mere bad manners, and to litigation in the field of trivialities. * * * Obviously, where, as here, the claim is actionable and has resulted in substantial damages apart from those due to mental distress, the danger of fictitious claims is reduced, and we are not here concerned with mere bad manners or trivialities but tortious conduct resulting in substantial invasions of clearly protected interests. * * *

Recovery of damages for mental suffering in the instant case does not mean that in every case of breach of contract the injured party may recover such damages. Here the breach also constitutes a tort. Moreover, plaintiff did not seek by the contract involved here to obtain a commercial advantage but to protect herself against the risks of accidental losses, including the mental distress which might follow from the losses. Among the considerations in purchasing liability insurance, as insurers are well aware, is the peace of mind and security it will provide in the event of an accidental loss, and recovery of damages for mental suffering has been permitted for breach of contracts which directly concern the comfort, happiness or personal esteem of one of the parties. * * *

It is not claimed that plaintiff's mental distress was not caused by defendant's refusal to settle or that the damages awarded were excessive in the light of plaintiff's substantial suffering.

The judgment is affirmed.

TRAYNOR, C.J., and McCOMB, TOBRINER, MOSK and BURKE, JJ., concur.

Notes

1. *The Insurer's Contractual Right to Control Defense and Settlement.* Most standard liability policies give the insurance company the "right and duty to defend the suit," and many policies provide that the company may "investigate and settle any claim or 'suit' at [the company's] discretion." As Professor Charles Silver has explained:

> These contract provisions are generally interpreted as granting the company plenary and exclusive control of the defense. Ordinarily, the company

can select counsel to defend the insured, discharge appointed counsel and name a replacement without the insured's consent, bargain with appointed counsel over fees, monitor counsel and direct litigation strategy, require counsel to inform the company of settlement demands and procedural developments, direct counsel to initiate settlement discussions, settle claims without an insured's consent and decline to settle claims over an insured's objection, and file appeals.

Charles Silver, *Does Insurance Defense Counsel Represent the Company or the Insured?*, 72 Tex. L. Rev. 1583, 1594–95 (1994).

Why would insurers, under standard liability policies, be unwilling to yield to insureds the ability to choose defense counsel, select defense strategy, and make settlement decisions? Why might it be in insureds' interests (in at least some situations) to agree to give insurers control over the defense and settlement of the case?

2. *Evaluating Settlement Demands In the Absence of Insurance.* To understand why courts have imposed certain standards on insurers when evaluating settlement offers, one must first appreciate some basics about settlement evaluation when no insurance is involved. In the absence of insurance, whether and when a defendant will accept a plaintiff's "demand" to settle will turn in large part on the expected costs of going to trial. These costs consist of the expected judgment if defendant loses multiplied by the expected probability of loss at trial, plus the additional attorneys' fees and court costs that defendant will incur by going to trial. Consider the following example, drawn from Kent Syverud, *The Duty to Settle*, 76 Va. L. Rev. 1113, 1128–29 (1990). Plaintiff demands $50,000 to settle her tort suit. Defendant evaluates the chances of a plaintiff verdict at 80%, the chances of a no-liability verdict at 20%, and the amount of the expected verdict (if plaintiff wins) as $40,000. Defendant also realizes that he will spend another $20,000 in fees and costs if the case goes to trial. Thus, defendant's full expected costs of turning down the settlement demand and proceeding to trial are: (.8 x $40,000) + $20,000 = $52,000. The defendant would rationally accept the plaintiff's demand.

3. *How Liability Insurance Affects the Evaluation of Settlement Offers.* Drawing again from Professor Syverud's analysis, suppose that the defendant in the above example has liability insurance of $100,000. Both the insurer and the defendant have a common interest in defeating the tort claim entirely. But their interests diverge with respect to settlement demands. Suppose again that the expected costs of going to trial are $52,000, and that the plaintiff submits a settlement demand of $99,000. What will the insurer prefer—accepting or rejecting the offer? What will the insured defendant prefer?

Now suppose that the plaintiff has a 90% chance of obtaining a liability verdict, and that the expected judgment amount should the plaintiff win is $200,000. Now the expected value of the plaintiff's claim is $180,000. The plaintiff demands to settle the case for $99,000. If the insurer rejects the demand and goes on to trial, it will risk only an additional $1000 (plus costs of defense) and will still have a small chance (10%) that it will win altogether. What will the insurer prefer? What will the insured defendant prefer?

The presence of a policy limit—$100,000 in our example—thus creates a conflict of interest with respect to settlement demands within policy limits. There are other sources of conflict between insurers and insureds with respect to settlement, and these also are explored in Professor Syverud's article.

In the *Crisci* case, was there a conflict of interest between Mrs. Crisci and the insurer?

4. *The Judicially Imposed Duty to Settle.* Most jurisdictions, many of them following *Crisci* explicitly, have recognized an extracontractual duty to settle on the part of liability insurers. Like the *Crisci* court, most jurisdictions hold that a claim for breach of the duty to settle sounds in tort; the factfinder in this tort action will be asked to evaluate whether the insurer's conduct comported with the required standard. Most jurisdictions use one or more of the following standards: (1) The insurer must act with reasonable care in evaluating settlement demands; (2) The insurer must act with good faith in evaluating settlement demands; (3) The insurer must give equal consideration to the interests of the insured and the insurer when evaluating settlement demands; and (4) The insurance company, when evaluating a settlement demand, must view the situation as it would if there were no policy limit applicable to the claim. The last standard was suggested by then-Professor, now-Judge Robert Keeton, in *Liability Insurance and Responsibility for Settlement*, 67 Harv. L. Rev. 1136 (1954). Some courts have added a requirement that the insurer have acted "recklessly" or with some gross absence of care. For instance, in Pavia v. State Farm Mutual Automobile Ins. Co., 82 N.Y.2d 445, 626 N.E.2d 24, 605 N.Y.S.2d 208 (1993), the court held that the insured must show a " 'gross disregard' of the insured's interests—that is, a deliberate or reckless failure to place on equal footing the interests of its insured with its own interests when considering a settlement offer."

Commentators and courts have considered a version of strict liability: the insurer will be liable any time it rejects a within-limits demand and the trial results in a verdict in excess of policy limits. No state has adopted this, however.

What are the benefits of a judicially imposed duty to settle? What are the costs? One obvious cost is that insurers, when defending tort suits against insureds, spend money and effort "to document the reasonableness of the insurer's behavior as much as to assist the insurer in resolving the underlying litigation." Syverud, *supra*, at 1165–66. Another potential cost is that insurers will essentially overpay some tort claims—a cost passed on to all insureds— when there is considerable ambiguity about how a jury in the later duty-to-settle suit will assess the insurer's conduct. These concerns are parallel to "overdeterrence" concerns raised in other tort contexts. Is the zone of uncertainty greater as to duty-to-settle contexts than as to, say, predictions about whether particular product design decisions will be found negligent by a jury?

Consider a modified strict liability standard proposed by Professor Syverud: The insurer will be liable for a verdict in excess of policy limits if the insurer refused to pay a sum equal to the value placed on the case by a neutral arbitrator, mediator, or settlement judge. The practical import of this proposal increases as more and more courts employ or mandate alternative dispute resolution.

For additional discussion of the rationale for duty to settle, see Kenneth S. Abraham, Distributing Risk 188–95 (1986); Kyle D. Logue, *Solving the Judgment–Proof Problem*, 72 Tex. L. Rev. 1375 (1994); Charles Silver, *A Missed Misalignment of Interests: A Comment on Syverud*, 77 Va. L. Rev. 1585 (1991). Syverud, *supra*. One commentator finds unpersuasive the theoretical and practical arguments for a judicially imposed duty to settle. *See* Alan O. Sykes,

Judicial Limitations on the Discretion of Liability Insurers to Settle or Litigate: An Economic Critique, 72 Tex. L. Rev. 1345 (1994).

5. *No Direct Claim Against Insurer By the Tort Claimant.* If an insurer unreasonably fails to respond to a settlement initiative made by the tort plaintiff, may the tort plaintiff directly sue the insurer? The judicially-developed duty to settle is a duty that the insurer owes to the insured defendant, not to the tort plaintiff. Insurance codes in virtually all states, however, also prohibit insurers from engaging in various unfair or fraudulent settlement practices. In 1979, the California Supreme Court interpreted the California insurance code as allowing a direct cause of action to tort plaintiffs themselves for "unfair claims settlement practices" by an insurer. Royal Globe Ins. Co. v. Superior Court, 23 Cal.3d 880, 153 Cal.Rptr. 842, 592 P.2d 329 (1979). Most other state courts did not interpret their own codes similarly, and *Royal Globe* was the subject of much criticism. The core criticism stemmed from the concern that recognizing a duty on the insurer's part to deal reasonably with the tort plaintiff would conflict with the duty that the insurer unquestionably owes to the insured to defend it against the tort lawsuit. Is such a concern warranted? Why?

A differently constituted Supreme Court of California, however, held, in a 5–2 decision given only prospective effect, that violations of the California Insurance Code do not by themselves give a right of action against the insurance company either to the insured or to a claimant against the insured. Moradi–Shalal v. Fireman's Fund Ins. Cos., 46 Cal.3d 287, 250 Cal.Rptr. 116, 758 P.2d 58 (1988). The court in *Moradi–Shalal,* however, went out of its way to declare that "apart from administrative remedies [to enforce the provisions of the insurance code], the courts retain jurisdiction to impose civil damages or other remedies against insurers in appropriate common law actions based on such traditional theories as fraud, infliction of emotional distress, and (as to the insured) either breach of contract or breach of the implied covenant of good faith and fair dealing." 46 Cal.3d at 304–05, 250 Cal.Rptr. at 127, 758 P.2d at 68–69.

6. *Strategic Opportunities for Plaintiffs.* Assume you are a plaintiff's lawyer representing a plaintiff injured in an intersectional collision; the plaintiff has severe brain damage and probably will need expensive care throughout her lifetime. The other driver has liability limits of $50,000, and there is no other possible defendant. Although accounts differ somewhat on who was at fault and by how much, the stronger evidence suggests that the defendant was probably more at fault. The other driver is virtually judgment-proof beyond her liability insurance.

Your jurisdiction recognizes the extracontractual duty to settle. If the insurer does not respond reasonably to a within-limits demand, then the insurer will be liable to the insured for any tort judgment in excess of policy limits.

You have several options: (1) Make a policy limits demand of $50,000, spelling out all the facts and giving the insurer ample time to respond; or (2) Make a policy limits demand of $50,000, giving the insurer a limited time to respond, in the hopes that the insurer will reject or fail to answer the demand, and that a later jury will find the insurer's rejection or response unreasonable. If this occurs, the insurer will be liable to the insured for the amount of the excess judgment, and your excess judgment will become collectable, not just a piece of paper. Indeed, most jurisdictions allow the insured defendant to "assign" away his or her cause of action against an insurance company. This means that, if the jury in the tort suit were to award an excess judgment against the insured defendant, you could approach the insured defendant and propose a deal: the plaintiff will "covenant not to execute" on the tort judgment, and in exchange the insured defendant will assign to your plaintiff the insured defendant's cause of action against the insurance company for breach of the duty to settle. Your plaintiff then can sue the insurance company directly, as assignee of the insured defendant. (Under an even more stream-lined approach that is often employed, the plaintiff and defendant agree to settle the case for an excess amount—such as $2,000,000 on our facts—the parties enter into a covenant not to execute and assignment of the insured's rights to the tort plaintiff, and then the tort plaintiff sues the insurer for breach of the duty to settle, seeking to collect this $2 million excess judgment.)

Would you pursue the second option? When would you send the demand letter, and how much time would you give the insurer? Remember that all this will be to no avail if the jury does not find that the insurer's failure to respond, or rejection, was unreasonable. In some cases, judges or juries have found that a 10–day or two-week limit did not present a reasonable offer to settle, especially if the demand was sent soon after the suit was filed. *See* Ashbrook v. Kowalick, 332 F.Supp. 78 (E.D.Pa.1971); Kriz v. Government Employees Ins. Co., 42 Or.App. 339, 600 P.2d 496 (1979). But sometimes plaintiffs have succeeded with demands of one or two week duration. *See* Critz v. Farmers Ins. Group, 230 Cal.App.2d 788, 41 Cal.Rptr. 401 (1964).

Suppose you gave a two-week limit, and the insurer rejected the demand. Two weeks later, however, the insurer switches course and offers the policy limits. Should you reject this and continue with your effort to obtain an amount in excess of policy limits? Most courts hold that, if a carrier's refusal is unreasonable, this "locks the insurer in by foreclosing it from later avoiding excess liability by offering its policy limits in settlement." Allan D. Windt, Insurance Claims and Disputes, Vol. 1 at 346 (3d ed. 1995). So, if you turn down the offered policy limits, and if you eventually prove that the carrier's initial rejection was unreasonable, you will succeed in obtaining more than $50,000. Should you turn down the sure $50,000 (the offered limits) in favor of this chance? What factors would you take into account in making a recommen-dation to the client?

A plaintiff's lawyer might have a strategic opportunity in a slightly different type of case: when the insurer doubts that there is coverage at all under the insurance policy. For instance, suppose that the plaintiff was shot by a neighbor with a gun following an argument. The plaintiff's lawyer files the case and pleads negligence; the insurance company provides a defense (because the complaint states a potentially covered claim) but reserves its right to contest coverage of the incident. The policy limits are $20,000. The plaintiff's lawyer makes a demand for $20,000. If the injury was only negli-gently inflicted, then the insurer would pay the demand because this is reasonable in light of the potential tort judgment against the insured. But if the injury was intentionally inflicted, then the policy does not cover it and in theory the insurer owes nothing. But whether the injury was or was not intentionally inflicted has not yet been adjudicated, and the insurer now is faced with the settlement demand.

Courts are still enunciating standards for this thorny problem. If the insurer turns out to be incorrect about the coverage issue, some courts hold that the insurer has breached the duty to settle even if its coverage decision was based on a good faith appraisal of the facts at the time. For further discussion, *see* Windt, *supra*, at 321–22; Stephen S. Ashley, *Coverage Doubts and the Insurer's Duty to Settle*, 4 Bad Faith L.Rep. 27 (1988). If you were in-house counsel to the insurer in the above example, what would you advise the insurer to do with respect to the $20,000 demand from the plaintiff if the potential excess verdict against the insured defendant is extremely high?

C. OTHER ISSUES RELATING TO LIABILITY INSURANCE

1. Do We "Overconsume" Liability Insurance?

KENT D. SYVERUD, ON THE DEMAND FOR LIABILITY INSURANCE *

72 Tex. L. Rev. 1629 (1994).

Liability insurance pervades economic life in the United States. Before Americans buy a cottage or a company, counsel a patient or a parishioner, design a product or provide a service, serve on the board of a corporation or a child-care center, drive a car or discipline a subordinate, we habitually consider both the possible attendant legal liability and how to insure against it. Fortunately, when Americans ponder potential liability (as we are more prone to do than people in any other country), we usually discover an abundance of liability insurance companies ready and willing to sell coverage against an astounding array of legal liabilities. Then we often choose policies with liability limits in the hundreds of thousands or millions of dollars.   * * *

* * *

Are these facts cause for alarm or for celebration? Insurance and tort law scholars disagree. Some argue that the spread of liability insurance promotes victim compensation while forcing insureds (through premiums) to take into account the full costs of their actions, including the costs of increased risks to others. Others see the growth of liability insurance as a wasteful byproduct of our tort law and civil jury system—an unpredictable lottery that usually results in overcompensation for minor injuries, under-compensation for serious injuries, and a waste of money through the costs of processing claims.

* * *

This finger-pointing by both the plaintiffs' bar and the insurance industry obscures one important insight. Each side portrays itself as the protector of the public interest against the greed and hypocrisy of the other, but, in truth, both sides benefit from the expansion of liability insurance and from the inflation of insurance premiums necessary to increase such expansion. Plaintiffs' lawyers and liability insurers are necessary and complementary players in the tort law industry. Their mutual interest is to increase demand for that industry's product (lawsuits and insurance covering them). Just as the United Auto Workers and the automobile industry are both happy when people buy more cars, lawyers and insurers ought to celebrate when people buy more insurance.

The mystery is why the rest of us go along. Why do insurance consumers continue, year in and year out, to demand more liability insurance? This Essay suggests an unorthodox answer, an answer that turns on the unusual determinants of a consumer's demand for liability insurance. It suggests that the expansion of liability insurance in the United States is caused, not by some dark conspiracy, but by lawyers and insurers rationally and openly pursuing what appears to be in their interest, but what is probably against the collective interest of insurance consumers. In a sentence, insurers and attorneys, with the cooperation and encouragement of legal and political institutions, have successfully, though perhaps unwittingly, driven us to overconsume liability insurance. This Essay advances a tentative theory explaining how and why this happens.

My argument rests on three propositions. * * * [F]irst, and perhaps most counterintuitively, an increase in the consumption of liability insurance tends inevitably to cause an increase in legal liability; second, increased consumption of liability insurance is strongly in the interest of both plaintiffs' attorneys and liability insurers; and third, because of unique determinants of the demand for liability insurance, insurance consumers themselves contribute to the expansion of liability insurance. Taken together, these propositions suggest that, even though insurance consumers as a group have an interest in preventing the expansion of liability insurance, because they are less effective at promoting their interests than attorneys and insurers, we see a rapid increase in the scope and amount of potential liability that is insured. This expansion then helps to drive up actual liability in the form of settlements and judgments, which in turn further increases the demand for insurance. This effect is perceived as a crisis only when the cost of insurance reaches some intolerably large fraction of the average consumer's budget. Even in the absence of such a "crisis," however, American insurance consumers arguably spend too much on liability insurance.

* * *

I. Liability Insurance Promotes Liability

The obvious relationship between legal liability and insurance is well known—liability and uncertainty about potential liability drive the liability insurance market. No one would buy insurance to cover conduct that is clearly immune from liability, and no one would sell insurance to cover conduct that necessarily required the payment of damages. If, however, the legal consequences of the conduct are uncertain—if a possibility exists that significant legal costs and damage awards may accompany the conduct—consumers may demand, and, therefore, producers may supply, insurance to cover the conduct. Liability insurance, it is clear, is promoted by liability. This is the world view that informs most insurers, lawyers, judges, and students of tort litigation.

A second important aspect of the relationship between liability and insurance is often overlooked—liability insurance promotes liability. When we expand the conduct covered by insurance, or when we increase the amount of potential liability that is insured against, we cause the amount of money paid out in legal fees, settlements, and judgments to increase. There are two straightforward mechanisms of this causation.

First, the more widely a particular activity is insured, the more likely it is to give rise to a lawsuit. Americans with a grievance may sue for many reasons—out of spite, a desire to obtain vindication, or a hope to change behavior. But mostly we sue to obtain money. * * *

Second, what is true in the absolute is also true at the margins—the larger the amount (or fraction) of potential liability that is insured, the larger the awards and settlements. Thus, as policy limits increase, larger judgments and settlements tend to result. If doctors buy liability policies calling for insurers to pay the first $1,000,000 of any valid malpractice claim, the amount of awards and settlements will tend to be greater than when the policy limit is only $100,000. This increase occurs because the amount of insurance affects both the litigants in their negotiations and the factfinders in their judgments.

* * *

II. INSURERS AND ATTORNEYS ALIKE BENEFIT FROM EXPANDING LIABILITY INSURANCE

* * *

A. Attorneys

Tort lawyers, and particularly plaintiffs' tort lawyers, *like* liability insurance, although they have little positive to say about liability insurance companies. A lawyer is more likely to sue an insured potential defendant than an uninsured potential defendant, even if both of the targets took identical precautions to avoid injuries to third parties. This is true simply because an insured claim is more valuable than an uninsured one.

* * *

Given that most lawyers would like to have more valuable claims, anything that increases the number of valuable claims would appear to be in the interests of the bar. It should thus cause no surprise when employment discrimination lawyers welcome rather than oppose employment discrimination insurance or when bar associations favor increasing the statutory minimum policy limits in automobile and medical malpractice policies. Liability insurance expands the market from which lawyers earn their livelihood, benefiting both the enterprising individual and the bar as a whole. To the extent that attorneys can influence the production or consumption of liability insurance, they should rationally seek to promote rather than discourage it.

* * *

B. Liability Insurers

Liability insurance companies, like attorneys, have great incentives to promote the expansion of liability insurance. However, unlike attorneys, they also have incentives to prevent lawsuits against their insureds, but they can do little to manage the moral hazard that liability insurance creates for plaintiffs' attorneys.

The first point—that liability insurers desire to expand the liability insurance market—is the easiest to demonstrate. The liability insurance market in the United States is, by and large, highly competitive. Hundreds of companies sell most lines of insurance. Only a few lines are dominated by a single underwriter (medical malpractice insurance in some states being the most prominent example), and even those exceptional markets are characterized by relatively low entry costs for other insurers who wait on the sidelines. Brokerage firms, ranging in size from small entrepreneurs to Fortune 500 corporations, aggressively compare policies and prices and, if necessary, help create new products for their customers. In such an environment, claims that liability insurance prices and supply are set by a monopolistic cartel are usually unpersuasive.

In such a competitive market, a liability insurer may rationally perceive increased sales to be the best method of increasing profits (and increasing the size of the company and the status and compensation of its managers). By selling more liability insurance, the managers may believe that they will make the company grow and increase absolute profits even though competition keeps profit margins low.

* * *

[O]ne good way to sell "more" liability insurance is to increase premium income without disproportionately increasing the fraction of the premium dollar that is paid out to settle claims. This, I believe, is precisely the type of expansion that many liability insurers seek through their marketing efforts. Specifically, many insurers are anxious to encourage current customers to increase their liability policy limits, thus increasing the premium income from a line of insurance and a set of insureds with which the underwriters are already most familiar. For the same reason, insurers promote the purchase of insurance by voluntarily uninsured persons who engage in a type of activity commonly underwritten by the insurer. Of course, some entrepreneurial, risk-taking insurers and brokers will also expand their business by underwriting new risks. The successful lines thereby created will then expand further through the methods described above.

Insurers, like attorneys, will therefore seek expansion of liability insurance. The future interests of insurers and attorneys largely converge—their antagonism towards each other is reserved for the situations after insurance has been purchased and a suit filed. When such a situation occurs, insurers and plaintiffs' attorneys are most at odds when the awards in individual cases are particularly large or when the amount of liability was unforeseen by the insurer at the time it fixed the premium. To a remarkable extent, these rare cases are the ones that dominate public debate. * * *

* * *

Finally, it bears emphasis that liability insurers cannot afford to be too successful in discouraging suits against insureds. Few liability insurers, for example, seek statutory immunity for all defendants (unless the cases involve a line of insurance, such as pollution coverage, in which the insurers have great exposure from policies already in force and have no desire to continue selling such policies). Put simply, fear of potential liability is a necessary condition for the existence of a demand for the product. Insurers seek to make potential liability predictable, but not to make it predictably nil. * * *

III. The Demand for Liability Insurance

If liability is an evil (from the point of view of insurance consumers), and if the expansion of liability insurance promotes growth in the amount of liability, consumers as a group should oppose the expansion of liability insurance. For example, physicians should encourage as many doctors as possible to remain uninsured and should fight to keep the average policy limits in malpractice policies low. Participants in traditionally uninsured activities (such as clergy who counsel their parishioners) should discourage colleagues from breaking ranks to buy insurance. Steps like these would help to keep down both liability and liability insurance premiums.

Unfortunately, liability insurance is often purchased by individuals rather than by groups. An individual's demand for liability insurance is determined not by what is in the collective interests of all potential defendants, but rather by the interests and preferences of the individual. Avoiding ruinous personal liability—and the bankruptcy it may entail— ranks high among those preferences. Thus, although an individual physician might think it quite desirable that most doctors buy malpractice policies with low limits, or better yet "go bare" and tell the world about it, she might nevertheless find it rational personally to purchase as much liability insurance as possible. In a world in which most doctors have no insurance and most jurors know it and act accordingly, the doctor with a lot of insurance gets a lot of security at a lower price. The individual benefits from having more than the average amount of liability insurance; hence, some individuals will continuously try to buy more than average amounts. This behavior becomes a self-defeating exercise—for the result is quite simply that the liability insurance supply will tend to create its own demand. And, as noted above, the insurers have incentives to increase the supply.

* * *

IV. Implications and Objections

* * *

The implications [of my thesis] are manifold, but three stand out. First, if liability insurers and the plaintiffs' bar dominate the political debate over tort reform and liability insurance reform in a particular jurisdiction, it is unlikely that any reforms enacted will significantly lower liability insurance costs or liability insurance consumption. The interests of the insurers and the bar are aligned toward expanding future liability insurance consumption; the reforms that they support will rarely be designed to prevent such expansion. Opposition will come only from parties who do not share an interest in the expansion—namely, from organized groups of insurance consumers who are able to recognize their collective interest and, perhaps, from first-party insurers whose products compete with the tort system to provide compensation to injured persons. When these possible opponents are absent or poorly organized, one would expect that legislative efforts at tort or liability insurance reform are particularly unlikely to reduce liability insurance consumption. This dynamic may contribute, for example, to the high levels of consumption of automobile liability insurance in many states.

Second, it may sometimes be appropriate for public and legal institutions to intervene to lower the amount of liability insurance that consumers would choose to purchase in unregulated markets. * * * This Essay suggests that sometimes legislatures should consider specifying maximum policy limits as well, thereby limiting the ability of a few highly risk-averse insureds to propel, however unintentionally, a relentless expansion of liability insurance and tort liability.

Third, other means are available to reduce liability insurance consumption. For example, we could * * * require defendants to disclose their liability insurance coverage to civil juries. The assumption of current practice, which forbids disclosure, is that jurors are likely to ignore the law in determining both liability and the amount of damages if they know whether and to what extent the defendant is insured. As noted earlier, rules forbidding disclosure encourage jurors to act on assumptions about a particular defendant's coverage based on general experience; the defendant with little or no insurance is harmed by such assumptions, whereas the defendant who has more than the typical amount of insurance benefits. By requiring full disclosure, we would deter insureds from buying (and insurance companies from selling) too much coverage due to fear that juries might find them liable for large amounts of damages. We would also, however, encourage people to buy little insurance or to go uninsured so that they could advertise their vulnerability in any subsequent jury trials. To some extent, the latter incentive's adverse effect on victim compensation could be limited by financial responsibility laws and statutes requiring persons engaged in certain activities to purchase minimum amounts of liability coverage.

I favor this last reform and would urge that we disclose liability insurance coverage to civil juries. The fear that jurors intentionally ignore the law in finding liability or damages is probably exaggerated anyway. Jurors today continue to do their best under appalling circumstances to follow the law in most civil cases. I believe that knowing about insurance would not drastically affect outcomes—or at least that after one hundred years of operating under the opposite assumption, it is time to test where the truth actually lies. To the extent that liability insurers and insureds are concerned that disclosure promotes liability, changing the rule and requiring disclosure would significantly reduce incentives to buy and to sell high-limit liability policies.

Notes

Several scholars responded to Professor Syverud's thesis. *See* Randall R. Bovbjerg, *Liability and Liability Insurance: Chicken and Egg, Destructive Spiral, or Risk and Reaction*, 72 Tex. L. Rev. 1655 (1994); Steven W. Pottier &

Robert C. Witt, *On the Demand for Liability Insurance: An Insurance Economics Perspective*, 72 Tex. L. Rev. 1681 (1994). Randall R. Bovbjerg, a Senior Research Associate at the Urban Institute and the author of many studies on the tort liability system, argues that the right question for analysis is not whether there is "too much" liability insurance but whether there is "too much" liability. If the rules governing potential tort liability are appropriate, then plenty of liability insurance against such potential liability is a good thing, not a bad thing. "If more liability were a good thing, then so too would be more (liability-inducing) coverage. Assuming appropriate levels of liability, more coverage would mean broader funding.... Syverud's surface assertion that there is over-insurance hence seems to rest on an underlying conclusion that there is too much tort recovery, a judgment that should really be established by direct discussion about liability." Bovbjerg, *supra*, at 1672. Chapter 14 will engage in this "direct discussion" when it considers existing and proposed reforms of the traditional tort liability system.

2. Interaction of Liability Insurance and First–Party Insurance Sources: Subrogation

First-party insurers often assert rights of subrogation in tort litigation. Consider an example. A fire breaks out in the insured's home and is not quenched until it has caused $50,000 to the dwelling and to insured contents. The insured has a property loss limit of $100,000, and recovers $48,000 from the insurer (the amount of damage, less the deductible). The fire began because a neighbor negligently allowed a trash fire to get out of control and spread to the insured's house. The property insurer will assert a right of subrogation against the negligent neighbor. Such a right is derivative: it allows the insurer to step into the shoes of the insured and make a claim for the insured's loss, to the extent the insurer has paid that loss. Most property insurance policies contain express subrogation clauses; when the policies do not include such clauses, most courts will allow subrogation on equitable grounds.

Subrogation interacts with the collateral source rule to achieve two aims: visiting upon negligent actors the full cost of the injuries they cause, and avoiding duplicative recoveries by the injured person. In the fire example, for instance, the collateral source rule would allow the insured to recover the full $50,000 from the negligent neighbor, notwithstanding that the insured already had recovered $48,000 from the property insurer. The insurer's subrogation interest will allow it to recoup that payment. Thus, the negligent neighbor still bears the full cost of his conduct, and the insured is not overcompensated for his loss.

The theory and workings of subrogation are relatively simple in this fire example. Subrogation can present, however, some complex theoretical and practical issues in tort litigation. Consider another example. The insured is a 16–year old girl who is an insured under her mother's health insurance policy. The girl sustains serious head injuries in a car accident, and will require expensive therapy and personal assistance for many years, perhaps even throughout her life. By the end of the first year following the accident, the health insurer has paid hospital and medical bills totalling $250,000; the health insurance has a total cap of $1 million as to any single insured. The girl's parents, as guardians, file a lawsuit on the girl's behalf against the driver whose negligence caused the accident. The driver has liability limits of $300,000. The liability insurer, after a short investigation, determines that this is a policy-limits case, and is willing to tender the full $300,000 to settle the claim. The health insurer, however, has notified the parents that it will seek subrogation to the extent of the $250,000 it has already paid.

What options does the plaintiff's lawyer have? She could try to settle the lawsuit for the full $300,000 liability limits and not notify the health insurer of the settlement. This option is unattractive for many reasons: the settlement might require judicial approval and the health insurer could intervene in the proceeding, thus rendering impossible a back-door deal that cuts out the health insurer; the liability insurer might be unwilling to settle without assurance that all subrogation interests are adequately dealt with; and a back-door deal would likely be deemed a breach by the insured of the insured's duties under the health insurance policy, thus forfeiting rights to further coverage under the health policy.

So the plaintiff's lawyer's options do not look promising unless there is some chink in the health insurer's assertion of a subrogation right. In fact, several types of chinks exist in different jurisdictions. First, some jurisdictions hold that the health insurer has no subrogation right unless the health insurance policy contains an explicit clause entitling it to subrogation; such jurisdictions do not recognize an equitable right of subrogation for health insurers. *See* Robert H. Jerry II, Understanding Insurance Law 602-03 (2d ed. 1996). Why are most jurisdictions willing to recognize equitable subrogation as to property insurance (as in the fire example) but not necessarily as to health insurance?

Second, even if the jurisdiction recognizes an equitable right of subrogation for health insurers, or even if the health policy contains a subrogation clause, a number of jurisdictions hold that the right does not exist unless the injured person has first been "fully compensated" for the insured loss by the tort recovery. *See, e.g.*, Powell v. Blue Cross and Blue Shield, 581 So.2d 772 (Ala.1990). If we apply this full compensation requirement to the fire example, it is easy to see that the insured, after payment of the tort recovery ($50,000) and the insurance funds ($48,000), has been fully compensated for his loss of $50,000; thus the insurer is entitled to subrogation above that amount. But, in the personal injury example, even the girl's receipt of the full $300,000 liability limits does not come close to "full compensation." Thus the health insurer will not receive any subrogation.

Given that one aim of subrogation is to prevent duplicative recoveries, does the "full compensation" requirement seem justifiable? How would a health insurer try to prove that a plaintiff's settlement exceeded "full compensation" for the insured loss?

There are at least two other approaches to this thorny problem of health insurance and personal injury settlements. Some jurisdictions take an approach opposite to that just outlined, and hold that, when a personal injury claimant settles with the tort defendant, the settlement amount is conclusively presumed to equal full compensation. Other jurisdictions attempt some type of allocation. For more detail, *see* Jerry, *supra*, at 607–09.

3. *Evaluation of Tort Claims By Liability Insurance Companies*

Over 90% of all tort claims are settled. When the tort claim is asserted against an insured defendant, the claim will generally not settle unless the insurance carrier agrees to the settlement. Thus, a critical issue is how insurance companies evaluate tort claims. This issue was the focus of a classic study, excerpted below, about how the formal rules of law are translated into practice by insurance adjusters in routine automobile-related tort litigation.

H. L. ROSS, SETTLED OUT OF COURT (1980)[2]
pp. 98–99, 234–237, 239–240.

Evaluation of a claim depends on understandings concerning the liability of the insured and the injuries and other damages suffered by the claimant. Just as evaluation is intimately linked with negotiation and investigation, so the question of liability, though logically prior, is intimately linked with all other aspects of evaluation, and the separation made here is analytical.

The formal law of negligence liability, as stated in casebooks from the opinions of appellate courts, is not easily applied to the accident at Second and Main. It deals with violation of a duty of care owed by the insured to the claimant and is based on a very complex and perplexing model of the "reasonable man," in this case the reasonable driver. Moreover, in the vast majority of accidents it would be erroneous to characterize the driving of either the insured or the claimant as "unreasonable," a fact that has gradually altered the law's ideal driver into a hypercautious, pokey, and infuriating roadway menace. It is not with this intellectual model, however, that claims men must deal. In their day-to-day work, the concern with liability is reduced to the question of whether either or both parties violated the rules of the road as expressed in common traffic laws. Taking the doctrine of negligence *per se* to an extreme doubtless unforeseen by the makers of the formal law, adjusters tend to define a claim as one of liability or of no liability depending only on whether a rule was violated, regardless of intention, knowledge, necessity, and other such qualifications that might receive sympathetic attention even from a traffic court judge. Such a determination is far easier than the task proposed in theory by the formal law of negligence.

To illustrate, if Car A strikes Car B from the rear, the driver of A is assumed to be liable and B is not. In the ordinary course of events, particularly where damages are routine, the adjuster is not concerned with *why* A struck B, or with whether A violated a duty of care to B, or with whether A was unreasonable or not. These questions are avoided, not only because they may be impossible to answer, but also because the fact that A struck B from the rear will satisfy all supervisory levels that a payment is

---

2. Aldine Pub. Co., New York, reprinted with permission.

in order, without further explanation. Likewise, in the routine case, the fact that A was emerging from a street governed by a stop sign will justify treating this as a case of liability, without concern for whether the sign was seen or not, whether there was adequate reason for not seeing the sign, etc. In short, in the ordinary case the physical facts of the accident are normally sufficient to allocate liability between the drivers. Inasmuch as the basic physical facts of the accident are easily known—and they are frequently ascertainable from the first notice—the issue of liability is usually relatively easy to dispose of. In fact, many adjusters claim to be able to predict the matter of liability with considerable accuracy from the moment they receive the notice of the accident. I interpret this as evidence of the mechanical and superficial way in which liability is determined; and if endless squabbles and large numbers of court cases are to be avoided, mechanical and superficial formulas are a necessity here as elsewhere for the vast bulk of routine cases. * * *

The formal criteria might lead to the expectation that relatively few people injured in an automobile accident would receive reparation. Most drivers may be thought to be ordinarily prudent people, and even where one is not, formal law embodies the difficulty of affirmative proof of unreasonable behavior. Moreover, to the extent that numbers of negligent drivers are on the highway, an equivalent number of negligent claimants might be expected, who ought to recover nothing. On these assumptions one would expect most claimants to be denied completely, the balance recovering something more than their economic losses. In contrast, the actual picture of recoveries shows that most people injured in traffic accidents are paid, and those who are seriously injured are paid in the large majority of cases. The amount of recoveries fits the formal model only for small claims; where injuries are serious, most claimants fail to recover even their out-of-pocket losses.[3]

The reason the distribution predicted by knowledge of the formal law does not fit the observed distribution of claims settlements is that other factors influence the settlement process. Some of these have been described in this book. Among them are the attitudes and values of the involved personnel, organizational pressures, and negotiation pressures. They exert a direct effect on the enormous majority of bodily claims. * * *

The personalities—attitudes and opinions—of the personnel are perhaps the least significant of the factors mentioned. Generally speaking, adjusters approach their work with conventional business values. Other things equal, they will seek low, conservative settlements, although a sense of fairness makes them disinclined to settle for less than net out-of-pocket losses in a case that is deemed to warrant any settlement at all. The goal of paying no more and no less than these tangible losses is often achieved in routine cases settled directly with the claimant. This is a settlement that many adjusters would characterize as ideal. However, many settlements are made for amounts quite different from the ideal, reflecting pressures and constraints of the employee role and the negotiating situation. Personal dispositions may affect the style with which an adjuster

---

3. See Alfred F. Conard, James N. Morgan, Robert W. Pratt, Jr., Charles E. Voltz, and Robert L. Bombaugh, *Automobile Acci-* *dent Costs and Payments: Studies in the Economics of Injury Reparation* (University of Michigan Press, 1964), pp. 181–236.

responds to external demands, but they seem to be relatively unimportant in determining the outcome of claims.

Organizational pressure would seem to be a more important factor than personality in affecting the outcome of claims. Pressures from the supervisory structure can even lead adjusters to violate some of the most important company rules, such as those forbidding nuisance payments. Perhaps unexpectedly the most insistent of organizational pressures is not to keep payments low, but to close files quickly. The closing of files represents for adjusters something of the same kind of central goal as the attainment of good grades represents for the college student, or number of placements for an employment counselor, or a high clearance rate for policemen.[4] * * * [T]he chief effect of this pressure on the behavior of claims men is to increase the number and raise the level of payments. This effect is unexpected and unrecognized by many claims department executives, who are insulated from the front lines by organizational distance, but it is understandable as a means to alleviate specific and recurring pressures experienced by adjusters from their supervisors. The pressure to close files quickly also causes adjusters to simplify their procedures of investigation, as well as their thinking in evaluation. Although the textbooks and manuals propose elaborate and time-consuming routines, the case load prescribes short cuts and approximations. * * *

Another important factor affecting settlement outcomes, particularly with represented claimants, is the medium of negotiation. Negotiation is a social process with a strong implicit rule structure and a repertory of tactics different from those available in litigation. In the case at hand, the most effective tactics threaten recourse to the expense of formal trial, * * *.

As a consequence of these and other pressures, the tort law in action is differentiated from the formal law by its greater simplicity, liberality, and inequity. * * *

The law of damages is also simplified in action. Although the measurement of special damages appears rather straightforward even in formal doctrine, some further simplification occurs in action when, for instance, life table calculations are used to compute future earnings. More important, the measurement of pain, suffering, and inconvenience is thoroughly routinized in the ordinary claim. The adjuster generally pays little attention to the claimant's privately experienced discomforts and agonies; I do not recall ever having read recitals of these matters in the statements, which are the key documents in the settlement process and in which all matters considered relevant to the disposition of a claim are recorded. The calculation of general damages is for the most part a matter of multiplying the medical bills by a tacitly but generally accepted arbitrary constant. This practice is justified by claims men on the theory that pain and suffering are very likely to be a function of the amount of medical treatment experienced. There is of course a grain of truth in this theory,

---

4. See Howard S. Becker, Blanche Geer, and Everett Hughes, *Making the Grade: The Academic Side of College Life* (John Wiley, 1968); Peter M. Blau, *The Dynamics of Bureaucracy* (University of Chicago Press, 1955); and Jerome H. Skolnick, *Justice Without Trial* (John Wiley, 1966); on students, employment counselors, and policemen, respectively.

but it also contains several sources of error. Types of injury vary considerably in the degree of pain and suffering, the necessity for treatment, and the fees charged for treatment; and the correlations between these elements are low. I believe that the more important reason for the use of the formula is again that all levels of the claims department find it acceptable in justifying payment over and beyond special damages. The formula provides a conventional measurement for phenomena that are so difficult to evaluate as to be almost unmeasurable. It provides a rule by which a rule-oriented organization can proceed, though the rule is never formalized. This simplification also meets the comparable needs of plaintiffs' attorneys and is acceptable to them as well. Because of the mutual acceptability of the formula, attorneys will try to capitalize on it by adding to the use and cost of medical treatment, a procedure known as "building" the file, and adjusters will argue concerning the reasonableness of many items that purport to be medical expenses and thus part of the base to which the formula is applied. The procedure is still far less complicated—and less sensitive—than that envisaged in the formal law. Thus again it appears that, relative to the formal law, the law in action is simple and mechanical. Although more individual consideration occurs in larger cases, the principle of simplification governs to a great degree the entire range of settled claims.

Chapter 14

TORT REFORM, AND NONTORT COMPENSATION PROGRAMS

A. INTRODUCTION

This chapter examines a number of existing and proposed schemes, other than traditional tort, for addressing the problems of accidental injury and disease. The chapter begins by discussing the many legislative tort reforms enacted during the past twenty years. The chapter then considers various existing and proposed nontort compensation programs, such as workers' compensation, automobile no-fault, social security disability, proposals for entirely replacing tort with a no-fault compensation system, and New Zealand's decision, in 1972, to abolish tort for most personal injuries and to replace it with a comprehensive no-fault compensation program.

Because all these existing and proposed alternatives to traditional tort are aimed at addressing disabilities caused by injury or illness, we should consider at the outset some basic data about (1) injury, disease, and disability in the United States, and (2) what the sources and amounts of payments are for injury, disease, and disability.

Injury, Disease, and Disability. An injury or disease might be so minor that it results in nothing but the most temporary of consequences, such as a scrape that heals within a day or a mild throat irritation that resolves within a week. Or injury and disease could lead to more substantial temporary or permanent consequences. Usually the terms "impairment" and "disability" are used to describe these consequences. Consider a serious knee injury that, for the first six weeks, prevents the individual from using the knee or leg at all. After surgery and rehabilitation, the knee eventually returns to a level of functioning, but will never have the strength or mobility it once had. Often the term "impairment" is used to refer to the person's organ-level or person-level reduced ability to function as measured by standard medical norms. For instance, the organ-level impairment would be the knee's reduced range of motion and strength; the person-level impairment would be the person's reduced mobility and capacity to bend or stoop.

The term "disability" often is used to refer to the consequences of the impairment on a particular person's life. For instance, the knee injury just described would produce a different level of disability for an accountant than for a professional tennis player. Both would have the same impairment, as measured by standard medical norms, but the consequences on work or social roles would be very different.

Reliable measures of impairment and disability in the United States are difficult to obtain. If we focus just on impairments, then by some estimates half the United States population has some type of medical impairment. A more useful approach is to focus on disability and to define disability as the reduced ability or inability to function in some major life activity (such as going to school, working, or performing basic daily activities such as dressing and eating), due to impairment. As of 1990, about 36 million Americans had some such disability. Of these, about 2 million were in institutions, such as homes for persons with mental disabilities, or nursing homes. *See* National Academy of Social Insurance, Preliminary Status Report of the Disability Policy Panel 57–58 (1994).

Sources of Payment for Disability. If we consider both cash payments and medical care, the sources of payment for disability include, in addition to the tort system, the following: social security disability, workers' compensation, a number of specialized compensation programs such as veterans' disability and black lung disability programs, and private health and disability insurance. Payments from these nontort programs dwarf those made by tort. Tort provides only about 10% or 11% of total payments for disability. *See* Kenneth S. Abraham & Lance Liebman, *Private Insurance, Social Insurance, and Tort Reform: Toward a New Vision of Compensation for Illness and Injury,* 93 Colum.L.Rev. 75, 78 (1993).

B. TORT REFORM

Since the early to mid–1970s, the tort system has been the subject of an intense academic, legislative, and cultural debate. Tort's critics have charged it with failing to address adequately any of the systemic goals at which it aims. The following is a summary of the criticisms and the tort reforms enacted since the mid–1970s.

1. *General Criticisms of Tort*

Critics claim that tort is a failure when considered in light of the three major systemic goals at which tort aims: deterrence, loss-spreading, and corrective justice. The following is a summary of the criticisms. After this summary, we will look at the empirical evidence that relates to these general criticisms, so that we will be in a better position to evaluate the criticisms and to decide whether (and what sort of) reform is warranted.

a. *Deterrence*

Critics claim that tort is a failure when considered as a system for deterring unreasonably dangerous conduct. According to the basic deterrence model, liability rules require actors to internalize the full costs of their conduct and thus in theory deter conduct whose costs outweigh its benefits. *See generally* Steven Shavell, An Economic Analysis of Accident Law 5–32 (1987). But tort's critics argue that social controls other than tort provide deterrence, and that tort arguably fails to produce meaningful deterrent effects. Government regulation, market forces (*e.g.*, consumer desire for airbags and product safety features), and instincts for self-preservation (*e.g.*, a consumer's or driver's own desire to avoid being hurt) also have deterrent effects that would continue even if tort were eliminated. And tort fails to produce optimal reductions in unsafe conduct for a number of reasons: lack of knowledge about tort liability; the unpredictability of potential tort liability; psychological factors that lead people to discount the threat of potential liability; and widespread liability insurance that, even if priced partly according to the risks that the insured poses, still blunts the deterrent impact of potential tort liability. Indeed, not only does tort fail to add meaningfully to the reduction of unreasonably unsafe conduct, it also manages to overdeter some desirable although risky social conduct because it holds out the prospect of occasional, unpredictable, and possibly "incorrect" enormous verdicts. For fuller accounts of these criticisms, *see* Stephen D. Sugarman, *Doing Away With Tort Law*, 73 Cal. L. Rev. 555 (1985); Richard J. Pierce, Jr., *Encouraging Safety: The Limits of Tort Law and Government Regulation*, 33 Vand. L. Rev. 1281 (1980); Daniel W. Shuman, *The Psychology of Deterrence in Tort Law*, 42 U. Kan. L. Rev. 115 (1993).

Others have argued that tort law to some degree or at least in certain arenas (such as products liability) has induced desirable safety-related changes and promotes a meaningful degree of deterrence, notwithstanding the presence of factors that somewhat reduce the deterrent impact of tort. *See* American Law Institute, Reporters' Study on Enterprise Responsibility for Personal Injury, Vol. 1, at 32 (1991) (citing some evidence of deterrent effects); Steven P. Croley & Jon D. Hanson, *What Liability Crisis? An Alternative Explanation for Recent Events in Products Liability*, 8 Yale J. Reg. 1 (1991); Gary T. Schwartz, *Reality in the Economic Analysis of Tort Law: Does Tort Law Really Matter?*, 42 U.C.L.A. L.Rev. 377 (1994).

b. *Insurance*

Critics charge that tort also fails when considered as a scheme of forced insurance—that is, a system for spreading the impact of unprevented or unpreventable losses. Tort overcompensates smaller injuries, undercompensates larger injuries, and fails to produce "horizontal consistency"— that is, juries award significantly different damage awards to basically similar injuries. Added to these criticisms is the "lottery" nature of tort compensation: whether and how much a deserving victim recovers in tort depends on the fortuity of whether the defendant has liability insurance or funds to satisfy a judgment. (This element of fortuity is only slightly reduced by minimum insurance laws in some areas.) And tort is an extremely expensive form of insurance when compared to first-party insurance or social insurance. Much more of our "tort premium" goes to the payment of administrative overhead, court costs, and attorneys' fees than with any other form of insurance.

In addition, tort's insurance has a regressive impact on the poor. Both the rich and poor must pay when the prospect of tort liability increases the prices for goods and services. Yet, if the injured person has a high income, he receives more from tort than the person with a low income, despite the fact that both usually have paid a similar tort "premium" in the form of an increased price for or reduced availability of the good or service. A final criticism is the point outlined in more detail in Chapter 10: that tort forces us to buy a type of insurance—for pain and suffering—that most of us do not desire and would not purchase if given a choice. For detail on these criticisms, *see* George L. Priest, *The Current Insurance Crisis and Modern Tort Law*, 96 Yale L.J. 1521 (1986); Alan Schwartz, *Proposals for Products Liability Reform: A Theoretical Synthesis*, 97 Yale L.J. 353 (1988).

These criticisms have generated a number of replies. Professor Jane Stapleton argues that to view tort as an insurance system is a misconception of tort in theory and in reality. *See* Jane Stapleton, *Tort, Insurance and Ideology*, 58 Modern L.Rev. 820 (1995). Professors Hanson and Logue accept the notion that tort law does and should serve an insurance function, and they argue that tort in fact is superior in some respects to first-party insurance mechanisms. *See* Jon D. Hanson & Kyle D. Logue, *The First-Party Insurance Externality: An Economic Justification for Enterprise Liability*, 76 Cornell L.Rev. 129 (1990). Others have argued that the tort-as-insurance arguments do not convincingly make the case for eliminating nonpecuniary damages. *See* Steven P. Croley & Jon D. Hanson, *The Nonpecuniary Costs of Accidents: Pain-and-Suffering Damages in Tort Law*, 108 Harv. L.Rev. 1787 (1995); Ellen S. Pryor, *The Tort Law Debate, Efficiency, and the Kingdom of the Ill: A Critique of the Insurance Theory of Compensation*, 79 Va.L.Rev. 91 (1993).

c. *Corrective Justice*

Critics contend that, in view of many of the points already noted (such as over-and under-compensation and the blunting effect of liability insurance) tort cannot be justified from a corrective justice perspective. As Professor Sugarman has argued, the "current system functions whimsically and doesn't accord with anyone's sense of justice. The much-vaunted individualized attention to victims in practice sanctions flagrant horizontal inequity because of settlement practices, trial theatrics, and other reasons already discussed." Sugarman, *supra*, at 604. Others argue that tort law does function to resolve disputes arising from perceived violations of social norms, *see* Stephen D. Smith, *The Critics and the Crisis: A Reassessment of Current Conceptions of Tort Law*, 72 Cornell L.Rev. 765 (1987), and that tort law's reliance on jury adjudication comports with a view of tort law as enforcing community standards of financial responsibility and just compensation, *see* Catherine Pierce Wells, *Tort Law As Corrective Justice: A Pragmatic Justification for Jury Adjudication*, 88 Mich.L.Rev. 2348 (1990).

2. *Empirical Evidence*

The following discussion focuses on a number of empirical issues that have been especially important in the debate over whether tort meaningfully advances any of its major goals. Consider how each point relates to the various systemic goals of tort, and what type of tort reform might be responsive to the issue.

a. *Overcompensating Small Injuries, Undercompensating Large Injuries*

One of the most consistent findings of many studies is that the tort system, via both settlement and trial, yields overcompensation as to smaller injuries and undercompensation of larger injuries. Many of these studies have compared actual settlement amounts with independent assessments of the value of the claim. Many small injury victims, of course, never file a claim and receive no compensation. But some who do are overcompensated, given the nuisance value to the defendant or its insurer of paying off the claim.

Factors that might explain undercompensation relative to the true value of a case include inadequate insurance or defendant solvency; the plaintiff's need for money and the inability to bear the delay of going to trial; uncertainties about the value of the claim; and cognitive or psychological factors that result in a discounting of higher damages.

For discussion of the issues, *see* Patricia Munch, Costs and Benefits of the Torts System If Viewed As a Compensation System 14, 38–39, 76–81 (1977); Marc Galanter, *Real World Torts: An Antidote to Anecdote*, 55 Md.L.Rev. 1093, 1116–20 (1996); Michael J. Saks, *Do We Really Know Anything About the Behavior of the Tort Litigation System—And Why Not?*, 140 U.Pa.L.Rev. 1147, 1216–20 (1992).

b. Vertical Consistency and Horizontal Inconsistency

Another persistent finding from a number of studies relates to how well jury verdicts correspond to the severity of injuries. Most studies find that jury awards over time reflect a high degree of "vertical consistency"— that is, juries tend to award higher damage amounts for more serious injuries, and lower damage amounts for less serious injuries. But jury awards over time do a poorer job of achieving "horizontal consistency"— that is, giving roughly similar damage awards for roughly similar injuries (after accounting for other reasons that might explain the variation).

To illustrate by an example, consider an injury severity scale from 1 to 9, with 1 and 2 corresponding to insignificant and temporary injury, and 8 and 9 corresponding, respectively, to permanent grave injury and to death. Juries over time are consistent in awarding higher amounts for each successive level of severity. But the variation of awards within any given category is very high, even after accounting for legitimate reasons for variation (such as the reducing effect of a finding of contributory negligence). For instance, one study found that awards for level 8 injuries ranged from a low of $147,000 to a high of $18,100,000, and that all awards in the top quartile for this severity level were at least six times as high as awards in the bottom quartile. Some of the variation could be explained by legitimate factors, such as variation in the plaintiff's age or pre-injury earnings. "No amount of adjusting, however, is likely to fully account for the extreme values." Randall R. Bovbjerg, Frank A. Sloan & James F. Blumstein, *Valuing Life and Limb in Tort: Scheduling "Pain and Suffering,"* 83 Nw. U. L. Rev. 908, 919–24 (1989). *See also* Saks, *supra,* at 1274–77 (discussing variation in awards).

c. Number of Claims and Size of Verdicts

The tort reform debate has frequently included contentions that too many frivolous tort claims are filed and that too many excessive verdicts are returned in favor of plaintiffs. Anecdotal evidence—descriptions of seemingly ridiculous claims or recoveries—has played a large role in this portion of the debate. Some of the circulated anecdotes, it is worth noting, were either fabricated or distorted in a crucial way. Nonetheless, as with any system, one can tell tort stories of greed, abuse, and excessiveness. But "if we want to know how the system is really performing, and we are not merely trying to provoke people to despise it or fear losing it, then we must do more than fling anecdotes back and forth." Saks, *supra*, at 1160.

Attention often has focused on increases in the number of filings in state and federal courts; the Justice Department Study in 1986, for instance, cited a 758% growth rate in the filing of federal products liability cases from 1974 to 1985. Several points are worth noting about the filing rates. First, tort filings in state courts increased about 9%, while population in the counted jurisdictions increased 8%, suggesting that state court tort litigation was basically in pace with population growth. Saks, *supra*, at 1205–07. Second, in federal courts, over the past ten years, little growth has occurred in garden-variety tort suits such as auto, slip and fall, premises liability. In state courts, non-auto-filings have been flat. *See* Galanter, *supra*, at 1103–09. Third, rates of filing have increased in products liability and medical malpractice, as well as mass latent injury cases. Much of the increase in products liability can be ascribed to asbestos, the Dalkon Shield, and Bendectin. American Law Institute, Reporters' Study on Enterprise Responsibility for Personal Injury, Vol. 1 at 60–63.

A more important shortcoming of arguments based on filing rates is that such rates, standing alone, do not tell us enough.

> Any assessment of whether the propensity to sue is increasing, decreasing, or remaining the same can be made only in relation to the waxing or waning of the pool of injuries from which suits properly arise. Any inference about whether the average size of awards or settlements has gone up, down, or remained level, in real terms, depends upon knowing what the pool of injuries looks like. If the pool of injuries has increased and the inherent seriousness of the injuries or the cost of repairing them has increased, one should not be surprised to find a commensurate increase in cases or awards. If the pool has shrunk either in size or cost of injuries, even a seemingly level number of filings or payments should in real terms be regarded as an increase.

Saks, *supra*, at 1173–74.

The most rigorous studies of the injury pool have taken place in the medical malpractice arena. Medical experts examined large numbers of hospital records to determine how many injuries had been the result of treatment, and how many of these had been the result of negligent treatment. Given these base rates compared with filing rates, studies estimate that at most 10% of negligently injured patients ever seek compensation, and only 1 in 6 of those with serious, permanent injuries ever seek compensation. Studies conducted outside the medical malpractice area also suggest base injury rates that are far greater than the claims rate. Saks, *supra*, at 1178–89.

What about the contention that the tort system produces too many excessive settlements and verdicts? As noted, most studies continue to show a pattern of overcompensation of smaller injuries and undercompensation of larger injuries. With respect to jury verdicts, two factors are at issue: whether the jury finds liability, and the amount of damages awarded. As to liability findings, there is a considerable body of research into the rationality of jury decisions, including comparisons with decisions by other methods (such as by judges). In general the research "supports the conclusion that juries make reasonable and rational decisions," and that rates of decisional error by other means or in other fields are not significantly lower. Saks, *supra*, at 1237–39.

As to damages awards, adequate study into the issue requires controlling for variables such as changes in severity of injury and inflation. Once this is done, the data show that there has been only a slight, if any, general increase in damages awards during the period leading up to the tort crisis. Saks, *supra*, at 1253. But there has been a significant increase in the number of very large jury awards, even if the average amount paid per claim across the board has not increased much. American Law Institute Reporters' Study, *supra*, at 64–66. More information is necessary, of course, to judge whether this increase reflects inappropriately high verdicts or instead results from other factors, such as changes in "case mix" (the number of serious injury cases filed), or higher survival rates (and thus higher long-term care and rehabilitation expenses) for injuries that in the past would have proved fatal.

Professor Neil Vidmar, analyzing the empirical evidence about jury awards in the medical malpractice area, concludes that the data do "not support the widely made claims that jury damage awards are based on the depths of defendants' pockets, sympathies for plaintiffs, caprice, or excessive generosity." N. Vidmar, Medical Malpractice and the American Jury 259 (1995).

d. Uncertainty and Overdeterrence

A critical though sometimes overlooked issue is the level of uncertainty that the tort system creates for individuals and corporations as they make decisions about which activities to engage in, which safety-related precautions to adopt, and how much liability insurance to purchase (or how to self-insure). If actors are highly uncertain about whether and how much they will be liable for a given action, then this uncertainty obviously interferes both with optimal deterrence and with optimal insurance. Even liability insurers, whose very livelihood depends on risk, dislike unpredictable or uncertain liability:

> Insurers do not support abolition of liability, for liability is their business. Many do not even object in principle to growth in liability. In this respect, they (partly) resemble attorneys. However, they vehemently object to unpredictable change, for they have to pay for the changed risk from unchanged, previously collected premiums. The two types of uncertainty that they appear to dislike the most are (1) tort law's unlimited damages and (2) its propensity to change legal rules over time with what appears to them to be essentially retroactive effect.

Randall R. Bovbjerg, *Liability and Liability Insurance: Chicken and Egg, Destructive Spiral, or Risk and Reaction?*, 72 Tex. L. Rev. 1655, 1668 (1994).

If actors resolve uncertainty by assuming error in favor of the victim (incorrect liability findings or excessive damage awards), then actors might be "overdeterred"; that is, fail to engage in risky though socially desirable conduct or engage in risk-reduction whose costs outweigh its benefits. And the price of liability insurance will increase as well. Disagreement persists about whether tort law has overdeterred in various areas, such as medical practice, aviation, pharmaceuticals, and products in general. Many argue that the withdrawal or limited availability of certain goods and services reflects overdeterrence. *See* The Liability Maze; The Impact of Liability Law on Safety and Innovation (Peter W. Huber & Robert E. Litan eds. 1991); George L. Priest, *The Current Insurance Crisis and Modern Tort Law*, 96 Yale L.J. 1521 (1986). Professors Croley and Hanson offer a different view. They argue that the reduction of certain goods and services instead reflects that consumers were no longer willing to pay the full cost of the product or service once tort law forced consumers to internalize the full cost of the product. *See* Steven P. Croley & Jon D. Hanson, *What Liability Crisis? An Alternative Explanation for Recent Events in Products Liability*, 8 Yale J. Reg. 1, 84–90 (1991). For other criticisms of the overdeterrence contention, *see* Galanter, *supra*, at 1145–49.

e. High Transaction Costs

There is general agreement that the tort system is expensive to administer. According to one respected study, each dollar expended on auto tort litigation was divided as follows: 52 cents in net compensation to the claimant; 24 cents to plaintiff's legal fees and expenses; 13 cents to defendants' fees and expenses; and 13 cents to various other costs. Non-auto tort liability cases delivered even less to victims: 43 cents was paid to the plaintiff in compensation; 20 cents went to plaintiff's legal fees and expenses; 18 cents went to defendants' fees and expenses; and 20 cents was absorbed by other costs. Deborah R. Hensler, et al., Trends in Tort Litigation: The Story Behind the Statistics 26–29 (1987). In asbestos cases, even less went to plaintiffs and more to transaction costs.

By contrast, first-party insurance (such as medical and private disability), and social insurance such as social security disability, deliver to the insured a far greater percentage of each dollar expended by the system. Thus, if the tort system is justified solely on an insurance rationale, it is too expensive. The high administrative overhead of the tort system must be justified on the basis of deterrence or corrective justice rationales.

f. Insurance Availability and Affordability

Policymakers have given much attention to two "crises" of insurance availability and affordability. The first occurred in the mid–1970s in the context of medical malpractice liability insurance. Numerous medical malpractice insurers withdrew from some state markets or raised prices significantly; some physicians could not find insurance at any price; and some doctors as a result slowed down certain medical services and lobbied for emergency legislation. Most states passed tort reform legislation aimed at alleviating the crisis.

The immediate crisis abated within two years as a result of several factors: new physician-run insurance associations entered the market; many states mandated that other private insurers participate in "joint underwriting associations" that provide coverage to physicians unable to procure it otherwise; there was a decline in the degree to which claims filing increased; and insurance increasingly was written on a "claims-made" rather than "occurrence" basis. Claims-made policies cover only claims that are made during the year of coverage; occurrence policies provide coverage for any malpractice incident that occurred during the year of coverage. Suppose, for instance, that an insurer provides occurrence-based cover for the year of 1970. The patient does not discover her impairment until 1973, sues in 1974 (given a "discovery" exception to the normal two-year statute of limitations), and receives a settlement in 1976. The insurer must cover the settlement. The "long tail" nature of much medical malpractice liability (the long time between occurrence, discovery, and claim recovery) means that occurrence-based exposures are harder to predict.

For more detail on the medical malpractice crisis, *see* Patricia Danzon, Medical Malpractice: Theory, Evidence, and Public Policy (1985); Frank A. Sloan, Randall R. Bovbjerg & Penny B. Githens, Insuring Medical Malpractice (1991); Paul Weiler, Medical Malpractice on Trial (1991).

The second insurance crisis occurred in the mid–1980s and involved not just medical malpractice in particular but also the general commercial general liability insurance market for products and services across the economy. Premiums rose sharply in this period; coverage reportedly became unavailable at any price as to certain products and services (such as IUDs and day care), forcing the withdrawal of some goods and services altogether. Forty-six states passed tort reform legislation aimed at responding to the crisis.

Within several years, there was a slowdown in the rapid rise of insurer losses and premium increases. But many contend that high premiums and reduced availability of insurance are still basic features of the landscape, resulting in higher prices for, and reduced availability of, products and services.

Disagreement persists over the origins of, meaning of, and proper response to the insurance crises. Some have argued that the problems largely resulted from insurance "cycles" (aggressively underwriting new risks at times of high interest on premium investment) or from collusion by insurers to manufacture a crisis. One prominent explanation, offered by a 1986 Department of Justice Report, is that the crisis resulted from sharp increases in the number of tort claims filed and in the number of plaintiff recoveries. *See* Report of the Tort Policy Working Group on the Causes, Extent and Policy Implications of the Current Crisis in Insurance Availability and Affordability (1986).

Still another influential account contends that the problem lies with the increased tendency to view tort law as an appropriate insurance mechanism, rather than a means of achieving deterrence. But tort, according to this view, is a poor *insurance* mechanism for many reasons: unlike first-party insurance, it is difficult for a liability insurer to segregate high-risk from low-risk insured risks (for instance, the tort premium on a lawnmower is the same no matter whether the purchaser of the lawnmower is careless or careful, and first-party insurance by contrast can do a better job of distinguishing between various levels of risk posed by insureds); it contains no deductibles or co-insurance requirements such as first-party insurance contains to discourage overuse; it forces the purchase of pain and suffering insurance; and it is regressive in its impact on the poor. *See* George L. Priest, *The Current Insurance Crisis and Modern Tort Law*, 96 Yale L.J. 1521 (1986). Professor Priest argues that, since tort law is inferior to first-party insurance sources as an insurance mechanism, tort doctrines cannot and should not be justified in light of an insurance goal. Rather, tort liability doctrines can and should be justified only in light of the deterrence aim. When deterrence considerations cannot justify an expansion of tort liability, then the expansion should be rejected.

A contrary account is offered by Professors Croley and Hanson:

> Recent events in consumer product markets—in particular, the withdrawal of some products and price increases for others—are largely the welcome result of efficient changes in products liability law. Expanded manufacturer liability has resulted in the internalization of two significant externalities. [These two externalities were the nonpecuniary costs of product injuries, and the pecuniary costs of accidents for which consumers already were insured.] [These externalities] led consumers and manufacturers to under-invest in accident prevention.
>
> Following the expansion of manufacturer liability, * * * product prices rose to reflect more closely real costs. Once price increases forced consumers to internalize the full costs of product accidents, consumption patterns changed, and the market for some products disappeared altogether.

Steven P. Croley & Jon D. Hanson, *What Liability Crisis? An Alternative Explanation for Recent Events in Products Liability*, 8 Yale J. Reg. 1, 9 (1991).

3. *Legislative Tort Reform*

a. *The Reforms*

The first wave of legislative tort reform, which occurred in the mid–1970s, was primarily in response to the perceived liability-insurance crisis stemming from medical malpractice, and the reforms usually related specifically to that area. The second wave of tort reform, consisting of legislation passed by over forty states in the mid–1980s, applied more generally. It was prompted by a perceived liability-insurance crisis that took the form of rapidly increasing commercial and municipal liability insurance premiums, withdrawals of insurance coverage for some products and services, and the withdrawal of some products and services from the market altogether.

Although over forty states passed reform legislation in 1986, that year does not mark the end of the reform movement. Rather, many states have passed additional measures in the past few years, and calls for further tort reform continue at the state level.

At the federal level, a number of tort reform bills have been introduced over the years. Not until 1994, however, did tort reform at the federal level seem to have serious prospects of success. Tort reform was one part of the Republican Party's "Contract With America," and both the House and Senate passed tort reform bills; the House version was significantly more dramatic. President Clinton vetoed the resulting bill. Thus, legislative tort reform remains primarily a state phenomenon.

The most commonly enacted tort reforms, many of which have been discussed earlier in this book, thus far are the following: caps on nonpecuniary damages; modification of the collateral source rule; modifications of joint and several liability; restrictions on punitive damages; and changes in the substantive standards governing product liability claims. Other reforms enacted by some states include: sanctions for filing frivolous suits; limits on attorneys' contingency fees; and provisions encouraging or requiring the periodic payment of judgments.

Still high on the tort reformers' national and state agendas are the following desired changes: abolition of joint and several liability; national product liability reform, including a "governmental compliance defense"; and restrictions on contingency fees.

b. *The Effects of the Reforms*

Our empirical information about how the tort system actually works in practice is still very incomplete. The lament applies as well to an empirically informed appraisal of the effects of tort reform legislation. Perhaps most helpful in this respect is the work of Patricia Danzon, who studied the effects of the medical malpractice tort reforms of the mid–1970s. She found that several reforms had an appreciable effect on the number of claims filed: alterations of the collateral source rule and tighter controls on the statute of limitations (that is, eliminating or greatly restricting the "discovery rule" exception to the usual two-year statute of limitations). Several reforms appreciably reduced the amounts paid out on claims: caps on noneconomic damages, alterations of the collateral source rule, and arbitration procedures. Patricia M. Danzon, New Evidence on the Frequency and Severity of Medical Malpractice Claims (1986).

Some limited evidence about the effects of the 1986 reforms has appeared. For instance, one study compared the reforms enacted in each state with subsequent changes in losses and premiums reported by insurers, and found that the reforms have indeed reduced the severity of insurer losses and slowed the increase in insurance premiums. Thus, the study concluded, the reforms achieved the objective of "defusing the problem of insurance availability and affordability." Glenn Blackmon & Richard Zeckhauser, State Tort Reform Legislation: Assessing Our Control of Risks, in Tort Law and the Public Interest 272, 273 (Peter H. Schuck, ed. 1991).

We know little, however, about the safety, distributional, or compensatory effects of these reforms. Several analysts have criticized the thrust of the 1986 reforms, contending that they are not tailored to address many of the particular concerns that prompted cries of a crisis. Robert Rabin,

Some Reflections on the Process of Tort Reform, 25 San Diego L. Rev.13 (1988); Joseph Sanders & Craig Joyce, *"Off To The Races": The 1980s Tort Crisis and the Law Reform Process*, 27 Hous. L. Rev. 207 (1990). A recent analysis contends that certain tort reforms will have a disparate negative impact on women. For instance, limiting recoveries for punitive damages and noneconomic damages in medical malpractice and medical device litigation will adversely affect women because women more often than men receive such damage findings. Thomas Koenig & Michael Rustad, *His and Her Tort Reform: Gender Injustice in Disguise*, 70 Wash. L. Rev. 1 (1995).

C. AN INTRODUCTION TO NONTORT COMPENSATION PROGRAMS

1. *Why Study Nontort Programs?*

The tort liability structure forms just one, albeit crucial, strand in the complex fabric that American society has developed for addressing the problems of injury and disease. Other strands include no-fault schemes such as workers' compensation and automobile no-fault; private first-party insurance sources such as health insurance, long-term care insurance, and disability insurance; social insurance such as social security disability insurance and the federal-state rehabilitation system; and federal and state "disability-rights" statutes mandating reasonable accommodation in employment settings, schools, etc.

Even if one were altogether satisfied with current American tort doctrine, these nontort programs would deserve attention because they represent a large proportion of the total dollars paid for illness and injury, and because they present intriguing and critical policy issues in their own right. According to one study, tort payments constitute only about 10% of all benefits paid for illness and injury; nontort sources (including private and social insurance and workers' compensation) account for the rest. *See* J. O'Connell & J. Guinivan, *An Irrational Combination: The Relative Expansion of Liability Insurance and Contraction of Loss Insurance*, 49 Ohio St. L.J. 757, 766 (1988).

Of course, there is much dissatisfaction with the traditional tort system, as the tort reform debates of the past twenty years attest. Therefore these nontort programs also have attracted attention because they represent potential models for more substantial tort reform. For instance, policymakers and legislatures, when considering the desirability of additional no-fault compensation schemes in, for instance, the medical injury context, have looked to workers' compensation as at least a partial sketch of the potential benefits and drawbacks of such a scheme.

2. *Program Categories and Purposes*

When examining the disability fabric, it is helpful to realize that each of these compensation programs can be placed into one of three general categories, corresponding to the basis upon which the program awards compensation: fault, cause, or loss. (This categorization is developed in Kenneth S. Abraham & Lance Liebman, *Private Insurance, Social Insur-*

ance, and Tort Reform: Toward a New Vision of Compensation for Illness and Injury, 93 Colum. L. Rev. 75 (1993).)

Generally, tort represents a fault-based compensation approach. By contrast, cause-based compensation programs do not depend on a finding of fault, but they do limit benefits to losses resulting from particular causes. Examples include workers' compensation (which requires an injury or disease causally linked to employment); automobile no-fault (which requires losses caused by automobile accidents); the National Vaccine Injury Compensation Fund (which requires an injury caused by the administration of a vaccine); and service-connected veteran's benefits.

The third category consists of programs that do not require either fault or a particular causal origin, and instead are based solely on whether a covered individual has sustained a loss of a certain sort. These include primarily (1) private health, life, and disability insurance; and (2) social insurance such as Medicare, Medicaid, and Social Security disability insurance (SSDI). Under all these programs, if a person is covered and if the loss is covered, then benefits are payable without regard to the causal source or fault. For instance, an individual disabled by a car accident may receive SSDI, but so too may an individual disabled by multiple sclerosis.

It is also useful to appreciate the amount of benefits delivered by each of the three categories. Annually, the tort system pays about $50 billion to its beneficiaries. Cause-based systems in combination pay approximately $55 billion. Loss-based programs pay far more: private insurance pays about $220 billion annually, and social insurance in excess of $235 billion. Abraham & Liebman, *supra*, at 78–85.

Just as the basis of compensation differs among various programs, so does the primary systemic purpose or purposes of the programs. As Professors Abraham and Liebman have shown, any program will aim at one or more of four primary goals. The first is corrective justice: identifying wrongful injurious conduct and requiring correction of that wrong by compensation of the victim. The second is deterring unreasonably unsafe conduct, usually defined as conduct whose social costs outweigh its social benefits. Third is the aim of insurance. That is, even if all wrongful injurious conduct were corrected, and even if all unreasonably unsafe conduct were deterred, some injuries and illnesses still would occur. There will be victims of multiple sclerosis and cerebral palsy; there will be victims of car accidents even when people drive as safely as possible in well-designed cars. The mechanism of insurance helps cushion these losses both by spreading them over time (the individual pays a series of smaller insurance premiums over time and thus can more easily absorb the large loss) and by spreading them among many people.

Finally, a compensation program might aim at income redistribution. For instance, federal "supplemental security income" makes payments to those (1) who are considered disabled and (2) whose income falls below a certain level. The aim is to provide some basic subsistence-level income for those who are both disabled and poor. On the whole, the American disability fabric is not primarily occupied with income redistribution, and instead is more understandable in light of the other three goals.

In most programs, only one or two of these goals will dominate. For instance, social insurance (such as social security disability insurance) cannot be viewed as aimed at deterrence because the costs of such insurance are not linked at all to the origin of or responsibility for the loss. By contrast, workers' compensation, though not fault-based, includes deterrence as an aim because insurance premiums or self-insurance costs are linked to the employer's actual injury costs, thus creating incentives to reduce injuries when it is cost-justified to do so. For more detail on these goals and how they relate to the various programs, *see* Abraham & Liebman, *supra*, at 86–94.

When considering any existing or proposed compensation program in light of these goals, keep in mind that two other mechanisms in theory can be used in service of the goal of optimal deterrence: direct government safety regulation, and the marketplace (consumers' own preferences for safety, translated into willingness to pay for safety). Thus, when considering whether an existing or proposed nontort compensation program would produce too little deterrence, one needs to consider whether the marketplace or direct government regulation could take up the deterrence slack.

3. The "Accident Preference"

Analysts have long noted that both tort and cause-based nontort programs (such as workers' compensation and auto no-fault) are far more likely to allow compensation for traumatic injuries than for injuries resulting from disease, even "man-made" disease. As Professor Jane Stapleton has explained, tort law does not officially prefer accident over disease victims, but tort law's conceptual structure—particularly the requirement of actual cause—makes it far less likely that victims of man-made disease will recover in tort than will accident victims. *See* Jane Stapleton, Disease and the Compensation Debate 3, 10–11, 116 (1986).

As you read the following materials, consider a number of questions about this "accident preference." How do the various existing and proposed nontort compensation programs address the issue of disease? For instance, do they allow compensation for some diseases but not others, and if so why? Are there theoretical reasons for distinguishing so-called "man-made" diseases (such as asbestos-related disease, cancers and immunological disorders arising from chemical exposure) from diseases that (at least given current knowledge) are so-called "natural" diseases? If so, how should a particular nontort program address the practical problems of distinguishing between these two categories? Does the overall fabric of American compensation programs (including tort and nontort) provide adequate compensation for disabilities due to disease?

D. CAUSE–BASED COMPENSATION PROGRAMS

The most prominent existing cause-based compensation schemes are workers' compensation and automobile no-fault. These are cause-based because they do not require a showing of fault, but instead turn on whether the injury or disease had a particular causal origin (arising out of and in the course and scope of employment; arising out of use of an automobile). Other cause-based compensation schemes include the National Childhood

Vaccine Injury fund and, in a few states, limited medical no-fault coverage for babies born with severe neurological problems.

The design of any cause-based compensation program must come to grips with several questions. First, what will be the causal trigger? If the causal trigger is vague and often contestable, then the system will be plagued by the high administrative costs of making that determination from case to case. And, if the causal trigger is too broad, then the system will allocate to a particular activity or industry costs that have nothing to do with that activity or industry.

A second question that a cause-based system must confront is whether the system will entirely supplant tort within a particular sphere, or instead will simply be added on to tort. As we will see, workers' compensation generally supplants tort entirely with regard to most work-related injuries. With respect to auto no-fault, sometimes it is simply added to existing tort remedies, but in some states supplants tort at least for less severe injuries. Whether the causal scheme supplants or simply supplements tort obviously affects many issues, including the cost of the system and its deterrent consequences.

A third question is how the cause-based system will be funded, including the degree to which system costs will be tied to the riskiness of a particular actor's conduct. For instance, in workers' compensation, employers pay insurance premiums that are tied in part to the number and severity of work-related injuries.

As you read the following materials about workers' compensation, auto no-fault, and other existing and proposed no-fault programs, consider how each system addresses these basic design questions. For more detailed exploration of these questions, *see* American Law Institute, Reporters' Study on Enterprise Responsibility for Personal Injury, Vol. II, 441–83 (1991).

1. *Workers' Compensation*

FENWICK v. OKLAHOMA STATE PENITENTIARY

Supreme Court of Oklahoma, 1990.
792 P.2d 60.

HODGES, JUSTICE.

This case arose after James R. Fenwick (Claimant) sought workers' compensation for permanent partial disability. The Workers' Compensation Court found that Claimant had not suffered an accidental injury. The Oklahoma Court of Appeals reversed the Workers' Compensation Court, and this Court granted the Petition for Writ of Certiorari. The issue on appeal is whether the claimant's mental stress, which arose out of an isolated incident, without any accompanying physical injury is compensable under the Workers' Compensation Act. We find that it is not.

On August 8, 1979, Claimant, while working as a psychological assistant at the Oklahoma State Penitentiary, encountered a situation where four women were being held hostage by an inmate. Claimant negotiated the release of three of the hostages in exchange for himself. Subsequently, the fourth woman was released. After being held hostage for approximately four and one-half hours, Claimant was released without physical injury.

Although Claimant took two days off work immediately following the hostage incident, he continued to work in the same position until October 1, 1982. At that time he resigned to take a similar job with the Carl Albert Community Mental Health Center.

On July 9, 1982, Claimant filed his Form 3 seeking disability compensation. The State Insurance Fund paid for Claimant's medical and psychiatric treatment until April, 1986. Then on January 6, 1987, Claimant filed a Form 9 seeking permanent partial disability.

Claimant was diagnosed by Dr. Nolan L. Armstrong as suffering from major depression, generalized anxiety disorder, and post-traumatic stress disorder. He was diagnosed by Dr. Larry M. Prater as suffering from post-traumatic stress disorder and personality disorder. Although Claimant complains of periodic shakiness, headaches, tingling in the hands, discomfort in the pit of his stomach, and several other physical disorders, none of the diagnosis included physical injury.

An employee is entitled to compensation, regardless of fault, when the employee suffers disability or death "resulting from an accidental personal injury ... arising out of and in the course of his employment."[1] The causation of the claimant's mental disorders are not disputed leaving the question of accidental personal injury as the only issue.

A definition of injury is provided in the Workers' Compensation Act (the Act) itself.[2] This definition is more repetitive of the requirements set out under section 11 than it is definitive. Since the definition in the Act is not comprehensive, it has been the duty of the courts to further define "accidental personal injury."

This Court has long recognized that "[a] disease of the mind or body which arises in the course of employment, with nothing more" is not an accidental injury and, thus, not compensable. * * * Claimant argues that the additional element requirement of "nothing more" is satisfied by the fact that the event which caused his stress is a definite and identifiable occurrence. This is not the case. This Court has consistently held that physical injury must be present for a disability to be compensable. * * * Just as physical symptoms such as pain, tingling of the limbs, and nausea do not constitute accidental injury, * * * neither does mental stress. Because there is no evidence in the present case that Claimant suffered any physical injury, * * * he has not shown that he suffered an accidental injury. Therefore, his disability is not compensable under the Act.

* * *

1. Okla.Stat. tit. 85, § 11 (1981).

2. Okla. Stat. tit. 85, § 3(7)(1981) provides: "Injury or personal injury" means only accidental injuries arising out of and in the course of employment and such disease or infection as may naturally result therefrom and occupational disease arising out of and in the course of employment as herein defined. Provided, only injuries having as their source a risk not purely personal but one that is reasonably connected with the conditions of employment shall be deemed to arise out of the employment.

[Previous cases have] involved mental stress or physical pain unaccompanied by a physical injury and caused by an identifiable event which occurred at a definite time. Yet, in all previous cases, the claimant's disability was not compensable. The present case presents the same situation. Here we have a disability without any evidence of a physical injury, caused by an identifiable event which occurred at a definite time.

For the first time in 1977, the American Medical Association (AMA) included a chapter on the evaluation of mental disorders in its guidelines.[9] Then in 1985, the Legislature mandated that the AMA's guidelines were to be used by physicians when evaluating impairment.[10] The legislative intent behind this mandate was to provide some consistency in the evaluations of mental disorders accompanied by physical injury. Had the Legislature intended to make disabilities from mental disorders without accompanying physical injury compensable, they would have changed the statutory definition of injury * * * rather than only including a method for consistently evaluating mental disorders.

It has long been the rule that disability, either mental or physical, which is not accompanied by a physical injury is not compensable under the Act. * * * This rule is based on the statutory definition of injury. * * * This definition has remained substantially unchanged since 1915 * * * even though the Act has frequently been amended. In fact, the Act has been amended annually since the establishment of this rule.

* * *

Since the Legislature has not substantially changed the statutory definition of injury, nor has it enacted any statute which would conflict with our prior decision, we must presume that the Legislature is in agreement with our judicial interpretation. Therefore, without a legislative mandate, we decline to alter the rule that disability unaccompanied by physical injury is not compensable under the Act. The Workers' Compensation Court was correct in ruling that Claimant was not entitled to compensation.

* * * COURT OF APPEALS' OPINION VACATED; ORDER OF THE WORKERS' COMPENSATION COURT SUSTAINED.

* * *

Dissenting Opinion by KAUGER, J., joined by OPALA, V.C.J., and DOOLIN, J.

* * *

The claimant, who offered himself as a hostage to secure the release of three female hostages while attempting to mediate a crisis at the Oklahoma State Penitentiary on August 8, 1979, first suffered serious psychological problems in December of that year when he experienced marital dysfunc-

---

9. American Medical Association, Guides to Evaluation of Permanent Impairment, p. 149 (AMA 1977).

10. Okla.Stat. tit. 85, § 3(11)(Supp.1985) provides in part: [A]ny examining physician shall evaluate impairment in substantial accordance with such guides to the evaluation of permanent impairment as have been officially approved by a majority of the Workers' Compensation Court. These guides may include, but shall not be limited to, the "Guides to the Evaluation of Permanent Impairment" published in 1971 by the American Medical Association. . . .

tion and extreme anxiety. Because of Fenwick's mental condition, he left the stress of the prison job, and accepted a position with a community mental health center. It is undisputed that in order to continue even at this occupation, he needs the benefit of counseling.

The State Insurance Fund recognized that Fenwick had been harmed—it paid for his medical and psychiatric treatment for almost four years. It was only after he filed a claim for permanent partial disability that the Fund denied that he had been injured in the course of his employment. * * * Recovery would surely have been granted to the hostage's survivors had he been killed while being held hostage; however, he is denied recovery for a life-altering trauma.

* * *

There are three types of psychic injury: 1) a mental stimulus which causes a physical injury; 2) a physical trauma which causes a nervous injury; and 3) a mental stimulus which causes a nervous injury. * * * Here, recovery is denied not because of lack of evidence of injury, but on the basis that there was no evidence of bleeding, bruising, or tearing, or of lasting physical injury, i.e., accidental personal injury. * * * It is undisputed that the Act has never specifically excluded recovery for mental stress in the absence of physical injury. Nor has it specifically provided that physical trauma is a prerequisite to recovery for mental stress. The Court has engrafted this requirement to its definition of personal injury just as the Court had engrafted sovereign immunity into the common law— * * * by judicial fiat, not by legislative enactment.

* * *

An increasing number of courts are recognizing that recovery is proper for mental injuries not associated with physical impact. There is already visible a distinct majority position supporting compensability for nervous injuries. * * * The courts which find that mental injuries may be compensable absent physical impact reason that there is no valid justification for distinguishing between mental disorders—whether caused by physical impact or injury caused or aggravated by emotional stimuli—in view of the policy of workmens' compensation statutes to provide for work-related disabilities. * * * Courts which do not allow compensation for disabling mental disorders resulting from a work-related emotional stimulus reason that an emotional stimulus is not an "accident" or "injury" within the meaning of the compensation statutes. * * * Some states prohibit recovery for mental or nervous injury by statutorily excluding such events from the definition of an injury arising out of the employment. * * * Although we have relied on this premise to deny recovery in the past, the Oklahoma Act does not specifically exempt mental or neurological illness from its application. * * * Denial of recovery for purely psychological injuries has been a judicial limitation rather than a statutory one. * * * Twenty-six jurisdictions, with similar statutes, allow recovery for properly documented cases of mental disability caused by on-the-job stress and strain. * * *

Adoption of the majority rule will not disrupt the ordinary evidentiary burden. Rule 20 * * * of the Act sets forth the requirements for expert medical testimony. The difficulty of requiring physicians to appear at trials is recognized. The Rule provides the standards necessary for verified reports. Reports prepared for trial must contain a statement that "the evaluation is in substantial accordance with the latest 'Guides to the Evaluation of Permanent Impairment'." * * * Chapter 14 of the Guide is devoted to the consideration of mental and behavioral disorders. The Guide provides a method of evaluation of diseases causing psychiatric impairment, and it is attached hereto as Appendix I.

The use of the Guide as an evaluative tool is also required by 85 O.S.Supp.1988 § 3(11). * * * This section defines "permanent impairment" as "any anatomical or functional abnormality or loss after reasonable medical treatment has been achieved, which abnormality or loss the physician considers to be capable of being evaluated at the time the rating is made." This definition, like those of "injury or personal injury" and "occupational disease" does not specifically exclude mental injuries. Instead, its reference to "any abnormality" encompasses the physical as well as mental condition of the claimant.

* * *

The nature of compensable injuries has changed since workers' compensation laws were originally enacted. What was once a severed limb or debilitating lung disease has become a stress-induced heart attack or a permanent psychic injury. Out of a total of 29,030 workers surveyed in 1900, only 5,115 were white-collar workers. The other 23,915 were manual and farm laborers. By 1970 the figures had changed. Of 79,802 laborers surveyed, 37,857 of those counted were in white-collar jobs. The rest, 41,868 were manual and farm workers. By 1987 in Oklahoma, there were only 40,400 agricultural workers compared to 1,104,783 wage and salary earners. * * * Blue-collar workers have gone from 40 percent of the national workforce in 1950 to 30 percent in 1982. The service sector has grown from 55 percent of the workforce to over 70 percent. Over two-thirds of today's laborers are found in the fields of accounting, banking, engineering, consumer services, education, health care, legal work, transportation, wholesale, and retail trade. * * * Instead of recognizing this shift, the majority mechanically transfers the non-physical injury concept designed to deter false claims by blue collar workers in routine industrial jobs to an environment where psychic trauma is a routine component of working conditions.

In the past, before the recognition of the relationship of mental and nervous injuries to physical symptoms and behavior, there was an understandable basis, i.e., apparently insoluble evidentiary difficulties, for denying recoveries based on such injuries, both in tort and in workers' compensation law. That justification is no longer valid. The present Act predicates indemnification based, not on the label assigned to the injury—whether mental or physical, but upon the employee's inability to work because of impairments flowing from his/her employment conditions. * * *

A human being is not constituted of mere blood, bones, muscles, ligaments, and tissues. He/she also has a nervous system, a brain and a psyche. * * * The majority opinion ignores one of the major portions of the body—the nervous system. Mental stimuli may cause either physical or mental disease, and there is no creditable distinction, nor can a valid line be drawn under contemporary medical standards, between what is totally psychological and what is purely physical. * * * No reason is suggested, and none appears, why injury in the form of debilitating depression, insomnia, and headaches, as well as injury to the cardiovascular system * * * and other internal organs caused by work induced mental or emotional stress and strain, should not be covered if the cause and effect are established by competent evidence.

* * *

Notes

1. *History*. Workers' compensation programs exist in all fifty states and also for federal workers. Their origins trace back to nineteenth century Europe. The first European legislation dealing with industrial accidents was enacted in Prussia in 1838 and made railroads strictly liable to passengers and employees for all accidents occurring in the course of their operations except those arising from an act of God or the negligence of the claimant. In subsequent years legislation was passed requiring employers in certain industries to contribute to local "sickness-association funds." Finally in 1884, Germany (the modern German state having been formed in 1871) adopted the first modern comprehensive compensation scheme. The German plan included also provision for disability arising from old age and causes not specifically covered under the heading of industrial accidents. *See* 1 A. Larson, Workmen's Compensation Law § 5.10 (1989).

In 1897 the Workmen's Compensation Act introduced the idea of accident compensation independent of tort into Great Britain. This legislation, as gradually extended, was consolidated in the Workmen's Compensation Act of 1925, 15 & 16 Geo. 5, c. 84. In 1946 Great Britain adopted (effective in 1948) a comprehensive scheme of National Insurance which replaced the Workmen's Compensation Act. The principal act is now the Social Security Act of 1975. Under this legislation, benefits are paid by the state. Of interest to the tort lawyer is the fact that an award under the social insurance scheme does not bar a common-law action by a worker against the employer. Rather, in assessing damages for loss of earnings in the tort action, one half of the value of the insurance benefits received are deducted. Law Reform (Personal Injuries) Act, 1948, 11 & 12 Geo. 6, c. 41, § 2. In the case of death, there is no deduction. In addition, since 1969, all private employers are compelled to maintain insurance to cover their possible liability to their workers. The current situation in Great Britain is described in P. Winfield and J. Jolowicz, Tort 35–37, 205–23 (14th ed. W. Rogers 1994).

The first workers' compensation act passed in this country was that of New York in the first decade of this century. After some initial uncertainty about whether the acts would pass constitutional muster, *see* Ives v. South Buffalo Ry. Co., 201 N.Y. 271, 94 N.E. 431 (1911)(invalidating the 1910 New York act on due process grounds); New York Central R.R. Co. v. White, 243 U.S. 188, 37 S.Ct. 247, 61 L.Ed. 667 (1917)(upholding the 1914 New York act), within short order most states had passed a workers' compensation statute, and constitutional challenges proved unavailing. The main impetus behind the acts was the widespread belief that tort law was a deficient vehicle for compensating and deterring the injury toll of an increasingly industrialized society. Several common-law tort doctrines combined to make especially unlikely a worker's recovery in tort: contributory negligence, the "fellow-servant rule" (under which the employer generally was not liable for injuries caused by the fault of another employee), and assumption of the risk.

2. *Basic Features.* Although workers' compensation statutes vary in a number of particulars, all statutes share basic similarities.

Quid Pro Quo. All workers' compensation acts reflect a basic quid-pro-quo. The employer agrees to provide (by insurance or self-insurance) certain no-fault benefits (medical benefits, cash disability benefits, and sometimes vocational rehabilitation benefits) for virtually all work-related injuries and for many occupational diseases. The benefits are payable without a showing of the employer's fault, and the employee's own fault (save certain limited exceptions, such as willful injury or intoxication) does not bar or limit recovery. The employer (or its insurer) is supposed to pay the benefits immediately as they are due, and penalties accrue for delay or unjustified opposition to the claim.

In exchange for these benefits, the employee gives up his or her common law right to sue in tort for the full spectrum of tort damages. Instead, for virtually all work-related injuries, the workers' compensation benefit structure is the employee's exclusive remedy (the "exclusivity" doctrine). There are some exceptions to the exclusivity doctrine; for instance, some states allow the employee's family to sue in tort if the employee dies as a result of gross negligence.

Compulsory Coverage. In most states, workers' compensation is compulsory for the great majority of wage and salary workers. (The most common coverage exclusions are for domestic workers and farmworkers.) In recent years, workers' compensation has covered approximately 87% of all wage and salary workers. *See* 65 Social Security Bulletin, Fall 1993, at 68. A few states allow the employer to "opt out" of the system. If the employer does opt out, it is fully exposed to tort suits by employees. Indeed, Texas, one of the few opt-out states, removes the defense of contributory negligence from any employer who opts out. Tex.Lab.Code Ann. § 406.033(a) (West 1996).

Benefits But Not "Full" Compensation. Workers' compensation benefits are of three types: medical, cash for disability, and (in some states) vocational rehabilitation. Until recently, the medical benefits under all state workers' compensation programs had few of the restrictions now common to private health insurance—deductibles, coinsurance provisions, and various managed care features, such as restrictions on choice of physician. Now, many states are allowing utilization review and restrictions on choice of physician. *See* Alliance of American Insurers, Survey of Workers' Compensation Laws 31–33 (1994).

Cash disability benefits are available both for partial and for total disability, and both for temporary and for permanent disabilities. The benefits are not aimed at complete compensation for lost earnings, but instead at replacing some substantial portion of the employee's lost earning capacity.

Administrative Adjudication. All workers' compensation programs replace tort's adjudicative approach with an administrative decisionmaking scheme. If a dispute over benefits arises, the dispute first is heard by an administrative hearing officer, whose decision may be appealed at one or more administrative levels. The final administrative decision—such as the decision of the state workers's compensation commission—usually is subject to judicial review.

3. *The Work–Relation Requirement.* In *Fenwick,* the prison guard's claim foundered on the work-relation test—the requirement that the injury be one

"arising out of and in the course of" the employment. All workers' compensation programs contain a work-relation requirement, and Oklahoma's statutory wording is typical. To understand the theoretical reasons for the work-relation requirement, consider the basic systemic aims of workers' compensation. First, worker's compensation has been viewed as serving a social justice aim: industry—and those who consume its products and services—should bear the cost of industry-related injury just as it does any other cost of business. Second, worker's compensation aims at deterrence. Workers' compensation internalizes to the employer at least many of the costs of untaken yet cost-justified safety precautions, thus inducing the employer to take cost-justified preventative steps. An extensive literature supports the conclusion that workers' compensation results in significant safety advantages not produced by the private market or regulatory structures. *See* Michael J. Moore & W. Kip Viscusi, Compensation Mechanisms for Job Risks 121–35 (1990). Third, workers' compensation in essence forces the purchase of insurance for income-replacement and medical costs arising from work-related injuries.

From either a justice-based or deterrence-based perspective, why would a work-relation test of some sort be necessary? Given the systemic aims that underlie workers' compensation in general and the work-relation requirement in particular, should Fenwick's injury have been covered?

4. *Mental Disabilities.* As the opinions in *Fenwick* note, mental disabilities in general have received less coverage under workers' compensation than have physical injuries. If a physical injury results in a mental disability (such as depression following a back injury), then usually the mental disability is covered. But coverage is much less likely when the precipitating event is not a physical injury. Several rationales might be advanced for such restrictions: a concern about the quality of proof available with respect to the existence and causal source of mental disabilities; the view that mental disabilities in general are not work-related or cannot reliably be proven to be; and concerns about the predictability and insurability of mental disabilities as distinct from physical disabilities.

Do these rationales convincingly support *some* form of restriction on coverage for mental disabilities? If so, do they convincingly support the approach embodied in the Oklahoma statute—the requirement of a physical injury? Some jurisdictions have tried other approaches to mental disabilities: (1) allow coverage if the source of the mental impairment is a sudden or shocking event; (2) allow coverage if the mental disability stems from employment-related stress which exceeds that of ordinary life; (3) allow coverage but only if the claimant can satisfy a high causal threshold, such as showing that the employment contributed to the impairment by at least 50%; or (4) allow coverage for most work-related mental disabilities but exclude particular types of claims, such as mental disabilities arising from bona fide personnel actions. For more detail, *see* Ellen S. Pryor, *Mental Disabilities and the Disability Fabric,* in Mental Disorder, Work Disability, and the Law 153 (R.J. Bonnie & J. Monahan, eds., Univ. Of Chicago 1997).

Which of these coverage approaches seems defensible in theory and workable in practice?

5. *Occupational Disease.* Earlier versions of workers' compensation statutes restricted recoveries to "accidental injury." Thus, the statutes contained large gaps for the victims of occupational diseases, such as victims of asbestos-related illnesses arising from longer-term exposure to asbestos. All workers'

compensation programs now cover at least some occupational diseases. Drawing the appropriate boundaries, however, has posed both theoretical and practical difficulties. From a theoretical perspective, coverage for disease should be restricted to work-related diseases, for the same theoretical reasons that explain the work-relation requirement in general. The challenge is devising a theoretically sound and practically workable causal test.

> The real source of the problem is the inherent mismatch between the characteristics of such disease conditions and the nature of the liability systems through which sufferers of these diseases might seek compensation, whether the basis of liability is fault or simply cause. * * * [E]ven if a disease such as lung cancer is clearly attributable to a variety of exposures in the workplace, it is even more likely to be caused by a variety of other toxic substances to which the worker is exposed in his daily life. Given the practical difficulties posed by a lengthy latency period between initial exposure and ultimate manifestation of the disease, together with the logical difficulties of using epidemiological statistics to establish causal connections in individual cases, any program offering benefits that rest on proof of cause (rather than simply loss) will likely reject more claims than it accepts and will actually attract an even smaller proportion of such claims in the first instance.

American Law Institute, Reporters' Study on Enterprise Responsibility for Personal Injury, Vol. I, at 112 (1991).

Common formulations of the work-relation test are (1) the disease must be "peculiar to the occupation," Conn. Gen. Stat. § 5223; (2) the disease must be characteristic of and peculiar to the employment, but excluding ordinary diseases of life to which the public is equally exposed, N.C Stat. 97–532.

Even if the worker can show that the disease has an occupational link, what if some portion of the disease is linked to nonoccupational factors? Again, jurisdictions differ. One approach is either-or in nature: the worker must prove that the work "significantly contributed to" the disease; if so the claim is covered, and if not no partial benefits are due. Other jurisdictions reduce the compensation award by a percentage reflecting nonoccupational factors. See Price v. Lithonia Lighting Co., 256 Ga. 49, 343 S.E.2d 688 (1986).

Given the problems with the causal test for occupational disease, would it be preferable to eliminate workers' compensation coverage for occupational disease claims and create a single "loss-based" compensation program for the most seriously disabling and fatal diseases, regardless of whether the disease was causally linked to the workplace? What would be the drawbacks of such an approach? For an argument along these lines, see Leslie I. Boden, *Problems in Occupational Disease Compensation,* in Current Issues in Workers' Compensation 313 (J. Chelius ed., 1986). For a detailed analysis of occupational disease and workers' compensation, see Peter S. Barth & H. Allan Hunt, Workers' Compensation and Work–Related Illnesses and Diseases (1980).

6. *Exclusivity, and Tort Options.* Workers' compensation carves out a no-fault system that generally displaces tort, by means of the exclusivity doctrine. Most courts, legislatures, and analysts have consider the exclusivity principle to be central to the viability of workers' compensation. Why? The exclusivity principle also applies to tort claims brought by family members of the injured worker. For instance, a spouse's tort claim for loss of consortium is generally disallowed, *see, e.g.*, Mardian Construction Co. v. Superior Court, 157 Ariz. 103,

754 P.2d 1378 (Ariz.Ct.App.1988), as are wrongful death actions by family members, *see, e.g.*, Morrill v. J & M Construction Co., 635 P.2d 88 (Utah 1981).

Despite general agreement over the importance of exclusivity, challenging issues continue to arise about the shape and the solidity of the boundary between tort and workers' compensation. One such "boundary" issue is raised by Fenwick's situation: may a worker sue in tort if the worker is or would be unsuccessful in recovering workers' compensation benefits? Several guidelines have emerged. If an injury is "covered"—that is, arises out of and in the course and scope of employment—but is simply not compensable, then the exclusivity doctrine bars a tort suit. Depending on the jurisdiction, examples of such covered but noncompensable injuries include: a back injury that causes pain but does not impair earning capacity; an injury to the worker's reproductive system that does not produce any rated impairment under the state's impairment schedule.

If the injury is not "covered"—that is, it does not arise out of and in the course and scope of employment—then the worker is not barred. Suppose, for instance, that the employer provides a remote parking facility and negligently fails to notify workers that there has been a series of assaults and robberies in the parking lot. A worker is physically assaulted when he arrives at the parking lot one evening. Many jurisdictions consider an injury sustained while driving to and from work, or in parking lots, to be outside the course and scope of employment. Thus, the worker in theory could sue the employer in tort.

Does this distinction between "covered but noncompensable" and "noncovered" flow from any of the purposes of workers' compensation and the need for an exclusivity rule? How does the distinction apply to Fenwick's injury; that is, would the exclusivity doctrine bar a tort claim by Fenwick? (Of course, even if the exclusivity doctrine would not bar a tort claim by Fenwick, the tort claim might run into other obstacles, such as governmental immunity or rules restricting recoveries for emotional distress.)

How does the exclusivity doctrine apply to claims of injury arising from sexual harassment? A leading case is Byrd v. Richardson–Greenshields Securities, Inc., 552 So.2d 1099 (Fla.1989).

> Our analysis must begin with the premise, now well established in our law, that workers' compensation generally is the sole tort remedy available to a worker injured in a manner that falls within the broad scope and policies of the workers' compensation statute. * * * This statute expresses a plain legislative intent that any potential liability arising from "injury or death" is abolished in favor of the exclusive remedy available under workers' compensation. However, if the liability arises from something other than "injury or death," the other potential bases of liability remain viable.

> * * *

> * * * [W]e cannot find that acts constituting sexual harassment were ever meant to fall under workers' compensation. Moreover, we have an equal obligation to honor the intent and policy of other enactments and, accordingly, may not apply the exclusivity rule in a manner that effectively abrogates the policies of other law. * * *

> There can be no doubt at this point in time that both the state of Florida and the federal government have committed themselves strongly to outlawing and eliminating sexual discrimination in the workplace, including the related evil of sexual harassment. The statutes, case law, and

administrative regulations uniformly and without exception condemn sexual harassment in the strongest possible terms. We find that the present case strongly implicates these sexual harassment policies and, accordingly, may not be decided by a blind adherence to the exclusivity rule of the workers' compensation statute alone. Our clear obligation is to construe both the workers' compensation statute and the enactments dealing with sexual harassment so that the policies of both are preserved to the greatest extent possible. [The court reviews the federal and state statutes outlawing workplace sexual harassment.]

* * *

In light of this overwhelming public policy, we cannot say that the exclusivity rule of the workers' compensation statute should exist to shield an employer from all tort liability based on incidents of sexual harassment. The clear public policy emanating from federal and Florida law holds that an employer is charged with maintaining a workplace free from sexual harassment. Applying the exclusivity rule of workers' compensation to preclude any and all tort liability effectively would abrogate this policy, undermine the Florida Human Rights Act, and flout Title VII of the Civil Rights Act of 1964.

This, we cannot condone. Public policy now requires that employers be held accountable in tort for the sexually harassing environments they permit to exist, whether the tort claim is premised on a remedial statute or on the common law.

We find this conclusion harmonizes with the policies and scope of workers' compensation. As often has been noted, workers' compensation is directed essentially at compensating a worker for lost resources and earnings. This is a vastly different concern than is addressed by the sexual harassment laws. While workplace injuries rob a person of resources, sexual harassment robs the person of dignity and self esteem. Workers' compensation addresses purely economic injury; sexual harassment laws are concerned with a much more intangible injury to personal rights. * * * To the extent these injuries are separable, we believe that they both should be, and can be, enforced separately.

522 So.2d at 1100–04.

Most courts, like *Byrd,* have allowed workers to pursue tort and civil rights claims for sexual harassment. *E.g.,* O'Connell v. Chasdi, 400 Mass. 686, 511 N.E.2d 349 (1987). A few, however, hold that workers' compensation is the exclusive avenue for mental anguish claims resulting from sexual harassment. *See* Knox v. Combined Insurance Co., 542 A.2d 363 (Me.1988). Would allowing tort and civil rights claims for sexual harassment undermine the purposes behind the exclusivity doctrine?

Suppose that sexual harassment caused a worker to experience anxiety or depression debilitating enough to cause at least a temporary disability and the need for medical and psychological treatment. According to the *Byrd* court's analysis, would the worker's injury be covered by workers' compensation? In Ramada Inn Surfside v. Swanson, 560 So.2d 300 (Fla.Ct.App.1990), the court was faced with such a claim. Citing *Byrd* and its reasoning, the court held that workers' compensation covered the claim. Do you agree with this reading of *Byrd?* If the result is correct as an interpretation of *Byrd,* do you see any problems with this way of addressing the relation of workers' compensation and sexual harassment claims?

For analysis of the interplay between tort and worker's compensation with respect to mental anguish and other nonphysical injuries, *see* Jean C. Love, *Actions for Nonphysical Harm: The Relationship Between the Tort System and No–Fault Compensation (With an Emphasis on Workers' Compensation)*, 73 Cal. L. Rev. 857 (1985).

Another category of boundary issues relates to the statutory and judicially crafted exceptions to the exclusivity doctrine. Most states allow tort recovery if the employer caused the injury intentionally. But this exception is quite narrow because in many states "intent" is interpreted to mean actual subjective intent to injure, as distinct from knowledge with substantial certainty, which can suffice to establish intent for purposes of tort law generally. *See, e.g.*, Bardere v. Zafir, 102 App. Div.2d 422, 477 N.Y.S.2d 131, aff'd on other grounds, 63 N.Y.2d 850, 472 N.E.2d 37, 482 N.Y.S.2d 261 (1984). For instance, West Virginia provides an exception only if the employer "consciously, subjectively and deliberately formed [the intent] to produce the specific result of injury or death." W.Va.Code § 23–4–2(c)(2). Why have courts and legislatures been reluctant to use the "knowledge with substantial certainty" formulation when drawing the boundary of the exclusivity doctrine?

Another exception is the "dual capacity" doctrine that courts fashioned in limited instances. If the employer acted in dual capacities—for instance, as both product manufacturer of the product that injured the worker, and as the worker's employer—then some courts allowed the worker to sue the employer in tort in the manufacturer's capacity. *See* Bell v. Industrial Vangas, Inc., 30 Cal.3d 268, 179 Cal.Rptr. 30, 637 P.2d 266 (1981). After some initial judicial acceptance of the doctrine, however, most courts now reject the dual capacity doctrine when the injury results from a product manufactured or sold by the employer. *See* Schump v. Firestone Tire and Rubber Co., 44 Ohio St.3d 148, 541 N.E.2d 1040 (1989). Following the *Bell* decision, California eliminated the dual capacity doctrine by statute. *See* Cal. Labor Code § 3602(a) (West 1996).

7. *Tort Suits Against Third Parties.* Consider the following scenario. A worker sustains a serious arm injury when using an industrial tool that is not equipped with a handguard. When the employer first purchased the tool from the manufacturer, the tool came with a handguard that could be attached and removed, depending on the uses to which the tool was put. The employer fails to attach the handguard when appropriate or to instruct workers about this, and eventually the handguard is simply lost. The worker sues the manufacturer, alleging negligent design and failure to warn, as well as products liability claims grounded in a section 402A theory. Suppose that the jury finds liability on the manufacturer's part and awards tort damages of $500,000. The total medical and disability benefits paid by the workers' compensation insurer amount to $150,000.

Until recently, most jurisdictions handled this scenario in the following way: (1) the manufacturer was not allowed to bring a claim against the employer for contribution; and (2) the employer (or employer's insurer) could bring a claim for subrogation against the manufacturer, requiring the manufacturer to repay the $150,000 in worker's compensation benefits. Thus, even if the employer's own negligence was a contributing factor in bringing about the injury, the manufacturer paid the full bill for the injury, and the employer could be relieved of even its workers' compensation bill. *See* Arthur Larson,

Third–Party Action Over Against Workers' Compensation Employer, 1982 Duke L.J. 483.

It is not difficult to understand the reluctance to allow the manufacturer's claim for contribution. "If contribution or indemnity is allowed, the employer may be forced to pay his employee—through the conduit of the third-party tortfeasor—an amount in excess of his statutory workers' compensation liability. This arguably thwarts the central concept of workers' compensation. * * *" Lambertson v. Cincinnati Corp., 312 Minn. 114, 119, 257 N.W.2d 679, 684 (1977). What are the drawbacks of the traditional approach?

Some jurisdictions and commentators have endorsed other approaches. Under one approach, the manufacturer could indeed bring a contribution claim against the employer and try to establish a percentage of fault or responsibility; the employer's contribution, however, would be capped by the amount of workers' compensation benefits. So, in our example, if the employer was found 80% responsible for the injury, the employer would owe contribution to the manufacturer not in the amount of $400,000 (80% of the tort damages) but only for the sum of $150,000. Note, though, that this approach would expose the employer to litigation costs, which might be considerable since the suit would need to determine percentages of fault for the accident. For discussion of the approach, *see* Paul Weiler, *Workers' Compensation and Product Liability: The Interaction of a Tort and Non–Tort Regime*, 50 Ohio St. L.J. 825 (1989).

A second approach would simply reduce the plaintiff's total tort judgment against any third party, dollar for dollar, by the amount of the benefits paid in workers' compensation. So, in our example, the manufacturer would not be allowed to bring a contribution claim, but would be liable to the claimant only for $350,000. The employer (or workers' compensation insurer) would not be allowed to recoup, via subrogation, the amount of benefits paid out. For endorsement of the approach, *see* Model Uniform Product Liability Act § 114(A).

This approach avoids litigation costs for the employer, and it also allocates some of the loss to the employer, rather than shifting it to the manufacturer. This is an attractive result when the employer has been partially at fault. But what if the accident involves no employer fault? Then the employer, under this approach, still would be unable to obtain subrogation from the product manufacturer, and the product manufacturer will bear less than the full costs of the accident. This may seem unappealing, yet the only way out is to have some type of factfinding about the employer's fault in each case, and this of course will raise again the problem of litigation costs. A few states do predicate this dollar-for-dollar approach on a finding of employer fault. *See* Witt v. Jackson, 57 Cal.2d 57, 17 Cal.Rptr. 369, 366 P.2d 641 (1961). Which of the approaches seems most likely to achieve appropriate allocation of accident costs at an acceptable level of transaction costs?

8. *Disability Benefits.* Throughout the 1980s and early 1990s, many employers, insurers, and analysts contended that the workers' compensation system was in need of serious reform. One item high on the reform agenda has been the escalating costs of medical benefits, which during the 1980s and early 1990s exceeded the rate of growth in non-workers' compensation health care costs. As noted earlier, many states now have implemented some type of managed care approach. It is still too early to draw firm conclusions about whether these reforms have lowered costs while still providing effective medical care.

Another key target of reformers has been the approach for calculating and awarding cash disability benefits. Both employers and employees have had complaints: the cost of providing disability benefits continued to increase rapidly, yet the actual amount of benefits delivered to workers was often well below the recommendation, made by the 1972 National Commission on State Workmen's Compensation Laws, that workers' compensation replace two-thirds of a worker's lost wages. Analysts have contended that these dual deficiencies are in large part the product of an excessively costly and inefficient system for measuring and awarding one category of disability benefits: "permanent partial" disability benefits ("PPD"). (The other categories are temporary total, temporary partial, and permanent total.)

To understand PPD benefits and the problems they have generated, consider a worker whose left hand is amputated after an industrial accident. He is unable to work at all for six months; during that time he will receive weekly or bi-weekly workers' compensation checks for temporary total disability. The amount of such benefits is based on the worker's "average weekly wage" before injury; depending on how generous the state's benefits are, the worker will receive from 66 ⅔% to 80% of his average weekly wage (subject to maximum caps or minimum benefit levels). During months 7 through 11 post-injury, the worker is able to return to a modified-duty position, earning less than he did before injury; he still undergoes another prosthetic surgery and some rehabilitation. During these 4 months, he will receive temporary partial disability payments, which also are based on the degree to which the injury has diminished his average weekly wages.

By month 12, the worker has reached medical stabilization. He still is working in the "light duty" position. The question now is what amount he should receive for the permanent though partial disability the injury has caused him. Until the legislative reforms of recent years, two approaches dominated.

First, some jurisdictions based awards of PPD, for all types of injuries, on an assessment of how the disability affects the worker's lost-earning capacity. For instance, the administrative judge might determine, based on medical and vocational reports and given the worker's particular education, age, and background, that the worker has suffered a 30% loss of his wage-earning capacity. Suppose, too, that the jurisdiction specifies that the maximum duration of PPD payments is 450 weeks. The worker then would receive either (1) a lump sum award equal to the present value of 30% times his average pre-injury weekly wage, multiplied by 450; or (2) weekly or biweekly checks equal to 30% of that average weekly wage.

Second, some jurisdictions used an anatomical "schedule" for determining PPD for at least some injuries—for instance, loss of a thumb might receive 75 weeks of compensation. The schedules usually applied only to anatomical members such as arm, hand, finger, leg, foot, toe, eye, ear; the schedules did not apply to "general" injuries such as back injuries, respiratory disabilities, etc. If the worker had only a partial loss of a thumb or a leg, then the worker received some portion of the scheduled amount. If the injury is a "general" one not governed by the schedule, then the PPD benefits depend on an assessment of how the injury has reduced the worker's wage-earning capacity. Thus, most schedule jurisdictions actually use two approaches: schedules for specific injuries, and lost-earning assessment for general injuries. Disputes often arose over whether an injury was really specific (thus governed only by the schedule) or whether it had "extended to and affected" some nonscheduled body part and thus had become a general injury.

In a schedule jurisdiction, then, our worker would receive the specified amount of compensation—such as an amount equal to 311 (number of weeks for loss of hand) times two-thirds of the average pre-injury weekly wage. Under the schedule approach, it would not matter whether the worker's occupation and training heavily required use of the hand (the worker is an artist or mechanic) or whether the worker will suffer little permanent wage loss as a result of the injury (the worker is an accountant).

What are the benefits and drawbacks of, respectively, the schedule approach and the lost wage-earning approach?

In both schedule and nonschedule jurisdictions, lengthy disputes over PPD have been common. Lawyers are often hired; administrative appeals and judicial review are common; and expert assessments of disability frequently diverge significantly.

In response, many jurisdictions have significantly altered the traditional approaches. Although the particulars vary somewhat among jurisdictions, the Texas reforms are representative of the newer approach. Consider again the worker with the amputated hand. In the Texas scheme, once the worker reaches maximum medical improvement—that is, once no further substantial medical recovery from the injury can be expected—the worker will be evaluated according to a comprehensive "impairment rating schedule." Texas has adopted the American Medical Association's schedule, known as the *Guides to the Evaluation of Permanent Impairment*, now in its fourth edition. The schedule consists of several hundred pages, and provides evaluative protocols for rating—in terms of a single "whole person" percentage—the anatomical impairment that an injury has produced. The schedule does not try to measure lost earning capacity, but only the "impairment." According to the *Guides,* a hand amputation translates into a 100% impairment of the hand, which in turn translates into a 90% impairment of the "upper extremity," which in turn translates into the final, whole-person impairment of 54%. In Texas, each percentage of whole-person impairment entitles the worker to 3 weeks of compensation at the rate of 70% of the worker's average weekly wage. Thus, our worker will be entitled to 162 weeks of compensation in the amount just noted. This amount is payable even if the worker has gone back to work at the full wages he once was earning. The percentage of impairment is the sole consideration. And Texas, like many states, resolves differences in ratings by giving presumptive weight to the rating provided by a "designated" physician— one agreed to by the parties or chosen by the administrative agency.

The aim here is to substitute a predictable, "objective" measurement method—the impairment rating schedule—for the unpredictable and disputed ratings generated by previous schedules and lost earnings assessments. But there is an obvious danger. What if the worker's injury, given his education, occupation, age, and background, prevents him from returning to the workforce, even after the allotted 162 weeks? Texas provides a "supplemental" form of benefits to address this scenario. If, after 162 weeks following the date of medical stabilization, our worker has not returned to work or is earning less than 80% of his previous average weekly wages, then the worker is entitled to additional benefits based on his lost earnings. The worker must show good faith efforts to obtain a job.

What are the possible benefits and disadvantages of reforms such as that of Texas, compared to the two more traditional approaches just described?

The early returns on recent legislative reforms directed at disability and medical payments indicate that costs have declined, and that more compensation dollars are being delivered to workers for each dollar expended for administrative overhead. *See* Jack Schmulowitz, *Workers' Compensation: Coverage, Benefits, and Costs, 1992–93,* in 1996 Workers' Compensation Yearbook, at I–33 (J. Burton ed. 1996). Still, important questions will remain unanswered until further study, including the distributional equity of payments and the measurement accuracy, in practice, of the *AMA Guides* or other comprehensive impairment schedules. Although almost 40 states now mandate or recommend use of the *Guides* for use in workers' compensation claims, virtually no empirical study has been conducted as to whether measurements produced by the *Guides* correlate to lost-earning capacity in the short or long run.

In addition, exclusive and rigid reliance on the *Guides* is troubling because (1) the *Guides,* though quite comprehensive, do not yet rate all impairments and still have gaps; (2) the *Guides* often require the physician to base the impairment rating on an assessment of how well the person can carry out "activities of daily living," but are not very precise about the activities that should be considered or what constitutes normal activity; (3) may lead to impairment ratings that reflect sexual bias. For instance, the first three editions of the *Guides* (some states still require use of the second or third edition) contained examples in which the relevant "activities of daily living" included, for women, the following: caring for children and home, going shopping, doing kitchen work, working as a seamstress, mopping, cleaning, performing household duties. Examples of daily activities performed by men, by contrast, included actively participating in sports, engaging in tennis and hiking, and playing 18 holes of golf regularly. For more detail on these problems with the *Guides, see* Ellen S. Pryor, *Flawed Promises: A Critical Evaluation of the American Medical Association's Guides to the Evaluation of Permanent Impairment (Book Review),* 103 Harv. L. Rev. 964 (1990).

> [A]ny effort to create a compensation schedule will involve important normative judgments about the types of functions that matter in evaluating impairments, and the significance of loss of these functions. Medically or scientifically authored ratings schemes can offer useful insights into the nature and measurement of various sorts of losses. Hence, when developing loss assessment systems, legislatures and administrative bodies can and should learn much from consultation with the medical community. But policymakers should appreciate that the search for an "objective," "accurate," or purely "medical" system is and always will be fruitless. And they must resist the seductive but false hope that use of a scientifically or medically authored ratings system can bypass the need to make the hard choices necessary for any loss assessment system.

Id., at 976.

Workers have filed constitutional challenges to the workers' compensation reforms of recent years, but generally these have been unavailing. *See* Texas Workers' Compensation Comm'n v. Garcia, 893 S.W.2d 504 (Tex.1995); Bradley v. Hurricane Restaurant, 670 So.2d 162 (Fla.Dist.Ct.App.1996).

2. *Automobile No–Fault*

Before beginning a look at auto no-fault, it is important to address briefly several other strands in the current fabric for compensating auto injuries: financial responsibility and compulsory insurance laws; unsatisfied judgment funds; and uninsured and underinsured motorist coverage. As you read these materials, consider whether any one of these strands, or some combination of them, can effectively address the persistent concern about victims of insolvent or uninsured drivers.

a. *Financial Responsibility and Compulsory Insurance Laws, Unsatisfied Judgment Funds, and Uninsured Motorists Coverage*
Compulsory Insurance and Financial Responsibility Laws

Beginning in the 1920s, every state eventually enacted some form of "financial responsibility" or "compulsory insurance" legislation. These statutes usually require that every motorist have a certain minimum level of liability insurance, or be able to demonstrate—in lieu of having such insurance—the financial ability to satisfy a tort judgment, up to some point. Although over the years many states have improved enforcement of such laws, the minimum amounts are not high enough to ensure basic coverage for many severe injuries. The minimum levels are commonly $20,000/$40,000/$10,000 (the first figure is the coverage amount for a single bodily injury; the second figure is the total amount required for the aggregate bodily injury if more than one person is injured in a single accident; and the third figure is the amount for property damage). Some states go higher, such as to 30/60/10, and a few are lower, such as 10/20/10.

The enactment of compulsory insurance laws has raised thorny problems relating to the availability and affordability of insurance. Consider, for instance, a driver who has had two previous accidents, lives in an urban area, is under the age of 25, and drives a sports car. On the basis of these factors this driver and others who share these characteristics form a "risk pool" with a far greater chance than some other drivers of being involved in a serious accident. Without any regulatory constraints, private insurers either will not write coverage for this driver or will charge a rate considerably higher than those for many other drivers. This problem of differential risks creates competing political interests: drivers who fall in the riskier categories demand available and affordable insurance, especially because insurers' risk classifications (based on age, geography, and sometimes even credit history) may seem subjective or contestable; insurers warn that heavy regulation of rates will force insurers out of the market and thus reduce coverage for less risky drivers; and less risky drivers wish to avoid paying increased premiums for the risks posed by the risky drivers.

What are the potential benefits and disadvantages of allowing significantly different rates to be charged to different categories of insureds?

States have varied in their approaches to these competing demands, and all approaches have posed some problems. One approach, taken by just a handful of states, is to allow private insurers to operate with little regulation of rates. Three basic categories then emerge: many drivers will be charged basically standard rates; other drivers will pay high-risk rates; and a few drivers will be unable to obtain coverage at all in the "voluntary" market (that is, insurance voluntarily provided by private insurers). The state thus also creates a mechanism, often known as an "assigned risk plan," that will provide insurance for this "involuntary" market. Usually an assigned risk pool works as follows. The state requires that each insurer be assigned some proportion of the uninsurable drivers; the proportion depends on the total volume of auto insurance that the insurer writes in the state. A driver who is unable to obtain insurance in the standard voluntary market is then able to obtain insurance as an assigned risk, and must pay higher premiums. (The person will be altogether ineligible under certain circumstances, such as drug use, felony conviction, or habitual violation of law.) Usually insurers sustain net losses on these assigned risks, even given higher premiums, and so the hope is that the size of the "involuntary market" or assigned risk pool is small.

Some have argued that this approach—minimal rate regulation—works best. Most drivers find coverage at standard rates, a smaller percentage must pay higher-risk rates, and a still-smaller percentage is unable to obtain insurance except through the involuntary system. Insurers are able to engage in risk differentiation among lower and higher risk insureds. In addition, although insurers are required to write insurance for a proportion of the assigned risks, insurers still can achieve an overall adequate return on auto insurance because, by slightly increasing the rates charged to all insureds, insurers can offset the losses that will be posed by the small percentage of assigned risks. For more detail as to these conclusions, see Note, *Withdrawal Restrictions in the Automobile Insurance Market,* 102 Yale L.J. 1431 (1993). Others criticize the approach because they maintain that regulation of rates is necessary to prevent excessive profits, or because they dispute the insurers' risk classifications, such as those based on geography, age, or sex.

Many other states, therefore, have taken an approach that more heavily regulates rates charged for auto insurance. The New Jersey experience is instructive. New Jersey enacted a compulsory insurance law in 1972, yet New Jersey strictly regulated the rates that insurers could charge in both the "voluntary" and the "involuntary" market. Because insurers were required to participate in providing coverage—at regulated rates—to the involuntary market, many insurers sought to withdraw from writing automobile insurance in the state, contending that they could not make an adequate profit. The state then enacted restrictions on insurers' ability to exit the auto insurance market. For instance, an insurer in some instances might be forced to give up other, more profitable lines of insurance if it chose to exit the auto insurance market. For more detail on the New Jersey experience, *see* Note, *supra*; Comment, *Automobile Insurance Reform in New Jersey: Could a Pure No–Fault System Provide a Final Solution?*, 25 Seton Hall L. Rev. 1219 (1995).

Although the debate over these various mechanisms will continue, consider a few points that emerge from this brief description. First, absent restrictions, insurers will engage in considerable risk differentiation among drivers, differentiation that may depend on geography, age, sex, marital status, use of the auto, driver education, and driving record. Higher-risk insureds will pay higher rates (or will simply opt not to carry insurance and risk the consequences). Second, regulation of rates in the voluntary market has seemed to increase the number of drivers to whom insurers are unwilling to sell coverage at the regulated rate. Put another way, the number of drivers in the "voluntary market" decreases and the number in the "involuntary" market increases. Why? Third, under any system, the state needs some mechanism for providing insurance to the involuntary market. These mechanisms end up transferring, to the voluntary market or to state coffers, the costs of higher risk insureds.

Unsatisfied Judgment Funds and Uninsured/Underinsured Motorist Coverage

A response to the problem of unsatisfied tort judgments has been the creation of state funds for compensating victims injured by insolvent drivers. The notion originated in the Canadian province of Manitoba, and spread to other Canadian provinces. North Dakota was the first state to follow this approach. Under the North Dakota scheme, any resident who obtains a judgment for auto injuries and is unable to collect the judgment is able to obtain payments from the fund up to certain specified limits. Other states do not require the victim to obtain a tort judgment, but only to show that the other party was legally liable. Only a few states have adopted such funds. For more detail, *see* Robert E. Keeton & Alan I. Widiss, Insurance Law § 4.10 & n.8 (1988).

Uninsured and underinsured motorist coverage is a feature of the liability insurance offered in most states. Basically, it works as follows. If the insured under a liability policy is injured by another party, and if that other party is underinsured or uninsured (or was a hit and run driver), then the injured person can recover against his own insurance company, up to the limits of the coverage, if he can show that the other party would have been liable for the injuries.

This coverage originated from the voluntary efforts of insurers seeking to avoid the imposition of compulsory insurance laws. Eventually all states required that uninsured coverage either be provided or offered. Many states have enacted similar provisions relating to underinsured motorist coverage. For more detail, *see* Robert E. Keeton & Alan I. Widiss, Insurance Law § 4.9 (1988).

b. History of Auto No–fault

Early consideration of no-fault concepts was not limited to the employment arena. A study published in 1932, by the Committee to Study Compensation for Automobile Accidents of the Columbia University Council for Research in the Social Sciences, examined thousands of auto liability cases and criticized several features of the tort liability system: serious injuries were underpaid, less serious injuries were overpaid, delay and gaps in liability coverage were common. The study proposed making automobile insurance compulsory and imposing upon the owners of motor vehicles a limited absolute liability for personal injuries or death arising out of the operation of their vehicles. The plan adopted the compensation schedules used in the workers' compensation schemes of New York and Massachusetts. As under workers' compensation, the remedy under the proposed automobile compensation scheme was to be exclusive. The Columbia Plan, as might be expected, generated a great amount of often bitter controversy.

Although never enacted into law, the Columbia Plan was the influential forerunner of a plan adopted in 1946 in the Canadian province of Saskatchewan (10 Geo. 6, c. 11), a plan that has been frequently amended since its initial adoption.

In 1965, Professor and now Judge Robert E. Keeton and Professor Jeffrey O'Connell published their Basic Protection for the Traffic Victim (hereafter *Basic Protection*), which proposed an auto no-fault system. Their proposed scheme applied to all injuries except severe injuries; a person with a severe injury retained the right to sue in tort. For anyone with a nonsevere injury, the no-fault scheme would be the only recourse. Under the no-fault scheme, benefits were to be paid by the injured person's own insurer, not the insurer of other individuals. Payment of benefits did not require a showing of anyone's fault. But benefits did not include payment for pain and suffering; rather, benefits were limited to net economic loss. An insured could buy a policy with greater protection (such as coverage for pain and suffering), but the premiums for this would be higher.

Almost contemporaneous with the publication of *Basic Protection*, another publication appeared that strongly argued against auto no-fault. W. Blum & H. Kalven, Jr., Public Law Perspectives on a Private Law Problem (1965). Blum and Kalven argued that a no-fault auto system would place on motorists both the costs of accidents caused by motorist fault and those not caused by motorist fault. In their view, there was no defensible reason for placing on motorists the costs of non-fault accidents. Rather, such costs in principle should be borne by the population as a whole, through the general tax and welfare system. And this result deserved rejection, in their view, because it simply created a form of social insurance for the victims of auto accidents, leaving victims of other injuries or illnesses uncovered or at least uncovered to such a degree. Do you find this criticism convincing?

In 1970, Massachusetts became the first state to adopt a no-fault plan. The Massachusetts plan went into effect in 1971. Since then several dozen additional states have adopted some version of auto no-fault.

c. *Current Types of Auto No–fault*

Currently, auto no-fault schemes vary in important ways. No state has entirely replaced the tort system with no-fault for all auto-related injuries. The no-fault schemes that do exist, as Professor Robert Jerry has shown, fall into several categories. *See* R. Jerry, Understanding Insurance Law § 132 (2d ed. 1996). One category is "add on" no-fault, which exists in approximately eleven states. These states simply add a requirement that each driver must have some level of no-fault coverage that will pay him directly in the event of injury. The tort system, however, remains fully in operation, and the injured driver still can pursue the other driver in tort.

Approximately thirteen states have true no-fault for injuries that do not exceed a particular level of seriousness, defined either in terms of monetary damages caused or medical severity. That is, if the case falls below the threshold, then the person may not sue in tort and is limited to the no-fault benefits. Most of these states use a monetary threshold.

When the threshold is higher, more cases will fall within the no-fault scheme; when the threshold is lower, more cases will remain within the traditional tort realm.

These no-fault schemes usually provide for five categories of benefits: (1) loss of income or wage-earning capacity; (2) the value of personal services that the insured would have otherwise performed for the family; (3) in death cases, losses that the survivors suffer as measured by income or earnings that the decedent would have provided; (4) medical and rehabilitative expenses; and (5) funeral expenses. R. Jerry, *supra,* at 851.

A third category of no-fault is a choice system. Under such a system, the insured driver would choose whether to be covered under the traditional tort system or under no-fault. This approach is discussed more fully in note 4 below; currently, only a few states have a limited form of choice. *See* R. Jerry, *supra,* at 852–53.

The following is an excerpt of New York's auto no-fault statute, along with a problem and questions relating to auto no-fault statutes.

MCKINNEY'S CONSOLIDATED LAWS OF NEW YORK ANNOTATED INSURANCE LAW
CHAPTER 28 OF THE CONSOLIDATED LAWS ARTICLE 51—COMPREHENSIVE MOTOR VEHICLE INSURANCE REPARATIONS

§ 5102. Definitions

In this chapter: (a) "Basic economic loss" means, up to fifty thousand dollars per person of the following combined items * * *: [All necessary medical care, including psychiatric and rehabilitative services; lost earnings; expenditures made to obtain services in lieu of those that the injured person would have performed for income; and other reasonable and necessary expenses up to $25 a day.]

* * *

(c) "Non-economic loss" means pain and suffering and similar non-monetary detriment.

(d) "Serious injury" means a personal injury which results in death; dismemberment; significant disfigurement; a fracture; loss of a fetus; permanent loss of use of a body organ, member, function or system; permanent consequential limitation of use of a body organ or member; significant limitation of use of a body function or system; or a medically determined injury or impairment of a non-permanent nature which prevents the injured person from performing substantially all of the material acts which constitute such person's usual and customary daily activities for not less than ninety days during the one hundred eighty days immediately following the occurrence of the injury or impairment.

* * *

(j) "Covered person" means any pedestrian injured through the use or operation of, or any owner, operator or occupant of, a motor vehicle which has in effect the financial security required by article six or eight of the vehicle and traffic law or which is referred to in subdivision two of section three hundred twenty-one of such law; or any other person entitled to first party benefits.

§ 5103.   Entitlement to first party benefits; additional financial security required

(a) Every owner's policy of liability insurance issued [in compliance with the state compulsory insurance law] shall also provide for * * * the payment of first party benefits to:

(1) Persons, other than occupants of another motor vehicle or a motorcycle, for loss arising out of the use or operation in this state of such motor vehicle. * * *

(2) The named insured and members of his household, other than occupants of a motorcycle, for loss arising out of the use or operation of (i) an uninsured motor vehicle or motorcycle, within the United States, its territories or possessions, or Canada; and (ii) an insured motor vehicle or motorcycle outside of this state and within the United States, its territories or possessions, or Canada.

* * *

(b) An insurer may exclude from coverage required by subsection (a) hereof a person who:

(1) Intentionally causes his own injury.

(2) Is injured as a result of operating a motor vehicle while in an intoxicated condition or while his ability to operate such vehicle is impaired by the use of a drug. * * *

* * *

§ 5104.   Causes of action for personal injury

(a) Notwithstanding any other law, in any action by or on behalf of a covered person against another covered person for personal injuries arising out of negligence in the use or operation of a motor vehicle in this state, there shall be no right of recovery for non-economic loss, except in the case of a serious injury, or for basic economic loss.

§ 5106.   Fair claims settlement

(a) Payments of first party benefits and additional first party benefits shall be made as the loss is incurred. Such benefits are overdue if not paid within thirty days after the claimant supplies proof of the fact and amount of loss sustained. If proof is not supplied as to the entire claim, the amount which is supported by proof is overdue if not paid within thirty days after such proof is supplied. All overdue payments shall bear interest at the rate of two percent per month. If a valid claim or portion was overdue, the claimant shall also be entitled to recover his attorney's reasonable fee, for services necessarily performed in connection with securing payment of the overdue claim, subject to limitations promulgated by the superintendent in regulations.

Notes

1. *Application of the Statute.* Consider the following accident scenario. Sarah and John are injured in a two-car collision. Sarah is the owner and driver of one of the cars; the car is insured through GoodHands, and Sarah is the named insured on the policy. John is the driver of the other car but is not its owner; a friend of John's—Bill—is the car's owner and gave John permission to drive Bill's car. John does not own a car. Bill's car is insured through AutoSure insurance company.

Sarah sustains a severe sprain to her back, and is bedridden for about two weeks. She receives medical care, including physical therapy, that eventually totals $14,000. She returns to work at a reduced schedule for several months before resuming her previous duties in full. She experiences considerable pain even now, as well as limitations on her ability to exercise vigorously, garden, etc. Her total lost wages equal $25,000.

John sustains a shattered hip that requires several surgeries. He is in and out of rehabilitation for almost a year, and never will be able to perform the full duties of his previous job. Instead, he undergoes vocational therapy and additional training, and now has a new job that is less physically demanding. The new job pays slightly more than his previous one, but he has experienced lost earnings of $40,000 as a result of surgeries, rehabilitation, etc. The total cost of his medical and rehabilitative treatment is about $85,000.

Sarah's Injuries

a. Is GoodHands required to pay for Sarah's medical and rehabilitative expenses? If so, when must GoodHands pay? For instance, may GoodHands take its time in paying and wait, say, one year from the date of injury before paying?

b. Suppose that Sarah and John were arguably negligent, but that the accident was not the result of anyone's intoxication or willful injury. Can GoodHands successfully contest any obligation to pay for Sarah's injuries by claiming that John was negligent or that Sarah was negligent?

c. Is GoodHands required to pay any amount for Sarah's pain and suffering or for her reduced ability to exercise, garden, etc.?

d. May Sarah sue John in tort for any or all of her injuries?

e. Suppose that Sarah's total medical expenses and lost earnings actually end up exceeding $50,000, and instead total $80,000. May she sue John in tort for any or all of this $80,000? For pain and suffering?

John's Injuries

a. Is AutoSure required to pay for John's medical and rehabilitative expenses?

b. Is AutoSure required to pay for John's pain and suffering?

c. Is John permitted to sue Sarah in tort for any or all of his injuries, including pain and suffering? Notice that, if John is permitted to sue Sarah in tort, then Sarah's policy with GoodHands—specifically, the liability insurance component of the policy—will be on the hook for this.

2. *Evaluating No–Fault.* From the standpoint of timely, certain, and complete compensation, what are the advantages and disadvantages of New York's no-fault scheme as compared to traditional tort? From the standpoint

of deterrence, does the no-fault scheme achieve less of the desirable level of deterrence than the tort system? In addressing this question, consider how auto insurance rates will be set under, respectively, the traditional tort system and under a no-fault scheme such as that of New York, under which more severe injuries can remain in the tort system. Will motorists be freer, under the no-fault scheme, from having to pay premiums linked to faulty behavior, and will any difference in pricing be practically significant to the behavior of motorists?

The empirical and analytical studies addressing the deterrent impact of no-fault have reached mixed results. One study concluded that no-fault schemes which partially supplant tort "substantially increase[d] accident losses, at least as evidenced by comparing the fatal accidents of states which have and have not adopted no-fault." Elizabeth M. Landes, *Insurance, Liability, and Accidents: A Theoretical and Empirical Investigation of the Effect of No–Fault Accidents*, 25 J. Law & Econ. 49, 65 (1982). Landes' conclusions were disputed in O'Connell & Levmore, *A Reply to Landes: A Faulty Study of No–Fault's Effect on Fault*, 48 Mo. L. Rev. 649 (1983). Subsequent studies have found that the adoption of no-fault has not had a significant effect on auto fatality rates. The studies are summarized in Michael J. Trebilcock, *Incentive Issues in the Design of "No–Fault" Compensation Systems*, 39 U. Tor. L.J. 19 (1989).

Some analysts, after reviewing the evidence, conclude that no-fault may lower the levels of deterrence. "Even with extensive risk-rating of premiums under a no-fault * * * scheme, it is possible that safety incentives would be attenuated relative to tort-third-party insurance regimes, where tort law still operates to stigmatize certain kinds of conduct and arguably helps to reinforce socially responsible attitudes to risk-taking." Trebilcock, *supra*, at 33. Others, including Professor O'Connell, contend that no-fault—even if it reduces incentives in certain ways—will increase safety incentives in other ways—for instance, drivers will know that they will not be able to recover for their own pain and suffering and thus will have reason to take this internalized cost into account when driving. *See* J. O'Connell, S. Carroll, M. Horowitz, A. Abrahamse & D. Kaiser, *The Costs of Consumer Choice for Auto Insurance in States Without No–Fault Insurance*, 54 Md. L. Rev. 281 (1995). Professor Jennifer H. Arlen concludes that replacing tort with no-fault would have the following effects: insurance premiums would diminish and thus the number of motorists and the frequency of their driving would increase, and the drivers on the road can be expected to use less care than under a negligence system. Jennifer H. Arlen, *Compensation Systems and Efficient Deterrence*, 52 Md. L. Rev. 1093, 1111–14 (1993). Whether no-fault is desirable thus turns on whether these deterrence-related costs are outweighed by no-fault's benefits of administrative cost savings and improved equity and certainty of payment.

As to timeliness of compensation payments, several studies have confirmed that no-fault claimants, with or without attorneys, receive compensation more rapidly than tort claimants. The studies are summarized in Robert H. Joost, Automobile Insurance and No–Fault 2d 53–55 (1992). Experience in all states confirms that simply "adding on" no-fault benefits, without carving any limitations on the right to sue in tort, increases the cost of auto insurance premiums.

The public reaction to no-fault has also been mixed. Since 1980, some states have repealed no-fault, others have enacted it, and still others have modified their no-fault plans. *See* R. Jerry, *supra*, p. 937, at 853.

3. *Retaining Tort for Severe Injuries.* As already noted, some states provide for some no-fault benefits in addition to full rights under the tort system. The New York statute does not simply add on no-fault benefits, but instead supplants the tort system in certain cases with the no-fault system.

Assuming the desirability of no-fault for some injuries, what is the rationale for retaining tort as to more severe injuries? Is the rationale linked to the aim of compensation? The aim of deterrence? Or is the retention of tort for more severe injuries difficult to justify theoretically and thus reflective of a political compromise? Professors Keeton and O'Connell, in their initial land-mark proposal, suggested retaining tort for more severe injuries. They explained that this would "retain most of whatever deterrent value tort liability engenders under the present system," and that it would also have a chance of political survival, in contrast to complete abolition of tort for auto-related injuries. *See* Robert E. Keeton & Jeffrey O'Connell, Basic Protection for the Traffic Victim 270–71 (1965).

If one is theoretically attracted to a two-tier approach, the remaining question is whether the two tiers can be effectively administered in practice. If the threshold is vague, then the threshold itself will generate litigation; if the doorway to tort is too wide or malleable, then injuries that in theory should be handled via no-fault will instead become tort claims. In light of these considerations, what is your evaluation of the threshold that the New York statute establishes? Can you suggest improvements?

4. *Choosing No–Fault Pain and Suffering; Choosing No–Fault.* Under the New York scheme, pain and suffering damages are available only if a tort suit is available; pain and suffering are not included in no-fault benefits. Professors Keeton and O'Connell proposed that motorists be allowed to purchase, for an added premium, coverage for pain and suffering as part of the no-fault coverage. "We suspect that most persons who might as an initial proposition think these benefits desirable are likely to change their minds when the cost of providing them is separately stated in the insurance premiums. But * * * the proposed arrangement * * * leaves the extent of its use to free development in the market place." R. Keeton & J. O'Connell, *supra*, at 362. Yet this feature has not been included in most states' no-fault laws. In theory, insurers could offer such no-fault benefits without authorizing legislation, so long as regulators would approve premium increases reflecting the higher costs of providing such insurance. Yet insurers have not offered such coverage in any state. Why? Might insurers fear that pain and suffering losses would be difficult to predict as an actuarial matter? If this is the concern, then insurers could experiment with some form of "schedule" that would specify particular benefit amounts depending on the severity of injury.

Scholars have proposed a choice approach: allowing motorists to choose whether or not to be covered by the tort system or by no-fault benefits only. *See* J. O'Connell, S. Carroll, M. Horowitz, A. Abrahamse & D. Kaiser, *The Costs of Consumer Choice for Auto Insurance in States Without No–Fault Insurance,* 54 Md. L. Rev. 281 (1995); J. O'Connell & R. Joost, *Giving Motorists a Choice Between Fault and No–Fault Insurance,* 72 Va. L. Rev. 61 (1986). A motorist could choose to be governed totally by no-fault, or instead to be covered by full tort liability protection that would allow the motorist to sue in tort. It is easy to see how this could work if all the injured persons in a given accident were covered by no-fault coverage, or if all the injured persons were covered by the full tort insurance. Suppose, for instance, that Driver A and Driver B both had opted for no-fault coverage; then each would recover only against his own no-fault insurer. If both drivers had chosen the full tort insurance, then Driver A would proceed against B and pursue the insurance provided by the insurer for Driver B, and Driver B would likewise pursue Driver A and his insurance carrier.

But what if Driver A had chosen the no-fault coverage, and Driver B had purchased full tort coverage? If we allowed Driver B to sue Driver A in such situations, then individuals purchasing no-fault coverage also would have to purchase liability coverage against the possibility of tort suits. And this would increase the overall costs of insurance to drivers wishing to opt only for no-fault coverage.

O'Connell and Joost propose a modified form of uninsured motorist coverage to handle this type of situation. Individuals such as Driver B, who purchase full tort insurance, would be covered by a policy that contains an extended form of uninsured motorist coverage. Driver B thus would recover full tort benefits against his own insurance carrier rather than from either Driver A or Driver A's insurance carrier. Driver B, of course, would pay more for his insurance than Driver A. Driver A would not have to pay for full tort coverage for himself, and he would not need to purchase liability coverage covering "full-tort" drivers because these drivers would proceed against their own uninsured motorist coverage.

Pennsylvania and New Jersey have enacted a form of "choice" legislation. In New Jersey, auto owners are required to purchase no-fault insurance along with liability coverage, but they have two choices with respect to the no-fault coverage. If an owner chooses option 1, he retains the right to sue in tort for full tort damages (including pain and suffering) as to any injury, including less severe injuries. If an owner chooses option 2, he may sue in tort only if he meets a threshold that is quite similar to the one contained in the New York statute and excerpted above. The choice must be made in writing, on a form approved by the Insurance Commissioner. An owner who chooses option 2 will pay a smaller premium.

What factors might go into an individual's choice, under either the choice proposal made by O'Connell and Joost, or New Jersey's choice approach? Would the wealth of the individual affect the choice? The individual's level of insurance coverage under other insurance, such as private medical and disability insurance? The individual's level of risk aversion?

3. *Other Cause–Based Compensation Programs and Proposals*

a. *The National Childhood Vaccine Injury Act*

Several other cause-based compensation schemes currently exist, including the National Childhood Vaccine Injury Act of 1986 (the Vaccine Act), and no-fault medical schemes enacted by Virginia and Florida for babies who are born with severe brain or neurological damage. The Vaccine Act (discussed briefly in Chapter Nine *supra,* at p. 691) provides no-fault compensation benefits to a narrow category of victims: children injured by exposure to particular government-mandated vaccines. The Act is financed by an excise tax on each dose of vaccine given. The injured claimant may pursue the statutory remedy in federal district court, where a special master gathers the evidence and renders a decision. The claimant must prove that he or she suffers an injury from a vaccine listed in the Act, and that the adverse reaction took place within the exposure period designated. Once the claimant makes this proof, he or she is entitled to no-fault benefits that consist of all actual medical and rehabilitative expenses, as well as compensation for lost earnings and damages for pain and suffering up to $250,000. Once the master renders a benefit decision, the claimant is entitled to reject it and pursue tort remedies instead. But, if the claimant chooses the tort route, he will face several obstacles, including the "learned intermediary doctrine" (which requires the manufacturer only to give adequate warning to the learned intermediary, such as the doctor) and immunity of the manufacturer from punitive damages if it complied with federal legislation. Since the adoption of the Vaccine Act, virtually no vaccine victims have rejected the statutory benefits and opted for a tort remedy. A recent analysis concludes that the Act has "achieved its goal of protecting the nation's vaccine supplies while providing compensation for the unavoidable injuries resulting from the administration of vaccines. * * *" Theodore H. Davis, Jr. & Catherine B. Bowman, *No–Fault Compensation for Unavoidable Injuries: Evaluating the National Childhood Vaccine Injury Compensation Program*, 16 U. Dayton L. Rev. 277, 279 (1991).

b. Proposals for Medical No–fault or Mass Tort Compensation Schemes

Scholars and policymakers have also considered nontort alternatives for compensating medical injuries and mass tort injuries, especially mass tort claims resulting from toxic substances. Consider the following analysis of how a more general medical no-fault program could be devised, particularly given the difficulty of distinguishing between losses caused by a medical incident ("iatrogenic losses") versus losses due to other causes, such as preexisting illness.

Under a standard no-fault scheme the victims of all medical accidents would be eligible for compensation because of the nature of the losses they suffered, not because their injuries were fortuitously produced by the carelessness of a doctor or a nurse * * *

* * *

* * * The current social judgment embedded in the tort system is that victims who are injured by demonstrably careless treatment will collect *full* compensation, whether their injuries are modest or grave, economic or non-economic, covered by collateral sources or uninsured. That judgment seemed appropriate as long as the issue was conceived as how to achieve corrective justice between innocent patient and careless doctor in deciding which party should bear the burden of the patient's injuries. But once we recognize that the compensation burden is borne collectively by patients through the premiums they pay their health insurers, who then pay the fees of doctors, who in turn pay liability premiums to malpractice insurers, who finally pay benefits to patients who are injured, the individualistic corrective justice idea appears to be an anachronism. * * *

* * * [F]unds should first meet the pecuniary needs of injured victims. Money should be provided to pay for medical treatment and physical or vocational rehabilitation. In addition, income should be made avail-

able to replace lost earnings. Finally, rather than cap or scale down pain and suffering damages, following the example of workers' compensation, non-economic redress should be confined to those who were severely and permanently disabled, with limited benefits specified in an age-adjusted schedule of physical impairments. * * *

* * * [L]egally mandated compensation would be available only to the minority of injured patients whose disability endures for some reasonably extended time. In the case of no-fault patient insurance, a time-based screening criterion is essential if only to ease the difficulty of disentangling the medical costs and lost earnings that are specifically attributable to the iatrogenic injury, on the one hand, from those losses that would normally be expected to flow from the underlying illness and its treatment and recuperation, on the other. Something like a six-month dividing line would be a reasonable transition point from the short-term disability protection that individuals can be expected to secure for themselves and the long-term disability benefits (Social Security Disability Insurance, for example) that the community mandates for everyone's protection. * * *

* * *

Opponents of no-fault respond that these administrative savings cannot be extrapolated from the occupational setting. Indeed, they argue, in the medical context determining the actual *cause* of the patient's injury is typically as difficult as determining the doctor's fault. If that is the case, there would be higher administrative costs under no-fault because much larger numbers of patients would be making claims. * * *

* * * In practice it would likely be too costly and burdensome to have a patient compensation program try in each case to isolate precisely which of the immediate economic consequences were attributable to the original unhealthy condition and which to the iatrogenic injury, even after determining that such an injury had in fact occurred. Instead, the program would have to feature an across-the-board rule that no-fault insurance would be available only after a certain period of disability had elapsed, perhaps six months. Not only would such a rule avoid this troublesome aspect of the causal inquiry, but as we saw earlier it would also concentrate the program's resources on longer-term disability that should be the proper focus of mandatory insurance under either a fault or no-fault liability criterion. * * *

American Law Institute, Reporters' Study on Enterprise Responsibility for Personal Injury, Vol. II, at 492–509 *.

E. LOSS–BASED PROGRAMS AND PROPOSALS

1. *Social Security Disability*

As noted at the outset of this chapter, the major loss-based programs in the United States are the social security disability system and private health care insurance. These systems are not fault-based (coverage does not require a showing of fault) or cause-based (coverage does not depend on a causal link such as work relation or arising out of the use of an auto). Rather, coverage depends on whether the person is enrolled in the program and whether the person has sustained the type of loss covered.

Social Security disability insurance (SSDI) was added to the Social Security program in 1956. It pays cash benefits to workers (and to their eligible spouses, children, and survivors) who have been employed for the requisite number of quarters and who are found to be disabled. "Disability" is defined as "inability to engage in any substantial gainful activity by reason of any medically determinable physical or mental impairment which can be expected to result in death or has lasted or can be expected to last for a continuous period of not less than 12 months", 42 U.S.C. § 423 (1990). The program is not means-tested; that is, it does not depend on the claimant's financial need. Monthly benefits are based on the worker's annual taxable earnings, averaged over most of the worker's adult years; the payment is subject to a maximum family benefit amount. Supplemental security income (SSI), added to the Social Security program in 1972, pays additional benefits to individuals who fall below a certain income level and are disabled.

Statutes and regulations set out extremely detailed substantive and procedural requirements governing the determination of disability. A multi-layered administrative decisional process, including a hearing by an administrative law judge, is responsible for the determination of disability. The results of the administrative decisional process are reviewable in federal district court.

One might suppose that, since the program does not require proof of fault or causation, the program has been relatively free of decisional controversies and difficulties. Yet the social security disability program has been the subject of intense political, scholarly, and judicial controversy over the past twenty years. Points of controversy have included the following: the increase in numbers and size of disability payments and whether funding is adequate; the fairness of the decisional criteria and processes, including when a disability recipient may be cut off on the grounds that he or she is no longer disabled; the extreme inefficiencies and delay in making decisions; the standards governing disability for children with disabilities; and the standards governing mental disabilities. For more detail on these issues, *see* Jerry L. Mashaw, Bureaucratic Justice (1983); Richard J. Pierce, Jr., *Political Control Versus Impermissible Bias in Agency Decisionmaking Lessons from Chevron and Mistretta*, 57 U.Chi. L.Rev. 481 (1990); Ellen S. Pryor, *Compensation and the Ineradicable Problems of Pain*, 59 Geo.Wash.L.Rev. 239 (1991). For a detailed analysis of the role the SSD program plays, see Matthew Diller, *Entitlement and Exclusion: the Role of Disability in the Social Welfare System*, 44 U.C.L.A. L.Rev. 361 (1996).

Professor Deborah Stone, in her classic study of disability policy, offers insights into why the design and administration of disability programs remain so difficult even when they do not require adjudication of fault or causal origin.

[T]here are important reasons why a concept of disability based on clinical criteria * * * cannot be perfectly objective and why, therefore, as a determination mechanism, it is highly flexible and inevitably subject to manipulation. Moreover, these problems with clinical criteria are not unique to Social Security; they plague all of the many redistributive programs that use certified disability, based on a notion of clinical impairment, as their eligibility criterion.

First, clinical tests can provide a measure of some phenomenon, but no single test can tell whether a person is "impaired" (whatever that means) or "disabled" or still able to work. Someone has to *decide* what level of any measurement is indicative of inability to function and how the information from different tests ought to be combined. Should disability be presumed when someone meets any two of a set of criteria, or any three?

* * *

* * * Nowadays, social psychologists have systematic techniques for collecting and merging the opinions of experts into one single opinion or prediction. But no matter how primitive or how sophisticated such techniques are, the resulting judgments are still only the product of personal opinion. * * * Ultimately, the question of which groups of people should be included in a disability benefit program is a political judgment, and the decision to set criteria in a certain fashion is a choice among competing alternatives, not something dictated by the clinical measurements themselves. And the manipulation of criteria by physicians, lawyers, and officials to include or exclude whole classes of individuals is far more potent than any strategic behavior on the part of individual applicants.

A second reason why clinical criteria cannot protect eligibility decisions from manipulation is that the diagnostic decisions on which judgments of impairment rest are themselves subject to an enormous degree of uncertainty. The evaluation of impairment rests on physicians' observations and interpretations of basic clinical findings; the medical history (elicited by interviewing the patient); auscultation (listening to chest sounds through a stethoscope); blood pressure, pulse, and temperature measurements; electrocardiograms; X-rays; and laboratory tests (especially urinalyses, blood cell counts, and blood chemistry analyses). These building blocks of clinical practice are as much art as science, and numerous studies have demonstrated significant variations among physicians and laboratory technicians in interpreting them.

* * *

In fact, a third problem with clinical criteria is that patients do have an enormous degree of influence over the results of many clinical tests. A number of important methods of disability determination, including cardiac "stress tests" and pulmonary function tests, require the subjects to perform in some way; the result is dependent on their efforts. It is also well known that the physiologic constitution of an individual changes over short periods of time, and the same test performed at intervals may yield different results. Digestion, emotion, work, and weather cause changes in body chemistry and therefore also in the outcome of laboratory tests.

Thus, one can trace in one particular type of disability—respiratory disease—a hierarchy of criteria from highly subjective to more objective. But ultimately, even the most objective criteria are subject to manipulation, and in the end the decision about what constitutes a legitimate medical impairment is still a matter of judgment. Given, this analysis of factors that influence clinical judgment, it is not surprising to find substantial inconsistencies in disability determination in a program whose definition rests on clinical judgment.

Deborah Stone, The Disabled State 127–33 (1984).*

2. *Comprehensive Loss–Based Compensation: Doing Away With Tort Law; the New Zealand System*

Scholars have proposed a more dramatic reform than the cause-based and loss-based programs just described: some type of general loss-based compensation plan that would replace tort and that would apply to both partial and total disabilities. One proposal, made by Professor Richard Pierce, would create a new federal agency that would compensate victims of accidents and disease and regulate safety in all areas of the economy. Compensation would not depend on fault, and the amount of compensation due for particular injuries or diseases would be determined according to formulas and schedules similar to those used in workers' compensation programs. Funding for the agency and its compensation would depend in part on general tax revenues, but the agency also would assess costs against various types of industries, based on the number and severity of accidents caused. For more detail, *see* Richard J. Pierce, Jr., *Encouraging Safety: The Limits of Tort Law and Government Regulation*, 33 Vand. L. Rev. 1281 (1980).

Professor Stephen Sugarman has set out one of the most detailed critiques of tort and proposals for comprehensive tort replacement. The basics of his proposal include the following. All Americans would be assured income for periods of temporary and permanent disability, and would also receive medical expense protection that would include traditional medical needs, rehabilitation, and assistant care. Safety regulation should remain the province of regulatory agencies, but individuals might be afforded private rights of action against injurers, not for compensatory but for injunctive relief against plainly and unreasonably dangerous conduct. *See* S. Sugarman, Doing Away With Personal Injury Law (1989).

In 1972, New Zealand eliminated tort as a scheme for compensating personal injury, and replaced it with a comprehensive no-fault compensation program. The Accident Compensation Act abolished tort remedies for "personal injury by accident," a phrase interpreted to exclude ordinary sickness but to include occupational disease. As originally enacted, the Act covered only "earners," that is, people who worked for a wage or salary or self-employed persons. Before the act became effective in 1974, however, it

* Reprinted with permission.

was amended to include homemakers and other non-earners. The Act also included periodic payments for permanent partial incapacity, and lump sums of up to NZ$17,000 for loss or impairment of bodily functions and up to NZ$10,000 for loss of amenities or capacity to enjoy life, including disfigurement, pain and suffering, and nervous shock. Non-earners receive all the benefits of the Act with the important exception that they are not awarded anything for loss of earnings. Loss of earnings are computed at 80% of earnings over a base period with an upper limit that has been periodically increased. Initially the upper limit on wages that would be considered under the plan was NZ$150 per week, but that soon escalated. It had reached NZ$600 by Dec. 17, 1982 and has increased further since. Initially, a very high percentage of New Zealand workers had wages within these limits, although the method of adjustment lagged behind changes in the value of money and this has only exacerbated the problem caused by the widening of income disparities that has accompanied New Zealand's deregulation of its economy. In the case case of certain low-wage workers, compensation is provided at 90% of earnings over the base period.

To finance the scheme, which is administered by the New Zealand Accident Compensation Commission, an Earners Fund and a Motor Vehicle Fund were established. The Earners Fund is financed by levies on employers as a certain percentage of their payroll costs. Rates vary according to industry and occupation. Self-employed persons are taxed at a flat 1% of earnings. The Motor Vehicle Fund is financed by a levy on automobile owners. Unless an "earner" injured in an automobile accident was injured while acting in the course of employment, he is compensated from the Motor Vehicle Fund. When the Act was amended to include non-earners— that is, people not covered by the Earners Fund—a supplementary fund, dependent upon sums appropriated from general revenues, was established to provide compensation for non-earners for all accidents not covered by the Motor Vehicle Fund.

Criticisms of the scheme over the years have included its increasing costs, and its exclusion for nonoccupational illnesses. On all these matters, see G. Palmer, Compensation for Incapacity (1979). Geoffrey Palmer was, for a time, a law professor, first in the United States and then in his native New Zealand. He subsequently entered politics and was elected to the New Zealand Parliament. After having served as Deputy Prime Minister and Minister of Justice, he became Prime Minister of New Zealand in August, 1989. The increased costliness of the New Zealand scheme has presented some problems. These and the proposed solutions are discussed extensively in R. Miller, *The Future of New Zealand's Accident Compensation Scheme*, 11 U.Haw.L.Rev. 1 (1989). *See also* L. Klar, *A Commentary on the New Zealand Accident Compensation Scheme*, 26 Alberta L.Rev. 319 (1988). For earlier discussions of the New Zealand experience in American periodical literature, see W. Pedrick, *Palmer's* Compensation for Incapacity: *The New Zealand and Australian "No Fault" Story*, 1981 Utah L.Rev. 115; Note, *The Accident Compensation Act of 1972: "No–Fault" Compensation for Personal Injury in New Zealand*, 3 Suffolk Transnational L.J. 203 (1979). For a critical assessment of the possible adoption of a New Zealand type plan in the United States, *see* J. Henderson, *The New Zealand Accident Compensation Reform*, 48 U.Chi.L.Rev. 781 (1981). Another recent comparative law discussion of tort reform is J. O'Connell and D. Partlett, *An America's Cup for Tort Reform? Australia and America Compared*, 21 J.L. Reform 443 (1988).

In 1992, New Zealand significantly modified the accident compensation scheme. First, the scope of the scheme's application was cut back. Coverage now requires injury by "an accident" rather than just by "accident." The latter formulation was interpreted to extend coverage when the disability or problem was accidental even if the injury could not be linked to a particular external event or cause, or when the person suffered injury from witnessing a physical injury to another person. These instances no longer are covered. Second, the 1992 amendments cut back on benefits. Lump-sum payments for nonpecuniary losses now are not available, and instead are replaced by a more modest "independence allowance." Third, mental injury now is not compensable unless it results from an independent physical injury. Fourth, the pre–1992 scheme allowed compensation for injuries resulting from medical, surgical, or dental "misadventure," without further definition or restriction. The 1992 amendments include a two-page definition of a compensable "medical misadventure" that essentially requires a showing of negligence. The 1992 amendments created an additional source of funding from premiums charged to health professionals. This change, along with the move to essentially a negligence requirement for victims of medical accidents, reflects a move toward deterrence objectives in the medical arena. For analysis of the 1992 changes, *see* Richard S. Miller, *An Analysis and Critique of the 1992 Changes to New Zealand's Accident Compensation Scheme*, 52 Md. L. Rev. 1070 (1993).

Chapter 15

NUISANCE

BROWN v. COUNTY COMMISSIONERS OF SCIOTO COUNTY

Court of Appeals of Ohio, 1993.
87 Ohio App.3d 704, 622 N.E.2d 1153.

HARSHA, PRESIDING JUDGE.

Jack D. Brown and Barbara Brown filed a complaint which alleged that the Scioto County Commissioners had failed to properly maintain and operate a sewage treatment plant and thereby created a nuisance and trespass to the Browns' neighboring property. After the trial court granted the commissioners' motion for summary judgment, Barbara Brown took this appeal.

* * *

For the sum of $50,000, the Browns purchased a house located approximately one-quarter of a mile from the sewage treatment plant. They moved into the house on March 12, 1978. Prior to moving into the house, they did not perceive any odor from the plant. However, within the first week after they moved in, they noticed some odor coming from the plant. The odor was not very noticeable the first few years, but became worse and more frequent during the early 1980s. The odor was particularly bad when the weather was hot and humid or when the wind was blowing in a particular direction. The worst period for the noxious odors emanating from the sewage treatment plant was the summer of 1983, when there was an odor comparable to having their septic tank cleaned. The extreme odor during that period lasted twenty-four hours every day and prompted the Browns to file their initial complaint. Additionally, the odors from the plant increased the number of insects of all kinds on the Browns' property, requiring them to call an exterminating company two or three times a month during one period of time. The Browns became nauseated due to the odors, and in 1984, a physician indicated that it was a "probability" that appellant's stomach problems, including loss of appetite, were related to the treatment plant odors. The odors made it uncomfortable and, at times, impossible to be outside their house.

According to Jack D. Brown, the sewage treatment plant emitted germs and bacteria that rotted the ears off two rabbits that the Browns owned. Although unsure of the exact date, the Browns had their home listed for sale at $65,000 and a woman interested in purchasing it was driven away by the plant odors. Although the Browns and several neighbors complained to appellees, as well as state and federal officials, no action was taken by appellees to remedy the problems associated with their operation and maintenance of the sewage treatment plant.

Appellees operated the sewage treatment plant from its inception under a lease with the state. The lease was extended for a few brief periods until it was determined that the state could more efficiently operate the plant. Accordingly, appellees relinquished operation and maintenance of the plant to the state on June 1, 1985. During appellees' period of operation of the plant, the condition of the plant was deplorable. The Ohio Environmental Protection Agency cited the plant for violations concerning the level of bacteria and suspended solids contained in the effluent discharged into an adjacent stream. Most of the equipment was old and worn out. A comminutor, which was utilized to break down the raw sewage, had not been operable for several months, and the screen used to filter the sewage through the treatment process had a large hole in it. One of the two oxidation ditches was idle and the other ditch was only operating at twenty-five to fifty percent of its capacity. The idle oxidation ditch had become septic, breeding anaerobic bacteria that emitted the gaseous substance causing the noxious odors.

When appellees operated the sewage treatment facility, they rarely stocked an inventory of spare parts for the plant machinery. Consequently, there were occasions when an old part malfunctioned and the plant would be shut down until a new part was back-ordered. The plant shutdowns caused untreated sewage to remain idle and contributed to the noxious odors.

* * *

Appellees * * * contended that the Browns had failed to introduce evidence which would preclude summary judgment on their nuisance and trespass claims. We will initially consider appellant's claim for relief based upon nuisance. Appellees asserted that there was no genuine issue of material fact as to the existence of either an absolute nuisance, a qualified nuisance, a public nuisance, or a private nuisance.

As stated by Professor Keeton in Prosser & Keeton, The Law of Torts (5th Ed.1984) 616, Section 86: "There is perhaps no more impenetrable jungle in the entire law than that which surrounds the word 'nuisance.'" Nuisance describes two separate fields of tort liability that through the accident of historical development are called by the same name. See Restatement of the Law 2d, Torts (1979) 84, Introductory Note. One of these two fields of liability bears the name of public nuisance and covers the invasion of public rights, i.e., rights common to all members of the public. Historically, public nuisance was criminal in nature and recovery in damages is limited to those who can show particular harm of a kind different from that suffered by the general public. Id.

The other field of liability is called private nuisance. This tort covers the invasion of the private interest in the use and enjoyment of land. As such, plaintiff's action must always be founded upon her interest in the land. Id. * * *

Restatement of the Law 2d, Torts (1979) 87, Section 821B, defines public nuisance as an unreasonable interference with a right common to the general public. Conduct does not become a public nuisance merely because it interferes with a large number of people. At common law, there must be some interference with a public right which is common to all members of the general public. In addition to common-law public nuisance, Ohio has adopted statutes and administrative regulations which define certain conduct as being a public nuisance. These statutes amount to a legislative declaration that the proscribed conduct is an unreasonable interference with a public right.

Restatement of the Law 2d, Torts (1979) 100, Section 821D, defines private nuisance as a nontrespassory invasion of another's interest in the private use and enjoyment of land. Section 822 of Restatement of the Law 2d, Torts provides that in order to be actionable, the invasion must be either (a) intentional and unreasonable, or (b) unintentional and caused by negligent, reckless or abnormally dangerous conduct (negligent and reckless conduct carry with them a degree of unreasonableness; abnormally dangerous activity is not treated in the same sense, but the balancing effort necessary to determine liability has the same effect). Id. at 113–115.

While the law in Ohio is far from clear in this area, absolute nuisance and nuisance per se seem to be the same. The essence of these two characterizations of nuisance is that no matter how careful one is, such activities are inherently injurious and cannot be conducted without damaging someone else's property or rights. They are based upon either intentional conduct or abnormally dangerous conditions, and as such the rule of absolute liability applies. A modern example would be a neighborhood "crack house."

Conversely, qualified nuisance is premised upon negligence. It consists of a lawful act that is so negligently or carelessly done as to have created an unreasonable risk of harm which in due course results in injury to another. Obviously, both public and private nuisances may be either absolute or qualified.

* * *

Having reviewed the appropriate law, we look first to see if appellant has presented sufficient evidence to allow her complaint to proceed in the area of either common law or statutory public nuisance. * * *

Since a pollution control facility operates under the sanction of law, it cannot be a common-law public nuisance.

* * *

In any event, Ohio Adm. Code 3745–15–07(A) states:

> "Except as provided in paragraph (B) of this rule, the emission or escape into the open air from any source or sources whatsoever, of smoke, ashes, dust, dirt, grime, acids, fumes, gases, vapors, odors, or any other substances or combinations of substances, in such manner or in such amounts as to endanger the health, safety or welfare of the

public, or cause unreasonable injury or damage to property, is hereby found and declared to be a public nuisance. It shall be unlawful for any person to cause, permit or maintain any such public nuisance."

* * *

Appellees did not argue below nor do they argue on appeal that subsection (A) is not applicable * * *. Accordingly, there remains a genuine issue of material fact as to whether their conduct constitutes a public nuisance pursuant to Ohio Adm. Code 3745–15–07(A). In this regard, the evidence indicated that appellees maintained the plant in "deplorable" condition, with numerous Ohio EPA violations.

* * *

A public nuisance as such does not afford a basis for recovery of damages in tort unless there is particular harm to the plaintiff that is of a different kind than that suffered by the public in general. See Restatement of the Law 2d, Torts (1979) 94, Section 821C(1). When the particular harm involved consists of interference with the use and enjoyment of land, the landowner may recover either on the basis of the particular harm to her resulting from the public nuisance or on the basis of private nuisance. See Restatement of the Law 2d, Torts (1979) 93, Section 821B, Comment h. Here appellant contends that she lost an opportunity to sell her property and was unable to use and enjoy it. This is a sufficiently distinct or particular harm from the public right so as to allow recovery under a statutory public nuisance theory.

However, just as the appellees' sewage disposal plant cannot be a common-law public nuisance because of the governmental authorization to operate, it likewise cannot be an absolute statutory nuisance. * * * In order for a duly licensed and regulated sanitary landfill to be found liable for maintaining a nuisance, negligence must be established, i.e., a qualified nuisance. * * *

As stated above, appellant introduced no evidence that appellees were not licensed to operate the sewage disposal plant. * * * [S]he failed to raise a genuine issue of material fact as to the presence of absolute public nuisance, but may proceed on the theory of qualified statutory nuisance.

We turn now to the cause of action for private nuisance. * * * [A]ppellant did not present sufficient evidence to withstand a motion for summary judgment on the issue of absolute private nuisance.

A civil action based upon the maintenance of a qualified private nuisance is essentially an action in tort for the negligent maintenance of a condition, which, of itself, creates an unreasonable risk of harm, ultimately resulting in injury. In such a case, negligence must be alleged and proven to warrant a recovery.

Appellees contend that there was no evidence of a qualified nuisance since there was no indication that appellant suffered any injury during the period when appellees operated the plant. * * * However, there was evidence that a prospective purchaser was lost due to the offensive odors from the plant. There was also evidence that appellant suffered nausea and was unable to fully use her property. To entitle adjoining property owners to recover damages for the maintenance of a nuisance, it is not necessary that they should be driven from their dwellings, or that the defendants' acts create a positive unhealthy condition; it is enough that their enjoyment of life and property is rendered uncomfortable, for in some circumstances discomfort and annoyance may constitute a nuisance. See, generally, 61 American Jurisprudence 2d (1981) 950, Pollution Control, Section 531. Accordingly, there remains a genuine issue of material fact as to whether appellees' conduct constituted a qualified private nuisance.

* * *

Additionally, construing the evidence most strongly in appellant's favor, we are persuaded that her evidence of loss of at least one prospective purchaser, increase in insects necessitating extermination expenses, nausea, and inability to use her property fully constituted sufficient evidence to raise a genuine issue of material fact as to whether appellees' interference with her property was substantial and unreasonable. Accordingly, a genuine issue of material fact remains on the question of qualified private nuisance.

Appellees further claim that there was no showing of trespass. The essential elements necessary to state a cause of action in trespass are: (1) an unauthorized intentional act, and (2) entry upon land in the possession of another. Traditionally, an invasion of the exclusive possession of land by intangible substances, such as an airborne pollutant, was usually held by the courts not to constitute a trespass since a trespass involved a physical invasion by tangible matters. See Annotation, Recovery in Trespass for Injury to Land Caused by Airborne Pollutants (1980), 2 A.L.R. 4th 1054. However, there has been a growing trend among jurisdictions to hold that the test for whether an invasion of a property interest is a trespass does not depend upon whether the intruding agent is an intangible or tangible substance, but whether the intrusion interferes with the right to the exclusive possession of property. Id. at 1055. However, odors emanating from a facility, see Born v. Exxon Corp. (Ala.1980), 388 So.2d 933, or mere diminution of value, see Maddy v. Vulcan Materials Co. (D.Kan.1990), 737 F.Supp. 1528, are insufficient to state a trespass claim even under the modern view.

The Supreme Court of Alabama in Born cited its previous decision in Borland v. Sanders Lead Co., Inc. (Ala.1979), 369 So.2d 523, 530, to note the following distinction between trespass under the modern trend and nuisance at 388 So.2d at 934:

> "For an indirect invasion to amount to an actionable trespass, there must be an interference with plaintiff's exclusive possessory interest; that is, through the defendant's intentional conduct, and with reasonable foreseeability, some substance has entered upon the land itself, affecting its nature and character, and causing substantial actual damage to the res. For example, if the smoke or polluting substance emitting from a defendant's operation causes discomfort and annoyance to the plaintiff in his use and enjoyment of the property, then the plaintiff's remedy is for nuisance; but if, as a result of the defendant's operation, the polluting substance is deposited upon the plaintiff's property, thus interfering with his exclusive possessory

interest by causing substantial damage to the res, then the plaintiff may seek his remedy in trespass, though his alternative remedy in nuisance may co-exist."

There is no summary judgment evidence of the polluting substance, i.e., noxious odors, depositing particulate matter on appellant's real property or causing physical damage to it. We are persuaded that under either the traditional or modern views, since appellant has failed to adduce summary judgment evidence of physical damage to her real property, appellees were entitled to summary judgment on appellant's trespass claim.

* * *

Appellant's assignment of error is sustained in part and overruled in part. Accordingly, the summary judgment entered by the common pleas court is affirmed as to appellant's claims of absolute nuisance, common-law public nuisance, trespass to real property, and injunctive relief, and is reversed and remanded for further proceedings consistent with this opinion * * *.

Judgment affirmed in part, reversed in part, and cause remanded.

PETER B. ABELE and STEPHENSON, JJ., concur.

Notes

1. Nuisance cases typically involve conflicts in land use and, therefore, while historically a tort, the law has very close ties to property and land use law. The topic is often taught in property courses related to land use and environment. As we have seen, it has close ties historically and today to the law of trespass to land. It also relates today to zoning law, the law of covenants regarding land use, and statutory law related to water and air pollution and hazardous waste. Its modern importance in those contexts is beyond the scope of this course. We provide a mere introduction to this fascinating topic.

2. *Nuisance and Trespass*

a. One of the leading modern cases pointing out the distinction between law of trespass and that of nuisance is Martin v. Reynolds Metals Co., 221 Or. 86, 342 P.2d 790 (1959), *cert. denied* 362 U.S. 918, 80 S.Ct. 672, 4 L.Ed.2d 739 (1960). The case involved the emission of very fine particulate matter and fluoride gases from the smoke stack of an aluminum reduction plant. Plaintiffs claimed that the air pollutants interfered with the use of their nearby land to raise livestock. According to the *Martin* court, "a possessor's interest in land * * * may under the appropriate circumstances, be violated by a ray of light, by an atomic particle, or by a particulate of fluoride." The *Martin* court also rejected the distinction between direct and indirect trespass. At the same time the *Martin* court declared that whether an invasion amounted to trespass depended upon the substantiality of the invasion and that this could not be determined solely by looking at the defendant's conduct but required an examination of the nature of the plaintiff's interest in the land. It thus seemed to inject into the context of trespass some of the balancing features associated with nuisance.

b. In Wilson v. Interlake Steel Co., 32 Cal.3d 229, 185 Cal.Rptr. 280, 649 P.2d 922 (1982), the court held that an action based on noise emissions must be brought in nuisance and not in trespass. An earlier nuisance suit seeking an injunction had been dismissed by the trial court on the basis of a statute prohibiting the enjoining, in a private nuisance suit, of a business operating in an area zoned for commercial use. The Supreme Court of California, in remanding the instant case, held that dismissal of the earlier suit did not necessarily preclude the award of damages in the later action.

    c. In a part of *Borland v. Sanders Lead Co., Inc.* not quoted in *Brown*, the court stated:

> The *Martin* Court pointed out that trespass and nuisance are separate torts for the protection of different interests invaded—trespass protecting the possessor's interest in exclusive possession of property and nuisance protecting the interest in use and enjoyment. The Court noted, and we agree, that the same conduct on the part of a defendant may, and often does, result in the actionable invasion of both interests.

> The confusion surrounding trespass and nuisance is due in a large part to the influence of common law forms of action. The modern action for trespass to land stemmed inexorably from the common law action for trespass which lay when the injury was both direct and substantial. Nuisance, on the other hand, would lie when injuries were indirect and less substantial. *See* Winfield, *Nuisance as a Tort,* 4 Camb.L.J., 189, 201–06 (1931). A fictitious "dimensional" test arose, which obviated the necessity of determining whether the intrusion was "direct" and "substantial." If the intruding agent could be seen by the naked eye, the intrusion was considered a trespass. If the agent could not be seen, it was considered indirect and less substantial, hence, a nuisance. * * *

> * * * Whether an invasion of a property interest is a trespass or a nuisance does not depend upon whether the intruding agent is "tangible" or "intangible." Instead, an analysis must be made to determine the interest interfered with. If the intrusion interferes with the right to exclusive possession of property, the law of trespass applies. If the intrusion is to the interest in use and enjoyment of property, the law of nuisance applies. As previously observed, however, the remedies of trespass and nuisance are not necessarily mutually exclusive.

Borland v. Sanders Lead Co., 369 So.2d 523, 527, 529 (Ala.1979). As noted in *Brown*, the Alabama court rejects the distinction, as do most modern decisions, between direct and indirect harm in determining whether a trespass had been committed. Is the distinction between direct invasion—for which no substantial damage must be shown—and indirect invasion an easier distinction to apply? Is it clear that the deposit of some small amounts of lead particulates, involved in *Borland*, interferes with the plaintiffs' right to exclusive possession of their land? Would the deposit of leaves in *Turner v. Coppola*, discussed in note 4, *infra* p. 964, be a direct or an indirect invasion. Would Ms. Turner have had a cause of action for trespass in Alabama? Would an invasion of light as in *Amphitheaters, Inc. v. Portland Meadows*, note 3, *infra* p. 964, constitute a direct invasion? Would extremely bright lights interfere with the right to exclusive possession of land?

    d. In Bradley v. American Smelting & Refining Co., 104 Wash.2d 677, 691, 709 P.2d 782, 791 (1985), the court stated:

> When airborne particles are transitory and quickly dissipate, they do not interfere with a property owner's possessory rights and, therefore, are properly denominated as nuisances. * * * When, however, the particles or

substance accumulates [sic] on the land and does [sic] not pass away, then a trespass has occurred.

3. Nuisances resulting solely from the defendant's negligence are relatively easy to resolve because, by definition, had the defendant exercised due care the nuisance would be abated. This, apparently was the situation in *Brown*.

4. Nuisance claims premised only on the defendant's negligent conduct are relatively rare. When the plaintiff is seeking an injunction against future continuation of an alleged nuisance the claim, almost by definition, seems to be that the nuisance is intentional. Is it not a consequence of the plaintiff's bringing suit that the defendant knows that his conduct is claimed to be affecting the plaintiff and yet intentionally continues the allegedly harmful course of conduct? *See* Hall v. Phillips, 231 Neb. 269, 436 N.W.2d 139 (Neb.1989). As the court in Morgan v. High Penn Oil Co., 238 N.C. 185, 191, 77 S.E.2d 682, 688 (1953) notes "Most private nuisances *per accidens* or in fact are intentionally created or maintained and are redressed by the courts without proof of negligence."

5. *Restatement (Second) of Torts* § 825 addresses the question of what constitutes intentional conduct in nuisance actions as follows:

§ 825. Intentional Invasion—What Constitutes

An invasion of another's interest in the use and enjoyment of land or an interference with the public right, is intentional if the actor

(a) acts for the purpose of causing it, or

(b) knows that it is resulting or is substantially certain to result from his conduct.

In addition, comment d. contains the following provision:

Continuing or recurrent invasions. Most of the litigation over private nuisances involves situations in which there are continuing or recurrent invasions resulting from continuing or recurrent conduct; and the same is true of many public nuisances. In these cases the first invasion resulting from the actor's conduct may be either intentional or unintentional; but when the conduct is continued after the actor knows that the invasion is resulting from it, further invasions are intentional.

GRACELAND CORP. v. CONSOLIDATED LAUNDRIES CORP.

Supreme Court of New York, Appellate Division, 1958.
7 A.D.2d 89, 180 N.Y.S.2d 644, aff'd 6 N.Y.2d 900,
190 N.Y.S.2d 708, 160 N.E.2d 926 (1959).

BREITEL, J. Defendant laundry appeals from a judgment granting to plaintiff apartment house owner a permanent injunction and nominal damages following a trial at Special Term. Involved is the obstruction by the laundry of the north sidewalk of East 94th Street, between First and Second Avenues in the City of New York. The laundry parks and stores its trucks on the pedestrian sidewalk in front of its own building. Plaintiff owns three partially renovated "new law" tenement houses on the same side of the street adjacent to the laundry. The issue in the case is whether the owner is entitled to enjoin the illegal use of the sidewalk by the laundry.

The laundry contends that, although it be assumed that its use is illegal (which it denies), and that such use constitutes a public nuisance, nevertheless, the adjacent owner is debarred from any private remedy because it cannot satisfy the legal requirement of showing special damage.

In substance the judgment should be affirmed, although it should be modified to make clear that the laundry is permitted to use the sidewalk for loading and unloading its commercial vehicles for reasonable periods of time under the provisions of the Administrative Code of the City * * *. Under the rules which obtain in regard to bringing private actions to enjoin a public nuisance, the owner has made a sufficient showing.

The laundry has operated at the site in question for some 25 years. It claims to have used the sidewalk in the same manner for 10 years. The owner purchased its property in late 1955 and remodeled the lower stories in early 1956. The property is used and rented as a multiple dwelling, and the owner claims that its rental value has been adversely affected by the obstruction of the adjacent sidewalk. To prove this the owner offered the testimony of a real estate expert and the rentals obtained from the entire property.

The laundry is, even by city standards, a large one. It uses large trucks, and the photographs submitted in evidence show that these trucks and some passenger automobiles are parked and stored on the public sidewalk. It is clear that this occurs while the trucks are not being loaded or unloaded. The effect is to block the sidewalk substantially with respect to access to the owner's premises, but not to preclude entirely pedestrian traffic. The court found, and it is not seriously disputed, that the practice is a continual one.

While it is variously argued that the laundry does no more than have its trucks "stand" while being loaded and unloaded, that is not the issue in the case. Such standing or parking is a permitted use. The issue turns on the finding supported by the evidence that the laundry "parks" and "stores" its vehicles on the pedestrian sidewalk.

The obstruction of a public street or sidewalk beyond the reasonable uses permitted to abutting owners is a public nuisance. (Administrative Code, §§ 82d7–15.0, 755(2)–4.0; Penal Law, §§ 1530, 1532.) In the absence of special damage to another, such public nuisance is subject only to correction at the hands of public authority. It is equally clear, however, that one who suffers damage or injury, beyond that of the general inconvenience to the public at large, may recover for such nuisance in damages or obtain injunction to prevent its continuance. This is old law. (Callanan v. Gilman, 107 N.Y. 360 * * *.)

While there has been suggestion that the obstruction of a street must be total before there is a remedy, the cases do not support such a total requirement. There must, of course, be a substantial impairment of the use of the street. This is exemplified by the very illustrations and the earlier precedents cited in the *Callanan* case (*supra*). Moreover, when the question has come up sharply, the courts have granted an injunction to a plaintiff although the obstruction was not total. * * *

As a matter of logic and common sense, the preceding analysis could hardly be otherwise. The key to the private remedy is special damage, and substantial obstruction may accomplish that result just as effectively, in some cases, as total obstruction. Of course, in other cases, it may well be that only total obstruction will be sufficient to incur special damage.

On the matter of special damage, moreover, there is no requirement that there be directness of such damage, or that there be any particular quantum, before there is a right to a private remedy, such as injunction * * *provided it is established that the plaintiff must have sustained some material injury peculiar to himself. * * *

In the cases, almost always involved was a conflict between merchants or a conflict between a merchant and an owner of a private dwelling. In this case the apartment house owner partakes of both merchant and owner of a private dwelling. Thus, in this case the owner provides dwellings for a price to members of the public. There was expert evidence, although it was hardly necessary, that a multiple dwelling the adjacent sidewalk to which is illegally obstructed by trucks and passenger automobiles will suffer depreciated rentals, and thereby reduce its value. This, of course, provides the commercial damage which has been stressed in some of the cases. But it is important to note that insofar as the owners of private dwellings are concerned there has not been such a necessity. In other words, a man may suffer special damage in his dwelling apart from commercial or even visible pecuniary damage, and that is just as actionable as the commercial damage suffered by a merchant from a diversion of potential customers.

The laundry has stressed, in a phrase not unfamiliar to the law, that the present owner has "come to the nuisance", that is, it purchased the building knowing of the obstruction of the adjacent sidewalk by the laundry of at least 10 years standing. Considering the illegality of the use by the laundry this is hardly a persuasive position. Nor is it one addressed to any equity that the court is obliged to recognize. (Campbell v. Seaman, 63 N.Y. 568, 584 * * *). Interestingly enough, in the *Campbell* case, there was some evidence that the defendant's brickyard had been such, albeit not continuously, for some 25 years, the precise period of the laundry's ownership. Of greater significance is that the factor of "coming to the nuisance", and factor is all that it is, is most often applied to private rather than to public nuisance * * *.

The laundry has also stressed that the owner's proper remedies lie with the Police Department of the City. One may not conjecture as to why that remedy has not sufficed during the period of the owner's interest in the adjacent property or the decade preceding. But it does not follow that because equity will decline to exercise its power where there is an adequate remedy at law, meaning an action at law, that, therefore, its doors are closed to petitioners because of the existence of an administrative remedy, an appropriate criminal proceeding—or even the availability of self-help. * * * It suffices, in any event, that equity, traditionally, in this country and in England, has granted injunctions in cases of public nuisance, although even from the days of the common law, indictment lay, and still lies, for a public nuisance * * *. Indeed, if the situation were otherwise, there never could be an injunction to restrain a public nuisance, because, by its very nature and nomenclature, a public nuisance is one for which there is a public remedy * * *.

[Order affirmed as modified.]

Settle order.

VALENTE, J. (dissenting). * * *

I dissent and would reverse the judgment and dismiss the complaint because plaintiff did not prove any special injury resulting from the alleged unreasonable use of the public streets which was peculiar to plaintiff as distinct from that suffered by the general public. * * *

The conduct of which plaintiff complains is singularly a matter for correction by the appropriate law enforcement agencies. It is not without significance that no reported cases involving grants of injunctions in similar matters have appeared in the books for many years. Quite clearly, the authorities have dealt with such complaints in adequate fashion. We should not open the door to pleas to a court of equity for injunctive relief unless there is sufficient evidence of special damage over and above the inconvenience to the general public. The showing in the instant case falls far short of the well-settled legal requirements.

It must also be pointed out that plaintiff became the owner of the three adjoining apartment houses in 1955. Defendant operates a large commercial laundry on East 94th Street between First and Second Avenues in the Borough of Manhattan, City of New York. It had continuously operated that laundry for 25 years before plaintiff purchased its properties. Plaintiff's agent admitted that he knew, during the last 10 years, that defendant had been backing up its trucks perpendicularly for loading and unloading. With knowledge of this practice, plaintiff nevertheless purchased the property. The requirement of a clear demonstration of special damage becomes even more warranted under such circumstances.

Notes

1. A somewhat similar case, decided the other way, is Hay v. Oregon Dep't of Transp., 301 Or. 129, 719 P.2d 860 (1986). The court found neither a public nor a private nuisance. The case involved the defendant allowing parking on the plaintiff's beach. For a study of the historical origins and development of public nuisance, see J. Spencer, *Public Nuisance—A Critical Examination*, [1989] Camb.L.J. 55.

2. The crash of the Exxon Valdez resulted in numerous suits by individuals allegedly harmed by the resulting oil spill. In In re the Exxon Valdez, 1994 WL 182856 (D.Alaska), *affirmed* 104 F.3d 1196 (9th Cir.1997), the court confronted a claim by native Americans for non-economic injury to their subsistence way-of-life based on the theory that the spill was a maritime public nuisance. The court granted Exxon a summary judgment on this claim.

The Alaska Natives' non-economic subsistence claims are not "of a kind different from [those] suffered by other members of the public exercising the right common to the general public that was the subject of Interference." Restatement (Second) or Torts § 821C(1). Although Alaska Natives may have suffered to a greater degree than members of the general public, "differences in the intensity with which a public harm is felt does not justify a private claim for public nuisance." *See*, Restatement (Second) of Torts § 821C(1)(stating, in comment b, that it is not enough to suffer the same kind of harm, but to a greater degree). All Alaskans have the right to lead subsistence lifestyles, not just Alaska Natives. All Alaskans, and not just Alaska Natives, have the right to obtain and share wild food, enjoy uncontaminated nature, and cultivate traditional, cultural, spiritual, and psychological benefits in pristine natural surroundings. Neither the length of time in which Alaska Natives have practiced a subsistence lifestyle nor the manner in which it is practiced makes the Alaska Native subsistence lifestyle unique. These attributes of the Alaska Native lifestyle only make it different in degree from the same subsistence lifestyle available to all Alaskans. The Alaska Natives do not have a viable, maritime, public nuisance claim, as their claim is only different in degree, but not in kind, from that suffered by the general population of Alaska.

In re the Exxon Valdez at 2–3. Do you agree? Would the native Americans have a claim if others were not permitted to engage in a subsistence way-of-life?

IMPELLIZERRI v. JAMESVILLE FEDERATED CHURCH

Supreme Court of New York, Onondaga County, 1979.
104 Misc.2d 620, 428 N.Y.S.2d 550.

JOHN R. TENNEY, JUSTICE.

Anthony and Luana Impellizerri are seeking an injunction to restrain the Jamesville Federated Church from playing its carillon. They contend that the playing of the carillon is an invasion of privacy and a nuisance. The carillon is a series of bells which are played in various musical arrangements. It is played three times a day and four times on Sundays at regular hours for a period of approximately four minutes each time. Many attempts have been made to compromise. The speakers have been moved, playing time curtailed and the sound intensity reduced to no avail. Plaintiffs want it stopped. There is no dispute as to the facts and neither party has requested a hearing.

Life is full of sounds. The same sound can be pleasant in one moment and unpleasant in another. Children at play can be a refreshing sound to some and an annoyance to others. Unwanted sound is called noise, and it can produce unwanted effects. It may even reach the point where it becomes a restrainable pollutant. * * * However, there are many noises which are part of life and which all of us have to learn to accept. Plaintiffs admit that on occasion the normal village and traffic sounds drown out the bells.

In an industrial society, there are many noises which the courts have considered and have found not subject to restraint; trains and whistles, low flying planes, manufacturing noises, loud music * * *.

The plaintiffs contend that the volume of the bells affects their son who has a neurological disease and is kept awake. Luana Impellizerri claims she has migraine headaches and muscle spasms as the result of an accident which are aggravated by the bells. Generally, the claim is that conversation is disrupted, and the sounds cause severe anxiety and emotional stress to plaintiffs.

Bells in one form or another are a tradition throughout the world. In the Koran, they are considered the music of God. In the Christian world, every church is proud of its bells. The bells are rung for joy, for sadness, for warnings and for worship.

There are people who find total beauty in the sounds of bells in the Tower of Parliament in London or the daily ritual ringing at the Cathedral of Notre Dame in Paris. There is little question that the sound is often deafening when these bells start to ring, but for the general enjoyment of the public, it is considered acceptable.

It is often said that what is beauty to one may be ugly to another. A person with a special problem or an extra sensitive ear will be upset by any but the purest sound. That is not enough to justify the interference of the law.

The right to make a reasonable use of one's property has been long protected. Such a right is limited only if it unreasonably interferes with the rights of others.

There must be a material interference with the physical comfort and financial injury before there can be a nuisance. Stated another way, an early Massachusetts case held that the test should be the "common care of persons of ordinary prudence" and not as to those with "peculiar condition[s]". Rogers v. Elliott, 146 Mass. 349, 15 N.E. 768, 772 (1888). The alleged nuisance must be such as would cause an unwanted effect on the health and comfort of an ordinary person in the same or a similar situation. * * *

It seems that the plaintiffs have a special problem because of their own special condition. There are no other complainants, although there are several neighbors who live closer to the church than plaintiffs. It cannot be said that the ringing of the bell is such that would produce an unwanted effect on the ordinary person in the same circumstances.

Plaintiffs also argue that the playing of the music is an infringement on their right to religious freedom. This argument has no merit. The music is played without words although it is the music of well-known Christian hymns. There is no attempt to preach or impose any unwanted views.

Therefore, the plaintiffs' motion for an injunction is denied, and the defendant's cross-motion to dismiss the complaint is granted.

Notes

1. In Rogers v. Elliott, 146 Mass. 349, 15 N.E. 768 (1888), discussed by the court, the plaintiff alleged that he had been suffering from sun stroke. His physician asked the pastor of the adjoining church to keep the church bells from being rung as the noise was interfering with the patient's recovery. The action was dismissed.

2. In Langan v. Bellinger, 203 A.D.2d 857, 611 N.Y.S.2d 59 (1994) the plaintiff objected to the chiming of the hour by the Presbyterian Church clarion. Defendant presented affidavits from 15 residents, some living closer to the church than the plaintiffs, saying they enjoyed the bells. Suppose there were fifty householders within two blocks of the church and fifteen found the

bells as offensive as did the plaintiff but the other thirty-five were indifferent. Private nuisance? Public nuisance?

3. Perhaps an extreme case of an idiosyncratic plaintiff (and defendant) is Amphitheaters, Inc. v. Portland Meadows, 184 Or. 336, 198 P.2d 847 (1948). The plaintiff owned a drive-in theater which was adjacent to the defendant's stock car race track at which night racing was held. When the automobile racing was held, the floodlights from the race track cast sufficient light upon the plaintiff's movie screen so as to interfere with the quality of the picture. On one occasion, the admission price to the drive-in theater had to be returned. The amount of light reaching the screen was equivalent to the light of a full moon on a cloudless night. The court held that, *vis-à-vis* the drive-in theater, the race track was not a nuisance. It also held that the casting of light upon the plaintiff's property did not constitute a trespass. Recall the idiosyncratic nature of mother mink discussed in *Foster v. Preston Mill Co.,* p. 606, *supra,* in connection with our discussion of strict liability for the miscarriage of dangerous activities. In a later Oregon case, Lunda v. Matthews, 46 Or.App. 701, 613 P.2d 63 (1980), it was held that, once a nuisance is established, the plaintiff may recover the damages proximately caused by the nuisance even if some of these damages arise because of some unique qualities of the plaintiff. In that case, one of the plaintiffs suffered from bronchitis and he claimed damages for the worsening of his illness owing to the cement dust emitted from the defendant's operations.

4. A case refusing to recognize a cause of action in nuisance for what the court felt was a *de minimis* interference with the use and enjoyment of land is Turner v. Coppola, 102 Misc.2d 1043, 424 N.Y.S.2d 864 (1980). The plaintiff claimed that the trees of the defendants, her neighbors, overhung her property. Furthermore, the leaves of these trees fell upon her lawn. The court declared that the plaintiff could resort to self-help to prune away the tree limbs that encroached on her property. What if the defendants threatened the plaintiff with violence if she tried to touch their trees? The court held that the falling of leaves on the plaintiff's property did not constitute a trespass.

5. As noted in *Brown* a plaintiff's private nuisance action must be founded upon an interest in land. *Restatement (Second) of Torts* § 821E lists the parties who can bring a nuisance action:

§ 821E. Who Can Recover for Private Nuisance

For a private nuisance there is liability only to those who have property rights and privileges in respect to the use and enjoyment of the land affected, including

> (a) possessors of the land,
>
> (b) owners of easements and profits in the land, and
>
> (c) owners of nonpossessory estates in the land that are detrimentally affected by interferences with its use and enjoyment.

6. Nuisance claims have traditionally involved the conflicting interests of adjacent landowners. Should successor landowners be permitted to sue previous owners on a nuisance theory for damage the previous owners did to the property? This question arose in Philadelphia Electric Company v. Hercules, Inc., 762 F.2d 303 (3d Cir.1985). The defendant had operated a hydrocarbon resin manufacturing plant on the property and the Pennsylvania Department of Environmental Resources compelled the plaintiff to expend over $400,000 in

a subsequent clean up due to resin seepage into the Delaware river. Judge Higginbotham dismissed the plaintiff's claim against the prior owners with the following discussion:

> The parties have cited no case from Pennsylvania or any other jurisdiction, and we have found none, that permits a purchaser of real property to recover from the seller on a private nuisance theory for conditions existing on the very land transferred, and thereby to circumvent limitations on vendor liability inherent in the rule of caveat emptor. In a somewhat analogous circumstance, courts have not permitted tenants to circumvent traditional limitations on the liability of lessors by the expedient of casting their cause of action for defective conditions existing on premises (over which they have assumed control) as one for private nuisance. * * * PECO cannot recover in private nuisance for the violation of a duty Hercules may have owed to others—namely, its neighbors.

> We believe that this result is consonant with the historical role of private nuisance law as a means of efficiently resolving conflicts between neighboring, contemporaneous land uses. * * * Neighbors, unlike the purchasers of the land upon which a nuisance exists, have no opportunity to protect themselves through inspection and negotiation. The record shows that PECO acted as a sophisticated and responsible purchaser—inquiring into the past use of the Chester site, and inspecting it carefully. We find it inconceivable that the price it offered Gould did not reflect the possibility of environmental risks, even if the exact condition giving rise to this suit was not discovered.

> Where, as here, the rule of caveat emptor applies, allowing a vendee a cause of action for private nuisance for conditions existing on the land transferred—where there has been no fraudulent concealment—would in effect negate the market's allocations of resources and risks, and subject vendors who may have originally sold their land at appropriately discounted prices to unbargained-for liability to remote vendees. * * * Such an extension of common law doctrine is particularly hazardous in an area, such as environmental pollution, where Congress and the state legislatures are actively seeking to achieve a socially acceptable definition of rights and liabilities. We conclude that PECO did not have a cause of action against Hercules sounding in private nuisance.

Philadelphia, 762 F.2d at 313–315. *Accord*, 55 Motor Avenue Company v. Liberty Industrial Finishing Corp., 885 F.Supp. 410 (E.D.N.Y.1994).

BOOMER v. ATLANTIC CEMENT COMPANY, INC.

Court of Appeals of New York, 1970.
26 N.Y.2d 219, 309 N.Y.S.2d 312, 257 N.E.2d 870.

BERGAN, JUDGE.

Defendant operates a large cement plant near Albany. These are actions for injunction and damages by neighboring land owners alleging injury to property from dirt, smoke and vibration emanating from the plant. A nuisance has been found after trial, temporary damages have been allowed; but an injunction has been denied.

The public concern with air pollution arising from many sources in industry and in transportation is currently accorded ever wider recognition

NUISANCE Ch. 15

accompanied by a growing sense of responsibility in State and Federal Governments to control it. Cement plants are obvious sources of air pollution in the neighborhoods where they operate.

But there is now before the court private litigation in which individual property owners have sought specific relief from a single plant operation. The threshold question raised by the division of view on this appeal is whether the court should resolve the litigation between the parties now before it as equitably as seems possible; or whether, seeking promotion of the general public welfare, it should channel private litigation into broad public objectives.

A court performs its essential function when it decides the rights of parties before it. Its decision of private controversies may sometimes greatly affect public issues. Large questions of law are often resolved by the manner in which private litigation is decided. But this is normally an incident to the court's main function to settle controversy. It is a rare exercise of judicial power to use a decision in private litigation as a purposeful mechanism to achieve direct public objectives greatly beyond the rights and interests before the court.

Effective control of air pollution is a problem presently far from solution even with the full public and financial powers of government. In large measure adequate technical procedures are yet to be developed and some that appear possible may be economically impracticable.

It seems apparent that the amelioration of air pollution will depend on technical research in great depth; on a carefully balanced consideration of the economic impact of close regulation; and of the actual effect on public health. It is likely to require massive public expenditure and to demand more than any local community can accomplish and to depend on regional and interstate controls.

A court should not try to do this on its own as a by-product of private litigation and it seems manifest that the judicial establishment is neither equipped in the limited nature of any judgment it can pronounce nor prepared to lay down and implement an effective policy for the elimination of air pollution. This is an area beyond the circumference of one private lawsuit. It is a direct responsibility for government and should not thus be undertaken as an incident to solving a dispute between property owners and a single cement plant—one of many—in the Hudson River valley.

The cement making operations of defendant have been found by the court at Special Term to have damaged the nearby properties of plaintiffs in these two actions. That court, as it has been noted, accordingly found defendant maintained a nuisance and this has been affirmed at the Appellate Division. The total damage to plaintiffs' properties is, however, relatively small in comparison with the value of defendant's operation and with the consequences of the injunction which plaintiffs seek.

The ground for the denial of injunction, notwithstanding the finding both that there is a nuisance and that plaintiffs have been damaged substantially, is the large disparity in economic consequences of the nuisance and of the injunction. This theory cannot, however, be sustained without overruling a doctrine which has been consistently reaffirmed in several leading cases in this court and which has never been disavowed here, namely that where a nuisance has been found and where there has been any substantial damage shown by the party complaining an injunction will be granted.

The rule in New York has been that such a nuisance will be enjoined although marked disparity be shown in economic consequence between the effect of the injunction and the effect of the nuisance.

The problem of disparity in economic consequence was sharply in focus in Whalen v. Union Bag & Paper Co., 208 N.Y. 1, 101 N.E. 805. A pulp mill entailing an investment of more than a million dollars polluted a stream in which plaintiff, who owned a farm, was "a lower riparian owner". The economic loss to plaintiff from this pollution was small. This court, reversing the Appellate Division, reinstated the injunction granted by the Special Term against the argument of the mill owner that in view of "the slight advantage to plaintiff and the great loss that will be inflicted on defendant" an injunction should not be granted (p. 2, 101 N.E. p. 805). "Such a balancing of injuries cannot be justified by the circumstances of this case", Judge Werner noted (p. 4, 101 N.E. p. 805). He continued: "Although the damage to the plaintiff may be slight as compared with the defendant's expense of abating the condition, that is not a good reason for refusing an injunction" (p. 5, 101 N.E. p. 806).

Thus the unconditional injunction granted at Special Term was reinstated. The rule laid down in that case, then, is that whenever the damage resulting from a nuisance is found not "unsubstantial", viz., $100 a year, injunction would follow. This states a rule that had been followed in this court with marked consistency * * *.

* * * Thus if, within Whalen v. Union Bag & Paper Co., *supra* which authoritatively states the rule in New York, the damage to plaintiffs in these present cases from defendant's cement plant is "not unsubstantial", an injunction should follow.

Although the court at Special Term and the Appellate Division held that injunction should be denied, it was found that plaintiffs had been damaged in various specific amounts up to the time of the trial and damages to the respective plaintiffs were awarded for those amounts. The effect of this was, injunction having been denied, plaintiffs could maintain successive actions at law for damages thereafter as further damage was incurred.

The court at Special Term also found the amount of permanent damage attributable to each plaintiff, for the guidance of the parties in the event both sides stipulated to the payment and acceptance of such permanent damage as a settlement of all the controversies among the parties. The total of permanent damages to all plaintiffs thus found was $185,000. This basis of adjustment has not resulted in any stipulation by the parties.

This result at Special Term and at the Appellate Division is a departure from a rule that has become settled; but to follow the rule literally in these cases would be to close down the plant at once. This court is fully agreed to avoid that immediately drastic remedy; the difference in view is how best to avoid it.*

One alternative is to grant the injunction but postpone its effect to a specified future date to give opportunity for technical advances to permit defendant to eliminate the nuisance; another is to grant the injunction conditioned on the payment of permanent damages to plaintiffs which would compensate them for the total economic loss to their property present and future caused by defendant's operations. For reasons which will be developed the court chooses the latter alternative.

If the injunction were to be granted unless within a short period—e.g., 18 months—the nuisance be abated by improved methods, there would be no assurance that any significant technical improvement would occur.

The parties could settle this private litigation at any time if defendant paid enough money and the imminent threat of closing the plant would build up the pressure on defendant. If there were no improved techniques found, there would inevitably be applications to the court at Special Term for extensions of time to perform on showing of good faith efforts to find such techniques.

Moreover, techniques to eliminate dust and other annoying by-products of cement making are unlikely to be developed by any research the defendant can undertake within any short period, but will depend on the total resources of the cement industry nationwide and throughout the world. The problem is universal wherever cement is made.

For obvious reasons the rate of the research is beyond control of defendant. If at the end of 18 months the whole industry has not found a technical solution a court would be hard put to close down this one cement plant if due regard be given to equitable principles.

On the other hand, to grant the injunction unless defendant pays plaintiffs such permanent damages as may be fixed by the court seems to do justice between the contending parties. All of the attributions of economic loss to the properties on which plaintiffs' complaints are based will have been redressed.

The nuisance complained of by these plaintiffs may have other public or private consequences, but these particular parties are the only ones who have sought remedies and the judgment proposed will fully redress them. The limitation of relief granted is a limitation only within the four corners of these actions and does not foreclose public health or other public agencies from seeking proper relief in a proper court.

It seems reasonable to think that the risk of being required to pay permanent damages to injured property owners by cement plant owners would itself be a reasonable effective spur to research for improved techniques to minimize nuisance.

---

* Respondent's investment in the plant is in excess of $45,000,000. There are over 300 people employed there.

The power of the court to condition on equitable grounds the continuance of an injunction on the payment of permanent damages seems undoubted. * * *

Thus it seems fair to both sides to grant permanent damages to plaintiffs which will terminate this private litigation. * * *

The judgment, by allowance of permanent damages imposing a servitude on land, which is the basis of the actions, would preclude future recovery by plaintiffs or their grantees * * *.

This should be placed beyond debate by a provision of the judgment that the payment by defendant and the acceptance by plaintiffs of permanent damages found by the court shall be in compensation for a servitude on the land.

Although the Trial Term has found permanent damages as a possible basis of settlement of the litigation, on remission the court should be entirely free to re-examine this subject. It may again find the permanent damage already found; or make new findings.

The orders should be reversed, without costs, and the cases remitted to Supreme Court, Albany County to grant an injunction which shall be vacated upon payment by defendant of such amounts of permanent damage to the respective plaintiffs as shall for this purpose be determined by the court.

JASEN, JUDGE (dissenting).

I agree with the majority that a reversal is required here, but I do not subscribe to the newly enunciated doctrine of assessment of permanent damages, in lieu of an injunction, where substantial property rights have been impaired by the creation of a nuisance.

It has long been the rule in this State, as the majority acknowledges, that a nuisance which results in substantial continuing damage to neighbors must be enjoined. (Whalen v. Union Bag & Paper Co., 208 N.Y. 1, 101 N.E. 805; Campbell v. Seaman, 63 N.Y. 568; see, also, Kennedy v. Moog Servocontrols, 21 N.Y.2d 966, 290 N.Y.S.2d 193, 237 N.E.2d 356.) To now change the rule to permit the cement company to continue polluting the air indefinitely upon the payment of permanent damages is, in my opinion, compounding the magnitude of a very serious problem in our State and Nation today.

In recognition of this problem, the Legislature of this State has enacted the Air Pollution Control Act (Public Health Law, Consol. Laws, c. 45, §§ 1264 to 1299–m) declaring that it is the State policy to require the use of all available and reasonable methods to prevent and control air pollution (Public Health Law § 1265).

The harmful nature and widespread occurrence of air pollution have been extensively documented. Congressional hearings have revealed that air pollution causes substantial property damage, as well as being a contributing factor to a rising incidence of lung cancer, emphysema, bronchitis and asthma.

The specific problem faced here is known as particulate contamination because of the fine dust particles emanating from defendant's cement plant. The particular type of nuisance is not new, having appeared in many cases for at least the past 60 years. * * * It is interesting to note that cement production has recently been identified as a significant source of particulate contamination in the Hudson Valley. This type of pollution, wherein very small particles escape and stay in the atmosphere, has been denominated as the type of air pollution which produces the greatest hazard to human health. We have thus a nuisance which not only is damaging to the plaintiffs, but also is decidedly harmful to the general public.

I see grave dangers in overruling our long-established rule of granting an injunction where a nuisance results in substantial continuing damage. In permitting the injunction to become inoperative upon the payment of permanent damages, the majority is, in effect, licensing a continuing wrong. It is the same as saying to the cement company, you may continue to do harm to your neighbors so long as you pay a fee for it. Furthermore, once such permanent damages are assessed and paid, the incentive to alleviate the wrong would be eliminated, thereby continuing air pollution of an area without abatement.

It is true that some courts have sanctioned the remedy here proposed by the majority in a number of cases, but none of the authorities relied upon by the majority are analogous to the situation before us. In those cases, the courts, in denying an injunction and awarding money damages, grounded their decision on a showing that the use to which the property was intended to be put was primarily for the public benefit. Here, on the other hand, it is clearly established that the cement company is creating a continuing air pollution nuisance primarily for its own private interest with no public benefit.

This kind of inverse condemnation * * * may not be invoked by a private person or corporation for private gain or advantage. Inverse condemnation should only be permitted when the public is primarily served in the taking or impairment of property. * * * The promotion of the interests of the polluting cement company has, in my opinion, no public use or benefit.

Nor is it constitutionally permissible to impose servitude on land, without consent of the owner, by payment of permanent damages where the continuing impairment of the land is for a private use. * * * This is made clear by the State Constitution (art. I, § 7, subd. [a]) which provides that "[p]rivate property shall not be taken for *public use* without just compensation" (emphasis added). It is, of course, significant that the section makes no mention of taking for a *private* use.

In sum, then, by constitutional mandate as well as by judicial pronouncement, the permanent impairment of private property for private purposes is not authorized in the absence of clearly demonstrated public benefit and use.

I would enjoin the defendant cement company from continuing the discharge of dust particles upon its neighbors' properties unless, within 18 months, the cement company abated this nuisance.

It is not my intention to cause the removal of the cement plant from the Albany area, but to recognize the urgency of the problem stemming from this stationary source of air pollution, and to allow the company a specified period of time to develop a means to alleviate this nuisance.

I am aware that the trial court found that the most modern dust control devices available have been installed in defendant's plant, but, I submit, this does not mean that *better* and more effective dust control devices could not be developed within the time allowed to abate the pollution.

Moreover, I believe it is incumbent upon the defendant to develop such devices, since the cement company, at the time the plant commenced production (1962), was well aware of the plaintiffs' presence in the area, as well as the probable consequences of its contemplated operation. Yet, it still chose to build and operate the plant at this site.

In a day when there is a growing concern for clean air, highly developed industry should not expect acquiescence by the courts, but should, instead, plan its operations to eliminate contamination of our air and damage to its neighbors.

FULD, C.J., and BURKE and SCILEPPI, JJ., concur with BERGAN, J.

JASEN, J., dissents in part and votes to reverse in a separate opinion.

BREITEL and GIBSON, JJ., taking no part.

Notes

1. In recent years the nuisance issues raised in this chapter have given rise to a very large body of published scholarship in both law and economics. Much of it starts with the Coase Theorem, discussed in Chapter Eight, page 611, *supra.* Coase's article, *The Problem of Social Cost,* 3 J.L. & Econ. 1 (1960), has had an enormous affect upon the thinking regarding nuisance law, as well as many other areas of tort law. *See, e.g.,* Louis Kaplow and Steven Shavell, *Property Rules Versus Liability Rules: An Economic Analysis,* 109 Harv. L. Rev. 713 (1996); James E. Krier and Stewart J. Schwab, *Property Rules and Liability Rules: The Cathedral In Another Light,* 70 N.Y.U. L. Rev. 440 (1995); Herbert Hovenkamp, *Marginal Utility and the Coase Theorem,* 75 Cornell L. Rev. 783 (1990); Jeff L. Lewin, *Compensated Injunctions and the Evolution of Nuisance Law,* 71 Iowa L.Rev. 775 (1986); Mitchell Polinsky, *Resolving Nuisance Disputes: The Simple Economics of Injunctive and Damage Remedies,* 32 Stan.L.Rev. 1075 (1980).

2. *Boomer,* like *Impellizerri* involve intentional activity on the part of the defendant. Confronted with these situations, courts must balance the benefits of the activity against its harms. The *Restatement (Second) of Torts* contains a number of provisions on this issue.

§ 826. Unreasonableness of Intentional Invasion

An intentional invasion of another's interest in the use and enjoyment of land is unreasonable if

(a) the gravity of the harm outweighs the utility of the actor's conduct, or

(b) the harm caused by the conduct is serious and the financial burden of compensating for this and similar harm to others would not make the continuation of the conduct not feasible.

§ 827. Gravity of Harm—Factors Involved

In determining the gravity of the harm from an intentional invasion of another's interest in the use and enjoyment of land, the following factors are important:

(a) The extent of the harm involved;

(b) the character of the harm involved;

(c) the social value that the law attaches to the type of use or enjoyment invaded;

(d) the suitability of the particular use or enjoyment invaded to the character of the locality; and

(e) the burden on the person harmed of avoiding the harm.

§ 828. Utility of Conduct—Factors Involved

In determining the utility of conduct that causes an intentional invasion of another's interest in the use and enjoyment of land, the following factors are important:

(a) the social value that the law attaches to the primary purpose of the conduct;

(b) the suitability of the conduct to the character of the locality; and

(c) the impracticability of preventing or avoiding the invasion.

§ 829. Gravity vs. Utility—Conduct Malicious or Indecent

An intentional invasion of another's interest in the use and enjoyment of land is unreasonable if the harm is significant and the actor's conduct is

(a) for the sole purpose of causing harm to the other; or

(b) contrary to common standards of decency.

§ 829a. Gravity vs. Utility—Severe Harm

An intentional invasion of another's interest in the use and enjoyment of land is unreasonable if the harm resulting from the invasion is severe and greater than the other should be required to bear without compensation.

§ 830. Gravity vs. Utility—invasion Avoidable

An intentional invasion of another's interest in the use and enjoyment of land is unreasonable if the harm is significant and it would be practicable for the actor to avoid the harm in whole or in part without undue hardship.

§ 831. Gravity vs. Utility—conduct Unsuited to Locality

An intentional invasion of another's interest in the use and enjoyment of land is unreasonable if the harm is significant, and

(a) the particular use or enjoyment interfered with is well suited to the character of the locality; and

(b) the actor's conduct is unsuited to the character of that locality.

3. In Carpenter v. Double R Cattle Co., 108 Idaho 602, 701 P.2d 222, 224 (1985), the court refused to adopt *Restatement (Second) of Torts* § 826(b) and concluded the defendant's feed lot was not a nuisance because its utility outweighed the costs. In a dissenting opinion, Justice Bistline accused the majority of adhering to "ideas on the law of nuisance that should have gone out with the use of buffalo chips as fuel."

> The majority's rule today suggests that part of the cost of industry, agriculture or development must be borne by those unfortunate few who have the fortuitous luck to live in the immediate vicinity of a nuisance producing facility. Frankly, I think this naive economic view is ridiculous in both its simplicity and its outdated view of modern economic society. The "cost" of a product includes not only the amount it takes to produce such a product but also includes the external costs: the damage done to the environment through pollution of air or water is an example of an external cost. In the instant case, the nuisance suffered by the homeowners should be considered an external cost of operating a feedlot and producing beef for public consumption. I do not believe that a few should be required to pay this extra cost of doing business by going uncompensated for a nuisance of this sort. If a feedlot wants to continue, I say fine, providing compensation is paid for the serious invasion (the odors, flies, dust, etc.) of the homeowner's interest. My only qualification is that the financial burden of compensating for this harm should not be such as to force the feedlot (or any other industry) out of business. The true cost can then be shifted to the consumer who rightfully should pay for the entire cost of producing the product he desires to obtain.

Carpenter, 701 P.2d at 229.

How do you think Justice Bistline would resolve the case if the financial burden of compensating for the harm would force the feedlot out of business? What would you propose? Consider the solution of the Arizona Supreme Court when confronted with a similar situation.

SPUR INDUSTRIES, INC. v. DEL E. WEBB DEVELOPMENT CO.

Supreme Court of Arizona, 1972.
108 Ariz. 178, 494 P.2d 700.

CAMERON, VICE CHIEF JUSTICE.

From a judgment permanently enjoining the defendant, Spur Industries, Inc., from operating a cattle feedlot near the plaintiff Del E. Webb Development Company's Sun City, Spur appeals. Webb cross-appeals. Although numerous issues are raised, we feel that it is necessary to answer only two questions. They are:

1. Where the operation of a business, such as a cattle feedlot is lawful in the first instance, but becomes a nuisance by reason of a nearby residential area, may the feedlot operation be enjoined in an action brought by the developer of the residential area?

2. Assuming that the nuisance may be enjoined, may the developer of a completely new town or urban area in a previously agricultural area be required to indemnify the operator of the feedlot who must

move or cease operation because of the presence of the residential area created by the developer?

* * * The area in question is located in Maricopa County, Arizona, some 14 to 15 miles west of the urban area of Phoenix, on the Phoenix–Wickenburg Highway, also known as Grand Avenue. About two miles south of Grand Avenue is Olive Avenue which runs east and west. * * *

Farming started in this area about 1911. In 1929, with the completion of the Carl Pleasant Dam, gravity flow water became available to the property located to the west of the Agua Fria River, though land to the east remained dependent upon well water for irrigation. By 1950, the only urban areas in the vicinity were the agriculturally related communities of Peoria, El Mirage, and Surprise located along Grand Avenue. Along 111th Avenue, approximately one mile south of Grand Avenue and 1½ miles north of Olive Avenue, the community of Youngtown was commenced in 1954. Youngtown is a retirement community appealing primarily to senior citizens.

In 1956, Spur's predecessors in interest, H. Marion Welborn and the Northside Hay Mill and Trading Company, developed feedlots, about ½ mile south of Olive Avenue, in an area between the confluence of the usually dry Agua Fria and New Rivers. The area is well suited for cattle feeding and in 1959, there were 25 cattle feeding pens or dairy operations within a 7 mile radius of the location developed by Spur's predecessors. In April and May of 1959, the Northside Hay Mill was feeding between 6,000 and 7,000 head of cattle and Welborn approximately 1,500 head on a combined area of 35 acres.

In May of 1959, Del Webb began to plan the development of an urban area to be known as Sun City. For this purpose, the Marinette and the Santa Fe Ranches, some 20,000 acres of farmland, were purchased for $15,000,000 or $750.00 per acre. This price was considerably less than the price of land located near the urban area of Phoenix, and along with the success of Youngtown was a factor influencing the decision to purchase the property in question.

By September 1959, Del Webb had started construction of a golf course south of Grand Avenue and Spur's predecessors had started to level ground for more feedlot area. In 1960, Spur purchased the property in question and began a rebuilding and expansion program extending both to the north and south of the original facilities. By 1962, Spur's expansion program was completed and had expanded from approximately 35 acres to 114 acres. * * *

Accompanied by an extensive advertising campaign, homes were first offered by Del Webb in January 1960 and the first unit to be completed was south of Grand Avenue and approximately 2½ miles north of Spur. By 2 May 1960, there were 450 to 500 houses completed or under construction. At this time, Del Webb did not consider odors from the Spur feed pens a problem and Del Webb continued to develop in a southerly direction, until sales resistance became so great that the parcels were difficult if not impossible to sell. Thomas E. Breen, Vice President and General Manager of the housing division of Del Webb, testified at deposition as follows:

"Q   Did you ever have any discussions with Tony Cole at or about the time the sales office was opened south of Peoria concerning the problem in sales as the development came closer towards the feed lots?

"A   Not at the time that that facility was opened. That was subsequent to that.

"Q   All right, what is it that you recall about conversations with Cole on that subject?

"A   Well, when the feed lot problem became a bigger problem, which, really, to the best of my recollection, commenced to become a serious problem in 1963, and there was some talk about not developing that area because of sales resistance, and to my recollection we shifted—we had planned at that time to the eastern portion of the property, and it was a consideration.

"Q   Was any specific suggestion made by Mr. Cole as to the line of demarcation that should be drawn or anything of that type exactly where the development should cease?

"A   I don't recall anything specific as far as the definite line would be, other than, you know, that it would be advisable to stay out of the southwestern portion there because of sales resistance.

"Q   And to the best of your recollection, this was in about 1963?

"A   That would be my recollection, yes.

＊   ＊   ＊   ＊   ＊   ＊   ＊   ＊

"Q   As you recall it, what was the reason that the suggestion was not adopted to stop developing towards the southwest of the development?

"A   Well, as far as I know, that decision was made subsequent to that time.

"Q   Right. But I mean at that time?

"A   Well, at that time what I am really referring to is more of a long-range planning than immediate planning, and I think it was the case of just trying to figure out how far you could go with it before you really ran into a lot of sales resistance and found a necessity to shift the direction.

"Q   So the plan was to go as far as you could until the resistance got to the point where you couldn't go any further?

"A   I would say that is reasonable, yes."

By December 1967, Del Webb's property had extended south to Olive Avenue and Spur was within 500 feet of Olive Avenue to the north. ＊ ＊ ＊

Del Webb's suit complained that the Spur feeding operation was a public nuisance because of the flies and the odor which were drifting or being blown by the prevailing south to north wind over the southern portion of Sun City. At the time of the suit, Spur was feeding between 20,000 and 30,000 head of cattle, and the facts amply support the finding of the trial court that the feed pens had become a nuisance to the people who resided in the southern part of Del Webb's development. The testimony indicated that cattle in a commercial feedlot will produce 35 to 40 pounds of wet manure per day, per head, or over a million pounds of wet manure per day for 30,000 head of cattle, and that despite the admittedly good feedlot management and good housekeeping practices by Spur, the resulting odor and flies produced an annoying if not unhealthy situation as far as the senior citizens of southern Sun City were concerned. There is no doubt that some of the citizens of Sun City were unable to enjoy the outdoor living which Del Webb had advertised and that Del Webb was faced with sales resistance from prospective purchasers as well as strong and persistent complaints from the people who had purchased homes in that area.

It is noted, however, that neither the citizens of Sun City nor Youngtown are represented in this lawsuit and the suit is solely between Del E. Webb Development Company and Spur Industries, Inc.

MAY SPUR BE ENJOINED?

The difference between a private nuisance and a public nuisance is generally one of degree. A private nuisance is one affecting a single individual or a definite small number of persons in the enjoyment of private rights not common to the public, while a public nuisance is one affecting the rights enjoyed by citizens as a part of the public. To constitute a public nuisance, the nuisance must affect a considerable number of people or an entire community or neighborhood. City of Phoenix v. Johnson, 51 Ariz. 115, 75 P.2d 30 (1938).

Where the injury is slight, the remedy for minor inconveniences lies in an action for damages rather than in one for an injunction. * * * Moreover, some courts have held, in the "balancing of conveniences" cases, that damages may be the sole remedy. See Boomer v. Atlantic Cement Co., 26 N.Y.2d 219, 309 N.Y.S.2d 312, 257 N.E.2d 870 * * *.

Thus, it would appear from the admittedly incomplete record as developed in the trial court, that, at most, residents of Youngtown would be entitled to damages rather than injunctive relief.

We have no difficulty, however, in agreeing with the conclusion of the trial court that Spur's operation was an enjoinable public nuisance as far as the people in the southern portion of Del Webb's Sun City were concerned.

It is clear that as to the citizens of Sun City, the operation of Spur's feedlot was both a public and a private nuisance. They could have successfully maintained an action to abate the nuisance. Del Webb, having shown a special injury in the loss of sales, had a standing to bring suit to enjoin the nuisance. * * * The judgment of the trial court permanently enjoining the operation of the feedlot is affirmed.

MUST DEL WEBB INDEMNIFY SPUR?

A suit to enjoin a nuisance sounds in equity and the courts have long recognized a special responsibility to the public when acting as a court of equity. * * *

In addition to protecting the public interest, however, courts of equity are concerned with protecting the operator of a lawfully, albeit noxious, business from the result of a knowing and willful encroachment by others near his business.

In the so-called "coming to the nuisance" cases, the courts have held that the residential landowner may not have relief if he knowingly came into a neighborhood reserved for industrial or agricultural endeavors and has been damaged thereby:

> "Plaintiffs chose to live in an area uncontrolled by zoning laws or restrictive covenants and remote from urban development. In such an area plaintiffs cannot complain that legitimate agricultural pursuits are being carried on in the vicinity, nor can plaintiffs, having chosen to build in an agricultural area, complain that the agricultural pursuits carried on in the area depreciate the value of their homes. The area being primarily agricultural, any opinion reflecting the value of such property must take this factor into account. The standards affecting the value of residence property in an urban setting, subject to zoning controls and controlled planning techniques, cannot be the standards by which agricultural properties are judged.

> "People employed in a city who build their homes in suburban areas of the county beyond the limits of a city and zoning regulations do so for a reason. Some do so to avoid the high taxation rate imposed by cities, or to avoid special assessments for street, sewer and water projects. They usually build on improved or hard surface highways, which have been built either at state or county expense and thereby avoid special assessments for these improvements. It may be that they desire to get away from the congestion of traffic, smoke, noise, foul air and the many other annoyances of city life. But with all these advantages in going beyond the area which is zoned and restricted to protect them in their homes, they must be prepared to take the disadvantages." Dill v. Excel Packing Company, 183 Kan. 513, 525, 526, 331 P.2d 539, 548, 549 (1958). * * *

Were Webb the only party injured, we would feel justified in holding that the doctrine of "coming to the nuisance" would have been a bar to the relief asked by Webb, and, on the other hand, had Spur located the feedlot near the outskirts of a city and had the city grown toward the feedlot, Spur would have to suffer the cost of abating the nuisance as to those people locating within the growth pattern of the expanding city:

> "The case affords, perhaps, an example where a business established at a place remote from population is gradually surrounded and becomes part of a populous center, so that a business which formerly was not an interference with the rights of others has become so by the encroachment of the population * * *."

We agree, however, with the Massachusetts court that:

> "The law of nuisance affords no rigid rule to be applied in all instances. It is elastic. It undertakes to require only that which is fair and reasonable under all the circumstances. In a commonwealth like this, which depends for its material prosperity so largely on the continued growth and enlargement of manufacturing of diverse variet-

ies, 'extreme rights' cannot be enforced.   * * *."   Stevens v. Rockport Granite Co., 216 Mass. 486, 488, 104 N.E. 371, 373 (1914).

There was no indication in the instant case at the time Spur and its predecessors located in western Maricopa County that a new city would spring up, full-blown, alongside the feeding operation and that the developer of that city would ask the court to order Spur to move because of the new city. Spur is required to move not because of any wrongdoing on the part of Spur, but because of a proper and legitimate regard of the courts for the rights and interests of the public.

Del Webb, on the other hand, is entitled to the relief prayed for (a permanent injunction), not because Webb is blameless, but because of the damage to the people who have been encouraged to purchase homes in Sun City. It does not equitably or legally follow, however, that Webb, being entitled to the injunction, is then free of any liability to Spur if Webb has in fact been the cause of the damage Spur has sustained. It does not seem harsh to require a developer, who has taken advantage of the lesser land values in a rural area as well as the availability of large tracts of land on which to build and develop a new town or city in the area, to indemnify those who are forced to leave as a result.

Having brought people to the nuisance to the foreseeable detriment of Spur, Webb must indemnify Spur for a reasonable amount of the cost of moving or shutting down. It should be noted that this relief to Spur is limited to a case wherein a developer has, with foreseeability, brought into a previously agricultural or industrial area the population which makes necessary the granting of an injunction against a lawful business and for which the business has no adequate relief.

It is therefore the decision of this court that the matter be remanded to the trial court for a hearing upon the damages sustained by the defendant Spur as a reasonable and direct result of the granting of the permanent injunction. Since the result of the appeal may appear novel and both sides have obtained a measure of relief, it is ordered that each side will bear its own costs.

Affirmed in part, reversed in part, and remanded for further proceedings consistent with this opinion.

Notes

1. Restatement (Second) of Torts § 840D provides: "The fact that the plaintiff has acquired or improved his land after a nuisance interfering with it has come into existence is not in itself sufficient to bar his action, but is a factor to be considered in determining whether the nuisance is actionable." How is this factor incorporated into the *Spur* opinion? What are the arguments against allowing the defendant to prevail on a "coming to the nuisance" defense every time the plaintiff moves near the defendant's activity? The issue is discussed in Donald Wittman, *First Come, First Served: An Economic Analysis of "Coming to the Nuisance,"* 9 J. Legal Studies 557 (1980).

2. Guido Calabresi and A. Douglas Melamed, *Property Rules, Liability Rules, and Inalienability: One View of the Cathedral*, 85 Harv.L.Rev. 1089 (1972), point out that nuisance situations can be resolved in one of four ways:

a. The complaining "victim" can stop the nuisance by securing an injunction.

b. The complaining "victim" can receive damages for the loss incurred as a result of the invasion.

c. The court can hold that there is no nuisance thus placing the cost of the loss upon the complaining "victim".

d. The court can find that there is an invasion but that the complaining "victim" must bear the cost of removing the offensive activity.

Go back over the cases you have read in this chapter and identify which fit into which category.

How should the courts decide which rule to apply? If one applies an economic analysis, does it make any difference? To the contesting parties? To society as a whole?

3. Robert Rabin, *Nuisance Law: Rethinking Fundamental Assumptions*, 63 Va.L.Rev. 1299 (1977), does a particularly good job of tracing through this analysis as applied to Amphitheaters, Inc. v. Portland Meadows, 184 Or. 336, 198 P.2d 847 (1948), discussed p. 964, *supra*.

4. The Arizona court applied a somewhat more conventional approach in Armory Park Neighborhood Ass'n v. Episcopal Community Services, 148 Ariz. 1, 712 P.2d 914 (1985), a case dealing with the effects upon the neighborhood of the defendant providing free meals to indigents.

Chapter 16

MISREPRESENTATION AND TORTIOUS INTERFERENCE WITH CONTRACT AND PROSPECTIVE CONTRACT

This chapter considers two areas of tort liability that currently play a significant role in much business litigation. The first area is liability for misrepresentation, including intentional or fraudulent misrepresentations, negligent misrepresentations, and "innocent" misrepresentations. The second area relates to liability that may be incurred when an actor induces another individual to breach a contract or not to enter into a contract or prospective business relation.

A. MISREPRESENTATION

1. Introduction

Consider the following two scenarios:

Example 1. A farmer applies for a loan from a bank, pledging as collateral most of his farm machinery. The bank agrees to lend the farmer $1,000,000, but on one condition: the farmer must obtain a letter from a lawyer certifying that there are no prior liens on the machinery. The farmer asks a friend of his, who is a lawyer, to prepare a letter. The lawyer does so, and gives the letter to the farmer. The letter states that the lawyer "conducted a thorough search" and that "the machinery is free and clear of all liens." But the lawyer never conducted such a search, and the machinery indeed did have prior liens. The farmer defaults on the loan, and the bank is unable to obtain the collateral because it is pledged to other creditors.

Example 2. A weight control clinic enrolls clients and recommends that they take a dietary supplement manufactured by the clinic. The clinic's literature claims that the supplement provides "full nutritional needs" and is "safe, with no side effects." A client of the clinic suffers an adverse reaction to a dose of the supplement that has been tainted with a toxic substance.

These two simple scenarios pose a number of themes that the materials in this chapter will explore.

Personal Injury Versus Purely Economic Loss. Misrepresentations can lead either to personal injury or to purely economic loss. Liability for misrepresentation exists for both contexts, although this chapter will concentrate on purely economic losses. Briefly, however, we should note that, with respect to personal injury contexts, if a defendant intentionally or negligently gives false information, and if a person suffers physical harm as a result of reasonably relying on this information, then the defendant is liable for full tort damages. *See* Restatement (Second) of Torts § 311 (1965). In a somewhat later doctrinal development, courts also developed a theory of liability for personal injury based on "innocent" misrepresentations; that is, false statements of fact that were not made either fraudulently or as a result of lack of due care. Section 402B of the Restatement of Torts (Second) provides for a cause of action in such cases if (1) the defendant is engaged in the business of selling chattels, (2) the defendant misrepresents a material fact relating to the quality or character of the chattel, and (3) physical harm is caused by justifiable reliance on the misrepresentation.

On the facts of Example 2, the plaintiff might not be able to show either that the clinic made the false statement with knowledge of its falsity, or that the clinic made the statement without having taken reasonable care. But in any event the clinic would be subject to liability if the jurisdiction had adopted the theory of liability based on section 402B.

In the remainder of this chapter, we will primarily consider the use of misrepresentation theories to recover for purely economic losses. Recall that, as we saw in Chapter 10, tort law has been reluctant to impose a general rule of negligence with respect to purely economic losses—this is the so-called "economic loss" doctrine. Several reasons for this reluctance have been prominent, and these reasons were explored in Chapter 10.

Nonetheless, despite the general "economic loss rule," tort law has developed rules of liability for many areas of purely economic loss, including the body of misrepresentation law. As you consider this area of law in more detail, consider whether and to what extent the reasons for tort's traditional economic loss rule do or do not apply to misrepresentation contexts.

The Defendant's State of Mind. The examples illustrate that a misrepresentation might be the product of different states of mind and different motives. A defendant might have made the statement knowing it to be false, with or without a purpose to harm. Or a defendant might have been reckless about the truth of the statement, or negligent. Finally, a defendant might have made a statement that is false even though the speaker neither knew this nor could have known it was false, even by exercising reasonable care. These differences are reflected in the law of misrepresentation, which has developed three theories of liability: fraud, negligent misrepresentation, and innocent misrepresentation.

Reliance, Justified Reliance, Materiality, and Contributory Negligence. The examples raise the issues of reliance, materiality, justified reliance, and contributory negligence. Should it matter whether the bank in Example 1 could have easily obtained a second opinion? Should it matter whether the client of the weight loss clinic was reasonable in believing that the vitamin supplement was safe, or should it be enough to show that she did in fact believe it to be safe? Even if she can state a prima facie case, should the defendant be able to raise a contributory negligence defense against the client?

Who May Sue. The examples also raise the issue of *who* may sue for misrepresentation. The bank was not in contractual privity with the lawyer; rather, the lawyer was in a contractual, lawyer-client relationship with the farmer. Should the law of misrepresentation extend to "third parties" such as the bank? If so, should it matter whether the defendant knew about third party's likely reliance on the letter?

One additional point should be noted at the outset. Misrepresentations by one contracting party have often formed the basis of a claim by the other party for recission of the contract. If a person is merely seeking rescission of a transaction, he may be entitled to relief on the basis of negligent or even innocent misrepresentations. Indeed rescission, under these circumstances, is merely part of the general question of when a reasonable mistake can justify equitable relief. *See* H. McClintock, Equity 253–55 (1948). The following materials, however, focus on the use of misrepresentation theories as a basis for affirmative relief in tort.

2. *Fraudulent Misrepresentation*

The oldest form of misrepresentation-based tort liability is that for fraudulent misrepresentation, sometimes known as "deceit" or "intentional misrepresentation." The following gives some history about this theory.

1 T. STREET, THE FOUNDATIONS OF LEGAL LIABILITY
374–377 (1906).

Deceit consists of the fraudulent imposition of damage, and this damage commonly takes the form of pecuniary loss or risk of pecuniary loss. The idea which is at the root of liability in deceit is that of a detriment imposed by fraud. It corresponds with the conception of *dolus* in the roman law. Let us proceed to discover the process by which the common law was led to grasp this notion of liability arising from dishonesty.

One of the very oldest of common-law writs is the writ of deceit *(breve de deceptione)*.[1] Consideration of the scope of this early writ shows where legal evolution in the field of fraud began. The first form of deceit which was recognized by the common law as a ground of legal liability was that which embodied a deception of the court and a consequent perversion of the ordinary course of legal proceeding. Of such a wrong the common law could take notice because it was an interference with the administration of royal justice. The wrong was viewed as an offense against the king as well as a wrong against the individual who happened to be damaged. Hence the wrongdoer had to pay a fine to the king as well as damages to the individual. False personation in court proceedings, whereby actions were brought without authority or judgments recovered against persons ignorant

---

1. The writ of deceit was already known in the time of John. 2 Poll. & Mait. Hist. Eng.Law, 2d ed., 535, citing Select Civil Pleas, pl. III (A.D.1201).

of the pendency of a suit, was the most common grievance for which the writ of deceit was used.

Deceit was one of the first of common-law actions to feel the stimulus of the statute specially authorizing the issuance of writs *in consimili casu*[2] with writs already formed; and under the influence of that statute, the action of deceit or case in the nature of deceit began to be used for many other purposes than that of recovering damages for deceitful practices in court proceedings. Illustrations of the extended use of the action on the case in the nature of deceit are found in situations like these: If one who had been retained as legal counsel fraudulently colluded with his client's adversary; or if one who had been retained of counsel to be at court on a certain day, failed to come, whereby the cause was lost; or if a man who professed skill in a common calling like that of a smith, lamed the horse that he had undertaken to shoe; or if a farrier undertook to cure a graveled horse, but on the contrary killed him; in all these cases, it was held, an action on the case in the nature of deceit lay at common law.

Reference to the authorities * * * will show that the old writ of deceit was entirely merged in or superseded by the action on the case in the nature of deceit and that in the latter form it became the general common-law remedy for fraudulent acts of any kind which result in actual damage. The remedy was broad enough to cover such wrongs as malicious prosecution and abuse of legal process, and, indeed, much of the old law on these topics is tucked away under the heading 'Deceit' in the old books.

———

The Restatement of Torts (Second), section 525, sets out the following elements of the modern cause of action for fraudulent misrepresentation:

(1) A misrepresentation of fact, opinion, intention, or law is made.

(2) The misrepresentation is made fraudulently. "Fraudulently made" means that the one who makes the misrepresentation

    (a) knows or believes that the matter is not as he represents it to be, or

    (b) does not have the confidence in the accuracy of his representation that he states or implies, or

    (c) knows that he does not have the basis for his representation that he states or implies.

(3) The misrepresentation is made for the purpose of inducing another to act or to refrain from action in reliance upon it.

(4) The other justifiably relies on it to his or her detriment.

———

VMARK SOFTWARE, INC. v. EMC CORPORATION

Appeals Court of Massachusetts, 1994.
37 Mass.App.Ct. 610, 642 N.E.2d 587.

2. [Ed. note] See Chapter One, p. 22f, supra.

Before FINE, PORADA and LAURENCE, JJ.

LAURENCE, JUSTICE.

A common but foreseeable frustration of modern life—the failure of new computer hardware or software to work properly—produced this commercial altercation, which the parties unfortunately failed to anticipate by a contractual dispute resolution mechanism that might have avoided their time-consuming and expensive litigation. The controversy arose out of the June 1990 grant by VMark Software, Inc. (VMark), of a license to EMC Corporation (EMC) to use VMark's software product, a relational database management system called "uniVerse." * * * EMC looked upon uniVerse as a vital product for its expanding business. According to VMark's representations, UniVerse would enable EMC to replace existing computer hardware that no longer had the capacity to meet its computing needs, while allowing it to retain its valuable application software, which UniVerse would render compatible with many different types of more efficient or versatile hardware.

When uniVerse failed to function as VMark had represented and EMC had anticipated, despite at least twenty remedial efforts by VMark, EMC unilaterally declared the license agreement terminated and refused to pay the license fee. VMark's suit to recover that fee provoked a counterclaim by EMC seeking damages for VMark's failure to deliver a functional product, founded upon counts for breach of contract, breach of warranty, promissory estoppel, misrepresentation, and [statutory violations].

Following a ten-day bench trial, a judge of the Superior Court—in a fifty-five page opinion containing 144 separate findings of fact that are unchallenged by the parties—ruled against VMark on its claim for payment, against EMC on its breach of warranty, misrepresentation, and [statutory] counts, but for EMC on its breach of contract and promissory estoppel claims. The judge awarded EMC $316,901 in what he termed "reliance damages." * * * That figure essentially reflected the net cost to EMC of certain Digital Equipment Corporation (DEC) computer hardware EMC had purchased in reliance on VMark's supplying it with a software product that would be fully functional in conjunction with that hardware.

Neither party was satisfied with the judge's determinations, and both appealed. VMark challenges the judge's award of reliance damages on either of EMC's theories. VMark argues that the license agreement contained damage limitation provisions restricting EMC's damages to those attributable to VMark's negligence.... EMC's principal cross-appeal argument is that the judge's adverse rulings on its misrepresentation and [statutory] charges are inconsistent with his undisputed subsidiary findings which establish the requisite elements of those claims in EMC's favor. * * *

Our analysis persuades us that the judge properly ruled in EMC's favor but should have done so on the basis of EMC's misrepresentation and [statutory] claims. Our conclusion makes it unnecessary to expound upon VMark's arguments against the judgment entered in favor of EMC on its breach of contract and promissory estoppel counts.

Background Facts. The following narrative is based upon the judge's findings. In early 1990, EMC foresaw its imminent need for expanded computing capability. A manufacturer of add-on computer products known as "peripherals," EMC sought an improved software product for managing its financial reporting, order management, production, and inventory tracking. At that time, EMC used a Prime computer system for those needs, but that system had become "saturated," forcing EMC to investigate various alternative systems to handle its expanding business data more quickly and efficiently. EMC required a system that would support both dynamic files * * * and alternate indices, * * * standard features of EMC's original Prime system. After a preliminary exploration of alternatives, EMC became interested in the possibility of replacing its Prime system with a "DEC Ultrix" system. EMC, however, used and wanted to continue to use a business applications software called "Madic" for its accounting, inventory, manufacturing, and financial needs, which was incompatible with the DEC Ultrix system.

EMC consequently sought a product that would enable it to retain the Madic software while using it on the DEC Ultrix hardware. VMark had developed and was licensing such a product, uniVerse, which it marketed to users, like EMC, who sought to move their applications software designed for a Prime system to other, more flexible or capacious systems. One advertised feature of the uniVerse software was its supposed ability to convert existing data files that run in a Prime environment to files that run in a uniVerse environment. UniVerse also was designed to support alternate indices and dynamic files, functions required by EMC.

In the spring of 1990, EMC approached VMark as a potential licensee of uniVerse. EMC gathered information about uniVerse and its capabilities through product demonstrations, reference checks, and a thorough review of uniVerse's operating manuals. During this process, EMC told VMark that its primary concerns in using uniVerse to replace its Prime system with a DEC system were processing its business data more quickly and efficiently, being able to continue to use dynamic files and alternate indices in its database, and being able to convert to the DEC system by October, 1990, because of the limitations of its Prime system.

VMark officials assured EMC that the uniVerse product supported the use of both dynamic files and alternate indices, that the conversion from Prime to uniVerse would be straightforward and nonproblematic, and that the conversion process could be completed before the end of the summer. At one of the demonstrations, the VMark sales representative additionally assured EMC that, if uniVerse did not function as promised, VMark would be responsible for the cost of the DEC hardware. By late June, 1990, EMC, relying on VMark's several representations as to uniVerse's performance and capabilities, had decided to obtain a license for uniVerse and to purchase the DEC Ultrix computer system. EMC would not have purchased the DEC hardware had it not also acquired what it perceived to be fully functional uniVerse software.

At the time VMark personnel made their several representations regarding uniVerse, they were confident of EMC's successful application of the software but knew that there had been some prior problems with the performance of uniVerse when used with a DEC Ultrix system. They were also aware that such a combined system had thus far operated more slowly than it was designed to do; that there had been relatively little experience with uniVerse's ability to support the alternate indices function, which even the developer of uniVerse was concerned might not work as represented to EMC; that VMark had not actually attempted to use uniVerse to achieve compatibility between Madic application software and DEC hardware; and that difficulties had been encountered with the ability of uniVerse operationally to convert dynamic files to the DEC/uniVerse system. The necessary conversion process required, at the then-current stage of development, an extra, time-consuming step that both VMark's creator and its engineering vice president recognized would make it difficult to meet EMC's initially desired timetable.

None of these problems was explicitly communicated by VMark to EMC during the demonstration and negotiation period. Instead, in keeping with VMark's apparent general policy of not mentioning or minimizing negative factors regarding uniVerse's capabilities to prospective customers, VMark personnel assured EMC that there would be no serious performance or conversion problems. Nor did the manuals and technical documents supplied by VMark to EMC highlight any of these problems relating to the use of uniVerse.

Unaware of these difficulties, and encouraged to act quickly by VMark's June 26, 1990, offer to give a twenty percent discount on the license fee if EMC signed up before the end of June, EMC soon thereafter executed a license agreement for the uniVerse software. This agreement contained various provisions limiting VMark's warranties and damage liability, which VMark asserts preclude any recovery by EMC.   * * *

Despite VMark's assurance that the conversion and transfer of EMC's data stored in its Prime system to the DEC system via uniVerse would occur uneventfully, difficulties in using uniVerse to load and convert EMC's data were encountered almost immediately. When EMC performed test functions in uniVerse on the few files that were successfully converted, the results were not uniformly complete or accurate. The DEC/uniVerse system turned out to operate much more slowly than the Prime system. None of VMark's repeated efforts to solve the various performance problems over the summer and fall of 1990 succeeded in overcoming them. By December, 1990, EMC concluded that uniVerse was too unreliable to permit EMC to conduct business activities on it. By that time VMark, after failing to correct the defects in the software despite delivering over twenty different but equally unsatisfactory versions of uniVerse to EMC, also conceded that uniVerse was not yet a fully functional product for EMC's purposes.

VMark told EMC at that point that its future efforts had to be directed to correcting fundamental problems with the software and that it would be unable to address EMC's specific performance issues until sometime thereafter. Immediately following that concession by VMark of uniVerse's inability to perform as represented, EMC halted the uniVerse conversion effort and purchased a larger Prime system to address its computing needs. EMC communicated this action to VMark and demanded reimbursement for the cost of the DEC hardware and for the time EMC employees had spent on the failed conversion effort. VMark refused EMC's claim, demanded payment under the license agreement, and the instant litigation ensued as described earlier.[7]

The parties and the judge devoted most of their trial and appellate energies to the question of the extent to which the license agreement, particularly its liability limitation provisions, restricts EMC's ability to recover damages for VMark's undisputed breach of its limited contractual warranty obligations to deliver a functional product conforming to specifications and to repair any defects so that the product would work as promised. Discussion of those contractual and quasi-contractual issues is not necessary in view of our determination that the judge's damage award in favor of EMC was correct because of VMark's actionable misrepresentations regarding uniVerse. The damage award did not, however, go far enough, and EMC is entitled to additional recovery.

1. [Intentional] Misrepresentation. Although the judge entered judgment for VMark on count IV (intentional misrepresentation) of EMC's counterclaim, [the facts found by the trial judge] demonstrate that VMark did make material misstatements during its negotiations with EMC, which relied on them to its detriment.[9] * * *

The judge found, on undisputed evidence (much of it from VMark's own witnesses) that prior to execution of the license agreement: (a) VMark made glowing representations (at sales presentations, product demonstrations, and in product manuals) regarding the capabilities of the uniVerse software, particularly its supposed ability to make EMC's Madic applications software compatible with the DEC Ultrix hardware system, to convert EMC's data from Prime to a DEC system easily in a few weeks, and to support computer functions (including dynamic files and alternate indices) essential to EMC's business operations; (b) EMC considered those representations to be material to its decision to license uniVerse, purchase the DEC computer, and undertake the substantial conversion process; (c) VMark knew that EMC considered those representations material and that EMC needed to replace its Prime computer system with a DEC system, while retaining its Madic software, within a relatively short period of time; (d) the uniVerse software did not at the time work as represented by VMark; (e) VMark knew (or should have known) when it made the unqualified representations to EMC regarding uniVerse's capabilities that the software still had defects and shortcomings which created doubt that it would function as successfully as had been represented, particularly with respect to (i) uniVerse's performance on DEC Ultrix systems, (ii) its ability to convert dynamic files, and (iii) its ability to support the alternate indices

7. "Experienced lawyers often caution clients not to sue customers who refuse to pay an invoice because of a reasonable complaint about the product. This case may be cited as an illustration of the soundness of that advice." Alcan Aluminum Corp. v. Carlton Aluminum of New England, Inc., 35 Mass.App.Ct. 161, 162 n. 4, 617 N.E.2d 1005 (1993).

9. The familiar elements of an action for misrepresentation are that the defendant made a false representation of a material fact for the purpose of inducing the plaintiff to rely upon it, and that the plaintiff did rely upon the representation as true, to his damage. The party making the representation need not know that the statement is false if the fact represented is susceptible of actual knowledge.

function; (f) VMark in good faith expected uniVerse eventually, when fine-tuned, to function as represented; (g) VMark did not disclose uniVerse's known problems to EMC so as to modify its unqualifiedly positive statements about uniVerse; (h) VMark feared that if EMC were told about uniVerse's current performance problems, EMC might not license the software; (i) as further inducement to EMC's entering into the license transaction and attempted corroboration of VMark's positive representations regarding uniVerse's capabilities, VMark promised that it would buy back from EMC the DEC hardware if uniVerse did not perform as represented; and (j) EMC reasonably relied on VMark's representations, promises, assurances, and product specifications regarding uniVerse, which were material influences on its decision to license the uniVerse software and purchase the DEC computer equipment. * * *

These specific findings by the judge satisfy EMC's burden in sustaining its claim of actionable [intentional] misrepresentation by Vmark.[11] EMC was accordingly entitled to all damages it had suffered as a proximate result of VMark's misleading representations, * * * including all "out of pocket" expenses incurred in connection with the transaction, so as to restore the status quo ante, as if the transaction had never occurred. * * * Under this standard, the judge correctly awarded EMC $316,901, representing the remaining value of the DEC computer equipment which it would not have purchased but for VMark's misleading representations regarding uniVerse, and which it was unable to sell in mitigation of its damages.

The judge should have applied the same measure of recovery with respect to the value of the lost time of EMC's employees in the failed conversion process. He found that EMC had reasonably committed these employee resources in July, 1990, in reliance upon VMark's assurances as to the ease of implementation of conversion and had discontinued that commitment only in December, 1990, when uniVerse's inability to perform as represented was acknowledged by VMark. Just as the DEC computer hardware had no value to EMC in the circumstances, the time of those EMC employees dedicated to the futile attempt to convert to the DEC system was wasted and had no value to EMC because of uniVerse's ongoing inability to function as promised. Damages for misrepresentation should have included the costs of the hours fruitlessly spent by EMC employees trying to make the defective computer system work. * * * EMC's evidence that it incurred costs of $65,208 for employees diverted to the unsuccessful conversion effort and that the time spent by such employees produced no benefit to EMC was undisputed and should have been accepted as the basis for the additional award.

* * *

[The court rules that Vmark's conduct was not so egregious as to justify statutory penalty damages for the statutory claims made by EMC.]

---

11. VMark's reliance on the damage limitation and integration clauses of the agreement to bar EMC's recovery for misrepresentation is misplaced. The Massachusetts authority just cited, particularly Bates, establishes that a party may not escape liability for misrepresentation by resort to such provisions.

VMark's earnest efforts to make good on its contractual obligation by overcoming its product's recognized problems and making it perform to expectations do not, of course, create a defense to the tort claim. Establishing liability for misrepresentation does not require a showing that the defendant even knew that the statements made were false, let alone that the defendant actually intended to deceive the plaintiff. See Zimmerman v. Kent, 31 Mass.App.Ct. at 77, 81–82, 575 N.E.2d 70; Restatement (Second) of Torts § 526 comment (e); Prosser & Keeton, The Law of Torts § 107 (5th *623 ed. 1984).

* * *

Accordingly, the judgment dated September 28, 1992, is to be modified by striking the second and third paragraphs and inserting the following:

"That judgment enter for the defendant EMC Corporation on counts IV and VI of its counterclaim against VMark Software, Inc., in the total amount of $382,109 plus interest."

* * *

As modified, the judgment is affirmed * * *.

Notes

1. *Falsity, Fraud, Purpose, and Intent.* Under the Restatement formulation, *supra*, p. 983 the second element requires proof of a particular state of mind with regard to the statement's truth or falsity. This is often known as the scienter requirement. The third element requires proof that the defendant had the purpose to induce reliance; some courts require either "purpose or intent" to induce reliance. Notice that the plaintiff does not need to prove that the defendant intended or had a purpose *to cause harm* to the plaintiff. The scienter requirement can be established by proof that the defendant knew the statement was false. But, as the Restatement reflects, something less than knowledge of falsity can suffice. For example, the defendant states that something is true but knows that he has no present basis for making that statement, although he hopes that the statement might be true or that subsequent events will make it true. This may in fact be the most accurate description of what happened in the *EMC* case.

Footnote 9 of the Court's opinion sets out the elements under Massachusetts law of the cause of action for fraudulent misrepresentation. The court's formulation requires purpose to induce reliance, but as stated in this opinion the Massachusetts formulation is cryptic about the scienter requirement. Massachusetts, however, like all other states, does require scienter.

Given the evidence as recounted in the court's opinion, and using the Restatement formulation, what arguments could EMC make to establish each element of the cause of action for fraudulent misrepresentation? Could Vmark make any plausible arguments that one or more of the elements were not established?

2. *Breach of Contract Versus Fraudulent Misrepresentation.* As in the main case, fraudulent misrepresentation claims often are joined with claims for breach of contract. It is important to appreciate several features of the relationship between the causes of action.

First, and most obviously, the contract claim might exist without a misrepresentation claim, and vice versa. The misrepresentation cause of action does not require a contractual relationship, and breaches of contract can occur without misrepresentation.

Second, different remedies are available for the two causes of action. The issue of remedies is taken up in the next note. Third, despite the analytical distinctions, in particular cases there may be factual overlap between the two causes of action, and courts have devoted considerable attention to deciding whether, in a given case, the plaintiff has proven only breach of contract or also a misrepresentation case. An illustrative case is Smehlik v. Athletes and Artists, Inc., 861 F.Supp. 1162 (W.D.N.Y.1994), in which a professional hockey player sued the agency that had represented him in connection with efforts to obtain a contract. According to the plaintiff, the agency had represented (1) that the agency could obtain a contract for him with the Sabres for the 1991/92 season; (2) that it could "make a deal right away;" (3) that it would arrange for him to participate in the Sabres' 1991 training camp; and (4) that it would make all necessary arrangements to enable him to attend the Sabres' 1991 training camp, which required obtaining a release from his Czech hockey club.

> A mere "promissory statement [ ] as to what will be done in the future" may give rise only to a breach of contract claim. [citation omitted] However, a false representation of a present fact may give rise to a separable claim for fraudulent inducement, and generally speaking, if a promise is "made with a preconceived and undisclosed intention of not performing it, it constitutes a misrepresentation of material existing fact" upon which an action for fraudulent inducement may be predicated. * * * Thus, it is clear that a cause of action for fraudulent inducement may be sustained on the basis of an allegation that the defendant made a promise to undertake some action separate and apart from his obligations under the express terms of the contract, if it is also alleged that he made the promise with no intention of making good on that commitment.
>
> What is much less clear is whether a cause of action for fraud may properly be sustained on the basis of an allegation that the defendant made a promise to perform under the express terms of the contract while intending not to abide by its terms. The New York courts are split on this issue. * * * The Second Department has recently stated, for example, that where a fraud claim "is premised upon an alleged breach of contractual duties and the supporting allegations do not concern representations which are collateral or extraneous to the terms of the parties' agreement, a cause of action sounding in fraud does not lie." McKernin v. Fanny Farmer Candy Shops, Inc., 176 A.D.2d 233, 574 N.Y.S.2d 58, 59 (2d Dept.1991)(citing Mastropieri v. Solmar Construction Co., Inc., 159 A.D.2d 698, 553 N.Y.S.2d 187 (2d Dept.1990)) * * * On the other hand, the Third Department has recently held that "a party who is fraudulently induced to enter a contract may join a cause of action for fraud with one for breach of the same contract" where the misrepresentations alleged are "misstatements of material fact or promises [to perform under the contract] made with a present, albeit undisclosed, intent not to perform them." Shlang v. Bear's Estates Development of Smallwood, N.Y., Inc., 194 A.D.2d 914, 599 N.Y.S.2d 141, 142–143 (3d Dept.1993) * * *

Id. at 1171–72.

One reason for the requirement that the fraudulent promise relate to action separate from the actions promised in the contract is the concern that ordinary breach of contract claims will be converted into claims for fraudulent misrepresentation. The resulting litigation, it is feared, would be more lengthy, expensive, and uncertain in outcome (because it requires the factfinder to look into the defendant's state of mind and not just to the more objective circumstances of whether a breach has occurred). Note, however, that even in the jurisdictions which do not impose the "separate from the contract" requirement the plaintiff must prove that the defendant made the promise with a present intent not to perform. In practice, would this requirement allay concerns about excessive use of the misrepresentation theory in breach of contract contexts?

Aside from the practical concerns just noted, is there any theoretical reason why we should exempt, from the tort cause of action, a fraudulent promise about future performance as distinct from a fraudulent statement about present facts?

3. *Remedies.* Because fraudulent misrepresentation is a tort, tort's general damage principle is usually thought to apply: restoring the plaintiff, to the degree money can do so, to the position plaintiff occupied before the wrongful act. Applying this general principle to misrepresentation scenarios has raised a number of interesting damages issues.

The first is whether the "benefit of the bargain" or the "out-of-pocket" measure should be used to compensate for the plaintiff's pecuniary harm. Both these terms appear in the law of contracts. (Both measures receive extensive discussion in 2 D. Dobbs, Law of Remedies (546–56 2d ed.)). The benefit of the bargain approach compensates for the difference in value between what the plaintiff actually received and what the plaintiff would have received if the defendant's representations had been true. The out-of-pocket measure compensates for the difference between what the plaintiff gave up (paid) and the value of what plaintiff actually received.

To take a simple example, suppose a piece of furniture is represented to be an antique; the buyer pays $3000 for it. If the furniture were really an antique, it would be worth $6000. In fact, however, the piece is not an antique and is worth only $2000. The out-of-pocket measure of damages is $1000; the benefit of the bargain measure is $4000. Another example that arises not infrequently is life insurance. Suppose a person has paid premiums totalling $20,000 on a life insurance policy that is represented to cover a spouse and that pays $1 million on death. The spouse dies, but the policy contains an exclusion whose terms were misrepresented when the policy was purchased. The out-of-pocket measure is $20,000, but the benefit of the bargain would yield the $1 million.

Most courts allow a plaintiff who succeeds on a fraudulent misrepresentation claim to recover under either measure. (A good number of courts, however, only allow the out-of-pocket measure if the claim is for negligent, rather than fraudulent, misrepresentation.) *See* D. Dobbs, *supra*, at 553–54. Some courts generally use only the out-of-pocket measure, but will allow the benefit of the bargain measure if the out-of-pocket measure seems particularly inappropriate. *See* B.F. Goodrich v. Mesabi Tire Co., 430 N.W.2d 180 (Minn. 1988).

A second damages issue relates to "consequential" pecuniary damages; that is, damages in addition to those measured by the out-of-pocket or benefit of bargain measure and sustained, allegedly, as a consequence of the defendant's misrepresentation. For instance, suppose that the spouse in the life insurance example is unable to pay her mortgage and loses her home as a result of the insurer's nonpayment (and original misrepresentation). Or suppose that the defendant misrepresents the quality of a product, and the plaintiff receives not just the lower benefit of the bargain but also sustains lost profits.

In general, tort law places fewer restrictions on the recovery of consequential damages than does contract law. Thus, courts in misrepresentation cases generally allow consequential damages, in addition to those damages measured by the out-of-pocket or benefit of bargain standards. In the *EMC* case, for instance, the judge allowed EMC to recover for the value of employee time spent in trying to make the defective system work.

A third damages issue is whether mental anguish should be allowed. The majority of courts and the Restatement take the position that mental anguish is not recoverable for misrepresentation, even for fraudulent misrepresentation. One recent case explains the divergent views on the issue.

> Some courts take the approach that the purpose of fraud or deceit cases is to put the plaintiff in the position that he would have been in had he not been defrauded. For example, in Cornell v. Wunschel, 408 N.W.2d 369, 382 (Iowa 1987), in considering damages on a claim for fraudulent misrepresentation, the court noted that emotional distress damages "are not ordinarily contemplated in a business transaction." Since deceit is an economic tort and resembles more a contract claim than a tort claim, the court held that emotional distress damages were not recoverable in fraud actions. Other courts, by contrast, have stressed that fraud is a tort cause of action and that even though it may arise out of a contractual dispute, intentional or reckless conduct justifies a broadened scope of damages. * * *

> We hold that, upon proof of intentional misrepresentation, a plaintiff may recover "emotional damages that are the natural and proximate result" of the defendant's conduct. * * * While the underlying dispute here is contractual in nature, defendants are alleged to have committed an intentional tort when they misrepresented the payoff amount of the note. Whether or not the tort was committed in a contractual context is not dispositive; mental suffering is a "natural and proximate" consequence of intentional fraud and should be a compensable injury. * * *

Osbourne v. Capital City Mortgage Corp., 667 A.2d 1321, 1328 (D.C.App.1995).

Consider again the arguments explored in Chapter 10 for and against recovery of mental anguish damages in personal injury torts. Which of these arguments applies to the question of mental anguish recoveries when the plaintiff has suffered pecuniary loss from an intentional misrepresentation?

4. *Justifiable Reliance.* Most courts require that the plaintiff have relied in fact on the representation, and that the reliance be justifiable. According to the Restatement, justifiable reliance requires that the matter misrepresented be a "material" one; materiality is defined as follows:

(2) The matter is material if

> (a) a reasonable man would attach importance to its existence or nonexistence in determining his choice of action in the transaction in question; or

(b) the maker of the representation knows or has reason to know that its recipient regards or is likely to regard the matter as important in determining his choice of action, although a reasonable man would not so regard it.

Restatement (Second) Torts § 538 (1965). The option set out in (a) employs the objective "reasonable man" standard, but option (b) offers a way to bypass the objective standard. For example, if A wishes to induce B to buy stock in a corporation, knows that B believes heavily in astrology, and tells B that the horoscope favors the purchase, then B can establish justifiable reliance even if B's behavior does not comport with that of the reasonable person. For this and other examples and explanations, *see* Restatement (Second) Torts § 538, comment f and illustrations.

Why retain an objective standard for all occasions when the maker of the representation does not know or have reason to know of the recipient's unusual beliefs or qualities?

5. *Opinion*

The area of opinion has posed special challenges for the law of misrepresentation. An early and much-cited discussion of the subject appeared in Judge Learned Hand's opinion in Vulcan Metals Co. v. Simmons Manufacturing Co., 248 Fed. 853 (C.C.N.Y. 1918). Simmons Manufacturing had allegedly made a number of representations about the qualities of certain tools, dies, and equipment sold by Simmons for the manufacture of vacuum cleaners. The representations included statements that the machines were perfect in even small details, that water power was the most economical and efficient way of operating a vacuum cleaner, and that it was simple, long-lived, easily operated, and effective, etc.

[The case raises], therefore, the question of law how far general 'puffing' or 'dealers' talk' can be the basis of an action for deceit.

The conceded exception in such cases has generally rested upon the distinction between 'opinion' and 'fact'; but that distinction has not escaped the criticism it deserves. An opinion is a fact, and it may be a very relevant fact; the expression of an opinion is the assertion of a belief, and any rule which condones the expression of a consciously false opinion condones a consciously false statement of fact. When the parties are so situated that the buyer may reasonably rely upon the expression of the seller's opinion, it is no excuse to give a false one. Bigler v. Flickinger, 55 Pa. 279. And so it makes much difference whether the parties stand 'on an equality.' For example, we should treat very differently the expressed opinion of a chemist to a layman about the properties of a composition from the same opinion between chemist and chemist, when the buyer had full opportunity to examine. The reason of the rule lies, we think, in this: There are some kinds of talk which no sensible man takes seriously, and if he does he suffers from his credulity. If we were all scrupulously honest, it would not be so; but, as it is, neither party usually believes what the seller says about his own opinions, and each knows it. Such statements, like the claims of campaign managers before election, are rather designed to allay the suspicion which would attend their absence than to be understood as having any relation to objective truth. It is quite true that they induce a compliant temper in the buyer, but it is by a much more subtle process than through the acceptance of his claims for his wares.

* * *

In the case at bar, since the buyer was allowed full opportunity to examine the cleaner and to test it out, we put the parties upon an equality. It seems to us that general statements as to what the cleaner would do, even though consciously false, were not of a kind to be taken literally by the buyer. As between manufacturer and customer, it may not be so; but this was the case of taking over a business, after ample chance to investigate. Such a buyer, who the seller rightly expects will undertake an independent and adequate inquiry into the actual merits of what he gets, has no right to treat as material in his determination statements like these. The standard of honesty permitted by the rule may not be the best; but, as Holmes, J., says in Deming v. Darling, 148 Mass. 504, 20 N.E. 107, 2 L.R.A. 743, the chance that the higgling preparatory to a bargain may be afterwards translated into assurances of quality may perhaps be a set-off to the actual wrong allowed by the rule as it stands.

Id. at 856–58. Was Judge Hand suggesting that an average individual consumer would not be "in equality" with the commercial seller and thus would have a cause of action for representations of the sort that Simmons made? What does the following rationale, set out in the Restatement, suggest should be the outcome if Simmons made such representations to an average individual consumer?

The law assumes that the ordinary man has a reasonable competence to form his own opinion as to the advisability of entering into those transactions that form part of the ordinary routine of life. The fact that one of the two parties to a bargain is less astute than the other does not justify him in relying upon the judgment of the other. This is true even though the transaction in question is one in which the one party knows that the other is somewhat more conversant with the value and quality of the things about which they are bargaining. Thus the purchaser of an ordinary commodity is not justified in relying upon the vendor's opinion of its quality or worth. For example, one who is purchasing a horse from a dealer is not justified in relying upon the dealer's opinion, although the latter has a greater experience in judging the effect of the factors which determine its value.

Restatement (Second) of Torts § 542, comment d (1965).

Doctrinally, therefore, courts treat opinions differently than representations of fact, although the precise doctrinal contours diverge somewhat among the jurisdictions. Some courts announce that "pure opinion" cannot as a matter of law serve as a representation for purposes of the law of misrepresentation, unless certain circumstances exist. *See* Transport Ins. Co. v. Faircloth, 898 S.W.2d 269 (Tex.1995). Others courts, and the Restatement, focus not on whether an opinion can constitute a misrepresentation, but on the circumstances when "justifiable reliance" on an opinion can be established. Although these two approaches appear to concentrate on different "elements" of the cause of action, the approaches are fundamentally the same because each allows the recipient to recover if certain circumstances are present. These circumstances include: (1) the maker purports to have special knowledge that the recipient does not have; (2) the maker is in a fiduciary relation with the recipient; or (3) the maker has some special reason to expect that the recipient will rely on the opinion. *See* Restatement (Second) of Torts § 542 (1965).

6. *Statements of Law.* Statements about law also have posed challenges for the law of misrepresentation. Obviously, the litigants in such a context might be a lawyer and the client. If so, the client may have, in addition to the misrepresentation cause of action, a claim for breach of contract, breach of fiduciary duty, or professional negligence. The client might be able to recover under all theories, or perhaps only one or two.

The older view was that misrepresentations of law could not form the basis of a misrepresentation action. Consider two common types of representations of law: a prediction or assertion about a legal outcome ("We will win the case"), and a conclusion about an issue of law ("The procedures that the city followed comply with all applicable state law"; "Exclusion A of the insurance policy excludes coverage in this case"). Under the older view, such representations could not form the basis of a tort cause of action because the recipient should know that no lawyer or layperson can be certain of a legal outcome or issue, and thus the recipient cannot justifiably rely on such statements. *See* Prosser & Keeton on Torts § 109 (5th ed.1984). Does this rationale convince you that none of the statements just noted should form the basis of a misrepresentation cause of action?

Most jurisdictions now recognize that misrepresentations of law in some circumstances can form the basis of a tort cause of action. Common circumstances include when the opinion contains a material misstatement of fact, when the maker of the opinion purports to have special knowledge of the matter, or when the maker stands in a fiduciary relationship with the recipient. Even when these circumstances are present, however, the question of justifiable reliance will usually be for the factfinder. *See generally* Restatement (Second) of Torts § 545 (1965); *see* Nagashima v. Busck, 541 So.2d 783, 783–84 (Fla.App.1989)(discussing traditional approach in this area, exceptions to it, and modern approach).

Consider again the two types of statements mentioned at the beginning of this note: predictions of a legal outcome and conclusions about a legal issue. Would a recipient be justified in relying on any or all of the statements given as examples?

7. *Concealment.* Suppose the defendant has not made a representation, but instead has remained silent about or has concealed some material fact. If a defendant actively conceals a fact—for instance, a defendant puts temporary caulk over a serious crack—then usually courts will treat this conduct as equivalent to a representation. The more difficult cases are those that involve mere nondisclosure. Many such cases arise from real estate transactions. A number of jurisdictions have passed legislation relating to what must be disclosed in real estate transactions. But the common law of misrepresentation continues to grapple with the issue. In Strawn v. Canuso, 140 N.J. 43, 657 A.2d 420 (N.J.1995), the court addressed the misrepresentation claims filed by purchasers of new homes that had been constructed near a hazardous waste dump site.

> Only gradually has the law of real property assimilated other principles of law. * * * For years, "[c]ourts continued to cling to the notion that a seller had no duty whatsoever to disclose anything to the buyer."

* * * That attitude endured, though the purchase of a home "is almost always the most important transaction [one] will ever undertake."

* * *

Other jurisdictions have limited the doctrine of caveat emptor. In California, when the seller knows of facts materially affecting the value or desirability of property and the seller also knows that such facts are not known to, or within the reach of the diligent attention and observation of the buyer, the seller is subject to a duty to disclose those facts to the buyer.

* * *

Under some formulations of the duty the seller must also know or suspect that the buyer is acting in ignorance. Different jurisdictions limit relief in other ways. Wisconsin, for example, only imposes disclosure duties on professional sellers. * * *

* * *

We need not debate the outer limits of the duty to disclose. Some courts have gone well beyond the confines of this case. In Reed v. King, 145 Cal.App.3d 261, 193 Cal.Rptr. 130 (1983), the court imposed a duty on the seller to disclose that a property had been the scene of a mass murder several years earlier. And in New York's so-called "poltergeist case," the purchaser argued that the presence of such spirits in his new home was a material element of the sale that should have been disclosed. The court agreed and imposed a duty on the seller to disclose that the property had been haunted. * * *

* * *

In the absence of such legislation or other regulatory requirements affecting real estate brokers, the question is whether our common-law precedent would require disclosure of off-site conditions that materially affect the value of property.

* * *

As noted, the principal factors shaping the duty to disclose have been the difference in bargaining power between the professional seller of residential real estate and the purchaser of such housing, * * * and the difference in access to information between the seller and the buyer * * *. Those principles guide our decision in this case.

The first factor causes us to limit our holding to professional sellers of residential housing (persons engaged in the business of building or developing residential housing) and the brokers representing them. Neither the reseller of residential real estate nor the seller of commercial property has that same advantage in the bargaining process. Regarding the second factor, professional sellers of residential housing and their brokers enjoy markedly superior access to information. Hence, we believe that it is reasonable to extend to such professionals a similar duty to disclose off-site conditions that materially affect the value or desirability of the property.

* * *

* * * [A] purchaser may establish a common-law claim by showing that the seller's or the broker's nondisclosure of material facts induced the purchaser to buy.

* * *

* * * In the case of on-site conditions, courts have imposed affirmative obligations on sellers to disclose information materially affecting the value of property. * * * There is no logical reason why a certain class of sellers and brokers should not disclose off-site matters that materially affect the value of property.

* * *

The duty that we recognize is not unlimited. We do not hold that sellers and brokers have a duty to investigate or disclose transient social conditions in the community that arguably affect the value of property. In the absence of a purchaser communicating specific needs, builders and brokers should not be held to decide whether the changing nature of a neighborhood, the presence of a group home, or the existence of a school in decline are facts material to the transaction. Rather, we root in the land the duty to disclose off-site conditions that are material to the transaction. * * * That duty is consistent with the development of our law and supported by statutory policy.

Id. at 53–63, 657 A.2d at 425–30.

Should a individual who is selling his own home, without assistance from real estate agents, be subject to liability for failing to disclose that the home is infested with termites or that the home has asbestos in it? Should individual or professional sellers of real estate be obligated to disclose factors that might taint the value of the property to the average buyer—for instance, that the property was the site of a mass murder?

Outside the real estate context, there is no general duty to disclose, unless special circumstances are present. These can include the presence of a fiduciary relationship or some other legal duty. *See* Restatement (Second) of Torts § 551 (1965).

8. *Third-Party Recipients*

The defendant might make the misrepresentation directly to the recipient, who then acts in reliance on it. This is the typical pattern in fraudulent misrepresentation cases. But a third party also might act in reliance on the misrepresentation, even though the defendant did not make the representation directly to him. Most courts allow such a third party to establish fraudulent misrepresentation, so long as the maker "intends or has reason to expect" that the substance of the misrepresentation will be communicated to the third party and will influence the conduct of the third party. Restatement (Second) of Torts § 533 (1965). The question of misrepresentation-based liability to third parties has arisen most often, and has posed the most difficult questions, in the context of negligent rather than intentional misrepresentation. Thus, we will take up the third-party question in more detail in the next subsection.

3. *Negligent Misrepresentation*

a. *Elements and Development*

Section 552 of the Restatement (Second) of Torts outlines the cause of action for negligent misrepresentation:

One who, in the course of his business, profession or employment, or in any other transaction in which he has a pecuniary interest, supplies false information for the guidance of others in their business transactions, is subject to liability for pecuniary loss caused to them by their justifiable reliance upon the information, if he fails to exercise reasonable care or competence in obtaining or communicating the information.

The cause of action for negligent misrepresentation includes many of the same elements as the cause of action for fraudulent misrepresentation: there must be a misrepresentation, there must be justifiable reliance, and the plaintiff must have suffered harm as a result of the reliance. The primary difference between the two causes of action relates to the defendant's state of mind. Negligent misrepresentation, unlike fraudulent misrepresentation, requires only that the plaintiff show the defendant failed to exercise reasonable care with regard to whether or not the representation was true.

As the common law of misrepresentation developed, it was initially doubtful whether a cause of action for negligent misrepresentation would be recognized at all. In Derry v. Peek, 14 App. Cas. 337 (House of Lords 1889), Lord Herschell's opinion explained:

> First, in order to sustain an action of deceit, there must be proof of fraud, and nothing short of that will suffice. Secondly, fraud is proved when it is shewn that a false representation has been made (1) knowingly, or (2) without belief in its truth, or (3) recklessly, careless whether it be true or false.

> * * *

> In my opinion making a false statement through want of care falls far short of, and is a very different thing from, fraud, and the same may be said of a false representation honestly believed though on insufficient grounds.

Derry v. Peek was immediately interpreted by the English legal profession to stand for the proposition that, absent privity of contract or some special relationship such as attorney/client or trustee/beneficiary, no action would lie for negligent misrepresentation, 34 Solicitors J. 140 (1889); and the Court of Appeal so held, shortly thereafter, in Le Lievre v. Gould, [1893] 1 Q.B. 491 (C.A.).

Derry v. Peek received a more guarded reaction in the United States. A number of United States cases allowed a cause of action for negligent misrepresentation in certain circumstances, such as cases involving certificates of title abstractors. *See, e.g.,* Anderson v. Spriestersbach, 69 Wash. 393, 125 P. 166 (1912).

In 1890, Parliament responded to *Derry v. Peek* by enacting the Directors Liability Act of 1890 (53 & 54 Vict., c. 64), now incorporated in the Companies Act of 1948 (11 & 12 Geo. 6, c. 38, § 43). Under this statute persons who have suffered damages as a result of acting upon incorrect statements negligently inserted in a prospectus issued by the promoters or directors of a company are given an action for damages.

In Hedley Byrne & Co. v. Heller & Partners Ltd., [1964] A.C. 465, (1963) [1963] 3 W.L.R. 101, 2 All E.R. 575, the House of Lords declared that all *Derry v. Peek* had held was that the allegation of outright fraud made in that case had not been proved rather than that an action for negligent misrepresentation would not lie on the facts of that case. Their Lordships further declared that there was no warrant for misunderstanding the *ratio decidendi* of *Derry v. Peek* after the speeches of Viscount Haldane and Lord Shaw in Nocton v. Lord Ashburton, [1914] A.C. 932. Whether this is so or not, the Court of Appeal's decision in *Candler v. Crane, Christmas, supra,* note 1, indicates that not many eyes were opened in 1914. Indeed, Lord Devlin, who was one of the law lords who decided *Hedley Byrne,* had failed to show this acumen in a book published as recently as 1961. P. Devlin, Law and Morals 15 (1961). Even Denning, L.J., (now Lord Denning), who dissented in *Candler v. Crane, Christmas,* was unaware of the true state of affairs. He thought that *Derry v. Peek* had ruled on the question of negligent misrepresentation but that it had only decided that on the specific facts present in *Derry* an action would not lie. [1951] 2 K.B. at 164, 177. That is, that *Derry* did not involve representations made by persons with special skills.

b. *Extent of Liability to Third–parties*

ROBERT R. BILY v. ARTHUR YOUNG & COMPANY.

Supreme Court of California,
In Bank.
1992.
3 Cal.4th 370, 11 Cal.Rptr.2d 51, 834 P.2d 745.
As Modified on Denial of Rehearing Nov. 12, 1992.

LUCAS, CHIEF JUSTICE.

We granted review to consider whether and to what extent an accountant's duty of care in the preparation of an independent audit of a client's financial statements extends to persons other than the client.

Since Chief Judge Cardozo's seminal opinion in Ultramares Corp. v. Touche (1931) 255 N.Y. 170, 174 N.E. 441 (Ultramares), the issue before us has been frequently considered and debated by courts and commentators. Different schools of thought have emerged. At the center of the controversy are difficult questions concerning the role of the accounting profession in performing audits, the conceivably limitless scope of an accountant's liability to nonclients who may come to read and rely on audit reports, and the effect of tort liability rules on the availability, cost, and reliability of those reports.

* * * We conclude that an auditor * * * owes no general duty of care regarding the conduct of an audit to persons other than the client. An auditor may, however, be held liable for negligent misrepresentations in an audit report to those persons who act in reliance upon those misrepresentations in a transaction which the auditor intended to influence, in accordance with the rule of section 552 of the Restatement Second of Torts, as adopted and discussed below. Finally, an auditor may also be held liable to

reasonably foreseeable third persons for intentional fraud in the preparation and dissemination of an audit report.

I.
Summary of Facts and Proceedings Below

* * *

[Osborne Computer Corporation was the first company to sell a personal computer, and by fall 1982 was one of the fastest growing enterprises in the history of American business. The plaintiffs were investors who had purchased "warrants" from Osborne before Osborne undertook a public offering of its shares, which was planned for early 1983. The warrants entitled the purchasers to buy large blocks of shares once the company went public. The company sold these warrants in order to obtain the funds to secure bridge financing to complete the process of going public. Arthur Young & Co., an accounting firm, performed the audit of Osborne's balance sheets for 1981 and 1982 and issued an unqualified or "clean" statement about these financial statements. All but one of the investors claimed that their investments in the warrants were made in reliance on Arthur Young's unqualified audit opinion. Osborne's new line of computers, however, contained bugs and, soon after IBM came out with its own personal computers in 1983, Osborne filed for bankruptcy.

The investors sued Arthur Young on grounds of professional negligence, negligent misrepresentation, and intentional misrepresentation. The jury found for the plaintiff on the professional negligence count, but found for defendant on the two theories of misrepresentation. The jury awarded $4,300,000 in damages; the trial court entered judgment for plaintiffs; and the court of appeals affirmed the judgment.]

II.
The Audit Function in Public Accounting

Although certified public accountants (CPA's) perform a variety of services for their clients, their primary function, which is the one that most frequently generates lawsuits against them by third persons, is financial auditing. (Hagen, Certified Public Accountant's Liability for Malpractice: Effect of Compliance with GAAP and GAAS (1987) 13 J.Contemp. Law 65, 66 [hereafter Hagen]; Siliciano, Negligent Accounting and the Limits of Instrumental Tort Reform (1988) 86 Mich.L.Rev.1929, 1931 [hereafter Siliciano].) "An audit is a verification of the financial statements of an entity through an examination of the underlying accounting records and supporting evidence." (Hagen, supra, 13 J.Contemp. Law at p. 66.) "In an audit engagement, an accountant reviews financial statements prepared by a client and issues an opinion stating whether such statements fairly represent the financial status of the audited entity." (Siliciano, supra, 86 Mich.L.Rev. at p. 1931.)

In a typical audit, a CPA firm may verify the existence of tangible assets, observe business activities, and confirm account balances and mathematical computations. It might also examine sample transactions or records to ascertain the accuracy of the client company's financial and accounting systems * * *.

For practical reasons of time and cost, an audit rarely, if ever, examines every accounting transaction in the records of a business. The planning and execution of an audit therefore require a high degree of professional skill and judgment. Initially, the CPA firm plans the audit by surveying the client's business operations and accounting systems and making preliminary decisions as to the scope of the audit and what methods and procedures will be used. The firm then evaluates the internal financial control systems of the client and performs compliance tests to determine whether they are functioning properly. Transactions and data are sampled, vouched for, and traced. Throughout the audit process, results are examined and procedures are reevaluated and modified to reflect discoveries made by the auditors. * * *

The end product of an audit is the audit report or opinion. The report is generally expressed in a letter addressed to the client. The body of the report refers to the specific client-prepared financial statements which are attached. In the case of the so-called "unqualified report" (of which Arthur Young's report on the company's 1982 financial statements is an example), two paragraphs are relatively standard.

In a scope paragraph, the CPA firm asserts that it has examined the accompanying financial statements in accordance with GAAS. GAAS are promulgated by the American Institute of Certified Public Accountants (AICPA), a national professional organization of CPA's, whose membership is open to persons holding certified public accountant certificates issued by state boards of accountancy. * * *

* * *

The generality of these statements is somewhat mitigated by the Statements on Auditing Standards (SAS), which are periodic interpretations of the standards issued by the Auditing Standards Board of the AICPA. * * *

In an opinion paragraph, the audit report generally states the CPA firm's opinion that the audited financial statements, taken as a whole, are in conformity with GAAP and present fairly in all material respects the financial position, results of operations, and changes in financial position of the client in the relevant periods. * * *

* * *

* * * [A]udits of financial statements and the resulting audit reports are very frequently (if not almost universally) used by businesses to establish the financial credibility of their enterprises in the perceptions of outside persons, e.g., existing and prospective investors, financial institutions, and others who extend credit to an enterprise or make risk-oriented decisions based on its economic viability. The unqualified audit report of a CPA firm, particularly one of the "Big Six," is often an admission ticket to venture capital markets—a necessary condition precedent to attracting the kind and level of outside funds essential to the client's financial growth and survival. As one commentator summarizes: "In the first instance, this unqualified opinion serves as an assurance to the client that its own perception of its financial health is valid and that its accounting systems are reliable. The audit, however, frequently plays a second major role: it

assists the client in convincing third parties that it is safe to extend credit or invest in the client." (Siliciano, supra, 86 Mich.L.Rev. at p. 1932.)

* * *

III.

APPROACHES TO THE PROBLEM OF AUDITOR LIABILITY TO THIRD PERSONS

The complex nature of the audit function and its economic implications has resulted in different approaches to the question whether CPA auditors should be subjected to liability to third parties who read and rely on audit reports. Although three schools of thought are commonly recognized, there are some variations within each school and recent case law suggests a possible trend toward merger of two of the three approaches.

A substantial number of jurisdictions follow the lead of Chief Judge Cardozo's 1931 opinion for the New York Court of Appeals in Ultramares, supra, 174 N.E. 441, by denying recovery to third parties for auditor negligence in the absence of a third party relationship to the auditor that is "akin to privity." (See part III(A), post.) In contrast, a handful of jurisdictions, spurred by law review commentary, have recently allowed recovery based on auditor negligence to third parties whose reliance on the audit report was "foreseeable." (See part III(B), post.)

Most jurisdictions, supported by the weight of commentary and the modern English common law decisions cited by the parties, have steered a middle course based in varying degrees on Restatement Second of Torts section 552, which generally imposes liability on suppliers of commercial information to third persons who are intended beneficiaries of the information. (See part III(C), post.) * * *

In this section we will review and briefly analyze each of the recognized approaches to the problem before us.

A. *Privity of Relationship*

In Ultramares, * * * the New York Court of Appeals, speaking through Chief Judge Cardozo * * * found the auditor owed no duty to the third party creditor for an "erroneous opinion." In an often quoted passage, it observed: "If liability for negligence exists, a thoughtless slip or blunder, the failure to detect a theft or forgery beneath the cover of deceptive entries, may expose accountants to a liability in an indeterminate amount for an indeterminate time to an indeterminate class. The hazards of a business conducted on these terms are so extreme as to enkindle doubt whether a flaw may not exist in the implication of a duty that exposes to these consequences." (Ultramares, supra, 174 N.E. at p. 444.)

Although acknowledging the demise of privity of contract as a limitation on tort liability in the context of personal injury and property damage, the court distinguished between liability arising from a "physical force" and "the circulation of a thought or the release of the explosive power resident in words." (Ultramares, supra, 174 N.E. at p. 445.) * * *

* * *

[I]n Credit Alliance v. Arthur Andersen & Co. (1985) 65 N.Y.2d 536, 493 N.Y.S.2d 435, 483 N.E.2d 110, * * * the New York court promulgated the following rule for determining auditor liability to third parties for negligence: "Before accountants may be held liable in negligence to non-contractual parties who rely to their detriment on inaccurate financial reports, certain prerequisites must be satisfied: (1) the accountant must have been aware that the financial reports were to be used for a particular purpose or purposes; (2) in the furtherance of which a known party or parties was intended to rely; and (3) there must have been some conduct on the part of the accountants linking them to that party or parties, which evinces the accountants' understanding of that party or parties' reliance." * * *

* * *

The evolution of the New York rule illustrates a primary difficulty of articulating a standard of auditor liability to third parties: As one moves from privity of contract to privity of relationship, a wide variety of possible circumstances and relationships emerges. From preengagement communications with its client, an auditor may acquire full knowledge of third party recipients of the audit report and a specific investment or credit transaction that constitutes the "end and aim" of the audit. As a consequence, the auditor is placed on notice of a specific risk of liability that accompanies the audit engagement. Yet, under the Credit Alliance test, the auditor appears to have no liability in this situation in the absence of further, distinct conduct "linking" the auditor to the third party in a manner that "evinces [auditor] understanding" of third party reliance. (Credit Alliance v. Arthur Andersen & Co., supra, 493 N.Y.S.2d at p. 443, 483 N.E.2d at p. 118.)

The New York court offers no rationale for the distinct "linking" element of its rule nor does it specify what conduct is required to satisfy this element, although direct communications between auditor and third party were deemed sufficient on the facts. One might question whether "linking" conduct should be necessary if, as in the example given in the previous paragraph, the auditor knows his engagement is for the express purpose of benefiting an identifiable class of third parties. * * *

[T]he "linking conduct" element appears to require not only that the existence of the third person be known to the auditor, but that the auditor either directly convey the audit report to the third person or otherwise act in some manner specifically calculated to induce reliance on the report. * * * In this regard, a mere "unsolicited phone call" by the third party to the auditor is insufficient. The auditor must be aware of a "particular purpose" for the audit engagement and must act to further that purpose. * * * This additional showing is not required by the Restatement test, which is discussed in part III(C), post.

From the cases cited by the parties, it appears at least nine states purport to follow privity or near privity rules restricting the liability of auditors to parties with whom they have a contractual or similar relationship. * * * The more recent of the cited cases generally follow the New York rule as reformulated in Credit Alliance.

B. Foreseeability

Arguing that accountants should be subject to liability to third persons on the same basis as other tortfeasors, Justice Howard Wiener advocated rejection of the rule of Ultramares in a 1983 law review article. (Wiener, Common Law Liability of the Certified Public Accountant for Negligent Misrepresentation (1983) 20 San Diego L.Rev. 233 [hereafter Wiener].) In its place, he proposed a rule based on foreseeability of injury to third persons. Criticizing what he called the "anachronistic protection" given to accountants by the traditional rules limiting third person liability, he concluded: "Accountant liability based on foreseeable injury would serve the dual functions of compensation for injury and deterrence of negligent conduct. Moreover, it is a just and rational judicial policy that the same criteria govern the imposition of negligence liability, regardless of the context in which it arises. The accountant, the investor, and the general public will in the long run benefit when the liability of the certified public accountant for negligent misrepresentation is measured by the foreseeability standard." (Id. at p. 260.) Under the rule proposed by Justice Wiener, "[f]oreseeability of the risk would be a question of fact for the jury to be disturbed on appeal only where there is insufficient evidence to support the finding." (Id. at pp. 256–257.)

Following in part Justice Wiener's approach, the New Jersey Supreme Court upheld a claim for negligent misrepresentation asserted by stock purchasers against an auditor who had rendered an unqualified audit report approving fraudulently prepared financial statements. (Rosenblum v. Adler (1983) 93 N.J. 324, 461 A.2d 138.) The court found no reason to distinguish accountants from other suppliers of products or services to the public and no reason to deny to third party users of financial statements recovery for economic loss resulting from negligent misrepresentation. * * * From its review of the purpose and history of the audit function, it concluded: "The auditor's function has expanded from that of a watchdog for management to an independent evaluator of the adequacy and fairness of financial statements issued by management to stockholders, creditors, and others." [ ] Noting the apparent ability of accounting firms to obtain insurance against third party claims under the federal securities laws, the court posited the same or similar protection would be available for common law negligent misrepresentation claims. * * *

From a public policy standpoint, the court emphasized the potential deterrent effect of a liability-imposing rule on the conduct and cost of audits: "The imposition of a duty to foreseeable users may cause accounting firms to engage in more thorough reviews. This might entail setting up stricter standards and applying closer supervision, which should tend to reduce the number of instances in which liability would ensue. Much of the additional cost incurred either because of more thorough auditing review or increased insurance premiums would be borne by the business entity and its stockholders or its customers." (Rosenblum v. Adler, supra, 461 A.2d at p. 152.)

* * *

Two other state high courts—those of Wisconsin and Mississippi—have endorsed foreseeability rules. * * *

In the nearly 10 years since it was formally proposed, the foreseeability approach has not attracted a substantial following. And at least four state supreme courts have explicitly rejected the foreseeability approach in favor of the Restatement's "intended beneficiary" approach since the New Jersey court's decision in Rosenblum. * * *

* * *

C. The Restatement: Intent to Benefit Third Persons

Section 552 of the Restatement Second of Torts covers "Information Negligently Supplied for the Guidance of Others." It states a general principle that one who negligently supplies false information "for the guidance of others in their business transactions" is liable for economic loss suffered by the recipients in justifiable reliance on the information. (Id., subd. (1).) But the liability created by the general principle is expressly limited to loss suffered: "(a) [B]y the person or one of a limited group of persons for whose benefit and guidance he intends to supply the information or knows that the recipient intends to supply it; and (b) through reliance upon it in a transaction that he intends the information to influence or knows that the recipient so intends or in a substantially similar transaction." (Id., subd. (2).) To paraphrase, a supplier of information is liable for negligence to a third party only if he or she intends to supply the information for the benefit of one or more third parties in a specific transaction or type of transaction identified to the supplier.

Comment (h) to subdivision (2) of section 552, Restatement Second of Torts, observes that the liability of a negligent supplier of information is appropriately more narrowly restricted than that of an intentionally fraudulent supplier. It also notes that a commercial supplier of information has a legitimate concern as to the nature and scope of the client's transactions that may expand the supplier's exposure liability. As the comment states: "In many situations the identity of the person for whose guidance the information is supplied is of no moment to the person who supplies it, although the number and character of the persons to be reached and influenced, and the nature and extent of the transaction for which guidance is furnished may be vitally important. This is true because the risk of liability to which the supplier subjects himself by undertaking to give the information, while it may not be affected by the identity of the person for whose guidance the information is given, is vitally affected by the number and character of the persons, and particularly the nature and the extent of the proposed transaction." (Ibid., italics added.)

To offer a simple illustration of comment (h) to subdivision (2) of section 552, Restatement Second of Torts, an auditor engaged to perform an audit and render a report to a third person whom the auditor knows is considering a $10 million investment in the client's business is on notice of a specific potential liability. It may then act to encounter, limit or avoid the risk. In contrast, an auditor who is simply asked for a generic audit and report to the client has no comparable notice.

The authors of the Restatement Second of Torts offer several variations on the problem before us as illustrations of section 552. For example, the auditor may be held liable to a third party lender if the auditor is informed by the client that the audit will be used to obtain a $50,000 loan, even if the specific lender remains unnamed or the client names one lender and then borrows from another. (Com. (h), illus. 6, 7.) However, there is no liability where the auditor agrees to conduct the audit with the express understanding the report will be transmitted only to a specified bank and it is then transmitted to other lenders. (Com. (h), illus. 5.) Similarly, there is no liability when the client's transaction (as represented to the auditor) changes so as to increase materially the audit risk, e.g., a third person originally considers selling goods to the client on credit and later buys a controlling interest in the client's stock, both in reliance on the auditor's report. (Com. (j) and illus. 14.)

Under the Restatement rule, an auditor retained to conduct an annual audit and to furnish an opinion for no particular purpose generally undertakes no duty to third parties. Such an auditor is not informed "of any intended use of the financial statements; but * * * knows that the financial statements, accompanied by an auditor's opinion, are customarily used in a wide variety of financial transactions by the [client] corporation and that they may be relied upon by lenders, investors, shareholders, creditors, purchasers and the like, in numerous possible kinds of transactions. [The client corporation] uses the financial statements and accompanying auditor's opinion to obtain a loan from [a particular] bank. Because of [the auditor's] negligence, he issues an unqualifiedly favorable opinion upon a balance sheet that materially misstates the financial position of [the corporation] and through reliance upon it [the bank] suffers pecuniary loss." (Rest.2d Torts, § 552, com. (h), illus. 10.) Consistent with the text of section 552, the authors conclude: "[The auditor] is not liable to [the bank]." (Ibid.)

Although the parties debate precisely how many states follow the Restatement rule, a review of the cases reveals the rule has somewhat more support than the privity of relationship rule and much more support than the foreseeability rule. * * *

In attempting to ascertain the presence of an intent to benefit third parties from the facts of particular audit engagements and communications with auditors, the Restatement rule inevitably results in some degree of uncertainty. Dean William L. Prosser, the Reporter for the Restatement, reflected on the difficulty of formulating a comprehensive rule in this area: "The problem is to find language which will eliminate liability to the very large class of persons whom almost any negligently given information may foreseeably reach and influence, and limit the liability, not to a particular plaintiff defined in advance, but to the comparatively small group whom the defendant expects and intends to influence. Neither the Reporter, nor, it is believed, the Advisers nor the Council, is entirely satisfied with the language of Subsection (2); and if anyone can do better, it will be most welcome." (Rest.2d Torts, Tent.Draft No. 11 (Apr. 15, 1965) § 552, p. 56.)

* * *

IV.
ANALYSIS OF AUDITOR'S LIABILITY TO THIRD PERSONS FOR AUDIT OPINIONS
A. Negligence

* * *

* * * [W]e decline to permit all merely foreseeable third party users of audit reports to sue the auditor on a theory of professional negligence. Our holding is premised on three central concerns: (1) Given the secondary "watchdog" role of the auditor, the complexity of the professional opinions rendered in audit reports, and the difficult and potentially tenuous causal relationships between audit reports and economic losses from investment and credit decisions, the auditor exposed to negligence claims from all foreseeable third parties faces potential liability far out of proportion to its fault; (2) the generally more sophisticated class of plaintiffs in auditor liability cases (e.g., business lenders and investors) permits the effective use of contract rather than tort liability to control and adjust the relevant risks through "private ordering"; and (3) the asserted advantages of more accurate auditing and more efficient loss spreading relied upon by those who advocate a pure foreseeability approach are unlikely to occur; indeed, dislocations of resources, including increased expense and decreased availability of auditing services in some sectors of the economy, are more probable consequences of expanded liability.

* * *

1. Liability Out of Proportion to Fault

An auditor is a watchdog, not a bloodhound. * * * As a matter of commercial reality, audits are performed in a client-controlled environment. The client typically prepares its own financial statements; it has direct control over and assumes primary responsibility for their contents. * * * The client engages the auditor, pays for the audit, and communicates with audit personnel throughout the engagement. Because the auditor cannot in the time available become an expert in the client's business and record-keeping systems, the client necessarily furnishes the information base for the audit.

The client, of course, has interests in the audit that may not be consonant with those of the public. "Management seeks to maximize the stockholders' and creditors' confidence in the company, within the bounds of [GAAP and GAAS]; whereas, the public demands a sober and impartial evaluation of fiscal performance." * * *

Client control also predominates in the dissemination of the audit report. Once the report reaches the client, the extent of its distribution and the communications that accompany it are within the exclusive province of client management. Thus, regardless of the efforts of the auditor, the client retains effective primary control of the financial reporting process.

Moreover, an audit report is not a simple statement of verifiable fact that * * * can be easily checked against uniform standards of indisputable accuracy. Rather, an audit report is a professional opinion based on numerous and complex factors. As discussed in part II above, the report is based on the auditor's interpretation and application of hundreds of professional standards, many of which are broadly phrased and readily subject to different constructions. Although ultimately expressed in shorthand form, the report is the final product of a complex process involving discretion and judgment on the part of the auditor at every stage. Using different initial assumptions and approaches, different sampling techniques, and the wis-

dom of 20–20 hindsight, few CPA audits would be immune from criticism.
* * *

Although the auditor's role in the financial reporting process is second-ary and the subject of complex professional judgment, the liability it faces in a negligence suit by a third party is primary and personal and can be massive. The client, its promoters, and its managers have generally left the scene, headed in most cases for government-supervised liquidation or the bankruptcy court. The auditor has now assumed center stage as the remaining solvent defendant and is faced with a claim for all sums of money ever loaned to or invested in the client. Yet the auditor may never have been aware of the existence, let alone the nature or scope, of the third party transaction that resulted in the claim.

The character of the damages claimed from the auditor—economic loss resulting from investment and credit decisions—introduces further uncer-tainties into the negligence suit against the auditor. An award of damages for pure economic loss suffered by third parties raises the spectre of vast numbers of suits and limitless financial exposure. * * *

Investment and credit decisions are by their nature complex and multifaceted. Although an audit report might play a role in such decisions, reasonable and prudent investors and lenders will dig far deeper in their "due diligence" investigations than the surface level of an auditor's opin-ion. And, particularly in financially large transactions, the ultimate deci-sion to lend or invest is often based on numerous business factors that have little to do with the audit report. The auditing CPA has no expertise in or control over the products or services of its clients or their markets; it does not choose the client's executives or make its business decisions; yet, when clients fail financially, the CPA auditor is a prime target in litigation claiming investor and creditor economic losses because it is the only available (and solvent) entity that had any direct contact with the client's business affairs. * * *

* * *

2. The Prospect of Private Ordering

Courts advocating unlimited auditor liability to all foreseeably injured third parties often analogize the auditor's opinion to a consumer product, arguing that the demise of privity as a barrier to recovery for negligence in product manufacture implies its irrelevance in the area of auditor liability as well. * * * Plaintiffs advance similar arguments. The analogy lacks persuasive force for two reasons. Initially, as noted above, the maker of a consumer product has complete control over the design and manufacture of its product; in contrast, the auditor merely expresses an opinion about its client's financial statements—the client is primarily responsible for the content of those statements in the form they reach the third party.

Moreover, the general character of the class of third parties is also different. Investors, creditors, and others who read and rely on audit reports and financial statements are not the equivalent of ordinary con-sumers. Like plaintiffs here, they often possess considerable sophistication in analyzing financial information and are aware from training and experi-ence of the limits of an audit report "product" that is, at bottom, simply a broadly phrased professional opinion based on a necessarily confined examination.

In contrast to the "presumptively powerless consumer" in product liability cases, the third party in an audit negligence case has other options—he or she can "privately order" the risk of inaccurate financial reporting by contractual arrangements with the client. * * * For example, a third party might expend its own resources to verify the client's financial statements or selected portions of them that were particularly material to its transaction with the client. Or it might commission its own audit or investigation, thus establishing privity between itself and an auditor or investigator to whom it could look for protection. In addition, it might bargain with the client for special security or improved terms in a credit or investment transaction. Finally, the third party could seek to bring itself within the Glanzer exception to Ultramares by insisting that an audit be conducted on its behalf or establishing direct communications with the auditor with respect to its transaction with the client. * * *

As a matter of economic and social policy, third parties should be encouraged to rely on their own prudence, diligence, and contracting power, as well as other informational tools. This kind of self-reliance promotes sound investment and credit practices and discourages the careless use of monetary resources. If, instead, third parties are simply permitted to recover from the auditor for mistakes in the client's financial statements, the auditor becomes, in effect, an insurer of not only the financial statements, but of bad loans and investments in general.[13]

3. *The Effect on Auditors of Negligence Liability to Third Persons*

Courts and commentators advocating auditor negligence liability to third parties also predict that such liability might deter auditor mistakes, promote more careful audits, and result in a more efficient spreading of the risk of inaccurate financial statements. For example, the New Jersey Supreme Court reasoned: "The imposition of a duty to foreseeable users may cause accounting firms to engage in more thorough reviews. This might entail setting up stricter standards and applying closer supervision, which would tend to reduce the number of instances in which liability would ensue. Much of the additional cost incurred because of more thorough auditing review or increased insurance premiums would be borne by the business entity and its stockholders or its customers.... Accountants will also be encouraged to exercise greater care leading to greater diligence in audits." (Rosenblum v. Adler, supra, 461 A.2d at p. 152.)

We are not directed to any empirical data supporting these prognostications. From our review of the cases and commentary, we doubt that a

---

13. The dissent argues that unsophisticated third parties who rely on audit reports are left unprotected by our decision. In our view, the argument itself poses a dilemma. If a third party possesses sufficient financial sophistication to understand and appreciate the contents of audit reports (which often include complex financial data and accounting language as well as technical terms like "Generally Accepted Accounting Principles" and "Generally Accepted Auditing Stan-

dards"), he or she should also be aware of their limitations and of the alternative ways of privately ordering the relevant risks. If, on the other hand, a third party lacks the threshold knowledge to understand the audit report and its terms, he or she has no reasonable basis for reliance. In either event, there is no sound basis to extend potentially unlimited liability based on any alleged lack of sophistication.

significant and desirable improvement in audit care would result from an expanded rule of liability. Indeed, deleterious economic effects appear at least as likely to occur.

In view of the inherent dependence of the auditor on the client and the labor-intensive nature of auditing, we doubt whether audits can be done in ways that would yield significantly greater accuracy without disadvantages. (Siliciano, supra, 86 Mich.L.Rev. at pp. 1963–1968.) Auditors may rationally respond to increased liability by simply reducing audit services in fledgling industries where the business failure rate is high, reasoning that they will inevitably be singled out and sued when their client goes into bankruptcy regardless of the care or detail of their audits. As a legal economist described the problem: "The deterrent effect of liability rules is the difference between the probability of incurring liability when performance meets the required standard and the probability of incurring liability when performance is below the required standard. Thus, the stronger the probability that liability will be incurred when performance is adequate, the weaker is the deterrent effect of liability rules. Why offer a higher quality product if you will be sued regardless whenever there is a precipitous decline in stock prices?" (Fischel, The Regulation of Accounting: Some Economic Issues (1987), 52 Brooklyn L.Rev. 1051, 1055.) Consistent with this reasoning, the economic result of unlimited negligence liability could just as easily be an increase in the cost and decrease in the availability of audits and audit reports with no compensating improvement in overall audit quality. * * *

In light of the relationships between auditor, client, and third party, and the relative sophistication of third parties who lend and invest based on audit reports, it might also be doubted whether auditors are the most efficient absorbers of the losses from inaccuracies in financial information. Investors and creditors can limit the impact of losses by diversifying investments and loan portfolios. They effectively constitute a "broad social base upon which the costs of accounting errors can be spread." (Siliciano, supra, 86 Mich.L.Rev. at p. 1973.) In the audit liability context, no reason appears to favor the alleged tortfeasor over the alleged victim as an effective distributor of loss. * * *

* * *

For the reasons stated above, we hold that an auditor's liability for general negligence in the conduct of an audit of its client financial statements is confined to the client, i.e., the person who contracts for or engages the audit services. Other persons may not recover on a pure negligence theory. * * *

* * *

There is, however, a further narrow class of persons who, although not clients, may reasonably come to receive and rely on an audit report and whose existence constitutes a risk of audit reporting that may fairly be imposed on the auditor. Such persons are specifically intended beneficiaries of the audit report who are known to the auditor and for whose benefit it renders the audit report. While such persons may not recover on a general negligence theory, we hold they may * * * recover on a theory of negligent misrepresentation [as set out in Restatement (Second) of Torts section 552].

* * *

C. *Intentional Misrepresentation*

As Chief Judge Cardozo recognized in Ultramares, supra, 174 N.E. 441, the liability of auditors to third parties presents different policy considerations when intentional fraud is involved. The secondary position of the auditor in the presentation of financial statements, the moral force of the argument against unlimited liability for mere errors or oversights and the uncertain connection between investment and credit losses and the auditor's report pale as policy factors when intentional misconduct is in issue. By joining with its client in an intentional deceit, the auditor thrusts itself into a primary and nefarious role in the transaction.

* * *

We are directed to no authority that would immunize auditors from liability to third parties for intentional misrepresentation; the general rule appears to be to the contrary. (Rest.2d Torts, § 531 ["One who makes a fraudulent misrepresentation is subject to liability to the persons or class of persons whom he intends or has reason to expect to act or to refrain from action in reliance upon the misrepresentation, for pecuniary loss suffered by them through their justifiable reliance in the type of transaction in which he intends or has reason to expect their conduct to be influenced."].)

[The court directs judgment against one set of investors. The court reverses and remands the claim of the certain plaintiffs to the Court of Appeals with instructions to decide whether the trial court improperly refused their requested fraud-related instructions.]

PANELLI, ARABIAN, BAXTER and GEORGE, JJ., concur.

KENNARD, JUSTICE, dissenting.

I dissent.

* * *

The effect of these holdings is to give negligent accountants broad immunity for their professional malpractice in rendering audit opinions.

In defining the scope of duty in negligence cases, courts must balance competing concerns. The burden imposed by the duty should bear some reasonable relation to the moral fault of the negligent party and should not be so onerous that those held liable are unwilling or financially unable to engage in socially beneficial activity. On the other hand, tort liability is itself socially beneficial to the extent that it provides both an incentive for due care, thereby preventing avoidable injuries, and compensation for those who have been injured. Courts should not define a legal duty so narrowly as to preclude these positive effects of tort liability, as the majority has done in this case.

Lenders and investors use the reports prepared by independent auditors so widely, and rely on them so heavily, that it is difficult to conceive how our complex modern capital markets would function if they were no longer available or no longer able to inspire confidence. In weighing the competing policy considerations that factor into a decision defining the scope of the accountant's duty in this context, a court must seek to fashion a rule that, without making the provision of auditing services prohibitively risky, ensures that the quality of those critically important services will be maintained at a high level. Such a rule is necessary so that lenders and investors will continue to have confidence in audited financial reports and so that the usual and foreseeable users of audit reports will receive fair compensation when they have been victimized by the occasional failure of an accountant to meet prevailing professional norms.

In my view, the law that has existed in this state until today strikes the proper balance. Until today, California law had recognized that accountants owe a duty of care to all persons who reasonably and foresee-ably rely on accountants' professional opinions. * * * Extending the duty to all such users provides a necessary incentive for due care in the conduct of audits and in the preparation of audit reports, and ensures fair compen-sation to innocent victims of auditors' negligence. Unlike the majority, I am not persuaded that the duty so defined has excessively burdened the accounting profession, or that it has caused or is likely to cause a signifi-cant reduction in the availability of auditing services. Even if these unfortunate consequences could be demonstrated, the remedy should come in the form of carefully crafted legislation, not wholesale curtailment of legal duty.

* * *

The majority asserts that holding negligent accountants liable to foreseeable users of audit opinions will subject accountants to "a claim for all sums of money ever loaned to or invested in the client", and result in "vast numbers of suits and limitless financial exposure" * * *. The majority uses such assertions to justify its claim that liability to foreseeable users of audit opinions would be out of proportion to fault.

The majority's characterizations of the scope of the liability that until now has existed in this state are gross exaggerations, yet typical of the hyperbole that seems to infect any debate of accountants' negligence liability to third parties. Such liability is indeterminate (like virtually all other forms of tort liability), but it is not limitless. Because liability has extended only to those business transactions conducted in reliance on the audited financial statements, and because audited financial statements become obsolete within a few years at most, the accountant's liability exposure has been finite and reasonably predictable in duration. Liability continues only so long as the audited financial statements reasonably influence business decisions. The amount of the potential liability is also measurable. Because it depends on the client's investment and borrowing potential, the scope of liability is necessarily proportional to the size and growth rate of the audited business.

* * *

Customer demand is not sufficient to ensure the quality of independent audits. What clients of auditing services want above all is not a careful audit but an unqualified opinion to satisfy investors, lenders, and others concerned with the clients' financial health. Indeed, defendant itself acknowledges that a client "may, for reasons of its own, actively seek to publish less than accurate financial information." Accountants are strongly motivated to satisfy their clients because it is they who pay the accountants' fees and provide future business. The accountant is thus caught between client pressure to produce an unqualified opinion and the moral and ethical obligation to maintain high standards of care and thoroughness. It is vital that accountants resolve this conflict in favor of careful auditing. The threat of liability to third parties reinforces the accountant's independence from the client, thereby helping to prevent loyalty to the client from consciously or unconsciously interfering with the accountant's professional judgment.

* * *

[T]here is no competent evidence before this court establishing that liability insurance is unavailable or prohibitively expensive for accountants who perform audits. Finally, even if such evidence were to be presented, the proper means of addressing the problem would be carefully crafted legislation such as I have previously discussed.

* * *

Mosk, J., concurs.

Notes

1. *Lawyers and the Third–Party Issue.* "One of the major trends in attorney liability over recent years has been the increase in malpractice and related suits brought against attorneys by non-clients. * * * Attorneys, once secure from non-client malpractice claims by the long-standing requirement of proof of an attorney-client relationship, suddenly find themselves being sued by unlikely plaintiffs." Timothy L. Hall, *Legal Malpractice in Mississippi: Suits By Non–Clients*, 64 Miss. L. J. 1 (1994). The question of attorney liability to nonclients has proved no less vexing than that of accountant liability. As in the accounting context, negligence claims against lawyers in theory could take one or both of two forms: professional negligence, and negligent misrepresentation. A client who receives bad advice from a lawyer may be able to pursue both theories. In fact, however, most clients rely primarily on the professional negligence theory. *See* 1 R. Mallen & J. Smith, Legal Malpractice 510 (4th ed. 1996). The question of liability to nonclients can likewise arise whether the complaint alleges professional negligence, negligent misrepresentation, or both. In considering the question, several examples should be useful.

Example A. Attorney prepares a will for a client who wants to bequeath half the estate to his spouse and half to his best friend. The will is not executed properly, and so when the client dies the estate is distributed according to the laws of intestacy. The friend thus receives nothing, and sues the lawyer on a theory of professional negligence.

Example B. Attorney for a defendant in a personal injury claim offers the plaintiff (who is not yet represented by counsel) $20,000 to settle the case, telling the plaintiff that "most cases of this sort don't settle for as much as this." The plaintiff accepts the offer, and then learns that the settlement value of the case was considerably more, given clear liability and high damages. She sues the attorney for negligent and intentional misrepresentation.

Example C. An attorney prepares an opinion letter for client, declaring that certain real property has no easements and is not burdened by any lien. The client shows the letter to prospective purchasers, one of whom relies on it and buys the land, only to discover that it does have several easements that diminish its value to him. He sues the attorney for negligent misrepresentation and for professional negligence.

Example D. A woman hires a lawyer to represent her in a personal injury claim arising from an injury she sustained in an accident. Only the woman, and not her husband, signs the contract with the lawyer. The lawyer never advises the client or her husband that the husband might have a claim for loss of consortium. The statute of limitations expires on the husband's potential claim for loss of consortium.

How do the policy concerns discussed by both opinions in *Bily* apply to the context of attorney liability to nonclients? Does the attorney liability context raise concerns different from those discussed in *Bily*? For instance, lawyers owe an undivided duty of loyalty and duties of confidentiality to their clients. Do these affect the analysis?

Which of the approaches outlined in *Bily* would you consider most desirable as a general rule for attorney liability to third parties? Does any one approach seem workable or defensible with respect to all four examples given above? If you believe that there are occasions when no attorney liability to third-parties should be recognized as a matter of law, can you articulate a "bright line" definition of those occasions?

The law in this area continues to evolve. Some courts have applied the New York "near privity" test, and a few have used a general foreseeability test. *See* R. Mallen & J. Smith, *supra*, §§ 7.10–.14. The outcome is now fairly predictable in a few fact patterns. First, in almost all jurisdictions, beneficiaries of wills are allowed to sue the attorney who did not prepare the will properly. (Sometimes the courts allow recovery only along contract lines, on the theory of third-party beneficiary; others allow the claim to be grounded in negligence.) Second, the ambit of attorney liability to third parties does not generally extend to adversaries. *See* Onita Pacific Corp. v. Trustees of Bronson, 315 Or. 149, 843 P.2d 890 (1992); United Bank of Kuwait v. Enventure Energy Enhanced Oil, 755 F.Supp. 1195 (S.D.N.Y.1989).

2. *Contributory Negligence.* Contributory negligence is not a defense—either as an absolute bar or in a comparative way—as to intentional misrepresentation claims. Some jurisdictions, however, have allowed a contributory negligence defense (now a comparative defense in most jurisdictions) to claims of negligent misrepresentation. Courts and commentators continue to disagree about whether and when such a defense should be recognized when the claim concerns the tort liability of an accountant or attorney. *See, e.g.*, Greenstein, Logan & Co. v. Burgess Marketing, Inc., 744 S.W.2d 170 (Tex.App.—Waco 1987, writ denied)(stating that the defense should be available only if the client's negligence caused the accountant's failure to perform the contract).

In considering the question, it is useful to appreciate that the contributory negligence argument might arise from several different categories of fact patterns. First, a plaintiff's negligence might have contributed to the alleged error in the audit in the first instance. For instance, suppose the client keeps sloppy records and that the accountant alleges that this sloppiness contributed to the error in the audit. Should this form of "pre-error" negligence by the client be allowed to form the basis of a comparative negligence defense?

Second, the plaintiff's alleged negligence might be in relying on the results of the audit or the professional advice. For instance, in a case brought by investors such as in *Bily*, the accounting firm might argue that the plaintiffs had or could reasonably have obtained independent information that would have indicated problems with the finances of the audited company. These same allegations, of course, would be relevant to a different aspect of the case: whether or not the plaintiff can prove "justifiable reliance." Still, a defendant who loses on the "no justifiable reliance" point still might try the comparative negligence argument and seek a comparative reduction in the damages. Does it seem likely that a defendant could ever persuade a factfinder that the plaintiff "justifiably relied" and yet was "unreasonable" in relying? In any event, courts have not been sympathetic to comparative negligence arguments that fit this fact pattern.

Third, the plaintiff's negligence might increase the size of the losses caused by the audit. This would be akin to the failure to mitigate (although some jurisdictions now treat the failure to mitigate as a species of contributory negligence). Courts have been willing to allow such conduct to form the basis of a comparative defense.

3. *Statutory Remedies for Financial Misrepresentations.* In the United States, in recent years, a number of statutes have, either expressly or by judicial construction, provided remedies for misrepresentations made in the course of certain kinds of transactions. Among the principal such statutory schemes is the one that, as a result of judicial construction, arises under § 10(b) of the Securities Exchange Act of 1934 (15 U.S.C. § 77j(b)),[3] and SEC Rule 10b–5 issued under the authority of that statutory provision. Disagreeing with a number of lower courts, the Supreme Court ruled that an action for damages based upon Rule 10b–5 cannot be maintained on a showing merely of negligence. Some kind of scienter is necessary, perhaps even as culpable as "an intent to deceive, manipulate, or defraud." Ernst & Ernst v. Hochfelder, 425 U.S. 185, 96 S.Ct. 1375, 47 L.Ed.2d 668 (1976). In a subsequent case, Basic, Inc., v. Levinson, 485 U.S. 224, 108 S.Ct. 978, 99 L.Ed.2d 194 (1988), the Court reaffirmed that the standard of materiality in actions brought under Rule 10b–5, was whether there was a substantial likelihood that a reasonable investor would consider the matter important in deciding what course of conduct to pursue. *See* TSC Industries, Inc. v. Northway, Inc., 426 U.S. 438, 96 S.Ct. 2126, 48 L.Ed.2d 757 (1976). The *Basic, Inc.* case involved the possible liability of a corporation for falsely denying that any preliminary discussions concerning a merger were taking place. The major problem facing the plaintiffs, who sold their shares for a lower price than they would have received if they had continued to hold the shares until a merger was eventually agreed upon, was to show that they had relied on the company's misrepresentations. The Court, by a 5–2 majority, adopted the so-called "fraud on the market theory"—namely, that an investor who buys or sells stock at the market price does so in reliance upon the "integrity of that price. Because most publicly available information is reflected in market price, an investor's reliance on any public material misrepresentations, therefore, may be presumed

---

3. Section 10 of the 1934 Act specifies the information required in a prospectus and au-   thorizes the SEC to issue rules relating thereto.

for purposes of a Rule 10b–5 action." 485 U.S. at 247, 108 S.Ct. at 992, 99 L.Ed.2d at 218. The defendant could rebut the presumption by showing that the plaintiff would have sold his stock for other reasons regardless of the misrepresented facts or that the market-makers were aware of the falsity of the statement, so that the stock was, in point of fact, not artificially underpriced.

Under some other statutory schemes, however, liability will lie for negligent misrepresentation and even, occasionally, for innocent misrepresentation. For example, under the Securities Act of 1933 (15 U.S.C. § 77a *et seq.*), issuers can be held liable for material innocent misrepresentations contained in registration statements; other persons, such as accountants, can be held liable for any material misrepresentations they might make if they are unable to show an absence of negligence on their part. (15 U.S.C. § 77k). Such liability can also extend to the failure to state facts that are reasonably necessary to prevent the statements that have been made from being misleading. This is a subject that is pursued further in a course on securities regulation.

In a fairly recent English case, Caparo Industries PLC v. Dickman, [1989] 1 Q.B. 653, 2 W.L.R. 316, 1 All E.R. 798 (C.A.1988), the Court of Appeal held that the auditors of a public company who had negligently conducted their audit owed a duty of care to the plaintiffs who were already shareholders in the company and who, on the basis of the defendants' audit, made a successful takeover bid for the company, but declared that no such duty would be owed to other investors who may have purchased shares on the strength of the auditors' report. The House of Lords, however, reversed; no such duty was owed to existing shareholders who purchased additional shares. [1990] 2A. C. 605, 1 All E.R. 568, 2 W.L.R. 358. In an earlier New Zealand case, however, Scott Group Ltd. v. McFarlane, [1978] 1 N.Z.L.R. 553, it was held that such a duty extended to potential investors as well as existing shareholders.

These new developments in the field of negligent misrepresentation have generated a substantial body of secondary literature. *See, e.g.,* J. Siliciano, *Negligent Accounting and the Limits of Instrumental Tort Reform,* 86 Mich. L.Rev. 1929 (1988); J. Bagby and J. Runhka, *The Controversy over Third–Party Rights: Toward More Predictable Parameters of Auditor Liability,* 22 Georgia L.Rev. 149 (1987); D. Causey, Jr., *Accountants' Liability in an Indeterminant Amount for an Indeterminant Time to an Indeterminant Class: An Analysis of* Touche Ross & Co. v. Commercial Union Ins. Co., 57 Miss.L.J. 379 (1987); R. Gormley, *The Foreseen, the Foreseeable, and Beyond—Accountants' Liability to Nonclients,* 14 Seton Hall L.Rev. 528 (1984). As can be gathered from the titles of some of these articles, much of the scholarly criticism has been critical of the more expansive extensions of accountants' liability.

B. TORTIOUS INTERFERENCE WITH CONTRACT AND PROSPECTIVE CONTRACTUAL RELATIONS

The tort causes of action for intentional interference with contract and intentional interference with prospective contractual relations are only several strands in a much larger and quite complex fabric regulating the protection of economic interests. Some of the other strands in the fabric are also common law in origin, such as the cause of action for breach of contract itself, as well as tort claims for misrepresentation. Many other crucial strands of the fabric are statutory, including the antitrust laws and the many statutes regulating intellectual property, such as the laws relating to trademark, copyright, and patents.

Protection for trademarks derives from the Lanham Act, 15 U.S.C. §§ 1051–1128 (1994). The Act makes actionable the deceptive or misleading use of trademarks and unfair competition with respect to trademarks. The statute protects many forms of marks, symbols, designs, and other product-identifying features. Federal law also includes an elaborate system for protecting patents, a system that includes a procedure for obtaining a new patent and substantive rights and remedies for the possessor of a patent. *See* 35 U.S.C. §§ 100–293 (1994). Federal law also protects copyrights, and expressly preempts state law with respect to some copyright issues. *See* 17 U.S.C. § 301 (1994). As we shall see in the following case, litigation arising out of economic injury often includes a mixture of common law and statutory claims.

The cause of action for tortious interference with contract is outlined in section 766 of the Restatement (Second) Torts (1965):

> "One who intentionally and improperly interferes with the performance of a contract (except a contract to marry) between another and a third person by inducing or otherwise causing the third person not to perform the contract, is subject to liability to the other for the pecuniary loss resulting to the other from the failure of the third person to perform the contract."

Section 766B outlines the cause of action for tortious interference with prospective contractual relations:

> "One who intentionally and improperly interferes with another's prospective contractual relation (except a contract to marry) is subject to liability to the other for the pecuniary harm resulting from loss of the benefits of the relation, whether the interference consists of (a) inducing or otherwise causing a third person not to enter into or continue the prospective relation or (b) preventing the other from acquiring or continuing the prospective relation."

Most authorities agree that intent for purposes of this tort, as with other intentional tort claims, can be established either by proof of subjective purpose or knowledge with substantial certainty. The additional element—an "improper" interference—was not included as an element under the first Restatement's formulation of the tort. Rather, the first Restatement placed the burden on the defendant to prove that the interference was in some way proper or privileged. The second Restatement declines to take a position on who bears the burden of proof on the issue of whether the interference was proper or improper.

DELLA PENNA v. TOYOTA MOTOR SALES, U.S.A., INC.

Supreme Court of California, 1995.
11 Cal.4th 376, 45 Cal.Rptr.2d 436, 902 P.2d 740.

ARABIAN, JUSTICE.

We granted review to reexamine, in light of divergent rulings from the Court of Appeal and a doctrinal evolution among other state high courts, the elements of the tort variously known as interference with "prospective economic advantage," "prospective contractual relations," or "prospective economic relations," and the allocation of the burdens of proof between the parties to such an action. We conclude that those Court of Appeal opinions requiring proof of a so-called "wrongful act" as a component of the cause of action, and allocating the burden of proving it to the plaintiff, are the better reasoned decisions; we accordingly adopt that analysis as our own, disapproving language in prior opinions of this court to the contrary. Such a requirement, incorporating the views of several other jurisdictions, much of the Restatement Second of Torts, the better reasoned decisions of the Court of Appeal, and the views of leading academic authorities, sensibly redresses the balance between providing a remedy for predatory economic behavior and keeping legitimate business competition outside litigative bounds. We do not in this case, however, go beyond approving the requirement of a showing of wrongfulness as part of the plaintiff's case; the case, if any, to be made for adopting refinements to that element of the tort—requiring the plaintiff to prove, for example, that the defendant's conduct amounted to an independently tortious act, or was a species of anticompetitive behavior proscribed by positive law, or was motivated by unalloyed malice—can be considered on another day, and in another case.

* * *

I

John Della Penna, an automobile wholesaler doing business as Pacific Motors, brought this action for damages against Toyota Motor Sales, U.S.A., Inc., and its Lexus division, alleging that certain business conduct of defendants both violated provisions of * * * California's state antitrust statute * * *, and constituted an intentional interference with his economic relations. The impetus for Della Penna's suit arose out of the 1989 introduction into the American luxury car market of Toyota's Lexus automobile. Prior to introducing the Lexus, the evidence at trial showed, both the manufacturer, Toyota Motor Corporation, and defendant, the American distributor, had been concerned at the possibility that a resale market might develop for the Lexus in Japan. Even though the car was manufactured in Japan, Toyota's marketing strategy was to bar the vehicle's sale on the Japanese domestic market until after the American rollout; even then, sales in Japan would only be under a different brand name, the "Celsior." Fearing that auto wholesalers in the United States might re-export Lexus models back to Japan for resale, and concerned that, with production and the availability of Lexus models in the American market limited, re-exports would jeopardize its fledgling network of American Lexus dealers, Toyota inserted in its dealership agreements a "no export" clause, providing that the dealer was "authorized to sell [Lexus automobiles] only to customers located in the United States. [Dealer] agrees that it will not sell [Lexus automobiles] for resale or use outside the United States. [Dealer] agrees to abide by any export policy established by [distributor]."

Following the introduction into the American market, it soon became apparent that some domestic Lexus units were being diverted for foreign sales, principally to Japan. To counter this effect, Toyota managers wrote to their retail dealers, reminding them of the "no-export" policy and explaining that exports for foreign resale could jeopardize the supply of Lexus automobiles available for the United States market. In addition, Toyota compiled a list of "offenders"—dealers and others believed by Toyota to be involved heavily in the developing Lexus foreign resale market—which it distributed to Lexus dealers in the United States. American Lexus dealers were also warned that doing business with those whose names appeared on the "offenders" list might lead to a series of graduated sanctions, from reducing a dealer's allocation to possible reevaluation of the dealer's franchise agreement.

During the years 1989 and 1990, plaintiff Della Penna did a profitable business as an auto wholesaler purchasing Lexus automobiles. * * * By late 1990, however, plaintiff's sources began to dry up, primarily as a result of the "offenders list." * * *

In February 1991, plaintiff filed this lawsuit against Toyota Motors, U.S.A., Inc., alleging both state antitrust claims * * * and interference with his economic relationship with Lexus retail dealers. [The trial court granted Toyota's motion for nonsuit on the state antitrust claim, and modified the standard jury instruction for tortious interference with prospective economic relations to require the plaintiff to show that the interference was "wrongful." The jury returned a verdict for Toyota; the Court of Appeal reversed the ensuing judgment and ordered a new trial on the ground that plaintiff's burden of proof did not encompass proof of a "wrongful" act and that the modified jury instruction was therefore erroneous.]

II

A

Although legal historians have traced the origins of the so-called "interference torts" as far back as the Roman law, the proximate historical impetus for their modern development lay in mid–19th century English common law. * * * The opinion of the Queen's Bench in Lumley v. Gye (1853) 2 El. & Bl. 216, a case that has become a standard in torts casebooks, is widely cited as the origin of the two torts—interference with contract and its sibling, interference with prospective economic relations[2]— in the form in which they have come down to us. The plaintiff owned the Queen's Theatre, at which operas were presented. He contracted for the services of a soprano, Johanna Wagner, to perform in various entertainments between April 15 and July 15, [1852] with the stipulation that Miss Wagner would not perform elsewhere during that time without his permission.

In an action on the case, the theater owner alleged that Gye, the owner of a rival theater, knowing of the Wagner–Lumley agreement, "maliciously" interfered with the contract by "enticing" Wagner to abandon her agreement with Lumley and appear at Gye's theater. Gye's demurrer to

---

2. Throughout this opinion, in an effort to avoid both cumbersome locutions and clumsy acronyms ("IIPEA"), we use the phrase "interference with economic relations" to refer to the tort generally known as "intentional interference with prospective contractual or economic relations" and to distinguish it from the cognate form, "intentional interference with contract."

the complaint was overruled by the trial court, a ruling that was affirmed by the justices of the Queen's Bench on the then somewhat novel grounds that (1) "enticing" someone to leave his or her employment was not limited to disrupting the relationship between master and servant but applied to a "dramatic artiste" such as Miss Wagner, and (2) "wrongfully and maliciously, or, which is the same thing, with notice, interrupt[ing]" a personal service contract, regardless of the means the defendant employed, was an actionable wrong. (2 El. & Bl. at p. 224, per Crompton, J.)

The opinion in Lumley dealt, of course, with conduct intended to induce the breach of an existing contract, not conduct intended to prevent or persuade others not to contract with the plaintiff. That such an interference with prospective economic relations might itself be tortious was confirmed by the Queen's Bench over the next 40 years. * * * Temperton v. Russell (1893) 1 Q.B. 715 (Temperton). * * *

As a number of courts and commentators have observed, the keystone of the liability imposed in Lumley, supra, 2 El. & Bl. 215, and Temperton, supra, 1 Q.B. 714, to judge from the opinions of the justices, appears to have been the "malicious" intent of a defendant in enticing an employee to breach her contract with the plaintiff, and damaging the business of one who refused to cooperate with the union in achieving its bargaining aims. While some have doubted whether the use of the word "malicious" amounted to anything more than an intent to commit an act, knowing it would harm the plaintiff * * *, Dean Keeton, assessing the state of the tort as late as 1984, remarked that "[w]ith intent to interfere as the usual basis of the action, the cases have turned almost entirely upon the defendant's motive or purpose and the means by which he has sought to accomplish it. As in the cases of interference with contract, any manner of intentional invasion of the plaintiff's interests may be sufficient if the purpose is not a proper one." (Prosser & Keeton on Torts (5th ed. 1984) * * * § 130, p. 1009).

It was, legal historians have suggested, this early accent on the defendant's "intentionality" that was responsible for allying the interference torts with their remote relatives, intentional torts of a quite different order—battery, for example, or false imprisonment. * * *

One consequence of this superficial kinship was the assimilation to the interference torts of the pleading and burden of proof requirements of the "true" intentional torts: the requirement that the plaintiff need only allege a so-called "prima facie tort" by showing the defendant's awareness of the economic relation, a deliberate interference with it, and the plaintiff's resulting injury. * * * By this account of the matter—the traditional view of the torts and the one adopted by the first Restatement of Torts— the burden then passed to the defendant to demonstrate that its conduct was privileged, that is, "justified" by a recognized defense such as the protection of others or, more likely in this context, the defendant's own competitive business interests. * * *

These and related features of the economic relations tort and the requirements surrounding its proof and defense led, however, to calls for a reexamination and reform as early as the 1920's. * * *

Because the plaintiff's initial burden of proof was such a slender one, amounting to no more than showing the defendant's conscious act and plaintiff's economic injury, critics argued that legitimate business competition could lead to time consuming and expensive lawsuits (not to speak of potential liability) by a rival, based on conduct that was regarded by the commercial world as both commonplace and appropriate. The "black letter" rules of the Restatement of Torts surrounding the elements and proof of the tort, some complained, might even suggest to "foreign lawyers reading the Restatement as an original matter [that] the whole competitive order of American industry is prima facie illegal." * * *

Calls for a reformulation of both the elements and the means of establishing the economic relations tort reached a height around the time the Restatement Second of Torts was being prepared for publication and are reflected in its departures from its predecessor's version. Acknowledging criticism, the American Law Institute discarded the prima facie tort requirement of the first Restatement. A new provision, section 766B, required that the defendant's conduct be "improper," and adopted a multifactor "balancing" approach, identifying seven factors for the trier of fact to weigh in determining a defendant's liability. The Restatement Second of Torts, however, declined to take a position on the issue of which of the parties bore the burden of proof, relying on the "considerable disagreement on who has the burden of pleading and proving certain matters" and the observation that "the law in this area has not fully congealed but is still in a formative stage." * * * In addition, the Restatement Second provided that a defendant might escape liability by showing that his conduct was justifiable and did not include the use of "wrongful means." * * *

B

In the meantime, however, an increasing number of state high courts had traveled well beyond the Second Restatement's reforms by redefining and otherwise recasting the elements of the economic relations tort and the burdens surrounding its proof and defenses. In Top Service Body Shop, Inc. v. Allstate Ins. Co. (1978) 283 Or. 201, 582 P.2d 1365 (Top Service), the Oregon Supreme Court, assessing this "most fluid and rapidly growing tort," noted that "efforts to consolidate both recognized and unsettled lines of development into a general theory of 'tortious interference' have brought to the surface the difficulties of defining the elements of so general a tort without sweeping within its terms a wide variety of socially very different conduct." Id. 582 P.2d at p. 1368, fn. omitted.

Recognizing the force of these criticisms, the court went on to hold in Top Service, supra, that a claim of interference with economic relations "is made out when interference resulting in injury to another is wrongful by some measure beyond the fact of the interference itself. Defendant's liability may arise from improper motives or from the use of improper means. They may be wrongful by reason of a statute or other regulation, or a recognized rule of common law, or perhaps an established standard of a trade or profession. No question of privilege arises unless the interference would be wrongful but for the privilege; it becomes an issue only if the acts charged would be tortious on the part of an unprivileged defendant." * * *

* * *

Over the past decade or so, close to a majority of the high courts of American jurisdictions have imported into the economic relations tort variations on the Top Service line of reasoning, explicitly approving a rule that requires the plaintiff in such a suit to plead and prove the alleged interference was either "wrongful," "improper," "illegal," "independently tortious" or some variant on these formulations. * * *

III

[The Court explains that California trial and appeals courts recently have required plaintiffs to prove "wrongfulness" and have allowed defendants to escape liability by showing that the conduct was not "independently wrongful."] * * * These developments, of course, closely reflect a nearly concurrent change in views both within the American Law Institute and in other jurisdictions. In the face of [these developments], we are thus presented with the opportunity to consider whether to expressly reconstruct the formal elements of the interference with economic relations tort to achieve a closer alignment with the practice of the trial courts, emerging views within the Court of Appeal, the rulings of many other state high courts, and the critiques of leading commentators. We believe that we should. * * *

IV

In searching for a means to recast the elements of the economic relations tort and allocate the associated burdens of proof, we are guided by an overmastering concern articulated by high courts of other jurisdictions and legal commentators: The need to draw and enforce a sharpened distinction between claims for the tortious disruption of an existing contract and claims that a prospective contractual or economic relationship has been interfered with by the defendant. Many of the cases do in fact acknowledge a greater array of justificatory defenses against claims of interference with prospective relations. Still, in our view and that of several other courts and commentators, the notion that the two torts are analytically unitary and derive from a common principle sacrifices practical wisdom to theoretical insight, promoting the idea that the interests invaded are of nearly equal dignity. They are not.

The courts provide a damage remedy against third party conduct intended to disrupt an existing contract precisely because the exchange of promises resulting in such a formally cemented economic relationship is deemed worthy of protection from interference by a stranger to the agreement. Economic relationships short of contractual, however, should stand on a different legal footing as far as the potential for tort liability is reckoned. Because ours is a culture firmly wedded to the social rewards of commercial contests, the law usually takes care to draw lines of legal liability in a way that maximizes areas of competition free of legal penalties.

A doctrine that blurs the analytical line between interference with an existing business contract and interference with commercial relations less than contractual is one that invites both uncertainty in conduct and unpredictability of its legal effect. The notion that inducing the breach of an existing contract is simply a subevent of the "more inclusive" class of acts that interfere with economic relations, while perhaps theoretically unobjectionable, has been mischievous as a practical matter. Our courts should, in short, firmly distinguish the two kinds of business contexts, bringing a greater solicitude to those relationships that have ripened into agreements, while recognizing that relationships short of that subsist in a zone where the rewards and risks of competition are dominant.

Beyond that, we need not tread today. It is sufficient to dispose of the issue before us in this case by holding that a plaintiff seeking to recover for alleged interference with prospective economic relations has the burden of pleading and proving that the defendant's interference was wrongful "by some measure beyond the fact of the interference itself." * * * (Top Service, supra, 582 P.2d at p. 1371.) It follows that the trial court did not commit error when it modified [the California standard jury instruction] to require the jury to find that defendant's interference was "wrongful." And because the instruction defining "wrongful conduct" given the jury by the trial court was offered by plaintiff himself, we have no occasion to review its sufficiency in this case. The question of whether additional refinements to the plaintiff's pleading and proof burdens merit adoption by California courts—questions embracing the precise scope of "wrongfulness," or whether a "disinterested malevolence," in Justice Holmes's words * * *, is an actionable interference in itself, or whether the underlying policy justification for the tort, the efficient allocation of social resources, justifies including as actionable conduct that is recognized as anticompetitive under established state and federal positive law * * *—are matters that can await another day and a more appropriate case.

CONCLUSION

We hold that a plaintiff seeking to recover for an alleged interference with prospective contractual or economic relations must plead and prove as part of its case-in-chief that the defendant not only knowingly interfered with the plaintiff's expectancy, but engaged in conduct that was wrongful by some legal measure other than the fact of interference itself. The judgment of the Court of Appeal is reversed and the cause is remanded with directions to affirm the judgment of the trial court.

Lucas, C.J., and Kennard, Baxter, George and Werdegar, JJ., concur.

Mosk, Justice, concurring.

I concur in the judgment.

* * *

Like the majority, I would reverse the Court of Appeal's judgment in this regard. As I shall explain, I believe that any instructional error was not prejudicial.

I

With the dissonance caused by such terms as "malice," "justification," and "privilege", the common law on the tort of intentional interference with prospective economic advantage, both in American jurisdictions generally and in California specifically, is fast approaching incoherence.   * * *

* * *

Why * * * should the interfered-with party receive favor, while the interfering party is disfavored, by virtue of their respective status? Why should the interfered-with party's acquisitive efforts be elevated to a kind of property interest, good against the world, while those of the interfering party are deemed illegitimate? * * * Reason supports the conclusion that, even when there is a breach of contract, the interfered-with party should not be preferred over the interfering party: the breach may be "efficient." * * * Reason practically compels the same conclusion when there is no breach because there is no contract.   * * *

Further, liability under the tort may threaten values of greater breadth and higher dignity than those of the tort itself.

One is the common law's policy of freedom of competition. " 'The policy of the common law has always been in favor of free competition, which proverbially is the life of trade. So long as the plaintiff's contractual relations are merely contemplated or potential, it is considered to be in the interest of the public that any competitor should be free to divert them to himself by all fair and reasonable means. * * * In short, it is no tort to beat a business rival to prospective customers. Thus, in the absence of prohibition by statute, illegitimate means, or some other unlawful element, a defendant seeking to increase his own business may cut rates or prices, allow discounts or rebates, enter into secret negotiations behind the plaintiff's back, refuse to deal with him or threaten to discharge employees who do, or even refuse to deal with third parties unless they cease dealing with the plaintiff, all without incurring liability.' "   * * *

C

[Another] reason for the common law's near-incoherence on the tort of intentional interference with prospective economic advantage may be discovered in its focus on the interfering party's motive, that is, why he seeks whatever it is that he seeks through his interference, and on his moral character as revealed thereby.

* * *

Even if it were not inappropriate, the focus on the interfering party's motive surely has a tendency to yield untoward results.   * * *

* * * It may be hard for a trier of fact to discern the interfering party's motive because of factors peculiar to the latter. * * * That is true when the interfering party is an individual: a person's mind and heart typically reveal themselves and conceal themselves at one and the same time. It is truer still when the interfering party is a group of individuals: many minds and hearts are then involved, and they cannot simply be added

up. And, of course, it is truest when the interfering party is a corporation or similar entity: the "mind" and "heart" of such a one is purely fictive.

* * *

The untoward results of the focus on the interfering party's motive may present themselves in individual cases in the form of arbitrary and capricious outcomes. * * * In matters in which the trier of fact believes it has discerned good motive or at least persuades itself it has, an interfering party who has both engaged in objectively bad conduct and produced objectively bad consequences may evade liability for injury. By contrast, in matters in which it adopts a contrary view, an interfering party who has neither engaged in such conduct nor produced such consequences may be made to pay for what is simply damnum absque injuria. In a word, much may depend on mere appearances and perceptions and on nothing more.

Such untoward results, however, will not confine themselves to individual cases but will spread generally to deter what should be encouraged * * * and also to encourage what should be deterred. The example of the interfering party who has both engaged in objectively bad conduct and produced objectively bad consequences, but has nevertheless evaded liability, may lure others to follow in his steps, and thereby cause detriment to society as a whole. Conversely, the example of the interfering party who has neither engaged in such conduct nor produced such consequences, but has still been made to pay, may serve to turn aside others, and thereby deny the community the benefit of good acts and good effects or at least the freedom to do as one chooses when he does no injury. Moreover, the example of both may lead to further social costs, as "properly motivated actors" take "precautions ... to avoid liability" that they should not be exposed to * * *, and actors otherwise motivated fabricate schemes to escape responsibility that they deserve.

II

With all this said, we are put to the question: What are we to do about the tort of intentional interference with prospective economic advantage?

It would be unreasonable to choose to do nothing. As stated, in this regard the common law is approaching incoherence. It is not about to turn to consistency of its own accord.

It would also be unreasonable to choose abolition. Such a course commands little support among courts or commentators. That is unsurprising. Most agree that the interfering party should not be granted general immunity, but should be exposed to liability under at least some circumstances. * * *

In view of the foregoing, the only reasonable choice is reformulation. Indeed, an undertaking of this sort is compelled by the almost unanimous agreement, referred to above, that the interfering party should be not be allowed to interfere with impunity at all times and under all circumstances.

To this end, we should clearly define the tort, basing it on stable and circumscribed ground. * * * Our focus should be on objective conduct and consequences. Further, our concern should be with such conduct and consequences as are unlawful.

* * *

Thus reformulated, the tort requires objective, and unlawful, conduct or consequences.

It follows that the tort may be satisfied by intentional interference with prospective economic advantage by *independently tortious means.* * * *

The interfering party is properly liable to the interfered-with party in such a situation. That is most plainly true when the independently tortious means the interfering party uses are tortious as to the interfered-with party himself. By the tort's very nature, the interfered-with party is an intended (or at least known) victim of the interfering party. * * * But it is true as well when the independently tortious means the interfering party uses are independently tortious only as to a third party. Even under these circumstances, the interfered-with party remains an intended (or at least known) victim of the interfering party—albeit one that is indirect rather than direct. * * * In this situation, the means in question are independently tortious as to the third party "if those elements that pertain to" the interfering party "are present" even if those that pertain to the third party are not: "For instance, fraudulent misrepresentations made" by the interfering party to a "third party are improper means of interference ... whether or not the third party can show reliance injurious to himself." * * *

It also follows that the tort may be satisfied by intentional interference with prospective economic advantage through restraint of trade, including monopolization. * * *

* * *

III

Let us turn now to the case at bar.

* * *

On appeal, Della Penna contended, inter alia, that the instructions were prejudicially erroneous because they required "wrongfulness." The Court of Appeal agreed, and reversed.

Under the tort as reformulated, it is plain that the Court of Appeal erred. To be sure, the instructions appear erroneous. They did not expressly require objective, and unlawful, conduct or consequences. Neither, it seems, did they do so impliedly. Any error, however, was not prejudicial. The reason is manifest. To the extent that they were satisfied by mere "wrongfulness"—which, at Della Penna's request, was defined under a kind of "'business ethics' standard" as behavior "outside the realm of legitimate business transactions" because of "method" or "motive"— they were satisfied by far too little. For to that extent they did not demand the use of independently tortious means or restraints of trade. It is true that their focus on motive—"[w]rongfulness may lie ... by virtue of an improper motive"—might threaten an arbitrary and capricious outcome in a given case. The same is true of their use of the term "wrongful" and its cognates, which are inherently ambiguous * * *. But, in spite of the foregoing, there is simply no basis to conclude that the outcome here was either arbitrary or capricious.

IV

It is evident in the analysis presented above that, on many points, I agree with the majority's discussion of the tort of intentional interference with prospective economic advantage and Della Penna's claim against Toyota asserting such a cause of action.

On two major points, however, I am compelled to state my disagreement.

First, I would not adopt the "standard" of "wrongfulness." As I have noted, the term and its cognates are inherently ambiguous. They should probably be avoided. They should surely not be embraced. * * *

Second, if I were to adopt such a "standard," I would not allow it to remain undefined. * * * Formerly, the interfering party as defendant was left "knowing he was entitled to some defense, but not knowing what defenses would be accounted sufficient." * * * Now, it appears, the interfered-with party as plaintiff will find himself in a similar position, knowing he may assert a claim, but not knowing the substance of a crucial element. This is hardly an improvement. Any definition of the "standard," of course, should avoid suggesting that the interfering party's motive might be material for present purposes. As I have explained, the focus on this issue is inappropriate. * * *[14]

Notes

1. *Privileges and Burden of Proof.* The case illustrates the complexity of the interrelated topics of "improper interference," privilege, and burden of proof. With respect to other intentional torts, the absence of justification or privilege is an affirmative defense for the defendant. In seeming contrast to other intentional torts, the Second Restatement's formulation of both interference torts includes the requirement that the interference be not just intentional but improper. Yet, as we have seen, the comments to the Second Restatement acknowledge that the caselaw is unsettled as to whether the plaintiff or defendant bears the burden of proof with respect to showing that the interference was improper or unprivileged. *See* Restatement (Second) Torts § 767, comment b (1965).

Courts in theory could adopt one of three approaches to the privilege-burden of proof question: (1) require only that the plaintiff show an intentional interference, placing on defendant the burden of proving that the interference was privileged and proper; (2) require that the plaintiff also show the interference was "improper," meaning that the plaintiff must both show some level of impropriety and negate any possible justification or excuse; or (3) require that the plaintiff show that the interference was "improper" in some sense, but

---

14. Of course, to hold that the interfering party's motive is not material for present purposes does not mean that such motive cannot amount to relevant evidence, that is, "evidence, including evidence relevant to the credibility of a witness or hearsay declarant, having any tendency in reason to prove or disprove any disputed fact that is of consequence to the determination of the action." (Evid.Code, § 210.)

leave the burden of proof on the defendant with respect to at least some privileges. To illustrate (3), courts might allow the plaintiff to satisfy the requirement of "improper" by showing that the interference was motivated partly by malice, and yet allow the defendant to escape liability by proving that the interference fell within the privilege of fair competition because it was motivated at least in part by a competitive goal and involved no illegal means. The current trend is to move away from (1), but much of the caselaw is still murky about whether the second or third approach applies.

Which of the three approaches does the *Della Penna* court identify as applying to tortious interference with prospective business relations? Assuming that a court is persuaded to reject the first approach, what rationales might explain choosing (3) over (2); that is, does it make sense to parse the general topic of whether the interference was proper into a burden that is partly the plaintiff's (a showing of improper) and partly the defendant's (a showing that the conduct was privileged)?

2. *The Meaning of "Improper."* The Restatement (Second) of Torts enumerates several factors that are relevant to determining if an interference was improper:

(a) the nature of the actor's conduct,

(b) the actor's motive,

(c) the interests of the other with which the actor's conduct interferes,

(d) the interests sought to be advanced by the actor,

(e) the social interests in protecting the freedom of action of the actor and the contractual interests of the other,

(f) the proximity or remoteness of the actor's conduct to the interference and

(g) the relations between the parties.

How does this multifactored approach differ from the concurring opinion's recommendations about what plaintiff should be required to prove?

In Leigh Furniture & Carpet Co. v. Isom, 657 P.2d 293, 304 (Utah 1982), the court stated that the plaintiff could satisfy the requirement of proving an improper interference by proving that the defendant interfered either "for an improper purpose or by improper means." An improper means would be shown if the plaintiff proved that the defendant's means of interference violated statutory or regulatory standards, common law standards, or an "established standard of a trade or profession." *Id.* at 308 (quoting Top Serv. Body Shop, Inc. v. Allstate Ins. Co., 283 Or. 201, 582 P.2d 1365, 1371 & n. 11 (1978)). Plaintiff could prove an improper purpose by showing that the defendant's ill will predominated over all legitimate economic motivations. A plaintiff, therefore, could prevail on the tort claim by showing an improper purpose even if the means were proper. Recently, the Utah Supreme Court expressed reservations about the wisdom of the two-part test:

The author of this opinion has grave doubts about the future vitality of Leigh 's improper-purpose prong, especially in the context of commercial dealings. * * * [T]he operative test set out in Leigh—a test under which all relevant considerations are issues of fact, which insulates improper-purpose findings from meaningful appellate review—gives no guidance as to which activities qualify as "commercial conduct" and provides no standards by which a court or jury can determine when to apply the improper-purpose test to "commercial conduct." Absent such standards, Leigh's improper-purpose test creates a trap for the wary and unwary alike: business practices that are found to be "proper means" by a finder of fact and may otherwise be regarded as wholly legitimate under our capitalistic economic system may be recast through a jury's unguided exercise of its moral judgment into examples of spite or malice. For example, the enforcement of a binding, valid contractual noncompete provision can result in liability under Leigh merely upon a jury finding of some ill-defined "improper purpose." For these reasons, the author of this opinion thinks Leigh's improper-purpose test should be revisited and recast to minimize its potential for misuse. However, neither [party] has asked this court to modify Leigh's improper-purpose prong. Therefore, the issue of whether lawful means can result in liability for an improper purpose is not before the court today.

Pratt v. Prodata, Inc., 885 P.2d 786, 789 n. 3 (Utah 1994) (Zimmerman, C.J.).

Iowa also makes use of an "improper purpose" standard, but under the Iowa formulation the plaintiff must show that "the sole or predominant purpose of the actor's conduct was to financially injure or destroy the plaintiff." *See* Willey v. Riley, 541 N.W.2d 521, 527 (Iowa 1995). Would this formulation satisfy the concerns expressed about the "purpose" inquiry by the Utah Supreme Court?

3. *The Interference Torts in the Employment Context.* The traditional rule is that a party cannot be liable for interfering with its own contract. This requirement that the interference be by a "third-party" and not a party to the contract has arisen in a number of employment cases. For example, in McGanty v. Staudenraus, 321 Or. 532, 901 P.2d 841 (1995), plaintiff sued her former employer, a collection agency, as well as the individual who was the president and owner of the agency; the president and owner had been her immediate supervisor. He allegedly had made unwelcome sexual advances and comments, and plaintiff sued on a variety of theories, including tortious interference with contract. Applying the law of respondeat superior, the court reasoned that the supervisor had been acting as the employer if he had made the advances during the course and scope of his employment. Thus, the supervisor could not be a third-party to the contract for the purposes of the tort of intentional interference.

Another issue that often arises when intentional interference is alleged in connection with an employment relationship is whether a contract for employment at will can serve as the basis for the tort cause of action. A number of courts have answered affirmatively. New York courts have cautioned that a plaintiff should not "be allowed to evade the employment at-will rule and relationship by recasting his cause of action in the garb of a tortious interference with his employment." Ingle v. Glamore Motor Sales, Inc., 73 N.Y.2d 183, 189, 535 N.E.2d 1311, 1313–14, 538 N.Y.S.2d 771, 774 (1989). Yet New York courts nonetheless allow an at-will employee to maintain a claim for tortious interference in limited circumstances; if, for instance, the defendant used wrongful means (such as fraud or misrepresentation) to effect the termination, the defendant acted with malice, or the means used violated a duty to the plaintiff. *See generally* Finley v. Giacobbe, 79 F.3d 1285 (2d Cir.1996).

4. *Litigation as the Basis for the Interference Torts?* Suppose that the means of the alleged interference is a lawsuit. In applying the interference torts in such contexts, courts have tended to look to the law of malicious

prosecution and vexatious litigation for guidance. As one court explained, "these kindred torts have also had to address the competing policies of deterrence of groundless litigation and protection of good faith access to the courts." Blake v. Levy, 191 Conn. 257, 464 A.2d 52 (Conn.1983). Thus, some courts have imported the standards governing vexatious litigation into the interference torts when plaintiff bases the latter on litigation. These standards often require that plaintiff show that the lawsuit was initiated maliciously, was initiated without probable cause, and terminated in the plaintiff's favor.

5. *The Pennzoil–Texaco Verdict.* In a now-famous chapter in the history of American civil litigation, Pennzoil sued Texaco in Texas state court for interfering with Pennzoil's contractual relations with Getty Oil Co. The underlying events behind the suit began with Pennzoil's and Getty's negotiations over an acquisition by Pennzoil of Getty Oil. The two companies drafted a memorandum of agreement, which stated that it was subject to approval by the Getty board. Yet the memorandum was signed by parties who controlled a majority of the outstanding shares of Getty, and eventually the Getty board voted to accept Pennzoil's proposal of $110 per share on the condition that the Pennzoil also pay a "stub" of $5 per share. There was evidence that Pennzoil then accepted the counteroffer. Yet Getty eventually accepted an offer from Texaco of $125 per share and signed a merger agreement with Texaco that gave Texaco control over Getty.

The jury returned a verdict for Pennzoil of $7.53 billion compensatory damages and $3 billion in punitive damages. The Court of Appeals affirmed the liability aspects of the case and the award of compensatory damages, but reduced the punitive damage award to $1 billion. Texaco, Inc. v. Pennzoil Co., 729 S.W.2d 768 (Tex.App.1987) *cert. denied* 485 U.S. 994, 108 S.Ct. 1305, 99 L.Ed.2d 686 (1988). After the Texas Supreme Court declined review, Texaco filed for bankruptcy and appealed to the United States Supreme Court. While this appeal was pending, the parties settled the case for $3 billion, the largest settlement or judgment in history.

Chapter 17

INTENTIONAL INFLICTION OF EMOTIONAL DISTRESS

TEXAS & PACIFIC RAILWAY v. JONES

Court of Civil Appeals of Texas, 1897.
39 S.W. 124.

HUNTER, J. On the 5th day of April, 1892, appellee Jessie Jones, about 45 minutes before train time, walked into the waiting room of appellant's station at Millsap, Tex., carrying some bundles in her arms, which she laid down on the seat, and sat down by them, intending to purchase a ticket to a small station on appellant's road, and to become a passenger on appellant's train, which was soon to arrive. She was called across the street by a friend, and, leaving her bundles in her seat, she left the waiting room, went across, the street, and returned in about 15 minutes, when she found her bundles had been thrown out of the waiting room on the platform. She inquired of the station agent's wife, who was at the ticket window, where her bundles were, when the agent's wife told her she knew nothing about them, and cared nothing about them, nor about her either, and then and there used insulting and abusive language about appellee, accusing her of being indecent, in having undressed before men, and of stealing her scissors, and continued the abuse for some 10 minutes, so that persons on the platform heard the abusive and insulting language, and saw the agent's wife throw the bundles out the window. The appellant's agent was in the ticket office, within a few feet of his wife, and heard, or could have heard, his wife's language and made no effort to protect appellee, or restrain his wife in her rude and abusive conduct towards her. Appellee was behaving herself properly at the time, and did nothing to call forth the abuse. Appellee was much humiliated and mortified in feelings from the abusive and insulting language used, had a severe headache consequent upon the nervous excitement produced thereby, and was made sick, and cried, and suffered pain and mental anguish by reason thereof, and was damaged in the amount of the verdict found by the jury, to wit, $450.

* * *

On her right to recover damages for mental suffering, we think that it was the duty of the appellant's station agent to protect appellee from insult and abuse from all persons while she was at its station, waiting to become a passenger on its train, whether she received physical injuries or did not.

1031

Leach v. Leach (Tex.Civ.App.) 33 S.W. 703. In the Leach Case there was no bodily injury, but only the mental suffering of a virtuous woman consequent upon an unwarranted proposal for sexual intercourse; and the supreme court refused a writ of error in that case. The right of a lady passenger to be secure from personal insult and abuse in the waiting room of a railroad station, and the correlative obligation of the railroad company, who has invited her there, to protect her in such right while there, is as clear in the one case as in the other. * * * We find no error in the judgment, and it is affirmed.

Notes

1. A later Texas case held that, in determining whether the behavior of the carrier's employees was tortious, the age as well as the sex of the plaintiff must be taken into account. Fort Worth & Rio Grande Railway v. Bryant, 210 S.W. 556 (Tex.Civ.App.1919)("obscene, vulgar, and profane language" actionable by ten year old girl but not by her father). Nevertheless there are cases allowing recovery by grown men. *See* Lipman v. Atlantic Coast Line Railroad, 108 S.C. 151, 93 S.E. 714 (1917). The first of the carrier cases seems to have been Chamberlain v. Chandler, 5 Fed.Cas. 413 (Ct.Cl.Mass.1823)(ship's captain insulted and mistreated passengers). The *Restatement of Torts* § 48 (1934) summarized these early cases by providing for the liability of a common carrier "for the offense reasonably suffered" by its passengers "through the insulting conduct of its servants while otherwise acting within the scope of their employment." The Restatement added a *caveat* as to whether this liability extends to "public utilities other than common carriers and to the possessors of land who for their business purposes hold it open as a place of public resort." In 1965, the American Law Institute extended the liability to public utilities (Restatement (Second) of Torts § 48), but retained a *caveat* as to whether "this Section may also be applicable to possessors of land whose premises are held open to the public for a business or other purpose." The extension of liability to public utilities whose employees, such as telephone repairmen or meter readers, often enter their customers' residences seems particularly warranted. Liability for insulting behavior has also been imposed upon innkeepers who were required, at least by English common law, to serve anyone who was prepared to pay the innkeeper's charges and deport himself properly.

2. In 1934, the American Law Institute confined recovery for conduct "intended or * * * likely to cause only mental or emotional disturbance" to cases of assault and the common carrier situations just discussed. *Restatement of Torts* § 46. As we shall soon see, this situation has now changed.

3. Even when recovery for intentional infliction of emotional distress was not generally recognized, recovery was occasionally had in some other limited types of circumstances. Thus, in Wilkinson v. Downton, [1897] 2 Q.B. 57, a practical joker told the plaintiff that her husband had been badly injured in an accident. She rushed off in a cab to get her husband. "The effect of this statement upon the plaintiff was a violent shock to her nervous system, producing vomiting and other more serious and permanent physical consequences at one time threatening her reason, and entailing weeks of suffering and incapacity as well as expense to her husband for medical attendance." The court would only allow the plaintiff to recover her cab fare on a fraud count. It

nevertheless upheld a jury award of £100 for injuries caused by nervous shock because the defendant had "wilfully done an act calculated to cause physical harm to the plaintiff * * * and has in fact thereby caused physical harm to her." *Wilkinson* is often classed as a case of "intangible battery." *Cf.* Price v. Yellow Pine Paper Mill Co., 240 S.W. 588 (Tex.Civ.App.1922), where an injured employee was carried to his home over his objections, and his wife, on seeing him bloody and battered, became ill and miscarried. On developments in English law, *see* R. Townshend–Smith, *Harassment as a Tort in English and American Law: The Boundaries of* Wilkinson v. Downton, 24 Anglo–Am.L.Rev. 299 (1995).

Another cruel practical joke case is Nickerson v. Hodges, 146 La. 735, 84 So. 37 (1920). The plaintiff, who died while the case was pending, was a spinster who had an obsession about finding a pot of gold coins supposedly buried by her ancestors on or near some land which had passed into the ownership of one of the defendants. Some twenty years earlier the plaintiff had actually been institutionalized "in an insane asylum, to the knowledge" of the defendants. What the defendants did was to bury an old pot containing rocks at a place where Miss Nickerson and those who were helping her in the search would find it. When the pot was found, arrangements were made to have it opened at a local bank in which Miss Nickerson had left the pot for safekeeping. A sizeable crowd attended the opening. When the pot proved to contain rocks and dirt, Miss Nickerson flew into a rage and had to be physically restrained from assaulting some of the defendants. The defendants claimed, *inter alia,* that they were trying to show Miss Nickerson that her obsession was a folly.

Section 306 of the *Restatement of Torts* tried to accommodate, at least the result in cases like *Wilkinson,* by providing that "[a]n act may be negligent, as creating an unreasonable risk of bodily harm * * * if the actor intends to subject, * * * or should realize that his act involves an unreasonable risk of subjecting, the other to an emotional disturbance of such a character as to be likely to result in illness or other bodily harm." *See also id.* § 312 which is a companion provision. The provisions have been retained *verbatim* in the *Restatement (Second).* A case going beyond § 306 was Blakeley v. Shortal's Estate, 236 Iowa 787, 20 N.W.2d 28 (1945). In that case, Shortal, a farmer, had recently been divorced. A day or so following "a sale" and division of the property with his ex-wife, Shortal went to the neighboring Blakeley farm and asked to spend the night. The next morning, after breakfast, Shortal asked for paper and pencil because he felt that "in the division of his property he had been beaten out of some money." At noon the plaintiff and her husband went to town to do some shopping. When they returned at four, the plaintiff opened the kitchen door to find Shortal lying in pools of blood. He had killed himself with a skinning knife belonging to the plaintiff's son. In bringing an action for mental and physical shock, the only allegations of physical injury were difficulty in sleeping, nervousness, and restlessness. The trial court granted a directed verdict for the defendant. The Supreme Court of Iowa reversed and directed that the case be submitted to the jury to decide whether Shortal could be said to have willfully inflicted shock and fright in subjecting the plaintiff to "the gory and ghastly sight."

STATE RUBBISH COLLECTORS ASSOCIATION
v. SILIZNOFF

Supreme Court of California, 1952.
38 Cal.2d 330, 240 P.2d 282.

TRAYNOR, JUSTICE.

On February 1, 1948, Peter Kobzeff signed a contract with the Acme Brewing Company to collect rubbish from the latter's brewery. Kobzeff had been in the rubbish business for several years and was able to secure the contract because Acme was dissatisfied with the service then being provided by another collector, one Abramoff. Although Kobzeff signed the contract, it was understood that the work should be done by John Siliznoff, Kobzeff's son-in-law, whom Kobzeff wished to assist in establishing a rubbish collection business.

Both Kobzeff and Abramoff were members of the plaintiff State Rubbish Collectors Association, but Siliznoff was not. The by-laws of the association provided that one member should not take an account from another member without paying for it. Usual prices ranged from five to ten times the monthly rate paid by the customer, and disputes were referred to the board of directors for settlement. After Abramoff lost the Acme account he complained to the association, and Kobzeff was called upon to settle the matter. Kobzeff and Siliznoff took the position that the Acme account belonged to Siliznoff, and that he was under no obligation to pay for it. After attending several meetings of plaintiff's board of directors Siliznoff finally agreed, however, to pay Abramoff $1,850 for the Acme account and join the association. The agreement provided that he should pay $500 in thirty days and $75 per month thereafter until the whole sum agreed upon was paid. Payments were to be made through the association, and Siliznoff executed a series of promissory notes totaling $1,850. None of these notes was paid, and in 1949 plaintiff association brought this action to collect the notes then payable. Defendant cross-complained and asked that the notes be cancelled because of duress and want of consideration. In addition he sought general and exemplary damages because of assaults made by plaintiff and its agents to compel him to join the association and pay Abramoff for the Acme account. The jury returned a verdict against plaintiff and for defendant on the complaint and for defendant on his cross-complaint. It awarded him $1,250 general and special damages and $7,500 exemplary damages. The trial court denied a motion for a new trial on the condition that defendant consent to a reduction of the exemplary damages to $4,000. Defendant filed the required consent, and plaintiff has appealed from the judgment.

Plaintiff's primary contention is that the evidence is insufficient to support the judgment. Defendant testified that shortly after he secured the Acme account, the president of the association and its inspector, John Andikian, called on him and Kobzeff. They suggested that either a settlement be made with Abramoff or that the job be dropped, and requested Kobzeff and defendant to attend a meeting of the association. At this meeting defendant was told that the association "ran all the rubbish from that office, all the rubbish hauling," and that if he did not pay for the job they would take it away from him. " 'We would take it away, even if we had to haul for nothing.' * * * [O]ne of them mentioned that I had better pay up, or else." Thereafter, on the day when defendant finally agreed to pay for the account, Andikian visited defendant at the Rainier Brewing Company, where he was collecting rubbish. Andikian told defendant that " 'We will give you up till tonight to get down to the board meeting and make some kind of arrangements or agreements about the Acme Brewery, or otherwise we are going to beat you up.' * * * He says he either would hire somebody or do it himself. And I says, 'Well, what would they do to me?' He says, well, they would physically beat me up first, cut up the truck tires or burn the truck, or otherwise put me out of business completely. He said if I didn't appear at that meeting and make some kind of an agreement that they would do that, but he says up to then they would let me alone, but if I walked out of that meeting that night they would beat me up for sure." Defendant attended the meeting and protested that he owed nothing for the Acme account and in any event could not pay the amount demanded. He was again told by the president of the association that "that table right there [the board of directors] ran all the rubbish collecting in Los Angeles and if there was any routes to be gotten that they would get them and distribute them among their members * * *." After two hour of further discussion defendant agreed to join the association and pay for the Acme account. He promised to return the next day and sign the necessary papers. He testified that the only reason "they let me go home, is that I promised that I would sign the notes the very next morning." The president "made me promise on my honor and everything else, and I was scared, and I knew I had to come back, so I believed he knew I was scared and that I would come back. That's the only reason they let me go home." Defendant also testified that because of the fright he suffered during his dispute with the association he became ill and vomited several times and had to remain away from work for a period of several days.

Plaintiff contends that the evidence does not establish an assault against defendant because the threats made all related to action that might take place in the future; that neither Andikian nor members of the board of directors threatened immediate physical harm to defendant. * * * We have concluded, however, that a cause of action is established when it is shown that one, in the absence of any privilege, intentionally subjects another to the mental suffering incident to serious threats to his physical well-being, whether or not the threats are made under such circumstances as to constitute a technical assault.

In the past it has frequently been stated that the interest in emotional and mental tranquillity is not one that the law will protect from invasion in its own right. * * * As late as 1934 the Restatement of Torts took the position that "The interest in mental and emotional tranquillity and, therefore, in freedom from mental and emotional disturbance is not, as a thing in itself, regarded as of sufficient importance to require others to refrain from conduct intended or recognizably likely to cause such a disturbance." Restatement, Torts, § 46, comment c. The Restatement explained the rule allowing recovery for the mere apprehension of bodily harm in traditional assault cases as an historical anomaly, § 24, comment c, and the rule allowing recovery for insulting conduct by an employee of a common carrier as justified by the necessity of securing for the public comfortable as well as safe service. § 48, comment c.

The Restatement recognized, however, that in many cases mental distress could be so intense that it could reasonably be foreseen that illness or other bodily harm might result. If the defendant intentionally subjected the plaintiff to such distress and bodily harm resulted, the defendant would be liable for negligently causing the plaintiff bodily harm. Restatement, Torts, §§ 306, 312. Under this theory the cause of action was not founded on a right to be free from intentional interference with mental tranquillity, but on the right to be free from negligent interference with physical well-being. A defendant who intentionally subjected another to mental distress without intending to cause bodily harm would nevertheless be liable for resulting bodily harm if he should have foreseen that the mental distress might cause such harm.

The California cases have been in accord with the Restatement in allowing recovery where physical injury resulted from intentionally subjecting the plaintiff to serious mental distress. * * *

The view has been forcefully advocated that the law should protect emotional and mental tranquillity as such against serious and intentional invasions * * * and there is a growing body of case law supporting this position. * * * In recognition of this development the American Law Institute amended section 46 of the Restatement of Torts in 1947 to provide: "One who, without a privilege to do so, intentionally causes severe emotional distress to another is liable (a) for such emotional distress, and (b) for bodily harm resulting from it."

In explanation it stated that "The interest in freedom from severe emotional distress is regarded as of sufficient importance to require others to refrain from conduct intended to invade it. Such conduct is tortious. The injury suffered by the one whose interest is invaded is frequently far more serious to him than certain tortious invasions of the interest in bodily integrity and other legally protected interests. * * *."

There are persuasive arguments and analogies that support the recognition of a right to be free from serious, intentional, and unprivileged invasions of mental and emotional tranquillity. If a cause of action is otherwise established, it is settled that damages may be given for mental suffering naturally ensuing from the acts complained of, * * * and in the case of many torts, such as assault, battery, false imprisonment, and defamation, mental suffering will frequently constitute the principal element of damages. * * * In cases where mental suffering constitutes a major element of damages it is anomalous to deny recovery because the defendant's intentional misconduct fell short of producing some physical injury.

It may be contended that to allow recovery in the absence of physical injury will open the door to unfounded claims and a flood of litigation, and that the requirement that there be physical injury is necessary to insure that serious mental suffering actually occurred. The jury is ordinarily in a better position, however, to determine whether outrageous conduct results in mental distress than whether that distress in turn results in physical injury. From their own experience jurors are aware of the extent and character of the disagreeable emotions that may result from the defendant's conduct, but a difficult medical question is presented when it must be determined if emotional distress resulted in physical injury. See, Smith, Relation of Emotions to Injury and Disease, 30 Va.L.Rev. 193, 303–306. Greater proof that mental suffering occurred is found in the defendant's conduct designed to bring it about than in physical injury that may or may not have resulted therefrom.

That administrative difficulties do not justify the denial of relief for serious invasions of mental and emotional tranquillity is demonstrated by the cases recognizing the right of privacy. Recognition of that right protects mental tranquillity from invasion by unwarranted and undesired publicity. Melvin v. Reid, 112 Cal.App. 285, 289, 297 P. 91 * * * As in the case of the protection of mental tranquillity from other forms of invasion, difficult problems in determining the kind and extent of invasions that are sufficiently serious to be actionable are presented. Also the public interest in the free dissemination of news must be considered. Nevertheless courts have concluded that the problems presented are not so insuperable that they warrant the denial of relief altogether.

In the present case plaintiff caused defendant to suffer extreme fright. By intentionally producing such fright it endeavored to compel him either to give up the Acme account or pay for it, and it had no right or privilege to adopt such coercive methods, in competing for business. In these circumstances liability is clear.

* * *

The judgment is affirmed.

Notes

1. The subject of invasion of privacy is discussed in Chapter Nineteen, *infra.*

2. Although Traynor, J.'s, discussion is wide-ranging, is it not the case that *Siliznoff* involved conduct that, while not an assault (either criminally or civilly) because the threat of physical harm was not immediate enough, was nevertheless arguably criminal, namely attempted extortion? Under this view of the matter *Siliznoff* could be viewed as another limited exception to the no-liability rule. The bill collector cases, to be considered at p. 1060ff, *infra,* would, under this approach, constitute another limited exception to the no-liability rule. After finishing the chapter one might consider whether this piecemeal approach might have been better. As noted by Traynor, J., however, the *Restatement* took a more expansive approach, the ramifications of which will be considered in the next few cases.

KORBIN v. BERLIN

District Court of Appeal of Florida, 1965.
177 So.2d 551.

CARROLL, JUDGE.

This appeal is from an order dismissing an amended complaint in an action brought by a six year old girl through her guardian and next friend.

It was alleged in the amended complaint that at a certain time and place the defendant "Willfully and maliciously approached the said plaintiff * * * and made the following statement to her: 'Do you know that your mother took a man away from his wife? Do you know God is going to punish them? Do you know that a man is sleeping in your mother's room?' She then again repeated, 'God will punish them.'" It was alleged the statements were knowingly false, "made maliciously, willfully and with utter disregard to the feelings of the six-year-old Plaintiff," and it was further alleged that the statements were made "for the purpose of causing the plaintiff-child undue emotional stress, mental pain and anguish." Resultant injuries were alleged, and damages were sought.

In our opinion the trial judge was in error in holding that a cause of action was not stated, and we reverse * * *.

The law in this state with reference to the cause of action declared on is dealt with in the cited cases. Thus, in Kirksey v. Jernigan, supra (45 So.2d at 189), the Supreme Court said:

> "This court is committed to the rule, and we re-affirm it herein, that there can be no recovery for mental pain and anguish unconnected with physical injury in an action arising out of the negligent breach of a contract whereby simple negligence is involved. * * *

> "But we do not feel constrained to extend this rule to cases founded purely in tort, where the wrongful act is such as to reasonably imply malice, or where, from the entire want of care of attention to duty, or great indifference to the persons, property, or rights of others, such malice will be imputed as would justify the assessment of exemplary or punitive damages. * * *"

Later, in Slocum v. Food Fair Stores of Florida, supra (100 So.2d at 397–398) it was said:

> "A most cogent statement of the doctrine covering tort liability for insult has been incorporated in the Restatement of the Law of Torts, 1948 supplement, sec. 46, entitled 'Conduct intended to cause emotional distress only.' It makes a blanket provision for liability on the part of 'one, who, without a privilege to do so, intentionally causes severe emotional distress to another,' indicating that the requisite intention exists 'when the act is done for the purpose of causing the distress or with knowledge * * * that severe emotional distress is substantially certain to be produced by [such] conduct.' Comment (a), sec. 46, supra. Abusive language is, of course, only one of the many means by which the tort could be committed.

> "However, even if we assume, without deciding, the legal propriety of that doctrine, a study of its factual applications shows that a line of demarcation should be drawn between conduct likely to cause mere 'emotional distress' and that causing 'severe emotional distress,' so as to exclude the situation at bar. Illus. 5, sec. 46, supra. * * *

> "This tendency to hinge the cause of action upon the degree of the insult has led some courts to reject the doctrine in toto. Wallace v. Shoreham Hotel Corp., D.C.Mun.App., 49 A.2d 81. Whether or not this is desirable, it is uniformly agreed that the determination of

whether words or conduct are actionable in character is to be made on an objective rather than subjective standard, from common acceptation. The unwarranted intrusion must be calculated to cause 'severe emotional distress' to a person of ordinary sensibilities, in the absence of special knowledge or notice. * * *"

The complaint in the instant case met the requirements for validity as outlined in Kirksey v. Jernigan, supra, as quoted above. This is so because the claim presented here for damages "for mental pain and anguish unconnected with physical injury" did not arise "out of the negligent breach of a contract whereby simple negligence is involved" but from action "founded purely in tort, where the wrongful act is such as to reasonably imply malice," or "great indifference" to the rights of others. The alleged tortious injury did not occur incident to violation of a contract obligation, but in the course of a tortious act, which, if the facts so established, was a slander of the plaintiff's mother.

In the later Slocum case, the Supreme Court showed readiness to apply the rule discussed and quoted * * *. However, in the Slocum case it was held the words used were not of such consequence.

Therefore, the determinative question here is whether what was said to the child was intended or reasonably calculated to cause the child "severe emotional distress." The alleged statements and the manner and circumstances under which they were communicated to the child leave little room to doubt they were made with a purpose and intent to shame her, and to shock the sensibilities of this child of tender years. Relating, as they did, to the child's mother, the content and import of the statements were such that it can not be said as a matter of law that this alleged deliberately harmful act was not one "calculated to cause 'severe emotional distress' to a person [child] of ordinary sensibilities." See Slocum v. Food Fair Stores of Florida, supra.

Accordingly, the order dismissing the amended complaint is reversed and the cause is remanded for further proceedings.

SWANN, JUDGE (dissenting).

I dissent on the authority of Slocum v. Food Fair Stores of Florida, Inc., Fla.1958, 100 So.2d 396, and Mann v. Roosevelt Shop, Inc., Fla.1949, 41 So.2d 894.

Notes

1. Suppose it proves to be true that the girl's mother, in some manner of speaking, "took a man away from his wife?" Should recovery be permitted then? Would allowing recovery interfere not only with the defendant's "freedom of speech" but also the "free exercise" of her religion? If the truth of the charge is a defense, is the court then merely expanding the class of potential plaintiffs in defamation actions to include the young children of persons who have been defamed?

2. In Slocum v. Food Fair Stores of Florida, Inc., 100 So.2d 396 (Fla. 1958), relied on in *Korbin,* one of the defendant's employees was asked the price of an item he was in the process of marking. He was alleged to have responded: "If you want to know the price, you'll have to find out the best way

you can * * * you stink to me." The Supreme Court of Florida upheld the dismissal of the complaint.

3. Undoubtedly in reaction to the potential constitutional issues and the reluctant attitude adopted by courts in cases like *Slocum*, § 46 was again revised in 1965 with the publication of the *Restatement (Second) of Torts*. Section 46(1) of the *Restatement (Second)* now provides:

> One who by extreme and outrageous conduct intentionally or recklessly causes severe emotional distress to another is subject to liability for such emotional distress, and if bodily harm to the other results from it, for such bodily harm.

Thus, the intentional infliction of severe emotional distress is by itself no longer sufficient for liability. The severe emotional distress must be caused by "extreme and outrageous conduct." At the same time the *Restatement (Second)* extended liability to recklessly caused severe emotional distress; the 1948 revision only extended to intentionally caused severe emotional distress. As the subsequent cases to be presented indicate, it is not at all clear that these changes avoid the constitutional problems.

4. Several states still have so-called insult statutes. *See* Miss.Code 1972 Ann., § 95–1–1; Va.Code § 18.2–416 (1996); W.Va.Code, 55–7–2 (1994). Statutes of this type had their origin in the anti-dueling codes of the nineteenth century. Generally they provide for liability for words which from their "usual construction and common acceptance" are considered as "insults" and lead to violence and breach of the peace. For a variety of reasons, including very definitely the possible conflict with a speaker's First Amendment rights, in modern times these statutes have tended to be construed as imposing no more than a statutory remedy for defamation, the subject which will be discussed in the next chapter.

PAUL v. WATCHTOWER BIBLE AND TRACT SOCIETY OF NEW YORK, INC.

United States Court of Appeals, Ninth Circuit, 1987.
819 F.2d 875, cert. denied 484 U.S. 926, 108 S.Ct. 289, 98 L.Ed.2d 249.

REINHARDT, CIRCUIT JUDGE:

Janice Paul, a former member of the Jehovah's Witness Church, appeals from the grant of summary judgment in favor of defendants, the corporate arms of the Governing Body of Jehovah's Witnesses. Paul contends that she is being "shunned" by adherents of the Jehovah's Witness faith. She initially filed suit in state court, setting forth various tort claims. Defendants removed the action on the ground of diversity. Because the practice of shunning is a part of the faith of the Jehovah's Witness, we find that the "free exercise" provision of the United States Constitution and thus of the Washington State Constitution precludes the plaintiff from prevailing. The defendants have a constitutionally protected privilege to engage in the practice of shunning. Accordingly, we affirm the grant of summary judgment, although for reasons different from those of the district court. * * *

I. FACTS

Janice Paul was raised as a Jehovah's Witness. Her mother was very active in the Church and, from the age of four, Paul attended church meetings. In 1962, when Paul was 11 years old, her mother married the overseer of the Ephrata, Washington congregation of Jehovah's Witnesses. In 1967, Paul officially joined the Witnesses and was baptized.

According to Paul, she was an active member of the congregation, devoting an average of 40 hours per month in door-to-door distribution of the Witnesses' publications. In addition to engaging in evening home bible study, she attended church with her family approximately 20 hours per month. She eventually married another member of the Jehovah's Witnesses.

In 1975, Paul's parents were "disfellowshiped" from the Church. According to Paul, her parents' expulsion resulted from internal discord within their congregation. The Elders of the Lower Valley Congregation told Paul that she and her husband should not discuss with other members their feeling that her parents had been unjustly disfellowshiped. That advice was underscored by the potential sanction of her own disfellowship were she to challenge the decision.

Sometime after the Elders' warning, Paul decided that she no longer wished to belong to the congregation, or to remain affiliated with the Jehovah's Witnesses. In November 1975, Paul wrote a letter to the congregation withdrawing from the Church.

The Witnesses are a very close community and have developed an elaborate set of rules governing membership. The Church has four basic categories of membership, non-membership or former membership status; they are: members, non-members, disfellowshiped persons, and disassociated persons. "Disfellowshiped persons" are former members who have been excommunicated from the Church. One consequence of disfellowship is "shunning," a form of ostracism. Members of the Jehovah's Witness community are prohibited—under threat of their own disfellowship—from having any contact with disfellowshiped persons and may not even greet them. Family members who do not live in the same house may conduct necessary family business with disfellowshiped relatives but may not communicate with them on any other subject. Shunning purportedly has its roots in early Christianity and various religious groups in our country engage in the practice including the Amish, the Mennonites, and, of course, the Jehovah's Witnesses.

"Disassociated persons" are former members who have voluntarily left the Jehovah's Witness faith. At the time Paul disassociated, there was no express sanction for withdrawing from membership. In fact, because of the close nature of many Jehovah's Witness communities, disassociated persons were still consulted in secular matters, e.g. legal or business advice, although they were no longer members of the Church. In Paul's case, for example, after having moved from the area, she returned for a visit in 1980, saw Church members and was warmly greeted.

In September 1981, the Governing Body of Jehovah's Witnesses, acting through the defendants—Watchtower Bible and Tract Society of Pennsylvania, Inc., and the Watchtower Bible and Tract Society of New York, Inc.— issued a new interpretation of the rules governing disassociated persons. The distinction between disfellowshiped and disassociated persons was, for all practical purposes, abolished and disassociated persons were to be treated in the same manner as the disfellowshiped. The September 15, 1981 issue of *The Watchtower,* an official publication of the Church, contained an article entitled "Disfellowshiping—how to view it." The article included the following discussion:

THOSE WHO DISASSOCIATE THEMSELVES

* * * Persons who make themselves 'not of our sort' by deliberately rejecting the faith and beliefs of Jehovah's Witnesses should appropriately be viewed and treated as are those who have been disfellowshiped for wrongdoing.

The Watchtower article based its announcement on a reading of various passages of the Bible, including 1 John 2:19 and Revelations 19:17–21. The article noted further that "[a]s distinct from some personal 'enemy' or worldly man in authority who opposed Christians, a * * * disassociated person who is trying to promote or justify his apostate thinking or is continuing in his ungodly conduct is certainly not one to whom to wish 'Peace' [understood as a greeting]. (1 Tim. 2:1, 2)." Finally, the article stated that if "a Christian were to throw in his lot with a wrongdoer who * * * has disassociated himself, * * * the Elders * * * would admonish him and, if necessary, 'reprove him with severity.' " (citing, *inter alia,* Matt. 18:18, Gal. 6:1, Titus 1:13).

Three years after this announcement in *The Watchtower,* Paul visited her parents, who at that time lived in Soap Lake, Washington. There, she approached a Witness who had been a close childhood friend and was told by this person: "I can't speak to you. You are disfellowshiped." Similarly, in August 1984, Paul returned to the area of her former congregation. She tried to call on some of her friends. These people told Paul that she was to be treated as if she had been disfellowshiped and that they could not speak with her. At one point, she attempted to attend a Tupperware party at the home of a Witness. Paul was informed by the Church members present that the Elders had instructed them not to speak with her.

Upset by her shunning by her former friends and co-religionists, Paul, a resident of Alaska, brought suit in Washington State Superior Court alleging common law torts of defamation, invasion of privacy, fraud, and outrageous conduct. Defendants, Watchtower Bible and Tract Associations, removed the action to federal court pursuant to 28 U.S.C. § 1441 (1982). Watchtower moved to dismiss for lack of subject matter jurisdiction and for failure to state a claim under Washington law. Fed.R.Civ.P. 12(b)(1) & (6). In the alternative, Watchtower sought summary judgment. Fed.R.Civ.P. 56(b).

The district court denied the 12(b)(1) motion to dismiss for lack of subject matter jurisdiction and the 12(b)(6) motion to dismiss for failure to state a claim, but granted the motion for summary judgment. The court ruled that it had jurisdiction over the case because the state court properly had jurisdiction originally. * * * The court also held that Paul's affidavits did not set forth facts that would establish a prima facie case for relief. Moreover, the court ruled that even if the practice of shunning was actionable, the court was prohibited from ruling on the issue on the ground of ecclesiastical abstention. That doctrine prohibits courts from determining issues of canon law. *See generally Serbian Eastern Orthodox Diocese v. Milivojevich,* 426 U.S. 696, 96 S.Ct. 2372, 49 L.Ed.2d 151 (1976).[1]

II. The Plaintiff's Cause of Action

Janice Paul seeks relief against the Church and several Church officials under Washington state law and pleads various causes of action in tort. She claims in essence that the practice of shunning invades interests that the state does or should protect through its tort law.

* * *

We note at the outset that in this case the actions of Church officials and members were clearly taken pursuant to Church policy. * * * Although shunning is intentional, the activity is not malum in se. The state is legitimately concerned with its regulation only to the extent that individuals are directly harmed.

One state has recently recognized a cause of action in tort arising from the practice of shunning. Although it did not purport to create a new tort, the Supreme Court of Pennsylvania, in *Bear v. Reformed Mennonite Church,* 462 Pa. 330, 341 A.2d 105 (1975), noted that certain interests protected by the state may be invaded when shunning occurs. As the Court stated:

> the "shunning" practice of appellee church and the conduct of the individuals may be an excessive interference within areas of "paramount state concern," i.e. the maintenance of marriage and family relationship, alienation of affection, and the tortious interference with a business relationship. * * *

Id. at 107.

Under Washington tort law there are at least three basic categories of intentional conduct that are relevant here: conduct causing emotional distress, conduct causing alienation of affections, and conduct causing harm to reputation. Paul claims to have suffered injuries in all three categories as a result of the intentional actions of the Jehovah's Witnesses. Under Washington law, "intangible-emotional" harm is, at least in some circumstances, sufficient to support a claim in tort. * * *

Federal courts are not precluded from affording relief simply because neither the state Supreme Court nor the state legislature has enunciated a clear rule governing a particular type of controversy. Were we able to invoke only clearly established state law, litigants seeking to protect their rights in federal courts by availing themselves of our diversity jurisdiction would face an inhospitable forum for claims not identical to those resolved in prior cases. Equally important, a policy by the federal courts never to

---

1. The doctrine of ecclesiastical abstention is not pertinent here. * * * Ecclesiastical abstention thus provides that civil courts may not redetermine the correctness of an interpretation of canonical text or some decision relating to government of the religious polity. Rather, we must accept as a given whatever the entity decides. * * *

This limited abstention doctrine is not relevant here because Paul is not alleging that

the new rules governing disassociation are improper under Church law. * * * Nor does she seek relief for having been "wrongfully" disfellowshiped. Rather, she seeks relief for the harms she has suffered as a result of conduct engaged in by the Jehovah's Witnesses that is presumably consistent with the governing law of the Church. Accordingly, the doctrine of *Serbian Orthodox Diocese* does not apply.

advance beyond existing state court precedent would vest in defendants the power to bar the successful adjudication of plaintiffs' claims in cases with novel issues; defendants could ensure a decision in their favor simply by removing the case to federal court. Congress, in providing for removal, certainly did not intend to provide such a weapon to defendants.

Nonetheless, we need not decide here whether Washington courts would ultimately rule that Paul has set forth a prima facie claim for relief in tort because the defendants, in any event, possess an affirmative defense of privilege—a defense that permits them to engage in the practice of shunning pursuant to their religious beliefs without incurring tort liability. Were shunning considered to be tortious conduct, the guarantee of the free exercise of religion would provide that it is, nonetheless, privileged conduct. In theory, we could examine the question whether the shunning of a former member of a church is, in itself, tortious; however, we will follow the practice of Washington courts which safeguard the free exercise of religion through the recognition of substantive defenses to torts, rather than by negating the plaintiff's cause of action itself (i.e. ruling that the conduct in question is not tortious). *See Carrieri v. Bush,* 69 Wash.2d 536, 419 P.2d 132, 137 (1966). The Washington practice, in addition to being the governing rule here is, in our view, the most sensible juridical approach.
* * *

III.   THE DEFENDANTS' PRIVILEGE

Shunning is a practice engaged in by Jehovah's Witnesses pursuant to their interpretation of canonical text, and we are not free to reinterpret that text.[2] Under both the United States and Washington Constitutions, the defendants are entitled to the free exercise of their religious beliefs.

State laws whether statutory or common law, including tort rules, constitute state action. Clearly, the application of tort law to activities of a church or its adherents in their furtherance of their religious belief is an exercise of state power. When the imposition of liability would result in the abridgement of the right to free exercise of religious beliefs, recovery in tort is barred.

The Jehovah's Witnesses argue that their right to exercise their religion freely entitles them to engage in the practice of shunning. The Church further claims that assessing damages against them for engaging in that practice would directly burden that right.

We agree that the imposition of tort damages on the Jehovah's Witnesses for engaging in the religious practice of shunning would constitute a direct burden on religion. The free exercise claim here is unlike the one in *Braunfeld v. Brown;* 366 U.S. 599, 81 S.Ct. 1144, 6 L.Ed.2d 563 (1961). In *Braunfeld,* the United States Supreme Court upheld Sunday closing laws even though it acknowledged that Sunday closings made the practice of their religious beliefs more expensive for Saturday Sabbatarians, by forcing them to close their businesses two days a week—Saturday (per religious compulsion) and Sunday (per state compulsion). In upholding the Pennsylvania statute, the Court stated that "to strike down ... legislation which imposes only an indirect burden on the exercise of religion, i.e. legislation

---

2. *See supra* note 1.

which does not make unlawful the religious practice itself, would radically restrict the operating latitude of the legislature." *Id.* at 606, 81 S.Ct. at 1147.

* * * In the Court's view, the law did not regulate or prohibit Saturday closings, (in which case it would have constituted a direct burden on Saturday Sabbatarians) but only Sunday operations. From this, the Court concluded that the statute did not directly regulate or prohibit a religious practice (Saturday closings) but merely regulated a non-religious one (Sunday business operations); accordingly, any effect on the religious practice was, in the Court's view, "indirect."[4]

Here, by contrast, shunning is an actual practice of the Church itself, and the burden of tort damages is direct. Permitting prosecution of a cause of action in tort, while not criminalizing the conduct at issue, would make shunning an "unlawful act." * * * The Church and its members would risk substantial damages every time a former Church member was shunned. In sum, a state tort law prohibition against shunning would directly restrict the free exercise of the Jehovah's Witnesses' religious faith.[5]

* * *

We find the practice of shunning not to constitute a sufficient threat to the peace, safety, or morality of the community as to warrant state intervention. The test for upholding a direct burden on religious practices is as stringent as any imposed under our Constitution. Only in extreme and unusual cases has the imposition of a direct burden on religion been upheld. *See, e.g., Reynolds v. United States,* 98 U.S. (8 Otto) 145, 25 L.Ed. 244 (1878)(polygamy); *Hill v. State,* 38 Ala.App. 404, 88 So.2d 880 (1956)(snake handling). The harms suffered by Paul as a result of her shunning by the Jehovah's Witnesses are clearly not of the type that would justify the imposition of tort liability for religious conduct. No physical assault or battery occurred. Intangible or emotional harms cannot ordinarily serve as a basis for maintaining a tort cause of action against a church for its practices—or against its members. * * *

A religious organization has a defense of constitutional privilege to claims that it has caused intangible harms—in most, if not all, circumstances. * * *

Providing the Church with a defense to tort is particularly appropriate here because Paul is a former Church member. Courts generally do not scrutinize closely the relationship among members (or former members) of a church. Churches are afforded great latitude when they impose discipline on members or former members. * * *

---

4. The reasoning of *Braunfeld* has been substantially undermined by subsequent cases. * * * In any event, for reasons set forth in the text immediately following, *Braunfeld* is not controlling.

5. At oral argument, both counsel seem to agree on the principle that if the behavior of the religious organization in question were criminal, the state would have a sufficient interest to overcome first amendment protections. This position is clearly incorrect. Whether a state labels a particular type of behavior criminal or whether it enables private citizens to enforce substantive rules of behavior through tort laws is not dispositive of the constitutional question. * * *

The members of the Church Paul decided to abandon have concluded that they no longer want to associate with her. We hold that they are free to make that choice. The Jehovah's Witnesses' practice of shunning is protected under the first amendment of the United States Constitution and therefore under the provisions of the Washington state constitution.

IV. CONCLUSION

We affirm the district court's grant of summary judgment in favor of the defendants, Watchtower Bible Societies of New York and Philadelphia. Although we recognize that the harms suffered by Janice Paul are real and not insubstantial, permitting her to recover for intangible or emotional injuries would unconstitutionally restrict the Jehovah's Witnesses free exercise of religion. The First Amendment of the United States Constitution and therefore the protections of the Washington Constitution provide the Jehovah's Witnesses' with a defense to the plaintiff's cause of action— the defense of privilege. The constitutional guarantee of the free exercise of religion requires that society tolerate the type of harms suffered by Paul as a price well worth paying to safeguard the right of religious difference that all citizens enjoy. Affirmed.

Note

1. Bear v. Reformed Mennonite Church, 462 Pa. 330, 341 A.2d 105 (1975), which was briefly discussed in the court's opinion in *Paul,* involved a case brought by a man who alleged that he had been excommunicated from the church and that as part of the excommunication process all members of the church had been ordered to "shun" him. As a result, he complained that his business was collapsing, since he was unable to hire workers, obtain loans, or market his products. Furthermore, he alleged that neither his wife nor his children would speak to him. The Supreme Court of Pennsylvania, in a very brief opinion, reversed the trial court's granting of a demurrer to the complaint. The Pennsylvania Supreme Court only held that the plaintiff had pleaded sufficient facts to entitle him to proceed with his action. It expressly stated that it did not rule out the possibility that "the First Amendment may present a complete and valid defense to the allegations of the complaint." On the general subject, *see* Comment, *Damned If You Do, Damned If You Don't: Religious Shunning and the Free Exercise Clause,* 137 U.Pa.L.Rev. 27 (1988).

2. In an important more recent case, Guinn v. the Church of Christ of Collinsville, Oklahoma, 775 P.2d 766 (Okl.1989), the Supreme Court of Oklahoma partially upheld an award of damages against the defendant church. The plaintiff had been confronted by the elders of the church with an allegation that she had been engaging in fornication. The initial confrontation was in a laundromat in front of her children. She admitted having an affair. The elders then requested that she appear before the church and repent of her sin and that she refrain from seeing her companion. After several other meetings, the elders told the plaintiff that if she did not repent they would initiate a withdrawal of fellowship process against her. This process involved the elders informing the congregation of her sexual involvement. After seeking legal advice, she wrote the elders imploring them not to publicize her sexual involvement and resigning from the church. Apparently the Church of Christ does not permit a member to disassociate from it. She was therefore publicly branded a fornicator. A letter was sent to four other Church of Christ congregations in the area advising them that the Collinsville church had

withdrawn its fellowship from the plaintiff and the reasons for its having done so. The membership of the Church of Christ comprised about five percent of the population in the Collinsville area. The majority of the Oklahoma Supreme Court ruled that both compensatory and punitive damages could be awarded for invasion of privacy and intentional infliction of emotional distress for the actions of the elders subsequent to the plaintiff's attempt to resign from the church. It held that, regardless of church doctrine, the plaintiff had a right to resign from the church. A judgment for substantial damages was vacated, and the case was returned to the trial court, because it was not clear from the jury's award to what extent it had taken into account the actions of the elders prior to the plaintiff's attempt to resign from the church. One judge dissented on the issue of whether punitive damages could be awarded, and two judges would not have allowed any award of damages at all. Having joined the church voluntarily, they argued, the plaintiff was obliged to accept the consequences, including the church doctrine refusing to recognize any attempt at disassociation. The case is somewhat unclear because there is some basis in the record to support the conclusion that the plaintiff had admitted her sexual dalliance under some promise of confidentiality. The major thrust of the case would thus appear to be one involving an invasion of privacy, a subject that will be discussed in Chapter 19, *infra,* in which emotional distress is merely one component of the damage award. In Hadnot v. Shaw, 826 P.2d 978 (Okla.1992), the court reaffirmed its holding that, after excommunication or expulsion or the voluntary withdrawal of an individual from membership in the church, a church no longer enjoys any general immunity from tort liability in an action brought by former members who alleged that the church had publicly explained their expulsion from the local Mormon church as being based on grounds of "fornication."

3. The reluctance of courts to get involved in ecclesiastical doctrinal disputes is well illustrated by O'Connor v. Diocese of Honolulu, 77 Haw. 383, 885 P.2d 361 (1994), in which the plaintiff, the publisher of a lay religious newspaper who had been excommunicated by the local Catholic Bishop for supporting the late Archbishop Marcel Lefebre, unsuccessfully sought to bring an action seeking *inter alia,* damages for mental distress, on a variety of theories. The courts are reluctant to intervene in the activities of religious bodies even when the content of the religious belief in question is not in dispute. For example, in Murphy v. I.S.K.Con. of New England, Inc., 409 Mass. 842, 571 N.E.2d 340 (1991), the court vacated a substantial judgment and dismissed that portion of the complaint based on a theory of intentional infliction of emotional distress when the supporting evidence was that the plaintiff's daughter had, when a minor, as a member of the Hare Krishna religion been exposed to the church's teaching on the inferior status of women and its claims that the "earthly family was a perversion of the Krishna family." It was not for the courts "to consider the propriety of constitutionally protected religious beliefs." Nevertheless, in Wollersheim v. Church of Scientology, 15 Cal.App.4th 1426, 6 Cal.Rptr.2d 532 (1992), it was held that, even accepting that the church's practices of "auditing," "disconnect" and "fair game" were religious practices, they nevertheless could be the basis of an action for intentional infliction of emotional distress when it was found that they were conducted in a coercive environment and were thus not truly "voluntary." The jury awarded a total of $30,000,000 in compensatory and punitive damages. This award was reduced on appeal to $500,000 in compensatory damages and $2,000,000 in punitive damages. Before its final disposition in the Califor-

nia Court of Appeals, the case reached the United States Supreme Court which, 499 U.S. 914, 111 S.Ct. 1298, 113 L.Ed.2d 234 (1991), vacated the initial California appellate judgment for reconsideration on the punitive damage issue, in the light of Pacific Mutual Life Insurance Company v. Haslip, 499 U.S. 1, 111 S.Ct. 1032, 113 L.Ed.2d 1 (1991), discussed in Chapter 10, *supra* at p. 792f. As already indicated, on reconsideration, the California Court of Appeal held that the punitive damage award met the *Haslip* criteria. On the general subject of religion and the tort of intentional infliction of emotional distress, *see* P. Hayden, *Religiously Motivated "Outrageous" Conduct: Intentional Infliction of Emotional Distress as a Weapon Against "Other People's Faiths,"* 34 Wm. & Mary L.Rev. 580 (1993).

HUSTLER MAGAZINE v. FALWELL

Supreme Court of the United States, 1988.
485 U.S. 46, 108 S.Ct. 876, 99 L.Ed.2d 41.

CHIEF JUSTICE REHNQUIST delivered the opinion of the Court.

Petitioner Hustler Magazine, Inc., is a magazine of nationwide circulation. Respondent Jerry Falwell, a nationally known minister who has been active as a commentator on politics and public affairs, sued petitioner and its publisher, petitioner Larry Flynt, to recover damages for invasion of privacy, libel, and intentional infliction of emotional distress. The District Court directed a verdict against respondent on the privacy claim, and submitted the other two claims to a jury. The jury found for petitioners on the defamation claim, but found for respondent on the claim for intentional infliction of emotional distress and awarded damages. We now consider whether this award is consistent with the First and Fourteenth Amendments of the United States Constitution.

The inside front cover of the November 1983 issue of Hustler Magazine featured a "parody" of an advertisement for Campari Liqueur that contained the name and picture of respondent and was entitled "Jerry Falwell talks about his first time." This parody was modeled after actual Campari ads that included interviews with various celebrities about their "first times." Although it was apparent by the end of each interview that this meant the first time they sampled Campari, the ads clearly played on the sexual double entendre of the general subject of "first times." Copying the form and layout of these Campari ads, Hustler's editors chose respondent as the featured celebrity and drafted an alleged "interview" with him in which he states that his "first time" was during a drunken incestuous rendezvous with his mother in an outhouse. The Hustler parody portrays respondent and his mother as drunk and immoral, and suggests that respondent is a hypocrite who preaches only when he is drunk. In small print at the bottom of the page, the ad contains the disclaimer, "ad parody—not to be taken seriously." The magazine's table of contents also lists the ad as "Fiction; Ad and Personality Parody."

Soon after the November issue of Hustler became available to the public, respondent brought this diversity action in the United States District Court for the Western District of Virginia against Hustler Magazine, Inc., Larry C. Flynt, and Flynt Distributing Co. Respondent stated in his complaint that publication of the ad parody in Hustler entitled him to recover damages for libel, invasion of privacy, and intentional infliction of emotional distress. The case proceeded to trial.[1] At the close of the evidence, the District Court granted a directed verdict for petitioners on the invasion of privacy claim. The jury then found against respondent on the libel claim, specifically finding that the ad parody could not "reasonably be understood as describing actual facts about [respondent] or actual events in which [he] participated." App. to Pet. for Cert. C1. The jury ruled for respondent on the intentional infliction of emotional distress claim, however, and stated that he should be awarded $100,000 in compensatory damages, as well as $50,000 each in punitive damages from petitioners.[2] Petitioners' motion for judgment notwithstanding the verdict was denied.

On appeal, the United States Court of Appeals for the Fourth Circuit affirmed the judgment against petitioners. *Falwell v. Flynt*, 797 F.2d 1270 (C.A.4 1986). The court rejected petitioners' argument that the "actual malice" standard of *New York Times Co. v. Sullivan*, 376 U.S. 254, 84 S.Ct. 710, 11 L.Ed.2d 686 (1964), must be met before respondent can recover for emotional distress. The court agreed that because respondent is concededly a public figure, petitioners are "entitled to the same level of first amendment protection in the claim for intentional infliction of emotional distress that they received in [respondent's] claim for libel." 797 F.2d, at 1274. But this does not mean that a literal application of the actual malice rule is appropriate in the context of an emotional distress claim. In the court's view, the *New York Times* decision emphasized the constitutional importance not of the falsity of the statement or the defendant's disregard for the truth, but of the heightened level of culpability embodied in the requirement of "knowing * * * or reckless" conduct. Here, the *New York Times* standard is satisfied by the state-law requirement, and the jury's finding, that the defendants have acted intentionally or recklessly.[3] The Court of Appeals then went on to reject the contention that because the jury found that the ad parody did not describe actual facts about respondent, the ad was an opinion that is protected by the First Amendment. As the court put it, this was "irrelevant," as the issue is "whether [the ad's] publication was sufficiently outrageous to constitute intentional infliction of emotional distress." *Id.*, at 1276. Petitioners then filed a petition for rehearing en banc, but this was denied by a divided court. Given the importance of the constitutional issues involved, we granted certiorari.

This case presents us with a novel question involving First Amendment limitations upon a State's authority to protect its citizens from the intentional infliction of emotional distress. We must decide whether a public figure may recover damages for emotional harm caused by the publication of an ad parody offensive to him, and doubtless gross and

---

1. While the case was pending, the ad parody was published in Hustler magazine a second time.

2. The jury found no liability on the part of Flynt Distributing Co., Inc. It is consequently not a party to this appeal.

3. Under Virginia law, in an action for intentional infliction of emotional distress a plaintiff must show that the defendant's con-

duct (1) is intentional or reckless; (2) offends generally accepted standards of decency or morality; (3) is causally connected with the plaintiff's emotional distress; and (4) caused emotional distress that was severe. 797 F.2d, at 1275, n. 4 (citing *Womack v. Eldridge*, 215 Va. 338, 210 S.E.2d 145 (1974)). [Ed. note] This case will be presented at p. 1053, *infra*.

repugnant in the eyes of most. Respondent would have us find that a State's interest in protecting public figures from emotional distress is sufficient to deny First Amendment protection to speech that is patently offensive and is intended to inflict emotional injury, even when that speech could not reasonably have been interpreted as stating actual facts about the public figure involved. This we decline to do.

At the heart of the First Amendment is the recognition of the fundamental importance of the free flow of ideas and opinions on matters of public interest and concern. * * * We have therefore been particularly vigilant to ensure that individual expressions of ideas remain free from governmentally imposed sanctions. The First Amendment recognizes no such thing as a "false" idea. *Gertz v. Robert Welch, Inc.,* 418 U.S. 323, 339, 94 S.Ct. 2997, 3007, 41 L.Ed.2d 789 (1974). * * *

The sort of robust political debate encouraged by the First Amendment is bound to produce speech that is critical of those who hold public office or those public figures who are "intimately involved in the resolution of important public questions or, by reason of their fame, shape events in areas of concern to society at large." *Associated Press v. Walker,* decided with *Curtis Publishing Co. v. Butts,* 388 U.S. 130, 164, 87 S.Ct. 1975, 1996, 18 L.Ed.2d 1094 (1967)(Warren, C.J., concurring in result). * * *

Of course, this does not mean that *any* speech about a public figure is immune from sanction in the form of damages. Since *New York Times Co. v. Sullivan, supra,* we have consistently ruled that a public figure may hold a speaker liable for the damage to reputation caused by publication of a defamatory falsehood, but only if the statement was made "with knowledge that it was false or with reckless disregard of whether it was false or not." *Id.,* 376 U.S., at 279–280, 84 S.Ct., at 726. False statements of fact are particularly valueless; they interfere with the truth-seeking function of the marketplace of ideas, and they cause damage to an individual's reputation that cannot easily be repaired by counterspeech, however persuasive or effective. * * * But even though falsehoods have little value in and of themselves, * * * a rule that would impose strict liability on a publisher for false factual assertions would have an undoubted "chilling" effect on speech relating to public figures that does have constitutional value. "Freedoms of expression require 'breathing space.' " *Philadelphia Newspapers, Inc. v. Hepps,* 475 U.S. 767, 772, 106 S.Ct. 1558, 1561, 89 L.Ed.2d 783 (1986)(quoting *New York Times,* 376 U.S., at 272, 84 S.Ct., at 721). This breathing space is provided by a constitutional rule that allows public figures to recover for libel or defamation only when they can prove *both* that the statement was false and that the statement was made with the requisite level of culpability.

Respondent argues, however, that a different standard should apply in this case because here the State seeks to prevent not reputational damage, but the severe emotional distress suffered by the person who is the subject of an offensive publication. * * * In respondent's view, and in the view of the Court of Appeals, so long as the utterance was intended to inflict emotional distress, was outrageous, and did in fact inflict serious emotional distress, it is of no constitutional import whether the statement was a fact or an opinion, or whether it was true or false. It is the intent to cause injury that is the gravamen of the tort, and the State's interest in preventing emotional harm simply outweighs whatever interest a speaker may have in speech of this type.

Generally speaking the law does not regard the intent to inflict emotional distress as one which should receive much solicitude, and it is quite understandable that most if not all jurisdictions have chosen to make it civilly culpable where the conduct in question is sufficiently "outrageous." But in the world of debate about public affairs, many things done with motives that are less than admirable are protected by the First Amendment. In *Garrison v. Louisiana*, 379 U.S. 64, 85 S.Ct. 209, 13 L.Ed.2d 125 (1964), we held that even when a speaker or writer is motivated by hatred or ill-will his expression was protected by the First Amendment:

> "Debate on public issues will not be uninhibited if the speaker must run the risk that it will be proved in court that he spoke out of hatred; even if he did speak out of hatred, utterances honestly believed contribute to the free interchange of ideas and the ascertainment of truth." *Id.*, at 73, 85 S.Ct., at 215.

Thus while such a bad motive may be deemed controlling for purposes of tort liability in other areas of the law, we think the First Amendment prohibits such a result in the area of public debate about public figures.

Were we to hold otherwise, there can be little doubt that political cartoonists and satirists would be subjected to damages awards without any showing that their work falsely defamed its subject. Webster's defines a caricature as "the deliberately distorted picturing or imitating of a person, literary style, etc. by exaggerating features or mannerisms for satirical effect." Webster's New Unabridged Twentieth Century Dictionary of the English Language 275 (2d ed. 1979). The appeal of the political cartoon or caricature is often based on exploration of unfortunate physical traits or politically embarrassing events—an exploration often calculated to injure the feelings of the subject of the portrayal. The art of the cartoonist is often not reasoned or evenhanded, but slashing and one-sided. One cartoonist expressed the nature of the art in these words:

> "The political cartoon is a weapon of attack, of scorn and ridicule and satire; it is least effective when it tries to pat some politician on the back. It is usually as welcome as a bee sting and is always controversial in some quarters." Long, The Political Cartoon: Journalism's Strongest Weapon, The Quill, 56, 57 (Nov.1962).

Several famous examples of this type of intentionally injurious speech were drawn by Thomas Nast, probably the greatest American cartoonist to date, who was associated for many years during the post-Civil War era with Harper's Weekly. In the pages of that publication Nast conducted a graphic vendetta against William M. "Boss" Tweed and his corrupt associates in New York City's "Tweed Ring." It has been described by one historian of the subject as "a sustained attack which in its passion and effectiveness stands alone in the history of American graphic art." M. Keller, The Art and Politics of Thomas Nast 177 (1968). Another writer explains that the success of the Nast cartoon was achieved "because of the emotional impact of its presentation. It continuously goes beyond the bounds of good taste and conventional manners." C. Press, The Political Cartoon 251 (1981).

Despite their sometimes caustic nature, from the early cartoon portraying George Washington as an ass down to the present day, graphic depictions and satirical cartoons have played a prominent role in public and political debate. Nast's castigation of the Tweed Ring, Walt McDougall's characterization of presidential candidate James G. Blaine's banquet with the millionaires at Delmonico's as "The Royal Feast of Belshazzar," and numerous other efforts have undoubtedly had an effect on the course and outcome of contemporaneous debate. Lincoln's tall, gangling posture, Teddy Roosevelt's glasses and teeth, and Franklin D. Roosevelt's jutting jaw and cigarette holder have been memorialized by political cartoons with an effect that could not have been obtained by the photographer or the portrait artist. From the viewpoint of history it is clear that our political discourse would have been considerably poorer without them.

Respondent contends, however, that the caricature in question here was so "outrageous" as to distinguish it from more traditional political cartoons. There is no doubt that the caricature of respondent and his mother published in Hustler is at best a distant cousin of the political cartoons described above, and a rather poor relation at that. If it were possible by laying down a principled standard to separate the one from the other, public discourse would probably suffer little or no harm. But we doubt that there is any such standard, and we are quite sure that the pejorative description "outrageous" does not supply one. "Outrageousness" in the area of political and social discourse has an inherent subjectiveness about it which would allow a jury to impose liability on the basis of the jurors' tastes or views, or perhaps on the basis of their dislike of a particular expression. An "outrageousness" standard thus runs afoul of our longstanding refusal to allow damages to be awarded because the speech in question may have an adverse emotional impact on the audience. * * *

Admittedly, these oft-repeated First Amendment principles, like other principles, are subject to limitations. We recognized in *Pacifica Foundation,* that speech that is " 'vulgar,' 'offensive,' and 'shocking' " is "not entitled to absolute constitutional protection under all circumstances." 438 U.S., at 747, 98 S.Ct., at 3039. * * * But the sort of expression involved in this case does not seem to us to be governed by any exception to the general First Amendment principles stated above.

We conclude that public figures and public officials may not recover for the tort of intentional infliction of emotional distress by reason of publications such as the one here at issue without showing in addition that the publication contains a false statement of fact which was made with "actual malice," *i.e.,* with knowledge that the statement was false or with reckless disregard as to whether or not it was true. This is not merely a "blind application" of the *New York Times* standard, see *Time, Inc. v. Hill,* 385 U.S. 374, 390, 87 S.Ct. 534, 543, 17 L.Ed.2d 456 (1967), it reflects our considered judgment that such a standard is necessary to give adequate "breathing space" to the freedoms protected by the First Amendment.

Here it is clear that respondent Falwell is a "public figure" for purposes of First Amendment law.[5] The jury found against respondent on his libel claim when it decided that the Hustler ad parody could not "reasonably be understood as describing actual facts about [respondent] or actual events in which [he] participated." App. to Pet. for Cert. Cl. The Court of Appeals interpreted the jury's finding to be that the ad parody "was not reasonably believable," 797 F.2d, at 1278, and in accordance with our custom we accept this finding. Respondent is thus relegated to his claim for damages awarded by the jury for the intentional infliction of emotional distress by "outrageous" conduct. But for reasons heretofore stated this claim cannot, consistently with the First Amendment, form a basis for the award of damages when the conduct in question is the publication of a caricature such as the ad parody involved here. The judgment of the Court of Appeals is accordingly reversed.

JUSTICE WHITE, concurring in the judgment.

As I see it, the decision in *New York Times v. Sullivan,* 376 U.S. 254, 84 S.Ct. 710, 11 L.Ed.2d 686 (1964), has little to do with this case, for here the jury found that the ad contained no assertion of fact. But I agree with the Court that the judgment below, which penalized the publication of the parody, cannot be squared with the First Amendment.

Note

For a similar case, *see* Dworkin v. Hustler Magazine, Inc., 867 F.2d 1188 (9th Cir.1989), *cert. denied* 493 U.S. 812, 110 S.Ct. 59, 107 L.Ed.2d 26 (1989). On the general subject of the constitutional problems raised by the tort of intentional infliction of emotional distress, *see* Note, *First Amendment Limits on Tort Liability for Words Intended to Inflict Severe Emotional Distress,* 85 Colum.L.Rev. 1749 (1985). The next few cases will present a sampling of situations in which the courts have tangled with the question of when the intentional infliction of emotional distress is actionable. Do you think these cases adequately take into account the constitutional considerations which were the focus of *Paul* and *Falwell?* What do you think of a doctrine that permits so-called "ordinary people," but not public figures, to recover for the intentional infliction of emotional distress by virtue of speech-related activities? What result would you expect if Falwell's mother had brought suit?

WOMACK v. ELDRIDGE

Supreme Court of Virginia, 1974.
215 Va. 338, 210 S.E.2d 145.

I'ANSON, CHIEF JUSTICE.

Plaintiff, Danny Lee Womack, instituted this action against the defendant, Rosalie Eldridge, to recover compensatory and punitive damages for mental shock and distress allegedly caused by the defendant's willful, wanton, malicious, fraudulent and deceitful acts and conduct toward him. The question of punitive damages was stricken by the trial court and the jury returned a verdict for the plaintiff in the amount of $45,000. The trial

---

5. Neither party disputes this conclusion. Respondent is the host of a nationally syndicated television show and was the founder and president of a political organization formerly known as the Moral Majority. He is also the founder of Liberty University in Lynchburg, Virginia, and is the author of several books and publications. Who's Who in America 849 (44th ed. 1986–1987).

court set aside the verdict *non obstante veredicto* on the ground that there could be no recovery for emotional distress in the absence of "physical damage or other bodily harm." We granted plaintiff a writ of error. Defendant did not assign cross-error, although the record shows she excepted to many rulings in the court below and several of them are relied upon in her brief and argument before us.

Plaintiff assigned numerous errors, but the controlling question is whether one who by extreme and outrageous conduct intentionally or recklessly causes severe emotional distress to another is subject to liability for such emotional distress absent any bodily injury.

The evidence shows that defendant had been engaged in the business of investigating cases for attorneys for many years. She was employed by Richard E. Seifert and his attorney to obtain a photograph of the plaintiff to be used as evidence in the trial of Seifert, who was charged with sexually molesting two young boys. On May 27, 1970, about 8 a.m., defendant went to plaintiff's home and upon gaining admittance told him that she was a Mrs. Jackson from the newspaper and that she was writing an article on Skateland. Defendant asked plaintiff, who was a coach at Skateland, if she could take a picture of him for publication with the article, and he readily consented.

Shortly thereafter defendant delivered the photograph to Seifert's counsel while he was representing Seifert at his preliminary hearing. Seifert's counsel showed plaintiff's photograph to the two young boys and asked if he was the one who molested them. When they replied that he was not, counsel withdrew the photograph and put it in his briefcase. However, the Commonwealth's Attorney then asked to see the photograph and requested additional information about the person shown in it. Defendant was then called to the stand and she supplied the plaintiff's name and address. Plaintiff's photograph in no way resembled Seifert, and the only excuse given by defendant for taking plaintiff's picture was that he was at Skateland when Seifert was arrested. However, the offenses alleged against Seifert did not occur at Skateland.

The Commonwealth's Attorney then directed a detective to go to plaintiff's home and bring him to court. The detective told plaintiff that his photograph had been presented in court; that the Commonwealth's Attorney wanted him to appear at the proceedings; and that he could either appear voluntarily then or he would be summoned. Plaintiff agreed to go voluntarily. When called as a witness, plaintiff testified as to the circumstances under which defendant had obtained his photograph. He also said that he had not molested any children and that he knew nothing about the charges against Seifert.

A police officer questioned plaintiff several times thereafter. Plaintiff was also summoned to appear as a witness before the grand jury but he was not called. However, he was summoned to appear several times at Seifert's trial in the circuit court because of continuances of the cases.

Plaintiff testified that he suffered great shock, distress and nervousness because of defendant's fraud and deceit and her wanton, willful and malicious conduct in obtaining his photograph and turning it over to Seifert's attorney to be used in court. He suffered great anxiety as to what people would think of him and feared that he would be accused of molesting the boys. He had been unable to sleep while the matter was being investigated. While testifying in the instant case he became emotional and incoherent. Plaintiff's wife also testified that her husband experienced great shock and mental depression from the involvement.

* * *

In the case at bar, reasonable men may disagree as to whether defendant's conduct was extreme and outrageous and whether plaintiff's emotional distress was severe. Thus, the questions presented were for a jury to determine. A jury could conclude from the evidence presented that defendant willfully, recklessly, intentionally and deceitfully obtained plaintiff's photograph for the purpose of permitting her employers to use it as a defense in a criminal case without considering the effect it would have on the plaintiff. There is nothing in the evidence that even suggests that plaintiff may have been involved in the child molesting cases. The record shows that the only possible excuse for involving the plaintiff was that Seifert was arrested at the place where plaintiff was employed. A reasonable person would or should have recognized the likelihood of the serious mental distress that would be caused in involving an innocent person in child molesting cases. If the two boys had hesitated in answering that the man in the photograph was not the one who had molested them, it is evident that the finger of suspicion would have been pointed at the plaintiff.

* * *

Judgment reversed, jury verdict reinstated, and final judgment.

MEITER v. CAVANAUGH

Court of Appeals of Colorado, 1978.
40 Colo.App. 454, 580 P.2d 399.

PIERCE, JUDGE.

Defendant appeals from an adverse judgment entered upon a jury verdict, alleging that plaintiff failed to establish a prima facie case of intentional infliction of emotional distress by outrageous conduct. Defendant also argues that the evidence is insufficient to justify the award of $5,500 in actual and $10,000 in exemplary damages. We affirm the judgment in its entirety.

* * *

In March of 1973, plaintiff and defendant entered into a specific performance contract, under which plaintiff was to purchase defendant's home. Plaintiff wanted to buy the house for her grandchildren and recently widowed daughter-in-law. The contract provided that defendant would have a right to retain possession of the property on a rental basis for a period not to exceed six weeks after the delivery of the deed. Since the deed was delivered at the closing on April 12, 1973, defendant's rental period ended on May 25, and plaintiff was entitled to exclusive possession on May 26.

Sometime in late May or early June, plaintiff went to the house to inquire about the surrender of possession. Defendant informed her, for the first time, that he would be unable to move until the end of his children's school term, sometime in early June. Plaintiff explained that her daughter-in-law desperately needed a place to stay. Defendant became quite belligerent, and responded, "Well, as far as that's concerned, you can move [her furniture] up in that shanty. When I get out, you can roll it down the hill."

During another early June encounter, defendant told plaintiff, "I'm an attorney. I know my rights. I'll move when I'm damn well ready." He also called plaintiff, who was visibly bandaged after recent cancer surgery, a "sick old woman."

On June 7, 1973, defendant mailed a letter to plaintiff notifying her that he was considering legal action. The letter implied that defendant had some special influence with the court:

"I am sure the local court known personally to me over the years, will appreciate my problem * * *. In fact, he may just break our contract, which would satisfy me and I will repay every cent of your money."

Meanwhile, plaintiff had to find another home for her daughter-in-law, and she purchased one on June 13, 1973. When defendant finally vacated in early July, plaintiff found that the premises had been damaged. Some windows were broken, a few sliding doors were untracked, and the lock on the back door was broken. Several outdoor light fixtures had been removed, and a built-in barbeque had been dismantled. After repairing some of this damage, plaintiff sold the house in December.

I.

The first question we must address is whether this conduct was sufficiently "outrageous" to withstand defendant's motions for a directed verdict and judgment notwithstanding the verdict. We hold that it was.

* * *

II.

Defendant argues that the award of damages was excessive and unsupported by the evidence. Again, we disagree.

The amount of damages is within the sole province of the jury, and an award will not be disturbed unless it is completely unsupported by the record. * * *

Here, there was evidence that plaintiff spent over $900 in repairing the damage to the house. There was also evidence that she suffered a loss exceeding $1,700 in re-selling the house, as well as incurring a substantial sum in brokerage fees. These out-of-pocket expenses, in addition to the damages attributable to the mental distress alone, were sufficient to support the award. The individual acts, or failures to act, which resulted in these expenditures, could be considered by reasonable jurors to be part of the total scheme of outrageous conduct directed at this plaintiff by this defendant. The isolated fact that plaintiff may not have incurred medical expenses immediately after the incidents does not require reversal. * * *

Nor does the fact that these out-of-pocket expenses may have been recoverable in an action for breach of the lease preclude their recovery in tort. * * *

Since the award of actual damages was supported by the record, and since the exemplary damages are not manifestly exorbitant, we affirm the judgment as to exemplary damages as well. * * *

* * *

The judgment is affirmed.

COYTE, JUDGE, concurring in part and dissenting in part:

I agree that the conduct of defendant toward the plaintiff constituted outrageous conduct. However, I feel that the award of damages is excessive and not supported by the evidence, where to justify the award, the majority has to point to the consequential damages suffered by plaintiff because of defendant's breach of contract. The cause should be remanded for a new trial on the damage issue but limited to mental suffering and the consequential damages flowing from the mental suffering and not the breach of contract.

HOOD v. NAETER BROTHERS PUBLISHING CO.

Court of Appeals of Missouri, 1978.
562 S.W.2d 770.

CLEMENS, PRESIDING JUDGE.

Action for damages for allegedly outrageous conduct by a newspaper in publishing plaintiff's name as witness to a murder. The trial court sustained defendants' motion for summary judgment and plaintiff has appealed.

Plaintiff pleaded he was an employee of a liquor store and was working on the evening of August 7, 1976 when the store was robbed by two masked black men. Plaintiff witnessed the fatal shooting of a fellow employee. The next day the Cape Girardeau police department released its report to the press, giving details of the robbery, including plaintiff's name and address. At this time, plaintiff, a recent resident of Cape Girardeau, was not listed in the telephone directory. The following day defendant Naeter Brothers published a front-page article, written by defendant Don Smith, reporting the robbery and murder in the "Southeast Missourian." The article identified plaintiff as a witness and printed his address. The two suspects were still at large.

Plaintiff further pleaded that as a result of the publication he has been in constant fear, has been forced to change his residence repeatedly, has become suspicious of all black persons and has been under the care of a psychiatrist.

Plaintiff contends defendants' publication of his name and address constituted outrageous conduct because defendants knew or should have known the killers were still at large. He argues that the issue of culpability is for a jury to determine and, accordingly, the trial court erred in granting summary judgment for defendant.

The issue is whether the alleged acts constitute outrageous conduct as a matter of law. We say no. In Pretsky v. Southwestern Bell Telephone Co., 396 S.W.2d 566, 568 (Mo.1965), our supreme court adopted § 46 of the Restatement of the Law of Torts and its comment (d):

* * *

Comment (d) gives guidance on the meaning of "extreme" and "outrageous."

"(d) Extreme and outrageous conduct. The cases thus far decided have found liability only where the defendant's conduct has been extreme and outrageous * * *. Liability has been found only where the conduct has been so outrageous in character, and so extreme in degree, as to go beyond all possible bounds of decency, and to be regarded as atrocious, and utterly intolerable in a civilized community. Generally, the case is one in which the recitation of the facts to an average member of the community would arouse his resentment against the actor, and lead him to exclaim, 'Outrageous!'

The liability clearly does not extend to mere insults, indignities, threats, arrogancies, petty oppression, or other trivialities. The rough edges of our society are still in need of a good deal of filing down, and in the meantime plaintiffs must necessarily be expected and required to be hardened to a certain amount of rough language, and to occasional acts that are definitely inconsiderate and unkind * * *."

Cases from other jurisdictions illustrate the type of conduct held to be outrageous. In Blakeley v. Shortal's Estate, 236 Iowa 787, 20 N.W.2d 28 (1945), the court upheld recovery against decedent's estate where the deceased slit his throat in plaintiff's kitchen and plaintiff suffered shock upon finding the body. And in Great Atlantic and Pacific Tea Co. v. Roch, 160 Md. 189, 153 A. 22 (1931), the court affirmed a jury verdict for plaintiff where defendant delivered a dead rat in a package instead of the bread plaintiff had ordered.[a]

Missouri cases involving outrageous conduct have dealt with creditors harassing debtors. In Liberty Loan Corp. of Antioch v. Brown, 493 S.W.2d 664[4] (Mo.App.1973), the court upheld a verdict for plaintiff where defendant made harassing, abusive and threatening phone calls to plaintiff in order to collect a debt. In Warrem v. Parrish, 436 S.W.2d 670[6] (Mo. 1969), the court upheld a count of plaintiff's petition alleging outrageous conduct where plaintiff pleaded that defendant, in order to collect a debt, put plaintiff's car on a lift for three hours, threatened plaintiff and refused to return the car until payment was made.

In contrast, in *Pretsky, supra,* at 396 S.W.2d 566 the court ruled plaintiff failed to state a cause of action for outrageous conduct where she alleged defendant's employee gained entrance to her house by falsely stating there was trouble on her telephone line and that he must enter to

a. [Ed. note] In *Roch,* the plaintiff alleged, and the evidence introduced supported the allegation, that she had suffered physical injuries as a result of her fright. The physical injuries included those suffered when she fainted and fell to the floor on seeing the dead rat.

correct the problem. The court followed § 46 of the Restatement and held defendant's conduct was not actionable, ruling:

> "The facts pleaded do not constitute what could be considered to be extreme and outrageous conduct * * *" and the petition "does not contain averments which invoke substantive principles of law which entitle plaintiff to relief."[b]

Similarly, in Nelson v. Grice, 411 S.W.2d 117[4] (Mo.1967), the court held no outrageous conduct was shown. There, defendants had leased property to plaintiff on which he ran a grocery store. Subsequently, defendants built a second building on the property and told plaintiff he could rent it at the same rate. Instead, defendants raised the rent, harassed plaintiff and operated their own store in competition. As a result, plaintiff suffered a heart attack and attempted suicide. The supreme court, based on that part of Restatement quoted in *Presky, supra,* reversed a jury verdict for plaintiff, holding no outrageous conduct was shown.

We hold the conduct alleged here is not of the extreme and outrageous nature contemplated by § 46 of the Restatement. The publication of the name and address of the sole witness to a violent crime at a time when the criminals are at large may be unwise but it does not go beyond the bounds of human decency. Furthermore, the published information was a matter of public record and readily available to all interested persons.[1]

We hold the trial court did not err in rendering summary judgment against plaintiff.

Judgment affirmed.

Notes

1. In Hyde v. City of Columbia, 637 S.W.2d 251 (Mo.Ct.App.1982), the court upheld a cause of action based on a negligent publication theory by a woman whose name, as the victim of a kidnaping, and address were revealed by the defendant city to the defendant newspaper which then published the information. The plaintiff alleged that her unknown assailant thereafter "terrorized her on seven different occasions." With regard to the action against the newspaper, the court held that the police report upon which the newspaper's story was based was not a "public record," and that the "dictum" of the *Hood* case that such reports were matters of public record was ill-advised. Whether the *Hyde* court's conclusion, that police reports about private persons are not matters of public record or interest, can support an action against a newspaper now seems questionable in the light of The Florida Star v. B.J.F. 491 U.S. 524, 109 S.Ct. 2603, 105 L.Ed.2d 443 (1989), which will be discussed at p. 1237, *infra*, when we consider the tort of invasion of privacy.

2. In Harris v. Jones, 281 Md. 560, 380 A.2d 611 (1977), the defendant, the plaintiff's supervisor at a factory, had ridiculed and mimicked the plaintiff

---

b. [Ed. note] In *Pretsky*, the plaintiff also unsuccessfully sought relief under § 48 of the *Restatement (Second) of Torts* dealing with gross insults by servants of common carriers or public utilities. There were no allegations of any insults. The plaintiff relied exclusively on the entry under false pretenses.

1. Plaintiff complains of the dissemination of his name and address to the public. Although neither party has raised the first amendment issue, the case of Cox Broadcasting Corp. v. Cohn, 420 U.S. 469, 95 S.Ct. 1029, 43 L.Ed.2d 328 (1975), is relevant. [p. 1229, *infra.*] * * *

who had a severe stuttering problem. The defendant's conduct was held not to be actionable. The court did not feel compelled to decide whether the supervisor's conduct was "extreme or outrageous" because it concluded that the plaintiff had made an insufficient showing that the humiliation he had suffered had led to "severe emotional distress." For the emotional distress to be sufficiently severe, the court opined that it must be a *"severely* disabling emotional response." In Pankratz v. Willis, 155 Ariz. 8, 744 P.2d 1182 (App.1987), the court concluded that all that was required was that the distress be severe; not that it be in any way disabling. The *Pankratz* case involved a father's action against his former wife's parents for their complicity in their daughter's absconding from the United States with the child born during the plaintiff's marriage to the defendants' daughter.

3. Solicitations to sexual intercourse are generally held not to be actionable. *See* C. Magruder, *Mental and Emotional Disturbance in the Law of Torts,* 49 Harv.L.Rev. 1033, 1055 (1936)(" * * * the view being, apparently, that there is no harm in asking.") Nevertheless, repeated solicitations, under some instances, have been held to be actionable. *See, e.g.,* Samms v. Eccles, 11 Utah 2d 289, 358 P.2d 344 (1961); Mitran v. Williamson, 21 Misc.2d 106, 197 N.Y.S.2d 689 (1960). The fact that the solicitation or other sexual advance was made in a context in which the person making the solicitation or advances is in a position of actual or apparent power over the person who is the object of the solicitation or advances is a relevant factor. *See e.g.* Howard University v. Best, 484 A.2d 958 (D.C.1984)(Dean with supervisory power over plaintiff faculty member); McDaniel v. Gile, 230 Cal.App.3d 363, 281 Cal.Rptr. 242 (1991)(Attorney threatened to withhold legal services from client). It has been held, however, that a single solicitation by a professor for oral sex in return for a higher grade, where there was no evidence of any retaliation against the student who rebuffed the solicitation, was not enough to support a claim for intentional infliction of emotional distress, even if it might support an action based on some other theory against either the individual defendant or the defendant community college. Slaughter v. Waubonsee Community College, 1994 WL 663596 (N.D.Ill.1994). These cases are but a small subset of a much larger set of cases, namely those alleging sexual harassment, particularly in the workplace. Harassment on a religious, sexual, or racial basis in the workplace, when condoned by the employer, is a form of discrimination prohibited by Title VII of the Civil Rights Act of 1964, as amended, 42 U.S.C. §§ 2000e *et seq.* (1988). The more difficult cases concern harassment based upon verbal conduct. Robinson v. Jacksonville Shipyards, Inc., 760 F.Supp. 1486 (M.D.Fla. 1991), which involved a claim largely based on the presence of nude pin-ups in the workplace, has received a fair amount of notoriety. The question of verbal harassment in the workplace is a vast subject raising questions that are far beyond the purview of a first-year tort class. For conflicting perspectives, *compare* E. Volokh, *Freedom of Speech and Appellate Review in Workplace Harassment Cases,* 90 Nw.U.L.Rev. 1009 (1996), *with* B. Wolman, *Verbal Sexual Harassment on the Job as Intentional Infliction of Emotional Distress,* 17 Cap.U.L.Rev. 245 (1988). *See also* K. Browne, *Title VII as Censorship: Hostile–Environment Harassment and the First Amendment,* 52 Ohio St.L.J. 481 (1991).

4. As the discussion in the *Hood* case makes clear, many of the cases in which a cause of action for the intentional infliction of severe emotional distress has been sustained have involved bill collectors. A good illustration is

Ford Motor Credit Co. v. Sheehan, 373 So.2d 956 (Fla.App.1979). The relevant facts of that case were as follows:

> On October 28, 1974, Sheehan purchased a Ford automobile which was financed by Ford Credit pursuant to the terms of a retail installment contract. Later, Sheehan moved to various locations and became delinquent on his account. Ford Credit was unable to locate Sheehan and assigned the account to a central recovery office maintained by it in Michigan. On May 1, 1975, Sheehan's mother, who lived in Coventry, Rhode Island, received a telephone call from a woman who identified herself as being employed by Mercy Hospital in San Francisco, California. She was advised that one or both of Sheehan's children had been involved in a serious automobile accident and that the caller was attempting to locate Sheehan. The mother supplied information to the caller concerning his home and business addresses and phone numbers located in Jacksonville, Florida.

> Sheehan testified that on May 1, 1975, he returned a call to his mother's home in Rhode Island, spoke to his sister, and as a result of information received in that telephone conversation, placed calls during a seven-hour period to hospitals and police departments in San Francisco, California until he finally discovered the information was false. The following day, Sheehan's automobile was repossessed by Search International, an independent contractor with Ford Credit.

There was no indication that any physical harm was sustained by the plaintiff. The court affirmed a judgment, entered on a jury verdict, awarding $4,000 in compensatory damages and $11,000 in punitive damages. The Supreme Court of Florida refused to review the case. 379 So.2d 204 (Fla.1979). The plaintiff in *Sheehan* also relied on a Florida statute prohibiting, *inter alia*, anyone while collecting a debt to "willfully communicate with the debtor or any other member of his family with such frequency as can reasonably be expected to harass the debtor or his family, or willfully engage in other conduct which can reasonably be expected to abuse or harass the debtor or any member of his family." West's Fla.Stat.Ann. § 559.72(7). The district court of appeal held the statute inapplicable to the case before it because the phone call had been made from Michigan. On the other hand, in Public Finance Corp. v. Davis, 66 Ill.2d 85, 4 Ill.Dec. 652, 360 N.E.2d 765 (1976), it was held that the following conduct which accompanied the finance company's judicial foreclosure of its security interest was not actionable:

> Count I of the amended counterclaim alleges the conduct of Public Finance which Davis claims entitles her to recover. Stripped of the conclusions, it is charged that on or about September 1, 1974, Davis informed Public Finance she was no longer employed, was on public aid and did not have enough money to make regular payments on her obligations; that in order to collect the account Public Finance from September 1, 1974, to April 4, 1975, called Davis several times weekly, frequently more than once a day; that in order to collect the account agents of Public Finance went to Davis' home one or more times a week; that on October 15, 1974, when Davis' daughter was in the hospital, an agent of Public Finance, in order to collect the account, called the defendant at the hospital; that on that day Davis informed the agent of the severity of her daughter's condition, that she, herself, was sick and nervous and asked

that Public Finance refrain from calling her at the hospital; that on the same day an agent of Public Finance again called Davis at the hospital; that after an employee of Public Finance induced Davis to write a check and promised that the check would not be processed, Public Finance phoned an acquaintance of Davis and informed her that Davis was writing bad checks; that in November 1974 an employee of Public Finance called at Davis' home and after being told that Davis had no money with which to make a payment, with Davis' permission, used her phone to call Public Finance and to describe and report the items of Davis' household goods; that on that day the employee "failed or refused" to leave Davis' home until her son entered the room.

The Illinois Supreme Court felt that "a creditor must be given some latitude to pursue reasonable methods of collecting debts even though such methods may result in some inconvenience, embarrassment or annoyance to the debtor." The court felt that the finance company's conduct was neither abrasive enough nor prolonged enough to subject it to liability. Two justices dissented to the denial of a rehearing of the case. For other debt collector cases, *see* 87 A.L.R.3d 201 (1978). An illustrative recent case is Etchart v. Bank One, 773 F.Supp. 239 (D.Nev.1991) in which the court refused to grant summary judgment in an action for intentional infliction of emotional distress based on a bank's refusal to provide written notice that the plaintiff no longer owed the bank anything and the bank's failure to stop reporting the outstanding debt to a credit reporting agency after settlement of earlier litigation between the parties. The outrageousness of the defendants' conduct and the severity of the plaintiff's emotional distress were issues for the jury.

5. Not only are there state statutes regulating the conduct of bill collectors, such as the one involved in the *Sheehan* case which also regulates approaches to a debtor's employer and the public dissemination of the fact of a debtor's indebtedness, but there is also federal legislation on the subject. Under the Fair Debt Collection Practices Act of 1977, 15 U.S.C. § 1692 *et seq.*, certain types of debt collectors are forbidden to communicate with a consumer at "any unusual time or place." Such a debt collector is required to assume, in the absence of knowledge of circumstances to the contrary, that times before 8:00 a.m. and after 9:00 p.m. are not convenient. Among other prohibitions, the debt collector may not communicate with third parties about the consumer more than once, unless requested to do so by that third person, nor may the debt collector use any symbol or words on the envelope of a mail communication that indicate that the debt collector is in the debt collection business. The debt collector is also forbidden to communicate with a consumer by post card. The Act provides for the civil liability of a debt collector who fails to comply with the provisions of the Act. The debt collector may only escape liability if it can show that any violations of the Act were both unintentional *and* the result of what the Act calls a "bona fide error." The Act was amended in 1986 to cover the activities of lawyers who regularly engage in debt collection. The Court has held that the Act applies even to lawyers regularly engaging in debt collection litigation. Heintz v. Jenkins, 514 U.S. 291, 115 S.Ct. 1489, 131 L.Ed.2d 395 (1995).

STAR v. RABELLO

Supreme Court of Nevada, 1981.
97 Nev. 124, 625 P.2d 90.

SPRINGER, JUSTICE.

Respondent Rabello sued appellant Star for special, general and punitive damages for assault and battery. Rabello also sued as Guardian ad Litem for her daughter, Lisa Rabello, who was a witness to the attack, for intentional infliction of emotional distress. Star counterclaimed for assault and battery, alleging that Rabello initiated the fight. * * *

At trial, both sides presented conflicting evidence as to who started the fight and who was the more aggressive during its course. After hearing testimony from fifteen witnesses, the trial judge dismissed Star's counterclaim, stating that Rabello's version of the fight was corroborated by two disinterested witnesses. He then found that Star precipitated the fight, and awarded Rabello special, general and punitive damages. He also awarded Lisa Rabello, Rabello's daughter, $300.00 in general damages for intentional infliction of emotional distress.

Star appeals from the damages awarded to Lisa Rabello, arguing that Lisa should not be entitled to recovery under an intentional infliction of emotional distress cause of action. We agree.

The fight occurred at Lisa's school after the opening of a school play. Star testified that she knew Lisa was present at the time. As a result of witnessing the altercation and her "embarrassment" at being the daughter of one of the participants, Lisa has suffered from intermittent headaches, sleeplessness and an upset stomach.

There are no reported cases in this jurisdiction concerning the intentional infliction of emotional distress—the tort of "outrage." * * *

Recovery on the part of a third party witness to an outrageous act is permitted if that third party is a close relative of the person against whom the outrage was directed. Restatement of Torts 2d § 46(2). Most plaintiffs who have been permitted recovery *as bystanders,* however, have witnessed acts which were not only outrageous but unquestionably violent and shocking.

Prosser's analysis of witness recovery indicates that the outrage requirement is more difficult to meet when the act has been directed against a third party in cases in which the plaintiff has been a mere witness to the occurrence. * * *

Thus, recovery has been allowed when a husband watched his wife die because the doctor refused to treat her, Grimsby v. Samson, 85 Wash.2d 52, 530 P.2d 291 (1975), and when an illegitimate five year old sued her father's estate after she had witnessed her father kill her mother, was kept in a room with the body for seven days, and was forced to watch her father commit suicide, Mahnke v. Moore, 197 Md. 61, 77 A.2d 923 (1951). Recovery was denied when, after a boundary line dispute, plaintiff's husband was verbally abused and assaulted with a pitchfork by an irate neighbor. Wiehe v. Kukal, 225 Kan. 478, 592 P.2d 860 (1979).

In urging that Star's conduct was sufficiently outrageous to sustain her cause of action, Rabello relies on three cases.[1] In each case, the defendant had knowledge that the witness was either pregnant or had recently given birth and was in a weakened state. Knowledge of a witness's condition tends to increase the outrageous nature of the act.

There is very little case law relating to recovery based on the mere observation of outrageous acts aimed at third parties. In instances where recovery has been allowed, the observed conduct has been outrageous in the extreme. Although the trial judge found that Star's conduct was outrageous, we rule, as a matter of law, that an assault of the kind presented in this appeal is insufficient to warrant recovery by a witness to such an assault; accordingly, the judgment in favor of Lisa must be reversed.

* * *

The judgment in favor of Sandra Rabello is affirmed; the judgment in favor of Lisa Rabello is reversed.

Note

The *Restatement (Second)* also permits witnesses who are not close relatives to recover but only if they can show that "such distress results in bodily harm." Garland v. Herrin, 724 F.2d 16 (2d Cir.1983), was an action brought by the parents of a girl who, while the parents were asleep in their bedroom, had been bludgeoned to death by her boyfriend in one of the other bedrooms of the house. The trial court had held that the parents were sufficiently "present" within the meaning of *Restatement (Second) of Torts* § 46(2) to be entitled to recover, 554 F.Supp. 308 (S.D.N.Y.1983), but the Second Circuit reversed.

---

1. Jeppsen v. Jensen, 47 Utah 536, 155 P. 429 (1916)(defendant, while in plaintiff's home and in front of her children, threatened her husband with a gun); Lambert v. Brewster, 97 W.Va. 124, 125 S.E. 244 (W.Va.1924) (plaintiff witnessed forcible assault on her father); Rogers v. Williard, 144 Ark. 587, 223 S.W. 15 (1920)(defendant threatened to shoot plaintiff's husband).

Chapter 18

DEFAMATION

A. COMMON–LAW DEVELOPMENT

STANDIFER v. VAL GENE MANAGEMENT
SERVICES, INC.

Court of Appeals of Oklahoma, 1974.
527 P.2d 28.

BRIGHTMIRE, PRESIDING JUDGE.

This is a slander action. The trial court disposed of it by granting defendant a summary judgment. Whether he was correct in doing so is the only issue presented for review. We think he was and affirm.

In her petition, plaintiff stated that through the mouth of its agent, 24–year-old redheaded Sharon Gayle Wright, defendant corporation maliciously spoke and published to several people certain slanderous, false and defamatory words about plaintiff, "to-wit: That the plaintiff was a constant troublemaker; that the plaintiff was not a fit tenant; that the plaintiff was harassing her; that the plaintiff had 'cussed her out'; that the plaintiff was disruptive in nature and was bothering the other tenants; and various and numerous statements tending to degrade the plaintiff * * * and * * * spoken * * * to blacken and injure the honesty, virtue, integrity, morality and reputation of * * * plaintiff and to thereby expose her to public contempt and ridicule." As a "direct * * * result" of all this she "was compelled to move from her residence of many years and incurred [these] actual damages * * * Moving expense—$375.00; Telephone—$15.00; Automobile expense—$20.00; and additional rent—$80.00." She asked for these amounts plus $5,000 general damages and $25,000 punitive damages.

A demurrer challenging the sufficiency of the petition was overruled. Defendant's short answer did nothing more than deny the allegations regarding slander.

Following the taking of agent Wright's deposition and plaintiff's, defendant filed an amended answer adding that if the alleged statements were made, they "are true."

A pretrial conference was held a short time later. And then defendant filed a motion for summary judgment stating in substance that plaintiff's deposition testimony generally supported the factual allegations in her petition and "assuming that all the statements said to have been made by defendant were in fact made, they are insufficient as a matter of law to be the foundation for recovery."

A short time later the court agreed and in sustaining the motion said:

"The remarks under consideration, although undeniably vulgar and offensive, do not fall within any of the various categories of publications recognized by the Oklahoma statute to be slanderous *per se* * * *."

The first question to be resolved is whether under District Court Rule 13, 12 O.S.1971, Ch. 2, App., the pleadings and depositions on file in this case require a finding that no substantial controversy as to any material fact exists and if not whether under the admitted facts defendant is entitled to judgment as a matter of law.

This question involves consideration of one or two more basic issues: (1) is the alleged publication slanderous per se; or if not, (2) has special resulting damage been adequately alleged?

To start our probe of these points we quote the statute defining slander—12 O.S.1971 § 1442:

"Slander is a false and unprivileged publication, other than libel, which:

"1. Charges any person with crime, or with having been indicted, convicted or punished for crime.

"2. Imputes in him the present existence of an infectious, contagious or loathsome disease.

"3. Tends directly to injure him in respect to his office, profession, trade or business, either by imputing to him general disqualification in those respects which the office or other occupation peculiarly requires, or by imputing something with reference to his office, profession, trade or business that has a natural tendency to lessen its profit.

"4. Imputes to him impotence or want of chastity; or,

"5. Which, by natural consequences, causes actual damage."

We can dismiss from consideration those paragraphs numbered one through four as being irrelevant because not alleged by plaintiff.

Slander is one of the two torts comprising the law of defamation. In general it is an oral publication while its mate, libel, is generally a written one. The distinction between the two developed haphazardly in old English courts from as far back as Runnymede. Their decisional expediencies were influenced considerably by the rise and fall in popularity of the actions at various points in time and—during the 14th and 15th centuries—by the ecclesiastical courts' punishment of defamation as a "sin." A jurisdictional dispute between church and common law courts was temporarily resolved by allowing the latter tribunals to act if "temporal" damage could be proved and if not then the defamation was deemed a "spiritual" matter for the church to handle. In its early development slander was thought to be within the province of ecclesiastical law prompting secular courts to hold the action would not lie without proof of "temporal" damages. Eventually proof of actual damage became an essential element of slander. Then in deference to reality courts began to recognize various exceptions such as imputations of a crime, of a loathsome disease, and those adversely affecting plaintiff's trade, business, or profession—exceptions which required no proof of damages.[1] This historical distinction between libel and slander eventually found its way into the statutory law of this area while Oklahoma was still Indian Territory, along with—as can be seen above—the addition of a fourth category regarding imputation of unchastity or impotency to one.

To compare our libel statute with the one defining slander is to dramatize the distinction and underscore the former's much larger "temporal" base. It is 12 O.S.1971 § 1441 and reads:

"Libel is a false or malicious unprivileged publication by writing, printing, picture, or effigy or other fixed representation to the eye, *which exposes any person to public hatred,* contempt, ridicule or obloquy, *or which tends to deprive him of public confidence, or to injure him in his occupation,* or any malicious publication as aforesaid, designed to blacken or vilify the memory of one who is dead, and tending to scandalize his surviving relatives or friends." (emphasis ours)

At once it can be seen libel has quite a bit broader statutory definition than slander. That the historical basis for the difference is irrational is beside the point. The statute being what it is must determine human rights until otherwise legally changed.

Turning now to the case at bar, it is conceded that plaintiff has not attempted to plead or complain of any statement which would be actionable slander without proof of damages under the first four numbered paragraphs of § 1442. These are the only "per se" slanders actionable in this state. All others are "per quod." Thus if an action she has it must be in terms of paragraph five requiring pleading and proof of "actual damage."

The words said to have been spoken by defendant's agent were, we think, defamatory on their face in that they have a clear tendency to injure plaintiff's reputation. By natural import they diminish the esteem, respect, and confidence in which she is held by others. They would, had the publication been written, be actionable without proof of damages.

But it was not written and so—because they neither charge a crime, impute disease or sexual irregularity, nor tend to injure plaintiff in respect to any known office or calling—it matters not how grossly defamatory or insulting the words may be they are actionable only upon proof of "special damage." * * *

---

1. Holdsworth, Defamation in the Sixteenth and Seventeenth Centuries, 40 L.Q.Rev. 302, 397 (1924), 41 L.Q.Rev. 13 (1925); Carr, The English Law of Defamation, 18 L.Q.Rev. 255, 388 (1902); Veeder, History and Theory of the Law of Defamation, 3 Col.L.Rev. 546 (1903), 4 Col.L.Rev. 33 (1904).

The next question then is does plaintiff claim actual damages which the slander "by natural consequences" caused?

The phrase "by natural consequences" is another way of saying there must be a causal connection between the slanderous statement and the damage sought—one that is reasonably direct.

As mentioned earlier the special damages plaintiff says she sustained as a "direct result" of the defamation were various items relating to moving from defendant's apartment to another.

The only conceivable basis upon which the moving expenses could be the natural consequences of the alleged slander would be that the defamation published to plaintiff's fellow tenants caused them to react toward and treat her in such a manner as to significantly interfere with the enjoyment of her habitation and effectuate a constructive ouster therefrom.

Such causal connection is not perceptible on the face of plaintiff's petition. And since this would not necessarily foreclose proof of the consequence at trial we will examine the record to see if it discloses any admission by plaintiff fatally inconsistent with a cause and effect relationship between the slander and the move.

* * *

Interpreting the foregoing in a light most favorable to plaintiff we can see no way the alleged defamation could have caused the move for the simple reason plaintiff was unaware of it until after she vacated defendant's apartment where she presumably would still be had she had not been asked to move. The cause of the move was a request by the manager to do so—a request involving neither a tortious nor anti-contractual act— not the defamation. Injured reputation there may have been but unless it in some way precipitated the change of apartments the latter could not be a natural consequence of the former.

We therefore hold the facts admitted by plaintiff disclose she is without an actionable cause for lack of special damages hence the trial court did not err in awarding defendant a summary judgment.

Affirmed.

Notes

1. The Oklahoma statute defining slander, quoted in the court's opinion, in large part tracks the common law. *See Restatement (Second) of Torts* §§ 570–74.

2. The provision making it slander per se to say of someone that he is impotent is somewhat unusual. As will be seen in the next principal case, at common law, slander imputing lack of chastity was not actionable without proof of special damages. In 1891 Parliament enacted the Slander of Women Act, 54 & 55 Vict. c. 51, making it slander per se to impute lack of chastity to a woman. By statute or common law a similar change was accepted in the United States. *See, e.g.,* Hollman v. Brady, 16 Alaska 308, 233 F.2d 877 (9th Cir.1956); Biggerstaff v. Zimmerman, 108 Colo. 194, 114 P.2d 1098 (1941). *See also* A. King, *Constructing Gender: Sexual Slander in Nineteenth Century America,* 13 Law & Hist. Rev. 63 (1995). In 1937 *Restatement of Torts* § 574 limited the lack of chastity category to women. The *Restatement (Second)*

provision, published in 1977, extends this category of slander per se to all "serious sexual misconduct" including the lack of chastity of men and homosexuality. It remains to be seen whether the majority of courts will follow this extension.

3. The Oklahoma statutory codification of libel, quoted in *Standifer,* includes defamation of the dead. This is an extension of the common law. In most jurisdictions an action will *not* lie for defamation of the dead. *See, e.g.,* Lee v. Weston, 402 N.E.2d 23 (Ind.App.1980).[1] For the contention that such a cause of action should be generally recognized, *see* Note, *Dead But Not Forgotten: Proposals for Imposing Liability for Defamation of the Dead,* 67 Tex.L.Rev. 1525 (1989). Defamation by the dead is another matter. It has, for example, been held that the estate of the testatrix was liable for defamatory statements made in her will. Brown v. Du Frey, 1 N.Y.2d 190, 151 N.Y.S.2d 649, 134 N.E.2d 469 (1956).

4. As noted in *Standifer,* if the slander does not fall within one of the per se categories, an action will not lie without allegation and proof of special damages. In many jurisdictions such allegations and proof must be quite specific and detailed. Special damages are pecuniary losses flowing from the defamatory statement, but not all such pecuniary losses will qualify as special damages. The pecuniary loss must be more than a consequence of the defamatory statement; it must be the direct result of the plaintiff's lowered reputation in the community that has been brought about by the defendant's statement. A classic case is Terwilliger v. Wands, 17 N.Y. 54, 72 Am.Dec. 420 (1858). The defendant had told third persons that the plaintiff was having intercourse with the wife of a man serving time in the state penitentiary. The plaintiff's proof showed that he had become distraught, was unable to work, and that he had incurred medical expenses. All this was held not to be a sufficient showing of special damages.

> Where there is no proof that the character has suffered from the words, if sickness results it must be attributed to apprehension of loss of character, and such fear of harm to character, with resulting sickness and bodily prostration, cannot be such special damages as the law requires for the action. The loss of character must be a substantive loss, one which has actually taken place.

17 N.Y. at 63. Citing a leading treatise of the period, examples of special damages were "loss of a marriage, loss of hospitable gratuitous entertainment, preventing a servant or bailiff from getting a place, the loss of customers by a tradesman." *Id.* at 60.

5. With regard to the category of slander per se involving imputation of criminal conduct, many of the older cases declared that the crime must be one involving moral turpitude or, in the alternative, an indictable offense. More recent authority has held that imputation of *any* criminal conduct is enough, whether punishable by imprisonment or fine. Starobin v. Northridge Lakes Development, 94 Wis.2d 1, 287 N.W.2d 747 (1980). This shift is partially reflected in the Restatements. *Restatement of Torts* § 571 required the crime to be indictable at common law and punishable by death or imprisonment

---

1. One should also note that, in perhaps as many as one half of the states, a defamation action still will not survive the death of either the plaintiff or the defendant. For an examination of developments in this area, *see* Note, *Defamation, Survivability, and the Demise of the Antiquated "Actio Personalis" Doctrine,* 85 Colum.L.Rev. 1833 (1985).

rather than a fine. *Restatement (Second) of Torts* § 571 requires either that the conduct charged be punishable by imprisonment or involve moral turpitude.

6. The category of slander per se involving the imputation of loathsome or infectious diseases is generally restricted to venereal diseases and leprosy. *Cf. Restatement (Second) of Torts* § 572 and comments.

JONES v. JONES

House of Lords, 1916.
[1916] 2 A.C. 481.

* * *

VISCOUNT HALDANE. My Lords, the question in this appeal is whether the appellant, who was plaintiff in the action, can recover general damages for an untrue verbal imputation of immoral conduct with a married woman. He is a certificated teacher and is the senior master of a council school in Wales. It is not in dispute that the imputation of such conduct, if believed, would be seriously prejudicial to a person in his position, and might lead to the loss of an appointment which, concerned as it is with the teaching of the young, implies in the person who holds it freedom from reproach of this kind. At the same time it must be remembered that the position of a certificated teacher is not unique in this respect, for there are many other appointments that are held on a similar condition, express or implied.

The school in which the appellant was employed was looked after by his aunt, as caretaker, and she was in the habit of employing the husband of a Mrs. Ellen Roberts to do some of the cleaning. The respondent, Mrs. Jones, is found by the jury before which the action was tried to have spoken words imputing moral misconduct between the appellant and Mrs. Roberts. Mrs. Jones was the defendant in the action, and her husband was joined as being liable for his wife's tort.[a] The jury found further, in response to questions from Lush J., who tried the case, that the words "were spoken of him in the way of his calling, that is, in such a way as to imperil the retention of his office," and further that "the words imputed that he was unfit to hold his office." It is, however, clear that there was no evidence that any words were used which referred to his office or his conduct in it, and the first part of the finding cannot be relied on as anything more than an inference. Nor was there any evidence of the use of words which could, by the terms used, bear out the second part of the finding. It was, moreover, not alleged that the appellant had been dismissed or otherwise pecuniarily injured in his calling, and indeed there was no evidence whatever of special damage. The jury, however, assessed general damages, at 10*l*. Upon these findings Lush J. reserved the question of law, whether the appellant was entitled to judgment, and afterwards, having heard arguments, delivered a considered opinion, as the result of which, after examining the authorities, he decided for the appellant. In the course of the argument before him, counsel for the present respondents admitted that the local educational authority would naturally not allow a teacher to

---

a. [Ed. note] At common law a husband was responsible for his wife's torts. This is no longer the case. See Chapter Twenty-two, *infra*.

remain in the school and teach children if he were carrying on an immoral intercourse. But he said that his admission was meant to have nothing in it distinctive of the office of a teacher, and that he admitted only what would apply equally in the case of other offices.

The Court of Appeal reversed the judgment of Lush J. and entered judgment for the respondents.

After examining the authorities, I have come to the conclusion that the Court of Appeal were right, and that the judgment of Lush J., notwithstanding the care which he had obviously bestowed on it, cannot be supported. He seems to have regarded the decided cases as having laid down a broad principle, which could be legitimately extended to a case like the present. My Lords, I think that is not so. The action for slander has been evolved by the Courts of common law in a fashion different from that which obtains elsewhere. As one of the consequences the scope of the remedy is in an unusual degree confined by exactness of precedent. It is not for reasons of mere timidity that the Courts have shown themselves indisposed to widen that scope, nor do I think your Lordships are free to regard the question in this case as one in which a clear principle may be freely extended. * * * There is a difference between slander and libel which has been established by the authorities, and which is not the less real and far-reaching because of the fact that it is explicable almost exclusively by the different histories of the remedies for two wrongs that are in other respects analogous in their characters. The greater importance and scope of the action for libel was mainly attributable to the appearance of the printing press. The Court of Star Chamber quickly took special cognizance of libel, regarding it not merely as a crime punishable as such, but as a wrong carrying the penalty of general damages. After the Star Chamber was abolished by the Long Parliament much of the jurisdiction which its decisions had established and developed in cases of libel survived, and was carried on by the Courts of common law to whom it passed.

The history of the action for slander is radically different. Slander never became punishable in the civil Courts as a crime. In early days the old local Courts took cognizance of it as giving rise to claims for compensation. When these Courts decayed, the entire jurisdiction in cases of defamation appears to have passed, not to the Courts of the King, but, at first at all events, to the Courts of the Church. However, after the Statute of Westminster the Second had enabled novel writs in consimili casu to be issued, the action on the case for spoken words began to appear as one which the Courts of the King might entertain. Subsequently to the Reformation, when the authority of the Courts of the Church received a heavy blow and began to wane, the Courts of the King commenced the full assertion of a jurisdiction in claims arising out of spoken defamation concurrent with that of the spiritual tribunals. As might have been expected of civil Courts, whose concern had been primarily with material rights and not with discipline as such, the new jurisdiction in claims based on slander appears to have been directed to the ascertainment of actual damage suffered and to a remedy limited to such damage. This explains the restricted character of the development of the remedy and the tendency to confine its scope by the assertion that actual damage was the gist of the action. * * * The rule thus established was to some extent relaxed in its form by decisions which in certain nominate cases treated particular types of slander as so injurious by their very nature that the suffering of actual damage might be presumed and need not be proved. These exceptional types of slander comprised imputations of the commission of serious criminal offenses, imputations of suffering from certain noxious diseases, and imputations of special forms of misconduct which would manifestly prejudice a man in his calling. But, as a general principle, as to the actionable character of words spoken of a man to his disparagement in his calling the Courts, with an exception to which I will refer later, appear on the balance of authority to have laid down the limitation that the words must have been actually spoken of him "touching" or "in the way" of that calling. In *Lumby v. Allday*[1] Bayley B. said: "Every authority which I have been able to find, either shows the want of some general requisite, as honesty, capacity, fidelity & c., or connects the imputation with the plaintiff's office, trade, or business." In speaking of the imputation of such a want of "general requisite" as actionable in itself I think that Bayley B. was referring to certain decisions which show that, in the case of a trader, the Courts construed language which might affect his credit to be presumed to be directed against his credit as a trader, although no express "colloquium" touching his trade had been proved. The Courts, who leaned specially to the protection of traders, appear to have made this presumption almost, if not quite, as matter of law for the security of commerce. But Bayley B. observed that the words must be such as to have "a natural" as distinguished from a merely probable tendency to damage the plaintiff's reputation in his calling. In *Jones v. Littler*[2] Parke B. laid down this exception to much the same effect. A brewer was alleged to have been locked up for debt. It was found that in the "colloquium" he had been referred to as a brewer. But Parke B. said that "even if" the words "were spoken of him in his private character, I think the case of *Stanton v. Smith*[3] is an authority to shew that the words would have been actionable, because they must necessarily affect him in his trade." * * * This readiness to make a presumption as regards language which might affect the credit of a trader of damage arising from words alleging insolvency, notwithstanding that the imputation is not in terms made about him in his capacity of trader, has not been extended to other callings. There is indeed at least one other illustration of such readiness disclosed by the books in the case of a clergyman who holds a benefice or an ecclesiastical position of temporal profit which may, by the very terms on which it is held, be put in peril of forfeiture by the slander. But this is an exception which has no application, notwithstanding peril of injury to his reputation in his calling, if the clergyman does not hold his benefice or position actually on these terms. Subject to the carefully-guarded exceptions to which I have referred, the rule is that laid down in Comyns' Digest, "Action upon the Case for Defamation" (D. 27): "But words not actionable in themselves, are not actionable, when spoken of one in an office, profession or trade, unless they touch him in his office, & c." In *Doyley v. Roberts*[1] Tindal C.J. applied the

1. 1 Cr. & J. 301, 305.
2. 7 M. & W. 423, 426.
3. 2 Ld.Raym. 1480.
1. 3 Bing.N.C. 835.

law as laid down in this passage by refusing relief to an attorney of whom it was falsely said that he had defrauded his creditors and been horsewhipped off the course at Doncaster. That this is the basic principle which limits the cases in which the common law permits general damages to be awarded was laid down in striking language in the judgment of the Court of King's Bench in *Ayre v. Craven*[2], delivered by Lord Denman C.J. "Some of the cases," he said, "have proceeded to a length which can hardly fail to excite surprise; a clergyman having failed to obtain redress for the imputation of adultery; and a schoolmistress having been declared incompetent to maintain an action for a charge of prostitution. Such words were undeniably calculated to injure the success of the plaintiffs in their several professions; but not being applicable to their conduct therein, no action lay." There a physician had been accused of adultery, but the words did not in terms connect the imputation with anything done by him when acting in a professional capacity. * * *

My Lords, I think that these authorities and others which were referred to in the arguments at the Bar have settled the law too firmly to admit of our extending the exceptions which have been made further than the decided cases go. * * * If we were to admit that an action for slander can lie in the case of a schoolmaster who has not proved either that the words were spoken of him "touching or in the way of his calling," or that he has suffered the actual damage which is the historical foundation of the action, and is even now its normal requisite, I think we should be overruling *Ayre v. Craven* and other decisions of great authority, and should be doing what only the Legislature can do to-day. It required an Act of Parliament, the Slander of Women Act, 1891, to enable a woman to recover general damages for an imputation of unchastity. In my opinion it would require an analogous Act to enable the present appellant to recover such damages for an imputation of adultery which was not obviously directed to his reputation as a schoolmaster. I am therefore of opinion that we have no option to do anything but dismiss this appeal with costs.

LORD SUMNER. My Lords, the facts of this case are of a familiar kind. The appellant, Mr. David Jones, is headmaster of the Llidiardau Council school, Rhoshirwaen, Pwllheli. He is an unmarried man and lives with his aunt. In May, 1914, Ellen Jones, who is a farmer's wife, told Elizabeth Jones, and, as was alleged, Eliza Griffiths too, that Mr. David Jones had committed adultery with Ellen Roberts. What is more, she added that Ellen Roberts herself had told her so. This came to the appellant's ears, and no doubt not to his alone, and he sued Ellen Jones and her husband for slander. A Carnarvon common jury awarded him 10*l.*, which seems to show that they thought it an ordinary matter, but it is only fair to him to say that the defendants did not venture to support the charge, and for their part had no merits whatever. It is accordingly just the sort of case in which a contention fundamentally challenging long-settled law would be brought before your Lordships.

Lush J. at the trial put to the jury, with other questions, these two: "Were they (the words charged) spoken of him (the plaintiff) in the way of his calling, i.e., in such a way as to imperil the retention of his office?" and

2.   2 Ad. & E. 2, 7.

"Did they impute that he was unfit to hold his office?" The jury said "Yes" to both. Evidence of the suggested tendency to affect the plaintiff in his office was not called, an admission having been made by counsel for the defendants. Of this admission two versions exist. The difference in form is slight, and no difference in substance was intended, but I think that the one actually made before verdict, in the hearing of the jury, is the one that should prevail. The substance of it, according to the shorthand note, is:—

"Lush J.: 'Can you suggest, Mr. Artemus Jones, that if a schoolmaster, in a place like this, is found misconducting himself with a married woman he is not likely to suffer in his employment?'

"Mr. Artemus Jones (for the defendants): 'I submit that he would suffer no more than a man following any other occupation, and I submit again that in order to get this evidence in, the foundation-stone must be laid—that the words were spoken of him in the way of his profession.'

"Lush J.: 'But you don't want evidence to show that he would not be kept in his employment if he misconducted himself in this way, but it does not follow that the words were spoken of him in the way of his profession.'

"Mr. Montgomery (for the plaintiff): 'This is a fact upon which evidence ought to be given.'

"Lush J.: 'Then you may take it that it would be injurious.' "

The words of the slander itself made no allusion to the appellant's calling at all, and Elizabeth Jones, to whom they were spoken, when asked in cross-examination "The words were spoken to you not in reference to his position as a schoolmaster at all?" said "Not at all." * * * The question, therefore, comes to be this: "In the absence of proof of special damage, of which none was given, is an imputation of adultery made against a man, who is in fact a schoolmaster but is not spoken of as such, a matter which is actionable per se?"

* * *

Thirdly, except in the case of slanders imputing incontinence to beneficed clergymen of the Church of England and slanders imputing insolvency to persons who in fact are tradesmen (which last is probably not a real exception), no plaintiff, at least since the time of Comyns' Digest, has ever recovered damages for a spoken imputation of incontinence, unless he either showed that the words were spoken of him in his calling or proved actual damage. Earlier cases, so far as they seem to be to the contrary, can, I think, be accounted for. They are often badly or too briefly reported; they are often cases in which after verdict the necessary allegation and proof that the words were spoken of and touched the plaintiff in his calling were presumed as a matter of course. How is this blank in the authorities to be explained, if the appellant's proposition be sound? For three centuries the Courts have been dealing with such imputations. They are, and long have been,—such is the weakness of our nature—a favourite weapon in the armoury of controversialists, male and female, in private life, and mankind has so often acted on the proverb that "hard words break no bones," that special damage has rarely been proved to have occurred. My

Lords, before these considerations can be answered, it must be shown that the law has long been grievously misunderstood, and that requires cogent proof indeed.

* * *

Order of the Court of Appeal affirmed and appeal dismissed with costs.

Notes

1.   The Artemus Jones referred to in Lord Sumner's speech is probably the plaintiff in the famous case of Hulton & Co. v. Jones, [1910] A.C. 20, a case that will be referred to and discussed in some of the subsequent cases and their accompanying notes.   Artemus Jones, the plaintiff in that case, was a barrister, apparently of Welsh origin.

2.   For a more recent discussion of the history of libel and slander, see J. M. Kaye, *Libel and Slander—Two Torts or One?*, 91 L.Q.Rev. 524 (1975).   With the coming of the Protestant Reformation and the decline of the ecclesiastical courts, the petty complaints, most of which were about oral statements that would now be classified as slander, increasingly were brought to the common-law courts.   Since much of this litigation was regarded as a nuisance not only was the special damage requirement imposed but the courts developed a doctrine known as *mitiore sensu,* under which, if a statement were capable of an innocent as well as a defamatory meaning, the more innocent meaning would be ascribed to it even if that meaning were the least plausible.   The most extreme of these early cases is the ludicrous Holt v. Astgrigg, Cro.Jac. 184, 79 Eng.Rep. 161 (K.B.1608).   The complaint alleged that the defendant had said: "Sir Thomas Holt struck his cook on the head with a cleaver, and cleaved his head; the one part lay on one shoulder, and another part on the other."   It was held that this was not slander per se for imputing the crime of murder to the plaintiff because "it is not averred that the cook was killed."   See also the perhaps more subtle Miles v. Jacob, Hob. 6, 80 Eng.Rep. 156 (Ex.Ch.1610), in which the words were "Thou hast poisoned Smith."   It was held that the words were not actionable for "it doth not appear by the words that he poisoned him willingly, neither that Smith was dead at the time the words spoken."

The Star Chamber's concern with defamation was undoubtedly stimulated by the development of the printing press and the circulation of religious and political tracts.   It was concerned on the whole with socially more important contexts and most, though not all, of the matters brought before it concerned written statements.   Star Chamber was most interested in prosecuting criminal libel, in which the defendant was prosecuted for undermining public confidence in authority, but it also provided remedies for aggrieved private persons.   Star Chamber was abolished in 1641 and, on the restoration of the monarchy in 1660, Charles II promised not to reestablish it.   The common law courts thus came to take on this jurisdiction as well.   In the process the *mitiore sensu* rule fell into disuse.

Kaye contends that in the latter part of the seventeenth century the options for the courts were to make all defamation actionable without proof of special damages where aggravating circumstances were present or to treat libel cases differently by in effect making written defamation a new category of slander per se.   Eventually the latter alternative prevailed.   The early history of the law of defamation is also discussed in R. Post, *The Social Foundations of Defamation Law: Reputation and the Constitution*, 74 Calif.L.Rev. 691 (1986).

It has been more or less taken for granted by most observers that the slander per se categories are fixed even if there is room for movement within the commonly recognized categories. In Ward v. Zelikovsky, 263 N.J.Super. 497, 623 A.2d 285 (App.Div.1993), however, the court created a new category of slander per se to cover charges of social and ethnic bigotry. At a board meeting of a condominium association the defendant shouted "Don't listen to these people * * * She's a bitch * * * These people hate jews." Do you think that expansion of the categories of slander per se to include charges of racial or ethnic bigotry is a wise development? The Supreme Court of New Jersey did not and reversed. 136 N.J. 516, 643 A.2d 972 (1994). It also held that, in the context in which they were made, the statements were mere invective. A factual charge of bigotry could be defamatory but, if the action is brought as one of slander, special damages must be shown.

3. *Who can be a plaintiff?* As will be illustrated in many of the cases that we shall subsequently consider, it is uncontroversial that corporations and other juridical entities, so long as they have standing to sue, may bring an action for statements that injure their reputation. It has been held, however, both in Great Britain and the United States, that public bodies cannot bring a civil action for defamation. *See* Derbyshire County Council v. Times Newspapers, Ltd., 1993 App.Cas. 534, 2 W.L.R. 449, 1 All E.R. 1011; City of Chicago v. Tribune Co., 307 Ill. 595, 139 N.E. 86 (1923). Allowing a civil action by a public body would be too great an inhibition on the freedom of speech of the citizens. A prosecution for criminal libel is more politically difficult to bring and provides the defendant with greater procedural protection, as well as a much lower exposure to monetary damages.

4. *Criminal libel.* Criminal libel was an indictable offense at common law. As already indicated, it was aimed at suppressing sedition and later extended to reach written materials likely to lead to breaches of the peace. There never was any such thing as criminal slander. Unlike the situation with regards to civil actions for libel, for a considerable period of time, truth was *not* a defense to criminal libel. The old saw was, "the greater the truth, the greater the libel." That state of the law was largely altered in England by the Libel Act of 1843, 6 & 7 Vict. c. 96, § 6, and eventually in most American jurisdictions, to make truth a defense if the matter was published for a proper motive. Previously in Fox's Libel Act, 32 Geo. 3, c. 60 (1792), in order to prevent judges from taking from the jury the issue of the defamatory nature of a publication, juries were empowered to bring in a general verdict in prosecutions for criminal libel. Finally, in Garrison v. Louisiana, 379 U.S. 64, 85 S.Ct. 209, 13 L.Ed.2d 125 (1964), as part of the "revolution" precipitated by the Supreme Court's insistence that constitutional considerations be taken into consideration in defamation litigation, it was held that truth is an absolute defense in a prosecution for criminal libel. In contrast to criminal libel, with some qualifications that will be touched on in some of the succeeding principal cases, and their accompanying notes, truth seems to have always been accepted as a defense to a tort action for defamation whether for libel or slander. A good discussion of the law of criminal libel in England is contained in, The Law Commission, Working Paper No. 84, Criminal Libel (1982), which proposed the abolition of criminal libel and its replacement with a few narrowly focused statutory crimes.

5. An attempt to abolish the distinction between libel and slander was made in Thorley v. Lord Kerry, 4 Taunt. 355, 128 Eng.Rep. 367 (Ex.Ch. 1812), but Lord Chief Justice Mansfield felt the distinction was too firmly established although "[i]f the matter were for the first time to be decided at this day, I should have no hesitation in saying, that no action could be maintained for written scandal which could not be maintained for the words if they had been spoken."

6. *Mitiore sensu* may be dead but it is not quite completely buried. In Hewitt v. Wasek, 35 Misc.2d 946, 231 N.Y.S.2d 884 (1962), the defendant had said that the plaintiff, a married woman, was having an affair with a married man. The court held that special damages had to be alleged. The statement did not necessarily impute lack of chastity because it could be taken to mean the woman and the man were having an affair that was "both romantic and platonic."

7. The most open-ended of the slander per se categories is that involving imputations affecting the business, trade, profession, or office of the plaintiff. Nevertheless, as the *Jones* case indicates, making the connection between the statement and the trade or profession is not always easy. In Gunsberg v. Roseland Corp., 34 Misc.2d 220, 225 N.Y.S.2d 1020 (1962), an employee of the defendant had said to the plaintiff, who was a patron at the defendant's dance hall: "Get out of here you silly, stupid senile bum; you are a troublemaker and should be confined to an asylum." The plaintiff was a stockbroker. It was held that the statement did not injure him in his trade or profession and was thus not actionable without allegation and proof of special damages.

8. *Pleading an action for defamation.* In an action for defamation the customary practice is for the plaintiff (a) to insert a verbatim description of the actual defamatory statements in his complaint, (b) to allege the publication of the defamatory statement to third parties, (c) to explain how the statements in question relate to him and why they are defamatory, and (d) to make a claim for damages. If the defamation is of the type for which special damages must be alleged and proved, (e) these special damages must be described in the complaint with some specificity. Insofar as the plaintiff's complaint includes a request for punitive damages, he must in most cases, also (f) allege actual malice in the sense of knowledge of falsity or reckless disregard of truth or falsity. At common law, actual malice could also be established by showing ill-will toward the plaintiff or a desire to injure him on the part of the defendant. As we shall see below, common-law malice is probably now no longer by itself a sufficient basis upon which to premise an award of punitive damages. Pleading an action for defamation has, however, continued to have a certain technical character and the following special technical vocabulary has developed to describe various components of the complaint:

The Inducement. Sometimes neither the defamatory character of a publication nor its connection with the plaintiff is evident from the actual words used in the allegedly defamatory statement. The plaintiff will therefore have to allege in his complaint the facts that are necessary to support his claim that the statements are defamatory and that they refer to him. The portion of the complaint in which these extrinsic facts are alleged is called the *inducement.* An alternate terminology sometimes used is to state that these extrinsic facts are "alleged by way of inducement."

The Colloquium. The *colloquium* is that portion of the complaint in which the plaintiff, making use if necessary of the facts alleged in the inducement, states that the allegedly defamatory statements were about him.

The Innuendo. The *innuendo* is that portion of the complaint in which the plaintiff explains what is defamatory about the statements made about him. Some courts speak of the plaintiff making this showing "by way of innuendo." In this usage the courts are referring to the method by which the plaintiff makes out the defamatory meaning rather than to some discreet portion of the complaint. The meaning which the plaintiff attempts to engraft upon the allegedly defamatory statement must be a reasonable one. In this regard, it is a question for the court, in the first instance, whether reasonable people could so construe the challenged statement. It is then for the jury to decide whether, in point of fact, those to whom the communication was addressed did understand it in a defamatory sense.

HINSDALE v. ORANGE COUNTY PUBLICATIONS, INC.

Court of Appeals of New York, 1966.
17 N.Y.2d 284, 270 N.Y.S.2d 592, 217 N.E.2d 650.

DESMOND, CHIEF JUDGE.

The plaintiffs in these two libel actions demand damages because of an article published in defendant's newspaper. Their complaints have been dismissed for insufficiency on the ground that the newspaper story was not libelous per se and that no special damages are pleaded as is required when the words are libelous *per quod* but not per se.

On July 7, 1964 defendant's daily newspaper *The Times Herald Record* (of Middletown, N.Y.) contained this:

"Mr. and Mrs. Paul M. Hinsdale of Balmville Gardens, Newburgh, have announced the engagement of their son, Robert W., to Concetta Kay Rieber of 43 Knox Drive, New Windsor.

"Miss Rieber, a native of Brooklyn, was educated in Brooklyn and Newburgh schools. She is employed by Jack Wilkins Associates, Inc., at Newburgh.

"Her fiance attended Newburgh and Connecticut schools. He is the president of the Jack Wilkins Associates insurance agency.

"The wedding is set for August."

Plaintiff Hinsdale's complaint asserts that at the time of the publication defendant knew or by reasonable diligence could have learned that Mr. Hinsdale was and is married and the father of two children, and that Concetta Kay Rieber was and is married and the mother of three sons, and that there was and is no engagement to marry between Robert Hinsdale and Mrs. Rieber. The Hinsdale pleading alleges that defendant's newspaper was of general circulation not only in Middletown, New York, but also in the City of Newburgh and its environs, that plaintiff lives and is in business in Newburgh and that he has been defamed by the newspaper announcement and held up to public disgrace, scorn and ridicule.

The Rieber complaint, besides repeating some of Hinsdale's allegations, says that Mr. and Mrs. Rieber live in New Windsor, that the wife was and is employed in the City of Newburgh, that because of the newspaper item Mrs. Rieber's reputation has been damaged and an evil opinion of her induced in the minds of the people of the community and that because of her pain, shock, fright and physical and mental suffering the husband has been deprived of his wife's services and society and put to expense, etc.

Special Term, although it dismissed the complaints, conceded that the facts in Sydney v. Macfadden Newspaper Pub. Corp. (242 N.Y. 208, 151 N.E. 209, 44 A.L.R. 1419) were "practically identical" to those in the present cases, holding that the controlling decision was the earlier one of O'Connell v. Press Pub. Co. (214 N.Y. 352, 108 N.E. 556). *O'Connell,* so the court reasoned, was not overruled by *Sydney* which expresses the rule that for a libel per se to be actionable without special damages the damage must arise from the publication itself "without any reference to extrinsic facts, except those generally known to a substantial number of the community of the general reading public." The court thought, apparently, that these complaints did not meet the *O'Connell* test. The Appellate Division unanimously affirmed and gave plaintiffs leave to replead, a permission of which they did not make use. We granted plaintiffs leave to appeal to this court.

It is not defamatory to say of a man or woman that he or she is engaged to be married but an announcement that an already married male or female is about to be married to a new partner imputes a violation of commonly accepted rules of marital morality, a deviation from community norms. It does not necessarily charge sexual immorality but to many minds it suggests a disregard of existing commitments and obligations * * * Surely such an announcement about a seemingly happily married person comes as a surprise and shock to relatives and acquaintances. To publicize an imminent marriage between two already married persons who work in the same office and live in the same lightly populated area would normally cause a local scandal of considerable size. This announcement amounted, therefore, to a written accusation which tended to hold plaintiffs up to "ridicule, contempt, shame, disgrace or obloquy, to degrade [them] in the estimation of the community, * * * to diminish [their] respectability" * * *

* * * Other courts in this State and elsewhere have agreed that a false statement as to a married person that he or she is about to be or has been divorced is defamatory * * *.

Printed material is, because of the relative permanency of its impact, more readily held to be defamatory per se than are oral utterances of similar import * * * We conclude, therefore, that printed statements like those in this newspaper announcement about married people are libelous per se, that is, that, without a showing of "special" damage, they raise a presumption of inevitable actual damage to reputation * * *.

But the newspaper article here complained of does not itself refer to the fact (alleged in the complaint and now conceded) that the "engaged" couple were in truth already married to others and living with their respective spouses. Defendant says—and the courts below agreed—that since the published material needs the allegation of existing facts the libel, if any, is not per se but *per quod* and, lacking any allegation of special damages, is not actionable. The authority cited for this "rule" is O'Connell v. Press Pub. Co. * * *.

The Sydney v. Macfadden Newspaper Pub. Corp. * * * decision would seem to control here. The plaintiff was a well-known actress of the day, known professionally under her maiden name of Doris Keane but married to one Basil Sydney. That latter fact was alleged in the complaint but nowhere alluded to in the newspaper column which was held to be libelous per se. The offending newspaper article said that Doris Keane was the "latest lady love" of Fatty Arbuckle, a movie comedian of the day whose claims to fame did not include a reputation for virtuous life. The columnist intimated that Doris Keane and Arbuckle were to marry. Defendant argued that the extrinsic fact of plaintiff's marriage could not be considered in determining whether the article was libelous per se. This court, however, rejected that argument. * * *

Defendant would have it that the *Sydney* decision (supra) turned on the taking of judicial notice that Arbuckle, a famous actor, was a person of bad repute. Not so. The dissenting opinion in *Sydney* not only analyzes the majority holding as permitting the allegation and proof of the fact of plaintiff's married status but says that the dissenter would have voted with the majority had the latter put its ruling on judicial notice of Fatty Arbuckle's reputation. The dissent correctly characterizes *Sydney* as a flat holding that such extrinsic facts as that the libeled person is already married can be alleged and proved to make a publication libelous per se. * * *.

We come now to the O'Connell v. Press Pub. Co. case * * * and the disputed and controversial "O'Connell rule" ("whatever it might mean", Henn, Libel by Extrinsic Fact, 47 Cornell L.Q. 14, 34). If the *O'Connell* case means that a libel per se action cannot stand if extrinsic facts must be read with it or into it, then *O'Connell* is directly opposed to the numerous decisions of our court above cited * * *.

Actually, the *O'Connell* decision (supra) is not in point here and not inconsistent with *Sydney* (supra). The reason for refusing to give it effect in *Sydney* was, it would seem, that *O'Connell* involved not "libel by extrinsic fact" but an effort to give defamatory meaning to the published words by ascribing to them an unnatural and unreasonable innuendo or ascribed meaning. The news article complained of in O'Connell's case discussed a Federal court criminal prosecution not against O'Connell but against certain sugar importers in which it was charged that the latter had arranged for fraudulent underweighing of sugar to avoid import duties. The newspaper story reported that O'Connell as a witness before the Grand Jury had testified that he had invented a steel spring device and that an officer of the corporation which was later indicted had referred plaintiff to an employee, also later indicted. The complaint in O'Connell's libel action alleged that these references to him meant that he had engaged in criminal conduct through the use of his invention on the weighing scales. The defendant moved to dismiss the complaint, alleging that the article was not a libel on its face but required the showing of extrinsic fact. This court held the complaint insufficient but not, it would seem, on that particular ground. * * * The *O'Connell* decision, therefore, must be understood as one dealing with the attempted use of an innuendo not justified by the words themselves. It is not, therefore, applicable here nor does it control or overrule the *Sydney* and other cases which allow not the utilization of innuendos but the pleading of extrinsic facts.

We conclude, therefore, that the complaint sufficiently alleges a publication libelous per se. It will be for a jury to say what damages (be they substantial or nominal) the several plaintiffs are entitled to.

The order appealed from should be reversed and the motions to dismiss the complaints denied, with costs in all courts.

Notes

1. In 1937, *Restatement of Torts* § 569 adopted what we have seen was the position developed at English common law, namely that all libel was actionable without allegation and proof of special damages. The late Dean Prosser, the Reporter for the *Restatement (Second)*, was of the opinion that the majority of American jurisdictions did not follow the English rule but instead distinguished between libel per se, actionable without allegation and proof of special damages, and libel per quod which was only actionable upon such allegation and proof. As to what fell within the libel per se category, there was some uncertainty. Some jurisdictions required the libel to be clear on its face, others required the libel to fall within the slander per se categories, and perhaps others required the libel to be both clear on its face and within the slander per se categories. *Restatement (Second) of Torts* § 569, and accompanying note (Tent.Draft No. 11, 1965). Dean Prosser proposed changing § 569 to restrict liability for libel "without proof of special harm" to those situations where either the defamatory meaning is apparent from the publication itself, "without reference to extrinsic facts by way of inducement," or the statement falls within the slander per se categories. Prosser's proposal was attacked as being against the weight of authority by Lawrence H. Eldredge, one of the advisers to the project, who was then still active at the Philadelphia Bar. *See* 42 ALI Proceedings 411–16 (1965); 43 ALI Proceedings 434–37, 444–45 (1966). Eldredge and Prosser then took their dispute to the law reviews. *See* L. Eldredge, *Spurious Rule of Libel Per Quod*, 79 Harv.L.Rev. 733 (1966); L. Eldredge, *Variation on Libel Per Quod*, 25 Vand.L.Rev. 79 (1972); W. Prosser, *More Libel Per Quod*, 79 Harv.L.Rev. 1629 (1966). Professor Henn interjected, in the article cited by Desmond, C.J., that the situation, particularly in New York, was more confused than Prosser was prepared to admit. H. Henn, *Libel by Extrinsic Fact*, 47 Cornell L.Q. 14 (1961).

As a consequence of the *Hinsdale* decision, Prosser abandoned the struggle. Except for minor changes in wording *Restatement (Second) of Torts* § 569, published in 1977, is identical to the original provision in the *Restatement*. All libel is actionable without allegation and proof of special damages. The Reporter's notes, reprinted in *Restatement (Second) of Torts* Appendix § 569 (1981), at p. 382, indicated that most state court decisions in the immediate aftermath of *Hinsdale* followed that case. This is not to say that, in many of those states which had previously adopted the distinction, it does not continue to be applied. For example, West's Ann.Cal.Civ.Code § 45a, which was added in 1945, provides that a plaintiff must allege and prove that he has suffered special damages, unless the defamatory language is libelous on its face. A statement is a "libel on its face" if it is "defamatory of the plaintiff without the necessity of explanatory matter, such as an inducement, innuendo, or other extrinsic fact."

2. It is not necessary that an allegedly defamatory statement be one that would lower the plaintiff's reputation in the entire community. It is enough if the statement would lower the plaintiff's esteem within what might be called a "significant" segment of "respectable society." Thus it has been held to be libelous to include the name of a Kosher butcher shop in an advertisement for bacon. Braun v. Armour & Co., 254 N.Y. 514, 173 N.E. 845 (1930). In a similar vein, the publication of the picture of a teetotaling nurse in a whiskey advertisement was held to be libelous in Peck v. Tribune Co., 214 U.S. 185, 29 S.Ct. 554, 53 L.Ed. 960 (1909), although it would seem that a modern court would want some extrinsic facts about the plaintiff's religious background and social circle before so concluding today. It has for example been more recently held that it is not defamatory to falsely write that a husband and wife were separated and getting a divorce. *See* Andreason v. Guard Publishing Co., 260 Or. 308, 489 P.2d 944 (1971). In Meyerson v. Hurlbut, 98 F.2d 232 (D.C.Cir. 1938), *cert. denied* 305 U.S. 610, 59 S.Ct. 69, 83 L.Ed. 388, it was held defamatory to call a businessman a "price cutter," but such a holding seems unlikely today. It has been argued that society is becoming more fragmented and that judges should be more open about the extent to which they are engaging in a process of social idealization. *See* L. Lidsky, *Defamation, Reputation, and the Myth of Community,* 71 Wash.L.Rev. 1 (1996).

3. The cases are uniform in holding that it is not defamatory to call someone an informer. The decisions are based more on the public policy of encouraging cooperation with the police than on the assumption that no decent person would think ill of such a person. An amusing example is Byrne v. Deane, [1937] 1 K.B. 818 (C.A.). In that case, what appeared to be slot machines—they are identified as "diddler" machines—were on the premises of a golf club owned and operated by the defendants. Someone told the police about the machines and the machines were removed. The plaintiff was a member of the club. Someone posted the following doggeral verse at the spot where the machines had been:

> For many years upon this spot
> You heard the sound of a merry bell
> Those who were rash and those who were not
> Lost and made a spot of cash
> But he who gave the game away
> May he byrnn in hell and rue the day
> > Diddleramus

Although the defendants had not posted the verse, the court was prepared to hold them responsible for publishing it, since they were aware that the verse had been posted and allowed it to remain. Nevertheless, the Court of Appeal reversed a judgment for the plaintiff. *See also* Connelly v. McKay, 176 Misc. 685, 28 N.Y.S.2d 327 (1941).

4. Some of the earlier cases held that it was not defamatory falsely to call someone a communist, but, with the post World War II hardening of attitudes, most courts treated such allegations as defamatory. *See* W. Prosser, The Law of Torts 744 (4th ed. 1971). This conclusion seemed particularly sound after the successful prosecution of the Communist leadership under the Smith Act.

See Dennis v. United States, 341 U.S. 494, 71 S.Ct. 857, 95 L.Ed. 1137 (1951). An interesting case is Grant v. Reader's Digest Association, 151 F.2d 733 (2d Cir.1945), *cert. denied,* 326 U.S. 797, 66 S.Ct. 492, 90 L.Ed. 485 (1946). In that case, the plaintiff was falsely accused of being the "legislative representative of the Massachusetts Communist Party." Learned Hand, J., writing for the court of appeals, held that people might infer that someone who represented the Communist Party as a legislative lobbyist shared the views of that party. As we have seen, the portion of the complaint in which the plaintiff spells out the defamatory implications of the statements made about him is called the *innuendo.*

5. Suppose that a headline and photograph accompanying a story are capable of a defamatory meaning but that when the entire article is read it is clear that there has been no defamation. What is the appropriate context: the headline and the photograph or the headline, the photograph, and the entire story? Compare *Restatement (Second) of Torts* § 563, Comment, *d,* with Charleston v. News Group Newspapers, [1995] 2 App.Cas. 65, 2 W.L.R. 450, 2 All E.R. 313.

6. So long as the statement is false and defamatory, it is no defense that the persons to whom the defamatory communication was communicated did not believe the statement. That people do not believe the statement may have some effect on the damages awarded, but it does not affect liability. It is the tendency of the type of statement in question to injure a person in the plaintiff's position that is relevant. Moreover, a statement which is not initially believed may, over time, come to affect the plaintiff's reputation quite substantially, especially if it is repeated. It is a fairly common belief that "where there is smoke, there is fire." It should finally be noted that the republication of defamatory material, except in some limited circumstances to be discussed below in connection with a consideration of the defenses available in defamation actions, is itself defamatory, even if the statement is attributed to the original source.

YOUSSOUPOFF v. METRO–GOLDWYN–MAYER PICTURES, LTD.

Court of Appeal, 1934.
50 T.L.R. 581.

LORD JUSTICE SCRUTTON.—An English company called Metro–Goldwyn–Mayer Pictures, Limited, which produces films circulated to the cinemas in this country, and which, according to its solicitor and chairman, is controlled by a firm of similar name in America, produced in this country a film which dealt with the alleged circumstances in which the influence of a man called Rasputin, an alleged monk, on the Czar and Czarina brought about the destruction of Russia. The film also dealt with the undoubted fact that Rasputin was ultimately murdered by persons who conceived him to be the evil genius of Russia.

In the course of that film a lady who had relations of affection with the person represented as the murderer was represented as having also had relations, which might be either relations of seduction or relations of rape, with the man Rasputin, a man of the worst possible character. When the film was produced in this country the plaintiff alleged that reasonable people would understand that she was the woman who was represented as having had these illicit relations. The plaintiff is a member of the Russian Royal House, Princess Irina Alexandrovna of Russia, and she was married after the incidents in question to a man who undoubtedly was one of the persons concerned in the killing of Rasputin. She issued a writ for libel against the English company. The English company declined to stop presenting the film. The action for libel proceeded. It was tried before one of the most experienced Judges on the Bench and a special jury, the constitutional tribunal for trying actions of libel, and, after several days' hearing, and after the jury had twice gone to see the film itself, they returned a verdict for the plaintiff with £25,000 damages.

The defendants now appeal from that verdict, and, as I understand the argument put before us by Sir William Jowitt and Mr. Wallington, for the defendants, it falls under three heads. First of all, they say that there was no evidence on which a jury, properly directed, could find that reasonable people would understand the Princess Natasha of the film to be Princess Irina, the plaintiff. That was the first point—the question of identification. Secondly, they say that if we are to take the Princess Natasha of the film to be identified with the Princess Irina, the plaintiff, there was no evidence on which a jury, reasonably directed, could find the film to be defamatory of the plaintiff. Thirdly, they say: "Assuming both of those points are decided against us, the damages were excessive. They were such as no jury, properly directed, could give in the circumstances of the case."

I deal with each of those three points in turn. First of all, there is the question of identification. Now, if this case had been heard before 1910 there would undoubtedly have been scope for very elaborate arguments, and this Court would probably have had to reserve judgment to consider the numerous authorities which would have been cited. But since the decision in 1910 in a case which is always identified with the name of Mr. Artemus Jones, and since a subsequent decision of this Court in which somewhat similar principles were applied in a case which is identified with the name of General Corrigan, of the Mexican Army, there is, fortunately, no difficulty about the law. In Hulton and Co., Limited v. Jones (26 *The Times* L.R. 128; [1910] A.C. 20) a Manchester paper published by Messrs. Hulton published what was supposed to be an amusing article about a gentleman named Artemus Jones, who, on one side of his life, was a blameless churchwarden at Peckham and, on the other side of his life, indulged in wild careers unfitted for such a churchwarden at Le Touquet. A Mr. Artemus Jones—there may be several—conceived that that article was a libel upon him, and he brought an action for libel. The editor and proprietors of the paper said, rightly or wrongly, that they had never heard of Mr. Artemus Jones as an existing being, and that they had not the slightest intention of libelling him. There was some unfortunate doubt whether the gentleman who wrote the article had not a personal grudge against the real Mr. Artemus Jones,[a] but, at any rate, the proprietors and publishers of the paper said: "We are innocent of any intention to injure Mr. Artemus Jones, of whom we never heard."

---

a. [Ed. note.] There was some evidence that the plaintiff had at one time been employed by the defendant newspaper, but it was accepted by counsel that the publishers were unaware of who Artemus Jones was and that they thought it was a fictitious name.

The case resulted in this way. In spite of a very careful judgment by Lord Justice Moulton in the Court of Appeal, counterbalanced by an equally learned and convincing judgment of Lord Justice Farwell in the Court of Appeal, the House of Lords unanimously came to the conclusion which is expressed in the first lines of the headnote in this way: "In an action for libel it is no defence to show that the defendant did not intend to defame the plaintiff, if reasonable people would think the language to be defamatory of the plaintiff"; and the Lord Chancellor quoted in his judgment this passage from the summing-up: "The real point upon which your verdict must turn is, ought or ought not sensible and reasonable people reading this article to think that it was a mere imaginary person such as I have said—Tom Jones, Mr. Pecksniff as a humbug, Mr. Stiggins, or any of that sort of names that one reads of in literature used as types? If you think any reasonable person would think that"—that is to say that it was mere type and did not mean anybody—"it is not actionable at all. If, on the other hand, you do not think that, but think that people would suppose it to mean some real person—those who did not know the plaintiff of course would not know who the real person was, but those who did know of the existence of the plaintiff would think that it was the plaintiff—then the action is maintainable."

A somewhat similar point was raised in the case where General Corrigan got damages—Cassidy v. Daily Mirror Newspapers, Limited (45 *The Times* L.R. 485; [1929] 2 K.B. 331). General Corrigan, who some-times called himself Cassidy, being at a race meeting, conceived the idea of being photographed with a young lady to whom he said he was engaged. This photograph was sent up as an object of interest to a daily paper, which at once inserted it. Now, it so happened that the General was in fact married to a lady who lived in a London suburb, and was visited by the suburban ladies in the vicinity, who had hitherto considered that she was an honest married woman. When they took in the daily paper and saw that the gentleman describing himself as the husband of the lady was representing himself as being engaged to somebody else they very natural-ly, as respectable women, conceived evil ideas of the lady whom they had hitherto thought to be an honest woman and whom they now suspected of being a kept woman. Thereupon the lady brought an action against the paper, and the paper said what before 1910 would have been the sort of thing you would expect them to say: "Why, good gracious, madam, we never heard of you. We had no intention of libelling you. We did not know you existed, and all we have done is to publish an interesting photograph, stating that the gentleman in the photograph says he is engaged to the lady in the photograph." Just as *Hulton and Co., Limited v. Jones (supra)* had caused a difference of opinion with a very excellent judgment by Lord Justice Moulton, so again the case of the General did cause a difference of opinion with again, if I may say so, a very excellent judgment of my brother Greer, but, unfortunately, the majority of the Court, myself and Lord Russell, took another view, and this Court is now bound by the view laid down by the Lord Chancellor in the *Hulton* case *(supra)* and by the case of General Corrigan, and we follow the law that though the person who writes and publishes the libel may not intend to libel a particular person and, indeed, has never heard of that particular person, the plaintiff, yet, if evidence is produced that reasonable people knowing some of the circumstances, not necessarily all, would take the libel complained of to relate to the plaintiff, an action for libel will lie.

That, therefore, was the class of evidence put before the jury in this case. On the one side, various people, some of them representatives of England in Russia at the time of these occurrences, some of them people who had been merely reading books about Russia and thought they knew something about it, were called to say that they saw the film, and they understood it to relate to the present plaintiff, the Princess Irina. On the other side, other people who knew something about Russia, or who did not know anything about Russia, were called to say that they saw the film, that they did not think it related to the plaintiff, and they gave their views as to whom they did think the characters in the film related.

There was evidence [on] each side. I think counsel for the defendants agree that it would have been impossible for the [judge] to have stopped the case because the film was not capable of a defamatory meaning, and the jury, who are a tribunal particularly suited to try an action for libel, for the reason that I am going to allude to under the second head, came to the view that reasonable people would take the film to relate to the plaintiff in the action. It is not my business to express an opinion on the matter. It was the jury's business, and the only question for me is whether there was evidence on which the jury might come to the conclusion to which they have come. That being my position, I can quite see that there is a great deal of evidence on which the jury might take the view that the plaintiff was identified reasonably with the Princess Natasha.

* * *

Therefore, on the first point, I come to the conclusion that we cannot possibly interfere with the verdict of the jury, who are the constitutional tribunal, when they think, as they obviously have thought, that reasonable people, not all reasonable people but many reasonable people, would take the film representing Princess Natasha as also representing and referring to the plaintiff in the action, the Princess Irina. * * *

Now the second point is this, and it takes some courage to argue it, I think: suppose that the jury are right in treating Princess Irina, the plaintiff, as the Princess Natasha in real life, the film does not contain anything defamatory of her. There have been several formulæ for describing what is defamation. The learned Judge at the trial uses the stock formula "calculated to bring into hatred, ridicule, or contempt," and because it has been clearly established some time ago that that is not exhaustive because there may be things which are defamatory which have nothing to do with hatred, ridicule, or contempt he adds the words "or causes them to be shunned or avoided." I, myself, have always preferred the language which Mr. Justice Cave used in Scott v. Sampson (8 Q.B.D. 491), a false statement about a man to his discredit. I think that satisfactorily expresses what has to be found. It has long been established that, with one modification, libel or no libel is for the jury, and the Court very rarely interferes with a finding by the jury that a particular statement is a libel or is no libel. The only exception is that it has been established with somewhat unfortunate results that a Judge may say: "No reasonable jury could possibly think this a libel, and consequently I will not ask the jury the question whether it is a libel or not." In a case in which that was conclusively established the law and the facts got so far from each other that the majority of the Judges—there was a great difference of opinion—held that a certain circular issued by a firm of brewers to their customers saying that they would not take the cheques of a particular bank was not capable of a defamatory meaning, though, in fact, it resulted in a run of a quarter of a million on the bank immediately it was issued.

Fortunately, however, in this case we have not to deal with that exception because it is not suggested that the Judge in this case could have withdrawn the question of this libel from the jury on the point that it was not capable of a defamatory meaning. When you get the matter going to the jury it is extremely rare that the Court interferes with the finding of the jury whether a thing is libel or no libel. That has resulted from the action of Parliament in Mr. Fox's Libel Act in settling a dispute between Lord Mansfield and another eminent Judge as to the powers of the Judge in dealing with questions of libel. Lord Mansfield was of opinion that if a libel came before the Courts the Judge was to say whether it was a libel, and it was only for the jury to assess damages or to find guilty or not guilty on the direction. That was considered so contrary to the constitution with regard to juries that Parliament intervened and passed an Act, known as Mr. Fox's Libel Act, by which the matter was left to the jury. * * *

If libel alone is for the jury on those lines, why is it said that the jury in this case have come to a wrong decision? I desire to approach this argument seriously if I can, because I have great difficulty in approaching it seriously. I understand the principal thing argued by the defendants is this: "This procedure, as it contains some spoken words, is slander and not libel. Slanders are not as a rule actionable unless you prove special damage. No special damage was proved in this case. Consequently, the plaintiff must get within the exceptions in which slander is actionable without proof of special damage." One of those exceptions is the exception which is amplified in the Slander of Women Act, 1891—namely, if the slander imports unchastity or adultery to a woman—and this is the argument as I understand it: "To say of a woman that she is raped does not impute unchastity." From that we get to this, which was solemnly put forward, that to say of a woman of good character that she has been ravished by a man of the worst possible character is not defamatory. That argument was solemnly presented to the jury, and I only wish the jury could have expressed, and that we could know, what they thought of it, because it seems to me to be one of the most legal arguments that were ever addressed to, I will not say a business body, but a sensible body.

That, really, as I understand it, is the argument upon which is based the contention that no reasonable jury could come to the conclusion that to say of a woman that she had been ravished by a man of very bad character when as a matter of fact she never saw the man at all and was never near him is not defamatory of the woman.

I really have no language to express my opinion of that argument. I therefore come, on the second point, to the view that there is no ground for interfering with the verdict of the jury (assuming the identification to stand, as I have assumed), that the words and the pictures in the film are defamatory of the lady whom they have found to be Princess Irina.

Then one comes to the third point, and that is the amount of damages. It is the law that in libel, though not in slander, you need not prove any particular damage in order to recover a verdict. What, then, is the position, the jury being the tribunal in libel or no libel, and, following from that, the tribunal as to the damages caused by libel, whose verdict is very rarely interfered with by the Court of Appeal? What have the jury to do? They have to give a verdict of amount without having any proof of actual damage. They need not have any proof of actual damage. They have to consider the nature of the libel as they understand it, the circumstances in which it was published, and the circumstances relating to the person who publishes it, right down to the time when they give their verdict, whether the defence made it true, and, if so, whether that defence has ever been withdrawn—the whole circumstances of the case. It is not the Judge who has to decide the amount. The constitution has thought, and I think there is great advantage in it, that the damages to be paid by a person who says false things about his neighbour are best decided by a jury representing the public, who may state the view of the public as to the action of the man who makes false statements about his neighbour, the plaintiff.

It is for that reason that it is extremely rare for the Court of Appeal to interfere with the verdict of the jury as to the amount of damages when the libel is established. It is very often the case that the individual Judges of the Court of Appeal, if they had been asked their verdict on the amount of damages, would have given a smaller sum. Sometimes they would have given a larger sum, but the question is not what amount the Judges would have given. The question is what amount the jury, as representing the public, the community, have fixed, and it is extremely rare to have that amount interfered with by the Court. A test has been formulated, and it is this, as has been correctly stated several times: the Courts will interfere only if the amount of damages is such that in all the circumstances no twelve reasonable men could have given it. If the Court comes to that view, it will interfere with the verdict, but even then it cannot fix the amount itself, but must send the case back to another jury who may very easily repeat the first verdict, and the Court cannot go on sending the case back to a jury until at last they get a verdict with which the Judges agree. Those are the reasons which justify the relation of the Court of Appeal to the amount of damages found by juries.

Applying that test to this case, * * * I find it quite impossible to say that the amount of damages here is such that no reasonable jury could have given it. There is the position of the plaintiff, a high position, although the Royal Family of Russia have fallen from their high position. There is the amount of publicity given by circulating the film through a large circle of cinemas to be seen at cheap prices by an enormous number of people. Apparently in this case there were performances for a week in more than 16, possibly 20, cinemas. Looking at all those matters, I come to the conclusion that, if the jury were properly directed, this Court cannot possibly interfere with the amount of the damages, even if any individual member of it, or all three members, had thought that if they had been on the jury they might have given a smaller sum.

* * *

For these reasons, in my opinion, this appeal should be dismissed, with costs.

* * *

LORD JUSTICE SLESSER.—This action is one of libel and raises at the outset an interesting and difficult problem which, I believe, to be a novel problem, whether the product of the combined photographic and talking instrument which produces these modern films does, if it throws upon the screen and impresses upon the ear defamatory matter, produce that which can be complained of as libel or as slander.

In my view, this action, as I have said, was properly framed in libel. There can be no doubt that, so far as the photographic part of the exhibition is concerned, that is a permanent matter to be seen by the eye, and is the proper subject of an action for libel, if defamatory. I regard the speech which is synchronized with the photographic reproduction and forms part of one complex, common exhibition as an ancillary circumstance, part of the surroundings explaining that which is to be seen.

* * *

SIR PATRICK HASTINGS.—The appeal will be dismissed, with costs?

LORD JUSTICE SCRUTTON.—Yes.

Notes

1. Hulton and Co. v. Jones, [1910] A.C. 20, discussed by Scrutton, L.J., was followed in Corrigan v. Bobbs–Merrill Co., 228 N.Y. 58, 126 N.E. 260 (1920). *See also* Hanson v. Globe Newspaper Co., 159 Mass. 293, 34 N.E. 462 (1893), particularly the dissenting opinion of Holmes, J. For a more recent case see Michaels v. Gannett Co., 10 A.D.2d 417, 199 N.Y.S.2d 778 (1960). In an article about a restauranteur against whom a tax lien had been filed, the defendants mistakenly published the plaintiff's address, the plaintiff having the same name.

It is common knowledge of course that many fictional characters in what clearly purport to be works of fiction—unlike the film involved in the *Youssoupoff* case, which purported to be a dramatization of an actual historical event— are modeled upon real persons. People who claim that they are in point of fact the model upon whom some fictional character is based have brought many defamation actions against authors. A well publicized case is Bindrim v. Mitchell, 92 Cal.App.3d 61, 155 Cal.Rptr. 29 (1979), *cert. denied* 444 U.S. 984, 100 S.Ct. 490, 62 L.Ed.2d 412 (1979). The particular problem such plaintiffs face, of course, is proving that they can be identified by the reader as the model for the character in question. Subsidiary questions after the constitutionalization of the law of defamation to which we will turn shortly, include the question whether the author intentionally or recklessly or negligently misstated the allegedly defamatory facts. A considerable secondary literature has examined this question. *See, e.g.,* Note, *"Clear and Convincing" Libel: Fiction and the Law of Defamation,* 92 Yale L.J. 520 (1983); Comment, *Fiction Based on*

Fact: Writers' Liability for Libel or Invasion of Privacy, 14 U.C.Davis 1029 (1981); Comment, *Defamation and Fiction: The Case for Absolute First Amendment Protection,* 29 Am.U.L.Rev. 571 (1980).

The Defamation Act of 1952, 15 & 16 Geo. 6 & 1 Eliz. 2 c. 66, permitted a person who has innocently defamed another to make an offer of amends including publication of a suitable correction and an apology, and where copies of the defamatory publication had been distributed the taking of reasonable steps to notify the persons to whom the original statement has been distributed that the words have been alleged to defame the aggrieved party. If the offer was accepted no defamation action might be brought; if the offer of amends was rejected, proof of innocent publication is a defense. For a fuller discussion of this and more recent British legislation *see* note 6, p. 1131f, *infra,* where the general subject of retraction statutes is discussed. In the United States, a number of statutes have been passed absolving broadcasters from liability for innocent misrepresentation. *See* L. Eldredge, The Law of Defamation 86–90 (1978); D. Remmers, *Recent Legislative Trends in Defamation by Radio,* 64 Harv.L.Rev. 727, 739–46 (1951). Even where the defendant is unable to show lack of fault in publishing defamatory material, some of these statutes limit the plaintiff to recovery of actual damages only.

2. While lack of intent to defame was no defense at common law, liability would not arise unless the publication to third parties were intended or at least the result of negligence. There was no liability for "accidental" publication. For a fairly recent case, *see* Smith v. Jones, 335 So.2d 896 (Miss.1976), in which the plaintiff's sons eavesdropped on the defendant's phone conversation with their mother. There was no liability because the defendants spoke "with the reasonable expectation that they would be heard by the plaintiff only." A letter to a child accusing him of theft, however, can be reasonably expected to be brought to the child's parent. *See, e.g.,* Hedgpeth v. Coleman, 183 N.C. 309, 111 S.E. 517 (1922).

3. The absolute liability of one who intentionally or negligently publishes defamatory material would impose a heavy burden on libraries, newspaper and magazine distributors, and newsstand and bookshop operators. To hold such persons liable they must, at the very least, be shown to have some knowledge of the defamatory content of the publication in question. *See, e.g.,* Balabanoff v. Fossani, 192 Misc. 615, 81 N.Y.S.2d 732 (1948); Weldon v. Times Book Co., 28 T.L.R. 143 (C.A.1911).

What about the Internet? The few cases that have thus far reached the courts have reached inconsistent results. In Cubby, Inc. v. CompuServe, Inc., 776 F.Supp. 135 (S.D.N.Y.1991), the court held that the defendant was merely a distributor who did not exercise any editorial control over a discussion forum available on its services. On the other hand in Stratton Oakmont, Inc. v. Prodigy Services Co., 1995 WL 323710, 23 Media L.Rep. 1794 (N.Y.Sup.1995), the court found that the defendant both represented itself as exercising and actually had the capability of exercising substantial editorial control over the bulletin board and therefore held that the defendant was not a mere distributor. On this and other problems for the law of defamation raised by this new technology, *see* Note, *Catching Jellyfish in the Internet: The Public–Figure Doctrine and Defamation on Computer Bulletin Boards, 21 Rutgers Computer & Tech.L.J. 461 (1995).*

4. Dictating a letter about a third party to a secretary is also generally considered to be a publication. *See* Ostrowe v. Lee, 256 N.Y. 36, 175 N.E. 505

(1931), also holding that dictating a letter is libel because of the transcription. If the person dictating the letter and the person taking the dictation are both employed by a common employer, and the letter pertains to the business of that employer, the publication may however be qualifiedly privileged. *See* p. 1114ff, *infra*.

5. As Slesser, L.J., noted, the *Youssoupoff* case was one of the first involving the question of whether a motion picture film was libel or merely slander. In holding it to be libel, courts have been impressed with the permanent nature of the film as well as the fact that the medium appeals to the visual sense. The more difficult case has involved radio and now television. Some early cases held radio to be slander. *See, e.g.,* Meldrum v. Australian Broadcasting Co., [1932] Vict.L.R. 425; Summit Hotel Co. v. National Broadcasting Co., 336 Pa. 182, 8 A.2d 302 (1939); Kelly v. Hoffman, 137 N.J.L. 695, 61 A.2d 143 (1948). *Contra* Sorensen v. Wood, 123 Neb. 348, 243 N.W. 82 (1932), *appeal dismissed* 290 U.S. 599, 54 S.Ct. 209, 78 L.Ed. 527 (1933); Coffey v. Midland Broadcasting Co., 8 F.Supp. 889 (W.D.Mo.1934). A few states also passed statutes making radio broadcasting slander. *See* L. Eldredge, The Law of Defamation 87–88 (1978). In Hartmann v. Winchell, 296 N.Y. 296, 73 N.E.2d 30 (1947), the New York Court of Appeals held that a radio broadcast read from a written script was libel. Subsequently in Shor v. Billingsley, 4 Misc.2d 857, 158 N.Y.S.2d 476 (1956), *affirmed* 4 A.D.2d 1017, 169 N.Y.S.2d 416 (1957), ad lib remarks on television were held to be libel. The *Restatement of Torts* took no position on the subject but *Restatement (Second) of Torts* § 568A now declares that radio or television broadcasts are libel regardless of whether a script is used. Radio and television are also classified as libel in Great Britain under the Defamation Act of 1952, *supra*. The act was amended in 1968 to extend the same treatment to words published in the course of the performance of a play.

6. Someone in possession of real or personal property, who fails to remove a defamatory statement affixed to his property by third persons within a reasonable time after notice, is himself liable for publishing the defamatory material. *See* Hellar v. Bianco, 111 Cal.App.2d 424, 244 P.2d 757 (1952)(defamatory statement about female plaintiff permitted to remain on wall in men's room toilet); Restatement (Second) of Torts § 577(2). *See also* Byrne v. Deane, [1937] 1 K.B. 818 (C.A.), discussed at p. 1082, *supra*.

7. *Multiple Publication.* At common law each sale or delivery of a copy of a newspaper, magazine, or book was considered a separate publication, creating a new and distinct cause of action. *See* Duke of Brunswick v. Harmer, 14 Q.B. 185, 117 Eng.Rep. 75 (1849). This was the position taken by *Restatement of Torts* § 578, *Comment (b)*. Most states have, however, now moved to some form of single publication rule as exemplified by *Restatement (Second) of Torts* § 577A(3) which provides that "[a]ny one edition of a book or newspaper or any one radio or television broadcast exhibition of a motion picture or similar aggregate communication is a single publication." The Uniform Single Publication Act, which was first propagated in 1952 and has been adopted in seven states, has similar provisions. *See* Unif. Single Publication Act, 14 U.L.A 377 (1990). Under the single publication rule, only one action for all damages suffered in all jurisdictions can be maintained and a judgment on the merits operates as a bar to any other action between the same parties in all jurisdictions. With regard to a motion picture, such as was involved in the *Youssoupoff* case, a single publication rule does not seem to deal with the problem presented by the *Youssoupoff* case in which the movie was shown repeatedly in

a number of theaters. Accepting the *Restatement's* declaration that any "exhibition of a motion picture" is a single publication, then each showing of the film, and certainly each showing in a separate theater, would be a new publication. In point of fact, the issue, for most purposes, is largely a theoretical one. Modern rules of pleading and common sense would dictate that a plaintiff bring only one action and modern rules of collateral estoppel and res judicata would probably make the judgment in that action dispositive in any future action. Some states have insisted on maintaining the common law multiple publication rule for venue purposes in order to preserve the possibility that citizens of that state can bring an action in the courts of that state rather than being forced to bring the action in the defendant's principal place of business or in the jurisdiction in which a publication was printed. *See* Lewis v. Reader's Digest Association, 162 Mont. 401, 512 P.2d 702 (1973). The choice between a multiple and a single publication rule might also have a decisive impact on when the statute of limitations begins to run. *See* Finnegan v. Squire Publishers, Inc., 765 S.W.2d 703 (Mo.Ct.App.1989) in which the court held that the plaintiff's cause of action against a newspaper accrued in Kansas, where the article was published and later distributed in Missouri as well as Kansas. The court therefore ruled that Kansas' one-year statute of limitations would apply, rather than Missouri's two-year statute. *See also* Givens v. Quinn, 877 F.Supp. 485 (W.D.Mo.1994), in which the court held that only one cause of action would lie against the author of the syndicated column but opined that separate causes of action could be brought against each newspaper that reprinted her column.

8. In Keeton v. Hustler Magazine, Inc., 465 U.S. 770, 104 S.Ct. 1473, 79 L.Ed.2d 790 (1984), the statute of limitations on the plaintiff's claim for defamation had run in every jurisdiction except New Hampshire. The case was brought in the United States District Court for the District of New Hampshire on a diversity-of-citizenship basis. The only contact that the parties or the claim had with New Hampshire was the fact that some 10,000 to 15,000 copies of *Hustler* magazine were sold in New Hampshire each month. The plaintiff claimed to have been libeled in five separate issues of the magazine published between September 1975 and May 1976. The case had been dismissed by the lower courts on the ground that New Hampshire's interest in the litigation was too attenuated to permit an assertion of personal jurisdiction over *Hustler* magazine. The lower courts were influenced by the fact that New Hampshire followed the single-publication rule so that if the plaintiff succeeded in her claim she would be entitled to recover damages for the nationwide publication of the magazine, which, as noted, was time-barred in every jurisdiction but New Hampshire, which had an unusually long, six-year limitations period for libel actions. A unanimous Supreme Court reversed and held that there was sufficient contact with the forum state to permit the exercise of personal jurisdiction.

On the same day that *Keeton v. Hustler Magazine, Inc.* was decided, the court also handed down its decision in Calder v. Jones, 465 U.S. 783, 104 S.Ct. 1482, 79 L.Ed.2d 804 (1984), which involved some related jurisdictional issues. The plaintiff, a California resident, claimed that she had been libeled in an article written and edited by the two individual defendants in Florida. The article had been published in a national magazine with a large circulation in California, the *National Enquirer,* which was also a defendant in the case. The individual defendants were a reporter employed by the *Enquirer,* who resided in Florida and traveled frequently to California on business, and the president and editor of the *Enquirer,* who was also a Florida resident and who had only been to California twice, once on a pleasure trip prior to the publication of the article and once after the article's publication to testify in an unrelated trial. The question presented was whether the individual defendants could be served under California's "long-arm" statute. The Superior Court of California granted the individual defendants' motion to quash the service of process, but the California Court of Appeal reversed, noting that the defendants, under the allegations of the complaint, had intended to, and did, cause tortious injury to the plaintiff in California. The fact that these effects were caused by activities conducted outside of California did not prevent California from asserting jurisdiction over the case. A unanimous Supreme Court of the United States affirmed this decision.

BURTON v. CROWELL PUBLISHING CO.

United States Court of Appeals, Second Circuit, 1936.
82 F.2d 154.

L. HAND, CIRCUIT JUDGE.

This appeal arises upon a judgment dismissing a complaint for libel upon the pleadings. The complaint alleged that the defendant had published an advertisement—annexed and incorporated by reference—made up of text and photographs; that one of the photographs was "susceptible of being regarded as representing plaintiff as guilty of indecent exposure and as being a person physically deformed and mentally perverted"; that some of the text, read with the offending photograph, was "susceptible of being regarded as falsely representing plaintiff as an utterer of salacious and obscene language"; and finally that "by reason of the premises plaintiff has been subjected to frequent and conspicuous ridicule, scandal, reproach, scorn, and indignity." The advertisement was of "Camel" cigarettes; the plaintiff was a widely known gentleman steeple-chaser, and the text quoted him as declaring that "Camel" cigarettes "restored" him after "a crowded business day." Two photographs were inserted; the larger, a picture of the plaintiff in riding shirt and breeches, seated apparently outside a paddock with a cigarette in one hand and a cap and whip in the other. This contained the legend, "Get a lift with a Camel"; neither it, nor the photograph, is charged as part of the libel, except as the legend may be read upon the other and offending photograph. That represented him coming from a race to be weighed in; he is carrying his saddle in front of him with his right hand under the pommel and his left under the cantle; the line of the seat is about twelve inches below his waist. Over the pommel hangs, a stirrup; over the seat at his middle a white girth falls loosely in such a way that it seems to be attached to the plaintiff and not to the saddle. So regarded, the photograph becomes grotesque, monstrous, and obscene; and the legends, which without undue violence can be made to match, reinforce the ribald interpretation. That is the libel. The answer alleged that the plaintiff had posed for the photographs and been paid for their use as an advertisement; a reply, that they had never been shown to the plaintiff after they were taken. On this showing the judge held that the advertisement did not hold the plaintiff up to the hatred, ridicule, or contempt of fair-minded people, and that in any event he consented to its use and might not complain.

We dismiss at once so much of the complaint as alleged that the advertisement might be read to say that the plaintiff was deformed, or that he had indecently exposed himself, or was making obscene jokes by means of the legends. Nobody could be fatuous enough to believe any of these things; everybody would at once see that it was the camera, and the camera alone, that had made the unfortunate mistake. If the advertisement is a libel, it is such in spite of the fact that it asserts nothing whatever about the plaintiff, even by the remotest implications. It does not profess to depict him as he is; it does not exaggerate any part of his person so as to suggest that he is deformed; it is patently an optical illusion, and carries its correction on its face as much as though it were a verbal utterance which expressly declared that it was false. It would be hard for words so guarded to carry any sting, but the same is not true of caricatures, and this is an example; for, notwithstanding all we have just said, it exposed the plaintiff to overwhelming ridicule. The contrast between the drawn and serious face and the accompanying fantastic and lewd deformity was so extravagant that, though utterly unfair, it in fact made of the plaintiff a preposterously ridiculous spectacle; and the obvious mistake only added to the amusement. Had such a picture been deliberately produced, surely every right-minded person would agree that he would have had a genuine grievance; and the effect is the same whether it is deliberate or not. Such a caricature affects a man's reputation, if by that is meant his position in the minds of others; the association so established may be beyond repair; he may become known indefinitely as the absurd victim of this unhappy mischance. Literally, therefore, the injury falls within the accepted rubric; it exposes the sufferer to "ridicule" and "contempt." Nevertheless, we have not been able to find very much in the books that is in point, for although it has long been recognized that pictures may be libels, and in some cases they have been caricatures, in nearly all they have impugned the plaintiff at least by implication, directly or indirectly uttering some falsehood about him. * * *

The defendant answers that every libel must affect the plaintiff's character; but if by "character" is meant those moral qualities which the word ordinarily includes, the statement is certainly untrue, for there are many libels which do not affect the reputation of the victim in any such way. * * *

A more plausible challenge is that a libel must be something that can be true or false, since truth is always a defense. It would follow that if, as we agree, the picture was a mistake on its face and declared nothing about the plaintiff, it was not a libel. We have been able to find very little on the point. In Dunlop v. Dunlop Rubber Co. (1920) 1 Irish Ch. & Ld.Com. 280, 290–292, the picture represented the plaintiff in foppish clothes, and the opinion seems to rely merely upon the contempt which that alone might have aroused, but those who saw it might have taken it to imply that the plaintiff was in fact a fop. In Zbyszko v. New York American, 228 App.Div. 277, 239 N.Y.S. 411, however, though the decision certainly went far, nobody could possibly have read the picture as asserting anything which was in fact untrue; it was the mere association of the plaintiff with a gorilla that was thought to lower him in others' esteem. Nevertheless, although the question is almost tabula rasa, it seems to us that in principle there should be no doubt. The gravamen of the wrong in defamation is not so much the injury to reputation, measured by the opinions of others, as the feelings, that is, the repulsion or the light esteem, which those opinions engender. We are sensitive to the charge of murder only because our fellows deprecate it in most forms; but a head-hunter, or an aboriginal American Indian, or a gangster, would regard such an accusation as a distinction, and during the Great War an "ace," a man who had killed five others, was held in high regard. Usually it is difficult to arouse feelings without expressing an opinion, or asserting a fact; and the common law has so much regard for truth that it excuses the utterance of anything that is true. But it is a non sequitur to argue that whenever truth is not a defense, there can be no libel; that would invert the proper approach to the whole subject. In all wrongs we must first ascertain whether the interest invaded is one which the law will protect at all; that is indeed especially important in defamation, for the common law did not recognize all injuries to reputation, especially when the utterance was oral. But the interest here is by hypothesis one which the law does protect; the plaintiff has been substantially enough ridiculed to be in a position to complain. The defendant must therefore find some excuse, and truth would be an excuse if it could be pleaded. The only reason why the law makes truth a defense is not because a libel must be false, but because the utterance of truth is in all circumstances an interest paramount to reputation; it is like a privileged communication, which is privileged only because the law prefers it conditionally to reputation. When there is no such countervailing interest, there is no excuse; and that is the situation here. In conclusion therefore we hold that because the picture taken with the legends was calculated to expose the plaintiff to more than trivial ridicule, it was prima facie actionable; that the fact that it did not assume to state a fact or an opinion is irrelevant; and that in consequence the publication is actionable.

Finally, the plaintiff's consent to the use of the photographs for which he posed as an advertisement was not a consent to the use of the offending photograph; he had no reason to anticipate that the lens would so distort his appearance. If the defendant wished to fix him with responsibility for whatever the camera might turn out, the result should have been shown him before publication. Possibly any one who chooses to stir such a controversy in a court cannot have been very sensitive originally, but that is a consideration for the jury, which, if ever justified, is justified in actions for defamation.

Judgment reversed; cause remanded for trial.

Notes

1. The picture involved in the *Burton* case was part of the record on appeal, and two of the editors of this casebook have a copy in their files. The picture makes it look very much as if the plaintiff were exposing himself in a bizarre and grotesque manner. The trial judge was not sympathetic, finding that no right-minded person would hold the plaintiff up to ridicule, hatred, or contempt and that, in any event, the plaintiff had consented to its use. On appeal, the plaintiff's attorneys argued that grotesque phalli had been used on the stage in ancient Greece and that, given the suggestion of the photograph, people might be prepared to think that the plaintiff was engaging in similar

conduct. Appellant's Brief at pp. 11–12. If the court had been prepared to accept this contention, the case would easily have fit into the traditional format. For reasons of prudishness or whatever, the circuit court of appeals was unwilling to view the photograph in this light.

2. The leading case on ridicule as defamation is Triggs v. Sun Printing and Publishing Association, 179 N.Y. 144, 71 N.E. 739 (1904). In that case the defendant newspaper published a series of sarcastic articles about Professor Oscar L. Triggs, a well-known professor of English at the University of Chicago who, among other things, favored a simpler style of English than was then currently fashionable. Triggs had turned down a substantial offer to give public lectures to the audiences who went to view the plays of a touring Shakespearean company. In bringing the action, Triggs' counsel argued that the articles implied that Triggs was an illiterate buffoon who was not professionally qualified to fill his high academic post and that such false factual implications made the articles libelous. The following extract is from one of the articles:

> The Shakespeare legend should be allowed to delude no more. Prof. Triggs * * * can be depended upon to reduce this man Shakespeare to his natural proportions, club the sawdust out of that wax figger of literature and preach to eager multitudes the superiority of the modern playrights, with all the modern improvements * * *. The so-called poetry and imagination visible in this Stratford Charlatan's plays must be torn out, deracinated, the fellow * * * would call it, in his fustian style * * *. If these plays are to be put upon the stage, they must be rewritten; and Prof. Triggs * * * is the destined rewriter, amender and reviser. The sapless, old-fashioned rhetoric must be cut down. The fresh and natural contemporary tongue, pure Triggsian, must be substituted. For example, who can read with patience these tinsel lines? 'Madam, an hour before the worshipped sun peered forth the golden window of the east, a troubled mind drave me to walk abroad.' This must be translated into Triggsian * * * somewhat like this: 'Say, lady, an hour before sun-up I was feeling wormy and took a walk around the block' * * *. Here is more Shakespearian rubbish:

> 'O, she doth teach the torches to burn bright!

> Her beauty hangs upon the cheek of night,

> As a rich jewel in an Ethiop's ear.'

How much more forcible in clear, concise Triggsian: 'Say, she's a peach! A bird!' * * * Hear 'Pop' Capulet drivel: 'Go to, go to, You are a saucy boy!' In the Oscar * * * dialect, this is this: 'Come off, kid. You're too fresh.' * * * Compare the dropsical hifalutin:

> 'Night's candles are burnt out, and jocund day

> Stands tiptoe on the misty mountain's tops,'

with the time-saving Triggsian version: 'I hear the milkman.' * * *

The downfall of Shakespeare is only a matter of time and Triggs.

179 N.Y. at 148–50, 71 N.E. at 740–41. The New York Court of Appeals held that Triggs stated a good cause of action for libel but focused only on the ridicule. The court seemingly held that the ridicule alone made out the libel in the circumstances of the case before it.

3. Relying on cases like *Burton* and *Triggs,* the late Dean Prosser proposed adding to the *Restatement (Second)* a new section providing that "[a] defamatory communication may consist of words or other matter which ridicule another." *Restatement (Second) of Torts* § 567A (Tent.Draft No. 11, 1965). This provision was also included in Tentative Draft No. 20, 1974. In adding the section on ridicule Prosser was building on *Restatement of Torts* § 566, which provided that "[a] defamatory communication may consist of a statement of opinion based upon facts known or assumed by both parties to the communication," and which it was proposed to retain in the *Restatement (Second).* In illustrating § 566, the *Restatement* gave as an example a political speech in which "A * * * accurately relates certain conduct of his opponent blocking reform measures advocated by A. In the course of his argument, A declares that any person who would so conduct himself is no better than a murderer." The *Restatement* concluded that A has defamed his opponent. In preparing for the *Restatement (Second)* the illustration was changed to be a discussion involving the accurate description of a neighbor's abuse of his wife and followed by the "no better than a murderer" characterization. In reaching these conclusions on defamatory opinions on known facts, the American Law Institute glossed over two problems. The first is that there was only sparse case support for the position and no consideration was given to free speech considerations. English law seems to have been more solicitous of the defendant's freedom of speech. *See* Slim v. Daily Telegraph, [1968] 2 Q.B. 157, 2 W.L.R. 599, 1 All E.R. 497 (C.A.). *See also* A. Goodhart, *Restatement of the Law of Torts, Volume III: A Comparison Between American and English Law,* 89 U.Pa.L.Rev. 265, 273–84 (1944). The second, and conceptually more difficult one, is that, *contra* Hand J., in the *Burton* case, *Restatement of Torts* § 558 states that "[t]o create liability for defamation there must be an unprivileged publication of *false* and defamatory matter." (Emphasis supplied). An attempt, in May 1974, to delete the proposed §§ 566 and 567A from the *Restatement (Second)* failed. In June 1974, however, Gertz v. Robert Welch, Inc., 418 U.S. 323, 94 S.Ct. 2997, 41 L.Ed.2d 789 (1974), reprinted *infra,* p. 1151, made it clear that the mere expression of opinion could not be the subject of an action for defamation and the provisions in question were dropped from the *Restatement (Second).* The controversy and the issues are discussed in G. Christie, *Defamatory Opinions and the Restatement (Second) of Torts,* 75 Mich.L.Rev. 1621 (1977). *See also* Note, *Fact and Opinion After* Gertz v. Robert Welch, Inc.: *The Evolution of a Privilege,* 34 Rutgers L.Rev. 81 (1981). Actually distinguishing between what is fact and what is opinion can often be very difficult. We will address that question in note 6, p. 1166, *infra,* following the presentation of the *Gertz* case.

4. The controversy noted above may have in part been influenced by what was once the fairly common practice of defendants, in defamation actions brought by well-known people against newspaper and other media defendants, of making the so-called "rolled-up plea" of "truth and fair comment." In most jurisdictions, the fair comment defense was only available if there were no misstatements of fact in the defendants' statements about the plaintiff. The leading case was Post Publishing Co. v. Hallam, 59 Fed. 530 (6th Cir.1893)(per Taft, J.), although there was a minority, as we shall see, prepared to excuse good-faith misstatements of fact at least in the context of political campaigns. *See* Coleman v. MacLennan, 78 Kan. 711, 98 P. 281 (1908). The recognition of the relevancy of a fair comment defense in a context in which there are no misstatements of fact suggests that, without the defense, some expressions of

opinion or instances of ridicule might be actionable merely qua opinion or ridicule but that the courts will protect such material if the opinion or ridicule does not go too far. It was sometimes said that, to be fair, the comment had to have some basis in fact and be the "honest" opinion of the critic and not published solely to harm the plaintiff. Although the issue of fair comment could be raised in an action brought by a public figure or official whose public life was being criticized, it most often figured in actions brought by artists, authors, and musical performers who were angry at the criticisms of their work published by the media. In point of fact, there are very few cases in which a defendant was held liable for expressing a derogatory opinion in the absence of there being a false implication of fact in the opinion,[2] and fewer still in which the comment was held to be "unfair." When literary, musical, or artistic endeavors were concerned some very biting criticism was routinely held non-actionable. In Cherry v. Des Moines Leader, 114 Iowa 298, 86 N.W. 323 (1901), the following review by a music critic of a group called the Cherry Sisters was held not to be actionable.

> Effie is an old jade of 50 summers, Jessie a friskie filly of 40, and Addie, the flower of the family, a capering monstrosity of 35. Their long skinny arms, equipped with talons at the extremities, swung mechanically, and anon waved frantically at the suffering audience. The mouths of their rancid features opened like caverns, and sounds like the wailings of damned souls issued therefrom. They pranced around the stage with a motion that suggested a cross between the danse du ventre and a fox trot,—strange creatures with painted faces and hideous mien. Effie is spavined, Addie is string halt, and Jessie, the only one who showed her stockings, has legs with calves as classic in their outlines as the curves of a broom handle.

5. We have already seen, in the previous chapter, that public officials and public figures cannot recover for ridicule or the expression of offensive and derogatory opinions by alleging that the defendant has, by his outrageous verbal conduct, intentionally inflicted severe emotional distress. *See* Hustler Magazine v. Falwell, 485 U.S. 46, 108 S.Ct. 876, 99 L.Ed.2d 41 (1988), reprinted at p. 1048, *supra*.

FAWCETT PUBLICATIONS, INC. v. MORRIS

Supreme Court of Oklahoma, 1962.
377 P.2d 42, *cert. denied*, 376 U.S. 513, 84 S.Ct. 964, 11 L.Ed.2d 968.

JACKSON, JUSTICE.

In the trial court, plaintiff Dennit Morris sued Fawcett Publications, Inc., the publisher of "True" Magazine, and Mid–Continent News Company, its distributor, for damages for libel. The suit grew out of an article in a 1958 issue of "True" Magazine entitled "The Pill That Can Kill Sports", concerning the use of amphetamine and other similar drugs by athletes throughout the country.

---

2. For example, unless one is commenting on facts known to all parties to the conversation if one says "in my opinion, X is a thief" one is implying that he knows of facts which would justify the opinion.

Plaintiff alleged in his petition that he was a member of the 1956 Oklahoma University football team; that the article imputed to him a crime against the laws of the state of Oklahoma and was libelous per se; and asked for general damages in the amount of $100,000, and punitive damages in the amount of $50,000.

At the conclusion of the evidence, the trial court instructed the jury to return a verdict against Fawcett, leaving only the amount of the damages for jury determination. Mid–Continent's motion for directed verdict in its favor was sustained.

The jury returned a verdict for plaintiff and against Fawcett in the amount of $75,000 for actual damages.

Fawcett is a foreign corporation without a service agent in this state, and service was had upon Fawcett herein by serving the Secretary of State pursuant to statute. On appeal, Fawcett, for its first proposition, argues that the court had no jurisdiction for the reason that Fawcett was not "doing business" in the state within the meaning of 18 O.S.1961, Sections 1.17 and 472, which authorize service upon the Secretary of State.

From uncontradicted evidence in the record, it appears that Fawcett had contracted with Mid–Continent to distribute its magazines in a portion of the State of Oklahoma. The "territory" is not described in the contract, and is left for all practical purposes to the discretion of Fawcett. Magazines were to be forwarded to Mid–Continent without specific orders, in amounts entirely within the discretion of Fawcett. Mid–Continent agreed to distribute not only the magazines and books named in the contract, but all "other matter" which Fawcett might choose to forward. All prices, sales dates and release dates were to be fixed by Fawcett and were subject to change at any time by Fawcett. Mid–Continent agreed to keep dealer records acceptable to Fawcett, showing "initial distribution, re-orders, pickups, returns and net sales". Provision was made for "returns", and credit thereon, and Mid–Continent agreed to dispose of unsold copies in any manner Fawcett should direct. Mid–Continent agreed to distribute to its retail dealers all "advertising, dealers' helps, posters, circulars, and other material" which Fawcett chose to supply. It agreed to furnish Fawcett a complete list of its dealers, showing address and line of business, and showing each dealer's "draw" of each of Fawcett's magazines, publications and other matter. The contract was for 10 years, but could be terminated by either party "at any time with or without cause by giving ten (10) days written notice" to the other party.

Fawcett also employed a "traveling representative" whose duty it was to call on both wholesalers and retailers, to "check up" on the manner of distribution, display and sale of Fawcett's publications and other matter. * * *

* * *

Considering the terms of the contract, and the activities of Fawcett's "traveling representative", we are forced to the conclusion that for all practical purposes Mid–Continent was little more than a mere conduit through which Fawcett exercised its own free and unhampered discretion as to all pertinent details of the business. Such being the case, * * *

Fawcett was doing business in Oklahoma within the meaning of 18 O.S. 1961 §§ 1.17 and 472. It follows that service upon the Secretary of State was authorized in this case, and that the court had jurisdiction of the defendant so served. Defendant's first proposition is therefore without merit.

The remaining propositions urged on appeal go to the merits of the case, and we therefore summarize the alleged libelous publication. The article is approximately seven full pages in length; was studiously prepared after what purports to be painstaking research; and starts at pages 44 and 45 of the magazine. Across the center of pages 44 and 45, we find in large letters and bold type the following:

"The Pill That Can kill Sports".

In the upper left hand corner of page 44 are these words: "Simply by using a phony letterhead, the author purchased by mail enough drugs to hop up over 100 football teams." Immediately under this statement is the following: "A SHOCKING REPORT:", which is emphasized by a red line underneath. In the middle of pages 44 and 45 is a picture of five bottles of pills; the sixth bottle is of the shape and type commonly used for hypodermic needle injections; and there are two hypodermic needles. In the upper right hand corner of page 45 is found the following:

"You can go to jail for selling amphetamine to a truck driver or injecting it into a racehorse, yet this same drug is being handed out to high school and college athletes all over the country."

In the lower half of page 45, and flowing over onto page 44, is pictured a heavily loaded dual-wheeled truck bearing the sign or label on its side, "DOPE". In the body of the truck are two individuals labeled "Avarice" and "Ignorance" shovelling out dope to athletes, including football players, who are running behind the truck and catching the pills. Another person is handing out pills to a football player from the cab of the truck. Above the engine of the truck are these words: "Victory at any Cost".

Across the center of pages 46 and 47 is a picture of a stable with the heads of horses appearing from the windows. In front of the horses are what appear to be uniformed officials and trainers. Underneath this picture is printed the following: "Racehorses are scrupulously guarded against doping violations, yet the same drugs are given freely to young athletes."

While the article is too lengthy to be quoted, a few excerpts which appear to be fairly representative of the entire article are quoted as follows:

"Definite proof that doping was a common practice came on September 13, 1956, when I received this report from the USOA's attorney, John T. McGovern. 'I have communicated with record executives of Olympic, university, A.A.U. organizations, athletic directors and others * * * At every point of contact I was informed * * * that substantially the entire population in schools and colleges have been using this type drug * * *'.

* * *

"The *amphetamines are administered to athletes by* hypodermic injection, *nasal spray,* or in tablets or capsules, but pills are the most common form, at least according to those athletic figures who are willing to talk.

* * *

"There is, however, one statistic which is available, and which strongly indicates that consumption is rapidly increasing. Recently *I was able to buy 30 cc.'s of dextroamphetamine sulphate for 95 cents.* This amount—*enough to hop up an entire football team*—cost three times this much a few years ago. Also, I was able to buy a thousand amphetamine pills for $1.40 less than a third of the 1954 price. When sales go up, prices go down.

"*Speaking of football teams,* during the 1956 season, *while Oklahoma was increasing its sensational victory streak,* several *physicians observed Oklahoma players being sprayed in the nostrils with an atomizer. And during a televised game, a close-up showed Oklahoma spray jobs to the nation.* 'Ten years ago,' Dr. Howe observed acidly, 'when that was done to a horse, the case went to court. Medically, there is no reason for such treatment. If *players* need therapy, they shouldn't be on the field.'

* * *

"*The 'lifter'* (amphetamine user) can and *does become heroic, boisterous, pugnacious, or vicious.*

* * *

"*These results are what make amphetamines useful in the field of athletics.* They promote aggression, increase the competitive spirit, and work the same as the epinephrine (adrenalin) produced in your body. The adrenal cortex, however, is wiser than victory-hungry coaches and athletes, * * *." (Emphasis supplied.)

The article refers to several nationally known brutal crimes as being committed by users of amphetamine.

Plaintiff's evidence at the trial shows that the substance administered to Oklahoma players and members of the 1956 football team was "spirits of peppermint", a harmless substance used for the relief of "cotton mouth", or dryness of mouth, resulting from prolonged or extreme physical exertion; that plaintiff did not use amphetamine or any other narcotic drug, and there was no evidence that any other member of the team used amphetamine or narcotic drugs.

Plaintiff's evidence further shows that plaintiff was fullback on the alternate squad of the 1956 football team; that he played in all games during the 1956 season, except two, when he was "side-lined" because of injuries; that the team won all ten regular games during the season and won the Bowl game at the end of the season in Miami, Florida; that plaintiff played in the Bowl game; that plaintiff was a sophomore in 1956 and continued to play on the team in 1957 and 1958; and that he was a member of the University baseball team while at the university. That there were sixty or seventy members of the team in 1956.

Plaintiff's evidence further shows that many people asked plaintiff about the article in True, beginning shortly after its publication, and continuing until shortly before trial.

* * *

Having concluded that the article is defamatory and libelous on its face we think it follows that the article is *libelous per se.* * * *

* * *

The additional and final legal argument presented under Fawcett's second proposition is that a defamatory publication concerning a large group is not libelous per se as to an unnamed member of that group. In this connection it appears that the courts have generally held that defamatory words used broadly in respect to a large class or group will not support a libel action by an individual member of the group. 70 A.L.R.2d 1382. This doctrine appears to stem from the early decision of Sumner v. Buel, 12 Johns 475 (New York 1815), wherein the court concluded that a *civil* action would not lie for a libelous publication against all of the nine officers of three named rifle companies, because of the uncertainty as to who was libeled. In that case the court said:

> "* * * A writing which inveighs against mankind in general, or against a particular order of men, is no libel, nor is it even indictable. It must descend to particulars and individuals, to make it a libel. (3 Salk. 224, 1 Ld.Raym. 486)."

We have examined the cited [English] case, * * * In our examination of the case * * * it is apparent that it was a criminal case, [and] * * * it appears * * * that the reason why the indictment was set aside was because the jurors were unable from the proof to determine who had been libeled. * * *

Thus it is quite apparent that the case is not authority for the proposition that plaintiff in a suit based upon a libelous publication against nine identifiable officers of three named rifle companies could not recover in a libel action. In 34 Columbia Law Review, beginning at page 1332, is a very thorough and studiously prepared article entitled "Liability for Defamation of a Group." In the article it is said of Sumner v. Buel, supra, that "the misinterpretation of a dictum in an early English criminal libel case (King v. Alme, supra) gave rise to the doctrine that because of the absence of specific mention of any person, no action would lie for a statement of this nature."

* * *

From our examination of the authorities we have reached the conclusion that the English courts have never barred recovery in Group libel cases unless the group is extremely large. In Ortenberg v. Plamondon et al., Quebec Court of Appeals, 35 Can. Law Times 262, American Annotated Cases, Ann.Cas.1915C, Page 347, it was held that a member of the Jewish race in Quebec, consisting of 75 families out of a total city population of

80,000 people, could maintain an action of defamation of the entire group even though he was not assailed individually, but only as a member of the group.

* * *

While there is substantial precedent from other jurisdictions to the effect that a member of a "large group" may not recover in an individual action for a libelous publication unless he is referred to personally, we have found no substantial reason why *size* alone should be conclusive. We are not inclined to follow such a rule where, as here, the complaining member of the group is as well known and identified in connection with the group as was the plaintiff in this case. * * *

We hold, in answer to Fawcett's second proposition, that since the article is libelous on its face without the aid of extrinsic facts to make it so, it is libelous per se; that the article libels every member of the team, including the plaintiff, although he was not specifically named therein; that the average lay reader who was familiar with the team, and its members, would necessarily believe that the regular players, including the plaintiff, were using an amphetamine spray as set forth in the article; that the article strongly suggests that the use of amphetamine was criminal; and that plaintiff has sufficiently established his identity as one of those libeled by the publication.

In reaching the conclusion that plaintiff has established his identity in the mind of the average lay reader as one of those libeled, we are mindful that a full-back on the alternate squad of a university team who has played in nine out of eleven all victorious games in one season will not be overlooked by those who were familiar with the team, and the contribution made by its regular players. It should be remembered that plaintiff was a constant player, and not a part of the "changing" element of that group.

* * *

The judgment in favor of plaintiff and against Fawcett Publications, Inc., is affirmed; and the action of the trial court in sustaining the motion for directed verdict and entering judgment for the defendant, Mid–Continent News Company, is also affirmed.

Notes

1. The case was decided by a divided court. Halley, J., dissented on the ground that the article was not libelous per se of Morris. Oklahoma is one of the states, now most probably a minority, that despite the *Hinsdale* case, p. 1078, *supra,* and *Restatement (Second) of Torts* § 569 still retains a libel per se/libel per quod distinction. *See* Akins v. Altus Newspapers, Inc., 609 P.2d 1263 (Okl.1977), *as modified on denial of rehearing* (1980). Three other judges concurred in part and dissented in part in the *Morris* case, but published no opinion so that, given the many issues in the case, it is not clear what they dissented to.

2. How many members of the 1956 Oklahoma University football team could have brought an action? Morris seems to be the only one who actually did, but if the entire team brought an action and were sustained in the contention that the article libelled them, the damages would be very great

indeed. Is this an argument for restricting the ability of members of a group to bring an action for statements that defame the group to which they belong? For a discussion of this general subject, *see* Note, *Group Defamation: Five Guiding Factors*, 64 Tex.L.Rev. 591 (1985).

3. In Owens v. Clark, 154 Okl. 108, 6 P.2d 755 (1931), discussed in an omitted portion of the *Morris* case, "certain members" of the Oklahoma Supreme Court were accused of making the Oklahoma courts an instrument for "looting" citizens of their property. It was held, by a special court, that the statement did not defame each of the nine members of the court. In the early case of Foxcroft v. Lacy, Hob. 89, 80 Eng.Rep. 239 (Ex.Ch.1613), the defendant had said, of seventeen men involved as defendants in a conspiracy suit in Star Chamber, that "[t]hese defendants are those that helped to murder Henry Farrar." It was held that each of the seventeen had been defamed.

4. It has been said that English law has never adequately found a means of handling group defamation. *See* Salmond & Heuston, Torts 145, n. 71 (21st ed. by R. Heuston and R. Buckley, 1996). The editor cites "a curious unreported case in which a newspaper thought it prudent to settle an action brought by 134 valuers of the London County Council." The leading modern English case is Knupffer v. London Express Newspaper, Ltd., [1944] A.C. 116. In that case, the defendant newspaper had published an article accusing "an emigre group called * * * [the] Young Russia" party of being "quislings on whom Hitler flatters himself he can build a pro-German movement within the Soviet Union." The group, founded in France, and at the time headquartered in the United States, had some two thousand members. There were 24 members in Great Britain. The plaintiff was the British representative of the party. The House of Lords held, as a matter of law, that the article could not be interpreted as referring to the plaintiff. Lord Porter asked:

> Can an individual sue in respect of words which are defamatory of a body or class of persons generally? The answer as a rule must be 'No,' but the inquiry is really a wider one and is governed by no rule of thumb. The true question always is: 'Was the individual, or were the individuals, bringing the action personally pointed to by the words complained of?'

Id. at 124. Several of their lordships agreed that a charge that "all lawyers were thieves" was not actionable by any lawyers but mere "vulgar generalizations." But Lord Porter allowed that "I can imagine it being said that each member of a body, however large, was defamed where the libel consisted in the assertion that no one of the members of the community was elected as a member unless he had committed a murder."

5. Civil remedies in cases like Ostenberg v. Plamondon, 35 Can. Law Times 262, 37 Am. & Eng.Ann. Cases (1915c) 347 (1914) present difficulties. In theory in England and some American jurisdictions, group defamation could be handled by public prosecution for criminal libel. As a practical matter this is hardly an effective remedy. A British Government Report states:

> It is also a criminal libel to libel any sect, company, or class if it is proved that the object is to excite the hatred of the public against the class libelled. As far as we know there has been no prosecution for this offense this century and probably today any proceedings resulting from incitement to racial hatred would be taken under the Race Relations legislation.

Report of the Committee on Defamation, Cmd. 5909, at ¶ 434(b) (1975).

In Beauharnais v. Illinois, 343 U.S. 250, 72 S.Ct. 725, 96 L.Ed. 919 (1952), an Illinois statute prohibiting the publishing of any publication portraying "depravity, criminality, unchastity, or lack of virtue of a class of citizens of any race, color, creed or religion" and which exposes such citizens "to contempt, derision or obloquy or which is productive of breach of the peace or riots" was applied to a scurrilous leaflet attacking the "encroachment, harassment and invasion of white people * * * by the Negro," etc. In upholding the conviction, the Court, per Frankfurter, J., relied on Chaplinsky v. New Hampshire, 315 U.S. 568, 62 S.Ct. 766, 86 L.Ed. 1031 (1942), which permitted a person to be prosecuted for uttering "fighting words," *i.e.* words calculated to incite an immediate breach of the peace. Justices Black, Douglas, Jackson, and Reed dissented in *Beauharnais*. Collin v. Smith, 578 F.2d 1197 (7th Cir.1978), *cert. denied* 439 U.S. 916, 99 S.Ct. 291, 58 L.Ed.2d 264, in which the Seventh Circuit affirmed a district court decision, *inter alia,* ruling unconstitutional an ordinance of Skokie, Illinois prohibiting the "dissemination of any materials * * * which promotes or incites hatred against persons by reason of their race, national origin, or religion, and is intended to do so * * *," seems, however, clearly inconsistent with *Beauharnais* and with any attempt, in a jurisdiction recognizing common law crimes, to prosecute on a criminal libel basis. The result in the Skokie litigation is not of course universally applauded. K. Lasson has criticized the decision as well as the conclusions which the current editors draw from that litigation in, *Racial Defamation as Free Speech: Abusing the First Amendment*, 17 Colum.Hum.Rts.L.Rev. 11 (1985); *Group Libel versus Free Speech: When Big Brother* Should *Butt In*, 23 Duquesne L.Rev. 77 (1984). The limitations that the first amendment imposes upon attempts to punish inflammatory and scurrilous attacks on distinct classes of citizens is of course much too large and important a subject to be capable of adequate treatment in a first year course on torts. One may still wonder, however, whether the attempt to deal with scurrilous and offensive verbal attacks on discrete classes of citizens through the mechanism of criminal libel laws may not be an instance of the cure being worse than the disease.

6. The most frequently cited case on group defamation is Neiman–Marcus v. Lait, 13 F.R.D. 311 (S.D.N.Y.1952). In a book called "U.S.A. Confidential," the authors talked of "whores" or "call girls" or "party girls." They went on to say that *"some* Neiman models are call girls" commanding a price of "a hundred bucks a night." (Emphasis supplied). They then proceeded: "The salesgirls are good, too—pretty and often much cheaper—twenty bucks on average." They continued by discussing the men's store at Neiman's. "You wonder how all the faggots got to the wild and wooly. You thought those with talent ended up in New York or Hollywood and the plodders got government jobs in Washington. Then you learn the nucleus of the Dallas fairy colony is composed of many Neiman dress and millinery designers imported from New York and Paris, who sent for their boy friends when the men's store expanded. Now *most* of the sales staff are fairies, too." (Emphasis supplied). On this aspect of the case the plaintiffs fell into three classes (a) all nine of the models at the store as of the time of publication of the book; (b) fifteen of the twenty-five salesmen on behalf of themselves and of the class; and (c) thirty saleswomen out of 382, again suing on behalf of themselves and of the class. The court held that the models and salesmen had a cause of action, even though the authors did not say that all of them engaged in the activities charged, but that none of the saleswomen did. Even though all were seemingly charged, the group was too big. The court felt that "no reasonable man would take the

writers seriously and conclude from the publication a reference to any individual saleswoman."

B. COMMON–LAW DEFENSES

CRANE v. NEW YORK WORLD TELEGRAM CORP.

Court of Appeals of New York, 1955.
308 N.Y. 470, 126 N.E.2d 753.

FULD, JUDGE.

On December 6, 1951, there appeared in a column of The *NEW YORK WORLD-TELEGRAM AND THE SUN,* a newspaper of wide daily circulation, this item:

> " 'John Crane, former president of the UFA now under indictment, isn't waiting for his own legal developments. Meanwhile his lawyers are launching a $,$$$,$$$ defamation suit.' "

The present action for libel followed; the individual defendant is the columnist who wrote the piece, the corporate defendant, the owner and publisher of the paper. The answer which defendants interposed includes two separate defenses, one complete, the other partial, both based on the premise and hypothesis that the charge is true in that plaintiff, though never "indicted" by a grand jury, had been accused of a number of indictable crimes by various people. By the motion under consideration, an order is sought striking both defenses as insufficient in law.

Plaintiff alleges that the publication was false and defamatory, that defendants knew or could have ascertained its falsity by the exercise of reasonable care and that they were guilty of "actual malice and wrongfully and wilfully intended to injure the plaintiff." Claiming, among other things, great injury to credit and reputation and an inability to secure or retain employment, he asks damages of $100,000.

Defendants deny all these allegations, except that of publication, and allege two separate defenses. The first of these purports to establish the truth of the publication. While nowhere stating that plaintiff was indicted by a grand jury—and, concededly, he never was—it asserts, nevertheless, that he was "under indictment" in an alleged nonlegal sense of that term; more specifically, it recites that he had been accused of various crimes by private individuals and was, in fact, guilty of those crimes. In support of the publication's truth under such a construction, it sets forth in considerable detail the substance of the New York City Fire Department scandals and investigations of 1950–1951, in which plaintiff, then president of an association of firemen, and others are depicted as playing a prominent part.

Little purpose would be served by repeating these allegations at any length. It is enough to observe that—while many of them touch on the derelictions of other firemen and relate to matters in which it is not clear that plaintiff was involved—it is recited that plaintiff misappropriated proceeds from the sale of tickets to the annual Firemen's Balls; that he had been accused of criminal activity by fellow firemen and others; and that, in testifying before a New York County grand jury and a committee of the United States Senate, he had admitted, without waiving immunity, facts which established his guilt of larceny and bribery.

* * *

The court at Special Term granted plaintiff's motion, directing that both defenses be stricken as insufficient in law, * * * on the ground that they had no relation to the truth of the publication. In the absence of qualifying language, the court said, the term "indictment" could be understood by reasonable people "in only one sense, namely, as a charge by a grand jury of the commission of a crime." The Appellate Division took a different view; it reversed, holding that "indictment" is reasonably susceptible to both the meaning "of an accusation by a grand jury, and of an accusation generally", and that it was for a jury to say in what sense it would be understood by the reader. The appeal is here by permission of the Appellate Division on certified questions.

In our judgment, the publication complained of, when considered in context as it must be, could reasonably be read and interpreted in only one way, that is, as charging that plaintiff had been indicted by the grand jury for some crime. * * * There can be no question that the "ordinary meaning" of the term "indictment" is that of the legal process, usually before a grand jury, whereby a person is formally charged with crime and a criminal prosecution begun. * * *

If, as defendants claim, the word permits of a looser, a highly rhetorical, use to signify an accusation by private persons, that sense of the term is so rare, as contrasted with the legal process of indictment, that no reader would so understand or accept it without some qualifying language to indicate that the ordinary meaning was not intended. An example would be a statement that John Doe stands "indicted in the court of public opinion." * * *

* * *

* * * A plea of truth as justification must be as broad as the alleged libel and must establish the truth of the precise charge therein made. * * *

Defendants contend, however, that, even though the complete defense be held insufficient, its allegations may properly be repeated in their entirety in the second numbered defense, as a partial defense in mitigation of damages, when coupled with the further allegations that "the facts" were widely known, that plaintiff's general reputation was bad, and that all such matters were known to defendants, relied upon by them and made them believe in the truth of the item in question. Before proceeding to a consideration of that defense, we examine some of the relevant principles governing damages in libel actions, as well as their mitigation or reduction by the proof of acts which fall short of those charged in the libel.

* * * Well settled is the basic rule that the amount of plaintiff's recovery may be reduced by proof of facts "tending but failing to prove the truth" of the libel's charge. * * * That proof is relevant in mitigation of punitive damages, for it may negative actual malice by showing that defendant, though mistaken, had reasonable grounds for belief in the truth of the charge contained in the publication. * * * And, turning to compensatory damages, such evidence may serve to reduce them as well, * * * on the theory that, if the actual facts "gave some color of verity to the statements contained in the published article, plaintiff would not be entitled to receive the same damages as if his reputation was beyond unfavorable criticism or comment." * * * But, of necessity, the facts that go to make up a partial defense in mitigation and reduction must *tend to prove the truth of the precise charge* made by the publication. * * *

In the case before us, however, the facts alleged are entirely unrelated to the truth of the charge that plaintiff had been indicted; they tend at most to prove that plaintiff had engaged in criminal activity and had been accused of wrong-doing by his fellow firemen. * * *

The situation might be different had defendants acknowledged that they had charged plaintiff with having been indicted and then proceeded to claim that they believed that to be true because plaintiff had been before the grand jury and had testified to his commission of crime. In such a case, those facts would tend, perhaps, toward proof of a belief in the charge actually made, but that is not this case. Here, by their very pleading, defendants seek to give a different and broader meaning to the published charge than reason permits. They do not even claim that they believed that plaintiff had been indicted * * *.

Defendants advance the additional contention that the pleading should be upheld and sustained, even if it does not tend to prove truth, because *some* of the facts alleged—as to particular acts of misconduct and bad reputation—may, nevertheless, be relevant to negative actual malice or reduce the value of plaintiff's injured reputation. Those allegations, the argument runs, may be used for that purpose irrespective of the form in which they are pleaded * * *.

Considerable doubt exists whether any of the matter pleaded is proper, for the rule is clear that, while defendant may offer proof of plaintiff's bad general reputation prior to the publication, to reduce the value of the injured interest, he may not plead or prove for that purpose "specific acts, or instances, of plaintiff's misconduct" having no connection with the charge of the libel. * * * Such specific misconduct, we have seen, may be admitted only if it also tends but fails to prove the truth of the libel's charge. * * *

However, regardless of what facts defendants might properly plead and prove, we may not approve the kind of pleading embodied in the second separate defense.

The entire thrust and purport of that defense is to establish defendants' belief in the truth of a different charge than the one made by the writing. Of the specific instances of misconduct alleged, which amount almost to a complete history of the Fire Department scandals, a considerable proportion would be inadmissible in evidence, as conclusory, irrelevant or prejudicial. The same is true of the list of newspaper headlines appended to the answer. Some of the items refer to the derelictions of fellow firemen with no suggestion that plaintiff was involved, while others purport to establish his guilt of divers acts on the basis of mere conjecture and rumor. * * * These allegations are certainly improper, and it is unthinkable that a defense, otherwise insufficient, should be saved and upheld by the device of simply adding a recital that plaintiff "enjoyed" a bad general reputation.[1]

* * *

We are not here deciding what facts defendants may adduce and prove in reduction of compensatory damages under the general denial, and nothing that we now say is to be taken as precluding defendants from seeking to amend their answer so as to plead properly matters in reduction of compensatory damages or in mitigation of those that are punitive in character. Nor are we suggesting that a partial defense must be pleaded in any particular form or that its purpose must be labeled. * * * All that we are holding is that the defense, aimed at establishing the truth of a charge different from that made in the publication, cannot stand. And it may not be saved by virtue of the fact that some of the items alleged might be pleaded properly in a different defense or that some of them might be proved at the trial.

* * *

Order reversed, etc.

Notes

1. *Jennings v. Telegram–Tribune Co.* 164 Cal.App.3d 119, 210 Cal.Rptr. 485 (1985) involved an action brought by a locally prominent architect against the San Louis Obispo Telegram–Tribune. Plaintiff had pleaded no contest to "'willfully and knowingly' failing to file federal income tax returns" for two calendar years. The defendant newspaper published a number of brief articles on plaintiff's difficulties. Plaintiff claimed that these articles contained a number of false and defamatory statements including statements that he had been "convicted of tax fraud" and that he had "pleaded no contest to income tax evasion charges." It was held that the statements in question were substantially fair and true reports of the criminal proceedings in which the plaintiff had been involved. Is *Jennings* inconsistent with *Crane*?

2. At common law truth was an affirmative defense which had to be raised and proved by the defendant. If the defamation consisted of charging the plaintiff with criminal conduct, the defense of truth had to be established only by the ordinary civil preponderance of the evidence standard. *See Restatement (Second) of Torts* § 581A, Comment *f.*

3. While one cannot justify a statement charging the plaintiff with having committed armed robbery by showing that the plaintiff has been convicted of embezzlement, slight discrepancies are permitted. For example, if, in *Crane,* the defendant had been able to show that criminal charges had been filed against the plaintiff by way of presentment, it probably would have succeeded in establishing the substantial truth of its charge that the plaintiff had been indicted.

4. In the light of the Supreme Court's injection of constitutional considerations into the law of defamation, a matter which we shall consider in the last section of this chapter, it is now undoubtedly part of the plaintiff's affirmative case in most, and perhaps even in all, defamation actions to establish the falsity

---

1. Proof of bad reputation is, of course, admissible under the general denial. * * *

of the defendant's allegedly defamatory statements. We shall discuss this specific question again at p. 1189 *infra*.

LEE v. PAULSEN

Supreme Court of Oregon, 1975.
273 Or. 103, 539 P.2d 1079.

DENECKE, JUSTICE.

The plaintiff teacher brought this defamation action against the defendants who are school officials and school board members. The trial court granted defendants' motion for an involuntary nonsuit upon the ground that the publication was absolutely privileged.

The plaintiff was a nontenured teacher. He was notified his contract was not going to be renewed. Plaintiff's attorney wrote the school district's attorney asking to be provided with the specific reasons for the nonrenewal of the contract and for a public hearing. The district's attorney replied by letter furnishing the specific reasons. He further stated that no evidence would be provided by the district at the hearing and no school officials or board members could be questioned. Plaintiff read this letter.

At the public hearing or meeting the plaintiff's attorney requested that the reasons, as contained in the letter sent to him, be stated by the board. The statements were made and this publication is charged as defamation. We will assume for the purposes of this decision that the publication is defamatory.

The cases and scholars agree that there is an absolute privilege for publications that are consented to. * * *

It should be remembered that usually the question of whether or not a defamatory statement is privileged, either absolutely or conditionally, depends upon the balance that the court strikes between competing interests. In Ramstead v. Morgan, 219 Or. 383, 387, 347 P.2d 594 (1959), we held the communication involved was absolutely privileged because the relationship occasioning the communication was so important that the law freed the publishing party from liability regardless of the fact that the publishing party might use the occasion to publish defamatory and malicious statements. The important interest in *Ramstead* was having citizens communicate with the organized Bar concerning possible misconduct of attorneys. We were of the opinion that this interest was so important that the communication should be absolutely privileged.

* * *

In the consent cases Harper and James point out that no public interest is being served by encouraging publication which is free from the threat of being the subject of a defamation suit.

The reason for the imposition of the privilege when the plaintiff consents or requests the publication "is based upon the unwillingness of the courts to let the plaintiff 'lay the foundation of a lawsuit for his own pecuniary gain.' " Harper and James, supra at 400, quoting from Richardson v. Gunby, 88 Kan. 47, 54, 127 P. 533 (1912).

* * *

Shinglemeyer v. Wright, 124 Mich. 230, 82 N.W. 887, 890 (1900), illustrates this rationale. In a private conversation between the parties the defendant charged the plaintiff with stealing his wheel. Plaintiff called a policeman. When he came she told him that the defendant had accused her of stealing his wheel and, in effect, asked him to hear the defendant's version. Defendant told the officer that the plaintiff had stolen his wheel. Plaintiff brought a slander action based upon the defendant's statement to the officer.

The court held for defendant, stating:

> "In regard to the statement by defendant in the presence of the officer Henry, it was not a publication for which the law gives a remedy. She herself solicited the statement, and sent for the officer for the express purpose of having the defendant repeat the statement in his presence. It would not have been stated to him except by her invitation." * * *

We emphasize that in both the present case and *Shinglemeyer v. Wright,* supra, when the plaintiff requested the publication he or she knew the exact language that would be used in the publication. This knowledge is essential in order for the publication to be absolutely privileged except in the circumstances present in Christensen v. Marvin, Or., 539 P.2d 1082 decided this date.

* * *

Nelson v. Whitten, 272 F. 135 (E.D.N.Y., 1921) illustrates the opposite circumstances. The plaintiff had been employed by the defendant as master of a vessel. Plaintiff asked defendant for a letter respecting his services. The defendant wrote in part:

> "As to your qualifications as a captain I can say you were an excellent housekeeper. Your knowledge of navigation is exceedingly meager.
>
> "I am so much in doubt as to your loyalty and integrity that I could not conscientiously give a recommendation to any one desiring to employ you." 272 F. at 136.

The letter was published to a third party and plaintiff brought a libel action. The defendant defended upon the ground that the plaintiff had consented. The court held for plaintiff stating, "Because of a request for such statement, plaintiff did not invite defendant to make public anything false and defamatory." 272 F. at 136.

In the present case the plaintiff did invite the defendant to make public a statement which plaintiff believed was false and defamatory. Defendants are absolutely privileged unless the publication falls within an exception to the rule that consent to publication creates an absolute privilege.

Plaintiff claims his case does fall within the exception stated in § 584, Restatement of Torts.

"The republication of false and defamatory matter of another by one who has previously published it is not privileged although the person defamed in an honest effort to ascertain the source of the original defamatory publication procures the republication." § 584.

The drafters of the Restatement (Second) have recommended that the section be broadened to read:

"An honest inquiry or investigation by the person defamed to ascertain the existence, source, content or meaning of a defamatory publication is not a defense to an action for its republication by the defamer." Restatement (Second), Torts, Tentative Draft No. 20 (1974) § 584, p. 158.

Assuming that the recommendation made in the Tentative Draft No. 20 correctly states the law, the plaintiff's case does not fall within the exception.

Cases cited by the reporter in Tentative Draft No. 20 in support of § 584 illustrate the intent of the section.

In Thorn v. Moser, 1 Denio (N.Y.) 488 (1845), plaintiff's agent had "heard that the defendant had charged this crime upon the plaintiff." 1 Denio (N.Y.) supra, at 488. He went to the defendant to inquire and defendant repeated the charge. In affirming a judgment for the plaintiff, the court commented: "An attempt by a person who deems himself injured to ascertain truly what slanderous imputations had already been cast upon him, could hardly be allowed to justify their renewal." * * * The agent's inquiry was to verify the existence and learn the content of a defamatory publication.

In Smith v. Dunlop Tire & Rubber Co., 186 S.C. 456, 458, 196 S.E. 174 (1938), one of the defendants stated to the plaintiff and his manager, "By God, I thought you birds were down here getting fat off of Dunlop. Now I know it." The plaintiff said he did not understand. The defendant replied, "you have been stealing." The court held the statement was not privileged. Plaintiff's inquiry was to determine the meaning of a possible defamatory publication.

In the present case, the request to the defendants to read the reasons for failure to renew, as stated in the defendants' letter previously sent plaintiff's attorney, was not "to ascertain the existence, source, content or meaning of a defamatory publication." * * *

Plaintiff contends one purpose in having the reasons read was to get a clarification of the reason, "Unprofessional conduct toward children." That contention cannot be substantiated. The school district's attorney informed the plaintiff and his attorney well before the meeting that the defendants and other school officials would not be open to questioning or offer any further explanation.

It must be remembered that the plaintiff is contending that this reading of the reasons for the defendants' refusal to renew plaintiff, which plaintiff requested, damaged his reputation.

The trial court commented, in regard to plaintiff's attorney requesting the reading of the statement, "you had no thought of setting up for entrapment in a libel suit." As we stated, the reason behind the rule that consent creates an absolute privilege is to prevent a plaintiff from "setting up" a lawsuit. However, it is not essential that the plaintiff in a particular case have that subjective intent. * * *. Affirmed.

Notes

1. In *Lee v. Paulsen,* the court declared that, for consent to publication to be a defense, the person defamed must be aware of the "exact language that would be used in the publication * * * except in the circumstances present in" Christensen v. Marvin, 273 Or. 97, 539 P.2d 1082 (1975). In that case, decided on the same day as *Lee v. Paulsen,* a school teacher whose contract was not going to be renewed asked the school board for a statement of reasons. Unlike the situation in *Lee,* the plaintiff in *Christensen* did not know the exact language of what the school board would say but she had more than enough reason to know that the reasons would be unflattering. Citing what is now *Restatement (Second) of Torts* § 583, Comment *d* and Illustration *2,* the court held that the plaintiff's consent barred her action.

On the general subject of the pitfalls that the law of defamation may present to those providing employment references *see* Note, *Contracting Around the Law of Defamation and Employment References,* 79 Va.L.Rev. 517 (1993). In an important recent English case, a plaintiff who was unable to bring an action for defamation against a person giving an unfavorable employment reference because of the successful invocation of "qualified privilege", was held to be entitled to bring an action based on a negligence theory against the person providing the reference. Spring v. Guardian Assurance Plc, [1995] 2 A.C. 296, 3 W.L.R. 354, 3 All E.R. 129. Do you think it was wise to treat a negligently given employment reference as just another type of negligent misrepresentation?

2. Defenses to defamation actions are classified as either absolute or qualified. Most of the absolute defenses are classified as privileges as are all of the qualified defenses. Most of the absolute defenses or privileges relate to statements made in the course of the participation in or the reporting of official or other public proceedings and will be discussed after the next principal case. We may mention at this stage, however, the absolute privilege, in most jurisdictions, to report suspected criminal conduct to the prosecuting authorities. *See Restatement (Second) of Torts* § 587. The court, in *Lee v. Paulsen,* referred to a case where it had extended the privilege to cover complaints to the "Organized Bar." *See also* Wiener v. Weintraub, 22 N.Y.2d 330, 292 N.Y.S.2d 667, 239 N.E.2d 540 (1968)(bar grievance committee). If the plaintiff has any redress in such situations his remedy would be an action for malicious prosecution, a subject to be discussed in Chapter Twenty, *infra.* New York is one of the few states that continues to grant only a qualified privilege to reports furnished to prosecutorial authorities, on the ground that such reports are not part of judicial proceedings. *See* Pecue v. West, 233 N.Y. 316, 135 N.E. 515 (1922); Toker v. Pollak, 44 N.Y.2d 211, 405 N.Y.S.2d 1, 376 N.E.2d 163 (1978). A letter to the President, with copies to other officials, that criticized a prospective appointee to federal office was held not to be absolutely privileged under the right "to petition" clause. McDonald v. Smith, 472 U.S. 479, 105 S.Ct. 2787, 86 L.Ed.2d 384 (1985).

Of the absolute defenses available in defamation actions concerning private matters, as we have seen, two, truth and consent, are usually not classified as privileges. For practical purposes, it makes little difference whether an absolute defense is classified as a privilege or not; the practical consequences are the same. One absolute defense that is classified as a privilege and is also available in litigation not involving public matters concerns inter-spousal communications. Arguably, before the married women's property acts of the nineteenth century, it was also possible to argue that inter-spousal communication was not a publication, but that analytical approach is clearly not available today.

3. At common law a qualified privilege could be defeated by a showing of malice. One way of showing malice is by demonstrating that the speaker's *dominant* motive in uttering the defamatory statement was not to protect the interest which underlies the granting of the privilege but rather to hurt the plaintiff. Another way is by establishing excessive publication. For example, if one person asks another for information about the character of her fiance, the respondent's statements to her may be privileged but publication of the statement to the mutual friends of the parties would clearly be excessive, that is beyond the purposes for which the privilege was created. *See Restatement (Second) of Torts* § 604. The plaintiff bears the burden of showing that the defendant acted with malice. *See* Lundquist v. Reusser, 7 Cal.4th 1193, 875 P.2d 1279, 31 Cal.Rptr.2d 776 (1994).

Restatement of Torts § 601 took the position that a defendant's lack of reasonable grounds for belief in the truth of the statements he has made defeated a claim of qualified privilege even if the circumstances were such as to give rise to the privilege. English law was more favorable to the defendant. The House of Lords has made it clear than an honest belief in the truth of the statement made, even if that belief is unreasonable, will permit the defendant to invoke a qualified privilege. See Horrocks v. Lowe, [1975] A.C. 135 (1974), [1974] 2 W.L.R. 282, 1 All E.R. 662. *See also* Clark v. Molyneux, 3 Q.B.D. 237 (1877)(C.A.). In the light of the constitutional developments, to which we shall turn shortly, most American jurisdictions have now undoubtedly adopted the English position, and that is the position taken by *Restatement (Second) of Torts* § 600.

4. The qualified privilege of self defense, i.e., to defend oneself against the defamatory remarks of others, has some analogues to the defense of consent and to the qualified privilege that arises for statements made in defense of one's personal interests. A good case is Shenkman v. O'Malley, 2 A.D.2d 567, 157 N.Y.S.2d 290 (1956), in which the president of the Brooklyn Dodgers responded in kind to some defamatory charges, about the Dodgers' unwillingness to pay for medical services, made by a physician who had treated one of the team's star ballplayers. An example of a qualified privilege arising in the course of an attempt to protect one's interests is presented by Faber v. Byrle, 171 Kan. 38, 229 P.2d 718 (1951). One of the statements involved in that case was the defendant's statement to the plaintiff's brother that the plaintiff was stealing his gasoline and that the defendant feared for his life if he said anything to the plaintiff. The statement was held to be qualifiedly privileged.

WATT v. LONGSDON

Court of Appeal, 1929.
[1930] 1 K.B. 130.

SCRUTTON L.J. This case raises, amongst other matters, the extremely difficult question equally important in its legal and social aspect, as to the circumstances, if any, in which a person will be justified in giving to one partner to a marriage information which that person honestly believes to be correct, but which is in fact untrue, about the matrimonial delinquencies of the other party to the marriage. The question becomes more difficult if the answer in law turns on the existence or non-existence of a social or moral duty, a question which the judge is to determine, without any evidence, by the light of his own knowledge of the world, and his own views on social morality, a subject matter on which views vary in different ages, in different countries, and even as between man and man.

The Scottish Petroleum Company, which carried on business, amongst other places, in Morocco, had in Casa Blanca, a port in Morocco, a manager named Browne, and a managing director named Watt. The company had in England a chairman named Singer, who held a very large proportion of shares in the company, and also another director, Longsdon, a young man under thirty years of age. The latter had been in Morocco in business and friendly relations with Watt and Browne, and was a friend of Mrs. Watt, who had nursed him in an illness. * * * Under these circumstances Longsdon in England received at the beginning of May from Browne in Casa Blanca a letter stating that Watt had left for Lisbon to look for a job, that he had left a bill for 88l. for whisky unpaid, and that he had been for two months in immoral relations with his housemaid, who was now publicly raising claims against him for money matters. The woman was described as an old woman, stone deaf, almost blind, and with dyed hair. A number of details were given which Browne said Watt's cook had corroborated. The information was mixed up with an allegation that Watt had been scheming to compromise or seduce Mrs. Browne. The letter concluded: "From a letter shown to me by Mr. Watt I know how bitterly disappointed Mrs. Watt is, and how very much troubled she is. It would therefore perhaps be better not to show her this letter as it could only increase most terribly her own feelings in regard to her husband. These awful facts might be the cause of a breakdown to her, and I think she has enough to cope with at present. Mr. Singer, however, should perhaps know." On May 5, Longsdon, without making inquiries, sent Browne's letter on to Singer, the chairman of the board of directors. At the trial Watt's counsel put in Longsdon's answer to interrogatory 5 that he believed the statements in the letter to be true. On May 5 Longsdon wrote a long letter to Browne, in which he said that he had long suspected Watt's immorality, but had no proof; that he thought it wicked and cruel that Mrs. Watt, a very old friend of the writer's, should be in the dark when Watt might return to her—did not Browne agree?—that he (Longsdon) would not speak until he had a sworn statement in his possession, "and only with such proof would I speak, for an interferer between husband and wife nearly always comes off the worst." Could Browne get a sworn statement? "It may even be necessary for you to bribe the women to do such, and if only a matter of a few hundred francs I will pay it and of course the legal expenses." Longsdon's letter describes one of the women who was to make this sworn statement as "a prostitute all her life," a description not contained in Browne's letter. Watt returned to England in May. Without waiting for the sworn statement, on May 12, Longsdon sent the letter to Mrs. Watt. Mr. and Mrs. Watt separated, and Mrs. Watt instituted proceedings for divorce, which apparently are still pending.

Mr. Watt then instituted proceedings against Longsdon for libel—namely (1.) the publication of Browne's letter to Singer; (2.) the publication of the same letter to Mrs. Watt; (3.) Longsdon's letter of May 5 to Browne. * * * The plaintiff also put in at the trial the defendant's answers to interrogatories that his only information on the subject was derived from Browne's letter, that he made no further inquiries, and that he believed that all the statements in Browne's letter, and in the defendant's letter of May 12 were true. The defendant did not justify, but pleaded privilege. The case was tried before Horridge J. and a jury. The learned judge held that all three publications were privileged, and that there was no evidence of malice fit to be left to the jury. He therefore entered judgment for the defendant. The plaintiff appeals.

The learned judge appears to have taken the view that the authorities justify him in holding that if "there is an obvious interest in the person to whom a communication is made which causes him to be a proper recipient of a statement," even if the party making the communication had no moral or social duty to the party to whom the communication is made, the occasion is privileged. * * *

By the law of England there are occasions on which a person may make defamatory statements about another which are untrue without incurring any legal liability for his statements. These occasions are called privileged occasions. A reason frequently given for this privilege is that the allegation that the speaker has "unlawfully and maliciously published," is displaced by proof that the speaker had either a duty or an interest to publish, and that this duty or interest confers the privilege. But communications made on these occasions may lose their privilege: (1.) they may exceed the privilege of the occasion by going beyond the limits of the duty or interest, or (2.) they may be published with express malice, so that the occasion is not being legitimately used, but abused. * * * The classical definition of "privileged occasions" is that of Parke B. in *Toogood v. Spyring*[8] a case where the tenant of a farm complained to the agent of the landlord, who had sent a workman to do repairs, that the workman had broken into the tenant's cellar, got drunk on the tenant's cider, and spoilt the work he was sent to do. The workman sued the tenant. Parke B. gave the explanation of privileged occasions in these words: "In general, an action lies for the malicious publication of statements which are false in fact, and injurious to the character of another (within the well-known limits as to verbal slander), and the law considers such publication as malicious, unless it is fairly made by a person in the discharge of some public or private duty, whether legal or moral, or in the conduct of his own affairs, in matters where his interest is concerned. In such cases, the occasion prevents the inference of malice, which the law draws from unauthorized communications, and affords a qualified defence depending upon the absence of actual malice. If fairly warranted by any reasonable occasion or exigency, and honestly made, such communications are protected for the common convenience and welfare of society; and the law has not

---

8. 1 C.M. & R. 181.

restricted the right to make them within any narrow limits." It will be seen that the learned judge requires: (1.) a public or private duty to communicate, whether legal or moral; (2.) that the communication should be "fairly warranted by any reasonable occasion or exigency"; (3.) or a statement in the conduct of his own affairs where his interest is concerned. * * * This adds to the protection of his own interest * * * the protection of the interests of another where the situation of the writer requires him to protect those interests. This, I think, involves that his "situation" imposes on him a legal or moral duty. The question whether the occasion was privileged is for the judge, and so far as "duty" is concerned, the question is: Was there a duty, legal, moral, or social, to communicate? As to legal duty, the judge should have no difficulty; the judge should know the law; but as to moral or social duties of imperfect obligation, the task is far more troublesome. The judge has no evidence as to the view the community takes of moral or social duties. All the help the Court of Appeal can give him is contained in the judgment of Lindley L.J. in *Stuart v. Bell*[1]: "The question of moral or social duty being for the judge, each judge must decide it as best he can for himself. I take moral or social duty to mean a duty recognized by English people of ordinary intelligence and moral principle, but at the same time not a duty enforceable by legal proceedings, whether civil or criminal. My own conviction is that all or, at all events, the great mass of right-minded men in the position of the defendant would have considered it their duty, under the circumstances, to inform Stanley of the suspicion which had fallen on the plaintiff." Is the judge merely to give his own view of moral and social duty, though he thinks a considerable portion of the community hold a different opinion? Or is he to endeavour to ascertain what view "the great mass of right-minded men" would take? It is not surprising that with such a standard both judges and text-writers treat the matter as one of great difficulty in which no definite line can be drawn. * * * A conspicuous instance of the difficulties which arise when judges have to determine the existence of duties, not legal, but moral or social, by the inner light of their own conscience and judgment and knowledge of the world, is to be found in the case of *Coxhead v. Richards*.[2] A correct appreciation of what was the difference of opinion in that case is, in my opinion, of great importance in the decision of the present case. The short facts were that Cass, the mate of a ship, wrote to Richards, an intimate friend of his, a letter stating that on a voyage from the Channel to Wales, which was going to continue to Eastern ports, the captain, Coxhead, had by his drunkenness endangered the safety of the ship, and the lives of the crew; and Cass asked Richards' advice what he should do in view of the risk of repetition of this danger on the voyage to the East. Richards, after consulting "an Elder Brother of the Trinity House, and an eminent shipowner," sent this letter to Ward, the owner of the ship. Richards did not know Ward, and had no interest in the ship. The owner dismissed the captain, who thereupon brought an action against Richards. The judge at the trial directed the jury, if they should think that the communication was strictly honest, and made solely in the execution of what he believed to be a duty, to find for the defendant. They did so, while finding that the plea of

1. [1891] 2 Q.B. 341, 350.   **2.** 2 C.B. 569.

justification failed. The plaintiff then moved for a new trial, on which motion the Court after two hearings was equally divided. It is not very clear whether the judges differed on a general principle, or on its application to the facts of the case. I understand Tindal C.J. to have taken the view that if a man has information materially affecting the interests of another, and honestly communicates it to that other, he is protected, though he has no personal interest in the subject matter, and that his protection arises from "the various social duties by which men are bound to each other," and that it was the duty of the defendant to communicate this information to the owner. Erle J. appears to put the matter on "information given to protect damage from misconduct," "the importance of the information to the interest of the receiver," and says that a person having such information is justified in communicating it to the person interested, though the speaker did not stand in any relation to the recipient, and was a volunteer. He does not expressly refer to any social duty. On the other hand, Coltman and Cresswell JJ. both appear to me to hold that in such circumstances there was no moral duty, for that any tendency that way was counterbalanced by the moral duty not to slander your neighbour. In the subsequent case of *Bennett v. Deacon*[1] the same four judges repeated the same division of opinion, where Deacon, a man to whom the plaintiff owed 25*l.*, volunteered to a tradesman, who was about to deal with the plaintiff, the statement that unless the tradesman was paid ready money he would lose the goods, and his money, or price, for he (Deacon) was about to seize the goods of the plaintiff for debt. I think it is clear that Tindal C.J. and Erle J. thought that a volunteer, with no personal interest, would be protected in giving information apparently material to the interest of the recipient, and that Coltman and Cresswell JJ. thought he would not. How far either set of judges meant to lay down a general principle applicable to all such cases is not very clear. They certainly differed in its application to the particular facts of those cases. I myself should have thought, and I think most of the judges who have considered the case * * * did think, that in the particular facts of *Coxhead v. Richards* Richards, if he believed the statements in the letter to be true, had a moral duty to forward them to the shipowner, who had obviously a vital interest in them, if they were true. * * *

Lastly, in *Stuart v. Bell* there was again a difference of opinion, though not an equal division of the judges, as in *Coxhead v. Richards*. Stanley, the explorer, and his valet, Stuart, were staying with the mayor of Newcastle, Bell. The Edinburgh police made a very carefully worded communication to the Newcastle police that there had been a robbery in Edinburgh at an hotel where Stuart was staying, and it might be well to make very careful and cautious inquiry into the matter. The Newcastle police showed the letter to the mayor, who after consideration showed it to Stanley, who dismissed Stuart. Stuart sued the mayor. Lindley and Kay L.JJ. held that the mayor had a moral duty to communicate, and Stanley a material interest to receive the communication; Lopes L.J. held that in the circumstances there was no moral duty to communicate, though in some circumstances there might be such a duty in a host towards a guest. I myself

---

1. (1846) 2 C.B. 628.

should have agreed with the majority, but the difference of opinion between such experienced judges shows the difficulty of the question.

In my opinion Horridge J. went too far in holding that there could be a privileged occasion on the ground of interest in the recipient without any duty to communicate on the part of the person making the communication. But that does not settle the question, for it is necessary to consider, in the present case, whether there was, as to each communication, a duty to communicate, and an interest in the recipient.

First as to the communication between Longsdon and Singer, I think the case must proceed on the admission that at all material times Watt, Longsdon and Browne were in the employment of the same company, and the evidence afforded by the answer to the interrogatory put in by the plaintiff that Longsdon believed the statements in Browne's letter. In my view on these facts there was a duty, both from a moral and a material point of view, on Longsdon to communicate the letter to Singer, the chairman of his company, who, apart from questions of present employment, might be asked by Watt for a testimonial to a future employer. Equally, I think Longsdon receiving the letter from Browne, might discuss the matter with him, and ask for further information, on the ground of a common interest in the affairs of the company, and to obtain further information for the chairman. I should therefore agree with the view of Horridge J. that these two occasions were privileged, though for different reasons. Horridge J. further held that there was no evidence of malice fit to be left to the jury, and, while I think some of Longsdon's action and language in this respect was unfortunate, as the plaintiff has put in the answer that Longsdon believed the truth of the statements in Browne's and his own letter, * * * I should not try excess with too nice scales, and I do not dissent from his view as to malice. As to the communications to Singer and Browne, in my opinion the appeal should fail, but as both my brethren take the view that there was evidence of malice which should be left to the jury, there must, of course, be a new trial as to the claim based on these two publications.

The communication to Mrs. Watt stands on a different footing. I have no intention of writing an exhaustive treatise on the circumstances when a stranger or a friend should communicate to husband or wife information he receives as to the conduct of the other party to the marriage. I am clear that it is impossible to say he is always under a moral or social duty to do so; it is equally impossible to say he is never under such a duty. It must depend on the circumstances of each case, the nature of the information, and the relation of speaker and recipient. It cannot, on the one hand, be the duty even of a friend to communicate all the gossip the friend hears at men's clubs or women's bridge parties to one of the spouses affected. On the other hand, most men would hold that it was the moral duty of a doctor who attended his sister in law, and believed her to be suffering from a miscarriage, for which an absent husband could not be responsible, to communicate that fact to his wife and the husband. * * * Using the best judgment I can in this difficult matter, I have come to the conclusion that there was not a moral or social duty in Longsdon to make this communication to Mrs. Watt such as to make the occasion privileged, and that there must be a new trial so far as it relates to the claim for publication of a libel to Mrs. Watt.

[The judgments of Greer and Russell, L.JJ. have been omitted]

Notes

1. When a person against whom a defamation action has been brought claims a privilege on the ground that his statement was made to protect the interests of third parties there are three important factors to consider. The first is the importance of the interest in question. When life or serious bodily harm is thought to be at risk, as in Coxhead v. Richards, 2 C.B. 569, 135 Eng.Rep. 1069 (1846), discussed in *Watt,* even a third party with no interest of his own in the matter will have a qualified privilege to come forward with information. A similar privilege has been recognized when a person's significant property interests have been involved. *See* Doyle v. Clauss, 190 App.Div. 838, 180 N.Y.S. 671 (1920) (letter advising employer that an employee was embezzling the employer's money). The second factor is the relationship of the person claiming the privilege to the person whose interests are purportedly being protected. An "immediate" family member of the person whose interests are involved, *see Restatement (Second) of Torts* § 597, will have a privilege in circumstances where a friend or other busybody will not. This was one of the points involved in *Watt. See also* Burton v. Mattson, 50 Utah 133, 166 P. 979 (1917)(unsolicited letter advising wife that husband engaged in adulterous relationship).[3] The third important factor is whether the defamatory communication has been solicited by the person whose interests are at stake or an immediate family member of that person, such as the parent of a person about to be married. *See Restatement (Second) of Torts* § 595(2)(a). *See also* Rude v. Nass, 79 Wis. 321, 48 N.W. 555 (1891)(defendant's letter had been solicited on behalf of father of girl whom plaintiff had been charged with seducing).

2. In addition to the common interests of employees of a common employer recognized in *Watt—see also* Ponticelli v. Mine Safety Appliance Co., 104 R.I. 549, 247 A.2d 303 (1968)(employer's statement to former co-workers of the reasons [alleged padding of production figures] for discharging that employee privileged on ground of discouraging similar conduct in other employees)—a common interest has been recognized among the members of a labor union. *See* Gabauer v. Woodcock, 520 F.2d 1084 (8th Cir.1975), *cert. denied* 423 U.S. 1061, 96 S.Ct. 800, 46 L.Ed.2d 653 (1976). *See also* Bereman v. Power Publishing Co., 93 Colo. 581, 27 P.2d 749 (1933)(statement about strike breakers in union newspaper; privilege not defeated because paper distributed to a few persons who are not union members). Among the other types of common interest that have been recognized is that of the members of a church. *See* Slocinski v. Radwan, 83 N.H. 501, 144 A. 787 (1929).

BARR v. MATTEO

Supreme Court of the United States, 1959.
360 U.S. 564, 79 S.Ct. 1335, 3 L.Ed.2d 1434.

MR. JUSTICE HARLAN announced the judgment of the Court, and delivered an opinion, in which MR. JUSTICE FRANKFURTER, MR. JUSTICE CLARK, and MR. JUSTICE WHITTAKER join.

* * *

---

3. In Nelson v. Whitten, 272 Fed. 135 (E.D.N.Y.1921), discussed in *Lee v. Paulsen, supra,* p. 1111, the court stressed that the former employer who made the defamatory statement had not been obliged to give the statement. Neither the plaintiff nor anyone else had invited the defendant to write anything that might be false or defamatory.

This is a libel suit, brought in the District Court of the District of Columbia by respondents, former employees of the Office of Rent Stabilization. The alleged libel was contained in a press release issued by the office on February 5, 1953, at the direction of petitioner, then its Acting Director. The circumstances which gave rise to the issuance of the release follow.

In 1950 the statutory existence of the Office of Housing Expediter, the predecessor agency of the Office of Rent Stabilization, was about to expire. Respondent Madigan, then Deputy Director in charge of personnel and fiscal matters, and respondent Matteo, chief of the personnel branch, suggested to the Housing Expediter a plan designed to utilize some $2,600,-000 of agency funds earmarked in the agency's appropriation for the fiscal year 1950 exclusively for terminal-leave payments. The effect of the plan would have been to obviate the possibility that the agency might have to make large terminal-leave payments during the next fiscal year out of general agency funds, should the life of the agency be extended by Congress. In essence, the mechanics of the plan were that agency employees would be discharged, paid accrued annual leave out of the $2,600,000 earmarked for terminal-leave payments, rehired immediately as temporary employees, and restored to permanent status should the agency's life in fact be extended.

Petitioner, at the time General Manager of the agency, opposed respondents' plan on the ground that it violated the spirit of the Thomas Amendment, 64 Stat. 768,[2] and expressed his opposition to the Housing Expediter. The Expediter decided against general adoption of the plan, but at respondent Matteo's request gave permission for its use in connection with approximately fifty employees, including both respondents, on a voluntary basis.[3] Thereafter the life of the agency was in fact extended.

Some two and a half years later, on January 28, 1953, the Office of Rent Stabilization received a letter from Senator John J. Williams of Delaware, inquiring about the terminal-leave payments made under the plan in 1950. Respondent Madigan drafted a reply to the letter, which he did not attempt to bring to the attention of petitioner, and then prepared a reply which he sent to petitioner's office for his signature as Acting Director of the agency. Petitioner was out of the office, and a secretary signed the submitted letter, which was then delivered by Madigan to Senator Williams on the morning of February 3, 1953.

---

2. This statute, part of the General Appropriation Act of 1951, provided that:

"No part of the funds of, or available for expenditure by any corporation or agency included in this Act, including the government of the District of Columbia, shall be available to pay for annual leave accumulated by any civilian officer or employee during the calendar year 1950 and unused at the close of business on June 30, 1951 * * *."

3. The General Accounting Office subsequently ruled that the payments were illegal, and respondents were required to return them. Respondent Madigan challenged this determination in the Court of Claims, which held that the plan was not in violation of law. Madigan v. United States, 142 Ct.Cl. 641 [1958].

On February 4, 1953, Senator Williams delivered a speech on the floor of the Senate strongly criticizing the plan, stating that "to say the least it is an unjustifiable raid on the Federal Treasury, and heads of every agency in the Government who have condoned this practice should be called to task." The letter above referred to was ordered printed in the Congressional Record. Other Senators joined in the attack on the plan. Their comments were widely reported in the press on February 5, 1953, and petitioner, in his capacity as Acting Director of the agency, received a large number of inquiries from newspapers and other news media as to the agency's position on the matter.

On that day petitioner served upon respondents letters expressing his intention to suspend them from duty, and at the same time ordered issuance by the office of the press release which is the subject of this litigation, and the text of which appears in the margin.[5]

Respondents sued, charging that the press release, in itself and as coupled with the contemporaneous news reports of senatorial reaction to the plan, defamed them to their injury, and alleging that its publication and terms had been actuated by malice on the part of petitioner. Petitioner defended, *inter alia,* on the ground that the issuance of the press release was protected by either a qualified or an absolute privilege. The trial court overruled these contentions, and instructed the jury to return a verdict for respondents if it found the release defamatory. The jury found for respondents.

Petitioner appealed, raising only the issue of absolute privilege. The judgment of the trial court was affirmed by the Court of Appeals, which held that "in explaining his decision [to suspend respondents] to the general public [petitioner] * * * went entirely outside his line of duty" and that thus the absolute privilege, assumed otherwise to be available, did not attach. * * * We granted certiorari, vacated the Court of Appeals' judgment, and remanded the case "with directions to pass upon petitioner's claim of a qualified privilege." * * * On remand the Court of Appeals held

---

5. "William G. Barr, Acting Director of Rent Stabilization today served notice of suspension on the two officials of the agency who in June 1950 were responsible for the plan which allowed 53 of the agency's 2,681 employees to take their accumulated annual leave in cash.

"Mr. Barr's appointment as Acting Director becomes effective Monday, February 9, 1953, and the suspension of these employees will be his first act of duty. The employees are John J. Madigan, Deputy Director for Administration, and Linda Matteo, Director of Personnel.

" 'In June 1950,' Mr. Barr stated, 'my position in the agency was not one of authority which would have permitted me to stop the action. Furthermore, I did not know about it until it was almost completed.

" 'When I did learn that certain employees were receiving cash annual leave settlements and being returned to agency employment on a temporary basis, I specifically notified the employees under my supervision that if they applied for such cash settlements I would demand their resignations and the record will show that my immediate employees complied with my request.

" 'While I was advised that the action was legal, I took the position that it violated the spirit of the Thomas Amendment and I violently opposed it. Monday, February 9th, when my appointment as Acting Director becomes effective, will be the first time my position in the agency has permitted me to take any action on this matter, and the suspension of these employees will be the first official act I shall take.'

"Mr. Barr also revealed that he has written to Senator Joseph McCarthy, Chairman of the Committee on Government Operations, and to Representative John Phillips, Chairman of the House Subcommittee on Independent Offices Appropriations, requesting an opportunity to be heard on the entire matter."

that the press release was protected by a qualified privilege, but that there was evidence from which a jury could reasonably conclude that petitioner had acted maliciously, or had spoken with lack of reasonable grounds for believing that his statement was true, and that either conclusion would defeat the qualified privilege. Accordingly it remanded the case to the District Court for retrial. * * * At this point petitioner again sought, and we again granted certiorari, * * * to determine whether in the circumstances of this case petitioner's claim of absolute privilege should have stood as a bar to maintenance of the suit despite the allegations of malice made in the complaint.

The law of privilege as a defense by officers of government to civil damage suits for defamation and kindred torts has in large part been of judicial making, although the Constitution itself gives an absolute privilege to members of both Houses of Congress in respect to any speech, debate, vote, report, or action done in session. This Court early held that judges of courts of superior or general authority are absolutely privileged as respects civil suits to recover for actions taken by them in the exercise of their judicial functions, irrespective of the motives with which those acts are alleged to have been performed, * * * and that a like immunity extends to other officers of government whose duties are related to the judicial process. * * * Nor has the privilege been confined to officers of the legislative and judicial branches of the Government and executive officers of the kind involved in Yaselli. In Spalding v. Vilas, 161 U.S. 483, 16 S.Ct. 631, 40 L.Ed. 780, petitioner brought suit against the Postmaster General, alleging that the latter had maliciously circulated widely among postmasters, past and present, information which he knew to be false and which was intended to deceive the postmasters to the detriment of the plaintiff. This Court sustained a plea by the Postmaster General of absolute privilege, * * *.

* * * The matter has been admirably expressed by Judge Learned Hand:

> "It does indeed go without saying that an official, who is in fact guilty of using his powers to vent his spleen upon others, or for any other personal motive not connected with the public good, should not escape liability for the injuries he may so cause; and, if it were possible in practice to confine such complaints to the guilty, it would be monstrous to deny recovery. The justification for doing so is that it is impossible to know whether the claim is well founded until the case has been tried, and that to submit all officials, the innocent as well as the guilty, to the burden of a trial and to the inevitable danger of its outcome would dampen the ardor of all but the most resolute, or the most irresponsible, in the unflinching discharge of their duties. Again and again the public interest calls for action which may turn out to be founded on a mistake, in the face of which an official may later find himself hard put to it to satisfy a jury of his good faith. There must indeed be means of punishing public officers who have been truant to their duties; but that is quite another matter from exposing such as have been honestly mistaken to suit by anyone who has suffered from their errors. As is so often the case, the answer must be found in a balance between the evils inevitable in either alternative. In this

instance it has been thought in the end better to leave unredressed the wrongs done by dishonest officers than to subject those who try to do their duty to the constant dread of retaliation. * * *

"The decisions have, indeed, always imposed as a limitation upon the immunity that the official's act must have been within the scope of his powers; and it can be argued that official powers, since they exist only for the public good, never cover occasions where the public good is not their aim, and hence that to exercise a power dishonestly is necessarily to overstep its bounds. A moment's reflection shows, however, that that cannot be the meaning of the limitation without defeating the whole doctrine. What is meant by saying that the officer must be acting within his power cannot be more than that the occasion must be such as would have justified the act, if he had been using his power for any of the purposes on whose account it was vested in him. * * *" Gregoire v. Biddle, 2 Cir., 177 F.2d 579, 581.

We do not think that the principle announced in Vilas can properly be restricted to executive officers of cabinet rank, and in fact it never has been so restricted by the lower federal courts. The privilege is not a badge or emolument of exalted office, but an expression of a policy designed to aid in the effective functioning of government. The complexities and magnitude of governmental activity have become so great that there must of necessity be a delegation and redelegation of authority as to many functions, and we cannot say that these functions become less important simply because they are exercised by officers of lower rank in the executive hierarchy.

To be sure, the occasions upon which the acts of the head of an executive department will be protected by the privilege are doubtless far broader than in the case of an officer with less sweeping functions. But that is because the higher the post, the broader the range of responsibilities and duties, and the wider the scope of discretion, it entails. It is not the title of his office but the duties with which the particular officer sought to be made to respond in damages is entrusted * * * which must provide the guide in delineating the scope of the rule which clothes the official acts of the executive officer with immunity from civil defamation suits.

Judged by these standards, we hold that petitioner's plea of absolute privilege in defense of the alleged libel published at his direction must be sustained. The question is a close one, but we cannot say that it was not an appropriate exercise of the discretion with which an executive officer of petitioner's rank is necessarily clothed to publish the press release here at issue in the circumstances disclosed by this record. * * * The integrity of the internal operations of the agency which he headed, and thus his own integrity in his public capacity, had been directly and severely challenged in charges made on the floor of the Senate and given wide publicity; and without his knowledge correspondence which could reasonably be read as impliedly defending a position very different from that which he had from the beginning taken in the matter had been sent to a Senator over his signature and incorporated in the Congressional Record. * * * It would be an unduly restrictive view of the scope of the duties of a policy-making executive official to hold that a public statement of agency policy in respect to matters of wide public interest and concern is not action in the line of duty. That petitioner was not *required* by law or by direction of his superiors to speak out cannot be controlling in the case of an official of policy-making rank, for the same considerations which underlie the recognition of the privilege as to acts done in connection with a mandatory duty apply with equal force to discretionary acts at those levels of government where the concept of duty encompasses the sound exercise of discretionary authority.

The fact that the action here taken was within the outer perimeter of petitioner's line of duty is enough to render the privilege applicable, despite the allegations of malice in the complaint * * *

We are told that we should forbear from sanctioning any such rule of absolute privilege lest it open the door to wholesale oppression and abuses on the part of unscrupulous government officials. It is perhaps enough to say that fears of this sort have not been realized within the wide area of government where a judicially formulated absolute privilege of broad scope has long existed. It seems to us wholly chimerical to suggest that what hangs in the balance here is the maintenance of high standards of conduct among those in the public service. To be sure, as with any rule of law which attempts to reconcile fundamentally antagonistic social policies, there may be occasional instances of actual injustice which will go unredressed, but we think that price a necessary one to pay for the greater good. And there are of course other sanctions than civil tort suits available to deter the executive official who may be prone to exercise his functions in an unworthy and irresponsible manner. We think that we should not be deterred from establishing the rule which we announce today by any such remote forebodings.

Reversed.

MR. JUSTICE BLACK, concurring.

I concur in the reversal of this judgment but briefly summarize my reasons because they are not altogether the same as those stated in the opinion of Mr. Justice Harlan.

* * *

The effective functioning of a free government like ours depends largely on the force of an informed public opinion. This calls for the widest possible understanding of the quality of government service rendered by all elective or appointed public officials or employees. Such an informed understanding depends, of course, on the freedom people have to applaud or to criticize the way public employees do their jobs, from the least to the most important.

* * * So far as I am concerned, if federal employees are to be subjected to such restraints in reporting their views about how to run the government better, the restraint will have to be imposed expressly by Congress and not by the general libel laws of the States or of the District of Columbia. How far the Congress itself could go in barring federal officials and employees from discussing public matters consistently with the First Amendment is a question we need not reach in this case. * * *

MR. CHIEF JUSTICE WARREN, with whom MR. JUSTICE DOUGLAS joins, dissenting.

The principal opinion in this case purports to launch the Court on a balancing process in order to reconcile the interest of the public in obtaining fearless executive performance and the interest of the individual in having redress for defamation. Even accepting for the moment that these are the proper interests to be balanced, the ultimate disposition is not the result of a balance. On the one hand, the principal opinion sets up a vague standard under which no government employee can tell with any certainty whether he will receive absolute immunity for his acts. On the other hand, it has not given even the slightest consideration to the interest of the individual who is defamed. It is a complete annihilation of his interest.

* * *

I.

The history of the privileges conferred upon the three branches of Government is a story of uneven development. Absolute legislative privilege dates back to at least 1399. This privilege is given to Congress in the United States Constitution and to State Legislatures in the Constitutions of almost all of the States of the Union. The absolute immunity arising out of judicial proceedings existed at least as early as 1608 in England.

But what of the executive privilege? Apparently, the earliest English case presenting the problem of immunity outside the legislative and judicial branches of government is Sutton v. Johnstone, 1 T.R. 493, decided in 1786. There, the plaintiff, captain of a warship, sued the commander-in-chief of his squadron for charging plaintiff, maliciously and without probable cause, with disobedience of orders and putting him under arrest and forcing him to face a court-martial. The Court of Exchequer took jurisdiction of the case but was reversed, 1 T.R. 510, on the ground that purely military matters were not within the cognizance of the civil courts. During the next century several other military cases were decided.

In Chatterton v. Secretary of State for India, [1895] 2 Q.B. 189, the defendant had been apprised that his action with respect to the plaintiff would be made the subject of a parliamentary inquiry. In the communication alleged to be libelous, the defendant told his Under Secretary what answer should be made if the question were asked him in Parliament. The court affirmed dismissal of the complaint relying on Fraser on The Law of Libel and Slander (1st ed.), p. 95, where the author, with no citations, observed, after relating the history of the military cases:

> "For reasons of public policy the same protection would, no doubt, be given to anything in the nature of an act of state, e.g., to every communication relating to state matters made by one minister to another, or to the Crown."

This was the actual birth of executive privilege in England.

Such was the state of English law when, the next year, this Court decided Spalding v. Vilas, supra. In granting the Postmaster General absolute immunity for "matters committed by law to his control or supervision," this Court relied exclusively on the judicial privilege cases and the English military cases. Thus, leaving aside the military cases, which are unique, the executive privilege in defamation actions would appear to be a judicial creature of less than 65 years' existence. Yet, without statute, this relatively new privilege is being extended to open the possibility of absolute privilege for innumerable government officials.

* * *

I would not extend Spalding v. Vilas to cover public statements of lesser officials. Releases to the public from the executive branch of government imply far greater dangers to the individual claiming to have been defamed than do internal libels. * * *

Giving officials below cabinet or equivalent rank qualified privilege for statements to the public would in no way hamper the internal operation of the executive department of government, nor would it unduly subordinate the interest of the individual in obtaining redress for the public defamation uttered against him. * * *

II.

* * *

It is clear that public discussion of the action of the Government and its officials is accorded no more than qualified privilege. In most States, even that privilege is further restricted to situations in which the speaker is accurate as to his facts and where the claimed defamation results from conclusions or opinions based on those facts. Only in a minority of States is a public critic of Government even qualifiedly privileged where his facts are wrong. Thus, at best, a public critic of the Government has a qualified privilege. Yet here the Court has given some amorphous group of officials—who have the most direct and personal contact with the public—an absolute privilege when their agency or their action is criticized. In this situation, it will take a brave person to criticize government officials knowing that in reply they may libel him with immunity in the name of defending the agency and their own position. * * *

* * *

I would affirm.

MR. JUSTICE STEWART, dissenting.

My brother Harlan's opinion contains, it seems to me, a lucid and persuasive analysis of the principles that should guide decision in this troublesome area of law. Where I part company is in the application of these principles to the facts of the present case.

I cannot agree that the issuance by the petitioner of this press release was "action in the line of duty." * * *

* * *

MR. JUSTICE BRENNAN, dissenting.

I think it is demonstrable that the solution of Mr. Justice Harlan's opinion to the question whether an absolute privilege should be allowed in these cases is not justified by the considerations offered to support it, and unnecessarily deprives the individual citizen of all redress against malicious defamation. Surely the opinion must recognize the existence of the deep-rooted policy of the common law generally to provide redress against defamation. But the opinion in sweeping terms extinguishes that remedy, if the defamation is committed by a federal official, by erecting the barrier of an absolute privilege. In my view, only a qualified privilege is necessary here, and that is all I would afford the officials. A qualified privilege would be the most the law would allow private citizens under comparable circumstances. * * *

* * *

There is an even more basic objection to the opinion. * * * It denies the defamed citizen a recovery by characterizing the policy favoring absolute immunity as "an expression of a policy designed to aid in the effective functioning of government." * * * To come to this conclusion, and to shift the line from the already extensive protection given the public officer by the qualified privilege doctrine, demands the resolution of large imponderables which one might have thought would be better the business of the Legislative Branch. * * *

* * *

Notes

1. In Westfall v. Erwin, 484 U.S. 292, 108 S.Ct. 580, 98 L.Ed.2d 619 (1988), the court held that the absolute state tort law immunity for actions taken by federal officials within the outer perimeter of their official duties only extended to the exercise of discretionary functions. Congress responded by enacting the Federal Employees Liability Reform and Tort Compensation Act of 1988 (popularly known as the "Westfall Act"), 102 Stat. 4563 (1988), which amended the Federal Tort Claims Act (F.T.C.A.) to provide for the substitution of the United States as the party defendant in all tort actions against federal employees that fall within the coverage of the F.T.C.A. 28 U.S.C. § 2679. The F.T.C.A. will be discussed in chapter 22, *infra.* Actions for defamation do not, however, fall within the coverage of the F.T.C.A.

2. With regard to the legislative privilege several questions deserve brief consideration. The first is when is a legislator acting in a legislative capacity? The Supreme Court has held that, while the privilege extends to committee meetings and the insertion of material in the Congressional Record, the privilege does not extend to press releases or news letters sent to a legislator's constituents. *See* Hutchinson v. Proxmire, 443 U.S. 111, 99 S.Ct. 2675, 61 L.Ed.2d 411 (1979). The privilege also protects legislative staff members insofar as the staff members are assisting a legislator in the performance of what might be called a "legislative act." *Cf.* Gravel v. United States, 408 U.S. 606, 92 S.Ct. 2614, 33 L.Ed.2d 583 (1972). Witnesses before legislative bodies are granted an absolute privilege at least if their remarks are germane to the issue under legislative consideration. *See Restatement (Second) of Torts* § 590A.

The other question worth mentioning is that some states distinguish between state legislators, who are granted an absolute privilege, and the members of subordinate legislatures such as city councils and school boards, who are only granted a qualified privilege. With a few exceptions—*see, e.g.,*

McClendon v. Coverdale, 57 Del. 568, 203 A.2d 815 (1964); Mills v. Denny, 245 Iowa 584, 63 N.W.2d 222 (1954)—the cases granting members of subordinate legislative bodies only a qualified privilege are from the nineteenth or early twentieth centuries. The predominant view is that members are entitled to an absolute privilege. *See* Board of Education v. Buffalo Council of Supervisors, 52 A.D.2d 220, 383 N.Y.S.2d 732 (1976); Larson v. Doner, 32 Ill.App.2d 471, 178 N.E.2d 399 (1961). *See also Restatement (Second) of Torts* § 590.

3. With regard to the absolute privilege of the judiciary, the issue sometimes arises whether a judge, who has made a defamatory statement, was acting in a judicial capacity. In Murray v. Brancato, 290 N.Y. 52, 48 N.E.2d 257 (1943), a lower court judge sent his opinions, in which he defamed a defense attorney, to the New York Law Journal and to the West Publishing Company for inclusion in the New York Supplement. In a 4–3 decision, it was held that while publication in the official reports (New York Miscellaneous Reports) was privileged, the judge exceeded his privilege by sending the opinions to the New York Law Journal and to West. *Cf.* Douglas v. Collins, 243 App.Div. 546, 276 N.Y.S. 87 (1934), *affirmed without opinion* 267 N.Y. 557, 196 N.E. 577 (1935)(judge's remarks after court had adjourned and he had stepped down from the bench not privileged). *Murray v. Brancato* now seems to be a questionable decision. Indeed, in Beary v. West Publishing Co., 763 F.2d 66 (2d Cir.1985), the federal court of appeal ruled that the full and accurate report of a case in an unofficial report (New York Supplement 2d Advance Sheets) was absolutely privileged. The federal court relied on § 74 of the New York Civil Rights Law which, *inter alia*, provides that no action can be maintained for "a fair and true report of any judicial proceeding." The New York Court of Appeals in *Murray v. Brancato*, had noted the possible application of § 74 but did not rule on the issue because it had not been raised in the pleadings and because the prevailing majority had doubts whether it applied to the publication by the judge himself.

The absolute privilege extends to statements made by parties, witnesses, jurors, and attorneys in the course of judicial proceedings, although the privilege they may claim is restricted by a requirement that the statements have some relevance to the judicial proceedings in question. *See Restatement (Second) of Torts* §§ 586–89. Under English law, there does not seem to be any relevancy requirement. *See* Salmond & Heuston, Torts 161–62 (21st ed. R. Heuston and R. Buckley, 1996).

4. Prior to *Barr v. Matteo,* most states distinguished between major executive officers such as governors and the state equivalents of federal cabinet officers, on the one hand, and lesser executive officials on the other. Only the former were granted an absolute privilege; lesser officials were granted only a qualified privilege. Since *Barr v. Matteo,* the situation on the state level is less clear. This uncertainty is reflected in a series of New York decisions. In Lombardo v. Stoke, 18 N.Y.2d 394, 276 N.Y.S.2d 97, 222 N.E.2d 721 (1966), an absolute privilege was granted to the New York City Board of Higher Education. The court relied on an earlier case recognizing an absolute privilege on the part of the Borough President of Queens. Sheridan v. Crisona, 14 N.Y.2d 108, 249 N.Y.S.2d 161, 198 N.E.2d 359 (1964). The court in *Lombardo* left open the question of whether the president of a municipal college was also able to claim an absolute privilege. In Stukuls v. State of New York, 42 N.Y.2d 272, 397 N.Y.S.2d 740, 366 N.E.2d 829 (1977), the court held that the acting president of the State University College at Cortland could only claim a qualified privilege. But then, in Ward Telecommunications and Computer

Services, Inc. v. State of New York, 42 N.Y.2d 289, 397 N.Y.S.2d 751, 366 N.E.2d 840 (1977), the court held that members of the staff of the Comptroller of New York State were absolutely privileged.

5. *The Reporting Privilege.* Reports of official proceedings, if accurate, are absolutely privileged. The privilege has been extended to cover "public meetings." A report of a stockholders' meeting, that was not open to the public, has been held not to be privileged. *See* Kimball v. Post Publishing Co., 199 Mass. 248, 85 N.E. 103 (1908)(distinguishing an earlier case, Barrows v. Bell, 73 Mass. (7 Gray) 301 (1856) holding a report of a meeting of the Massachusetts Medical Society to be privileged). In the light of the constitutional developments, to which we are about to turn, however, it is questionable whether a case like *Kimball* would be followed today. Indeed, in Edwards v. National Audubon Society, Inc., 556 F.2d 113 (2d Cir.1977), *cert. denied* 434 U.S. 1002, 98 S.Ct. 647, 54 L.Ed.2d 498, the New York Times reported the charges and countercharges between the plaintiff scientists and the Audubon Society on the issue of whether the use of DDT was affecting bird life. The court of appeals held that the Times articles were privileged as "neutral reportage" of a public dispute. *See also* Krauss v. Champaign News Gazette, Inc., 59 Ill.App.3d 745, 17 Ill.Dec. 78, 375 N.E.2d 1362 (1978). The *Edwards* case was rejected by another circuit in Dickey v. CBS, Inc., 583 F.2d 1221 (3d Cir.1978). *Edwards* was not applied by a later case, Cianci v. New Times Publishing Co., 639 F.2d 54 (2d Cir.1980), in which the court held that "a jury could well find that the New Times did not simply report the charges [of rape] but espoused or concurred in them. * * *" The *Edwards* case was rejected by the New York state courts in Hogan v. Herald Co., 84 A.D.2d 470, 446 N.Y.S.2d 836 (4th Dept.1982), *affirmed on opinion below* 58 N.Y.2d 630, 458 N.Y.S.2d 538, 444 N.E.2d 1002. A California case has, however, applied an analogous privilege based on state-law grounds. Stockton Newspapers, Inc. v. Superior Court, 206 Cal.App.3d 966, 254 Cal.Rptr. 389 (1988)(report of a claim of official misconduct against the plaintiff, who was a public official, made by a third party). The scope of any such privilege in California is undoubtedly rather limited. It certainly does not include situations in which the newspaper itself participated in creating the event which it is purporting to report or situations involving private parties. *See* Brown v. Kelly Broadcasting Co., 48 Cal.3d 711, 771 P.2d 406, 257 Cal.Rptr. 708 (1989). For a general discussion of the broader aspects of the subject, *see* J. Wade, *The Tort Liability of Investigative Reporters*, 37 Vand.L.J. 301 (1984). It should finally be noted that in Farmers Educational & Cooperative Union v. WDAY, Inc., 360 U.S. 525, 79 S.Ct. 1302, 3 L.Ed.2d 1407 (1959), the Court construed the Federal Communications Act (47 U.S.C. § 315(a)) to absolutely immunize broadcasters for defamatory remarks made by candidates for public office if the broadcaster permits such candidates to use its facilities.

There has been some controversy over whether the mere filing of a complaint is such a public act as to permit a newspaper that accurately reports the substance of the complaint to claim the reporting privilege. Relying on cases like Sanford v. Boston Herald–Traveler Corp., 318 Mass. 156, 61 N.E.2d 5 (1945), *Restatement (Second)* § 611, Comment *e,* continues to take the position that the mere filing of a complaint does not give rise to a reporting privilege. Some official action on the complaint is necessary. *See also* Stern v. Piper, [1996] 3 All E.R. 385 (C.A.). New York has for many years taken the opposite position—*see* Campbell v. New York Evening Post, Inc., 245 N.Y. 320, 157 N.E. 153 (1927)(relying on a statutory provision)—and the modern trend is clearly in this direction. *See* Johnson v. Johnson Publishing Co., 271 A.2d 696 (D.C.App. 1970); *cf.* O'Brien v. Franich, 19 Wash.App. 189, 575 P.2d 258 (1978); Hurley v. Northwest Publications, Inc., 273 F.Supp. 967 (D.Minn.1967), *affirmed* 398 F.2d 346 (8th Cir.1968). A reportorial privilege to reprint complaints and other material on file in public record offices may now indeed be constitutionally required.

. That is not to say that there may not be some circumstances where the reporting privilege may not be applicable. For example, in Williams v. Williams, 23 N.Y.2d 592, 298 N.Y.S.2d 473, 246 N.E.2d 333 (1969), at the instigation of the defendants, an action was instituted against the plaintiff by his former employer charging him with misappropriating money and other derelictions while he was an employee. After the filing of the complaint, the defendants circulated copies of the complaint among the trade. The New York Court of Appeals, with two judges dissenting, held that this public circulation of the complaint could not claim the protection of the reporting privilege. The court held, however, that the trial of the libel action should await the results of the employer's action against the plaintiff. The *Williams* case was distinguished in Stover v. Journal Pub. Co., 105 N.M. 291, 731 P.2d 1335 (App.1985), *cert. denied* 484 U.S. 897, 108 S.Ct. 230, 98 L.Ed.2d 189 (1987). In the *Stover* case the defendant newspaper had been a defendant in another action. In the course of that other action, the newspaper, pursuant to the trial court's order, filed an affidavit from a witness whose testimony the defendant intended to use in that other action. The affidavit indicated that Stover, who was a candidate for sheriff, and a former governor of New Mexico, who was a candidate for the United States Senate, had connections with Mafia figures. The attorneys for the former governor advised the trial court that they intended to call a press conference and to release the affidavit which had been filed with the court in order to rebut the contents of that affidavit as it applied to the former governor. The newspaper then filed an unopposed motion to unseal the affidavit. The affidavit was unsealed and the newspaper, on the following day, published an article concerning the affidavit and the denials of Stover and others. Stover then brought his action for defamation against the newspaper. It was held that the newspaper's article was a fair and accurate report of the affidavit which had been filed with the trial court in the other action and that consequently the newspaper article was absolutely privileged. The *Williams* case was distinguished. Unlike the situation in *Williams*, the newspaper had not instigated the other judicial proceedings in which the affidavit had been filed; rather it was an unwilling defendant. The newspaper pointed out that the affidavit had been unsealed and was readily available for public examination. Indeed, the contents of the affidavit had already been the subject of reports presented by several local television stations.

6. *Retraction.* A timely retraction is of course normally relevant on the issue of damages. A few states, *e.g.,* West's Ann.Cal.Civ.Code § 48a; Or.Rev. Stat. § 30.160, provide that unless a retraction is demanded and refused, the plaintiff may not recover any general damages from a media defendant. The California statute, which applies only to newspapers and broadcasters, expressly limits the plaintiff in such a situation to his "special damages." The Oregon statute extends also to magazine publishers. Although the California and Oregon statutes have withstood constitutional attack in the courts of those states, a somewhat similar Montana statute was held unconstitutional in Madison v. Yunker, 180 Mont. 54, 589 P.2d 126 (1978). The Montana statute went further than the other statutes in conditioning even the right to bring an

action for actual damages on a prior request for a retraction. It should finally be noted that, in Miami Herald Publishing Co. v. Tornillo, 418 U.S. 241, 94 S.Ct. 2831, 41 L.Ed.2d 730 (1974), a unanimous Court struck down a Florida statute requiring newspapers to publish a reply by any candidate for public office whom the newspaper had attacked.

In Great Britain, under § 4 of the Defamation Act of 1952, a person who published material "defamatory of another" and who claimed that "the words were published by him innocently of another" could make an "offer of amends." An offer of amends was defined to include an offer to publish "a suitable correction" and "a sufficient apology" and to take steps to notify persons to whom the person making the offer of amends knew the allegedly defamatory material had been distributed. If the party alleged to be defamed accepted the offer, a jury trial was avoided and, if the parties were unable to agree, the courts were given jurisdiction to award legal costs and other reasonable expenses incurred by the party allegedly defamed. If the party defamed rejected a timely offer of amends, the making of the offer served as a defense to an action of defamation if the defendant could show that he acted with reasonable care and that "the words complained of were published by him innocently in relation to the plaintiff." Sections 2, 3, and 4 of the Defamation Act of 1996 continue and expand the "offer to make amends" procedure. If the offer is accepted, a jury trial is avoided and the courts are empowered, in the absence of agreement by the parties, to determine the appropriate damages to be paid to the plaintiff. If an offer to make amends is not accepted and the defendant is prepared to waive all other defenses, the defendant can plead the offer to make amends as a complete defense if the defendant neither knew nor had reason to believe (a) that the material referred to the plaintiff or was likely to be understood as referring to the plaintiff *and* (b) that the material was both false and defamatory. The burden of showing defendant's knowledge of falsity or reason to believe that the material was false is apparently on the plaintiff.

7. *Alternative remedies.* It has often been urged that there should be alternate remedies for defamation. The principal such remedy that has been suggested over the years involves the use of declaratory judgment proceedings to establish the falsity of derogatory statements that have been made about the plaintiff. Given the constitutionalization of much of the law of defamation, we will postpone our discussion of these possible alternative remedies until p. 1190, *infra,* because all these proposed remedies themselves raise some first amendment issues.

C. CONSTITUTIONAL DEVELOPMENTS

NEW YORK TIMES CO. v. SULLIVAN

Supreme Court of the United States, 1964.
376 U.S. 254, 84 S.Ct. 710, 11 L.Ed.2d 686.

MR. JUSTICE BRENNAN delivered the opinion of the Court.

We are required in this case to determine for the first time the extent to which the constitutional protections for speech and press limit a State's power to award damages in a libel action brought by a public official against critics of his official conduct.

Respondent L. B. Sullivan is one of the three elected Commissioners of the City of Montgomery, Alabama. He testified that he was "Commissioner of Public Affairs and the duties are supervision of the Police Department, Fire Department, Department of Cemetery and Department of Scales." He brought this civil libel action against the four individual petitioners, who are Negroes and Alabama clergymen, and against petitioner the New York Times Company, a New York corporation which publishes the New York Times, a daily newspaper. A jury in the Circuit Court of Montgomery County awarded him damages of $500,000, the full amount claimed, against all the petitioners, and the Supreme Court of Alabama affirmed. 273 Ala. 656, 144 So.2d 25.

* * *

Of the 10 paragraphs of text in the advertisement, the third and a portion of the sixth were the basis of respondent's claim of libel. They read as follows:

Third paragraph:

"In Montgomery, Alabama, after students sang 'My Country, 'Tis of Thee' on the State Capitol steps, their leaders were expelled from school, and truckloads of police armed with shotguns and tear-gas ringed the Alabama State College Campus. When the entire student body protested to state authorities by refusing to re-register, their dining hall was padlocked in an attempt to starve them into submission."

Sixth paragraph:

"Again and again the Southern violators have answered Dr. King's peaceful protests with intimidation and violence. They have bombed his home almost killing his wife and child. They have assaulted his person. They have arrested him seven times—for 'speeding,' 'loitering' and similar 'offenses.' And now they have charged him with 'perjury'—a *felony* under which they could imprison him for *ten years*. * * *"

Although neither of these statements mentions respondent by name, he contended that the word "police" in the third paragraph referred to him as the Montgomery Commissioner who supervised the Police Department, so that he was being accused of "ringing" the campus with police. He further claimed that the paragraph would be read as imputing to the police, and hence to him, the padlocking of the dining hall in order to starve the students into submission. As to the sixth paragraph, he contended that since arrests are ordinarily made by the police, the statement "They have arrested [Dr. King] seven times" would be read as referring to him; he further contended that the "They" who did the arresting would be equated with the "They" who committed the other described acts and with the "Southern violators." Thus, he argued, the paragraph would be read as accusing the Montgomery police, and hence him, of answering Dr. King's protests with "intimidation and violence," bombing his home, assaulting his person, and charging him with perjury. Respondent and six other Montgomery residents testified that they read some or all of the statements as referring to him in his capacity as Commissioner.

It is uncontroverted that some of the statements contained in the two paragraphs were not accurate descriptions of events which occurred in

Montgomery. Although Negro students staged a demonstration on the State Capitol steps, they sang the National Anthem and not "My Country, 'Tis of Thee." Although nine students were expelled by the State Board of Education, this was not for leading the demonstration at the Capitol, but for demanding service at a lunch counter in the Montgomery County Courthouse on another day. Not the entire student body, but most of it, had protested the expulsion, not by refusing to register, but by boycotting classes on a single day; virtually all the students did register for the ensuing semester. The campus dining hall was not padlocked on any occasion, and the only students who may have been barred from eating there were the few who had neither signed a preregistration application nor requested temporary meal tickets. Although the police were deployed near the campus in large numbers on three occasions, they did not at any time "ring" the campus, and they were not called to the campus in connection with the demonstration on the State Capitol steps, as the third paragraph implied. Dr. King had not been arrested seven times, but only four; and although he claimed to have been assaulted some years earlier in connection with his arrest for loitering outside a courtroom, one of the officers who made the arrest denied that there was such an assault.

On the premise that the charges in the sixth paragraph could be read as referring to him, respondent was allowed to prove that he had not participated in the events described. Although Dr. King's home had in fact been bombed twice when his wife and child were there, both of these occasions antedated respondent's tenure as Commissioner, and the police were not only not implicated in the bombings, but had made every effort to apprehend those who were. Three of Dr. King's four arrests took place before respondent became Commissioner. Although Dr. King had in fact been indicted (he was subsequently acquitted) on two counts of perjury, each of which carried a possible five-year sentence, respondent had nothing to do with procuring the indictment.

Respondent made no effort to prove that he suffered actual pecuniary loss as a result of the alleged libel.[3] One of his witnesses, a former employer, testified that if he had believed the statements, he doubted whether he "would want to be associated with anybody who would be a party to such things that are stated in that ad," and that he would not re-employ respondent if he believed "that he allowed the Police Department to do the things that the paper say he did." But neither this witness nor any of the others testified that he had actually believed the statements in their supposed reference to respondent.

The cost of the advertisement was approximately $4800, and it was published by the Times upon an order from a New York advertising agency acting for the signatory Committee. The agency submitted the advertisement with a letter from A. Philip Randolph, Chairman of the Committee,

---

3. Approximately 394 copies of the edition of the Times containing the advertisement were circulated in Alabama. Of these, about 35 copies were distributed in Montgomery County. The total circulation of the Times for that day was approximately 650,000 copies. [Ed. note] The *Times* argued that the Alabama courts had no basis for asserting jurisdiction over it, but the Court, in note 4 to its opinion that has been omitted, upheld the Alabama courts' ruling that the *Times* waived this objection by making a general appearance.

certifying that the persons whose names appeared on the advertisement had given their permission. Mr. Randolph was known to the Times' Advertising Acceptability Department as a responsible person, and in accepting the letter as sufficient proof of authorization it followed its established practice. * * * Each of the individual petitioners testified that he had not authorized the use of his name, and that he had been unaware of its use until receipt of respondent's demand for a retraction. The manager of the Advertising Acceptability Department testified that he had approved the advertisement for publication because he knew nothing to cause him to believe that anything in it was false, and because it bore the endorsement of "a number of people who are well known and whose reputation" he "had no reason to question." Neither he nor anyone else at the Times made an effort to confirm the accuracy of the advertisement, either by checking it against recent Times news stories relating to some of the described events or by any other means.

Alabama law denies a public officer recovery of punitive damages in a libel action brought on account of a publication concerning his official conduct unless he first makes a written demand for a public retraction and the defendant fails or refuses to comply. * * * Respondent served such a demand upon each of the petitioners. None of the individual petitioners responded to the demand, primarily because each took the position that he had not authorized the use of his name on the advertisement and therefore had not published the statements that respondent alleged had libeled him. The Times did not publish a retraction in response to the demand, but wrote respondent a letter stating, among other things, that "we * * * are somewhat puzzled as to how you think the statements in any way reflect on you," and "you might, if you desire, let us know in what respect you claim that the statements in the advertisement reflect on you." Respondent filed this suit a few days later without answering the letter. The Times did, however, subsequently publish a retraction of the advertisement upon the demand of Governor John Patterson of Alabama, who asserted that the publication charged him with "grave misconduct and * * * improper actions and omissions as Governor of Alabama and Ex–Officio Chairman of the State Board of Education of Alabama." When asked to explain why there had been a retraction for the Governor but not for respondent, the Secretary of the Times testified: "We did that because we didn't want anything that was published by The Times to be a reflection on the State of Alabama and the Governor was, as far as we could see, the embodiment of the State of Alabama and the proper representative of the State and, furthermore, we had by that time learned more of the actual facts which the ad purported to recite and, finally, the ad did refer to the action of the State authorities and the Board of Education presumably of which the Governor is the ex-officio chairman * * *." On the other hand, he testified that he did not think that "any of the language in there referred to Mr. Sullivan."

* * * The jury was instructed that, because the statements were libelous *per se,* "the law * * * implies legal injury from the bare fact of publication itself," "falsity and malice are presumed," "general damages need not be alleged or proved but are presumed," and "punitive damages may be awarded by the jury even though the amount of actual damages is

neither found nor shown." An award of punitive damages—as distinguished from "general" damages, which are compensatory in nature—apparently requires proof of actual malice under Alabama law, and the judge charged that "mere negligence or carelessness is not evidence of actual malice or malice in fact, and does not justify an award of exemplary or punitive damages." He refused to charge, however, that the jury must be "convinced" of malice, in the sense of "actual intent" to harm or "gross negligence and recklessness," to make such an award, and he also refused to require that a verdict for respondent differentiate between compensatory and punitive damages. The judge rejected petitioners' contention that his rulings abridged the freedoms of speech and of the press that are guaranteed by the First and Fourteenth Amendments.

In affirming the judgment, the Supreme Court of Alabama sustained the trial judge's rulings and instructions in all respects. * * * In sustaining the trial court's determination that the verdict was not excessive, the court said that malice could be inferred from the Times' "irresponsibility" in printing the advertisement while "the Times in its own files had articles already published which would have demonstrated the falsity of the allegations in the advertisement"; from the Times' failure to retract for respondent while retracting for the Governor, whereas the falsity of some of the allegations was then known to the Times and "the matter contained in the advertisement was equally false as to both parties"; and from the testimony of the Times' Secretary that, apart from the statement that the dining hall was padlocked, he thought the two paragraphs were "substantially correct." * * * The court reaffirmed a statement in an earlier opinion that "There is no legal measure of damages in cases of this character." * * * It rejected petitioners' constitutional contentions with the brief statements that "The First Amendment of the U.S. Constitution does not protect libelous publications" and "The Fourteenth Amendment is directed against State action and not private action." * * *

Because of the importance of the constitutional issues involved, we granted the separate petitions for certiorari of the individual petitioners and of the Times. * * * We reverse the judgment. We hold that the rule of law applied by the Alabama courts is constitutionally deficient for failure to provide the safeguards for freedom of speech and of the press that are required by the First and Fourteenth Amendments in a libel action brought by a public official against critics of his official conduct. We further hold that under the proper safeguards the evidence presented in this case is constitutionally insufficient to support the judgment for respondent.

I.

We may dispose at the outset of two grounds asserted to insulate the judgment of the Alabama courts from constitutional scrutiny. The first is the proposition relied on by the State Supreme Court—that "The Fourteenth Amendment is directed against State action and not private action." That proposition has no application to this case. Although this is a civil lawsuit between private parties, the Alabama courts have applied a state rule of law which petitioners claim to impose invalid restrictions on their constitutional freedoms of speech and press. It matters not that that law has been applied in a civil action and that it is common law only, though supplemented by statute. * * *

The second contention is that the constitutional guarantees of freedom of speech and of the press are inapplicable here, at least so far as the Times is concerned, because the allegedly libelous statements were published as part of a paid, "commercial" advertisement. The argument relies on Valentine v. Chrestensen, 316 U.S. 52, 62 S.Ct. 920, 86 L.Ed. 1262, * * *.

The publication here was not a "commercial" advertisement in the sense in which the word was used in Chrestensen. It communicated information, expressed opinion, recited grievances, protested claimed abuses, and sought financial support on behalf of a movement whose existence and objectives are matters of the highest public interest and concern. * * *

II.

Under Alabama law as applied in this case, a publication is "libelous per se" if the words "tend to injure a person * * * in his reputation" or to "bring [him] into public contempt"; the trial court stated that the standard was met if the words are such as to "injure him in his public office, or impute misconduct to him in his office, or want of official integrity, or want of fidelity to a public trust * * *." The jury must find that the words were published "of and concerning" the plaintiff, but where the plaintiff is a public official his place in the governmental hierarchy is sufficient evidence to support a finding that his reputation has been affected by statements that reflect upon the agency of which he is in charge. Once "libel per se" has been established, the defendant has no defense as to stated facts unless he can persuade the jury that they were true in all their particulars. * * * His privilege of "fair comment" for expressions of opinion depends on the truth of the facts upon which the comment is based. * * * Unless he can discharge the burden of proving truth, general damages are presumed, and may be awarded without proof of pecuniary injury. A showing of actual malice is apparently a prerequisite to recovery of punitive damages, and the defendant may in any event forestall a punitive award by a retraction meeting the statutory requirements. Good motives and belief in truth do not negate an inference of malice, but are relevant only in mitigation of punitive damages if the jury chooses to accord them weight. * * *

The question before us is whether this rule of liability, as applied to an action brought by a public official against critics of his official conduct, abridges the freedom of speech and of the press that is guaranteed by the First and Fourteenth Amendments.

Respondent relies heavily, as did the Alabama courts, on statements of this Court to the effect that the Constitution does not protect libelous publications. Those statements do not foreclose our inquiry here. None of the cases sustained the use of libel laws to impose sanctions upon expression critical of the official conduct of public officials. * * * In the only previous case that did present the question of constitutional limitations upon the power to award damages for libel of a public official, the Court was equally divided and the question was not decided. Schenectady Union Publishing Co. v. Sweeney, 316 U.S. 642, 62 S.Ct. 1031, 86 L.Ed. 1727 (1942).

The general proposition that freedom of expression upon public questions is secured by the First Amendment has long been settled by our decisions.

Thus we consider this case against the background of a profound national commitment to the principle that debate on public issues should be uninhibited, robust, and wide-open, and that it may well include vehement, caustic, and sometimes unpleasantly sharp attacks on government and public officials. * * * The present advertisement, as an expression of grievance and protest on one of the major public issues of our time, would seem clearly to qualify for the constitutional protection. The question is whether it forfeits that protection by the falsity of some of its factual statements and by its alleged defamation of respondent.

Authoritative interpretations of the First Amendment guarantees have consistently refused to recognize an exception for any test of truth—whether administered by judges, juries, or administrative officials—and especially one that puts the burden of proving truth on the speaker. * * * As Madison said, "Some degree of abuse is inseparable from the proper use of every thing; and in no instance is this more true than in that of the press." 4 Elliot's Debates on the Federal Constitution (1876), p. 571. * * *

Injury to official reputation affords no more warrant for repressing speech that would otherwise be free than does factual error. * * *

If neither factual error nor defamatory content suffices to remove the constitutional shield from criticism of official conduct, the combination of the two elements is no less inadequate. This is the lesson to be drawn from the great controversy over the Sedition Act of 1798, 1 Stat. 596, which first crystallized a national awareness of the central meaning of the First Amendment. * * * That statute made it a crime, punishable by a $5,000 fine and five years in prison, "if any person shall write, print, utter or publish * * * any false, scandalous and malicious writing or writings against the government of the United States, or either house of the Congress * * *, or the President * * *, with intent to defame * * * or to bring them, or either of them, into contempt or disrepute; or to excite against them, or either or any of them, the hatred of the good people of the United States." The Act allowed the defendant the defense of truth, and provided that the jury were to be judges both of the law and the facts. Despite these qualifications, the Act was vigorously condemned as unconstitutional in an attack joined in by Jefferson and Madison. * * *

Although the Sedition Act was never tested in this Court,[16] the attack upon its validity has carried the day in the court of history. Fines levied in its prosecution were repaid by Act of Congress on the ground that it was unconstitutional. See, e.g., Act of July 4, 1840, c. 45, 6 Stat. 802, accompanied by H.R.Rep. No. 86, 26th Cong., 1st Sess. (1840). Calhoun, reporting to the Senate on February 4, 1836, assumed that its invalidity was a matter "which no one now doubts." Report with Senate bill No. 122, 24th Cong., 1st Sess., p. 3. Jefferson, as President, pardoned those who had been convicted and sentenced under the Act and remitted their fines, stating: "I

---

16. The Act expired by its terms in 1801.

discharged every person under punishment or prosecution under the sedition law, because I considered, and now consider, that law to be a nullity, as absolute and as palpable as if Congress had ordered us to fall down and worship a golden image." Letter to Mrs. Adams, July 22, 1804, 4 Jefferson's Works (Washington ed.), pp. 555, 556. The invalidity of the Act has also been assumed by Justices of this Court. * * * These views reflect a broad consensus that the Act, because of the restraint it imposed upon criticism of government and public officials, was inconsistent with the First Amendment.

There is no force in respondent's argument that the constitutional limitations implicit in the history of the Sedition Act apply only to Congress and not to the States. It is true that the First Amendment was originally addressed only to action by the Federal Government, and that Jefferson, for one, while denying the power of Congress "to controul the freedom of the press," recognized such a power in the States. See the 1804 Letter to Abigail Adams quoted in Dennis v. United States, 341 U.S. 494 * * *.

What a State may not constitutionally bring about by means of a criminal statute is likewise beyond the reach of its civil law of libel. The fear of damage awards under a rule such as that invoked by the Alabama courts here may be markedly more inhibiting than the fear of prosecution under a criminal statute. * * * Alabama, for example, has a criminal libel law which subjects to prosecution "any person who speaks, writes, or prints of and concerning another any accusation falsely and maliciously importing the commission by such person of a felony, or any other indictable offense involving moral turpitude," and which allows as punishment upon conviction a fine not exceeding $500 and a prison sentence of six months. Alabama Code, Tit. 14, § 350. Presumably a person charged with violation of this statute enjoys ordinary criminal-law safeguards such as the requirements of an indictment and of proof beyond a reasonable doubt. These safeguards are not available to the defendant in a civil action. The judgment awarded in this case—without the need for any proof of actual pecuniary loss—was one thousand times greater than the maximum fine provided by the Alabama criminal statute, and one hundred times greater than that provided by the Sedition Act. And since there is no double-jeopardy limitation applicable to civil lawsuits, this is not the only judgment that may be awarded against petitioners for the same publication.[18] Whether or not a newspaper can survive a succession of such judgments, the pall of fear and timidity imposed upon those who would give voice to public criticism is an atmosphere in which the First Amendment freedoms cannot survive. * * *

The state rule of law is not saved by its allowance of the defense of truth. * * * A rule compelling the critic of official conduct to guarantee the truth of all his factual assertions—and to do so on pain of libel judgments virtually unlimited in amount—leads to a comparable "self-censorship." Allowance of the defense of truth, with the burden of proving

---

18. The Times states that four other libel suits based on the advertisement have been filed against it by others who have served as Montgomery City Commissioners and by the Governor of Alabama; that another $500,000 verdict has been awarded in the only one of these cases that has yet gone to trial; and that the damages sought in the other three total $2,000,000.

it on the defendant, does not mean that only false speech will be deterred.[19] Even courts accepting this defense as an adequate safeguard have recognized the difficulties of adducing legal proofs that the alleged libel was true in all its factual particulars.   * * * Under such a rule, would-be critics of official conduct may be deterred from voicing their criticism, even though it is believed to be true and even though it is in fact true, because of doubt whether it can be proved in court or fear of the expense of having to do so. * * * The rule thus dampens the vigor and limits the variety of public debate.   It is inconsistent with the First and Fourteenth Amendments.

The constitutional guarantees require, we think, a federal rule that prohibits a public official from recovering damages for a defamatory falsehood relating to his official conduct unless he proves that the statement was made with "actual malice"—that is, with knowledge that it was false or with reckless disregard of whether it was false or not. An oft-cited statement of a like rule, which has been adopted by a number of state courts, is found in the Kansas case of Coleman v. MacLennan, 78 Kan. 711, 98 P. 281 (1908).   * * *

Such a privilege for criticism of official conduct is appropriately analogous to the protection accorded a public official when *he* is sued for libel by a private citizen.   In Barr v. Matteo, * * * this Court held the utterance of a federal official to be absolutely privileged if made "within the outer perimeter" of his duties.   The States accord the same immunity to statements of their highest officers, although some differentiate their lesser officials and qualify the privilege they enjoy.   But all hold that all officials are protected unless actual malice can be proved.   The reason for the official privilege is said to be that the threat of damage suits would otherwise "inhibit the fearless, vigorous, and effective administration of policies of government" and "dampen the ardor of all but the most resolute, or the most irresponsible, in the unflinching discharge of their duties."   Barr v. Matteo, supra, * * * Analogous considerations support the privilege for the citizen-critic of government.   It is as much his duty to criticize as it is the official's duty to administer.   * * * As Madison said, * * * "the censorial power is in the people over the Government, and not in the Government over the people."   It would give public servants an unjustified preference over the public they serve, if critics of official conduct did not have a fair equivalent of the immunity granted to the officials themselves.

We conclude that such a privilege is required by the First and Fourteenth Amendments.

III.

We hold today that the Constitution delimits a State's power to award damages for libel in actions brought by public officials against critics of their official conduct.   Since this is such an action,[23] the rule requiring

19. Even a false statement may be deemed to make a valuable contribution to public debate, since it brings about "the clearer perception and livelier impression of truth, produced by its collision with error." Mill, On Liberty (Oxford: Blackwell, 1947), at 15; see also Milton, Areopagitica, in Prose Works (Yale, 1959), Vol. II, at 561.

23. We have no occasion here to determine how far down into the lower ranks of government employees the "public official" designation would extend for purposes of this

proof of actual malice is applicable. While Alabama law apparently requires proof of actual malice for an award of punitive damages, where general damages are concerned malice is "presumed." Such a presumption is inconsistent with the federal rule. * * * Since the trial judge did not instruct the jury to differentiate between general and punitive damages, it may be that the verdict was wholly an award of one or the other. But it is impossible to know, in view of the general verdict returned. Because of this uncertainty, the judgment must be reversed and the case remanded. * * *

Since respondent may seek a new trial, we deem that considerations of effective judicial administration require us to review the evidence in the present record to determine whether it could constitutionally support a judgment for respondent. This Court's duty is not limited to the elaboration of constitutional principles; we must also in proper cases review the evidence to make certain that those principles have been constitutionally applied. This is such a case * * *.

Applying these standards, we consider that the proof presented to show actual malice lacks the convincing clarity which the constitutional standard demands, and hence that it would not constitutionally sustain the judgment for respondent under the proper rule of law. The case of the individual petitioners requires little discussion. Even assuming that they could constitutionally be found to have authorized the use of their names on the advertisement, there was no evidence whatever that they were aware of any erroneous statements or were in any way reckless in that regard. The judgment against them is thus without constitutional support.

As to the Times, we similarly conclude that the facts do not support a finding of actual malice. The statement by the Times' Secretary that, apart from the padlocking allegation, he thought the advertisement was "substantially correct," affords no constitutional warrant for the Alabama Supreme Court's conclusion that it was a "cavalier ignoring of the falsity of the advertisement [from which], the jury could not have but been impressed with the bad faith of The Times, and its maliciousness inferable therefrom." The statement does not indicate malice at the time of the publication; even if the advertisement was not "substantially correct"— although respondent's own proofs tend to show that it was—that opinion was at least a reasonable one, and there was no evidence to impeach the witness' good faith in holding it. The Times' failure to retract upon respondent's demand, although it later retracted upon the demand of Governor Patterson, is likewise not adequate evidence of malice for constitutional purposes. Whether or not a failure to retract may ever constitute such evidence, there are two reasons why it does not here. *First,* the letter written by the Times reflected a reasonable doubt on its part as to whether the advertisement could reasonably be taken to refer to respondent at all. *Second,* it was not a final refusal, since it asked for an explanation on this point—a request that respondent chose to ignore. Nor does the retraction upon the demand of the Governor supply the necessary proof. It may be

rule, or otherwise to specify categories of persons who would or would not be included. * * * Nor need we here determine the boundaries of the "official conduct" concept. * * *

doubted that a failure to retract which is not itself evidence of malice can retroactively become such by virtue of a retraction subsequently made to another party. But in any event that did not happen here, since the explanation given by the Times' Secretary for the distinction drawn between respondent and the Governor was a reasonable one, the good faith of which was not impeached.

Finally, there is evidence that the Times published the advertisement without checking its accuracy against the news stories in the Times' own files. The mere presence of the stories in the files does not, of course, establish that the Times "knew" the advertisement was false, since the state of mind required for actual malice would have to be brought home to the persons in the Times' organization having responsibility for the publication of the advertisement. * * * We think the evidence against the Times supports at most a finding of negligence in failing to discover the misstatements, and is constitutionally insufficient to show the recklessness that is required for a finding of actual malice. * * * We think the evidence was constitutionally defective in another respect: it was incapable of supporting the jury's finding that the allegedly libelous statements were made "of and concerning" respondent. Respondent relies on the words of the advertisement and the testimony of six witnesses to establish a connection between it and himself. Thus, in his brief to this Court, he states:

> "The reference to respondent as police commissioner is clear from the ad. In addition, the jury heard the testimony of a newspaper editor * * *; a real estate and insurance man * * *; the sales manager of a men's clothing store * * *; a food equipment man * * *; a service station operator * * *; and the operator of a truck line for whom respondent had formerly worked * * *. Each of these witnesses stated that he associated the statements with respondent * * *." (Citations to record omitted.)

There was no reference to respondent in the advertisement, either by name or official position. A number of the allegedly libelous statements—the charges that the dining hall was padlocked and that Dr. King's home was bombed, his person assaulted, and a perjury prosecution instituted against him—did not even concern the police; despite the ingenuity of the arguments which would attach this significance to the word "They," it is plain that these statements could not reasonably be read as accusing respondent of personal involvement in the acts in question. The statements upon which respondent principally relies as referring to him are the two allegations that did concern the police or police functions: that "truckloads of police * * * ringed the Alabama State College Campus" after the demonstration on the State Capitol steps, and that Dr. King had been "arrested * * * seven times." These statements were false only in that the police had been "deployed near" the campus but had not actually "ringed" it and had not gone there in connection with the State Capitol demonstration, and in that Dr. King had been arrested only four times. The ruling that these discrepancies between what was true and what was asserted were sufficient to injure respondent's reputation may itself raise constitutional problems, but we need not consider them here. Although the statements may be taken as referring to the police, they did not on their face make even an oblique reference to respondent as an individual. Support for the asserted reference must, therefore, be sought in the testimony of respondent's witnesses. But none of them suggested any basis for the belief that respondent himself was attacked in the advertisement beyond the bare fact that he was in overall charge of the Police Department and thus bore official responsibility for police conduct; to the extent that some of the witnesses thought respondent to have been charged with ordering or approving the conduct or otherwise being personally involved in it, they based this notion not on any statements in the advertisement, and not on any evidence that he had in fact been so involved, but solely on the unsupported assumption that, because of his official position, he must have been. This reliance on the bare fact of respondent's official position was made explicit by the Supreme Court of Alabama. * * *

This proposition has disquieting implications for criticism of governmental conduct. * * *

The judgment of the Supreme Court of Alabama is reversed and the case is remanded to that court for further proceedings not inconsistent with this opinion.

Reversed and remanded.

MR. JUSTICE BLACK, with whom MR. JUSTICE DOUGLAS joins (concurring).

I concur in reversing this half-million-dollar judgment against the New York Times Company and the four individual defendants. In reversing the Court holds that "the Constitution delimits a State's power to award damages for libel in actions brought by public officials against critics of their official conduct." * * * I base my vote to reverse on the belief that the First and Fourteenth Amendments not merely "delimit" a State's power to award damages to "public officials against critics of their official conduct" but completely prohibit a State from exercising such a power. * * *

* * *

MR. JUSTICE GOLDBERG, with whom MR. JUSTICE DOUGLAS joins (concurring in the result).

* * *

In my view, the First and Fourteenth Amendments to the Constitution afford to the citizen and to the press an absolute, unconditional privilege to criticize official conduct despite the harm which may flow from excesses and abuses. * * * The right should not depend upon a probing by the jury of the motivation[2] of the citizen or press. * * *

* * *

We must recognize that we are writing upon a clean slate. * * * It may be urged that deliberately and maliciously false statements have no conceivable value as free speech. That argument, however, is not responsive to the real issue presented by this case, which is whether that freedom of speech which all agree is constitutionally protected can be effectively

---

2. The requirement of proving actual malice or reckless disregard may, in the mind of the jury, add little to the requirement of proving falsity, a requirement which the Court recognizes not to be an adequate safeguard. * * *

safeguarded by a rule allowing the imposition of liability upon a jury's evaluation of the speaker's state of mind. If individual citizens may be held liable in damages for strong words, which a jury finds false and maliciously motivated, there can be little doubt that public debate and advocacy will be constrained. And if newspapers, publishing advertisements dealing with public issues, thereby risk liability, there can also be little doubt that the ability of minority groups to secure publication of their views on public affairs and to seek support for their causes will be greatly diminished. * * *

* * *

This is not to say that the Constitution protects defamatory statements directed against the private conduct of a public official or private citizen. Freedom of press and of speech insures that government will respond to the will of the people and that changes may be obtained by peaceful means. Purely private defamation has little to do with the political ends of a self-governing society. The imposition of liability for private defamation does not abridge the freedom of public speech or any other freedom protected by the First Amendment.[4] * * *

* * *

For these reasons, I strongly believe that the Constitution accords citizens and press an unconditional freedom to criticize official conduct. It necessarily follows that in a case such as this, where all agree that the allegedly defamatory statements related to official conduct, the judgments for libel cannot constitutionally be sustained.

Notes

1. *Sullivan's* requirement that the plaintiff prove either knowledge of falsity or reckless disregard of falsity was extended to cover actions brought by relatively low-ranking public officials or former public officials, at least when the action was based upon statements about the plaintiff's official conduct. *See* Rosenblatt v. Baer, 383 U.S. 75, 86 S.Ct. 669, 15 L.Ed.2d 597 (1966)(former supervisor of county recreation facility). The Court has, however, remarked that, while it "has not provided precise boundaries for the category of 'public official,' it cannot be thought to include all public employees. * * *" Hutchinson v. Proxmire, 443 U.S. 111, 119 n. 8, 99 S.Ct. 2675, 2680 n. 8, 61 L.Ed.2d 411, 421 n. 8 (1979).

2. The Court also made clear that recklessness could only be proven by some showing of conscious indifference to truth; a *mere* failure to investigate is not enough. *See* St. Amant v. Thompson, 390 U.S. 727, 88 S.Ct. 1323, 20 L.Ed.2d 262 (1968); Beckley Newspapers Corp. v. Hanks, 389 U.S. 81, 88 S.Ct. 197, 19 L.Ed.2d 248 (1967)(per curiam).

3. The Court, following the lead of some lower courts, also soon extended the scope of application of the *Sullivan* standard to statements concerning at least the non-private aspects of the lives of public figures, even those who were

---

4. In most cases, as in the case at bar, there will be little difficulty in distinguishing defamatory speech relating to private conduct from that relating to official conduct. I recognize, of course, that there will be a gray area. The difficulties of applying a public-private standard are, however, certainly, of a different genre from those attending the differentiation between a malicious and nonmalicious state of mind. * * *

not involved in politics. *See* Curtis Publishing Co. v. Butts, 388 U.S. 130, 87 S.Ct. 1975, 18 L.Ed.2d 1094 (1967); Associated Press v. Walker, reported *sub. nom.* Curtis Publishing Co. v. Butts. Justice Harlan suggested in *Butts* and *Walker* that public figures who were not public officials might be able to recover on a showing of only gross negligence but he later abandoned that position in the *Rosenbloom* case. Concurrently in a privacy case, the Court also indicated that a relatively unknown person could, by accidental involvement in an event of major newsworthiness, become a public figure, at least with regard to matters involving the newsworthy event. *See* Time, Inc. v. Hill, 385 U.S. 374, 87 S.Ct. 534, 17 L.Ed.2d 456 (1967).

4. The last case in the expansive period of the application of *Sullivan* was Rosenbloom v. Metromedia, Inc., 403 U.S. 29, 91 S.Ct. 1811, 29 L.Ed.2d 296 (1971). In that case the plaintiff was a magazine distributor. The police had arrested him and seized some of his magazines on the ground that they were obscene. In reporting these events, the defendant Philadelphia radio station stated that the police had "confiscated 3000 obscene books." The plaintiff claimed that at most the station could have said that the materials seized were "allegedly" obscene. The plaintiff brought suit in the federal courts for the return of the materials. In reporting these developments, the defendant described the proceeding as one in which the defendant sought an injunction "ordering * * * [the authorities and the media] to lay off the smut literature racket." In the same vein the report declared: "The girlie-book peddlers say the police crack down and continued reference to their borderline literature as smut or filth is hurting their business." The report continued that "if the injunction is not granted * * * it could signal an even more intense effort to rid the city of pornography." Shortly thereafter the plaintiff complained to the radio station that "his magazines were 'found to be completely legal and legitimate by the United States Supreme Court.'" The newscaster for the station replied that the district attorney had said the magazines were obscene. The plaintiff replied that he had a statement from the district attorney that the magazines were "legal." At that point the conversation was terminated. There was no request for a retraction or correction and none was made. Subsequently, in a criminal prosecution against the plaintiff, a state court jury acquitted the plaintiff under instructions from the trial judge who ruled that, as a matter of law, the nudist magazines distributed by the plaintiff were not obscene. At this point the plaintiff brought his defamation action in the federal courts on the basis of diversity of citizenship. The district court refused to apply the *Sullivan* standards and the jury found for the plaintiff. The jury awarded the plaintiff $25,000 in compensatory damages and $725,000 in punitive damages. On remittitur, the trial judge reduced the punitive damages to $250,000. The United States Court of Appeals for the Third Circuit reversed and the Supreme Court affirmed.

Although five of the eight justices who heard the case voted to affirm (Justice Douglas did not participate in the decision of the case), there was no opinion for the Court. Writing for himself and two other Justices (Chief Justice Burger and Justice Blackmun), Justice Brennan began by noting that the Pennsylvania law of defamation tracked the *Restatement of Torts*. Justice Brennan then continued:

> We turn then to the question to be decided. Petitioner's argument that the Constitution should be held to require that the private individual prove only that the publisher failed to exercise "reasonable care" in publishing defamatory falsehoods proceeds along two lines. First, he

argues that the private individual, unlike the public figure, does not have access to the media to counter the defamatory material and that the private individual, unlike the public figure, has not assumed the risk of defamation by thrusting himself into the public arena. Second, petitioner focuses on the important values served by the law of defamation in preventing and redressing attacks upon reputation.

We have recognized the force of petitioner's arguments, Time, Inc. v. Hill, *supra,* 385 U.S., at 391, 87 S.Ct., at 543–544, and we adhere to the caution expressed in that case against "blind application," of the *New York Times* standard. * * * Analysis of the particular factors involved, however, convinces us that petitioner's arguments cannot be reconciled with the purposes of the First Amendment, with our cases, and with the traditional doctrines of libel law itself. Drawing a distinction between "public" and "private" figures makes no sense in terms of the First Amendment guarantees. The *New York Times* standard was applied to libel of a public official or public figure to give effect to the Amendment's function to encourage ventilation of public issues, not because the public official has any less interest in protecting his reputation than an individual in private life. While the argument that public figures need less protection because they can command media attention to counter criticism may be true for some very prominent people, even then it is the rare case where the denial overtakes the original charge. Denials, retractions, and corrections are not "hot" news, and rarely receive the prominence of the original story. When the public official or public figure is a minor functionary, or has left the position that put him in the public eye, *see* Rosenblatt v. Baer, *supra,* the argument loses all of its force. In the vast majority of libels involving public officials or public figures, the ability to respond through the media will depend on the same complex factor on which the ability of a private individual depends: the unpredictable event of the media's continuing interest in the story. Thus the unproved, and highly improbable, generalization that an as yet undefined class of "public figures" involved in matters of public concern will be better able to respond through the media than private individuals also involved in such matters seems too insubstantial a reed on which to rest a constitutional distinction. Furthermore, in First Amendment terms, the cure seems far worse than the disease. If the States fear that private citizens will not be able to respond adequately to publicity involving them, the solution lies in the direction of ensuring their ability to respond, rather than in stifling public discussion of matters of public concern.[15]

Further reflection over the years since *New York Times* was decided persuades us that the view of the "public official" or "public figure" as assuming the risk of defamation by voluntarily thrusting himself into the public eye bears little relationship either to the values protected by the First Amendment or to the nature of our society. We have recognized that "[e]xposure of the self to others in varying degrees is a concomitant of life in a civilized community." Time, Inc. v. Hill, *supra,* * * * Voluntarily or not, we are all "public" men to some degree. Conversely, some aspects of the lives of even the most public men fall outside the area of matters of public or general concern. * * * Thus, the idea that certain "public"

---

15. Some States have adopted retraction statutes or right-of-reply statutes. * * * [Ed. note] The Court has since declared right of reply statutes unconstitutional in the *Tornillo* case, discussed in note 6, p. 1132, *supra.*

figures have voluntarily exposed their entire lives to public inspection, while private individuals have kept theirs carefully shrouded from public view is, at best, a legal fiction. In any event, such a distinction could easily produce the paradoxical result of dampening discussion of issues of public or general concern because they happen to involve private citizens while extending constitutional encouragement to discussion of aspects of the lives of "public figures" that are not in the area of public or general concern.

* * *

Moreover, we ordinarily decide civil litigation by the preponderance of the evidence. Indeed, the judge instructed the jury to decide the present case by that standard. In the normal civil suit where this standard is employed, "we view it as no more serious in general for there to be an erroneous verdict in the defendant's favor than for there to be an erroneous verdict in the plaintiff's favor." In re Winship, 397 U.S. 358, 371, 90 S.Ct. 1068, 1076, 25 L.Ed.2d 368 (1970)(Harlan, J., concurring). In libel cases, however, we view an erroneous verdict for the plaintiff as most serious. Not only does it mulct the defendant for an innocent misstatement—the three-quarter-million-dollar jury verdict in this case could rest on such an error—but the possibility of such error, even beyond the vagueness of the negligence standard itself, would create a strong impetus toward self-censorship, which the First Amendment cannot tolerate. These dangers for freedom of speech and press led us to reject the reasonable-man standard of liability as "simply inconsistent" with our national commitment under the First Amendment when sought to be applied to the conduct of a political campaign. Monitor Patriot Co. v. Roy, 401 U.S. 265, 276, 91 S.Ct. 621, 627, 28 L.Ed.2d 35 (1971). The same considerations lead us to reject that standard here.

* * *

* * * We thus hold that a libel action, as here, by a private individual against a licensed radio station for a defamatory falsehood in a newscast relating to his involvement in an event of public or general concern may be sustained only upon clear and convincing proof that the defamatory falsehood was published with knowledge that it was false or with reckless disregard of whether it was false or not. * * *

Justice Black concurred on familiar grounds. Justice White also concurred on the ground that the case involved a "report and comment upon the official actions of public servants," i.e. the police. Justice Harlan in dissent argued that the concerns of the majority could be met by prohibiting the award of presumed damages in any defamation action. Justice Marshall, writing for himself and Justice Stewart, joined in this proposal but also contended that punitive damages should not be allowed in defamation actions. Anticipating the Gertz case to which we shall shortly turn, all three dissenters concluded that public officials and public figures should continue to have to meet the standards enunciated in Sullivan but that plaintiffs like George Rosenbloom who did not fit into either category should be able to recover for genuinely injurious defamation upon a showing of negligence.

5. In imposing the requirement that the plaintiff must, at least in some defamation actions, show that the defendant was aware of the falsity of his statements or at the very least consciously indifferent to the truth or falsity of his statements the Court has obviously made the defendant's state of mind, or

the state of mind of those for whom the defendant is legally accountable, a relevant consideration. In Herbert v. Lando, 441 U.S. 153, 99 S.Ct. 1635, 60 L.Ed.2d 115 (1979), the plaintiff was, *inter alia*, reported, in a television program produced by CBS, to have accused his superiors of war crimes to explain his relief from military command in Vietnam. Lando, the individual defendant who prepared the report for CBS, also subsequently repeated the charges in an article published in the Atlantic Monthly. Herbert brought his defamation action against Lando, CBS, and the Atlantic Monthly. During the taking of depositions, Lando refused to answer questions concerning a variety of issues. In deciding whether Lando could refuse to answer the questions asked him, the Court relied upon and quoted the following summary of the matters in controversy prepared by the United States Court of Appeals for the Second Circuit:

1. Lando's conclusions during his research and investigations regarding people or leads to be pursued, or not to be pursued, in connection with the '60 Minutes' segment and the Atlantic Monthly article;

2. Lando's conclusions about facts imparted by interviewees and his state of mind with respect to the veracity of persons interviewed;

3. The basis for conclusions where Lando testified that he did reach a conclusion concerning the veracity of persons, information or events;

4. Conversations between Lando and Wallace about matter to be included or excluded from the broadcast publication; and

5. Lando's intentions as manifested by his decision to include or exclude certain material.

Lando claimed he had a constitutional privilege to refuse to answer on the ground that the first amendment prohibited "inquiry into the state of mind of those who edit, produce or publish, and into the editorial process." The district court rejected the claim of privilege and ordered Lando to answer the questions. A divided court of appeals reversed. The Supreme Court granted certiorari and in turn reversed the court of appeals. The opinion of the Court was written by Justice White and joined by five other Justices including Justice Powell, who also wrote a concurring opinion. Both Justice White and Justice Powell reminded district courts of their power to insist on relevancy as a means of preventing the abuse of discovery procedures. Justice Brennan dissented in part. He concluded that questions pertaining to Lando's state of mind were permissible but not questions concerning Lando's conversations with Wallace during the editorial process. Justice Stewart in dissent thought the questions asked Lando were too broadranging to be relevant. Moreover, inquiry into the publisher's motives was clearly irrelevant. Justice Marshall also dissented. He contended that discovery requests in such litigation should be governed by strict standards of relevance. He furthermore argued that, while a journalist's state of mind could be probed, he "would foreclose discovery in defamation cases as to the substance of editorial conversation." For scholarly comment on various aspects of the case, *see* M. Franklin, *Reflections on* Herbert v. Lando, 31 Stan.L.Rev. 1035 (1979); J. Friedenthal, Herbert v. Lando: *A Note on Discovery,* 31 Stan.L.Rev. 1059 (1979).

6. *Fictionalized Quotations.* In Masson v. New Yorker Magazine, Inc., 501 U.S. 496, 111 S.Ct. 2419, 115 L.Ed.2d 447 (1991), the Court was confronted with a case in which Janet Malcolm, a co-defendant and free lance journalist, wrote a story about the plaintiff, Jeffrey Masson, and his disputes with Anna

Freud, the daughter of Sigmund Freud, and Dr. Kurt Eissler, the director of the Sigmund Freud Archives. The story was first published in two parts in the *New Yorker* and then in expanded form as a book. Masson had for a time been projects director of the Freud Archives but soon became disillusioned with Freudian Psychology. After Masson expressed his disillusionment in a public lecture delivered at the meeting of a professional association, he was terminated. In her story Malcolm used what purported to be a number of direct quotes which, however, could not be found in the tapes of her extensive interviews with Masson. For example, Masson was quoted as saying that, after his book was published, the psychoanalytic establishment "will say that Masson is a great scholar, a major analyst—after Freud he's the greatest analyst who ever lived." These statements did not appear in the tapes. The most germane portion of the tapes contain statements that "no analyst in the county . . . will say a single word in favor of Masson's work," that for a time Masson thought that it was "me and Freud against the world, or me and Freud and Anna Freud and Kur[t] Eissler * * * [and a few others] against the rest of the world. Not so, it's me. It's me alone." The tapes also contained an exchange between Masson and Malcolm in which Masson said "analysis stands or falls with me now," to which Malcolm replied "[w]ell that's a very grandiose thing to say," and Masson rejoined: "Yeah, but it's got nothing to do with me. It's got to do with the thing I discovered." The Court also discussed 5 additional instances of variances between the quotations attributed to Masson and the transcript of the tapes. The district court granted the defendants summary judgment and the court of appeals affirmed, 895 F.2d 1535 (9th Cir.1989). According to the Ninth Circuit, so long as the quotations in Malcolm's story were a reasonable interpretation of the interview the deviation between the material on the tapes and the published story did not establish either knowledge of falsity or reckless disregard of truth or falsity. The Court reversed as to all but one of the misquotations (having to do with why Masson at one time changed his middle name) and remanded. The Ninth Circuit's doctrine was too favorable to the defendant. Accepting that minor alterations of interviews to correct for mistakes of grammar or syntax were permissible, the Court concluded that "a deliberate alteration of the words uttered by a plaintiff does not equate with knowledge of falsity for purposes of New York Times Co. V. Sullivan * * * unless the alteration results in a material change in meaning." Justices White and Scalia dissented on that point. According to them, if a publication contains deliberate misquotations and the misquotations are defamatory, the plaintiff is entitled to go to the jury on the issue of whether the defendant made the statements with knowledge of falsity or with reckless disregard of truth or falsity.

7. Even leaving aside the problem of deliberate misquotation, establishing that the defendant was consciously or recklessly indifferent to the truth or falsity of statements is not always an easy matter. An instructive illustration is the involved litigation that gave rise to Tavoulareas v. Piro, 817 F.2d 762 (D.C.Cir.1987)(en banc), *cert. denied* 484 U.S. 870, 108 S.Ct. 200, 98 L.Ed.2d 151. The case involved a story that appeared in *The Washington Post* in which it was asserted that the plaintiff, William Tavoulareas, had used his influence as the president of Mobil Corporation to "set up" his son Peter, who was also a plaintiff in the litigation, as a partner in a shipping firm with a multimillion dollar management services contract with Mobil. The jury returned a verdict for the plaintiffs but this was vacated by the trial judge who awarded judgment notwithstanding the verdict to the *Post* and to its reporters and editors who

had been joined as defendants. A divided panel of the court of appeals reinstated the jury's verdict but the full court vacated that portion of the panel opinion and set the case for rehearing en banc. The full court of appeals, sitting en banc, affirmed in its entirety the district court's decision. The opinion for the court was filed by Judge Kenneth Starr and senior Judge J. Skelly Wright. The court of appeals first found that some of the most damning allegations in the *Post* story were substantially true. The court noted that ill-will towards the plaintiff or other bad motives are not elements of actual malice as that has been defined by the Supreme Court. Nevertheless, while admitting such evidence will undoubtedly have some chilling effect on honestly believed speech, the court was not prepared to rule out the possibility that, under some circumstances, the probative value of the evidence of ill-will, in establishing an intent to inflict harm through falsehood, would be sufficiently high that the value of admitting such evidence would outweigh that risk. The court found that the evidence of ill-will or bad motive in the case before it, however, lacked such high probative value. An extremely interesting part of the court's opinion was its dealing with the plaintiff's contention that an inference of reckless disregard for truth or falsity could be drawn from the fact that reporters were under managerial pressure to produce high impact stories. In the *Tavoulareas* case, a *Post* editor had testified at trial that he was looking for stories that would cause a person reading the *Post* to exclaim "holy shit".[a] The court held that, "managerial pressure to produce such stories cannot, as a matter of law, constitute evidence of actual malice." 817 F.2d at 796. In Harte–Hanks Communications, Inc. v. Connaughton, 491 U.S. 657, 109 S.Ct. 2678, 105 L.Ed.2d 562 (1989) the Court, citing *Lando* and *Tavoulareas,* declared that "it cannot be said that evidence concerning motive or care never bears any relation to the actual malice inquiry." Although "courts must be careful not to place too much reliance on such factors, a plaintiff is entitled to prove the defendant's state of mind through circumstantial evidence."

8. *Role of trial judge and jury.* As *Gertz* and the other Supreme Court cases described in this section indicate, the question of who is a public figure is a question of law to be decided by the court. *See also Restatement (Second) of Torts* § 580A, Comment *c.* When the issue at least is knowledge of falsity or reckless indifference to truth or falsity, the plaintiff must prove his case by "clear and convincing evidence" and not merely by the preponderance of the evidence. This is how the Court's declaration in *New York Times v. Sullivan* that constitutional malice must be shown with "convincing clarity" was interpreted by the lower federal courts and the state courts in cases such as Yiamouyiannis v. Consumers Union, 619 F.2d 932, 940 (2d Cir.1980), *cert. denied* 449 U.S. 839, 101 S.Ct. 117, 66 L.Ed.2d 46 and Burns v. Times Argus Association, Inc., 139 Vt. 381, 430 A.2d 773 (1981). This interpretation of *New York Times v. Sullivan* has been expressly accepted in a number of subsequent decisions of the Court. *See e.g.,* Bose Corp. v. Consumers Union of United States, Inc., 466 U.S. 485, 104 S.Ct. 1949, 80 L.Ed.2d 502 (1984). The Court in the *Bose* case also made clear that *New York Times v. Sullivan* made the issue of actual or constitutional malice one of "constitutional fact", that is a fact as to which a trial court deciding whether to accept a jury verdict or an appellate court reviewing a trial court decision must exercise an "independent judgment." It is not enough for there to be a reasonable basis for the decision being reviewed if the reviewing court is not convinced that the decision on this

a. The evidence on this point is examined more fully in the earlier panel opinion of the District of Columbia Circuit, Tavoulareas v. Piro, 759 F.2d 90, 120–21 (D.C.Cir.1985).

issue was the correct one. In ruling on a motion for summary judgment, however, the Court has more recently declared, in a case which arose in the federal courts, that, while a plaintiff may not avoid the granting of the motion if the evidence supporting his claim is "merely colorable", the motion should not be granted if there is "sufficient evidence favoring the non-moving party for a jury to return a verdict for that party." At this stage of litigation the trial judge is not to "weigh the evidence and determine the truth of the matter." But, at least in the federal courts, whether there is enough evidence to support a jury verdict in favor of the plaintiff must be determined in the light of the plaintiff's burden of proving constitutional malice by clear and convincing evidence. Anderson v. Liberty Lobby, Inc., 477 U.S. 242, 106 S.Ct. 2505, 91 L.Ed.2d 202 (1986). Several states, however, have expressly held that, in ruling on a motion for summary judgment, the trial court is merely to consider whether there is a "genuine issue of fact" and not to take into account the plaintiff's heightened burden of persuasion, because to do so would involve weighing the evidence which is the jury's prerogative. *See e.g.*, Dairy Stores, Inc. v. Sentinel Pub. Co., 104 N.J. 125, 516 A.2d 220 (1986); Moffatt v. Brown, 751 P.2d 939 (Alaska 1988). This of course makes it easier for the plaintiff to resist the granting of the motion.

GERTZ v. ROBERT WELCH, INC.

Supreme Court of the United States, 1974.
418 U.S. 323, 94 S.Ct. 2997, 41 L.Ed.2d 789.

Mr. Justice Powell delivered the opinion of the Court.

This Court has struggled for nearly a decade to define the proper accommodation between the law of defamation and the freedoms of speech and press protected by the First Amendment. With this decision we return to that effort. We granted certiorari to reconsider the extent of a publisher's constitutional privilege against liability for defamation of a private citizen. * * *

I

In 1968 a Chicago policeman named Nuccio shot and killed a youth named Nelson. The state authorities prosecuted Nuccio for the homicide and ultimately obtained a conviction for murder in the second degree. The Nelson family retained petitioner Elmer Gertz, a reputable attorney, to represent them in civil litigation against Nuccio.

Respondent publishes American Opinion, a monthly outlet for the views of the John Birch Society. Early in the 1960's the magazine began to warn of a nationwide conspiracy to discredit local law enforcement agencies and create in their stead a national police force capable of supporting a communist dictatorship. As part of the continuing effort to alert the public to this assumed danger, the managing editor of American Opinion commissioned an article on the murder trial of officer Nuccio. For this purpose he engaged a regular contributor to the magazine. In March of 1969 respondent published the resulting article under the title "FRAME–UP: Richard Nuccio And The War On Police." The article purports to demonstrate that the testimony against Nuccio at his criminal trial was false and that his prosecution was part of the communist campaign against the police.

In his capacity as counsel for the Nelson family in the civil litigation, petitioner attended the coroner's inquest into the boy's death and initiated actions for damages, but he neither discussed officer Nuccio with the press nor played any part in the criminal proceeding. Notwithstanding petitioner's remote connection with the prosecution of Nuccio, respondent's magazine portrayed him as an architect of the "frame-up." According to the article, the police file on petitioner took "a big, Irish cop to lift." The article stated that petitioner had been an official of the "Marxist League for Industrial Democracy, originally known as the Intercollegiate Socialist Society, which has advocated the violent seizure of our government." It labelled Gertz a "Leninist" and a "Communist-fronter." It also stated that Gertz had been an officer of the National Lawyers Guild, described as a communist organization that "probably did more than any other outfit to plan the Communist attack on the Chicago police during the 1968 Democratic convention."

These statements contained serious inaccuracies. The implication that petitioner had a criminal record was false. Petitioner had been a member and officer of the National Lawyers Guild some 15 years earlier, but there was no evidence that he or that organization had taken any part in planning the 1968 demonstrations in Chicago. There was also no basis for the charge that petitioner was a "Leninist" or a "Communist-fronter." And he had never been a member of the "Marxist League for Industrial Democracy" or the "Intercollegiate Socialist Society."

The managing editor of American Opinion made no effort to verify or substantiate the charges against petitioner. Instead, he appended an editorial introduction stating that the author had "concluded extensive research into the Richard Nuccio case." And he included in the article a photograph of petitioner and wrote the caption that appeared under it: "Elmer Gertz of the Red Guild harrasses Nuccio." Respondent placed the issue of American Opinion containing the article on sale at newsstands throughout the country and distributed reprints of the article on the streets of Chicago.

Petitioner filed a diversity action for libel in the United States District Court for the Northern District of Illinois. He claimed that the falsehoods published by respondent injured his reputation as a lawyer and a citizen. Before filing an answer, respondent moved to dismiss the complaint for failure to state a claim upon which relief could be granted, apparently on the ground that petitioner failed to allege special damages. But the court ruled that statements contained in the article constituted libel *per se* under Illinois law and that consequently petitioner need not plead special damages. * * *

After answering the complaint, respondent filed a pretrial motion for summary judgment, claiming a constitutional privilege against liability for defamation. It asserted that petitioner was a public official or a public figure and that the article concerned an issue of public interest and concern. For these reasons, respondent argued, it was entitled to invoke the privilege enunciated in New York Times Co. v. Sullivan. * * * Under this rule respondent would escape liability unless petitioner could prove publication of defamatory falsehood "with 'actual malice'—that is, in the knowledge that it was false or with reckless disregard for whether it was true or not." * * * Respondent claimed that petitioner could not make such a showing and submitted a supporting affidavit by the magazine's managing editor. The editor denied any knowledge of the falsity of the statements concerning petitioner and stated that he had relied on the author's reputation and on his prior experience with the accuracy and authenticity of his contributions to American Opinion.

The District Court denied respondent's motion for summary judgment in a memorandum opinion of Sept. 16, 1970. The court did not dispute respondent's claim to the protection of the *New York Times* standard. Rather, it concluded that petitioner might overcome the constitutional privilege by making a factual showing sufficient to prove publication of defamatory falsehood in reckless disregard of the truth. During the course of the trial, however, it became clear that the trial court had not accepted all of respondent's asserted grounds for applying the *New York Times* rule to this case. It thought that respondent's claim to the protection of the constitutional privilege depended on the contention that petitioner was either a public official under the *New York Times* decision or a public figure under Curtis Publishing Co. v. Butts, * * * apparently discounting the argument that a privilege would arise from the presence of a public issue. After all the evidence had been presented but before submission of the case to the jury, the court ruled in effect that petitioner was neither a public official nor a public figure. It added that, if he were, the resulting application of the *New York Times* standard would require a directed verdict for respondent. Because some statements in the article constituted libel *per se* under Illinois law, the court submitted the case to the jury under instructions that withdrew from its consideration all issues save the measure of damages. The jury awarded $50,000 to petitioner.

Following the jury verdict and on further reflection, the District Court concluded that the *New York Times* standard should govern this case even though petitioner was not a public official or public figure. It accepted respondent's contention that that privilege protected discussion of any public issue without regard to the status of a person defamed therein. Accordingly, the court entered judgment for respondent notwithstanding the jury's verdict. This conclusion anticipated the reasoning of a plurality of this Court in Rosenbloom v. Metromedia, Inc. * * *

Petitioner appealed to contest the applicability of the *New York Times* standard to this case. Although the Court of Appeals for the Seventh Circuit doubted the correctness of the District Court's determination that petitioner was not a public figure, it did not overturn that finding. It agreed with the District Court that respondent could assert the constitutional privilege because the article concerned a matter of public interest, citing this Court's intervening decision in Rosenbloom v. Metromedia, Inc., *supra*. The Court of Appeals read *Rosenbloom* to require application of the *New York Times* standard to any publication or broadcast about an issue of significant public interest, without regard to the position, fame, or anonymity of the person defamed, and it concluded that respondent's statements concerned such an issue. After reviewing the record, the Court of Appeals endorsed the District Court's conclusion that petitioner had failed to show by clear and convincing evidence that respondent had acted with "actual malice" as defined by *New York Times*. There was no evidence that the managing editor of American Opinion knew of the falsity of the accusations made in the article. In fact, he knew nothing about petitioner except what he learned from the article. The court correctly noted that mere proof of failure to investigate, without more, cannot establish reckless disregard for the truth. Rather, the publisher must act with a "high degree of awareness of * * * probable falsity." St. Amant v. Thompson, 390 U.S. 727, 731, 88 S.Ct. 1323, 1325, 20 L.Ed.2d 262 (1968). * * * The evidence in this case did not reveal that respondent had cause for such an awareness. The Court of Appeals therefore affirmed * * *. For the reasons stated below, we reverse.

II

The principal issue in this case is whether a newspaper or broadcaster that publishes defamatory falsehoods about an individual who is neither a public official nor a public figure may claim a constitutional privilege against liability for the injury inflicted by those statements. The Court considered this question on the rather different set of facts presented in Rosenbloom v. Metromedia, Inc. * * * Rosenbloom, a distributor of nudist magazines, was arrested for selling allegedly obscene material while making a delivery to a retail dealer. The police obtained a warrant and seized his entire inventory of 3,000 books and magazines. He sought and obtained an injunction prohibiting further police interference with his business. He then sued a local radio station for failing to note in two of its newscasts that the 3,000 items seized were only "reportedly" or "allegedly" obscene and for broadcasting references to "the smut literature racket" and to "girlie-book peddlers" in its coverage of the court proceeding for injunctive relief. He obtained a judgment against the radio station, but the Court of Appeals for the Third Circuit held the *New York Times* privilege applicable to the broadcast and reversed. * * *

This Court affirmed the decision below, but no majority could agree on a controlling rationale. The eight Justices who participated in *Rosenbloom* announced their views in five separate opinions, none of which commanded more than three votes. The several statements not only reveal disagreement about the appropriate result in that case; they also reflect divergent traditions of thought about the general problem of reconciling the law of defamation with the First Amendment. One approach has been to extend the *New York Times* test to an expanding variety of situations. Another has been to vary the level of constitutional privilege for defamatory falsehood with the status of the person defamed. And a third view would grant to the press and broadcast media absolute immunity from liability for defamation. * * *

* * *

III

We begin with the common ground. Under the First Amendment there is no such thing as a false idea. However pernicious an opinion may seem, we depend for its correction not on the conscience of judges and juries but on the competition of other ideas. But there is no constitutional value in false statements of fact. Neither the intentional lie nor the careless error materially advances society's interest in "uninhibited, robust, and wide-open" debate on public issues. * * *

Although the erroneous statement of fact is not worthy of constitutional protection, it is nevertheless inevitable in free debate. * * * The First Amendment requires that we protect some falsehood in order to protect speech that matters.

The need to avoid self-censorship by the news media is, however, not the only societal value at issue. If it were, this Court would have embraced long ago the view that publishers and broadcasters enjoy an unconditional and indefeasible immunity from liability for defamation. * * * Such a rule would indeed obviate the fear that the prospect of civil liability for injurious falsehood might dissuade a timorous press from the effective exercise of First Amendment freedoms. Yet absolute protection for the communications media requires a total sacrifice of the competing value served by the law of defamation.

The legitimate state interest underlying the law of libel is the compensation of individuals for the harm inflicted on them by defamatory falsehoods. We would not lightly require the State to abandon this purpose. * * *

Some tension necessarily exists between the need for a vigorous and uninhibited press and the legitimate interest in redressing wrongful injury. * * * To that end this Court has extended a measure of strategic protection to defamatory falsehood.

The *New York Times* standard defines the level of constitutional protection appropriate to the context of defamation of a public person. Those who, by reason of the notoriety of their achievements or the vigor and success with which they seek the public's attention, are properly classed as public figures and those who hold governmental office may recover for injury to reputation only on clear and convincing proof that the defamatory falsehood was made with knowledge of its falsity or with reckless disregard for the truth. This standard administers an extremely powerful antidote to the inducement to media self-censorship of the common law rule of strict liability for libel and slander. And it exacts a correspondingly high price from the victims of defamatory falsehood. Plainly many deserving plaintiffs, including some intentionally subjected to injury, will be unable to surmount the barrier of the *New York Times* test. Despite this substantial abridgement of the state law right to compensation for wrongful hurt to one's reputation, the Court has concluded that the protection of the *New York Times* privilege should be available to publishers and broadcasters of defamatory falsehoods concerning public officials and public figures. * * * We think that these decisions are correct, but we do not find their holdings justified solely by reference to the interest of the press and broadcast media in immunity from liability. Rather, we believe that the *New York Times* rule states an accommodation between this concern and the limited state interest present in the context of libel actions brought by public persons. For the reasons stated below, we conclude that the state interest in compensating injury to the reputation of private individuals requires that a different rule should obtain with respect to them.

Theoretically, of course, the balance between the needs of the press and the individual's claim to compensation for wrongful injury might be struck on a case-by-case basis. * * * But this approach would lead to unpredictable results and uncertain expectations, and it could render our duty to supervise the lower courts unmanageable. Because an *ad hoc* resolution of the competing interests at stake in each particular case is not feasible, we must lay down broad rules of general application. Such rules necessarily treat alike various cases involving differences as well as similarities. Thus it is often true that not all of the considerations which justify adoption of a given rule will obtain in each particular case decided under its authority.

With that caveat we have no difficulty in distinguishing among defamation plaintiffs. The first remedy of any victim of defamation is self-help—using available opportunities to contradict the lie or correct the error and thereby to minimize its adverse impact on reputation. Public officials and public figures usually enjoy significantly greater access to the channels of effective communication and hence have a more realistic opportunity to counteract false statements than private individuals normally enjoy.[9] Private individuals are therefore more vulnerable to injury, and the state interest in protecting them is correspondingly greater.

More important than the likelihood that private individuals will lack effective opportunities for rebuttal, there is a compelling normative consideration underlying the distinction between public and private defamation plaintiffs. An individual who decides to seek governmental office must accept certain necessary consequences of that involvement in public affairs. He runs the risk of closer public scrutiny than might otherwise be the case. And society's interest in the officers of government is not strictly limited to the formal discharge of official duties. * * *

Those classed as public figures stand in a similar position. Hypothetically, it may be possible for someone to become a public figure through no purposeful action of his own, but the instances of truly involuntary public figures must be exceedingly rare. For the most part those who attain this status have assumed roles of especial prominence in the affairs of society. Some occupy positions of such persuasive power and influence that they are deemed public figures for all purposes. More commonly, those classed as public figures have thrust themselves to the forefront of particular public controversies in order to influence the resolution of the issues involved. In either event, they invite attention and comment.

Even if the foregoing generalities do not obtain in every instance, the communications media are entitled to act on the assumption that public officials and public figures have voluntarily exposed themselves to increased risk of injury from defamatory falsehoods concerning them. No such assumption is justified with respect to a private individual. * * * He has relinquished no part of his interest in the protection of his own good name, and consequently he has a more compelling call on the courts for

9. Of course, an opportunity for rebuttal seldom suffices to undo harm of defamatory falsehood. Indeed, the law of defamation is rooted in our experience that the truth rarely catches up with a lie. But the fact that the self-help remedy of rebuttal, standing alone, is inadequate to its task does not mean that it is irrelevant to our inquiry.

redress of injury inflicted by defamatory falsehood. Thus, private individuals are not only more vulnerable to injury than public officials and public figures; they are also more deserving of recovery.

For these reasons we conclude that the States should retain substantial latitude in their efforts to enforce a legal remedy for defamatory falsehood injurious to the reputation of a private individual. The extension of the *New York Times* test proposed by the *Rosenbloom* plurality would abridge this legitimate state interest to a degree that we find unacceptable. And it would occasion the additional difficulty of forcing state and federal judges to decide on an *ad hoc* basis which publications address issues of "general or public interest" and which do not—to determine, in the words of Mr. Justice Marshall, "what information is relevant to self-government." Rosenbloom v. Metromedia, Inc. * * * We doubt the wisdom of committing this task to the conscience of judges. Nor does the Constitution require us to draw so thin a line between the drastic alternatives of the *New York Times* privilege and the common law of strict liability for defamatory error. The "public or general interest" test for determining the applicability of the *New York Times* standard to private defamation actions inadequately serves both of the competing values at stake. On the one hand, a private individual whose reputation is injured by defamatory falsehood that does concern an issue of public or general interest has no recourse unless he can meet the rigorous requirements of *New York Times*. This is true despite the factors that distinguish the state interest in compensating private individuals from the analogous interest involved in the context of public persons. On the other hand, a publisher or broadcaster of a defamatory error which a court deems unrelated to an issue of public or general interest may be held liable in damages even if it took every reasonable precaution to ensure the accuracy of its assertions. And liability may far exceed compensation for any actual injury to the plaintiff, for the jury may be permitted to presume damages without proof of loss and even to award punitive damages.

We hold that, so long as they do not impose liability without fault, the States may define for themselves the appropriate standard of liability for a publisher or broadcaster of defamatory falsehood injurious to a private individual. This approach provides a more equitable boundary between the competing concerns involved here. It recognizes the strength of the legitimate state interest in compensating private individuals for wrongful injury to reputation, yet shields the press and broadcast media from the rigors of strict liability for defamation. At least this conclusion obtains where, as here, the substance of the defamatory statement "makes substantial danger to reputation apparent." This phrase places in perspective the conclusion we announce today. Our inquiry would involve considerations somewhat different from those discussed above if a State purported to condition civil liability on a factual misstatement whose content did not warn a reasonably prudent editor or broadcaster of its defamatory potential. Cf. Time, Inc. v. Hill. * * * Such a case is not now before us, and we intimate no view as to its proper resolution.

IV

Our accommodation of the competing values at stake in defamation suits by private individuals allows the States to impose liability on the publisher or broadcaster of defamatory falsehoods on a less demanding showing than that required by *New York Times*.   This conclusion is not based on a belief that the considerations which prompted the adoption of the *New York Times* privilege for defamation of public officials and its extension to public figures are wholly inapplicable to the context of private individuals.   Rather, we endorse this approach in recognition of the strong and legitimate state interest in compensating private individuals for injury to reputation.   But this countervailing state interest extends no further than compensation for actual injury.   For the reasons stated below, we hold that the States may not permit recovery of presumed or punitive damages, at least when liability is not based on a showing of knowledge of falsity or reckless disregard for the truth.

The common law of defamation is an oddity of tort law, for it allows recovery of purportedly compensatory damages without evidence of actual loss.   Under the traditional rules pertaining to actions for libel, the existence of injury is presumed from the fact of publication.   Juries may award substantial sums as compensation for supposed damage to reputation without any proof that such harm actually occurred.   The largely uncontrolled discretion of juries to award damages where there is no loss unnecessarily compounds the potential of any system of liability for defamatory falsehood to inhibit the vigorous exercise of First Amendment freedoms.   Additionally, the doctrine of presumed damages invites juries to punish unpopular opinion rather than to compensate individuals for injury sustained by the publication of a false fact.   More to the point, the States have no substantial interest in securing for plaintiffs such as this petitioner gratuitous awards of money damages far in excess of any actual injury.

We would not, of course, invalidate state law simply because we doubt its wisdom, but here we are attempting to reconcile state law with a competing interest grounded in the constitutional command of the First Amendment.   * * * We need not define "actual injury," as trial courts have wide experience in framing appropriate jury instructions in tort action.   Suffice it to say that actual injury is not limited to out-of-pocket loss.   Indeed, the more customary types of actual harm inflicted by defamatory falsehood include impairment of reputation and standing in the community, personal humiliation, and mental anguish and suffering.   Of course, juries must be limited by appropriate instructions, and all awards must be supported by competent evidence concerning the injury, although there need be no evidence which assigns an actual dollar value to the injury.

We also find no justification for allowing awards of punitive damages against publishers and broadcasters held liable under state-defined standards of liability for defamation.   In most jurisdictions jury discretion over the amounts awarded is limited only by the gentle rule that they not be excessive.   Consequently, juries assess punitive damages in wholly unpredictable amounts bearing no necessary relation to the actual harm caused.   And they remain free to use their discretion selectively to punish expressions of unpopular views.   Like the doctrine of presumed damages, jury discretion to award punitive damages unnecessarily exacerbates the danger of media self-censorship, but, unlike the former rule, punitive damages are wholly irrelevant to the state interest that justifies a negligence standard for private defamation actions.   * * * In short, the private defamation plaintiff who establishes liability under a less demanding standard than that stated by *New York Times* may recover only such damages as are sufficient to compensate him for actual injury.

V

Notwithstanding our refusal to extend the *New York Times* privilege to defamation of private individuals, respondent contends that we should affirm the judgment below on the ground that petitioner is either a public official or a public figure. There is little basis for the former assertion. Several years prior to the present incident, petitioner had served briefly on housing committees appointed by the mayor of Chicago, but at the time of publication he had never held any remunerative governmental position. Respondent admits this but argues that petitioner's appearance at the coroner's inquest rendered him a "de facto public official." Our cases recognized no such concept. Respondent's suggestion would sweep all lawyers under the *New York Times* rule as officers of the court and distort the plain meaning of the "public official" category beyond all recognition. We decline to follow it.

Respondent's characterization of petitioner as a public figure raises a different question. That designation may rest on either of two alternative bases. In some instances an individual may achieve such pervasive fame or notoriety that he becomes a public figure for all purposes and in all contexts. More commonly, an individual voluntarily injects himself or is drawn into a particular public controversy and thereby becomes a public figure for a limited range of issues. In either case such persons assume special prominence in the resolution of public questions.

Petitioner has long been active in community and professional affairs. He has served as an officer of local civil groups and of various professional organizations, and he has published several books and articles on legal subjects. Although petitioner was consequently well-known in some circles, he had achieved no general fame or notoriety in the community. None of the prospective jurors called at the trial had ever heard of petitioner prior to this litigation, and respondent offered no proof that this response was atypical of the local population. We would not lightly assume that a citizen's participation in community and professional affairs rendered him a public figure for all purposes. Absent clear evidence of general fame or notoriety in the community, and pervasive involvement in the affairs of society, an individual should not be deemed a public personality for all aspects of his life. It is preferable to reduce the public figure question to a more meaningful context by looking to the nature and extent of an individual's participation in the particular controversy giving rise to the defamation.

In this context it is plain that petitioner was not a public figure.   * * *

We therefore conclude that the *New York Times* standard is inapplicable to this case and that the trial court erred in entering judgment for respondent. Because the jury was allowed to impose liability without fault and was permitted to presume damages without proof of injury, a new trial is necessary. We reverse and remand for further proceedings in accord with this opinion.

It is so ordered.

Reversed and remanded.

MR. JUSTICE BLACKMUN, concurring.

I joined Mr. Justice Brennan's opinion for the plurality in Rosenbloom v. Metromedia, Inc. * * *. I did so because I concluded that, given New York Times Co. v. Sullivan * * * and its progeny * * * the step taken in *Rosenbloom,* extending the *New York Times* doctrine to an event of public or general interest, was logical and inevitable. A majority of the Court evidently thought otherwise * * *.

The Court today refuses to apply *New York Times* to the private individual, as contrasted with the public official and the public figure. It thus withdraws to the factual limits of the pre-*Rosenbloom* cases. It thereby fixes the outer boundary of the *New York Times* doctrine and says that beyond that boundary, a State is free to define for itself the appropriate standard of a media's liability so long as it does not impose liability without fault. As my joinder in *Rosenbloom's* plurality opinion would intimate, I sense some illogic in this.

The Court, however, seeks today to strike a balance between competing values where necessarily uncertain assumptions about human behavior color the result. Although the Court's opinion in the present case departs from the rationale of the *Rosenbloom* plurality, in that the Court now conditions a libel action by a private person upon a showing of negligence, as contrasted with a showing of willful or reckless disregard, I am willing to join, and do join, the Court's opinion and its judgment for two reasons:

1. By removing the spectres of presumed and punitive damages in the absence of *New York Times* malice, the Court eliminates significant and powerful motives for self-censorship that otherwise are present in the traditional libel action. * * *

2. The Court was sadly fractionated in *Rosenbloom.* A result of that kind inevitably leads to uncertainty. I feel that it is of profound importance for the Court to come to rest in the defamation area and to have a clearly defined majority position that eliminates the unsureness engendered by *Rosenbloom's* diversity. If my vote were not needed to create a majority, I would adhere to my prior view. A definitive ruling, however, is paramount. * * *

For these reasons, I join the opinion and the judgment of the Court.

MR. CHIEF JUSTICE BURGER, dissenting.

The doctrines of the law of defamation have had a gradual evolution primarily in the state courts. In New York Times Co. v. Sullivan and its progeny this Court entered this field.

Agreement or disagreement with the law as it has evolved to this time does not alter the fact that it has been orderly development with a consistent basic rationale. In today's opinion the Court abandons the traditional thread so far as the ordinary private citizen is concerned and introduces the concept that the media will be liable for negligence in publishing defamatory statements with respect to such persons. Although I agree with much of what Mr. Justice White states, I do not read the

Court's new doctrinal approach in quite the way he does. I am frank to say I do not know the parameters of a "negligence" doctrine as applied to the news media. Conceivably this new doctrine could inhibit some editors, as the dissents of Mr. Justice Douglas and Mr. Justice Brennan suggest. But I would prefer to allow this area of law to continue to evolve as it has up to now with respect to private citizens rather than embark on a new doctrinal theory which has no jurisprudential ancestry.

* * *

MR. JUSTICE DOUGLAS, dissenting.

The Court describes this case as a return to the struggle of "defin[ing] the proper accommodation between the law of defamation and the freedoms of speech and press protected by the First Amendment." * * * I would suggest that the struggle is a quite hopeless one, for, in light of the command of the First Amendment, no "accommodation" of its freedoms can be "proper" except those made by the Framers themselves.

Unlike the right of privacy which, by the terms of the Fourth Amendment, must be accommodated with reasonable searches and seizures and warrants issued by magistrates, the rights of free speech and of a free press were protected by the Framers in verbiage whose prescription seems clear. * * *

* * *

Since in my view the First and Fourteenth Amendments prohibit the imposition of damages upon respondent for this discussion of public affairs, I would affirm the judgment below.

MR. JUSTICE BRENNAN, dissenting.

I agree with the conclusion, expressed in Part V of the Court's opinion, that, at the time of publication of respondent's article, petitioner could not properly have been viewed as either a "public official" or "public figure"; instead, respondent's article, dealing with an alleged conspiracy to discredit local police forces, concerned petitioner's purported involvement in "an event of 'public or general interest.' " Rosenbloom v. Metromedia, Inc. * * * I cannot agree, however, that free and robust debate—so essential to the proper functioning of our system of government—is permitted adequate "breathing space," * * * when, as the Court holds, the States may impose all but strict liability for defamation if the defamed party is a private person and "the substance of the defamatory statement 'makes substantial danger to reputation apparent.' " * * * I adhere to my view expressed in Rosenbloom v. Metromedia, Inc., *supra,* that we strike the proper accommodation between avoidance of media self-censorship and protection of individual reputations only when we require States to apply the New York Times Co. v. Sullivan * * * knowing-or-reckless-falsity standard in civil libel actions concerning media reports of the involvement of private individuals in events of public or general interest.

* * *

Since petitioner failed, after having been given a full and fair opportunity, to prove that respondent published the disputed article with knowledge of its falsity or with reckless disregard of the truth * * *, I would affirm the judgment of the Court of Appeals.

MR. JUSTICE WHITE, dissenting.

For some 200 years—from the very founding of the Nation—the law of defamation and right of the ordinary citizen to recover for false publication injurious to his reputation have been almost exclusively the business of state courts and legislatures. Under typical state defamation law, the defamed private citizen had to prove only a false publication that would subject him to hatred, contempt or ridicule. Given such publication, general damages to reputation were presumed, while punitive damages required proof of additional facts. The law governing the defamation of private citizens remained untouched by the First Amendment because until relatively recently, the consistent view of the Court was that libelous words constitute a class of speech wholly unprotected by the First Amendment, subject only to limited exceptions carved out since 1964.

But now, using that amendment as the chosen instrument, the Court, in a few printed pages, has federalized major aspects of libel law by declaring unconstitutional in important respects the prevailing defamation law in all or most of the 50 States. That result is accomplished by requiring the plaintiff in each and every defamation action to prove not only the defendant's culpability beyond his act of publishing defamatory material but also actual damage to reputation resulting from the publication. Moreover, punitive damages may not be recovered by showing malice in the traditional sense of ill will; knowing falsehood or reckless disregard of the truth will now be required.

I assume these sweeping changes will be popular with the press, but this is not the road to salvation for a court of law. As I see it, there are wholly insufficient grounds for scuttling the libel laws of the States in such wholesale fashion, to say nothing of deprecating the reputation interest of ordinary citizens and rendering them powerless to protect themselves. I do not suggest that the decision is illegitimate or beyond the bounds of judicial review, but it is an ill-considered exercise of the power entrusted to this Court, particularly when the Court has not had the benefit of briefs and argument addressed to most of the major issues which the Court now decides. I respectfully dissent.

* * *

II

* * *

The central meaning of *New York Times,* and for me the First Amendment as it relates to libel laws, is that seditious libel—criticism of government and public officials—falls beyond the police power of the State. * * * In a democratic society such as ours, the citizen has the privilege of criticizing his government and its officials. But neither *New York Times* nor its progeny suggest that the First Amendment intended in all circumstances to deprive the private citizen of his historic recourse to redress published falsehoods damaging to reputation or that, contrary to history and precedent, the Amendment should now be so interpreted.   * * *

* * *

V

In disagreeing with the Court on the First Amendment's reach in the area of state libel laws protecting nonpublic persons, I do not repudiate the principle that the First Amendment "rests on the assumption that the widest possible dissemination of information from diverse and antagonistic sources is essential to the welfare of the public, that a free press is a condition of a free society." Associated Press v. United States, 326 U.S. 1, 20, 65 S.Ct. 1416, 1425, 89 L.Ed. 2013 (1945).   * * * I continue to subscribe to *New York Times* and those decisions extending its protection to defamatory falsehoods about public persons. My quarrel with the Court stems from its willingness "to sacrifice good sense to a syllogism"[39]—to find in the *New York Times* doctrine an infinite elasticity. Unfortunately, this expansion is the latest manifestation of the destructive potential of any good idea carried out to its logical extreme.

* * *

I fail to see how the quality or quantity of public debate will be promoted by further emasculation of state libel laws for the benefit of the news media. If anything, this trend may provoke a new and radical imbalance in the communications process.   * * * It is not at all inconceivable that virtually unrestrained defamatory remarks about private citizens will discourage them from speaking out and concerning themselves with social problems. This would turn the First Amendment on its head.   * * *

* * *

In our federal system, there must be room for allowing the States to take diverse approaches to these vexing questions.   * * * Whether or not the course followed by the majority is wise, and I have indicated my doubts that it is, our constitutional scheme compels a proper respect for the role of the States in acquitting their duty to obey the Constitution. Finding no evidence that they have shirked this responsibility, particularly when the law of defamation is even now in transition, I would await some demonstration of the diminution of freedom of expression before acting.

* * *

Notes

1.   Most of Justice White's long dissent has been omitted. In describing the modern law of defamation, Justice White relied upon *Restatement (Second) of Torts* Tentative Draft No. 12, 1966. In particular he relied upon § 569 of the Tentative Draft No. 12, which distinguished between libel that was clear on its face and libel that was not. In our discussion, *supra,* p. 1081, we saw that at one time the drafters of the *Restatement (Second)* had proposed making libelous statements that were not defamatory on their face actionable without proof of special damages only if they fell within the slander per se categories. (Note

---

39. O. Holmes, The Common Law 36 (1881).

Justice White's statement that the law of defamation of the several states was "in transition.") By the time of the *Gertz* decision, however, the drafters of the *Restatement (Second)* had abandoned that position and reverted to the English common-law position. *See Restatement (Second) of Torts* § 569 (Tent. Draft No. 20, 1974), and as we have already seen this is the position taken by the final version of the *Restatement (Second)*.

2. It should be noted that Justice Powell, in writing the opinion of the Court in *Gertz,* spoke in terms of actions against a "publisher or broadcaster." It is thus possible to argue that *Gertz* only applies in actions by private figures against the news media; actions by private figures against non-media defendants would thus be governed by the traditional common law. In the portion of his dissent reprinted above, Chief Justice Burger indicates his view that Justice Powell was only speaking about actions against "news media." Justice Powell's opinion was also interpreted in this manner in M. Nimmer, *Introduction—Is Freedom of the Press a Redundancy: What Does It Add to Freedom of Speech?*, 26 Hastings L.J. 639 (1975). *See also* M. Nimmer, *Speech and Press: A Brief Reply,* 23 U.C.L.A.L.Rev. 120 (1975). Moreover, former Justice Stewart publicly expressed the view that the media are in fact granted special protection by the First Amendment. *See* P. Stewart, *"Or of the Press,"* 26 Hastings L.J. 631 (1975). And Justice Stewart joined in Justice Powell's opinion for the Court in *Gertz.* Nevertheless, by the time *Gertz* was decided, the Court had already rejected the notion that the press has any special privileges not enjoyed by the rest of society. *See* Branzburg v. Hayes, 408 U.S. 665, 92 S.Ct. 2646, 33 L.Ed.2d 626 (1972). *See also Herbert v. Lando,* discussed at p. 1148, *supra.* Moreover, as is conceded by Professor Nimmer, it is generally agreed that the founding fathers used the terms "freedom of speech" and "freedom of the press" interchangeably and that when they spoke about the "press" they were probably adverting to Blackstone's idea of "no prior restraint," *i.e.* to the freedom to publish. *See* L. Levy, Legacy of Suppression (1960); D. Lange, *The Speech and Press Clauses,* 23 U.C.L.A.L.Rev. 77 (1975).[a] Moreover, if the press does have special privileges, who constitutes the press? What about a professor researching a book? *Cf.* United States v. Doe, 460 F.2d 328 (1st Cir.1972), *cert. denied* 411 U.S. 909, 93 S.Ct. 1527, 36 L.Ed.2d 199 (1973)(professor at Harvard denied any privileges not enjoyed by citizens at large to refuse to answer questions before a grand jury concerning the leakage of the "Pentagon Papers.") Nevertheless, a few state courts have restricted *Gertz* to actions by private figures against the media. *See* Harley–Davidson Motorsports, Inc. v. Markley, 279 Or. 361, 568 P.2d 1359 (1977). *See also* Denny v. Mertz, 106 Wis.2d 636, 318 N.W.2d 141 (1982); Rowe v. Metz, 195 Colo. 424, 579 P.2d 83 (1978); Calero v. Del Chemical Corp., 68 Wis.2d 487, 228 N.W.2d 737 (1975).

a. It is hard to tell exactly what regulation of speech is permitted by the first amendment because, as has often been very persuasively argued, there is a very strong and persuasive case that the first amendment was intended principally as a proposition about federalism, namely that regulation of speech was a matter for the states and not for Congress. *See* W. Van Alstyne, *Congressional Power and Free Speech: Levy's Legacy Revisited* (Book Review), 99 Harv.L.Rev. 1089 (1986). This is a review of L. Levy, Emergence of a Free Press (1985), which is in effect a second edition of Levy's *Legacy of Suppression* cited in the text. *See also* P. Kurland, *Public Policy, the Constitution and the Supreme Court,* 12 N.Ky.L.Rev. 181 (1985). This reading, which may very well be totally correct, may help explain why it is difficult to apply against the states, whom the founding fathers did believe had some authority to regulate speech, a provision which the founding fathers may well have thought absolutely prohibited any regulation by the Congress.

Most state courts that have considered the question, however, have concluded that no such distinction is possible. *See, e.g.,* Jacron Sales Co. v. Sindorf, 276 Md. 580, 350 A.2d 688 (1976); Ryder Truck Rentals v. Latham, 593 S.W.2d 334 (Tex.Civ.App.1979). *See also* Gray v. Allison Division, General Motors Corp., 52 Ohio App.2d 348, 370 N.E.2d 747 (1977). This is the position taken by the *Restatement (Second) of Torts* §§ 558, 580B, Comment *e*. We will return to this question again when we examine Dun & Bradstreet, Inc. v. Greenmoss Builders, Inc., 472 U.S. 749, 105 S.Ct. 2939, 86 L.Ed.2d 593 (1985) at p. 1176, *infra.*

3. On the same day that the Court decided *Gertz,* it also decided Old Dominion Branch No. 496, National Association of Letter Carriers v. Austin, 418 U.S. 264, 94 S.Ct. 2770, 41 L.Ed.2d 745 (1974). In that case the three plaintiff letter carriers who were among a group of fifteen out of 435 who were not members of the defendant union, were described as "scabs" in the union newsletter and then likened to Esau, Judas, and Benedict Arnold. The newsletter continued by quoting Jack London's definition of a "scab" as "a traitor to his God, his country, his family and his class." The plaintiffs had recovered substantial damages for defamation in the trial courts and the Supreme Court of Virginia had affirmed. The Supreme Court of the United States, however, reversed. Writing through Justice Marshall, the Court, with three dissents, held that the *Sullivan* standards were applicable because the statements in question had been made in the course of what was arguably a "labor dispute." Although most of the opinion of the Court discusses the applicability of the *Sullivan* standards, the Court went on to hold in the alternative that the statements in the newsletter were in any event not actionable because they involved mere expressions of opinion and the use of epithets. Can the *Old Dominion* case be confined to labor disputes or is it an indication that the newsworthiness issue cannot be avoided? Can debate about labor matters be freer than debate about politics, foreign relations, or social issues like abortion? The *Old Dominion* case, together with the immediate *post-Gertz* developments, is discussed in G. Christie, *Injury to Reputation and the Constitution: Confusion Amid Conflicting Approaches,* 75 Mich.L.Rev. 43 (1976). Decisions of the Court since *Old Dominion* rejecting content based regulation of speech activities makes it even harder to restrict *Old Dominion's* extension of the *Sullivan* standard in actions involving private figures as plaintiffs to the labor relations area. *See* G. Christie, *Underlying Contradictions in the Supreme Court's Classification of Defamation,* 1981 Duke L.J. 811.

4. While most state courts have accepted the distinction drawn in *Gertz* between public officials and public figures on the one hand and private persons on the other, some courts have refused to join the Court in its retreat from *Rosenbloom v. Metromedia, Inc.* and have continued to require a showing of intended falsehood or reckless disregard for truth, at least when the defamatory statement concerns an issue of public interest. *See, e.g.,* Walker v. Colorado Springs Sun, Inc., 188 Colo. 86, 538 P.2d 450 (1975), *cert. denied* 423 U.S. 1025, 96 S.Ct. 469, 46 L.Ed.2d 399, as extended by Diversified Management, Inc. v. Denver Post, Inc., 653 P.2d 1103 (Colo.1982); AAFCO Heating & Air Conditioning Co. v. Northwest Publications, Inc., 162 Ind.App. 671, 321 N.E.2d 580 (1974), *cert. denied* 424 U.S. 913, 96 S.Ct. 1112, 47 L.Ed.2d 318 (1976); Schaefer v. State Bar, 77 Wis.2d 120, 252 N.W.2d 343 (1977); Dairy Stores, Inc. v. Sentinel Pub. Co., 104 N.J. 125, 516 A.2d 220 (1986). See *also* Gay v. Williams, 486 F.Supp. 12 (D.Alaska 1979). New York has adopted an intermediate position. In a case reminiscent of *Rosenbloom v. Metromedia, Inc.,* the

New York Court of Appeals held that when a private individual is defamed in an article whose

> content * * * is arguably within the sphere of legitimate public concern, which is reasonably related to matters warranting public exposition * * * [the plaintiff] must establish, by a preponderance of the evidence, that the publisher acted in a grossly irresponsible manner without due consideration for the standards of information gathering and dissemination ordinarily followed by responsible parties.

Chapadeau v. Utica Observer–Dispatch, Inc., 38 N.Y.2d 196, 199, 379 N.Y.S.2d 61, 64, 341 N.E.2d 569, 571 (1975). Recent compilations of how the various states have handled this question are contained in Lansdowne v. Beacon Journal Pub. Co., 32 Ohio St.3d 176, 186–87, 512 N.E.2d 979, 989–90 (1987)(concurring opinion); Rouch v. Enquirer & News of Battle Creek, 427 Mich. 157, 187–89, 398 N.W.2d 245, 259–60 (1986).

5. On retrial, the jury awarded Gertz $100,000 in compensatory damages and $300,000 in punitive damages. The Seventh Circuit affirmed, finding more than enough evidence that the article was published with "utter disregard for truth or falsity." 680 F.2d 527 (7th Cir.1982), *cert. denied*, 459 U.S. 1226, 103 S.Ct. 1233, 75 L.Ed.2d 467 (1983).

6. *Fact vs. Opinion.* Actually deciding what is opinion and what is fact can sometimes be a very difficult task whose difficulty has been highlighted now that the Court has held that the distinction between fact and opinion is one of constitutional significance. It has long been recognized that the expression of some opinions clearly gives rise in the minds of a reasonable reader or listener to the conclusion that the speaker or writer has a factual basis for the statement that has been made. The Court, in Milkovich v. Lorain Journal Co., 497 U.S. 1, 110 S.Ct. 2695, 111 L.Ed.2d 1 (1990) has rebuked those who sought to read *Gertz* as providing a blanket immunity, on first amendment grounds, to all expressions of opinion. If an allegedly defamatory opinion reasonably implies a statement that is "sufficiently factual to be susceptible of being proved true or false," the so-called opinion is actionable provided the other hurdles to bringing an action for defamation are met.

But the awareness that some so-called expressions of opinion are capable of being interpreted as implicit statements of fact only begins to illustrate the difficulty that can sometimes be experienced in deciding what is opinion rather than fact. An important case is Ollman v. Evans, 750 F.2d 970 (D.C.Cir. 1984)(en banc), in which the eleven judges who heard the case issued seven different opinions. The case involved nationally syndicated columnists Evans and Novak who had commented on a proposal to name the plaintiff, who had been a professor at New York University, as Chairman of the Department of Government and Politics at the University of Maryland. The columnists tried to draw a distinction between the plaintiff's qualifications as a scholar which they were prepared to recognize was not the crucial issue, and his allegedly active support for what they termed "political marxism". Nevertheless the columnists did include a statement from someone identified as a "political scientist in a major eastern university whose scholarship and reputation as a liberal are well known" that the plaintiff had "no status within the profession but is a pure and simple activist." On what they considered to be the main issue, the columnists had declared, partially using quotations that purported to be from the plaintiff's own work, that the plaintiff believed that the classroom should be a place to convert students to socialism and to dismantle the students' "bourgeois ideology" and that " 'our prior task' before the revolution he writes 'is to make more revolutionaries' ". The majority of the court of appeals held that all these statements represented mere statements of opinions. Writing for the majority of the court, Judge Kenneth Starr surveyed the several methods that had been put forward for distinguishing between fact and opinion. Some courts had treated the matter as a judgment call to be made by the judiciary and others have focused upon the lack of verifiability of the allegedly defamatory statements. Other courts have adopted a multifactor test under which they attempted to analyze the statements in question in the context of the totality of the circumstances in which they appeared. Judge Starr himself started by analyzing common usage, that is whether the language had a precise core of meaning or whether the statement in question was indefinite and ambiguous. He then considered the verifiability of the statement in question. Next he turned to the full textual context in which the statement appeared, that is the entire article. Finally, he considered the broader social context or setting in which the statement appeared. Judge Robert Bork, in the concurring opinion in which three other judges joined, felt that all of the allegedly libelous statements at issue were expressions of opinion but that the majority had not adequately explained why. Judge Bork rejected the suggestion that the Supreme Court had imposed any sharp dividing line between opinions which are not actionable as libel and facts which are. Judge Antonin Scalia, who after his elevation to the Supreme Court, was one of the Justices joining the Court's opinion in *Milkovich*, dissented from the conclusion that the statements about the plaintiff having no status in the profession was merely an opinion as to which no action would lie. Judges Patricia Wald and Harry Edwards both concurred with Judge Scalia. The *Ollman* case gave rise to voluminous literature on this difficult subject. *See e.g.,* Note, *The Fact–Opinion Determination in Defamation,* 88 Colum.L.Rev. 809 (1988); Comment, *The Fact/Opinion Distinction: an Analysis of the Subjectivity of Language in Law,* 70 Marq.L.Rev. 673 (1987); Note, *The Fact–Opinion Dilemma and First Amendment Defamation Law,* 13 Wm. Mitchell L.Rev. 545 (1987); Comment, *Structuring Defamation Law to Eliminate the Fact–Opinion Determination: A Critique of* Ollman v. Evans, 71 Iowa L.Rev. 913 (1986). Since the Court's decision in *Milkovich*, whether the statement in question is capable of verification or falsification has undoubtedly taken on greater importance.

TIME, INC. v. FIRESTONE

Supreme Court of the United States, 1976.
424 U.S. 448, 96 S.Ct. 958, 47 L.Ed.2d 154.

Mr. Justice Rehnquist delivered the opinion of the Court.

Petitioner is the publisher of Time, a weekly news magazine. The Supreme Court of Florida affirmed a $100,000 libel judgment against petitioner which was based on an item appearing in Time that purported to describe the result of domestic relations litigation between respondent and her husband. We granted certiorari * * * to review petitioner's claim that the judgment violates its rights under the First and Fourteenth Amendments to the United States Constitution.

I

Respondent, Mary Alice Firestone, married Russell Firestone, the scion of one of America's wealthier industrial families, in 1961. In 1964, they separated, and respondent filed a complaint for separate maintenance in the Circuit Court of Palm Beach County, Fla. Her husband counterclaimed for divorce on grounds of extreme cruelty and adultery. After a lengthy trial the Circuit Court issued a judgment granting the divorce requested by respondent's husband. In relevant part the court's final judgment read:

> "This cause came on for final hearing before the court upon the plaintiff wife's second amended complaint for separate maintenance (alimony unconnected with the causes of divorce), the defendant husband's answer and counterclaim for divorce on grounds of extreme cruelty and adultery, and the wife's answer thereto setting up certain affirmative defenses. * * *

> * * *

> "According to certain testimony in behalf of the defendant, extramarital escapades of the plaintiff were bizarre and of an amatory nature which would have made Dr. Freud's hair curl. Other testimony, in plaintiff's behalf, would indicate that defendant was guilty of bounding from one bedpartner to another with the erotic zest of a satyr. The court is inclined to discount much of this testimony as unreliable. Nevertheless, it is the conclusion and finding of the court that neither party is domesticated, within the meaning of that term as used by the Supreme Court of Florida. * * *

> * * *

> "In the present case, it is abundantly clear from the evidence of marital discord that neither of the parties has shown the least susceptibility to domestication, and that the marriage should be dissolved.

> * * *

> "The premises considered, it is thereupon

> "ORDERED AND ADJUDGED as follows:

> "1. That the equities in this cause are with the defendant; that defendant's counterclaim for divorce be and the same is hereby granted, and the bonds of matrimony which have heretofore existed between the parties are hereby forever dissolved.

> * * *

> "4. That the defendant shall pay unto the plaintiff the sum of $3,000 per month as alimony beginning January 1, 1968, and a like sum on the first day of each and every month thereafter until the death or remarriage of the plaintiff." App. 523–525, 528.

Time's editorial staff, headquartered in New York, was alerted by a wire service report and an account in a New York newspaper to the fact that a judgment had been rendered in the Firestone divorce proceeding. The staff subsequently received further information regarding the Florida decision from Time's Miami bureau chief and from a "stringer" working on a special assignment basis in the Palm Beach area. On the basis of these four sources, Time's staff composed the following item which appeared in the magazine's "Milestones" section the following week:

> "DIVORCED. By Russell A. Firestone, Jr., 41, heir to the tire fortune: Mary Alice Sullivan Firestone, 32, his third wife; a onetime Palm Beach schoolteacher; on grounds of extreme cruelty and adultery; after six years of marriage, one son; in West Palm Beach, Fla. The 17–month intermittent trial produced enough testimony of extra-marital adventures on both sides, said the judge, 'to make Dr. Freud's hair curl.' "

Within a few weeks of the publication of this article respondent demanded in writing a retraction from petitioner, alleging that a portion of the article was "false, malicious and defamatory." Petitioner declined to issue the requested retraction.[1]

Respondent then filed this libel action against petitioner in the Florida Circuit Court. Based on a jury verdict for respondent, that court entered judgment against petitioner for $100,000, and after review in both the Florida District Court of Appeal, 279 So.2d 389 and the Supreme Court of Florida, the judgment was ultimately affirmed. 305 So.2d 172 (1974). Petitioner advances several contentions as to why the judgment is contrary to decisions of this Court holding that the First and Fourteenth Amendments of the United States Constitution limit the authority of state courts to impose liability for damages based on defamation.

II

Petitioner initially contends that it cannot be liable for publishing any falsehood defaming respondent unless it is established that the publication was made "with actual malice," as that term is defined in New York Times Co. v. Sullivan * * *. Petitioner advances two arguments in support of this contention: that respondent is a "public figure" within this Court's decisions extending *New York Times* to defamation suits brought by such individuals * * *; and that the Time item constituted a report of a judicial proceeding, a class of subject matter which petitioner claims deserves the protection of the "actual malice" standard even if the story is proved to be defamatorily false or inaccurate. We reject both arguments.

In *Gertz v. Robert Welch, Inc.* * * * we have recently further defined the meaning of "public figure" * * *. Respondent did not assume any role of especial prominence in the affairs of society, other than perhaps Palm Beach society, and she did not thrust herself to the forefront of any particular public controversy in order to influence the resolution of the issues involved in it.

Petitioner contends that because the Firestone divorce was characterized by the Florida Supreme Court as a "cause célèbre," it must have been a public controversy and respondent must be considered a public figure. But in so doing petitioner seeks to equate "public controversy" with all controversies of interest to the public. Were we to accept this reasoning, we would reinstate the doctrine advanced in the plurality opinion in

---

1. Under Florida law the demand for retraction was a prerequisite for filing a libel action, and permits defendants to limit their potential liability to actual damages by complying with the demand. Fla.Stat.Ann. §§ 770.01–770.02 (1963).

Rosenbloom v. Metromedia, Inc. * * *. In *Gertz*, however, the Court repudiated this position, stating that "extension of the *New York Times* test proposed by the *Rosenbloom* plurality would abridge [a] legitimate state interest to a degree that we find unacceptable." * * *

Dissolution of a marriage through judicial proceedings is not the sort of "public controversy" referred to in *Gertz*, even though the marital difficulties of extremely wealthy individuals may be of interest to some portion of the reading public. Nor did respondent freely choose to publicize issues as to the propriety of her married life. She was compelled to go to court by the State in order to obtain legal release from the bonds of matrimony. We have said that in such an instance "[r]esort to the judicial process * * * is no more voluntary in a realistic sense than that of the defendant called upon to defend his interests in court." Boddie v. Connecticut, 401 U.S. 371 (1971). Her actions, both in instituting the litigation and in its conduct, were quite different from those of General Walker in *Curtis Publishing Co., supra*.[3] She assumed no "special prominence in the resolution of public questions." * * * We hold respondent was not a "public figure" for the purpose of determining the constitutional protection afforded petitioner's report of the factual and legal basis for her divorce.

For similar reasons we likewise reject petitioner's claim for automatic extension of the *New York Times* privilege to all reports of judicial proceedings. It is argued that information concerning proceedings in our Nation's courts may have such importance to all citizens as to justify extending special First Amendment protection to the press when reporting on such events. We have recently accepted a significantly more confined version of this argument by holding that the Constitution precludes States from imposing civil liability based upon the publication of truthful information contained in official court records open to public inspection. Cox Broadcasting Corp. v. Cohn, 420 U.S. 469 (1975).[a]

Petitioner would have us extend the reasoning of *Cox Broadcasting* to safeguard even inaccurate and false statements, at least where "actual malice" has not been established. But its argument proves too much. It may be that all reports of judicial proceedings contain some informational value implicating the First Amendment, but recognizing this is little different from labeling all judicial proceedings matters of "public or general interest," as that phrase was used by the plurality in *Rosenbloom*. Whatever their general validity, use of such subject-matter classifications to determine the extent of constitutional protection afforded defamatory falsehoods may too often result in an improper balance between the competing interests in this area. It was our recognition and rejection of this weakness in the *Rosenbloom* test which led us in *Gertz* to eschew a subject-matter test for one focusing upon the character of the defamation plaintiff. * * *

---

3. Nor do we think the fact that respondent may have held a few press conferences during the divorce proceedings in an attempt to satisfy inquiring reporters converts her into a "public figure." Such interviews should have had no effect upon the merits of the legal dispute between respondent and her husband or the outcome of that trial, and we do not think it can be assumed that any such purpose was intended. Moreover, there is no indication that she sought to use the press conferences as a vehicle by which to thrust herself to the forefront of some unrelated controversy in order to influence its resolution. See *Gertz v. Robert Welch, Inc.* * * *

a. [Ed. note] This case will presented at p. 1229, *infra*.

Presumptively erecting the *New York Times* barrier against all plaintiffs seeking to recover for injuries from defamatory falsehoods published in what are alleged to be reports of judicial proceedings would effect substantial depreciation of the individual's interest in protection from such harm, without any convincing assurance that such a sacrifice is required under the First Amendment. And in some instances such an undiscriminating approach might achieve results directly at odds with the constitutional balance intended. Indeed, the article upon which the *Gertz* libel action was based purported to be a report on the murder trial of a Chicago police officer. * * * Our decision in that case should make it clear that no such blanket privilege for reports of judicial proceedings is to be found in the Constitution.

It may be argued that there is still room for application of the *New York Times* protections to more narrowly focused reports of what actually transpires in the courtroom. But even so narrowed, the suggested privilege is simply too broad. Imposing upon the law of private defamation the rather drastic limitations worked by *New York Times* cannot be justified by generalized references to the public interest in reports of judicial proceedings. The details of many, if not most, courtroom battles would add almost nothing toward advancing the uninhibited debate on public issues thought to provide principal support for the decision in *New York Times*. * * * And while participants in some litigation may be legitimate "public figures," either generally or for the limited purpose of that litigation, the majority will more likely resemble respondent, drawn into a public forum largely against their will in order to attempt to obtain the only redress available to them or to defend themselves against actions brought by the State or by others. There appears little reason why these individuals should substantially forfeit that degree of protection which the law of defamation would otherwise afford them simply by virtue of their being drawn into a courtroom. The public interest in accurate reports of judicial proceedings is substantially protected by *Cox Broadcasting Co., supra*. As to inaccurate and defamatory reports of facts, matters deserving no First Amendment protection * * *; we think *Gertz* provides an adequate safeguard for the constitutionally protected interests of the press and affords it a tolerable margin for error by requiring some type of fault.

III

Petitioner has urged throughout this litigation that it could not be held liable for publication of the "Milestones" item because its report of respondent's divorce was factually correct. In its view the Time article faithfully reproduced the precise meaning of the divorce judgment. But this issue was submitted to the jury under an instruction intended to implement Florida's limited privilege for accurate reports of judicial proceedings. * * * By returning a verdict for respondent the jury necessarily found that the identity of meaning which petitioner claims does not exist even for laymen. The Supreme Court of Florida upheld this finding on appeal, rejecting petitioner's contention that its report was accurate as a matter of law. Because demonstration that an article was true would seem to preclude finding the publisher at fault, * * * we have examined the predicate for petitioner's contention. We believe the Florida courts properly could have found the "Milestones" item to be false.

For petitioner's report to have been accurate, the divorce granted Russell Firestone must have been based on a finding by the divorce court that his wife had committed extreme cruelty toward him *and* that she had been guilty of adultery. This is indisputably what petitioner reported in its "Milestones" item, but it is equally indisputable that these were not the facts. Russell Firestone alleged in his counterclaim that respondent had been guilty of adultery, but the divorce court never made any such finding. Its judgment provided that Russell Firestone's "counterclaim for divorce be and the same is hereby granted," but did not specify that the basis for the judgment was either of the two grounds alleged in the counterclaim. The Supreme Court of Florida on appeal concluded that the ground actually relied upon by the divorce court was "lack of domestication of the parties," a ground not theretofore recognized by Florida law. The Supreme Court nonetheless affirmed the judgment dissolving the bonds of matrimony because the record contained sufficient evidence to establish the ground of extreme cruelty. * * *

Petitioner may well argue that the meaning of the trial court's decree was unclear, but this does not license it to choose from among several conceivable interpretations the one most damaging to respondent. Having chosen to follow this tack, petitioner must be able to establish not merely that the item reported was a conceivable or plausible interpretation of the decree, but that the item was factually correct. We believe there is ample support for the jury's conclusion, affirmed by the Supreme Court of Florida, that this was not the case. * * *

* * * Petitioner has argued that because respondent withdrew her claim for damages to reputation on the eve of trial, there could be no recovery consistent with *Gertz*. Petitioner's theory seems to be that the only compensable injury in a defamation action is that which may be done to one's reputation, and that claims not predicated upon such injury are by definition not actions for defamation. But Florida has obviously decided to permit recovery for other injuries without regard to measuring the effect the falsehood may have had upon a plaintiff's reputation. This does not transform the action into something other than an action for defamation as that term is meant in *Gertz*. In that opinion we made it clear that States could base awards on elements other than injury to reputation, specifically listing "personal humiliation, and mental anguish and suffering" as examples of injuries which might be compensated consistently with the Constitution upon a showing of fault. Because respondent has decided to forgo recovery for injury to her reputation, she is not prevented from obtaining compensation for such other damages that a defamatory falsehood may have caused her.

* * * There was competent evidence introduced to permit the jury to assess the amount of injury. Several witnesses[6] testified to the extent of respondent's anxiety and concern over Time's inaccurately reporting that she had been found guilty of adultery, and she herself took the stand to elaborate on her fears that her young son would be adversely affected by

---

6. These included respondent's minister, her attorney in the divorce proceedings, plus several friends and neighbors, one of whom was a physician who testified to having to administer a sedative to respondent in an attempt to reduce discomfort wrought by her worrying about the article.

this falsehood when he grew older. The jury decided these injuries should be compensated by an award of $100,000. We have no warrant for re-examining this determination. * * *

IV

Gertz established, however, that not only must there be evidence to support an award of compensatory damages, there must also be evidence of some fault on the part of a defendant charged with publishing defamatory material. No question of fault was submitted to the jury in this case, because under Florida law the only findings required for determination of liability were whether the article was defamatory, whether it was true, and whether the defamation, if any, caused respondent harm.

The failure to submit the question of fault to the jury does not of itself establish noncompliance with the constitutional requirements established in *Gertz,* however. Nothing in the Constitution requires that assessment of fault in a civil case tried in a state court be made by a jury, nor is there any prohibition against such a finding being made in the first instance by an appellate, rather than a trial, court. The First and Fourteenth Amendments do not impose upon the States any limitations as to how, within their own judicial systems, factfinding tasks shall be allocated. If we were satisfied that one of the Florida courts which considered this case had supportably ascertained petitioner was at fault, we would be required to affirm the judgment below.

But the only alternative source of such a finding, given that the issue was not submitted to the jury, is the opinion of the Supreme Court of Florida. That opinion appears to proceed generally on the assumption that a showing of fault was not required, but then in the penultimate paragraph it recites:

"Furthermore, this erroneous reporting is clear and convincing evidence of the negligence in certain segments of the news media in gathering the news. * * * Pursuant to Florida law in effect at the time of the divorce judgment (Section 61.08, Florida Statutes), a wife found guilty of adultery could not be awarded alimony. Since petitioner had been awarded alimony, she had not been found guilty of adultery nor had the divorce been granted on the ground of adultery. A careful examination of the final decree prior to publication would have clearly demonstrated that the divorce had been granted on the grounds of extreme cruelty, and thus the wife would have been saved the humiliation of being accused of adultery in a nationwide magazine. This is a flagrant example of 'journalistic negligence.' " * * *

It may be argued that this is sufficient indication the court found petitioner at fault within the meaning of *Gertz.* Nothing in that decision or in the First or Fourteenth Amendment requires that in a libel action an appellate court treat in detail by written opinion all contentions of the parties, and if the jury or trial judge had found fault in fact, we would be quite willing to read the quoted passage as affirming that conclusion. But without some finding of fault by the judge or jury in the Circuit Court, we would have to attribute to the Supreme Court of Florida from the quoted language not merely an intention to affirm the finding of the lower court, but an intention to find such a fact in the first instance.

* * *

It may well be that petitioner's account in its "Milestones" section was the product of some fault on its part, and that the libel judgment against it was, therefore, entirely consistent with *Gertz*. But in the absence of a finding in some element of the state court system that there was fault, we are not inclined to canvass the record to make such a determination in the first instance. * * * Accordingly, the judgment of the Supreme Court of Florida is vacated and the case remanded for further proceedings not inconsistent with this opinion.

So ordered.

Notes

1. Justice Stevens did not participate in the "consideration or decision" of the case. Justice Powell, writing for himself and Justice Stewart, joined the opinion of the Court but wrote in a separate opinion that, given the "opaqueness" of the trial court's decree in the divorce proceedings, "there *was* substantial evidence supportive of Time's defense that it was not guilty of actionable negligence." Justice Brennan dissented on the ground that the First Amendment protected the erroneous reporting of the results of a judicial proceeding and that there could be liability only under the circumstances outlined in *Rosenbloom v. Metromedia, Inc.* Justice White dissented for the reasons outlined in his dissent in *Gertz* and for the further reason that, "in any event, the requisite fault was properly found below." Justice Marshall dissented on the ground that "Mary Alice Firestone * * * [was] a 'public figure' within the meaning of our prior decisions."

2. Mrs. Firestone apparently decided not to proceed with the case on retrial on the ground that she felt vindicated by the original verdict. *See* Editor & Publisher, Sept. 16, 1978, p. 11.

3. "Defining public figures is much like trying to nail a jellyfish to the wall." Rosanova v. Playboy Enterprises, Inc., 411 F.Supp. 440, 443 (S.D.Ga. 1976), affirmed 580 F.2d 859 (5th Cir.1978)(plaintiff held to be a public figure because of newspaper and other media reports that he was associated with organized crime).

4. Since *Firestone,* the Court, on June 26, 1979, handed down two further decisions on the question of who is a public figure. Hutchinson v. Proxmire, 443 U.S. 111, 99 S.Ct. 2675, 61 L.Ed.2d 411 (1979) and Wolston v. Reader's Digest Association, 443 U.S. 157, 99 S.Ct. 2701, 61 L.Ed.2d 450 (1979). *Hutchinson* involved a professor whose work on the emotional behavior of animals had been funded by the federal government. Some of this research involved the study of behavior patterns such as the clenching of jaws when the animals were exposed to certain stressful stimuli. The Court ruled that Hutchinson was a private figure; the public interest in the expenditure of government funds did not cause Hutchinson to be a public figure. Other related aspects of the *Hutchinson* case were discussed, *supra,* at p. 1144.

The *Wolston* case involved the nephew of Myra and Jack Noble, who were arrested in 1957 on charges of spying for the Soviet Union and who later pleaded guilty to charges of espionage. After the Nobles' arrest Wolston was summoned before several grand juries. Having failed to appear before the grand jury in July of 1958, Wolston was held in contempt; given a suspended sentence; and placed on three year's probation conditioned on his cooperation with grand jury investigations of Soviet espionage. A number of newspapers reported these events. Nevertheless, although Wolston was identified as a Soviet agent in an FBI report in 1960, he was never prosecuted. Aside from the investigation in the late 1950's, Wolston had led a life of obscurity. In 1974 the defendants published a book entitled *KGB* that named Wolston, among others as a Soviet agent in the United States. Wolston thereupon brought a defamation action. The district court classified Wolston as a public figure and granted summary judgment for Reader's Digest; the court of appeals affirmed. The Supreme Court, however, reversed, and held that Wolston was a private figure. The Court declared:

> Petitioner's failure to appear before the grand jury and citation for contempt no doubt were 'newsworthy,' but the simple fact that these events attracted media attention also is not conclusive of the public-figure issue. A private individual is not automatically transformed into a public figure just by becoming involved or associated with a matter that attracts public attention. To accept such reasoning would in effect re-establish the doctrine advanced by the plurality opinion in *Rosenbloom v. Metromedia, Inc.,* * * *.

5. Despite *Hutchinson* and *Wolston,* the chief prosecution witness in the famous "Scottsboro Boys" trial of 1931 and 1933 was held to have remained a public figure for the purposes of a television dramatization in 1976 of the 1933 trial. Street v. National Broadcasting Co., 645 F.2d 1227 (6th Cir.1981), *cert. granted* 454 U.S. 815, 102 S.Ct. 91, 70 L.Ed.2d 83 (1981), *cert. dismissed* by stipulation of the parties, 454 U.S. 1095, 102 S.Ct. 667, 70 L.Ed.2d 636 (1981). Earlier in Meeropol v. Nizer, 560 F.2d 1061 (2d Cir.1977), *cert. denied* 434 U.S. 1013, 98 S.Ct. 727, 54 L.Ed.2d 756 (1978), the children of Julius and Ethel Rosenberg, who were executed in 1953 for transmitting defense secrets to the Soviet Union, were deemed public figures with regard to a book published in 1973 about their parents' trial. On the other hand, a dissident shareholder and former corporate counsel of a publicly held company was not a public figure in the context of newspaper reports of management turnover at the company. Denny v. Mertz, 106 Wis.2d 636, 318 N.W.2d 141 (1982). In Dameron v. Washington Magazine, Inc., 779 F.2d 736 (D.C.Cir.1985), *cert. denied* 476 U.S. 1141, 106 S.Ct. 2247, 90 L.Ed.2d 693 (1986), an air traffic controller who was on duty at Dulles airport at the time an airliner crashed with 92 fatalities was held to be an involuntary public figure with respect to an article concerning the cause of the crash. On the other hand, a woman, who had dinner with Dr. Martin Luther King the night before his assassination and who the defendant in his book had alleged had had an affair with Dr. King, was held not to be a public figure for purposes of her defamation action against the defendant. Although the plaintiff had been a civil rights activist and had run for elected office, the court stressed that the subject matter of her defamation action was not related to any such public conduct. Naantaanbuu v. Abernathy, 816 F.Supp. 218 (S.D.N.Y.1993). The court nevertheless granted summary judgment in favor of the defendant because the defamation action involved a matter of public interest and, under New York law (see p. 1166, *supra*), could only proceed if the defendant acted in a "grossly irresponsible manner." The earlier history of the *Milkovich* case, (*supra* p. 1166) is also instructive on the difficulty the courts have had in deciding who is a public figure. In Milkovich

v. News–Herald, 15 Ohio St.3d 292, 473 N.E.2d 1191 (1984), *cert. denied* 474 U.S. 953, 106 S.Ct. 322, 88 L.Ed.2d 305 (1985), the plaintiff, a head wrestling coach at a public high school who had been censured by the state athletic association after a fight had broken out at a meet when the referee had disqualified a wrestler on the coach's team, was held to be neither a public official nor a public figure.[a] This latter ruling was made despite the fact that the plaintiff was a nationally prominent high school wrestling coach who was well-known in the area. Dissenting from the denial of certiorari, Justice Brennan, joined by Justice Marshall, characterized the Ohio court's holding that the plaintiff was not a public figure "for purposes of discussion about the controversy" as "simply nonsense". 474 U.S. at 964, 106 S.Ct. at 330, 88 L.Ed.2d at 314. When the Ohio Supreme Court considered a companion case arising out of the same article, brought by the superintendent of the local public school system, it held that the school superintendent was a public official and that, furthermore, the alleged defamation was the expression of opinion. Scott v. News–Herald, 25 Ohio St.3d 243, 496 N.E.2d 699 (1986).

DUN & BRADSTREET, INC. v. GREENMOSS BUILDERS, INC.

Supreme Court of the United States, 1985.
472 U.S. 749, 105 S.Ct. 2939, 86 L.Ed.2d 593.

JUSTICE POWELL announced the judgment of the Court and delivered an opinion, in which JUSTICE REHNQUIST and JUSTICE O'CONNOR joined.

In *Gertz v. Robert Welch, Inc.,* * * * we held that the First Amendment restricted the damages that a private individual could obtain from a publisher for a libel that involved a matter of public concern. More specifically, we held that in these circumstances the First Amendment prohibited awards of presumed and punitive damages for false and defamatory statements unless the plaintiff shows "actual malice," that is, knowledge of falsity or reckless disregard for the truth. The question presented in this case is whether this rule of *Gertz* applies when the false and defamatory statements do not involve matters of public concern.

I

Petitioner Dun & Bradstreet, a credit reporting agency, provides subscribers with financial and related information about businesses. All the information is confidential; under the terms of the subscription agreement the subscribers may not reveal it to anyone else. On July 26, 1976, petitioner sent a report to five subscribers indicating that respondent, a construction contractor, had filed a voluntary petition for bankruptcy. This report was false and grossly misrepresented respondent's assets and liabilities. That same day, while discussing the possibility of future financing with its bank, respondent's president was told that the bank had received the defamatory report. He immediately called petitioner's regional office, explained the error, and asked for a correction. In addition, he requested the names of the firms that had received the false report in order to assure them that the company was solvent. Petitioner promised to look

---

a. The Ohio Supreme Court divided 4–3 in the case. The three dissenters felt that the statements in question were merely opinions. Two of the dissenters thought that Milkovich was a public figure.

into the matter but refused to divulge the names of those who had received the report.

After determining that its report was indeed false, petitioner issued a corrective notice on or about August 3, 1976, to the five subscribers who had received the initial report. The notice stated that one of respondent's former employees, not respondent itself, had filed for bankruptcy and that respondent "continued in business as usual." Respondent told petitioner that it was dissatisfied with the notice, and it again asked for a list of subscribers who had seen the initial report. Again petitioner refused to divulge their names.

Respondent then brought this defamation action in Vermont state court. It alleged that the false report had injured its reputation and sought both compensatory and punitive damages. The trial established that the error in petitioner's report had been caused when one of its employees, a 17–year–old high school student paid to review Vermont bankruptcy pleadings, had inadvertently attributed to respondent a bankruptcy petition filed by one of respondent's former employees. Although petitioner's representative testified that it was routine practice to check the accuracy of such reports with the businesses themselves, it did not try to verify the information about respondent before reporting it.

After trial, the jury returned a verdict in favor of respondent and awarded $50,000 in compensatory or presumed damages and $300,000 in punitive damages. Petitioner moved for a new trial. It argued that in *Gertz v. Robert Welch, Inc.,* * * * this Court had ruled broadly that "the States may not permit recovery of presumed or punitive damages, at least when liability is not based on a showing of knowledge of falsity or reckless disregard for the truth," and it argued that the judge's instructions in this case permitted the jury to award such damages on a lesser showing. The trial court indicated some doubt as to whether *Gertz* applied to "non-media cases," but granted a new trial "[b]ecause of * * * dissatisfaction with its charge and * * * conviction that the interests of justice require[d]" it. App. 26.

The Vermont Supreme Court reversed. 143 Vt. 66, 461 A.2d 414 (1983). Although recognizing that "in certain instances the distinction between media and nonmedia defendants may be difficult to draw," the court stated that "no such difficulty is presented with credit reporting agencies, which are in the business of selling financial information to a limited number of subscribers who have paid substantial fees for their services." * * * Relying on this distinguishing characteristic of credit reporting firms, the court concluded that such firms are not "the type of media worthy of First Amendment protection as contemplated by *New York Times* * * * and its progeny." * * * It held that the balance between a private plaintiff's right to recover presumed and punitive damages without a showing of special fault and the First Amendment rights of "nonmedia" speakers "must be struck in favor of the private plaintiff defamed by a nonmedia defendant." * * * Accordingly, the court held "that as a matter of federal constitutional law, the media protections outlined in *Gertz* are inapplicable to nonmedia defamation actions." *Ibid.*

Recognizing disagreement among the lower courts about when the protections of *Gertz* apply, we granted certiorari. * * * We now affirm, although for reasons different from those relied upon by the Vermont Supreme Court.

II

As an initial matter, respondent contends that we need not determine whether *Gertz* applies in this case because the instructions, taken as a whole, required the jury to find "actual malice" before awarding presumed or punitive damages. The trial court instructed the jury that because the report was libelous *per se,* respondent was not required "to prove actual damages * * * since damage and loss [are] conclusively presumed." * * * It also instructed the jury that it could award punitive damages only if it found "actual malice." *Id.,* at 20. Its only other relevant instruction was that liability could not be established unless respondent showed "malice or lack of good faith on the part of the Defendant." *Id.,* at 18. Respondent contends that these references to "malice," "lack of good faith," and "actual malice" required the jury to find knowledge of falsity or reckless disregard for the truth—the "actual malice" of *New York Times Co. v. Sullivan,* * * *—before it awarded presumed or punitive damages.

We reject this claim because the trial court failed to define any of these terms adequately. It did not, for example, provide the jury with any definition of the term "actual malice." In fact, the only relevant term it defined was simple "malice." And its definitions of this term included not only the *New York Times* formulation but also other concepts such as "bad faith" and "reckless disregard of the [statement's] possible consequences." App. 19. The instructions thus permitted the jury to award presumed and punitive damages on a lesser showing than "actual malice." Consequently, the trial court's conclusion that the instructions did not satisfy *Gertz* was correct, and the Vermont Supreme Court's determination that *Gertz* was inapplicable was necessary to its decision that the trial court erred in granting the motion for a new trial. We therefore must consider whether *Gertz* applies to the case before us.

III

* * *

In *Gertz,* we held that the fact that expression concerned a public issue did not by itself entitle the libel defendant to the constitutional protections of *New York Times*. These protections, we found, were not "justified solely by reference to the interest of the press and broadcast media in immunity from liability." 418 U.S., at 343, 94 S.Ct., at 3008. Rather, they represented "an accommodation between [First Amendment] concern[s] and the limited state interest present in the context of libel actions brought by public persons." * * * Nothing in our opinion, however, indicated that this same balance would be struck regardless of the type of speech involved.

IV

We have never considered whether the *Gertz* balance obtains when the defamatory statements involve no issue of public concern. To make this determination, we must employ the approach approved in *Gertz* and balance the State's interest in compensating private individuals for injury to their reputation against the First Amendment interest in protecting this type of expression. This state interest is identical to the one weighed in *Gertz*. There we found that it was "strong and legitimate." * * *

The First Amendment interest, on the other hand, is less important than the one weighed in *Gertz*. We have long recognized that not all speech is of equal First Amendment importance. It is speech on "'matters of public concern' "that is "at the heart of the First Amendment's protection." *First National Bank of Boston v. Bellotti,* 435 U.S. 765, 776, 98 S.Ct. 1407, 1415, 55 L.Ed.2d 707 (1978), citing *Thornhill v. Alabama,* 310 U.S. 88, 101, 60 S.Ct. 736, 743, 84 L.Ed. 1093 (1940). * * * In contrast, speech on matters of purely private concern is of less First Amendment concern. * * * As a number of state courts, including the court below, have recognized, the role of the Constitution in regulating state libel law is far more limited when the concerns that activated *New York Times* and *Gertz* are absent.[6]

While such speech is not totally unprotected by the First Amendment, see *Connick v. Myers, supra,* 461 U.S., at 147, 103 S.Ct., at 1690, its protections are less stringent. In *Gertz,* we found that the state interest in awarding presumed and punitive damages was not "substantial" in view of their effect on speech at the core of First Amendment concern. * * * This interest, however, *is* "substantial" relative to the incidental effect these remedies may have on speech of significantly less constitutional interest. The rationale of the common-law rules has been the experience and judgment of history that "proof of actual damage will be impossible in a great many cases where, from the character of the defamatory words and the circumstances of publication, it is all but certain that serious harm has resulted in fact." W. Prosser, Law of Torts § 112, p. 765 (4th ed. 1971) * * * As a result, courts for centuries have allowed juries to presume that some damage occurred from many defamatory utterances and publications. * * * This rule furthers the state interest in providing remedies for defamation by ensuring that those remedies are effective. In light of the reduced constitutional value of speech involving no matters of public concern, we hold that the state interest adequately supports awards of presumed and punitive damages—even absent a showing of "actual malice."

V

The only remaining issue is whether petitioner's credit report involved a matter of public concern. In a related context, we have held that "[w]hether * * * speech addresses a matter of public concern must be determined by [the expression's] content, form, and context * * * as revealed by the whole record." *Connick v. Myers, supra,* 461 U.S., at 147–148, 103 S.Ct., at 1690. These factors indicate that petitioner's credit

---

6. As one commentator has remarked with respect to "the case of a commercial supplier of credit information that defames a person applying for credit"—the case before us today—"If the first amendment requirements outlined in *Gertz* apply, there is some-thing clearly wrong with the first amendment or with *Gertz*." Shiffrin, The First Amendment and Economic Regulation: Away From a General Theory of the First Amendment, 78 Nw.U.L.Rev. 1212, 1268 (1983).

report concerns no public issue.[8] It was speech solely in the individual interest of the speaker and its specific business audience. * * * This particular interest warrants no special protection when—as in this case— the speech is wholly false and clearly damaging to the victim's business reputation. * * * Moreover, since the credit report was made available to only five subscribers, who, under the terms of the subscription agreement, could not disseminate it further, it cannot be said that the report involves any "strong interest in the free flow of commercial information." * * * There is simply no credible argument that this type of credit reporting requires special protection to ensure that "debate on public issues [will] be uninhibited, robust, and wide-open." * * *

In addition, the speech here, like advertising, is hardy and unlikely to be deterred by incidental state regulation. * * * It is solely motivated by the desire for profit, which, we have noted, is a force less likely to be deterred than others. * * * Arguably, the reporting here was also more objectively verifiable than speech deserving of greater protection. * * * In any case, the market provides a powerful incentive to a credit reporting agency to be accurate, since false credit reporting is of no use to creditors. Thus, any incremental "chilling" effect of libel suits would be of decreased significance.[9]

VI

We conclude that permitting recovery of presumed and punitive damages in defamation cases absent a showing of "actual malice" does not violate the First Amendment when the defamatory statements do not involve matters of public concern. Accordingly, we affirm the judgment of the Vermont Supreme Court.

It is so ordered.

CHIEF JUSTICE BURGER, concurring in the judgment.

* * *

I dissented in *Gertz* because I believed that, insofar as the "ordinary private citizen" was concerned, * * * the Court's opinion "abandon[ed] the traditional thread," *id.*, at 354–355, 94 S.Ct., at 3014, that had been the theme of the law in this country up to that time. I preferred "to allow this area of law to continue to evolve as it [had] up to [then] with respect to private citizens rather than embark on a new doctrinal theory which [had]

---

8. The dissent suggests that our holding today leaves all credit reporting subject to reduced First Amendment protection. This is incorrect. The protection to be accorded a particular credit report depends on whether the report's "content, form, and context" indicate that it concerns a public matter. We also do not hold, as the dissent suggests we do, * * * that the report is subject to reduced constitutional protection because it constitutes economic or commercial speech. We discuss such speech, along with advertising, only to show how many of the same concerns that argue in favor of reduced constitutional protection in those areas apply here as well.

9. The Court of Appeals for the Fifth Circuit has noted that, while most States provide a qualified privilege against libel suits for commercial credit reporting agencies, in those States that do not there is a thriving credit reporting business and commercial credit transactions are not inhibited. *Hood v. Dun & Bradstreet, Inc.*, 486 F.2d 25, 32 (1973), cert. denied, 415 U.S. 985, 94 S.Ct. 1580, 39 L.Ed.2d 882 (1974). The court cited an empirical study comparing credit transactions in Boise, Idaho, where there is no privilege, with those in Spokane, Washington, where there is one. 486 F.2d, at 32, and n. 18.

no jurisprudential ancestry." *Ibid.* *Gertz,* however, is now the law of the land, and until it is overruled, it must, under the principle of *stare decisis,* be applied by this Court.

The single question before the Court today is whether *Gertz* applies to this case. The plurality opinion holds that *Gertz* does not apply because, unlike the challenged expression in *Gertz,* the alleged defamatory expression in this case does not relate to a matter of public concern. I agree that *Gertz* is limited to circumstances in which the alleged defamatory expression concerns a matter of general public importance, and that the expression in question here relates to a matter of essentially private concern. I therefore agree with the plurality opinion to the extent that it holds that *Gertz* is inapplicable in this case for the two reasons indicated. No more is needed to dispose of the present case.

I continue to believe, however, that *Gertz* was ill-conceived, and therefore agree with Justice White that *Gertz* should be overruled. * * * The great rights guaranteed by the First Amendment carry with them certain responsibilities as well.

Consideration of these issues inevitably recalls an aphorism of journalism that "too much checking on the facts has ruined many a good news story."

JUSTICE WHITE, concurring in the judgment.

Until *New York Times Co. v. Sullivan,* * * * the law of defamation was almost exclusively the business of state courts and legislatures. Under the then prevailing state libel law, the defamed individual had only to prove a false written publication that subjected him to hatred, contempt, or ridicule. Truth was a defense; but given a defamatory false circulation, general injury to reputation was presumed; special damages, such as pecuniary loss and emotional distress, could be recovered; and punitive damages were available if common-law malice were shown. General damages for injury to reputation were presumed and awarded because the judgment of history was that "in many cases the effect of defamatory statements is so subtle and indirect that it is impossible directly to trace the effects thereof in loss to the person defamed." Restatement of Torts § 621, Comment *a,* p. 314 (1938). The defendant was permitted to show that there was no reputational injury; but at the very least, the prevailing rule was that at least nominal damages were to be awarded for any defamatory publication actionable *per se.* * * *

* * *

I joined the judgment and opinion in *New York Times.* I also joined later decisions extending the *New York Times* standard to other situations. But I came to have increasing doubts about the soundness of the Court's approach and about some of the assumptions underlying it. I could not join the plurality opinion in *Rosenbloom,* and I dissented in *Gertz,* asserting that the common-law remedies should be retained for private plaintiffs. I remain convinced that *Gertz* was erroneously decided. I have also become convinced that the Court struck an improvident balance in the *New York Times* case between the public's interest in being fully informed about public officials and public affairs and the competing interest of those who have been defamed in vindicating their reputation.

In a country like ours, where the people purport to be able to govern themselves through their elected representatives, adequate information about their government is of transcendent importance. That flow of intelligence deserves full First Amendment protection. Criticism and assessment of the performance of public officials and of government in general are not subject to penalties imposed by law. But these First Amendment values are not at all served by circulating false statements of fact about public officials. On the contrary, erroneous information frustrates these values. They are even more disserved when the statements falsely impugn the honesty of those men and women and hence lessen the confidence in government. As the Court said in *Gertz:* "[T]here is no constitutional value in false statements of fact. Neither the intentional lie nor the careless error materially advances society's interest in 'uninhibited, robust, and wide-open' debate on public issues." * * * Yet in *New York Times* cases, the public official's complaint will be dismissed unless he alleges and makes out a jury case of a knowing or reckless falsehood. Absent such proof, there will be no jury verdict or judgment of any kind in his favor, even if the challenged publication is admittedly false. The lie will stand, and the public continue to be misinformed about public matters. This will recurringly happen because the putative plaintiff's burden is so exceedingly difficult to satisfy and can be discharged only by expensive litigation. Even if the plaintiff sues, he frequently loses on summary judgment or never gets to the jury because of insufficient proof of malice. If he wins before the jury, verdicts are often overturned by appellate courts for failure to prove malice. Furthermore, when the plaintiff loses, the jury will likely return a general verdict and there will be no judgment that the publication was false, even though it was without foundation in reality.[2] The public is left to conclude that the challenged statement was true after all. Their only chance of being accurately informed is measured by the public official's ability himself to counter the lie, unaided by the courts. That is a decidedly weak reed to depend on for the vindication of First Amendment interests * * *.

* * *

2. If the plaintiff succeeds in proving a jury case of malice, it may be that the jury will be asked to bring in separate verdicts on falsity and malice. In that event, there could be a verdict in favor of the plaintiff on falsity, but against him on malice. There would be no judgment in his favor, but the verdict on falsity would be a public one and would tend to set the record right and clear the plaintiff's name.

It might be suggested that courts, as organs of the government, cannot be trusted to discern what the truth is. But the logical consequence of that view is that the First Amendment forbids all libel and slander suits, for in each such suit, there will be no recovery unless the court finds the publication at issue to be factually false. Of course, no forum is perfect, but that is not a justification for leaving whole classes of defamed individuals without redress or a realistic opportunity to clear their names. We entrust to juries and the courts the responsibility of decisions affecting the life and liberty of persons. It is perverse indeed to say that these bodies are incompetent to inquire into the truth of a statement of fact in a defamation case. I can therefore discern nothing in the Constitution which forbids a plaintiff to obtain a judicial decree that a statement is false—a decree he can then use in the community to clear his name and to prevent further damage from a defamation already published.

The *New York Times* rule thus countenances two evils: first, the stream of information about public officials and public affairs is polluted and often remains polluted by false information; and second, the reputation and professional life of the defeated plaintiff may be destroyed by falsehoods that might have been avoided with a reasonable effort to investigate the facts. In terms of the First Amendment and reputational interests at stake, these seem grossly perverse results.

* * *

In *New York Times,* instead of escalating the plaintiff's burden of proof to an almost impossible level, we could have achieved our stated goal by limiting the recoverable damages to a level that would not unduly threaten the press. Punitive damages might have been scrutinized as Justice Harlan suggested in *Rosenbloom, supra,* 403 U.S., at 77, 91 S.Ct., at 1836, or perhaps even entirely forbidden. Presumed damages to reputation might have been prohibited, or limited, as in *Gertz.* Had that course been taken and the common-law standard of liability been retained, the defamed public official, upon proving falsity, could at least have had a judgment to that effect. His reputation would then be vindicated; and to the extent possible, the misinformation circulated would have been countered. He might have also recovered a modest amount, enough perhaps to pay his litigation expenses. At the very least, the public official should not have been required to satisfy the actual malice standard where he sought no damages but only to clear his name. In this way, both First Amendment and reputational interests would have been far better served.

We are not talking in these cases about mere criticism or opinion, but about misstatements of fact that seriously harm the reputation of another, by lowering him in the estimation of the community or to deter third persons from associating or dealing with him. * * *

I still believe the common-law rules should have been retained where the plaintiff is not a public official or public figure. As I see it, the Court undervalued the reputational interest at stake in such cases. I have also come to doubt the easy assumption that the common-law rules would muzzle the press. But even accepting the *Gertz* premise that the press also needed protection in suits by private parties, there was no need to modify the common-law requirements for establishing liability and to increase the burden of proof that must be satisfied to secure a judgment authorizing at least nominal damages and the recovery of additional sums within the limitations that the Court might have set.[3]

It is interesting that Justice Powell declines to follow the *Gertz* approach in this case. I had thought that the decision in *Gertz* was intended to reach cases that involve any false statements of fact injurious to reputation, whether the statement is made privately or publicly and whether or not it implicates a matter of public importance. Justice Powell, however, distinguishes *Gertz* as a case that involved a matter of public concern, an element absent here. Wisely, in my view, Justice Powell does not rest his application of a different rule here on a distinction drawn

3. The Court was unresponsive to my suggestion in dissent, 418 U.S., at 391–392, 94 S.Ct., at 3032, that the plaintiff should be able to prove and obtain a judgment of falsehood without having to establish any kind of fault.

between media and nonmedia defendants. On that issue, I agree with Justice Brennan that the First Amendment gives no more protection to the press in defamation suits than it does to others exercising their freedom of speech. None of our cases affords such a distinction; to the contrary, the Court has rejected it at every turn. It should be rejected again, particularly in this context, since it makes no sense to give the most protection to those publishers who reach the most readers and therefore pollute the channels of communication with the most misinformation and do the most damage to private reputation. If *Gertz* is to be distinguished from this case, on the ground that it applies only where the allegedly false publication deals with a matter of general or public importance, then where the false publication does not deal with such a matter, the common-law rules would apply whether the defendant is a member of the media or other public disseminator or a nonmedia individual publishing privately. Although Justice Powell speaks only of the inapplicability of the *Gertz* rule with respect to presumed and punitive damages, it must be that the *Gertz* requirement of some kind of fault on the part of the defendant is also inapplicable in cases such as this.

As I have said, I dissented in *Gertz,* and I doubt that the decision in that case has made any measurable contribution to First Amendment or reputational values since its announcement. Nor am I sure that it has saved the press a great deal of money. Like the *New York Times* decision, the burden that plaintiffs must meet invites long and complicated discovery involving detailed investigation of the workings of the press, how a news story is developed, and the state of mind of the reporter and publisher. See *Herbert v. Lando,* 441 U.S. 153, 99 S.Ct. 1635, 60 L.Ed.2d 115 (1979).[a] That kind of litigation is very expensive. I suspect that the press would be no worse off financially if the common-law rules were to apply and if the judiciary was careful to insist that damages awards be kept within bounds. A legislative solution to the damages problem would also be appropriate. Moreover, since libel plaintiffs are very likely more interested in clearing their names than in damages, I doubt that limiting recoveries would deter or be unfair to them. In any event, I cannot assume that the press, as successful and powerful as it is, will be intimidated into withholding news that by decent journalistic standards it believes to be true.

The question before us is whether *Gertz* is to be applied in this case. For either of two reasons, I believe that it should not. First, I am unreconciled to the *Gertz* holding and believe that it should be overruled. Second, as Justice Powell indicates, the defamatory publication in this case does not deal with a matter of public importance. Consequently, I concur in the Court's judgment.

JUSTICE BRENNAN, with whom JUSTICE MARSHALL, JUSTICE BLACKMUN, and JUSTICE STEVENS join, dissenting.

This case involves a difficult question of the proper application of *Gertz v. Robert Welch, Inc.,* * * * to credit reporting—a type of speech at some remove from that which first gave rise to explicit First Amendment

a. [Ed. note] discussed at p. 1148, *supra.*

restrictions on state defamation law—and has produced a diversity of considered opinions, none of which speaks for the Court. * * *

* * *

II

The question presented here is narrow. Neither the parties nor the courts below have suggested that respondent Greenmoss Builders should be required to show actual malice to obtain a judgment and actual compensatory damages. Nor do the parties question the requirement of *Gertz* that respondent must show fault to obtain a judgment and actual damages. The only question presented is whether a jury award of presumed and punitive damages based on less than a showing of actual malice is constitutionally permissible. *Gertz* provides a forthright negative answer. To preserve the jury verdict in this case, therefore, the opinions of Justice Powell and Justice White have cut away the protective mantle of *Gertz*.

* * *

A

* * *

The free speech guarantee gives each citizen an equal right to self-expression and to participation in self-government. * * * This guarantee also protects the rights of listeners to "the widest possible dissemination of information from diverse and antagonistic sources." *Associated Press v. United States,* 326 U.S. 1, 20, 65 S.Ct. 1416, 1424, 89 L.Ed. 2013 (1945).[9] Accordingly, at least six Members of this Court (the four who join this opinion and Justice White and The Chief Justice) agree today that, in the context of defamation law, the rights of the institutional media are no greater and no less than those enjoyed by other individuals or organizations engaged in the same activities. See *ante,* * * * (opinion concurring in judgment).[10]

B

Eschewing the media/nonmedia distinction, the opinions of both Justice White and Justice Powell focus primarily on the content of the credit report as a reason for restricting the applicability of *Gertz.* Arguing that at most *Gertz* should protect speech that "deals with a matter of public or general importance," * * * Justice White, without analysis or explanation, decides that the credit report at issue here falls outside this protected category. The plurality opinion of Justice Powell offers virtually the same conclusion with at least a garnish of substantive analysis.

* * *

9. In light of the "increasingly prominent role of mass media in our society, and the awesome power it has placed in the hands of a select few," *Gertz,* 418 U.S., at 402, 94 S.Ct., at 3037 (White, J., dissenting), protection for the speech of nonmedia defendants is essential to ensure a diversity of perspectives.

See J. Barron, Freedom of the Press for Whom? (1973). * * *

10. Justice Powell's opinion does not expressly reject the media/nonmedia distinction, but does expressly decline to apply that distinction to resolve this case.

In professing allegiance to *Gertz,* the plurality opinion protests too much. As Justice White correctly observes, Justice Powell departs completely from the analytic framework and result of that case: "*Gertz* was intended to reach cases that involve any false statements * * * whether or not [they] implicat[e] a matter of public importance." *Ante,* * * * (concurring in judgment).[11] Even accepting the notion that a distinction can and should be drawn between matters of public concern and matters of purely private concern, however, the analyses presented by both Justice Powell and Justice White fail on their own terms. Both, by virtue of what they hold in this case, propose an impoverished definition of "matters of public concern" that is irreconcilable with First Amendment principles. The credit reporting at issue here surely involves a subject matter of sufficient public concern to require the comprehensive protections of *Gertz.* Were this speech appropriately characterized as a matter of only private concern, moreover, the elimination of the *Gertz* restrictions on presumed and punitive damages would still violate basic First Amendment requirements.

(1)

The five Members of the Court voting to affirm the damages award in this case have provided almost no guidance as to what constitutes a protected "matter of public concern." * * *

In evaluating the subject matter of expression, this Court has consistently rejected the argument that speech is entitled to diminished First Amendment protection simply because it concerns economic matters or is in the economic interest of the speaker or the audience. * * *

The credit reporting of Dun & Bradstreet falls within any reasonable definition of "public concern" consistent with our precedents. Justice Powell's reliance on the fact that Dun & Bradstreet publishes credit reports "for profit," * * * is wholly unwarranted. Time and again we have made clear that speech loses none of its constitutional protection "even though it is carried in a form that is 'sold' for profit." *Virginia Pharmacy Bd.,* 425 U.S., at 761, 96 S.Ct., at 1825. * * * More importantly, an announcement of the bankruptcy of a local company is information of potentially great concern to residents of the community where the company is located; * * * such a bankruptcy "in a single factory may have economic repercussions upon a whole region." And knowledge about solvency and the effect and prevalence of bankruptcy certainly would inform citizen opinions about

---

11. One searches *Gertz* in vain for a single word to support the proposition that limits on presumed and punitive damages obtained only when speech involved matters of public concern. *Gertz* could not have been grounded in such a premise. Distrust of placing in the courts the power to decide what speech was of public concern was precisely the rationale *Gertz* offered for rejecting the *Rosenbloom* plurality approach. * * * It would have been incongruous for the Court to go on to circumscribe the protection against presumed and punitive damages by reference to a judicial judgment as to whether the speech at issue involved matters of public concern. At several points the Court in *Gertz* makes perfectly clear the restrictions

of presumed and punitive damages were to apply in all cases. * * *

Indeed, Justice Powell's opinion today is fairly read as embracing the approach of the *Rosenbloom* plurality to deciding when the Constitution should limit state defamation law. The limits imposed, however, are less stringent than those suggested by the *Rosenbloom* plurality. Under the approach of today's plurality, speech about matters of public or general interest receives only the *Gertz* protections against unrestrained presumed and punitive damages, not the full *New York Times Co. v. Sullivan* protections against any recovery absent a showing of actual malice.

questions of economic regulation. It is difficult to suggest that a bankruptcy is not a subject matter of public concern when federal law requires invocation of judicial mechanisms to effectuate it and makes the fact of the bankruptcy a matter of public record. * * *

Speech about commercial or economic matters, even if not directly implicating "the central meaning of the First Amendment," * * * is an important part of our public discourse. * * *

Given that the subject matter of credit reporting directly implicates matters of public concern, the balancing analysis the Court today employs should properly lead to the conclusion that the type of expression here at issue should receive First Amendment protection from the chilling potential of unrestrained presumed and punitive damages in defamation actions.

(2)

Even if the subject matter of credit reporting were properly considered—in the terms of Justice White and Justice Powell—as purely a matter of private discourse, this speech would fall well within the range of valuable expression for which the First Amendment demands protection. Much expression that does not directly involve public issues receives significant protection. Our cases do permit some diminution in the degree of protection afforded one category of speech about economic or commercial matters. "Commercial speech"—defined as advertisements that "[do] no more than propose a commercial transaction," *Pittsburgh Press Co. v. Pittsburgh Comm'n on Human Relations,* 413 U.S. 376, 385, 93 S.Ct. 2553, 2558, 37 L.Ed.2d 669 (1973)—may be more closely regulated than other types of speech. Even commercial speech, however, receives substantial First Amendment protection. * * *

* * *

The credit reports of Dun & Bradstreet bear few of the earmarks of commercial speech that might be entitled to somewhat less rigorous protection. In *every* case in which we have permitted more extensive state regulation on the basis of a commercial speech rationale the speech being regulated was pure advertising—an offer to buy or sell goods and services or encouraging such buying and selling. Credit reports are not commercial advertisements for a good or service or a proposal to buy or sell such a product. We have been extremely chary about extending the "commercial speech" doctrine beyond this narrowly circumscribed category of advertising because often vitally important speech will be uttered to advance economic interests and because the profit motive making such speech hardy dissipates rapidly when the speech is not advertising. * * *

It is worth noting in this regard that the common law of most States, although apparently not of Vermont, 143 Vt. 66, 76, 461 A.2d 414, 419 (1983), recognizes a qualified privilege for reports like that at issue here. See Maurer, Common Law Defamation and the Fair Credit Reporting Act, 72 Geo.L.J. 95, 99–105 (1983). The privilege typically precludes recovery for false and defamatory credit information without a showing of bad faith or malice, a standard of proof which is often defined according to the *New York Times* formulation. See, *e.g., Datacon, Inc. v. Dun & Bradstreet, Inc.,* 465 F.Supp. 706, 708 (N.D.Tex.1979). The common law thus recognizes that credit reporting is quite susceptible to libel's chill; this accumulated learning is worthy of respect.

Even if Justice Powell's characterization of the credit reporting at issue here were accepted in its entirety, his opinion would have done no more than demonstrate that this speech is the equivalent of commercial speech. The opinion, after all, relies on analogy to advertising. Credit reporting is said to be hardy, motivated by desire for profit, and relatively verifiable. * * * But this does not justify the elimination of restrictions on presumed and punitive damages. State efforts to regulate commercial speech in the form of advertising must abide by the requirement that the regulatory means chosen be narrowly tailored so as to avoid any unnecessary chilling of protected expression. * * *[16]

* * *

(3)

Even if not at "the essence of self-government," *Garrison v. Louisiana,* 379 U.S. 64, 74–75, 85 S.Ct. 209, 216, 13 L.Ed.2d 125 (1964), the expression at issue in this case is important to both our public discourse and our private welfare. That its motivation might be the economic interest of the speaker or listeners does not diminish its First Amendment value. * * * Whether or not such speech is sufficiently central to First Amendment values to require actual malice as a standard of liability, this speech certainly falls within the range of speech that *Gertz* sought to protect from the chill of unrestrained presumed and punitive damage awards.

Of course, the commercial context of Dun & Bradstreet's reports is relevant to the constitutional analysis insofar as it implicates the strong state interest "in protecting consumers and regulating commercial transactions," *Ohralik v. Ohio State Bar Assn.,* 436 U.S. 447, 460, 98 S.Ct. 1912, 1920, 56 L.Ed.2d 444 (1978). * * * The special harms caused by inaccurate credit reports, the lack of public sophistication about or access to such reports, and the fact that such reports by and large contain statements that are fairly readily susceptible of verification, all may justify appropriate regulation designed to prevent the social losses caused by false credit reports. And in the libel context, the States' regulatory interest in protecting reputation is served by rules permitting recovery for actual compensatory damages upon a showing of fault. Any further interest in deterring potential defamation through case-by-case judicial imposition of presumed and punitive damages awards on less than a showing of actual malice simply exacts too high a toll on First Amendment values. Accordingly, Greenmoss Builders should be permitted to recover for any actual damage it can show resulted from Dun & Bradstreet's negligently false credit report, but should be required to show actual malice to receive presumed or punitive damages. Because the jury was not instructed in accordance with

16. Indeed Justice Powell has chosen a particularly inept set of facts as a basis for urging a return to the common law. Though the individual's interest in reputation is certainly at the core of notions of human dignity, * * * the reputational interest at stake here is that of a corporation. Similarly, that this speech is solely commercial in nature undercuts the argument that presumed damages should be unrestrained in actions like this one because actual harm will be difficult to prove. If the credit report is viewed as commercial expression, proving that actual damages occurred is relatively easy. * * *

these principles, we would reverse and remand for further proceedings not inconsistent with this opinion.

Notes

1. Is *Dun & Bradstreet v. Greenmoss Builders* consistent with *Gertz* case? Recall that in *Gertz* the court rejected the *Rosenbloom* "public or general interest" distinction because "[w]e doubt the wisdom of committing this task to the conscience of judges." It should be noted that Justice Powell's plurality opinion in *Dun & Bradstreet* was only joined in by two other justices whereas Justice Brennan's dissent represented the votes of four justices including himself. Justice Brennan's opinion was by far the longest opinion filed in the case. It is hoped that the extracts printed above give the reader a fairly accurate feel for the arguments that he presented.

2. It is obvious that, with the change in personnel on the Court, there is a fair amount of uncertainty as to what direction the Court will take in the future. For example, in Philadelphia Newspapers, Inc. v. Hepps, 475 U.S. 767, 106 S.Ct. 1558, 89 L.Ed.2d 783 (1986) the Court by only a five-four vote held that *Gertz* required that the burden of persuasion in a defamation action brought by a private figure against a newspaper about articles of public concern, on the issue of truth, be placed on the plaintiff. The *Restatement (Second) of Torts* § 580B, Comment *j* (1977) thought that, after *New York Times* and its progeny, this was a foregone conclusion. If the plaintiff must show that the defendant intentionally published a false statement, or was recklessly indifferent or negligent with regard to that statement, it does not seem to make much sense to place the burden of persuasion on the question of truth or falsity on the defendant. Writing per Justice O'Connor, the Court, moreover, made the following curious reservation in a footnote:

> We also have no occasion to consider the quantity of proof of falsity that a private-figure plaintiff must present to recover damages. Nor need we consider what standards would apply if the plaintiff sues a non-media defendant, *see* Hutcheson v. Proxmire, 443 U.S. 111, 133, n. 16, 99 S.Ct. 2675, 61 L.Ed.2d 411 (1975), or if the state were to provide a plaintiff with the opportunity to obtain a judgment that declared the speech at issue to be false but not give rise to liability for damages.

Id. at 779, n. 4, 106 S.Ct. at 1565, 89 L.Ed.2d at 794. Justice Brennan, joined by Justice Blackburn, both of whom otherwise concurred in the majority opinion, wrote that, while the Court reserved the question whether the doctrine it announced applied to non-media defendants, he continued to adhere to the view he expressed in *Dun & Bradstreet v. Greenmoss Builders* that such a distinction is irreconcilable with the fundamental principles of the first amendment.

3. Justice Powell's plurality opinion in *Dun & Bradstreet v. Greenmoss Builders* said nothing about whether, in litigation between private persons not involving matters of public concern, the states are free to return to the common law doctrine that someone who publishes a statement that turns out to be defamatory of another is strictly liable if the statement turns out to be false. Nevertheless, as we have just seen, Justice White, in his concurring opinion in that case (*supra*, p. 1184), opined that the logic of the plurality opinion rendered the *Gertz* requirement of fault inapplicable. And, indeed a few state courts have shown themselves prepared so to read *Dun & Bradstreet v. Greenmoss Builders*. For example, although the case before it involved a

matter of public interest, the Arizona Supreme Court, in Dombey v. Phoenix Newspapers, Inc., 150 Ariz. 476, 481, 724 P.2d 562, 567 (1986), declared that the decisions of the United States Supreme Court "establish that when a plaintiff is a private figure and the speech is of private concern, the states are free to retain common law principles." *See also* Nelson v. Lapeyrouse Grain Corp., 534 So.2d 1085, 1092 n. 2 (Ala.1988) (dictum); Cox v. Hatch, 761 P.2d 556, 559–60 (Utah 1988)(dictum). In Ross v. Bricker, 770 F.Supp. 1038, 1043–44, (D.Vi.1991), the court also so interpreted *Dun & Bradstreet v. Greenmoss Builders*, but ruled that the Virgin islands would continue to follow the *Gertz* standards. On the other hand a federal district court in a diversity case ruled, in what might be considered an alternate holding rather than dictum, that North Carolina law could be interpreted as having recognized, in a limited class of libel cases between private parties, liability without proof of negligence. Sleem v. Yale University, 843 F.Supp. 57, 63–64 (M.D.N.C.1993).

4. *Alternative remedies.* Justice White is not the first person to claim that many people, and particularly political figures, are more interested in establishing that derogatory statements made about them are false than in recovering any damages. Among such proposals are: M. Franklin, *A Declaratory Judgment Alternative to Current Libel Law,* 74 Calif.L.Rev. 809 (1986) and D. Barrett, *Declaratory Judgments for Libel: A Better Alternative,* 74 Calif.L.Rev. 847 (1986). On the general subject, *see also* R. Smolla and M. Gaertner, *The Annenberg Libel Reform Proposal: The Case for Enactment,* 31 Wm. & Mary L.Rev. 25 (1989). Barrett's proposal tracks H.R. 2846, 99th Cong., 1st Sess. (1985) that was introduced by Representative Charles Schumer. That bill only covered actions by public officials or public figures who are the "subject of a publication or broadcast which is published or broadcast in the print or electronic media." It permitted either the plaintiff or the defendant in such an action to designate the action as one for declaratory judgment in which no proof of the state of mind of the defendant is required and in which no damages are to be awarded. At the same time the Schumer bill prohibited punitive damages "in any action [for defamation] arising out of a publication or broadcast which is alleged to be false and defamatory" and provided for a one year statute of limitations on any such actions. Awards of attorneys' fees to prevailing parties were permitted. The Franklin proposal was not restricted to media defendants or to actions brought by public officials or public figures. Franklin's proposal would rule out the award of punitive damages in any "action for libel, or slander or false-light invasion of privacy." In an action for declaratory judgment no proof of the state of mind of the defendant would be required but no damages would be awarded. With some exceptions, Franklin would also allow the award of attorneys' fees to the prevailing party.

One *assumption* in all these proposals is that by eliminating the state of mind of the defendant as an issue and by eliminating damages the cost of either bringing or defending defamation actions would not be so great as either to discourage people from seeking redress or to have a chilling effect on potential defendants' willingness to speak out. These proposals also assume that awarding attorneys' fees to the prevailing party will not reintroduce those same inhibiting concerns. In the very famous litigation between Arial Sharon and *Time Magazine* in 1984–1985, Judge Abraham Sofaer sent the case to the jury with a tripartite instruction. The jury was to first decide if Sharon had been defamed. If the jury concluded that he had been, the jury was then to decide if Sharon had proved that the defamatory statements made about him were false. If the jury decided this question in the affirmative as well, it was then to decide on the question of constitutional or actual malice. The jury decided these questions seriatim and reported its conclusions as it reached them. It eventually decided the first two questions in the affirmative. *See* New York Times Sat. Jan., 1985, p. 1, col. 5. The jury subsequently ruled that Sharon had not proved that *Time Magazine* published the article knowing it was false or with serious doubts about its truth. In effect Judge Sofaer allowed Sharon to have a declaratory judgment that false derogatory statements had been made about him. In the absence of statute one may have some doubts about the propriety of this procedure. It certainly introduces a greater judicial involvement in the jury's deliberations than is customary in defamation actions and goes against the spirit of Fox's libel act (32 Geo. 3, c. 60 (1792)) empowering juries to bring in general verdicts in criminal libel prosecutions. Although that statute only applied to criminal prosecutions, it has been taken in England to make the question of "libel or no libel" a jury question in civil actions and the usual practice there as in the United States has been to use general verdicts in defamation actions. It is also not at all clear that the greater volume of actions that a newspaper or other frequent defendants in defamation actions may expect to be brought against them will not cumulatively lead to the incurring of costs equal to those now being incurred when the potential recovery is much greater but the procedural hurdles which the plaintiff must overcome are much greater. M. Massing, *The Libel Chill: How Cold is It out There?* Colum.J.Rev., May/June 1985 at 31 is a frequently cited source for the proposition that the costs of defending libel actions can seriously threaten the media, particularly smaller newspapers. One incident that he described involved the Alton, Illinois *Telegraph* which was threatened with bankruptcy by a $9.2 million verdict in a defamation action. The defendant in that case decided to settle the action with the help of its libel insurer rather than take the chance that the entire award might be upheld on appeal.

Chapter 19

PRIVACY

ROBERSON v. ROCHESTER FOLDING BOX CO.

Court of Appeals of New York, 1902.
171 N.Y. 538, 64 N.E. 442.

[Reprinted at p. 8, *supra*]

Notes

1.   S. Warren and L. Brandeis, *The Right to Privacy*, 4 Harv.L.Rev. 193 (1890), has been one of the most frequently cited law review articles ever written.   The conventional wisdom has been that the article was prompted by Warren's annoyance over the manner in which the wedding of his daughter was covered by the press.   *See* W. Prosser, *Privacy*, 48 Cal.L.Rev. 383 (1960); H. Kalven, Jr., *Privacy in Tort Law—Were Warren and Brandeis Wrong?*, 31 Law & Contemp. Probs. 326, 329 n. 22 (1966).   More recent and more exhaustive scholarship contends that if there was any impetus for Warren and Brandeis' article, it was press criticism of Warren's father-in-law, Thomas Bayard, Sr., who had been a United States Senator from Delaware and who had been Secretary of State in the first Cleveland administration.   *See* J. Barron, *Warren and Brandeis, The Right to Privacy*, 4 Harv.L.Rev. 193 (1890): Demystifying a Landmark Citation, *13 Suffolk U.L.Rev. 875 (1979).   Barron points out that Warren's daughter was only seven years old in 1890.   A cousin of Warren's had been married in 1890, but the press coverage had been fairly sedate.*

2.   As previously noted, p. 15, *supra*, the New York legislature in 1903 responded to the decision in *Roberson* by enacting what, after reenactment in 1909, became §§ 50–51 of the New York Civil Rights Law.   The complete current wording of these provisions is as follows:

§ 50.   Right of privacy

A person, firm or corporation that uses for advertising purposes, or for the purposes of trade, the name, portrait or picture of any living person without having first obtained the written consent of such person, or if a minor of his or her parent or guardian, is guilty of a misdemeanor.

§ 51.   Action for injunction and for damages

Any person whose name, portrait, picture or voice is used within this state for advertising purposes or for the purposes of trade without the written consent first obtained as above provided may maintain an equitable action in the supreme court of this state against the person, firm or corporation so using his name, portrait, picture or voice, to prevent and restrain the use thereof; and may also sue and recover damages for any injuries sustained by reason of such use and if the defendant shall have knowingly used such person's name, portrait, picture or voice in such manner as is forbidden or declared to be unlawful by section fifty of this article, the jury, in its discretion, may award exemplary damages. But nothing contained in this article shall be so construed as to prevent any person, firm or corporation from selling or otherwise transferring any material containing such name, portrait, picture or voice in whatever medium to any user of such name, portrait, picture or voice, or to any third party for sale or transfer directly or indirectly to such a user, for use in a manner lawful under this article; nothing contained in this article shall be so construed as to prevent any person, firm or corporation, practicing the profession of photography, from exhibiting in or about his or its establishment specimens of the work of such establishment, unless the same is continued by such person, firm or corporation after written notice objecting thereto has been given by the person portrayed; and nothing contained in this article shall be so construed as to prevent any person, firm or corporation from using the name, portrait, picture or voice of any manufacturer or dealer in connection with the goods, wares and merchandise manufactured, produced or dealt in by him which he has sold or disposed of with such name, portrait, picture or voice used in connection therewith; or from using the name, portrait, picture or voice of any author, composer or artist in connection with his literary, musical or artistic productions which he has sold or disposed of with such name, portrait, picture or voice used in connection therewith. Nothing contained in this section shall be construed to prohibit the copyright owner of a sound recording from disposing of, dealing in, licensing or selling that sound recording to any party, if the right to dispose of, deal in, license or sell such sound recording has been conferred by contract or other written document by such living person or the holder of such right. Nothing contained in the foregoing sentence shall be deemed to abrogate or otherwise limit any rights or remedies otherwise conferred by federal law or state law.

In 1979, an additional provision was added. As amended in 1991, it provides:

§ 50–b. Right of privacy; victims of sex offenses

1. The identity of any victim of a sex offense, as defined in article one hundred thirty or section 255.25 of the penal law, shall be confidential. No report, paper, picture, photograph, court file or other documents, in the custody or possession of any public officer or employee, which identifies such a victim shall be made available for public inspection. No such public officer or employee shall disclose any portion of any police report, court file, or other document, which tends to identify such a victim except as provided in subdivision two of this section.

2. The provisions of subdivision one of this section shall not be construed to prohibit disclosure of information to:

a. Any person charged with the commission of a sex offense, as defined in subdivision one of this section, against the same victim; the counsel or guardian of such person; the public officers and employees charged with the duty of investigating, prosecuting, keeping records relating to the offense, or any other act when done pursuant to the lawful discharge of their duties; and any necessary witnesses for either party; or

b. Any person who, upon application to a court having jurisdiction over the alleged sex offense, demonstrates to the satisfaction of the court that good cause exists for disclosure to that person. Such application shall be made upon notice to the victim or other person legally responsible for the care of the victim, and the public officer or employee charged with the duty of prosecuting the offense; or

c. Any person or agency, upon written consent of the victim or other person legally responsible for the care of the victim, except as may be otherwise required or provided by the order of a court.

3. The court having jurisdiction over the alleged sex offense may order any restrictions upon disclosure authorized in subdivision two of this section, as it deems necessary and proper to preserve the confidentiality of the identity of the victim.

4. Nothing contained in this section shall be construed to require the court to exclude the public from any stage of the criminal proceeding.

As we shall see, p. 1229ff *infra,* attempts to prohibit the publication of the names of the victims of sexual offenses have had difficulty passing constitutional muster. We shall thus have occasion to consider whether a narrowly drawn statute like § 50–b is able to avoid the pitfalls of more broadly worded provisions. For a detailed discussion of the New York statute, *see* L. Savell, *Right of Privacy—Appropriation of a Person's Name, Portrait, or Picture for Advertising or Trade Purposes without Prior Written Consent: History and Scope in New York,* 48 Albany L.Rev. 1 (1983). We have already noted, note 1, p. 15, *supra,* the rejection of *Roberson* in Pavesich v. New England Life Insurance Co., 122 Ga. 190, 50 S.E. 68 (1905).

3. In an article written in 1960 the late Dean Prosser categorized and summarized the development of the law up until that time as follows:

What has emerged from the decisions is no simple matter. It is not one tort, but a complex of four. The law of privacy comprises four distinct kinds of invasion of four different interests of the plaintiff, which are tied together by the common name, but otherwise have almost nothing in common except that each represents an interference with the right of the plaintiff, in the phrase coined by Judge Cooley, "to be let alone." Without any attempt to exact definition, these four torts may be described as follows:

1. Intrusion upon the plaintiff's seclusion or solitude, or into his private affairs.

2. Public disclosure of embarrassing private facts about the plaintiff.

3. Publicity which places the plaintiff in a false light in the public eye.

4. Appropriation, for the defendant's advantage, of the plaintiff's name or likeness.

It should be obvious at once that these four types of invasion may be subject, in some respects at least, to different rules; and that when what is said about any one of them is carried over to another, it may not be at all applicable, and confusion may follow.

W. Prosser, *Supra* Note 1, at 389. Prosser's characterization of the tort has become extremely influential and it may be helpful to keep it in mind in analyzing the remaining cases presented in this chapter. Arguing *contra* Prosser, that there really is a core notion of privacy, is E. Bloustein, *Privacy as an Aspect of Human Dignity: an Answer to Dean Prosser,* 39 N.Y.U.L.Rev. 962 (1964). Bloustein also has attacked what might be characterized as the suggestion in Kalven, *supra* note 1, that privacy is a "trivial tort." *See* E. Bloustein, *Privacy, Tort Law, and the Constitution: Is Warren and Brandeis' Tort Petty and Unconstitutional as Well?,* 46 Tex.L.Rev. 611 (1968). For a stimulating discussion of the philosophical foundation of the notion of privacy, see C. Fried, *Privacy,* 77 Yale L.J. 475 (1968). *See also* R. Gavison, *Privacy and the Limits of Law,* 89 Yale L.J. 421 (1980); J. Reiman, *Privacy, Intimacy and Personhood,* 6 Phil. & Pub. Aff. 26 (1976). A good analysis of the various interests that have been subsumed under the rubric "privacy" is contained in H. Gross, *The Concept of Privacy,* 42 N.Y.U.L.Rev. 34 (1967). For a lively discussion of the dangers to individual privacy posed by modern technological innovations, *see* A. Miller, The Assault on Privacy: Computers, Data Banks, and Dossiers (1971). For a different view as to where the legal lines should be drawn, *see* G. Christie, *The Right to Privacy and the Freedom to Know: A Comment on Professor Miller's the Assault on Privacy,* 119 U.Pa.L.Rev. 970 (1971). On the comparative aspects of privacy, *see* H. Krause, *the Right to Privacy in Germany— Pointers for American Legislation?,* 1965 Duke L.J. 481; J. Weeks, *the Comparative Law of Privacy,* 12 Clev.-Mar.L.Rev. 484 (1963). English Law has not been very sympathetic to attempts to develop a right of privacy. *See* G. Dworkin, *The Younger Committee Report on Privacy,* 36 Mod.L.Rev. 399 (1973). *See also* W. Pratt, Privacy in Britain (1979).

More recent critical discussions of the judicial creation of the tort of privacy include D. Zimmerman, *Requiem for a Heavyweight: A Farewell to Warren and Brandeis's Privacy Tort,* 68 Cornell L.Rev. 291 (1983); R. Bezanson, *The Right to Privacy Revisited: Privacy, News, and Social Change, 1890–1990,* 80 Cal.L.Rev. 1133 (1992); Comment, *Privacy in Photographs: Misconception Since Inception,* 18 John Marshall L.Rev. 969 (1985). The Zimmerman article is a fairly comprehensive review of the law of privacy as of 1983. She concluded that the interests sought to be protected by the "so-called right to privacy" might better be served by narrowly drawn statutory provisions that focus on the point of origin of the information in question rather than the ultimate dissemination of that information to the public at large. She also advocates adequate sanctions for the breach of "special confidential relationships". Bezanson also maintains that the principal focus of the common-law tort of privacy should be the protection of confidentiality with perhaps a more expanded notion of the range of confidentiality.

CANTRELL v. FOREST CITY PUBLISHING CO.

Supreme Court of the United States, 1974.
419 U.S. 245, 95 S.Ct. 465, 42 L.Ed.2d 419.

MR. JUSTICE STEWART delivered the opinion of the Court.

Margaret Cantrell and four of her minor children brought this diversity action in a Federal District Court for invasion of privacy against the Forest City Publishing Co., publisher of a Cleveland newspaper, the Plain Dealer, and against Joseph Eszterhas, a reporter formerly employed by the

Plain Dealer, and Richard Conway, a Plain Dealer photographer. The Cantrells alleged that an article published in the Plain Dealer Sunday Magazine unreasonably placed their family in a false light before the public through its many inaccuracies and untruths. The District Judge struck the claims relating to punitive damages as to all the plaintiffs and dismissed the actions of three of the Cantrell children in their entirety, but allowed the case to go to the jury as to Mrs. Cantrell and her oldest son, William. The jury returned a verdict against all three of the respondents for compensatory money damages in favor of these two plaintiffs.

The Court of Appeals for the Sixth Circuit reversed, holding that, in the light of the First and Fourteenth Amendments, the District Judge should have granted the respondents' motion for a directed verdict as to all the Cantrells' claims. * * *

I

In December 1967, Margaret Cantrell's husband Melvin was killed along with 43 other people when the Silver Bridge across the Ohio River at Point Pleasant, W.Va., collapsed. The respondent Eszterhas was assigned by the Plain Dealer to cover the story of the disaster. He wrote a "news feature" story focusing on the funeral of Melvin Cantrell and the impact of his death on the Cantrell family.

Five months later, after conferring with the Sunday Magazine editor of the Plain Dealer, Eszterhas and photographer Conway returned to the Point Pleasant area to write a follow-up feature. The two men went to the Cantrell residence, where Eszterhas talked with the children and Conway took 50 pictures. Mrs. Cantrell was not at home at any time during the 60 to 90 minutes that the men were at the Cantrell residence.

Eszterhas' story appeared as the lead feature in the August 4, 1968, edition of the Plain Dealer Sunday Magazine. The article stressed the family's abject poverty; the children's old, ill-fitting clothes and the deteriorating condition of their home were detailed in both the text and accompanying photographs. As he had done in his original, prize-winning article on the Silver Bridge disaster, Eszterhas used the Cantrell family to illustrate the impact of the bridge collapse on the lives of the people in the Point Pleasant area.

It is conceded that the story contained a number of inaccuracies and false statements. Most conspicuously, although Mrs. Cantrell was not present at any time during the reporter's visit to her home, Eszterhas wrote, "Margaret Cantrell will talk neither about what happened nor about how they are doing. She wears the same mask of non-expression she wore at the funeral. She is a proud woman. Her world has changed. She says that after it happened, the people in town offered to help them out with money and they refused to take it." Other significant misrepresentations were contained in details of Eszterhas' descriptions of the poverty in which the Cantrells were living and the dirty and dilapidated conditions of the Cantrell home.

The case went to the jury on a so-called "false light" theory of invasion of privacy. In essence, the theory of the case was that by publishing the false feature story about the Cantrells and thereby making them the objects of pity and ridicule, the respondents damaged Mrs. Cantrell and her son William by causing them to suffer outrage, mental distress, shame, and humiliation.

II

In Time, Inc. v. Hill, 385 U.S. 374, the Court considered a similar false-light, invasion-of-privacy action. The New York Court of Appeals had interpreted New York Civil Rights Law, McKinney's Consol.Laws, c. 6, §§ 50–51 to give a "newsworthy person" a right of action when his or her name, picture or portrait was the subject of a "fictitious" report or article. Material and substantial falsification was the test for recovery. * * * Under this doctrine the New York courts awarded the plaintiff James Hill compensatory damages based on his complaint that Life Magazine had falsely reported that a new Broadway play portrayed the Hill family's experience in being held hostage by three escaped convicts. This Court, guided by its decision in New York Times Co. v. Sullivan, * * * which recognized constitutional limits on a State's power to award damages for libel in actions brought by public officials, held that the constitutional protections for speech and press precluded the application of the New York statute to allow recovery for "false reports of matters of public interest in the absence of proof that the defendant published the report with knowledge of its falsity or in reckless disregard of the truth." * * * Although the jury could have reasonably concluded from the evidence in the *Hill* case that Life had engaged in knowing falsehood or had recklessly disregarded the truth in stating in the article that "the story re-enacted" the Hill family's experience, the Court concluded that the trial judge's instructions had not confined the jury to such a finding as a predicate for liability as required by the Constitution. * * *

The District Judge in the case before us, in contrast to the trial judge in Time, Inc. v. Hill, did instruct the jury that liability could be imposed only if it concluded that the false statements in the Sunday Magazine feature article on the Cantrells had been made with knowledge of their falsity or in reckless disregard of the truth. No objection was made by any of the parties to this knowing-or-reckless-falsehood instruction. Consequently, this case presents no occasion to consider whether a State may constitutionally apply a more relaxed standard of liability for a publisher or broadcaster of false statements injurious to a private individual under a false-light theory of invasion of privacy, or whether the constitutional standard announced in Time, Inc. v. Hill applies to all false-light cases. Cf. Gertz v. Robert Welch, Inc. * * *. Rather, the sole question that we need decide is whether the Court of Appeals erred in setting aside the jury's verdict.

III

At the close of the petitioners' case-in-chief, the District Judge struck the demand for punitive damages. He found that Mrs. Cantrell had failed to present any evidence to support the charges that the invasion of privacy "was done maliciously within the legal definition of that term." The Court of Appeals interpreted this finding to be a determination by the District Judge that there was no evidence of knowing falsity or reckless disregard of the truth introduced at the trial. Having made such a determination, the

Court of Appeals held that the District Judge should have granted the motion for a directed verdict for respondents as to all the Cantrells' claims. * * *

The Court of Appeals appears to have assumed that the District Judge's finding of no malice "within the legal definition of that term" was a finding based on the definition of "actual malice" established by this Court in New York Times Co. v. Sullivan * * *. As so defined, of course, "actual malice" is a term of art, created to provide a convenient shorthand expression for the standard of liability that must be established before a State may constitutionally permit public officials to recover for libel in actions brought against publishers. As such, it is quite different from the common-law standard of "malice" generally required under state tort law to support an award of punitive damages. In a false-light case, common-law malice—frequently expressed in terms of either personal ill will toward the plaintiff or reckless or wanton disregard of the plaintiff's rights—would focus on the defendant's attitude toward the plaintiff's privacy, not toward the truth or falsity of the material published. * * *

Although the verbal record of the District Court proceedings is not entirely unambiguous, the conclusion is inescapable that the District Judge was referring to the common-law standard of malice rather than to the New York Times "actual malice" standard when he dismissed the punitive damages claims. For at the same time that he dismissed the demands for punitive damages, the District Judge refused to grant the respondents' motion for directed verdicts as to Mrs. Cantrell's and William's claims for compensatory damages. And, as his instructions to the jury made clear, the District Judge was fully aware that the Time, Inc. v. Hill meaning of the New York Times "actual malice" standard had to be satisfied for the Cantrells to recover actual damages. Thus, the only way to harmonize these two virtually simultaneous rulings by the District Judge is to conclude, contrary to the decision of the Court of Appeals, that in dismissing the punitive damages claims he was not determining that Mrs. Cantrell had failed to introduce any evidence of knowing falsity or reckless disregard of the truth. * * *

Moreover, the District Judge was clearly correct in believing that the evidence introduced at trial was sufficient to support a jury finding that the respondents Joseph Eszterhas and Forest City Publishing Co. had published knowing or reckless falsehoods about the Cantrells. There was no dispute during the trial that Eszterhas, who did not testify, must have known that a number of the statements in the feature story were untrue. In particular, his article plainly implied that Mrs. Cantrell had been present during his visit to her home and that Eszterhas had observed her "wear[ing] the same mask of nonexpression she wore [at her husband's] funeral." These were "calculated falsehoods," and the jury was plainly justified in finding that Eszterhas had portrayed the Cantrells in a false light through knowing or reckless untruth.

* * *

For the foregoing reasons, the judgment of the Court of Appeals is reversed and the case is remanded to that court with directions to enter a judgment affirming the judgment of the District Court as to the respondents Forest City Publishing Co. and Joseph Eszterhas.

It is so ordered.

Reversed and remanded.

MR. JUSTICE DOUGLAS, dissenting.

I adhere to the views which I expressed in Time, Inc. v. Hill, 385 U.S. 374 (1967). * * * Freedom of the press is "abridged" in violation of the First and Fourteenth Amendments by what we do today. This line of cases, which of course includes New York Times Co. v. Sullivan, * * * seems to me to place First Amendment rights of the press at a midway point similar to what our ill-fated Betts v. Brady, 316 U.S. 455 (1942) did to the right to counsel. The press will be "free" in the First Amendment sense when the judge-made qualifications of that freedom are withdrawn and the substance of the First Amendment restored to what I believe was the purpose of its enactment.

A bridge accident catapulted the Cantrells into the public eye and their disaster became newsworthy. To make the First Amendment freedom to report the news turn on subtle differences between common-law malice and actual malice is to stand the Amendment on its head. Those who write the current news seldom have the objective, dispassionate point of view—or the time—of scientific analysts. They deal in fast-moving events and the need for "spot" reporting. The jury under today's formula sits as a censor with broad powers—not to impose a prior restraint, but to lay heavy damages on the press. The press is "free" only if the jury is sufficiently disenchanted with the Cantrells to let the press be free of this damages claim. * * * Whatever might be the ultimate reach of the doctrine Mr. Justice Black and I have embraced, it seems clear that in matters of public import such as the present news reporting, there must be freedom from damages lest the press be frightened into playing a more ignoble role than the Framers visualized.

I would affirm the judgment of the Court of Appeals.

Notes

1. In Time, Inc. v. Hill, 385 U.S. 374, 87 S.Ct. 534, 17 L.Ed.2d 456 (1967), the Court noted that on their face §§ 50–51 of the New York Civil Rights Law

> proscribe only conduct of the kind involved in *Roberson*, that is, appropriation and use in advertising or to promote the sale of goods, of another's name, portrait or picture without his consent. An application of that limited scope would present different questions of violation of the constitutional protections for speech and press.
>
> The New York courts have, however, construed the statute to operate much more broadly. * * *

385 U.S. at 381, 87 S.Ct. at 538–39, 17 L.Ed.2d at 463. Nevertheless, the Court noted that the New York Court of Appeals had held, in Spahn v. Julian Messner, Inc., 18 N.Y.2d 324, 274 N.Y.S.2d 877, 221 N.E.2d 543 (1966), that "truth is a complete defense in actions under the statute based upon reports of newsworthy people or events." *Spahn* involved the partially fictionalized (though not unflattering) biography of a well-known baseball player. Furthermore, the New York court had also held that "minor errors" were not

actionable. The Court in *Hill* went on to hold that, accepting this construction of the New York statutes, no action could constitutionally lie unless there were proof of knowledge of falsity or reckless disregard for truth. An interesting part of the Court's opinion, written by Justice Brennan, is footnote 7, the pertinent parts of which read as follows:

> This case presents no question whether truthful publication of such matter could be constitutionally proscribed.
>
> It has been said that a 'right of privacy' has been recognized at common law in 30 States plus the District of Columbia and by statute in four States. See Prosser, Law of Torts 831–832 (3d ed. 1964). Professor Kalven notes, however, that since Warren and Brandeis championed an action against the press for public disclosure of truthful but private details about the individual which caused emotional upset to him, "it has been agreed that there is a generous privilege to serve the public interest in news. * * * What is at issue, it seems to me, is whether the claim of privilege is not so overpowering as virtually to swallow the tort. What can be left of the vaunted new right after the claims of privilege have been confronted?" Kalven, "Privacy in Tort Law—Were Warren and Brandeis Wrong?" 31 Law & Contemp.Prob. 326, 335–336 (1966).

2. Justice Stewart, in *Cantrell*, leaves open the question whether the *Gertz* standard may not be applicable in false-light privacy cases brought by private figures. Declaring that the *Gertz* negligence standard does replace the *Hill* standard in such cases is Rinsley v. Brandt, 446 F.Supp. 850 (D.Kan.1977), which was followed in Tomson v. Stephan, 696 F.Supp. 1407, 1413 (D.Kan. 1988). *See also* Wood v. Hustler Magazine, Inc., 736 F.2d 1084 (5th Cir.1984), *cert. denied* 469 U.S. 1107, 105 S.Ct. 783, 83 L.Ed.2d 777 (1985). *See also* A. Hill, *Defamation and Privacy Under the First Amendment,* 76 Colum.L.Rev. 1205, 1274 (1976); J. Phillips, *Defamation, Invasion of Privacy and the Constitutional Standard of Care,* 16 Santa Clara L.Rev. 77, 99 (1975). On the other hand, in Dodrill v. Arkansas Democrat Co., 265 Ark. 628, 590 S.W.2d 840 (1979) *cert. denied* 444 U.S. 1076, 100 S.Ct. 1024, 62 L.Ed.2d 759 (1980), the court held that until the Supreme Court held otherwise it was obliged to follow *Hill* and apply the *Sullivan* standard in false-light privacy cases. This position has been taken by the majority of courts that have considered the question. *See* Colbert v. World Pub. Co., 747 P.2d 286 (Okl.1987); Machleder v. Diaz, 618 F.Supp. 1367, 1373 n. 4 (S.D.N.Y.1985), *reversed on other grounds* 801 F.2d 46 (2d Cir.1986). *Restatement (Second) of Torts* § 652E also applies the *Sullivan* standard to false-light privacy cases. In this regard, it should be noted that in *Gertz,* Justice Powell, who wrote for the Court, specifically said, in conjunction with explaining why private figures could recover in defamation actions merely on a showing of "fault," "[o]ur inquiry would involve considerations somewhat different from those discussed above if a State purported to condition civil liability on a factual misstatement whose content did not warn a reasonably prudent editor or broadcaster of its defamatory potential. *Cf.* Time, Inc. v. Hill, * * * Such a case is not now before us, and we intimate no view as to its proper resolution." *See* p. 1157, *supra.*

3. Because of the similarities with defamation, most of the restrictions applied against plaintiffs in defamation actions have been applied to plaintiffs in false-light invasion of privacy actions. *See* Fellows v. National Enquirer, Inc., 42 Cal.3d 234, 228 Cal.Rptr. 215, 721 P.2d 97 (1986) which, in a false-light invasion of privacy action, applied the California doctrine that, if a false

statement is not defamatory on its face, recovery is only permitted upon allegation and proof of special damages.

4. In Renwick v. News and Observer Pub. Co., 310 N.C. 312, 312 S.E.2d 405 (1984), *cert. denied* 469 U.S. 858, 105 S.Ct. 187, 83 L.Ed.2d 121 the court declared that North Carolina would not recognize actions for false-light invasion of privacy. Recovery for the dissemination of false information about a person may only be had in actions for libel or slander. Do you approve of this approach? *See* D. Zimmerman, *False Light Invasion of Privacy: The Light That Failed*, 64 N.Y.U.L.Rev. 364 (1989) which strongly approves of the approach taken in cases like *Renwick*. In Godbehere v. Phoenix Newspapers, Inc., 162 Ariz. 335, 783 P.2d 781 (1989) the court would not permit a false-light invasion of privacy action to be brought for publications relating to the public life or duties of public officials.

NADER v. GENERAL MOTORS CORP.

New York Court of Appeals, 1970.
25 N.Y.2d 560, 307 N.Y.S.2d 647, 255 N.E.2d 765.

FULD, CHIEF JUDGE.

On this appeal, taken by permission of the Appellate Division on a certified question, we are called upon to determine the reach of the tort of invasion of privacy as it exists under the law of the District of Columbia.

The complaint, in this action by Ralph Nader, pleads four causes of action against the appellant, General Motors Corporation, and three other defendants allegedly acting as its agents. The first two causes of action charge an invasion of privacy, the third is predicated on the intentional infliction of severe emotional distress and the fourth on interference with the plaintiff's economic advantage. This appeal concerns only the legal sufficiency of the first two causes of action, which were upheld in the courts below as against the appellant's motion to dismiss * * *.

The plaintiff, an author and lecturer on automotive safety, has, for some years, been an articulate and severe critic of General Motors' products from the standpoint of safety and design. According to the complaint—which, for present purposes, we must assume to be true—the appellant, having learned of the imminent publication of the plaintiff's book "Unsafe at any Speed," decided to conduct a campaign of intimidation against him in order to "suppress plaintiff's criticism of and prevent his disclosure of information" about its products. To that end, the appellant authorized and directed the other defendants to engage in a series of activities which, the plaintiff claims in his first two causes of action, violated his right to privacy.

Specifically, the plaintiff alleges that the appellant's agents (1) conducted a series of interviews with acquaintances of the plaintiff, "questioning them about, and casting aspersions upon [his] political, social * * * racial and religious views * * *; his integrity; his sexual proclivities and inclinations; and his personal habits" (Complaint, par. 9[b]); (2) kept him under surveillance in public places for an unreasonable length of time (par. 9[c]); (3) caused him to be accosted by girls for the purpose of entrapping him into illicit relationships (par. 9[d]); (4) made threatening, harassing and obnoxious telephone calls to him (par. 9[e]); (5) tapped his telephone and eavesdropped, by means of mechanical and electronic equipment, on his private conversations with others (par. 9[f]); and (6) conducted a "continuing" and harassing investigation of him (par. 9[g]). These charges are amplified in the plaintiff's bill of particulars, and those particulars are, of course, to be taken into account in considering the sufficiency of the challenged causes of action. * * *

The threshold choice of law question requires no extended discussion. In point of fact, the parties have agreed—at least for purposes of this motion—that the sufficiency of these allegations is to be determined under the law of the District of Columbia. The District is the jurisdiction in which most of the acts are alleged to have occurred, and it was there, too, that the plaintiff lived and suffered the impact of those acts. It is, in short, the place which has the most significant relationship with the subject matter of the tort charged. * * *

Turning, then, to the law of the District of Columbia, it appears that its courts have not only recognized a common-law action for invasion of privacy but have broadened the scope of that tort beyond its traditional limits. * * * Thus, in the most recent of its cases on the subject, Pearson v. Dodd (133 U.S.App.D.C. 279, 410 F.2d 701, *supra*), the Federal Court of Appeals for the District of Columbia declared (p. 704):

> "We approve the extension of the tort of invasion of privacy to instances of *intrusion,* whether by physical trespass or not, into spheres from which an ordinary man in a plaintiff's position could reasonably expect that the particular defendant should be excluded." (Italics supplied.)

It is this form of invasion of privacy—initially termed "intrusion" by Dean Prosser in 1960 (Privacy, 48 Cal.L.Rev. 383, 389 et seq.; Torts, § 112)—on which the two challenged causes of action are predicated.

Quite obviously, some intrusions into one's private sphere are inevitable concomitants of life in an industrial and densely populated society, which the law does not seek to proscribe even if it were possible to do so. "The law does not provide a remedy for every annoyance that occurs in everyday life." (Kelley v. Post Publishing Co., 327 Mass. 275, 278, 98 N.E.2d 286, 287 (1951)). However, the District of Columbia courts have held that the law should and does protect against certain types of intrusive conduct, and we must, therefore, determine whether the plaintiff's allegations are actionable as violations of the right to privacy under the law of that jurisdiction. To do so, we must, in effect, predict what the judges of that jurisdiction's highest court would hold if this case were presented to them. * * * In other words, what would the Court of Appeals for the District of Columbia say is the character of the "privacy" sought to be protected? More specifically, would that court accord an individual a right, as the plaintiff before us insists, to be protected against any interference whatsoever with his personal seclusion and solitude? Or would it adopt a more restrictive view of the right, as the appellant urges, merely protecting the individual from intrusion into "something secret," from snooping and prying into his private affairs?

The classic article by Warren and Brandeis (The Right to Privacy, 4 Harv.L.Rev. 193)—to which the court in the *Pearson* case referred as the source of the District's common-law action for invasion of privacy (410 F.2d, at p. 703)—was premised, to a large extent, on principles originally developed in the field of copyright law. The authors thus based their thesis on a right granted by the common law to "each individual * * * of determining, ordinarily, to what extent his thoughts, sentiments and emotions shall be communicated to others" (4 Harv.L.Rev., at p. 198). Their principal concern appeared to be not with a broad "right to be let alone" (Cooley, Torts [2d ed.], p. 29) but, rather, with the right to protect oneself from having one's private affairs known to others and to keep secret or intimate facts about oneself from the prying eyes or ears of others.

In recognizing the existence of a common-law cause of action for invasion of privacy in the District of Columbia, the Court of Appeals has expressly adopted this latter formulation of the nature of the right. * * * And, in *Pearson,* where the court extended the tort of invasion of privacy to instances of "intrusion," it again indicated, contrary to the plaintiff's submission, that the interest protected was one's right to keep knowledge about oneself from exposure to others, the right to prevent *"the obtaining of the information* by improperly intrusive means" * * *. In other jurisdictions, too, the cases which have recognized a remedy for invasion of privacy founded upon intrusive conduct have generally involved the gathering of private facts or information through improper means. * * *

It should be emphasized that the mere gathering of information about a particular individual does not give rise to a cause of action under this theory. Privacy is invaded only if the information sought is of a confidential nature and the defendant's conduct was unreasonably intrusive. Just as a common-law copyright is lost when material is published, so, too, there can be no invasion of privacy where the information sought is open to public view or has been voluntarily revealed to others. * * * In order to sustain a cause of action for invasion of privacy, therefore, the plaintiff must show that the appellant's conduct was truly "intrusive" and that it was designed to elicit information which would not be available through normal inquiry or observation.

The majority of the Appellate Division in the present case stated that *all of "[t]he activities complained of"* in the first two counts constituted actionable invasions of privacy under the law of the District of Columbia * * *. We do not agree with that sweeping determination. At most, only two of the activities charged to the appellant are, in our view, actionable as invasions of privacy under the law of the District of Columbia * * *. However, since the first two counts include allegations which are sufficient to state a cause of action, we could—as the concurring opinion notes— merely affirm the order before us without further elaboration. To do so, though, would be a disservice both to the judge who will be called upon to try this case and to the litigants themselves. In other words, we deem it desirable, nay essential, that we go further and, for the guidance of the trial court and counsel, indicate the extent to which the plaintiff is entitled to rely on the various allegations in support of his privacy claim.

In following such a course, we are prompted not only by a desire to avoid any misconceptions that might stem from the opinion below but also by recognition of the fact that we are dealing with a new and developing area of the law. Indeed, we would fail to meet our responsibility if we were to withhold determination—particularly since the parties have fully briefed and argued the points involved—and thereby thrust upon the trial judge the initial burden of appraising the impact of a doctrine still in the process of growth and of predicting its reach in another jurisdiction.

Turning, then, to the particular acts charged in the complaint, we cannot find any basis for a claim of invasion of privacy, under District of Columbia law, in the allegations that the appellant, through its agents or employees, interviewed many persons who knew the plaintiff, asking questions about him and casting aspersions on his character. Although those inquiries may have uncovered information of a personal nature, it is difficult to see how they may be said to have invaded the plaintiff's privacy. Information about the plaintiff which was already known to others could hardly be regarded as private to the plaintiff. Presumably, the plaintiff had previously revealed the information to such other persons, and he would necessarily assume the risk that a friend or acquaintance in whom he had confided might breach the confidence. If, as alleged, the questions tended to disparage the plaintiff's character, his remedy would seem to be by way of an action for defamation, not for breach of his right to privacy. * * *

Nor can we find any actionable invasion of privacy in the allegations that the appellant caused the plaintiff to be accosted by girls, with illicit proposals, or that it was responsible for the making of a large number of threatening and harassing telephone calls to the plaintiff's home at odd hours. Neither of these activities, howsoever offensive and disturbing, involved intrusion for the purpose of gathering information of a private and confidential nature.

As already indicated, it is manifestly neither practical nor desirable for the law to provide a remedy against any and all activity which an individual might find annoying. On the other hand, where severe mental pain or anguish is inflicted through a deliberate and malicious campaign of harassment or intimidation, a remedy is available in the form of an action for the intentional infliction of emotional distress—the theory underlying the plaintiff's third cause of action. But the elements of such an action are decidedly different from those governing the tort of invasion of privacy, and just as we have carefully guarded against the use of the prima facie tort doctrine to circumvent the limitations relating to other established tort remedies * * *, we should be wary of any attempt to rely on the tort of invasion of privacy as a means of avoiding the more stringent pleading and proof requirements for an action for infliction of emotional distress. * * *

Apart, however, from the foregoing allegations which we find inadequate to spell out a cause of action for invasion of privacy under District of Columbia law, the complaint contains allegations concerning other activities by the appellant or its agents which do satisfy the requirements for such a cause of action. The one which most clearly meets those requirements is the charge that the appellant and its codefendants engaged in unauthorized wiretapping and eavesdropping by mechanical and electronic means. The Court of Appeals in the *Pearson* case expressly recognized that such conduct constitutes a tortious intrusion and other jurisdictions have reached a similar conclusion. * * * In point of fact, the appellant does not dispute this, acknowledging that, to the extent the two challenged counts charge it with wiretapping and eavesdropping, an actionable invasion of privacy has been stated.

There are additional allegations that the appellant hired people to shadow the plaintiff and keep him under surveillance. In particular, he claims that, on one occasion, one of its agents followed him into a bank, getting sufficiently close to him to see the denomination of the bills he was withdrawing from his account. From what we have already said, it is manifest that the mere observation of the plaintiff in a public place does not amount to an invasion of his privacy. But, under certain circumstances, surveillance may be so "overzealous" as to render it actionable. * * * Whether or not the surveillance in the present case falls into this latter category will depend on the nature of the proof. A person does not automatically make public everything he does merely by being in a public place, and the mere fact that Nader was in a bank did not give anyone the right to try to discover the amount of money he was withdrawing. On the other hand, if the plaintiff acted in such a way as to reveal that fact to any casual observer, then, it may not be said that the appellant intruded into his private sphere. In any event, though, it is enough for present purposes to say that the surveillance allegation is not insufficient as a matter of law.

Since, then, the first two causes of action do contain allegations which are adequate to state a cause of action for invasion of privacy under District of Columbia law, the courts below properly denied the appellant's motion to dismiss those causes of action. It is settled that, so long as a pleading sets forth allegations which suffice to spell out a claim for relief, it is not subject to dismissal by reason of the inclusion therein of additional nonactionable allegations. * * *

We would but add that the allegations concerning the interviewing of third persons, the accosting by girls and the annoying and threatening telephone calls, though insufficient to support a cause of action for invasion of privacy, are pertinent to the plaintiff's third cause of action—in which those allegations are reiterated—charging the intentional infliction of emotional distress. However, as already noted, it will be necessary for the plaintiff to meet the additional requirements prescribed by the law of the District of Columbia for the maintenance of a cause of action under that theory.

The order appealed from should be affirmed, with costs, and the question certified answered in the affirmative.

BREITEL, JUDGE (concurring in result).

There is no doubt that the first and second causes of action are sufficient in alleging an invasion of privacy under what appears to be the applicable law in the District of Columbia * * *. This should be the end of this court's proper concern with the pleadings, the only matter before the court being a motion to dismiss specified causes of action for insufficiency.

Thus it is not proper, it is submitted, for the court directly or indirectly to analyze particular allegations in the pleadings, once the causes of action are found sufficient, in order to determine whether they would alternatively sustain one cause of action or another, or whether evidence offered in support of the allegations is relevant only as to one rather than to another cause of action. Particularly, it is inappropriate to decide that several of the allegations as they now appear are referable only to the more restricted tort of intentional infliction of mental distress rather than to the common-law right of privacy upon which the first and second causes of action depend. The third cause of action is quite restricted. Thus many of the quite offensive acts charged will not be actionable unless plaintiff succeeds in the very difficult, if not impossible, task of showing that defendants' activities were designed, actually or virtually, to make plaintiff unhappy and not to uncover disgraceful information about him. The real issue in the volatile and developing law of privacy is whether a private person is entitled to be free of certain grave offensive intrusions unsupported by palpable social or economic excuse or justification.

True, scholars, in trying to define the elusive concept of the right of privacy, have, as of the present, subdivided the common law right into separate classifications, most significantly distinguishing between unreasonable intrusion and unreasonable publicity * * * This does not mean, however, that the classifications are either frozen or exhausted, or that several of the classifications may not overlap.

Concretely applied to this case, it is suggested, for example, that it is premature to hold that the attempted entrapment of plaintiff in a public place by seemingly promiscuous ladies is no invasion of any of the categories of the right to privacy and is restricted to a much more limited cause of action for intentional infliction of mental distress. Moreover, it does not strain credulity or imagination to conceive of the systematic "public" surveillance of another as being the implementation of a plan to intrude on the privacy of another. Although acts performed in "public", especially if taken singly or in small numbers, may not be confidential, at least arguably a right to privacy may nevertheless be invaded through extensive or exhaustive monitoring and cataloguing of acts normally disconnected and anonymous.

* * *

It is not unimportant that plaintiff contends that a giant corporation had allegedly sought by surreptitious and unusual methods to silence an unusually effective critic. If there was such a plan, and only a trial would show that, it is unduly restrictive of the future trial to allocate the evidence beforehand based only on a pleader's specification of overt acts on the bold assumption that they are not connected causally or do not bear on intent and motive.

* * *

There is still further difficulty. In this State thus far there has been no recognition of a common law right of privacy, but only that which derives from a statute of rather limited scope * * *. Consequently, this court must undertake the hazardous task of applying what is at present the quite different law of the District of Columbia. True, this may be the court's burden eventually, if the case were to return to it for review after trial, especially if the plaintiff were to prevail upon such a trial. However, there is no occasion to advance, now, into a complicated, subtle and still-changing field of law of another jurisdiction, solely to determine before trial the relevancy and allocability among pleaded causes of action or projected but not yet offered items of evidence.   * * *

* * *

Notes

1.   In Pearson v. Dodd, 410 F.2d 701 (D.C.Cir.1969), *cert. denied* 395 U.S. 947, 89 S.Ct. 2021, 23 L.Ed.2d 465, the defendants, Drew Pearson and Jack Anderson, had published a number of nationally syndicated newspaper columns concerning then Senator Thomas Dodd's relations with lobbyists representing "foreign interests."   The defendants obtained their information from xerox copies of materials in Dodd's files.   The xerox copies had been made by former employees of Dodd with the assistance of some of Dodd's current employees. In his complaint, Dodd charged the defendants with invasion of privacy and conversion.   Although Dodd charged Pearson and Anderson with aiding and abetting in the unauthorized removal of documents from Dodd's files, it was undisputed that it could only be shown that Pearson and Anderson received the documents knowing that the documents were removed and copied without Dodd's permission.   The district court denied Dodd's request for summary judgment on the privacy count but granted Dodd's request for summary judgment on the conversion count.   The court of appeals reversed on the conversion count because "appellants committed no conversion of the physical documents."   Recognizing that the ambit of legal protection had expanded, principally through the avenue of "common-law copyright," the court of appeals nevertheless held that no relief was possible here because "[i]nsofar as we can tell, none of it [i.e. the information] amounts to literary property, to scientific invention, or to secret plans formulated * * * for the conduct of commerce. Nor does it appear to be information held in any way for sale * * * analogous to the fresh news copy produced by a wire service."   On the privacy count, after the discussion that was relied on in *Nader,* the court of appeals affirmed the district court's refusal to grant partial summary judgment in favor of Dodd.   Obtaining information from an intruder was not itself intrusion.

2.   One of the leading cases on intrusion is Hamberger v. Eastman, 106 N.H. 107, 206 A.2d 239, 11 A.L.R.3d 1288 (1964), a case mentioned several times in omitted portions of the majority's and Breitel, J.'s opinions in *Nader.* There was no trespass in *Hamberger* because the defendant landlord had placed the listening device in the wall of the bedroom before the plaintiffs took possession of the premises.   Other cases holding that there may be liability for intrusion include Roach v. Harper, 143 W.Va. 869, 105 S.E.2d 564 (1958)(factually very similar to *Hamberger*) and Fowler v. Southern Bell Telephone & Telegraph Co., 343 F.2d 150 (5th Cir.1965)(tapping of a telephone; issue to be determined on remand was whether defendants acted at behest of federal agents acting within outer limits of their authority).

A frequently cited case is Dietemann v. Time, Inc., 449 F.2d 245 (9th Cir.1971).   In that case, two reporters for *Life* magazine, pursuant to an arrangement with the Los Angeles District Attorney's office, visited the plaintiff for the purpose of obtaining, in the words of the trial judge, "facts and pictures" concerning the plaintiff's "practice of healing with clay, minerals, and herbs" and with "some equipment which could at best be described as gadgets, not equipment which had anything to do with the practice of medicine."   Using the name of a friend of the plaintiff's as a ruse to obtain entrance to his home, the male reporter surreptitiously photographed the plaintiff while he was examining the female reporter. One of these photographs was subsequently published in *Life* as part of a story entitled "Crackdown on Quackery." The plaintiff's conversation with the female reporter was transmitted by a radio transmitter hidden in her purse to an automobile occupied by another employee of *Life* magazine and employees of the District Attorney's office and the State Department of Public Health. A few days later the plaintiff was arrested on a charge of practicing medicine without a license. A *Life* photographer was present and took many photographs. The district court ruled that the surreptitious photographing of the plaintiff in his home on the first occasion was an actionable invasion of the plaintiff's privacy and the court of appeals affirmed. As to the second set of photographs the defendant claimed they were obtained by consent. The plaintiff, however, claimed he had permitted the photographing because he thought the *Life* photographer was a police officer. There was no ruling on this issue. How would you decide it? The whole subject is discussed in Note, *Press Passes and Trespasses: Newsgathering on Private Property*, 84 Colum.L.Rev. 1298 (1984).

It should be noted that, when the basis of the action is intrusion, the tort is complete when the intrusion is committed. It is not necessary for the plaintiff to show that any information gathered as a result of the intrusion has been published to third parties, although such factors will obviously be relevant on the issue of damages.

An interesting recent case is Howell v. New York Post, Inc., 81 N.Y.2d 115, 612 N.E.2d 699, 596 N.Y.S.2d 350 (1993). The plaintiff was a patient in a private psychiatric hospital who alleged that it was essential for her recovery to keep her hospitalization secret from all but her immediate family. One of the other patients was a woman who was the subject of intense public interest because she had been the live-in lover of a man accused of killing his six-year old daughter. A photographer employed by the defendant trespassed on the grounds of the hospital and, using a telephoto lens, took a photograph of this other woman who happened to be walking on the hospital grounds in the company of the plaintiff. The hospital's medical director phoned the defendant to ask it not to publish any photographs of the patients but the defendant published the photograph as part of a news story about the "live-in lover." The plaintiff brought an action based on invasion of privacy, intentional and negligent infliction of emotional distress, trespass, and harassment. The Supreme Court (in New York the trial court) dismissed all causes of action other than those based on intentional infliction of emotional distress. On the cross appeals, the appellate division also dismissed the causes of action for intentional infliction of emotional distress. The case was then appealed to the New York Court of Appeals solely on the issue of the propriety of the dismissal of the privacy and intentional infliction of emotional distress counts. That court affirmed. It noted that the limited right of privacy recognized by statute in New York only covered the use of a photograph for advertising or trade purposes and held that the use of the photograph as part of a newsworthy article was not covered by the statute, nor did such "privileged conduct" constitute, in the case before the court, the tortious intentional infliction of emotional distress. The court noted that it had taken an extremely restrictive approach to intentional infliction of emotional distress claims and that all such claims that had thus far reached the court had been found not to be based on conduct that was sufficiently outrageous.

3. Since 1968, under Title III of the Omnibus Crime Control and Safe Streets Act (18 U.S.C. §§ 2510–20), it is now a federal crime for anyone not a party to the communication to intercept any wire or oral communication or to disclose or use its contents. A civil action for damages is granted to those whose conversations have been intercepted, disclosed, or used. (18 U.S.C. § 2520). The statutory protection extends to all "oral communication uttered by a person exhibiting an expectation that such communication is not subject to interception under circumstances justifying such expectation." 18 U.S.C. § 2510(2). To avoid the constitutional problems presented when a conversation is carried on loudly where it may be overheard without the use of any electronic or mechanical listening or amplifying devices, it has been held that there cannot be a justifiable expectation that a conversation will not be recorded by third parties unless the conversation was conducted under circumstances justifying an actual expectation of privacy. *See* United States v. Carroll, 337 F.Supp. 1260 (D.D.C.1971).

4. About one third of the states have so-called "Peeping Tom" criminal statutes. At least one-half of these statutes require a trespass upon the victim's property before a criminal charge may be brought. As such they present relatively little constitutional difficulty. The remaining statutes permit a construction that does not require a physical intrusion unto the land of another. *See, e.g.,* LSA–Rev.Stat. § 14:284; Mich.Comp.Laws Ann. § 750.167 ("window peeper"); N.C.Gen.Stat. § 14–202 (secretly peeping "into any room occupied by a female person"). There is very little case authority on these statutes and that which does exist largely involves trespassing "peepers." *See, e.g.,* State v. Bivins, 262 N.C. 93, 136 S.E.2d 250 (1964); Butts v. State, 97 Ga.App. 465, 103 S.E.2d 450 (1958). Despite the oft-cited Katz v. United States, 389 U.S. 347, 88 S.Ct. 507, 19 L.Ed.2d 576 (1967), which allowed the defendant to object to the use of conversations recorded by a listening device placed in a phone booth, on the ground that the defendant had a reasonable expectation of privacy, it has been held that a criminal defendant cannot object to non-trespassory visual surveillance conducted with the aid of strong binoculars. *See* Commonwealth v. Hernley, 216 Pa.Super. 177, 263 A.2d 904 (1970), *cert. denied,* 401 U.S. 914, 91 S.Ct. 886, 27 L.Ed.2d 813 (1971); State v. Manly, 85 Wn.2d 120, 530 P.2d 306 (1975). *But see* United States v. Kim, 415 F.Supp. 1252 (D.Hawai'i 1976). It seems doubtful that a civil action for intrusion could constitutionally lie for any non-trespassory visual observations, particularly if the observations are made from a public place or the defendant's own premises, even if binoculars are used, and almost inconceivable that an action could lie if the observations are made with the naked eye. *Cf.* Texas v. Brown, 460 U.S. 730, 103 S.Ct. 1535, 75 L.Ed.2d 502 (1983)(discussing ambit of "plain view" doctrine); United States v. Lee, 274 U.S. 559, 47 S.Ct. 746, 71 L.Ed. 1202 (1927)(examination of a boat by searchlight is not an unconstitutional search and declared to be similar to use of a "field glass"). With regard to observation by overflying aircraft, *see* Florida v. Riley, 488 U.S. 445, 109 S.Ct. 693, 102 L.Ed.2d 835 (1989).

5. On the subject of surveillance by governmental authorities, see G. Christie, *Government Surveillance and Individual Freedom: A Proposed Statutory Response to* Laird v. Tatum *and the Broader Problem of Government Surveillance of the Individual,* 47 N.Y.U.L.Rev. 871 (1972).

6. As has already been noted, this chapter has been organized around the late Dean Prosser's division of the law of privacy into four separate categories, which do not pretend to exhaust the total range of activities which might be

said to affect human privacy. The purpose of Prosser's analytical suggestion was to make what would otherwise be a subject of infinite scope sufficiently manageable. There will always, however, be some centrifugal tendencies. Whether these tendencies are desirable is another question. For example, in Phillips v. Smalley Maintenance Services, Inc., 435 So.2d 705 (Ala.1983), a woman employee had been discharged for refusing to have oral and other forms of sex with her supervisor. She was awarded damages in federal court for wrongful discharge under Title VII, 42 U.S.C. § 2000e *et seq.*, of the Civil Rights Act of 1964. The plaintiff had joined to her federal claim a claim for damages for invasion of privacy. The United States Court of Appeals for the Eleventh Circuit certified to the Alabama Supreme Court the question whether Alabama law recognized a cause of action for invasion of privacy on the assumed facts of the case. The Alabama court held that it did despite the fact that there was nothing resembling a trespassory invasion of physical space or a public disclosure of embarrassing information about the plaintiff. Rather, the court held that an action would lie for invasion of the plaintiff's "emotional sanctum". Subsequently, the "intrusion" into one's emotional space was found not to be sufficiently "offensive" to be actionable in Logan v. Sears, Roebuck & Co., 466 So.2d 121 (Ala.1985), where a customer overheard a Sears employee, who had phoned him to inquire whether he had paid his bill, tell someone "[t]his guy is as queer as a three-dollar bill." The customer was in fact a homosexual. A lack of sufficient offensiveness was also found in McIsaac v. WZEW–FM Corp., 495 So.2d 649 (Ala.1986), which involved a less extreme form of sexual harassment than *Phillips*. On the other hand, in K–Mart Corp. v. Weston, 530 So.2d 736 (Ala.1988), a jury verdict for the plaintiff was upheld where a customer was told, in front of other customers, that he could not use a check-cashing card because his wife had given K–Mart a bad check. The check had been returned due to a bank error. The action had also been brought, in the alternative, on a defamation theory. Finally, in Hogin v. Cottingham, 533 So.2d 525 (Ala.1988), an attorney who, on behalf of a client, tried unsuccessfully to identify a young girl, whose picture was published in a Birmingham newspaper, by making inquiries at the girl's school was sued by the girl's irate parents "for invasion of privacy, outrageous conduct and intentional or reckless infliction of emotional distress". The trial court awarded the defendant summary judgment. The Supreme Court of Alabama reversed (5–3) on the privacy claim, affirmed the awarding of summary judgement on the other claims, and remanded the case for trial. What constitutes the invasion of privacy? Wanting to know the girl's name and address or trying, unsuccessfully, to secure that information from her school? Does the case raise constitutional questions?

We have already seen, chapter 17, *supra,* other instances in which actions for what normally would be considered the intentional infliction of severe emotional distress by outrageous conduct are sometimes framed, in the alternative, as actions for invasion of privacy. *See e.g.*, Guinn v. Church of Christ of Collinsville, 775 P.2d 766 (Okl.1989), discussed at p. 1046, *supra.* That case is perhaps a less extreme expansion of the scope of an invasion of privacy action because it arguably involved the publication of embarrassing information that had been secured under a promise of confidentiality. Should labelling the complaint as one for the invasion of privacy make it easier for the plaintiff to recover than if the action were labelled as one for the intentional infliction of severe emotional distress? Should it be possible by doing so to avoid the strictures of Hustler Magazine, Inc. v. Falwell, 485 U.S. 46, 108 S.Ct. 876, 99

L.Ed.2d 41 (1988), presented at p. 1048, *supra?* Do all these centrifugal tendencies confirm once again that the concept of privacy is capable of encompassing a good part of both morality and law?

GALELLA v. ONASSIS

United States Court of Appeals, Second Circuit, 1973.
487 F.2d 986.

Before SMITH, HAYS and TIMBERS, CIRCUIT JUDGES.

J. JOSEPH SMITH, CIRCUIT JUDGE:

Donald Galella, a free-lance photographer, appeals from a summary judgment dismissing his complaint against three Secret Service agents for false arrest, malicious prosecution, and interference with trade (S.D.N.Y., Edward C. McLean, Judge), the dismissal after trial of his identical complaint against Jacqueline Onassis and the grant of injunctive relief to defendant Onassis on her counterclaim and to the intervenor, the United States, on its intervening complaint and a third judgment retaxing transcript costs to plaintiff (S.D.N.Y., Irving Ben Cooper, Judge), 353 F.Supp. 196 (1972). In addition to numerous alleged procedural errors, Galella raises the First Amendment as an absolute shield against liability to any sanctions. The judgments dismissing the complaints are affirmed; the grant of injunctive relief is affirmed as herein modified. Taxation of costs against the plaintiff is affirmed in part, reversed in part.

Galella is a free-lance photographer specializing in the making and sale of photographs of well-known persons. Defendant Onassis is the widow of the late President, John F. Kennedy, mother of the two Kennedy children, John and Caroline, and is the wife of Aristotle Onassis, widely known shipping figure and reputed multimillionaire. John Walsh, James Kalafatis and John Connelly are U.S. Secret Service agents assigned to the duty of protecting the Kennedy children under 18 U.S.C. § 3056, which provides for protection of the children of deceased presidents up to the age of 16.

Galella fancies himself as a "paparazzo" (literally a kind of annoying insect, perhaps roughly equivalent to the English "gadfly.") Paparazzi make themselves as visible to the public and obnoxious to their photographic subjects as possible to aid in the advertisement and wide sale of their works.[2]

Some examples of Galella's conduct brought out at trial are illustrative. Galella took pictures of John Kennedy riding his bicycle in Central Park across the way from his home. He jumped out into the boy's path, causing the agents concern for John's safety. The agents' reaction and interrogation of Galella led to Galella's arrest and his action against the agents; Galella on other occasions interrupted Caroline at tennis, and invaded the children's private schools. At one time he came uncomfortably close in a power boat to Mrs. Onassis swimming. He often jumped and postured around while taking pictures of her party notably at a theater opening but also on numerous other occasions. He followed a practice of bribing apartment house, restaurant and nightclub doormen as well as

---

2. The newspapers report a recent incident in which one Marlon Brando, annoyed by Galella, punched Galella, breaking Galella's jaw and infecting Brando's hand.

romancing a family servant to keep him advised of the movements of the family.

After detention and arrest following complaint by the Secret Service agents protecting Mrs. Onassis' son and his acquittal in the state court, Galella filed suit in state court against the agents and Mrs. Onassis. Galella claimed that under orders from Mrs. Onassis, the three agents had falsely arrested and maliciously prosecuted him, and that this incident in addition to several others described in the complaint constituted an unlawful interference with his trade.

Mrs. Onassis answered denying any role in the arrest or any part in the claimed interference with his attempts to photograph her, and counterclaimed for damages and injunctive relief, charging that Galella had invaded her privacy, assaulted and battered her, intentionally inflicted emotional distress and engaged in a campaign of harassment.

The action was removed under 28 U.S.C. § 1442(a) to the United States District Court. On a motion for summary judgment, Galella's claim against the Secret Service agents was dismissed, the court finding that the agents were acting within the scope of their authority and thus were immune from prosecution. At the same time, the government intervened requesting injunctive relief from the activities of Galella which obstructed the Secret Service's ability to protect Mrs. Onassis' children. Galella's motion to remand the case to state court, just prior to trial, was denied.

Certain incidents of photographic coverage by Galella, subsequent to an agreement among the parties for Galella not to so engage, resulted in the issuance of a temporary restraining order to prevent further harassment of Mrs. Onassis and the children. Galella was enjoined from "harassing, alarming, startling, tormenting, touching the person of the defendant * * * or her children * * * and from blocking their movements in the public places and thoroughfares, invading their immediate zone of privacy by means of physical movements, gestures or with photographic equipment and from performing any act reasonably calculated to place the lives and safety of the defendant * * * and her children in jeopardy." Within two months, Galella was charged with violation of the temporary restraining order; a new order was signed which required that the photographer keep 100 yards from the Onassis apartment and 50 yards from the person of the defendant and her children. Surveillance was also prohibited.

Upon notice of consolidation of the preliminary injunction hearing and trial for permanent injunction, plaintiff moved for a jury trial—nine months after answer was served, and to remand to state court. The first motion was denied as untimely, the second on grounds of judicial economy. Just prior to trial Galella deposed Mrs. Onassis. Under protective order of this court, the defendant was allowed to testify at the office of the U.S. Attorney and outside the presence of Galella.

After a six-week trial the court dismissed Galella's claim and granted relief to both the defendant and the intervenor. Galella was enjoined from (1) keeping the defendant and her children under surveillance or following any of them; (2) approaching within 100 yards of the home of defendant or her children, or within 100 yards of either child's school or within 75 yards of either child or 50 yards of defendant; (3) using the name, portrait or picture of defendant or her children for advertising; (4) attempting to communicate with defendant or her children except through her attorney.

We conclude that grant of summary judgment and dismissal of Galella's claim against the Secret Service agents was proper. Federal agents when charged with duties which require the exercise of discretion are immune from liability for actions within the scope of their authority. Ordinarily enforcement agents charged with the duty of arrest are not so immune. * * * The protective duties assigned the agents under this statute, however, require the instant exercise of judgment which should be protected. The agents saw Galella jump into the path of John Kennedy who was forced to swerve his bike dangerously as he left Central Park and was about to enter Fifth Avenue, whereupon the agents gave chase to the photographer. Galella indicated that he was a press photographer listed with the New York City Police; he and the agents went to the police station to check on the story, where one of the agents made the complaint on which the state court charges were based. Certainly it was reasonable that the agents "check out" an individual who has endangered their charge, and seek prosecution for apparent violation of state law which interferes with them in the discharge of their duties.

* * *

Discrediting all of Galella's testimony the court found the photographer guilty of harassment, intentional infliction of emotional distress, assault and battery, commercial exploitation of defendant's personality, and invasion of privacy. Fully crediting defendant's testimony, the court found no liability on Galella's claim. Evidence offered by the defense showed that Galella had on occasion intentionally physically touched Mrs. Onassis and her daughter, caused fear of physical contact in his frenzied attempts to get their pictures, followed defendant and her children too closely in an automobile, endangered the safety of the children while they were swimming, water skiing and horseback riding. Galella cannot successfully challenge the court's finding of tortious conduct.[11]

Finding that Galella had "insinuated himself into the very fabric of Mrs. Onassis' life * * *" the court framed its relief in part on the need to prevent further invasion of the defendant's privacy. Whether or not this accords with present New York law, there is no doubt that it is sustainable under New York's proscription of harassment.

Of course legitimate countervailing social needs may warrant some intrusion despite an individual's reasonable expectation of privacy and freedom from harassment. However the interference allowed may be no greater than that necessary to protect the overriding public interest. Mrs. Onassis was properly found to be a public figure and thus subject to news coverage. * * * Nonetheless, Galella's action went far beyond the reasonable bounds of news gathering. When weighed against the *de minimis*

---

11. Harassment is a criminal violation under New York Penal Law § 240.25 (McKinney's Consol.Laws, c. 40, 1967) when with intent to harass a person follows another in a public place, inflicts physical contact or engages in any annoying conduct without legitimate cause. Galella was found to have engaged in this proscribed conduct. Conduct sufficient to invoke criminal liability for harassment may be the basis for private action. * * *

public importance of the daily activities of the defendant, Galella's constant surveillance, his obtrusive and intruding presence, was unwarranted and unreasonable. If there were any doubt in our minds, Galella's inexcusable conduct toward defendant's minor children would resolve it.

Galella does not seriously dispute the court's finding of tortious conduct. Rather, he sets up the First Amendment as a wall of immunity protecting newsmen from any liability for their conduct while gathering news. There is no such scope to the First Amendment right. Crimes and torts committed in news gathering are not protected. * * *

* * *

Injunctive relief is appropriate. Galella has stated his intention to continue his coverage of defendant so long as she is newsworthy, and his continued harassment even while the temporary restraining orders were in effect indicate that no voluntary change in his technique can be expected. New York courts have found similar conduct sufficient to support a claim for injunctive relief. Flamm v. Van Nierop, 56 Misc.2d 1059, 291 N.Y.S.2d 189 (1968).[20]

The injunction, however, is broader than is required to protect the defendant. Relief must be tailored to protect Mrs. Onassis from the "paparazzo" attack which distinguishes Galella's behavior from that of other photographers; it should not unnecessarily infringe on reasonable efforts to "cover" defendant. Therefore, we modify the court's order to prohibit only (1) any approach within twenty-five (25) feet of defendant or any touching of the person of the defendant Jacqueline Onassis; (2) any blocking of her movement in public places and thoroughfares; (3) any act foreseeably or reasonably calculated to place the life and safety of defendant in jeopardy; and (4) any conduct which would reasonably be foreseen to harass, alarm or frighten the defendant.

Any further restriction on Galella's taking and selling pictures of defendant for news coverage is, however, improper and unwarranted by the evidence. * * *

Likewise, we affirm the grant of injunctive relief to the government modified to prohibit any action interfering with Secret Service agents' protective duties. Galella thus may be enjoined from (a) entering the children's schools or play areas; (b) engaging in action calculated or reasonably foreseen to place the children's safety or well being in jeopardy, or which would threaten or create physical injury; (c) taking any action which could reasonably be foreseen to harass, alarm, or frighten the children; and (d) from approaching within thirty (30) feet of the children.

* * *

20. The defendant in *Flamm* was sued for intentional infliction of emotional distress. He was charged with having dashed at the plaintiff in a threatening manner in various public places with threatening gestures, grimaces, leers, distorted faces and malign looks, accompanied by ridiculous utterances and laughs, driven his automobile behind that of the plaintiff at a dangerously close distance; walked behind or beside or in front of the plaintiff on the public streets; and consistently telephoned the plaintiff at home and place of business and hung up or remained on the line in silence.

As modified, the relief granted fully allows Galella the opportunity to photograph and report on Mrs. Onassis' public activities. Any prior restraint on news gathering is miniscule and fully supported by the findings.

* * *

TIMBERS, CIRCUIT JUDGE (concurring in part and dissenting in part):

With one exception, I concur in the judgment of the Court and in the able majority opinion of Judge Smith.

With the utmost deference to and respect for my colleagues, however, I am constrained to dissent from the judgment of the Court and the majority opinion to the extent that they modify the injunctive relief found necessary by the district court to protect Jacqueline Onassis and her children, Caroline B. and John F. Kennedy, Jr., from the continued predatory conduct of the self-proclaimed paparazzo Galella.

* * *

In the instant case, after a six week trial at which 25 witnesses testified, hundreds of exhibits were received and a 4,714 page record was compiled, Judge Cooper filed a careful, comprehensive 40 page opinion, 353 F.Supp. 194, which meticulously sets forth detailed findings of fact and conclusions of law. * * *

* * *

* * * I feel very strongly that such findings should not be set aside or drastically modified by our Court unless they are clearly erroneous; and I do not understand the majority to suggest that they are.

But here is what the majority's modification of the critical distance provisions of the injunction has done:

DISTANCES GALELLA IS REQUIRED TO MAINTAIN	AS PROVIDED IN DISTRICT COURT INJUNCTION	AS MODIFIED BY COURT OF APPEALS MAJORITY
From home of Mrs. Onassis and her children	100 yards	No restriction
From children's schools	100 yards	Restricted only from entering schools or play areas*
From Mrs. Onassis personally	50 *yards*	25 *feet* and not to touch her
From children personally	75 *yards*	30 *feet**

In addition to modifying the distance restrictions of the injunction, the majority also has directed that Galella be prohibited from blocking Mrs. Onassis' movement in public places and thoroughfares; from any act "foreseeably or reasonably calculated" to place Mrs. Onassis' life and safety

---

* As pointed out below, the majority appears further to have modified the injunction by limiting the protection of the children to the "grant of injunctive relief to the *government* modified to prohibit any action interfering with Secret Service agents' protective duties." (emphasis added). The district court injunction was not so limited. It granted injunctive relief for the protection of the children as specifically prayed for *by Mrs. Onassis*. The distinction introduced by the majority * * * substantially reduces the protection provided for the children.

in jeopardy (and similarly with respect to her children); and from any conduct which would "reasonably be foreseen" to harass, alarm or frighten Mrs. Onassis (and similarly with respect to her children).

With deference, I believe the majority's modification of the injunction in the respects indicated above to be unwarranted and unworkable. * * *

* * *

Notes

1. Galella was subsequently held in contempt for violating the modified injunction in 1981. Galella v. Onassis, 533 F.Supp. 1076 (S.D.N.Y.1982). In settlement of the contempt proceedings, Galella agreed to pay Mrs. Onassis $10,000 and to give up forever his legal right to take pictures of Mrs. Onassis or her two children. See N.Y. Times, Mar. 25, 1982, at A25, col. 1.

2. In Gill v. Hearst Publishing Co., 40 Cal.2d 224, 253 P.2d 441 (1953), a couple, who embraced at the Farmer's Market in Los Angeles, were photographed by a wandering photographer. The photograph appeared in several widely circulated magazines. The couple was denied recovery on the ground that, by acting voluntarily in public, they relinquished any right to prevent a photograph of their actions from being published in a magazine. Would a contrary decision be constitutionally sound? See also Gautier v. Pro–Football, Inc., 304 N.Y. 354, 107 N.E.2d 485 (1952). The unsuccessful plaintiff was performing as an animal trainer during halftime at a Redskins–Giants football game and was televised, as part of the halftime festivities, by the company telecasting the game. The Gautier case presents some different considerations because the plaintiff's complaint as a professional performer is not so much that he was televised but that he was not paid for being televised. Cf. the Zacchini case, infra p. 1250. On the general subject, see Comment, Privacy in Photographs: Misconception Since Inception, 18 John Marshall L.Rev. 968 (1985).

3. In Blumenthal v. Picture Classics, 235 App.Div. 570, 257 N.Y.S. 800 (1935), affirmed on procedural grounds 261 N.Y. 504, 185 N.E. 713, inclusion of a six second sequence of the plaintiff selling bread and photographed through the glass window of a bakery in a documentary about New York City was held actionable. The case does not appear to have been followed.[1] Moreover, the possible suggestion in that case that motion pictures are different than print media is no longer constitutionally sustainable. See Joseph Burstyn, Inc. v. Wilson, 343 U.S. 495, 72 S.Ct. 777, 96 L.Ed. 1098 (1952).

4. The New York Penal Law Provisions cited (supra, p. 1213) in note 11 of the court's opinion in Galella is part of a set of statutes that has been amplified over the years and now consists of four provisions, N.Y. Penal Law §§ 240.25, 240.26, 240.30 and 240.31 (Mckinney)(Supp. 1996) that cover first and second degree harassment and first and second degree aggravated harassment. Aggravated harassment in the first degree is a class E felony; aggravated harassment in the second degree is a class A misdemeanor; and harassment in the first degree is a class B misdemeanor. Second degree harassment is only a "violation." All these provisions cover a variety of conduct, some of which includes physical threats. Several provisions, however, present serious consti-

1. The majority's opinion in *Blumenthal* is extremely cursory. A subsequent New York lower court case has tried to explain *Blumen-* thal as involving some element of fictionalization. *See* Sarat Lahiri v. Daily Mirror, 162 Misc. 776, 295 N.Y.S. 382 (1937).

tutional problems. Harassment in the first degree (§ 240.25) includes repeatedly following a person in public places and second degree aggravated harassment (§ 240.30) includes making telephone calls with intent to harass and "no purpose of legitimate communication" and the making, with intent to harass, of any communications in a manner likely to cause annoyance or alarm. Second degree harassment (§ 240.26) includes "a course of conduct or repeatedly committed acts which alarm or seriously annoy * * * [an]other person and which serve no legitimate purpose." There is an exception for activities covered by federal labor relations laws. A provision of an earlier version of this statutory scheme that made it a violation, punishable by 15 days imprisonment, to threaten someone with physical contact or, to use "abusive or obscene language" in a public place was struck down as unconstitutional in a prosecution of a woman who called a mentally retarded woman a "bitch," referred to the woman's mentally retarded son as a "dog", and who said that she "would beat the crap out of [the complainant] some day or night on the street." People v. Dietze, 75 N.Y.2d 47, 549 N.E.2d 1166, 550 N.Y.S.2d 595 (1989). There have been few recent convictions under any of these statutes as the courts have insisted on extremely outrageous behavior usually with strong implications of physical threat. *But see* People v. Miguez, 147 Misc.2d 482, 556 N.Y.S.2d 231 (1990), where the court submitted the question of whether daily telephone calls over a five-month period from a woman to the man she loved constituted aggravated harassment. On the other hand, soliciting, at 3:00 a.m., three young women whom the defendant mistakenly took for prostitutes did not constitute harassment. People v. Malausky, 127 Misc.2d 84, 485 N.Y.S.2d 925 (1985).

An illustration of what might be the basis of a tort action for stalking or harassment is Summers v. Bailey, 55 F.3d 1564 (11th Cir.1995). In that case the plaintiff had purchased a store from the defendant. A few years later, in the midst of bankruptcy proceedings, the plaintiff, who had been operating the store with her husband, negotiated the sale of the store to a third party. The defendant did not approve of this resale. It was alleged that he appeared at the store with a large hand gun, that he would park outside the store for hours and tell the plaintiff and her customers that he wanted her out of the store, that he would follow her in his truck when she ran errands, that he sometimes parked on her property, and that he followed her as she departed from her house. The plaintiff brought her action on grounds of malicious abuse and use of process, intentional infliction of emotional distress, and invasion of privacy. The district court granted summary judgment as to all plaintiff's causes of action, but the court of appeals held that the plaintiff was entitled to go to trial on her invasion of privacy claim. Certainly there seems here to be not only some element of trespass or intrusion but also a reasonable apprehension of physical violence. A common type of case involves insurance investigators who follow the plaintiff on the public streets and observe the plaintiff while he engages in public activities. These actions are normally unsuccessful. *See* Forster v. Mancheser, 410 Pa. 192, 189 A.2d 147 (1963). Figured v. Paralegal Technical Services, 231 N.J.Super. 251, 555 A.2d 663 (1989). The *Figured* case contains a good discussion of the law. In McLain v. Boise Cascade Corp., 271 Or. 549, 533 P.2d 343 (1975), the court reached the same result even though the investigators may have trespassed on the far corner of the plaintiff's land. The plaintiff was seeking worker's compensation for a back injury. Surveillance conducted in a manner that might frighten a reasonable person might, however, be actionable. *See* Pinkerton Nat'l Detective Agency, Inc. v. Stevens, 108 Ga.App. 159, 132 S.E.2d 119 (1963).

In September 1996, Congress made interstate stalking a federal crime. The statute, 18 U.S.C. § 2261A, however, requires that the person stalked should be put in reasonable fear of death or serious bodily injury to himself or to a member of his immediate family.

SIDIS v. F–R PUBLISHING CORP.

Circuit Court of Appeals, Second Circuit, 1940.
113 F.2d 806.

Before SWAN, CLARK, and PATTERSON, CIRCUIT JUDGES.

CLARK, CIRCUIT JUDGE.

William James Sidis was the unwilling subject of a brief biographical sketch and cartoon printed in The New Yorker weekly magazine for August 14, 1937. Further references were made to him in the issue of December 25, 1937, and in a newspaper advertisement announcing the August 14 issue. He brought an action in the district court against the publisher, F–R Publishing Corporation. His complaint stated three "causes of action" * * * Defendant's motion to dismiss the first two "causes of action" was granted, and plaintiff has filed an appeal from the order of dismissal. * * *

William James Sidis was a famous child prodigy in 1910. His name and prowess were well known to newspaper readers of the period. At the age of eleven, he lectured to distinguished mathematicians on the subject of Four–Dimensional Bodies. When he was sixteen, he was graduated from Harvard College, amid considerable public attention. Since then, his name has appeared in the press only sporadically, and he has sought to live as unobtrusively as possible. Until the articles objected to appeared in The New Yorker, he had apparently succeeded in his endeavor to avoid the public gaze.

Among The New Yorker's features are brief biographical sketches of current and past personalities. In the latter department, which appears haphazardly under the title of "Where Are They Now?" the article on Sidis was printed with a subtitle "April Fool." The author describes his subject's early accomplishments in mathematics and the wide-spread attention he received, then recounts his general breakdown and the revulsion which Sidis thereafter felt for his former life of fame and study. The unfortunate prodigy is traced over the years that followed, through his attempts to conceal his identity, through his chosen career as an insignificant clerk who would not need to employ unusual mathematical talents, and through the bizarre ways in which his genius flowered, as in his enthusiasm for collecting streetcar transfers and in his proficiency with an adding machine. The article closes with an account of an interview with Sidis at his present lodgings, "a hall bedroom of Boston's shabby south end." The untidiness of his room, his curious laugh, his manner of speech, and other personal habits are commented upon at length, as is his present interest in the lore of the Okamakammessett Indians. The subtitle is explained by the closing sentence, quoting Sidis as saying "with a grin" that it was strange, "but, you know, I was born on April Fool's Day." Accompanying the biography is a small cartoon showing the genius of eleven years lecturing to a group of astounded professors.

It is not contended that any of the matter printed is untrue. Nor is the manner of the author unfriendly; Sidis today is described as having "a certain childlike charm." But the article is merciless in its dissection of intimate details of its subject's personal life, and this in company with elaborate accounts of Sidis' passion for privacy and the pitiable lengths to which he has gone in order to avoid public scrutiny. The work possesses great reader interest, for it is both amusing and instructive; but it may be fairly described as a ruthless exposure of a once public character, who has since sought and has now been deprived of the seclusion of private life.

The article of December 25, 1937, was a biographical sketch of another former child prodigy, in the course of which William James Sidis and the recent account of him were mentioned. The advertisement published in the New York World–Telegram of August 13, 1937, read: "Out Today. Harvard Prodigy. Biography of the man who astonished Harvard at age 11. Where are they now? by J.L. Manley. Page 22. The New Yorker."

The complaint contains a general allegation, repeated for all the claims, of publication by the defendant of The New Yorker, "a weekly magazine of wide circulation throughout the United States." Then each separate "cause" contains an allegation that the defendant publicly circulated the articles or caused them to be circulated in the particular states upon whose law that cause is assumed to be founded. Circulation of the New York World–Telegram advertisement is, however, alleged only with respect to the second "cause," for asserted violation of New York law.

1. Under the first "cause of action" we are asked to declare that this exposure transgresses upon plaintiff's right of privacy, as recognized in California, Georgia, Kansas, Kentucky, and Missouri. Each of these states except California grants to the individual a common law right, and California a constitutional right, to be let alone to a certain extent. The decisions have been carefully analyzed by the court below,[3] and we need not examine them further. None of the cited rulings goes so far as to prevent a newspaper or magazine from publishing the truth about a person, however intimate, revealing, or harmful the truth may be. Nor are there any decided cases that confer such a privilege upon the press. Under the mandate of Erie R. Co. v. Tompkins, 304 U.S. 64, 58 S.Ct. 817, 82 L.Ed. 1188, 114 A.L.R. 1487, we face the unenviable duty of determining the law of five states on a broad and vital public issue which the courts of those states have not even discussed.

All comment upon the right of privacy must stem from the famous article by Warren and Brandeis on The Right of Privacy in 4 Harv.L.Rev. 193. The learned authors of that paper were convinced that some limits ought to be imposed upon the privilege of newspapers to publish truthful items of a personal nature. * * *

* * *

3. Judge Goddard's decision is reported in 34 F.Supp. 19. * * * [Ed. note] Among the cases mentioned as having been considered by Judge Goddard is Melvin v. Reid, 112 Cal.App. 285, 297 P. 91 (1931), discussed in the *Briscoe* case, *infra* p. 1221.

It must be conceded that under the strict standards suggested by these authors plaintiff's right of privacy has been invaded. Sidis today is neither politician, public administrator, nor statesman. Even if he were, some of the personal details revealed were of the sort that Warren and Brandeis believed "all men alike are entitled to keep from popular curiosity."

But despite eminent opinion to the contrary, we are not yet disposed to afford to all of the intimate details of private life an absolute immunity from the prying of the press. Everyone will agree that at some point the public interest in obtaining information becomes dominant over the individual's desire for privacy. Warren and Brandeis were willing to lift the veil somewhat in the case of public officers. We would go further, though we are not yet prepared to say how far. At least we would permit limited scrutiny of the "private" life of any person who has achieved, or has had thrust upon him, the questionable and indefinable status of a "public figure." * * *

William James Sidis was once a public figure. As a child prodigy, he excited both admiration and curiosity. Of him great deeds were expected. In 1910, he was a person about whom the newspapers might display a legitimate intellectual interest, in the sense meant by Warren and Brandeis, as distinguished from a trivial and unseemly curiosity. But the precise motives of the press we regard as unimportant. And even if Sidis had loathed public attention at that time, we think his uncommon achievements and personality would have made the attention permissible. Since then Sidis has cloaked himself in obscurity, but his subsequent history, containing as it did the answer to the question of whether or not he had fulfilled his early promise, was still a matter of public concern. The article in The New Yorker sketched the life of an unusual personality, and it possessed considerable popular news interest.

We express no comment on whether or not the news worthiness of the matter printed will always constitute a complete defense. Revelations may be so intimate and so unwarranted in view of the victim's position as to outrage the community's notions of decency. But when focused upon public characters, truthful comments upon dress, speech, habits, and the ordinary aspects of personality will usually not transgress this line. Regrettably or not, the misfortunes and frailties of neighbors and "public figures" are subjects of considerable interest and discussion to the rest of the population. And when such are the mores of the community, it would be unwise for a court to bar their expression in the newspapers, books, and magazines of the day.

Plaintiff in his first "cause of action" charged actual malice in the publication, and now claims that an order of dismissal was improper in the face of such an allegation. We cannot agree. If plaintiff's right of privacy was not invaded by the article, the existence of actual malice in its publication would not change that result. Unless made so by statute, a truthful and therefore non-libelous statement will not become libelous when uttered maliciously. * * * A similar rule should prevail on invasions of the right of privacy. * * *

* * *

2. The second "cause of action" charged invasion of the rights conferred on plaintiff by §§ 50 and 51 of the N.Y. Civil Rights Law. * * * The statute forbids the use of a name or picture only when employed "for advertising purposes, or for the purposes of trade." In this context, it is clear that "for the purposes of trade" does not contemplate the publication of a newspaper, magazine, or book which imparts truthful news or other factual information to the public. Though a publisher sells a commodity, and expects to profit from the sale of his product, he is immune from the interdict of §§ 50 and 51 so long as he confines himself to the unembroidered dissemination of facts. Publishers and motion picture producers have occasionally been held to transgress the statute in New York, but in each case the factual presentation was embellished by some degree of fictionalization. * * * The New Yorker articles limit themselves to the unvarnished, unfictionalized truth.

The case as to the newspaper advertisement announcing the August 14 article is somewhat different, for it was undoubtedly inserted in the World–Telegram "for advertising purposes." But since it was to advertise the article on Sidis, and the article itself was unobjectionable, the advertisement shares the privilege enjoyed by the article. * * *

* * *

Affirmed.

Note

The Harvard Law Record, April 14, 1978, p. 1, col. 3 (Vol. 66, no. 8), reports the continued notoriety of the descendants and other surviving relatives of Helen Palsgraf.

<h2 style="text-align:center">BRISCOE v. READER'S DIGEST ASSOCIATION</h2>

Supreme Court of California, 1971.
4 Cal.3d 529, 93 Cal.Rptr. 866, 483 P.2d 34.

PETERS, JUSTICE.

Plaintiff Marvin Briscoe filed suit against defendant Reader's Digest Association, alleging that defendant had willfully and maliciously invaded his privacy by publishing an article which disclosed truthful but embarrassing private facts about plaintiff's past life. A demurrer was sustained without leave to amend, and plaintiff has appealed from the ensuing judgment. Thus, we are presented simply with a pleading problem—does the complaint state a cause of action?

The allegations of the complaint may be summarized as follows: On December 15, 1956, plaintiff and another man hijacked a truck in Danville, Kentucky. "[I]mmediately subsequent to said incident, plaintiff abandoned his life of shame and became entirely rehabilitated and has thereafter at all times lived an exemplary, virtuous and honorable life * * * he has assumed a place in respectable society and made many friends who were not aware of the incident in his earlier life."

"The Big Business of Hijacking," published by defendant 11 years after the hijacking incident, commences with a picture whose caption reads,

"Today's highwaymen are looting trucks at a rate of more than $100 million a year. But the truckers have now declared all-out war." The article describes various truck thefts and the efforts being made to stop such thefts. Dates ranging from 1965 to the time of publication are mentioned throughout the article, but none of the described thefts is itself dated.

One sentence in the article refers to plaintiff: "Typical of many beginners, Marvin Briscoe and [another man] stole a 'valuable-looking' truck in Danville, Ky., and then fought a gun battle with the local police, only to learn that they had hijacked four bowling-pin spotters." There is nothing in the article to indicate that the hijacking occurred in 1956.

As the result of defendant's publication,[1] plaintiff's 11–year-old daughter, as well as his friends, for the first time learned of this incident. They thereafter scorned and abandoned him.

Conceding the truth of the facts published in defendant's article, plaintiff claims that the public disclosure of these private facts has humiliated him and exposed him to contempt and ridicule. Conceding that the *subject* of the article may have been "newsworthy," he contends that the use of his *name* was not, and that the defendant has thus invaded his right to privacy.

The concept of a legal right to privacy was first developed by Warren and Brandeis in their landmark law review article, * * *. Try as they might, Warren and Brandeis had a difficult time tracing a right of privacy to the common law. In many respects a person had less privacy in the small community of the 18th century than he did in the urbanizing late 19th century or he does today in the modern metropolis. Extended family networks, primary group relationships, and rigid communal mores served to expose an individual's every deviation from the norm and to straitjacket him in a vise of backyard gossip. Yet Warren and Brandeis perceived that it was mass exposure to public gaze, as opposed to backyard gossip, which threatened to deprive men of the right of "scratching wherever one itches." * * *

Acceptance of the right to privacy has grown with the increasing capability of the mass media and electronic devices with their capacity to destroy an individual's anonymity, intrude upon his most intimate activities, and expose his most personal characteristics to public gaze.

In a society in which multiple, often conflicting role performances are demanded of each individual, the original etymological meaning of the word "person"—mask—has taken on new meaning. Men fear exposure not only to those closest to them; much of the outrage underlying the asserted right to privacy is a reaction to exposure to persons known only through business or other secondary relationships. The claim is not so much one of total secrecy as it is of the right to *define* one's circle of intimacy—to choose who shall see beneath the quotidian mask. Loss of control over which "face" one puts on may result in literal loss of self-identity * * * and is humiliat-

---

1. The article was a condensed version of an article which originally appeared in the December 10, 1967, issue of Chicago's American Magazine, published by the Chicago American Publishing Company. It is not alleged that this first publication injured plaintiff. Defendant concedes that this first publication does not absolve it from responsibility.

ing beneath the gaze of those whose curiosity treats a human being as an object.

A common law right to privacy, based on Warren and Brandeis' article, is now recognized in at least 36 states. * * * California has recognized the right to privacy for 40 years. (Melvin v. Reid (1931) 112 Cal.App. 285, 297 P. 91.)

The right to keep information private was bound to clash with the right to disseminate information to the public. * * * The instant case, pitting a rehabilitated felon's right to anonymity against a magazine's right to identify him, compels us to consider the character of these competing interests.

The central purpose of the First Amendment "is to give to every voting member of the body politic the fullest possible participation in the understanding of those problems with which the citizens of a self-governing society must deal. * * * "(A. Meiklejohn, Political Freedom: The Constitutional Powers of the People (1960) p. 75.) Nor is freedom of the press confined to comment upon public affairs and those persons who have voluntarily sought the public spotlight. * * * The scope of the privilege thus extends to almost all reporting of recent events, even though it involves the publication of a purely private individual's name or likeness. * * *

Particularly deserving of First Amendment protection are reports of "hot news," items of possible immediate public concern or interest. The need for constitutional protection is much greater under these circumstances, where deadlines must be met and quick decisions made, than in cases where more considered editorial judgments are possible. * * * Most factual reporting concerns current events. * * *

* * *

In general, therefore, truthful reports of *recent* crimes and the names of suspects or offenders will be deemed protected by the First Amendment.[10]

The instant case, however, compels us to consider whether reports of the facts of *past* crimes and the identification of *past* offenders serve these same public-interest functions.

We have no doubt that reports of the facts of past crimes are newsworthy. Media publication of the circumstances under which crimes were committed in the past may prove educational in the same way that reports of current crimes do. The public has a strong interest in enforcing the law, and this interest is served by accumulating and disseminating data cataloguing the reasons men commit crimes, the methods they use, and the ways in which they are apprehended. Thus in an article on truck hijack-

---

10. We do not mean to imply that the First Amendment gives the media the unmitigated right to publish the identity of suspected offenders or victims. In some jurisdictions, for example, the Legislature has decided that the rehabilitative goals of the juvenile law are so important as to override the right of the press to identify juvenile defendants. * * *

Similarly, some states have prohibited the naming of rape victims in news reports. * * *

ings, Reader's Digest certainly had the right to report the *facts* of plaintiff's criminal act.

However, identification of the *actor* in reports of long past crimes usually serves little independent public purpose. Once legal proceedings have terminated, and a suspect or offender has been released, identification of the individual will not usually aid the administration of justice. Identification will no longer serve to bring forth witnesses or obtain succor for victims. Unless the individual has reattracted the public eye to himself in some independent fashion, the only public "interest" that would usually be served is that of curiosity.

There may be times, of course, when an event involving private citizens may be so unique as to capture the imagination of all. In such cases—e.g., the behavior of the passengers on the sinking *Titanic,* the heroism of Nathan Hale, the horror of the Saint Valentine's Day Massacre—purely private individuals may by an accident of history lose their privacy regarding that incident for all time. There need be no "reattraction" of the public eye because the public interest never wavered. An individual whose name is fixed in the public's memory, such as that of the political assassin, never becomes an anonymous member of the community again. But in each case it is for the trier of fact to determine whether the individual's infamy is such that he has never left the public arena; we cannot do so as a matter of law.

* * *

Another factor militating in favor of protecting the individual's privacy here is the state's interest in the integrity of the rehabilitative process. Our courts recognized this issue four decades ago in Melvin v. Reid, * * * There, plaintiff had been a prostitute. She was charged with murder and acquitted after a long and very public trial. She thereafter abandoned her life of shame, married, and assumed a place in respectable society, making many friends who were not aware of the incidents of her earlier life.

Seven years after the trial defendants made a movie based entirely on Mrs. Melvin's early life. They used only facts found in the public record, and did not falsify or create false innuendoes regarding that period of her life. Defendants used Mrs. Melvin's true maiden name in the film.

The Court of Appeal, in a decision cited ceaselessly since, held that the *subject* of the film was protected. No cause of action accrues from the use of "incidents of a life * * * so public as to be spread upon a public record," the court reasoned, since these matters "cease to be private." * * * The court took a different view of defendants' use of Mrs. Melvin's *name.* Although that, too, had been spread upon a public record, the court held that defendants' use of plaintiff's name was improper. The lapse of time between the incidents in issue and the making of the film was a relevant, but not conclusive, factor to the court. * * * The plaintiff was held to have stated a cause of action for invasion of privacy.

One of the premises of the rehabilitative process is that the rehabilitated offender can rejoin that great bulk of the community from which he has been ostracized for his anti-social acts. In return for becoming a "new man," he is allowed to melt into the shadows of obscurity.

We are realistic enough to recognize that men are curious about the inner sanctums of their neighbors—that the public will create its heroes and villains. We must also be realistic enough to realize that full disclosure of one's inner thoughts, intimate personal characteristics, and past life is neither the rule nor the norm in these United States. We have developed a variegated panoply of professional listeners to whom we confidentially "reveal all"; otherwise we keep our own counsel. The masks we wear may be stripped away upon the occurrence of some event of public interest. But just as the risk of exposure is a concomitant of urban life, so too is the expectation of anonymity regained. It would be a crass legal fiction to assert that a matter once public never becomes private again. Human forgetfulness over time puts today's "hot" news in tomorrow's dusty archives. In a nation of 200 million people there is ample opportunity for all but the most infamous to begin a new life.

Plaintiff is a man whose last offense took place 11 years before, who has paid his debt to society, who has friends and an 11-year-old daughter who were unaware of his early life—a man who has assumed a position in "respectable" society. Ideally, his neighbors should recognize his present worth and forget his past life of shame. But men are not so divine as to forgive the past trespasses of others, and plaintiff therefore endeavored to reveal as little as possible of his past life. Yet, as if in some bizarre canyon of echoes, petitioner's past life pursues him through the pages of Reader's Digest, now published in 13 languages and distributed in 100 nations, with a circulation in California alone of almost 2,000,000 copies.

In a nation built upon the free dissemination of ideas, it is always difficult to declare that something may not be published. * * * The right to know and the right to have others *not* know are, simplistically considered, irreconcilable. But the rights guaranteed by the First Amendment do not require total abrogation of the right to privacy. The goals sought by each may be achieved with a minimum of intrusion upon the other.

In Time, Inc. v. Hill, * * * the United States Supreme Court considered some of these same balancing problems with regard to a different form of invasion of privacy, that of placing the individual in a false light in the public eye. The New York statute construed in *Time* did not create a right of action for the truthful report of newsworthy people or events. The Supreme Court stated, however, that "[t]his limitation to newsworthy persons and events does not of course foreclose an interpretation * * * to allow damages where 'Revelations may be so intimate and so unwarranted in view of the victim's position as to outrage the community's notions of decency.' * * *"[a] * * * Thus a truthful publication is constitutionally protected if (1) it is newsworthy and (2) it does not reveal facts so offensive as to shock the community's notions of decency.

We have previously set forth criteria for determining whether an incident is newsworthy. We consider "[1] the social value of the facts published, [2] the depth of the article's intrusion into ostensibly private

a. [Ed. note] This quote is taken from footnote 7 of the Court's opinion. A more relevant part of that footnote is reprinted at p. 1200, *supra*. Does the extract quoted by the Supreme Court of California accurately capture the Supreme Court of the United States' meaning? Is the implication found by the California court a valid one?

affairs, and [3] the extent to which the party voluntarily acceded to a position of public notoriety. * * *"

On the assumed set of facts before us we are convinced that a jury could reasonably find that plaintiff's identity as a former hijacker was not newsworthy. First, as discussed above, a jury could find that publication of plaintiff's identity in connection with incidents of his past life was in this case of minimal social value. There was no independent reason whatsoever for focusing public attention on Mr. Briscoe as an individual at this time. A jury could certainly find that Mr. Briscoe had once again become an anonymous member of the community. Once legal proceedings have concluded, and particularly once the individual has reverted to the lawful and unexciting life led by the rest of the community, the public's interest in knowing is less compelling.

Second, a jury might find that revealing one's criminal past for all to see is grossly offensive to most people in America. Certainly a criminal background is kept even more hidden from others than a humiliating disease * * * or the existence of business debts * * *. The consequences of revelation in this case—ostracism, isolation, and the alienation of one's family—make all too clear just how deeply offensive to most persons a prior crime is and thus how hidden the former offender must keep the knowledge of his prior indiscretion.

Third, in no way can plaintiff be said to have voluntarily consented to the publicity accorded him here. He committed a crime. He was punished. He was rehabilitated. And he became, for 11 years, an obscure and law-abiding citizen. His every effort was to forget and have others forget that he had once hijacked a truck.

Finally, the interests at stake here are not merely those of publication and privacy alone, for the state has a compelling interest in the efficacy of penal systems in rehabilitating criminals and returning them as productive and law-abiding citizens to the society whence they came. A jury might well find that a continuing threat that the rehabilitated offender's old identity will be resurrected by the media is counter-productive to the goals of this correctional process.

Mindful that "the balance is always weighted in favor of free expression" * * * and that we must not chill First Amendment freedoms through uncertainty,[18] we find it reasonable to require a plaintiff to prove, in each case, that the publisher invaded his privacy with reckless disregard for the fact that reasonable men would find the invasion highly offensive.[19]

We do not hold today that plaintiff must prevail in his action. It is for the trier of fact to determine (1) whether plaintiff had become a rehabilitat-

---

18. Because the categories with which we deal—private and public, newsworthy and nonnewsworthy—have no clear profile, there is a temptation to balance interests in ad hoc fashion in each case. Yet history teaches us that such a process leads too often to discounting society's stake in First Amendment rights. * * *

However, there is little uncertainty here. A publisher does have every reason to know, *before* publication, that identification of a man as a former criminal will be highly offensive to the individual involved. It does not require close reading of "Les Miserables" or "The Scarlet Letter" to know that men are haunted by the fear of disclosure of their past and destroyed by the exposure itself.

19. In alleging malice and willfulness in his complaint, plaintiff has complied with this initial requirement.

ed member of society, (2) whether identifying him as a former criminal would be highly offensive and injurious to the reasonable man, (3) whether defendant published this information with a reckless disregard for its offensiveness, and (4) whether any independent justification for printing plaintiff's identity existed. We hold today only that, as pleaded, plaintiff has stated a valid cause of action, sustaining the demurrer to plaintiff's complaint was improper, and that the ensuing judgment must therefore be reversed.

* * *

Notes

1. Is it relevant that the *Reader's Digest* article was a condensed reprint of an article in the "Chicago American Magazine" and that no action was brought against the publishers of that magazine? Suppose one of Briscoe's neighbors who was curious about him had gone back to Kentucky and examined the files of the United States District Court for the Eastern District of Kentucky (the court in which Briscoe had been convicted). Could that neighbor have been subject to an invasion of privacy action? What if the neighbor told someone else? Suppose he advised all of Briscoe's neighbors to visit the office of the Clerk of the United States District Court for the Eastern District of Kentucky? The *Briscoe* case has been reprinted in Torts casebooks. Any privacy problems?

2. Melvin v. Reid, 112 Cal.App. 285, 297 P. 91 (1931), has become a classic case. The facts of the case were set forth in *Briscoe*. The essence of the court's reasoning is set forth in the following paragraphs from its opinion:

> In the absence of any provision of law, we would be loath to conclude that the right of privacy as the foundation for an action in tort, in the form known and recognized in other jurisdictions, exists in California. We find, however, that the fundamental law of our state contains provisions which, we believe, permit us to recognize the right to pursue and obtain safety and happiness without improper infringements thereon by others.

> Section 1 of article 1 of the Constitution of California provides as follows: "All men are by nature free and independent, and have certain inalienable rights, among which are those of enjoying and defending life and liberty; acquiring, possessing, and protecting property; and pursuing and obtaining safety and happiness."

> The right to pursue and obtain happiness is guaranteed to all by the fundamental law of our state. This right by its very nature includes the right to live free from the unwarranted attack of others upon one's liberty, property, and reputation. Any person living a life of rectitude has that right to happiness which includes a freedom from unnecessary attacks on his character, social standing, or reputation.

> The use of appellant's true name in connection with the incidents of her former life in the plot and advertisements was unnecessary and indelicate, and a willful and wanton disregard of that charity which should actuate us in our social intercourse, and which should keep us from unnecessarily holding another up to the scorn and contempt of upright members of society.

We have seen that the trial court in *Sidis* considered *Melvin v. Reid* but did not follow it. *Melvin v. Reid* was also not followed in Barbieri v. News–Journal Co., 56 Del. 67, 189 A.2d 773 (1963). *Barbieri* is a seldom cited case but it is a good illustration that, even before the entry of the United States Supreme Court into the defamation and privacy arena, there was a judicial reluctance to engage in supervision of the press. *Barbieri* involved a 1961 article reporting the introduction of legislation making whipping a mandatory punishment for certain crimes. The article mentioned the plaintiff by name as having been the last person flogged in the state, the flogging having occurred in 1952. In declining to follow *Melvin v. Reid,* The Delaware Supreme Court said:

> With deference to the California Court of Appeal, we must express a serious doubt whether [the] basis of the decision—the unnecessary and indelicate use of plaintiff's name—is a sound one on which to sustain an action for invasion of privacy. Such a rule would in reality subject the public press to a standard of good taste—a standard too elusive to serve as a workable rule of law. We agree that the producer of the picture in the Melvin case was guilty of a breach of good taste; and we add that we think that the articles here involved evidenced a lack of feeling for the plaintiff. Indeed, the articles did not even credit the plaintiff with the rehabilitation he had apparently achieved, whether because of ignorance or indifference or for other reasons, we cannot say. As plaintiff's counsel says, what did plaintiff's name add to the story? The point was the gradual disuse of the whipping post.

> But we cannot agree to impose upon the public press a legal standard founded on such considerations. There must be something more than the mere publication of facts of record relating to a matter of public interest. In the Melvin case, in our opinion, there was the fact of exploitation of plaintiff's private life for commercial profit in a medium—the motion picture—almost inevitably entailing a certain amount of distortion to capture the attention of the public. If the facts of the murder trial had been set forth in a collection of studies of criminal cases, a different result would be indicated. * * *

We have already seen, *supra,* p. 1216, note 3, that motion pictures cannot any longer be considered a different sort of medium. Indeed, unless a verbatim transcript of the entire public record is presented, is there not inevitably an element of editorialization in any report?

3. On remand from the Supreme Court of California's decision overturning the trial court's granting of a demurrer, the *Briscoe* case was removed to the United States District Court for the Central District of California. On July 18, 1972, Lydrick, J., granted the defendant's motion for summary judgment. The court ruled, *inter alia,* that the "publication disclosed no private facts about or concerning the plaintiff, Marvin Briscoe," and that "said publication did not invade plaintiff Marvin Briscoe's privacy." (*See* Briscoe v. Reader's Digest Association, Inc., 1972 WL 7259 (C.D.Cal.1972). In Hall v. Post, 323 N.C. 259, 372 S.E.2d 711 (1988), the court reversed a decision by the intermediate appellate court that, in reliance on *Briscoe,* held that an adopted child and her adopted mother had a cause of action against the newspaper which reported the attempts of the child's natural mother to locate her some seventeen years after the child had been abandoned and adopted. If it had not been reversed, would the lower court decision have been open to attack on constitutional grounds? In Wasser v. San Diego Union, 191 Cal.App.3d 1455, 236

Cal.Rptr. 772 (1987), the plaintiff had brought suit against his principal and the school district over the validity of an evaluation report. In reporting this event the newspaper revealed that the plaintiff had, some eleven years before, been the defendant in a criminal prosecution in which he was acquitted of murdering his previous wife. Distinguishing *Briscoe*, the court held that this latter information was newsworthy as a matter of law.

COX BROADCASTING CORP. v. COHN

Supreme Court of the United States, 1975.
420 U.S. 469, 95 S.Ct. 1029, 43 L.Ed.2d 328.

MR. JUSTICE WHITE delivered the opinion of the Court.

The issue before us in this case is whether, consistently with the First and Fourteenth Amendments, a State may extend a cause of action for damages for invasion of privacy caused by the publication of the name of a deceased rape victim which was publicly revealed in connection with the prosecution of the crime.

I

In August 1971, appellee's 17–year-old daughter was the victim of a rape and did not survive the incident. Six youths were soon indicted for murder and rape. Although there was substantial press coverage of the crime and of subsequent developments, the identity of the victim was not disclosed pending trial, perhaps because of Ga.Code Ann. § 26–9901 (1972),[1] which makes it a misdemeanor to publish or broadcast the name or identity of a rape victim. In April 1972, some eight months later, the six defendants appeared in court. Five pleaded guilty to rape or attempted rape, the charge of murder having been dropped. The guilty pleas were accepted by the court, and the trial of the defendant pleading not guilty was set for a later date.

In the course of the proceedings that day, appellant Wassell, a reporter covering the incident for his employer, learned the name of the victim from an examination of the indictments which were made available for his inspection in the courtroom. That the name of the victim appears in the indictments and that the indictments were public records available for inspection are not disputed. Later that day, Wassell broadcast over the facilities of station WSB–TV, a television station owned by appellant Cox Broadcasting Corp., a news report concerning the court proceedings. The report named the victim of the crime and was repeated the following day.

In May 1972, appellee brought an action for money damages against appellants, relying on § 26–9901 and claiming that his right to privacy had

---

1. "It shall be unlawful for any news media or any other person to print and publish, broadcast, televise, or disseminate through any other medium of public dissemination or cause to be printed and published, broadcast, televised, or disseminated in any newspaper, magazine, periodical or other publication published in this State or through any radio or television broadcast originating in the State the name or identity of any female who may have been raped or upon whom an as-sault with intent to commit rape may have been made. Any person or corporation violating the provisions of this section shall, upon conviction, be punished as for a misdemeanor."

Three other States have similar statutes. See Fla.Stat.Ann. §§ 794.03, 794.04 (1965 and Supp.1974–1975); S.C.Code Ann. § 16–81 (1962); Wis.Stat.Ann. § 942.02 (1958). * * *

been invaded by the television broadcasts giving the name of his deceased daughter. Appellants admitted the broadcasts but claimed that they were privileged under both state law and the First and Fourteenth Amendments. The trial court, rejecting appellants' constitutional claims and holding that the Georgia statute gave a civil remedy to those injured by its violation, granted summary judgment to appellee as to liability, with the determination of damages to await trial by jury.

On appeal, the Georgia Supreme Court, in its initial opinion, held that the trial court had erred in construing § 26–9901 to extend a civil cause of action for invasion of privacy and thus found it unnecessary to consider the constitutionality of the statute. * * * The court went on to rule, however, that the complaint stated a cause of action "for the invasion of the appellee's right of privacy, or for the tort of public disclosure"—a "common law tort exist[ing] in this jurisdiction without the help of the statute that the trial judge in this case relied on." * * * Although the privacy invaded was not that of the deceased victim, the father was held to have stated a claim for invasion of his own privacy by reason of the publication of his daughter's name. The court explained, however, that liability did not follow as a matter of law and that summary judgment was improper; whether the public disclosure of the name actually invaded appellee's "zone of privacy," and if so, to what extent, were issues to be determined by the trier of fact. Also, "in formulating such an issue for determination by the fact-finder, it is reasonable to require the appellee to prove that the appellants invaded his privacy with wilful or negligent disregard for the fact that reasonable men would find the invasion highly offensive." * * * The Georgia Supreme Court did agree with the trial court, however, that the First and Fourteenth Amendments did not, as a matter of law, require judgment for appellants. The court concurred with the statement in Briscoe v. Reader's Digest Assn., Inc., * * * that "the rights guaranteed by the First Amendment do not require total abrogation of the right to privacy. The goals sought by each may be achieved with a minimum of intrusion upon the other."

Upon motion for rehearing the Georgia court countered the argument that the victim's name was a matter of public interest and could be published with impunity by relying on § 26–9901 as an authoritative declaration of state policy that the name of a rape victim was not a matter of public concern. This time the court felt compelled to determine the constitutionality of the statute and sustained it as a "legitimate limitation on the right of freedom of expression contained in the First Amendment." The court could discern "no public interest or general concern about the identity of the victim of such a crime as will make the right to disclose the identity of the victim rise to the level of First Amendment protection." * * *

We postponed decision as to our jurisdiction over this appeal to the hearing on the merits. * * * We conclude that the Court has jurisdiction, and reverse the judgment of the Georgia Supreme Court.

II

* * *

In light of the prior cases, we conclude that we have jurisdiction to review the judgment of the Georgia Supreme Court rejecting the challenge under the First and Fourteenth Amendments to the state law authorizing damage suits against the press for publishing the name of a rape victim whose identity is revealed in the course of a public prosecution. The Georgia Supreme Court's judgment is plainly final on the federal issue and is not subject to further review in the state courts. Appellants will be liable for damages if the elements of the state cause of action are proved. They may prevail at trial on nonfederal grounds, it is true, but if the Georgia court erroneously upheld the statute, there should be no trial at all. Moreover, even if appellants prevailed at trial and made unnecessary further consideration of the constitutional question, there would remain in effect the unreviewed decision of the State Supreme Court that a civil action for publishing the name of a rape victim disclosed in a public judicial proceeding may go forward despite the First and Fourteenth Amendments. * * *

III

Georgia stoutly defends both § 26–9901 and the State's common-law privacy action challenged here. Its claims are not without force, for powerful arguments can be made, and have been made, that however it may be ultimately defined, there *is* a zone of privacy surrounding every individual, a zone within which the State may protect him from intrusion by the press, with all its attendant publicity. Indeed, the central thesis of the root article by Warren and Brandeis * * * was that the press was overstepping its prerogatives by publishing essentially private information and that there should be a remedy for the alleged abuses.

More compellingly, the century has experienced a strong tide running in favor of the so-called right of privacy. * * *

These are impressive credentials for a right of privacy, but we should recognize that we do not have at issue here an action for the invasion of privacy involving the appropriation of one's name or photograph, a physical or other tangible intrusion into a private area, or a publication of otherwise private information that is also false although perhaps not defamatory. The version of the privacy tort now before us—termed in Georgia "the tort of public disclosure," * * *—is that in which the plaintiff claims the right to be free from unwanted publicity about his private affairs, which, although wholly true, would be offensive to a person of ordinary sensibilities. Because the gravamen of the claimed injury is the publication of information, whether true or not, the dissemination of which is embarrassing or otherwise painful to an individual, it is here that claims of privacy most directly confront the constitutional freedoms of speech and press. The face-off is apparent, and the appellants urge upon us the broad holding that the press may not be made criminally or civilly liable for publishing information that is neither false nor misleading but absolutely accurate, however damaging it may be to reputation or individual sensibilities.

It is true that in defamation actions, where the protected interest is personal reputation, the prevailing view is that truth is a defense; and the message of New York Times Co. v. Sullivan * * * and like cases is that the defense of truth is constitutionally required where the subject of the publication is a public official or public figure. What is more, the defamed public official or public figure must prove not only that the publication is false but that it was knowingly so or was circulated with reckless disregard for its truth or falsity. Similarly, where the interest at issue is privacy rather than reputation and the right claimed is to be free from the publication of false or misleading information about one's affairs, the target of the publication must prove knowing or reckless falsehood where the materials published, although assertedly private, are "matters of public interest." Time, Inc. v. Hill, * * *[19]

The Court has nevertheless carefully left open the question whether the First and Fourteenth Amendments require that truth be recognized as a defense in a defamation action brought by a private person as distinguished from a public official or public figure. *Garrison* [*v. Louisiana* (1964)] held that where criticism is of a public official and his conduct of public business, "the interest in private reputation is overborne by the larger public interest, secured by the Constitution, in the dissemination of truth," * * * but recognized that "different interests may be involved where purely private libels, totally unrelated to public affairs, are concerned; therefore, nothing we say today is to be taken as intimating any views as to the impact of the constitutional guarantees in the discrete area of purely private libels." * * * In similar fashion, Time, Inc. v. Hill, *supra,* expressly saved the question whether truthful publication of very private matters unrelated to public affairs could be constitutionally proscribed. * * *

Those precedents, as well as other considerations, counsel similar caution here. In this sphere of collision between claims of privacy and those of the free press, the interests on both sides are plainly rooted in the traditions and significant concerns of our society. Rather than address the broader question whether truthful publications may ever be subjected to civil or criminal liability consistently with the First and Fourteenth Amendments, or to put it another way, whether the State may ever define and protect an area of privacy free from unwanted publicity in the press, it is appropriate to focus on the narrower interface between press and privacy that this case presents, namely, whether the State may impose sanctions on the accurate publication of the name of a rape victim obtained from public records—more specifically, from judicial records which are maintained in connection with a public prosecution and which themselves are open to public inspection. We are convinced that the State may not do so.

In the first place, in a society in which each individual has but limited time and resources with which to observe at first hand the operations of his government, he relies necessarily upon the press to bring to him in convenient form the facts of those operations. Great responsibility is accordingly placed upon the news media to report fully and accurately the

19. In another "false light" invasion of privacy case before us this Term, Cantrell v. Forest City Publishing Co., * * * we observed that we had, in that case, "no occasion to consider whether a State may constitutionally apply a more relaxed standard of liability for a publisher or broadcaster of false statements injurious to a private individual under a false-light theory of invasion of privacy, or whether the constitutional standard announced in Time, Inc. v. Hill applies to all false-light cases. Cf. Gertz v. Robert Welch, Inc. * * *."

proceedings of government, and official records and documents open to the public are the basic data of governmental operations. Without the information provided by the press most of us and many of our representatives would be unable to vote intelligently or to register opinions on the administration of government generally. With respect to judicial proceedings in particular, the function of the press serves to guarantee the fairness of trials and to bring to bear the beneficial effects of public scrutiny upon the administration of justice.

Appellee has claimed in this litigation that the efforts of the press have infringed his right to privacy by broadcasting to the world the fact that his daughter was a rape victim. The commission of crime, prosecutions resulting from it, and judicial proceedings arising from the prosecutions, however, are without question events of legitimate concern to the public and consequently fall within the responsibility of the press to report the operations of government.

The special protected nature of accurate reports of judicial proceedings has repeatedly been recognized. * * *

* * *

Thus even the prevailing law of invasion of privacy generally recognizes that the interests in privacy fade when the information involved already appears on the public record. The conclusion is compelling when viewed in terms of the First and Fourteenth Amendments and in light of the public interest in a vigorous press. The Georgia cause of action for invasion of privacy through public disclosure of the name of a rape victim imposes sanctions on pure expression—the content of a publication—and not conduct or a combination of speech and nonspeech elements that might otherwise be open to regulation or prohibition. * * *

By placing the information in the public domain on official court records, the State must be presumed to have concluded that the public interest was thereby being served. * * *

We are reluctant to embark on a course that would make public records generally available to the media but forbid their publication if offensive to the sensibilities of the supposed reasonable man. Such a rule would make it very difficult for the media to inform citizens about the public business and yet stay within the law. The rule would invite timidity and self-censorship and very likely lead to the suppression of many items that would otherwise be published and that should be made available to the public. At the very least, the First and Fourteenth Amendments will not allow exposing the press to liability for truthfully publishing information released to the public in official court records. If there are privacy interests to be protected in judicial proceedings, the States must respond by means which avoid public documentation or other exposure of private information. Their political institutions must weigh the interests in privacy with the interests of the public to know and of the press to publish. Once true information is disclosed in public court documents open to public inspection, the press cannot be sanctioned for publishing it. In this instance as in others reliance must rest upon the judgment of those who decide what to publish or broadcast. * * *

Appellant Wassell based his televised report upon notes taken during the court proceedings and obtained the name of the victim from the indictments handed to him at his request during a recess in the hearing. Appellee has not contended that the name was obtained in an improper fashion or that it was not on an official court document open to public inspection. Under these circumstances, the protection of freedom of the press provided by the First and Fourteenth Amendments bars the State of Georgia from making appellants' broadcast the basis of civil liability.[27]

Reversed.

Mr. Chief Justice Burger concurs in the judgment.

Mr. Justice Powell, concurring.

I join in the Court's opinion, as I agree with the holding and most of its supporting rationale. My understanding of some of our decisions concerning the law of defamation, however, differs from that expressed in today's opinion. Accordingly, I think it appropriate to state separately my views.

I am in entire accord with the Court's determination that the First Amendment proscribes imposition of civil liability in a privacy action predicated on the truthful publication of matters contained in open judicial records. But my impression of the role of truth in defamation actions brought by private citizens differs from the Court's. The Court identifies as an "open" question the issue of "whether the First and Fourteenth Amendments require that truth be recognized as a defense in a defamation action brought by a private person as distinguished from a public official or a public figure." *Ante,* at [1232]. In my view, our recent decision in Gertz v. Robert Welch, Inc. * * * largely resolves that issue.

* * *

* * * Of course, no rule of law is infinitely elastic. In some instances state actions that are denominated actions in defamation may in fact seek to protect citizens from injuries that are quite different from the wrongful damage to reputation flowing from false statements of fact. In such cases, the Constitution may permit a different balance to be struck. And, as today's opinion properly recognizes, causes of action grounded in a State's desire to protect privacy generally implicate interests that are distinct from those protected by defamation actions. But in cases in which the interests sought to be protected are similar to those considered in *Gertz,* I view that opinion as requiring that the truth be recognized as a complete defense.

Mr. Justice Douglas, concurring in the judgment.

I agree that the state judgment is "final," and I also agree in the reversal of the Georgia court. On the merits, the case for me is on all fours with New Jersey State Lottery Comm'n v. United States, 491 F.2d 219 (C.A.3 1974), vacated and remanded, 420 U.S. 371 (1975). For the reasons I stated in my dissent from our disposition of that case, there is no power

---

27. Appellants have contended that whether they derived the information in question from public records or instead through their own investigation, the First and Fourteenth Amendments bar any sanctions from being imposed by the State because of the publication. Because appellants have prevailed on more limited grounds, we need not address this broader challenge to the validity of § 26–9901 and of Georgia's right of action for public disclosure.

on the part of government to suppress or penalize the publication of "news of the day."

Mr. Justice Rehnquist, dissenting.

Because I am of the opinion that the decision which is the subject of this appeal is not a "final" judgment or decree, as that term is used in 28 U.S.C. § 1257, I would dismiss this appeal for want of jurisdiction.

Notes

1.　United States v. New Jersey Lottery Commission, 420 U.S. 371, 95 S.Ct. 941, 43 L.Ed.2d 260 (1975), cited by Justice Douglas, involved the constitutionality of a federal statute prohibiting the broadcast of advertising for or information about lotteries. The application of the statute to forbid broadcast of the winning numbers in the New Jersey State Lottery was challenged. The FCC ruled against New Jersey's contention that the statute was inapplicable to state-run lotteries but the Third Circuit reversed. While the case was pending in the Supreme Court, Congress amended the statute to exclude state-run lotteries and the Court remanded the case for a determination of mootness. Justice Douglas dissented. The winning numbers in lotteries were news and Congress could not forbid their dissemination by radio broadcast.

2.　Shortly after the decision of the *Cox Broadcasting* case, its scope was tested in Virgil v. Time, Inc., 527 F.2d 1122 (9th Cir.1975), *cert. denied* (with Justices Brennan and Stewart dissenting), 425 U.S. 998, 96 S.Ct. 2215, 48 L.Ed.2d 823 (1976). The *Virgil* case involved a story in *Sports Illustrated* about the sport of "body surfing." The plaintiff, Virgil, was described as the most daredevil of all the body surfers. Among the details of Virgil's life revealed in the article were that he dove headfirst down a flight of stairs to impress some "chicks;" and that he would take construction jobs and "dive off billboards or drop loads on myself so that I could collect unemployment compensation so that I could surf at the Wedge." The article reported that, according to Virgil's wife, Virgil ate "spiders and other insects and things." The article noted that "[p]erhaps because most of his time was spent engaged in such activity, Virgil never learned how to read." The author of the article obtained his information from long talks with Virgil and from conversations with his wife and friends. The plaintiff admitted he talked freely with the reporter but claimed he "revoked all consent" upon learning that the article was not confined to describing his physical prowess. The plaintiff learned about the contents of the article and first made known his desire not to have references to his private life in the article during a conversation with a Time, Inc. "checker" who was trying to verify the factual correctness of the article. The district court had refused Time, Inc.'s motion for summary judgment and Time, Inc. brought an interlocutory appeal. In disposing of the case, the court of appeals concluded:

> Talking freely to a member of the press, knowing the listener to be a member of the press, is not then in itself making public. Such communication can be said to anticipate that what is said will be made public since making public is the function of the press, and accordingly such communication can be construed as consent to publicize. Thus if publicity results it can be said to have been consented to. However, if consent is withdrawn prior to the act of publicizing, the consequent publicity is without consent.

The court of appeals noted that the Court in *Cox Broadcasting* had refused to reach the broad question of whether " 'truthful publication may ever be subject to civil or criminal liability.'" Accordingly, unless the information were "newsworthy * * * the publicizing of private facts is not protected by the First Amendment." The case was therefore remanded for reconsideration in light of the views expressed by the court of appeals. On remand, the district court granted Time, Inc.'s motion for summary judgment on the grounds first that the information about Virgil was not so offensive and second that, even if it were so offensive, the facts revealed were newsworthy. 424 F.Supp. 1286 (S.D.Cal.1976). While the court of appeals had questioned whether the "identity of Virgil as the one to whom such facts apply is a matter of public interest," the district court held that "compelling need" was not the test for newsworthiness. Moreover, unlike *Briscoe,* there was no "serious danger that revelation of the person's identity will lead to stigmatization and possible ostracism." If the information had been gained in the course of a confidential relationship would it matter that the information was newsworthy? In this regard it should be noted that the Supreme Court has held that the First Amendment is no bar to an action for damages for breach of a promise of confidentiality, even if the information revealed is newsworthy. Cohen v. Cowles Media Co., 501 U.S. 663, 111 S.Ct. 2513, 115 L.Ed.2d 586 (1991). The question of when confidential information contained in medical records may be revealed because of pressing countervailing considerations is a complex one. *See e.g.* Doe v. City of New York, 15 F.3d 264 (2d Cir.1994)(revelation plaintiff's infection with HIV); W. v. Ed, [1990] Ch. 359, 2 W. L.R. 471, 1 A11 E.R. 835 (C.A.)(Mass killer applying for release from mental institution objecting to revelation of report of examining psychiatrist.) *Cf.* the discussion at p. 481 *supra*, of the duty of mental health care professionals to those who may come in contact with their patients.

The Ninth Circuit had occasion to apply *Virgil* in Capra v. Thoroughbred Racing Ass'n of No. America, Inc., 787 F.2d 463 (9th Cir.1986), *cert. denied* 479 U.S. 1017, 107 S.Ct. 669, 93 L.Ed.2d 721. That case involved a man who, after having been convicted of a federal offense for fixing horse races, was allowed to participate in the witness protection program in exchange for testifying in other federal proceedings. Under the program, he, his wife, and his son were given new names, appropriate documents, and resettled in a new location. The wife, using her new name, subsequently applied on her own behalf and on behalf of her son for an "open claiming license" from the California horse racing authorities. This license would allow her to race horses and to purchase horses in claiming races throughout California. The defendants were asked to conduct the customary investigation of applicants. During the course of that investigation, the defendants learned the wife's former name and that she was married to the convicted felon. Her application for a license was denied and the defendants issued a press release with regard to the denial of the application in which were revealed the former identity of the wife and her husband and the location in which they presently lived. The entire family brought an action for invasion of privacy. The district court granted summary judgment for the defendants on the ground that the information published was newsworthy. Citing *Virgil* and some intermediate appellate court decisions in the California state courts, the court of appeals held that the plaintiffs had made a case for the jury. In addition to the other factors that should be considered under *Virgil* and the California cases, the jury "must consider the social value of the facts published in light of the public's interest in protecting persons willing to testify," a "concern * * * not present in *Virgil.*" In the light of the decisions of the Supreme Court of the United States subsequent to *Cox*

Broadcasting, which will be discussed in the next note, is this decision a sound one?

3. In Oklahoma Publishing Co. v. District Court, 430 U.S. 308, 97 S.Ct. 1045, 51 L.Ed.2d 355 (1977), the Court relied upon *Cox Broadcasting* to strike down, in a *per curiam* decision, a state trial court's pretrial order enjoining the publication of the name or photograph of an eleven year old boy charged with second degree murder in a juvenile proceeding. Finally, in Smith v. Daily Mail Publishing Co., 443 U.S. 97, 99 S.Ct. 2667, 61 L.Ed.2d 399 (1979), the Court struck down a West Virginia statute making it a crime to publish the name of a youth charged as a juvenile offender without a written order of the court. The case was somewhat distinguishable from *Cox Broadcasting* and *Oklahoma Publishing* in that the newspaper did not get its information from court records but rather from "routine newspaper reporting techniques" such as asking questions of witnesses and police officers. In his concurrence, Justice Rehnquist relied on the fact that the statute only applied to newspapers and was thus unconstitutional on equal protection grounds.

The Court returned to the question in The Florida Star v. B.J.F., 491 U.S. 524, 109 S.Ct. 2603, 105 L.Ed.2d 443 (1989). That case involved an action brought under West's Fla.Stat.Ann. § 794.03, which made it unlawful "to print, publish or broadcast * * * in any instrument of mass communication the name, address or other identifying fact or information of the victim of any sexual offense * * *." In 1983 B.J.F. reported to the sheriff's department of Duval County that she had been robbed and sexually assaulted by an unknown assailant. The department prepared a report on the incident which identified the plaintiff by her full name. The department then placed the report in its press room. The department did not restrict access either to the press room or to the reports made available there. Although there apparently was a sign in the press room declaring that the names of rape victims were not matters of public record and were not to be published (*see* White, J.,'s dissent), a reporter-trainee from the newspaper who had been sent to the press room copied the police report verbatim, including the plaintiff's full name.[a] The newspaper then prepared a one paragraph article on the incident which also included the plaintiff's full name. In printing the victim's full name, the newspaper violated its own internal policy of not publishing the names of victims of sexual offenses. Plaintiff brought the action using her full name, but the Florida District Court of Appeal, *sua sponte,* revised the caption to refer to the plaintiff by her initials and the Supreme Court of the United States did likewise. The case was tried to a jury which awarded the plaintiff $75,000 in compensatory damages and $25,000 in punitive damages. The plaintiff had already settled an action against the sheriff's department for $2,500. The trial judge set off this amount against the compensatory damages but otherwise entered judgment on the basis of the jury verdict. This judgment was affirmed in a brief opinion by the District Court of Appeal. After the Supreme Court of Florida denied discretionary review the case was appealed to the Supreme Court of the United States which reversed. The opinion for the Court was written by Justice Marshall who wrote for himself and four other justices. Justice Scalia concurred in part and concurred in the judgment. Justice White dissented in an opinion in which he was joined by Chief Justice Rehnquist and Justice O'Connor. Justice Marshall refused the invitation to declare that "truthful publica-

a. The reporter-trainee apparently indicated that she was aware that names were not to be published. *Ibid.*

tion may never be punished consistent with the First Amendment." Rather he concluded:

> Our holding today is limited. We do not hold that truthful publication is automatically constitutionally protected or that there is no zone of personal privacy within which the State may protect the individual from intrusion by the press or even that a State may never punish publication of the name of a victim of a sexual offense. We hold only that where a newspaper publishes truthful information which it has lawfully obtained, punishment may lawfully be imposed, if at all, only when narrowly tailored to a state interest of the highest order and that no such interest is satisfactorily served by imposing liability under § 794.03 * * * under the facts of this case.

In his discussion Justice Marshall observed that "[d]espite the strong resemblance this case bears to *Cox Broadcasting,* that case cannot be fairly read as controlling here," because the name of the rape victim in *Cox Broadcasting* was obtained from "courthouse records that were open to public inspection." Rather Justice Marshall thought the case was governed by *Smith v. Daily Mail, supra* this note, which involved information that had been "lawfully obtained." Justice Marshall declared that, to the extent sensitive information rests in private hands, the government might under some circumstances forbid its nonconsensual acquisition and thereby bring the publication of any such information obtained without consent outside of the *Daily Mail* principle. The government had even greater powers with regard to information in its possession. It could provide a damage remedy against the government or against its officials who had mishandled the information. Justice Marshall also noted that, having made the information publicly available, it was hard to see what interest the state was advancing by trying to punish its publication. He finally noted the inhibiting effect of imposing liability upon "those who rely on the government's implied representations of the lawfulness of dissemination" of information that is made publicly available. Justice Marshall noted some other objections to the Florida statute. First, the Florida statute seemed to impose liability upon a disseminator of the proscribed information regardless of any fault. Second, the statute only applied to "an instrument of mass communication" which meant that the statute did not cover the dissemination of the identities of victims of sexual offenses by other entities and individuals. Justice Scalia found this last consideration decisive and thought it sufficient to decide the case on that basis alone. In his dissent Justice White attempted to distinguish *Daily Mail* because the disclosure in that case involved "the name of the perpetrator of an infamous murder of a fifteen-year-old student." He thought the rights of those who are accused of crimes are different from those who are the victims of crimes. He concluded:

> I do not suggest that the Court's decision today is a radical departure from a previously charted course. The Court's decision has been foreshadowed. In *Time, Inc. v. Hill* * * * we observed that—after a brief period early in the century when Brandeis' view was ascendant—the trend in "modern" jurisprudence has been to eclipse an individual's right to maintain private any truthful information that the press wished to publish. More recently, in *Cox Broadcasting,* * * * we acknowledged the possibility that the First Amendment may prevent a State from ever subjecting the publication of truthful yet private information to civil liability. Today, we hit the bottom of the slippery slope.

I would find the place to draw the line higher on the hillside: a spot high enough to protect B.J.F.'s desire for privacy and peace-of-mind in the wake of a horrible personal tragedy.   * * *

In a footnote he noted that the Court did not address the problems presented by the award of punitive damages but he acknowledged that this was a more troublesome issue.

Re-examine § 50–b of the New York Civil Rights Law reprinted at p. 1193, *supra.* Does that statute adequately meet the concerns expressed by Justice Marshall in his opinion for the Court in *The Florida Star v. B.J.F.?*

Why is the Court unwilling to declare that the publication of truthful information which has not been obtained unlawfully is under all circumstances privileged, at least with regard to an action for invasion of privacy. In his opinion for the majority, Justice Marshall alluded to possible national security concerns that might warrant the punishment of those who publish truthful information, but these concerns are not present in an action for invasion of privacy. It is worth noting that, in Butterworth v. Smith, 494 U.S. 624, 110 S.Ct. 1376, 108 L.Ed.2d 572 (1990), a unanimous Court struck down as unconstitutional a Florida statute that prohibited a person who had testified before a grand jury from ever disclosing his testimony except in response to the order of a court. The Court held that, after the term of the grand jury had expired, the witness was free to make whatever truthful statement he wished of information he had acquired on his own.

4. An approach to the problem of information gathering that presents fewer constitutional problems is not to restrict the ability to gather information but to restrict the uses that may be made of the information obtained. For example, it might be made illegal to deny consumer credit on the basis of arrests, convictions or bankruptcies that have occurred sufficiently far in the past. The Fair Credit Reporting Act of 1970, however, takes the tack of prohibiting consumer reporting agencies from furnishing reports containing arrests, convictions, or judgments more than seven years old and bankruptcies more than ten years old (15 U.S.C. § 1681c, as amended). On some of the problems presented by the Act, see G. Christie, *The Right to Privacy and the Freedom to Know: A Comment on Professor Miller's* The Assault on Privacy, 119 U.Pa.L.Rev. 970, 975–80 (1971). Another approach is not to try to restrict access to information or even dissemination of information but rather to make sure that the information is accurate. Thus, the Fair Credit Reporting Act has provisions requiring the notification of the consumer that information may be obtained about him (15 U.S.C. § 1681d(a)). The Act also provides procedures by which a consumer can find out what information has been obtained about him (15 U.S.C. §§ 1681g(a), 1681m(b)) and procedures whereby consumer credit records can be corrected (15 U.S.C. § 1681i). The subsequent Federal Privacy Act of 1974, 5 U.S.C. § 552a, also contains procedures whereby an individual may find out if the Government is keeping records about him—he may also be able to obtain this information under the Freedom of Information Act, 5 U.S.C. § 552, as amended. Moreover, procedures also exist, under the Privacy Act, whereby an individual can seek correction of government records concerning him.

5. The problem of providing a legal remedy for publication of private facts in breach of a traditionally recognized confidential relationship presents somewhat different considerations. Consider Commonwealth v. Wiseman, 356 Mass. 251, 249 N.E.2d 610 (1969), *cert. denied* 398 U.S. 960, 90 S.Ct. 2165, 26

L.Ed.2d 546 (1970), *decree modified in minor respects* 360 Mass. 857, 275 N.E.2d 148 (1971). For a more detailed discussion of the case and its background, see Comment, *The "Titicut Follies" Case: Limiting the Public Interest Privilege,* 70 Colum.L.Rev. 359 (1970). Wiseman had obtained official permission to make an educational documentary film of the Massachusetts Correctional Institute at Bridgewater. The permission was subject to certain conditions designed to protect the privacy of the inmates and patients. Wiseman in due course produced a film about the criminally insane entitled *Titicut Follies.* The film is not without sympathy for the staff, who were struggling with excruciatingly difficult problems in an obsolete institution with inadequate resources, or for the depressing plight of the inmates, but it shows inmates in pathetic and embarrassingly indecent situations. The film contains scenes of forced nose feeding, skin searches of naked patients, and pathetic attempts of prisoners to hide their genitals. Unknown to the Massachusetts authorities, the film was shown at two film festivals, in one of which it won first prize as the best documentary film of the year. Wiseman contracted for the commercial distribution of the film, and it was first shown in New York where it was advertised as making " 'Marat Sade' look like 'Holiday on Ice.' " The Attorney General of Massachusetts, concluding that the film went beyond the scope of the consent granted by Massachusetts authorities and that the film was an unauthorized invasion of the inmates' privacy, brought suit to enjoin future exhibitions. Wiseman argued that the distribution of the film was in the public interest as a means of bringing the plight of the inmates to the public's attention. The Supreme Judicial Court of Massachusetts agreed with the trial court that Wiseman had not adequately complied with the conditions of the permission to make the film, one of which was to photograph only inmates legally competent to sign releases. Treating Wiseman as primarily a collector of information who had breached the conditions under which he was allowed to make the film, one can see little difficulty with the legal system's providing remedies to protect the interests of the inmates. Furthermore, regardless of the conditions that were or were not imposed, perhaps a court should have held that no one may grant permission to photograph mentally incompetent inmates within a state institution unless the photographs are necessary for treatment of the patients or would aid in the efficient administration of the institution such as for identification purposes. What is curious, however, is that the appellate court modified the trial court's decree that the film be destroyed, in order to permit exhibition to specialized audiences, such as "legislators, judges, lawyers, sociologists, social workers, doctors, psychiatrists, students in these or related fields, and organizations dealing with the social problems of custodial care and mental infirmity," provided that "a brief explanation that changes and improvements have taken place in the institution" be included in the film. Relying on this modification of the original decree the film was shown from time to time at a number of law schools and other educational institutions. Does the court's order imply that some people's right to know is better than others? An earlier federal district court decision, Cullen v. Grove Press, Inc., 276 F.Supp. 727 (S.D.N.Y.1967), denied relief to guards at Bridgewater who sought to enjoin the film's showing in New York. The restrictions on the distribution of *Titicut Follies* have now been lifted by the Massachusetts' courts. See N.Y. Times, Saturday, August 3, 1991, § 1, p. 6, col. 6. The passage of time was a decisive factor. What if all the inmates portrayed in the film had not died. Should that have been the decisive factor? For the actual order, *see* Commonwealth v. Wiseman, Civ. Action No. 87538 (Mass., Superior

Ct., Suffolk Cty., July 29, 1991). (Wiseman, however, was not permitted to reveal the names of inmates who appeared in the film.)

TAGGART v. WADLEIGH–MAURICE LTD.

United States Court of Appeals, Third Circuit, 1973.
489 F.2d 434, *cert. denied* 417 U.S. 937, 94 S.Ct. 2653, 41 L.Ed.2d 241 (1974).

OPINION OF THE COURT

GIBBONS, CIRCUIT JUDGE.

This is an appeal from the grant of defendants' motion for summary judgment. The pleadings, affidavits, and depositions on file establish that the appellant Taggart is an employee of Port–O–San, a corporation engaged in the business of furnishing and servicing portable latrines. Taggart was sent by his employer to Bethel, New York in August, 1969 to service such portable latrines furnished by Port–O–San to the promoters of the Woodstock music festival. While he was servicing the Port–O–San latrines he was, according to his complaint and deposition, diverted from that work and engaged in conversation by agents of defendant Wadleigh–Maurice, Ltd., who were filming the festival, and photographed by sound motion picture. Wadleigh–Maurice, Ltd. during the course of the festival took over 315,000 feet of film (about 120 hours of viewing). From this 315,000 feet of film a feature length "documentary" was assembled, which defendant Warner Bros. Inc. undertook to distribute for commercial viewing. There is no dispute that the festival, the preparation of the film, and its distribution to theatres were all undertaken for commercial profit-making purposes. In those parts of the 315,000 feet of film chosen for inclusion in the "documentary" and thereby given widespread public dissemination is a sequence of approximately two minutes depicting Taggart emptying latrines. Taggart's deposition discloses the circumstances in which he was photographed:

"Q. Basically, at the time you were at Woodstock and you were approached by these two men, had you ever seen them before?

A. No, I never did.

Q. Did you know who they were?

A. No, I have no idea.

Q. How did they engage you in conversation?

A. Well, as I said before, as I was working these two men just came up and started talking to me. What are you doing there, I think was the key sentence. What are you doing there, they said.

Q. You responded to the conversation that ensued?

A. Yes. From there on, I went on about my business, about doing my work. As I was, they spoke to me and asked me what was this, and so forth.

Q. Did you respond to anything they asked you?

A. I responded to the questions they asked me.

Q. You mentioned before that they had cameras. How big were the cameras they had? Can you show us?

A. They looked like the little square box or something like that.

MR. FARLEY: Indicating about six inches long.

A. Maybe rectangular.

Q. Do you have a home movie camera yourself at home?

A. I have one, yes. It would be not in that category. It would be more like my son's. Thomas has one with a zoom thing on it and stuff like that.

Q. The camera that the man was holding, was that similar to the camera your son has?

A. It would be something like that.

Q. So the cameras were like home movie type cameras?

A. Yes.

Q. Did you see any of those large cameras that they used to depict when they show the news?

A. No.

Q. You didn't see anything like that?

A. No. Whatever it was they had was strapped. They had them in a strap on their neck.

Q. A strap to hold the camera?

A. Yes, a little bit of a strap.

Q. In the general vicinity through these days you were at the festival, were there many people with cameras of various types?

A. As I recall, I saw different types of cameras. I wouldn't say there was a wholesale thing with cameras there, you know.

Q. At any time did anyone ask your permission to take the picture?

A. Well, not that they asked me. Nobody came up to me and said, can I take your picture, nothing like that. They just came up and started talking. As they were talking—

Q. Was one talking to you and the other took the picture?

A. It was a combination. I don't know if I'm making myself clear here * * *

* * *

Q. In relation to the two men taking your picture did you know that they were taking it for any public released [sic]?

A. No. I had no idea of that."

Taggart contends that the sequence in which he was interrogated while performing his necessary though not necessarily pleasant employment was edited into the "documentary" in such a way as to achieve, at his expense, a comic effect. That this may well have been the intended and actual effect is supported by evidence in the record of the reaction of critics. For example, Kathleen Carroll, the critic, stated "[T]he funniest scene shows the latrine attendant proudly demonstrating his job." Craig McGregor, writing in the New York Times, April 19, 1970, stated "* * * and the man who is the real schizophrenic hero of Woodstock, the Port–O–San man, who empties the latrines of the beautiful people and has one son there at Woodstock and another flying a DMZ helicopter in Vietnam." Taggart contends that while he was engaged in his ordinary work he was without warning, and without consent, drawn into a conversation and photographed so that the sequence could be used as a key part of the theme of the "documentary" which was being prepared as a commercial enterprise.

When Taggart learned that he had been included in the commercial film he protested to the defendants, but they refused to delete the scene and proceeded to distribute the film nationwide. As a result, he alleges, he has suffered mental anguish, embarrassment, public ridicule, and invasion of his right to privacy which has detrimentally affected his social and family life and his employment. His deposition supports his contention that such ongoing damaging effects have occurred and are continuing. In this diversity civil action he seeks damages and an injunction against continued distribution of the offending scene. * * *

Moving for summary judgment, the defendants placed principal reliance on Man v. Warner Bros. Inc., 317 F.Supp. 50 (S.D.N.Y.1970). In that case Man, a professional musician, was at Woodstock, where at 4 A.M. he mounted the stage and played "Mess Call" on his Flugelhorn. His performance was photographed by the Wadleigh–Maurice camera crews, and was edited into the documentary without his consent. He brought a diversity action for injunctive relief pursuant to New York's right of privacy statute * * * and moved for a preliminary injunction. The defendant made a cross motion for summary judgment, which was granted. * * * In justification for the grant of summary judgment the court pointed out (1) that a professional musician who mounts a stage to give a performance before an audience of 400,000 is a public figure, (2) that in any event the depiction of his performance was merely a factual depiction of his participation in a newsworthy event, and (3) that plaintiff's forty-five second performance was *de minimis*.

The transcript of the argument on the motion for summary judgment in this case discloses that the district court appreciated several distinctions between this case and *Man*. First, Taggart was not a professional musician performing before an audience of 400,000. He was an ordinary working man going about his lowly task. Second, the reaction of the critics suffices to prevent the entry of summary judgment on a *de minimis* basis. The latrine sequence apparently makes a significant and memorable contribution to the film's overall impact. Thus, if summary judgment is to be sustained, it must be sustained solely because Taggart was a participant in a newsworthy event, and as such, outside the protection of § 51 or some other statutory or common law right of privacy. The district judge recognized, however, that it would be one thing to photograph Taggart as he went about his duties at a newsworthy event and to include such a photograph in a factual description of the event, but quite another thing to deliberately draw him out in conversation for the purpose of making him an inadvertent performer in a sequence intended to be exploited for its artistic effect. Recognizing this distinction, the district judge viewed the offending film sequence, and ruled:

"I react, as Mr. Dershowitz's remarks indicate, as the reasonable man might react after seeing the film. I come to a different conclusion after having seen the film than I did from reading just the dialogue. It was not so much a drawing out as to expose him to a substantial participation in the film. The event fits in a perspective of moving from one aspect of this festival to the next. He was not diverted from the work he was doing and brought, so to speak, upon the stage and made somebody separate and apart from the fellow who was working at the time they focused the camera on him. It is a very difficult line to draw.

I believe as you do, as I indicated before the luncheon recess, that there still is an area left where somebody does set out deliberately to make somebody participate in gaining a profit without compensation to him. But there is still an area where that is not protected by the First Amendment cases. I do not think that falls on this side of the line. I feel that summary judgment is indicated and I will grant the motion." (Tr. at 32).

The difficulty with this ruling is that it chooses between Taggart's version, that he was drawn out and made an involuntary performer, and the defendants' version, that he was a mere participant in a newsworthy event. The sequence which * * * [the judge] viewed undoubtedly was significant evidence in support of the defendants' position. But it was only evidence to be weighed against Taggart's testimony and the reaction of the critics. * * *

Clearly, then, the record presents disputed fact issues. We can affirm the grant of summary judgment on such a record only if we are prepared to hold that as a matter of law the defendants are entitled to judgment even if Taggart was deliberately drawn out as a performer in a commercial film. Such a ruling would leave very little to § 51 or to any similar statutory or common law right of privacy. It would be predicated upon a more absolutist interpretation of the first amendment than has yet been espoused by a majority of the Supreme Court. * * * We realize that requiring the defendants to defend in a trial rather than to obtain summary judgment puts them to additional expense, and arguably subjects their first amendment rights, should those rights ultimately be held to prevail over Taggart's right to privacy, to that much extra "chill." In the context of the problem—their commercial exploitation of Taggart's allegedly induced performance—this degree of "chill" seems to us *de minimis* when compared with the unsatisfactory alternative of ruling on a potentially serious conflict between legally protected rights without a complete record.

Judge Van Dusen, dissenting, urges that where "constitutional fact" is involved a district court may on a motion for summary judgment, or an appellate court may on appeal, resolve disputed fact issues. * * * Just as disputed facts in a nonjury case are determined by trial and not on summary judgment motion, a trial judge's decision to instruct the jury with the *New York Times* standard or an appellate court's de novo review of "constitutional fact" are both made after a full trial on the contested factual issues. Properly viewed these represent nothing more than the application of a governing legal standard to undisputed facts or to facts that are viewed in a light more favorable to one party. They do not involve the resolution of such credibility issues as whether or not Taggart was drawn out or was a willing participant. The label "constitutional fact" does not permit even an appellate court reviewing a full record to resolve credibility issues.

The judgment of the district court will be reversed and the case remanded for further proceedings consistent with this opinion.

Van Dusen, Circuit Judge (dissenting):

I respectfully dissent and would affirm the granting of summary judgment by the district court.

The court has today characterized the issue before the district court as whether Mr. Taggart was "drawn out" and made an involuntary performer or whether he was a mere participant in a newsworthy event and concluded that such factual determinations are for the jury. If this case involved only the application of the New York statute to the factual situation presented here, I would agree that summary judgment was improperly granted.

However, the central issue before the district court was whether the rule of Time, Inc. v. Hill * * * applied to the facts of this case. The question of whether or not Mr. Taggart was a participant in a newsworthy event, even if properly characterized as one of fact, involves a constitutional decision as to the proper application of a First Amendment standard. It must, therefore, be considered one of "constitutional fact" which the Supreme Court has said to be subject to de novo review. Rosenbloom v. Metromedia, * * *. It follows that at trial such issues are properly decided by the judge on a motion for summary judgment, where there are no other genuine issues of material fact.

* * *

There is no question that the Woodstock festival itself was an event of public interest nor that Mr. Taggart, by his presence there, was a participant in it. Furthermore, counsel for appellant has conceded in oral argument that if Mr. Taggart had only been filmed and not interviewed, this action would be barred. I fail to see why the mere fact of the brief questions asked should alter that result.

There may arise cases where a reporter or film maker conducts an interview in such a way as to lose the constitutional privilege of Time, Inc. v. Hill, *supra*. For example, where an incident is staged, as in the television series "Candid Camera," it would not seem to be an event of public interest. But here Mr. Taggart was simply filmed going about his ordinary occupation and asked a few questions that directly related to his participation in, and opinions on, a clearly newsworthy event. This is a common and important technique of investigative reporting and should enjoy the same constitutional protection as would a written or filmed account of that event. I would affirm the district court's granting of summary judgment.

Notes

1. We have already discussed the question of the degree of scrutiny which courts should exercise over factual issues arising in the course of litigation over the scope of the first amendment in connection with our discussion of defamation where these questions are presented more frequently. It, therefore, may be helpful to review the discussion at p. 1150f, *supra.* There is no question that the Court has made many factual issues which arise in the course of such litigation questions of "constitutional fact" as to which a trial court deciding whether to accept a jury verdict or an appellate court reviewing a lower court decision must exercise an "independent judgment". On the other hand, the Court has also made clear that, in deciding whether to grant summary judgment, the trial court is only to ask whether a reasonable jury could decide in the plaintiff's favor. The more searching independent judgment doctrine only comes into play once the jury has rendered its verdict. *See* Anderson v. Liberty Lobby, Inc., 477 U.S. 242, 106 S.Ct. 2505, 91 L.Ed.2d 202 (1986). The Court has of course recognized that the question of credibility is a particularly difficult one for an appellate court to handle. *See* Bose Corp. v. Consumers Union of United States, Inc., 466 U.S. 485, 104 S.Ct. 1949, 80 L.Ed.2d 502 (1984).

2. We have already briefly considered p. 1216, *supra,* the question whether the incidental inclusion of someone in a documentary motion picture is an invasion of someone's privacy. *See* Blumenthal v. Picture Classics, 235 App. Div. 570, 257 N.Y.S. 800 (1935), *aff'd on procedural grounds,* 261 N.Y. 504, 185 N.E. 713. The clear implication of *Taggart v. Wadleigh–Maurice Ltd.* is that is not. In Town and Country Property Inc. v. Riggins, 249 Va. 387, 457, S.E.2d 356 (1995), the plaintiff, a former professional football player, recovered, under a Virginia statute modeled after the New York statute that has been discussed in many of the cases of this chapters, $50,000 in compensatory and punitive damages in the following circumstances. As a result of a divorce settlement, the plaintiff had conveyed to his ex-wife his interest in the former matrimonial home that was located in the Virginia suburbs of Washington D.C. His ex-wife became a sales representative of the defendant realty company. When she decided to sell the house she prepared a flyer that exhorted real estate brokers to "come see John Riggins' former home." Three type sizes were used with "John Riggins' " in the largest type size and "former home" in the smallest. The court held that the use of the plaintiff's name "was not relevant to dissemination of information to consumers about the physical condition, architectural features, or quality of the home." Are these the only relevant considerations? The question of commercial appropriation of a person's name, likeness, etc. will be further pursued in the next two cases.

GRANT v. ESQUIRE, INC.

United States District Court, Southern District of New York, 1973.
367 F.Supp. 876.

WHITMAN KNAPP, DISTRICT JUDGE.

The essential facts relevant to the cross motions for summary judgment in this diversity action are not in dispute, and are relatively simple. Back in 1946, Esquire published an article about the clothing tastes and habits of six Hollywood stars, including plaintiff Cary Grant. This article was illustrated with posed pictures of these stars, obtained with their consent. The caption under Mr. Grant's picture was as follows:

"Hollywood Luminary Cary Grant—Cary Grant, ever coming up with the unexpected in pictures (as witness his roles in films from Gunga Din to Notorious with Ingrid Bergman), leans to conservative dress in his private life. Accordingly you see him in his favorite town suit of blue-striped unfinished worsted. The jacket, designed with slightly extended shoulders, has long rolled lapels which emphasize a trim waistline. The shirt, of off-white silk shantung, has a full collar. The black and white small-figured tie is typical of his taste in neckwear. He designs his own easygoing dress shirts, by the way. Made with a fly front, they fasten informally with buttons. As a concession to usage, they have studs but these purely decorative devices go only through the flap of the shirt."

It is to be observed that the foregoing caption provides the reader—in succinct form—with a fair amount of information about Mr. Grant's habits and life style. A considerable segment of the population might well consider this both interesting and informative.

In 1971, Esquire republished the same picture with one modification: everything below the collar line had been replaced with the figure of a model clothed in a cardigan sweater-jacket. Under the picture was the following caption:

"To give a proper good riddance to the excesses of the Peacock Revolution we have tried a little trickery. And what better way to show the longevity of tradition than by taking the pictures of six modish men that appeared in Esquire in 1946 and garbing the ageless enchantment of these performers in the styles of the Seventies. Above, Cary Grant in a descendant of the classic cardigan, an Orlon doubleknit navy, rust, and buff sweater-coat (Forum, $22.50)."

It is to be observed that neither the picture nor the caption tells the reader anything about Mr. Grant. One is not told whether Mr. Grant ever wore a cardigan sweater jacket, or anything else about him except his one-time appearance in the pages of Esquire. Mr. Grant's face serves no function but to attract attention to the article. Presumably the model who posed for the torso got a professional fee for his part in the enterprise. The question presented is whether Esquire had the right to compel Mr. Grant to contribute his face for free.

It is plaintiff's claim that the 1971 Esquire article gives rise to three causes of action: for libel; for invasion of plaintiff's statutory right of privacy; and, while not made explicit in the complaint, for violation of plaintiff's "right of publicity."

Defendants contend that the complaint fails to state any claim as a matter of state law; and that, in any event, all of its claims are barred by the First Amendment and must therefore be dismissed.

It is readily apparent that these claims and contentions pose two basic questions: 1) Has plaintiff stated one or more valid claims under state law? 2) If so, is there a constitutional bar to plaintiff's enforcement of such otherwise valid state claim?

I.

Turning to state law, there is no difficulty in disposing of the claim for libel. * * *

* * * The publication * * * is not, as a matter of law, libelous. The first cause of action is accordingly dismissed.

Plaintiff's remaining state claims rest on § 51 of the New York Civil Rights Law * * * and upon the somewhat related common law "right of publicity". * * *

The two key expressions in this section are "for advertising purposes" and "for the purposes of trade". We shall first consider the expression "for advertising purposes". As to that, the Court rules as a matter of law that the article on its face does not constitute an advertisement. * * *

Plaintiff contends, however, that he should be allowed to prove that defendants had some covert arrangement with each other which converted the Esquire article into a paid advertisement for the co-defendant Forum. As to that, it seems highly unlikely—in light of the detailed affidavits submitted by defendants on this motion—that plaintiff will be able to establish such a contention. However, the facts—if any—being wholly within defendants' control, plaintiff should have the opportunity to establish its case by pre-trial discovery if he can. * * *

The statutory phrase "for the purposes of trade" is not so easily disposed of. The statutory right to recover damages for the use of one's name for the purpose described in that phrase has had a development influenced by and intertwined with a somewhat disparate common law right known as the right of publicity. * * * The "right of publicity" is somewhat akin to the exclusive right of a commercial enterprise to the benefits to be derived from the goodwill and secondary meaning that it has managed to build up in its name. * * *

* * *

As above indicated, two distinct interests appear to be protected under the general rubric of a "right to privacy". The first protects that right in its more conventional sense, and permits a private individual to recover damages for injured feelings and general embarrassment if for purposes of trade he is unjustifiably subjected to the harsh and—to him—unwelcome glare of publicity. * * * The second—almost the obverse of the first— protects public figures from having the publicity value of their names and reputations unlawfully appropriated by others. * * * It is the second of these aspects that plaintiff Grant seems particularly to be invoking in this litigation.

There is obvious difficulty in defining a "right of privacy" for public personages. Moreover, plaintiff Grant has complicated the difficulty by asserting that he does not want anyone—himself included—to profit by the publicity value of his name and reputation.

To obviate at least the latter difficulty, let us shift our focus from the reticent Mr. Grant and consider the problem from the point of view of one who makes no bones about the commercial exploitation of publicity, the famous English fashion model, Leslie Hornby, commonly known as "Twiggy". Two things are clear in her case: (a) she has amassed a small fortune by exploiting the publicity value of her looks, name and reputation; and (b) in the process, she has become a public personage. In the latter capacity she has become fair game for the media. If she should appear, for example, at the opera in a Givenchy creation she could not complain if her photograph appeared in a newspaper, a magazine, or on television in connection with a story about the opera, about fashions, or about the life and times of Twiggy herself. However, it by no means follows that publishers could present an apparently posed picture of Twiggy and—without her consent—use it in competition with other pictures for which she had professionally posed or in competition with (or in substitution for) the professionally posed pictures of other models. *A fortiori,* no magazine could without her consent crop her head off a posed photograph and superimpose it on the torso of another model.

The question then arises whether the rights of plaintiff Grant—because of his renunciation of any desire to exploit the commercial value of his own name and fame—should be any different than those of Twiggy. We think not. If the owner of Blackacre decides for reasons of his own not to use his land but to keep it in reserve he is not precluded from prosecuting trespassers.

It follows that—absent any constitutional prohibition[a]—the motion for summary judgment will be denied as to the "for purposes of trade" phase of the complaint, and the jury will be asked to decide whether defendant Esquire has appropriated plaintiff Grant's picture for purposes of trade—e.g. merely to attract attention—or whether the picture was used in the course of some legitimate comment on a public figure or subject of public interest with which plaintiff has voluntarily associated himself. * * *

A word about damages. If the jury decides in plaintiff Grant's favor he will of course be entitled to recover for any lacerations to his feelings that he may be able to establish. More importantly, however, he will be able to recover the fair market value of the use for the purposes of trade of his face, name and reputation. The Court has no present suggestion as to how this should be proved. However, the Court can take judicial notice that there is a fairly active market for exploitation of the faces, names and reputations of celebrities, and such market—like any other—must have its recognized rules and experts. One element of damage will probably be the fact—if it be a fact—that Mr. Grant has never sanctioned his commercial use as a photographic model. There may well be a recognized first-time value (which diminishes with use) which the jury might find defendants to have appropriated.

With respect to the "advertising" phase of plaintiff's claim, he would, of course, be entitled to punitive damages should he be able to establish that defendants had secretly and deliberately used his likeness in a commercial advertisement. Punitive damages would not be available under the

a. [Ed. note] In portions of the opinion that have been omitted the court found that there were no such prohibitions.

other phases of his claim as nothing in the affidavits submitted would appear to support a finding of bad faith.

* * *

ZACCHINI v. SCRIPPS–HOWARD BROADCASTING CO.

Supreme Court of the United States, 1977.
433 U.S. 562, 97 S.Ct. 2849, 53 L.Ed.2d 965.

Mr. Justice White delivered the opinion of the Court.

Petitioner, Hugo Zacchini, is an entertainer. He performs a "human cannonball" act in which he is shot from a cannon into a net some 200 feet away. Each performance occupies some 15 seconds. In August and September 1972, petitioner was engaged to perform his act on a regular basis at the Geauga County Fair in Burton, Ohio. He performed in a fenced area, surrounded by grandstands, at the fair grounds. Members of the public attending the fair were not charged a separate admission fee to observe his act.

On August 30, a freelance reporter for Scripps–Howard Broadcasting Co., the operator of a television broadcasting station and respondent in this case, attended the fair. He carried a small movie camera. Petitioner noticed the reporter and asked him not to film the performance. The reporter did not do so on that day; but on the instructions of the producer of respondent's daily newscast, he returned the following day and video-taped the entire act. This film clip approximately 15 seconds in length, was shown on the 11 o'clock news program that night, together with favorable commentary.[1]

Petitioner then brought this action for damages, alleging that he is "engaged in the entertainment business," that the act he performs is one "invented by his father and * * * performed only by his family for the last fifty years," that respondent "showed and commercialized the film of his act without his consent," and that such conduct was an "unlawful appropriation of plaintiff's professional property." * * * Respondent answered and moved for summary judgment, which was granted by the trial court.

The Court of Appeals of Ohio reversed. The majority held that petitioner's complaint stated a cause of action for conversion and for infringement of a common-law copyright, and one judge concurred in the judgment on the ground that the complaint stated a cause of action for appropriation of petitioner's "right of publicity" in the film of his act. All three judges agreed that the First Amendment did not privilege the press to show the entire performance on a news program without compensating petitioner for any financial injury he could prove at trial.

---

1. The script of the commentary accompanying the film clip read as follows:

"This * * * now * * * is the story of a *true spectator* sport * * * the sport of human cannonballing * * * in fact, the great *Zacchini* is about the only human cannonball around, these days * * * just happens that, *where* he is, is the Great Geauga County Fair, in Burton * * * and believe me, although it's not a *long* act, it's a thriller * * * and you really need to see it *in person* * * * to appreciate it. * * *" (Emphasis in original.) App. 12.

Like the concurring judge in the Court of Appeals, the Supreme Court of Ohio rested petitioner's cause of action under state law on his "right to the publicity value of his performance." * * * The opinion syllabus, to which we are to look for the rule of law used to decide the case, declared first that one may not use for his own benefit the name or likeness of another, whether or not the use or benefit is a commercial one, and second that respondent would be liable for the appropriation over petitioner's objection and in the absence of license or privilege, of petitioner's right to the publicity value of his performance. * * * The court nevertheless gave judgment for respondent because, in the words of the syllabus:

> "A TV station has a privilege to report in its newscasts matters of legitimate public interest which would otherwise be protected by an individual's right of publicity, unless the actual intent of the TV station was to appropriate the benefit of the publicity for some non-privileged private use, or unless the actual intent was to injure the individual."

We granted certiorari * * * to consider an issue unresolved by this Court: whether the First and Fourteenth Amendments immunized respondent from damages for its alleged infringement of petitioner's state-law "right of publicity." * * * Insofar as the Ohio Supreme Court held that the First and Fourteenth Amendments of the United States Constitution required judgment for respondent, we reverse the judgment of that court.

I

* * *

Even if the judgment in favor of respondent must nevertheless be understood as ultimately resting on Ohio law, it appears that at the very least the Ohio court felt compelled by what it understood to be federal constitutional considerations to construe and apply its own law in the manner it did. In this event, we have jurisdiction and should decide the federal issue; for if the state court erred in its understanding of our cases and of the First and Fourteenth Amendments, we should so declare, leaving the state court free to decide the privilege issue solely as a matter of Ohio law. * * *

II

The Ohio Supreme Court held that respondent is constitutionally privileged to include in its newscasts matters of public interest that would otherwise be protected by the right of publicity, absent an intent to injure or to appropriate for some nonprivileged purpose. If under this standard respondent had merely reported that petitioner was performing at the fair and described or commented on his act, with or without showing his picture on television, we would have a very different case. But petitioner is not contending that his appearance at the fair and his performance could not be reported by the press as newsworthy items. His complaint is that respondent filmed his entire act and displayed that film on television for the public to see and enjoy. This, he claimed, was an appropriation of his professional property. The Ohio Supreme Court agreed that petitioner had "a right of publicity" that gave him "personal control over commercial display and exploitation of his personality and the exercise of his talents."

This right of "exclusive control over the publicity given to his performances" was said to be such a "valuable part of the benefit which may be
attained by his talents and efforts" that it was entitled to legal protection.
It was also observed, or at least expressly assumed, that petitioner had not
abandoned his rights by performing under the circumstances present at the
Geauga County Fair Grounds.

The Ohio Supreme Court nevertheless held that the challenged invasion was privileged, saying that the press "must be accorded broad latitude
in its choice of how much it presents of each story or incident, and of the
emphasis to be given to such presentation. No fixed standard which would
bar the press from reporting or depicting either an entire occurrence or an
entire discrete part of a public performance can be formulated which would
not unduly restrict the 'breathing room' in reporting which freedom of the
press requires." Under this view, respondent was thus constitutionally
free to film and display petitioner's entire act.

The Ohio Supreme Court relied heavily on *Time, Inc. v. Hill,* * * * but
that case does not mandate a media privilege to televise a performer's
entire act without his consent. * * *

Time, Inc. v. Hill, which was hotly contested and decided by a divided
Court, involved an entirely different tort from the "right of publicity"
recognized by the Ohio Supreme Court. As the opinion reveals in *Time,
Inc. v. Hill,* the Court was steeped in the literature of privacy law and was
aware of the developing distinctions and nuances in this branch of the law.
* * * The Court was aware that it was adjudicating a "false light" privacy
case involving a matter of public interest, not a case involving "intrusion,"
* * * "appropriation" of a name or likeness for the purposes of trade,
* * * or "private details" about a non-newsworthy person or event * * *.
It is also abundantly clear that *Time, Inc. v. Hill* did not involve a
performer, a person with a name having commercial value, or any claim to
a "right of publicity." This discrete kind of "appropriation" case was
plainly identified in the literature cited by the Court and had been
adjudicated in the reported cases.

The differences between these two torts are important. First, the
State's interests in providing a cause of action in each instance are
different. "The interest protected" in permitting recovery for placing the
plaintiff in a false light "is clearly that of reputation, with the same
overtones of mental distress as in defamation." Prosser, *supra,* 48 Cal-
if.L.Rev., at 400. By contrast, the State's interest in permitting a "right of
publicity" is in protecting the proprietary interest of the individual in his
act in part to encourage such entertainment. As we later note, the State's
interest is closely analogous to the goals of patent and copyright law,
focusing on the right of the individual to reap the reward of his endeavors
and having little to do with protecting feelings or reputation. Second, the
two torts differ in the degree to which they intrude on dissemination of
information to the public. In "false light" cases the only way to protect
the interests involved is to attempt to minimize publication of the damaging matter, while in "right of publicity" cases the only question is who gets
to do the publishing. An entertainer such as petitioner usually has no
objection to the widespread publication of his act as long as he gets the

commercial benefit of such publication. Indeed, in the present case petitioner did not seek to enjoin the broadcast of his act; he simply sought compensation for the broadcast in the form of damages.

Nor does it appear that our later cases * * * require or furnish substantial support for the Ohio court's privilege ruling. These cases, like *New York Times* emphasize the protection extended to the press by the First Amendment in defamation cases, particularly when suit is brought by a public official or a public figure. None of them involve an alleged appropriation by the press of a right of publicity existing under state law.

Moreover, *Time, Inc. v. Hill, New York Times, Metromedia, Gertz,* and *Firestone* all involved the reporting of events; in none of them was there an attempt to broadcast or publish an entire act for which the performer ordinarily gets paid. It is evident, and there is no claim here to the contrary, that petitioner's state-law right of publicity would not serve to prevent respondent from reporting the newsworthy facts about petitioner's act. Wherever the line in particular situations is to be drawn between media reports that are protected and those that are not, we are quite sure that the First and Fourteenth Amendments do not immunize the media when they broadcast a performer's entire act without his consent. The Constitution no more prevents a State from requiring respondent to compensate petitioner for broadcasting his act on television than it would privilege respondent to film and broadcast a copyrighted dramatic work without liability to the copyright owner, * * * or to film and broadcast a prize fight, * * * or a baseball game, * * * where the promoters or the participants had other plans for publicizing the event. There are ample reasons for reaching this conclusion.

The broadcast of a film of petitioner's entire act poses a substantial threat to the economic value of that performance. As the Ohio court recognized, this act is the product of petitioner's own talents and energy, the end result of much time, effort, and expense. Much of its economic value lies in the "right of exclusive control over the publicity given to his performance"; if the public can see the act free on television, it will be less willing to pay to see it at the fair. The effect of a public broadcast of the performance is similar to preventing petitioner from charging an admission fee. * * * Moreover, the broadcast of petitioner's entire performance, unlike the unauthorized use of another's name for purposes of trade or the incidental use of a name or picture by the press, goes to the heart of petitioner's ability to earn a living as an entertainer. Thus, in this case, Ohio has recognized what may be the strongest case for a "right of publicity"—involving, not the appropriation of an entertainer's reputation to enhance the attractiveness of a commercial product, but the appropriation of the very activity by which the entertainer acquired his reputation in the first place.

Of course, Ohio's decision to protect petitioner's right of publicity here rests on more than a desire to compensate the performer for the time and effort invested in his act; the protection provides an economic incentive for him to make the investment required to produce a performance of interest to the public. This same consideration underlies the patent and copyright laws long enforced by this Court. * * *

These laws perhaps regard the "reward to the owner [as] a secondary consideration," * * * but they were "intended definitely to grant valuable, enforceable rights" in order to afford greater encouragement to the production of works of benefit to the public. * * * The Constitution does not prevent Ohio from making a similar choice here in deciding to protect the entertainer's incentive in order to encourage the production of this type of work. * * *

There is no doubt that entertainment, as well as news, enjoys First Amendment protection. It is also true that entertainment itself can be important news. *Time, Inc. v. Hill.* But it is important to note that neither the public nor respondent will be deprived of the benefit of petitioner's performance as long as his commercial stake in his act is appropriately recognized. Petitioner does not seek to enjoin the broadcast of his performance; he simply wants to be paid for it. Nor do we think that a state-law damages remedy against respondent would represent a species of liability without fault contrary to the letter or spirit of *Gertz v. Robert Welch, Inc.* * * * Respondent knew that petitioner objected to televising his act, but nevertheless displayed the entire film.

We conclude that although the State of Ohio may as a matter of its own law privilege the press in the circumstances of this case, the First and Fourteenth Amendments do not require it to do so.

Reversed.

MR. JUSTICE POWELL, with whom MR. JUSTICE BRENNAN and MR. JUSTICE MARSHALL join, dissenting.

Disclaiming any attempt to do more than decide the narrow case before us, the Court reverses the decision of the Supreme Court of Ohio based on repeated incantation of a single formula: "a performer's entire act." * * * I doubt that his formula provides a standard clear enough even for resolution of this case. In any event, I am not persuaded that the Court's opinion is appropriately sensitive to the First Amendment values at stake, and I therefore dissent.

Although the Court would draw no distinction, * * * I do not view respondent's action as comparable to unauthorized commercial broadcasts of sporting events, theatrical performances, and the like where the broadcaster keeps the profits. There is no suggestion here that respondent made any such use of the film. Instead, it simply reported on what petitioner concedes to be a newsworthy event, in a way hardly surprising for a television station—by means of film coverage. The report was part of an ordinary daily news program, consuming a total of 15 seconds. It is a routine example of the press' fulfilling the informing function so vital to our system.

The Court's holding that the station's ordinary news report may give rise to substantial liability has disturbing implications, for the decision could lead to a degree of media self-censorship. * * * Hereafter, whenever a television news editor is unsure whether certain film footage received from a camera crew might be held to portray an "entire act," he may decline coverage—even of clearly newsworthy events—or confine the broadcast to watered-down verbal reporting, perhaps with an occasional still picture.

The public is then the loser. This is hardly the kind of news reportage that the First Amendment is meant to foster. * * *

In my view the First Amendment commands a different analytical starting point from the one selected by the Court. Rather than begin with a quantitative analysis of the performer's behavior—is this or is this not his entire act?—we should direct initial attention to the actions of the news media: what use did the station make of the film footage? When a film is used, as here, for a routine portion of a regular news program, I would hold that the First Amendment protects the station from a "right of publicity" or "appropriation" suit, absent a strong showing by the plaintiff that the news broadcast was a subterfuge or cover for private or commercial exploitation.

I emphasize that this is a "reappropriation" suit, rather than one of the other varieties of "right of privacy" tort suits identified by Dean Prosser * * * In those other causes of action the competing interests are considerably different. The plaintiff generally seeks to avoid any sort of public exposure, and the existence of constitutional privilege is therefore less likely to turn on whether the publication occurred in a news broadcast or in some other fashion. In a suit like the one before us, however, the plaintiff does not complain about the fact of exposure to the public, but rather about its timing or manner. He welcomes some publicity, but seeks to retain control over means and manner as a way to maximize for himself the monetary benefits that flow from such publication. But having made the matter public—having chosen, in essence, to make it newsworthy—he cannot, consistent with the First Amendment, complain of routine news reportage. * * *

Since the film clip here was undeniably treated as news and since there is no claim that the use was subterfuge, respondent's actions were constitutionally privileged. I would affirm.

Mr. Justice Stevens, dissenting.

* * *

As I read the state court's explanation of the limits on the concept of privilege, they define the substantive reach of a common-law tort rather than anything I recognize as a limit on a federal constitutional right. The decision was unquestionably influenced by the Ohio court's proper sensitivity to First Amendment principles, and to this Court's cases construing the First Amendment; indeed, I must confess that the opinion can be read as resting entirely on federal constitutional grounds. Nevertheless, the basis of the state court's action is sufficiently doubtful that I would remand the case to that court for clarification of its holding before deciding the federal constitutional issue.

Notes

1. Is it crucial for this decision that Zacchini performed at a county fair to which no one was admitted unless he paid an admission fee? Suppose Zacchini had not been paid for the particular performance that was filmed but did make his living from performing that act? Do you think Man v. Warner Brothers,

Inc., 317 F.Supp. 50 (S.D.N.Y.1970), discussed in the *Taggart* case at p. 1243, *supra,* was correctly decided?

2. Generally, just as one cannot defame the dead, so one cannot invade the privacy of the dead. *See Restatement (Second) of Torts* § 652I. The question has arisen, however, whether the right of commercial appropriation of a famous person's name, likeness, etc., is descendible to his heirs or otherwise survives the person's death. In Factors Etc., Inc. v. Pro Arts, Inc., 579 F.2d 215 (2d Cir.1978), *cert. denied* 440 U.S. 908, 99 S.Ct. 1215, 59 L.Ed.2d 455 (1979), the court, applying what it believed to be New York law, enjoined the sale of posters bearing Elvis Presley's photograph. The court noted that Presley had commercially exploited his name and likeness in his lifetime. A few months later a different federal court refused to rule that either the making of a large bronze statue of Elvis Presley *or* the distribution of an eight-inch replica to anyone who contributed twenty-five dollars or more to the project infringed Factors Etc., Inc.'s license, given in Presley's lifetime, to exploit his name or likeness. Memphis Development Foundation v. Factors Etc., Inc., 616 F.2d 956 (6th Cir.1980), *cert. denied* 449 U.S. 953, 101 S.Ct. 358, 66 L.Ed.2d 217. Because the court felt that the matter was governed by Tennessee law, the Second Circuit reluctantly followed the Sixth Circuit's decision in Factors Etc., Inc. v. Pro Arts, Inc., 652 F.2d 278 (2d Cir.1981), *cert. denied* 456 U.S. 927, 102 S.Ct. 1973, 72 L.Ed.2d 442 (1982). On the other hand in the Estate of Elvis Presley v. Russen, 513 F.Supp. 1339 (D.N.J.1981), it was held that Elvis Presley's right of publicity would be descendible under New Jersey law. And, in State ex rel. Elvis Presley v. Crowell, 733 S.W.2d 89 (Tenn.App.1987), it was held that, under Tennessee law, Elvis Presley's right to control his name and image had in fact descended to his estate at his death. This latter decision by a Tennessee state court of course meant that the Sixth Circuit's decision in the *Memphis Development* case had been incorrect. However, in a somewhat ironic twist, the Second Circuit has now decided that its 1978 interpretation of New York law, in the first *Pro Arts* case, was also incorrect. It concluded that there is no descendible right of publicity under new York law. Pirone v. MacMillan, 894 F.2d 579 (2d Cir.1990)(the plaintiffs included the two daughters of Babe Ruth).

In Lugosi v. Universal Pictures, 25 Cal.3d 813, 160 Cal.Rptr. 323, 603 P.2d 425 (1979), the court held that the late Bela Lugosi had not commercially exploited his name and likeness in association with the character of Dracula and therefore his heirs had no such right of exclusive commercial exploitation. Accord, Guglielmi v. Spelling–Goldberg Productions, 25 Cal.3d 860, 160 Cal. Rptr. 352, 603 P.2d 454 (1979) (plaintiff was the nephew and "legal heir" of Rudolph Valentino). The California legislature responded to these decisions by enacting Cal.Civ.Code § 990 in 1984 giving persons to whom the deceased may have passed his right by contract or by establishing a trust or by testamentary disposition or, in the absence of such arrangements, by the deceased's next of kin the right to control the use of "a deceased personality's name, voice, signature, photograph or likeness * * * on or in products, merchandise, or goods or for purposes of advertising or selling, or soliciting purchases of, products, merchandise, goods, or services * * *." with minimum damages of $750 for any unauthorized use. Uses in connection with news, public affairs, sports broadcasts or political campaigns are expressly defined as uses for which consent is not required. The use of a personality's name, etc. in a play, book, magazine, musical composition, film, radio or television program, other than an advertisement or commercial announcement, is also not prohibited as is any material that is "of political or newsworthy value" or "[s]ingle and original works of fine art." There is no requirement that the personality have commercially exploited any aspects of his public persona. In Martin Luther King, Jr., Center for Social Change, Inc. v. American Heritage Products, Inc., 250 Ga. 135, 296 S.E.2d 697 (1982) responding to a question certified by the Eleventh Circuit as to Georgia law, the Supreme Court of Georgia held that a descendible right of publicity exists under Georgia law and, furthermore, that it was not necessary that "the owner have commercially exploited the right before it can survive his death". The case involved a suit to prohibit the defendant from manufacturing and selling plastic busts of the late Dr. Martin Luther King, Jr. In Southeast Bank, N.A. v. Lawrence, 66 N.Y.2d 910, 498 N.Y.S.2d 775, 489 N.E.2d 744 (1985), the personal representative of the late Tennessee Williams brought a suit to enjoin the defendants from renaming their theatre on West 48th Street in Manhattan the "Tennessee Williams". The lower courts granted the plaintiff's motion for preliminary injunction but the New York Court of Appeals reversed. It held that the matter was governed by Florida law, because at the time of his death Williams was domiciled in Florida and it interpreted West's Fla.Stats.Ann. § 540.08 as giving a descendible right of publicity only to a person to whom a license had been issued during the decedent's lifetime or to the decedent's surviving spouse and children. It cited Loft v. Fuller, 408 So.2d 619 (Fla.App.1981) for the proposition that the statute was not to be extended beyond its "contours". The New York Court of Appeals expressly refused to rule on the question decided in the New York lower courts, namely "whether a common-law descendible right of publicity exists in this State."

Chapter 20

FALSE IMPRISONMENT AND MISUSE OF LEGAL PROCESS

A. FALSE IMPRISONMENT

SERPICO v. MENARD, INC.

United States District Court, Northern District of Illinois, 1996.
927 F.Supp. 276.

GETTLEMAN, DISTRICT JUDGE.

The moral of this case is never to put someone else's nuts in your pocket. Plaintiff's amended complaint concerns an incident in which defendant accused plaintiff of shoplifting a machine nut from one of defendant's Menards [sic] stores. In his amended complaint plaintiff alleges that defendant: falsely arrested/imprisoned him (Count I); intentionally inflicted emotional distress upon him (Count II); and violated the Illinois Consumer Fraud and Deceptive Business Practices Act, 815 ILCS 50⅗ et seq. (Count III). After filing an answer and affirmative defenses to the amended complaint, defendant filed a motion for judgment on the pleadings pursuant to Fed.R.Civ.P. 12(c).

FACTS

On December 12, 1994, plaintiff, who is seventy years old, went to one of defendant's stores located at Hall Plaza in Chicago to pick up supplies that he needed to fix a broken sprinkler system for his employer. The first item plaintiff looked for and located was a nut. After picking out a nut, which had a value of less than 70 cents, plaintiff asked several of defendant's employees where he could locate pipe wrap.

During his search for the pipe wrap plaintiff put the "solitary, little nut" in his pocket so that he would not drop the nut or misplace it while he searched for the pipe wrap. Plaintiff found and picked up some pipe wrap, went to a cash register and paid for the pipe wrap, but forgot to remove or pay for the nut he had put in his pocket. Plaintiff then proceeded to exit the store without paying for the nut. After plaintiff exited, one of defendant's representatives stopped plaintiff and forced him to accompany the representative to a closed room within the store. In the room, defendant's representative demanded that plaintiff empty his pockets. Plaintiff proceeded to remove the nut, money, and a cash register receipt for the pipe wrap.

Defendant refused to listen to plaintiff's explanation that he had merely forgotten to pay for the nut. Defendant's representative then took plaintiff's picture and displayed it on a bulletin board along with numerous other pictures labeled as criminals who had stolen merchandise, and called the Chicago Police Department to have an officer come to defendant's store to file a criminal complaint against plaintiff for shoplifting. The police officer tried to dissuade defendant's store manager from filing a complaint against plaintiff, telling the manager that plaintiff did not intend to steal the nut and that plaintiff had made an honest mistake. Nonetheless, the manager insisted on filing a criminal complaint, and the police took plaintiff to the station where he was fingerprinted.

As a result of defendant's insistence that plaintiff be prosecuted for theft of the 70 cent nut, plaintiff was forced to retain a lawyer. The lawyer called defendant's store manager who told the attorney that defendant intended to prosecute plaintiff for shoplifting. When plaintiff's employer learned what had happened, one of its representatives called defendant's store manager, vouched for plaintiff's integrity, stated that plaintiff had not intended to steal the item, and explained that the employer always reimbursed plaintiff for all purchases plaintiff made for repairs for the employer (thus negating any motive or intent by plaintiff to steal the nut).

After further calls and investigation, the vice president of plaintiff's employer told a manager at defendant's corporate headquarters that the store manager had decided that plaintiff had not intended to steal the nut. Defendant's corporate headquarters, however, told plaintiff's attorney that regardless of whether plaintiff intended to steal the nut, defendant still intended to prosecute plaintiff because it was defendant's company policy to prosecute every case. Despite defendant's repeated insistence on having plaintiff prosecuted for shoplifting, on the date set for plaintiff's criminal trial no one from defendant's company appeared, and the judge dismissed the charges.

After the trial date William Payne, defendant's "legal enforcement manager," sent plaintiff a letter dated April 10, 1995, making a "civil restitution settlement demand." In the April 10 letter Payne wrote that plaintiff had been apprehended for concealing and taking unpaid merchandise from the store on December 12, 1994. The letter further stated that under "Illinois Statutes" Chapter 38 Sections 16A–3 & 16A–7, any person who commits retail theft (shoplifts) can be sued civilly by the owner of the property. The letter offered that to avoid additional time and expense to plaintiff of defending a law suit, defendant was "willing to settle the matter for [defendant's] actual costs in processing [plaintiff's] case." Defendant offered to settle all civil claims against plaintiff for $100. The letter noted that settlement of defendant's civil claim did not prevent local authorities from proceeding with a criminal prosecution.

Defendant, through Payne, then sent plaintiff a follow up letter dated May 16, 1995, giving plaintiff "final notice" to "amicably settle" the matter, stating that if defendant did not receive a $100 payment by May 30,

1995, defendant would file a lawsuit. Plaintiff filed the instant case against defendant on June 14, 1995. Defendant has not filed a counterclaim or otherwise made good on its "legal enforcement manager's" threat to sue plaintiff for the 70 cent nut.

* * *

FALSE ARREST/IMPRISONMENT

Defendant raises two arguments in support of its motion for judgment on the pleadings as to plaintiff's claim for false arrest/imprisonment. First, defendant asserts that it had probable cause to arrest and detain plaintiff. Under Illinois law, a claim for false arrest must allege the restraint of an individual's liberty without probable cause. * * * Probable cause is an absolute defense to an action for false arrest and false imprisonment. * * *

The existence of probable cause is a question of law for the court to determine. * * * Under Illinois law, probable cause is defined as "a state of facts that would lead a [person] of ordinary caution and prudence to believe, or to entertain an honest and strong suspicion, that the person arrested committed the offense charged." * * * "It is the state of mind of the one commencing the [arrest or imprisonment], and not the actual facts of the case or the guilt or innocence of the accused which is at issue." * * * In the instant case plaintiff was detained and turned over to the police for alleged retail theft actionable under § 16A–3 of the Illinois Criminal Code of 1961 * * *, which provides in part: A person commits the offense of retail theft when he or she knowingly: (a) Takes possession of, * * * any merchandise * * * offered for sale in a retail mercantile establishment with the intention of retaining such merchandise or with the intention of depriving the merchant permanently of the possession, * * * of such merchandise without paying the full retail value. * * *

Therefore, the issue presented by defendant's motion is whether plaintiff's allegations can support a finding that a person of ordinary caution and prudence would not believe or even entertain an honest and strong suspicion that plaintiff took the nut without intending to pay for it. They can. It is hard to imagine that under the facts alleged any person of ordinary caution could strongly suspect that plaintiff intended to pay for the more expensive pipe wrap but also intended to steal the 70 cent nut. Of particular import is the allegation that the police officer believed, and told defendant that he believed, that it was an honest mistake. Accordingly, the court concludes that if plaintiff proves the allegations of the complaint, he will establish that defendant did not have probable cause to arrest and detain him.

Next, defendant argues that it is entitled to judgment on its affirmative defense based on section 16A–6 because even if it did not have probable cause, its actions were reasonable under sections 16A–4 and 5 of the Criminal Code. Section 16A–4 provides:

If any person: (a) conceals upon his or her person or among his or her belongings, unpurchased merchandise displayed, held, stored or offered for sale in a retail mercantile establishment; and (b) removes that merchandise beyond the last known station for receiving payments for that merchandise in that retail mercantile establishment such person shall be presumed to have possessed, carried away or transferred such merchandise with the intention of retaining it or with the intention of depriving the merchant permanently of the possession, use or benefit of such merchandise without paying the full retail value of such merchandise.

Section 16A–5 provides:

Any merchant who has reasonable grounds to believe that a person has committed retail theft may detain such person, on or off the premises of a retail mercantile establishment, in a reasonable manner and for a reasonable length of time for all or any of the following purposes: (a) To request identification; (b) To verify such identification; (c) To make reasonable inquiry as to whether such person has in his possession unpurchased merchandise and, to make reasonable investigation of the ownership of such merchandise; (d) To inform a peace officer of the detention of the person and surrender that person to the custody of a peace officer;

* * *

Section 16A–6 provides that: A detention as permitted in this Article does not constitute an arrest or an unlawful restraint, as defined in Section 10–3 of the Code, nor shall it render the merchant liable to the person so detained.

Whether defendant's detention of plaintiff was permitted under the Article depends on whether it was "reasonable." 720 ILCS $\frac{5}{16}$A–5. It was most likely reasonable for defendant to stop plaintiff initially, because under section 16A–4 it could presume that plaintiff intended to "steal" the nut. Under section 16A–5, however, defendant had to have reasonable grounds to believe that plaintiff committed retail theft and could only detain plaintiff a reasonable amount of time to make that determination. Defendant has the burden of proving that the actions of its security force were "reasonable." * * * Whether defendant's agents acted "reasonably" in continuing to detain plaintiff after refusing to hear plaintiff's explanation and after the police officer told defendant that plaintiff did not intend to steal the nut is a question for the jury to determine. * * *

Accordingly, the court concludes that under the facts alleged, defendant is not entitled to a finding as a matter of law that the entire length of detention at defendant's store and then at the police station was reasonable and permitted under the statute. Therefore, defendant's motion for judgment on the pleadings on Count I is denied.

[The court's discussion of the claim under intentional infliction of emotional distress and the claim for violation of the Illinois Consumer Fraud and Deceptive Trade Practices Act is omitted. The court found that no reasonable jury could find the acts of the defendant "so severe that no reasonable man could be expected to endure it" and dismissed the claim. The consumer fraud claim was dismissed because plaintiff was not a purchaser of the nut.]

Notes

1. Frequently, when a customer is detained by store security personnel, the customer is questioned about the alleged theft and is given the opportunity to sign statements admitting liability for the theft of store merchandise. In a subsequent criminal trial this evidence may be offered against the customer to establish guilt when charged with shoplifting or theft. Customers have challenged the admissibility of these statements claiming that the security personnel were acting to enforce the state criminal law and were, therefore, subject to constitutionally imposed restrictions on the use of their state-granted authority. The United States Supreme Court in Colorado v. Connelly, 479 U.S. 157, 107 S.Ct. 515, 93 L.Ed.2d 473 (1986), required police involvement before these protections would be violated. Based on this decision, some states which had previously excluded these statements because the store security personnel were acting pursuant to a state statutory authority have reversed their position. *See, e.g.*, State v. Muegge, 178 W.Va. 439, 360 S.E.2d 216 (1987), rev'd on this issue by State v. Honaker, 193 W.Va. 51, 59, 454 S.E.2d 96, 104 (1994).

In Bowman v. State, 468 N.E.2d 1064 (Ind.App.1984), it was held that, when an off-duty police officer working as a security guard detains someone for investigation under a shoplifting statute, the person detained is "not in 'custody'," so as to bring into play the warnings required by Miranda v. Arizona, 384 U.S. 436, 86 S.Ct. 1602, 16 L.Ed.2d 694 (1966). The court declared that "the short duration allowed for such 'custody' and the authority given civilians under the statute indicates official custody was neither contemplated nor authorized by the legislature."[1]

One possibility is to bring an action under 42 U.S.C. § 1983 which grants a federal remedy against those who, under color of state law, deprive people of their rights under the Constitution and laws of the United States. We shall briefly discuss such actions in the next chapter devoted to "Constitutional Torts." The other possibility is a common law tort action for false imprisonment (or false arrest). In Alvarado v. City of Dodge City, 238 Kan. 48, 708 P.2d 174 (1985) the court held that an off-duty police officer working as a private security guard who detained someone under a shoplifting statute was in point of fact acting under color of state law but the court also held, probably mistakenly, that there was no cause of action under 42 U.S.C. § 1983 because "the Kansas tort actions for false imprisonment, battery and defamation provide an adequate post-deprivation remedy sufficient to satisfy the requirements of due process under the Fourteenth Amendment." It has been suggested in cases like *People v. Raitano*, 81 Ill.App.3d 373, 36 Ill.Dec. 597, 401 N.E.2d 278 (1980), that constitutional prohibitions may not apply to persons acting pursuant to shoplifting statutes on the ground that these statutes are "merely a codification of the common law shopkeepers' privilege." Such a statement shows first the plasticity of the term "common law"—the shopkeepers' privilege is, as we shall see in the succeeding notes, a quite recent development—and is also almost certainly incorrect. We have already seen in *New York Times v. Sullivan, supra*, p. 1136, that the enforcement of a state's common law clearly is state action and clearly can be subject to constitutional restraints. *See also Tennessee v. Garner*, discussed in note 2, *infra*.

---

1. *But see* Owen v. State, 490 N.E.2d 1130 (Ind.App.1986) which distinguished between off-duty police officers who were subject to the *Miranda* requirements and private persons who were not.

2. False arrest may usefully be considered a subcategory of false imprisonment. What makes the detention of a person an arrest, rather than merely an imprisonment, is the assertion of state authority to detain someone because that person is suspected of having committed a crime. Generally, both police officers and private persons may arrest someone pursuant to a warrant that is valid on its face. Arrests pursuant to a warrant will be discussed briefly in *Boose v. City of Rochester,* the next principal case. The major tort problems arise when the arrest is made without a warrant. The common law on the subject is summarized in *Restatement (Second) of Torts, §§* 119, 120, and 121. At common law a private person could arrest another without a warrant for the commission of a felony if the person arrested had in fact committed the felony for which he had been arrested or if a felony had in fact been committed and the person making the arrest reasonably believed that the other had committed that felony. A private person could also arrest a person without a warrant for the commission of a misdemeanor *if* the person arrested had, in the presence of the person making the arrest, committed a breach of the peace. A police officer could arrest a person without a warrant in all the circumstances in which a private person could make an arrest. In addition, a police officer could arrest someone without a warrant for a crime constituting a felony, even if no such felony had been committed, if the officer reasonably believed that such a felony had been committed and that the person arrested had committed the felony. Most states now have statutes governing the matter. Subject to the requirement of probable cause (or reasonable belief) many of these statutes enlarge the circumstances in which an arrest can be made. In Minnesota, for example, an officer may arrest someone for the commission of any misdemeanor committed in the officer's presence and, in certain circumstances, for some other misdemeanors even if not committed in the officer's presence. Minn.Stat.Ann. § 629.34 (Supp.1996)(West). In New York a police officer has the authority to arrest anyone whom the officer has "reasonable cause" to believe has committed any crime whether the crime was committed in the officer's presence or not and a private person has the power to arrest anyone who has committed any offense in his/her presence. N.Y. Crim.Proc. §§ 140.10, 140.30 (McKinney).

Shoplifting came to be considered a problem because, if the amount thought to be stolen was relatively small, the crime involved would be petty larceny which is only a misdemeanor. Since the commission of such a crime usually does not involve a breach of the peace, under common law neither a police officer nor a private citizen would have any authority to arrest without a warrant. If the amount thought to have been taken was sufficient to make the suspected crime a felony, the situation was somewhat eased. But, if in fact the person arrested had not taken the goods nor had the goods been taken by any other person, a private person would have had no authority to make an arrest regardless of how reasonable the belief that a felony had been committed or that the person arrested had been the one who committed the felony.

At common law, one could use reasonable force in making the arrest. If the offense for which the person being arrested was a felony, even deadly force could be used if resort to such force was reasonably believed to be necessary in order to effect the arrest. *See Restatement (Second) of Torts § 131.* In Tennessee v. Garner, 471 U.S. 1, 105 S.Ct. 1694, 85 L.Ed.2d 1 (1985), however, the Court held that deadly force could only be used in the course of arresting a fleeing felon when there are reasonable grounds to believe that the fleeing felon poses a serious risk of death or serious harm to others. The use of deadly force could not be justified merely because it was necessary to resort to such force in order to apprehend the fleeing felon. In the *Garner* case, the Court upheld the reinstatement of a claim under 42 U.S.C. § 1983, a subject to be discussed in the next chapter, against a police officer who shot a fleeing felon who had broken into a dwelling house at night. The Court held that the fact that the person shot had broken into a dwelling house at night did not by itself prove that he was dangerous. Justice O'Connor dissented. She noted that a large percentage of rapes and robberies are committed by burglars (i.e., those who break and enter into dwellings).

3. Reacting to the perceived problem of how to deal with shoplifters, some courts began to permit the detention of suspected shoplifters under circumstances in which, under the common law, the shopkeeper would have had no right to arrest the suspect. For example, in Collyer v. Kress Co., 5 Cal.2d 175, 54 P.2d 20 (1936), the court held that a seventy-year-old man who was detained, questioned, and searched did not have a cause of action for false imprisonment against the store and its personnel. The defendants' conduct was held to be reasonable under the circumstances. Plaintiff had been seen by several persons putting a string of Christmas tree lights in his pocket. Plaintiff claimed that he had bought the items but had asked that they not be wrapped. Whether this was true or not, a jury had acquitted him in a criminal prosecution. Building on cases like *Collyer,* the *Restatement (Second) of Torts* added the following new provision which had not appeared in the original *Restatement.*

§ 120A. Temporary Detention for Investigation

One who reasonably believes that another has tortiously taken a chattel upon his premises, or has failed to make due cash payment for a chattel purchased or services rendered there, is privileged, without arresting the other, to detain him on the premises for the time necessary for a reasonable investigation of the facts.

Many states either judicially adopted the *Restatement (Second)* provision or adopted statutes like the Illinois statute noted in the *Serpico* case, above. Consider the following two representative statutes.

Minn.Stat.Ann.[2] § 629.366 Theft in business establishments; detaining suspects

Subdivision 1. Circumstances justifying detention. (a) A merchant or merchant's employee may detain a person if the merchant or employee has reasonable cause to believe:

(1) that the person has taken, or is taking, an article of value without paying for it, from the possession of the merchant in the merchant's place of business or from a vehicle or premises under the merchant's control;

(2) that the taking is done with the intent to wrongfully deprive the merchant of the property or the use or benefit of it; or

(3) that the taking is done with the intent to appropriate the use of the property to the taker or any other person.

(b) Subject to the limitations in paragraph (a), a merchant or merchant's employee may detain a person for any of the following purposes:

---

2. (Supp.1996)(West).

(1) to require the person to provide identification or verify identification;

(2) to inquire as to whether the person possesses unpurchased merchandise taken from the merchant and, if so, to receive the merchandise;

(3) to inform a peace officer; or

(4) to institute criminal proceedings against the person.

(c) The person detained shall be informed promptly of the purpose of the detention and may not be subjected to unnecessary or unreasonable force, nor to interrogation against the person's will. A merchant or merchant's employee may not detain a person for more than one hour unless:

(1) the merchant or employee is waiting to surrender the person to a peace officer, in which case the person may be detained until a peace officer has accepted custody of or released the person; or

(2) the person is a minor, or claims to be, and the merchant or employee is waiting to surrender the minor to a peace officer or the minor's parent, guardian, or custodian, in which case the minor may be detained until the peace officer, parent, guardian, or custodian has accepted custody of the minor.

(d) If at any time the person detained requests that a peace officer be summoned, the merchant or merchant's employee must notify a peace officer immediately.

Subd. 2. Arrest. Upon a charge being made by a merchant or merchant's employee, a peace officer may arrest a person without a warrant, if the officer has reasonable cause for believing that the person has committed or attempted to commit the offense described in subdivision 1.

Subd. 3. Immunity. No merchant, merchant's employee, or peace officer is criminally or civilly liable for any action authorized under subdivision 1 or 2 if the arresting person's action is based upon reasonable cause.

N.C.Gen.Stat. § 14–72.1 Concealment of merchandise in mercantile establishments.

(a) Whoever, without authority, willfully conceals the goods or merchandise of any store, not theretofore purchased by such person, while still upon the premises of such store, shall be guilty of a misdemeanor and, upon conviction, shall be punished as provided in subsection (e). Such goods or merchandise found concealed upon or about the person and which have not theretofore been purchased by such person shall be prima facie evidence of a willful concealment.

* * *

(c) A merchant, or his agent or employee, or a peace officer who detains or causes the arrest of any person shall not be held civilly liable for detention, malicious prosecution, false imprisonment, or false arrest of the person detained or arrested, where such detention is in a reasonable manner for a reasonable length of time, if in detaining or in causing the arrest of such person, the merchant, or his agent or employee, or the peace officer had at the time of the detention or arrest probable cause to believe that the person committed the offense created by this section. If the person being detained by the merchant, or his agent or employee, is a minor 16 years of age or younger, the merchant or his agent or employee, shall call or notify, or make a reasonable effort to call or notify the parent or guardian of the minor, during the period of detention.

(d) Whoever, without authority, willfully transfers any price tag from goods or merchandise to other goods or merchandise having a higher selling price or marks said goods at a lower price or substitutes or superimposes thereon a false price tag and then presents said goods or merchandise for purchase shall be guilty of a misdemeanor and, upon conviction, shall be punished as provided in subsection (e).

Nothing herein shall be construed to provide that the mere possession of goods or the production by shoppers of improperly priced merchandise for checkout shall constitute prima facie evidence of guilt.

* * *

4. In addition to false imprisonment actions brought by customers against stores, frequently actions are being brought by employees against their employers for conduct during the course of a loss prevention investigation. In these cases a key issue becomes whether the claim is barred by the exclusivity provisions of the state's worker's compensation statute. *See* Fermino v. Fedco, Inc., 7 Cal.4th 701, 872 P.2d 559, 30 Cal.Rptr.2d 18 (1994)(holding a false imprisonment not to be part of the normal employer-employee relationship and, therefore, a tort cause of action is not barred by the California worker's compensation statute). *But see,* Dunn v. United States, 516 F.Supp. 1373 (E.D.Pa.1981).

5. The essence of the common law tort of false imprisonment is the intentional confinement of another person, without that person's consent within boundaries set by the actor.[3] Confinement may be accomplished by physical barriers, by physical force, or by the threat of physical force. A display of actual authority by a police officer or of purported authority by someone such as a railroad conductor ordering a passenger to remain on a train will also be enough to sustain the action. These situations in which confinement is achieved through a purported exercise of authority might perhaps be considered as situations involving the implicit threat of physical force. A person who is under a legal duty to release another from a place of confinement will also be liable for false imprisonment if he intentionally refuses to try to release him. *See* Bennett v. Ohio Dep't of Rehabilitation and Correction, 60 Ohio St.3d 107, 573 N.E.2d 633 (1991)(false imprisonment claim properly pled when State parole board wrongly held prisoner for six months after the end of sentence term). Also a shopkeeper who, upon discovering that a customer is locked in the store's washroom, refuses to take steps to release the customer will be liable for false imprisonment. *Cf.* Talcott v. National Exhib. Co., 144 App.Div.

---

3. "Imprisonment is the restraint of a man's liberty whether it be in the open field, or in the stocks or cage in the street, or in a man's own house, as well as in the common goal. And in all these places the party so restrained is said to be a prisoner, so long as he has not his liberty freely to go at all times to all places whither he will, without bail or mainprize." Termes de la Ley (c.1520), quoted in Winfield and Jolowicz on Tort 59 (13 ed. by W. Rogers 1989). The *Restatement (Second) of Torts* treats the subject of false imprisonment in §§ 35 *through* 45A.

337, 128 N.Y.S. 1059 (2d Dept.1911)(ballpark failed to advise patron of alternate exit after main gate locked because of the crush of the crowd). Confinement may also be accomplished by means of duress in the form of a physical threat to one's own property or to a third person. Consider, for example, the case in which one person takes another's purse to prevent her from leaving a place and she remains because there is a large amount of money in her purse. She has been falsely imprisoned. *See* Ashland Dry Goods Co. v. Wages, 302 Ky. 577, 195 S.W.2d 312 (1946). For the tort to lie, the confinement must be complete, that is to say there must be no reasonable escape route *known* to the person confined. *See* Talcott v. National Exhib. Co., *supra*. A reasonable escape route is one whose use does not involve any serious risk of physical injury or extreme degree of social embarrassment. One who is intentionally confined in a building is not obliged to incur the risk of injury by jumping out of an open second-story window nor would a person whose clothes have been taken as a prank while he was taking a shower be required to leave the building naked. An interesting, though not very often litigated question, is how large must the area of confinement be and still constitute a "prison". In Allen v. Fromme, 141 App.Div. 362, 126 N.Y.S. 520 (1st Dept.1910), a law student who was confined to the city of New York during vacation time under invalid civil process was held to have a cause of action for false imprisonment. A more recent example is presented by Helstrom v. North Slope Borough, 797 P.2d 1192 (Alaska 1990), in which it was held that confinement within the Borough was sufficient to constitute false imprisonment.

The traditional common law definition of false imprisonment has been thought to require that the person confined be conscious of the confinement. *See* Herring v. Boyle, 1 Cr.M. & R., 141 Eng.Rep. 1126 (Exch. 1834). *But see* Meering v. Grahame–White Aviation Co., 122 L.T. 44 (C.A.1920), criticized in Winfield and Jolowicz on Tort 59–60 (13th ed. by W. Rogers 1989). In *Herring,* a headmaster refused to allow a mother to take home her son because the mother had not paid the school fees. The mother eventually secured the release of her son through a writ of habeas corpus. An action for false imprisonment was dismissed because the boy was unaware that he was being detained against his mother's wishes. *The Restatement (Second of Torts)* §§ 35, 42, broadens the common law, permitting an action for false imprisonment for physical confinement of a person to either (1) one who knows or is conscious of the confinement or (2) one who is harmed by the confinement. One of the examples given under § 42 is that of a child six days old who was locked in the vault of a bank for two days and suffers from hunger and thirst and whose health is affected by the confinement. Would not such a person have a cause of action against the persons confining him under a negligence theory? Does the *Restatement Second* 's attempt to broaden the scope of the action serve many practical needs?

6. Note that in *Serpico* the plaintiff tried to use two other claims, in addition to the false imprisonment claim. In these cases several other torts are frequently pled. In addition to a claim for intentional infliction of emotional distress, which is quite common in these cases, other possibilities, as already noted, include a Section 1983 claim. If the confinement is followed by court action, a malicious prosecution claim is frequently added, as noted in the next section of this chapter. If there is any touching or threatened touching, an assault or battery claim may be included. For an example of a case asserting multiple, alternative claims and also dealing with the issue of governmental

immunity, to be taken up in Chapter 24, *see* Sena v. Commonwealth, 417 Mass. 250, 629 N.E.2d 986 (1994).

B. MALICIOUS PROSECUTION AND RELATED TORTS

BOOSE v. CITY OF ROCHESTER

Supreme Court of New York, Appellate Division, 1979.
71 A.D.2d 59, 421 N.Y.S.2d 740.

SIMONS, JUSTICE Presiding:

Plaintiff commenced this action for malicious prosecution alleging that defendant, acting through its police officers, wrongfully procured her indictment for assault second degree. At the conclusion of plaintiff's case, the Trial Court dismissed the cause of action for malicious prosecution, but permitted the trial to proceed. At the close of the evidence, the court solicited a motion to conform the pleadings to the proof and it then submitted the cause to the jury for recovery based upon negligence and false imprisonment. The jury returned a verdict of $6,000 in plaintiff's favor and defendant appeals.

Plaintiff was arrested for two crimes apparently committed by others. In the first instance, the perpetrator of the crime identified herself to police by use of plaintiff's name, and a warrant was issued charging "Gloria Jean Booth" with obstruction of governmental administration, a misdemeanor. In the second instance, the police had no identification but assuming that the crime was committed by the same defendant, they procured a warrant for "Jane Doe Booze" and arrested plaintiff for assault second degree. The charge was subsequently submitted to the Grand Jury and an indictment was handed up, later to be superseded by a no bill and dismissal.

At the root of the case is plaintiff's right to damages, by whatever legal theory, for injury occasioned to her because of the alleged inadequate investigation by the police into the identity of a criminal defendant before obtaining a warrant and making an arrest. The jury in this trial was asked to decide in essence, whether the police had been negligent in their preparation of plaintiff's assault case. Plaintiff may not recover under broad general principles of negligence, however, but must proceed by way of the traditional remedies of false arrest and imprisonment and malicious prosecution. Her right to be free of restraint or unjustified and unreasonable litigation is limited by the obvious policy of the law to encourage proceedings against those who are apparently guilty of criminal conduct and to let finished litigation remain undisturbed and unchallenged. To that end, plaintiff's recovery must be determined by established rules defining the torts of false arrest and imprisonment and malicious prosecution, rules which permit damages only under circumstances in which the law regards the imprisonment or prosecution as improper and unjustified * * *.

At the time of these events plaintiff was 23 years old, employed by Eastman Kodak Company and a part-time college student. She resided at 167 Pennsylvania Avenue in Rochester with her mother and seven sisters and she had an older, married sister who lived one or two houses away.

On June 22, 1975 one Miguel Pabon was driving down Pennsylvania Avenue near the Boose home when someone in a group of children threw a rock at his car. Mr. Pabon stopped and got out. Intending to find the child's parent, he followed the child as it ran to a nearby house. A "fair number" of people came out of the house, including one woman with a hammer and another with a club, and they started to chase him. Mr. Pabon tried to run to his car but before he could safely reach it he was assaulted and robbed. The next day, after reporting the incident to the police, he went to the house on Pennsylvania Avenue to investigate with Sergeant Scacchetti and Officer Zigarowicz of the Rochester police. A young lady came to the door and Mr. Pabon identified her as the one who had hit him. When she was asked, she answered that her name was "Gloria Jean Boosey" but Officer Scacchetti testified that a confrontation soon began to develop and the men decided to leave rather than risk "having a riot on [their] hands". Officer Scacchetti returned to the house on several subsequent occasions to investigate but no one answered the door. He described the person who gave her name as Gloria Jean Boose as 18 or 19 years of age.

Several months later, on October 16, 1975, a warrant was issued on the basis of these facts charging "Gloria Jean Booth" with obstruction. At trial Officer Scacchetti admitted that plaintiff was not the person whom he had met on Pennsylvania Avenue in June and who identified herself as "Gloria Jean Boosey".

A second incident occurred on August 20, 1975. On that day Anthony Kasper was driving his car down Pennsylvania Avenue when a young child threw a rock at him. Mr. Kasper also got out of his car to locate the child's parents and when he did so he was assaulted by two females, one heavy set and around 40 years of age, and the other between 14 and 17 years old. Before the Grand Jury and during the trial, Mr. Kasper identified one Ossie Boose as the older woman and as the individual who had hit him with a board causing his injuries. She was the mother of the child and, as it turns out she is plaintiff's mother.

On October 23, 1975 a warrant was procured based upon this August incident charging "Jane Doe Booze" with assault, second degree. Officer Scacchetti explained that a Jane Doe warrant was used because Kasper had not identified the defendant to him and he (Scacchetti) "assumed that it was one of the two (females, the younger one) from the previous (incident) * * *." It is this charge on which plaintiff was indicted and which is the basis of this action. At the trial Officer Scacchetti admitted that he was unsure at the time that he procured the warrants in October whether Gloria Jean Boose was the person he actually wanted or whether it was some other person in the Pennsylvania Avenue house.

Plaintiff appeared at the police station in response to these warrants at about 10:30 a.m. on October 30, 1975. She was booked, photographed and fingerprinted and then held in a cell until release on her own recognizance at about 5:00 p.m. Officer Scacchetti was in the building at the time and he was notified of her arrest, but he did not investigate further to determine whether the right person had been taken into custody. Plaintiff was first served with the obstruction warrant and later that afternoon, she was served with the Jane Doe warrant for assault.

Plaintiff was arraigned the next morning and a preliminary examination was requested but never took place, apparently because of plaintiff's failure to appear. The Monroe County Grand Jury indicted her for assault second degree January 30, 1976 and she was arraigned in County Court on the indictment February 5, 1976. It subsequently appeared that there was no identification testimony before the Grand Jury, and the indictment was superseded by a no bill dated February 17. County Court dismissed the indictment on February 18, 1976 and this action followed.

It will be helpful at the outset to recite the difference between the torts of false arrest and imprisonment and malicious prosecution as they have been defined by the Court of Appeals in Broughton v. State of New York, 37 N.Y.2d 451, 373 N.Y.S.2d 87, 335 N.E.2d 310: "* * * The tort of malicious prosecution protects the personal interest of freedom from unjustifiable litigation * * *. The essence of malicious prosecution is the perversion of proper legal procedures. Thus, it has been held that some sort of prior judicial proceeding is the *sine qua non* of a cause of action in malicious prosecution * * *. Such a judicial proceeding may be either an evaluation by a Magistrate of an affidavit supporting an arrest warrant application, or an arraignment or an indictment by a Grand Jury. The elements of the tort of malicious prosecution are: (1) the commencement or continuation of a criminal proceeding by the defendant against the plaintiff, (2) the termination of the proceeding in favor of the accused, (3) the absence of probable cause for the criminal proceeding and (4) actual malice * * *."

Further than that, however, an action for false arrest and imprisonment was not made out on the facts. An arrest made pursuant to a warrant valid on its face and issued by a court having jurisdiction of the crime and person is privileged * * * and this is so even though the process may have been erroneously or improvidently issued * * *. The arresting officer having reasonably carried out the instruction on the warrant, the appropriate remedy to challenge an unlawful arrest is malicious prosecution * * *.

There are exceptions to this privilege. As we have noted, an arrest is not privileged if the issuing court lacks jurisdiction * * *.

Further, if there is more than one individual with the same name, the arresting officer must exercise reasonable care and due diligence in executing the warrant * * *. This is not a misnomer case, however, because plaintiff was the person intended to be apprehended under the warrant. The police error was in determining the true identity of the party to be named in the warrant, not in determining that plaintiff was the person named.

Finally, it has been held that an arresting officer may not insulate himself from liability for false arrest or imprisonment by procuring the issuance of a warrant based upon his own false or unsubstantiated evidence * * *. In executing his affidavit, Officer Scacchetti did not knowingly supply any false evidence to support issuance of the warrant. He erroneously assumed on the basis of his limited knowledge that the same defendant who was involved in the Kasper assault was involved in the Pabon matter. The gravity of that mistake could be tested by an action for malicious prosecution, but it did not give plaintiff a cause of action for false imprisonment. * * *

Turning now to malicious prosecution, we hold that the Trial Court erroneously dismissed that cause of action. Plaintiff's uncontroverted evidence established the initiation of a criminal proceeding against her by defendant which terminated in her favor. The evidence also established *prima facie* that the proceeding was commenced without probable cause and with actual malice.

Probable cause consists of such facts and circumstances as would lead a reasonably prudent man in like circumstances to believe plaintiff guilty * * *. A mistake of fact as to the identity of a criminal may be consistent with probable cause if the defendant acted reasonably under the circumstances and in good faith * * *, but failure to make inquiry of plaintiff or further inquiry about her when a reasonable man would have done so may be evidence of a lack of probable cause * * *. In short, a defendant may be said to act with probable cause to arrest only if a reasonable man in the same position would believe, and defendant did in fact believe, that he had sufficient information to justify initiating a criminal proceeding against plaintiff without further investigation or inquiry * * *.

Plaintiff's arrest for assault was based upon affidavits made without any verification of her identity. Kasper could not name his assailant and Officer Zigarowicz, who interviewed him before preparing a police report, listed two female defendants, one in her forties and another named Roxanne, 14 to 16 years old, residing at an address listed as 173 Pennsylvania Avenue. This information differed significantly from the information Scacchetti acquired after the Pabon incident. He testified that the girl involved in that assault and identified as Gloria Jean Boose appeared to him to be 18 or 19 years of age and she resided at 167 Pennsylvania Avenue (where seven other Boose children resided). Furthermore, Scacchetti testified that he harbored some doubt that the name of Gloria Jean Boose given to him on June 22 during the Pabon incident was correct and he had returned to Pennsylvania Avenue several times to inquire further. Because of this doubt Scacchetti applied for the "Jane Doe Booze" warrant, rather than naming Gloria Jean Boose, but he did so without checking further or resolving the discrepancies in Officer Zigarowicz's report because he assumed that the August assault must have involved the same person as the Pabon incident in June. Plaintiff's name "stuck" in his mind.

It was defendant's contention that further investigation might prove futile or dangerous. The jury was entitled to weigh this claim, but it could also consider that the investigation had been dormant for several months and that nothing in the evidence indicated a need for plaintiff's prompt arrest. * * * Whatever the jury's resolution of those competing contentions, the evidence established, prima facie, that the police procured a warrant for plaintiff's arrest without probable cause to believe her to be the guilty party and the issue should have been submitted to the jury to decide.

There is a further contention to be addressed. The general rule is that a Grand Jury indictment is *prima facie* evidence of probable cause. The plaintiff in a malicious prosecution action must meet this evidence with proof that defendant has not made a full and complete statement of the facts either to the Grand Jury or the District Attorney, has misrepresented or falsified the evidence or else kept back evidence which would affect the result * * *. The rule is based upon the reasoning that the Grand Jury acts judicially and it may be presumed that it has acted regularly on the matter. The burden is placed upon plaintiff, therefore, to rebut this presumption. One may well question whether there is any basis for application of the rule in this case when the Grand Jury superseded its original indictment three weeks later with a no-bill * * *, but be that as it may, there was evidence at the trial that the prosecution was transferred by the police to the District Attorney for Grand Jury action naming plaintiff as the defendant although the police knew that there was no evidence identifying her and in fact no witness testified before the Grand Jury to supply that evidence. This was sufficient to overcome any presumption in defendant's favor because of the Grand Jury indictment.

The remaining element necessary to prove the cause of action is malice. Malice means "malice in fact" or "actual malice", not malice implied by law * * *. The only justification for a criminal proceeding is to bring an offender to justice and malice exists if the jury can find from the evidence that defendant commenced the proceeding because of a wrong or improper motive, something other than a desire to see the ends of justice served * * *. Thus, plaintiff is not required to prove that defendant was motivated by spite or ill will, although such proof will satisfy the legal requirements * * *. The existence of malice may be presumed by proof that probable cause was lacking or by proof of defendant's reckless or grossly negligent conduct * * *. Indeed, it has been said that it is difficult to conceive how a prosecution initiated without probable cause could be initiated with any other than bad motives * * *. The issue is a matter for the jury, however, * * * and it may infer malice from the lack of probable cause insofar as it tends to show that defendant did not believe in the guilt of the accused and that he did not initiate the proceedings for a proper purpose * * *. It has been held that malice exists where a prosecution is commenced to discover who might have committed a crime * * *. Viewing the evidence in a way most favorable to plaintiff, as we must on this appeal, the jury in this case might well have inferred from it that defendant's officers had arrested this plaintiff without probable cause and with actual malice for just that purpose.

The judgment should be reversed and a new trial granted.

Notes

1. *See* Sheldon Appel Co. v. Albert & Oliker, 47 Cal.3d 863, at 871, 765 P.2d 498, at 501–02, 254 Cal.Rptr. 336, at 340(1989):

> The common law tort of malicious prosecution originated as a remedy for an individual who had been subjected to a maliciously instituted criminal charge, but in California, as in most common law jurisdictions, the tort was long ago extended to afford a remedy for malicious prosecution of a civil action.

* * *

Although the malicious prosecution tort has ancient roots, courts have long recognized that the tort has the potential to impose an undue "chilling effect" on the ordinary citizen's willingness to report criminal conduct or to bring a civil dispute to court, and, as a consequence, the tort has traditionally been regarded as a disfavored cause of action. * * * In a number of other states, the disfavored status of the tort is reflected in a requirement that a plaintiff demonstrate some "special injury" beyond that ordinarily incurred in defending a lawsuit in order to prevail in a malicious prosecution action. (*See* O'Toole v. Franklin (1977) 279 Or. 513, 569 P.2d 561, 564, fn. 3 [listing 17 states adhering to special-injury rule]; Friedman v. Dozorc (1981) 412 Mich. 1, 312 N.W.2d 585, 596 [applying special-injury rule].) Even in jurisdictions, like California, which do not impose a special-injury requirement, the elements of the tort have historically been carefully circumscribed so that litigants with potentially valid claims will not be deterred from bringing their claims to court by the prospect of a subsequent malicious prosecution claim.

2. Since a malicious prosecution action may not be brought without a showing that the original proceeding was instituted without probable cause and since want of probable cause will justify a finding of malice, how important an element is the requirement of actual malice? The *Restatement (Second) of Torts* uses the term "improper purpose" in place of the traditional term "malice". In § 669 the *Restatement (Second)* specifically declares that "lack of probable cause for the initiation of criminal proceedings, insofar as it tends to show that the accuser did not believe in the guilt of the accused, is evidence that he did not initiate the proceedings for a proper purpose". If there is probable cause will a showing of malice permit the bringing of a malicious prosecution action? Consider that *Restatement (Second) of Torts* § 669A specifically provides that an "improper purpose" is *not* evidence of lack of probable cause.

3. In *Boose* the action had to be brought against the city for the actions of its police officers because a prosecuting attorney cannot be the subject of a malicious prosecution action for any criminal proceedings instituted in the prosecuting officer's official capacity. *See Restatement (Second) of Torts* § 656. A similar absolute privilege attaches to judges who might hear, or rule on, any issues involved in the proceedings. An instructive case is Belcher v. Paine, 136 N.H. 137, 612 A.2d 1318 (1992). Plaintiffs were indicted for aggravated felonious sexual assault. After the indictments were nol prossed by the defendant, the County Attorney, the plaintiffs filed an action for malicious prosecution. The New Hampshire Supreme Court affirmed summary judgment for the defendant based upon his claim of absolute privilege from civil liability whenever the claimed activity is "functionally related to the initiation of criminal process or to the prosecution of criminal charges."

4. The defendant in a malicious prosecution action can relitigate the question of the plaintiff's guilt. Moreover, in the civil action the question of guilt will be resolved by the preponderance-of-the-evidence standard, not the beyond-a-reasonable-doubt standard. *See Restatement (Second) of Torts* § 657 and Comments; Wal–Mart Stores, Inc. v. Blackford, 264 Ga. 612, 449 S.E.2d 293 (1994).

5. A defendant who can establish that he relied in good faith upon the advice of an apparently disinterested attorney given upon a "full disclosure of the facts," will conclusively establish probable cause. *See Restatement (Second)*

of Torts § 666. An instructive case is Peoples Bank & Trust Co. v. Stock, 181 Ind.App. 483, 392 N.E.2d 505 (1979). That was a case for malicious "civil" prosecution, a cause of action that has arisen by analogy to the malicious prosecution of criminal proceedings. In *Stock* the bank had agreed to serve as executor of an estate at the request of an attorney representing the deceased's former wife. In that capacity it prevented, for a substantial period of time, the payment of the proceeds of the deceased's insurance policy to the named beneficiary, the woman with whom the deceased had been living at the time of his death. The court held that the attorney was not a disinterested party upon whom the bank could rely.

6. The question of probable cause and the question of whether the prior proceedings terminated in favor of the plaintiff are among the issues to be decided by the court. *See Restatement (Second) of Torts* § 673; Solitro v. Moffatt, 523 A.2d 858 (R.I.1987).

BANK OF LYONS v. SCHULTZ

Supreme Court of Illinois, 1980.
78 Ill.2d 235, 35 Ill.Dec. 758, 399 N.E.2d 1286.

WARD, JUSTICE:

The plaintiff, Mary Schultz, brought an action in October 1975 in the circuit court of Cook County against the Bank of Lyons for malicious prosecution for damages allegedly sustained as a result of two suits filed against her by the bank, both of which were decided in her favor. The trial court dismissed her complaint and the appellate court reversed. * * * We granted the bank's petition for leave to appeal.

The plaintiff's claim of malicious prosecution by the bank is founded upon the following events. In April of 1962 the bank filed a creditor's suit against the plaintiff and her late husband, Alvin Schultz, who died during the pendency of that suit. As the beneficiary of his life insurance policies the plaintiff was to receive $61,533.27. The bank filed a suit in equity in June 1963 petitioning for an accounting and for an injunction to restrain distribution of the insurance proceeds to the plaintiff. The trial court issued a preliminary injunction enjoining the insurance companies from making payments to the plaintiff and ordering that the funds be deposited with the clerk of the circuit court. The trial court, however, following the recommendation of a master in chancery to whom the matter was referred, dissolved the injunction on July 2, 1963, and dismissed the complaint in equity. The plaintiff was also granted leave to file a suggestion of her damages on account of the injunction's issuance as provided for in section 12 of the Injunction Act (Ill.Rev.Stat.1963, ch. 69, par. 12). She was subsequently awarded $2,369.67 on her suggestion of damages to cover interest she would have earned on the insurance proceeds held by the clerk of the court, attorneys' fees and costs.

Seventeen days after the injunction was dissolved, the bank was given leave to amend the complaint in its pending creditor's suit by adding a second count, and in it the bank again prayed for an accounting and for a preliminary injunction prohibiting distribution of the insurance proceeds. A preliminary injunction was entered on July 19, but almost two years later, on September 24, 1965, the court dismissed the second count, stating that the injunction had been wrongfully issued. The court also dissolved this injunction and ordered the clerk of the court to release to the plaintiff those insurance proceeds in excess of $30,000. The plaintiff was also given leave to file a suggestion of damages under section 12.

In November of 1965 the bank, with leave of court, filed another count to its creditor's suit. This third count alleged conversion and unlawful withholding of funds based on claims that the bank had been induced to issue cashier's checks to Alvin Schultz without consideration and that the bank had erroneously credited the plaintiff's account in the amount of $10,200. A master in chancery found, however, that the bank failed to prove a *prima facie* cause of action, and the circuit court, following the recommendation of the master, dismissed this third count. This was in September 1969.

The court also ordered the release of the balance of the insurance proceeds to the plaintiff. The bank appealed, and the appellate court remanded to the trial court to determine whether the plaintiff was a holder in due course. * * * On remand the trial court found the plaintiff was a holder in due course and again dismissed the third count.

On June 21, 1972, the trial court dismissed count I of the bank's creditor's suit because of a failure to allege fraud. No appeal was taken by the bank. On August 1, 1972, the plaintiff filed her second suggestion of damages pursuant to the September 1965 order and, on March 6, 1973, was awarded a total of $24,103.52, representing unearned interest on the proceeds of insurance, attorneys' fees and costs. Upon the bank's appeal, the appellate court affirmed. * * *

Plaintiff filed this suit for malicious prosecution in October 1975, claiming $49,848.13 in compensatory damages for the forfeiture of her interest in a house which she had owned jointly with her late husband, Alvin Schultz, which interest was foreclosed, she alleged, as a result of the injunction which prevented her from using the insurance proceeds to make mortgage payments. She also claimed $300,000 in punitive damages.

It appears that the plaintiff's complaint for malicious prosecution was dismissed by the trial court on the ground that the damages claimed should have been requested when she filed her second statutory suggestion of damages, and that recovery was barred under the doctrine of *res judicata,* and, further, because she failed to allege an arrest of her person, seizure of property, or some other special injury. The appellate court, in reversing, held that the wrongful issuance of the preliminary injunction constituted a seizure of property for purposes of establishing a cause of action for malicious prosecution and that the plaintiff's claim for compensatory and punitive damages was not barred by the doctrine of *res judicata.*

In this jurisdiction a plaintiff, in a suit for malicious prosecution founded on the defendant's wrongful bringing of a civil suit, must show that the suit he claims was wrongfully filed was terminated in his favor. He must also prove that it was brought maliciously and without probable cause and, further, he must establish evidence of his arrest, the seizure of his property, or some other special injury which exceeds the usual expense and annoyance and inconvenience of defending a lawsuit. * * *

Clearly as a result of the preliminary injunctions the plaintiff was prevented from using the insurance proceeds for a period of more than nine years. There have been holdings in jurisdictions, which have the same requirements for malicious prosecution as we do, to the effect that an injunction may constitute a sufficient interference with property for purposes of bringing a malicious prosecution suit. * * *

We are not persuaded by the bank's contention that there must be an actual seizure of property, as opposed to an interference with it, before a cause of action for malicious prosecution can arise. There obviously can be harm from interference with one's property. In principle the harm may be the same in both cases. Even in jurisdictions which appear to focus on whether there has been a seizure of property rather than an interference, there have been holdings that events resembling those here amounted to seizures. For example, in Multiple Realty, Inc. v. Walker (1969), 119 Ga.App. 393, 167 S.E.2d 380, the court determined there had been a seizure where the plaintiff's funds were held in the registry of the court and not released until a writ of attachment was dissolved. In Balsiger v. American Steel & Supply Co. (1969), 254 Or. 204, 458 P.2d 932, it was held that though there had been no actual seizure, causing a petition for bankruptcy to be filed constituted interference with the debtor's property so as to satisfy the requirement of a seizure. * * *

Here injunctions were issued during the pendency of the suit filed by the bank in 1962 restraining the distribution of over $60,000 to the plaintiff, $30,000 of which was not released until 1973, more than nine years after her husband's death. This constituted an interference with the plaintiff's property interests sufficient to satisfy the requirement of a seizure or special injury in bringing an action for malicious prosecution.

We do not consider there is merit to the bank's contention that the plaintiff could have claimed damages for the loss of her house under section 12 of the Injunction Act, and that, as she did not do so, her claim for malicious prosecution is barred under the doctrine of *res judicata*. It is clear that the damages recoverable under section 12 are limited to damages actually suffered during the life or pendency of the injunction. * * * The plaintiff in her complaint for malicious prosecution sets out that her statutory right to redeem following the foreclosure did not expire until the second injunction obtained by the bank had been dissolved and, assuming for this discussion that damages of this character could be recovered under section 12, she could not claim under that section, as she did not sustain this loss during the pendency of the injunction. Too, as we have observed, to have a cause of action for malicious prosecution, the suit which was wrongfully brought must have been determined in favor of the plaintiff. At the time the second injunction obtained by the bank had been dissolved, and when the plaintiff filed her second suggestion of damages, no cause of action for malicious prosecution could have arisen because the litigation brought against her by the bank had not yet been concluded in her favor.

For the reasons given, the judgment of the appellate court is affirmed and the cause is remanded to the circuit court for further proceedings not inconsistent with this opinion.

Notes

1. As will be seen in the next principal case, the requirement that no cause of action will lie for malicious institution of civil proceedings unless there is some interference with the plaintiff's person or property or some other form of special damage is sometimes called the "English" rule.

2. Ohio and Illinois have recently reaffirmed their use of the special damages rule, emphasizing the need to strike an appropriate balance between the interest in discouraging frivolous and vexatious law suits, on the one hand, but not chilling resort to the courts to settle disputes peacefully, on the other. *See* Robb v. Chagrin Lagoons Yacht Club, Inc., 75 Ohio St.3d 264, 662 N.E.2d 9 (1996)(involving repeated litigation growing out of disciplinary action and finally expulsion of some members of a private yacht club); Levin v. King, 271 Ill.App.3d 728, 208 Ill.Dec. 186, 648 N.E.2d 1108 (1995), *appeal dismissed*, 163 Ill.2d 560, 212 Ill.Dec. 422, 657 N.E.2d 623 (1995)(involving litigation growing out of a dispute over building a housing project).

O'TOOLE v. FRANKLIN

Supreme Court of Oregon, 1977.
279 Or. 513, 569 P.2d 561.

LINDE, JUSTICE.

I

In a number of recent decisions, this court has followed the "English rule," first adopted in this state in 1896, that an action for the malicious prosecution of civil proceedings requires a showing of "special injury" beyond the trouble, cost, and other consequences normally associated with defending oneself against unfounded legal charges. * * * The present appeal asks us to reconsider this rule.

The appeal is from an order sustaining a demurrer to plaintiffs' complaint for failure to state a cause of action. The complaint alleged, in summary, that appellants are practicing physicians and partners in the Medford Clinic; that in July 1974, the respondent attorneys commenced a medical malpractice action against them on behalf of the respondent Mathis, alleging that the physicians had administered certain drugs to Mr. Mathis in 1972; that upon learning of this action the physicians informed Mr. Mathis and his attorneys that they had not treated Mathis during the period in question and repeatedly asked that the action be dismissed, but that it was not dismissed until January 1975; and that the action was prosecuted maliciously and without probable cause despite respondents' knowledge that the physicians had not administered any drugs to Mathis. The first count of the complaint continued with an allegation that prosecution of the malpractice action injured appellants' professional reputation "to their special injury in the sum of $50,000," and that they were entitled to exemplary and punitive damages in the sum of $200,000. A second count added allegations of negligence on the part of Mathis in not informing his attorneys that appellants did not treat him during the period in question, and on the part of the attorneys in not properly investigating the case and advising Mathis that he had no just claim against them, but rather inciting him to commence the malpractice action. It also added a demand for $50,000 general damages for "emotional disturbance and anguish." Upon respondents' demurrer, the trial court held that these allegations did not state a cause of action against either Mathis or his attorneys, and appellants declined to plead further.

II

On appeal, the doctors argue first that the asserted damage to their professional reputations from the unfounded charge of malpractice should be recognized as the kind of extraordinary harm contemplated by the "special injury" required for the tort of wrongful (or "malicious") prosecution of a civil action.[4] It may be conceded that "special" is not the most self-explanatory of terms. This court has found the requirement satisfied when the chosen proceeding itself involved immediate interference with the person, property, income, or credit of the subsequent complainant, apart from the ultimate judgment, as in the use of garnishment * * *, attachment * * *, or involuntary bankruptcy * * *. That is consistent with decisions of other courts which follow the English rule. * * * This view focuses on the defendant's responsibility for his choice, as plaintiff in the earlier action, to trigger the interfering procedure; in the later action the "special injury is determined by the manner of the defendant's prosecution of the original case rather than by any happenstance of the plaintiff's situation." * * * But beyond immediate legal interference, the court has also recognized exceptionally sensitive proceedings as actionable if maliciously instituted, e.g., insanity proceedings * * *, and it has left open the possibility that "special injury" might be claimed when a defendant is on notice that the claimant whom he wrongfully subjected to legal proceedings was uniquely vulnerable to being harmed thereby, beyond the ordinary hardships of similar cases. * * *

The present plaintiffs have pleaded neither of these elements; their claim of "special injury" to professional reputation is one that would be common to most professional malpractice actions. They offer a two-step argument for nevertheless recognizing this injury as a basis of liability for malicious civil proceedings: One, that recovery for injury to reputation from bad-faith litigation is the necessary counterpart of the litigant's privilege against liability for defamation; and two, that a remedy for an injury to reputation in some form is required by the constitution. If such an injury is not recognized as "special," they argue, then the requirement of a "special injury" should be abandoned altogether.

The Restatement of Torts, as appellants point out, recognizes that a plaintiff's privilege to accuse a defendant finds its limits in the defamed party's potential recovery for "wrongful initiation of the proceedings," Restatement, Torts, § 587, Comment a. Recovery for injury to reputation in such an action is not inconsistent with Oregon cases, if the elements of the action are otherwise made out; the difference is that the Restatement does not adopt "special injury" as one of the elements. Restatement, Torts, §§ 674, 681(b) * * *. Appellants' main argument is that this court should also drop that element from the tort of malicious prosecution of civil

---

4. The Restatement of Torts describes the tort as "wrongful civil proceedings," includ-   ing their "initiation, continuation or procurement." Restatement of Torts § 674.

proceedings. The case is fairly and candidly presented as a suggestion for a judicial change in the established rule on policy grounds.

The "English rule" requiring some direct interference or other extraordinary injury is followed, at last count, by seventeen American jurisdictions, including Oregon. Twenty-three states impose no such condition on the tort; the remainder have not decided the issue. The rule has been criticized by Dean Prosser and, as we have said, rejected by the Restatement of Torts. The argument is that the mere award of costs to the successful defendant, without the attorney fees included in England, is not full compensation for an unfounded lawsuit, which is true; and that while honest litigants should be encouraged to seek justice, "surely there is no policy in favor of vexatious suits known to be groundless, which are a real and often a serious injury". Prosser, The Law of Torts 851, § 120 (4th ed., 1971). Adequate protection for bona fide litigants, according to this view, exists in "the heavy burden of proof upon the plaintiff, to establish both lack of probable cause and an improper purpose," *ibid.*

While the first proposition may be conceded, the second has seemed doubtful to other eminent authority. The question is not whether a plaintiff should sue only in good faith, but under what circumstances he must be prepared to defend his good faith in a countersuit. As Judge Edgerton put it in reaffirming the English rule for the District of Columbia, "[s]ome sort of balance has to be struck between the social interests in preventing unconscionable suits and in permitting honest assertion of supposed rights. These interests conflict because a suit which its author thinks honest may look unconscionable to a jury." Soffos v. Eaton, 80 U.S.App.D.C. 306, 152 F.2d 682, 683 (1945). The "special interest" rule is not squarely addressed to misgivings whether that balance is adequately protected by the burden of proof and by the inferences allowed a jury in malicious prosecution cases, and we might not in the first instance adopt the rule for that reason. But this case is not the first instance, and the rule as we have stated it does make some contribution insofar as it holds a plaintiff to notice of circumstances or procedures that subject a defendant to immediate interference or extraordinary risk of harm.

Nor do we accept the argument that the litigant's privilege against a libel action constitutionally compels a malicious prosecution action specifically for injury to reputation. * * *

This court is not unprepared to reconsider an old common law rule that may have been overtaken by important changes in the conditions that originally gave it birth, or in related areas of law, or by complications and inconsistencies that call for clarification. The law of malicious prosecution is not immune * * *. But readiness to take account of extrinsic changes or intrinsic flaws in common law premises is not equivalent to legislating from year to year. Such a view is sometimes urged, not only because courts were responsible for the original rule, but also on the ground that they are institutionally better equipped for the rational and systematic development of private law; for legislatures are said to give attention to this development only sporadically at the initiative of special interests, and individuals who may someday be claimants in civil litigation seldom recognize a shared interest in the law in advance of such litigation. See Peck, *The Role of the*

Courts and Legislatures in the Reform of Tort Law, 48 Minn.L.Rev. 265 (1963) and sources there cited.[5] But the legislative process is not inappropriate, given adequate time and preparation, for studying and resolving the competing and the common interests at stake in private law, and this state's legislative assembly has in fact addressed itself in recent years to major issues of civil liability. These include two recent examinations of medical malpractice actions, the same problem that we are invited to address by changing the common law action of malicious prosecution. * * * That this common law action would offer no remedy against baseless malpractice actions in the absence of "special injury" has been well known; the court reaffirmed the requirement as recently as 1969, 1971, 1975, and 1976 in the cases referred to above. No newly demonstrated flaw or major change in related law or in external conditions justifies our departure from these recent holdings now. The demurrer to the first count of appellants' complaint was correctly sustained.

III

The second count of appellants' complaint presents a different problem. This count alleged that defendant attorneys were "negligent" in not ascertaining the facts of their erroneous malpractice action and in "maintaining and counseling said action of defendant Mathis against plaintiffs when they knew such action was not legal and just."

The negligence alleged here was toward plaintiffs themselves, not derivative from negligence toward the attorneys' client; and the possibility of an injured third party's action against a negligent attorney was left open in Metzker v. Slocum, 272 Or. 313, 317, 537 P.2d 74 (1975), when the court found the complaint in that case insufficient to support such an action. * * * But when it takes a "special injury" to recover for the *malicious* pursuit of an unfounded civil action, it would be incongruous to base a recovery on mere carelessness without the same requirement. That is equally true of this count against the client, Mathis.

Appellants rely on the statutory duties imposed on attorneys by ORS 9.460 in order to protect members of the public in appellants' position. This statute enjoins attorneys to

> (3) Counsel or maintain such actions, suits, or proceedings or defenses only as may appear to him legal and just, except the defense of a person charged with a public offense;

and

---

5. Professor Peck argued that courts are more familiar with the actual functions of legal rules in litigation, that they are less likely to adopt a proposed rule favoring one interest without consideration of its impact on related concerns, and that they have as much opportunity as legislatures to take account of known empirical materials. On the other hand, certain legislative techniques are not available to a court, for instance specifying minimum or maximum amounts of recovery. Nor does an appeal briefed by two parties on specific facts, despite occasional briefs *amicus curiae,* equal the public participation in legislative hearings and direct communications.

The fact that proposed reforms in private law can be better *prepared* by long-term commissions, academic groups, and possibly judges (*see* Cardozo, *A Ministry of Justice,* 35 Harv.L.Rev. 113 (1921)) than in *ad hoc* legislative bills does not mean that the ultimate choice whether or not to *enact* the proposed readjustment of interests is not properly a legislative decision.

(7) Not encourage the commencement or continuance of an action, suit or proceeding from any motives of passion or interest; * * *.

It is true that the duties expressed in these provisions of the Oregon State Bar act run to members of the public beyond an attorney's clients. In the present case, the complaint did not in fact allege that defendants were motivated by the "passion or interest" proscribed by subsection (7), but the allegation quoted above does appear to invoke subsection (3). Taken by itself, it asserts a violation of that subsection by pursuit of an action *known* to be wrongful and unjust. If it stood alone, it would appear to go beyond negligence to allege a deliberate breach of a duty imposed by statute to protect members of the public against the precise kind of injury of which plaintiffs complain.

Violations of duties of this kind often do give rise to private rights of action independent of the common law. * * * And of course, the professional duties imposed by ORS 9.460 bind attorneys independently of any "special injury" to anyone. However, in the present case the allegation of the attorneys' knowledge was pleaded expressly as a specification of negligence, not as an intentional and deliberate breach of a statutory duty to plaintiffs. As stated above, we reject a theory of liability for negligence toward persons wrongfully sued that would reach injuries not protected against malicious prosecution of civil proceedings. Accordingly, the demurrer was properly sustained.

Affirmed.

Notes

1. As the court notes in the *O'Toole* case, the "English rule" is a minority position, followed by about one-third of the states. 1 Harper, James & Gray, The Law of Torts, § 4.8, at 4.69 (3d Ed. 1995). *See also*, L. Anderson, *"Special Injury" in the Torts of Malicious Prosecution and Injurious Falsehood: Will They Get You Into or Keep You Out of Court?*, 26 For the Defense 22 (May 1984) in which it is stated that sixteen jurisdictions still require some form of special injury, thirty jurisdictions follow the "American" rule, and five jurisdictions have yet to rule on the issue. Even some of the minority states will permit an action to be brought for wrongful instigation of civil proceedings when the defendant is accused of having brought repetitious civil actions against the plaintiff for the purposes of harassment, as for example a landlord bringing multiple unsuccessful eviction actions to rid himself of a tenant whom he does not like. *See, e.g.,* Weisman v. Middleton, 390 A.2d 996 (D.C.App.1978)(tenant had tried to organize other tenants to complain about landlord's maintenance of the building), relying on Soffos v. Eaton, 152 F.2d 682 (D.C.Cir.1945); *cf.* Timeplan Loan & Investment Corp. v. Colbert, 108 Ga.App. 753, 134 S.E.2d 476 (1963).

2. While, as we have seen in the *O'Toole* case, a lawyer can be subject to an action for the wrongful institution of civil proceedings, it has been recognized that the line between zealous advocacy and wrongful institution of civil proceedings or misuse of legal process is a difficult one. *Restatement (Second) of Torts* § 674, Comment *d* tries to resolve the problem in the following statement which is not without its own difficulties:

     d. Attorneys. An attorney who initiates a civil proceeding on behalf of his client or one who takes any steps in the proceeding is not liable if he has probable cause for his action (*see* § 675); and even if he has no probable cause and is convinced that his client's claim is unfounded, he is still not liable if he acts primarily for the purpose of aiding his client in obtaining a proper adjudication of his claim. (See § 676).[6] An attorney is not required or expected to prejudge his client's claim, and although he is fully aware that its chances of success are comparatively slight, it is his responsibility to present it to the court for adjudication if his client so insists after he has explained to the client the nature of the chances.

If, however, the attorney acts without probable cause for belief in the possibility that the claim will succeed, and for an improper purpose, as, for example, to put pressure upon the person proceeded against in order to compel payment of another claim of his own or solely to harass the person proceeded against by bringing a claim known to be invalid, he is subject to the same liability as any other person. There is one situation that sometimes arises in civil proceedings but does not occur in criminal proceedings. An attorney who initiates civil proceedings on a contingent-fee basis with his client is not for that reason to be charged with an improper motive or purpose, since the contingent fee is a legitimate arrangement and the interest of the attorney in receiving it is merely the ordinary interest of a professional man in being paid for his services. But by obtaining the authority of the client to bring the action he procures its initiation; and if he does so without probable cause and for an improper purpose other than the fee, he is subject to liability under the rule stated in this Section. An attorney may also be subject to liability if he takes an active part in continuing a civil proceeding properly begun, for an improper purpose and without probable cause.

In Junot v. Lee, 372 So.2d 707 (La.App.1979), the court affirmed dismissal of an action against an attorney for instituting multiple proceedings in a custody dispute on the ground that given the increased overruling of older cases in recent years it was reluctant, except in "a clear case," to permit an action to be brought against an attorney who "urges a position which has little or no chance of success under current jurisprudence." One of the few cases in which a physician has been able to win an action for wrongful institution of civil proceedings or, as it was called in that case, "malicious prosecution," against an attorney is Raine v. Drasin, 621 S.W.2d 895 (Ky.1981). *See also*, Nelson v. Miller, 227 Kan. 271, 607 P.2d 438 (1980), limited in Goss v. Reid, 242 Kan. 782, 751 P.2d 131 (1988)(no malicious prosecution action against attorney who erroneously and without prior attempt to contact her had named the plaintiff a defendant in a suit to quiet title where no money judgment was sought against her); Peerman v. Sidicane, 605 S.W.2d 242 (Tenn.App.1980). These cases are discussed in H. Hirsch, *Physician Countersuit—To Sue or Better Not to Sue*, 34 Medical Trial Techniques Quarterly 59 (Winter 1987). Earlier discussions include H. Greenbaum, *Physician Countersuits: A Cause Without Action*, 12 Pac.L.J. 745 (1981); S. Reuter, *Physician Countersuits: A Catch–22*, 14 U.S.F.L.Rev. 203 (1980).

3. An interesting new development is the common law creation of the tort of "malicious defense". The New Hampshire Supreme Court recognized this

---

6. [Ed. note] *Restatement (Second) of Torts* § 676 provides as follows:

To subject a person to liability for wrongful civil proceedings, the proceeding must have been initiated or continued primarily for a purpose other than that of securing the proper adjudication of the claim on which they are based.

new cause of action building upon the suggestions made in Van Patten & Willard, *The Limits of Advocacy: A Proposal for the Tort of Malicious Defense in Civil Litigation*, 35 Hastings L.J. 891 (1994). This variation on the malicious prosecution action is composed of essentially the same elements. The plaintiff must prove the following: (1) acting without probable cause, the defendant forwarded a defense "without any credible basis in fact and such action is not warranted by existing law or established equitable principles or a good faith argument for the extension, modification or reversal of existing law", (2) the defendant had knowledge of the lack of merit for the defense, (3) the defendant acted primarily for a purpose other than the adjudication of the defense (*i.e.*, to vexate, injure, harass, or delay the opponent), (4) the proceedings are terminated in favor of the party claiming malicious defense, and (5) injury or damage to the claimant. Aranson v. Schroeder, 140 N.H. 359, 671 A.2d 1023 (1995).

4. Some states now deal with these abuse of process causes of action in statutes. An example is the statute passed by Georgia in 1989 (Ga. Code Ann.):

§ 51–7–80 Definitions.

As used in this article, the term:

(1) "Civil proceeding" includes any action, suit, proceeding, counterclaim, cross-claim, third-party claim, or other claim at law or in equity.

(2) "Claim" includes any allegation or contention of fact or law asserted in support of or in opposition to any civil proceeding, defense, motion, or appeal.

(3) "Defense" includes any denial of allegations made by another party in any pleading, motion, or other paper submitted to the court for the purpose of seeking affirmative or negative relief, and any affirmative defense or matter asserted in confession or avoidance.

(4) "Good faith," when used with reference to any civil proceeding, claim, defense, motion, appeal, or other position, means that to the best of a person's or his or her attorney's knowledge, information, and belief, formed honestly after reasonable inquiry, that such civil proceeding, claim, defense, motion, appeal, or other position is well grounded in fact and is either warranted by existing law or by reasonable grounds to believe that an argument for the extension, modification, or reversal of existing law may be successful.

(5) "Malice" means acting with ill will or for a wrongful purpose and may be inferred in an action if the party initiated, continued, or procured civil proceedings or process in a harassing manner or used process for a purpose other than that of securing the proper adjudication of the claim upon which the proceedings are based.

(6) "Person" means an individual, corporation, company, association, firm, partnership, society, joint-stock company, or any other entity, including any governmental entity or unincorporated association of persons with capacity to sue or be sued.

(7) "Without substantial justification," when used with reference to any civil proceeding, claim, defense, motion, appeal, or other position, means that such civil proceeding, claim, defense, motion, appeal, or other position is:

(A) Frivolous;

(B) Groundless in fact or in law; or

(C) Vexatious.

(8) "Wrongful purpose" when used with reference to any civil proceeding, claim, defense, motion, appeal, or other position results in or has the effect of:

(A) Attempting to unjustifiably harass or intimidate another party or witness to the proceeding; or

(B) Attempting to unjustifiably accomplish some ulterior or collateral purpose other than resolving the subject controversy on its merits.

§ 51–7–81   Liability for abusive litigation.

Any person who takes an active part in the initiation, continuation, or procurement of civil proceedings against another shall be liable for abusive litigation if such person acts:

(1) With malice; and

(2) Without substantial justification.

§ 51–7–82 Defenses.

(a) It shall be a complete defense to any claim for abusive litigation that the person against whom a claim of abusive litigation is asserted has voluntarily withdrawn, abandoned, discontinued, or dismissed the civil proceeding, claim, defense, motion, appeal, civil process, or other position which the injured person claims constitutes abusive litigation within 30 days after the mailing of the notice required by subsection (a) of Code Section 51–7–84 or prior to a ruling by the court relative to the civil proceeding, claim, defense, motion, appeal, civil process, or other position, whichever shall first occur; provided, however, that this defense shall not apply where the alleged act of abusive litigation involves the seizure or interference with the use of the injured person's property by process of attachment, execution, garnishment, writ of possession, lis pendens, injunction, restraining order, or similar process which results in special damage to the injured person.

(b) It shall be a complete defense to any claim for abusive litigation that the person against whom a claim of abusive litigation is asserted acted in good faith; provided, however, that good faith shall be an affirmative defense and the burden of proof shall be on the person asserting the actions were taken in good faith.

(c) It shall be a complete defense to any claim for abusive litigation that the person against whom a claim of abusive litigation is asserted was substantially successful on the issue forming the basis for the claim of abusive litigation in the underlying civil proceeding.

Sections 51–7–84 and 51–7–85 deal with procedural aspects, damages recoverable, and makes the remedy exclusive.

5. Thus far, as in *O'Toole,* no one has been able to win an action against an attorney for negligently instituting civil proceedings. This has been so even in states which have abandoned the special injury requirement for actions for wrongful institution of civil proceedings. In Bird v. Rothman, 128 Ariz. 599, 627 P.2d 1097, *cert. denied,* 454 U.S. 865, 102 S.Ct. 327, 70 L.Ed.2d 166 (1981),

the action was brought by an architect who had brought his action against two attorneys who instigated a malpractice action against him. After upholding dismissal of a malicious prosecution count because of the presence of probable cause, the court turned to the negligence count and declared:

> * * * Our courts must be held open to litigating parties without fear or subsequent prosecution for calling upon the court to decide a contested issue. The lawyer's role in this process is unlike that of other professionals. His relationship with the opposing party is by its very nature adverse, not mutually beneficial. The party who is forced to defend a groundless lawsuit may institute disciplinary proceedings against the offending lawyer, as well as bringing a malicious prosecution action.

> Since we hold that there can be no liability in negligence for an attorney who allegedly brings a groundless suit against another party, the summary judgment on this count was properly granted.

> In summary, despite appellant's arguments that negligence suits, such as the underlying suit in this action, against architects and engineers have a significant impact on malpractice liability insurance rates and serve to impugn the reputation of conscientious professionals, we are persuaded that in the absence of proof of malicious prosecution on the part of the injured party or his attorney, the interest of freedom of access to our courts compels the conclusions we have reached. * * *

In another case brought by a physician, Nelson v. Miller, 227 Kan. 271, 607 P.2d 438 (1980), the court, relying upon *Restatement (Second) of Torts* § 674, Comment *d,* quoted above, reversed the dismissal by the trial court of "the claim * * * based upon a theory of malicious prosecution of a civil action." The court, however, upheld dismissal of a claim based upon "professional negligence." The essence of the court's opinion is contained in the following extract:

> * * * The traditional rule has been that an attorney will be held liable for negligence only to his client. The rationale of that rule is that there can be no action against an attorney for professional negligence in the absence of some privity of contract between the plaintiff and the attorney. More recently, the strict requirement of privity of contract has been eased in situations where an attorney has rendered services which he should recognize as involving a foreseeable injury to some third-party beneficiary of the contract. These cases usually involve the negligence of attorneys in will drafting and in the examination of real estate titles. We have been cited no cases, and we have found none, where an attorney has been held liable to his client's adversary in prior civil litigation on the basis of professional negligence alone.

> In representing their clients, lawyers are expected to use the legitimate sidearms of a warrior. It is only when a lawyer uses the dagger of an assassin that he should be subjected to discipline or to personal liability. We believe that the public is adequately protected from harassment and abuse by an unprofessional member of the bar through the means of the traditional cause of action for malicious prosecution. We, therefore, hold in accordance with established law, that an attorney cannot be held liable for the consequence of his professional negligence to his client's adversary. We further hold that a violation of the Code of Professional Responsibility does not alone create a cause of action against an attorney in favor of a third party. The remedy provided a third-party adversary is solely through

an action for malicious prosecution of a civil action. It follows that the district court was correct in dismissing the plaintiff's second cause of action based upon a theory of professional negligence.

In Comment, *Attorney Professional Responsibility: Competence Through Malpractice Liability,* 77 N.W.U.L.Rev. 633 (1982), the argument is made that an attorney should be held liable for failure to meet the level of conduct (including fairness to adversaries, etc.) contained in the American Bar Association's Model Code of Professional Responsibility. On some of the more technical problems involved in bringing an action for the malicious instigation of civil proceedings, *see* C. Aragon, *Favorable Termination in Malicious Prosecution of Civil Proceedings,* 15 S.W.U.L.Rev. 65 (1984) which discusses the not uncommon situation where the prior case was discontinued without a ruling on the "merits."

Chapter 21

CONSTITUTIONAL TORTS

It was one of the glories of the common law that everyone, except the king himself, was answerable in the courts of law to those whom he had legally wronged.[a] The king's ministers could be, and often were, hauled before the courts by those whom they had allegedly wronged. As we shall see, over the course of years, certain privileges arose which immunized some public servants from some types of litigation arising out of their attempts to perform their official duties. For example, since the English Bill of Rights, (1 W. & M. Sess. 2, c. 2 (1689)), "the freedom of speech and debates or proceedings in Parliament ought not to be impeached or questioned in any court or place out of Parliament." Compare Article 1, § 6, cl. 1 of the United States Constitution which provides that members of Congress "shall in all cases, except Treason, Felony, or Breach of the Peace, be privileged from Arrest during their Attendance at the Session of their respective Houses, and in going to or returning from the same; and for any Speech or Debate in either House, they shall not be questioned in any other Place." Judges also came to be immune from suit for anything they may have done in the course of performing their judicial function.

The common-law notion that even government ministers are answerable in the courts of law for their torts, like the freedom of debate in Parliament, was carried over to this country. Over the course of time, however, there came to be a common perception that the threat of a tort action was less likely to deter an official who abused his authority in the United States than was the case in Great Britain. Policemen and federal law enforcement officials are the public servants most likely to be involved in this type of litigation and it came to be considered that the poor and underprivileged, who were most likely to suffer from police abuse, would be unable to find sympathy among state court jurors. There thus came to be increasing pressure to find some method for bringing these actions into federal courts. In Bell v. Hood, 327 U.S. 678, 66 S.Ct. 773, 90 L.Ed. 939

a. Although it was often said that the king can do no wrong, the reason the king was not personally answerable in the courts of law was a conceptual one, namely how could a person be a judge in a legal action involving himself? This formalistic problem arose because the judges were the servants of the king and pronounced judgment in his name. Since at least Magna Carta (1215), a subject who was aggrieved by the Crown could file a "petition of right" seeking redress for injuries. The granting of the petition was totally a matter of discretion. The most famous of these petitions was the "Petition of Right" of 1628 in which Parliament presented Charles I with a list of grievances.

(1946) the question was presented whether conduct on the part of FBI agents which might provide the basis for a "common law action in trespass under state law" might also be actionable in the federal courts as an action arising "under the Constitution or laws of the United States" under the Congress' grant of federal question jurisdiction to the United States District Courts. The Court, in *Bell* held that this question was itself a federal question and remanded the case to the lower federal courts. It did not, however, itself express any opinion on this matter.

Beginning in 1961, however, first in cases involving state officers or those who acted under color of state law and then later, from 1971, in cases involving federal officials, a new category of tort litigation, "constitutional torts", was born and has since rapidly expanded. By 1976 it was estimated that "one out of three 'private' federal question suits filed in the federal courts was a civil rights action against the state or a local official." C. Whitman, *Constitutional Torts,* 79 Mich.L.Rev. 5, 6 (1980). Not all of these suits were tort actions, of course. Perhaps one half involved petitions by state prisoners seeking some change in the conditions of their incarceration. Unfortunately, the statistics kept by the Administrative Office of the United States Courts do not break down the data on the caseload of the federal courts in such a way as to permit the reader to arrive at an accurate determination of how many cases were constitutional tort actions brought against state officials or those who acted under color of state law or constitutional tort actions brought against federal officials. In 1988 almost 240,000 civil cases were commenced in the United States District Courts. Of these, almost 102,000 or 38% involved federal questions and of the federal question cases, over 9,000 involved "other civil rights" and over 23,500 involved prisoner petitions concerned with "civil rights". Presumably litigation in which damages or other remedies are sought for conduct that amounts to a constitutional tort would be subsumed within these categories. Annual Report of the Director of the Administrative Office of the Federal Courts (1988), at 180–82 (Table C2). In 1995, over 248,000 civil cases were filed in the federal courts, of which over 153,000 involved federal questions. Of the federal question cases, over 40,000 involved prisoners' petitions concerned with "other civil rights" and over 15,000 involved "other civil rights" brought by non-prisoners. Judicial Business of the United States Courts (1995), at 138–39 (Table C2).

It is impossible in a first year course on torts to exhaustively treat the important subject of constitutional torts. Many law schools cover the subject in narrowly-focused upper-class courses or seminars. The most that we can do is sketch out the history and development of the notion of constitutional torts in the United States and to highlight some of the important questions that have arisen, particularly those which have close analogues in the common-law torts which form the background out of which the constitutional torts have evolved.

A. ACTIONS AGAINST STATE OFFICIALS AND OTHERS ACTING UNDER "COLOR OF STATE LAW"

1. *Historical Development*

Rev.Stat. § 1979, more commonly referred to as 42 U.S.C. § 1983, first enacted in 1871 as part of the "Ku Klux" Act, provides that:

every person who, under color of statute, ordinance, regulation, custom, or usage, of any State or Territory * * * or the District of Columbia subjects, or causes to be subjected, any citizen of the United States or other person within the jurisdiction thereof to the deprivation of any rights, privileges, or immunities secured by the Constitution and laws, shall be liable to the party injured in an action at law, suit in equity, or other proper proceeding for redress.

In *Monroe v. Pape,* 365 U.S. 167, 81 S.Ct. 473, 5 L.Ed.2d 492 (1961), the Court held that the actions of officials—in that case thirteen Chicago police officers who allegedly broke into petitioners' home in the early morning, routed them from bed, made them stand naked in the living room, and ransacked every room emptying drawers and ripping mattress covers—were activities conducted "under color of" state law, despite the fact that what these officers did was clearly in violation of the constitution and laws of Illinois and that legal redress was theoretically available in the Illinois courts for this outrageous conduct.[a] At the same time, the Court held that 42 U.S.C. § 1983 did not impose liability on a municipal corporation (in the case before them, the city of Chicago). Justice Frankfurter dissented from the holding that conduct which is forbidden by state law might nonetheless be "under color of" state law. For the position that Justice Frankfurter's view of the meaning of "under color" of the state law is without historical support *see* S. Winter, *The Meaning of "Under Color" of Law,* 91 Mich. L.Rev. 323 (1992).

Once the Court had held that state officials who acted unlawfully were nonetheless acting "under color" of state law, the modern constitutional tort was born. In Monell v. New York City Dept. of Social Services, 436 U.S. 658, 98 S.Ct. 2018, 56 L.Ed.2d 611 (1978), the Court overruled that portion of *Monroe v. Pape* which held that municipalities were not subject to liability under § 1983. Municipalities could be liable under § 1983 when the acts complained of were acts done in execution of official policy or were the acts of senior officials who might be said to make the policy of the municipality. In Pembaur v. City of Cincinnati, 475 U.S. 469, 106 S.Ct. 1292, 89 L.Ed.2d 452 (1986) the Court held that a single decision of a high-ranking official with final authority over the issue involved—in that case the County Prosecutor—could be considered the making of a "policy" for which a governmental entity may be liable in an action under § 1983. The mere fact that a government employee has been delegated final decision-making authority over an issue does not by itself, however, establish that such a person can make governmental policy. *See* City of St. Louis v. Praprotnik, 485 U.S. 112, 108 S.Ct. 915, 99 L.Ed.2d 107 (1988) where the Court held that the director of the city's "Community Development Agency" was not a municipal policymaker despite his authority to initiate transfers and layoffs and despite the fact that the director was given substantial discretion in making these decisions. It would have been a different case if, through a series of decisions, "a 'custom or usage' had been established" of which the persons delegating the authority "must have been aware". The Court has continued to hold, however, that Congress, in § 1983, did not provide the specific authorization required by

---

a. *See also* Patsy v. Board of Regents of Fla., 457 U.S. 496, 102 S.Ct. 2557, 73 L.Ed.2d 172 (1982)(no requirement to exhaust state administrative procedures).

the Court's reading of the eleventh amendment in order to permit a suit in the federal courts against the state. *See* Quern v. Jordan, 440 U.S. 332, 99 S.Ct. 1139, 59 L.Ed.2d 358 (1979).[b] It should finally be noted that, in fleshing out the scope of the tort created by § 1983, the Court has held in Maine v. Thiboutot, 448 U.S. 1, 100 S.Ct. 2502, 65 L.Ed.2d 555 (1980), that the language in § 1983 covering "deprivation of any rights, privileges and immunities secured by the Constitution and laws" covered all federal law and not just those federal statutes concerned with "equal rights." The Court has since ruled that actions for violations of the Commerce Clause may also be brought under § 1983. Dennis v. Higgins, 498 U.S. 439, 111 S.Ct. 865, 112 L.Ed.2d 969 (1991). The two dissenters argued that the Commerce Clause is only concerned with delimiting the regulatory power of the state and federal governments and not the creation of "rights."

2. *Attorneys Fees and Non-Compensatory Damages*

Under an amendment to 42 U.S.C. § 1988, enacted in 1976, *attorneys' fees* can now be granted to prevailing parties in actions under § 1983 and related statutes. While prevailing plaintiffs are almost routinely granted counsel fees, the Court has construed the statutory authorization to permit prevailing defendants to recover counsel fees only when the plaintiff's action was "frivolous, unreasonable or without foundation." Christianburg Garment Co. v. EEOC, 434 U.S. 412, 98 S.Ct. 694, 54 L.Ed.2d 648 (1978). In City of Riverside v. Rivera, 477 U.S. 561, 106 S.Ct. 2686, 91 L.Ed.2d 466 (1986) the Court held that the fee awarded to a prevailing plaintiff is not required to be proportional to the actual monetary award that was recovered.

The Court has held that *punitive damages* are available in § 1983 actions against individuals upon a showing that "the defendant's conduct * * * [was] motivated by evil motives or intent, or when it involves reckless or callous indifference to the federally protected rights of others." Smith v. Wade, 461 U.S. 30, 103 S.Ct. 1625, 75 L.Ed.2d 632 (1983). Punitive damages are not available, however, in § 1983 actions against municipalities. City of Newport v. Fact Concerts, Inc., 453 U.S. 247, 101 S.Ct. 2748, 69 L.Ed.2d 616 (1981). In Carey v. Piphus, 435 U.S. 247, 98 S.Ct. 1042, 55 L.Ed.2d 252 (1978), the Court held, in an action brought by school children who claimed they had been suspended without being given the proper procedural safeguards, that there could be no *presumed damages* in § 1983 actions, at least where the claim was based upon a denial of procedural due process. Subsequently, in Memphis Community School District v. Stachura, 477 U.S. 299, 106 S.Ct. 2537, 91 L.Ed.2d 249 (1986), the Court amplified this holding by ruling that there could be no recovery of damages for the abstract deprivation of rights although it left open the possibility that presumed damages might possibly be appropriate in circumstances where compensatory damages are difficult to measure.

b. In Will v. Michigan Dept. of State Police, 491 U.S. 58, 109 S.Ct. 2304, 105 L.Ed.2d 45 (1989) the Court held (5–4) that a state was not a "person" under § 1983 so that a § 1983 action against a state could not even be brought in a state court in a state which had completely waived its sovereign immunity.

3. *The Role of State Courts and State Law*

It was soon held by a number of state courts, *see e.g.*, Clark v. Bond Stores, Inc., 41 A.D.2d 620, 340 N.Y.S.2d 847 (1973); Ingram v. Moody, 382 So.2d 522 (Ala.1980), that § 1983 actions were also cognizable in the state courts. This state court practice was recognized and accepted by the Court in a number of cases. *See e.g.*, Martinez v. California, 444 U.S. 277, 100 S.Ct. 553, 62 L.Ed.2d 481 (1980)(n. 7 of Court's opinion); Maine v. Thiboutot, 448 U.S. 1, 100 S.Ct. 2502, 65 L.Ed.2d 555 (1980)(n. 1 of Court's opinion). The Court has ruled, however, that, if a § 1983 action is brought in the state courts, the states may not apply provisions of state law which would impose restrictions upon the plaintiff that would not be applicable if the action had been brought in the federal courts. *See* Felder v. Casey, 487 U.S. 131, 108 S.Ct. 2302, 101 L.Ed.2d 123 (1988). In the *Felder* case the restriction was a state statute which provided that no action could be brought against any state governmental subdivision, agency, or officer unless the claimant had provided a written notice of claim within 120 days of the alleged injury or could demonstrate that the defendant had actual notice of the claim and had not been prejudiced by lack of written notice. Subsequently, in Howlett v. Rose, 496 U.S. 356, 110 S.Ct. 2430, 110 L.Ed.2d 332 (1990), the Court held that a school district for which sovereign immunity had been waived for state law claims is subject to suit in state court under § 1983. State courts may not entertain state law actions but refuse to entertain similar federal claims.

The relationship between state law and federal law in § 1983 actions is complicated by the fact that in 42 U.S.C. § 1988, Congress has specifically declared, that, where federal law is not "suitable" to achieve the purposes of the various civil rights statutes or "are deficient in the provisions necessary to furnish suitable remedies * * *, the common law, as modified and changed by the constitution and statutes of the State wherein the court having jurisdiction of such * * * causes is held, so far as the same is not inconsistent with the Constitution and laws of the United States, shall be extended to and govern the said courts in the trial and disposition of the cause * * *." This portion of § 1988 dates from 1866. Relying on § 1988, in Wilson v. Garcia, 471 U.S. 261, 105 S.Ct. 1938, 85 L.Ed.2d 254 (1985), the Court held that the characterization of § 1983 actions for purposes of applying a statute of limitations would be governed by federal law, but state law would provide the appropriate limitation period. The Court went on to hold that § 1988 required the selection in each state of a single statute of limitations for all § 1983 claims rather than the use of different statutes of limitations depending upon the nature of the particular § 1983 claim involved. It then finally held, in *Garcia*, that all § 1983 claims should be characterized as "personal injury actions" for purposes of applying statutes of limitations. Subsequently, in Owens v. Okure, 488 U.S. 235, 109 S.Ct. 573, 102 L.Ed.2d 594 (1989), the Court held that, in a state with more than one statute of limitations for personal injury actions, § 1983 actions are to be governed by the residual or general personal injury statute of limitations rather than the statute of limitations for enumerated, intentional torts. Finally, in Hardin v. Straub, 490 U.S. 536, 109 S.Ct. 1998, 104 L.Ed.2d 582 (1989), the Court held that a Michigan provision tolling the three-year limitation period for personal injury actions during the period a person is under a legal disability—in the instant case, the petitioner was incarcerated in prison—was not inconsistent with the purposes of § 1983 and should be applied in the case at bar. The lower court had recognized that it was normally obligated to apply state tolling provisions but felt that, in cases like the instant case in which the application of the state tolling provision could lead to a very lengthy tolling period, such a potentially long delay would be contrary to the federal policy of attempting to deal with § 1983 claims as promptly as was practicable. The Court disagreed.

Despite the statement in *Monroe v. Pape* that resort to § 1983 does not require exhaustion of available state remedies, the Court has shown a reluctance to allow the § 1983 action to become a substitute for state tort law when the defendant is a state official whose official actions are alleged to have injured the plaintiff. For example, in Paul v. Davis, 424 U.S. 693, 96 S.Ct. 1155, 47 L.Ed.2d 405 (1976), the Court held that, what was in substance a claim that the defendant police chiefs had libelled the plaintiff in a flyer about shoplifters, could not be brought under § 1983. *See also* Siegert v. Gilley, 500 U.S. 226, 111 S.Ct. 1789, 114 L.Ed.2d 277 (1991), where the Court held that a defamatory letter in response to a request for information about his job performance could not be the basis of an action against a federal official under the federal equivalent of a § 1983 action that will be discussed shortly. Furthermore in Ingraham v. Wright, 430 U.S. 651, 97 S.Ct. 1401, 51 L.Ed.2d 711 (1977), the Court held that students who had been "paddled" did not have an eighth amendment ("cruel and unusual punishment") claim, because they were not being punished for commission of a crime and that whatever due process claims the students might have because of the manner in which the paddlings were administered could be redressed under Florida statutory and common law.

4. Actions Based on a Negligence Theory

A question with which the Court has wrestled for a considerable length of time is whether a § 1983 action can be based on a negligence theory. The Court deliberately left the question open in Parratt v. Taylor, 451 U.S. 527, 101 S.Ct. 1908, 68 L.Ed.2d 420 (1981), which involved a claim by a state prisoner whose mail-ordered hobby materials were negligently lost when the normal procedures for the receipt of mailed packages had not been followed by prison officials. The Court held that the prisoner did not have a § 1983 claim based on a deprivation of "due process of law" because he had an adequate state remedy against the offending officials. The case thus seemed to suggest, at least when merely negligence was involved, that, contrary to *Monroe v. Pape,* whether a person had a valid § 1983 claim depended upon the adequacy of state remedies although the actual holding in *Parratt* appears to have been that the § 1983 wrong, if any, would not have been the negligent loss of the hobby materials but a failure to provide some kind of adequate state remedy for this loss.

The Court has now expressly overruled *Parratt* in Daniels v. Williams, 474 U.S. 327, 106 S.Ct. 662, 88 L.Ed.2d 662 (1986), where the Court held that injuries suffered by an inmate in a state prison as a result of the negligence of the state prison authorities were not redressable in a § 1983 action based on a "deprivation of due process of law." The Court expressly noted that it had "no occasion to consider whether something less than intentional conduct such as recklessness or 'gross negligence,' is enough to trigger the protections of the Due Process Clause." *Id.* at n. 3. In a case decided on the same day, Davidson v. Cannon, 474 U.S. 344, 106 S.Ct. 668, 88 L.Ed.2d 677 (1986), the Court held that negligence could not be the basis of a § 1983 claim for depriving a person of rights under the due process clause, regardless of whether the rights involved were procedural or substantive. In *Daniels* the plaintiff was injured in the Richmond, Va. city jail when he slipped on a pillow negligently left on the stairs by one of the jailers. The plaintiff argued that the respondent's conduct had deprived him of due process because the respondent claimed that he was "entitled to the defense of sovereign immunity in a state tort suit." In *Davidson* the plaintiff claimed that the New Jersey prison authorities had negligently failed to respond to his written note advising them that he had been threatened by a fellow inmate who subsequently attacked him. Justice Brennan, in a concurring opinion, agreed "that merely negligent conduct by a state official does not constitute a deprivation of liberty under the Due Process Clause" but he believed that the case should be remanded so that the court of appeals could review the district court's holding that the respondent's conduct was not reckless. Justice Blackman, joined by Justice Marshall, agreed that the case should be remanded for consideration of the recklessness issue, but he also believed that, under the circumstances involved in *Davidson,* namely the failure to protect someone in the custody of the state, a § 1983 action would also lie for mere negligence.

Six weeks after *Daniels* and *Davidson* were decided the Court was again confronted with the issue in Whitley v. Albers, 475 U.S. 312, 106 S.Ct. 1078, 89 L.Ed.2d 251 (1986). In *Whitley* the plaintiff was an inmate in the Oregon State Penitentiary who was shot by prison guards while he was trying to protect elderly prisoners during the course of a prison riot during which a guard had been taken hostage. The plaintiff based his claim on both the eighth amendment right not to be subjected to "cruel or unusual punishment" and more generally on the deprivation of "a protected liberty interest without due process of law." The Court reinstated the district court's grant of summary judgment to the defendants. No action would lie for mere negligence and, in the circumstances, there was insufficient evidence from which to infer "a wanton willingness to inflict unjustified suffering" on the plaintiff. Justice Marshall, joined by Justices Brennan, Blackmun, and Stevens, dissented. In their view, there was enough evidence of wantonness to take the case to the jury. In a more recent case a transsexual brought an analogous action against federal prison officials for placing him in the general prison population where he alleged he was injured by other inmates. Farmer v. Brennan, 511 U.S. 825, 114 S.Ct. 1970, 128 L.Ed.2d 811 (1994). The Court held that the prison officials would only be liable if it could be shown that they knew that a prisoner faced a substantial risk of serious harm and then exhibited deliberate indifference to that risk. The Court adopted the "subjective" recklessness test of the criminal law.

The extensive litigation under § 1983 has generated a very extensive literature. This literature includes P. Schuck, Suing Government: Citizen

Remedies for Official Wrongs (1983); H. Monaghan, *State Law Wrongs, State Law Remedies, and the Fourteenth Amendment,* 86 Colum.L.Rev. 976 (1986); S. Schwab & T. Eisenberg, *Explaining Constitutional Tort Litigation: The Influence of the Attorney Fees Statute and the Government as Defendant,* 73 Cornell L.Rev. 719 (1988); (Hon.) H. Blackmun, *Section 1983 and the Federal Protection of Human Rights—Will the Statute Remain Alive or Fade Away,* 60 N.Y.U.L.Rev. 1 (1985)(Justice Blackmun disputed the contention that the federal courts are being overwhelmed by these actions); T. Eisenberg, *Section 1983: The Final Foundations and an Empirical Study,* 67 Corn.L.Rev. 482 (1982); R. Cass, *Damage Suits Against Public Officers,* 129 U.Pa.L.Rev. 1110 (1981); C. Whitman, *Constitutional Torts,* 79 Mich.L.Rev. 5 (1980). For a discussion of the interplay between the liability of municipalities and the liability or immunity of the officials who act for the municipality, *see* M. Brown, *Correlating Municipal Liability and Official Immunity under Section 1983,* 1989 Ill.L. Forum 625. For a critical reaction to the Court's refusal to permit a constitutional tort action to be brought in negligence, *see* W. Burnham, *Separating Constitutional and Common–Law Torts: A Critique and a Proposed Constitutional Theory of Duty,* 73 Minn.L.Rev. 515 (1989).

B. ACTIONS AGAINST FEDERAL OFFICIALS

In 1971 the Court finally decided the question left open in *Bell v. Hood, supra* p. 1287. The case in which this important issue was resolved was Bivens v. Six Unknown Named Agents of Federal Bureau of Narcotics, 403 U.S. 388, 91 S.Ct. 1999, 29 L.Ed.2d 619 (1971). Like *Bell v. Hood* and *Monroe v. Pape,* the case involved an improper arrest and consequent search. It was alleged that agents of the Federal Bureau of Narcotics, acting under a claim of federal authority, entered Bivens' apartment and arrested him for alleged narcotics violations. They manacled him in front of his wife and children and threatened to arrest the entire family. The agents then searched the apartment "from stem to stern." He was eventually taken to the Federal Court House in Brooklyn, N.Y., where he was interrogated, booked and subjected to a "visual strip search." The complaint was dismissed by the district court on the ground, *inter alia,* that it failed to state a cause of action. The Second Circuit affirmed. The respondents argued that Bivens had a remedy under state law to which he should have resorted by bringing an action in the state courts. They were forced to admit, however, that, if the action had been brought in the state courts, the Department of Justice would, as a matter of policy, have removed the case to federal court under 28 U.S.C. § 1442(a)(1) which permits removal to the federal courts of any civil action or criminal prosecution commenced in a state court against an officer of the United States for any acts "under color of such office" or "on account of any right, title or authority claimed under any Act of Congress for the apprehension or punishment of criminals or the collection of the revenue." Respondent's point, however, was that all such actions would be governed by state law. Writing for the majority, Justice Brennan declared that "[t]he interests protected by state laws regulating trespass and the invasion of privacy, and those protected by the Fourth Amendment's guarantee against unreasonable searches and seizures, may be inconsistent or even hostile. Thus, we may bar the door against an unwelcome private intruder or call the police if he persists in seeking entrance. The availability of such alternate means for the protection of privacy may lead the State to restrict imposition of liability for any consequent trespass * * *." In a footnote (n. 8) Justice Brennan noted that, while no state had as yet limited the common-law doctrine that one may use reasonable force to resist arrest by a private person, some states had made it unlawful to resist an unlawful arrest when the arrest is made by a person known to be an officer of the law. He then concluded that "petitioner's complaint states a cause of action under the Fourth Amendment * * * [for which the] petitioner is entitled to receive money damages for any injuries he has suffered as a result * * *."

The district court in *Bivens* had also ruled that the respondents were immune from liability by virtue of their official position. The Court did not rule on that question but, rather, reversed the judgment below and remanded the case for further proceedings. Justice Harlan concurred in a separate opinion. There were three dissenters. Chief Justice Burger believed that "an entirely different remedy is necessary but it was one that in my view is as much beyond judicial power as the step the Court takes today * * *." The Chief Justice felt that "Congress should develop an administrative or 'quasi-judicial' remedy against the government itself to afford compensation and restitution for persons whose Fourth Amendment rights had been violated * * *." Justice Black, whose opinion for the Court in *Bell v. Hood* had left the question now being decided open, thought that it was up to Congress to create a remedy. Even if the Court "had the legislative power to create a remedy" there were important reasons why the Court should decline to do so. He particularly stressed the plethora of "lawsuits" with which "[t]he courts of the United States as well as those of the States are choked * * *." Justice Blackmun also dissented. He relied principally on the reasons expressed by Chief Judge Lumbard who wrote the opinion for the court of appeals (409 F.2d 718 (2d Cir.1969)). Judge Lumbard stressed that the framers of the fourth amendment did not seem to contemplate a new federal cause of action and that, while the federal courts now had the power under their general grant of jurisdiction to provide a federal remedy, they should only do so if the provision of such a remedy "is essential to insure the vitality of a constitutional right."

On remand of the *Bivens* case to the Second Circuit, that court held that no absolute immunity, such as that recognized in *Barr v. Matteo, supra* p. 1120, for defamatory remarks made by federal officials acting within the outer perimeter of their official duties, would apply. Federal law enforcement officers, however, were entitled to defend damage actions based upon unconstitutional searches and seizures by showing good faith and reasonable grounds for believing that they were acting properly. 456 F.2d 1339 (2d Cir.1972). The case was then returned to the district court. The question of immunities is common to both actions pursuant to § 1983 brought against those acting "under color of state law" and to *Bivens*-type actions brought against federal officials. The resolution of the question has been much influenced by common-law developments which cover a wide variety of torts. The question will be discussed at length in *Butz v. Economou, infra* and in the notes following that case.

In November 1981, Deputy Attorney General Edward C. Schmults testified before the Subcommittee on Agency Administration of the Senate Judiciary Committee that there were over 2,000 *Bivens*-type actions against federal officials pending in the federal courts at the time. Deputy Attorney General Schmults further testified that as of that time only nine money judgments against federal officials had ever been entered in any of these actions. Of these nine judgments some had been reversed on appeal; in a few others appeals were pending. Interestingly, the *Bivens* case itself is not mentioned in the list of successful actions. The largest judgment that had been entered was in Dellums v. Powell, 566 F.2d 167 (D.C.Cir.1977), which was a class action on behalf of some 2,000 people whose demonstration on the steps of the United States Capitol against the Vietnamese war was broken up by the police. The defendants included the Chiefs of the District of Columbia and United States Capitol police. According to Mr. Schmults a judgment of $2,500,000 was eventually entered in favor of 1,200 plaintiffs. The judgment, together with accrued interest, was eventually paid through congressional appropriations. The pattern in almost all the cases in which the plaintiffs had been successful had been for the damages to run between 1,000 to 7,500 dollars. *See Federal Tort Claims Act: Hearings Before Subcomm. on Agency Administration of the Senate Comm. on the Judiciary*, 97th Cong., 1st Sess. 2–18 (1981)(statement of Dep. Att'y Gen. Schmults). Unfortunately there are no subsequent figures as to how many of the "other civil rights" actions filed annually in the federal courts, *see* statistics discussed at p. 1288, *supra*, are *Bivens*-type actions against federal officials.

In 1974, the Federal Tort Claims Act was amended to provide that "with regard to acts or omissions of investigative or law enforcement officers of the United States" claims could be brought against the United States "arising * * * out of assault, battery, false imprisonment, false arrest, abuse of process, or malicious prosecution." 28 U.S.C. § 2680(h), as amended. The Federal Tort Claims Act is among the subjects that will be discussed in the next chapter. While the 1974 amendment was enacted with *Bivens* in the background, the immediate precipitating factor was a series of actions brought against federal agents who, by mistake, broke into the wrong houses at night during raids for drugs in Collinsville, Illinois in 1973. The agents were operating without warrants. At that time, since-repealed legislation specifically authorized agents, under certain circumstances, to "break open an outer or inner door or window of a building" in search of "controlled substances." 84 Stat. 1274 (1970). This was the so-called "no-knock" authority. On the 1974 amendment and its background, see J. Boger, M. Gitenstein, and P. Verkuil, *The Federal Tort Claims Act Intentional Tort Amendment: An Interpretative Analysis*, 54 N.C.L.Rev. 497 (1976).

In 1988, in the "Westfall Act," (Federal Employees Liability Reform and Tort Compensation Act of 1988, 102 Stat. 4563 (1988)) Congress provided for the substitution of the United States as the party defendant in all actions, against federal employees, whose subject matter falls within the coverage of the Federal Tort Claims Act (28 U.S.C. § 2679). The Westfall Act, however, specifically declares that the provisions making the remedy against the United States the exclusive remedy do *not* apply to actions against federal employees "for a violation of the Constitution of the United States" (28 U.S.C. § 2679(b)(2)A). The statute codified the result the Court had earlier reached in Carlson v. Green, 446 U.S. 14, 100 S.Ct. 1468, 64 L.Ed.2d 15 (1980), where the Court specifically noted the possibility of recovery of punitive damages and the availability of a jury in *Bivens*-type actions and also established a uniform federal rule of survival for all such actions. While the availability of a Federal Tort Act claim against the United States does not pre-empt a *Bivens*-type action, it has been asserted that the federal courts are becoming increasingly reluctant to infer a *Bivens*-type action when the plaintiff's case is based upon a general claim of maladministration of a federal program, particularly if Congress has provided any kind of a remedial scheme, even if it is inadequate in particular cases. *See* B. Grey, *Preemption of* Bivens *Claims: How Clearly Must Congress Speak,* 70 Wash.U.L.Q. 1087 (1992), commenting on, *inter alia,* Schweiker v. Chilicky, 487 U.S. 412, 108 S.Ct. 2460, 101 L.Ed.2d 370 (1988). *See also* La Compania Ocho, Inc. v. United States Forest Service, 874 F.Supp. 1242 (D.N.M.1995). If there had ever been any doubt about the matter, the Court has now unanimously held that an independent federal agency, even if it has otherwise waived sovereign immunity, cannot be the subject of a *Bivens*-type action. Federal Deposit Insurance Corp. v. Meyer, 510 U.S. 471, 114 S.Ct. 996, 127 L.Ed.2d 308 (1994). Such actions can only be brought against federal officials.

Academic discussions of *Bivens*-type actions against federal officials have usually been conducted in a larger context that includes § 1983 actions against state officials. *See* p. 1293f, *supra. See also* Note, *The Limits of Implied Constitutional Damages Actions: New Boundaries for* Bivens, 55 N.Y.U.L.Rev. 1238 (1980). A comprehensive recent review of the history and development of *Bivens*-type actions is W. Kratzke, *Some Recommendations Concerning Tort Liability of Government and its Employees for Torts and Constitutional Torts,* 9 Admin.L.J.Am.U. 1105 (1996).

C. IMMUNITIES

BUTZ v. ECONOMOU
Supreme Court of the United States, 1978.
438 U.S. 478, 98 S.Ct. 2894, 57 L.Ed.2d 895.

Mr. Justice White delivered the opinion of the Court.

This case concerns the personal immunity of federal officials in the Executive Branch from claims for damages arising from their violations of citizens' constitutional rights. Respondent filed suit against a number of officials in the Department of Agriculture claiming that they had instituted an investigation and an administrative proceeding against him in retaliation for his criticism of that agency. The District Court dismissed the action on the ground that the individual defendants, as federal officials, were entitled to absolute immunity for all discretionary acts within the scope of their authority. The Court of Appeals reversed, holding that the defendants were entitled only to the qualified immunity available to their counterparts in state government. * * * Because of the importance of immunity doctrine to both the vindication of constitutional guarantees and the effective functioning of government, we granted certiorari. * * *

I

Respondent controls Arthur N. Economou and Co., Inc., which was at one time registered with the Department of Agriculture as a commodity futures commission merchant. Most of respondent's factual allegations in this lawsuit focus on an earlier administrative proceeding in which the Department of Agriculture sought to revoke or suspend the company's registration. On February 19, 1970, following an audit, the Department of Agriculture issued an administrative complaint alleging that respondent, while a registered merchant, had willfully failed to maintain the minimum financial requirements prescribed by the Department. After another audit, an amended complaint was issued on June 22, 1970. A hearing was held before the Chief Hearing Examiner of the Department, who filed a recommendation sustaining the administrative complaint. The Judicial Officer of the Department, to whom the Secretary had delegated his decisional authority in enforcement proceedings, affirmed the Chief Hearing Examiner's decision. On respondent's petition for review, the Court of Appeals for the Second Circuit vacated the order of the Judicial Officer. It reasoned that "the essential finding of willfulness * * * was made in a proceeding instituted without the customary warning letter, which the Judicial Officer conceded might well have resulted in prompt correction of the claimed insufficiencies." * * *

While the administrative complaint was pending before the Judicial Officer, respondent filed this lawsuit in Federal District Court. Respondent sought initially to enjoin the progress of the administrative proceeding, but he was unsuccessful in that regard. On March 31, 1975, respondent filed a second amended complaint seeking damages. Named as defendants were the individuals who had served as Secretary and Assistant Secretary of Agriculture during the relevant events; the Judicial Officer and Chief Hearing Examiner; several officials in the Commodity Exchange Authority; the Agriculture Department attorney who had prosecuted the enforcement proceeding; and several of the auditors who had investigated respondent or were witnesses against respondent.

The complaint stated that prior to the issuance of the administrative complaints respondent had been "sharply critical of the staff and operations of Defendants and carried on a vociferous campaign for the reform of Defendant Commodity Exchange Authority to obtain more effective regulation of commodity trading." * * * The complaint also stated that some time prior to the issuance of the February 19 complaint, respondent and his company had ceased to engage in activities regulated by the defendants. The complaint charged that each of the administrative complaints had been issued without the notice or warning required by law; that the defendants had furnished the complaints "to interested persons and others without furnishing respondent's answers as well"; and that following the issuance of the amended complaint, the defendants had issued a "deceptive" press release that "falsely indicated to the public that [respondent's] financial resources had deteriorated, when Defendants knew that their statement was untrue and so acknowledge[d] previously that said assertion was untrue." * * *

The complaint then presented 10 "causes of action," some of which purported to state claims for damages under the United States Constitution. For example, the first "cause of action" alleged that respondent had been denied due process of law because the defendants had instituted unauthorized proceedings against him without proper notice and with the knowledge that respondent was no longer subject to their regulatory jurisdiction. The third "cause of action" stated that by means of such actions "the Defendants discouraged and chilled the campaign of criticism [plaintiff] directed against them, and thereby deprived the [plaintiff] of [his] rights to free expression guaranteed by the First Amendment of the United States Constitution."

The defendants moved to dismiss the complaint on the ground that "as to the individual defendants it is barred by the doctrine of official immunity * * *." * * * The defendants relied on an affidavit submitted earlier in the litigation by the attorney who had prosecuted the original administrative complaint against respondent. He stated that the Secretary of Agriculture had had no involvement with the case and that each of the other named defendants had acted "within the course of his official duties." * * *

The District Court, apparently relying on the plurality opinion in Barr v. Matteo, * * * held that the individual defendants would be entitled to immunity if they could show that "their alleged unconstitutional acts were within the outer perimeter of their authority and discretionary." * * * After examining the nature of the acts alleged in the complaint, the District Court concluded: "Since the individual defendants have shown that their alleged unconstitutional acts were both within the scope of their authority and discretionary, we dismiss the second amended complaint as to them." * * *

The Court of Appeals for the Second Circuit reversed the District Court's judgment of dismissal with respect to the individual defendants. * * * The Court of Appeals reasoned that Barr v. Matteo, supra, did not "represen[t] the last word in this evolving area," * * * because principles governing the immunity of officials of the Executive Branch had been elucidated in later decisions dealing with constitutional claims against state officials. * * * These opinions were understood to establish that officials of the Executive Branch exercising discretionary functions did not need the protection of an absolute immunity from suit, but only a qualified immunity based on good faith and reasonable grounds. The Court of Appeals rejected a proposed distinction between suits against state officials sued pursuant to 42 U.S.C. § 1983 and suits against federal officials under the Constitution, noting that "[o]ther circuits have also concluded that the Supreme Court's development of official immunity doctrine in § 1983 suits against state officials applies with equal force to federal officers sued on a cause of action derived directly from the Constitution, since both types of suits serve the same function of protecting citizens against violations of their constitutional rights by government officials." * * * The Court of Appeals recognized that under Imbler v. Pachtman, 424 U.S. 409, 96 S.Ct. 984, 47 L.Ed.2d 128 (1976), state prosecutors were entitled to absolute immunity from § 1983 damages liability but reasoned that Agriculture Department officials performing analogous functions did not require such an immunity because their cases turned more on documentary proof than on the veracity of witnesses and because their work did not generally involve the same constraints of time and information present in criminal cases. * * * The court concluded that all of the defendants were "adequately protected by permitting them to avail themselves of the defense of qualified 'good faith, reasonable grounds' immunity of the type approved by the Supreme Court in Scheuer and Wood." * * * After noting that summary judgment would be available to the defendants if there were no genuine factual issues for trial, the Court of Appeals remanded the case for further proceedings.

II

The single submission by the United States on behalf of petitioners is that all of the federal officials sued in this case are absolutely immune from any liability for damages even if in the course of enforcing the relevant statutes they infringed respondent's constitutional rights and even if the violation was knowing and deliberate. Although the position is earnestly and ably presented by the United States, we are quite sure that it is unsound and consequently reject it.

* * *

The Government places principal reliance on Barr v. Matteo * * *.

* * *

Barr does not control this case. It did not address the liability of the acting director had his conduct not been within the outer limits of his duties, but from the care with which the Court inquired into the scope of his authority, it may be inferred that had the release been unauthorized, and surely if the issuance of press releases had been expressly forbidden by statute, the claim of absolute immunity would not have been upheld. The inference is supported by the fact that Mr. Justice Stewart, although agreeing with the principles announced by Mr. Justice Harlan, dissented and would have rejected the immunity claim because the press release, in his view, was not action in the line of duty. * * * It is apparent also that a quite different question would have been presented had the officer ignored an express statutory or constitutional limitation on his authority.

Barr did not, therefore, purport to depart from the general rule, which long prevailed, that a federal official may not with impunity ignore the limitations which the controlling law has placed on his powers. The immunity of federal executive officials began as a means of protecting them in the execution of their federal statutory duties from criminal or civil actions based on state law. * * * A federal official who acted outside of his federal statutory authority would be held strictly liable for his trespassory acts. For example, Little v. Barreme, 2 Cranch 170, 2 L.Ed. 243 (1804), held the commander of an American warship liable in damages for the seizure of a Danish cargo ship on the high seas. Congress had directed the President to intercept any vessels reasonably suspected of being en route *to* a French port, but the President had authorized the seizure of suspected vessels whether going *to* or *from* French ports, and the Danish vessel seized was en route *from* a forbidden destination. The Court, speaking through Mr. Chief Justice Marshall, held that the President's instructions could not "change the nature of the transaction, or legalize an act which, without those instructions, would have been a plain trespass." * * * Although there was probable cause to believe that the ship was engaged in traffic with the French, the seizure at issue was not among that class of seizures that the Executive had been authorized by statute to effect. * * *

* * *

As these cases demonstrate, a federal official was protected for action tortious under state law only if his acts were authorized by controlling federal law. * * * Since an unconstitutional act, even if authorized by statute, was viewed as not authorized in contemplation of law, there could be no immunity defense. * * *

* * * Kendall v. Stokes, 44 U.S. (3 How.) 87, 11 L.Ed. 506 (1845), addressed a different situation. The case involved a suit against the Postmaster General for erroneously suspending payments to a creditor of the Post Office. Examining and, if necessary, suspending payments to creditors were among the Postmaster's normal duties, and it appeared that he had simply made a mistake in the exercise of the discretion conferred upon him. He was held not liable in damages since "a public officer, acting to the best of his judgment and from a sense of duty, in a matter of account with an individual [is not] liable in an action for an error of judgment." * * * Having "the right to examine into this account" and the right to suspend it in the proper circumstances, * * * the officer was not liable in damages if he fell into error, provided, however, that he acted "from a sense of public duty and without malice." * * *

Four years later, in a case involving military discipline, the Court issued a similar ruling, exculpating the defendant officer because of the failure to prove that he had exceeded his jurisdiction or had exercised it in a malicious or willfully erroneous manner * * *. Wilkes v. Dinsman, 48 U.S. (7 How.) 89, 131, 12 L.Ed. 618 (1849).

In Spalding v. Vilas, 161 U.S. 483, 16 S.Ct. 631, 40 L.Ed. 780 (1896), on which the Government relies, the principal issue was whether the malicious motive of an officer would render him liable in damages for injury inflicted by his official act that otherwise was within the scope of his authority. * * *

Spalding made clear that a malicious intent will not subject a public officer to liability for performing his authorized duties as to which he would otherwise not be subject to damages liability. But Spalding did not involve conduct manifestly or otherwise beyond the authority of the official, nor did it involve a mistake of either law or fact in construing or applying the statute. It did not purport to immunize officials who ignore limitations on their authority imposed by law. * * * It is also evident that Spalding presented no claim that the officer was liable in damages because he had acted in violation of a limitation placed upon his conduct by the United States Constitution. If any inference is to be drawn from Spalding in any of these respects, it is that the official would not be excused from liability if he failed to observe obvious statutory or constitutional limitations on his powers or if his conduct was a manifestly erroneous application of the statute.

Insofar as cases in this Court dealing with the immunity or privilege of federal officers are concerned, this is where the matter stood until Barr v. Matteo. There, as we have set out above, immunity was granted even though the publication contained a factual error, which was not the case in Spalding. The plurality opinion and judgment in Barr also appear— although without any discussion of the matter—to have extended absolute immunity to an officer who was authorized to issue press releases, who was assumed to know that the press release he issued was false and who therefore was deliberately misusing his authority. Accepting this extension of immunity with respect to state tort claims, however, we are confident that Barr did not purport to protect an official who has not only committed a wrong under local law, but also violated those fundamental principles of fairness embodied in the Constitution. Whatever level of protection from state interference is appropriate for federal officials executing their duties under federal law, it cannot be doubted that these officials, even when acting pursuant to congressional authorization, are subject to the restraints imposed by the Federal Constitution.

The liability of officials who have exceeded constitutional limits was not confronted in either Barr or Spalding. Neither of those cases supports the Government's position. Beyond that, however, neither case purported to abolish the liability of federal officers for actions manifestly beyond their line of duty; and if they are accountable when they stray beyond the plain limits of their statutory authority, it would be incongruous to hold that they may nevertheless willfully or knowingly violate constitutional rights without fear of liability.

Although it is true that the Court has not dealt with this issue with respect to federal officers, we have several times addressed the immunity of state officers when sued under 42 U.S.C. § 1983 for alleged violations of constitutional rights. These decisions are instructive for present purposes.

III

Pierson v. Ray, 386 U.S. 547, 87 S.Ct. 1213, 18 L.Ed.2d 288 (1967), decided that § 1983 was not intended to abrogate the immunity of state judges which existed under the common law and which the Court had held applicable to federal judges in Bradley v. Fisher, 13 Wall. 335 (1872). Pierson also presented the issue "whether immunity was available to that segment of the executive branch of a state government that is * * * most frequently exposed to situations which can give rise to claims under § 1983—the local police officer." Scheuer v. Rhodes, 416 U.S. at 244–245, 94 S.Ct., at 1690 [1974]. Relying on the common law, we held that police officers were entitled to a defense of "good faith and probable cause," even though an arrest might subsequently be proved to be unconstitutional. We observed, however, that "[t]he common law has never granted police officers an absolute and unqualified immunity, and the officers in this case do not claim that they are entitled to one." 386 U.S. at 555.

In Scheuer v. Rhodes, supra, the issue was whether "higher officers of the executive branch" of state governments were immune from liability under § 1983 for violations of constitutionally protected rights. * * * There, the Governor of a State, the senior and subordinate officers of the state National Guard, and a state university president had been sued on the allegation that they had suppressed a civil disturbance in an unconstitutional manner. We explained that the doctrine of official immunity from § 1983 liability, although not constitutionally grounded and essentially a matter of statutory construction, was based on two mutually dependent rationales:

> "(1) the injustice, particularly in the absence of bad faith, of subjecting to liability an officer who is required, by the legal obligations of his position, to exercise discretion; (2) the danger that the threat of such liability would deter his willingness to execute his office with the decisiveness and the judgment required by the public good." * * *

The opinion also recognized that executive branch officers must often act swiftly and on the basis of factual information supplied by others, constraints which become even more acute in the "atmosphere of confusion, ambiguity, and swiftly moving events" created by a civil disturbance. * * * Although quoting at length from Barr v. Matteo, we did not believe that there was a need for absolute immunity from § 1983 liability for these high-ranking state officials. Rather the considerations discussed above indicated:

> "[I]n varying scope, a qualified immunity is available to officers of the executive branch of government, the variation being dependent upon the scope of discretion and responsibilities of the office and all the circumstances as they reasonably appeared at the time of the action on which liability is sought to be based. It is the existence of reasonable grounds for the belief formed at the time and in light of all the circumstances, coupled with good-faith belief, that affords a basis for qualified immunity of executive officers for acts performed in the course of official conduct." 416 U.S. at 247–248, 94 S.Ct., at 1692.

Subsequent decisions have applied the Scheuer standard in other contexts. In Wood v. Strickland, 420 U.S. 308, 95 S.Ct. 992, 43 L.Ed.2d 214 (1975), school administrators were held entitled to claim a similar qualified immunity. A school board member would lose his immunity from a § 1983 suit only if "he knew or reasonably should have known that the action he took within his sphere of official responsibility would violate the constitutional rights of the student affected, or if he took the action with the malicious intention to cause a deprivation of constitutional rights or other injury to the student." * * * In O'Connor v. Donaldson, 422 U.S. 563, 95 S.Ct. 2486, 45 L.Ed.2d 396 (1975), we applied the same standard to the superintendent of a state hospital. In Procunier v. Navarette, 434 U.S. 555, 98 S.Ct. 855, 55 L.Ed.2d 24 (1978), we held that prison administrators would be adequately protected by the qualified immunity outlined in Scheuer and Wood. We emphasized, however, that, at least in the absence of some showing of malice, an official would not be held liable in damages under § 1983 unless the constitutional right he was alleged to have violated was "clearly established" at the time of the violation.

None of these decisions with respect to state officials furnishes any support for the submission of the United States that federal officials are absolutely immune from liability for their constitutional transgressions. On the contrary, with impressive unanimity, the Federal Courts of Appeals have concluded that federal officials should receive no greater degree of protection from *constitutional* claims than their counterparts in state government. * * *

* * *

The Government argues that the cases involving state officials are distinguishable because they reflect the need to preserve the effectiveness of the right of action authorized by § 1983. * * *

* * *

The presence or absence of congressional authorization for suits against federal officials is, of course, relevant to the question whether to infer a right of action for damages for a particular violation of the Constitution. * * *

But once this analysis is completed, there is no reason to return again to the absence of congressional authorization in resolving the question of immunity. Having determined that the plaintiff is entitled to a remedy in damages for a constitutional violation, the court then must address how best to reconcile the plaintiff's right to compensation with the need to protect the decisionmaking processes of an executive department. Since our decision in Scheuer was intended to guide the federal courts in resolving this tension in the myriad factual situations in which it might arise, we see no reason why it should not supply the governing principles for resolving this dilemma in the case of federal officials. The Court's opinion in Scheuer relied on precedents dealing with federal as well as state officials, analyzed the issue of executive immunity in terms of general policy considerations, and stated its conclusion, quoted supra, in the same universal terms. The analysis presented in that case cannot be limited to actions against state officials.

* * * To create a system in which the Bill of Rights monitors more closely the conduct of state officials than it does that of federal officials is to stand the constitutional design on its head.

IV

* * *

Our opinion in Bivens put aside the immunity question; but we could not have contemplated that immunity would be absolute. If, as the Government argues, all officials exercising discretion were exempt from personal liability, a suit under the Constitution could provide no redress to the injured citizen, nor would it in any degree deter federal officials from committing constitutional wrongs. Moreover, no compensation would be available from the Government, for the Tort Claims Act prohibits recovery for injuries stemming from discretionary acts, even when that discretion has been abused.

The extension of absolute immunity from damages liability to all federal executive officials would seriously erode the protection provided by basic constitutional guarantees. The broad authority possessed by these officials enables them to direct their subordinates to undertake a wide range of projects—including some which may infringe such important personal interests as liberty, property, and free speech. It makes little sense to hold that a Government agent is liable for warrantless and forcible entry into a citizen's house in pursuit of evidence, but that an official of higher rank who actually orders such a burglary is immune simply because of his greater authority. Indeed, the greater power of such officials affords a greater potential for a regime of lawless conduct. Extensive Government operations offer opportunities for unconstitutional action on a massive scale. In situations of abuse, an action for damages against the responsible official can be an important means of vindicating constitutional guarantees.

Our system of jurisprudence rests on the assumption that all individuals, whatever their position in government, are subject to federal law:

* * *

This is not to say that considerations of public policy fail to support a limited immunity for federal executive officials. We consider here, as we did in Scheuer, the need to protect officials who are required to exercise their discretion and the related public interest in encouraging the vigorous exercise of official authority. Yet Scheuer and other cases have recognized that it is not unfair to hold liable the official who knows or should know he is acting outside the law, and that insisting on an awareness of clearly established constitutional limits will not unduly interfere with the exercise of official judgment. We therefore hold that, in a suit for damages arising from unconstitutional action, federal executive officials exercising discretion are entitled only to the qualified immunity specified in Scheuer, subject to those exceptional situations where it is demonstrated that absolute immunity is essential for the conduct of the public business.

* * * Insubstantial lawsuits can be quickly terminated by federal courts alert to the possibilities of artful pleading. Unless the complaint states a compensable claim for relief under the Federal Constitution, it should not survive a motion to dismiss. Moreover, the Court recognized in Scheuer that damages suits concerning constitutional violations need not proceed to trial, but can be terminated on a properly supported motion for summary judgment based on the defense of immunity. * * * In responding to such a motion, plaintiffs may not play dog in the manger; and firm application of the Federal Rules of Civil Procedure will ensure that federal officials are not harassed by frivolous lawsuits.

V

Although a qualified immunity from damages liability should be the general rule for executive officials charged with constitutional violations, our decisions recognize that there are some officials whose special functions require a full exemption from liability. * * * In each case, we have undertaken "a considered inquiry into the immunity historically accorded the relevant official at common law and the interests behind it." Id., at 421.

In Bradley v. Fisher, the Court analyzed the need for absolute immunity to protect judges from lawsuits claiming that their decisions had been tainted by improper motives. The Court began by noting that the principle of immunity for acts done by judges "in the exercise of their judicial functions" had been "the settled doctrine of the English courts for many centuries, and has never been denied, that we are aware of, in the courts of this country." 13 Wall, at 347.   * * *

The principle of Bradley was extended to federal prosecutors through the summary affirmance in Yaselli v. Goff, 275 U.S. 503, 48 S.Ct. 155, 72 L.Ed. 395 (1927) * * *.

We recently reaffirmed the holding of Yaselli v. Goff in Imbler v. Pachtman, supra, a suit against a state prosecutor under § 1983.   * * *

Despite these precedents, the Court of Appeals concluded that all of the defendants in this case—including the Chief Hearing Examiner, Judicial Officer, and prosecuting attorney—were entitled to only a qualified immunity.   The Court of Appeals reasoned that officials within the Executive Branch generally have more circumscribed discretion and pointed out that, unlike a judge, officials of the Executive Branch would face no conflict of interest if their legal representation was provided by the Executive Branch. The Court of Appeals recognized that "some of the Agriculture Department officials may be analogized to criminal prosecutors, in that they initiated the proceedings against [respondent], and presented evidence therein," * * * but found that attorneys in administrative proceedings did not face the same "serious constraints of time and even information" which this Court has found to be present frequently in criminal cases.   * * *

We think that the Court of Appeals placed undue emphasis on the fact that the officials sued here are—from an administrative perspective— employees of the Executive Branch.   Judges have absolute immunity not because of their particular location within the Government but because of the special nature of their responsibilities.   This point is underlined by the fact that prosecutors—themselves members of the Executive Branch—are also absolutely immune.   * * *

The cluster of immunities protecting the various participants in judge-supervised trials stems from the characteristics of the judicial process rather than its location.   * * *

At the same time, the safeguards built into the judicial process tend to reduce the need for private damages actions as a means of controlling unconstitutional conduct.   The insulation of the judge from political influence, the importance of precedent in resolving controversies, the adversary nature of the process, and the correctability of error on appeal are just a few of the many checks on malicious action by judges.   Advocates are restrained not only by their professional obligations, but by the knowledge that their assertions will be contested by their adversaries in open court. Jurors are carefully screened to remove all possibility of bias.   Witnesses are, of course, subject to the rigors of cross-examination and the penalty of perjury.   Because these features of the judicial process tend to enhance the reliability of information and the impartiality of the decisionmaking process, there is a less pressing need for individual suits to correct constitutional error.

We think that adjudication within a federal administrative agency shares enough of the characteristics of the judicial process that those who participate in such adjudication should also be immune from suits for damages.   The conflicts which federal hearing examiners seek to resolve are every bit as fractious as those which come to court. * * * Moreover, federal administrative law requires that agency adjudication contain many of the same safeguards as are available in the judicial process. * * *

There can be little doubt that the role of the modern federal hearing examiner or administrative law judge within this framework is "functionally comparable" to that of a judge. His powers are often, if not generally, comparable to those of a trial judge: * * *

We also believe that agency officials performing certain functions analogous to those of a prosecutor should be able to claim absolute immunity with respect to such acts. The decision to initiate administrative proceedings against an individual or corporation is very much like the prosecutor's decision to initiate or move forward with a criminal prosecution. An agency official, like a prosecutor, may have broad discretion in deciding whether a proceeding should be brought and what sanctions should be sought. * * *

The discretion which executive officials exercise with respect to the initiation of administrative proceedings might be distorted if their immunity from damages arising from that decision was less than complete. * * * While there is not likely to be anyone willing and legally able to seek damages from the officials if they do not authorize the administrative proceeding, * * * there is a serious danger that the decision to authorize proceedings will provoke a retaliatory response. An individual targeted by an administrative proceeding will react angrily and may seek vengeance in the courts. A corporation will muster all of its financial and legal resources in an effort to prevent administrative sanctions. "When millions may turn on regulatory decisions, there is a strong incentive to counter-attack."[39]

The defendant in an enforcement proceeding has ample opportunity to challenge the legality of the proceeding. An administrator's decision to proceed with a case is subject to scrutiny in the proceeding itself. The respondent may present his evidence to an impartial trier of fact and obtain an independent judgment as to whether the prosecution is justified. His claims that the proceeding is unconstitutional may also be heard by the courts. Indeed, respondent in this case was able to quash the administrative order entered against him by means of judicial review. * * *

We believe that agency officials must make the decision to move forward with an administrative proceeding free from intimidation or harassment. Because the legal remedies already available to the defendant in such a proceeding provide sufficient checks on agency zeal, we hold that those officials who are responsible for the decision to initiate or continue a proceeding subject to agency adjudication are entitled to absolute immunity from damages liability for their parts in that decision.

We turn finally to the role of an agency attorney in conducting a trial and presenting evidence on the record to the trier of fact. We can see no substantial difference between the function of the agency attorney in presenting evidence in an agency hearing and the function of the prosecutor who brings evidence before a court. In either case, the evidence will be

---

39. Expeditions Unlimited Aquatic Enterprises, Inc. v. Smithsonian Institution, 184   U.S.App.D.C. 397, 401, 566 F.2d 289, 293 (1977), cert. pending, , 76 418.

subject to attack through cross-examination, rebuttal, or reinterpretation by opposing counsel. Evidence which is false or unpersuasive should be rejected upon analysis by an impartial trier of fact. If agency attorneys were held personally liable in damages as guarantors of the quality of their evidence, they might hesitate to bring forward some witnesses or documents. * * * Apart from the possible unfairness to agency personnel, the agency would often be denied relevant evidence. * * * Administrative agencies can act in the public interest only if they can adjudicate on the basis of a complete record. We therefore hold that an agency attorney who arranges for the presentation of evidence on the record in the course of an adjudication is absolutely immune from suits based on the introduction of such evidence.

VI

There remains the task of applying the foregoing principles to the claims against the particular petitioner-defendants involved in this case. Rather than attempt this here in the first instance, we vacate the judgment of the Court of Appeals and remand the case to that court with instructions to remand the case to the District Court for further proceedings consistent with this opinion.

So ordered.

MR. JUSTICE REHNQUIST, with whom THE CHIEF JUSTICE, MR. JUSTICE STEWART, and MR. JUSTICE STEVENS join, concurring in part and dissenting in part.

I concur in that part of the Court's judgment which affords absolute immunity to those persons performing adjudicatory functions within a federal agency, * * * those who are responsible for the decision to initiate or continue a proceeding subject to agency adjudication, * * * and those agency personnel who present evidence on the record in the course of an adjudication * * *. I cannot agree, however, with the Court's conclusion that in a suit for damages arising from allegedly unconstitutional action federal executive officials, regardless of their rank or the scope of their responsibilities, are entitled to only qualified immunity even when acting within the outer limits of their authority. The Court's protestations to the contrary notwithstanding, this decision seriously misconstrues our prior decisions, finds little support as a matter of logic or precedent, and perhaps most importantly, will, I fear, seriously "dampen the ardor of all but the most resolute, or the most irresponsible, in the unflinching discharge of their duties," Gregoire v. Biddle, 177 F.2d 579, 581 (C.A.2 1949)(Learned Hand, J.).

Most noticeable is the Court's unnaturally constrained reading of the landmark case of Spalding v. Vilas, * * *. The Court in that case did indeed hold that the actions taken by the Postmaster General were within the authority conferred upon him by Congress, and went on to hold that even though he had acted maliciously in carrying out the duties conferred upon him by Congress he was protected by official immunity. But the Court left no doubt that it would have reached the same result had it been alleged the official acts were unconstitutional.

"We are of the opinion that the same general considerations of public policy and convenience which demand for judges of courts of superior jurisdiction immunity from civil suits for damages arising from acts done by them in the course of the performance of their judicial functions, apply to a large extent to official communications made by heads of Executive Departments when engaged in the discharge of duties imposed upon them by law. The interests of the people require that due protection be accorded to them in respect of their official acts." * * *

* * *

Indeed, the language from Spalding quoted above unquestionably applies with equal force in the case at bar. No one seriously contends that the Secretary of Agriculture or the Assistant Secretary, who are being sued for $32 million in damages, had wandered completely off the official reservation in authorizing prosecution of respondent for violation of regulations promulgated by the Secretary for the regulation of "futures commission merchants," 7 U.S.C. § 6 (1976 ed.). * * * This is precisely what the Secretary and his assistants were empowered and required to do. That they would on occasion be mistaken in their judgment that a particular merchant had in fact violated the regulations is a necessary concomitant of any known system of administrative adjudication; that they acted "maliciously" gives no support to respondent's claim against them unless we are to overrule Spalding.

The Court's attempt to distinguish Spalding may be predicated on a simpler but equally erroneous concept of immunity. At one point the Court observes that even under Spalding "an executive officer would be vulnerable if he took action 'manifestly or palpably' beyond his authority or ignored a clear limitation on his enforcement powers." * * * From that proposition, which is undeniably accurate, the Court appears to conclude that anytime a plaintiff can paint his grievance in constitutional colors, the official is subject to damages unless he can prove he acted in good faith. After all, Congress would never "authorize" an official to engage in unconstitutional conduct. That this notion in fact underlies the Court's decision is strongly suggested by its discussion of numerous cases which supposedly support its position, but all of which in fact deal not with the question of what level of immunity a federal official may claim when acting within the outer limits of his authority, but rather with the question of whether he was in fact so acting. * * *

Putting to one side the illogic and impracticability of distinguishing between constitutional and common-law claims for purposes of immunity, which will be discussed shortly, this sort of immunity analysis badly misses the mark. It amounts to saying that an official has immunity until someone alleges he has acted unconstitutionally. But that is no immunity at all: The "immunity" disappears at the very moment when it is needed. The critical inquiry in determining whether an official is entitled to claim immunity is not whether someone has in fact been injured by his action; that is part of the plaintiff's case in chief. The immunity defense turns on * * * whether the official was acting within the outer bounds of his authority. Only if the immunity inquiry is approached in this manner does it have any meaning. That such a rule may occasionally result in individual injustices has never been doubted, but at least until today, immunity has been accorded nevertheless. * * *

Barr v. Matteo * * * unfortunately fares little better at the Court's hand than Spalding. Here the Court at least recognizes and reaffirms the minimum proposition for which Barr stands—that executive officials are absolutely immune at least from actions predicated on common-law claims as long as they are acting within the outer limits of their authority. * * * Barr is distinguished, however, on the ground that it did not involve a violation of "those fundamental principles of fairness embodied in the Constitution." * * * But if we allow a mere allegation of unconstitutionality, obviously unproved at the time made, to require a Cabinet-level official, charged with the enforcement of the responsibilities to which the complaint pertains, to lay aside his duties and defend such an action on the merits, the defense of official immunity will have been abolished in fact if not in form. The ease with which a constitutional claim may be pleaded in a case such as this, where a violation of statutory or judicial limits on agency action may be readily converted by any legal neophyte into a claim of denial of procedural due process under the Fifth Amendment, will assure that. The fact that the claim fails when put to trial will not prevent the consumption of time, effort, and money on the part of the defendant official in defending his actions on the merits. * * *

It likewise cannot seriously be argued that an official will be less deterred by the threat of liability for unconstitutional conduct than for activities which might constitute a common-law tort. The fear that inhibits is that of a long, involved lawsuit and a significant money judgment, not the fear of liability for a certain type of claim. Thus, even viewing the question functionally—indeed, *especially* viewing the question functionally—the basis for a distinction between constitutional and common-law torts in this context is open to serious question. Even the logical justification for raising such a novel distinction is far from clear. That the Framers thought some rights sufficiently susceptible of legislative derogation that they should be enshrined in the Constitution does not necessarily indicate that the Framers likewise intended to establish an immutable hierarchy of right in terms of their importance to individuals. The most heinous common-law tort surely cannot be less important to, or have less of an impact on, the aggrieved individual than a mere technical violation of a constitutional proscription.

* * *

The Court also looks to the question of immunity of state officials for causes arising under § 1983 * * *. * * * [E]ven a moment's reflection on the nature of the Bivens-type action and the purposes of § 1983, as made abundantly clear in this Court's prior cases, supplies a compelling reason for distinguishing between the two different situations. In the first place, as made clear above, a grant of absolute immunity to high-ranking executive officials on the federal side would not eviscerate the cause of action recognized in Bivens. The officials who are the most likely defendants in a Bivens-type action have generally been accorded only a qualified immunity. But more importantly, Congress has expressly waived sovereign immunity

for this type of suit. This permits a direct action against the Government
* * *. And the Federal Government can internally supervise and check its
own officers. The Federal Government is not so situated that it can
control state officials or strike this same balance, however. Hence the
necessity of § 1983 and the differing standards of immunity. * * *

* * *

My biggest concern, however, is not with the illogic or impracticality of
today's decision, but rather with the potential for disruption of Government that it invites. The steady increase in litigation, much of it directed
against governmental officials and virtually all of which could be framed in
constitutional terms, cannot escape the notice of even the most casual
observer. From 1961 to 1977, the number of cases brought in the federal
courts under civil rights statutes increased from 296 to 13,113. See
Director of the Administrative Office of the United States Courts Ann. Rep.
189, Table 11 (1977); Ann.Rep. 173, Table 17 (1976). It simply defies logic
and common experience to suggest that officials will not have this in the
back of their minds when considering what official course to pursue. It
likewise strains credulity to suggest that this threat will only inhibit
officials from taking action which they should not take in any event. It is
the cases in which the grounds for action are doubtful, or in which the
actor is timid, which will be affected by today's decision.

The Court, of course, recognizes this problem and suggests two solutions. First, judges, ever alert to the artful pleader, supposedly will weed
out insubstantial claims. * * * That, I fear, shows more optimism than
prescience. Indeed, this very case, unquestionably frivolous in the extreme, belies any hope in that direction. And summary judgment on
affidavits and the like is even more inappropriate when the central, and
perhaps only, inquiry is the official's state of mind. * * *

The second solution offered by the Court is even less satisfactory. The
Court holds that in those special circumstances "where it is demonstrated
that absolute immunity is essential for the conduct of the public business,"
absolute immunity will be extended. * * * But this is a form of "absolute
immunity" which in truth exists in name only. If, for example, the
Secretary of Agriculture may never know until inquiry by a trial court
whether there is a possibility that vexatious constitutional litigation will
interfere with his decisionmaking process, the Secretary will obviously
think not only twice but thrice about whether to prosecute a litigious
commodities merchant who has played fast and loose with the regulations
for his own profit. Careful consideration of the rights of every individual
subject to his jurisdiction is one thing; a timorous reluctance to prosecute
any of such individuals who have a reputation for using litigation as a
defense weapon is quite another. Since Cabinet officials are mortal, it is
not likely that we shall get the precise judgmental balance desired in each
of them, and it is because of these very human failings that the principals
of Spalding, 161 U.S. at 498, 16 S.Ct., at 637, dictate that absolute
immunity be accorded once it be concluded by a court that a high-level

executive official was "engaged in the discharge of duties imposed upon [him] by law."*

* * *

Notes

1. Does not the continued vitality of *Barr v. Matteo,* reprinted *supra* p. 1120, now depend on the Court's continued adherence to the holding in Paul v. Davis, 424 U.S. 693, 96 S.Ct. 1155, 47 L.Ed.2d 405 (1976), discussed at p. 1292, *supra,* that defamatory statements made by officials acting in their official capacity only give rise to common-law actions? This may be a hard position for the Court to maintain. *See* G. Christie, *Injury to Reputation and the Constitution: Confusion Amid Conflicting Approaches,* 75 Mich.L.Rev. 43 (1976).

2. Do you think that Justice Rehnquist's attempts to distinguish between state officials subject to § 1983 actions and federal officials subject to *Bivens*-type actions are persuasive?

3. On remand, the claims against all the defendants in the *Economou* case were dismissed by the district court in two separate decisions: Economou v. Butz, 466 F.Supp. 1351 (S.D.N.Y.1979) and Economou v. Butz, 84 F.R.D. 678 (S.D.N.Y.1979). More recently, in an action brought against a court reporter for failure to provide a transcript to a person seeking to appeal a criminal conviction, the Court held that court reporters are not entitled to the absolute immunity granted to judges. Antoine v. Byers & Anderson, Inc., 508 U.S. 429, 113 S.Ct. 2167, 124 L.Ed.2d 391 (1993). As indicated in the *Economou* case, prosecutors are entitled to absolute immunity, but only when engaged in prosecutorial functions. Thus in Burns v. Reed, 500 U.S. 478, 111 S.Ct. 1934, 114 L.Ed.2d 547 (1991), the Court held that a prosecutor enjoyed absolute immunity for matters arising in the course of a probable cause hearing but did not enjoy absolute immunity for legal advice he had given the police. Subsequently, in Buckley v. Fitzsimmons, 509 U.S. 259, 113 S.Ct. 2606, 125 L.Ed.2d 209 (1993), the Court held that a prosecutor engaged in trying to determine if a footprint left at the scene of a crime was that of the plaintiff was engaged in an investigatory function which, as a type of administrative function, did not entitle him to absolute immunity. In that case, the plaintiff also claimed that the defendant prosecutor had, by defaming him in a press conference, denied him a fair trial by turning the jury against him and leading the jury to deadlock rather than acquit him. The Court held that this activity of the prosecutor was also not entitled to absolute immunity. Of course, when denied absolute immunity, a prosecutor can still claim the normal qualified immunity enjoyed by government officials. The absolute immunity of persons serving in a quasi-judicial role has been extended by the lower courts to court-appointed media-

---

* The ultimate irony of today's decision is that in the area of common-law official immunity, a body of law fashioned and applied by judges, absolute immunity within the federal system is extended only to judges and prosecutors functioning in the judicial system. * * * Similarly, where this Court has interpreted 42 U.S.C. § 1983 in the light of common-law doctrines of official immunity, again only judges and prosecutors are accorded absolute immunity. * * * If one were to hazard an informed guess as to why such a distinction in treatment between judges and prosecutors, on the one hand, and other pub-

lic officials on the other, obtains, mine would be that those who decide the common law know through personal experience the sort of pressures that might exist for such decision-makers in the absence of absolute immunity, but may not know or may have forgotten that similar pressures exist in the case of nonjudicial public officials to whom difficult decisions are committed. But the cynical among us might not unreasonably feel that this is simply another unfortunate example of judges treating those who are not part of the judicial machinery as "lesser breeds without the law."

tors. *See* Wagshal v. Foster, 28 F.3d 1249 (D.C.Cir.1994), *cert. denied*, ___ U.S. ___, 115 S.Ct. 1314, 131 L.Ed.2d 196 (1995).

4. Even prior to *Monroe v. Pape*, discussed *supra* p. 1289, decided in 1961, the Court had held that an action brought under § 1983 and a companion statute would not lie against a state legislator who, it was alleged, had called the plaintiff before a California state senate legislative committee not "for a legislative purpose" but "to intimidate and silence the plaintiff and deter and prevent him from effectively exercising his constitutional rights of free speech. * * *" Tenney v. Brandhove, 341 U.S. 367, 71 S.Ct. 783, 95 L.Ed. 1019 (1951). Subsequently, in Davis v. Passman, 442 U.S. 228, 99 S.Ct. 2264, 60 L.Ed.2d 846 (1979), the Court was confronted with a claim by a former deputy administrative assistant of the defendant-Congressman that she had been discharged because he preferred to have a man in that position. A majority of the Court held that the plaintiff had stated a valid *Bivens*-type claim for violation of her rights, under the due process clause of the fifth amendment, not to be subject to discrimination based on sex. The Court did not, however, rule on whether the defendant could successfully claim that his conduct was immunized by the "speech or debate" clause of the Constitution. Since the court of appeals had not ruled on that issue, the Court remanded the case for further proceedings. If there were any further proceedings, there is no report of them. More recently, in Forrester v. White, 484 U.S. 219, 108 S.Ct. 538, 98 L.Ed.2d 555 (1988), the Court held that a state court judge who allegedly demoted and later discharged a probation officer on account of her sex did not enjoy absolute immunity in a resulting § 1983 action.

In Pulliam v. Allen, 466 U.S. 522, 104 S.Ct. 1970, 80 L.Ed.2d 565 (1984), the Court, in a 5–4 decision, held that, although one could not bring an action against a judge for damages arising out of the judge's exercise of a judicial role, the plaintiff could sue her for an injunction and, having obtained the injunction, could be awarded attorney's fees. Although at common law one could not obtain an injunction against a judge, the majority noted that errant judges could and were controlled by writs of prohibition and mandamus issued by King's Bench. The Court relied on the common-law practice to support its conclusion that there was no inconsistency in allowing a judge to be immune from damage actions while making her susceptible to suits seeking prospective "collateral relief."

5. In Halperin v. Kissinger, 606 F.2d 1192 (D.C.Cir.1979), *affirmed by an equally divided court* 452 U.S. 713, 101 S.Ct. 3132, 69 L.Ed.2d 367 (1981)(Justice Rehnquist not sitting), it was held that former President Nixon could be liable in damages for his role in authorizing, while he was President, unlawful wiretapping of the plaintiff's telephone. The plaintiff at the time in question was a member of the staff of the National Security Council and was suspected of leaking classified material to the press. Relying on *Butz v. Economou* and Scheuer v. Rhodes, 416 U.S. 232, 94 S.Ct. 1683, 40 L.Ed.2d 90 (1974), the court of appeals refused to accord Mr. Nixon any absolute immunity while serving as President. Mr. Nixon would be liable if he acted with " 'actual malice' "(Wood v. Strickland, 420 U.S. 308, 95 S.Ct. 992, 43 L.Ed.2d 214 (1975)), or "failed to meet a statutory or constitutional obligation that was clear under the circumstances as understood at the time." The issue, however, reached the Court again. Nixon v. Fitzgerald, 457 U.S. 731, 102 S.Ct. 2690, 73 L.Ed.2d 349 (1982). With the entire Court sitting, the majority, in a 5–4 decision, held that a President is entitled to absolute immunity for acts within the "outer perimeter" of his official responsibilities. In a companion case, Harlow v.

Fitzgerald, 457 U.S. 800, 102 S.Ct. 2727, 73 L.Ed.2d 396 (1982), the Court held that presidential assistants should enjoy only a qualified privilege. Chief Justice Burger, the sole dissenter, argued that presidential assistants should share the President's immunity. In a subsequent case, the Court held that President Nixon's Attorney General, John Mitchell, was entitled to a qualified but not an absolute immunity in an action brought by someone the warrantless tapping of whose phone had been authorized by Mitchell on national security grounds (a suspected plot to kidnap a presidential advisor and sabotage government buildings). Mitchell v. Forsyth, 472 U.S. 511, 105 S.Ct. 2806, 86 L.Ed.2d 411 (1985). The Court nevertheless reversed the decision below which had affirmed the district court's denial of summary judgment in favor of Mitchell. In his opinion concurring in the result, Justice Stevens declared that sometimes cabinet officials are exercising the "President's powers," and he thought that this is what Mitchell had done. Accordingly, he believed that Mitchell was entitled to absolute immunity. More recently, in Jones v. Clinton, 72 F.3d 1354 (8th Cir.1996), *cert. granted,* ___ U.S. ___, 116 S.Ct. 2545, 135 L.Ed.2d 1066, a § 1983 action was brought against the President, by a former state employee, for alleged sexual harassment while he was Governor of Arkansas. The Eight Circuit held that a sitting President was not entitled to immunity for his unofficial acts. Two of the three circuit judges also held that a sitting President was not automatically entitled to have all such actions stayed, barring exigent circumstances, until the conclusion of the President's term of office. The majority felt that the district court had amply authority to schedule the proceedings to avoid interfering with the proper performance of the President's duties. One awaits the Supreme Court's resolution of these issues.

6. In Owen v. City of Independence, Missouri, 445 U.S. 622, 100 S.Ct. 1398, 63 L.Ed.2d 673 (1980), a majority of the Court held that a municipality against which an action had been brought under § 1983 could not take advantage of any qualified immunity based upon the good-faith and absence of malice of the officials for whose conduct the municipality was responsible. The qualified immunity was only applicable in actions against the individual officials.

7. When the defendant in the typical § 1983 or *Bivens*-type action is an individual, does not the question of liability merge into the question of immunity more than it does in, say, defamation? Consider again the issue raised at p. 1292 *supra,* whether civil-rights actions may be based upon negligence.

8. Over the years, the Court has decided a number of other cases involving the question of immunities. In Briscoe v. LaHue, 460 U.S. 325, 103 S.Ct. 1108, 75 L.Ed.2d 96 (1983), the Court held (6–3) that a policeman who, as a witness, had lied at the plaintiff's criminal trial was entitled to immunity in a § 1983 action. In Cleavinger v. Saxner, 474 U.S. 193, 106 S.Ct. 496, 88 L.Ed.2d 507 (1985), however, the Court held 6–3 that the members of a prison "Discipline Committee" are only entitled to a qualified rather than an absolute immunity. Subsequently, in Malley v. Briggs, 475 U.S. 335, 106 S.Ct. 1092, 89 L.Ed.2d 271 (1986), the Court held that a police officer who applied for a warrant which was then issued by a judge only had a qualified immunity. The Court adopted the common-law rule applied in cases of malicious prosecution, namely that one who procures the issuance of a warrant will be liable if the complaint was maliciously made and without probable cause. Citing *Harlow v. Fitzgerald, supra,* the Court in *Malley* declared that an action could be brought

against an officer who procures an arrest warrant "if, on an objective basis, it is obvious that no reasonably competent officer would have concluded that a warrant should issue * * *."

9.   The question of immunities is discussed in some of the literature cited at p. 1293f, *supra,* in the course of our discussion of the history and general features of constitutional torts.   More narrowly focused discussions centered on the question of immunities include K. Blum, *Qualified Immunity: A User's Manual,* 26 Ind.L.Rev. 187 (1993);   D. Rudovsky, *The Qualified Immunity Doctrine in the Supreme Court: Judicial Activism and the Restriction of Constitutional Rights,* 138 U.Pa.L.Rev. 23 (1989);   Note, *Qualified Immunity for Government Officials: The Problem of Unconstitutional Purpose in Civil Rights Litigation* 95 Yale L.J. 126 (1985);   Comment, *Tort Immunity of Federal Executive Officials: The Mutable Scope of Absolute Immunity,* 37 Okla.L.Rev. 285 (1984);   Comment, *Rejecting Absolute Immunity for Federal Officials,* 71 Cal.L.Rev. 1707 (1983);   Note, *An Examination of Immunity for Federal Executive Officials,* 28 Villanova L.Rev. 956 (1983).

Chapter 22

IMMUNITIES

A. GOVERNMENTAL IMMUNITIES

1. *Suits Against the United States*

I.M. GOTLIEB, TORT CLAIMS AGAINST THE UNITED STATES[1]

30 Geo.L.J. 462, 462–64 (1942).

Deeply rooted in the history of the common law in England was the immunity of the sovereign from the processes of the law. In theory, however, even in the thirteenth century, the idea of some man or body of men above the law was objectionable to the English concept of justice. The adherence to such a doctrine would indeed have been incompatible with anything but absolute monarchy and the recognition of the divine right of kings. * * *

Notwithstanding this theoretical elevation of the position of the law, even in relation to the king, there was no established or orderly method whereby the courts could restrain an erring king. * * *

Much the same immunity was extended to the feudal lords through the courts Baronial and Manorial, largely because of their status in their own communities.

The much repeated phrase, "The King can do no wrong" would seem from the foregoing explanation to denote more the lack of adequate redress at law than the absence of capacity to violate the law. * * * Certainly, the sovereign's immunity from suit was adverse to the belief on the part of those seeking to augment parliamentary power that the king should not be able to disregard the rights of his subjects. The emergence of the sovereign as against the feudal hierarchy perhaps made necessary an exclusion from the ordinary processes governing lesser individuals. The agitation for the availability of tort remedy against the sovereign, or the state, to any considerable degree, is a more mature development of the law.

---

1. Reprinted with the permission of the publisher, c. 1942 The Georgetown Law Journal Association. Most footnotes omitted.

This doctrine of sovereign immunity has been incorporated into American law. Unlike all other employers, the state bears no legal responsibility for the torts of its agents. In *Gibbons v. United States*,[2] Mr. Justice Miller followed the time-honored pattern when he stated that "no government has ever held itself liable to individuals for misfeasance, laches, or unauthorized exercise of power by its officers or agents."[3]

This decision in 1868 enunciates the right of the national Government to immunity from suit more as a matter of public policy, although later decisions imply this might be a derivation from its inherent sovereignty as the natural successor to Crown prerogatives. * * *

Practically every country of western Europe has to some extent long admitted such liability. In this category are several of the British colonies and dominions, like Canada, Australia, New Zealand and South Africa.

Dissatisfaction with sovereign immunity from suit grew with the increasing scope of governmental activities. The compelling reasons for excluding the sovereign from suit without his consent in Anglo–Norman times no longer exists, and on the contrary, strong arguments of justice and logic may be adduced to support such liability. The expanding activities of the Federal Government touch upon the life of every citizen in such an intimate manner that the denial of consent to suit in tort constitutes a patent injustice to *bona fide* claimants whose only present recourse, excepting scattered statutes of very limited scope, is by way of a private relief bill.

The private relief bills either directly appropriate a specified sum to meet the claim or refer the claimant to the Court of Claims or a Federal District Court for determination of the claim. This remedy is excessive in cost and delay, inequitable in operation and is unduly burdensome on the Claims Committees of Congress. It has been characterized by several Claims Committees and individual members of Congress as unsatisfactory, and an outright failure.

Notes

1. A good discussion of English law is contained in L. Jaffe, *Suits Against Governments and Officers: Sovereign Immunity*, 77 Harv.L.Rev. 1 (1963).

2. Gotlieb reported that, in the 76th Congress (1939–40), almost 1,700 private claim bills were introduced of which a little over half were based on tort. Six hundred fifty of these bills were enacted into law including 262 based on tort. Over 95% of the private laws based on tort were for $7,500 or less. In the immediately preceding Congresses as many as over 2,300 private claims bills had been introduced in a single Congress. *See* Dalehite v. United States, 346 U.S. 15, 25 n. 9, 73 S.Ct. 956, 962, 97 L.Ed. 1427, 1435 (1953).

3. The leading academic proponent of expanded liability in tort for all levels of government (federal, state, municipal) was Professor Edwin M. Borchard of Yale, who wrote a series of articles on the subject in the 1920s. E. Borchard, *Government Liability in Tort*, 34 Yale L.J. 1, 129, 229 (1924–25); 36 Yale L.J. 1, 757, 1039 (1926–27); 28 Colum.L.Rev. 577, 734 (1928).

4. The Court of Claims was established in 1855 to hear claims founded "upon statutes or any law of Congress, or upon any regulation of an executive

---

2. 8 Wall. 269 (U.S. 1868).   **3.** *Id.* at 274.

department, or upon any contract, express or implied." 10 Stat. 612. This was the first major abrogation of the doctrine of sovereign immunity by the federal government. As originally constituted, the Court of Claims was to report periodically to the Congress. In cases in which it ruled in favor of the claimant, the court was to include draft bills carrying out its decisions for the consideration of Congress. In 1863, however, the Court of Claims was authorized actually to render judgment against the United States. 12 Stat. 765, 766. In 1887, under the Tucker Act, the Court of Claims' jurisdiction was enlarged to cover claims for "damages, liquidated or unliquidated, in cases not sounding in tort." 24 Stat. 505. The Tucker Act also gave concurrent jurisdiction to the United States District Courts for all such claims that did not exceed $1,000 and to the now defunct circuit courts for claims between $1,000 and $10,000. The Court of Claims has now been renamed the United States Claims Court. Its jurisdiction is now codified at 28 U.S.C. § 1491. The concurrent jurisdiction of the district courts, now raised to $10,000, is codified in 28 U.S.C. § 1346(a)(2). Over the next forty years Congress authorized suits against the government for patent infringement (1910), maritime torts (1920), and damage caused by public vessels (1925). In 1922, Congress enacted the Small Tort Claims Act which provided for the administrative settlement of property damage claims of up to $1,000. 42 Stat. 1066. This Act was repealed by the Federal Tort Claims Act, 60 Stat. 842, 846 (1946), to which we shall shortly turn and which subsumed its provisions. Although enacted in 1946, the Federal Tort Claims Act covered all claims occurring "on and after January 1, 1945." On the history of the United States' acceptance of liability in tort as well as for a discussion of the Federal Tort Claims Act itself, see K. Davis & R. Pierce, 3 Administrative Law Treatise §§ 19.1 et seq. (2d ed. 1994).

THE "FEDERAL TORT CLAIMS ACT"

60 Stat. 842 (1946), as amended and codified in Title 28, United States Code.

§ 1346. United States as Defendant

(b) Subject to the provisions of chapter 171 of this title,[4] the district courts, together with the United States District Court for the District of the Canal Zone and the District Court of the Virgin Islands, shall have exclusive jurisdiction of civil actions on claims against the United States, for money damages, accruing on and after January 1, 1945, for injury or loss of property, or personal injury or death caused by the negligent or wrongful act or omission of any employee of the Government while acting within the scope of his office or employment, under circumstances where the United States, if a private person, would be liable to the claimant in accordance with the law of the place where the act or omission occurred.

§ 2674. Liability of United States

The United States shall be liable, respecting the provisions of this title relating to tort claims, in the same manner and to the same extent as a private individual under like circumstances, but shall not be liable for interest prior to judgment or for punitive damages.

* * *

4. [Ed. note] Chapter 171 of Title 28 is entitled "Tort Claims Procedure," and in- cludes 28 U.S.C. §§ 2671–80.

With respect to any claim under this chapter, the United States shall be entitled to assert any defense based upon judicial or legislative immunity which otherwise would have been available to the employee of the United States whose act or omission gave rise to the claim, as well as any other defenses to which the United States is entitled. [added in 1988]

§ 2680. Exceptions

The provisions of this chapter and section 1346(b) of this title shall not apply to—

(a) Any claim based upon an act or omission of an employee of the Government, exercising due care, in the execution of a statute or regulation, whether or not such statute or regulation be valid, or based upon the exercise or performance or the failure to exercise or perform a discretionary function or duty on the part of a federal agency or an employee of the Government, whether or not the discretion involved be abused.

(b) Any claim arising out of the loss, miscarriage, or negligent transmission of letters or postal matter.

(c) Any claim arising in respect of the assessment or collection of any tax or customs duty, or the detention of any goods or merchandise by any officer of customs or excise or any other law-enforcement officer.

(d) Any claim for which a remedy is provided by sections 741–752, 781–790 of Title 46, relating to claims or suits in admiralty against the United States.

(e) Any claim arising out of an act or omission of any employee of the Government in administering the provisions of sections 1–31 of Title 50, Appendix.[5]

(f) Any claim for damages caused by the imposition or establishment of a quarantine by the United States.

[(g) Repealed. Sept. 26, 1950, ch. 1049, § 13(5), 64 Stat. 1043.][6]

(h) Any claim arising out of assault, battery, false imprisonment, false arrest, malicious prosecution, abuse of process, libel, slander, misrepresentation, deceit, or interference with contract rights: *Provided,* that, with regard to acts or omissions of investigative or law enforcement officers of the United States Government, the provisions of this chapter and section 1346(b) of this title shall apply to any claim arising, on or after the date of the enactment of this proviso, out of assault, battery, false imprisonment, false arrest, abuse of process, or malicious prosecution. For the purpose of this subsection, "investigative or law enforcement officer" means any officer of the United States who is empowered by law to execute searches, to seize evidence, or to make arrests for violations of Federal law.

(i) Any claim for damages caused by the fiscal operations of the Treasury or by the regulation of the monetary system.

---

5. [Ed. note] This is the Trading with the Enemy Act.

6. [Ed. note] This now repealed provision excepted injuries incurred by persons, ships, or property in transit through the Panama Canal and is now covered by the more broadly worded exception "m."

(j) Any claim arising out of the combatant activities of the military or naval forces, or the Coast Guard, during time of war.

(k) Any claim arising in a foreign country.

(*l*) Any claim arising from the activities of the Tennessee Valley Authority.

(m) Any claim arising from the activities of the Panama Canal Company.

(n) Any claim arising from the activities of a Federal land bank, a Federal intermediate credit bank, or a bank for cooperatives.

Notes

1. We have already had occasion to discuss the background to the amendment of exception "h" in 1974, at p. 1296, *supra*. In 1988, Congress declared that exception "h" "shall not apply to any claim arising out of a negligent or wrongful act or omission of * * * [medical personnel of the Department of Veterans affairs] while furnishing medical care or treatment * * *" 38 U.S.C. § 4116(f).

The Court has made clear that, while the Government cannot be liable for intentional torts committed by government employees who are not law enforcement officers, it may be liable if its negligence makes possible the commission of an intentional tort by a government employee. *See* Sheridan v. United States, 487 U.S. 392, 108 S.Ct. 2449, 101 L.Ed.2d 352 (1988). In that case a person who had been shot by an obviously intoxicated off-duty serviceman brought an action against the Government alleging that the Government was negligent in allowing the serviceman to leave the hospital with a loaded rifle in his possession. The Court ruled that such an action was not one arising out of an assault or battery within the meaning of exception "h." In an earlier case, United States v. Shearer, 473 U.S. 52, 105 S.Ct. 3039, 87 L.Ed.2d 38 (1985), four Justices had expressed the contrary view, namely that the assault or battery exception could not be avoided by couching the complaint in terms of negligent supervision. The three dissenting Justices in *Sheridan* (Justice O'Connor, joined by Chief Justice Rehnquist and Justice Scalia) urged the reaffirmation of that position.

2. *Shearer, supra,* involved a wrongful death action brought by the mother of a soldier who had been kidnapped and murdered by a fellow serviceman. The Court was unanimous in holding that the Government was not liable under the doctrine of Feres v. United States, 340 U.S. 135, 71 S.Ct. 153, 95 L.Ed. 152 (1950), namely that the Tort Claims Act does not permit a serviceman to bring an action for injuries that "arise out of or are [incurred] in the course of activity incident to service." Most of the Court did not feel obligated to speculate on the scope of exception "h." The *Feres*, doctrine was also applied in United States v. Johnson, 481 U.S. 681, 107 S.Ct. 2063, 95 L.Ed.2d 648 (1987). In Taber v. United States, 45 F.3d 598 (2d Cir.1995), the court includes an interesting survey of the history and evolution of the *Feres* doctrine.

3. 28 U.S.C. §§ 2671–79 are the other provisions of the "Tort Claims Procedure" (ch. 171, Title 28 of the United States Code). These provisions were also part of the Federal Tort Claims Act of 1946 although there have been significant amendments since 1946. We shall discuss some of these provisions in the succeeding notes.

4. Under 28 U.S.C. § 2679(b)(1), if the tort arises from acts or omissions of a government employee acting within the scope of employment, the remedy against the United States is exclusive. The federal employee is immunized from state tort liability. *Cf.* Barr v. Matteo, 360 U.S. 564, 79 S.Ct. 1335, 3 L.Ed.2d 1434 (1959). The Supreme Court, in Westfall v. Erwin, 484 U.S. 292, 108 S.Ct. 580, 98 L.Ed.2d 619 (1988), had held that the immunity described in *Barr* would only apply if the employee's alleged negligence was not only in the scope of employment, but also involved an element of discretionary behavior. The Court rejected the government's argument for absolute immunity in all circumstances. Congress immediately responded by amending § 2679(b) in 1988 which, in its present form as just noted, makes the action against the United States the exclusive remedy. *See also* the discussion at p. 1296f, *supra.* An exclusive remedy for actions arising out of the operation of a motor vehicle was first added in 1961 and then, as just noted, extended to other actions in 1988. The exclusive remedy against the government provided by U.S.C. § 2679(b) has, since 1988, been expressly declared not to prevent civil actions against government employees for violations of the Constitution or for violations of federal statutes. 28 U.S.C. § 2679(b)(2). There is a similar exclusive remedy provision with regard to malpractice actions brought against the Veterans Administration. 38 U.S.C. § 7316(a). A judgment in an action against the United States has always been a complete bar to a similar tort action against the employee. 28 U.S.C. § 2676. The statutory provisions making the remedy against the United States exclusive operate to prevent an action against the negligent employee even in situations in which an action against the United States is precluded by one of the exclusions contained in 28 U.S.C. § 2680, such as that the tort occurred in a foreign country. *See* United States v. Smith, 499 U.S. 160, 111 S.Ct. 1180, 113 L.Ed.2d 134 (1991).

5. 28 U.S.C. § 2672 retained the authorization contained in the Small Tort Claims Act of 1922 to settle administratively claims against the United States. The limit on claims was raised to $2,500 in 1959. Then, in 1966, the upper limit on the amount of administrative settlements was removed and submission of claims for administrative settlement became mandatory. 28 U.S.C. § 2675(a). Settlements by agency heads are now to be made in accordance with regulations prescribed by the Attorney General and all settlements "in excess of $25,000" must be approved by the Attorney General or a designee of the Attorney General. 28 C.F.R. § 14.10 (1996). The Attorney General had already been granted authority in 1948, to "arbitrate, compromise or settle any claim * * * after the commencement of an action thereon." 28 U.S.C. § 2677. Administrative settlements of $2,500 or less are paid out of the agency's appropriation; settlements in excess of $2,500, as well as all settlements of pending court cases made by the Attorney General, are paid in the same way that court judgments are paid which is, namely, under a standing appropriation under 31 U.S.C. § 1304. Payment is secured by filing a copy of the judgment with the General Accounting Office. Prior to 1977, the standing appropriation only covered judgments not in excess of $100,000. Thus, prior to 1977, any judgment for more than $100,000 could only be paid after Congress had specifically appropriated the money to pay the judgment in question.

6. All claims brought under the Federal Tort Claims Act must be filed with the appropriate federal agency within two years after the claim accrues. 28 U.S.C. § 2401(b). Since, as noted, the Act now allows administrative settlement of claims, regardless of amount, the statute of limitations for any claim presented to a federal agency within the two-year period is tolled for a

period of six months after the claim is denied by the agency. For a discussion of the mechanics of presenting claims against the federal government, *see* D. Tillman, *Presenting a Claim under the Federal Tort Claims Act*, 43 La.L.Rev. 961 (1983); Note *Federal Tort Claims Act: Notice of Claim Requirement*, 67 Minn.L.Rev. 513 (1982).

7. If the plaintiff obtains an award of damages under the Federal Tort Claims Act, the Act limits attorneys' fees to 25% of the judgment or settlement obtained in an action filed in the courts and to 20% of the award obtained on claims settled administratively. 28 U.S.C. § 2678. Prior to 1966, the limits were 20% for court cases and 10% for claims settled administratively. It is a crime, punishable by fine of up to $2,000 or imprisonment of up to one year or both, for an attorney to demand or receive a greater fee.

8. In Molzof v. United States, 502 U.S. 301, 112 S.Ct. 711, 116 L.Ed.2d 731 (1992), the Court held that the prohibition on awarding punitive damages, contained in § 2674, did not preclude a claim for damages for future medical expenses, even though the claimant (who died while the appeal was pending) was eligible for free treatment in a Veteran's Administration hospital, or for loss of enjoyment of life, if those damages were available under the applicable state law. The Court said that Congress intended the exception to apply only to "punitive damages" as understood under traditional common law principles—based upon intentional or egregious misconduct and the purpose of which is to punish.

LAIRD v. NELMS

Supreme Court of the United States, 1972.
406 U.S. 797, 92 S.Ct. 1899, 32 L.Ed.2d 499.

Mr. Justice Rehnquist delivered the opinion of the Court.

Respondents brought this action in the United States District Court under the Federal Tort Claims Act, 28 U.S.C. §§ 1346(b), 2671–2680. They sought recovery for property damage allegedly resulting from a sonic boom caused by California-based United States military planes flying over North Carolina on a training mission. The District Court entered summary judgment for petitioners, but on respondents' appeal the United States Court of Appeals for the Fourth Circuit reversed. That court held that, although respondents had been unable to show negligence "either in the planning or operation of the flight," they were nonetheless entitled to proceed on a theory of strict or absolute liability for ultrahazardous activities conducted by petitioners in their official capacities. That court relied on its earlier opinion in United States v. Praylou, 208 F.2d 291 (1953), which in turn had distinguished this Court's holding in Dalehite v. United States, 346 U.S. 15 (1953). We granted certiorari. * * *

Dalehite held that the Government was not liable for the extensive damage resulting from the explosion of two cargo vessels in the harbor of Texas City, Texas, in 1947. The Court's opinion rejected various specifications of negligence on the part of Government employees that had been found by the District Court in that case, and then went on to treat petitioners' claim that the Government was absolutely or strictly liable because of its having engaged in a dangerous activity. The Court said with respect to this aspect of the plaintiffs' claim:

"[T]he Act does not extend to such situations, though of course well known in tort law generally. It is to be invoked only on a 'negligent or wrongful act or omission' of an employee. Absolute liability, of course, arises irrespective of how the tortfeasor conducts himself; it is imposed automatically when any damages are sustained as a result of the decision to engage in the dangerous activity." 346 U.S. at 44, 73 S.Ct. at 972.

This Court's resolution of the strict-liability issue in Dalehite did not turn on the question of whether the law of Texas or of some other State did or did not recognize strict liability for the conduct of ultrahazardous activities. It turned instead on the question of whether the language of the Federal Tort Claims Act permitted under any circumstances the imposition of liability upon the Government where there had been neither negligence nor wrongful act. The necessary consequence of the Court's holding in Dalehite is that the statutory language "negligent or wrongful act or omission of any employee of the Government," is a uniform federal limitation on the types of acts committed by its employees for which the United States has consented to be sued. Regardless of state law characterization, the Federal Tort Claims Act itself precludes the imposition of liability if there has been no negligence or other form of "misfeasance or nonfeasance," 346 U.S. at 45, 73 S.Ct. at 972, on the part of the Government.

It is at least theoretically possible to argue that since Dalehite in discussing the legislative history of the Act said that "wrongful" acts could include some kind of trespass, and since courts imposed liability in some of the early blasting cases on the theory that the plaintiff's action sounded in trespass, liability could be imposed on the Government in this case on a theory of trespass which would be within the Act's waiver of immunity. We believe, however, that there is more than one reason for rejecting such an alternate basis of governmental liability here.

The notion that a military plane on a high-altitude training flight itself intrudes upon any property interest of an owner of the land over which it flies was rejected in United States v. Causby, 328 U.S. 256, 66 S.Ct. 1062, 90 L.Ed. 1206 (1946). There this Court, construing the Air Commerce Act of 1926, 44 Stat. 568, as amended by the Civil Aeronautics Act of 1938, 52 Stat. 973, 49 U.S.C. § 401, said:

"It is ancient doctrine that at common law ownership of the land extended to the periphery of the universe—*Cujus est solum ejus est usque ad coelum*. But that doctrine has no place in the modern world. The air is a public highway, as Congress has declared. Were that not true, every transcontinental flight would subject the operator to countless trespass suits. Common sense revolts at the idea. To recognize such private claims to the airspace would clog these highways, seriously interfere with their control and development in the public interest, and transfer into private ownership that to which only the public has a just claim." 328 U.S. at 260–261, 66 S.Ct., at 1065.

Thus, quite apart from what would very likely be insuperable problems of proof in connecting the passage of the plane over the owner's air space with any ensuing damage from a sonic boon, this version of the trespass theory is ruled out by established federal law. Perhaps the precise holding of United States v. Causby, supra, could be skirted by analogizing the pressure wave of air characterizing a sonic boom to the concussion that on occasion accompanies blasting, and treating the air wave striking the actual land of the property owner as a direct intrusion caused by the pilot of the plane in the mold of the classical common-law theory of trespass.

It is quite clear, however, that the presently prevailing view as to the theory of liability for blasting damage is frankly conceded to be strict liability for undertaking an ultrahazardous activity, rather than any attenuated notion of common-law trespass. * * *

More importantly, however, Congress in considering the Federal Tort Claims Act cannot realistically be said to have dealt in terms of either the jurisprudential distinctions peculiar to the forms of action at common law or the metaphysical subtleties that crop up in even contemporary discussions of tort theory. * * * The legislative history discussed in Dalehite indicates that Congress intended to permit liability essentially based on the intentionally wrongful or careless conduct of Government employees, for which the Government was to be made liable according to state law under the doctrine of respondeat superior, but to exclude liability based solely on the ultrahazardous nature of an activity undertaken by the Government.

A House Judiciary Committee memorandum explaining the "discretionary function" exemption from the bill when that exemption first appeared in the draft legislation in 1942 made the comment that "the cases covered by that subsection would probably have been exempted * * * by judicial construction" in any event, but that the exemption was intended to preclude any possibility "that the act would be construed to authorize suit for damages against the Government growing out of a legally authorized activity, such as a flood-control or irrigation project, where no wrongful act or omission on the part of any Government agent is shown, and the only ground for suit is the contention that the same conduct by a private individual would be tortious * * *." Hearings on HR 5373 and HR 6463 before the House Committee on the Judiciary, 77th Cong., 2d Sess., ser. 13, pp. 65–66 (1942).

Shortly after the decision of this Court in Dalehite, the facts of the Texas city catastrophe were presented to Congress in an effort to obtain legislative relief from that body. Congress, after conducting hearings and receiving reports, ultimately enacted a bill granting compensation to the victims in question. * * * At no time during these hearings was there any effort made to modify this Court's construction of the Tort Claims Act in Dalehite. Both by reason of stare decisis and by reason of Congress' failure to make any statutory change upon again reviewing the subject, we regard the principle enunciated in Dalehite as controlling here.

Since Dalehite held that the Federal Tort Claims Act did not authorize suit against the Government on claims based on strict liability for ultrahazardous activity, the Court of Appeals in the instant case erred in reaching a contrary conclusion. * * *

Our reaffirmation of the construction put on the Federal Tort Claims Act in Dalehite makes it unnecessary to treat the scope of the discretionary-function exemption contained in the Act, or the other matters dealt with by the Court of Appeals.

Reversed.

Mr. Justice Douglas, having heard the argument, withdrew from participation in the consideration or decision of this case.

Mr. Justice Stewart, with whom Mr. Justice Brennan joins, dissenting.

While the doctrine of absolute liability is not encountered in many situations even under modern tort law, it was nevertheless well established at the time the Tort Claims Act was enacted, and there is nothing in the language or the history of the Act to support the notion that this doctrine alone, among all the rules governing tort liability in the various States, was considered inapplicable in cases arising under the Act. The legislative history quoted by the Court relates solely to the "discretionary function" exception contained in § 2680, an exception upon which the Court specifically declines to rely. As I read the Act and the legislative history, the phrase "negligent or wrongful act or omission" was intended to include the entire range of conduct classified as tortious under state law. The only intended exceptions to this sweeping waiver of governmental immunity were those expressly set forth and now collected in § 2680. * * *

The rule announced by the Court today seems to me contrary to the whole policy of the Tort Claims Act. For the doctrine of absolute liability is applicable not only to sonic booms, but to other activities that the Government carries on in common with many private citizens. Absolute liability for injury caused by the concussion or debris from dynamite blasting, for example, is recognized by an overwhelming majority of state courts. A private person who detonates an explosion in the process of building a road is liable for injuries to others caused thereby under the law of most States even though he took all practicable precautions to prevent such injuries, on the sound principle that he who creates such a hazard should make good the harm that results. Yet if employees of the United States engage in exactly the same conduct with an identical result, the United States will not, under the principle announced by the Court today, be liable to the injured party. Nothing in the language or the legislative history of the Act compels such a result, and we should not lightly conclude that Congress intended to create a situation so much at odds with common sense and the basic rationale of the Act. * * *

For the reasons stated, I would hold that the doctrine of absolute liability is applicable to conduct of employees of the United States under the same circumstances as those in which it is applied to the conduct of private persons under the law of the State where the conduct occurs. That holding would not by itself be dispositive of this case, however, for the petitioners argue that liability is precluded by the "discretionary function" exception in the Act. While the Court does not reach this issue, I shall state briefly the reasons for my conclusion that the exception is inapplicable in this case.

No right of action lies under the Tort Claims Act for any claim "based upon an act or omission of an employee of the Government, exercising due care, in the execution of a statute or regulation, whether or not such statute or regulation be valid, or based upon the exercise or performance or the failure to exercise or perform a discretionary function or duty on the part of a federal agency or an employee of the Government, whether or not the discretion involved be abused." 28 U.S.C. § 2680(a).

The Assistant Attorney General who testified on the bill before the House committee indicated that this provision was intended to create no exceptions beyond those that courts would probably create without it * * *.

The Dalehite opinion seemed to say that no action of a Government employee could be made the basis for liability under the Act if the action involved "policy judgment and decision." 346 U.S., at 36, 73 S.Ct., at 968. Decisions in the courts of appeals following Dalehite have interpreted this language as drawing a distinction between "policy" and "operational" decisions, with the latter falling outside the exception. That distinction has bedeviled the courts that have attempted to apply it to torts outside routine categories such as automobile accidents, but there is no need in the present case to explore the limits of the discretionary function exception.

The legislative history indicates that the purpose of this statutory exception was to avoid any possibility that policy decisions of Congress, of the Executive, or of administrative agencies would be second-guessed by courts in the context of tort actions. There is no such danger in this case, for liability does not depend upon a judgment as to whether Government officials acted irresponsibly or illegally. Rather, once the creation of sonic booms is determined to be an activity as to which the doctrine of absolute liability applies, the only questions for the court relate to causation and damages. Whether or not the decision to fly a military aircraft over the respondents' property, at a given altitude and at a speed three times the speed of sound, was a decision at the "policy" or the "operational" level, the propriety of that decision is irrelevant to the question of liability in this case, and thus the discretionary function exception does not apply.

Notes

1. Dalehite v. United States, 346 U.S. 15, 73 S.Ct. 956, 97 L.Ed. 1427 (1953), was "a test case representing some 300 separate personal and property claims in the aggregate amount of two hundred million dollars," 346 U.S. at 17, 73 S.Ct. at 959, consolidated for trial in the Southern District of Texas. The district court found for the plaintiffs but the Court of Appeals for the Fifth Circuit reversed. In a 4–3 decision, with two Justices (Clark and Douglas) not participating, the Supreme Court affirmed the court of appeals. Justice Reed wrote the opinion of the Court and was joined by Chief Justice Vinson and Justices Burton and Minton. Justice Jackson wrote for the dissenters and was joined by Justices Black and Frankfurter. The claims arose when fertilizer loaded on two ships in Texas City, Texas for shipment to France, as part of the Marshall Plan program, exploded and literally levelled the town and killed many people. *Inter alia*, the complaint alleged negligence in the storage and loading of the fertilizer. As noted in Justice Rehnquist's opinion for the Court in *Laird v. Nelms*, Congress passed an act to compensate the victims of the disaster. 69 Stat. 707 (1955). Under the act, however, the maximum amount that could be paid on any claim, whether for property damage or personal injury or wrongful death was $25,000, a grossly inadequate sum for those suffering major damage.

2. A few years after the *Dalehite* case, the Court decided another frequently-cited case construing the Federal Tort Claims Act. In that case, Indian Towing Co. v. United States, 350 U.S. 61, 76 S.Ct. 122, 100 L.Ed. 48 (1955), the plaintiffs claimed damages for cargo that had been damaged when a tugboat towing a barge went aground owing to the alleged negligence of the Coast Guard in maintaining a navigation light on the upper Mississippi. The district court dismissed and the Fifth Circuit affirmed. In a 5–4 decision, the Court, writing through Justice Frankfurter, reversed. The fact that private parties did not engage in the activity in question did not preclude liability under the Federal Tort Claims Act. The Government argued that 28 U.S.C. § 2674, *supra* p. 1318, imposing liability "in the same manner and to the same extent as a private individual under like circumstances * * *" precluded this result. By this time Chief Justice Vinson had died and been succeeded by Chief Justice Warren. The three remaining members of the *Dalehite* majority dissented in an opinion written by Justice Reed. They were joined by Justice Clark who had not participated in *Dalehite*.

3. Determination of what is a discretionary function under 28 U.S.C. § 2680(a) has proved to be a difficult task. See United States v. Gaubert, 499 U.S. 315, 111 S.Ct. 1267, 113 L.Ed.2d 335 (1991), in which the Supreme Court held that the action was immune if it involved any significant element of discretion, even if the action was at the "ministerial" level, not the policy making level. An important and illuminating case is Payton v. United States, 679 F.2d 475 (en banc 5th Cir. Unit B[7] 1982). In that case the complaint alleged that a federal prisoner who had been convicted of "attacking or ravishing multiple females of all ages" was released from custody despite extensive medical reports describing him as a homicidal psychotic. Shortly after his release, he brutally murdered and horribly mutilated three women including the appellant's decedent. The district court granted the government's motion to dismiss on the ground that it lacked jurisdiction because the conduct involved the exercise of a "discretionary function." 468 F.Supp. 651 (S.D.Ala.1979). This ruling was reversed 636 F.2d 132 (5th Cir.1981). Establishing guidelines for the release of federal prisoners was a discretionary function but the application of those guidelines to concrete cases was not. The panel noted that in 1973 the Federal Parole Board had replaced earlier guidelines, which had focussed upon a relatively unstructured assessment of the extent of a prisoner's rehabilitation, with guidelines requiring construction of a matrix focusing on the severity of the crime and nine personal characteristics statistically determined to bear on the risk of repeat behavior. The panel observed, as had previous courts, that, if *Dalehite* were taken literally, any federal official with decision-making power would be performing a discretionary function. *Dalehite,* accordingly, could not be interpreted in such an absolute fashion. The panel noted that the attempt to interpret discretionary function by distinguishing between the planning level and the operational level was not particularly helpful in deciding difficult cases because the distinction was conclusory. A rehearing en banc was then successfully sought by the United States. While the divided en banc court, per Hatchett, J., agreed that the complaint stated a cause of action, it held that the Government's only possible liability arose from its alleged failure to consult its own records and its alleged

---

7. This case arose in what is now the Eleventh Circuit. The old Fifth Circuit was divided on October 1, 1981. Cases submitted for decision prior to that date were handled "as though this Act had not been enacted."

P.L. 96–452, Oct. 14, 1980, § 9(3), 94 Stat. 1995. Petitions for rehearing en banc in such cases "shall be reheard as if the Act had not been enacted." *Ibid.*

failure to ascertain the nature and extent of the prisoner's mental problems. The decision to release the prisoner was the exercise of a discretionary function that could not be challenged. Fay, J., the writer of the panel opinion, and two other judges dissented from the retreat from the panel decision. Tjoflat, J., and three other judges dissented from the recognition of any possible cause of action.

4. The *Payton* case is a difficult one. The notion underlying 28 U.S.C. § 2680(a) is that there is some core of governmental activity that is beyond any sort of judicial examination. Taking the cliche that the state is *"parens patriae,"* the discretionary power of the government over the citizenry has an analogue in the discretion a parent may exercise in the upbringing of a child. As we shall see in section C, *infra,* even in jurisdictions in which an unemancipated minor may bring an action against its parents, a parent is not legally answerable for choosing where to live or for deciding not to send the child to private school even if the parent can afford to do so.

5. The original panel in *Payton* referred to Cohen v. United States, 252 F.Supp. 679 (N.D.Ga.1966), *reversed on other grounds* 389 F.2d 689 (5th Cir.1967), and Fleishour v. United States, 244 F.Supp. 762 (N.D.Ill.1965), *affirmed* 365 F.2d 126 (7th Cir.), *certiorari denied* 385 U.S. 987, 87 S.Ct. 597, 17 L.Ed.2d 448 (1966), in which prisoners were allowed to bring an action against the United States for the negligence of prison officials in protecting the plaintiffs against assaults by other prisoners. The panel also referred to Fair v. United States, 234 F.2d 288 (5th Cir.1956), in which wrongful death actions were successfully brought for the deaths of three persons who were shot by a homicidal, mentally disturbed Air Force officer who had been allegedly negligently released from an Air Force hospital. Are these cases distinguishable from *Payton?* The Eleventh Circuit, en banc, in *Payton,* distinguished the *Fair* case on the ground that it involved not the decision to treat the officer but rather negligence in treating an officer whom the government had undertaken to treat.

6. The court in *Payton* also referred to Johnson v. State of California, 69 Cal.2d 782, 73 Cal.Rptr. 240, 447 P.2d 352 (1968), and Tarasoff v. Regents of the University of California, 17 Cal.3d 425, 131 Cal.Rptr. 14, 551 P.2d 334 (1976). It did not, however, refer to Thompson v. County of Alameda, 27 Cal.3d 741, 167 Cal.Rptr. 70, 614 P.2d 728 (1980), reprinted at p. 473, *supra,* in which the Supreme Court of California discussed *Johnson* and *Tarasoff* and held that the county was immune from liability for deciding to release a juvenile offender and in selecting the juvenile's mother as his custodian. Is the *Payton* case distinguishable from *Thompson? See also,* Hurst v. Ohio Dep't of Rehabilitation. & Correction, 72 Ohio St.3d 325, 650 N.E.2d 104 (1995). The Ohio court held that the public duty doctrine immunized the parole decision process and the manner in which parole violations should be handled.

7. Compare two cases involving accidents in Yellowstone National Park. In Smith v. United States, 546 F.2d 872 (10th Cir.1976), a fourteen year old boy fell into a super-heated thermal pool. The district court held for the United States on the grounds that the plaintiff sought to hold the government liable for the exercise of a discretionary function and that furthermore the boy's recovery was barred by contributory negligence. The court of appeals disagreed on the discretionary function aspect of the case. Even if the decision to leave the section of the park in which the injury occurred as an "'undeveloped' natural area" was the exercise of a discretionary function, the decision

not to post warning signs in the area was not the exercise of a discretionary function. The court of appeals nevertheless upheld the district court's conclusion that the action was barred by the plaintiff's contributory negligence. Martin v. United States, 546 F.2d 1355 (9th Cir.1976), *certiorari denied* 432 U.S. 906, 97 S.Ct. 2950, 53 L.Ed.2d 1078 (1977), involved the death of a hitchhiker who was killed by a grizzly bear. The government's liability was premised upon the decision to close the garbage dumps at which the grizzly bears had been feeding. In reversing a judgment in favor of the plaintiffs, the court of appeals held that the decision to close the dumps was made at the planning level. The court also noted that the deceased, who had not paid the required visitor's fee, had disregarded advice to go to the Ranger Station or the Visitor's Center and had camped in an unauthorized place. This showed that the plaintiff and his companion put themselves in a position in which they could not receive any warning. Furthermore the facts showed that the deceased had been contributorily negligent.

8. The Court reaffirmed the validity of *Dalehite* in United States v. S.A. Empresa de Viacao Aerea Rio Grandense (Varig Airlines), 467 U.S. 797, 104 S.Ct. 2755, 81 L.Ed.2d 660 (1984), a consolidation of two cases. The plaintiffs in *Varig* sought damages from the United States on the ground that the Federal Aviation Authority and its predecessor had been negligent in issuing type certificates for two types of aircraft. The claim was based on the contention that the planes were certified although they did not comply with certain FAA regulations, in one case regulations concerning the lavatory trash receptacle and, in the other, regulations concerning gasoline burning cabin heaters. In both cases, a substantial number of lives were lost owing to fire which engulfed the aircraft. The Court unanimously held that the discretionary function exception precluded a tort action based upon the FAA's conduct in certifying the aircraft in question for use in commercial aviation. The Court noted that the FAA relied principally on the employees of the aircraft manufacturers to comply with its regulations in the design of aircraft. The FAA's decision to utilize a "spot-check" program for reviewing the information supplied by the aircraft manufacturers was an exercise of discretion and could not be challenged in the Court. The claim that, in administering this spot-check program, the FAA's inspectors failed to check particular items was also barred by the discretionary function exception. The Court's decision in *Varig* was heavily relied upon in Allen v. United States, 816 F.2d 1417 (10th Cir.1987), *cert. denied* 484 U.S. 1004, 108 S.Ct. 694, 98 L.Ed.2d 647 (1988). In *Allen* "nearly 1200 named plaintiffs * * * sued the United States alleging some 500 deaths and injuries as a result of radioactive fall-out from open-air atomic bomb tests held in Nevada in the 1950s and 1960s." The district court "selected and tried twenty-four 'bellwether' claims, in order to find a common framework for the rest." In a 225 page opinion the district court entered judgment in favor of the Government in fourteen of the claims and against the Government in nine, with one claim left outstanding. On appeal by the Government, the Tenth Circuit reversed. The Atomic Energy Commission had statutory authority, subject to annual presidential authorization, to "conduct experiments * * * in the military application of atomic energy." In making these tests the AEC was "authorized and directed to make arrangements * * * for the protection of health * * *." The court held that, in conducting these tests, the AEC was exercising a discretionary function and that, therefore, an action against the United States for damages allegedly arising out of these tests was barred by the doctrine of sovereign immunity. The Supreme Court has

made it clear, however, that the mere fact that an agency is exercising a regulatory function does not automatically immunize the United States from liability. Failure of agency personnel to follow applicable requirements established by statute or regulation can be the basis for an action under the Federal Tort Claims Act. *See* Berkovitz v. United States, 486 U.S. 531, 108 S.Ct. 1954, 100 L.Ed.2d 531 (1988). Applying the test set forth in *Berkovitz*, the court in Domme v. United States, 61 F.3d 787 (10th Cir.1995), held that an employee of a federal contractor could not sue on a claim that a laboratory workplace was unsafe because the charges fell within the discretionary function exception.

2. *Suits Against the States*

The doctrine of sovereign immunity was also invoked by the various states. As the role of government became more pronounced the pressures to abolish the state's immunity from suit increased. The first abolitions of sovereign immunity were by statute. New York, one of the earliest states to abolish sovereign immunity, did so in 1920. In what is now N.Y.Jud.Ct. of Claims Act § 8 (McKinney), "[t]he state hereby waives its immunity from liability and action and hereby assumes liability and consents to have the same determined in accordance with the same rules of law as apply to actions in the supreme court against individuals or corporations * * *." In other states abolition was more gradual with the initial steps being confined to the waiver of sovereign immunity in a limited number of situations such as the dangerous condition of public property or the negligent operation of motor vehicles. Those dissatisfied with the pace of legislative modification of the common-law doctrines gradually turned to the courts. The courts in many states had already developed a distinction between so-called proprietary functions and governmental functions. This doctrine developed primarily in connection with the immunity of municipalities and other units of local government, but it was sometimes also applied against the states. We shall discuss the distinction between so-called governmental and proprietary functions at p. 1339f, *infra*. Increasingly, however, litigants sought the complete abolition of sovereign immunity by judicial decision. One of the earliest and most famous judicial abolitions of sovereign immunity was Muskopf v. Corning Hosp. Dist., 55 Cal.2d 211, 11 Cal.Rptr. 89, 359 P.2d 457 (1961). The decision in *Muskopf* eventually led in 1963 to the adoption of a comprehensive legislative treatment of the subject (West's Cal.Gov.Code Ann. § 810 *et seq.*), portions of which will be presented below.

In the last thirty years the momentum for change has increased. At the present time, over three-fourths of the states have either totally abolished the doctrine of sovereign immunity or substantially modified it. In many states the courts have taken the lead as they did in California, after which the legislature responded with some kind of tort claims act. For example, the Kansas legislature initially responded to the judicial abrogation of sovereign and other governmental immunity in Carroll v. Kittle, 203 Kan. 841, 457 P.2d 21 (1969), by re-establishing sovereign immunity except where liability is imposed by statute, but it did not re-establish the governmental immunity of lesser units of government. L.1970, c. 200. The constitutionality of this statute was upheld in Brown v. Wichita State Univ., 219 Kan. 2, 547 P.2d 1015 (1976), *appeal dismissed for want of jurisdiction* 429 U.S. 806, 97 S.Ct. 41, 50 L.Ed.2d 67 (1976). The unsuccessful claim was, *inter alia,* that the distinction between suits against the state and suits against local government was irrational. Kansas then subsequently enacted a comprehensive tort claims act applicable to the state and to local governmental entities. Kan.Stat.Ann. 75–6101–6115.

Another example is Mayle v. Pennsylvania Dept. of Highways, 479 Pa. 384, 388 A.2d 709 (1978), which was followed by a statute declaring that "* * * the Commonwealth and its officials and employees acting within the scope of their duties shall continue to enjoy sovereign and official immunity from suit except as the General Assembly shall specifically waive the immunity * * *." 1 Pa.Cons.Stat.Ann. § 2310 (Purdon). At the same time, the General Assembly waived sovereign immunity for a limited number of tort claims. These are now contained in 42 Pa.Cons.Stat.Ann. §§ 8521–28 (Purdon). The types of claims for which sovereign immunity were waived were: vehicle liability; medical/professional liability; care, custody or control of personal property; injuries arising out of a condition of real estate owned by the Commonwealth and of commonwealth roads, but any liability for the condition of highways arising from pot holes or sink holes or other similar conditions created by natural elements is limited to personal injury; injuries arising out of the care and custody of animals, not including injuries caused by wild animals except as otherwise provided; injuries arising out of sales of liquor by the Pennsylvania Liquor Control Board in violation of the Pennsylvania Dram Shop Act; injuries caused by acts of members of the Pennsylvania National Guard; and in certain circumstances, injuries from "toxoids and vaccines" distributed by the Commonwealth. Damages are limited to a maximum of $250,000 for any one claimant and $1 Million in aggregate for any one incident. There are similar provisions concerning the governmental immunity of local governmental units. 42 Pa.Cons.Stat.Ann. §§ 8541–42, 8553 (Purdon). Liability is limited to an aggregate of $500,000 for any one incident. The constitutionality of this legislation, which continues municipal immunity for claims not specifically provided for, was upheld in Carroll v. County of York, 496 Pa. 363, 437 A.2d 394 (1981).

The Missouri legislature responded more drastically to the judicial abolition of sovereign immunity in Jones v. State Highway Comm'n, 557 S.W.2d 225 (Mo.1977). In Vernon's Ann.Mo.Stat. § 537.600 it re-imposed immunity for both the state itself and for other units of government except with regard to claims arising from automobile accidents or out of the dangerous condition of government property. It also permitted governmental entities to buy insurance to cover tort claims and waived immunity to the extent they had done so. In all situations where a suit is permitted, either because the claim involves an automobile accident or the dangerous condition of governmental property or because insurance has been obtained, the maximum liability is $100,000 per person and $1,000,000 per accident. Vernon's Ann.Mo.Stat. § 537.610. North Dakota is the most recent state in which its supreme court abolished sovereign immunity. Bulman v. Hulstrand Constr. Co., 521 N.W.2d 632 (N.D.1994). The legislative response is discussed in Case Comment, *Sovereign Immunity*, 71 N.D.L.Rev. 761 (1995).

There are a few states that still purport to uphold the doctrine of sovereign immunity. For example, the Arkansas constitution declares that "[t]he State of Arkansas shall never be made defendant in any of her courts." Ark.Const.Art. 5, § 20. By statute, the same immunity is given to all governmental subdivisions. Ark.Stat. § 21–9–301. As a practical matter, however, it is impossible totally to immunize a governmental entity from all claims that may be filed against it, nor is it practical to require such claimants to resort to special legislation, which in many cases is difficult to obtain because of state constitutional prohibitions against private acts, an inhibition which is not contained in the U.S. Constitution. Thus, despite the assertion of complete immunity which we have just noted, Arkansas provides for a state claims commission which is authorized to indemnify state employees for all actual damages, but not punitive damages, which they may be obliged to pay owing to acts committed in the course of their official duties. Ark.Stat. § 21–9–202. Moreover, units of local government are required to maintain liability insurance and are authorized to settle tort claims made against them. Ark.Stat. §§ 21–9–302, 303.

A number of states other than those already mentioned have limitations on the amount of damages recoverable. *See, e.g.,* Ill.—S.H.A. ch. 705, § 5⁰⅝ ($100,000 per claimant other than claims arising out of the operation of motor vehicles); Me.Rev.Stat.Ann. tit. 14, § 8105 ($300,000 aggregate per occurrence); N.C.Gen.Stat. § 143–291(a) ($150,000 per injured person).

CALIFORNIA GOVERNMENT CODE ANNOTATED (WEST)

DIVISION 3.6 CLAIMS AND ACTIONS AGAINST PUBLIC ENTITIES AND PUBLIC EMPLOYEES
Stat. 1963, c. 1681

PART 2, CHAPTER 1
ARTICLE 2
LIABILITY OF PUBLIC ENTITIES

§ 815. Liability for injuries generally; immunity of public entity; defenses

Except as otherwise provided by statute:

(a) A public entity is not liable for an injury, whether such injury arises out of an act or omission of the public entity or a public employee or any other person.

(b) The liability of a public entity established by this part (commencing with Section 814) is subject to any immunity of the public entity provided by statute, including this part, and is subject to any defenses that would be available to the public entity if it were a private person.

§ 815.2. Injuries by employee within scope of employment; immunity of employee

(a) A public entity is liable for injury proximately caused by an act or omission of an employee of the public entity within the scope of his employment if the act or omission would, apart from this section, have given rise to a cause of action against that employee or his personal representative.

(b) Except as otherwise provided by statute, a public entity is not liable for an injury resulting from an act or omission of an employee of the public entity where the employee is immune from liability.

§ 815.4. Injuries by independent contractors

A public entity is liable for injury proximately caused by a tortious act or omission of an independent contractor of the public entity to the same extent that the public entity would be subject to such liability if it were a private person. Nothing in this section subjects a public entity to liability for the act or omission of an independent contractor if the public entity would not have been liable for the injury had the act or omission been that of an employee of the public entity.

§ 815.6. Mandatory duty of public entity to protect against particular kinds of injuries

Where a public entity is under a mandatory duty imposed by an enactment that is designed to protect against the risk of a particular kind of injury, the public entity is liable for an injury of that kind proximately caused by its failure to discharge the duty unless the public entity establishes that it exercised reasonable diligence to discharge the duty.

Law Revision Commission Comment

This section declares the familiar rule, applicable to both public entities and private persons, that failure to comply with applicable statutory or regulatory standards is negligence unless reasonable diligence has been exercised in an effort to comply with those standards. * * *

In the sections that follow in this division, there are stated some immunities from this general rule of liability. See, for example, Section 818.2.

§ 818. Exemplary damages

Notwithstanding any other provision of law, a public entity is not liable for damages awarded under Section 3294 of the Civil Code or other damages imposed primarily for the sake of example and by way of punishing the defendant.

§ 818.2. Adoption or failure to adopt or enforce enactment

A public entity is not liable for an injury caused by adopting or failing to adopt an enactment or by failing to enforce any law.

(Added by Stats.1963, c. 1681, p. 3268, § 1.)

Law Revision Commission Comment

This section would be unnecessary except for a possible implication that might arise from Section 815.6, which imposes liability upon public entities for failure to exercise reasonable diligence to comply with a mandatory duty imposed by an enactment. This section recognizes that the wisdom of legislative or quasi-legislative action, and the discretion of law enforcement officers in carrying out their duties, should not be subject to review in tort suits for damages if political responsibility for these decisions is to be retained.

The New York courts recognize a similar immunity in the absence of statute. Under the Federal Tort Claims Act, this immunity falls within the general immunity for discretionary acts.[8]

§ 818.4. Issuance, denial, suspension or revocation of permit, license, etc.

A public entity is not liable for an injury caused by the issuance, denial, suspension or revocation of, or by the failure or refusal to issue, deny, suspend or revoke, any permit, license, certificate, approval, order, or similar authorization where the public entity or an employee of the public entity is authorized by enactment to determine whether or not such authorization should be issued, denied, suspended or revoked.

Legislative Committee Comment—Senate

This section, like Section 818.2, would be unnecessary but for a possible implication that might arise from Section 815.6. It recognizes another immunity that has been recognized by the New York courts in the absence of statute. Under the Federal Tort Claims Act, the immunity would be within the general discretionary immunity. Direct review of this type of action by public entities is usually available through writ proceedings or other proceedings to review administrative action or inaction.

Under this section, for example, the State is immune from liability if the State Division of Industrial Safety issues or fails to issue a safety order and a city is immune if it issues or refuses to issue a building permit, even though negligence is involved in issuing or failing to issue the order or permit.[9]

§ 818.5. Injury Caused by Omission of Lienholder's Name From Ownership Certificate for Motor Vehicle

The Department of Motor Vehicles is liable for any injury to a lienholder or good faith purchaser of a vehicle proximately caused by the department's negligent omission of the lienholder's name from an ownership certificate issued by the department. The liability of the department under this section shall not exceed the actual cash value of the vehicle.

§ 818.6. Failure to inspect, or negligent inspection of, property

A public entity is not liable for injury caused by its failure to make an inspection, or by reason of making an inadequate or negligent inspection, of

---

8. [Ed. note] Under § 820.2 in the California act "[e]xcept as otherwise provided by statute, a public employee is not liable for an injury resulting from his act or omission where the act or omission was the result of the exercise of the discretion vested in him, whether or not such discretion be abused." Under § 821, a public employee "is not liable for an injury caused by his adoption of or failure to adopt an enactment or by his failure to enforce an enactment." Finally, a public employee who acts in "good faith, without malice, and under the apparent authority of an enactment that is unconstitutional, invalid or inapplicable" is only liable for any injuries he may thereby cause, "to the extent that he would have been liable had the enactment been constitutional, valid and applicable." § 820.6.

9. [Ed. note] A similar immunity is extended to public employees by § 821.2.

any property, other than its property (as defined in subdivision (c) of Section 830), for the purpose of determining whether the property complies with or violates any enactment or contains or constitutes a hazard to health or safety.

Legislative Committee Comment—Senate

Like Sections 818.2 and 818.4, this section would be unnecessary but for Section 815.6. It recognizes another immunity that has been recognized by the New York courts in the absence of statute. Because of the extensive nature of the inspection activities of public entities, a public entity would be exposed to the risk of liability for virtually all property defects within its jurisdiction if this immunity were not granted.

So far as its own property is concerned, a public entity may be held liable under Chapter 2 (commencing with Section 830) for negligently failing to discover a dangerous condition by conducting reasonable inspections, or a public entity may be held liable under Section 815.6 if it does not exercise reasonable diligence to comply with any mandatory legal duty that it may have to inspect its property.

The immunity provided by this section covers negligent failure to make an inspection and negligence in the inspection itself. For example, the section makes the public entity immune from liability if its employee negligently fails to detect a defect in a building being inspected; but the section does not provide immunity where a public employee inspecting a building under construction negligently causes a plank to fall on a workman.[10]

§ 818.8. Misrepresentations by employees

A public entity is not liable for an injury caused by misrepresentation by an employee of the public entity, whether or not such misrepresentation be negligent or intentional.

(Added by Stats.1963, c. 1681, p. 3269, § 1.)

Legislative Committee Comment—Senate

This section provides public entities with an absolute immunity from liability for negligent or intentional misrepresentation. A similar immunity is provided public employees by Section 822.2, except that an employee may be held liable if he is guilty of actual fraud, corruption or actual malice. This section will provide, for example, a public entity with protection against possible tort liability where it is claimed that an employee negligently misrepresented that the public entity would waive the terms of a construction contract requiring approval before changes were made.

§ 818.9. Advice to small claims court litigants

A public entity, its employees, and volunteers shall not be liable because of any advice provided to small claims court litigants pursuant to Section 117.18 of the Code of Civil Procedure.

---

10. [Ed. note] A similar immunity is extended to public employees by § 821.4.

Notes

1. As has been indicated, immunities similar to those given public entities have been given to public employees. Could the employees nevertheless be subject to an action brought under 42 U.S.C. § 1983 for conduct for which suit could not be brought under California law? What about § 1983 actions against public entities other than the states, such as municipalities? *See* Chapter 21, *supra.*

2. In other portions of Division 3.6, it is provided that neither a public entity nor a public employee is liable for failure to provide police protection (§ 845) nor for injuries due to the parole of prisoners[11] or escape of prisoners (§ 845.8) nor for the failure to provide fire protection (§ 850ff).

3. However much it may be desirable to subject public bodies to the same sort of liability as is imposed on private bodies, it has proven impossible to do so. Thus, in New York in which as we have seen, *supra* p. 1330, the state has assumed the same liability as private persons, something like the discretionary function exception contained in the Federal Tort Claims Act has been recognized by judicial construction. *Cf.* Weiss v. Fote, 7 N.Y.2d 579, 200 N.Y.S.2d 409, 167 N.E.2d 63 (1960). In other words, the special responsibility of government for the public welfare has led to treating governmental bodies as somehow different from private persons. *See, e.g.,* Estate of Arrowwood v. State, 894 P.2d 642 (Alaska 1995)(immunity, involving failure to close a snow-covered roadway).

3. Suits Against Other Governmental Entities

RUSSELL v. THE MEN OF DEVON

Court of King's Bench, 1788.
2 T.R. 667, 100 Eng.Rep. 359.

This was an action upon the case against the men dwelling in the county of Devon, to recover satisfaction for an injury done to the waggon of the plaintiffs in consequence of a bridge being out of repair, which ought to have been repaired by the county; to which two of the inhabitants, for themselves and the rest of the men dwelling in that county, appeared, and demurred generally.

LORD KENYON, CH.J. If this experiment had succeeded, it would have been productive of an infinity of actions. And though the fear of introducing so much litigation ought not to prevent the plaintiff's recovering, if by law he is entitled, yet it ought to have considerable weight in a case where it is admitted that there is no precedent of such an action having been before attempted. Many of the principles laid down by the plaintiff's counsel cannot be controverted; as that an action would lie by an individual for an injury which he has sustained against any other individual who is bound to repair. But the question here is, whether this body of men, who are sued in the present action, are a corporation, or quà a corporation, against whom such an action can be maintained. If it be reasonable that they should be by law liable to such an action, recourse must be had to the Legislature for that purpose. But it has been said that this action ought to be maintained by borrowing the rules of analogy from the Statutes of Hue

---

11. *Cf.* Thompson v. Alameda County, reprinted *supra,* p. 473.

and Cry: But I think that those statutes prove the very reverse. The reason of the Statute of Winton was this; as the hundred were bound to keep watch and ward, it was supposed that those irregularities which led to robbery must have happened by their neglect. But it was never imagined that the hundred could have been compelled to make satisfaction, till the statute gave that remedy; and most undoubtedly no such action could have been maintained against them before that time. Therefore when the case called for a remedy, the Legislature interposed; but they only gave the remedy in that particular case, and did not give it in any other case in which the neglect of the hundred had produced any injury to individuals. And when they gave the action, they virtually gave the means of maintaining that action; they converted the hundred into a corporation for that purpose; but it does not follow that, in this case where the Legislature has not given the remedy, this action can be maintained. And even if we could exercise a legislative discretion in this case, there would be great reason for not giving this remedy; for the argument urged by the defendant's counsel, that all those who become inhabitants of the county, after the injury sustained and before judgment, would be liable to contribute their proportion, is entitled to great weight. It is true indeed that the inconvenience does happen in the case of indictments; but that is only because it is sanctioned by common law, the main pillar of which, as Lord Coke says is unbroken usage. Among the several qualities which belong to corporations, one is, that they may sue and be sued; that puts it then in contradistinction to other persons. I do not say that the inhabitants of a county or hundred may not be incorporated to some purposes; as if the King were to grant lands to them, rendering rent, like the grant to the good men of the town of Islington. But where an action is brought against a corporation for damages, those damages are not to be recovered against the corporators in their individual capacity, but out of their corporate estate: but if the county is to be considered as a corporation, there is no corporation fund out of which satisfaction is to be made. Therefore I think that this experiment ought not to be encouraged; there is no law or reason for supporting the action; and there is a precedent against it in Brooke: though even without that authority I should be of opinion that this action cannot be maintained.

ASHHURST, J. It is a strong presumption that that which never has been done cannot by law be done at all. And it is admitted that no such action as the present has ever been brought, though the occasion must have frequently happened. But it has been said that there is a principle of law on which this action might be maintained, namely, that where an individual sustains an injury by the neglect or default of another, the law gives him a remedy. But there is another general principle of law which is more applicable to this case, that it is better that an individual should sustain an injury than that the public should suffer an inconvenience. Now if this action could be sustained, the public would suffer a great inconvenience; for if damages are recoverable against the county, at all events they must be levied on one or two individuals, who have no means whatever of reimbursing themselves; for if they were to bring separate actions against each individual of the county for his proportion, it is better that the plaintiff should be without remedy. However there is no foundation on which this action can be supported; and if it had been intended, the Legislature would have interfered and given a remedy, as they did in the case of hue and cry. Thus this case stands on principle: but I think the case cited from Brooke's Abridgment is a direct authority to shew that no such action could be maintained; and the reason of that case is a good one, namely, because the action must be brought against the public.

BULLER, J. and GROSE, J. assented.

Judgment for the defendants.

Notes

1. Although *Russell v. The Men of Devon* is often cited in connection with the assertion that "The King can do no wrong," the case itself has nothing to do with the liability of the Crown or the British Government. It merely concerns the issue whether, in the absence of an Act of Parliament, an unincorporated entity—the county of Devon (or Devonshire)—can be subject to suit as if it had legal personality such as a corporate body would have. Under English law, incorporated local governmental bodies, such as boroughs with corporate status by royal charter or by prescription (*e.g.,* the City of London), and which had the capacity to sue and be sued, were treated like private corporations. These incorporated local governmental bodies were not treated as surrogates for the Crown or its Ministers. The major early examples of other corporate entities recognized by English law were charitable corporations, like the Colleges of Oxford and Cambridge, and later the great trading corporations, like the East India Company. Since the Crown regarded all corporate bodies as exercising powers that were in derogation of the rights and privileges of the Crown itself, the rights and privileges of corporations in early English law were defined and limited by the Crown in royal charters or, as in the case of a few ancient entities like the City of London, by prescription.

This view of the status of municipal corporations was carried over to colonial America and at the time of the American Revolution the analogy between municipal corporations and private corporations was still strong. With the rise of general corporation laws in the nineteenth century—prior to which time incorporation involved separate legislative action—the analogy between municipal corporations and private corporations came to be seen as less appropriate. Instead, either by judicial decision or by the amendment of state constitutions, municipal corporations came more and more to be seen as exercising general governmental powers and therefore to share, to some extent, in the immunities of state governments. Indeed, as noted in footnote 8 of the court's opinion in Mayle v. Pennsylvania Dept. of Highways, 479 Pa. 384, 388 A.2d 709 (1978), the immunity of local government was sometimes completely merged with that of state government. In the areas with which we are now concerned, a key decision was Mower v. Leicester, 9 Mass. 247 (1812), in which the court distinguished a municipal corporation from a private corporation and, on the basis of an inappropriate reliance upon *Russell v. The Men of Devon,* tort liability against a municipal corporation was denied.[12] On the general history

---

12. Curiously the *Mower* case was brought against "The Inhabitants of Leicester" although the report makes clear that the Town of Leicester was incorporated. In the course of its very brief decision the court said: "Corporations created for their own benefit stand on the same ground in this respect as individuals. But *quasi* corporations, created by the legislature for purposes of public policy, * * * are not liable to an action for such neglect, unless the action be given by statute." With regard to the court's

of the developments, see J. Herget, *The Missing Power of Local Governments: A Divergence Between Text and Practice in Our Early State Constitutions,* 62 Va.L.Rev. 999 (1976).

2. Despite the developments described in the preceding note, the Eleventh Amendment, which has been construed to forbid suit in the federal courts against states without their consent, was never applied to prevent suit against municipalities in the federal courts. For example, suits against municipal corporations based upon violations of the contract clause of the United States Constitution have been brought in the federal courts from almost the beginning of the Republic. The highwater mark of this litigation was in the second half of the nineteenth century. *See* C. Fairman, Vol. 6, Pt. 1, History of the Supreme Court of the United States 918–1116 (1971).

3. From the point of view of the potential tort claimant, the immunity from suit of local governments was even more intolerable than that of the federal or state governments. Not only were people more likely to be affected by the activities of local government, but, even leaving aside their usually more limited financial capability, local governments did not have the same freedom to make *ex gratia* payments to accident victims as did higher levels of government.

4. Almost all of the states have now either abolished municipal immunity or substantially limited its scope. *See* Note, *Municipal Immunity in Virginia,* 68 Va.L.Rev. 638, n. 2 (1982); *Municipal Tort Liability for Erroneous Issuance of Building Permits: A National Survey,* 58 Wash.L.Rev. 537, 540–47 (1983). More recently, several additional states have abolished governmental immunity by judicial decision. *See e.g.,* Haverlack v. Portage Homes, Inc., 2 Ohio St.3d 26, 442 N.E.2d 749 (1982); McCall v. Batson, 285 S.C. 243, 329 S.E.2d 741 (1985).[13] Even a state like Arkansas, which purports to maintain the traditional governmental immunity of local governmental entities, requires such entities to maintain liability insurance and authorizes them to settle tort claims against them. Ark.Code Ann. §§ 21–9–303. As we have also seen, Missouri, which has waived governmental immunity for local governments only in accidents involving motor vehicles or the dangerous condition of government property, nevertheless permits these entities to purchase insurance and to assume liability up to the extent of the insurance coverage with a limit of $100,000 per person and $1,000,000 per accident. Vernon's Ann.Mo.Stat. § 537.610. North Carolina is another state which allows local governmental entities to waive governmental immunity to the extent of insurance coverage. *See* N.C.Gen.Stat. §§ 115C–42 (local boards of education), 153A–435 (counties), and 160A–485 (cities).

5. Many states, which otherwise take a restrictive view of the extent to which governmental immunity has been waived, will nevertheless permit an action against a local governmental entity if the activity involved is considered to be a proprietary as opposed to a governmental function, although some

---

statement that "[t]his question is fully discussed in the case of *Russell et al. vs. The Men of Devon,* * * * and the reasoning there is conclusive against the action," the editor of the report, D. A. Tyng, in a footnote states "* * * it is not very obvious how this decision can have any other tendency than to show that, upon principle, the action may be maintained here."

13. Both of these cases were followed by legislative enactment of tort claim acts. *See*

Ohio Rev.Code § 2744.01 *et seq.* (Anderson) (enacted in 1985) and S.C.Code § 15–78–10 *et seq.* (Law. Co-op.) (enacted in 1986). Because the *McCall* case also abolished the state's sovereign immunity, S.C.Code § 15–78–10 *et seq.* also covers tort claims against the state. Ohio had already provided for tort claims against the state in 1975. *See* Ohio Rev.Code § 2743.01 *et seq.* (Anderson).

states, such as South Carolina, which in 1985 finally abolished governmental immunity in the *McCall* case, *supra,* refused to recognize the distinction as a means of ameliorating the effect of the traditional doctrine. *See* Boyce v. Lancaster City Nat. Gas Auth'y, 266 S.C. 398, 223 S.E.2d 769 (1976).

The governmental/proprietary distinction is, to say the least, a difficult one. In Austin v. City of Baltimore, 286 Md. 51, 405 A.2d 255 (1979), a wrongful death action was brought for the death of a child who drowned, allegedly from inadequate supervision during a trip to a state park, while she was a camper at a day camp run by the City of Baltimore. Relying on cases holding that maintenance of a public swimming pool and park was a governmental function, the Court of Appeals of Maryland held that operation of a day camp was also a governmental function.[14] In this regard one might note that, under the Illinois Local Governmental and Governmental Employees Tort Immunity Act, which was enacted in response to the judicial abolition of local governmental immunity in Molitor v. Kaneland Community Unit District No. 302, 18 Ill.2d 11, 163 N.E.2d 89 (1959), *certiorari denied* 362 U.S. 968, 80 S.Ct. 955, 4 L.Ed.2d 900 (1960) "[n]either a local public entity nor a public employee is liable for an injury where the liability is based on the existence of a condition of any public property intended to be used as a park, playground or open area for recreational purposes unless such local entity or public employee is guilty of willful and wanton injury proximately causing such injury." Ill.—S.H.A. ch. 745, §§ 10/3–106, 10/3–108. Under § 3–108 there is no liability for failure to supervise an activity on public property but there is an exception for swimming pools. In Virginia, it has been held that operation of a swimming pool is a proprietary function. Hoggard v. City of Richmond, 172 Va. 145, 200 S.E. 610 (1939). The Supreme Court of Virginia reasoned from cases holding the operation of a municipal water works to be a proprietary function. In a later case, Freeman v. City of Norfolk, 221 Va. 57, 266 S.E.2d 885 (1980), the court held that, while the maintenance of public streets and buildings is a proprietary function, the design of public streets and buildings is a governmental function. In 1981 Virginia enacted a state tort claims act which is, in many ways, quite similar to the Federal Tort Claims Act (Va.Code 1950, §§ 8.01–195.1–195.8),[15] but Virginia has thus far not done anything to abrogate the traditional governmental immunity of municipalities and thereby relieve the courts of the burden of distinguishing between proprietary and governmental functions in suits against these entities.

Some states have passed statutes that confer immunity on public as well as private owners of land or facilities generally open to the public without charge for recreational use. Ohio Rev. Code Ann. § 1533.181; LiCause v. City of Carton, 42 Ohio St.3d 109, 537 N.E.2d 1298 (1989).

In Muskopf v. Corning Hospital District, 55 Cal.2d 211, 11 Cal.Rptr. 89, 359 P.2d 457 (1961), in which, as already noted, *supra* p. 1330, the Supreme Court of California judicially abrogated all governmental immunities, Traynor, J., noted that, in California, "a community theater in a public park," "a public

---

14. In 1987 Maryland adopted a local government tort claims act which gives some relief from the doctrine of governmental immunity by requiring local governments to defend and to pay the judgments entered in actions against their employees up to a limit of $200,000 per individual claim and $500,-000 for the total number of claims arising from the same occurrence. Md.Code, Cts. & Jud.Proc., § 5–402–04.

15. One important difference is that Virginia imposes a limitation of $25,000 per claim ($75,000 for claims arising after July 1, 1988) or the maximum limits of any insurance policies covering the claim.

golf course," "an electric lighting plant" and "the furnishing of impure water," had all been previously classified as proprietary functions for which tort liability would lie in California. In Roman Catholic Diocese of Vermont, Inc. v. City of Winooski Housing Authority, 137 Vt. 517, 408 A.2d 649 (1979), a case involving a claim for damages caused to adjacent property by vibrations from a pile driver, construction of a federally subsidized housing project was labeled proprietary.[16]

A variation on the government-proprietary function approach is based on a duty analysis. Courts following this approach agree that governmental acts are immune from tort liability but the immunity arises out of the lack of duty to the individual injured. The duty, rather, is owed to the public at large. *See* Hurst v. Ohio Dep't of Rehabilitation & Correction, 72 Ohio St.3d 325, 650 N.E.2d 104 (1995)(no liability for negligence in not informing state-wide law enforcement agencies of a parole violation order); *see also,* Allison Gas Turbine Div., General Motors Corp. v. District of Columbia, 642 A.2d 841 (D.C.App. 1994); P.W. and R.W. v. Kansas Dept. of Social and Rehabilitation Services, 255 Kan. 827, 877 P.2d 430 (1994).

B. CHARITABLE IMMUNITY

The doctrine of charitable immunity is a distinctly American innovation. It had its origins in some dicta in three mid-nineteenth century cases which were overruled by the House of Lords in Mersey Docks & Harbour Board of Trustees v. Gibbs, 11 H.L.Cas. 686, 11 Eng.Rep. 1500 (1866). The principal question with which these cases were concerned was whether trustees were liable for the negligence of the employees of the trust—a question which the House of Lords in *Mersey* answered in the affirmative. None of the English cases were concerned with whether or not a charity enjoyed a blanket immunity from tort liability. Nevertheless, relying on Holliday v. Parish of St. Leonard, 11 C.B. (N.S.) 192, 142 Eng.Rep. 769 (1861), which had held that commissioners of public works who served gratuitously would only be liable if they had been negligent in selecting the persons to carry on those works and which had been already overruled in *Mersey,* it was held, in McDonald v. Massachusetts Gen. Hosp., 120 Mass. 432 (1876), that a charitable corporation was not liable for the torts of its employees, at least when the plaintiff was a charitable patient.

At one time, some form of charitable immunity operated in most states. One of the principal justifications of charitable immunity was the contention that it was contrary to the intent of the donors of funds contributed to charitable organizations to expend those funds for the payment of tort judgments. *See, e.g.,* Parks v. Northwestern University, 218 Ill. 381, 75 N.E. 991 (1905). This is the so-called "trust-fund" theory. The theory was buttressed by the assertion that, in performing their charitable functions, private charities were rendering the same sort of services as were public entities which were at that time generally immune from suit. A subsidiary justification was that the beneficiaries of charitable organizations should not be able to "bite the hand that feeds them."

---

16. In 1985, the Vermont legislature enacted legislation which makes towns responsible for the defective condition of bridges and culverts subject to a maximum of $75,-000 per claim or the upper limits of any applicable insurance policy, Vt.Stat.Ann. tit. 19, § 985, but did not otherwise modify the common law. The limit was raised to $100,-000 per claim, effective in 1993.

But this latter argument is of limited validity when applied to paying patients at a non-profit (i.e. charitable) hospital, and it is of no validity at all when applied to members of the general public who have been injured by the activities of the charity's employees and yet have never received any service or benefits from the charity or used its facilities.

The first major complete judicial abrogation of the doctrine of charitable immunity was President and Directors of Georgetown College v. Hughes, 130 F.2d 810 (D.C.Cir.1942). Since then the doctrine has been totally or partially abolished in most states. Undoubtedly the availability of liability insurance has influenced this development. A few states continue to bar actions by beneficiaries. After the complete judicial abrogation of charitable immunity in New Jersey, in Collopy v. Newark Eye and Ear Infirmary, 27 N.J. 29, 141 A.2d 276 (1958), the legislature responded, in 1959, by reinstating the immunity from liability based on negligence as to the beneficiaries of all charitable, including religious, organizations except hospitals. The liability to anyone who is a beneficiary "to whatever degree" of a charitable hospital is limited to $10,000 per occurrence. N.J.Stat.Ann. 2A:53A–7 and 53A–8 (West). In Maine, since 1966, the purchase of liability insurance is a waiver of immunity to the extent of the insurance coverage. Me.Rev.Stat.Ann. tit. 14, § 158 (West).

With the decision of Fitzer v. Greater Greenville South Carolina Young Mens Christian Association, 277 S.C. 1, 282 S.E.2d 230 (1981), which totally abrogated the doctrine of charitable immunity in South Carolina, it does not appear as if any state still maintains the doctrine in anything like its former vigor. In Note, *The Quality of Mercy: "Charitable Torts" and Their Continuing Immunity*, 100 Harv.L.Rev. 1382, 1385–86 (1987), it is stated that "[b]y the beginning of 1986, thirty-three jurisdictions had abrogated the doctrine for some kinds of charities, and sixteen of the thirty-three had abandoned it altogether." The note declared "[e]ighteen jurisdictions retain one or another form of partial immunity. These forms range from old distinctions between strangers and beneficiaries, or between paying and non-paying beneficiaries, to more modern devises such as legislative limits on damages." This note is one of the few recent comprehensive textual treatments of the subject.

In recent years a number of states have resurrected, usually by statute, some qualified immunity for charitable organizations and people that volunteer to perform charitable services. These developments are surveyed in *Developments in the Law–Nonprofit Corporations*, Part VI. Special Treatment and Tort Law, 105 Harv. L. Rev. 1677 (1992). An example is Chapter 84 of the Texas Code Ann. [Civ. Prac. & Rem.]:

§ 84.002. Findings and Purposes

The Legislature of the State of Texas finds that:

(1) robust, active, bona fide, and well-supported charitable organizations are needed within Texas to perform essential and needed services;

(2) the willingness of volunteers to offer their services to these organizations is deterred by the perception of personal liability arising out of the services rendered to these organizations;

(3) because of these concerns over personal liability, volunteers are withdrawing from services in all capacities;

(4) these same organizations have a further problem in obtaining and affording liability insurance for the organization and its employees and volunteers;

(5) these problems combine to diminish the services being provided to Texas and local communities because of higher costs and fewer programs;

(6) the citizens of this state have an overriding interest in the continued and increased delivery of these services that must be balanced with other policy considerations; and

(7) because of the above conditions and policy considerations, it is the purpose of this Act to reduce the liability exposure and insurance costs of these organizations and their employees and volunteers in order to encourage volunteer services and maximize the resources devoted to delivering these services.

§ 84.003. Definitions

In this chapter:

(1) "Charitable organization" means:

(A) any organization exempt from federal income tax under Section 501(a) of the Internal Revenue Code of 1986 * * * by being listed as an exempt organization in Section 501(c)(3) or 501(c)(4) of the code, * * * if it is a nonprofit corporation, foundation, community chest, or fund organized and operated exclusively for charitable, religious, prevention of cruelty to children or animals, youth sports and youth recreational, or educational purposes, excluding private primary or secondary schools, alumni associations and related on-campus organizations, or is organized and operated exclusively for the promotion of social welfare by being primarily engaged in promoting the common good and general welfare of the people in a community;

* * *

(2) "Volunteer" means a person rendering services for or on behalf of a charitable organization who does not receive compensation in excess of reimbursement for expenses incurred, and such term includes a person serving as a director, officer, trustee, or direct service volunteer.

§ 84.004. Volunteer Liability

* * *

(b) Except as provided by Subsection (c) of this section [cases resulting from use of motor vehicles covered by insurance] and Section 84.007 of this Act [covering several specific exceptions to the immunity, including "an act or omission that is intentional, wilfully or wantonly negligent, or done with conscious indifference or reckless disregard for the safety of others"], a volunteer who is serving as a direct service volunteer of a charitable organization is immune from civil liability for any act or omission resulting in death, damage, or injury if the volunteer was acting in good faith and in the course and scope of his duties or functions within the organization.

* * *

§ 84.005. Employee Liability

Except as provided in Section 84.007 of this Act, in any civil action brought against an employee of a nonhospital charitable organization for damages based on an act or omission by the person in the course and scope of the person's employment, the liability of the employee is limited to money damages in a maximum amount of $500,000 for each person and $1,000,000 for each single occurrence of bodily injury or death and $100,000 for each single occurrence for injury to or destruction of property.

§ 84.006. Organization Liability

[Identical to the preceding provision applicable to employees.]

C. FAMILY IMMUNITIES

1. *Interspousal Immunity*

BURNS v. BURNS

Supreme Court of Mississippi, en banc, 1988.
518 So.2d 1205.

PRATHER, JUSTICE, for the Court:

At issue in this appeal is the question of continuance of the judicially imposed rule of interspousal immunity in Mississippi. The Circuit Court of Alcorn, on a motion for judgment on the pleadings, dismissed a complaint filed by Betty Burns, against her husband, Erit Lamar Burns for an alleged assault and battery. The court ruled that the complaint was barred by the doctrine of interspousal immunity. This Court reverses the dismissal of that complaint. * * *

The only facts before the Court are that on August 1, 1984, Erit Burns allegedly assaulted and battered his wife Betty Burns. Thereafter, Betty Burns sued in circuit court to recover for her injuries. In oral argument before this Court, counsel for the parties revealed that Mr. Burns and Mrs. Burns have separated and have filed for divorce in chancery court. * * *

Interspousal tort immunity is an ancient common law doctrine founded on the theory of the legal unity of husband and wife. 1 W. Blackstone, Commentaries 433.

Appellant now implores this Court to reevaluate the viability of this judicially created doctrine and to judicially abrogate the doctrine in response to the present needs of society. * * *

Three reasons traditionally assigned as justification for the doctrine of interspousal immunity are: (A) the legal unity of the husband and wife recognized at common law; (B) the promotion of peace and harmony in the home; and (C) the avoidance of fraudulent or collusive claims.

A.

The common law unity concept which prohibited suits between spouses for any claim is no longer viable. * * *

By discarding "the common law unity concept," this Court would imply no denigration to the spiritual and emotional unity which is recognized by virtue of marital vows. * * *

It is this concept of legal unity, which constituted a woman a chattel to her husband, that can no longer operate to bar one spouse from suing the other for intentional tortious claims.

As noted, in Mississippi spouses are able to sue each other for breach of contract and to protect property rights, * * * but they may not sue each other for tortious injury, negligent or intentional. * * * The inconsistency of this approach is clear in view of Mississippi Constitution Art. 3, section 24, which reads in pertinent part:

> All courts shall be open; and every person for an injury done him in his * * * person * * * shall have a remedy by due course of law, and right and justice shall be administered without sale, denial or delay.

B.

The idea that maintenance of interspousal immunity will promote the public interest in domestic tranquility is wholly illusory. If one spouse commits against the other an act which, but for the immunity, would constitute a tort, the desired state of matrimonial tranquility is necessarily destroyed. But common sense suggests the peace is destroyed by the act of the offending spouse, not the lawsuit filed by the other. Beyond that, maintenance of the immunity surely cannot prevent injured spouses from harboring ill will and anger. Seen in this light, our traditional rule of interspousal immunity appears incapable of achieving the end claimed for it. Instead it leaves injured spouses without adequate or complete remedies. It is also noted that remedies incident to divorce and criminal prosecution are not adequate for the protection sought in this type of intentional tort.

It is this Court's opinion that the doctrine of interspousal tort immunity cannot be maintained on the ground that it promotes marital peace and harmony.

C.

The third argument espoused in support of the doctrine is that to allow such suits would encourage fraud and collusion. The Supreme Court of California, in abrogating the interspousal immunity rule reasoned:

> It would be a sad commentary on the law if we were to admit that the judicial processes are so ineffective that we must deny relief to a person otherwise entitled simply because in some future case a litigant may be guilty of fraud or collusion. Once that concept were accepted,

then all causes of action should be abolished. Our legal system is not that ineffectual.

Klein v. Klein, 58 Cal.2d 692, 26 Cal.Rptr. 102, 376 P.2d 70 (1962).

All of the reasoning and analysis of these opinions from our sister states equally applies to our consideration of the possible fraud or collusion argument within this state, and this Court is of the opinion such fraud argument lacks validity.   * * *

Looking to the above arguments, this Court is sufficiently persuaded that there is no justification to preserve and leave intact the interspousal immunity doctrine. In fact to do so repudiates the constitutional guarantee of equal protection of the laws. United States Constitution, Amendment XIV.   * * *

This time honored rule no longer fits the reasoning and rationale of today's mores as evidenced by the abrogation of the rule in whole or in part, in 44 of the states.   * * *

This Court hereby abrogates the rule of interspousal immunity. Therefore, this Court reverses the decision of the trial judge and remands the case for further proceedings consistent with this opinion.

REVERSED AND REMANDED.

[The dissent by Justice Griffin, relying upon the traditional reasons, is omitted.]

Notes

1.   Historically, the common law doctrine of interspousal immunity was an absolute bar to any legal actions between spouses. The doctrine reflected social and legal conceptions of marriage, particularly the notion that upon marriage the wife's legal rights merged with those of the husband—the husband had complete control over any legal rights of the marital unit, and there could be no torts between them since they were viewed as a unit, not as two separate legal persons. Although the Married Women's Property Acts of the mid-nineteenth century gave married women the right to enter into contracts, own property, and sue and be sued, the courts generally construed these acts narrowly and held that they did not abolish the interspousal immunity doctrine in tort law. One of the leading early cases construing the Married Women's Property Acts as not permitting tort suits between spouses is Thompson v. Thompson, 218 U.S. 611, 31 S.Ct. 111, 54 L.Ed. 1180 (1910)(construing District of Columbia law). Interspousal immunity was abolished in the District of Columbia in 1976 by D.C. Code 1981, § 30–201. For a good treatment of the historical development in this area, *see* C. Tobias, *Interspousal Tort Immunity in America*, 23 Ga. L. Rev. 359 (1989).

2.   By 1996, 48 states had abolished the doctrine of interspousal immunity, either completely or at least in certain types of cases. Florida, in Waite v. Waite, 618 So.2d 1360 (1993), and Delaware, in Beattie v. Beattie, 630 A.2d 1096 (1993), were the last two states to abolish the doctrine. Two states, Georgia and Louisiana, preserve the doctrine by statute. *See* Ga. Code § 19–3–877 (1994); La. Rev. Stat. Ann. § 9:291. Nevertheless, the Georgia courts have made some exceptions to the application of the doctrine, refusing to apply it in wrongful death cases, Jones v. Jones, 259 Ga. 49, 376 S.E.2d 674 (1989), or in situations where the traditional policy reasons for applying it are not

present, such as where there is no marital harmony to preserve or there is no possibility of collusion. Shoemake v. Shoemake, 200 Ga.App. 182, 407 S.E.2d 134 (1991). Thus, Louisiana appears to be the only state that retains completely the doctrine of interspousal immunity in tort actions.

3. Among the states abolishing interspousal immunity, some have only partially abrogated the doctrine, ruling narrowly that it does not apply in certain types of cases. *See, e.g.,* Rupert v. Steinne, 90 Nev. 397, 528 P.2d 1013 (1974)(abolishing the doctrine in Nevada for automobile accident cases); Asplin v. Amica Mut. Ins. Co., 121 R.I. 51, 394 A.2d 1353 (1978) (holding that there is no interspousal immunity in Rhode Island tort actions where one or both of the spouses has died, since marital harmony can no longer be disrupted by the action); Stoker v. Stoker, 616 P.2d 590 (Utah 1980)(abolishing the doctrine in Utah for intentional tort cases). The abolition of the doctrine in Utah has followed an interesting path. While the *Stoker* case abolished the doctrine for cases involving intentional torts, the Utah courts have not been presented with a case requiring a decision as to whether this abolition extends to negligence cases as well—an issue the courts have expressly declined to decide in subsequent intentional tort suits between spouses. *See, e.g.,* Noble v. Noble, 761 P.2d 1369 (Utah 1988). However, an Arizona court of appeals, applying Utah law of interspousal immunity to a Utah couple involved in an auto accident in Arizona, ruled that the rationale for abolishing the doctrine in intentional tort cases as articulated in *Stoker* applied equally to negligence cases, and allowed the wife's negligence action against her husband to proceed. *See* Lucero v. Valdez, 180 Ariz. 313, 884 P.2d 199 (1994). For a review of the current state of the law of interspousal immunity, *see* 2 Automobile Accident Law and Practice § 25.06 (Keith C. Miller ed., 1995).

4. In states where interspousal immunity has been abolished, the issue arises as to whether the immunity can effectively be reestablished by contract in the insurance setting by including a provision excluding coverage of spouses in the policy. Since many of the cases litigated, including most auto accident cases, involve an insurance policy to cover the judgment, the validity of such exclusions becomes crucial to the ability of one spouse to sue the other and collect damages. Traditionally, the rule has been that the parties to an insurance contract are free to negotiate for any terms that are mutually agreed upon, so long as the terms do not violate public policy, and therefore such exclusions are permissible. *See, e.g.,* Walker v. American Family Mut. Ins. Co., 340 N.W.2d 599 (Iowa 1983). However, in Mutual of Enumclaw Insurance Co. v. Wiscomb, 97 Wash.2d 203, 643 P.2d 441 (1982), a clause in an automobile liability policy, excluding coverage for intrafamily torts, was declared void as against public policy, at least where the evidence reveals that "the parties * * * have not truly bargained for such an exclusion." Legislation in New York takes a different approach, requiring that no insurance policy providing liability coverage for "culpable conduct" shall include liability to the spouse of the insured unless there is an "express provision relating specifically thereto * * * in the policy." N.Y.-McKinney's Ins. L. § 3420(g). For further discussion of the effect of such exclusionary clauses in insurance policies, *see* 2 Automobile Accident Law and Practice § 25.02[1] (Keith C. Miller ed., 1995).

5. Although interspousal immunity in tort actions has largely been abolished, the policies underlying the doctrine can still sometimes be seen at work in courts' handling of suits between spouses. This is particularly true of suits between spouses for intentional infliction of emotional distress. The concern that allowing suits between spouses would lead to litigation of countless marital

squabbles, once used to justify continuation of the interspousal immunity doctrine, now manifests itself in the establishment of a requirement of an especially high level of outrageous conduct to maintain an action against a spouse for intentional infliction of emotional distress. Some courts have applied "special caution" in deciding such actions where spouses are involved, and held that defense motions for summary judgment should be viewed sympathetically in order to avoid "excessive and frivolous litigation intruding into the marital lives of the parties." *See* Henriksen v. Cameron, 622 A.2d 1135 (Me. 1993). The notion is that all marriages have ups and downs, but the hurt feelings caused by these travails are a part of married life and generally should not be actionable. As one court stated, to maintain an action against a spouse for intentional infliction of emotional distress, there must be conduct "considerably more egregious than that experienced in the rough and tumble of everyday life." Whelan v. Whelan, 41 Conn. Supp. 519, 588 A.2d 251 (1991). Thus, courts have rejected claims based on conduct such as adultery and verbal abuse. *See* Browning v. Browning, 584 S.W.2d 406 (Ky.Ct.App.1979); Hakkila v. Hakkila, 112 N.M. 172, 812 P.2d 1320 (App.1991). In Pryzbyla v. Pryzbyla, 87 Wis.2d 441, 275 N.W.2d 112 (App.1978), the court rejected a claim for intentional infliction of emotional distress by a husband against his wife who had an abortion against his wishes and after allegedly deceiving him into believing she would not seek an abortion. The court ruled that the exercise by a woman of her constitutionally protected right to terminate her pregnancy cannot serve as the basis for such a claim.

Actions for intentional infliction of emotional distress have been allowed for conduct such as conspiring to murder a spouse, Vance v. Chandler, 231 Ill.App.3d 747, 173 Ill.Dec. 525, 597 N.E.2d 233 (1992), and against a husband, falsely representing to his wife that he was HIV-positive, Whelan v. Whelan, 41 Conn. Supp. 519, 588 A.2d 251 (1991). For an excellent survey of how courts have dealt with claims for intentional infliction of emotional distress, as well as other torts, between spouses after the abolition of interspousal immunity, see S. Benson & L. Knisken, *Interspousal Tort Liability: Abrogation of Interspousal Immunity*, 68 Fla. B.J. 62 (1994).

2. *Parent–Child Immunity*

The immunity that prevents personal injury actions[17] between an unemancipated child and its parents developed in the United States in the latter part of the nineteenth century and the early part of the twentieth century. It has no precedential basis in English law, although it should be pointed out that there were also no English cases at the time supporting the right of a child to sue its parent. Rather, there was a complete dearth of cases. *See* Prosser & Keeton on Torts § 122 at 904 (5th ed. 1984). The first of the American cases was Hewellette v. George, 68 Miss. 703, 9 So. 885 (1891), which involved an action by a minor daughter against the estate of her mother for wrongfully having incarcerated her in an insane asylum. The daughter had married, but she had separated from her husband and had returned to live at home. The court held that any right the daughter had to recover damages was dependent on "[w]hether she had resumed her former place in her mother's house, and the relationship, with

---

17. There never was any immunity that operated to prevent actions involving property.

its reciprocal rights and duties, of a minor child to her parent * * *." As noted, the immunity only applies between parents and unemancipated (minor) children.

The most frequently cited discussion of the concept of emancipation is probably Gillikin v. Burbage, 263 N.C. 317, 139 S.E.2d 753 (1965). Briefly, a child becomes completely emancipated automatically, by operation of law, when the child marries or when the child achieves majority unless, in this latter instance, the child is so infirm in body or mind that it cannot support itself and continues to live, unmarried, in the parents' home. The law will also consider a child completely emancipated when a parent abandons the child or fails to discharge his legal duty to support the child. Finally, a parent can completely emancipate a child by surrendering all right to the services and earnings of the child together with a surrender of the right to the custody and control of the child. Merely surrendering the right to the child's earnings is not enough.

The first judicial abrogation of the doctrine of parent-child immunity occurred in Goller v. White, 20 Wis.2d 402, 122 N.W.2d 193 (1963),[18] and a number of other states soon followed that lead. In 1977 the American Law Institute promulgated § 895G of the *Restatement (Second) of Torts* in which it declared that there was no immunity between parent and child but that the "[r]epudiation of * * * tort immunity does not establish liability for an act or omission that, because of the parent-child relationship, is otherwise privileged * * *." The state of the law was described as follows in Rousey v. Rousey, 528 A.2d 416 (D.C.App.1987):

> Many states have since followed the lead of *Goller v. White* and the Restatement, so that a substantial majority of states have now abandoned the doctrine in whole or in part. To date eleven states have abrogated it entirely or have declined to adopt it; eleven have abrogated it in automobile negligence cases; five have abrogated it in automobile negligence cases in which the parent has liability insurance; and seven have abrogated it except in cases in which the parent's alleged tortious act involves an exercise of parental authority over the child, or ordinary parental discretion with respect to such matters as food, care, and education.

Rousey itself completely abolished the immunity adding another jurisdiction to the first category. For those jurisdictions that have been prepared to abolish the doctrine totally, the sticking point has been the degree to which a parent should be subjected to an action for decisions that the parent may have made in the exercise of parental authority. This is a question which concerned the court in *Goller v. White*. It is presented in the next principal case.

---

18. Some 30 years earlier an intermediate appellate court in Missouri held that a parent could bring a tort action against a minor child. Wells v. Wells, 48 S.W.2d 109 (Mo. App.1932). The court seems to have believed that the immunity doctrine had never been adopted in Missouri. Subsequent Missouri cases, however, held that, in point of fact, the immunity existed in Missouri. *See* Kohler v. Rockwell Int'l Corp., 600 S.W.2d 647 (Mo. App.1980) and cases cited therein. The continued viability of the immunity doctrine was substantially reaffirmed by the Supreme Court of Missouri in Kendall v. Sears, Roebuck and Co., 634 S.W.2d 176 (Mo.1982).

BRUNNER v. HUTCHINSON DIVISION, LEAR–SIEGLER, INC.

United States District Court, District of South Dakota, 1991.
770 F.Supp. 517.

BATTEY, DISTRICT JUDGE.

This case arises from an injury to plaintiff's ward, Jeremiah Brunner, age 2½ at the time of the injury, which occurred on the Brunner family farm near Vale, South Dakota. The injury was the result of contact between the infant Brunner and machinery manufactured by defendant and third-party plaintiff Hutchinson Division, Lear–Siegler, Inc. (Lear–Siegler). Lear–Siegler subsequently filed a third-party complaint seeking indemnity and/or contribution from third-party defendants Brad Brunner and H.L. Brunner & Sons.

Third-party defendants have made a motion for summary judgment alleging that Lear–Siegler is barred by the doctrine of parental immunity from bringing a contribution claim against Jeremiah's father and his business partnership. Lear–Siegler defends against the summary judgment motion on the grounds that the State of South Dakota has never recognized the doctrine of parental immunity, and, to the contrary, has statutorily mandated access to the courts to all persons. This Court does not accept third-party defendants' arguments that the doctrine of parental immunity operates in this jurisdiction to shield a parent from a cause of action by the parent's offspring. For reasons set forth below, this Court prefers to adopt the more modern approach of the Restatement (Second) of Torts s 895(g)(1977), which simply recognizes that in limited circumstances a parent is privileged from liability with respect to certain causes of action. Among those causes of action for which a parent is privileged is a claim of negligent supervision, a cause of action that is not recognized at law in the State of South Dakota. Accordingly, the Court grants the third-party defendants' motion for summary judgment. * * *

On the day of the accident Jeremiah was accompanying his father, Brad Brunner, as the elder Brunner carried out his day's labors on the Brunner farm. Among the chores Brad Brunner had scheduled for that day was the removal of corn from a storage bin for transportation to the cattle feedlot. The grain was to be removed from the bin and loaded onto the truck with the assistance of a mechanical auger, a screw device which scoops and pushes the grain from the silo through a series of rotating blades. The elder Brunner positioned the truck to receive the grain, switched the augers on, and took Jeremiah into the farm house to turn the boy over to his mother.

Jeremiah's mother, Laurie Brunner, was ill and unable to care for her son at that time so the responsibility of supervising Jeremiah fell to Brad Brunner, who brought the boy back to the truck and sat with him in the cab while the augers were operating. Brad Brunner concedes that he was under no time constraints which required him to move the grain immediately. During the course of the unloading, Brad Brunner found it necessary to leave the truck to inspect the operation of the augers. Before leaving the truck, Brunner told the boy to stay in the truck, he locked the door of the truck, and walked over to where the sweep auger was operating to determine that everything was operating properly.

Brad Brunner entered an adjoining grain bin, losing visual contact with the truck and his son. Upon exiting the bin, Mr. Brunner found Jeremiah standing near the portable grain auger. He had suffered a traumatic amputation of the right hand. At the time of his injury, Jeremiah Brunner was approximately 70 percent permanently hearing impaired, and today he wears hearing aids. Jeremiah continues to live with his mother and father and two siblings on the farm near Vale.

DISCUSSION

In the motion for summary judgment, third-party defendants ask the Court to dismiss the third-party complaint based upon the doctrine of parental immunity, despite the absence of any legal authority establishing, or for that matter disparaging, the operation of such immunity in this jurisdiction. In the alternative, third-party defendants request this Court to certify the question to the Supreme Court of South Dakota pursuant to SDCL 15–24A. * * *

The question presented by the defendant's motion of whether a parent is immune from suit, either directly or upon a third-party claim of contribution, for certain acts arising out of the prosecution of parental functions is one of first impression for this jurisdiction. * * * [Kloppenburg v. Kloppenburg, 66 S.D. 167, 280 N.W. 206 (1938)]

Of historical note, the doctrine of parental immunity has no roots in the general common law adopted by many states at the time of their political organization, but instead has its origins in the Mississippi case of Hewellette v. George, 68 Miss. 703, 9 So. 885 (1891). In refusing to permit a suit by a minor daughter against her mother for false imprisonment, the Hewellette court relied exclusively on public policy arguments stating:

> [t]he peace of society, and of the families composing society, and a sound public policy, designed to subserve the repose of families and the best interests of society, forbid to the minor child a right to appear in court in the assertion of a claim to civil redress for personal injuries suffered at the hands of the parent. The state, through its criminal laws, will give the minor child protection from parental violence and wrong-doing * * *.

Hewellette, 9 So. at 887. Forty-two states followed Mississippi's lead and adopted some form of parental immunity. See Hollister, Parent–Child Immunity: A Doctrine in Search of Justification, 50 Fordham L.Rev. 489, 494 (1981–82).

Among the various rationale that have provided the basis for the parental immunity doctrine are included: (1) the disruption of domestic tranquility and the family as the basic social unit of American society; (2) the threat to parental discipline and control; (3) the proliferation of fraudulent and collusive suits; and, (4) the depletion of family resources. * * *

These policy arguments, however, have not proven capable of withstanding judicial or scholarly scrutiny over time and have been found to be insufficient to justify the continued application of the doctrine. With respect to the family harmony justification, some courts have argued that family harmony and parental authority is more seriously disrupted when a victim of another's negligence is permitted to go uncompensated. * * * Other courts point to the illogic of permitting a child to sue one or both parents in contract and property disputes but not in tort. The domestic tranquility argument is further undermined by the modern prevalence of liability insurance which shifts the controversy and burden of providing compensation to a third-party insurer. * * *

The danger of fraud or collusion is widely regarded as too specious to serve as a basis for a total ban on parent-child tort actions by reason that judges and juries are regarded as capable of detecting fraudulent and collusive claims. * * * Finally, with respect to the potential for the depletion of family resources arising out of intra-family lawsuits, it is argued that the presence of insurance eliminates this risk, and to the extent the risk exists, it overlooks the compelling question of compensating the child for its injuries. * * *

Although the overwhelming majority of states at one time followed the doctrine of parental immunity, judicial support for the doctrine eroded quickly after a 1963 Wisconsin decision which entirely abrogated parental immunity, except in cases where the allegedly tortious conduct involved "an exercise of parental authority ... [or] ordinary parental discretion with respect to the provision of food, clothing, housing, medical and dental services, and other care." Goller v. White, 20 Wis.2d 402, 122 N.W.2d 193, 198 (1963). Fourteen years later, the American Law Institute, specifically endorsing the Goller approach, published section 895G of the Restatement (Second) of Torts, completely rejecting general parent-child tort immunity: (1) A parent or child is not immune from tort liability to the other solely by reason of that relationship. (2) Repudiation of general tort immunity does not establish liability for an act or omission that, because of the parent-child relationship, is otherwise privileged or is not tortious. Restatement (Second) of Torts s 895G comment j (1977).

Numerous states have reexamined the question of parent-child tort immunity in the wake of the Goller decision and the Restatement's abrogation of general immunity. To date, a substantial majority of jurisdictions have abrogated the doctrine either partially or completely. Of the states which have reconsidered parental immunity, few have eliminated the doctrine entirely.[19] Three states have declined to adopt parental immunity or have replaced it with a reasonable parent standard.[20] Most jurisdictions have retained the doctrine, but have limited its application to certain circumstances. The principal variations relating to tort actions include: parental immunity or privilege only where the exercise of parental authority or discretion is somehow involved;[21] parental immunity except where the

---

19. [Ed. note] Citing cases from the following states: Hawaii, Nevada, New Hampshire, New York, Pennsylvania, and South Carolina.

20. Gibson v. Gibson, 3 Cal.3d 914, 92 Cal.Rptr. 288, 479 P.2d 648 (1971); Anderson v. Stream, 295 N.W.2d 595 (Minn.

1980); Miller v. Leljedal, 71 Pa.Cmwlth. 372, 455 A.2d 256 (1983).

21. [Ed. note] Citing cases from Alaska, Arizona, Delaware, Iowa, Kentucky, Maine, Michigan, New Jersey, Texas, and Wisconsin.

injury was caused by negligence in a motor vehicle accident;[22] parental immunity except to the extent of liability insurance;[23] some cases deny immunity when the child's injury occurred in the course of the parent's vocational or business activities;[24] most other states continue to adhere to the traditional rule of immunity for simple negligence torts.[25] In no case is the immunity held to apply to intentional, willful, or malicious torts.

Over the years, the Goller decision's exemptions for parental conduct involving parental authority and discretion have been criticized as being susceptible to arbitrary distinctions. See Gibson v. Gibson, 3 Cal.3d 914, 92 Cal.Rptr. 288, 479 P.2d 648, 653 (1971); compare Lemmen v. Servais, 39 Wis.2d 75, 158 N.W.2d 341 (1968)(failure to warn a child to watch for traffic was within parental discretion and immune under Goller) with Cole v. Sears Roebuck & Co., 47 Wis.2d 629, 177 N.W.2d 866 (1970) (allowing a two-year old child to play on a swing set was not within the Goller immunity). The California Supreme Court has rejected the Goller approach on the ground that it would theoretically provide a parent a carte blanche right to act negligently toward a child in certain circumstances. California adopted an approach which imposes upon a parent the duty to act as a reasonable parent in all cases. * * * The reasonable parent standard, however, also has found criticism for its attempt to apply a uniform standard of acceptable parental conduct across the economic, educational, cultural, religious, and ethnic spectrum. See Holodook v. Spencer, 36 N.Y.2d 35, 364 N.Y.S.2d 859, 324 N.E.2d 338 (1974). The Holodook court stated that to apply the reasonable parent standard "would be to circumscribe the wide range of discretion a parent ought to have in permitting his child to undertake responsibility and gain independence." Holodook, 324 N.E.2d at 346.

In spite of judicial criticism of the Goller opinion, and the adoption of alternative standards in select jurisdictions, the Goller formula retains vitality, even in jurisdictions that have abrogated parental immunity. * * * Notwithstanding the total abrogation of parental immunity in paragraph (1) of section 895G of the restatement [sic], paragraph (2), when read in connection with comments (j) and (k) of section 895G, has served as a legal basis independent of the parental immunity doctrine for adopting the Goller formula. Paragraph (2) of section 895G declares that certain parental acts are privileged by reason of the parent-child relationship. For example, the Restatement (Second) recognizes as privileged certain disciplinary acts which would be tortious if directed at a third party, e.g., a parent who spanks a child would be privileged from being sued by the child for battery. Comment (j) cites Goller with approval, and designates as the "better law" the trend entirely abrogating parent child immunity, while comment (k) specifically singles out the exercise of parental authority and discretion as among the essential elements of parenthood to be preserved.

22. [Ed. note] Citing cases from Alaska, Arizona, Connecticut, Kansas, Maine, Montana, North Dakota, New Mexico, North Carolina, Oklahoma, Rhode Island, Virginia, Washington, and West Virginia.

23. [Ed. note] Citing cases from Delaware, Florida, Massachusetts, Idaho, and Oklahoma.

24. [Ed. note] Citing cases from Texas and Colorado.

25. [Ed. note] Citing cases from Alabama, Arkansas, Colorado, Georgia, Idaho, Illinois, Indiana, Louisiana, Maryland, Mississippi, Missouri, Nebraska, Ohio, Oregon, Tennessee, and Wyoming.

Accordingly some jurisdictions have adopted the Goller formula, not as an exception to the general abrogation of parental immunity as originally promulgated by the Goller court, but as a distinct parental privilege under paragraph (2) of section 895G. Winn v. Gilroy, 296 Or. 718, 681 P.2d 776 (1984)(parental authority and discretion privileges adopted pursuant to Restatement).

South Dakota has never explicitly adopted or rejected the parental immunity doctrine and, absent authority endorsing the concept, this Court does not believe the Supreme Court of South Dakota would adopt the doctrine. Most persuasive is the fact that the vast majority of states have been abrogating or curtailing the application of the doctrine. Further, this Court holds that the rule expressed in Goller and the Restatement (Second) embodies the more persuasive reasoning.

A general exploration of statutory and judicial law relating to duties which arise out of the family relationship, and which, if breached, may form the basis of legal action, indicates that the legislature and the courts of this state interfere only to a very limited degree in family relations with the result that few legal duties exist by reason of the parent-child relation which, if breached, would entail legal consequences for the parent. * * *

In the past, the law has interposed itself into the realm of domestic relations only for the limited purpose of establishing a parental duty of support and guidance to a child personally. With respect to third parties, absent circumstances indicating an intentional tort on the part of the child or entrustment with a dangerous instrumentality on the part of the parent, South Dakota law does not recognize a third-party's claim against a parent based upon the parent's negligent supervision of the child. Accordingly, it would not seem logical that South Dakota would recognize a claim by a child against the parent for negligent supervision. While the foregoing authority admittedly concerns the duty of a parent to prevent injury to a third person by exercising proper supervision over a child, as distinguished from the instant case which involves the duty owed by a parent to a child, the rationale in either case rests upon the parent's exercise of supervision. If there is good rationale for the rule that a parent owes no duty to third parties for negligent supervision of the child, it seems a logical corollary that there is no duty owed by the parent to the child. * * *

In addition to strong legal authority indicating a general policy disfavoring state involvement in the family relationship, persuasive policy arguments also exist in favor of the adoption of a general parental privilege in the realm of parental authority and discretion. This Court is concerned with preventing official interference in matters involving parent-child relationships, protection of family integrity and harmony, and the protection of parental discretion in the discipline and care of a child. With respect to the parental exercise of supervision, the Court is mindful of the Holodook court's admonition that there are conceivably: few, if any, accidental injuries to children which could not have been prevented or substantially mitigated, by keener parental guidance, broader foresight, closer protection, and better example. Indeed, a child could probably avoid most physical harm were he under his parent's constant surveillance and instruction, though detriment more subtle and perhaps more harmful than physical injury might result.   If the instant negligent supervision claims were allowed, it would be the rare parent who could not conceivably be called to account in the courts for his conduct toward his child, either by the child directly or by virtue of [a claim for contribution].   Holodook, 324 N.E.2d at 343.   Raising a child is a unique and delicate function which involves reciprocal responsibilities between parent and child which do not exist between a child and a stranger.   Principles of freedom and democracy are closely interwoven with preserving the integrity of family decision making. Objective standards of proper child rearing, such as California's reasonable parent standard, are inimical to these values and likely impossible to formulate.   * * *   Moreover, objective standards encourage judicial second-guessing of a parent's own highly personal determination of the best methods of raising a child or infringe on a parent's individual conclusion regarding the level of trust to place in a child in a given situation.

The prevalence of insurance is often cited as a justification for subjecting parents to liability to suit by their children as insurance shifts the adversarial nature of the proceedings from the parent to the insurer, and places upon the insurer the burden of compensation.   This argument is flawed in the basic assumption that parents will always be properly and adequately insured against the category of claim made by the child or the child's ward.   Unlike automobile insurance, other forms of insurance are not compulsory by statute.   Parents who rent a home or apartment may not have a comprehensive homeowner's policy which would include tort liability coverage.   A child whose parents are adequately covered by insurance might be expected to prosecute their claims eagerly, but vulnerability to a countersuit for contribution will certainly make uninsured parents reluctant to assert claims against negligent third parties.   Thus, the net effect of permitting a child's cause of action against the parent, and by implication a third party plaintiff's claim for contribution, could deter a child from suing an insured tortfeasor. Conversely, where a child of an uninsured parent does sue a third party and the parent is ultimately held liable for contribution, family discord and strife must inevitably result. The whole purpose of insurance becomes distorted when the presence of insurance encourages new kinds of liability.   The effect of judicial activity in this connection will quite simply occur at a cost to society in the form of increased premiums and the necessity of purchasing insurance coverage to guard against new forms of liability.   * * *

The Court is not persuaded that the conduct of third-party defendant Brad Brunner on the day of the injury transgressed the boundaries of the privilege accorded acts of parental authority and discretion.   Defendant nowhere alleges that Brad Brunner acted willfully or maliciously toward Jeremiah, but instead attempts to distinguish Brunner's supervision of Jeremiah as being different from mere negligence on the grounds that the father "physically brought" his son into a dangerous area.   Whether an act is one involving a discharge of parental authority and discretion does not rest upon the presence or absence of an affirmative act on the part of the parent.   If such were the case, then any parent who takes a child to a playground and lets the child play upon such potentially hazardous equipment as a tall slide or a teeter-totter would be open to suit either directly or upon contribution.   For that matter, every time a parent plugged in an iron, operated a toaster, or boiled a pot of water on the stove the parent would be subject to potential liability were a child injured by contact with these daily household hazards. It simply becomes all too easy to circumvent the parental privilege by characterizing the parent's conduct as an affirmative step toward placing the child in danger. The fact that Jeremiah Brunner was in his father's company for purposes of supervision sufficiently implicates functions of parental authority and discretion as to fall within that privilege. * * *

Having determined that third-party defendant Brad Brunner is not civilly liable for his role in this matter, it follows that neither he, nor his partnership, may be liable upon a claim of contribution. * * *

By parental authority, the Court contemplates an exercise or act involving discipline, supervision, or guidance of a child. An exercise of discretion would tend to concern a parent's decisions concerning food and clothing, the home environment, medical care, and other necessities. Jilani v. Jilani, 767 S.W.2d 671 (Tex.1988). The scope of these privileges is likely to be as broad as the circumstances in which they may arise. For example, a parent's negligent operation of an automobile is generally not deemed sufficiently related to an exercise of parental authority or discretion as to fall within the privilege. * * * On the other hand, the question of whether or not to install a pool in the family backyard, obviously an indulgence and not a necessity, has been deemed sufficiently related to parental discretion respecting the sort of home to provide as to bar a minor child's claim based on injuries sustained diving into the pool. McCallister v. Sun Valley Pools, Inc., 100 Mich.App. 131, 298 N.W.2d 687, 691 (1980); Haddrill v. Damon, 149 Mich.App. 702, 386 N.W.2d 643 (1986)(a parent may determine in the exercise of reasonable parental authority that a child may or may not ride a dirt bike). It is apparent that a parent's responsibility for physical conditions in the home, for food, medical care, toys and recreation, and general supervision falls within a range of distinct issues that need not be incorporated into a general verbal formula until the need arises to address them. Nonetheless, the construction given the privilege must be sufficiently broad as to respect the importance of maintaining parental freedom in the exercise of authority and discretion, and as to give effect to the underlying policy consideration of preventing the substitution of judicial discretion for parental judgment. Accordingly, it is:

ORDERED that the third-party defendant's motion for summary judgment is GRANTED.

Notes

1. Gibson v. Gibson, 3 Cal.3d 914, 92 Cal.Rptr. 288, 479 P.2d 648 (1971), in which, as noted in *Brunner,* the reasonable parent standard finds its genesis, involved an unemancipated child bringing an action against his father. The child's father had "negligently stopped the car [which was towing a Jeep] on the highway and negligently instructed James [the child] to go out on the roadway to correct the position of the Jeep's wheels. While following these directions, James was injured when another vehicle struck him."

2. In Thoreson v. Milwaukee & Suburban Transport Co., 56 Wis.2d 231, 201 N.W.2d 745 (1972), a mother left her three-year old son "in the living room in her home in Milwaukee, watching television, while she went to a neighbor's

home." The boy left the house and ran "into the street from in front of a parked car into the path" of a bus owned by the defendant. The bus company recovered a judgment of contribution against the mother, entered upon a jury verdict, of 40% of the amounts recovered against it by the boy. It is not clear whether the mother was insured against this liability. In affirming this judgment, the court declared:

> In deciding *Goller,* the first exception to the abolishment of immunity involved the exercise of parental authority over the child. This exception embraces the area of discipline. The second exception involved the parents' duty to provide food, clothing, housing, medical and dental services and other care. In this area, parents are allowed discretion in performing their legal duties. We think * * * that the rule of *ejusdem generis* should be applied in interpreting the words "other care" and that the exception does not extend to the ordinary acts of upbringing, whether in the nature of supervision or education, which are not of the same legal nature as providing food, clothing, housing, and medical and dental services. The care sought in the exclusion is not the broad care one gives to a child in day-to-day affairs. If this were meant, the exclusion would be as broad as the old immunity was. The exclusion is limited to legal obligations, and a parent who is negligent in other matters cannot claim immunity simply because he is a parent.

Is there now much difference between Wisconsin and California?

3. In Holodook v. Spencer, 36 N.Y.2d 35, 364 N.Y.S.2d 859, 324 N.E.2d 338 (1974), the New York Court of Appeals quite candidly assigned as a principal reason for denying the child's cause of action for negligent supervision the fact that a major consequence of recognizing such a cause of action would be actions against parents for contribution by those who had tortiously injured a child. The court noted "that, except in cases of great wealth, it [the family] is a single economic unit. * * *"

4. As the traditional immunities recede, the possible types of action that a child might have against its parents are practically infinite and raise some very serious issues of public policy. *See* R. Beal, *"Can I Sue Mommy?" An Analysis of a Woman's Tort Liability for Prenatal Injuries to her Child Born Alive,* 21 San Diego L.Rev. 325 (1984). In Carpenter v. Bishop, 290 Ark. 424, 720 S.W.2d 299 (1986), the court held that a wrongful death action could not be brought on behalf of an eight and a half month old viable fetus when the mother negligently drove an automobile into a bridge abutment killing herself and the fetus. Even if the fetus was a person under the wrongful death statute, the action was barred by the parental immunity doctrine. *See also* Stallman v. Youngquist, 125 Ill.2d 267, 126 Ill.Dec. 60, 531 N.E.2d 355 (1988), where the court ruled that a child injured while *in utero* by her mother's allegedly negligent driving could not bring an action against her mother regardless of whether the parent-child immunity had continued viability in Illinois. *But see* Grodin v. Grodin, 102 Mich.App. 396, 301 N.W.2d 869 (1980). Some of these issues were explored in more depth in Chapter 12, although without explicit treatment of the intra-family immunity doctrine. The complex social policies that are involved in such cases are perhaps better treated in the context of family law in which it may be possible to consider these issues from a broader perspective than is possible when the problem is treated as just one more instance of a personal injury. *Cf.* Peters, *Rethinking Wrongful Life: Bridging the Boundary Between Tort and Family Law,* 67 Tul. L. Rev. 397 (1992).

                              *

Index

References are to Pages

†

0-314-21113-6

90000

9 780314 211132